The **Rough Guide** to

# Southeast Asia ON A BUDGET

this edition written and researched by

Laura Bennitt, Tom Burns, Emily Butler, Róisín Cameron, Ben Connor, Michelle Doran, Paul Gray, Hilary Heuler, Ciara Kenny, Lorna North, Nicholas Owen, Emily Paine, Lesley Reader, Lucy Ridout and Henry Stedman

NEW YORK • LONDON • DELHI

www.roughguides.com

# Contents

◄◄ KRABI REGION, THAILAND ◄ ROYAL PALACE, PHNOM PENH

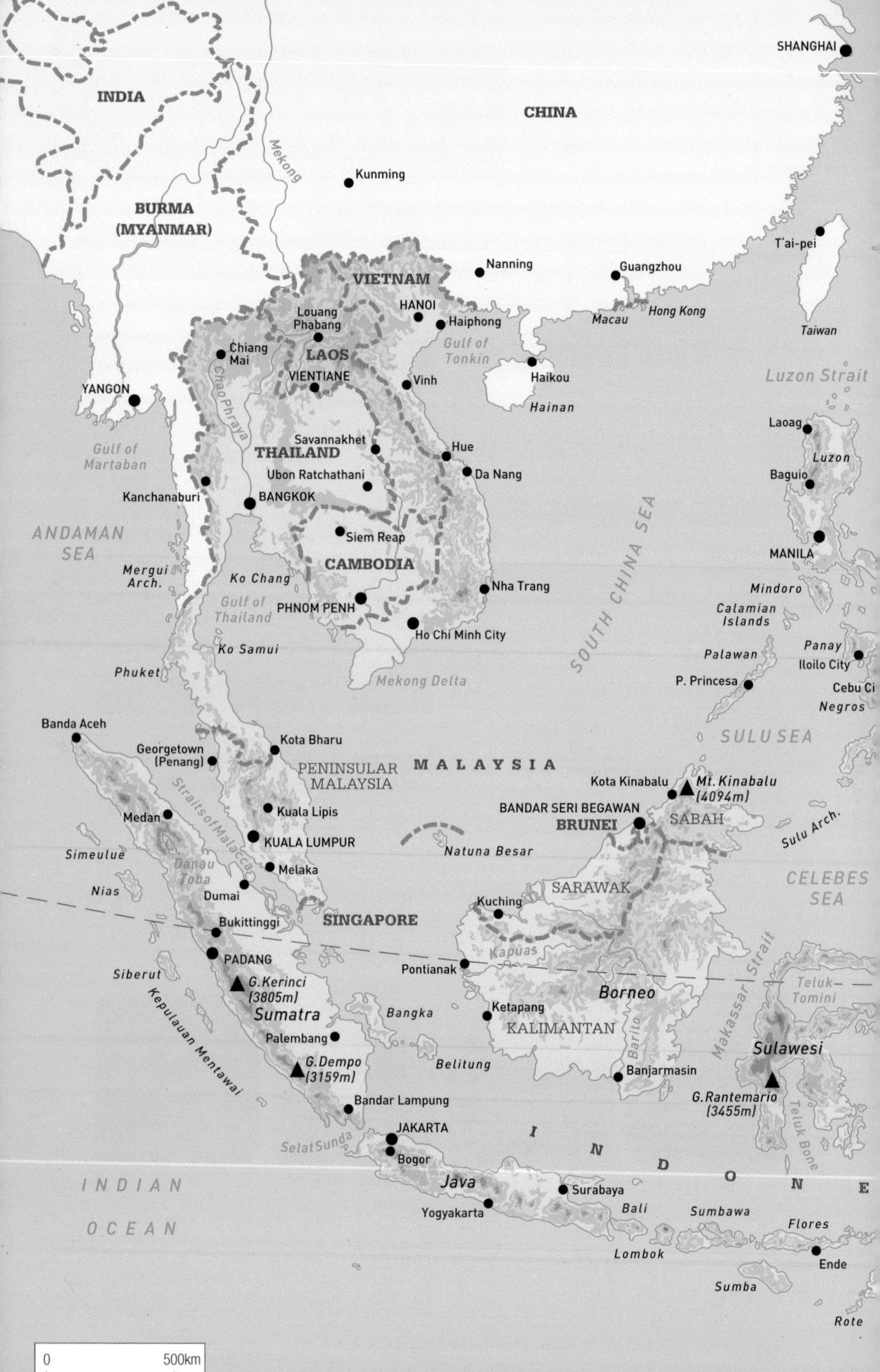

INDIA
CHINA
SHANGHAI
Mekong
Kunming
BURMA (MYANMAR)
T'ai-pei
Nanning
Guangzhou
VIETNAM
HANOI
Louang Phabang
Haiphong
Macau
Hong Kong
Taiwan
Chiang Mai
LAOS
Gulf of Tonkin
Haikou
YANGON
VIENTIANE
Vinh
Hainan
Luzon Strait
Chao Phraya
Laoag
Gulf of Martaban
Savannakhet
THAILAND
Hue
Luzon
Ubon Ratchathani
Da Nang
Baguio
Kanchanaburi
BANGKOK
ANDAMAN SEA
Siem Reap
SOUTH CHINA SEA
MANILA
CAMBODIA
Mergui Arch.
Ko Chang
Nha Trang
Mindoro
Gulf of Thailand
PHNOM PENH
Calamian Islands
Ho Chi Minh City
Panay
Ko Samui
Palawan
Iloilo City
Phuket
Mekong Delta
P. Princesa
Cebu Ci
Negros
Banda Aceh
SULU SEA
Kota Bharu
Georgetown (Penang)
PENINSULAR MALAYSIA
MALAYSIA
Kota Kinabalu
Mt. Kinabalu (4094m)
Straits of Malacca
Kuala Lipis
BANDAR SERI BEGAWAN
Medan
BRUNEI
SABAH
KUALA LUMPUR
Sulu Arch.
Natuna Besar
Simeulue
Danau Toba
Melaka
CELEBES SEA
Nias
SARAWAK
Dumai
Kuching
Bukittinggi
SINGAPORE
Kapuas
PADANG
Pontianak
Makassar Strait
Teluk Tomini
Siberut
G. Kerinci (3805m)
Borneo
Kepulauan Mentawai
Sumatra
Bangka
Ketapang
KALIMANTAN
Barito
Sulawesi
Palembang
G. Dempo (3159m)
Belitung
Banjarmasin
G. Rantemario (3455m)
Bandar Lampung
Teluk Bone
JAKARTA
I
Selat Sunda
Bogor
N
D
INDIAN OCEAN
O
Java
N
Surabaya
E
Bali
Sumbawa
Yogyakarta
Flores
Lombok
Ende
Sumba
Rote
0
500km

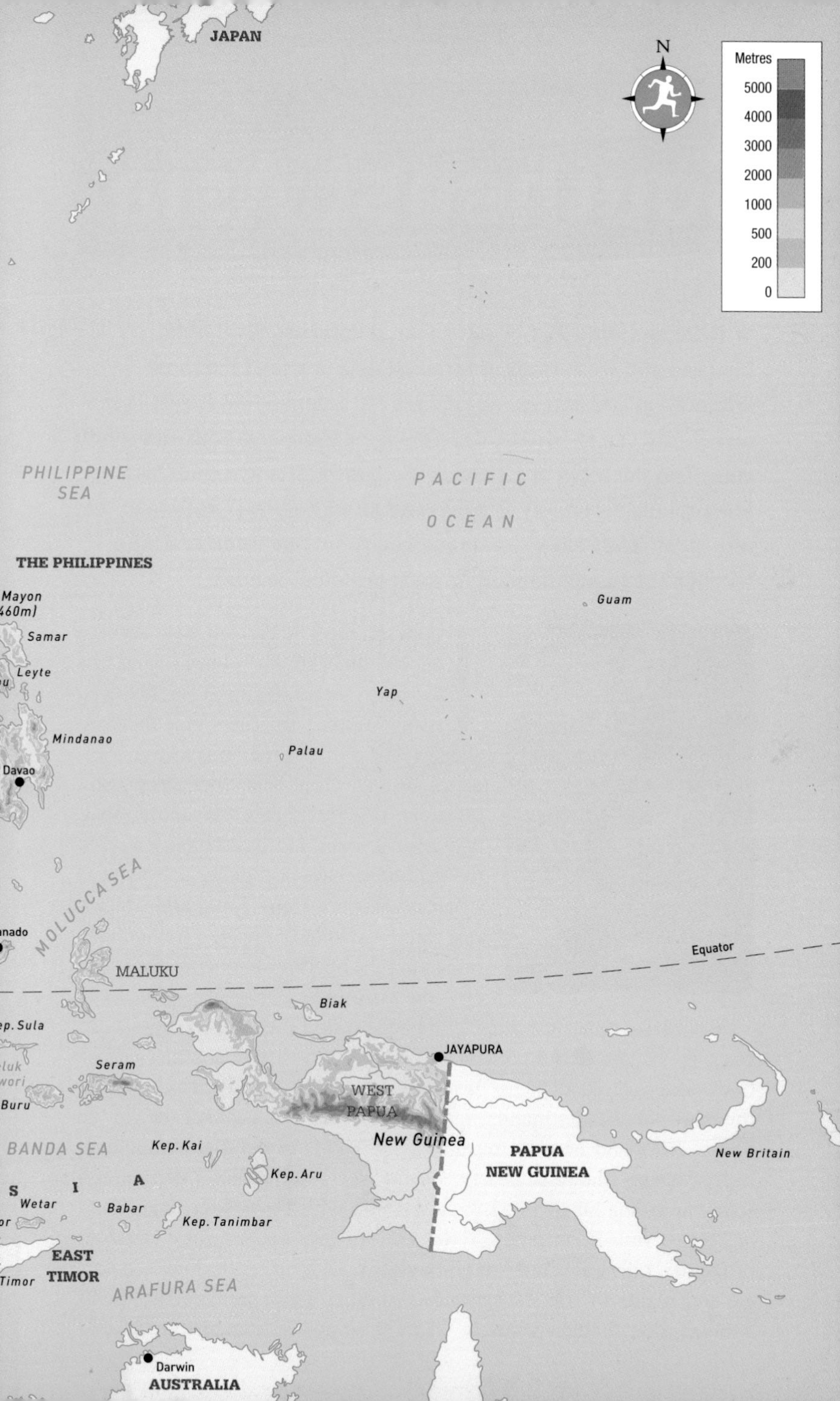

JAPAN
N
Metres
5000
4000
3000
2000
1000
500
200
0
PHILIPPINE SEA
PACIFIC OCEAN
THE PHILIPPINES
Mayon
2460m)
Guam
Samar
Leyte
bu
Yap
Mindanao
Palau
Davao
MOLUCCA SEA
anado
Equator
MALUKU
Biak
ep. Sula
JAYAPURA
Seram
eluk
wori
Buru
WEST PAPUA
New Guinea
PAPUA NEW GUINEA
New Britain
BANDA SEA
Kep. Kai
Kep. Aru
S
I
A
Wetar
Babar
Kep. Tanimbar
or
EAST TIMOR
Timor
ARAFURA SEA
Darwin
AUSTRALIA

Introduction to

# Southeast Asia

**With its tempting mix of volcanoes, rainforest, ricefields, beaches and coral reefs, Southeast Asia is one of the most stimulating and accessible regions for independent travel in the world. You can spend the day exploring thousand-year-old Hindu ruins and the night at a rave on the beach; attend a Buddhist alms-giving ceremony at dawn and go white-water rafting in the afternoon; chill out in a bamboo beach hut one week and hike through the jungle looking for orang-utans the next.**

In short, there is enough here to keep anyone hooked for months, and the average cost of living is so low that many Western travellers find they can afford to take their time. The region comprises Brunei, Cambodia, Indonesia, Laos, Malaysia, the Philippines, Singapore, Thailand and Vietnam, and, as useful gateways to the region, we have also included Southeast Asian neighbours **Hong Kong and Macau**; we have excluded Burma (Myanmar), respecting the boycott on tourism requested by Aung San Suu Kyi.

There are some classic routes through the region – with some suggestions given in our itineraries section (see p.17) – but there are endless variations. Many travellers begin their trip in Bangkok, and Thailand remains the most popular destination in Southeast Asia, with some of the world's best beaches and islands, hill towns and plenty of cultural stimulation. Neighbouring **Malaysia** boasts equally nice beaches, good diving, and some rewarding jungle hikes. East Malaysia, which shares the large island of Borneo with Indonesia's Kalimantan province and the little kingdom of **Brunei**, offers adventurous (if costly) travel by river through the jungle and nights in tribal longhouses. Another convenient starting point is **Singapore**; though relatively pricey it combines a fascinating mix of

## Local transport

Tuk-tuk, bemo, jeepney, sawngthaew, moto, cyclo – the names are endless, as are the types of vehicle, which can be anything from modern mini-vans to three-wheel buggies. You'll soon become familiar with the different ones as you travel around, particularly in the more remote parts of the region. Noisy, bumpy and often jam-packed with people, these vehicles are a world away from the slick, air-conditioned transport systems you'll find in Asia's big cities. In some places the larger vehicles run as buses on fixed routes – bemos in some Indonesian towns for example – but more often they are share-taxis or taxis. Negotiate the fare before you get in, make sure you know whether you're chartering the whole vehicle or just a seat in one, and, as you would anywhere in the world, take sensible precautions when travelling alone and at night.

old and new. From Singapore or Malaysia it's a boat ride or short flight to **Indonesia**. It could take you a lifetime to explore this vast and varied archipelago, with fantastic volcanic landscapes, an unparalleled diversity of tribal cultures, decent beaches and diving and lots of arts and crafts.

Travelling northeastward out of Thailand takes you into **Laos**, where there are memora-

LONGTAIL BOATS, ANDAMAN COAST, THAILAND

## Street food

Southeast Asia boasts some of the world's tastiest cuisines, and the really good news for those travelling on a budget is that the cheapest is often the best, with markets and roadside hawkers unbeatable places to try local specialities. Night markets, in particular, are great for tasting different dishes at extremely low prices – sizzling woks full of frying rice, swirling clouds of spice-infused smoke and rows of glistening fried insects all make for an unforgettable gastronomic experience. With each country, each region and even each town having its own specialities, there's so much variety your tastebuds will never get bored.

ble long-distance boat journeys, some fine old temples and a traditional rural culture. Neighbouring **Vietnam** offers impressive old Chinese towns, two vibrant, rapidly changing and very different cities and some stunning scenery, from the northern mountains to the southern waterways of the Mekong. **Cambodia** is now firmly established on the tourist trail, mainly because of the fabulous temple ruins at Angkor. From here it's possible to complete the entire circuit overland back to Thailand.

Northeast of Indonesia, a flight away from mainland Southeast Asia, and consequently less visited, **the Philippines** boasts some of the best beaches and most dramatic diving in the whole region, making it well worth the detour from the main tourist trail.

# When to go

Southeast Asia sits entirely within the tropics and so is broadly characterized by a hot and humid climate that varies little throughout the year, except during the two annual monsoons. The **southwest monsoon** arrives in west-coast regions at around the end of May and brings daily rainfall to most of Southeast Asia by mid-July (excepting certain east-coast areas, explained opposite). From then on you can expect overcast skies and regular downpours until October or November. This is not a great time to travel in Southeast Asia, as west-coast seas are often too rough for swimming, some islands become inaccessible and poorly maintained roads may get washed out. However, rain showers often last just a couple of hours a day and many airlines and guesthouses offer decent discounts at this time. The **northeast monsoon** brings drier, slightly cooler weather to most of Southeast Asia (east-coast areas excepted) between November and February, making this period the best overall time to travel in the region. The main exceptions to the above pattern are the east-coast regions of Vietnam, Thailand and Peninsular Malaysia, which get rain when the rest of tropical Asia is having its driest period, but stay dry during the southwest monsoon. If you're planning a long trip to Southeast Asia, this means you can often escape the worst weather by hopping across to the other coast. Indonesia and Singapore are hit by both monsoons, attracting the west-coast rains from May through October, and the east-coast rains from November to February.

BOAT ON THE MEKONG, VIETNAM

BALINESE RICE TERRACES

# Ideas Architectural wonders

**CITY SKYLINE, HONG KONG**
One of the most eye-popping urban vistas on earth. **See p.164**

**ANGKOR WAT, CAMBODIA**
The immense Hindu temple complex is nothing short of magnificent. **See p.108**

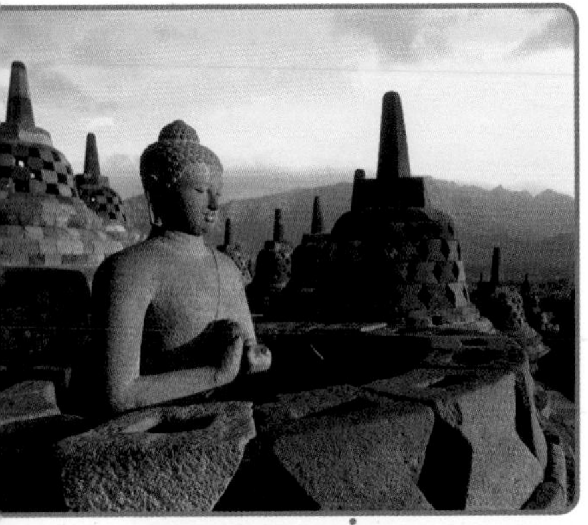

**BOROBUDUR, INDONESIA**
The biggest Buddhist stupa in the world, covered in delicately sculpted reliefs. **See p.235**

**ROYAL CITY OF HUE, VIETNAM** A majestic citadel and grand imperial mausoleums dotted along the Perfume River. **See p.959**

**BANGKOK'S GRAND PALACE, THAILAND** Exuberant murals, a highly revered Buddha image and Thailand's holiest temple. **See p.755**

**LOUANG PHABANG, LAOS** An enchanting and beautifully preserved city. **See p.429**

# Ideas The great outdoors

**TAMAN NEGARA NATIONAL PARK, MALAYSIA** One of the world's oldest rainforests, teeming with wildlife. **See p.531**

**BANAUE RICE TERRACES, THE PHILIPPINES** The stairways to heaven; for the best view, trek through them to Batad. **See p.696**

**HA LONG BAY, VIETNAM** A famously dramatic landscape of weird rock formations, hidden bays and gloomy caves. **See p.984**

**BORACAY, THE PHILIPPINES** In a country awash with perfect white sand beaches, Boracay's White Beach still stands out as one of the best. **See p.671**

**KHAO SOK NATIONAL PARK, THAILAND** Humid jungle overshadowed by stunning limestone crags. **See p.862**

**ORANG-UTANS, INDONESIA AND MALAYSIA** Observe their antics at Bukit Lawang in Sumatra and Sepilok in Sabah. **See pp.258 & p.599**

# Ideas Activities

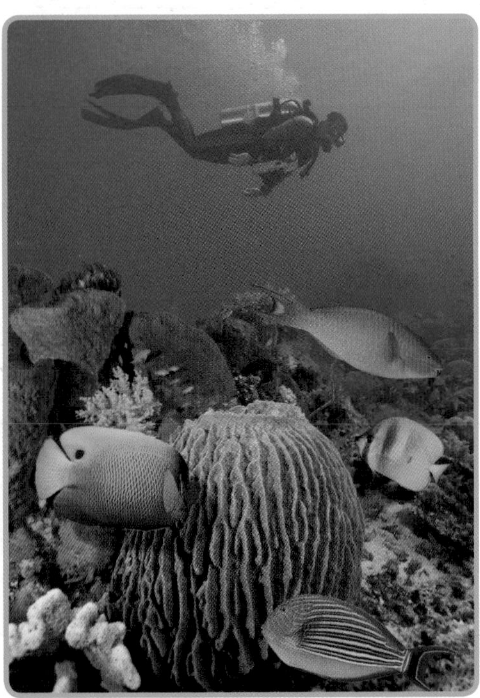

**DIVING** The region is home to some of the world's best dive sites, and it's a great place to learn. Indonesia, Malaysia, Thailand and the Philippines all have some stunning marine life.

**CLIMBING MOUNT KINABALSU, MALAYSIA** Southeast Asia's highest peak, a challenging but straightforward two-day hike. **See p.595**

**TREKKING AROUND SA PA, VIETNAM** Invigorating day hikes to ethnic minority villages. **See p.993**

**TAKING THE SLOW BOAT DOWN THE MEKONG, LAOS** The perfect way to absorb Lao life and landscapes. **See p.451**

**SEA-KAYAKING IN THE KRABI REGION, THAILAND** Discover your own lonely bays and mysterious lagoons. **See p.874**

**PARTYING ON KO PHA NGAN, THAILAND** Home of the classic backpacker full moon parties. **See p.851**

# ITINERARIES

# ITINERARIES

# Southeast Asia itineraries



**You can't expect to fit everything Southeast Asia has to offer into one trip and we don't suggest you try. On the following pages are a selection of itineraries that guide you through the different countries, picking out a few of the best places and major attractions along the way. For those taking a big trip through the region you could join a few together – across from northern Thailand into Laos and down the mighty Mekong, for example. There is, of course, much to discover off the beaten track, so if you have the time it's worth exploring the smaller towns and villages further afield, finding your own deserted island, perfect hilltown or just a place you love to rest up and chill out.**

## BANGKOK AND NORTHERN THAILAND

❶ **BANGKOK** Immerse yourself in Thailand's frenetic capital, with its grand palaces, noisy tuk-tuks and thriving, crowded markets. See p.755

❷ **AYUTTHAYA** Rent a bicycle and explore the remarkable, extensive ruins of this ancient capital. See p.784

❸ **KANCHANABURI** A mix of charming rafthouses, waterfalls and lush hills, this place is a popular and chilled-out backpackers' haunt. see p.778

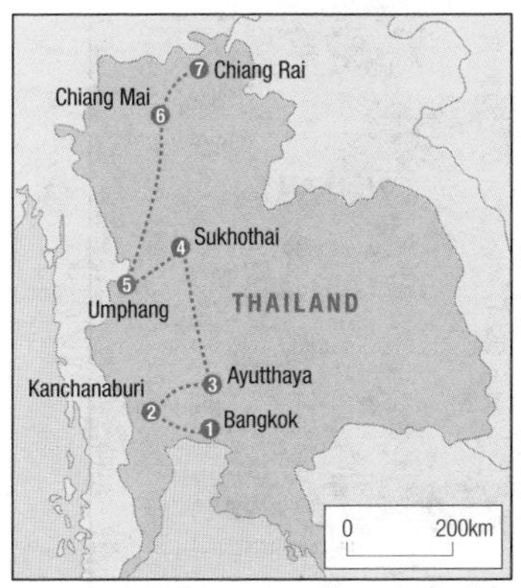


❹ **SUKHOTHAI** Elegant temple remains in Old Sukhothai attest to its former glory. See p.791

❺ **UMPHANG** If you fancy breaking free of the tourist route, head for this lovely, isolated place surrounded by majestic trekking-friendly mountains. See p.796

❻ **CHIANG MAI** The complete backpacker package: vibrant markets, hill treks to ethnic minority villages, glorious temples and delectable cuisine. See p.799

❼ **CHIANG RAI** The place to come for trekking – from gentle riverside ambles to strenuous mountain scrambles – either on an elephant or on your legs. See p.817

## LAOS AND CAMBODIA

❶ **HOUAYXAI TO LOUANG PHABANG** An unmissable two-day trip down the Mekong River ends in lovely Louang Phabang, the city of golden spires. See p.451 & p.429

❷ **VIENTIANE** A charming capital boasting a number of interesting temples, good restaurants and the chance to indulge in a relaxing herbal sauna. See p.418

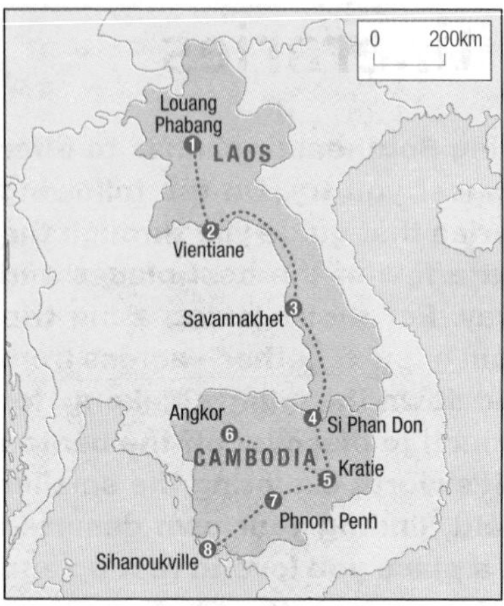


❸ **SAVANNAKHET** Provincial capital, drawing the crowds for its lovely French colonial architecture, narrow lanes and pretty shop-houses. **See p.452**

❹ **SI PHAN DON** Four thousand islands scattered across the Mekong, this is a relaxing rural stop before picking up a minibus to Stung Treng in Cambodia. **See p.463**

❺ **KRATIE** The unassuming town of Kratie is home to a colony of rare freshwater Irrawaddy dolphins. **See p.132**

❻ **PHNOM PENH** A pleasant sprawl of shop-houses and boulevards, lustrous palaces and engrossing museums. **See p.89**

❼ **ANGKOR** Another boat-trip takes you from Cambodia's capital to Siem Reap and the world-famous temples of Angkor. From here it's a straightforward journey to Bangkok, or back to Phnom Penh to continue. **See p.103**

❽ **SIHANOUKVILLE** Cambodia's only proper beach resort provides travel-worn tourists a chance to relax, party and sun-worship on its sandy beaches, before heading on to Vietnam. **See p.121**

## VIETNAM

❶ **HO CHI MINH CITY** Vietnam's bustling second city and most travellers' first taste of Vietnam; an effervescent collusion of French colonial style and brash, cosmopolitan youth. **See p.904**

❷ **MEKONG DELTA** Interconnecting canals and rivers cut through lush rice paddies; hop on a boat to visit one of the region's vibrant floating markets. **See p.918**

❸ **PHU QUOC** Vietnam's largest island, a restful place fringed with sandy beaches and an offshore archipelago perfect for diving and snorkelling. **See p.926**

❹ **DA LAT** Vietnam's premier hill station and the gateway to the Central Highlands. **See p.932**

❺ **MUI NE** Watersports hub with a vast stretch of golden, palm-shaded beach, laid-back backpacker hangouts and sand dunes. **See p.941**

❻ **NHA TRANG** Vietnam's pre-eminent party town, with a popular municipal beach, boat-trips to nearby islands, diving, snorkelling and nearby Cham architecture. **See p.944**

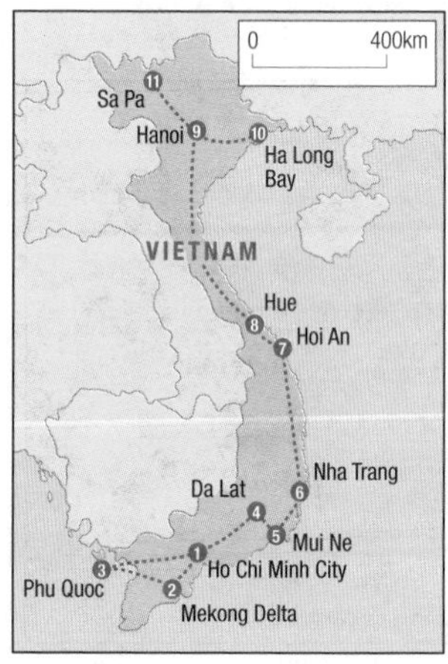

❼ **HOI AN** Charmingly seductive sixteenth-century merchant town, offering excellent shopping opportunities and an attractive beach. See p.949

❽ **HUE** Tranquil yet engaging city famous for its nineteenth-century imperial architecture, and as a base for tours to the DMZ. See p.959

❾ **HANOI** Vietnam's historical, political and cultural capital, an animated maze of old merchant streets and grand French colonial architecture. See p.968

❿ **HA LONG BAY** UNESCO World Heritage site featuring two thousand limestone karsts jutting out of shimmering turquoise waters that teem with boats. See p.984

⓫ **SA PA** Bustling market town nestled in the northern mountains, that's a popular base for tours to ethnic minority villages, or as the starting point for a hair-raising trip back to Hanoi through the dramatic landscape of Vietnam's northwestern circuit. See p.993

## THAILAND'S BEACHES AND ISLANDS

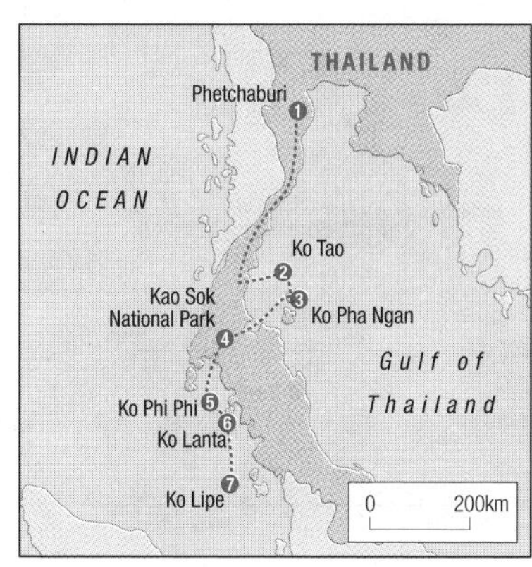


❶ **PHETCHABURI** Retains an old-world charm with historic shop-houses, fascinating wats and Rama IV's fabulous hilltop palace. See p.843

❷ **KO TAO** Rough, mountainous, jungle interiors, secluded east and south coast beaches, a tastefully developed west coast beach life and numerous dive schools to choose from. See p.855

❸ **KO PHA NGAN** Famous for its pre, post, in-between and actual full moon parties, Ko Pha Ngan also offers a few, as yet, untainted paradise beaches. See p.851

❹ **KHAO SOK NATIONAL PARK** Tropical jungle, dotted with dramatic limestone crags, this is one of the most bio-diverse places on the planet. See p.862

❺ **KO PHI PHI** An ugly tourist village that's host to undeniably fun all-night parties is offset by beautiful Long Beach and Viking Beach, great snorkelling and diving and the magnificent Maya Bay. See p.875

❻ **KO LANTA** Manages to combine a relaxed island get-away experience with a dynamic and upbeat nightlife (if you know where to look). See p.876

❼ **KO LIPE** While rapidly becoming over developed you will still find pockets of paradise here, and the beautiful Ko Tarutao National Marine Park is yours to explore. See p.882

## SINGAPORE AND MALAYSIA

❶ **SINGAPORE** An easy introduction to Southeast Asia, with an array of tourist-friendly pleasures: shopping, markets, zoos, temples and delicious food. See p.701

❷ **MELAKA** An old colonial town with a fascinating mix of cultures, Melaka makes an ideal first stop in Malaysia from either Singapore or Indonesia. See p.552

❸ **KUALA LUMPUR** Visit the thriving capital, packed with modern architecture, monuments, galleries and markets. See p.493

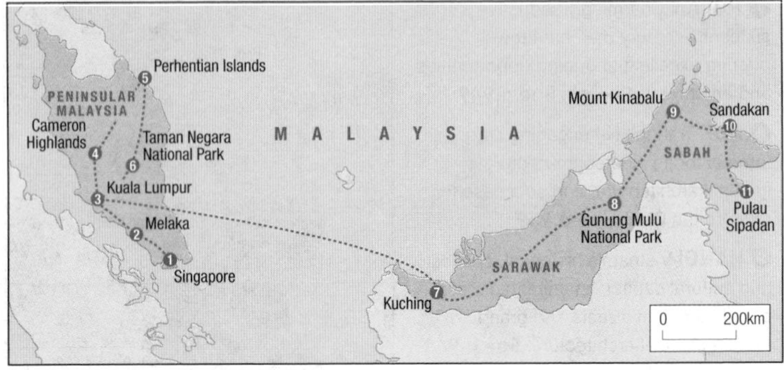


❹ **CAMERON HIGHLANDS** The cooling heights of the Cameron Highlands entice the crowds at weekends who come to enjoy the spectacular, lush scenery. **See p.507**

❺ **PERHENTIAN ISLANDS** A pair of stunning small islands, with white sand beaches and buckets of charm, this is the perfect place to kick back and relax. **See p.541**

❻ **TAMAN NEGARA NATIONAL PARK** Explore the spectacular and ancient rainforests of Malaysia's interior. Taking the Jungle Railway from Kota Bharu in the northeast is a meandering, scenic way to reach it. **See p.531**

❼ **KUCHING** Sarawak's capital is an attractive, relaxed city that makes a good base for visits to Iban longhouses. **See p.567**

❽ **GUNUNG MULU NATIONAL PARK** Sarawak's premier national park, and home to the largest limestone cave system in the world, as well as the impressive Pinnacles. **See p.585**

❾ **KINABALU NATIONAL PARK** An exhausting, exhilarating trek up Mount Kinabalu, the highest peak in Southeast Asia, is rewarded with breathtaking views from the summit at sunrise. **See p.595**

❿ **SANDAKAN AND AROUND** While not an appealing city in itself, Sandakan makes a great base to discover Sabah's rich wildlife at Sepilok's Orang-utan Rehabilitation Centre, Turtle Islands National Park and along the Kinabatangan River. **See p.597**

⓫ **PULAU SIPADAN** One of the top dive sites in the world, the waters around here teem with spectacular marine life. **See p.601**

## INDONESIA

❶ **BUKIT LAWANG AND DANAU TOBA** There's plenty to discover among the beautiful scenery of northern Sumatra: Bukit Lawang is home to the famous orang-utan centre, while further south lies the vast lake Danau Toba, with pleasant island resorts and fascinating traditional villages. **See p.258 & p.263**

❷ **JAKARTA** Whether you're travelling from Sumatra or Singapore, you may end up in the frenetic capital, where it's worth taking time to explore the interesting museums and enjoy the vibrant nightlife. **See p.209**

❸ **YOGYAKARTA** The cultural heart of Java, with a fascinating walled royal city, Yogya is a centre for Javanese arts and also the best place to base yourself for visiting the magnificent temples of Borobudur and Prambanan. **See p.226**

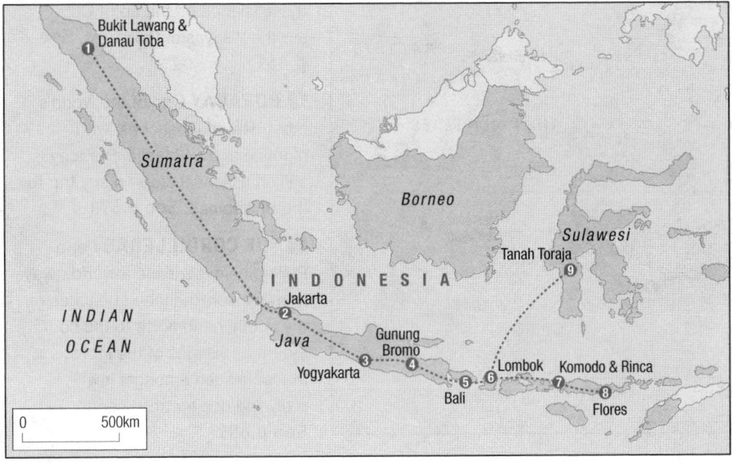




❹ **GUNUNG BROMO** A vast volcanic crater, with the still smoking Gunung Bromo rising up from its base; the pre-dawn hike up the crater rim is well worth the effort for the dramatic sunrise views over a spectacular landscape. **See p.247**

❺ **BALI** The laid-back Hindu island is still the most popular destination in the archipelago, with great nightlife, perfect surf, beautiful scenery and the chilled-out cultural centre of Ubud. **See p.278**

❻ **LOMBOK** Just a short hop from Bali, head to the awesome Gunung Rinjani for a few days' trekking, or to the Gili Islands, just off the northwest coast, for some fabulous diving. **See p.328**

❼ **KOMODO AND RINCA** Close encounters with the fearsome Komodo dragon. Overnight trips can be organized from Labuanbajo on Flores, or from Lombok. **See p.354**

❽ **FLORES** A fertile, mountainous island, Flores has one of the most alluring landscapes in the country. The three craters of Kelimutu each contain a lake of vibrantly different colours. **See p.355**

❾ **TANAH TORAJA** You'll probably have to backtrack to Bali before travelling up to Sulawesi, where the major attraction is the highlands of Tanah Toraja, home to a fascinating culture and flamboyant festivals. **See p.386**

## THE PHILIPPINES

❶ **MANILA** The Philippine capital can appear sprawling and seedy, but it has a compelling energy all of its own. It's also the most convenient gateway to some of the country's more inaccessible areas. **See p.621**

❷ **PALAWAN** A prehistoric landscape of underground rivers, giant lizards, shockingly beautiful limestone islands and some of the best wreck diving in the world. **See p.676**

❸ **CEBU CITY** The Philippines' second city is nearly as frenetic as Manila, and an inevitable stop as you island-hop around the Visayas. **See p.655**

❹ **CAMIGUIN** Easily reached from Cebu City, this small volcanic island offers some of the country's most appealing adventure activities and a laid-back bohemian arts scene. **See p.683**

❺ **MALAPASCUA AND BANTAYAN** For a slice of island living complete with limited electricity and captivating sunsets

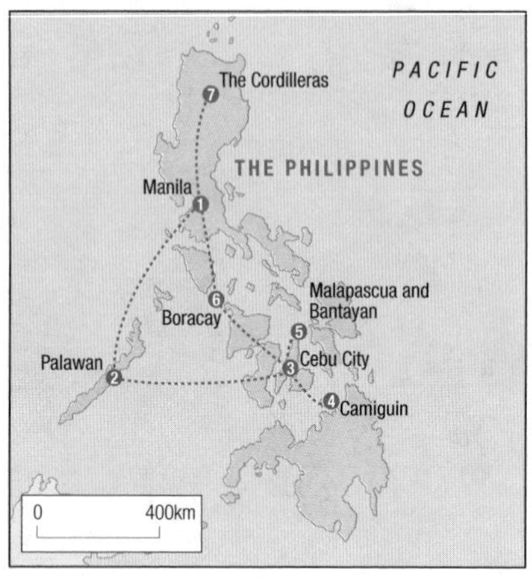


these islands off the tip of Cebu are the Visayas at their best. See p.661

❻ **BORACAY** One of the world's most beautiful beaches, with nightlife to rival Manila, Boracay is still an essential stop on any trip to the Philippines. See p.671

❼ **THE CORDILLERAS** For a Philippine experience a world away from the sun-drenched beaches of the south, head north to the cool mountain villages of the Igorot tribes, nestled amongst jaw-dropping rice terrace scenery. See p.689

# BASICS

# Basics

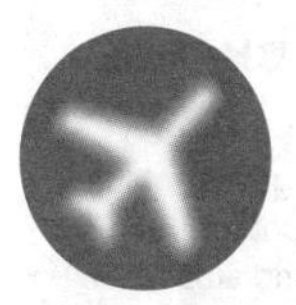

# Getting there

**The quickest and easiest way to get to Southeast Asia is by air. One of the cheapest options is to buy a flight to one of the region's gateway cities, such as Singapore or Bangkok, and make onward travel arrangements from there. If you're keen to combine your trip with a visit to India or China, you could consider a stopover or open-jaw ticket, which flies you into one country and out of another, allowing you to explore overland in between. If you're planning a multi-stop trip, then a Round-the-World or Circle Asia/Pacific ticket offers good value; the cheapest and most popular routes include one or more "surface sectors" where you have to make your way between point A and point B by road, rail or sea or by a locally bought flight. Another good option is the Asean Air Pass, put together by the national airlines of Brunei, Indonesia, Malaysia, the Philippines, Singapore, Thailand and Vietnam, which allows stopovers in two to six of these countries, with a minimum stay of three nights and a maximum of three months for each one. As an alternative to air travel, you could consider taking one of the world's classic overland trips, the Trans-Siberian railway, through Russia and Mongolia to China, and from there to Indochina.**

The biggest factor affecting the price of a ticket is the time of year you wish to travel. **High season** for many Asian destinations is over Christmas, when much of the region is experiencing its driest period, and during the UK summer holidays. It's best to book well in advance for a ticket in high season. Some airlines and travel agents charge more than others, so it's always good to shop around. Discount flights agents often offer the best deals. You can also get good deals if you are a **student** or **under 26** with discount agents such as STA and the Canadian company Travel CUTS.

Flying into Southeast Asia on a one-way ticket is fairly inexpensive and gives you plenty of options for onward travel, but it can cause **problems at immigration**. Many officials like to see proof of onward or return transport, fearing that you may stay illegally in their country. Some will be happy if you show proof of sufficient funds to keep you going (about £1350/US$2600), others will be more satisfied if you can give details of a convincing onward route, with dates. Some travellers get round all this by buying the cheapest return flight available and then cashing in the return sector, but read the small print before going for this option. RTW/Circle Asia tickets will also eliminate any immigration hassle.

In some countries, you may have to apply for a **visa** in advance if arriving on a one-way ticket, rather than being granted one automatically at immigration, so always check with the relevant embassy before you leave. If you are continuing overland, you need to research visa requirements at the border crossings before leaving home. Details on **overland transport** from

### FLY LESS – STAY LONGER! TRAVEL AND CLIMATE CHANGE

Climate change is perhaps the single biggest issue facing our planet. It is caused by a build-up in the atmosphere of carbon dioxide and other greenhouse gases, which are emitted by many sources – including planes. Already, **flights** account for three to four percent of human-induced global warming: that figure may sound small, but it is rising year on year and threatens to counteract the progress made by reducing greenhouse emissions in other areas.

Rough Guides regard travel as a **global benefit**, and feel strongly that the advantages to developing economies are important, as are the opportunities for greater contact and awareness among peoples. But we also believe in travelling responsibly, which includes giving thought to how often we fly and what we can do to redress any harm that our trips may create.

We can travel less or simply reduce the amount we travel by air (taking fewer trips and staying longer, or taking the train if there is one); we can avoid night flights (which are more damaging); and we can make the trips we do take "climate neutral" via a carbon-offset scheme. **Offset schemes** run by climatecare.org, carbonneutral .com and others allow you to "neutralize" the greenhouse gases that you are responsible for releasing. Their websites have simple calculators that let you work out the impact of any flight – as does our own. Once that's done, you can pay to fund projects that will reduce future emissions by an equivalent amount. Please take the time to visit our website and make your trip climate neutral, or get a copy of the *Rough Guide to Climate Change* for more detail on the subject.

**www.roughguides.com/climatechange**

neighbouring Southeast Asian countries are given in the introduction to each chapter.

## FLIGHTS FROM THE UK AND IRELAND

It's usually more expensive to fly **from the UK and Ireland** non-stop than to change planes in Europe or Asia en route. Some European airlines offer competitive fares to Asia from **regional airports** such as Glasgow, Manchester, Dublin and Belfast, though none of them are direct flights.

One of the cheapest and most useful **gateways** to Southeast Asia is **Bangkok**. London–Bangkok flights start at about £350 one-way, £500 return, rising to at least £450/£650 during peak times (July, Aug, Dec), and take a minimum of twelve hours. Another inexpensive and popular gateway city is **Singapore**. London–Singapore flights start at £330 one-way, £480 return, or £450/£600 during peak times (mid-July to Sept), and take at least twelve hours.

If you want to go to China as well as Southeast Asia, consider buying a flight to **Hong Kong**. London–Hong Kong flights start at about £300 one-way, £420 return or £390/£550 during peak times (mid-June to Sept, Christmas, Chinese New Year, and Easter), and take at least eleven hours. Hong Kong gives you easy and inexpensive local transport options into Guangdong province, from where you could continue west into Vietnam, and on into Laos.

If you're planning to fly direct from London to either Vientiane or Phnom Penh, you will have to change planes in Bangkok or Singapore, as there are currently no long-haul flights to these destinations. It's also much faster and easier to get visas for Vietnam in Bangkok than in London, so it's worth building in a stopover just for that.

Stopover tickets could be a London–Singapore return with a stay in Bangkok (of up to three months) for about £500. Open-jaw options might include a flight from London to **Delhi** and then out of Bangkok or Singapore a few months later. A one-year open RTW ticket from London taking in Bangkok, Singapore, Perth, Sydney, Auckland and Los Angeles starts at as little as £700. The cheapest time to begin your RTW trip is usually April to June. A typical **Circle Asia** from London to Bali and back might include a flight from London to

Bangkok, then a surface sector from Bangkok to Singapore, followed by flights from Singapore to Bali, then Bali to London; total cost from £580. An **Asean Air Pass** beginning and ending in most Southeast Asian countries starts at £399 for three stopovers, £549 for four and £699 for five.

## FLIGHTS FROM THE USA AND CANADA

There's no way around it, **flights from North America** to Southeast Asia are long. With the exception of non-stop services to Singapore, Bangkok and Hong Kong from the US West Coast, all flights, including so-called "direct flights", will require a stop somewhere along the way. But this means you can take advantage of the **stopovers** offered by many airlines.

Numerous airlines run daily flights to **Bangkok** from major East- and West-coast cities, usually making one stop. Flying time from the West Coast via Asia is approximately seventeen hours, and from New York via Europe it's around nineteen hours. From the US West Coast, expect to pay from US$1100. From the East Coast, prices start at about US$825. From Canada, the flight takes around sixteen hours (from Vancouver via Tokyo) or around twenty (from Montreal via Europe). Prices are around CAN$1400 from Vancouver, and CAN$1600 from Toronto. **Singapore** is served from New York, Los Angeles, and San Francisco; flying eastbound is more direct but is still at least 22 hours' travelling time. Prices start around US$1450 from New York; from Washington, Miami, or Chicago prices start at US$1300; from Los Angeles, San Francisco or Seattle $1000. From Toronto or Montréal, prices go from CAN$1275 and from Vancouver CAN$1200.

Fly via **Hong Kong** if you wish to visit China. The cheapest low-season fare from the US West Coast is around US$700 round-trip and the flight takes at least fourteen hours. From the East Coast most flights to Hong Kong stretch to twenty-two hours, and include a connection. The cheapest published fares from New York are around US$850. The best options for flights **from Canada** to Hong Kong include non-stop flights from Vancouver (13hr) and direct flights from Toronto and Montréal (21hr). Fares from Canada's West Coast start at around CAN$1200.

From New York to Singapore with a stopover in Hong Kong (of up to three months) fare start from $1500. A RTW itinerary might be San Francisco–Bali–Singapore surface to Bangkok–Cairo–Athens surface to London–San Francisco for US$1850. A typical Circle Pacific ticket might be New York–Hong Kong–Bangkok–Jakarta–Bali–Los Angeles–New York for US$1200. For an Asean Air Pass departing and finishing in most Southeast Asian countries, prices start at $780 for three stopovers, $1070 for four and $1360 for five.

## FLIGHTS FROM AUSTRALIA AND NEW ZEALAND

The cheapest way to get to Southeast Asia **from Austalia and New Zealand** is to buy a one-way flight to one of the region's gateways such as Denpasar (Bali), Jakarta, Singapore, Kuala Lumpur, Bangkok or Hong Kong, and carry on from there by air, sea or overland.

Airfares from east-coast **Australian gateways** are all pretty much the same, although they're cheaper from Darwin and Perth. **From New Zealand**, you can expect to pay about NZ$150–300 more from Christchurch and Wellington than from Auckland. Single fares to Indonesia, Malaysia, the Philippines and Brunei start at roughly AUS$800/NZ$1100, while to Thailand, Indochina and Hong Kong you can expect to pay from AUS$900/NZ$1000 single. If you're thinking of entering Indonesia on a one-way fare, make sure you have a valid onward ticket (air or ferry) out of the country.

An open-jaw sample price could be: Darwin to Kuala Lumpur on the outward leg and Bangkok to Darwin on the return at around AUS$800. A RTW ticket from Sydney to Singapore, taking in London, New York, Los Angeles and Auckland, starts at around AUS$2400/NZ$3000. An Asean Air Pass beginning and ending in most Southeast Asia countries costs from around AUS$415/NZ$510 for three coupons, AUS$570/NZ$700 for four coupons, AUS$730/NZ$890 for five coupons.

## AIRLINES, AGENTS AND OPERATORS

### Online booking

ⓦ**www.expedia.co.uk** (UK), ⓦ**www.expedia.com** (US), ⓦ**www.expedia.ca** (Canada)
ⓦ**www.lastminute.com** (UK)
ⓦ**www.opodo.co.uk** (UK)
ⓦ**www.orbitz.com** (US)
ⓦ**www.travelocity.co.uk** (UK), ⓦ**www.travelocity.com** (US), ⓦ**www.travelocity.ca** (Canada)
ⓦ**www.travelonline.co.za** (South Africa)
ⓦ**www.zuji.com.au** (Australia), ⓦ**www.zuji.co.nz** (New Zealand)

### Airlines

**Air Canada** UK ⓣ0871/220 1111, Republic of Ireland ⓣ01/679 3958, US and Canada ⓣ1-888/247-2262, Australia ⓣ1300/655 767, New Zealand ⓣ0508/747 767; ⓦwww.aircanada.com.
**Air China** UK ⓣ020/7744 0800, US ⓣ1-800/982-8802, Canada ⓣ416/581-8833, Australia ⓣ02/9232 7277; ⓦwww.airchina.com.cn.
**Air India** UK ⓣ020/8560 9996 or 8745 1000, US ⓣ1-800/223-7776, Canada ⓣ1-800/625-6424, Australia ⓣ02/9283 4020, New Zealand ⓣ09/631 5651; ⓦwww.airindia.com.
**Air New Zealand** UK ⓣ0800/028 4149, US ⓣ1-800/262-1234, Canada ⓣ1-800/663-5494, New Zealand ⓣ0800/737 000, Australia ⓣ0800/132 476; ⓦwww.airnz.co.nz.
**Air Pacific** UK ⓣ020/626 4283, US and Canada ⓣ1-800/227-4446, Australia ⓣ1800/230 150, New Zealand ⓣ0800/800178; ⓦwww.airpacific.com.
**All Nippon Airways (ANA)** UK ⓣ0870/837 8811, US and Canada ⓣ1-800/235-9262, Republic of Ireland ⓣ1850/200 058; ⓦwww.anaskyweb.com.
**Asiana Airlines** UK ⓣ020/7514 0200, US ⓣ1-800/227-4262, Australia ⓣ02/9767 4343; ⓦwww.flyasiana.com.
**ATA (American TransAir)** US ⓣ1-800/435-9282, ⓦwww.ata.com.
**British Airways** UK ⓣ0844/493 0787, Republic of Ireland ⓣ1890/626 747, US and Canada ⓣ1-800/AIRWAYS, Australia ⓣ1300/767 177, New Zealand ⓣ09/966 9777, South Africa ⓣ114/418 600; ⓦwww.ba.com.
**Cathay Pacific** UK ⓣ020/8834 8888, US ⓣ1-800/233-2742, Canada ⓣ1-800/2686-868, Australia ⓣ13 17 47, New Zealand ⓣ09/379 0861, South Africa ⓣ11/700 8900; ⓦwww.cathaypacific.com.
**China Airlines** UK ⓣ020/7436 9001, US ⓣ1-917/368-2003, Australia ⓣ02/9231 5588, New Zealand ⓣ09/308 3364; ⓦwww.china-airlines.com.
**China Eastern Airlines** UK ⓣ0870/760 6232, US ⓣ626/538/1500, Canada ⓣ604-689/8998, Australia ⓣ02/9290 1148; ⓦwww.chinaeastern.co.uk.
**China Southern Airlines** US ⓣ1-888/338-8988, Australia ⓣ02/9231 1988; ⓦwww.cs-air.com.
**Continental Airlines** UK ⓣ0845/607 6760, Republic of Ireland ⓣ1890/925 252, US and Canada ⓣ1-800/523-3273, Australia ⓣ1300/737 640, New Zealand ⓣ09/308 3350, International ⓣ1800/231 0856; ⓦwww.continental.com.
**Delta** UK ⓣ0845/600 0950, Republic of Ireland ⓣ1850/882 031 or 01/407 3165, US and Canada ⓣ1-800/221-1212, Australia ⓣ1300/302 849, New Zealand ⓣ09/977 2232; ⓦwww.delta.com.
**Emirates** UK ⓣ0844/800 2777, US and Canada ⓣ1-800/777-3999, Australia ⓣ1300/303 777, New Zealand ⓣ05/0836 4728, South Africa ⓣ0861/364 728; ⓦwww.emirates.com.
**Etihad Airways** UK ⓣ0870/241 7121, US ⓣ1-8888/ETIHAD, Canada ⓣ1-416/221-4744, South Africa ⓣ11/3439 140; ⓦwww.etihadairways.com.
**EVA Air** UK ⓣ020/7380 8300, US and Canada ⓣ1-800/695-1188, Australia ⓣ02/8338 0419, New Zealand ⓣ09/358 8300; ⓦwww.evaair.com.
**Garuda Indonesia** UK ⓣ020/7467 8661, US ⓣ1-212/279-0756, Canada ⓣ1-416/924-3175, Australia ⓣ1300/365 330 or ⓣ02/9334 9900, New Zealand ⓣ09/3661862; ⓦwww.garuda-indonesia.com.
**Gulf Air** UK ⓣ0870/777 1717, Republic of Ireland ⓣ0818/272 828, US ⓣ1-888/359-4853, Australia ⓣ1300/366 337, South Africa ⓣ11/268 8909; ⓦwww.gulfairco.com.
**JAL (Japan Air Lines)** UK ⓣ0845/774 7700, Republic of Ireland ⓣ01/408 3757, US and Canada ⓣ1-800/525-3663, Australia ⓣ1300/525 287, New Zealand ⓣ0800/525 747, South Africa ⓣ11/214 2560; ⓦwww.jal.com or ⓦwww.japanair.com.
**KLM (Royal Dutch Airlines)/Northwest** UK ⓣ0870/507 4074, Republic of Ireland ⓣ1850/747 400, US and Canada ⓣ1-800/225-2525, Australia ⓣ1300/392 192, New Zealand ⓣ09/921 6040, South Africa ⓣ0860/247 747; ⓦwww.klm.com.
**Korean Air** UK ⓣ0800/413 000, Republic of Ireland ⓣ01/799 7990, US and Canada ⓣ1-800/438-5000, Australia ⓣ02/9262 6000, New Zealand ⓣ09/914 2000; ⓦwww.koreanair.com.
**Lufthansa** UK ⓣ0871/945 9747, Republic of Ireland ⓣ01/844 5544, US ⓣ1-800/3995-838,

Canada ⓣ1-800/563-5954, Australia ⓣ1300/655 727, New Zealand ⓣ0800/945 220, South Africa ⓣ0861/842 538; ⓦwww.lufthansa.com.
**Malaysia Airlines** UK ⓣ0871/423 9090, Republic of Ireland ⓣ01/6761 561, US ⓣ1-800/5529-264, Australia ⓣ13 26 27, New Zealand ⓣ0800/777 747, South Africa ⓣ11-8809 614; ⓦwww.malaysia-airlines.com.
**Northwest/KLM** UK ⓣ0870/507 4074, US ⓣ1-800/225-2525, Australia ⓣ1300/767-310; ⓦwww.nwa.com
**Philippine Airlines** UK ⓣ01293/596 680, US ⓣ1-800/435-9725, Canada ⓣ604/276 6015, Australia ⓣ612/9279 2020, New Zealand ⓣ09/308 5206; ⓦwww.philippineairlines.com.
**Qantas** UK ⓣ0845/774 7767, Republic of Ireland ⓣ01/407 3278, US and Canada ⓣ1-800/227-4500, Australia ⓣ13 13 13, New Zealand ⓣ0800/808 767 or 09/357 8900, South Africa ⓣ11/441 8550; ⓦwww.qantas.com.
**Qatar Airways** UK ⓣ020/7399 2577, US ⓣ1-877/777-2827, Canada ⓣ1-888/366-5666, Australia ⓣ386/766 400, South Africa ⓣ11/523 2928; ⓦwww.qatarairways.com.
**Royal Brunei** UK ⓣ020/7584 6660, Australia ⓣ1300/721 271, New Zealand ⓣ09/977 2209; ⓦwww.bruneiair.com.
**Singapore Airlines** UK ⓣ0844/800 2380, Republic of Ireland ⓣ01/671 0722, US ⓣ1-800/742-3333, Canada ⓣ1-800/663-3046, Australia ⓣ13 10 11, New Zealand ⓣ0800/808 909, South Africa ⓣ11/880 8560 or 11/880 8566; ⓦwww.singaporeair.com.
**Thai Airways** UK ⓣ0870/606 0911, US ⓣ1-212/949-8424, Australia ⓣ1300/651 960, New Zealand ⓣ09/377 3886, South Africa ⓣ11/268 2580; ⓦwww.thaiair.com.
**United Airlines** UK ⓣ0845/844 4777, US ⓣ1-800/864-8331, Australia ⓣ13 17 77; ⓦwww.united.com.
**US Airways** UK ⓣ0845/600 3300, Republic of Ireland ⓣ1890/925 065, US and Canada ⓣ1-800/428-4322; ⓦwww.usair.com.
**Vietnam Airlines** UK ⓣ020/3263 2062, US ⓣ1-415/677-8909, Canada ⓣ1-416/927-0275, Australia ⓣ02/9283 1355; ⓦwww.vietnamairlines.com.
**Virgin Atlantic** UK ⓣ0870/574 7747, US ⓣ1-800/821-5438, Australia ⓣ1300/727 340, South Africa ⓣ11/340 3400; ⓦwww.virgin-atlantic.com.

## Agents

**North South Travel** UK ⓣ01245/608 291, ⓦwww.northsouthtravel.co.uk. Friendly, competitive travel agency, offering discounted fares worldwide. Profits are used to support projects in the developing world, especially the promotion of sustainable tourism.
**Trailfinders** UK ⓣ0845/058 5858, Republic of Ireland ⓣ01/677 7888, Australia ⓣ1300/780 212; ⓦwww.trailfinders.com. One of the best-informed and most efficient agents for independent travellers.
**STA Travel** UK ⓣ0871/2300 040, US ⓣ1-800/781-4040, Australia ⓣ134 782, New Zealand ⓣ0800/474 400, South Africa ⓣ0861/781 781; ⓦwww.statravel.com. Worldwide specialists in independent travel; also student IDs, travel insurance, car rental, rail passes, and more. Good discounts for students and under-26s.

## Tour operators

An organized tour is worth considering if you're after a more energetic holiday, have ambitious sightseeing plans and limited time, are uneasy with the language and customs, or just don't like travelling alone. The specialists listed below can also help you get to more remote areas and organize activities that may be difficult to arrange yourself, such as extended overland tours that take in several countries, white-water rafting, diving, cycling and trekking. Some also arrange volunteering opportunities. Unless otherwise stated, the prices below generally refer to the land tour only, so you'll need to factor in extra for flights.

### From the UK and Ireland

**Destinations Worldwide Holidays** Dublin ⓣ01/862 0070, ⓦwww.destinations.ie. Specialists in Far Eastern and exotic destinations.
**Earthwatch Institute** UK ⓣ01865/318 831, ⓦwww.earthwatch.org. Volunteer work on projects in Southeast Asia and throughout the world. A wide range of opportunities to assist archeologists, biologists and community workers, staying with local people. Prices start at £795 for one week; £1500 for two weeks.
**Exodus** UK ⓣ020/8675 5550, ⓦwww.exodus.co.uk. Overland trips aimed at 18–45-year olds, including "Cycle Indochina and Angkor Wat" (£1700).
**Explore Worldwide** UK ⓣ0844/499 0901, Dublin ⓣ01/677 9479, ⓦwww.explore.co.uk. Heaps of options throughout Southeast Asia, including tours that explore the Angkor ruins in Cambodia and the jungles of Borneo.
**Gecko Travel** ⓣ023 9225 8859, ⓦwww.geckotravel.com. Offers numerous tours of Thailand and most of Southeast Asia, from £1000 for two weeks.
**Intrepid Travel** UK ⓣ 020 3147 7777, ⓦwww.intrepidtravel.com. They offer a wide range of

## AVERAGE DAILY TEMPERATURES AND RAINFALL

This climate chart lists average maximum daily temperatures and average monthly rainfall for the capital cities of Southeast Asia. Bear in mind, however, that each country has myriad micro-climates, determined by altitude and proximity to the east or west coast amongst other factors; for more detail, see the when to go box in the introduction of each chapter.

| | Jan | Feb | Mar | Apr | May | June | July | Aug | Sept | Oct | Nov | Dec |
|---|---|---|---|---|---|---|---|---|---|---|---|---|
| **Bandar Seri Begawan, Brunei** | | | | | | | | | | | | |
| max (°C) | 30 | 30 | 31 | 32 | 32.5 | 32 | 31.5 | 32 | 31.5 | 31.5 | 31 | 31 |
| max (°F) | 86 | 86 | 88 | 89.5 | 90.5 | 89.5 | 89 | 89.5 | 89 | 89 | 88 | 88 |
| Rainfall (mm) | 133 | 63 | 71 | 124 | 218 | 311 | 277 | 256 | 314 | 334 | 296 | 241 |
| **Bangkok, Thailand** | | | | | | | | | | | | |
| max (°C) | 28 | 28 | 29 | 30 | 31 | 31 | 30 | 31 | 31 | 30 | 29 | 28 |
| max (°F) | 82.5 | 82.5 | 84 | 86 | 88 | 88 | 86 | 88 | 88 | 86 | 84 | 82.5 |
| Rainfall (mm) | 66 | 28 | 33 | 36 | 58 | 112 | 147 | 147 | 170 | 178 | 206 | 97 |
| **Hanoi, Vietnam** | | | | | | | | | | | | |
| max (°C) | 17 | 18 | 20 | 24 | 28 | 30 | 30 | 29 | 28 | 26 | 22 | 19 |
| max (°F) | 62.5 | 64.5 | 68 | 75 | 82.5 | 86 | 86 | 84 | 82.5 | 79 | 71.5 | 66 |
| Rainfall (mm) | 18 | 28 | 38 | 81 | 196 | 239 | 323 | 343 | 254 | 99 | 43 | 20 |
| **Hong Kong & Macau** | | | | | | | | | | | | |
| max (°C) | 18 | 17 | 19 | 24 | 28 | 29 | 31 | 31 | 29 | 27 | 23 | 20 |
| max (°F) | 64.5 | 62.5 | 66 | 75 | 82.5 | 84 | 88 | 88 | 84 | 80.5 | 73.5 | 68 |
| Rainfall (mm) | 33 | 46 | 74 | 137 | 292 | 394 | 381 | 367 | 257 | 114 | 43 | 31 |
| **Jakarta, Indonesia** | | | | | | | | | | | | |
| max (°C) | 29 | 29 | 30 | 31 | 31 | 31 | 31 | 31 | 31 | 31 | 30 | 29 |
| max (°F) | 84 | 84 | 86 | 88 | 88 | 88 | 88 | 88 | 88 | 88 | 86 | 84 |
| Rainfall (mm) | 300 | 300 | 211 | 147 | 114 | 97 | 64 | 43 | 66 | 112 | 142 | 203 |
| **Kuala Lumpur, Malaysia** | | | | | | | | | | | | |
| max (°C) | 32 | 33 | 33 | 33 | 33 | 32 | 32 | 32 | 32 | 32 | 31 | 31 |
| max (°F) | 89.5 | 91.5 | 91.5 | 91.5 | 91.5 | 89.5 | 89.5 | 89.5 | 89.5 | 89.5 | 88 | 88 |
| Rainfall (mm) | 159 | 154 | 223 | 276 | 182 | 119 | 120 | 133 | 173 | 258 | 263 | 223 |
| **Manila, the Philippines** | | | | | | | | | | | | |
| max (°C) | 28 | 28 | 30 | 31 | 32 | 30 | 29 | 29 | 29 | 29 | 29 | 28 |
| max (°F) | 82.5 | 82.5 | 86 | 88 | 89.5 | 86 | 84 | 84 | 84 | 84 | 84 | 82.5 |
| Rainfall (mm) | 35 | 25 | 25 | 35 | 130 | 260 | 415 | 415 | 340 | 210 | 145 | 80 |
| **Phnom Penh, Cambodia** | | | | | | | | | | | | |
| max (°C) | 25 | 27 | 28 | 29 | 29 | 29 | 29 | 29 | 29 | 28 | 27 | 26 |
| max (°F) | 77 | 80.5 | 82.5 | 84 | 84 | 84 | 84 | 84 | 84 | 82.5 | 80.5 | 79 |
| Rainfall (mm) | 10 | 10 | 45 | 80 | 120 | 150 | 165 | 160 | 215 | 240 | 135 | 55 |
| **Singapore** | | | | | | | | | | | | |
| max (°C) | 31 | 32 | 32 | 32 | 32 | 32 | 31 | 31 | 31 | 31 | 31 | 30 |
| max (°F) | 88 | 89.5 | 89.5 | 89.5 | 89.5 | 89.5 | 88 | 88 | 88 | 88 | 88 | 86 |
| Rainfall (mm) | 146 | 155 | 182 | 223 | 228 | 151 | 170 | 163 | 200 | 199 | 255 | 258 |
| **Vientiane, Laos** | | | | | | | | | | | | |
| max (°C) | 28 | 30 | 33 | 34 | 32 | 32 | 31 | 31 | 31 | 31 | 29 | 28 |
| max (°F) | 82.5 | 86 | 91.5 | 93 | 89.5 | 89.5 | 88 | 88 | 88 | 88 | 84 | 82.5 |
| Rainfall (mm) | 5 | 15 | 38 | 99 | 267 | 302 | 267 | 292 | 302 | 109 | 15 | 3 |

holidays, including adventure and overland, plus a "basix" range for more budget-conscious travellers, and have now joined forces with Guerba Expeditions.

**Imaginative Traveller** UK ⓣ0845/077 880, ⓦwww.imaginative-traveller.com. Broad selection of tours to less-travelled parts of Asia, including walking, cycling, camping, cooking and snorkelling. There's a fifteen-day "Journey through Laos" tour as well as the 22-day "Bangkok to Ho Chi Minh City by bike" tour.

**Symbiosis** UK ⓣ01845/123 2844, ⓦwww.symbiosis-travel.com. Environmentally aware outfit that offers specialist interest holidays in Southeast Asia, cycling trips, and trekking through jungles and longhouse communities of Sarawak and Sabah.

## From the US and Canada

**Adventure Center** ⓣ1-800/228-8747, ⓦwww.adventure-center.com. Offering extremely affordable Southeast Asian tours. "Hanoi to Singapore" is a 43-day trip taking in well-known and off-the-beaten-track destinations, and includes the limestone landscapes of Ha Long Bay and the temples at Angkor (from $2580). You can also do a 22-day bicycle tour from Bangkok to Ho Chi Minh City for $1535.

**Adventures Abroad** ⓣ1-800/665-3998 or 604/303-1099, ⓦwww.adventures-abroad.com. Specializing in small-group tours, such as a nineteen-day tour of Cambodia and Vietnam for $2589. A 45-day tour of Thailand, Burma, Laos, Vietnam and Cambodia costs $7538. Other combinations include Burma, Laos, Vietnam and Cambodia for $5960.

**Geographic Expeditions** ⓣ1-800/777-8183 or 415/922-0448, ⓦwww.geoex.com. Specialists in "responsible tourism" with a range of customized tours and/or set packages. Their trips are perhaps a bit more demanding of the traveller than the average specialist, although each tour is rated from easy to rigorous.

**Mountain Travel-Sobek** ⓣ1-888/687-6235, ⓦwww.mtsobek.com. Tours to Laos, Vietnam, Thailand and Cambodia.

**Pacific Holidays** ⓣ212/629-3888, ⓦwww.pacificholidaysinc.com. Inexpensive tour group. Trips include a fifteen-day "Best of Southeast Asia" sightseeing tour of Bangkok, Bali, Singapore, Hong Kong from $2070.

## From Australia and New Zealand

**The Adventure Travel Company** New Zealand ⓣ09/379 9755, ⓦwww.adventuretravel.co.nz. NZ's one-stop shop for adventure travel and agents for Intrepid, Peregrine, Guerba Expeditions and a host of others.

**Adventure World** Australia ⓣ02/8913 0755, ⓦwww.adventureworld.com.au, New Zealand ⓣ09/524 5118, ⓦwww.adventureworld.co.nz. Agents for a vast array of international adventure travel companies.

**Allways Dive Expeditions** Australia ⓣ1800/338 239, ⓦwww.allwaysdive.com.au. All-inclusive dive packages to prime locations through Southeast Asia.

**Earthwatch** ⓣ03/9682 6828, ⓦwww.earthwatch.org/australia. Volunteer work on projects in Indonesia and Thailand.

**Intrepid Adventure Travel** Australia ⓣ1300/360 667, ⓦwww.intrepidtravel.com. Small-group tours to China and Southeast Asia with an emphasis on cross-cultural contact and low-impact tourism.

**Peregrine Adventures** Australia ⓣ03/9662 2700, ⓦwww.peregrine.net.au. Affordable small-group adventure travel company and agent offering a range of graded trips.

**Pro Dive Travel** Australia ⓣ02/9281 5066 or 1800/820 820, ⓦwww.prodive.com.au. Dive packages to Southeast Asia.

**San Michele Travel** Australia ⓣ02/9299 1111 or 1800/22 22 44, ⓦwww.asiatravel.com.au. Customized rail tours throughout Southeast Asia.

**Silke's Travel** Australia ⓣ1800/807 860 or 02/8347 2000, ⓔsilke@silkes.com.au. Specially tailored packages for gay and lesbian travellers.

**The Surf Travel Co** Australia ⓣ02/9527 4722 or 1800/687 873, New Zealand ⓣ09/473 8388, ⓦwww.surftravel.com.au. A well-established surf travel company that can arrange airfares, accommodation and yacht charter in Indonesia, as well as give the low-down on the best surf beaches in the region.

**Travel Indochina** Australia ⓣ1300/365 355, ⓦwww.travelindochina.com.au. Offers low-impact tour packages, using mid- to top-range hotels.

# Getting around

**Local transport across Southeast Asia is uniformly good value compared to public transport in the West, and is often one of the highlights of a trip, not least because of the chance to fraternize with local travellers. Overland transport between neighbouring Southeast Asian countries is also fairly straightforward so long as you have the right paperwork and are patient; full details on cross-border transport options are given throughout the guide. Travelling between countries by bus, train or boat is obviously more time-consuming than flying, but it's also cheaper and can be more satisfying.**

## LOCAL TRANSPORT

Not surprisingly, the ultra-modern enclaves of Singapore and Hong Kong boast the fastest, sleekest and most efficient transport systems in the region. Elsewhere **long-distance buses** are the chief mode of travel in Southeast Asia, which though often frequent, can be fairly nerve-wracking. Standards vary across the region, and often between different companies that cover the same route. At the bottom end seats are usually cramped and the whole experience is often uncomfortable, so wherever possible, try to book a pricier but more comfortable a/c bus for overnight journeys – or take the train. Shorter bus journeys can be very enjoyable, however, and are often the only way to get between places. Buses come in various shapes and sizes; full details of all these idiosyncrasies are given in each chapter.

**Trains** are generally the most comfortable way to travel any distance. Thailand and Peninsular Malaysia both have decent train networks and rolling stock, while Indonesia's is a notch below them, but still a better option than buses on Java. Vietnam's train system is good for some journeys, and again it's often worth paying extra for more comfort on longer routes.

**Taxis** come in many forms, including the infamous **tuk-tuk** (three-wheeled buggies with deafening two-stroke engines), elegant rickshaws powered by a man on a bicycle, or simply a bloke on a motorbike (usually wearing a numbered vest); only conventional taxis in the major cities have meters, so all prices must be bargained for and fixed before you set off. In many riverine towns and regions, it's also common to travel by taxi boat.

Regular **ferries** connect all major tourist islands with the mainland, and often depart several times a day, though some islands become inaccessible during the monsoon. In some areas, **flying** may be the only practical way to get around. Tickets are reasonably priced, especially if the route is covered by one of the region's growing number of low-cost airlines – see p.36 for a list.

In most countries, **timetables** for any transport other than trains and planes are vague or non-existent; the vehicle simply leaves when there are enough passengers to make the journey profitable for the driver. The best strategy is to turn up early in the morning when most local people begin their journeys. For an idea of frequency and duration of transport services between the main towns, check the **"Moving On"** details in each chapter. **Security** is an important consideration on public transport: see p.50 for more advice.

Throughout Southeast Asia it's possible to rent your own transport, though in Vietnam you can't rent self-drive cars. **Cars** are available in all major tourist centres, and range from flimsy Jimnys to a/c 4x4s; you will need your international driver's licence. If you can't face the traffic yourself, you

## MAJOR BORDER CROSSINGS, OVERLAND AND SEA ROUTES

The following is an overview of those land and sea crossings that are both legal and straightforward ways for tourists to travel between the countries of Southeast Asia. The information is fleshed out in the accounts of relevant border towns within the Guide. Long-distance tourist buses often run between major destinations, making cross-border travel simpler and quicker, but there are also numerous options by local transport.

### To Brunei

**From Malaysia** Boats to Brunei depart daily from Lawas and Limbang in northern Sarawak, and from Pulau Labuan in Sabah, itself connected by boat to Kota Kinabalu. From Miri in Sarawak, several buses travel daily to Kuala Belait, in Brunei.

### To Cambodia

**From Vietnam** Four border crossings: at Moc Bai to Bavet (buses run from HCMC to Phonm Penh); two crossings just north of Chau Doc on the Bassac River (by bus and boat); and from near Ha Tien over the border (Prek Chang) to Kep (by xe om only).

**From Thailand** Six border crossings: from Aranyaprathet to Poipet (with connections to Siem Reap and Phnom Penh); the coastal crossing at Hat Lek, near Trat, then to Cham Yeam; two border crossings near Pailin (the easier Phsa Prom and the more remote Daung Leum); and two more recently opened crossings from northeast Thailand – the Chong Chom–O'Smach border pass near Kap Choeng in Thailand's Surin province and the little-used Sa Ngam–Choam crossing.

**From Laos** It's possible to cross from Laos on the Mekong at Voen Kham to Stung Treng (by boat or minibus from Si Phan Don).

### To Hong Kong and Macau

**From China** By train from Beijing to Hong Kong (via Guangzhou in Canton). Boats from China dock at China Ferry Terminal.

### To Indonesia

**From Malaysia and Singapore** Several routes by boat from Malaysia and Singapore to ports in Sumatra including: Penang to Medan; Melaka to Dumai or Pekanbaru; Johor Bahru and Singapore to Pulau Batam and Pulau Bintan, in Indonesia's Riau archipelago (and on to Sumatra); and from Port Klang, near Kuala Lumpur, to Dumai. By bus from Kuching (Sarawak) to Pontianak (Kalimantan). By ferry from Tawau (Sabah) to Pulau Nunukan in northeastern Kalimantan.

### To Laos

**From Thailand** Five legal border crossings (by various combinations of road, rail and river transport): Chiang Khong to Houayxai; Nong Khai to Vientiane; Nakhon Phanom to Thakhek; Mukdahan to Savannakhet; and Chong Mek to Pakxe.

**From Vietnam** Six legal border crossings: the Lao Bao Pass, 240km from Savannakhet (buses from Hue and Da Nang to Savannakhet); at Cau Treo, 105km from Vinh (buses from Da Nang to Savannakhet and Vientiane); the Bo Y crossing 80km from Kon Tum (buses to Attapu); Tay Trang crossing, near Dien Bien Phu to Muang Khoua (no tourist buses); Nam Can to Nong Het, east of Phonsavan in Laos (buses from Vinh to Phonsavan); and the more remote, seldom used Na Meo, east of Xam Nua.

**From China** By bus from Jinghong in China's southwestern Yunnan province to Oudomxai and Louang Namtha.

**From Cambodia** By bus or boat from Phnom Penh to Stung Treng on the Mekong at Voen Kham, with minibuses going from Stung Treng to Si Phan Don.

**Contd...**

### To Malaysia and Singapore

**From Thailand** Though there are buses and trains from Bangkok via Hat Yai into Malaysia, these routes are currently advised against because of political unrest in southern Thailand; check the latest situation before travelling (see p.883). The western routes are safer, particularly from Satun, from where you can take local transport to Kuala Perlis and Pulau Langkawi or Alor Setar; also by ferry from Ko Lipe to Pulau Langkawi.

**From Indonesia** Several routes by boat from Sumatra including: Medan to Penang; Dumai to Melaka; from Pulau Batam and Pulau Bintan in the Riau archipelago to Johor Bahru and Singapore. From Kalimantan, you can take a bus from Pontianak to Kuching in Sarawak. Or you can cross into Sabah on a two-hour ferry from Pulau Nunukan to Tawau, two days' bus ride southeast of Kota Kinabalu.

**From Brunei** Direct boats from Bandar Seri Begawan to Limbang and Lawas (Sarawak), and Pulau Labuan (just off Sabah). Also, buses from Bandar Seri Begawan to Miri in Sarawak (via Seria and Kuala Berait).

### To Thailand

**From Malaysia and Singapore** Travel to some areas of southern Thailand (such as Hat Yai) is not recommended (see p.883); check the latest situation before travelling. The best route is by boat from Kuala Perlis and Pulau Langkawi to Satun.

**From Laos** There are five border crossings:
Houayxai to Chiang Khong; Vientiane across the first Friendship Bridge to Nong Khai; Thakhek to Nakhon Phanom; Savannakhet to Mukdahan; and Pakxe to Chong Mek.

**From Cambodia** Six border crossings: Poipet to Aranyaprathet; by bus and boat from Sihanoukville via Koh Kong and Hat Lek to Trat in east Thailand. By bus across the two border crossings from Pailin (easiest at Phsa Prom and one further north at Daung Lem) to Chanthaburi province in northeast Thailand; via the Chong Chom–O'Smach border pass to Surin; and the little-used Sa Ngam–Choam crossing.

**From Vietnam** By bus from Vietnam, via the Lao Bao Pass, Savannakhet in Laos and then across the Second Friendship Bridge to Thailand.

### To Vietnam

**From Laos** Six border crossings: the Lao Bao Pass and the Cau Treo pass, near Vinh (buses via both from Vientiane and Savannakhet to Da Nang or Hue); the Bo Y crossing (from Attapu to Kon Tum in Vietnam's Central Highlands); Tay Trang (from Muang Ngoi to Dien Bien Phu); Nong Het (from Phonsavan to Vinh); and the remote, seldom used Na Meo crossing (east of Xam Nua).

**From Cambodia** Four crossings: Moc Bai (buses from Phnom Penh, and from Moc Bai on to Ho Chi Minh City); two crossings just north of Chau Doc in the Mekong Delta (boat or bus); and the Xa Xia /Ha Tien border crossing near Kep and Kampot in Cambodia to Ha Tien in Vietnam.

**From China** By direct train from Beijing to Hanoi. Or by bus from Kumming to Lao Cai and then by train to Hanoi. By bus from Guangzhou via Mong Cai or via Huu Nghi from Pingxiang or Nanning.

can often hire a **car with driver** for a small extra fee. One of the best ways to explore the countryside is to rent a **motorbike**. They vary from small 100cc Yamahas to more robust trail bikes and can be rented from guesthouses, shops or tour agencies. Check the small print on your insurance policy, and buy extra cover locally if necessary. **Bicycles** are also a good way to travel, and can be rented from guesthouses or larger-scale rental places.

## Low-cost regional airlines

The airlines listed below are some of the best-known options for getting from country to country. There are also numerous smaller airlines serving internal destinations; check

### A NOTE ON BURMA

Burma (Myanmar), which borders Thailand on the west, and shares a short stretch of border with Laos, is not covered by this book, respecting the boycott on tourism requested by the Nobel Peace prize winner and pro-democracy leader Aung San Suu Kyi, who is currently under house arrest. For more on the politics and ethics of visiting Burma visit Ⓦwww.tourismconcern.org.uk.

the "Directory" sections in the relevant chapters for these.

**Air Asia** Ⓦwww.airasia.com. Frequent daily flights from Bangkok to Chiang Mai, Hanoi, Jakarta, Macau, Phnom Penh, Phuket and Singapore, from Kuala Lumpur to Bali, Bangkok and Jakarta, and from Jakarta to Bali.

**Bangkok Airways** Bangkok (Ⓣ02/265 5555), Ⓦwww.bangkokair.com. Twice-daily flights from Bangkok to Chiang Mai, Phnom Penh and Phuket, and daily flights to Ho Chi Minh and Macau.

**Garuda** Ⓦwww.garuda-indonesia.com. Indonesia's national airline. Frequent flights from Denpasar and Jakarta to Kuala Lumpur and Singapore, plus numerous domestic and regional destinations. Note, however, that Garuda, and all Indonesian airlines, are currently on the EU list of airlines with poor safety records.

**Jet Star Asia** Singapore (Ⓣ6822 2288) Ⓦwww.jetstarasia.com. Daily flights from Singapore to Bangkok, Ho Chi Minh City, Hong Kong, Jakarta, Kuala Lumpur, Macau and Manila, and less frequent flights to Bali, Phnom Penh and Siem Reap.

**Lao Airlines** Vientiane (Ⓣ021/212053) Ⓦwww.laoairlines.com. Frequent flights from Vientiane and Louang Phabang to Bangkok, Chiang Mai, and Hanoi; and flights to Siem Reap and Phnom Penh.

**Nok Air** Bangkok (Ⓣ02/627 2000), Ⓦwww.nokair.com. Frequent daily flights from Bangkok to Chiang Mai and Phuket, and less frequent flights to Hanoi.

**Silk Air** Singapore (Ⓣ6223 8888), Ⓦwww.silkair.com. Daily flights from Singapore to Phnom Penh and Phuket, and less frequent flights to Chiang Mai.

**Thai Airways** Bangkok (Ⓣ02/545 3690), Ⓦwww.thaiair.com. Frequent daily flights from Bangkok to Hanoi, Ho Chi Minh City, Hong Kong, Jakarta, Kuala Lumpur, Macau, Manila, Phnom Penh, Phuket, Singapore, Vientiane.

**Tiger Airways** Singapore (Ⓣ6538 4437), Ⓦwww.tigerairways.com. Daily flights from Singapore to Bangkok, Ho Chi Minh City, Kuala Lumpur, Macau, Manila and Phuket, and less frequent flights to Hanoi and Padang.

**Vietnam Airlines** Hanoi (Ⓣ04/832 0320). Ⓦwww.vietnamairlines.com.vn. Twice-daily flights from Hanoi to Hong Kong, Singapore and Vientiane, and daily flights to Bangkok, Jakarta, Kuala Lumpur and Phnom Penh.

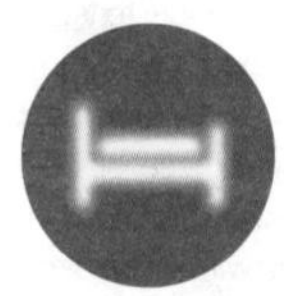

# Accommodation

**You'll rarely have a problem finding inexpensive accommodation in Southeast Asia, particularly if you stick to the main tourist areas. The mainstay of the travellers' scene are guesthouses (also known as bungalows, homestays or backpackers') which can be anything from a bamboo hut to a three-storey concrete block.**

## GUESTHOUSES AND HOTELS

A standard **guesthouse** room will be a simple place with one or two beds, hard mattresses, thin walls and a fan – some, but not all, have a window (usually screened against mosquitoes), and the cheapest ones share a bathroom. Always ask to see several rooms before opting for one, as standards can vary widely within the same establishment. For a **basic double room** with shared bathroom in a guesthouse that's in a capital city or tourist centre, rates start at about US$3 in Indonesia, US$5 in Laos, US$6 in Thailand, Cambodia and the Philippines, US$7 in Malaysia and Vietnam; the highest prices are in Singapore (from US$15 a double) and Hong Kong (from US$25). In smaller towns and beach resorts, rates can be significantly lower, and prices everywhere are usually negotiable during low season. **Single rooms** tend to cost about two-thirds the price of a double, but many guesthouses also offer dormitory beds, which can cost as little as US$2 a night. More specific costings for accommodation are given in the introduction to each chapter. Most clued-up places provide useful **facilities**, such as restaurants, travellers' noticeboards, internet, safes for valuables, baggage-keeps, tour-operator desks and their own poste restantes. At most guesthouses, **check-out time** is noon, which means that during high season you should arrive to check in at about 11.30am to ensure you get a room: few places will draw up a "waiting list", and they rarely take advance bookings unless they know you already.

If you venture to towns that are completely off the tourist circuit, the cheapest accommodation is usually the bland and sometimes seedy **cheap urban hotels** located near bus and train stations. These places are designed for local businesspeople rather than tourists and often double as brothels; they tend to be rather soulless, but are usually inexpensive and clean enough.

For around US$15–30 almost anywhere in Southeast Asia except Singapore and Hong Kong, you can get yourself a comfortable room in an upmarket guesthouse or small **mid-range hotel**. These are often very good value, offering pleasantly furnished rooms, with private hot-water bathroom, and quite possibly a/c, a fridge and a TV as well. Some of these also have a swimming pool. And for $60, you'll get the kind of **luxury** you'd be paying well over $100 for in the West.

## BATHROOMS

Usually, bathrooms with Western-style facilities such as sit-down toilets and cold-water showers are provided. But in rural areas, on some beaches, and in some of the cheapest accommodation, you'll be using a **traditional Asian bathroom**, where you wash using the scoop-and-slosh method. This entails dipping a plastic scoop or bucket into a huge vat or basin of water (often built into the bathroom wall) and then sloshing the water over yourself. The basin functions as a water supply only and not a bath; all washing is done outside it and the basin should not be contaminated by soap or shampoo. **Toilets** in these places will be Asian-style squat affairs, flushed manually with water scooped from the pail that stands alongside; **toilet paper** tends to clog these things up so if you want to avoid an embarrassing situation, learn to wash yourself like the locals do.

## VILLAGE ACCOMMODATION

In the more remote and rural parts of Southeast Asia, you may get the chance to stay in **village accommodation**, be it the headman's house, a family home, or a traditional longhouse. Accommodation in these places usually consists of a mattress on the floor in a communal room, perhaps with a blanket and mosquito net, but it's often advisable to take your own net and blanket or sleeping

### ACCOMMODATION PRICE CODES

All accommodation reviewed in this guide has been graded according to the following **price codes**, in US dollars, which represent the cost of the cheapest double room available in high season. Where a price range is indicated, this means that the establishment offers rooms with varying facilities – as explained in the write-up.

❶ $5 and under
❷ $6–10
❸ $11–15
❹ $16–20
❺ $21–25
❻ $26–40
❼ $41–60
❽ $61–80
❾ $81 and over

bag. As a sign of appreciation, your hosts will welcome gifts, and a donation may be in order, too. But in reality, the chance of encountering this kind of arrangement is quite rare. Some countries such as Laos forbid tourists from sleeping in homes that aren't approved by the government as tourist accommodation.

### HOSTELS

Iit's not worth becoming an HI member just for your trip to Southeast Asia, as there are so few **youth hostels** in the region, and prices don't necessarily compare favourably with other budget options. The one exception is Hong Kong, whose seven youth hostels offer the cheapest accommodation in the territory.

### CAMPING

As accommodation is so inexpensive in Southeast Asia and there are few campsites, there's no point taking a tent. The only times when you may need to **camp** are in the national parks or when trekking, and you may be able to rent gear locally – check the Guide for details. Bungalow owners usually take a dim view of beach campers. Beaches, especially in tourist areas, are often unsafe at night, particularly for women by themselves.

## Food and drink

**One of the highlights of a trip to Southeast Asia is its fabulous cuisine: from fresh Thai green curries to Lao làp (a "salad" of minced meat mixed with garlic, chillies, shallots, aubergine, galangal and fish sauce), the variation of fresh, interesting dishes is endless.**

Each country has its own national dish, but they also demonstrate influences from abroad – Vietnamese cuisine, for example, has many Chinese elements – and in large Southeast Asian cities it's always possible to find establishments specializing in Western and Indian food. Fresh fruit is always available (see box p.40). Eating customs differ from country to country; see the separate chapters for further information on these. You can't buy alcohol in Brunei, but in other countries, the most popular tipple is beer, rather than wine.

### WATER

Most **water** that comes out of taps in Southeast Asia has had very little treatment, and can contain a whole range of bacteria and viruses – always stick to bottled, boiled or sterilized water. Except in the furthest-flung corners of Southeast Asia, **bottled water** is on sale everywhere. Be wary of salads and vegetables that have been washed in tap water, and bear in mind that **ice** is not always made from sterilized water.

The only time you're likely to be out of reach of bottled water is trekking into remote areas, in which case you must boil or sterilize your water.

### GENERAL PRECAUTIONS

Most health problems experienced by travellers are a direct result of food they've eaten. Avoid eating uncooked vegetables and fruits that cannot be peeled, and be warned that you risk ingesting worms and other parasites from dishes containing raw meat or fish. Cooked food that has been sitting out for an undetermined period of time should also be treated with suspicion. Avoid

## TROPICAL FRUITS OF SOUTHEAST ASIA

You'll find fruit offered everywhere – neatly sliced in glass boxes on hawker carts, blended into delicious shakes at night-market stalls, and served as dessert in restaurants. These are the region's less familiar fruits:

**Custard apple (soursop)** Knobbly, grey-green skin hiding creamy, almond-coloured blancmange-like flesh and many seeds.

**Durian** The most prized, and expensive, fruit with a greeny-yellow, spiky exterior. Inside, it divides into segments of thick, yellow-white flesh that give off a disgustingly strong stink that's been compared to a mixture of mature cheese and caramel.

**Guava** Green, textured skin and sweet, crisp flesh that can be pink or white and is studded with tiny edible seeds.

**Jackfruit** Large, pear-shaped fruit with a thick, bobbly, greeny-yellow shell protecting sweet, yellow flesh. Green, unripe jackfruit is sometimes cooked as a vegetable in curries.

**Mangosteen** The size of a small apple, with smooth, purple skin and a fleshy inside that divides into succulent, white segments that are sweet though slightly acidic.

**Papaya (paw-paw)** Similar in size and shape to a large melon, with smooth, green skin and yellowy-orange flesh.

**Pomelo** Looks rather like a grapefruit, though it is slightly drier and sweeter and has less flavour.

**Rambutan** The bright-red soft, spiny exterior has a white, opaque fruit of delicate flavour, similar to a lychee.

**Salak (snakefruit)** Teardrop-shaped, the *salak* has a brown, scaly skin like a snake's and a bitter taste.

**Sapodilla (sapota)** Small, brown, rough-skinned ovals look a bit like kiwi fruit and conceal a grainy, yellowish pulp that tastes almost honey-sweet.

**Star fruit (carambola)** A waxy, pale-green fruit with a fluted, almost star-like shape. It resembles a watery, crunchy apple. The yellower the fruit, the sweeter its flesh.

sharing glasses and utensils. The amount of money you pay for a meal is no guarantee of its safety; in fact, food in top hotels has often been hanging around longer than food cooked at roadside stalls. Use your common sense – eat in places that look clean, avoid reheated food and be wary of shellfish.

# Health

**The vast majority of travellers to Southeast Asia suffer nothing more than an upset stomach, so long as they observe basic precautions about food and water hygiene (see p.39), and research pre-trip vaccination and malaria prophylactic requirements.**

The standard of **local healthcare** varies across the region, with Laos having the least advanced system (best to get across the border and go to a Thai hospital) and Singapore boasting world-class medical care. If you have a minor ailment, it's usually best to head for a pharmacy – most have a decent idea of how to treat common ailments and can provide many medicines without prescription. Otherwise, ask for the nearest doctor or hospital. Details of major hospitals are given throughout the Guide and there's an overview of local healthcare under "Medical care and emergencies" in the introduction to each country. If you have a serious accident or illness, you may need to be evacuated home or to Singapore, so it's vital to arrange **health insurance** before you leave home.

When planning your trip, **visit a doctor** at least two months before you leave, to allow time to complete any recommended courses of vaccinations or anti-malarial tablets. For up-to-the-minute **information**, call the Travellers' Health phone lines or visit a travel clinic. In the UK, pick up the Department of Health's free publication, *Health Advice for Travellers*, available at the post office, or by calling ⓣ0800/555 777. The content of the booklet, which contains immunization advice, is available at ⓦwww.dh.gov.uk.

## GENERAL PRECAUTIONS

Bacteria thrive in the tropics, and the best way to combat them is to keep up standards of personal hygiene. Frequent **bathing** is essential and hands should be washed before eating, especially in countries where food is traditionally eaten with the hands. Cuts or scratches can become infected very easily and should be thoroughly cleaned, disinfected and bandaged to keep dirt out.

Ask locally before **swimming** in freshwater lakes and rivers, including the Mekong River, as tiny worms carrying diseases such as bilharzia infect some tracts of freshwater in Southeast Asia. The worm enters through the skin and may cause a high fever after some weeks, but the recognizable symptoms of stomach pain and blood in the urine only appear after the disease is established, which may take months or even years. At this point, some damage to internal organs may have occurred.

Many countries in Southeast Asia have significant **AIDS** problems. Condoms are available at pharmacies throughout Southeast Asia, though the quality is not always reliable: it's best to bring a supply with you, take special care with expiry dates and bear in mind that condoms don't last as long when kept in the heat. Blood transfusions, intravenous drug use, acupuncture, dentistry, tattooing and body piercing are also high-risk.

## INOCULATIONS

There are no compulsory vaccinations required for entry into any part of Southeast Asia, but health professionals strongly recommend that travellers to all Southeast Asian destinations get **inoculations** against the following common and debilitating diseases: typhoid, hepatitis A, tetanus and polio. In addition, you may be advised to have some of the following vaccinations, for example, if travelling during the rainy season or if planning to stay in remote rural areas: rabies, hepatitis B, Japanese encephalitis, diphtheria, meningitis and TB. If you're only going to Hong Kong and Macau, you may not have to get any inoculations. All shots should be recorded on an **International Certificate of Vaccination** and carried with your passport when travelling abroad; some immigration officials levy "fines" for those without a certificate. If you've been in an area infected with yellow fever during the fourteen days before your arrival in Southeast Asia, you will need a certificate of vaccination against the disease.

Some of the **illnesses** you can pick up in Southeast Asia may not show themselves immediately. If you become ill within a year of returning home, tell your doctor where you have been.

## MALARIA

The whole of Southeast Asia lies within a **malarial zone**, although in many urban and developed tourist areas there is little risk (see below). Most health professionals advise that travellers on a multi-country trip through Southeast Asia should take full precautions against malaria, which is a potentially fatal and very dangerous disease. Information regarding malaria is constantly being updated, so it's absolutely essential to get medical advice.

Malaria is caused by a parasite in the saliva of the anopheles mosquito that is passed into the human when bitten by the mosquito. There are many strains of the disease, and some are resistant to particular prophylactic drugs. The following are the most common anti-malarial tablets: chloroquine (Avloclor or Nivaquine) and proguanil (Paludrine), mefloquine (Lariam), doxycycline (Vibramycin) and Malarone™ (atovaquone-proguanil). The first three can be bought from pharmacies, but may have to be ordered in if you are going for a long trip, while the final three require a prescription from your doctor. All the malaria prevention medicines must be started before you travel, so make sure you visit the doctor or pharmacy in good time. Mefloquine has to be started two-and-a-half weeks before travel, chloroquine and proguanil should be started a week before, and Malarone and doxycycline one to two days before travelling. It's absolutely essential to finish your course of anti-malarial drugs, as there is some time delay between being bitten and the parasites emerging into the blood: taking all your medicine will cover the incubation time, eliminating the risk of infection.

None of the drugs is one hundred percent effective, and it is equally important for the **prevention of malaria** to stop the

### MALARIAL OR NOT?

Areas infected with malaria are constantly changing, so find out what the current situation is from your doctor before travelling.

**Brunei** Extremely low malarial risk.

**Cambodia** Malarial in all forested and hilly rural areas, in Siem Reap and along the Thai and Laos borders. Phnom Penh, Sihanoukville and Battambang are malaria-free.

**Hong Kong and Macau** Extremely low malarial risk.

**Indonesia** Malarial, except on Bali.

**Laos** Very malarial.

**Malaysia** Malarial but low risk on the Peninsula.

**Philippines** Malarial except on the majority of the Visayas Islands (except Romblon Island).

**Singapore** Extremely low malarial risk.

**Thailand** Generally low malaria risk, but very high risk along the Burma, Cambodia and Laos borders as well as northern Kanchanaburi province, and parts of Trat province (but low risk on Ko Chang).

**Vietnam** Malarial, but low risk in Hanoi, Ho Chi Minh City, the coast between them and the northern Red River Delta.

mosquitoes biting you. Mosquitoes are mainly active from dusk until dawn, and during this time you should wear trousers, long-sleeved shirts and socks and smother yourself and your clothes in mosquito repellent containing the chemical compound DEET: shops all over Southeast Asia stock it. DEET is strong stuff, and if you have sensitive skin a natural alternative is citronella (sold as Mosi-guard in the UK), made from a blend of eucalyptus oils. At night, you should either sleep under a mosquito net sprayed with DEET or in a room with screens across the windows. Accommodation in tourist spots nearly always provides screens or a net (check both for holes), but if you're planning to go way off the beaten track, you can either take a net with you or buy one locally from department stores in capital cities. Mosquito coils – widely available in Southeast Asia – also help keep the insects at bay.

The **symptoms** of malaria are fever, headache and shivering, similar to a severe dose of flu and often coming in cycles, but a lot of people have additional symptoms. You will need a blood test to confirm the illness, and the doctor will prescribe the most effective treatment locally. If you develop flu-like symptoms any time up to a year after returning home, you should inform a doctor and ask for a blood test.

## DENGUE FEVER

A nasty disease that's becoming more and more widespread is **dengue fever**, a virus carried by mosquitoes, which bite day and night. There's no vaccine or tablet available to prevent the illness, which causes fever, headache and joint and muscle pains, as well as possible internal bleeding and circulatory-system failure. There is no specific drug to cure it, and the only treatment is lots of rest, liquids and Panadol (or any other acetaminophen painkiller, *not* aspirin, which can increase chances of haemorrhaging), though more serious cases may require hospitalization. It is vital to get an early medical diagnosis and get treatment.

## HEAT PROBLEMS

Travellers who are unused to tropical climates regularly suffer from **sunburn** and **dehydration**. The important thing is to make sure that you drink enough water and to limit your exposure to the sun. As you sweat in the heat you lose salt, so you may want to add some extra to your food. A more serious result of the heat is **heatstroke**, indicated by high temperature, dry red skin and a fast, erratic pulse. As an emergency measure, try to cool the patient off by covering them in sheets or sarongs soaked in cold water and turn the fan on them; they may need to go to hospital, though. **Heat rashes**, **prickly heat**, and **fungal infections** are also common: wear loose cotton clothing, dry yourself carefully after bathing and use medicated talcum powder.

## STOMACH PROBLEMS

If you travel in Asia for an extended period of time, you are likely to come down with some kind of stomach bug. For most, this is just a case of **diarrhoea**, caught through bad hygiene, or unfamiliar or affected food, and is generally over in a couple of days; **dehydration** is one of the main concerns if you have diarrhoea, so rehydration salts dissolved in clean water provide the best treatment. **Gastroenteritis** is a more extreme version, but can still be cured with the same blend of rest and rehydration. You should be able to find a local brand of **rehydration salts** in pharmacies in most Southeast Asian towns, but you can also make up your own by mixing three teaspoons of sugar and one of salt to a litre of water. You will need to drink as much as three litres a day to stave off dehydration. Eat non-spicy, non-greasy **foods**, such as young coconut, unbuttered toast, rice, bananas and noodles, and steer away from alcohol, coffee, milk and most fruits. Since diarrhoea purges the body of the bugs, taking blocking **medicines** such as Imodium is not recommended unless you have to travel.

The next step up from gastroenteritis is **dysentery**, diagnosable from blood and mucus in the (often blackened) stool. Dysentery is either amoebic or bacillary, with the latter characterized by high fever and vomiting. Serious attacks will require antibiotics, and hospitalisation.

**Giardia** can be diagnosed by foul-smelling farts and burps, abdominal distension, evil-smelling stools that float, and diarrhoea without blood or pus. Don't be over-eager with your diagnosis though, and treat it as normal diarrhoea for at least 24 hours before resorting to flagyl antibiotics.

## VIRUSES

The frequency with which travellers suffer from these infectious diseases makes a very strong case for inoculation (see p.41). **Hepatitis A** or **E** is a waterborne viral infection spread through water and food. It causes jaundice, loss of appetite, and nausea and can leave you feeling wiped out for months. Seek immediate medical help if you think you may have contracted hepatitis. The Havrix vaccination lasts for several years, provided you have a booster the year after your first jabs. **Hepatitis B** is transmitted by bodily fluids, during unprotected sex or by intravenous drug use.

**Cholera** and **typhoid** are generally spread when communities rely on sparse water supplies. The initial symptoms of cholera are a sudden onset of watery, but painless diarrhoea. Later, nausea, vomiting and muscle cramps set in. Cholera can be fatal if adequate fluid intake is not maintained. Copious amounts of liquids, including oral rehydration solution, should be consumed and medical treatment should be sought immediately. Like cholera, typhoid is also spread in small, localized epidemics. Symptoms can vary widely, but generally include headaches, fever and constipation, followed by diarrhoea. Vaccination against typhoid is recommended for all travellers to Southeast Asia.

## BITES AND STINGS

The most common irritations for travellers come from tiny pests whose most serious evil is the danger of infection to or through the bitten area, so keep bites clean. **Fleas, lice** and **bed bugs** adore grimy sheets, so examine your bedding carefully, air and beat the offending articles and then coat yourself liberally in insect repellent. Scabies, which cause severe itching by burrowing under the skin and laying eggs, might affect travellers who stay overnight in hilltribe villages.

**Ticks** are nasty pea-shaped bloodsuckers that attach themselves to you if you walk through long grass. A dab of petrol, alcohol, tiger balm or insect repellent, or a lit cigarette, should make them let loose and drop off; whatever you do, don't pull them off, as their heads can remain under the skin, and cause infection. Bloodsucking **leeches** can be a problem in the jungle and in fresh water. Get rid of them by rubbing them with salt, though anti-tick treatments also work. Apply **DEET** to the tops of your boots and around the lace-holes.

Southeast Asia has many species of both land and sea **snakes**, so wear boots and socks when hiking. If **bitten**, the number one rule is not to panic. Stay still in order to slow the venom's entry into the bloodstream. Wash and disinfect the wound, apply a pressure bandage as tightly as you would for a sprain, splint the affected limb, keep it below the level of the heart and get to hospital as soon as possible. **Scorpion** stings are very painful but usually not fatal; swelling usually disappears after a few hours.

If stung by a **jellyfish**, the priority treatment is to remove the fragments of tentacles from the skin – without causing further discharge of poison – which is easiest done by applying vinegar to deactivate the stinging capsules. The best way to minimize the risk of stepping on the toxic spines of sea urchins, sting rays and stone fish is to wear thick-soled shoes, though these cannot provide total protection; sea-urchin spikes should be removed after softening the skin with a special ointment (likely to be Tiger Balm), though some people recommend applying urine to help dissolve the spines; for sting-ray and stone-fish stings, alleviate the pain by immersing the wound in very hot water – just under 50°C – while waiting for help.

**Rabies** is transmitted to humans by the bite of infected animals; **tetanus** is an additional danger from such bites. All animals should be treated with caution, particularly monkeys, cats and dogs. Be extremely cautious with wild animals that seem inexplicably tame, as this can be a symptom. If you do get bitten, scrub the wound with a strong antiseptic and then alcohol and get to a hospital as soon as possible. Do not attempt to close the wound. The incubation period for the disease can be as much as a year or as little as a few days; once the disease has taken hold, it will be fatal.

## Medical resources for travellers

### UK and Ireland

**Hospital for Tropical Diseases Travel Clinic** ⓣ0845/155 5000 or ⓣ020/7387 4411, ⓦwww.thehtd.org.
**MASTA (Medical Advisory Service for Travellers Abroad)** ⓦwww.masta-travel-health.com or ⓣ0870/606 2782 for the nearest clinic.
**Travel Medicine Services** ⓣ028/9031 5220.
**Tropical Medical Bureau** Republic of Ireland ⓣ1850/487 674, ⓦwww.tmb.ie.

### US and Canada

**CDC** ⓣ1-800/311-3435, ⓦwwwn.cdc.gov/travel. Official US government travel health site.
**International Society for Travel Medicine** ⓣ1-770/736-7060, ⓦwww.istm.org. Has a full list of travel health clinics.
**Canadian Society for International Health** ⓣ613/241-5785, ⓦwww.csih.org. Extensive list of travel health centres.

### Australia, New Zealand and South Africa

**Travellers' Medical and Vaccination Centre** ⓦwww.tmvc.com.au, ⓣ1300/658 844. Lists travel clinics in Australia, New Zealand and South Africa.

# Culture and etiquette

**Although the peoples of Southeast Asia come from a huge variety of ethnic backgrounds and practise a spread of religions, they share many social practices and taboos, many unfamiliar to Westerners. You will get a much friendlier reception if you do your best to be sensitive to local morals, particularly when it comes to dress. Social and religious customs specific to each country are dealt with in the relevant chapters.**

## DRESS

Appearance is very important in Southeast Asian society, and dressing neatly is akin to showing respect. Clothing – or the lack of it – is what bothers Southeast Asians most about tourist behaviour. You need to **dress modestly** whenever you are outside a tourist resort, and in particular when entering religious buildings and people's homes, and when dealing with people in authority, especially when applying for visa extensions. For women, that means below-knee-length skirts or trousers, a bra and sleeved tops; for men, long trousers. "Immodest" clothing includes thongs, shorts, vests, and anything that leaves you with bare shoulders. Most Southeast Asian people find **topless** and nude bathing extremely unpalatable. If you wash your own clothes, hang out your **underwear** discreetly.

## VISITING TEMPLES, MOSQUES AND SHRINES

Besides dressing conservatively, always take your **shoes** off when entering temples, pagodas and mosques. **Monks** are forbidden to have any close contact with women, which means, as a female, you mustn't sit or stand next to a monk, even on a bus, nor brush against his robes, or hand objects directly to him. When giving something to a monk, the object should be placed on a nearby table or passed to a layman who will then hand it to the monk. All **Buddha images** are sacred, and should never be clambered over. When sitting on the floor of a monastery building that has a Buddha image, never point your feet in the direction of the image.

When visiting a **mosque**, women must cover their shoulders and possibly their heads as well (bring a scarf or shawl).

Many religions prohibit **women** from engaging in certain activities – or even entering a place of worship – during menstruation. If attending a **religious festival**, find out beforehand whether a dress code applies.

### SOCIAL PRACTICES AND TABOOS

In Buddhist, Islamic and Hindu cultures, various parts of the body are accorded a particular status. The **head** is considered the most sacred part of the body and the **feet** the most unclean. This means that it's very rude to touch another person's head – even to affectionately ruffle a child's hair – or to point your feet either at a human being or at a sacred image. Be careful not to step over any part of people who are sitting or lying on the floor (or the deck of a boat), as this is also considered rude. If you do accidentally kick or brush someone with your feet, apologize immediately and smile as you do so.

**Public displays** of sexual affection like kissing or cuddling are frowned upon across the region, though friends (rather than lovers) of the same sex often hold hands or hug in public.

Most Asians dislike **confrontational behaviour**, such as arguing or shouting, and will rarely show irritation of any kind.

## Religion

**Religion pervades every aspect of life in most Southeast Asian communities, dictating social practices to a much greater extent than in the West. All the world's major faiths are represented in the region, but characteristic across much of Southeast Asia is the syncretic nature of belief, so that many Buddhists, Hindus and Muslims incorporate animist rituals into their daily devotions as well as occasional elements of other major faiths.**

### BUDDHISM

Buddhists follow the teachings of Gautama Buddha who, in his five-hundredth incarnation, was born in present-day Nepal as **Prince Gautama Siddhartha**, to a wealthy family some time during the sixth century BC. At an early age, Siddhartha renounced his life of luxury to seek the ultimate deliverance from worldly suffering and strive to reach **Nirvana**, an indefinable, blissful state. After several years he attained enlightenment and then devoted the rest of his life to teaching the Middle Way that leads to Nirvana.

His **philosophy** built on the Hindu theory of perpetual reincarnation in the pursuit of perfection, introducing the notion that desire is the root cause of all suffering and can be extinguished only by following the eightfold path or Middle Way. This **Middle Way** is a highly moral mode of life that encourages compassion and moderation and eschews self-indulgence and anti-social behaviour. But the key is an acknowledgement that the physical world is impermanent and ever-changing, and that all things – including the self – are therefore not worth craving. Only by pursuing a condition of complete detachment can human beings transcend earthly suffering.

In practice, most Buddhists aim only to be **reborn** higher up the incarnation scale rather than set their sights on Nirvana. Each reincarnation marks a move up a kind of ladder, with animals at the bottom, women figuring lower down than men, and monks coming at the top. The rank of the reincarnation is directly related to the good and bad actions performed in the previous life, which accumulate to determine one's **karma** or destiny – hence the obsession with **"making merit"**. Merit-making can be done in all sorts of ways, including giving alms to a monk or, for a man, becoming a monk for a short period.

### Schools of Buddhism

After the Buddha passed into Nirvana in 543 BC, his doctrine spread relatively quickly across India. His teachings, the Tripitaka, were written down in the Pali language and became known as the **Theravada School of Buddhism** or "The Doctrine of the Elders". Theravada is an ascetic form of Buddhism, based on the principle that each individual is wholly responsible for his or her own accumulation of merit or sin and subsequent enlightenment; it is prevalent in **Thailand**, **Laos** and **Cambodia** as well as in Sri Lanka and Burma.

The other main school of Buddhism practised in Southeast Asia is **Mahayana Buddhism**, which is current in **Vietnam**, and in **ethnic Chinese communities** throughout the region, as well as in China itself, and in Japan and Korea. The ideological rift between the Theravada and Mahayana Buddhists is as vast as the one that divides Catholicism and Protestantism. Mahayana Buddhism attempts to make Buddhism more accessible to the average devotee, easing the struggle towards enlightenment with a pantheon of Buddhist saints or bodhisattva who have postponed their own entry into Nirvana in order to work for the salvation of all humanity.

## CHINESE RELIGIONS

The **Chinese communities** of Singapore, Hong Kong, Macau, Malaysia, Vietnam and Thailand generally adhere to a system of belief that fuses Mahayana Buddhist, Taoist and Confucianist tenets, alongside the all-important ancestor worship.

### Ancestor worship

One of the oldest cults practised among both city dwellers and hilltribes people who migrated into Southeast Asia from China is that of **ancestor worship**, based on the fundamental principles of filial piety and of obligation to the past, present and future generations. Practices vary, but all believe that the spirits of deceased ancestors have the ability to affect the lives of their living descendants, rewarding those who remember them with offerings, but causing upset if neglected. At funerals and subsequent anniversaries, paper money and other **votive offerings** are burnt, and special food is regularly placed on the ancestral altar.

### Confucianism

The teachings of **Confucius** provide a guiding set of moral principles based on piety, loyalty, humanitarianism and familial devotion, which permeate every aspect of Chinese life. Confucius is the Latinized name of K'ung-Fu-Tzu, who was born into a minor aristocratic family in China in 551 BC and worked for many years as a court official. At the age of 50, he set off around the country to spread his ideas on social and political reform. His central tenet was the importance of **correct behaviour**, namely selflessness, respectfulness and non-violence, and loyal service, reinforced by ceremonial rites and frequent offerings to heaven and to the ancestors.

After the death of Confucius in 478 BC, the doctrine was developed by his disciples, and by the first century AD, Confucianism had absorbed elements of Taoism and evolved into a **state ideology** whereby kings ruled under the Mandate of Heaven. Social stability was maintained through a fixed hierarchy of relationships encapsulated in the notion of filial piety. Thus children must obey their parents without question, wives their husbands, students their teacher, and subjects their ruler.

### Taosim

Taoism is based on the **Tao-te-ching**, the "Book of the Way", traditionally attributed to **Lao Tzu** ("Old Master"), who is thought to have lived in China in the sixth century BC. A philosophical movement, it advocates that people follow a central path or truth, known as Tao or "The Way", and cultivate an understanding of the nature of things. The Tao emphasizes effortless action, intuition and spontaneity; it cannot be taught, nor can it be expressed in words, but can be embraced by virtuous behaviour. Central to the Tao is the duality inherent in nature, a tension of complimentary opposites defined as **yin** and **yang**, the female and male principles. Harmony is the balance between the two, and experiencing that harmony is the Tao.

In its pure form Taoism has no gods, but in the first century AD it corrupted into an organized religion venerating a deified Lao Tzu, and developed highly complex rituals. The vast, eclectic pantheon of Taoist **gods** is presided over by the Jade Emperor, who is assisted by the southern star, the north star, and the God of the Hearth. Then there is a collection of immortals, genies and guardian deities, including legendary and historic warriors, statesmen, and scholars. Confucius is also honoured as a Taoist saint.

## ISLAM

**Islam** is the youngest of all the major religions, and in Southeast Asia is practised mainly in **Indonesia**, **Malaysia**, **Singapore** and **Brunei**. It was founded by **Mohammed** (570–630AD), a merchant from Mecca in Arabia, who began, at the age of 40, to receive messages from Allah (God). On these revelations Mohammed began to build a new religion: Islam or "Submission", as the faith required people to submit to God's will. Islam quickly gained in popularity not least because its revolutionary concepts of equality in subordination to Allah freed people from the feudal Hindu caste system that had previously dominated parts of the region.

The Islamic religion is founded on the **Five Pillars**, the essential tenets revealed by Allah to Mohammed and collected in the **Koran**, the holy book that Mohammed dictated before he died. The first is that all Muslims should profess their faith in Allah with the phrase "There is no God but Allah and Mohammed is his prophet". The act of praying is the second pillar. Five daily prayers can be done anywhere, though Muslims should always face Mecca when praying, cover the head, and ritually wash feet and hands. The third pillar demands that the faithful should always give a percentage of their income to charity, whilst the fourth states that all Muslims must observe the fasting month of **Ramadan**. This is the ninth month of the Muslim lunar calendar, when the majority of Muslims fast from the break of dawn to dusk, and also abstain from drinking and smoking. The reason for the fast is to intensify awareness of the plight of the poor. The fifth pillar demands that every Muslim should make a pilgrimage to Mecca at least once in their lifetime.

## HINDUISM

**Hinduism** was introduced to Southeast Asia by Indian traders more than a thousand years ago, and spread across the region by the Khmers of Cambodia who left a string of magnificent castle-temples throughout northeast Thailand, Laos and most strikingly at Angkor in Cambodia. The most active contemporary Hindu communities live in **Singapore** and **Malaysia**, and the Indonesian island of **Bali** is also a very vibrant, if idiosyncratic, Hindu enclave.

Central to Hinduism is the belief that life is a series of reincarnations that eventually leads to spiritual release. The aim of every Hindu is to attain **enlightenment** (moksa), which brings with it the union of the individual and the divine, and liberation from the painful cycle of death and rebirth. Moksa is only attainable by pure souls, and can take hundreds of lifetimes to achieve. Hindus believe that everybody is reincarnated according to their **karma**, this being a kind of account book that registers all the good and bad deeds performed in the past lives of a soul. Karma is closely bound up with caste and the notion that an individual should accept rather than challenge their destiny.

A whole variety of **deities** are worshipped, the most ubiquitous being Brahma, Vishnu and Shiva. **Brahma** is the Creator, represented by the colour red and often depicted riding on a bull. As the Preserver, **Vishnu** is associated with life-giving waters; he rides the garuda (half-man, half-bird) and is honoured by the colour black. Vishnu also has several avatars, including Buddha – a neat way of incorporating Buddhist elements into the Hindu faith – and Rama, hero of the Ramayana story. **Siwa**, the Destroyer or, more accurately, the Dissolver, is associated with death and rebirth, and with the colour white. He is sometimes represented as a phallic pillar or lingam. He is the father of the elephant-headed deity **Ganesh**, generally worshipped as the remover of obstacles.

## ANIMISM

**Animism** is the belief that all living things – including plants and trees – and some non-living natural features, such as rocks and waterfalls, have **spirits**. It is practised right across Southeast Asia, by everyone from the Dayaks of Sarawak and the hilltribes of Laos to the citydwellers of Bangkok and Singapore, though rituals and beliefs vary significantly. As with Hinduism, the animistic faiths teach that it is necessary to live in harmony with the spirits; disturb this harmonious balance, by upsetting a spirit for example, and you risk bringing misfortune upon yourself, your household or your village. For this reason, animists consult, or at least consider, the spirits before almost everything they do, and you'll often see small **offerings** of flowers or food left by a tree or river to appease the spirits that live within.

# Travel essentials

## COSTS

Your **daily budget** in Southeast Asia depends both on where you're travelling and on how comfortable you want to be. You can survive on £7/US$15 a day in most parts of Laos, Indonesia, Malaysia, Thailand and Vietnam, on around £9/$18 a day in Cambodia, on £10/$20 in the Philippines, on £12/$23 in Hong Kong and Brunei, and on £18/$32 in Singapore, but for this money you'll be sleeping in very basic accommodation, eating at simple food stalls, and travelling on local non-a/c buses. In some countries, prices for tourist accommodation and foreigners' restaurants are quoted in **US dollars**, though the local equivalent is always acceptable.

Travellers soon get so used to the low cost of living in Southeast Asia that they start **bargaining** at every available opportunity, much as local people do. Most buyers start their counterbid at about 25 percent of the vendor's opening price, and the bartering continues from there. But never forget that the few pennies you're making such a fuss over will go a lot further in a local person's hands than in your own.

**Price tiering** exists in some parts of Southeast Asia, with foreigners paying more

### PRICES

At the beginning of each chapter you'll find a guide to "rough costs" including food, accommodation and travel. Prices are quoted in US dollars. Within the chapter itself prices are quoted either in local currency, or dollars or euros, if these are the currencies in which prices are quoted on the ground.

than locals for public transport, hotels, and entry fees to museums and historical sites. Remember prices vary within individual countries, especially when you enter more remote areas.

Very few **student discounts** are offered on entry prices,

**Tipping** isn't a Southeast Asian custom, although some upmarket restaurants expect a gratuity, and most expensive hotels add service taxes.

## CRIME AND PERSONAL SAFETY

For the most part, travelling in Southeast Asia is safe and unthreatening, though, as in any unfamiliar environment, you should keep your wits about you. The most common hazard is opportunistic theft, which can easily be avoided with a few sensible precautions. Occasionally, political trouble flares in the region, as it has done recently in parts of Indonesia, so before you travel you may want to check the official government advice on international troublespots (see box below). Most experienced travellers find this official advice less helpful than that offered by other travellers – the online travellers' forums listed on p.56 are useful. In some countries, there are specific year-round dangers such as banditry (parts of Laos), kidnapping (southern Philippines), and unexploded ordnance (Laos, Cambodia, Vietnam); details of these and how to avoid them are described in the introduction to the relevant country.

### General precautions

As a tourist, you are an obvious target for opportunistic **thieves** (who may include your fellow travellers), so don't flash expensive cameras or watches around. Carry traveller's cheques, cash and important documents (airline tickets, credit cards and passport) under your clothing in a **money belt** – the all-too-obvious bum-bags are easy to cut off in a crowd. It's a good idea to keep $100 cash, photocopies of the relevant pages of your passport, insurance details and travellers' cheque receipts separate from the rest of your valuables.

Ensure that **luggage** is lockable (you can buy gadgets to lock backpacks), and never keep anything important in outer pockets. A **padlock** and chain, or a cable lock, is useful for doors and windows at inexpensive guesthouses and beach bungalows, and for securing your pack on **buses**, where you're often separated from your belongings. If your pack is on the top of the bus, make sure it is attached securely, and keep an eye on it whenever the bus pulls into a bus station. Be especially aware of pickpockets on buses, who usually operate in pairs: one will distract you while another does the job. On **trains**, either cable lock your pack or put it under the bottom bench-seat, out of public view. Be wary of accepting food and drink from strangers on long overnight bus or train journeys: it may be drugged so as to knock you out while your bags are stolen.

### OFFICIAL ADVICE ON INTERNATIONAL TROUBLESPOTS

The following sites provide useful advice on travelling in countries that are considered unstable or unsafe for foreigners.

**Australian Department of Foreign Affairs**

Ⓦ www.dfat.gov.au. Advice and reports on unstable countries and regions.

**British Foreign and Commonwealth Office**

Ⓦ www.fco.gov.uk. Constantly updated advice for travellers on circumstances affecting safety in over 130 countries.

**Canadian Foreign Affairs Department**

Ⓦ www.fac-aec.gc.ca. Country-by-country travel advisories.

**US State Department Travel Advisories**

Ⓦ travel.state.gov/travel/warnings.html. Website providing "consular information sheets" detailing the dangers of travelling in most countries of the world.

Some guesthouses and hotels have **safe-deposit boxes** or lockers, which solve the problem of what to do with your valuables while you go swimming. The safest lockers are those that require your own padlock, as valuables sometimes get lifted by hotel staff. Padlock your luggage when leaving it in hotel or guesthouse rooms.

Violent crime against tourists is not common in Southeast Asia, but it does occur. Obvious precautions include securing locks at night, and not travelling alone at night in an unlicensed taxi, tuk-tuk or rickshaw. Think carefully about motorbiking alone in sparsely inhabited and politically sensitive border regions. If you're going hiking on your own for a day, inform hotel staff of your route, so they can look for you if you don't return when planned.

### Con-artists and scams

**Con-artists** try their luck with tourists, but are usually fairly easy to spot. Always treat **touts** with suspicion – if they offer to take you to a great guesthouse/jewellery shop/untouristed village, you can be sure there'll be a huge commission in it for them, and you may end up being taken somewhere against your will. A variation on this theme involves taxi drivers assuring you that a major sight is closed for the day, so encouraging you to go with them on their own special tour.

Some, but by no means all, **travel agencies** in the backpackers' centres of Southeast Asia are fly-by-night operations. Although it's not necessarily incriminating if a travel agent's office seems to be the proverbial hole in the wall, it may be a good idea to reject those that look too temporary in favour of something permanent and thriving. In Vietnam in particular travel agents and guesthouses will copy the name of a successful and reputable company, so always double-check the address to check it is actually the place that's recommended.

### Reporting a crime

If you are a victim of theft or violent crime, you'll need a **police report** for insurance purposes. Try to take someone along with you to the police station to translate, though police will generally do their best to find an English speaker. Allow plenty of time for any involvement with the police, whose offices often wallow in bureaucracy; you may also be charged "administration fees" for enlisting their help, the cost of which is open to sensitive negotiations. You may also want to contact your **embassy** – see the "Directory" section of the nearest capital city for contact numbers. In the case of a medical emergency, you will also need to alert your **insurance company**.

### Drugs

**Drugs** penalties are tough throughout the region – in many countries there's even the possibility of being sentenced to death – and you won't get any sympathy from consular officials. Beware of drug scams: either being shopped by a dealer or having substances slipped into your luggage. If you are arrested, or end up on the wrong side of the law for whatever reason, you should ring the consular officer at your embassy immediately.

## TRAVELLERS WITH DISABILITIES

Aside from Hong Kong and Singapore, which have wheelchair-accessible public transport, most Southeast Asian countries make few provisions for people with disabilities. Pavements are usually high, uneven, and lacking dropped kerbs, and public transport is not wheelchair-friendly. On the positive side, however, most disabled travellers report that help is never in short supply, and wheelchair users with collapsible chairs may be able to take cycle rickshaws and tuk-tuks, balancing their chair in front of them. Also, services in much of Southeast Asia are very inexpensive for Western travellers, so you should be able to afford to hire a car or minibus with driver for a few days, stay at better-equipped hotels, and even take some internal flights. You might also consider hiring a local tour guide to accompany you on sightseeing trips – a native speaker can facilitate access to temples and museums, or perhaps book a package holiday – see below for useful contacts. Carry a doctor's letter about any drug prescriptions with you when passing through airport customs, as this will ensure you don't get hauled up for narcotics transgressions.

### Contacts for travellers with disabilities

#### In the UK and Ireland

**Access Travel** ⓣ01942/888 844, ⓦwww.access-travel.co.uk. Flights, transfer and accommodation.

**Holiday Care** ⓣ0845 124 9971, ⓦwww.holidaycare.org.uk. Provides free lists of accessible accommodation abroad.

**Irish Wheelchair Association** ⓣ01/833 8241, ⓦwww.iwa.ie. Useful information provided about travelling abroad with a wheelchair.

#### In the USA and Canada

**Access-Able** ⓦwww.access-able.com. Online resource for travellers with disabilities.

**Directions Unlimited** ⓣ1-800/533-5343 or 914/241-1700. Tour operator specializing in custom tours for people with disabilities.

**Society for the Advancement of Travelers with Handicaps (SATH)** ⓣ212/447-7284, ⓦwww.sath.org. Organization that actively represents travellers with disabilities.

#### In Australia and New Zealand

**National Disability Services** ⓦwww.nds.org.au. Also offices nationwide.

**Disabled Persons Assembly** ⓣ04/801 9100, ⓦwww.dpa.org.nz. Resource centre with lists of travel agencies and tour operators for people with disabilities.

## ELECTRICITY

In most parts of the region, electricity is supplied at 220 volts, though socket type varies from country to country, so you should bring a travel plug with several adapters. Specific details are given in the Accommodation section in the introduction to each chapter. Power cuts are common, so bring a torch. ⓦwww.kropla.com is a useful website giving details of how to plug your lap-top in when abroad, and information about electrical systems in different countries.

## GAY AND LESBIAN TRAVELLERS

Homosexuality is broadly tolerated in Southeast Asia, if not exactly accepted. Thailand and the Philippines have the most public and developed **gay scene** in Southeast Asia, and gay travellers are generally made to feel welcome in both places. Indonesia, Cambodia, Laos and Vietnam all have less obvious gay communities, but they do exist and homosexuality is not illegal in any of them. The situation is less rosy in more conservative Malaysia, and travellers should be especially discreet – despite this, there are gay bars and meeting places in Kuala Lumpur and Penang. In Singapore, though there is a gay scene, sodomy is illegal, and the government gives mixed messages on its attitude to homosexuality.

The tourist-oriented gay sex industry is a tiny but highly visible part of Southeast Asia's gay scene, and is most obvious in Thailand where gay venues are often nothing more than brothels.

For detailed **information** on the gay scene in Southeast Asia, check out the **websites** ⓦwww.utopia-asia.com, which is an excellent resource for gay travellers to all regions of Asia and has travellers' reports on gay scenes across the region, and the website ⓦwww.fridae.com, which has gay city guides for the region.

### Contacts for gay and lesbian travellers

#### In the UK

**ⓦwww.gaytravel.co.uk** Online gay and lesbian travel agent.

**Madison Travel** ⓣ01273/202 532, ⓦwww.madisontravel.co.uk. Packages to gay- and lesbian-friendly destinations.

#### In the USA and Canada

**Damron Company** ⓣ1-800/462-6654 or 415/255-0404, ⓦwww.damron.com. Publisher of Damron Accommodations, which lists 1000 accommodations for gays and lesbians worldwide.

**International Gay & Lesbian Travel Association** ⓣ1-800/448-8550, ⓦwww.iglta.com. Keeps a list of gay- and lesbian-friendly travel agents and accommodation.

#### In Australia and New Zealand

**Gay and Lesbian Travel** ⓦwww.galta.com.au. Directory for gay and lesbian travel worldwide.

**Gay Travel** ⓦwww.gaytravel.com. Trip planning and bookings.

**Tearaway Travel** ⓣ03/9510 6344, ⓦwww.tearaway.com. Gay-specific travel agent.

## INSURANCE

Wherever you're travelling to in Southeast Asia, you must have adequate travel insurance. Before buying a policy, check that you're not already covered: student health coverage often extends during vacations and for one term beyond the date of last enrolment, and your home insurance policy may cover your possessions against loss or theft even when overseas.

Most policies exclude so-called dangerous sports unless an extra premium is paid: in Southeast Asia, this can mean scuba diving, white-water rafting and bungee jumping, though probably not trekking. Read the small print and benefits tables of prospective policies carefully.

You should definitely take **medical coverage** that includes both hospital treatment and medical evacuation; be sure to ask for the 24-hour medical emergency number. Keep all medical bills and, if possible, contact the insurance company before making any major outlay. Very few insurers will arrange on-the-spot payments in the event of a major expense – you will usually be reimbursed only after going home, so a credit/debit card could be useful to tide you over.

When securing **baggage cover**, make sure that the per-article limit will cover your most valuable possession. If you have anything stolen, get a copy of the police report, otherwise you won't be able to claim. Always make a note of the policy details and leave them with someone at home in case you lose the original.

## INTERNET

Internet access has become widespread in Southeast Asia, and there are now internet cafés in even the poorest nations such as Cambodia and Laos, while backpackers' areas such as Thanon Khao San in Bangkok and Kuta in Bali have dozens of them. Rates are nearly always very competitive. WiFi is also increasingly available in some guesthouses and malls in big cities.

## LAUNDRY

There are hardly any coin-operated laundries in Southeast Asia, but nearly every guesthouse and hotel will wash your clothes for a reasonable price.

## LEFT LUGGAGE

Every guesthouse and hotel will store luggage for you, though sometimes only if you make a reservation for your anticipated return; major train stations and airports also have left-luggage facilities.

## MAIL

Travellers can receive mail in any country in Southeast Asia via **poste restante**. The system is universally fairly efficient, but tends only to be available at the main post office in cities and backpackers' centres, not in small towns and villages. Most post offices hold letters for a maximum of one month, though some hold them for up to three, and others seem to hold them forever. Mail should be addressed: Name (family name underlined or capitalized), Poste Restante, GPO, Town or City, Country. It will be filed by family name, though it's always wise to check under your

### ROUGH GUIDES TRAVEL INSURANCE

Rough Guides has teamed up with Columbus Direct to offer you **travel insurance** that can be tailored to suit your needs. Products include a low-cost **backpacker** option for long stays; a **short break** option for city getaways; a typical **holiday package** option; and others. There are also annual **multi-trip** policies for those who travel regularly. Different sports and activities (trekking, skiing, etc) can be usually be covered if required.

See our website (ⓦwww.roughguides.com/website/shop) for eligibility and purchasing options. Alternatively, UK residents should call ⓣ0870/033 9988; Australians should call ⓣ1300/669 999 and New Zealanders should call ⓣ0800/55 9911. All other nationalities should call ⓣ+44 870/890 2843.

first initial as well. To collect mail, you'll need to show your passport and may have to pay a tiny fee. For a small fee, you can arrange for poste restante mail to be forwarded from one GPO to another, though you usually have to apply for this service in person.

## MONEY

The easiest way to carry your money is in the form of plastic; ATMs are fairly widespread, except in parts of Cambodia and Laos (where ATMs only accept MasterCard). All banks charge a handling fee of about 1.5 percent per transaction when you use your debit card at overseas ATMs.

Top hotels and a growing number of restaurants, shops and travel agents accept American Express, Visa, MasterCard and Diners Club credit cards. However, surcharging of up to five percent is rife, and theft and forgery are major industries – always demand the carbon copies and destroy them immediately. It's sensible not to rely on plastic alone; you may want to consider **traveller's cheques** in US dollars, UK pound sterling, euro or the local currency. Hold on to the **receipt** (or proof of purchase), as some exchange places require seeing it before cashing your cheques. Most **international airports** have exchange counters, which is useful, as you can't always buy Southeast Asian currencies before leaving home. Tourist centres also have convenient **exchange counters** where rates can compare favourably with those offered by the banks, but always establish any **commission** first – the places that display promising rates may charge a hefty fee, and be careful of some common scams, including by miscalculating amounts (especially when there are lots of zeros involved), using a rigged calculator, folding over notes to make the amount look twice as great, and removing a pile of notes after the money's been counted.

### Wiring money

**Wiring money** through a specialist agent is a fast but expensive way to send and receive money abroad. The money wired should be available for collection, usually in local currency, from the company's local agent within twenty minutes of being sent via Western Union or MoneyGram; both charge on a sliding scale, so sending larger amounts of cash is better value.

**American Express MoneyGram** UK and Republic of Ireland ⓣ0800/6663 9472, US and Canada ⓣ1-800/926-9400, Australia ⓣ1800/230 100, New Zealand ⓣ09/379 8243 or 0800/262 263, ⓦwww.moneygram.com.

**Western Union** UK ⓣ0800/833 833, Republic of Ireland ⓣ1800/395 395, US and Canada ⓣ1-800/325-6000, Australia ⓣ1800/649 565, New Zealand ⓣ09/270 0050, ⓦwww.westernunion.com.

## PHONES

You should be able to **phone** home from any city or large town in Southeast Asia. One of the most convenient ways of phoning home from abroad is over the internet, with a provider such as Yahoo or Skype, enabling you to make internet calls at the price of a local call, and free computer to computer calls. See ⓦwww.voice.yahoo.com or ⓦwww.skype.com for details. Alternatively, though much more expensive, take a **telephone chargecard** from your phone company back home, to charge calls to your account.

In most places national telecommunications offices or post offices tend to charge less than private telephone offices and guesthouses for international calls. In phone centres where there's no facility for reverse-charge calls, you can almost always get a "**call-back**". Ask the operator for a minimum (one-minute) call abroad and get the phone number of the place you're calling from; you can then be called back directly at the phone centre.

### Mobile phones

If you want to use your **mobile phone** in Southeast Asia, you'll need to check with your phone provider whether it will work abroad, and what the call charges are. Generally speaking, UK, Australian and New Zealand mobiles should work fine in Southeast Asia. However, with US mobile phones only tri-band models are likely to work outside the States.

You are likely to be charged extra for incoming calls when abroad, as the people

## IDD CODES

To phone abroad from the following countries, you must first dial the international access code, then the IDD country code, then the area code (usually without the first zero), then the phone number:

**International access codes when dialling from:**

Australia ⓣ0011
Brunei ⓣ00
Cambodia ⓣ001
Canada ⓣ011
Hong Kong ⓣ001
Indonesia ⓣ001
Ireland ⓣ00
Laos ⓣ00
Macau ⓣ00
Malaysia ⓣ00
New Zealand ⓣ00
Northern Ireland ⓣ048
Philippines ⓣ00
Singapore ⓣ001
Thailand ⓣ001
UK ⓣ00
USA ⓣ011
Vietnam ⓣ00

**IDD country codes**

Australia ⓣ61
Brunei ⓣ673
Cambodia ⓣ855
Canada ⓣ1
Hong Kong ⓣ852
Indonesia ⓣ62
Ireland ⓣ353
Laos ⓣ856
Macau ⓣ853
Malaysia ⓣ60
New Zealand ⓣ64
The Philippines ⓣ63
Singapore ⓣ65
Thailand ⓣ66
UK ⓣ44
USA ⓣ1
Vietnam ⓣ84

calling you will be paying the usual rate. For further information about using your phone abroad, check out ⓦwww.telecomsadvice.org.uk/features/using_your_mobile_abroad.htm. If you're in the country for a while it's often worth buying a local pre-pay SIM card.

# TOURIST INFORMATION

Although some Southeast Asian countries have no dedicated tourist information offices abroad, there's plenty of information available on the internet.

## Tourist offices abroad

Local tourist information services are described in the introduction to each chapter.

**Brunei** contact your nearest Bruneian embassy or consulate (see p.56).

**Cambodia** See ⓦwww.mot.gov.kh. Tourist offices are developing, but slowly.

**Hong Kong and Macau** ⓦwww.discoverhongkong.com. Australia and New Zealand ⓣ02/9283 3083; Canada ⓣ416/599-6636; UK and Ireland ⓣ020/7533 7100; USA ⓦwww.discoverhongkong.com/usa, New York ⓣ212/421-3382; Los Angeles ⓣ310/208-4582. ⓦwww.macautourism.gov.mo; Australia ⓣ02/9264 1488; New Zealand ⓣ09/308 5206; UK and Ireland ⓣ020/8877 4517.

**Indonesia** ⓦwww.tourismindonesia.com; contact the relevant consulate or embassy (see p.57).

**Laos** A few, basic tourist offices abroad. Attempting to contact and extract information from Lao embassies often results in frustration. The most useful information is ⓦwww.visit-laos.com.

**Malaysia** ⓦwww.tourism.gov.my; Australia ⓣ02/9299 4441, Perth ⓣ09/481 0400; Canada ⓣ604/689-8899; New Zealand contact the embassy (see p.57); UK and Ireland ⓣ020/7930 7932; USA Los Angeles ⓣ323/689-9702; New York ⓣ212/754-1114.

**The Philippines** ⓦwww.wowphilippines.com.ph; Australia ⓣ02/9283 0711; Canada ⓣ416/924-3569; New Zealand contact the Sydney office (see above) or the consulate in Auckland (see p.57); UK and Ireland ⓣ020/7835 1100; USA Chicago, IL ⓣ312/782-2475; New York ⓣ212/575-7915; San Francisco ⓣ415/956-4060.

**Singapore** ⓦwww.visitsingapore.com; Australia ⓣ02/9290 2888; Canada contact nearest office in the USA (see below); New Zealand ⓣ09/262 3393; UK and Ireland ⓣ020/7437 0033; USA Los Angeles ⓣ323/677-0808; New York ⓣ212/302-4861.

**Thailand** ⓦwww.tourismthailand.org; Australia ⓣ02/9247 7549; Canada contact nearest office in the USA (see below); New Zealand ⓣ09/358 1191; UK and Ireland ⓣ020/7499 7679; recorded information available on ⓣ0870/900 2007; USA Los Angeles ⓣ323/382-2353; New York ⓣ212/432-0433.

**Vietnam** ⓦwww.vietnamtourism.com; contact the relevant embassy (see opposite)

### Useful websites

For country specific websites see the relevant country introduction.

**AsianDiver** ⓦwww.asiandiver.com. Online version of the divers' magazine, with good coverage of Southeast Asia's diving sites, including recommendations and firsthand diving stories.

**Internet Travel Information Service** ⓦwww.itisnet.com. Specifically aimed at budget travellers, this site is a really useful resource of current info on many Southeast Asian countries, regularly updated by travellers and researchers. Up-to-the-minute info on airfares, border crossings, visa requirements and hotels.

**Open Directory Project** ⓦwww.dmoz.org/Recreation/Travel. Scores of backpacker-oriented links, including a lot of Asia-specific ones, plus travelogues and message boards.

**Tales of Asia** ⓦwww.talesofasia.com. Reliable practical advice on border crossings, overland travel and assorted off-road adventures; mainly Cambodia, though it covers several other countries as well.

**Travel-Library.com** ⓦwww.travel-library.com. Great site, which has lively pieces on dozens of travel topics, from the budget travellers' guide to sleeping in airports to how to travel light. Good links too.

**Tourism Concern** ⓦwww.tourismconcern.org.uk. Website of the British organization that campaigns for responsible tourism. Plenty of useful links to politically and environmentally aware organizations across the world, and a particularly good section on the politics of tourism in Burma.

### Travellers' forums

**Rough Guides** ⓦwww.roughguides.com. Interactive site for independent travellers, with forums, bulletin boards, travel tips and features, plus online travel guides.

**Virtual Tourist** ⓦwww.virtualtourist.com. Interactive site that allows travellers to post reviews and photos of destinations, accommodation, restaurants, and travel-related advice.

## TIME ZONES

The region is covered by two time zones: Cambodia, west Indonesia (Java, Sumatra, Kalimantan Barat and Kalimantan Tengah), Laos, Thailand and Vietnam are **7 hours ahead of GMT**, 12 hours ahead of New York, 15 hours ahead of LA, three hours behind Sydney and five hours behind Auckland. Brunei, Hong Kong and Macau, east Indonesia (Bali, Lombok, Nusa Tenggara, Sulawesi and south and east Kalilmantan), Malaysia the Philippines and Singapore are all **8 hours ahead of GMT**, 13 hours ahead of New York, 16 hours ahead of LA, 2 hours behind Sydney and 4 hours behind Auckland. No countries in the region use daylight saving time.

## VISAS

Country-specific advice about visas, entry requirements, border formalities and visa extensions is given in the introduction at the beginning of each chapter. As a broad guide, the only countries in Southeast Asia for which citizens of the EU, USA, Canada, Australia and New Zealand need to buy a visa in advance if arriving by air and staying less than thirty days are: **Vietnam** (no entry without advance visa) and the **Philippines** (21 days maximum on arrival). However, different rules usually apply if you're staying more than thirty days or arriving overland; in **Indonesia** you can only get a thirty-day visa on arrival at certain designated air and seaports (see p.194). However, as all visa requirements, prices and processing times are subject to change, it's always worth double-checking with embassies. Nearly every country requires that your passport be valid for at least six months from your date of entry. Some also demand proof of onward travel (such as an air ticket) or sufficient funds to buy a ticket.

### Embassies and consulates abroad

It's usually straightforward to get visas for your next port of call while you're on the road in Southeast Asia. Details of **neighbouring Southeast Asian embassies** are given in the Directory section of each capital city within the Guide.

**Brunei** ⓦwww.brunet.bn/gov/mfa/abroad.htm; Australia: 16 Bulwarra Close, O'Mally, ACT 2606, Canberra ⓣ02/6290 1801; Canada: 395 Laurier Avenue East, Ottawa, Ontario K1N 6R4 ⓣ613/234 5656; New Zealand: Contact the embassy in Canberra; UK and Ireland: 19–20 Belgrave Square, London SW1X 8PG ⓣ020/7581 0521; USA:

Watergate Hotel, Suite 300, 2600 Virginia Avenue, Washington DC 20037 ⓣ 202/342 0159.
**Cambodia** ⓦ www.cambodia.gov.kh/unisql1/egov/english/country.embassy.html; Australia: 5 Canterbury Crescent, Deakin, ACT 2600 ⓣ 02/6237 1259; Canada: Contact the embassy in Washington; France: 4 Rue Adolphe Yvon, 75116 Paris ⓣ 01/45 03 47 20. New Zealand: Contact the embassy in Canberra; UK and Ireland: Contact the embassy in France (see above); USA: 4500 16th St, Washington DC 20011 ⓣ 202/726-8042; 866 UN Plaza, Suite 420, New York 10017 ⓣ 212/223-0676; 422 Ord St, Los Angeles, California 90112 ⓣ 213/625-7777.
**Hong Kong and Macau** Contact your nearest Chinese embassy ⓦ www.fmprc.gov.cn/eng/wjb/zwjg/default.htm; Australia: 15 Coronation Drive, Yarralumla, ACT 2600 ⓣ 02/6273 4780; 539 Elizabeth St, Surry Hills, Sydney ⓣ 02/9699 2216; plus offices in Melbourne ⓣ 03/9804 3683 and Perth ⓣ 08/9481 3278; Canada: 515 St Patrick's St, Ottawa, Ontario K1N 5H3 ⓣ 613/791 0511; Ireland: 40 Ailesbury Rd, Dublin 4 ⓣ 01/269 1707; New Zealand: 2-6 Glenmore Street, Wellington, ⓣ 04/472 1382; UK: 31 Portland Place, London W1; ⓣ 020/7299 4049; USA: 2300 Connecticut Ave NW, Washington DC 20008 ⓣ 202/328 2500.
**Indonesia** ⓦ www.indonesianembassy.org.uk/link_indo_embassy.html; Australia: 8 Darwin Ave, Yarralumla, Canberra, ACT 2600 ⓣ 02/6250 8600; 20 Harry Chan Ave, Darwin, NT 5784 ⓣ 089/41 0048; 72 Queen Rd, Melbourne, VIC 3004 ⓣ 03/9525 2755; 134 Adelaide Terrace, East Perth, WA 6004 ⓣ 08/9221 5858; 236–238 Maroubra Rd, Maroubra, NSW 2035 ⓣ 02/9344 9933; Canada: 287 Maclaren Street, Ottawa, Ontario ⓣ 613/236-7403; New Zealand: 70 Glen Rd, Kelburn, Wellington, PO Box 3543 ⓣ 04/475 8697; UK and Ireland: 38 Grosvenor Square, London ⓣ 020/7499 7661; USA: 2020 Massachusetts Avenue NW, Washington DC 20036 ⓣ 202/775 5200.
**Laos** It's much easier to apply for a visa in Bangkok than in the West ⓦ www.laoembassy.com; Australia: 1 Dalman Crescent, O'Malley, Canberra, ACT ⓣ 02/6286 4595; Canada: Contact embassy in Washington; France: 74 Ave Raymond Poincaré, Paris ⓣ 01/45 53 02 98; New Zealand: Contact embassy in Canberra; UK and Ireland: Contact embassy in France or Thailand: USA: 2222 S Street NW, Washington DC 20008 ⓣ 202/332 6416.
**Malaysia** ⓦ www.kln.gov.my; Australia: 7 Perth Ave, Yarralumla, Canberra, ACT 2600 ⓣ 02/6273 1543; Canada: 60 Boteler St, Ottawa, Ontario ⓣ 613/241-5182; New Zealand: 10 Washington Ave, Brooklyn, Wellington ⓣ 04/385 2439; UK and Ireland: 45 Belgrave Square, London SW1 ⓣ 020/7235 8033; USA: 3516 International Court, N.W. Washington DC ⓣ 202 572 9700.
**The Philippines** ⓦ www.dfa.gov.ph/posts/pemb.htm; Australia:1 Moonah Place, Yarralumla, Canberra, ACT 2600 ⓣ 02/6273 2535; Philippine Centre, Level 1 27–33 Wentworth Ave, Sydney, NSW 2000 ⓣ 02/9262 7377; Canada: 130 Albert Street, Suite 606, Ottawa ⓣ 613/233 1121; New Zealand: 50 Hobson St, Thorndon, Wellington ⓣ 04/4729 848; 8th Floor, 121 Beach Rd, Auckland 1 ⓣ 09/303 2423; UK and Ireland: 9a Palace Green, London W8 ⓣ 020/7937 1600; USA: 1600 Massachusetts Ave NW, Washington DC ⓣ 202/467 9300.
**Singapore** ⓦ www.mfa.gov.sg; Australia: 17 Forster Crescent, Yarralumla, Canberra, ACT ⓣ 02/6271 2000; Canada: 999 West Hastings St, Suite 1820, Vancouver ⓣ 604/669-5115; New Zealand: 17 Kabul St, Khandallah, Wellington, PO Box 13-140 ⓣ 04/479 0850; UK and Ireland: 9 Wilton Crescent, London SW1 ⓣ 020/7235 8315; USA 3501 International Place NW, Washington DC ⓣ 202/537 3100.
**Thailand** ⓦ www.thaiembassy.org; Australia: 111 Empire Circuit, Yarralumla, Canberra ACT 2600 ⓣ 02/6273 1149; consulates in Adelaide, Brisbane, Melbourne, Perth and Sydney; Canada: 180 Island Park Drive, Ottawa, Ontario ⓣ 613/722 4444; New Zealand: 2 Cook St, PO Box 17-226, Karori, Wellington ⓣ 04/4768 618; UK and Ireland: 30 Queens Gate, London SW7 ⓣ 020 7589 2944; USA: 1024 Wisconsin Ave NW, Suite 401, Washington DC ⓣ 202/944 3600, ⓦ www.thaiembdc.org.
**Vietnam** ⓦ www.vnembassy.net; Australia: 6 Timbarra Crescent, O'Malley, Canberra, ACT 2606 ⓣ 02/6286 6059; Canada: 470 Wilbrod St, Ottawa, Ontario ⓣ 613/236-0772; New Zealand: Contact embassy in Canberra; UK and Ireland: 12–14 Victoria Rd, London W8 ⓣ 020/7937 1912; USA: 1233 20th St NW, Suite 400, Washington DC ⓣ 202/861 0737, ⓦ www.vietnamembassy-usa.org.

## WOMEN TRAVELLERS

Southeast Asia is generally a safe region for women to travel around alone. That said, it pays to take the normal precautions, especially late at night when there are few people around on the streets; after dark, take licensed taxis rather than cycle rickshaws and tuk-tuks.

Be aware that the Asian perception of Western female travellers is of sexual availability and promiscuity. This is particularly the case in the traditional Muslim areas of Indonesia and Malaysia, as well as southern

Thailand and the southern Philippines, where lone foreign women can get treated contemptuously however decently attired. Most Southeast Asian women **dress modestly** and it usually helps to do the same, avoiding skimpy shorts and vests, which are considered offensive (see also p.45). Some Asian women travelling with white men have reported cases of serious harassment – something attributed to the tendency of Southeast Asian men to automatically label all such women as prostitutes. These incidents are most common in Vietnam. Be wary of invitations to drink with a man or group of men if there are no other women present. To many Southeast Asian men, simply accepting such an invitation will be perceived as tacit agreement to have sex, and some Southeast Asian men will see it as their right to rape a woman who has "led them on" by accepting such an invitation and then refused to follow through. Women should also take care around Buddhist monks. It should go without saying that monks who touch women (an act that is strictly against the Buddhist precepts) or who suggest showing you around some isolated site – such as a cave – should be politely but firmly rebuffed. The key is to stay aware without being paranoid.

# Brunei

## HIGHLIGHTS

**OMAR ALI SAIFUDDIEN MOSQUE, BANDAR:** take your shoes off and step into the magnificent mosque

**KAMPUNG AYER:** explore this vast village on stilts in the middle of a river

**SUNGAI TEMBURONG:** take a boat ride past mangrove-lined riverbanks, spotting crocodiles and proboscis monkeys along the way

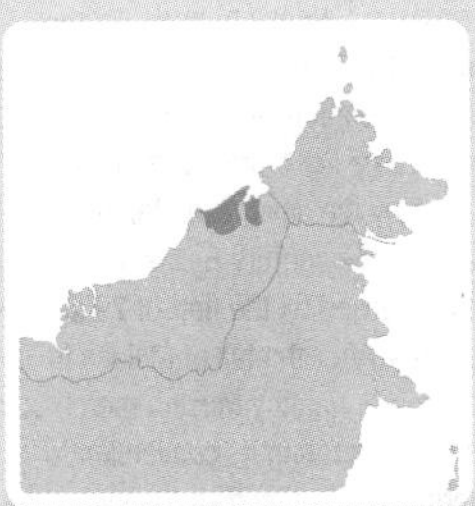

## ROUGH COSTS

**DAILY BUDGET** Basic US$18/ Occasional treat US$47

**DRINK** Cup of tea US$2 (no alcohol is served in Brunei)

**FOOD** Satay with nasi goreng US$3

**HOSTEL/BUDGET HOTEL** US$7/ US$22

**TRAVEL** Bus: Bandar Seri Begawan–Kuala Belait (85km; 2hr 30min) US$5; Boat: Muara–Pulau Labuan (35km; 1hr) US$11

## FACT FILE

**POPULATION** 379,000

**AREA** 5765 sq km

**LANGUAGE** Bahasa Malaysia, though English is also widely spoken

**RELIGION** Muslim, with Christian minorities

**CURRENCY** Brunei dollars (B$)

**CAPITAL** Bandar Seri Begawan

**INTERNATIONAL PHONE CODE** ⓣ+ 63

**TIME ZONE** GMT + 8hr

# Introduction

**Surrounded by Sarawak on Borneo's northern coast, the tiny but thriving sultanate of Brunei combines notable wealth with Islamic conservatism. Most famous as the home of one of the world's richest men, for many Brunei is just a stopover on a long-haul flight. However, for those with a bit of time and some cash to spend, the state does offer a few hidden surprises. With its decorative architecture and obvious riches, the capital, Bandar Seri Begawan, can often feel a world away from its Malaysian neighbours rather than just a short border hop. Further afield, the remote Ulu Temburong National Park offers untouched virgin rainforest teeming with flora and fauna. And for diving enthusiasts, the Brunei coast is rich in rarely frequented underwater treasures.**

Budget travel is difficult here; accommodation is more expensive than Sarawak and Sabah, and a hire car is essential if you wish to travel around. Many of Brunei's pulling points can be found on a much grander scale, for a fraction of the cost, in the neighbouring Malaysian states. But for those looking for a sense of serenity off the beaten track, Brunei is a good stamp in the passport.

Resident Bruneians experience a quality of life that is unlike anywhere else in Southeast Asia; education and healthcare are free; houses, cars and even pilgrimages to Mecca are subsidized; and taxation on personal income is unheard of. The explanation for this is simple: oil. First discovered in 1903 at the site of the town of Seria, Brunei's wealth is all down to the natural resources pumping through its veins.

## WHEN TO VISIT

The climate is hot and humid, with average temperatures in the high twenties all year round. Lying 440km north of the equator, Brunei has a tropical weather system so, even if you visit outside the wet season (usually Sept to Jan), there's every chance you'll get caught in some rain.

## CHRONOLOGY

**c. Seventh century** Chinese records suggest that a forerunner to the Brunei state – referred to as "Po ni" – has trading relations with China.

**Fourteenth century** For a brief period the region is taken over by the Javanese Majapahit Empire; by the end of the century Brunei is independent and governed by the first of 29 sultans.

**Fifteenth century** After the fall of Melaka in 1511 (see p.552), many wealthy Muslim merchants decamp to Brunei, accelerating its conversion to Islam, and bolstering its position as a trading centre.

**Sixteenth century** Brunei's golden age: its influence stretches along Borneo's northern and western coasts, and as far as the modern-day Philippines.

**1578** Spain wins a sea battle and their forces take the Brunei capital, only to be chased out days later by a cholera epidemic.

**1839** Fortune-seeker James Brooke arrives near Kuching, helps the sultan to quell an uprising, and demands the governorship of Sarawak in return; Brunei's contraction begins, as Brooke and his successors take land.

**January 1846** British gunboats quell a court coup; in return Pulau Labuan is ceded to the British crown.

**1888** The British declare Brunei a protected state, with responsibility for its foreign affairs.

**1890** The cession of the Limbang region, literally splitting Brunei in two.

**1903** The discovery of oil; three years later, the British set up a Residency in Brunei.

**1941–45** The Japanese occupation; after their defeat it becomes a British Protectorate again.

**1959** The British withdraw – but still control defence and foreign affairs – and a new constitution is established.

**1962** A pro-democratic armed coup is crushed by the British Army. The sultan starts ruling by decree under emergency powers that largely remain in place today.

**1963** Brunei is the only Malay state that chooses to remain a British dependency rather than join the Malaysian Federation.

**October 5, 1967** Following the voluntary abdication of his father, the current sultan, Sultan Hassanal Bolkiah (see p.68), takes the throne.

**1970s** As oil prices escalate, Bruneians – especially the sultan – grow rich.

**January 1, 1984** Brunei gains full independence from Britain.

**1991** A conservative, religious ideology is introduced, which presents the sultan as defender of faith; the sale of alcohol is banned.

**1998** The sultan's brother (and finance minister) is sued for embezzling B$3bn of state funds: the court reduces his living expenses to a meagre US$300,000 a month.

**2004** The sultan revives Brunei's legislative council after two decades; though the constitution allows for fifteen elected members, for now all members are appointed.

# Basics

## ARRIVAL

Brunei can be reached by air, land or sea. Some long-haul **flights** (principally between the UK and Australia) have stopovers at Brunei International Airport, while Royal Brunei Airlines and Malaysia Airlines run connecting flights from surrounding Sabah and Sarawak; there are also regular flights to other regional hubs, including Singapore, KL, Bangkok, Hong Kong and Manila, with Singapore Airlines, Malaysia Airlines, Thai Airways, Dragonair and Philippines Airlines. **Boats** to Brunei depart daily from Lawas and Limbang (see p.588)

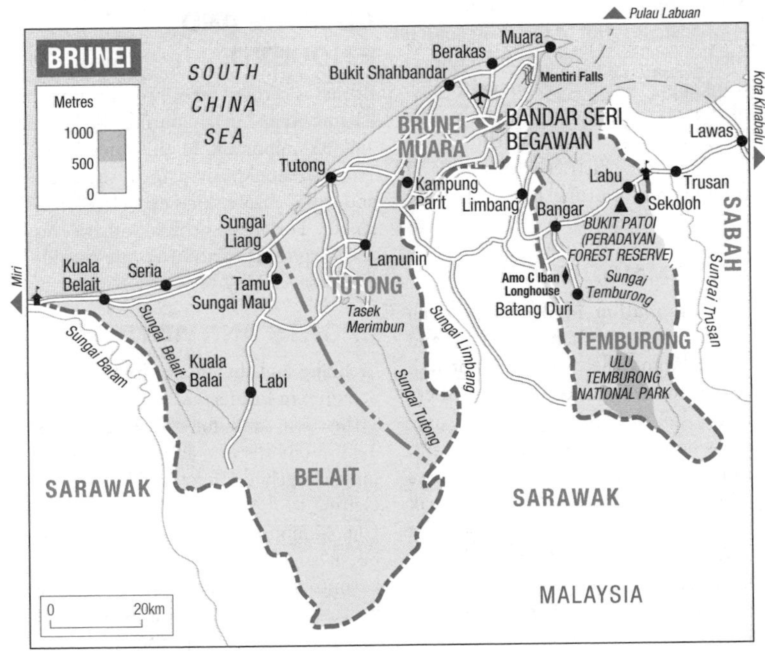

in northern Sarawak, and from Pulau Labuan (see p.595), en route from Kota Kinabalu in Sabah. Travelling overland, Bandar Seri Begawan can be reached by **bus** from Miri in Sarawak (see p.584), though the route from Sabah involves taking a bus to Lawas and on to Bangar in the Temburong district, from where it's a short connecting boat trip to Bandar.

## VISAS

US citizens can travel for ninety days in Brunei without a visa, while UK and New Zealand travellers are granted thirty days; Canadians, Australians, South Africans and citizens of most European countries are allowed fourteen days. All other visitors must apply for visas at local Brunei diplomatic missions (see p.56) or, failing that, at a British consulate.

## GETTING AROUND

If you intend to explore Brunei in any depth, you've got little option but to **rent a car**. **Bus** services are non-existent south of the main coastal roads, while **taxis** are expensive. Apart from short hops across Sungai Brunei in Bandar's water taxis, the only time you're likely to use a **boat** is to get to the Temburong district, which is cut off from the rest of Brunei by the Limbang corridor of Sarawak.

## ACCOMMODATION

**Accommodation** in Brunei is much more expensive than in Sabah and Sarawak, and the country is not well set up for backpackers, though there is a hostel in Bandar. There are some areas however where local Malay and Murut villages and Iban longhouses offer **homestay programmes** – speak to Brunei Tourism (see p.68) for current areas. The villages don't have fixed accommodation prices, but as a rough guide expect to pay around B$3–7.

## FOOD AND DRINK

The **food** in Brunei is very similar to that of Malaysia, though unlike Sabah and Sarawak you'll find a good deal of Indian and Bangladeshi dishes here. Brunei does have its own signature dish, *ambuyat* – a glutinous, sticky mass, which is made from the pith of the sago tree mixed with water. It's generally pretty tasteless and rather chewy, and is served with dips such as sambal to give it a bit of flavour. It can found at the night markets and on some restaurant menus. It is illegal to buy **alcohol** in Brunei but tourists can bring in two bottles of wine/spirits and twelve cans of beer, which must be declared.

**Cafés** are generally open from 7am to 9pm and **restaurants** from 11am to 10pm, usually waiting until the last customer leaves. There are a number of **night markets** around the capital with hawker stalls that are open until the early hours.

## CULTURE AND ETIQUETTE

Brunei is certainly more conservatively Islamic than neighbouring Malaysia and it's important to dress modestly. Women should cover their shoulders and legs – ensure skirts are below knee-length. For men, t-shirts with sleeves and long shorts or trousers are considered respectable.

## SPORTS AND ACTIVITIES

Trekking and diving are the two main activities in Brunei.

The best area for **trekking** is the Temburong district, an area of pristine jungle largely undiscovered by tourists. Getting to the principal national park, Ulu Temburong, independently can be an adventure in itself as obtaining permits and insurance is often a lengthy process; most people visit as part of a tour from Bandar. Trips usually include a visit to the Iban longhouse at Batang Duri and proboscis monkey spotting.

**Diving** off the coast of Brunei is becoming increasingly popular, with draws including colourful coral pinnacles, sunken ships (some of which are casualties from World War II) and disused oil rigs. In terms of marine life, divers can come face to face with tropical species including rays, and hammerhead and grey-tip sharks.

See p.68 for details of operators in Bandar running trekking and diving trips.

## COMMUNICATIONS

**Postcards** to anywhere in the world cost 50c, aerogrammes 45c and overseas **letters** 75c–B$1.20 (depending upon the destination) for every 10g. There are a number of **internet cafés** around Bandar, charging around B$1 per hour. Most internet cafés now also have headsets so you can chat for hours using VoIP/Skype. Otherwise, **local calls** cost 10c flat fee from phone boxes and are free from private phones. **International** (IDD) **calls** can be made through hotels, from booths at Bandar's Telekom office (see p.70) or from card phones. Phonecards (B$10, B$20, B$50 and B$100) can be bought from the Telekom office, post office and shops. To phone abroad from Brunei, dial ⓣ00 + IDD country code + area code minus first 0 + subscriber number.

## CRIME AND SAFETY

Brunei has very little crime and travellers rarely experience any trouble. Note that the possession of **drugs** – whether hard or soft – carries a hefty prison sentence, and trafficking is punishable by the death penalty. If you are caught smuggling drugs into or out of the country, at the very best you will face a long stretch in a foreign prison; at worst, you could be hanged.

### EMERGENCY NUMBERS

Ambulance ⓣ991
Fire brigade ⓣ995
Police ⓣ993

## MEDICAL CARE AND EMERGENCIES

**Medical services** in Brunei are excellent; staff speak good English and use up-to-date techniques. Tourists must pay for medical services upfront, the cost obviously depending upon the level of treatment required.

Each province has its own **hospital**. Tourists are usually advised to go to RIPAS Hospital in Bandar (see p.70), but there are also hospitals in Tutong (ⓣ04/221336), Belait (ⓣ03/332366) and Temburong (ⓣ05/221526).

Oral **contraceptives** and condoms are available at pharmacies.

## INFORMATION AND MAPS

In addition to Brunei Tourism's offices (see p.68), the excellent *Explore Brunei* and *Places of Interest* leaflets are good sources of **information**, available at most hotels. Local tour operators (see p.68) can also be helpful.

### BRUNEI ON THE NET

ⓦ**www.bruneitourism.travel** Brunei Tourism's website has a wealth of information – from seven-star hotels to local markets.
ⓦ**www.brudirect.com** Daily local and international news.
ⓦ**www.onebrunei.com** News and a yellow pages directory covering every service you'll ever need.
ⓦ**www.bruneidiary.info** Lists events happening in and around the sultanate.

Nelles East Malaysia **map** has the best coverage of Brunei, while *Explore Brunei* includes a reasonable map of Bandar city centre.

## MONEY AND BANKS

Brunei's **currency** is the Brunei dollar, which is divided into 100 cents; you'll see it written as B$, or simply as $. The Brunei dollar has parity with the Singapore dollar, and both are legal tender in either country. Notes come in B$1, B$5, B$10, B$50, B$100, B$500, B$1000 and B$10,000 denominations; coins are in denominations of 1, 5, 10, 20 and 50 cents (c). At the time of writing, the **exchange rate** was B$2.89 to the British pound or B$1.35 to the US dollar, and RM2.3 to B$1.

There's no shortage of **ATMs** in Bandar, and this is a good place to get out cash if you're thinking of heading further afield. Most accept all types of credit and debit card but note that some charge for withdrawing cash. You can get **money wired** to you via any of the major banks.

Sterling and US dollar **traveller's cheques** can be cashed at banks, licensed moneychangers and some hotels. Major **credit cards** are accepted in most hotels and large shops. Banks will **advance cash** against major credit cards, and with MasterCard, Visa, American Express or any bank card bearing a Maestro, Plus or Cirrus logo.

## OPENING HOURS AND HOLIDAYS

**Government offices** in Brunei open Mon–Thurs and Sat 7.45am–12.15pm and 1.30–4.30pm; **shopping centres** open daily 10am–10pm. **Banking hours** are Mon–Fri 9am–4pm and Sat 9–11am. **Post offices** are open Mon–Thurs & Sat 8am–4.30pm.

Most of Brunei's **public holidays** have no fixed dates and change annually according to the lunar calendar, so check with the tourist office. During **Ramadan**, Muslims spend the ninth month of the Islamic calendar fasting in the daytime; during this time it is culturally sensitive for tourists not to eat or smoke blatantly in public during daylight hours.

### Public holidays

**Jan 1** New Year's Day
**Jan/Feb** Chinese New Year
**Feb/March** Hari Raya Haji
**Feb 23** National Day
**Feb/March** Birthday of the Prophet Mohammed
**May 31** Armed Forces' Day
**July 15** Sultan's Birthday
**July/Aug** Israk Mikraj
**Aug/Sept** First day of Ramadan
**Sept** Anniversary of Revelation of the Koran
**Oct/Nov** Hari Raya Aidilfitri
**Nov/Dec** Hari Raya Aidiladha
**Dec 25** Christmas Day
**Dec/Jan** Hijrah (Islamic New Year)

## FESTIVALS

**National Day** (Feb 23). The sultan and 35,000 other Bruneians watch parades and fireworks at the Sultan Hassanal Bolkiah National Stadium, just outside Bandar.

**Armed Forces' Day** (May 31). Bandar's square hosts parades and displays.

**Sultan's Birthday** (July 15). Kicks off a fortnight of parades, lantern processions, traditional sports competitions and fireworks.

**Hari Raya Aidilfitri** (Oct/Nov). The end of the Ramadan fasting period, when the sultan declares his home, the Istana Nurul Iman, an open house to the public.

# Bandar Seri Begawan

The capital of Brunei, **BANDAR SERI BEGAWAN** (also known as BSB or simply Bandar), is a striking juxtaposition of modern buildings and traditional stilt houses, home to nearly a quarter of the Sultanate's population. As capitals go, the city has very few tourist attractions and the main sights can easily be covered in a day. However, Bandar's large, sweeping streets and sense of space provide a welcome contrast to the chaos of most Southeast Asian cities.

As recently as the middle of the nineteenth century, Bandar was little more than a sleepy water village, but with the discovery of oil came its evolution into the attractive, clean and modern waterfront city of today. It's also home to one of the world's richest men, the Sultan of Brunei, whose displays of wealth are visible in the numerous opulent buildings – most obviously, the magnificent Omar Ali Saifuddien Mosque, which dominates the skyline.

## What to see and do

**Downtown Bandar** is hemmed in by water. To the east is Sungai Kianggeh; to the south, the wide Sungai Brunei; and to the west, Sungai Kedayan, which runs up to the Edinburgh Bridge. The classical Omar Ali Saifuddien Mosque is Bandar's most obvious point of reference, cradled by the floating village of Kampung Ayer. Bandar is a fairly small place and easily navigable on foot – the wide, empty streets make it a pleasant place to amble around.

### The Omar Ali Saifuddien Mosque

At the very heart of both the city and the sultanate's Muslim faith is the magnificent **Omar Ali Saifuddien Mosque** (Mon–Wed, Sat & Sun 8am–noon, 1–3.30pm & 4.30–5.30pm; Fri 4.30–5.30pm; closed Thurs to non-Muslims). Built in classical Islamic style, it was commissioned by and named after the father of the present sultan, and completed in 1958. Because the mosque is something of a national showcase, non-Muslims are made to feel more welcome here than at most mosques in the region. Topping the cream-coloured building is a 52-metre-high golden dome, whose curved surface is adorned with a mosaic comprising over three million pieces of Venetian glass. It is sometimes possible to obtain permission to ride the elevator up the 44-metre-high minaret, and look out over the water village below. The usual dress codes – modest attire, and shoes to be left at the entrance – apply when entering the mosque.

### Kampung Ayer

From the mosque, it's no distance to Bandar's **Kampung Ayer**. Stilt villages have occupied this stretch of the Sungai Brunei for hundreds of years, and today it's home to an estimated thirty thousand people, their dwellings connected by a maze of wooden promenades. These villages have their own clinics, mosques, schools, a fire brigade and a police station; the homes have piped water, electricity and TV. The waters, however, are distinctly unsanitary, and the houses are susceptible to fire, evidence of which is apparent today.

The meandering pathways of Kampung Ayer make it an intriguing place to explore on foot – enter via the bridge just behind the Yayasan Complex. For a real impression of its dimensions though, it's best to charter a water taxi a half-hour round trip will cost around B$20 per person.

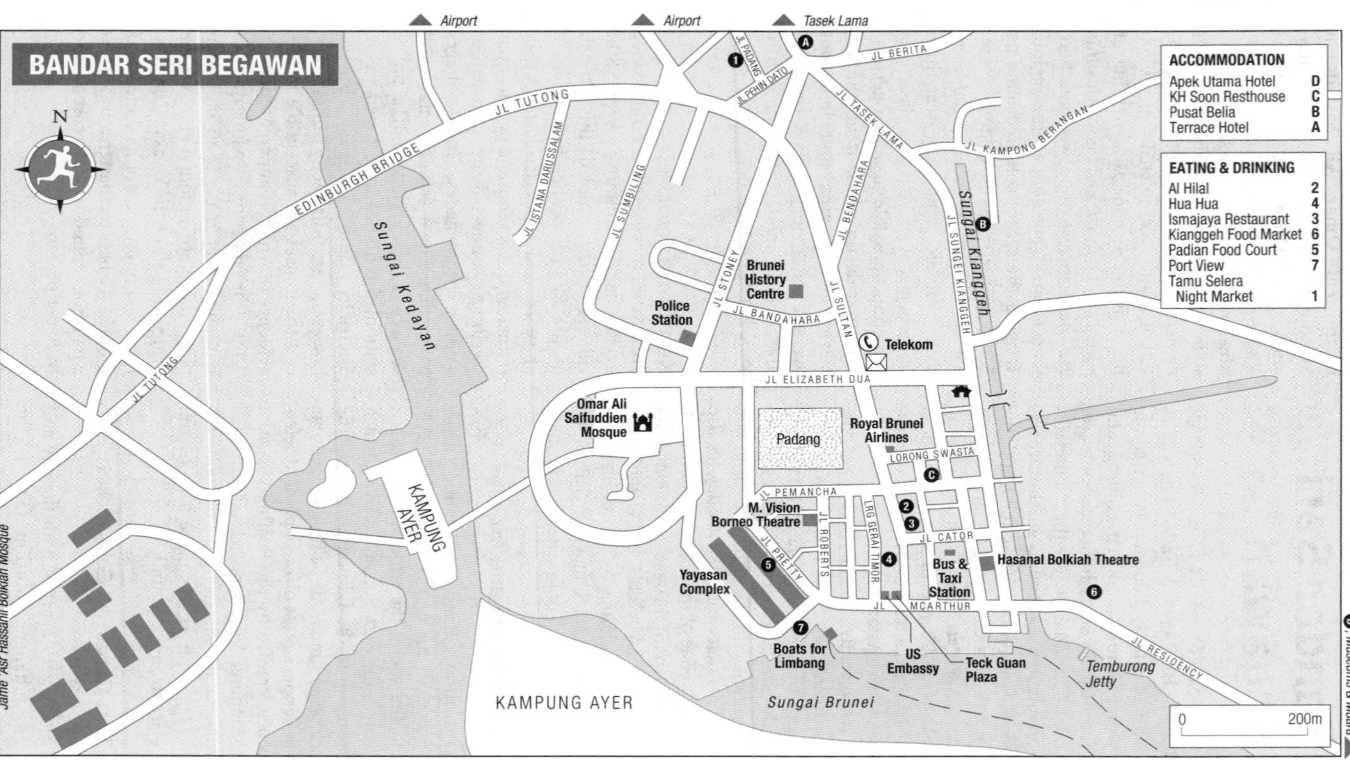
BANDAR SERI BEGAWAN
ACCOMMODATION
Apek Utama Hotel D
KH Soon Resthouse C
Pusat Belia B
Terrace Hotel A
EATING & DRINKING
Al Hilal 2
Hua Hua 4
Ismajaya Restaurant 3
Kianggeh Food Market 6
Padian Food Court 5
Port View 7
Tamu Selera Night Market 1
Airport
Airport
Tasek Lama
Gadong, Airport, Simpang
Istana Nurul Iman & Jame 'Asr Hassanil Bolkiah Mosque
D, Museums & Muara
Limbang
Temburong
JL TUTONG
EDINBURGH BRIDGE
JL ISTANA DARUSSALAM
JL SUMBILING
JL STONEY
JL PADANG
JL PEHIN DATO
JL BERITA
JL TASEK LAMA
JL KAMPONG BERANGAN
JL BENDAHARA
JL SULTAN
JL SUNGEI KIANGGEH
Sungai Kianggeh
Sungai Kedayan
JL BANDAHARA
JL ELIZABETH DUA
Brunei History Centre
Police Station
Telekom
Omar Ali Saifuddien Mosque
Padang
Royal Brunei Airlines
LORONG SWASTA
JL PEMANCHA
M. Vision
Borneo Theatre
JL ROBERTS
LRG GERAI TIMOR
JL CATOR
JL PRETTY
JL MCARTHUR
Bus & Taxi Station
Hasanal Bolkiah Theatre
Yayasan Complex
Boats for Limbang
US Embassy
Teck Guan Plaza
Temburong Jetty
JL RESIDENCY
KAMPUNG AYER
KAMPUNG AYER
Sungai Brunei
0 200m
N

### The Brunei Museum and Malay Technology Museum

The **Brunei Museum** (Mon–Thurs, Sat & Sun 9am–5pm, Fri 9–11.30am & 2.30–5pm; free), about 5km east of Sungai Kianggeh on Jalan Residency (Central Line bus #11 & Eastern Line #39), has several outstanding galleries. The undoubted highlight is the **Islamic Art Gallery** where, among the riches on display, are beautifully illuminated antique copies of the Koran from around the world, exquisite prayer mats, and quirkier items such as a pair of ungainly wooden slippers. In the inevitable **Oil and Gas Gallery**, exhibits, graphics and captions recount the story of Brunei's oil reserves, from the drilling of the first well in 1928 to current extraction and refining techniques. Also interesting, though tantalizingly sketchy, is the **Muslim Life Gallery**, whose dioramas allow glimpses of social traditions, such as the sweetening of a newborn baby's mouth with honey or dates, and the disposal of its placenta in a *bayung*, a palm-leaf basket which is either hung on a tree or floated downriver.

Close by, the three galleries of the Malay Technology Museum (Mon–Thurs, Sat & Sun 9am–5pm, Fri 9–11.30am & 2.30–5pm; free) focus on handicrafts, architecture and house building. It includes some interesting reconstructions of water village life, and explores original indigenous techniques of hunting and gathering.

### The Jame 'Asr Hassanil Bolkiah Mosque

Many people reckon that the **Jame 'Asr Hassanil Bolkiah (State) Mosque** (also known as the Kiarong Mosque; Mon–Wed & Sun 8am–noon, 2–3pm & 5–6pm; closed Thurs & Fri to non-Muslims), set in harmonious gardens near the commercial suburb of Gadong, has a distinct edge over the Omar Ali Saifuddien Mosque, both in style and grandeur. With its sea-blue roof, golden domes and slender minarets, this is Brunei's largest mosque, constructed to commemorate the silver jubilee of the sultan's reign in 1992. Circle Line buses (#1, #22) skirt the grounds of the mosque en route to Gadong.

### The Istana Nurul Iman

The **Istana Nurul Iman**, the official residence of the sultan, is sited along the banks of the Sungai Brunei, 4km west of the capital. Bigger than either Buckingham Palace or the Vatican, the istana is a monument to self-indulgence, with 1788 rooms and a royal banquet hall that can seat 4000. Its design is a sinuous blend of traditional and modern, with Islamic motifs, such as arches and domes, and sloping roofs fashioned on traditional longhouse designs, combined with all the mod cons you'd expect of a homeowner whose fortune is estimated at $22bn.

Unfortunately, the palace is rarely open to the general public, though the sultan declares an open house every year during Hari Raya. If it's shut, head to **Taman Persiaran Damuan**, a kilometre-long park sandwiched between Jalan Tutong and Sungai Brunei, which offers the best view, or fork out for a boat trip (B$15 for 30min) to see the palace lit up at night from the water.

All westbound buses travel along Jalan Tutong, over the Edinburgh Bridge and past the istana.

## Arrival

**By bus** The central bus station, where all buses terminate, is below the multi-storey car park on Jl Cator. It's right in the centre of town, and less than a five-minute walk from most of the accommodation and Jl Sultan, the main drag for restaurants.

**By boat** Boats from Limbang dock centrally, beside the Customs and Immigration Station at the junction of Jl Roberts and Jl McArthur. Boats from Pulau Labuan and Lawas dock at Serasa Wharf in Muara, 25km northeast of the city; regular buses run from here to Bandar and usually wait for the ferry to arrive.

## THE SULTAN OF BRUNEI

Brunei's twenty-ninth sultan, **Hassanal Bolkiah** (his full title is 31 words long), is reported to be the world's richest monarch, worth a cool $22bn. Not shy of spending money, his list of assets includes: the 1788-room Istana Nurul Iman; family homes in London, LA, New York and Paris; two Boeings; five aircraft hangars to house his five thousand cars; and climate-controlled stables for his two hundred polo ponies. His yearly expenditure lists US$2.52m on badminton lessons, US$2.5m on masseuses and acupuncturists and nearly US$100,000 on guards for his exotic birdcages.

This information all became public after he accused his younger brother, Prince Jefri, of siphoning off US$16bn during his thirteen years as finance minister. A court battle ensued and after fifteen years it finally ruled in the sultan's favour. Jefri was dealt a crushing blow and ordered to hand over two hotels, three houses, diamonds, cherished paintings and cash. But when your older brother is the prime minister, defence minister, finance minister, Supreme Commander of the Armed Forces, Supreme Head of Islam and chief of police, as well as sultan, who was he to argue?

**By air** The plush Brunei International Airport (Lapangan Terbang Antarabangsa; ⓣ02/331747) is 8km north of the city. There are free public phones to your right beyond passport control (useful if you need to book a room), and to the left, as you walk out of the arrivals concourse and into the car park, is a tourist information booth and a scattering of ATMs. If you are here on a long stopover (as on flights between the UK and Australia), half-day tours of the city are surprisingly easy to arrange. Taxis can be flagged down outside the arrivals hall. They cost B$16 into the city centre, with a B$5 surcharge if arriving after 9pm, plus a further B$1 for each piece of luggage in the boot. Alternatively, bear right as you exit arrivals, into the free parking zone where you can catch a bus (#23, 24, 36 & 38; every 15min; 6.30am–6pm; B$1) into town.

## Information and tours

**Tourist information** Brunei Tourism has an office on the same road as the bus station Jl Cantor (ⓣ02/382822 or 382832, ⓦwww.bruneitourism.travel). There's also a small information booth at the airport.

**Tour operators** Sunshine Borneo Tours and Travel, 2nd Floor, Unit 1, Block C, Abdul Razak Complex, Gadong (ⓣ02/446509 or 441791 ⓦwww.exploreborneo.com), has dozens of leaflets on attractions in the city and around the state, and owner Anthony Chieng offers good advice. He also runs numerous tours, including a two-day excursion to the Temburong district (B$245). Mona Florafauna Tours Enterprise (ⓣ2230761, ⓔmft@brunet.bn) offers good budget deals on trekking, while for diving, recommended operators include Intrepid Tours, Unit 105, 1st Floor PBBMB Building, Jl Sungai Kianggeh (ⓣ02/221685) and Naquina NQ Inbound Tours (ⓣ02/8873416). Reef dives start from B$185, wreck dives B$205.

## City transport

**Buses** Local buses leave from the bus station on Jl Cator (every 15–20min; 6.30am–6pm; B$1). Routes are clearly displayed in the bus station, with explanatory maps. There are three lines – northern, eastern and central – each of which crosses the city centre. Note however that the bus system shuts down around 6pm, which can be infuriating.

**Taxis** Fares for regular, metered taxis start at B$4, with a night-time surcharge; from the city centre to the Brunei Museum costs about B$6. If you need to book a taxi call ⓣ02/222214.

**Water taxis** The most common form of city transport are the motorized canoes that whizz up and down the Sungai Brunei. Nicknamed "flying coffins" because of their shape and speed, water taxis charge B$2 for a short hop. The jetty below the intersection of Jl Roberts and Jl McArthur is the best place to catch one.

## Accommodation

Brunei is almost bereft of budget accommodation, with the *Pusat Belia* (youth hostel) being the only real cheap option in town.

**Apek Utama Hotel** Simpang 229, Kampung Pintu Malim, Jl Kota Batu ⓣ02/220808. Located

3km out of town (bus #39), this hotel is a firm favourite with travellers. It's pretty simple, but rooms are clean and all have a/c. There's a DVD room and the helpful owner has a large stock of films, as well as a wealth of knowledge on tours around the area. Doubles B$30 ❺

**KH Soon Resthouse** Jl Pemancha ⓣ02/222052, ⓣkhsoon-resthouse.tripod.com. Located right by the bus station this is a good, cheap option smack bang in the centre. Rooms are small and somewhat lacking in character, but all have a/c and attached bathrooms. ❻

**Pusat Belia** Jl Sungei Kianggeh ⓣ02/223936, ⓦwww.bruneiyouth.org.bn. By far the cheapest option, with four-bed dorms and sparklingly clean if somewhat spartan facilities. There's a huge pool downstairs for guests to use and an internet café next door. Reception closes at 10pm, but is very rarely manned. Ask at the internet café to contact them for you – they're usually not far away. Dorm B$10 per person per night.

**Terrace Hotel** Jl Tasek Lama ⓣ02/243554, ⓦwww.terracebrunei.com. A comfier if more expensive option than the basic budget places. Rooms at the *Terrace* are large and bright, with big double beds, cable TV, in-room kettles and a small outdoor pool. It's right opposite the night market so good for midnight feasts. ❼

## Eating

Fortunately, Bandar's restaurants are more reasonably priced than its hotels. The best place to get tasty, freshly made food is at the night markets.

**Al Hilal** Jl Sultan. Indian food heaven and good for vegetarians. If you ask for it, they've probably got it here; don't miss the pakoras, jalebi, dosais and rotis, to name but a few. Open from breakfast until early hours when the last customer leaves. Mixed veg and rice from B$4.

**Hua Hua** 48 Jl Sultan. Steamed chicken with sausage is one of the highlights, and it's a good place to get freshly squeezed juice for breakfast. Daily 7am–9pm. B$2.50–12.

**Ismajaya Restaurant** Jl Sultan. This Indian eatery does great roti canai and can make dishes to order. Open from 8am until early hours. From B$3.

**Kianggeh Food Market** Jl Residency. This cluster of stalls located along the riverside serves good, cheap soto ayam, satay, nasi campur and other Malay staples (around B$4).

**Port View** The jetty, western end of Jl McArthur. Western and Malay food in a relaxing setting overlooking the harbour and Kampung Ayer. There are sometimes live bands (Sat 10pm–2am). Main courses are around B$15.

**Tamu Selera Night Market** Jl Padang. Located opposite the *Terrace* hotel, the night market is home to over twenty stalls serving a mix of Malay and international food. Roti John is a popular snack amongst locals and the nearest thing you'll get to a kebab in Brunei. B$2.

## Entertainment

Bandar isn't a heaving mass of entertainment when it comes to fun after dark, though the Hassanal Bolkiah Cinema (Jl Sungai); ⓣ02/22084 and M Vision Theatre (Jl Roberts); ⓣ02/236316 show English-speaking movies. There are also arcades in the shopping malls at Gadong (see p.70) as well as the Mall Cineplex. To get to Gadong take bus #1, 22 or 55, although the last bus leaves at 5.30pm so you may need to take a taxi back (B$35). Some travellers have been known to hitch, which is generally considered safe in Brunei, but as always with hitching use your common sense.

**TREAT YOURSELF**

Stepping into the **Empire Hotel & Country Club** on Muara-Tutong Highway, Kampung Jerudong (ⓦwww.theempirehotel.com), with its high ceilings, marble floors and trimmings dripping in gold, may mistakenly make you think you've set foot inside the palace. Set in 445 acres, the hotel has eight swimming pools and an enviable position overlooking the South China Sea. It's a pleasant trip out of the centre (about a half-hour taxi ride away) and a good chance to witness opulence, if not necessarily taste, first hand. If you really feel like splashing out then a room will set you back from B$500 upwards – assuming your budget won't stretch that far, afternoon tea is a good alternative, costing the princely sum of B$20. Sadly, all the facilities are reserved for guests, but you may get the chance to rub shoulders with some *Dynasty* stars, which is worth the B$25 cab ride alone.

## Shopping

**Bookshops** English-language books can be found at: Best Eastern Books, G4 Teck Guan Plaza, Jl Sultan; Paul & Elizabeth Book Services, 2nd Floor, Yayasan Complex, Jl Pretty; and Times Bookshop, 1st Floor, Yayasan Complex, Jl Pretty.
**Shopping malls** The Yayasan Complex (Jl Pretty; 10am–10pm) and Centrepoint and The Mall complexes (same hours) in Gadong will tire any hardened shopper.

## Directory

**Airlines** MAS, 144 Jl Pemancha ⓣ02/224141; Philippine Airlines, 1st Floor, Wisma Haji Fatimah, Jl Sultan ⓣ02/222970; Royal Brunei Airlines, RBA Plaza, Jl Sultan ⓣ02/242222; Singapore Airlines, 49–50 Jl Sultan ⓣ02/227253; Thai Airways, 4th Floor, Kompleks Jalan Sultan, 51–55 Jl Sultan ⓣ02/242991.
**Car rental** Most hire cars can be booked for collection at the airport. Avis ⓣ02/442284; Azizah Car Rental ⓣ02/229388; Budget ⓣ02/345573; Hertz ⓣ02/452244.
**Embassies and consulates** Australia, Level 6, DAR Takaful IBB Utama, Jl Pemancha ⓣ02/229435; Canada, 5th Floor, Jalan McArthur Building, 1 Jl McArthur ⓣ02/220043; Indonesia, Simpang 528, Lot 4498, Sungei Hanching Baru, Jl Muara ⓣ02/330180; Malaysia, Lot 27 & 29, Simpang 396–397, Kampong Sungai Akar, Jl Kebangsaan ⓣ02/381095; New Zealand, 35a Seri Lambak Shopping Centre, Jl Berakas ⓣ02/331010; Philippines, no. 17, Simpang 126, Km 2, Jl Tutong ⓣ02/241466; Singapore, no. 8, Simpang 74, Jl Subok ⓣ02/262741; Thailand, Lot 25251, Simpang 683, Jl Tutong ⓣ02/653108; UK, Unit 2.01, Block D, Yayasan Complex, Sultan Hassanal Bolkiah ⓣ02/222231; USA, 3rd Floor, Teck Guan Plaza, Jl Sultan ⓣ02/220384.
**Exchange** There are many cash-only moneychangers on Jl McArthur, and a variety of banks with ATMs on Jl Sultan, including the Standard Chartered, which doesn't charge for withdrawing cash.
**Hospitals** The Raja Isteri Pengiran Anak Saleha Hospital (RIPAS; ⓣ02/242424) is across Edinburgh Bridge on Jl Putera Al-Muhtadee Billah; or there's the private Hart Medical Clinic at 47 Jl Sultan (ⓣ02/225531).
**Immigration** The Immigration Office is on Jl Menteri Besar (Mon–Thurs & Sat 7.45am–12.15pm & 1.35–4.30pm; ⓣ02/383106). Take Circle Line bus #1 to get there.
**Internet** LA Cyber Café, Floor 2, Yayasan Complex; A2 Teen Cybercafé, 1st floor, Yayasan Complex; Cyber Café, Jl Sungei Kianggeh next to *Pusat Belait*.
**Laundry** Superkleen, opposite *Brunei Hotel*, Jl Pemancha.
**Pharmacies** Yin Chee Dispensary, Jl Bunga Kuning; Danzarac Pharmacare 47 Ground Floor, Jl Sultan; Khong Lin Dispensary, G3A, Wisma Jaya, Jl Pemancha.
**Police** Central Police Station, Jl Stoney ⓣ02/222333.
**Post office** The GPO (Mon–Thurs & Sat 8am–4.30pm) is at the intersection of Jl Elizabeth Dua and Jl Sultan.
**Telephones** The Internet café next door to the *Pusat Belia* has headsets where you can chat using Skype/VoIP. You can also make IDD calls at Telekom (daily 8am–midnight), next to the GPO on Jl Sultan, or from public phones with a phonecard.

## Moving on

**By bus** All buses out of Bandar depart from the bus terminal on Jl Cantor. See box opposite for details of the border crossing to Miri in Sarawak.
**Destinations:** Miri, Sarawak (via Seria and Kuala Belait; every 30min until 5pm; 5hr 30min) Muara (every 30min; 30min); Seria (every 30min until 5pm; 2hr).
**By boat** Boats to Limbang in Sarawak leave when full from beside the Customs and Immigration Station at the junction of Jl Roberts and Jl McArthur (B$10). Boats to Pulau Labuan, Sabah (B$15) and to Lawas, Sarawak (B$16), leave from Serasa Ferry Terminal at Muara, 25km northeast of Bandar; buses to Muara cost B$2. If you're travelling on from Labuan to Kota Kinabalu, note that there are connecting boats timed to meet the arriving ferries. Speedboats to Bangar in Temburong (B$7) depart from the wharf at Jalan Residency, 2km east of the centre.
**Destinations:** Bangar (7am–5pm; 45min); Lawas, Sarawak (daily 11.30am; 2hr); Limbang (6am–6pm; 30min); Pulau Labuan, Sabah (daily 7.30am & 4.40pm; 1hr 30min).
**By air** From the bus station in central Bandar take Northern (#23 & 24), or Eastern (#36 & 38) buses (every 15min: 6.30am–6pm; B$1) to the airport. For flight information, call ⓣ02/331747. Brunei airport departure tax is B$5 for flights to East Malaysia and B$12 to West Malaysia, Singapore and all other destinations.
**Destinations:** Bangkok, Thailand (3 weekly; 2hr); Hong Kong (2 daily; 3hr); Kota Kinabalu, Sabah (daily; 20min); Kuala Lumpur, Malaysia (daily;

**INTO MALAYSIA: MIRI**

Buses to **Miri** in Sarawak (via Seria and Kuala Belait) leave from the bus station on Jalan Cator. If you leave Bandar by 10.30am at the latest you will make all the connections and arrive in Miri by 3pm. There are two immigration stops – one leaving Brunei and the second on entering Sarawak. First take a bus to Seria (every 30min: 6.30am–5pm; B$6; 2hr), where a connecting bus waits to take passengers on to Kuala Belait (every 30min: 6.30am–8pm; B$1; 30min). At the ticket office at Kuala Belait (to the left of where the bus stops), you can buy your ticket straight through to Miri and pick up your immigration card. You then get on a third bus (7am, 9am, 10.30am, 1pm & 3pm; B$10.20; 2hr), which will take you over the border, from where you join another bus to take you onto Miri. Although it sounds complicated it's a hassle-free journey, all routes are perfectly timed and staff are on hand to help.

2hr 20min); Kuching, Sarawak (3 weekly; 1hr 10min); Manila, Philippines (daily; 2hr); Singapore (2 daily; 2hr).

# Bangar and the Temburong district

The sparsely populated and seldom visited **Temburong** district is Brunei's great expanse of untouched jungle, and the country's greatest natural attraction. Temburong's main town, **Bangar**, is the gateway to the pristine forest that lies within – protected in **Ulu Temburong National Park** and **Peradayan Forest Reserve** – and the contact point for visits to **Malay and Murut kampungs** or an **Iban longhouse** (for an account of the ethnic minorities of Borneo, see p.485). The majority of visitors to the area come on organized tours from Bandar, which often work out cheaper and less time-consuming than trying to organize it themselves.

## BANGAR

**BANGAR** sits on the Sungai Temburong, reachable only on a hair-raising speedboat journey from Bandar. Boats scream through narrow mangrove estuaries that are home to crocodiles and proboscis monkeys, swooping around corners and narrowly missing vessels travelling the opposite way, before shooting off down Sungai Temburong. After such a lead-up, the town of Bangar is something of a disappointment; its main street, which runs west from the jetty to the town mosque, is lined only with a handful of coffee shops and provision stores. Across the bridge is the town's grandest building, its new District Office, whose waterfront **café** is the town's best place to eat, serving a range of traditional Malay dishes. If you get stuck here **overnight**, try the *Pusat Belia* (youth hostel; ☎02/5221694), with four basic and somewhat sparse but clean dorm rooms for B$10. Or there's the equally basic government-run resthouse, *Rumah Peringgahan Kerajaan*, Jalan Batang Duri (☎02/5221239), which also offers beds for B$10. Bangar does have its own **tourist office** (13–14 Kedai Rakyat; ☎02/5221439), which can help with details of getting around the area, though it's best to try to organize tours through the office in Bandar.

## ULU TEMBURONG NATIONAL PARK

The lowland rainforest of **Ulu Temburong National Park** is home to rich flora and fauna with Borneo's famous proboscis monkey being a guaranteed sight on any trip. Unless you're visiting the park on an organized trip from Bandar, you will need to obtain a permit from the Forestry Department (☎02/2381687, ⓔforestrybrunei@hotmail.com) – a process that can take several days.

From Bangar, it's a twenty-minute drive south to the jetty at the small kampung of **Batang Duri**. There's no public transport to this spot; either hitch a lift (quite a safe practice in Brunei) or take a taxi (B$15). From here you'll have to charter a longboat (1hr 30min; B$150) to **Ulu Temburong Park Headquarters**. This upstream stretch of Sungai Temburong is very shallow, and when the water level is low you may have to get out and help pull the boat over rocks. It is possible to stay overnight at the park; enquire at the Forestry Department for overnight permits and latest availability.

The forest can be explored by various walkways or, for a bird's-eye view, via the near-vertical **treetop canopy**, a climb that will test your nerves to the limit. The canopy is the highest of its type in Borneo, and the view from the top is breathtaking: you can see Brunei Bay to the north and Gunung Mulu Park in Sarawak to the south.

## IBAN HOMESTAYS

Besides being a good base for exploring the park, staying in an **Iban longhouse** is an excellent opportunity to absorb the local culture. Iban homestays are also the only bargain accommodation to be found in the whole country. From Bangar, take a taxi (20min; B$15) to the Iban longhouse, Amo C, on the Batang Duri road. If you aren't visiting on a tour and wish to stay overnight, it's best to prearrange your visit through the tourist information office in BSB or Bangar (13–14 Kedai Rakyat; ☎02/5221439).

When visiting an Iban longhouse it's always best to take some small gifts; try to find out in advance how many families are in the longhouse as presents will get divided equally. Guests sleep on the veranda, the communal area for the families who live in the longhouse. Mats are placed on the floor here – it's polite not to walk on them as they're the Iban equivalent of a couch. Travellers should pay for their stay and contribute some money towards meals. There are no set prices and you should pay what you think is a fair amount for your stay. A rough framework is B$3 for breakfast, B$6 for lunch and dinner and B$5 for staying the night, but it's up to your discretion. The Iban are extremely hospitable people and are quite shy when it comes to asking for money so be sure not to take advantage and skip off without paying; being generous will keep this longhouse from posting prices, as has happened at several in Malaysia.

Around the longhouse there are some pleasant **trails** into the forest that the Ibans use for hunting. You will need a guide, which can be arranged with a

### INTO MALAYSIA: LIMBANG AND LAWAS

If you're planning to **cross into Sarawak** – either to Limbang or to Lawas – you'll first have to make for the immigration post beside the turning for Kampung Puni, 5km west of Bangar. **Limbang** is easiest and cheapest to reach: after a B$5–10 taxi ride from Bangar, take a ferry (B$1) across the river at Kampung Puni, which marks the border with Malaysia, and then catch one of the connecting buses (6.30am–5pm; B$2) that run into Limbang. The only way to get to **Lawas** is to catch the Lawas Express bus which starts in Limbang at 8am, reaches Bangar around 9am and pulls into Lawas at 1pm. Going the other way from Lawas, it arrives at Bangar around 3pm, terminating in Limbang about an hour later.

travel agent in Bandar (around B$20–30 per person for a day-trip; B$50 overnight). If you choose an overnight trip, take your own gear and see if the people at the longhouse can help you prepare some food for the trip.

## MALAY AND MURUT HOMESTAYS

East of Bangar on the road to Lawas is the Labu region of Temburong. Again, the only way to get here is by taxi from Bangar. Rice paddies line the road on one side, while thick forest lines the other. About 15km further along this road from Bangar you come to the **Peradayan Forest Reserve**, where you can make the strenuous three-hour hike along a wooden path up Bukit Patoi. From the top of the hill there are great views across Brunei's spectacular, largely undisturbed rainforests south towards Sarawak. There are no facilities in the park.

About five kilometres beyond the reserve, a road to the right leads to **SEKOLOH**, a Malay and Murut village comprising a few dozen elevated dwellings. This area sometimes offers **homestays** and visitors are usually welcome here – but it's best to check ahead with the tourist office in Bangar (see p.68). The villagers take turns putting people up, thereby sharing the "fun" of having foreigners in their isolated kampung. Similar to the Iban longhouse, there is no set price as to what to pay and you should donate what you think the stay is worth; as a rough guide, work on the basis of B$5 for an overnight stay. Besides walking around the kampung, meeting people, eating and relaxing, there's little to do. Nevertheless, a visit to a homestay like this one gives you a rare insight into the lifestyle of traditional, rural Bruneians, and it's well worth making the effort to go for that alone.

# Cambodia

## HIGHLIGHTS

**ANGKOR WAT:** lose yourself among the soaring towers of these spectacular temple ruins

**RATTANAKIRI PROVINCE:** from Banlung, explore jungles, chunchiet villages and a volcanic lake

**KRATI:** glimpse the silver heads of rare Irrawaddy dolphins

**ROYAL PALACE AND SILVER PAGODA, PHNOM PENH:** marvel at the gleaming golden spires and vivid Ramayana murals

**SIHANOUKVILLE:** relax on pristine white-sand beaches, then enjoy the vibrant nightlife

## ROUGH COSTS

**DAILY BUDGET** Basic US$18/ Occasional treat US$25

**DRINK** Angkor beer (US$1)

**FOOD** Noodle soup from a street stall (*geauttev*; US$0.75); fried rice at a local restaurant (*bai chaa*; US$2)

**HOSTEL/BUDGET HOTEL** US$2–4/ US$4–10

**TRAVEL** Phnom Penh–Sihanoukville (230km): Bus 4hr, US$4; Share taxi/minibus, 3hr 30min, US$5

## FACT FILE

**POPULATION** 14 million

**AREA** 181,035 sq km

**LANGUAGE** Khmer

**RELIGIONS** Theravada Buddhism (95 percent), Islam, Christianity, Animism

**CURRENCY** Riel (r), US dollars

**CAPITAL** Phnom Penh

**INTERNATIONAL PHONE CODE** ⓣ+855

**TIME ZONE** GMT +7hr

# Introduction



**Having left its troubled past largely behind, Cambodia is fast becoming one of Southeast Asia's hottest destinations. Lured by ancient temples, relatively unspoilt beaches and a host of natural wonders to explore, tourists have been flocking to the country in increasing numbers over the past decade; 2007 saw two million foreign visitors, the Cambodian government proudly proclaims. With tourism infrastructure improving fast, modern Cambodia promises soon to rival its better-known neighbours in both accessibility and attractions.**

The Kingdom of Cambodia occupies a modest wedge of land, almost completely hemmed in by Vietnam, Laos and Thailand. Most visitors head for the stunning **Angkor** ruins, a collection of over one hundred temples dating back to the ninth century. Once the seat of power of the Khmer Empire, Angkor is royal extravagance on a grand scale, its imposing features enhanced by a dramatic setting of lush jungle greenery and verdant fields. The complex is acknowledged as the most exquisite example of ancient architecture in Southeast Asia, and has been declared a World Heritage Site by UNESCO.

The capital, **Phnom Penh**, is also an alluring attraction in its own right. Wide, sweeping boulevards and elegant, if neglected, French colonial-style facades lend the city a romantic appeal. However, there's also stark evidence that you're visiting one of the world's poorest countries. Halfway between Angkor and Phnom Penh, it's worth stopping off for a day at **Kampong Thom**, to make a side trip to the **pre-Angkor ruins** of Sambor Prei Kuk where there is scarcely another tourist in sight.

Miles of unspoilt beaches and remote islands offer sandy seclusion along the **southern coastline**. Although **Sihanoukville** is the main port of call, it's easy enough to commandeer transport to nearby hidden coves and offshore islands. **Ratanakiri** province in the northeastern corner of the country, with its hilltribes and volcanic scenery, is also becoming increasingly popular with visitors, while neighbouring **Mondulkiri** is less well known, but equally impressive, offering dramatic woodlands, villages and mountains. In the central plains, **Battambang**, Cambodia's second city, is a sleepy provincial capital, and the gateway to a region rich in Khmer Rouge history.

## WHEN TO GO

Cambodia's **monsoon climate** creates two distinct seasons. The southwesterly monsoon from May to October brings heavy rain, humidity and strong winds, while the northeasterly monsoon from November to April produces dry, hot weather, with average temperatures rising from 25°C in November to around 32°C in April. The best months to visit are December and January, as it's dry and relatively cool, though Angkor is at its most stunning during the lush rainy season.

## CHRONOLOGY

**First century AD** The area to the west of the Mekong Delta, along the trading route from India to China, begins to become an important commercial settlement, known by the Chinese as Funan.

**Sixth century** Now known as Chenla, the region is occupied by small, disparate fiefdoms operating

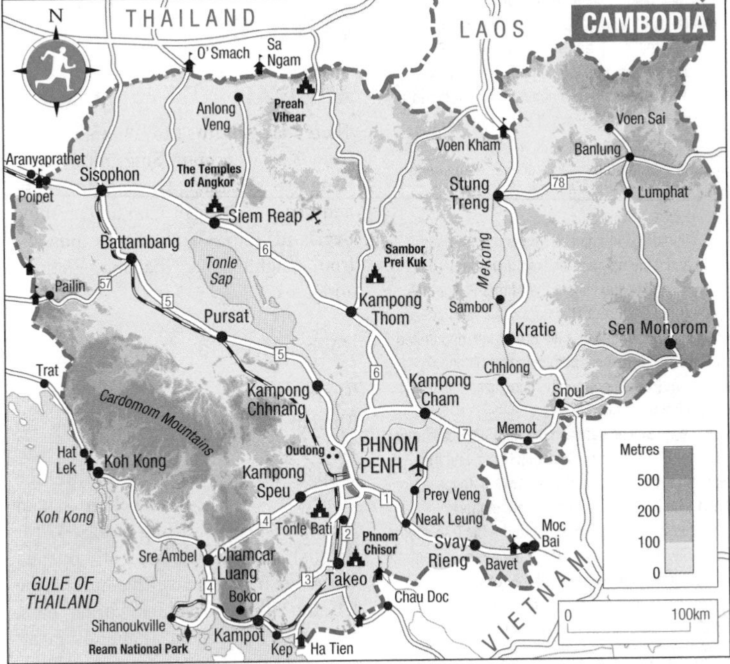


independently. The temples of Sambor Prei Kuk date from this time.

**Early ninth century** Rival Chenla kingdoms are united by Jayavarman II, and the Khmer Empire's greatest period, known as the Angkorian period, begins. Jayavarman II establishes the religious cult of the devaraja (god-king). The empire lasts for 39 successive kings.

**c.1181–1219** The reign of Jayavarman VII, the last major Angkor king. After reclaiming Angkor from the Champa empire he embarks on a massive programme of construction, culminating in the creation of Angkor Thom.

**Fourteenth century** The Thai army mounts raids on Cambodian territory, virtually destroying Angkor Thom.

**Mid-fifteenth century** The capital of Angkor is abandoned in favour of more secure locations to the south; the Khmer Empire is in irreversible decline.

**1594** The Khmer capital falls to the Thais; vast swathes of land are lost in tribute payments to both Siam and Vietnam.

**1863** King Norodom, wanting to reduce Thai control and secure his own position, exchanges mineral and timber rights with the French in return for military protection.

**1904** King Norodom dies; the following three kings are chosen by the French.

**1941** Eighteen-year-old Prince Norodom Sihanouk succeeds King Monivong; World War II interrupts French control and Japan invades.

**1945** Following the Japanese surrender, King Sihanouk campaigns for independence; France, preoccupied by Vietnam, grants it.

**May 1954** Independence is formally recognized by the Geneva Conference. Sihanouk abdicates the throne, installing his father Norodom Suramarit as king, to fight in the elections.

**1955** Sihanouk's party, The People's Socialist Community, wins every seat in the newly formed parliament. Political opposition is ruthlessly repressed, and communist elements, the "Khmers Rouges", flee to the countryside.

**1960** Sihanouk's father dies and he appoints himself Chief of State, in a further gesture of despotic power.

**1960s** Despite publicly declaring neutrality over the Vietnam conflict, Sihanouk allows the North Vietnamese to use Cambodian soil for supplying the Viet Cong.

**1969–73** The US covertly bombs Cambodia's eastern provinces, where they believe Viet Cong guerrillas are hiding. Thousands of Cambodian civilians are killed or maimed.

**1970** General Lon Nol and Prince Sisowath Matak depose Sihanouk. The Viet Cong are ordered to leave, but instead push deeper into Cambodia, pursued by US and South Vietnamese troops. As the country turns into a battlefield, the Khmer Rouge regroup and begin taking control of large areas.

**April 17, 1975** Khmer Rouge forces march into Phnom Penh to the cheers of the Cambodian people. Under Communist party leader Pol Pot, they institute a brutal regime to eradicate all perceived opposition, killing between one and two million people (see p.93).

**1978** Invading Vietnamese forces reach Phnom Penh and a Vietnamese-backed government led by Hun Sen is established; the Khmer Rouge flee to the jungle near the Thai border. A rival Chinese-backed government-in-exile is created, dominated by the Khmer Rouge, and headed by Sihanouk; the international community recognizes this in opposition to Vietnam.

**1987** Negotiations between the Hun Sen government and the coalition led by Sihanouk begin, and the Vietnamese agree to start withdrawing troops.

**1991** The Paris Peace Accords are signed. Sweeping powers are granted to the UN Transitional Authority in Cambodia (UNTAC) to supervise control of the country and implement free elections, but under UNTAC there is little disarmament.

**1993** Despite assassinations and intimidation tactics, there is a nearly ninety percent turnout at the elections; a fragile coalition between the royalist FUNCINPEC party, led by Prince Norodom Ranariddh, and Hun Sen's Cambodian People's Party (CPP) is agreed. Sihanouk is reinstated as constitutional monarch in August.

**1994** The Khmer Rouge are outlawed, and though they still control the north and northwest, an amnesty begins to attract some defections.

**1996** Notorious senior Khmer Rouge commander Ta Mok arrests Pol Pot and sentences him to life imprisonment; more defections follow.

**April 1998** As Cambodian troops encroach on the last Khmer Rouge strongholds, Pol Pot dies, possibly of a heart attack, or possibly executed by his own cadre.

**July 1998** Hun Sen's CPP wins another election; an alliance is negotiated, with Hun Sen as sole prime minister.

**2004** King Sihanouk abdicates and invites one of his sons, Norodom Sihamoni, to replace him as king. In October Phnom Penh is the site of grand and ancient royal ceremonies last performed on Sihanouk's coronation in 1941.

**2008** UN-backed war crimes trials of former Khmer Rouge leaders begin. The first to stand trial is Kaing Guek Eav (also known as Duch), head of S21 prison in Phnom Penh (see p.93). Four other senior Khmer Rouge are due to stand trial later in the year.

# Basics

## ARRIVAL

There are **flights** to Phnom Penh from Kuala Lumpur, Singapore, Seoul, Bangkok, Vientiane, Ho Chi Minh City, and several cities in China. Travelling **overland** into Cambodia is possible from neighbouring Thailand, Vietnam and Laos.

### Overland from Thailand

There are six entry points from Thailand: the border crossing at **Aranyaprathet**, east of Bangkok, near Poipet; two crossings at **Pailin**; the coastal border at **Hat Lek** to Cham Yeam, west of Koh Kong (see p.837 for details); and the more recently opened crossings in northeast Thailand, at the **Chong Chom–O'Smach** border pass, near Kap Choeng in Thailand's Surin province (see p.826), and the little-used **Sa Ngam–Choam** border in Si Saket province.

### Overland from Laos

From Laos, there are two crossing points in the far south, close to Stung Treng, one by road, the other by river (see p.469).

### Overland from Vietnam

From Vietnam, four crossings are open to foreigners: one northwest of Ho Chi Minh City at **Moc Bai** to Bavet, south-east of Phnom Penh (see p.917), and two near **Chau Doc**, northwest of Can Tho on the Bassac river (see p.925); and one east of Kep along the coast, known as the **Ha Tien** crossing (see p.931).

## VISAS

All foreign nationals, except Malaysians, Lao and Singaporeans, need a **visa** to enter Cambodia. **Tourist visas**, valid for thirty days, cost $20 and are issued on arrival at Pochentong Airport in Phnom Penh and at the airport at Siem Reap; two passport photos are required. It's also possible to obtain a visa on arrival at all overland border crossings, although Cambodian border officials have been known to inflate the price. To avoid the risk, you may prefer to take care of your tourist visa online in advance (Ⓦevisa.mfaic.gov.kh), though these e-visas are not valid at all overland crossing points – check the map on the website for details. **E-visas** cost $25 and can take up to thirty days to process; you'll need to provide scans of your passport and a digital photograph.

**Extending a tourist visa** is a painless process in Phnom Penh, but impossible elsewhere in Cambodia, so if you're planning a long trip into the provinces think about whether you'll need an extension before you go. Extensions are issued at the Department of Immigration, Pochentong Road, opposite the airport in Phnom Penh (Mon–Fri 8–10.30am & 2.30–4.30pm). You'll need one passport photo and next-day service costs $45. Given the location of the offices, it's easier to take advantage of the extension services offered by travel agents and guesthouses; they can do the running around for you and charge just a couple of dollars' commission. A tourist visa can only be extended once, for one month. You are charged $5 per day for overstaying your visa.

## GETTING AROUND

**Transport** in Cambodia is all part of the adventure. Some of the roads are in a terrible state, although this is slowly changing, and urban traffic patterns, or lack thereof, can make your head spin. **Boats** can only operate when the water is high enough, and the **train** system is so decrepit that for years it has only been used for freight. Fortunately, Cambodia is not a big country and its fairly functional **bus** system is expanding rapidly, while **share taxis** operate where the buses don't run.

### AIRPORT DEPARTURE TAX

Cambodian **airport tax** from both Pochentong and Siem Reap is currently $25 for international departures, and $6 for domestic departures.

### Buses

**Buses and coaches**, operated by a number of private companies, are the cheapest and most comfortable way to get around Cambodia. While they don't yet run on all routes, buses are available between major cities and towns and a rapidly expanding list of smaller ones. The main drawback is that they are usually slower than shared taxis or minibuses, and occasionally much slower – Kampot to Phnom Penh by bus takes up to six hours, for example, while by taxi it can be done in three. Check the route to decide whether saving the couple of dollars is really worth it. With new bus companies opening up all the time, frequencies between routes vary from month to month. It's safe to assume that for most routes there are many buses per day – significant exceptions to this are noted in the "Moving on" sections of the text.

### Share taxis and minibuses

**Share taxis** – often scarcely adequate two-wheel-drive Toyotas – and their battered **minibus** counterparts, are the country's most ubiquitous form of transport. Taxis operate on nearly every route a bus would, and many more, usually cramming four people into the front seat and four into the back; minibuses tend to be similarly cramped and aren't particularly comfortable either. **Prices** vary according to distance, but they tend to be slightly more expensive than buses, so many people use them as a last resort. Timetables don't exist for shared transport: they leave as soon as they're full, from early in the morning normally through to about 1 or 2pm. Drivers don't like to travel at night, so for long-distance destinations the majority move off first thing, around 6 or 7am.

## Local transport

Motorcycle taxis, commonly called **motos**, are the most convenient way of getting around town and are inexpensive – short journeys cost 2000–4000r. Their baseball-capped drivers are highly skilled at spotting customers, often before they even realize they need a ride. English-speaking drivers can usually be found outside hotels, guesthouses and other tourist spots, though they may well charge a small premium for being able to communicate. Non-English-speaking drivers will often nod enthusiastically in a show of understanding, only to proceed to the nearest guesthouse or tourist site. You can hire a moto for the day to visit sights in and around towns all over the country: for trips within a twenty-kilometre radius, a daily rate of $6 is a pretty good deal for both sides; over that, around $10 is the norm.

Three-wheeled **cyclos** (cycle rickshaws) are a more relaxing way to trundle around Phnom Penh, but are only practical for shorter trips. Cyclo fares are subject to negotiation, usually costing a little more than motos (4000–8000r), and a little more still in the midday heat or pouring rain. Another option is **tuk-tuks**, motorbike-drawn rickshaws that ply the roads of most major cities; they can comfortably carry up to four people, and cost around 4000–12,000r per trip. With motos, cyclos and tuk-tuks, it's best to agree a fare in advance.

**Taxis** aren't really used for short hops around town. There is one metered taxi service in Phnom Penh, which you must book in advance. Otherwise, cars are rented by the day, or by the journey.

## Vehicle rental

Renting a **motorbike** is the most practical self-drive option for Cambodia's poor provincial roads. At the rental shops in Phnom Penh, you can pick up a fairly good 250cc trials bike ($10 per day), which should be able to handle most terrain. **Cars** tend to come with a driver. They're almost exclusively white Toyota Camrys, and cost around $40 per day.

If you do intend to **self-drive** any vehicle in Cambodia, bear in mind that road conditions are unpredictable. Your journey may take much longer than you anticipate, you should never travel alone, and it's a good idea to carry food and water. Really, it's only practical if you've had extensive experience of driving in Southeast Asia already.

Officially, vehicles drive on the right, but **traffic regulations** in Cambodia are flexible and you may encounter people driving on the left. Traffic on the roads from Phnom Penh to Sihanoukville and Kampong Cham is heavy and hectic, but much lighter elsewhere.

**Bicycles** are available to rent cheaply, and except in Phnom Penh, where traffic is intimidating, cycling is a pleasant way to explore.

## Trains

Although plans to restore sections of Cambodia's dilapidated **train** network have recently been announced, including a rail link to Poipet, it is unlikely to include much in the way of passenger services.

## Boats

**Boats** are an easy way to travel to areas on the Tonle Sap and the south coast, though boat routes along the Mekong River have recently been dropped due to the improvement of the road system that runs parallel to the river. On the whole, Malaysian-made express boats are used – a cross between an old school bus and a torpedo. The ride is more comfortable (and much faster) than in a taxi, but conditions are still fairly cramped so don't expect the luxury that the foreigner prices imply. Many tourists opt to sit on the roof for the views.

### Planes

There is only one domestic route in Cambodia: Siem Reap Airways flies between Phnom Penh and Siem Reap for around $90 one-way. All other routes are currently suspended.

## ACCOMMODATION

There are guesthouses or basic hotels in every provincial town, with a wide range of styles from traditional wooden houses to modern concrete blocks. In general, expect to have an en-suite cold-water shower, with towel and toilet paper. The cheapest **hotel** rooms go for a bargain $5 and almost always have cable TV – a Cambodian necessity.

Tourist-oriented **budget guesthouses** are springing up in towns across the country, though you'll find most of them in Phnom Penh, Siem Reap and Sihanoukville. It's possible to get a bed for $2 if you don't mind basic facilities. Most establishments offer a range of rooms; the cheapest usually have one bed – although it is often a double (*graiy thom*) – and a fan. A dollar or so more expensive are those with attached bathrooms and two beds. Throughout the country, you'll pay $5 more per night for a/c. Price codes given in the text relate to the cost of the cheapest room, but most establishments will offer more luxurious rooms as well. You'll also find a number of **mid-range guesthouses** in the main towns, offering better-appointed accommodation with hot water, for $10–15. It's always worth negotiating at these, especially in low season (May–Oct).

**Camping** is theoretically illegal in Cambodia, but is a possibility in some places – for example, on the beaches and islands of the south coast. In the dry season, all you need is a mosquito net and hammock for a comfortable night's sleep.

**Electricity** is usually supplied at 220 volts, through plugs of the two-flat-pin variety. Power cuts and power surges are common, and hotels and guesthouses often have back-up generators.

### ADDRESSES

Many roads in Cambodia have no names, and those that do are often known by a number rather than a name, so for example, 50 Street 125 means building number 50 on Street 125. Throughout the chapter, where street names are non-existent, we have located places by describing their location or giving a nearby landmark.

## FOOD AND DRINK

Cambodian food is heavily influenced by China, with **stir-fries** featuring on most menus. Some dishes are similar to Thai cuisine, but with herbs being used for flavouring rather than spices. Chilli is usually served on the side rather than blended into the dish. Even **curry dishes**, such as the delicious coconut milk and fish *amok*, tend to be served very mild. **Rice** is the staple food, while **noodles** are eaten more for breakfast – when they're served as a soup – and as a snack. Hygiene standards may not match what you're used to, but produce is always fresh. At street stalls though, given the lack of refrigeration it's as well to make sure the food is piping hot. If you have a choice, pick somewhere that's busy.

### Where to eat

The cheapest Khmer cuisine is to be found at **street stalls** and **markets**, which is where you'll find dishes more like the ones the locals eat at home. There are usually one or two dishes on offer at each stall – perhaps pigs' organ soup, fried noodles or a tasty filled baguette. If you're ordering soup, you can pick and choose the ingredients to taste. These stalls are dirt cheap – you can certainly get a meal for less than $1 – though the portions tend to be on the small side. Some baguette and noodle stalls are open throughout the day, but many more crop up around sunset.

**Khmer restaurants** are the next step up, recognizable by their beer signs outside. In the evenings, the better ones fill up early on, and most places close soon after 9pm. Buying a selection of dishes to share is the norm: each dish costs $1.50–3 and there's also a small cover charge. In these restaurants, as in beer gardens, drinks are purchased from "beer girls" (see "Drinks" below).

**Western restaurants** are plentiful in Phnom Penh, Siem Reap and Sihanoukville, though standards vary enormously. They usually cost more than Khmer restaurants, with meals at $3–5, and the more upmarket restaurants charge $5–10. Western-oriented restaurants tend to stay open later than their Khmer counterparts, usually closing around 11pm, or even later if they double as bars.

Many **guesthouses** also do meals – typically noodles, rice and pasta – for about the same price as Khmer restaurants. It's easy to make do with guesthouse food after a hard day's sightseeing, but for authentic Cambodian culinary colour, you'll need to be more adventurous.

## Khmer food

A standard **meal** in Cambodia consists of rice, plus two or three other dishes, either a fish or meat dish, and a steaming bowl of soup. Flavours are dominated by fish sauce, herbs – especially lemongrass (particularly in soup) – coconut milk and tamarind.

If you only try one Khmer dish, it should be *amok dt'ray*, a delightful fish curry with a rich coconut-milk sauce baked in banana leaves – you'll stand the best chance of finding it in Siem Reap. Most fish served in Cambodia is freshwater, and close to the Tonle Sap it is particularly abundant. Fish turns up on every menu, in popular dishes such as *dt'ray chorm hoy* (steamed fish), *dt'ray aing* (grilled fish) and *sumlar mjew groueng dt'ray* (Cambodian fish soup with herbs).

For **snacks**, try *noam enseum j'rook* (sticky rice, soy beans and pork served in a bamboo tube) or *noam enseum jake* (sticky rice and banana). Baguettes (*noam pang*) are always a handy snack food, especially when travelling. Vendors have a selection of fillings, normally pork pâté, sardines, pickled vegetables and salad.

There are some surprisingly tasty **desserts** to be found at street stalls, markets and some restaurants, many of them made from rice and coconut milk. They're very cheap, so you could try a selection. Succulent **fruits** are widely available at the markets. Rambutan, papaya, pineapple, mangosteen and dragonfruit are delicious, and bananas incredibly cheap. Durians grow in abundance in Kampot, and are, according to Cambodians, the world's finest; they're in season from late March.

## Drinks

If you want to reduce the chance of stomach problems, don't drink the **water** and don't take **ice** out on the streets, although it's generally safe in Western bars and restaurants. Bottled, sealed water is available everywhere. Other thirst-quenchers are the standard international **soft drinks** brands, available in bottles or cans, and a few local variants. Freshly squeezed sugar-cane juice is another healthy roadside favourite, although the tastiest Khmer beverage has to be *dteuk krolok*, a sweet, milky fruit shake, to which locals add an egg for extra nutrition.

**Coffee** is often served iced and black, with heaps of sugar; if you order it white, it comes with a slug of condensed milk already in the glass. Chinese-style **tea** is commonly drunk with meals, and is served free in most restaurants. You'll only find Western tea in tourist restaurants.

The local brew is Angkor **beer**, a fairly good drop, owing in part to the use of Australian technology at the Sihanoukville brewery. International brands, such as Tiger, Fosters and Heineken, are also on offer at restaurants and beer gardens and are purchased from so-called **beer girls**. Each brand has its own beer girls, so if you want a particular brand you have to order from the corresponding beer girl. Once you've ordered, a tray of cans is brought to your table and a beer girl will keep coming back to open the cans and top up your glass.

## CULTURE AND ETIQUETTE

Cambodians are extremely conservative, and regardless of their means do their very best to keep clean; you'll gain more respect if you're well turned out and modest in your dress. Men should wear tops and women avoid skimpy tops and tight shorts. Particularly offensive to Cambodians is any display of public affection between men and women: even seeing foreigners holding hands is a source of acute embarrassment. Cambodia shares many of the same attitudes to **dress** and **social taboos** as other Southeast Asian cultures (see p.45).

**Tipping** is common only in Western restaurants, where a couple of thousand riel is generally adequate.

## SPORTS AND OUTDOOR ACTIVITIES

Cambodia's lack of tourist infrastructure, combined with the continuing danger of landmines, has made trekking and mountain biking difficult (if not downright dangerous) in the past. However, an increasing number of opportunities are appearing for travellers hankering to get outdoors.

For **trekking**, the place to be is the northeast, particularly Banlung and Sen Monorom, where local guides can lead groups or individuals on overnight excursions into the surrounding jungle and Virachey National Park (p.138). Another good place to hike is in the forested mountains around Kampot, where the closure of Bokor's access road has boosted the popularity of overnight treks up to the abandoned French colonial resort (p.127).

For **diving**, a number of PADI dive shops have opened up in Sihanoukville, all of which offer certification courses, fun dives and "discover diving" outings for beginners (see p.121).

**Mountain biking** is a bit more difficult to organize, although for those with some cash to spare, several companies in Phnom Penh organize bike trips down to the coast and into the surrounding villages. Pepy (Ⓣ023/222804, Ⓦwww.pepyride.org) leads tours in support of local education programmes, though you should contact them in advance.

## COMMUNICATIONS

To send anything by **mail** it's best to use the main post office in Phnom Penh, as all mail from the provinces is consolidated here anyway. International post is often delivered in around a week, but can take up to a month, depending on the destination. **Poste restante** is available at the Phnom Penh, Siem Reap and Sihanoukville post offices.

To **phone abroad** from Cambodia, dial Ⓣ001 + IDD country code + area code minus first 0 + subscriber number. For international directory enquiries, call Ⓣ1201. Making a phone call in Cambodia, is expensive, however – about double the amount you'd pay in Bangkok, for example. The cheapest and easiest way to call abroad is via the internet, a service offered by most internet cafés. Calls to landlines in the US and Europe cost 200r–400r/min, while calls to mobiles cost around 1,500r/min. Both domestic and international calls (IDD) can also be made from guesthouses, hotels, post offices and public phone booths. Phone cards are usually on sale at the shop nearest to the phone booth.

The cost of **internet access** in Phnom Penh and Siem Reap has been sent tumbling by an improved telephone system and an influx of internet cafés. Surfing the net costs 400r/hr on average. Internet access is available in most other major cities, although it can cost up to three times as much as in Phnom Penh and is unreliable.

## CRIME AND SAFETY

The **security situation** in Cambodia has improved significantly over the last few years. Areas that were once plagued with bandit activity or by the threat of unpredictable Khmer Rouge factions are now safe to travel in. In spite of recent crackdowns, however, there is still a culture of guns in Cambodia, and there have been incidents of armed robbery against locals and tourists alike. All areas covered in this book are safe to travel to and within overland, but you should remain alert to the fact that Cambodia, as well as being one of the most mined countries in the world, also has a terrible legacy of unexploded ordinances (UXO). See below for more.

**Gun crime** is actually more frequent in Phnom Penh than anywhere else in the country, and reaches a peak at festival times, most notably Khmer New Year. Even so, the threat is small, so it shouldn't stop you enjoying the nightlife.

There are plenty of civilian and military **police** hanging around, whose main function appears to be imposing arbitrary fines or tolls for motoring "offences". Of the two, the **civilian police**, who wear blue or khaki uniforms, are more helpful. Military police wear black-and-white armbands. If find yourself in need of actual police assistance, your best bet are the **tourist police** offices in major cities; they generally speak some English.

### Landmines

The war has ended, but the killing continues. Years of guerrilla conflict have left Cambodia the most densely mined country in the world. The statistics are horrendous: up to six million **landmines** in the country; over fifty thousand amputees; and a further one thousand mine victims every year. The worst affected areas are the province of Battambang and the border regions adjacent to Thailand in the northwest, namely Banteay Meanchey, Pailin and Preah Vihear provinces.

Although the risk is very real for those who work in the fields, the threat to tourists is minimal. The main **tourist areas** are clear of mines, and even in the heavily mined areas, towns and roads

### CAMBODIA ON THE NET

**www.bayonpearnik.com** Travel information, listings and local gossip with a humorous twist, produced and written by expats.

**www.canbypublications.com** Online version of the free tourist guides available in Phnom Penh, Sihanoukville and Siem Reap, full of up-to-date information about food, lodging and transport.

**www.talesofasia.com** Reliable practical advice on border crossings, overland travel and assorted off-road adventures; mainly Cambodia, though it covers several other countries as well.

are safe. The main danger occurs when striking off into fields or forests, so the simple solution is to stick to known safe paths. If you must cross a dubious area, try to use a local guide, or at least ask the locals "*mian min dtay*?" ("Are there mines here?"). Look out for the red mine-warning signs, and on no account touch anything suspicious-looking.

## MEDICAL CARE AND EMERGENCIES

For serious **medical emergencies**, consider flying to Bangkok, although clinics and hospitals in Phnom Penh are equipped to deal with most ailments (see p.98). Sihanoukville and Siem Reap have limited facilities, but generally medical facilities outside Phnom Penh are poor. If you're stuck in the provinces and require emergency evacuation to Phnom Penh, contact International SOS on ⓣ023/216911. General emergency telephone numbers are listed in the box below, but whatever the emergency, it's probably best to contact the English-speaking operators, available 24 hours.

Street-corner **pharmacies** throughout Cambodia are well stocked with basic supplies, and money rather than a prescription gives easy access to anything available, though beware of out-of-date medication. Standard shop hours (see p.88) apply at most of these places, but some stay open in the evening. More reputable operations with English- and French-speaking pharmacists can be found in Phnom Penh, where a wider variety of specialized drugs are available. Some even offer 24-hour service (see p.99).

### EMERGENCY NUMBERS

Police ⓣ117
Fire ⓣ118
Ambulance ⓣ119
Police assistance (English, French and Italian spoken) ⓣ023/724793 or 012/942484

## INFORMATION AND MAPS

Cambodia is beginning to recognize the importance of tourism to its economy, and is establishing a network of basic **tourist offices**. These offices, however, are desperately starved of resources and generally don't have much information, so it's better to ask at local guesthouses.

International Travel Maps publishes a useful 1:800,000 **map**. If you're travelling around the region, you could try the 1:2,000,000 regional map of Vietnam, Cambodia and Laos published by UBD or Bartholomew. Bear in mind, however, that all these maps are based on dated surveys: the existence of a road is no guarantee as to condition; many of the older roads featured no longer exist; and new roads are not shown.

## MONEY AND BANKS

Cambodia's unit of currency is the **riel**, abbreviated to "r". **Notes** come in denominations of 50, 100, 200, 500, 1000, 2000, 5000, 10,000, 20,000, 50,000 and 100,000, although the bigger notes are seldom seen, as dollars tend to be used for larger transactions. **US dollars** are accepted everywhere; you can pay in dollars rather than riel at guesthouses, restaurants, tourist sites, even street stalls. In fact, it's possible to get by in Cambodia without actually changing any foreign currency into riel at all. Coins are not used, however, so all of your small change will come back to you in local currency, and smaller transactions are almost always priced in riel; the standard rate used is $1 = 4000r. **Thai baht**, abbreviated to "B", are also widely used in the border areas, and on the main trade routes from Thailand.

It's best to change your currency into dollars before you enter Cambodia, although banks in Phnom Penh and Siem Reap will exchange most currencies. **ATMs** are easy to find in most cities, particularly at branches of ANZ Royal Bank, where for a

## KHMER

Khmer is the national language of Cambodia. Unusually for the region, it is not a tonal language, which theoretically makes it easier to master. However, the difficulty lies with pronunciation, as there are both vowels and consonant clusters that are pronounced unlike any sounds in English. What follows here is a phonetic approximation widely used for teaching Khmer. (People and places throughout this chapter follow the commonly used romanized spellings rather than the phonetic system used below.)

### Pronunciation

Most consonants follow English pronunciation, except the following:

**bp** a sharp "p" sound, between the English "b" and "p"
**dt** a sharp "t" sound, between the English "d" and "t"
**hs** soft "h"
**n'y/ñ** as in "canyon"
**a** as in "ago"
**aa** as in "bar"
**ai** as in "Thai"
**ao** as in "Lao"
**ay** as in "pay"
**ee** as in "see"
**eu** as in the expression of disgust "uugh"
**i** as in "fin"
**o** as in "long"
**oa** as in "moan"
**oo** as in "shoot"
**ou** similar to "cow"
**OO** as in "look"
**u** as in "fun"

### Greetings and basic phrases

| | |
|---|---|
| Hello | *soo-a s'day* |
| How are you? | *sok sa-bai jee-a dtay?* |
| Fine, thanks | *sok sa-bai jee-a dtay* |
| Goodbye | *lee-a hou-ee* |
| Excuse me | *soam dtoah* |
| Please | *soam* |
| Thank you | *or-gOOn* |
| Can you speak English? | *nee'ak jeh ni-yee-ay pee-a-saa ong-klayh reu dtay?* |
| I don't understand | *k'nyom s'dup meun baan dtay* |
| Yes (male) | *baht* |
| Yes (female) | *jahs* |
| No | *dtay* |
| Where is the? | *… noo-ee-naa?* |
| Ticket | *som-bot* |
| Airport | *jom nort yoo-un hoh/aa- gaah-sa-yee-un-taan* |
| Boat (no engine) | *dtook* |
| Boat (with engine) | *karnowt* |
| Bus/coach | *laan tom/laan krong* |
| Taxi | *dtak-see* |
| Car | *laan toit* |
| Bicycle | *gong* |
| Bank | *tor-nee-a-gee-a* |
| Post office | *bprai-sa-nee* |
| Passport | *li-keut ch'lorng dain* |
| Hotel | *son-ta-gee-a* |
| Motorbike taxi | *moto/motodub* |
| Restaurant | *poa-cha-nee-ya-taan* |
| Please stop here | *soam chOOp tee neeh* |
| Left/right | *ch'wayng/s'dam* |
| Do you have any rooms? | *nee'ak mee-un bon-dtOOp dtay?* |
| How much is it? | *t'lai bpon maan?* |
| Cheap/expensive | *taok/t'lai* |
| Single room A/c | *bon-dtOOp graiy moo-ay maa-seen dtro-chey-at* |

small fee you can withdraw money via Cirrus/Maestro. **Credit-card cash advances** are available in Phnom Penh, Siem Reap, Sihanoukville and Battambang, but don't rely on them as a source of cash, as systems are unreliable. Branches of the Canadia Bank give commission-free cash advances

| | |
|---|---|
| Electric fan | *dong-harl* |
| Mosquito net | *mOOng* |
| Toilet paper | *gra-daah* |
| Telephone | *dtoo-ra-sup* |

**Emergencies**

| | |
|---|---|
| Help! | *choo-ee!* |
| Are there any mines here? | *mee-un meen dtay?* |
| Accident | *kroo-ah t'nak* |
| Please call a doctor | *soam hao kroo bphet moak* |
| Hospital | *moo-un dtee bphet* |
| Police station | *bpohs bpoli* |

**Numbers**

| | |
|---|---|
| 1 | *moi* |
| 2 | *bpee* |
| 3 | *bai* |
| 4 | *bpoo-oun* |
| 5 | *bprahm* |
| 6 | *bprahm-moi* |
| 7 | *bprahm bpee/ bprahm bpeul* |
| 8 | *bprahm-bai* |
| 9 | *bprahm- bpoo-oun* |
| 10 | *dop* |
| 11, 12, 13, etc | *dop moi/moi don dop, dop bpee/bpee don dop, dop bai/ bai don-dop* |
| 20 | *m'pay* |
| 30, 40, 50, etc | *saam seup, sai seup, haa seup* |
| 100 | *moi roy* |
| 101 | *moi roy moi* |
| 200, 300, 400, etc | *bpee roy, bai roy, bpoo- oun roy* |
| 1000 | *moi bpoa-un* |
| 10,000 | *moi meun* |

**Food and drinks glossary**

| | |
|---|---|
| *lerk gai-o* | Cheers! |
| *dtai bon-lai soam* | Only vegetables, please |
| *k'nyom niam sait dtey, sait dt'ray* | I don't eat meat or fish |
| *k'nyom chong…* | I'd like… |

**Rice and noodles**

| | |
|---|---|
| *geautiev* | noodle soup |
| *mee chaa* | fried noodles |
| *bai* | cooked rice |
| *bai chaa* | fried rice |

**Fish, meat and vegetables**

| | |
|---|---|
| *bong-kong* | shrimp/prawn |
| *bon-lai* | vegetables |
| *bpayng boh* | tomato |
| *bpoat* | corn |
| *dom-loang barang* | potato |
| *dt'ray* | fish |
| *dtee-a* | duck |
| *dtray-meuk* | squid |
| *g'daam* | crab |
| *moa-un* | chicken |
| *sait goa* | beef |
| *sait j'rook* | pork |
| *sait* | meat |

**Basics**

| | |
|---|---|
| *bpong* | egg |
| *bpong moa-un chien* | fried eggs |
| *m'tayh* | chilli |
| *dtao-oo* | tofu |
| *nOOm-bpung* | bread |
| *om-beul* | salt |
| *plai cher* | fruit |
| *s'gor* | sugar |

**Drinks**

| | |
|---|---|
| *bee-yair* | beer |
| *dteuk dtai* | tea |
| *dteuk groatch-grobaight* | orange juice |
| *dteuk doang* | coconut milk |
| *dteuk k'nai choo* | palm wine |
| *dteuk sot moi dorb* | bottle of water |
| *dteuk om bpow* | sugar-cane juice |
| *dteuk sot* | drinking water |
| *ka-fei dteuk doh goa* | coffee with milk |
| *gaa-fay khmao* | coffee (black) |
| *ot dak dteuk kork* | no ice |

on Visa and MasterCard. **Traveller's cheques** can be changed at most banks for a small commission, normally two percent.

The easiest way to get **money wired** to you in Cambodia is via the branches of the Acleda Bank, agents for Western Union in Cambodia, or via

MoneyGram, handled by Canadia Bank and Cambodia Commercial Bank; all have branches in major towns.

On the whole, food and accommodation is slightly more expensive in Cambodia than in its neighbouring countries, however, it's possible to live quite **cheaply** if you stay in the cheapest guesthouses and eat only at the markets and street stalls A **two-tier pricing system** is beginning to develop and tourists are being asked to pay a hefty premium for some transport and entrance fees. Unlike in neighbouring Vietnam, however, you're unlikely to be ripped off for local services, with motos, pick-ups, accommodation and food charged at the Cambodian price.

## OPENING HOURS AND HOLIDAYS

**Opening hours** vary, and even posted "official" times tend to be flexible, as many people juggle more than one job. In theory, **office hours** are Monday to Saturday 7.30am to 5.30pm, with a siesta of at least two hours from around 11.30am. **Banking hours** are generally Monday to Friday 8.30am to 3.30pm, and many banks are also open on Saturday morning. **Post offices** (7am–5pm, or later), markets, **shops** (7am–8pm, or later), travel agents and many tourist offices open every day.

### Public holidays

**January 1** International New Year's Day
**January 7** Victory Day over the Genocidal Regime, celebrating the liberation of Phnom Penh in 1979 from the Khmer Rouge
**March 8** International Women's Day
**April 12/13–15 (variable)** Bonn Chaul Chhnam (Khmer New Year)
**May 1** Labour Day
**May (variable)** Bonn Chroat Preah Nongkoal, the "Royal Ploughing Ceremony"
**May (variable)** Visakha Bochea commemorates the birth of Buddha
**June 1** International Children's Day
**June 18** Her Majesty the Queen's Birthday
**September 24** Constitution and Coronation Day
**Late September** Bonn P'chum Ben, "Ancestors' Day"
**September 24** Constitution and Coronation Day
**October 23** Anniversary of the Paris Peace Accords commemorates the 1991 Paris conference on Cambodia
**October 30–November 1** King Sihanouk's Birthday
**November 9** Independence Day
**Early November** Bonn Om Tuk, "Water Festival"
**December 10** UN Human Rights' Day

## FESTIVALS

Festivals tend to be fixed by the lunar calendar, so dates vary from year to year.

**Bonn Chaul Chhnam** (mid-April) Khmer New Year is the most significant festival of the year, a time when families get together, homes are spring-cleaned and people flock to the temples with elaborate offerings of fruits, flowers, cakes, rice and drinks.

**Bonn P'chum Ben** (late Sept) "Ancestors' Day" is one of the most important events in the festive calendar, and the beginning of festival season. Families make offerings to their ancestors in the days leading up to it, and celebrations take place in temples on the day itself.

**Bonn Om Tuk** (early Nov) The "Water Festival" is celebrated every year when the current of the Tonle Sap, which swells so much during the rainy season that it actually pushes water upstream, reverses and flows back into the Mekong River. The centre of festivities is Phnom Penh's riverbank, where everyone, including the royal family, gathers to watch boat racing, an illuminated boat parade and fireworks.

# Phnom Penh and around

Cambodia's capital, **PHNOM PENH**, sprawls west from the confluence of the Mekong and Tonle Sap rivers. When approaching from the airport, the city is a confusing mess, its main boulevards choked with motos and other traffic and lined with generic low-rise, concrete blocks. Despite initial impressions, however, the heart of Phnom Penh has a strong appeal. The French influence is evident in the colonial shophouses lining the boulevards, with the occasional majestic monument or public building animating the cityscape. The Phnom Penhois are open and friendly, and the city itself is small enough to get to know quickly. Phnom Penh may not have much in the way of tourist attractions – the majority of sights can be covered in a day or two – but many visitors end up lingering, if only to soak up the unique indolent atmosphere of this neglected city.

## What to see and do

Phnom Penh **city centre** can be loosely defined as the area between Monivong Boulevard and the Tonle Sap River, stretching as far north as Chroy Chung Va Bridge, and as far south as Sihanouk Boulevard. Its tourist hub is the scenic Sisowath Quay, from where most of the sights and monuments are easily accessible.

### Sisowath Quay and around

The heart of Phnom Penh life is a small, fairly nondescript square of land at the junction of **Sisowath Quay** and Street 184, in front of the Royal Palace. It's here that Cambodians used to congregate to listen to declarations and speeches from the monarch, and where Khmer families still gather in the evenings and at weekends. Picnics, games, kite-flying and perhaps a cup of *dteuk k'nai choo* are the order of the day. Running to the north and south, Sisowath Quay is lined with tall palms on one side, and bars, cafés and restaurants on the other. In the middle of the day the area is largely deserted but as evening draws in, it is transformed into a popular and lively social centre – the people of Phnom Penh enjoy the simple pleasures of the fine river views from the riverbank, while expats, tourists and well-to-do locals do the same from the luxury of the bars across the road. You can hire a boat for a short cruise up the Tonle Sap, particularly popular around sunset – boats can be rented along the shore for about $10/hr.

### The Royal Palace

Behind the park, set back from the riverbank on Sothearos Boulevard, stand the **Royal Palace** and adjacent Silver Pagoda (both daily 8–11am & 2–5pm; 25,000r entry to both), the city's finest examples of twentieth-century Khmer-influenced architecture. Both are one-storey structures – until the Europeans arrived, standing above another's head (the most sacred part of the body) was strictly prohibited.

You'll catch glimpses of the glistening, golden Royal Palace buildings behind the high daffodil-yellow perimeter walls. The buildings are at once simple and ornate – the main building structures follow uncomplicated geometry, but are crowned with highly decorative roofs.

The **palace** itself is strictly off-limits, but it's possible to visit several buildings within the compound, even when the king is around – a blue flag flies when he is in residence.

Visitors enter via the Silver Pagoda (see p.92) and are directed to the palace compound first, an oasis of order and calm. Head straight for the main building in the centre of the compound,

# PHNOM PENH

| EATING & DRINKING | |
|---|---|
| Boat Noodle | 23 |
| California 2 | 9 |
| Cantina | 9 |
| Capitol | L |
| Elsewhere | 20 |
| Foreign Correspondents' Club | 13 |
| Frizz | 9 |
| Garden Centre Café | 5 |
| Gold Fish River | 3 |
| Happy Herb's Bistro | 12 |
| Heart of Darkness | 14 |
| Howie's | 15 |
| Java Café | 22 |
| Lazy Gecko | 1 |
| Lumbini | 19 |
| The Magic Sponge | 2 |
| Mamak's Corner | 6 |
| Martini | 24 |
| Nature and Sea | 21 |
| Nouveau Pho de Paris | 17 |
| Pink Elephant | 11 |
| Ponlok | 10 |
| Pontoon | 4 |
| Riverside Bistro | 8 |
| Royal India | 18 |
| Sam Doo | 7 |
| Walkabout Hotel | 16 |

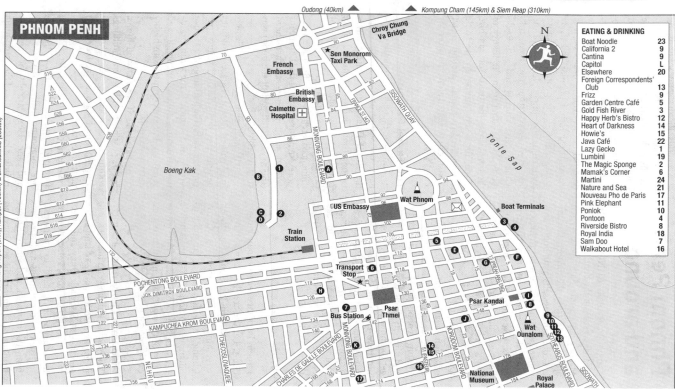

Oudong (40km)
Kompung Cham (145km) & Siem Reap (310km)
Pochentong Airport (3km), Kampot (150km) & Sihanoukville (230km)
N
Chroy Chung Va Bridge
Sen Monorom Taxi Park
French Embassy
British Embassy
Calmette Hospital
Tonle Sap
Boeng Kak
Wat Phnom
US Embassy
Boat Terminals
Train Station
Transport Stop
Psar Thmei
Bus Station
Psar Kandal
Wat Ounalom
National Museum
Royal Palace
SISOWATH QUAY
MONIVONG BOULEVARD
FRANCE ST (47)
POCHENTONG BOULEVARD
JOK DIMITROV BOULEVARD
KAMPUCHEA KROM BOULEVARD
TCHECOSLOVAQUEIE
NEHRU
CHARLES DE GAULLE BOULEVARD
NORODOM BOULEVARD
51 (PASTEUR)
13 (PREAH ANG ENG)
SOTHEAROS BOULEVARD
SISOWATH

## PHNOM PENH

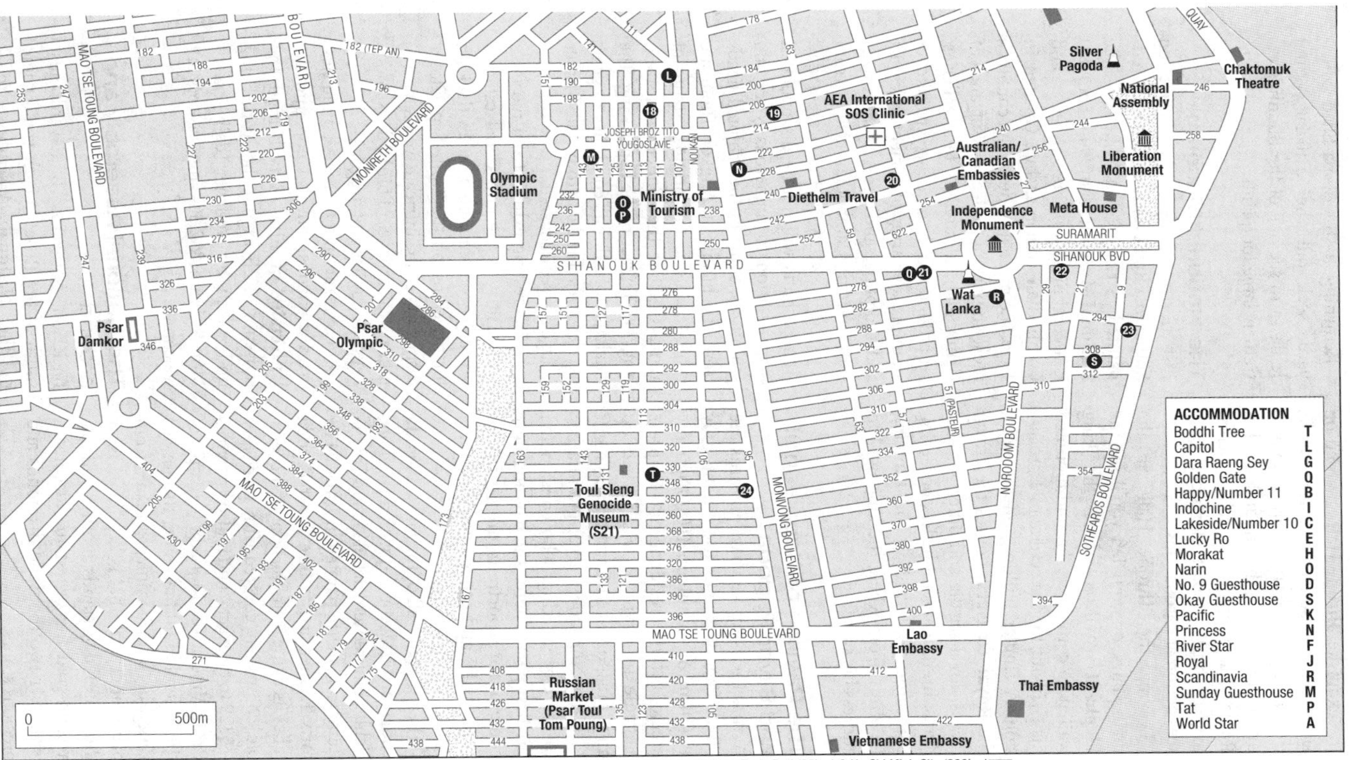
ACCOMMODATION
Boddhi Tree T
Capitol L
Dara Raeng Sey G
Golden Gate Q
Happy/Number 11 B
Indochine I
Lakeside/Number 10 C
Lucky Ro E
Morakat H
Narin O
No. 9 Guesthouse D
Okay Guesthouse S
Pacific K
Princess N
River Star F
Royal J
Scandinavia R
Sunday Guesthouse M
Tat P
World Star A
Chaktomuk Theatre
Silver Pagoda
National Assembly
Liberation Monument
Meta House
Australian/ Canadian Embassies
Independence Monument
Wat Lanka
AEA International SOS Clinic
Diethelm Travel
Ministry of Tourism
Olympic Stadium
Psar Olympic
Psar Damkor
Toul Sleng Genocide Museum (S21)
Russian Market (Psar Toul Tom Poung)
Lao Embassy
Thai Embassy
Vietnamese Embassy
QUAY
SURAMARIT
SIHANOUK BVD
SOTHEAROS BOULEVARD
NORODOM BOULEVARD
51 (PASTEUR)
MONIVONG BOULEVARD
SIHANOUK BOULEVARD
MAO TSE TOUNG BOULEVARD
JOSEPH BROZ TITO YOUGOSLAVIE
NOUKAN
MONIRETH BOULEVARD
182 (TEP AN)
BOULEVARD
500m
Monivong Bridge, Tonle Bati (35km) & Ho Chi Minh City (220km)
Choeung Ek (12km)

the exquisite **Throne Hall**, guarded on either side by statues of naga. Inside, the ceiling is adorned with colourful murals recounting the Hindu legend of Ramayana. The throne itself, watched over by busts of past monarchs, only sees action at coronations.

Leaving the Throne Hall via the main stairs, on your left you'll see the **Elephant Pavilion** where the king waited on coronation day and mounted his elephant for the ceremonial procession. A similar building on the right, the **Royal Treasury**, houses the crown jewels, royal regalia and other valuable items. In front and to the left, bordering Sothearos Boulevard, is the **Dancing Pavilion**, from where the king used to address his subjects.

## The Pavilion of Napoleon III and Silver Pagoda

Across the complex, back towards the Silver Pagoda stands the quaint, grey **Pavilion of Napoleon III**. Originally erected at the residence of Empress Eugénie in Egypt, it was packed up and transported to Cambodia as a gift to King Norodom, great-grandfather to the current king, who constructed the first palace here. The pavilion now contains royal portraits, dresses for the royal ballet and other royal paraphernalia.

The internal wall of the **Silver Pagoda courtyard** is decorated with a fabulous, richly coloured and detailed mural of the Ramayana myth, painted in 1903–04 by forty Khmer artists. The Silver Pagoda takes its name from the floor of the temple, completely covered with silver tiles – 5329 to be exact – and is also known as Preah Vihear Keo Morakot ("Temple of the Emerald Buddha"), after the famous **Emerald Buddha** image, made from baccarat crystal, that is kept here. Near the central dais stands another Buddha, a solid-gold life-size statue, decorated with over two thousand diamonds and precious stones.

Returning to the stupa-filled courtyard, seek out the artificial Mount Kailassa to see one of the Buddha's extremely large footprints.

## The National Museum

Just north of the Royal Palace on Sothearos Boulevard, the grand, red-painted structure that houses the **National Museum** (daily 8am–5pm; $3) is a combination of French design and Cambodian craftsmanship. Opened in 1920, the museum houses the country's most important collections of ancient Cambodian culture. Its four galleries, set around a tranquil courtyard, shelter an impressive array of ancient relics, art and sculpture, and general craftsmanship covering Cambodian history from the sixth century to the present day. Angkor buffs will not be disappointed – in addition to numerous relics and sculptures, some of the sculpted heads from the bridge at Angkor Thom are exhibited, as is the original statue of Yama God of the Underworld from Angkor's Terrace of the Leper King. The catalogue of exhibits continues to grow as treasures hidden from the Khmer Rouge are rediscovered.

An interesting exhibit from more recent history is the king's boat cabin, a portable wooden room used by the king for travelling on the Tonle Sap. Closer inspection of the intricate wooden carvings reveals images of birds, dogs, monkeys, crocodiles and dragons.

After examining the antiquities, art aficionados can also pop into the **University of Fine Arts** behind the museum to check out the work being undertaken by students (daily except Mon 8–11am & 2.30–5pm; visitors are welcome).

## The National Assembly and around

Back on Sothearos Boulevard, just south of the Royal Palace, you'll come to the **National Assembly**. You'll know if the Assembly is in session by the excessive police presence and a row of black limousines. Just beyond, on the other side of the road, there's a park, in the middle of which stands the **Liberation Monument**, sometimes called the Cambodia–Vietnamese Friendship Monument, commemorating the defeat of the Khmer Rouge in 1979. The southern tip of the park is crossed by Sihanouk Boulevard, lined with colonial-era buildings. Following Sihanouk Boulevard west brings you to **Independence Monument**, on the roundabout at the junction with Norodom Boulevard, built in 1958 to celebrate Cambodia's independence from France.

### Toul Sleng Genocide Museum (S21)

As the Khmer Rouge were starting their reign of terror, Toul Svay Prey Secondary School, in a quiet Phnom Penh neighbourhood about 2km from Sisowath Quay, was transformed into a primitive prison and interrogation centre. Corrugated iron and barbed wire were installed around the perimeter, and classrooms were divided into individual cells, or housed rows of prisoners secured by shackles. From 1975 to 1979, an estimated twenty thousand victims were imprisoned in **Security Prison 21**, or S21 as it became known. Teachers, students, doctors, monks and peasants suspected of anti-revolutionary behaviour were brought here, often with their spouses and children. They were subjected to horrific tortures, and then killed or taken to extermination camps outside the city.

The prison is now a **museum** (daily 7.30am–5.30pm; $2) and a monument to the thousands of Cambodians who suffered at the hands of the Khmer Rouge. It's been left almost exactly as it was found by the liberating Vietnamese forces – the fourteen victims found hideously disfigured in the individual

### THE KHMER ROUGE

Born of radical communism and wartime opportunism, the **Khmer Rouge** defined the darkest period in Cambodia's history, leaving a legacy that will last for generations. The rag-tag band of communist guerrillas, led by French-educated Saloth Sar (subsequently known as **Pol Pot**), first began to garner popular support during the American bombings of eastern Cambodia. After King Sihanouk was deposed (see p.77), the Khmer Rouge took advantage of the chaos to seize territory, eventually marching into Phnom Penh to the cheers of Cambodians longing for peace. But the party, known simply as *Angkar*, immediately began to act on their deranged designs to create a socialist utopia by transforming the country into an agrarian collective. The entire population of Phnom Penh and other provincial capitals was forcibly removed to the countryside to begin new lives as peasants working on the land. They were the lucky ones. Pol Pot ordered the mass extermination of intellectuals, teachers, writers, educated people, and their families. Even wearing glasses was an indication of intelligence, a "crime" punishable by death. The brutal regime lasted four years before invading Vietnamese forces captured Phnom Penh in 1978; by this time, between one and three million Cambodians had perished in the genocide.

Driven into the jungle, the Khmer Rouge installed themselves near the Thai border and continued to wage guerrilla warfare against the occupation government, supported by an international community fearful of communist expansionism. It wasn't until Ieng Sary, Pol Pot's trusted number two, defected in 1996, causing a split in the Khmer Rough ranks, that the tide began to turn. Pol Pot himself was found dead two years later, having been convicted by his own troops of murder. To this day no one knows for sure how he died.

cells have been buried in the school playground. It's a thoroughly depressing sight, and it's not until you see the pictures of the victims, blood stains on the walls and instruments of torture that you get any idea of the scale of suffering endured by the Cambodian people.

### Wat Phnom

The most popular of Phnom Penh's temples, **Wat Phnom** (dawn–dusk; $1), atop the city's only hill, was originally founded in 1372 by a local widow, Lady Penh. The current construction, dating from 1927, sees hundreds of Cambodians converge daily for elephant rides, photos and perhaps a prayer or two. Weekends and holidays are especially busy.

At the eastern entrance, lions and naga images beckon the visitor to the top of the staircase, where a gold-painted bas-relief depicts the victory of King Jayavarman VII over the Champa army in the twelfth century. Inside the temple, a resplendent Maitreya Buddha ("Buddha of the Future") looks down from the central dais, and murals illustrate tales of the Buddha's life and the Ramayana. Behind the main sanctuary, the stupa of fifteenth-century Khmer King Ponhea Yat remains the highest point in Phnom Penh, a fact not lost on the French, who commandeered the shrine as a watchtower.

On the northern side of the hill nestles a temple to the spirit **Preah Chau**, popular among the Chinese and Vietnamese communities. Gifts of raw meat and eggs are offered to the stone lions outside in return for protection from enemies.

### Wat Ounalom

Set back slightly from the river at the northern junction of Sothearos Boulevard and Sisowath Quay, **Wat Ounalom** ("Eyebrow Temple") is the centre of modern-day Khmer Buddhist teaching, led by Supreme Patriarch Taep Vong, respectfully referred to by the novices as "The King of Monks". The main temple building, built in 1952, is a modern reincarnation of the original, built in the fifteenth century. The building to the right is the main residence for the monks, and the five-hundred-year-old stupa behind the temple encases one of the Buddha's eyebrows, after which the temple is named. Just in front stands a monument to those killed during the Pol Pot regime. It's pleasant to stroll around the complex – many of the monks are learning English, and are happy to tell you what they know about the temple and its history. The best time to visit is at 6pm, when they congregate in the main sanctuary to chant their prayers.

## Arrival

**By bus** Most buses draw up near the southwest corner of the central market, Psar Thmei, from where you can catch a moto or a tuk-tuk into the centre of town. The Sen Monorom bus arrives at Olympic Stadium.

**By share taxi or minibus** Share taxis and minibuses will either pull up at the transport stops – just northwest of the central market or at Psar Damkor 3km southwest of the centre – or will drop you off along the way into town.

**By boat** Express boats dock at the terminal just east of the post office on Sisowath Quay.

**By air** Pochentong Airport, Cambodia's international gateway, lies 6km west of the city centre. Licensed taxis and motos operate from a counter directly outside the terminal building; taxis charge a flat fee of $7 and motos $2 for the journey into the city centre.

## Information

**Tourist information** The airport has a tourist information desk (opening hours variable), with a list of hotels and travel agents. Most guesthouses and hotels have reliable information; *Capitol Guesthouse* (see opposite) has set itself up as the tourist guru in the absence of official information, though, naturally, they will try and peddle their own tours. The free *Phnom Penh Visitors' Guide* has a wealth of information on activities and sights around the city, plus a useful map; you'll find it in restaurants, internet cafés and bars.

**Tour agencies** There is a wealth of tour agencies around Phnom Penh, but most are geared towards large groups. For independent budget travellers the best bet is often to arrange a tour through a guesthouse: *Capitol*, *Okay* and *Royal* all offer tour services, and the list is growing fast.

## City transport

Phnom Penh has no public bus service; a trial on two routes in the city met with considerable scepticism.
**Motos** Motorcycle taxis, or motos, are the most convenient way of getting around the city and are inexpensive. Expect to pay 2000–4000r for a short hop, or up to 8000r for a longer journey. Prices go up after dark and in the rain. You can also hire a moto-driver for a day – explain to the driver exactly where you want to go and negotiate a price beforehand. A good English-speaker will charge around $6–7 per day for his services as driver and guide.
**Tuk-tuks** Tuk-tuks are everywhere in Phnom Penh, and for groups of two or more they are usually the cheapest (though not the quickest) way to get around. Negotiate the fare in advance, and expect to pay around 4000–12,000r.
**Cyclos** If you're not in a hurry, cyclos are handy for short trips. Fares are subject to negotiation – usually 4000–8000r.
**Taxis** Taxis are not hailed on the street – you can either book them over the phone or pick one up at Monivong Boulevard near the central market, where they tend to gather. Negotiate the fare in advance. Taxis are also available for hire for the day: expect to pay around $40. Baileys Taxi Service (ⓣ012/012890) offers a 24hr taxi service with experienced, reliable English-speaking drivers.

## Accommodation

The best area for budget accommodation is Boeung Kak, which has become something of a backpackers' ghetto filled with rooms for $2–3. For a less touristy atmosphere, try the centre of town.

### The riverfront

**Indochine** 251 Sisowath Quay ⓣ023/427292 Friendly Khmer-owned hotel right on the river, offering spacious, good-value, en-suite rooms. ❷
**River Star** 185 Sisowath Quay ⓣ023/990501, ⓦwww.riverstarhotel.com. Corner building with five floors of rooms, some with balconies and view of the river. Newish rooms have TV and a/c. ❹

### Central Phnom Penh

**Capitol** 14 St 182 ⓣ023/724104. The *Capitol* empire is the Phnom Penh equivalent of Bangkok's Khao San Road, comprising *Capitol Guesthouse* and nearby clones *Monorom Inn* and *Hello*. Backpackers arrive here by the busload for the cheap accommodation, food and tours. Indeed, it offers the most comprehensive selection of inexpensive tours in Phnom Penh, and can help arrange onward transport. If minibussing all the central sights in one day is your bag, sign up here. Rooms are a bit cell-like, but plentiful. ❶
**Dara Raeng Sey** 45 St 118 ⓣ023/428181. This rambling corner building is a good location for both the riverfront and the old French Quarter. Rooms have either fan or a/c as well as TV, though some are window-less. Staff are very friendly and helpful. ❷
**Lucky Ro** 122 St 110 ⓣ023/986559. Small, friendly hotel with good-sized, clean and tidy rooms, all with TV and en suite; those with a/c have hot water. ❶
**Morakat** 33 St 107 ⓣ012/963077. Just off the main thoroughfare, a welcoming hotel with clean, presentable rooms, all with en-suite bathrooms, a/c, TV and fridge. ❷
**Narin** 50 St 125 ⓣ023/991955. One of the long-standing budget guesthouses in Phnom Penh. Rooms are clean and quite adequate; the best part is the pleasant terrace restaurant, which is a good place to meet up with other travellers. ❶
**Pacific** 234 Monivong Blvd ⓣ023/218592. Recently refurbished, this hotel has a pleasant reception area with seating and a lobby bar; rooms are large, bright and nicely furnished, with sturdy Cambodian wood furniture. The room rate includes breakfast in the downstairs restaurant. ❺
**Princess** 302 Monivong Blvd ⓣ023/801089. A stylish and efficient modern hotel. Rooms are large, light and well equipped. ❻
**Royal** 91 St 154 ⓣ023/218026. Bustling family-run guesthouse in the centre of town with a small shop and ATM. Rooms come with cable TV, fridge and en-suite facilities plus optional a/c. ❶
**Sunday Guesthouse** 97 St 141 ⓣ012/848858. Friendly guesthouse with helpful staff and a communal backpacker atmosphere. There are nightly video screenings in the restaurant, where internet is also available, and clean fan or a/c rooms. ❷
**Tat** 52 St 125 ⓣ012/921211. Decently sized, bright rooms in this cheerful guesthouse mostly come with en-suite facilities. The lounge has internet, communal TV and video, and the rooftop restaurant serves cheap Cambodian and Western food. ❶

### South of Sihanouk Road

**Boddhi Tree** 50 St 113 ⓣ023/211397, ⓦwww.boddhitree.com. You'll feel more like a friend of the family than a tourist at this well-decked-out little guesthouse in an old wooden house opposite Toul Sleng Genocide Museum. Gorgeous, individually decorated rooms have shared bath, and tasty meals are served in the bustling, leafy courtyard. ❸

**Golden Gate** 9 St 278 ⓣ023/721161. A variety of rooms available in two buildings, but the impressive lobby outclasses the rooms themselves. Similar accommodation is available next door at the smaller *Golden Bridge* and *Golden Sun* hotels. ❸

**Okay Guesthouse** 3 St 258 ⓣ012/300804. Some of the cheapest accommodation to be had this close to the river, offering cramped $1 dorm beds as well as more spacious a/c rooms in a newer building. The bustling backpackers' café downstairs is a popular place to meet people and arrange tours. ❶

**Scandinavia** 4 St 282 ⓣ023/214498. Nicely renovated small hotel with swimming pool, restaurant, library and bar. Rooms are clean and have TV, a/c and some funky modern lighting fixtures Located just up the street from the *Goldiana*. ❻

### Boeng Kak and around

**Happy/Number 11** off St 93 ⓣ012/884506. Homely and scrupulously clean lakeside guesthouse, full of potted plants. The simple rooms have immaculate communal bathrooms and the great terrace restaurant dishes up Cambodian, Thai and Vietnamese fare. Shared stereo and TV, and a free pool table. ❶

**Lakeside/Number 10** off St 93 ⓣ023/430621. A guesthouse offering budget rooms in a spectacular spot, with a large terrace overlooking Boeng Kak. Free pool table, plus videos, hammocks and sunset views. ❶

**Number 9** off St 93 ⓣ012/327466. The most picturesque of the lakeside guesthouses, with basic en-suite rooms set around a small, lily-filled lagoon. Free pool, videos and a relaxing deck restaurant serving the usual travellers' fare. ❶

**World Star Hotel** 56 Monivong Blvd ⓣ023/427220. Recently refurbished mid-range hotel, boasting a fitness centre and sauna. ❸

## Eating

Street stalls, where budget travellers can fill up on noodle dishes or filled baguettes, spring up in different places at various times of day: markets are a good place for a daytime selection, and the riverside in the early evening. The more fashionable street-corner restaurants are concentrated just south of the junction of Sihanouk and Monivong boulevards. Phnom Penh is also filled with innumerable reasonably priced restaurants aimed at expats and tourists, with more springing up all the time; expect to pay $3–6 per dish.

### Khmer and Asian restaurants

**Boat Noodle** 8B St 294. Attractive balcony restaurant serving tasty noodle dishes, sometimes accompanied by live music.

**Frizz** Sisowath Quay. Small but excellent restaurant, similar to a Korean barbecue, where you cook your own Cambodian meat and vegetable dishes on charcoal braziers. Also offers Khmer cooking classes.

**Gold Fish River** Sisowath Quay, at the junction with St 106. In a lovely location out over the Tonle Sap, with a menu of Khmer food that's consistently good. Curried frog and stir-fried squid are just two tasty options, and they can rustle up French fries, too.

**Lumbini** 51 St 214, near the intersection with St 63. There's a good ambience and friendly service at this moderately priced north Indian place. Besides curries, the extensive menu includes a selection of tandoori dishes, bhajis, Nepali dishes and vegetarian options.

**Mamak's Corner** 18 St 114. Nasi goreng, roti pratha, satay and other Malaysian delights for $2 a plate, tasting as good as anything you'd buy at a KL street stall.

**Nouveau Pho de Paris** 258 Monivong Blvd. Busy Chinese, Cambodian and Vietnamese restaurant, with plenty of vegetarian options and a picture menu to help you choose. Huge steaming bowls of *pho* are popular and the crispy fried duck mouth-watering.

**Ponlok** 319 Sisowath Quay. Illustrated menus in English and French make ordering good Khmer food here easy. Attentive service and a busy, breezy balcony.

**Royal India** 21 St 111, just south of *Capitol Guesthouse*. The most consistently good North Indian food in town, all at economical prices and served with a smile at this simple restaurant. The menu is comprehensive and halal, including chicken and mutton curries which come with rice or naan bread. Freshly made vegetarian samosas, and tasty sweet lassis.

**Sam Doo** 56–58 Kampuchea Krom Blvd. The basic surroundings belie the delicious fare: juicy Sichuan prawns come with a spicy dressing and *dim sum*, for which *Sam Doo* is especially reputed.

### Western restaurants

**California 2** 317 Sisowath Quay. This guesthouse restaurant has the best Baja fish tacos in town, and possibly the whole region.

**Cantina** 347 Sisowath Quay. Operated by long-time Phnom Penh icon Hurley Scroggins, this no-frills place on the riverfront delivers some of the best (and only) Mexican food in the country.

**Capitol** 14 St 182. Cheap and cheerful travellers' fare at this busy street-corner café.

**Foreign Correspondents' Club (FCC)** 363 Sisowath Quay ⓣ023/724014. Fine – if pricey – dining in this famous riverside colonial building. Bar snacks also available, or just pop in for a soothing ale.

**Garden Centre Café** 60–61 St 108 ⓣ023/991850. Moderately priced food from the MSG-free menu includes home-made bread, granola breakfasts, burgers, and baked goods; on weekends, the special features a generous helping of a roast and a veggie option, plus choice of salads. Closed Mon.

**Happy Herbs Bistro** 345 Sisowath Quay. Cheap pizza and pasta. A large "Special" pizza will fill you up or share it between two.

**Java Café** 56 Sihanouk Blvd. Soups, salads, bagels on a cosy balcony overlooking the Independence Monument, where you can also browse the rotating art exhibitions. A great place to unwind on a hot afternoon.

**Lazy Gecko** 23 St 93, near Boeng Kak. This friendly and inexpensive travellers' eatery serves up delicious banana pancakes, ice-cream sundaes and even a couple of Khmer favourites. It's also a hub of backpacker activity, offering everything from films to day-long excursions.

**Nature and Sea** On the corner of Sts 51 & 278. Organic salads, sandwiches and crepes served up on a balcony filled with bamboo and potted plants.

**Riverside Bistro** 273 Sisowath Quay. Pavement terrace partially shielded from the passing shoe-shine boys by a jungle of potted plants. Reasonably priced European and Khmer dishes, plus a pool table.

## Drinking and nightlife

For most Khmers, nightlife centres around an early evening meal out, followed by a tuneful burst of karaoke: the southern end of Monivong Blvd has a particular concentration of the larger, glitzy joints. However, Western nightlife tastes are more than catered for, and you'll always find a crowd in established favourites such as the *FCC*, *Heart of Darkness* and *Walkabout*, many going strong well into the wee hours.

### Bars

**Elsewhere** 175 St 51 ⓣ023/211348. Normally a relaxed bar set in the garden of an elegant colonial-style building, this place wakes up the first Friday of every month to host legendary parties. Closed Tues.

**Foreign Correspondents' Club (FCC)** 363 Sisowath Quay ⓣ023/724014. No, it's not really a foreign correspondents' club, but a Southeast Asian version of Bogart's bar in the film *Casablanca*. The balmy air, whirring ceiling fans and spacious armchairs invite one to spend a hot afternoon getting slowly, purposefully smashed. Prices are relatively high but worth it.

**Howie's** 32 St 51. Located near the *Heart of Darkness*, *Howie's* is the place to go after the former invariably disappoints. It's worth arriving early to stake out a table on the sidewalk outside.

**The Magic Sponge** 12 St 93. Locally described as an "adolescent's paradise", the *Sponge* offers darts, board games, poker nights and PlayStation in a seductively cosy rendition of an English pub.

**Pink Elephant** 343 Sisowath Quay. Relaxed, backpacker-oriented bar on the river, with cheap drinks, free pool and board games. Popular after a *Happy Herbs* pizza next door. 9am–late.

**Pontoon** western end of 108 St. Phnom Penh's only "floating bar" is a favourite among the expat crowd, with regular visiting DJs, a beautiful amber bar, an intriguing range of cocktails and comfy couches to lose yourself in. Open until midnight Sun–Thurs, and until late Fri & Sat.

**Walkabout Hotel** Corner of 51 & 174 sts. A 24hr bar with pool table, restaurant and sports TV. Surrounded by bordellos and teeming with "taxi girls", *Walkabout* is decidedly sleazy during the early evening, but it's *the* place to congregate when the clubs close at around 3am.

### Clubs

**Heart of Darkness** 26 St 51. Overrated, but it's been here for ages and is one of those places everybody has to visit once. Buy a T-shirt, but wait until you get home to wear it. Nightly from 8pm.

**Martini** 48 St 95. Western-style disco and girly bar, with movies on the big screen, inexpensive food on the menu and plenty of company available. 7pm–3am.

## Entertainment

**Cinemas** Your chance to watch films in Phnom Penh is pretty limited, with just a few options. The French Cultural Centre (St 184, just east of Monivong Blvd; free) screens French films with English subtitles: check local listings for details. Meta House, 6 St 264, offers free open-air film screenings (Thurs–Sun), as well as live music and art exhibitions. Otherwise, select your own laser-disc movie at Movie Street Video Centre, 116

Sihanouk Blvd, and watch it in their comfortable screening rooms ($5 per person).

**Kick-boxing** A popular Phnom Penh Sunday-afternoon outing used to be a trip to the kick-boxing, but now the stadium has been closed there's no set venue. If you want to watch a bout, and it's sometimes as much fun to watch the crowd as the competitors, ask at your guesthouse for details. Otherwise, do as many Cambodians do and watch it on TV.

**Traditional arts** Unfortunately, cultural events in Phnom Penh are few and far between. The ancient tradition of Cambodian classical dance, which originated in the twelfth century, was all but wiped out in the 1970s, and performances at the Chaktomuk Theatre on Sisowath Quay are still infrequent – check the listings in the Friday edition of the *Cambodia Daily*. The theatre is also the venue for occasional Khmer plays and musical shows.

## Shopping

**Bookshops** The *FCC* stocks a wide range of English and French books, including novels, as well as books on Cambodia and Angkor, while Monument Books (111 Norodom Blvd; ⓣ023/217617) has a large collection of new books. Secondhand books are sold at The London Book Centre (51 St 240; ⓣ023/214258), which has over 5000 titles in English, French and German.

**Markets** A trip to one of the capital's numerous markets is essential, if only to buy the red-checked *krama* (traditional chequered scarf), popular with Khmers and visitors alike. The markets are liveliest in the morning; many vendors have a snooze at midday for a couple of hours and things wind down by 5pm. Vendors at the Art Deco Psar Thmei (just ask moto drivers for "psar"), at the eastern end of Kampuchea Krom Blvd, are wise to the apparently limitless funds of all *barangs* (Westerners), and will price their wares accordingly. Electronic goods, T-shirts, shoes and wigs are all in abundance here. Although the drugs, guns and ammunition are no longer available, a stroll around the Russian Market (Psar Toul Tom Poung), in the southern end of town at the junction of 163 and 440 streets, remains a colourful experience. It's a good balance of tourist-oriented curios and stalls for locals, with jewellery, gems, CDs, food stalls, souvenirs, furniture and motorbike parts all grouped in their own sections. Don't expect an easy bargain – you'll have to work hard to pay the locals' price.

**Supermarkets** Bayon Supermarket, 135 Monivong Blvd (7am–8pm); Lucky Supermarket, 160 Sihanouk Blvd (8am–9pm); Pencil Supermarket, 15 St 214 (7am–9pm); Big A on Monivong between 178 & 184 sts (8am–9pm). There are also minimarts, which stock a remarkable variety of imported goods, attached to some petrol filling stations of Caltex Star Mart and Total La Boutique.

## Directory

**Airline offices** Bangkok Airways, 61A St 214 ⓣ023/426624; China Southern Airlines, 53 Preah Monivong, Phnom Penh Hotel ⓣ023/430877; Dragonair, A4–A5 Regency Square, 168 Monireth Blvd ⓣ023/424300; Lao Airlines, 58C Sihanouk Blvd ⓣ023/222956; Malaysia Airlines, 1st Floor, Diamond Hotel, 172–184 Monivong Blvd ⓣ023/426688; Siem Reap Airways, 65 St 214 ⓣ023/720055; Silk Air, 313 Sisowath Quay ⓣ023/426808; Thai Airways, 294 Mao Tse Toung Blvd, suite 8B ⓣ023/214359; Vietnam Airlines, 41 St 214 ⓣ023/363396.

**Banks and exchange** ATMs dispense riel or dollars or both; there are two at the airport and many more downtown. Traveller's cheques can be cashed at virtually any bank around town for a commission of two percent. The best rates for changing foreign currency into riel can be found with the moneychangers in and around Psar Thmei. Western Union Money transfer is available at: the Cambodia Asia Bank branches at 539 Monivong Blvd; Pencial Supermarket, 483 Sisovath Blvd and 252 Monivong Blvd; Russey Keo, 301 St 6A; and Singapore Bank, St 214.

**Bicycle rental** *Capitol Guesthouse* (see p.95); 8000r per day.

**Dentists** International SOS Dental Clinic, 161 St 51 (ⓣ023/216911) has English-speaking staff.

**Embassies and consulates** Australia, 11 St 254 ⓣ023/213470; Canada, 11 St 254 ⓣ023/213470 ext. 426; Laos, 15–17 Mao Tse Toung Blvd ⓣ023/997931; Thailand, 196 Norodom Blvd ⓣ023/726306; UK, 29 St 75 ⓣ023/427124; USA, 1 St 96 ⓣ023/728000; Vietnam, 436 Monivong Blvd ⓣ023/726284.

**Hospitals and clinics** For any travel-related illness, tests or vaccinations, head for AEA International SOS Clinic at 161 St 51 (ⓣ023/216911) or the Tropical & Travellers' Medical Clinic, 88 St 108 (ⓣ023/366802). The Naga Clinic at 11 St 254 (ⓣ011/211300) also has English- and French-speaking doctors. The main hospital is Calmette Hospital, 3 Monivong Blvd (ⓣ023/426948).

**Immigration department** For visa extensions, it's easier to go to one of the travel agents in town or to your guesthouse – they'll charge a couple of dollars. The Department of Immigration (ⓣ012/581558) is now well out of town on Russian

Blvd opposite the airport, although you'll need to go there for other immigration queries. The office is open Mon–Fri 8–10.30am & 2.30–4.30pm.

**Internet** There are outlets all over town, with access around 4000r/hr.

**Motorbike rental** Lucky! Lucky!, 413 Monivong Blvd (☎023/212788), charges $4 per day for a 110cc moped, $10 per day for a 250cc off-road bike, with discounts on rentals of a week or longer. Helmets are provided but no insurance. It's worth paying the 500r to park in the many moto compounds around the city – thieves are rather partial to unattended Hondas.

**Newspapers and magazines** The best selection of international newspapers and magazines can be found at the *FCC*, although many bars will carry copies of Cambodia's English-language dailies, the *Cambodian Daily* and *Phnom Penh Post*.

**Pharmacies** Drug stores are literally everywhere. Trained English-speaking pharmacists are available at Pharmacie de la Gare, corner of Monivong and Pochentong boulevards (daily 8.30am–6pm). It's arguably the best in Cambodia, stocking a good selection of Western pharmaceuticals. Credit cards are accepted.

**Post office** The main post office is east of Wat Phnom, on St 13 between sts 98 and 102 (daily 6.30am–9pm. Poste restante pick-up is at the far left-hand counter (300r per item).

**Tourist police** ☎023/724793 or 012/942484.

## Moving on

**By bus** Most buses out of Phnom Penh operate scheduled departures from the bus station near the northwest corner of the central market. To connect with the express boat to Koh Kong from Sihanoukville, be sure to get an early bus – you'll have to leave Phnom Penh by 8am to make the connection. Note that the bus to Sen Monorom leaves from Olympic Stadium.

**Destinations:** Battambang (5hr); Ho Chi Minh City, Vietnam (6hr); Kampong Cham (3hr); Kampong Thom (4hr); Koh Kong (6hr); Kratie (7hr); Poipet (8hr); Sen Monorom (10hr); Siem Reap (6hr); Sihanoukville (4hr); Stung Treng (9hr).

**By share taxi or minibus** Journeys from Phnom Penh to Kratie, Kampot and Sen Monorom are considerably quicker by taxi than bus. Share taxis and minibuses head out throughout the morning from Psar Thmei for destinations north of Phnom Penh: Kampong Thom, Stung Treng, Siem Reap, Kampong Cham, Kratie, Battambang, and through to Sisophon and Poipet. If you're going a long way, get there early, by 6 or 7am, as drivers like to complete the trip in daylight. For destinations closer to town you'll easily be able to get a share taxi out until early afternoon, after which departures become less frequent as fewer people will be travelling. For the southern destinations of Sihanoukville and Kampot, shared transport leaves from Psar Damkor, southwest of the city centre; fares to the coast are in the region of 20,000r. Taxis are the only option for travellers headed to Bavet, on the Vietnam border; they leave in the mornings from the Psar Olympic, south of the Olympic Stadium. For Sen Monorom, the taxi park is on St 80, at the northern end of Monivong; transport leaves daily at 7am.

**Destinations:** Bavet (for Vietnam; 3hr); Kampot (4hr); Kratie (4hr 30min); Sen Monorom (8hr); Sihanoukville (3hr 30min); Sisophon (6hr); Stung Treng (6hr 30min).

**By boat** From the new passenger boat terminal (aka the tourist docks) on the river near the main post office, express boats take around 5hr to power up the Tonle Sap River to Siem Reap, subject to variations in the river's flow (tickets cost $25 for foreigners, though some guesthouses sell tickets for a few dollars less). Boats leave at 7am and have allocated seating; you can buy your ticket at the dock the day before or on the morning of departure.

**Destination:** Siem Reap (1–2 daily; 5hr).

**By air** The airport is easily reached in under half an hour by moto (8000r) or taxi (20,000–28,000r). Both domestic carriers operate flights to Siem Reap (40min) – this seems to be the only profitable route in the country. All other routes had been suspended at the time of writing. Flight schedules change regularly, so check with a travel agent for the latest timetable.

**Destination:** Siem Reap (6 daily; 45min).

# AROUND PHNOM PENH

Escaping into Phnom Penh's surrounding **countryside** for some peace and fresh air is very easy – it doesn't take long to get out past the shanty-town suburbs, and the majority of roads that extend from the capital are in fairly good condition, making the excursions listed here an easy day or even half-day trip.

### Choeung Ek (The Killing Fields)

A visit to **CHOEUNG EK** (daily 7.30am–5.30pm; $2), 15km southwest of Phnom Penh and signposted from Monireth Boulevard, is a sobering experience. It was here in 1980 that the bodies of

### INTO VIETNAM

The popular 245-kilometre trip from Phnom Penh to HCMC has become easier and cheaper over the last few years, and it's now possible to get **public transport all the way**. Guesthouses run minibuses for around $12 (check prices at *Capitol* and *Narin*, see p.95). On this trip, you'll have to walk 500m or so across the border, complete the necessary formalities and change to transport from the guesthouse's associate in HCMC. Several bus companies also operate full-sized buses all the way to HCMC for $10–12, or to Chao Doc for $7. The alternative is to get yourself a place in a share taxi ($8) to **Bavet**, and then minibus it to HCMC (US$4) after crossing the border; there are plenty of touts at Bavet to help you out. However you get to the border, allow plenty of time to clear **immigration**: it can take two hours or more. The border closes at 5pm. The city-to-city trip takes about eight or nine hours, including immigration formalities, and be aware that visas are not available at the border. You can pick one up at the Vietnamese Embassy at the southern end of Monivong Boulevard in Phnom Penh (Mon–Fri 8–11am & 2–4pm) for around $50, depending on your nationality and how quickly you need it, but guesthouses can usually organize this for slightly less. The only place to get a same-day visa is in Sihanoukville.

The route through **Chau Doc** is more complicated than crossing at Bavet; you'll have to get to Neak Leung and then take a boat down the Mekong to the border, where you can pick up a moto for the short ride to the immigration point on the Bassac River. Again, you'll need to be in possession of a valid visa.

For details of the border crossing at Prek Chak (Ha Tien), see the box on p.130.

8985 people, victims of Pol Pot and his Khmer Rouge comrades, were exhumed from 86 mass graves. A further 43 graves have been left untouched. Many of those buried here had suffered prolonged torture at S21 prison in Phnom Penh, before being led to their deaths at Choeung Ek. Men, women and children were beaten to death, shot, beheaded, or tied up and buried alive.

The site is dominated by a tall, white, hollow stupa that commemorates all those who died from 1975 to 1979, displaying thousands of unearthed skulls on glass shelves. A pile of the victims' ragged clothing lies scattered underneath. A pavilion has a small display of the excavation of the burial pits and a hand-written sign nearby (in Khmer and English) outlines the Khmer Rouge atrocities, a period described as "a desert of great destruction which overturned Kampuchean society and drove it back to the stone age". Although Choeung Ek is by far the most notorious of the killing fields, scores of similar plots can be found all over Cambodia, many with no more than a pile of skulls and bones as a memorial. **Transport** to Choeung Ek can be arranged at *Capitol Guesthouse* (see p.95), or take a moto for $4 return (30min).

### Royal Tombs of Oudong

The ancient capital of **OUDONG**, 40km to the northwest of Phnom Penh, served as the seat of power for successive Cambodian kings for over two hundred years until, in 1866, it was sacked by King Norodom, who transferred his court to Phnom Penh. Nowadays, visitors come to see the hill of Phnom Oudong, dotted with stupas harbouring the ashes and spirits of bygone royalty along its east–west ridge. A long line of food and drink stalls marks your arrival. Continue to the end of the road, where a staircase will lead you up to the larger of two ridges. You can then descend via the staircase at the eastern end of the ridge to complete the circuit.

At the top of the staircase at the western edge of the hill sits what's left of Vihear Preah Atharas, also known as **Wat Preah Thom**, which houses a giant stone Buddha. The **royal stupas** themselves are higher on the ridge to the northeast. The first and most interesting is the yellow stupa, decorated with elephants, garudas and lotus-flower motifs, that houses the ashes of King Sisowath Monivong, who died in 1941. The adjacent Tray Troeng chedi is said to house the ashes of King Ang Duong and his wife. The third stupa, Damrei Sam Poan, was built by King Chey Chetar II for the former King Soriyopor. At the end of the ridge, a further stupa is just being completed, designed to house Buddha relics currently contained in Preah Sack Kyack Moni chedi outside Phnom Penh train station.

From the royal stupas, the eastern staircase descends to a small, dusty monument displaying the bones and skulls of those killed at a nearby Khmer Rouge detention centre. **To get to Oudong** by rented Honda or bicycle, follow Route 5 northwards from Phnom Penh for about 37km, turn left at a large picture of Oudong and follow the road for a few kilometres to the western staircase. Guesthouses and hotels in Phnom Penh organize tours for $5. A taxi here and back costs $30, a moto around $13.

### Phnom Chisor and around

Originally known as Suryaparvata in honour of the monarch Suryavarman I, the eleventh-century temple of **Phnom Chisor** looks east from its hilltop vantage point, 35km south of Phnom Penh across the green palm and paddy plains of Takeo province. There are two routes to the top of the hill, both of which are best climbed in the cooler early-morning temperatures. The track that skirts around the hill is an easier climb and gets you to the top in about twenty minutes.

The modern pagodas and shrines that surround Phnom Chisor are of little interest, so make straight for the main courtyard of the ancient temple. Eight edifices surround the main sanctuary tower dedicated to Shiva. Although the buildings were badly damaged by American bombing raids in the 1970s, you can still see some of the sculptural reliefs. The most impressive of these is to be found in the former library, where there is a pediment carved with a dancing Shiva figure set above a lintel, showing Indra riding a three-headed elephant.

The site lies off National Route 2 – a few kilometres along a dirt track that bears left at Prasat Neang Khmau. You can **hire a moto** for around $15 in Phnom Penh, or a **taxi** for about $35.

A side-trip to **Tonle Bati**, Phnom Penh's nearest Angkorian site, about 40km south of the capital, should be included in the price. Tonle Bati's two temples date back to the twelfth century, and their leafy garden setting and nearby lake can make for a pleasant afternoon out (daily 8am-4pm; $3). *Capitol Guesthouse* (see p.95) runs a **tour** to both destinations for $8.

## Central Cambodia

**Central Cambodia** is a forgotten territory stretching from north of Phnom Penh through sparsely populated countryside right up to the Thai border. The region is hardly a popular tourist destination: the most that visitors usually see of it is the rice paddies that stretch either side of National Route 6, the major trunk road between the capital and Siem Reap, which cuts across the southern part of the area. But for those itching to get off the tourist trail, central Cambodia has a few ancient temple sites worth visiting, and compared to Angkor Wat they're practically deserted. The starting point is invariably **Kampong Thom**, the only town of any size hereabouts, and thus your last taste of comfort for a few days if you're planning a foray into the interior. Thankfully, it's no major expedition if you want to see **Sambor Prei Kuk**, where there are three groups of well-preserved brick-built temples.

## KAMPONG THOM

**KAMPONG THOM**, located about midway between Phnom Penh and Siem Reap on National Route 6, is the gateway to the pre-Angkor temple ruins of **Sambor Prei Kuk**, 30km northeast, as well as to the holy mountain of Phnom Santuk, 20km south, and a number of local archeological sights. The town itself is little more than a busy transport stop, but it's full of friendly people, has a good choice of decent accommodation and several respectable restaurants. The main features are a **double-bridge** over the Sen River – where the old one has been left alongside the new – and gaudy Wat Kampong Thom, the local **pagoda**, with massive leopard and rhino statues standing guard outside.

### Arrival and information

**By bus** Buses generally stop across from the market on the main road, not far from the taxi transport stop. If you arrive on the bus from Phnom Penh to Siem Reap (17,000r), or vice-versa (16,000r), tell the driver you want to get off en-route. You won't have to walk more than 500m from here to reach a hotel or guesthouse, but there are plenty of moto drivers around if you need one.

**By share taxi or minibus** The transport stop is in the square behind the Department of Arts and Culture, east of the main road. Taxis from Phnom Penh (17,000r) arrive at the south side of the square, while transport from Siem Reap (15,000r) comes in at the north.

**Tourist information** The friendly tourist office is in the wooden building just off the southeast corner of the transport stop.

### Accommodation

The best budget accommodation is east of the transport stop on Pracheathipatay.

**Ponloeu Thmey Guesthouse** ⓣ012/910896. Tidy en-suite rooms in a four-storey modern building, 500m south of the market on the main road. Optional fan or a/c. ❶

**Santepheap Guesthouse** 23 Pracheathipatay ⓣ012/739118. Traditional wooden house with a shady courtyard and simply furnished fan rooms, some with shared facilities. ❶

**Stung Sen Royal Garden** 6 Krom 3rd ⓣ062/961228. The best hotel in town, on the main road overlooking the river. The comfy rooms all have TV, a/c and hot water. ❹

### Eating

Kampong only has two real restaurants, both serving Cambodian and Chinese fare. Inexpensive food stalls at the market, on the main road just south of the bridge, are open from early morning to mid-afternoon, and the night market sets up outside the east entrance to the market from late afternoon.

**Arunras Hotel** On the main road. Serves great soups and stir-fries, although it occasionally gets rowdy; its sister restaurant next door is the best place in town for breakfast, serving up excellent rice and noodle soups.

**Stung Sen** Huge restaurant, just south of the *Stung Sen Royal Garden Hotel*, dishing up generous portions of stir-fried pork with vegetables. You can feel a bit lost here when it's quiet.

### Directory

**Banks and exchange** You can change money in the market, or at the Acleda Bank, about 500m south of the market on the opposite side of the road. At the time of writing there were no ATMs.

**Hospital** The hospital is on Pracheathepatay, west of the *Arunras Hotel*.

**Internet** There is a shop with several terminals available (at 4000r/hr) on the main road just north of the market, and another around 200m south.

**Post office** The post office and Camintel office, for international calls, are in the same building next door to the seven-storey *Arunras Hotel* on the main road.

### Moving on

**By bus** Buses to Phnom Penh and Siem Reap leave from the main road across from the market.

**Destinations:** Phnom Penh (8 daily; 4hr); Siem Reap (8 daily; 2hr)

**By share taxi or minibus** These leave between around 6am and 2pm – the earlier you get to the transport stop, in the square behind the Department of Arts and Culture, east of the main road, the better.

**Destinations:** Kampong Cham (2hr); Phnom Penh (4hr); Siem Reap (2hr).

## SAMBOR PREI KUK

**Sambor Prei Kuk** is the site of a Chenla-era capital, the seventh-century Ishanapura, and once boasted hundreds of temples; built of brick, most have crumbled or been smothered by the encroaching forest, but three fine sets of towers have been cleared and are worth the excursion. You'll have to sign in at the entrance booth and pay a fee of $2. The site is divided into the north (closest to the entrance booth), central (more recent than the other two, being ninth century) and south groups. If you've come with a driver, he may well know of temples that have recently been uncovered, as new sites are being cleared all the time.

The north group, known as **Prasat Sambor Prei Kuk**, is distinguished by the reliefs of the central sanctuary tower. These depict **flying palaces** and are the home of the gods who look after the temples. In spite of their age, you can make out figures and the floors of the palace. Also look out for the rather cute reliefs of winged horses and tiny human faces. The rubble piles around the site are ruins of the numerous other towers that once stood here.

Only the main sanctuary tower, **Prasat Tor**, still remains of the central group, and it's particularly photogenic, sprouting vegetation and reproduction lions flanking the entrance steps. Carvings of intricate foliage patterns – for which Sambor Prei Kuk is highly regarded – are still visible on the south lintel.

The south group, also called **Prasat Neak Pean**, was the most important temple at Ishanapura. Inside the brick-walled enclosure, you'll be able to spot flying palaces on the octagonal towers and – in the building east of the central tower – large medallion-shaped reliefs.

**To get to** Sambor Prei Kuk, your best best is a moto. The site is about 15km east of National Route 64 and is easily reached ($6 round trip) from Kampong Thom; the road is good and the journey takes around an hour.

# Angkor

The world-renowned temples of **Angkor**, in northwest Cambodia, stand as an impressive monument to the greatest ancient civilization in Southeast Asia. Spiritually, politically and geographically, Angkor was at the heart of the great Khmer Empire. During the Angkorian period, the ruling god-kings (*devarajas*) built imposing temples as a way of asserting their divinity, leaving a legacy of more than one hundred temples built between the ninth and fifteenth centuries.

The nearest town to the temples is **Siem Reap**, which has established itself as the base from which to make your way round Angkor, a tradition begun by American Frank Vincent Jr, who borrowed three elephants from the governor of Siem Reap in 1872 to explore the ruins. These days, there are plenty of motos, tuk-tuks and taxis on hand for the journey.

## SIEM REAP

**SIEM REAP** is Cambodia's most touristy town, and has sacrificed some of its charm and authenticity as a result. However, Western luxuries are freely available, there are plenty of English-speaking locals and the selection of bars and restaurants seems infinite. **Transport** around town is limited to motos (4000r) or to tuk-tuks (4000–8000r).

For those with some time on their hands, the area surrounding Siem Reap does offer more to see than just temples. One popular excursion is to a floating village on the **Tonle Sap**, Southeast Asia's largest lake, where houses, shops, basketball courts and crocodile farms are all built on barges (round trip to the lakeshore: $4 moto, $6 tuk-tuk). But beware: guides in Siem Reap have seriously capitalized on village tours, and at this point you're likely to run across as many tourist boats as villagers. A boat from the shore to the village is expensive as well ($10–20/person depending on the size of your group.

Those interested in giving back to the community might consider donating blood at the Angkor Children's Hospital, where you'll get a free t-shirt for your pains along with that warm fuzzy feeling (Ⓣ063/963409, Ⓦwww.fwab.org).

## Arrival

**By share taxi or pick-up** You'll probably be dropped at the smart new market, Psar Leu, to the east of the city, a hectic transport hub.
**By boat** Boats cruise into the port, around 12km south of Siem Reap (the distance varies with the level of the lake), passing hundreds of floating houses. Guesthouse reps will be keen to offer a free ride into town, so it's a good idea to decide beforehand where you want to stay; otherwise, there are motos (12,000r) and taxis (20,000r).
**By air** Guesthouse touts meet planes at the airport, 6km west of town; or you can take a registered taxi from the booth in the airport (20,000r).

## Information and tours

**Tourist information** There is a tourist information office (Mon–Fri 8.30am–noon & 2.30–5.30pm; Ⓣ063/964347) opposite the *Grand Hôtel d'Angkor*, on Tosamut Blvd, but you'll find they're only interested in selling you a tour. You'd do better to check out the free town guides: the *Siem Reap Visitors' Guide* can be found at shops, bars and guesthouses.
**Tours** Organized tours, even those not targeting large overseas groups, tend to be pricey. The cheapest way to go is to arrange your own transport and hire a guide through your guesthouse or the tourist information office; they charge around $20 a day. Be sure to get one certified by the Khmer Angkor Tour Guide Association (KATGA), which requires its members to pass an examination on temple history. For a more inclusive package, Exotissimo (Ⓣ063/964323, Ⓦwww.exotissimo.com) can provide cars or vans ($25/$35 a day) and guides ($35 a day).

**TREAT YOURSELF**

If you're feeling templed-out, Siem Reap is a great place to try a spa treatment. One of the best is **Body Tune** (Ⓣ063/764141 Ⓦwww.bodytune.co.th), just east of Psar Chas, where you can rejuvenate with Thai and Swedish massage, aromatherapy and body scrubs (from $15/hr).

## Accommodation

Most budget accommodation is largely concentrated in two areas: just east of the river, off National Route 6 (also known as Airport Road), and on the sidestreets west of Sivatha St. The latter is also home to a concentration of mid-range establishments, which offer TV, a/c and en-suite facilities for $15–20.

### East of the river

**Big Lyna Villa** 659 Wat Bo Village, off Achasvar St Ⓣ063/964807. The most delightful rooms in this old wooden house are the large wood-panelled affairs upstairs. There's also a big balcony and a garden for lazing about. ❸
**European** Near junction of National Route 6 and Wat Bo St Ⓣ012/582237. Large and extremely clean rooms at this calm, homey guesthouse, tucked away on a sidestreet filled with budget accommodation. ❶
**Golden Banana** East of Psar Chas Ⓣ012/888366, Ⓦwww.golden-banana.com. Western-managed, gay-friendly place in a quiet neighbourhood a five-minute walk over the bridge next to Psar Chas. The lovely, artistically decorated bungalows, set in a pleasant garden, feature a/c, TV and Wi-Fi. Breakfast is included in the leafy courtyard cafe. ❺
**Green Town** 182 Wat Bo Village, between Wat Bo and Achasvar streets Ⓣ063/964974. Range

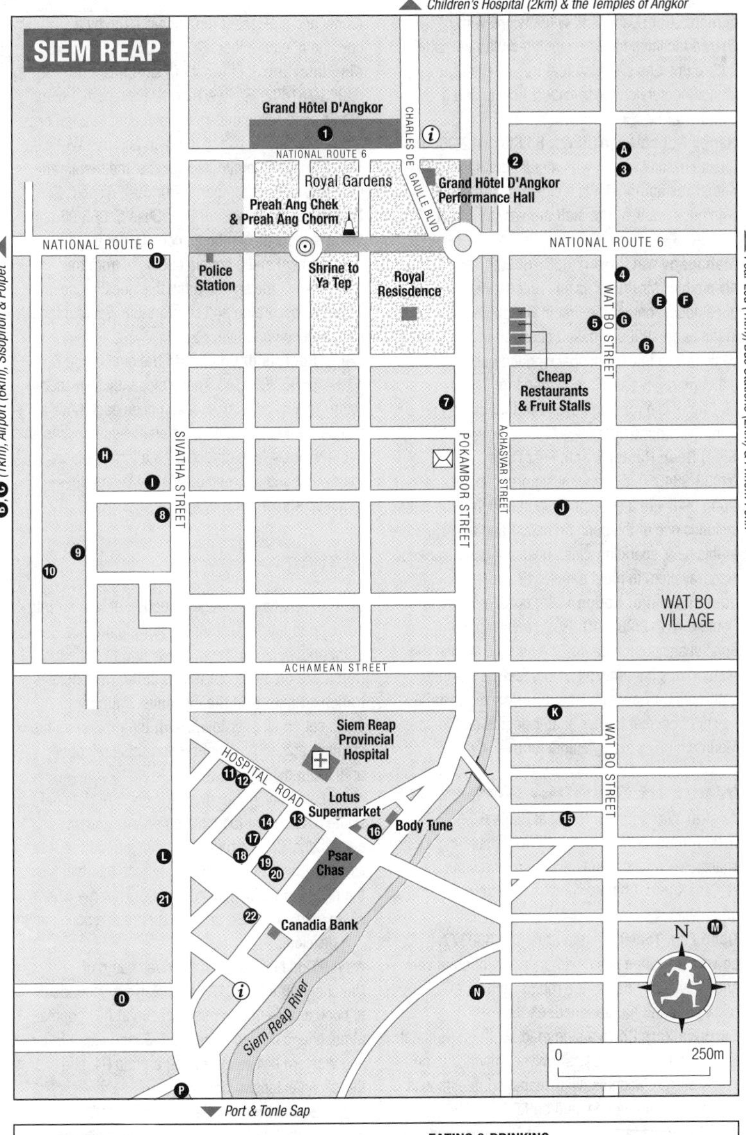


**ACCOMMODATION**

| | |
|---|---|
| Angkor Wat | H |
| Big Lyna Villa | K |
| Dead Fish Tower | L |
| Earthwalkers | B |
| European | F |
| Golden Angkor | D |
| Golden Banana | N |
| Green Garden Home | I |
| Green Town | J |
| Happy Guesthouse | E |
| Mahogany | G |
| Mandalay Inn | P |
| Red Piano | O |
| Secrets of Elephants | C |
| Siem Reap Hostel | M |
| Yaklom Angkor Lodge | A |

**EATING & DRINKING**

| | |
|---|---|
| Angkor What? | 19 |
| Arun | 2 |
| Bayon | 4 |
| Blue Pumpkin | 12 |
| Butterflies Garden | 15 |
| Café Indochine | 8 |
| Chivit Thai | 5 |
| Dead Fish Tower | L |
| Elephant Bar | 1 |
| FCC | 7 |
| Forest Hut | 21 |
| Hawaii Pizza | 6 |
| Ivy | 22 |
| Kampucino Pizza | 16 |
| Khmer Kitchen | 14 |
| Linga Bar | 20 |
| New Delhi | 11 |
| Red Piano | 18 |
| Sawasdee Food Garden | 3 |
| Soup Dragon | 13 |
| Sugar Palm | 9 |
| Temple Bar | 17 |
| Zone One | 10 |

of rooms from basic and windowless with shared facilities to well-appointed with en-suite bathrooms and a/c. Also features a restaurant, a booking service for transport tickets and a communal TV. ❶

**Happy Guesthouse** Off Wat Bo St ⓣ012/960879. Clean en-suite rooms with a quiet courtyard and Khmer restaurant, down a sidestreet bursting with guesthouses. The staff are very helpful and friendly. ❶

**Mahogany** Wat Bo St ⓣ063/760909. The hospitable "Mr Prune" is still running his guesthouse, one of the first in Siem Reap to open in the early 1990s. It hasn't changed much, offering basic rooms in a traditional wooden building, although renovations are planned for 2009. Mr Prune also runs an adventure tour company from the ground floor.

**Siem Reap Hostel** East of Psar Chas ⓣ063/964660, ⓦwww.thesiemreaphostel.com. Dorm beds are a bit expensive at $10, but the price includes use of the pool, breakfast and free bicycles at this new, sparkling-clean hostel. A good place for solo travellers to meet people. ❷

**Yaklom Angkor Lodge** 100m north of National Route 6 ⓣ012/983510, ⓦwww.yaklom.com. Spacious accommodation in a cottage around the restaurant's gardens; all rooms feature en-suite bathrooms, TV and a/c. The decor makes tasteful use of chunchiet fabrics, water gourds and *khapas*. Mountain bikes are available for hire. ❹

### West of Sivatha Street

**Angkor Wat** South of National Route 6 ⓣ063/963809. Modern family-run guesthouse with spacious en-suite rooms and a small restaurant serving Khmer/Chinese food and Western breakfasts. ❷

**Dead Fish Tower** Sivatha St ⓣ012/630377. Lower mid-range place with a variety of creatively and individually decorated rooms, and an excellent restaurant and bar attached. ❶

**Earthwalkers** Down a side road south off National Route 6 ⓣ012/967901, ⓦwww.earthwalkers.no. This well-run, Scandinavian-managed guesthouse offers a swimming pool and buffet breakfast, included in the rates. Immaculate $5 dorm beds as well as en-suite rooms. ❶

**Golden Angkor** Near National Route 6/Sivatha St intersection ⓣ063/964039. Hotel accommodation at guesthouse prices; though far from lavish, rooms at this friendly place have hot showers, TV, fridge and a/c. ❸

**Green Garden Home** Just off Sivatha St ⓣ012/890363, ⓦwww.greengardenhome.com. Friendly guesthouse with a variety of ample-sized rooms and a pleasant terrace area, run by a budding photographer. ❷

**Mandalay Inn** Southwest of Psar Chas ⓣ063/761662, ⓦwww.mandalayinn.com. Rooms at this good-value mid-range place feature fan or a/c, hot water, TV, use of the gym and free Wi-Fi. If you're tiring of Cambodian cuisine, the restaurant here also does a number of Burmese dishes. ❷

**Red Piano** Southwest of Psar Chas ⓣ063/963240, ⓦwww.redpianocambodia.com. Under the same management and a couple of blocks from the restaurant of the same name, this guesthouse is tastefully decorated and comfortable. Several family rooms sleep up to five. ❹

**Secrets of Elephants** National Route 6 ⓣ063/964328. These elegantly furnished rooms in a traditional wooden house each have a unique theme, based on a different Southeast Asian country. Set in lush gardens, it's a terrific place to unwind, and the restaurant downstairs does fantastic Khmer cuisine. ❸

## Eating

Siem Reap boasts a huge selection of restaurants catering to tourist tastes; for something more authentic, head for the markets and the cheap fruit stalls on the eastern side of the river near National Route 6. In the evenings, impromptu stalls set up all over town, with the market as the culinary epicentre. Most restaurants stay open until around 11pm.

**Arun** East bank of the river, just north of National Route 6. Excellent food, huge portions and an educational picture menu; it's also a handy spot to listen to Khmer music wafting across the river from the nightly traditional dancing at the nearby *Grand Hôtel d'Angkor*. Their *amok* – served in a coconut – is delicious.

**Bayon** One block east of the river, south of National Route 6 ⓣ012/855219. It's a good idea to book a table during peak season at this popular, atmospheric garden restaurant. Good-value Khmer and Western dishes are priced around $4, and there's an extensive drinks menu.

**Butterflies Garden** East of Psar Chas ⓣ063/761211. Khmer, Western and Asian fusion cuisine served in a tropical garden draped in a net and filled with live butterflies. Part of a project to provide restaurant training to disadvantaged Khmer youth, but also an enchanting dining experience.

**Café Indochine** Sivatha St. This upmarket French-run restaurant in a traditional wooden house has some excellent Khmer dishes on offer ranging from $4 to $9. Ask about the daily specials.

**Chivit Thai** Opposite *Bayon*. More than just the usual Thai and Khmer menu at a reasonable $2–5, with relaxed veranda and Thai-style seating.
**FCC** Pokambor St ☎063/760280. Many of the dishes on the menu at the *Foreign Correspondents' Club* (*FCC*) in Phnom Penh can be had here, too. Relaxed seating will ensure that you linger long after your meal is finished, if you can get it; big tour groups tend to congregate here.
**Forest Hut** Sivatha St, just south of *Dead Fish Tower*. A wide selection of both Khmer and Western food is on offer here, but the Khmer food stands out.
**Hawaii Pizza** Off Wat Bo St. Fantastic food at a good price; Cambodian and Italian food and salads are all on the menu, plus great sandwiches. Turns into a popular bar in the late evening. Pizzas $4–6.
**Kampucino Pizza** By Psar Chas. The picturesque riverside location sells this newly expanded place, which is more restaurant than pizza parlour, despite its name. Offers all-day brunch breakfasts, as well as a wide range of pastas, grills and salads.
**Khmer Kitchen** Off Hospital Rd. This perennially packed, family-run restaurant is becoming something of a legend in Siem Reap for its great Khmer home-cooking with the odd modern twist. A good place to sample anything you've been wanting to try, and nothing is over $3.
**New Delhi** Opposite Siem Reap Provincial Hospital. Vegetarian and non-veg Indian dishes in a converted shop-house. There is other Indian food to be had in Siem Reap, but this is the best.
**Sawasdee Food Garden** One block east of the river, north of National Route 6. Fantastic Thai food in a relaxed garden setting. Dishes around $1–4.
**Soup Dragon** Hospital Rd. Fantastic Vietnamese, Cambodian and Western food, including a good selection for veggies. The fish barbecue and salad is highly recommended. Moderately priced at $3–5, friendly staff and nicely decorated.
**Sugar Palm** One block south of Sivatha St. Exquisite Khmer food served on the stylish balcony bar of an old wooden house, decorated entirely in tiger-striped palm wood. Mains $4–6.

## Nightlife

Siem Reap is a bustling place, with bars targeted at foreigners opening up all over town, especially around Psar Chas: you can easily while away a week or so visiting a different venue each evening. Plenty of bars stay open until the last customer leaves.
**Angkor What?** One block northwest of Psar Chas. Popular, trendy bar, with DJs cranking out lively tunes. A good place to socialize and meet people.
**Blue Pumpkin** Near the Siem Reap Provincial Hospital. Free Wi-Fi in a chic upstairs a/c lounge. Cocktails and food available too.
**Dead Fish Tower** Sivatha St. Wacky decor featuring meandering stairways to multiple levels as well as a crocodile pit make this place a world-class challenge to navigate while drunk. Live music and excellent food will ensure that you come back a second time.
**Elephant Bar** At the *Grand Hôtel d'Angkor*. Start your evening off in style in the luxurious cellar bar, with happy-hour half-price drinks (daily 7–9pm); a ready supply of free bar snacks may mean you won't need dinner.
**Ivy** By Psar Chas. Very much an expat hangout, with free use of the pool table and $1 beer.
**Linga Bar** On a small side-street northwest of Psar Chas. Gay-managed lounge bar with a mixed clientele and a generous list of cocktails, high on the list of Siem Reap's most stylish places to sip a cosmopolitan.
**Red Piano** Northwest of Psar Chas. Attractive bar-restaurant with stylish *Tomb Raider*-style decor generously decked out with ferns; you can also sample an Angelina Jolie cocktail or two.
**Temple Bar** Northwest of Psar Chas. One of Siem Reap's more popular watering holes, with a DJ and nightly Apsara classical dancing upstairs (7.30pm). Stays open very late.
**Zone One** Northwest of Psar Chas. Siem Reap's most popular disco, playing Western favourites and Cambodian hip-hop to a mixed crowd of locals, tourists and expats.

## Directory

**Airlines** Bangkok Airways, 571 National Route 6 ☎063/380191; Lao Airlines, 114 National Route 6 ☎063/963283; Siem Reap Airways, 571 National

### DANCE AND MUSIC

Siem Reap is a good place to take in a cultural performance of classical **Khmer dance**, often known as "Apsara dancing", packaged with dinner by several of the hotels. The most popular is the nightly event staged by the *Grand Hôtel d'Angkor*, incorporating dinner and a show for $32, though you can catch much cheaper (often free) performances at various restaurants around town – try *Temple Bar* or *Butterflies Garden*.

Route 6 ⓣ063/965427; Vietnam Airlines, 342 National Route 6 ⓣ063/964488.

**Banks and exchange** ATMs are everywhere. Acleda Bank, next to *Angkor Hotel*, National Route 6; Canadia Bank, southwest of Psar Chas; Mekong Bank, Sivatha St (with an exchange booth operating outside the bank Mon–Fri 6.30–8.30am & 4–6pm, Sat 6.30–8.30am).

**Hospital and clinics** International SOS (c/o their Phnom Penh clinic on ⓣ023/216911) has a doctor on call in Siem Reap and can arrange emergency evacuations. The Naga Medical Centre, 593 National Route 6 (ⓣ016/964500) has English- and French-speaking staff. The basic, government-run Siem Reap Provincial Hospital, 500m north of Psar Chas (ⓣ063/760705), should be approached only as a last resort.

**Internet** Expect to pay around 2000–4000r/hr to get online at one of the many internet cafés. Hotels generally charge their guests a bit more.

**Post office** Pokambor St (daily 7.30am–5.30pm) offers facilities for poste restante and domestic and international calls.

**Supermarkets** Stock up on bottles of spirits, Rizlas and a scattering of Western luxuries at Lotus Market, opposite Psar Chas.

**Telephones** Cheap international calls via the internet can be made at many internet cafés, as well as at the post office.

**Tourist police** Junction of Sivatha St and National Route 6 ⓣ063/760215.

### Moving on

**By bus** Public buses bound for Bangkok, Battambang, Phnom Penh and other destinations within Cambodia leave rather inconveniently from a string of bus stations about 2km northeast of town. Travel agents in Siem Reap can book you tickets, but you still have to trek out to catch the bus. Note that on the Bangkok route, the buses tend to arrive at Poipet at around 1pm, convenient if you're hooking up with onward road transport, but leaving little time to catch the train from Aranyaprathet; to do the latter, you'd be advised to get an early ride out to Poipet.

**Destinations:** Bangkok (1 daily; 10hr); Battambang (5hr); Kampong Cham (5hr); Kampong Thom (2hr); Phnom Penh (6hr); Poipet (6hr); Sisophon (4hr).

**By boat** Boats leave from the port at 7am for Phnom Penh ($25) and Battambang ($15). When the water level is really low (Feb–May) the express boats for Phnom Penh moor some way out, and you'll be taken out to them on smaller craft. You'll need to book your ticket at least a day ahead – two days ahead March–Nov – when often just one boat runs on each route. If you get your ticket at a travel agent or from the boat company offices (they have several premises around the centre, each displaying a large sign of a boat), you'll need to find your own transport to the port (12,000r by moto; allow at least 30min on the truly dreadful road), but if you buy from a guesthouse or hotel, a minibus will collect you, which may mean setting out as early as 5.30am, as the vehicle will pick up passengers from various locations before heading down to the port.

**Destinations:** Battambang (daily; 3hr 30min); Phnom Penh (daily; 5–6hr).

**By air** Besides flights to Phnom Penh, there are an increasing number of international departures to Bangkok, HCMC and Vientiane, and further afield to Kuala Lumpur, Singapore and Hong Kong. If you're staying at a hotel, they'll generally drive you to the airport free of charge.

**Destinations:** Bangkok (9 daily); HCMC (6 daily); Phnom Penh (6 daily).

## THE TEMPLES OF ANGKOR

In 802, Jayavarman II united the warring Chenla factions and declared himself universal god-king, becoming the first of a succession of 39 monarchs to reign over what was then the most powerful kingdom in Southeast Asia. So the **Angkor era** was born, a period marked by imaginative building projects, the design and construction of inspirational **temples** and palaces, the creation of complex irrigation systems and the development of magnificent walled cities. However, as resources were channelled into ever more ambitious construction projects, Angkor became a target for attack from neighbouring **Siam**. Successive invasions culminated in the sacking of Angkor in the fifteenth century and the city was abandoned to the jungle. Although Khmers knew of the lost city, it wasn't until the West's "discovery" of Angkor by a French missionary in the nineteenth century that international interest was aroused.

### What to see and do

More than one hundred Angkorian monuments are spread over some

3000 square kilometres of countryside around Siem Reap. The best-known monuments are the vast Hindu temple of **Angkor Wat** and the walled city of **Angkor Thom**, while jungle-ravaged **Ta Phrom** and exquisitely decorated **Banteay Srei** are also popular sites. The **Roluos** ruins are significant as the site of the empire's first capital city and as a point of comparison with the later architectural styles of **Banteay Kdei** and **Ta Keo**. Many of the artefacts on display at the temples of Angkor are not originals – **thefts** of the valuable treasures have been a problem since the 1970s. Attempts have been made to protect the most valuable by moving them to the National Museum in Phnom Penh, or to the Angkor Conservation Office in Siem Reap, and replacing them with copies.

## Angkor Wat

Built in the twelfth century as a mausoleum and temple for King Suryavarman II, **Angkor Wat** represents the height of Khmer art, combining architectural harmony, grand proportions and detailed artistry. Approaching along the sandstone causeway across a broad moat and through the western gate, you're teased with glimpses of the central towers, but it's not until you're through the gate that the full magnificence of the temple comes into view. The causeway, extending 300m across the flat, open compound, directs the eye to the proud temple and its most memorable feature, the distinctive conical-shaped towers, designed to look like lotus buds.

If you can resist the urge to head straight for the main temple building, the entry **gopura** is worth exploring for its exceptional carvings and an eight-armed Vishnu image with a Buddha head, an interesting marriage of Buddhism and Hinduism. Built as a Hindu temple dedicated to Vishnu,

### VISITING THE TEMPLES

The temples are officially open daily from 5am till 6pm, although Banteay Srei closes at 5pm.

**Transport**

There are a number of transport options to get to and around Angkor Wat from Siem Reap: your choice will depend on your time-frame, your budget and which temples you intend to visit. Hiring a taxi is one of the quickest ways to go ($20/day) and is handy for reaching far-away temples like Banteay Srei. For one person, a moto ($8/day) can serve a similar purpose; tuk-tuks ($10/day) are somewhat slower. If you have time and are content to stay within a smaller area, a bicycle ($2/day) can also be a very pleasant way to explore – the distances are manageable, and the terrain is almost completely flat.

**Entry passes**

**Entry passes** are required to enter the Angkor area, and must also be shown at several of the temples. At the main entrance, on the Siem Reap–Angkor Wat road, three categories of pass are available, valid for one day ($20), three days ($40) or seven days ($60); additionally, one-day passes can be bought at Angkor Wat and Bakong (Roluos). Most people find it adequate to buy the three-day pass, which gives enough time to see all the temples in the central area and to visit the outlying temples at Roluos and Banteay Srei. If you're short on time, you can just about cover Angkor Wat, the Bayon, Ta Phrom and Banteay Srei in one full day. For three- and seven-day tickets, you'll need to furnish a **passport photo** of yourself – these can be taken for free at the main entrance but the long line means you'll waste precious time if you don't come with one. Children under 12 are admitted free, but you must take their passport with you as proof of age. Entry passes must be used on consecutive days.

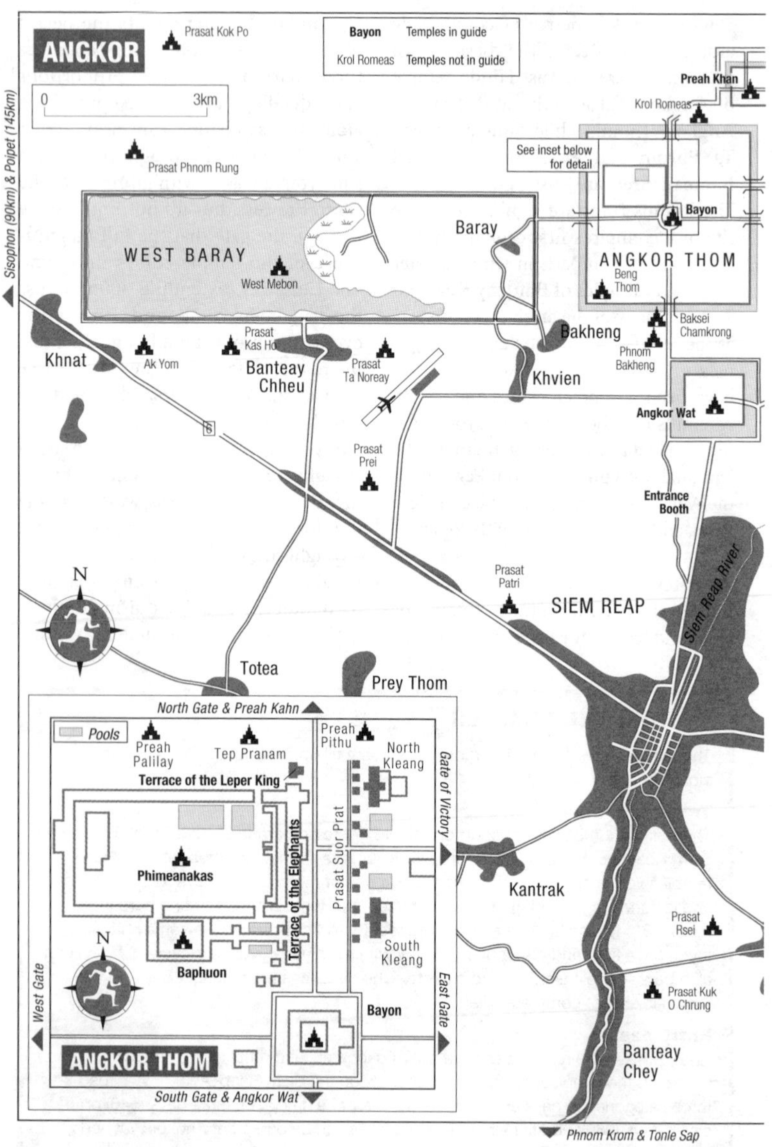


Angkor Wat was later converted to a Buddhist monastery.

Continuing east along the causeway, you'll pass between the wat's library buildings and two ponds, and mount a flight of steps to the **Terrace of Honour**. The terrace is the gateway to the extraordinary **Gallery of Bas Reliefs**, a covered gallery which extends around the perimeter of the first level. The carvings cover almost the entire wall – 700m long, 2m high – depicting religious narratives,

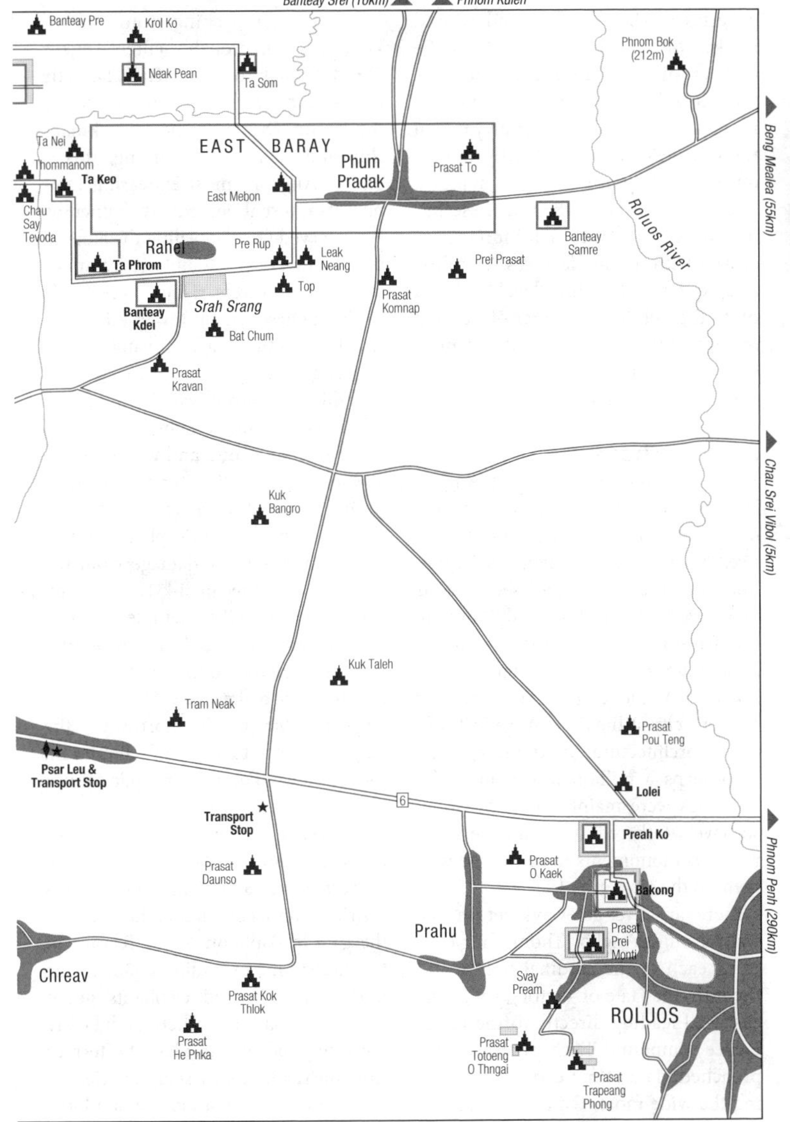


battle scenes and Hindu epics. The best-known carving, **The Churning of the Ocean of Milk**, in the East Gallery, depicts the myth of creation: gods (*devas*) and evil spirits (*asuras*) churn the ocean for a thousand years to produce the elixir of immortality, creating order out of chaos. The detail and sharpness of the images make this one of the greatest stone sculptures ever created.

As you approach the central chamber, you'll pass through the cruciform galleries linking the first and second levels. On the right-hand side is the **Gallery of One Thousand Buddhas**, though only a handful of figures now remain. The walls of the courtyard on the next level are carved with numerous detailed *apsaras*, celestial nymphs. There are a total of 1850 of these figures in Angkor Wat, each individually carved with unique features. The final steep climb to the third level is closed off to the public. A number of Buddha images look down from the central sanctuary on top at the seat of the ancient Khmer Empire.

## Angkor Thom

**Angkor Thom**, 2km north of Angkor Wat, was the last and greatest capital of the Angkor era, built during the late twelfth and early thirteenth centuries. The immense city is enclosed by four defensive walls, 8m high and 3km long on each side. This in turn is surrounded by a 100m wide moat. Certainly more spectacular and extravagant than any Western city at the time, Angkor Thom was an architectural masterpiece, home to perhaps a million inhabitants. The buildings were mainly made of wood, so have weathered away, but the stone religious monuments remain as a testament to the city's grand scale.

There are five gateways set in the walls around Angkor Thom, four covering each of the cardinal points and the fifth, the Gate of Victory, set in the east wall leading directly to the Royal Palace compound. Each gateway is approached via a **stone causeway** crossing the wide moat. On each causeway, 54 god images on the left and 54 demons on the right depict the myth of the Churning of the Ocean of Milk, as featured in the East Gallery of Angkor Wat. Each of the five sandstone gopuras is crowned with four large heads, facing the points of the compass, flanked by an image of the Hindu god Indra riding a three-headed elephant.

If you're approaching from Angkor Wat, you will probably enter Angkor Thom through the South Gate. Directly north, at the centre of the walled city, is the **Bayon**. Despite its poor workmanship and haphazard sculpting, this is one of Angkor's most endearing temples, its unusual personality defined by large carved faces adorning the sides of its 54 towers. The temple is pyramid-shaped, the towers rising successively to the highest central tower. Although small, it's actually a confusing temple to navigate, largely owing to its complex history. Bayon was built on top of an earlier monument, follows an experimental layout, and was added to at various times. It is thought to have been completed in the early thirteenth century, but its chaotic plan was further complicated by damage from the Siamese invasion in 1431. Although originally a Buddhist temple, it has a Hindu history too, and themes of both religions can be found in the reliefs adorning the galleries.

Lying 200m to the northwest, the neighbouring temple of **Baphuon**, though now no more than a pile of rubble, was, at its peak, when the tower was covered in bronze, even more impressive than the Bayon. Restoration work is being carried out and access is restricted until completion. Just beyond the gate to Baphuon is the **Terrace of the Elephants**, extending 300m to the north. Three-headed elephants guard the stairway at the southern end; before ascending, be sure to view the terrace from the road, where a sculpted frieze of hunting and fighting elephants adorns the facade. The terrace, which originally housed wooden pavilions, would have been used by the king to address his public and as a ceremonial viewing platform.

Immediately north of here is the **Terrace of The Leper King**, named after the statue of a naked figure that was discovered here (and is now in Phnom

Penh's National Museum – a copy stands on the platform). It's uncertain who the Leper King was or even where the name originates from, though an inscription on the statue suggests that it may represent Yama, the god of the underworld and judge of the dead, giving rise to the theory that the terrace was used as a royal crematorium. Superb sculptures of a variety of figures and sea creatures grace the sides of the terrace, while the original wall, also adorned with beautiful carvings, can be accessed via a viewing passageway. You'll need a torch to see the detail.

The two terraces mark what would have been the western edge of the Royal Palace. The timber buildings have since disintegrated, leaving just the temple mountain of **Phimeanakas** and the king's and queen's **bathing pools**. Now little more than a pyramid of stones, Phimeanakas was the palace chapel, crowned with a golden tower and probably completed in the early eleventh century. The western staircase has a handrail to aid the short, steep climb to the upper terrace. From the top, there's a good view of Baphuon to the south through the trees, and to the north, the royal baths.

### Phnom Bakheng

The hilltop temple of **Phnom Bakheng**, south of Angkor Thom, is the oldest building in this area; it was constructed following Yasorvarman's move westwards from Roluos. The state temple was built from the rock of the hill on which it stands. It originally boasted 108 magnificent towers set on a spectacular pyramid, although only part of the central tower now remains. The five diminishing terraces rise to a central sanctuary adorned with female divinities, which once housed the lingam of the god Yashodhareshvara. Bakheng, however, is visited less for its temple than for the view from the hilltop, Angkor Wat soaring upwards from its jungle hideout to the east. At sunset, the best time to visit for great views of Angkor, it becomes a circus of tourists and vendors, with elephant rides on offer, one-dollar drinks and souvenir T-shirts piled up on the ancient stones.

### Preah Khan

Just beyond the northeast corner of Angkor Thom's perimeter wall stands **Preah Khan**, a tranquil site surrounded by dense foliage. The twelfth-century temple served as the temporary residence of King Jayavarman VII while he was rebuilding Angkor Thom, damaged in an attack by the Siamese. A systematic tour of the temple is impossible, as routes are blocked with piles of fallen stones, trees or archeological excavation. Most people enter from the western entrance, but it's worth continuing all the way to the eastern edge of the temple. Here you'll find an unusual two-storey structure, with circular columns supporting the second floor of square columns and windows, unique in Khmer architecture. Not far from here, at the southern end of the east gopura, a photogenic battle of wood and stone is being fought as an encroaching tree grows through the ruins: the tree appears to be winning. Mostly shady, Preah Khan is a good one to visit during the hotter hours of the day.

### Ta Keo

About 2km east of the Bayon, **Ta Keo** scores well on the height points, but is awarded nothing for decoration. This towering replica of Mount Meru, which was never finished, is bereft of the usual Angkor refineries. It's commonly believed that it was struck by lightning, a truly bad omen.

### Ta Phrom

The stunning twelfth-century temple-monastery of **Ta Phrom**, 1km southeast of Ta Keo, has a magical appeal. Rather than being cleared and restored like most of the other Angkor monuments, it's been left to the jungle and appears roughly as it did to the Europeans who rediscovered these ruins in the nineteenth century. Roots and trunks intermingle with the stones and seem almost part of the structure, and the temple's cramped corridors reveal half-hidden reliefs, while valuable carvings litter the floor.

Jayavarman VII originally built Ta Phrom as a Buddhist monastery, although Hindu purists have since defaced the Buddhist imagery. The temple was once surrounded by an enclosed city. An inscription found at the site testifies to its importance: over twelve thousand people lived at the monastery, maintained by almost eighty thousand people in the surrounding villages.

### Banteay Kdei

Southeast of Ta Phrom and one of the quieter sites in this area, **Banteay Kdei** is a huge twelfth-century Buddhist temple, constructed under Jayavarman VII. It's in a pretty poor state of repair, but the crumbling stones create an interesting architecture of their own. Highlights are the carvings of female divinities and other figures in the niches of the second enclosure, and a frieze of Buddhas in the interior court. Opposite the east entrance to Banteay Kdei is the **Srah Srang** or "Royal Bath", a large lake which was probably used for ritual ablutions.

### Roluos group

Not far from the small town of **Roluos** are three of Angkor's oldest temples: **Bakong**, **Preah Ko** and **Lolei**. Signposts mark the way from National Route 6, about 13km east of Siem Reap; Lolei is 1km north of the road, while Preah Ko and Bakong lie to the south, a couple of kilometres down the track. The relics date from the late ninth century, the dawn of the Angkorian era, and a time when the emphasis was on detail rather than size. All three temples are characterized by innovative construction methods, architecture and ornamentation.

South of National Route 6, the first temple you come to is **Preah Ko**, built by Indravarman I as a funerary temple for his ancestors. It's in poor condition, but is charming; the highlights are the six brick towers of the central sanctuary, which sit on a low platform at the centre of the inner enclosure. Before the central sanctuaries are three ruined sculptures of the sacred bull Nandin, the mount of Shiva. Male figures are carved into the three eastern towers, while those on the smaller western towers are female.

Cambodia's earliest temple-mountain, **Bakong**, a kilometre or so south of Preah Ko, is made up of five tiers of solid sandstone surrounded by brick towers. Entering from the east across the balustraded causeway you'll come into the inner enclosure through a ruined gopura; originally eight brick towers surrounded the central sanctuary, but only five remain standing. In the heart of the enclosure is a five-tiered pyramid, which you can climb on any of the four sides. Twelve small sanctuaries are arranged symmetrically around the fourth tier, and above you on the summit is the well-preserved central sanctuary – if you're wondering why it's in such good nick, it's because it was rebuilt in 1941.

Return to the main road for the sanctuary of **Lolei**, built by Yashovarman I on an artificial island. Its four collapsing brick-and-sandstone towers are only worth visiting for the Sanskrit inscriptions in the door jambs that detail the work rosters of the temple "slaves"; a few carvings remain but are badly eroded.

### Banteay Srei

The pretty tenth-century temple of **Banteay Srei** is unique amongst its Angkorian peers. Its miniature proportions, unusual pinkish colour and intricate ornamentation create a surreal effect, enhanced by its astonishing state of preservation. The journey to the site, about 30km northeast of Angkor Wat, takes about an hour. Tour groups start arriving en masse from 8.30am, and because of its small size, it gets crowded quickly. Hiring a car or a moto from Siem Reap, you could arrive here an hour or so beforehand, when you'll have the temple to yourself.

The sharp and detailed carving above the doorway of the east gopura is a prelude to the delights within. From the entry tower, across the moat, the tops of the three intricate central towers and two libraries are visible over the low enclosure wall. The reddish sandstone against the green backdrop of the jungle is a magnificent sight, as if you've stumbled across a fairytale city. Inside the enclosure wall, there's a riot of intricate decoration and architecture with elegant pillars and exquisite frontons; walls are covered with carved foliage and guardian divinities, and panels are extravagantly decorated with scenes from Hindu mythology. It's a magical, miniature fantasyland; the central towers have midget doors barely a metre tall, though getting in is academic now, as they're roped off prohibiting entry – not so much to preserve the site as to prevent a tourist jam inside.

# Western Cambodia

The flat stretch of land that fans out from Phnom Penh to the border with Thailand is sandwiched between the **Cardamom Mountains** in the southwestern corner of the country and the **Dangrek Range** in the north. A perfect hideout, these frontier hills were home to the Khmer Rouge guerrillas for nearly twenty years from 1979. However, the government has been firmly in control of the area for years now, and travellers have returned. The towns within the former occupied territories, such as the remote frontier outpost of **Pailin**, are not attractive places, as you might expect after twenty years of war and isolation, but the countryside is stunning in places and has a Wild West appeal. Many of the residents are ex-soldiers who have spent most of their lives living in the jungle; sticking to the roads and paths is essential, as this is the most densely mined area in the country. Stretching across the vast central plain is the **Tonle Sap**, which swells to over 8000 square kilometres during the rainy season, and is the region's primary focus of transport, livelihood and leisure. The area's commercial hub is **Battambang**, an agreeable town bearing traces of its French colonial days. Its northern neighbour, **Sisophon**, makes a convenient stopping-off point on the route into Thailand.

## BATTAMBANG

**BATTAMBANG** is one of Cambodia's biggest cities, but it's a world apart from Phnom Penh's urban bustle, enjoying an unhurried pace and a reputation for friendliness. The city, however, is keen not to get left behind in the country's recent surge of development and modernization. French-colonial-era terraces on the riverside are rapidly filling with private English-language schools and mobile-phone shops. The busiest Battambang gets, however, is at the central market, Psar Nat, where **gemstones** from the town of Pailin, southwest of the city, are cut and traded. Don't expect to pick up a bargain unless you know what to look for – the better stones are shipped straight to Thailand. The local **museum** (Mon–Fri 8–11am & 2–5pm; 4000r) is well worth a visit, as are two **temples** near the town centre – Wat Phephittham and Wat Dhum Rey Sor.

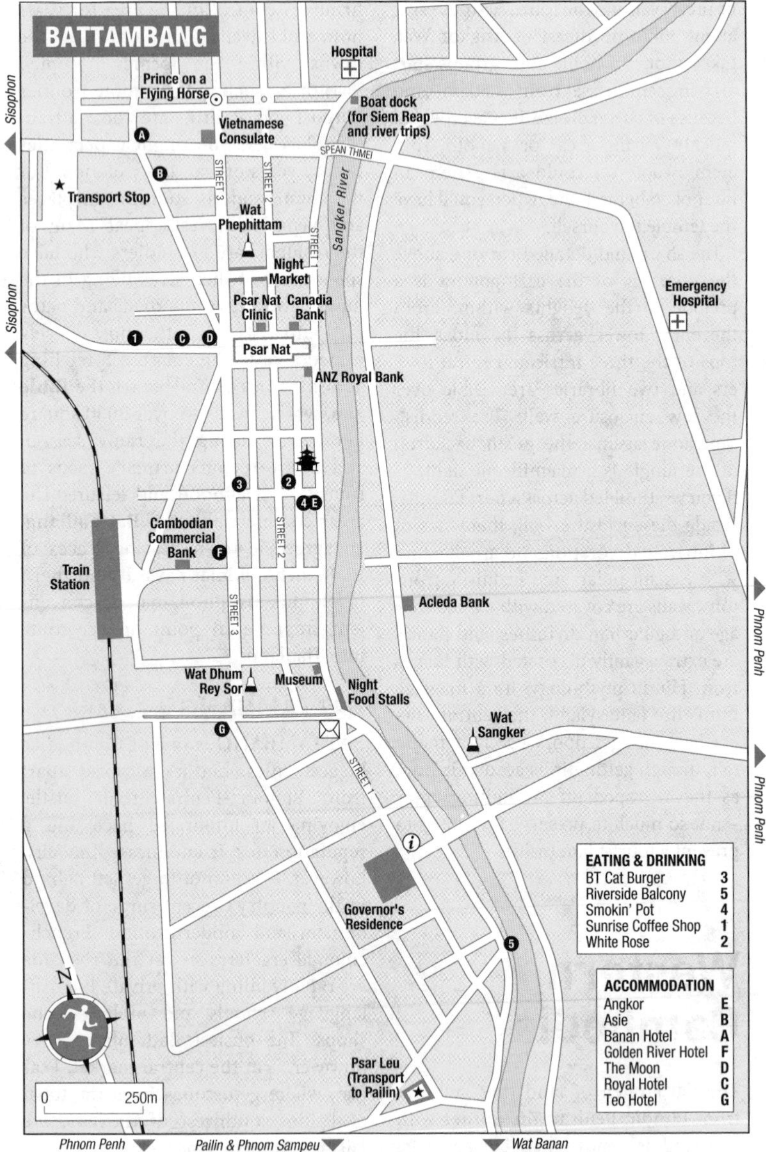


## Arrival and information

**By bus** Buses arrive near the transport stop in the northwest of town, just off National Route 5.

**By share taxi or pick-up** These arrive at the transport stop as well; arriving from the south, they'll drop you at Psar Nat if you ask.

**By boat** The boat dock is on the river, just opposite the hospital, a few hundred metres from the centre of town; hotel reps and English-speaking moto drivers meet the boats, so you'll have no trouble getting to your accommodation speedily.

**Tourist information** There is a tourist office across the street from the Governor's Residence that can provide maps of the area and basic information.

## Accommodation

An abundance of hotels and guesthouses makes for competitively priced accommodation, with decent rooms available for $4–5 per night, all with cable TV, en-suite bathroom and fan, unless otherwise stated.

**Angkor** St 1 ⓣ053/952310. Overlooking the river, this hotel has one of the nicest situations in Battambang, so it's a shame the rooms don't quite live up to the location: though clean and en suite, with a/c, TV and fridge, they're a bit run-down. ❸

**Asie** North of the market, towards the transport stop ⓣ016/944955. A modern hotel, where the rooms have cold-water en-suite facilities, fan and TV. Some a/c rooms available. ❶

**Banan Hotel** Just northeast of the transport stop ⓣ053/953242. The poshest place in town, though its brand-new rooms are still good value. All the usual amenities plus lots of gleaming wood. ❸

**Golden River Hotel** St 3, south of the market ⓣ012/838605. This friendly, helpful place, run by an Australian/Khmer family, enjoys a good, central location. Some of the single rooms are a bit small. ❶

**The Moon** Just west of Psar Nat ⓣ015/530201. Basic guesthouse with a central location beside the market and cheap but noisy rooms. ❶

**Royal Hotel** Western end of the market ⓣ016/912034. This smart hotel is probably the best value in Battambang, offering modern rooms with cable TV, fridge and en-suite facilities. The rooftop is home to both the cheapest rooms and a cheerful travellers' restaurant. ❶

**Teo Hotel** St 3, on the southern edge of the commercial district ⓣ053/952288. Not as expensive as it looks from the outside, but is a bit of a distance from the town-centre action. Double rooms include a telephone in addition to the usual facilities, and the restaurant boasts an enormous menu of Khmer offerings. ❷

## Eating and drinking

In the evening, a buzzing night market opens up on the street south of Wat Phephittam. For delicious noodle dishes, desserts and fruit shakes, head down to the riverfront opposite the post office, where street stalls set up in the afternoon and serve late into the evening.

**BT Cat Burger** St 3, south of Psar Nat. Offers an eclectic menu featuring beef, fish, chicken and pork burgers, as well as a huge variety of milk teas and juices.

**Riverside Balcony** St 1, near Psar Leu. In an idyllic spot overlooking the river, this Swiss-run bar serves a range of beers and cocktails as well as some Western snacks on a tastefully designed terrace. They have a pool table, too. Closed Mon.

**Smokin' Pot** ⓣ012/821400. Behind the *Angkor Hotel*. Despite its name, serves nothing more than good Khmer, Thai and "Western comfort" food such as muesli and English fry-ups. It does, however, also offer cookery classes at around $8 a day – call ahead to reserve a place.

**Sunrise Coffee Shop** Just west of the *Royal Hotel*, west of the market. A backpackers' hangout serving delicious Western breakfasts, creative sandwiches and coffee, plus bicycle rental (6000r/day) and a book exchange. The perfect place to while away a hot Cambodian afternoon.

**White Rose** St 2. Hard to beat for economical Khmer dishes, and serving up tasty fare from early morning until around 9pm.

## Directory

**Banks and exchange** ATMs are plentiful – try ANZ Royal Bank near Psar Nat. Banks offering exchange include Canadia Bank, near Psar Nat, and the Cambodian Commercial Bank, near the train station.

**Hospital** The provincial hospital is at the northern end of the riverside, but has limited facilities. The Emergency Hospital east of the river has English-speaking Italian doctors.

**Internet** Available all over town – there are several places along St 3 south of the market.

**Post office** On the riverside, and has stamps and a national telephone facility.

## Moving on

**By bus** Buses leave from the transport stop or pick you up at your hotel if you arrange it beforehand with the staff.

**Destinations:** Phnom Penh (6hr); Poipet (4hr); Siem Reap (5hr), Sisophon (1hr 30min).

**By share taxi and minibus** These leave from the transport stop, unless you're going to Pailin, in which case you should join a share taxi in the south of town, near the start of Route 10 at Psar Leu (20,000r). They leave from early morning until midday – it's a dusty journey.

**Destinations:** Pailin (2–3hr); Phnom Penh (6hr); Poipet (3hr); Siem Reap (daily; 4hr), Sisophon (1hr 30min).

**By boat** Boats depart daily at 7am for Siem Reap (4–8hr); the foreigner price is $15. The trip takes much longer in the dry season.

## AROUND BATTAMBANG

Two popular places to visit near Battambang are **Phnom Sampeu** and **Wat Banan**. Since they are both located to the southwest of the city, they can be combined conveniently into a day-trip by moto (about $5). The entrance ticket is $2 for both places.

### Phnom Sampeu

Around 15km along the road that heads west from Battambang, you'll see two lopsided hills rising from the plain. They supposedly resemble a sinking boat, with **Phnom Sampeu** as the broken hull and Phnom G'daong as the broken sail bobbing around in the water. An unshaded ten-minute hike up the north-east side of Phnom Sampeau takes you to **Wat Sampeau**, where you can explore various temple buildings and big caves. The site was used to great advantage by the government forces in their skirmishes with the Khmer Rouge. Across the ridge are the temple of Prasat Brang, built in 1964, and a small decorative stupa.

If your moto-driver doesn't know it, ask children in the area to show you the complex of **caves**, known as Laang Lacaun ("Theatre Cave"), nearby. The caves were the site of atrocities committed by the Khmer Rouge – the victims, whose smashed skulls are collected in an ornate metal cage, were thrown into the deep cave from a hole above. Lying nearby is an immense reclining Buddha statue. An adjacent cave, trailing eerily downwards into the darkness, is apparently still full of the scattered bones of victims; it's thought that more than ten thousand people died in these caves. Once, they had a pleasanter role, however: the larger cave was used for plays and theatrical productions, its approaching slope providing the seats for the audience.

### Wat Banan

The best preserved of the temples around Battambang, **Wat Banan** can be reached from Wat Sampeu by a pleasant back-country road. If your moto driver doesn't know the way, offer one of the local kids a dollar to show you – it's just a few kilometres. As you approach, you'll see some distinctive Angkor Wat-like towers; the temple lies immediately at the top of a steep laterite stairway, which ascends a seventy-metre-high hill.

It's known that Wat Banan was consecrated as a Buddhist temple, but scholars are uncertain who built the temple or exactly when it was completed – estimates put this between the tenth and thirteenth centuries. Five corn-on-the-cob towers remain, all in a somewhat collapsed state. You'll likely be accompanied on the climb by young kids hoping for a tip by telling you a bit about the temple. It's certainly worth the steep clamber up to see the detailed lintels, beheaded *apsaras*, and views out over endless paddies, with Phnom Sampeu clearly visible to the north.

## PAILIN

Some 80km southwest of Battambang, **PAILIN** is a dusty little frontier town. The only link to the rest of the country is the unsurfaced National Route 57 from Battambang, and once you arrive there's really no reason to be here unless you're crossing the border into Thailand. The town has a wild and edgy atmosphere, and was one of the most heavily mined regions of the country: high up and surrounded by jungle, it was long a Khmer Rouge stronghold, supplied with food and weapons from the nearby Thai border (see box, p.120).

### What to see and do

Pailin became famous for its **gem-mining**, though the land is now pretty much mined out. All you're likely to see today are a few dealers in the **market**, ready to hand over cash for rough, uncut stones pulled from the ground.

### THE KHMER AND PAILIN

Pailin's reputation as a former centre of Khmer activity rests largely on **Ieng Sary**, who managed a highly organized, well-disciplined group of guerrilla soldiers. He created a prosperous town, gutting the countryside of gems and logs for miles around and selling them to Thailand for an estimated $10m a month, until in a surprise move he defected – with over three thousand of his soldiers – to the government side in 1996. Granted immunity, he now lives comfortably in Phnom Penh; his move precipitated the demise of the Khmer Rouge, which finally disappeared when Brother Number 2, Nuon Chea, surrendered in 1998; he still lives in a house in town.

The carving of the legend The Churning of The Ocean of Milk that covers the outer wall of **Wat Ratanasaoporn**, on the way into town, is the pagoda's only feature; its claim to fame is that most of the monks were defrocked in 2000 for entertaining local taxi girls. The adjacent hill of **Phnom Yat** houses a small pagoda, its outer wall decorated with startling images of people being tortured in hell – tongues are pulled out with pliers, women drowned, people stabbed with forks and heads chopped off.

## Arrival

**By share taxi** The only way to get to Pailin is by shared taxi from Battambang, a trip that generally takes 2–3hr. You arrive at the market in the centre of town, which is where you come to get transport back to Battambang.

## Accommodation

Pailin offers a pretty limited selection of accommodation, but at least it's cheap.

**Kim Young Heng Guest House** ⓣ012/736904. Located a few steps up the hill from the market behind the restaurant of the same name, with a range of fan and a/c rooms, some bright and appealing, others windowless cells. ❶

**Le Manoir de Pailin** ⓣ012/640763. The best hotel in town and by far the best value, a little west of the centre, towards the border. Rooms here are clean and pleasant, with chunky wood furniture, hot-water en-suite bathrooms and TV. ❶

**Punleu Pich Guest House** ⓣ016/796708. Opposite the market, offering the cheapest (though most basic) rooms in town. ❶

## Eating

Eating in Pailin is no gastronomic delight, but there are plenty of stalls in the market and cheap restaurants nearby.

**Hang Meas** Hotel restaurant with an English-language menu. Does a selection of Khmer and Thai dishes as well as eggs and bread for breakfast.

**Kim Young** Turns out tasty Khmer food just up from the market and has an English menu. Try the sweet-and-sour fish and morning glory with garlic.

## Moving on

**By share taxi** to: Battambang (2–3hr); Thailand (see box, p.120).

## SISOPHON

**SISOPHON** has emerged from the shadow of the Khmer Rouge to become an increasingly important staging post for Thai–Cambodian trade. Thai goods are trucked into the town and transferred to trains for the slow journey to Phnom Penh. Travellers, too, are passing through in increasing numbers from the Poipet border crossing (see p.120), though they don't tend to hang around – Sisophon is a pretty nondescript town, but it's a handy place to break your journey, especially if you're not going to make the border before it closes or if you've crossed late and can't get on to Battambang or Siem Reap.

While US dollars and riel are accepted in Sisophon, many transactions are in **baht**.

### INTO THAILAND AT PAILIN

The easier of the two borders in the Pailin area to cross is the one at **Phsa Prom** (7am–8pm), 20km from town and only a half-hour ride by share taxi (B50) or moto (B100, depending on your bargaining skills). The road passes deforested hillsides and small farming plots along the way. At the border itself, a small market and three rather incongruous casinos entertain an almost exclusively Thai clientele – the Thai side of the border is known as Ban Pakkard. If you're crossing the border here, take a share taxi to Chanthaburi (B140; see p.836), then another bus to Bangkok, or Trat (for Ko Chang). Coming into the country from here, expect the same immigration scams you'll get at any other Cambodian border crossing, though you'll probably have the advantage of not being caught in a crush of tourists. The other border access point to Thailand, the Daung Lem border crossing at **Ban Laem** is considerably further north (See p.837).

## Arrival

**By bus** A new bus station was being built at the time of writing, east of the market and of the road to Battambang. This will soon be the pick-up and drop-off point for all buses.

**By share taxi or minibus** Share taxis and pick-ups from Phnom Penh stop at the northern edge of town; from everywhere else they pull into the transport stop near the market in the centre; motos (1000r) will be on hand to ferry you to a guesthouse or hotel.

## Accommodation

Accommodation in Sisophon is nothing to write home about.

**Golden Crown Hotel** ⓣ012/695752. Centre of town, near the market. Enjoying one of the best locations in Sisophon, this sparkling new building offers the usual en-suite rooms with TV. ❶

**Neak Meas Hotel** ⓣ012/216422. Another centrally located place, where all rooms have a/c, hot water, TV and fridge; be warned, though, that it also functions as an "entertainment centre", with girls hovering outside the VIP karaoke rooms at the hotel entrance in the evening. ❸

**Rong Roeung Hotel** ⓣ092/260515. Cheap option where there is a choice of spartan a/c or fan rooms but no hot water. ❶

**Sarat Tong Guest House** ⓣ017/475100. On the north side of the main road heading east out of town. A collection of en-suite rooms in a small, family-run guesthouse. ❶

### INTO THAILAND AT POIPET

From Sisophon, it's a two-hour bus or taxi ride to the border crossing at **Poipet**. Six to seven buses pass through every afternoon, most en-route from Siem Reap (10,000r). Thai visas are arranged on the spot. From the border, take a tuk-tuk to Aranyaprathet, from where you can head on to Bangkok by train (2 daily; 6hr) or bus (4 daily, last one 5pm; 4hr 30min). For advice on coming into Cambodia at Aranyaprathet, see the box on p.837.

## Eating and drinking

In the late afternoon and early evening, stalls selling basic Khmer food, desserts and fruit juices open on the south side of Independence Park, a block north of the transport stop.

**Phkay Proek** Just downhill from the *Phnom Svay Hotel*. Surprisingly good, inexpensive restaurant, serving Western breakfasts, fabulous pancakes and good Chinese/Khmer food. Daily 6am–9pm.

**Suon Kamson** On a corner near the park. Inexpensive Khmer, Thai and Western food illustrated on an extensive English picture menu. Occasional live music jazzes up the atmosphere.

## Moving on

**By bus** to: Battambang (1hr 30min); Phnom Penh (6hr); Poipet (2hr); Siem Reap (4hr); Thailand (see box, opposite).

**By share taxi or minibus** to: Battambang (1hr 30min); Phnom Penh (6hr); Poipet (1hr 30min); Siem Reap (3hr 30min); Thailand (see box opposite).

# The southwest

To the southwest of Phnom Penh, a series of mountain ranges, known as the Cardamom and Elephant mountains, rise up imposingly from the plains, as if shielding Cambodia's only stretch of coast from the world. Indeed, only a few places along the coast are accessible by road. The most popular destination is the beach resort of **Sihanoukville**, whose sandy shores are the launching point for trips to **Ream National Park** and remote and sparsely populated islands in the Gulf of Thailand. Further east along the coast are the city of **Kampot** and the quaint coastal village of **Kep**. On Cambodia's western border, **Koh Kong** serves as a transit point for visitors arriving from or leaving for Thailand.

The accessible areas of the southwest are well served by public **transport**. National Routes 3 and 4 are in a fairly good state of repair, while comfortable express boats ply the sea routes.

## SIHANOUKVILLE

The closest that Cambodia gets to a full-blown beach resort, **SIHANOUKVILLE** is a town on the make. Five-star resorts and shopping complexes are mushrooming on every available plot of land, locally-run beach bars making way for Cambodia's upmarket vision of its tourism destiny. Fortunately for budget travellers, that vision has yet to be fully realized, and Sihanoukville still has plenty of long sandy beaches, fresh seafood and affordable facilities to go around. It's certainly a good place to relax and unwind, especially if you've been travelling hard on the provincial Cambodian roads. Moreover, lazy days on the beach can be complemented by an evening of partying at one of the town's vibrant nightspots. If you're visiting during high season or a holiday weekend, though, be prepared to battle the crowds.

### What to see and do

The **town** itself is inland, with its centre around the market; sprawling over a large peninsula, it's ringed by beaches with many of the mid-range hotels. Towards the port is the backpacker area up on **Weather Station Hill**, 2km from the town centre. Here, you'll find plenty of guesthouses, cheap Western-oriented restaurants and a smattering of bars. Sihanoukville's main attraction is its beaches, which are more accessible here than anywhere else in the country.

#### The Town

The **Angkor Brewery** is located just north of the town centre. Free tours, with an open bar, can be arranged through *Marlin* guesthouse, among others (Wed 3pm). Other than that, the town's sights are limited, although the main pagoda, **Wat Leu**, atop Phnom Sihanoukville, north of the town, is a worthy excursion with panoramic views and a colourful vihara interior. To get here, take the turning off from National Route 4 at the brewery. **Wat Khrom**, on Santepheap Street, is set in a tranquil spot among Bodhi trees, with views across the sea and surrounding countryside.

#### Beaches

**Victory Beach** is the nearest to Weather Station Hill, a comparatively quiet stretch of sand sporting only a few bars and rows of wooden deckchairs. Just up the road is the almost completely undeveloped **Hawaii Beach**, although a nearby construction site has rendered it somewhat less tranquil than before. It's worth making the trip 2km south of the town to **Serendipity** and **Ochheuteal beaches**, the most impressive of Sihanoukville's seaside offerings, where you can enjoy not only long stretches of golden sand but also a buzzing bar and restaurant scene. These two popular beaches also have a broad range of accommodation, all concen-

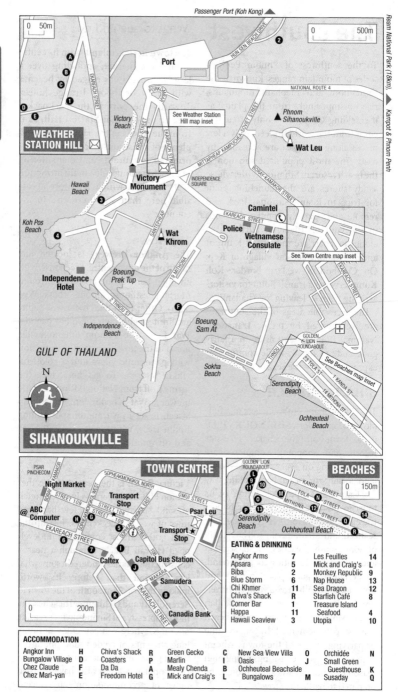

Passenger Port (Koh Kong)
Ream National Park (18km), Kampot & Phnom Penh

# SIHANOUKVILLE

WEATHER STATION HILL
0 50m
EKAREACH STREET

0 500m
Port
HUN SEN BEACH DRIVE
NATIONAL ROUTE 4
PORKOMBAR
See Weather Station Hill map inset
Phnom Sihanoukville
Wat Leu
Victory Beach
KRONG STREET
EKAREACH STREET
MITTAPHEAP KAMPUCHEA-SOVIET STREET
BORAY-KAMAKOR STREET
Victory Monument
INDEPENDENCE SQUARE
Hawaii Beach
Camintel
Koh Pos Beach
SANTEPHEAP
Wat Khrom
Police
Vietnamese Consulate
See Town Centre map inset
19 MITHONA
Boeung Prek Tup
Independence Hotel
2 THNOU ST
Boeung Sam At
Independence Beach
GOLDEN LION ROUNDABOUT
GULF OF THAILAND
Sokha Beach
23 TOLA ST
1 KANDA ST
14 MITHONA ST
See Beaches map inset
Serendipity Beach
Ochheuteal Beach
N

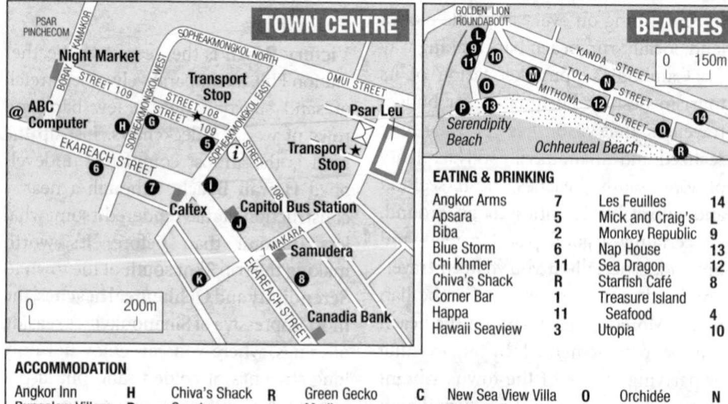


**EATING & DRINKING**

| | | | |
|---|---|---|---|
| Angkor Arms | 7 | Les Feuilles | 14 |
| Apsara | 5 | Mick and Craig's | L |
| Biba | 2 | Monkey Republic | 9 |
| Blue Storm | 6 | Nap House | 13 |
| Chi Khmer | 11 | Sea Dragon | 12 |
| Chiva's Shack | R | Starfish Café | 8 |
| Corner Bar | 1 | Treasure Island Seafood | 4 |
| Happa | 11 | Utopia | 10 |
| Hawaii Seaview | 3 | | |

**ACCOMMODATION**

| | | | | | | | | | |
|---|---|---|---|---|---|---|---|---|---|
| Angkor Inn | H | Chiva's Shack | R | Green Gecko | C | New Sea View Villa | O | Orchidée | N |
| Bungalow Village | D | Coasters | P | Marlin | I | Oasis | J | Small Green Guesthouse | K |
| Chez Claude | F | Da Da | A | Mealy Chenda | B | Ochheuteal Beachside Bungalows | M | Susaday | Q |
| Chez Mari-yan | E | Freedom Hotel | G | Mick and Craig's | L | | | | |

trated at the western end of the three-kilometre strand. Continuing west, the next along is the less-visited Sokha Beach, after which comes **Independence Beach**. The beach is named after a seven-storey 1960s monolith, the *Independence Hotel*, which sits at its western end and has been recently renovated and reincarnated as a new luxury resort. Independence Beach itself is set on a gently curved bay, with a line of drinks stalls and shaded huts. As it sweeps round, rocks and small, secluded bays allow some privacy. As at the other beaches, deckchairs and inner tubes are available for $1.

### Offshore islands

**Boat trips** to Sihanoukville's offshore islands are organized by most guesthouses. A day-trip to **Bamboo Island** costs around $10 – including a barbecue and snorkelling equipment – and camping trips for two to three days can also be arranged ($50 per head). A variety of dive shops in town offer **diving trips** (see p.125). Some also offer "Discover Scuba Diving" trips for first-timers.

## Arrival and information

**By bus** Buses arrive at the busy transport stop in the centre of Sihanoukville, on St 108.

**By share taxi or minibus** Pick-ups and taxis usually terminate at the transport stop on St 108 or opposite the Psar Leu, and most town-centre accommodation is within walking distance.

**By boat** Boat arrivals from Koh Kong speed into the passenger port 4km to the northwest of the town centre on Hun Sen Beach Drive around midday; guesthouse reps meet the boats and will give you a free ride if you're going to stay with them. Otherwise, catch a moto into town for around 6000r.

**Tourist information** The *Sihanoukville Visitors' Guide* is a comprehensive, regularly updated tourist guide, available from guesthouses and bars around town.

## City transport

**By moto** Motos and tuk-tuks are the principal form of local transport. For motos, reckon on 2000–3000r from town to the beaches or Weather Station Hill, and about twice that for tuk-tuks.

## Accommodation

Sihanoukville is not short of accommodation, although hotels tend to fill up quickly at weekends and holidays. While the town centre is the transport hub and boasts some decent guesthouses, its distance from the beaches means that many travellers opt to stay elsewhere. Budget accommodation is available all over town with a concentration on Weather Station Hill above Victory beach, but the recent influx of girlie bars has made the area a bit sleazy at night. It's also possible to find some reasonably priced rooms around Ochheuteal Beach – these include a handful of dirt-cheap cells in beach bars, some of which even offer free accommodation in exchange for your patronage. You can find a few of these in the area around Chiva's Shack.

### The town centre

**Angkor Inn** Sopheakmongkol West, just off Ekareach St ⓣ016/896204. Well-regarded budget guesthouse offering plain, but cool and tidy rooms with en-suite facilities, as well as internet and a roof garden; the friendly owner goes by the name of "Mom". ❶

**Freedom Hotel** Sopheakmongkol West ⓣ012/257953. Western-run place with good-value fan and a/c rooms (monthly rates available) and one of the town's best bars on the ground floor. ❶

**Marlin** Ekareach St ⓣ012/512016. Conveniently located, Western-run place, where all rooms have a/c and hot-water bathrooms. Popular bar and Sri Lankan restaurant downstairs. ❸

**Oasis** Ekareach St ⓣ012/638947. Offers massive rooms and a range of facilities, plus a big bar and restaurant and a three-metre-wide TV screen. Rates negotiable based on length of stay. ❷

**Small Green Guesthouse** 7 Makara St ⓣ034/399052. Newly renovated rooms with TV, a/c and hot water, plus a restaurant serving international cuisine prepared by a Swedish chef. ❸

### Weather Station Hill

**Bungalow Village** Weather Station Hill, towards Victory Beach ⓣ012/806155. Rustic bungalows set in tropical gardens, all with attached cold-water en-suite bathrooms. Nightly film screenings in the restaurant. ❶

**Chez Mari-yan** Weather Station Hill ⓣ034/933709. Wooden bungalows with lovely views over Victory Beach, connected by rustic walkways that tumble down the hillside. Tasty food on the classy restaurant deck. ❶

**Da Da** Weather Station Hill ⓣ016/724862. Friendly, family-run place, with ocean views, offering six large, clean en-suite rooms. Close to budget eateries. ❶

**Green Gecko** Weather Station Hill ⊕012/560944, ⓦwww.greengeckocambodia.com. A friendly place with basic, cheap rooms, over 500 free movies, a large library and a café. ❶

**Mealy Chenda** West of Ekareach St, above Victory Beach ⊕034/933472. Legendary on the budget circuit, and still popular despite increasing competition thanks to its low prices and sociable atmosphere. Accommodation is en-suite. A limited number of rooms have sea views, and there's a travellers' restaurant with 2000r draft beer. ❶

## The southern beaches

**Chez Claude** On the hill between Independence and Sokha beaches ⊕012/824870. Individually designed timber bungalow suites and rooms, all en-suite, on the hill overlooking the bay. Bungalows boast private balconies looking out to sea. There's a French restaurant, and the owners arrange diving trips. ❸

**Chiva's Shack** South end of Ochheuteal Beach ⊕012/360911. Very basic $2 rooms above a beach bar, popular with those on a seriously tight budget. You're right on the sand, but don't expect much peace, quiet or privacy. ❶

**Coasters** Serendipity Beach ⊕034/933776. Idyllic rooms in quaint little bungalows overlooking the beach; all have en-suite facilities, fans and balconies. The bar-restaurant serves breakfast, drinks and fantastic food. Booking advised. ❸

**Mick and Craig's** Between the Golden Lion Roundabout and Serendipity Beach ⊕016/302325. Cheap and cheerful rooms at the back of a popular travellers' café, remarkably inexpensive for the location. ❷

**New Sea View Villa** Just back from Serendipity Beach ⊕092/759753. A range of big, clean rooms offering the best value in the neighbourhood, though they tend to fill up fast. Pleasant little restaurant out front. ❷

**Ochheuteal Beachside Bungalows** Behind Ochheuteal Beach ⊕012/916298. Not exactly beachside, but only 70m away. The attractive thatched rooms have verandas and a/c, and some have hot water. There's an excellent restaurant. ❸

**Orchidée** One block back from Ochheuteal Beach on Tola St ⊕034/933639, ⓦwww.orchidee-guesthouse.com. Fully equipped, spacious rooms, with a pleasant breakfast terrace, a shady garden setting and a pool. ❸

**Susaday** Ochheuteal Beach ⊕034/933907. Within a towel's throw of the beach, this French-owned guesthouse offers smallish but spotless, secure rooms, all with fan and bathroom, some with a/c. ❷

# Eating and drinking

Sihanoukville has a good selection of Western-oriented restaurants and bars. In town, most places are clustered along Ekareach St at the junction with Sopheakmongkol East, home of the night market. Most of the Western places stay open beyond midnight, and a couple only shut when the last person leaves.

## Restaurants and cafés

**Angkor Arms** Ekareach St. Real English-pub atmosphere, with friendly staff and a wide range of Khmer and Western food, including fish and chips and pork chops. Draft beer, cocktails and sports on cable TV. 9am–late.

**Apsara** Cnr of St 109 and Sopheakmongkol East. Locals swear by this town-centre restaurant, specializing in Khmer and Chinese food, but the double-pricing system makes it expensive for foreigners at around $10 a plate.

**Chi Khmer** Behind *Happa*. Fine Khmer cuisine in a small, intimate bamboo garden; mains $3–6.

**Corner Bar** Weather Station Hill. Popular bar/restaurant serving sandwiches, great pizzas and other Western dishes from $3. Delivery service, too. Open 24hr.

**Happa** Between Golden Lion Roundabout and Serendipity Beach. Stylish Japanese teppanyaki restaurant, where food is grilled in front of you and served with a choice of mouth-watering sauces. Tapas-style dishes $2–4. Open for dinner only.

**Hawaii Seaview** Right on Hawaii Beach. Seafood restaurant that's open all day but popular early evening for sunset views of Koh Pos Island.

**Les Feuilles** one block back from Ochheuteal Beach, on Tola St. There's an excellent French/Khmer menu at this bar-restaurant, which is especially popular with weekending French expats. The steaks are the pick of the extensive menu, and come with a choice of sauces, including a creamy blue-cheese dressing.

**Mick and Craig's** Between the Golden Lion Roundabout and Serendipity Beach. Choice Western grub for the discerning budget traveller. Serves sandwiches, quiches and grills from $4. Open all day and bar open till late.

**Sea Dragon** Ochheuteal Beach. In a nice spot, with very reasonably priced seafood specials. Serves breakfast, lunch and dinner.

**Starfish Café** Off 7 Makara, behind Samudera Supermarket. Delicious Western breads, cakes, scones and other goodies to eat in a garden setting, or takeaway.

**Treasure Island Seafood** Between Hawaii and Independence beaches. A gem of a restaurant serving Chinese food with the emphasis on succulent seafood and fish, set on its own small, secluded beach, ideal for watching the sunset. Moderately priced and friendly, with seafood dishes around $7. Open for lunch and dinner.

### Bars and clubs

All bars and clubs are open daily and some stay open 24 hours.

**Biba** Hun Sen Beach Drive, Dom Thmei Village. Khmer disco very popular among locals, though a little way out of town.

**Blue Storm** Ekareach St. The nightclub for *really* loud Khmer, Thai and other Asian music.

**Chiva's Shack** South end of Ochheuteal Beach. Happening beach bar with full-moon parties and a bizarre musical selection ranging from Bob Dylan to heavy metal.

**Monkey Republic** Between Golden Lion Roundabout and Serendipity Beach. Convivial English-run pub popular among both tourists and expats, still going strong on nights when other bars fall quiet. One of the only places in Cambodia offering Marmite and Vegemite.

**Nap House** Serendipity Beach. Cosy outdoor bar featuring bench swings, conversation-level music and occasional dancing.

**Utopia** Between Golden Lion Roundabout and Serendipity Beach. Popular beachside club attracting a better mix of locals and travellers than some of the discos in town.

## Directory

**Banks and exchange** ATMs are readily available near Caltex downtown. Canadia Bank, Ekareach St, east of 7 Makara St for cash on MasterCard and MoneyGram; First Union Commercial Bank, on the corner of Ekareach and Sopheakmongkol streets.

**Diving** To arrange a trip, contact: Claude at *Chez Claude* (ⓣ012/824870); EcoSea Dive (ⓣ012/654104); Scuba Nation (ⓣ023/211850, ⓦwww.divecambodia.com); or The Dive Shop (ⓣ016/214007, ⓦwww.diveshopcambodia.com). All except *Chez Claude* have offices around Serendipity Beach.

**Hospitals and clinics** Sihanoukville Public Hospital (ⓣ012/555086) is on Ekareach St, between the town centre and Golden Lion roundabout; it has very limited facilities.

**Internet** Try ABC Computer or the Camintel office, both on Ekareach St west of the town centre.

**Motorbike rental** If lazing on the beach doesn't provide enough excitement, and you want to explore Sihanoukville and the area, the best option is to rent a motorcycle. Most guesthouses provide this service: a 125cc bike goes for about $4–5 per day and a 250cc for $7–8. You'll probably need to leave your passport as security, and make sure you lock your moto when you leave it – thefts are common.

**Police** On Ekareach St between Independence Square and the town centre (ⓣ034/933222 or ⓣ012/826273).

**Post office** The main post office is one block behind Krong St, off Victory Beach; poste restante is available. You can get stamps and post items at the smaller branch office opposite the market.

**Supermarkets** Samudera Supermarket, 7 Makara St, 50m from Ekareach St.

**Telephone services** International calls can be made from any of the internet cafes around town. Domestic calls are best made from the cheap-rate booths around the market.

## Moving on

**By bus** At the time of writing there were no public buses to Kampot or Kep, although G'Day Mate on Ekareach St was running an express bus to Kep (daily; $6.50). The bus service to Koh Kong should improve dramatically once the new bridges are finished, hopefully some time in 2008.

**Destinations:** Koh Kong (2 daily, 6hr); Phnom Penh (12 daily, 4hr).

**By share taxi or minibus** to: Kampot (2hr); Koh Kong (6hr); Phnom Penh (3hr 30min).

**By boat** to: Koh Kong, via Koh S'dach (daily; 4hr).

# REAM NATIONAL PARK

**Ream National Park**, also known as Preah Sihanouk National Park, located 18km east of Sihanoukville, is one of the most accessible national parks in Cambodia, and a great place to explore the country's unique, unspoilt natural environment. Its 21,000 hectares include evergreen and mangrove forests, sandy beaches, coral reefs, offshore islands and a rich diversity of flora and fauna. To get to the **park headquarters** you'll need to join a group from a guesthouse (about $15 per person depending on number in the group), or take a taxi or moto ($7) from Sihanoukville along National Route 4 to Ream village, turning right down the track next to the airport.

The rangers at the park headquarters (☎012/875096) are extremely helpful, and can arrange **boat trips** (about $30 for the boat, or $5 per person for large groups) along the Prek Toek Sap estuary, to the fishing village of Thmor Tom, and perhaps on to the islands of Koh Thmei and Koh Ses. The river is bordered by mangroves, and you're likely to see kingfishers, sea eagles and maybe monkeys along the way.

## KOH S'DACH

The small island of **KOH S'DACH** is the fishing capital of Cambodian waters, just off Koh Kong province in the Gulf of Thailand. If you're rushing between Sihanoukville and Thailand, there's little here to warrant an overnight stop, but with time on your hands, the area is worth exploring.

The real reason for stopping here is to get out in a boat to explore the coast – just off the north shore of Koh S'dach you'll find brilliantly coloured coral within paddling distance. A cluster of **islands** nearby – Koh Samai, Koh Samot, Koh Chan and Koh Totang – are all within a boat's row. A fishing boat to the islands is open to negotiation: $20 a day seems the going rate. Alternatively, you can hop in one of the small, fibreglass boats that go across to the mainland (around 4000r) where there are also some fine, deserted beaches. Note that all transactions on the island are in **baht**. The pathway from the port to the small market area is the centre of activity on the island, where fishermen gather to gamble at streetside games of cards or dice.

The only way **to get to** Koh S'Dach is by the express boat, which stops briefly as it surges between Koh Kong and Sihanoukville. The fare is a flat $10 to or from either of these destinations and it takes about two hours.

The island's **guesthouse** is within easy walking distance of the jetty. As you leave the pier, go along to the left for about ten minutes until you reach the *Koh S'Dach* (❷), a collection of basic concrete bungalows. You can buy simple **food** at the market area, and at the stalls around the port. A well-stocked village store sells beer, snacks and sundries.

## KOH KONG

Boat schedules and border opening times used to conspire to make an overnight stop in **KOH KONG** a necessity. Since the border post extended its hours to 8pm, you no longer have to stay, though a few days exploring the surrounding area is well rewarded. One option is to hire a small boat and head to the waterfalls at **Tatai**, a fifty-minute trip upstream under the cliffs of the Cardamom Mountains. Several **islands** lie near to the town, the largest of which is **Koh Kong Island** itself (not to be confused with the mainland town of Koh Kong), which has pristine stretches of sand on the seaward side. It costs B500 to hire a six-person boat out.

Situated on the eastern bank of the Kah Bpow River, Koh Kong was historically an insular outpost, its prosperity based on fishing, logging and smuggling. These days, however, it's the border that brings in the trade. A new bridge, nearly 2km long, crosses the river, and a left turn shortly after the bridge takes you to **Beach 2000**, a popular weekend spot for locals. Despite the fact that much of the rich sandalwood forest has been transported to Thailand, the area around the town remains beautiful and unspoilt. This remote outpost owes its identity more to Thai influences than Khmer culture: most people speak Thai, baht is the favoured currency and Beer Chang is the drink of choice.

Koh Kong town is not a large place, and you can get around on foot, but motos are not expensive at just 1000r a trip. There's an Acleda Bank on the north side of the market, or you can change baht and dollars at the market itself.

## Arrival

**By bus** Buses usually drop off downtown, near the central roundabout. If you are heading to the border, you will sometimes have to change buses in Koh Kong.

**By share taxi or minibus** If coming by road from Sihanoukville, you will need to change buses at Sre Ambel, 155km away. You can either stop off in town or head straight through to the border. If you're stopping in Koh Kong, get out at the market or the port, from where you can easily walk to guesthouse accommodation.

**By boat** From the dock, it's a 5min walk to the market in the town centre.

## Accommodation

Accommodation options have improved remarkably in recent years, with the opening of two smart yet inexpensive hotels on the riverfront.

**Asean** Just north of the jetty, set back from the river ☎035/936667. The town's newest hotel has spotlessly clean a/c rooms, some with hot water, many with views over the river. ❷

**The Dugout Hotel** Just north of the central roundabout ☎035/936220. Western-run guesthouse with a pool, a pleasant courtyard and clean, airy rooms. ❷

**Koh Kong Guest House** South of the jetty ☎016/286669. Clean fan rooms with shared bathrooms, some with river views, in a charming, polished wooden house. Offers the cheapest rates in town, and the riverfront balcony restaurant does Khmer, Thai and spaghetti. ❶

**Otto's** On a side road south of the jetty ☎012/924249. Rooms here are pretty simple, with shared bathrooms, though they tend to vary in quality. The upstairs terrace acts as a combination of lounge, bar and inexpensive restaurant and is especially popular with Germans. ❶

**Phoumint Koh Kong** Just north of the jetty on the riverbank ☎011/760259. Even some of the cheapest rooms here have fine river views. The best ones are large and comfy with a/c and hot-water bathrooms. ❶

**Rasmey Buntham Guest House** Southeast of the market ☎016/798884. Features good-sized rooms set around a central lobby, with a pleasant patio. Staff can help with travel arrangements, and offer a free pick-up from the border if you phone ahead. ❶

## Eating and drinking

All the guesthouses listed above have attached restaurants and turn out reasonable Khmer food.

**Baan Peakmai** On the road that runs past the east side of the market, three blocks to the north. Offers the nicest ambience in town, with a covered terrace around a garden. Serves good Khmer, Thai and Western food, including many vegetarian dishes, at reasonable prices.

**Bob Bar** Southeast of the roundabout. Friendly English-run café offering a somewhat pricey selection of Western food including apple pie and pork chops.

**Phoumint Koh Kong** Just north of the jetty on the riverbank. Good seafood restaurant with fantastic river views.

**Sunset Lounge** On the river, a 10min walk south of the jetty. Relaxed bar right on the water and a great place to watch the sunset. The owner can organize boat trips to the islands.

## Moving on

**By boat** an express boat leaves at 8am for Sihanoukville ($20) via Koh S'dach. This can be an unpleasant experience in stormy weather.

**Destinations:** Koh S'dach (daily; 2hr); Sihanoukville (daily; 4hr).

**By bus** Buses to Phnom Penh and Sihanoukville (both $9) leave from the transport stop about 1km north of the central roundabout. It's the same bus; Sihanoukville passengers alight and switch buses near Sre Ambel. The journey will become much faster once bridges across the route's four river crossings are completed.

**Destinations:** Phnom Penh (6hr); Sihanoukville (6hr).

# KAMPOT

**KAMPOT**, with its riverside location, backdrop of misty Bokor Mountains

### INTO THAILAND: KOH KONG

From **Koh Kong**, it's a twelve-kilometre share taxi or moto ride (B100) to the border crossing at Cham Yeam (daily 7am–8pm). Thai visas are arranged on the spot. From Hat Lek, on the Thai side of the border, minibuses leave for Trat (see p.836), 91km northwest, roughly every 45 minutes between 6am and 5pm (1hr–1hr 30min); Trat has regular connections on to Ko Chang.

and terraces of French shop-houses, is one of the most attractive of Cambodia's provincial towns. It's also the staging post for side trips to Kep, and a pleasant place to spend an afternoon browsing round the market, strolling along the Teuk Chhou River, heading into the mountains to explore caves or taking a boat cruise out to the rapids. The river marks the western boundary of the town, with the new market to the north and the roundabout in the centre.

**Bokor**, the French colonial ghost-town perched high in the mountains above Kampot, is currently being renovated into a five-star resort; the road is closed until at least 2010, though it is still possible to hike up (two days return). Excursions can be arranged through Sok Lim Tours across from *Blissful Guesthouse* for around $50/person.

## Arrival

**By share taxi or minibus** You will be dropped either at the market or at the transport stop in the southeast of town, off the road to Kep.

## Accommodation

**Blissful Guesthouse** On a quiet side street about 1km south of the traffic circle ⓣ012/513024. Popular Western-run place with inexpensive, immaculate rooms; all beds have mosquito nets. There's also a comfy chill-out room upstairs and a travellers' restaurant downstairs in the beautiful garden. Tends to fill up fast in high

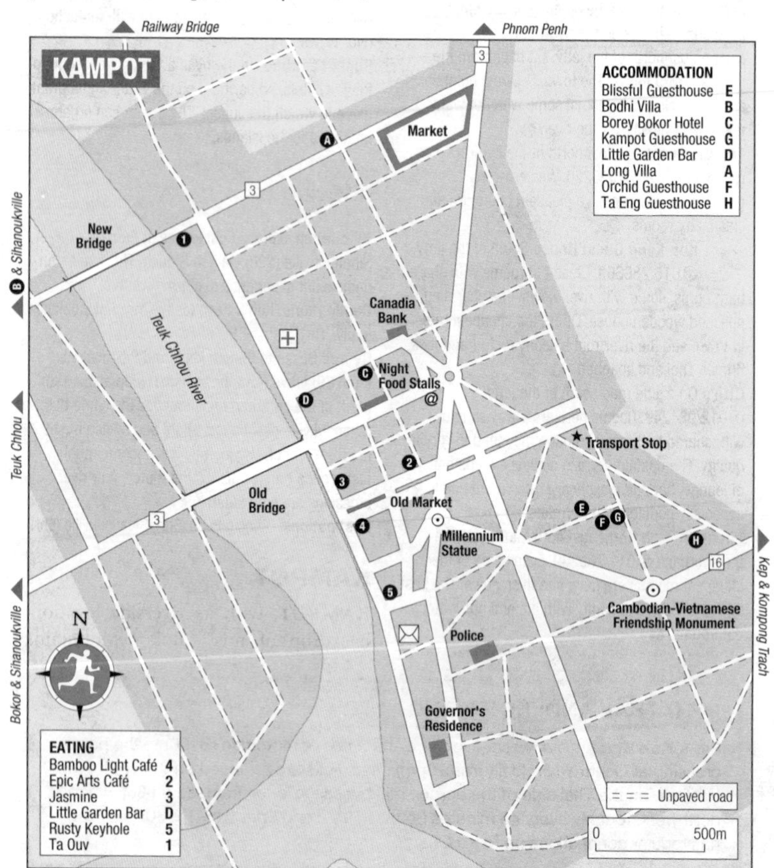

season and doesn't reserve rooms, so be sure to arrive early. ❶

**Bodhi Villa** 2km north of town, on the west side of the river ⓣ012/728884. A relaxed, communal space, set in an old meditation centre on the water. Accommodation ranges from floating bungalows to mattresses on the deck, and there's even a recording studio out back. Popular with long-termers. ❶

**Borey Bokor Hotel** Between the roundabout and the river ⓣ092/978168. The main hotel in town, with brand-new en-suite rooms, equipped with cable TV and a/c. ❸

**Kampot Guesthouse** On a quiet sidestreet about 1km south of the traffic circle, opposite *Blissful* ⓣ012/512931. Sprawling place with a variety of accommodation, some en suite. The rooms are a bit shabby, but it's one of the only guesthouses to offer dorm beds ($3), and the garden restaurant is lovely. ❶

**Little Garden Bar** Along the river ⓣ012/256901, ⓦwww.littlegardenbar.com. Cozy little guesthouse tastefully decorated using natural materials, in an old colonial building above a leafy riverside garden patio. Rooms all en suite. ❷

**Long Villa** In the north of town, west of the market ⓣ092/251418. Cosy en-suite rooms in a wooden villa with a pleasant patio restaurant out front. ❶

**Orchid Guesthouse** On a quiet side street about 1km south of the traffic circle, opposite *Blissful* ⓣ092/226996. Rooms and small bungalows in a pleasant, orchid-filled garden. Helpful staff also run a variety of tours of the area, and can arrange moto rental. ❶

**Ta Eng Guesthouse** On the road towards Kep ⓣ012/330058. One of the original guesthouses in town; the comfy rooms here all have en-suite showers, and the friendly owner speaks French and English. ❶

## Eating and drinking

The best street food to be had is between the Old Bridge and the central traffic circle, where noodle, dessert and shake stalls appear in the evenings. Nightlife is limited to the usual karaoke places, the most popular of which are across the river towards the railway bridge, although many of the Western restaurants offer a range of cocktails.

**Bamboo Light Café** Along the riverfront. Western breakfasts and sandwiches, as well as some tempting Sri Lankan and Indian dishes.

**Epic Arts Café** East of the old market. Part of a project benefiting the disabled, this cute little café serves tasty home-made baked goods and milkshakes, as well as breakfast and lunch.

**Jasmine** Along the riverfront. Stylish if somewhat pricey Western-run restaurant featuring Khmer, Thai and Western food along with a selection of Californian wines.

**Little Garden Bar** Along the riverfront. Khmer and Western food, including pizza, served up in a relaxing little garden patio; also has a rooftop bar.

**Rusty Keyhole** Along the riverfront. Cheap and tasty salads and sandwiches, plus Premier League football on TV.

**Ta Ouv** East bank of the river near the market. Inexpensive, delicious Khmer seafood, with a peaceful setting overlooking the river for a late afternoon beer or two.

## Moving on

**By bus** Two buses run daily to Phnom Penh ($4) via Kep ($2; 45min), but the route is circuitous and the trip can take up to six hours.

**By share taxi or minibus** Taxis to Phnom Penh ($5) and Sihanoukville ($4) leave regularly from the transport stop.

**Destinations:** Phnom Penh (3hr); Sihanoukville (2hr).

**By moto or tuk-tuk** A moto to Kep costs around $3, a tuk-tuk $7; the journey takes 45 minutes.

# KEP

Some 25km southeast of Kampot, **KEP** itself may not have much of a beach, but its breezy seaside character and palm-shaded walks are seductive nonetheless. The town is renowned throughout Cambodia for its delicious, inexpensive seafood, freshly plucked from the clean waters, and the laid-back atmosphere can come as a relief after the hordes and hassle of Sihanoukville. Kep is really no more than a fishing village during the week, but at weekends Khmer tourists descend on it from the capital, and the pace picks up a notch.

Approaching Kep from Kampot, you'll see the remains of magnificent **colonial villas** and holiday homes half-hidden in the shrubs along the three-kilometre seafront. As you come into town, past the food stalls, you'll round the headland and see the large Vietnamese island of **Phu Quoc** rising offshore in the Gulf of Thailand. The sovereignty of the island has long been in dispute, however, and the white statue of a woman at Kep Beach looks out towards the island, yearning for the day when it will be returned to Cambodia.

One of the highlights of a trip to Kep is a boat tour to one of the nearby islands, such as quaint **Koh Tonsay** ("Rabbit Island"), its tranquil stretch of palm-fringed beach perfect for a day or two of concentrated relaxation. Boat trips can be arranged at any of the guesthouses in Kep or Kampot, or down on the beach in Kep. A place on a boat to Koh Tonsay costs about $6, or $20 if you want to charter one yourself. There are rustic bamboo cottages on the beach where you can stay for $5, and plenty of local families around to cook for you.

### INTO VIETNAM: HA TIEN

The border crossing at Prek Chang (**Ha Tien**), near Kep, was opened to foreigners in 2007 (daily 7am–6pm), allowing beachlovers to travel through Thailand, Cambodia and Vietnam without ever leaving the coast. You can hire a moto to the border from Kep for around $8–12 ($13–15 for a tuk-tuk) for the hour-long trip. Bear in mind that travelling in both directions you need to be in possession of a visa, as they are not available on the spot for either country. On the Vietnam side, you can hire a moto ($3) to either Ha Tien or Ba Hon, from where you can catch a boat to the island of Phu Quoc or a bus to Ho Chi Minh City. Tour companies in Kampot can assist with transport.

## Accommodation

There's plenty of accommodation in Kep but it still fills up in high season. There are no truly budget rooms, but the northern end of town does offer a range of affordable and attractive hillside bungalows.

**Botanica** 2km north of the crab market ⓣ016/562775. The least expensive bungalows in town, en suite with thatched roofs, set in a pleasant garden. Bicycles available for 1000r/day to compensate for the distance from town. ❷

**Kep Seaside Guesthouse** On the main road into town, down a side road on the right ⓣ012/684241. Good-value rooms right on the beach, with en-suite facilities; also has a small restaurant serving Western and Khmer food. The owners are friendly and speak English. ❷

**Le Bout du Monde** On the hill behind *Vanna Bungallows* ⓣ011/964181. Artistic little bungalows, some ingeniously fashioned entirely of bamboo and detailed with loving care. All are en suite with private balconies festooned with hanging plants. ❷

**Vanna Bungallows** On the hill behind the town ⓣ012/755038. Bungalows perched on the hillside with terrific sea views, surrounded by lush gardens. The restaurant serves a wonderful vegetable soup, among other things. ❷

### TREAT YOURSELF

**Veranda Natural Resort** ⓣ012/888619, ⓦwww.veranda-resort.com. Located on the hill behind the town, this stylish complex of bungalows connected by elevated wood-and-stone walkways offers a range of sophisticated rooms from $25–60, as well as a good restaurant, an atmospheric bar and spectacular views.

## Eating

Kep is heaven for the seafood connoisseur. The crab market on the first stretch of seafront on the way in from Kampot is the place for crab; further on, the stalls around the centre cook up grilled fish, chicken and other delights, but only during the day.

**Botanica** 2km north of the crab market. Attached to the guesthouse of the same name, this "world kitchen" serves up tasty and creative dishes from around the globe.

**Kimly** Next to the crab market. Known by locals as the pick of the crabshacks, this place is always busy dishing out fresh seafood for around $3 a plate, and the menu is in English.

**Riel Bar** Just off the road to Kampot. Bakery, restaurant and bar specializing in Asian, Western and North African fare. There's a twenty percent discount if you pay in riel.

**Veranda** On the hill behind town. The food is pricey, but go for a drink and a stunning view of the islands from the expansive balcony.

## Moving on

**By bus** Buses pass through Kep en-route to Phnom Penh, but the journey is long and circuitous.
**Destinations:** Phnom Penh (daily; 5hr); Sihanoukville (daily; 2hr 30min).
**By moto or tuk-tuk to:** Kampot (45min; $3 moto $7 tuk-tuk).

# Eastern Cambodia

As you travel east from the Mekong River to the Vietnamese border, the people become poorer and the infrastructure worsens. The Mekong is the overland gateway to this region, punctuated by the very different towns of **Kampong Cham**, **Kratie** and **Stung Treng**. Travellers are beginning to make the journey here and beyond to the remote hilly provinces of Ratanakiri and Mondulkiri (see p.135). Others pass by en route to and from Laos.

During the **American War**, the eastern provinces were heavily bombed by the US to flush out the Viet Cong from the Ho Chi Minh Trail. These attempts proved largely unsuccessful, and thousands of Cambodian civilians were killed, wounded or left homeless by the attacks. It was during this period that the Khmer Rouge began gathering strength and momentum in the area. Pol Pot used the remote northeastern provinces to hide from Sihanouk's troops, while receiving support from his communist brothers in the Viet Minh.

Nowadays, the Mekong towns, Kampong Cham in particular, are forward-looking and relatively prosperous, having integrated well with modern-day Cambodia.

## KAMPONG CHAM AND AROUND

The northeast's largest city and capital of the province of the same name, **KAMPONG CHAM**, 120km northeast of Phnom Penh, is a busy transport hub, though with a very relaxed atmosphere. It has become even more laid-back since the huge Japanese-funded bridge across the Mekong was completed, rendering ferry services obsolete. Improved roads in the region mean that it's no longer necessary to stop over here, but the city has a distinctive charm and it would be a shame to pass it by.

### What to see and do

It's well worth taking a casual stroll along the banks of the massive Mekong, about 1.5km wide here, to look at the delightful but crumbling colonial buildings. **Wat Pra Tohm Nah Day Doh** on the riverbank about a kilometre south of the bridge also merits a view; fronted by a huge standing Buddha, its grounds are scattered with intriguing statues of people and animals, while a forest of miniature stupas stabs up into the sky.

#### Wat Nokor

The most interesting sight around town is **Wat Nokor**, about 2km north of the centre just off Route 7, an unusual fusion of ancient and modern Khmer religious architecture with a new temple built in and around the eleventh-century ruins. It's a fascinating juxtaposition of old and new, the luminous blues, pinks, oranges and greens of the wall paintings framed by ancient laterite walls still painted black from the days of Khmer Rouge occupation. Look out for striking sights like the bright pink Buddha images tucked into the monochrome sandstone stupa.

#### Phnom Bpros and Phnom Srei

About 12km further out of town past Wat Nokor rise the twin temple hills of

**Phnom Bpros** and **Phnom Srei**, "Man and Woman Mountains". According to legend, in ancient times women had to ask men to marry them. Fed up with this, the women challenged the men to see who could build the best temple by daybreak – the winners would win the right to be proposed to. When the women realized they were lagging behind, they built a huge fire, which the men took to be the rising sun. The men headed for bed while the women carried on building, producing a magnificent temple and winning the right to receive marriage proposals. Both Phnom Bpros and Phnom Srei afford fine views of the area. To get here, rent a motorbike in town or negotiate with a moto driver.

### Day-trips along the river

Several interesting places around Kampong Cham can be reached **by boat**. One trip follows a tributary of the Mekong to the **Maha Leap Pagoda**, an old wooden structure with gilt-adorned teak columns that was somehow spared by the Khmer Rouge. Just upstream from the pagoda is **Proek Changkran**, a weaving village where silk is woven on traditional handlooms. Silk traders from around the country come here to purchase fine, detailed cloth. You can hire local boatmen by the boat jetty for a day out (expect to pay about $10/hr); ask at the *Mekong Crossing Restaurant* (see below) for more details. If you're travelling alone, most of these sites can be reached more cheaply by moto.

### Arrival

**By bus** Buses from Phnom Penh (12,000r) – an easy 3hr trip – arrive at the depot northwest of the market.
**By share taxi or minibus** Taxis and minibuses arrive at the market.

### Accommodation

**Bophear** One block back from the river, behind the *Mekong Hotel* ⓣ012/857919. Clean fan rooms with shared bathrooms go for just $2 at this guesthouse, which has bicycles for rent as well. ❶
**Mekong Hotel** On the riverfront a short way north of the bridge ⓣ042/941536. The best-value accommodation in town, with spotless, sizeable rooms with TV, some with a/c. ❷
**Nava** Near the market ⓣ012/205615. Offers clean, smallish twin-bed rooms, with bathroom and TV. ❶
**Phnom Prosh Hotel** Just up the road from ANZ Bank ⓣ042/941444. Large modern hotel with an attached restaurant and comfortable, reasonably priced en-suite rooms with TV. ❷

### Eating and drinking

Given its size, eating options are rather limited in Kampong Cham, and some places close by around 9pm so don't leave it too late to eat. Around the market, you'll find some decent food stalls and noodle shops, with drink stalls along the riverfront.
**Hao An** At the corner of Pasteur and Monivong. Has a vast selection of delicious dishes from 8000r, and easy ordering from the full-colour picture menu.
**Lazy Mekong Daze** Along the riverfront. English breakfasts, Western meals and Khmer food in this cosy riverside hangout.
**Mekong Crossing** Round the corner from the *Mekong Hotel*. Serves a huge breakfast plate of eggs, bacon, chips and baked beans, and also has a short menu of Khmer and Western dishes available throughout the day and evening.

### Moving on

**By bus** Buses serve Kratie (18,000r), but it's a long, roundabout journey, and you're better off taking a taxi ($5) for this stretch.
**Destinations:** Kratie (4hr); Phnom Penh (3hr); Siem Reap (5hr); Stung Treng (6hr 30min).
**By share taxi or minibus** to: Kratie (2hr 30min); Phnom Penh (2hr); Stung Treng (4hr).

## KRATIE AND AROUND

Life ticks by slowly in **KRATIE** (pronounced "Kracheh"). This tiny, indolent town on the Mekong is an unexpected delight. Away from the blemish of the modern market, Kratie is a wonderful hotchpotch of colonial terraces and traditional old Khmer buildings – sturdy wooden structures, with dark-red roof tiles and often a decorative flourish of colour. There's not much for visitors to do in the town itself, which stretches lazily along the west bank of the river, but it makes a good base for exploring the surrounding countryside.

About 11km north of Kratie following the river road, **Phnom Sambok** is set in a grotto of lush-green vegetation on a twin-peaked hill. The dense trees hide a meditation commune on the first level and a small temple on the higher summit. Around 10km further north on the same road, a sign marks your arrival at **Kampie**, the best riverside vantage point from which to view the rare freshwater **Irrawaddy dolphins**, of which it's thought that no more than a hundred remain in the Mekong. A small group of these snub-nosed dolphins live in this area of rapids, and can usually be seen at any time of day, being particularly evident when the water is low. The only way to visit these places is to hire a moto (12,000r) or a taxi ($10) from Kratie. If you can spare a full day, you could also include a visit to **Sambor**, some 35km north of Kratie, the site of an ancient pre-Angkorian capital (24,000r by moto, $20 by taxi).

## Arrival

**By bus** Most buses draw up along the riverside, just west of the market.

**By share taxi or minibus** Taxis will usually drop you off en-route; otherwise the transport stop is one block north of the market.

## Accommodation

**Heng Heng II** Just south of the dock ⓣ011/282821. Pleasant rooms in a renovated building facing the river, with en-suite bathrooms and TV. ❶

**Santepheap Hotel** Opposite the boat dock ⓣ072/971537. Rooms here are well appointed and feature en-suite bathrooms and TV, some also boasting hot water and a/c. ❷

**Star Guesthouse** Opposite the southwest corner of the market ⓣ012/753401. Offers cheap, central en-suite rooms with fan. The owners speak good English, can arrange motos or dolphin tours and also run a popular café downstairs. ❶

**U Hong** North side of the market ⓣ011/674088. Cheap, serviceable en-suite rooms above a busy café with internet. Owners also arrange onward transport. ❶

## Eating and drinking

Snack and drink stalls set up every evening by the riverside.

**Heng Heng I** On the riverfront, just south of the dock. Good range of fish and Khmer/Chinese dishes, including a pretty decent sweet-and-sour vegetable dish. Open from early morning to mid-evening.

**Mekong Restaurant** Just south of the boat dock, round the corner from *Red Sun Falling*. Offers competent, if unexciting, renditions of the standard range of Khmer dishes, with an English-language menu.

**Red Sun Falling** Just south of the boat dock. Western-run place that has a short menu of Khmer dishes chalked up on a blackboard, a range of beers and cocktails and a cosy ambience. They also arrange dolphin tours.

**Star Guesthouse** Opposite the southwest corner of the market. A popular international restaurant with a picture menu designed to teach about Khmer food. Also boasts a wide range of cocktails and rather upscale palm wine.

## Moving on

**By bus** Buses to Kampong Cham and Phnom Penh leave at around 7.30am (25,000r), though they take significantly longer than taxis. You can also buy a bus ticket direct to Banlung, but you have to switch to a minibus in Stung Treng.

**Destinations:** Banlung (daily; 6hr); Kampong Cham (daily; 4hr); Phnom Penh (daily; 7hr); Stung Treng (daily; 2hr).

**By share taxi or minibus** Share taxis and minibuses, which leave from the transport stop just north of the market, are the quickest way to travel between Kratie and Kampong Cham.

**Destinations:** Banlung (5hr); Kampong Cham (2hr 30min); Phnom Penh (4hr 30min); Stung Treng (2hr).

# STUNG TRENG

For most people, **STUNG TRENG** is just a staging post on the overland trek to Rattanakiri (see p.135) or on the way to Laos, but the surrounding countryside is beautiful and can be explored by boat, moto or bicycle. Hotel and guesthouse owners can arrange visits to a silk weaving centre, fruit orchards, lakes and waterfalls, and boat trips to remote villages. More and more travellers are hanging around here for a few days.

One of the most popular outings is a Mekong trip to the **Laos border** (the Sekong joins the Mekong 2km west of town; the border crossing itself is at Voen Kham), offering the possibility of some dolphin-spotting and a glimpse at the waterfalls that make the river impassable here. Back in town, the charm of Stung Treng is in seeking out your own entertainment – sipping a cool drink at the riverfront, or wandering around the market with its chunchiet products.

## Arrival

**By share taxi or minibus** All road transport arrives and leaves from the transport stop on the riverfront.

## Accommodation

**Dara Guesthouse** Opposite the taxi stand ⓣ011/693429. Tidy en-suite rooms with mosquito nets for only $3, plus a restaurant with the usual Asian fare. Owner speaks French but not much English. ❶

**Riverside Guest House** Virtually opposite the boat terminal and taxi stand ⓣ012/439454. The most convenient place to stay in town, where the few simple, adequate rooms are often full. Its owner, Mr T, also happens to be the best fixer in town and can arrange border transport, river trips and excursions to a range of interesting destinations in the local area. ❶

**Sekong Hotel** A 5min walk west along the riverside ⓣ012/757468. A notch up in price from the other riverside guesthouses, offering bright and spacious rooms facing the water. ❸

**Tonle** 10min west of the transport stop, on the river ⓣ074/973638. Run by a Swiss NGO training locals in eco-tourism, this attractive, homely little guesthouse has three immaculate rooms and a Khmer/French restaurant, all serviced by trainees. Usually closed weekends, but you can still stay if you call ahead. ❷

## Eating

The market in Stung Treng is exceptional, serving delicious Khmer food of the type people cook at home: throughout the day and into the evening, you can fill up easily for less than $1.

**Richie's** Along the riverfront. The only real non-hotel restaurant is an attractive little place serving a selection of curries in coconut shells.

**Riverside Guest House** Opposite the boat terminal and taxi stand. Numbers Western breakfasts, spaghetti and pancakes among its offerings, which you can enjoy downstairs or in the neat rooftop restaurant and bar.

## Moving on

**By bus** to: Kampong Cham (7hr); Kratie (2hr); Phnom Penh (9hr).

### INTO LAOS: DOM KRALOR/VOEN KHAM

There are two border crossings to Laos, fairly close to each other: the cheaper road crossing at **Dom Kralor**, and the more expensive but more scenic river crossing to **Voen Kham**. **Minibuses** are available up to the Dom Kralor border, but if you opt for the latter, hotel and guesthouse owners will help fix you up with a **boat** ($40 for the boat) for the trip from Stung Treng into Laos. Opt for an ordinary boat; in a speedboat, there's little chance of enjoying the scenery as you hurtle by, legs cramped up and clinging on for dear life. Another alternative is to take a minibus from Stung Treng to Si Phan Don (Four Thousand Island, see p.463; $10; 2 daily) or on to Pakxe ($12).

If you plan to cross the border, you'll need to be in possession of a Laos visa, though Cambodia visas are available upon arrival ($20 and one photo). As with all Cambodia border crossings, immigration officials ask for a $2–3 fee to stamp your passport. If you ask for the official's name and demand a receipt, you may find they back down on this request. Coming from Laos, you can either get a group together to hire a taxi from Si Phan Don to Stung Treng ($20), or call ahead to *Riverside Guest House* for a minibus pickup ($5/person).

**By share taxi or minibus** Share taxis and pick-ups leave from the transport stop at around 7.30am and then intermittently through the day, depending on demand. The *Riverside Guest House* can also help arrange transport.

**Destinations:** Banlung (3hr); Kampong Cham (4hr); Kratie (2hr); Laos border (1hr; see box opposite); Phnom Penh (6hr 30min).

# Northeast Cambodia

Eastwards from the Mekong towns, Cambodia's remote eastern uplands remain stuck in their own isolated world, largely untouched by the march of development. Tucked away in the remote northeastern corner, hilly **Ratanakiri** province is bordered by Vietnam to the east and Laos to the north. If you like nature and wildlife, this is the place to be. The rainy season leaves the area dripping with greenery and alive with exotic animals and rushing waterfalls. The rich and fertile lands are covered with plantations: rubber, coffee, sugar cane, bananas, cashew nuts and pineapples all grow in abundance. The upland forests are also home to around twelve distinct groups of **chunchiets**, who comprise over eighty percent of the province's population. They now forego traditional dress for modern clothing, but remain among the most deprived people in Cambodia, with poor education and health care, and practically no way of making a living other than their traditional slash and burn farming.

The province of **Mondulkiri** is Ratanakiri's forgotten southern neighbour, in the far east of the country, bordering Vietnam. It's less visited but can claim similar attractions: a high proportion of chunchiet, waterfalls and beautiful landscapes – its forested highlands are interrupted occasionally by grassy fields and gentle hills that would look more at home in rural England. The climate is not dissimilar either: the temperature is a mere 18°C on average in the dry season, with chilly nights.

## BANLUNG AND AROUND

The sprawling town of **Banlung,** approximately 600km northeast of Phnom Penh, only became the provincial capital in 1979, replacing the Khmer Rouge capital of Voen Sai (which had in turn replaced Lumphat, which had been devastated by American bombs). The town is a good base for trips into the surrounding area to see chunchiet villages and unspoilt countryside.

### What to see and do

Banlung may be the provincial capital, but not a lot happens here. At its heart is the **market**, especially lively in the early morning when the chunchiet come in to sell fresh produce and forest foods on the scruffy patch of land nearby.

#### Yeak Laom Lake

Chunchiets aside, Banlung is chiefly known for **Yeak Laom Lake**, 4km east of town (4000–8000r by moto), created by a volcanic eruption many thousands of years ago. The lake's three-kilometre circumference is lined with stands of bamboo and dense green forest, its remarkable tranquillity interrupted only by the occasional birdcall. A swim in the clean, turquoise waters is a good way to cleanse yourself of the penetrating dust from Banlung's red dirt roads. The committee responsible for managing the lake and its surroundings is comprised of Tampoun villagers, the indigenous inhabitants of the area. Along the banks of the lake is the Chunchiet Cultural Centre; built in traditional Tampoun style, it houses a collection of memorabilia and examples of craftwork.

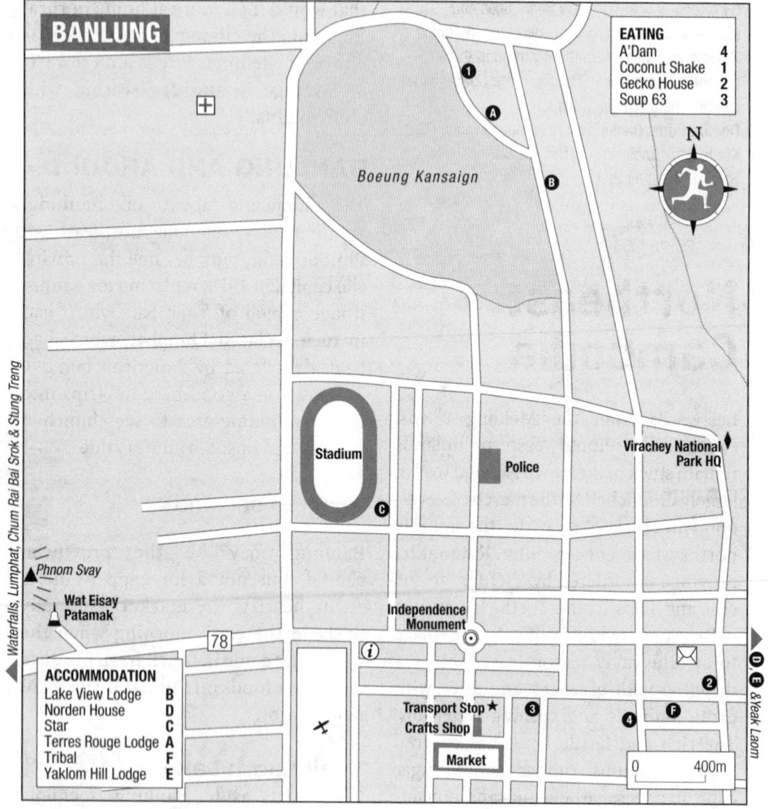


## Veal Rum Plan

About 14km from Banlung is a bizarre clearing in the forest covered by an almost circular area of flat stone – the remains of a cooled lava flow. The area is known in English as Field of Stone and in Khmer as **Veal Rum Plan**. Rum Plan, so the legend goes, was a young boy who fell to his death from a tree onto the black rock while trying to retrieve his kite. His spirit is believed to live on, protecting the plateau and surrounding trees.

## Eisey Patamak Mountain and the waterfalls

On the western fringe of Banlung, the easy ten-minute climb up **Eisey Patamak Mountain**, behind the temple of the same name, is well worth it for the glorious views of the O Traw Mountains. Locals even claim it's possible to see the mountains of Laos to the north, and Vietnam to the east. All this is lost on the five-metre-long Reclining Buddha, which lies at the summit, its eyes closed.

Beyond Wat Eisey Patamak, a turning leads to Banlung's two most impressive sets of waterfalls: **Ka Chhang** and **Chha Ong**. At Chha Ong, water sprays from a rock overhang into a small jungle clearing. It lacks a decent pool for a swim, but brave visitors shower under the smaller column of water – be careful, though, as it's slippery. To get there, follow the Stung Treng road past the airport and continue for about 2km. A small road to the right leads to Chhaa Ong, and the one on the left goes to Ka Chhang.

### Jungle excursions

Aside from treks into Virachey National Park (see p.138), many local guides offer overnight excursions into the surrounding **jungle** – prices depend on the group size, but usually end up being around $15–20 a day per person. If you've time to spare, you could also ask about elephant rides at your guesthouse. Nearby villagers are only too happy to give these animals a break from hard work and let them stroll around with tourists on board. Expect to pay $10/hr for a ride.

## Arrival

**By bus, share taxi or minibus** All road transport arrives at the transport stop near the market; National Route 78 from Stung Treng is passable year-round but in wet weather it becomes incredibly slippery and gets churned up, causing delays.

## Accommodation

Accommodation choices are getting better as the town attracts more visitors. As well as functional and reasonably priced concrete blocks in the centre, there are some stylish wooden bungalows surrounded by greenery on the outskirts of town.

**Lake View Lodge** On the road around Boeung Kansaign ⓣ012/408190. Cosy en-suite rooms in the old governor's house, now polished and gleaming, set in a quiet courtyard by the lake. The owner speaks excellent English and arranges tours of the area, including multi-day treks. ❶

**Norden House** Along the road to Yeak Laom lake ⓣ012/448950. Less than a kilometre from Yeak Laom, these brand-new stylish bungalows sit in a well-manicured garden with attached restaurant and bar. ❹

**Star** Close to the stadium on the main road ⓣ012/958322. A big wooden house covered in dark wood and antlers, this hotel has the feel of a hunting lodge but its en-suite rooms, with TV and a/c, are comfortable enough. The friendly owner arranges tours. ❶

TREAT YOURSELF

**Terres Rouges Lodge** ⓣ075/974051, ⓦwww.ratanakiri-lodge.com. Hidden away in Ratanakiri is what some describe as the best hotel in Cambodia – an idyllic wooden house on Boeung Kansaign lake, where black-and-white photos, gleaming Art Nouveau furniture and jungle decor make you feel like you've stepped back into another era. Rooms, luxuriously appointed using chunchiet fabrics, go for $32–75.

**Tribal** One block south of the post office and just over two blocks east of the market ⓣ075/974074. An attractive addition to Banlung's accommodation scene, catering for all budgets in a colourful, sociable compound just away from the town centre. ❶

**Yaklom Hill Lodge** 6km east of town, beyond the Hill Tribe Monument ⓣ011/725881, ⓦwww.yaklom.com. An eco-lodge with fourteen sturdily built wooden bungalows on stilts with ample verandas, all surrounded by dense greenery. The simple but stylish rooms all have attached bathrooms, and breakfast is included in the price. Electricity – and hot showers – from 6pm to 9pm. ❷

## Eating

Most of the hotels and guesthouses also have decent restaurants. Stop by the market at night to explore Banlung's amazing dessert stalls, which offer an unusually wide selection of sweets.

**A'Dam** Two blocks south of the main road, east of the market. A wooden balcony perched in the treetops, serving Khmer and Chinese food and some of the cheapest beer in town. Also has a pool table.

**Coconut Shake** On the road around Boeung Kansaign lake, just past *Terres Rouges*. BBQ beef, fantastic coconut shakes and a lovely lake view enjoyed from a quiet terrace.

**Gecko House** East of the market, across from *Tribal*. Laid-back corner bar and restaurant serving good Khmer food and pizza. Popular with expats.

**Soup 63** Two blocks east of the market. There are only two things on the menu at this simple place: Khmer "soup chhnangdey" (add your own ingredients) and grill-it-yourself beef with vegetables. Both are excellent.

## Directory

**Banks and exchange** There's nowhere to change traveller's cheques in town and no ATM yet, so come with enough cash in small dollar bills to get you through.

**Post office** Telephone, fax and postal facilities are available at the post office, on the right-hand side of the road out towards Yeak Laom lake.

**Internet** There are several internet cafés in town – try Cyber-Sophat next to the market – but rates are expensive at $2–3 per hour.

## Moving on

Hotel and guesthouse owners can help to sort out onward transport.

**By bus** A pickup (5000r) makes the dusty trip between Banlung and Voen Sai when full. Hour Lean also runs a daily bus to Phnom Penh via Stung Treng and Kratie.

**Destinations:** Kratie (daily; 5hr); Phnom Penh (daily; 11hr); Stung Treng (daily; 3hr 30min); Voen Sai (45min).

**By share taxi and minibus** Transport goes to Stung Treng (30,000r) and then on to Kratie (25,000r).

**Destinations:** Kratie (5hr); Stung Treng (3hr).

# VOEN SAI AND VIRACHEY NATIONAL PARK

The road north of Banlung winds its way past numerous chunchiet villages until, after around 38km, it reaches the village of **VOEN SAI**, located on the San River, the headquarters of Virachey National Park and one of the most accessible villages in the region.

Covering over 800,000 acres, **Virachey National Park** is a haven for a variety of endangered species, including tigers, deer, rare hornbills, and kouprey, the almost-extinct jungle cow. Rangers have made real progress in the reduction of logging and poaching of rare animals, but face a continuing struggle – the price commanded by a tiger on the open market could feed a whole family for a generation. Overnight **treks** in the park (including a visit to a chunchiet village, a night in a hammock and a ride downriver on a bamboo raft) can be organized through the park headquarters in Banlung, northeast of the market (Mon–Fri 8–11.30am & 2–5pm; ☎012/172 6817) or through the Office of Environmental Capacity in Stung Treng (☎012/939158). Prices are around $20 per person per day.

Voen Sai itself is home to an unusual mix of **ethnic minorities**, predominantly Lao and Chinese, but also Kreung. A small boat (1500r) connects Voen Sai with villages on the opposite bank – to the right, there is a small Lao settlement, and to the left a Chinese community. It's best to visit these places with a local guide, as you'll need someone to act as an interpreter and smooth the way. The easiest way to get to **Voen Sai** is to rent a moto from Banlung ($10); you can also get a pickup. It's also possible to access the park by taking a daily shared boat from Stung Treng (15,000r per person).

# SEN MONOROM AND AROUND

Provincial capitals don't get more remote or inaccessible than **SEN MONOROM**, 420km from Phnom Penh and the only place to stay in remote Mondulkiri province. The town extends for a short way down either side of a low hill topped by an airstrip, now used only for NGO flights. It's a friendly little place with a small-town atmosphere, and it makes a good base from which to explore the surrounding countryside and chunchiet villages.

## What to see and do

Locals will direct you to the **Monorom Falls** (Sihanouk Falls), a peaceful nook on the edge of the jungle where a ten-metre-high cascade of water drops into a swirling plunge pool. You can either walk the few kilometres here or hire a moto along the easy road. The path ends at the top of the waterfall, where brave souls hurl themselves into the deep water during the rainy season. The more safety-conscious scramble down through the foliage for a refreshing swim. The more distant but spectacular **Bou Sraa Falls**, about 40km northeast from Sen Monorom, can be reached by moto by way of a stunningly beautiful forest trail. The falls themselves are a dramatic two-tiered affair, with more than thirty metres of water gushing into a jungle-clad gorge.

There are hundreds of chunchiet villages around Sen Monorom, but some villages are not keen on foreign visitors, so it's best to take a local to act as a guide and interpreter. One of the largest and easiest villages to access is **Phulung**, inhabited by Phnong, the majority chunchiet group in Mondulkiri. The curious huts have woven wooden walls and thatched roofs almost to the floor. Three or more families often live in just one hut, but you'll be lucky to see more than a handful of people during daytime, as they're all out working in the fields. Phulung is also the starting point for half- or full-day elephant treks in the area ($15–30), which you can arrange through guesthouses in Sen Monorom.

## Arrival and information

**By bus** An Hour Lean bus runs daily to Sen Monorom from Olympic Stadium in Phnom Penh ($10), via Kampong Cham, but it's a good deal slower than a taxi or pick-up.

**By share taxi or pick-up** These run either direct from Phnom Penh (8hr) or from the Mekong at Kampong Cham (6hr). You will get *very* dusty in a pick-up, unless you sit in the cab. The road is pretty good in parts but terrible in others; there were plans to surface it, though the timeline for this is uncertain.

**Tourist information and guides** To see most sights, you'll need to engage the help of a guide. You can book reliable guides at your guesthouse or at the tourist office behind the post office (the white building just off the airstrip). They don't come cheap, though, starting at around $20/day. Another good place to get local information – and the only place to find internet – is at the *Green House* in the centre of town (Ⓣ012/190 5659, Ⓦwww.mondolkiritrekking.com). Staff here can organize guides and local elephant treks, and can also arrange rental of 250cc trail bikes for $15/day. Expect to pay $10 for a moto to get to Bou Sraa.

## Accommodation

There are an expanding number of places to stay in Sen Monorom:

**Bou Sraa Guesthouse** Centre of town, next to *Holiday Guesthouse* Ⓣ012/527144. Rooms of varying sizes; more expensive ones have hot water. ❶

**Holiday Guesthouse** On the left as you enter town, past *Pich Kiri* Ⓣ012/936606. Single and double rooms, all of which have attached bathrooms. ❶

**Nature Lodge** 2km north of town Ⓣ011/494449. An idyllic little eco-lodge offering both cabins and camping opportunities out in the woods, with an MSG-free kitchen and a hydro-electric power supply. ❶

**Pich Kiri** On the left as you enter town Ⓣ012/932102. Well-maintained and convenient hotel with a choice of rooms, either in the main house or bungalows around the verdant gardens. Terrific food is served at the restaurant, and friendly staff can help book excursions in the area. ❶

## Eating

Proper restaurants in Sen Monorom are somewhat limited, but there are plenty of noodle shops at the market and near the transport stop.

**Bananas** 5min down the hill from the centre. Dishes up tasty Western dishes in an attractive setting.

**Chom Nor Tmey** The most popular Khmer restaurant in town, attracting locals and tourists.

**Green House** Off the main road in the centre of town. Made entirely of bamboo, this is a nice little place to have an afternoon drink. Also a good spot to book guides of the area or elephant tours (see above).

**Mahogany** Classier and a bit pricier than the rest, specializing in Nepalese dishes as well as the usual Khmer and Western.

**Pitch Kiri** On the left as you enter town. Terrific Khmer and Western fare in this friendly place, set in a lush garden. Perfect for enjoying a beer while your food is cooked.

# Hong Kong and Macau

## HIGHLIGHTS

**WONG TAI SIN TEMPLE:** an absorbing glimpse of modern-day Taoist worship

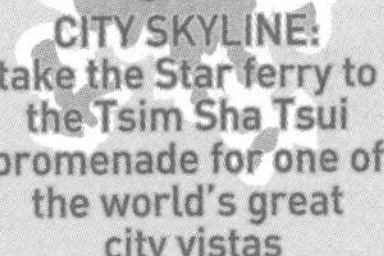

**MACANESE CUISINE:** discover Portuguese classics with a Chinese twist

**CITY SKYLINE:** take the Star ferry to the Tsim Sha Tsui promenade for one of the world's great city vistas

**TIAN TAN BUDDHA:** the view of forested Lantau is breathtaking

**MACAU TOWER:** stand on the glass panels in the viewing gallery and set your heart a flutter

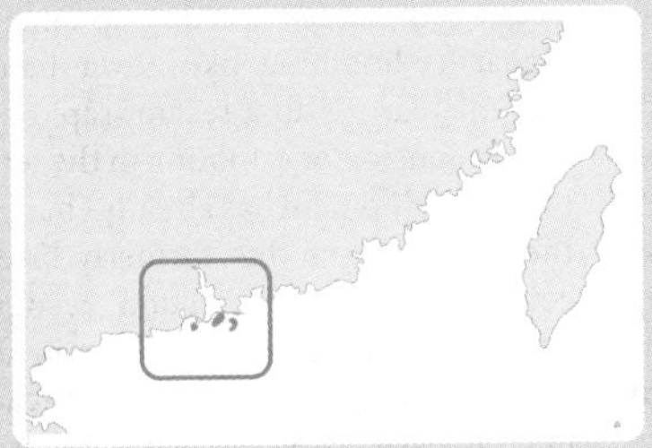

## ROUGH COSTS

**DAILY BUDGET** Basic US$23/ Occasional treat US$29

**FOOD** Noodle soup, fried rice US$3-6

**DRINK** Tsingtao US$3 in restaurants, US$5 in bars

**HOSTEL/BUDGET HOTEL** US$8–37

**TRAVEL** Bus Central-Stanley US$0.60–1.35; MTR Tsim Sha Tsui-Central US$1; Ferry Central-Lantau HK$1.40

## FACT FILE

**POPULATION** 7 million in Hong Kong; 520,000 in Macau

**AREA** 1,104 sq km for Hong Kong; 28.6 sq km for Macau

**LANGUAGE** Cantonese, English in Hong Kong; Cantonese, some Portuguese and English in Macau.

**CURRENCY** Hong Kong dollar (HK$); pataca (ptca/M$/MOP/ MOP$) in Macau.

**INTERNATIONAL PHONE CODE** ⓣ852 in Hong Kong (01 from Macau); ⓣ853 in Macau.

**TIME ZONE** GMT +8hr

# Introduction

**One of the great world city-states, Hong Kong is an extraordinary, complex and crowded territory of seven million people. The view of Hong Kong Island's skyscrapers across the harbour from Kowloon, is one of the most stunning urban panoramas on earth, but if the sheer energy of its street and commercial life feels overwhelming, it's easy to escape to surprisingly beautiful hiking trails and inviting beaches. Tiny Macau offers similar contrasts, with a myriad of traditional temples firmly resisting the ever-increasing number of glitzy casinos.**

Since their **handover** to China, in 1997 for Hong Kong and 1999 for Macau, the people of both cities have found themselves in a unique position: subject to the ultimate rule of Beijing, they live in a semi-democratic capitalist enclave – a "Special Administrative Region (SAR) of China". Hong Kong's per capita **GNP** doubled in the first decade of Chinese rule yet the inequality of incomes is staggering: the conspicuous consumption of the few hundred super-rich (all Cantonese), for which Hong Kong is famous, tends to mask the fact that most people work long hours and live in crowded, tiny apartments. There is a lot of wealth, but Hong Kong is also an expensive place to live. Best comparison is to London's City district – most people who work there earn large salaries compared to the average Londoner, but only the very top ones are truly "super-rich". The average expat in HK also does well on perks, such as enjoying accommodation allowances.

Sixty kilometres west from Hong Kong across the Pearl River Delta, the tiny former Portuguese trading enclave of **Macau** may seem a geographic and economic midget compared to its high-rise cousin but it's catching up quickly. Macau is booming like never before – thanks largely to a recent, rapid and vast expansion of gambling in the territory. Development has already changed the character of this formerly sleepy colonial backwater beyond recognition (and ambitious plans for a bridge to Hong Kong look set to go ahead), but old Macau is still very much in evidence and the historic centre boasts UNESCO World Heritage status. With a colonial past predating that of Hong Kong by nearly three hundred years, Macau's historic buildings – from old

## WHEN TO GO

Hong Kong and Macau's **climate** is subtropical. The best time to visit is between October and April, when the weather is cooler, humidity levels drop and the flowers are in bloom. In January and February, it can get quite rainy and cold. The temperature and humidity start to pick up in mid-April and between late June and early September readings of 30°C and 95 percent humidity or more are the norm. During typhoon season, from May to September, ferry and airline timetables are often disrupted by bad weather. If a category T8 typhoon is on its way, offices and shops will close and public transport will shut down. You are best off heading back to your hotel and closing the windows and curtains.

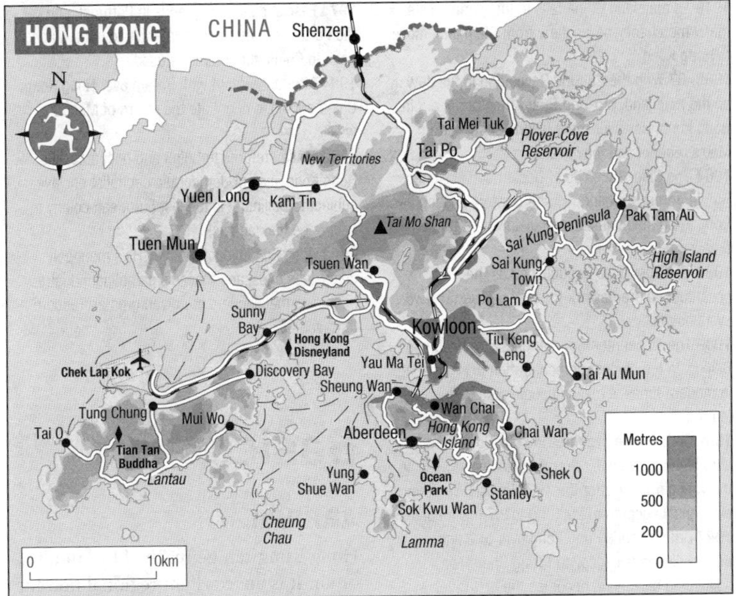


fortresses to Baroque churches to faded mansion houses – are plentiful and almost every tiny backstreet holds a surprise. South of the main city, on **Taipa** and **Coloane**, are beaches and quiet villages where you can sample a unique cuisine blending Asian, European and African influences.

Although many travellers base themselves in Hong Kong and cover Macau just on a day-trip, a short visit means you risk seeing nothing but busy streets and excessively lavish casinos. With the development of Macau's airport into a hub for cheap regional flights, it's worth stopping off here en route from Hong Kong to the rest of Asia or vice versa.

## CHRONOLOGY

### Hong Kong

**Early eighteenth century** British merchants arrive in China's Guangzhou province, and take a cue from the Portuguese, trading silk and tea from the region.

**1757** Co Hong, a Guangzhou merchants' guild, wins the exclusive rights to sell Chinese products to foreign traders, who are allowed to live in Guangzhou for six months each year.

**1773** The first British shipload of opium arrives from India and demand for the drug explodes in China, despite Beijing's opposition.

**1839** The first Opium War starts. Commissioner of Guangzhou, Lin Zexu, forces the British to surrender their opium, before ceremonially burning it.

**1840** A naval expeditionary force is dispatched from London; it blockades ports and seizes assets up and down the Chinese coast for a year.

**1842** The Treaty of Nanking cedes to Britain "in perpetuity" a small offshore island called Hong Kong.

**1860** After more blockades and a march on Beijing during the second Opium War, China grants Britain the Kowloon peninsula.

**1898** As the Qing dynasty declines, Britain secures a 99-year lease on one thousand square kilometres of land north of Kowloon, known as the New Territories.

**1907** The drug trade is voluntarily dropped as Hong Kong merchants switch from trade to manufacturing.

**1941–45** Japanese forces occupy Hong Kong along with the rest of eastern China.

**1949** As mainland China falls to the communists, many merchants, particularly from Shanghai, move to Hong Kong.
**1966–67** With the Cultural Revolution in full flow on the mainland, pro-Red Guard riots break out in Hong Kong. However there is little support from Mao's regime, and they fizzle out.
**1984** The Sino-British Joint Declaration is signed. Britain agrees to relinquish the territory as long as Hong Kong maintains a capitalist system for at least fifty years.
**1988** The Basic Law is published as the constitutional framework for the one country, two systems policy.
**1989** The Tiananmen Square massacre occurs in Beijing. In the biggest demonstration in Hong Kong in modern times, a million people take to the streets in protest.
**1992** Chris Patten becomes the last Governor and introduces a series of reforms, including increasing the voting franchise for the 1995 Legislative Council elections (Legco) from 200,000 to 2.7 million people.
**1997** Britain hands Hong Kong over to China. Beijing disbands Legco, and Tung Chee Hwa, a shipping billionaire, becomes the first Chief Executive of the Hong Kong Special Administrative Region (SAR) of the People's Republic of China. Within days, the Asian Financial Crisis begins and Hong Kong's economy goes into recession.
**July 1, 2003** 500,000 protestors take to the streets against a proposed anti-subversion bill that will restrict civil liberties; in September the bill is withdrawn.
**March 2005** Chief executive Tung Chee Hwa resigns; he is succeeded by Donald Tsang.
**2008** Beijing rules out direct democratic elections until at least 2017.

### Macau

**1557** The Portuguese persuade local Chinese officials to rent them a strategically placed peninsula at the mouth of the Pearl River Delta, known as Macao, which meants "the goddess of the sea". As the only foreigners permitted to trade with China, the Portuguese become sole agents for merchants across a whole swathe of east Asia and the Portuguese in Macau grow immensely wealthy.
**1641** The Portuguese lose Melaka in Malaysia to the Dutch; Macau's trading links are cut and its fortunes wane.
**1842** Once the British claimed Hong Kong to the east, Macau's status as a backwater is definitively settled.
**1847** Licensed gambling is introduced as a desperate means of securing some kind of income.
**1974** Fascist dictatorship ends in Portugal, and the Portuguese attempt unilaterally to hand Macau back to China; the offer is refused.
**1984** After agreement with Britain over Hong Kong, China agrees to negotiate the return of Macau as well.
**1999** Macau returns to China and becomes, like Hong Kong, a semi-democratic capitalist enclave subject to Beijing; it is the last European colony in Asia to be handed back.
**2002** Hong Kong tycoon Stanley Ho's monopoly on casinos ends, and Macau's gambling industry booms as mainlanders are given greater freedom to travel.

# Basics

## ARRIVAL

Hong Kong can be reached by land, sea or air. It is an excellent regional hub for flights arriving from the US, Europe or Asia, as it regularly features as a stop-over on an around-the-world ticket. Trains from Guangzhou in China arrive at Hung Hom station on the Kowloon peninsula. It's a short bus ride from there to the Star Ferry terminus, where you can catch a ferry over to Hong Kong island.

**Boats** from China arrive at the China Ferry Terminal on Canton Road, also in Kowloon, not far from the guesthouses on Nathan Road. Some ferries from Macau dock here, but most will set you down at the Macau Ferry Terminal on the western end of Hong Kong Island's northern shore. From here you can catch a bus, train or tram to the rest of the territory.

The new Hong Kong airport, **Chek Lap Kok**, is situated on Lantau Island. It is linked to the island and to Kowloon by a high-speed train, the Airport Express Link (AEL) and by buses.

Most people reach Macau by **ferry** from Hong Kong. Ferries dock at the Jetfoil Terminal just north of the city centre, and you can catch a bus from there into town. Some ferries also run to the Cotai Strip on Taipa, though these mainly cater for the casinos there.

Macau's airport is also on Taipa, and many budget carriers have started flying there from Southeast Asia. There is a bus into town from here.

## VISAS

Most nationalities need only a valid passport to enter **Hong Kong**, although the length of time you can stay varies. Citizens of the United Kingdom get 180 days, whereas most European nationalities (including Irish citizens), along with travellers from Canada, Australia, New Zealand and the United States, can stay for up to 90 days. South Africans are only allowed 30 days. The easiest way to **extend your stay** is to go to Macau and come back, getting another stamp in your passport. A trip to China and back (for which you'll need to get a visa in advance, see p.176) will also gain you a new stamp. For a longer stay, you'll need to apply for a visa in advance of your visit from the **Immigration Department**, Immigration Tower, 7 Gloucester Rd, Wan Chai, Hong Kong (Ⓣ2824 6111 Ⓦwww.immd.gov.hk), or from a Chinese consulate abroad. All nationalities except British need a work visa for employment; allow four to six weeks for most visa applications.

To enter **Macau**, citizens of Britain, Ireland, Australia, New Zealand, Canada, the US and most Western European countries need only a valid passport. British citizens can stay for six months, Europeans for 90 days and others listed for 30 days. The simplest way to **extend your stay** is to go to Hong Kong and re-enter Macau at a later date.

## GETTING AROUND

Hong Kong's public transport system is efficient, comfortable, extensive and cheap, although it can be extremely crowded during rush hours. The MTR (Mass Transit Railway) system and the main bus routes are easy to use and most signs are in English as well as Chinese, although don't expect staff to speak much English. The same is true with taxi drivers. It's a good idea to get someone to write down your destination (and where you've come from for the return) in Chinese characters. If you get stuck, tourist maps also print the Chinese characters for the main tourist places. See p.169 for details of public transport in Hong Kong; see p.183 for details of public transport in Macau.

## ACCOMMODATION

Hong Kong boasts some of the most luxurious hotels in Asia – if not the world – as well as some of the seediest guesthouses. Sky-high property prices mean that cheaper accommodation is not nearly as plentiful as in other Asian cities, or as good value. **Guesthouses** – flats converted to hold as many tiny private rooms as possible – are mostly in Tsim Sha Tsui at the southern tip of Kowloon and Causeway Bay on the island's north shore. The majority are crammed into a couple of huge, warren-like apartment blocks, *Mirador Mansions* and *Chungking Mansions*. Quality and cleanliness vary greatly from guesthouse to guesthouse, but all the rooms will be small and some will have no windows. English is not always spoken. These two blocks are also crammed with shops, travel agents and restaurants. Most guesthouses will be able to sort out visas for China, though rates vary. An alternative is to stay at a **youth hostel**, where rates are as low as HK$50 for members or HK$80 for non-members. They are mostly in quite out-of-the-way locations, which offers peace and quiet you won't find elsewhere but can make them impractical. **Electricity** throughout the territory is usually supplied at 220 volts.

**Accommodation** in Macau is generally more expensive, as there is a dearth of cheap hostels. Most guesthouses cater

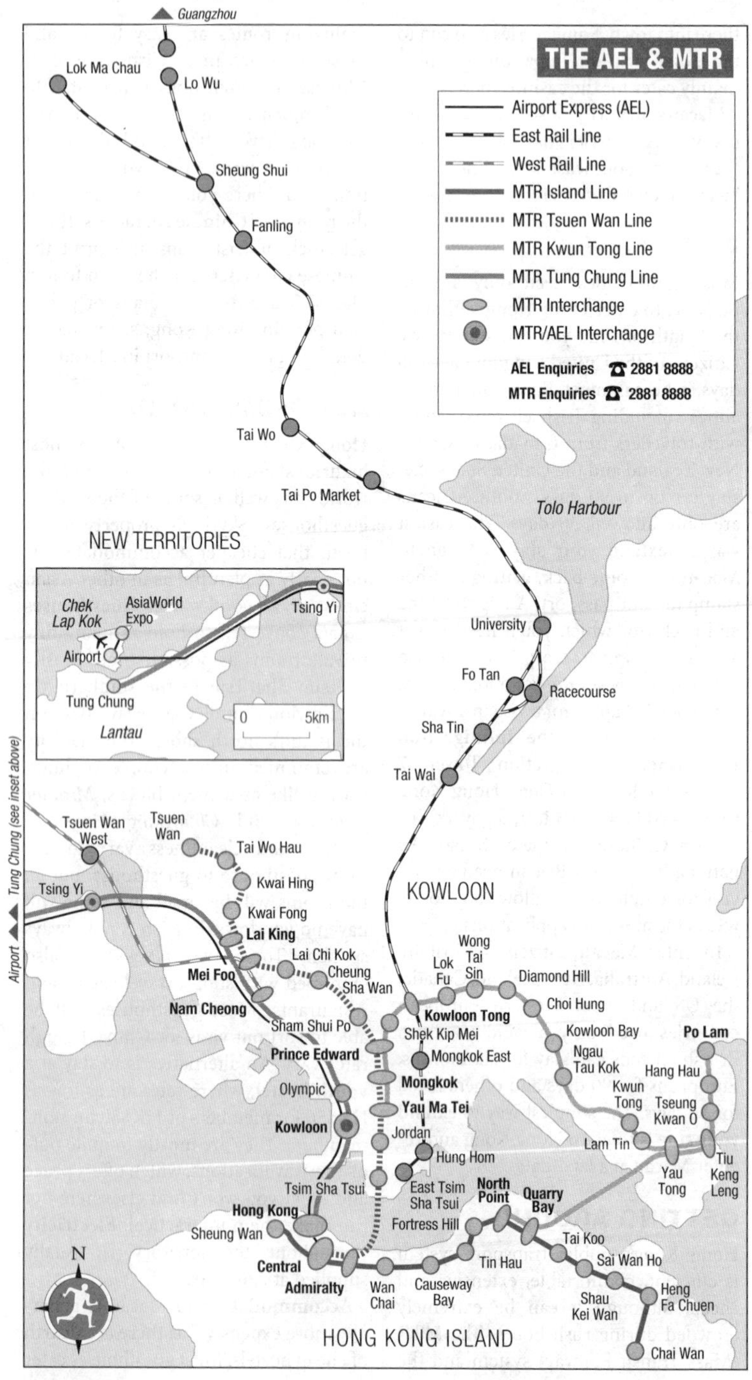
THE AEL & MTR
Airport Express (AEL)
East Rail Line
West Rail Line
MTR Island Line
MTR Tsuen Wan Line
MTR Kwun Tong Line
MTR Tung Chung Line
MTR Interchange
MTR/AEL Interchange
AEL Enquiries 2881 8888
MTR Enquiries 2881 8888
Guangzhou
Lok Ma Chau
Lo Wu
Sheung Shui
Fanling
Tai Wo
Tai Po Market
Tolo Harbour
NEW TERRITORIES
Chek Lap Kok
AsiaWorld Expo
Airport
Tsing Yi
Tung Chung
Lantau
0
5km
University
Fo Tan
Racecourse
Sha Tin
Tai Wai
Airport
Tung Chung (see inset above)
Tsuen Wan West
Tsuen Wan
Tai Wo Hau
Kwai Hing
Kwai Fong
Tsing Yi
Lai King
Lai Chi Kok
Mei Foo
Cheung Sha Wan
Nam Cheong
Sham Shui Po
KOWLOON
Lok Fu
Wong Tai Sin
Diamond Hill
Choi Hung
Kowloon Tong
Shek Kip Mei
Kowloon Bay
Po Lam
Prince Edward
Mongkok East
Ngau Tau Kok
Hang Hau
Mongkok
Kwun Tong
Tseung Kwan O
Olympic
Yau Ma Tei
Kowloon
Jordan
Lam Tin
Hung Hom
Yau Tong
Tiu Keng Leng
Tsim Sha Tsui
East Tsim Sha Tsui
North Point
Quarry Bay
Hong Kong
Sheung Wan
Fortress Hill
Tai Koo
Central
Tin Hau
Sai Wan Ho
Admiralty
Wan Chai
Causeway Bay
Shau Kei Wan
Heng Fa Chuen
HONG KONG ISLAND
Chai Wan
N

for mainland tourists and won't speak English, making it difficult to book in advance. There is more space available in Macau though, so you do generally get more for your money but prices often shoot up at weekends.

## FOOD AND DRINK

As one of the great culinary capitals of the world, Hong Kong boasts not only a superb native cuisine – Cantonese – but also perhaps the widest range of international restaurants of any city outside Europe or North America. This is due in part to the cosmopolitan nature of the population, but perhaps more importantly, to the incredible seriousness attached to dining by the local Chinese. In Macau, the territory's native cuisine, Macanese food, is a tempting blend of Portuguese and Asian. In both Hong Kong and Macau, the **water** is fit for drinking.

### Hong Kong

As well as the joys of *dim sum* – a Hong Kong speciality meaning "little eats" – the city offers the full gamut of Chinese regional cuisines, from Beijing to Shanghai to Szechuan (Sichuan), and many smaller localities. It also offers excellent Indian and Malaysian curry houses, Japanese sushi bars, Vietnamese restaurants, British pub-style food and numerous cheap **street stalls** (*dai pai dongs*), which are often the best value for money of all. However, the stalls are becoming rarer as the government cracks down on outdoor canteens, refusing to issue or renew licences. You'll also find the local Chinese fast-food chains, *Café de Coral* and *Fairwood*, alongside *McDonald's*, *Pizza Hut* and *KFC*. The choice is seemingly limitless, and all budgets are catered for. English or picture **menus** are widely available. Nearly all non-fast food restaurants will add a ten percent **service charge** to your bill.

The kind of **snacks** you'll find at the *dai pai dongs*, or street stalls, and many indoor food halls and canteens (called *cha chan tengs*), include fish, beef and pork balls, stuffed buns, grilled chicken wings, spiced noodles, fresh and dried squid, spring rolls, *congee* (rice porridge served with an oily, doughnut-type stick), cooked intestines, tofu pudding and various sweets. Some *dai pai dongs* have simple tables and chairs and serve slightly more elaborate food, such as seafood, mixed rice and noodle dishes, stews and soups, and bottled beer. A large meal here will cost at most HK$55–65.

The most common Chinese food in Hong Kong is **Cantonese**, from China's southern Guangdong province. Dishes consist of extremely fresh food, quickly cooked and only lightly seasoned. Popular ingredients are fruit and vegetables, fish and shellfish, though the cuisine is also known for its more unusual ingredients – things like fish maw and chicken's feet. Cantonese restaurants also have the best selection of **dim sum**, a late breakfast or midday meal consisting of small flavoured buns, dumplings and pancakes, washed down with copious amounts of tea (see p.153 for a list of the most common dishes). In the more traditional *dim sum* restaurants, the food is wheeled in trolleys through the restaurant: they'll come to your table and you select what you want. Most dishes cost the same, around HK$25–45 each, and you'll find it hard to spend more than HK$120 a head. Restaurants that specialize in *dim sum* open early in the morning, from around 7am, and serve right through lunch up until around 5pm; many regular Cantonese restaurants also serve *dim sum*, usually 10–11am until 3pm. It's best to go in a group so that you can order a number of items to share.

**Beijing** food is heavier than Cantonese cooking, based around a solid diet of wheat and millet buns, noodles, pancakes and dumplings, accompanied by the savoury tastes of dark soy sauce and bean paste, white onions and cabbage. Mongol and Muslim influences include hotpots and grilled roast meats. Combined with exotic items imported by foreign merchants, these rather basic ingredients were turned into sophisticated marvels such as Peking duck.

**Shanghai** cuisine is characterized by little, delicate forms and light, fresh, sweet flavours, sometimes to the point of becoming precious – tiny meatballs are steamed in a rice coating and called "pearls" for example.

**Szechuan** food is the antithesis of Shanghai cuisine. There's a heavy use of chillies and pungent, constructed flavours using dried orange peel, aniseed, ginger and spring onions. The cooking methods themselves rely on unusual techniques, such as dry frying and smoking.

In most Chinese restaurants, the usual **drink** with your meal is **jasmine tea**, often brought to your table as a matter of course. **Beer** is also popular. All restaurants are non-smoking.

Drinking in bars is mainly an expat pursuit, and is ludicrously expensive outside of Happy Hour, which usually only lasts until 8 or 9pm. The main drinks are bottled lagers, including Chinese Tsingtao and fancy cocktails. Bars are usually open till 2 or 3am, and will become non-smoking in 2009.

### Macau

The Portuguese elements of **Macanese food** include fresh bread, cheap imported wine and good coffee, as well as an array of dishes ranging from *caldo verde* (vegetable soup) to *bacalhau* (dried salted cod). *Bacalhau* forms the base for several tasty dishes, which can come baked, grilled, casseroled or poached. There's also the Brazilian *feijoadas*, a heavy stew with beans, pork, sausages, cabbage and potatoes. One of Macau's most interesting Portuguese colonial dishes is **African chicken**, a concoction of Goan and east African influences, comprising chicken grilled with peppers and spices. Macau is also justly acknowledged for the exceptional quality of its sweet, flaky custard tarts or *natas*. Straightforward **Cantonese restaurants**, often serving *dim sum* for breakfast and lunch, are also plentiful.

Most restaurants in Macau don't open as late as they do in Hong Kong – although bars do. If you want to eat later than 10pm, you'll probably end up either in a hotel (many of which have 24-hour coffee bars that also serve snacks) or in the new bar/restaurant area, the NAPE (Novos Aterros do Porto Exterior). Costs, however, are nearly always lower than across the water, with bills even in smart venues usually not exceeding MOP$150–250 per head.

Drinking here is not quite as expensive as in Hong Kong, but not far off. Most of it takes place in the casinos, and bars can often feel very empty even at weekends, though they stay open till late.

## CULTURE AND ETIQUETTE

Generally speaking, Hong Kong and Macau people are not as concerned as other Asian cultures about covering the skin – girls often wear skirts as short as those in the West. Having said that, however, don't think of **bathing topless** on any of Hong Kong's beaches: you'll draw a lot of attention to yourself, offend some people and, in any case, it's illegal. In general, Hong Kong residents mind their own business, and although they may come across as unfriendly compared to other Asian countries, it also means you very rarely get hassled (Nathan Road being the exception). However, if you're struggling to order food, local residents will often step in and translate for you.

## SPORTS AND ACTIVITIES

Hong Kong residents in particular are keen sporting spectators. **Horse-racing**, inseparable from gambling and therefore illegal in China, is a national pastime, and there are two racecourses in the territory with weekly meets during the season (see p.159). The other huge sporting draw is the **Rugby Sevens**, which takes place over three days at the end of March. As the name implies, teams have seven players instead of fifteen, and this international tournament has become a major fixture in Hong Kong's calendar.

In spite of its image as little more than a city-state, Hong Kong offers some amazing opportunities for **outdoor activities**, from hillwalking to scuba diving. Just an hour's ferry-ride away from the city, you can spend an entire day climbing mountains on well-maintained paths without seeing a single other person. The island of Cheung Chau offers great windsurfing. For anyone seeking more extreme activities, the Macau Tower offers the highest commercial **bungy** platform in the world (see p.180).

## COMMUNICATIONS

From Hong Kong, **airmail** takes three days to a week to reach Britain or North America. Letters sent **poste restante** will arrive at the GPO building in Central (see p.176). To send parcels, turn up at the post office with the goods you want to send and the staff will help you pack them. You can buy boxes, paper and tape at the post office. You'll also need to fill out a customs declaration form. Parcels go by surface mail unless you specify otherwise. **Airmail** sent from **Macau** to Europe and North America takes between five days and a week to arrive. **Poste restante** is delivered to Macau's main post office.

**Local calls** from private phones in **Hong Kong** are free; most shops and restaurants will let you use theirs for nothing. There are no area codes. Public **phones** usually cost HK$1 for five minutes, and every pay and cardphone has instructions in English. **Phone cards** come in units of HK$50, HK$100, HK$200 and HK$300, and are available from PCCW Service Centres, tourist offices and convenience stores such as 7-11 and Circle K. You can make **international calls** from International Direct Dialling (IDD) phones or one of the several **PCCW Service Centres** in the territory. Collect or reverse-charge calls and home-direct calls can be made free of charge from these centres, which also offer fax services. To phone abroad from Hong Kong, dial ⓣ001 + IDD country code + area code minus first 0 + subscriber number. For directory enquiries in English, call ⓣ1081. Hong Kong SIM cards can be bought for less than HK$50 and calls from mobiles are cheap.

In Macau, local calls are free from **private phones**, MOP$1 from payphones. Cardphones work with CTM cards, issued by the Macau State Telecommunication Company, on sale in hotels or at the back of the main post office in Largo do Senado (open 24hr), where you can also make direct calls. **Macau phone numbers** have no area codes: just dial the number given. Instructions on most phones are in English as well as Portuguese. For **calls to Hong Kong**, dial ⓣ01 followed by the eight-digit number. You can make **international calls** from public phones or from the telephone office at the back of the main post office. Dial ⓣ00 + IDD country code + area code minus first 0 + subscriber number. There's also a **Home Direct** service (*Pais Directo*), which gives you access to an operator in the country you're calling. Vending machines at the ferry terminal sell SIM cards from MOP$50.

## HONG KONG AND MACAU ON THE NET

**www.discoverhongkong.com** – The Hong Kong Tourist Board's website is packed with information, and most of their leaflets can be downloaded.
**www.macautourism.gov.mo** – Not quite as good as the Hong Kong one but still very handy. It also features a list of guesthouses.
**www.hkoutdoors.com** – For an insight into Hong Kong's hidden side, as well as practical information.

**Internet access** is available in Hong Kong at the Hong Kong Central Library; at most branches of the *Pacific Coffee Company* and other internet cafés (see p.176); and at most hostels. In Macau, internet access is available free at the Macau Business Tourism Centre on Largo do Senado, but is not usually offered by budget hotels.

## CRIME AND SAFETY

You're very unlikely to encounter any trouble in Hong Kong or Macau. The main thing to look out for is **pickpockets**: it's best to keep money and wallets in inside pockets, carry handbags around your neck and be careful when getting on and off packed buses and trains. The only other problems you might encounter are in strip bars where the emphasis is on buying very expensive drinks for the "girls": if you get drunk and refuse or are unable to pay, the bar heavies will soon make sure you find your wallet.

There is a fairly heavy **police** street presence in Hong Kong – they are on the look-out for illegal immigrants largely from the mainland – and everyone is required to carry some form of **identification** at all times: for a traveller this means your passport. Most officers can speak some English, and will quickly radio help for you if they can't understand and you have a major problem. It is very unwise to have anything to do with **drugs** of any description.

## EMERGENCY NUMBERS

In both Hong Kong and Macau, dial ⓣ999 for fire, police and ambulance.

## MEDICAL CARE AND EMERGENCIES

**Pharmacies** (daily 9am–6pm) can help with minor injuries or ailments and will prescribe basic medicines. Contraceptives and antibiotics are also available over the counter. All pharmacies are registered and, in Hong Kong at least, are usually staffed by English-speakers.

For a **doctor in Hong Kong**, look in the local phone directories' *Yellow Pages* under "Physicians and Surgeons". You'll have to pay for a consultation and any medicines that are prescribed; be sure to get a receipt so that you can make an insurance claim when you get home. **Hospital** treatment is very expensive, making it important to have some form of medical insurance. Emergency room visits will also cost you; fifteen public hospitals have 24-hour casualty departments. See p.176 for hospital addresses. Note that both doctors and **dentists** are known as "doctor" in Hong Kong.

If you need a **doctor** in Macau, go straight to the 24-hour emergency department at the public Centro Hospitalar Conde São Januário, or to the private Hospital Kiang Wu (see p.188). Casualty visits cost around MOP$200. As in Hong Kong, you'll have to pay for a consultation and any medicines; get a receipt for insurance purposes.

## MONEY AND BANKS

Hong Kong's unit of **currency** is the Hong Kong dollar (HK$), divided into one hundred cents. Bank notes are issued by the Hong Kong and Shanghai Banking Corporation (HSBC), the Standard Chartered Bank and the Bank of China, and are of slightly different design and size, but they're all interchangeable. **Notes** come in denominations of HK$10, HK$20, HK$50, HK$100, HK$500 and HK$1000; there's a nickel-and-bronze HK$10 coin; silver coins come as HK$1, HK$2 and HK$5; and bronze coins as 10c, 20c and 50c. At the time of writing, the exchange rate was around HK$14 to the **pound sterling**, and it's pegged at HK$7.78 to the US dollar. There's no black market and money, in any amount, can be freely taken in and out of the territory. All major **credit cards** are accepted in Hong Kong, but watch out for the three- to five-percent commission that lots of travel agencies and shops try to add to the price. **ATM machines** will take American Express, MasterCard and Visa, as well as debit cards.

The unit of **currency** in Macau is the pataca (abbreviated to MOP$ in this book; often seen as M$, MOP or ptca), which is in turn broken down into 100 avos. **Notes** come in denominations of MOP$20, 50, 100, 500 and 1000ptca; **coins** come as 10, 20 and 50 avos, and 1, 5 and 10ptca. The pataca is worth fractionally less than the HK dollar. At the time of writing, the **exchange rate** was £1 = 15ptca and US$1 = 7.7ptca. HK dollars are freely accepted as currency in Macau, and a lot of visitors from Hong Kong don't bother changing money at all. All the **major credit cards** are accepted in the larger hotels, but most guesthouses and restaurants want cash. If you need to get money, most ATMs in the centre of town will accept foreign credit cards. If you want to get money sent from overseas, you'd be better off doing it in Hong Kong, where they are more efficient and experienced.

## OPENING HOURS

In Hong Kong, **offices** are open Monday–Friday 9am–5pm, and some open Saturday 9am–1pm; **shops**, daily 10am–7/8pm, though later in tourist areas. **Banks** are open Monday–Friday 9am–4.30pm, Saturday 9am–12.30pm. **Post office** opening hours are Monday–Friday 9.30am–5pm, Saturday 9.30am–1pm (the main post offices in Central and Tsim Sha Tsui are also open 8am–6pm on Sat and 9am–2pm on Sun). All government offices close on public holidays and some religious festivals.

In Macau, government **offices** open Monday–Friday 9am–1pm and 3–5/5.30pm, Saturday 8.30/9am–1pm. **Shops** and businesses are usually open for longer and don't close for lunch. **Banks** generally open Monday to Friday from 9am until 4 or 4.30pm, but close by 12.30pm on Saturdays. All government offices close on public holidays and some religious festivals.

### Public holidays

Hong Kong's public holidays are changing as China jettisons the old colonial holidays in favour of its own celebrations. For now, the following public holidays are observed. Sundays are also classed as public holidays.

Macau does not observe the HKSAR Establishment Day.

**January 1** New Year
**January/February** Chinese New Year (three days' holiday)
**March/April** Easter (holidays on Good Friday, Easter Saturday and Easter Monday)
**April** Ching Ming Festival
**May 1** Labour Day
**May** Buddha's Birthday
**June** Tuen Ng (Dragon Boat) Festival
**July 1** HKSAR Establishment Day
**September** Mid-Autumn Festival
**October 1** Chinese National Day

## CANTONESE

Cantonese is the national language of Hong Kong, with Mandarin a fast-growing second. English is widely spoken among the well educated and many in the tourist trade (although not many taxi drivers), otherwise, people speak only basic English. The vast majority of people in Macau speak Cantonese and many also speak Portuguese and English.

Cantonese is a tonal language, which means that the tone a speaker gives to a word will determine its meaning. As a simple two-letter word can have up to nine different meanings depending on the pitch of the voice, the romanized word is really only an approximation of the Chinese sound.

### Pronunciation

oy as in boy
ai as in fine
i as in see
er as in urn
o as in pot
ow as in now
oe as in oh
or as in law

### Words and phrases

| | |
|---|---|
| Good morning | *joe sun* |
| Hello/how are you? | *lay hoe ma?* |
| Thank you/excuse me | *m goy* |
| Goodnight | *joe tow* |
| Goodbye | *joy geen* |
| I'm sorry | *doy m joot* |
| Can you speak English? | *lay sik m sik gong ying man?* |
| Yes | *yow* |
| No | *mo* |
| I don't understand | *ngor m ming bat* |
| What is your name? | *lay gew mut yeh meng?* |
| My name is... | *ngor gew...* |
| I am from England /America | *ngor hai ying/ may gwok yan* |
| Where is this place? (while pointing to the place name or map) | *ching mun, leedi day fong hai been do ah?* |
| Train | *for chair* |
| Bus | *ba-see* |
| Ferry | *do lun schoon* |
| Taxi | *dik-see* |
| Airport | *fay gay cherng* |
| Hotel | *jow deem* |
| Hostel | *loy gwun* |
| Restaurant | *charn Teng* |
| Toilets | *chee saw* |
| Police | *ging chat* |

### Numbers

The number two changes when asking for two of something – **lerng wei** (a table for two) – or stating something other than counting – **lerng mun** (two dollars).

| | |
|---|---|
| 1 | *yat* |
| 2 | *yee* |
| 3 | *saam* |
| 4 | *say* |
| 5 | *mm* |
| 6 | *lok* |
| 7 | *chat* |
| 8 | *bat* |
| 9 | *gow* |
| 10 | *sap* |
| 11, 12, 13, etc | *sap yat, sap yee, sap saam* |
| 20, 21, 22, 23, etc | *yee sap, yee sap yee, yee sap saam* |
| 30, 40, 50, etc | *saam sap, say sap, mm sap* |
| 100 | *yat bat* |
| 1000 | *yat cheen* |

### Food and drinks glossary

#### Ordering food

| | |
|---|---|
| *Mai daan* | Bill/check |
| *Fai tzee* | Chopsticks |
| *La sow ho choy* | House speciality |
| *Gay dor cheen?* | How much is that? |
| *Ngor hi fut gow toe/ngor tzee sik soe* | I'm a Buddhist/ vegetarian |

| | |
|---|---|
| *Ngor serng yew...* | I would like... |
| *Choy daan/toe choy/Ying man choy daan* | Main/set menu/ English menu |

**Drinks**

| | |
|---|---|
| *Beh tsow* | Beer |
| *Ga fay* | Coffee |
| *Char* | Tea |
| *Kong tuen soy* | Mineral water |
| *Poe toe tsow* | Wine |

**Staple foods**

| | |
|---|---|
| *Sun jeem* | Bamboo shoots |
| *Dow* | Beans |
| *Dow ah* | Bean sprouts |
| *Ow yok* | Beef |
| *Hat dow see* | Black bean sauce |
| *Man tow* | Buns (plain) |
| *Bow tzee* | Buns (filled) |
| *Yew gaw* | Cashew nuts |
| *Gai* | Chicken |
| *Lar jew* | Chilli |
| *Hi* | Crab |
| *Aap* | Duck |
| *Suen yue* | Eel |
| *Yue* | Fish |
| *Dai suen* | Garlic |
| *Gerng* | Ginger |
| *Lok yip soe choy* | Green vegetables |
| *Leen sum* | Lotus root |
| *Mei jing* | MSG |
| *Mor goo* | Mushrooms |
| *Meen tew* | Noodles |
| *Taan beng* | Pancake |
| *Far sun* | Peanut |
| *Jew yok* | Pork |
| *Toe dow* | Potato |
| *Ha* | Prawns |
| *Bak faan* | Rice (boiled) |
| *Chow faan* | Rice (fried) |
| *Jook* | Rice porridge congee |
| *Yeem* | Salt |
| *Seh yok* | Snake |
| *Dow foo* | Tofu |
| *Daan chow faan* | Egg fried rice |
| *Law bat yue daan tong* | Fish ball soup with white radish |
| *Mun yue* | Fish casserole |
| *Dai suen lar jew chow yok peen* | Fried shredded pork with garlic and chilli |
| *For war* | Hotpot |
| *Yok choon* | Kebab |
| *Tong meen* | Noodle soup |
| *Dai suen chow ha* | Prawn with garlic sauce |
| *How aap* | Roast duck |
| *Wong dow yok peen* | Sliced pork with yellow bean sauce |
| *Tong choe pai gwut* | Sweet and sour spare ribs |
| *Chek dow taan beng* | Sweet bean paste pancakes |
| *Wun dung tong* | Wonton soup |

**Vegetables and eggs**

| | |
|---|---|
| *Dai suen larjew chow ke tzee* | Aubergine with chilli and garlic sauce |
| *Dun herng goo fungus* | Braised mountain |
| *Dow foo soe choy* | Fried beancurd with vegetables |
| *Herng la ke tzee tew* | Spicy braised aubergine |
| *Soe choy tong* | Vegetable soup |

**Dim Sum (Yum Cha)**

| | |
|---|---|
| *Char sew bao* | Barbecue pork bun |
| *Hai yok ha* | Crab and coriander dumpling |
| *Daan tat* | Custard tart |
| *Zar meen beng goon* | Doughnut |
| *Faan sue woo gow* | Fried taro and mince dumpling |
| *Gow tzee* | Joazi steamed pork dumplings |
| *Leen yong goe* | Lotus paste bun |
| *Yuet beng* | Moon cake sweet bean paste in flaky pastry |
| *Sew mai* | Pork and prawn dumpling in ornate wrapping |
| *Ha peen* | Prawn crackers |
| *Ha gow* | Prawn dumpling |
| *Tzee ma ha* | Prawn paste on fried toast |
| *Wo teet* | Shanghai fried and vegetable dumpling |
| *Chun goon* | Spring roll |

**October** Chung Yeung Festival
**December 25 and 26** Christmas Day and the next working day
**Additional Macau public holidays**
**November 2** All Souls Day
**December 8** Feast of Immaculate Conception
**December 20** Macau SAR Establishment Day
**December 22** Winter Solstice

## FESTIVALS

With roots going back hundreds (even thousands) of years, many of Hong Kong's festivals are highly symbolic and are often a mixture of secular and religious displays and devotions. On these occasions, there are dances and Chinese opera performances at the temples, plenty of noise, and a series of offerings left in the temples – food and paper goods that are burned as gifts to the dead. The normal Chinese holidays are celebrated in Macau, plus some Catholic festivals introduced from Portugal, such as the procession of Our Lady of Fatima from São Domingos Church annually on May 13 (although this is no longer a public holiday).

As the Chinese use the lunar calendar and not the Gregorian calendar, many of the region's festivals fall on different days, even different months, from year to year; for exact details, contact the Hong Kong or Macau tourist offices (see p.169 and p.188).

**Chinese New Year** (Jan/Feb) The most important festival, celebrated in Hong Kong and Macau; the entire population takes time out to celebrate and there are spectacular firework displays over the harbour.
**Tin Hau Festival** (late April or May) Particular to Hong Kong in honour of the Goddess of Fishermen, when large seaborne festivities take place at Joss House Bay on Sai Kung Peninsula.
**Tai Chiu (Bun) Festival** (May) Held on Cheung Chau island.
**Tuen Ng (Dragon Boat) Festival** Early June. In Hong Kong, with races along the coast in long, narrow boats.
**Mid-Autumn Festival** September. Chinese festival, almost as popular as Chinese New Year, and celebrations are more public in Hong Kong and Macau.

# Hong Kong

The territory of **HONG KONG**, whose name means fragrant harbour, comprises an irregularly shaped peninsula abutting the Pearl River Delta to the west, and a number of offshore islands, which cover more than a thousand square kilometres in total. The southern part of the peninsula, known as **Kowloon**, and the island immediately south of it, **Hong Kong Island**, are the principal urban areas of Hong Kong. They were ceded to Britain "in perpetuity", but were returned to China at midnight on June 30, 1997. Since then, it has been renamed the **Hong Kong Special Administrative Region** (SAR) of the People's Republic of China.

The island of Hong Kong offers not only traces of the old colony – from English place names to ancient trams trundling along the shore – but also superb modern architecture and futuristic cityscapes, as well as plentiful opportunities for **hiking** and bathing on the **beaches** of its southern shore. Kowloon, in particular its southernmost tip, **Tsim Sha Tsui**, boasts a countless number of shops, offering a greater variety of goods per square kilometre than anywhere in the world, and is also the budget accommodation centre of Hong Kong. The **offshore islands**, including **Lamma** and **Lantau**, are well worth a visit for their fresh fish restaurants, scenery and tranquillity.

## HONG KONG ISLAND

As the oldest colonized part of Hong Kong, its administrative and business centre and site of some of the most expensive real estate in the world, **Hong Kong Island** is, in every sense, the heart of the whole territory. Despite its size, just 15km from east to west and 11km from north to south, the island encompasses the best the territory has to offer in one heady hit: lavish temples to consumer excess, the vivid sights and smells of a Chinese wet market and (away from the north shore's steel and concrete mountains) surprising expanses of sandy beach and forested nature reserves.

### What to see and do

On the northern shore of Hong Kong Island, overlooking Victoria Harbour and Kowloon on the mainland opposite, lies the territory's major financial and commercial quarter, known as **Central**. East of Central are **Wan Chai** and lively **Causeway Bay**, while in the opposite direction the **Western District** is rather older and more traditional in character. Towering over the city, **The Peak** is a highlight of any trip to the city, offering magnificent views.

On its south side, Hong Kong Island straggles into the sea in a series of dangling peninsulas and inlets. The atmosphere is far quieter here than on the north shore. You'll find not only separate towns such as **Aberdeen** and **Stanley** with a flavour of their own, but also beaches, such as that at **Repulse Bay**, and much farther east, at the remote and pretty village of **Shek O**. Buses are plentiful to all destinations on the southern shore, and Aberdeen is linked to Central by a tunnel under The Peak. Nowhere is more than an hour from Central.

#### Central

Central extends out from the Star Ferry Pier a few hundred metres in all directions. Easily recognizable from the tramlines that run up and down here, Des Voeux Road used to mark Hong Kong's seafront before the days of reclamation. East along **Des Voeux Road**, you'll find Statue Square on your left towards the shore, and, immediately south, the magnificently hi-tech, "inside-out" **Hong Kong and Shanghai Bank** building, designed by Sir Norman

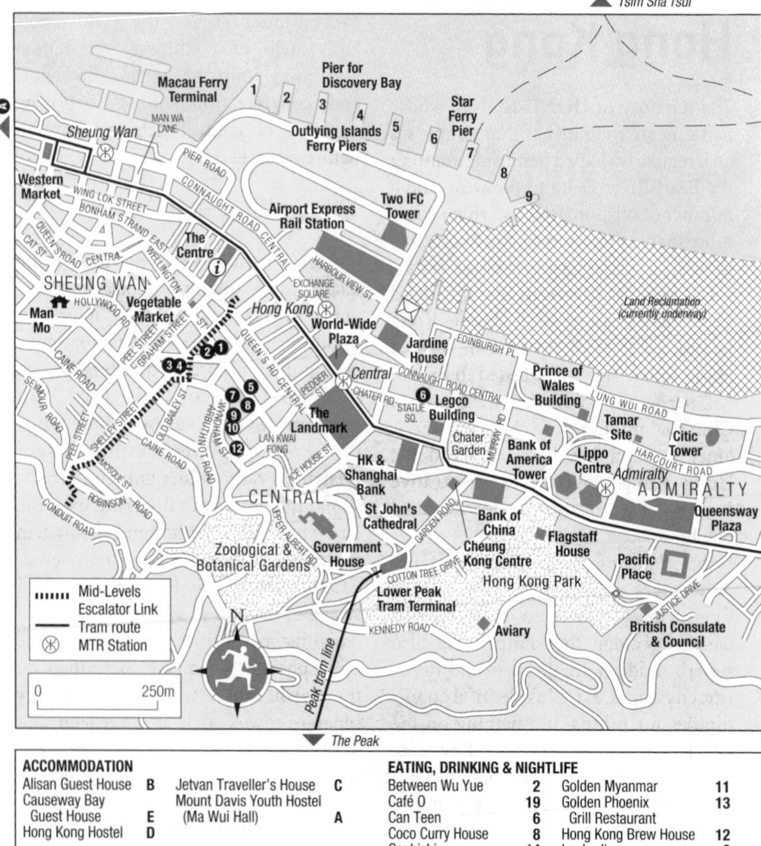


| ACCOMMODATION | | | |
|---|---|---|---|
| Alisan Guest House | B | Jetvan Traveller's House | C |
| Causeway Bay Guest House | E | Mount Davis Youth Hostel (Ma Wui Hall) | A |
| Hong Kong Hostel | D | | |

| EATING, DRINKING & NIGHTLIFE | | | |
|---|---|---|---|
| Between Wu Yue | 2 | Golden Myanmar | 11 |
| Café O | 19 | Golden Phoenix Grill Restaurant | 13 |
| Can Teen | 6 | Hong Kong Brew House | 12 |
| Coco Curry House | 8 | Le Jardin | 9 |
| Genbishi | 14 | | |

Foster – at the time of construction one of the most expensive office blocks ever built. A few hundred metres east is the 300m-high blue glass geometric shard of the **Bank of China** tower, which ignores all the normal feng shui sensitivities and

## CENTRAL'S ELEVATED WALKWAYS

Inland from the shore, the main west–east roads are Connaught Road, Des Voeux Road and Queen's Road respectively, though pedestrians are better off concentrating on the extensive system of **elevated walkways**. Coming off the Star Ferry upper deck will lead you straight into the walkways. First off to your right is the entrance to the **IFC Mall**, while carrying straight on takes you inland. **Hong Kong MTR** station is under the IFC Mall; **Central station** is reached by heading in a straight line then dropping down to Pedder Street just before Worldwide Plaza, while **Exchange Square**'s three marble-and-tinted-glass towers sit atop the **Bus Station**. A further branch of the elevated walkway runs northwest from here, parallel with the shore and along the northern edge of Connaught Road all the way to the Macau Ferry Terminal and Sheung Wan MTR.

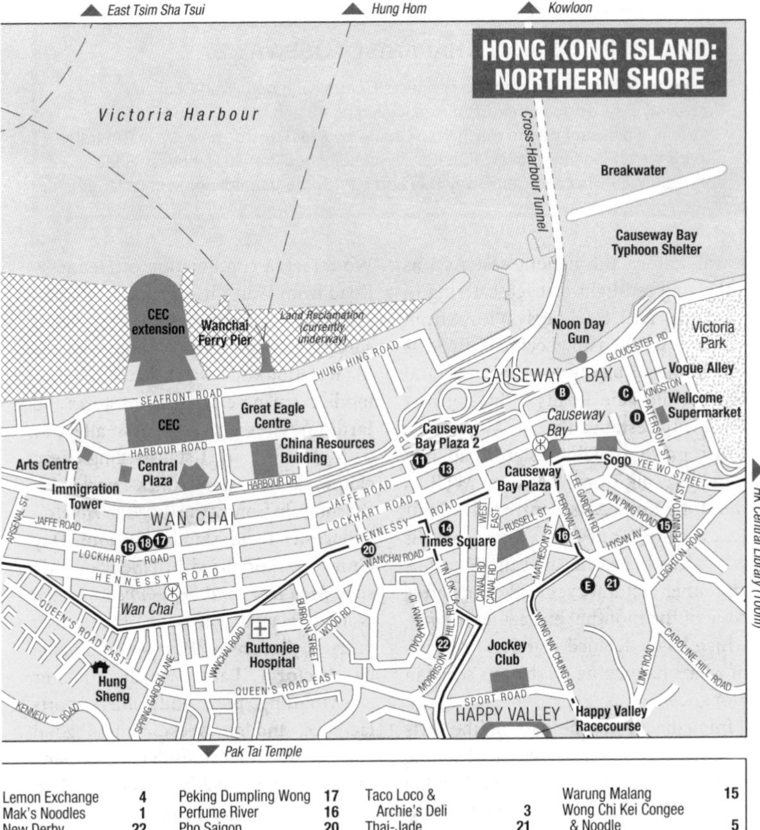


| | | | | | | | |
|---|---|---|---|---|---|---|---|
| Lemon Exchange | 4 | Peking Dumpling Wong | 17 | Taco Loco & Archie's Deli | 3 | Warung Malang | 15 |
| Mak's Noodles | 1 | Perfume River | 16 | Thai-Jade | 21 | Wong Chi Kei Congee & Noodle | 5 |
| New Derby | 22 | Pho Saigon | 20 | Tsim Chai Kee Noodles | 2 | | |
| Pearl Vietnamese Restaurant | 7 | Sabah | 18 | Tsui Wah Restaurant | 5 | | |
| | | Schnurrbart | 10 | | | | |

is accordingly feared and disliked in Hong Kong.

South of Queen's Road the land begins to slope seriously upwards. The **Mid-Levels Escalator Link** is a giant series of escalators that runs 800m straight up the hill (downwards only 6am–10am; upwards 10.20am–midnight) servicing the expensive **Mid-Levels** residential area, as well as the thriving restaurant district of **SoHo**. Nearby **Lan Kwai Fong** is another eating and drinking area. A short but steep walk away are the **Hong Kong Zoological and Botanical Gardens** (daily 6am–10pm; free), a pleasant refuge though nothing spectacular. From the eastern exit of the Botanical Gardens, a ten-minute walk along Garden Road brings you to the rather more impressive **Hong Kong Park** (daily 6am–11pm; free); there's also an entrance just to the east of the Lower Peak Tram Terminal (see p.160), and from the north, on Supreme Court Road – follow signs from Admiralty MTR Station, through the Pacific Place shopping mall. The highlight here is the wonderful **Edward Youde Aviary** (daily 9am–5pm; free), where you find yourself in a cool, shady rainforest setting.

## Wan Chai

In the 1950s and 1960s, **Wan Chai** – the area stretching east of Central

### TRANSPORT TO WAN CHAI AND CAUSEWAY BAY

The MTR train route and tramline connects Central with both Wan Chai and Causeway Bay, as do numerous buses, including #2 and #111. If you're in Tsim Sha Tsui, a pleasant way to reach Wan Chai is by Star Ferry or, if you're in Central, aboard the endearingly rickety (but non-air-conditioned) trams. Hennessy Road connects Wan Chai and Causeway Bay and carries the tram for some of its length.

– was known throughout east Asia as a thriving red-light district, catering in particular for US soldiers on leave from Korea and Vietnam. Lockhart Road is still home to plenty of strip clubs and **bars**, while Jaffe Road to the north is lined with **restaurants**.

Just north of Gloucester Road, ten minutes' walk from Wan Chai MTR, is the **Hong Kong Arts Centre** (2 Harbour Road, daily 10am–8pm; free) which is worth visiting for its art galleries, films and other cultural events. Pick up a free copy of the monthly magazine *Artslink*, which has a detailed diary and reviews of what's happening on the arts scene in Hong Kong.

Immediately to the east of the Arts Centre stands a vast set of gleaming modern buildings that have changed the face of Wan Chai beyond all recognition. The **Hong Kong Convention and Exhibition Centre (CEC)** (1 Expo Drive, opening hours vary according to events) on the seafront is probably the biggest and best of its kind in Asia. When there are no events going on, you can visit the centre's extraordinary interior. The centre is at the end of a seafront promenade to Causeway Bay, which will eventually extend the other way to the Star Ferry but is still under construction.

## Causeway Bay

East of Wan Chai, **Causeway Bay** is a lively district packed with shops, restaurants and, on weekends, seemingly most of Hong Kong's seven million citizens. It's centred between the eastern end of Lockhart Road and the western edge of Victoria Park. Trams run here along Yee Wo Street, a continuation of Hennessy Road from Wan Chai.

The main activity in Causeway Bay is shopping. Within a few minutes of the MTR station you'll find a couple of ultra-modern Japanese department stores and **Jardine's Crescent**, a narrow alleyway packed with market stalls selling cheap clothes, jewellery and knick-knacks. On the shore, in front of the *Excelsior Hotel* on Gloucester Road, stands the **Noon Day Gun** – immortalized in Noel Coward's song *Mad Dogs and Englishmen* – which is fired every day at noon. The eastern part of Causeway Bay is dominated by **Victoria Park**, which contains a swimming pool and other sports facilities, and on weekdays is a good place to watch local residents practising their t'ai chi. On public holidays such as Chinese New Year there are fairs here, and it's a good place to wander with celebrating locals.

Heading inland from Hennessy Road, on the corner of Matheson and Russell streets, is Causeway Bay's most famous shopping plaza, the half-moon shaped **Times Square**, fronted by a huge video screen, a packed courtyard, thirteen floors of shops and restaurants and a cinema. Just to the west of Times Square lies **Bowrington Road Market** and the streets of market stalls surrounding it, worth dropping in on in the morning (if you're not squeamish) to see poultry, fish and meat being hacked about on a huge scale.

## Happy Valley

The low-lying area extending inland from the shore south of Wan Chai and

**TREAT YOURSELF**

Hong Kong's blend of East and West is in evidence everywhere, and what better way to celebrate it than with a multicultural **afternoon tea**? Most of the smart hotels offer a variation on the theme, but the best of all can be found at the *JW Marriott* at Pacific Place. For HK$220 (including service charge) you'll feast on an all-you-can-eat buffet of *dim sum*, cucumber sandwiches, cakes and waffles, while watching the world go by through floor-to-ceiling windows with harbour views. Sit back and enjoy the luxury!

Causeway Bay is known as Happy Valley, and means only one thing for the people of Hong Kong: horseracing, or more precisely, gambling. The **Happy Valley Racecourse**, which dates back to 1846, was for most of Hong Kong's history the only one in the territory. A night at the races is a quintessential, and extremely cheap Hong Kong experience, as long as you don't gamble away your budget. The racing season runs from September until June, with meetings once or twice a week Entrance to the public enclosure is just HK$10. There's a racing museum (Tues–Sun 10am–5pm, race days 10am–12.30pm; free), and HKTB (see p.169) runs a "Come Horse-racing Tour" (from HK$620), which includes transport to and from the track, entry to the Members' Enclosure and a buffet meal at the official Jockey Club – plus a HK$30 betting voucher. Happy Valley can be reached from Central or Causeway Bay on a spur of the tramline, or on bus #1 from Central.

### Western District

Almost entirely Chinese-inhabited, Western District's crowded residential streets and traditional shops form a striking contrast to Central. **Sheung Wan**, immediately adjacent to Central, spreads south up the hill from the seafront at the modern Shun Tak Centre, which houses the Macau Ferry Terminal and the Sheung Wan MTR Station. The Shun Tak Centre is a fifteen-minute walk along the elevated walkway from Exchange Square in Central, though you'll get more flavour of the district by following the tramlines along Des Voeux Road. Head south to **Bonham Strand East** for an intriguing range of peculiar specialist shops such as seafood wholesalers, piled high, rather pathetically, with mounds of dried seahorses and shark fins.

Running from part-way up the Mid-Levels escalator to the Western District is **Hollywood Road**. The big interest here is the array of **antique and curio shops**. The antique shops extend into the small alley, Upper Lascar Row, commonly known as **Cat Street**, where you'll find wall-to-wall curiosity stalls – a good hunting ground for portable, kitschy Chinese keepsakes. Nearby **Ladder Street**, which runs north–south across Hollywood Road, is a relic from the nineteenth century when a number of such stepped streets existed to help sedan-chair carriers get their loads up the steep hillsides. On Hollywood Road, adjacent to Ladder Street, the 150-year-old **Man Mo Temple** (daily 7am–5pm) is one of the most atmospheric small temples in Hong Kong.

### The Peak

The uppermost levels of the 552-metre hill that towers over Central and Victoria Harbour have always been known as Victoria Peak (or simply "The Peak"), and, in colonial days, the area was populated by upper-class expats. Aside from its exclusive residential area, the Peak makes a good vantage point offering some extraordinary panoramic views over the city and harbour below, as well as some pleasant, leisurely walks.

The Peak Tram drops you at the terminal in the **Peak Tower**. This building and the **Peak Galleria** across the road are full of souvenir shops and

### GETTING TO THE PEAK

Half the fun of the Peak is the ascent on the **Peak Tram**, which climbs 373 vertical metres to the terminus in eight minutes. To find the Lower Peak Tram Terminal in Central, you can catch bus #15C (HK$4) from the Star Ferry. On foot, it's on Garden Road a little way up the hill from St John's Cathedral. The Peak Tram itself (daily 7am–midnight; HK$22 one-way, HK$33 return) runs every ten to fifteen minutes. You can also catch bus #15 (HK$9.20) to the Peak from just in front of the Star Ferry or from Exchange Square, which is a slower but still scenic route. Finally, minibus #1 (HK$8) runs from under the IFC building.

mainly pricey bars and restaurants, some with spectacular views. The Peak Tower charges HK$20 to access its viewing gallery, or you can buy a ticket that combines the tram and the terrace (HK$37 one-way, HK$48 return). Alternatively the Peak Galleria has a free terrace, where you can look out over the harbour on one side and green hills on the other. From the Peak Tower Tram Terminal area, Mount Austin Road leads up to the very top of The Peak, where you'll find the **Victoria Peak Garden**, formerly the site of the Governor's residence. Follow Harlech Road, due west of the terminal area, for a delightful rural stroll through trees; after half an hour the road runs into Lugard Road, which heads back towards the terminal around the northern rim of the Peak, giving magnificent views over Central and Kowloon.

An excellent way to descend the Peak is to **walk**, the simplest route being to follow the sign pointing to Hatton Road, from opposite the picnic area on Harlech Road. The walk is along a very clear path all the way through trees, eventually emerging after about 45 minutes in Mid-Levels, near the junction between Kotewall Road and Conduit Road. Catch bus #13 or minibus #3 from Kotewall Road to Central, or you can walk east for about 1km along Conduit Road until you reach the top end of the Mid-Levels Escalator (see p.157), and follow that down into Central (remember that after 10am it only runs uphill).

## Aberdeen

Situated on the quiet south side of Hong Kong Island, **Aberdeen** is the largest separate town on the island, with a population of more than sixty thousand, a dwindling minority of whom still live on **sampans** (small motorized boats) **and junks** in the narrow harbour that lies between the main island and the offshore island of Ap Lei Chau. The boat people who live here are following a tradition that certainly preceded the arrival of the British in Hong Kong, although their ancient way of life is now facing extinction. In the meantime, a time-honoured and enjoyable tourist activity in Aberdeen is to take a **sampan tour** around the harbour. From the bus stop, just head towards the ornamental park by the waterfront until you reach a sign advertising "Water Tours". On the way you will also be accosted by a swarm of unlicensed boat owners offering tours. The trip offers great photo opportunities of the old house-boats jammed together, complete with dogs, drying laundry and outdoor kitchens. Along the way, you'll also pass boat yards and floating restaurants, which are especially spectacular when lit up at night. To reach Aberdeen, catch **bus** #7 or #70 from Central, or #72 from Causeway Bay (30min). There's also a **boat** connection between here and nearby Lamma Island (see p.165).

## Ocean Park

**Ocean Park**, a gigantic theme and adventure park (daily 10am–6pm; summer

10am–11pm; HK$208 including all rides; www.oceanpark.com.hk), covers an entire peninsula east of Aberdeen. You can easily spend a day here, though in summer make sure you arrive early to avoid queues. The park houses an impressive collection of marine life, including sharks and jellyfish; new, hi-tech habitats for four giant pandas, which were a gift from China to celebrate ten years of rule. and a selection of aviaries, as well as roller coasters. The park also plays an active role in wildlife conservation and breeding. A huge expansion programme is underway, with plans to add killer whale shows, polar bears and a hotel, though the park will remain open right through to completion in 2010. A special **bus** service, the #629, runs from Central Star Ferry Pier (9.35am–10.55pm; HK$10.60) and from Admiralty MTR (9am–4pm; HK$10.60) to Ocean Park. Otherwise, any bus going through the Aberdeen Tunnel will do, including buses #70, #75, #90, #97 and #M590 from Exchange Square in Central; #72, #92, #96 and #592 from Causeway Bay; #973 from Tsim Sha Tsui. Get off immediately after the Aberdeen Tunnel and follow the signs.

### Repulse Bay and beyond

Popular with locals, but rather packed and polluted, are the beaches of **Deep Water Bay** and **Repulse Bay** just east of Ocean Park. The bay's unusual name may stem from the British fleet's repulsion of pirates there in 1841. Repulse Bay has a **Tin Hau Temple** (dedicated to the goddess of the sea), surrounded by a wide variety of statues and a longevity bridge, the crossing of which is said to add three days to your life. South of Repulse Bay, you'll find the more secluded but narrower beaches of **Middle Bay** and **South Bay**, fifteen and thirty minutes' walk respectively farther along the coast. You can reach Repulse Bay on **buses** #6, #61, #66 or #260 from Central, minibus #40 from Causeway Bay, or on bus #973 from Tsim Sha Tsui East. Between Aberdeen (to the west) and Stanley (to the east) there are frequent buses that pass all of the bays mentioned above.

### Stanley

Straddling the neck of Hong Kong's southernmost peninsula, **Stanley** is a moderately attractive residential village, with large numbers of pubs and restaurants catering to expatriates. A little way to the north of the bus stop is **Stanley Beach**, which has a watersports centre where you can hire kayaks (8.30am–5pm, closed Wed; from HK$16 per hour). Walk downhill from the bus stop and you'll soon find **Stanley Market**, selling cheap clothes and tourist souvenirs. To the west, on Stanley Main Road, there are vast numbers of seafront restaurants, bars and burger kiosks, the cheapest of which are in the Waterfront Mart. If you continue walking west from the restaurants, you'll come to another **Tin Hau Temple**, built in 1767. Inside, there's a large, blackened tiger skin, the remains of an animal shot near here in 1942 – a poignant symbol of how the area has changed. In a direct feng shui-friendly line from the temple to the shore is **Murray House**, built in 1843 for the British Army and originally sited in Central. Murray House was recently rebuilt in Stanley (having been knocked down to make way for the Bank of China) using salvaged stonework and elements from other historical buildings. Today, it houses a few decent restaurants offering alfresco dining with pleasant sea views. All the buses mentioned going to Repulse Bay also go to Stanley, and you can take minibus #52 between Aberdeen and Stanley.

### Shek O

In the far east of the island, **Shek O** is Hong Kong's most remote and exclusive settlement – house numbers on Shek O Road refer not to location but to when the owner became a member of the golf club and therefore allowed to build here. There's a strong surf pounding the wide, white **beach** and, during the week, it's more or less deserted. The beach is just a few minutes' walk east from the bus stop, beyond a small roundabout. For lunch, stop at the excellent *Chinese-Thai* restaurant. on the left just before the roundabout. If you take the small lane on the left that runs right through the restaurant area, you'll pass first the local temple and then a variety of shops and stalls.

Reaching Shek O is one of the best things about it. You need to get to **Shau Kei Wan** on the northeastern shore of Hong Kong Island, either by tram or MTR. From the bus terminal outside the MTR station, catch bus #9 to Shek O, a great journey over hills (30min) during which you'll be able to spot first the sparkling waters of the Tai Tam Reservoir, then Stanley (far to the southwest) and finally Shek O itself, appearing down below.

Alternatively, jump off the bus at Cape Collinson, just after a tiny roundabout, and from there you can walk to Shek O along the **Dragon's Back**, possibly Hong Kong's most famous hike. Once off the bus head into Shek O Country Park, follow signs to Shek O Peak, and you're on the Hong Kong trail. The tourist office brochure *Discover Hong Kong Nature* has full details. The hike takes 2–3 hours and boasts spectacular views.

**Big Wave Bay**, a 15-minute walk from Shek O, offers windsurfing and plenty of shops hiring equipment.

## KOWLOON

A four-kilometre strip of the mainland grabbed by the British in 1860 to add to their offshore island, **Kowloon** was part of the territory ceded to Britain "in perpetuity" and was accordingly developed with gusto and confidence. With the help of land reclamation and the diminishing significance of the border between Kowloon and the New Territories at Boundary Street, Kowloon has, over the years, just about managed to accommodate the vast numbers of people who have squeezed into it. Today, areas such as Mongkok, jammed with soaring tenements, are among the most densely populated urban areas in the world (in places shoehorning 100,000 people into each square kilometre).

While Hong Kong Island has mountains and beaches to palliate the effects of urban claustrophobia, Kowloon has just more shops, more restaurants and more hotels. It's hard to imagine that such a relentlessly built-up, crowded and commercial place could possibly have any cachet among the travelling public – and yet it does. The **view** across the harbour to Hong Kong Island, wall-to-wall with skyscrapers, is one of the most unforgettable city panoramas you'll see anywhere, especially at night.

### What to see and do

**Tsim Sha Tsui** is the tourist heart of Hong Kong, and **Nathan Road** – full of shops and budget hotels – is its main artery, leading down to the harbour and to the phenomenal view south over Hong Kong Island. The part of Kowloon north of Tsim Sha Tsui – encompassing **Yau Ma Tei** and **Mongok** – is more rewarding to walk around, with authentic Chinese neighbourhoods and interesting markets.

### Tsim Sha Tsui

The **Star Ferry Pier**, for ferries to Hong Kong Island, is right on the southwestern tip of the **Tsim Sha Tsui** peninsula. East of here, along the southern shore, are a number of hi-tech, modern museums and galleries built on reclaimed land. The **Hong Kong Cultural Centre**, about 100m east of the Star Ferry Pier, contains concert halls, theatres and galleries, including, in an adjacent wing, the **Museum of Art** (Mon–Wed, Fri & Sun 10am–6pm, Thurs & Sat

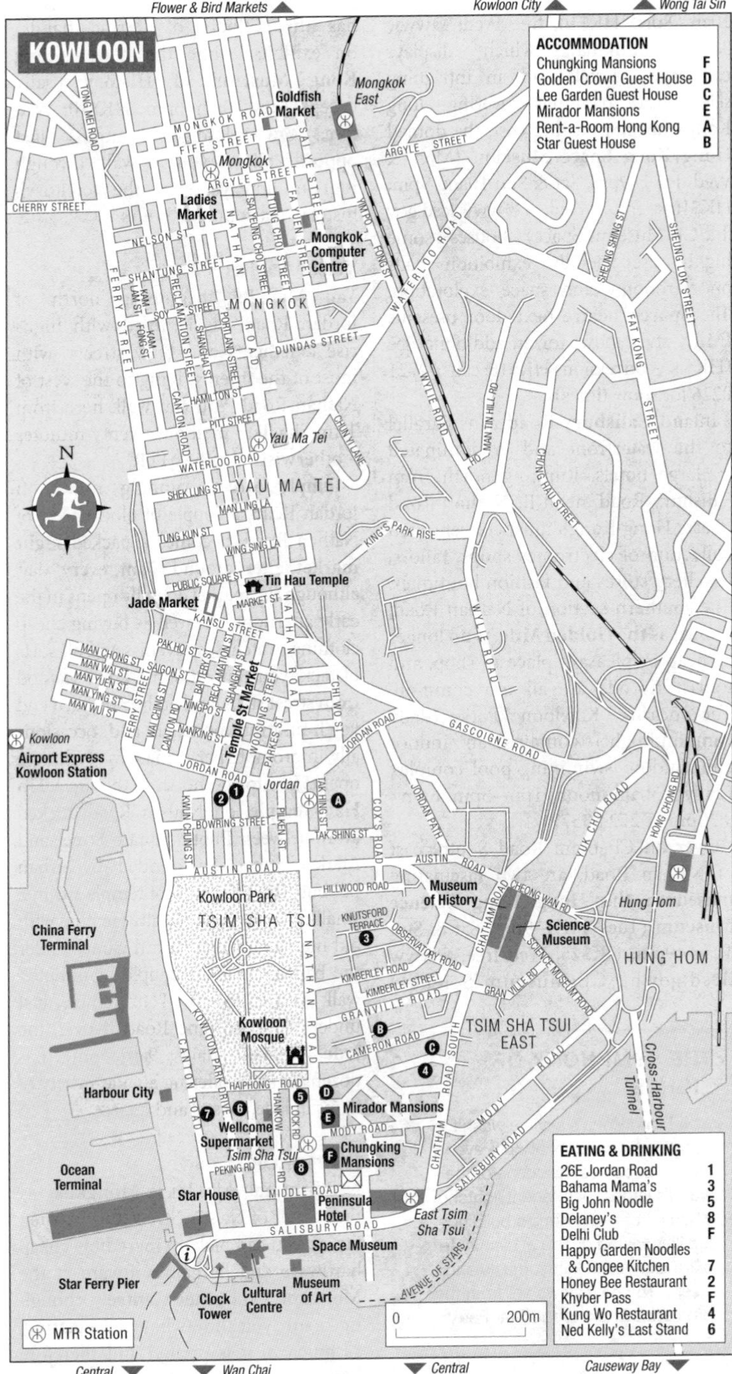
KOWLOON
ACCOMMODATION
Chungking Mansions F
Golden Crown Guest House D
Lee Garden Guest House C
Mirador Mansions E
Rent-a-Room Hong Kong A
Star Guest House B
EATING & DRINKING
26E Jordan Road 1
Bahama Mama's 3
Big John Noodle 5
Delaney's 8
Delhi Club F
Happy Garden Noodles & Congee Kitchen 7
Honey Bee Restaurant 2
Khyber Pass F
Kung Wo Restaurant 4
Ned Kelly's Last Stand 6
Flower & Bird Markets
Kowloon City
Wong Tai Sin Temple (2km)
Goldfish Market
Mongkok East
Mongkok
Ladies Market
Mongkok Computer Centre
MONGKOK
Yau Ma Tei
YAU MA TEI
Tin Hau Temple
Jade Market
Temple St Market
Kowloon Airport Express Kowloon Station
Jordan
Kowloon Park
TSIM SHA TSUI
Museum of History
Science Museum
Hung Hom
HUNG HOM
China Ferry Terminal
Kowloon Mosque
TSIM SHA TSUI EAST
Harbour City
Mirador Mansions
Wellcome Supermarket
Tsim Sha Tsui
Chungking Mansions
Ocean Terminal
Star House
Peninsula Hotel
East Tsim Sha Tsui
Space Museum
Star Ferry Pier
Clock Tower
Cultural Centre
Museum of Art
Cross-Harbour Tunnel
MTR Station
0 200m
Central
Wan Chai
Central
Causeway Bay

10am–8pm; HK$10, free Wed; ⓦwww.lcsd.gov.hk/hkma), which displays calligraphy, scrolls and an intriguing selection of paintings covering Hong Kong's history. Further east, the domed **Hong Kong Space Museum** (Mon & Wed–Fri 1–9pm, Sat & Sun 10am–9pm; HK$10, free Wed; ⓦwww.lcsd.gov.hk/CE/Museum/Space) houses some highly user-friendly exhibition halls on astronomy and space exploration. The **Space Theatre** next door presents IMAX-style shows for an additional fee (HK$32, concessions HK$16; call ⓣ2721 0226 for show times).

Inland, **Salisbury Road** runs parallel to the waterfront and is dominated by large hotels. Running north from Salisbury Road, neon-lit **Nathan Road** boasts Hong Kong's most concentrated collection of electronics shops, tailors, jewellery stores and fashion boutiques. The southern section of Nathan Road, known as **the Golden Mile**, is no longer a cheap or pleasant place to shop, and tourist rip-offs are all too common. The nearby Kowloon Park (daily 6am–midnight) contains an indoor and outdoor swimming-pool complex (daily 6.30am–noon, 1pm–5pm, 6pm–9:30pm; ⓣ2724 3577).

Over on Chatham Road South, east of Nathan Road, are two fascinating museums: the **Hong Kong Science Museum** (Tues–Fri 1–9pm, Sat & Sun 10am–9pm; HK$25, Wed free; ⓦwww.lcsd.gov.hk/CE/Museum/Science) has three floors of terrific hands-on exhibits; while the newer **Hong Kong Museum of History** (daily except Tues 10am–6pm; HK$10, Wed free; ⓦwww.lcsd.gov.hk/hkmh) just opposite allows you to walk through four million years of the territory's history in a couple of hours.

## THE SYMPHONY OF LIGHTS

As if Hong Kong's skyline wasn't spectacular enough, at 8pm every night it becomes the scene of the world's largest permanent lightshow, when 44 of Hong Kong's buildings are illuminated during a 14-minute extravaganza of lights, music and lasers. The best views are from the promenade next to the Star Ferry.

## Yau Ma Tei

**Yau Ma Tei**, beginning north of Jordan Road, is jammed with high-rise tenements and busy streets, with most of the interest lying to the west of Nathan Road. You can walk here from Tsim Sha Tsui in about twenty minutes – otherwise take the MTR.

**Temple Street**, running north off Jordan Road, a couple of blocks west of Nathan Road, becomes a packed **night market** after around 7pm every day, although the market actually opens in the early afternoon. As well as buying cheap clothing, watches, souvenirs and all sorts of tack, you can eat some great seafood from street stalls, and at the northern end you'll find fortune-tellers and, occasionally, impromptu performances of Chinese opera. Just to the north is the local **Tin Hau Temple**, off Nathan Road, tucked away between Public Square Street and Market Street. Surrounded by urban hubbub, this tiny, ancient temple sits in a small concrete park, usually teeming with old men gambling on card games under the banyan trees. A couple of minutes' walk west of the Tin Hau Temple, just under the Gascoigne Road flyover, the **Jade Market** (daily 9am–6pm) has dozens of stalls offering a wide variety of items in jade, crystal and quartz.

## Mongkok

North of Yau Ma Tei is **Mongkok**. At the corner of Nelson Street and Fa Yuen Street, you can pick up incredibly cheap hardware and bargain software at the **Mongkok Computer Centre** – though make sure you know what you're getting, as much of it is pirated and therefore illegal. A few hundred metres north of here in the direction of Prince Edward MTR are two traditional markets. Just to the north of Prince Edward Road are the **Flower Market** (daily 7am–8pm), in Flower Market Road, and the **Bird Market** (daily 7am–8pm), at the eastern end of the same street, where it meets the MTR flyover. The flower market is at its best on Sundays and in the run-up to Chinese New Year, when many people come to buy chrysanthemums and orange trees to decorate their apartments for good luck. The bird market is set in a Chinese-style garden. As well as the hundreds of birds on sale here, along with their intricately designed bamboo cages, there are live crickets – whose fate is bird-feed. Many local men bring their own songbirds here for an airing, and the place gives a real glimpse into a traditional area of Chinese life. **Tung Choi Street** to the south houses a myriad of goldfish and pet shops. Whereas goldfish and birds are popular pets among the older generations, cats and particularly dogs are becoming increasingly fashionable among younger Hong Kong residents, as many decide that having children is too expensive. Hong Kong now has one of the lowest birthrates in the world.

### Outer Kowloon

Head a few hundred metres north of Mongkok and you reach **Boundary Street**, which marks the border between Kowloon and the New Territories – though these days the distinction is fairly meaningless.

The main tourist attraction in this area is well to the northeast of Boundary Street. The **Wong Tai Sin Temple** (daily 7am–5.30pm; small donation) is a huge thriving place packed with more worshippers than any other temple in Hong Kong (especially during Chinese New Year). Big, bright and colourful, it offers a glimpse into the practices of modern Chinese religion: solemn devotees kneel and pray, burn incense, rattle fortune-telling sticks in jars, and present food and drink to the Taoist deities, while mainland tourists cheerfully snap away with digital cameras. Fortune-tellers, some of whom speak English, have booths near the exit and offer palm and face readings. The temple can be reached directly from the Wong Tai Sin MTR Station.

One stop further on, Diamond Hill MTR takes you to the beautiful **Chi Lin Nunnery** (daily 9am–4.30pm) and **Nan Lian Garden** (daily 7am–9pm; free). The nunnery is built of wood, without the use of a single nail, in contrast to the tower blocks looming all around it. The Nan Lian Garden includes a carp pond, golden pagoda and a small bonsai collection.

## THE OUTLYING ISLANDS

The **outlying islands** of Hong Kong offer a delightful combination of seascape, old fishing villages and relative rural calm, almost entirely free of motor vehicles (except for the taxis and buses on Lantau Island). The islands are conveniently connected to Central by frequent ferries. Although most tourists come on day-trips, there is some accommodation on the islands (see p.172).

### Lamma Island

Lying just to the southwest of Aberdeen, **Lamma** is the closest island to Hong Kong Island, with a population of less than ten thousand, no cars, a spine of greenery-clad hills, a few sandy beaches, and lots of seafood restaurants. There are two possible **ferry** crossing points, from Central to either Yung Shue Wan or Sok Kwu Wan or from Aberdeen to Yung Shue Wan. By far, the best way to appreciate the island is to take a boat to either Yung Shue Wan or Sok Kwu Wan, then walk to the other side and catch the boat back.

**Yung Shue Wan** is a small village, where life is punctuated by bursts

## FERRIES TO THE ISLANDS

The following is a selection of the most useful island **ferry services**. Most offer slow and fast ferries. Schedules differ slightly on Saturdays and Sundays (services generally start later in the morning), when prices also rise:

**To Cheung Chau**

**From Outlying Islands Ferry Piers** (Pier 5): first boat out 6.15am, last boat back 11.45pm (at least hourly; 1hr; HK$11.30 slow, HK$22.20 fast), plus infrequent services through the night.

There are also some infrequent sailings between Mui Wo on Lantau and Cheung Chau.

**To Yung Shue Wan, Lamma Island**

**From Outlying Islands Ferry Piers** (Pier 4): first boat out 6.30am, last boat back 11.30pm (roughly every 20–30min; 40min; HK$11.80 slow, HK$16.80 fast).

**From Aberdeen** (via Pak Kok Tsuen): first boat out 6.30am, last boat back 7.45pm (roughly every 60–90min; 30min; HK$12.80).

**To Sok Kwu Wan, Lamma Island**

**From Outlying Islands Ferry Piers** (Pier 4): first boat out 7.20am, last boat back 10.40pm (11 daily; 50min; HK$14.80).

**To Mui Wo (Silvermine Bay), Lantau Island**

**From Outlying Islands Ferry Piers** (Pier 6): first boat out 6.10am, last boat back 11.30pm (at least hourly; 30–50min; HK$11.30 slow, HK$22.20 fast), also one returning at 3.40am. Some sailings go via Peng Chau.

**To Peng Chau**

**From Outlying Islands Ferry Piers** (Pier 6): first boat out 7am, last boat back 11.30pm (roughly hourly; 50min; HK$11.30).

of activity each time a ferry arrives. To walk to Sok Kwu Wan from here (1hr), follow signs for **Hung Shing Yeh Beach**. The beach itself is overlooked by the power plant, but offers a couple of pleasant restaurants. On from the beach, the path climbs quite sharply up to a little summit, where a pavilion commands views over the island. Thirty minutes' walk further on will take you to **Sok Kwu Wan**, which comprises a row of seafood restaurants with terraces built out over the water. Lamma is still reputed for its seafood, but the restaurants are mainly oriented towards large parties and are not cheap. Some run their own ferries.

Tucked among the restaurants in Sok Kwu Wan is a booth promoting the **Lamma Fisherfolk's Village** (daily 10am–sunset; from HK$40; Ⓦwww.fisherfolks.com.hk). The village itself is actually a fish-farm that has been converted into a museum of sorts, with insights into the lives of local fishermen.

The street beyond the restaurants will take you on a well-signposted loop round the eastern side of the island. This includes **Mo Tat Wan** beach, which is wide and peaceful. The loop brings you back out by the Tin Hau Temple. Be aware that timetabled ferries from Sok Kwu Wan are not as reliable as those from Yung Shue Wan.

### Cheung Chau Island

Another great little island where you can spend a few hours strolling around and then have dinner, **Cheung Chau** is just south of Lantau and an hour from Hong Kong by ferry. Despite its minuscule size of 2.5 square kilometres, Cheung Chau is the most crowded of all the outer islands, with a population of some twenty thousand. The narrow strip between its two headlands is jam-packed with tiny shops, markets and seafront restaurants. Seafood here is both cheaper and less tour-group oriented than on Lamma. As well as romantic dinners and late-night ferry rides home, the island offers some interesting **walks**. It also features several temples, the most important being the two-hundred-year-old **Pak Tai Temple**, a few hundred metres northwest of the ferry pier, along Pak She Street. For a few days in late April or early May the temple is the site of one of Hong Kong's liveliest and most spectacular festivals, the **Tai Chiu (Bun) Festival**.

The main beach on the island, the scenic but crowded **Tung Wan Beach**, is due west of the ferry pier. Windsurfers (from HK$90 per hour) and kayaks (from HK$60 per hour) are available for rent at the nearby windsurfing club (Ⓦwww.ccwindc.com.hk). To walk round the southern half of the island, follow signs from here for the **Mini Great Wall**, actually a ridge. The path leads past some interesting rock formations. As a general rule, paths branching off to the right take you back towards the village, while left forks keep you going round the coast. Past the cemetery, follow signs down to **Pak Tso Wan** for a peaceful, secluded beach. If you fancy a change from walking, you can cover the last section between **Sai Wan** and the ferry pier by public *kaido* (a tiny passenger boat). A similar signposted circular walk covers the northern half of the island. Each loop from the village takes about three hours.

## Lantau Island

With wild countryside, monasteries, old fishing villages and seriously secluded beaches, **Lantau Island** – twice the size of Hong Kong Island – offers the best quick escape from the city. Former governor Crawford Murray MacLehose declared all areas of Lantau more than 200m above sea level a country park; building is still prohibited here, so in spite of the new airport and Disneyland already on the island, Lantau should remain relatively peaceful.

The road west from Mui Wo, the point of arrival, passes along the southern shore, which is where Lantau's most accessible beaches are located. **Cheung Sha Beach**, with a couple of cafés and a hotel, is the most appealing, and buses #1, #2, and #4 from Mui Wo all pass by here.

In the western part of the island, the **Po Lin Monastery** (daily 10am–5.30pm; free) lies high up on the Ngong Ping Plateau. It's the largest temple in the whole territory of Hong Kong, and although it was only established in 1927,

### HONG KONG OUTDOORS

Hong Kong is not just a heaving metropolis and when you've had enough of the people and skyscrapers it's easy to escape. Lamma and Cheung Chau provide easy, paved walks around headlands. Lantau, especially in the southwest corner, offers spectacular mountains and sea views. For the more adventurous, Sai Kung and Plover Cove in the New Territories to the north plunge into rural wilderness just an hour from Central. The free Hong Kong Tourist Board brochure **Discover Hong Kong Nature** provides basic maps and information on how to get there. Alternatively, you can buy detailed Ordnance Survey maps from any branch of Dymocks for around HK$80. Decent trainers are enough for any walks. If you don't fancy heading off into the wilderness alone, Walk Hong Kong (Ⓣ9103 1386, Ⓦwww.walkhongkong.com) offer excellent and highly informative guided walks, while Kayak and Hike (Ⓣ9300 5197, Ⓦwww.kayak-and-hike.com) do just that. Paul Etherington, who runs Kayak and Hike, is happy to offer general advice to anyone wanting to discover the hidden beauties of Hong Kong.

## GETTING TO LANTAU

Until recently the only way to reach Lantau was by ferry, and this is still the most picturesque. The point of arrival is **Mui Wo,** otherwise known as **Silvermine Bay**, 30-60 minutes' ferry ride from Central. Some of the Mui Wo boats stop at the small island of Peng Chau en route. There are also a few daily ferries that connect Mui Wo with Cheung Chau. Mui Wo itself is not much to speak of, but has a bus station linking it with the attractions elsewhere on the island.

Alternatively, you can now catch the **MTR to Tung Chung**, which also has a bus terminus, and is the arrival point for the **Ngong Ping 360 cable car** up to the Tian Tan Buddha.

it is a very vibrant, busy temple. Busloads of tourists arrive here by the hour, in particular to pay their respects to the bronze **Tian Tan Buddha**, the largest seated bronze outdoor Buddha in the world, and to eat in the huge vegetarian **restaurant** (11.30am–4.30pm); it costs HK$60 for a filling multi-course meal, while the "deluxe" version served in an air-con annexe costs HK$100 – meal tickets are available from the office at the bottom of the steps to the Buddha and include entry to the exhibition at the top. Tickets for the exhibition alone cost HK$23. The Po Lin Monastery is often referred to in bus schedules as Ngong Ping and can be reached by bus #2 from Mui Wo; it's a spectacular forty-minute ride through the hills (the last bus back to Mui Wo leaves at 7.20pm) Bus #23 from Tung Chung also goes there.

Since 2006, there has been an alternative, even more impressive way of accessing the Buddha: the Ngong Ping 360 cable car (10am–6pm Mon–Fri, 10am–6.30pm Sat, 9am–6.30pm Sun; HK$58 one-way, HK$88 return). The ride takes about half an hour.

Right on the far northwestern shore of Lantau is the fascinating little fishing village of **Tai O**. This remote place, constructed over salt flats and a tiny offshore island, has become a popular tourist spot particularly at weekends, but still retains much of its old character. The picturesque walk to **Lung Ngam Monastery** across the Sun Kei bridge takes you through the village, past houses built out of old boats and out to hillside views and mangroves. You can reach Tai O by bus #1 from Mui Wo (last bus back 12.10am), by bus #21 from the Po Lin Monastery (one an hour, last service out to Tai O is at 5pm) or by bus #11 from Tung Chung.

### Disneyland

The Disneyland here is not as popular with locals as Ocean Park, due to its smaller size and higher cost. The park is divided into four "lands", each with its own theme, though Space Mountain is its only "big" ride. A separate MTR line runs to the resort, branching off the Tung Chung line out of Hong Kong Station (6.15am–12.45am; approx 30min from Kowloon or Hong Kong stations; HK$18), where there is a Disneyland ticket counter. Alternatively, morning and evening buses are available. Bus #R11 runs from North Point via Central, Causeway Bay and Wan Chai (HK$38, 9am & 9.20am, also 9.40am at weekends, return 15–45 mins after the evening fireworks) and bus #R21 runs from Hung Hom via Jordan and Tsim Sha Tsui (HK$32, 8.50am & 9.10am, also 9.30am at weekends, return 15–45mins after the fireworks). Admission costs HK$295 during the week and HK$350 at weekends.

## Arrival

**By train** The main land route into Hong Kong is by train. Express trains from China arrive at Hung Hom MTR Station (☎2947 7888), east of Tsim Sha

Tsui. You can transfer to the MTR East Rail line for one stop to East Tsim Sha Tsui Station, a short walk from Nathan Road and the heart of Tsim Sha Tsui. Alternatively, signposted walkways lead to an adjacent bus terminal and taxi rank. The Star Ferry Pier for boats to Central is a 15-minute walk round the harbour, or you can catch bus #5C, which goes via Tsim Sha Tsui.

A cheaper alternative is to take a local train from Guangzhou to the Chinese border city of Shenzhen, from where you walk across the border to Lo Wu on the Hong Kong side and pick up the frequent MTR trains to East Tsim Sha Tsui (50min). There are now regular daily bus services from Guangzhou and Shenzhen operated by CTS (ⓦwww.ctshk.com); these take about one hour longer than the direct train and drop you off at Hung Hom, Sheung Wan, Wan Chai and Causeway Bay.

**By ferry** The Macau Ferry Terminal is in the Shun Tak Centre, on Hong Kong Island, from where the Sheung Wan MTR Station is directly accessible; Macau ferries run frequently throughout the day and take an hour. The China Ferry Terminal is in the west of Tsim Sha Tsui, just ten minutes' walk from Nathan Road. Ferries from Xiamen (20hr), Guangzhou (2–3hr), Shekou (45min) and Zhuhai (1hr 10min), plus a few from Macau, dock here.

**By air** Chek Lap Kok Airport (known officially as Hong Kong International Airport; ⓣ2181 8888 ⓦwww.hongkongairport.com) is 34km west of Central on the north coast of Lantau Island.

The high-speed Airport Express rail service (AEL; ⓦwww.mtr.com.hk), accessed directly from arrivals (every 10min; 5.50am–1.15am), whisks you to Hong Kong Station in Central in 23 minutes (HK$100), via Tsing Yi (12min; HK$60) and Kowloon (20min; HK$90). There are taxi ranks, bus stops and hotel-shuttle bus stops at the AEL stations, plus a left-luggage service at Hong Kong Station (6am–1am) in Central.

Frequent Airbuses run from the airport (6am–midnight); the airport customer-service counters sell tickets (exact money only if you pay on the bus). The #A11 goes to Causeway Bay on Hong Kong Island via Sheung Wan, Central, Admiralty and Wan Chai, while the #A12 goes to Central (HK$40). The cheaper E11 also covers Central and Causeway Bay (HK$21). Bus #A21 goes to Hung Hom MTR Station via Tsim Sha Tsui, Jordan, Yau Ma Tei and Mongkok (HK$33). All the buses have equivalent night services.

**Taxis** into the city are metered and reliable, but get the tourist office in the arrivals area of the airport to write down the name of your destination in Chinese characters, so that you can show it to the taxi driver. It costs roughly HK$280 to get to Tsim Sha Tsui (20–30min), and about HK$340 for Hong Kong Island (30–50min). There may be extra charges for luggage and for tunnel tolls – on some tunnel trips the passenger pays the return charge too. Rush-hour traffic can slow down journey times considerably.

## Information

**Tourist information** The Hong Kong Tourism Board (HKTB; ⓦwww.discoverhongkong.com) has an office in the arrivals area of the airport (daily 7am–11pm, information and internet available 24hr), at the Star Ferry Pier in Tsim Sha Tsui (daily 8am–8pm) and in Causeway Bay MTR station, near exit F (daily 8am–8pm). There's also an HKTB multilingual telephone service (ⓣ2508 1234).

**Listings publications** Countless leaflets on what to do including *Where* magazine and *City Life* can be picked up at HKTB outlets (see above). Among the unofficial free listings magazines (which you can pick up from most bars and some cafés and restaurants), *HK Magazine* (ⓦwww.aziacity.com/hk), published every Friday, contains excellent up-to-date information on restaurants, bars, clubs, concerts and exhibitions, as do the fortnightly *BC* (ⓦwww.bcmagazine.net) and *List* (ⓦwww.thelist.com.hk) magazines.

## City transport

**MTR** The MTR (Mass Transit Railway) is Hong Kong's train system, which operates from roughly 6am to 1am. The Island Line (marked dark blue on maps) runs along the north shore of Hong Kong Island, from Sheung Wan in the west to Chai Wan in the east, taking in useful stops such as Central, Wan Chai and Causeway Bay. The Tsuen Wan Line (red) runs from Central, under the harbour, through Tsim Sha Tsui and on to Mongkok. The Tung Chung Line (yellow) follows much of the same route as the Airport Express, linking Central and Lantau. Finally the East Rail Line starts at Tsim Sha Tsui East and runs via Hung Hom up to Lo Wu and Lok Ma Chau on the border with China. You can buy single-journey tickets (HK$4.50–36.50) from machines in the stations, or a slightly better-value Octopus Card (see p.170). You can also buy 3-day tourist MTR passes for HK$50.

**Trams** A great way to travel along the north shore of Hong Kong Island. All trams except those going to Happy Valley run between Causeway Bay and Central. You board at the back, and drop the money in the driver's box (HK$2; no change given) when you get off.

**Buses** The single- and double-decker air-conditioned buses that run around town are

## THE OCTOPUS CARD

The rechargeable stored-value **Octopus Card** (ⓣ2266 2222 for information) can be used for travel on the MTR, the Airport Express, trams, ferries, buses and green minibuses. There's talk of putting readers in taxis, and you can also use it at convenience stores, supermarkets and some fast-food restaurants. You pay a deposit of HK$50 to get the plastic card, and an initial HK$100 credit, then add value to it by feeding it and your money into machines in the MTR. Your fare is electronically deducted each time you use the card – just swipe it over the yellow sensor pad. Buses, trams and minibuses don't give change, so it avoids you overpaying, and when you leave just hand it back in at the airport and you'll get back any remaining credit and your deposit, minus HK$7 if you've had it less than three months.





essential for many destinations along the south of Hong Kong Island. You pay as you board and exact change is required; the amount is often posted up on the timetables at bus stops. The main bus terminal in Central is at Exchange Square, a few minutes' walk west of the Star Ferry Pier, though some buses also start from the ferry piers concourse. In Tsim Sha Tsui, the main bus terminal is right in front of the Star Ferry Pier.

**Taxis** Taxis in Hong Kong are not expensive. Note that there is a toll to be paid (around HK$10) on any trips through a tunnel and drivers are allowed to double this, and do, on the grounds that they have to get back again. Many taxi drivers do not speak English, so be prepared to show the driver the name of your destination written down in Chinese. If you get stuck, gesture to the driver to call the dispatch centre on the two-way radio; someone there will speak English.

**Ferries** One of the most enjoyable things to do in Hong Kong is to ride the Star Ferry between Kowloon and Hong Kong Island. You can ride upper deck (HK$2.20) or lower deck (HK$1.70). Ferries run every few minutes between Tsim Sha Tsui and Central (daily 6.30am–11.30pm; 8min), and between Tsim Sha Tsui and Wan Chai (daily 7.20am–10.50pm). For ferries to the outlying islands, see p.166.

## A FEW USEFUL LOCAL BUS ROUTES

**From Central**

#6 and #6A to Stanley via Repulse Bay
#15 to The Peak
#70 to Aberdeen

**From Tsim Sha Tsui Star Ferry Pier**

#8A and #5C to East Tsim Sha Tsui and Hung Hom MTR stations
#1 and #1A to Mongkok including the Bird and Flower Markets

## Accommodation

### Kowloon

Most of the accommodation listed below is within fifteen minutes' walk of the Star Ferry Pier – conveniently central, though very touristy.

**Golden Crown Guest House** 5th Floor, Golden Crown Court, 66–70 Nathan Rd ⓣ2369 1782, ⓦwww.goldencrownhk.com. The owners of this clean but cramped place speak very little English, but the prices are reasonable if you want to avoid Chungking Mansions. ❼

**Lee Garden Guest House** 8th Floor, 36 Cameron Rd ⓣ2367 2284, ⓦwww.starguesthouse.com.hk. Friendly owner Charlie Chan and his son Raymond offer a comfortable range of clean, small singles, doubles and triples, that feel more like a hotel than a guesthouse. They also own the *Star Guest House* at 6th Floor, 21 Cameron Rd ⓣ2723 8951. ❻

**Rent-a-Room** Flat A, 2nd floor, Knight Garden, 7–8 Tak Hing Street ⓣ2366 3011, ⓦwww.rentaroomhk.com. This swish and swanky hotel offers decent-sized rooms at very reasonable prices, as well as a whole range of facilities including internet access, money changing and laundry. They also have rooms available long-term. Security is top-notch. Prices go up at weekends and public holidays. Dorm HK$160. ❽

### Chungking Mansions

Chungking Mansions, an apartment block at 36–44 Nathan Road, is a noisy, crowded, hodgepodge of shops, restaurants and guesthouses swarming with people from all over the world. Above the second floor, the building is divided into five blocks, lettered

A to E, each served by two tiny, stuffy lifts, usually attended by long queues. It has a poor reputation, but the very real fear of SARS and bird flu led to a massive clean-up, and fire safety and hygiene are both at acceptable levels. CCTV has been added and there are even plans to redo the outside. For a full list of the guesthouses here check out ⓦwww.chungking-mansions.hk. Block A is the noisiest block in Chungking Mansions.

**Dragon Inn** 3rd Floor, Block B ⓣ2368 2007, ⓦwww.dragoninn.info. Well-organized, friendly and secure hostel-cum-travel agent with singles, doubles and triples. Some brand-new rooms verge on the luxurious, while the older ones are cheaper. ❻

**New Shanghai Guest House** Flat 2, 16th floor, Block D ⓣ2311 2515. The owner here speaks no English, but the en-suite rooms are enormous by Hong Kong standards, and it's located in one of the quietest blocks, making it a peaceful haven. ❻

**Park Guesthouse**, Flat 1, 15th Floor, Block A ⓣ2368 1689. The rooms here are light and airy, and there are plenty of them, but some are so small the beds have indents to allow for pillars. Make sure you know what you're getting before you pay. ❻

**Peking (and New Peking) Guest House** Flat 2, 12th Floor, Block A ⓣ2723 8320. This 23-room hostel has excellent security and offers good value for money, as well as cheap internet access. ❻

**Tom's Guesthouse** Flat 5, 8th Floor, Block A ⓣ2722 4956. Run by friendly management who speak very good English, this hostel offers double rooms for not much more than the price of two dorm beds elsewhere. The smallest singles are also very cheap. *Tom's* has another branch at Flat 1, 16th Floor, Block C (ⓣ2722 6035). ❹

**Travellers' Hostel** 16th Floor, Block A ⓣ2368 7710. A time-worn, shabby retreat for backpackers with mixed six-bed dorms and some singles, with or without a/c. Shared bathrooms. They also have a kitchen and internet access, both available 24hrs. ❹

**Welcome Guest House** 7th Floor, Block A ⓣ2721 7793, ⓦwww.guesthousehk.net. A recommended first choice, offering a/c rooms with or without shower. Nice clean rooms, each with TV and telephone, luggage storage, laundry service and China visas available. The management are very friendly and helpful, and there are discounts for students, YHA members and long stays. They also own the *Spring Guest House* at Flat 5, 15th Floor, Block A ⓣ2367 1598. ❺

## Mirador Mansions

This is the big apartment block at 54–64 Nathan Rd, on the east side, in between Carnarvon Road and Mody Road, right opposite the Tsim Sha Tsui MTR Station. Dotted around in among the residential apartments are large numbers of guesthouses. Once seen as superior to *Chungking Mansions*, *Mirador Mansions* has now fallen behind its neighbour and although acceptable, it is somewhat more run-down. The main lifts stop working late at night and you'll have to head further into the building to find others.

**Cosmic Guest House** Flat A1, 12th Floor ⓣ2369 6669, ⓦwww.cosmicguesthouse.com. A Mirador institution offering some of the best, cheap dorms you'll find and a huge number of rooms for both short- and long-term stays. Rooms in the newly-renovated block are tiny and may not have windows, though they do sparkle with cleanliness. Dorms cannot be booked in advance. ❻

**Garden Hostel** Flat F4, 3rd Floor ⓣ2311 1183, ⓦwww.gardenhostel.com.hk. A great place to meet fellow-travellers, friendly and laid-back with free washing machines, Kung Fu lessons, lockers and even a patio garden. Dorms are noisy but cheap; discounts available for long stays. Not to be confused with the *New Garden*, whatever the touts may say. ❺

**Man Hing Lung Hotel** Flat F2, 14th Floor ⓣ2311 8807. A friendly place tucked at the back of *Mirador Mansions* (turn left out of the lift) offering internet access and China visas. Rooms on the same floor as reception are nicer than those on the 12th floor. 4 of the 14 rooms share bathrooms. ❺

**USA Hotel Group** Flat F1, 13th Floor ⓣ2311 2523, ⓦwww.usahotel.com.hk. Comprising the *USA*, *Kowloon* and *New Garden Hostels*, there's plenty of choice to be had here and though not the cheapest, the rooms are luxurious by *Mirador* standards. There are some rumours of deposits not being returned and rates varying from those quoted though, so make sure you get bookings in writing and a receipt for any money handed over. They have only one cheap dorm, but it is possibly the worst you'll find anywhere. The more expensive 3-bed dorms are quite swish. ❼

## Hong Kong Island

The budget rooms on Hong Kong Island are mostly in Causeway Bay, some near Sogo and others towards Leighton Road. They are generally more expensive than in Kowloon, but quieter.

**Alisan Guest House** Flat A, 5th Floor, Hoi To Court, 275 Gloucester Road ⓣ2838 0762, ⓦhome.hkstar.com/~alisangh. One of the few places in Hong Kong bridging the gap between hostel and hotel, the *Alisan* offers excellent service and security. Some rooms don't have windows, others have harbour views. The entrance is at 23 Cannon Street. ❼

**Causeway Bay Guest House** Flat B 1st Floor, Lai Yee Building, 44 Leighton Rd ⓣ2895 2065, ⓦwww.cbgh.net This easy-to-find guesthouse offers seven small but decent rooms. The staff are friendly, but they may not take bookings at weekends or during holidays. ❼

**Hong Kong Hostel** 3rd Floor Block A, 47 Paterson St ⓣ2392 6868, skype hkkostel, ⓦwww.hostel.hk. This efficient hostel is the cheapest place to stay in Causeway Bay, with decent three-bed dorms. Internet is free, but laundry is expensive. It's hard to find as there are no signs outside and the entrance looks like it's part of a shopping centre. Other landlords in the building claim the hostel violates laws on commercial use of residential buildings, and although the owner maintains this is not aimed at him it would be wise to call and check they're still in operation before arriving. Phone bookings do not require advance payment. Dorm HK$150 ❼

**Jetvan Traveller's House** Flat A, 4th Floor, Fairview Mansion, 51 Paterson St ⓣ2890 8133, ⓦwww.jetvan.com. The reception area here feels like someone's living room, thanks to the large leather sofa and constant ironing that takes place. Staff speak very good English, there is internet access and all rooms have a TV and telephone. ❼

**Mount Davis Youth Hostel (Ma Wui Hall)** Mt Davis Path, Mt Davis ⓣ2817 5715, ⓦwww.yha.org.hk. Perched on top of a mountain, this place has superb views over the harbour and is unbelievably peaceful. Facilities are basic but adequate and it can get cold in winter. There are some private rooms, though none ensuite. The hostel is closed between midnight and 7am and stays are limited to six nights. It is not conveniently located, but there is a free shuttle bus that runs from Sheung Wan MTR station. Single-sex dorms (❷), with HK$30 extra for non-HI members. Private rooms rates rise at weekends. ❻

### Outlying islands

There is no budget accommodation on either Cheung Chau or Lamma but as soon as you step off the ferry on either place, you will see a selection of signs and small booths advertising holiday rooms, which are affordable, but not cheap enough or convenient enough for anything other than escape from the city. There is only one convenient hostel on Lantau.

**S G Davis Hostel Ngong Ping**, Lantau Island ⓣ2985 5610, ⓦwww.yha.org.hk. Bus #2 from Mui Wo (see p.168) and #23 from Tung Chung MTR will take you to the Ngong Ping Terminal, then follow the signs for the tea garden. This is a great base for hill-walking on Lantau, but requires a bit of planning, as it is closed completely (including to residents) between 10am and 4pm every day and the nearest eating places in Ngong Ping close at 6pm (including a 7-11 selling microwave meals). There is a supermarket a bus ride away in Tung Chung though, and the hostel has a kitchen. Dorms HK$50 for HI members, HK$80 for non-members. ❷

## Eating

Most cheap eating in Central can be found along Wellington Street, and up the hill from there along either side of the Mid-Levels escalator as it heads towards SoHo. Further east, you'll find plenty of choice on Jaffe Road and in the streets near Times Square.

### Central

**Between Wu Yue** 26 Cochrane St (facing the escalator) ⓣ2815 5520. Some of the best Beijing dumplings you'll find are served almost before you've ordered them. A local favourite is pork dumplings in hot and sour soup, but veggie options are also available. Soup HK$21.

**Can Teen** M20–28 Prince's Building, Chater Rd ⓣ2524 6792. A smart, modern and cheap lunch stop serving a range of tasty dishes including sushi, Chinese rice- and noodle-based fare, sweet pastries and fresh juices. They also have branches in the IFC Mall, Citibank Plaza, the Admiralty Centre and Telford Plaza. Roasted meat and rice, HK$30.

**Coco Curry House** 8 Wing Wah Lane ⓣ2523 6911. As soon as you get half-way up this little cul-de-sac known as "Rat Alley" you will be accosted by vast numbers of people waving menus, in spite of the fact that all the restaurants here appear to work together. The tasty curries are best enjoyed with the superb Malay roti that the chef prepares with great theatre out front. Curry and rice HK$60.

**Lemon Exchange** 45 Cochrane St This hole-in-the-wall next to the escalator serves wonderfully refreshing smoothies and fruit juices (HK$15), as well as snack food such as burgers and chips.

**Mak's Noodles** 77 Wellington St ⓣ2854 3810. The noodles here are famous for their silky texture and fine taste, which comes from using duck eggs rather than the usual chicken. Portions are not large, but the staff are friendly. They have another branch on Jardine's Bazaar in Causeway Bay. Soup HK$25.

**Pearl Vietnamese Restaurant** 7 Wo On Lane, D'Aguilar St ⓣ2522 4223. Conveniently just round the corner from Lan Kwai Fong, this poky little place serves very tasty food. Rice with fish HK$55.

**Taco Loco & Archie's Deli** 7 & 9 Staunton St ☎2522 1262. Run out of the same kitchen, these tiny places tucked next to the escalator offer very good food if you're after a change from Asian cuisine. Service can be slow, but Archie's burgers are well worth the wait. Burger and chips HK$60.

**Tsim Chai Kee Noodles** 98 Wellington St ☎2850 6471. Eating here is a typical Hong Kong lunch experience. You may have to wait, but only a short while as vast numbers of people are seated wherever there's space, fed one of only three options on the menu and whizzed out again. You may be left feeling slightly dazed, but the noodle soup with dumplings is excellent and very cheap. Soup HK$15.

**Tsui Wah Restaurant** 15–19 Wellington St ☎2525 6338. This fast-food café serves Chinese, Malaysian and Western dishes, as well as cheap sandwiches. The European dinner sets are probably the best value around. They also have branches at 20–22 Cannon Street and 493–495 Jaffe Road. Hainan chicken set HK$50.

**Wong Chi Kei Congee & Noodle** 15B Wellington St ☎2869 1331. Originally from China then Macau, the Hong Kong branch of this restaurant offers a cheap and incredibly varied menu. You could eat here every night and not get bored. Fried rice HK$25.

## Wan Chai and Causeway Bay

**Cafe O** 1 Capital Place, 18 Luard Rd ☎3543 0224. Tasty pizzas up to a metre long, freshly cooked while you wait, as well as a selection of sandwiches, lasagne and salads. Pizza HK$26.

**Genbishi** 3 Tang Lung St ☎2827 7228. There is an English menu in this Japanese restaurant, but it still takes a fair bit of guesswork. The sushi and seafood are cheaper than you'll find elsewhere and it all tastes good, even if you get it wrong. They're located just off Canal Road, more or less behind Times Square. Noodles with salmon HK$40.

**Golden Myanmar** 379–389 Jaffe Rd ☎2838 9305. The food here may not win any Michelin stars, but it offers a taste of Burma, which stands apart from anything else you'll find in Hong Kong. Curry HK$60.

**Golden Phoenix Grill Restaurant** 415-421 Jaffe Rd ☎2891 6832. Come here for steaks served on sizzling platters. They are so hot that when sauce is poured over them, waiters will ask you to shield yourself with your napkin. Their definition of a fillet or sirloin might not be quite what you'd expect, but given the amazing value of their dinner sets who can argue? They also have a branch at 9A Hillwood Road, in Tsim Sha Tsui. Steak set HK$57.

**Peking Dumpling Wong** 118 Jaffe Rd ☎2527 0289. The fried dumplings here are not to be missed and come with a variety of fillings, all at good prices. A plate of rice and a plate of dumplings will serve two if you're on a really tight budget, or you can enjoy feeling greedy – you probably won't want to share once they arrive anyway. Dumplings HK$25, fried rice HK$30.

**Perfume River** 89 Percival St ☎2576 2240. The best Vietnamese dishes in Hong Kong, along with cold Vietnamese beer and happy, friendly staff. The lemon grass chicken and pork (HK$50) comes highly recommended.

**Pho Saigon** 319 Hennessy Rd ☎2833 6833. An unassuming little place that serves filled baguettes as well as the usual Vietnamese food at affordable prices. Pho soup HK$40.

**Sabah** 98–108 Jaffe Rd ☎2143 6626. Sit and watch the chef flinging roti dough around while you eat your Malaysian curry (HK$68). The atmosphere is laid-back and the noodle and rice dishes (HK$55) make an affordable meal.

**Thai-Jade** 50 Leighton Rd ☎2808 0734. The atmosphere here feels almost like you're eating at home, as it's friendly and unpretentious. There's a wide variety of affordable dishes, all served with an orchid on the plate. The food is delicious, though beer is on the pricey side for a restaurant. Chicken and rice HK$60.

**Warung Malang** 2/F, Flat B2, Dragon Rise Building, 9-11 Pennington St ☎2915 7859. Come here on a Sun to get a true sense of the other expat community in Hong Kong: the amahs, or domestic helpers. Most are Filipina or Indonesian, and Dragon Rise Building caters for the latter. The restaurant is squashed in a tiny room marked members only and you'll probably see people eating their food in the bookshop next door, making themselves at home. Selection of dishes around HK$50.

## Kowloon

You don't have to walk far in Kowloon to find a source of cheap food. Temple Street and the surrounding area are particularly good spots and you can take your pick from a multitude of stalls and cafés, most of which offer outdoor seating. Walk up Canton Road towards Kowloon Park Drive for more restaurant-like options.

**26E Jordan Road** ☎2199 7468. One of many places popular with locals, you won't find any English spoken here, though there is a comprehensible menu. Noodle dishes come as cheaply as HK$10, and the ingredients are fresh and tasty. A perfect place for any meal, as they're open 24hrs.

**Big John Noodle** 18 Lock Rd. Just across the road from Chungking Mansions, this tiny place is always busy. Find a stool to perch on and enjoy a full English breakfast, sandwiches, noodles, or afternoon tea, including excellent cheesecake. Open Mon–Sat 8am–7.30pm. Noodle soup HK$24.

**Happy Garden Noodles & Congee Kitchen** 72 Canton Rd ⓣ2377 2604. Reading the extensive menu here will take you a while, especially as most of it is affordable. Service is friendly and efficient, and they're open till 1am. Grilled meat and rice HK$30.

**Honey Bee Restaurant** 237–247 Temple St ⓣ2735 0780. A mix of Japanese, Malaysian and European food, with very good value set lunches and reasonable mains. The sizzling fried *teppanyaki* (HK$45) is excellent. Despite the restaurant claiming not to, they may add a service charge on public holidays.

**Kung Wo Restaurant** 27 Prat Avenue ⓣ2739 1880 & 21 Lock Rd ⓣ2623 4680. This clean and friendly place offers good, cheap noodles, rice and snacks just round the corner from the museums. Order a main course and you can get a drink or dessert half-price. Soup and rice dishes HK$26.

### Chungking Mansions

**Delhi Club** 3rd Floor, C Block ⓣ2368 1682. Not quite as tasty as the Khyber Pass (below), the Delhi Club wins out on decor and still provides a decent curry. It has no sign outside, presumably assuming (more-or-less rightly) that everyone knows where it is. Curries around HK$50.

**Khyber Pass** 7th Floor, E Block ⓣ2721 2786. Generally reckoned by travellers and residents alike to be the best curry house in Chungking Mansions. There is also a decent selection of vegetarian food on offer. Ignore the sign on the door that says "Members only". Curries from around HK$35.

## Nightlife

The most concentrated collection of bars is in Central, spreading from the long-standing popular **Lan Kwai Fong** to the network of streets leading into and including the new and upmarket **SoHo** area. Rubbing shoulders with the "hostess bars" in Jaffe and Lockhart Roads in **Wan Chai** are a dozen or more earthier clubs and bars where beer-swilling antics are the norm. **Tsim Sha Tsui's** nightlife scene is rather sparse. The best place to head for if you're after a night out rather than just a drink or two is Knutsford Terrace (just off Kimberley Rd).

### Hong Kong Island

**Hong Kong Brew House** 33 Wyndham St, Lan Kwai Fong, Central ⓣ2522 559. Quaff down the decent premises-brewed ale and munch on peanuts while you take in Lan Kwai Fong's neon-lit hubbub beneath you. A great spot from which to people-watch as you plan your evening out.

**Le Jardin** 10 Wing Wah Lane, Lan Kwai Fong, Central ⓣ2526 2717. Tucked away on a small raised terrace at the end of the lane, up some stairs behind *Coco's*, this place is basically a covered patio filled with greenery.

**New Derby** 80–82 Morrison Hill Rd, Happy Valley ⓣ2893 9123. If you're after somewhere more peaceful to drink, this pub offers a quiet atmosphere and reasonably-priced food.

**Schnurrbart** 29 D'Aguilar Street, Lan Kwai Fong, Central ⓣ2523 4700. Sit at the bar in this German establishment, and you will be able to people-watch on D'Aguilar Street itself. The staff are wonderfully friendly. They have another branch at 9–11 Prat Avenue in Tsim Sha Tsui.

### Kowloon

**Bahama Mama's** 4–5 Knutsford Terrace, just north of Kimberly Rd, Tsim Sha Tsui ⓣ2368 2121. A good atmosphere with plenty of space for pavement drinking. There's a beach-bar theme and outdoor terrace that prompts party crowd antics.

**Delaney's** 71–77 Peking Rd, Tsim Sha Tsui ⓣ2301 3980. Friendly Irish pub with draught beers, Guinness and Irish pub food; features pub quizzes and music challenges with free shooters to be won, as well as showing sporting events. Also at 18 Luard Rd, Wan Chai (ⓣ2804 2880).

### CHEAP DRINKS

Drinking in Hong Kong is expensive and a beer will normally set you back at least HK$50. Most bars however have a **happy hour**, where prices can fall by as much as fifty percent. These usually end around 8 or 9pm, but may last all day on Sunday. *HK Magazine* has a section devoted to places where you can get cheap or even free booze, as well as favourite happy hours. Many bars have Ladies' Nights, particularly on Wednesdays and Thursdays, where women can easily stay out all night without spending anything. Some clubs may also be free for women.

**Ned Kelly's Last Stand** 11A Ashley Rd, Tsim Sha Tsui ⓣ2376 0562. Very popular with both travellers and expats. Features excellent nightly ragtime jazz.

## Shopping

In Tsim Sha Tsui, Causeway Bay and Wan Chai, shop opening hours are generally 11am–11pm; in Central, it's 10am–7pm.

**Arts and crafts** For Chinese souvenirs, including fabrics, porcelain and clothes, visit Chinese Arts and Crafts, which has branches at the China Resources Building, 26 Harbour Rd, Wan Chai; 230 The Mall, One Pacific Place; 88 Queensway, Admiralty; JD Mall, 233 Nathan Rd; and Star House, 3 Salisbury Rd, Tsim Sha Tsui. There's also Yue Hwa Chinese Products Emporium, 55 Des Voeux Road Central, Central, plus 301–309 Nathan Rd, Yau Ma Tei. Try the "Low Price Shop" at 47 Hollywood Road (ⓣ2544 4235) for a mix of statues, *mahjong* sets and Mao memorabilia.

**Bookshops** Dymock's bookshop has branches in most shopping centres and is good for paperbacks and travel guides; the largest is in the IFC Mall. You can also try Page One in Times Square, Causeway Bay. Hip! on 6th Floor, Parekh House, 63 Wyndham Street, Central has the widest selection of guidebooks you'll find anywhere in Hong Kong. For cheap secondhand books, try the excellent Flows at 40 Lyndhurst Terrace or Collectables at 11 Queen Victoria St, both in Central, or The Chapter House, 10 Stanley Main St, Stanley.

**Clothes** Clothes can be good value in Hong Kong, particularly the local casual wear chain stores including Giordano, Wanko and Bossini, which have branches all over the city, but big-name foreign designer clothes are often expensive. For local fashion designs and cheap and unusual togs, head for Granville Road in Tsim Sha Tsui; the boutiques behind SOGO in Causeway Bay as well as nearby Island Beverley; and the Pedder Building on Pedder Street in Central. Beware of size labels – they're often way out. Stanley has the advantage over other markets in that you can usually try things on. For clothing repairs, there are many shops in World-Wide Plaza, Des Voeux Road, Central, including Perfect Fashion Alteration on the 3rd Floor.

**Computers** Both hardware and software can work out very cheap, though you'll need to make sure you get an international warranty. Pirated computer software is also big business, though these days it's more discreet. Recommended outlets include Star Computer City, Star House, 3 Salisbury Rd, Tsim Sha Tsui; 298 Computer Zone, 298 Hennessy Rd, Wan Chai; Golden Shopping Arcade, 156 Fuk Wah St, Sham Shui Po, Kowloon; and Mongkok Computer Centre, at the corner of Nelson and Fa Yuen streets, Mongkok.

**Department stores** Some of Hong Kong's longest-established department stores include the typically Chinese CRC Department Store, 92 Queen's Rd, Central and 488 Hennessy Rd, Causeway Bay; Wing On, 211 Des Voeux Road Central, Central (and other branches).

**Jewellery** There are literally thousands of jewellers in Hong Kong, and prices are relatively low. One place to start is Gallery One, 31–33 Hollywood Rd, Central, which has a huge selection of semi-precious stones and beads. If you're looking for jade, there's a special Jade Market in Kansu Street, Yau Ma Tei (see p.164), and if you'd rather make your own jewellery, head to the streets around exit A of Sham Shui Po MTR.

## Directory

**Airlines** The Hong Kong Airport website (ⓦwww.hongkongairport.com) has details of all airlines flying there. Air India ⓣ2522 1176; British Airways ⓣ2822 9000; Cathay Pacific ⓣ2747 1888; Dragonair ⓣ3193 3888; Hong Kong Airlines ⓣ2155 1888; JAL ⓣ2523 0081; Korean Air ⓣ2366 2001; Malaysia Airlines ⓣ2916 0088; Qantas ⓣ2822 9000; Singapore Airlines ⓣ2520 2233; Thai International ⓣ2876 6888; United Airlines ⓣ2810 4888; Virgin Atlantic Airways ⓣ2532 6060.

**Banks and exchanges** Banks and ATMS are found throughout Hong Kong. For traveller's cheques, American Express is located on the 31st Floor World Trade Centre, 280 Gloucester Rd, Causeway Bay ⓣ2808 2828 (report stolen cheques on ⓣ3002 1276), Mon-Fri 9am-6pm, Sat 9am-1pm.

**Embassies and consulates** Australia, 23rd Floor, Harbour Centre, 25 Harbour Rd, Wan Chai ⓣ2827 8881; UK, 1 Supreme Court Rd, Admiralty ⓣ2901 3000; Canada, 11th-14th Floor, 1 Exchange Square, Central ⓣ3719 4700; China, 7th Floor, China Resources Building, Lower Block, 26 Harbour Rd, Wan Chai ⓣ3413 2424; India, 16D, United Centre, 95 Queensway, Admiralty ⓣ2528 4028; Japan, 46th Floor, One Exchange Square, Central ⓣ2522 1184; Korea, 5th Floor, Far East Financial Centre, 16 Harcourt Rd, Central ⓣ2529 4141; New Zealand, Rm 6501, Central Plaza, 18 Harbour Rd, Wan Chai ⓣ2525 5044; The Philippines, 14th Floor, United Centre, 95 Queensway, Admiralty ⓣ2823 8500; Taiwan (for visas) Chung Hwa Travel Service, 40th Floor, East Tower, Lippo Centre, 89 Queensway, Admiralty ⓣ2525 8315; Thailand, 8th Floor, Fairmont House, 8 Cotton Tree Drive, Central

Ⓣ2521 6481; US, 26 Garden Rd, Central Ⓣ2523 9011; Vietnam, 15th Floor, Great Smart Tower, 230 Wan Chai Rd, Wan Chai Ⓣ2591 4510.

**Hospitals** There are 15 government hospitals offering emergency care, which costs HK$570 with an additional HK$3300 per day for overnight stays. They include the Ruttonjee Hospital, 266 Queen's Rd East, Wan Chai Ⓣ2291 2000, and the Queen Elizabeth Hospital, 30 Gascoigne Road, Kowloon Ⓣ2958 8888. For an ambulance, dial Ⓣ999.

**Internet** Free internet access for customers at most branches of *Pacific Coffee Company* cafés, including one on Nathan Road and in most shopping centres. All public libraries offer free internet access, though you may need to book in advance (Ⓣ2921 2675). Try the Central Library at 66 Causeway Rd, Causeway Bay (Thurs-Tues 10am-9pm, Wed 1-9pm) or City Hall Library on the 6th Floor, City Hall High Block, Central, just round the corner from the Star Ferry Pier (Mon–Thurs 10am–7pm, Fri 10am–9pm, Sat & Sun 10am–5pm).

**Laundry** On the ground floor of Golden Crown Court, Nathan Rd (one block north of *Mirador Mansions*; red entrance). There are also a couple on Tang Lung Street near Times Square in Causeway Bay. Dry cleaners are everywhere; if you get stuck try in the concourse of an MTR station. Some also do laundry.

**Left luggage** In the departure lounge at the airport (daily 6.30am–1am), at Hong Kong MTR Station (under the IFC Mall) and in the China Ferry Terminal in Tsim Sha Tsui. There are also lockers at Outlying Islands Pier 3 and at the Macau Ferry Terminal.

**Police** Crime hotline and taxi complaints Ⓣ2527 7177. For general police enquiries, call Ⓣ2860 6144.

**Post office** The General Post Office is at 2 Connaught Place, Central Ⓣ2921 2222 (Mon–Sat 8am–6pm and Sun 9am–5pm), just west of the Star Ferry Pier. Poste restante mail is delivered here (you can pick it up Mon–Sat 8am–6pm), unless specifically addressed to "Kowloon". The Kowloon main post office is at 405 Nathan Rd, Yau Ma Tei.

**Supermarkets** The best one on Hong Kong island is the 24-hr Wellcome in Causeway Bay, with entrances at 32-36 Patterson Street and 25-29 Great George Street. The bakery will stock you up for breakfast, picnics or snacks, and they also do reheatable deli-style meals. It can get crowded and chaotic but is very useful! In Central, another Wellcome is hidden in The Forum, upstairs off Exchange Square. Kowloon has two useful supermarkets on Hankow Road, a small 24hr Park'n'Shop at no. 8-10 and a decent-sized Wellcome (8am-10pm) buried in the basement of no. 28.

**Telephone services** For IDD calls, use a payphone (which take coins or stored-value cards). You can buy IDD call cards from convenience stores such as 7-11.

**Travel agents** Hong Kong is full of budget travel agents including: Shoestring Travel Ltd, Flat A, 4th Floor, Alpha House, 27 Nathan Rd, Tsim Sha Tsui Ⓣ2723 2306; China Touring Centre (HK), 703 Stag Building, 148–150 Queen's Rd, Central Ⓣ2545 0767; and Hong Kong Student Travel Ltd, 533 Star House, Tsim Sha Tsui Ⓣ2730 2800. For train tickets, tours, flights and visas to mainland China, try the Japan Travel Agency, Room 507–513, East Ocean Centre, 98 Granville Rd, Tsim Sha Tsui East (Ⓣ2368 7767 Ⓦwww.jta.biz/chinavisa), which does the best deals on visas, or the State-run CTS, whose main office is on the Ground Floor, CTS House, 78–83 Connaught Rd, Central (Ⓣ2851 1700 Ⓦwww.ctshk.com).

## Moving on

**By train and bus** The simplest route into China is by direct train from Hung Hom. There are services to Beijing (1 daily, 3.16pm; 24hr; from HK$574),

### CHINESE VISAS

To enter China, you'll need a **visa** – easily obtainable in Hong Kong. Any travel agency and most hotels, even the cheapest hostels, offer this service. A single-entry visa costs about HK$200 with a three-day wait, HK$250–300 if you want it the next day or HK$300–400 for the express same-day service. You can also get more expensive multiple-entry visas. Some passport-holders, including British and US, may have to pay significantly more. Depending on your nationality and passport, it's now also possible to make brief trips to Shenzhen only without a pre-arranged visa (you get a temporary one at the border), but check with the Ministry of Foreign Affairs, 7th Floor, Lower Block, China Resources Building, 26 Harbour Rd, Wan Chai (Mon–Fri 9am–noon & 2–5pm; Ⓣ3413 2300 for a recorded message or Ⓣ3413 2424 Ⓦwww.fmcoprc.gov.hk) as to whether you qualify.

Shanghai (1 daily, 3.16pm; 20hr; from HK$508), Guangzhou (roughly one an hr 7.28am–7.24pm; 1hr 30min, from HK$190; via Dongguan, 1hr, HK$145), and Zhaoqing (one daily, 12.30pm, 4hr; via Dongguang, 1hr, HK$145; Guangzhou East, 1hr 45min, HK$190; and Foshan, 3hrs, HK$210). Tickets are obtainable in advance from CTS offices (see opposite), or on the same day from the Hung Hom MTR Station. For more information, call ⓣ2947 7888. As a cheaper alternative, ride the MTR from East Tsim Sha Tsui up to Lo Wu or Lok Ma Chau (frequent; 50min; HK$36.50), walk into Shenzhen and pick up one of the hourly trains to Guangzhou – tickets can be easily purchased in Hong Kong dollars and cost about HK$100. Buses also run this route. Alternatively, hop on one of the CTS Guangzhou-bound buses that you can pick up from outside their offices in Mongkok or Wan Chai (7 daily; 2–3hr; HK$100; ⓦwww.ctshk.com). There is also a bus station on Scout Path just off Austin Road from where you can catch buses to several Chinese cities including Shenzhen and Guangzhou. They do not produce any information in English but staff at the terminus can help with bookings and enquiries.

**By boat** You can travel to several Chinese cities, the majority from the China Ferry Terminal in Tsim Sha Tsui, where tickets can be bought in advance from a branch of CTS or directly from the booths in the terminal itself. There are services to Shenzhen (Turbojet: 7 daily from Sheung Wan and 1 daily from Kowloon, HK$208, around 1hr; Hyfco Travel Agency, 7 daily, HK$105) and Zhuhai (Chu Kong Shipping; 8 daily; 1hr 10min; HK$180 depending on departure time) as well as several other destinations. Turbojets and catamarans to Macau leave from the Macau Ferry Terminal in Sheung Wan on Hong Kong Island (24hr service every 15min, 7am–8pm, at least every hour thereafter; HK$134-168, depending on departure time and service) and from the China Ferry Terminal (every 30mins 7am–7pm, 8pm and 9pm; HK$134–168). Ferry services to several Chinese destinations (as well as Macau) also operate from Chek Lap Kok Airport. Using this service, it's possible to transfer direct to China without passing through Hong Kong immigration (although you'll need a China visa for all destinations).

**By air** You can fly from Hong Kong into virtually all major Chinese cities on an ever-increasing number of Chinese and Hong Kong-based carriers, including Air China, China Airlines, Dragonair and Hong Kong Airlines. The airport website (ⓦwww.hongkongairport.com) has links to all operators, and destinations include Beijing (4hr); Chengdu (2hr 30min); Fuzhou (1hr 30min); Guangzhou (50min); Guilin (1hr 10min); Haikou (1hr 10min); Hangzhou (2hr); Nanjing (2hr); Shanghai (2hr); Wuhan (1hr 40min); Xiamen (1hr); and Xi'an (2hr 45min). You'll save substantially on ticket prices if you opt to fly from the nearby airports of Macau, Shenzhen or Guangzhou inside China. Macau airport in particular is becoming a mini-hub for budget airlines operating routes to Southeast Asia.

The quickest way to get to the airport is via the Airport Express (6am–12.45am) from either Hong Kong (HK$100) or Kowloon (HK$90) MTR stations. AEL ticket-holders can check in at Hong Kong MTR station up to 24hrs before their flight. Cheaper options include bus #A21 from Nathan Rd (HK$33), #A11 from Gloucester Rd in Causeway Bay and Connaught Road Central in Central (HK$40), #A12 from Connaught Road Central (HK$40), and #E11 from Hennessy Road in Causeway Bay and Connaught Road Central (HK$21). All the buses have equivalent night services and none gives change. Allow an hour to get to the airport; rush hour traffic can slow things down considerably. A taxi will set you back around HK$280 from Tsim Sha Tsui and HK$340 from Hong Kong Island.

# Macau

Macau comprises three distinct parts: the **peninsula**, which is linked by bridge to the island of **Taipa**, and beyond that the former island of **Coloane**, now joined to Taipa by an ever-widening strip of land reclamation.

The peninsula of Macau, the location of the original old city and most of the historic sights (as well as the city amenities), is entirely developed right up to the border with China in the north. Taipa and Coloane used to be just dots of land supporting a few small fishing villages and although the latter is still relatively tranquil, the opening of the new airport, a third bridge from the mainland and a huge reclamation and casino-building programme mean that Taipa has become a rather soulless city suburb. The old village and Coloane are, however, still well worth a visit.

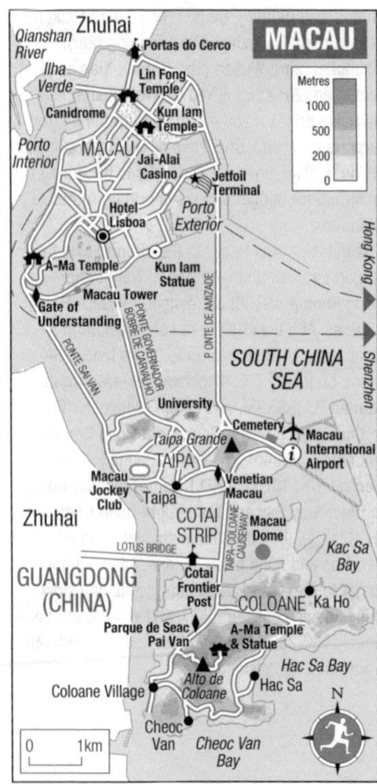


## MACAU PENINSULA

The peninsula is not large and it's possible to get around most of it on foot, though you'll need buses for the longer stretches.The town of Macau was born in the south of the peninsula, around the bay-front road known as the **Praia Grande**, and grew out from there. Sadly, these days, a stroll on the seafront is not what it once was, with the bay now being enclosed and reclamation work underway. The most important road today, **Avenida de Almeida Ribeiro**, cuts across from east (where it's known as Avenida do Infante d'Henrique) to west, taking in the *Hotel Lisboa*, one of Macau's most famous landmarks. The road exits on its western end at the **Porto Interior** (Inner Harbour), near the old docking port, from which foreigners can still depart for the mainland city of Shenzhen in Guangdong.

The western part of Almeida Ribeiro is also the budget-hotel area, and some of the streets immediately inland from here are worth poking around; **Rua da Felicidade**, for example, has been nicely restored and is now full of small hotels, friendly restaurants and stalls selling a colourful array of egg rolls, peanut and sesame snacks and marinated meat.

The northern part of the peninsula up to the border with China is largely residential, though it has a couple of points of interest. It's possible to walk the 3km from Almeida Ribeiro to the border, but the streets at this end of town are not particularly atmospheric, so it makes sense to resort to the local buses.

### Largo do Senado

The beautiful **Largo do Senado** (Senate Square) marks the downtown area and bears the unmistakable influence of southern Europe. At the northern end of the square, away from the main road, is the handsome seventeenth-century Baroque church, **São Domingos** (daily 10am–6pm; free), while to the south, facing the square from across the main road, stands the **Leal Senado** (daily 8am–8pm; free), generally considered the finest Portuguese building in the city. Step into the interior courtyard here to see wonderful blue-and-white Portuguese tiles around the walls, while up the staircase from the courtyard, you reach first a formal garden and then the richly decorated **senate chamber** itself. In the late sixteenth century, all of the colony's citizens would cram into this hall to debate issues of importance. The senate's title *leal* (loyal) was earned during the period when Spain occupied the Portuguese throne and Macau became the final stronghold of those loyal to the true king. Today, the senate chamber is still used by the municipal government of Macau. Adjacent to the chamber is the wood-carved **public library**, whose collection includes many fifteenth- and sixteenth-century books, which visitors are free to browse.

## São Paulo

A few hundred metres north of Largo do Senado stands Macau's most famous landmark, the church of **São Paulo**, once hailed as the greatest Christian monument in east Asia, but today surviving as no more than a facade. Constructed at the beginning of the seventeenth century, it dominated the city for two hundred years until its untimely destruction by fire in 1835. Luckily, however, the facade, which had always been considered the highlight of the building, did not collapse – richly carved and laden with statuary, the cracked stone still presents an imposing sight from the bottom of the steps leading up from the Rua de São Paulo. Next to the facade are the **Na Tcha Temple** and a small section of the old city walls, built nearly five hundred years ago.

## Museum of Macau

Immediately east of São Paulo looms another early seventeenth-century monument, the **Fortaleza do Monte** (daily 7am–7pm; free), which also houses the **Museum of Macau** (Tues–Sun 10am–6pm; MOP$15). The fort is an impressive pile, though it was only once used in a military capacity: to repel the Dutch in 1622, when it succeeded in blowing up the Dutch magazine with a lucky shot from a cannon ball.

## Around Praça Luis de Camões

Perhaps the nicest part of Macau lies a few hundred metres northwest of São Paulo around **Praça Luís de Camões** (also accessible on buses #17 from the *Hotel Lisboa*, and #18 from the Barrier Gate and Inner Harbour). North, facing the square, is the **Jardim Luís de Camões** (daily 6am–10pm; free), a delightful shady park built in honour of the great sixteenth-century Portuguese poet, Luís de Camões, who is thought to have been banished here for part of his life. Immediately east of the square lies the fascinating **Old Protestant Cemetery** (daily 8.30am–5.30pm; free), where all the non-Catholic traders, visitors, sailors and adventurers who happened to die in Macau in the early part of the nineteenth century were buried. The restored gravestones combine to form a vivid image of death in a maritime colony.

### THE MACAU MUSEUMS PASS

The Macau Museums Pass costs MOP$25 and is valid for five days in six museums, including the Museum of Macau, the Maritime Museum, the Arts Museum, the Grand Prix Museum and the Wine Museum and the Lin Zexu Museum.

## Colina da Guia

The Colina da Guia is Macau's highest hill, and its summit is crowned by the seventeenth-century **Guia Fortress**, the dominant feature of which is a charming whitewashed **lighthouse**, added in the nineteenth century and the oldest anywhere on the Chinese coast. It's still in operation, competing with the casinos to light up the sky at night. You can take a **cable car** (Tues–Sun 9am–6pm; MOP$2) up the hill from the Flora Garden, or you can climb the steps underneath it. At the top there are some superb views over the whole peninsula, including, on a clear day, a glimpse of Lantau Island far to the east. There's a tourist information counter and coffee bar (daily 9am–5.30pm) up here as well.

## Outer Harbour

Built on reclaimed land south of the Jetfoil terminal, **Fisherman's Wharf** is a rather bewildering array of amusements, shops and restaurants. It includes a fake volcano, a Roman amphitheatre and a fortress housing a war gaming centre, but dubious claims that it forms a "world-class entertainment centre" are not enough to prevent people wandering on after gawping at it. To the south, the 20m high bronze statue of **Kun Iam**, the Goddess of Mercy, forms a more elegant feature of the Outer Harbour. The seafront area in front of the statue, along Avenida Dr Sun Yat-Sen, has become Macau's main entertainment area, **the NAPE**, with arrays of bars and restaurants open until the small hours.

### Kun Iam Temple

On Avenida do Coronel Mesquita, cutting the peninsula from east to west about 2km north of Almeida Ribeiro, is the enchanting **Kun Iam Temple** (daily 7am–6pm, free), accessible on bus #12, 18 or 19 from the *Hotel Lisboa*. The complex of temples, dedicated to the Goddess of Mercy, is around four hundred years old. In 1844, the United States and China signed their first treaty of trade and co-operation here – you can still see the granite table they used. Around the central statue of Kun Iam, to the rear of the main temple, a crowd of statues represent the eighteen wise men of China, among whom, curiously, is Marco Polo (on the far left), depicted with a curly beard and moustache. The temple is well used by locals who come here to divine their future by shaking a cylinder of bamboo fortune sticks.

### Portas do Cerco: the Chinese border

You can catch bus #18 directly from the Kun Iam Temple to the **Portas do Cerco**, or Barrier Gate, the nineteenth-century stuccoed archway marking the border with China. These days, people cross the border through a customs and immigration complex to one side. A short walk to the west of the gate is the **Sun Yat-sen Memorial Park**, which gives interesting views over Zhuhai in the People's Republic, immediately across a small canal. Buses #3 or #10 will get you back to Almeida Ribeiro and the *Hotel Lisboa* from the gate.

### Rua Central

The small but hilly tongue of land south of Almeida Ribeiro is dotted with interesting buildings. The best way to start exploring this area is to walk up the steep Rua Central leading south from Almeida Ribeiro, just east of Largo do Senado. After five minutes you can detour off down a small road to your right, which leads you up to **Largo de Santo Augustino**, a pleasant square surrounded by colonial edifices, including the pastel-coloured early nineteenth-century church of Santo Agostinho. Back along Rua Central will lead you to another attractive church of the same era, the cream-and-white **São Lourenço**, standing amid palm trees, and then to **Largo do Lilau**, one of the earliest Portuguese residential areas.

### A-Ma Temple

The southwestern side of the Macau peninsula is known as the **Barra district**. Situated underneath Barra Hill overlooking the Inner Harbour, the celebrated **A-Ma Temple** may be six hundred-years-old in some sections. Dedicated to the goddess A-Ma, whose identity blurs from Queen of Heaven into Goddess of the Sea (who is also known as Tin Hau), the temple is an attractive jumble of altars among the rocks.

### Maritime Museum

Immediately across the road from the A-Ma Temple, on the seafront, stands the **Maritime Museum** (daily except Tues 10am–5.30pm; MOP$10, MOP$5 on Sundays), a well-presented, if rather static, collection covering old explorers, seafaring techniques, equipment, models and boats.

### Macau Tower

The futuristic spike rising 338m at the southern end of the peninsula is the **Macau Tower**, which offers (the near-ubiquitous smog permitting) impressive views out to sea and over China. It's also the site of the highest commercial bungy-jump in the world, at 233m. For this and other activities involving clambering round the outside of the tower, contact AJ Hackett (ⓣ8988 8656, ⓦwww.macautower.com.mo, from MOP$418). For the less adventurous, there are two observation decks (daily 10am–8pm, MOP$80) plus a revolving café and restaurant at the top. The road north from here up to the Praia Grande takes about fifteen minutes on foot, or there's a free shuttle bus to the *Hotel Lisboa*.

## TAIPA

Until the eighteenth century, **Taipa** was two islands separated by a channel, the silting up of which subsequently caused the two to merge into one. The same fate has now befallen Taipa and Coloane, except that this time land reclamation is the culprit – the two islands have been fused into one, to make space for large-scale development.

### Taipa Village

**Taipa Village** on the southern shore, with its old colonial promenade, is a pleasant place to wander. There isn't much more than a few streets to the modern village, where the buses stop, though you'll find some great restaurants around the central north–south alley, Rua do Cunha, and, to the west – on the right as you face the shore – a couple of temples in the vicinity of a quiet old square. Next to the Pak Tai Temple you can **rent bicycles,** or simply sit on the new square there and **people-watch**.

#### GETTING TO TAIPA AND COLOANE

Buses #11 and #33 go to Taipa Village from different stops on Almeida Ribeiro, while buses #21, #21A, #26 and #26A stop outside the *Hyatt Regency* on Taipa before going on to Coloane.

### Avenida da Praia

The island's real interest lies a few minutes' walk to the east of Taipa Village, in the former waterfront area. Here, as though frozen in time, is a superb old colonial promenade, the **Avenida da Praia**, complete with its original pale-green houses, public benches and street lamps. The beautifully restored mansions overlook what was the sea – but is now the back of the *Venetian Hotel*. The mansions are open to the public; one houses the **Taipa House Museum**, which gives you some idea of what bourgeois domestic life was like at the beginning of the twentieth century, though descriptions can be rather trite. Next door, the **House of the Islands** displays some old photos of Taipa and Coloane, while the **House of the Portuguese Regions** is a fairly dull celebration of pre-industrial Portuguese culture. The **Exhibition Gallery** next door hosts temporary art shows, while the final villa, the **House for Receptions**, is used for functions. Apart from the last one, the houses are all open from 10am till 6pm Tuesday to Sunday, and one ticket (MOP$5) is valid for all of them.

### The Venetian Macau and Cotai Strip

Macau's most extravagant casino to date is the **Venetian Macau**, worth a trip just to let your jaw drop. Built as a replica of Venice, it includes an artificial outdoor lake and an indoor canal, both with gondolas offering rides (MOP$100 outside, MOP$120 inside). You can also take a lift up to the top of the tower outside. Inside, the complex houses restaurants and shops as well as a rather uninspiring casino. The Grand Canal Shoppes, housed under a rather oppressive fake sky, are mainly affordable high-street shops, and include the likes of *McDonalds*. The Venetian runs free buses for all visitors to both border crossings, both ferry terminals, the airport and Sands casino.

The Venetian is the first establishment to be completed on the **Cotai Strip**, an area of reclaimed land billed as "Asia's Las Vegas". Huge casinos are being built right along it, it has its own ferry service and, in practice, its own border crossing. Existing casinos such as Sands are also building here, and only time will tell what impact this will have on tourism in Macau.

## COLOANE

Coloane peninsula is considerably bigger than Taipa, yet the village is smaller, leaving you with plenty of forested hills to explore and beaches to relax on. It's a pleasant place to spend a few hours, or even a leisurely day.

### A-Ma temple complex

The first attraction is the **Parque de Seac Pai Van** (Tues–Sun 9am–5.45pm; free), a large park with pleasant walks. On top of the nearby hill is a white marble **statue** of the goddess A-Ma; at almost twenty metres high it is the tallest A-Ma in the world. Just below lies a beautiful **A-Ma Temple** complex, which in itself is worth a trip to Coloane. A free shuttle bus runs up to the temple every half hour, leaving from the large ornamental gates just along the road from the main park entrance.

From behind the small eating-area opposite the temple you can join up with the **Coloane trail**, part of a network of well-signposted, straightforward walks around the peninsula. Follow the signs and a half-hour walk will take you down to **Hac-Sa Reservoir,** where you can hire pedalos at weekends; the path then continues across the road and down to the beach.

> **TREAT YOURSELF**
>
> Macau is renowned for its food, which blends Asian, European and African influences. The best food is not as expensive as you might think and is unlikely to cost you more than a meal out at home. Two of the most famous places worth splashing out on are *A Lorcha* and *Fernando's* (see p.184 & p.185).

### Coloane Village

Once past the park, the buses all stop at the roundabout in pretty **Coloane Village** on the western shore, overlooking mainland China just across the water. There's no beach, just mud, in which you'll see old men fishing with nets, but it's a pleasant spot for a coffee and a scrumptious Portuguese egg tart. To the north, you'll find a few junk-building sheds, while the street leading south from the village roundabout, one block back from the shore, contains a couple of interesting antique shops. You'll also find the unexpected yellow-and-white **St Francis Xavier Chapel**, which is fronted by a couple of appealing alfresco restaurants. A few hundred metres beyond this is the **Tam Kong Temple**, housing a metre-long whale bone, carved into the shape of a dragon boat.

### Beaches

Coloane's beaches are not spectacular, but they're pleasant and not usually crowded. With restaurants and a pool next to both of them, they're perfect for a spot of sunbathing away from the noise and people of Macau itself.

Cycling is a good way to travel the 3km to **Hac Sa Beach** on the eastern shore (otherwise, take bus #21A, #25, #26 or #26A), perhaps dropping in on **Cheoc Van Beach** to the south. Alternatively, you can walk most of the way round the headland between the two: from Hac Sa head for the row of white houses at the end of the beach, and from Cheoc Van follow the road until you reach a pink housing estate, and turn left just inside it. The beach at Hac Sa, tree-lined and stretching far off round the bay, is without doubt the best in Macau, despite the black colour of its sand, and both beaches have good facilities including showers and toilets, as well as some decent restaurants nearby (see p.185).

## Arrival

**By boat** Access to Macau for many visitors is by boat from Hong Kong. Every day, large numbers of vessels make the one-hour journey between Hong Kong and Macau's Ferry Terminal ("Terminal Maritimo"), in the east of town, at the Porto Exterior (Outer Harbour). The terminal is connected to the *Hotel Lisboa* and the budget-hotel area on Almeida Ribeiro by several buses, including #3A and #10. The boat services include a 24-hour Turbojet route (every 15min 5.50am–1am, then every 30min) from the Shun Tak Macau Ferry Terminal in Hong Kong, and catamarans departing from the China Ferry Terminal on Canton Road in Tsim Sha Tsui (every 30min 7am–7pm, then one at 8pm and one at 9pm, with later ferries till midnight on Saturdays, Sundays and public holidays ). Ticket prices vary, with evening and weekends being more expensive, but daytime economy class on Turbojet costs $134 from HK–Macau and MOP$142 on the way back. You may have to pay extra to check luggage in, as in theory you're only allowed one piece up to 10kg, and anything above that is charged at HK$10 per kg, minimum charge HK$20. Although you can just turn up, buy a ticket and go, it's advisable to book at weekends and around public holidays. Allow an hour before your sailing for queues with luggage and passport, but daytime tickets are valid on all boats earlier than the stated time, so if you show up early or check in quickly and there's a seat spare you can sail earlier. CotaiJet goes to Taipa not Macau.
**By air** The airport on Taipa Island, is connected by airport bus #AP1 to the Jetfoil Terminal and the Chinese border. You can also catch a **bus** from the airport straight to China. The bus companies have counters at the airport, or you can call China Travel Services (Macau) on ⓣ2886 1356. The airport has left luggage facilities.

## City transport

**Taxi** Taxis are cheap (MOP$11 minimum charge), although don't expect the drivers to speak English. It's best to get someone to write your destination in Chinese characters first. There's a MOP$2 surcharge if you're crossing to Taipa, and a MOP$3 one for each item of luggage in the boot.
**Bus** The flat bus fare on the peninsula is MOP$2.5; the maximum you'll pay to Taipa or Coloane is MOP$5; exact fares only are accepted. Some important bus interchanges include the Ferry Terminal (Terminal Maritimo), the *Hotel Lisboa*, Almeida Ribeiro, Praça Ponte e Horta (near the Porto Interior), Barra (near the Maritime Museum on the Porto Interior), the Barrier Gate (usually referred to by its Portuguese name, Portas do Cerco) and the islands Taipa and Coloane.

## Information

**Tourist information** The Macau Government Tourist Office ((MGTO; ⓦwww.macautourism.gov.mo) has offices in Hong Kong at the Macau Ferry Terminal, Room 1303, Shun Tak Centre (daily 9am–1pm & 2.15–5.30pm; ⓣ2857 2287); at the Visitor Information Centre at the Jetfoil Terminal in Macau (daily 9am–10pm; ⓣ2872 6416); at Taipa Airport (daily 9am–1.30pm, 2.15pm–7.30pm & 8.15pm–10pm; ⓣ2886 1436) and at Largo do Senado 9 in Macau (daily 9am–6pm; ⓣ8397 1120). They also have a Tourist Hotline ⓣ2833 3000. Look out for two useful, free news sheets, *Macau Where* and *Macau What's On*, which list upcoming cultural events. The MGTO puts out a range of leaflets on all the enclave's sights as well as useful maps, most of which have bus routes marked on them.
**Travel agencies** CTS, Nam Kwong Building, Avenida do Dr Rodrigo Rodriguez (ⓣ2870 0888, ⓦwww.cts.com.mo), can sort out China visas and tickets, as can most other tour operators.

## Accommodation

Guesthouses and cheap hotels are clustered at the western end of Almeida Ribeiro, spreading out from the Porto Interior, though there are one or two places in remote, tranquil spots on Coloane. Prices usually go up by at least MOP$50 at weekends and all hotels charge 15 percent tax, so make sure that's included in the price. Many also ask for key deposits of MOP$100 or so. Always ask for a receipt in return.

### USEFUL BUS ROUTES

**#3, #3A, #10 and #10A** from the Jetfoil Terminal to *Hotel Lisboa* and Almeida Ribeiro.
**#5, #18 and #10** from the Barra district in the southwest of the peninsula to Almeida Ribeiro and the Barrier Gate.
**#21 and #21A** from Almeida Ribeiro to Taipa Village and Coloane.
**#18** from the Macau Tower to *Hotel Lisboa*.

The Macau tourist office produces a leaflet with details of budget hotels.

### Macau peninsula

**Augusters Lodge** Rua do Dr Pedro Jose Lobo 24, 3rd floor ⓣ2871 3242, ⓦwww.augusters.de. The only real hostel in Macau, this ramshackle place will fit in a bed for you anywhere there's space – make sure when you book that you've got a bed in a dorm not the lobby. It's a great place to meet other travellers, and the staff are very friendly and speak excellent English. MOP$80 dorm bed, MOP$100 bed in two-bed dorm. ❸

**East Asia Hotel** Rua da Madeira 1 ⓣ2892 2433, reservations from Hong Kong ⓣ2540 6333. In the heart of old Macau, off Rua de Cinco de Outubro. Not the cheapest but with standards of cleanliness and service that may be lacking elsewhere. Singles, doubles and triples have a/c, en-suite bathroom and telephone, and are reasonably good value for money. ❼

**Hotel Central** Ave de Almeida Ribeiro 264 ⓣ2837 3888. The location is great, though the rooms are shabby verging on the grotty, and the cheap ones don't have windows. It's one of the cheapest of all the hotels, but far from the nicest. ❻

**Hou Kong Hotel** Travessa das Virtudes 1 ⓣ2893 7555. This hotel off Rua das Lorchas is clean and relatively quiet. Some of its cheapest rooms even have windows. ❻

**San Va Hospedaria** Rua da Felicidade 67 ⓣ2857 3701. A very basic 42-room hostel with shared facilities. Recommended for low rates and central location. Inspect a few rooms before you pay, as value-for-money varies greatly. The staff speak no English, but they have a list of useful questions on the desk for you to point at. ❹

**Vila Universal** Rua de Felicidade 73 ⓣ2857 3247. This efficiently-run place is clean and manages to make even its windowless rooms feel relatively light ❼

### Coloane

**Pousada de Juventude de Hac Sa & Pousada de Juventude de Cheoc Van** These two hostels in Coloane are amazingly cheap, with beds in very spacious dorms, and are right next to the beach, which makes them peaceful. Both are a little far away, but are on bus routes. There is a catch, however. Only holders of an HI card (and no other) are allowed to use them. Guests must apply to stay here at least eight working days in advance – either in person or by fax to the Directorate of Education and Youth Services, or DSEJ (Avenida de D. Joao IV 7-9, 1st floor, ⓣ2855 5533, ⓕ2896 0115, ⓦwww.dsej.gov.mo). Applications must include a form downloaded from the website and a photocopy of your HI card. The hostels are reserved for local groups during July and August and at other times priority is given to DSEJ and other local groups. MOP$20/30 dorm, MOP$30/50 in 4-bed, MOP$50/80 in two-bed ❶

**Camping** The DSEJ also runs a campsite at Hac Sa beach. HI card holders can theoretically just turn up and pitch their tent, but check first.

## Eating

Most restaurants in Macau serve Chinese and Portuguese food, but if you want something different head to the NAPE, although it will be pricier than anywhere else on Macau. The area features Lebanese, Vietnamese, Japanese and Mexican restaurants.

### Macau peninsula

**A Lorcha** Rua do Almirante Sergio 289 ⓣ2831 3193. Often labelled the best Portuguese restaurant in Macau, with an extensive menu of wonderfully cooked dishes. Standouts include the heart-stopping *serradura*, a spectacular cream and biscuit dessert. Closed Tues. Mains from MOP$68.

**A Vencedora** Rua do Campo 264 ⓣ2835 5460. Established in 1918, this cheap restaurant has a menu with a distinctly Macanese flavour, including plenty of fish options. The service is welcoming and friendly. Fishcakes MOP$45.

**Dragon Mama Cuisine** Rua da Felicidade 51 ⓣ2893 9929. This is the place to go for fresh, cheap, tasty noodles, rice and soups. There's a varied menu and portions are large. They're open for lunch and dinner, and the friendly staff speak reasonable English. Noodles MOP$27.

**Long Kei** Largo do Senado 7B ⓣ2857 3970. A 100-year-old traditional but inexpensive restaurant serving an impressive variety of Cantonese dishes. It's on the left as you face the square from Almeida Ribeiro. Pigeon MOP$50.

**Margeret's Café e Nata** Rua Comandante Mata e Oliveira ⓣ2871 0032. A Macau institution, with street-side benches where you can tuck into inexpensive, chunky sandwiches, baguettes, home-baked quiches and muffins. Macau's creamy egg tarts, or *natas*, don't get any better than the delights served here. Closed Wed. *Nata* MOP$6.

**Wong Chi Kei** Largo do Senado 17 ⓣ2833 1313. In spite of its smart appearance, this restaurant offers excellent food at minimal prices. The beer is also very cheap and there's a history of noodles on the placemat to educate you while you wait. Fried rice MOP$24.

## MACAU FOOD AND DRINKS GLOSSARY

**Basics and snacks**

| | |
|---|---|
| *Arroz* | Rice |
| *Batatas fritas* | French fries |
| *Legumes* | Vegetables |
| *Ovos* | Eggs |
| *Prego* | Steak roll |
| *Sandes* | Sandwiches |

**Soups**

| | |
|---|---|
| *Caldo verde* | cabbage and potato soup |
| *Sopa álentejana* | Garlic and bread soup with a poached egg |
| *Sopa de mariscos* | Shellfish soup |
| *Sopa de peixe* | Fish soup |

**Meat**

| | |
|---|---|
| *Almondegas* | Meatballs |
| *Bife* | Steak |
| *Chouriço* | Spicy sausage |
| *Coelho* | Rabbit |
| *Cordoniz* | Quail |
| *Costeleta* | Chop |
| *Galinha* | Chicken |
| *Porco* | Pork |
| *Salsicha* | Sausage |

**Fish and seafood**

| | |
|---|---|
| *Ameijoas* | Clams |
| *Bacalhau* | Dried and salted cod |
| *Camarões* | Shrimps |
| *Carangueijo* | Crab |
| *Gambas* | Prawns |
| *Linguado* | Sole |
| *Lulas* | Squid |
| *Meixilhões* | Mussels |

**Specialities**

| | |
|---|---|
| *Cataplana* | Seafood stew with bacon, sausage and peppers |
| *Cozido á Portuguesa* | Boiled casserole of mixed meats, eg pig's trotters rice and vegetables |
| *Galinha á Africana* | Chicken rolled or marinated in a pepper and chilli paste |
| *Galinha á Portuguesa* | Chicken with eggs, potatoes, onion and saffron in a mild, creamy curry sauce |
| *Feijoada* | Brazilian bean, pork, sausage, cabbage and potato stew |
| *Pasteis de bacalhau* | Deep-fried cod fishcakes |
| *Porco á álentejana* | Pork and clam stew |

**Desserts**

| | |
|---|---|
| *Arroz doce* | Rice pudding |
| *Nata* | Egg tart |
| *Pudim flán* | Crème caramel |

**Drinks**

| | |
|---|---|
| *Água mineral* | Mineral water |
| *Café* | Coffee |
| *Chá* | Tea |
| *Cerveja* | Beer |
| *Vinho* | Wine |
| *Vinho do Porto* | Port (red and white) |
| *Vinho verde* | A slightly sparkling white wine |

### Taipa

**Galo** Rua do Cunha 45, ☎2882 7423. Another good place to sample cheap but very tasty Portuguese food. They have another, more expensive branch called *DomGalo* in the NAPE. African Chicken, MOP$55.

**Panda** Rua Carlos Eugenio 4 ☎827 338. On a tiny alley leading east from the southern end of Rua da Cunha in Taipa Village. Reasonably priced Portuguese place, with a large selection of *bacalhau*.

### Coloane

**Fernando's** Hac Sa Beach ☎882 531. Not far from the bus stop. An institution amongst local expats, *Fernando's* has the casual, cheerful atmosphere of a Mediterranean bistro and great, reasonably priced Portuguese food. Advance booking recommended, especially at weekends. Mains from MOP$66.

**Lord Stow's Bakery** Coloane Town Square. A contender, with *Margaret's Café e Nata*, for Macau's best egg custard tart. You can sit and eat at the new *Lord Stow's Café* just around the corner. Alternatively, consume your treats on the benches overlooking the water. *Nata* MOP$6.

## Nightlife

Although drinking isn't a major pastime in Macau and can be expensive, a cluster of new bars and night-time cafés lies in the stretch of reclaimed land just southwest of the Jetfoil

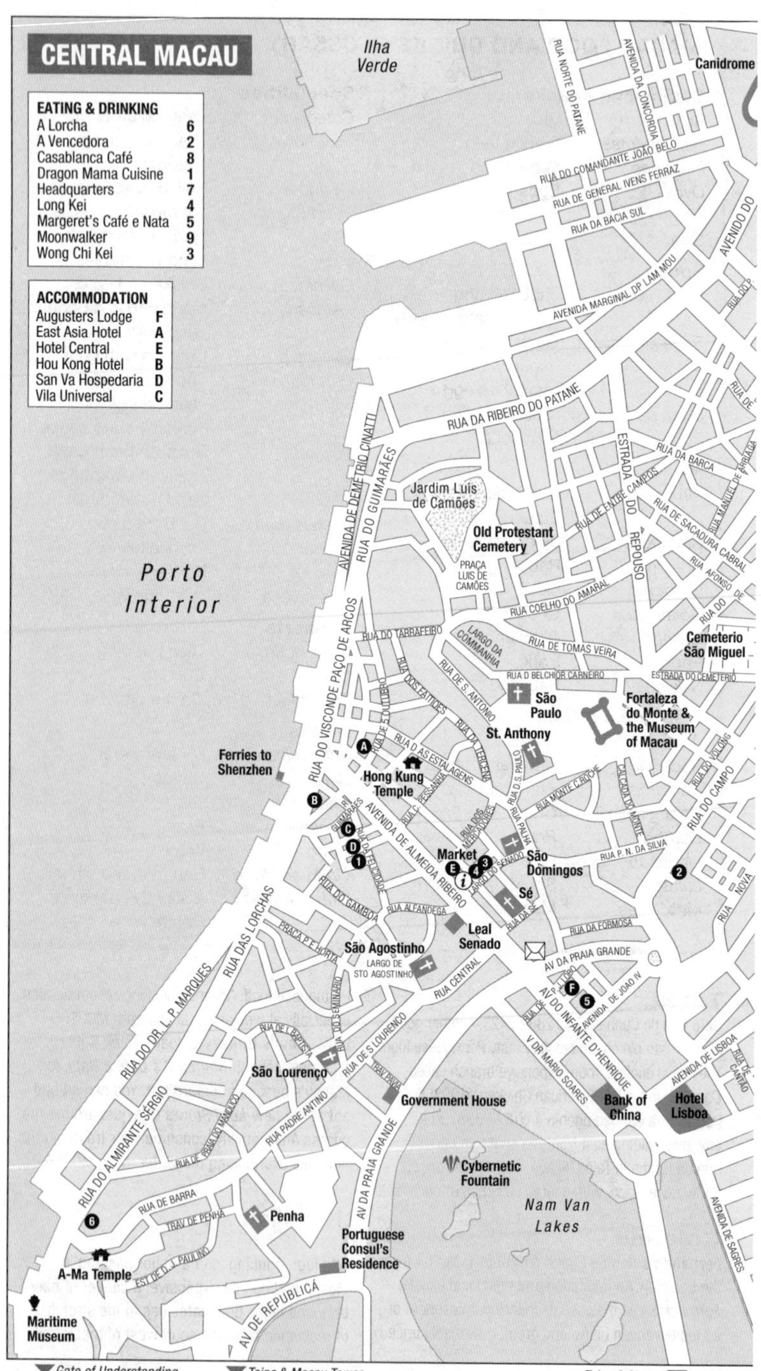
CENTRAL MACAU
EATING & DRINKING
A Lorcha 6
A Vencedora 2
Casablanca Café 8
Dragon Mama Cuisine 1
Headquarters 7
Long Kei 4
Margeret's Café e Nata 5
Moonwalker 9
Wong Chi Kei 3
ACCOMMODATION
Augusters Lodge F
East Asia Hotel A
Hotel Central E
Hou Kong Hotel B
San Va Hospedaria D
Vila Universal C
Ilha Verde
Canidrome
Porto Interior
Jardim Luis de Camões
Old Protestant Cemetery
Praça Luis de Camões
Cemeterio São Miguel
São Paulo
Fortaleza do Monte & the Museum of Macau
St. Anthony
Ferries to Shenzhen
Hong Kung Temple
Market
São Domingos
Sé
Leal Senado
São Agostinho
Largo de Sto Agostinho
São Lourenço
Government House
Bank of China
Hotel Lisboa
Cybernetic Fountain
Nam Van Lakes
Penha
Portuguese Consul's Residence
A-Ma Temple
Maritime Museum
Rua Norte do Patane
Avenida da Concordia
Rua do Comandante João Belo
Rua de General Ivens Ferraz
Rua da Bacia Sul
Avenida Marginal DP Lam Mou
Rua da Ribeiro do Patane
Avenida de Demetrio Cinatti
Rua do Guimarães
Estrada do Repouso
Rua da Barca
Rua de Entre Campos
Rua de Sacadura Cabral
Rua Coelho do Amaral
Rua do Tarrafeiro
Largo da Commanhia
Rua de Tomas Veira
Rua D Belchior Carneiro
Estrada do Cemeterio
Rua do Visconde Paço de Arcos
Rua dos Faitides
Rua de S. Antonio
Rua da Tercena
Rua D as Estalagens
Rua Monte C. Roche
Calcada do Monte
Rua do Campo
Avenida de Almeida Ribeiro
Rua da Felicidade
Rua do Gamboa
Rua Alfandega
Largo do Senado
Rua P. N. da Silva
Rua Nova
Rua da Formosa
Av da Praia Grande
Avenida de João IV
Av do Infante D'Henrique
V Dr Mario Soares
Avenida de Lisboa
Rua das Lorchas
Praça P E Horta
Rua Central
Rua do Seminario
Rua de S Lourenço
Trav Paiva
Rua do Dr. L. P. Marques
Rua do Almirante Sergio
Rua Padre Antino
Av da Praia Grande
Rua de Barra
Trav de Penha
Est de D. J. Paulino
Av de Republicá
Avenida de Sagres
Gate of Understanding
Taipa & Macau Tower
Taipa & Airport

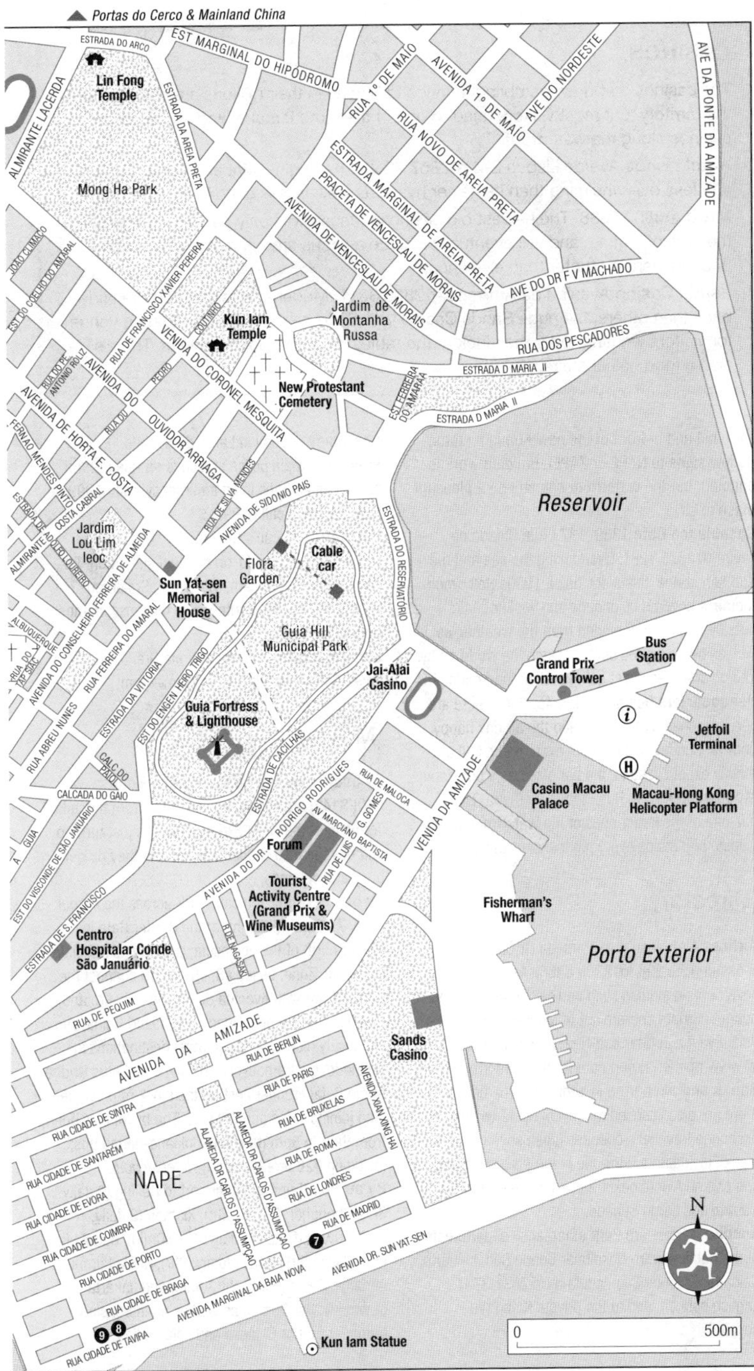
Portas do Cerco & Mainland China
Lin Fong Temple
Mong Ha Park
Kun Iam Temple
New Protestant Cemetery
Jardim de Montanha Russa
Reservoir
Jardim Lou Lim Ieoc
Sun Yat-sen Memorial House
Flora Garden
Cable car
Guia Hill Municipal Park
Guia Fortress & Lighthouse
Jai-Alai Casino
Grand Prix Control Tower
Bus Station
Jetfoil Terminal
Casino Macau Palace
Macau-Hong Kong Helicopter Platform
Forum
Tourist Activity Centre (Grand Prix & Wine Museums)
Fisherman's Wharf
Porto Exterior
Centro Hospitalar Conde São Januário
Sands Casino
NAPE
Kun Iam Statue
AVENIDA DA AMIZADE
AVENIDA DR. SUN YAT-SEN
AVENIDA MARGINAL DA BAIA NOVA
ESTRADA DO RESERVATÓRIO
AVENIDA DO CORONEL MESQUITA
AVENIDA DE HORTA E COSTA
RUA DOS PESCADORES
AVE DO DR F V MACHADO
0
500m
N

### CASINOS

The casinos that draw gambling fanatics to Macau in their millions are dotted about the territory, but most visitors head to one of the more famous (and accessible) casinos along the waterfront.

**Hotel Lisboa** Ave de Lisboa 2–4 ⓣ2857 7666. The original Macau casino is smaller and less overwhelming than its newer rivals, as well as less gaudily decorated.

**MGM** ⓣ8802 8888. The newest big casino in Macau was only partly in operation at the time of writing, and will eventually include a circus amongst other attractions. Security here is stricter than elsewhere.

**Sands Casino** Avenida da Amizade ⓣ2888 3311. Modern, hi-tech and more laid-back than others, the huge Sands Casino is likely to be the least intimidating venue for visitors wanting to try their luck at the tables or on the slot machines. There's also a food hall upstairs.





Terminal and in front of the new Kun Iam statue (follow signs to NAPE or ZAPE). Building work is ongoing, but the waterfront can still be a pleasant place to sit.

**Casablanca Café** 1369–1373 Rua Cidade de Tavira ⓣ2875 1281. Overlooking the sea and the Kun Iam statue, this place has a 1930s Hollywood theme. A covered colonnade and wicker chairs outside mean it's protected from the weather, as well as being a good spot to watch the world go by. Things don't really get going until around midnight.

**Headquarters** Rua de Madrid 45. Prices here are very reasonable for Macau and the all-day happy hour on Sunday makes them even better. Full of mainly expat clientele, the bar also has a pool table.

**Moonwalker** 1361 Rua Cidade de Tavira. This bar, one of the larger ones of the waterfront, hosts Filipino pop bands every night except Tuesday.

## Directory

**Airlines** Air Macau is at Alameda Dr Carlos D'Assumpcao 398 (ⓣ8396 6888). As well as several main airlines such as Thai Airways, many budget carriers operate out of Macau, including Air Asia, Eva Air, JetStar and Tiger Airways. Check out ⓦwww.macau-airport.com for more information.

**Banks and exchange** In addition to the banks, there are also licensed moneychangers which exchange traveller's cheques (open seven days a week), including a 24hr one in the *Lisboa Casino*, and two on Ave Almeida Ribeiro between *Hotel Central* and Largo Senado.

**Hospitals** There are 24hr emergency departments at the public Centro Hospitalar Conde São Januário, Calçada Visconde São Januário (ⓣ2831 3731; English spoken) and at the private Kiang Wu hospital.

**Pharmacy** Several in Largo do Senado.

**Police** The main police station is on Rua Central and operates 24hr. In an emergency, call ⓣ999; to report a crime call ⓣ993.

**Post office** Macau's General Post Office is in Largo do Leal Senado, on the east side (Mon–Fri 9am–5.30pm, Sat 9am–12.30pm). Small red booths all over the territory also dispense stamps from machines.

**Supermarkets** Pavilions at Praia Grande 421, (Mon–Sat 10am–9pm, Sun 11am–8pm).

## Moving on

**By boat** Tickets for **boats to Hong Kong** (MOP$142) are available in advance from the Jetfoil Terminal at the Porto Exterior. You can just turn up and buy the next available ticket, but they do get busy at weekends.

**By bus to China** You can **walk** across the border (daily 7.30am–midnight) at the Barrier Gate in the far north of the peninsula, into Zhuhai Special Economic Zone; buses #3, #5 and #9 connect the Barrier Gate with Avenida de Almeida Ribeiro and Rua da Praia Grande. Once in mainland China, you can easily pick up a bus to most destinations in Guangdong. Alternatively, cross via the Lotus Bridge at the Cotai Frontier Post on the block of reclaimed land joining Taipa and Coloane. The building is open from 9am to 8pm (take any Coloane-bound bus, including #26 or #21A, from *Hotel Lisboa*).

**By air** from Taipa Island airport to Beijing (2 daily; 3hr), Shanghai (7 daily; 2hr), Xiamen (2 daily; 1hr), Taiwan (frequent daily; 1hr 30min), Bangkok (5–6 daily; 2hr), Manila (daily; 2hr), Kuala Lumpur (4 daily), Seoul (daily; 4hr 30min) and Jakarta (4 weekly; 3hr 30min) as well as an increasing number of other Chinese and Asian cities.

# Indonesia

## HIGHLIGHTS

ORANG-UTANS: see these enchanting creatures at Bukit Lawang

EAST KALIMANTAN: explore Borneo's remote rivers and jungles

TANAH TORAJA, SULAWESI: gorgeous scenery, traditional architecture and festivals

UBUD: Bali's cultural capital with art galleries, dance performances and festivals

BOROBUDUR: the biggest Buddhist stupa in the world

GUNUNG RINJANI, LOMBOK: climb one of Indonesia's highest mountains

FACE THE DRAGONS: while Komodo gave its name to the world's largest lizard, Rinca is more atmospheric

## ROUGH COSTS

**DAILY BUDGET** Basic US$15–25/ Occasional treat US$30–50

**DRINK** US$4

**FOOD** US$5

**HOSTEL/BUDGET HOTEL** US$9

**TRAVEL** Bus: Denpasar-Yogyarta (15hr) up to US$30; Ferry Bali–Lombok (4hr) US$2.50

## FACT FILE

**POPULATION** 234.7 million

**AREA** 1,919,440 sq km

**LANGUAGE** Bahasa Indonesian, plus 500 local languages.

**RELIGIONS** Islam majority, plus Christian groups, Hinduism and animism and ancestor worship.

**CURRENCY** Indonesian rupiah (Rp)

**CAPITAL** Jakarta

**INTERNATIONAL PHONE CODE** ⓣ+61

**TIME ZONE** GMT + 7–9hr. Bali is one hour ahead of Java.

# Introduction

**The Indonesian archipelago spreads over 5200km between the Asian mainland and Australia, all of it within the tropics, and comprises between 13,000 and 17,000 islands. Its ethnic, cultural and linguistic diversity is correspondingly great – around 500 languages and dialects are spoken by its 200 million people, whose fascinating customs and lifestyles are a major attraction.**

There is a well-worn overland travellers' route across the archipelago which begins by taking a boat from Penang in Malaysia to **Medan** on Sumatra's northeast coast. From here, the classic itinerary runs to the **orang-utan sanctuary** at Bukit Lawang, the hill resort of **Berastagi**, and the lakeside resorts of **Danau Toba**. Further south, the area around **Bukittinggi** appeals because of its flamboyant Minangkabau architecture and dances. Many travellers then hurtle through to **Java**, probably spending no more than a night in the traffic-clogged capital **Jakarta** in their rush to the ancient cultural capital of

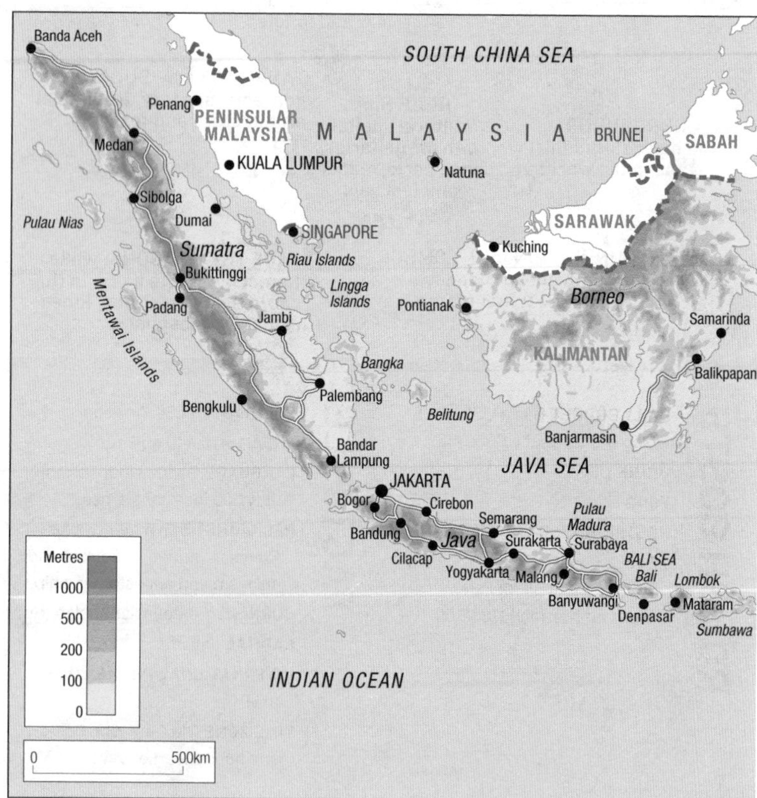

**Yogyakarta** – the best base for exploring the huge **Borobudur** (Buddhist) and **Prambanan** (Hindu) temples. Java's biggest natural attractions are its volcanoes, most famously East Java's **Gunung Bromo**, where most travellers brave a sunrise climb to the summit.

Just across the water from Java sits **Bali**, the long-time jewel in the crown of Indonesian tourism, a tiny island of elegant temples, verdant landscape and fine surf. The biggest resorts are the party towns of **Kuta** and adjacent **Legian**, with the more subdued beaches at **Lovina** and **Candi Dasa** appealing to travellers not hell-bent on nightlife. Most visitors also spend time in Bali's cultural centre **Ubud**, whose lifeblood continues to be painting, carving, dancing and music-making. The islands east of Bali – collectively known as **Nusa Tenggara** – are now attracting bigger crowds, particularly neighbouring **Lombok**, with its beautiful beaches and temples. East again, the **Komodo dragons** draw travellers to **Komodo** and **Rinca**, and then it's an easy hop across to **Flores**, which has the unforgettable coloured crater lakes of **Kelimutu**. South of Flores, **Sumba** is famous for its intricate fabrics, grand funeral ceremonies and extraordinary annual ritual war, the *pasola*.

North of Flores, **Sulawesi** is renowned for the idiosyncratic architecture and impressively ghoulish burial rituals of the highland Torajans. While west of Sulawesi, the island of Borneo plays host to the Indonesian state of **Kalimantan**, with opportunities for river travel in remote jungle.

## SAFETY IN INDONESIA

The militant Islamic Jemaah Islamiyah terrorist group has been responsible for numerous bombs in Indonesia, most notable, of course, the **Bali bomb** of 2002, which left over 200 dead and the country's entire tourist industry in tatters. Since then the *Marriott* hotel in Jakarta was bombed in August 2003, the Australian embassy in Jakarta in September 2004 and Bali again in October 2005. Terrorism remains a threat, though arguably no more than in much of the rest of the world.

At the time of writing, there was also specific advice still in place against travelling to a couple of ongoing troublespots in the country – the **Maluku islands** and **central Sulawesi**. Much of the trouble dates back to 1999, and the horrifying chaos of the elections of the newly independent state of East Timor. Riots in many parts of the archipelago pitched Muslims against their Christian neighbours, while locals in other provinces, inspired by the success of East Timor in winning its independence, began to fight for the secession of their own province. The **Maluku Islands** in particular were devastated by an internecine war that left thousands dead. A measure of calm is returning to the islands, and travellers are now trickling back.

The security situation can also be unpredictable in other troublespots such as **Aceh** in northern Sumatra, and the Poso region of **central Sulawesi** (see p.381 for more) – where the beheading of three Christian schoolgirls in October 2005 provoked some serious sectarian violence – though the situation in both places has improved dramatically. We also do not cover remote and little-visited **West Papua** (formerly known as Irian Jaya), whose ongoing separatist struggle has in the past resulted in violence against foreigners, or East Timor's neighbour, **West Timor**. If you insist on visiting Indonesia's more unsettled areas, make sure you are fully aware of the latest situation, and heed any warnings given out by your foreign office (see box p.50 for websites), as well as the local people who, along with your fellow travellers, are usually the best source of up-to-date information.

## CHRONOLOGY

**c. 800,000 years ago** Java Man, whose skull fragments were found near Solo in 1893, is the earliest evidence of hominoids in the region.

**Fifth century AD** Numerous small Hindu kingdoms pepper the islands.

**Seventh century** The Buddhist Srivijaya kingdom, based in Palembang in South Sumatra, control the Melaka straights for the next four hundred years. Its empire extends as far as Thailand and West Borneo.

**Ninth century** In central Java, it's an age of spectacular, competitive temple building: the Buddhist Saliendra kingdom erects the magnificent temple of Borobudur, while the rival Sanjaya empire builds the Hindu Prambanan temple complex.

**1292–1389** The Hindu Majapahit empire, based in East Java, rules over a vast area from Sumatra to Timor, the first time the archipelago's major islands are united.

**Fourteenth century** Islam, which had been introduced to Sumatra centuries earlier, spreads eastwards into Java as small coastal sultanates grow after the collapse of the Majapahit empire.

**Early sixteenth century** The Portuguese establish a virtual monopoly over the lucrative spice trade, taking control of the Moluccas (Maluku or Spice Islands).

**1602** The Dutch, who had arrived at the end of sixteenth century, establish the Dutch East India Company (VOC), which gains a monopoly over trade with the Moluccas. It starts building a loose but lucrative empire across the archipelago.

**1619** The VOC builds a fortress in Jakarta. The local population responds angrily, and the Dutch retaliate by razing the city and renaming it Batavia.

**Eighteenth century** The plains of Central Java, ruled by the Islamic Mataram Empire, are riven by dynastic disputes, known as the Three Wars of Succession. The last one (1746–57) divides the empire into three sultanates, two at Solo and one at Yogyakarta. The Dutch then subjugate the entire territory.

**1799** The VOC folds and the Dutch government (under a French Protectorate) takes possession of its territories.

**1811** The British, under Sir Thomas Stamford Raffles, attack and pick off the islands one by one, landing at Batavia in 1811.
**1816** With the end of the Napoleonic wars, the territories return to the Dutch who are soon embroiled in bloody disputes with opponents of their rule.
**1830** The Dutch devise the Cultural System whereby Javanese farmers must grow cash crops for sale in Europe at a huge profit. Java became one giant plantation, to the detriment of indigenous farmers.
**1870 onwards** The Dutch gradually implement more progressive policies, but this coincides with some devastating natural disasters. Later irrigation, healthcare and education programmes are started.
**1894–1920** The Dutch expand into previously independent territories: Lombok in 1894, Bali in 1906 and Aceh in 1908. By 1910 the Dutch have conquered nearly all of Indonesia; West Papua is the last to fall in 1920.
**1927** Achmed Sukarno founds the pro-independence Partai Nasional Indonesia (PNI). The Dutch outlaw the party and imprison Sukarno in 1931, later exiling him.
**1942–45** Japanese occupation.
**August 17, 1945** Sukarno reads a Declaration of Independence, but it is not recognized by the allies whom return the territory to the Dutch.
**1946–49** War with the Dutch, who withdraw in December 1949. The new Republic of Indonesia is established with Sukarno as president.
**1949–65** Sukarno presides over a system he calls guided democracy, in reality authoritarian rule. He forges ties with the Soviet Union, and is sympathetic to the communist party, against the Indonesian army.
**September 30, 1965** A group of communists (whom Sukarno is thought to be in cahoots with) abduct and execute a number of leading generals, claiming they are preventing an army-led coup. General Suharto eventually seizes control from them.
**1965–67** Suharto launches a purge against the communists, during which it's thought at least 500,000 people die. He restores relations with the West and aid pours into Indonesia. In 1967 Suharto is named acting president.
**1970s** Indonesia benefits from rising oil prices – its biggest export.
**December 1975** Indonesia invades East Timor, which had been granted independence by Portugal the previous year.
**1997** Southeast Asia's currency crisis. The value of the rupiah plummets. There are widespread demonstrations, and riots take place in all major cities.
**May 21, 1998** Suharto steps down after 32 years and his vice-president, B.J. Habibie, takes over. In early November there's more rioting, with demands Suharto is tried on charges of mismanagement and corruption.
**1999** Though the Indonesian Democratic Party of Struggle, led by Megawati Sukarnoputri, Sukarno's daughter, win the elections, Indonesia's parliament chooses Gus Dur as president with Megawati vice-president.
**1999** East Timor gains independence. Other far-flung Indonesian provinces begin to become more vocal – and violent – in their struggle for sovereignty.
**2002** Two bombs are left by Islamist terrorists in a nightclub and an Irish bar in Kuta, Bali, killing 202 people.
**2004–5** There are a series of bombings – at a hotel in Jakarta in August 2004, the Australian Embassy in September, and in October 2005 Bali is bombed again.
**December 26, 2004** A devastating tsunami hits the country leaving over 160,000 Indonesians dead or missing.
**January 2008** Suharto dies. His legacy is mixed: he oversaw the country's economic growth, but was accused of – and evaded prosecution for – massive corruption, and many human rights abuses, including the deaths of hundreds of thousands of people.

### WHEN TO GO

Climate-wise, the whole archipelago is tropical, with **temperatures** at sea level always between 21°C and 33°C, although cooler in the mountains. In theory, the year divides into a wet and dry season, though it's often hard to tell the difference. Very roughly, in much of the country, November to April are the wet months (Jan, and Feb, the wettest) and May through to October are dry. However, in northern Sumatra, this pattern is effectively reversed. The **peak tourist season** is between mid-June and mid-September and again over the Christmas and New Year season. This is particularly relevant in the major resorts, where prices rocket and rooms can be fully booked for days, and sometimes weeks, on end.

# Basics

## ARRIVAL

Jakarta's Soekarno-Hatta Airport and Bali's Ngurah Rai Airport are the main international air gateways into Indonesia, with direct flights from several Australian cities – there are flights to Bali from Sydney, Melbourne, Perth and Darwin. The archipelago also boasts international airports at Medan, Makassar, Manado, Surabaya and Yogyakarta – with connections mainly with other Southeast Asian airports.

The once-popular Kupang to Darwin flight, that allowed Australia-bound travellers to travel through the archipelago to West Timor without having to double back on themselves to catch their flight to Oz, has yet to recommence, though rumours persist that it will start again one day.

Indonesia has good ferry connections with Malaysia and Singapore and there are occasional cargo boats from the Philippines.

### From Malaysia and Singapore

A variety of ferries and speedboats depart from Penang (see p.522), on the west coast of Peninsular Malaysia, to **Medan** and from Melaka (see p.557) in southern Malaysia to **Dumai** or **Pekanbaru**. You can also take ferries from Johor Bahru (see p.557), in far southern Malaysia, and Singapore to Sumatra via the islands of **Batam** and **Bintan**; and from Port Klang (see p.505), near Kuala Lumpur, to **Tanjung Balai** and Dumai in Sumatra.

There are two entry points between **East Malaysia and Kalimantan**. You can catch a bus between the capital of Malaysian **Sarawak** at Kuching (see p.573) to West Kalimantan's capital, Pontianak; alternatively, you can cross from the East Malaysian state of **Sabah** by catching a two or three-hour ferry (see p.603) to **Pulau Nunukan** or **Tarakan** from Tawau, two days' bus ride southeast of Kota Kinabalu.

## VISAS

Citizens of Britain, Ireland, most of Europe, Australia, New Zealand, Canada and the USA can get thirty-day visas (around $35) on arrival from any of Indonesia's **official immigration gateways**, though it's worth checking before hand as Indonesian visa regulations are prone to change. Official gateways include major international airports – such as Jakarta, Denpasar (Bali), Yogyakarta, Solo, Surabaya and Medan – and several seaports, including Padan Bai in Bali, Tanjung Priok for Jakarta, Palau Batam and Palau Bintam (between Singapore and Sumatra), and Medan on Sumatra. If you're arriving if Indonesia through a more remote air or seaport, check whether you need to obtain a visa from an Indonesian consulate in advance. For a full list of official gateways see ⓦwww.indonesianembassy.org.uk.

You can get a **sixty-day visa**, but only by applying in advance from an Indonesian consulate; the cost is around $55 and the process takes about three days, though this varies from one consulate to the next. Neither the thirty- nor sixty-day visas are extendable, and you'll be **fined** US$20 for every day you overstay your visa, up to a maximum of fourteen days. After that, you'll get blacklisted from Indonesia for two years. Note that you must show your ticket out of the country when applying for a visa, whether you're applying at the embassy or the port.

Those entering the country via a **non-designated gateway** must get a visa from an Indonesian consulate (see p.57) before travelling. Further details on the latest situation can be found at www.indonesianembassy.org.uk.

## AIRPORT DEPARTURE TAX

The **airport departure tax** varies from airport to airport, but is approximately Rp100,000 on international flights, and Rp5000–30,000 for domestic flights.

# GETTING AROUND

Delays are common to all forms of transport – including major flights – caused by weather, mechanical failure, or simply not enough passengers turning up, so you'll save yourself a good deal of stress if you keep your schedule as flexible as possible.

## Buses, minibuses and trains

**Buses** are cheap, easy to book and leave roughly on time. But they're also slow, cramped and often plain terrifying: accidents can be devastating. Where there's a choice of operators on any particular route, ask local people which bus company they recommend. **Tickets** are sold a day or more in advance from the point of departure or bus company offices – which are not necessarily near the relevant **bus station** (*terminal*). Where services are infrequent it's a good idea to buy tickets as early as possible. Tell the driver your exact destination, as it may be possible to get delivered right to the door of your hotel. The average **long-distance bus** has padded seats but little leg- or headroom; it's worth forking out for a luxury bus, if available, which costs twice as much but will have reclining seats. You'll get regular meal stops at roadhouses along the way. On shorter routes, you'll use minibuses, widely known by their Balinese tag, **bemo**. Other names for local transport include *taksi* (bemo in Kalimantan), pete-petes (in Sulawesi), *travel* (share taxis in Flores) and *oplet*. Once on their way, they're faster than buses and cheaper; fares are handed over on board, and rarely advertised. You may also have to pay for any space your luggage occupies. It's almost impossible to give the **frequency** with which bemos and public buses run; if no frequency is given in the guide, they are frequent, roughly hourly. Journey times given are the minimum you can expect.

In resort areas such as Bali, a more pleasant option are **tourist shuttle buses** – though far more expensive than local services, these will take you between points as quickly as possible. The longest-established firm on Bali and Lombok is **Perama** (ⓦwww.peramatour.com). They have offices in most major tourist destinations and produce a useful leaflet outlining their routes. Typical fares for these are around Rp30,000–85,000.

In Java, **trains** can be a better option than buses. They're much more comfortable and reliable, the train stations are generally more centrally situated, and you're much less likely to get ripped off.

## Boats and ferries

Most Indonesians choose to travel between islands by boat, either on the state shipping line, Pelni, or on anything from cargo freighters to tiny fishing vessels. Public ferries run regularly on the shorter crossings between neighbouring islands, such as between Sumatra and Java, Java and Bali and Bali and Lombok, for example. In more visited areas you'll find tourist boat services, and combined long-distance bus and boat options.

For longer routes **Pelni** (ⓦwww.pelni.com) currently operates more than twenty **passenger liners**, most of which run on two-week or monthly circuits and link Java with ports on all the main island groups between Sumatra and Papua (see pp.196–197 for a map of the main routes). The best place for up-to-date information on routes is the **local Pelni office** (listed under "Moving on"

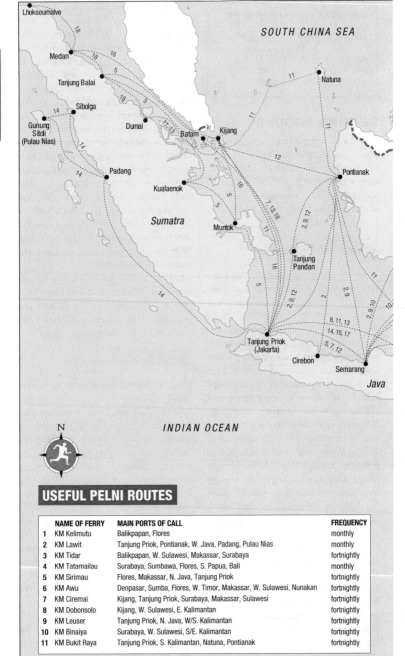

SOUTH CHINA SEA

Lhokseumalve

Medan

Tanjung Balai

Sibolga

Gunung Sitoli (Pulau Nias)

Dumai

Batam

Kijang

Natuna

Padang

Kualaenok

Pontianak

Sumatra

Muntok

Tanjung Pandan

Tanjung Priok (Jakarta)

Cirebon

Semarang

Java

INDIAN OCEAN

## USEFUL PELNI ROUTES

| | NAME OF FERRY | MAIN PORTS OF CALL | FREQUENCY |
|---|---|---|---|
| 1 | KM Kelimutu | Balikpapan, Flores | monthly |
| 2 | KM Lawit | Tanjung Priok, Pontianak, W. Java, Padang, Pulau Nias | monthly |
| 3 | KM Tidar | Balikpapan, W. Sulawesi, Makassar, Surabaya | fortnightly |
| 4 | KM Tatamailau | Surabaya, Sumbawa, Flores, S. Papua, Bali | monthly |
| 5 | KM Sirimau | Flores, Makassar, N. Java, Tanjung Priok | fortnightly |
| 6 | KM Awu | Denpasar, Sumba, Flores, W. Timor, Makassar, W. Sulawesi, Nunakan | fortnightly |
| 7 | KM Ciremai | Kijang, Tanjung Priok, Surabaya, Makassar, Sulawesi | fortnightly |
| 8 | KM Dobonsolo | Kijang, W. Sulawesi, E. Kalimantan | fortnightly |
| 9 | KM Leuser | Tanjung Priok, N. Java, W/S. Kalimantan | fortnightly |
| 10 | KM Binaiya | Surabaya, W. Sulawesi, S/E. Kalimantan | fortnightly |
| 11 | KM Bukit Raya | Tanjung Priok, S. Kalimantan, Natuna, Pontianak | fortnightly |

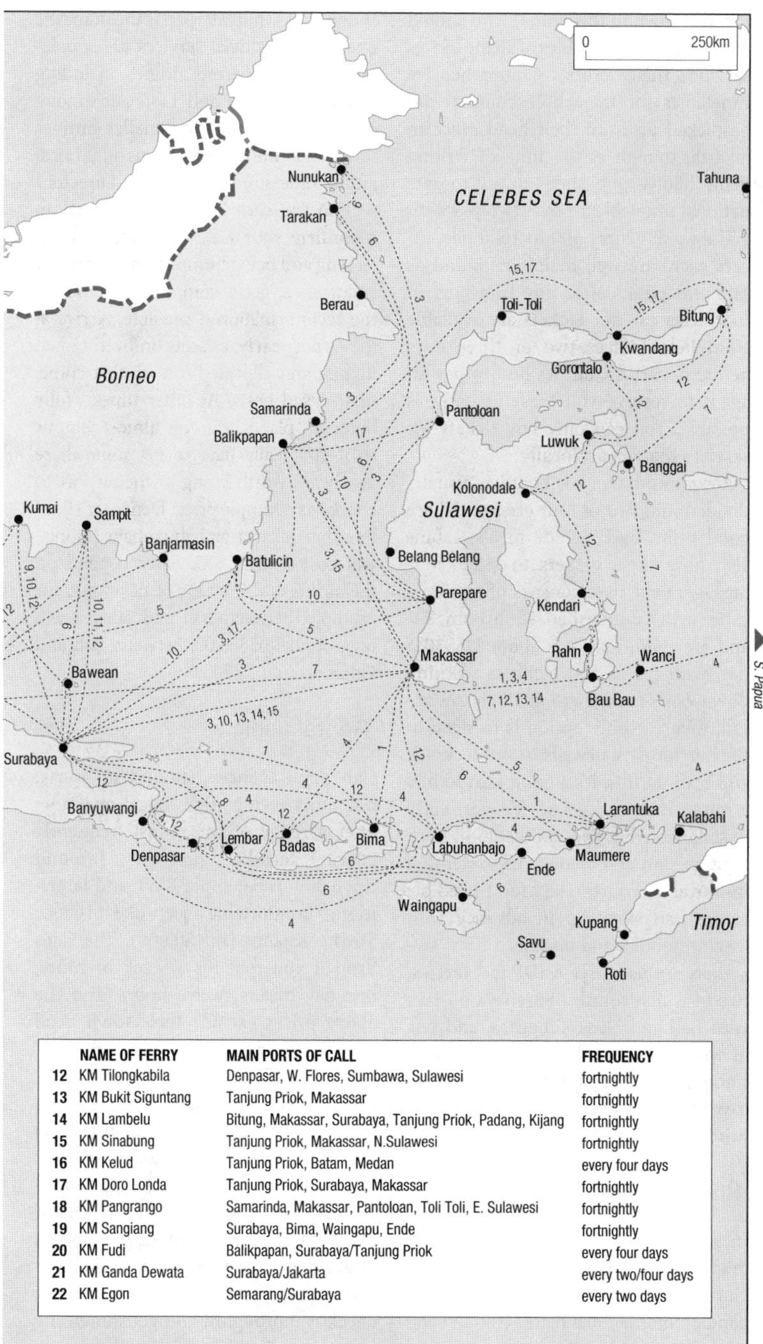


| | NAME OF FERRY | MAIN PORTS OF CALL | FREQUENCY |
|---|---|---|---|
| 12 | KM Tilongkabila | Denpasar, W. Flores, Sumbawa, Sulawesi | fortnightly |
| 13 | KM Bukit Siguntang | Tanjung Priok, Makassar | fortnightly |
| 14 | KM Lambelu | Bitung, Makassar, Surabaya, Tanjung Priok, Padang, Kijang | fortnightly |
| 15 | KM Sinabung | Tanjung Priok, Makassar, N.Sulawesi | fortnightly |
| 16 | KM Kelud | Tanjung Priok, Batam, Medan | every four days |
| 17 | KM Doro Londa | Tanjung Priok, Surabaya, Makassar | fortnightly |
| 18 | KM Pangrango | Samarinda, Makassar, Pantoloan, Toli Toli, E. Sulawesi | fortnightly |
| 19 | KM Sangiang | Surabaya, Bima, Waingapu, Ende | fortnightly |
| 20 | KM Fudi | Balikpapan, Surabaya/Tanjung Priok | every four days |
| 21 | KM Ganda Dewata | Surabaya/Jakarta | every two/four days |
| 22 | KM Egon | Semarang/Surabaya | every two days |

for each town in this guide) who should have complete timetables of all the ferries serving their ports. Comprehensive timetables for the whole country can be picked up from their head office in Jakarta, though at the time of writing Pelni hadn't published an up-to-date national timetable for over two years.

The vessels carry 500 to 1600 passengers each, are well maintained, and as safe and punctual as any transport in Indonesia can be. **Tickets** are available from Pelni offices two or three days before departure, but it's best to pay an agent to reserve you these as early as possible. You can only buy tickets for services that depart locally.

Accommodation on board is usually divided into two or four classes. All are good value, and include meals; cabins also have large lockers to store your luggage. First class consists of a private cabin with a double bed, washroom, TV and air conditioning – about US$30 a day, with prices and facilities working downwards from there. If all classes are full, then the only option is to sleep in the corridors, stairwells or on deck – if you plan on this, it's a good idea to buy a rattan mat, and get to the port early to stake out your spot on the floor. Lock luggage shut and chain it to something immovable. Fourth-class food is edible at best, so stock up in advance with instant noodles and biscuits.

There are also three **ASDP fast ferries,** two of which connect Surabaya on Java with Bali and Nusa Tenggara, and one of which sails north from Surabaya to Kalimantan. While not cheap the service is very good, and ferries take less than a third of the time of Pelni vessels.

## Planes

In some areas, **flying** may be the only practical way to get around. State-operated **Garuda** (Ⓦwww.garuda-indonesia.com) handles international flights (though you might also use them for transport within Indonesia), while Merpati is the domestic operator. Provincial services are supplemented by numerous airlines, including Mandala, Bouraq and Lion Air among others. Many of these smaller airlines serve a handful of destinations only. Local airline offices are listed in the Directory section for each town. It's essential to **reconfirm** your seat, as waiting lists can be long and being bumped off is a regular occurrence; get a computer printout of the reconfirmation if possible. Arrive at the airport **early**, as seats on overbooked flights are allocated on a first-come, first-served basis. At other times, "fully booked" planes can be almost empty, so if you really have to get somewhere it's always worth going to the airport to check. As a sample price: Denpasar (Bali) to either Jakarta or Labuanbajo (Flores) will cost around $75. Fares depend on the airline and the type of ticket but, for example, between Bali and Jakarta will be around Rp535,000; between Bali and Flores around Rp700,000.

## Rental vehicles

Car-rental agencies abound in tourist hot spots such as Bali. Local operators offer a range of cars, most frequently 800cc Suzuki Jimneys (around Rp90,000–100,000 per day), and larger, more comfortable jeep-like 1600cc Toyota Kijangs (Rp150,000). The rates drop if you rent for a week or more; one day means twelve hours, and the above prices exclude fuel. You'll need to produce an **international drivers' licence** before you rent. Rental motorbikes vary from small 100cc Yamahas to trail bikes. Prices start at Rp50,000 per day without insurance. Conditions are not suitable for inexperienced drivers, with heavy traffic on major routes; there are increasing numbers of accidents involving tourists, so don't take risks. Before you take a vehicle, check it thoroughly, and get something in writing about any existing damage.

Traffic in Indonesia **drives on the left** and there is a maximum speed limit of 70kph. Drivers must always carry an international driving licence and the vehicle registration documents. All motorcyclists must wear a helmet. In some places, certain roads change from two-way to one-way during the day, not publicized in any way that is comprehensible to foreigners. The **police** carry out regular spot checks, and you'll be **fined** for any infringements.

### Urban transport

In cities, colour-coded or numbered minibus **bemos** might run fixed circuits, or adapt their routes according to their customers. Rides usually cost a few hundred rupiah, but fares are never displayed, and you'll get overcharged at first. Other standbys include **ojek** (single-passenger motorbikes) and **becak** (cycle-rickshaws), which take two passengers. Jakarta also has motorized becak, called bajaj. Negotiating **fares** for these vehicles requires a balance of firmness and tact; try for around Rp3000 for an ojek for a trip around town, and Rp1500 a kilometre for a becak, though you'll have to pay more for the latter if there are any hills along the way. The drivers are also notoriously tough negotiators – never lose your temper with one unless you want a serious fight.

## ACCOMMODATION

Prices for the simplest double room start at around US$5, and in all categories are at their **most expensive** from mid-June through August, and in December and January. Single rooms are a rarity, so lone travellers will get put in a double at about 75 percent of the full price. Check-out time is usually noon. The cheapest accommodation has shared **bathrooms**, where you wash using a mandi (see p.38). Toilets in these places will be squat affairs, flushed manually with water scooped from the pail that stands alongside, so you'll have to provide toilet paper yourself.

The bottom end of Indonesia's accommodation market is provided by homestays and hostels. *Penginapan*, or **homestays**, are most often simply spare bedrooms in the family home, though there's often not much difference between these and losmen, *pondok* and *wisma*, which are also family-run operations. Rooms vary from whitewashed concrete cubes to artful bamboo structures – some are even set in their own walled gardens. Hard beds and bolsters are the norm, and you may be provided with a light blanket. Most losmen rooms have fans and cold-water bathrooms.

Almost any place calling itself a **hotel** in Indonesia will include at least a basic breakfast in the price of a room. Most of the middle and top-end places add a service-and-tax surcharge of between 10 and 22 percent to your bill, and upmarket establishments quote prices – and prefer foreigners to pay – in dollars, though they accept plastic or a rupiah equivalent. In popular areas such as Bali and Tanah Toraja, it's worth booking ahead during the peak seasons; some hotels will also provide transport to and from transit points if requested in advance. Bland and anonymous, cheap urban hotels are designed for local businesspeople rather than tourists, with tiny rooms and shared squat toilets and mandi. Moderately priced hotels often have a choice of fan or a/c rooms, almost certainly with hot water. Expensive hotels can be very stylish indeed, particularly in Bali.

In rural Indonesia, you may end up **staying in villages** without formal lodgings, in a bed in a family house. First ask permission from the local police or the kepala desa (village head). In exchange for accommodation and meals, you should offer cash or useful gifts, such as rice, salt, cigarettes or food, to the value of about US$1.50.

The only bathroom might be the nearest river. With such readily available and inexpensive alternatives, **camping** is only necessary when trekking.

Usually, **electricity** is supplied at 220–240 volts AC, but outlying areas may still use 110 volts. Most outlets take plugs with two rounded pins.



### ADDRESSES

A law banning the use of foreign words for business names, including those for **accommodation** and restaurants, has caused a few problems. Some hotels have circumvented the new rule by just adding the word "Hotel" in front of their name (this is an Indonesian as well as an English word), but others have had to start over. **Street names** are another cause of confusion, many having been renamed as historical or political figures fall in and out of fashion. Where relevant, we have included both new and old names for hotels and streets, as many people still refer to them by the old name, though the sign will show the new version.

## FOOD AND DRINK

Compared to other Southeast Asian cuisines, Indonesian meals lack variety. Coconut milk and aromatic spices at first add intriguing tastes to the meats, vegetables and fruits, but after a while everything starts to taste the same – spiced, fried and served with rice. Be particularly careful about food **hygiene** in rural Indonesia, avoiding poorly cooked fish, pork or beef.

**Rice** (*nasi*) is the favoured staple across much of the country, an essential, three-times-a-day fuel. Noodles are also widely popular. The seafood is often superb, and chicken, goat and beef are the main meats in this predominantly Muslim country. Vegetarians can eat well in Indonesia, though restaurant selections can be limited to *cap cay* – fried mixed vegetables. There's also plenty of tofu and the popular *tempe*, a fermented soya-bean cake.

### Indonesian food

The backbone of all Indonesian cooking, spices are ground and chopped together, then fried to form a paste, which is either used as the flavour-base for curries, or rubbed over ingredients prior to frying or grilling. Chillies always feature, along with *terasi* (also known as *belacan*), a fermented shrimp paste. Meals are often served with *sambal*, a blisteringly hot blend of chillies and spices.

Light meals and snacks include various rice dishes such as **nasi goreng**, a plate of fried rice with shreds of meat and vegetables and topped with a fried egg, and **nasi campur**, boiled rice served with a small range of side dishes. Noodle equivalents are also commonly available, as are **gado-gado**, steamed vegetables dressed in a peanut sauce, and sate, small kebabs of meat or fish, barbecued over a fire and again served with spicy peanut sauce. Indonesian bread (*roti*) is made from sweetened dough, and usually accompanies a morning cup of coffee.

Sumatran **Padang restaurants** are found right across Indonesia, the typically fiery food pre-cooked – not the healthiest way to eat – and displayed cold on platters piled up in a pyramid shape inside a glass-fronted cabinet. There are no menus; you either select your composite meal by pointing, or wait for the staff to bring you a selection and pay just for what you consume. You may encounter boiled *kangkung* (water spinach); *tempe*; egg, vegetable, meat or seafood curry; fried whole fish; potato cakes; and fried cow's lung.

### Where to eat

The cheapest places to eat in Indonesia are at the **mobile stalls** (*kaki lima*, or "five legs"), which ply their wares around the streets and bus stations during the day, and congregate at night markets after dark. You simply place your order and they cook it up on the spot. **Warung** are the bottom line in Indonesian restaurants, usually just a few tables, and offering much the same food as *kaki lima* for under a dollar a dish. **Rumah makan** are bigger, offer a wider range of dishes and comfort, and may even have a menu. Anything labelled as a **restaurant** will probably be catering to foreigners, with fully fledged service and possibly international food; many close by 8 or 9pm. Tourist restaurants will charge at least three times as much for the same dish you'd get in a warung. In addition, many of the moderate and all of the expensive establishments will add up to 21 percent service tax to the bill.

### Drinks

Most **water** that comes out of taps in Indonesia has had very little treatment, and can contain a whole range of bacteria and viruses. Drink only bottled, boiled or sterilized water. Boiled water (*air putih*) can be requested at accommodation and restaurants, and dozens of brands of **bottled water** (*air minum*) are sold throughout the islands. Indonesian **coffee** is among the best in the world, and drunk with copious amounts of sugar and, occasionally, condensed milk.

Alcohol can be a touchy subject in parts of Indonesia, where public drunkenness may incur serious trouble. There's no need to be overly paranoid about this in cities, however, and the locally produced **beers,** Anker and Bintang Pilsners, are good, and widely available at Chinese restaurants and bigger hotels. In non-Islamic regions, even small warung sell beer. **Spirits** are less publicly consumed, and may be technically illegal, so indulge with caution. Nonetheless, home-produced brews are often sold openly in villages. *Tuak* (also known as *balok*) or palm wine is made by tapping a suitable tree for its sap, comes in plain milky white or pale red varieties, and varies in strength. Far more potent are rice wine (variously known as *arak* or *brem*), and *sopi*, a distillation of *tuak*, either of which can leave you incapacitated after a heavy session.

## CULTURE AND ETIQUETTE

Indonesia is the world's most populous Muslim country but the practice of **Islam** across the archipelago has been shaped by centuries of interaction with Hinduism, Buddhism and other faiths, as well as traditional animist practices. As a result, Islam in Indonesia is far removed from the more austere practices of the Gulf states. In the capital Jakarta, it's possible to find mosques situated across the street from nightclubs that would make the raunchiest bar back home seem positively prudish. Although there are regional variations in accepted social norms, with Aceh among the most conservative provinces and Bali the most liberal, there are also differences within provinces. Commonsense is the best course of action. Outside the main tourist resorts, dress conservatively, especially if visiting religious sites, to avoid giving offence. Be especially sensitive during the Muslim fasting month of Ramadan.

Visitors to **Balinese temples** (*pura*) show respect to the shrines and dress modestly – so no skimpy clothing, bare shoulders or shorts – and often you'll be required wear a sarong and a ceremonial sash around your waist (usually provided by the most visited temples).

Indonesia shares the same **attitudes to dress and social taboos** as other Southeast Asian cultures (see p.45). In addition, Indonesians are generally very sociable, and dislike doing anything alone. It's normal for complete strangers engaged in some common

## TRADITIONAL DANCE AND MUSIC

Given the enormous cultural and ethnic mix that makes up Indonesia, it's hardly surprising that the range of traditional music and dance across the archipelago is so vast.

### Dance

Best-known are the highly stylized and mannered **classical dance performances** in Java and Bali, accompanied by the gamelan orchestra. Every step is minutely orchestrated, and the merest wink of an eye or arch of an eyebrow has significance. Ubud on Bali and Yogyakarta on Java are the centres for these dances, with shortened performances staged for Western visitors. Yogya is also the main place to catch a performance of **wayang kulit**, shadow puppet plays.

### Gamelan

A gamelan is an ensemble of tuned percussion, consisting mainly of gongs, metallophones and drums, made of bronze, iron, brass, wood or bamboo, with wooden frames, which are often intricately carved and painted. A complete **Javanese gamelan** is made up of two sets of instruments, one in each of two scales. The full ensemble also includes vocalists – a male chorus and female solo singers – and is led by the drummer in the centre. A large gamelan may be played by as many as thirty musicians, and is a communal form of music-making – there are no soloists or virtuosos. Most village halls and neighbourhoods in Central Java have a gamelan for use by the local community.

When the Dutch took control of **Bali** in the early twentieth century, the island's courts all but disappeared, and a new gamelan style took hold: *kebyar*, a fast, dynamic music, full of changes of tempo and sudden loud outbursts. It is this that makes much Balinese gamelan music today sound so different from the Javanese form.

**Sundanese** (West Javanese) *degung* is arguably the most accessible gamelan music for Western ears. Its musical structures are clear and well defined, and it is played by a small ensemble, but includes the usual range of gongs and metallophones found in all gamelan.

*By Jenny Heaton and Simon Steptoe*

enterprise – catching a bus, for instance – to introduce themselves and start up a friendship. **Sharing cigarettes** between men is in these circumstances a way of establishing a bond, and Westerners who don't smoke should be genuinely apologetic about refusing; it's well worth carrying a packet to share around even if you save your own "for later".

## SPORTS AND OUTDOOR ACTIVITIES

### Diving

Indonesia has many of the world's best **diving sites**, one of the finest of which is Pulau Bunaken off **Sulawesi**, where the vast diversity of tropical fish and coral is complemented by visibility that can reach over 30m. **Bali** has many good sites, including the famous Liberty wreck, and reputable tour operators at all major beach resorts; **Lombok**'s operators are limited to Senggigi and the Gili Islands. The best time for diving is between April and October. Most major beach resorts have dive centres, but once you get further afield you'll probably have to rely on live-aboard cruises or even on having your own gear. A day's diving with two tanks, lunch and basic equipment costs anything from $30 to $100. Be sure to enquire about the reputation of the dive operators before signing up, check their PADI or equivalent accreditation and, if possible, get first-hand recommendations from other divers. Be aware that it is down to you to check your equipment, and that the purity of an air tank can be suspect, and could cause serious injury. Also check your guide's credentials carefully, and bear in mind that you may be a long way from a decompression chamber.

### Surfing

Indonesia is also one of the world's premier surfing destinations, with an enormous variety of class waves and perfect breaks. The best-known waves are found on **Bali**, **G-Land** (Grajagan) on Java, but Sumba and the Mentawai Islands are increasingly popular. Pulau Nias off Sumatra was once a popular surfing destination, though it has yet to fully recover following an earthquake in 2005.

In June and July, during the best and most consistent surf, you can expect waves to be crowded, especially in Java and Bali. Several surf companies in Kuta in Bali offer all-in surf safaris to other destinations in Indionesia (see p.288). Try to bring your own board, and a padded board-bag, though in the popular surf spots you can rent some decent boards on the beach. Most public transport charges extra for boards, but many surfers simply rent motorbikes with board-carrying attachments.

For detailed reviews of surf breaks, see the book *Indo Surf and Lingo*, available from Ⓦwww.indosurf.com.au and from surfshops and bookshops in Bali. Good surf websites include Ⓦwww.baliwaves.com, Ⓦwww.wannasurf.com and Ⓦwww.balisurfreport.com.

### Trekking

There are endless **trekking** opportunities in Indonesia. The most popular volcano treks include **Gunung Batur** on Bali and **Gunung Bromo** on Java; more taxing favourites include **Gunung Rinjani** on Lombok and **Gunung Semeru** on Java. In Sumatra, the **Gunung Leuser National Park** is Southeast Asia's largest, and includes the famous Bukit Lawang orang-utan sanctuary. Many routes need **guides**, and not just to find the paths: turning up at a remote village unannounced can cause trouble, as people may mistrust outsiders, let alone Westerners. Guides are always available from local villages and tourist centres.

## COMMUNICATIONS

Aside from the usual services, many **post offices** (*kantor pos*) now offer internet and fax facilities. Indonesia's **poste restante** system is fairly efficient, but only in the cities; poste restante is officially held for a maximum of one month. **Overseas letters** to Western Europe and America take between seven and ten days to arrive.

In larger post offices, the parcels section is usually in a separate part of the building, and sending one is expensive and time-consuming. The cheapest way of sending mail home is by surface (under 10kg only). Don't seal the parcel before staff at the post office have checked what's inside it; in the larger towns, there's usually a parcel-wrapping service near the post office.

There are two types of **telephone** office in Indonesia: the ubiquitous government-run Telkom offices (often called Yantel, which are open 24hr), and privately owned wartels (usually 7am–midnight), which tend to be slightly more expensive, but are often conveniently located. Both also offer fax services, though the wartels rarely have a collect-call service.

Many payphones now take telephone cards only (*kartu telefon*), available in various denominations, bought from most local corner stores. In the big cities, there are also *kartu cip* phones that take microchip cards. Long-distance domestic calls (*panggilan inter-lokal*) are charged according to a zone system, with different rates; it's cheaper between 9pm and 6am.

Rates for **international calls** are fixed, though the premium charged by the private wartels varies. All calls at weekends and on national holidays are discounted by 25 percent. To **call abroad** from Indonesia, dial ⓣ001 or ⓣ008 + country code + area code (minus the first 0) + number. For international directory enquiries call ⓣ102; the international operator is ⓣ101. Some Telkom offices and airports also have home-country direct phones, from which you can call collect (reverse-charge calls), or settle up after the call; they cost more than IDD phones.

**Mobile phone** coverage is good across most of Java, Sumatra and Bali, but elsewhere is confined largely to the main cities and populated areas only. If you're spending more than a week or so in Indonesia, it's worth purchasing a pre-paid mobile phone card, which are available from most wartels from Rp10,000. The two dominant operators are Telkomsel and Indosat. There's a complicated registration process, so ask the sales assistant for help after you've purchased the card. You shouldn't have to pay to receive calls.

**Internet access** is becoming increasingly widespread in Indonesia, and there are now tourist-friendly internet offices and cafés in many towns and cities; prices vary widely from Rp5000 to Rp30,000 per hour. Free WiFi is also becoming more common in tourist cafés, shopping malls and more expensive hotels.

## CRIME AND SAFETY

The bombing of a nightclub in the tourist centre of Kuta on Bali in 2002, which left over 200 (mostly foreigners) dead, as well as foreign fatalities resulting from the suppression of independence movements in West Papua and Timor, and the urban violence that surrounded the political and religious upheavals of the past decade, all undermine the idea that Indonesia is a safe place to travel. However, it's also true that serious incidents involving Westerners are rare. **Petty theft**, however, is a fact of life, so don't flash around expensive jewellery or watches. Don't hesitate to check that doors and windows – including those in the bathroom – are secure before accepting **accommodation**; if the management seems offended by this, you probably don't want to stay there anyway. Some guesthouses and hotels have safe-deposit boxes.

If you're unlucky enough to get **mugged**, never resist and, if you disturb a thief, raise the alarm rather than try to take them on. Be especially aware of **pickpockets** on buses or bemos, who usually operate in pairs: one will distract you while another does the job. Afterwards, you'll need a **police report** for insurance purposes. In smaller villages where police are absent, ask for assistance from the headman. Try to take along someone to translate, though police will generally do their best to find an English speaker. You may also be charged "administration fees", the cost of which is open to sensitive negotiations. Have nothing to do with **drugs** in Indonesia: the penalties are tough, and you won't get any sympathy from consular officials. If arrested, ring your embassy immediately.

### EMERGENCY NUMBERS

Police ⓣ110
Ambulance ⓣ118
Fire ⓣ113

## MEDICAL CARE AND EMERGENCIES

If you have a minor ailment, head to a pharmacy (*apotik*), which can provide many medicines without prescription. Condoms (*kondom*) are available from pharmacists. Only in the main tourist areas will assistants speak English; in the village health posts, staff are generally ill-equipped to cope with serious illness. If you need an English-speaking doctor (*doktor*) or dentist (*doktor gigi*), seek advice at your hotel (some of the luxury ones have an in-house doctor) or at the local tourist office. You'll find a public hospital (*rumah sakit*) in major cities and towns, and in some places these are supplemented by private hospitals, many of which operate an accident and emergency department. If you have a serious accident or illness, you will need to be evacuated home or to Singapore, which has the best medical provision in Asia. It is, therefore, vital to arrange health insurance before you leave home.

## INFORMATION AND MAPS

There's a range of **tourist offices** in Indonesia, including government-run organizations, normally called **Dinas** (or Kantor) Pariwisata (Diparda). Though they can lack hard information, staff often speak some English, usually have a map of the town or district, and may advise about local transport options or arrange guides. Many private **tour operators** are also excellent, if sometimes partisan, sources of information. In remote locations, you can try asking the local police.

Good all-round maps include GeoCentre's 1:2,000,000 series and the Nelles Indonesia series. In the same league is Periplus' range of user-friendly city and provincial maps.

## MONEY AND BANKS

The Indonesian currency is the **rupiah** (abbreviated to "Rp"). **Notes** come in denominations of Rp500 (rare), Rp1000, Rp5000, Rp10,000, Rp20,000, Rp50,000 and even Rp100,000 (also rare); **coins**, mainly used for public telephones and bemos (minibuses), come in Rp25 (rare), Rp50, Rp100, Rp500 and Rp1000 denominations. Officially, rupiah are available outside Indonesia, but the currency's volatile value means that very few banks carry it. At the time of writing, the exchange rate was Rp17,300 to £1 and Rp9500 to US$1.

Sometimes prices for tourist services, such as diving or organized trips, are quoted in **dollars**, or increasingly in **euros**, particularly with European-run businesses, but you can pay in rupiah at whatever the exchange rate is on the day.

You'll find **banks** capable of handling foreign exchange in provincial capitals and bigger cities throughout Indonesia, and most bigger places have **ATMs**, which take at least one from Visa, MasterCard or Cirrus-Maestro. There are also privately run **moneychangers** in major tourist centres. You may be asked to supply a photocopy of your **passport**, or the receipt (or proof of purchase) that you get when you buy your traveller's cheques. Always count your money carefully, as unscrupulous dealers can rip you off, either by folding notes over to make it look as if you're getting twice as much, or by distracting you and then whipping away a few notes from your pile. Moneychangers in Kuta, Bali, are notorious for this.

In less-travelled regions, provincial banks won't cash traveller's cheques, but will take **US dollar notes**. Over-the-counter **cash advances** on Visa can be used for obtaining the full international rate.

## OPENING HOURS AND HOLIDAYS

As a rough outline, businesses such as airline offices open Mon–Fri 8am–4pm & Sat 8am–noon. Banking hours are Mon–Fri 8am–3pm & Sat 8am–1pm, but banks may not handle foreign exchange in the afternoons or at weekends. Moneychangers usually keep shop rather than bank hours. Post offices operate roughly Mon–Thurs 8am–2pm, Fri 8–11am and Sat 8am–1pm, though in the larger cities the hours are much

## BAHASA INDONESIAN

The national language of Indonesia is Bahasa Indonesia, although there are also over 250 native languages spoken throughout the archipelago. Bahasa Indonesia is a form of Bahasa Malay and, because it's written in Roman script, has no tones and uses a fairly straightforward grammar, it's relatively easy to learn.

### Pronunciation

**a** as in a cross between father and cup
**e** sometimes as in along; or as in pay; or as in get; or sometimes omitted (*selamat* pronounced "slamat")
**i** either as in boutique; or as in pit
**o** either as in hot; or as in cold
**u** as in boot
**ai** as in fine
**au** as in how
Most consonants are pronounced as in
**c** as in cheap
**g** always hard as in girl
**k** hard, as in English, except at the end of the word, when you should stop just short of pronouncing it.

### Greetings and basic phrases

| | |
|---|---|
| Good morning | *Selamat pagi* |
| Good day | *Selamat siang* |
| Good afternoon | *Selamat sore* |
| Good evening | *Selamat malam* |
| Goodbye | *Selamat tinggal* – (If the person you're addressing is staying). |
| Cheers | *Selamat minum* |
| Please (requesting) | *Tolong* |
| Please (offering) | *Silakan* |
| Thank you (very much) | *Terima kasih (banyak)* |
| You're welcome | *Sama sama* |
| Sorry/Excuse me | *Ma'af* |
| No worries/ Never mind | *Tidak apa apa* |
| Yes | *Ya* |
| No (with verb) | *Tidak (sometimes pronounced "tak")* - |
| Do you speak English? | *Bisa bicara bahasa Inggris?* |
| I don't understand | *Saya tidak mengerti* |
| I want/would like... | *Saya mau...* |
| I don't want it /No thanks | *Tidak mau* |
| Men/women | *Laki-laki/perempuan or wanita* |
| open/closed | *buka/tutup* |
| Where is the...? | *dimana...?* |
| airport | *lapangan terbang* |
| bank | *bank* |
| beach | pantai |
| bemo/bus station | *terminal* |
| city/city centre | *kota* |
| hospital | *sakit* |
| hotel | *losmen* |
| market | *pasar* |
| pharmacy | *apotik* |
| police station | *kantor polisi* |
| post office | *kantor pos* |
| shop | *toko* |
| telephone office | *wartel/kantor telkom* |
| bicycle | *sepeda* |
| bus | *bis* |
| car | *mobil* |
| entrance/exit | *masuk/keluar* |
| ferry | *ferry* |
| motorbike | *sepeda motor* |
| taxi | *taksi* |
| ticket | *karcis* |
| Stop! | *Estop!* |
| air conditioning | *AC* |
| bathroom | *kamar mandi* |
| breakfast | *makan pagi* |
| fan | *kipas* |
| hot water | *air panas* |
| mosquito net | *kelambu nyamuk* |
| toilet | *kamar kecil/wc (pronounced "way say")* |

### Numbers

| | |
|---|---|
| Zero | *Nol/kosong* |
| 1 | *Satu* |
| 2 | *Dua* |
| 3 | *Tiga* |
| 4 | *Empat* |
| 5 | *Lima* |
| 6 | *Enam* |
| 7 | *Tujuh* |
| 8 | *Delapan* |
| 9 | *Sembilan* |
| 10 | *Sepuluh* |

| | |
|---|---|
| 11, 12, 13, etc | *Sebelas, duabelas, tigabelas* |
| 20 | *Duapuluh* |
| 21, 22, etc | *Duapuluh satu, duapuluh dua, duapuluh, tiga* |
| 30, 40, etc | *Tigapuluh, Empatpuluh, Limapuluh* |
| 100 | *Seratus* |
| 200 | *Duaratus* |
| 1000 | *Seribu* |
| 10,000 | *Sepuluhribu* |
| 20,000 | *Duapuluhribu* |
| 100,000 | *Seratusribu* |
| 1,000,000 | *Sejuta* |
| 2,000,000 | *Dua juta* |

**Food and drinks glossary**

| | |
|---|---|
| *Daftar makanan* | Menu |
| *Enak* | Delicious |
| *Goreng* | Fried |
| *Panas* | Hot (temperature) |
| *Pedas* | Hot (spicy) |
| *Saya injin bayar* | I want to pay |
| *Saya seorang vegetaris* | I'm a vegetarian |
| *Saya tidak makan daging* | I don't eat meat |

**Meat, fish and basic foods**

| | |
|---|---|
| *Anjing* | Dog |
| *Ayam* | Chicken |
| *Babi* | Pork |
| *Bakmi* | Noodles |
| *Buiah* | Fruit |
| *Es* | Ice |
| *Garam* | Salt |
| *Gula* | Sugar |
| *Ikan* | Fish |
| *Itik* | Duck |
| *Jaja* | Rice cakes |
| *Kambing* | Goat |
| *Kare* | Curry |
| *Kepiting* | Crab |
| *Nasi* | Rice |
| *Samibal* | Hot chilli sauce |
| *Sapi* | Beef |
| *Soto* | Soup |
| *Telur* | Egg |
| *Tikkus* | Rat |
| *Udang* | Prawn |

**Everyday dishes**

| | |
|---|---|
| *Ayam bakar* | Fried chicken |
| *Bakmi goreng* | Fried noodles with vegetables and meat |
| *Cap cay* | Mixed fried vegetables |
| *Gado-gado* | Steamed vegetables served with a spicy peanut sauce |
| *Kue tiaw* | Singaporean stir-fry of flat rice noodles and meat |
| *Lumpia* | Spring rolls |
| *Murtabak* | Thick, dough pancake, often filled with meat |
| *Nasi ayam* | Boiled rice with chicken |
| *Nasi campur* | Boiled rice served with small amounts of vegetable, meat, fish and sometimes egg |
| *Nasi goreng* | Fried rice |
| *Nasi gudeg* | Rice with jackfruit and coconut-milk curry |
| *Nasi putih* | Plain boiled rice |
| *Nasi soto ayam* | Chicken-and-rice soup |
| *Pisang goreng* | Fried bananas |
| *Rendang* | Dry-fried beef and coconut-milk curry |
| *Rijsttaffel* | Dutch/Indonesian buffet of six to ten meat, fish and vegetable dishes with rice |
| *Sate* | Meat or fish kebabs served with a spicy peanut sauce |
| *Tahu goring telur* | Tofu omelette |
| *Urap-urap/urap timum* | Vegetables with coconut and chilli |

**Drinks**

| | |
|---|---|
| *Air jeruk* | Orange juice |
| *Air jeruk nipis* | Lemon juice |
| *Air minum* | Drinking water |
| *Arak* | Palm or rice spirit |
| *Bir* | Beer |
| *Brem* | Local rice beer |
| *Kopi* | Coffee |
| *Kopi susu* | White coffee |
| *Sopi* | Palm spirit |
| *Susu* | Milk |
| *Teh* | Tea |
| *Tuak* | Palm wine |

longer. Muslim businesses, including **government offices**, may also close at 11.30am on Fridays, the main day of prayer, and national **public holidays** see all commerce compulsorily curtailed.

**Ramadan**, a month of fasting during daylight hours, falls during the ninth Muslim month, which changes from year to year as it is based on a lunar calendar. Even in non-Islamic areas, Muslim restaurants and businesses shut down during the day, and in staunchly Islamic parts of rural Lombok, Sumatra and Kalimantan's Banjarmasin, you should not eat, drink or smoke in public at this time. **Idul Fitri**, also called *Hari Raya* or *Lebaran*, marks the end of Ramadan and is a two-day national holiday of noisy celebrations.

### Public holidays

Most of the national public holidays fall on different dates of the Western calendar each year, as they are calculated according to Muslim or local calendars.

**January 1** New Year's Day (*Tahun Baru*)
**Jan/Feb** Chinese New Year
**Muharam** (usually Jan) Muslim New Year
**March/April** *Nyepi*, Balinese New Year
**March/April** Good Friday and Easter Sunday
**Maulud Nabi Muhammad** (usually March or April) The anniversary of the birth of Mohammed
**May/June** *Waisak* Day Anniversary of the birth, death and enlightenment of Buddha
**May/June** Ascension Day of Jesus
**Lailat al Miraj** (usually between July and September) Ascension Day of Mohammed
**August 17** Independence Day (*Hari Proklamasi Kemerdekaan*) celebrates the proclamation of Indonesian Independence in 1945 by Dr Sukarno
**Idul Fitri** (usually Oct of Nov) The celebration of the end of Ramadan
**Idul Adha** (*Hajhl*, usually between Dec and Jan) Muslim Day of Sacrifice
**December 25** Christmas Day

## FESTIVALS

In addition to national public holidays, there are frequent **religious festivals** throughout Indonesia's Muslim, Hindu, Chinese and indigenous communities. Each of Bali's 20,000 temples has an anniversary celebration, for instance, and other ethnic groups may host elaborate marriages or funerals, along with more secular holidays. Many of these festivals change annually against the Western **calendar**.

**Erau Festival** Tenggarong, Kalimantan. September. A big display of indigenous Dayak skills and dancing.

**Funerals** Tanah Toraja, Sulawesi. Mostly May to September. With buffalo slaughter, bullfights and *sisemba* kick-boxing tournaments.

**Galungun** Bali. Takes place for ten days every 210 days to celebrate the victory of good over evil.

**Kasada** Bromo, East Java. Offerings are made to the gods and thrown into the crater. Held on the fourteenth day of Kasada, the twelfth month in the Tenggerese calendar year (Dec).

**Nyepi** throughout Bali. End of March or beginning of April. The major purification ritual of the year. In the lead-up, religious objects are paraded from temples to sacred springs or the sea for purification. The night before *nyepi*, the spirits are frightened away with drums, cymbals, firecrackers and huge papier-mâché monsters. On the day itself, everyone sits quietly at home to persuade any remaining evil spirits that Bali is completely deserted.

**Pasola** West Sumba. Held four times in February and March, the exact dates being determined by local priests, this festival to balance the upper sphere of the heavens culminates with a frenetic pitched battle between two villages of spear-wielding horsemen.

**Sekaten** Central Java. March or April. The celebration of the birthday of the prophet Mohammed, held in the royal courts of Central Java, includes a month-long festival of fairs, gamelan recitals, *wayang kulit* (Javanese shadow puppet performances) and *wayang orang* (a form of Javanese ballet) performances, culminating in a procession.

# Java

One of the most populous places in all of Asia, **Java** is characterized by great natural beauty. Its central spine is dominated by hundreds of volcanoes, many of which are still very evidently active, their fertile slopes supporting a landscape of glimmering ricefields spotted with countless small villages. To the south of this mountainous backbone is the homeland of the ethnic Javanese and the epicentre of their arts, culture and language, epitomized by the royal courts of **Yogyakarta** and **Solo**. Still steeped in traditional dance, music and art, these two cities are the mainstay of Java's tourist industry and offer first-rate facilities for travellers. They also provide excellent bases from which to explore the giant ninth-century Buddhist temple **Borobudur**, and the equally fascinating **Prambanan** complex, a contemporary Hindu site. To the east, the huge volcanic massif of **Gunung Bromo** is the other major stop on most travellers' itineraries, not least for the sunrise walk to its summit. But there are plenty more volcanic landscapes to explore, including the coloured lakes of the windswept **Dieng Plateau**, and the world's most famous – and destructive – volcano, **Krakatau**, off the west coast of Java. Less visited but very worthwhile destinations abound in the mountains around the West Java capital of **Bandung**. Aside from Yogyakarta (often refered to as "Yogya"), Java's cities are not that enticing, but **Jakarta**, the chaotic sprawl that is Indonesia's capital, does boast several worthwhile museums. And once you've exhausted the pleasures of Java you can easily move on to neighbouring islands – Sumatra is just ninety minutes' ferry ride from Merak in the west; Bali a mere half-hour from Banyuwangi in the east.

## JAKARTA

Bounded to the north by the Java Sea and the south by the low Bogor Hills, Indonesia's overwhelming capital, **JAKARTA**, has long been the focus of the country's changing political face, most dramatically with the student-led demonstrations against Suharto in 1998. Indonesia's most populous city, it has grown from a mere 900,000 inhabitants in 1945, to well over thirteen million (and over twenty million if you take into account the greater urban region known as Jabotabek). The capital sprawls over 661 square kilometres of northern Java. Unfortunately, few foreign visitors find the city as alluring as the local population do. However, the suburb of **Kota** in the north, the former heart of the old Dutch city, still retains a number of beautiful historic buildings, as does the neighbouring port of **Sunda Kelapa**. The capital also has some of the country's finest museums, including the **Maritime Museum**, the **Wayang Museum** and the National Museum.

### What to see and do

To head from north to south through the centre of Jakarta is to go forward in time, from the pretty, old Dutch city of Batavia, **Kota**, in the north, to the modern golf courses and amusement parks in the south. **Medan Merdeka**, a giant, threadbare patch of grass, marks the spiritual centre of Jakarta, if not exactly its geographical one, bordered to the west by the city's major north–south thoroughfare. The main commercial district and the budget accommodation enclave of **Jalan Jaksa** lie just a short distance to the south of Medan Merdeka.

#### Kota (Old Batavia)

The quaint old district of Kota was known as **Batavia** when it was the administrative centre of the Dutch trading empire. To reach Kota take the Busway (Rp3500), north along Jalan Gajah Mada, terminating

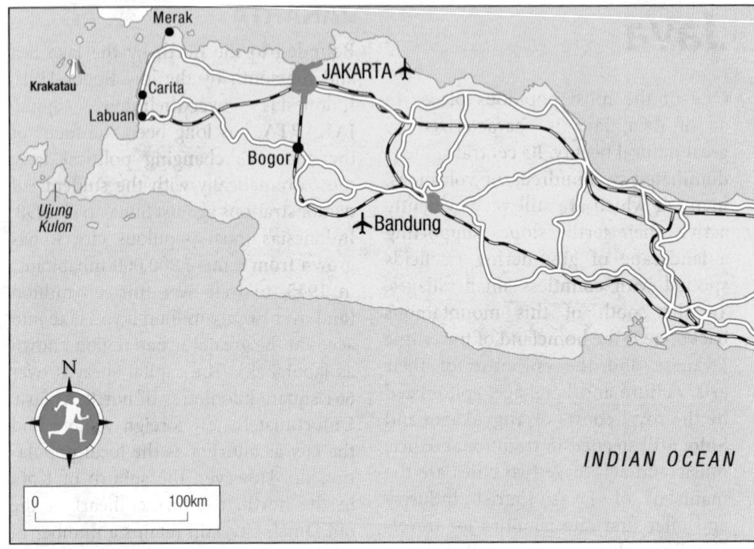


in front of **Kota train station**. North from Kota station along Jalan Lada, past the Politeknik Swadharma, you enter what was once the walled city of Batavia, whose centre, **Taman Fatahillah**, lies 300m to the north of the train station, an attractive cobbled square hemmed in by museums. On the south side, the largely disappointing **Jakarta History Museum** (Tues–Sun 9am–3pm; Rp2000), covers (in Indonesian only) the history of the city from the Stone Age, but only really gets as far as the seventeenth century. Upstairs is more interesting, with many of the rooms furnished as they would have been two hundred years ago. The finest exhibit is the ornate **Cannon Si Jagur**, which previously stood in the square and was built by the Portuguese to defend Melaka. On the side is the Latin inscription *Ex me ipsa renata sum* – "Out of myself I was reborn" – and the whole thing is emblazoned with sexual imagery, from the clenched fist (a suggestive gesture in Southeast Asia) to the barrel itself, a potent phallic symbol in Indonesia.

The more entertaining **Wayang Museum** (Tues–Sun 9am–3pm; Rp2000), to the west of the square, is dedicated to the Javanese art of puppetry and housed in one of the oldest buildings in the city. Puppets from right across the archipelago are displayed, and every Sunday between 10am and 2pm there is a free **wayang show**. While in the area, don't miss the chance to luxuriate in the stylish surroundings of the historic *Café Batavia*, on the northwestern corner of Taman Fatahillah. To the east of the square, the **Balai Seni Rupa** (Tues–Sun 9am–3pm; Rp2000), Jakarta's fine arts museum, and the **Ceramics Museum** house works by Indonesia's most illustrious artists.

## Sunda Kelapa

About 1km north of Taman Fatahillah lies the historic harbour of **Sunda Kelapa** (Rp1500 entrance), the most important in the Dutch empire. Although the bulk of the sea traffic docks at Tanjung Priok these days, a few of the smaller vessels, particularly some picturesque wooden schooners, still call in at this eight-hundred-year-old port. You can either walk here from Taman Fatahillah (about 20min) or hail an ojek (Rp10,000).

From the port, cross over the bridge to the west and turn right at the

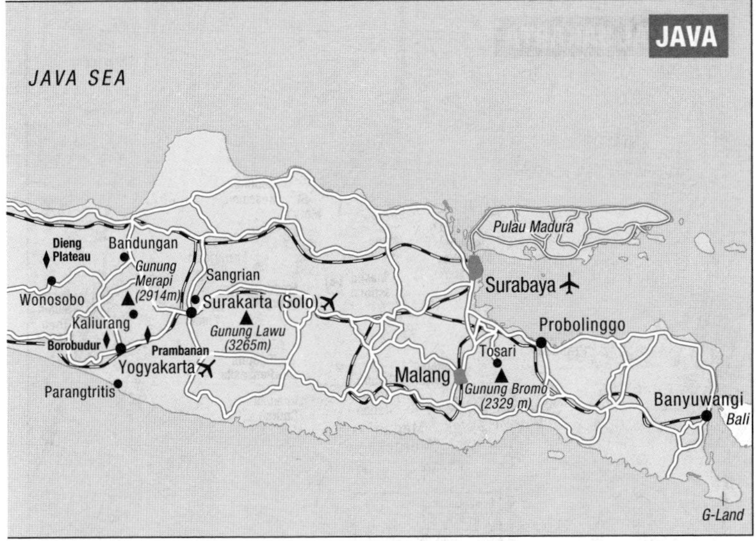


nineteenth-century watchtower, the **Uitkijk**, built to direct shipping traffic to the port. Here, buried in the chaotic Pasar Ikan (fish market) that occupies this promontory, is the entrance to the excellent **Museum Bahari**, or **Maritime Museum** (Tues–Sun 9am–3pm; Rp2000), housed in a warehouse dating from 1652, which charts the relationship between the Indonesian archipelago and the sea, beginning with the simple, early fishing vessels and continuing through the colonial years to the modern age. All kinds of sea craft are on display, from the Buginese *pinisi* to the *kora-kora* war boat from the Moluccas.

South from here, across the busy road, the *VOC Galangan* restaurant is a great place to take five minutes out with a cold drink. From here, keep the Kali Besar canal on your left until you come to the ornate two-hundred-year-old wooden drawbridge, **Jembatan Pasar Ayam**. The grand Dutch terrace houses on the streets south of here were once the smartest addresses in Batavia, the most famous being the Chinese-style **Toko Merah** (Red Shop) at no. 11 Jalan Kali Besar Barat – the former home of the Dutch governor general Van Imhoff. The Batavia bus station lies on the eastern side of the canal, from where you can catch a pale-blue minivan (Rp1000) back to Kota and the Busway.

## Medan Merdeka

The heart and lungs of Jakarta, **Medan Merdeka** is a square kilometre of sun-scorched grass in the centre of the city. At its centre stands the **Monas Tower**, a soaring 137-metre marble, bronze and gold torch, commissioned by Sukarno in 1962 to symbolize the indomitable spirit of the Indonesian people, and known as "Sukarno's last erection" in recognition of his world-famous philandering. You can take a lift up to its top for a city view (daily except last Mon of every month, 8.30am–5pm; Rp7500); the ticket includes entry to the **National History Museum** or Goblet Yard in Monas' basement, a series of 48 dioramas that depict the history of Jakarta.

The **National Museum** (Tues–Thurs, Sat & Sun 9am–3pm, Fri 8.30–11.30am; Rp750), on the western side of Medan Merdeka, is a fabulous place and a great introduction to Indonesia; the

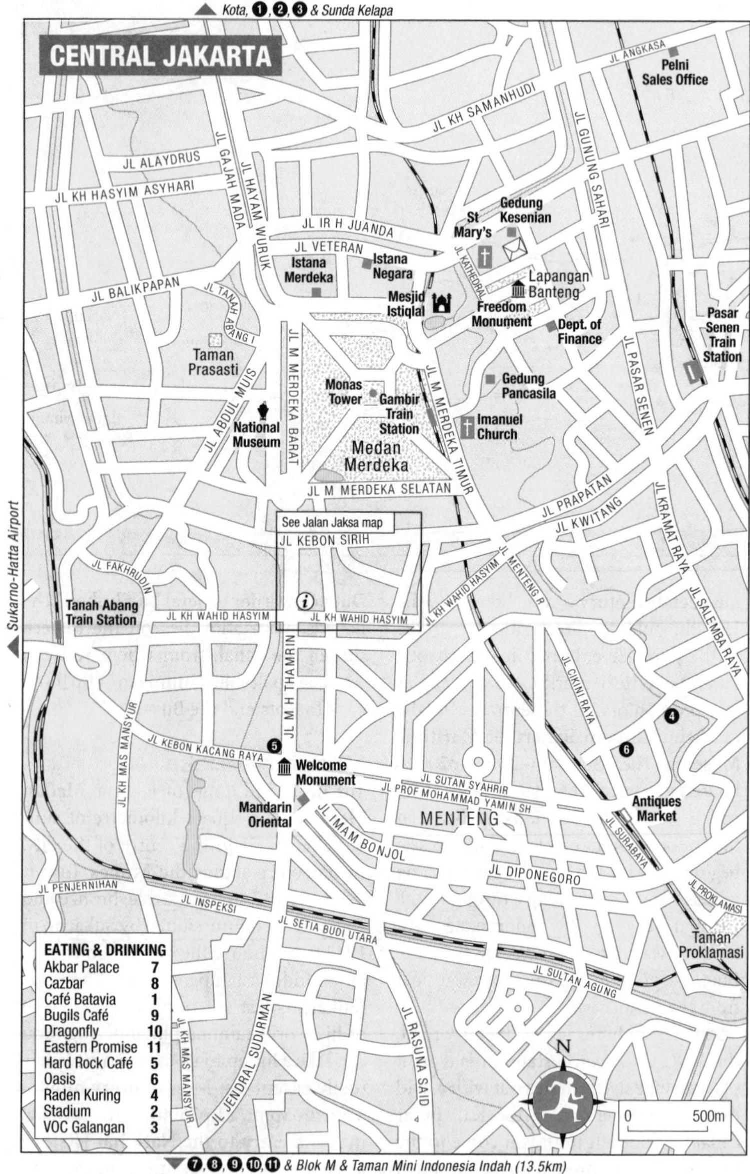


Indonesian Heritage Society conducts tours in English (Tues–Thurs 9.30am). Many of the country's top ruins have been plundered for their statues, which now sit, unmarked, in the museum courtyard. Other highlights include huge Dongson kettledrums, the skull and thighbone of Java Man, found near Solo in 1936, and the cache of golden artefacts discovered at the foot of Mount Merapi in 1990. There are also sometimes cultural performances such as dance and theatre here.

The dazzling white, if rather unprepossessing, **Mesjid Istiqlal** looms over the northeastern corner of Medan Merdeka. Completed in 1978, it is the largest mosque in Southeast Asia and can hold up to 250,000 people. For a donation, and providing you're conservatively dressed, the security guards will take you on an informal tour. At the foot of the minaret sits a 2.5-tonne wooden drum from east Kalimantan, the only traditional feature in this otherwise state-of-the-art mosque.

### Mini Indonesia

Eighteen kilometres south of Medan Merdeka, the **Taman Mini Indonesia Indah** (Sun–Tues 8am–5pm; Rp9000) is a huge theme park celebrating the archipelago's rich ethnic and cultural diversity. At its centre is a man-made lake, around which are 27 houses, each built in the traditional style of Indonesia's 27 provinces. The park also contains several **museums** (Rp2000 each), including the Science Museum; the Asmat Museum, housing woodcarvings from West Papua; and the Museum of Indonesia, with displays on the country's people, geography, flora and fauna. Neighbouring **Museum Purna Bhakti Pertiwi** (daily 9am–4pm; Rp5000) displays a fabulously opulent collection of gifts presented to President Suharto, including a whole gamelan orchestra made of old Balinese coins, a series of carved wooden panels depicting Suharto's life story, and an enormous rubber-tree root decorated with the nine gods of Balinese Hinduism. To get to all these attractions, catch **bus** #P10, #P11 or #P16 to Rambutan bus station, then minibus #T19 or #M55 to the Taman Mini entrance (1hr total).

## Arrival and information

**By bus** Jakarta's three major bus stations are all inconveniently situated. Each serves different destinations, although there are overlaps. Most buses from Central Java, East Java and Bali pull into Pulo Gadung station, 12km to the east of the city. From here catch bus #AC08, which passes the western end of Jl Cokroaminoto in Menteng, from where you can take a bajaj from the Batak church to the south end of Jl Jaksa (ask for Ujung Jl Jaksa). Buses from West Java use Kampung Rambutan station, 18km south of the city centre near Taman Mini. Buses #P10, #P11, #P16 and #AC10 all ply the route between Rambutan and the stop opposite the *Sari Pan Pacific Hotel* on Jl Thamrin (1hr 30min). Buses from the west of Sumatra arrive at Kalideres station 15km west of the centre. Buses #78 and #64 run from here to Jl Thamrin.

**By ferry** All Pelni ferries dock at Tanjung Priok harbour, 500m from the bus station of the same name. For Jl Jaksa, catch bus #P145 from the harbour bus station and alight at the junction of Jl Kebon Sirih and Jl MH Thamrin. A taxi to Jl Jaksa should cost Rp30,000 or so. Most ferries from Borneo dock at the Sunda Kelapa harbour, near the Kota district. Walk for twenty minutes or catch one of the light blue minivans (Rp1000) to the Kota bus station, then take the Busway down to the Sarinah stop, a five-minute walk away from Jl Jaksa along Jl Wahid Hasyim.

**By train** There are four central train stations (and dozens of minor suburban ones); Gambir station is the most popular and convenient. To walk to Jl Jaksa from here (15min), exit the station facing the National Monument and turn left. Follow the overhead railway line as far as Jl Kebon Sirih where the traffic's coming from your right. Turn right and proceed for 300m or so until you see the arch reading "Kawasan Wisata Malam" at the north end of Jaksa. Taxis are also available; avoid the touts and head for the Blue Bird taxi stand though you'll have to pay a Rp4500 surcharge.

Of the other stations, Kota, near old Batavia, is the busiest. Although Kota is on the same line as Gambir, some of the trains departing from Kota do not stop at Gambir, and vice versa. To reach Jl Jaksa from Kota, catch the Busway (which leaves from outside the station) to Sarinah (Rp3500), about a five-minute walk away from Jl Jaksa along Jl KH Wahid Hasyim.

**By air** Jakarta's Sukarno-Hatta Airport is 13km west of the city centre. The baggage reclamation area has currency exchange booths and hotel booking desks. Through customs, there's a small tourist office and more exchange booths, most of which close at 10pm; rates are 25 percent lower than in the city centre. DAMRI buses run from the airport every thirty minutes 3am–10pm (45min; Rp10,000) to Gambir train station and also to

Blok M in the south, Rawamangun (east) and Kemayoram (north). Turn left out of arrivals and walk about 200m to the bus stand. With taxis, in addition to the metered fare, passengers must pay the toll fees (about Rp8000) plus another Rp3000 guaranteed service fee; a taxi from the airport to Jl Jaksa costs about Rp120,000 in total. Blue Bird is the most reliable firm.

**Tourist information** The main tourist information office is in the Jakarta Theatre building, opposite Sarinah's department store on Jl Wahid Hasyim (Mon–Fri 10am–7pm; ⓣ021/315 4094), which has knowledgeable English-speaking staff.

## City transport

**Buses** The Busway system is the only bus service in Jakarta with designated stops. It runs between Kota and Blok M, and is the easiest and most useful service for tourists. With its own designated bus lane, it's also far quicker than other transport services. Buy your ticket (Rp3500 flat fare) before boarding from the ticket office at the station. Other useful stations include Sarinah (for Jl Jaksa) and Monumen (for the Monas Tower and National Museum).

Other buses operate a set-fare system, regardless of distance, but prices depend on the type of bus. The cheapest are the small, pale-blue minivans, which operate out of Kota bus station (their numbers are always preceded by "M") and the large coaches found all over the city; they all charge Rp1000. A/c buses cost Rp3500. To alight from the bus, hail the driver or conductor with "*kiri!*" (left) or rap the overhead rail with a coin.

**Bajaj** The two-stroke motorized rickshaws, or bajaj (pronounced "ba-jais"), monopolize the city's backstreets. Be sure to bargain very, very hard (for example, from Jl Jaksa to the post office, should be Rp8000); bajaj are banned from major thoroughfares such as Jl Thamrin, so you might get dropped off a long way from your destination.

**Taxis** Jakarta's taxis are numerous and, providing you know your way around the city, inexpensive. The most reputable firm is Blue Bird. Most drivers will use meters without being asked so fares depend on how long you spend stuck in one of Jakarta's many traffic jams (a half-hour ride should cost about Rp60,000), but don't expect drivers to speak English. The black limo-style Silver Bird taxis, part of the Blud Bird group, often have English-speaking drivers, but cost almost twice as much. Women should avoid travelling in taxis alone at night as there are increasing reports of assaults and robberies.

## Accommodation

Jakarta has relatively few budget hotels, so they fill up fast and should be booked ahead – prices start at Rp20,000 for a dorm bed. Nearly all budget places are on or around Jl Jaksa, the city's travellers' enclave to the south of Medan Merdeka. Jl Wahid Hasyim, at the southern end of Jl Jaksa, has a number of mid-priced places.

**Bloemsteen** Jl Kebon Sirih Timur I/174 ⓣ021/325389. One of the cleaner hostels around Jaksa, with spacious rooms, good bathrooms, and a pleasant, sunny balcony. ❶–❷

**Borneo** Jl Kebon Sirih Barat 37 ⓣ021/314 0095. Ramshackle and friendly hostel. ❷–❸

**Bumi Johar** Jl Johar 17–19 ⓣ021/314 5746. Two minutes' walk from Jl Jaksa, this small hotel has comfortable rooms with a/c and TVs. ❻

**Cipta** Jl Wahid Hasyim 53 ⓣ021/390 4701. Reasonable mid-priced hotel facing the south end of Jl Jaksa; every room is en suite, with a/c. ❻

**Delima** Jl Jaksa 5 ⓣ021/3190 4157. The oldest of the city's hostels, though looking tired now and some rooms could be cleaner. Dorms ❶; rooms ❶–❷

**Hostel 35** Jl Kebon Sirih Barat 35 ⓣ021/392 0331. Once part of *Borneo*, this hostel has some of the most attractive rooms rooms on the street, the most expensive with a/c and TVs. ❷–❸

**Le Margot** Jl Jaksa 15 ⓣ021/391 3830. The best value mid-priced hotel offering reasonable rooms with a/c, cable TV and hot water. The rooms overlooking the street are noisy at night. ❹

**Nick's Corner** (also called *Wisma Niki*) Jl Jaksa 16 ⓣ021/310 7814. Once one of Jl Jaksa's most popular hostels, this *wisma* is now looking very run down. Window-less dorms are available (❶); rooms ❸

**Rota International Hotel** Jl Wahid Hasyim 63 ⓣ021/315 2858. Airy hotel, with clean a/c rooms (all with TV) and friendly service. ❻

**Tator** Jl Jaksa 37 ⓣ021/323940. Many people's favourite, this spotless hotel has friendly staff and breakfast is included in the price. Some rooms have hot water. ❷–❸

**Yusran** Jl Kebon Sirih Barat Dalam VI/9 ⓣ021/314 0373. Perhaps Jaksa's best-kept secret, this pleasant budget hotel lies at the end of Gang 6 to the west of Jl Jaksa. Doubles are spotless and comfortable. More expensive rooms have a/c. ❶–❸

## Eating

Food is more expensive in the capital than anywhere else in Indonesia: *nasi goreng* can cost twice as much. Local street food thrives, particularly along Jl HA Salim (also known as Jl Sabang).

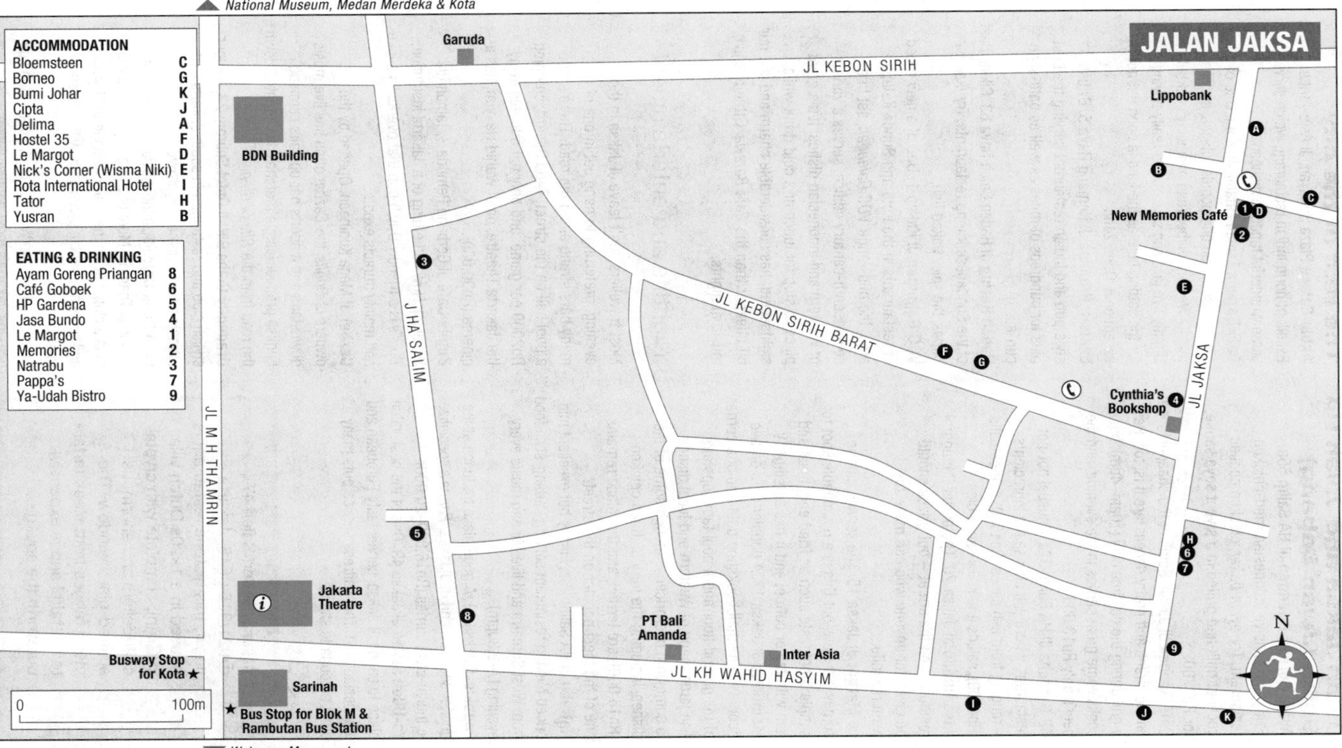
JALAN JAKSA
National Museum, Medan Merdeka & Kota
Gambir Train Station
Welcome Monument
N
JL KEBON SIRIH
JL KEBON SIRIH BARAT
JL JAKSA
J HA SALIM
JL M H THAMRIN
JL KH WAHID HASYIM
Garuda
BDN Building
Lippobank
New Memories Café
Cynthia's Bookshop
Jakarta Theatre
PT Bali Amanda
Inter Asia
Busway Stop for Kota ★
Sarinah
★ Bus Stop for Blok M & Rambutan Bus Station
0
100m
ACCOMMODATION
Bloemsteen C
Borneo G
Bumi Johar K
Cipta J
Delima A
Hostel 35 F
Le Margot D
Nick's Corner (Wisma Niki) E
Rota International Hotel I
Tator H
Yusran B
EATING & DRINKING
Ayam Goreng Priangan 8
Café Goboek 6
HP Gardena 5
Jasa Bundo 4
Le Margot 1
Memories 2
Natrabu 3
Pappa's 7
Ya-Udah Bistro 9

### Jalan Jaksa and Jalan HA Salim (Jalan Sabang)

**Ayam Goreng Priangan** Jl HA Salim 55a. Fairly inexpensive Indonesian fried-chicken restaurant. Try *ayam bakar*, chicken cooked in coconut milk and grilled in a sweet soya sauce, for Rp7700.

**Café Goboek** Jl Jaksa. Some of the cheapest food on the street, and pretty decent fare it is, too. Has a grill during the daytime only (10am–4pm), but cooks some great curries in the evening, and the beer's only Rp13,000.

**HP Gardena** Jl HA Salim 32a. Unusual hot-pot restaurant, where you choose the ingredients – ranging from fish cakes (Rp4500) to meatballs (Rp4500), salads and spicy sauce dips.

**Jasa Bundo** Jl Jaksa 20. The better Padang restaurant on the street – but prizes should be given for anyone who can make the waiters smile.

**Le Margot** Jl Jaksa 15. The service can be somewhat slow, but this is a reasonable spot for simple breakfasts such as fried egg, toast and jam with tea or coffee, and it has satellite TV.

**Memories** Jl Jaksa 17. A popular café on two floors with a small bookshop built into one corner of the ground floor and a pool table upstairs. The large menu of Western and local dishes is somewhat overpriced – though some of the dishes, including the fiery Sichuan chicken (Rp16,000), are terrific, and this place remains one of the most popular on the street.

**Natrabu** Jl HA Salim 29a. Flashy but excellent mid-priced Minang restaurant serving Padang-style food from West Sumatra and live Minang music every evening (7–9.30pm).

**Pappa's** Jl Jaksa 41. A good place for lunch at the quieter southern end of JlJaksa, *Pappa's* specializes in Indian-style curries (Rp16,000–20,000).

**Ya-Udah Bistro** Jl Jaksa 49. One of the best-value place to eat on Jl Jaksa, serves tasty European and Indonesian food. The waitress service puts many other emporia to shame.

> TREAT YOURSELF
>
> **Oasis** Jl Raden Saleh 47 ⓣ021/315 0646. Jakarta's finest, this historic restaurant is housed in a 1920s Dutch villa in Cikini, complete with crystal chandeliers and enormous stained-glass window. The menu ranges from steak tartare to rijsttaffel and is expensive but worth the splurge.

### The rest of the city

**Akbar Palace** Plaza Senayan, Jl Asia-Afrika. Excellent north Indian restaurant, which serves some wonderful tandoori dishes.

**Café Batavia** Taman Fatahillah, Kota. One of the city's most stylish and popular places, serving mainly Western dishes, and over sixty cocktails. Nightly live jazz and soul. You're really paying for the setting here as the food is good but not exceptional. Open 24hr.

**Eastern Promise** Jl Kemang Raya 5. British-style pub and Indian restaurant serving the best pies for hundreds of miles as well as balti-style curries.

**Raden Kuring** Jl Raden Saleh Raya 63, Cikini. Best of the Sundanese kuring restaurants. Try *ikan mas pepes*, the spicy baked fish.

**VOC Galangan** Jl Kakap 1. One of a new breed of restaurants in the Kota and Sunda Kelapa area, the mid-range *VOC Galangan*, set in a seventeenth-century edifice, serves a variety of Western and Indonesian dishes. It's a great place to stop for lunch or a cold drink while sightseeing, has considerable charm and is a fair bit cheaper than the *Café Batavia*. Often has live music at nights.

## Nightlife and entertainment

Most travellers don't leave Jl Jaksa in the evening, preferring to hang out in one of the many bars strung along the road. There's also a pool hall on the street, Tatto Bilyard, charging Rp2000 per game, and only ten minutes away the Jakarta Theatre, on Jl Wahid Hasyim, has a cinema (Rp30,000).

**Bugils Café** Jl Gerbang Pemuda 3, Taman Ria Senayan. Now something of a Jakarta institution, *Bugils* is a friendly Dutch pub that overlooks a lake and mainly attracts expats.

**Cazbar** Jl Mega Kuningan. Opened by the owners of *Bugils*, the *Cazbar* often has live music downstairs and a sports bar upstairs screeing English premier league matches. It's situated down the road from the *Ritz Carlton*.

**Dragonfly** Graha BIP, Jl Gatot Subroto 23. A super stylish club and restaurant in south Jakarta that attracts a fairly glamorous crowd.

**Hard Rock Café** Plaza Indonesia Entertainment X'nter, Jl Thamrin. More of a late-night restaurant than a club, but it's the nearest venue to Jl Jaksa and remains popular, particularly with Jakarta's teenyboppers.

**Stadium** Jl Hayam Wuruk 111. A full-on club and perhaps Jakarta's most popular venue.

## Shopping

While Jakarta has no particular indigenous craft of its own, the capital isn't a bad place to go souvenir shopping.

**Books** There are a couple of places in the basement of the smart Indonesia Plaza, including a branch of the excellent Periplus chain. For secondhand books, visit Cynthia's bookshop on Jl Jaksa, or the small store in the corner of *New Memories Café*.

**Market** The antiques market on Jl Surabaya, one block west of Cikini station in Jakarta's Menteng district, sells fine silver jewellery, and traditional Javanese wooden trunks and other pieces of furniture, as well as old records.

**Souvenirs** The entire fifth floor of the Sarinah department store is given over to souvenirs, with wayang kulit and wayang golek puppets, leather bags and woodcarvings a speciality. Batik fabrics are sold on the fourth floor.

## Directory

**Airlines** Air Canada, Jl Mega Kuningan Lot 5.1 Menara Rajawali 8th Floor ⓣ021/576 1629; Air France, Summitmas Tower, 9th floor, Jl Jend Sudirman ⓣ021/520 2262; Bouraq, Jl Angkasa 1–3, Kemayoran ⓣ021/628 8815; British Airways, Menara Bank, Jl Thamrin 5 ⓣ021/230 0277; Cathay Pacific, Gedung Bursa Efek, Jl Jend Sudirman Kav 52–53 ⓣ021/515 1747; China Airlines, Wisma Dharmala Sakti, Jl Jend Sudirman 32 ⓣ021/251 0788; Emirates, *Hotel Sahid Jaya*, 2nd floor, Jl Jend Sudirman 86 ⓣ021/520 5363; Eva Air, Price Waterhouse Centre, 10th floor, Jl Rasuna Said Kav C3 ⓣ021/520 5363; Garuda, Jl Merdeka Selatan 13 ⓣ021/231 0082, and at the BDN Building, Jl Thamrin 5; Gulf Air, Jl Jend Sudirman Kav 45–46, Wisma Danamon Aetna Life Lt 25 ⓣ021/577 0789; Japan Airlines, Jl Jend Sudirman Kav 3–4 Wisma Kyoei Prince Indonesia Lt 1–2 ⓣ021/572 3211; Jatayu, Jl Batu Tulis Raya 19B ⓣ021/345 8666; Kartika Airlines, Jl Medan Merdeka Timur 7 ⓣ021/345 2947; KLM, Summitmas II, 17th floor, Jl Jend Sudirman Kav 61–62 ⓣ021/252 6740; Korean Airlines, Jl Jend Sudirman Kav 28, Mayapada Tower 9th floor, ⓣ021/521 2175; Lufthansa, Panin Centre Building, 2nd floor, Jl Jend Sudirman 1 ⓣ021/570 2005; Malaysian Airlines, World Trade Centre, Jl Jend Sudirman Kav 29 ⓣ021/522 9682; Mandala, Jl Garuda 76 ⓣ021/424 6100, also Jl Veteran I 34 ⓣ021/381 1057; Merpati, Jl Angkasa 7, Blok B15 Kav 2 & 3 ⓣ021/654 8888; Pelita, Jl Abdul Muis 52-56A ⓣ021/231 2222; Philippine Airlines, 15th floor, World Trade Center Building, Jl Jend Sudirman Kav 29–31 ⓣ021/526 8668; Qantas Airways, Menara Bank, Jl Thamrin 5 ⓣ021/230 0277; Royal Brunei Airlines, World Trade Centre, 11th floor, Jl Jend Sudirman Kav 29–31 ⓣ021/521 1842; Singapore Airlines, Menara Kadin Indonesia, 8th floor, Jl HR Rasuna Said Blok X-5, Kav 2 & 3, ⓣ021/5790 3747; Thai International, BDN Building, ground floor, Jl Thamrin 5 ⓣ021/230 2552.

**Banks and exchange** Many of the banks, Sarinah, the post office and Gambir train station have their own ATM machines, which offer a better rate than any bank or moneychanger. Otherwise, Lippobank, just west of the northern end of Jl Jaksa on Jl Kebon Siri, offers the best rates in town, as well as credit-card advances. The AMEX representative is the Suman Leisure Group, Jl Tanah Abang III/28E, ⓣ021/344 6235; or PT Dwidaya Tour and Travel, Jalan KH Samanhudi, No. 22 A–B. The InterAsia moneychanger at Jl Wahid Hasyim 96a is reasonable for cash exchanges, but offers poor rates for traveller's cheques. PT Ayu in Toko Gunung Agung, Jl Kwitang Raya (Rp3000 bajaj from Jl Jaksa) gives consistently good rates for notes.

**Embassies and consulates** Australia, Jl H Rasuna Said Kav 15-16, ⓣ021/2550 5555; Britain, Jl Thamrin 75 ⓣ021/315 6254; Canada, Metropolitan Building 1, Jl Jend Sudirman Kav 29 ⓣ021/2550 7800; Malaysia, Jl Rasuna Said 1–3, Kuningan ⓣ021/522 4947; New Zealand, Jl Diponegoro 41 ⓣ021/330 680; Singapore, Jl Rasuna Said 2, Kuningan ⓣ021/520 1489; South Africa, Wisma GKBI Jl Sudirman ⓣ021/719 3304; Thailand, Jl Imam Bonjol 74 ⓣ021/390 4055; US, Jl Medan Merdeka Selatan 5 ⓣ021/360360.

**Hospitals and clinics** The MMC hospital on Jl Rasuna Said in Kuningan is the best in town (ⓣ021/520 3435). The private SMI (Sentra Medika International) clinic at Jl Cokroaminoto 16 in Menteng (ⓣ021/315 7747) is run by Australian and Indonesian doctors. Any *Praktek Umum* (public clinic) will treat foreigners cheaply.

**Internet** Perhaps the best, and certainly the best-value, internet café in the Jaksa area is Mnet, next to *Pappa's* on Jl Jaksa. Wi-Fi is available at *Starbucks* in the Jakarta Theatre building though you have to buy a pre-paid card.

**Post office** The GPO lies to the north of Lapangan Benteng (Mon–Sat 8am–8pm, Sun 9am–5pm), northeast of Medan Merdeka (catch bus #15 or #P15 from Jl Kebon Siri, to the north of Jl Jaksa). Poste restante is at counter no. 55. The *Sari Pan Pacific* will also handle mail.

**Telephones** The Indosat building, 21 Jl Medan Merdeka Barat, has IDD and HCD on its ground floor (cash only), as do the RTQ warpostel at Jl Jaksa 17 (8am–midnight) and the wartel on Jl Kebon Siri Barat. IDD calls can be made from the lobby of *Hotel Cipta* at any time as well as from *Pappa's*, Jl Jaksa, during opening hours.

**Travel agents** Good travel agencies on or near Jl Jaksa include the highly respected Global at no. 49 and PT Robertur Kencana at no. 20b, Lipta Marsada Pertala at no. 11 (☎021/326291), and PT Bali Amanda at Jl Wahid Hasyim 110a, which can book Pelni ferry tickets on the internet.

## Moving on

For addresses and telephone numbers of airlines and travel agents in Jakarta, see p.217.

**By bus** The capital has good bus connections to all points in Java, and many cities on neighbouring islands, too. There's usually a range of prices for every destination, depending on the type of bus you're travelling in, with frequent departures to all main destinations. Tickets bought from an agency in town are more expensive, but some of the buses leave from right outside the agency, saving a trip to the bus station, all of which are inconveniently located. Leave at least an 1hr 30min to get from the city centre to any bus station. It's advisable not to try to travel by bus at the end of Ramadan.

Most buses to Central Java, East Java and Bali depart from Pulo Gadung station. Buses to West Java, including Bogor and Bandung, use Rambutan Kampung station, 18km south of the city centre near Taman Mini. Alternatively to reach Bogor, catch #AC10 southbound to Universitas Kristen Indonesia (UKI) at Cawang and from there a local bus to the Bogor terminal. Buses to Carita (for Krakatau) and Labuan leave from the Kalideres station, 15km west of the city centre; buses #78 and #64 run between Jl MH Thamrin and Kalideres.

**Destinations** (Pulo Gadung station unless otherwise stated) to: Banda Aceh (60hr); Bandung (from Kampung Rambutan station; 4hr 30min); Bogor (from Kampung Rambutan station; every 15min; 1–2hr); Bukittinggi (30hr); Carita (from Kalideres; 3hr 30min); Denpasar (24hr); Labuan (from Kalideres; 3hr); Medan (from Pulo Gadung or Kalideres; 2 days); Merak (from Kalideres; 3hr); Padang (from Pulo Gadung or Kalideres; 32hr); Pangandaran (12hr); Solo (13hr); Surabaya (15hr); Yogya (12hr).

**By ferry** Pelni ferries sail from Tanjung Priok harbour. Bus #P125 runs from opposite the Sari Pan Pacific to Tanjung Priok bus station, 500m from the harbour. Allow at least 75 minutes for your journey from Jl Jaksa. For the latest timetable, call in at the ground floor of the Pelni head office at Jl Gajah Mada 14. The Pelni booking office is at Jl Angkasa 18 (Mon–Thurs 8am–noon & 1–2.30pm, Fri 8–11.30am & 1–2.30pm); catch bus #15 or #P15 to Pasar Senen station, then bus #10 to Angkasa. The Kapuas Express ferry runs from Godown 2 at the Sunda Kelapa harbour to Pontianak in Kalimantan (2 weekly; 19hr); tickets from PT Egel Tripelti, Rajawali Condominium Edelweiss Tower, Jl Rajawali Selatan 1/1b (☎021/640 9288). The harbourmaster's office is on the second floor of the Departemen Perhubungan at the end of Baruna III in Sunda Kelapa.

Fortnightly (except where stated) to: Balikpapan (3 days); Banda (4 days); Belawan, Medan (every 4 days; 48hr); Denpasar (39hr); Jayapura (7 days); Kijang (24–39hr); Kumai (3–4 days); Kupang (5 days); Larantuka (4 days); Makassar (48hr); Nias (48hr); Nunukan (5 days); Pontianak (every 3 days; 11–31hr); Pulau Batam (every 4 days; 24hr) Surabaya (24hr); Tarakan (5 days); Ternate (4 days).

**By train** Most of the trains travelling to West and Central Java begin at Gambir station, including those to Yogya, Surakarta (Solo), Bogor and Bandung. There are two special offices (daily 7.30am–7pm) selling tickets for the luxury trains, such as the Parahiyangan Express to Bandung and the Argolawu Express to Yogya and Solo. Although Kota station, near old Batavia, is on the same line as Gambir, some of the trains departing from Kota do not stop at Gambir, and vice versa. To reach Kota from Jl Jaksa, catch the Busway (Rp3500) to Sarinah, about a five-minute walk away. From there, buses continue south to the Welcome Monument. The other two train stations, Tanah Abang and Pasar Senen, are further out of town, have fewer services and rarely see tourists.

**Destinations:** (from Gambir station): Bandung (hourly; 2hr 20min); Bogor (every 20min; 1hr 30min); Cilacap (1 daily; 6hr 13min); Cirebon (18 daily; 5hr); Malang (1 daily; 18hr 5min); Solobapan, Solo (4 daily; 7hr–10hr 25min); Surabaya (5 daily; 9hr–14hr 30min); Yogyakarta (6 daily; 6hr 50min–8hr 40min).

**By air** All scheduled flights use Sukarno-Hatta Airport (☎021/550 5000). DAMRI buses depart for the airport from Gambir station every thirty minutes from 6am to 6pm (45min; Rp10,000). A taxi from town to the airport costs from Rp100,000.

**Destinations**: Banda Aceh (daily; 3hr 45min); Bandung (10 daily; 40min); Banjarmasin (5 daily; 1hr 40min); Denpasar (16 daily; 1hr 50min); Jayapura; (2 daily; 8hr); Makassar (12 daily; 2hr 20min); Manado (4 daily; 4hr 45min); Mataram (6 weekly; 3hr 15min); Medan (16 daily; 2hr 10min); Padang (7 daily; 1hr 40min); Pekanbaru (7 daily;

1hr 40min); Pontianak (9 daily; 1hr 30min); Pulau Batam (8 daily; 1hr 35min); Surabaya (33 daily; 1hr 20min); Solo/Surakarta (4 daily; 1hr 5min); Yogyakarta (22 daily; 1hr 5min).

### MERAK AND FERRIES TO SUMATRA

At the extreme northwestern tip of Java, **Merak** is the port for ferries across the Sunda Straits to Bakauheni on Sumatra. Ferries **to Sumatra** leave about every thirty minutes and take about two hours and thirty minutes; crowds of buses connect with the ferries to take you on to Bandar Lampung, Palembang or destinations further north in Sumatra. If you get stuck at Merak, try the *Hotel Anda*, Jl Florida 4, which has basic rooms with fan and mandi (☎0254/71041; ❶).

## KRAKATAU

At 10am on August 27, 1883, an explosion equivalent to 10,000 Hiroshima atomic bombs rent **Krakatau** island; the boom was heard as far away as Sri Lanka. As the eruption column towered 40km into the atmosphere, a thick mud rain began to fall over the area, and the temperature plunged by 5°C. Tremors were detected as far away as the English Channel and off the coast of Alaska. One single **tsunami** as tall as a seven-storey building, raced outwards, erasing 300 towns and villages and killing 36,417 people; a government gunboat was carried 3km inland and deposited up a hill 10m above sea level. Once into the open sea, the waves travelled at up to 700kph, reaching South Africa and scuttling ships in Auckland harbour. Two-thirds of Krakatau had vanished for good, and on those parts that remained not so much as a seed or an insect survived.

Today, the crumbled caldera is clearly visible west of the beaches near Merak and Carita, its sheer northern cliff face soaring straight out of the sea to nearly 800m. But it is the glassy black cone of **Anak Krakatau**, the child of Krakatau volcano, that most visitors want to see, a barren wasteland that's still growing and still very much active. It first reared its head from the seas in 1930, and now sits angrily smoking among the remains of the older peaks. To get here requires a **motorboat trip** (4–6hr) from Labuan or Carita, then a half-hour walk up to the crater, from where you can see black lava flows, sulphurous fumaroles and smoke. The easiest way to visit Krakatau is with the Black Rhino **tour** company in **Carita**.

### Carita

Boasting one of the most sheltered stretches of sea in Java, Carita is the best spot to arrange **tours** (day-trips $50) to Krakatau. Tours run by Black Rhino (☎0253/81072), across from the marina, are recommended, but don't fall for the unqualified guides who approach you on spec. **Buses** run from the Kalideres bus station in Jakarta to Lubuan (3hr); from here you can pick up a **colt** to Carita – don't get conned into taking transport round to the stop for colts, which is just two minutes' walk towards the seafront and round to the right. All **accommodation** in Carita is on or close to the main seaside road, known as Jalan Carita Raya or Jalan Pantai Carita. Prices shoot up at the weekend, when the town is invaded by jetskiers. Friendly staff, clean rooms and interesting decor make *Sunset View* (☎0253/81075; ❶) one of the best-value places on the west coast. *Carita Krakatau* (☎0253/83027; ❶–❷), behind the restaurant of the same name, is also recommended and offers spotless rooms with mandi, fan and breakfast.

The public parts of the beach in Carita are lined with **food** carts selling *murtabak*, sate and soto. *Carita Krakatau*, 30m towards Anyer from the marina, cooks a good fish steak for, while *Diminati*, opposite the entrance to the marina, boasts the cheapest cold beer in town and does an excellent *kakap* fish steak meal.

## BOGOR

Located 300m above sea level and just an hour's train journey south of Jakarta, **BOGOR** enjoys a cool, wet climate and is home to the famously lush Kebun Raya Bogor or **Botanical Gardens** (daily 8am–5pm; Rp9500, plus Rp2000 for the orchid house; catch bus #2 from the train station), which were founded by Sir Stamford Raffles in 1811. In the gardens, pathways wind between towering bamboo stands, climbing bougainvillea, a small tropical rainforest, and ponds full of water lilies and fountains. Perhaps the garden's best-known occupants are the giant rafflesia and *bungu bangkai*, two of the world's largest (and smelliest) flowers. Near the gardens' main entrance, the rather dilapidated **Zoological Museum** (daily 8am–4pm) houses some 30,000 specimens, including a complete skeleton of a blue whale, a stuffed Javan rhino and, most impressively, the remains of a huge coconut crab. **Wayang golek puppets** are made at a workshop to the northeast of the gardens; ask for Pak Dase's place. If you're interested in **gamelan** and Javanese gongs, visit Pak Sukarna's factory on Jalan Pancasan to the southwest of the gardens. Here the instruments are forged using traditional methods, and are also for sale.

### Arrival, local transport and information

**By bus** Buses from Jakarta's UKI at Cawang arrive at the bus terminal about 500m southeast of the gardens.
**By train** The train station, which is prone to rainy-season flooding, is about 500m northwest of the Botanical Gardens and close to some of the town's budget accommodation.
**Bemos** The main bemo stop is behind the bus terminal, but the best place to pick up bemos is by the train station. Bemo #2 runs between the station and the botanical gardens; #3 runs between the station and bus terminal.
**Tourist information** There's a small tourist information centre (Mon–Fri 9am–4pm) at the southern entrance to the gardens, and a second by the train station (8am–5pm).

### Accommodation

**Abu Pensione** Jl Mayor Oking 15 T0251/322893. With excessively friendly staff, river views and excellent breakfasts this is probably the best budget place to stay in Bogor; the pricier rooms here have hot water and a/c. Turn right out of the station, then right again a few hundred metres later down Jl Mayor Oking. ❷–❸
**Hotel Mirah** Jl Pangrango 9a T0251/328044. Has an inviting pool (open to non-guests for Rp15,000) and a/c en-suite rooms; from the station, catch bemo #3 and jump out by the hotel's sign on Jalan Salak. ❻–❾
**Pensione Firman** Jl Paledang 48 T0251/323246. Long the budget travellers' favourite accommodation with basic rooms, though the price includes breakfast. To reach it from the station, walk for 1km along Jl Paledang or catch #2 and jump out at the junction of Jl Juanda and Jl Paledang. ❷
**Wisma Karunia** Jl Sempur 35–37 T0251/323411. Friendly and quiet, with a range of rooms and breakfast included. ❷

### Eating

Along Jl Pengadillan, near the Telkom and train station, are bunches of night stalls, which set up after 6pm.
**Bogor Permai** Corner of Jl Jend Sudirman and Jl Sawojajar. A small food complex housing a fine delicatessen and the best bakery in Bogor. The *Bogor Permai* restaurant in the back of the building serves quality seafood and steaks from Rp35,000.
**Restoran Si Kabayan** Jl Bina Marga I 2. One of the best places to try genuine Sundanese food is in the garden here, where *ikan mas* is a speciality.
**Salak Sunset Café** 50m down from the *Pensione Firman* on Jl Paledang. The only traveller-oriented place in Bogor, overlooking the river and serving great pizzas as well as ice-cold beer. Open from 4pm.

### Moving on

**By bus** There are buses every fifteen minutes or so to Jakarta (1–2hr) and Bandung (3–4hr).
**By train** Express trains to Gambir, Jakarta (1hr).

## BANDUNG AND AROUND

Set 750m above sea level, and protected by a fortress of watchful volcanoes 190km southeast of Jakarta, **BANDUNG** is the third largest city in Indonesia and a centre of industry and traditional Sundanese arts – with plenty of cultural performances for tourists – though it suffers from incredible traffic pollution and uninteresting modern developments. Sundanese culture has remained intact here since the fifth century when the first Hindu Sundanese settled in this part of West Java. Modern Bandung's main tourist attraction is nearby **Tangkbuhan Prahu volcano**, from where there's a very pleasant two-hour forest walk down to the city, too.

The Dutch spotted the potential of this lush, cool plateau and its fertile volcanic slopes in the mid-seventeenth century, and set about cultivating coffee and rice here, settling in the area to live in the early nineteenth century. Several relics from the city's colonial era remain, including some of the elegant shops along Jalan Braga, and some fine buildings on Jalan Asia-Afrika.

## What to see and do

On Jalan Asia-Afrika, northeast of the alun-alun (town square), is the **Gedung Merdeka** building, which hosted the first Asia-Afrika Conference in 1955 and is known as the Asia-Afrika or Liberty building. Inside, a small museum (daily 8am–3pm; free) commemorates the conference. running north from here is **Jalan Braga**, the chic shopping boulevard of 1920s Bandung. There's still one bakery here that's tried to hang on to its history, and a few of the facades maintain their stylish designs. The side streets that run off Jalan Braga were notorious for their raucous bars and brothels – at night, a lot of the seediness remains.

A twenty-minute walk to the northeast, the impressive 1920s **Gedung Sate** building at Jl Diponegoro 22, is known as the Sate Building because the regular globules on its gold-leaf spire resemble meat on a skewer. The excellent **Geographical Museum** (Mon–Thurs 9am–2pm, Fri 9–11am, Sat 9am–1pm; free) is nearby at Jl Diponegoro 57, and displays mountains of fossils, as well as several full dinosaur skeletons, a four-metre mammoth skeleton and a replica of the skull of the famous Java Man.

About 750m west of the museum, Jalan Cihampelas, known to Westerners as **Jeans Street**, is lined with shops selling cheap T-shirts, bags, shoes and jeans. These are no longer such a bargain, and it's better to head to the shops at the south end of Jalan Dewi Sartika just before the Kebon Kelapa bus terminal, or the huge clothes market at the south end of Jalan Otista. The shopfronts on Jeans Street themselves are adorned with a kitsch kaleidoscope of colossal plaster superheroes, including Rambo, straddling spaceships and fluffy stucco clouds.

## Arrival and information

**By bus** Bus services to Bandung run from every major town in Java, including Jakarta. The main Leuwi Panjang bus terminal for buses from the west is 5km south of the city; the Cicaheum bus terminal for those from the east is at the far eastern edge of town. Local DAMRI buses serve both stations.

**By train** Bandung's civilized train station is located within walking distance of most budget accommodation, fairly close to the centre of town.

**By air** The airport is 3km northwest of the train station, served by plenty of taxis.

**Tourist information** Presently in a temporary office at the Masjid Agung, but purportedly moving permanently to a building on the western side of the alun-alun, the tourist office is run by the well-meaning Pak Ajid (Mon–Sat 9am–5pm; ⓣ022/420 6644). There is another office at the train station, and a regional office at Jl A Yani 277 (ⓣ022/721 0768).

## City transport

**Buses and minibuses** Bandung's white-and-blue DAMRI buses cost Rp2500 a journey, and ply routes between the bus terminals through the centre of town. Red angkots (minibuses) also run a useful circular route, via the train station and the alun-alun (town square), to the Kebun Kelapa bus terminal, which serves Cicaheum bus terminal, Dago, Ledeng and Lembang.

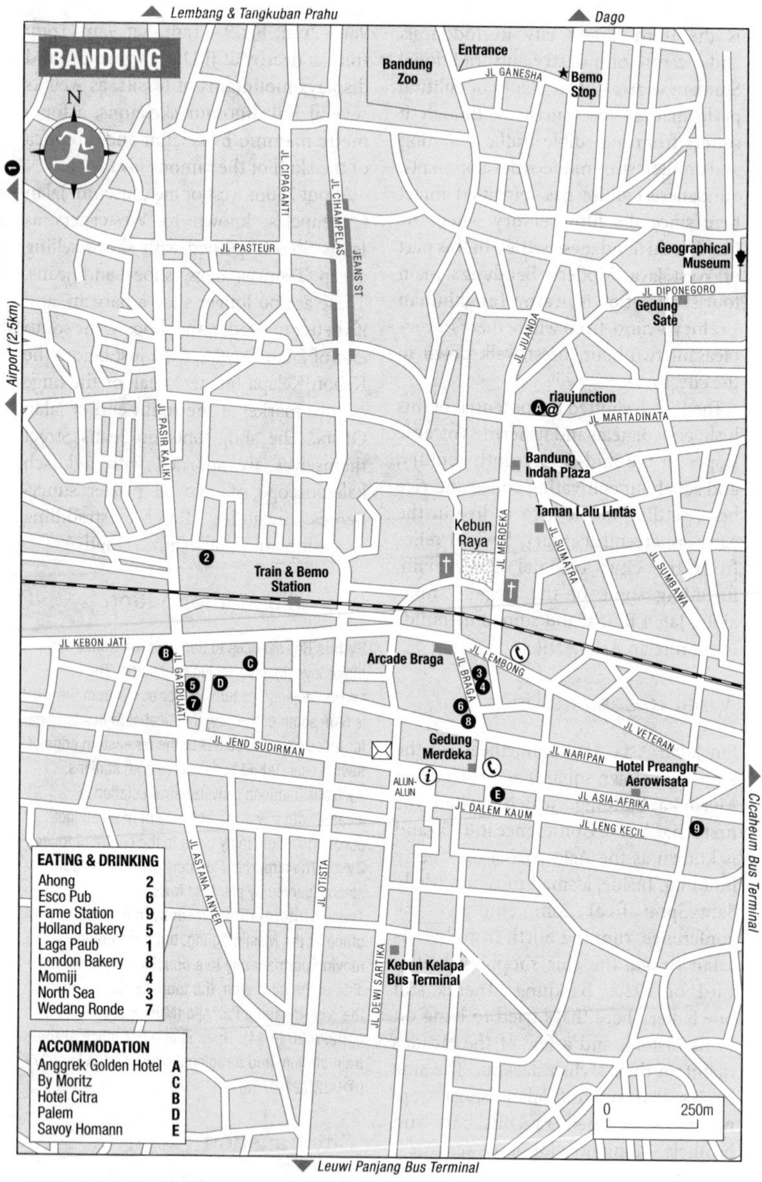


## Accommodation

Coming into town from the airport or bus terminals, it's best to get dropped off at the train station, which is close to all the cheap hostels.

**Anggrek Golden Hotel** Jl Martadinata 15 ⓣ022/420 5537. All rooms come with a/c, phone and hot water, but this hotel is beginning to show its age. ❻

**By Moritz** Jl Belakang Pasar/Luxor Permai 35 ⓣ022/420 5788. A popular travellers' hangout, but with a run-down feel, with singles and doubles, some en suite. ❷

**Hotel Citra** Jl Gardujati 93 ⓣ022/600 5061. Close to the train station, and one of the best bargains in Bandung, though a little noisy. Clean rooms with mandi, TV, fan and a/c. ❷

**Palem** Jl Belakang Pasar 117 ⓣ022/423 6277. Smart, clean and friendly hotel in central location. All rooms come with TV and bathroom, and rates include breakfast. Popular with locals so book ahead. ❸

**Savoy Homann** Jl Asia-Afrika 112 ⓣ022/423 2244. If you want colonial flavour then this is the place. Sizeable rooms, some with views of the courtyard gardens. ❽–❾

## Eating

There are food courts in the numerous shopping centres – the one on the second floor of Arcade Braga at the northern end of Jl Braga is good – and side streets near the square serve some of the best warung food.

**Ahong** Jl Kebon Kawang. Chinese place serving *kangkung* (water spinach) and *sapi* (beef) hotplate (Rp25,000).

**Holland Bakery** Jl Gardujati 66. A good selection of cakes and a welcome air-conditioned respite from the noise of the street outside, but serves only cold drinks.

**London Bakery** Jl Braga. Specializing in a range of coffees and teas, this is a modern European-type place with newspapers in English.

**Momiji** Jl Braga 64. A stylish Japanese restaurant. At Rp55,000, the delicious Bento boxes are the budget choice.

**Wedang Ronde** Jl Gardujati 52. Serves standard Indonesian food in clean and comfortable surroundings.

## Nightlife

Most of Bandung's nightlife is concentrated on Jl Braga but there are a couple of options elsewhere.

**Esco Bar** Jl Braga 71. A laid-back bar with cheap beer and live music on Thursday, Friday and Saturday nights.

**Fame Station** 11th Floor, Lippo Building, Jl Gatot Subroto 2. This bar attracts a young crowd and often features live music. 11am–2am; Rp25,000.

**Laga Pub** Jl Junjungan 164. Popular with expats for its live music and cheapish beer.

**North Sea** Jl Braga 82. A Dutch-owned emporium with a good reputation for food.

## Cultural performances

Bandung is the capital of Sundanese culture; pick up the *Jakarta and Java Kini* magazine from the tourist information office to find out about special performances.

**Bandung Zoo** In the north of town. Often has shows on Sunday mornings, usually either the Indonesian martial art *pencak silat*, or puppet shows.

**Panghegar hotel** Jl Merdeka 2. Stages Sundanese cultural performances in its restaurant (Wed & Sat).

**Ram fighting** The most spectacular local event is the ram fighting (*adu domba*), held every other Sunday at 10am near the Sari Ater hot spring, 30km from the city. Check ahead at the tourist office. Take a minibus from the train station to Lembang terminal, then a second minibus to Ciater (Rp5000). To the sound of Sundanese flutes and drums, the magnificently presented rams lunge at each other until one of them fades; there's no blood, just flying wool and clouds of dust.

## Directory

**Airlines** Bouraq, Jl Naripan 44 (ⓣ022/423 6436); Garuda, at the *Hotel Preangher Aerowisata* Jl Asia-Afrika 81 (ⓣ022/420 9468); Lion Air, Jl Dr Djundjunan 155B (ⓣ022/602 0333); Merpati, Jl Kebonjali Kav A-1 62 (ⓣ022/730 2746).

**Banks and exchange** The two Golden Megacorp moneychangers, at Jl Juanda 89 opposite the Telkom building and at Jl Otista 180, have excellent rates.

**Internet** Internet cafés are surprisingly sparse in such a big town, though there is a small warung internet next to the Bandung Indah Plaza on Jalan Merdeka (Rp4000/hr). Many shopping centres offer free Wi-Fi, including the Arcade on Jl Braga, Bandung Indah Plaza and riaujunction next to *Anggrek Golden Hotel*.

**Post office** Jl Asia-Afrika 49 at the corner of Jl Banceuy (Mon–Sat 8am–9pm).

**Telecom** Main Telkom office on Jl Lembang (24hr).

## Moving on

**By bus** to: Banyuwangi (daily; 24hr); Bogor (4hr 30min); Jakarta (from Leuwi Panjang terminal; 4hr 30min–5hr 30min); Pangandaran (2 daily; 5hr); Yogya (9hr 30min).

**By train** to: Banjar (hourly; 4hr); Jakarta (13 daily; 2hr 20min); Surabaya (10 daily; 12 hr); Yogyakarta (10 daily; at least 9hr).

**By air** to: Makassar (daily; 4hr 20min); Mataram (daily; 8hr 25min); Singapore (daily; 3hr); Solo (3 weekly; 1hr 30min); Surabaya (3 daily; 1hr 20min).

## TANGKUBAN PRAHU VOLCANO AND THE DAGO TEAHOUSE WALK

The mountainous region to the north of Bandung is the heart of the Parahyangan Highlands – the "Home of the Gods" – a highly volcanic area considered by the Sundanese to be the nucleus of their spiritual world. A very pleasant day out from Bandung on public transport takes you first to the 1830-metre-high **Tangkuban Prahu volcano**, the most visited volcano in West Java, 29km north of Bandung. Although it hasn't had a serious eruption for many years, the volcano still spews out vast quantities of sulphurous gases and at least one of its ten craters is still considered to be active. To get there from Bandung, take a Subang **minibus** from the train station (30min; Rp1500) and ask to be put down at the turn-off for the volcano, where there's a Rp35,000 entrance fee. From here you can either charter an ojek or minibus up the asphalt road to the summit (10min; Rp5000) or walk up – it's about 4km up the road, or there's a good footpath via the Domas Crater, which starts just over 1km up the road from the guard post, to the right by the first car park. The **information booth** at the summit car park has details about crater walks; guides will offer their services, but it's pretty obvious where you should and shouldn't go – just be sure to wear strong hiking boots. The main crater, **Kawah Ratu,** is the one you can see down into from the end of the summit road, a huge, dull, grey cauldron with a few coloured lakes. From the summit you can trek down to **Domas Crater**, site of a small working sulphur mine.

### The Dago Teahouse walk

On the return journey from Tangkuban Prahu to Bandung you'll pass through Lembang, where you can change on to a minibus for the resort of **MARIBAYA** (4km; Rp500). There are waterfalls near the entrance gate and hot springs, which have been tapped into a public pool. Further down is the largest **waterfall**, which you have to pay extra to see. An ugly iron bridge has been built right across the lip of the falls, and this is the starting point for a wonderful **walk down to the Dago Teahouse** on the edge of Bandung (6km; 2hr). The path winds downhill through a gorge and forests – just before the teahouse are tunnels used by the Japanese in World War II and the Dago waterfall, which lies among bamboo thickets. At the end of your walk is the teahouse, with private tables under their own thatched roofs, and superb views over Bandung city. From here, plenty of minibuses head back into the centre of town (15min; Rp500).

## THE DIENG PLATEAU

The **Dieng Plateau** lies in a volcanic caldera 2093m above sea level and holds a rewarding mix of multicoloured sulphurous **lakes**, craters that spew pungent gases, and some of the oldest **Hindu temples** in Java. The volcano is still active – in 1979, over 150 people died after a cloud of poisonous gas bled into the atmosphere – and the landscape up on this misty, windswept plain is sparse, denuded and terraced. The authorities have given the temple complex and surroundings a makeover, which has succeeded in increasing the number of local tourists, but has had a detrimental effect on the plateau's formerly isolated atmosphere. Indeed, many travellers are now turning their backs on Dieng, considering its flagging charms a poor return for the effort it takes to get here, though some still arrive on day-trips from Yogya, especially during the dry season. Nevertheless the temples here are interesting, as are the other sights up here, and the plateau is still a worthy destination for those seeking a different, chillier side to Java.

## What to see and do

Although travel agents run **day-trips** from Yogya, these involve eight hours' travelling for just one hour on the plateau, so it's better to spend a night up here, in the damp and isolated village of **Dieng**, just across the road from the plateau's main temple complex; bring warm clothes and waterproofs.

### The temples

It is believed that the Dieng Plateau was once a completely self-contained **retreat** for priests and pilgrims. Unfortunately, it soon became completely waterlogged, and the entire plateau was eventually abandoned in the thirteenth century, only to be rediscovered, drained and restored some six hundred years later. The eight temples left on Dieng today are a tiny fraction of what was once a huge complex built by the Sanjayas in the seventh and eighth centuries.

Of these temples, the five that make up the **Arjuna complex** (daily 6.15am–5.15pm; Rp12,000), standing in fields opposite Dieng village, are believed to be the oldest. They have been named after heroes from the Mahabharata tales, although these are not the original names. Three of the five were built to the same blueprint: square, with two storeys and a fearsome kala head above the main entrance. The northernmost of these two-storey temples, the **Arjuna Temple**, is the oldest on Java (*c.*680 AD), and was dedicated to Shiva. Next to Arjuna stands **Candi Srikandi**, the exterior of which is adorned with reliefs of Vishnu (on the north wall), Shiva (east) and Brahma (south). **Candi Gatutkaca** overlooks the Arjuna complex 300m to the southwest, and twenty minutes' walk (1km) south of here stands the peculiar-looking **Candi Bima**, named after the brother of Arjuna. Rows of faces stare impassively back at passers-by from the temple walls, a design based on the temples of southern India.

### The lakes

From Candi Bima, you can continue down the road for a kilometre or so to **Telaga Warna** (coloured lake; Rp6000), the best example of Dieng's coloured lakes, where sulphurous deposits shade the water blue, from turquoise to azure. The lake laps against the shore of a small peninsula that holds a number of meditational caves. It was in one of these caves, **Gua Semar**, that Suharto and Australian Prime Minister Gough Whitlam decided the future of Timor in 1974.

Of the other lakes on the plateau, **Telaga Nila** and **Telaga Dringo**, 12km west of Dieng village, are the prettiest and can be combined with seeing **Sumur Jalatunda**, a vast, vine-clad well just off the main road – for a small fee, small boys will show you a little-used path from the well to the two lakes. To get to these lakes and caves it's easiest to hire an **ojek** from Dieng village (Rp50,000 per day) or join a **tour** from *Dieng Homestay* (Rp25,000).

## Arrival

**By bus** From Yogya you need to change buses twice, going first to Magelang from the Jombor terminal (Rp6000 – infrequent bus #5 in Yogya takes you from the western end of Jl Sosro to the terminal), then to Wonosobo (Rp6000), and then to Dieng itself (Rp5000). The total journey time is around four to five hours.

## Accommodation and eating

The tiny village of Dieng lines Jl Raya Dieng, the road that runs along the plateau's eastern edge, and hosts the limited choice of some fairly grim accommodation.

**Bu Djono** next door to *Dieng Homestay* ⓣ0286/322755. Has shabby rooms but superior food – eat here. ❷

**Dieng Homestay** On the junction with the road to Wonosobo at Jl Raya Dieng 16 ⓣ0286/92823. Basic, cell-like rooms, and the mandi are excruciatingly cold; this is, however, the best of the budget bunch. ❶

## YOGYAKARTA

**YOGYAKARTA** (pronounced "Jogjakarta" and often just shortened to "Jogja") ranks as one of the best-preserved and most attractive cities in Java, and is a major centre for the classical **Javanese arts** of batik, ballet, drama, music, poetry and puppet shows. At its heart is Yogya's first family, the Hamengkubuwonos, whose elegant palace lies at the centre of Yogya's quaint old city, the **Kraton**, itself concealed behind high castellated walls. Tourists flock here, attracted not only by the city's courtly splendour but also by the nearby temples of **Prambanan** and **Borobudur**, so there are more hotels in Yogya than anywhere else in Java and, unfortunately, a correspondingly high number of touts, pickpockets and con artists.

**Sultan Hamengkubuwono I** (also known as **Mangkubumi**) established his court here in 1755, spending the next 37 years building the new capital, with the Kraton as the centrepiece and the court at Solo as the blueprint. In 1946, the capital of the newly declared Republic of Indonesia was moved to Yogya from Jakarta, and the Kraton became the unofficial headquarters for the republican movement. The royal household of Yogya continues to enjoy almost slavish devotion from its subjects and the current sultan, Hamengkubuwono X, remains an influential politician.

### What to see and do

The layout of Yogya reflects its character: modern and brash on the outside, but with a very ancient and traditional heart in the **Kraton**, the walled city. Set in a two-kilometre-wide strip of land between the rivers Kali Winongo and Kali Code, this is the focus of interest for most visitors. Kraton means "royal residence" and originally referred just to the **Sultan's Palace**, but today it denotes the whole of the walled city (plus Jalan Malioboro), a town of some ten thousand people. The Kraton has changed little in the two hundred years; both the palace, and the 5km of crenellated icing-sugar walls that surround it, date from the first sultan's reign.

#### Alun-alun Utara

Most people enter the Kraton through the northern gates by the main post office, beyond which lies the busy town square, Alun-alun Utara. As is usual in Java, the city's grand mosque, **Mesjid Agung** (visit outside of prayer times), built in 1773 by Mangkubumi, stands on the western side of the alun-alun. It's designed along traditional Javanese lines, with a multi-tiered roof on top of an airy, open-sided prayer hall. A little to the north of the mosque, just by the main gates, stands the **Sono Budoyo Museum**, Jl Trikoro 6 (Tues–Thurs 8.30am–1.30pm, Fri–Sun 8.30am–noon; Rp3000), which houses a fine exhibition of the arts of Java, Madura and Bali. The intricate, damascene-style wooden partitions from Northern Java are particularly eye-catching, as are the many classical gold and stone statues dating back to the eighth century.

#### Ngayogyokarto Hadiningrat – The Sultan's Palace

On the southern side of the alun-alun lies a masterpiece of understated Javanese architecture, the elegant collection of ornate kiosks and graceful pendopos (open-sided pavilions) that comprises the **Ngayogyokarto Hadiningrat** – the **Sultan's Palace**. It was designed as a scale model of the Hindu cosmos, and every plant, building and courtyard is symbolic; the sultans, though Muslim, held on to many Hindu and animist beliefs and thought that this design would ensure the prosperity of the royal house.

The palace is split into two parts. The first section, the **Pagelaran** (Mon–Thurs, Sat & Sun 8.30am–2pm, Fri 8.30am–noon; Rp3000, plus Rp1500

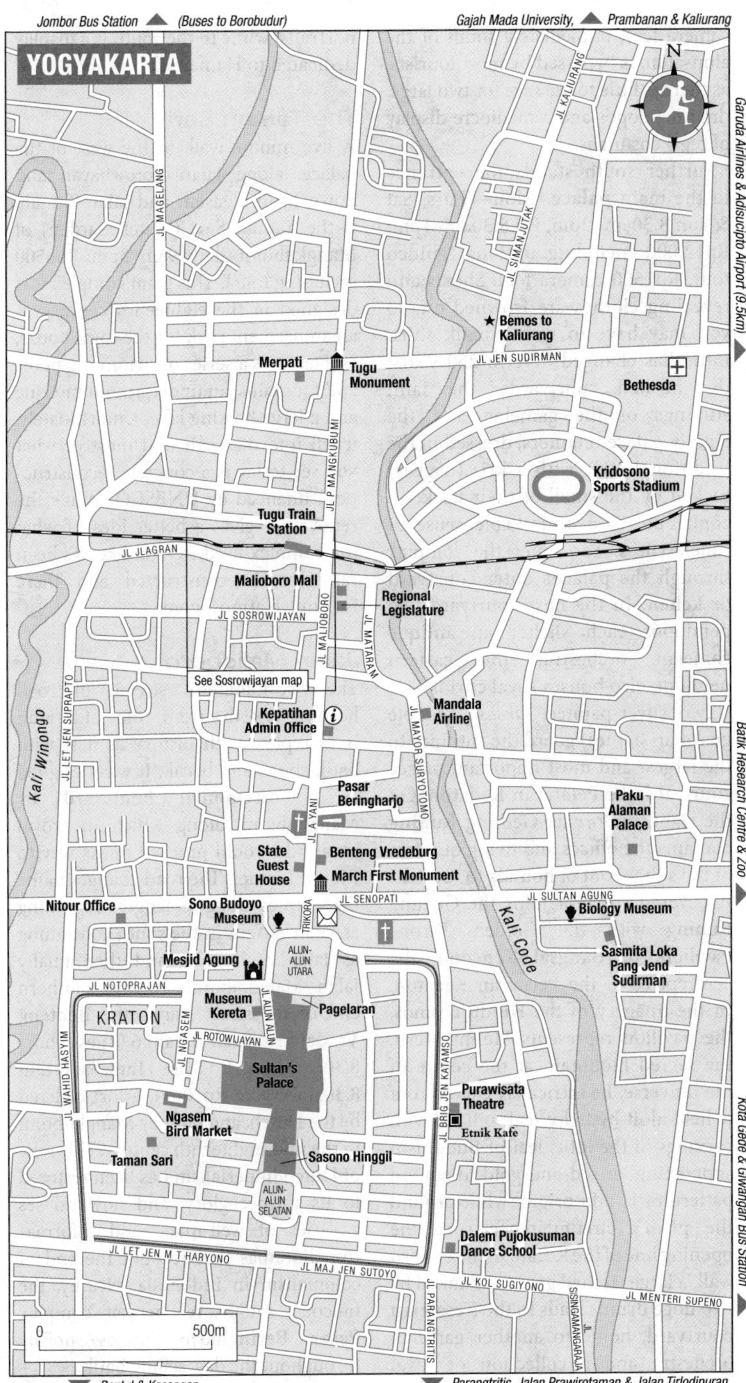

YOGYAKARTA
Jombor Bus Station
(Buses to Borobudur)
Gajah Mada University,
Prambanan & Kaliurang
Garuda Airlines & Adisucipto Airport (9.5km)
Batik Research Centre & Zoo
Kota Gede & Giwangan Bus Station
Bantul & Kasongan
Parangtritis, Jalan Prawirotaman & Jalan Tirlodipuran
JL KALIURANG
JL MAGELANG
JL SIMANJUTAK
Bemos to Kaliurang
JL JEN SUDIRMAN
Merpati
Tugu Monument
Bethesda
JL P MANGKUBUMI
Kridosono Sports Stadium
Tugu Train Station
JL JLAGRAN
Malioboro Mall
Regional Legislature
JL SOSROWIJAYAN
JL MALIOBORO
JL MATARAM
See Sosrowijayan map
Mandala Airline
Kepatihan Admin Office
Kali Winongo
JL LET JEN SUPRAPTO
JL MAYOR SURYOTOMO
Pasar Beringharjo
Paku Alaman Palace
JL A YANI
State Guest House
Benteng Vredeburg
March First Monument
JL SENOPATI
JL SULTAN AGUNG
Nitour Office
Sono Budoyo Museum
TRIKORA
Biology Museum
Kali Code
ALUN-ALUN UTARA
Sasmita Loka Pang Jend Sudirman
Mesjid Agung
JL NOTOPRAJAN
Museum Kereta
Pagelaran
KRATON
JL NGASEM
JL ALUN ALUN
JL ROTOWIJAYAN
JL WAHID HASYIM
Sultan's Palace
JL BRIG JEN KATAMSO
Purawisata Theatre
Etnik Kafe
Ngasem Bird Market
Taman Sari
Sasono Hinggil
ALUN-ALUN SELATAN
Dalem Pujokusuman Dance School
JL LET JEN M T HARYONO
JL MAJ JEN SUTOYO
JL KOL SUGIYONO
JL MENTERI SUPENO
JL PARANGTRITIS
SISINGAMANGARAJA
0
500m

camera fee), immediately south of the alun-alun, is bypassed by most tourists, as there is little to see save for two large, drab pendopos and a mediocre display of regal costumes.

Further south stands the entrance to the main **palace** (Mon–Thurs, Sat & Sun 8.30am–2pm, Fri 8.30am–1pm; Rp12,000 including optional guided tour, Rp1500 camera fee). Shorts and revealing clothes are frowned on, so you may have to rent a batik shirt. Little has changed here in 250 years: the hushed courtyards, the faint stirrings of the gamelan and the elderly palace retainers, dressed in the traditional style with a kris (dagger) tucked by the small of their back, all contribute to a remarkable sense of timelessness. You enter the complex through the palace's outer courtyard or **keben**. In the next courtyard two pendopos each shelter an antique gamelan orchestra; the eastern pendopo also houses royal curios.

Two silver-painted *raksasa* (temple guardian statues) guard the entrance to the largest and most important palace courtyard, the **Pelataran Kedaton**. On the right, the ornate **Gedung Kuning** contains the offices and living quarters of the sultan, out of bounds to tourists. A covered corridor joins the Gedung Kuning with the Golden Throne Pavilion, or **Bangsal Kencono**, the centrepiece of the Pelataran Kedaton. In the imagery of the Hindu cosmos, the pavilion represents Mount Meru, the sacred mountain at the centre of the universe. Its intricately carved roof is held aloft by hefty teak pillars, with carvings of the lotus leaf of Buddhism supporting a red-and-gold diamond pattern of Hindu origin, while around the pillar's circumference runs the opening line of the Koran. In the eastern wall, a large, arched gateway flanked by two huge drums leads to the **Kesatrian** courtyard, home to another gamelan orchestra and a collection of royal portraits, while to the south is a display dedicated to Hamengkubuwono IX.

### The Taman Sari

A five-minute walk to the west of the palace, along Jalan Rotowijayan and down Jalan Ngasem and Jalan Taman, is the **Taman Sari** (Water Garden) of Mangkubumi (daily 9am–3pm; Rp3500 including tour). This giant complex was designed in the eighteenth century as an amusement park for the royal house, and features a series of swimming pools and fountains, an underground mosque and a large boating lake. Unfortunately, it fell into disrepair and most of what you see today is a concrete reconstruction, financed by UNESCO. While the renovation gives a better idea of what the complex used to look like, it's been rather over-reconstructed and there isn't much atmosphere.

### Jalan Malioboro

The two-kilometre stretch of road heading north from the alun-alun is as replete with history as it is with batik shops and becak. It was designed as a **ceremonial boulevard** by Mangkubumi, along which the royal cavalcade would proceed on its way to Mount Merapi. The road changes name three times along its length, beginning as Jalan A Yani in the south continuing as Jalan Malioboro, and then finally Jalan Mangkubumi. At the southern end of the street stands the **Benteng Vredeburg**, Jalan A Yani 6 (Tues–Thurs 8.30am–1 pm, Fri 8.30–11am, Sat & Sun 8.30am–noon; Rp1000), a fort ordered by the Dutch, and built by Mangkubumi in the mid-eighteenth century. This relic of Dutch imperialism has been restored to its former glory, and now houses a series of well-made and informative dioramas that recount the end of colonialism in Indonesia. Nearby, the raucous, multi-level market complex **Pasar Beringharjo** buzzes noisily throughout the day, selling batik.

## Paku Alaman Palace

Yogyakarta's second court, **Paku Alaman Palace** (Tues, Thurs & Sun 9.30am–1.30pm; Rp5000), lies 50m to the northeast of the Biology Museum on the north side of Jalan Sultan Agung. As is traditional, the minor court of the city faces south as a mark of subservience to the main palace. The royal household of Paku Alam was created in 1812 by the British in a deliberate divide-and-rule tactic. The part that is open to general view – by the southeastern corner of the courtyard – houses a motley collection of royal artefacts, including a room filled with chariots, which unfortunately appear to be permanently shrouded in dust sheets.

## Arrival

**By bus** All inter-city buses arrive at the Giwangan station, just inside the city ring road a few kilometres southeast of the city centre. If you're arriving from Borobudur or elsewhere in the north, you can alight at Jombor terminal, around 3km north of the city centre, from where you can catch infrequent bus #5 (Rp2000) to the main post office. From near Giwangan, there are regular services into town, including bus #2 (Rp2000), which travels via Jl Prawirotaman, and #5, which goes to the western end of Jl Sosrowijayan.

**By train** Tugu train station lies just one block north of Jl Sosrowijayan, on Jl Pasar Kembang. A taxi to Jl Prawirotaman costs Rp18,000; or catch southbound bus #2 (Rp2000) from Jl Mataram, one block east of Jl Malioboro.

**By air** From Adisucipto Airport, 10km east of the city centre, walk 200m south of the terminal on to Jl Adisucipto, where you can flag down any bus (Rp2000) heading west to Yogya. A taxi costs Rp25,000.

## Information and tour operators

**Tourist information** Jl Malioboro 16 (Mon–Thurs 8am–7pm, Fri & Sat 8am–6pm; ☎0274/562811 x1222). It keeps plenty of information on local events, language and meditation courses.

**Tour operators** Yogya is full of tour companies offering trips to the nearby temples (Rp60,000 for a tour of both Prambanan and Borobudur), as well as further afield, such as the popular trips to Bali with an overnight stop in Cemoro Lawang to see the sunrise at Gunung Bromo:

**Annas** Jl Prawirotaman 7 ☎0274/386556. One of the larger companies operating in Prawirotaman offering the standard package of tours, including

### FROM YOGYAKARTA TO BALI

Two-day tours from Yogya to Denpasar are a popular option for travellers wanting to get to Bali's beaches quickly without missing one of the highlights of any trip to Indonesia: **Gunung Bromo**.

An a/c minibus picks you up from your hotel for the eight-hour drive to **Probolingo**, where you transfer to another minibus for the drive to **Cemoro Lawang**, which takes about an hour. A jeep will collect you from your hotel at 4am to see sunrise from the viewing point at **Gunung Penanjakan** before driving to **Gunung Bromo** itself. The jeep will drop you back at Cemoro Lawang at about 9am, where you'll have an hour or so at your hotel for breakfast, before a minibus takes you to Probolingo, where you'll transfer to another for the trip to **Denpasar**, which takes about ten hours, depending on ferry connections. It's also possible to be driven back from Probolingo to Yogya or Solo.

The standard two-day tour **costs** approximately Rp300,000 per person, including all accommodation and transport, except for the jeep ride (Rp80,000) and entrance fee to the national park (Rp20,000). You can walk to Gunung Bromo but you'll miss the view from Gunung Penanjakan.

There's little to choose between most operators. However, if you want to spend more time in East Java, Via Via's **five-day tour** to Bali also takes in the hilltown of Kalibaru and the sea turtles at Meru Betiri National Park. Two people will pay €230 each, three or four people €195 each.

day-trips to Borobodur, Prambanan and Merapi, as well as two/three-day trips to Mount Bromo with the option to be dropped off in Bali (Rp290,000).

**Great Tours** Jl Sosro 29 ⓣ0274/583221. Large operator in the Sosro area offering similar tours to Annas in Prawirotaman.

**Via Via Café** Jl Prawirotaman 30 ⓣ0274/386557. The most innovative of Yogya's operators. Tours include bicycle and hiking trips, walkabouts in Yogya with a local student, as well as a five-day trip to Bali taking in Mount Bromo, the hill town of Kalibaru and the Meru Betiri National Park (€230).

**Travel agents** Probably the most respected of Yogya's travel agents, and certainly one of the more reliable, is Intras Tour at Jl Malioboro 131 (ⓣ0274/561972), just a few metres south of the eastern end of Jl Sosro.

## City transport

**Buses** All city buses charge a set Rp2000 and begin and end their journeys at the Giwangan bus station. Most buses stop running at about 6pm, although the #15 runs to the main post office until 8pm. The most useful buses for travellers are the #4, which runs south down Jl Malioboro before heading to Kota Gede and the Giwangan bus station; and the #5, which runs between Giwangan and Jombor stations via Jl Sosro (when heading north) and the main post office (when returning to Giwangan).

**Becak** There are thousands of becak, and they are the most convenient form of transport. It should cost no more than Rp10,000 from Jl Sosro to the main post office (Rp20,000 from Jalan Prawirotaman).

**Horse-drawn carriages** Known as *andong*, they tend to queue up along Jl Malioboro, and are a little cheaper than becak.

**Taxis** Good value (Rp5000 minimum). You can usually find them hanging around the main post office, or ring Setia Kawan (ⓣ0274/412000).

**Bicycle rental** Yogya is a flat city, so you might want to rent a bicycle: try Bike 33 in Jl Sosro Gang I (Rp5000 per day); motorbikes are nearer Rp50,000 per day. Orange-suited parking attendants throughout the city will look after your bike for Rp1000 or so.

## Accommodation

A kilometre north of the Kraton, the budget travellers' mecca of Jl Sosrowijayan (known as Jl Sosro) runs west off Jl Malioboro to the south of Tugu train station. There's a more upmarket

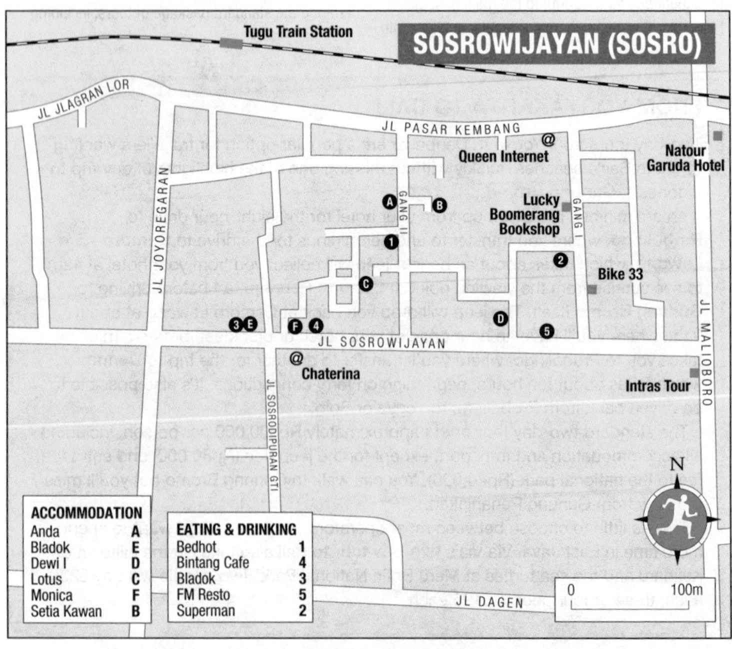

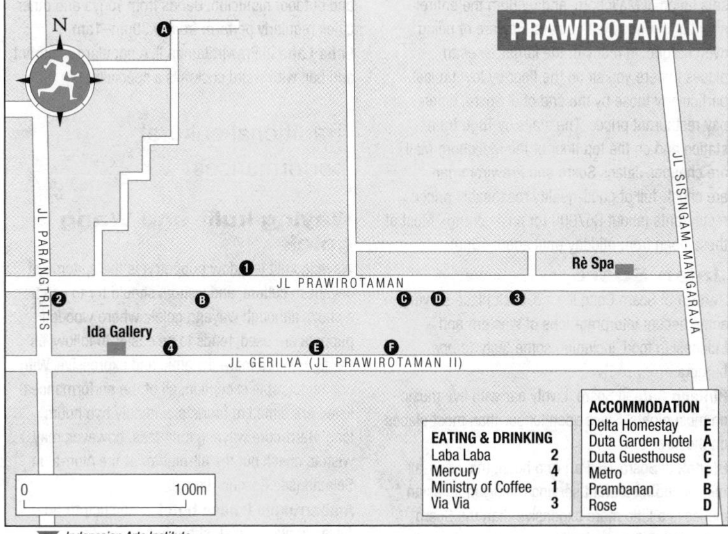




cluster of tourist hotels and restaurants on Jl Prawirotaman, in the suburbs southeast of the Kraton.

### Jalan Sosro and around

**Anda** Jl Sosro Gang II. Homely, inexpensive and highly recommended, with smart rooms (with shared balcony) and friendly owners. ❶

**Bladok** Jl Sosro 76 ⓣ0274/560452. One of the smarter options on Sosro, with dark but comfortable and clean rooms, all en suite, and a pool for guests only. ❷

**Dewi I** Jl Sosro ⓣ0274/516014. Largish, good-value losmen offering decent-sized, spotless rooms, some fairly charming with intricate wood carving, all at reasonable prices. ❷

**Lotus** Jl Sosro Wetan Gang I 167 ⓣ0274/515090. Light, airy and clean losmen, good value and with a pleasant balcony. ❶

**Monica** Jl Sosro GT1/192 ⓣ0274/580598. This shimmeringly clean hotel, built round a garden, is one of the most handsome on Jl Sosro. ❷–❸

**Setia Kawan** Jl Sosro GT1/127 ⓣ0274/512452. Run by the owners of the nearby *Bedhot* restaurant, this artistically decorated hotel offers a range of rooms and is highly recommended. Book ahead. ❷–❸

### Jalan Prawirotaman and around

**Delta Homestay** Jl Prawirotaman II MGIII/597A ⓣ081/7271047, ⓦwww.dutagardenhotel.com. Another quality place run by the same owners as the *Duta Guesthouse* and *Duta Garden*. This is their cheapest homestay, clean and efficient, rooms have fans, and there's a small pool. ❷

**Duta Garden Hotel** Jl Timuran MGIII/103 ⓣ0274/373482, ⓦwww.dutagardenhotel.com. Exceptionally beautiful cottage-style hotel smothered in a thick blanket of bougainvillea and roses, sister of *Duta Guesthouse*. Rooms are equally exquisite; bargain hard in the low season for a discount. ❻

**Duta Guesthouse** Jl Prawirotaman I 26 ⓣ0274/372064, ⓦwww.dutagardenhotel.com. Big hotel that is popular with tour groups; it has a good pool and does huge breakfasts. Popular with tour groups. ❺

**Metro** Jl Prawirotaman II 71 ⓣ0274/372364, ⓔcafeyg2@idola.net.id. A big hotel with a pool and restaurant, and a fairly grotty economy section in a different building at the end of the street. ❸

**Prambanan** Jl Prawirotaman I 14 ⓣ0274/376167, ⓦwww.prambanangh.be. A quiet hotel with bamboo-walled rooms, swimming pool and eager-to-please staff. Breakfast and afternoon tea included. ❸

**Rose** Jl Prawirotaman I 28 ⓣ0274/377991. The best value in Prawirotaman. Hearty breakfasts, a swimming pool and very cheap rooms. Bargain in the low season for an even better deal. ❷

## Eating and drinking

Yogya's specialities are *ayam goreng* and *nasi gudeg* (rice and jackfruit), and many foodstalls serve nothing else. Every evening a food market sets up on Jl Malioboro, and by 8pm the entire street is thronged with diners. Beware of being overcharged. In many of the larger *lesehan* places (where you sit on the floor by low tables), particularly those by the end of Jl Sosro, diners pay restaurant prices. The stalls by Tugu train station and on the top floor of the Malioboro Mall are cheaper. Jalans Sosro and Prawirotaman are chock-full of good-quality reasonably priced restaurants (about Rp7000 for nasi goreng). Most of these open from midday until about 10pm.

### Jalan Sosro

**Bedhot** Jl Sosro Gang II. Laid-back place serving some decent interpretations of Western and Indonesian food, including some tasty *tempe* burgers.

**Bintang Cafe** Jl Sosro. Lively bar with live music on most nights. Stays open longer than most places on the street.

**Bladok** Jl Sosro 76. Part of a hotel, this open-air mid-priced restaurant serving mainly Indonesian dishes is a little more expensive than the Sosro norm, but definitely worth it.

**FM Resto** Jl Sosro 10. Great atmosphere and live music; the most popular travellers' place in Yogya. The food is good and varied.

**Superman** JL Sosro Gang I/71. Popular restaurant in Sosro, with delicious pancakes, ice-cold beer and regular screenings of European football.

### Jalan Prawirotaman

**Mercury** Jl Parawirotaman II MG3/595. Beautiful, colonial-style restaurant serving surprisingly affordable mid-priced Indonesian and Western dishes.

**Ministry of Coffee** Jl Prawirotaman. The sort of café that wouldn't look out of place on one of the smarter high streets of Europe. Great coffee, fine snacks and cakes, and a wonderful escape from the hubbub outside. Free Wi-Fi.

**Via Via** Jl Prawirotaman 30 ☎0274/386557. A foreign-run and popular travellers' hangout. Good European and Indonesian food, though pricier than most. Also a good place to get information on what there is to do in Yogya. Free WiFi.

## Nightlife

Yogya's nightlife is really an early-evening life; very few places stay open beyond midnight, and most of the action happens between 7pm and 10pm, when the city's cultural entertainment is in full swing.

**Djogja Kafe** Jl Kyai Mojo 57. A popular nightspot with al fresco drinking and live music.

**Etnik Kafe** Jl Brigen Katamso ☎0274/375705. Not far from the Sultan's Palace, this combines a café and outdoor nightclub. Bands from Yogya and other cities regularly perform from 9.30pm–1am.

**Laba Laba** Jl Prawirotaman II. A popular restaurant and bar, with weird cocktails a speciality.

## Traditional cultural performances

### Waying kulit and Wang golek

Wayang kulit (shadow puppetry) is the epitome of Javanese culture, and visitors should try to catch a show, although wayang golek, where wooden puppets are used, tends to be easier to follow, as the figures are more dynamic and expressive. With one honourable exception, all of the performances listed are aimed at tourists, and only two hours long. Hard-core wayang kulit fans, however, may wish to check out the all-nighter at the Alun-alun Selatan (see Sasono Hinggil).

**Ambarrukmo Palace Hotel** Jl Adisucipto 66. A free wayang golek show in the hotel's restaurant is put on as an accompaniment to the food (Mon 8pm).

**Nitour** Jl KHA Dalan 71 ☎0274/376450. This centre, outside of the northern walls of the Kraton, puts on a wayang golek performance of the Ramayana tales. Daily except holidays 11am–1pm; Rp5000.

**Sasono Hinggil** Alun-alun Selatan. Yogya's only full-length wayang kulit performance runs from 9pm to 5.30am on the second Saturday of every month (Rp5000).

**Sono Budoyo Museum** Jl Trikora 1. The most professional and popular wayang kulit show, performed daily for 2hr (8pm; Rp20,000).

**Sultan's Palace** Good for a preview. On Saturday mornings (10am–noon), there's a practice-cum-performance of wayang kulit in the Sriminganti courtyard, and every Wednesday (10am–noon) a free wayang golek show. On Mon and Tues mornings between 10.30am and noon, free gamelan performances are given.

### Javanese dancing

The Ramayana dance drama is a modern extension of the court dances of the nineteenth century, which tended to use that other Indian epic, the Mahabharata, as the source of their story lines. The biggest crowd-pulling spectacle nearby is the summer time moonlit performances of the Ramayana ballet, at the open-air theatre at Prambanan Temple, and can be booked in Yogya (see p.237).

**Purawisata Theatre** Jl Brig Jen Katamso ☎0274/374089. Every night the Puriwisata Theatre puts on a 90min performance of the Ramayana. The story is split into two episodes, with each episode performed on alternate nights. On the last day of every month, the whole story is performed.

**Sultan's Palace** Every Sunday and Thursday, the Kraton Classical Dance School holds public rehearsals (10.30am–noon). No cover fee once you've paid to get into the palace. Well worthwhile.

## Shopping

Yogya is Java's souvenir centre, with keepsakes and mementoes from all over the archipelago finding their way into the city's shops and street stalls.

### Antiques, puppets and curios

There are a number of cavernous antique shops near Jl Prawirotaman dealing mainly in teak furniture from Jepara and the north, but they also sell woodcarvings, wayang kulit puppets and keris daggers.

**Ida Gallery** Jl Prawirotaman III ⓣ0274/382958. Set in a courtyard, this shop sells puppets and keris daggers, among other curios. You can also walk around the furniture restoration workshop at the back.

**Moesson Antik** Jl Prawirotaman. Near the *Ministry of Coffee*, this shop's collection ranges from simple tat to genuine antiques – great for a rummage even if you have no intention of buying.

**Samudra Raya** Jl Sosro GT1/32. This shop specializes in selling good-quality models of traditional Indonesian ships.

### Batik

With the huge influx of tourists over the last twenty years, Yogya has evolved a batik style that increasingly panders to Western tastes. However, there is still plenty of the traditional indigo-and-brown batik clothing – sarongs, shirts and dresses – for sale, especially on Jl Malioboro and in Pasar Beringharjo. For the best-quality – and most expensive – batiks in town, head to Jl Tirtodipuran, west of Jl Prawirotaman.

**Batik Research Centre** Jl Dr Sutomo 13 ⓣ0274/515953. Puts the craft in an historical context and provides examples of the several techniques and styles.

**Batik Plentong** Jl Tirtodipuran 48 ⓣ0274/373777. Large shop with friendly staff that stocks a wide selection of good-quality batik fabrics.

**Kerajinan Batik Winotosastro** Jl Tirtodipuran 54 ⓣ0274/375218. Large batik-seller, but with a smaller selection than Batik Plentong and with pushier staff.

### Books

**The Lucky Boomerang** and **Wan's Bookshop** Jl Sosro Gang I. Both stock second-hand English-language novels.

**Periplus** Lower ground floor of Malioboro Mall. Has a wide selection of English-language novels and histories of Indonesia, as well as guidebooks and maps.

### Leather and pottery

All around Yogya, and particularly in the markets, and some of the shops, along Jl Malioboro, hand-stitched, good-quality **leather** bags, suitcases, belts and shoes are for sale extremely cheaply. Much of it comes from the village of Manding, 12km south of Yogya. To see them being made and get a better deal than you would in town, catch a white Jahayu bus to Manding from Jl Parangtritis (25min; Rp3000).

**Javanese pottery** is widely available throughout Yogya. Again, the markets along Jl Malioboro sell ochre pottery, with huge Chinese urns, decorative bowls, erotic statues, whistles, flutes and other pottery instruments.

### Silver

The suburb of Kota Gede is the home of the silver industry in Central Java, famous for its fine filigree work. If your budget is limited, then the many stallholders along Jl Malioboro sell perfectly reasonable silver jewellery, much of it from East Java or Bali.

**MD Silver** Keboan Kotagede ⓣ0274/375063. Although smaller than Tom's, this workshop situated down an alley off Jl Pesegah KG is also cheaper.

**Tom's Silver** Jl Ngeksi Gondo 60 ⓣ0274/377800. Huge workshop which allows you to wander around and watch the smiths at work.

### Souvenirs

The main shopping area for inexpensive souvenirs is **Jalan Malioboro**, with batik pictures, leather bags, woodcarvings, silver rings and the traditional Yogyan batik headdresses (*blangkon*).

**Batik Keris** Jl A Yani 104 ⓣ0274/512492. Reputable shop offering a huge array of souvenirs from Yogya and elsewhere in Indonesia.

**Batik Mirota** Jl A Yani 9 ⓣ0274/588524. A Batik specialist that will tailor clothers but also offers other souvenirs.

## Directory

**Airlines** Batavia, Jl Urip Sumoharjo ⓣ0274/547373; Bouraq, Jl Menteri Supeno 58 ⓣ0274/383414; Garuda, *Ambarrukmo Palace Hotel* ⓣ0274/487983, and at the airport ⓣ0274/560108;

Lion Air, *Hotel Melia Purosani*, Jl Mayor Suryotomo 31 ⓣ0274/555028; Mandala, *Hotel Melia Purosani*, Jl Mayor Suryotomo 573 ⓣ0274/520603; Merpati, Jl Diponegoro 31 ⓣ0274/514272. All open: Mon–Fri 7.30am–5pm, Sat & Sun 9am–1pm.

**Banks and exchange** Yogya is one of the few places where the moneychangers offer a better deal than the banks, at least for cash. In particular, PT Gajahmas Mulyosakti, Jl A Yani 86a, and PT Dua Sisi Jogya Indah, at the southern corner of the Malioboro Mall, offer very competitive rates. PT Baruman Abadi in the *Natour Garuda Hotel*, Jl Malioboro 60, offers good rates and stays open longer (Mon–Fri 7am–7pm, Sat 7am–3pm). In Prawirotaman, the Agung moneychanger at Jl Prawirotaman 68 and Kresna at no. 18 offers the best rates. BNI, Jl Trikora 1, just in front of the post office, or BCA Jl Mangkubumi, both accept Visa and MasterCard at their ATMs.

**Batik courses** Right by the entrance to the Taman Sari is the workshop of Dr Hadjir (ⓣ0274/377835), who runs a three- to five-day course (US$25 for three days, plus US$5 for materials). His course is one of the most extensive and includes tutoring on the history of batik and the preparation of both chemical and natural dyes. The Batik Research Centre at Jl Kusumanegara 2 has intensive three-day courses for US$55. For the truly committed, they also run a three-month course.

**Cookery courses** The *Via Via* café, Jl Prawirotaman 24b, runs afternoon courses (Rp85,000).

**Dance and gamelan courses** Several places offer courses in gamelan. Mrs Tia of the Ndalem Pujokusirman dance school at Jl Brig Jen Katamso 45 (ⓣ0274/371271) invites foreigners to join her two-hour group lessons beginning at 4pm. At the northern end of the same street is the Puriwisata (ⓣ0274/374089), an open-air theatre and mini-theme park which holds Javanese dance courses for Rp50,000 per 3hr session. They also run a gamelan school (Rp50,000 per session).

**Hospitals and clinics** The Gading Clinic, south of the Alun-alun Selatan at Jl Maj Jen Panjaitan 25, has English-speaking doctors (ⓣ0274/375396). The main hospital in Yogya is the Bethesda, Jl Jen Sudirman 70 ⓣ0274/566300. Also Ludira Husada Tama Hospital, Jl Wiratama 4 ⓣ0274/620091.

**Internet** For Sosro, Cafe Rina, on the main street (Rp8000/hr), remains popular, but cheaper (Rp7000/hr) and open 24hr is Queen Internet, just a few metres west from the northern entrance to Gang I on Pasar Kembang. Metro Internet in the *Metro* guesthouse, Jl Prawitotaman II/71, is useful in Prawirotaman. If you have a laptop you can use free Wi-Fi at the *Ministry of Coffee* and *Via Via* café

**Language courses** Yogya is the place to learn Bahasa Indonesia. The two most established schools are *Alam Bahasa Indonesia*, Kompleks Kolombo 3, Jl Cendrawasih (ⓣ0274/589631, ⓦwww.alambahasa.com); and *Puri Bahasa Indonesia*, Jl Purwanggan 15 (ⓣ0274/588192, ⓦwww.puribahasa.net). One-to-one tuition typically costs US$8 per hour. Alternatively, *Via Via* café offers a three-hour course for Rp40,000.

**Post office** Jl Senopati 2, at the southern end of Jl Malioboro (Mon–Sat 6am–10pm, Sun 6am–8pm). The parcel office is on Jl Mayor Suryotomo (Mon–Sat 8am–3pm, Sun 9am–2pm). Parcel-wrappers loiter outside the office during these times.

**Swimming** The *Hotel Batik Yogyakarta*, south of Jl Sosro, allows non-guests to use their pool for Rp7000 (daily 9am–9pm). In Prawirotaman, you can use the *Rose Guesthouse*'s pool for Rp7000.

**Telephone** The main Telkom office at Jl Yos Sudarso 9 is open 24hr and has Home Direct phones, too. There's a wartel office at no. 30 Jl Sosro and another on Jl Parangtritis, south of Jl Prawirotaman Gang II.

## Moving on

**By bus** Long-distance buses leave from the Giwangan terminal. From Jl Sosro, catch city bus #4; from Jl Prawirotaman, catch #2 (all Rp2000).
**Destinations**: Frequent buses to Bandung (9hr 30min); Bogor (10hr 30min); Borobudur (2hr); Cilacap (5hr); Denpasar (15hr); Jakarta (11hr 30min); Magelang (1hr 30min); Prambanan (45min); Probolinggo (9hr); Solo (2hr); Surabaya (7hr 30min).

**By train** to: Bandung (5 daily; 6hr 30min); Jakarta (9 daily; 8hr 45min); Malang (1 daily; 6hr 50min); Solo (7 daily; 1hr 30min); Surabaya (6 daily; 4hr 50min).

**By air** to: Bandung (4 weekly; 1hr 15min); Denpasar (6 daily; 2hr 15min); Jakarta (22 daily; 1hr 5min); Surabaya (3 daily; 1hr).

# GUNUNG MERAPI AND KALIURANG

Marking the northern limit of the Daerah Istimewa Yogyakarta, symmetrical, smoke-plumed **Gunung Merapi** (Giving Fire) is an awesome 2914-metre presence in the centre of Java, visible from Yogyakarta, 25km away. This is Indonesia's most volatile volcano, and the sixth most active in the world. The Javanese worship the mountain as a life-giver, its lava enriching the soil and providing Central Java with its agricultural fecundity. Down the centuries its ability to annihilate has frequently been demonstrated. Thirteen hundred people died following a particularly vicious eruption in 1930, and as recently as 1994 an entire mountain village was incinerated by lava, which killed 64 people.

Nearly a kilometre up on Merapi's southern slopes is the village of **KALIURANG**, a tatty, downmarket but tranquil hill station and an extremely popular weekend retreat for Yogyakartans. A bus from Yogya's Giwangan station costs Rp2000; it's Rp3000 by bemo from behind the Terban terminal on Jalan Simanjutak. In Kaliurang, you can join a trekking group to the summit (organized by *Vogel's Hostel*, see below), a fairly arduous five-hour scramble through the snake- and spider-infested forest that beards Merapi's lower slopes. The tigers, which terrorized this forest as recently as the 1960s, have now all been killed off. During Merapi's dormant months (usually March to Oct) it's possible to climb all the way to the top, but at other times, when the volcano is active, you may have to settle for a distant view from the observation platform. All treks begin in the dark at 3am, when the lava, spilling over the top and tracing a searing path down the mountainside, can be seen most clearly. Bring warm clothes, a torch and sturdy boots (not sandals, which offer little protection against poisonous snakes).

### Accommodation

**Village Taman Eden** Jalan Astya Mulya ☎0274/895442. If you're looking for somewhere plusher, try this collection of reasonably luxurious villas of varying quality and price built round a central swimming pool. ❸–❺

**Vogel's Hostel** Jl Astya Mulya 76, Kaliurang ☎0274/895208. Organizes treks (Rp15,000 including breakfast) and is a good place for information. This is a great budget hostel, split into two parts: the rooms in the new extension are beautiful and good value, while those in the old building are spartan but inexpensive. The food, including Indonesian staples and Western snacks, is delicious, and there's a large travellers' library. ❶–❷

**Wisma Gadja Mada** Jl Wreksa 447 ☎0274/895225. A colonial-period guesthouse with villa-style accommodation. ❸–❹

## BOROBUDUR

Forty kilometres west of Yogya, surrounded on three sides by volcanoes and on the fourth by jagged limestone cliffs, is the largest monument in the southern hemisphere. This is the temple of **Borobudur**, greatest single piece of classical architecture in the entire archipelago. The temple is actually a colossal multi-tiered Buddhist stupa lying at the western end of a four-kilometre-long chain of temples (one of which, the nearby **Candi Mendut**, is also worth visiting), built in the ninth century by

### BOROBUDUR: A SHORT HISTORY

The world's largest Buddhist stupa was actually built on Hindu foundations, which began life in 775 AD as a large step pyramid. Fifteen years later, construction was abandoned as the Buddhist Saliendras drove the Sanjayas eastwards. The Saliendras then used the pyramid as the foundation for their own temple, beginning in around 790 AD and completing the work approximately seventy years later. Over 1.6 million blocks of a local volcanic rock (called andesite) were used, joined together without mortar. Sculpted reliefs adorned the lower galleries, covered with stucco and painted. Unfortunately, the pyramid foundation proved to be inherently unstable, cracks appeared, and the hill became totally waterlogged. After about a century, the Saliendras abandoned the site and for almost a thousand years Borobudur lay neglected. The English "rediscovered" it in 1815, but nothing much was done until 1973, when UNESCO began to take the temple apart, block by block, in order to replace the waterlogged hill with a concrete substitute. The project took eleven years and cost US$21million.

the Saliendra dynasty. At 34.5m tall, however, and covering an area of some 200 square metres, Borobudur is on a different scale altogether, dwarfing all the other *candi* in the chain.

## What to see and do

Borobudur is pregnant with symbolism, and precisely oriented so that its four sides face the four points of the compass; the **entrance** lies to the north (daily 6am–5.30pm; US$11, students US$7, Rp40,000 for guided tour, Rp3000 for the tourist train around the site plus Rp3000 for the rather poor museum; Ⓦwww.borobudurpark.com).

### The stupa

Unlike most temples, Borobudur was not built as a dwelling for the gods, but rather as a representation of the Buddhist cosmic mountain, Meru. Accordingly, at the base is the real, earthly world, a world of desires and passions, and at the summit is nirvana. Thus, as you make your way around the temple passages and slowly spiral to the summit, you are symbolically following the path to enlightenment.

Every journey to enlightenment begins in the squalor of the real world, and at Borobudur the first five levels – the square terraces – are covered with three thousand **reliefs** representing man's earthly existence. As you might expect, the lowest, subterranean level has carvings depicting the basest desires, best seen at the south-east corner. The reliefs on the **first four levels above ground** cover the beginning of man's path to enlightenment. Each of the ten series (one on each level on the outer wall and one on the inner wall) tells a story, beginning by the eastern stairway and continuing clockwise. Follow all the stories, and you will have circled the temple ten times – a distance of almost 5km. Buddha's own path to enlightenment is told in the upper panels on the inner wall of the first gallery. As you enter the **fifth level**, the walls fall away to reveal a breathtaking view of the surrounding fields and volcanoes. You are now in the Sphere of Formlessness, the realm of enlightenment: below is the chaos of the world, above is nirvana, represented by a huge empty stupa almost 10m in diameter. Surrounding this stupa are 72 smaller ones, each occupied by a statue of Buddha.

### Candi Mendut

Originally Borobudur was part of a chain of four temples joined by a sacred path. Two of the other three temples have been restored and at least one, **Candi Mendut** (daily 6.15am–5.15pm; Rp3000), 3km east of Borobudur, is worth visiting. Buses between Yogya and Borobudur drive right past Mendut (Rp5000 from Yogya, 1hr 20min; Rp1000 from Borobudur, 10min). Built in 800 AD, Mendut was restored at the end of the nineteenth century. The exterior is unremarkable, but the three giant **statues** sitting inside – of Buddha and the Bodhisattvas Avalokitesvara and Vajrapani – are exquisitely carved and startling in their intricacy.

## Arrival

Most people choose to see the site on a **day-trip** from Yogya, with plenty of agencies offer all-inclusive tours (see p.229).

**By bus** Buses from Yogya's Giwangan station call in at Jombor bus station (handy for Jl Sosro) before heading off to Borobudur village bus station (bus #5; 1hr 30min; Rp6000–8000), though you may have to change one more time in Muntilan. The entrance to the temple lies 500m southwest of the bus stop.

## Accommodation and eating

There are a number of hotels up in the village. Most people who stay in Borobudur overnight choose to eat in their hotel, though there are a couple of inexpensive *padang* places opposite the entrance to the temple grounds.

**Lotus Guesthouse** Jl Medang Kamulan 2 Ⓣ0293/788281. The most popular budget choice on the northern side of the park, with good views of the temple from the rooftop. ❷–❹

**The Manohara** ⓣ0293/788131. Actually in the temple grounds, just 100m or so south of the main entrance. It's expensive, but when you consider that entry into the temple is included, and it means staying in the smartest rooms around, the hotel seems fair value. ❼

**Rajasa** Jl Badrawati 2 ⓣ0293/788276. To the south, this quiet, unassuming place has beautiful views over the ricefields and some smart rooms, the most expensive having hot water, a/c and a bathtub. ❸–❹

## THE PRAMBANAN PLAIN

Nourished by the volcanic detritus of Mount Merapi and washed by innumerable small rivers, the verdant **Prambanan Plain** lies 18km east of Yogya, a patchwork blanket of sun-spangled paddy-fields and vast plantations sweeping down from the southern slopes of the volcano. As well as being one of the most fertile regions in Java, the plain is home to the largest concentration of ancient ruins on the island.

Over thirty **temples** and **palaces**, dating mainly from the eighth and ninth centuries, lie scattered over a thirty-square-kilometre area. The temples, a number of which have been fully restored, were built at a time when two rival kingdoms, the Buddhist Saliendra and the Hindu Sanjaya dynasties, both occupied Central Java. In 832 AD, the Hindu Sanjayas gained the upper hand and soon the great Hindu Prambanan temple complex was built. It seems that some sort of truce followed, with temples of both faiths being constructed on the plain in equal numbers.

### The Prambanan complex

As you drive east along Jalan Adisucipto from Yogya, you'll catch sight of three giant, rocket-shaped temples, each smothered in intricate narrative carvings, that suddenly loom up by the side of the highway. This is the **Prambanan complex** (daily 6am–6pm; $10, students $6, Rp50,000 for guided tour), the largest Hindu complex in Java and a worthy rival to Borobudur.

The Sanjayas began work on the three giants around 832 AD, finishing them 24 years later. They were built just a few hundred metres south of the once mighty Buddhist **Candi Sewu**. The three Prambanan temples were in service for just fifty years before they were abandoned. Restoration work began in the 1930s, and Prambanan was severely damaged by the May 2006 earthquake, but has since been substantially restored. At the time of writing, scaffolding remained on only one of the towers.

The complex consists of six temples in a raised **inner courtyard**, surrounded by **224 minor temples**, which now lie in ruins. The three biggest temples are dedicated to the three main Hindu deities: Shiva, whose 47-metre temple is the tallest of the three, Brahma (to the south of the Shiva temple) and Vishnu

### RAMAYANA BALLET PERFORMANCES

The highlights of the dancing year in Central Java are the phenomenal Ramayana ballets held during the summer months at the **Prambanan Open-Air Theatre**, to the west of the complex. The Ramayana story is performed just twice monthly from May to October, spread over the two weekends closest to the full moon. The story is split into four episodes, each evening from Friday to Monday (7.30–9.30pm). The second night is the best, with most of the characters making an appearance, and the action is intense. Tickets cost Rp40,000–150,000, depending on where you sit; plenty of agents in Yogya organize packages including entrance fees and transport.

From January to April and November to December Prambanan's **Trimurti Theatre** (ⓣ0274/496408), an indoor venue to the north of the open-air arena, performs the Ramayana ballet (Tues & Thurs 7.30–9.30pm; Rp40,000–150,000). Tickets are available on the door or from the tourist office in Yogya.

(north). Facing these are three smaller temples housing the animal statues – or "chariots" – that would accompany the gods: Hamsa the swan, Nandi the bull and Garuda the sunbird respectively.

The **Shiva Temple** is decorated with exceptional carvings, including a series along the inner wall of the first terrace walkway that recounts the first half of the Ramayana epic. At the top of the steps is the temple's inner sanctuary, whose eastern chamber contains a statue of Shiva, while in the west chamber is Shiva's elephant-headed son, Ganesh. A beautiful sculpture of Nandi the Bull stands inside the temple of Shiva's chariot. Just as painstakingly decorated, the first terrace of the **Brahma Temple** takes up the Ramayana epic where the Shiva Temple left off, while the carvings on the terrace of Vishnu's temple recounts stories of **Krishna**, the eighth of Vishnu's nine earthly incarnations.

## Temples north of Prambanan

The other ancient sites on the Prambanan Plain (dawn–dusk; free) are not as spectacular as the Shiva Temple, but you are almost certain to be the only person on site. The three temples immediately to the **north of Prambanan** are within easy walking distance of the Shiva Temple, reached via the children's park next to the museum. All three date from the late eighth century, just predating Borobudur. **Candi Lumbung** consists of sixteen small, crumbling temples surrounding a larger, but equally dilapidated, central temple. Separated from Lumbung by the unimpressive pile of rubble that is Candi Bubrah, Buddhist **Sewu** once consisted of 240 small shrines surrounding a large, central temple but has been severely looted. A ten-minute bike ride or thirty-minute walk to the east of Candi Sewu, **Candi Plaosan** is also surrounded by building debris, but the two-storey building still houses two stone Bodhisattvas.

## Temples south of Prambanan

The other worthwhile ruins lie to the **south of Prambanan** and are best tackled by bicycle. From the village, cycle down the path that begins by the small graveyard to a small village school on the left-hand side (10min). Turn left, and after five minutes you reach **Candi Sojiwan**, a plain, square temple, sparingly decorated with scenes from Buddhist folklore. Return to the main path and head south towards the foot of the Shiva Plateau. The path to the summit of the plateau and **Kraton Ratu Boko** (US$5) is unsuitable for bicycles, so ask to leave them at the house at the bottom. The ruins are in two parts: a series of bathing pools and, 400m to the west, the ceremonial gate that adorns many tourist posters. The views from the kraton are wonderful, as they are from **Candi Barong**, to the south – to get there, head west towards the main road, Jalan Raya Piyungan, where you turn left (south) and cycle for 1.5km until a signpost on your left points to Barong, 1km to the east. This *candi* is actually two hillside Buddhist temples mounted on a raised platform on the southern slopes of the plateau. A little way back along this path and to the south is **Banyunibo**, a pretty Buddhist shrine dedicated to Tara. From there, head back onto the main road and turn right; Prambanan village lies 2km away.

### Arrival

Most people visit the Prambanan temples on a **day-trip** from Yogya. with many tour companies offering all-inclusive packages (see p.229).

**By bus** It's easy enough to get there by local bus from Yogya's Giwangan bus station or Solo. Public buses drop passengers off in Prambanan village, a tiny huddle on the southern side of Jalan Adisucipto, a five-minute walk from the eastern entrance to the temple complex.

**By bike** If you come by bus you can't get to the other ruins on the plain, which is why some visitors cycle here from Yogya. Fume-choked Jl Adisucipto is the most straightforward route, but there's a quieter alternative that begins by heading north along Yogya's Jl Simanjutak and Jl Kaliurang until you reach the Mataram Canal, just past the main Gajah Mada University compound. Follow the canal path east for 12km (1hr), and you'll come out eventually near Candi Sari on Jalan Adisucipto. Prambanan village is 4km east of Candi Sari, along Jalan Adisucipto. *Via Via* café also organizes bike rides to Prambanan.

### Accommodation

You can stay in the village at one of the rudimentary losmen (❶).

**Prambanan Village Hotel** North of the open-air theatre ⓣ0274/496435. Provides more salubrious accommodation and houses a fine Japanese restaurant. ❻

## SURAKARTA (SOLO)

Sixty-five kilometres northeast of Yogya stands quiet, leafy low-rise **SURAKARTA**, or, as it's more commonly known, **SOLO**. This is the older of the two royal cities in Central Java, and its ruling family can lay claim to being the rightful heirs to the Mataram dynasty.

Not long after their establishment – in 1745 and 1757 respectively – Solo's two royal houses wisely stopped fighting and instead threw their energies into the arts, developing a highly sophisticated and graceful court culture. The gamelan pavilions became the new theatres of war, with each city competing to produce the more refined court culture – a situation that continues to this day.

### What to see and do

Like Yogya, Solo has two **royal palaces** and a number of museums, yet its tourist industry is nowhere near as developed. The city's main source of income is from textiles, and Solo has the biggest **batik market** on Java. Solo also makes an ideal base from which to visit the home of Java Man at Sangiran, as well as the intriguing temples Candi Ceto and Candi Sukuh.

#### Kasunanan Palace

Brought from Kartasura by Pakubuwono II in one huge day-long procession in 1745, the **Kasunanan Palace** (Mon–Thurs 9am–2pm, Sat & Sun 9am–3pm; Rp8000, plus Rp2000 camera fee) is Solo's largest and most important royal house. It stands within the kraton, just south of the alun-alun; guides are available free of charge and are definitely worth taking. Non-royals must enter the main body of the palace by the eastern entrance. This opens out into a large courtyard whose surrounding buildings house the palace's **kris** (dagger) collection, as well as a number of chariots, silver ornaments and other royal knick-knacks. An archway to the west leads into the susuhunan's living quarters. Many of the buildings in this courtyard are modern copies, the originals having burnt down in 1985. By the southwest corner of the town's main alun-alun, the three-storey Pasar Klewer (daily 9am–4pm), claims to be Java's largest **batik market**, and designs from all over Java can be found here.

#### Puro Mangkunegoro

The second royal house in Solo, the **Puro Mangkunegoro** (guided tours only Mon–Sat 8.30am–2pm, Sun 8.30am–1pm; Rp10,000 includes tour) stands 1km west of the kraton and, like Yogya's court of Paku Alam, faces south towards the Kasunanan Palace as a mark of respect. With its fine collection of antiques and curios, in many ways the Puro Mangkunegoro is more interesting than the Kasunanan Palace. It was built in 1757 to placate the rebellious Prince Mas Said (Mangkunegoro I), a nephew of Pakubuwono II, who was given a royal title, a court in Solo and rulership over four thousand of Solo's households in a peace deal. The palace hides behind a high white wall, entered through the gateway to the south. The vast **pendopo** (the largest in Indonesia) that fronts the palace shields four gamelan orchestras underneath its rafters, three of which can only be played on very special occasions. The pendopo's vibrantly painted roof features Javanese zodiac figures surrounding the main batik centrepiece that took three years to complete. A portrait of the current resident, Mangkunegoro IX, hangs by the entrance to the **Dalam Agung**, or living quarters, whose reception room has been turned into an extremely good museum, displaying ancient coins, ballet masks and chastity preservers.

### Radya Pustaka Museum

A kilometre west along Jalan Brig Jen Slamet Riyadi brings you to the **Radya Pustaka Museum** (Tues–Sun 8am–1pm; Rp1000). Built by the Dutch in 1890, this is one of the oldest and largest museums in Java, housing a large Dutch and Javanese library as well as collections of wayang kulit puppets, kris and scale models of the mosque at Demak and the cemetery at Imogiri.

## Arrival

**By bus** All buses terminate at the Tirtonadi bus station in the north of the city. Just across the crossroads by the northeastern corner of Tirtonadi is the minibus terminal, Gilingan. From the front of the *Hotel Surya*, overlooking Tirtonadi, orange angkuta #6 departs for the town centre, stopping at Ngapeman, the junction of Jl Gajah Mada and Jl Brig Jen Slamet Riyadi. A becak from the bus station to Jl Dahlan costs around Rp4000, while a taxi will cost about Rp7000.

**By train** You'll pay Rp4000 for a becak and approximately Rp7000 for a taxi from the Balapan train station, 300m south of Tirtonadi to Jl Dahlan. Avoid the pre-paid taxi stand inside the station which charges Rp20,000.

**By air** Adisumaryno Airport, Central Java's only international airport, is 10km west of Solo and just 2km north of Kartasura. There is no public transport direct to Solo, although a half-hourly minibus to Kartasura (Rp2000) goes along the main road alongside the runway, and from Kartasura you can catch a bus to Solo (Rp2000). A taxi from the airport to Solo will cost approximately Rp50,000.

## Information and tours

**Tourist information** Solo boasts three tourist offices, located at the airport, at Balapan train station and behind the Radya Pustaka Museum at Jl Brig Jen Slamet Riyadi 275. Only the latter (Mon–Sat 8am–6pm; ⓣ0271/711435) is of any real use, however, with English-speaking staff, details of events and a reasonable range of brochures.

**Tours** The cycling tours organized by *Warung Baru* (see p.242), Jl Dahlan 8, are very rewarding and usually includes a visit to a gamelan factory, bakery, tofu factory and even an *arak* manufacturer.

**Travel agents** Inta Tours & Travel Jl Brig Jen Slamet Riyadi 96 (ⓣ0271/654010) are recommended.

## City transport

**Taxis** The main taxi stand is situated by the Matahari department store; they are metered. The minimum fare is Rp4000.

**Becak** More reasonable than taxis: unlike the ones in Yogya, Solo's becak do not charge a higher rate if there is more than one person in the carriage. As ever, bargain hard.

**Bike rental** Being flat and, for a Javanese city, relatively free of traffic, cycling is an excellent way to get round the city. Bikes can be rented from many of the homestays for Rp15,000 per day.

## Accommodation

Some of the budget hotels are hidden in the kampung to the south of Jl Brig Jen Slamet Riyadi, and can be difficult to find. The simplest solution is to hire a becak to take you there, although, as usual, the driver's commission will result in a higher room rate.

**Cakra Homestay** Jl Cakra II/15, Kauman ⓣ0271/634743. This place is a bit of a secret delight, with its own pool, Javanese charm and furnishings, and even a gamelan orchestra – all tucked away behind high walls. Popular with those staying for a long time in Solo, though the rooms are basic with cold-water mandi only. ❷

**Dana** Jl Brig Jen Slamet Riyadi 286 ⓣ0271/711976; danasolo@indo.net.id. Large hotel with 49 a/c rooms, conveniently situated opposite the tourist office and museum. ❺

**Istana Griya** Jl Dahlan 22 ⓣ0271/632667. Highly efficient homestay tucked away down a quiet little gang with the smartest and best-value rooms in this price range. The friendly English-speaking owner organizes a number of tours. Internet available for Rp5000/hr. ❷

**Novotel** Jl Brig Jen Slamet Riyadi 272 ⓣ0271/724555 or 716800, ⓔreservation@novotelsolo.com. Luxury hotel with its own pool; gym; Indonesian, Japanese and Chinese restaurants; and plush a/c rooms. ❼–❽

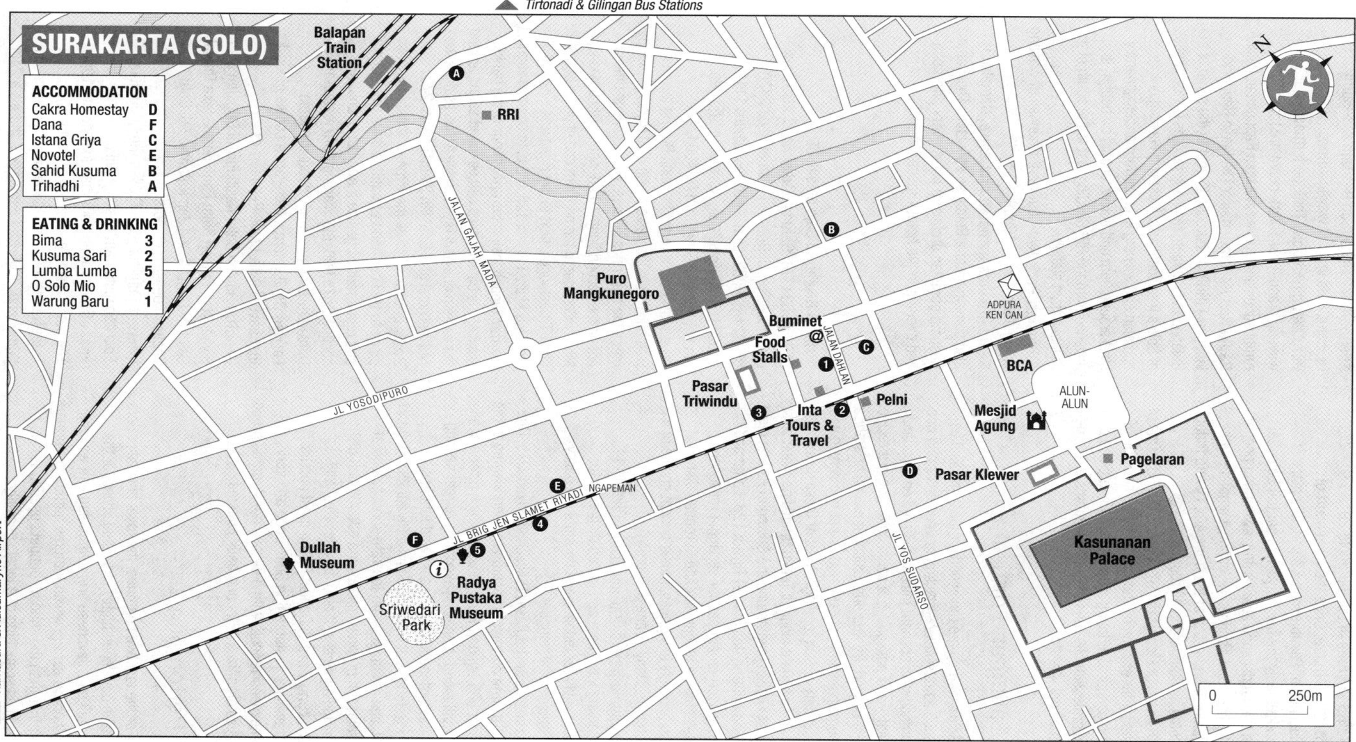

Tirtonadi & Gilingan Bus Stations
SURAKARTA (SOLO)
ACCOMMODATION
Cakra Homestay D
Dana F
Istana Griya C
Novotel E
Sahid Kusuma B
Trihadhi A
EATING & DRINKING
Bima 3
Kusuma Sari 2
Lumba Lumba 5
O Solo Mio 4
Warung Baru 1
Balapan Train Station
RRI
JALAN GAJAH MADA
Puro Mangkunegoro
Buminet
Food Stalls
JALAN DAHLAN
Pasar Triwindu
Inta Tours & Travel
Pelni
ADPURA KEN CAN
BCA
ALUN-ALUN
Mesjid Agung
Pagelaran
Pasar Klewer
Kasunanan Palace
JL YOSODIPURO
NGAPEMAN
JL BRIG JEN SLAMET RIYADI
JL YOS SUDARSO
Dullah Museum
Radya Pustaka Museum
Sriwedari Park
Karkasura & Adisumaryno Airport
0 250m

**Sahid Kusuma** Jl Sugiopranoto 20 ⓣ0271/646356. Once the royal court of Susuhunan Pakubuwono X's son, this place is undoubtedly the most stylish in central Solo. Set in five landscaped acres with a swimming pool at the back and pendopo reception, complete with gamelan orchestra, at the front. A/c, TV and fridge come as standard in all rooms. ❼–❾

**Trihadhi** Jl Monginsidi 97 ⓣ0271/637557. One of the better options by the train station, and one of the cheapest in town; a spotlessly clean place that is professionally run but homely. Rooms are large and cool. ❶–❸.

## Eating and drinking

Solo's warung are renowned for local specialities such as *nasi liwet* – chicken or vegetables and rice drenched in coconut milk and served on a banana leaf – and *nasi gudeg*, a variation on Yogya's recipe. For dessert, try *kue putu* (coconut cakes) or *srabi*, a combination of pancake and sweet rice served with a variety of fruit toppings. Most of these delicacies can be bought along Jl Teuku Umar, one block west of Jl Dahlan, and around the Sriwedari Park at night.

**Bima** Jl Brig Jen Slamet Riyadi 128. Large and swish ice-cream parlour serving a reasonable selection of Indonesian and European dishes at surprisingly low prices, plus a decent choice of ice creams. Daily 10am–9.30pm.

**Kusuma Sari** Jl Brig Jen Slamet Riyadi 111. Serving ice cream and grilled dishes, with, unusually for Indonesia, a no-smoking policy. Popular local hangout.

**Lumba Lumba** Pasar Pujosari, Jl Riyadi 275. One of a large number of restaurants and warung to the east of Sriwedari Park, most of which offer a similar, small menu. A shady, welcoming retreat serving standard Indonesian snacks and lunches.

**O Solo Mio** Jl Brig Jen Slamet Riyadi 253. A smart Italian restaurant with top-rate service, a great selection of wines, pizzas and other Italian dishes, including steaks. It also provides free WiFi.

**Warung Baru** Jl Dahlan 8. The most popular travellers' restaurant in Solo. Good and very inexpensive food, with delicious home-made bread. Also organizes tours and batik courses.

## Performing arts

For the last two centuries, the royal houses of Solo have developed highly individual styles for the traditional Javanese arts of gamelan and wayang. **Wayang orang**, which features human performers rather than the shadow puppets used in wayang kulit, is something of a local speciality.

**Kasunanan Palace** (Sun 9–11am & 3–5pm) Graceful, fluid style of wayang orang.

**Puro Mangkunegoro** Their performances of wayang orang (Wed 10am–noon) are more rumbustious and aggressive than Kasunanan Palace.

**Radio Republik Indonesia** The Radio Republik Indonesia (RRI), Jl Marconi 55, just to the south of the Balapan train station, regularly records performances of Solo's traditional arts, including wayang orang; gamelan and wayang kulit; performances generally start around 9pm and tickets should be bought in advance from the RRI Building just to the south of the Balapan train station.

**Sriwedari Park** Two-hour performances of wayang orang (Mon–Sat 8–10pm).

**Sahid Kusuma gamelan orchestra.** Gamelan is also something of a Solonese speciality. The Sahid Kusuma gamelan orchestra plays every afternoon and evening in the hotel's reception hall,

## Directory

**Airlines** Bouraq, Jl Gaja Madah 86 ⓣ0271/634376; Garuda, *Cakra Hotel*; also Bank Lippo Building, Jl Brig Jen Slamet Riyadi 328 ⓣ0271/630082; Lion Air, Jl Yosodipuro 111B ⓣ0271/722599; Silk Air, *Novotel*, Jl Brig Jen Slamet Riyadi 272 ⓣ0271/724604.

**Banks and exchange** The Bank BCA, in the vast BCA building at the eastern end of Jl Riyadi, currently offers the best rates in town. The exchange offices are on the second floor (10am–noon). The Golden Money Changer at the northern end of Jl Yos Sudarso, and PT Desmonda, next to the *Bima* restaurant at Jl Brig Jen Slamet Riyadi 128, are both open throughout the day, though their rates are inferior to the banks. Most of the banks, which can be found at and around the eastern end of Jl Riyadi, have ATMs, as does the *Novotel* hotel at Jl Brig Jen Slamet Riyadi 272.

**Batik courses** For all the hype of Yogya, the best place to try your hand at batik is Solo. Homestays and restaurants organize a number of courses costing Rp75,000: the *Warung Baru* restaurant on Jl Dahlan runs an extremely popular course.

**Ferries** On Jl Veteran, there are a couple of kiosks that have details of the Pelni ferries.

**Hospital** Rumah Sakit Kasih Ibu, Jl Brig Jen Slamet Riyadi 404, Rumah Sakit Panti Kosala (aka Rumah Sakit Dr Oen), Jl Brig Jen Katamso 55. Both have English-speaking doctors.

**Internet** Buminet on Jl Dahlan (Rp4,000/hour). *O Solo Mio* restaurant has free WiFi.

**Post office** Jl Jend Sudirman (daily 6am–10pm). The poste restante closes in the evening.

**Telephones** Just behind the Telkom offices on Jl Sumoharjo, Jl Mayor Kusmanto 3, there's a 24hr wartel office. There's also a wartel on Jl Brig Jen Slamet Riyadi to the west of Jl Yos Sudarso.

### Moving on

**By bus** To reach the bus station from the centre, catch a BERSERI bus (Rp1000) from the bus stop on Jl Brig Jen Slamet Riyadi, 100m east of Jl Dahlan. **Destinations**: Frequent buses to Bandung (12hr); Banyuwangi (12hr); Jakarta (12hr); Malang (7hr); Semarang (3hr); Surabaya (6hr); Yogyakarta (2hr).
**By train** to: Bandung (5 daily; 8hr 50min); Jakarta (5 daily; 10hr 30min); Malang (1 daily; 6hr 25min); Purworketo (6 daily; 3hr 15min); Surabaya (6 daily; 3hr 20min); Yogya (14 daily; 1hr 30min).
**By air** to: Jakarta (6 daily; 1hr 5min); Singapore (2 weekly; 2hr 20min); Surabaya (2 daily; 1hr 5min).

## SURABAYA

Polluted, noisy and sprawling, **SURABAYA** is the second-largest city in Indonesia, and the major port of East Java. With time and effort the city is comprehensible and even somewhat enjoyable, but for most tourists Surabaya is nothing more than a transport hub. If you do want to linger, the **Chinese** and **Arab quarters** to the north of the city centre, the fascinating **Kalimas harbour**, and the **zoo** and **museum** to the south are the most interesting sights.

### What to see and do

Surabaya's **Chinese quarter** hums with activity, an abundance of traditional two-storey shop-houses lining narrow streets, and minuscule red-and-gold altars glinting in shops and houses. The area centres on Jalan Slompretan, Jalan Bongkaran and the part of Jalan Samudra southwest of the three-hundred-year-old **Hok Teck Hian Temple** on Jalan Dukuh. The temple itself is a vibrant place with several tiny shrines spread over two floors, and Buddhist, Confucian and Hindu effigies.

The oldest and most famous mosque in Surabaya is **Mesjid Ampel**, located in the Arab area, the **kampung Arab** or **Qubah**, to the north of the Chinese quarter. The whole kampung, bounded by Jalan Nyanplungan, Jalan KH Mas Mansur, Jalan Sultan Iskandar Muda and Jalan Pabean Pasar, was originally settled by Arab traders and sailors who arrived in Kali Mas harbour. It's a maze of tidy, well-kept alleyways crammed with flowers, beggars and shops. The area isn't particularly tourist-friendly, and women will have to dress extremely conservatively and take a scarf to cover their heads.

One of the best places to visit in the city, **Surabaya Zoo** (Kebun Binatang Surabaya; daily 7am–6pm; Rp5000), lies 3km south of the city centre; take buses C, P1, P2 or either PAC bus. Spacious, and with over 3500 animals, it's surprisingly pleasant and, at least in parts, less distressing for animal-lovers than many Indonesian zoos. Highlights include the orang-utans and Komodo dragon.

### Arrival

**By bus** The main bus station is Bungusarih (also known as Purabaya), 6km south of the city. All long-distance and inter-island buses start and finish here, plus many of the city buses and bemos. Local buses into the city leave from the far end of the Bungusarih terminal: follow the signs for "Kota". Many of the C (Rp1000), P (Rp2000) and both PAC (Rp3500) buses serve Bungusarih. There's also a huge taxi rank here. Minimum fare of Rp4000; expect to pay about Rp20,000 to anywhere in town.
**By train** Surabaya has three main train stations. Gubeng station is in the east of town; it has a hotel reservation desk (daily 8am–8pm), but only for expensive places. Kota station is towards the north of the city centre, while Pasar Turi station is in the west of the city centre.
**By ferry** Arriving by sea, probably by Pelni ferry, you'll dock at Tanjung Perak in the far north of the city, served by C, P and PAC buses.
**By air** You can get a visa on arrival at Surabaya airport; all flights arrive at Juanda International Airport (ⓣ031/866 7642), 18km south of the city, where there's a tourist office. No public bus connects with the town centre, but there's a rank for fixed-price taxis (Rp70,000).

### Information and agencies

**Tourist information**The most useful tourist office is at Jl Jend Basuki Rachmat 119–121, opposite the *Hyatt* (Mon–Fri 7am–2pm; ⓣ031/534 4710).

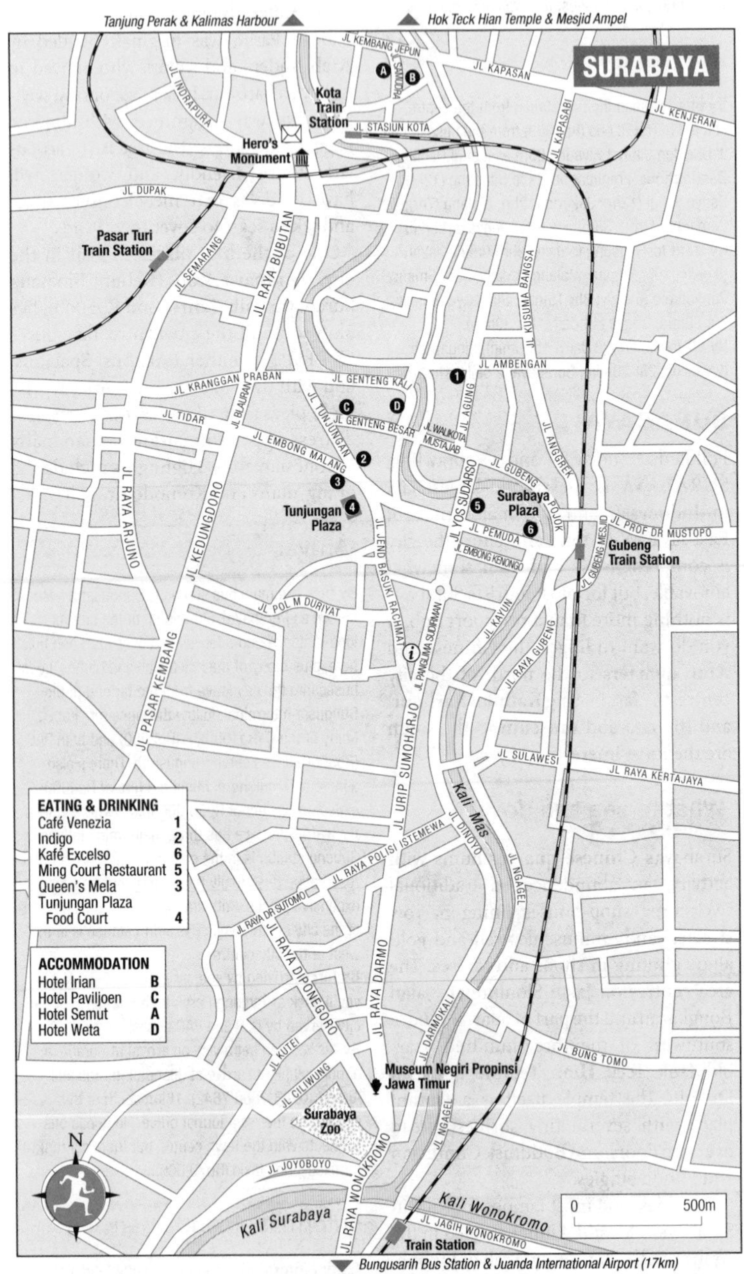
SURABAYA
Tanjung Perak & Kalimas Harbour
Hok Teck Hian Temple & Mesjid Ampel
Kota Train Station
Hero's Monument
Pasar Turi Train Station
Tunjungan Plaza
Surabaya Plaza
Gubeng Train Station
Kali Mas
Museum Negiri Propinsi Jawa Timur
Surabaya Zoo
Kali Surabaya
Kali Wonokromo
Train Station
Bungusarih Bus Station & Juanda International Airport (17km)
JL KEMBANG JEPUN
JL SAMUDRA
JL KAPASAN
JL KENJERAN
JL KAPASARI
JL INDRAPURA
JL STASIUN KOTA
JL DUPAK
JL SEMARANG
JL RAYA BUBUTAN
JL KUSUMA BANGSA
JL AMBENGAN
JL KRANGGAN PRABAN
JL GENTENG KALI
JL TUNJUNGAN
JL GENTENG BESAR
JL WALIKOTA MUSTAJAB
JL AGUNG
JL ANGGREK
JL TIDAR
JL BLAURAN
JL EMBONG MALANG
JL YOS SUDARSO
JL GUBENG POJOK
JL PROF DR MUSTOPO
JL PEMUDA
JL EMBONG KENONGO
JL GUBENG MESJID
JL RAYA ARJUNO
JL KEDUNGDORO
JL JEND BASUKI RACHMAT
JL POL M DURIYAT
JL PANGLIMA SUDIRMAN
JL KAYUN
JL RAYA GUBENG
JL PASAR KEMBANG
JL URIP SUMOHARJO
JL SULAWESI
JL RAYA KERTAJAYA
JL DINOYO
JL RAYA POLISI ISTEMEWA
JL NGAGEL
JL RAYA DR SUTOMO
JL RAYA DIPONEGORO
JL RAYA DARMO
JL DARMOKALI
JL BUNG TOMO
JL KUTEI
JL CILIWUNG
JL JOYOBOYO
JL RAYA WONOKROMO
JL JAGIH WONOKROMO
0 500m
N
EATING & DRINKING
Café Venezia 1
Indigo 2
Kafé Excelso 6
Ming Court Restaurant 5
Queen's Mela 3
Tunjungan Plaza Food Court 4
ACCOMMODATION
Hotel Irian B
Hotel Paviljoen C
Hotel Semut A
Hotel Weta D

**Travel agents** The following is a selection of the largest, best-established set-ups. Many agents in Surabaya offer all-inclusive tours to the sights of the region, either day-trips or longer, plus international bookings. Haryono Tours and Travel, Jl Sulawesi 27–29 ⓣ031/503 3000 or 503 4000; Orient Express, Jl Panglima Sudirman 62 ⓣ031/545 6666; Pacto, *Hyatt Regency Hotel*, Jl Jend Basuki Rakhmat 106–128 ⓣ031/546 0628.

## Accommodation

Much of the cheaper accommodation is slightly out of the centre, in the area north of Kota station, which isn't good either for buses (you'll need to figure out the bemos around here) or the central sights.

**Hotel Irian** Jl Samudra 16 ⓣ031/352 0953. A pleasant old-style bungalow, cool and with a choice of rooms. There are shared bathrooms and fan at the lower end and en-suite bathrooms in the more expensive rooms. ❶–❸

**Hotel Paviljoen** Jl Genteng Besar 94–98 ⓣ031/534 3449. The most popular budget hotel. Spotlessly clean rooms in an old colonial bungalow; the ones at the back have excellent verandas around a courtyard and all have attached cold-water mandi, while top-end rooms have a/c. This is an excellent choice if you want to be fairly central and have a bit of comfort. Southbound buses P1 and P2 stop just at the end of the street on Jl Tunjungan. ❷–❸

**Hotel Semut** Jl Samudra 9–15 ⓣ031/24578. All rooms have a/c and attached bathroom: cold water in the less expensive rooms and hot water in the pricier ones. There are deep, cool verandas looking into the garden, as well as a coffee shop and restaurant. ❸

**Hotel Weta** Jl Genteng Kali 3–11 ⓣ031/531 9494. With a small but attractive lobby area, friendly and helpful staff, and clean, attractive rooms with a/c and hot-water bathrooms, this is a central, good-value choice in this price range. Staff will always discuss discounts. ❺

## Eating and drinking

**Café Venezia** Jl Ambengan 16. Located on a busy and noisy corner; you can eat outside or in the high-ceilinged cool interior. There's a comprehensive menu of Indonesian, Chinese, Japanese, Korean and Western food, plus plenty of ice creams and sundaes.

**Indigo** *Hotel Majapahit Mandarin Oriental*, Jl Tunjungan 65. Just off the lobby of this stylish old-world hotel, this contemporary coffee shop serves excellent Indonesian, Chinese and Western dishes, including great pizzas. Upstairs is the *Sarkies* restaurant – probably the most elegant in town – serving Asian cuisines, with seafood a speciality.

**Kafé Excelso** This Indonesian chain has branches on the ground floor of Surabaya Plaza and in the second floor Tunjungan Plaza, and is very popular with well-heeled Indonesians and expatriates. They have an excellent choice of expensive Indonesian coffees (choose between Bali, Toraja, Sumatra or Java Arabica blends), plus iced coffee, salads, snacks, cakes and ice creams.

**Ming Court Restaurant** *Garden Palace Hotel*, Jl Yos Sudarso 11. This first-floor restaurant offers very good (and reasonably priced) Cantonese-style food, something quite rare among Chinese restaurants in Surabaya.

**Queen's Mela** *Sheraton Hotel*, Jl Embong Malang 25–31. Surabaya's only Indian restaurant. Stylish decor and delicious, but expensive, Mogul, North Indian and fusion food.

**Tunjungan Plaza Food Court** On the fifth floor of the biggest and brashest of the city's shopping plazas. There is a vast array of fast food available here in the largest food court in Surabaya: *KFC*, *McDonald's*, Singaporean noodles, Cajun grills, New Zealand ice cream, crepes and kebabs.

## Nightlife

There's no shortage of entertainment in Surabaya, although it's a lot easier to find a disco or cinema in the city than a wayang kulit show. The discos (daily 10pm–2am) alternate recorded music with live, and are generally fairly expensive.

**Desperadoes** *Shangri-La Hotel*, Jl Mayjen Sungkono 120. A Mexican-themed cocktail bar situated in one of Surabaya's premier five-star hotels. Also serves food. Sun–Thurs 6pm–1.30am, Fri & Sat 6pm–2.30am.

**Tavern Pub** *Hyatt Regency*, Jl Basuki Rachmat 106–128. British-style pub with nightly live bands. Sun–Thurs 5pm–1am, Fri & Sat 5pm–2am.

## Directory

**Airlines** The following airlines are found in the Hyatt Graha Bumi Modern (next to the *Hyatt Hotel*), Jl Jen Basuki Rachmat 106–128: British Airways, 5th Floor ⓣ031/547 1508; Cathay Pacific, 1st Floor ⓣ031/531 7421; Eva Air, 5th Floor ⓣ031/546 5123; Garuda, Level 4 ⓣ031/532 6321; Malaysia, 1st Floor ⓣ & ⓕ031/531 8632; Northwest, 5th Floor ⓣ031/531 7086; Qantas, 5th Floor ⓣ031/545 2322; Thai, 5th Floor ⓣ031/534 0861. Elsewhere are: Batavia, Jl Raya Gubeng 68E ⓣ031/504 9666; Bouraq,

Jl P Sudirman 70–72 ☎031/545 2918, and Jl Genteng Kali 63 ☎031/534 4940; Emirates, Lt Dasar, *Hyatt Regency*, Jl Jend Basuki Rachmat 106–128 ☎031/546 0000; Jatayu, Jl Diponegoro 54E ☎031/560018; KLM, World Trade Centre, Jl Pemuda 27–31 ☎031/531 5096; Lion Air, Jl Sulawesi 75 ☎031/503 6111; Mandala, Jl Diponegoro 91D ☎031/561 0777; Merpati, Jl Raya Darmo 111 ☎031/568 111; Pelita, Juanda Airport ☎031/866 7584; Singapore Airlines, 10th Floor, Menara BBD Tower, Jl Jend Basuki Rachmat 2–6 ☎031/531 9217; Trans Asia Airways Regency, Jl Jend Basuki Rachmat 106–128 ☎031/546 3181.

**Banks and exchange** All of the main Indonesian banks have huge branches in Surabaya, with exchange facilities.

**Consulates** Australia (actually a Western Australia trade office, not a consulate, but they'll help where possible), World Trade Center, Jl Pemuda 27–31 ☎031/531 9123; UK, c/o Hong Kong and Shanghai Bank, 3rd Floor, Graha Bumi Modern, Jl Jend Basuki Rachmat 106–128 ☎031/532 6381; USA, Jl Dr Sutomo 33 ☎031/567 6880.

**Hospitals** The following are respected and have staff and doctors who speak English and Dutch: Rumah Sakit Darmo, Jl Raya Darmo 90 ☎031/567 6253; Rumah Sakit Katolik St Vincentius A Paulo (known as "RKZ"), Jl Diponegoro 51 ☎031/567 7562.

**Immigration office** Jl Jend S. Parman 58a ☎031/853 1785.

**Internet** All the big plazas have at least one internet café (Rp3000–8000 per hr). Telkom Café on the lower ground floor of Tunjungan Plaza provides free Wi-Fi.

**Post office** The main post office for poste restante and parcels (Mon–Thurs 8am–3pm, Fri & Sat 8am–1pm) is at Jl Kebonrojo 10. To get there from the city centre, take a C, P1, P2, PAC1 or PAC2 bus from outside Tunjungan Plaza to the junction of Jl Kebonrojo and Jl Bubutan; to get back to the city, go along to the other end of Jl Kebonrojo and pick up the same buses on Jl Pahlawan. If you're just sending letters, a more central post office is at Jl Taman Apsaril 1 (Mon–Thurs 8am–12.30pm, Fri 8–11am, Sat 8am–noon), just off Jl Pemuda in the city centre.

**Telephones** The warpostel at Jl Genteng Besar 49 (daily 5am–11pm) has telephone, fax and letter services. One of the most convenient wartels (daily 24hr) is the one on the ground floor of Tunjungan Plaza. It's a bit tucked away, under the main steps leading down into Tunjungan 2, just behind *Kafé Excelso*. There's another 24hr wartel at Jl Walikota Mustajab 2–4.

## Moving on

Surabaya is the main air, sea, rail and road hub for East Java and has excellent connections across Indonesia and internationally.

**By bus** For bus journeys within East Java (including Probolinggo for Gunung Bromo), just buy your ticket on the bus, but be wary of overcharging. You will pay Rp200 to get into the departure area at Bungusarih station – the bays are clearly labelled. Long-distance journeys are completed by night buses (departing 2–6pm) from Bay 8 – the ticket offices for all the night-bus companies are in the bus station; book ahead. Central minibus companies run more expensive daily trips to the main Javan destinations, leaving from their offices.

**Destinations**: Banyuwangi (every 30min; 5–7hr); Bondowoso (hourly; 4hr); Bukittinggi (daily; 48hr); Denpasar (5 daily; 11hr); Jakarta (20 daily; 14hr); Madura (Sumenep; hourly; 5hr); Mataram (2 daily; 20hr); Medan (daily; 3 days); Padang (daily; 48hr); Pekanbaru (daily; 48hr); Probolinggo (every 30min; 2hr); Solo (every 30min; 5hr); Sumbawa Besar (daily; 26hr); Yogyakarta (every 30min; 7hr).

**By train** Some (but not all) trains from Gubeng station also pass through Kota station, which is towards the north of the city centre. Pasar Turi station serves destinations along the northern route across the island to Jakarta via Semarang.

**Kota station** to: Bandung (2 daily; 16–18hr); Banyuwangi (3 daily; 6–7hr); Malang (7 daily; 3hr); Jakarta (3 daily; 14–16hr); Yogyakarta (3 daily; 5–6hr).

**Pasar Turi station** to: Jakarta (4 daily; 12–16hr).

**Gubeng station** to: Bandung (3 daily; 16–18hr); Banyuwangi (2 daily; 6–7hr); Jakarta (2 daily; 14hr); Malang (daily; 2hr 20min); Pasuruan (2 daily; 1hr 30min); Probolinggo (2 daily; 2–4 hr); Yogyakarta (2 daily; 5hr 10min).

**By ferry (Pelni)** Tanjung Perak is the major port in East Java, and no fewer than fifteen of Pelni's ferry fleet call here on their routes through the archipelago. For details, see p.195. The main Pelni office is at Jl Pahlawan 112 (Mon–Thurs 9am–noon & 1–3pm, Fri–Sat 9am–noon; ☎031/353 9048).

**Destinations** fortnightly (except where stated) to: Banda (3 days); Banjarmasin (5 times fortnightly; 24hr); Batulicin (23hr); Denpasar (16hr); Dumai (3 days); Ende (3 days); Jayapura (6–7 days); Kaimana (monthly; 4 days); Ketapang (3 days); Kijang (48hr); Kumai (22hr); Kupang (44hr); Labuanbajo (48hr); Makassar (24hr); Nias (3 days); Nunukan (3 days); Padang (30–42hr); Pontianak (39hr); Rote (3 days); Sabu (3 days); Samarinda (3 days); Sibolga (3 days); Tanjung Priok (16–21hr); Tarakan (weekly; 3 days); Waingapu (48hr).

**By air** Some international flight destinations are reached direct, while others have connections via Jakarta or Denpasar; see p.245, for airline offices in Surabaya. Airport information: ⓣ 031/866 7642 or 866 7513. Taxis from Gubeng train station taxi rank to the airport are fixed at Rp30,000.
**Destinations**: Banda Aceh (daily; 10hr); Bandung (4 daily; 1hr–2hr 30min); Banjarmasin (2 daily; 2hr); Denpasar (12 daily; 1hr 10min); Gorontalo (4 weekly; 5hr); Jakarta (22 daily; 1hr 20min); Jayapura (5 daily; 9hr); Kendari (2 daily; 5hr); Kupang (3 daily; 6hr 35min); Makassar (11 daily; 1hr 30min); Manado (daily; 4hr); Mataram (5 daily; 1hr 30min); Medan (5 daily; 7hr); Palangkarya (daily; 5hr); Palu (2 daily; 6hr); Pekanbaru (daily; 6hr); Pontianak (4 daily via Jakarta; 6hr); Pulau Batam (3 daily; 3hr 25min); Samarinda (daily; 7hr); Solo (daily; 1hr 10min); Ternate (daily; 8hr 15min); Waingapu (3 weekly; 3hr 20min–5hr 35min); Yogya (8 daily; 50min).

## THE BROMO REGION

The **Bromo region** is best known for its awesome scenery; at its heart is a vast, ancient volcanic crater with sheer walls over 300m high. Within this crater, a host of picturesque mountains, including the dramatic, still-smoking Gunung Bromo (2329m), rises up from the Sea of Sand, the sandy plain at the crater's base. Hundreds of thousands of visitors come here each year to climb Bromo for the sunrise – a stunning sight, and less strenuous than many other Indonesian peaks.

### What to see and do

This unique landscape now comprises the Bromo-Tengger-Semeru National Park, whose highlights are the dramatic smoking crater of **Gunung Bromo**, **Gunung Penanjakan** – on the outside crater's edge and one of the favourite sunrise spots – and **Cemoro Lawang**, with its brilliant panoramic view of the crater. The park also contains the highest mountain in Java, **Gunung Semeru**, which can be climbed by experienced trekkers. Views are best in the dry season but, whatever time of year, you should bring warm clothes.

There are two main approaches to the Bromo region. The most popular is to head inland from **Probolinggo**, on the north coast, to the crater's edge at Cemoro Lawang, where most people stay in order to make the dawn trip to Gunung Bromo as easy as possible. Alternative access is from **Pasuruan**, also on the north coast, inland to the villages of Tosari and Wonokitri. These villages are linked by road to Gunung Penanjakan, so they offer an excellent approach for the sunrise from there. Many people visit Bromo as part of a trip from Yogya to Bali (see box p.229).

#### Gunung Bromo

There are a variety of excursions possible from Cemoro Lawang, the most popular being the climb to the top of **Gunung Bromo** (2392m); if you're lucky with the clouds, there may be an absolutely spell-binding sunrise. There's a Rp20,000 per person entry fee for the park. To get to the base of Gunung Bromo, you can walk (1hr; bring a torch and follow the white pillars through the Sea of Sand), get a horse (Rp10,000), or hire a jeep or ojek (Rp30,000). However you get there, you'll still have to manage the 249 concrete stairs up to the crater rim, from where there are great views down into the smoking crater and back across the Sea of Sand.

#### Gunung Penanjakan

The best spot for the sunrise across the entire Bromo area is **Gunung Penanjakan** (2770m). The whole crater area lies below, Bromo smoking and Semeru puffing up regular plumes while the sun rises dramatically in the east. You can **camp** up here if you wish, but you'll be invaded before dawn by the hordes. Otherwise, you can walk from Tosari or Wonokitri at around 4.30am or, more popular, take a jeep from Cemro Lawang at around 3.30am that will then drive across the Sea of Sand to Bromo before returning to Cemro Lawang (Rp75,000).

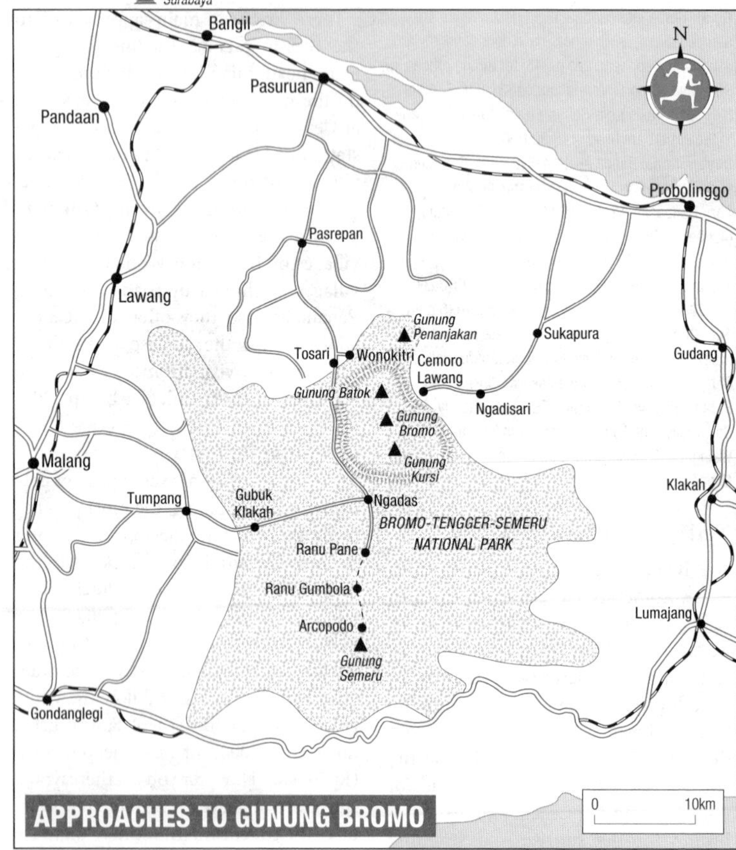

APPROACHES TO GUNUNG BROMO

## Gunung Semeru

Essentially a dry-season expedition (June–Sept or possibly Oct), the climb up **Gunung Semeru** (3676m), Java's highest mountain, is for fit, experienced trekkers only and requires good preparation and equipment. It takes at least three full days. The volcano is still active, with over 20,000 seismic events recorded in a typical year; it's vital to take a guide (ask at the PHPA office or your hotel) and heed local advice. The path starts at the village of **RANU PANE**, to the north of the mountain, accessible via a path across the Sea of Sand. In the village, you need to check in at the **PHPA office** and get your **permit** (Rp20,000). The PHPA office will also recommend porters (one per person at Rp50,000 each if you bargain). Bring your own sleeping bag and tent, and rent a cooking stove in Ranu Pane. In the village, trekkers can stay in the *Forest Guest House* (❶), where you'll need to cook for yourself, or there's a **campsite** near the PHPA office.

## Probolinggo

**PROBOLINGGO**, the most popular access poing for Bromo, is 100km southeast of Surabaya. From the **train station**, which is on the northern side of the alun-alun, there are connections to Banyuwangi, Malang and Surabaya.

The **bus terminal** is 6km southwest of town; yellow microlets run to the town centre. **Minibuses** for Cemoro Lawang leave from the terminal, and there are two buses daily – they are labelled "Sukapura" and "Ngadisari" on the front but also serve Cemoro Lawang. There are also frequent buses to Banyuwangi, Denpasar (Bali), Jakarta, Mataram (Lombok), Pasuruan, Solo and Yogyakarta.

The best **accommodation** is *Hotel Bromo Permai*, Jl Raya P Sudirman 237 (ⓣ0335/427451; ❷–❹), where staff can arrange chartered transport to Cemoro Lawang and have train information. To get here from the bus station, take a G or F yellow microlet and, from here to the terminal or station, a G. For **eating**, *Restaurant Malang*, Jl Raya P Sudirman 48, has an extensive menu of reasonably priced well-cooked Indonesian and Chinese dishes, plus plenty of drinks.

### Cemoro Lawang

The small village of **CEMORO LAWANG**, 46km from Probolinggo, is perched on the crater's edge and is the easiest place from which to set off on the pre-dawn excursion to Gunung Bromo itself. From the crater's edge in Cemoro Lawang, there are brilliant views of the entire area – best at the end of the road from the north coast and in front of *Lava View Lodge*. **Minibuses** (Rp15,000) from Probolinggo run up to the crater rim from 6am to 5.30pm; they do the return journey from 8am till 4pm. Several places advertise minibus and express-bus tickets, which are more expensive but more convenient.

The **national park office** (Kantor Taman Nasional Bromo Tengger Semeru; daily 24 hours) in Cemoro Lawang has displays about the area. *Hotel Yoschi* is the best place for local information, especially if you want to trek. The postal agent at the *Hotel Bromo Permai* charges a lot, so bring stamps with you. There's a wartel (daily 3am–10pm) on the left as you reach the top of the road, and a **health centre** in Ngadisari, Jl Raya Bromo 6, just by the checkpost.

## Accommodation

There's plenty of accommodation in Cemoro Lawang, Ngadisari (3km from the rim), Wonokerto (5km) and Sukapura (18km). You can **camp** anywhere: Penanjakan is popular, although you will get disturbed at sunrise, and there's a good site 200m along the rim from the *Lava View Lodge*. There are plenty of places to eat in the vicinity of Cemoro Lawang, and many of the hotels have restaurants.

**Café Lava Hostel** ⓣ0335/541020. A justly popular travellers' choice, close to the crater rim, on the main road into Cemoro Lawang. There are two standards of room, the less expensive ones being basic with shared cold-water mandi (often a long walk away) and the more expensive ones, which are spotless, with lovely sitting areas in an attractive garden. However, rooms get very cold during the winter months – ask for extra blankets. ❸

**Cemoro Indah** ⓣ0335/541197. On the crater's rim around to the right from the *Hotel Bromo Permai*. The main road into Cemoro Lawang forks about 200m before it reaches the crater rim; the left fork goes to the centre of the village, and the right fork to the *Cemoro Indah*. There's a big choice of rooms, from basic ones with cold-water shared mandi to stunningly positioned bungalows with hot water. The attached restaurant is equally well located. ❶–❻

**Hotel Yoschi** Jl Wonokerto 1, Wonokerto ⓣ0335/541014. A great place with many options: the cheaper rooms have shared bathroom, while the top-priced ones are actually cottages. The decor is attractive and the garden a delight. Staff provide plenty of good information on the area and sell maps of local hikes. You can also use the book exchange, book bus tickets, arrange local guides, charter transport and rent warm jackets. ❸–❼

**Lava View Lodge** ⓣ0335/541009. About 500m left along the crater's edge from the centre of Cemoro Lawang; go through the concrete area between the row of shops and *Hotel Bromo Permai* and follow the main track. This is a very popular choice, offering comfortable rooms – all have attached bathrooms, very good Indonesian buffet, live music and the views are brilliant, especially from the more expensive rooms and the restaurant. ❸–❻

### Pasuruan

Located 60km southeast of Surabaya, the port town of **PASURUAN** is a convenient stopping-off spot close to Bromo on the way to or from Tosari and Wonokitri. The main north-coast road is Jalan Raya.

**Buses** run every few minutes throughout the day between Pasuruan and Surabaya (1–2hr) and Pasuruan and Banyuwangi (6hr) The bus terminal at the eastern end of Jl Raya, about 1.5km from the alun-alun. Microlets run direct to Tosari, although there is no sign at the terminal. There are daily trains (1hr 30min) from Gubeng station in Surabaya. The train station is just north of Jl Raya, on Jl Stasiun.

*Hotel Pasuruan*, Jl Nusantara 46, has three standards of room, from cold-water bathroom and fan rooms up to those with a/c and hot water bathrooms (☎0343/424494; ❸–❹). Alternatively, try *Wisma Karya*, Jl Raya 160, which has a range of rooms behind an old colonial bungalow (☎0343/426655; ❷). The top-end rooms have a/c, but the cheaper ones with fan and attached cold-water mandi are adequate.

You can eat at the small **night market** around the alun-alun, or try the inexpensive Indonesian and Chinese food at *Rumah Makan Savera*, on Jl Raya 92a.

### Tosari and Wonokitri

Just over 40km south from Pasuruan, the small villages of **Tosari** and **Wonokitri** sit 2km apart on neighbouring ridges of the Bromo massif foothills. These are excellent choices for early access to **Gunung Penanjakan** and are less tourist-oriented than Cemoro Lawang. Microlets that go to one also go to the other, and both villages have accommodation. The road from Pasuruan divides 500m before Tosari: the right fork leads up to the market area of that village, and the left fork twists up to the next ridge and Wonokitri. Wonokitri is a compact, shabby town with good views, while Tosari is more spread out, with an attractive ridge to the northeast that leads to the *Hotel Bromo Cottages*. It's better to take one of the regular minibus direct from Pasuruan, which will take about an hour.

At the **national park checkpost** and information centre at the southern end of Wonokitri you pay the **admission fee** to the park (Rp20,000).

#### Accommodation

**Bromo Surya Indah** Wonokitri ☎0343/571049. Just before the Balinese-style village meeting hall, about 300m before the national park checkpost at the far end of the village; rooms have attached bathroom, clean bedding and good views. ❷

**Mekar Sari** Jl Raya 1, Tosari. A small rumah makan with a few simple rooms and a good roof terrace. ❶

**Penginapan Wulun Aya** Jl Bromo Cottage 25 Tosari ☎0343/57011. Small and clean with good views. ❶–❷

## BANYUWANGI

The town of **BANYUWANGI** has excellent transport links and is 8km south of **Ketapang**, from where ferries run to Gilimanuk in **Bali**. But buses travelling to or from Bali head straight to the ferry terminal so there's no need to stop at the town itself.

#### Arrival and information

**By bus** There are several bus terminals serving Banyuwangi. The main long-distance terminal is Sri Tanjung, 2km north of Ketapang.

**By boat** The ferry terminal is situated 8km north at Ketapang. Bemos will take you there from the town centre.

**Tourist information** A helpful East Java tourist office (daily 8am–7pm) is located inside the ferry terminal building.

#### Accommodation and eating

Many of the hotels have attached restaurants and there is a night market along Jl Pattimura offering warung food.

**Hotel Baru** Jl MT Hariyono 82–84 ☎0333/421369. Popular with travellers and sits in a quiet, central location ten minutes' walk from the post office. All rooms have attached mandi, and the more expensive ones have a/c. ③–④

**Hotel Blambangan**, Jl Dr Wahidin 4 ⓣ0333/421598. On the south side of the square, about 100m from the post office, this is in an old colonial bungalow with a two-storey building behind. All rooms are large with high ceilings, and those upstairs have balconies. ①–④

## Directory

**Banks and exchange** For exchange, go to BCA at Jl Jend Sudirman 85–87 or BNI at Jl Banetrang 46.

**Post office** Jl Diponegoro 1 (Mon–Thurs 8am–3pm, Fri 8–11am, Sat 8am–1pm, Sun & hols 8am–noon). On the west side of the sports field and has public internet access.

**Telephones** Just around the corner, off the southwest corner of the sports field, the 24hr Telkom office is at Jl Dr Sutomo 63, and there are plenty of wartels around town, including Jl Jaksa Agung Suprapto 130.

## Moving on

**By boat to Bali** 24-hour service; every 30min; 45min.

**By bus** If you're heading to Surabaya, you can either go around the north coast via Situbondo, or via Jember (further but more scenic); travel time on both routes is similar.

**Destinations**: Bandung (daily; 24hr); Jakarta (daily; 20–24hr); Madura (Sumenep, hourly; 12hr); Malang (hourly; 7hr); Pasuruan (5 hourly; 6hr); Probolinggo (5 hourly; 5hr); Situbondo (every 20min; 2–3hr); Solo (hourly; 11–13hr); Surabaya (every 30min; 5–7 hr); Yogyakarta (hourly; 12–14hr).

### GRAJAGAN: G-LAND

In the far southeastern corner of Java, the fishing village of **GRAJAGAN** has become famous for the world-class surf in Grajagan Bay, whose awesomely long left-handers, promising endless tubes and walls, are known as **G-Land**. A surf camp caters for surfers from April to October. Several tour operators on Bali and Lombok run all-inclusive trips. Prices start from US$300 for a six-night package at G-Land (see p.288). G-Land operators based in Kuta include Wanasari Wisata, Jl Pantai Kuta 8B (ⓣ0361/755588, ⓦwww.grajagan.com) and G-Land Surf Camp, Okie House, Poppies 2 (ⓣ0361/750320, ⓦwww.g-landsurfcamp.com).

# Sumatra

Although North Sumatra receives fewer tourists than it used to, there's plenty to see in the rugged central highlands, the homelands of the **Batak** who arrived over four thousand years ago and evolved almost completely in isolation from the rest of the island, developing languages and cultures that owe little to any outside influences.

The hill station of **Berastagi**, part of the Karo Batak territory, and the many waterside resorts around beautiful **Danau Toba** – Southeast Asia's largest lake and the spiritual home of the Toba Batak – throng with tourists every summer. The province also features the hugely popular orang-utan centre at **Bukit Lawang** – just a couple of hours' drive from the provincial capital of **Medan**, an entry point from Malaysia.

Getting around Sumatra on **public transport** can be gruelling – distances are huge, the roads tortuous and the driving hair-raising. There are plenty of road connections on to Java from even the smallest towns, but if you intend going by sea or air to make your trip less stressful, you'll need to plan carefully as only the large cities have airports, and ferry connections are generally irregular.

### MEDAN

**MEDAN**, Indonesia's fourth-largest city, occupies a strategic point on Sumatra's northeast coast and is a major entry point for boats and flights from Malaysia. It has acquired a reputation for being filthy and chaotic, but also holds some glorious examples of nineteenth-century colonial

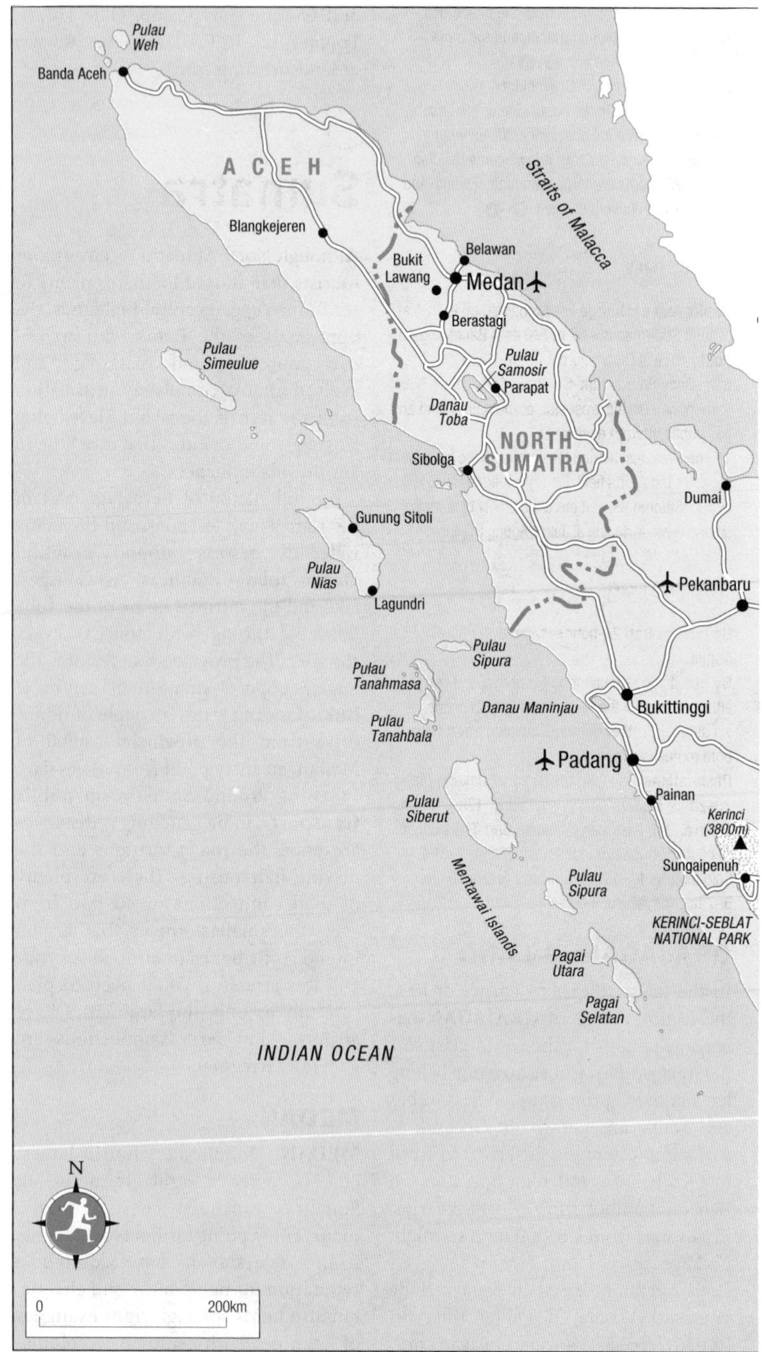
Pulau Weh
Banda Aceh
ACEH
Blangkejeren
Bukit Lawang
Belawan
Medan
Berastagi
Straits of Malacca
Pulau Simeulue
Pulau Samosir
Parapat
Danau Toba
NORTH SUMATRA
Sibolga
Dumai
Gunung Sitoli
Pulau Nias
Lagundri
Pekanbaru
Pulau Sipura
Pulau Tanahmasa
Pulau Tanahbala
Danau Maninjau
Bukittinggi
Padang
Painan
Pulau Siberut
Kerinci (3800m)
Sungaipenuh
Mentawai Islands
Pulau Sipura
KERINCI-SEBLAT NATIONAL PARK
Pagai Utara
Pagai Selatan
INDIAN OCEAN
N
0
200km

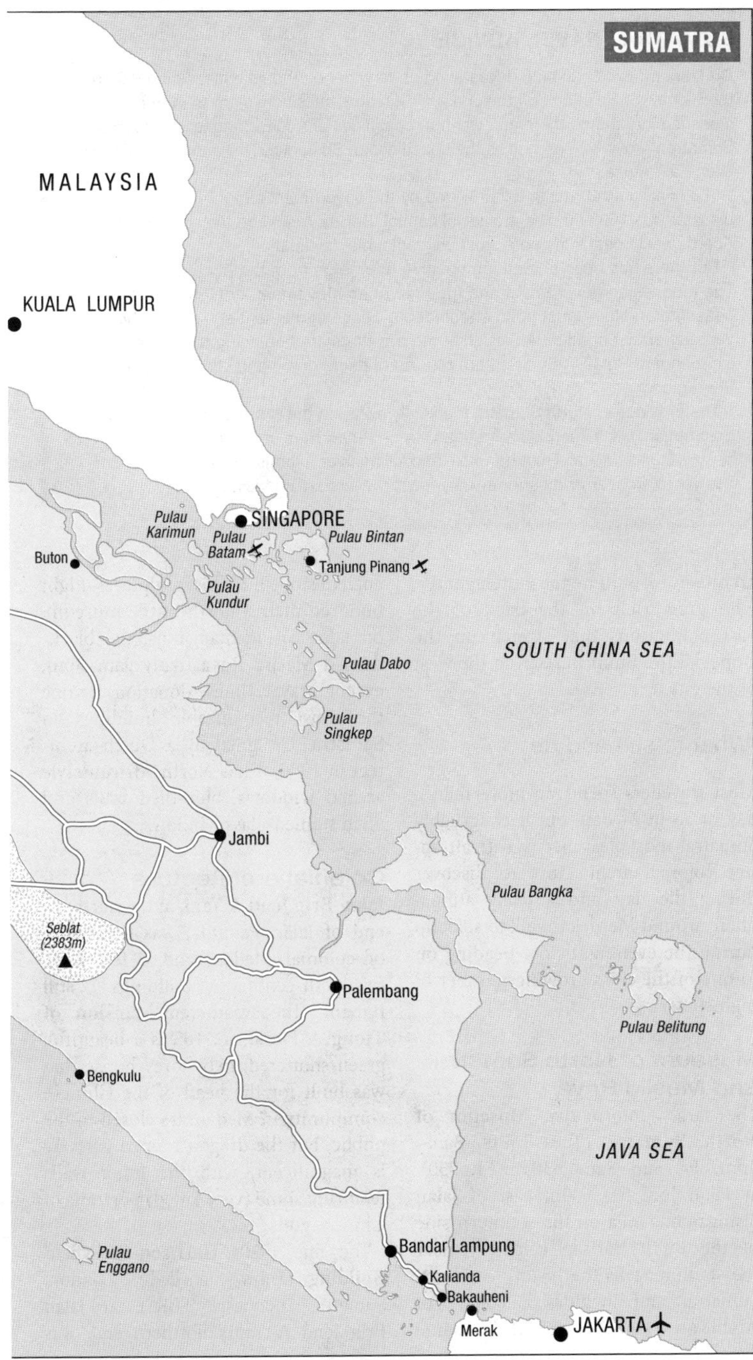
SUMATRA
MALAYSIA
KUALA LUMPUR
SINGAPORE
Pulau Karimun
Pulau Batam
Pulau Bintan
Buton
Tanjung Pinang
Pulau Kundur
SOUTH CHINA SEA
Pulau Dabo
Pulau Singkep
Jambi
Pulau Bangka
Seblat (2383m)
Palembang
Pulau Belitung
Bengkulu
JAVA SEA
Bandar Lampung
Pulau Enggano
Kalianda
Bakauheni
Merak
JAKARTA

## SUMATRA TRAVEL ADVICE

On **December 26, 2004**, a devastating underwater earthquake measuring 9.0 on the Richter Scale struck off the coast of Sumatra, causing a giant **tsunami** that smashed into the northern and western coastlines of Aceh – Indonesia's troubled Sumatran province – as well as the coastlines of Sri Lanka, Thailand, Malaysia and even East Africa.

The final "official" death toll provided by the government a month after the disaster was 166,000. The provincial capital, **Banda Aceh** and the villages on Aceh's west coast suffered almost unimaginable devastation.

But there has been something positive to emerge from the Aceh disaster. The Indonesian government and the Free Aceh Movement, or GAM, agreed a ceasefire and in August 2005 concluded a peace agreement ending the thirty-year separatist conflict. Although some travellers are beginning to venture back to Aceh and Pulau Weh, there are reports of rising crime and vigilante violence in the region.

The province of North Sumatra thankfully escaped the worst of the tsunami's destruction, but a second earthquake struck **Pulau Nias** on March 28, 2005, destroying its capital, Gunung Sitoli, and killing over a thousand people. Tourism has yet to recover, and currently very few travellers are choosing to visit.

architecture, built by the Dutch gentry, who grew rich on the back of the vast plantations that stretch up the slopes of the Bukit Barisan to the west of the city.

## What to see and do

Most travellers spend no more than a day or so in Medan, but it is agruably Sumatra's most pleasant city, with attractive colonial architecture to discover during the day, and a lively atmosphere around Merdeka Walk to soak up during the evening, before heading on to one of the city's growing number of nightspots.

### Museum of North Sumatra and Mesjid Raya

The large, informative **Museum of North Sumatra** (Tues–Thurs 8am–4pm, Fri–Sun 8am–3.30pm; Rp750), at Jalan Joni 51, 500m east of Jalan Sisingamangaraja on the southern side of the Bukit Barisan cemetery near the stadium, tells the history of North Sumatra, and includes a couple of Arabic gravestones from 8 AD and some ancient stone Buddhist sculptures. Eight hundred metres north of the museum, on Jalan Sisingamangaraja, the black-domed **Mesjid Raya** (daily 9am–5pm, except prayer times; donation) is one the most recognizable buildings in Sumatra. Designed by a Dutch architect in 1906, it has North African-style arched windows, blue-tiled walls and vivid stained-glass windows.

### Colonial architecture

**Jalan Brig Jend A Yani**, at the northern end of Jalan Pemuda, was the centre of colonial Medan, and a few early twentieth-century buildings still remain. The weathered **Mansion of Tjong A Fie** at no. 105 is a beautiful, green-shuttered, two-storey house that was built for the head of the Chinese community in Medan. It's closed to the public, but the dragon-topped gateway is magnificent, with the inner walls featuring some (very faded) portraits of Chinese gods.

The fine 1920s **Harrison-Crossfield Building** (now labelled "London, Sumatra, Indonesia TBK"), at Jalan Brig Jend A Yani's northern end, was

Indosat Telephone Office & Tanjung Belawan

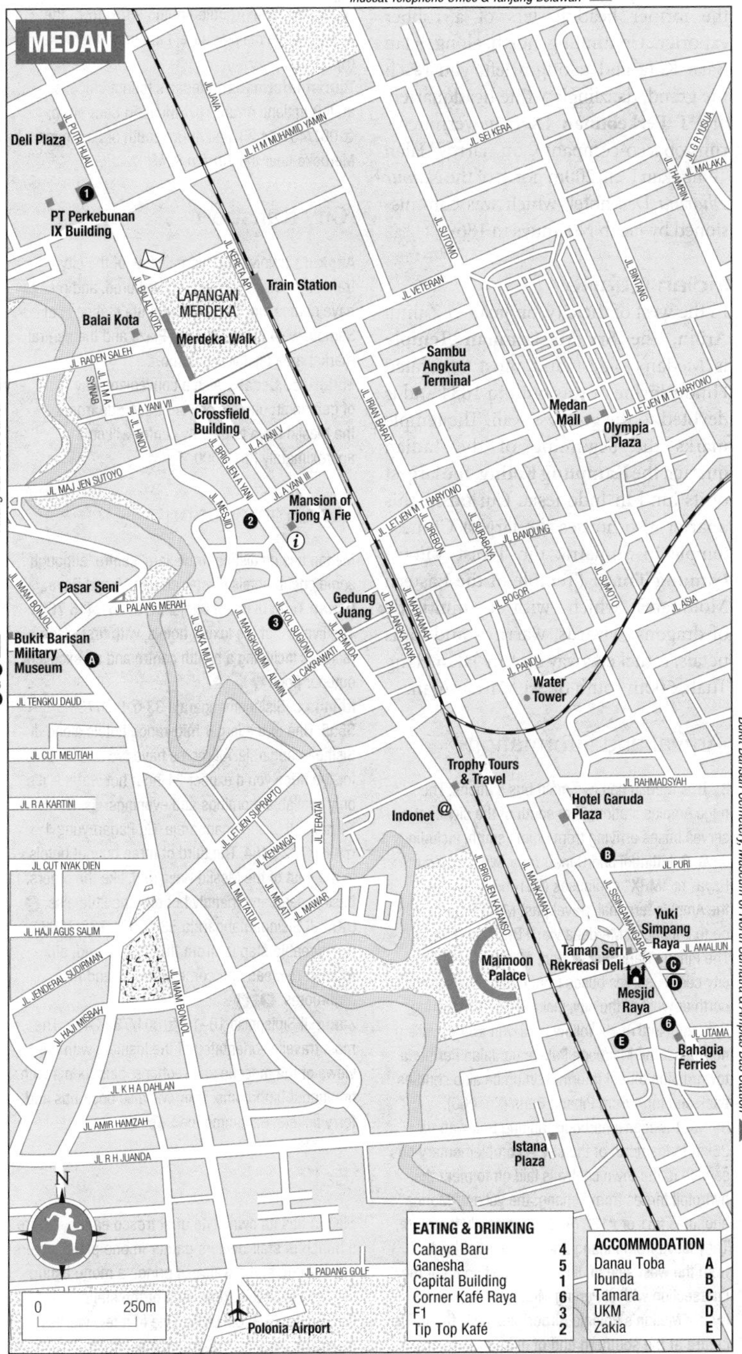
MEDAN
Deli Plaza
PT Perkebunan IX Building
Train Station
LAPANGAN MERDEKA
Balai Kota
Merdeka Walk
Sambu Angkuta Terminal
Harrison-Crossfield Building
Medan Mall
Olympia Plaza
Mansion of Tjong A Fie
Pasar Seni
Gedung Juang
Bukit Barisan Military Museum
Water Tower
Trophy Tours & Travel
Indonet
Hotel Garuda Plaza
Yuki Simpang Raya
Taman Seri Rekreasi Deli
Maimoon Palace
Mesjid Raya
Bahagia Ferries
Istana Plaza
Polonia Airport
Pinang Baris Bus Station
4 & 5
Bukit Barisan Cemetery, Museum of North Sumatra & Amplas Bus Station
0 250m
N
EATING & DRINKING
Cahaya Baru 4
Ganesha 5
Capital Building 1
Corner Kafé Raya 6
F1 3
Tip Top Kafé 2
ACCOMMODATION
Danau Toba A
Ibunda B
Tamara C
UKM D
Zakia E

the former headquarters of a rubber exporter. Continuing north along Jalan Balai Kota and taking a left, you reach the grand, dazzlingly white headquarters of **PT Perkebunan IX** (a government-run tobacco company), on narrow Jalan Tembakau Deli, 200m north of the *Natour Dharma Deli* hotel, which was commissioned by Jacob Nienhuys in 1869.

### Indian Quarter

In the west of the city, on Jalan H Zainul Arifin, the **Sri Mariamman Temple** is Medan's oldest and most venerated Hindu shrine. It was built in 1884 and is devoted to the goddess Kali. The temple marks the beginning of the Indian quarter, the **Kampung Keling**, the largest of its kind in Indonesia. Curiously, this quarter also houses the largest Chinese temple in Sumatra, the Taoist **Vihara Gunung Timur** (Temple of the Eastern Mountain), which, with its multitude of dragons, wizards, warriors and lotus petals, is tucked away on tiny Jalan Hang Tuah, 500m south of Sri Mariamman.

## Arrival and information

**By bus** Medan has two main bus stations. The huge Amplas station, 5km south of the city centre, serves buses arriving from points south, including Java, Bukittinggi and Danau Toba. White "Medan Raya" or "MRX" minibuses (Rp1000) leave from the Amplas terminal, travel past Mesjid Raya and on to Lapangan Merdeka via Jl Brig Jen A Yani. The Pinang Baris bus station, 10km west of the city centre, serves buses from destinations to the north or west of the city, including Bukit Lawang, Berastagi and Aceh. Yellow mini-van #64 travelling north past the Maimoon Palace up Jalan Permuda towards the tourist information office also shuttles back and forth from Pinang Baris (Rp1000).

**By boat** Medan's harbour, Tanjung Belawan, is 25km to the north of the city. A complementary bus service to the town centre is laid on to meet the hydrofoil ferries from Penang; the yellow "Morina" angkutas #81 or #122 (Rp2000) also ply the route. They leave from Pinang Baris bus station and from the west side of Jl Pemuda, just south of the intersection with Jl Perang Merah.

**By air** Medan's Polonia Airport lies near the town centre at the southern end of Jl Imam Bonjol. You'll have little trouble finding a taxi from the airport to the main square, Lapangan Merdeka (Rp35,000).

**Tourist information** Medan's tourist office is at Jl Brig Jend A Yani 107 (Mon–Fri 8am–4pm; ⓣ061/452 8436), just 400m south of Lapangan Merdeka near the *Tip Top Kafé*.

## City transport

**Angkuta** (minivans) The mainstay of the city transport network; they are numbered, and many have names too. The main angkuta station is at Sambu, west of the Olympia Plaza and the central market area on Jalan Sutomo.

**Motorized becaks** Also a convenient way of getting around the city centre. A ride from the Mesjid Raya to the city centre will cost approximately Rp10,000.

## Accommodation

Medan has no distinct travellers' centre, although some cheap hotels cluster around Mesjid Raya.

**Danau Toba** Jl Imam Bonjol 17 ⓣ061/415 7000. The liveliest of the luxury hotels, with first-class facilities including a health centre and an excellent outdoor pool. ❼

**Ibunda** Jl Sisingamangaraja 33 ⓣ061/734 5555. One of the larger mid-range hotels along Jl Sisingamangaraja. All rooms have a/c and TV, but for the price you'd expect 24-hour hot water – it's only available mornings and evenings. ❺

**Tamara** Jl Sisingamangaraja, Gg Pagaruyung 1 ⓣ061/732 2484. The third of three budget hotels to the east of the Mesjid Raya and, like the others, basic, cheap and friendly but offering little else. ❷

**UKM** Jl Sisingamangaraja 53 ⓣ061/736 7208. A noticeable step up from the bottom end, all rooms are clean and come with TVs and nice bathrooms. ❷–❸

**Zakia** Jl Sipisopiso 10–12 ⓣ061/732 2413. The most traveller-orientated of the losmen, with fine views of the mosque and rooftops, plus rooms with or without bathrooms. They will also book bus and ferry tickets. Recommended. ❶–❷

## Eating

Medan has its own style of al fresco eating, where a bunch of stall-owners gather in one place, chairs are put out, and a waitress brings a menu listing the food available from each of the stalls.

**Cahaya Baru** Jl Cik Ditiro. One of a few worthwhile places on the Indian quarter's main drag.

**Corner Café Raya** The closest thing Medan has to a travellers' café and is open 24 hours. Serves mainly western food, including English fry-up breakfasts, as well as jugs of Bintang for Rp65,000.
**Ganesha** Jl Cik Ditiro. Another good place in the Indian quarter, offering reasonable subcontinental cuisine.
**Merdeka Walk** Lapangan Merdeka. Medan's most popular evening eating spot – a new development with a lively ambience and a good selection of outdoor restaurants serving up mainly Indonesian food.
**Tip Top Kafé** Jl Brig Jen A Yani 92. Part restaurant, part Medan institution – this is a venerable old place that's been serving European and Indonesian food to Westerners and well-heeled locals for over eighty years. The large menu includes such "treats" as frog's legs, as well as an extensive selection of ice creams.

## Entertainment and nightlife

**Capital Building** Jl Putri Hijau 1A. There are several entertainment venues in this "exclusive" complex that's popular with affluent locals, including *Retro*, a pub, and *Classical*, a karaoke lounge with a pleasant bar, but some less salubrious private rooms. Follow the floodlights from Merdeka Walk.
**Deli Plaza** Jl Putri Hijau. Home to the city's best cinema.
**F1** Jl Kol Sugiono. Packed with clubbers on weekends, but deserted during the week, this disco plays thumping techno and is so dark you might consider bringing a torch.
**Tavern Pub** Jl Imam Bonjol 17. Part of the Danau Toba complex, this pub offers draught beer and live music.
**Yuki Simpang Raya** Jl Sisingamangaraja. A bowling alley (Rp6000 per game) and pool tables (Rp20000 per hour) are available in the basement of this shopping mall situated close to the travellers' hostels.

## Directory

**Airlines** Adam Airlines, Hotel Garuda Plaza Batavia, Jl S Parman Komplek Medan Bisnis Center A20 ☎061/453 7620; Bouraq, Jl Brig Jend Katamso 411 ☎061/455 2333; Cathay, Tiara Building, Jl Cut Mutiah ☎061/453 7008; Garuda, Jl S Monginsidi 34a (☎061/455 6777; includes city check-in), also at the *Natour Dharma Deli*, Jl Balai Kota (☎061/516 400), and the Tiara building, Jl Cut Mutiah ☎061/538527; Jatayu, Hotel Garuda Plaza, Jl Sisingamangaraja 18 ☎061/736 0888 and Jl Katamso 62a ☎061/452 8988; Lion Air, Hotel Garuda Plaza, Jl Sisingamangaraja 18 ☎061/735 1168; Mandala, Jl Brig Jend Katamso 37e ☎061/457 9100; MAS, *Hotel Danau Toba*, Jl Imam Bonjol 17 ☎061/451 9333; Merpati, Jl Brig Jend Katamso 72–122 ☎061/455 1888; Pelita, Polonia Airport ☎061/562241; Silk Air, Tiara Convention Centre, Jl Meutiah, ☎061/453 7744; SMAC, Jl Imam Bonjol 59 ☎061/564760.
**Banks** The BCA, at the corner of Jl Diponegoro and Jl H Zainul Arifin, offers by far the best rates in town, though it's only open for changing money between 10am and noon.
**Consulates** Australia, Jl Kartini No 32 ☎061/455780; Malaysia, Jl P Diponegoro 43 ☎061/453 1342; UK, Jl Kapt Pattimura 450 ☎061/8210 5259.
**Hospital** Dewi Maya Hospital, Jl Surakarta 2 ☎061/4574279.
**Internet** Try Indonet, Jl Brig Jen Katamso 32I, Nusanet in the basement of the Yuki Simpang Raya shopping plaza opposite the Mesjid Raya (Rp4000 per hr), or there's a Warposnet at the GPO on the northwest corner of Lapangan Merdeka (Mon–Sat 8am–11pm, Sun 8am–7pm). Free WiFi at the sports bar in the lobby of the *Hotel Garuda Plaza* on Jl Sisingamangaraja.
**Post office** Jl Balai Kota, on the northwest corner of Lapangan Merdeka (Mon–Fri 7.30am–8pm, Sat 7.30am–3pm). The poste restante is at counter 11.
**Telephones** Overseas calls from Indosat (7am–midnight), on Jl Jati at the intersection with Jl Thamrin (Rp2000–3000 by becak from the GPO). The *Tip Top Kafé* has a Home Country Direct telephone.

## Moving on

**By bus** Buses to points north and west of Medan (including Bukit Lawang and Aceh) depart from the Pinang Baris station (reached by angkuta "Koperasi" #64 heading west along Jl RH Jaunda or north along Jl Pemuda past the Maimoon Palace), while the Amplas station (reached by angkuta "Soedarko" #3 or #4 heading south along Jalan Palangka Raya) serves most other destinations with two important exceptions: travellers to Berastagi will find it much quicker to catch an angkuta to Padang Bulan (#60 or #41 from the Istana Plaza heading west on Jalan RH Juanda, or #10 heading north along Jl Pemuda), a lay-by in the southwestern corner of the city, from where buses (named Sinabung Jaya, Sutra and Karsima) leave every ten minutes. Travellers arriving from Bukit Lawang and heading to Berastagi can catch buses from Pinang Baris station, though invariably these stop in the lay-by at Padang Bulan, too.

**Destinations:** Banda Aceh (12hr); Berastagi (every 20min; 2hr); Bukit Lawang (every 20min until 6pm; 3hr); Bukittinggi (hourly; 18hr); Jakarta (hourly; 48hr); Kutacane (12 daily; 8hr); Padang (hourly; 20hr); Parapat (hourly, last at 6pm; 3hr); Sibolga (daily; 12hr).

**By boat** Medan's Tanjung Belawan serves ferries to Malaysia and other parts of Indonesia. There are currently two ferries sailing daily to Penang: the Perdana Expres and the Bahagia Expres. With both, transfer to the port from agencies such as Trophy Tours and Travel is free. The Pelni ship *KM Kelud* sails weekly to Jakarta via Batam. The main Pelni office is 7 to 8km from the centre on Jl Krakatau 17a (Ⓣ061/662 2526); most travellers buy tickets from one of the agents on Jl Pemuda, such as Trophy Tours and Travel at number 33d–e (Ⓣ061/415 5666). Tickets are a little more expensive from here but they do include a free shuttle to the docks. (Otherwise take yellow angkuta "Morina" #81 or #122 to the docks.)

**Destinations:** daily to Penang (4hr); Pulau Batam (18hr) and Jakarta (42hr).

**By air** to Banda Aceh (2 daily; 55min); Dumai (weekly; 1hr 25min); Gunung Sitoli (6 weekly; 1hr 10min); Jakarta (15 daily; 2hr 15min); Kuala Lumpur (17 daily; 1hr); Padang (3 daily; 1hr 10min); Pekanbaru (daily; 2hr); Penang (11 weekly; 40min); Pulau Batam (3 daily; 1hr 15min); Sibolga (6 weekly; 1hr); Singapore (2 daily; 1hr 30min).

## BUKIT LAWANG

The popular tourist resort of **BUKIT LAWANG**, tucked away on the easternmost fringes of the Gunung Leuser National Park, 78km north of Medan, is home to the **Orang-Utan Rehabilitation Centre**. On November 2, 2003, a flash-flood ripped through the heart of the resort leaving over two hundred dead, including five tourists. Although some hotels and restaurants have reopened, the devestating effects of the flood are still clearly visible along the eastern bank of the Sungai Bohorok.

### What to see and do

Despite its idyllic setting opposite the forest-clad slopes of Gunung Leuser, there's little to keep travellers in the town itself for more than a day or so. The main attractions are the **Orang-Utan Rehabilitation Centre** and the treks in the **Gunung Leuser National Park**.

### The Bohorok Orang-Utan Rehabilitation Centre

The reason for the existence of the tourist resort is the **Bukit Lawang Bohorok Orang-Utan Rehabilitation Centre**, founded in 1973 by two Swiss women, Monica Borner and Regina Frey, with the aim of returning captive and orphaned orang-utans into the wild, reteaching them the art of tree climbing and nest building before being freed into the nearby forest. Still under threat, the orang-utans should never be touched or fed by the public as this could spread disease and discourage their return to the wild – advice that is routinely disregarded by the "guides" who offer their services the moment you arrive at the bus terminal. For more information, take a look at Ⓦwww.orangutans-sos.org.

Since the flooding, the rehabilitation programme has been suspended, and though the centre is still open, it is more a tourist attraction than anything else. Visitors are allowed to watch the twice-daily (8.30am & 3.30pm), hour-long **feeding sessions** that take place on the hill behind the centre. All visitors must have a permit from the PHPA office (see opposite). The centre is reached by a small pulley-powered canoe that begins operating approximately one hour before feeding begins. All being well, you should see at least one orang-utan during the session, and to witness their gymnastics is to enjoy one of the most memorable experiences in Indonesia.

### Trekking

Bukit Lawang is the most popular base for organizing **treks** into the Gunung Leuser National Park, with plenty of guides based here. If you want only a short day-trek, a walk in the forest around Bukit Lawang is fine, and your chance of seeing monkeys, gibbons, macaques and, of course, orang-utans is very high. If you do decide to do a **long trek** from Bukit Lawang, the five- to seven-day walk to Ketambe is pleasant and passes through some excellent tracts of primary forest. Do check on the latest situation in Aceh, however, before attempting any trek of more than a couple of days. The three-day hike to Berastagi (see below) is also possible. You must have a **permit** (see below), for every day that you plan to spend in the park, and you must also have a **guide**, and should also be careful when choosing him. Guides supplied by the *Jungle Inn* have the best repuation. Fees are €15 for a three-hour trek, €25 for a day and €65 for three days, which should include a permit for the park. Whoever you decide to hire, they should never feed or touch the orang-utans. Make this clear before you set out.

### Tubing

**Tubing** – the art of sitting in the inflated inner tube of a tyre as it hurtles downstream, battered by the wild currents of the Bohorok – is popular though not without risk. The tubes can be rented from almost anywhere in Bukit Lawang for about Rp5000 per day, or your losmen may supply them for free. There is a bridge 12km downstream of the village, from where you can catch a bus back. If you're not a strong swimmer, consider tubing on a Sunday, when lifeguards are dotted along the more dangerous stretches of the river around Bukit Lawang.

### Arrival and information

**By bus** Buses from Medan's Pinang Baris bus station stop at the terminal, 1km from the Bohorok Visitor Centre. Motorized becaks travel the distance for Rp2000.

**Tourist information and permits** The permit office is part of the excellent Bohorok Visitor Centre (daily 8am–3pm), which is packed with information about the park. You can get a permit (Rp20,500 per day) to watch the feeding sessions at the orang-utan centre from the PHPA Permit Office (daily 7am–4pm), which overlooks the square to the east, by the visitor centre. Separate trekking permits (Rp4000 per day) are also available here.

### Accommodation and eating

Most of Bukit Lawang's restaurants are in the hotels. The exception is *Tony's Restaurant*, on the eastern shore of the river, which serves great pizzas, but the service is slow.

**Eco Lodge Bukit Lawang Cottages** ☎061/454 5061. Conveniently situated across a suspension bridge from the becak drop-off point, this resort is set in pleasant gardens and has clean rooms and a restaurant. The pricier "orang-utang" rooms have beautiful open-air bathrooms. Try bargaining. ❸

**Indra Inn** Small friendly place on the eastern shore of the river with basic rooms. The attached *Valley Café* is also popular. ❷

**Jungle Inn** ☎081375324015. Situated near the river crossing to the rehab centre, one of the few laid-back rough-and-ready places remaining, with great views from the higher rooms across the river to the forested hills. A good selection of rooms from the basic (❷) to the luxurious (❻).

**Rindu Alam Hotel and Restaurant** ☎061/882 2988. Characterless and expensive accomodation catering mainly for tours of Indonesian business people. ❻

### Moving on

You'll have to catch the bus back to **Medan's Pinang Baris station** for onward connections. The Medan buses start around 5am and are more or less half-hourly. Alternatively, it's possible to charter tourist minibuses to Berastagi. Bargain hard.

## BERASTAGI

Lying 1330m above sea level, 70km southwest of Medan and 25km due north of the shores of Danau Toba, **BERASTAGI** is a cold, compact little hill station in the centre of the Karo Highlands. It was founded by the Dutch in the 1920s as a retreat from the sweltering heat of Medan, and has been popular with tourists ever since. The town is set in a gorgeous bucolic landscape bookended

### THE KARO

Covering an area of almost five thousand square kilometres, from the northern tip of Danau Toba to the border of Aceh, the **Karo Highlands** comprise an extremely fertile volcanic plateau at the heart of the Bukit Barisan mountains. The plateau is home to over two hundred farming villages and two main towns: the regional capital, Kabanjahe, and the popular market town and tourist resort of **Berastagi**.

According to local legend, the Karo people were the first of the Batak groups to settle in the highlands of North Sumatra and, as with all Batak groups, the strongly patrilineal Karo have their own language, customs and rituals, most of which have survived, at least in a modified form, to this day. These include convoluted wedding and funeral ceremonies, both of which can go on for days, and the **reburial ceremony**, held every few years, where deceased relatives are exhumed and their bones are washed with a mixture of water and orange juice.

Today, over seventy percent of the Karo are Christian, fifteen percent Muslim and the rest adhere to the traditional Karo religion. Every member of Karonese society is bound by obligations to their clan, which are seen as more important than any religious duties.

by two huge but climbable **volcanoes**, Gunung Sibayak and Gunung Sinabung (see opposite), and provides a perfect base for **trekking**. It's little more than a one-street town, with nearly all accommodation running north of the bus station on Jalan Veteran.

## What to see and do

There are few attractions in the town itself, except for the three markets: the **general market**, which takes place five times a week (not Wed or Sun) behind the bus station; the daily **fruit market**, which also sells souvenirs, to the west of the roundabout, and the **Sunday market**, which takes place every other week on top of Gundaling Hill and attracts such novelty acts as the teeth-pulling man and the snake charmer. The hill also offers picturesque views of Gunung Sinabung.

### The Karo villages

During the Dutch invasion of 1904, most of the towns in the Karo Highlands were razed by the Karonese themselves to prevent the Dutch from appropriating them. But there are villages where you can still see the **traditional wooden houses** with their striking palm-frond gables.

The most accessible is **Peceren** (Rp1000 entrance fee), 2km northeast of Berastagi. Coming from the town, take the road to Medan and turn down the lane on your right after the *Rose Garden* hotel. There are six traditional houses here, but the village itself is probably the least picturesque. There are three more villages to the south of Berastagi, but many of the houses are slipping into a terrible state of repair. The first village, **Gurusinga**, lies about an hour due south of Berastagi. From the southern end of Jalan Veteran, take the road running southwest alongside the *Wisma Sibayak*. After about twenty minutes you'll come to a path by the "Expedisi C.V. Lakona" site. This path heads off through fields to Gurusinga, home to several traditional thatched longhouses. The path then continues to the village of **Lingga Tulu**. At the road at the end of the path, you can turn left and walk the 2km to the next village, **Lingga**, though flagging down a bemo is a better option. Finding a bemo heading back to Kabanjahe can be tricky so walk back to the main road and catch a **minibus** from there (last bus 5pm; Rp1000). From Kabanjahe, catch a bemo back to Berastagi (last bus 7pm; Rp1200).

## Arrival and information

**By bus** The bus station is at the southern end of Jl Veteran.

**Tourist information** The tourist office (Mon–Sat 8am–5pm) is just over the road from the post office but the information at the losmen is better.

## Accommodation

**Ginsata** Jl Veteran 27 ⓣ0628/91441. Quiet, unfussy hotel overlooking the main roundabout that's good if you want solitude. Rooms are basic and overpriced, though there's cheaper accommodation available in the cottage behind the hotel. ❶

**Losmen Sibayak** Jl Veteran 119 ⓣ0628/91095 or 91122. Younger sister of the Wisma Sibayak, under the same management but with a few added features such as a book exchange, Pelni ticket office, numerous tours, and a pizza restaurant. ❶

**Sibayak Multinational Guest House** Jl Pendidikan 93 ⓣ0628/91031. Yet another branch of the Sibayak chain, set in its own gardens to the north of town on the way to Sibayak. Even the cheapest rooms come with their own terrace and a hot shower; rooms in the old 1930s Dutch section of the house are larger and cost more. ❶–❷

**Wisma Sibayak** Jl Udara 1 ⓣ0628/91104. One of Sumatra's best and longest-established hostels: the walls are smothered with good information (though some is a little dated), the travellers' comments books are very useful, and the beds are clean. ❶

## Eating

There are few restaurants in Berastagi except for a handful of no-nonsense Chinese eateries on Jl Veteran. Several street stalls selling *ikan goreng*, or fried fish, spring up along Jl Veteran during the evening, and the hotels all have restaurants.

**Eropa** Jl Veteran. Situated on the western side of the street, this is the best of the mainly non-descript Chinese restaurants.

**Gundaling Restaurant** Sibayak Internasional Jl Merdeka. The restaurant at this luxury hotel serves reasonable Western and Indonesian dishes but is expensive.

**Losmen Sibayak** Jl Veteran 119. This hostel, as well as its two sister hostels, Wisma Sibayak and Sibayak Multinational, serve delicious pizzas and other traveller favourites.

## Directory

**Banks** The BNI bank, with ATM, is on Jl Veteran, and you can change US dollars and traveller's cheques at *Losmen Sibayak*.

**Pharmacy** There's a health centre on Jl Veteran, past the traffic police post.

**Police** The police office is situated by the war memorial, just of Jl Veteran.

**Post office** The post office (Mon–Thurs 7.30am–3pm, Fri 7.30–noon, Sat 7.30am–1pm) is next to the police station. The Telekom office is also here.

## Moving on

**By bus** Buses to Medan (frequent; 3hr) leave from the bus station at the southern end of Jl Veteran, while minibuses to the Karo villages leave from outside the *Wisma Sibayak* heading south down Jl Udara.

To get to **Danau Toba**, either take the *Losmen Sibayak*'s direct tourist bus – if you are a large enough group to make it worth their while – or three minivans (starting at 8am) from the road next to and just east of the Wisma Sibayak. The first van gets you to Kabenjahe (15min), the second – called either "Simas" or "Sepedan" – to Pematangsiantar, usually just called Siantar (3hr) and the third to the jetty at Parapat (1hr).

# VOLCANOES AROUND BERASTAGI

There are two active volcanoes more than 2000m high in the immediate vicinity around Berastagi: **Sibayak**, to the north of town, is possibly the most accessible volcano in the whole of Indonesia, and takes just four hours to climb up and three hours down, while the hike up **Sinabung**, to the southwest of town, is longer and tougher and involves an hour by car to the trailhead. The lists of missing trekkers plastered all around Berastagi prove that these climbs are not as straightforward as they may at first seem. The tourist office urges climbers always to take a guide – which you can hire from them or from your losmen – though for Sibayak a guide is unnecessary providing you're climbing with someone else and the visibility is good.

For both volcanoes, set off early in the morning. It's a good idea to take some food, too, particularly bananas and chocolate for energy, and warm clothing, and if you're looking to take advantage of the hot springs at the foot of Sibayak, your swimming costume and a towel, too. *Losmen Sibayak* offers various guided treks to both peaks.

### Gunung Sibayak

Before attempting your assault of **Sibayak** (2094m), pick up one of the *Wisma Sibayak*'s maps. Walk to *Sibayak Multinational Guest House* and continue along the road until you reach a large arch. Next to this arch is a café where you register your name and pay the hiking fee of Rp1500. From here, walk past the bemo station and you'll begin the series of up-and-down dips that leads to the summit. Near the top, look out for some rough steps cut into the embankment on your left. If you reach the end of the tarmac, you've gone too far.

Finding the path back down to the hot springs is the hardest part of the walk (if you're not certain of the way down, walk back down the way you came up). For those who wish to visit the hot springs, however, at the crater rim you'll see a cluster of antennae high up on a pinnacle. Facing the antennae, walk anticlockwise to about 3 o'clock and climb up to your right from there. At the top you'll see a path running along the rim. Turn right, and after about 50m you'll come to the first couple of broken steps – little more than concrete strips in the ground at this stage. As you follow the steps, you'll enter into a forest, pass through a grove of bamboo, before emerging at a geothermal plant. Below this is a series of **hot springs** (Rp2000) – a great reward for a hard trek. Afterwards, bemos leave occasionally for Berastagi (Rp2500); otherwise, you'll have to continue along the road for several kilometres to the junction with the main road and pick one up from there (Rp1000).

### Gunung Sinabung

Take a taxi to tiny **Danau Kawar** (1hr), where the path begins by the side of a restaurant to the north of the water, and continues through cabbage fields for approximately an hour, before entering fairly thick jungle. The walk becomes relentlessly tough soon after; having left the jungle you soon find yourself scrambling up some steep and treacherous rocky gullies. A couple of hours later, you'll be standing on the edge of a cliff looking down into **Gunung Sinabung**'s two craters. Take care when walking around up here, as the paths are crumbling and it's a long way down.

## PARAPAT

Situated at the point where the Trans-Sumatran Highway touches the eastern shore of lake Danau Toba (see opposite), **PARAPAT** is a town split in two. There's the **resort**, crammed with hotels and souvenir shops and, set on the hills away from the lake, the bus station, bank and telephone office. The main reason for visiting is to catch a ferry to the island of Samosir.

### Arrival

**By bus** Buses arriving in Parapat drive through the resort to Tigaraja harbour before heading back to the bus station. You can get a minivan to and from the bus station at any time for Rp1000.

### Accommodation

With over sixty hotels in Parapat, there's plenty of accommodation to choose from, though only a few fairly grotty places at the budget end of the market.

**Atsari Hotel & Bungalow** Jl Pulau Samosir 9 ☎0625/41219. One of Parapat's better value mid-range options. A good selection of rooms some with a/c and hot water. Will offer discounts. ❹

**Charley's** Jl Pekan Tiga Raja ☎0625/41277. Situated on the market square next to the ferry terminal, *Charley's* has a selection of cell-like rooms. ❶

**Hotel Riris** Jl Haranggaol 43 ☎0625/41392. Central location with some character but the cheapest rooms are probably best avoided. Even the more expensive rooms could do with a clean. ❷

**Inna Parapat** Jl Marihat 1 ☎0625/41012. One of Parapat's oldest hotels. All rooms come with hot water though a/c is only available in the deluxe rooms. Overpriced, and mainly aimed at Indonesian business parties. ❼

## Eating

For a tourist resort, there are surprisingly few restaurants in Parapat outside of the hotels, which tend to serve unremarkable food.

**Hong Kong** Jl Haranggaol 9–11. Good-value Chinese restaurant set back from the main road, with a selection of imported beers.

**Mariana** Jl Haranggaol 48. One of the many Padang-style Rumah Makan but with a more extensive selection than the rest, including great *beef rendang*. Also serves beer.

**Mitudo Café** Jl Pulau Samosir. Pleasant spot for a drink but dining options are fairly limited.

## Directory

**Banks** There's a Bank BNI ATM on Jl Sisingamangaraja. Bemos will drop you there from the ferry terminal (Rp2000).

**Pharmacies** Tobafarma, two doors down from *Hong Kong* restaurant on Jl Haranggaol, supplies basic medicines.

**Post office** Jl Sisingamangaraja, opposite the BNI ATM.

**Telecom** On the back road between the bus station and the quay; fifty percent cheaper than from Samosir.

**Travel agents** There are plenty of travel agents selling tickets for tourist minibuses to Medan (Rp60,000) and other destinations. Tickets purchased in Parapat are cheaper than those sold on Pulau Samosir.

## Moving on

**By bus** Berastagi, via Kabanjahe and Pematangsiantar (daily; 6hr); Bukittinggi (14hr); Jakarta (3 daily; 43hr); Medan (10 daily; 3hr); Padang (3 daily; 16hr); Sibolga (daily; 6hr).

**By ferry** Regularly to Tuk Tuk on Samosir Island (hourly 9.30am–7.30pm; 30min), and also Ambarita (hourly 8.45am–6.45pm; 45min).

# DANAU TOBA AND PULAU SAMOSIR

Lying right in the middle of the province, jewel-like **Danau Toba** is Southeast Asia's largest freshwater lake, and at 525m possibly the world's deepest, too. It was formed about 80,000 years ago by a colossal volcanic eruption: the caldera that was created eventually buckled under the pressure and collapsed in on itself, the high-sided basin that remained filling with water to form the lake. A second, smaller volcanic eruption, 50,000 years after the first, created an island the size of Singapore in the middle of the lake. This island, **Pulau Samosir**, is the cultural and spiritual heartland of the Toba Batak people and one of the most fascinating, pleasant and laid-back spots in Indonesia.

## What to see and do

Pulau Samosir is a pleasant place to relax for a few days amid stunningly beautiful scenary. Most tourists make for the eastern shores of Samosir where there's a string of enjoyable resorts, the main one being Tuk Tuk, where there are plenty of restaurants and bars. From here you can go trekking in the deforested hills in the centre of Samosir, or cycle or motorbike around the coastline, calling in at the tiny Batak villages with their flamboyant tombs and distinctive concave-roofed houses, and the island's cultural centre of **Simanindo**, on Samosir's northern shore.

### Tuk Tuk

The waters that lap the shores of **Tuk Tuk** are safe for **swimming**; the roped-off section of the lake by *Carolina's*, complete with pontoons, canoes and a diving board, is the most popular place. There are also a few activities on offer in Tuk Tuk, including cruises around Samosir (Rp80,000),

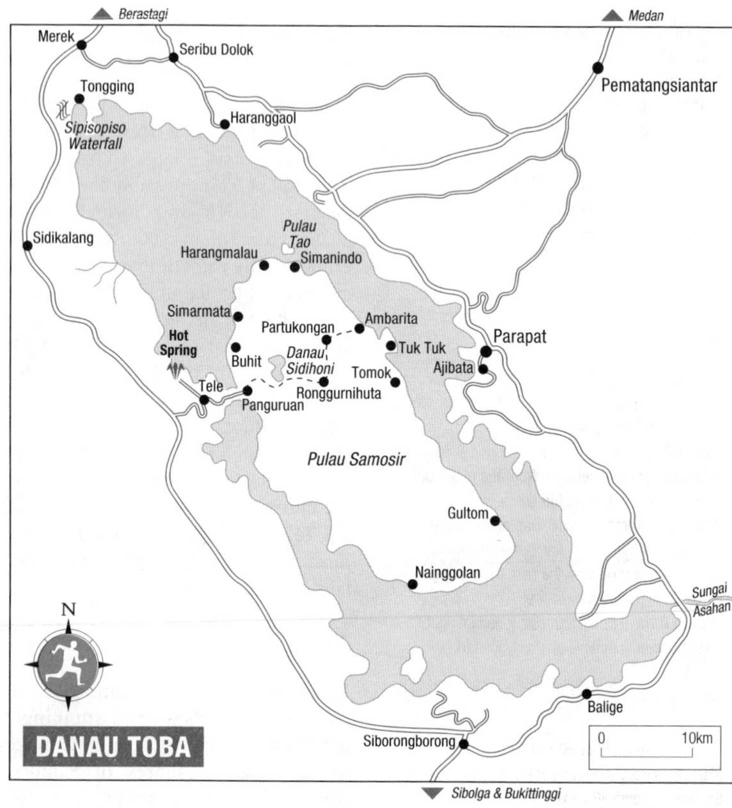


speedboat trips (Rp700,000 for half a day, or Rp210,000 per hour). You can also rent **bicycles** (Rp20,000 per day) and **motorbikes** (Rp70,000 per day including petrol), should you want to visit the more far-flung reaches of the island, which will allow you to visit Simalungun and the **hot springs** at Tele on the western side.

### Tomok

**Tomok**, 2km south of Tuk Tuk, is the most southerly of the resorts on the east coast; dozens of virtually identical souvenir stalls line the main street. Tomok's most famous sight is the early nineteenth-century stone **sarcophagus of Raja Sidabutar**, the chief of the first tribe to migrate to the island. The coffin has a Singa face – a part-elephant, part-buffalo creature of Toban legend – carved into one end, and a small stone effigy of the king's wife on top of the lid. On the way to Ambarita from Tomok, due west of Tuk Tuk, is the tiny village of **Garoga**, from where you can hike to the waterfall of the same name (after rainfall). Ask the locals for directions.

### Ambarita

In **Ambarita** there is a curious collection of stone chairs (daily 7am–5pm; Rp2000), one of which is mysteriously occupied by a stone statue. Most of the villagers will tell you that these chairs acted as the local law courts two hundred years ago; others say that the chairs are actually less than fifty years old, and the work of a local mason who copied drawings of the original.

### Simanindo

**Simanindo** lies at the northern end of the island, 15km beyond the town of Ambarita. The **Simanindo Museum** (daily 12.30–5pm; Rp5000) is housed in the former house of Raja Simalungun, and has some mildly diverting household implements, including spears, magical charms and a wooden *guri guri* (ashes urn). The large *adat* houses in the **traditional village**, through the stone archway, are unexceptional save for their thatched roofs – a rarity on Samosir. The museum and village also hold traditional Batak dancing performances every morning (10.30–11.10am at the museum, 11.45am–12.30pm in the village).

### Simarmata and Pangururan

Continuing round to the western side of the island, **Simarmata**, halfway between Simanindo and Pangururan, is one of the best-preserved Batak villages on Samosir. There's little to see in **Pangururan** itself, though there's a **hot spring** (Rp2000) across the bridge in the village of **Tele**.

### Trekking across Samosir

The hills in the centre of Samosir tower 700m above the lake, and at the heart of the island is a large plateau and **Danau Sidihoni**, a body of water about the size of a large village pond. It's a ten-hour walk from one side of the island to the other, but a stopover in one of the villages on the plateau is usually necessary. Most begin in Ambarita on the eastern shore, on the uphill path, from where it's two to three hours' climb to the tiny hilltop village of **Partukongan** – aka Dolok or "summit" – the highest point on Samosir. There are two homestays here, *John's* and *Jenny's*, and three losmen in the next village on the trail, **Ronggurnihuta**. The villagers can be a bit vague when giving directions, so take care and check frequently with passers-by that you're on the right trail. Ronggurnihuta is a three- or four-hour walk away, with **Pangururan** three to fours hours further on at the end of a torturously long downhill track (18km) that passes **Danau Sidihoni** on the way. Arrive in Pangururan before 5pm and you should be in time to catch the last bus back to the eastern shore; otherwise, stay at the *Wartel Wisata* (☎0626/20558; ❶) at Jl Dr TB Simatupang 42 by the bus stop.

#### TRAVEL TO AND FROM DANAU TOBA

Most tourists catch a ferry (ask to be dropped at your specific guesthouse) from the Tigaraja harbour in the resort of Parapat; there are ferries every hour during the day to Tuk Tuk, with the last at around 7.30pm, returning 8am–5pm (Rp7000 one way), often – but not always – calling in at the other ferry ports on the peninsula before they do so. There is still the five-times-a-day car ferry service from Tomok to Ajibata, south of Parapat.

## Accommodation

All accommodation is found on the Tuk Tuk peninsular. Over thirty losmen and hotels, numerous restaurants, bars, bookshops, travel agents and souvenir stalls stand cheek-by-jowl. Tell the ferryman which hotel you're going to and he'll drop you off at the nearest quay.

**Bagus Bay Homestay** ☎0625/451287. One of the finer budget options on Tuk Tuk, with excellent facilities, including a pool table, internet café, bike rental, badminton court, board games, bar, videos three times a night and a twice-weekly Batak dancing display, and a large menu. ❷–❸

**Carolina's** ☎0625/41520. Classy Batak-style bungalows, each with a lakeside view and their own little section of beach. The luxury rooms with fridge, hot water and TV are among the best on the island, but the cheaper rooms are poor value. ❶–❸

**Libertas** ☎0625/451035. Six smart, traditional-style bungalows, good facilities and a limited but varied menu of superb and enormous food, all cooked by the likeable and honest manager, Mr Moon. ❶–❷

**Romlan's** ☎0625/41557. Good value – if slightly scruffy – little guesthouse with some of the cheapest traditional bungalows on the island, many overlooking the water to Parapat. It's hard to find: turn down the track signposted to the Sumber Pulomas hotel, then take a right on the small grassy path leading to the reception. ❶

**Samosir Cottages** ☎0625/41050. The most popular traveller-orientated place on the peninsula, with rooms ranging from the basic to luxury bungalows (complete with hot water and a bathtub) overlooking the lake. Has a good restaurant, Internet access, satellite TV and a pool table. Recommended. ❶–❸

**Tabo Cottages** ☎0625/451318, Ⓦwww.tabo-cottages.com. The best mid-range option on the peninsular, attractive and efficiently run with a wide range of facilities. Rooms range from the comfy to the exquisite, with the best of them coming with a veranda and hammock; the food conjured up in the restaurant and bakery is terrific, too. Also provides helpful island maps. ❷–❺

## Directory

**Banks** None of the banks change money, but guesthouses and a handful of moneychanging shops often will.

**Internet** Many places offer internet, though at hugely inflated prices (usually Rp20,000–25,000 per hour); the quickest connection by far is *Bagus Bay Homestay*.

**Massage** The Sunshine Beauty and Wellness Studio at Tuk Tuk (☎081375748172) includes massage (Rp40,000) amongst its range of services.

**Telephone** There are many wartels where you can make (expensive) international calls.

**Tours** Many of the guesthouses, in particular *Bagus Bay Homestay* and *Tabo*, have their own travel agencies, which can book transport and tours.

# PADANG

A bustling port and university town, attractive **PADANG** is an important transport hub and famed throughout Indonesia for its spicy local cuisine, **Makanan Padang** (Padang food). Its climate is equally extreme: hot and humid and with the highest rainfall in Indonesia at 4508mm a year. Most tourists pause only briefly here, before aiming for the nearby hill town of Bukittinggi or the Mentawai Islands. The city's main sight is the very pleasant **Adityawarman Museum** (Tues–Sun 8.30am–4pm; Rp1500), housed in a traditional Minang house on Jalan Bundo Kandung and specializing in Minangkabau culture, with textiles, kris and finely worked basketware. For a good local shopping experience, ignore the large shopping centres and head instead for Pasar Raya in the city centre, a terrific general **market**. Bungus Beach, south of Padang, was once a popular tourist destination, but the hotels there are now derelict.

## Arrival and information

**By bus** The local bus terminal has moved to Aie Pacah, 10km east of the city, but few of the bus firms have actually adopted the new terminal as their home, leading to a rather confusing situation as to where exactly the buses arrive. Generally all buses stop at Minang Plaza, from where it's possible to catch an oplet (Rp2000) into the town centre.

**By boat** Pelni boats arrive at the port of Teluk Bayur, 7km south of town, from where you can take a oplet to the city centre. Pelni currently connect Padang with Pulau Nias and Jakarta.

**By air** Padang is a visa-free entry point to Indonesia. Tabing Airport is 9km north of the city centre. The bank and moneychangers are located at the front of the international arrivals building, and there's a taxi ticket office – collect the fixed-price ticket from the office and pay the driver on arrival (prices within the city are around Rp50,000). Out on the main road (200m walk from the terminal), buses #14a and #14b (Rp1000) stop just outside the airport gates: those heading to the left go into the city. Small white bemos (called "oplets" in Padang) also stop here bound for the oplet terminal in town for Rp2000.

**Tourist information** Jl Samudra 1 ☎0751/34186 (Mon–Fri 7.30am–4pm). Helpful English-speaking staff and a range of brochures.

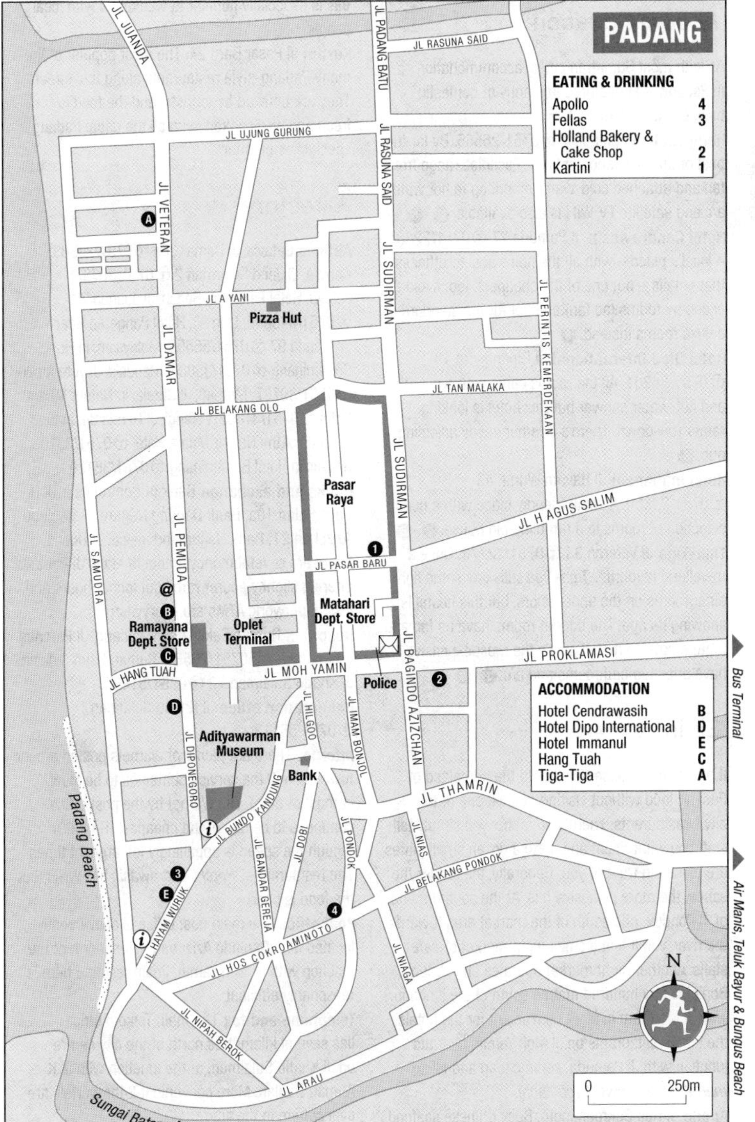


## City transport

Padang is quite compact and easy to negotiate by public transport, the exception being Pelabuhan Muara in the district of Batau Arau, for which you'll have to walk or grab a taxi.

**Buses and oplets (bemo)** Local buses (Rp2000) and oplets (Rp2000) run from 6am to 10pm. The oplet terminal is on Jl Moh Yamin, in the market area. Look out for the route number and destination signs suspended high above the oplet waiting area.

## Accommodation

As with most Sumatran cities, accommodation in Padang is aimed predominantly at domestic business travellers.

**Hang Tuah** Jl Pemuda 1 ☎0751/26556. By far the best of the mid-range options. Facilities range from fan and attached cold-water mandi up to hot water, a/c and satellite TV. WiFi is also available. ❷–❺

**Hotel Cendrawasih** Jl Pemuda 27 ☎0751/22894. A local's place – with all the noise and scruffiness that entails – but one of the cheapest, too. Avoid the economy rooms (no fan) and opt for the standard or deluxe rooms instead. ❷

**Hotel Dipo International** Jl Diponegoro 13 ☎0751/34261. All the rooms come with a/c, bath and hot-water shower but this hotel is looking rather run-down. There's a rather seedy adjoining pub. ❻

**Hotel Immanuel** Jl Hayam Wuruk 43 ☎0751/28560. A small friendly place with a good selection of rooms in a rambling old house. ❷–❻

**Tiga-Tiga** Jl Veteran 33 ☎0751/22173. Once a travellers' favourite, *Tiga-Tiga* stills has some light, airier rooms on the upper floors, but this hostel is showing its age. The budget rooms have no fan and feature outside mandi, while the most expensive have attached bathrooms and a/c. ❷–❸

## Eating

It makes little sense to come to the homeland of Padang food without visiting at least one of the city's restaurants. There's no menu: you simply tell staff you want to eat and up to a dozen small plates are placed in front of you. Generally, the redder the sauce, the more explosive it is. At the southern end of Jl Pondok, due south of the market area towards the river, you'll find a small night market of *sate* stalls. Another night market operates on Jl Imam Bonjol, a few hundred metres south of the junction with Jl Moh Yamin. More convenient for the hotels, the small restaurants on Jl Moh Yamin, near the junction with Jl Pemuda, serve cheap and filling *martabaks* and sweet *roti canai*.

**Apollo** Jl Hos Cokroaminoto. Busy Chinese seafood place, which fills up fast with locals at night, so come early.

**Fellas Resto** Jl Hayam Waruk 47. By far the best place in town for a beer. Live bands play to punters seated at outdoor tables and chairs. Also an extensive Japanese food menu. Remember to bring mosquito repellent. Open 4pm till late.

**Holland Bakery and Cake Shop** Jl Proklamasi 61b. With a good choice of cakes and sweet breads, this is especially popular at weekends with local people.

**Kartini** Jl Pasar Baru 24. The most popular of the many Padang-style restaurants along this street. They are unfazed by tourists, and the food is fresh and well cooked, with all the usual Padang specialities on offer.

## Directory

**Airlines** Batavia, Jl Damar 36a ☎0751/28383; Garuda, Jl Jend Sudirman 2 ☎0751/30737; Jatayu, Hotel Pangeran Beach, Jl Juanda 79 ☎0751/446890; Lion Air, Hotel Pangeran Beach, Jl Juanda 97 ☎0751/55555; Malaysian, in Hotel Bumiminang ☎0751/35888; Mandala, Jl Veteran 20C ☎0751/39737; Merpati, Jl Gereja, in Natour Muara Hotel ☎0751/31852; Pelangi, Jl Gereja 34, in the grounds of the Natour Muara Hotel ☎0751/38103; Silk Air, in Hotel Bumiminang ☎0751/38120.

**Banks and exchange** Bank of Central Asia, Jl H Agus Salim 10a; Bank Dagang Negara, Jl Bagindo Azizchan 21; Bank Negara Indonesia, Jl Dobi 1. There are several moneychangers along Jl Pemuda offering slightly poorer rates but longer hours and less paperwork. ATMs are everywhere.

**Hospitals** Rumah Sakit Umum Padang, Jl Perentis Kemerdekan ☎0751/26585; Rumah Sakit Selasih, Jl Khatib Sulaiman 72 ☎0751/51405.

**Immigration office** Jl Khatib Sulaiman ☎0751/55113.

**Internet** There are plenty of warnets posted around town, though the service continues to be slow in most of them. The Warnet by the post office continues to be one of the cheapest (Rp4000) though the speed is appallingly lethargic at times. The restaurant at *Hotel Cendrawasih* has Wi-Fi (but the food is poor).

**Post office** The main post office is conveniently located at Jl Bagindo Azizchan 7, just north of the junction with Jl Moh Yamin. Poste restante here is reasonably efficient.

**Telephone and fax** The main Telkom office lies several kilometres north of the city centre on Jl Khatib Sulaiman, at the junction with Jl K Ahmad Dahlan. More convenient 24hr wartels are everywhere in the city.

## Moving on

**By bus** Because few bus firms have adopted the Aie Pacah terminal, it's easier for travellers heading to Bukittinggi to catch a white oplet heading north along Jl Pemuda to the Minang Plaza, opposite from which you can catch a Kijang jeep – or "Travel" in the local parlance – to Bukittinggi

(Rp10,000). Similarly, those heading south should also head to the Minang Plaza, from where the Jakarta buses leave. Ask your hotel for the latest details. Alternatively, head to the travel agents on Jl Pemuda, north of the Ramayana Department Store, who sell minibus tickets to most destinations.

**Destinations:** Banda Aceh (4 daily; 30hr); Bandar Lampung (10 daily; 25hr); Bukittinggi (every 20min; 2hr 30min); Jakarta (10 daily; 30–35hr); Medan (10 daily; 20hr); Pekanbaru (10 daily; 8hr); Prapat (10 daily; 18hr); Sibolga (4 daily; 18hr).

**By boat** Blue oplets #432, #433 and #434 run to the harbour of Teluk Bayur.

The Pelni ticket office is at Jl Tanjung Priok 32 in Teluk Bayur (☎0751/61624).

**Destinations:** fortnightly to Balikpapan (4 days); Makassar (3 days); Nias (9–20hr); Sibolga (13hr–16hr); Surabaya (48hr); Tanjung Priok (30hr).

**By air** White oplets run north from Jl Pemuda out to Minang Plaza and towards the airport.

**Destinations:** Bandung (daily; 2hr–3hr 30min); Jakarta (4 daily; 45min); Medan (1–2 daily; 1hr 10min); Pekanbaru (3 weekly; 50min); Pulau Batam (daily; 1hr).

## BUKITTINGGI

Situated on the eastern edge of the Ngarai Sianok Canyon and with the mountains of Merapi and Singgalang rising to the south, **Bukittinggi** spreads for several kilometres in each direction. However, the central part of town, which is of most interest to visitors, is relatively compact and easy to negotiate. The most useful **landmark** is the clock tower at the junction of Jalan A Yani (the main thoroughfare) and Jalan Sudirman (the main road leading out of town to the south). Due north of the tower is the enormous **market**, the biggest in Sumatra, which swells to bursting point on Wednesdays and Saturdays. Jalan A Yani, 1km from north to south, is the tourist hub of Bukittinggi, and most of the sights, hotels, restaurants and shops that serve the tourist trade are on this street or close by. The surrounding area holds plenty of attractions, including craft villages, the rafflesia reserve at Batang Paluh, the beautiful Ngarai Sianok Canyon, and some fine examples of Minang culture.

### What to see and do

A few hundred metres to the north of the clock tower, **Fort de Kock** (daily 7.30am–6pm; Rp8000) was built by the Dutch in 1825 and is linked by a footbridge to the park, Taman Bundo Kanduang, on the hill on the other side of Jalan A Yani; there's little left of the original fort but some old cannons and parts of the moats. From here you can see Gunung Merapi, on the left, and the much more dramatic cone-shaped Gunung Singgalang to the right. The park's **museum** (Rp1000) is housed in a traditional *rumah gadang*, and features clothing, musical instruments, textiles, models of traditional houses, and stuffed freaks of nature,

### THE MINANG HIGHLANDS

The gorgeous mountainous landscape of the **Minang Highlands** features soaring rice terraces and easily accessible traditional culture. The highlands consist of three large valleys, with **Bukittinggi**, a bustling hill town, the administrative and commercial centre of the whole district. Located to the west of the main highland area, **Danau Maninjau** is an appealing destination.

The highlands around Bukittinggi are the cultural heartland of the **Minangkabau** (Minang) people. The Minang are staunchly matrilineal, one of the largest such societies extant, and Muslim. The most visible aspect of their culture is the distinctive architecture of their homes, with massive roofs soaring skywards at either end (to represent the horns of a buffalo). Typically, three or four generations of one family would live in one large house built on stilts, the *rumah gadang* (big house) or *rumah adat* (traditional house), a wood-and-thatch structure often decorated with fabulous wooden carvings.

including a two-headed buffalo and an eight-legged goat. Surrounding it is the inhumane zoo.

Much more pleasant is a trip to **Panorama Park** (daily 7am–7pm; Rp4000), perched on a lip of land overlooking the sheer cliff walls down into Ngarai Sianok Canyon, the best Bukittinggi sight by far. Beneath the park stretch 1400m of Japanese **tunnels** and rooms built with local slave labour during World War II as

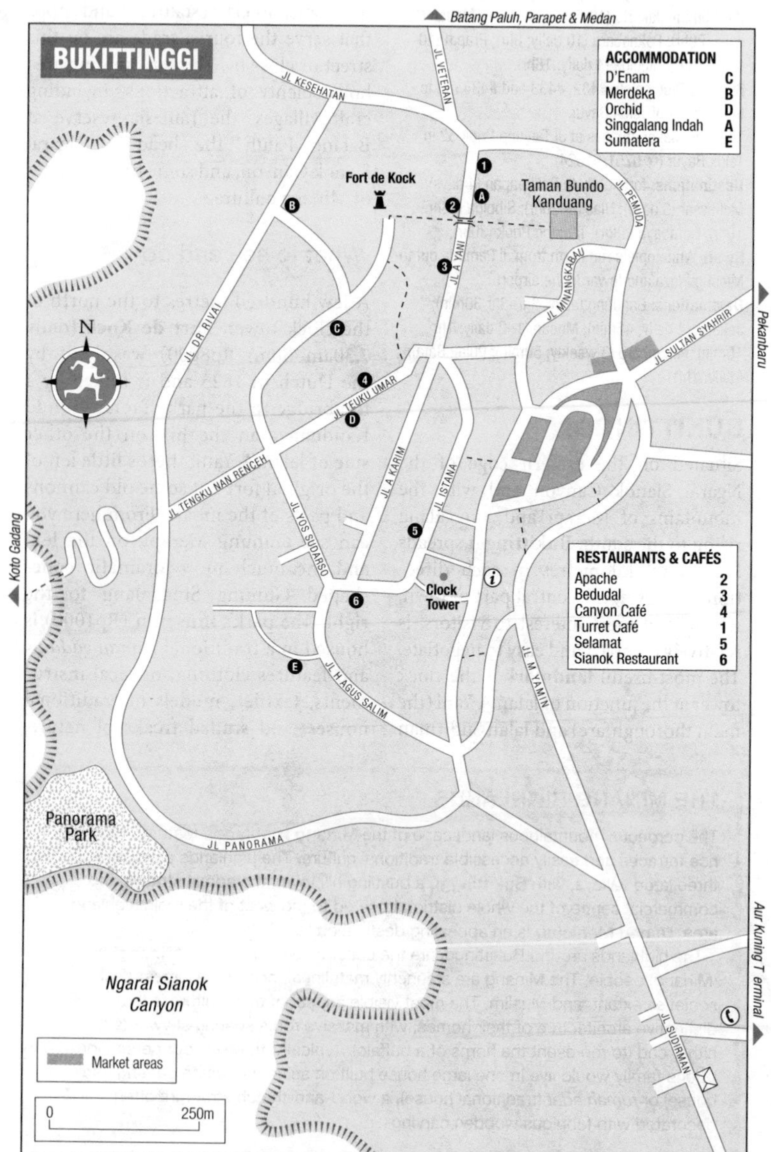

a potential fortress. You can venture down into these dank, miserable depths, although there's nothing really to see. The **Ngarai Sianok Canyon** is part of a rift valley that runs the full length of Sumatra – the canyon here is 15km long and around 100m deep, with a glistening river wending its way along the bottom.

### Koto Gadang

**Koto Gadang** is a small, attractive village situated on the western edge of the **Ngarai Sianok Canyon**, an hour or so from Bukittinggi, with plenty of small silver workshops and shops. Though you can get local transport to the village, many people try to find the route from Bukittinggi by foot that starts off down Jalan Tengku Nan Renceh, and then heads along a footpath to the footbridge across the river and up the steps on the other side of the canyon. Be aware that there's a well-orchestrated scam, with local people refusing to point the way and hapless tourists being led by young lads on a two-hour rough trek through the canyon, for which they expect payment.

### Batang Paluh

*Rafflesia arnoldi* is the largest flower in the world – up to 90cm across – has remarkable red-and-white colouring, and an appalling smell like rotting meat. One of the most accessible places in Sumatra to see this rare and extraordinary flower is at **Batang Paluh**, 13km north of Bukittinggi; take a local bus (Rp2000) and ask in the village. Enquire at the tourist office in Bukittinggi first as it generally flowers for a couple of weeks between August and December – but even in bud the plant is quite something.

### Batusangkar

Accessed via Padangpanjang, the largest town in the Tanah Datar Valley is **Batusangkar**, 39km southeast of Bukittinggi and served by frequent buses (1hr 30min). The Minang court of the fourteenth to nineteenth centuries was based in the valley, the gold and iron mines of ancient times the source of its riches. The entire area is awash with cultural relics, megaliths and places of interest.

The most worthwhile tourist destination was **Pagaruyung**, the reconstructed palace of the last Raja Alam of the Minangkabau, Sultan Arifin Muning Alam Syah, but it burnt down after being struck by lightening in 2007. There are many other examples of Minangkabau *rumah adat* in the town and the stunning surrounding countryside. Given the distances involved, most travellers visit Batusangkar on a day trip from Bukittingi. *Orchid* and other hostels will organize a tour, which generally involves riding behind someone on their motorcycle.

## Arrival and information

**By bus** A few tourist services may drop you at your hotel of choice (check when you book), but other long-distance buses terminate at the Aur Kuning terminal, 3km southeast of the town centre. Buses from Padang stop on the southern outskirts of town on Jl Sudirman before turning off for the terminal; you can get a red #14 or #19 bemo into the town centre from this junction, and all but one of the accommodation choices are within an easy walk of the route.

**Tourist information** Office by the clock tower (Mon–Sat 8am–4pm, closed Fri prayers).

## City transport

**Bemos** scurry around town in a circular route, with a flat fare of Rp2000. To get to the bus terminal, stop any red bemo heading north on Jalan A Yani, which will circle to the east of town and pass the main post office before turning for Aur Kuning.

## Accommodation

**D'Enam** Jl Yos Sudarso ⓣ0752/32240. Rooms in an airy bungalow. All are good value – some of the cheapest in Bukittinggi; there's also a lounge for residents and a laundry service next door. ❶–❷

**Merdeka** Jl Dr Rivai 20 ☎0752/23937. A small guesthouse in and around a colonial bungalow set in a good-sized garden – the large, cool rooms have high ceilings and cold-water mandi (though there's hot water in the most expensive rooms). Clean and pleasant. ❷

**Orchid** Jl Teuku Umar 11 ☎0752/32634. Clean, presentable rooms, many with balconies, and currently the most popular choice of travellers. The price includes breakfast, and the more expensive rooms have TVs and hot water. Fair value but the nearby mosque makes it a little noisy. ❷–❸

**Singgalang Indah** Jl A Yani 130 ☎0752/21576. Central though soulless, it's a good place for enquiring about silat classes. Only the top rooms (Rp120,000 and above) come with hot water. ❸–❺

**Sumatera** Jl Dr Setia Budhi 16e ☎0752/21309. Situated on a quiet road, the rooms have attached bathroom with hot water. The accommodation is adequate for this price but the real bonus is the balcony with its stunning views. ❸–❹

## Eating

A small night market sets up near the Jl A Yani/Jl Teuku Umar junction.

**Apache** Jl A Yani. Typical travellers' fare at reasonable prices. Good for people-watching and potato salad.

**Bedudal** Jl A Yani. A pleasant place with an extensive, good-quality menu of Western dishes including steaks, the speciality being pizzas and calzone.

**Canyon Café** Jl Teuku Umar. The most popular restaurant in Bukittinggi, with good Western food and a few local dishes, including *rendang*.

**Selamat** Jl Istana. One of the best Padang restaurants in town, they usually have eggs in coconut sauce, especially good for vegetarians, and are used to Westerners.

**Sianok Restaurant** *The Hills Hotel*, Jl Laras Datuk Bandaro. Expensive joint with Italian, Chinese, Indonesian, Minang and Western barbecue nights, special Minang lunches and daily afternoon tea.

**Turret Café** Jl A Yani. Mainly Western food with attractive furnishings, a relaxed atmosphere and an internet café attached (Rp10,000/hour).

## Traditional entertainment

**Minangkabau dance shows** Staged by local dance troupes (8.30pm; Rp20,000) nightly in a hall just behind *Hotel Jogya* on Jalan Moh Yamin; head up the small road on the left of the hotel and the hall is on the right. The dancing is accompanied by *talempong pacik*, traditional Minang music performed by a gamelan orchestra. Most shows also include a demonstration of *silek*, the Minang martial art taught to both young men and women, and the *tari piriang*, a dance that originated in the ricefields after harvest time when young people danced with the plates they had just eaten from: piles of crockery shards are trodden and even rolled in by the dancers.

**Buffalo fights** Were popular, and had been held twice-weekly, have been suspended in a bid to discourage gambling. It's possible that these, which are rarely gory, will resume; enquire at the tourist office.

## Directory

**Banks and exchange** Bank Rakyat Indonesia, Jl A Yani 3; Bank Negara Indonesia, Jl A Yani (with ATM); Bank Danamon Jl A Yani (with ATM); Bank Central Asia Jl Istana (with ATM). There's also an ATM by the clock tower. Several travel agents including PT Tigo Balai, Jl A Yani 100 (daily 8am–8pm; ☎0752/31996), change traveller's cheques and offer cash advances against Visa and MasterCard.

**Bookshops** Anyone heading into central and southern Sumatra, an English-language book desert, should stock up in the new and secondhand bookshops on Jl Teuku Umar and Jl A Yani.

**Car and motorbike rental** Enquire at your accommodation or any of the travel agents in town. Typical prices are Rp35,000 for a 12hr motorbike rental.

**Hospital** Rumah Sakit Dr Achmad Mochtar is on Jl Dr Rivai (☎0752/21013 or 33825). The tourist information offices will advise on English-speaking doctors in Bukittinggi.

**Internet** Fifals, on Jl Teuku Umar, currently has the fastest connection, though they charge a little more, too, at Rp15,000 per hour. Those on Jl A Yani, such as Harau, charge around Rp12,000 per hour.

**Post office** The main post office is inconveniently far from the town centre on Jl Sudirman.

**Telephone** The main telephone office is on Jl M Syafei towards the southern end of town, around the corner from the post office. There are also many wartels in town.

**Travel agents** Try Jogja Wisata Travel, Jl Yani 85 ☎0752/33507; PT Tigo Balai, Jl A Yani 100 ☎0752/31996; and Travina Tours and Travel Service, Jl A Yani 105 ☎0752/21281 – this is a good place to enquire about the many tours of the area on offer.

## Moving on

**By bus** Local buses (7am–5pm) for Bukit Paluh, Danau Maninjau, Batusangkar, Payakumbuh and Padang leave from the Aur Kuning terminal, where you'll also find the ticket offices. Long-distance buses (book ahead) also use Aur Kuning; destinations include Sibolga, Parapat, Medan, Pekanbaru, Palembang, Lubuklinggau (for the South Sumatra train service), Jakarta and Bandung. Tourist buses to Danau Toba are also on offer, through the travel agents in town (see opposite). Travel agents in Bukittinggi can also arrange Pelni and airline tickets from Padang, which is the closest port and airport.
**Destinations:** Aceh (2 daily; 25hr); Bandar Lampung (3 daily; 24hr); Bandung (1 daily; 34hr); Batusangkar (hourly; 1hr 30min); Bengkulu (1 daily; 16hr); Jakarta (1 daily; 35hr); Maninjau (hourly; 1hr 30min); Medan (3 daily; 18hr); Palembang (1 daily; 15hr); Pekanbaru (6 daily; 6hr); Prapat (daily; 14hr); Pulau Batam (daily; 24hr); Sibolga (2 daily; 12hr).

## DANAU MANINJAU

A very pleasant and hassle-free area for rest and relaxation on the way to or from Danau Toba, **Danau Maninjau** (Lake Maninjau) is situated 15km due west of Bukittinggi, although public transport on the road takes a long-winded 37km (1hr 30min) to get there. At an altitude of 500m, the lake is 17km long and 8km wide and set 600m below the rim of an ancient volcanic crater, with jungle-covered walls, almost sheer in places, providing a picturesque backdrop. The area of interest for tourists centres on the village of **MANINJAU**, just where the road from Bukittinggi reaches the lakeside road, and the village of **Bayur** 4km to the north.

### What to see and do

There's not that much to do here apart from relax and frolic in the lake, though you may like to try to track down a **rafflesia** in the jungle-clad hills behind the village, or visit the nearby **waterfall**. For either trip, Pak Juney, often found at the *Parantha Café*, is an excellent guide, very knowledgeable and fluent in English. Or you can go pig-hunting with dogs, a traditional local activity, on Wednesdays and Sundays; contact one of the little agents in town for details. Cycling around the lake is also popular: bikes can be rented for Rp30,000 per day from *Kafe Kawa*. Motorbikes (just about essential if you want to circumnavigate the entire lake) cost around Rp65,000 per day.

### Arrival and information

**By bus** From Bukittingi, buses will drop you at the small square opposite the police station at the foot of the mountain road, before continuing along the lakeside road to Bayur – ask the conductor to drop you at your hotel.
**Tourist information** There is no official tourist information office but Indo Wisata Travel (☎0752/61418), part of *Bagoes Café*, is a helpful spot.

### Accommodation

Accommodation is ranged along the east side of the lake, from about 500m south of the junction of the

### CLIMBING GUNUNG MERAPI

Access to 2890-metre **Gunung Merapi** (Fire Mountain) is from Koto Baru, 12km south of Bukittinggi. Typically, the climb, which is strenuous rather than gruelling if you're reasonably fit, takes five hours up and four down; most people climb at night to arrive at the top for the sunrise. The first four hours or so are through the forest and then across bare rocks leading to the summit. The top is actually a plateau area with the still-smoking crater in the middle. You may spot bats, gibbons and squirrels in the forest, but the main reason to go is the view across to Gunung Singgalang. Engage an experienced local **guide** through your losmen (around Rp100,000 per person) and take enough water and energy food, plus sturdy footwear and warm clothes for the top.

lakeside road with the road from Bukittinggi, to just north of the 5km marker.

**44** ⓣ0752/61238. Very inexpensive shoreside bungalows with attached mandi and a small restaurant. Rooms are simple – consisting of a mattress on the floor – though the family are very welcoming, and it's good value. ❶

**Arlen** ⓣ0815/358685. Far away from the "action" of Maninjau village, this is a great place to get away from it all, and has some of the smartest lakeside bungalows around. ❷

**Beach Guest House** ⓣ0752/61082. Popular place in a great location on the lakeside, with a small beach and hammocks. Offers two sorts of simple concrete rooms, some with attached mandi and a small veranda. Internet available. ❶

**Lili's** Attractive option with fine, shared-mandi bungalows and a tree house. A two-minute walk through the rice paddies from the main road. ❶

**Tan Dirih** ⓣ0752/61263. Small, tiled, spotless place with sunloungers on a terrace overlooking the lake. It's the best mid-range choice, and all rooms have TV, hot water and tubs. ❸

### Eating and drinking

**Bagoes Café** Good-quality Western and Indonesian restaurant specializing in fish from the lake. Has the best internet access in town.

**Kafe Kawa** Serving tasty and cheap food, this unassuming place lies just to the north of the village centre; also offers bike rental.

**Simple Café** Situated close to the road but with good views across the rooftops down to the lake. A vast, inexpensive menu offering all the usual Western and Indo-Chinese favourites. Bike rental available.

**Srikandi Café** This place at the southern end of Maninjau village has a large and varied menu of soups (pumpkin, curried apple, Thai *tom yam*), and main courses including stir-fries, *sate*, fish, steak, pizzas and burgers.

### Directory

**Bookshops** There are a couple of secondhand bookshops: Bacho Bookshop is the best.

**Internet** Bagoes Café is the best place for Internet and changing cash (but not traveller's cheques or plastic).

**Post office** The post office isn't far from the main junction on Jalan Telaga Biru Tanjung Raya.

**Telephone** The 24hr Telkom office is on the main street by the junction; the nearby bank sadly won't change money.

### Moving on

**By bus** There are regular buses back to Bukittinggi with the last departing at 5pm. If you want to go to Padang, either head back to Bukittinggi or take a minivan travelling to Lubukbasung, from where you can pick up Padang buses during the day. Alternatively, *Bagoes Café* can arrange tourist minibuses (Rp65,000).

**Destinations:** Bukittinggi (1hr 30min); Padang (2 daily; 3hr); Pekanbaru (daily; 8hr).

## THE MENTAWAI ISLANDS

The enticing rainforest-clad Mentawai Islands, 100km off the west Sumatran coast, are home to an ethnic group who are struggling to retain their identity in the modern world. There are over forty islands in the chain, of which the four main ones are Pulaus **Siberut**, **Sipora**, **North Pagi** and **South Pagi**. Only Pulau Siberut, the largest, at 110km long by 50km wide, is accessible to tourists; all visitors must be registered by the authorities. The islanders' traditional culture is based on communal dwelling in longhouses (*uma*) and subsistence agriculture, their religious beliefs centring on the importance of coexisting with the invisible spirits that inhabit the world. With the advent of Christian missionaries and the colonial administration in the early twentieth century, many of the islanders' religious practices were banned, but plenty of beliefs and rituals have survived and some villages have built new *uma*. However, the islanders are still under threat, not least from an Indonesian government seeking to integrate them into mainstream life.

### What to see and do

**Organized** tours of Mentawai are loudly marketed in Bukittinggi as a trip to see the "primitive" people and "stone-age" culture. Generally, Mentawai people welcome tourism as a way of validating and preserving their own culture, although they get little financial benefit from it. Be sure to read and obey guidelines about behaviour that are given to you, as the people have a complex system of taboo behaviour. Expect to pay at least US$250 per person for an eight-day trip from Bukittingi. Be aware that day one usually means a 3pm departure from Bukittinggi and day eight may well end at 10am when you get back to Bukittinggi. Most tours centre on the southeast of the island, where you'll be able to watch and join in with people going about their everyday activities, such as farming, fishing and hunting. The ceremonies of Siberut are something of a draw for tourists, but many are actually staged for them.

**Pulau Siberut** is the best-known, largest and most northerly of the Mentawai chain and the only one with anything approaching a tourist industry. Access to the island is by **overnight ferry** from Padang and, although it's possible, still, to visit the island independently, the vast majority of visitors go on tours arranged from Bukittinggi. Malaria is endemic on the island, so take your own net or borrow one from the tour company.

The main town of **MUARASIBERUT** is in reality a sleepy little shanty-style village on the coast and around the mouth of the river. Small, unstable "speedboats" ferry passengers and cargo around. The only accommodation in Muarasiberut is *Syahruddin's Homestay* (☎0759/21014; ❶) on the coast at the mouth of the river. There are no exchange facilities on the island. Mentawai is also known for **surfing**; see p.203 for information and resources on surfing in Indonesia.

### INTO MALAYSIA

Sumatra's major east-coast port is **Dumai**, 189km north of Pekanbaru and just across the Straits of Malacca from the Malaysian city of Melaka. Dumai is a visa-free entry point, and a fast ferry runs daily to and from Melaka (2hr 30min). Regular buses run between Dumai and Pekanbaru, but if you get stranded you can stay at the *City Hotel*, Jl Sudirman 445 (☎0765/21550; ❷); Pelita Air has an office at the airport (☎0765/31121).

## PEKANBARU

The booming oil town of **PEKANBARU** is a major gateway into Indonesia from Singapore, via **Pulau Batam** and **Pulau Bintan**. Most travellers head straight through but it's worth considering a journey break here – it's six hours west to Bukittinggi and another nine or ten hours east to Singapore. Pekanbaru's main street is Jalan Sudirman, which runs north–south from the river through the centre of town to the airport. Most hotels, restaurants and shops are within easy reach of this thoroughfare. Pekanbaru's **markets** are fun: Pasar Pusat is the food and household-goods market, and Pasar Bawah and Pasar Tengeh in the port area have an excellent range of Chinese goods, including ceramics and carpets.

### Arrival and information

**By bus** The long-distance bus terminal is on to Bandarraya Payung Sekaki (moved from Jl Nangka).

**By boat** Most express ferry services from Pulau Batam and Pulau Bintan dock at Buton, connected to Pekanbaru by a three-hour bus journey; buses arrive at the express-ferry offices at the northern end of Jl Sudirman or at the bus terminal. Slow ferries come into the main port area at the northern end of Jl Saleh Abbas in the Pasar Bawah market area, a couple of hundred metres west of Jl Sudirman.

**By air** All domestic and international flights (Singapore, KL, Melaka) touch down at Simpang Tiga Airport, 9km south of the city centre. There's a taxi desk outside arrivals. You'll pay a Rp10,000 airport surcharge plus the metered fare – ensure the driver uses the meter.

**Tourist information** The tourist information office is inconveniently sited at Jl Diponegoro

24 (Mon–Thurs 8am–2pm, Fri 8–11am, Sat 8am–12.30pm; ⓣ0761/31562).

## Accommodation

Accommodation in Pekanbaru is a dire subject: there's little charm or hospitality to most hotels, especially at the lower end of the scale, which bottoms out at Rp35,000.

**Anom** Jl Gatot Subroto 1–3 ⓣ0761/36083. Centrally located, about 100m from Jl Sudirman, *Anom* has spotlessly clean rooms opening off a central courtyard, some with hot water. Will also help guests book bus tickets. ❷

**Hotel Linda** Jl Nangka 145 ⓣ0761/36915. The best of the basic, noisy and poor-value places on Jl Nangka right opposite the old bus station. ❷

**Hotel Pangeran Pekanbaru** Jl Sudirman 371–73 ⓣ0761/853636. Upmarket hotel. Rooms with a/c and minibar, and boasts the best pool in the city. ❼

## Eating

Even if you stayed in the city for a month, you could have every meal at the brilliant Pasar Pusat **night market** (in the market area near Jl Bonjol) and not eat the same thing twice.

**Sederhana** Jl Nangka 121–12. One of many Padang-style restaurants that offer good-value but spicy eating in the area near the bus station.

## Directory

**Airlines** Batavia, Jl Jend Sudirman 312 ⓣ0761/856031; Garuda, in *Hotel Pangeran Pekanbaru*, Jl Sudirman 371–373 ⓣ0761/45063; Jatayu, in *Hotel Mutiara Merdeka*, Jl Yos Sudarso 12a ⓣ0761/855775; Lion Air, in *Hotel Mutiara Merdeka*, Jl Yos Sudarso 12 ⓣ0761/40670; Mandala, Jl Sudirman 3485 ⓣ0761/34777; Merpati, Jl Jend Sudirman 343 ⓣ0761/41555; Pelangi, Jl Pepaya 64c ⓣ0761/28896.

**Banks and exchange** All the main banks have branches in the city, including BCA, Jl Sudirman 448, and BNI 1946, Jl Sudirman 63.

**Post office** The main post office is at Jl Sudirman 229, but there's a more convenient post office for sending mail at Jl Sudirman 78, close to its northern end.

**Telephone and fax** The Telkom office is at Jl Sudirman 117, and there are wartel all over town, including Jl Gatot Subroto 6.

**Travel agents** PT Indah Wisata Tours and Travel, Jl Pangeran Hidayat 2 ⓣ0761/702441, sells minibus tickets to many Sumatran destinations, including Bukittinggi.

## Moving on

Pekanbaru has extremely good sea, land and air connections with the rest of island, as well as the rest of the archipelago.

**By bus** Long-distance buses to destinations throughout Sumatra and Java depart from the Bandarraya Payung Sekaki station. If you're heading to Bukittinggi, it's usually more economical to buy a minibus ticket (Rp70,000) from a travel agent such as PT Indah Wisata, as this avoids the trip to the bus terminal. Approach them directly or ask at your hotel.

**Destinations:** Bandar Lampung (10 daily; 24hr); Bukittinggi (10 daily; 6hr); Denpasar (daily; 4 days); Dumai (10 daily; 3hr); Jakarta (10 daily; 34hr); Maninjau (daily; 8hr); Mataram (Lombok, daily; 4 days); Medan (daily; 25–35hr); Padang (10 daily; 8hr); Prapat (daily; 22–30hr); Yogyakarta (4 daily; 42hr).

**By boat** High-speed bus and ferry services for Pulau Batam and Pulau Bintan for Singapore (see box opposite) leave from the ticket offices at the northern end of Jl Sudirman. You can also sail directly to Melaka from Pelabuhan Duku, beyond the eastern end of Jl Datuk (9am; 7hr). Tickets (Rp165,000) are available from PT Jasa Sarana Citra Bestari, Jl Tanjung Datuk 153 (ⓣ0761/858777) or, more expensively, from agencies around town.

**By air** to Jakarta (6 daily; 1hr–1hr 40min); Kuala Lumpur (4 weekly; 1hr); Medan (daily; 1hr 20min); Melaka (4 weekly; 40min); Padang (3 weekly; 40min); Pulau Batam (3–4 daily; 45min); Tanjung Pinang (4 weekly; 50min).

# BANDAR LAMPUNG

Occupying a stunning location in the hills overlooking Lampung Bay, from where you can see as far as Krakatau, **BANDAR LAMPUNG** is an amalgamation of Teluk Betung, the traditional port, and Tanjung Karang, the administrative centre on the hills behind. Local people continue to talk about Teluk Betung and Tanjung Karang, and when you're coming here from other parts of Sumatra your destination will usually be referred to as Rajabasa, the name of the bus terminal. Other than the views down onto Lampung Bay, there are few sights in town.

### INTO SINGAPORE

Though most people now fly between Singapore and Indonesia, there are several sea routes, via **Pulau Batam** or **Pulau Bitan**, Batam being more convenient, just 20km from Singapore at the closest point. **From Pekanbaru** most high-speed ferry services leave from the northern end of Jl Sudirman and involve a three-hour bus journey to Buton, where you transfer to the ferry for the trip to the islands (Rp190,000 to Batam and Rp215,000 to Bintan); there are typically two departures a day, one at around 7.30am and another at 5pm. The trip, including a two-hour wait at Buton, will take 9–12 hours.

At Batam most travellers arrive at the port of **Sekupang**, in a bay at the northwest of the island, from where boats from the international terminal run to Singapore (every 30min to Singapore's World Trade Center; 7.30am–7pm, Mon & Wed till 8pm). Batam's domestic terminal (200m away) operates services to and from Sumatran destinations such as Pekanbaru and Dumai, as well as running boats to Tanjung Pinang on Pulau Bintan. You can book at the Sekupang terminal, any travel agent or from the Pelni office at Jl Dr Cipto Mangunkusumo 4, Sekupang (☎0778/321070).

## Arrival and information

**By bus** Buses from the north arrive at the Rajabasa terminal, 7km north of the city. Catch a light blue "microlet" – the local name for bemos – into Pasar Bawah in town (24hr), or catch the bus (services finish at about 6pm) that goes to Pasar Bawah but then continues its circular route down Jl Raden Intan, along Jl A Yani and up Jl Kartini before going out to Rajabasa again. Coming to the city from Bakauheni or Kalianda, buses arrive at the Panjang terminal, about 1km east of Pasar Panjang. Some terminate there, while others go on to the Rajabasa terminal. Orange bemos run between Panjang terminal and Sukaraja terminal in the heart of Teluk Betung; from here, you can get a purple bemo into the city (Rp1000; until 10pm) as far as Pasar Bawah, or a large orange bus direct to Rajabasa via the eastern ring road.

**By train** Bandar Lampung is part of the triangular rail network that extends between Bandar Lampung, Palembang and Lubuklinggau. The train station is on Jalan Kotoraja, about 100m from Pasar Bawah.

**By air** Branti Airport is 25km north of the city; walk 200m onto the main road and catch a Branti–Rajabasa bus to Rajabasa terminal (Rp250) and take connections to the city from there. Fixed-price taxis from the airport into town will cost Rp30,000.

**Tourist information** The useful tourist office is Dinas Investasi Kebudayaan Dan Parwisata (or you could just ask for the Kantor Parwisata), Jl Jend Sudirman 29 (☎0721/261430).

## City transport

**Buses and bemos** DAMRI bus services (6am–6pm) operate between the two major terminals or up and down Jalan Randen Intan and Jalan Diponegoro. Bemo routes are less fixed than buses: tell them your destination as you enter. Most stop at about 9pm, but the light blue service runs 24 hours a day.

**Taxis** Meters start at Rp1350 and a fare across the city is under Rp15,000. Be firm with drivers about using the meter before you get in.

## Accommodation

Whilst Bandar Lampung has a good range of mid- to top-range hotels, offering pleasant and good-value accommodation, if you're on a very tight budget the situation is grim. In particular, the area around Pasar Bawah, while simply noisy during the day, gets unpleasant at night.

**Gading** Jl Kartini 72 ☎0721/255512. Offering a variety of rooms, conveniently located near the market area, it's a short walk from the bus route from Rajabasa terminal and is a large setup on a quiet alleyway in a busy area. ❷

**Lusy** Jl Diponegoro 186 (Karang–Betung buses and purple bemos pass the door) ☎0721/485695. The accommodation is very basic but clean, and all rooms have attached mandi. Some have fans and some a/c. ❶–❷

**Rarem** Jl Way Rarem 23 ☎261241. Tucked away behind Jl KHA Dahlan and on the green bemo route; super-clean rooms with shared mandi or private bath and a/c. The small garden is a haven of peace in the bustling city. ❷–❸

## Eating

There's a great range of places to eat at in Bandar Lampung, the highlight being a visit to Pasar Mambo, the night market, at the southern end of Jl Hassanudin, which operates from dusk until about 11pm.

**Bukit Randu** Perched on top of the hill of the same name with panoramic views of the city and Lampung Bay. The menu is so extensive that there's an information booth at the entrance.

**East Garden** Jl Diponegoro 106. Excellent and very wide-ranging Chinese/Indonesian place with lots of *tauhu* (tofu) and tempe dishes as well as soup, noodles, seafood and many iced fruit juices. Clean, inexpensive and excellent value – they've even got a take-away.

**Marcopolo Restaurant** At the Marcopolo Hotel. The outside terrace, with a fantastic view over the entire city and out into Lampung Bay, makes this a great place for Western, Chinese and Indonesian food, which ranges from rice and noodle dishes at Rp6000, up to pepper steak at Rp20,000.

**Pempek 56** Jl Salim Batubara 56. Just one of a huge range of *pempek* places along this road; they are named by the number on the street, and all serve inexpensive *pempek*, the grilled or fried Palembang speciality of balls made from sago, fish and flavourings, which are dished up with a variety of sauces.

## Directory

**Airlines** Merpati has an office at Jl Diponegoro 189 (☎0721/268486).

**Hospitals** Local hospitals include Rumah Sakit Bumi Waras, Jalan Wolter Moginsidi (☎0721/255032); Rumah Sakit Immanuel Way Halim, Jalan Sukarno Hatta B (☎0721/704900); and Rumah Sakit Abdul Muluk, Jalan Kapten Rivai (☎0721/703312).

**Immigration** The immigration office is at Jl Diponegoro 24 (☎0721/482607 or 481697).

**Internet** There's internet at the post office (open until 6pm).

**Post office** The post office is at Jl KHA Dahlan 21.

**Telephone** The main Telkom office is at Jl Kartini 1, and there's also a 24hr wartel at Jl Majapahit 14 – one of many in town.

## Moving on

**By bus** Long-distance buses depart from the Rajabasa terminal, situated 7km north of the city centre.

### FERRIES TO JAVA

Around 30km south of Kalianda, and 90km south of Bandar Lampung, lies Bakauheni, the departure point for ferries to Merak (see p.219), on Java's northwest tip. There's no reason to stay in Bakauheni itself. The town is served by regular buses from the Rajabasa and Panjang terminals in Bandar Lampung, and by bemos from Kalianda. There's also a 24hr wartel and a couple of shops. Ferries from Bakauheni operate round the clock (2hr 30min), leaving every thirty minutes during the day and less frequently at night. **High-speed ferries** (40min) also depart hourly from 7.40am to 5pm

**Destinations:** Bakauheni (every 30min; 2–3hr); Banda Aceh (3 daily; 3 days); Bukittinggi (6 daily; 24hr); Denpasar (4 daily; 3 days); Dumai (4 daily; 48hr); Jakarta (20 daily; 8hr); Kalianda (every 30min; 1–2hr); Medan (10 daily; 2 days); Padang (6 daily; 24hr); Parapat (10 daily; 2 days); Pekanbaru (6 daily; 24hr); Yogyakarta (20 daily; 24hr).

**By train** Trains to Palembang (3 daily; 6–8hr). depart from the station on Jalan Kotoraja.

# Bali

With its pounding surf, emerald-green rice terraces and exceptionally artistic culture, the small volcanic island of **Bali** – population 3.1million and the only Hindu society in Southeast Asia – has long been Indonesia's premier tourist destination. Although it suffers the predictable problems of congestion and commercialization, Bali's original charm is still much in evidence, its distinctive temples and elaborate festivals set off by the mountainous, river-rich landscape of the interior.

Bali's most famous and crowded resort is **Kuta**, an eight-kilometre sweep of golden sand, with plenty of accommodation and the best shopping and nightlife on the island. Surfing is fun here too, but experienced wave-riders head for the **surfing beaches** on the Bukit peninsula and along Bali's southwest coast. **Sanur** is a fairly sedate southern beach, but most backpackers prefer the tranquil island of **Nusa Lembongan,** the beaches of peaceful east-coast **Amed**, **Candi Dasa** and **Padang Bai**, or **Lovina** on the north coast. Immensely rich sea-life means that snorkelling and diving are big draws at all these resorts. Bali's other major destination is the cultural centre of **Ubud**, where traditional dances are staged every night and the streets are full of organic cafés and arts-and-crafts galleries. In addition, there are numerous elegant Hindu temples to visit, particularly at **Tanah Lot** and **Besakih**, and a good number of volcano hikes, the most popular being the route up **Gunung Batur**, with **Gunung Agung** only for the very fit.

**Transport** to and from Bali is efficient: the island is served by scores of international and domestic flights, which all land at **Ngurah Rai Airport** just south of Kuta, as well as round-the-clock ferries from Java, west across the Bali Strait from **Gilimanuk**, and from Lombok, east of **Padang Bai**. Pelni ferries from ports across Indonesia call at Benoa Harbour (p.195).

## DENPASAR

Bali's capital city, **DENPASAR** (sometimes known by its old name, Badung), has the island's best museum and several lively markets but lacks the tourist accommodation and other facilities of Kuta and Sanur, just 10km and 6km away respectively. Most visitors simply come for the day, or use Denpasar as a transport interchange, but a night in the city's traditional northern neighbourhoods offers an interesting chance to experience untouristed urban Bali.

### What to see and do

**Puputan Square** marks the heart of the downtown area. It commemorates the ritual fight to the death (*puputan*) on September 20, 1906, when the raja of Badung and hundreds of his subjects stabbed themselves to death rather than submit to the Dutch invaders. Overlooking the square on Jalan Mayor Wisnu, the **Bali Museum** (Museum

### BALI: A SHORT HISTORY

Bali was a more or less independent society of Buddhists and Hindus until the fourteenth century, when it was colonized by the strictly **Hindu** Majapahits from neighbouring Java. Despite the subsequent Islamicization of nearly all her neighbours, Bali has remained firmly Hindu ever since. In 1849, the Dutch started to take an interest in Bali, and by January 1909 had wrested control of the whole island. Following a short-lived Japanese occupation in World War II, and Indonesia's subsequent declaration of independence in 1945, Bali became an autonomous state within the Republic in 1949. But tensions with Java are ongoing and there is concern about wealthy entrepreneurs from Jakarta (and the West) monopolizing the financial benefits from Bali's considerable attractions, with the Balinese fearing they may lose control of their own homeland. These tensions were horrifically highlighted when Muslim extremists from Java bombed Kuta's two most popular nightclubs on October 12, 2002, killing over two hundred people and sending Bali's tourist-dependent economy into severe decline. A second attack, in October 2005, came just as the island was starting to recover. Reprisals and religious conflict have not ensued, however, due in part to Bali's impressively equanimous Hindu leadership; by mid-2008, tourist numbers were healthier than ever, though it will take a lot longer to redress the hardships caused by the bombings.

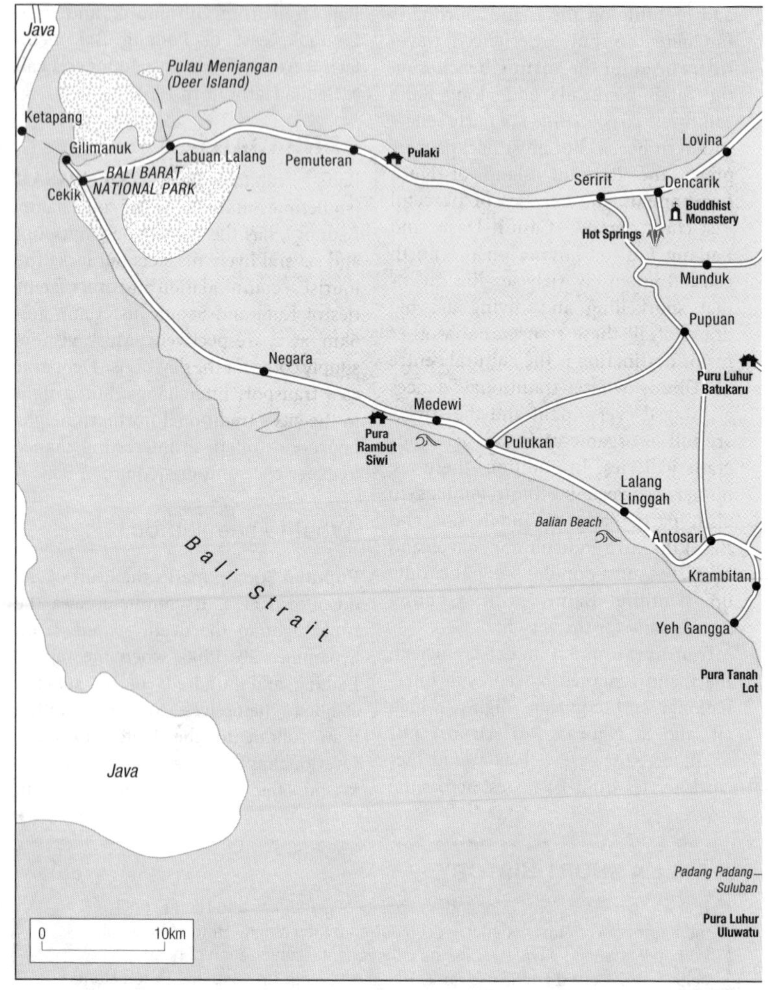


Negeri Propinsi Bali; Mon–Thurs & Sat 8am–3pm, Fri 8am–12.30pm; closed public hols; Rp2000, children Rp1000; on the turquoise Kereneng–Ubung bemo route) is Denpasar's top attraction and includes displays on prehistory, textiles and theatrical costumes as well as an exceptionally interesting exhibit on spiritual **rituals**, in the Gedung Karangasem building. Alongside the Bali Museum stands the modern state temple of **Pura Agung Jagatnata**, built in 1953.

The biggest of Denpasar's markets is **Pasar Badung**, which trades day and night from the three-storey covered stone-and-brick *pasar* (market) beside the Badung River, just off Jalan Gajah Mada. Its top-floor art market is crammed with good-value sarongs, batik cloth and ceremonial gear, but you may get landed with a self-appointed guide. Until it burnt down in 2007, the four-storey **Pasar Kumbasari**, across on the west bank of the river, also just

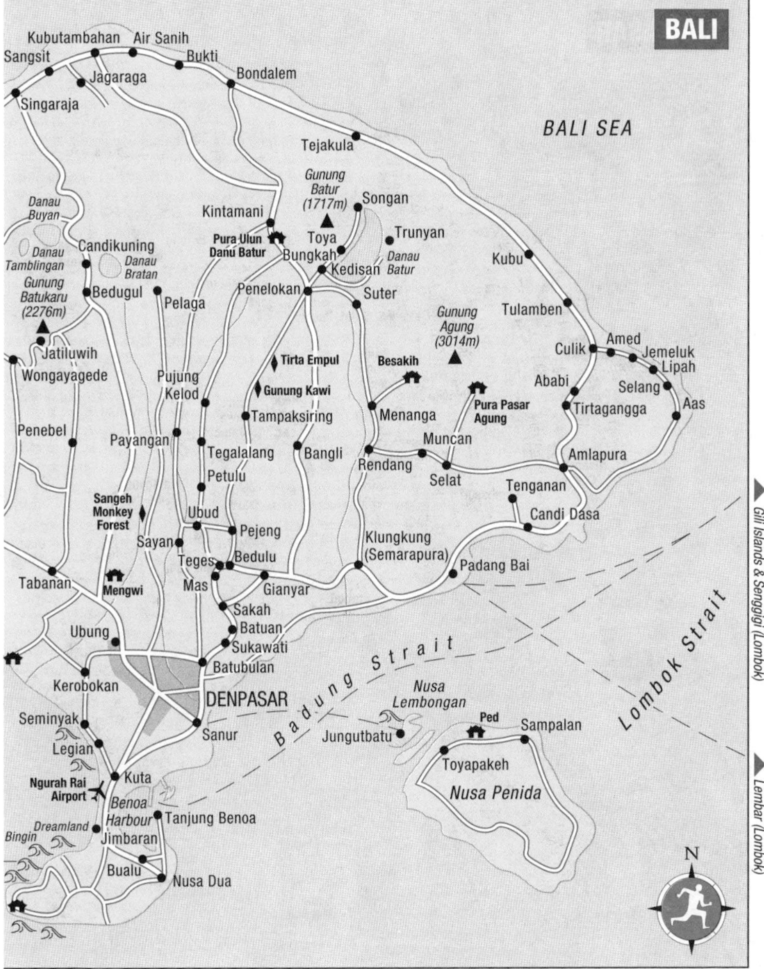




south off Jalan Gajah Mada, used to be another good source of cheap handicrafts and clothes; it's not yet clear when it will reopen.

## Arrival and information

**By bemo or public bus** Arriving in Denpasar by bemo or public bus, you'll be dropped at one of the city's four main terminals, from where trans-city bemos beetle into the centre and out to the other bemo stations. Coming from the south you'll arrive at Tegal; transport from the north, west and Java uses Ubung; bemos and buses from Ubud, the east and the north come in to Batubulan; and Sanur bemos arrive at Kereneng. No tourist shuttle buses serve Denpasar.

**By boat** All Pelni ships from the rest of Indonesia dock at Benoa Harbour (Pelabuhan Benoa), 10km southeast of Denpasar. Bemos meet the ships and take passengers into Denpasar, terminating near Sanglah hospital. A taxi from the port should cost about Rp35,000 to Denpasar, Kuta or Sanur.

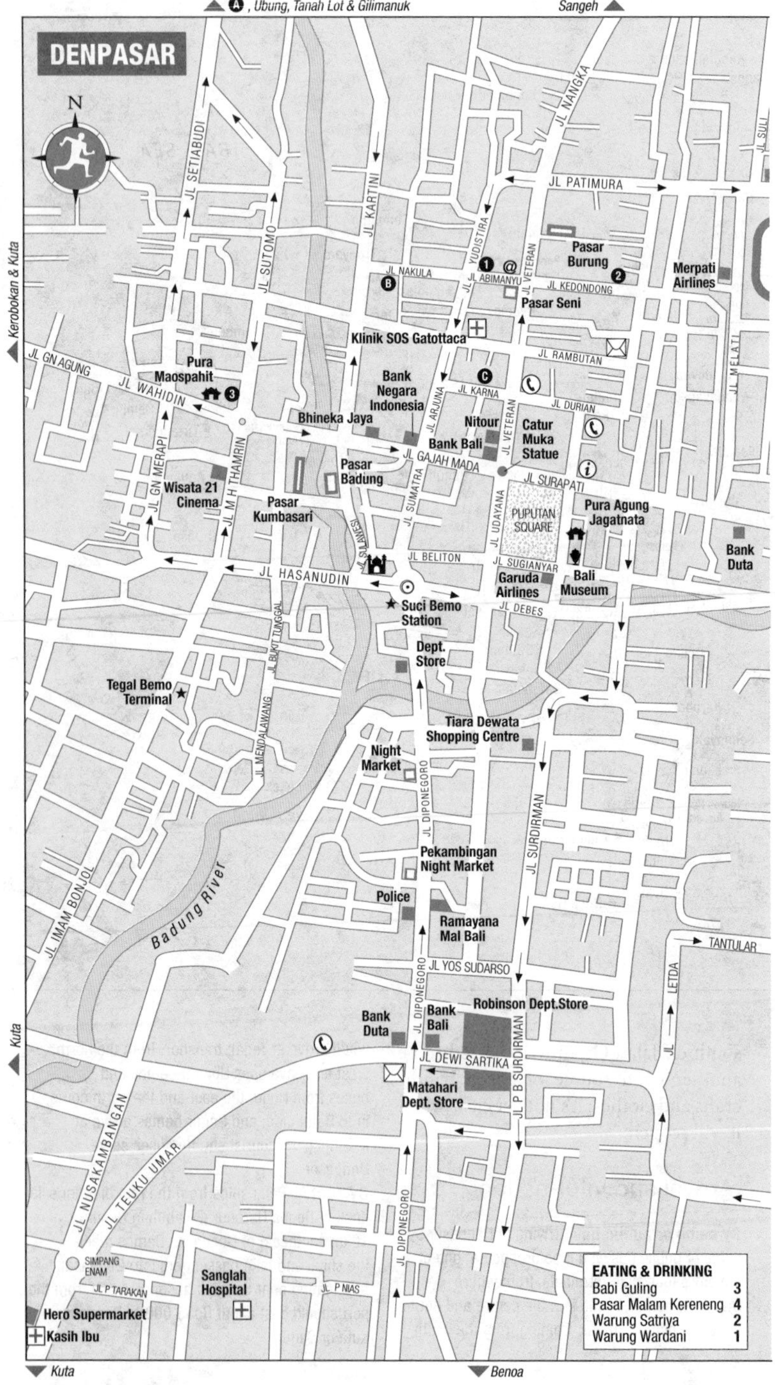
DENPASAR
A, Ubung, Tanah Lot & Gilimanuk
Sangeh
Kerobokan & Kuta
Kuta
Kuta
Benoa
JL SETIABUDI
JL SUTOMO
JL KARTINI
JL NANGKA
JL PATIMURA
JL SULI
JL YUDISTIRA
JL VETERAN
JL NAKULA
JL ABIMANYU
JL KEDONDONG
Pasar Burung
Merpati Airlines
Pasar Seni
Klinik SOS Gatottaca
JL RAMBUTAN
JL GN AGUNG
JL WAHIDIN
Pura Maospahit
Bank Negara Indonesia
JL KARNA
JL DURIAN
JL MELATI
Bhineka Jaya
Nitour
Catur Muka Statue
Bank Bali
JL ARJUNA
JL GAJAH MADA
JL SURAPATI
Pasar Badung
JL GN MERAPI
JL M H THAMRIN
Wisata 21 Cinema
Pasar Kumbasari
JL SUMATRA
JL UDAYANA
PUPUTAN SQUARE
Pura Agung Jagatnata
Bank Duta
JL SULAWESI
JL BELITON
JL SUGIANYAR
JL HASANUDIN
Garuda Airlines
Bali Museum
Suci Bemo Station
JL DEBES
JL BUKIT TUNGGAL
Dept. Store
Tegal Bemo Terminal
Tiara Dewata Shopping Centre
JL MENDALAWANG
Night Market
JL DIPONEGORO
Pekambingan Night Market
JL SURDIRMAN
JL IMAM BONJOL
Badung River
Police
Ramayana Mal Bali
TANTULAR
JL YOS SUDARSO
JL LETDA
Robinson Dept.Store
Bank Duta
Bank Bali
JL DEWI SARTIKA
JL P B SURDIRMAN
Matahari Dept. Store
JL NUSAKAMBANGAN
JL TEUKU UMAR
SIMPANG ENAM
JL P TARAKAN
Sanglah Hospital
JL P NIAS
Hero Supermarket
Kasih Ibu
EATING & DRINKING
Babi Guling 3
Pasar Malam Kereneng 4
Warung Satriya 2
Warung Wardani 1

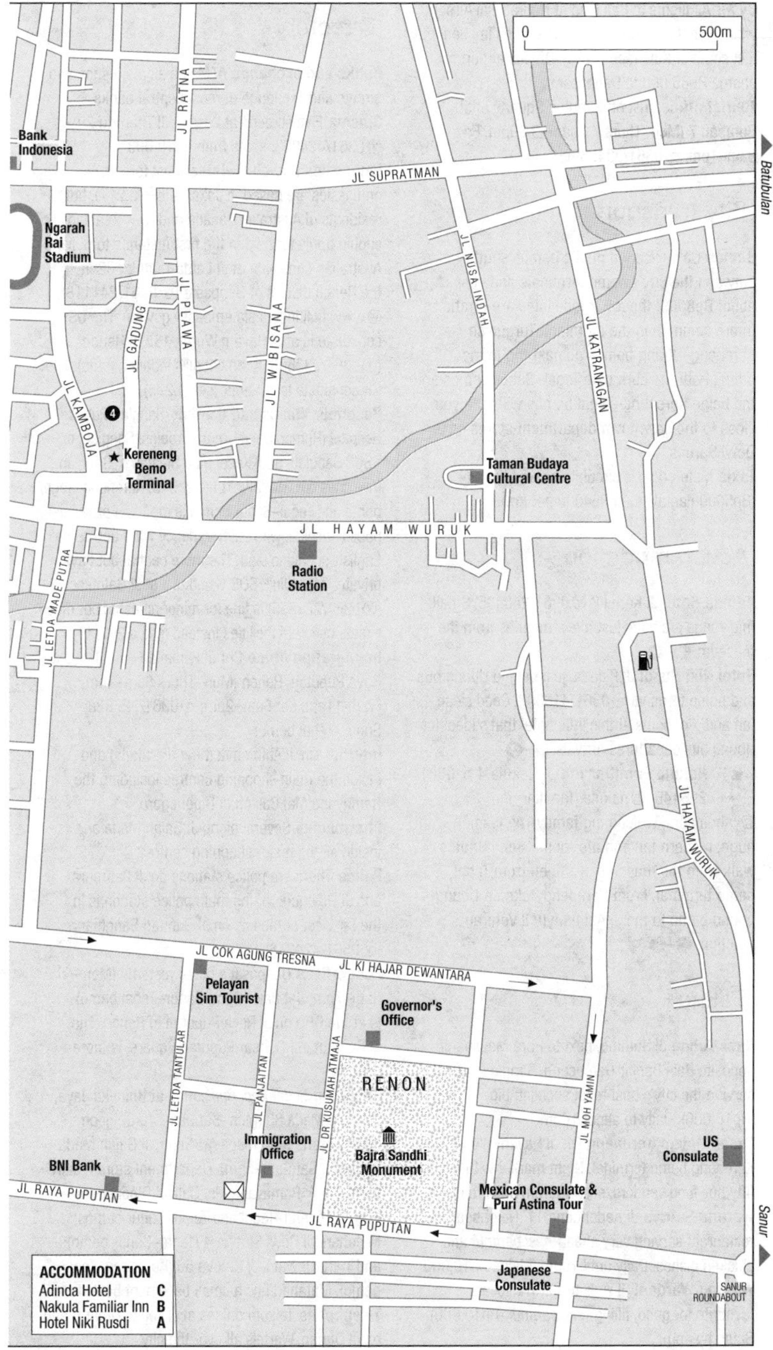
0
500m
Bank Indonesia
JL RATNA
JL SUPRATMAN
Batubulan
Ngarah Rai Stadium
JL NUSA INDAH
JL KATRANAGAN
JL PLAWA
JL GADUNG
JL WIBISANA
JL KAMBOJA
Kereneng Bemo Terminal
Taman Budaya Cultural Centre
JL HAYAM WURUK
Radio Station
JL LETDA MADE PUTRA
JL HAYAM WURUK
JL COK AGUNG TRESNA
JL KI HAJAR DEWANTARA
Pelayan Sim Tourist
Governor's Office
RENON
JL LETDA TANTULAR
JL PANJAITAN
JL DR KUSUMAH ATMAJA
JL MOH YAMIN
Immigration Office
Bajra Sandhi Monument
US Consulate
BNI Bank
JL RAYA PUPUTAN
Mexican Consulate & Puri Astina Tour
JL RAYA PUPUTAN
Sanur
Japanese Consulate
SANUR ROUNDABOUT
ACCOMMODATION
Adinda Hotel C
Nakula Familiar Inn B
Hotel Niki Rusdi A

**By air** All flights to Bali land at Ngurah Rai Airport, which is not in Denpasar as sometimes implied, but just south of Kuta (see p.288). Official airport taxis charge Rp65,000 to Denpasar.
**Tourist office** Just off Puputan Square, at Jl Surapati 7 (Mon–Thurs 7.30am–3.30pm, Fri 8am–1pm; ⓣ0361/234569).

## City transport

**Bemos** Colour-coded public bemos shuttle between the city's bemo terminals and cost about Rp3000, though frequencies are erratic (more common in the morning). Turquoise Kereneng–Ubung bemos go past the tourist office; both the dark blue Tegal–Sanur bemos and the beige Kereneng–Tegal bemos will take you close to the downtown department stores on Jl Dewi Sartika.
**Taxis** Metered taxis circulate around the city (Rp5000 flagfall, then Rp4000 per km).

## Accommodation

**Adinda Hotel** Jl Karna 8 ⓣ0361/240435. Small, mid-range a/c hotel just a few minutes from the museum. ❹–❻
**Hotel Niki Rusdi** Jl Pidada, just behind Ubung bus and bemo terminal ⓣ0361/416397. Good clean fan and a/c rooms at this little hotel that's ideal for Ubung bus departures/arrivals. ❷–❸
**Nakula Familiar Inn** Jl Nakula 4 ⓣ0361/226446, ⓔnakula_familiar_inn@yahoo.com. Welcoming family-run losmen with huge, modern fan and a/c rooms. Ten minutes' walk from the museum or fifteen from Tegal bemo terminal. From Kereneng, take an Ubung-bound bemo to the Jl Abimanyu/Jl Veteran junction. ❷–❸

## Eating

**Babi Guling** Jl Sutomo, next to Pura Maospahit, opposite Bale Banjar Gerenceng. Simple warung serving the city's best roast suckling pig (Rp10,000). Daily to about 10pm.
**Pasar Malam Kereneng** Off Jl Hayam Wuruk, at Kereneng bemo terminal. Night market with over fifty hot-food vendors, serving from dusk to dawn.
**Warung Satriya** Jl Kedondong 11. Neighbourhood restaurant serving very cheap *nasi campur* and chicken dishes. Daily until 10pm. Mains Rp10,000.
**Warung Wardani** Jl Yudistira 2. The locals' favourite for good, filling *nasi campur* (Rp10,000). Shuts by 4pm.

## Directory

**Banks and exchange** ATMs on all main shopping streets and exchange at most central banks.
**Cinema** Five screens at Wisata, Jl Thamrin 29 ⓣ0361/424023; seats from Rp10,000.
**Embassies and consulates** Most foreign embassies are based in Jakarta (see p.217), but residents of Australia, Canada and New Zealand should apply for help in the first instance to Bali's Australian consulate at Jl Letda Tantular 32 in the Renon district of Denpasar (ⓣ0361/241118, ⓦwww.bali.indonesia.embassy.gov.au). The US consulate is at Jl Hayam Wuruk 188 in Renon (ⓣ0361/233605, ⓔamcobali@indosat.net.id). The UK consulate is in Sanur (see p.295).
**Hospitals, clinics and dentists** Sanglah Public Hospital (Rumah Sakit Umum Propinsi Sanglah, or RSUP Sanglah) at Jl Kesehatan Selatan 1, Sanglah (five lines ⓣ0361/227911–227915; Kereneng–Tegal bemo and Tegal–Sanur bemo) is the main provincial public hospital, with an emergency ward and some English-speaking staff. The more central but tiny, private, 24hr Klinik SOS Gatotkaca at Jl Gatotkaca 21 (ⓣ0361/223555) is fine for minor ailments but most expats use Kuta facilities instead (see p.291).
**Immigration office** Cnr Jl Panjaitan and Jl Raya Puputan, Renon (Mon–Thurs 8am–4pm, Fri 8–11am, Sat 8am–2pm; ⓣ0361/227828; Sanur–Tegal bemo).
**Internet** On Jl Abimanyu (near Jl Nakula) and inside the main shopping centres including the Ramayana Mal Bali on Jl Diponegoro.
**Pharmacies** Several along Jl Gajah Mada and inside all the major shopping centres.
**Police** There are police stations on Jl Patimura and Jl Diponegoro; the main police station is in the far west of the city on Jl Gunung Sanghiang (ⓣ0361/424346).
**Post offices** Denpasar's poste restante (Mon–Fri 8am–7pm, Sat 8am–6pm; Sanur–Tegal bemo) is at the GPO on Jl Raya Puputan in Renon. The Jl Rambutan PO, near Puputan Square, is more central.
**Shopping** Local *kopi Bali* coffee at Bhineka Jaya, Jl Gajah Mada 80 (Mon–Sat 9am–4pm); good quality crafts from Mega Art Shop, Jl Gajah Mada 36 (Mon–Sat 9am–5pm). Department stores (daily 9am–9pm): Ramayana Mal Bali, Jl Diponegoro 103 (Kereneng–Tegal and Tegal–Sanur bemos); Matahari, Jl Dewi Sartika 4 (Tegal–Sanur bemo); and Tiara Dewata, Jl Sutoyo 55 (Kereneng–Tegal bemo). Matahari has a small basement bookstore.
**Telephones** Telkom offices at Jl Teuku Umar 6 and on Jl Durian. Wartels all over the city.

**Tourist driving licence** Available for cars or motorbikes (Rp200,000) in 20min from Pelayan Sim Tourist (Mon–Fri 8am–3pm, Sat 8am–1pm; ☎0361/243939) inside the Kantor Bersama Samsat on Jl Cok Agung Tresna in Renon. Take a passport and home driving licence.

## Moving on

**By bemo and public bus** Bemo and bus services operate out of four main terminals but are becoming less reliable on certain shorter routes because of the huge rise in motorbike ownership. Expect to wait for up to an hour between departures, especially in the afternoon; most don't run after 5pm. Bemos from Tegal run to destinations south of Denpasar; Batubulan is for Ubud, east and north Bali; and Ubung serves north and west Bali, Padang Bai (for Lombok) and Java. Sample fares include: Kuta Rp5000; Ubud Rp7000; Candi Dasa Rp10,000; and Padang Bai Rp20,000. No shuttle buses operate out of Denpasar.

**Batubulan terminal** to: Candi Dasa (2hr); Gianyar (1hr); Kintamani (1hr 30min); Kuta (eastern edge; Damri buses; 40min); Padang Bai (for Lombok; 1hr 40min); Sanur (western edge; 20min); Semarapura (1hr 20min); Singaraja (Penarukan terminal; 3hr); Ubud (50min).

**Kereneng terminal** to: Sanur (15–25min).

**Tegal terminal** to: Kuta (25min); Ngurah Rai Airport (35min); Sanur (25min).

**Ubung terminal** to: Bedugul (1hr 30min); Cekik (3hr); Gilimanuk (3hr 15min); Jakarta (24hr); Kediri (30min); Lalang Linggah (1hr 15min); Medewi (1hr 30min); Singaraja (Sukasada terminal; 3hr); Solo (15hr); Surabaya (10hr); Yogyakarta (15hr).

**By ferry (Pelni)** Pelni boat tickets for long-distance ferries to other Indonesian islands from Pelni offices at Jl Diponegoro 165 ☎0361/234680, Benoa Harbour ☎0361/723689 and in Kuta (see p.292).

**Destinations from Benoa harbour:** services twice a fortnight except where indicated to: Bima (Sumbawa; 3 fortnightly; 21–31hr); Bitung (Sulawesi; 5 days); Ende (Flores; 2 days); Kupang (West Timor; fortnightly; 26hr); Labuanbajo (Flores; 30hr); Makassar (Sulawesi; 2–4 days); Maumere (Flores; fortnightly; 3 days); Surabaya (Java; fortnightly; 23hr); Waingapu (Sumba; 26hr).

**By ferry (other)** Benoa Harbour to the Gili Islands (1–2 daily; 2hr–2hr 30min).

**By air** Domestic airline tickets from Nitour, Jl Veteran 5 (☎0361/234742, Ⓔnitourbali@denpasar.wasantara.net.id); international and domestic airline tickets from Puri Astina Tour, Jl Moh Yamin 1A, Renon (☎0361/223552, Ⓔastina@denpasar.wasantara.net.id). Garuda has a city check-in at Jl Sugianyar 5 (Mon–Thurs 7.30am–4.30pm, Fri 7.30am–5pm, Sat & Sun 9am–1pm; 24-hr national call centre ☎0804/180 7807 or ☎021/2351 9999 if calling from a mobile). For other airlines see p.291; for airport departures info see Kuta, p.292.

**By train** No trains on Bali, but train tickets for Java from Jl Diponegoro 150 Blok B4 ☎0361/227131.

# KUTA, LEGIAN AND SEMINYAK

Crammed with hotels, restaurants, bars, clubs, tour agencies and shops, the **KUTA-LEGIAN-SEMINYAK** conurbation, 10km southwest of Denpasar, is Bali's biggest, brashest beach resort. The beach itself is the finest on the island, its gentle curve of golden sand stretching for 8km, lashed by huge breakers that bring experienced and novice surfers flocking, though be wary of the strong undertow and always swim between the red- and yellow-striped flags. Everyone else comes to shop and to party, fuelled by a pumping nightlife that ranges from the trashy in Kuta to the chic in Seminyak and Petitenget, though drugs, prostitution and gigolos (known locally as Kuta cowboys or mosquitos because they jump from woman to woman) feature all over. Although the resort's party atmosphere was shattered in 2002, when Islamic extremists from Java bombed Kuta's two most popular clubs, and again when Kuta Square was attacked in 2005, the good-time vibe has resurfaced. A **Monument of Human Tragedy** now occupies the 2002 "Ground Zero" site.

Accommodation, shopping and restaurant options broadly fit the same geographical pattern, with Kuta the destination of the young and fun, Legian the choice for a calmer, family stay, and Seminyak favoured by those with style and/or money. **Kuta** stretches north from the Matahari department store in Kuta Square to Jalan Melasti, while its southern fringes, extending south from Matahari to the airport, are defined as **Tuban**; **Legian** runs from Jalan Melasti as far as Jalan Arjuna

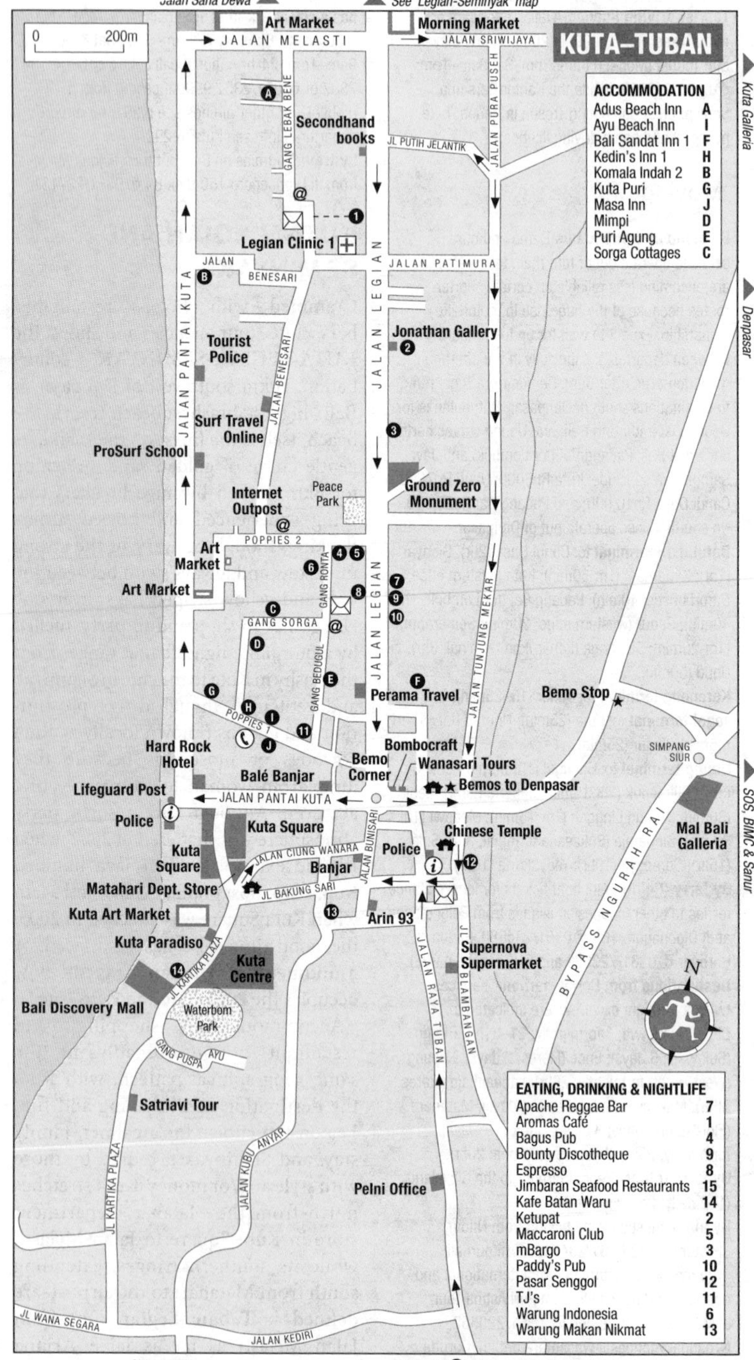

KUTA–TUBAN
Jalan Saha Dewa
See 'Legian-Seminyak' map
0 200m
Art Market
Morning Market
JALAN MELASTI
JALAN SRIWIJAYA
ACCOMMODATION
Adus Beach Inn A
Ayu Beach Inn I
Bali Sandat Inn 1 F
Kedin's Inn 1 H
Komala Indah 2 B
Kuta Puri G
Masa Inn J
Mimpi D
Puri Agung E
Sorga Cottages C
Kuta Galleria
Denpasar
SOS, BIMC & Sanur
GANG LEBAK BENE
Secondhand books
JL PUTIH JELANTIK
JALAN PURA PUSEH
Legian Clinic 1
JALAN BENESARI
JALAN PATIMURA
JALAN PANTAI KUTA
JALAN LEGIAN
Jonathan Gallery
Tourist Police
Surf Travel Online
ProSurf School
Ground Zero Monument
Internet Outpost
Peace Park
POPPIES 2
Art Market
GANG RONTA
JALAN TUNJUNG MEKAR
GANG SORGA
GANG BEDUGUL
Perama Travel
Bemo Stop
POPPIES 1
Hard Rock Hotel
Bombocraft
Bemo Corner
Wanasari Tours
SIMPANG SIUR
Balé Banjar
Bemos to Denpasar
Lifeguard Post
JALAN PANTAI KUTA
Police
Kuta Square
Chinese Temple
Mal Bali Galleria
JALAN CIUNG WANARA
JALAN BUNISARI
Police
Banjar
Matahari Dept. Store
JL BAKUNG SARI
Kuta Art Market
Arin 93
BYPASS NGURAH RAI
Kuta Paradiso
Supernova Supermarket
JL KARTIKA PLAZA
Kuta Centre
JL BLAMBANGAN
JALAN RAYA TUBAN
Bali Discovery Mall
Waterbom Park
N
GANG PUSPA AYU
Satriavi Tour
JALAN KUBU ANYAR
EATING, DRINKING & NIGHTLIFE
Apache Reggae Bar 7
Aromas Café 1
Bagus Pub 4
Bounty Discotheque 9
Espresso 8
Jimbaran Seafood Restaurants 15
Kafe Batan Waru 14
Ketupat 2
Maccaroni Club 5
mBargo 3
Paddy's Pub 10
Pasar Senggol 12
TJ's 11
Warung Indonesia 6
Warung Makan Nikmat 13
JL KARTIKA PLAZA
Pelni Office
JL WANA SEGARA
JALAN KEDIRI
Airport
Airport & 15
Nusa Dua

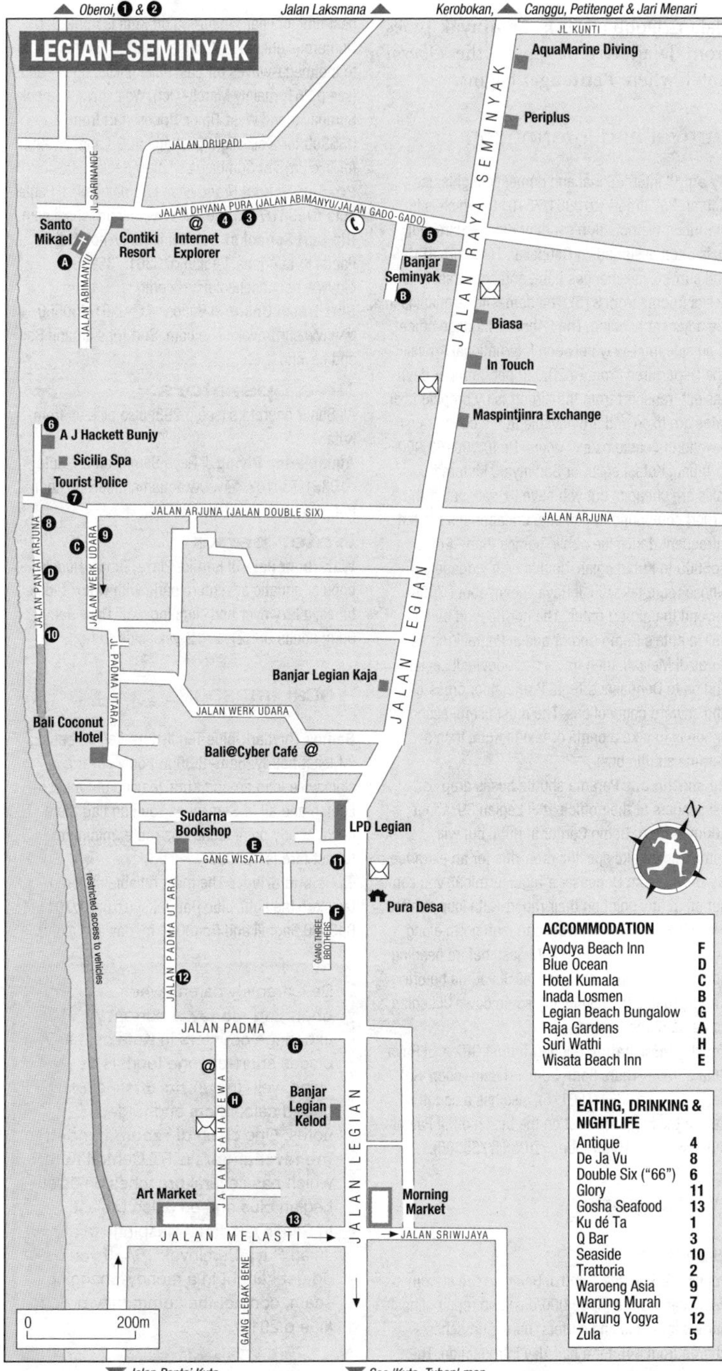
LEGIAN–SEMINYAK
Oberoi, 1 & 2
Jalan Laksmana
Kerobokan,
Canggu, Petitenget & Jari Menari
JL KUNTI
AquaMarine Diving
Periplus
JALAN RAYA SEMINYAK
JALAN DRUPADI
JL SARINANDE
JALAN DHYANA PURA (JALAN ABIMANYU/JALAN GADO-GADO)
Santo Mikael
Contiki Resort
Internet Explorer
Banjar Seminyak
JALAN ABIMANYU
Biasa
In Touch
Maspintjinra Exchange
A J Hackett Bunjy
Sicilia Spa
Tourist Police
JALAN ARJUNA (JALAN DOUBLE SIX)
JALAN ARJUNA
JALAN PANTAI ARJUNA
JALAN WERK UDARA
JL PADMA UTARA
Banjar Legian Kaja
JALAN LEGIAN
JALAN WERK UDARA
Bali Coconut Hotel
Bali@Cyber Café
Sudarna Bookshop
LPD Legian
GANG WISATA
Pura Desa
restricted access to vehicles
JALAN PADMA UT ARA
GANG THREE BROTHERS
JALAN PADMA
Banjar Legian Kelod
JALAN SAHADEWA
Art Market
Morning Market
JALAN MELASTI
JALAN SRIWIJAYA
GANG LEBAK BENE
0
200m
Jalan Pantai Kuta
See 'Kuta–Tuban' map
N
ACCOMMODATION
Ayodya Beach Inn F
Blue Ocean D
Hotel Kumala C
Inada Losmen B
Legian Beach Bungalow G
Raja Gardens A
Suri Wathi H
Wisata Beach Inn E
EATING, DRINKING & NIGHTLIFE
Antique 4
De Ja Vu 8
Double Six ("66") 6
Glory 11
Gosha Seafood 13
Ku dé Ta 1
Q Bar 3
Seaside 10
Trattoria 2
Waroeng Asia 9
Warung Murah 7
Warung Yogya 12
Zula 5

(Jalan Double Six); **Seminyak** goes from Jalan Arjuna up to the *Oberoi* hotel, where **Petitenget** begins.

## Arrival and information

**By air** All international and domestic flights use Ngurah Rai Airport (☎0361/751011), which is in the Tuban district, 3km south of Kuta Square, not, as is often assumed, in Denpasar. There are ATMs and currency exchanges here, and hotel-reservation desks (rooms from $15). The domestic terminal is in the adjacent building. The 24hr left-luggage office is outside, mid-way between International Arrivals and Departures (from Rp20,000 per item per day). Easiest transport from the airport is by prepaid taxi: rates are fixed and are payable at the counter just beyond the customs exit doors: Rp40,000–60,000 to Tuban, Kuta, Legian or Seminyak. Metered taxis are cheaper, but you have to walk out of the airport compound to hail one. Cheaper still are the infrequent dark-blue public bemos (5am–6pm; Rp5000 to Kuta/Legian, double with luggage), whose route takes in Jl Raya Tuban, about 700m beyond the airport gates. The northbound bemos go via Kuta's Bemo Corner and Jl Pantai Kuta as far as Jl Melasti, then travel back down Jl Legian and on to Denpasar's Tegal terminal for cross-city and onward connections. The most useful economy option is to take a bemo or taxi to Kuta, then a Perama shuttle bus.

**By shuttle bus** Perama shuttle buses drop passengers at their office at Jl Legian 39, about 100m north of Bemo Corner in Kuta, but will sometimes make specific drop-offs for an extra fee.

**By bemo** From Denpasar's Tegal terminal, you can get off at any point on their round-Kuta loop, which runs via Bemo Corner, west and then north along Jl Pantai Kuta, east along Jl Melasti before heading north up Jl Legian only as far as Jl Padma before turning round and continuing south down Jl Legian as far as Bemo Corner.

**Tourist information** Badung Tourist Office, Jl Raya Kuta 2 (Mon–Thurs 8am–3pm, Fri 8am–noon, Sat 8am–4pm; ☎0361/756175), also has a counter beside the lifeguard post on the beach off Jl Pantai Kuta (Mon–Fri 10am–3pm; ☎0361/755660).

## Watersports

### Surfing

Poppies 2, Poppies 1 and Jl Benesari are crammed with board rental (Rp50,000/day) and repair shops, surfwear outlets and surfers' bars. Surf schools charge from $45 for a half-day introduction. The best time of year for surfing off Kuta is April–Oct. Numerous agents in Kuta sell "surfari" surfing tours to the mega-waves off East Java (including G-Land (see p.251; mainly March–Oct), West Java, Lombok, Sumbawa and West Timor. Prices start from US$300 for a six-night package at G-Land, or $390 for five days at Sumbawa's Lakey Peak.

**Pro Surf School** *Grand Istana Rama* hotel, Jl Pantai Kuta ☎0361/7441466, Ⓦwww.prosurfschool.com.

**Rip Curl School of Surf** *Blue Ocean* hotel, Jl Pantai Kuta Arjuna, Legian ☎0361/735858, Ⓦwww.ripcurlschoolofsurf.com.

**Surf Travel Online** Jl Benesari ☎0361/750550, Ⓦwww.surftravelonline.com. Surf trips around Bali and beyond.

### Dive operators

All Sanur operators (see p.293) also pick up from Kuta.

**AquaMarine Diving** Jl Raya Seminyak 2A, Kuta ☎0361/730107, Ⓦwww.aquamarinediving.com. PADI five-star Gold Palm Resort.

### Water parks

**Waterbom Park** Jl Kartika Plaza, Tuban. Hugely popular aquatic adventure park, with water slides, tubes, a lazy river and climbing wall. Daily 9am–6pm; adults US$21, 2–12-year-olds $11.

## Local transport

**Bemos** The dark-blue Tegal-Kuta-Legian bemos (at least hourly; 5am–8.30pm) only cover a clockwise loop around Kuta, leaving out most of Legian and all of Seminyak. You can flag them down at any point along this route; minimum tourist fare is Rp3000.

**Taxis and drivers** The most reliable metered taxis are the light-blue Bali Taksi (☎0361/701111; Rp5000 flagfall and Rp4000/km, day and night).

> Be extremely careful when **changing money** at currency exchange counters in Kuta as many places short-change tourists by using well-known **rip-offs** including rigged calculators and folded notes. One chain of **recommended moneychangers** is PT Central Kuta, which has several branches on Jalan Legian plus one on Jalan Melasti. In Seminyak go to Maspintjinra at Jalan Raya Seminyak 16A. If you do get caught in a money-changing scam, contact the community police (see p.291).

The informal taxi service offered by the ubiquitous transport touts is rarely cheaper for short trips but can be worthwhile for longer journeys and day-trips (from Rp350,000/day). A recommended freelance English-speaking driver and guide is Wayan Artana (ⓣ0812/396 1296, ⓔiartana@hotmail.com).

**Car, motorbike and bicycle rental** Tour agents and touts through the resort offer cars (from Rp90,000/day), motorbikes (from Rp50,000) and bicycles (Rp25,000) for rent.

## Accommodation

The biggest concentration of cheap accommodation is in Kuta, along Poppies 1, Poppies 2 and Jl Benesari. Legian has good-value places with pools and a/c; Seminyak is sophisticated and pricey.

### Kuta

**Adus Beach Inn** Off Gang Lebak Bene ⓣ0361/755419. Very cheap, simple losmen rooms down a quiet but convenient lane. ❷

**Ayu Beach Inn** Poppies 1 ⓣ0361/752091, ⓦwww.ayubeachinn.baliklik.com. Well-located and efficiently run budget option with pool. Fan and a/c. ❸–❺

**Bali Sandat Inn 1** Jl Legian 120 ⓣ0361/753491. Clean, well-maintained fan and a/c rooms in the heart of the action. ❷–❹

**Kedin's Inn 1** Poppies 1 ⓣ0361/756771. Backpackers' favourite: large, attractive fan and a/c rooms plus a pool. ❷–❹

**Komala Indah 2** Jl Benesari ⓣ0361/754258. Good, simple, ultra-cheap fan and a/c rooms in a nice garden near the beach. ❶–❹

**Kuta Puri** Poppies 1 ⓣ0361/751903, ⓦwww.kutapuri.com. Terraced a/c rooms and more luxurious bungalows in a very spacious garden with a large pool. ❼

**Masa Inn** Poppies 1 #27 ⓣ0361/758507, ⓦwww.masainn.com. Well-priced hotel with a large pool, sociable garden area and plain but good a/c rooms. ❻

**Mimpi** Gang Sorga, off Poppies 1 ⓣ0361/751848, ⓔkumimpi@yahoo.com.sg. Just seven characterful, thatched, fan-cooled Balinese cottages in a shady garden with pool. ❹–❻

**Puri Agung** Gang Bedugul, off Poppies 1 ⓣ0361/750054. Welcoming little losmen with cheap, sprucely kept rooms packed into two storeys around a minuscule courtyard. ❷

**Sorga Cottages** Gang Sorga ⓣ0361/751897, ⓦwww.angelfire.com/nb/sorgacott. Good-value fan and a/c rooms in a three-storey block set round a small pool and a restaurant. ❸–❺

### Legian and Seminyak

**Ayodya Beach Inn** Gang Three Brothers ⓣ0361/752169, ⓔayodyabeachinn@yahoo.com. Cheap and friendly losmen with fifteen mostly fairly basic terraced fan rooms. ❷

**Blue Ocean** Jl Pantai Arjuna ⓣ0361/730289. Simply furnished fan rooms (some with kitchens) in a prime spot on the beachfront road. Surf school on the premises. ❹

**Hotel Kumala** (*Kumala Grand*) Jl Werk Udara ⓣ0361/732186, ⓔgkumala@indosat.net.id. Great-value place close to shore, with appealing a/c rooms and cottages, plus two pools. ❹–❻

**Inada Losmen** Gang Bima 9, off Jl Dhyana Pura and Jl Raya Seminyak ⓣ0361/732269, ⓔputuinada@hotmail.com. Top-value losmen on a quiet leafy lane, with a dozen large, clean rooms set round a garden yard. ❷

**Legian Beach Bungalow** Jl Padma ⓣ0361/751087, ⓔgading_lbb@yahoo.com. Inviting place with simple but pleasant fan and a/c rooms and bungalows set in a spacious garden with pool. ❷–❹

**Raja Gardens** Jl Dhyana Pura ⓣ0361/730494, ⓔjdw@eksadata.com. Six unusual, nicely furnished fan-cooled bungalows and a big pool one minute's walk from the beach. ❻

**Suri Wathi** Jl Sahadewa 12 ⓣ0361/753162, ⓔsuriwati@yahoo.com. Popular, family-run little hotel with well-priced fan and a/c rooms and bungalows, plus a decent pool. ❹–❻

**Wisata Beach Inn** Off Jl Padma Utara ⓣ0361/755987. Quiet little place with just four split-level fan bungalows (each sleeps four) and balconies on both floors. ❷–❸

## Eating

### Kuta and Tuban

**Aromas Café** Jl Legian. Classy Mexican, Indian and Indonesian veggie food, plus cakes and vegetable juices. Mains Rp25,000–45,000.

**Jimbaran Seafood Restaurants** Jimbaran Beach, 4km south of Kuta (about Rp30,000 by taxi). Over fifty seafood warung barbecue the day's catch at tables on the beach here (from Rp60,000 with trimmings); they open from noon but are best in candlelight.

**Kafe Batan Waru** Jl Kartika Plaza. Wholesome specialities from across Indonesia (mostly Rp40,000–70,000), including spicy, Manado-style chicken and *tenggiri* fish steaks in turmeric sauce.

**Ketupat** Jl Legian 109. Upscale, atmospheric spot serving dishes from around Indonesia

(Rp40,000–70,000), including prawns in spicy Sulawesi sauce, and lime-stewed chicken from Kalimantan.

**Maccaroni Club** Jl Legian 52. Lounge-style dining with mellow DJ sounds, comfy armchairs and free WiFi, plus twenty Absolut cocktails and predominantly Italian food (Rp30,000–80,000).

**Pasar Senggol** Jl Blambangan. Kuta's main night market is busy with hot-food stalls serving cheap local grub from around 5pm until the early hours.

**TJ's** Poppies 1. Popular Californian/Mexican restaurant with tables set around a water garden. Mid-priced menu of fajitas, buffalo wings and enchiladas (around Rp45,000), plus margaritas and strawberry daiquiris.

**Warung Indonesia** Gang Ronta. Welcoming, budget warung where *nasi campur* costs just Rp7500.

**Warung Makan Nikmat** just off Jl Kubu Anyar (50m west from the southern end of Gang Kresek or 300m west of Supernova). Locals crowd here at lunchtime for the bargain Rp6500 *nasi campur* assembled from fifty different east Java-style dishes. Shuts around 2.30pm.

### Legian and Seminyak

**Antique** Abimanyu Arcade 7, Jl Dhyana Pura. Creative, good-value, modern Asian cuisine, including a tasty chicken and *urap* combo, and chocolate passionfruit tart. Mains Rp32,000–45,000. Dinner only; closed Mon.

**Glory** Jl Legian 445. Long-running mid-priced tourists' favourite that's known for its huge Rp29,500 "outback breakfasts".

**Gosha Seafood** Jl Melasti 7. Lobster's a speciality at this very popular, mid-priced seafood restaurant.

**TREAT YOURSELF**

Looks are all at **Ku dé Ta** (next to the *Oberoi* hotel on Jl Laksmana, Seminyak), a dramatic, designer restaurant whose indoor-outdoor beachfront dining area frames a stunning sea view with tables and loungers perfectly angled to catch a flattering glimpse of the fashionable clientele. It's a favourite expat haunt, especially after 11pm when a club vibe takes over, but the modern-European food is variable considering the price (Rp190,000 for saffron risotto, Rp270,000 for prosciutto-wrapped veal cutlet) so many people prefer to soak up the setting over a long, lazy breakfast.

**Seaside** Jl Pantai Arjuna. Ocean views from the streetside benches and roof terrace plus a menu that includes tortillas, home-made soups. *mahi mahi* fish fillet and veggie mezze. Mains Rp35,000–65,000.

**Trattoria** Jl Laksmana. Outstanding, home-style Italian cuisine served from an extensive, constantly rotating menu. Most mains Rp35,000–45,000l; evenings only.

**Waroeng Asia** Jl Arjuna 23. Shady café that's an expat fave for its palate-tingling, well-priced Thai food. Most mains Rp25,000.

**Warung Murah** Jl Arjuna. *Nasi campur* place that's popular with economy-minded expats. From Rp12,000 for a plate of two meat servings, two veggies plus rice.

**Warung Yogya** Jl Padma Utara 79. Another busy, unpretentious Indonesian place, where *nasi campur* (veg or non-veg) costs Rp12,000 and juices Rp5000.

**Zula** Jl Dhyana Pura 5. Predominantly organic vegetarian food, with macrobiotic *nasi campur* (Rp48,000), daily grain specials and booster juices.

## Drinking and nightlife

For gigs and nightlightlife listings see the free fortnightly magazine *the beat* (Ⓦ www.beatmag.com).

### Kuta

**Apache Reggae Bar** Jl Legian 146. Kuta's primary reggae spot pounds to the sound of Rasta beats played by the four house bands and resident DJs. Daily 11pm–2am.

**Bagus Pub** Poppies 2. Large and loud tourist restaurant and video bar. Daily 9am–2am.

**Bounty Discotheque** Jl Legian. Infamous hub of Australian excess, housed in a replica of Captain Bligh's eighteenth-century galleon. DJs play hip-hop and dance music, there are live bands, and foam parties happen a lot. Jam jars (lethal, pint-sized cocktails) are of course the signature drink. Daily 6pm till late.

**Espresso** Jl Legian 83. Capacity crowds at this small and always rockin' live music bar where musical punters are often invited up on stage. Daily 8pm–3am.

**mBargo** Jl Legian. Great music from hip-hop and R&B DJs ensures packed dance floors at this trendy lounge bar and dance club. Opens at 8pm but kicks off around 1–4am.

**Paddy's Pub** Jl Legian 66. Part of the *Bounty* complex and just as popular, this open-sided place gets crammed with Australian drinkers and hosts frequent drinking competitions and foam parties. Daily 4pm–4am; happy hour 7.30–11pm.

## Legian and Seminyak

**De Ja Vu** Jl Pantai Arjuna ❼, Legian. Happening, sleek and slender beach-view lounge-bar whose in-house DJs spin progressive house, electro and chill-out sounds to big crowds. Daily 9pm–4am.

**Double Six ("66")** Jl Pantai Arjuna, Legian. Large, lively, Legian institution that's currently massive with the gay crowd who congregate here after 2am for the hardcore dance music; Rp30,000 including one free drink. Daily 11pm–6am

**Q Bar** Jl Dhyana Pura, Seminyak. Seminyak's main gay venue stages different events every night, including drag shows, cabarets and retro theme nights. Daily 4pm–2am.

## Directory

**Airlines** Except where stated, all the following offices are at Ngurah Rai Airport: Adam Air, Jl Raya Sesetan 12B, Denpasar ⓣ0361/227999; Air Asia ⓣ0804/133 3333; Batavia ⓣ0361/751011 ext 5336; Cathay Pacific ⓣ0361/753942; China Airlines ⓣ0361/757298; Garuda ⓣ0804/180 7807 or ⓣ021/2351 9999 if calling from a mobile (both 24-hr), city check-ins in Sanur, south Kuta/Tuban, and Denpasar; JAL, Jl Bypass Ngurah Rai 100X, Tuban ⓣ0361/757077; Jetstar, contact Jakarta ⓣ021/385 2288; Korean Air ⓣ0361/768377; Lion Air/Wings ⓣ0804/177 8899; Malaysia Air ⓣ0361/764 995; Mandala ⓣ0804/123 4567 or ⓣ021/5699 7000 from a mobile; Merpati, Jl Melati 51, Denpasar ⓣ361/235358; Qantas, *Inna Grand Bali Beach hotel*, Sanur ⓣ0361/288331; Qatar Airways, *Discovery Kartika Plaza* hotel, Tuban ⓣ0361 752222; Royal Brunei, Soka Bali Arcade 8, Jl Bypass Ngurah Rai, Tuban ⓣ0361/759736; Singapore Airlines/Silk Air ⓣ0361/768388; Sriwijaya Air, Jl Teuku Umar 97B, Denpasar ⓣ0361/228461; Thai Airways, *Inna Grand Bali Beach hotel*, Sanur ⓣ0361/288141; Trans Nusa/ Trigana/Pelita Air ⓣ0361/754421.

**Banks and exchange** There are ATMs every few hundred metres and a Moneygram agent at Bank Danamon just south of Poppies 2 on Jl Legian.

**Batik classes** Batik artist Heru gives three-day workshops (Rp500,000) at his home: Arin 93 Gallery, Gang Kresek 5, off Jl Bakung Sari, south Kuta (ⓣ0361/765087, ⓔarin93batik@hotmail.com).

**Bookshops** Several secondhand bookstores on Poppies 1, Poppies 2, Jl Benesari and Jl Padma Utara. New books from branches of Periplus at Discovery Shopping Centre, Jl Kartika Plaza; Mal Bali Galleria, Jl Bypass Ngurah Rai (eastern outskirts of Kuta); *Made's Warung 2* complex, Jl Raya Seminyak; and on Jl Kunti, Seminyak.

**Cinema** Galleria 21 Cineplex, Mal Bali Galleria, Jl Bypass Ngurah Rai, east Kuta (ⓣ0361/767021); tickets from Rp20,000. Programmes are listed in the tourist freebie *What's Up Bali* and in the weekly English-language newspaper *The Bali Times*. Soundtracks are usually original, with Indonesian subtitles.

**Dentist** Bali Dental Clinic 911, Mal Bali Galleria, Simpang Siur roundabout, Jl Bypass Ngurah Rai ⓣ0361/7449911.

**Embassies and consulates** See Denpasar, p.284.

**Festivals and events** The Kuta Karnival (ⓦwww.kutakarnival.com) is held in early September and features parades, surfing and skateboarding competitions and gigs by local bands.

**Hospitals and clinics** The nearest hospitals are in Denpasar; see p.284. Most expats use one of two reputable small, private 24hr hospitals on the outskirts of Kuta, both of which have English-speaking staff, A&E facilities, ambulance and medivac services: Bali International Medical Centre (BIMC), Jl Bypass Ngurah Rai 100X, near the Simpang Siur roundabout ⓣ0361/761263, ⓦwww.bimcbali.com; and nearby International SOS (Klinik SOS Medika), Jl Bypass Ngurah Rai 505x ⓣ0361/710505, ⓦwww.sos-bali.com. Consultations cost from Rp540,000. Smaller, cheaper clinics include Legian Clinic (24hr consultation and dental services), Jl Benesari ⓣ0361/758503; and La Walon Clinic, Poppies 1 ⓣ0361/757326.

**Internet** Countless Internet centres throughout the resort; most charge Rp200–300/minute.

**Left luggage** At the airport; at Internet Outpost on Poppies 2 (ⓣ0361/763392; daily 9am–1am; large locker Rp30,000/day or Rp150,000/week); and, for Perama customers, at the Perama office, Jl Legian 39, Kuta (daily 7am–10pm; ⓣ0361/751875; Rp10,000 a week or part thereof).

**Pharmacies** Inside the shopping malls and department stores; on every major shopping street; next to Legian Clinic 1 on Jl Benesari, Kuta; and at La Walon Clinic on Poppies 1.

**Police** The English-speaking community police, Satgas Pantai Desa Adat Kuta, have a 24hr office on the beach in front of *Inna Kuta Beach Hotel* ⓣ0361/762871. The government police station is at Jl Raya Kuta 141, south Kuta (ⓣ0361/751598).

**Post office** Kuta's GPO and poste restante is on indistinct, unsignposted Gang Selamat, between Jl Raya Kuta and Jl Blambangan (Mon–Sat 8am–5pm). There are many small postal agents elsewhere in the resort, including on the ground floor of Matahari Department Store in Kuta Square.

**Shopping** Generally, browse the Kuta end of Jl Legian for cheaper souvenirs and surfwear, and the Legian/Seminyak end of Jl Legian for designer clothes and homewares. Go to Matahari department store, Kuta Square (daily 10am–10pm), for necessities or the colossal seafront Discovery Shopping Mall (10am–11pm) on Jl Kartika Plaza Kuta/Tuban for a one-stop frenzy.
**Spas and massage** On the beach (Rp30,000 for 30min) and (from Rp75,000 for 60min plus) at: Jari Menari, Jl Raya Basangkasa 47, Seminyak (☎0361/736740, Ⓦwww.jarimenari.com); Sicilia Spa, Jl Arjuna (☎0361/736292, Ⓦwww.siciliaspa.com; and Putri Bali beauty salon, next to *Wisata Beach Inn*, off Jl Padma Utara ☎0361/755987.
**Telephones** The dozens of private wartels mostly open from 8am–midnight and offer calls at Rp7000/min whatever the destination. Most Internet cafés also have Skype (from Rp200/min).

## Moving on

**By shuttle bus** The easiest way to reach the main tourist destinations on Bali and Lombok is by tourist shuttle bus and the most reliable service is provided by Perama (daily 7am–10pm; ☎0361/751875, Ⓦwww.peramatour.com), whose tiny office is located 100m north of Bemo Corner at Jl Legian 39. Perama buses leave from here, but you can buy tickets on the phone and through other agents and can arrange a pick-up from your hotel for an extra Rp5000. Typical fares include Ubud Rp30,000; Lovina Rp85,000; and the Gili Islands Rp240,000 (including boat transfer).
**Destinations:** Bedugul (daily; 2hr 30min–3hr); Candi Dasa (3 daily; 3hr); Gili Islands (daily; 9hr 30min); Kintamani (daily; 2hr 30min); Lovina (daily; 4hr); Mataram (Lombok; 2 daily; 8hr 30min); Nusa Lembongan (daily; 2hr 30min); Padang Bai (3 daily; 2hr 30min); Sanur (4 daily; 30min); Senggigi (Lombok; 2 daily; 9hr); Ubud (4 daily; 1hr–1hr 30min).
**By bemo** Dark-blue bemos run from Kuta to Denpasar's Tegal terminal (25min; Rp5000). The easiest place to catch them is at the Jl Pantai Kuta/Jl Raya Tuban intersection, just east of the Bemo Corner junction. For destinations further afield, you'll need to get a cross-city bemo from Tegal to another bemo terminal (see p.285).
**By ferry** Many Kuta travel agents sell boat tickets to Lombok and Nusa Lembongan and these include transfers to the relevant port; Perama shuttle bus (see above) is the best known operator. For Gili Islands transport and accommodation contact Island Promotions, The Gili Paradise Shop, Poppies 1 #12 (☎0361/753241, Ⓦwww.gili-paradise.com). Pelni long-distance boat tickets to other Indonesian islands from Jl Raya Tuban 299, 500m south of Supernova Supermarket (☎0361/763963).
**By air** Domestic and international airline tickets from: Perama, Jl Legian 39, Kuta ☎0361/751875, Ⓦwww.peramatour.com; KCB Tours, Jl Raya Kuta 127 ☎0361/751517, Ⓦwww.kcbtours.com; and Satriavi Tour, *Bali Rani Hotel*, Jl Kartika Plaza ☎0361/751369 ext 179, Ⓦwww.aerowisata.com. Garuda sales and city check-in at the *Kuta Paradiso* hotel in Tuban (Mon–Fri 7.30am–4.30pm, Sat & Sun 9am–1pm; national call centre ☎0807/180 7807). For other airline offices, see p.291. Any hotel will arrange transport to the airport (about Rp50,000 from Kuta), though metered taxis are usually cheaper (about Rp25,000 from Kuta). During daylight hours, the dark-blue Tegal (Denpasar)–Kuta–Tuban bemo also passes close to the airport gates (Rp3000–5000) but frequencies are random. Airport departure tax is Rp150,000 for international departures and Rp30,000 for domestic flights.
**Destinations:** Bima (1–2 daily; 1hr 15min); Ende (weekly; 2hr); Jakarta (21 daily; 1hr 40min); Kupang (3 daily; 1hr 40min); Labuanbajo (10 weekly; 2hr 20min); Makassar (2 daily; 1hr 10min); Mataram (7–8 daily; 30min); Maumere (daily; 2hr 20min); Padang (3 weekly; 3hr 30min); Surabaya (13 daily; 45min); Waingapu (5 weekly; 1hr 10min); Yogyakarta (6 daily; 1hr 10min).

## THE BUKIT

Just south of Kuta, southern Bali bulges out into **the Bukit** ("hill"), a harsh, infertile limestone plateau whose craggy coastline challenges surfers with its world-class breaks, most famously at Uluwatu and Padang Padang. Where once only hard-core wave-riders would endure the pot-holed tracks to get to its secluded little **surf beaches**, party-hungry backpackers are now following suit as the roads get improved and tiny hotels are hollowed out of the clifftops, often accessible only via steep rock-cut steps. Take local advice on where it's safe to swim as currents can be treacherous round here.

There's almost no public transport on the Bukit, so you'll need to rent a car or bike from Kuta; to get to the beaches, simply follow signs for the temple, Pura Luhur Uluwatu, at Bali's southwestern-most point, until directed otherwise.

## Surf beaches

The first of the main surf beaches is **DREAMLAND**, with gloriously white if rather congested sands; it's currently being developed by a condo project which has jeopardized budget accommodation facilities. Access is via the ostentatious entrance to the Pecatu Indah development. Fast developing into the liveliest of the Bukit surf beaches, nearby **BINGIN** enjoys the same great coastal scenery and a superior choice of accommodation. **The break at Padang Padang** is considered to be one of the most exciting in Indonesia and there's plenty of roadside accommodation here, while close by **SULUBAN** is the location of the world-famous **Uluwatu surf breaks**.

## Pura Luhur Uluwatu

Revered since the tenth century as one of Bali's most important temples, **Pura Luhur Uluwatu** (daylight hours; Rp3000) commands a superb position on a rocky promontory 70m above the foaming surf, at the far southwestern tip of Bali, 2km south of Suluban, 18km from Kuta. As a directional temple, or *kayangan jagat*, Pura Luhur Uluwatu is the guardian of the southwest and is dedicated to the spirits of the sea; it's also a state rather than a village temple and so has influence over all the people of Bali, not just the local villagers or ancestors. Despite all this, the temple structure itself lacks magnificence, being relatively small, and its greyish-white coral bricks for the most part unadorned. Most tourists come to Pura Luhur at **sunset**, when the setting is at its most dramatic and there's a performance of the *Kecak* **and Fire Dance** (daily 6–7pm; Rp50,000).

### Accommodation

**Ayu Guna Inn** Padang Padang roadside ⓣ0815/575 6294, ⓔayugunabali@yahoo.com. Popular spot whose rice-barn-style bungalows all have a mattress, fan, balcony and private outside bathroom. ❸

**Full Moon Warung** Bingin cliffside. Reasonably comfy accommodation in four upstairs en-suite rooms that all open onto a wide seaview terrace. ❸

**The Gong** Suluban roadside ⓣ0361/769976, ⓔthegongacc@yahoo.com. This chilled and friendly surfers' favourite has six fan-cooled rooms, rents motorbikes and sells warung-style food and travellers' breakfasts. ❸

**Guna Mandala Inn** Padang Padang roadside ⓣ0361/847 0673. Spruce, modern place with twenty good, clean fan rooms and a restaurant. ❸

**Mama and Ketut** Bingin cliffside. Ultra-basic, thin-walled rooms with shared bathrooms. ❷

**Mamo Home Stay** Suluban roadside ⓣ0361/769882. Six large, solid, sparklingly maintained fan rooms set around the garden of the family home ❺

**Pondok Indah Gung and Lynie** Bingin clifftop ⓣ0361/847 0933. Welcoming place with a dozen rather tasteful fan rooms set round a garden, some of them in pretty coconut-wood-and-thatch bungalows. ❺

**Sunny** Padang Padang roadside ⓣ0361/769887 Seven unexpectedly huge brick and woven-bamboo huts. ❷

# SANUR

Nicknamed "Snore" because it lacks the clubs and all-night party venues of Kuta, **SANUR** is actually an appealingly sedate resort with a distinct village atmosphere, a fairly decent, five-kilometre-long sandy beach, and plenty of attractive budget accommodation. It's also a major centre for diving and the main departure point for boats to Nusa Lembongan, plus it's only 15km to Kuta or forty minutes' drive to Ubud.

Though the sea here is only properly swimmable at high tide (a big expanse of shore gets exposed at low tide, and the currents beyond the reef are dangerously strong), there are lots of inviting restaurants along the beach and you can walk or cycle the entire 5km from the *Inna Grand Bali Beach* in the north to *Hotel Sanur Beach* in the south along a seafront esplanade.

### Arrival

**By shuttle bus** Perama shuttle buses terminate at Warung Pojok minimarket, Jl Hang Tuah 31, north Sanur; bemos run from near here to Jl Danau Tamblingan.

**By bemo or public bus** The only direct bemos to Sanur leave at irregular intervals from Denpasar terminals at Kereneng (green; 15min; Rp5000) and Tegal (blue; 30min; Rp5000). Both routes cover north Sanur's Jl Bypass/Jl Hang Tuah junction, dropping passengers just outside the *Inna Grand Bali Beach* compound, before continuing via Jl Danau Beratan and Jl Danau Buyan and running all the way down Jl Danau Tamblingan to the *Trophy Pub Centre* in south Sanur. From Denpasar's Batubulan terminal, white Damri buses bound for Nusa Dua drop Sanur passengers at the *Sanur Paradise Plaza* hotel on Jl Bypass in north Sanur (20min; Rp6500).

**By boat** All boats from Nusa Lembongan arrive at the jetty at the eastern end of Jl Hang Tuah, north Sanur, from where it's a 200m walk west to the Perama pick-up or 400m to the bemo drop at the Jl Bypass junction.

**By air** Taxis charge Rp85,000 from Ngurah Rai airport to Sanur.

## Local transport

**Bemos** The Denpasar–Sanur bemos (see above), are also useful for getting around Sanur, especially for destinations along the 2km-long Jl Danau Tamblingan; a local ride costs Rp3000.

**Taxis and transport touts** Ubiquitous metered light-blue Bali Taksi cars (ⓣ0361/701111; Rp5000 flagfall, then Rp4000/km) are most reliable. Negotiate with transport touts for longer rides and day-trips.

**Car and motorbike rental** Easily arranged through transport touts and tour agencies. Reputable car rental, plus optional insurance, from JBA, inside the compound of the *Diwangkara Hotel*, Jl Hang Tuah 54, north Sanur (ⓣ0361/286501, ⓔjbadwkbl@denpasar.wasantara.net.id).

**Bicycles** Countless outlets along Jl Danau Tamblingan and the beachfront promenade (Rp20,000–35,000).

## Watersports and diving

Four-day PADI Open Water dive courses cost about $380; dive excursions to superior reefs beyond south Bali average $100.

**Blue Oasis Beach Club** Beachfront of *Hotel Sanur Beach*, south Sanur ⓣ0361/288011. Parasailing, wakeboarding and water-skiing, plus windsurfing courses ($25/hr).

**Blue Season Bali** Jl Tamblingan 69XX, central Sanur ⓣ0361/282574, ⓦwww.baliocean.com. PADI five-star IDC dive centre.

**Crystal Divers** Jl Danau Tamblingan 168, central Sanur ⓣ0361/287314, ⓦwww.crystal-divers.com. PADI five-star IDC dive centre; also runs liveaboards to distant sites.

**Jeladi Wilis Boat Co-operative** Beachfront of the *Inna Grand Bali Beach* hotel, north Sanur ⓣ0361/284206. Snorkelling trips ($20 per person/hr), boat charter, kayak, windsurf and jet-ski rental.

## Accommodation

**Agung & Sue Watering Hole 1** Jl Hang Tuah 37, north Sanur ⓣ0361/288289, ⓦwww.wateringholesanurbali.com. Traveller-friendly little hotel with good-quality fan and a/c rooms only 250m from the beach. Very handy for boats to Nusa Lembongan. ❸–❹

**Ari (formerly Luisa) Homestay** Jl Danau Tamblingan 40, central Sanur ⓣ0361/289673. Elementary but cheerful and very cheap rooms, some with hot water, behind the family shop. Large breakfasts included. ❷–❸

**Coco Homestay** Jl Danau Tamblingan 42, central Sanur ⓣ0361/287391, ⓔketutcoco@hotmail.com. Archetypal homestay offering just eight budget rooms behind the family art shop. ❷

**Hotel Bali Rita** Jl Danau Tamblingan 152, central Sanur ⓣ0361/282630, ⓔbalirita@hotmail.com. A dozen exceptionally good-value a/c bungalows, some with kitchens, in a spacious garden off the road. ❹–❻

**Jambu Inn** Jl Hang Tuah 57, north Sanur ⓣ0361/286501, ⓔjbadwkbl@denpasar.wasantara.net.id. Tiny, quiet place with just eight fan and a/c bungalows, many with a separate living area, set round a cute garden with pool and gazebo. ❸–❻

**Yulia Homestay 1** Jl Danau Tamblingan 38, central Sanur ⓣ0361/288089. Attractive, terraced, fan-cooled bungalows in a homestay compound filled with the owner's prize-winning songbirds. ❷–❸

## Eating

Inside the Sindhu Market at the Jl Danau Tamblingan/Jl Danau Toba intersection, central Sanur, the **night market** is good for cheap local eats from around 5pm through to the early hours.

**Beach Café** Beachfront walkway south off Jl Pantai Sindhu, central Sanur. Sea-view couches indoors plus tables on the sand make this a great spot for breakfast – eggs Benedict, frittatas, lattes and full English (Rp35,000) – as well as dinner "taster platters" from Rp65,000.

**Bonsai Café** Beachfront walkway just north of *La Taverna* hotel, access off Jl Danau Tamblingan, central Sanur. Breezy seafront restaurant and late-opening bar that serves standard *nasi goreng*, pizza, pasta and seafood (Rp30,000–90,000), plus cocktails.
**Café Batu Jimbar** Jl Danau Tamblingan 75A, central Sanur. Trendy surrounds and wholesome food – roast vegetable salads, minted lamb medallions, home-baked cakes and breads – plus live music Tues, Thurs & Sat from 8pm. Mains Rp35,000–150,000.
**Massimo** Jl Danau Tamblingan 228, south Sanur. South Italian restaurant serving more than fifty types of pizza (from Rp37,000) plus specialities from Lecce and delicious home-made *gelato* (Rp16,500).
**Warung Blanjong** Jl Danau Poso 78, south Sanur. Good, cheap Balinese dishes (Rp11,000–30,000), including lots of vegetarian options.

## Drinking and nightlife

**The Cat and the Fiddle** Opposite *Hotel Sanur Beach*, Jl Danau Tamblingan, south Sanur. There's live Irish music at least three nights a week at this Ireland-focused bar-restaurant.
**Jazz Bar & Grille** Komplek Pertokoan Sanur Raya 15, next to *KFC* at the Jl Bypass/Jl Hang Tuah crossroads, north Sanur. Some of Bali's best jazz, blues and pop bands play live sets nightly from about 9.30pm. Daily 10am–2am.
**Kafe Wayang** Komplek Pertokoan Sanur Raya 12–15, same building as *Jazz Bar & Grille*, north Sanur. Bar-restaurant that stages regular live contemporary Balinese music.
**Lazer Sports Bar** Opposite *Gazebo Hotel* at Jl Danau Tamblingan 68, central Sanur. Big-screen TV sports, pool tables and live MOR bands.

## Directory

**Banks and exchange** ATMs and exchange facilities all over the resort.
**Bookshops** Periplus, inside Hardy's Grosir supermarket, Jl Danau Tamblingan 193, central Sanur.
**Embassies and consulates** Most embassies are in Jakarta (see p.217), but there's a UK consulate at Jl Tirta Nadi 20A, Sanur ⓣ0361/270601, ⓔbcbali@dps.centrin.net.id, and US and Australian consulates in Denpasar (see p.284).
**Hospitals and clinics** All the big hotels provide 24hr medical service; try the the *Inna Grand Bali Beach* (ⓣ0361/288511), or the *Bali Hyatt* (ⓣ0361/288271). Expats tend to use the two international clinics on the edge of Kuta (see p.291); the nearest hospitals are all in Denpasar (see p.284).
**Internet** Internet centres every few hundred metres on all main roads.
**Pharmacies** Several on Jl Danau Tamblingan, including Guardian Pharmacy next to Hardy's Grosir.
**Police** The police station is on Jl Bypass in north Sanur, just south of the *Paradise Plaza* hotel (ⓣ0361/288597).
**Post office** Main post office is on Jl Danau Buyan, north-central Sanur. There are postal agents opposite *Respati* hotel at Jl Danau Tamblingan 66, central Sanur and inside the Trophy Centre on Jl Cemara in south Sanur.
**Telephones** Numerous private wartels in central Sanur, and Direct Dial public phones in the basement of the *Inna Grand Bali Beach*.

## Moving on

**By shuttle bus** Perama shuttle buses depart from Warung Pojok minimarket, Jl Hang Tuah 31 in north Sanur (ⓣ0361/285592 ⓦwww.peramatour.com); other Perama ticket outlets, where you may also be able to get picked up, include the more central Nagasari Tours, opposite *Griya Santrian* hotel at Jl Danau Tamblingan 102 (ⓣ0361/288096), and Tunas Tour, next to *Resto Ming* on the southern stretch of the same road at Jl Danau Tamblingan 105 (ⓣ0361/288581).
**Destinations:** Bedugul (1 daily; 2hr–2hr 30min); Candi Dasa (3 daily; 2hr–2hr 30min); Gili Islands (1 daily; 9hr); Kintamani (1 daily; 2hr 15min); Kuta/Ngurah Rai Airport (5 daily; 30min–1hr); Lovina (1 daily; 2hr 30min–3hr); Mataram (Lombok; 2 daily; 8hr); Padang Bai (3 daily; 1hr 30min–2hr); Senggigi (Lombok; 2 daily; 8hr 30min); Ubud (4 daily; 30min–1hr).
**By bemo or public bus** Travelling by bemo to anywhere entails going via the Denpasar terminals at Tegal (for Kuta connections; dark blue; 25min; Rp5000) or Kereneng (most other places; dark green;15–25min; Rp5000); both services operate at random frequencies during daylight hours. The alternative for Ubud connections is the white Damri bus service to Denpasar's Batubulan terminal (hourly until about 3pm), which picks up from near the *Sanur Paradise Plaza* hotel on Jl Bypass in north Sanur.
**By taxi** A taxi ride to central Kuta should cost about Rp45,000.
**By boat** Sanur is the main departure point for boats to Nusa Lembongan, which leave from the eastern end of Jl Hang Tuah in north Sanur (see box on p.296). Gili Cat, a catamaran service to Gili Trawangan and Lombok, runs free transfers to the

departure point in Padang Bai from its central Sanur office at Jl Danau Tamblingan 51 (Ⓣ0361/271680, Ⓦwww.gilicat.com).

**By air** Air tickets from JBA, inside the compound of the *Diwangkara Hotel*, Jl Hang Tuah 54, north Sanur Ⓣ0361/286501, Ⓔjbadwkbl@denpasar.wasantara.net.id; and Sumanindo Tour, Jl Danau Tamblingan 22, central Sanur Ⓣ0361/288570, Ⓔsumantravel@dps.centrin.net.id. Garuda sales and city check-in at *Hotel Sanur Beach*, south Sanur (Mon–Fri 7.30am–4.30pm, Sat & Sun 9am–1pm; 24-hour national call centre Ⓣ0804/180 7807 or Ⓣ021/2351 9999 if calling from a mobile). Most hotels and losmen will arrange a car to Ngurah Rai airport for around Rp70,000, or you can hail a metered taxi for about Rp60,000; Perama shuttle buses charge Rp15,000/person.

## NUSA LEMBONGAN

Southeast across the Badung Strait, encircled by a mixture of white-sand beaches and mangrove, the tiny island of **NUSA LEMBONGAN** (4km by 3km) is an ideal escape from the bustle of the south. Seaweed farming is the major occupation here, supplemented by the tourist income from surfers, snorkellers, divers and anyone seeking attractive beaches, a bit of gentle exploring and an addictively somnolent atmosphere.

### What to see and do

Ranged along the west coast for over 1km, the low-key village of **JUNGUTBATU** has plenty of losmen and restaurants. **Coconut Beach, Chelegimbai and Mushroom Bay** (Tanjung Sanghyang) to the southwest and **Dream Beach** around on the south coast offer more upmarket accommodation and Mushroom Bay is the destination for day-trippers from the mainland. This can disturb the peace in the middle of the day but does little to detract from the idyllic white sand and turquoise waters.

You can **walk** around the island in three to four hours, and **bicycles** (from Rp40,000 per day) and **motorbikes** (Rp25,000–30,000 per hour, Rp100,000–150,000 per day) are widely available for rent in Jungutbatu.

The **surf breaks** are reached from Jungutbatu, and there are several sites for **snorkelling** accessible by rented boat around the island and, further away, the Penida Wall and Crystal Bay, close to the neighbouring island of Nusa Penida, are also popular (Rp150,000–350,000 for two

### TRAVEL TO AND FROM NUSA LEMBONGAN

Drop off points for the boats from Sanur to Jungutbatu and Mushroom Bay depend on the tide – you'll wade ashore wherever you land.

**Public boats from Sanur** Public boats operate between Sanur and Jungatbutu and Mushroom Bay (8am & 10am from Sanur, 10am only for Mushroom Bay, 7am from Mushroom Bay, 8am from Jungutbatu; 1hr 30min–2hr; Rp33,000 to Jungutbatu, Rp43,000 to Mushroom Bay). Buy tickets in Sanur from the office at the beach end of Jalan Hang Tuah near the *Ananda Hotel* and from the beachfront office in Jungutbatu.

**Perama** Ⓣ0361/751875, Ⓦwww.peramatour.com. Operates a daily tourist shuttle boat between Sanur and Jungutbatu (10.30am from Sanur, 8.30am from Jungutbatu; 1hr 30min; Rp70,000); book one day ahead. These boats connect with buses serving other parts of Bali and Lombok which you can book through tickets for.

**Public Speedboat** One daily, leaves Sanur, at 4pm, Jungutbatu at 3pm (40min; Rp150,000 one-way, Rp250,000 return). Buy tickets from vendors on Sanur beach near Jalan Hang Tuah and at the ticket office in Jungutbatu.

**Scoot speedboat** Ⓣ0361/285522, Ⓦwww.scootcruise.com. Two speedboats daily, three in peak season (9.30am & 4pm plus 1.30pm peak season from Sanur Beach; 8.30am & 3pm plus 11.30am from Nusa Lembongan; $18 one way, $35 return; 40min). Tickets from their office at Jl Hang Tuah 27 or office in Jungutbatu (Ⓣ0361/780 2255).

hours for two people including equipment). World Diving also take snorkellers, if the site is suitable (Rp100,000 per person, including equipment; about 4hr). The area around the islands is popular for **diving**, although the sea can be cold with treacherous currents so it is important to dive with operators familiar with the area. Manta Point off the south coast of Nusa Penida is renowned for *mola mola*.

## Diving

**World Diving Lembongan** (ⓣ0812/390 0686, ⓦwww.world-diving.com). The most established company on the island, a PADI five-star international operator, based at *Pondok Baruna* resort in Jungutbatu. The PADI Open Water dive course costs about $370 and a one-day, two-dive package $70.

## Accommodation

### Jungutbatu

**Agung** ⓣ0366/24483. Basic rooms in a concrete building plus some two-storey thatched places. ❷

**Bungalo No. 7** ⓣ0366/24497, ⓦwww.bungalo-no7.com. Good-value rooms at the far southern end of the beach, all with balconies or verandas. There's a sunbathing area overlooking the beach. ❹

**Linda Bungalows** ⓣ0812/360 0867, ⓔbcwcchoppers@yahoo.com. Aussie-owned spotlessly clean place right next to the beach. Rooms are in well-built two-storey buildings with good-quality furnishings. ❷

**Nusa Indah** ⓣ0366/24480. Set back behind the *Surfer's Beach Café*, the bungalows here are new and good quality. ❸

**Pondok Baruna** ⓣ0812/390 0686, ⓦwww.world-diving.com. A few hundred metres south of the main accommodation area. Basic rooms overlook the beach, and World Diving Lembongan is based here. ❷–❸

TREAT YOURSELF

**Tanis Villas** ⓣ0361/743 2344, ⓦwww.tanisvillas.com. Excellent, well-furnished bungalows with good verandas, well-spaced in an attractive garden just behind the glorious sweep of white sand at Mushroom Beach. There's a lovely pool as well. ❼–❽

### Dream Beach

**Dream Beach Bungalows** ⓣ0812/398 3772. In peaceful isolation in the far south above a fantastic white-sand beach, the large, well-kept rooms have fans and cold-water bathrooms. Take care if swimming nearby as the waves can be big and there's an undertow. ❹–❻

## Eating

Most of the accommodation has restaurants right on the beach. All dish up international and Indo-Chinese favourites, local seafood and the usual travellers' food.

**Ketut's Warung** A short distance behind the beach in Jungutbatu accessed north of *Agung*. Worth searching out for excellent local and Thai dishes, such as *Tom Ha Gai* and *Tom Yum* (Rp20,000–25,000).

**Linda** *At Linda Bungalows*. Tasty, well-cooked food from a small menu supplemented by daily specials. Mains Rp20,000–35,000.

**Nyoman's Warung** On the road, about ten minutes' walk north of Jungutbatu. *Nyoman* serves splendid Balinese dishes, mostly fish, at great prices (Rp35,000 for a meal).

**Pondok Baruna** Jungutbatu. All the food here is good, but if you like it hot, their *ikan pepes* and *Baruna curry* (both Rp28,000) are especially recommended, and the lassis (Rp10,000) are to die for.

## Directory

**Banks and exchange** Moneychangers along the beach in Jungutbatu or at Bank Pembangunan Daerah Bali (Mon–Fri 10am–1pm); rates are dire so bring plenty of cash.

**Hospitals and clinics** Contact the health centre, *klinik*, in Jungutbatu through your accommodation.

**Internet** At several cafés and hotels, about Rp1000 per minute or Rp45,000 per hour.

**Telephones** Private wartel in a beachside shop towards the south of Jungutbatu.

# PURA TANAH LOT

Dramatically marooned on a craggy, wave-lashed rock sitting just off the coast about 30km northwest of Kuta, **Pura Tanah Lot** (Rp10,000) is Bali's most photographed sight. Framed by frothing white surf and glistening black sand, its elegant multi-tiered shrines have become the unofficial symbol of Bali and they attract huge crowds of visitors every day, particularly around sunset. The temple is said to have been founded in the sixteenth century by the wandering Hindu priest Nirartha and is one of the most holy places on Bali. Only bona fide devotees are allowed to climb the stairway carved out of the rock face and enter the compounds; everyone else is confined to the base of the rock.

Although there are occasional bright-blue **bemos** from Denpasar's Ubung terminal direct to Tanah Lot, you'll probably have to go via **Kediri**, 12km east of the temple on the main Denpasar–Tabanan road. All Ubung (Denpasar)–Gilimanuk bemos drop passengers at Kediri bemo terminal (about Rp3000; 30min), where you should change on to a Kediri–Tanah Lot bemo (more frequent in the morning; about Rp5000; 25min). Alternatively, join one of the numerous tours to Tanah Lot that operate out of all major tourist resorts.

If you get stuck between bemos, you can **stay** at the rudimentary but prettily located *Pondok Wisata Astiti Graha* (ⓣ0361/812955; ❷), 700m up the road from the Tanah Lot car park.

## SOUTHWEST SURF BEACHES

West of Tabanan, the Denpasar–Gilimanuk coast road passes a couple of appealingly low-key black-sand **surf beaches**, both of them served by Denpasar (Ubung)–Gilimanuk bemos. The current can be severe all along this coast, so check locally before swimming.

About 26km west of Tabanan, the village of **LALANG LINGGAH** gives access to **Balian beach**, where *Balian Segara* (ⓣ0859/3536 8404; ❸) has four simple, concrete en-suite bungalows just above the surf, and *Balian Surfer Homestay* (ⓣ0361/747 4633, ⓦwww.baliansurfer.com; ❸–❹) has homestay rooms 300m from the sea.

Twenty-five kilometres further west, **MEDEWI** beach (about 2hr by bemo from Ubung) is known for its light current and fairly benign waves, making it a popular spot for novice surfers. The cheapest accommodation here is the primitive *Homestay G'de* (ⓣ0812/397 6668; ❶), whose cheap warung sits right on the shore. About 600m east, *CSB Beach Inn* (ⓣ0813/3866 7288; ❹–❻) has large, well-kept fan and a/c rooms overlooking the shorefront ricefields.

## UBUD AND AROUND

**UBUD** is Bali's cultural hub, a seductive town set amid terraced rice-paddies and known for its talented classical dancers and musicians and for its prolific painters and craftspeople. Tradition is particularly important here and temple festivals happen almost daily. However, although it's fashionable to characterize Ubud as the real Bali, especially in contrast with Kuta, it's a major tourist destination and bears little resemblance to a typical Balinese town.

### What to see and do

Arty, high-minded Ubud has the best art **museums** and **commercial galleries** on the island and is also a recognized centre for **spiritual tourism**, with many opportunites to try out indigenous and imported healing therapies. Organic cafés, riverside bungalows and craft shops crowd its central marketplace, while the surrounding countryside is ideal for **walks** and **cycle rides**, and there's easy access to the northern volcanoes.

There is major (mostly tasteful) development along the central Jalan Monkey Forest, and Ubud's peripheries now encompass the neighbouring hamlets of Campuhan, Sanggingan, Penestanan, Nyuhkuning, Peliatan, Pengosekan and Padang Tegal.

#### Central Ubud

Ubud's oldest and most central art collection is the **Museum Puri Lukisan** on Jalan Raya Ubud (daily

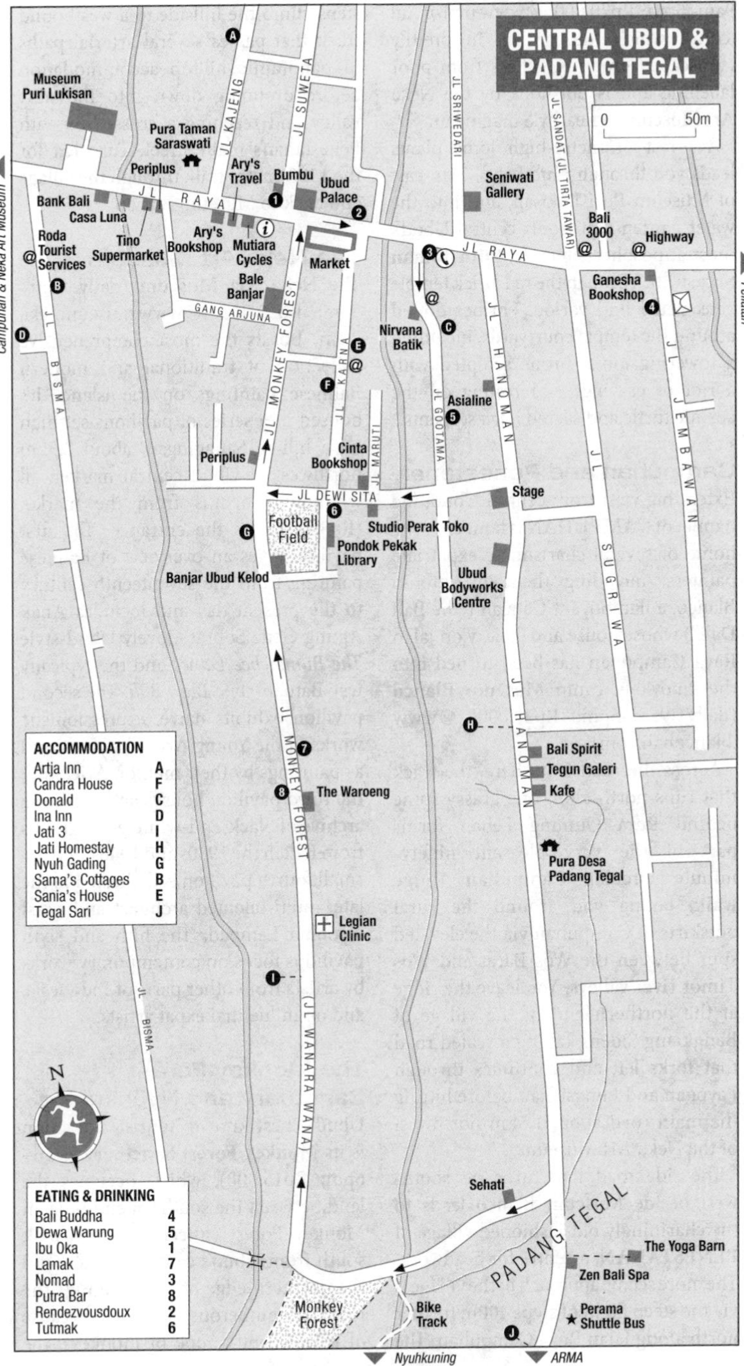
CENTRAL UBUD & PADANG TEGAL
0 50m
Ubud Botanic Garden
Campuhan & Neka Art Museum
Peliatan
Nyuhkuning
ARMA
Museum Puri Lukisan
Pura Taman Saraswati
Periplus
Ary's Travel
Bumbu
Ubud Palace
Bank Bali
Casa Luna
Roda Tourist Services
Tino Supermarket
Ary's Bookshop
Mutiara Cycles
Market
Bale Banjar
GANG ARJUNA
JL RAYA
JL KAJENG
JL SUWETA
JL SRIWEDARI
JL SANDAT (JL TIRTA TAWAR)
Seniwati Gallery
Bali 3000
Highway
Ganesha Bookshop
Nirvana Batik
JL BISMA
JL MONKEY FOREST
JL KARNA
JL MARUTI
JL GOOTAMA
JL HANOMAN
JL JEMBAWAN
JL SUGRIWA
Asialine
Periplus
Cinta Bookshop
JL DEWI SITA
Stage
Football Field
Studio Perak Toko
Pondok Pekak Library
Banjar Ubud Kelod
Ubud Bodyworks Centre
Bali Spirit
Tegun Galeri
Kafe
The Waroeng
Pura Desa Padang Tegal
Legian Clinic
(JL WANARA WANA)
Sehati
PADANG TEGAL
The Yoga Barn
Zen Bali Spa
Monkey Forest
Bike Track
Perama Shuttle Bus
N
ACCOMMODATION
Artja Inn A
Candra House F
Donald C
Ina Inn D
Jati 3 I
Jati Homestay H
Nyuh Gading G
Sama's Cottages B
Sania's House E
Tegal Sari J
EATING & DRINKING
Bali Buddha 4
Dewa Warung 5
Ibu Oka 1
Lamak 7
Nomad 3
Putra Bar 8
Rendezvousdoux 2
Tutmak 6

9am–5pm; Rp20,000; ⓦwww.mpl-ubud.com), which, though set in prettily landscaped grounds, suffers from poor labelling and is outshone by the Neka Art Museum in nearby Sanggingan.

A forest of metre-high lotus plants leads you through *Café Lotus*, 75m east of Museum Puri Lukisan, and into the water garden that fronts central Ubud's most atmospheric temple, **Pura Taman Saraswati**. Through the red-brick temple gate, you'll find various shrines dotted around the temple courtyards, including a towering lotus throne sculpted with a riot of carvings and resting on the cosmic turtle and sacred *naga* serpents.

### Campuhan and Penestanan

Extending west from central Ubud, the hamlet of **CAMPUHAN** is famous as the home of several charismatic expatriate painters, including the late Antonio Blanco, a flamboyant Catalan ("the Bali Dalí") whose house and gallery on Jalan Raya Campuhan has been turned into the enjoyably camp **Museum Blanco** (daily 9am–5pm; Rp20,000; ⓦwww.blancobali.com).

Across the road from here, the track that runs north along the grassy spine behind Pura Gunung Lebah forms part of the very pleasant ninety-minute circular **Campuhan Ridge walk**, taking you around the rural outskirts of Campuhan via the elevated spur between the Wos Barat and Wos Timor river valleys. You leave the ridge at the northern end of the village of Bangkiang Sidem, taking a sealed road that forks left and continues through Payogan and Lungsiakan before hitting the main road about 1.5km northwest of the Neka Art Museum.

The side road that turns off southwest beside Museum Blanco leads to the charmingly old-fashioned village of **PENESTANAN**, a centre for beadwork. The more scenic approach to the village is via the steep flight of steps 400m further north along Jalan Raya Campuhan. The steps climb the hillside to a westbound track that passes several arterial paths to panoramic hilltop accommodation before dropping down into the next valley and reaching a crossroads with Penestanan's main street. Turn left for the 1500-metre walk through the village and back to Museum Blanco.

### The Neka Art Museum

The **Neka Art Museum** (daily 9am–5pm; Rp20,000; ⓦwww.museumneka.com) boasts the most comprehensive collection of traditional and modern Balinese paintings on the island. It's housed in a series of pavilions set high on a hill in Sanggingan, about 2.5km northwest of Ubud central market; all westbound bemos from the market (Rp5000) pass the entrance. The first pavilion gives an overview of Balinese painting from the seventeenth century to the present day and includes Anak Agung Gede Sobrat's lovely Ubud-style *The Bumblebee Dance* and the typically wry Batuan-style *Busy Bali*. The second pavilion exhibits naive, expressionistic works in the Young Artists' style as well as paintings by their mentor, Arie Smit; the third pavilion houses an interesting archive of black-and-white photographs from Bali in the 1930s and 1940s; and the small fourth pavilion is dedicated to the late, multi-talented architect and artist Nyoman Lempad. The fifth and sixth pavilions focus on contemporary works by artists from other parts of Indonesia, and on influential expat artists.

### The Monkey Forest Sanctuary and Nyuhkuning

Ubud's best-known tourist attraction is its **Monkey Forest Sanctuary** (8am–6pm; Rp15,000), which occupies the land between the southern end of Jalan Monkey Forest (fifteen minutes' walk south from Ubud's central market) and the northern edge of Nyuhkuning. The focus of numerous day-trips because of its resident troupe of monkeys, the

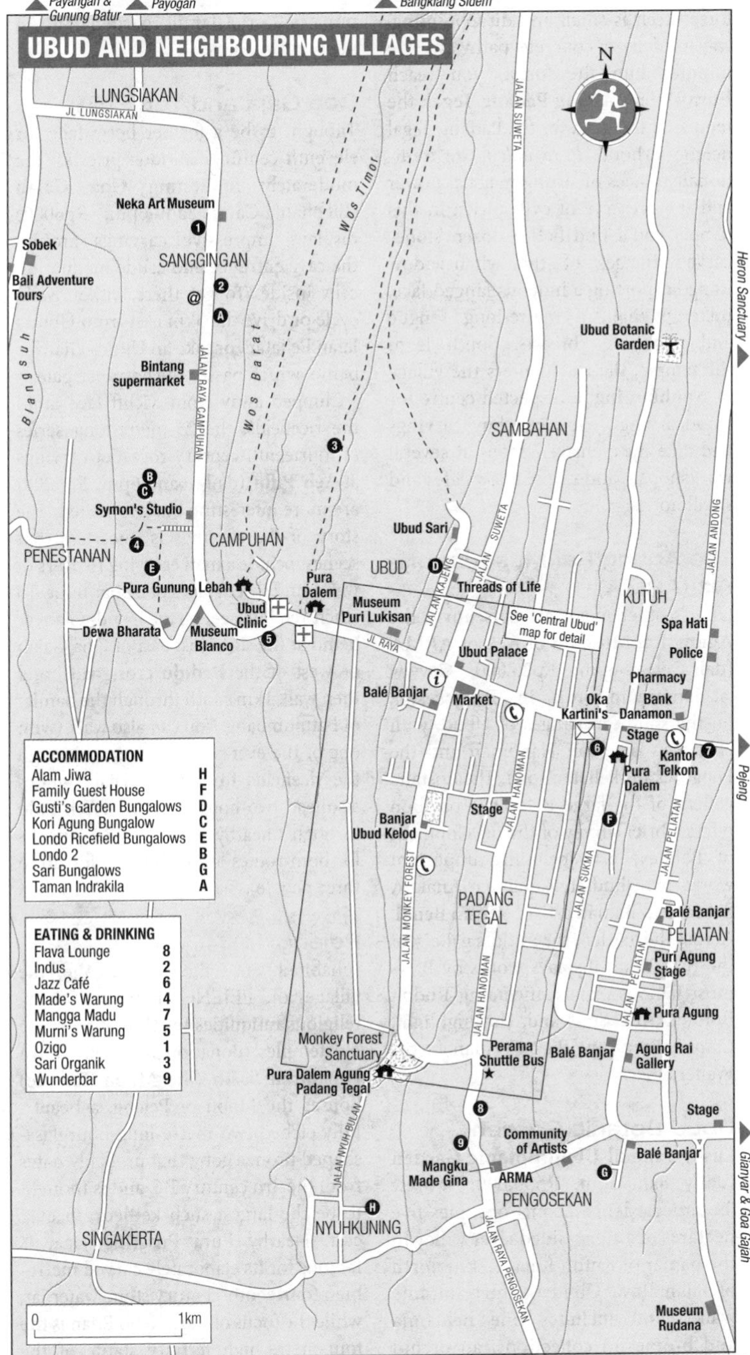

UBUD AND NEIGHBOURING VILLAGES
Payangan & Gunung Batur
Payogan
Bangkiang Sidem
LUNGSIAKAN
JL LUNGSIAKAN
Neka Art Museum
SANGGINGAN
Sobek
Bali Adventure Tours
Bintang supermarket
Symon's Studio
CAMPUHAN
PENESTANAN
Pura Gunung Lebah
Ubud Clinic
Déwa Bharata
Museum Blanco
Pura Dalem
Museum Puri Lukisan
UBUD
Ubud Sari
Threads of Life
See 'Central Ubud' map for detail
Ubud Palace
Balé Banjar
Market
SAMBAHAN
KUTUH
Ubud Botanic Garden
Heron Sanctuary
Spa Hati
Police
Pharmacy
Oka Kartini's
Bank Danamon
Stage
Kantor Telkom
Pura Dalem
Pejeng
Stage
Banjar Ubud Kelod
PADANG TEGAL
Balé Banjar
PELIATAN
Puri Agung Stage
Pura Agung
Monkey Forest Sanctuary
Pura Dalem Agung Padang Tegal
Perama Shuttle Bus
Balé Banjar
Agung Rai Gallery
Stage
Community of Artists
Balé Banjar
Mangku Made Gina
ARMA
PENGOSEKAN
Gianyar & Goa Gajah
NYUHKUNING
SINGAKERTA
Museum Rudana
Lodtunduh
Sukawati & Denpasar
JALAN SUWETA
JALAN RAYA CAMPUHAN
Wos Barat
Wos Timor
Blangsuh
JL RAYA
JALAN KAJENG
JALAN SUWETA
JALAN ANDONG
JALAN HANOMAN
JALAN SUKMA
JALAN PELIATAN
JALAN MONKEY FOREST
JALAN NYUH BULAN
JALAN RAYA PENGOSEKAN
0 1km
N
ACCOMMODATION
Alam Jiwa H
Family Guest House F
Gusti's Garden Bungalows D
Kori Agung Bungalow C
Londo Ricefield Bungalows E
Londo 2 B
Sari Bungalows G
Taman Indrakila A
EATING & DRINKING
Flava Lounge 8
Indus 2
Jazz Café 6
Made's Warung 4
Mangga Madu 7
Murni's Warung 5
Ozigo 1
Sari Organik 3
Wunderbar 9

forest itself is small and disappointing, traversed by a concrete pathway. Five minutes into the forest, you reach **Pura Dalem Agung Padang Tegal**, the temple of the dead for the Padang Tegal neighbourhood. *Pura dalem* are traditionally places of strong magical power and the preserve of evil spirits; in this temple you'll find half a dozen stone-carved images of the witch-widow Rangda sporting a hideous fanged face, unkempt hair, a metre-long tongue and pendulous breasts. South from the temple, the track enters the village of **Nyuhkuning**, a respected centre for woodcarving – you can buy carvings and take inexpensive lessons at several workshops – and site of a few cafés and small hotels.

### The Agung Rai Museum of Art (ARMA)

Ubud's other major art museum is the **Agung Rai Museum of Art**, or **ARMA** (daily 9am–6pm; Rp25,000; Ⓦwww.armamuseum.com), in Pengosekan, on the southern fringes of Ubud, with entrances on Jalan Hanoman and the Pengosekan–Peliatan road. The upstairs gallery of the large Bale Daja pavilion offers a brief survey of the development of Balinese art, including important works by Ubud-style painter Anak A Sobrat and Batuan artist I Wayan Bendi. Across the garden, the middle gallery of the Bale Dauh displays works by Bali's most famous expats, including Rudolf Bonnet, Arie Smit and, the highlight, *Calonnarang* by the German artist Walter Spies.

### Ubud Botanic Garden

Lush, tranquil **Ubud Botanic Garden** (daily 8am–6pm; Rp50,000; Ⓦwww.botanicgardenbali.com) occupies five hectares of a steep-sided river valley in the banjar of Kutuh Kaja, 1.7km north of Jalan Raya Ubud (a thirty-minute walk), and includes fine heliconia and bromeliad collections, an orchid nursery, an Islamic garden and a meditation court.

### Goa Gaja and Yeh Pulu

Thought to be a former hermitage for eleventh-century Hindu priests, the moderately interesting **Goa Gajah** (Elephant Cave; 8am–6pm; Rp6000) displays impressive carvings around the cave entrance and crude meditation cells inside. To get there, either walk, cycle or drive the 3km east from Ubud's Jalan Peliatan, or take an Ubud–Gianyar bemo, which passes the entrance gate.

Chipped away from a cliff face amid the ricefields, the 25-metre-long series of fourteenth-century rock-cut carvings at **Yeh Pulu** (daily 6am–6pm; Rp6000) are more interesting but less visited. The story of the carvings is uncertain, but scenes include a man carrying two jars of water, and three stages of a boar hunt. To reach Yeh Pulu, get off the Ubud–Gianyar bemo at the signs just east of Goa Gajah or west of the **Bedulu** crossroads, and then walk 1km south through the hamlet of Batulumbang. You can also walk (with one of the ever-present guides) through the ricefields from Goa Gajah; guides also lead two-hour treks from Yeh Pulu through nearby countryside (prices for both routes are Rp100,000 for up to three people).

### Pejeng

Inhabited since the Bronze Age, the village of PEJENG harbours many religious antiquities and three interesting old temples (donation required). **Pura Penataran Sasih** (the **Moon Temple**) houses the Moon of Pejeng, a beautifully etched two-metre-long hourglass-shaped bronze gong that probably dates from the 3rd century BC and is thought to be the largest such kettledrum ever cast. Nearby Pura Pusering Jagat is famous for its elaborately carved metre-high fourteenth-century stone water jar, while the focus of Pura Kebo Edan is the four-metre-high fertility statue of the

**Pejeng Giant**, complete with massive lifelike phallus. To reach Pejeng from Ubud, take a Gianyar-bound bemo to the Bedulu crossroads and then either wait for a Tampaksiring-bound one, or walk 1km to the temples.

### Gunung Kawi

Hewn from the rocky walls of the lush, enclosed valley of the sacred Pakrisan River, the eleventh-century royal *candi* (tomb-style memorials) at Gunung Kawi (daily 8am–5.30pm; Rp6000) occupy a lovely, impressive spot and don't get many visitors. They're signed about 400m north of **Tampaksiring's** bemo terminus (served by Gianyar–Bedulu–Tampaksiring bemos).

## Arrival

**By shuttle bus** Perama shuttle buses terminate at the Perama office at the southern end of Jl Hanoman in Padang Tegal, about 750m from the bottom of Jl Monkey Forest and 2.5km from the central market. There are no local bemos or metered taxis from this inconvenient spot, so you'll either have to pay Rp5000 extra for the Perama drop-off service, negotiate a ride with a transport tout, or walk. Independent shuttle bus operators (from Kuta or Lovina for example) may drop you off more centrally.

**By bemo** All public bemos terminate in front of Ubud's central marketplace, at the junction of Jl Raya and Jl Monkey Forest (signed as Jl Wanara Wana, but rarely referred to as such).

**By air** Taxis charge Rp175,000 from Ngurah Rai airport (see p.288) to Ubud.

## Information and tours

**Tourist Information** Jl Raya (daily 8am–8pm; ☎0361/973285) posts dance-performance schedules and details of upcoming festivals, runs inexpensive day-trips and sells shuttle bus tickets. It also dishes out the excellent free *Ubud Community* booklet. If you're planning to do any local walks or cycle rides, buy the *Bali Pathfinder* map from any bookstore.

**Walking, trekking and cycling tours** Guided cultural walks and sunrise volcano treks with Keep Walking Tours, c/o Bali Spirit, Jl Hanoman 44B (☎0361/970581, Ⓦwww.balispirit.com/tours). Sunrise treks up Gunung Batur and Gunung Agung with Bali Sunrise 2001, Jl Raya Tegalalang 88 (☎0818/552669, Ⓦwww.balisunrise2001.com). Traditional medicine walks with Herb Walk, (☎0361/975051, Ⓔsupadupa@dps.centrin.net.id). Downhill bicycle rides with Bike Baik Tours, (☎0813/3867 3852, Ⓦwww.balispirit.com/tours).

## Local transport

**Bicycle rental** From Rp20,000/day from the efficient Mutiara Cycles, next to the tourist office on Jl Raya, and from many streetside outlets along Jl Monkey Forest.

**Car and motorbike rental** Numerous places on Jl Monkey Forest rent out motorbikes and cars. Reputable car rental, plus optional third-party insurance, from Ary's Business and Travel Service (☎0361/973130, Ⓔarys_tour@yahoo.com) on Jl Raya.

**Transport touts and drivers** There are no metered taxis in Ubud, so you need to negotiate with the ubiquitous transport touts or hire a driver. Expect to pay Rp10,000–20,000 for local rides on a motorbike, a bit more in a car. A day-trip to Kintamani will cost Rp300,000 all-in, for up to four people. Recommended freelance drivers include Putu Purnawan (☎0816/471 6857, Ⓔputu09@yahoo.com) and Nyoman Suastika (☎0813/3870 1962, Ⓦnyoman-suastika.tripod.com).

**Bemos** You can use the public bemos for short hops around the area (Rp5000): for Campuhan/Sanggingan, just flag down any bemo heading west, such as the turquoise ones going to Payangan.

## Accommodation

Accommodation on the lanes around Jl Monkey Forest is both central and and peaceful. Peliatan, Penestanan, Campuhan/Sanggingan and Nyuhkuning have better views but are more remote.

### Central Ubud and Padang Tegal

Except where stated, see map on p.299.

**Artja Inn** Jl Kajeng 9 ☎0361/974425. Classic, peaceful losmen offering six simple but pleasant bamboo-walled cottages with cold-water mandi. ❷

**Candra House** Jl Karna 8 ☎0361/976529. Nine typical losmen rooms with fans and cold water inside a quiet but central family compound. Good breakfasts. ❷

**Donald** Jl Gootama 9 ☎0361/977156. Tiny, well-run and friendly homestay with four bungalows (two with hot water) in a secluded garden compound. ❷

**Gusti's Garden Bungalows** Jl Kajeng 27 ⓣ0361/973311, ⓔgustigarden@yahoo.com; see map p.301. Fifteen pleasant, better-than-average losmen rooms, all with hot water, set around a swimming pool. ❹

**Ina Inn** Off Jl Bisma ⓣ0361/973317, ⓦwww.inainn.com. Attractively furnished hot-water ricefield cottages plus a fine rooftop pool. Great value. ❹–❺

**Jati 3** Off Jl Monkey Forest ⓣ0361/973249, ⓔjati3_ubud@yahoo.com. Good-quality losmen-style bungalows in a courtyard, plus four huge, split-level, riverside bungalows with big windows. ❸–❹

**Jati Homestay** Jl Hanoman ⓣ0361/977701, ⓦwww.jatihs.com. Comfortable bungalows, with hot water, facing the rice paddies, plus art studio. Run by a family of painters. ❸–❹

**Nyuh Gading** Jl Monkey Forest ⓣ0361/973410. Seven standard bungalows set in a pretty garden behind a restaurant, plus one family house with kitchen. ❷–❺

**Sama's Cottages** Jl Bisma ⓣ0361/973481, ⓦwww.balilife.com/sama's. Simple but charming ultra-typical Ubud hideaway of eight fan-cooled brick cottages built on steep tiers in a river gully. Also has a tiny pool. ❹

**Sania's House** Jl Karna 7 ⓣ0361/975535, ⓔsania_house@yahoo.com. Hugely popular, well-run, but densely packed backpackers' favourite with good bungalows (some a/c) and a small pool. ❷–❻

**Tegal Sari** Jl Hanoman ⓣ0361/973318, ⓦwww.tegalsari-ubud.com. Exceptionally appealing, tastefully furnished rooms, all with both fan and a/c, strung out alongside the paddy-fields. Also has a pool, and provides free local transport. ❻–❽

### The outskirts

See map on p.301

> **TREAT YOURSELF**
>
> **Alam Jiwa** Nyuhkuning ⓣ0361/977463, ⓦwww.alamindahbali.com. You could spend all day soaking up the view at this charming hideaway, where the ten generously sized bungalows all enjoy dramatic vistas of ricefields and Gunung Agung from the bathtub and balcony. Upstairs rooms have fans, downstairs are a/c. Staff are charming plus there's a pool and free transport into central Ubud. ❽

**Family Guest House** Jl Sukma 39, Tebesaya, Peliatan ⓣ0361/974054. Friendly upscale homestay offering well-designed bungalows, a couple of enormous suites, and great breakfasts. ❹–❻

**Kori Agung Bungalow** Northern ridgetop, Penestanan ⓣ0361/975166. Six well-furnished rooms, each with a large terrace and some with nice westerly paddy-field views. Access via the Campuhan steps on Jl Raya Campuhan. ❹

**Londo Ricefield Bungalows** Southern ridgetop, Penestanan ⓣ0361/976548, ⓦwww.londobungalows.com. Ultra-friendly, family-run little place up on the ridge offering four large two-storey west-facing cottages; each sleeps four and has a kitchenette. ❸

**Londo 2** Northern ridgetop, Penestanan ⓣ0361/976764. Amazingly good-value if simple two-storey ridgetop bungalows (can sleep four) with kitchenettes and fine ricefield views. Access via the Campuhan steps on Jl Raya Campuhan. ❷

**Sari Bungalows** Off the southern end of Jl Peliatan, Br Kalah, Peliatan ⓣ0361/975541. The fifteen simple bungalows here are some of the cheapest in Ubud; they're away from the touristed area and many overlook the paddy-fields. ❷

**Taman Indrakila** Jl Raya Sanggingan, Sanggingan/Campuhan ⓣ0361/975017. Offering a five-star view at two-star prices, the six traditional-style cottage rooms, with fan, afford spectacular vistas over the Campuhan ridge. Also has a pool. ❺

## Eating

### Central Ubud

**Bali Buddha** Jl Jembawan 1. The café that started the Ubud trend for wholesome organic food serves great bread, healthy juices and raw-food meals, salads and pastas (Rp25,000–37,000). The noticeboard advertises yoga and language classes.

**Dewa Warung** Jl Gootama. This typical Balinese warung sells *cap cay*, *nasi campur* and *nasi goreng* at typical Balinese prices (around Rp6000), attracting both savvy foreigners and local lads.

**Ibu Oka** Jl Suweta. Considered by many to roast the best *babi guling* (suckling pig) in Bali, for Rp10,000 with rice and *sambal*. Daily 11am to about 2.30pm.

**Lamak** Jl Monkey Forest. The outstanding, creative, modern-Asian menu at this large, fashionable restaurant includes medallions of butterfish (Rp75,000), hot raspberry soufflé, and lots of vegetarian dishes. Well worth the money.

**Nomad** Jl Raya Ubud 35. Serving good-value travellers' food since 1979, including great home-made ravioli (Rp24,000), gado-gado and black rice pudding.

**Tutmak** Jl Dewi Sita. Expats' favourite for coffee and cakes, plus smoked salmon bagels (Rp60,000) and full English breakfasts (Rp35,000).

### The outskirts

**Indus** Jl Raya Sanggingan ⓣ0361/977684. Sample local *tenggiri* river fish plus home-made cakes, breads and healthy salads while enjoying fine views over the Campuhan ridge. Free shuttle from *Casa Luna* in central Ubud.

**Made's Warung** Penestanan ridge. Homely spot that serves well-priced travellers' favourites, including cheap juices (Rp6000) and good *nasi campur* (Rp12,500).

**Mangga Madu** Jl Gunung Sari 1, Peliatan. Cheap, popular Indonesian warung known for its tuna dishes – sweet and sour, fried, or curried. Also does veggie curry, *nasi campur* and *nasi pecel* (Rp6000–15,000).

**Murni's Warung** Jl Raya Campuhan. Multi-tiered restaurant built into the Wos River valley and serving curries, home-made soups and Indonesian specialities, as well as strawberry cheesecake and banana and caramel cake. Free Wi-Fi. Mains Rp20,000–65,000.

**Sari Organik** Off Jl Abangan, about 800m walk north along a path from the aqueduct on western Jl Raya Ubud: follow signs from *Abangan Bungalows*. Marooned in the ricefields, this ultra chilled-out café grows its own organic produce and serves great veggie kebabs, delicious chicken, and lots of salads. Mains Rp17,000–35,000. Daily 8am–8pm.

## Drinking and nightlife

The bar scene can be very quiet, so choose a live-music night to be sure of a decent crowd. Where phone numbers are given, free transport within the Ubud area is usually available.

**Flava Lounge** Jl Raya Pengosekan. It's open mike on Wed nights at this pizza and Mexican-food restaurant.

**Jazz Café** Jl Sukma 2, Peliatan ⓣ0361/976594; free transport from *The Waroeng* restaurant on Jl Monkey Forest. Quality live jazz Tues to Sat from 7.30pm.

**Ozigo** Jl Raya Sanggingan, Sangginan ⓣ0812/367 9736. Expat bar with a small dance floor, DJs, theme nights and live music nightly from 10pm.

**Putra Bar** Jl Monkey Forest. Ubud's most Kuta-style bar has a dance floor, sports TV and live music at weekends.

**Rendezvousdoux** Jl Raya Ubud 14. Live world music at this secondhand bookshop and café, usually followed by a jam session, every Thurs from 8pm.

**Wunderbar** Jl Raya Pengosekan. There's a pool table at this a/c bar-restaurant, and live music every Fri and Sat. Closed Mon.

## Traditional dance

Up to nine different traditional dance and music shows are staged every night in the Ubud area; the tourist office publishes the weekly schedule (also available at ⓦwww.ubud.com) and arranges free transport to outlying venues. Tickets cost Rp50,000–80,000 and can be bought at the tourist office, from touts, or at the door. If you have only one evening to catch a show, either choose the lively **Kecak** (Monkey Dance), or go for whatever is playing at the **Ubud Palace** (Puri Saren Agung), central Ubud's most atmospheric venue.

## Courses

**Batik** Nirvana Batik, Jl Gootama 10 (ⓣ0361/975415, ⓦwww.nirvanaku.com; $35/day).

**Cookery** At *Casa Luna* restaurant, Jl Raya Ubud (ⓣ0361/973282, ⓦwww.casalunabali.com; Rp250,000); and *Bumbu restaurant*, Jl Suweta 1 (ⓣ0361/974217, ⓔbumbu_bali@plasa.com; Rp150,000).

**Crafts** Classes in woodcarving, beadwork, painting, batik, basketry, kite-making, mask-painting, shadow-puppetry and traditional offerings at Museum Puri Lukisan, Jl Raya (ⓣ0361/971159, ⓦwww.mpl-ubud.com; Rp350,000); ARMA, Jl Raya Pengosekan (ⓣ0361/976659, ⓦwww.armamuseum.com; $22–50); and Pondok Pekak, Jl Dewi Sita (ⓣ0361/976194, ⓔpondok@indo.net.id; Rp50,000–200,000).

**Language** Indonesian and Balinese at Pondok Pekak Library, Jl Dewi Sita (ⓣ0361/976194, ⓔpondok@indo.net.id; Rp120,000/2hr).

**Music and dance** Sehati, Jl Monkey Forest (ⓣ0361/976341, ⓦwww.sehati-guesthouse.com; Rp50,000/hr).

**Silversmithing** At Studio Perak, Jl Gootama (ⓣ0812/365 1809, ⓦwww.studioperak.com; Rp175,000).

**Yoga** Several daily classes at The Yoga Barn, southern Jl Hanoman (ⓦwww.theyogabarn.com; Rp90,000); arrange via the holistic information centre, Bali Spirit, Jl Hanoman 44B (ⓣ0361/970992, ⓦwww.balispirit.com).

## Directory

**Banks and exchange** There are ATMs throughout Ubud and its environs. Many tour agents offer exchange services, but see p.288 for details of common scams. Western Union agents include the GPO, and Bank Mandiri on Jl Raya Ubud.

**Bookshops** New English-language books and maps at Ary's Bookshop, Jl Raya; Ganesha Bookshop, Jl Raya; and Periplus, Jl Monkey Forest, Jl Raya Ubud and inside Bintang Supermarket on Jl Raya Campuhan. Secondhand books at Cinta Bookshop, Jl Dewi Sita; Pondok Pekak, Jl Dewi Sita; and Rendezvousdoux Jl Raya Ubud 14.

**Hospitals and clinics** For minor casualties go to the Legian Clinic, Jl Monkey Forest (ⓣ0361/970805), or the Ubud Clinic, which also has a dental service, at Jl Raya Campuhan 36 (ⓣ0361/974911). Both are open 24hr, are staffed by English-speakers, and will respond to emergency call-outs. For anything serious, the nearest hospitals are in Denpasar (p.284).

**Internet** Highway, Jl Raya Ubud (high-speed connection and laptop hookups; open 24hr); Bali 3000, Jl Raya Ubud; Roda Tourist Services, Jl Bisma 3; and Ary's Business and Travel Service, Jl Raya Ubud.

**Pharmacies** On Jl Raya Ubud, Jl Monkey Forest and Jl Peliatan.

**Police** The main police station is on the eastern edge of town, on Jl Andong, but there's a more central police booth at the Jl Raya/Jl Monkey Forest crossroads.

**Post office** The GPO on Jl Jembawan (Mon–Sat 8am–5pm, Sun & hols 9am–4pm) keeps poste restante, and there's a parcel-packing service at the back. There are postal agents throughout Ubud.

**Shopping** Souvenirs, mass-market handicrafts, and sarongs at the central market, Jl Raya Ubud. Silver jewellery at Studio Perak Toko, Jl Raya Ubud and Jl Hanoman. Handicrafts at Asialine, Jl Hanoman 8; Tegun Galeri, Jl Hanoman 44; and Mangku Made Gina near ARMA on Jl Hanoman. Quirky, portable musical instruments at Adi Musical Instruments, Jl Hanoman 7. Also worthwhile are Sukawati art market, 8km south of Ubud (served by Ubud–Batubulan bemos), and the handicraft outlets that line the 12km Ubud–Tegalalang–Pujung road (best with own transport).

**Spas and massage** At Nur Salon, Jl Hanoman 28 (ⓣ0361/975352); Ubud Bodyworks Centre, Jl Hanoman 25 (ⓣ0361/975720, ⓦwww.ubudbodyworkscentre.com); and Balinese Traditional Healing Centre, Jl Jembawan 5 (ⓣ0852/3710 4401).

**Telephones** The government Kantor Telkom is at the eastern end of Jl Raya Ubud (daily 8am–9pm) and has credit-card phones outside. There are IDD direct-dial phones outside the GPO on Jl Jembawan and in front of the market; phone cards are sold at Bintang Supermarket, Jl Raya Campuhan. Most internet centres offer international phone services and many also have Skype.

## Moving on

**By shuttle bus** Perama runs buses to the island's main tourist destinations and Lombok. It does pick-ups from central Ubud and from its office on southern Jl Hanoman (ⓣ0361/973316, ⓦwww.peramatour.com). Tickets are also available from the tourist office and some travel agencies. If travelling to northwest Bali, take a shuttle bus to Lovina and then change on to the bemo system.

**Destinations:** Bedugul (1 daily; 1hr 30min); Candi Dasa (3 daily; 1hr 30min–2hr); Gili Islands (1 daily; 8hr); Kintamani (daily; 45min); Kuta/Ngurah Rai Airport (5 daily; 1hr–1hr 30min); Lovina (1 daily; 1hr 30min–2hr); Mataram (Lombok; 2 daily; 7hr); Nusa Lembongan (1 daily; 2hr 30min); Padang Bai (3 daily; 1hr–1hr 30min); Sanur (5 daily; 30min–1hr); Senggigi (Lombok; 2 daily; 7hr 30min).

**By bemo** East- and southbound bemos leave from the central market on Jl Raya; north- and westbound bemos leave from just round the corner on Jl Monkey Forest. Services should depart at least half-hourly from about 6am until around 2pm, then at least hourly until about 5pm. For destinations south, west and on to Java you'll need to change in Denpasar. For Padang Bai (for Lombok) and Candi Dasa change in Gianyar.

**Destinations:** Campuhan/Sanggingan (5–10min); Denpasar (Batubulan terminal; chocolate-brown or light blue; 50min) via Peliatan (5min) and Sukawati (30min); Gianyar (turquoise or orange; 20min) via Goa Gajah (10min); Kintamani (brown or bright blue; 1hr).

**By boat** Perama sells combination bus and boat tickets for the Gili Islands and Lombok.

**By air** Air tickets from Ary's Business and Travel Service, Jl Raya Ubud (ⓣ0361/973130, ⓔarys_tour@yahoo.com). The most economical way to get to Ngurah Rai airport is by shuttle bus (Rp30,000 per person); transport touts charge about Rp150,000 per car.

# BESAKIH

The major tourist draw in the east of Bali is undoubtedly the **Besakih** temple complex (daily 8am–5pm; Rp10,000, parking Rp2000), situated on the slopes of **Gunung Agung**, the holiest and highest mountain on the island.

Besakih is a schizophrenic place. It's the most venerated site on Bali for Balinese

Hindus, who believe that the gods occasionally descend to reside in the temple, during which times worshippers don their finery and bring them elaborate offerings. The complex's sheer scale is impressive, and on a clear day, with Agung towering dramatically behind, and with ceremonies in full swing, it is a wonderful place. However, Besakih is also a jumble of buildings, unremarkable in many ways, around which has evolved the habit of separating foreign tourists from their money as quickly as possible. Even the stark grandeur of Besakih's location is often shrouded in mist, leaving Agung in all-enveloping cloud and the splendid panorama back south to the coast an imaginary delight.

## What to see and do

The complex consists of more than twenty separate temples spread over a site stretching for more than 3km. The central temple is **Pura Penataran Agung**, the largest on the island, built on seven ascending terraces, and comprising more than fifty structures. Start by following the path just outside Pura Penataran Agung's wall, and then wander at will: the *meru* (multi-tiered shrine roofs) of **Pura Batu Madeg**, rising among the trees to the north, are enticing. **Pura Pengubengan**, the most far-flung of the temples, is a couple of kilometres through the forest.

Unless you're praying or making offerings, you're **forbidden to enter** the temples, and most remain locked unless there's a ceremony going on. However, a lot is visible through the gateways and over walls. The rule about wearing a sarong and sash appears to be inconsistently applied but you'll definitely need them if you're in skimpy clothing; **sarong and sash rental** are available, with negotiable prices, but it's much easier to take your own.

There are huge numbers of local **guides** at Besakih hoping to be engaged by visitors, but you don't need one to explore the complex; stick to the paths running along the walls outside the temples, wear a sarong and sash, and you'll be in no danger of causing religious offence. If you do hire a guide, you should use one who has an official guide badge and is wearing an *endek* shirt as uniform, and always establish the **fee** beforehand; Rp20,000 is reasonable. If you're escorted into one of the temples to receive a blessing from a priest you'll be expected to make a "donation" to the priest, the amount negotiable through your guide.

## Arrival and information

**Tours** Without your own transport, the easiest way of getting to Besakih is to take an organized tour, available from any of the tourist centres (from Rp200,000 per person), but anything offering less than an hour at the temple isn't worth it. If you're in a group, it's more economical to charter a car and driver for the day (Rp350–400,000) and put together your own itinerary.

**By public transport** Bemos from Semarapura (also known as Klungkung) go as far as Menanga from where there are ojek (Rp5,000–10,000) to the temple car park. In Semarapura bemos pass through Jl Gunung Rinjani just north of the main road in the town centre. Bemos also run from Amlapura via Selat to Rendang, with some going on to Menanga. Most bemos run in the morning and dry up in the afternoon. There are no public bemos north of Menanga to Penelokan.

**Tourist information** The tourist office (daily 8am–7pm), on the right just beyond the car park, is staffed by guides who will pressure you to make a donation and engage their services (both are unnecessary but difficult to resist).

**Map** There's a noticeboard with a map of the complex on the left as you approach Pura Penataran Agung, beyond all the shops that line the road up to the temple from the car park.

## Accommodation

**Lembah Arcca** On the road between Menanga and Besakih, a couple of km before the temple complex ⓣ0366/23076. Basic rooms with blankets and attached cold-water bathrooms. ❸

## CLIMBING GUNUNG AGUNG

At 3014m, **Gunung Agung** is the highest Balinese peak and visible from throughout eastern Bali. The spiritual centre of Bali, it is believed that the spirits of the ancestors of the Balinese people dwell there. Climbing is forbidden at certain times because of **religious festivals**. Weather-wise, the **dry season** (April to mid-Oct) is best; don't contemplate it during January and February, the wettest months. You'll need walking boots, a good head lamp, water and snacks; for the descent, a stout stick is handy.

### Routes

There are two main routes, both long and hard. From **Pura Pasar Agung**, it's at least a three-hour climb with an ascent of almost 2000m, so you'll need to set out at 3am or earlier to get to the top for sunrise. From **Besakih**, the climb is longer (5–7hr) and much more challenging; you'll need to leave between 10pm and midnight. A third, less used, route, from **Dukuh Bujangga Sakti**, inland from Kubu on the north coast, involves starting out in the afternoon, camping on the mountain and completing the three hours to the summit pre-dawn.

### Guides

This is a serious trek and it's essential to take a guide familiar with the route – check before you engage anybody. The local organization of trekking guides has people on standby at Pura Pasar Agung day and night (Rp350,000 for a guide for one or two people). At Besakih, arrange guides at the tourist office (Rp700,000 per guide, for two people). Their level of English is variable and some don't have much experience with tourists so you may feel more comfortable dealing with one of the experienced agencies.

Closest to **Pura Pasar Agung**, in Muncan, 4km east of Rendang, I Ketut Uriada (ⓣ0812/364 6426), has trained several local guides. Anybody in the village will direct you to his house. It's $30 for a guide for one or two people from Pura Pasar Agung or $50 from Besakih; larger groups may need more than one guide. I Ketut Uriada will help you arrange transport between Muncan and the start of the climb. Gung Bawa, Jl Sri Jaya Pangus 33, Selat (ⓣ0366/24379, ⓦgb-trekking.blogspot.com), charges Rp350,000 per person from Pura Pasar Agung and Rp500,000 per person from Besakih.

Inevitably, prices are higher if you arrange the trek from further afield. Options include: the *Pondok Lembah Dukuh* losmen in Ababi near Tirtagangga (Rp700,000 for two people including transport); M&G Trekking in Candi Dasa (ⓣ0363/41464 or 0813/315 3991, ⓔmgtrekking@hotmail.com; Rp890,000 per person, minimum of two people for the climb from Dukuh including transport); Bali Sunrise 2001 in Ubud (ⓣ0818/552669, ⓦwww.balisunrise2001.com; from $100 per person depending on the pick-up point), who pick-up pretty much anywhere on Bali; Perama (contact any of their offices, ⓦwww.peramatour.com; Rp750,000 per person, minimum two people); and the guiding operations in Toya Bungkah, which charge from $100 per person (minimum of two or four people).

## CANDI DASA

At the eastern end of Amuk Bay, **CANDI DASA** is a relaxed resort with a wide choice of accommodation and restaurants; it is a good centre for snorkelling, diving and exploring the east. Much of the beach in the centre of Candi Dasa washed away following the destruction of the offshore reef in the 1980s to produce lime for cement, though this process has been reversed a little thanks to the large sea walls that have been built into the sea to protect it, and there are many pockets of pretty, white sand. The beaches to the west and east of the centre are a respectable size.

The pretty lagoon in the centre of Candi Dasa, just across the main road from the temple, is a useful landmark. Most of the **accommodation** in Candi Dasa is spread about 1km along the main road running just behind the beach both east and west of the lagoon. East of this central section, **Forest Road** has some quiet guesthouses, and to the west, about 1km from the centre of Candi Dasa, the villages of **Senkidu** and **Mendira** are slightly detached but still convenient for the main facilities. Beyond this, **Buitan** is several kilometres from the centre.

## What to see and do

Candi Dasa is an ideal base for **diving**. The group of tiny islands lying just off the coast (Gili Tepekong, Gili Biaha and Gili Mimpang) offer excellent sites for experienced divers (currents can be strong), including walls, a pinnacle and the dramatic Tepekong Canyon. All the operators also arrange trips further afield to Padang Bai, Nusa Penida, Nusa Lembongan, Amed, Tulamben and Gili Selang.

The reef along the coast is gradually rejuvenating and there is some decent **snorkelling** just offshore, stretching for about 1km westwards from the area in front of *Puri Bagus Candidasa* hotel. Take care not to venture too far out be aware of your position as the currents can be hazardous. You can also go on snorkelling trips to more distant spots with local boat-owners (Rp200–300,000 for two hours for up to three people including equipment). Popular sites are off Gili Mimpang, Blue Lagoon towards Padang Bai on the western side of Amuk Bay and Pasir Putih to the east of Candi Dasa. Dive operators also take snorkellers along on dive trips ($15–30); always be clear whether or not equipment is included in the price.

There's also good trekking in the Candi Dasa area. One of the most popular trips is from Kastala to Tenganan, which involves about three hours of easy walking with excellent rice terrace views. Local guides are increasingly offering their services to visitiors; it's best to go by personnal recommendation if possible.

### Tenganan

Rejecting the Javanization of their land, the introduction of the caste system and the religious reforms that followed the Majapahit conquest of the island in 1343, the Bali Aga ("original Balinese") withdrew to their villages to live a life based around ritual and ceremony. The village of **TENGANAN** (admission by donation), near Candi Dasa, retains its strong adherence to traditional ways, and is the only place in Indonesia that produces *gringsing* or double *ikat*, a ceremonial cloth in brown, deep red, blue-black and tan, that can take many years to make and is prized throughout Bali as a protection against evil. However, despite the emphasis on tradition, you'll still see noisy motorbikes scurrying around and television aerials and satellite dishes crowding the skyline.

The annual month-long **Usaba Sambah festival** (May/June) is the most colourful time to visit but at all times the village is fascinating for anyone interested in crafts, a shoppers' paradise with textiles, baskets produced from *ata* grass and intricate pictures inscribed on lontar palms on sale in the village and at the stalls that line the car park. The road up to Tenganan is a pleasant three-kilometre **walk** from Candi Dasa; **ojek** (Rp5000) wait at the bottom of the road up to the village.

## Arrival and information

**By bus and bemo** You can be dropped anywhere along the main road through Candi Dasa.

**By shuttle bus** Perama will drop you at their office at the western end of the central area, or for Rp5000 per person extra at your hotel.

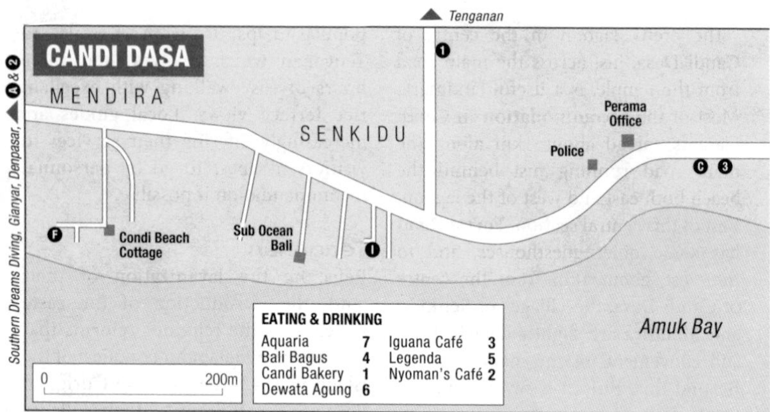


**By air** Official airport taxis from Ngurah Rai Airport charge Rp300,000.

**Tourist information** The tourist office close to the lagoon has erratic opening hours and staffing. The glossy magazine *Agung*, widely distributed across the island, is an excellent source of information and up-to-date maps about the east including Candi Dasa.

## Dive operators

Dive trips cost $60–80 depending on the distance; PADI Open Water ($360–400) and Advanced Open Water ($250–300) courses are widely available. Many operators charge extra for equipment rental ($5–15 per set per day) so check at the time of booking.

**Divelite** ⓣ0363/41660, ⓦwww.divelite.com. Offering fun dives and courses in Japanese, Indonesian and English.

**Pineapple Divers** At *Candi Beach Cottage* ⓣ0363/41760, ⓦwww.bali-pineapple-divers.com. Also arranges two- and three-day package tours of the dive sites around the island, including accommodation.

**Shangrila Scuba Divers** ⓣ0813/3733 5081, ⓦwww.divingatbalishangrila.com. At the *Bali Shangrila Beach Club* on the Forest Road and with a counter in town.

**Southern Dreams Diving** ⓣ0363/41506, ⓔsouthern@idola.net.id. On the road down to Buitan Beach, offering mostly trips for experienced divers.

**Sub Ocean Bali** ⓣ0363/41411, ⓦwww.suboceanbali.com. In Senkidu, providing courses up to Divemaster plus Nitrox diving.

## Accommodation

### Candi Dasa

**Agung Bungalows** ⓣ&ⓕ0363/41535. Located on the coast a couple of hundred metres west of the lagoon, the bungalows here have good-sized verandas, fans, hot and cold water. ❸

**Kelapa Mas** ⓣ0363/41369, ⓦwww.kelapamas.com. Justifiably popular and centrally located, a hundred metres west of the lagoon, offering a range of clean bungalows in a lovely garden on the seafront. Hot water and a/c are available. ❸–❻

TREAT YOURSELF

**Kubu Bali** ⓣ0363/41532, ⓦwww.damuhbali.com. Lovely, huge, well-furnished bungalows in central Candi Dasa, west of the lagoon, with deep verandas, widely spaced in a glorious garden ranging up the hillside to the delightful swimming pool at the top. ❽

**Seaside Cottages** ⓣ0363/41629, ⓦwww.balibeachfront-cottages.com. Several standards of decent accommodation, from basic budget bungalows with attached mandi to ones on the seafront, a couple of minutes' walk east of the Perama office, with a/c and hot water. ❷–❺

### Forest Road

**Genggong** Ten minutes' walk along Forest Rd ⓣ0363/41105. Bungalows and rooms in a two-storey block all with big balconies and verandas, with a/c available. The big draw is the large garden

and picturesque stretch of white-sand beach just over the wall. ❷–❹

**Puri Oka Beach Bungalows** Just over ten minutes' walk along Forest Road ⓣ0363/41092, ⓔpuri_oka@hotmail.com. Something of a work in progress, this long-established place is undergoing renovations. The basic bottom-end rooms currently offer amazing value for a place with a pool. ❸–❼

## Senkidu, Mendira and Buitan

**Amarta Beach Inn** Mendira ⓣ0363/41230. A couple of km west of the centre, on a side road leading down to the coast. Large, tiled bungalows, all with fans, facing the ocean. The more expensive rooms have hot water. There's a beachside restaurant and plenty of space for sunbathing. ❸–❹

**Bali Santi** Senkidu ⓣ0363/41611, ⓦwww.balisanti.com. Good-value, clean, well-maintained accommodation in a lovely garden with fine coastal views. ❷–❸

**Lumbung Damuh** Buitan; turning from the main road at the sign to *Royal Bali Beach Club* ⓣ0363/41553, ⓦwww.damuhbali.com. Four wooden *lumbung*-style cottages in a lush garden on Buitan's coast, several km west of the centre. Bedrooms, with small fridges, are upstairs and bathrooms with hot water are down. There is homecooked bread for breakfast and free use of boogie boards and canoes. ❻

## Eating, drinking and nightlife

Candi Dasa nightlife consists of the live music which alternates between *Legenda* and *Iguana Café*.

**Aquaria** Along a side road near the junction of Forest Rd and the main road ⓣ0363/41127, ⓦwww.aquariabali.com. Tiny restaurant attached to a small hotel with tables overlooking a pretty swimming pool and serving inventive food that is well above the norm. The fixed-price menu (Rp65,000 for three courses) changes daily and makes full use of local produce and offers vegetarian options. Also worth a visit for the lunchtime and snack menu.

**Bali Bagus** ⓣ0363/41363. Excellent value with set three-course meals from Rp39,950 at this central place east of the lagoon. Free transport in the Candi area.

**Candi Bakery** About 300m along the road to Tenganan. Serves the best iced coffee in Candi Dasa, as well as an appetizing selection of bread and cakes. Lunch and dinner includes some German dishes such as *Bratwurst*, *Sauerkraut* and *Bratkartoffel*. Main courses Rp18,000–25,000.

**Dewata Agung** Overlooking the lagoon ⓣ0363/41204. The extensive menu features the usual suspects but the food is well cooked and features a range of Balinese specialities. The set menus aren't the cheapest in town (Rp49,000) but they're worth it.

**Nyoman's Cafe** One of a trio of cheap-and-cheerful places on the road to Buitan beach, several km west of the centre, with a selection of Indonesian and Western favourites including local seafood (mains about Rp15,000).

## Directory

**Banks and exchange** Moneychangers on the main street. The closest international ATMs are in Amlapura, Padang Bai (if it is working) and Semarapura.

**Bike rental** Sub Ocean Bali in central Candi Dasa and Gloria Warung on Forest Road (Rp25,000 a day). Beware the busy traffic on the main road.
**Car and motorbike rental** Established rental companies include Safari (☎0363/41707) in the centre of town; and Candi Dasa Rent Car (☎0363/41225) at the start of Forest Rd (Rp90,000–100,000 per day for a Suzuki Jimney; Rp150,000 for a Kijang and Rp50,000–60,000 for a motorbike). The insurance included varies considerably. To put together your own day-trip, you'll be looking at Rp350,000–400,000 per day for vehicle, driver and petrol, depending on your itinerary. Negotiate with the touts along the main street, ask at your accommodation or approach the car rental companies. Ketut Lagun (☎0812/362 2076) is a recommended driver.
**Doctor** Dr Nisa will visit Candi Dasa (see opposite).
**Internet** On the main street (Rp400/min), although the dial-up connection is slow.
**Police** Just west of the Perama office.
**Post office** Near the lagoon (Mon–Fri 8.30am–noon).
**Spa and massage** Beach massages (Rp50,000 per hr). The spa at the small hotel Aquaria (☎0363/41127), reached via a small side road off Forest Rd, offers massage, scrubs, hot stone treatments and crystal massages and facials in the oceanfront spa from Rp150,000.
**Telephones** Warung telkom (daily 7am–10.45pm) next to *Kubu Bali* hotel.

### Moving on

**By shuttle bus** Plenty of places offer shuttle buses. Perama (☎0363/41114, ⓦwww.peramatour.com, 8am–9pm) is the most established operator.
**Destinations:** Amed (1 daily, min 2 people; 1hr–1hr 30min); Bedugul (daily; 2hr–2hr 30min); Kuta/Ngurah Rai Airport (3 daily; 3hr); Lovina (1 daily; 3hr–3hr 30min); Padang Bai (3 daily; 30min); Sanur (3 daily; 2hr–2hr 30min); Tirtagangga (1 daily; min 2 people; 1hr); Tulamben (1 daily, min 2 people; 2hr); Ubud (3 daily; 1hr 30min–2hr).
**By public bemo and bus** to: Amlapura (20min); Denpasar (Batubulan terminal; 2hr); Gianyar (1hr); Padang Bai (20min); Semarapura (40min).

## PADANG BAI

**PADANG BAI**, the port for Lombok, nestles in a small white-sand cove lined with fishing boats. Many travellers stay a night or two and the tiny village has developed into a laid-back resort. Jalan Silayukti is the main seafront road at the eastern end of the bay, while all the small roads leading from the seafront to the road across the top of the village are named, from west to east, Jalan Segara 1, Jalan Segara 2 and so on.

### What to see and do

If you find the main beach too busy, head to the bay of **Bias Tugal** (also known as Pantai Kecil), to the west, which is quieter (though a five-star hotel is planned); follow the road past the post office and, just as it begins to climb, take the roadway to the left. East over the headland from the main beach, if you take the left fork for a couple of hundred yards beyond the beachside *Topi Inn*, you reach the white-sand cove of **Blue Lagoon**, where there's the best snorkelling in the area. Several places in Padang Bai rent out **snorkelling equipment** (Rp20,000 per day); the water in the main bay is surprisingly clear.

Padang Bai is an excellent base for **diving** and the sites at Blue Lagoon attract eels, wrasses, turtles, flatheads and lion fish – plus there's a good chance of spotting sharks, and there are plenty of species that you won't see elsewhere in Bali. The operators also arrange dive trips further afield to Nusa Penida, Amed, Tulamben, Candi Dasa and Gili Selang

*Topi Inn,* Jl Silayukti (☎0363/41424, ⓦwww.topiinn.com), organizes an enormous range of **cultural and artistic workshops** (€8–10 per person, minimum of two people), including batik, weaving, basket-making, Balinese dance, sculpture, cooking and wayang kulit (puppets).

### Arrival and information

**By bemo** Bemos from Semarapura and Amlapura stop at the port entrance at the western end of the bay, and everything is within easy walking distance.
**By tourist shuttle bus** Perama buses stop at their office near the port entrance.
**By ferry** The public ferry from Lembar, Lombok, arrives in the port.

**By speedboat** The Gili Cat speedboat from the Gili Islands arrives at the jetty in the bay.
**By air** Official airport taxis from Ngurah Rai Airport charge Rp300,000.
**Tourist information** The closest tourist office is in Candi Dasa. The glossy magazine *Agung*, widely distributed across the island, is an excellent source of information and has an up-to-date map of the village.

## Dive operators

Dive trips are $40–90 for two dives depending on distance. PADI courses up to Divemaster are available (the PADI Open Water course is $300–320).
**Geko Dive** Jl Silayukti, on the seafront ⓣ0363/41516, ⓦwww.gekodive.com.
**Water Worx** Close to Geko on Jl Silayukti ⓣ0363/41220, ⓦwww.waterworxbali.com.

## Accommodation

**Bagus Inn** Jl Segara 6 ⓣ0363/41398. A good village choice offering small rooms with attached bathrooms in a friendly family compound. ❷
**Kembar Inn** Jl Segara 6 ⓣ0363/41364. Spotless place in the village with plenty of sitting areas and a buffet breakfast. A/c and hot water available. ❷–❻
**Made Homestay** Jl Silayukti ⓣ0363/41441, ⓔmades_padangbai@hotmail.com. Clean rooms with fan and attached cold-water bathrooms in a two-storey block convenient for both the beach and the village. ❷
**Marco Inn** ⓣ0813/3785 4486. Eight simple rooms set around a pretty garden plus a kitchen and a DVD/video room for guests. Accessed via a small passageway leading off the seafront road, about five minutes east of the ferry terminal. ❷
**Padang Bai Billabong** Jl Silayukti ⓣ0363/41399. Cheap as chips budget place with rooms set in a wild garden near the beach. ❷
**Parta** Gang Tongkol III, 7, in a small alley off Jl Segara 6 ⓣ0363/41475. Clean village place, offering some rooms with hot water and a/c, with a great communal sitting area on the top floor. ❶–❺
**Serangan Inn II** ⓣ0363/41425. Spotless place at the top of the village at the far eastern end of the road across the top of the village; take the road next to the market off the main road into town. There are good views and fine breezes on the verandas plus a/c and hot water in the pricier rooms. ❷–❻

## Eating and nightlife

**Ali in Bali** An Arabic lounge bar on the seafront, about five minutes east of the ferry terminal, with lots of drinks but just two items on the menu: a Dutch breakfast (Rp25,000) and Shoearma Doner Kebab (Rp29,000), spicy meat in tasty bread.
**Babylon Reggae Bar** Jl Segara 8. Perennially popular late-night drinking and music venue.
**Omang Omang** Jl Segara 8. The classiest dining in town with a small menu of well-cooked Western, Indonesian and Balinese food including splendid ice cream and desserts (mains mostly Rp28,000–59,000), and regular live music.
**Padang Bai Café** Tiny place on the seafront about five minutes walk east of the ferry terminal, that more than lives up to its promise of having the best seafood in town. Mains Rp25,000–30,000.
**Topi Inn** Jl Silayukti. There's a menu several centimetres thick and great bread, cakes, coffee and plenty of imaginative vegetarian dishes supplementing the more usual Western and Indonesian meals. Mains Rp23,000–38,000 and baguettes from Rp18,000.
**Zen Bar** On the road that runs just inland and behind the ferry terminal car park. Friendly staff, a huge screen showing an almost unbelievably eclectic range of music videos and a vast selection of drinks are served late into the night.

## Directory

**Banks and exchange** BRI Bank with an international ATM on the main road into Padang Bai, about 100m from the port entrance. Moneychangers on the main street.
**Car and motorbike rental** Ask at your accommodation or any of the seafront tourist counters. Rp150,000 per day for a Suzuki Jimney, Rp200,000 for a Kijang and Rp50,000 for a motorbike.
**Doctor** Dr Nisa (ⓣ0811/380645) is a highly regarded, English-speaking local doctor who will visit sick tourists privately. Can also be contacted at Water Worx dive centre on the seafront. The nearest hospitals are at Amlapura, Semarapura and Denpasar.
**Internet** Widely available (Rp300/min), although the dial-up connection is slow.
**Police** Near the port entrance.
**Post office** Near the port entrance.
**Telephones** Warung telkom (daily 7am–10pm) on the seafront.

## Moving on

**By bemo and bus** to: Amlapura (45min); Candi Dasa (20min); Denpasar (Batubulan terminal; 2hr); Semarapura (30min).
**By shuttle bus** The Perama office is on the main road into Padang Bai close to the port entrance (ⓣ0363/41419, ⓦwww.peramatour.com; 7am–7pm).
**Destinations:** Candi Dasa (3 daily; 30min); Gili Islands via ferry (1 daily; 5–6hr); Kuta/Ngurah Rai Airport (3 daily; 2hr 30min); Lovina (1 daily; 2hr 30min–3hr); Mataram via direct Perama boat (1 daily; 5hr) via ferry (daily; 6–7hr); Sanur (3 daily; 1hr 30min–2hr); Senggigi via ferry (1 daily; 5–6hr); Ubud (1 daily 2hr–2hr 30min).
**By direct Perama boat** to: Gili Islands (1 daily; 4hr); Senggigi (1 daily; 5hr).
**By ferry** to Lembar, Lombok (every 90min; 4hr–4hr 30min).
**By speedboat** to the Gili Islands (2hr 30min) with Gili Cat (ⓣ0361/271680, ⓦwww.gilicat.com) or book at *Made Restaurant* in front of *Made Homestay*.

## TIRTAGANGGA

**TIRTAGANGGA**'s draw is its **Water Palace** (daily 7am–7pm; Rp5000; ⓦwww.tirtagangga.com) with an impressive terraced garden full of pools, statues and fountains. However, the village is refreshingly cool and surrounded by paddy-fields which offer pleasant walks both long and short and glorious views of Gunung Agung to the west and Gunung Lempuyang to the east.

Nyoman Budiarsa's shop at *Genta Bali Warung* (ⓣ0363/22436) on the main road sells a map of local walks (Rp3000); an established **guide** is Komang Gede Sutama (contact him through *Good Karma* restaurant, near the main parking area).

For **accommodation** *Rijasa* (ⓣ0363/21873; ❷–❸), across the main road from the track leading to the Water Palace, is central and *Kusumajaya Inn* (ⓣ0363/21250, ⓔjaya.ttrg@yahoo.co.id; ❷) is about 300m north of the centre of Tirtagangga, perched on a hill with splendid ricefield views. For food search out *The* Rice Terrace Coffee Shop, attached to Puri Sawah guesthouse, one of the quietest spots in the village and signed from the bend just north of the centre. There's great Western and Indonesian food with plenty of vegetarian choices (around Rp28,000 for a main course). They also serve the best apple crumble in eastern Bali.

Tirtagangga is served by **minibuses** and **buses** plying between Amlapura and Singaraja. From Candi Dasa get off on the outskirts of Amlapura at the junction with the Singaraja road – minibuses wait here for passengers to the north. Perama charters are available from Candi Dasa.

### Ababi

**ABABI**, a lovely spot just north of Tirtagangga, is worth considering for its accommodation, reached along a left-hand turn signed from the main road just over a kilometre north of Tirtagangga or via footpaths from Tirtagangga itself. *Pondok Batur Indah* (ⓣ0363/22342; ❸) and *Pondok Lembah Dukuh* (ⓣ0813/3829 5142; ❷–❺) both have good value rooms.

## AMED, JEMELUK AND THE FAR EAST COAST

The stretch of coast in the far east of Bali from Culik to Aas is known as **AMED** although this is just one village here. Accommodation is mushrooming along the 11km stretch from Amed to Aas, as word spreads about the glorious coastline, clear water, peace and quiet and underwater attractions.

Access to Amed is from the small junction village of **Culik** just over 9km north of Tirtagangga on the Amlapura–Singaraja road. In Amed, 3km away, life centres on fishing and salt production, which you can see at close quarters. A kilometre east is the hamlet of Congkang, then **Jemeluk**, 6km from Culik, which attracts divers and snorkellers for the offshore coral terrace leading to a wall dropping to a depth of more than 40m. There's a high density of fish, with sharks, wrasses and parrotfish in the outer parts. From Jemeluk lies headland after headland: the beaches and villages of Bunutan and Lipah Beach are the most developed areas, though they remain low-key, lead on to Lean Beach, Selang, Ibus, Banyuning and eventually Aas, almost 15km from Culik.

As well as at Jemeluk, there's excellent **diving** at a wreck at Lipah Beach and a drift dive at Bunutan with the chance to see schools of barracuda and giant barrel sponges. Advanced divers can explore Gili Selang, the eastern tip of Bali, where a pristine reef, pelagics and exciting currents are the draw. Good **snorkelling** spots include Jemeluk, the wreck at Lipah Beach and a Japanese wreck near the coast at Banyuning.

## Arrival

**By shuttle bus** A Perama charter service runs from Candi Dasa (Rp75,000 per person, minimum two people).

**By bemo** From Culik, bemos run via Amed to Aas in the morning; hard bargaining should get a fare of around Rp25,000 to Lipah Beach. Later in the day you'll need to charter a bemo (aim for Rp25,000 per person). There's no public transport between Aas and Seraya.

**By ojek** From Culik, about Rp30,000 to Lipah Beach.

**By car or motorbike** It's a picturesque 30km from Amlapura to Aas via Ujung, Seraya and Kusambi. Allow at least ninety minutes for the trip. Take local advice on the road condition before setting off; rivers cross the road, which may become impassable in the rainy season.

## Dive operators

**Eco-Dive** Office in Jemeluk (moving in 2009 to between *Amed Café* and *Bamboo Bali* losmen in Jemeluk) ⓣ0363/23482, ⓦwww.ecodivebali.com. The staff have tremendous local knowledge and offer dives for experienced divers and PADI courses up to Divemaster level.

**Euro Dive** Office in Lipah ⓣ0363/23605, ⓦwww.eurodivebali.com. Offering all PADI courses up to Divemaster. Nitrox diving is available.

**Jukung Dive** Congkhang ⓣ0363/23469, ⓦwww.jukungdivebali.com. Premises include a pool and restaurant. PADI courses up to Divemaster level. "Dive and Massage" packages are available.

**Puri Wirata Dive School** Attached to *Puri Wirata* hotel in Bunutan ⓣ0363/23523, ⓦwww.diveamed.com. Offers dives for experienced divers and courses.

## Accommodation

All accommodation and restaurants line the main road along the coast.

### Amed, Congkang and Jemeluk

**Geria Giri Shanti** ⓣ0819/1665 4874, ⓦwww.geriagirishanti.com. Four spotless bungalows above the road in Congkang, all with fine verandas, cold water and fans. Hot water is planned. ❸

**Jukung Bali** ⓣ0363/23470, ⓦwww.jukungbali.com. A smashing little place in Congkang with big bungalows with cold-water garden bathrooms, fans and deep verandas, just a few feet from the beach in a pretty garden. ❻

### Bunutan

**Deddy's** ⓣ0363/23510. Three bungalows set on the hillside on the way into Bunutan from the west, with fans and cold water. Another three rooms near the beach have a/c and hot water. ❹–❻

**Prema Liong** ⓣ0363/23486, ⓦwww.bali-amed.com. Four two-storey thatched cottages up on the hillside in the centre of Bunutan with stunning views, fans, cold-water bathrooms and great lounging areas on deep verandas. There's an eccentric bell system to call the staff up to collect refreshment orders. ❻

### Lipah Beach

**Bayu Cottages** At the far eastern end of Lipah Beach ⓣ0363/23495, ⓦwww.bayucottages.com. Popular rooms on the hillside with fan and a/c, hot water bathrooms and an attractive pool. ❻

**Le Jardin** ⓣ0363/23507, ⓔlimamarie@yahoo.fr. Four bungalows in a lovely garden in the central part of Lipah Beach with the beach a short walk away. The so-called cold water is usually warm from the tank. ❻

### Lean, Selang, Banyuning and Aas

**Eka Purnama** ⓣ0813/3757 8060, ⓦwww.eka-purnama.com. On the hillside above the road between Banyuning and Aas, there are four bamboo bungalows with tiled roofs. All have large verandas looking seawards, fans and cold-water bathrooms. ❻

**Good Karma** On the beach at Selang ⓣ0812/368 9090. With budget wood, bamboo and thatch bungalows, all with fans and cold water bathrooms set in a shady garden, and larger, more expensive bungalows. ❸–❻

## Eating, drinking and nightlife

### Amed, Congkang and Jemeluk

**Divers Café** In the heart of Jemeluk overlooking the beach. Their *ikan pepes bakar* (spicy grilled fish) is particularly good.

**Villa Coral** At the far eastern end of the bay in Jemeluk. Quiet and friendly beachside café, with great offshore snorkelling nearby.

### Bunutan

**Aiona Garden of Health** ⓣ0813/3816 1730, ⓦwww.aionabali.com This small hotel at the western end of Bunutan has a vegetarian restaurant, open for lunch (noon–3pm) and dinner (5–7pm); reservations recommended.

**Anda Amed** The restaurant in this hotel in the centre of Bunutan has some creative and unusual choices, all of it tasty and well executed (mains Rp30,000–70,000). Probably the only hotel in Bali with pet ducks.

**Pazzo Restaurant and Bar** This is the closest that Amed has to nightlife, a busy bar with live music on Friday nights. The Indonesian and Western food is well cooked (mains Rp30,000–55,000), and there's an extensive drinks list and a pool table.

### Lipah Beach

**Le Jardin** In the heart of Lipah Beach, offering vegetarian (Rp25,000), fish (Rp35,000) and chicken (Rp40,000) dishes (7–10pm), depending on what is available that day, plus French cakes, ice cream and yogurt.

**Wawa Wewe** Serving a good selection of Indonesian and Western favourites, and sometimes cake as well, there's live music on Tuesdays and Saturdays in this place in the centre of Lipah Beach.

### Lean, Selang, Banyuning and Aas

**Baliku** Across the road from the beach at Banyuning ⓣ0828/372 2601. Indonesian and Western food (mains Rp22,000–42,000), free transport to the restaurant in the Amed area and if you dine here there's free use of the showers and pool.

**Komang John Café** At *Blue Moon Villas* on the headland beyond the beach at Selang. This place is laid-back and recommended for good food and drink and a friendly welcome (mains Rp45,000–50,000), and wine by the bottle).

## Directory

**Banks and exchange** Moneychangers in Lipah Beach, Bunutan and Jemeluk; the closest ATM is in Amlapura.

**Bicycle rental** Ask at your accommodation or *Amed Café* (Rp35,000 a day). The gradients over some of the headlands are a bit extreme.

**Motorbike rental** Ask at your accommodation or *Amed Café* (Rp50,000 a day).

**Hospital** The nearest hospital is in Amlapura.

**Internet and telephones** Warung telkoms with internet access in Lipah, at *Apa Kabar* hotel in Bunutan and *Amed Café* near Jemeluk but connections are slow.

**Massage and spa** Beach massages for Rp60,000 per hour. For more pampering, the "a" Spa (10am–7pm; ⓣ0813/3823 8846, ⓔaspatrad@yahoo.com), opposite *Pazzo Bar* in Bunutan, gives treatments in a lovely garden *bale*; the two-hour Traditional Lulur package is $33.

**Post office** The closest is in Amlapura.

## Moving on

**By bemo** To Culik from Aas in the mornings; hard bargaining should get a fare of around Rp25,000 from Lipah Beach. Later in the day you'll need to charter a bemo (aim for about Rp25,000 per person). There's no public transport between Aas and Seraya.

**By ojek** About Rp30,000 to Culik from Lipah Beach.

**By shuttle bus** A Perama charter service runs to Candi Dasa (Rp75,000 per person, minimum two people). Phone the Candi Dasa office to book (ⓣ0363/41114, ⓦwww.peramatour.com). *Amed Café* near Jemeluk also operates shuttle buses (3 daily; destinations include Padang Bai, €5; Ubud €10; the southern resorts plus the airport €10–15; and Lovina €12; ⓣ0363/23473).

**By car or motorbike** It's 30km from Aas around the far east to Amnalapura (see p.315).

**By boat to the Gili islands** Increasing numbers of skippers provide charters direct to the Gili Islands (Rp550,000 plus per person) from Amed. The boats are often small with single engines, they don't carry radios, and mobile phones may well be out of range in the middle of the Lombok Strait.

## TULAMBEN

The small village of **TULAMBEN**, about 10km northwest of Culik, is mainly a destination for diving and snorkelling. It's the site of the most popular dive in Bali, the Liberty wreck, attracting up to a hundred divers a day. The wreck lies about 30m offshore and is encrusted with hard and soft coral, gorgonians and hydrozoans, providing a wonderful habitat for around three hundred species of fish that live on the wreck and over a hundred species that visit from deeper water. The wreck is now pretty broken up and there are plenty of entrances letting you explore inside. Parts of it are in shallow water, making this a good snorkelling site, too. It's worth staying in the vllage to avoid the rush hours (11.30am–4pm) on the wreck, enjoy a night dive and explore some of the other excellent sites in the area – enough to dive for a week or more.

### Arrival

**By bus** Buses and minibuses between Amlapura and Singaraja pass through the village and will drop you where you want.
**By shuttle bus** A Perama charter service runs from Candi Dasa (Rp75,000 per person, minimum 2 people).

### Dive operators

These are the two most established operators in Tulamben. Both offer local dives to the wreck and all other Tulamben sites ($50 for two dives), trips to other sites on Bali (for example, $75 for two dives at Pulau Menjangan) and PADI courses ($350 for the PADI Open water course).
**Tauch Terminal** ⓣ0363/22911, or contact in southern Bali ⓣ0361/774504, ⓦwww.tulamben.com; see below.
**Tulamben Wreck Divers** ⓣ0363/23400, ⓦwww.tulambenwreckdivers.com.

### Accommodation

**Puri Aries** ⓣ0363/23402. Eight basic bungalows in a small compound above the main road. All have fan, cold-water bathrooms and verandas, and are fine if you don't need to be next to the sea. ❷
**Puri Madha** ⓣ0363/22921, ⓕ0363/23346. Near the Liberty wreck. Older rooms are basic with fan and cold-water bathrooms while newer ones are attractive and offer a/c and hot water as well as ocean views. ❷–❻

**TREAT YOURSELF**

**Tauch Terminal Resort** ⓣ0363/22911 or contact in southern Bali ⓣ0361/774504, ⓦwww.tulamben.com. Large, attractive, lively establishment that fronts a long section of beach, with landscaped gardens, a pretty pool, spa and busy dive centre. The rooms are the best in the area, and all have a/c and hot water, with good furnishings and balconies. ❽

### Directory

**Banks and exchange** Moneychanger on the main road, the closest ATM is in Amlapura.
**Hospital** The nearest hospital is in Amlapura.
**Internet** Available at a few spots including *Tulamben Wreck Divers* (2–9pm; Rp500/min) and *Tauch Terminal Resort*, where Wi-Fi is also available.
**Massage and spa** Beach massages are widely available. (Rp60,000/hr). For more pampering the spa at *Tauch Terminal* is open to all (noon–7pm) and a vast range of treatments is available (25min–2hr 40min; €10–49).
**Telephones** Warung telkom (8am–9pm) 250m east of the village.

### Moving on

**By bus** Buses and minibuses between Amlapura and Singaraja via Culik and Tirtagangga pass through the village and will pick you up.
**By shuttle bus** A Perama charter service runs to Candi Dasa (Rp75,000 per person, minimum two people). Phone the Candi Dasa office to book (ⓣ0363/41114, ⓦwww.peramatour.com).

## GUNUNG BATUR AND DANAU BATUR

The **BATUR** area, the most popular and dramatic volcanic scenery in Bali, was formed thirty thousand years ago when a gigantic volcano erupted. The rim of this vast crater remains clearly visible and it is the views from here that is the main draw. Confusingly, the entire area is sometimes referred to as **Kintamani**, although this is the name of just one of many villages. The highest points on the rim are **Gunung Abang** (2153m) on the eastern side, the third highest mountain in Bali, and **Gunung Penulisan** (1745m) on the northwest corner, with Pura Puncak Penulisan on its summit. Rising from the floor of this huge crater, **Gunung Batur** (1717m) is an active volcano with four craters of its own and **Danau Batur** lake nestled beside it. Many visitors come to the area to climb Gunung Batur, usually for the sunrise.

There's an **admission charge** to the area (Rp4000; Rp2000 per car or motorbike). The ticket offices are just south of Penelokan on the road from Bangli and at the junction of the road from Ubud and the rim road.

### The crater rim

The villages of **Penelokan**, **Batur** and **Kintamani** are spread for 11km along the rim of the vast ancient crater and virtually merge. The views across the stark volcanic landscape from **Penelokan** (1450m) are majestic. Danau Batur lies far below, while Gunung Batur and Gunung Abang tower on either side of the lake. The hoardes of day-trippers who pass through Penelokan attract an entourage of hawkers. The only way to avoid the circus is to come early or late, or stay overnight.

About 4km north of Penelokan, Pura Ulun Danu Batur (admission by donation; sarong rental available) is the second most important temple on the island after Besakih. It's a fascinating place to visit at any time as there are usually pilgrims making offerings and praying, and the mist that frequently shrouds the area adds to the atmosphere.

### Danau Batur and around

Situated at the bottom of the ancient crater, 500m below its rim, **Danau Batur** is the largest lake in Bali, 8km long and 3km wide, and one of the most glorious. Home of Dewi Danu, the goddess of the crater lake, it is especially sacred to the Balinese, and its waters are believed to percolate through the earth and reappear as springs in other parts of the island. Villages sit on the lake's shores – **Kedisan** is at the junction where the road from Penelokan reaches the lakeside **and Toya Bungkah** is further north on the western shore of the lake. Its hot springs, Toya Devasa (daily 8am–7pm; $6 including lunch), are clean and attractive, with a cold-water swimming pool and smaller hot-water pools.

## Arrival and information

**By bus** The main road through Penelokan, Batur and Kintamani is on the bus route between Singaraja (Penarukan) and Denpasar (Batubulan).
**By bemo** The villages along the rim are served by bemos from Ubud. The lakeside villages of Kedisan and Toya Bungkah are served by public bemos (Rp5000 with bargaining). You can also charter (aim for Rp20,000 per person).
**Hotel transport** Some of the Kedisan accommodation offers free pick-ups in the area.
**By shuttle bus** A Perama charter service runs from Ubud (Rp75,000 per person), Sanur or Kuta (Rp100,000 per person). Minimum two people.
**Tourist information** Yayasan Bintang Danu, a local organization, runs the tourist office in Penelokan (daily 10am–3pm; ⓣ0366/51730), almost opposite the turning down to Danau Batur.

## Accommodation

### On the rim

**Lakeview Hotel** ⓣ0366/51394, ⓦwww.indo.com/hotels/lakeview. Right on the edge of the crater rim in Penelokan, where the main road turns south away from the rim. There are no frills but it has stunning views, hot water and thick quilts. ❻–❼
**Miranda** 100m north of Kintamani market; all public transport along the rim passes the door ⓣ0366/52022. The rooms are clean and have

attached mandi and squat toilet. The owner, Made Senter, is an experienced trekking guide. ❷

### By the lake

**Hotel Astra Dana** ⓣ0366/52091. A dozen rooms by the lakeside at Kedisan; the most expensive have hot water and fabulous lake views. Free pick-ups from Penelokan. ❷

**Nyoman Mawar III** (also known as *Under the Volcano III*) ⓣ0813/3860 0081. Simple, clean bungalows close to the lake in Toya Bungkah with fabulous views. ❷

## Eating

**Arlina's** Toya Bungkah. A long-standing favourite with well-cooked Western and Indo-Chinese dishes and lake fish. Mains Rp15,000–28,000.

**Volcano Breeze** Toya Bungkah. On a quiet track down to the lake offering Western and Indonesian dishes.

**Warung Kopi** With glorious views of Gunung Batur and the lake from its perch on the crater rim about 300m towards Kintamani from Penelokan tucked



### CLIMBING GUNUNG BATUR

Batur remains **active** so check the current situation for climbing at ⓦwww.vsi.esdm.go.id – it's mostly in Indonesian but it is clear if a mountain is on alert. Climbing Batur is best in the **dry season** (April–Oct). The path becomes unpleasant in the wet and the views clouded over. However, the wet season isn't unrelenting, and you might be lucky and hit a few dry days.

There's a choice of **routes up Gunung Batur**. If you have your own wheels, the easiest route is to drive to **Serongga**, off the Yehmampeh road, west of Songan. From the car park, it's thirty minutes to an hour to the highest peak and largest crater, **Batur I**.

The most common walking routes up to Batur I are from **Toya Bungkah** and **Pura Jati**. The path from Pura Jati is shadeless and largely across old lava fields. From Toya Bungkah, numerous paths head up through the forest (one starts just south of *Arlina's* guesthouse); after about an hour you'll come out onto the bare slope of the mountain, from where you can follow the paths up to the warung perched on the crater rim. This is the steep bit, slippery with black volcanic sand. Allow two to three hours to get to the top from either start and about half that time to get back down.

A **medium-length trek** involves climbing to Batur I, walking around the rim and then descending by another route. The **long-trek** option, sometimes called the **Exploration** (about 8hr in total), involves climbing up to Batur I and descending via Batur II and Batur III.

In **daylight**, you don't need a guide from Toya Bungkah or Pura Jati if you've a reasonable sense of direction, but you shouldn't climb alone and you should let somebody responsible know where you are going. If you climb in the **dark**, which most people do to reach the top for the fabulous sunrise views, you'll need to leave around 4–5am and a guide is vital. For the longer treks you will need a guide.

#### Guides and trekking agencies

Local guides are organized into the **Association of Mount Batur Trekking Guides** (ⓣ0366/52362), with offices in Toya Bungkah and at Pura Jati, and anyone who climbs Batur is under intense pressure to engage them, but in spite of "fixed" prices supposedly displayed in the offices (from Rp200,000 per group of four people) they can be confusing to use. Be absolutely sure what is included (for example, is breakfast extra), which trek you are doing and whether the price you have agreed is per person or for the group. Many people find it is more straightforward to deal with their hotel or with the trekking agencies.

All hotels and the **trekking agencies** in Toya Bungkah arrange climbs. These include Jero Wijaya at *Lakeside Cottages* (ⓣ0366/51249, ⓦwww.lakesidebali.com) and *Arlina's* (ⓣ0366/51165). Both charge $20–25 per person for the short trek, or $35–38 for the long one. Bali Sunrise 2001 (ⓣ0818/552669, ⓦwww.balisunrise2001.com) arranges treks including pick-ups throughout Bali ($45–80 per person depending on pick-up point, the trek and whether overnight accommodation in Toya Bungkah is included). Usually minimum of two people.

behind the more expensive *Ramana*. There's a selection of Indoneseian mains at Rp15,000–25,000.
**Wibisana Penelokan** On the opposite side of the road to the view this is the cheapest eatery in the area with good-value Indonesian food (main courses about Rp11,000).



### Directory

**Banks and exchange** There's an international ATM in the car park of the *Lakeview* hotel, but otherwise it's difficult to change money so bring plenty of cash.
**Post office** Just off the main road 2km north of Penelokan.
**Telephones** There's a telephone office just off the main road 2km north of Penelokan and a warung telkom (8am–11pm) in Toya Bungkah.

### Moving on

**By bus** The main road through Penelokan, Batur and Kintamani is on the bus route between Singaraja (Penarukan) and Denpasar (Batubulan).
**By bemo** The villages along the rim are served by bemos to Ubud. The lakeside villages of Kedisan and Toya Bungkah are served by public bemos (Rp5000 with bargaining) to Penelokan. You can also charter (aim for Rp20,000 per person).
**By shuttle bus** A Perama charter service runs to Ubud (Rp75,000 per person), Sanur or Kuta (Rp100,000 per person). Minimum two people. Telephone the office where you want to go to book.

## DANAU BRATAN AND CANDIKUNING

Neither as big nor as dramatic as the Batur region, the **Danau Bratan** (Lake Bratan) area, sometimes just known as Bedugul, has impressive mountains, beautiful lakes, quiet walks and attractive and important temples.

Situated at 1200m above sea level and thought to be 35m deep in places, **Danau Bratan** is surrounded by forested hills and, like Danau Batur, is revered by Balinese farmers as the source of freshwater springs across a wide area of the island. The lake (and its goddess) are worshipped in the temple of **Pura Ulun Danu Bratan** (daily 7am–5pm; Rp10,000), one of the most photographed temples in Bali, which consists of several shrines, some dramatically situated on small islands that appear to float on the surface of the lake.

The lake nestles in the lee of Gunung Catur, on the main Denpasar–Mengwi–Singaraja road 53km north of Denpasar and 30km south of Singaraja; no direct route links it to Batur. There are the smaller, quieter lakes of Buyan and Tamblingan about 5km to the northwest, both worth exploring if you have time.

### Candikuning

The small village of **CANDIKUNING**, which sits above the southern shores of Danau Bratan, is home to one of the gems of central Bali, the **Bali Botanical Gardens** (Kebun Raya Eka Karya Bali; daily 8am–6pm; Rp3500), home to more than a thousand species of plants, including trees, bamboo and orchids, and a rich area for birdwatching. The entrance is a short walk from the market area, along a small side road. Inside the gardens is the wonderful **Bali Treetop Adventure Park** (Ⓣ0361/852 0680, Ⓦwww.balitreetop.com; $20) with five circuits of ropeways, bridges, platforms and zip lines constructed up to 20m off the ground. There's a circuit to suit every level of bravado including adrenaline junkies. Booking is recommended, weekends and holidays are best avoided and packages are available from the southern resorts including transport, lunch and a visit to Pura Ulun Danu Bratan.

Candikuning's daily **market**, Bukit Mungsu, is small but offers a vast range of fruit, spices and plants, including orchids.

### Arrival

**By bus** Candikuning is on the bus route between Denpasar (Ubung; 1hr 30min) and Singaraja (Sukasada; 1hr 30min).
**By shuttle bus** Perama services drop you at the *Sari Artha* losmen, just below Bukit Mungsu market on the main road in Candikuning.

## Accommodation

**Permata Firdaus** ⓣ0368/21531. Just off the road to the Botanical Gardens, offering six good-value, simple rooms with hot water. ❷

**Sari Artha Inn** ⓣ0368/21011. Just north of the market, there's a choice of rooms with or without hot water, all with verandas, set in a pretty garden but with no lake views. The Perama office is here. ❷–❸

## Eating

**Anda** Just across the road from the turning to the Botanical Gardens. This is one of the few places open in the evenings. There's tasty Indonesian and Chinese food.

**Crackers Bar and Top Deck Restaurant** Tucked away in Bukit Mungsu market, this is a quiet haven with a small menu of sandwiches, burgers and fish and chips (Rp18,000–35,000) alongside a big choice of drinks.

**Roti Bedugul** On the main road near Bukit Mungsu market. They make fabulous homebaked bread, sweet buns and cookies.

**Strawberry Stop** 2km north of Candikuning. Serving strawberries with cream or ice cream, milkshakes and pancakes all Rp8000–10,000.

## Directory

**Banks and exchange** Moneychangers in the market and the car park of Pura Ulun Danu Bratan temple.

**Telephones** Warung telkom in the market.

## Moving on

**By bus** to Denpasar (Ubung terminal; 1hr 30min) and Singaraja (Sukasada terminal; 1hr 30min).

**By shuttle bus** The Perama office (ⓣ0368/21011) is at the *Sari Artha* losmen, just below the market on the main road in Candikuning. There's one daily service to the north of the island and one to the south

**Destinations:** Kuta (2hr 30min–3hr); Lovina (1hr 30min); Sanur (2hr–2hr 30min); Ubud (1hr 30min).

# SINGARAJA AND AROUND

The second-largest Balinese city after Denpasar, **SINGARAJA** has an airy spaciousness created by broad avenues, large monuments and colonial bungalows set in attractive gardens. It's of most interest to travellers for its transport connections: if you're visiting the north you'll probably pass through at some point.

## Arrival and informaton

**By bemo and bus** There are three bemo and bus terminals in Singaraja. Sukasada (locally called Sangket), to the south of the town, serves Bedugul and Denpasar; Banyuasri, on the western edge of town, serves the west, including Lovina, Seririt and Gilimanuk; and Penarukan is for services eastwards along the north coast via Tulamben to Amlapura and along the Kintamani/Penelokan road for the Batur area and on to Bangli. Small bemos (flat rate Rp5000) ferry passengers between the terminals.

**Tourist information** The tourist office is south of the town centre at Jl Veteran 23 (Mon–Thurs 8am–3pm, Fri 8am–11am; ⓣ0362/25141, ⓦwww.northbalitourism.com).

## Accommodation

**Wijaya** Jl Sudirman 74 ⓣ0362/21915, ⓕ25817. Clean, tiled rooms conveniently close to Banyuasri terminal. A/c and hot water are available. ❷–❻

## Eating

There's a **night market** in the Jl Durian area, between Jl Dr Sutomo and the main market, Pasar Anyar, in the centre of the city, just opposite Bank Central Asia. Kampung Tinggi, just east of the bridge on the main road east out of Singaraja, is lined with stalls every afternoon (2–8pm), some of which have a basic written menu.

**Kafetaria Lima-Lima** Jl Jen Achmad Yani 55a. Cheap Indonesian food and drink. Mains about Rp6000.

**Surya** Jl Jen Achmad Yani 25. Padang food at Rp6–7000 per plate.

## Directory

**Banks and exchange** Bank Central Asia on Jl Dr Sutomo (exchange counter Mon–Fri 10am–2pm) is most convenient for exchange and there's also an international ATM. Several other ATMs, including Bank Danamon on Jl Jen Achmad Yani and at Hardy's supermarket.

**Hospitals** Rumah Sakit Umum (the public hospital), Jl Ngurah Rai ⓣ0362/41046. Many of Singaraja's medical facilities, including doctors and pharmacies, are concentrated nearby.

**Internet** Warnet, Jl Dewi Sartika 32A (6am–midnight; Rp4000/hr).
**Post office** The main post office, and poste restante is at Jl Gajah Made 156 (Mon–Thurs 8am–3pm, Fri 8am–1pm, Sat 8am–noon), and is also a Western Union agent. A smaller post office is south of *Wijaya* hotel at Jl Sudirman 68a, a short walk from Banyuasri terminal.
**Telephones** The main phone office is at the southern end of Jl Kartini.
**Supermarket** Hardy's (6am–10.30pm), the closest that Singaraja boasts to a mall, is three floors of local shops including a supermarket.

## Moving on

**By long-distance bus** All these buses leave from the offices listed. Menggala, Jl Jen Achmad Yani 76 (☎0362/24374), operates daily night buses to Surabaya (7pm; 8hr), arriving at Probolinggo and Pasuruan in East Java, access point for the Bromo region, in the middle of the night. Safari Dharma Raya, Jl Jen Achmad Yani 84 (☎0362/23460), runs daily buses to Jakarta (3pm; 24hr). Puspa Rama, Jl Jen Achmad Yani 90 (☎0362/22696), operates daily buses to Surabaya (7.30pm; 8hr) and Malang (7.30pm; 9–10hr). They also sell tickets for the daily bus that leaves Gilimanuk at 5pm for Yogyakarta (12hr).
**By bemo and bus**
**Banyuasri terminal** to: Gilimanuk (2hr 30min); Lovina (20min); Seririt (40min).
**Penarukan terminal** to: Amlapura (3hr); Culik (2hr 30min); Denpasar (Batubulan terminal; 3hr); Gianyar (2hr 20min); Penelokan (1hr 30min); Kubutambahan (20min); Tirtagangga (2hr 30min); Tulamben (1hr).
**Sukasada terminal** to: Bedugul (1hr 30min); Denpasar (Ubung terminal; 3hr).

# LOVINA

**LOVINA** stretches along 8km of black-sand beach, the largest resort in Bali outside the Kuta–Legian–Seminyak conurbation. While the peak season (June–Aug and Dec) is busy, Lovina remains far less frantic than the southern resorts, although there's some nightlife and activity centres on the beach, with snorkelling, diving

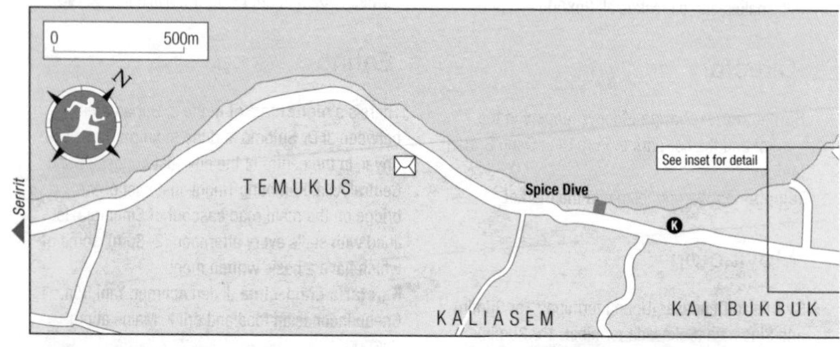


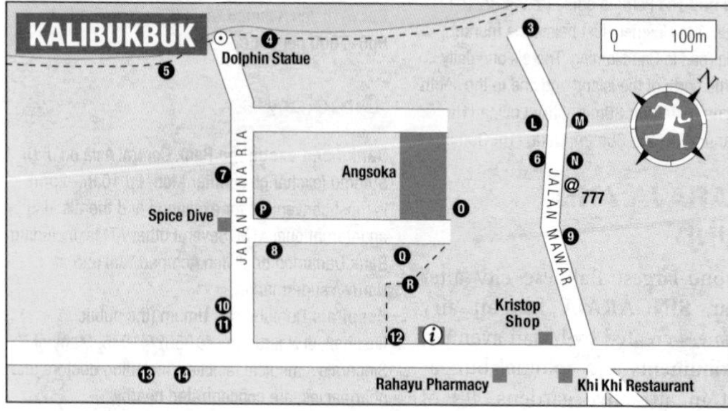

and dolphin-watching as diversions. It's also an ideal base for exploring the whole of the north coast and the volcanic areas inland.

Beginning 6km west of Singaraja, the resort encompasses six villages, from east to west: **Pemaron**, **Tukad Mungga**, **Anturan**, **Kalibukbuk** (including a side road, to the east of the centre, known as **Banyualit**), **Kaliasem** and **Temukus**.

**Kalibukbuk** is the centre of Lovina and chock full of accommodation, restaurants and tourist facilities. It is centred around two parallel side roads, Jalan Bina Ria and, a few hundred metres east, Jalan Mawar, also known as Jalan Ketapang or Jalan Rambutan. The entrance to Jalan Mawar is at the crossroads marked by traffic lights (the only ones in Lovina) virtually opposite *Khi Khi Restaurant* on the main road. A beachfront walkway links the ocean ends of Jalan Mawar and Jalan Bina Ria. East of here, in **TUKAD MUNGGA** (where the beach is known as Pantai Happy), the small fishing village of **Anturan** and along the **Banyualit** side road Jalan Laviana, 1.5km from the centre, it tends to be quiet despite the development of losmen and restaurants, and the villagers are well used to tourists wandering around. West of Kalibukbuk, restaurants and accommodation line the roadside in the villages of **Kaliasem** and **Temukus**. Road noise is the enemy here; only consider accommodation set far enough back to block the noise out.

## What to see and do

Lovina is famous (or infamous) for dawn trips to see the **dolphins** that frolic off the coast; opinions are evenly split between those who think it's grossly overrated and those who consider it one of the best things on Bali. It's pretty much

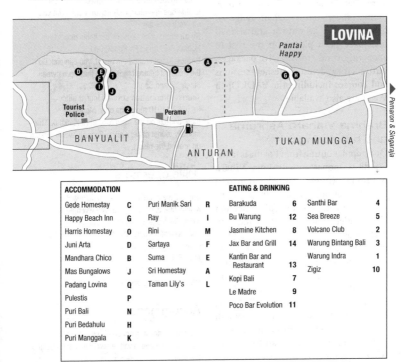

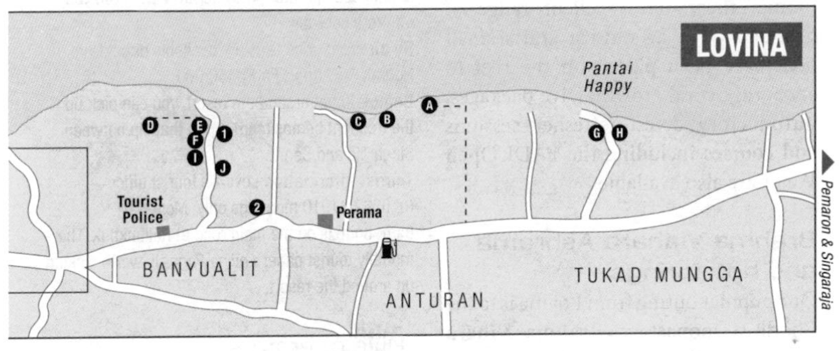


**ACCOMMODATION**

| | | | |
|---|---|---|---|
| Gede Homestay | C | Puri Manik Sari | R |
| Happy Beach Inn | G | Ray | I |
| Harris Homestay | O | Rini | M |
| Juni Arta | D | Sartaya | F |
| Mandhara Chico | B | Suma | E |
| Mas Bungalows | J | Sri Homestay | A |
| Padang Lovina | Q | Taman Lily's | L |
| Pulestis | P | | |
| Puri Bali | N | | |
| Puri Bedahulu | H | | |
| Puri Manggala | K | | |

**EATING & DRINKING**

| | | | |
|---|---|---|---|
| Barakuda | 6 | Santhi Bar | 4 |
| Bu Warung | 12 | Sea Breeze | 5 |
| Jasmine Kitchen | 8 | Volcano Club | 2 |
| Jax Bar and Grill | 14 | Warung Bintang Bali | 3 |
| Kantin Bar and Restaurant | 13 | Warung Indra | 1 |
| Kopi Bali | 7 | Zigiz | 10 |
| Le Madre | 9 | | |
| Poco Bar Evolution | 11 | | |

the luck of the draw, some days there is little to see while on others the dolphins cavort around and under the boats in a grand display. If you're happy to take a gamble, it's a good trip, and very, very occasionally **whales** have been spotted. Boats leave at 6am and cost Rp50,000 per person for the two-hour trip; book directly with the skippers on the beach or through your accommodation

The skippers also know the best spots on the local reef for **snorkelling** (Rp50,000; 1hr 30min–2hr), and dive operators will take snorkellers on dive trips further afield if they have space, which is more expensive but offers greater variety.

Situated between the main north coast diving areas, Lovina is an ideal base for **diving**, with fun dives in the Lovina area and further afield at Pulau Menjangan, Tulamben and Amed all available. The local reef, perhaps unfairly, has a reputation as being uninteresting, though there's an excellent range of fish, and tyres, an old car and a small boat have been placed on the reef to encourage coral growth. Dive packages, introductory dives, refresher sessions and courses including the PADI Open Water are also available.

### Brahma Viahara Ashrama and hot springs

One popular outing from Lovina is to the Buddhist monastery, **Brahma Vihara Ashrama** (rarely closed; donation includes sarong rental), 10km southwest of Lovina, a colourful confection in a wonderful hillside setting and with a glorious gold Buddha as the centrepiece in the main temple. Catch any westbound bemo to **Dencarik**, where a sign points inland to the monastery, and ojek wait to take you the last steep 5km. From the temple you can walk to the **hot springs** (daily 8am–6pm; Rp3000): head back downhill from the monastery and take the first road to the left. After a few hundred metres you'll reach a major crossroads and marketplace at the village of **Banjar Tega**. Turn left and after about 200m you'll see a sign for the "Air Panas Holy Hot Spring", from where it's a kilometre walk.

## Arrival, local transport and information

**By bus** Inter-island buses from Java to Singaraja pass through Lovina, as do Gilimanuk–Singaraja and Amlapura–Gilimanuk services and all buses from the west of the island. You can also come directly on Denpasar (Ubung)–Singaraja services via Pupuan, or on minibuses to Seirit before swapping onto local services. From the east of Bali, you'll come via Singaraja, from whose Banyuasri terminal it's a short bemo ride. As the accommodation is so spread out, it's worth knowing where you want to be dropped off.

**By shuttle bus** Perama buses drop off at their office (daily 8am–10pm; ⓣ0362/41161) in Anturan, a short walk from the Anturan accommodation. They charge an additional Rp5000 to be dropped off elsewhere. Check with other shuttle bus operators whether they will drop you off more centrally.

**By air** Fixed price taxis are available direct from Ngurah Rai Airport for Rp450,000.

**Bemos** To get around the resort, you can pick up the frequent bemos (4am–6pm) that zip between Singaraja and Seririt.

**Tourist information** Lovina's tourist office (ⓣ0362/41910 mornings only; Mon–Sat 8am–8pm) is on the main road at Kalibukbuk. The monthly tourist paper *Lovina Pages* is worth picking up around the resort.

## Dive operators

**Spice Dive** In Kaliasem and on Jl Bina Ria, Kalibukbuk ⓣ0362/41509, ⓦwww.balispicedive.com. The longest-established Lovina operator and the resort's only PADI five-star dive centre. PADI Open Water (€250), fun dives in the Lovina area, Pulau Menjangan, Tulamben and Amed are all available (€35–65) as are dive packages, introductory dives and refresher sessions.

## Accommodation

Most of the accommodation is on side roads leading to the beach with a few places right behind the beach.

### Tukad Mungga

**Happy Beach Inn** ⓣ0362/41017. Four functional rooms with attached cold-water bathrooms in a small garden close to the beach. ❷

**Puri Bedahulu** ⓣ0362/41731. Next to the beach at Pantai Happy. Comfortable bungalows with elegant Balinese carvings; hot water and a/c is available. ❷–❸

### Anturan

**Gede Homestay** ⓣ0362/41526. Good-quality accommodation in two rows of bungalows just behind the beach. There's a small restaurant and sunbathing area; a/c and hot water are available. ❷–❹

**Mandhara Chico** ⓣ0362/41271. Close to the beach, the best rooms are the two beachfront bungalows with verandas facing seawards; a/c and hot water are available. ❷–❸

**Sri Homestay** ⓣ0813/3757 0692. All the bungalows face the ocean and some have hot water. Access is via a track from the main road or via the beach. ❸–❹

### Banyualit

**Juni Arta** ⓣ0362/41885. Rather tucked away, access is via a path from the beach end of Jl Laviana, these are good-quality bungalows in a peaceful spot. ❷–❸

**Mas Bungalows** ⓣ0362/41773, ⓦwww.masbungalows.com. All rooms have hot water and are decorated with local textiles. A/c is available and there's a large pool. ❸–❹

**Ray** ⓣ0362/41088. Tiled rooms in a two-storey building with balcony or veranda looking out onto a decent garden. All have fan, hot water is available, and there's a small spa. ❸–❹

**Sartaya** ⓣ0362/42240, ⓔkembarsartaya@hotmail.com. Two rows of good-quality, clean bungalows, some with hot water and a choice of fan or a/c, facing each other across a small garden. ❷–❸

**Suma** ⓣ0362/41566, ⓦwww.sumahotel.com. A range of rooms, from fan and cold-water options up to ones with a/c and hot water. The pool is excellent, the gardens pretty and there's internet access for guests (Rp200/min). Booking recommended. ❸–❼

### Kalibukbuk

**Harris Homestay** ⓣ0362/41152. A popular budget gem tucked away off Jl Bina Ria. Just five simple rooms, all with fans and en-suite cold-water bathrooms. ❷

**Padang Lovina** ⓣ0362/41302, ⓔpadanglovina@yahoo.com. Central but quiet accommodation in a two-storey block just off Jl Bina Ria. Guests can use the pool at *Pulestis*. ❸–❻

**Pulestis** ⓣ0362/41035. With a grand entrance on Jl Bina Ria, this guesthouse offers comfortable rooms and a pool. ❷–❸ & ❻

**Puri Bali** ⓣ0362/41485, ⓦwww.puribalilovina.com. A variety of rooms, in an attractive, quiet garden on Jl Mawar with an excellent pool; more expensive ones, closer to the pool, have a/c and hot water. ❸–❺

**Puri Manik Sari** ⓣ&ⓕ0362/41089. Mostly fan-cooled bungalows with hot water in a pretty garden set far enough back from the road to avoid the noise. There's one with a/c. ❷–❸

**Rini** ⓣ0362/41386, ⓦhttp://rinihotel.homepage.dk. Several standards of extremely clean accommodation in a pretty garden on Jl Mawar. A/c and hot water are available, and there's a salt-water pool with a poolside restaurant. ❸–❻

**Taman Lily's** Jl Mawar ⓣ0362/41307, ⓦwww.balilovinahotel-tamanlilys.com. A row of six excellent-value, spotless bungalows, with fans or a/c, and hot water. ❹

### Kaliasem and Temukus

**Puri Manggala** ⓣ0362/41371, ⓔPurimanggala@hotmail.com. Neat, simple rooms in a small, friendly family compound. Hot water and a/c are available. ❷–❹

## Eating

### Banyualit

**Warung Indra** Friendly little place in Banyualit featuring a vast menu of Western and Indonesian standards; nothing is more than Rp20,000 and there are plenty of vegetarian choices.

### Kalibukbuk

**Barakuda** Jl Mawar. Specializes in well-cooked, good-value seafood served with one of eleven Balinese or Chinese sauces. The set meals are excellent value, from Rp85,000 for two. There are plenty of vegetarian, pork and chicken options as well.

**Bu Warung** This tiny place on the main road has a small, great-value menu of around a dozen well-cooked mains (Rp10,000–12,500). There are also sandwiches, pancakes and fried bananas.

**Jasmine Kitchen** Outstanding restaurant serving fabulous Thai food (mains up to Rp39,000) in relaxed surroundings just off Jl Bina Ria. Everything is delectable but desserts (Rp18,000) and coffee are exceptional.

**Kopi Bali** Jl Bina Ria Popular place with well-cooked food. With *nasi goreng* at Rp12,900, this is the place for big appetites with small budgets.

**Le Madre** Little spot on Jl Mawar serving excellent Italian food but with Indonesian and Balinese dishes as well. Service is friendly, and *focaccia* is baked daily. Mains Rp25,000–35,000; pizzas Rp28,000–40,000.

**Santhi Bar** Shady chill-out spot near the beach at the end of Jl Bina Ria. Drinks (alcoholic and non) are cheap and there's a good-value menu of Indonesian and Western food with mains up to Rp25,000.

**Sea Breeze** A great spot on the beach close to the Dolphin Statue for sunset drinks, with an excellent menu of Western, Indonesian and seafood dishes (mains Rp25,000–55,000), plus good cakes and desserts. Acoustic music regularly accompanies the setting sun.

**Warung Bintang Bali** At the end of Jl Mawar close to the beach, a relaxed and popular place with friendly staff and a big good-value menu of the usual travellers' fare with mains Rp18,000–24,000.

## Drinking and nightlife

**Jax Bar and Grill** On the main road, Kalibukbuk. Live music supplemented by good food and drinks.

**Kantin Bar and Restaurant** On the main road, Kalibukbuk. Close to *Jax*, this is another live music spot, with a good drinks list.

**Poco Bar Evolution** Jl Bina Ria, Kalibukbuk. Lively spot with regular live music and drinks late into the evening.

**Volcano Club** Lovina's main nightlife, on the main road near Banyualit; opening varies with the season – look out for local adverts.

**Zigiz** Jl Bina Ria, Kalibukbuk. Popular bar, serving up live music, a friendly atmosphere and plenty of drinks.

## Directory

**Banks and exchange** Moneychangers throughout the resort. There's an international BCA ATM on the main road in Kalibukbuk.

**Bicycle rental** On Jl Mawar next to Suga Gallery, Rp20,000 per day.

**Car and motorbike rental** Available throughout the resort from established firms and from people who'll approach you on the street (Rp90,000–100,000/day for a Suzuki Jimney and Rp150,000–200,000 for a Kijang). Motorbikes are also widely available (Rp30,000–40,000 per day). Established companies include Yuli Transport (Ⓣ0362/41184), on Jl Mawar, and Dupa, on the main road (Ⓣ0362/41397). To charter a vehicle plus driver, you'll be looking at Rp300,000–350,000 per day including petrol. Made Wijana (Ⓣ0813/3856 3027) is a recommended driver.

**Cookery classes** Adjani (Ⓣ0812/385 6802, Ⓔad-janibali@telkom.net) is well established and has an office in Kaliasem (Rp150,000–175,000 per person). *Barakuda* restaurant on Jl Mawar (Ⓣ0362/41405, Ⓔrestaurant_barakuda@hotmail.com), offers classes consisting of four main courses (Rp75,000–85,000 per person) or seven main courses (Rp135,000–175,000). In Banyualit, Penny's Cooking Classes can be booked at *Suma's* (Rp150,000 for four dishes). Putu's Cooking (Ⓣ0813/3856 3705) is advertised throughout the resort (Rp150,000 per person).

**Hospital** The closest hospital is in Singaraja.

**Internet** Offered by many places (8am–10pm; Rp400/min). 777 Internet on Jl Mawar and Spice Dive on Jl Bina Ria both burn CDs and DVDs, print and work with USB devices. They also offer telephone services.

**Pharmacy** Rayahu Pharmacy (9am–9pm) on the main road and there is a doctor attached.

**Police** Ⓣ0362/41010. On the main road to the east of Kalibukbuk.

**Post office** The post office with poste restante (Mon–Thurs 8am–3pm, Fri 8am–1pm, Sat 8am–noon) is about 1km west of Kalibukbuk. Several places in Kalibukbuk sell stamps.

**Spas and massages** Plenty of spas in addition to beach massages: Bali Samadhi Spa (Ⓣ0813/3855 8260, Ⓦwww.balisamadhi.com) is off Jl Mawar; Agung's (Ⓣ0362/42018, Ⓦwww.lovina-spa.com) on the road to *Damai Lovina Villas*; and Araminth Spa (Ⓣ0362/41901, Ⓦwww.arunaspa.com) on Jl Mawar. All have extensive spa menus, with prices from Rp60,000 for a massage.

**Yoga** At the Banana Plantation in Kaliasem (Mon–Thurs 8am; Ⓣ0819/1562 5525, Ⓔakarbali@peacemail.com; Rp50,000). Enquire at the Akar Shop in Jl Bina Ria.

## Moving on

**By shuttle bus and long-distance buses** The Perama office is at Anturan (daily 8am–10pm; Ⓣ0362/41161). See p.322 for long-distance buses from Singaraja. Perama book buses to other parts of Indonesia, including Jakarta, Surabaya and Yogyakarta, as well as within Bali and Lombok.

**Destinations:** Bedugul (1 daily; 1hr 30min); Candi Dasa (2 daily; 3hr–3hr 30min); Kuta, Bali/Ngurah Rai Airport (1 daily; 3hr); Mataram (daily; 7–8hr); Padang Bai (1 daily; 2hr 45min); Sanur (1 daily; 2hr 30min–3hr); Sengiggi (1 daily; 7hr 30min–8hr 30min); Ubud (1 daily; 3hr 30min–4hr).

**By bemo and bus** to: Gilimanuk (2hr 30min); Pemuteran (1hr 15min); Seririt (20min); Singaraja (Banyuasri terminal; 20min).

## BALI BARAT NATIONAL PARK

Bali's only national park, **Bali Barat National Park (Taman Nasional Bali Barat)**, protects some 190 square kilometres of savannah, forest and reef 20km west of Lovina, and is home to 160 species of bird, including the endangered **Bali starling**, Bali's one true endemic creature. A few trails are open to the public, but most visitors come to dive and snorkel the spectacular **Pulau Menjangan** reefs. All visitors must hire a guide and buy a permit, either through the **National Park headquarters** (daily 8am–5pm) in **CEKIK**, 3km south of Gilimanuk, or at the Pulau Menjangan jetty (see below). **Guides** charge Rp190,000–440,000 for a two- to seven-hour hike for up to two people. Permits cost Rp20,000 per person per day. All Ubung (Denpasar)–Gilimanuk **bemos** pass the park headquarters, as do all Singaraja–Gilimanuk bemos.

If your main interest is birdspotting, opt for the Prapat Agung Peninsula **trek** (1–2hr), or the Teluk Terima trail (2hr). The Gunung Klatakan–Gunung Bakingan **rainforest** trail (7hr) is more strenuous but lacking in wildlife.

Camping is forbidden in most of the park, but you can ask to pitch your tent on Labuan Lalang's beach or at the Cekik headquarters, though there are few facilities at either spot. The nearest **hotel** and restaurant is the basic *Pondok Wisata Lestari* (Ⓣ0365/61504; ❷–❺), 1.5km north of the headquarters on the road into Gilimanuk. Much pleasanter is the lovely little beach haven of **Pemuteran**, 28km east of Cekik (or just 15km from Labuan Lalang), served by Gilimanuk–Singaraja bemos, where the most affordable options are the attractive fan and a/c bungalows at *Rare Angon* (Ⓣ0362/94747, Ⓔrareangon@yahoo.co.id; ❹–❻) and *Jubawa Homestay* (Ⓣ0362/94745; ❺–❻). Snorkelling and dive trips to Menjangan are easily arranged here.

### Pulau Menjangan (Deer Island)

By far the most popular part of Bali Barat is **Pulau Menjangan (Deer Island)**, a tiny uninhabited island 8km off the north coast, whose shoreline is encircled by fabulous **coral reefs**, with drop-offs of up to 60m, first-class wall dives and superb visibility.

Guides, permits and boat transport should be arranged at the jetty in **Labuan Lalang**, 13km east of Cekik, on the Gilimanuk–Singaraja bemo route (30min from Gilimanuk or 2hr from Lovina). There's a small national park office here (daily 8am–3pm), and several warung. **Boats** to Pulau Menjangan can be hired any time up to 3pm; they hold ten people and cost Rp310,000 for a four-hour snorkelling tour – it's thirty minutes to the island. You'll also have to pay Rp60,000 for your guide (one per boat), plus Rp20,000 per person for the national park permit; snorkelling gear costs Rp50,000 a set. There are occasional reports of thefts from the boats while snorkellers are underwater, so leave your valuables elsewhere. Pulau Menjangan also features on day- and overnight tours for snorkellers (from US$40) and divers (from US$80) based in Pemuteran, Lovina, Kuta, Sanur or Candi Dasa.

## GILIMANUK

Situated on the westernmost tip of Bali, about 17km west of Labuan Lalang, the small, ribbon-like port town of **GILIMANUK** is of interest only for its ferry connections to East Java less than 3km away.

### Arrival and information

**By bus and bemo** The bus and bemo depot is across the road from the ferry terminal. The only

ATM for foreign cards is in the ferry terminal compound.

### Accommodation

Accommodation in Gilimanuk is grim.
**Nusantara Gilimanuk Guest House** Jl Raya Gilimanuk, about 800m south of the ferry terminal, just north of the mosque ⓣ0365/61405. One of the friendlier options, with a strikingly modern entrance, but basic fan and a/c rooms. ❹–❺

### Eating

**Asli Warung Men Tempeh** In the lot 500m north across the road from the mosque on Jl Raya. Famous throughout Bali for its fiery *ayam betutu* (steamed chilli chicken; Rp45,000). Daily 10am–4pm.

### Moving on

**By bus and bemo** Buses and bemos depart when full from the transport depot across the road from the ferry terminus.
**Destinations:** Amlapura (4hr); Cekik (10min); Denpasar (Ubung terminal; 3hr 15min); Kediri (for Tanah Lot; 2hr 45min); Medewi (1hr 45min); Labuan Lalang (25min); Lalang Linggah (2hr 15min); Lovina (2hr 15min); Padang Bai (5hr); Pemuteran (1hr); Singaraja (Banyuasri terminal; 2hr 30min).
**By boat** to Ketapang, East Java (24-hr service, every 20min; 45min).

# Lombok and the Gili Islands

Thirty-five kilometres east of Bali at its closest point, Islamic **Lombok** (80km by 70km) is populated by Sasak people. It differs considerably from its Hindu neighbour, with lots of wide-open spaces and unspoilt beaches, and much less traffic and pollution. Tourist facilities are less widespread and public transport sparser. The island's northern area is dominated by the awesome bulk of **Gunung Rinjani**, and trekking at least part of the way up is the reason many tourists come to Lombok. Most base themselves in the nearby villages of **Senaru** or **Sembalun Lawang**. Other visitors enjoy the cool foothills at tiny **Tetebatu** and **Sapit**. The other big draw are the beaches. The trio of **Gili Islands**, just off the northwest coast, attracts increasing numbers of visitors, while the resort of **Senggigi** on the west coast and south-coast **Kuta**, a popular surfing centre, also offer a range of tourist facilities. Lombok's capital and main city area **Ampenan-Mataram-Cakranegara-Sweta** has excellent transport connections and is a user-friendly Indonesian city.

## AMPENAN-MATARAM-CAKRANEGARA-SWETA

The **AMPENAN-MATARAM-CAKRANEGARA-SWETA** conurbation comprises four towns and stretches over 8km from west to east, but it's easy to get around and offers a good opportunity to experience Indonesian city life. At the western end of the city is the bustling old port town of **Ampenan**, the jumping-off point for Senggigi a few kilometres up the coast. Merging into Ampenan to the east, **Mataram** is the capital of West Nusa Tenggara province as well as the district of West Lombok and full of offices and government buildings. East again, **Cakranegara**, usually known as Cakra (pronounced "Chakra"), is the commercial heart of the island, with shopping centres, markets and workshops. **Sweta**, on the eastern edge of the city area, is the location of the island's main bus station. Most tourists come to the city for the day but an overnight stay is a good chance to try the city's restaurants in the evening and visit early morning markets.

### What to see and do

The vibrant **markets** offer a great chance to see local life. The Kebon Roek market in Ampenan and the market

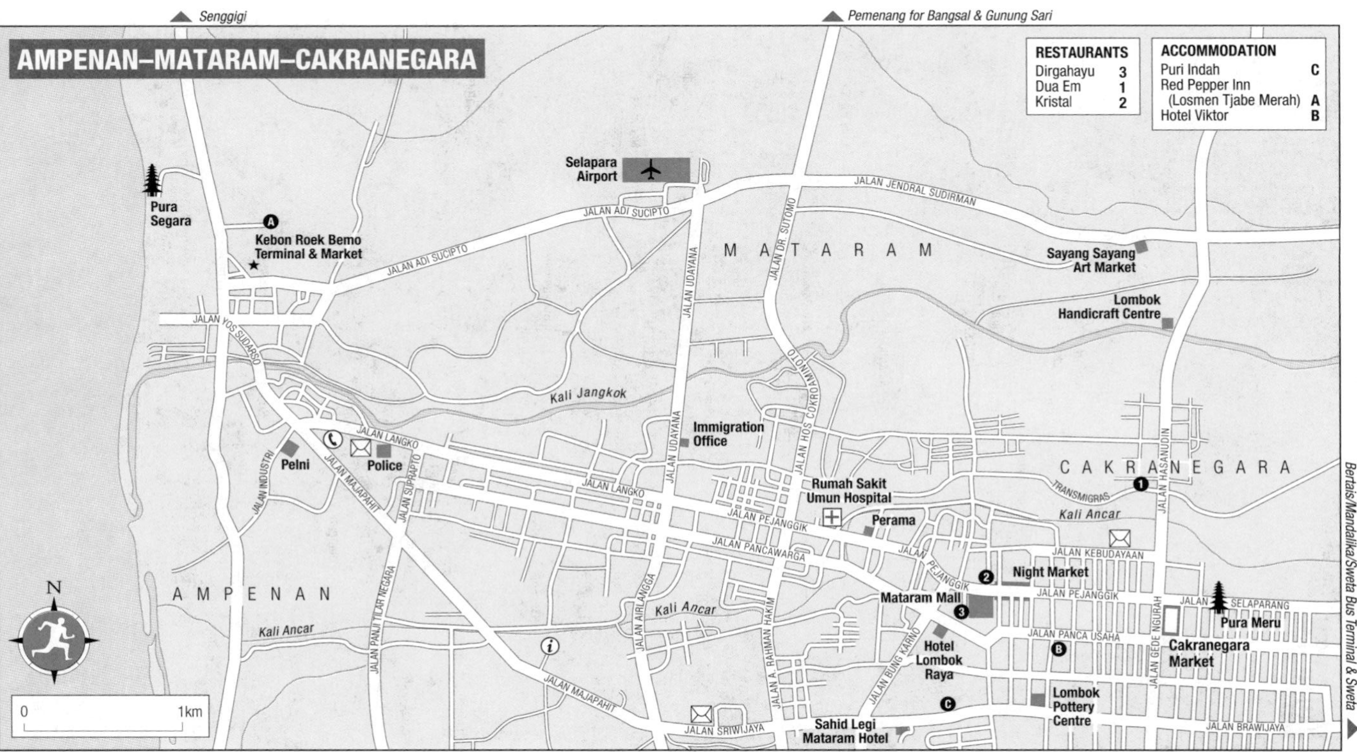
AMPENAN–MATARAM–CAKRANEGARA
RESTAURANTS
Dirgahayu 3
Dua Em 1
Kristal 2
ACCOMMODATION
Puri Indah C
Red Pepper Inn (Losmen Tjabe Merah) A
Hotel Viktor B
Senggigi
Pemenang for Bangsal & Gunung Sari
Bertais/Mandalika/Sweta Bus Terminal & Sweta
Lembar
Selapara Airport
Pura Segara
Kebon Roek Bemo Terminal & Market
MATARAM
CAKRANEGARA
AMPENAN
Sayang Sayang Art Market
Lombok Handicraft Centre
Kali Jangkok
Kali Ancar
Immigration Office
Police
Pelni
Rumah Sakit Umun Hospital
Perama
Night Market
Mataram Mall
Hotel Lombok Raya
Lombok Pottery Centre
Sahid Legi Mataram Hotel
Pura Meru
Cakranegara Market
JALAN JENDRAL SUDIRMAN
JALAN ADI SUCIPTO
JALAN DR. SUTOMO
JALAN UDAYANA
JALAN HOS COKROAMINOTO
JALAN YOS SUDARSO
JALAN LANGKO
JALAN INDUSTRI
JALAN MAJAPAHIT
JALAN SUPRAPTO
JALAN PANJI TILAR NEGARA
JALAN PEJANGGIK
JALAN PANCAWARGA
JALAN AIRLANGGA
JALAN A. RAHMAN HAKIM
JALAN SRIWIJAYA
JALAN BUNG KARNO
JALAN KEBUDAYAAN
JALAN PANCA USAHA
JALAN BRAWIJAYA
JALAN GEDE NGURAH
JALAN HASANUDIN
JALAN SELAPARANG
TRANSMIGRAS
N
0
1km

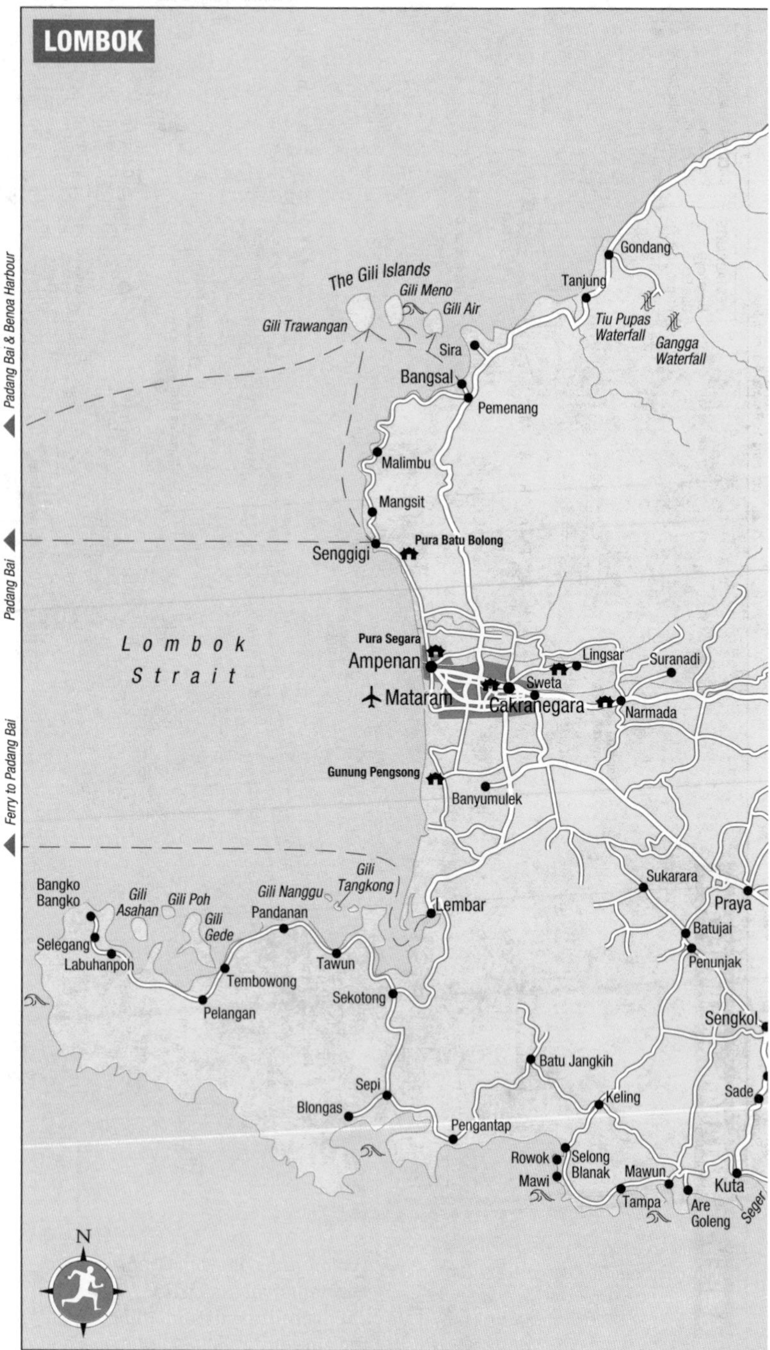
LOMBOK
Padang Bai & Benoa Harbour
Padang Bai
Ferry to Padang Bai
The Gili Islands
Gili Meno
Gili Air
Gili Trawangan
Sira
Bangsal
Pemenang
Tanjung
Gondang
Tiu Pupas Waterfall
Gangga Waterfall
Malimbu
Mangsit
Senggigi
Pura Batu Bolong
Lombok Strait
Pura Segara
Ampenan
Mataram
Lingsar
Suranadi
Sweta
Cakranegara
Narmada
Gunung Pengsong
Banyumulek
Gili Tangkong
Bangko Bangko
Gili Asahan
Gili Poh
Gili Nanggu
Gili Gede
Pandanan
Lembar
Selegang
Labuhanpoh
Tembowong
Tawun
Sekotong
Pelangan
Sukarara
Praya
Batujai
Penunjak
Sengkol
Batu Jangkih
Sepi
Blongas
Keling
Sade
Pengantap
Rowok
Selong Blanak
Mawi
Mawun
Tampa
Kuta
Are Goleng
Seger
N

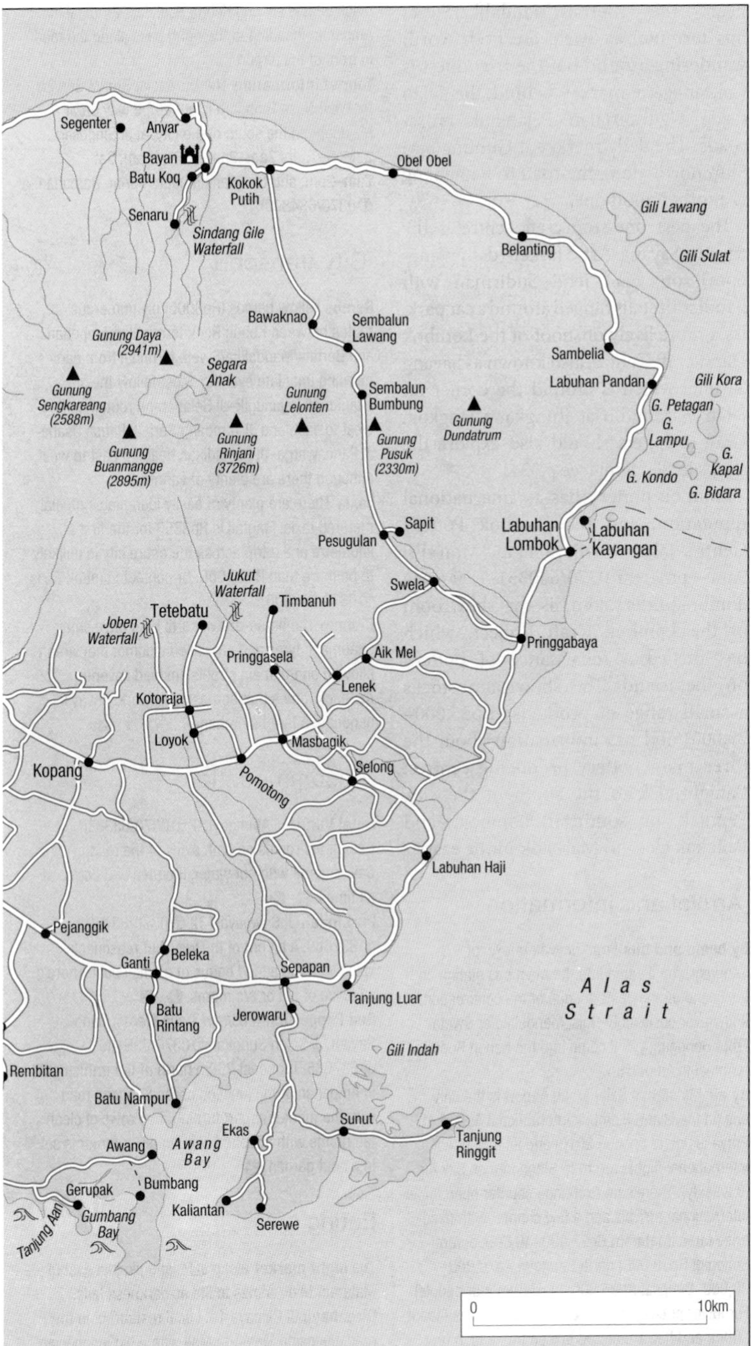
Segenter
Anyar
Bayan
Batu Koq
Kokok Putih
Obel Obel
Senaru
Sindang Gile Waterfall
Gili Lawang
Belanting
Gili Sulat
Bawaknao
Sembalun Lawang
Gunung Daya (2941m)
Segara Anak
Sambelia
Gunung Sengkareang (2588m)
Labuhan Pandan
Gili Kora
Gunung Lelonten
Sembalun Bumbung
G. Petagan
G. Lampu
Gunung Dundatrum
Gunung Pusuk (2330m)
Gunung Rinjani (3726m)
Gunung Buanmangge (2895m)
G. Kapal
G. Kondo
G. Bidara
Sapit
Labuhan Lombok
Labuhan Kayangan
Pesugulan
Swela
Ferry to Sumbawa
Jukut Waterfall
Timbanuh
Tetebatu
Joben Waterfall
Pringgabaya
Aik Mel
Pringgasela
Lenek
Kotoraja
Loyok
Masbagik
Kopang
Selong
Pomotong
Labuhan Haji
Pejanggik
Beleka
Ganti
Sepapan
Tanjung Luar
Batu Rintang
Jerowaru
Alas Strait
Gili Indah
Rembitan
Batu Nampur
Sunut
Tanjung Ringgit
Ekas
Awang
Awang Bay
Bumbang
Gerupak
Kaliantan
Serewe
Gumbang Bay
Tanjung Aan
0
10km

near the Bertais/Mandalika/Sweta bus terminal at Sweta are both worth wandering around but the friendliest is Cakranegara market behind the Jalan Gede Ngurah/Jalan Pejanggik crossroads. The daily market at Gunung Sari 5km north along the road to Pemenang is another good one.

The best one-stop craft centre is the Sayang Sayang Art Market (daily 9am–6pm), on Jalan Jend Sudirman with handicraft stalls ranged around a car park. It's a more lively offshoot of the Lombok Handicraft Centre, also known as Sayang Sayang, which is around the corner on Jalan Hasanudin at Rungkang Jangkok. Craft shoppers should also explore the shops in Senggigi (see p.334).

Lombok pottery has an international reputation, and the Lombok Pottery Centre, Jalan Sriwijaya 111a (Mon–Fri 9am–4pm; ⓣ0370/640351, ⓦwww.lombokpottery.com) is the showroom of the Lombok Craft Project, which has fuelled a renaissance of pottery on the island. The showroom stocks a small range of products (Rp25,000–75,000) and has information about the three main pottery producing centres: Banyumulek to the south of the city, Penujak in southern Lombok, and Penakak close to Masbajik in the east.

## Arrival and information

**By bemo and bus** From anywhere except Senggigi, you'll come into the main bus station on the island on the eastern edge of the conurbation, known variously as Bertais, Mandalika or Sweta. From Senggigi, you'll come into the Kebon Roek terminal in Ampenan.

**By air** Mataram's Selaparang Airport is the only one on the island (Lombok International Airport at Praya is due to open in 2010) and its only direct international flights are from Singapore on Silk Air (3 weekly). There's an exchange counter open for international arrivals and a taxi counter with fixed-price fares (Mataram Rp27,000–40,000; central Senggigi Rp50,000; north Senggigi Rp70,000–90,000; Bangsal Rp95,000; maximum four people). For lower prices walk out of the airport gates (about 200m) and hail a metered taxi on the road. A few black bemos serving Kebon Roek bus terminal in Ampenan (heading to the right) pass along the road in front of the airport.

**Tourist information** The Provincial Tourist Service for West Nusa Tenggara is out of the way off Jl Majapahit in the south of the city, at Jl Singosari 2 (Mon–Thurs 7am–2pm, Fri 7–11am, Sat 7am–2pm; shorter opening hours during Ramadan; ⓣ0370/634800).

## City transport

**Bemos** Yellow bemos (Rp3000) ply numerous routes between Kebon Roek terminal in Ampenan and Bertais/Mandalika/Sweta terminal from early morning until late evening. Most follow the Jl Langko–Jl Pejanggik–Jl Selaparang route heading west to east, and Jl Tumpang Sari–Jl Panca Usaha–Jl Pancawarga–Jl Pendidikan heading east to west, although there are plenty of variations.

**Taxis** There are plenty of easily identifiable official metered taxis. Flagfall is Rp3850 for the first kilometre and a trip across the entire city is unlikely to be more than Rp20,000. Or contact Lombok Taxis ⓣ0370/627000.

**Cidomo** The horse-drawn carts here have small pneumatic tyres and are called cidomo; they aren't allowed on the main streets, instead covering the back routes that bemos don't work. Always negotiate a fare beforehand.

## Accommodation

**Hotel Viktor** Jl Abimanyu 1 ⓣ0370/633830. Decent a/c rooms on both sides of the road in Cakra, some with hot water. Free tea and coffee at all times. ❷–❸

**Puri Indah** Jl Sriwijaya 132 ⓣ0370/637633, ⓕ637669. A bit out of the way, but reasonable value with the added bonus of a small pool. There's a choice of fan or a/c rooms. ❷–❸

**Red Pepper Inn** (*Losmen Tjabe Merah*) Gang Sawah, Jl Saleh Sungkar ⓣ0370/636150, ⓕ637635. Turn east 200m north of the traffic lights in Ampenan at the junction of the Senggigi road with the market/airport turning. Two rows of clean fan rooms with attached cold-water bathrooms set in a neat garden. ❷

## Eating

The **night market** along Jl Pejanggik, just east of Mataram Mall, comes to life as darkness falls.

**Dirgahayu** Jl Cilinaya 10. Local restaurant in the road alongside Mataram Mall with a big Indonesian

menu (take the dictionary). Excellent for cheap eats; *nasi campur* is Rp6000.
**Dua Em** Jl Transmigrasi 99. Traditional Sasak food. This one is for the adventurous; the food is beyond hot and all body parts are dished up. *Otak* is brains; *paru* is liver; *jeroan* is entrails; and *sate sum-sum* is bone marrow *sate* (main courses Rp20,000–25,000).
**Kristal** Jl Pejanggik 22a, Cakranegara. There's a big Chinese, Indonesian and seafood menu, including lots of vegetarian dishes. Mains Rp12,000–25,000.

## Directory

**Airlines** Airline ticket counters listed below are at the airport, unless otherwise stated: Batavia, Jl Pejanggik 88 ⓣ0370/648998; Citilink Garuda International, Jl Pejanggik 42–44 ⓣ0370/638259; Indonesia Air Transport ⓣ0370/639589; Lion Air/Wings Air ⓣ0370/662 7444, 24hr reservation 0804-1-778899; Merpati, Jl Pejanggik 69 ⓣ0370/621111, airport ⓣ0370/633637; Silk Air *Hotel Lombok Raya*, Jl Panca Usaha 11 ⓣ0370/628254, airport ⓣ0370/63624; Trigana Air ⓣ0370/616428.
**Banks and exchange** All the large Mataram and Cakra banks change money and traveller's cheques, and have international ATMs. The most convenient are BCA, Jl Pejanggik 67 ⓣ0370/622587; BNI, Jl Langko 64 ⓣ0370/622788; Bank Danamon, Jl Pejanggik ⓣ0370/622408. The main post office is a Western Union agent.
**Boats** Pelni, Jl Industri 1, Ampenan ⓣ0370/637212, ⓦwww.pelni.co.id (Mon–Fri 8am–3pm, Sat 8am–1pm).
**Car rental** The best choice and prices are in Senggigi (see p.337).
**Dentist** Dr Darmono, Jl Kebudayan 108, Mataram (ⓣ081/836 7749), speaks good English. Call to make an appointment. If you can't get through on his mobile, contact him 8am–4pm on ⓣ0370/636852 and from 4–9pm on ⓣ0370/643483. Clinic opening times are 8am–noon & 5–9pm.
**Hospitals** The public hospital, Rumah Sakit Umum, Jl Pejanggik 6, Mataram ⓣ0370/623498, has a daily (9am–11am) tourist clinic.
**Immigration office** Kantor Imigrasi, Jl Udayana 2, Mataram ⓣ0370/632520.
**Internet** Deddy's Internet (9am–9pm; Rp6000/hr), walk through the cassette shop at the front of Mataram Mall.
**Police** Senggigi Tourist Police ⓣ0370/632733.
**Post office** Lombok's main office is at Jl Sriwijaya 21, Mataram (Mon–Sat 8am–7pm, Sun 8am–noon). Another at Jl Langko 21, Ampenan (Mon–Sat 8am–7pm). For poste restante, the Senggigi post office is more used to dealing with tourists.
**Recompression chamber** Jl Adi Sucipto 13B (24-hr phone ⓣ0370/660 0333)
**Supermarket** Hero in the Mataram Mall (daily 10am–9pm).
**Telephones** Phone office, Jl Langko 23, Ampenan (daily 24hr).

## Moving on

**By public buses and bemos** Departures just north of the Kebon Roek terminal for Senggigi and at the Bertais/Mandalika/Sweta terminal for all other Lombok destinations.
**Destinations:** Bayan (for Gunung Rinjani; 2hr 30min); Labuhan Lombok (2hr); Lembar (30min); Pemenang (for the Gili Islands; 1hr); Pomotong (for Tetebatu; 1hr 15min); Praya (for Kuta; 30min);
**By shuttle bus** Perama have the biggest choice of departures. Their office is at Jl Pejanggik 66, Mataram ⓣ0370/635928, ⓦwww.peramatour.com.
**Destinations:** Bangsal (1 daily; 2hr; min 2 people); Candi Dasa (Bali; 1 daily; 5hr 30min–6hr); Kuta, Bali/Ngurah Rai Airport (Bali; 1 daily; 8hr 30min); Kuta, Lombok (2 daily; 2hr; min 2 people); Lovina (Bali; 1 daily; 10hr; min 2 people); Padang Bai (Bali; 1 daily; 4hr 30min–5hr); Sanur (Bali; 1 daily; 8hr); Senggigi (1 daily; 30min; min 2 people); Tetebatu (2 daily; 2hr; min 2 people); Ubud (Bali; 1 daily; 8hr).
**Inter-island buses** Buy tickets for inter-island departures at the Bertais/Mandalika/Sweta terminal. Perama can advise on fares and timings and can also book tickets for you.
**Destinations:** Bima (Sumbawa; 12hr); Denpasar (Bali; 6–8hr); Dompu (Sumbawa; 10hr); Jakarta (Java; 2 days); Labuanbajo (Flores; 24hr); Medan (4 days); Padang (Sumatra; 4 days); Ruteng (Flores; 36hr); Sape (Sumbawa; 14hr); Sumbawa Besar (Sumbawa; 6hr); Surabaya (Java; 20hr); Yogyakarta (Java; 22hr).
**By air** See above for airline contact details on Lombok. The departure tax is Rp30,000 (domestic), Rp100,000 (international).
**Destinations:** Denpasar (Bali; 12 daily; 30min); Jakarta (Java; daily; 3hr); Singapore (6 weekly; 2hr 30min); Surabaya (Java; 4 daily; 50min); Yogyakarta (Java; 1 daily; 1hr 15min).

## LEMBAR

Boats to and from Bali and Pelni ferries dock at **LEMBAR**, 22km south of Mataram. **Bemos** run between Sweta's Bertais/Mandalika/Sweta terminal and

Lembar. There's little accommodation here and no advantage in staying.

### Accommodation and eating

**Tidar** ⓣ0370/681444. Useful if you get stranded here, they are well used to travellers arriving at all hours. There are eight functional rooms and a restaurant with a small Indonesian menu (mains Rp5,000–15,000). It's a bold orange and black so easily spotted on the road from the port to the main road. ❷–❸

### Moving on

**By ferry (Pelni)**: All are fortnightly services unless otherwise stated: Baubau (Sulawesi; 61hr); Benoa (Bali; 4hr); Bima (Flores; 15hr); Bitung (Sulawesi; 4 days, 20hr); Kendari (Sulawesi; 73hr); Ende (Flores; 32hr); Kalabahi (Alor; 57hr); Kolonedale (Sulawesi; 92hr); Kupang (Timor; 44hr); Labuanbajo (Flores; 24hr); Lewoleba (Lembata; 64hr); Luwuk (Sulawesi; 4 days, 1hr); Makassar (Sulawesi; twice fortnightly; 37hr or 95hr); Maumere (Flores; 72hr); Nunukan (Kalimantan; 6 days, 20hr); Parepare (Sulawesi; 4 days, 18hr); Raha (Sulawesi; 66hr); Tarakan (Kalimantan; 6 days, 12hr); Waingapu (Sumba; 24hr).
**By ferry (other)** to: Padang Bai (Bali; every 90min; 4hr–4hr 30min).
**By bus/bemo** Bemo fares should be about Rp15,000 to the Ampenan-Mataram-Cakranegara-Sweta area, but you'll do well to bargain the drivers down to anything respectable.
**Taxi** Metered taxis are available at the port or just outside the gates all day and all night. Typical fares are Rp50,000–60,000 to Cakranegara.

## SENGGIGI

Covering a lengthy stretch of coastline, **SENGGIGI**, with sweeping bays separated by towering headlands, is an attractive and laid-back beach resort, offering a wide range of accommodation and restaurants, and low-key nightlife. The southern end of Senggigi is just 5km north of Ampenan, and there are a few places spread out along the next 4km until the main concentration of hotels that stretches for roughly 1km from the *Graha Senggigi* hotel to the *Sheraton Senggigi Beach Resort*. Low-density development continues for another 8km to the most northerly development, *Bulan Baru* at Lendang Luar. Proximity to the airport makes it an ideal first- or last-night destination but it is also a good base from which to explore the island. There are, however, plenty of hawkers in the central areas – keeping your cool and getting to know them is the best approach.

Plenty of operators cater for people who want to **dive** in the Gili Islands but stay in the comfort of Senggigi. Operators also take **snorkellers** on trips; mostly you go along with the divers and have to be fairly self-reliant in the water. Expect to pay US$15 including equipment and lunch. However Blue Marlin run guided snorkelling tours ($20 for one, $30 for two), a big advantage for the less confident.

### Arrival and local transport

**By bemo** Bemos from Ampenan run throughout the day (every 15–20min) along the main road as far as Lendang Luar.
**By shuttle bus** Perama shuttle buses drop passengers at their office in central Senggigi.
**By boat** The speedboats from Bali to the Gili islands also drop passengers, at Teluk Nara, north of Senggigi.
The direct Perama boat from Padang Bai arrives in central Senggigi.
**By air** From the airport, fixed-price taxis charge Rp50,000 to central Senggigi, Rp90,000 to north Senggigi.
**By taxi** Metered taxis are available at all hours. A ride from central Senggigi to Lendang Luar costs about Rp16,000 and to Mangsit Rp10,000–12,000.

### Dive operators

Qualified divers will pay $35 for the first dive and $30 for subsequent dives, and a PADI Open Water course is about $350. Most operators also have offices in the Gili islands.
**Blue Marlin** ⓣ0370/692003, ⓦwww.diveindo.com. At *Senggigi Beach Hotel* (ⓣ0370/693210), *Alang-Alang* (ⓣ0370/693911) and *Holiday Resort Lombok* (ⓣ0370/693719).
**Dive Indonesia** ⓣ0370/693367. Office in the Galleria in Senggigi.
**Dive Zone** ⓣ0370/660 3205, ⓦwww.divezone-lombok.com. There's a booking counter

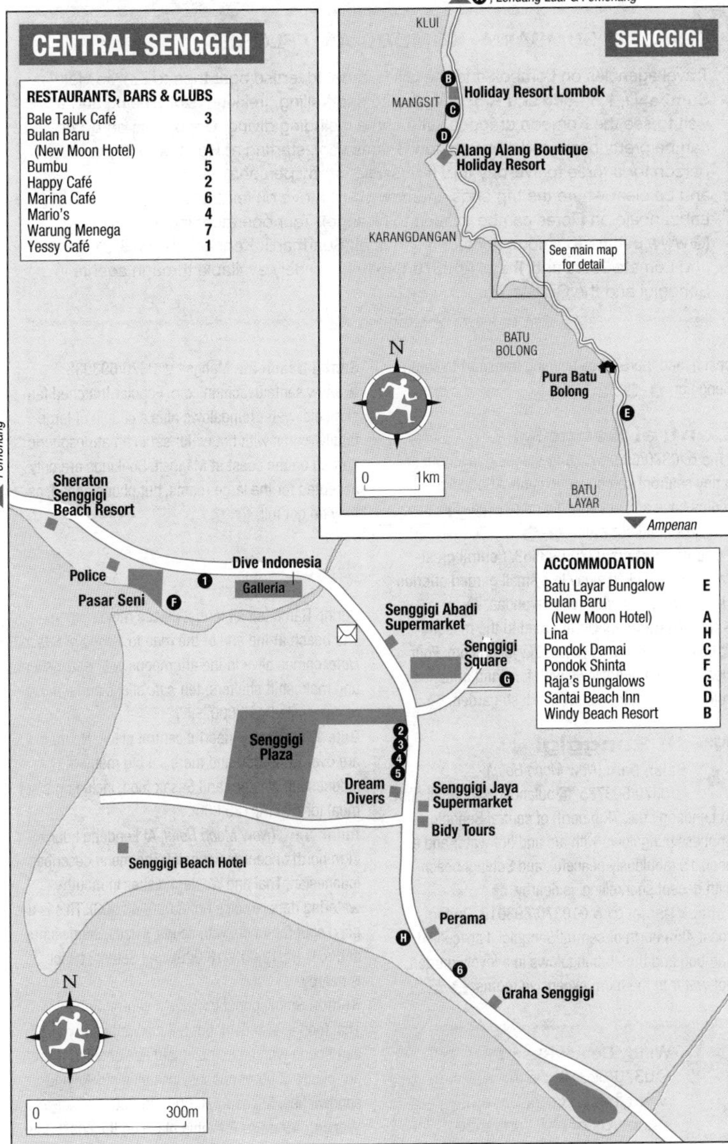


in Bidy Tours next to Senggigi Jaya Supermaket. Diving in the Kuta area and other parts of south Lombok.

**Dream Divers** ⓣ0370/693738, ⓦwww .dreamdivers.com. Also at the *Sheraton Senggigi Beach Resort* and *The Santosa* hotel in central Senggigi.

## Accommodation

### South Senggigi

**Batu Layar Bungalow** ⓣ0370/692235. Clean bungalows in an attractive garden, with fans and most have hot water. It's a short walk to the

### TRIPS TO SUMBAWA, KOMODO AND FLORES

Travel agencies on Lombok and the Gili Islands advertise boat trips to **Flores** via **Sumbawa**, **Komodo** and **Rinca**, including snorkelling, trekking, sightseeing and a visit to see the Komodo dragons, with some including diving. Conditions on board can be pretty basic and comforts few. Prices vary, starting at Rp1,000,000 per person for a three to five-day trip. If possible, go by personal recommendation, and be clear where the trip ends and how you'll move on (air transport out of Labuanbajo on Flores can be difficult to arrange). Tour operators include: Perama (Ⓦwww.peramatour.com; contact any office); Suarmanik Kencana (Ⓣ0376/21738); and Lomata Tours and Travel (Ⓣ0370/646494) – widely available through agents in Senggigi and the Gili islands.

beach, and there's free evening transport to central Senggigi. ❷–❸

## Central Senggigi

**Lina** Ⓣ0370/693237. Long-standing favourite in a tiny seafront compound in central Senggigi. All rooms have a/c, but only the more expensive have sea views and hot water. ❸–❹

**Pondok Shinta** Ⓣ0370/693563. Central great-value place tucked away in a small garden offering clean, fan rooms with good verandas. ❷

**Raja's Bungalows** Off the road to the mosque Ⓣ0812/373 4171, ⒺRajas22@yahoo.com. Four clean, budget bungalows with fans and attached cold-water bathrooms set in a lush garden. ❸

## North Senggigi

**Bulan Baru** (*New Moon Hotel*) Ⓣ0370/693785, Ⓔbulanbaru@hotmail.com. At Lendang Luar, 7km north of central Senggigi. Spotless bungalows with a/c and hot water and a pool. It's fabulously peaceful, and Setangi beach, with decent snorkelling, is nearby. ❹

**Pondok Damai** Ⓣ & Ⓕ0370/693019. On the coast 4km north of central Senggigi. Fan-cooled bamboo and thatch bungalows in a lovely garden; hot water in the more expensive rooms. ❹

**TREAT YOURSELF**

**Windy Beach Resort** Ⓣ0370/693191, Ⓦwww.windybeach.com. Several standards of well-furnished bungalows in a great garden with a stunning beachside pool (Rp20,000 for non-residents), 5km north of central Senggigi. All rooms have hot water and a/c is available. There are a couple of good spots for snorkelling nearby (you can rent equipment). ❻

**Santai Beach Inn** Mangsit Ⓣ0370/693038, Ⓦwww.santaibeachinn.com. Popular thatched fan and cold-water bungalows plus a couple of large family rooms with hot water set in an atmospheric garden on the coast at Mangsit. Bookings are only accepted for the large rooms, but phone ahead, as they do get full. ❸–❺

## Eating

During Ramadan all tourist places remain open. The beach at the end of the road to *Senggigi Beach Hotel* comes alive in the afternoons with *sate* sellers and makeshift shelters; ten *sate* sticks and a parcel of rice costs Rp15,000.

**Bale Tajuk Café** Cheerful central place. No mains are over Rp40,000 and there's a big menu of Indonesian, Western and Sasak food, including a set meal for two (Rp125,000).

**Bulan Baru** (*New Moon Hotel*) At Lendang Luar, 7km north of central Senggigi. The menu describes Indonesian, Thai and Western dishes in mouth-watering detail (mains Rp28,000–48,000). This is a good spot for lunch, with soups, salads, sandwiches and rolls (Rp12,000–16,000), and Setangi beach is nearby.

**Bumbu** Small, popular place in central Senggigi. Thai food is excellent, but tell the waiters if you can't cope with industrial quantities of chilli. There are plenty of other options, including steaks and sandwiches. Mains Rp20,000–40,000.

**Warung Menega** A simple place on the coast 3km south of Senggigi, easily spotted by the sign on the main road, with delectable seafood sold by weight or in good-value set meals (Rp70,000–140,000 including drinks).

**Yessy Café** central Senggigi, on the road between the Galleria and Pasar Seni Ⓣ0370/693148. Cheap drinks (Aussie wine Rp28,000 per glass, large Bintang Rp16,000) and a big menu of good value food (mains Rp27,000–34,000) make this a popular, lively spot.

## Drinking and nightlife

Senggigi is the only place on mainland Lombok with any sort of nightlife, but it is extremely sedate in keeping with the sensibilities of the local Muslim population. All these places are on the main road in central Senggigi.

**Happy Café** Cnr of entrance to Senggigi Plaza. Excellent live music in a friendly atmosphere, with a large bar, a vast drinks menu and an extensive menu of well-priced Indonesian, Chinese and Western food (mains Rp15,000–75,000).

**Marina Café** South of Perama office. Live music, sometimes featuring big bands from Jakarta, attracts a mix of local people, expats and tourists.

**Mario's** Near *Bale Tajuk Café, Bumbu* and *Happy Café*. Dark wood bar serving plenty of drinks plus a hefty menu of Indonesian and Western food with a German slant (mains Rp30,000–60,000). There are draft beers and excellent teas and coffees.

## Directory

**Banks and exchange** International ATM near Senggigi Abadi supermarket. Moneychangers (daily 10am–10pm) on the main street.

**Car and motorbike rental** Plenty of places rent vehicles with and without drivers. Check the insurance at the time of renting. Prices are: Suzuki Jimneys (Rp150,000/day), Kijangs (Rp250,000), motorbikes (Rp35,000–75,000 without insurance) and bicycles (Rp25,000–30,000). Chartering a vehicle with driver costs Rp250,000–300,000 per day with the customer paying for the fuel. It's best to go by personal recommendation. Highly recommended local drivers include Hasan Nur (ⓣ081/854 8227, ⓔhsn_y@yahoo.com), Made (ⓣ0370/667 9679 or 0812/372 5415) and Mudzakir (ⓣ0370/640170 or 0813/3977 5211).

**Doctor** *Senggigi Beach Hotel* ⓣ0370/693210 (24hr). See p.333 for hospitals in Ampenan-Mataram-Cakranegara-Sweta.

**Internet and telephones** Several internet cafés along the main street (daily 8am–10pm; Rp300/min), also offer telephone services. Planet Senggigi is reliable and can work with USB devices.

**Left luggage** Perama (Rp10,000/item/week), or most accommodation will store stuff if you're coming back to them.

**Police** Tourist Police ⓣ0370/632733, on the main road.

**Post office** In the centre of Senggigi (Mon–Thurs 7.30am–5pm, Fri & Sat 7.30am–4pm). Poste restante is available here.

**Shopping** The main road in Senggigi has several good quality craft shops selling a big range of items from across the island. The art market, Pasar Seni, at the north end of the main road in central Senggigi is full of small craft stalls.

**Supermarkets** In the centre, Senggigi Abadi and Senggigi Jaya (daily 8.30am–9.30pm), which sell necessities, postcards and souvenirs.

## Moving on

**By boat** Perama has an office in central Senggigi (6am–10pm; ⓣ0370/693007, ⓦwww.peramatour.com) which operates a daily boat to Gili Trawangan at 9am (1hr 30min; Rp70,000) and it then goes directly to Padang Bai (Rp200,000).

**By shuttle bus** Perama (ⓣ0370/693007, ⓦwww.peramatour.com, 6am–10pm) are the longest-standing of the companies offering tourist shuttles to Bali and Lombok; you can either use the public ferry or their direct boat to get to Bali.

**Destinations:** Bangsal (daily; 2hr; min 2 people); Candi Dasa (Bali; daily; 5hr 30min-6hr); Kuta, Bali/Ngurah Rai Airport (Bali; daily; 8hr 30min); Kuta, Lombok (2 daily; 2hr; min 2 people); Padang Bai (Bali; daily; 4hr 30min–5hr); Sanur (Bali; daily; 8hr); Tetebatu (2 daily; 2hr; min 2 people); Ubud (Bali; daily; 8hr).

**By air** It's a short taxi ride to Selaparang airport from Senggigi (about Rp30,000)..

# THE GILI ISLANDS

Strikingly beautiful, with glorious white-sand beaches lapped by warm, brilliant-blue waters, the three **Gili Islands** just off the northwest coast of Lombok are a magnet for visitors. Of the three, **Gili Trawangan** best fits the image of "party island", with heaps of accommodation, restaurants and nightlife. The smallest of the islands, **Gili Meno**, has absolutely no nightlife and a more limited choice of accommodation and, closest to the mainland, **Gili Air** offers a mix of the two, with plenty of facilities in the south, and more peace elsewhere.

Accommodation prices vary dramatically depending on the season: a bungalow costing Rp150,000 in February or October will cost Rp400,000 or even more from June to September and in December. Reservations are essential in

## TRAVEL TO AND FROM THE GILI ISLANDS

Whichever boat you use to get to the Gili Islands, you'll get wet feet; the boats anchor in the shallows and passengers wade to and fro.

### From Bangsal

The access port for the Gili Islands is **Bangsal**, 25km north of Senggigi, a cidomo (horse-drawn cart) ride or a shadeless 1.5-kilometre walk from **Pemenang**, 26km beyond the Ampenan-Mataram-Cakranegara-Sweta area and served by buses from Bertais/Mandalika/Sweta terminal. There is no bemo service along the coastal road north from Senggigi to Pemenang.

The ticket office (8am–4.30pm) is right on the seafront; there's a printed price list covering public boats, shuttles and charters. Buy your ticket only from there; ignore anybody who tries to persuade you otherwise. Everything on sale in Bangsal is also on sale on the Gili Islands, including water, mosquito coils and return boat tickets. Ideally, get your own bag on and off the boats, or negotiate with the porters beforehand – be clear whether you're talking about rupiah or dollars, for one bag or for the whole lot.

In Bangsal the *Taman Sari* (☎0370/646934; ❷), about 1 km from the coast on the road to Pemenang, has functional rooms.

**Public boats** Between Bangsal and Gili Air (Rp7000), Gili Meno (Rp7500) and Gili Trawangan (Rp8000), leaving when full (7.30am–4.30pm; 20–45min).

**Shuttle boats** 8.15am from Gili Trawangan and Gili Air and 4.30pm from Bangsal (Rp21,000 to Gili Air, Rp22,000 to Gili Meno, Rp23,000 to Gili Trawangan). You can also charter a boat for up to ten people, one way or return, or for trips to more than one island. Prices, from Rp135,000 for a one-way charter, are fixed and displayed in the ticket offices at Bangsal and on the islands.

Prices escalate after dark (Rp40,000 between Bangsal and Gili Trawangan and Rp25,000–30,000 between the islands), so most people charter then.

the high season or face a long, possibly fruitless, search for a bed.

None of the islands has a particular **crime** problem, although take reasonable precautions against theft. Women should take care during and after the Gili Trawangan parties – don't leave these alone. You'll be offered any and all drugs on the island. There are no police; it's the role of the kepala desa, the headman who looks after Gili Air and Gili Meno, and the kepala kampung on Gili Trawangan, to deal with any problems, so report any incidents to them initially. If you need to make a police report, go to the police on the mainland (at Tanjung or Ampenan).

For reliable Gili island information on Bali visit Island Promotions, Shop 12, Poppies Lane 1, Kuta (9am–10pm; ☎0361/753241, ⓦwww.gili-paradise.com). They can also book transport and accommodation and have a hotel booking site ⓦwww.gili-hotels.com.

### Gili Trawangan

Furthest from the mainland, the largest of the islands, **GILI TRAWANGAN** attracts the greatest number of visitors and is very developed. The southeast of the island is wall-to-wall bungalows, restaurants and dive shops, although it is still low-key and relaxing outside the high season. For quieter surroundings, head further north.

Island transport is by cidomo, or you can rent bicycles (Rp10,000–25,000 per hour). A **walk around the island**, less than 3km long by 2km at its widest part, takes four hours or less. Inland, the hundred-metre **hill** is the compulsory expedition at sunset – follow any of the tracks from the southern end of the island – for views of the Bali volcanoes with

### Senggigi and elsewhere on Lombok and Bali

Combination tickets for tourist shuttle buses and public ferries between the Gili Islands and all main tourist destinations on Bali and Lombok are widely advertised. Perama customers can use the Perama boat between Padang Bai and Senggigi/Gili islands or public ferries and buses. Other companies use public ferries.

There is no direct public or tourist shuttle boat for the return trip from the islands to Senggigi – you go to Bangsal and proceed overland (walk from the port at Bangsal to the gate on the main road, where you'll be collected by the shuttle bus operator).

**From Senggigi** Daily Perama boat at 9am (Rp70,000; 2hr). Charters are also available – approach the boat captains on the beach. It's a great trip but the boats are small and weather conditions sometimes make it impossible.

**From Serangan Harbour** to Gili Trawangan: Daily Mahi Mahi boat (Rp550,000; 2hr 30min); book through Island Promotions (ⓣ0818/0530 5632).

**From Benoa (Denpasar harbour, Bali)** to Gili Trawangan, Gili Meno, Gili Air. Daily Blue Water Express boat runs June to October (Rp690,000; 2hr; ⓣ0813/3841 8988, ⓦwww.bwsbali.com). Low season discounts apply.

**From Padang Bai (Bali)** to Gili Trawangan. Daily Gili Cat (Rp660,000; 2hr 30min; ⓣ0361/271680, ⓦwww.gilicat.com).

**From Amed (Bali)** Increasing numbers of skippers arrange charters to the islands. The boats are often small with single engines, don't carry radios, and mobile phones may well be out of range in the middle of the Lombok Strait. For the return trip talk to Dean on Gili Meno (see p.341) and Ozzy Shop (see p.343) on Gili Air who have twin-engined boats.

### Island hopping

The "**hopping island**" boat service is handy for day trips to other islands. It does one circuit – Air–Meno–Trawangan–Meno–Air – in the morning, and one in the afternoon. It's conveniently timetabled and fast. Prices and times are posted in ticket offices on the islands.



the sky blazing behind. The northern end of the east coast is popular for snorkelling: most people hang out here during the day, and there are plenty of restaurants nearby.

## Accommodation

### The east coast

**Beach Wind** ⓣ0812/376 4347, ⓔcae_beachwind@hotmail.com. Good-value bungalows with a hot water option. Prices include breakfast, which, party-goers may appreciate, is available until noon. ❻–❼

**Big Bubble** ⓣ0370/625020, ⓦwww.bigbubblediving.com. Well-decorated and maintained bungalows in the garden behind the dive shop. All have only cold water and a/c is an option; two price-brackets. ❹–❼

**Ozzy Homestay** ⓣ0812/371 8039. Good-quality rooms with verandas set in a quiet garden close to the main snorkelling area. All have cold water but there is a choice of fan or a/c. ❹–❻

**Sirwa** ⓣ0819/1724 6125. A row of small, basic bungalows, some with a/c, across the track from the main sunbathing beach. If they are full, consider *Sagita* (ⓣ0812/373 1832) to the north or *Emalia* (ⓣ0819/1713 4470) to the south. ❸–❹

### The village

**Edy Homestay** ⓣ0812/373 4469. Neat, clean rooms in a friendly compound, with a/c and hot water available. Breakfast is served at any time. Look at *Maulana* across the road if they are full. ❺–❼

**Marta's** ⓣ0812/372 2777, ⓔmartas_trawangan@yahoo.com. Great-quality two-storey accommodation, all with a/c and hot water, and lovely verandas with day beds looking onto a pretty garden with a pool. ❼

**Pondok Lita** ⓣ0370/648607. An excellent choice with rooms set around a small garden. They have fans and cold-water bathrooms, and there's one with a/c. ❸–❻

**Pondok Sederhana** ⓣ0813/3953 6047. A row of neat, fan, cold-water bungalows in a pretty fenced garden. ❺–❻

### The north coast

**Coral Beach 2** ⓣ0370/639946. Simple bungalows just behind the beach in the northeast. A/c and hot water are available. ❺–❼

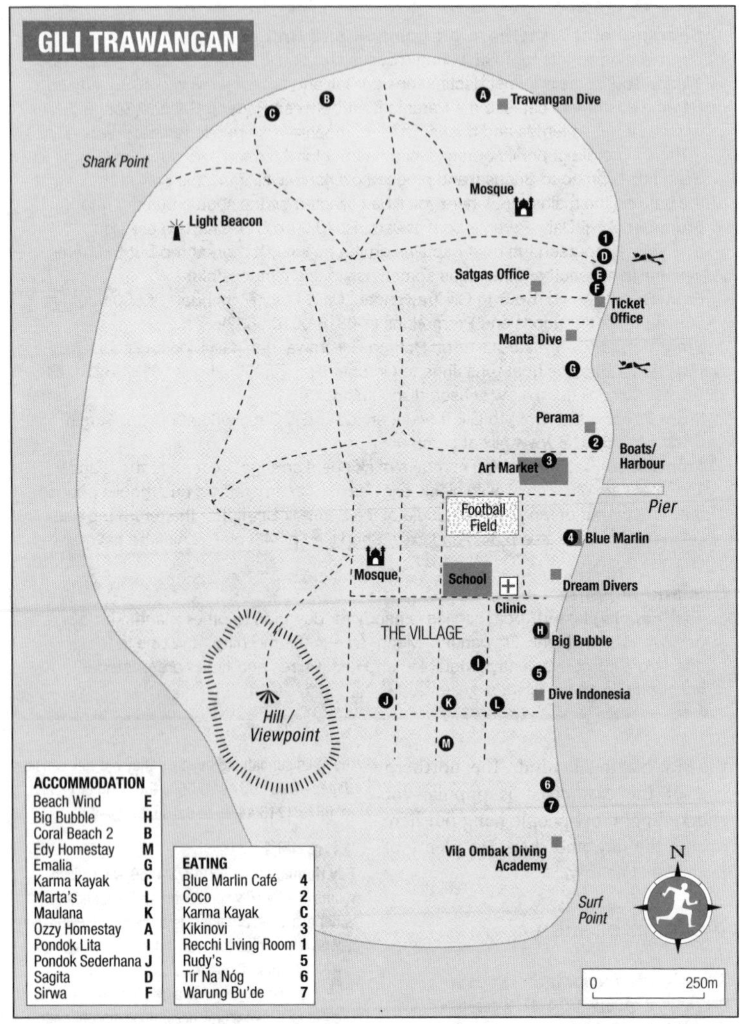


**Karma Kayak** ⓣ0818/0364 0538, ⓦwww.karmakayak.com. Excellent bungalows with a/c which are well built, thoughtfully designed and in a fabulous location in the far north of the island. A cidomo from the central area costs Rp15,000–20,000 and staff can contact drivers when necessary. 6–7

## Eating

**Blue Marlin Café** At the dive shop in the central area to the south of the pier, with tables near the pool or the beach. The menu is large and food well cooked – their barbecued seafood has a lot of fans. Mains around Rp45,000, baguettes and salads Rp30,000–35,000.

**Coco** East coast, near the Perama office. Illy coffee (Rp15,000–18,000), cakes including mango cheesecake and brownies (Rp6000–15,000), salads (Rp28,000–30,000) and baguettes (Rp25,000–38,000). There's even a loyalty card for addicts.

**Karma Kayak** A delightful spot in the far north of the island with excellent and imaginative tapas (Rp11,000–26,000). From May to mid-Sept, this is the prime sunset viewing spot.

**Kikinovi** East coast near the pier. A sparkly, grey-haired lady cooks up local food every lunchtime and sells it in the art market You point to what you want, and pay afterwards – Rp10,000–15,000 depending on her mood.
**Recchi Living Room** East coast. The surroundings are simple but the food is excellent and great value (mains Rp25,000–50,000) and includes Western (pizza, pasta, moussaka, steaks) and local options.
**Warung Bu'de** Bottom of the east coast. A favourite among expat divers on the island – good cheap eats at Rp5000 per plate in a tiny place just north of *Vila Ombak hotel.*

## Nightlife

Gili Trawangan is renowned for its many high season parties and full moon parties in the low season. All get going at about 11pm. Flyers around the island advertise venues.
**Blue Marlin Café** East coast. Monday party venue.
**Rudy's** East coast. Open late every day, with parties on Fridays.
**Tír Na Nóg** East coast. Popular Irish bar with beer, darts, movies and sports TV plus an ambitious menu which is great for comfort food such as bangers and mash (Rp35,000). The drinks list includes bottled Guinness and Irish whiskey. Outdoor *bale* (sitting platform with roof) all have individual TV screens and guests select their own DVDs from a vast choice. Wed party venue but open late the rest of the week as well.

## Directory

**Banks and exchange** No ATMs. Moneychangers line the main strip but rates are better on the mainland. Dive companies offer advances on Visa and MasterCard – useful in an emergency but you will pay ten percent for this.
**Bus tickets** Perama (daily 7am–10pm) is near the jetty and many other companies also advertise.
**Internet** Several places offer internet (Rp400/min; minimum 5min) but connection can be slow and unreliable.
**Medical aid** The *pak mantra* (nurse) at the clinic in the village is experienced with first aid and traveller's ailments – enquire through your accommodation first as the nurse is occasionally off the island. Theres' also Clinic Vila Ombak, just south of the hotel of the same name (daily 8am–5pm).
**Post** There's a postal agent in the *Pasar Seni.*
**Shopping** Several shops sell and exchange second-hand books and there's a small art market (*pasar seni*) for clothes and crafts.
**Telephones** Wartel (7am–midnight).

## Gili Meno

A similar oval shape to Gili Trawangan, **GILI MENO** is much smaller, about 2km long and just over 1km wide. This is the most tranquil island of the three, with a small local population and no nightlife. It takes a couple of hours to stroll around the island.

The **snorkelling** is good along the east coast; start at Royal Reef and drift down to Kontiki in the south. Take care – there may well be boats coming in and out to the harbour along here. The other option is to start at the yellow light beacon in the north of the island, swim left and the current will take you round to the west coast over the Meno Wall and you can get out at the old Bounty jetty part of the way down the west coast. Keep your fins on until you're in very shallow water, as there can often be quite an undertow; see p.342 for a warning about **offshore currents**. You can venture further afield by boat: ask on the beach (about Rp200,000 per person for a minimum of two people off Gili Meno, Rp350,000 for all three islands). Equipment is available on the island but a lot has seen (far) better days (Rp20,000 per day). See box on p.342 for **dive** operators on the island. For **boat trips** search out Dean (Ⓣ0813/3950 9859), one of the boat captains; he's often in front of the Blue Marlin dive shop. He'll take you on fishing trips, to see dolphins (best in March–Aug & Nov) and to see spring water in the sea off the north coast of Lombok (Rp200,000–Rp400,000 per person). You can charter him to Amed but see the warning on p.339.

### Accommodation

**Amber House** Ⓣ0813/3757 9728, Ⓔamber_house02pm@hotmail.com. Thatch and bamboo bungalows set slightly back from the beach towards the north of the island. A quiet choice, cheaper with salt-water showers and more expensive with fresh-water showers. ❷–❹

## SNORKELLING AND DIVING ON THE GILI ISLANDS

The **snorkelling and diving** around the Gili Islands is some of the best and most accessible in Lombok and, despite a lot of visitors, the reefs remain in reasonable condition. All the islands are fringed by coral reefs and visibility is generally around 15m. The fish life includes white-tip and black-tip reef sharks, sea turtles, manta rays, Napoleon wrasse and bumphead parrotfish.

There are good snorkelling spots just off all the islands' beaches. Snorkel gear is widely available for Rp25,000 per day, but the condition does vary. You can buy good-quality gear in the dive shops. Dive companies take snorkellers further afield for about US$10. The **offshore currents** around the island are strong and can be hazardous. Dive operators are aware of this, but if you're snorkelling or swimming off the beach it's easy to get carried out further than you intend and then be unable to get back to land. There has been at least one drowning in recent years.

The best **dive sites** involve short boat trips. There are plenty of **dive operators** on the islands, and there's a price agreement, so they all charge the same; however, they vary significantly in approach. Prices are: $35 for a single dive for a qualified diver ($30 for second dives and discounts for five or more), $60 for Discover Scuba, $350 for a PADI Open Water, $275 for a PADI Advanced Open Water course and $650 for Divemaster. Some operators are qualified to take people on the Instructor Development Course.

All divers pay a one-off **reef tax** of Rp30,000 (snorkellers pay Rp10,000) to the Gili Eco Trust, which works to protect the reefs around the islands.

The nearest hospital is in Mataram, where there is also a **recompression chamber** at Jl Adi Sucipto 13B (24-hr hotline ⓣ0370/660 0333).

### Dive operators

**Big Bubble** Gili Trawangan ⓣ0370/625020, ⓦwww.bigbubblediving.com. Friendly place owned by two British women. Groups are small so dives are planned to suit guests and take advantage of quiet sites. Join them for volleyball at the end of every afternoon on the court in front of the dive shop.

**Blue Marlin** Gili Trawangan ⓣ0370/632424, Gili Meno ⓣ0370/639980, Gili Air ⓣ0370/634387, ⓦwww.diveindo.com. British-owned, with an expertise in technical diving and offering courses up to PADI IDC (Instructor Development Courses) and IANTD (International Association of Nitrox and Technical Divers) Instructor Training Course level.

**Dive Indonesia** Gili Trawangan ⓣ0370/644174. Courses up to PADI IDC; all divers are loaned dive computers to use.

**Dream Divers** Gili Trawangan ⓣ0370/603 4496, Gili Air ⓣ0370/634547, ⓦwww.dreamdivers.com. Courses up to PADI IDC. Dive instruction offered in German and English.

**Manta Dive** Gili Trawangan ⓣ0370/643649, Gili Air ⓣ0813/5305 0462, ⓦwww.manta-dive.com. British owned company with highly respected local dive guides. Courses up to PADI Divemaster level are offered, and trips to the more distant Tunang Wall with some excellent coral – suitable for all levels.

**Trawangan Dive** North Gili Trawangan ⓣ0370/649220, ⓦwww.trawangandive.com. At the quieter part of the island, they pride themselves on taking good care of divers (fruit, water and towels on boats). They also offer technical diving and underwater photography courses.

**Vila Ombak Diving Academy** *Vila Ombak* hotel, Gili Trawangan ⓣ0370/638531, ⓦwww.hotelombak.com. Don't be deterred by its location one of the smarter hotels – prices are the same as elsewhere. All divers are provided with a computer attached to their regulator.

**Mallia's Child** ⓣ0370/622007, ⓦwww.gilimeno-mallias.com. Traditional beachside bungalows with fine sea views from the verandas. Just south of the harbour, all with fan and cold water. ❹–❻

**Royal Reef Resort** ⓣ & ⓕ0370/642340. Close to the harbour, these good-quality, well-furnished bungalows, set in a large garden, have fans and good verandas. ❺

**Sunset Gecko** ⓣ0813/5356 6774, ⓦwww.thesunsetgecko.com. Well-built, attractive wood and thatch accommodation in the quiet north just behind the beach and with some great views. ❷–❻

**Tao' Kombo'** ⓣ0812/372 2174, ⓔtao_kombo@yahoo.com. Set in a garden 200m behind the beach (take the turn inland just south of *Mallia's Child*) with a large bar. Four bungalows have fans and fresh-water showers. There are also two *brugak* (open-sided sleeping platforms) with mattress, screen, mosquito net and shared bathrooms. *Brugak* ❷; bungalows ❹

## Eating

**Balenta** In a brilliant location at the top of the island, specializing in Sasak food (Rp11,000–20,000).

**Bibi's** Attached to *Vila Nautilus* just south of the harbour, serving the best pizzas on the island (Rp35,000–45,000).

**Family** Offering the usual travellers' favourites near the harbour with great views across to Gili Air with the Lombok mountains rising behind.

**Jungle Bar** at *Tao' Kombo'*. One of the main late-night chill out spots, with cool music and plenty of drinks.

**Rust Bar** Close to the harbour – one of the late night drinking venues of choice.

## Directory

**Banks and exchange** No ATMs. Moneychangers at two kiosks, one south of *Mallia's Child* and one further north.

**Boat tickets** The office is under a tree in the harbour area of the east coast – by the red handpainted sign nailed to the tree.

**Bus tickets** The Perama agent is at the *Kontiki* hotel in the south of the island.

**Internet and telephone** The wartel (8am–10pm) is near the harbour and has internet access but connection can be slow and unreliable.

**Post** No postal service.

## Gili Air

Closest to the mainland, **GILI AIR** stretches about 1.5km in each direction and takes a couple of hours to walk round. It sits between lively, social Gili Trawangan and peaceful Gili Meno. Although **accommodation** is spread around most of the coast, it's concentrated on the southeast corner. It is quieter further north and it makes sense to engage a cidomo to reach the more far-flung spots when you arrive at the harbour in the south of the island.

The **beach** in the southeast corner is popular, with good **snorkelling**. Snorkelling gear is widely available for rent; try Ozzy's Shop on the east coast (Rp25,000 per day). For snorkelling further afield, **boat trips** are advertised pretty much everywhere (Rp70,000–75,000 per person including equipment; 9.30am–2.30pm) taking in sites off all three islands. See box opposite for **dive** operators on the island.

## Accommodation

**Abdi Fantastik** ⓣ0370/636421. In a fine location on the east coast; the wood and thatch bungalows have fans and mosquito nets, and there are sitting areas overlooking the water. ❹

**Coconut Cottages** ⓣ0370/635365, ⓦwww.coconuts-giliair.com. Attractive, clean bungalows in a garden haven set back from the east coast. All have hot water and a/c is available. Staff are lovely, and there's a great restaurant; *the* place for total relaxation. ❻

**Gili Air Santay** ⓣ0818/0375 8695, ⓦwww.giliair-santay.com. Popular, good-quality traditional cottages set 100m back from the east coast in a shady garden. *Brugak* on the beach for relaxing. ❸–❺

**Gita Gili** ⓣ0813/3955 3395. About ten minutes' walk up the east coast from the harbour, with thatch, wood and bamboo bungalows facing the sea. All have fans and attached cold-water bathrooms. ❹

**Gusung Indah** ⓣ0812/378 9054. At the top of the east coast, with two standards of bungalows facing seawards, some with squat toilets. There are good *brugak* and an excellent bar. *Sandy*, nearby, is similar although they also have two rather fine new A-frame places at the front. ❻

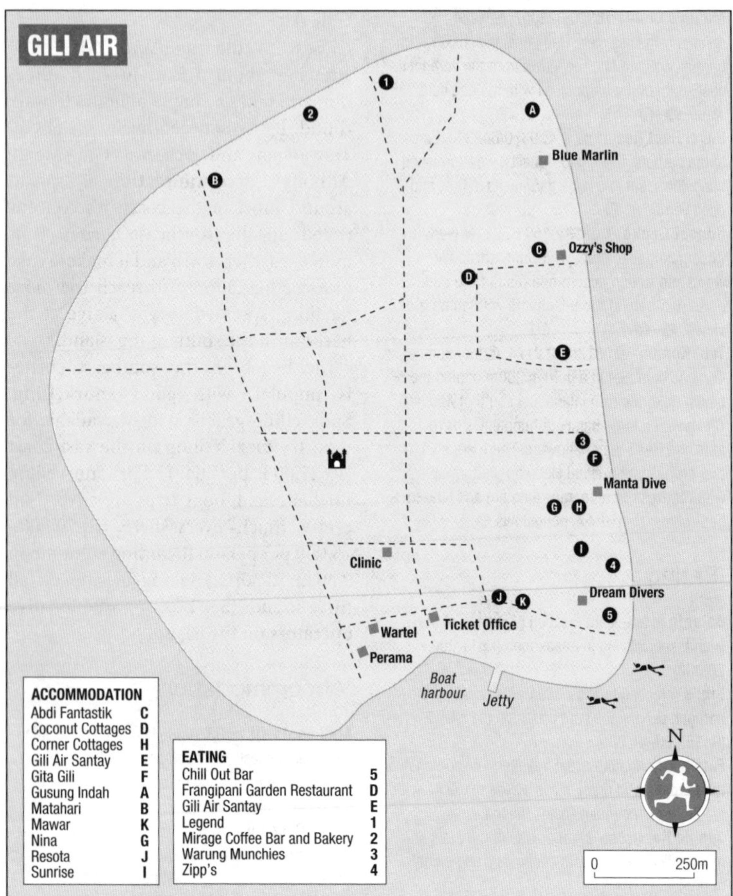


**Matahari** Good choice if you want total isolation on the far northwest coast. The older bungalows are showing their age but the new A-frame ones are clean and have great verandas. ❹–❻

**Mawar** ⓣ0813/6225 3995. Four clean bungalows a short walk inland from the harbour. All have fans and cold water, plus deep verandas with hammocks and decent furnishings. ❸

**Nina** ⓣ0819/1612 6343. Bamboo, thatch and wood cottages in a neat garden just on the edge of the southeast corner. All have fans and cold water and decent verandas. *Corner Cottages* offer similar cottages nearby. Access is through *Corner Cottages.* ❷

**Resota** ⓣ0859/3618 5928, ⓔmarini_resota@yahoo.co.uk. Traditionally built bungalows with deep verandas which are good for relaxing. Close to the harbour and near *Mawar.* ❸

**Sunrise** ⓣ & ⓕ0370/642370. On the southeast corner. Accommodation is in two-storey *lumbung* barns with sitting areas upstairs and down. The ones at the front have good sea views. All have fans and cold-water bathrooms. ❹–❺

## Eating

**Frangipani Garden Restaurant** *Coconut Cottages.* The most imaginative dining on the island with Western and local cuisine and seafood. A set menu (Rp100,000 for two) is a feast of Sasak food that needs to be ordered the day before.

**Gili Air Santay** The Thai food (Rp20,000–30,000) is highly recommended although it's only one section of a vast global menu.

**Mirage Coffee Bar and Bakery** A laid-back spot in the far north with home-made bread, sandwiches (Rp20,000–35,000), mezze including hummus (Rp45,000), brie on toast (Rp15,000) and full English breakfast (Rp35,000). This is an ideal sunset spot from June to Aug.
**Warung Munchies** On the east coast. Serving well-cooked food at good prices; all mains are under Rp30,000, and they do reasonable cake.

## Nightlife

**Chill Out Bar** In the southeast corner. A great spot to hang out during the day between forays into the water and to linger long into the night.
**Legend** Weekly parties on Wed in the high season at this bar towards the north. Dark Moon parties in Feb and Aug – enquire at your guesthouse.
**Zipp's** Next to the *Chill Out Bar*, the vibe is similar and it's a good place to hang out after dark.

## Directory

**Banks and exchange** No ATM but a few moneychangers near the habour and up the east coast – rates are poor.
**Bicycle rental** Ozzy Shop rents bicycles (Rp25,000 per day).
**Bus tickets** The Perama office (7am–1pm & 2–6pm; ⓣ0370/637816 or ⓣ0818/0527 2735) is next to *Villa Karang* hotel. Other companies also advertise shuttle tickets.
**Internet and telephone** There's a wartel (daily 8am–10pm) behind *Villa Karang* hotel and another at Ozzy Shop, where there is also internet access (Rp400 per min, minimum Rp4000) but connection is unreliable and often slow – it's known to be worse in cloudy weather for some unfathomable reason.
**Medical aid** There is a clinic inland from the harbour, with a nurse in attendance most days (7am–9am & 5–7pm) who is fine for first aid and has a limited supply of medicines. The closest hospital is in Mataram.
**Post** No post office.

# GUNUNG RINJANI AND AROUND

From a distance, **Gunung Rinjani** (3726m) appears to rise in solitary glory from the plains, but in fact the entire area is a throng of bare summits, wreathed in dense forest. The climb up Rinjani, taking in Danau Segara Anak, the magnificent crater-lake, measuring 8km by 6km, with the perfect cone of Gunung Baru rising from it, is the most energetic and rewarding trek on either Bali or Lombok. Climbs start from either Senaru **to the north of the mountain** or Sembalun Lawang to the northeast.

Trekking on Rinjani is not for the unfit. A guide is essential (see box, p.346) and you must register at the Rinjani Trek Centres at Senaru or Sembalun Lawang and pay the National Park admission fee (ⓦwww.rinjaninationalpark.com; Rp50,000). You'll need basic equipment; it's highly advisable to bring your own walking boots (not trainers), a head torch and food and drink (take loads of snacks and sweets even if food is provided). If you haven't got a seriously warm, windproof jacket with you, rent one. The Rinjani Trek Centres rent out radios but increasingly mobile telephones are being relied on as emergency back-up; make sure your party has one or the other.

### Gunung Rinjani

There are several possible **climbs** around Rinjani, and few trekkers reach the **summit**, most are satisfied with shorter, less arduous trips.

The **shortest trek** is **from Senaru** to the **crater rim**, from where there are classic views across Segara Anak to Gunung Baru, and back to Senaru (two days, one night). For a **longer trek**, a path continues from the crater rim (2hr) and descends into the crater to **the lake**, at 2050m. It is steep and scary at the top with metal handrails and some ropes but it gets better further down. You can bathe in the lakeside hot springs. From the lake, you can return the same way to Senaru (three days/two nights).

The shortest route to the **summit of Rinjani** is to climb **from Sembalun Lawang** on the northeast side of the mountain, starting on the track next to the Rinjani Trek Centre. It takes seven to eight hours to the overnight camp site called Plawangan II and you then attack the summit the next morning. It's an extraordinarily steep haul up to the summit (3–4hr up; 3hr back down to Plawangan II). You then descend to the lake to ease tired muscles in the hot springs and return to Sembalun Lawang (three days, two nights).

The most complete exploration of the mountain involves a one-way trip; ascending from Sembalun Lawang, taking in the summit, then the lake and descending to Senaru – this has the advantage of getting the most exhausting ascent over while you are fresh (four days/three nights).

### Batu Koq and Senaru

The small villages of **BATU KOQ** and **SENARU**, south of Bayan (about 86km from Mataram), are reached by bemo (Rp10,000) or ojek (Rp15,000–20,000) from Bayan, a few kilometres to the north. Buses from Mandalika/Bertais/Sweta and Labuhan Lombok terminate in Bayan.

Just south of Pondok Senaru, a small path heads east to the river and Sindang

## ORGANIZING THE TREK

If you want to climb Gunung Rinjani, an extremely useful first stop is one of the **Rinjani Trek Centres**: at the top of the village at the start of the path to Gunung Rinjani in Senaru, and in the centre of Sembalun Lawang (June–Sept daily 7am–5pm, at other times opening hours are more hit and miss). They provide information about climbing routes, can arrange all-inclusive trips and they register and collect the fee from everyone entering the National Park. If you want to put your trek together **independently**, it is possible to arrange a guide (Rp100,000 per day) and porters (Rp60,000) at the Trek Centres (all guides and porters should all be licensed) and rent equipment there, though you'll need to buy your own food and food for the porter and guide.

### Prices

Prices largely depend on your bargaining ability (though everyone quotes "published prices" you should still bargain). They should include guide, porters, equipment (including sleeping bags and tents) and meals. Return transport should be included in treks arranged in Senggigi. If time is limited it is possible to arrange the trek in Senggigi or on the internet but it is inevitably cheaper in Senaru or Sembalun Lawang. Typically **published prices** in Senaru or Sembalun are: from Rp1,500,000 for the two day/one night crater rim trip to Rp2,300,000 for the four day/three night summit and lake trek for one person; Rp900,000–1,400,000 per person for a party of two; and Rp823,000–1,175,00 per person for a party of three or more.

### Questions to ask

What exactly is included in the price?
How many porters and guides are included?
What is the menu?
Will the person you are talking to be going with you?
Will your group be part of a larger group or going independently?

### Trekking companies

The number of trekking **agencies** arranging all-inclusive treks is bewildering. In **Senggigi** check out John's Adventures (ⓦwww.lombok-rinjanitrek.com in Bidy Tours office), Rinjnai Trekking Club (ⓣ0370/693202, ⓦwww.info2lombok.com) and Planet Senggigi Internet (ⓣ0370/693921), all on the main street, and driver Made (ⓣ0370/6679679 or 0812/372 5415) who is also a registered trekking guide.

In **Senaru and Sembalun** check out the Rinjani Trek Centres and other local operators, including Lembah Rinjani in Sembalun (ⓣ0818/0365 2511).

Gile waterfall (Rp2000). The main fall is about 25m high. Tiu Kelep is another waterfall a further hour beyond the first. You should probably take a dip here; local belief is that you become a year younger every time you swim behind the falls.

It's worth visiting the traditional village at the end of the tarmacked road in Senaru, with houses of bamboo and thatch where the villagers still live a very simple life. A villager will show you around, and you'll be expected to make a donation and sign the visitors' book.

For gentle exercise through the immediate area, the Senaru Panorama Walk (3hr) or Rice Terraces and Waterfalls Walk (1hr 30min) are guided by local women; ask at the Rinjani Trek Centre.

## Accommodation and eating

All accommodation except *Rinjani Mountain Garden* is spread for several km along the road through Batu Koq and Senaru. Bemos go all the way so you can stop outside any of them. All will store your stuff while you climb and have small restaurants attached, serving simple Indonesian, Sasak and Western food.

**Bukit Senaru** Closest to the start of the path in Senaru. Well-spaced bungalows in a pleasant garden. They're bigger than many in the area, and have Western toilets. ❸

**Emy Guesthouse** At the Batu Koq end of the village ⓣ0817/575 0585. Four simple rooms with in a large house. All are adequate if not plush. ❷

**Gunung Baru** ⓣ0817/572 4863. Small set-up not far from the start of the trail in Senaru with a few simple, tiled bungalows. ❷

**Rinjani Mountain Garden** ⓣ0818/569730, ⓔrinjanigarden@hotmail.de. Luxury camping (all equipment provided) in a fabulous garden with great views, spotless showers (solar heated warm water) and a swimming pool. Less accessible than the other accommodation; head past the old mosque in Bayan and at the sharp left turn in the road go straight on along a small road for 4km to the village of Teres Genit. ❺

**Segara Anak** ⓣ0817/575 4551, ⓦrinjanitrekking.com. The first place on the road from Bayan, a couple of km from the start of the path. There are fine panoramas from the verandas of the more expensive bungalows. The same company owns *Rinjani Lodge* 50m further up the hill with equally fine views. ❷

## Sembalun Lawang and Sembalun Bumbung

Set in countryside that is unique in Lombok, the Sembalun area is a high, flat-bottomed mountain valley surrounded by hills. **SEMBALUN LAWANG** is accessed via a steep 16km road from Kokok Putih (by minibuses or ojek; Rp20,000) or an equally steep, 16km road north from Sapit on the other side of the mountains. Kokok Putih is accessible by bemo or minibus from Bayan or Labuhan Lombok.

The village of **SEMBALUN BUMBUNG** is 4km south of Sembalun Lawang with houses clustered around the mosque. Buses run through here between Sembalun Lawang and Aik Mel (Rp40,00); all buses between Labuhan Lombok and the Bertais/Mandalika/Sweta bus terminal pass through Aik Mel.

### Accommodation

**Lembah Rinjani** ⓣ0818/0365 2511. On the start of the track to Rinjani beside the Rinjani Trek Centre in Sembalun Lawang. Clean rooms with verandas facing Rinjani and they can provide hot water in a bucket for bathing. There's also a restaurant. ❹

**Paer Doe** ⓣ0852/3977 8818. Tiny homestay with four basic rooms in a pretty garden just opposite the football field in Sembalun Bumbung. ❷

**Pondok Sembalun** ⓣ0852/3956 1340. Next to *Lembah Rinjani* in Sembalun Lawang. Four simple, thatched rooms but no Rinjani views and a telephone mast in front. ❷

## TETEBATU

Set amid picturesque scenery on the southern slopes of Gunung Rinjani, 50km east of Sweta, the small village of **Tetebatu** is a cool, but not cold, quiet spot for a few days of relaxation. From here you can explore nearby waterfalls and craft village Pondok Tetebatu (see p.348), rent motorcycles (Rp50,000 per day self-drive or Rp80,000 with driver) or vehicle charters (Rp300,000–350,000 per day including driver and petrol). Guides for local treks can be arranged at all the accommodation – the most usual trek is through the local monkey forest to **Jukut Waterfall** (Rp75,000–100,000 per person; 4–6hr) or there are shorter two-hour treks closer to home (Rp50,000 per person).

On public transport, get off the bemo or bus at Pomotong on the main road and either take a bemo (Rp10,000) or an ojek (Rp15,000) to Tetebatu. Alternatively, from Mataram you can arrange a Perama charter (Ⓦwww.peramatour.com; Rp90,000 per person, minimum two people). Charter transport to other Lombok destinations is widely available (Rp300,000–400,000 depending on distance).

It isn't easy to change money locally and there's no public telephone or internet access.

## Accommodation and eating

Accommodation is on the main road north through the village and the road off to the east, Waterfall St. Most have restaurants attached – best views are from those at *Cendrawasih* and *Hakiki*. *Bale Bale Cafe* and *Salabuse* on the main road serve Indo-Chinese and Western dishes, plus some Sasak options (mains Rp12,000–30,000).

**Cendrawasih** Ⓣ0828/364 6158. Attractive traditional rice-barn style accommodation in a lush garden on Waterfall St. ❷

**Hakiki** Ⓣ0818/0373 7407. In the middle of paddy-fields at the eastern end of Waterfall St, two-storey traditional rice-barn style accommodation with excellent verandas. Some squat toilets and some Western toilets. ❷–❸

**Pondok Tetebatu** Ⓣ0819/1771 6445. On the main road, just north of the junction with Waterfall St. Small but clean tiled rooms in two rows facing across a small garden, with welcoming staff. ❷

## SAPIT

Situated at 1400m on the southern slopes of Gunung Pusuk, the small village of **SAPIT** is a quiet retreat with wonderful views down to the east coast. From Sapit the mountain road climbs 11.5km up along a forested ridge to the pass, surrounded by towering peaks and with great views back towards Sapit and ahead down to Sembalun Bumbung and on to Sembalun Lawang. It's 16km from Sembalun Lawang to Sapit (daily bus; 2–3hr) but the road is prone to landslides. There are ojek between Sapit and the Sembalun valley (Rp20,000–25,000). It's the same distance from the cross-island road, either via Aik Mel or Pringgabaya (Rp10,000 by bemo; more frequent from Aik Mel). There's accommodation at Hati Suci and nearby Balelangga (both Ⓣ0370/636545, Ⓦwww.hatisuci.tk; ❷–❸), which are run by the same family, and have simple bungalows in lovely gardens. Each has a small restaurant offering a basic menu (mains Rp17,000–20,000), and staff will direct you for **walks** to waterfalls and the monkey forest and, for the hardy, the fifteen-kilometre trek across to the Sembalun valley.

## LABUHAN LOMBOK

The port town of **LABUHAN LOMBOK** runs **ferries to Sumbawa** (every 40min; Rp12,5000) from the ferry terminal, Labuhan Kayangan, at the far end of the promontory, 3km around the south side of the bay (Rp3000 by local bemo or Rp5000 by ojek). **Buses** run regularly along the cross-island road between Labuhan Lombok and the Bertais/Mandalika/Sweta terminal at Sweta with some continuing on to the ferry terminal, and between Labuhan Lombok and Bayan; change at Kokok Puitih for the Sembalun valley. Travelling between Kuta and Labuhan Lombok involves changing at Praya and then Kopang, on the main road. A decent **place to stay** is *Hotel Melati Lima Tiga*, Jl Kayangan 14 (Ⓣ0376/23316; ❷), about 150m from the town centre on the road to the ferry terminal. There's a local Perama office on the coast side of the road to the harbour (Ⓣ0376/292 4534 and 0813/3991 1345).

## KUTA AND AROUND

The only tourist development on the south coast is KUTA, 54km from Mataram and 32km from Praya, a tiny fishing village situated behind a sweeping, white-sand beach. It's ideal for a few quiet days by the sea, especially if you like wild coastal scenery and turbulent surf. Apart from the Sunday and Wednesday markets, the area is extremely quiet.

Kuta days revolve around the beach or pool. You can hire surf boards at *Mimpi Manis* and Kimen Surf in the village (Rp20,000 per day) and arrange fishing trips from *Mimpi Manis* (3hr Rp250,000; full day Rp600,000) and they'll grill your catch for dinner. The only dive operator in the area, Dive Zone (ⓣ0370/660 3205, ⓦwww.divezone-lombok.com) at Novotel Lombok, knows of sites for all levels of experience.

The main road runs just inland from the beach and **accommodation** is spread for about 500m on the far side of the road, so don't expect cottages on the beach. There are also places in the village.

### Around Kuta

The glorious beaches of Seger and Tanjung Aan to the **east of Kuta** are, at a push, walkable, though bicycles are a good idea. Past Tanjung Aan, the small fishing village of **Gerupak**, just under 8km from Kuta, perches on the western shores of Gumbang Bay. From Gerupak, there are fine views across the bay to **Bumbang** on the eastern shore, and you can rent a canoe or motorboat to take you across. The thriving fishing village of **Awang**, 16km east of Kuta, is well worth the trip for the stunning views of **Awang Bay**, also known as Ekas Bay, a massive inlet, with great views across to Ekas on the southeast penninsula.

Along the coast **west of Kuta** you can explore half a dozen or more of the prettiest beaches on the island, but you'll need your own transport. The closest is **Are Goleng** a couple of kilometres out of Kuta, and heading west you come to **Mawun**, **Tampa**, **Mawi** and **Rowok** before reaching the small village of **Selong Blanak**, 15km from Kuta, from where you can cut inland to Keling and on to Praya (24km). Take a decent road map if you're exploring any further west from Selong Blanak and be aware that the road deteriorates badly the further west you go.

### Arrival

**By bemo** Coming from the west, buses run to Praya from Bertais/Mandalika/Sweta terminal in Sweta. From Praya, bemos either go as far Sengkol, where you can change, or right through to Kuta. From the east of Lombok, bemos run to Praya from Kopang on the main cross-island road. Bemos pass *Mimpi Manis* on their way into Kuta, then stop at the western end of the village – it's about ten minutes' walk to the accommodation.

**By shuttle bus** Perama offer tourist charters to Kuta (Rp90,000 per person, 2 people min) from Lembar or Mataram.

### Accommodation

All accommodation is spread a few hundred metres along the road that runs just behind the beach at the eastern end of the village or is in the village itself.

**Anda** ⓣ0370/654836. Clean, tiled budget rooms set in a shady garden on the road just behind the beach; a/c available. ❸

**G'day Inn** ⓣ0370/655342. Five well-kept rooms with attached cold-water bathrooms in a friendly family compound in the village; head east at the main village crossroads that are just inland from the market area. ❷

**Lamancha Homestay** ⓣ & ⓕ0370/655186. Family place in the village, a short walk from the beach, comprising three rooms with attached mandi and squat toilet. Located just beyond the *G'day Inn*. ❷

**Mimpi Manis** ⓣ081/836 9950, ⓦwww.mimpimanis.com. Just over 1.5km north of the beach on the way to Sade, this spotless place is run by a Balinese–English family. Choose between a/c or fan rooms or a two-storey house. There are DVD players, an extensive selection of films and safety boxes. ❷–❸

**Segare Anak** ⓣ0370/654846, ⓦwww.kutalombok.com. This long-standing favourite, on the road that runs behind the beach, has a big choice of rooms, some with a/c but all with cold water, set in a lovely garden with a dinky pool. Safe deposit boxes are available. ❷–❹

**Sekar Kuning** ☎0370/654856. Clean, cold-water, fan rooms in a small garden on the road that runs behind the beach. ❷

## Eating and nightlife

**Ashtari** At the top of the hill on the road west from Kuta – the views are spectacular, the food is excellent and the small vegetarian menu of sandwiches, salads and Indonesian dishes (mains around Rp18,000) is great value. Daliy 8.30am–6pm.

**Bong's Café** On the road between the beach and the village. The menu is vast (mains up to Rp35,000), taking in Mexican, German, Thai and Italian alongside the more usual choices; the food is fine and you've got to admire the ambition.

**Lombok Lounge** West of the main village crossroads that are just inland from the market area. Mains up to Rp35,000 on their menu of Indonesian and Western dishes featuring plenty of seafood.

**The Shore Bar** Far eastern end of the road that runs along the beach ☎0817/575 5653. Live music on Sat nights in the high season until about 2am. Free local transport.

## Directory

**Banks and exchange** *Anda* and *Surfer's Inn* change money. The closest ATM is in Praya.

**Bicycle rental** Rp25,000 per day from *Mimpi Manis*.

**Bus tickets** *Segare Anak* (☎0370/654846) are Perama agents.

**Internet** Available in Ketapang, corner of the road along the beach where it turns inland to the village, Anda and Segare Anak (Rp400–500/min).

**Motorcycle rental** Rp35,000–50,000 per day from *Mimpi Manis*.

**Post** *Segare Anak* is a postal agent and you can use them for poste restante; get mail addressed to you at *Segare Anak*, Kuta Beach, Lombok Tengah, Nusa Tenggara Barat 83573. The nearest post office is in Sengkol.

**Telephones** No public phone access.

## Moving on

**By bemo** From the western end of the village, bemos run to Praya.

**By charter transport** Ask at your accommodation. Most people use charters for one-way drops: Rp200,000 to Mataram/the airport, Rp250,000 to Senggigi, Rp300,000 to Bangsal.

**By shuttle bus** Perama offer tourist charters to Lembar or Mataram (Rp90,000 per person, 2 people min). Book at Segare Anak.

# Sumbawa

East of Lombok, the scorched, mountainous island of **Sumbawa** is often bypassed by travellers now the tourist boats sail between Lombok and Flores. However, it has some fine west-coast **beaches** and holds enough of interest for those curious about the history and ethnicity of **Nusa Tenggara**. Sumbawa is a strictly Muslim enclave and all travellers should dress conservatively.

Historically, the Sumbawan people in the western half of the island have always been influenced by the Balinese and the Sasaks of Lombok, while the Bimans in the east share linguistic and cultural similarities with the Makarese of Sulawesi and the peoples of Flores and Sumba.

**Ferries** to and **from Lombok** (90min) dock at Poto Tano, at the extreme western end of Sumbawa; buses meet all incoming ferries and run south from the harbour to **Sumbawa Besar** (2hr), and sometimes all the way to Bima (9hr), but it's easy to change at Sumbawa Besar if not. **Ferries** to and **from Flores** (6–9hr) and **Sumba** (6–9hr) use the port at Sape. **Pelni** ferries dock at Bima.

## SUMBAWA BESAR

**SUMBAWA BESAR**'s open streets are lined with crumbling white plaster buildings, bright blue and green wooden doors adorning its many shopfronts. It's the largest town on the island, and visitors wishing to break up the bus-run across the island could do worse

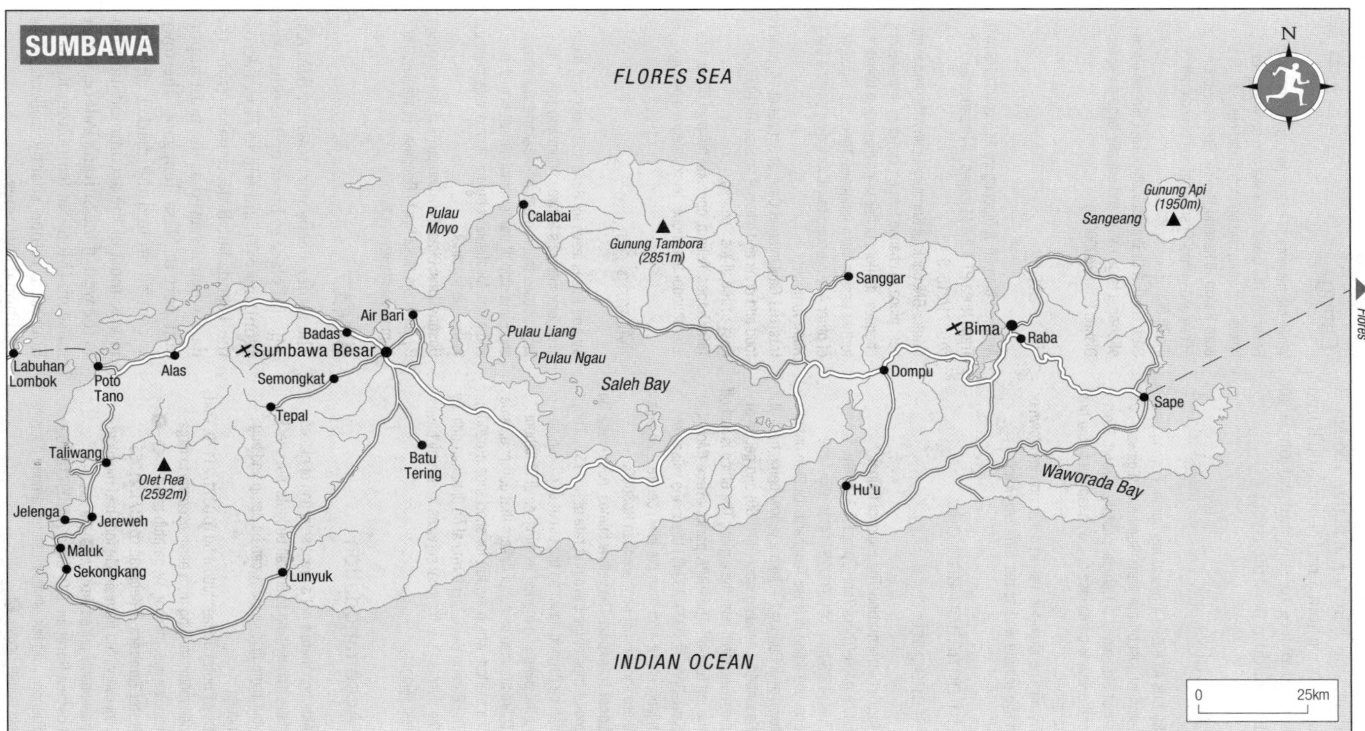
SUMBAWA
FLORES SEA
N
Pulau Moyo
Calabai
Gunung Tambora (2851m)
Gunung Api (1950m)
Sangeang
Sanggar
Flores
Air Bari
Badas
Sumbawa Besar
Labuhan Lombok
Poto Tano
Alas
Semongkat
Tepal
Pulau Liang
Pulau Ngau
Saleh Bay
Bima
Raba
Dompu
Sape
Batu Tering
Taliwang
Olet Rea (2592m)
Hu'u
Wawarada Bay
Jelenga
Jereweh
Maluk
Sekongkang
Lunyuk
INDIAN OCEAN
0
25km

than stop here for a night. Though it sprawls without a real centre, you'll find several places to stay and eat on Jalan Hasanuddin near the river.

## Arrival

**By bus** All buses arrive at the Sumer Payong bus terminal, just off the Trans-Sumbawa highway, about 3km along Jl Garuda, past the airport. Most of the yellow bemo (see below) head out to the bus terminal.
**By air** The airport is a short dokar ride into town or a five-minute walk to the *Tambora Hotel.*

## Information and city transport

**Tourist information** The regional tourist office (Mon–Thurs 7am–2pm, Fri 7–11am, Sat 7am–12.30pm; ☎0371/23714) is about the best you'll find in Nusa Tenggara: it's 2km out of town at Jl Bungur 1 – take a yellow bemo from Jl Hasanuddin heading west (Rp1750) and get off at the roundabout past the airport. The office is just off the left turn-off. The **PHPA parks office** (Mon–Sat 8am–3pm; ☎0371/23941) lies in the village of Nijang, about 4km from the town centre – an ojek there should cost no more than Rp3000.
**Local transport** The yellow bemos, *bemo kota*, do round-trips of the town (flat rate of Rp1750). They can be flagged down on the street or picked up at the Seketeng market terminal on Jl Setiabudi. There are also plenty of dokars that gather outside the market, which are fun for short trips (Rp2000). The Barang Barat bus terminal on Jl Kaharuddin by the river is used for local services to nearby towns and villages.

## Accommodation

Although there's not a great selection of places, there's something to suit all budgets, but check your room first as many can be damp and bug ridden.
**Dewi Hotel** Jl Hasanuddin 60 ☎0371/21170. Thirty one rooms ranging from basic *ekonomi* to large doubles with minibar, TV, bathtub and a/c. ❷–❺
**Hotel Tambora** Jl Kebayan ☎0371/21555. Has everything from simple four-bed rooms to (reasonably priced) luxury. ❷–❻
**Losmen Harapan** Jl Dr Cipto 7 ☎0371/21629. Friendly, with fan rooms clustered around a lovely old timber house. ❷

## Eating

While the majority of eating places in Sumbawa Besar are the usual local *warung* serving goat stews and sate, two options stand out.
**Ikan Bakar** Jl Hasanuddin 14. Great selection of seafood including scrumptious boiled crab (Rp30,000).
**Sadi Dadi** Jl Dr Wahidi 7. Popular, Chinese place offering a large menu and equally large portions. Dishes from Rp9000.

## Directory

**Airlines** Merpati Jl Diponegoro 115 ☎0371/21416 Trans Nusa PT Adhe Mitragas; Jl Hasanuddin 110 ☎0371/21565.
**Banks** BNI bank, Jl Kartini, has an ATM, and is the best place to change foreign currency or traveller's cheques; it offers better rates than most banks further east in Nusa Tenggara. There are a couple of other ATMs around town, including outside the *Hotel Tambora.*
**Internet** Gaul Internet Café, Jl Setiabudi 14, offers food and drink and internet access (Rp10,000/hr).
**Post office** Jl Yos Sudarso.
**Telephones** Telkom, opposite the post office, has international telephone, telex, telegram and fax.

## Moving on

**By bus** Buses leave for Bima and places en route at regular intervals between 6am and 1pm. The larger buses that run between Jakarta, Surabaya and Bima stop at the terminal almost hourly, day and night. Most yellow bemos, *bemo kota*, head out to the bus terminal.
**Destinations:** Bima (7hr); Dompu (5hr); Taliwang (3hr).
**By air** Trans Nusa flys to Denpasar (4 weekly; 1hr 45min) via Mataram (35 min).

# BIMA

The rather sleepy port town of **BIMA** is a useful place to break up the otherwise agonizing overland trip to Flores across the island, but little remains from the days when it served as the most important port in Nusa Tenggara. The town is centred around the market on Jalan Flores; most of the accommodation lies to the west of the **Sultan's Palace**, whose museum (Mon–Sat 8am–2pm; Rp3000) houses a rather shabby collection of traditional costumes.

## Arrival and information

**By bus** Most travellers arriving in Bima from the west or the airport end up at the bus terminal just south of town, a short dokar or bemo ride to the centre.

**By ferry** Pelni ferries dock at the harbour, 2km west of Bima and served by dokar.

**By air** The airport is 20km away on the main road to Sumbawa Besar. Buses stop in both directions, and taxis meet arrivals.

**Tourist office** Jl Sukarno Hatta, near the Telkom office. English-speaking and pretty helpful. Catch a bemo (Rp1750) heading east from the southern side of the sports field in the centre of town.

## Accommodation

**Hotel La'mbitu** Jl Sumbawa 4 ☎0371/42222. Facing the market and the best place to stay, with great-value standard rooms with TVs and hot water. ❸–❹

**Lila Graha** Jl Lombok ☎0371/42740. Similar to the *La'mbitu* but gloomier, scruffier, less friendly and inferior value. Still, it's fine if the *La'mbitu* is full; the new block is better. ❷–❺

**Losmen Komodo** Jl Sultan Ibrahim ☎0371/42070. Passable if you're looking for somewhere dirt cheap, though basic. ❶

## Eating

**Lila Graha** Jl Sumbawa. Unlike the rather poor hotel, the restaurant at the *Lila Graha* is the finest in town with good helpings of Chinese food (*kwe tiao goreng* noodles for Rp12,000), and a few Western dishes on offer too.

**Mawar** Jl Sulawesi. Standard Indonesian dishes but the service is friendly and prices low (Rp6000 upwards).

## Directory

**Airlines** Trans Nusa, Jl Sulawesi 26 ☎0374/647251; Merpati, next to *Hotel Parewa*, Jl Sukarno Hatta ☎0374/42897.

**Banks** The BNI on Jl Hasanuddin changes foreign currency and traveller's cheques and has the only ATM in town that will accept foreign cards.

**Internet** Komodo Explorer, Jl Sumbawa, has a few terminals (Rp12,000 per hr)

**Telephones** The Telkom office on Jl Sukarno Hatta has international telephone and fax. A yellow bemo (Rp2000) runs along Jl Sukarno Hatta from the market.

## Moving on

**By bus** There are several night-bus agents on Jl Pasar that offer a/c and standard buses to all major destinations, including Mataram and Sumbawa Besar. Kumbe terminal for buses to Sape (2hr) is in Raba, about 5km out of town and served by yellow bemos (Rp1750).

**Destinations:** Mataram via Sumbawa Besar (Bima terminal; 11hr); Sape (Kumbe terminal; 2hr); Sumbawa Besar (Bima terminal; 7hr).

**By ferry (Pelni)** If you need to catch one of the early-morning ferries from Sape to Labuanbajo, tell your hotel the night before and the bus to Sape should pick you up at 4am. Nearly all buses from Sape continue into town and stop outside the BNI bank on Jl Hasanuddin. The Pelni office is about 1.5km out of the centre at Jl Kesatria 2 (☎0374/42625), by the port; yellow bemos can drop you there to arrange tickets.

**Destinations:** Denpasar (monthly; 18hr/fortnightly; 24hr); Labuanbajo (fortnightly; 12hr); Makassar (fortnightly; 27hr); Surabaya (fortnightly; 34hr); Waingapu (fortnightly; 13hr).

**By air** Trans Nusa fly to Denpasar (4 weekly; 1hr 25min) via Mataram (4 weekly; 50min); Merpati fly daily to Denpasar (55min).

# SAPE

**SAPE** and the port of Bugis are seeing a few more travellers who choose to stay here rather than Bima, though it remains a quiet, dusty town where livestock wander the streets. Most of the town's facilities, including the **post office** and a **BNI Bank** with an ATM, are on the main road down to the port. In the port area, *Losmen Mutiara* (☎0374/71337; ❷–❹) offers good-value standard rooms in a new annexe. Nearby **Gili Banta** is a good day-trip, with nice beaches and a burgeoning turtle population. The best **place to eat** and stock up for the long ferry ride is the *Arema* restaurant, just up from the *Mutiara*, near the port entrance.

## Moving on

**By ferry** The ADSP ferry office is at the harbour (☎0374/71075). There is a daily direct ferry service to Labuanbajo on Flores (Mon & Wed–Sun 8am, Tues 3pm; 6–9hr), and one weekly service to

Waikelo on Sumba (Mon 8pm; 6–9hr). Neither is particularly comfortable, but on the Waikelo ferry it's worth trying to sneak upstairs to the much quieter crew area, where you could ask to kip down on one of the wooden benches, out of range of the livestock noises from the car deck below.



# Komodo and Rinca

Off the east coast of Sumbawa lies **Komodo National Park**, a group of parched but majestic islands that have achieved fame as the home of the Komodo dragon, or *ora* as it is known locally, which lives nowhere else but here and on a few neighbouring islands. The south coast of the main island is lined with impressive, mostly dormant volcanoes, the north with mainly dusty plains, irrigated to create rice paddies around the major settlements. The two most visited islands in the national park are **Komodo** and **Rinca.**

### THE KOMODO DRAGON

*Varanus komodoensis*, the **Komodo dragon**, is the largest extant lizard in the world. Unlike many rare species, the dragon is actually steadily increasing in numbers. The largest recorded specimen was well in excess of 3m long and weighed a mammoth 150kg, but most fully grown males are a more manageable 2m and around 60kg. The dragon usually strikes down prey with its immensely powerful tail or slices the leg tendons with scalpel-sharp fangs. Once the animal is incapacitated, the dragon eviscerates it, feeding on its intestines while it slowly dies. Contrary to popular belief, the dragon has neither poisonous breath nor bite, but its prey usually die of infected wounds.

## KOMODO

Most visitors to **Komodo Island** offload at the PHPA camp at **LOH LIANG,** where you'll find all the facilities. Although the practice of feeding live goats to the dragons stopped a long time ago, you may still feel as if you've stepped straight into *Jurassic Park* if your visit coincides with big tour groups. That said, the longer treks around the island, especially out of high season, should guarantee you some peace and quiet, and with a good guide you should have an excellent chance of enjoying the full primordial experience.

### Treks and excursions

The full day's walk to the top of **Gunung Ara**, the highest point on the island, from the PHPA camp doesn't promise dragon sightings, but is absolutely extraordinary. It's an arduous, excruciatingly hot march, but you'll see scores of unusual plants, animals and birdlife, such as sulphur-crested cockatoos, brush turkeys and the **megapode bird**, which builds huge ground nests where its eggs are incubated in warm dung. Bring water and wear decent boots.

There are also regular guided walks from the PHPA camp to **Banunggulung**, the river bed where the dragons used to be fed fresh goats daily, and to **Sebita**, one of the mangrove forests that are vital for providing shelter and food for the island's populations of bats, birds, crabs and fish.

The seas around Komodo, though home to spectacular coral reefs and an abundance of fish, are a far cry from the Gili Islands or Bali, and riptides, whirlpools, sea snakes, sea-wasp jellyfish and a healthy shark population make these waters potentially dangerous, so stick to recommended snorkelling locations such as the excellent **Pantai Merah**. Many boat operators will include at least one snorkelling stop on visits to the

### VISITING KOMODO AND RINCA

The best way to reach Komoda and Rinca is by organizing a trip **from Labuanbajo on Flores** (see p.356), although private (and more expensive) trips can be arranged in Sape. There are also trips advertised to Sumbawa, Komodo and Flores **from Lombok** (see box p.336 ). There are a host of agencies competing for tourists, so it's worth shopping around or asking others for recommendations. Most people are content with a **day-trip** to Rinca, which works out at about Rp500,000 for a boat (up to six people). A multi-day trip that includes both Komodo and Rinca is worth it if you have the time, however, if only to see for yourself just how different, scenically, the two islands are. A **two-day trip** including both islands, some snorkelling, meals and a night on the boat costs between Rp1–1.5 million per boat .

The PHPA charges Rp20,000 for **entry** to the park (both islands; valid for 3 days); in addition, there are **guide fees** (Rp10,000 per person). There's also a US$15 (for a stay of 1–3 days) **conservation contribution fee**. These fees are rarely included in the price negotiated with the boat owner/travel agent, so be sure to bring enough money and plenty of small change, hard to come by on the islands. On all excursions around the islands a guide is a necessity: they have sharp eyes and excellent knowledge of the area. Treks around the national park should reward you with sightings of wild horses, deer, wild pigs and, on Rinca, macaques, but trekking on both islands can be hot and tiring, so make sure you also bring decent footwear with you and take plenty of water.

The accommodation on Komodo and Rinca (❷) comprises wooden cabins, which are pretty basic. Many people bring their own food (which the cafés will happily cook for you) but the island's restaurants serve noodles, omelettes and pancakes. Don't be surprised to see several dragons sleeping near the cabins, drawn by the chance of leftovers.

island. If you visit between October and January, you may even be lucky enough to catch sight of migratory whales that pass through these waters.

## RINCA

With its proximity to Labuanbajo, **Rinca** is now receiving as many visitors as Komodo, if not more, and given that the dragon populations are denser and there's less cover, you're much more likely to catch sight of them here. Rinca consists mostly of parched grassland covering steep slopes, drought-resistant lontar palms and huge patches of flowering cacti and other hardy shrubs. The PHPA camp at **LOH BUAYA** has just eight cabins and a small café. There are a couple of well-marked treks and at the right time (mornings and late afternoons) you shouldn't have any problems spotting dragons, monkeys, buffalo, deer and wild pigs.

# Flores

A fertile, mountainous barrier between the Savu and Flores seas, **Flores** comprises one of the most alluring landscapes in the archipelago. The volcanic spine of the island soars to 2500m, and torrential wet seasons result in a lushness that marks Flores apart from its scorched neighbours. It also differs in its religious orientation – 95 percent of islanders are Catholic. The most spectacular natural sight in Flores is magnificent **Kelimutu**, a unique volcano near Moni, northeast of **Ende**. The three craters of this extinct peak each contain a lake, of vibrantly different and gradually changing colours. In the east of Flores, high-quality **ikat weaving** is still thriving. At the extreme west end of the island, **Labuanbajo** has some fine **coral gardens** nearby and is also the port for ferries to and **from Sumbawa**, and boats from Lombok.

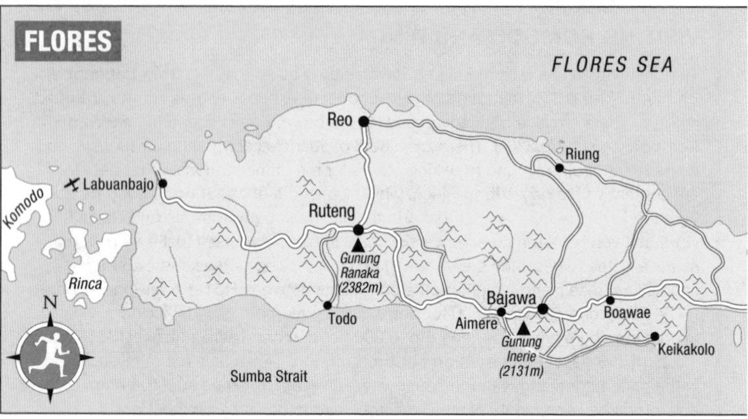


## LABUANBAJO

The once sleepy little port town of **LABUANBAJO** is experiencing a boom in tourism, serving as the gateway to Flores and as the main departure point for trips to **Komodo National Park** (see box p.354). **Ferries from Sumbawa** pass myriad beautiful green islands before docking at the port, where there's no shortage of touts and tour operators waiting to take passengers to losmen or further afield. You can stay in town or at one of the beach hotels within an hour's boat trip – a pleasant option, as most of these places offer a quiet getaway with unspoilt beaches and decent snorkelling. You can also easily organize **dive trips** from one of the dive shops in town; prices are around €55 for two dives. Divine Diving (Ⓣ0385/41948, Ⓦwww.divinediving.info) is a new Dutch-Indonesian owned outfit that's highly recommended, with new equipment and experienced divemasters.

### Arrival

**By ferry** The new passenger harbour lies near the northern end of the main street, on which almost all of the town's losmen and restaurants are situated.

**By air** The airport is about 2km away from the front; a bemo costs Rp5000.

### Accommodation

#### In town

**Chez Felix** Ⓣ0385/41032. Has great views from its restaurant and twelve clean and spacious rooms set around a neat garden, but it's quite a trek uphill from the main road; take the turning opposite the market area ❸–❺

**Gardena Hotel** Jl Sokarno Ⓣ0385/41258. Remains the most popular place in town, despite a rather unsmiling, overworked staff. Boasts nineteen bamboo bungalows, many with great views over the bay – the better ones are those higher up. ❸

**Golo Hilltop** Ⓣ0385/41337; Ⓦwww.golohilltop.com. Dutch-run and with lovely, smartly furnished rooms overlooking the bay, the *Golo* remains the top place to stay despite competition from more expensive rivals and an inconvenient location about 1km out of town (an ocek from the harbour is about Rp3000, though touts usually meet ferries and planes, waiting to whisk tourists away). They also run the nearby *Paradise Bar*, a romantic spot with intimate tables spread across the slope below the main bar. ❹–❻

#### On the beach

All beach accommodation places offer regular free boats to and from the harbour; if you're leaving first thing in the morning, you shouldn't have any problem connecting with the ferries west or the second bus to Ruteng. Running water and electricity may not always be available.

**Kawana Hotel** Office opposite the *Dewata Ayu* restaurant. Standing on its own islands north of Labuanbajo (45min by boat). With reasonable huts set back from the beach, and the price includes meals. ❺

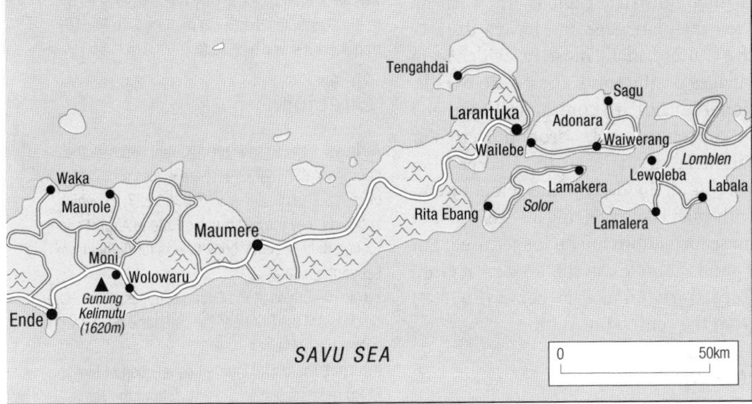




**Seraya Bungalows** Contact the *Gardena* for details. Again, a bungalow resort that can boast its own island just north of Labuanbajo (1hr by boat). Slightly cheaper than the *Kawana*, but with little difference in quality. Price includes meals although these can be bland. ❸, plus Rp20,000 transport

## Eating

**Lounge** Jl Sokarno. European-managed, swanky, pricey place that's good if you crave Western food such as onion rings (Rp15,000) or potato salad.
**Mata Hari** Jl Sokarno. Part of a hotel of the same name, serving fair portions of tasty food (fish sizzler Rp25,000) – though the view over the water is the main attraction.
**Pesona Bali** Highly recommended little restaurant just along from the *Gardena Hotel* on the main street with excellent fish dishes (grilled snapper Rp30,000) and a good view over the harbour.

## Directory

**Airlines** Trans Nusa (☎0385 41800) is towards the southern end of Jl Sokarno. Merpati's office (☎0385/21147) is on the way to the airport at Jl Eltari 6. IAT Air are just round the corner from the BNI at the southern end of town at Jalan Katamso 3 (☎0385/41008).
**Bank** Bank BNI at the south end of town has the town's only ATM; the BRI bank next to the post office changes most common currencies.
**Internet** The Telkom office has an internet service but only for those with their own laptop.
**Post office** On the main street.
**Telephone office** The Telkom office is a little way out of town, up the hill beyond the market, just past the Komodo national park conservation office; walk south from the harbour. For most phone calls, the wartels in town are just as good a bet.

## Moving on

**By bus** Tickets can be bought from all the hotels, or you can just hail a bus from the street.
**Destinations:** Bajawa (2 daily; 11hr); Ende (1 daily, 14hr); Ruteng (2 daily, 4–5hr).
**By ferry (Pelni)** Other ferries also operate, sometimes to Waikelo on Sumba (10–12hr), so it's worth asking at the port office for routes other than those mentioned.
**Destinations:** Bima (fortnightly; 12hr); Makassar (fortnightly; 20hr); Surabaya (fortnightly; 40hr); Waingapu (fortnightly; 10hr).
**By ferry (other)** to: Sape (daily; 6–9hr, or 17hr on Mon & Thurs as sails via Waingapu); Waingapu (2 weekly, 8hr).
**By air** Trans Nusa fly to: Denpasar (6 weekly; 1hr 25min), via Mataram (5hr 25min); and Kupang (5 weekly; 2hr 15min) via Ruteng (20min) and Ende (1hr 5min). Merpati fly to Denpasar (5 weekly; 1hr 35 min) via Bima (2 weekly; 45min) or Mataram (3 weekly; 1hr 15min).

## RUTENG

The first large town near Labuanbajo is **RUTENG**, 140km to the east. Surrounded by stark, forested volcanic hills and rolling rice-paddy plains, it's an archetypal hill town and a cool, relaxing place. The market just to the south is the central meeting point for the local **Manggarai** people, as Ruteng is their district capital. They speak their own language and have a distinctive culture that's most in evidence in villages on the south coast. Their traditional houses are conical and arranged in concentric circles around a circular sacrificial arena; even the rice paddies are round, divided up like spiders webs, with each clan receiving a slice. Most of these formations are no longer used, but a good example can still be seen at **Golo Cara**, thirty minutes by bemo (Rp5000) from the central bus station.

## Arrival

**By bus** Buses from Labuanbajo arrive at the central bus terminal. Buses from the east will drop you at the Puspasari terminal, 3km from town by bemo (Rp2000); the driver will stop where you ask.
**By air** The airport is 2km from the centre, served by bemo to and from the central bus terminal (Rp2000).

## Accommodation

**Hotel Dahlia** Jl Bhayangkara 18 ☎0385 21322. Best location for travellers, near a number of restaurants and airline offices, but rather soulless, housed in a new block and without showers. ❸–❺
**Hotel Sindha** Jl Yos Sudarso 26 ☎0385/21197. Best value in the town centre; standard rooms are looking a little tired now, but the new building next door is good value. ❸–❺
**Rima Hotel** Jl A Yani 14 ☎0385 22196. Far and away the nicest hotel, a chalet-style place with helpful staff, comfortable rooms and an upstairs restaurant with a nice balcony looking out over the town. ❷–❸

## Eating

**Agape Coffee House & Café** Jl Bhayangkara. Opposite the *Dahlia Hotel*, with a Western feel, different types of coffee on the menu and Bob Marley on the stereo. Not an exceptionally imaginative menu, with Indonesian staples (*nasi goring* Rp10,000) and a few mediocre attempts at Western dishes.
**Lestari** Jl Komodo. In terms of variety and comfort, this place is probably the best restaurant in Ruteng, serving plenty of fresh seafood. Fried squid Rp25,000.
**Merlin** Jl Bhayangkara. Very friendly place next to the *Dahlia*, that has a big menu – with English translations – and nice staff.

## Directory

**Airlines** Trans Nusa is on Jl Kartini opposite the church (☎0385 22322). There is also an IAT Air office at Jl Yos Sudarso 5 (☎0385 22772), which suggests they may start using Ruteng Airport soon, though they currently book tickets for flights from Labuanbajo only.
**Bank** The BRI on Jl Yos Sudarso, opposite the *Hotel Sindha*, and the BNI near the cathedral on Jl Kartini, both have ATMs.
**Internet** There's an internet connection at the RSPD radio station on Jl Pertiwi; from the *Rima Hotel* turn left at the traffic lights then first right. (Rp5000 per hour).
**Post office** Jl Baruk 6.
**Telephone office** Jl Kartini, open 24hr.

## Moving on

**By bus** Your hotel can arrange for the bus to pick you up to save you the hassle of getting back out to the terminal.
**Destinations:** Bajawa (several daily; 4–5hr); Labuanbajo (several daily; 4–5hr); Ende (1 daily; 8–10hr); Maumere (1 daily; 15hr); Moni (1 daily; 12hr).
**By shared taxi** Wandi at the *Merlin* restaurant (☎0385 22475) runs his own *travel* (shared taxi) operation and is very friendly, helpful and speaks good English: Bajawa (4hr); Labuanbajo (4hr).
**By air** to: Kupang (1 daily; 1hr 40min) via Ende (30min); Mataram (5 weekly; 5hr 5min) via Labuanbajo (20min) and Denpasar (2hr 5min).

# BAJAWA AND THE NGADA VILLAGES

The hill town of **BAJAWA** is one of the most popular tourist destinations in Flores, surrounded by lush slopes and striking volcanoes. **Gunung Inerie** is just one of the active volcanoes near Bajawa: it's an arduous but rewarding hike, and you can see all the way to Sumba from the summit if it's clear.

Bajawa is the largest town in the **Ngada district**, an area that maintains its status as the spiritual heartland of Flores. Here, despite the growing encroachment of curious travellers, indigenous animist religions flourish and the villages maintain fascinating houses, megalithic stones and interesting totemic structures. Up to 60,000 people in the Ngada district speak the distinct Ngada language, and a good proportion of the older generation don't understand basic Bahasa Indonesian.

Not for the faint-hearted are the local specialities of **moke**, a type of wine that tastes like methylated spirits, and **raerate** or "**rw**" (pronounced "air-vay"), dog meat marinated in coconut milk and then boiled in its own blood.

### NGADA ARCHITECTURE

In the centre of most villages in this district stand several **ceremonial edifices**, which represent the ancestral protection of, and presence in, the village. These include the **Ngadhu**, which resembles a man in a huge hula skirt, the thatched skirt sitting atop a crudely carved, phallic forked tree-trunk, which is imbued with the power of a male ancestor. The female part of the pairing, the **Bhaga**, is a symbol of the womb, a miniature house. The symbolic coupling is supplemented by a carved stake called a **Peo**, to which animals are tied before being sacrificed.

## What to see and do

The influx of tourists to the Ngada region has led to a booming **guide** industry in Bajawa. Many guides belong to the local guide association, whose members have excellent local knowledge and speak English, Indonesian and the local Bajawan language. For Rp120,000 a day per person (minimum four people), a guide will arrange transport, entrance to all the villages and often a traditional Bajawan meal. A day-tour should include at least **Bena** and **Wogo**, as well as the hot springs at **Soa**, but many guides now include a trip up to **Wawo Muda**, one of Indonesia's newest volcanoes. Most guides visit the hotels and restaurants looking for custom, so arranging an organized trip shouldn't pose a problem.

Alternatively you can **rent a motorbike** and explore the region for yourself. The market is a good place to look for people willing to hire out their wheels; expect to pay around Rp55,000 per day. An ocek (motorbike with driver) will be around Rp100,000–125,000 per day.

### Ngada villages

**BENA** (Rp5000) is the prettiest and most traditional of the Ngada villages. Lying about 13km south of Bajawa, to reach it take the turn off past the large church at Mangulewa, 5km east of Bajawa, from where a good road leads down to Bena. (The signposted road to Bena from just by the bus terminal at Bajawa is in a poor state of repair and is not recommended.) Here they have nine different clans, in a village built on nine levels with nine Ngadhu/Bhaga Mcouplings. It's the central village for the local area's religions and traditions, and one of the best places to see **festivals** such as weddings, planting and harvest celebrations.

Some of the finest megaliths and Ngadhu are at the twin villages of **WOGO BARU and WOGO LAMA,** the former lying 1km south of Mataloko (30min by bemo from Bajawa; Rp2000). Wogo Baru is a typically charming Ngada village, but the main attraction lies about 1.5km further down the road at Wogo Lama, where some distinctly eerie megaliths sit in a clearing.

### Hot springs and Wawo Muda

The most popular destination near Bajawa is the **hot springs** at **SOA**. The springs are set in magnificent surroundings and are a joy, especially in the chilly late afternoon. Buses and **bemos** from Bajawa bemo station run to Soa village (Rp2500), from where it's a two-kilometre walk to the springs. There are some quieter though equally seductive hot springs at Malanage 3km south of Bena on a bad road.

In the first few months of 2001 a new **volcano** erupted above the small village of Ngoranale, about 10km to the north of Bajawa. What had previously been just a large hill covered with pasture – one among many in this part of the world – suddenly burst its top, incinerating the vegetation in the newly formed crater and turning the trees into spindly blackened sticks. There are currently five small red lakes in the bottom of the crater. To visit **Wawo Muda**, catch a bemo to Ngoranale from the market (Rp2000) or the main road to the west of the *Hotel Anggrek*, then ask a villager to show you the start of the wide and easy-to-follow trail, which takes about an hour and a half to meander up to the summit.

## Arrival

**By bus** The bus terminal is 2km out of town at Watujaji. Regular bemos from the terminal to the town cost Rp2000.

**By air** The airport is around 20km out of town and about 6km outside of Soa. If you're lucky there maybe a bemo to Bajawa (Rp6000) waiting. Otherwise you'll have to catch a cab (Rp35,000).

## Accommodation

Accommodation in Bajawa is centred either around Jl Ahmad Yani as you come into town (handy for the town's main restaurants) or up just past the main market.

**Edelweiss** Jl Ahmad Yani 76 ⓣ0384/21345. Often busy, it offers quiet, clean and comfortable rooms, and offers good breakfasts and a daytime menu. ❷–❸

**Hotel Bintang Wisata** Next to the market on Jl Palapa ⓣ0384/21744. Suits those looking for more comfort: the rooms are a bit pricey but do offer hot water – handy, as it can get quite cold at night here. ❸–❻

**Hotel Kembang** Jl Martadimata 18 ⓣ0384/21072. The most popular place to stay up in the centre, this place has eight good-sized rooms set around a pretty garden. ❹–❺

**Korina** Jl Ahmad Yani 81 ⓣ0384/21162. Has very helpful and friendly staff with en-suite rooms set around a spacious lounge, and serves good breakfasts and a daytime menu. ❸

## Eating

There are a handful of restaurants around Jl Ahmad Yani. Many of the hotels also offer evening meals, although standards are pretty average.

**Borobudur** Around the corner from Jl Ahmad Yani on Jl Basuki Rahmat. Friendly and has a decent menu, with staples such as *nasi goreng* around Rp8000, but the decor is a bit stark.

**Lucas** Next to the *Korina*, The best restaurant on the street, deservedly popular, it serves wonderful sautéed pumpkin (Rp12,000) and fish and chips (Rp25,000).

## Directory

**Airlines** Trans Nusa's office is at Jl Satsinit Tubun 1 (ⓣ0384/21078); ask for Toko Cemerlang to find it.

**Banks** The BNI on the street west of the Borobudur restaurant and BRI on Jl Sukarno-Hatta both have ATMs and the BNI changes dollars and dollar traveller's cheques.

**Internet and telephones** The Telkom office on Jl Sukarno Hatta is open 24hr a day and also has an internet terminal (Rp10,000).

**Post office** The main one is up on the hill at the crossroads.

## Moving on

**By bus** Most buses come into town to look for passengers, but it's best to be on the safe side and go to them.

**Destinations:** Ende (several daily; 4hr); Labuanbajo (2 daily; 11hr); Moni (1 daily; 6hr); Ruteng (several daily; 4–5hr).

**By shared taxi** The *Hotel Virgo* to the north of the market operates a few *travel* (shared taxis) daily to Ende (4hr) and Ruteng (4hr).

**By air** The airport is around 25km from Bajawa. You may find a bemo to the airport (Rp6000), particularly when flights are due; ask around the Watujaji bus terminal. Otherwise you'll have to catch a cab (Rp35,000). Kupang (3 weekly; 55min).

# ENDE

Situated on a narrow peninsula with flat-topped Gunung Meja and the active volcano Gunung Ipi at its sea end, the port of **ENDE** is the largest town on Flores and provides access for Kelimutu and Moni. Ende suffered severe damage in the 1992 earthquake that razed Maumere and killed several hundred people here. The town is pretty much back on its feet now, though it still looks fairly ramshackle and tired, with little to attract the tourist other than banks and **ferries** to other destinations. Black-sand **beaches** stretch down both east and west coasts: the Bajawa road runs right along the seafront, so just catch a bemo out to Ndao bus terminal and the beach begins right there. The town is also an ideal starting point for exploring villages that specialize in **ikat** weaving. **NGELLA** is a weaving village about 30km east from Wolowana bus terminal in Ende, near the coast: take a bemo or truck (Rp5000).

The cheaper losmen and some restaurants are spread out along Jl A Yani and around the airport roundabout, whilst the rest are down in the old town; travelling between the two areas is easily done by bemo (Rp2000) or ojek (Rp2000–3000).

## Arrival

**By bus** Buses from the east arrive 4km further on from the airport at the Wolowana bus terminal, served by bemo or ojek from the town centre. Buses from the west arrive at Ndao bus terminal, which is on the beach about 2km west of the centre of town; bemos are in plentiful supply.

**By ferry** Ipi harbour on the southeastern coast of the peninsula is used for all long-distance boats; the ferry and harbour master's offices are on the road that leads down to the harbour.

**By air** The airport is just north of the town, close to Ipi harbour, on Jl Jenderal Ahmad Yani.

## Accommodation

Most people use Ende as a simple overnight stop, in which case the losmen near the airport on Jl A Yani are fine.

**Dwi Putra** Jl Sudarso ☎0381/21685. Useful for those who prefer to stay in the town itself, this place has fairly decent standard rooms. ❷–❻

**Hotel Merpati** Jl A Yani ☎0381/25535. Just up from the *Ikhlas*, with ten newish en-suite rooms, some doubles, all arranged around a cosy reception area. ❷–❹

**Losmen Ikhlas** Jl A Yani 65 ☎0381/21695. Offers what may be the best value in Nusa Tenggara; their superior rooms are a bargain and it is deservedly popular, so book ahead. ❶–❷

**Safari** Jl A Yani 65 ☎0381/21997. Next to the *Ikhlas* and offering a bit more choice with a/c VIP and superior rooms with showers and TV. ❷–❺

## Eating

**Bangkalan II** Jl Ahmad Yani. Up near the airport roundabout and offering cheap and good helpings of Padang food (around Rp6000).

**Istana Bambu** Jl Kemakmuran 30a. The best option in the town centre, serving a good range of Chinese dishes and delicious fresh juices (*kwe tiao goreng* Rp12,000).

**Telaga Raya Baru** Smart Padang food place near the airport roundabout (around Rp7000).

## Directory

**Airlines** Merpati, Jl Nangka 10 ☎0381/21355; Trans Nusa, Jl Keli Mutu 39 ☎0381/24333 or 24222.

**Bank** The BRI and Danamon banks – two blocks up from the sea on Jl Sukarno – have ATMs.

**Internet** The most reliable internet café is Pemkabende, up the hill at Jl Diponegoro 4 (Rp6000/hr).

**Post office** Way out up the hill on Jl Basuki Rahmat (☎0381/86318).

## Moving on

**By bus** to: Bajawa (several daily; 4hr); Labuanbajo (1 daily; 18hr); Maumere (several daily; 6hr); Moni (several daily; 1hr 30min); Ruteng (several daily; 10hr).

**By ferry (Pelni and ASDP)** The Pelni ferries *KM Awu* and *KM Wilis* stop here on their route around the islands, and there's also an ASDP ferry serving Sumba on a continuous loop (via Timor) once a week. The Pelni office at Jl Kathedral 2 (☎0381/21043) can help with Pelni and ASDP tickets.

**Destinations:** Denpasar (fortnightly; 44hr); Labuanbajo (fortnightly; 20hr); Makassar (fortnightly; 64hr); Maumere (fortnightly; 40hr); Surabaya (fortnightly; 58hr); Waingapu (fortnightly; 8hr).

**By air** Trans Nusa fly to: Kupang (6 weekly; 50min); Maumere (11 weekly; 20min). Merpati fly to: Denpasar (5 weekly; 1hr 55min); Kupang (7 weekly; 40min), Waingapu (1 weekly; 40min).

## KELIMUTU AND MONI

Stunning **Kelimutu** volcano, with its three strangely coloured crater lakes, is without doubt one of the most startling natural phenomena in Indonesia. The picturesque village of **Moni**, 40km northeast of Ende, stretches along the road from the lower slopes of the volcano down to the valley floor, and makes a great base from which to take a hike up to Kelimutu and around.

### Kelimutu

The summit of **Kelimutu** (1620m) is a startling lunar landscape with, to the east, two vast pools separated by a narrow ridge. The waters of one are a luminescent green that changes to a milky jade in the sun; the other is the colour of Coca-Cola. A few hundred metres to the west, in a deep depression, is a huge brown lake that resembles a big bowl of chocolate. The lakes' colours are due partly to the levels of certain **minerals** that dissolve in them. As the waters erode the caldera they lie in, they uncover bands of different compounds and, as the levels of these compounds are in constant flux, so are the colours. Just as important, however, is the level of oxygen dissolved in the water. When their supply is low, the lakes look green. Conversely, when they are rich in oxygen, they range between deep red to black. In the 1960s, the lakes were red, white and blue, and locals predict that within years they will have returned to these hues.

Every morning at around 4am tourists ride by ocek (Rp35,000 for the return journey) from their hotel in Moni to Kelimutu; make sure you organize this the night before, and tell the driver if you intend to walk back to save him waiting. Just before the car park near the summit you have to pay a park fee of Rp20,000. The best view is from the south crater rim, looking north over the two sister lakes; the trails that run around other rims are extremely dangerous – tourists have disappeared up here. The **walk** back down to Moni, which takes about three hours, with rolling grassy meadows flanking extinct volcanic hills, and views all the way to the sea, is a joy, especially in fine weather. Practically the whole walk is downhill, but always bring water and wear good boots. A shortcut by the PHPA post cuts off a good 4km from the road route, takes you through some charming local villages and past the **waterfall** (*air terjun*) less than 1km from central Moni, which is a great spot for a dip after what can be a very hot walk. A little further down is a hot spring, the perfect place to soak weary feet.

### Moni

Nestling among scores of lush rice paddies, the village of **MONI** exudes a definite lazy charm. Full of cheap places to stay and home to several decent restaurants, it's a relaxed place to spend a few days, with great walking in the surrounding hills. Some fetching pieces of ikat are often available from the losmen, though prices are better at the market further down the hill, where Tuesday seems to be the best trading day. There is no bank, post office, internet or Telkom in Moni, despite the increasing number of tourists, but you can make phone calls at the tiny **wartel** between the *Maria* and *John homestays*.

**Buses** from Ende (1hr 30min) and Maumere (4hr) stop here regularly throughout the day, and there's one bus daily to Bajawa, though you should ask your losmen to book it otherwise it may be full by the time it gets to Moni.

#### Accommodation

Most of the losmen are laid out along the hill at the top of the village, with most concentrated around the two main bends in the road. Many of the cheap homestays offer the same rates and have very similar rooms.

**Arwanty** Just up the hill. Three huge bungalows, each with a double bed, en-suite shower, rest area and balcony; unfortunately, they're looking a little tired now and the creatures that scurry around the roof at night will keep you awake. ❷–❸

**Bintang Restaurant** Opposite Watugona. This friendly restaurant now has a few smart rooms that are good value ❷

**Sao Ria Wisata** Right above the village. A cut above the rest, a collection of very smart thatched bungalows next to a fine restaurant. ❷–❸

**Watugona Bungalows** This central place is currently the most popular choice, with five clean rooms, all with mosquito nets. Rooms range in size but a good breakfast is included. ❷

## Eating

For such a small isolated village, the cuisine in Moni is impressive.

**Bintang Restaurant** Offers very tasty and filling potato cakes (*croquet*; Rp15,000), and has great views across the valley.

**Keli mutu** At the top of town by the *Sao Wisata*. Serves some delicious meals including a few Western staples and curries (Rp18,000 per plate).

**Nusa Bunga** Further down the hill. Has an all you can eat buffet for Rp50,000, though you'll need to give them a bit of notice before you indulge.

# MAUMERE

On the north coast of Flores, roughly equidistant between Ende and Larantuka, **MAUMERE** was once the visitor centre and best diving resort on the island. In 1992, a devastating earthquake and tsunami destroyed most of the town, and it still seems to be trying to get back on its feet. However, improved transport links and regular air services are steadily making it one of the main stops on trips around the Nusa Tenggara; from here, you can even organize tours that take in all of Flores' attractions. Diving is also improving with dive centres offering dives to see fresh coral emerging from the sea bed after its destruction. Maumere is the capital of the Sikka district, which stretches all the way to the east coast. It's especially renowned for its **weaving**, which characteristically has maroon, white and blue geometric patterns, in horizontal rows on a black or dark-blue background.

The main square and market are just up from the seafront but don't expect a massive amount of activity.

## Arrival

**By bus** Buses from Ende, Moni and other destinations in the west are served by the Ende bus terminal, a couple of km down Jl Gajah Mada southwest of town. Plenty of bemos go from here to the centre.

**By air** Most accommodation will offer you a lift from the airport if you book to stay with them; shared taxis or minibuses into town are around Rp30,000.

## Accommodation

Many travellers bypass the accommodation on offer in Maumere and instead opt for the out-of-town beachside establishments, especially if they've come here for the diving or snorkelling.

### Maumere

**Hotel Gardena** Jl Patirangga 28 ⓣ0382/22644. By far the best of all the budget options, with a warm welcome from the staff and clean rooms, ensuring this is still the travellers' favourite. Includes a decent breakfast. ❸

**Hotel Maiwali** Jl Don Thomas 6 ⓣ0382/21220. Offers a wide range of rooms – from simple *ekonomis* to gorgeous superior rooms in a new annexe at the back – but the cheaper rooms inside the building are a bit grim. ❷–❻

**Hotel Wini Rai I** Jl Gajah Mada 50 ⓣ0382/21388. Handy for the bus terminal, this hotel has some big, clean and very comfortable rooms towards the top end. Surprisingly, some of the better rooms are those set around the lobby. ❷–❻

### On the coast

These places typically offer a full day's diving with food for between $55 and $70 or accommodation only from $20. Both are near the village of Waiara, 9km from Maumere You could try to contact them beforehand to see if there's any chance of a lift from Maumere. Otherwise, charter a bemo or taxi for around Rp40,000, or take a Larantuka-bound bus and ask to be dropped off near the resort.

**Sao Wisata** Jl Sawista, Waiara ⓣ0382/21555, ⓦwww.saowisata.com. Definitely one of the smartest outfits on the coast, this dive resort has a/c and fan cottages and cabins, all with private showers, and a swimming pool on the beachfront. US$75, includes two dives and hire of all gear. Accommodation only ❹

**Sea-World Club** Jl Sawista, Waiara ⓣ0382/21570, ⓦwww.sea-world-club.com. Another smart beachside dive resort, this one German-run, offering thatched wooden bungalows with a sense of privacy. US$60 includes two dives and hire of diving gear. Accommodation only ❹

## Eating

**Golden Fish** Jl Hasanuddin. Really fresh seafood (much of it kept live in tanks on the ground floor) and great views over the bay. Fried squid Rp35,000.

**Sarinah** Jl Raja Centis. Best of the bunch near the market, with a fair range of fish and seafood (Rp15,000–35,000) as well as cold beer.

**Sunga Indah** Jl Raja Centis. Next door to the *Sarinah*, a large and well-run Padang food place (Rp6000 per plate).

## Directory

**Airlines** Merpati, Jl Don Thomas 18 (ⓣ0382/21342); Trans Nusa, Jl Anggrek 2, by the northwest corner of the Gelora Samador stadium (ⓣ0382/21393).

**Banks** The two biggest banks are the BRI on Jl A Yani and the BNI on Jl Sukarno Hatta; both change money. You will also find ATMs here, as well as at a couple of other smaller banks in the town centre.

**Internet** Comtel Internet café is down near the seafront on Jl Bandeng, and offers a surprisingly reliable – if occasionally slow – service for Rp12,000 per hr.

**Post office** Jl A Yani near the sports field.

**Telephone office** The Telkom office is just above and across the road from the BNI bank.

## Moving on

**By bus** Buses to Moni, Ende, and all points west leave from the Ende bus terminal. Most buses meander around the town centre for at least an hour before heading off to make absolutely sure there's no one left in town who might be thinking of leaving.

**Destinations:** Bajawa (1 daily; 10hr); Ende (several daily; 6hr); Moni (several daily; 3hr); Ruteng (1 daily; 15hr).

**By share taxi** Share taxis (called *travel*) can be arranged by your hotel and cost Rp50,000 to Moni.

**By ferry (Pelni)** Tickets can be bought at the Pelni office by the middle gate of the harbour (ⓣ0382/21013).

**Destinations:** Bima (monthly; 24hr); Kalabahi (fortnightly; 15hr); Makassar (fortnightly; 24hr).

**By ferry (other)** There are several private ferries running passengers once a week to Surabaya, including *KM Kirana* and *KM Mentari*; tickets can be bought from the *Hotel Benggoan I*, just up the hill from the central market on Jalan Moa Toda. There is also the *KM Dharma Kencana*, with tickets available from their office at Jalan Nong Meak 30 (ⓣ0382/23399).

**By air** Merpati fly to: Denpasar (7 weekly; 2hr 10min), via Waikabubak (4 weekly; 40min) or Waingapu (3 weekly 40min); Kupang (1 daily; 45min). Trans Nusa fly to: Denpasar (3 weekly; 2hr 10min); Kupang (8 weekly; 45min).

# Sumba

Sumba is a land with a split personality. The east of the island is rocky, parched and fairly mountainous; the west is contrastingly fertile and green, with rolling hills and a long rainy season. **Waingapu**, the capital, is well known for producing the finest *ikat* fabric in the whole of Indonesia. A little further out at **Rende** and **Melolo** are stone tombs with bizarre carvings, and other villages right out on the east coast offer the chance to see quality weaving and traditional structures near some deserted beaches. The main town in the west is **Waikabubak**, where characteristic houses with thatched roofs soar to an apex over 15m above the ground.

Access to Sumba is either by **ferry** from Ende in Flores to Waingapu or from Sape in Sumbawa to Waikelo, or by **air** to either Waingapu or Waikabubak (the airport is at Tambolaka). Most people choose to fly out of **Waingapu** rather than Waikabubak, which has a very chequered record for reliability and cancellations.

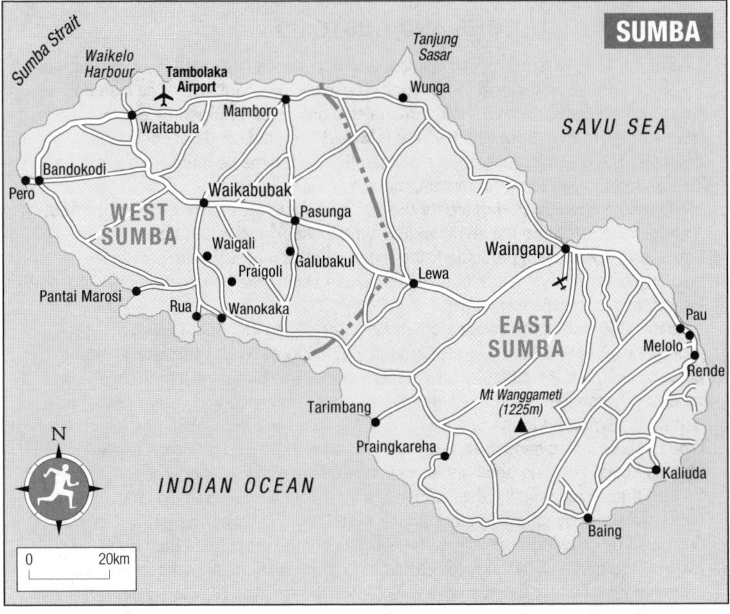


## WAINGAPU

It may be the largest port and town on Sumba, but **WAINGAPU** is far from a modern metropolis. Pigs and chickens roam the backstreets and locals still walk around barefoot, with *ikat* tied around their heads and waists. The older half of the hourglass-shaped town is centred around the port, and the newer part around the bus terminal and market, where the government has channelled development in recent years. It's only a fifteen-minute walk between the two, but an endless army of bemos do the circular trip (Rp1750). The bay to the west of town has a harbour at the extreme point of either shore; all ferries dock at the **western harbour**, requiring an eight-kilometre journey around the bay to town. The eastern harbour in the old town is now just used for fishing boats. It's also worth taking a trip 15km up to the **huge pasola statues** on the main road to the southwest from where there are some spectacular views over the bay and surrounding countryside.

### What to see and do

**PRAILU** is the most visited of the local **ikat-weaving villages**, just a ten-minute bemo hop away. After signing in at the large, traditional house (Rp5000), you can inspect weavings that weren't good enough to be bought by the traders. The **ikat** blankets of east Sumba are ablaze with symbolic dragons, animals, gods and headhunting images. The cloth worn by men is called the **hinggi**, and is made from two identical panels sewn together into a symmetrical blanket. One is worn around the waist and another draped across one shoulder. These are the most popular souvenirs, as they make great wall hangings. Small blankets of medium quality usually retail for under $50 but will mainly use only chemical dye. Most pieces retailing at up to US$100 will use a *campur* (mix) of traditional vegetable **dyes** and manufactured chemical dyes. For larger, high-quality pieces, you

### SUMBA'S TRADITIONS AND CUSTOMS

One of the main reasons to visit Sumba is to experience first-hand the extraordinary agrarian **animist cultures** in the villages. These villages comprise huge clan houses set on fortified hills, centred around megalithic graves and topped by a totem made from a petrified tree, from which villagers would hang the heads of conquered enemies. The national government insisted that all totems be removed back in the 1970s, and though some do remain, many have disappeared.

The most important part of life for the Sumbanese is death, when the mortal soul makes the journey into the spirit world. Sumbanese **funerals** can be extremely impressive spectacles, particularly if the deceased is a person with prestige, inspiring several days' worth of slaughter and feasting, the corpse wrapped in hundreds of exquisite *ikat* cloths.

Ostensibly, visiting the villages often involves nothing more than hiring a motorbike (available from town for around Rp70,000 per day; your hotel is the best place to ask), but the difficulty for **Western visitors** to Sumba is that traditions and taboos in Sumbanese village life are still very powerful and sit ill at ease with the demands of modern tourism. A visitor to a Sumbanese village must first take the time to share *sirih pinang* (**betel nut**) with both the *kepala desa* (village headman) and his hosts. Bringing betel nut is seen as a peace offering (enemies would rarely turn up brandishing gifts), while its use is a sign of unity; Sumbanese ritual culture sets great store by returning blood to the earth, and the bright-red gobs of saliva produced by chewing *sirih* represent this. (The central purpose of the Pasola festival, see p.368, is similarly to return blood to the soil.) Many villages that are on the regular trail for tourists have supplanted the tradition of sharing betel with a simple request for money, but if you come with gifts (betel nuts, cigarettes) you'll be far more welcome.

can pay anything from $100 to $1000. A tight weave, clean precise motifs and sharp edges between different colours are all signs of a good piece. Dealers in the towns will often give you better prices than those in the villages.

## Arrival

**By bus** Buses from Waingapu and the west use the terminal 5km west of town; a bemo from here costs around Rp1750. The bus terminal near the market in the new town serves the rest of east Sumba, with buses from Melolo, Rende and Baing.

**By ferry** Passengers arriving at the main western harbour can get any bemo to drop them at the hotel of their choice (Rp1750).

**By air** The airport is about 10km to the southeast on the road to Rende. Representatives from the main hotels are usually on hand to ferry tourists into town – as long as you agree to look at their hotel first; if they're not there, head out to the main road and flag a bus down or take a cab (Rp20,000).

## Accommodation

All the accommodation below is in the newer part of town near the bus terminal and market. All the hotels can offer transport to the airport if required.

**Hotel Elvin** Jl A Yani ⓣ 0387/61462. Split into two halves, with a plush renovated section housing smart a/c rooms with verandas, and a cheaper, older section with large, basic rooms. ❷

**Hotel Merlin** Jl Dil Panjaitan 25 ⓣ 0387/61300. Looks as if it ought to be more expensive than it is, but the staff's experience with large tour groups can make them indifferent to the independent traveller. Rooms are tiled and clean but the road outside is very, very noisy. ❷–❹

**Hotel Sandle Wood** Jl Dil Panjaitan 23 ⓣ 0386/61887. One of the more expensive options in town; nevertheless, it offers good value for money, and you'll receive a warm welcome from the helpful staff. ❷–❹

## Eating

You're almost spoilt for choice for food, with warung lining the main road linking the old and new towns. Check out the new food court **Komplek Ruko** on the road between the old and new towns, opposite the *Hotel Elvin*.

**Nazareth** Jl Lalamentik. Popular Chinese restaurant and justfiably so with a fairly good choice of food at reasonable prices (noodle dishes Rp11,000–20,000).

**Restu Ibu** Long-established restaurant with a fine reputation, on the way into the old town and serving no-nonsense Indonesian staples (Rp7000–15,000).

**Steak House** Komplex Ruko. Unusual – especially for Sumba – Western-style restaurant with a large menu of decent Western dishes (Rp15,000–35,000).

## Directory

**Airlines** Merpati office, Jl Sukarno 4 near the sports field ☎0387/61323; Trans Nusa, Jl A Yani 8 ☎0387/61363.

**Banks** There are several banks in the new part of town, but the BRI on Jl A Yani, the road between the new and old towns, has the only ATM that accepts foreign cards. The BNI on Jl Ampera has the best rates for cash and traveller's cheques.

**Post office** Jl Hasanuddin, in the old town.

**Telephone office** Telkom office, Jl Cut Nyak Dien.

## Moving on

**By bus** to: Melolo and Rende (several daily; 2hr); Waikabubak (several daily; 4hr 30min).

**By ferry (Pelni)** The Pelni office (☎0387/61665) is down at the bottom of the hill near the old harbour.

**Destinations:** Bima (fortnightly; 13hr); Denpasar (fortnightly; 30hr); Ende (fortnightly; 10hr).

**By ferry (other)** The ASDP office is at Jl Wanggameti (☎0387/61533), 4km out of town on the main road to Waikabubak.

**Destinations:** Aimere (weekly; 10hr); Ende (weekly; 10hr).

**By air** Merpati fly to: Denpasar (3 weekly, 1hr 10min); Kupang (5 weekly, 1hr 5min–2hr); Maumere (4 weekly, 45min). Trans Nusa fly to: Denpasar (3 weekly, 1hr 55mins); Kupang (3 weekly; 50min–1hr 5min); Mataram (3 weekly; 5hr 5min); Tambolaka (aka Waikabubak; 3 weekly; 25min).

# WAIKABUBAK

Surrounded by lush green meadows and forested hills, tiny **WAIKABUBAK** is a small town enclosing several small kampung with slanting thatched roofs and megalithic **stone graves**, where life proceeds according to the laws of the spirits. Kampung **Tarung**, on a hilltop just west of the main street, has some excellent megalithic graves and is regarded as one of the most significant spiritual centres on the island. The **ratu** (king) of Tarung is responsible for the annual **wula padu** ceremony, which lasts for a month at the beginning of the Merapu New Year in November. The ceremony commemorates the visiting spirits of important ancestors, who are honoured with the sacrifice of many animals and entertained by singing and dancing. Kampung **Praijiang**, a five-tiered village on a hilltop surrounded by rice paddies, is another fine kampung, several kilometres east of town. You can catch a bemo (Rp1750) to the bottom of the hill. Waikabubak enjoys an extended rainy season that lasts way into May, when the countryside can be drenched by daily downpours and it can get chilly at night. Most things that you will need in Waikabubak are either on the main street of Jalan Ahmad Yani, or within several minutes' walk of it.

## Arrival

**By bus** The bus terminal is in the southeast of the town and serves Waingapu as well as all areas of western Sumba including Bandokodi and Pero; trucks and bemos also stop here.

**By ferry** (from Waikelo) The weekly ferry from Sape in Sumbawa arrives in Waikelo harbour, served by buses from the main terminal (Rp5000).

**By air** Waikabubak Airport at Tambolaka is a good 90min drive from the north of town towards Waikelo harbour; buses (Rp5000) and taxis (Rp70,000) meet arriving planes. In Pasola season (see box, p.368), flights are more reliable but are often booked for months in advance, so if you're coming at this time make sure you have a reservation.

## Accommodation

For such a small town, the choice of places to stay in Waikabubak is pretty good.

**Hotel Aloha** Jl Sudirman 26 ☎0387/21245. Efficient, friendly and a worthy rival to the *Artha*. Has a fair restaurant, too. ❷

**Hotel Artha** Jl Veteran ☎0387/21112. Has big, clean rooms with fans, set around a garden courtyard, and very helpful and friendly staff. Best value and most popular in town. ❶–❸

**Hotel Manandang** Jl Pemuda 4 ⓣ0387/21197. Boasts a variety of huge rooms around a well-kept garden; a bit pricey by local standards but clean and efficient. ❷–❻

**Pelita** Jl A Yani 2 ⓣ0387/21104. The renovated wing is smart but overpriced; the *ekonomi* section grim and only for those counting every last rupiah. ❶

## Eating

As well as these, and the hotels' restaurants, there are a handful of warung scattered around town.

**Fanny** Jl Bhayangkara. Clean, tidy, smiling and friendly, and serving some lovely Chinese and local dishes (Rp8000–25,000). Popular and highly recommended.

**Gloria** Opposite the petrol station. Worth the 1km walk along the main road west out of town. Boasts a reasonable choice of curries (chicken curry Rp15,000).

## Directory

**Airlines** Trans Nusa (ⓣ0387/22563) is in the *Hotel Aloha*.

**Banks** The BNI bank at the junction of Jl A Yani and Jl Sudirman and the BRI bank on Jl Gajah Mada both change money, and the latter has an ATM.

**Post office** Jl Sudirman, just west of the BNI bank.

**Telephone office** The 24hr Telkom office is a few hundred metres south of the bus station.

## Moving on

**By bus** to: Bandokodi and Pero (daily; 4hr); Waingapu (several daily; 4hr 30min).

**By ferry** (from Waikelo) The weekly ferry to Sape (7hr) in Sumbawa operates from Waikelo harbour, served by buses from the main terminal (Rp5000).

**By air** to: Denpasar (3 weekly, 1hr); Kupang (4 weekly; 1hr 45min); Waingapu (4 weekly; 25min).

# KODI AND PERO

In the extreme west of Sumba lie the increasingly popular areas of **Kodi** and **Pero**. The Kodi district, with its centre in the village of **Bandokodi**, is particularly well known for the towering roofs that top the traditional houses. It is also one of the main **pasola** venues in west Sumba. There is one direct bus a day from Waikabubak to Bandokodi; otherwise, you'll have to take a bus to **Waitabula** in the north and then wait for a bus to fill up for the trip around the coast. As the trip between Bandokodi and Waikabubak takes approximately four hours, and the last bus back to Waitabula is at 2pm, a stopover in Pero is in order.

## Pero

The Waikabubak bus will usually take you all the way to **PERO**, a seaside village with a solitary losmen. The village is not

### THE PASOLA

By far the best-known and most dazzling festival in Nusa Tenggara, the **Pasola** is one of those rare spectacles that actually surpasses all expectations. It takes place in **Kodi** and **Lamboya** in February and in **Wanokaka** and Gaura in March; most hotels can give you a rough idea of the date. This brilliant pageant of several hundred colourfully attired, spear-wielding horsemen in a frenetic and lethal pitched battle is truly unforgettable. It occurs within the first two moons of the year, and is set off by the mass appearance of a type of sea worm which, for two days a year, turn the shores into a maelstrom of luminous red, yellow and blue. The event is a rite to balance the upper sphere of the heavens and the lower sphere of the seas. The Pasola places the men of each village as two teams in direct opposition; the spilling of their blood placates the spirits and restores balance between the two spheres. The proceedings begin several weeks before the main event, with villages hurling abuse and insults at their neighbours in order to get their blood up. The actual fighting takes place on the special Pasola fields where the battle has been fought for centuries.

constructed in traditional Sumbanese style, but its rough, cobbled street flanked by colourful wooden houses has a certain charm. Numerous kampung with teetering high roofs and mossy stone tombs dot the surrounding countryside, only a short walk away. The *Homestay Story* (full-board only; ❷), about half way towards the sea on the right, offers basic but clean rooms and massive portions of really tasty food. There are a lot of mosquitoes and no nets are provided, so come prepared. The main surfers' beach, a desolate long stretch where high waves all the way from Antarctica crash onto the steeply sloping sand, is down to the right, but the currents and undertow are ferocious. There's a more sheltered beach down to the left over the river.

# Kalimantan

Dense tropical jungle, murky rivers teeming with traffic, lined with villages and with wildlife so abundant it becomes part of the norm, Kalimantan is a jungle-cloaked landmass which appeals to those looking to venture into undiscovered territory. Occupying the southern two-thirds of the island of Borneo, Kalimantan remains largely untouched by tourism. With few roads, the interior's **great rivers** are its highways and a trip up one of them will give you a taste of traditional Dayak life and introduce you to lush areas of dense jungle. More intrepid explorers can spend weeks on end navigating their way through seldom-ventured parts, and

### VISAS

If you're visiting Kalimantan from outside of Indonesia you must make sure you have a valid visa before entering. **Balikpapan** is the only airport in Kalimantan that will offer visas on arrival, usually for thirty days. If travelling overland from Malaysian Borneo, you can now pick up a thirty-day visa from the consulate in **Kuching**, Sarawak. In Sabah you can get them from the consulate in **Kota Kinabalu** or **Tawau**, and it may be possible to get sixty-day ones, but it seems to be at their discretion.

a visit to one of the national parks could bring you face-to-face with wild **orang-utans** (see box, p.374). The provincial capitals of **Pontianak**, **Palangkaraya** and **Samarinda** are expensive dusty towns which offer little aside from their services. However, once out of the crowded, populated areas Kalimantan's character starts to unfold.

For the independent traveller, Kalimantan can be expensive and a bit of a mission; time, patience, knowledge of Bahasa and effort are certainly required. But if you're looking for a true sense of Borneo, then these obstacles are a small price to pay.

## PONTIANAK

The capital of West Kalimantan, or Kalbar (short for "Kalimantan Barat"), **PONTIANAK** is a sprawling, grey industrial city of over half a million people. Lying right on the equator on the confluence of the Landak and Kapuas Kecil rivers, it is a hot and noisy place, often smoky from the vast forest fires that recurrently rage inland. Most travellers stay just long enough to stock up on supplies before heading for a trip up the Sungai Kapuas, flying on to Balikpapan or moving straight on to Kuching (see p.567).

### What to see and do

Pontianak has very little to offer in itself. To get your bearings, take a **boat** up the river (35,000Rp per hour) from behind the Kapuas Indah building. Along the river, there are still several old buildings of interest: the eye-catching **Istana Kadriyah**, built in 1771, and the traditional Javanese four-tiered roof of **Mesjid Jami** stand near each other on the eastern side of the Kapuas Kecil, just over the Kapuas bridge from the main part of town.

### THE DAYAK

**Dayak** is an umbrella name for all of Borneo's indigenous peoples. In Dayak religions, evil is kept at bay by attracting the presence of helpful spirits, or scared away by protective tattoos, carved spirit posts (*patong*), and lavish funerals. Shamans also intercede with spirits on behalf of the living. Although now you'll often find ostensibly Christian communities with inhabitants clutching mobile phones and watching satellite TV, the Dayak are still well respected for their jungle skills and deep rooted traditions.

Traditionally **headhunting** was an important method of exerting power and settling disputes. It was believed that when cutting off someone's head the victim's soul is forced into the service of its captor. It was not practised now, but in 1997, West Kalimantan's Dayak exacted fearsome revenge against Madurese transmigrants. An estimated 1400 people were killed in a horrific purge of ethnic cleansing which involved headhunting and cannabilism. Similar violence reoccurred between the Malays and the Madurese in the Sampit region of South Kalimantan in 2001. The situation is relatively peaceful now, and headhunting is once again relegated to the past.

### Museum Negeri Pontianak

On Jalan Jend A Yani, 1.5km south of the town centre (Rp2500 by taksi), the museum **Negeri Pontianak** (Tues–Sun 8am–3pm; donation) contains a comprehensive collection of Dayak tribal masks, weapons and musical instruments. Just round the corner from the museum, on Jalan Sutoyo, is an impressive replica of a **Dayak longhouse**.

### Equator monument

Pontianak's twelve-metre-high **equator monument** (Tugu Khatulistiwa) is on the northern side of the Kapuas, 5km west of the Siantan bus terminal. From the terminal catch any *taksi* (Rp3500) but ask if they're heading that far. The monument is on the left after the Pertamina petroleum depot. The exhibit is not much to look at but it's interesting to see the equator line turning into a drainage ditch on the western side of the visitor centre. You can amuse yourself here by stepping between hemispheres to your heart's content.

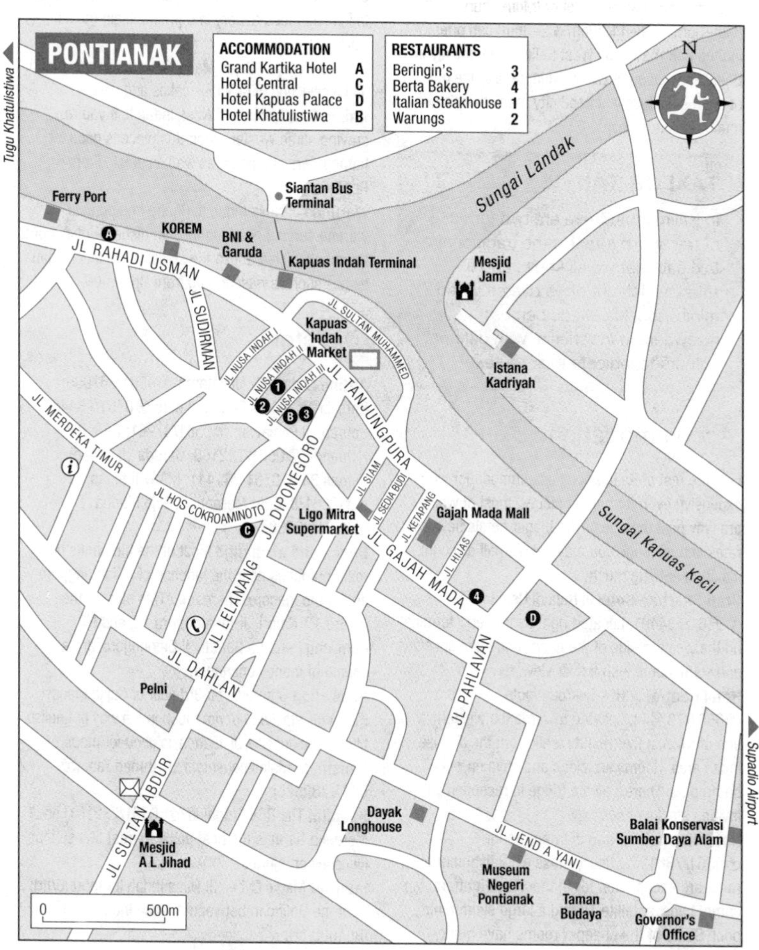

## Arrival and information

**By bus** Most buses that serve Pontianak arrive at the Kapuas Indah terminal, perched on the water's edge in the Chinese quarter. Buses also arrive into the Siantan bus terminal on the eastern side of the river.

**By boat** The main ferry port where the Pelni and other passenger boats arrive is a few hundred metres north of the *Kartika Hotel* on Jl Pa'Kasih.

**By air** Supadio Airport lies 18km south of the city centre. Taksis (Rp15,000) run to the Kapuas Indah terminal in the centre of town from the road just outside the airport, or you can catch a cab using the pre-pay taxi desk just inside the terminal (Rp70,000).

**Tourist information** Jl Johor (Mon–Thurs 8am–3pm, Fri 8–11.30am & 2–3pm) can offer limited information on West Kalimantan, mostly in Bahasa. It's about a twenty-minute taxi ride out of town so unless you need city maps there's not much reason to go.

### TAXI OR TAKSI?

In Kalimantan there are two forms of transport: a **taxi** is the traditional taxi cab that we all know; and a **taksi**, which are often overcrowded minibuses, known as bemos elsewhere in Indonesia, with different colours to indicate their route.

## Accommodation

Like the rest of Kalimantan, accommodation is expensive even for budget places, most of which are way past their best. The bigger hotels have set rates and although you may get a small discount it's often nothing much.

**Grand Kartika Hotel** Jl Rahadi Usman ⓣ0561/734401. Located right by the ferry terminal on the western side of the river; rooms are spacious and some come with a river view. ❹

**Hotel Central** Jl Hos Cokroaminoto ⓣ0561/737444. Located towards the western end of town, a five-minute walk from the Jl Nusa Indah area. Rooms are clean and have en-suite bathrooms. There's also a fridge in reception with inviting stocks of beer. ❸

**Hotel Kapuas Palace** Jl Imam Bonol ⓣ0561/736122. Luxury-class establishment but rates are exceptional for the facilities it offers: big comfy beds, satellite TV and a large swimming pool. Some of the cheaper rooms have quirky extras like lights that don't turn out, and TVs that don't work. ❻–❼

**Hotel Khatulistiwa** Jl Diponegoro ⓣ0561/736793. A large hotel, somewhat reminiscent of a 1960s holiday camp chalet, with large, clean rooms. Prices are reasonable (if you don't mind squat toilets). ❷

## Eating

There are plenty of street stalls dotted around town, especially down near the market and ferry dock. There's also a booming population of bakeries and coffee houses, and a handful of places that serve Western food.

**Beringin's** Jl Diponegoro. This is the largest of four places around town. The friendly owner offers good Indonesian food at very low prices. Main meals from Rp10,000.

**Berta Bakery** Jl Gajah Mada. Sells tasty fresh bread, and a selection of delicious cakes and pastries.

**Italian Steakhouse** Jl Nusa Indah II. If you're craving some Western food this place is good for hamburgers and pasta as well as steak. From Rp15,000

**Warungs** Jl Nusa Indah II. Cheap and popular warung serving good Indonesian dishes – check out the menus listed above the stalls. Usual Indonesian dishes such as *nasi goreng* from Rp10,000.

## Directory

**Airlines** Adam Air, Jl Veteran ⓣ0561/767999; Batavia Air, Jl Hos Cokroaminoto ⓣ0561/73448; Bouraq, Jl Pahlawan ⓣ0561/37261; DAS Jl Ir H Juanda ⓣ0561/732160; Garuda, Jl Rahadi Usman 8a ⓣ0561/741441; MAS, Jl Sidas 8 ⓣ0561/30069; Merpati, Jl Gaja Madha ⓣ0561/36568.

**Banks and exchange** Most of the big banks have main branches near the junction of Jl Tanjungpura and Jl Diponegoro. There are ATMs all over the centre. PT Safari, Jl Tanjungpura 12, and PT Gemilang Perdana Serjati, Jl Diponegoro, are a couple of money changers.

**Book shop** Gramedia on 3rd floor of Gajah Mada mall. Well stocked but not much in the way of English titles. Toko Juanda, Jl Juanda, is good for maps.

**Consulate** Malay consulate, Jl Ahmad Yani (ⓣ 0561/732986).

**Hospital** The RSV Antonius (ⓣ 0561/732101) on Jl Merdeka Barat is the best place to treat any serious illnesses or injuries.

**Internet** Magic Cyber, Jl Nusa Indah II (Rp5000/hr); Centrine Online in between Jl Nusa Indah I & II (Rp4000/hr).

## SUNGAI KAPUAS

Journeying along Indonesia's longest river, the **Sungai Kapuas**, is an adventure that few travellers embark on, and means travelling with the locals and sharing deck space with whatever is being carted in that direction. Starting in **Pontianak** and ending in **Putussibau**, the five-day trip involves meandering along the murky river, cruising past local stilt villages and getting an insight into local life. Public boats leave from behind the Kapuas Indah Building and depart early in the morning so it's best to enquire the night before, or get there about 6am. The houseboat will provide a thin mattress to sleep on, and snacks are served on board – expect to pay about Rp90,000 for five days. Once at Putussibau you can catch the bus (Rp100,000; 20hr) or fly back to Pontianak.

If you want to travel in more luxurious style, you can take a tourist house boat up to Putussibau; try contacting local English-speaking guide, Alex Afdhal (☎081/732340).

**Post office** Jl Sultan Abdur Rahman 49 (Mon–Sat 7.30am–9:30pm, Sun 8am–2pm). Poste restante at the back of the building.

**Shopping** Ligo Mitra Supermarket, Jl Gajah Mada, is useful or self-caterers. Gajah Mada mall, off Jl Gajah Mada, has Western-style outlets on three floors. Matahari department store, Jl Nusa Indachi; Ayani Megamall, on Jl A Yani; Market on Jl Rahadi Usman.

**Telephones** Telkom, Jl Teuku Umar 15, is open 24hr.

### Moving on

**By bus** An army of agents at Kapuas Indah terminal, where most buses leave from, can supply you with tickets for Kuching in Sarawak (Rp140,000–200,000), or for interior towns such as Sintang and Putussibau. Alternatively, you can cross the river to the Siantan bus terminal, where you'll find more agents and buses. Buses to Sarawak tend to run either in the morning or late at night.

**Destinations:** Kuching (several daily; 10hr); Putussibau (1 daily; 20hr); Sintang (1 daily; 12hr).

**By ferry** There are lots of agents on jalans Gajah Mada and Diponegoro who can organize tickets for the express boats to Jakarta and Surabaya; PT Indo Pacific Jasaprataura at Jl Gajah Mada 2a is one of the better ones. For Pelni ferries, you can buy tickets at their office at Jl Sultan Abdur Rahman 12 (Mon–Thurs 8.30am–3pm, Fri & Sat 8.30am–noon; ☎0561/748124). The place may look closed but the ticket office is round to the right-hand side on the ground floor.

**Destinations:** Jakarta (weekly; 36hr); Semarang (fortnightly; 38hr); Surubaya (fortnightly; 42hr); Tanjung Priok (fortnightly; 38hr).

**By air** To get to the airport, take a *taksi* from the Kapuas Indah terminal (Rp15,000) or catch a cab (Rp70,000).

**Destinations:** Balikpapan (several daily) via Jakarta with Batavia, Lion, Garuda, Adam Air (3hr with transit); Jakarta (several daily with Merpati, Garuda, Batavia and Adam Air; 1hr 15min); Ketapang (Kalstar; 1 daily; 30min); Kuching (Batavia air; 4 weekly; 45min).

## BALIKPAPAN

Built around a huge petroleum complex, **BALIKPAPAN** is Kalimantan's wealthiest city, its 500,000 residents enjoying a high standard of living thanks to massive oil reserves offshore. Although there's nothing much to see here, Balikpapan is one of the most likely places you'll end up in if you want to explore Kalimantan's eastern and central areas. The intersection of the main roads Jalan Ahmed Yani and Jalan Sudirman serves as the city's core, where you'll find hotels, restaurants and the best shops but, as almost everything is imported from Java or Sumatra, prices are generally much higher here than in the rest of Kalimantan.

### Arrival and information

**By bus** Buses arrive at Terminal Batu Ampar, 6km north from the centre. Take blue *taksi* #3 (Rp2500) to get into town.

**By boat** Boats from Java, Sumatra and Sulawesi berth at the Pelni docks, 2.5km west of the centre on Jl Sudirman. *Taksis* #3 and #6 both go here.

## AT HOME WITH THE ORANG-UTANS

Over the past few decades, Indonesia has lost about eighty percent of its original forest habitat. Illegal logging is still the number one culprit and visitors to Kalimantan will hear the gurgling chainsaws, and see the evidence of their mighty wrath, with sparse patches of forest dotted along the riverbanks. But expanding palm oil plantations are a huge problem as well. This means the loss of the natural habitat of one of the world's most beautiful creatures, the **orang-utan**. Kalimantan is one of the few areas that still has orang-utans roaming free. **Gunung Palung National Park**, in West Kalimantan, and **Kutai National Park**, in East Kalimantan, are a couple of areas where tourists have a chance of seeing them in the wild. Time, effort, cash and determination are definitely required, but it's well worth it.

### Gunung Palung National Park

Previously only an area for research, this national park is now open to the public, and is thought to be home to a couple of thousand wild orang-utans. If you do wish to visit here independently, be armed with patience and plenty of Bahasa. A permit must be obtained (call or fax a week in advance) from Unit Taman Nasional Gunung Palung, Jl Kh. Wahid Hasyim 41 A, Ketapang (Ⓣ0534/33539, Ⓕ0534/32720). **From Pontianak**, take a speedboat to Ketapang (7am; 6hr; Rp140,000). Visit the park office to collect your permit (Rp30,000) and meet your compulsory guide (Rp200,000 per day). From here it's a two-hour bus ride, followed by a five-hour hike to the research centre, Cabang Panti. Harvard University has an established research site here and sometimes offers accommodation. Call ahead to check (Harvard University, Jl Parit Haji Husin 1, Gang Cakra 31, Pontianak; Ⓣ0561/710118). A **guided tour** is a good option – speak to the tourist office in Pontianak about the best tours, or Mr Alex Afdhal (Ⓣ0561/7004449 or 0812/5768066, Ⓔalexafdhal@yahoo.com) offers a five-day tour including jungle trek for $370, including all food, transport and accommodation.

### Kutai National Park

East Kalimantan suffered from prolific logging back in the 1970s, and the 3000-square-kilometre Kutai National Park was established in 1982 to try and prevent further decline, but fires then destroyed sixty percent of the protected area. Nowadays the forest is recovering and is reasonably accessible. **From Samarinda** head to Bontang by bus (3hr 30min; Rp30,000). The bus station is 3km from the centre, but there will be *taksis* to take you into town or to the park. First you need to register at the park headquarters (Balai Taman Nasional Kutai; Mon–Thurs 7.30am–4pm, Fri 8–11am; Ⓣ0548/27218); again bring copies of your passport. Hire a guide from park headquarters (Rp100,000 per day, plus costs). Boats can be chartered to get round the park; expect to pay about Rp250,000. There is basic accommodation (❷), which park headquarters can help you with. In Bontang there is *Hotel Equator*, Jl Komp Pupuk Kaltim (Ⓣ0548/21506; ❹) and *Hotel Kartika*, Jl Yani 37 (Ⓣ0548/21012; ❸).

**By air** Sepinggan Airport is 8km east of the city (15min by taxi, Rp35,000), or green #7 *taksi* takes you to the Damai terminal, then the blue #5 or #6 bus into town (Rp2500).

**Tourist information** Jl Marsma R Iswahyudi 121 Ⓣ0542/761111, Ⓔparawisata@balikpapan.go.id (Mon–Thurs 8am–5pm). Located 5km out of town, take blue *taksi* #6 out to the bus terminal, then green *taksi* #7 towards the airport. Ask the driver to drop you at the Kantor Parawisata. Staff speak very little English and most of the literature is in Bahasa.

**Guides** For more concise information on tours in East Kalimantan, as well as across Borneo, Kiswono (Ⓣ0542/7204517, Ⓔtour@indosat.net.id) is a great English-speaking guide and a mine of information. He runs several tours ranging from short day-trips to three-week jungle treks crossing from East to West Kalimantan. Day-trips from Rp300,000; three-week jungle treks from Rp25,000,000.

## Accommodation

Accommodation is mainly clustered into two groups: at the central intersection of JlA Yani and Jl Sudirman; and a few km north up Jl A Yani. Decent budget accommodation is hard to find.

**Hotel Aida** Jl A Yani 12 ⓣ0542/421006. At the north end of Jl A Yani this sprawling place has clean, decent-sized rooms. ❷–❹

**Hotel Buana Lestari** Jl Jend Sudirman 418 ⓣ0542/737175. Good central location and bit more upmarket, rooms are spacious and tidy. ❺

**Hotel Gajah Mada** Jl Sudirman 14 ⓣ0542/734634. By far the best value of the hotels at the main intersection. Good-sized rooms, and a really handy location. ❸–❻

**TREAT YOURSELF**

If Balikpapan's lacklustre hotels leave you crying out for a bit of R&R, head to the **Hotel Pacific** (Jl Ahmad Yani; ⓣ0542/750888). The squashy beds, ample pillows and big bathtubs will help you feel human again. Free internet and a fabulous breakfast are a bonus. From ❺

## Eating

There are some cheap warung along the coast road, at the Pelni harbour and next to the post office west on Jl Sudirman.

**Balikpapan Plaza Foodcourt** On the lower ground floor of the Balikpapan Plaza, Jl Sudirman. Great for those who struggle with Bahasa, the foodcourt has pretty pictures of the food on offer. It's cheap and serves great *gado-gado.* Rp10,000.

**Bondy** Jl A Yani. This gorgeous, tiered open-air restaurant serves great Indonesian and Western dishes at pretty decent prices. For seafood lovers you even get to pick your own fish. From Rp30,000.

**Seafood Corner** Off Jl Sudirman, nr *Gaja Madha* hotel. For a tasty treat this restaurant serves fresh seafood and Western food. Lovely location right on the waterfront, and there's a cool bar next door to end the evening with a nightcap. From Rp40,000.

**Terminal Rasa** Jl Sudirman. A massive food court near the Gelora cinema, worth a look for its huge choice and tasty Indonesian staples.

## Directory

**Airline offices** Batavia, Jl Sudirman ⓣ0542/739230; DAS, Jl Marsma R Iswahyudi ⓣ0542/764362; Garuda, at the *Adika Bahtera Hotel* on Jl Sudirman ⓣ0542/422301; Kalstar Jln Sudirman ⓣ0542/737473; Lion Air, Jl Sudirman 271 ⓣ0542/441006; Mandala, Jl Sudirman at Komplek Permai ⓣ0542/410708; Merpati, Jl Sudirman 22 ⓣ0542/424452; Silk Air, also at the *Hotel Benakutai* on Jl A Yani ⓣ0542/419555; Permai (ⓣ0542/749422).

**Banks and exchange** There are scores of ATMs, and big branches of BNI, BCA and BRI on Jl Sudirman.

**Bookshops** Gramedia, 2nd Floor, Balikpapan Plaza, is Kalimantan's best-stocked bookshop but don't expect much English reading material unless you're an oil worker or botanist.

**Hospital** Public Hospital (Rumah Sakit Umum) is halfway up Jl Yani (ⓣ0542/434181).

**Internet** There's a good Internet café beneath the main BRI building on Jl Sudirman, and Datanet, Jl Sudirman (both Rp8000/hr).

**Pharmacies** The Kimia Farma has two 24hr pharmacies with consultation services. One is on Jl Sudirman near the Terminal Rasa, the other Jl A Yani 95; and Guardian Pharmacy, ground floor, Balikpapan Plaza

**Police** Jl Wiluyo ⓣ0542/421110.

**Post** The main post office with poste restante and EMS counters is at Jl Sudirman 31.

**Telephones** The main Telkom office is up Jl Yani near the hospital but wartels are scattered all over town.

## Moving on

**By bus** Buses to and from Samarinda (several daily; 3hr) use Terminal Batu Ampar, 6km north from the centre and served by *taksi* #3 (Rp2000 into town). Tell the driver you want to go to Batu Ampar as not all travel that far out. Buses to Benjarmasin (twice daily; 15hr) leave from the bus station near the pier on Jl Monginsidi – take blue *taksi* #6 to get here.

**By boat** Several Pelni ferries run from the Pelni docks, 2.5km west of the centre on Jl Sudirman, to Sulawesi, Java and Sumatra. Tickets are available from the Pelni office (Jl Yos Sudarso 1; ⓣ0542/424171) at the harbour or from one of the many travel agents in the centre. There are also non-Pelni ferries to Surabaya and Sulawesi. The helpful Agung Sedayu agency on Jl Sudirman can assist with details for all the ferry operators.

**Destinations:** Makassar (weekly; 26hr/fortnightly; 28hr/ monthly; 30hr); Nunukan (fortnightly; 52hr);

Pantoloan (2 fortnightly; 12 or 17hr); Surabaya (5 fortnightly, 1 weekly; either 27hr, 38hr or 46hr); Tanjung Priok (fortnightly; 69hr); Tarakan (2 fortnightly; 24hr or 42hr); Tolitoli (fortnightly; 27hr).

**By air** To get to the airport, blue *taksi* #6 will take you out to the bus terminal, then green *taksi* #7 towards the airport (Rp2500 each journey; 45min total). Taxis will cost Rp35,000.

**Destinations:** Jakarta (many daily with Adam Air, Air Asia, Batavia, CityLink, Garuda, Kartika, Lion, Mandala, Sriwijaya, Wings Air; 2hr); Makassar (daily with Garuda, Merpati; 1hr 10min); Manado (daily with Batavia; 2hr 30min); Pontianak (via Jakarta, Lion Air, Garuda, Adam Air; 3hr including transit); Surabaya (many daily with Bouraq, CityLink, Garuda, Lion, Merpati, Mandala and Batavia; 1hr 25min); Tarakan (daily with Bouraq and Merpati; 2hr).

## SAMARINDA

Some 120km north of Balikpapan, the tropical port town of **SAMARINDA** is 50km upstream from the sea, where the Sungai Mahakam is 1km wide and deep enough to be navigable by ocean-going ships. It has become increasingly prosperous since large-scale logging of Kalimantan Timur's interior began in the 1970s, its western riverfront abuzz with mills. There's not much to see here; indeed, the town remains a rather sprawling smelly mess, with open sewers, and though it's a convenient place to stock up for trips heading further up the Mahakam, Tenggarong is a nicer, more relaxed place to start your journey upriver.

### Arrival and information

**By bus** Buses from the north terminate 5km northeast of the city at Terminal Bontang, from where you catch a brown *taksi* to the centre. *Taksis* use Terminal Banjarmasin on the south bank of the Mahakam; cross over the road to the pier and catch a boat directly across to Pasar Pagi (Rp1000). Larger buses from Tenggarong, Balikpapan and Kota Bangun use Terminal Sungai Kunjang, on the north side of the river and 5km west of the centre – take a green *taksi* into town.

**By boat** The Mahakam river ferries use the Sungai Kunjang docks (green *taksi* into town). All ocean-going vessels use the docks east of the centre along Jl Sudarso.

**By air** The airport is 2km north of the centre – a taxi into town will cost Rp10,000, or an ojek Rp3000.

**Tourist information** The Dinas Pariwisata, or provincial tourist office, is on the corner of Jl Awang Long and Jl Sudirman. They stock a few maps of the town and some literature on East Kalimantan, but mainly written in Bahasa.

**Guides** You'll need to find a guide in Samarinda if you're heading further upstream than Long Bagun on the Mahakam. The best are accredited by the Dinas Pariwisata, so ask there or try at *Hotel Pirus* or the *Hotel Hidayah*. Prices vary enormously, so check the details of what you're paying for; expect to pay between Rp100,000 and Rp150,000 per day just for a guide. Alternatively, contact Kiswono in Balikpapan; he's well connected and may have some suggestions (see p.374).

### Accommodation

As you're only likely to stop here for a night or two before heading up the Sungai Mahakam, you're better off staying near the centre, within easy reach of all Samarinda's services. Unfortunately, there's little decent budget accommodation in town.

**Hidayah 2** Jl KH Khalid 25 ⓣ0541/741712. The eighteen decent fan rooms are fine for a night or two. They can also help organize river trips. ❸–❹

**Hotel Latansa** Jl Sudirman ⓣ0541/746312. Some cheap rooms but they're pretty shabby. ❷

**Hotel Pirus** Jl Pirus 30 ⓣ0541/741873. A better-value choice with good-sized rooms with showers, a/c and TVs, and friendly staff. ❸–❹

### Eating

There's a bounty of cheap warung around Jl Awang Long and the Mesra Indah store.

**The Hadayani** Jl Abul Hasan, just north of the Mesra Indah store. It can't decide whether it's a florist or a restaurant, but they have a big enough menu (and one with pictures for the tourists) and serve delicious *gado-gado* and *mie goreng*.

**Lezat Baru Chinese Restaurant** Jl Mulawarman, near the Ramayana shopping mall. An unpretentious place serving simple rice dishes – fans of the big prawn won't go hungry. Mains from Rp10,000.

**The Tepian** Jl Awang Long, near the *Pirus h*otel. A large seafood restaurant, favoured by locals, it serves scores of fish and dishes including Samarinda's giant river prawn. Mains from Rp15,0000.

## Directory

**Airline offices** Bouraq, Jl Mulawarman 24 ☎0541/732532; DAS, Jl Gatot Subroto 92 ☎0541/735250; KAL Star, Jl Gatot Subroto ☎0541/742110; MAF, Jl Rahuia Rahaya, northwest of the airport off Jl Let Jend Parman ☎0541/43628; Merpati, Jl Sudirman 23; Star Air in *Hotel MJ*, Jl KH Khalid 1 ☎0541/410337;
**Banks and exchange** The BCA on Jl Sudirman has fair rates. ATMs are everywhere.
**Internet** Kaltimnet on the ground floor of the *MJ Hotel* is open 24 hr (Rp10,500/hr). There's also Cybercafe in the Mesra Indah mall.
**Pharmacies** Rumah Sakit Bhakti Nugraha on Jl Basuki Rachmat ☎0541/741363.
**Police** Jl Bhayangkara, ☎0541/741340.
**Post office** Corner of Jl Gajah Mada and Jl Awang Long, near the tourist office.
**Telephones** There are wartels all over town; the Wartel Palapa Sakti, Jl Dermaga, has good rates, and doubles up as a money changer.
**Travel agents** Mesra Tours, Jl KH Khalid 1, *Hotel Mesra* (☎0541/738787) can provide information on further tours around East Kalimantan. Duta Miramar, Jl Sudirman 20 (☎0541/743385), Travel Waperisama ☎0541/743124 can arrange domestic flights.

## Moving on

**By bus** Buses to the north depart from Terminal Bontang – to get here, take a brown *taksi* from J Bhayangkara. *Taksis* (minibuses) to Tenggarong (1hr–1hr 30min) use Terminal Banjarmasin on the south bank of the Mahakam. However, larger buses to Tenggarong and Kota Bangun (3hr), further up the Mahakam, use Terminal Sungai Kunjang, on the north side of the river and 5km west of the centre. There are regular departures until mid-afternoon. Buses from Balikpapan (Rp25,000) also pull into Terminal Sungai Kunjang. Green "A" *taksis* run between here and Jl Gajah Mada, outside Pasar Pagi (Rp2000).
**Destinations:** Balikpapan (several daily; 2hr 30min); Kota Bangun (several daily; 3hr); Tenggarong (several daily; 1hr 30min).
**By boat** The Mahakam river ferries use the Sungai Kunjang docks (green *taksi* from town). All ocean-going vessels use the docks east of the centre along Jl Sudarso: Pelni runs twice monthly from here to Surabaya via Sulawesi. You can get tickets at their office at Jl Yos Sudarso 76 (☎0541/741402).
**Destinations:** Kota Bangun (morning only; 10hr); Long Bagun (seasonally – depending on water level; 2 daily, 40hr–4 days); Long Iram (1–2 daily;

### ALONG THE SUNGAI MAHAKAM

Borneo's second-longest river, the **Mahakam**, winds southeast for over 900km from its source far inside the central ranges on the Malaysian border, before emptying into the Makassar Straits through a multi-channelled delta.

There's an established three-day circuit taking in the historic town of **Tenggarong** and the Benuaq Dayak settlements at **Tanjung Issuy** and adjacent **Mancong**. With a week to spare, scanty forest and less cosmetic communities inland from the Middle Mahakam townships of **Melak** and **Long Iram** are within range; ten days is enough to include a host of Kenyah and Benuaq villages, venturing up the changing Mahakam through the rapids towards **Long Iram** and **Long Bagun**.

Whatever your plans, bring as little as possible with you. A change of clothes, wet-weather gear, decent footwear, a torch and first-aid kit are adequate for the Lower and Middle Mahakam, as there are accommodation and stores along the way. After Tenggarong, there are **no banks** on the Mahakam capable of changing money. **Guides** are essential beyond Long Bagun if you can't speak the language. Balikpapan or Samarinda are good places to hire a guide, though there are a few opportunities to pick one up along the way.

Crowded, basic **public ferries** are the cheapest way to tackle the Lower and Middle reaches of the Mahakam. If you plan to disembark before the boat's ultimate destination, make sure that the pilot, not the ticket collector, knows.

Ferries leave Samarinda's **Terminal Sungai Kunjang** every morning for towns as far upstream as Long Iram. Unless you're a real boat enthusiast, take a bus to **Kota Bangun**, and hire a *ces* (a motorized one-person wide canoe) to start your journey from there. It's possible to go as far as Muara Muntai in one of the motorized boats, stay overnight there, then continue on in the morning.

30hr); Melak (daily; 24hr); Muara Muntai (daily; 14hr); Surabaya (fortnightly; 3 days); Tenggarong (daily; 3hr).

**By air** To reach the airport, which is 2km out of town, take a taxi (Rp35,000) or an ojek (Rp3000). **Destinations:** DAS: Berau, Datadawai, Long Apung, Tanjung Selor (several weekly); KAL Star: Tarakan, Nunukan, Berau (2 daily).

INDONESIA KALIMANTAN

# TENGGARONG

On from Samarinda, the river is broad and slow, with sawmills and villages peppering the banks. **TENGGARONG** is 45km and three hours upstream – or just an hour by road. This small, neat and very prosperous country town was, until 1959, the seat of the Kutai Sultanate, whose territory encompassed the entire Mahakam basin and adjacent coastline. It's a good place to stay if you want to escape big cities, and a convenient location to start trips up the Mahakam (see box, p.377).

## What to see and do

The former palace, just opposite the **ferry dock** on Jalan Diponegoro, is now **Museum Negeri Mulawarman** (Tues–Sun 9am–2pm; Rp2500), and includes statuary from Mahakam's Hindu period (pre-fifteenth century), and replicas of fourth-century conical stone ***yupa***, which are Indonesia's oldest written records. Dayak pieces include Benuaq weaving, Kenyah beadwork and Bahau *hudoq* masks. It's worth visiting the Kalimantan theme park on nearby **Pulau Kumara** (daily 9am–5pm; ferry Rp3000; entrance fee Rp10,000). Although it's all rather Disney-esque, the longhouse and temple reconstructions provide an interesting insight into Kalimantan life, while a ride on Indonesia's only **Alpine ski lift** gives great views over the river and town.

## Arrival and information

**By bus** The bus terminal is 5km south of town, beyond the huge road bridge. *Taksis* run between here and the town for Rp2000.

**By boat** Boats arrive at their pier on the southern end of Jl Sudirman.

**Tourist information** The tourist information centre is at the back of the marketplace on Jl Dioponegoro ⓣ0541/61042.

**Guides** Rio at the *Hotel Anda Dua* speaks excellent English and is a good contact for finding a local guide.

## Accommodation

Tenggarong is a cheaper, more relaxed and quieter place to stay than Samarinda.

**Hotel Anda Dua** Near the canal at Jl Sudirman 129 ⓣ0541/661409. Welcoming and has decent rooms. English-speaking owner Rio can provide tour information and advice on how to get further up river. ❷

**Hotel Fatma** Jl KH Ahmed Muksin 39 ⓣ0541/661356. Has good *ekonomi* rooms and a balcony overlooking the river. ❷

**Hotel Karya Tapin** Jl Maduningrat ⓣ0541/661258. Another good option set a couple of streets back from the Mahakam; rooms are basic but clean and have en-suite showers. ❹

## Eating

Cheap, tasty and popular these warungs are dotted along Jl Cut Nya Din and do a selection of freshly cooked food (Rp5000).

**Sate Madura Pamekasan** Next to the canal. Heaven for *sate* lovers – you can choose from chicken, goat and liver. It's also one of the few places that serves beer.

**Tepian Pandam** Opposite the museum. Highly recommended, with a great location right on the river and offering excellent Chinese food; fresh grilled prawns are a speciality (from Rp10,000).

## Directory

**Banks and exchange** There's an ATM at the Lippobank on Jl Sudirman, north of the docks.

**Post office** Jl Ahmed Yani (Mon–Sat 7.30am–9.30pm, Sun 8am–2pm).

**Travel agents** Rio at *Hotel Anda Dua* can offer advice on tours. PT Duta Miramar, Jln Kartini can help with domestic flight bookings.

## Moving on

**By bus** Minibuses to Samarinda run fairly often (Rp8000), but if you're going straight on to

Balikpapan by bus, ask them to drop you off at the junction with the main Balikpapan road in Loa Janan, just before you get to Samarinda; buses are rarely full so will stop if you flag them down. For buses to Kota Bangun (Rp15,000; every 30min 7am–5.30pm; 2hr), you'll need to wait by the junction beyond the bus terminal – check at the terminal first.

**Destinations:** Balikpapan (several daily, 3hr 30min): Kota Bangun (several daily, until 5pm; 2hr); Samarinda (several daily; 1hr).

**By boat** Daily passenger boats travelling from Samarinda cruise through Tenggarong, Kota Bangun (morning, before 7am); Long Bagun (seasonally, depending on water level; 8hr): Long Iram (1–2 daily; 28hr); Melak (daily; 22hr): Muara Muntai (daily; 12hr); Samarinda (daily; 1 hr); Surabaya (fortnightly; 3 days); .

## KOTA BANGUN

The river narrows perceptibly as it continues to **KOTA BANGUN**, a small town, three hours from Samarinda by bus. A single short stretch of tarmac marks the centre of the town's commercial area. Market stalls and warung line the street either side of the main pier. There are plenty of opportunities to charter private boats from the town to explore villages upstream. Expect to pay around Rp300,000 for a trip up to Muara Muntai.

Aside from coming here to head up the Mahakam, there isn't any reason to visit Kota Bangun. It's essential to arrive by 3pm so you'll reach the river villages before dark.

### Arrival and information

**By bus** Buses arrive at the road junction just up from the pier.

**By boat** All the river ferries stop at the one pier.

**Tours** Local boatmen hang around the river just off the main road, they can act as a guide for a couple of hours to get you up the Mahakam river.

### Accommodation

**Losmen Muzirat** Jl Mesjid Raya t081/2553 2287. If you do get stuck in town, the only option is to stay at the losmen, which offers basic, spartan rooms with shared mandis. ❶

### Eating

There are a couple of warungs dotted along the main (and only) road in town; the best one is back towards the main junction where the bus first turns into town, which serves simple *mie/nasi goreng* dishes for Rp4000.

### Moving on

**By bus** There are eight buses a day to and from Samarinda (3 hr).

**By boat** Motorized canoes (*ces*) can be chartered to head further up the Mahakam: Muara Muntai (2hr; Rp300,000); Tanjung Issuy (3–6 hr, depending on water level, Rp400,000).

## MUARA MUNTAI

Beyond Kota Bangun, there's a definite thickening of the forest along the banks as the river enters the marshy lakelands. Sadly, even here the jungle isn't as lush as it used to be and the effects of years of logging is evident. Around four hours from Kota Bangun, and fourteen from Samarinda, is the 8km boardwalk stilt village of **MUARA MUNTAI**. A massive fire here in July 2004 destroyed over 250 homes, but it has now been completely restored and is back to the wooden village it once was, complete with losmen, convenience stores and even its own hospital. Muara Muntai is the last place along the Mahakam to buy any supplies, though prices are often more expensive than in Samarinda.

### Arrival

**By boat** House boat or chartering a *ces* is the only option to reach Muara Muntai (2hr from Kota Bangun).

### Accommodation

**Penginapan Adi Guna** Walk up the jetty and turn right; this losmen is above where the big "photocopying" sign is. Rooms are basic, but serve the purpose. Also serves simple dishes of *mie* or *nasi goreng*. ❶

## TANJUNG ISSUY

**Tanjung Issuy** is the first Dayak village on the Mahakam and a boat ride away from Muara Muntai (chartered *ces* Rp200,000; 1–3 hr depending on water level). The river ride takes you further into the jungle, passing hornbills, sweeping kingfishers and pot-bellied proboscis monkeys along the way. Tanjung Issuy is a small township of gravel lanes, timber houses and fruit trees. Turn right off the jetty, past a couple of lumber yards, stores and workshops, and follow the street around to **Losmen Louu Taman Jamrud**, a restored Dayak longhouse which is maintained as tourist accommodation (❶). It's a bit like staying in a longhouse in a museum, but the place is surrounded by carved wooden patong posts (spirit posts) and does give you a sense of the community. Out the back is a six-tier mausoleum where Tanjung Issuy's founder was laid to rest in 1984, decorated with carvings of dragons, hornbills and scenes from reburial ceremonies. Moving on from Tanjung Issuy, you can either return to Muara Muntai, or hire a *ces* to take you across the northwest towards Mancong (Rp200,000).

## TARAKAN

A twenty-four-kilometre spread of low hills just off the coast north-east of Tanjung Selor, Pulau Tarakan floats above extensive oil reserves: offshore rigs dot the horizon, while the west-coast town of **TARAKAN** is surrounded by smaller-scale "nodding donkey" pumps. Though it's a surprisingly brisk, busy place, just a stone's throw from **Pulau Nunukan** and the open **border with Malaysia**, Tarakan is very much a transit town with little to do.

### Arrival and information

**By boat** The port is 2km south of the town centre, which can be reached by *taksi* (Rp3000).
**By air** The airport is 2km north of town, Rp35,000 by taxi.

### Accommodation

There are numerous places to stay, mostly east down Jl Sudirman within 150m of the centre.
**Barito** Jl Sudirman 133 ☎0551/21181. Has tidy rooms and although slightly more expensive the rate includes free breakfast. ❸
**Hotel Taufiq** Jl Yos Sudarso ☎ 0551/21347. Good budget option in the centre of town, rooms are clean and spotless. ❷–❸
**Tarakan Plaza** Jl Yos Sudarso 1 ☎0551/21870. More expensive again, but rooms are comfortable and provide a good rest stop. Some staff speak English and the hotel has a bar. ❺

### Eating

Warungs are dotted along Jl Yos Sudarso.
**Rumah Makan Cahaya** Jl Sudirman. A popular Chinese restaurant, serving large portions of seafood and the usual *nasi goreng*.

### Directory

**Airlines** Bouraq, 8 Jl Yos Sudarso (☎0551/21248); DAS, 9 Jl Sudirma (☎0551/51578); Garuda, 33 Jl Sebengkok (☎0551/21130); Merpati, 8 Jl Yos Sudarso (☎0551/21875).
**Banks and exchange** The BNI bank just south of the intersection and across from the police station on Jl Sudarso has good exchange rates and ATMs.
**Pharmacies** Tarakan Plaza, Jl Sudirman.
**Post office** Jl Yos Sudarso (Mon–Sat 7.30am–9.30pm, Sun 8am–2pm).
**Travel agents** Wisma Murni Travel (☎0551/21697) at the *Hotel Wisata* can book boats as well as flights to Nunukan and Samarinda. PT Angkasa Express (☎0551/51789) can also book tickets for air and boat.

### Moving on

**By boat** Ferries to and from Berau and Nunukan use the Tengkayu jetty while Mulundung harbour, 500m further down, is served by Pelni's ferries to Balikpapan, Nunukan, Sulawesi and Java. The Pelni office is here too.
**Destinations:** Balikpapan (2 fortnightly; 24hr or 48hr); Berau (3 weekly; 10hr); Makassar (2 fortnightly; 38hr or 60hr); Nunukan (4 daily; 6–12hr); Tanjung Selor (14 daily; 1–2hr); Tewau, Malaysia (Indomaya Expres, daily except Sun; 3hr); Tolitoli (fortnightly; 24hr).

### INTO MALAYSIA: TAWAU

The border crossing into Malaysia lies between **Tarakan** and the Malaysian town of **Tawau** in Sabah (see p.602). It's open every day except Sunday. From Tarakan, the *Indomaya Express* fast ferry departs for Tawau from Mulundung harbour daily (except Sun) at 7.30am (3hr; Rp150,000), leaving for the return journey at 11am.

**By air** There are regular flights to Balikpapan with Kartika, Mandala, Batavia. DAS flies to Berau, Long Bawan, Nunukan, Tanjung Selor Nunukan. Speak to a local travel agent for current schedules.

# Sulawesi

**Sulawesi** sprawls in the centre of the Indonesian archipelago, a bizarre outline resembling a one-thousand-kilometre letter "K", and one of the country's most compelling regions. Nowhere in Sulawesi is much more than 100km from the sea, though an almost complete covering of mountains not only isolates its four separate peninsulas from one another, but also traditionally made them difficult to penetrate individually. Invaders were hard pushed to colonize beyond the coast and, despite echoes of external forces, a unique blend of cultures and habitats has developed. The south is split between the highland **Torajans** and the lowland **Bugis**, there are various isolated tribes in the central highlands, and the Filipino-descended **Minahasans** are in the far north.

The most settled part of the island, the south, is home to most of Sulawesi's fifteen million inhabitants, and the energetic capital, the port of **Makassar**. Rich in history, the southern plains rise to the mountain vastness of **Tanah Toraja**, whose beautiful scenery and unusual architecture and festivals are the island's chief tourist attraction. Those after a more languid experience can soak up sun and scenery on the **Togian Islands**, and there's fabulous diving at **Pulau Bunaken**, out from the northern city of **Manado**. In many areas, Sulawesi's roads are well covered by **public transport**, though freelance Kijang (pick-up trucks) and minibuses are often faster and better value than scheduled buses. Where these fail you'll find ferries, even if services are unreliable.

## MAKASSAR

At Sulawesi's southwestern corner and facing Java and Kalimantan, **MAKASSAR** (also known as Ujung Pandang) is a large, hot and crowded port city with good transport links between eastern and western Indonesia, and several attractions. More than anything, Makassar offers an introduction to Sulawesi's largest ethnic group, the **Bugis**, who continue

### TROUBLE IN SULAWESI

Between 1998 and 2001, violent unrest and bloody fighting between Christians and Muslims in and around the town of **Poso** claimed over two thousand lives. A peace deal signed in 2001 helped to bring some sort of peace to the region, though sporadic attacks – including bombings and beheadings – since then have insured tensions still occasionally boil over. Although people have been travelling through the area for the past couple of years, the situation is still far from stable. If you insist on travelling through Poso, make sure you check the local situation first: contact your foreign office for up-to-date advice and try to find out if any other travellers have made the trip recently.

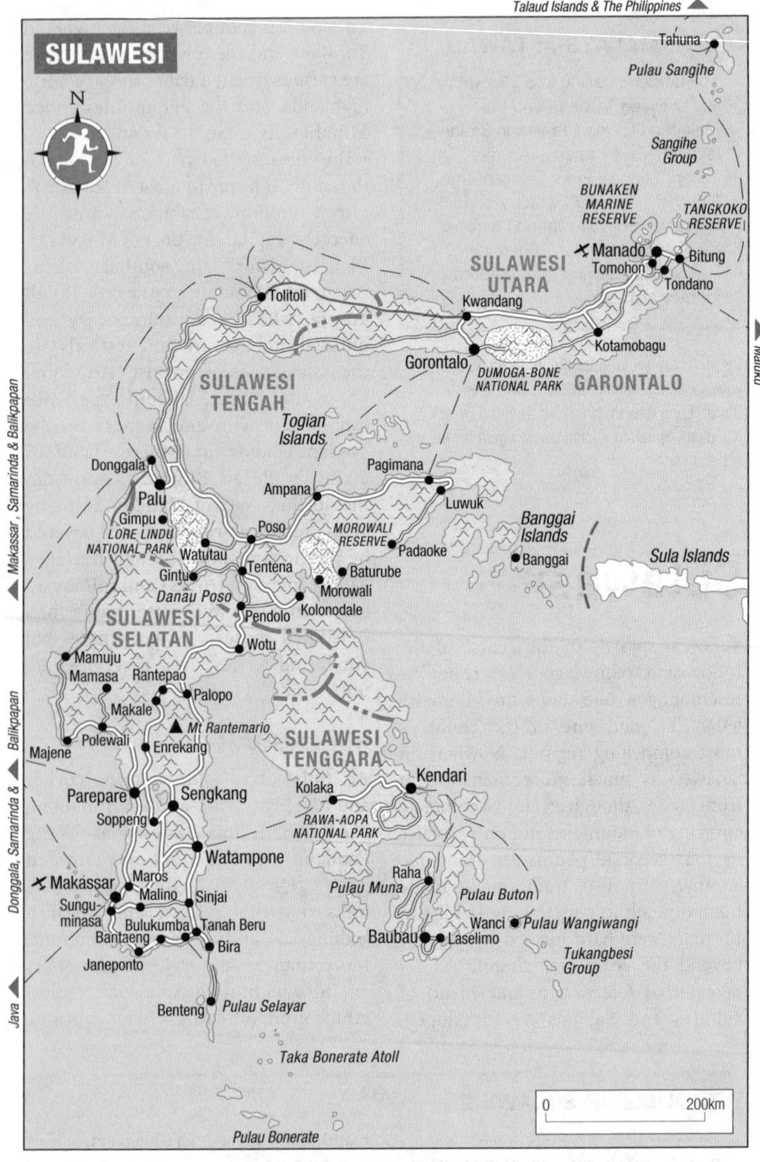


to export their goods and presence well beyond Sulawesi in *prahu*, distinctive vessels with steep, upcurved prows. The city has a long and distinguished history as a crucial trading port and coastal defence.

## What to see and do

A monument to Sulawesi's colonial era, **Fort Rotterdam** on Jalan Ujung Pandang (daily 7.30am–6pm; free – ignore the guard asking for "donations";

La Galigo museum same times, Rp1700) was established as a defensive position in 1545 and enlarged a century later when the Dutch commander Cornelius Speelman rechristened it in memory of his home town. The fort's high, thick walls are its most impressive feature and worth climbing to get a look at the tall, white buildings inside. On the northwest side, Speelman's House is the oldest surviving building, and nestles next to one half of La Galigo Museum, whose most interesting item is a prehistoric megalith from Watampone.

The **Museum Kota Makassar** (Tues–Thurs 8am–2pm, Fri 8–11am, Sat & Sun 9am–2pm; free), on Jalan Balaikota, one block east of the post office, gives a run-through of the city's history with a number of mildly diverting old photos, maps and official documents. Northwest from here, and bordered by north-oriented Jalan Nusantara and Jalan Irian, the **Chinese quarter** is worth a look for its half-dozen brightly coloured temples, which cluster along the lower reaches of Jalan Sulawesi.

**Pasar Sentral** (Central Market) was once the city's main shopping district, and although the mega malls now steal much of its custom, it remains a thriving place, and is also the main terminal for pete-petes. From here you can catch a pete-pete 3km north up Jalan Sudarso to where Bugis *prahu* from all over Indonesia unload and embark cargo at **Paotere harbour** (Rp1000 admission). Though the smell and lack of sanitation can be a bit much on a hot day, it's quite a spectacle when the harbour is crowded, the red, white and green *prahu* lined up along the dock.

## Arrival

**By air** Hasanuddin Airport is 25km northeast of the city. A taxi to the town centre takes 40min (fixed fare Rp70,000, pay at the booth on the left of the exit hall). You can also take a pete-pete (bemo; Rp2000) to Terminal Daya and a second one from there to the centre of town.

**By bus** Buses from Rantepao and the north pull into the huge Terminal Daya (also called Terminal Panaikang) 16km to the east on the way to the airport, from where you can catch a metered taxi (around Rp30,000) or pete-pete (Rp2000) into the centre. Most south-coast buses arrive at Terminal Tamalate on Jl Gowa Raya (an extension of Jl Sudirman), 5km south of the centre, but some use Terminal Mallengkeri, also on Jl Gowa Raya, or Sungguminasa, 10km southeast of Makassar. There's no shortage of pete-petes for the brief trip into town (Rp2000).

**By ferry** The Pelni harbour is less than 1km northwest of the Pasar Sentral on Jl Nusantara, served by becaks and taxis. Other boats dock at Paotere harbour, 3km north of the centre; becaks will take you into town for around Rp6000.

## City transport

**Pete-petes/bemos** Bemos (called pete-petes here), charge Rp2000, and most terminate at or near Pasar Sentral. They are colour coded for different destinations and have their routes written on the windscreen. The most common and most useful are those out to Panakkukang (from where you can get out to Terminal Daya) and Tamalate.

**Becak** Makassar's becak drivers are annoyingly persistent and often ignorant of your destination; a fare of Rp2000 per km is reasonable, more if it's raining.

## Accommodation

There are very few cheap places to stay in Makassar, but mid-range hotels (Rp100,000–160,000 for a double) are decent value.

**Asoka** Jl Latumahina 21/38 ⓣ0411/873476. Four gorgeous rooms and one suite in a huge house just around the corner from the *Imperial Aryaduta Hotel*. ❺

**Hotel Bali** Jl Sungai Pareman III 15–17 ⓣ0411/320071. Sparkling clean and friendly, this is a good-value hotel down a small gang in a busy quarter of Makassar. ❸

**New Legend** Jl Jampea 5g ⓣ0411/313777, ⓦwww.newlegendhostel.com. The city's backpacker favourite, now all done up and renovated but still friendly, well located and with good value a/c rooms and a small dorm (Rp45,000). Best value in the city. ❷–❸

**Wisma Mulia** Jl Sungai Pareman III 1 ⓣ0411/3650967. New, a/c place down a small gang, reasonably priced though the standard rooms lack windows; useful, however, if the *Hotel Bali*, 50m up the road, is full. ❸–❹

**TREAT YOURSELF**

Even if you can't afford to stay for the night, an excellent shelter from the weather and the hurly burly outside is provided by the **Hotel Pantai Gapura**, Jl Pasar Ikan 10 (☎0411/350222, ⓦwww.pantaigapura.com). It's a real away-from-it-all kind of place, with beautiful wooden bungalows on stilts over the sea and a smart reception area where you can sit and take tea. The VIP suite has two bedrooms, gazebo, terrace, Jacuzzi, dining room, kitchen, lounge and its own security staff. Check the website for special offers. ⑦–⑨

## Eating and drinking

For a taste of local colour head down the coast road past the *Imperial Aryaduta Hotel* towards the huge ornate gatehouses that mark the start of Jl Metro to the **Tanjung Bunga food stalls.** Along the parade for about 1km are dozens of bars, cafés and warung selling a mouthwatering variety of cheap snacks and drinks.

**Mam's** Jl Layaligo 31A, just off Jl Sudirman. This mid-price "cakery" is great for mid-morning iced coffee or afternoon tea, and serves exquisite Black Forest gateaux and some quintessentially European dishes from chicken in a basket to spaghetti.

**Nelayan** Jl Ali Malaka 25. A busy but brilliant fish restaurant combining Manado and Makassar cooking styles. Choosing which fish to have from the icebox outside is infinitely easier than selecting from the vast array of sauces and extras that immediately fill your entire table.

**Patene** Jl Sulawesi 48. In the centre of the Chinese quarter, this restaurant is open all day, and despite its shabby appearance offers excellent (and inexpensive) noodles, soups and fish.

**Sentosa** Jl Penghibur 26. The number one Bakso restaurant in Makassar is a must. Rice comes wrapped in banana leaves (*burasa*) and they're famous for their *es pisang ijo* (banana milk shake). Just a few metres down the road, *Bakso Kota* and *Bakso Yosda* provide similar food and stiff competition.

## Directory

**Airlines** Batavia Air, Jl A Yani 35E ☎0411/3655255; Garuda, Slamet Riyadi, just up from the post office ☎0411/43654737; Lion Air, Jl Jend A Yani No B 22–24 ☎0411/350777; Merpati, Jl Gunung Bawakaraeng 109 ☎0411/442471; Sriwijaya Air, Jl Boulevard Raya 23, Panakukang ☎0411/424800.

**Banks and exchange** Most banks have ATMs, with many located along the northern side of Medan Karebosi. BCA has the best rates for cash exchange, whilst BNI has the best for traveller's cheques. The best moneychanger in town is Haji La Tunrung, in the building by the seafront at the southern end of Jl Nusantara.

**Hospitals** Stella Maris, Jl Penghibur ☎0411/854341. Your best chance in southern Sulawesi for correct diagnosis and treatment by English-speaking staff.

**Immigration** Jl Tentara Pelajar 2 8–12 ☎0411/315439. Officials here can be obstructive, and it's not the easiest place in Indonesia to get a visa extended.

**Internet** By far the most pleasant and efficient of the many Internet places is the Surf@Cybercafe, above the *Pizza Ria* on Jl Yani (Rp6900/hr). Also good is Xpress Café by the Haji La Tunrung moneychangers.

**Police** Main office is on Jl Ahmad Yani.

**Post office** Jl Slamet Riyadi near Fort Rotterdam.

**Shopping** The huge MTC Karebosi on the northeast corner of Karebosi Square is a good place to cool off and shop for bargains.

**Telephone** International wartel booths on the western side of Medan Karebosi on Jl Kajaolaliddo, and also on Jl Bali, west of Pasar Sentral.

**Travel agents** The most efficient agent is Ante Express, Jl Dr Wahidin Sudirohusodo 34A (☎0411/318648), who are helpful and are agents for most national and international carriers; Caraka Travelindo, Jl Samalona 12 (☎0411/318877), is also reasonable, with English speakers.

## Moving on

**By bus** Buses for Tanah Toraja and many other destinations right up to Manado leave from Terminal Daya; catch a pete-pete from Pasar Sentral (Rp2000); make sure the driver knows where you're going. Some bus operators will pick you up in town if you organize your tickets through an agent.

**Destinations:** Ampana (28hr); Bira (5hr); Mamasa (15hr); Manado (2–3 days); Palu (29hr); Polewali (7hr); Rantepao (8hr); Tentena (19hr).

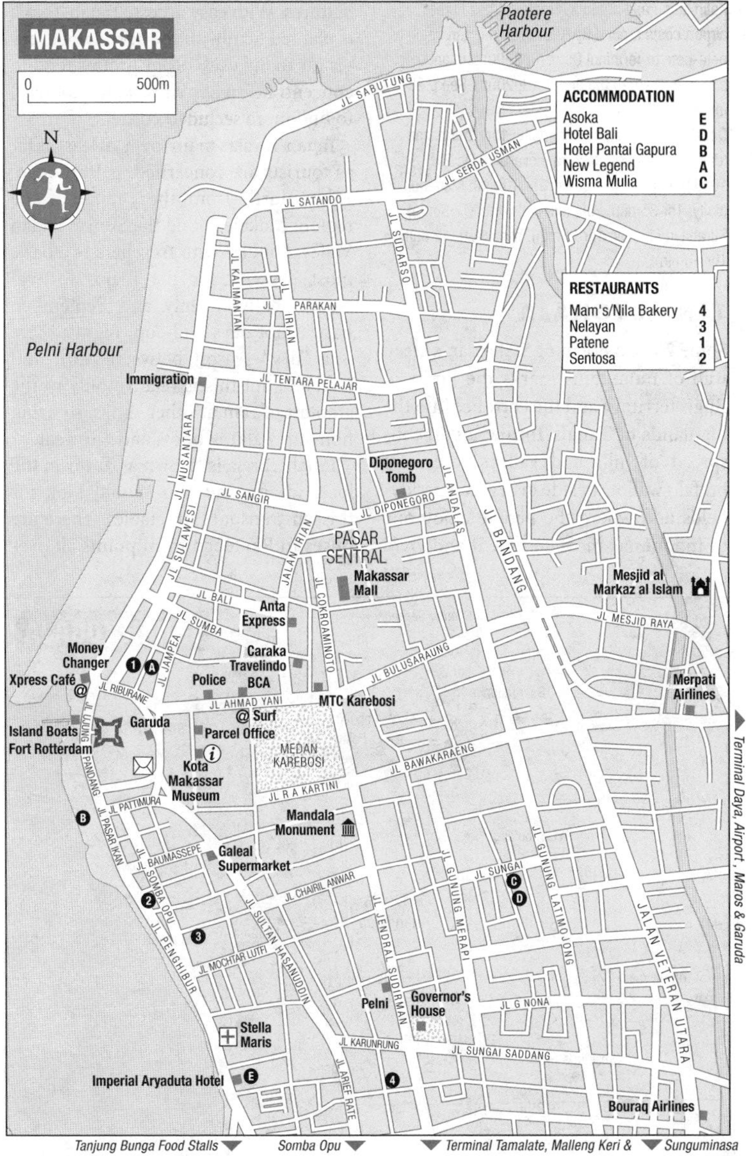


**By ferry (Pelni)** From the Pelni harbour, ferries run to ports all over Sulawesi, plus Java, Sumatra, Kalimantan, Bali and Nusa Tenggara. The Pelni office is at Jl Sudirman 38 (☎0411/331411); tickets (Mon–Fri 8am–4pm) on ground level through a side door. **Destinations:** Balikpapan (2 fortnightly; 20hr or 37hr; 1 monthly; 31hr); Bima (fortnightly; 27hr); Denpasar (2 fortnightly; 20hr or 48hr); Maumere (fortnightly; 31hr); Larantuka (fortnightly; 27hr); Nunukan (1 weekly, 72hr; 1 fortnightly, 69hr); Surabaya (5 fortnightly; 24–27hr); Tanjung Priok (3 fortnightly; 45hr, 51hr or 78hr); Tarakan (2 fortnightly; 40hr or 60hr).

**By air** Hasanuddin Airport is the busiest in eastern Indonesia, with flights to Nusa Tenggara, Java,

Kalimantan and abroad. A metered taxi to the airport costs around Rp70,000, or you can catch a pete-pete to Terminal Daya (Rp2000) and another one from there to the airport (Rp2000). See p.384 for airline offices.

**Destinations:** Balikpapan (daily; 1hr); Denpasar (daily; 1hr 20min); Jakarta (several daily; 2hr 10min); Kupang (3 weekly; 2hr 10min); Manado (daily; 1hr 35min); Palu (several weekly; 55min); Surabaya (4 daily; 1hr 25min); Yogyakarta (2 daily; 1hr 40min).

## TANAH TORAJA

Some 250km north of Makassar, a steep wall of mountains marks the limits of Bugis territory and the entrance into the highlands of **Tanah Toraja**, a gorgeous spread of hills and valleys where fat buffalo wallow beside lush green paddy-fields and where the people enjoy one of Indonesia's most confident and vivid cultures. With easy access, Tanah Toraja is planted firmly on the agenda of every visitor to Sulawesi. Tour groups tend to concentrate on key sites, so it's not hard to find more secluded corners.

Tanah Toraja's main town, at least as far as tourists are concerned, is **Rantepao**, 18km north from the capital of the region, Makale, along the Sungai Sadan Valley. Popular with travellers as a base, most descend for the major **festival season** between July and September. Expect hot days and cool nights; there is a "dry" season between April and October, but this is relative only to the amount of rain at other times, so bring non-slip walking boots and rainwear.

Tanah Toraja is known as **Tator** in the local idiom, and you should look for this on transport timetables. There are **buses** to Rantepao from points all over

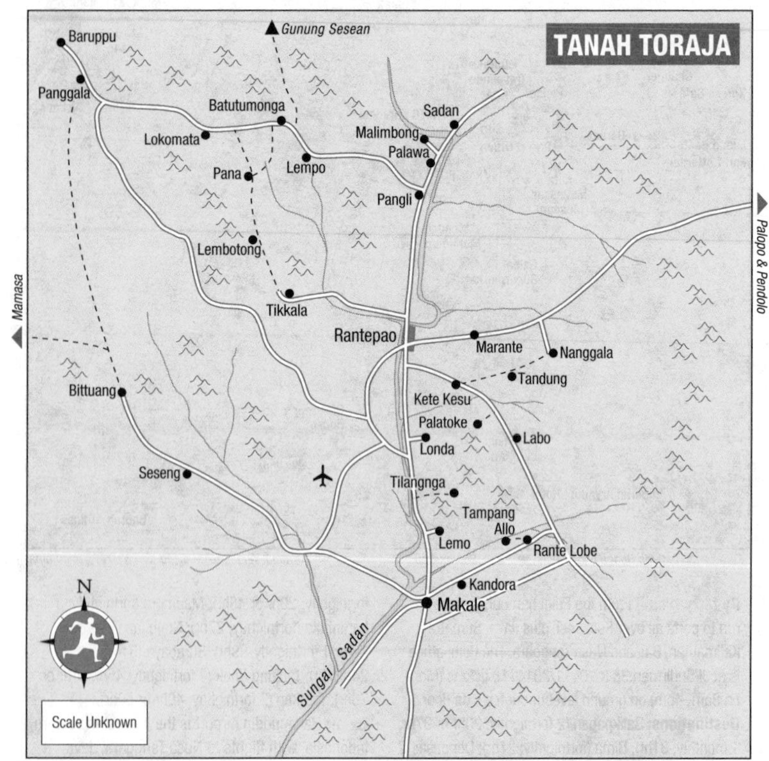

## TORAJA CULTURE AND FESTIVALS

Anthropologists place Torajan **origins** as part of the Bronze Age exodus from Vietnam; Torajans say that their ancestors descended from heaven by way of a stone staircase, which was later angrily smashed by the creator Puang Matua after his laws were broken. These laws became the root of **aluk todolo**, the way of the ancestors. Only a fraction of Torajans now follow the old religion, the strict practice of which was prohibited after headhunting and raunchy life-rites proved unacceptable to colonial and nationalist administrations. But its trappings are still an integral part of Torajan life: everywhere you'll see extraordinary **tongkonan** and **alang**, traditional houses and rice-barns, while the Torajan social calendar remains ringed with exuberant ceremonies involving pig and buffalo sacrifices. Torajans are masters at promoting their culture, positively encouraging outsiders to experience their way of life.

### Torajan festivals

Ceremonies are divided into *rambu tuka*, or smoke ascending (associated with the east and life), and *rambu solo*, smoke descending (west and death). A typical *rambu tuka* ceremony is the **dedication of a new tongkonan**.

The biggest of all Torajan ceremonies are **funerals**, the epitome of a *rambu solo* occasion. Held over several days in a special field, it starts with the parading of the oval coffin. At the end of the first afternoon you'll see **buffalo fights**. The following day – or days, if it's a big funeral – is spent welcoming guests, who troop village by village into the ceremonial field, led by a noblewoman dressed in orange and gold, bearing gifts of *balok*, pigs trussed on poles and buffalo. The next day, the **major sacrifice** takes place: the nobility must sacrifice at least 24 buffalo, with one hundred needed to see a high-ranking chieftain on his way. Horns decorated with gold braid and ribbons, the buffalo are tied one by one to a post and their throats slit, the blood caught in bamboo tubes and used in cooking. Finally, the coffin is laid to rest in a west-oriented house-grave or rockface mausoleum, with a **tau-tau**, a life-sized wooden effigy of the deceased, positioned in a nearby gallery facing outwards, and – for the highest-ranking nobles – a megalith raised in the village ground.

### Attending Torajan ceremonies

Witnessing a traditional ceremony is what draws most visitors to Tanah Toraja, particularly during the "peak festival season" in the agriculturally quiet period from June to September. Take a **gift** for your hosts – a carton of cigarettes, or a jerry can of *balok* (palm wine) – and hand it over when they invite you to sit down with them – gift-giving is an integral part of Torajan ceremonies. Do not sit down uninvited, or take photos without asking; dress modestly and wear **dark clothing** for funerals – a black T-shirt with blue jeans is perfectly acceptable, as are thong sandals. Most importantly, spend time at the ceremony, drinking coffee and *balok* with your hosts, as too many tourists just breeze in and out.

Sulawesi. From Makassar, buses leave day and night from Terminal Daya.

### Rantepao

**RANTEPAO** is a prosperous market town on the rocky banks of **Sungai Sadan**, home to both the Sadan Toraja and, for half the year, swarms of foreigners. However unfavourably you view this, Rantepao has excellent facilities and a couple of sites within walking distance. Sadly though, its popularity has yet to spur the local administration into a long-overdue cleanup – the dusty, litter-strewn streets detract from the town's gorgeous setting between the mountains, and the river seems to take the brunt of large-scale waste disposal.

Rantepao stretches for 1km along the eastern bank of the Sadan. The central **crossroads** is marked by a miniature tongkonan on a pedestal: north from here, Jalan Mappanyuki is a short run of souvenir shops, bus agents and restaurants; Jalan Ahmad Yani points south towards Makale past more of the same before becoming Jalan Pong Tiku; east is Jalan Diponegoro and the Palopo road; while westerly Jalan Landorundun heads over to the riverside along the bottom edge of a large exhibition ground.

Rantepao's main **market** – the biggest in Tanah Toraja and located 2.5km northeast of the centre at Terminal Bolu – is a must: where else could you pick up a bargain buffalo then celebrate your purchase with a litre or two of palm wine? It operates on a six-day cycle, and an entry fee of Rp10,000 is demanded of foreigners.

An easy hour's walk from Rantepao takes you across the river to the summit of **Bukit Singki** for a fine view over Rantepao. On the way you'll come across hamlets such as **Pa'bontang** marked by stately tongkonan, and at **Tambolang** a white mausoleum stands below a cliff-side niche sporting rows of tau-tau and coffins.

## Arrival

**By bus** Long-distance buses will either drop you off at your accommodation or in the vicinity of the exhibition ground or crossroads. Cars and bemos from Palopo, however, will probably terminate at Terminal Bolu, 2.5km northeast from the centre. It's an easy Rp2000 bemo ride into town from here.

## WALKS AROUND TANAH TORAJA

There's a morbid attraction to many of Tanah Toraja's sights, which feature ceremonial animal slaughter, decaying coffins and dank mausoleums spilling bones. **Entry fees** of around Rp10,000 are common at sites. If you speak a little Indonesian, **guides** are seldom necessary for hiking or visiting villages, though to visit a ceremony outsiders should really have an **invitation**, which guides can provide. As more participants means greater honour, however, it's also possible to turn up at an event and hang around the sidelines until somebody offers to act as your host.

**Bemos** to most places originate at Rantepao's Terminal Bolu, though those heading south can be hailed on Jalan Ahmad Yani. Accommodation and tour agents also rent out **motorbikes** (Rp10,000 per hour, Rp50,000 per day), or **minibus/car and drivers** (Rp300,000 per day including driver). Hikers heading off to villages should carry cigarettes, if only to initiate conversations.

Many tour agents, restaurants and hotels in Rantepao can set you up with a guide. Prices start at around Rp100,000–150,000 a day depending on how many people and your itinerary. Competition is fierce and most agents are experienced and reliable, but it's worth asking around.

### South to Makale

**Makale** is the administrative capital of Tanah Toraja. It's a small town set around a large pond and public square. Tanah Toraja's most famous sites lie off the 18km Rantepao–Makale road. Just south of Rantepao, a concrete statue of a pied buffalo marks the road east to four much-restored tongkonan at **Kete Kesu** (4km; Rp10,000). The central one is said to be the oldest in the district. An adjacent rante ground (ceremonial ground) sports a dozen megaliths, the tallest about 3m high. A path leads up the hill past hanging and no-longer-hanging coffins mortised into the side of the truncated peak.

Some of the other sights to the south of Rantepao can be combined to form a pleasant half-day's stroll – there are usually plenty of people around to ask the way. The walk begins 9km from Rantepao at the turn-off to **Lemo** (Rp3000 by car from the main crossroads in Rantepao; Rp10,000 to visit Lemo). Lemo lies 1km from

**By air** From the airport at Rantetayo you'll probably have to end up chartering a taxi (Rp100,000) or an ocek (Rp25,000–30,000) to Rantepao.

## Accommodation

Accommodation is scattered across town, with some offering excellent value for money, though a few aren't that easy to find.

**Duta 88** Jl Sawerigading 12 ⓣ0423/23477. Seven beautiful, tightly packed traditional-style bungalows in a pretty garden set around a rice barn. Good value and a brilliant location. ❷

**Hotel Indra Toraja 1** Jl Landorundun 63 T0423/21163, ⓔindrahotel63@yahoo.com. Chain hotels that maintain pretty good standards and are always busy. The *Indra Toraja I* is smart, friendly and central. *Indra Toraja II* (Jl Monginsidi) ❹

**Pia's Poppies** Jl Lorong Merpati, off Jl Pong Tiku ⓣ0423/21121. Unusual, eccentric, very welcoming and good value, this is a lovely little place with a tranquil garden and rooms with individually designed rock-pool bathrooms. Well worth the walk south out of town. ❷

**Pondok Wisata** Jl Penbangunan 23 ⓣ0423/21595. Pleasant, central, backstreet homestay, that's nothing special but fairly priced. ❸

**Wisma Irana** Jl Abdul Gani 16 ⓣ0423/21371. Lovely clean rooms in a Torajan-motifed wisma located in a quiet lane west of the main street. Rooms are clean and reasonably priced and the breakfasts are huge. ❷

## Eating and drinking

All restaurants, including Chinese and Western-style places, offer local Torajan dishes such as *Piong* (chicken, fish, pork or buffalo cooked over an open fire in bamboo shoots with coconut, herbs and spices) and *Pamarassan* (again chicken, fish, pork or buffalo cooked in black Torajan spice), though most will ask for at least two hours' notice.



the road and is famous for its much-photographed *tau-tau*, set 30m up on a flat cliff-face and mutely staring over the fields with arms outstretched. There are also several dozen square-doored mausoleums bored straight into the rock face. From the centre of Lemo a wide track continues for 2km to **Tilangnga**, home to a swimming hole in the forest (Rp10,000). Above the church at Tilangnga another path branches off towards **Londa**, about an hour's walk away. A shaded green well underneath tall cliffs, overhung with a few coffins and a fantastic collection of very lifelike tau-tau, Londa (Rp10,000) boasts two caves whose entrances are piled high with more coffins and bones, all strewn with offerings of tobacco and booze. You'll need a guides with pressure lamps (Rp15,000) to venture inside the labyrinth. From Londa it's a twenty-minute walk back to the highway and a bemo back to Rantepao (Rp2000).

### East to Nanggala

You can see almost all the main features of Tanah Toraja at **Marante**, a spread-out village 6km east from Rantepao on the Palopo road. Close to the road is a fine row of tongkonan; behind, a path leads to where tau-tau and weathered coffins face out over a river (Rp5000). **Nanggala**, about 11km along the Palopo road and then 2km south, is a stately village with a dozen brilliantly finished tongkonan; sadly, most of them have had their traditional roofs replaced with tin.

There's a very pleasant five-hour walk due west to **Kete Kesu** from here, via **Tandung** village and a couple of small lakes, and if you're lucky you may even see a flying fox or two.

### North to Sadan

For something a bit different, spend a day making the slow haul from Rantepao's bemo terminal north to **Sadan**. Seven kilometres along the way you pass **Pangli**, famed for its *balok*. Not much further, a rante ground with thirty upright stones marks the short track to **Palawa**, whose tongkonan are embellished with scores of buffalo horns stacked up their tall front posts, while in the hills beyond the village are babies' graves, wooden platforms in the trees. Five kilometres more brings you to a fork in the road: east is **Sadan** itself, with another market every six days; west is riverside **Malimbong**, famous for its *ikat*.

**Christo** Jl Landorundun. Clean and popular Chinese place, not exceptional but reasonable value and serving decent portions.

**Mambo** Jl Sam Ratulangi. A very popular place near the river, with a huge Western, Chinese and Indonesian menu (guacamole with crackers Rp15,000) and beer in frosted glasses. The food itself, however, isn't as good as at *Mart's Café*, nearby.

**Mart's Café** Jl Sam Ratulangi. A popular choice, with some great dishes from guacamole to a steak hotplate (Rp30,000). Best in town.

**Riman** Jl Andi Mappanyuki 113. Friendly enough staff, and with a few (old) secondhand books for sale, but again, the food isn't great.

**Sururan** Jl Ahmad Yani 115. Great location by the post office, this good-value Chinese restaurant offers big helpings at reasonable prices (*kwe tiau goreng* Rp14,000) served by friendly staff.

## Directory

**Banks and exchange** The BNI and Danamon banks, next to each other on Jl Diponegoro, and the BRI on Jl Ahmad Yani, all have ATMs. There is also an official moneychanger on Jl Lamdorundun with longer opening hours.

**Hospital** The best doctors are at Elim Hospital, Jl Ahmad Yani.

**Internet** Cyber Computer, just up from the Danamon bank on Jl Ahmad Yani, has a reasonably fast service (Rp6000/hr). PMC on Jl Mappanyuki is slower and more expensive (Rp10,000/hr).

**Post office** Jl Ahmad Yani 111 just south of the main crossroads.

**Telephones** The Telkom office next to the post office at Jl Ahmad Yani 113 (8am–late) stays open the longest and has the best rates for international calls.

**Travel agencies** Lebonna, Jl Sam Ratulangi (☎0423/23520) rents out motorbikes and cars and their prices are reasonable. Toraja Permai, near the Abadi supermarket at Jl Mappanyuki 10 (☎0423/21784), is useful for flight tickets and they are the main agents for DAS airlines.

## Moving on

**By bus** For Makassar, use Litha bus agent, across from the Abadi supermarket on Jl Andi Mappanyuki, who run basic, comfortable and luxury buses (daily 7.30am–9pm; 8hr). Agents along Jl Andi Mappanyuki can arrange tickets for other destinations.

**Destinations:** Makassar (8hr); Palu (21hr); Pendolo (8hr); Tentena (11hr).

**By bemo** Bemos leave Jl Ahmad Yani every few minutes for Makale, and just as often from Jl Diponegoro for Terminal Bolu.

**By air** DAS fly three times a week to Makassar, on Tues & Thurs at 1pm, Fri at 10.30am. Tickets can be bought from their agent, Toraja Permai (see above).

# AMPANA

If you're heading **to the Togian Islands from the south**, then the chances are you'll have to spend the night in the dusty and ramshackle port of **AMPANA**. You can hide away here in the excellent *Oasis Hotel,* Jl Kartini 5 (☎0464/21058; ❷–❹), boasting en-suite a/c and fan rooms and perfectly placed on the seafront near the port. If that's full, try the *Irama,* just up the road at Jl Kartini 11 (☎0464/21055; ❷), with fairly basic rooms with mandi. For **food**, the huge *Green Garden Café* at the *Oasis* has an upstairs terrace where you can watch the sunset. There's an unreliable **internet** café opposite the *Irama*, and an equally unreliable **ATM** at Bank BRI one block further west.

**For the Togian Islands, ferries** run almost daily to **Wakai** (for Kadidiri) and **Bomba**, and there are services three times a week to **Gorontalo**, the latter stopping at Wakai and other Togian islands en route.

Heading south, there's one **bus** in the evening at 10pm to Palopo (for Rantepao; Rp175,000). Alternatively, you can break up the journey and travel in the daytime by catching a minibus to Poso (9am; tickets from various offices one block south of the harbour), from where there are several buses to Palopo in the afternoon. Book in advance for either option and arrange for a pick-up from the *Oasis*, which is more pleasant than waiting at the main petrol station just west of town.

# THE TOGIAN ISLANDS

The **Togian Islands** form a fragmented, 120-kilometre-long crescent across

### TRAVEL TO AND AROUND THE TOGIAN ISLANDS

There are **ferries** to the islands from **Ampana** (almost daily at 10am; 4–5hr; Rp30,000–40,000) and **Gorontalo**. Two ferries from Gorontalo stop at most of the major islands before leaving Wakai for Ampana: The *KM Tuna Tomini*, leaves Gorontalo at 7pm on Thurs, for Wakai (10–12hr; Rp41,500–65,000, Rp200,000 extra for a cabin) before continuing on to Ampana (16hr); the *KM Puspita Sari* leaves on Weds at 8pm serving Wakai (16hr; Rp95,000) as well as other Togian destinations including Dolong (10hr; Rp75,000), Malenge (12hr; Rp82,500) and Katupat (14hr; Rp90,000) and on to Ampana (20hr; Rp100,000); it's worth trying to book one of the crew's cabins (Rp200,000) from Gorontalo for a good night's sleep.

A ferry runs from Wakai to **Dolong** (Walea Kodi) twice a week via Katupat and **Malenge** (off Talata Koh), then back again. Other ferries do operate to other islands from Wakai, but schedules are unpredictable. For resorts in **Kadidiri**, the main diving resort island near Wakai, the owners usually run small boats to their accommodation from Wakai for free if you plan to stay there. Elsewhere, there's bound to be something along eventually if you can afford to wait, or you can **charter** a motorized outrigger at about Rp150,000–200,000 an hour.

the shallow blue waters of Tomini Bay, their steep grey sides weathered into sharp ridges capped by coconut palms and hardwoods. The exceptional **snorkelling and diving** around the islands features turtles, sharks, octopus, garden eels, and a mixed bag of reef and pelagic fish species. On the down side, there are also nine depots in the Togians dealing in the live export of seafood to restaurants in Asia; many of these operations employ cyanide sprays, which stun large fish but kill everything else – including coral.

From west to east, **Batu Daka**, **Togian** and **Talata Koh** are the Togians' three main islands, with **Walea Kodi** and **Walea Bahi** further east. The main settlements here are **Bomba** and **Wakai** on Batu Daka, and **Katupat** on Togian. Wakai is something of a regional hub, with transport out to smaller islands. There are no vehicle roads or widespread electricity in the Togians and, with all travel by boat, you'll find it pays not to be on too tight a schedule; most accommodation places offer day-trips and shared transfers. Tourism in the islands is budget-oriented but good, and prices usually include meals. July through to September are the coolest months, when winds can interrupt ferries. Diving is usually good all year round, though visibility in December can be variable.

## Bomba

Three hours from Ampana and at the western end of Batu Daka, **BOMBA** comprises two dozen houses and a mosque facing north across a pleasant bay. There's a long beach 5km west of town, but it's the sea that warrants a visit here, with the Togians' best snorkelling an hour away at **Catherine reef**. The coast near here is interesting, too, with the possibility of seeing crocodiles in remote inlets, and some islets east of Bomba completely covered by villages, their sides reinforced with hand-cut coral ramparts. Bomba can be reached only from Wakai by chartering a boat or by taking the public boat from Ampana.

## Wakai and Kadidiri

At the eastern end of Batu Daka, about five hours from Ampana and two from Bomba, **WAKAI** is similar to the dock area at Ampana. Half an hour by motorized outrigger from Wakai, **Kadidiri** is one of the nicest of the islands, 3km long and with fine beaches, with a couple of good resorts.

## Accommodation

### Bomba

**Island Retreat** ⓣ0852/41158853, ⓦwww.togian-island-retreat.com; contact them at least two weeks in advance to arrange for them to pick you up. Just a little way to the south of Bomba, this American-run place is the smartest place on the Togians and the food is fantastic. They also run a diving operation (US$50 for two dives). ❻

### Kadidiri

Both these places have attached dive centres and can organize all manner of dive courses and diving and snorkelling trips, as well as shuttles to and from Wakai.

**Black Marlin** ⓣ0435/831869. Next door to *Paradise*, it has several smart cabins set back from the beach but is not quite as welcoming or social. ❸–❹, meals included

**Paradise Bungalows** (no number). Undergoing extensive refurbishment and now has some beautiful bungalows with private garden showers. ❸–❹, meals included

# GORONTALO

**GORONTALO**, capital of its own province, is a pleasant, sleepy Muslim city with useful ferry links to the Togian Islands, Pagimana and Ampana, and buses to Manado. It's centred on the Mesjid Baitur Rahim, which stands at a wide crossroads. Many streets have been renamed and, though the streets themselves carry the new names, many shops and offices display the old ones. The two main north–south streets are Jalan A Yani, on which you'll find most banks and accommodation and some restaurants, and Jalan Sutoyo, which runs south from the delicious food stalls that make up the busy evening market.

## Arrival

**By bus** Buses from Manado, Palu and Makassar use Terminal Andalas, 3km and a short microlet ride north of the centre (Rp2000), or, if you're unlucky, at the very remote Terminal Isimu, a full 30km from the town centre but linked by plenty of transport.

**By ferry** The harbour is 20min from the centre by *bentur* (motorized rickshaw; Rp7500), which have sadly replaced the more sedate dokars.

**By air** Limboto Airport lies 32km north of town. A taxi costs Rp80,000 into town.

## Accommodation

**Melati Hotel** Jl Monginsidi 33 ⓣ0435/822934, ⓔmelatihotelgtlo@hotmail.com. By some distance the best place in town, run by the same family for four generations, and extraordinarily helpful and efficient. Rooms vary in quality but those in the new wing are smart and clean. ❷–❹; dorms ❶

**Mini Saronde** Jl Kalengkongan 17 ⓣ0435/822677. Across the sports field from the *Melati*, this also has decent a/c rooms and friendly staff. ❷–❹

## Eating

**Agung** Jl Gajah Mada. Two blocks down from the Melati. Chinese place, nothing special but friendly and convenient.

**Cikia** Corner of Jl 23 Januari and Jl Tribrata. It serves wonderful *milu siram* (corn soup) with chillies, onions, garlic and fish.

**Toko Brantas** Jl Hasanuddin. Opposite the mosque. Has delicious pastries. For a more filling meal, try the selection of Chinese noodle dishes (Rp10,000–15,000).

## Directory

**Airlines** Lion Air, Jl Basuki Rachmat 17A ⓣ0435/830035; Merpati, Jl 23 Januari 19 ⓣ0435/21736; Sriwijaya, Jl Agus Salim 18 ⓣ0435/827878.

**Banks and exchange** The BNI and Danamon banks on Jl A Yani both have ATMs.

**Internet** The best internet café is at the *Hotel Melati* (Rp5000/hr).

**Post office** Corner of Jl A Yani and Jl 23 Januari.

**Telephone** The main Telkom office is 2km out of town; the Internet café at the *Hotel Melati* has several phone booths for international calls.

## Moving on

**By bus** Makassar (at least 1 daily; 3 days); Manado (8hr).

**By car** Kijangs to Manado leave from their offices on Jl Andalas, north past the bus station (Rp85,000–125,00 depending on your seat; Rp680,000 gets you the whole car).

**By ferry (Pelni):** The Pelni office is at Jl 23 Januari No. 31 (ⓣ0435/821089).

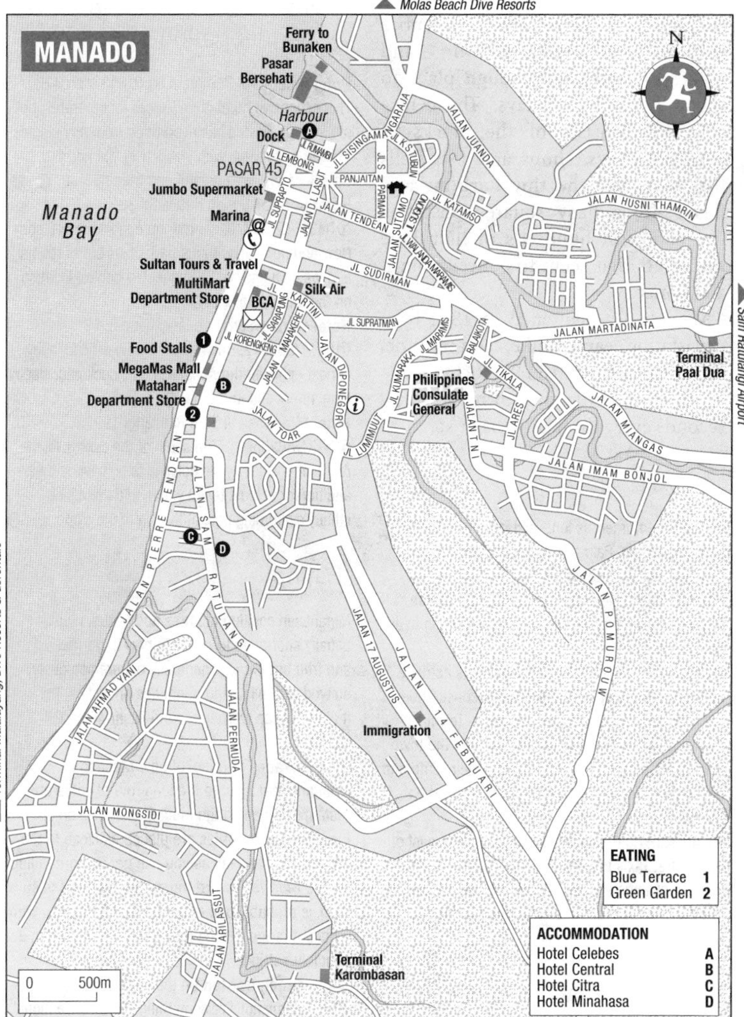


**Destinations:** Bitung (fortnightly; 10hr); Luwuk and Makassar (fortnightly; 10hr).

**By ferry (other)** There are two boats that serve the Togian Islands and Ampana (see box p.390).

**By air** Makassar (2 daily with Sriwijaya or Lion Air; 1hr 30min).

## MANADO

Capital of Sulawesi Utara, **MANADO** is mainly seen as a stopping-off point for spectacular **diving and snorkelling** at the Bunaken Marine reserve. You can either base yourself in Manado and do day-trips to the reefs, base yourself just outside Manado at one of the dive resorts that offer all-inclusive packages, or, the cheapest but least reliable option, base yourself on Pulau Bunaken itself (see p.396).

The town itself is enjoying a bit of a boom – huge new malls, shops and office complexes stretch a good couple of kilometres along the entire seafront south of the harbour – and makes an agreeable enough place to spend a couple of days. The centre of town consists of the blocks of markets, alleys, shops and fish stalls that surround the tiny **harbour** and **Pasar 45**, a busy square constantly jammed with hundreds of light-blue **microlets** that seem to converge on it all at once.

Manado was flattened in 1844 by a devastating **earthquake**, and tremors measuring up to 5.0 on the Richter scale continue to rattle the town for a few seconds every three months or so.

## Arrival

**By bus** The numerous long-distance buses that serve Gorontalo, Palu and Makassar use the Terminal Malalayang about 6km south along the coast. From the Minahasa highlands, buses use Terminal Karombasan, with microlets running to Jl Sam Ratulangi.

**By ferry** The regional Pelni ferry port is actually in Bitung on the opposite, southern, coast. There are regular buses from the harbour to Terminal Paal Dua, from where microlets run into the town centre. All microlets (Rp1750) have their route and destination displayed on the roof or painted on the outside.

**By air** Sam Ratulangi Airport is 12km northeast of the centre. Taxis to town cost Rp40,000–70,000, or you can arrange a pick-up from your hotel. Some of the bigger dive centres have representatives on hand.

## Information and activities

**Tourist information and guides** The official tourist office is useless; instead head to Sultan Tours and Travel (Ⓣ0812/4404882) below the Indag Souvenir shop on Jl Sam Ratulangi, who are very helpful with information about Manado, Bunaken and Tangkoko. Monal here can help with organizing tours around Sulawesi, and is a mine of local information.

**Dive operators** Day-trips from the mainland start at around US$70 for two dives, plus US$30 for full equipment. Blue Banter (Ⓦwww.bluebanter-manado.com), on the second floor of the *Ritzy Hotel* on the seafront, is a well-established and professional outfit.

## Accommodation

**Hotel Celebes** Jl Rumambi 8a Ⓣ0431/870425. This expansive hotel (the *Celebes* incorporates the old *Smiling Hostel*) has everything from tiny singles to luxurious rooms with views over the harbour. Good location, with helpful and friendly staff. ❷–❼

**Hotel Central** Jl Sam Ratulangi 33 Ⓣ0431/851234, Ⓔcentral_manado@hotmail.com. New and popular, with a smart, clean set of rooms and, as its name would suggest, a central location on the main drag. ❹–❼

**Hotel Citra** Jl Sam Ratulangi, lane 8, 12 Ⓣ0431/863812. Down a quiet flower-filled lane almost opposite the *Minahasa*, this secluded, sleepy hotel offers cheap rooms. ❷

**Hotel Minahasa** Jl Sam Ratulangi 199 Ⓣ0431/862559. 1.5km south of the centre. All the rooms in this lovely old colonial hotel have showers and hot (or at least tepid) water, and there's an infinity swimming pool at the top of the slope. ❹–❻

## Eating

Minahasan cooking features dog (*rintek wuuk*, usually shortened to *rw*, or "airvay"), rat (*tikkus*) and fruit bat *(paniki)*, generally unceremoniously stewed with blistering quantities of chillies. Try it at the cheap warung around Pasar 45 and Jl Sudirman.

**Blue Terrace** For a feel of how Manado is changing, head out to the long row of cafés and restaurants behind the MegaMas centre on Jl Pierre Tendean. Tables are placed as close to the edge of the sea wall as you can get without falling in. The *Blue Terrace*, at the northern end of this strip, is probably one of the coolest hangouts, with a decent range of food (fish steak Rp20,000) in a candlelit setting.

**Green Garden** On the main Jl Sam Ratulangi. For something more conventional, this is a great place, a huge establishment with an equally large menu of Chinese dishes, with fish very much at the forefront. Fried squid Rp20,000.

## Directory

**Airlines** Batavia, Jl P Tendean, Kawasan MegaMas B1A-1/20 Ⓣ0431/877878; Garuda, Jl P Tendean Komplek Ⓣ0431/852154; Lion Air, Komp ITC Marina Plaza, Blok Bunaken 18 Ⓣ0431/8880022; Merpati, Jl Martadinata 30 PAL II Ⓣ0431/842000; Silk Air, Jl Sarapung 5 Ⓣ0431/863744; Sriwijaya Air Jl Walter Mongonsidi, Komp. Bahu Mal Blok S-18 Ⓣ0431/837667.

**Banks and exchange** There are lots of ATMs around town. The best place to change cash and traveller's cheques is BCA on Jl Sam Ratulangi.
**Hospital** Public hospital 6km south of the city near Terminal Malalayang (☎0431/853191); microlets to the bus terminal pull in here.
**Immigration** Jl 17 Augustus ☎0431/863491.
**Internet** The best place is the Telkom office, (24hr; Rp6000/hr), but it's often full. The post office, just across the road, also has a few terminals, though it's slower. More expensive but smarter, The Gateway, part of the Marina complex, charges Rp6000 for 30min, Rp3000 for every 15min thereafter.
**Post office** Jl Sam Ratulangi 21. Also has wartel for international calls and internet café (see above).
**Swimming pool** At the *Swahid Kawanua Hotel*, Jl Sudirman 30 (Rp15,000 to non-residents).
**Telephone services** The main Telkom office is on Jl Sam Ratulangi, just to the north of the post office.
**Travel agents** Safari Tours and Travel (☎0431/857637, ⓦwww.manadosafaris.com) offer flights and tours; their office is on the main Jl Sam Ratulangi, just to the north of Garuda.

### Moving on

**By bus** Buses for Gorontalo leave about 5.30am; those to further afield leave around lunchtime.
**Destinations:** Gorontalo (8–10hr); Makassar (2–3 days); Palu (24hr).
**By car** For Gorontalo there is the more comfortable car option, leaving from the CV Garuda Permai office on Jl Kartini (at least 4 daily, usually before 10am; Rp85,000–125,000 depending on where you sit).
**By ferry** The nearest Pelni office is in Bitung (☎0438/835818). Bunaken (daily except Sun; 1hr).
**By air** Balikpapan (daily with Garuda or Batavia; 2hr 30min); Jakarta (several daily with Batavia, Garuda, Lion Air and Merpati; 2hr 10min); Makassar (several daily with Garuda, Lion, Merpati and Sriwijaya; 1hr 35min); Singapore (4 weekly with Silk Air; 3hr 30min).

## BUNAKEN MARINE RESERVE

Northwest of Manado, a 75-square-kilometre patch of sea is sectioned off as **Bunaken Marine Reserve** and promoted as Indonesia's official scuba centre, where **coral reefs** around the reserve's four major islands drop to a forty-metre shelf before falling into depths of 200m and more, creating stupendous reef walls abounding with Napoleon (maori) wrasse, barracuda, trevally, tuna, turtles, manta rays, whales and dolphin. Set aside concerns about snakes and sharks and avoid instead the metre-long Titan trigger-fish, sharp beaked and notoriously pugnacious when guarding its nest; and small, fluorescent-red anemone fish, which are prone to giving divers a painful nip.

You can visit the reserve in two ways, either on day-trips from Manado, which can be arranged privately, or through dive operations, or by staying at budget accommodation within the reserve on Pulau Bunaken. If you need any training

### THE TARSIERS OF TANGKOKO

An ever-popular trip from Manado is to the **Tangkoko National Park**, home of the world's smallest primate, the **tarsier**. These nocturnal tree-dwelling monkeys resemble bushbabies or aye-ayes with their large saucer eyes and long, thin fingers. The beach-side forest of Tangkoko is also home to troops of black macaque, hornbills and couscous, all of which you should see.

Tangkoko is difficult to get to by pubic transport, involving a bus to Bitung from Terminal Paal Dua (Rp7,600) followed by a microlet to Girian (Rp2000) and a pick-up to Tangkoko. Alternatively, a charter from Manado is around Rp200,000–250,000. There are a couple of basic homestays at Tangkoko; go for *Tangkok Ranger* (☎0813/40407690; ❸–❺ per day including three meals), the friendliest of the bunch. Guides are compulsory to visit the park; various candidates will approach you at your hotel or you can walk for ten minutes from the homestays to the park entrance and pick one up there. Expect to pay around Rp85,000 per person.

or qualified assistance you might be better off opting for one of the pricier, professional dive operators in Manado itself, or with one of the larger operators – such as Froggies or Two Fish (see opposite) – on Pulau Bunaken. If you're already certified, however, you'll save money by shopping around the budget operators on the island, though you must check the **reliability** of rental gear and **air quality**, the two biggest causes for concern here.

The best **weather conditions** are between June and November, with light breezes, calm seas and visibility underwater averaging 25m and peaking beyond 50m. Try to avoid the westerly storms between December and February and less severe, easterly winds from March until June.

## Pulau Bunaken and around

About an hour by ferry out from Manado, **Pulau Bunaken** is a low-backed, five-kilometre-long comma covered in coconut trees and ringed by sand and mangroves. Entry into the national park currently costs Rp150,000, which buys a tag valid for one year. Bunaken's homestays usually arrange free transport to and from the island for its guests; if you haven't already organized this in Manado, take a **public ferry** from the harbour immediately to the north of the fish market (daily at 2pm, get there 30min early; return 7.30am; Rp25,000 for tourists); there are also plenty of private boat owners (Rp200,000 is a typical starting price, though it can be many times this). Either way, you end up at **Bunaken village** on the island's south-eastern tip.

Off the west beach between Bunaken village and Liang beach, **Lekuan 1**, **2** and **3** are exceptionally steep, deep walls, and the place to find everything from gobies and eels to deep-water sharks. Further around on the far western end of the island, there are giant clams and stingrays at **Fukui**, while **Mandolin** is good for turtles and occasional mantas, and **Mike's Point** attracts sharks and sea snakes.

### Dive operators

The standard of dive operators on Bunaken is high by Indonesian standards. If you can, check that the operators are part of the North Sulawesi Watersports Association (Ⓦwww.divenorthsulawesi.com), which is trying to promote environmentally responsible diving in Bunaken. Dives usually around US$50–75 per day (two dives), though each operator has their own deals. A discount on your accommodation is also usually offered.

**Bastiano's** (see opposite) Based on Liang Beach and said to be the best of the local dive operators, with a wealth of experience and a pro-active policy to preserving the national park.

**Froggies** (see opposite) The most well-known and established of the diving operators on Bunaken, situated on Liang Beach. Expensive, but good value nevertheless. €65 for two dives.

**Immanuel's** Part of *Daniel Homestay* on Pangalisang Beach. Friendly and popular with budget divers. €20 per dive.

**Living Colour** Ⓣ0812/4306063, Ⓦwww.livingcoloursdiving.com. One of the larger and more efficient operators on Bunaken, situated at Pangalisang Beach, with a good reputation for both equipment and environmental awareness. €50 for two dives.

**Two Fish Divers** Ⓣ0811/432805, Ⓦwww.twofishdivers.com. Pangalisang-based outfit run by British couple Nigel and Tina, with good equipment and high standards. US$55 for two dives.

### Accommodation

There is plenty of accommodation on the island, either close to the main village on the east side on Pangalisang beach, or west along Liang beach. With all accommodation on Bunaken, prices are per person and include three meals per day.

#### Pangalisang

**ChaCha Dive Lodge** Ⓦwww.bunakenchacha.com. Ten beautiful wooden bungalows with fans and mosquito nets. They also offer discounts for long stays, and dive packages that include accommodation. Check their website for details. All inclusive ⑨

**Daniel's** One of the first you come to from the village, a more traditionally Indonesian place than the others round here – friendly, relaxed and reasonable value. ❸

**Living Colour** Ⓣ0812/4306063, Ⓦwww.livingcoloursdiving.com. Finnish-owned and run, smart wooden bungalows stretching up the hill and a lovely, lazy, cheerful atmosphere. ❼

**Lorenso's I & II** Ⓔlorenso@sulawesi-info.com. *Lorenso's I* is the cheapest on the island but is rather tatty; *Lorenso's II* is perhaps the best value, with a variety of rooms and a large beachfront restaurant. Neither offer diving, however, so guests are usually sent to *Living Colour* next to *Lorenso II*. *Lorenso's I* ❷–❸; *Lorenso's II* ❷–❻

**Two Fish Divers** Ⓣ0811/432805, Ⓦwww.twofishdivers.com. Efficient, friendly and run by a UK couple who are both PADI instructors. Internet access (US$1 for 15 min). ❹–❻

## Liang beach

**Bastianos** Ⓣ0431/853566, Ⓦwww.bastianos.com. A worthy rival to nearby *Froggies*, with smart wooden bungalows, internet access, a spa with massage and reasonable prices. ❻ full-board

**Froggies** Ⓣ0431/850210, Ⓦwww.divefroggies.com. Fine, long-established, and still maintaining high standards for both accommodation and diving. Only evening meals and breakfast (and soft drinks) are included. ❼

**Panorama** Ⓔpanorama@sulawesi-dive-quest.com. Best place for budget travellers on Liang, though can be a little dirty when it gets busy. ❷

# Laos

## HIGHLIGHTS ✪

SLOW BOAT ON THE MEKONG: chug down the vast river on a wooden cargo boat
LOUANG PHABANG: a fabulous UNESCO World Heritage site: a great place to explore
VANG VIANG: enjoy a great range of outdoor activities at this spectacular natural playground
PLAIN OF JARS: one of the world's greatest archeological mysteries
WAT SISAKET, VIENTIANE: visit this wonderful historic monastery
WAT PHOU: discover the mighty religious site of the Khmer ruins

## ROUGH COSTS

**DAILY BUDGET** Basic US$15/ Occasional treat US$25–30

**DRINK** Beer Lao (US$1)

**Food** Noodle soup (US$1)

**HOSTEL/BUDGET HOTEL** US$2–5

**TRAVEL** Bus: Vientiane–Louang Phabang (390 km; 10–12hr; US$6; Slow boat: Houayxai–Louang Phabang (2 days; US$15).

## FACT FILE

**POPULATION** 5.6 million

**AREA** 236, 800sq km

**LANGUAGE** Lao

**RELIGIONS** Theravada Buddhism (two thirds)

**CURRENCY** Kip (K)

**CAPITAL** Vientiane

**INTERNATIONAL PHONE CODE** ⓣ856

**TIME ZONE** GMT +7hr

# Introduction

**For a long time Laos was largely unknown to Western travellers. However, since the 1990s, a steady flow of visitors has trickled into this poverty-stricken, old-fashioned country, encouraging the development of some traveller-oriented services. For many, a journey through Laos consists of a whistle-stop tour through the two main towns of Vientiane and Louang Phabang, with perhaps a brief detour to the mysterious Plain of Jars or ancient Wat Phou. Those willing to explore further and brave difficult roads and basic, candlelit accommodation will be rewarded with a rugged natural landscape and an ethnically diverse people not much changed over the centuries.**

Laos's lifeline is the **Mekong River**, which runs the length of the landlocked country and in places serves as a boundary with Thailand. Set on a broad curve of the Mekong, **Vientiane** is Southeast Asia's most modest capital city, and provides a smooth introduction to Laos, offering a string of cosmopolitan cafés to compensate for a relative lack of sights. From here, most tourists dash north to tiny, cultured **Louang Phabang**, once the heart and soul of the ancient kingdom of **Lane Xang** and now the country's most enticing destination, with a spellbinding panoply of gilded temples and weathered shophouses. However, it's worth stopping off en route at **Vang Viang** where you can spend a few days trekking and cycling through the rice paddies, exploring the many caves and floating down the river in a tractor inner tube.

The wild highlands of the **far north** are the best for trekking: Louang Namtha and Muang Sing have good agents that can arrange treks to hilltribe villages. From here, you can travel by bus to **Houayxai**, an entry point popular with travellers arriving from Thailand in search of a slow boat for the picturesque journey south to Louang Phabang. Some of the most dramatic scenery in Laos is in the northeast, especially round the town of **Nong Khiaw**. Following Routes 6 and 7 south brings you to the bustling town of **Phonsavan**, set beside the **Plain of Jars**, a moonscape of bomb craters dotted with ancient funerary urns. In the south, the vast majority of travellers zip down Route 13, stopping off in the major southern towns: genial and cultural **Savannakhet** – also a handy border crossing with Thailand, and offering buses to Vietnam, too – and the important transport hub of **Pakxe**. Further south, near the former royal seat of **Champasak**, lie the ruins of **Wat Phou**, one of the most important Khmer temples outside Cambodia. South again, the countless river islands of **Si Phan Don** lie scattered across the Mekong, boasting scores of traditional

### WHEN TO VISIT

November to February are the most pleasant months to travel in lowland Laos, when daytime temperatures are agreeably warm and evenings slightly chilly; at higher elevations, temperatures can drop to freezing point. In March, temperatures begin to climb, peaking in April, when the lowlands are baking hot and humid. The rains begin in May and last until September, rendering many of Laos's unsealed roads impassable.

fishing communities and the chance to spot the rare Irrawaddy dolphin.

## CHRONOLOGY

**Iron-age** The Plain of Jars in the northeast dates from around 2000 years ago, and is the earliest known indigenous culture in Laos.
**First century AD** Indian traders introduce Buddhism to Southeast Asia; between the sixth and ninth centuries, upper Laos is dominated by the Theravada Buddhist culture of the Mon people, known as Dvaravati.
**Ninth century** The Hindu Khmer Empire of Angkor expands across the whole region, building dozens of Angkor-style temples.
**1353** With Khmer support, exiled prince Fa Ngum takes Louang Phabang (then called Xiang Dong Xiang Thong). He establishes the Lane Xang Hom Khao empire, the "Kingdom of a Million Elephants and the White Parasol", and extends its borders north and south.
**1512** The golden Buddha image, the Pha Bang, is brought to Xiang Dong Xiang Thong from Vientiane by King Visoun (1500–20), establishing it as the symbol of a unified Buddhist kingdom.
**1563** With the Burmese empire encroaching, the capital is moved to Vientiane, but the Pha Bang statue is left, and Louang Phabang is renamed after it. Burmese warrior-kings reduce the kingdom of Lane Xang to vassalage within a decade.
**1637–94** The reign of Sourinyavongsa, and the Golden Age of Lane Xang. After his death the region divides into three principalities.
**1778** The kingdom of Siam takes Vientiane, capturing hundreds of prisoners, and the precious Pha Bang statue. Over the next century, Siam and Vietnam compete to control fragmented Lao principalities.
**1893** French vice-consul in Louang Phabang Auguste Pavie persuades the northern kingdom to pay tribute to France. For half a century, Laos is a French colony, and the country's present-day borders take shape.
**World War II** The Japanese occupy Laos.
**1945** Prince Phetsarath forms a government known as the Lao Issara, or "Free Laos", and deposes the pro-French king, but it isn't recognized by the Potsdam Agreement at the end of the war.
**March 1946** French reoccupation forces take Vientiane and Louang Phabang. Thousands of Lao Issara supporters flee to Thailand, where Phetsarath establishes a government-in-exile.
**1947** The Kingdom of Laos – under French control – is unified under the royal house of Louang Phabang. The Lao Issara, supported by Ho Chi Minh's Viet Minh, launch guerrilla raids on French convoys and garrisons.
**July 1949** France concedes greater independence to the Vientiane government. The Lao Issara disbands and its more moderate members join the new Royal Lao Government (RLG).
**1950** Souphanouvong (Phetsarath's younger brother) founds the resistance group Pathet Lao ("the Land of the Lao"), which calls for an independent Laos and co-operation with the Vietnamese and Khmer against the French.
**1953** The Viet Minh seize parts of Laos and give them to the Pathet Lao. Lao independence is granted in October, but control of the country is divided between Pathet Lao and the Royal Lao Government.
**May 1954** The Geneva conference reaffirms Lao independence under the Royal Lao Government; the Pathet Lao are allotted the provinces of Phongsali and Houa Phan.
**1955–1960** The US, which didn't sign the Geneva accords, supports the Royal Lao Army against the Pathet Lao. Laos is the centre of a Cold War showdown as the US and Soviet Union arm opposing sides, and the country becomes increasingly unstable.
**1961** At a second Geneva conference a coalition government is formed and all foreign military agree to leave Laos; while publicly supporting this, all sides ignore it, keeping Laos at war.
**1964–73** In 1964 prime minister Souvannaphouma, dependent on the US, permits "armed reconnaissance" flights over Laos against the North Vietnamese, who are using the Ho Chi Minh Trail in Lao territory to infiltrate South Vietnam. During this secret war the US drops 2,093,100 tons of bombs on Laos in a decade.
**April 1974** Following the Paris Peace Accords, a coalition government is formed in Laos, including both Souvannaphouma and Souphanouvong.
**1975** After communist victories in Phnom Penh and Saigon, Pathet Lao forces take Vientiane in a bloodless coup on August 23, and the Lao People's Democratic Republic (PDR) is proclaimed on December 2. A rigid, socialist regime is established and up to 50,000 royalists are sent to malaria-ridden labour camps.
**1977** The royal family are arrested and exiled to Houa Phan province, ending the centuries-old Lao monarchy.
**1986** Prime minister Kaysone Phomvihane implements the New Economic Mechanism, essentially a market economy, though there are no political reforms, and dissenters are still arrested.
**1992** Diplomatic relations are re-established with the US.

**1997** Laos becomes a member of the Association of Southeast Asian Nations (ASEAN) but the Asian economic crisis is a major setback for Laos.
**2004** Vientiane hosts ASEAN members at the country's first major summit.
**2007** In the US, ten members of the Hmong minority – many of whom had fought with the US against the communists and then emigrated – are arrested and accused of trying to overthrow the Lao government.



# Basics

## ARRIVAL

Travelling to Laos **by air** from Europe, the US, Canada, Australia or New Zeland you will have to fly first to Bangkok, Thailand, and then get a connecting flight on to Vientiane's Wattay International Airport or Louang Phabang with Thai Airways or Bangkok Airways.

There are flights to both Vientiane and Louang Phabang from: Bangkok and Chiang Mai in Thailand; Hanoi and Ho Chi Minh City in Vietnam; Phnom Penh, and Siem Reap in Cambodia; and Kunming in China. Budget airlines include Bangkok Airways, Lao Airlines, Thai Airways, Bangkok Airways and Vietnam Airlines. Laos has **borders** with Thailand, Vietnam, Cambodia, China and Burma, though foreigners cannot cross the border from Burma.

### Overland from Cambodia

Although the border crossing between Cambodia and Laos at Voen Kham is not "officially" open, a steady stream of Western travellers continue to get through in both directions without incident (see p.134).

### Overland from China

From the town of Jinghong in China's southwestern Yunnan province, daily buses travel to and from Oudomxai and Louang Namtha. The last town on the Chinese side is the village of Mo Han and the first Lao village you come to is Boten. The river route from China to Laos is currently only open to cargo boats.

### Overland from Thailand

There are currently five points along the Thai border where Westerners are permitted to cross into Laos: Chiang Khong (see p.821) to Houayxai; Nong Khai (see p.831) to Vientiane; Nakhon Phanom (see p.832) to Thakhek; Mukdahan (see p.832) to Savannakhet; and Chong Mek (see p.823) to Pakxe. For visa information, see below.

### Overland from Vietnam

There are six border points between Laos and Vietnam where tourists can cross overland. The **Lao Bao Pass** (see p.967), roughly 240km from Savannakhet, is the most popular. There's also an international bus link between Savannakhet and Da Nang, which can take up to 24hr (see p.959). Border crossings have opened at **Bo Y** near Kon Tum in the Central Highlands (see p.941) and **Tay Trang** near Dien Bien Phu in the far northwest (see p.999), which offer two interesting but challenging routes. There are additional crossings close to the Vietnamese city of Vinh at **Cau Treo** (see p.967) and **Nong Het** (east of Phonsavan in Laos, see p.967), and the more remote, seldom used **Na Meo** (east of Xam Nua). It's worth noting that there have been several complaints from travellers using buses coming from Laos to the Vietnam border. Due care should be taken with operators; try and ask fellow travellers about the more reliable ones.

## VISAS

**Visas** are required for all foreign visitors to Laos except Thais. A thirty-day visa-on-arrival is available for $35 (US dollars, cash only, plus one photo) to travellers flying into Vientiane's Wattay Airport or Louang Phabang Airport. This visa is also available to travellers crossing one of the five routes across the Mekong from Thailand. The fee is $35 and one to two photos are required, depending on the border crossing point.

For a longer visa, you will have to apply in advance at a Lao embassy (see p.57) or through a travel agency. Many visitors do this while staying in Bangkok or Hanoi. In **Bangkok**, you can apply for a fifteen- or thirty-day tourist visa directly from the Lao embassy (see p.774); for B1000–1600 (depending on your nationality), fifteen-day visas are not significantly cheaper. You will need two passport photos, and if you apply before noon, it may be ready the same afternoon. An alternative option is to apply through a travel agent in Bangkok;

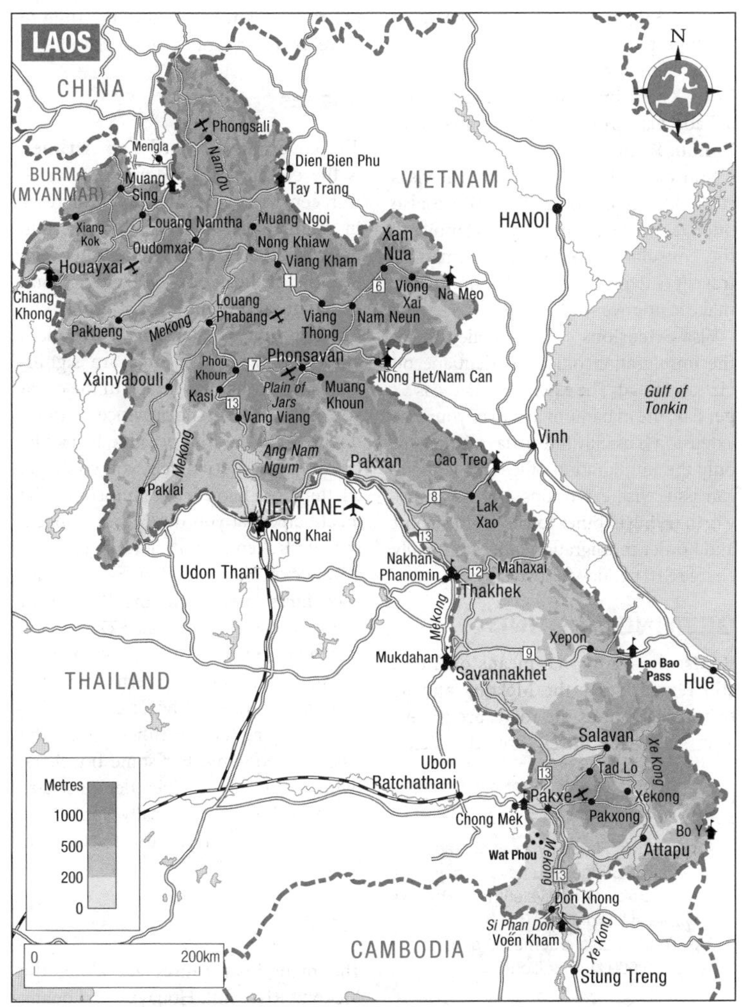

they charge B750 for a fifteen-day tourist visa, and B1200–1800 for a thirty-day tourist visa; allow three working days for processing. There is a Lao consulate in Khon Kaen in northeastern Thailand (see p.828) that can also issue visas, though fees and processing times are variable.

Travellers from Vietnam can get visas for Laos at the Lao embassy in **Hanoi** or at the consulates in **Ho Chi Minh City** and **Da Nang,** as well as at the six border crossings. A thirty-day visa costs around $50, and requires two passport photographs.

Travellers who cross into Laos from Voen Kham in Cambodia must obtain a Laos visa from the Lao embassy in **Phnom Penh**.

Non-extendible, five-day transit visas ($25–30; three working days) are also offered at the Lao embassy in Hanoi and the consulate in Kunming, China, for travellers flying to Bangkok who wish to make a stopover in Vietiane.

**Visa extensions** can be applied for at the immigration office in Vientiane on Hatsady Road. The extension charge is $2 per day; the maximum length of your visa extension is usually fifteen days. Officially, only the immigration office in Vientiane can issue visa extensions, but it's always worth trying in other towns. Both airport and border immigration offices generally charge $10 per day for overstays.

## GETTING AROUND

**Boats**, the traditional means of travel, still regularly ply the Mekong and its tributaries, but as the roads are gradually surfaced, **buses** are displacing riverboats as the main mode of transportation. Regardless of whether you go by road or river, you only need to travel for a week or two in Laos before realizing that timetables are irrelevant, and estimated times of arrival pointless. It is possible to fly although, obviously it is not the most economic mode of transport and tracking down the airline office in some towns can be a hassle, particularly with the language barrier. With the improving road conditions and the attraction of meandering down the river it is worth taking the time to travel by these modes rather than fly.

### AIRPORT DEPARTURE TAX

When leaving Laos by air or via the Friendship Bridge, you have to pay a **departure tax** equivalent to $10, payable in US dollars, Thai baht or kip. There is also a domestic airport tax of 20,000 kip per flight.

### Planes

The government-owned **Lao Airlines**, is the country's only domestic carrier. In recent years, there's been an increase in maintenance of aircraft on certain domestic routes, namely flights between Vientiane and Louang Phabang, and Vientiane and Phonsavan.

The airline only accepts **US dollars cash**, and foreigner fares are significantly more than for locals. In the event you're stuck out in the provinces without dollars, it should be possible to pay by credit card. Alternatively, you could get a letter from Lao Airlines informing the local bank that you need to exchange a traveller's cheque for dollars or get a cash advance on Visa in dollars. Sample one-way **fares** are: Vientiane–Phonsavan $56; Vientiane–Xam Nua $77; Louang Phabang–Vientiane $64; and Vientiane–Pakxe $100. Most Western embassies still have travel advisories warning against flying Lao Airlines, given the hassle of booking. For some travellers, flying with Lao Airlines demonstrates bravado, but it's not really something you want to do if you don't absolutely have to.

### Boats

The main boat **routes** are along the Mekong River link Houayxai to Louang

Phabang, and Pakxe to Champasak and Si Phan Don. Smaller passenger **boats** also cruise up the Nam Ou River, linking Louang Phabang to Phongsali, and vessels still travel the remote Louang Phabang–Vientiane route, a journey that takes four days to a week.

The **slow boats** (*heua sa*) that ply the Mekong routes are built to carry cargo and don't have seats, leaving passengers to grab any spot they can find on the floor. Along the Houayxai to Louang Phabang route, boats for foreign passengers have been fitted out with seats, and there is an overnight stop at Pakbeng, the halfway point. The stops on this route are few and far between, so it's a good idea to bring extra water and food.

On the Mekong, **speedboats** (*heua wai*) are a more costly but faster alternative to the plodding cargo boats. Connecting towns along the river from Vientiane all the way to the Chinese border, these five-metre terrors accommodate up to eight passengers and can shave hours off a river journey. Fares for speedboats cost two to three times the slow-boat fare. Crash helmets are handed out before journeys and life-jackets are occasionally available. Think twice about taking a speedboat, though: the Mekong has some tricky stretches, and can be particularly rough late in the rainy season. Fatal accidents occur with an alarming frequency. You must insist on a life-jacket and helmet, and be sure to bring earplugs.

On the northern routes, the **fares** are posted but foreigners pay significantly more than locals. Southern routes are more haphazard: fares are not posted and you just bargain for and buy your ticket on the spot.

## Buses

**Buses** in Laos range from a/c tourist coaches on the Vientiane–Louang Phabang route to the rattling wrecks that serve the outlying provinces. Cramped, overloaded and extremely slow, the latter can be profound tests of endurance and patience.

There are no public toilets in Laos so passengers relieve themselves by the road during breaks on long journeys. Keep in mind that some areas still have unexploded ordnance about (see p.412), so it's not a good idea to go too far off the road.

**Ordinary buses** run between major towns, and occasionally link provincial hubs with their surrounding areas. Buses plying long-distance routes tend to be in poor shape and can be either regular buses or souped-up tourist vans. In a few remote areas, converted Russian flat-bed trucks, once the mainstay of travel in Laos, still operate.

Except for buses out of major towns – where you buy a **ticket** from the bus station before boarding – it's common practice to pay on board. **Timetables** exist but it's best to get to the bus station well before your scheduled departure, especially if you want a decent seat.

Where there's no fixed departure time, you should get to the bus station between 6 and 7am, when most Lao passengers travel. There are generally few departures after midday. Occasionally, buses won't even depart if there aren't enough passengers. It's also possible to flag down a bus from the side of the road, provided it's not full.

## Sawngthaews

In most provinces, the lack of a bus network is made up for by **sawngthaews** – converted flat-bed trucks – into which drivers cram as many passengers as they can get onto two benches in the back. They usually depart from the regular bus station, and only leave when there are enough passengers to make the trip worthwhile. If there aren't enough passengers, the driver may try to cajole extra kip out of passengers in order to get things going. The fare is paid at the end of the ride (but agreed at the beginning) and foreigners are routinely over-charged. To catch a sawngthaew in remote areas simply flag it down from the side of the road and tell the driver where you're headed.

### Jumbos and tuk-tuks

Transport within Lao towns is by motorized *samlaw* (literally "three wheels"), which function as shared taxis for four or five passengers. There are two types of *samlaw*: **jumbos** and **tuk-tuks**. Jumbos are homemade three-wheelers consisting of a two-wheeled carriage welded to the front half of a motorcycle. Tuk-tuks are just bigger, sturdier jumbos, and Lao tend to refer to these vehicles interchangeably. To catch one, flag it down and tell the driver where you're going. You pay at the end of the ride, but make sure you agree the fare upfront. Payment is according to the number of passengers, the distance travelled and your bargaining skills. Rates vary depending on a number of circumstances, but figure on around 5000K per kilometre.

### Vehicle rental

Self-drive car rental is possible in Laos, but unless you're experienced with local driving habits, it's easier to hire a **car and driver**. In most major towns tour agencies have a/c vans and 4WD pick-up trucks, and can provide drivers as well. Prices can be as much as $80–100 per day. Always clarify who pays for fuel and repairs and the driver's food and lodging, and be sure to ask what happens in case of a major breakdown or accident. A much cheaper alternative for short distances or day-trips is to simply charter a tuk-tuk or sawngthaew. If you do have experience with driving in the region and want to do it yourself, you'll find car and pick-up truck rental service in Vientiane.

Renting a **motorbike** costs between $10–20 per day. At the time of writing, tourists were not allowed to rent either bicycles or motorbikes in Louang Phabang, apparently for their own safety, but more likely for the increase of business it provides for the tuk-tuk drivers. 250cc dirt bikes are available in Vientiane but elsewhere you'll be limited to 100cc step-throughs such as the Honda Dream. A licence is not required and insurance is not available, so make sure you have travel insurance coverage. Before zooming off, check the bike thoroughly for any damage and take it for a test run. Few rental places will have a helmet on offer, but it doesn't hurt to ask. Helmets in Thailand are cheaper, so it's a good idea to buy one there. **Bicycles** can also be rented from guesthouses and tourist-oriented shops for around $1–2 per day. Sunglasses are essential and proper shoes, long trousers and a long-sleeved shirt will provide some protection if you take a spill.

## ACCOMMODATION

Inexpensive **accommodation** can be found all over Laos. For a basic double room, prices start at around $2 in the provinces and $8 in Vientiane. Moving up the scale, $25 lands you a cosy room in a restored French villa. The higher standards of accommodation are in the larger Mekong towns, particularly Vientiane and Louang Phabang. Remote towns and villages lag far behind.

**Standards** and **room types** can vary widely within the same establishment so always ask to see several rooms before choosing one. In the north, many towns only have **electricity** for a few hours in the evening, so you should weigh the added cost of a/c against the number of hours you'll have power to use it. Electrical wiring in budget guesthouses is usually an accident waiting to happen; even turning on the light can sometimes require caution. Electricity is supplied at 220 volts AC. Two-pin sockets are the norm.

En-suite showers and flush toilets are now found in most tourist-quality hotels. At local hotels, showers and toilets are communal and will probably be Asian-style.

The distinction between a **guesthouse** and a **hotel** is blurred in Laos. Either can denote anything ranging from a bamboo-and-thatch hut to a multi-storey concrete building. As rooms are so cheap, few guesthouses offer dorm accommodation. Guesthouses and budget hotels don't take advance bookings unless they know you already. In order to secure a good room, it helps to check-in mid-morning, just after people begin checking out.

**Mid-range hotels** are common in medium-sized towns, and are mostly four or five storey, offering large rooms with tiled floors and en-suite bathrooms from $5. The beds are usually hard but the sheets and quilts are clean. Hot water is not always available.

Once you cross the $20 threshold, you enter a whole new level of comfort. In the former French outposts on the Mekong, this translates into an atmospheric room in a restored **colonial villa** or recently built accommodation with cable TV, fridge, air conditioning and a hot-water shower. Colonial-era hotels only have a limited number of rooms, so book ahead if you are visiting in December and January.

If you find yourself stuck in a remote town or village overnight, someone will usually put you up in the absence of a guesthouse. You should fix the price for your food and lodging ahead of time – around 10,000K ($1) per person, or twice that if they feed you is a fair rate.

## FOOD AND DRINK

Fiery and fragrant, with a touch of sour, **Lao food** owes its distinctive taste to fermented fish sauces, lemon grass, coriander leaves, chillies and lime juice and is closely related to Thai cuisine. Eaten with the hands along with the staple sticky rice, much of Lao cuisine is roasted over an open fire and served with fresh herbs and vegetables. Pork, chicken, duck and water buffalo all end up in the kitchen, but freshwater fish is the main source of protein. An ingredient in many recipes is *nâm pa*, or fish sauce, which is used like salt. Most Lao cooking includes fish sauce so you may want to order "*baw sai nâm pa*" ("without fish sauce").

Vientiane and Louang Phabang boast the country's best food, with excellent Lao food and international cuisine, but in remote towns you'll often only find noodles. Although Laos is a Buddhist country, very few Lao are **vegetarian**. It's fairly easy, however, to get a vegetable dish or a vegetable fried rice.

As for **hygiene**, Laos kitchens are often just a shack without proper lighting or even running water, and, in many northern towns, there's no electricity to run refrigeration. As a rule, sticking to tourist-class restaurants or well-frequented street stalls is the safest bet

### ADDRESSES

Lao **addresses** can be confusing because property is usually numbered twice to show firstly which lot it stands in, and then to signify where it is on that lot. In addition, some cities have several conflicting address systems. To avoid unnecessary confusion, numbers have been omitted from addresses given in the guide text, and locations are described as far as possible using landmarks. Only a handful of cities in Laos actually have street names, signs are rare, and many roads change names from block to block. Use street names to find a hotel on a map in the guide text, but when asking directions or telling a tuk-tuk driver where to go, refer to a landmark, monastery or prominent hotel.

but it is by no means a guarantee of not getting an upset stomach: try to avoid cooked food that has been left standing.

Dishes containing raw meat or raw fish are considered a delicacy in Laos, but people who eat them risk parasites.

## Where to eat

The **cheapest** places for food are markets, street stalls and noodle shops. Despite their name, **morning markets** (*talat sâo*) remain open all day and provide a focal point for noodle shops (*hân khãi fõe*), coffee vendors, fruit stands and sellers of crusty French loaves. In Louang Phabang and Vientiane, vendors hawking pre-made dishes gather in **evening markets** (*talat láeng)* towards late afternoon. Takeaways such as grilled chicken (*pîng kai),* spicy papaya salad (*tam màk hung*) and minced pork salad (*làp mu*) are commonly available.

Some **noodle shops** and street stalls feature a makeshift kitchen surrounded by a handful of tables and stools. Most stalls will specialize in only one general food type, or even only one dish, for example a stall with a mortar and pestle, unripe papayas and plastic bags full of pork rinds will only offer spicy papaya salads. Similarly, a noodle shop will generally only prepare noodles with or without broth. A step up from street stalls and noodle shops are *hân kin deum*, literally "eat-drink shops", where you'll find a somewhat greater variety of dishes, as well as beer and whisky. Outside of Vientiane, street stalls and noodle shops rarely stay open beyond 8pm.

Most proper **restaurants** (*hân ahãn*) are run by ethnic Vietnamese and Chinese. Since the Lao seldom eat Lao food outside the home, there are few Lao-food restaurants. Many local eateries don't have menus – in Lao or English – so it's a good idea to memorize a few stock dishes such as fried rice (*khao phat*). Restaurants catering more to foreigners usually have an English menu and offer fried noodles and fried rice as well as a variety of Lao, Chinese and Thai dishes.

## Lao food

Most Lao meals feature **sticky rice** (*khào niaw*), which is served in a lidded wicker basket (*típ khào)* and eaten with the hands. Typically, the rice will be accompanied by a fish or meat dish and soup, with a plate of fresh vegetables, such as string beans, lettuce, basil and mint, served on the side. Grab a small chunk of rice from the basket, squeeze it into a firm wad and then dip it into one of the dishes. At the end of your meal, it's thought to be bad luck not to replace the lid. Plain, steamed, white rice (*khào jâo*) is eaten with a fork and spoon; chopsticks (*mâi thu*) are reserved for noodles.

So that a variety of tastes can be enjoyed during the course of a meal, Lao meals are eaten **communally**, with each dish, including the soup, being served at once, rather than in courses. If you're eating a meal with steamed white rice, only put a small amount of one dish onto your rice at a time; when the meal is accompanied by sticky rice, it's normal to simply dip a ball of rice into the main servings. For two of you, order two or three dishes, plus your own rice.

If Laos were to nominate a **national dish**, a strong contender would be *làp*, a "salad" of minced meat mixed with garlic, chillies, shallots, aubergine, galingale and fish sauce. *Làp* is either eaten raw (*díp*) – a culinary experience you may want to avoid – or *súk* (cooked). Another quintessentially Lao dish is *tam màk hung* (or *tam sòm*), a spicy salad made with shredded green papaya, garlic, chillies, lime juice, fish paste (*pa dàek)* and, sometimes, dried shrimp and crab. Each vendor will have their own particular recipe, but it's also acceptable to pick out which ingredients

– and how many chilli peppers – you'd like. Usually not too far away from any *tam màk hung* vendor, you'll find someone selling *pîng kai*, basted grilled chicken. Fish, *pîng pa*, is another grilled favourite, with whole fish skewered and barbecued.

When the Lao aren't filling up on glutinous rice, they're busy eating *fõe*, the ubiquitous **noodle soup**. Although primarily eaten for breakfast, *fõe* can be enjoyed at any time of day, and, outside of towns, may well be the mainstay of your diet. The basic bowl of *fõe* consists of a light broth, to which is added thin rice noodles and slices of meat (usually beef, water buffalo or grilled chicken) and is served with a plate of lettuce, mint and coriander leaves and bean sprouts. Also on offer at many noodle shops is *mi*, a yellow wheat noodle served in broth with slices of meat and a few vegetables. It's also common to eat *fõe* and *mi* without broth (*hàeng*), and at times fried (*khùa*).

The best way to round off a meal is with **fresh fruit** (*màk mâi*), as the country offers a wide variety, including guavas, lychees, rambutans, mangosteen and pomelos. Puddings don't figure on many restaurant menus, although some offer desserts such as banana in coconut milk (*nâm wãn màk kûay*). Markets often have a food stall specializing in inexpensive **coconut-milk desserts**, generally called *nâm wãn*. Look for a stall displaying a dozen bowls, containing everything from water chestnuts to fluorescent green and pink jellies, from which one or two items are selected and then added to a sweet mixture of crushed ice, slabs of young coconut meat and coconut milk.

## Drinks

The Lao don't drink **water** straight from the tap and nor should you; contaminated water is a major cause of sickness. Plastic bottles of drinking water (*nâm deum*) are sold countrywide for around 2000K. Noodle shops and inexpensive restaurants generally serve free pitchers of weak tea or boiled water (*nâm tóm*), which is fine, although perhaps not as foolproof. Most **ice** in Laos is produced in large blocks under hygienic conditions, but it can become less pure in transit or storage, so be wary. Brand-name soft drinks are widely available for around 6000K per bottle or 10,000K per can. More refreshing are the **fruit shakes** (*màk mâi pan*) available in larger towns, which consist of your choice of fruit blended with ice, liquid sugar and sweetened condensed milk. Freshly squeezed fruit juices, such as lemon (*nâm màk nao*) and coconut juice (*nâm màk phao*) are a popular alternative, as is sugar-cane juice (*nâm oi*).

The Lao drink very strong **coffee**, or *kafeh hâwn*, which is served with sweetened condensed milk and sugar. If you prefer your coffee black, and without sugar, ask for *kafeh dam baw sai nâm tan*. Black **tea** is available at most coffee vendors and is what you get, mixed with sweetened condensed milk, when you request *sá hâwn*.

### Alcohol

**Beer Lao** (*Bia Lao*) is a very enjoyable, cheap brew, at 10,000k per bottle. In Vientiane and Louang Phabang, draft Beer Lao known as *bia sót* is available at bargain prices by the litre; there are dozens of *bia sót* outlets in the capital, most of which are outdoor beer gardens with thatch roofs. Some foreign beers are also available country-wide. Drunk with equal gusto is *lào-láo*, a clear **rice alcohol** with the fire of a blinding Mississippi moonshine. Although the government distils its own brand, Sticky Rice, which is sold nationally, most people indulge in local brews. *Lào-láo* is usually sold in whatever bottle the distiller had around at the time (look twice before you buy that bottle of Fanta) and is sold at drink shops and general stores for around 5000K per 750ml. Drunk from a large earthenware jar with thin bamboo straws, the rice alcohol *lào hái* is fermented by households in the countryside and is weaker *than lào-láo*, closer to a wine in taste. Drinking *lào hái*, however, can be risky, as unboiled water is sometimes added during fermentation. Several brand-name rice whiskies, with a lower alcohol content than *lào-láo*, are available for around 10,000k per bottle at local general stores.

## CULTURE AND ETIQUETTE

Laos by and large shares the same attitudes to dress and **social taboos** as other Theravada Buddhist Southeast Asian cultures; see p.45, for details. The lowland Lao traditionally **greet** each other with a *nop* – bringing their hands together in a prayer-like gesture. The status of the persons giving and returning the *nop* determines how they will execute it, so most Lao prefer to shake hands with Westerners. If you do receive a *nop* as a gesture of greeting or thank you, it is best to reply with a smile and nod of the head, the customary way for strangers to show that they mean well.

Take care to respect Lao attitudes to religion by sticking to basic temple etiquette; don't dress too provocatively, and always remove your shoes before entering the temple. It can also cause offence to photograph the monks and images of Buddha.

**Tipping** isn't a Lao custom, although upmarket restaurants in Vientiane expect a gratuity of around ten percent.

## SPORTS AND OUTDOOR ACTIVITIES

Laos's landscape is a sports haven: mountainous highlands and ethnic villages for trekkers; well paved, traffic-free routes for bike enthusiasts; and rivers for rafters and kayakers. Outdoor activities and adventure companies include **Diethelm Travel Laos** (ⓣ021/215920, ⓦwww.diethelmtravel.com) and **Xplore-Asia** (ⓦwww.xplore-asia.com), which organizes kayaking, rafting, trekking and cycling trips.

### Trekking

**Trekking** is the most popular activity. Centres in the northern provinces such as Louang Namtha (p.445) and Muang Sing (p.447) can arrange a few days hiking through forests and sleeping at village homestays, offering the opportunity to experience authentic Lao life.

Companies like Green Discovery (ⓣ021/ 215920, ⓦwww.greendiscoverylaos.com; branches in Vientiane, Louang Phabang Louang Namtha, Pakxse and Vang Viang), will lead you through spectacular wildlife on eco-tours that cross through national parkland called **National Biodiversity Conservation Areas** (NBCA), which are host to a wealth of diverse flora and fauna.

### Cycling

**Cycling** is an increasingly popular way to explore Laos. As well as going on organized trips provided by companies such as Green Discovery and Xplore Asia, it is possible to rent fairly good mountain bikes in towns like Vang Viang (p.426) and set off on your own adventure around the countryside.

### Water sports

Daring watersports fans can opt for **whitewater rafting** trips out of Louang Phabang on the northern rivers such as the Nam Ou, the Nam Xuang and the Nam Ming. Those who prefer a more relaxed paddle can **kayak** down river at a slower pace whilst taking in the lovely views of Vang Viang (p.426), Muang Ngoi (p.440) and Si Phan Don (p.463).

### Caving and rock climbing

**Caving** and **rock climbing** is best at Vang Viang, where Laos's first bolted cliff face has several routes available for all abilities from beginner to advanced. There is plenty of caving throughout Laos with so many limestone karsts, particularly in Vang Viang. Remember to take a head torch and some good footwear.

## COMMUNICATIONS

**Mail** takes one to two weeks in or out of Laos. **Poste restante** services are available in Vientiane and Louang Phabang; always address mail using the country's official name, "Lao PDR", rather than "Laos". It's not advisable to ship anything of value home from Laos; if you're going to Thailand, wait and send it from there. When sending **parcels**, leave the package open for inspection; incoming **parcels** are also subject to inspection.

The best place to make **overseas telephone calls** is the local Telecom Office (8am–9pm); elsewhere, international calls can sometimes be placed at the post office. To **call abroad** from Laos, dial ⓣ00 + IDD country code + area code minus first 0 + subscriber number. Calls cost approximately $3 per minute to the UK and North America, $1.50 to New Zealand and less than $1 to Australia. There's no facility for collect or reverse-charge calls, but you can often get a "call back" for a small fee: ask the operator for the minimum call abroad and then get the person you're calling to ring you back.

Public **card-phones** are wired for both domestic and international calls. Phone booths are usually stationed outside post offices in provincial capitals, and occasionally elsewhere in larger towns. Phonecards (*bat tholasap*; $2.50–6) are sold at shops and post and telephone offices in several denominations of time "units"; these are units of time rather than money. Because of high charges for overseas calls and the low amount of time units available, it's difficult to make an overseas call that lasts for more than a few minutes before you're cut off. Local calls can be made at hotels and guesthouses for a small fee. **Regional codes** are given throughout the chapter: the "0" must be dialled before all long-distance calls.

**Internet cafés** are springing up all over the place, even in the most unlikely, rural parts. It won't be long before an internet connection becomes a normality in even the most remote of places. **Charges** range from 100K to 400K per minute, or 10,000K per hour.

## CRIME AND SAFETY

Laos is a relatively **safe country** for travellers. For the most part, if you keep your wits about you, you shouldn't have any problems.

If you have anything stolen, you'll need to get the police to write up a report for your insurance: bring along a translator if you can. Women should be wary of Lao monks and novices who try to lure them into an isolated part of the monastery. There have been incidents, especially in Louang Phabang, where

### LAOS ON THE NET

ⓦ**www.ecotourismlaos.com** Award-winning website with clear and comprehensive trekking info.

ⓦ**www.greendiscoverylaos.com** Tour company website that specializes in active and adventurous trips also with useful local information.

ⓦ**www.vientianetimes.com** Website for the Laotian English-language paper, providing latest news stories about the country.

monks or novices have attempted to rape foreign women.

### Banditry

The section of **Route 13** between Kasi and Vang Viang continues to be the target of Hmong bandits and insurgents. Although the risk is very small, it's a good idea to ask around before taking a bus that traverses this route. South of Route 7 lies the **Xaisomboune Special Zone**, an administrative district controlled by the army and considered unsafe. **Route 6** from Muang Khoun to Pakxan in the eastern part of the Special Zone should be avoided. Likewise, take extra precautions and ask around before setting out on Route 7 between Phonsavan and Phou Khoun.

### Unexploded ordnance

The Second Indochina War left Laos with a legacy of **bombs**, **land mines** and **mortar shells** that will haunt the country for decades to come, despite the efforts of de-mining organizations. Round, tennis-ball sized anti-personnel bomblets, known as "bombi", are the most common type of **unexploded ordnance** (UXO), and large bombs, ranging in size from 100kg to 1000kg, also abound. Ten provinces have one or more districts severely contaminated with UXO. Listed in descending order of contamination they are: Savannakhet, Xiang Khouang, Salavan, Khammouan, Xekong, Champasak, Saisomboun, Houa Phan, Attapu and Louang Phabang. Another five provinces have at least one district with significant contamination: Louang Namtha, Phongsali, Bolikhamxai, Vientiane province and Vientiane prefecture.

Although most towns and tourist sites are free of UXO, 25 percent of villages remain contaminated. As accidents often occur while people are tending their fields, the risk faced by the average visitor is extremely limited. Nonetheless, the number-one rule is: don't be a trailblazer. When in rural areas, always stay on well-worn paths, even when passing through a village, and don't pick up or kick at anything if you don't know what it is.

### Drugs

It is **illegal** to smoke ganja and opium in Laos although it continues to be available in some places. Tourists who use illegal drugs risk substantial "fines" if caught by police, who do not need a warrant to search you or your room. Wide-scale government crack-downs on drug tourism have been effective

## MEDICAL CARE AND EMERGENCIES

You'll find **pharmacies** in all the major towns and cities. Pharmacists in Vientiane and Louang Phabang are quite knowledgeable and have a decent supply of medicines.

Healthcare in Laos is so poor as to be virtually non-existent. The nearest **medical care** of any competence is in neighbouring Thailand, and if you find yourself afflicted by anything more serious than travellers' diarrhoea, it's best to head for the closest Thai border crossing and check into a hospital. A clinic attached to the Australian embassy in Vientiane is mainly for embassy personnel, but can be relied upon in extreme emergencies.

## INFORMATION AND MAPS

The **National Tourism Authority of Laos** (NATL) operates offices in a few major towns, but the staff are generally untrained and speak little English. Sodetour and Diethelm, two privately owned companies with offices in most major towns, can provide more reliable data. Word-of-mouth information from other travellers is often the best source, as conditions in Laos change with astonishing rapidity.

**EMERGENCY NUMBERS**

In **Vientiane** dial the following numbers: fire ☎190, ambulance ☎195, police ☎191. There are no emergency numbers for the rest of the country.

Good **maps** for Laos are difficult to find. The best road map of Laos is the *Laos 2002 Guide Map* published by Golden Triangle Rider and available at bookstores in Thailand. The latest edition of Nelles 1:1,500,000 map of Vietnam, Laos and Cambodia is adequate for orientation but not very good for pinpointing towns or villages. Likewise, the Bartholomew 1: 2,000,000 Vietnam, Cambodia and Laos map is not always reliable.

## MONEY AND BANKS

Lao currency is the **kip** and is available in 50,000K, 20,000K, 10,000K, 5000K, 2000K, 1000K and 500K notes. There are no coins in circulation. In addition, the Thai baht and US dollar operate parallel to the kip. Although a 1990 law technically forbids the use of foreign currencies to pay for local goods and services, many hotels, restaurants and tour operators actually quote their prices in dollars, and accept payment in either **baht** or **dollars**. The government-owned airline, Lao Airlines, only accepts payment in US dollars cash.

After several years of hyper-inflation inflation has settled but many Lao are suffering real hardship, as prices continue to rise while salaries remain the same.

At the time of writing, the official **exchange rate** was 8,735 kip to the US dollar, 265 kip to the Thai baht.

**Traveller's cheques** are a safe way to carry your money, but it's a good idea to have a decent supply of US dollars or Thai baht in **cash** if you intend to spend time in the remoter parts of the country. Major **credit cards** are accepted at many hotels, upmarket restaurants and shops in Vientiane and Louang Phabang. **Cash advances** on Visa cards and, less frequently, MasterCard are possible in most major towns. Only recently have **ATMs** started to pop up around the country, many of them still only accepting MasterCard. Those with Visa cards should not rely on them. At the time of writing, there were ATMs in Louang Phabang, Vientiane, Vang Viang, Odomxai, Louang Namtha and Pakxe – more are due to open. Bear in mind that you cannot change kip back into dollars or baht when leaving the country – and that duty-free shops only accept dollars and baht.

### Costs

Given the volatility of the kip, **prices** for accommodation and travel in this chapter have been given in their more stable dollar equivalents. Indeed, many hotels and guesthouses have opted to fix their rates to the dollar. The prices quoted in kip for transport, museum entrance fees and so on were correct at the time of research and have been retained to give a relative idea of costs, though in practice many of these prices will be higher.

While restaurants and some shops have fixed prices, you should always **bargain** in markets and when chartering transport (fares on passenger vehicles are fixed). Room rates can be bargained for in low season. As the Lao in general – with the exception of some tourist businesses in Vientiane and Louang Phabang – are less out to rip off tourists than their counterparts in Thailand and Vietnam, they start off the haggling by quoting a fairly realistic price and expect to come down only a little. **Price tiering** does exist in Laos, with foreigners paying more than locals for airfares, bus fares, speed-boat tickets and entry to museums and famous sites.

## LAO

The main language of Laos is Lao. The spoken Lao of Vientiane is very similar to Thai spoken in Bangkok, though there are pockets of Laos where no dialect of Lao, much less the Vientiane version, will be heard. Since economic liberalization, English has become the preferred foreign tongue, and it's quite possible to get by without Lao in the towns. Out in the countryside, you will need some Lao phrases.

### Pronunciation

The dialect of Lao spoken in Vientiane, which has been deemed the official language of Laos, has six tones. Thus, depending on its tone, the word "*sang*" can mean either "elephant", "craftsman", "granary", "laryngitis", a species of bamboo, or "to build".

a as the "ah" as in "autobahn"
ae as the "a" in "cat"
ai as in "Thai"
aw as in "jaw"
ao as in "Lao"
e as in "pen"
eu as in French "fleur"
i as in "mimi"
ia as in "India"
o as in "flow"
oe as in "Goethe"
u (or ou) as the "ou" in "you"
ua (or oua) as the "ua" in "truant"
b as in "big"
d as in "dog"
f as in "fun"
h as in "hello"
j (or CH) as in "jar"
k as in "skin" (unaspirated)
kh as the "k" in "kiss"
l as in "luck"
m as in "more"
n as in "now"
ng as in "singer" (this combination sometimes appears at the beginning of a word)
ny as in the Russian "nyet"
p as in "speak" (unaspirated)
ph as the "p" in "pill"
s (or x) as in "same"
t as in "stop" (unaspirated)
th as the "t" in "tin"
w (or v) as in "wish"
y as in "yes"

### Words and phrases in Lao

Questions in Lao are not normally answered with a yes or no. Instead the verb used in the question is repeated for the answer. For example: "Do you have a room?" ("*mí hàwng wàng baw*"), would be answered "Have" ("*mí*") in the affirmative or "No have" ("*baw mí*") in the negative.

### Greetings and basic phrases

| | |
|---|---|
| Hello | *sabai di* |
| Goodbye | *lá kawn* |
| Goodbye (in reply) | *sok di* |
| How are you? | *sabai di baw* |
| I'm fine | *sabai di* |
| Please | *kaluna (rarely used)* |
| Thank you | *khop jai* |
| Do you speak English? | *jâo wâo phasã angkit dâi baw* |
| I don't understand | *khói baw khào jai* |
| Yes | *lâew* |
| No | *baw* |
| right/left | *khwã/sâi* |
| Where are you from? | *jâo má tae sãi* |
| Hospital | *dae* |
| I need a doctor | *khói tâwng kan hã mãw* |
| Where is the...? | *...yu sãi* |
| Can you help me? | *jâo suay khói dâi baw* |
| Police station | *sathani tamluat* |
| Do you have any rooms? | *mí hàwng wàng baw* |
| Can I have the bill? | *khãw sek dae* |

### Numbers

| | |
|---|---|
| 0 | *sun* |
| 1 | *neung* |
| 2 | *sãwng* |
| 3 | *sãm* |
| 4 | *si* |
| 5 | *hà* |
| 6 | *hók* |
| 7 | *jét* |

| | |
|---|---|
| 8 | *pàet* |
| 9 | *kâo* |
| 10 | *síp* |
| 11, 12, etc | *síp ét, síp sãwng* |
| 20 | *sao* |
| 21, 22, 23, etc | *sao ét, sao sãwng, sao sãm* |
| 30, 40, 50, etc | *sãm síp, si síp, hà síp* |
| 100 | *hôi* |
| 1000 | *phán* |

### Food and drinks glossary

*khói kin sîn baw dâi* — I can't eat meat
*soen sàep* — Bon appetit
*hân ahãn* — restaurant

**Fish, meat and vegetables**

*jeun khai* — omelette
*kai* — chicken
*khai dao* — egg, fried
*khào jâo* — rice, steamed
*khào ji* — bread
*khào niaw* — rice, sticky
*kûng* — shrimp
*màk phét* — chilli
*mu* — pork
*nâm pa* — fish sauce
*nâm tan* — sugar
*nóm sòm* — yoghurt
*pa* — fish
*pa dàek* — fish paste
*pét* — duck
*phõng sú lot* — MSG
*pu* — crab
*sìn ngúa* — beef
*tâo hû* — bean curd

**Fruit**

*màk kûay* — banana
*màk len* — tomato
*màk mo* — watermelon
*màk muang* — mango
*màk náo* — lime/lemon
*màk nat* — pineapple
*phák* — vegetables

**Noodles**

*fõe* — rice noodle soup
*fõe hàeng* — rice noodle soup without broth
*fõe khùa* — fried rice noodles
*khào piak sèn* — rice noodle soup, served in chicken broth
*khào pûn* — flour noodles with sauce
*mi hàeng* — yellow wheat noodles without broth
*mi nâm* — yellow wheat noodle soup

**Everyday dishes**

*khào ji pateh* — bread with Lao-style pâté and vegetables
*khào ji sai boe* — bread with butter
*khào khùa or khào phát* — fried rice
*khào khùa sai kai* — fried rice with chicken
*khùa khing kai* — chicken with ginger
*khùa phák baw sai sìn* — stir-fried vegetables
*làp mu* — minced pork
*man falang jeun* — chips
*mu phát bai hólapha* — pork with basil over rice
*pîng kai* — grilled chicken
*pîng pa or jeun pa* — grilled fish
*tam màk hung* — spicy papaya salad
*tôm yam pa* — spicy fish soup with lemon grass
*yam sìn ngúa* — spicy beef salad
*yáw díp* — spring rolls, fresh
*yáw jeun* — spring rolls, fried

**Drinks**

*bia* — beer
*bia sót* — beer, draught
*kafeh* — coffee
*kafeh dam* — black coffee
*kafeh nóm hawn* — hot Lao coffee (with milk and sugar)
*kafeh nóm yén* — iced coffee (with milk and sugar)
*lào-láo* — rice whisky
*màk kuay pan* — banana shake
*màk mai pan* — fruit shake
*nâm deum* — water
*nâm kâwn* — ice
*nâm màk phâo* — coconut juice
*nâm sá* — tea
*nâm yén* — water, cold
*nóm* — milk
*sá jin* — tea, Chinese

## OPENING HOURS AND HOLIDAYS

While official hours for **government offices** are 8am–noon and 1–5pm Monday to Friday, very little gets done between 11am and 2pm. **Post offices** are generally open 8am–5pm Monday to Friday, 8am–4pm on Saturday and 8am–noon on Sunday. **Banking hours** are usually 8.30am–noon and 1–4pm, Monday to Friday nationwide; exchange kiosks keep longer hours but are rare. The hours of private **businesses** vary, but almost all are closed on Sunday. During the heat of the day many shop owners will partly close their doors and snooze, but it is perfectly acceptable to wake them up. All government businesses close on public holidays, though some shops and restaurants may stay open. The only time when many private businesses do close – for three to seven days – is during Chinese New Year (new moon in late Jan to mid-Feb), when the ethnic-Vietnamese and Chinese populations of Vientiane, Thakhek, Savannakhet and Pakxe celebrate with parties and temple visits. Temples are usually open from 8am–noon and 1–4pm.

Morning food and drink **stalls** are up and running at about 7am, while night stalls are usually open from 6–10pm. Most **restaurants** are open daily until about 10pm.

### Public holidays

**January 1** New Year's Day
**January 6** Pathet Lao Day

### PEOPLE

The **Lao Loum** (or lowland Lao) make up the majority in Laos: between fifty percent and sixty percent of the population. They prefer to inhabit river valleys and practise Theravada Buddhism as well as some animist rituals. Of all the ethnicities found in Laos, the culture of the lowland Lao is dominant, mainly because it is they who hold political power. Their language is the official language, their religion is the state religion and their holy days are the official holidays.

#### Mon-Khmer groups

The **Khamu** of northern Laos, speakers of a Mon-Khmer language, are the most numerous of the indigenes, and have assimilated to a high degree.

Another Mon-Khmer-speaking group that inhabits the north are the **Htin**. Owing to a partial cultural ban on the use of any kind of metal, the Htin excel at fashioning bamboo baskets and fish traps.

#### Highland groups

The **Lao Soung** (literally the "high Lao") live at the highest elevations and include the Hmong, Mien, Lahu and Akha.

The **Hmong** are the most numerous, with a population of approximately 200,000. Hmong apparel is among the most colourful to be found in Laos and their silver jewellery is prized by collectors. Their written language uses Roman letters and was devised by Western missionaries.

#### Southern peoples

The Bolaven Plateau in southern Laos is named for the **Laven** people, a Mon-Khmer-speaking group whose presence predates that of the Lao. The Laven were very quick to assimilate the ways of the southern Lao. Other Mon-Khmer-speaking minorities found in the south, particularly in Savannakhet and Salavan, include the **Bru**, who are skilled builders of animal traps; the **Gie-Trieng**, who are expert basket weavers; the **Nge**, who produce textiles featuring stylized bombs and fighter planes; and the **Katu**, a very warlike people.

**January 20** Army Day
**March 8** Women's Day
**March 22** Lao People's Party Day
**April 13–16** Lao New Year
**May 1** International Labour Day
**June 1** Children's Day
**August 13** Lao Isara
**August 23** Liberation Day
**October 12** Freedom from France Day
**December 2** National Day

## FESTIVALS

All major **festivals**, whether Buddhist or animist, feature parades, music and dancing, not to mention the copious consumption of *lào-láo*. Because the Lao calendar is dictated by both solar and lunar rhythms, the dates of festivals change from year to year. Tourists are usually welcome to participate in the more public Buddhist festivals, but at hilltribe festivals, you should only watch from a distance.

Festivals of most interest to tourists include:

**Lao New Year** (April 13–16). Most stunningly observed in Louang Phabang, where there's a big procession and sand stupas are erected in monastery grounds. In Vientiane and almost everywhere else in the country, you'll be ambushed by young people carrying pails of water and armed with squirt guns. Also known as the "Rocket Festival".

**Bun Bang Fai** (May). A rainmaking ritual that predates Buddhism in Laos, and involves launching crude rockets, accompanied by plenty of bawdy jokes and props.

**Lai Heua Fai** (full moon in Oct). A festival of lights, again most magically celebrated in Louang Phabang, where each neighbourhood builds a large float, festoons it with lights, and parades it first through the streets and then on the Mekong.

**That Louang Festival** (full moon in Nov). In the days leading up to this, Vientiane's great stupa becomes the centrepiece of a fairground, where vendors, musicians and other performers gather for the annual celebrations.

# Vientiane and around

Hugging a bend of the Mekong River, the low-rise capital of Laos is a quaint and easygoing place, looking more like a rambling collection of villages than a city. However, in the mere decade and a half since Laos reopened its doors to foreign visitors, **VIENTIANE** has changed with dizzying rapidity. Happily, most of the changes have been for the better: there's an excellent selection of restaurants and accommodation to chose from, and the city still retains much of its placid charm.

## What to see and do

Two days is sufficient to see Vientiane's sights; the museum of Lao art, housed at the Haw Pha Kaew should be high on your list. The placid Buddhist monastery known as **Wat Sisaket** offers a good half-day diversion, and you should take a ride out to **That Louang**, Laos's most important religious building, to admire the effects of a sunset on its golden surface. If the weather isn't too steamy, many visitors opt for a soak in one of Vientiane's **herbal saunas**, and then top it off with a traditional massage. A popular day-trip destination is **Xiang Khouan** or the "**Buddha Park**", a Hindu-Buddhist fantasy in ferro-concrete on the banks of the Mekong, while a couple of hours north of the capital, the laid-back town of **Vang Viang**, set amid spectacular scenery on the road to Louang Phabang, has become a travellers' favourite.

A plaza surrounding **Nam Phou Fountain** marks the heart of downtown Vientiane, where you'll find the greatest concentration of accommodation, restaurants and shops catering to visitors. The fountain creates a pleasant public space in which both locals and visitors congregate to cool off after the sun goes down.

### The National Museum

North of Nam Phou, on Samsenthai Road, the **National Museum** (daily 8am–noon & 1–4pm; 10,000K) deals primarily with the events, both ancient and recent, that led to the "inevitable victory" of the proletariat in 1975. Inside, scenes portray Lao patriots liberating the motherland from Thai and Burmese feudalists, and French colonialists bullwhipping villagers. Black-and-white photographs tell the story of the struggle against "the Japanese fascists" and "American imperialists".

### Wat Sisaket

Towards the eastern end of Setthathilat Road, the street running parallel to and just south of Samsenthai Road, stands **Wat Sisaket** (daily 8am–noon & 1–4pm; 5000K), the oldest wat in Vientiane. Constructed by King Anouvong (Chao Anou) in 1818, it was the only monastery to survive the Siamese sacking ten years later. Surrounded by a tile-roofed cloister, the *sim* (building housing the main Buddha image) contains some charming, though badly deteriorating, murals. A splendidly ornate candle holder of carved wood situated before the altar is a fine example of nineteenth-century Lao woodcarving. Outside, the cloister holds countless niches from which peer diminutive Buddhas.

### The Presidential Palace and Haw Pha Kaew

Opposite Wat Sisaket stands the **Presidential Palace**, an impressive French Beaux Arts-style building, built to house the French colonial governor, and now used mainly for government ceremonies. Just east of the palace, the **Haw Pha Kaew** (daily 8am–noon & 1–4pm; 5000K), once the king's personal Buddhist temple, now functions as a **museum of art and**

**antiquities**. The temple is named for the Emerald Buddha, or Pha Kaew, which was pilfered by the Siamese in 1779 and carried off to their capital, where it remains today. The museum houses the finest collection of Lao art in the country, one of the most striking works being a Buddha in the "Beckoning Rain" pose (standing with arms to the sides and fingers pointing to the ground) and sporting a jewel-encrusted navel. Also of note are a pair of eighteenth-century terracotta *apsara*, or celestial dancers, and a highly detailed "naga throne" from Xiang Khouang that once served as a pedestal for a Buddha image.

### Lane Xang Avenue and Patouxai

Seedy **Lane Xang Avenue**, leading off north from Setthathilat Road, is reputedly modelled on France's Champs Elysées and **Patouxai** on the Arc de Triomphe. Popularly known as *anusawali* (Lao for "monument"), this massive ferro-concrete Arch of Victory (daily 8am–noon & 1–4pm; 3000K), 1km from the Presidential Palace, was built in the late 1950s to commemorate casualties of war on the side of the Royal Lao Government. The view of Vientiane from the top is worth the climb. A handful of hawkers shelter by a ceiling adorned with reliefs of the Hindu deities; the walls depict characters from the Ramayana, the epic Hindu story of battles between good and evil.

### That Louang

One-and-a-half kilometres east of Patouxai stands the Buddhist stupa, **That Louang** (daily except Mon & public holidays 8am–noon & 1–4pm; 3000K), Laos's most important religious building, and its national symbol. The original That Louang is thought to have been built in the mid-sixteenth century by King Setthathilat, whose statue stands in front, and was reported to have looked like a gold-covered "pyramid". Today's structure dates from the 1930s: the tapering golden spire of the main stupa is 45m tall and rests on a plinth of stylized lotus petals; it's surrounded on all sides by thirty short, spiky stupas. Within the cloisters are kept a collection of very worn Buddha images, some of which may have been enshrined in the original Khmer temple that once occupied the site.

## Arrival

**By bus** Most buses from the south, including Savannakhet and Pakxe, arrive at Vientiane's main bus station, next to the Morning Market (Talat Sao) on Khou Viang Road, 1.5km from Nam Phou Fountain. Most transport from the north, including Louang Phabang, via Vang Viang, arrives at the Khoua Louang bus stand (Khiw Lot Khua Luang), 2km northwest of the city centre, close to Nong Douang Market (the Talat Laeng or Evening Market).
**By air** Wattay International Airport is 6km west of downtown Vientiane. Airport facilities include visa-on-arrival ($35 plus one photo; see p.402 for details) and exchange services. The cheapest way of getting into town is to take a tuk-tuk or jumbo, a three-wheeled motorized taxi ($2), or a taxi ($6). Alternatively, walk out to Louang Phabang Avenue, a few hundred metres from the terminal, and hail an eastbound sawngthaew (10,000K), which will drop you off anywhere along the route to the main bus station next to the Morning Market.

## Information and tours

**Tourist information** The fairly helpful Lao National Tourism Authority (NTAL; Mon–Fri 8am–5pm; ⓣ021/212248 or 212356) operates out of an imposing building on Lane Xang Avenue, near the Morning. Phimphone minimarkets, *Scandinavian Bakery* and *Le Croissant d'Or* (see p.423) maintain more useful noticeboards, displaying information on everything from language classes to motorbikes for sale. Helpful maps can be bought from Monument Books on Nokeo Koummane Rd.
**Tour agencies** Recommended tour agencies include: Boualian Lao Travel Company, 346 Samsenthai Rd ⓣ021/213061; Diethelm Travel, Nam Phou Fountain ⓣ021/215920; Inter-Lao Tourisme, Setthathilat Rd ⓣ021/214832; Green Discovery, Nam Phou Fountain ⓣ 021/ 251564/ 223022, ⓦwww.greendiscoverylaos.com; Lane Xang,

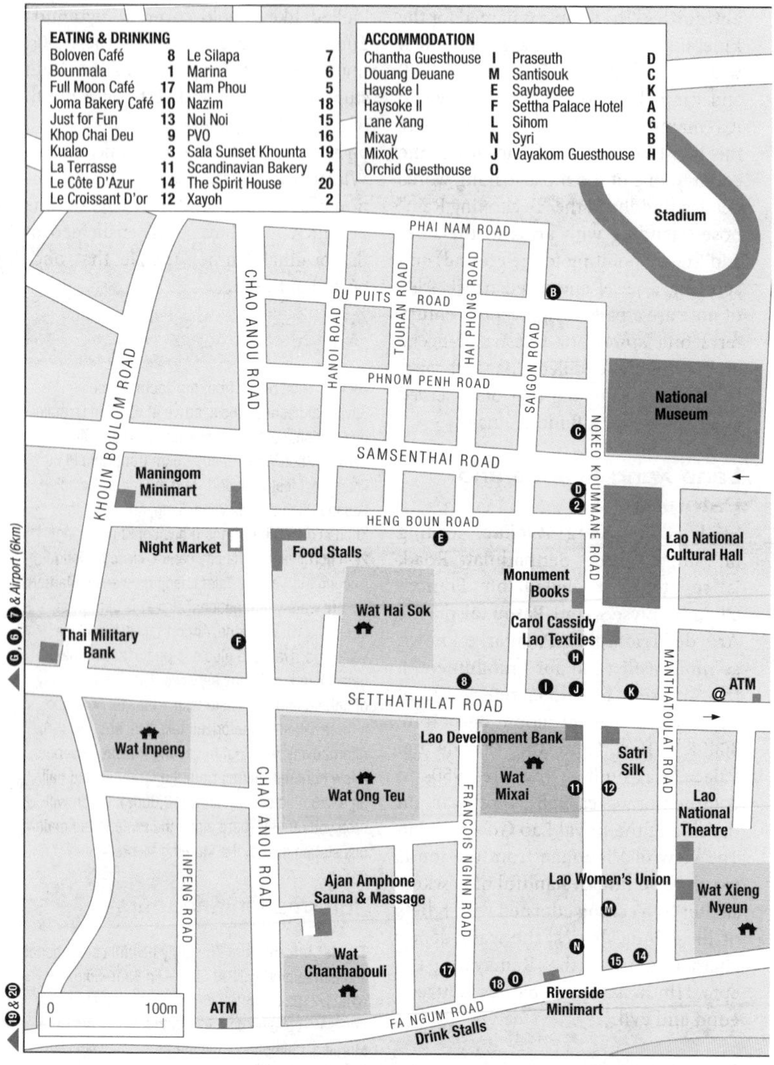


Pangkham Rd ☎021/213198; Lao Tourism, Lane Xang Ave ☎021/216671; Lao Travel Service, Lane Xang Ave ☎021/216603 or 216604; Phudoi Travel, Phonxai Rd ☎021/413888;

## City transport

**Bicycles and motorbikes** Bikes are $2 per day at many guesthouses and shops. Motorbikes are also easy to find ($6–10 per day) and easy to ride in Vientiane's bucolic traffic; the longest established rental shops are next door to each other on Samsenthai Road, near Pangkham Road – PVO (☎021/214444) and Boualian Travel (☎021/213061).

**Car rental** Cars and and pick-up trucks can be rented for self-drive trips into the provinces at Asia Vehicle Rental (☎021/217493) and Boualian Lao Travel Company (☎021/213061) on Samsenthai Road. Rates are approximately $55 per day.

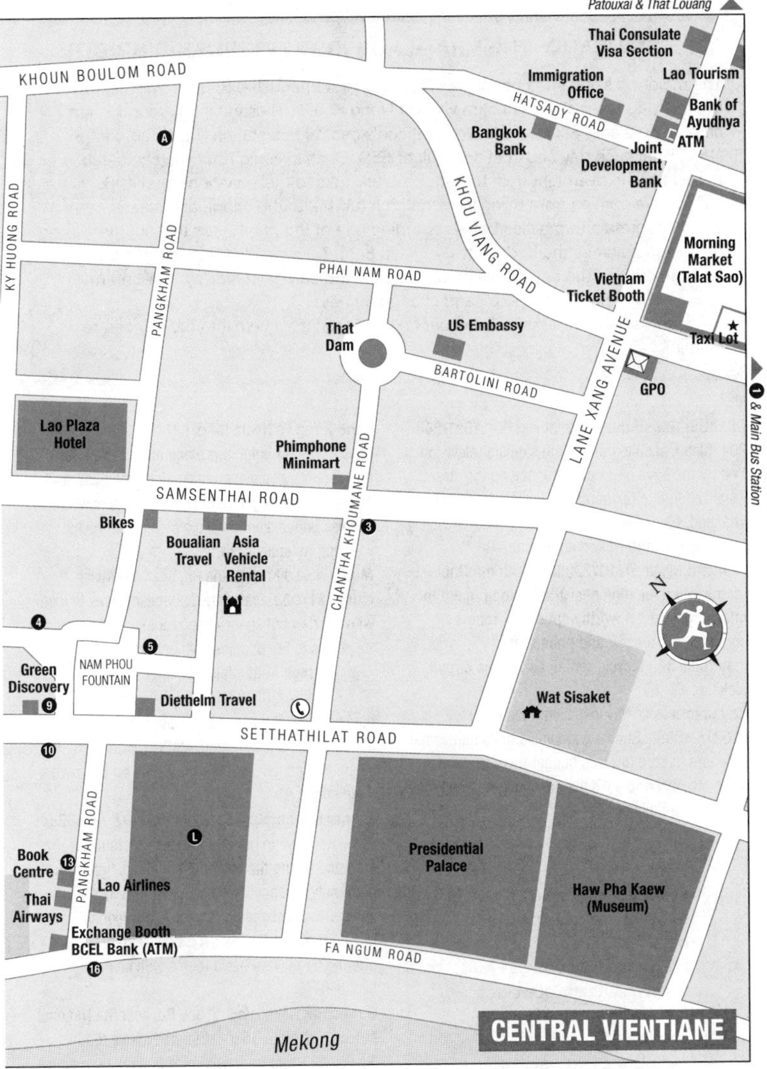


**Tuk-tuks and jumbos** Shared tuk-tuks generally ply frequently travelled routes, such as Lane Xang Avenue between the Morning Market and That Louang and along Louang Phabang Avenue heading out from the city centre, and charge around 10,000K for destinations within the city. There are usually a few tuk-tuks parked and waiting for foreign passengers near Nam Phou.

**Taxis** A fleet of unmetered taxis, none with a/c, gathers outside the Morning Market, in the car park on the Khou Viang Road side of the market. Prices are negotiable; drivers will accept Thai baht and American dollars as well as Lao kip.

## Accommodation

The majority of budget accommodation centres around Nam Phou, within the general area formed by Khoun Boulom Road and Lang Xang Avenue. All the hotels below are within walking distance of the city centre and Nam Phou.

## INTO THAILAND: THE THAI–LAO FIRST FRIENDSHIP BRIDGE

The major crossing into Laos is the Thai–Lao First Friendship Bridge, which spans the Mekong River at a point 5km west of Nong Khai in Thailand, and around 20km east of Vientiane. Six buses leave Vientiane's central bus station (Talat Sao) for Nong Khai each day and cost 15,000k or 55B. Once in Nong Khai you can catch the bus or the overnight train to Bangkok. Tuk-tuks to these stations cost 40B.

If you are coming from Nong Khai, catch a tuk-tuk to the bridge and clear Thai immigration formalities before boarding one of the **minibuses** that shuttle passengers across the bridge (every 15min 8am–7.30pm; B20), stopping at **Lao immigration** on the opposite side of the river. You can get a 30-day visa-on-arrival ($35 plus one passport photo), and change money.

After crossing, tuk-tuks ($3) and car taxis ($5) run from here into the city centre (30min).

**Chantha Guesthouse** Setthathilat Rd ⓣ021/243 204. Clean, ensuite rooms with satellite television. Two rooms have a balcony overlooking the street. Small, adequate restaurant serving simple food attached. ❷

**Douang Deuane** Nokeo Koummane Rd, near Wat Mixai ⓣ021/222301–3. Comfortable rooms and a location near the Mekong make this mid-range hotel a worthy option. All rooms en suite with a/c, TV and phone. Offers motorbike and bicycle rental, as well as airport pick-up. ❹–❺

**Haysoke II** Near *Haysoke I*, on Chao Anou Rd ⓣ021/240888. Similar good value to its namesake but more geared towards budget travellers and more atmospheric – it's the only budget option in a colonial-era building. ❶–❷

**TREAT YOURSELF**

If you fancy splurging on a luxurious night's sleep, head to the stunning colonial-era hotel, **Settha Palace Hotel** (6 Pangkham Rd ⓣ021/217581, ⓦwww.setthapalace.com). It has all the usual features of a five-star establishment, including a pool set in a serene garden adorned with overhanging foliage. They have created an ambient setting that would cure you from any of the aches and pains of roughing it, while the restaurant, *La Belle Epoque*, serves fine French cuisine and seasonal Lao dishes. They also own an authentic London black cab which they use to deliver their guests to the airport. ❽

**Lane Xang** Fa Ngum Rd ⓣ021/214102. Once Laos's premier hotel, this place has a retro Fifties feel, a pool, spacious grounds along the quay, and 109 fantastically good-value rooms. The downside is noise on weekends – it's a popular venue for wedding receptions. ❺

**Mixay** Nokeo Koummane Rd, near Wat Mixai ⓣ021/217023. One of the cheapest places in town, with spartan but super-cheap rooms ranging from $2 dorms to fan doubles with bath ($6). ❶

**Mixok** Setthathilat Rd, opposite Wat Mixai ⓣ021/251606. A favourite with backpackers; it has a slightly more intimate feel about it than Mixay. Cheap, restful rooms with clean, shared facilites. Great location on the town's main street. ❶

**Orchid Guesthouse** Fa Ngum Rd ⓣ021/252825. Given its position right on the main restaurant strip and facing the Mekong, the prices here are extremely reasonable. ❹

**Praseuth** Samsenthai Rd, near the National Museum ⓣ021/217932. A friendly establishment offering large, very basic rooms with shared facilities. ❷

**Santisouk** Nokeo Koummane Rd, near the National Museum ⓣ021/215303. Situated above the *Santisouk Restaurant*, with nine budget a/c rooms and an upstairs balcony. ❷

**Saybaydee** Setthathilat Rd. Cheap dorms, single, double and triple rooms on the main road. It is one of the few budget hostels in the area and is a comfortable cheap option for an overnight stay. ❶

**Sihom** Sihom Rd, along the dirt alley to the west of *Le Silapa Restaurant* ⓣ021/214562. Eleven tastefully decorated rooms, some with a/c and satellite TV. The a/c rooms are only $1 more than the fan-equipped rooms. ❷

**Syri** Saigon Rd ⓣ021/212682. A large house on a quiet lane in the Chao Anou residential district, with spacious double and triple a/c rooms and a nice balcony. Motorbikes and bikes for rent. ❸

**Vayakorn Guesthouse** Nokeo Koummane Rd ⓣ021/214911. Peaceful, spotless rooms with ensuite and satelite TV. Good value for a mid-range guesthouse. ❸

## Eating

There are restaurants catering to virtually every taste, from sauerkraut to Korean BBQ, in Vientiane. Aside from tourist restaurants, there are a number of cheap travellers' cafés along Fa Ngum Road and riverside food stalls offering Lao staples such as tam *màk hung* (spicy papaya salad), *pîng kai* (grilled chicken) and fruit shakes. A night market sets up on Khoun Boulom Road and along Heng Boun Road in the early evening, and there's a more extensive version at Dong Palane Market on Ban Fai Road near Wat Ban Fai. Most of Vientiane's restaurants open for lunch and then again for dinner; no-frills eateries are usually open throughout the day, closing around 9pm.

### Breakfast, bakeries and cafés

**Joma Bakery Café** Setthathilat Rd, just west of Nam Phou Fountain. The best sandwiches in town, great desserts, and good quiches and coffee. Canadian-managed with fast, friendly service. The breakfasts here are particularly delicious.

**Le Croissant d'Or** Nokeo Koummane Rd, just around the corner from *Joma Bakery Café*. The pastries and croissants here are as great as the other big two bakeries, and you can always get a seat.

**Scandinavian Bakery** Nam Phou. Vientiane's most popular bakery offers sandwiches and a wide selection of pastries and cookies. Usually completely overrun with tourists.

### Asian Food

**Bounmala** Khou Viang Rd, near Wat Phaxai. Classic, inexpensive Lao-beer-and-roast-chicken joint under a tin roof. Also worth sampling is the roast beef, served with *khào pun* (flour noodles in a sauce), star fruit and lettuce.

**Kualao** Samsenthai Rd. Lao food with traditional music and dance performances in a restored colonial-era house. Tends to cater mostly to large tour groups. Definitely overpriced but worth it if you're looking for some music and entertainment. ❷–❻.

**Noi Noi** Fa Ngum Rd. Very cheap Lao, Thai and Western dishes: this is the best one of the row of five popular travellers' cafés facing the river here.

### Vietnamese and Indian

**Nazim** Fa Ngum Rd. Indian restaurant facing the Mekong with inside and sidewalk seating. Strong on vegetarian dishes, and immensely popular with backpackers.

**PVO** Samsenthai Rd. Highly recommended, great-value eatery, serving fantastic sandwiches, spring rolls, *nâm neuang* and *baw* bun on the spot or to go.

### Western food

**Boloven Café** Setthathilat Rd, opposite Francois Nginn Rd. Features European fare and coffee from the plateau for which it is named. The picture windows afford a pleasant view of a particularly leafy stretch of Setthathilat Road.

**La Terrasse** Nokeo Koummane Rd, near Wat Mixai. Outstanding steaks, pizza, a fair approximation of Mexican food and salads at prices lower than most of the other Western joints. Nightly BBQ from 7.30pm. Closed Sun.

**Le Côte D'Azur** Fa Ngum Rd, near Nokeo Koummane Rd. One of Vientiane's better restaurants, boasting terrific service and a great menu of Provençal-style seafood and pasta, plus a large selection of excellent pizzas. Closed Sun lunchtime.

**Le Silapa** Sihom Rd, west of the Thai Military Bank. French food served in a beautifully restored colonial shop-house. The food here is not cheap but they do feature a good-value $5 set lunch.

**Nam Phou** On edge of the plaza. Offers Continental cuisine, with outdoor seating that makes the most of the new incarnation of Vientiane's old fountain. Moderately expensive for Vientiane but worth a splurge for the charming al fresco dining.

**Xayoh** Corner of Samsenthai and Nokeo Koummane, facing the Lao National Cultural Hall. This is Vientiane's latest, greatest yuppie-style bistro serving burgers and salads as well as coffees and desserts.

### Vegetarian

**Just for Fun** Pangkham Rd. Time your meal at this tiny, clean vegetarian-friendly restaurant to avoid the lunchtime crowds, as the tasty over-rice dishes are very good value. Also does some of the best chocolate cake in town and a great selection of herbal teas. Closed Sun.

## Nightlife

Vientiane's location along an east–west stretch of the Mekong positions it for spectacular sunsets, and makeshift stalls selling bottles of Beer Lao and fruit shakes set up on the riverfront sidewalk every afternoon. Dance clubs along Louang Phabang Avenue, just beyond the *Novotel*, play Thai pop and international dance mixes and cater to well-heeled teenagers. They don't usually get going until after 9pm, and are unplugged by 2am at the latest.

## Bars and clubs

**Full Moon Café** Francois Nginn Rd. Good ambience created by the design conscious décor, chilled music and really pleasant staff. Happy hour is 6–9pm.
**Khop Chai Deu** Nam Phou Fountain. Popular outdoor café with cheap pitchers of draft beer and passable Lao, Indian, and Western food. Full of tourists, yes, but still the most fun place in town.
**Marina** Louang Phabang Ave, 3km west of the centre. The best of a number of big discos on the edge of town for Lao teenagers, with a good dance floor and a separate bar.
**Sala Sunset Khounta** Fa Ngum Rd. Known to some simply as "The End of the World" and others as "The Sunset Bar", the original spot for sundowners in Vientiane was expanded owing to its immense popularity with expats and tour groups, but it still ends up crowded at sunset. Get here early to sample the *tam kûay tani*, a spicy salad of green bananas, eggplant and chillies.

**TREAT YOURSELF**

The classy bar, **The Spirit House** (105 Fa Ngum Rd, ⓦwww.thespirithouselaos.com) is definitely in a league of its own, with contemporary interior design, picturesque riverside beer garden and extensive cocktail menu. They also serve posh snacks and lunches.

## Shopping

Besides the Morning Market, most textile, souvenir and antique shops are found on Samsenthai and Setthathilat roads and along the lanes running between them. However, the vast majority of the "antiques" on offer are cheap imitations, as are many "silk" and "silver" items. If you're heading north, it's best to save your shopping for Louang Phabang.
**Books** Monument Books (ⓣ021/243708) on Nokeo Koummane Rd; The Vientiane Book Centre, Pangkham Rd (ⓣ021/212031).
**Morning Market** (Talat Sao). Some good bargains in homespun cotton clothing ($2–5) and handicrafts: shoulder bags (*nyam*) are cheap and functional, as are hand-woven *pha biang*, a long, scarf-like textile.
**Tailoring** Although the selection of fabrics is sometimes limited, the tailors along Pangkham Road, just north of Nam Phou, are amazingly cheap and fast. If you find some silk or cotton fabric in the Morning Market, you can bring it here and have a shirt made in a day or two for about $10.
**Textiles and silk** Shops specializing in traditional textiles and authentic silk include Satri Silk (ⓣ021/219295), Carol Cassidy Lao Textiles (ⓣ021/212123) and the Lao Women's Union's The Art of Silk, located on Manthatoulat Road near Wat Xieng Nyeun.

## Directory

**Airline offices** Lao Airlines, Pangkham Rd ⓣ021/212053, or at Wattay International Airport, Louang Phabang Ave ⓣ021/512028; Thai Airways International, Pangkham Rd ⓣ021/216143; Vietnam Airlines, Samsenthai Rd, mezzanine floor of the Lao Hotel Plaza ⓣ021/217562.
**Banks and exchange** Lao and Thai banks, many of which are located on Lane Xang Ave, exchange traveller's cheques and do cash advances on Visa and MasterCard; a few local banks also maintain exchange booths around the city centre; BCEL on the corner Pangkham Street has an ATM that accepts Visa and MasterCard. There's also an ATM on Setthathilat Rd opposite Joma Bakery that only accepts Mastercard and domestic cards. The representative agent for American Express is Diethelm Travel, on the corner of Setthathilat Rd and Nam Phou Fountain.
**Bowling** Lao Bowling Centre; Khoun Boulom Rd; 12,000K per person per game.
**Embassies and consulates** Australia, Nehru Rd ⓣ021/413600 or 413805; Cambodia, near That Khao, Thadua Rd ⓣ021/315251; China, near Wat Nak Noi, Wat Nak Rd ⓣ021/315100 or 315103; Indonesia, Phon Kheng Rd, Ban Phon Sa-at ⓣ021/413908-10; Malaysia, near Wat Phaxai, That Louang Rd ⓣ021/414205–6; Philippines, near Wat Nak, Salakoktane Rd ⓣ021/215826; Thailand (visa section), across from the NTAL building, Lane Xang Ave ⓣ021/214582; United States, near That Dam, Bartholonie Rd ⓣ021/212580–1; Vietnam, near Wat Phaxai, That Louang Rd ⓣ021/413400–2.
**Hospitals and clinics** Australian Clinic, Nehru Rd ⓣ021/413603 by appointment only, with vaccinations on Thursdays; International Clinic, Mahosot Hospital Compound, Fa Ngum Rd ⓣ021/214022, open 24hr; Mahosot Hospital, Mahosot Rd ⓣ021/214018; Setthathilat Hospital, Phon Sa-at Rd ⓣ021/450197; Swedish Clinic, near Swedish Embassy, near Wat Nak, Sok Pa Louang Rd ⓣ021/315015.

**Immigration department** Hatsady Rd, near the junction with Lane Xang Ave ☎021/212520; open Mon–Fri 8am–noon & 1–4pm.

**Internet** There are dozens of small internet centres scattered all around city centre that charge 100K per minute and close at about 10pm.

**Language courses** Centre de Langue Française, Lane Xang Ave ☎021/215764; Lao-American Language Center, Phon Kheng Rd, Ban Phon Sa-at ☎021/414321.

**Laundry** Guesthouses will be happy to do your laundry for around 10,000K a kilo.

**Massage and herbal sauna** A massage costs about $3 per hour and saunas $1 at: Ajan Amphone, next to Wat Chanthabouli, Chao Anou Rd (Mon–Fri 2–5pm, Sat & Sun 10am–7pm); Hôpital de Médicine Traditionnelle, near Wat Si Amphon has massages for $2, saunas for $1.

**Pharmacies** The best pharmacies are on Mahosot Rd in the vicinity of the Morning market.

**Post office** The GPO is on the corner of Khou Viang Rd and Lane Xang Ave. Poste restante is held for up to three months (Mon–Fri 8am–5pm, Sat 8am–4pm, Sun 8am–noon).

**Swimming** Lane Xang Hotel, Fa Ngum Rd ($2 per day); Lao Plaza Hotel, Samsenthai Rd ($5); Novotel, Louang Phabang Ave ($5); Royal Dokmaideng Hotel, Lane Xang Ave ($3); Sok Pa Louang Swimming Pool ($1).

**Telephones** International calls and faxes at Telecom, Setthathilat Rd (daily 7am–10pm).

**Visa Services** Boualian Lao Travel, 346 Samsenthai Rd (☎021/213061), will arrange Lao visa extensions and visa for Vietnam, Cambodia, China and Thailand.

## Moving on

**By bus** Talat Sao, near the Morning market, is the station for all buses going within the region; the Khoua Louang bus stand or northern station, 2km northwest of centre for all buses going north, and the southern bus station, 8km south of centre, for all those going south and long-haul VIP bus services. International and VIP buses are booked through guesthouses and tour agencies and will collect you from where you are staying. These services are sometimes the simplest, most time-effective way to get around for long distances and are worth the extra money.

**From Talat Sao central bus station:** Friendship Bridge (every 45min); Nong Khai, Thailand (6 daily; 1hr); Udon Thani (6 daily; 3hr 30min); Vang Viang (local, 6 daily; 3hr 30min; VIP 2 daily; 2hr 30min).

**From Khoua Louang, Northern bus station:** Louang Namtha (1 daily; 20hr); Louang Phabang (5 daily; 10–12hr); Phonsavan (2 daily; 10–12hr); Xam Nua (1 daily; 8hr); Oudomxai (1 daily; 19hr).

**From Southern bus station:** Attapu (2 daily; 23hr); Lak Xao (3 daily; 9hr); Paksan (12 daily; 2hr); Paxke (local, 3 daily; 14hr; VIP, 4 leave at 8.30pm; 9hr); Savannakhet (8 daily; 8hr); Thakhek (10 daily; 6hr).

**By boat** Slow boats to Louang Phabang (2–3 week; 4 days–1 week; $20 per person) leave from Tha Hua Kao Liaw pier, located on the Mekong River, 10km west of the centre of Vientiane; tuk-tuks cost 40,000K from the centre. There's no boat service going south.

**By train** Overnight trains to Bangkok leave between 5 and 7pm from Nong Khai, Thailand. Take a taxi or tuk-tuk to the Friendship Bridge; once on the Thai side, hire a share taxi to the train station 20 baht.

**By air** A tuk-tuk to Wattay International airport costs 10,000K.

**Destinations:** Bangkok, Thailand (2 daily; 1hr); Chiang Mai, Thailand (6 weekly; 2hr); Hanoi, Vietnam (10 weekly; 1hr 10min); Houayxai (3 weekly; 1hr 20min); Kunming, China (2 weekly; 3hr); Louang Namtha (4 weekly; 1hr 10min); Louang Phabang (2–3 daily; 40min); Oudomxai (6 weekly; 50min); Pakxe (5 weekly; 1hr 20min); Phnom Penh, Cambodia (8 weekly; 2hr 30min); Phonsavan (10 weekly; 40min); Siem Reap, Cambodia (2 weekly; 2hr 30min); Xam Nua (4 weekly; 1hr 10min).

## BUDDHA PARK

Located on the Mekong River 27km from downtown Vientiane, **Xiang Khouan** or the "**Buddha Park**" (daily 8am–5pm; 10,000K), is Laos's quirkiest attraction. This collection of massive ferro-concrete sculptures, which lie dotted around a wide riverside meadow, was created under the direction of Luang Phu Boonlua Surirat, a self-styled holy man who claimed to have been the disciple of a cave-dwelling Hindu hermit in Vietnam. Upon returning to Laos, Boonlua began the sculpture garden in the late 1950s as a means of spreading his philosophy of life and his ideas about the cosmos. Besides the brontosaurian reclining Buddha that dominates the park, there are concrete statues of every conceivable deity in the Hindu-Buddhist pantheon. After the revolution, Boonlua was forced to flee across the Mekong to Nong Khai in Thailand, where he established an even more elaborate version of his philosophy in concrete at Sala Kaeo Kou, also known as Wat Khaek. To **get to the park**, either take bus #14 from Vientiane's main bus station (every 40min), or hire a tuk-tuk to do the round trip, including a wait of an hour or so, for $8–10.

## VANG VIANG AND AROUND

Just 155km north of the capital lies the spectacular limestone karst valley of **VANG VIANG**, which is known for its lovely **caves** and nearby ethnic minority villages. Most backpackers stop here for a few days, floating down the river in large tractor inner tubes, stopping off at various bamboo-structured bars for a Beer Lao or a whisky bucket. Admittedly, Vang Viang is not the epicentre for Lao culture, but its beautiful riverside setting makes the town a perfect rest stop from a gruelling sightseeing itinerary. Chill out in a hammock, rent a bike, explore the scenery or socialize in one of the waterside bars. Remember that because of the licensing laws, everything shuts down at 11pm.

### What to see and do

A popular way to spend the day is to float down the Nam Xong on huge tractor inner **tubes**. There are some fabulous views to enjoy, and just enough rapids and tiny islands to keep things interesting. Some people stop for shots of *lào-láo* while floating down the river, but be warned that alcohol and tubing don't mix; there have been a number of drownings on tube trips in recent years. The best launching point is the village of Pakpok, about 4km north of Vang Viang, which makes for a two- to three-hour trip. Longer (10km) tube trips start from Ban Pha Thao off Route 13. Tubes (60,000K per day), **bicycles** (20,000K per day) and **motorcycles** ($7 per day) can be rented at many places around town. A number of restaurants and guesthouses advertise tubing and caves as an organized tour but the groups can be uncomfortably large so ask if there's a maximum limit.

#### The caves

If you decide to visit the **caves** on your own, you can find hand-drawn maps at most restaurants and guesthouses. You'll also find that locals are more than happy to point you in the right direction. There is usually someone posted at each cave to collect a small entrance fee. Likewise, there is normally someone collecting a toll from foreigners who cross the bamboo footbridge heading west towards the caves.

#### Tham Phou Kham cave

Six kilometres west of Vang Viang, **Tham Phou Kham** (10,000K) makes a rewarding half-day trip that takes in some fine scenery. Cross the river by the bamboo footbridge near the Nam Song and follow the road to Na Thong, 4km west. Follow the signs along the trail until it forks off through the rice fields towards the cliff-face, 1km away. It's a short, steep climb to the entrance. In the main cavern reclines a bronze Buddha; bring a torch if you want to explore the tunnels branching off the main gallery. Outside the cave, the perfectly blue stream is a great spot for a swim; you can buy cool drinks and fruit nearby.

#### Tham Pha Thao cave and Pha Thao

**Tham Pha Thao** is 10km north of Vang Viang: stretching for more than 2km, the tunnel-like cave is pitch-black, filled with huge stalactites and stalagmites, and is the most satisfying caving trip you can make from Vang Viang. It's best visited near the end of the rainy season, when the water level is perfect for a swim in the subterranean swimming pool 800m into the cave. Bear in mind that you'll be up to your chest in water at times, so travel light and don't bring anything valuable. In the height of the dry season, it's possible to go beyond the pool and explore the full length of the cave. The cave is near the Hmong village of **Pha Thao**, which lies 13km north of Vang Viang. Turn left after the bridge just beyond the Km10 marker on Route 13 – a road sign points the way to the "Nam Xong-Pha Thao Irrigation Project" – and either ford the river or hail a boat for a few thousand kip. Once across, head for the village at the base of the cliff, where you'll find a few simple restaurants. The villagers will point the way to the cave mouth.

## Arrival

**By bus** For buses to and from Vientiane and Louang Phabang, the station is behind the old airstrip, within walking distance of most accommodation. The a/c tourist buses and private minivans drop passengers at *Thavisouk Bungalows*.

## Accommodation

Despite its small size, Vang Viang is the best-value spot for accommodation in the country. However, most of the town's guesthouses are modern, concrete monstrosities and despite the huge number of choices, finding a friendly, family-run guesthouse in Vang Viang is not that easy.

**Bungalow Thavonsouk** At the bamboo bridge. Superbly located deluxe en-suite bungalows spread along the banks of the Nam Xong River. Prices depend on the size and quality of bungalow: some are quite luxurious. ❹–❻

**Chaleune** Located on the main drag, this basic place has good views from the common veranda. It also has some of the cheapest rooms in town. ❶

**Dok Khoun I, II** Clean, tiled rooms, many en suite and with hot water, in modern, multi-storey buildings at three locations around town. Reasonably good value and quality but devoid of personality or atmosphere. ❶–❷

**Kien Thong** On the street with the *Vieng Keo* restaurant at one end and the *Phaykham* at the other ⓣ023/511069. Popular, friendly two-storey guesthouse with twenty clean doubles, most with hot water and en-suite bathrooms. ❶

**May Lyn** Across the Nam Song from Vang Viang, a 10min walk from the main town reachable by a suspension bridge ⓣ020/604 095. *May Lyn* is owned by a charming Irishman and is set away from the main tourist attractions. It is set in a well-tended garden, and also has a very welcome sauna. ❶–❷

**Nana** Alley by the *Vieng Keo* ⓣ023/511036. Fourteen clean, en-suite doubles, all with hot water and some with a/c. The upstairs rooms are best, and there's a pleasant terrace on the second floor. Same quality as the *Dok Khoun II* across the road but much more personality. ❸

**Ngeunphanith** ⓣ023/511150. Centrally located on the main road above one of the popular television bars; rooms are clean but the standard of each room varies so check them out first. ❶

**Pan's Place** ⓣ023/511484, ⓔneilenolix@hotmail.com. This place is in a good location at the quieter end of town and backing onto the old airstrip near the bus station. Cheap, clean and comfy rooms with a sweet café out the front and the chilled *Jeska Bar* out the back. Friendly vibe. ❶

**Pany** Alley by the *Vieng Keo*. Roomy, en-suite doubles with wood floors in a modern two-storey house. Very clean, and an excellent deal for the money. ❶

**Phoubane** South of the market, just in from the river road ⓣ023/511037. A pleasant, leafy compound, with decent rooms, some en suite. Extremely good value. ❶

**Phou Kham** Directly behind the *Dok Khoun I*. Two-storey house with gaudy pillars but the rooms are better value than many similar places. Several of the upstairs rooms have good views of the karsts. ❶

**Sivixay** Main road opposite the *Bountang* ⓣ023/511030. These two modern buildings set in a large compound are not much to look at but contain seventeen very decent, tiled en-suite doubles with hot water. ❶

## Eating

The quality and selection of international restaurants in Vang Viang depends on what seems to be a cyclic purge – sometimes having restaurants and bars to rival those of Vientiane, before they are shut down and replaced by mediocre pizzerias.

**Luang Prabang Bakery** Decent pastries and breakfast with good coffee to wake you up from the night before.

**Nazim** Part of the Nazim chain, serving decent Indian and Malay dishes for about $2.

**Organic Farm Café** This place serves up delicious mulberry pancakes, excellent fruit shakes and hearty cooked breakfasts. It has a

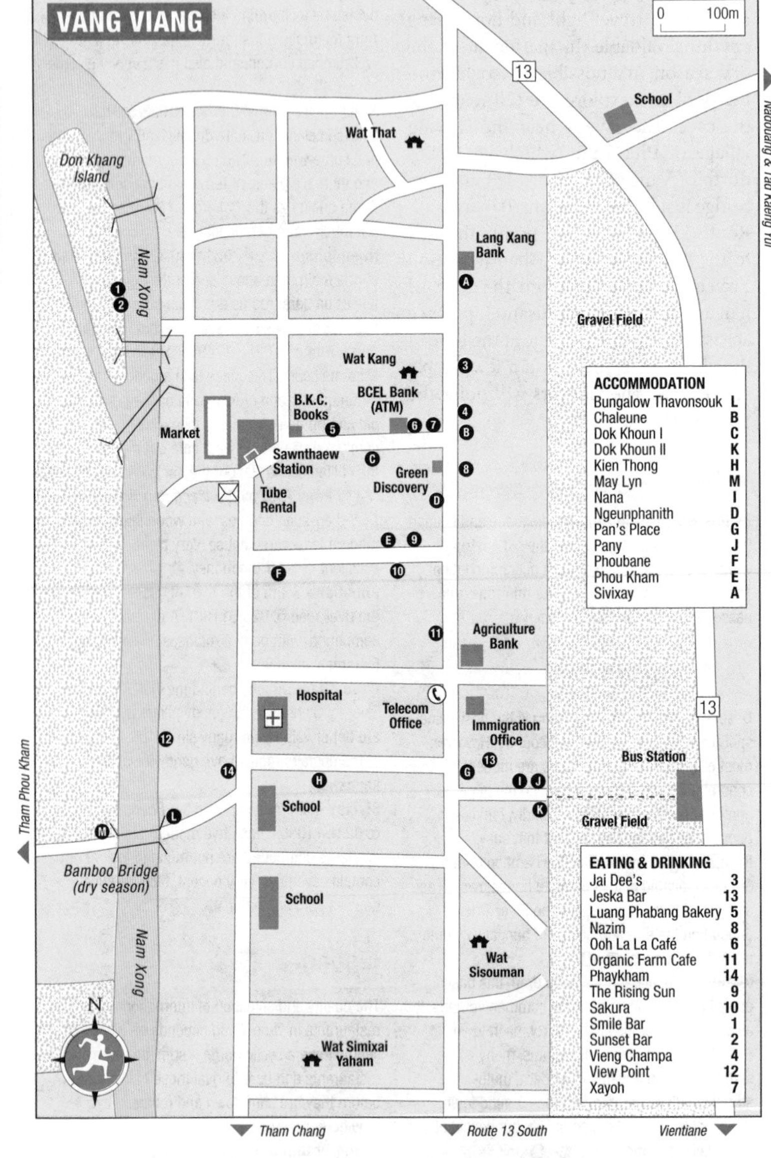


pleasant outdoor terrace where you can sit in the morning and watch the town slowly start to wake up.

**Phaykham** Just three houses north of the turn-off to the *Sunset*, this has a big deck offering spectacular views over the river and the majestic peaks beyond. The food is not as impressive as the view but serves simple sandwiches and Lao dishes.

**The Rising Sun** Owned by a Cornish expat, *The Rising Sun* serves decent British pub grub; fry-up breakfasts, steak and chips and even Cornish pasties.

**Vieng Champa** If you are beginning to feel horribly uncultured for taking advantage of all the Western food joints, you can find authentic, tasty Lao food at this restaurant.

### DRUGS IN VANG VIANG

Rolling up, kicking back and losing yourself in the tranquil setting might seem like a good idea to those partial to a spliff, but remember that this is **illegal**: plain-clothed police officers wait around smoker hot spots (bars and the river), ready to issue a $500 fine.

Vang Viang is also a "happy" place. Many restaurants keep a special menu listing food and drink options mixed with marijuana, opium or mushrooms. Naturally, if consumed in excess, the experience can rapidly become the opposite of "happy" and can cause bad trips and extreme vomiting.

**View Point** As the name suggests, this place boasts a beautiful view across the river and serves Lao and Western dishes.

**Xayoh** Popular bar and restaurant on the town's main corner with a pleasant open seating area serving the usual Western and Lao fare.

## Drinking

The river bars down the tubing stretch of the Nam Song is where the boozing normally begins and then once back on land, the town has several good drinking holes available, even if they do all close down at 11pm.

**Jai Dee's** A reliable choice for a good party atmosphere, consisting of the two main ingredients: good music and booze buckets.

**Jeska Bar** Chilled out, open-air bar, round the back of *Pan's Place* guesthouse, decorated with floor cushions and twinkly fairy lights.

**Ooh La La Cafe** Bucket-fuelled venue with good music, drink and food. The bar is run by the flirtatious matriarch, Mama Lao.

**Sakura** Similar to Jai Dee's, with a dance floor and staff that used to be punters but who have stayed on, because they just couldn't leave.

**Smile Bar** The most popular bar in Vang Viang, by the river where the tubers exit. Partyers dance round the fire whilst a long-standing DJ spins the decks (or just presses play). Great atmosphere and location.

**Sunset Bar** Riverside bar, most popular in the early evening when soaking tubers leave the river and huddle round the fire. The perfect, peaceful pitstop before the evening's parties kick off.

## Directory

**Banks** There's a BCEL bank on the main street opposite the *Dok Khoun I* guesthouse which has an ATM that accepts MasterCard; Lang Xang Bank on the town's main north–south road, and an Agriculture Bank on the same street further south.

**Bicyles and motorbikes** These are very easy to find at dozens of outlets along the main strip. Bikes ($2 per day); motorbikes ($5 per day).

**Book shop** B.K.C Bookshop has the best selection of secondhand titles.

**Hospital** Very near the centre of town on the road parallel to the river (Ⓣ023/511604).

**Internet** Available at dozens of outlets, all charging 200K per minute.

**Post office** Right next to the town market.

**Telephones** The telecom office (Mon–Fri 8am–noon & 1–5pm) is on the opposite corner from Agricultural Bank, which handles international calls.

**Tour Companies** Green Discovery Ⓣ023/511440, Ⓦwww.greendiscovery.com; LV Natural Tours, Xplore-Asia Ⓦwww.xplore-asia.com.

## Moving on

**By bus** Louang Phabang (5 daily; 6hr); Phonsavan (1 daily; 7 hr); Vientiane (10 daily; 3hr).

**By sawngthaew** Ones to surrounding villages leave from the stand right off the central market in Vang Viang.

# Louang Phabang and around

Nestling in a slim valley shaped by lofty, green mountains and cut by the swift Mekong and Khan rivers, **LOUANG PHABANG** exudes tranquillity and grandeur. A tiny mountain kingdom for more than a thousand years and designated a World Heritage site in 1995, it is endowed with a legacy of ancient, red-roofed temples and French-Indochinese architecture, not to mention some of the country's most refined cuisine, its richest culture and most sacred Buddha image. The very name Louang Phabang conjures up the classic image of Laos – streets of ochre colonial houses and swaying palms, lines of saffron-robed monks gliding through the morning mist, and longtail boats racing down the Mekong. This is where the first proto-Lao nation took root. It's the most Lao city in Laos, the only one where ethnic Lao are in the majority and where the back streets and cobblestoned lanes have a distinctly village-like feel. Conveniently, Louang Phabang is also the **transport hub** of northern Laos, with road, river and air links – both domestic and international – all leading to the city.

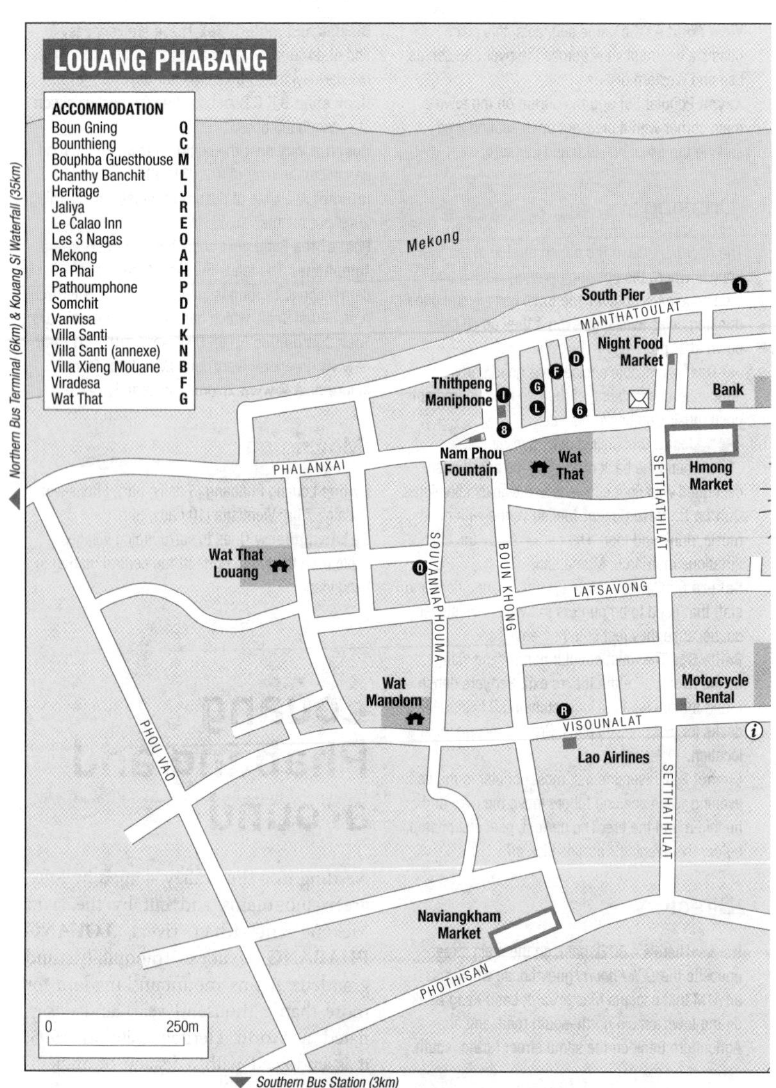

## What to see and do

Louang Phabang's **old city** is largely concentrated on a tongue of land, approximately 1km long and 0.25km wide, with the confluence of the Mekong and Nam Khan rivers at its tip. This peninsula is dominated by a steep and forested hill, **Phou Si** ("Sacred Hill"), crowned with a Buddhist stupa that can be seen for miles around. Most of Louang Phabang's architecture of merit – monasteries and French-influenced mansions – is to be found on the main thoroughfare, **Xiang Thong**, between the tip of the peninsula and Setthathilat Road. Beyond Setthathilat Road, near the Mekong, lies the old silversmithing district, **Ban Wat That**, centred on its monastery, Wat That.

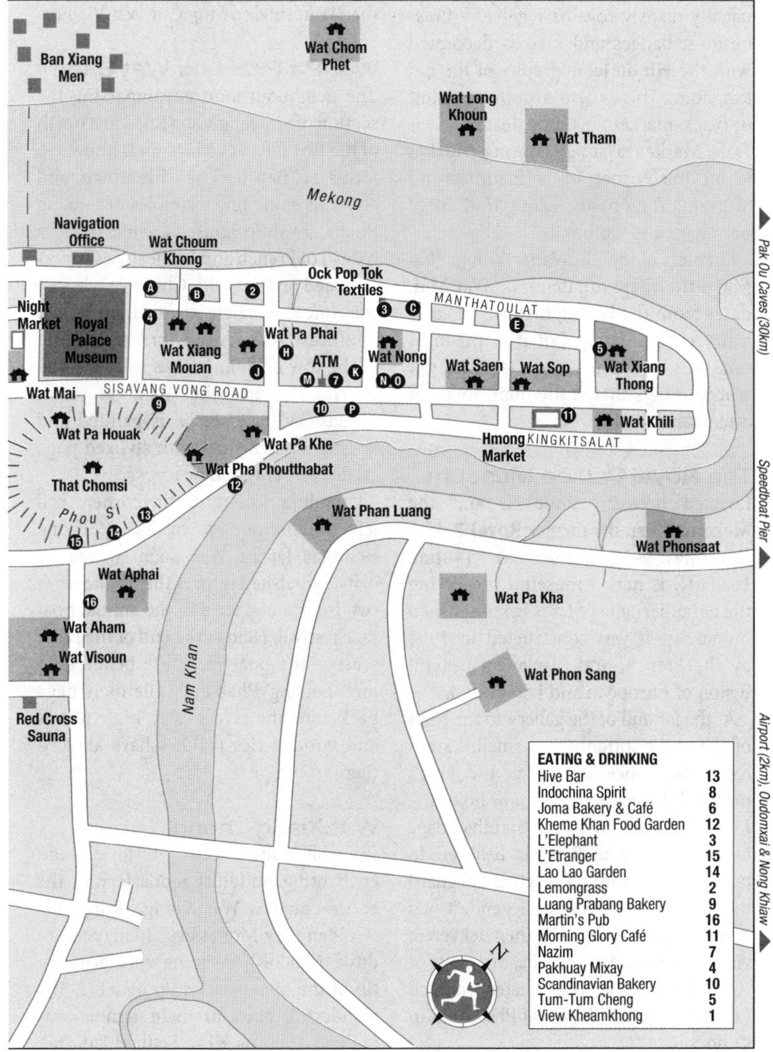

### Dala Market, Hmong Market and Wat Mai

A good place to start your tour of the old city is the dry-goods market, **Dala Market**, on Setthathilat Road. Wild chicken calls, resembling tin whistles, are on display beside bags of saltpetre and sulphur which, when mixed with ground charcoal, produce homemade gunpowder. Stalls selling gold and silver jewellery double as pawn shops and usually display royalist regalia — brass buttons, badges and medals decorated with the Hindu iconography of the old kingdom. This is also a popular haunt of black-market currency dealers. Near Dala Market, a small **Hmong Market** is on the corner of Setthathilat and Sisavang Vong roads, selling traditional hats, bags and clothes.

Further along Sisavang Vong, Wat Mai Suwannaphumaham, or **Wat Mai**, dates from the late eighteenth or early nineteenth century, but it is the *sim's* relatively modern facade with its gilt stucco reliefs that is the main focus of attention.

### The Royal Palace Museum

Located between Phou Si and the Mekong River, the former **Royal Palace** (Mon–Fri 8.30am–noon & 1–4pm; 10,000K) is now a museum preserving the paraphernalia of Laos's extinguished monarchy. It was constructed in 1904 by the French, and displays a tasteful fusion of European and Lao design.

At the far end of the gallery to the right of the main entrance is a small, barred room that once served as the king's personal shrine room, and now holds the **Pha Bang**, the most sacred Buddha image in Laos. The Pha Bang is believed to possess miraculous powers that safeguard the country. According to legend, it was crafted in the heavens and then delivered, via Sri Lanka and Cambodia, to the city of Xiang Dong Xiang Thong, later renamed Louang Phabang (the Great Pha Bang) in its honour.

The most impressive room inside the palace is the dazzling **Throne Hall**, its high walls spangled with mosaics of multicoloured mirrors. On display here are rare articles of royal regalia: swords of hammered silver and gold, an elaborately decorated fly-whisk and even the king's own *howdah* (elephant saddle). Also on exhibit is a cache of small crystal, silver and bronze Buddha images taken from the inner chamber of the "Watermelon Stupa" at Wat Visoun.

### Wat Pa Phai and Wat Saen

The neighbourhood encompassing the section of Sisavang Vong Road just north of the Royal Palace Museum is known to locals as "Ban Jek" or **Chinatown**, and contains some fine examples of Louang Phabang shop-house architecture, a hybrid of French and Lao features superimposed on the South Chinese style that was once prevalent throughout urban Southeast Asia. A left turn at the end of the row of shop-houses will take you to **Wat Pa Phai**, the "Bamboo Forest Monastery", whose *sim* is painted and lavishly embellished with stylized naga (water serpent) and peacocks.

Doubling back up to the corner, turn left to continue down Xiang Thong Road as far as **Wat Saen**, where an ornate boatshed houses the monastery's two **longboats**, used in the annual boat race festival. Held at the end of the rainy season, the boat races are believed to lure Louang Phabang's guardian naga back into the rivers after high waters and flooded rice paddies have allowed them to escape.

### Wat Xiang Thong

Probably the most historic and enchanting Buddhist monastery in the entire country, **Wat Xiang Thong**, the "Golden City Monastery" (daily 8am to dusk; 10,000K), near the northernmost tip of the peninsula, is unmissable. The wonderful, graceful main temple was built in 1560 by King Setthathilat and, unlike nearly every other temple in Louang Phabang, was neither razed by Chinese marauders nor over-enthusiastically restored. You'll need to stand at a distance to get a view of the roof, the temple's most outstanding feature. Elegant lines curve and overlap, sweeping nearly to the ground, and evoke a bird with outstretched wings or, as the locals say, a mother hen sheltering her brood.

On the other side of the monastery grounds is the **Funerary Carriage Hall** (daily 8am to dusk) or *haw latsalot*. Built in 1962, the hall's wide teakwood panels are deeply carved with depictions of Rama, Sita, Ravana and Hanuman, characters from the Lao version of the Ramayana. Check out the carved window shutters on the building's left side where Hanuman, the King of the Monkeys, is depicted in pursuit of the fairer sex. Inside, the principal article on display is the *latsalot*, the royal funerary carriage, used to transport the mortal remains of King Sisavong Vong to cremation. The vehicle is built in the form of several bodies of parallel naga, whose jagged fangs and dripping tongues heralded the king's final passage through Louang Phabang. Atop the carriage are three gilded urns in which the royal corpse was kept in foetal position until the cremation.

### Phou Si

**Phou Si** ("Sacred Hill") (20,000K) is both the geographical and spiritual centre of the city. The hill's peak affords a stunning panorama of the city, and can be reached by three different routes. The first and most straightforward is via the stairway directly opposite the main gate of the Royal Palace Museum. You should ask to be let into the adjacent *sim*, which is sometimes padlocked shut. Known as **Wat Pa Houak**, this fine little temple contains the city's most fascinating murals, which depict Lao, Chinese, Persian and European inhabitants of Louang Phabang. From the *sim*, it's a steep but shady climb to the peak. The second approach is on the other side of the hill, up a zigzag stairway flanked by whitewashed naga. The third, rambling but more atmospheric, approach is via **Wat Pha Phoutthabat** near Phou Si's northern foot (across from *Saynamkhan Guest House*). There are actually three monasteries in this temple compound, and the most interesting structure is the *sim* of **Wat Pa Khe**, a tall, imposing building with an unusual inward-leaning facade. Behind and to the left of the *sim* is a stairway leading to the "**Buddha's footprint**", a larger-than-life stylized footprint. The shrine housing the footprint is rarely open. The path meanders up past monks' stone quarters and the remains of an old anti-aircraft gun, to the summit, crowned by the stupa **That Chomsi**.

### Outside the Old City

The older parts of the city may have a higher concentration of monasteries and old buildings, but there is plenty to see beyond Setthathilat Road. **Wat That**, officially known as Wat Pha Mahathat, is situated on a rise next to the *Phou Si Hotel* and is reached via a stairway flanked by some impressive seven-headed naga. At the top of the stairs is perhaps the most photographed window in all of Louang Phabang. Framed in ornately carved teak, it's a blend of Lao, Chinese and Khmer design.

**Wat Visoun** and Wat Aham share a parcel of land on the opposite side of Phou Si from the Royal Palace Museum. The *sim* of the former was once lavishly decorated but was razed in 1887. The looters made off with many treasures stored within, but what they left behind is now on display in the throne room of the Royal Palace Museum (see opposite). Neighbouring **Wat Aham** features a delightfully diminutive *sim* and a couple of mould-blackened *that*. A small fee is sometimes collected from foreign visitors for access to these monasteries.

## Arrival

**By bus** Louang Phabang has three bus stations, all served by shared tuk-tuks into town (10,000K). Buses from Vientiane, Vang Viang and other points south along Route 13 stop at the southern bus station, 3km south of the centre. Buses and sawngthaews from the north arrive at the northern bus station, 6km north of town, while buses from Xainyabouli terminate at the Pakkhon depot near the southern bus station.

**By boat** Slow boats dock at the Navigation Office landing behind the former Royal Palace in the old city, an easy walk from most guesthouses. Speedboats dock at a separate landing in the village of Ban Don, 7km north of the city (30,000K by tuk-tuk).

**By air** The airport is 2km northeast of the city. If you're arriving on an international flight, you can get a fifteen-day visa on arrival here. There are also exchange facilities. Arrivals on domestic flights don't need to pass immigration. Tuk-tuks (20,000K) will ferry you into town.

## Information and agencies

**Tourist information** Lao National Tourism Administration, 3 Visounalat Road, next to the Red Cross Sauna (Mon–Fri 8am–5pm; ⓣ071/212487).

**Tour agencies** Sisavang Vong Rd is lined with tour agencies. These ones offer community-based eco-tourism, biking, kayaking, elephant trekking and more: All Lao Travel Service, 13 Sisavang Vong Rd ⓣ856/2535223, ⓦwww.alllaoservice.com; Green Discovery, 37 Sisavang Vong Rd ⓣ071/212093, ⓦwww.greendiscoverylaos.com; Tiger Trail, Sisavang Vong Rd ⓣ856/252655, ⓦwww.laos-adventures.com.

## City transport

**Bicycles** Reputedly for the tourist's protection, bicycles and motorbikes have been banned from tourists' use. **Tuk-tuks** To get out to the bus stations or airport, you'll have to rely on the town's small fleet of tuk-tuks, which can be flagged down easily on most busy streets. Typically, a ride anywhere in town is 10,000K per person.

## Accommodation

Accomodation in Louang Phabang is pricey and if you are a single traveller, the cheapest room you can expect to find is around $5. The old city is still home to a dwindling number of budget options. Less expensive areas are Ban Wat That, located between Wat That and the Mekong River, and the area east of Nam Phou Fountain in the grid of streets and lanes between the Nam Phou Fountain on Xiang Thong Road and Visounnalat Road to the east.

Prices tend to rise around December but you can get good discounts in low season (May–Oct). It's an early-to-bed-early-to-rise town, so always ask what time guesthouse doors are locked at night.

### The Old City

**Bounthieng** Souvannakhamphong Rd ⓣ071/252488. If you're in the market for a colonial-era guesthouse facing over the Mekong this is the place for you. The more expensive upstairs rooms have balconies looking over the river. ❸

**Boupha Guesthouse** Sisavang Vong Rd, ⓣ 071/252 405. This is probably as cheap as you will find on the main drag. It is excellent value, with a friendly owner. The rooms are basic and have shared bathroom facilities. A great budget option. ❶–❷.

**Heritage** near Wat Pa Phai ⓣ071/252537. This used to be one of the best value places In town but the growing prices are making it lose its charm with the cheapest room at $10. All the rooms have en-suite facilities. ❷

**Le Calao Inn** Manthatoulat Rd ⓣ071/212100. Housed in a century-old colonial mansion, this place has only six rooms, all with private veranda overlooking the Mekong. ❸

**Mekong** Manthatoulat Rd ⓣ071/212752. This well-located guesthouse is the pick of the bunch of inexpensive digs along the Mekong River, with budget rooms, including some en suite, in a big 1960s building. Great shared veranda on the second floor. ❸

**Pa Phai** Opposite Wat Pa Phai ⓣ071/212752. A quirky little guesthouse with a pleasant patio set on a quiet street right off Sisavang Vong Rd. ❷–❸

**Pathoumphone** Kingkitsalat Rd ⓣ071/212946. Decent rooms, some with shared facilities, are spread out across three houses and offer views of the Nam Khan River and the mountains. ❸

### Ban Wat That

**Chanthy Banchit** Ban Wat That ⓣ071/ 252 538. A Swiss-owned guesthouse with cosy wood panelled rooms, stylishly décorated. Clean shared bathroom facilities. ❷

**Vanvisa** Ban Wat That ⓣ071/212925. This yellow 1960s villa is a charming guesthouse, and the owner is very friendly and welcoming. ❷

TREAT YOURSELF

The receiver of rave reviews, **Les 3 Nagas** (☎071/253888, ⓦwww.alilahotels.com/3nagas), on Sisavang Vong Rd, styles itself as a boutique hotel and lives up to the claim. Rooms have direct Internet access, and are tastefully decorated and comfortable with polished wooden floorboards, clay roofs and simple, elegant furniture. All the rooms are en suite with kingsize beds and open onto a private terrace that overlooks either the street or the gardens. Aside from the impressive decor, the hotel prides itself on the pleasant service and the hotel's two outstanding restaurants, the slightly more formal *Les 3 Nagas* and the open air *Mango Tree* restaurant, both of which serve delicious Western and Asian cuisine. ❽

**Viradesa** Ban Wat That ☎071/252026. A wide range of cheap rooms and dorms; the cheapest room is $8, while the $2 dorms are a steal. There is also a good restaurant attached serving reasonably priced Lao food and basic Western dishes such as sandwiches and omelettes. ❶–❷

**Wat That** Ban Wat That ☎071/212913. This tiny wooden house contains four basic, but surprisingly spacious rooms with clean, shared facilities. There's a restaurant in the garden that serves up pancakes, sandwiches and great fruit shakes. ❷

### East of Nam Phou Fountain

**Jaliya** Visounalat Rd ☎071/252154. Across from Lao Airlines (see p.436), the dozen en-suite rooms tucked away behind this shop-house travel agency are clean and comfortable, and all face onto a private garden. ❷

**Somchit** Latsavong Rd ☎071/212522. A lovely wooden house, good-value with decent shared facilities. ❷

## Eating and drinking

Louang Phabang prides itself on its food, and the city boasts more restaurants than anywhere in the country outside of Vientiane. Most of the city's tourist cafés are located along a 500-metre strip of Sisavang Vong Road that expats sarcastically call "Thang Falang" or "White Man's Way", and tend to be fairly pricey by Lao standards. Much cheaper meals can be found at the delightful riverside restaurants along Ounkham Road. The best way to dine is to head to the night market and join the communal tables, sampling all the local treats in a casual, buzzing atmosphere.

### Cafés

**Joma Bakery & Café** Sisavang Vong Rd. This is one of the best places in town for breakfast, although a little expensive, with good service and delicious pastries, quiches and sandwiches. The cool a/c interior makes a comforting break from the outside heat.

**L'Etranger Books and Tea** South side of Phousi Hill. A good place to have a drink; there's a chilled-out area, complete with cushions, upstairs. They show non-mainstream films every evening at 7pm.

**Morning Glory Café** Sisavang Vong Rd. Closed on Tues. Fantastic breakfasts: strong coffee, bacon, omelettes, fruit and muesli will get you going for the day. They also serve delicious lunches.

**Scandinavian Bakery** Sisavang Vong Rd. Very popular place, and a handy spot to catch up on the Bangkok newspapers and watch the news on satellite TV.

### Restaurants

**L'Elephant** Straight towards the Mekong from the Villa Santi. A cross between Southern California and Casablanca, this has a great atmosphere, as well as some of the best vegetarian food in town.

**Indochina Spirit** Xiang Thong Rd, near the Nam Phou Fountain. A popular restaurant in Louang Phabang, this charming antique house with a lovely alfresco patio and traditional music should be right at the top of anyone's dining list.

**Kheme Khan Food Garden** Kingkitsalat Rd. High on the bank of the Nam Khan River behind Phou Si, this is a great venue for traditional Lao food, with lovely views of the Nam Kham. The keng kai *màk nao*, a soup served with chicken, and the

#### LOCAL SPECIALITIES

You shouldn't miss out on having a traditional Lao meal. At the top of the list should be **aw lam**, a bitter-sweet soup, heavy on aubergines and mushrooms. Other local specialities include **jaew bong**, a condiment of red chillies, shallots, garlic and dried buffalo skin, and **phak nâm**, a type of watercress particular to the area and widely used in salads.

*sai-ua* Louang Phabang, or Lao-style sausages, are standouts.

**Nazim** Sisavang Vong Rd. Decent Indian restaurant, one of a chain throughout Laos serving delicious meat and vegetarian curries.

**Pakhuay Mixay** Near Wat Xiang Mouan. The main draw is the garden atmosphere, in a quiet residential corner of the old city, away from the bustle of Xiang Thong Rd, but the Lao cuisine served here is worth seeking out on its own merits.

**Tum-Tum Cheng** Cooking School and Restaurant, Sisavang Vong Rd, near Wat Xiang Thong. This restaurant serves tasty Lao food in a cool, old colonial building and offers popular Lao cooking lessons (www.tumtumcheng.com).

**View Kheamkhong** Ounkham Rd. Lovely outdoor restaurant right on the banks of the Mekong River with inexpensive, delicious food. The Gong Bao-style cashew chicken is to die for.

## Nightlife

**The Bowling Alley** Believe it or not, the place to be after the bars close at 11pm is the ten-pin bowling alley, which stays open til 2am. As the night wears on, revellers become steadily worse at bowling. Tuk-tuks will be waiting outside *Hive* and *Lao Lao Garden* to take you there.

**Hive Bar** Behind Phou Si Hill, Latsavong Rd. A Happy Hour runs at this bar from 6–9pm, offering two-for-one deals on classic cocktails. Chilled-out background music and an ambient setting.

**Lao Lao Garden** Next door to *Hive*. Come here to enjoy the cocktails, the lively atmosphere and the fantastic Lao barbecue.

**Lemongrass** Next to Wat Xiang Mouan. Particularly welcoming to gay travellers, this bar has a sophisticated feel to it. Wne and cocktails are the tipples to quaff.

**Martin's Pub** On the south side of Phou Si hill, down the road opposite *Hive Bar*. Although it looks nothing like an English pub, it serves beer and Western food and is a good place to catch an evening film in the downstairs lounge.

## Entertainment

**Royal Ballet Theatre** The Royal Palace Museum ☎071/212200. Demonstrations of classical Lao dance are given three times a week (Mon, Wed & Fri 6.30pm). Performances include excerpts of the Lao version of the Ramayana (the *Pha Lak Pha Lam*) and cost $8–20 per person depending on the seat.

## Shopping

Many of the town's souvenir shops are on Sisavang Vong Road, especially in the neighbourhood known as "Ban Jek", near the Royal Palace Museum. The night markets are on the side streets near the Royal Palace Museum (5pm–10pm), selling, among other items, silk, lamps, Beer Lao T-shirts, Hmong silver.

**Paper lanterns** Ban Khili (opposite Wat Sop) offers a good selection of originally designed traditional mulberry paper lanterns, including collapsible models.

**Silverware** Items worth looking out for are paraphernalia for betel chewing: round or oval boxes for storing white lime, cone-shaped containers for betel leaves and miniature mortars used to pound areca nuts. Hilltribe silver jewellery is usually bold and heavy, and most is the handiwork of the Hmong. New silver of superior quality should be bought directly from Louang Phabang's expert silversmiths. The best known of these is Thithpeng Maniphone, whose workshop is located just down the small lane opposite Wat That. Other silversmiths are located near the Royal Palace Museum and opposite Wat Aham. Gold jewellery shops can be found on Chao Sisouphan Road.

**Textiles** There are now many upmarket boutiques specializing in high-quality Lao textiles. Ock Pop Tok Textiles, next to *L'Elephant* (see p.435), is typical of the kind of chic shops popping up around this end of town. More basic Lao textile products are cheapest at the Hmong Market and at Talat Dala where *nyam* – shoulder bags – and the all-purpose *pha khao ma*, a chequered, wrap-around sarong used by Lao men, are all very inexpensive.

**Woodcarving** Traditionally religious in nature, and Buddha images can be found everywhere, but these are now supplemented by souvenirs such as carved wooden hangers for displaying textiles.

## Directory

**Airlines** Lao Airlines, Visounalat Rd (☎071/212172), for domestic and international flights.

**Banks and exchange** There are several exchange places along Xiang Thong Rd, including the main branch of Lane Xang Bank opposite the Hmong Market, which changes traveller's cheques and can do cash advances on Visa; Lane Xang Bank also maintains an exchange bureau (daily 8.30am–4pm) on Latsavong Rd; cash and traveller's cheques only.

**Hospitals and clinics** The main hospital is on Setthathilat Rd; an International Clinic (☎071/252049) is around the corner on the hospital's western side. In case of a serious illness, you should fly direct to Thailand, where there are many good hospitals.

**Internet** Internet cafés can be found along Sisavang Vong Rd east of the Royal Palace Museum, as well as on Setthathilat Rd. Most places charge 200K per minute and will stay open as late as midnight as long as there are customers at the terminals.

**Massage and herbal sauna** The Red Cross Sauna (daily 5–9pm) on Visounalat Rd (Ⓣ071/252856) has traditional Lao massage at $3 per hour (reserve ahead) and an excellent sauna for $1 (bring a sarong).

**Post office** The GPO (Mon–Fri 8am–noon & 1–5pm, Sat 8am–noon) is located on the corner of Xiang Thong and Setthathilat roads. Poste restante is kept for three months.

**Telephones** International calls and faxes at Telecom (daily 8am–9pm), behind the GPO. No collect calls, but a callback service is available. International direct dial-phones are located outside the GPO, and phonecards are available at many convenience stores.

**Volunteering** Next to the *3 Nagas Restaurant* off main road Ⓣ071/254937, Ⓦwww.bigbrothermouse.com. Big Brother Mouse is a new project that is creating schemes to teach and encourage Laos children to read and write. Go and visit the centre, help them proofread texts, hang out with the children, buy books and donate them to the cause.

## Moving on

**By bus or sawngthaew** Southbound buses leave from the Southern bus station, and those heading north leave from the Northern bus station. Take a tuk-tuk to both of these (10,000K).

**Destinations:** Muang Nan (3 daily; 3hr); Nam Bak (2 daily; 2hr); Nong Khiaw (3 daily; 3hr); Oudomxai (5 daily; 4hr); Pakmong (5 daily; 2hr); Phonsavan (1 daily; 8hr); Vang Viang (8 daily; 6–7hr); Viang Kham (daily; 4hr); Vientiane (10 daily, final departure 5pm; 10–12hr).

**By boat** Slow boats set off from the Navigation Office behind the Royal Palace Museum: Speedboats leave from a separate landing in the village of Ban Don, 7km north of the city (20,000K by tuk-tuk). The eight-seat speedboats travel to points north and south along the Mekong River, as well as for destinations along the Nam Ou River. Passengers sign up for their destinations, and the boats leave when full. Arrive early to get a seat, although there's no guarantee that every destination is served every day. Alternatively, you can charter a speedboat. In fact, the boatmen will practically insist that you do just that.

For Nong Khiaw (see p.439) you will have to negiotiate chartering a boat, so try to get a group together. The boat will cost about 880,000K.

**Destinations:** Houayxai (slow boat, 2 days; speed boat, 3–4hr; Pakbeng (slow boat; 1 day); Nong Khiaw (passenger boat; 6–8hr); Muong Noi (passenger boat; 7–9hr).

**By air** The easiest way to get to the airport is by tuk-tuk ($1 per person). International destinations include Siem Reap, Cambodia, Bangkok and Chiang Mai in Thailand and Hanoi, Vietnam.

**Destinations:** Pakxe (2 weekly; 2hr); Phonsavan (3 weekly; 1hr 30min); Vientiane (3 daily; 40min).

# DAY-TRIPS FROM LOUANG PHABANG

You haven't seen Louang Phabang until you **cross the Mekong** to Xiang Men and climb up to Wat Chom Phet, a hilltop monastery that offers superior views of the city's gilded temples at sunset. The popular **Pak Ou Caves** and the nearby **Kouang Si waterfall** – a good spot for a picnic and splashing around in turquoise waters – are both wonderful excursions.

## Xiang Men

A half-day trip to the sleepy village of **XIANG MEN** gives you a chance to view Louang Phabang from across the river. A passenger ferry operates between Louang Phabang and Xiang Men and leaves from the landing west of the Royal Palace Museum. You could also strike a deal with one of the many boats to be found along the riverbank: the short journey should cost around 5000K per person and you can ask to be let off at **Wat Long Khoun**, once used by Louang Phabang's kings as a pre-coronation retreat. Check out the two Chinese door guardians painted either side of the main entrance to the *sim* and the murals within. An easy climb to the top of the hill behind Wat Long Khoun brings you to the *sim* and stupas of **Wat Chom Phet**, a disused monastery best visited at dusk, when the views of the sunset are spectacular.

## Kouang Si

The best day-trip from Louang Phabang is the picturesque, multi-level **Kouang**

**Si waterfall** (entry 15,000K), tumbling 60m before spilling through a series of crystal-blue pools. A large landslide has altered the setting somewhat but it shouldn't be long before nature sets things right again. Vendors near the lower pool sell *tam màk hung*, fruit and drinks. The steep path on the opposite side of the falls leads to a grassy meadow filled with brilliantly coloured butterflies. The path can get quite slippery, so be very careful.

There are several options for reaching the waterfall, situated 35km southwest of Louang Phabang. The most scenic route is by **boat** down the Mekong River – many of the same boat drivers running trips to the Pak Ou caves will also offer to take you to the falls. This entails taking a tuk-tuk for the last portion of the journey, something that is handled by the boat driver and usually worked into his fee: check when negotiating your fare. Boatmen hang out along the Mekong riverside and charge \$15–20 for a boat that can accommodate up to ten people and a further \$2 for the tuk-tuk. You can also do the whole journey by **tuk-tuk** from Louang Phabang; if you can assemble a group, this is a cheap option (\$10 return). Drivers, who can be found at the Hmong Market, will wait for you while you visit the falls.

### The Pak Ou Caves and Whisky Village

Numerous caves punctuate the limestone cliffs around Pak Ou – the confluence of the Mekong and Nam Ou rivers, some 25km out of Louang Phabang. The best-known caves are the "**Buddha Caves**", Tham Ting and Tham Phoum. They have been used for centuries as a repository for old and unwanted Buddha images that can no longer be venerated on an altar, and the hundreds upon hundreds of serenely smiling images covered in dust and cobwebs make an eerie scene. **Tham Ting**, the lower cave, just above the water's surface, is light enough to explore without artificial light but the upper cave is unlit, so bring a torch, or better still, a handful of candles to enhance the spooky effect. A 10,000K entrance fee is collected at the lower cave (50,000K if you plan to take photographs).

On the opposite bank of the river is a village that for thousands of years produced stoneware jars but has now found that distilling liquor is more lucrative. The inhabitants of Ban Xang Hai, referred to by English-speaking boatmen as the **Whisky Village**, are quite used to thirsty visitors stopping by for a pull on the bamboo straw. The liquor is made from fermented sticky rice, and pots filled with hooch are lined up on the beach awaiting transport up or down the river.

Both sites can be seen in a couple of hours, and boatmen hired in Louang Phabang usually treat it as a package, assuming that after you've seen a cave-full of Buddhas you'll be ready for a good, stiff drink. Boats are easily arranged at the slow-boat landing in Louang Phabang and cost \$10 for up to five people to hire for the trip there and back. The ride upriver takes less than an hour.

# The northeast

Difficult to reach and short on proper tourist sites, the remote **northeast** is one of the least-visited parts of Laos. This area was heavily bombed during the Second Indochina War, particularly at the strategic **Plain of Jars**, which takes its name from the fields of ancient, giant funerary urns –the northeast's main tourist draw. For most visitors a trip to the north-east means a flying visit to the town of **Phonsavan** to see the nearby Jar sites. Very few travellers make it here; however, since the opening to foreigners of the Vietnamese border crossings at Na Meo (due east of **Xam Nua**), those who do can now continue their journey into Vietnam.

There is a direct bus from Louang Phabang to Phonsavan (along Routes 1 and 7) from where you can start exploring the region. Alternatively, you can fly into Xam Nua or Phonsavan.

## NONG KHIAW

Resting at the foot of a striking red-faced cliff, amid towering blue-green limestone escarpments, the dusty town of **NONG KHIAW** on the banks of the Nam Ou River lies smack in the middle of some of the most dramatic scenery in Indochina, and is fast becoming a popular tourist destination. Part of Nong Khiaw's attraction lies in reaching the town itself – taking a slow boat up the picturesque Nam Ou from Louang Phabang is one of the best **river journeys** in Laos.

Although the old town stretches 1km along a dirt road parallel to Route 1, all of Nong Khiaw's **tourist facilities** are located by the big bridge over the Nam Ou. Here, at the western end of the bridge, you'll find the boat mooring, the bus lot, and most of the guesthouses and restaurants. At the eastern end of the bridge on the opposite bank are more guesthouses and restaurants and the village of **Ban Lao**. You can also rent good moutain bikes from the Nong Khiaw River Resort for $4.

### Arrival

**By bus** From Louang Phabang, the journey is under three hours up Route 13. Sawngthaews will drop you near the boat landing.

**By boat** The most scenic route to Nong Khiaw from Louang Phabang is the six-hour boat trip up the Nam Ou, a stunning journey through rural Laos. Since most locals prefer to travel to Nong Khiaw by road, catching a passenger boat on the Nam Ou isn't easy: the best method is get a group of fellow travellers together and hire a passenger boat ($50 for 10 people).

### Accommodation and eating

**Manypoon** At the top of the main street, near the bridge. Good-value place with seven simple rooms in a lovely house with a small garden. The upstairs rooms are the best and there's a small balcony with a great view east. ❶

**Phanoy Guesthouse and Restaurant** Just on the other side of the bridge. This place has en-suite bungalows and a restaurant looking out onto the river with a good menu. It also has a small book exchange and bicycles for $1. ❶–❷

**Phaybourn** Route 1, a short walk from the bridge. Built for tour groups, the rooms here are a cut above the rest, especially those in the new wing that all feature en-suite bathrooms. ❶–❷

**Sunset** Across the river. This is a popular choice largely because of its excellent restaurant and fantastic sun-deck overlooking the river. The guesthouse itself is clean and well run, and the owner is friendly and informative. ❷

### INTO VIETNAM FROM THE NORTHEAST

There are two official border crossings into Vietnam from northeastern Laos although they are still infrequently used due to lack of available transport and road difficulties on the Vietnamese side.

**Na Meo Crossing for Thanh Hoa province**

To get to Na Meo from Xam Nua, the nearest big town, catch the daily sawngthaew (4hr) or regular trucks from Vieng Xai (2hr). Xam Nua can be reached from Phonsavan (1 daily; 8hr). Make sure you have obtained your visa before arrival whichever country you are heading for. Be prepared to pay a small fee for crossing ($1).

**Nong Het to Nam Can**

From Phonsavan you can get to Nong Het on the four-times a day bus (4hr). Probably more time-efficient is the bus from Phonsavan direct to Vinh (4 weekly; 11hr). Those crossing into Laos can obtain a 30-day visa upon arrival but you'll need to arrange a Vietnamese visa in advance.

**Vinat Restaurant** On the other side of the bridge just beyond the *Phanoy* restaurant. Set on a shady terrace serving good Lao and Thai dishes.

## Moving on

**By bus** Louang Phabang via Pakmong (3 daily; 3hr).

**By boat** Boats leave regularly for Muong Noi until about 2pm and cost 20,000K per person. Those going to Louang Phabang can hire a boat for 10 people at about $80 (5hr).

# MUONG NOI

Hidden away on a peninsula on the Nam Ou about an hour's boat ride from Nong Khiaw, **MUONG NOI** is the perfect place for a few days' peace and quiet among beautiful scenery.

All the accommodation and most of the restaurants are built on the river banks, where people tend to just while away their days sleeping, eating, reading and relaxing.

However, there are options for the more energetic: kayaking down the river, trekking through buffalo-ridden rice fields; and fishing with the locals at sunset.

## Arrival and information

**By boat** Boats from Nong Khiaw will arrive at the landing at the north end of the village. If you are coming in dry season, you may have to get out half-way and walk around part of the island as the boat tries to navigate through the shallow water.

**Tourist information** There is no tourist office as such but Mr Kong Keo, the local English teacher, can provide information about treks to local villages. Follow the signs to his house as you alight at the pier and walk down through the village.

**Tours** Lao Youth Travel (Ⓦwww.laoyouthtravel.com), near the boat landing, can organize treks and kayaking tours.

## Accommodation and eating

Muong Noi has lots of cheap wood or bamboo bungalows built on stilts with shared bathroom facilities. Electricity only runs from 6–10pm. All accommodation lines one strip along the river bank. You may want to shop around to find your perfect bungalow but they all follow the same sort of set-up, most with restaurants attached serving noodle and rice dishes and pancake, omelette and baguette-style breakfasts.

**Banana Guesthouse and Restaurant** This is one of the best options with clean bungalows set amongst a grove of banana trees and a decent restaurant to go with it. ❶

**KaiKeo Bungalows** These bungalows are right at the end of the strip and if there is enough demand, food can be prepared for you and eaten on the balcony looking out onto the river. ❶

**Nicksa's Guesthouse** The owner of this decent guesthouse speaks good English. The restaurant here is a popular one serving a variety of dishes. Try the pumpkin curry. ❶

**Riverview Bungalows** This is the place with the most character, run by charismatic Mama Joumne who will absolutely insist you have a shot of *Lào-láo* with your breakfast. Her rooms are pleasant too (or perhaps it is the rice whisky helping you sleep). ❶

## Moving on

**By boat** Boats back to Nong Khiaw from the boat landing leave regularly.

# PHONSAVAN

Faced with the prospect of a long, and potentially dangerous road trip via Route 7 or Routes 1 and 6, many visitors

### SAFETY IN XIANG KHOUANG PROVINCE

Occasional attacks by bandits or insurgents have given **Xiang Khouang** province an uncertain reputation. Because the Lao government is so intent on controlling information, news of these attacks rarely reaches the international media unless a foreigner is killed, though they have decreased since 2004. That said, hundreds of tourists visit the area each month without incident. Of more immediate danger are the **mines, bombis and bombs** littering the province. The three main Jar sites have been cleared of unexploded ordnance (UXO), but it's advisable to stick to the paths.

opt for a flight into **PHONSAVAN**, which also gives an unforgettable view of the treeless flatlands and crater-ridden landscape of the Plain of Jars. The capital of **Xiang Khouang province**, Phonsavan has emerged as the most important town on the Plain of Jars since the total devastation of the region in the Second Indochina War. Hastily rebuilt in the aftermath of decades of fighting, Phonsavan is only now beginning to recover economically, thanks in a large part to international interest in the world-famous **jar sites** scattered around the perimeter of the plain. Although most visitors come only to see these, the Xiang Khouang Plateau is a place of great natural beauty and its backroads are well worth exploring. The Mines Advisory Group is well worth visiting (see p.442).

## Arrival and information

**By bus** The station is 3km southwest of town. Tuk-tuks and guesthouse owners will be waiting to drop you in town, free of charge if you stay at their establishment.

**By air** Tuk-tuks cost 10,000K per person for the 4km ride from the airport into town. Alternatively, you can get a free lift with one of the hotel reps. There is an exchange kiosk at the airport.

**Tours** There is a Provincial Tourism Office near Kong Keo Guesthouse but it's best to organize your trips around the Jar sites at your guesthouse. They usually cost around $10–15 depending on the amount of people.

## Accommodation

Phonsavan boasts many guesthouses and hotels, most of which line Route 7, east of the dry-goods market. Electricity is 24hr.

**Daophouan** Across from the GPO ⓣ061/312171. The eleven rooms in this three-storey building are a notch above others in the same category and all are en suite with hot water. Good quality but a bit pricey. ❹

**Dokkhoun** Route 7, east of the dry-goods market ⓣ061/312189. Two separate buildings with clean, tiled en-suite doubles with hot water. The mid-range rooms here are better value than the budget ones. ❷

**TREAT YOURSELF**

**Auberge de la Plaine des Jarres** (ⓣ061/312044). On a hill southeast of town, this very classy lodge has deluxe two-room cabins with fireplaces, and private bathrooms that overlook the town. Equipped with roaring log fires – perfect in a town at high altitude, where evening temperatures plummet – the rooms are extremely comfortable. The views from the restaurant are absolutely spectacular; a lovely setting to enjoy a delicious French dinner. ❻

**Hay Hin** Route 7, east of centre ⓣ061/312252. This long-standing guesthouse has just the basics – a bed and a toilet – but at least it's fairly clean and cheap. ❶

**Kong Keo** Off Route 7, next to the old airstrip ⓣ061/211354. *Kong's* definitely wins for personality and atmosphere: in the evenings you can enjoy sitting round the campfire, swigging at *lào-láo*. The rooms aren't bad either. There are wooden bungalows or clean and slightly warmer rooms to choose from. ❶–❷

**Nice Guesthouse** Route 7, next to *Dokkhoun*. This guesthouse is true to its name with clean rooms, bathrooms and a communal balcony. ❷

**Vanaloune** Route 7, next to the *Phonekeo Restaurant* ⓣ061/312070. Old and basic but better value than a lot of other places in the same price range. The bathrooms are tiled and clean but without hot water. ❶

**Vinhtong** Route 7, another block further east of the *Dokkhoun* ⓣ061/212622. Popular, basic place with tiled floors and en-suite bathrooms with hot water. There are also some bigger units out back, costing slightly more. ❶

## Eating

Eating out options aren't great, you may want to go to a pricey hotel for a good meal. If you're a fan of *fõe* (rice noodle soup, usually garnished with fresh coriander, mint and basil), you're in luck – Phonsavan seems to thrive on it.

**Kong Keo** This guesthouse serves up tasty, warming curries, eaten on your lap around the fire.

**Maly Hotel** West of the museum. Although possibly too expensive to stay here, the restaurant is probably the best in town serving Lao and Western food ($3–5).

**Nang Sila** 600m west of the dry-goods market. Well thought of by the locals and the best place to come for *fõe*.
**Phonkeo** On the corner of the turning to *Kong Keo's*. Cheap and friendly restaurant with good Lao dishes.
**Phonexay** On Route 7. The food is pretty average but it is a good meeting place for lone travellers.
**Sangah** Opposite the *Phonexay* and fairly same similar in terms of its noodle and rice dishes.

## Directory

**Airlines** Lao Airlines is about 500m south of the main junction, next to Lao Development Bank (Ⓣ061/212027).
**Banks** Lao Development Bank (Mon–Fri 8.30am–3.30pm). Two branches, one south of the junction, one on Route 7. Travel agencies also exchange money.
**Internet** Hot Net and *Phoukham Guesthouse*, both on Route 7, 500K/min.
**Mines Advisory Group office (MAGS)** On Route 7 (8am–4pm, Mon–Fri, Ⓦwww.magclearsmines.org). This team of de-miners have been working In the fields to stop the bombs from exploding. The office is a good place to learn about the effects and devastation of the war.
**Market** The two markets are at the main junction on opposite sides of Route 7. The Dry Market sells clothes and other consumer goods and the Wet Market, behind the Post Office, sells fresh food.
**Travel Agencies** Diethelm Tours, Indochina Travel both on Route 7.

## Moving on

**By bus** If you are travelling to anywhere within the Xiang Khuang province then you will need to go to the sawngthaews station next to the Dry Market. All other main destinations leave from the main bus station, 2km away.
**Destinations:** Muang Kham (4–5 daily; 1hr 30min); Muang Khoun (2–3 daily; 1hr); Nam Neun (1–2 daily; 6hr); Louang Phabang (1 daily; 8hr); Xam Neua (1 daily; 8hr); Vang Viang (3 daily; 6hr); Vientiane (1 daily, 9hr); Nong Het (for Vietnamese border) (daily; 4hr); Vinh, Vietnam (4 weekly; 11hr).
**By air** Louang Phabang (3 weekly; 1hr); Vientiane (5 weekly; 1hr 30min).
**Tuk-tuk** The tuk-tuk stand is on the main road just opposite the *Daophouan Guesthouse*.
**Vehicle rental** For journeys further afield, four-wheel-drives can be hired through most hotels and travel agencies. Most guesthouses can handle bookings.

# THE PLAIN OF JARS

The fifteen-kilometre-wide stretch of grassy meadows and low rolling hills around Phonsavan takes its name from the clusters of chest-high urns found here. Scattered across the **Plain of Jars** and on the hills beyond, the ancient jars, which are thought to be around two thousand years old, testify to the fact that Xiang Khouang province, with its access to key regional trade routes, its wide, flat spaces and temperate climate, has been considered prime real estate in Southeast Asia for centuries. The largest jars measure 2m in height and weigh as much as ten tonnes. Little is known about the Iron-Age megalithic civilization that created them, but in the 1930s, bronze and iron tools as well as coloured glass beads, bronze bracelets and cowrie shells were found at the sites, leading to the theory that the jars were funerary urns, originally holding cremated remains. More recent discoveries have also revealed underground burial chambers. During the **Second Indochina War**, the region was bombed extensively. American planes levelled towns and forced villagers to take to the forest, as the two sides waged a bitter battle for control of the Plain of Jars, which represented a back door to northern Vietnam. The plain was transformed into a wasteland, the treeless flatlands and low rolling brown hills dramatically pockmarked with craters.

## What to see and do

Of the dozens of jar sites that give the Plain of Jars its name, three groups have become tourist attractions, largely because they are accessible and have a greater concentration of jars. All three of these jar sites and old **Xiang Khouang** can be seen in a day, with hotels and tour companies pitching the four spots as a **package**. The cheapest visiting option is to book a vehicle and guide through one of the local guesthouses ($30–40 for a van). Hiring a vehicle for a do-it-yourself tour isn't allowed.

### Site 1

Of the three main groups, the closest one, **Thong Hai Hin** ("Stone Jar Plain") – known as Site 1 – is just 2km southwest of town, has over two hundred jars and is the most visited. There's a 4000K entrance fee at the pavilion. From here, a path leads up to **Hai Cheaum** ("Cheaum Jar"), a massive two-metre-high jar named after a Tai-Lao hero. Nearby is another group of jars, one of which has a crude human shape carved onto it. In the hill off to the left is a large cave that the Pathet Lao used during the war – and which, according to local legend, was used as a kiln to cast the jars. Erosion has carved two holes in the roof of the cave – natural chimneys that add weight to the kiln theory. It may also have been used as a crematorium.

### Site 2

**Site 2** is located about 10km southwest of the village of Lat Houang, which is on the road to Muang Khoun. There is a 10,000K entry charge. The site is based on two adjacent hills called Phou Salato. Nearly a hundred jars are scattered across the twin hills here, lending the site the name **Hai Hin Phou Salato** ("Salato Hill Stone Jar").

### Site 3

Site 3, the most atmospheric of the three sites, lies 4km up the road from Site 2, just beyond the village of Ban Xiang Di. Here you'll see Wat Xiang Di, a simple wooden monastery that holds a bomb-damaged Buddha. A path at the back of the monastery leads up a hill through several fields to the site, **Hai Hin Lat Khai**, where there are more than a hundred jars on a hillside with sweeping views of the plain below.

### Muang Khoun (Xiang Khouang)

A ghost of its former self, **MUANG KHOUN**, old Xiang Khouang, 35km southeast of Phonsavan, was once the royal seat of the minor kingdom of Xiang Khouang, renowned in the sixteenth century for its 62 opulent stupas, whose sides were said to be covered in treasure. Years of bloody invasions, pillaging and a monsoon of bombs that lasted nearly a decade during the Second Indochina War taxed this town so heavily that, by the time the air raids stopped, next to nothing was left of its exquisite temples. Although the town has been rebuilt and renamed, all that remains of the kingdom's former glory are a few evocative ruins, usually visited as part of a day-trip to the jar sites. A path alongside the market leads up to the blackened hilltop stupa of **That Dam**, the base of which has been tunnelled straight through by treasure-seekers. Continuing on the main road beyond the market, you'll pass the ruins of a villa, the only reminder that this town was once a temperate French outpost of ochre colonial villas and shop-houses, and arrive at the ruins of sixteenth-century Wat Phia Wat. Brick columns reach skywards around an impressive, seated Buddha of great size, a mere hint at the temple architecture for which the city was renowned.

## The far north

Decades of war and neglect have kept this isolated region in far northern Laos from developing and have unwittingly preserved a way of life that has virtually vanished in neighbouring countries. The hills and mountains up here have long been the domain of a scattering of **animist tribal peoples**, including the Hmong, Mien and Akha, and it is largely the chance to experience first-hand these near-pristine cultures that draws visitors to the region today.

By far the most popular route out of Louang Phabang is the road through **Oudomxai** and **Louang Namtha** to **Muang Sing**, a laid-back Tai Leu town lying within the borders of the Golden Triangle, once the world's most notorious opium-producing zone. Muang Sing is a popular base for trekking, owing to its decent accommodation and easy access to Akha, Mien and Tai Dam villages. Travellers en route to **China** are allowed to cross at **Boten**, reached by bus from Louang Namtha or Oudomxai. From Muang Sing, the road leads southwest to the village of **Xiang Kok** on the Mekong, the launching point for speedboats to Houayxai, an official border crossing with **Thailand**. Many travellers exit Laos here after completing their trip around the north, but it's also possible to come full circle and return to Louang Phabang via a memorable **Mekong boat journey**. The usual direction of the loop is counter-clockwise (Louang Phabang–Oudomxai–Muang Sing–Xiang Kok–Houayxai–Louang Phabang), but a clockwise route, heading north up the Mekong to Xiang Kok first, avoids the crowds on the Mekong slow boat and means you don't constantly run into the same travellers at every stop.

## OUDOMXAI

Most travellers heading north to Muang Sing and Louang Namtha begin their journey in Louang Phabang and head up Route 13 to **OUDOMXAI** (Muang Xai), an important transport hub at the junction of Route 1 and Route 4. Although there's no reason to visit Oudomxai, if you travel around the north, chances are you'll end up having to stop-over here at some point, like it or not. From Oudomxai, **public transport** runs in all directions. Most vehicles leave early morning (8–10am), but there are some afternoon departures.

Oudomxai is a popular springboard into Laos for Chinese tourists and traders, and the town's hotels and karaoke lounges readily accept Chinese yuan. Few stay longer than a night here, but with 24-hour electricity, laundry service, hot water and internet cafés, it does have its uses.

### Arrival and Information

**By bus** Buses from all destinations arrive at the station, east of the Phu That stupa. A fairly short walk will get you onto the main street.

**By air** The airport is 3km east of town; there are 3 weekly flights from Vientiane. Tuk-tuks will drop you off.

**Tourist Information** There is a very helpful Oudomxay Provincial Tourism Office (8am–noon & 1.30–4pm) just beyond the bridge with information about treks in the area.

### Accommodation

Oudomxai's position as a transportation hub means the town gets its share of Chinese truckers, who treat the town as a last-chance saloon – hence, many of the hotels are involved in the sex trade. A dozen newer guesthouses are on the east side of the river, on or just off the main road, though most of them are noisy, badly built and poorly maintained.

**Kongchai Guesthouse** Up the first alley east of the Linda and 20m further north ⓣ081/211141. Features simple but clean and reasonably priced rooms with en-suite bathrooms and hot water. The rooms at the front of the building overlook the football field and have views of the mountains. ❷

**Linda Guesthouse** ⓣ081/312147. Around the corner from *Phouxay* this cheap option has a choice of fan or a/c, but if you choose the latter, make sure it works – the top-floor rooms tend to get hot in the afternoons. ❶

**Phouxay Hotel** ⓣ081/312140. Down a lane to the West of Phou Xay Hill. Although It looks like a prison from the outside it Is one of the better backpacker-oriented places, offering clean rooms with fan or a/c, en-suite bathroom and hot water. ❶

**Vongprachit Guesthouse** ⓣ081/312 455. Centrally located near Wat Phou That with clean rooms and hot showers. A good budget choice. ❶–❷

## Eating

There are plenty of restaurants in Oudomxai, particularly Chinese-run places.
**Kanya's Food and Drink** Just off the main street. Good rice and noodles dishes and very cold beer.
**Keomoung Khoun** Pleasant restaurant on the main street with a large array of Lao food.
**Singphet Restaurant** Friendly staff but forgiving slow service – the breakfasts are tasty, when they eventually arrive.

## Directory

**Bank** The Lane Xang bank is 500m north of the market just past the *Misay* restaurant. BCEL is west of the bus station and has an ATM that only accepts MasterCard. Both exchange foreign currency and traveller's cheques, and accept Visa.
**Internet** Several internet cafés are located on the main street.
**Massage** Lao Red Cross Massage, off the main road, turning by the petrol station. Massage ($3) and sauna ($1); 3–7pm.

## Moving on

**By bus** From the main bus station.
**Destinations:** Boten (2 daily; 4hr); Louang Namtha (3 daily; 3–4hr); Louang Phabang (3 daily; 4hr); Nong Khiaw (2 daily; 3 hr); Pakbeng (2 daily; 4hr); Phongsali (daily; 9–11hr); Vientiane (daily; 19hr). Jinghong, China, via Boten (1 daily; 12hr).
**By air** To Vientiane (3 weekly; Tues, Thurs & Sat; 1hr 30min).

# LOUANG NAMTHA

Straddling Route 3, four hours' drive northwest of Oudomxai, **LOUANG NAMTHA** was heavily contested during Laos's civil war, which is to say that it was razed to the ground. Once the fighting stopped, the surrounding hills were stripped of their trees and the mammoth logs were trucked away to China. Now, the valley is making a comeback as a booming tourist area with rafting, kayaking and trekking activities.

In the town itself there's little to do except drop by the **Louang Namtha Provincial Museum** (Mon–Fri 8.30am–noon & 1–3.30pm; 5000K), housed in a green-roofed building behind the Kaysone Monument. The real reason to come to Louang Namtha though is an active one: walk or cycle to nearby Hmong and Leten villages, take a trek in the hills, or go kayaking or rafting on the Nam Tha and Nam Ha rivers. Louang Namtha is also a launch base for passenger boat trips down the Nam Tha River to Houayxai.

## Arrival

**By bus** If arriving from within the province, you will be dropped at the bus stop on the main road about 1km walk from all the guesthouses. Buses from further away arrive at the bus station 10km out of town. A tuk-tuk should cost 10,000K from here.
**By air** The airport is located 7km south of the main town. Sangthaews serve the town; there are no tuk-tuks at the airport.

## Accommodation

Louang Namtha has the best selection of accommodation and restaurants north of Louang Phabang, with over twenty guesthouses and hotels.
**Dalasavath Guesthouse** ☎086/211299. This Chinese-run place has a selection of rooms, some with bamboo walls, the others with concrete, it might be worth going for the slightly more expensive ones as they are in better condition. It has a popular restaurant too. ❶
**Gold Source Guesthouse** One street back from the main road near and on the same side as the police station ☎086/211253. A pleasant guesthouse with small rooms and shared bathrooms. The pleasant staff speak English. ❶
**Khammanivong** Main road 50m south of Lao Airlines. Ten simple but clean rooms with shared bathrooms in an attractive wooden house. All the rooms have wood floors, large windows, and Lao textile quilts. There are hot showers and the rear balcony has mountain views. ❷
**Luang Namtha Guesthouse** North up the road running along the west side of the bus field ☎086/312087. Several types of accommodation available, including large rooms in a huge modern house, nicely built thatched bungalows out back, and another concrete hotel-style building. The latter's rooms are the cheapest, but the bungalows overlooking the pond and the main house are good value for money. ❶–❷
**Many Chan** Main street In the centre ☎086/312209. Eight rooms on the second floor of a wooden house, with toilets and hot shower below. The rooms

are spartan but very clean. This is the favourite backpacker hotel in town so it fills up very quickly. ❶

**Soulivong** On the corner one block east of the GPO ⓣ086/312253. This large three-storey house with a peaked blue roof has clean rooms with tile floors and en-suite bathrooms with hot water. The rooms on the 2nd and 3rd floors are the best. ❶

## Eating

**Banana Restaurant** This seems to be the place weary trekkers convene after an exhausting day to refuel on the wide selection of dishes at this place. It serves Western breakfast and appetizing Thai and Lao dishes.

**Dalasavath** Another travellers' favourite attached to the guesthouse of the same name. The pen-style seating is a good place for a drink after a long trek.

**House Lao Restaurant** On the main street, at the north end of town opposite the *Sinsavanh Guesthouse*. The flashiest option in town, this marvellous Lao-style restaurant, completely built of wood, is far too nice for its poor location, but the Lao specialities make it a must.

**Many Chan** A decent, inexpensive travellers' café at this guesthouse on the main street.

**Panda Restaurant** This used to be a small shack but, due to its increasing popularity has expanded to a proper restaurant near the Morning Market. The food is tasty and freshly prepared and includes Thai, Lao and Western dishes. A very friendly family run the restaurant.

## Directory

**Banks and exchange** For currency exchange, head to BCEL on the main road, which accepts cash, traveller's cheques, Visa and also has an ATM that accepts MasterCard; there's also a Lane Xang Bank on the main street just north of Lao Airlines which can exchange foreign currency and traveller's cheques.

**Bicycle rental** Bicycles ($5 per day) can by rented from The Bicycle Shop on the main street.

**Internet** KNT Internet, opposite Green Discovery, 300K/min. Green Mountain Internet Café, main street, next to *Many Chan* guesthouse.

**Lao herbal saunas** Luang Namtha Herbal Sauna, West of House Lao Restaurant; Herbal Sauna and Massage, on the main road between *Dalasavatha* and *Khammanivong*, cross the bamboo bridge. ($1 sauna; $3 massage).

**Post office** Main Street (daily; 8am–noon & 1.30–4pm).

**TREAT YOURSELF**

Northern Laos's most famous eco-style resort is the **Boat Landing** (ⓣ086/312398, ⓦwww.theboatlanding.com), which is situated 6km south of the centre on the banks of the Nam Tha River. It's fantastic value at $17–45 a room, and treks and rafting can also be arranged here. The restaurant serves the best food in the area, with a wide choice of northern specialities – the spicy Lao purees are particularly worth trying. ❻

### TREKKING, RAFTING AND KAYAKING AROUND LOUANG NAMTHA

**Trekking** in the National Biodiversity Conservation Area must be booked through a licensed agent or through the Louang Namtha Guide Services Office, who offer a full range of one-, two- and three-day guided treks. The GSO (daily 8am–noon & 1–5pm) is located opposite the south side of the Kaysone Monument, just off the main street. Groups have a four-person minimum and a six- to eight-person maximum limit and generally work out about $10 per person per day. Not all the tours leave daily, so the GSO should be your first stop after checking in to your hotel. The GSO also has a wall display showing the villages that can be visited and which tribal peoples inhabit them, as well as a big topographical map of the NBCA.

For **kayaking** and **rafting** trips, see the Wildside Outdoor Adventures office on the main street. Wildside has a number of river packages on the Nam Tha and Nam Ha, ranging from one to four days and with stays in tribal villages en route. Prices vary and are significantly cheaper when there are more people joining the tour, but you're generally looking at about $20 a day. Programmes vary, so see Wildside for information on tours, departures and group sizes as soon as you get to town.

**Telephone** Lao Telecom for international calls. Main Street.
**Travel agencies and tours** Green Discovery (☎086/211484, ⓦwww.greendiscoverylaos.com) located on the main street. Organizes trekking, kayaking, rafting and cycling trips. Nam Ha Ecotoursim Project (☎086/211534) is next door to the tourism office, behind the post office. Offers slightly cheaper eco-treks and other sustainable tourism excursions.

## Moving on

**By bus** From the main bus station 10km out of town.
**Destinations:** Houayxai (2 daily; 5 hr); Jing Jong, China (1 daily; 11hr); Louang Phabang (1 daily; 8hr); Vientiane (1 daily; 22hr).
**By sawngthaew** From the small bus station, 1km west from town.
**Destinations:** Muang Sing (6 daily; 2hr); Oudomxai (3 daily; 3–4hr); Boten for China border (6 daily; 2hr).
**By boat** During the wet season, travellers heading for Houayxai have the option of going by boat. The Nam Tha is navigable from about July until January. You must hire a boat outright ($140 for a boat that holds up to ten people). If water levels are high, it's a one-day trip but if the water is low it takes half a day longer, with an overnight stop in Na Lae. Boatmen usually only go as far as Paktha, where the Nam Tha meets the Mekong. From there, you get a speedboat for the last 36km stretch along the Mekong to Houayxai (1hr; B300 per person). It's very important to strike a clear deal with the boatman, as they have been known to want to renegotiate the fare once en route.
**By air** There are daily flights to Vientiane and Louang Phabang.

# MUANG SING AND AROUND

**MUANG SING**, located some 60km northwest of Louang Namtha, is a full-on backpacker haven. Residents have opened dozens of guesthouses and restaurants to cater to tourists and trekkers in search of exotic **hilltribes** in traditional garb.

However, it's still an agreeable and friendly little town where great, sway-backed sows drag their teats down the main road and young novice monks play *kataw* and ride bicycles around the monastery grounds.

### INTO CHINA: BOTEN

Travellers with a valid visa for China can take a Chinese-operated bus in the morning from Louang Namtha bus station to the border crossing at Boten (daily 8am–5pm) and on to Jinghong in China (daily; 11hr). Sawngthaews only go as far as the border (4 daily; 2hr). Those coming down from China can get a 30-day Lao visa on arrival.

## What to see and do

Hidden behind the *Muangsing Guesthouse*, the ancient-looking **Wat Sing Jai** has a wonderfully rustic *sim*, painted in festive bright hues with a huge Buddha image inside.

Muang Sing's morning **market** was famous for its colourfully dressed vendors and shoppers, though nowadays camera-toting tourists almost outnumber the locals, who are more likely to be wearing track suits and Nike knock-offs. If you want to take a photo of a vendor, it's only polite to buy something first and try to have a little conversation. The market convenes very early, just after sunrise, and winds down by noon, though goods are on sale all day long.

To get a look at lifestyles beyond the town limits, you can join a one, two- or three-day **trek** through the surrounding mountains to remote and unspoilt hilltribe villages where daily life has barely changed in centuries.

## Arrival and information

**By bus and sawngthaews** The bus station is in the northwest of town, in front of the large market that sells fresh produce but you may well be dropped off on the main street.
**Tourist information** There is a very helpful visitor information office on the main street. Trekking must be booked through the Muang Sing Guide Services Office (GSO).

## Accommodation

Although Muang Sing is still pretty rustic, the town has a fair range of hotel options.

**Adima** 8km north of town, on the road to the Chinese frontier ☎086/212372. Muang Sing's first eco-tourist resort, featuring bamboo architecture in a rural setting. There's a choice of rooms in two big thatched bungalows with grass roofs or in A-frame cabins. The nice bamboo restaurant with a deck overlooking the fields is worth visiting even if you stay in town. ❷

**Charmpadeang** Northeast corner of the market ☎086/212374. The best of the four budget hotels facing the market. Rooms on the second floor have terrific views over the rice fields towards the mountains. ❶

**Danneua** Main road just north of the *Muangsing Guesthouse* ☎086/212369. Typical of the newer places, this is an unsightly concrete building, but the eight upstairs rooms are clean and modern and have en-suite bathrooms. There's a nice wide balcony overlooking the main drag. ❶

**Muangsing Guesthouse** Main street near Wat Sing Jai. This very friendly, family-run place is the backpacker favourite. One- and two-bed rooms with shared bath or ensuite facilities. The sitting area on the roof is also good for sunsets. Perhaps not recommended for style or particular comfort but the proprietor is always cheery and jolly and for this it is worth the stay. ❶

**Saengdeuang** Main road, 100m north of the Exhibition building ☎086/212376. This large, well-built, two-storey building has eight rooms and a clean restaurant downstairs. But the real draw are the thatched bungalows with shake roofs out back. The bungalow rooms have wooden floors, big windows and en-suite bathrooms. ❶

**Singcharean** ☎081/212347. West off the main road from the Phou lu. Muang Sing's biggest tourist hotel with 22 rooms aimed at package-tour groups from France. Institutional and devoid of atmosphere, but if you need something clean and modern with an en-suite bathroom, this fits the bill. ❷

**Tai Lue** This was the first guesthouse in Muang Sing and still holds its appeal. It is an attractive building with a veranda and small basic rooms with shared bathrooms. It is run by the same jolly man as *Muang Sing Guesthouse* across the road.❶

## Eating

Muang Sing's restaurant scene consists of several laid-back traveller's cafés. A good place to grab a noodle soup in the morning is at the market near the bus station.

**Ethnic Restaurant** Just off the main street, next door to the sauna. Owned by the same man who works in the tourist office, this restaurant has low tables and comfortable cushion seats and serves tasty Lao dishes.

**Muang Sing View Restaurant** Attached to the Lao sauna place at the south end of the main street. Has a very nice covered deck with a superb view over the rice fields.

**Phou lu Guesthouse** The restaurant here is extremely pleasant and serves fresh fish brought in from fish-farms in nearby China.

**Tai Leu Guesthouse** Friendly restaurant beneath the guesthouse. Service is a little slow but warmly delivered.

**Viengxay** Popular tourist restaurant on the main street serving a decent pad thai, rice and noodle dishes.

**Vieng Phone** Right next to *Viengxay* on the main street, similar sort of set up, atmosphere and menu.

## Directory

**Banks** You can exchange cash and traveller's cheques at BCEL opposite the *Viengxai* guesthouse or the Lane Xang Bank service unit on the south side of the market square.

**Bicycles** Available from *Anousone* restaurant opposite the museum for 12,000K and Tai Leu guesthouse for 10,000K.

### THE GOLDEN TRIANGLE

Historically, the Golden Triangle has been one of Asia's main illegal **opium-producing areas**, and incorporates Laos, as well as Burma and Thailand. Muang Sing played a large part as a busy way station and market during the twentieth century. Now, opium cultivation seems to be reducing in Laos, as traffickers are focusing their efforts on the lucrative methamphetamine trade. GTZ, a German federal corporation that helps run opium prevention, reduction and rehabilitation programmes, has a project office on the western edge of town. A small but informative free exhibition there (Mon–Fri 9am–4pm) documents their work.

### TREKKING ETIQUETTE

Always trek in **groups**, as there have been assaults on Western tourists in rural areas. If you are approached by armed men and robbery is clearly their intent, do NOT resist. Most hilltribe peoples are **animists**. Offerings to the spirits, often bits of food, left in what may seem like an odd place, should never be touched or tampered with. The Akha are known for the elaborate gates that they construct at the entrances to their villages. These gates have special meaning to the Akha and should also be left alone. Many hill folk are willing to be photographed, but old women, particularly of the Hmong and Mien tribes, are not always keen, so ask first. Passing out sweets to village kids is a sure way to generate mobs of young beggars. Likewise, the indiscriminate handing out of medicine, particularly antibiotics, does more harm than good. Unless you are a trained doctor, you should never attempt to administer medical care.

**Lao massage** A traditional Lao massage parlour and herbal sauna (10,000K) is located on the main road, 100m south of the town's market.
**Market** There is one market in the centre of town which sells local textiles and another northwest of the town facing the bus station that sells the usual consumer goods and fresh produce.
**Post office** Directly opposite the market; the telecom office is located west of the main road, on the street running parallel to the stream.

### Moving on

The Chinese border north of Muang Sing is not open to Westerners.
**By sawngthaew** Sawngthaews wait in the station in front of the market northwest of town and leave when full. Most vehicles depart in the morning but it's still possible to find one leaving at around 2pm.
**Destinations:** Louang Namtha (4 daily; 2hr 30min); Xiang Kok (2 daily; 2hr 30min).

## VILLAGES AND TREKKING AROUND MUANG SING

Muang Sing is located in the centre of a flat, triangular plain surrounded on all three sides by high mountains. There are scores of hilltribe settlements both in the valley and all through the surrounding mountains populated by Tai Leu, Tai Dam, Akha, Mien and Hmong people. The Tourist Authority runs a GSO (Guide Services Office) in Muang Sing to provide licensed guides. Visitors are not allowed to wander in and out of hilltribe villages unescorted, and locals are fined if caught guiding foreigners on unauthorized treks. The GSO-organized tours are professional and environmentally friendly, and help to reduce the villagers' resentment, who came to realize that they were the attraction yet were receiving no financial gain from the daily parade of gawkers.

## HOUAYXAI

The town of **HOUAYXAI**, situated on a hilly stretch of the Mekong River, is a favourite border crossing for people moving between Laos and Thailand. Travellers arriving in Houayxai can strike up or down the Mekong by boat, or bus overland up Route 3 to Louang Namtha. Those exiting Laos here can obtain a thirty-day **visa-on-arrival** from Thai immigration in Chiang Khong (daily 8am–5.30pm; see p.821) on the Thai side. Once in Chiang Khong, there are direct buses on to Chiang Rai and Chiang Mai.

### What to see and do

Houayxai's main sight is the hilltop **Wat Chom Khao Manilat**, boasting a tall, Shan-style building of picturesquely weathered teakwood, now used as a classroom for novice monks. There's also a traditional Lao herbal **sauna** run by the Red Cross in Bokeo (daily 5–9pm;

sauna 8000K; massage 25,000K for 1hr), located just past the wooden bridge as you go north up the main road.

## Arrival

**By boat** If arriving from Chiang Khong in Thailand you will embark at the ferry pier, which is right in the centre of town; the slow-boat pier is about 500m north of the centre. You can obtain a 30-day visa for Laos upon arrival. There are two speedboat piers; the southbound pier for boats heading to Louang Phabang is 2km downriver and the northbound pier for boats to Xieng Kok is 27km out of town (15,000K by tuk-tuk into town).

**By bus** The bus station is 3km south of town (10,000K by tuk-tuk into town).

## Accommodation

There are a dozen choices of accommodation in Houayxai, all on the main road just uphill from the ferry landing. Since the older hotels haven't lowered their prices, the newer places are actually better value for money.

**Arimid Guesthouse** ⓣ084/211040. These bungalows are at the north end of town, close to the bank and the slow-boat pier. A very nice setting with a restaurant and helpful staff. ❶–❷

**Friendship Guesthouse** On the main road at the south end of town ⓣ084/211219. This is a good place to stay with clean rooms at a reasonable price. There is also a fairly speedy internet café attached. ❶–❷

**Phonevichith Guesthouse** North of town, 2min walk from the slow-boat pier ⓣ084/211765. If you want somewhere close to the slow-boat pier, a little out of town with a lovely view of the Mekong, this guesthouse has individual ensuite bungalows and a pleasant restaurant attached. ❶

**Savanh Bokeo** This is a cheap deal in town, with its large two-, three- and four-bed rooms and shared facilities in a nice, old wooden house north of the ferry landing. ❶

**Sabaydee Guesthouse** Huay Xai. Offers the top value in town with spotless rooms with tiled, en-suite bathrooms. The four corner units give terrific views of the Mekong. ❷

**Thanormsub Guesthouse** ⓣ084/211095. Just about opposite *Sabaydee* is this blue-roofed house with fourteen very clean, tiled rooms with en-suite bathrooms and hot water. Some rooms are available with a/c. ❶

**Thaweesinh Hotel** ⓣ021/211502. A four-storey concrete building with a nice rooftop patio, this place is clean and modern and therefore popular with group tours. Rooms range from windowless singles ($2) to a/c doubles with TV ($8). ❶–❷

## Eating and drinking

**Bar Who?** Main road, near *Nut Pop* restaurant. Relaxed lounge with good music and ambient lighting. Feels almost like a trendy European bar.

**Mouang Neua** This restaurant opposite the *Thaweesinh Hotel* has an English menu and specializes in tourist fare – the vegetable omelette is a must.

**Nutpop** Lovely setting with a leafy wooded decking area and delicious fish and meat dishes.

**Riverview Restaurant** This large restaurant on the river is a good place to catch the sunset. It has a large menu of decent Lao and Korean food.

## Directory

**Bank** Lao Development Bank at the north end of town behind the *Arimid* guesthouse (8.30am–3.30pm Mon–Fri). Exchanges baht, dollars, traveller's cheques and can do cash advances. There is also an exchange booth at immigration.

**Internet** *Friendship Guesthouse* has the best internet facilities. 400k/min.

**Massage and Sauna** The Red Cross Sauna (5–9pm daily) offers traditional massage ($3/hr) and herbal sauna ($1). It is just beyond the wooden bridge towards the north end of town.

**Post office** South end of town (8am–10pm Mon–Fri).

**Travel agency** Bokeo Travel, 114 Mekong River Bank Road.

## Moving on

You will either be leaving from the ferry landing for Chiang Khong in Thailand; the slow-boat pier down the Mekong; the southbound pier for speedboats to Pakbeng and Louang Phabang; the northbound pier for Xieng Kok or the bus station 3km north of town. For buses you can either arrange transport at a tour agents or book it at the bus station, which is normally cheaper.

**By boat** to Thai border (8am–5.30pm; 5min); Louang Namtha (passenger boat 1–2 days); Louang Phabang (slow boat 2 days; speedboat 6hr); Pakbeng (slow boat 1 day; speedboat 3hr); Xiang Kok (speedboat 4hr).

**By bus** to: Louang Namtha (2 daily; 7hr); Louang Phabang (1 daily; 15hr); Odomxai (1 daily; 11hr); Vientiane (1 daily; 23hr).

### TAKING THE SLOW BOAT DOWN THE MEKONG TO LOUANG PHABANG

Slow boats take two days to complete the journey from Houayxai to **Louang Phabang**, stopping overnight at the village of **Pakbeng** (see below).

Despite the general lack of comfort, most travellers agree that the two-day journey by **slow boat** (*heua sa*) to the old royal capital is one of those once-in-a-lifetime experiences. Every morning, slow boats leave from the slow-boat pier, 1km upriver from the Chiang Khong ferry landing, and arrive at Pakbeng in the late afternoon. The following morning the boat continues on to Louang Phabang, arriving around dusk. Fares ($8 to Pakbeng, $15 to Louang Phabeng) are payable in Thai baht, dollars or kip. Some of the boats have been converted to take only foreign passengers, and while the level of comfort is passable, these new boats are lacking in the romance department. There are still genuine cargo boats doing the run, however, so it just depends on which boat is making the trip the day you want to depart. Bring along food and bottled water, as none is available on board. A closed-in area on the stern serves as the toilet. During high season it's not unusual for the boatmen to pack as many as eighty tourists into a single vessel. If this isn't your cup of tea, simply do the trip in reverse, upriver from Louang Phabang to Houayxai, where the same boat is virtually empty.

**Speedboats** (*heua wai*) also make the journey from Houayxai to Pakbeng ($15) and Louang Phabang ($30); although they are potentially dangerous – they seem to crash into rocks with an alarming frequency. Crash helmets and life-vests are supposed to be provided, and don't forget to bring earplugs. The speedboat landing is located 2km downriver for boats going south. Speedboats going upriver to Xiang Kok now leave from the Nam Keng landing, 27km north of town. The road to Nam Keng is paved and the fare is B100. It's important to arrive at the landings as early as possible in order to get a boat – if there are no other passengers, it may be necessary to hire the boat outright. Provided you have sunglasses, sunblock, and good earplugs, you might find the ride is quite fun – at least for the first hour or so.

## PAKBENG

A single-lane dirt road winding up the side of a mountain makes up the bustling, frontier riverport of **PAKBENG**, the halfway point between Houayxai and Louang Phabang and the only sizeable town along the 300km stretch of river between them. As slow boats don't travel the Mekong after dark, a night here is unavoidable if you're travelling this way. Stumbling off the slow boat at the end of a long day, the ramshackle settlement of wood-scrap, corrugated tin and hand-painted signs that constitutes the port area can be a bit of a culture shock. Since Pakbeng is many travellers' first night in Laos, the expression on a lot of faces is "What have I got myself into?" Don't worry; Pakbeng is only typical of the northern backwoods. You'll be sipping lattes in Louang Phabang in no time.

### Arrival and information

**By boat** You will arrive at the boat landing or the floating speedboat landing, which are both a short walk from the guesthouses.

**Electricity** There is only power from 6–10pm.

### Accommodation and eating

Once the boat pulls in, don't waste any time securing a room. From the landing, the majority of guesthouses are just up the hill, well before you reach the actual town of Pakbeng itself. The budget options are all pretty much the same, comprising very basic wooden rooms with beds, mosquito nets and fans, with shared cold-water washrooms out back. Electricity seems to be seasonal: reliable in the rainy season, not so reliable in the dry. Most guesthouses in Pakbeng have a generator on standby just in case.

**Donevilasak** ☎081/212315. At the top of the hill. Divided into two buildings, this place used to be one of the best but is being surpassed by competition. Still offers an adequate night's sleep. ❶–❷

**Monsavan** This is a good cheap option if you don't mind hearing your neighbours' every move. The simple rooms are fine for a stopover. ❶

**Phuylathda Guesthouse** ☎020/5181095. Just beyond the boat landing. This guesthouse is run by a charming lady and has clean, comfortable rooms with cold water shared bathroom. ❶

**Vatsana Guesthouse** This is a good one for those on a really strict budget with its four-person dorm. Basic, with shared bathroom facilities and cold water. ❶

### Eating

Considering this is a stopover town, the choices of restaurants aren't half bad. In the morning, takeaway submarine sandwich-makers line the road down to the boat landing.

### Moving on

**By boat** If you're continuing to Louang Phabang on the boat, you should be down at the landing before 8am. Some captains stop briefly at the caves at Pak Ou (see p.438) before Louang Phabang, charging each passenger who disembarks for a look a couple of thousand kip extra. This does work out cheaper than chartering a boat from Louang Phabang, but leaves little time for exploring.

**By bus** Sawngthaews up Route 2 from Pakbeng to Oudomxai leave from the foot of the hill between 8am and 9am. The 150-kilometre-long road passes through Hmong and Tai Leu villages, and takes about four hours.

# South central Laos

Many travellers see very little of **south central Laos**, spending just a night or two in the town of Savannakhet before pressing on to the far south or **crossing the border** into Vietnam. The two principal settlements of south central Laos – Thakhek and Savannakhet – both lie on the Mekong River, and both offer straightforward border crossings into Thailand. Route 8 between Vientiane and Thakhek is the best and easiest overland route to Vietnam, the paved road snaking through mountains, rainforests and the Phu Pha Man "stone forest" before winding down to the city of Vinh. **Savannakhet** has been described as southern Laos's Louang Phabang, its inhabitants living comfortably among the architectural heirlooms handed down by the French, and is a pleasant enough place. East from Savannakhet, Route 9 climbs steadily until it eventually bisects another route of more recent vintage: the **Ho Chi Minh Trail.** The trail was used by the North Vietnamese Army to infiltrate and finally subdue its southern neighbour, and is still littered with lots of war junk, some of it highly dangerous. The safest way to view these rusting relics is to use the town of **Xepon** as a base. Journeying further east leads to the **Vietnam border crossing** at Daen Sawan, popularly known as "Lao Bao".

## SAVANNAKHET

The town of **SAVANNAKHET**, known locally as "Sawan", is southern Laos's most-visited provincial capital. Its popularity is due in part to its central location on the overland routes between Vientiane and Pakxe, and Thailand and Vietnam. Travellers doing the "Indochina loop" – through Cambodia, Vietnam, Laos and Thailand – have the option of taking the 240-kilometre-long Route 9 on their way between Laos's two neighbours, hence the presence of both a **Thai** and a **Vietnamese consulate**. But Savannakhet also has its own appeal, with impressive architecture inherited from the French colonial period and narrow streets and shop-houses of ochre-coloured stucco that are reminiscent of parts of Hanoi. A large percentage of the

### INTO VIETNAM: THE KAEW NUA CROSSING

Halfway between Pakxan and Thakhek, at the junction town of **Ban Viang Kham**, 88km south of Pakxan, Route 8 heads across central Laos to the Kaew Nua Pass, which marks the border with Vietnam, before switchbacking down to the city of Vinh on the coast of Vietnam. Most travellers pass through here on direct, a/c buses running the Vientiane/Vinh route, but the paved road traces a centuries' old trading route to Vietnam zigzagging through ruggedly beautiful countryside.

The rag-tag **buses** that make the trip to the frontier town Lak Xao from Thakhek and Vientiane (daily; 8hr) stop at its market. The **Vietnamese border**, known as **Kaew Nua Pass** (or Nam Phao in Lao), is 35km from Lak Xao and best reached by hiring a tuk-tuk (20,000K each) from the market. For those crossing into Laos from Vietnam, there's usually a tuk-tuk on hand for hire into Lak Xao.

**Crossing the border** (daily 7.30am–5pm) is generally hassle-free, but start your journey early. Sort out your Vietnamese visa in advance; Laos 30-day visa is issued on arrival. Watch out for the minibus touts who will try and charge you the earth to get to Vinh, try to get it down to at least half that. A small exchange kiosk sits in the Lao terminal, but don't expect to get a decent rate. The settlement on the Vietnamese side of the border is **Cau Treo**, 105km west of Vinh on Highway 8; see p.967 for details.



town's population is ethnic Vietnamese, though most have been living here for generations and consider themselves to be Lao in habit and temperament.

## What to see and do

As you head inland from the ferry landing, you soon come to the town square, dominated by the octagonal spire of **St Teresia Catholic Church**, built in 1930. Check out the old teakwood confessional and, high up on the walls, a set of hardwood plaques, with Vietnamese mother-of-pearl inlay work, depicting the fourteen Stations of the Cross. Not surprisingly, the biblical characters have distinctly Asian faces.

Roads laid out on a neat grid surrounding the square constitute the **Old French Quarter**, and are lined with some fine examples of European-inspired architecture. Aside from wandering about admiring the crumbling buildings and the town's pleasant wats and Chinese temples, there's not much more to do in Savannakhet but watch the sun set over the Mekong. Neither of the town's museums offers much in the way of enticement: housed in a peeling colonial-era mansion on Tha He Road, about 1km south of the ferry landing, the unswept, rundown **provincial museum** (daily 8am–noon & 2–4pm; 5000K) mostly contains dusty photographs of former communist party leader Kaysone Phomvihane (1920–92), Savannakhet's most revered native son, but is almost always closed; the **Dinosaur Museum** on Khanthabouli Road isn't really very interesting except for the opportunity to chat with the friendly curators.

### INTO THAILAND: SAVANNAKHET TO MUKDAHAN

The newly built **Second Friendship Bridge** allows Thai-Lao bus services to cross over into Thailand from Savannakhet. Foreigners must not use the passenger ferry that runs across the Mekong between Savannakhet and Mukdahan in Thailand. There is an exchange kiosk in the ferry terminal. When crossing after 6pm or on Sundays, immigration on both sides sometimes charges extra. Lao 30-day visa available on arrival.

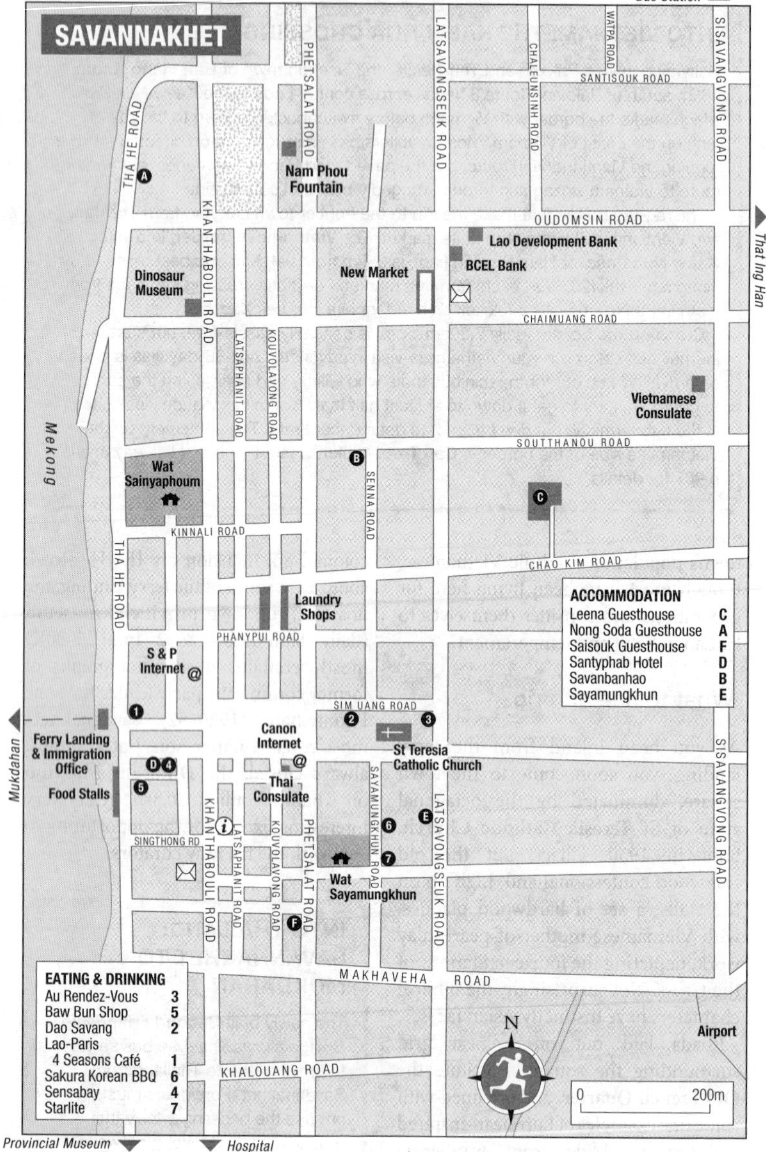


### That Ing Hang

Outside of town is a much-revered Buddhist stupa, the **That Ing Hang**, which can be reached by bicycle. Follow Route 13 north for 13km until you see a sign on the right and follow this road for a further 3km. The stucco work that covers the stupa is crude yet appealing, especially the whimsical rosettes which dot the uppermost spire. Off to one side of the stupa stands an amusing sandstone sculpture of a lion, grinning like a Cheshire cat, which could only have been hauled here from one of the Khmer ruins downriver. The stupa is best visited during its annual festival in February when thousands make the pilgrimage here; it can be a bit of a letdown during the rest of the year.

## Arrival and information

**By bus** Most buses offload at the station on the north side of Savannakhet. A/c buses from Vientiane drop passengers at a separate stand nearby, known locally as khiw Sensabay. Tuk-tuks make the 2km run from the bus stations into the city centre (10,000K),

**By air** The airport is on the southeastern side of town, not far from the centre. Most flights are private charters only.

**Tourist information** There is a Tourism Authority (☎041/212755) on Latsaphanit Road, just south of the square. They offer eco-friendly treks.

## City transport

**Tuk-tuks** As Savannakhet is incredibly spread out, you'll find that tuk-tuks are a better idea than trying to walk the long blocks outside the old quarter.

**Bicycle rental** $1 per day from *Sensabay* restaurant and some guesthouses.

**Vehicle rental** Both the *Savanbanhao* and the *Nanhai Hotel*, a block north of the Lao May Bank, have vans with drivers for hire. Self-drive at either place is not an option, though you can rent motorcycles for $5 a day at the Canon Internet shop on the town square.

## Accommodation

Savannakhet has a very good choice and range of accommodation; the most convenient and atmospheric are in the Old French Quarter. Many hotels in Savannakhet have their own travel agencies that can organize tours of the Ho Chi Minh Trail (see p.457).

**Leena Guesthouse** Chao Kim Rd, 200m east off Latsavongseuk Rd ☎041/212404. Huge two-storey building in a quiet residential area with twelve clean, en-suite rooms, some with a/c. ❶

**Nong Soda Guesthouse** Tha He Rd. This place is a short walk north from the customs pier. Good-value rooms with a/c and hot water. You can also rent bicycles ($2) and motorbikes ($8 per day). ❷

**Saisouk Guesthouse** Phetsalat Rd, a block south of Wat Sayamungkhun ☎041/212207. Homestay-style guesthouse in a lovely wooden house in a quiet area. Shared facilities and no hot water, but if you're looking for a friendly, relaxed atmosphere with genuinely nice people, this is the place for you. ❶

**Savanbanhao** Senna Rd, four blocks north of the church ☎041/212202. Six large houses set in a big walled compound. Unfriendly service and no atmosphere at all, but a wide range of good-value rooms with en-suite bathrooms and hot water. ❶–❷

**Sayamungkhun** Latsavongseuk Rd ☎041/212426. A large house on the main street close to the old quarter, with sixteen spacious, en-suite, a/c rooms. Excellent value, and one of the few guesthouses in a heritage building. ❶

## Eating and drinking

The food and service at all of Savannakhet's travellers' cafés is notably poor, but the town does have some good restaurants if you know where to look. One local noodle dish worth seeking out is **baw bun** (Vietnamese rice noodles served with chopped-up spring rolls and beef). In the evening, shops selling soft drinks and a few *tam màk hung* vendors crop up on the riverbank in front of Wat Sainyaphoum, a pleasant spot to catch the sunset over Thailand and mingle with the locals. The fruit shakes are in a class of their own – look for the blenders.

**Au Rendez-Vous Café** 179 Latsavongseuk Rd. Somewhat lacking in atmosphere and friendliness but a standard menu of Lao and Western favourites that will hit the spot.

**Baw Bun Shop** Fourth shop-house from the river, in the alley behind *Santyphab Hotel*. If it's *baw bun* you're after, this is the place, but it's only open in the morning.

**Lao-Paris 4 Seasons Café** Tha He Rd, near the immigration office. All the travellers seem to end up at this Vietnamese shop-house near the river. Alright for sandwiches and coffee, but the service is slow and unfriendly.

**Sakura Korean BBQ** Sayamungkhun Rd. Great Korean-style barbecue with a good selection of meat and fish to choose from.

**TREAT YOURSELF**

If you fancy blowing the budget on well-cooked and well-presented French cuisine, try the fantastic restaurant, **Dao Savang**, located on the square. It serves generous glasses of red wine for $3 and a hearty steak for $6.

A refreshing break from the usual traveller café get-up.

**Sensabay** Next to *Santyphab Hotel*. Popular backpacker spot with quite tasty Western and Asian food but slow service. The fried chicken is worth trying.

**Starlite** Sayamungkhun Rd behind Wat Sayamungkhun. Very good Korean barbecue steamboat with a choice of beef or fish, and lots of fresh veggies and glass noodles.

## Directory

**Airlines** Lao Airlines (☎041/212140) is at the airport, southeast of the city centre.

**Banks and exchange** There are two banks near the intersection of Latsavongseuk and Oudomsin roads. The Lao Development Bank faces Oudomsin Rd, and the BCEL faces Latsavongseuk Rd (Mon–Fri 8.00am–3.30pm).

**Consulates** Thai: on Kouvolavong Rd on block south of the square (Mon–Fri 8.30am–noon & 2–3.30pm; ☎041/212373); tourist visas costs $7 and require two photos. Provided you apply before noon, the visa will be ready the next afternoon. Vietnamese: on Sisavangvong Rd (Mon–Fri 7.30–11am & 1.30–4.30pm; ☎041/212418); visas cost $50, require two photos and take five working days.

**Hospitals and clinics** The biggest hospital is located on Khanthabouli Rd, near the provincial museum; a 24hr clinic operates on Phetsalat Rd, a block south of the *Hoongthip Hotel*. The biggest pharmacy is on the corner of Oudomsin and Senna roads.

**Internet** Most of the internet places are to be found on Ratsavong Rd and charge around 4000K a minute.

**Laundry** Fast and cheap at the laundry shops along Kouvolavong Rd, north of the town square.

**Market** Talat Nyai (New Market) sells all sorts of goods and is located at the north end of Savannakhet.

**Massage** The Red Cross on Kouvolavong Rd opposite the Chinese temple offers traditional massage for $3.

**Post and telephone** The GPO is on Khanthabouli Rd, a few blocks south of the town square (Mon–Fri 8am–noon & 1–5pm, Sat & Sun 8–11am). The Telcom building with overseas phone and fax service (daily 8am–10pm) is just behind it. There is a post office branch near the BCEL Bank, on the corner of Chaimuang and Latsavongseuk roads.

## Moving on

**By bus** The main bus station is 2km north of town. **Destinations:** Attapu (1 daily; 9 hr); Daen Sawan/Lao Bao, Vietnam (4 daily; 5hr); Da Nang, Vietnam (6 weekly; 10hr); Dong Ha, Vietnam (1 daily; 8hr); Hanoi, Vietnam (1 weekly; 20hr); Hue, Vietnam (6 weekly; 8hr); Mukhdahan, Thailand (9 daily; 30min); Vientiane (16 daily; 8hr); Xepon (4 daily; 2hr); Thakhek (8 daily; 2hr); Pakxe (5 daily; 5hr); Xekong (1 daily, 8hr).

**By boat** The boat landing to get across to Mukdahan, Thailand is just west of the main square (6 daily Mon–Fri, 3 daily on weekends).

# ROUTE 9: THE HO CHI MINH TRAIL AND THE VIETNAMESE BORDER

Route 9 weaves east through a series of drab towns from Savannakhet to the **Lao Bao border crossing** into Vietnam. The road ends its Lao journey at the Lao Bao Pass before heading on to Dong Ha, where it connects with Vietnam's Highway 1. While most travellers barrel through on the direct buses, the frontier is not without sites of interest. Muang Phin can be used as a base for the Dong Phou Viang NBCA and there are **Ho Chi Minh Trail** sites open for tourism on both sides of the border.

## Xepon

A picturesque village in the foothills of the Annamite Mountains, 40km from the Vietnamese border, **XEPON** is a pleasant rural stopover between Vietnam and Savannakhet. The old town of Xepon was obliterated during the Second Indochina War – along with every house in the district's two hundred villages – and was later rebuilt here 6km west of its original location, on the opposite bank of the Xe Banghiang River. The old city had been captured by communist forces in 1960 and became an important outpost on the Ho Chi Minh Trail. As such, it was the target of a joint South Vietnamese and American invasion in 1971, Operation Lam Son 719 (see box opposite), aimed at disrupting the flow of troops and supplies headed for communist forces in South Vietnam.

**Buses** arriving from Savannakhet or the Lao Bao border stop at the market, from where it's a short walk uphill to the government **guesthouse** ($1/bed), which offers dormitory-style accommodation. If you don't mind the 1.5-kilometre walk, the forestry department runs a somewhat nicer dorm-style guesthouse ($2 /bed) at the edge of town. To get here, take a left at the second road west of the market and follow the road to the foot of the hill. A small **restaurant** across from the market offers noodles, omelettes and stir-fries. There are no **official exchange** services in Xepon, but cash can always be exchanged. Sawngthaews run up to Ban Dong as well as the border-town of Daen Sawan, where you can continue by motorcycle taxi to the Lao Bao border post.

## The Ho Chi Minh Trail at Ban Dong

Halfway between Xepon and the Vietnam border is the town of **BAN DONG**, the site of one of America's most ignominious defeats during the war, and a popular stop on tours of the **Ho Chi Minh Trail**. Situated in the foothills of the Annamite Mountains, bomb craters and spent ordnance still litter the landscape more than a quarter of a century after the war. If you're travelling by public transport, it's best to visit Ban Dong in the morning, as few late-afternoon sawngthaews ply this stretch of Route 9 and Ban Dong has no guesthouses, although there are some bamboo-and-thatch drink shops.

## Daen Sawan

Route 9 ends its journey through Laos in the village of **DAEN SAWAN**, 1km from the Lao immigration office. For a remote border town, Daen Sawan is relatively tourist-friendly, with food, accommodation and exchange services. The *Friendly guesthouse* (❶) has basic rooms with shared bathrooms and a helpful owner. Attached to the guesthouse is the popular *Loung Aloune*

### OPERATION LAM SON 719

In 1971, US President Richard Nixon ordered an attack on the **Ho Chi Minh Trail,** in order to cut off supplies to communist forces. Although US ground troops were prohibited by law from crossing the border from Vietnam into Laos and Cambodia, the US command saw this as a chance to test the strengths of Vietnamization, the policy of turning the ground war over to the South Vietnamese. For the operation, code-named **Lam Son 719**, it was decided that ARVN (Army of the Republic of Vietnam) troops were to invade Laos and block the trail with US air support. The objective was **Xepon**, a town straddled by the Trail, which was 30–40km wide at this point. In early February 1971, ARVN troops and tanks pushed across the border at Lao Bao and followed Route 9 into Laos. Like a caterpillar trying to ford a column of red ants, the South Vietnamese troops were soon engulfed by superior numbers of North Vietnamese (NVA) regulars. ARVN officers stopped halfway to Xepon and engaged the NVA in a **series of battles** that lasted over a month. US air support proved ineffectual, and by mid-March, scenes of frightened ARVN troops retreating were being broadcast around the world.

The most tangible relics of Operation Lam Son 719 are two rusting **American tanks** that sit on the outskirts of Ban Dong, on Route 9. The easiest tank to find lies five minutes' walk off the road that cuts south out of town towards Taoy. Shaded by a grove of jack-fruit trees, it rests atop a small hill east of the road, partially dismantled for its valuable steel. As of 1998, UXO-Lao (the Lao National Unexploded Ordnance Programme) has cleared Ban Dong of unexploded war debris, but it's still a good idea to ask a villager to show you the way, as you should always take extra care when leaving a well-worn path.

**restaurant**. There's a Lao May Bank in town, as well as a branch at the Lao immigration office on the border. The rates are not good, so only change what you need: $20 is more than enough to get you to Savannakhet, via Xepon. From Daen Sawan, you can hire a motorcycle taxi for the final 1km ride to the Lao immigration office. If you've entered Laos from Vietnam, there are four buses a day to Savannakhet (3hr) from Daen Sawan, the last leaving at 2pm, and four daily (1hr) to Xepon.

# The far south

Bordered by Thailand, Cambodia and Vietnam, the far south conveniently divides into two regions, with **Pakxe**, the most important market town and the access point for the Chong Mek **border crossing** into Thailand, as the hub. In the west, the Mekong River corridor is scattered with dozens of ancient Khmer temples, including **Wat Phou**, one of the most important Angkorian ruins outside Cambodia, and the main tourist attraction in southern Laos. From the nearby town of **Champasak**, it makes sense to go with the flow of the river south to **Si Phan Don**, where the Mekong's 1993km journey through Laos rushes to a thundering conclusion in a series of tiny riverine islands at the Cambodian border; the waters here are home to a dwindling number of very rare Irrawaddy **dolphins**. In the east of the region, the fertile highlands of the **Bolaven Plateau** separate the Mekong corridor from the Annamite Mountains that form Laos's border with Vietnam. Much of the area east of the Mekong lies off the beaten track and involves hard journeys on bumpy roads. One city well worth making the effort to see, though, is **Attapu**, known as the garden city for its pleasant atmosphere and laid-back pace.

## PAKXE

Located at the confluence of the Xe Don and the Mekong rivers, roughly halfway between the Thai border and the Bolaven Plateau, **PAKXE** is the far south's biggest city, and its commercial and transport hub. For travellers, it is a necessary stopover en route to Si Phan Don and Cambodia, and makes a more comfortable base than Pakxong for exploration of the Bolaven Plateau and nearby NBCAs. There is also a border crossing to Thailand just west of Pakxe at Chong Mek, making it a logical entry or exit point for travellers doing a north–south tour of Laos.

### INTO VIETNAM: LAO BAO BORDER CROSSING

A short distance from the Lao immigration office is the **Lao Bao border crossing** (daily 7am–11am & 1pm–7pm) into **Vietnam**. Travellers to Vietnam must have a valid visa, and the crossing is not always hassle-free. Vietnamese officials may send you back if your visa is not stamped for "Lao Bao". Motorcyclists have also reported problems, with officials sometimes unwilling to allow larger bikes to enter. On the Vietnamese side, there are motorcycle taxis to take you down the hill to Lao Bao town (see p.967) where buses leave for the 20km journey to Khe Sanh every thirty minutes, with some going straight through to Dong Ha on Route 1, where bus or train connections can be made to Hanoi and Hue; see p.967 for details. Accommodation is available in Lao Bao town.

This border is 255km from Savannakhet from which you can catch two daily buses to Daen Sawan and from there motorbike taxis for the final 1km to the border or take direct buses with a stop at immigration to Da Nang (4 weekly; 10hr) or Hue (3 weekly; 8hr). Travellers must have a valid visa for Vietnam.

## What to see and do

Pakxe only has two real tourist attractions, both just east of the town centre on Route 13 and easily reached by tuk-tuk. The first is the **Champasak Palace Hotel**, a majestic eyesore resembling a giant cement wedding cake. Legend has it that the late Prince Boun Oum na Champasak, a colourful character who was the heir to the Champasak kingdom and one of the most influential southerners of the twentieth century, needed a palace this size so that he could accommodate his many concubines. The palace is now a hotel. The second attraction, 500m further along Route 13, is the **Champasak Provincial Museum** (Mon–Fri 8–11.30am & 2–4pm; 5000K), which houses some fine examples of ornately carved pre-Angkorian sandstone lintels taken from sites around the province. Upstairs is a selection of local tribes' costumes and jewellery.

## Arrival and Information

**By bus** There are two separate bus stations, both of which are served by tuk-tuks to hotels (5000K). Buses to and from Savannakhet and the north use the Northern bus station, 7km north of the city on Route 13.

Buses to and from points south and east use the Southern bus station, 8km southeast of town on Route 13. If you are arriving from Champasak you will probably be dropped at the Dao Heung Market (Morning Market), where most of the sawngthaews leave from.

**By boat** The boat landing is behind the post office on the N.11 Road, but boats are rarely used.

**By air** The airport lies 2km northeast of the city on Route 13, from where tuk-tuks (8000K) run into town.

**Tourist Information** Provincial Tourism Office, 8am–noon and 1.30–4pm, near The Lao Airlines Office (see p.460). Good for general information and organizing village treks around the region.

## Accommodation

Most of the budget hotels are north of the Central Market, along Route 13.

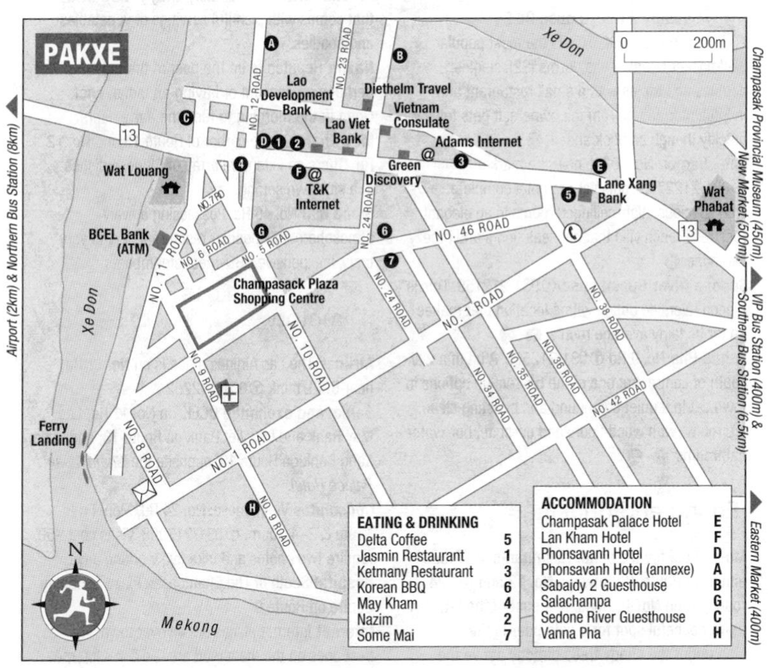

## INTO THAILAND: CHONG MEK

To get to the **Lao–Thai border crossing** at Chong Mek, go to the New Market and catch a sawngthaew for the forty-kilometre trip to the border crossing at Vangtao (daily 8.30am–4pm), which takes around one hour. The fare is 10,000K or B50 per person if the vehicle is full, more if not. The expansive market that straddles the border thrives on weekends. After crossing into Thailand, sawngthaews will be waiting to shuttle you to **Ubon Ratchathani**, which has plentiful road and rail links (see p.872). There are also two direct **Chong Mek-to-Bangkok** a/c buses that leave from the market at 4pm and 5pm respectively.

There are also four daily direct buses from Pakxe to Ubon Ratchathani that take three hours.



**Champasak Palace Hotel** Route 13 ☎031/212263. The top hotel in Pakxe, with ninety rooms. It was obviously fit for a prince, and is great value at $35 for a double. ❻`

**Lan Kham Hotel** Route 13 ☎031/213314. Fairly modern building with clean rooms. Centrally located with motorbike ($10) and bicycle ($1) hire. ❺

**Phonsavanh Hotel** Corner of Route 13 and No. 12 Rd ☎031/202842. Budget travellers should head here: it's a dump, but the staff are friendly, the location's good and it has a certain seedy charm. Ask about the *Phonsavanh's* annexe a short walk down No. 12 Rd, which has newer rooms for the same low price. ❶

**Sabaidy 2 Guesthouse** Rd 24 ☎031/212992. This is the most popular backpacker haunt. It has dorms ($2), singles, doubles and triples with a small restaurant and helpful information from the owners. It gets full very quickly though so book ahead. ❶

**Salachampa** No. 10 Rd, near the market ☎031/212273. A colonial-era hotel complete with spacious, high-ceilinged rooms in an elegant, restored French villa that has teak floors and breezy verandas. ❸

**Sedone River Guesthouse** ☎031/212158. This is a good riverside option with a location that makes up for Its fairly average rooms. ❶–❷

**Vanna Pha** No. 9 Rd ☎031/212502. A bit of a walk south of centre, but one of the best-value options in town set in a quiet compound and boasting clean, a/c rooms with wood floors and en-suite, hot-water bathrooms. ❶–❷

## Eating and drinking

Most of the town's better restaurants are found either on Route 13 between No. 12 and No. 24 roads, or on No. 46 Road, just east of the latter. A more peaceful spot for a cold beer is the stall under the shady trees directly above the boat landing, where you can look out over the Mekong River.

**Delta Coffee** Route 13. A great café for Western food set out on a terrace spilling onto the street. Their extensive menu has a large section devoted to different variations of coffee. Their pasta dishes are highly recommended.

**Jasmin Restaurant** Route 13. One of the two Indian restaurants situated competitively side by side serving Indian and Malay dishes.

**Ketmany Restaurant** Route 13. Good place for an ice cream and the usual selection of Thai and Lao food.

**Korean BBQ** Road 46. Tasty array of BBQ meat that comes with plentiful servings of vegetables and noodles.

**Nazim** Reputed to be the best of the Indians, perhaps on account of having an Indian chef. Open in the morning to feed the early risers.

**May Kham** On the corner of Route 13 and No. 12 Rd. Offers an extensive array of Chinese dishes in a sit-down setting.

**Some Mai** No. 46 Rd. Possessing a lively atmosphere, this popular restaurant serves very tasty, inexpensive BBQ-meat steamboats.

## Directory

**Airlines** The Lao Airlines office is on No. 11 Rd, near BCEL bank ☎031/212252.

**Banks and exchange** BCEL, on No. 11 Rd; Lao May Bank and Lao Viet Bank on Route 13; and Lane Xang Bank on Route 13, opposite the *Champasak Palace Hotel*.

**Consulates** Vietnamese: No. 24 Rd, Mon–Fri 8–11am & 2–4.30pm; ☎031/212058. Visas cost $50, require two photos and take five working days.

**Hospital** South of The Champasak Plaza Shopping Centre on Route 9.

**Internet** Internet places are all over town. The best ones on the main road are @d@m's Internet (international calls can be made here), and SD Internet.

**Post office** At the corner of No. 8 Rd and No. 1 Rd; daily 7.30am–9pm.

**Telephone services** International calls and faxes at Telecom, on the corner of No. 1 and No. 38 Rds; daily 8am–9pm.

**Tour agencies** Green Discovery ⓣ031/252908, ⓦwww.greendiscoverylaos.com; Sodetour, corner of Route 13 and No. 24 Rd ⓣ031/212122; Lane Xang Travel ⓦwww.xplore-asia.com, Route 13, below the *Phonesavanh Hotel* ⓣ031/212002; Inter-Lao Tourisme, in the lobby of the *Champasak Palace Hotel* ⓣ031/212778.

## Moving on

**By bus** Most towns in the far south are only served by one or two buses a day, from the Southern bus station, which tend to leave early in the morning. Buses for towns to the east, including Tad Lo, Xekong and Attapu also depart from Pakxe's Southern station. An express van departs for Attapu from the Southern bus station daily in the early afternoon – arrive early, as seating is limited.

**Destinations:** Attapu (2 daily; 4–7hr); Champasak (3 daily; 1hr 30min); Chong Mek (hourly; 45min); Muang Sen (2 daily; 5hr 30min); Nakasang (5 daily; 3hr); Pakxong (hourly; 2hr); Salavan (5 daily; 3hr); Savannakhet (5 daily; 4hr); Tad Lo (3 daily; 2–3hr); Thakhek (4 daily; 6hr); Vientiane (4 daily; 12hr); Xekong (2 daily; 4–5hr).

**By VIP bus** Comfortable, a/c buses, booked through travel agencies. They leave from the VIP bus station/ evening market station just off Route 13.

**Destinations:** Vientiane (1 daily; 10hr); Ubon Ratchathani Thailand (4 daily; 3hr).

**By sawngthaew** The sawngthaew lot is at the Dao Heung (Morning Market). Sawngthaews head in all directions, including Champasak and the Thai border. Northbound buses also use the sawngthaew lot, although these also pull into the Northern bus station before leaving town.

**By boat** Passenger boats to Si Phan Don ($17) and Champasak ($6) leave from the boat landing at 8am. If you miss this it is possible to charter a private boat but this can be very expensive.

**By air** to: Phnom Penh, Cambodia (2 weekly; 1hr 20min); Siem Reap, Cambodia (3 weekly; 1hr); Vientiane (1 daily; 1hr 20min); Louang Phabang (2 weekly; 1hr 40min).

# CHAMPASAK

From Pakxe, daily passenger boats ply the 40km stretch of the Mekong south, past misty green mountains and riverbanks loaded with palm trees, to the charming riverside town of **CHAMPASAK**. An increasingly popular backpacker resort, Champasak also serves as the gateway to **Wat Phou** and the **Khmer** ruins, although it is also possible to visit Wat Phou as a day-trip from Pakxe. Buses from Pakxe also head to Champasak three times a day. Meandering for 4km along the right bank of the Mekong, Champasak is now an unassuming town, but was once the capital of a Lao kingdom, whose territory stretched from the Annamite Mountains into present-day Thailand. A former **palace of Prince Boun Oum na Champasak**, the scion of the royal family of Champasak and a one-time prime minister, can be seen below Wat Phou.

## Arrival and information

**By bus** Buses and sawngthaews (7000K) will let you off at Champasak's tiny roundabout.

**By boat** The boat and ferry dock lies about 2km north off the roundabout; tuk-tuks are available at the dock.

**Tourist Information** The Champasak District Visitor Information Centre 8am–4.30pm, near the post office. They can organize tours around the region.

## Accommodation and eating

**Anouxa Guesthouse** ⓣ031/213272. Right between the boat landing and the town. Several clean individual bungalows run by a helpful family who are happy to advise and suggest places to visit. There's also a good restaurant and bicycle rental. ❷

**Kham Khong** ⓣ031/213248. 2km south of the roundabout. A collection of rather tatty bungalows and a restaurant with a deck overlooking the Mekong. ❷

**Kham Phouy** ⓣ0031/252700 Roomy doubles and triples, along with wooden, en-suite bungalows in the garden. ❶

**Saythong** Just south of the roundabout ⓣ031/920 092. Basic rooms with shared facilities in an old wooden house, above a restaurant overlooking the Mekong. ❶

**Souchittra Guesthouse** ⓣ031/212366. Across the street from *Saythong* with basic rooms in the old house with a clean, shared bath or self-contained bungalows on the lawn overlooking the Mekong serving tasty Lao dishes. ❷

**Vongpaseud** ☎031/920038. Owned by an extremely lively, jolly man, this place has a very fun vibe. There are simple ensuite rooms and a great restaurant on the river serving tasty Lao dishes. ❷

## Directory

**Bank** Lao Development Bank is just off the roundabout and does exchange, traveller's cheques and cash advances. Mon–Fri 8.30am–3.30pm.

**Internet** Internet Nam Ohy just beyond *Vongpaseud* Guesthouse has two computers and charges 300K/min.

**Post office** Just north of the roundabout (daily; 8.30am–3pm).

## Moving on

**By bus or sawngthaew** to: Pakxe (3 daily; 2hr; hail from main road); Si Phan Don, you'll have to cross the river to Ban Muang and wait for a bus heading south on Route 13.

**By boat** to: Pakxe (book at *Vongpaseud* for cheapest deal, around 50,000K each for 7–8 people; 1hr 30min); Ban Muang (15min; 5000K).

**Tuk-tuks** Can be hired for the 8km journey to Wat Phou. The drivers charge $6 for up to six passengers, and wait for you while you visit the ruins.

# WAT PHOU

The most evocative Khmer ruin outside Cambodian borders, the World Heritage site of **Wat Phou** (daily 8.30am–4.30pm; 5000K), 8km southwest of Champasak, should be at the top of your southern Laos must-see list. A romantic and rambling complex of pre-Angkorian temples dating from the sixth to the twelfth centuries, Wat Phou occupies a setting of unparalleled beauty in a lush river valley. Unlike ancient Khmer sites of equal size or importance found in neighbouring Thailand, Wat Phou has yet to be over-enthusiastically restored, so walking among the half-buried pieces of sculpted sandstone gives a good idea of what these sites once looked like.

Wat Phou, which in Lao means "Mountain Monastery", is actually a series of ruined temples and shrines at the foot of Lingaparvata Mountain. Although the site is now associated with Theravada Buddhism, sandstone reliefs indicate that the ruins were once a **Hindu place of worship**. When viewed from the Mekong, it's clear why the site was chosen. A phallic stone outcropping is easily seen among the range's line of forested peaks: this would have made the site especially auspicious to worshippers of Shiva, a Hindu god often symbolized by a phallus.

## What to see and do

Approaching from the east, a **stone causeway** – once lined with low stone pillars – leads up to the first set of ruins. On either side of the causeway there would have been reservoirs, which probably represented the oceans that surrounded the mythical Mount Meru, home of the gods of the Hindu pantheon. Just beyond the causeway, on either side of the path, stand two megalithic structures of sandstone and laterite, which may have served as segregated **palaces**, one for men and the other for women.

Continuing up the stairs, you come upon a ruined temple containing the finest examples of decorative **stone lintels** in Laos. Although much has been damaged or is missing, sketches done at the end of the nineteenth century show the temple to have changed little since then.

Up the hill behind the temple is a **shallow cave** with a constant drip of water that collects on its ceiling. This water is considered highly sacred, as it has trickled down from the peak of Lingaparvata. Foreign visitors should resist the temptation to wash with this water, which would be akin to having a bathe in the baptismal font.

If you follow the base of the cliff in a northerly direction, a bit of sleuthing will lead you to the enigmatic **crocodile**

## A SHORT HISTORY OF WAT PHOU

Archeologists tend to disagree on who the original founders of the site were and when it was first consecrated. The oldest parts of the ruins are thought to date back to the sixth century and were most likely built by the ancient Khmer. The site is highly sacred to the ethnic Lao and is the focus of an annual festival (Jan or Feb) that attracts thousands of pilgrims.

The **Khmer**, ancestors of modern-day Cambodians, were the founders of a highly sophisticated culture. From its capital, located at Angkor in Cambodia, a long line of kings reigned with absolute authority. With cultural trappings inherited from earlier Khmer kingdoms, which in turn had borrowed heavily from India, the Khmer rulers at Angkor venerated deities from the **Hindu** and **Buddhist** pantheons. Eventually, a new and uniquely Khmer cult was born, the devaraja or god-king, which propagated the belief that a Khmer king was actually an incarnation of a certain Hindu deity on earth.

In 1177, armies from the rival kingdom of **Champa**, taking advantage of a period of political instability, were able to sack Angkor, leaving the empire in disarray. Convinced that the old state religion had somehow failed to protect the kingdom from misfortune, the new Khmer leader Jayavarman VII embraced Mahayana Buddhism and went on to expand his empire to include much of present-day Thailand, Vietnam and Laos. But after his death, the empire began to decline and by 1432 was so weak that the **Siamese** also gave Angkor a thorough sacking. They pillaged the great stone temples of the Angkorian god-kings and force-marched members of the royal Khmer court, including classical dancers, musicians, artisans and astrologers, back to Ayutthaya, then the capital of Siam. To this day, much of what Thais perceive as Thai culture, from the sinuous moves of classical dancers to the flowery language of the royal Thai court, was actually acquired from the Khmer. Much of the Khmer culture absorbed by the Siamese was passed on to the Lao, including the gracefully curving lines of written Lao.

**stone**, which may have been used as an altar for pre-Angkor-period human sacrifices. A few metres away to the north is the **elephant stone**, a huge, moss-covered boulder carved with the face of an elephant, probably dating from the nineteenth century.

## SI PHAN DON

In Laos's deepest south, just above the border with Cambodia, the muddy stream of the Mekong is carved into a fourteen-kilometre-wide web of rivulets, creating a landlocked archipelago. Known as **Si Phan Don**, or "Four Thousand Islands", this labyrinth of islets, rocks and sandbars has acted as a kind of bell jar, preserving traditional southern lowland Lao culture from outside influences. Local life unravels slowly and peacefully: fishermen head out at sunset silhouetted against the sky's colourful backdrop and cast their nets out across the water, while children play and run about the village, overlooked by their parents and grandparents who sit and watch the world go by. The archipelago is home to rare flora and fauna, including a species of **freshwater dolphin**. Southeast Asia's largest **waterfalls** are also located here.

### Don Khong

The largest of the Four Thousand Islands group, **Don Khong** draws a steady stream of visitors. It boasts a venerable collection of Buddhist temples, good-value accommodation and interesting fresh-fish cuisine.

Don Khong has only two settlements of any size, the port town of **Muang Sen** on the island's west coast, and the east-coast

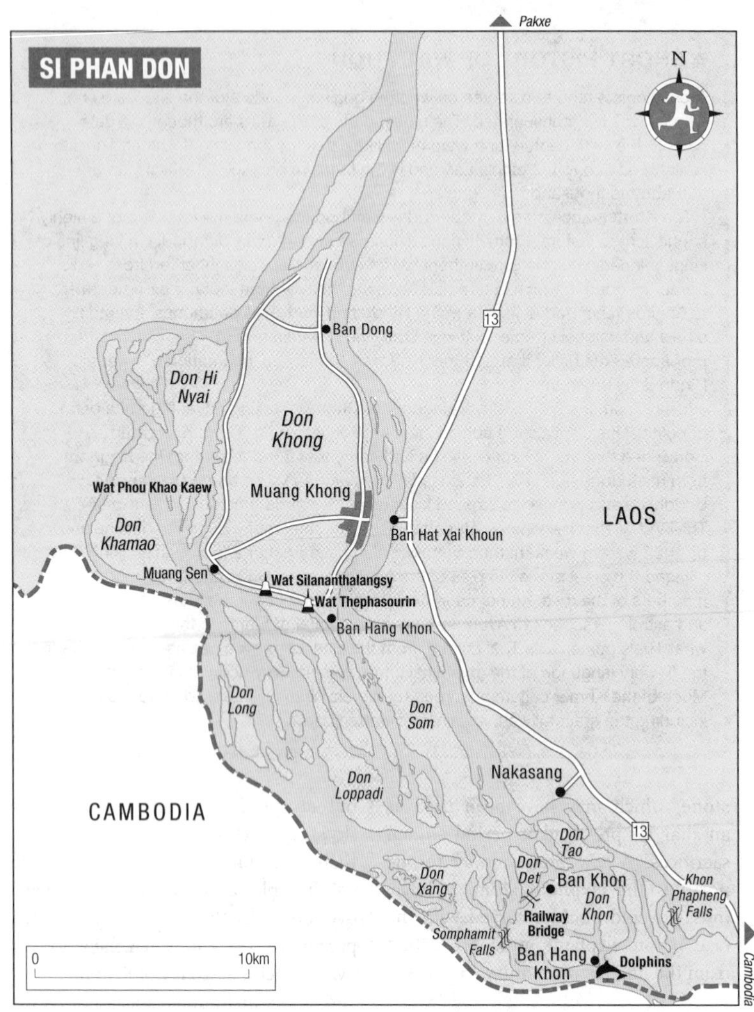


town of **Muang Khong**, where most of the accommodation and cafés are. Like all Si Phan Don settlements, both Muang Sen's and Muang Khong's homes and shops cling to the bank of the Mekong for kilometres, but barely penetrate the interior, which is reserved for rice fields.

## What to see and do

The best way to explore the island is to rent a bicycle – the flat terrain and almost complete absence of motor vehicles make for ideal cycling conditions.

### Excursion 1

Follow the river road south from Muang Khong, and cross the wooden bridge: stick to the narrow path along the river, not the road that parallels it slightly inland. A couple of kilometres south of Muang Khong lies the village of **BAN NA**, where the real scenery begins. The trail snakes between thickets of bamboo, past traditional southern Lao wooden houses. Near the tail of the island the path forks: a veer to the left will lead you to the tiny village of **BAN HANG KHONG** and a dead end. Keeping to the right will put you at the gates of Wat Thephasourin, parts of which were constructed in 1883. From here the path soon skirts the edge of a high riverbank, at intervals opening up views of the muddy Mekong. The dense canopy of foliage overhead provides welcome shade as you pass through **BAN SIW**, with quaint little houses, decorated with wood filigree, and inviting bamboo-and-thatch drink shops lining the path. The village monastery, Wat Silananthalangsy, is also worth a look. The path widens at the approach to Muang Sen, Don Khong's sleepy port, which makes a welcome stop for rest and refreshment before heading east via the unshaded eight-kilometre stretch of road that leads back to Muang Khong.

### Excursion 2

For another interesting trip, head due west from Muang Khong, on the road that bisects the island. Just before reaching the town of **MUANG SEN** on the western side of the island, turn right at the crossroads and head north. Follow this road up and over a low grade and after about 4km you'll cross a bridge. Keep going another 1.5km and you'll notice large black boulders beginning to appear off to the left. Keeping your eyes left, you'll see a narrow trail leading up to a ridge of the same black stone. Park your bike at the foot of the ridge, and, following the trail up another 200m to the right, you'll spot the teak buildings of **Wat Phou Khao Kaew**, an evocative little forest monastery situated atop a stone bluff overlooking the Mekong. A fractured pre-Angkorian stone lintel lies at the base of its central stupa, which possibly dates the whole structure to the middle of the seventh century. Nearby sits a charming miniature *sim*, flanked by plumeria trees. A curious collection of carved wooden deities that somehow found their way downriver from Burma decorate the ledges.

## Arrival

**By bus** Seven buses from Pakxe stop at Ban Hat Xai Khoun, from where you can catch the ferry across to Don Khong. The other five pass through Ban Hat Xai Khoun on their way to Nakasang.
**By boat** The boats will leave you off at the main boat landing at Muang Khong near all the guesthouses.
Don Khong has 24-hour electricity.

## Accommodation

Most of the accommodation is concentrated in Muang Khong, which is on the quieter side of the island and provides a good launching point for excursions around the Si Phan Don area.

### Muang Khong

**Auberge Sala Done Khong** ⓣ031/212077. Smart option, south of the ferry landing. This nicely restored French-era villa has a/c and hot water, catering largely to a package-tour clientele. ❻
**Done Khong Guest House** ⓣ031/214010. Adjacent to the ferry landing. Basic rooms with shared facilities, and a popular restaurant. ❷
**Done Khong II** 300m from the ferry landing on the road to Muang Sen. Set in an airy teak house with verandas offering commanding views of the countryside, its accommodation ranges from dorm beds to comfortable en-suite doubles. ❶–❷
**Mr Pon's Guesthouse** ⓣ031/214037. Located along the waterfront, and has a popular restaurant. Mr Pon himself speaks very good English and is a wealth of information about tours and the island. ❸
**Phoukhong Guesthouse** ⓣ031/213673. A small and friendly guesthouse next door to *Mr Pon's* with a restaurant on the riverfront. They also have internet connection. ❶
**Villa Kang Khong** ⓣ031/213539. 100m west of the Muang Khong ferry landing. Offers great service at bargain prices in a colonial-era teak house. ❷

### Muang Sen

**Say Khong** Directly above the boat dock. Spacious fan doubles and triples, and a balcony, excellent for viewing Mekong sunsets. ❶

## Eating and drinking

**Done Khong Guesthouse** This restaurant probably serves the tastiest Lao dishes on the island. Don't forget to try out the fish.

**The Mekong Restaurant** This place claims to do a traditional Canadian breakfast which basically means coffee and an average pancake. Some of their other dishes are worth a meal here though.

**Mr Pon's** Attached to the guest house of the same name. Ideally situated with a river view and popular with travellers.

**Phoukhong Guesthouse** The friendly neighbour of *Mr Pon's* with a similar menu and view.

**Souksan Restaurant** Serves Chinese food and has a fantastic river view. The restaurant stands on stilts above the river.

## Directory

**Bank** The Agricultural Promotion Bank at the south end of town just past the big Buddha exchanges dollars, baht and traveller's cheques (9.30am–4pm).

**Bicycles** Several of the guesthouses and shops facing the Mekong offer bicycles (10,000K per day) for rent. Motorbikes are available at Villa Kang Khong for $10.

**Internet** Alpha Internet (8am–9pm; 1000K/min). *Phoukong Guesthouse* (1000K/min).

**Post office** just south of the bridge Telecom, about 200m west of the ferry landing. International calls are available. Mon–Fri 8am–noon & 1–4pm, Sat 8am–noon.

## Moving on

**By bus** Buses for Pakxe and Champasak depart from in front of the Big Buddha in Muang Khong (3 in the early morning starting in Muang Sen; 2–3hr). An a/c minibus leaves around 11am and is booked through guesthouses. For Voen Kham on the Cambodian border take the car ferry back to Route 13 and catch the bus coming from Pakxe, which usually passes through at about 8.30am. Alternatively arrange a minibus through to Stung Treng in Cambodia (see p.133).

**By boat** Boats to Don Khon, Don Det and Nakasang should cost $4 and can be arranged through the guesthouses.

## Don Khon and Don Det

The tropical islands of **Don Khon** and **Don Det**, 15km downstream from Don Khong, are fringed with swaying coconut palms and planted with jade- and emerald-coloured rice paddies. Besides being a picturesque little haven, they also offer some leisurely trekking.

The more popular island for backpackers to stay on is Don Det, Don Khon catering for more mid-range budgetters. Despite plans to construct yet more travellers' cafes, introduce 24hr electricity and internet services, Don Det maintains its rustic charm. Simple wooden bungalows with hammocks out the front line each side of the island, coaxing people into staying here for days. It certainly is hard to leave.

It's possible to do Don Khon–Don Det–Khon Phapheng, Southeast Asia's largest **waterfall** situated to the east of Don Khon, as a day-trip from Don Khong, although ideally they are both worth a few days' visit. The boat for the day-trip costs 10,000K per person, and you can see both waterfalls and the defunct railway in one day. The boat can't go directly to Khon Phapheng Falls, so the boatman will take you to the right bank, where a tuk-tuk (another 10,000K

### FISH AND WHISKY

Fish is a staple in Si Phan Don. Recipes range from the traditional **làp pa** (a Lao-style salad of minced fish mixed with garlic, chillies, shallots and fish sauce) to tropical fish steamed in coconut milk. Be sure to try the island speciality **mók pa**, fish steamed in banana leaves, which has the consistency of custard and takes an hour to prepare.

The local **lào-láo** has gained a reputation as one of the best **rice whiskies** in Laos. For those who haven't taken a shine to Lao white lightning, Muang Khong has devised a gentler blend known as the "Lao cocktail", a mix of wild honey and *lào-láo* served over ice.

per person) will be waiting to take the passengers on the thirty-kilometre round-trip to the falls (10,000K admission). Afterwards, your boatman will take you back to Don Khong.

## What to see and do

A delightfully sleepy place with a timeless feel about it, **BAN KHON**, located on Don Khon east of the bridge, is the islands' largest settlement. To explore the remnants of Laos's old French railway, head to the southern side of the foot of the bridge back behind some houses, where you'll find the rusty remains of the locomotive that once hauled French goods and passengers between piers on Don Khon and Don Det, bypassing the rapids that block this stretch of the river.

### Walking

Linked by a bridge and traversed by a trail, Don Khon and Don Det can be easily explored on foot. The fee is 9000K for a day or a ten-day pass; there's a ticket booth at the southern end of the railway bridge near the trail-heads for the falls and dolphin pools. A short walk west of the bridge stands the village monastery, Wat Khon Tai. Taking the southerly path behind the wat for 1.5km, you'll come to a low cliff overlooking **Somphamit Falls**, a series of high rapids that crashes through a jagged gorge.

Another good walk is from Don Khon to Don Det across the bridge and along the three-kilometre elevated trail to the small village at the northern end of the island. A Stonehenge-like structure that was used for hoisting cargo from the train onto awaiting boats is all that remains of the railway's northern terminus.

### Dolphin spotting from Ban Hang Khon

From Ban Khon, follow the easterly former railway trail adjacent to the high school through rice paddies and thick forest and eventually, after 4km, you'll reach the village of **BAN HANG KHON**, the jumping-off point for **dolphin-spotting** excursions. The April–May dry season, when the Mekong is at its lowest, is the optimum time of year to catch a glimpse of this highly endangered species (early mornings and late afternoons are best), and boats can be hired out from the village to see them. Visitors should bear in mind that the security situation on the Cambodian side of the river is variable. If boatmen refuse to shuttle you out to see the dolphins, don't insist: they will know what the current situation is. Boats cost $5 and you're obliged to pay for the boat regardless of whether you see any dolphins.

The bluish-grey freshwater **Irrawaddy dolphin** (*Orcaella brevirostris*) known as *pa kha*, are rare in Lao waters, as most are unable to swim beyond the Khon Phapheng Falls near the Lao–Cambodian border. Over the past century their numbers in the Mekong have dwindled dramatically, from thousands to little more than one hundred today. Gill-net fishing and, across the border, the use of poison, electricity and explosives are to blame. In the past, fishermen were reluctant to cut costly nets to free entangled dolphins, but Lao villagers are now compensated for their nets – part of an initiative begun by the Lao Community Fisheries and Dolphin Protection Project.

### Khon Phapheng Falls

Despite technically being the largest waterfall in Southeast Asia, **Khon Phapheng**, to the east of Don Khon, is not all that spectacular. Indeed, it's best described as a low but wide cliff that just happens to have a huge volume of water running over it. The vertical drop is highest during the March–May dry season. A tourist pavilion above the falls provides an ideal place to sit and enjoy the view. Most tourists do the falls as a package from Don Khon but it is also possible to get there by sawngthaew from Ban Hat Xai Khoun (opposite Muang Khong) or Nakasang (4000K). An admission charge of 10,000K is made for foreigners.

## Arrival

**By boat** To get to Don Khon or Don Det, the cheapest option from Muang Khong is to take the ferry (5000K) across the river to Ban Hat Xai Khoun and then get a bus to Nakasang, where you can get a boat to Don Khon or Don Det ($1–2). The boats depart from the landing a short walk from the market. Alternatively, you can join a Don Khon day-trip and negotiate a one-way, discounted price for the boat trip to Don Khon. The asking price is $4 for up to three passengers.

## Accommodation

Head for the budget accommodation on Don Det, and then work out whether you prefer a sunrise or sunset-located lodging. Typically, you can expect a bamboo and wood hut with a small veranda and hammock overlooking the river. Bathing facilities are usually shared. Candles are used for lighting at places without generators.

### Don Det (sunset side)

All the bungalows below are dotted along a stretch at the north end of the island near the restaurants and bars. Follow the signed path that cuts down the water's edge from the main road and take your pick.

**Mr B's Sunset Bungalows** ⓣ030/5345109. A popular choice with efficient service and a good restaurant. It may be a little too orderly for some, who might prefer the rustic charm of the island's other guesthouses. ❶

**Sunset Guesthouse** ⓣ020/5730137. With only 4 bungalows, this place gets full quickly and attracts sunset seekers who want to chill out in the afternoon and into the evening. A fun, social spot. ❶

**Tena Guesthouse** ⓣ020/2700115. Several bungalows with balconies overlooking the stunning view. In a quiet and peaceful spot. ❶

**Thon Don Family Guesthouse** This place has a lovely family feel to it. All the communication is done via charades as "mama" speaks no English .❶

### Don Det (sunrise side)

The sunrise bungalows are dotted along the east side of the island, the majority being at the north end where all the restaurants and bars are.

**King Kong's** Further south down the island. More removed from the long line of guesthouses and therefore quieter. ❶

**Mama Thanon Guesthouse** This guesthouse is run by charismatic "mama" who is worth the stay in itself. Some of her rooms have electricity and private bathrooms. ❶

**Mr Tho's Bungalows** ⓣ030/5345865. This place is at the quieter end of the island and has a good book exchange service for those who are ploughing through their reading material. ❶

**Nouphit Guesthouse** ⓣ020/5494928. This place is a pleasing set up with well-made, restful bungalows, an English-speaking owner and a great restaurant attached to it. ❶

### Don Khon

**Bounphan Riverside Guesthouse** ⓣ020/656 5298. This guesthouse is good value and has a choice of a shared or private bathroom. ❶

**Pan's Guesthouse** ⓣ030/346939. Although friendly, Pan's Is little over-priced considering it's not on the waterfront. Internet here for 1000K/min. ❷

**Somphamit** Riverside bamboo bungalows, some more comfortable than others. ❶

**Souksanh** This is a good budget option with simple, cheap rooms. ❶

## Eating and drinking

An increasing number of Western-style restaurants are popping up on the islands, serving pizza and sandwiches. To avoid this, most bungalow places on the islands have a restaurant serving Lao food and the usual travellers' fare. Remember that food, not accommodation, is the real money-earner here, so do take at least some meals at the bungalow you stay at.

### Don Det

**Jasmin Indian and Malay Restaurant** This Indian restaurant chain has made it onto the island and is a popular meeting point for dinner in the evening. Due to the large intake of customers, the service is quite slow.

**Jone Nee Guesthouse** Serves up a good green curry but given its exposed location on the northern tip of the island, meal times can be a pretty windy affair.

**The Pool Room** Not particulary original but is good if you need a pizza or pasta fix. Unsuprisingly, it also has a pool table.

**The Reggae Bar** Using a small, frail monkey as a way of luring in customers seems to work in this reggae-themed restaurant but only because people feel sorry for it as. If you can bear the monkey's whimpering then this is a good place for dinner or a beer, and maybe a competitive game of chess with the owner.

**The Sunset Bar** Attached to the *Sunset Guesthouse*. Not so good for dinner as the service is a little slow, but this is the place to be for an evening drink and chilled out music. Try the *lào-láo* mojito.

### Don Khon

**Chanthounma's Restaurant** Along the water's edge near the bridge. This pleasant restaurant run by a charming couple is a great spot for lunch, serving cheap rice and noodle dishes and fresh spring rolls.

**Seng Ahloune Restaurant** As long as you avoid this place when the tour groups decend for lunch, this restaurant at the foot of the bridge serves up tasty and filling dishes of both Lao and Western variety.

## Directory

**Banks and exchange** There are no banks on either island but traveller's cheques, dollars and baht are exchangable at some guesthouses and tour agencies. The nearest Lao Development Bank is at Ban Khinak back on Route 13.

**Bike Rental** Bicylces are for rent at many guesthouses on each island for 10,000K per day.

**Electricity** There is only electricity from 6pm till 11pm on the islands.

**Internet** On Don Det there are two internet oulets opposite the turning for the sunset side that charge 800–1000K/min. On Don Khon head for *Pan's Restaurant* and *Auberge Sala Done Kong*, 1000K/min.

**Telephone** International calls can be made from Natural Travel on Don Det for 6000K/min.

**Tours** Lane Xang Travel (Ⓦwww.xplore-asia.com) attached to *The Pool Bar* on Don Det can arrange boating, rafting, kayaking and trekking tours. Other tour agents that organize transport to Thailand, Cambodia and Vietnam are signposted around the islands.

## Moving on

**By boat and bus** Take a boat from the islands to the nearby village of Nakasang (15min; 15,000K) from where buses leave between 8–10am; most journeys heading north will go via Pakse. Minibuses are available to Stung Treng, Cambodia.

**Destinations:** Pakxe (2hr); Champasak (3hr) Savannakhet (8hr); Thakhek (12hr); Vientiane (17hr).

**Sawgthaews** To Pakxe (hourly between 6–10am, 2–3hr).

## THE BOLAVEN PLATEAU AND TAD LO FALLS

High above the hot Mekong River Valley stands the natural citadel of the **Bolaven Plateau** – hilly, roughly circular in shape, and with an average altitude of 600m – dominating eastern Champasak province and overlooking the provinces of Salavan, Xekong and Attapu to the east. Rivers flow off the high plateau in all directions and then plunge out of lush forests along the Bolaven's edges in a series of spectacular waterfalls, some more than 100m high. The provincial capitals of Pakxe, Salavan, Xekong and Attapu surround the Bolaven, but the main settlement on the plateau itself is the town of **Pakxong**. South of Route 23 between Pakxe and Pakxong is the Dong Hua Sao NBCA.

### Tad Lo Falls

The ten-metre-high **Tad Lo Falls**, on the banks of the Xe Set River, draw a steady stream of visitors, providing the perfect setting for a few days' relaxation and the opportunity to ride an elephant along the breezy western flank

### INTO CAMBODIA: VOEN KHAM

The easiest way to get into Cambodia via the Voen Kham crossing is to take a direct bus that leaves either from the islands or from Pakxe. Most people arrange a minibus to Stung Treng (see p.133). However, to do it alone you need to hire a boat at the southern end of Don Khon that takes you down the Mekong. Cambodian **visas** are available on arrival. Immigration officials on both sides ask for a $2–3 fee to stamp your passport, just one of many scams that operate at all land borders into Cambodia. If you ask for the official's name and demand a receipt, you may find they back down on this request.

of the fertile Bolaven Plateau. In the hot season, the pools surrounding Tad Hang, the lower falls, are a refreshing escape from the heat; be sure to clear the water before 8pm, however, when the floodgates of a dam upstream unleash a torrent of water without warning. Elephant treks ($5/2hr) through the forested hills around Tad Lo are easy to arrange through any of the guesthouses in Tad Hang.

## Arrival and information

**By bus** The Tad Lo Falls are two hours northeast of Pakxe by bus and about 30km southwest of Salavan; the road is mostly dirt but is flat and in good condition.

The turn-off for Tad Lo is 88km northeast of Pakxe, just beyond the village of Lao Ngam; buses will drop you at the turn-off, from where it's a 1.5km tuk-tuk ride (5000K per person) along a dirt road to Tad Hang.

**Information** Opposite *Tim's Guesthouse* is the Visitor Information Centre.

## Accommodation and eating

**Sailomyen Guesthouse** Cheap place to stay, set above the river on raised bungalows with hammocks on the balcony. The walls are rather thin but the setting and value is brilliant. ❶

**Samly Guesthouse** A modest guesthouse next door to the more popular *Tim's* (see below), which has all the basic needs with cheap wooden bungalows and friendly owners. ❶

**Sypaseuth Guesthouse** ☎034/211890. This place offers cheap rooms overlooking the river. The restaurant is a good place to have dinner with standard Lao dishes and several Western dishes for $1–3. ❶

**Tad Lo Resort** ☎031/212105 ext 3325. High on a hill overlooking Tad Hang perches *Tad Lo Resort*, the best accommodation in the area, with thirteen rooms in an assortment of bungalows. The restaurant attached serves well-cooked Lao, Thai and Western dishes for around $5. ❺–❻

**Tim's Guesthouse** This is the place where all the travellers come to relax in the evenings and listen to the owner's jazz selection. The rooms are nothing special: wooden bungalows with shared bathrooms but the restaurant serves good food, there is a book exchange and you can use the internet for 1000K a minute. You can also rent motorbikes for $8. If you want your laundry done though, go next door to *Samly* as *Tim's* is very expensive. ❶–❷

## Moving on

**By bus** Find a tuk-tuk driver to take you back to the highway (5000K), where you can pick up a bus to Salavan or Pakxe that leaves hourly between 7.30am–2pm. If heading to Xekong or Attapu get a ride from the highway to Ban Beng and from there get the bus onwards.

# THE XE KONG RIVER VALLEY

The **Xe Kong** is one of Laos's great rivers, starting high in the Annamite Mountains from the eastern flanks of 2500m-high Mount Atouat and flowing southwestward around the southern edge of the Bolaven Plateau and then across the plains of Cambodia to join the Mekong at Stung Treng. The main towns along the Xe Kong in Laos are **Xekong** and **Attapu**, which are linked by a paved road. Roads into the vast forest interior are still extremely poor but various tributaries link the Xe Kong to no less than four of Laos's most pristine NBCAs.

### Xekong

In 1984, a wide expanse of jungle was cleared of trees and flattened, heralding the birth of **XEKONG**. Founded partly because nearby Ban Phon was deemed no longer habitable after an unexploded ordnance (UXO), Xekong has something of a frontier feel about it, but it is the departure point for a very scenic journey downriver to Attapu. Three major branches of the Ho Chi Minh Trail snaked through the jungle surrounding Xekong, making this area one of the most heavily bombed in Laos, and an astonishing amount of UXO still blankets this province, so you mustn't go off exploring here. In addition, there is a disturbing beasty lurking in Xekong's waterways: the *pa pao* is a **blowfish** with a piranha-like appetite and, according to locals, a particular fondness for lopping off the tip of the male member.

### Arrival

**By bus** Buses to and from Pakxe operate from the dirt lot outside the Morning Market, about 1km from the main market (2000K by tuk-tuk). Heading into town, you'll pass a branch of the Lao Development Bank, where you can exchange cash and traveller's cheques, and the post office and the Telecom building, where international calls can be made.

### Accommodation and eating

**Pa Thip Restaurant** Opposite Sekong *Souksamlane*. This place serves decent food for up to $3. They also offer basic rooms for $3. Motorbikes are available for $10 and bicylces for $5.

**Sekong Souksamlane** ⓣ031/212022. Located 500m downriver from the market and has decent, if somewhat over-priced rooms. Cheap restaurants surround the hotel, but the hotel restaurant cooks up rather good Thai food too. ❶–❷

**Woman Fever Kosmet Centre Guesthouse** ⓣ020563 8286. Near the *Sekong Souksamlane* on the river road. Not the best name for a guesthouse but a good budget option nonetheless. ❶

**Vangxang Savanh Sekong Hotel** ⓣ038211797. Large complex that feels rather uninhabited. This is where you catch the boat to Attapu. It's situated on the river and has a reasonably good restaurant attached to it.

### Moving on

**By bus** Attapu (every 2hr from 8am–4pm, 2hr); Pakse (2 daily; 3–4hr, then sawngthaews/buses come from Attapu up until 1pm; Salavan (4 daily, 3–4hr);

**By boat** to Attapu, see below for details.

## Down the Xe Kong River

The scenic **Xe Kong River**, which meanders through little-visited countryside, provides a strong incentive to hire a boat for the journey south to Attapu. Emerging from high in the Annamite Mountains, the Xe Kong meanders south by southwest until it eventually joins the Mekong River north of Stung Treng in Cambodia. Motorized pirogues make the four-hour journey through gentle rapids and past lushly forested riverbanks. At around $60 per boat, it's expensive, but well worth it. Late in the dry season, the trip can take seven hours, and the shallow waters require passengers to walk some short stretches – at this time of year, captains will only take two passengers, thereby increasing the price per person. To find a captain, ask at the *Pa Thip Restaurant* the night before or walk down to the Vangxang Savanh Sekong Hotel in the early morning to organize a trip.

## Attapu

Despite its name literally translating as "buffalo shit", Attapu is a cosy settlement of almost twenty thousand people, most of whom are Vietnamese, Chinese or Lao. Occuping a bend in the Xe Kong River, with coconut palms and banana trees shading spacious wooden houses with generous balconies, high on stilts, the town is known throughout southern Laos as the "garden city". Although it was near this distant outpost that the Ho Chi Minh Trail diverged, with one artery running south towards Cambodia and the other into South Vietnam, Attapu somehow eluded the grave effects of war and remains an easygoing place that's ideal for leisurely wandering. This region of Laos has the country's highest rate of malaria, so heed the advice on p.42.

### Arrival

**By bus** You will be deposited in a dirt field on the southwestern outskirts of the city, a two-kilometre walk or tuk-tuk ride from the centre (10,000K). If you're on the express bus from Pakxe, don't automatically get off here, as the bus may continue into town.

**By boat** On arrival, walk up the ramp and follow the road into town to the Lao Development Bank, which is a good point of orientation.

### Accommodation

**Aloonsotsai** ⓣ036/211250. Clean, good value rooms. The friendly staff speak no English. ❷

**Attapeu Palace** ⓣ036/211204,
Looking slightly out of place in this remote town, this large hotel has spacious rooms, some with TVs and fridges. It also has internet for 1000K/min. The restaurant, however is pretty poor. ❷–❸

**Phoutthavong Guesthouse** ⓣ020/9818440. Close to the town, sitting one block back from the Sekong River. Tidy rooms with a/c and hot water. ❷

**Souksomphone** ⓣ036/211046. A modern building opposite the bank, with seven clean, spacious rooms although slightly unenthusiastic staff. ❶

## Eating

Attapu does not boast a flourishing culinary scene but it does have one or two restaurants worth a try. The market is also a good place to buy a few Laotian particulars.

**Ban Laek Tee Neung** ⓣ020/5913580. This is the best place to eat in Attapu – just off the street with the post office and *Attapu Palace*. It has an appetizing Korean-style barbecue serving good *laap* and noodle dishes.

**Thi Thi Vietnamese Restaurant** ⓣ020/211303. As the name suggests, this restaurant serves a good variety of Vietnameses dishes between $1–3.

## Directory

**Bank** Lao Development Bank, exchanges baht and dollars and traveller's cheques (Mon–Fri 8.30am–3.30pm).

### INTO VIETNAM: BO Y

The newest and least trodden crossing into Vietnam is down route 18B through the Attapu province. There are three weekly buses to Kon Tum, Vietnam, leaving from Attapu. You'll need to arrange a Vietnamese visa in advance. Whether you can get Lao visas on arrival is still unclear, so if you are taking this route it's wise to get one in advance.

**Bike rental** *Attapu Palace* and *Aloonsotsai* hotels rent motorbikes for $10 per day and bicycles for $5.

**Internet** *Attapu Palace* 1000K/min.

**Market** Near the bridge, best in the morning.

**Post office** Opposite *Attapu Palace*. Also has Western Union (Mon–Fri 8–11.30am).

## Moving on

**By bus** All buses from Attapu leave from the bus station in the dirt field.

**Destinations:** Pak Song (4 daily, 4–5hr); Pakxe (4 daily; 5–6hr); Savannakhet (1 daily, at 6am, 9–10 hr); Xekong (4 daily, 2–3hr); Kontum, Vietnam (3 weekly; 12hr).

**By boat** Up the Xe Kong River to Xekong ($40); can be arranged through the *Souksomphone*.

# Malaysia

## HIGHLIGHTS

**PULAU PERHENTIAN:** palm-fringed white sand, crystal clear waters – an earthly paradise

**PULAU PANGKOR:** a tiny, laid-back island bursting with rural charm

**TAMAN NEGARA:** trek through this breathtaking rainforest, the oldest in the world

**CAMERON HIGHLANDS:** gloriously cool emerald green tea plantations and rolling fields

**MELAKA:** explore this beautiful, culturally rich city

**MOUNT KINABALU:** with a summit like a pyramid of black glass, the dawn trek up is a must

**GUNUNG MULU:** the world's largest system of limestone caves

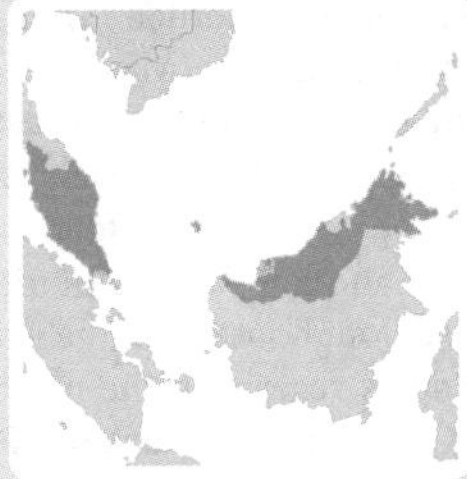

## ROUGH COSTS

**DAILY BUDGET** Basic US$15 / Occasional treat US$25

**DRINK** Beer US$2.50 (from US$0.50 on tax-free Langkawi to US$3.50 in stricter Muslim areas)

**FOOD** *Mee Goreng* (noodles) US$1

**HOSTEL/BUDGET HOTEL** US$2.50–5

**TRAVEL** Bus: Kuala Lumpur–Melaka (144km) US$3; Ferry: Kuala Kedah–Pulau Langkawi (51km) US$7; Train: Kota Bharu–Jerantut (131km) US$7.

## FACT FILE

**POPULATION** 24.8 million

**AREA** 328,600 sq km

**LANGUAGE** Bahasa Malay (also English, Tamil, Hokkien, Cantonese, Mandarin)

**RELIGIONS** Islam, Hinduism and Chinese religions

**CURRENCY** Malaysian Ringgit (RM)

**CAPITAL** Kuala Lumpur

**INTERNATIONAL PHONE CODE** +60

**TIME ZONE** GMT+8hr

# Introduction

**Malaysia may not be as obvious a hotspot on the classic backpacker's route as, say, Thailand, but it is just as full of charm and beauty. Its rich cultural heritage is apparent both in its traditional village areas and in its commitment to religious plurality. The dominant cultural force is undoubtedly Islam, but the country's diverse population of indigenous Malays, Chinese and Indians has spawned a fabulous juxtaposition of mosques, temples and churches, a panoply of festivals and a wonderful mixture of cuisines. The Malays insist that their food combines the best flavours and dishes of the surrounding countries – and after a few meals from a sizzling street stall, you're likely to agree. Malaysia also boasts beautiful beaches, the world's oldest tropical rainforest and some breathtakingly lush tea plantations.**

First impressions of Malaysia's hi-tech, fast-growing capital, **Kuala Lumpur (KL)**, are likely to be of a vibrant and colourful, if crowded, place. Less than three hours' journey south lies the birthplace of Malay civilization, **Melaka**. Further up the coast is the first British settlement, the island of **Penang**, and its fascinating capital, Georgetown, full of undiscovered corners. For a taste of Old England and walks through emerald-green scenery, head for the hill stations of the **Cameron Highlands**.

North of Penang, the premier tourist destination is **Pulau Langkawi**, a popular, palm-fringed, duty-free island. Routes down the Peninsula's east coast are laid-back, with stops at sleepy mainland villages, such as **Cherating**, and the truly stunning islands of Pulau Perhentian and Pulau Tioman. The state capitals of **Kota Bharu**, in the northeast, and **Kuala Terengganu**, further south, are great stops for soaking up Malay culture, while the unsullied tropical rainforests of **Taman Negara National Park** offer innumerable trails, animal hides, a high canopy walkway and rushing waterfalls.

Across the sea, East Malaysia comprises the Bornean states of **Sarawak** and **Sabah**. For most travellers, their first taste of Sarawak is Kuching, the old colonial capital, and then the Iban longhouses of the Batang Ai and Batang Lupar river systems, or the Bidayuh communities closer to the Kalimantan border. The best time to visit is in late May to early June when the Iban and the Bidayuh celebrate their harvest festivals with ribald parties. Sibu, much further to the north, is another starting point for visits to Iban longhouses and the idyllic Pelagus Rapids region. In the north of the state, **Gunung Mulu National Park** is the principal destination, its extraordinary razor-sharp limestone needles providing demanding climbing.

The main reason for a trip to Sabah is to conquer the 4101-metre granite peak of **Mount Kinabalu**, though the lively modern capital **Kota Kinabalu** and its offshore islands have their moments, too. Sabah also has wonderful wildlife, including turtles, orang-utans, proboscis monkeys and hornbills, while oceanic **Pulau Sipadan** has a host of sharks, fish and turtles, as well as one of the world's top coral-reef dives.

> **WHEN TO VISIT**
>
> **Temperatures** in Malaysia constantly hover around 30°C (22°C in highland areas), and humidity is high all year round. The monsoon season brings heavy and prolonged downpours to the east coast of Peninsular Malaysia, the northeastern part of Sabah and the western end of Sarawak from November to February; boats to most of the islands do not run during the height of the monsoon. The Peninsula's west coast experiences fewer major thunderstorms during the months of April and May. The ideal time to visit depends on what you're looking for – for tropical heat and a buzzing atmosphere, May to September is the time to go. For those prepared to risk a few showers for fewer crowds, the months bordering the monsoon, March–April and October–November, are good options.

## CHRONOLOGY

**200 AD onwards** Indian traders arrive in the region, bringing Hindu and Buddhist practices.
**Seventh–thirteenth centuries** The Buddhist Srivijaya empire is predominant. Based in Sumatra it stretches across into modern-day Malaysia.
**c.1390** Sumatran prince Paramesvara flees to Singapore, then on to Melaka, where he founds the Melaka Sultanate.
**Fifteenth century** Well-placed, and with a deep harbour, Melaka flourishes as a trading centre. Islam is adopted as the dominant religion, and over the next century the Melaka Sultanate expands along the west coast of the Peninsula and to Singapore and most of east-coast Sumatra.
**1511** The Portuguese take Melaka and Sultan Mahmud Shah flees. They retain it for 130 years.
**1526** The Portuguese raze the Sultan's new court of Johor on Pulau Bentam. Johor's court moves frequently during a century of assaults by Portugal and Aceh.
**1641** The Dutch East India Company take Melaka. The Johor court aligns itself with them, and are the predominant Malay kingdom for the next century.
**Sixteenth–nineteenth centuries** As trade with China grows, many Chinese merchants come to Melaka, and marry Malay women, creating the unique Baba-Nyonya culture.
**1786** The British establish a trading fort at Penang (Georgetown).
**1819** Sir Stamford Raffles establishes a British trading station in Singapore, which weakens both Melaka and Penang, forcing the Dutch to relinquish the former to the British, and leaving the latter to decline.
**1824** The British and Dutch agree to split the territories between them, giving the Dutch Indonesia, and making the British the only Western power in the Peninsula.
**1826** The British unify Melaka, Penang and Singapore into one administration, the Straits Settlements, with Singapore replacing Penang as its capital in 1832.
**1839** British explorer James Brooke arrives in Kuching, helps the Sultan of Brunei suppress a rebellion, and demands to be given Sarawak in return.
**1874** By this time there are large Chinese communities in many towns. Struggles between Chinese clan groups are rife, and Malay factions frequently become involved, causing a string of civil wars. The British intervene after they sign the Pangkor Treaty with the Perak Malay chief, Rajah Abdullah, formalizing British intervention in the political affairs of the Malay people.
**1880s** The name British Malaya comes into use. The Malay sultans' powers are gradually eroded, while the introduction of rubber estates makes British Malaya one of the most productive colonies in the world.
**1888** Sarawak, Sabah and Brunei are made British protectorates.
**1896** The Peninsula states under British control are given the title the Federated Malay States, with Kuala Lumpur the regional capital.
**1909–19** British control in the Peninsula expands to the northern Malay states of Kedah and Perlis in 1909; Johor (1914) and Terengganu – previously under Thai control – in 1919.
**1930s** As Chinese immigration increases, so do Chinese-Malay tensions. The Malayan Communist Party is founded in 1930, with significant support in the Chinese community, and demands an end to British rule and the perceived privileges of the Malays. The Singapore Malay Union is formed in response, which advocates a Malay supremacist line.
**1942–45** Japanese occupation. Up to fifty thousand people – mainly Chinese – are killed in the two weeks following the British surrender of Singapore. Chinese activists in the MCP organize much of the resistance.

**1946** The British introduce the Malayan Union, which gives Chinese and Indian inhabitants equal rights to Malays. In response Malayan nationalists form the United Malays National Organization (UMNO), arguing that Malays should retain special privileges.
**1948** The Federation of Malaya replaces the Malay Union. It re-establishes the power of the Malay sultans, and Chinese and Indians only qualify as citizens if they have lived there for fifteen years and speak Malay or English. Sarawak and North Borneo are made British Crown Colonies.
**1948–60** Known as "The Emergency", in reality civil war between the Chinese, identified with the MCP under its leader, Chin Peng, and the Malays. The violence peaks in 1950–51.
**1955** UMNO's leader, Tunku Abdul Rahman, wins the first federal elections by co-operating with moderate Chinese and Indian parties and campaigning for *merdeka* (freedom) – an independent Malaya.
**August 31, 1957** Britain grants independence to Malaya, and Rahman becomes the first prime minister. Under the new constitution nine Malay sultans alternate as king. The UMNO remains the most influential party.
**September 1963** North Borneo (renamed Sabah), Sarawak and Singapore join Malaya to form the Federation of Malaysia. Brunei refuses to join.
**August 1965** Following tensions between the Malay-dominated UMNO Alliance Party in KL and Lee Kuan Yew in Singapore, Singapore leaves the Federation.
**1969** When the UMNO Alliance loses parliamentary elections, Malays in major cities react angrily and rioting breaks out. Hundreds of people, mostly Chinese, are killed. Rahman keeps the country under a state of emergency for nearly two years,
**1970** Rahman resigns, handing over to Tun Abdul Razak, also from UMNO, who though less authoritarian, introduces a form of positive discrimination for ethnic Malays, known as *bumiputra*, which gives them favoured positions in business and professions.
**1981** New UMNO leader Dr Mahathir Mohammed becomes prime minister.
**1998** Dr Mahathir sacks his Deputy Prime Minister Anwar Ibrahim, who is then imprisoned on trumped-up charges of homosexual activity and corruption (he is released in 2004).
**2003** Mahathir hands over the premiership to Abdullah Badawi.
**March 2008** Badawi and the UNMO scrape to victory in elections with a tiny majority in parliament.

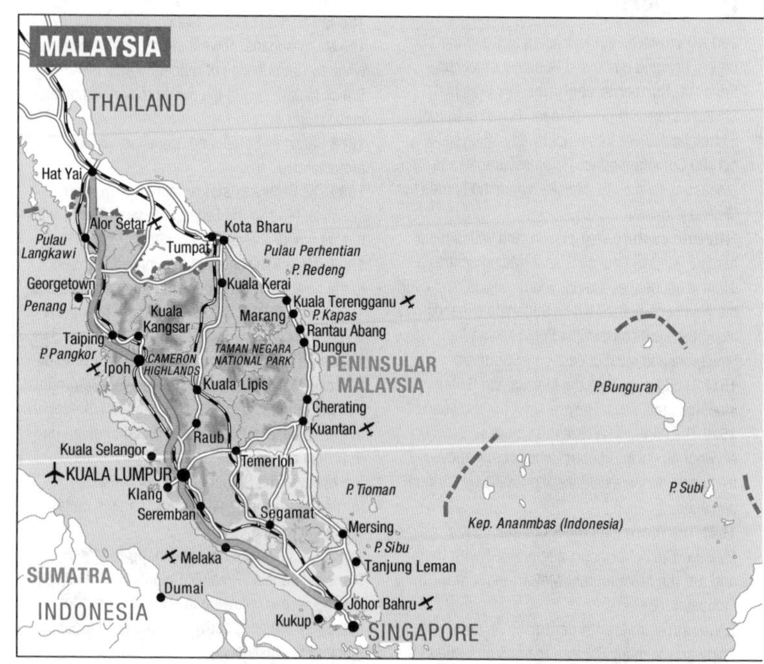

# Basics

## ARRIVAL

By far the most common airport to fly into is Kuala Lumpur International Airport (®www.klia.com.my), to which there are international flights from most countries. The new Low Cost Carrier Terminal is located close to KLIA, and Air Asia, Asia's premier low-cost airline, operates from here. Between them, these terminals handle almost all international flights. Penang also has an international airport, but in reality there are only a few flights from Australia and other parts of Asia that stop here – the overwhelming majority of flights land in Kuala Lumpur. From KL, onwards travel to any destination is hassle-free – Air Asia has recently been adding many new domestic routes, and prices are spectacularly low. As Malaysia is not too large and the bus and train routes are extremely efficient, even crossing the entire length of the Peninsula can be done overnight. For a list of the main airlines operating out of KL and their contact details, see p.504.

Malaysia has land borders with Thailand, Singapore, Brunei and Indonesian Kalimantan. There are regular boats from Bandar Seri Bagawan in Brunei to Lawas and Limbang in Sarawak and to Pulau Labuan in Sabah. Full details of routes are given in the accounts of relevant departure points.

### From Indonesia

A variety of ferries and speedboats depart from Indonesia to Malaysia: from Medan (see p.251), in north Sumatra, to Penang; from Dumai (see p.275), south of Medan, to Melaka; from Pulau Batam (see p.277), in the Riau archipelago, to Johor Bahru; and from Tanjung Balai

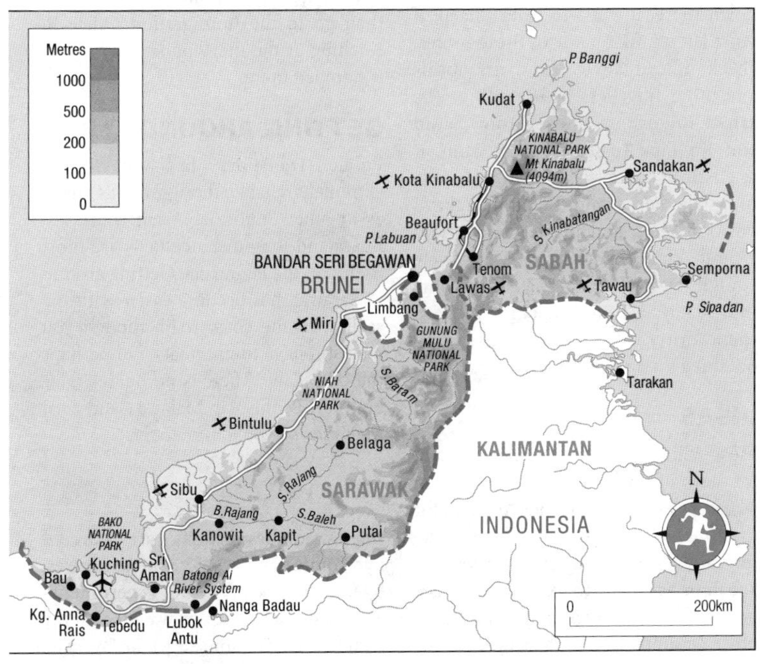

in Sumatra, to Port Klang; and from Tarakan (see p.381) in northeastern Kalimantan to Tawau in Sabah.

There is a land border at Entikong, 100km south of Kuching in Sarawak; buses run from Pontianak in southern Kalimantan through here to Kuching (see p.370).

### From Thailand

Travelling from Thailand to Malaysia used to be fairly straightforward; currently, however, political unrest has made it more dangerous and some routes are strongly advised against. Martial law has been declared in Songkhla, Pattani, Yala and Narathiwat provinces, and travelling in these regions is advised against. This makes the city and transport hub of Hat Yai and several of the main border crossings to Malaysia essentially out of bounds: this includes travelling by rail from Hat Yai (and Bangkok) to Butterworth via Padang Besar, and down the east coast to Kota Bharu; if you plan on taking any of these routes, check official advice, and ask locals and other travellers before going. The safest routes are those from Satun and Ko Lipe (p.883). From Satun, it is possible to travel by local transport to Kuala Perlis and Pulau Langkawi or Alor Setar, and the ferry from Ko Lipe to Pulau Langkawi is a relatively straightforward route. If you do come into Malaysia from Thailand, you can spend thirty days here without having obtained a visa beforehand.

## VISAS

Most nationalities do not need a **visa** for stays of fewer than two months in Malaysia, but passports must be valid for three months beyond your date of departure, and for six months if you're going to Sabah or Sarawak. To **extend your visa**, go to a local immigration department office or simply cross into Singapore (or Thailand) and back. A one-month extension should be no problem, and a three-month extension may be possible.

Tourists travelling from the Peninsula to Sarawak and Sabah must be cleared again by immigration. Visitors **to Sabah** can remain as long as their original two-month stamp is valid. Visitors **to Sarawak** – whether from Sabah or the Peninsula – receive a new, one-month stamp that is rarely extendible. If you start your trip in Sarawak and then fly to the mainland, be sure to get your passport stamped by immigration with the usual two-month pass. If an officer isn't available to do this, then go to the Immigration Office in Kuching at the first opportunity to get it stamped there.

### AIRPORT DEPARTURE TAX

**Departure tax** is RM6 for domestic flights, and RM45 on international flights, including those to Brunei and Singapore. If you're buying your ticket from an agent in, say, the UK, tax will usually be included in the overall price.

## GETTING AROUND

Public **transport** in Malaysia is extremely reliable, though not as cheap as in other Southeast Asian countries. Buses and long-distance taxis are most useful on the Peninsula. Getting around in Sarawak has become easier with the sealing of the coast road, though you may still have to use boats and perhaps the odd plane. There is no boat service between Peninsular Malaysia and East Malaysia, so you'll have to fly.

### Buses

Inter-state destinations are covered by comfortable, a/c **express buses**, operated either by the government's Transnasional, (Ⓦwww.nadi.com.my/transportation_home.asp) or by state or private bus companies; each company has an office at the bus station, which is where you buy your ticket. Since prices are fairly similar on all routes, it matters little which company you opt for.

Buses for long-distance routes (over 3hr) typically leave in clusters in the early morning and late evening, while shorter routes are served throughout the day. In most cases, you can just turn up, though on popular routes like KL to Penang (8hr; RM22.50), or during public and school holidays, you should reserve ahead. Local buses usually operate from a separate station, serve routes within the state and are cheaper, but also slower, less comfortable and without a/c; buy your ticket on the bus.

Several buses run across Sabah, but they're outnumbered by the more uncomfortable, and seldom faster, **minibuses** that leave when full from the same terminals; Kota Kinabulu to Sandakan will cost RM15 by bus and RM20 by minibus. Landcruisers and outsized jeeps are also common; they take eight passengers and cost less than a taxi but more than a bus. Modern a/c buses in Sarawak ply the trans-state coastal road between Kuching and the Brunei border, via Sibu (RM30), Bintulu and Miri (RM70).

## Long-distance taxis

Most towns in Peninsular Malaysia have a **long-distance taxi** rank. The four-seater taxis are generally very reliable and a lot quicker than the buses; they charge fixed-price fares, which are 50–100 percent more than the regular bus fare (KL to Butterworth costs RM35, KL to Kota Bharu RM45). You have to wait until the car is full, but this is rarely long in big towns. As a foreigner, you may be pressured to charter the whole car (at four times the one-person fare).

## Trains

The Peninsula's **train** service, operated by Keretapi Tanah Melayu (KTM; Ⓦwww.ktmb.com.my), is limited, relatively expensive and very slow. However, it is the best way to reach some of the more interesting places in the interior. A free timetable for the whole country is available from major train stations, although in reality the trains are usually at least two hours behind.

There are only **two main lines** through Peninsular Malaysia, both originating in Thailand at the southern town of Hat Yai. The west coast route from Thailand via Padang Besar on the Malaysian border runs south through Butterworth (for Penang), Ipoh, Tapah Road (for the Cameron Highlands) and KL, where you usually have to change trains before continuing on to Singapore. The scenery along this route is rather monotonous: a highway parallels the rails for much of the journey and the landscape is more urban than rural, though there are stretches of rubber and palm oil plantations.

However, serious fans of rail travel need not despair. Between KL and Singapore the train route splits at Gemas, 58km northeast of Melaka, from where a second line runs north through the mountainous interior – a section known as the **Jungle Railway** – via Kuala Lipis and skirting Kota Bharu to the northeastern border town of Tumpat. Note that the train from Gemas going north is a night train, so if you've come to see the jungle views, do this stretch from north to south. East Malaysia's only rail line is the bone-shaking 55-kilometre link between Kota Kinabalu and Tenom in Sabah; only the stretch between Beaufort and Tenom is worth considering (see p.593).

**Express trains** run on the west coast line only and stop at principal stations; ordinary trains, labelled *M* on the timetables, run on both lines and stop at virtually every station. Both trains have three classes: second-class is fine for most journeys, and the only real advantage of first-class travel is the air con; third-class is more crowded.

The likelihood is that whatever you ask for, as a foreigner you'll be sold the most expensive possible ticket anyway. On overnight sleepers, only first- and second-class fare is available, though you can opt for air con or not in second class. From KL to Butterworth costs RM67/59/17 for first/second/third class travel on an overnight express train. Seat reservations can be booked at Ⓦwww.ktmb.com.my.

## Ferries and boats

**Ferries** sail to all the major islands off Malaysia's east and west coasts, but during the monsoon (Nov–Feb), east-coast services are vastly reduced. There are no ferry services from the Peninsula to East Malaysia, so you'll have to fly. Once you're **in Sarawak**, the most usual method of travel is by turbo-charged express boat along the river systems; they run to a fairly regular timetable.

On the smaller tributaries, travel is by longboat, which you may have to charter. This mode of travel can get very expensive, as diesel prices multiply alarmingly the further into the interior you travel. Longboat travel is becoming increasingly obsolete as isolated riverside longhouse communities are getting connected to the road network – mostly by way of logging tracks hacked out of the jungle by timber concessionaires. This makes them accessible by 4WD and trucks, if not yet by buses, taxis and cars. **Sabah** has no express boats, but regular ferries connect Pulau Labuan with its west-coast towns. Ferries **to Indonesia** from eastern Sabah ports are being increasingly used by travellers.

## Planes

The cheapest airline with the most domestic flight routes is **Air Asia** (Ⓦwww.airasia.com, Ⓣ1300 889 933, or Ⓣ603 86604343 from outside Malaysia), which has been going from strength to strength in recent years. Prices change according to season, but it's often possible to get domestic flights for as little as RM18 (before tax). As flights are quick and efficient – it is just 55 minutes from KL to Langkawi as opposed to an eleven-hour bus journey – it's well worth checking out. Other popular airlines with domestic and Southeast Asian flights include: Malaysia Airlines (Ⓦwww.malaysiaairlines.com); Riau Airlines (Ⓦwww.riau-airlines.com); Silk Air (Ⓦwww.silkair.com) and Berjaya Air (Ⓦwww.berjaya-air.com), who operate flights to Pulau Tioman, Pulau Pangkor, Pulau Redang and Singapore from KL (Ⓦwww.berjaya-air.com).

If you buy an international Malaysia Airlines flight (excluding flights from Singapore or Brunei), you can get a **Discover Malaysia Pass**: US$199 for five flights within the country including one flight to Sabah or Sarawak. The passes are valid for 28 days; dates can be changed for free and you can alter the route for US$25. For details, and other useful air passes, see Ⓦwww.airtimetable.com/airpass_asia.htm.

Flights to East Malaysia operate mainly out of Kuala Lumpur, with Johor Bahru providing additional services to Kuching and Kota Kinabalu. Within Sarawak and Sabah, there are numerous nineteen-seater Twin-Otter and Fokker flights from Miri to other towns in the state's northern interior, such as Lawas and Limbang. MASWings (Ⓦwww.maswings.com.my) is a subsidiary of Malaysian Airlines that offers cheap internal flights around Sarawak and Sabah. Small aircraft also fly from Kota Kinabalu to Kudat, Sandakan and Tuwau.

## Vehicle rental

The condition of the roads in Peninsular Malaysia is generally excellent, making **driving** there a viable prospect for tourists, though not so in Sabah and Sarawak where the roads are rougher and susceptible to flash flooding.

Malaysians drive on the left, and wearing seat belts in the front is compulsory. Keep in mind that drivers flash their headlights when they are claiming the right of way, *not* the other way around, as is common practice in the West. Malaysians are, on the whole, reasonable drivers who *don't* share the Southeast Asian habit of keeping their hands permanently over their horns, which makes for a refreshing change and will give your eardrums time to recover if you've come from, say, Vietnam. The **speed limit** is 110km/hr on highways, 90km/hr on trunk roads and 50km/hr in built-up areas; speed traps are common, and fines are up to RM300. The North–South Highway is the only toll road – you can reckon on paying approximately RM1 for every 7km travelled.

To rent a vehicle, you must be 23 or over and have held a clean driving licence for at least a year; a national driving licence should be sufficient. Avis, Budget, Hertz and National have offices in major towns and at the airports (book two days ahead). **Rates** start at RM120 (£22/US$42) per day or RM700 (£120/US$230) per week; local companies charge the same. **Motorbike rental** is more informal, usually offered by guesthouses and shops in touristy areas (around RM30 per day). You may need to leave your passport as a deposit, but it's unlikely you'll have to show any proof of eligibility – officially, you must be over 21 and have an appropriate driving licence. Wearing helmets is compulsory and the laws are strictly enforced. **Bicycles** can be rented for about RM5 a day.

## ACCOMMODATION

Malaysia may not have the cheapest **accommodation**, but it does have some of the most atmospheric accommodation in Southeast Asia – and you still get pretty good deals on simple rooms. Fans of colonial-era architecture will find an abundance of options, and unlike in neighbouring countries, many of these are in the mid range – with all the amenities but without the shockingly high tariffs.

It is possible to find double rooms for under RM30, and there are dorms (from RM8) in the majority of guesthouses. Sarawak and Sabah are a little more expensive: dorms cost from RM20 and for a very basic double, you'll be looking at RM40 upwards. Sabah is the pricier of the two, and you'll often have to pay RM60 for a very ordinary place. Official **youth hostels** in Malaysia are often hopelessly far-flung and no cheaper than the guesthouses, and there are few official campsites.

A single room usually contains one double bed, while a double has two double beds or two single beds. Room rates can rise dramatically during the major holiday periods – Christmas, Easter, Chinese New Year and Hari Raya Haji (which marks the end of the annual Muslim pilgrimage to Mecca) – but as a general rule it's always worth bargaining. At the budget end of the market, you'll have to share a bathroom. Older places sometimes have mandi (see p.38) instead of showers.

The mainstay of the travellers' scene in Malaysia are the **guesthouses**, now increasingly being called "backpackers", located in popular tourist areas and usually good places to meet other people and pick up information. They can range from simple beachside A-frame huts to modern multi-storey apartment buildings. Almost all offer dormitory beds (from RM8) and basic double rooms (from RM 20). Prices on the east coast can drop to as little as RM10 for a double room, but on the islands you're unlikely to get anything, particularly at peak season, for less than RM25.

The **cheapest hotels** in Malaysia are usually Chinese-run and cater for a predominantly local clientele. They're generally clean and there's never any need to book in advance, but they can be noisy and some of the cheapest ones double as brothels (especially those called **Rumah Persinggahan**). Ordinary rooms start at RM20 and will have a washbasin, fan and a hard mattress; there's usually an a/c option, too. Bathrooms are shared.

**Mid-range hotels** have sprung mattresses, en-suite bathrooms, a/c and TV. Prices range from RM40 to RM100, but a genuine distinction is made between single rooms and doubles. Also in the mid-range category are the excellent-value Government Resthouses (**Rumah Rehat**): rooms are large, en-suite and well- equipped. In many towns they have been replaced by **Seri Malaysia** hotel chain (Ⓦwww.serimalaysia.com.my), which offer a uniformly good standard for RM100 per night.

The most atmospheric accommodation in Malaysia is in the stilted **longhouses**, found on the rivers of Sarawak and Sabah. These can house dozens of families, and usually consist of three elevated sections reached by a simple ladder. The snag is that it's getting increasingly hard to stay in them as an independent traveller – most tourists can only stay at longhouses as part of an organized tour. Also, the traditional, wooden longhouse design is fast disappearing and being replaced by more utilitarian concrete – although still long – structures.

**Electricity** in Malaysia is supplied at 220 volts, and plugs have three prongs like British ones.

## FOOD AND DRINK

Malaysians are justifiably proud of their cuisine. The range and mix of cultures in the country is strongly evident in the delicious fusion of flavours and styles, and even the fussiest eaters are guaranteed to find something to suit their taste (while the less fussy are in for a gastronomic feast).

The **cuisine** is inspired by the three main communities, Malay, Chinese and Indian. Food everywhere is remarkably good value – basic noodle or rice-based meals at a street stall can be had for around RM2.50–4, and a full meal with drinks in a decent restaurant will seldom cost more than RM40 a head. Food hygiene standards are generally quite high – within reason, you can try anything anywhere and expect to get away without gastroenteritis.

### The cuisines

**Malay cuisine** is based on rice, often enriched with *santan* (coconut milk), which is served with a dazzling variety of curries, vegetable stir-fries and sambals, a condiment of chillies and shrimp paste.

The most famous dish is satay – virtually Malaysia's national dish – which comprises skewers of barbecued meat dipped in spicy peanut sauce. The classic way to sample Malay curries is to eat *nasi campur*, a buffet (usually served at lunchtime) of steamed rice supplemented by up to two dozen accompanying dishes, including *lembu* (beef), *kangkong* (greens), fried chicken, fish steaks and curry sauce, and various vegetables. Another popular dish is *nasi goreng* (mixed fried rice with meat, seafood and vegetables). For breakfast, the most popular Malay dish is *nasi lemak*, rice cooked in coconut milk and served with *sambal ikan bilis* (tiny fried anchovies in hot chilli paste).

In **Sabah**, there's the Murut speciality of *jaruk* – raw wild boar fermented in a bamboo tube, but the most famous Sabah dish is *hinava*, or raw fish pickled in lime juice. In **Sarawak**, you're most likely to eat with the indigenous Iban group sampling wild boar with jungle ferns and sticky rice; although they have been known to prepare some boiled monkey for guests, it's not a regular item on the menu. A particular favourite in Kuching are bamboo clams, small pencil-shaped slivery delicacies that only grow in the wild in mangrove-dense riverine locations. These are called "monkey's penises" by the locals.

Typical **Nyonya dishes** (the distinctive fusion cuisine formed by the descendants of Chinese and Malay intermarriage) incorporate elements from Chinese, Indonesian and Thai cooking. Chicken, fish and seafood form the backbone of the cuisine, and unlike Malay food, pork is used. Noodles (*mee*) flavoured with chillies, and rich curries made from rice flour and coconut cream, are common. A popular breakfast dish is *laksa*, noodles in spicy coconut soup served with seafood and beansprouts, lemon grass, pineapple, pepper, lime leaves and chilli. Other popular Nyonya dishes include *ayam buah keluak*, chicken cooked with Indonesian "black" nuts; and *otak-otak*, fish mashed with coconut milk and chilli and steamed in a banana leaf.

**Chinese food** dominates in Malaysia – fish and seafood is nearly always outstanding, with prawns, crab, squid and a variety of fish on offer almost everywhere. Noodles, too, are ubiquitous, and come in wonderful variations – thin, flat, round, served in soup (wet) or fried (dry). Malaysians eat noodles any time of the day or night, and a particular favourite is a dish called *hokkien mee*: fat, white noodles with *tempe* (a cheese-like food made of the soya residue from tofu-making) in a rich soy sauce whipped up in three minutes flat by a wok chef at the side of the road. *Koey teow goreng*, flat rice noodles simply fried with chicken or seafood and local greens, is another popular staple dish.

The dominant style is Cantonese and the classic lunch is *dim sum*, a variety of steamed and fried dumplings served in bamboo baskets. Standard dishes include chicken in chilli or with cashew nuts; buttered prawns, or prawns served with a sweet and sour sauce; spare ribs; and mixed vegetables with tofu (beancurd) and beansprouts. For something a little more unusual, try a steamboat, a Chinese-style fondue filled with boiling stock in which you cook meat, fish, shellfish, eggs and vegetables; or a claypot – meat, fish or shellfish cooked over a fire in an earthenware pot.

There isn't a big dessert culture in Malaysia, but *ais kacang*, shaved ice with fruit syrup, often served with sweet red beans and condensed milk, is deliciously refreshing, particularly in the heat. Most Malaysian towns also have a good bakery or two (often conveniently situated in the train station), with tasty specialities such as pineapple cakes and shredded chicken rolls.

**North Indian food** tends to rely more on meat, especially mutton and chicken, and breads – *naan*, *chapatis*, *parathas* and *rotis* – rather than rice. The most famous style of North Indian cooking is *tandoori* – named after the clay oven in which the food is cooked. A favourite breakfast is *roti canai* (flaky pancake and *daal*) or *roti kaya* (pancake spread with egg and local jam). **Southern Indian food** tends to be spicier and more reliant on vegetables. Its staple is the *dosa* (pancake), often served at breakfast as a *masala dosa*, stuffed with onions, vegetables and chutney. Indian Muslims serve the similar *murtabak*, a grilled *roti* pancake with egg and minced meat. Many South Indian cafés serve *daun pisang* at lunchtime, usually a vegetarian meal where rice is served on banana leaves with vegetable curries. It's normal to eat a banana-leaf meal with your right hand, though restaurants will always have cutlery.

## Where to eat

To eat inexpensively go to **hawker stalls**, traditionally simple wooden stalls on the roadside, with a few stools to sit at. They serve standard Malay noodle and rice dishes, satay, Indian fast food such as *roti canai*, plus more obscure regional delicacies. Most are scrupulously clean, and the food is cooked in front of you. Avoid dishes that look as if they've been standing around or have been reheated, and you should be fine. Hawker stalls don't have menus and you don't have to sit close to the stall you're patronizing: find a free table, and the vendor will track you down when your food is ready. You may find that the meal should be paid for when it reaches your table, but the usual form is to pay when you're finished. Most outdoor stalls open at around 11am, usually offering the day's *nasi campur* selection; prices are determined by the

## PEOPLES

With a pivotal position on the maritime trade routes between the Middle East, India and China, Malaysia has always attracted immigration. The region also had many indigenous tribes, Orang Asli ("the first people"). On the Peninsula, the Malays form just over fifty percent of the population, the Chinese nearly 38 percent, Indians ten percent and the Orang Asli around one percent; in Sarawak and Sabah, the indigenous tribes account for around fifty percent of the population, the Chinese 28 percent, with the other 22 percent divided amongst Malays, Indians and Eurasians. Although many of Malaysia's ethnic groups are now nominally Christian or Muslim, many of their old **animist** beliefs and ceremonies still survive.

### The Malays

The **Malays** first moved to the west coast of the Malaysian Peninsula from Sumatra in early times, but the growth in power of the Malay sultanates from the fifteenth century onwards – coinciding with the arrival of Islam – established Malays as a significant force. They developed an aristocratic tradition, courtly rituals and a social hierarchy that still have an influence today. The main contemporary change for Malays in Malaysia was the introduction after independence of the *bumiputra* policy, which was designed to make it easier for the Malays, the Orang Asli of the Peninsula and other indigenous groups to compete in economic and educational fields against the high-achieving Chinese and Indians. Malays now hold most of the top positions in government and in state companies.

### The Chinese and Straits Chinese

The first significant **Chinese** community established itself in Melaka in the fifteenth century. However, the ancestors of the majority of Chinese now living in Peninsular Malaysia emigrated from southern China in the nineteenth century to work in the tin-mining industry. In Sarawak and Sabah, the Chinese played an important part in opening up the interior. Chinatowns developed throughout the region, and Chinese traditions became an integral part of a wider Malayan culture. The Malaysian Chinese are well-represented in parliament. One of the few examples of regional intermarrying is displayed in the Peranakan or "Straits-born Chinese" heritage of Melaka and Penang. When male Chinese immigrants married local Malay women, their male offspring were termed "Baba" and the females "Nyonya" (or Nonya). **Baba–Nyonya** society adapted elements from both cultures: the descendants of these sixteenth-century liaisons have a unique culinary and architectural style.

### The Indians

The first large wave of **Tamil** labourers arrived in the nineteenth century. But an embryonic entrepreneurial class from **north India** soon followed and set up businesses in Penang. Although Indians comprise only ten percent of Malaysia's population, their impact is felt everywhere.

### The Orang Asli

The **Orang Asli** are the indigenous peoples of Peninsular Malaysia , thought to have migrated here around fifty thousand years ago. They mostly belong number of dishes you choose on top of your rice, usually about RM2–3 per portion. Hawker stalls often stay open late – the early ones will close around 10pm, while some can continue until 2 or 3am.

Few streets exist without a *kedai kopi*, a **coffee house** or **café** usually run by Chinese or Indians. Most open at 7am or 8am; closing times vary from 6pm to midnight. Basic Chinese coffee houses serve noodle and rice dishes all day, as well as cakes. The culinary standard might not be very high, but a filling one-plate meal only costs a couple of dollars.



to three distinct groups, of which there are various tribes. Though most tribes retain some cultural traditions, government drives have encouraged many tribespeople to integrate. The largest group is the **Senoi** (pop. 40,000), who live in the forested interior of Perak, Pahang and Kelantan states and are divided into two main tribes, the Semiar and the Temiar. They follow animist customs and practise shifting cultivation. The dark-skinned **Semang** (or Negritos; pop. 2000) live in the northern areas of the Peninsula and share a traditional nomadic, hunter-gatherer culture. The so-called **Aboriginal Malays** live south of the Kuala Lumpur–Kuantan road.

### Sarawak's peoples

Nearly fifty percent of **Sarawak's population** is made up of various indigenous Dyak and Orang Ulu groups – including the Iban, Bidayuh, Kayan, Kenyah, Kelabit and Penan tribes, many of whom live in longhouses and maintain a rich cultural legacy.The **Iban**, a stocky, rugged people, make up nearly one-third of Sarawak's population. Iban longhouse communities are found in the Batang Ai river system in the southwest, and along the Rajang, Katibas and Baleh rivers. These communities are quite accessible, their inhabitants always hospitable and keen to show off their traditional dance, music, textile-weaving, blow-piping, fishing and game-playing. In their time, the Iban were infamous headhunters, but this tradition has been replaced by that of *berjelai*, or "journey", whereby a young man leaves the community to prove himself in the outside world – returning to his longhouse with television sets, generators and outboard motors, rather than heads.The southernmost of Sarawak's indigenous groups are the **Bidayuh**, who traditionally lived away from the rivers, building their longhouses on the sides of hills. Culturally, they are similar to the Iban. Most of the other groups in Sarawak are classed as **Orang Ulu** (people of the interior). They inhabit the more remote inland areas, on the upper Rajang, Balui, Baram and Linau rivers. The most numerous, the **Kayan** and the **Kenyah**, are longhouse-dwellers, animists and shifting cultivators. The **Kelabit** live in longhouses on the highland plateau that separates north Sarawak from Kalimantan, and are Christian. The semi-nomadic **Penan** live in the upper Rajang and Limbang areas and rely on hunting and gathering. The state government's resettlement programme – a controversial policy not entirely unconnected with the logging industry – is now largely complete, and few Penan still live their traditional lifestyle.

### Sabah's peoples

The **Dusun**, or Kadazan/Dusun, account for around a third of Sabah's population. Traditionally agriculturists, they inhabit the western coastal plains and the interior. Although most Dusun are now Christians, remnants of their animist past are still evident. The mainly Muslim **Bajau** tribe drifted over from the southern Philippines some two hundred years ago, and now constitute ten percent of Sabah's population, living in the northwest. They are agriculturists and fishermen, noted for their horsemanship and their rearing of buffalo. The **Murut** inhabit the area between Keningau and the Sarawak border, in the southwest.

If available, full meals of meat, seafood and vegetables cost about RM5.

On the whole, proper **restaurants** are places to savour particular delicacies found nowhere else, like shark's-fin dishes (although you may want to consult your moral conscience before sampling these), bird's-nest soup and high-quality seafood. In many restaurants, the food is not necessarily superior to that served at a good café or hawker stall – you're just paying for a/c and tablecloths. Tipping is not expected and bills arrive complete with service charge and government tax. Restaurants are usually open from 11.30am to 2.30pm and from 6 to 10.30pm.

### Drinking

**Tap water** is said to be safe to drink in Malaysia, though it's wise to stick to bottled water (RM2 a litre). Using ice for drinks is generally fine, too, making the huge variety of seasonal fresh fruit drinks available in hawker centres and street corners even more pleasant. You'll often find that sweet condensed milk is added to tea and coffee unless you ask for it without. In city centres, look out for the sweetened soy milk, fresh fruit juices and sugar-cane juice touted on street corners.

Only in certain places on the east coast of the Malaysian peninsula is drinking alcohol outlawed. Elsewhere, alcohol is available in bars, restaurants, Chinese *kedai kopi*, supermarkets and sometimes at hawker's stalls. Anchor and Tiger **beer** (lager) are locally produced and are probably the best choices, although Carlsberg and Heineken are being marketed heavily. Locally produced whisky and rum are cheap enough, too, though pretty rough. The **brandy**, which is what some local Chinese drink, tends to be better. **Wine** is becoming more common and competitively priced, too. There is a thriving bar scene in KL, Kuching and Penang; less so in other towns. Fierce competition keeps happy hours a regular feature (usually 5–7pm), bringing the beer down to around RM5 a glass. Some bars open all day (11am–11pm), but most tend to double as clubs, opening in the evenings until 2 or 3am. All-night clubs are a relatively new development.

## CULTURE AND ETIQUETTE

The Malays like to please and in general are likely to be some of the kindest and most helpful people you'll come across. The flipside of their desire to please, however, can be that they don't necessarily furnish you with negative information. If there's a bus leaving at the time you require, surely you'd be happy to know that. Why upset you by telling you that it's categorically fully booked for the next week? Frustration can be alleviated by asking every obvious question you can think of before making any decisions.

The vast majority of Malaysians are Muslims, but there are also significant numbers of Hindus, Buddhists, Confucianists and animists among the population. For an introduction to all these faiths, see p.46.

**Islam** in Malaysia today is relatively liberal. Although most Muslim women don headscarves, few wear a veil, and some taboos, like not drinking alcohol, are ignored by a growing number of Malays. There are stricter, more fundamentalist Muslims – in Kelantan the local government is dominated by them – but in general, Islam here has a moderate and modern outlook. There are clear hints of other religions within Malaysian tradition as well – the traditional Malay wedding ceremony, for example, has clear **Hindu** influences, and talking to people about their day-to-day beliefs and superstitions often suggests the influence of **Chinese animistic religions**. Just like the cultures, religions tend to overlap fairly easily in Malaysia – whereas an individual will obviously have his or her religion, cultures and tit-bits from other belief systems are seamlessly incorporated into day-to-day life.

Malaysia shares the same attitudes to dress and social taboos as other Southeast Asian cultures; see p.45 for details.

## SPORTS AND OUTDOOR ACTIVITIES

The varied terrain of Malaysia means activities such as **cycling**, **golf** and **horse-riding** are possible across the country. Cycling in towns isn't all that advisable as traffic is fairly unpredictable and people expect you to be able to duck and swerve to avoid their manoeuvres, but in more regional areas it's a great way to explore. Cycle rental is available in many guesthouses for around RM5 per day. On the islands, **canoeing** is also a great way to go from cove to cove, and again, canoe rental is usually available from guesthouses for RM5–10 per day. For both cycling and canoeing, be sure to wear plenty of sunscreen – in the equatorial sunshine, it's far too easy to get burnt to a cinder without even realizing it.

### Snorkelling and diving

The crystal-clear waters of Malaysia and its abundance of tropical fish and coral make **snorkelling and diving** a must for any underwater enthusiast. This is particularly true of East Sabah's islands, which include Sipadan and Mabul, and the Peninsula's east-coast islands of Perhentian, Redang, Kapas and Tioman. Pulau Tioman offers the most choice for schools and dive sites. Make sure that the dive operator is registered with PADI (Professional Association of Diving Instructors) or equivalent; dive courses cost from RM750 for a four-day PADI Open Water course to RM1800 for a Divemaster course. If you're already certified, it's possible to rent all the necessary equipment for a day's worth of diving for RM80–100.

### Trekking

The majority of **treks**, either on the Malaysian Peninsula or in Sarawak and Sabah, require some forethought and preparation, and you should be prepared for trails and rivers to become much more difficult to negotiate when it rains. That said, although the rainy season (Nov–Feb) undoubtedly slows your progress on some of the trails, conditions are less humid and the parks and adventure tours not oversubscribed. Most visitors trek in the large national parks to experience the remaining primary jungle and rainforest at first hand. For these, you often need to be accompanied by a guide, which can either be arranged through tour operators in KL, Kuching, Miri and Kota Kinabulu, or at the parks themselves. For inexperienced trekkers, Taman Negara National Park (see p.531) is probably the best place to start, while Sarawak's Gunung Mulu National Park (see p.585) offers sufficient challenges for most tastes. Few people who make it across to Sabah forego the chance of climbing Mount Kinabalu (see p.595) – not a task to be undertaken lightly, however. Details of essential trekking equipment are given in each relevant account.

## COMMUNICATIONS

Overseas **mail** takes around four to seven days to reach its destination in Malaysia. Packages are expensive to send, with surface/sea mail taking two months to Europe, longer to the USA, and even air mail taking a few weeks. There's usually a shop near the post office that will wrap your parcel for RM5 or so. Each Malaysian town has a General Post Office (GPO), with a poste restante/general delivery section, where mail is held for two months. GPOs also forward mail (for one month) free of charge if you fill in the right form.

There are **public telephone boxes** in most towns in Malaysia; local calls cost 10 sen for an unlimited amount of time. Making long-distance calls can be surprisingly complicated, and even with the same phone companies, different rules seem to apply for different regions. The most common card for overseas calls is the Telecom Malaysia card. In some regions this only works in Telecom Malaysia phones, whereas elsewhere it will work in any card phone. Similarly, although the card is supposedly activated by dialling a freephone number and then typing in the PIN printed on the card, sometimes it will only work if you put a nominal coin into the phone first.

Not all phones will give callers an English-speaking option. Non PIN cards are available for the ubiquitous Uniphone (yellow), the green Cityphone, the government Kadfon (blue) or the orange Telecom Malaysia phone. Cards of RM10, RM20, RM50 and RM100 are sold at Shell and Petronas stations, newsagents and most 7-Elevens. Uniphone only takes RM20 or RM50 cards. Check for an international logo on the phone booth before dialling overseas.

To call **abroad** from Malaysia, dial ☏00 + IDD country code + area code minus first 0 + subscriber number.

**Collect** (reverse charge) calls can be made from hotels or from a **Telekom** office (open office hours), though these are found only in larger towns. In KL, Penang and Kota Kinabalu there are also **Home Country Direct** phones – press the appropriate button and you'll be connected with your home operator, who can either arrange a collect call or debit you. Many businesses in Malaysia have mobile phone numbers; they are prefixed ☏011 or 010 and are expensive to call.

**Internet cafés** are plentiful and often found in smaller towns and many hotels (even tiny, remote hostels) also provide internet access. Prices are very competitive, ranging between RM3 and RM10 per hour. Connections are usually pretty good.

## CRIME AND SAFETY

If you lose something in Malaysia, you're more likely to have someone running after you with it than running away. The most common crimes are perpetrated by **pickpockets** and snatch thieves. Take care if you rent a motorbike not to leave anything valuable in the basket on the handlebars. The ferry from Butterworth to Georgetown (Penang) is notorious for pickpockets who work in teams: a common tactic is for one to strike up a conversation to create a diversion, while the other works at your pack or pockets.

**Theft** from dormitories by other tourists is also a relatively common complaint. It's a good idea to keep one credit or debit card with you and another in your room. In the more remote parts of Sarawak or Sabah there is little crime, and you needn't worry unduly about carrying more cash than usual. If you do need to report a crime in Malaysia, head for the nearest **police station**, where there'll be someone who speaks English – you'll need a copy of the police report for insurance purposes. In many major tourist spots, there are specific tourist police stations. It is very unwise to have anything to do with **drugs** of any description in Malaysia or Singapore. The penalties for trafficking drugs in or out of either country are extreme – foreigners have been executed in the past.

### EMERGENCY NUMBERS

Police/Ambulance ☏999
Fire Brigade ☏994

## MEDICAL CARE AND EMERGENCIES

The levels of hygiene and **medical care** in Malaysia are higher than in much of the rest of Southeast Asia; staff almost everywhere speak good English and use up-to-date techniques. There's always a pharmacy in main towns, which is well stocked with brand-name drugs. Oral contraceptives and condoms are sold over the counter. Pharmacists can help with simple complaints, though if you're in any doubt get a proper diagnosis from a private clinic. Opening hours are usually Monday to Saturday 9.30am to 7pm; pharmacies in shopping malls stay open later. **Private clinics** are found even in the smallest towns; a visit costs around RM30, excluding medication. The **emergency department** of each town's general hospital will see foreigners for the token fee of RM1, though costs rise rapidly if continued treatment or overnight stays are necessary. See the "Listings" sections at the end of major town accounts for addresses of pharmacies and hospitals.

## INFORMATION AND MAPS

Tourism Malaysia (Ⓦwww.tourism.gov.my) operates a **tourist office** in most major towns, but is not that useful for areas off the beaten track. Locally run **visitor centres**, found in most major towns, are more geared up to independent travellers' needs. You can also book permits and accommodation for the **national parks** at these centres.

The best general **maps** of Malaysia are Macmillan's 1:2,000,000 *Malaysia Traveller's Map* and the more detailed Nelles 1:650,000 *West Malaysia* (not including Sabah and Sarawak). Also check out the *Rough Guide Malaysia* Map. The best detailed relief map of Sarawak is the Land and Survey Department's 1:500,000 issue, available in the bookshop at the Kuching *Holiday Inn*. The best coverage of Sabah is on maps produced by Nelles. **City maps** can usually be picked up in the visitor centres.

### MALAYSIA ON THE NET

**Ⓦwww.tourism.gov.my** The Malaysian Tourist Board's website. Provides excellent, up-to-date information.

**Ⓦwww.virtualmalaysia.com** Another official website, which provides good information.

**Ⓦwww.visitorsguide.com.my** A visitors' guide to the country.

## MONEY AND BANKS

Malaysia's unit of **currency** is the Malaysian ringgit, divided into 100 sen. You'll see the ringgit written as "RM" (as it is throughout this Guide), or simply as "$" (M$), and often hear it called a "dollar". Notes come in RM1, RM5, RM10, RM20, RM50, RM100, RM500 and RM1000 denominations; coins are minted in 1 sen, 5 sen, 10 sen, 20 sen, 50 sen and M$1 denominations. At the time of writing, the **exchange rate** was around RM6.90 to £1, with the ringgit fixed against the US dollar at RM3.80. There is no black market.

Sterling and US dollar **traveller's cheques** can be cashed at Malaysian banks, licensed moneychangers and some hotels. Ban Hin Lee Bank (BHL) doesn't charge any commission for changing American Express traveller's cheques, but can only be found in major cities.

Licensed moneychangers' kiosks in bigger towns tend to open until around 6pm, and sometimes at weekends; some hotels will **exchange** money at all hours. It's not difficult to change money in Sabah or Sarawak, though if travelling by river in the interior, you should carry a fair bit of cash in smallish denominations.

Major **credit cards** are accepted in most hotels and large shops, but beware of illegal surcharges. Banks will advance cash against major credit cards, and with American Express, Visa and MasterCard as well as Cirrus, Plus and Maestrobank (debit) cards, you can withdraw money from automatic teller machines (ATMs) in big cities and many towns.

## BAHASA MALAYSIA

The national language of Malaysia is Bahasa Malaysia, which is simple enough to learn. You'll be able to get by with English in all but the most remote areas. Nouns have no genders and don't require an article, while the plural form is constructed just by saying the word twice; thus "child" is *anak*, while "children" is *anak anak*. Doubling a word can also indicate "doing"; for example, *jalan jalan* is used to mean "walking". Verbs have no tenses either. Sentence order is the same as in English, though adjectives usually follow the noun.

### Pronunciation

The **pronunciation** of Bahasa Malaysia is broadly the same as the English reading of Roman script, with a few exceptions:

**a** as in cup
**c** as in **ch**eap
**e** as in end
**g** as in girl
**i** as in boutique
**j** as in joy
**k** hard, as in English, except at the end of the word, when you should stop just short of pronouncing it.
**o** as in got
**u** as in boot
**ai** as in fine
**au** as in how
**sy** as in shut

### Greetings and basic phrases

**Selamat** is the all-purpose greeting derived from Arabic, which communicates general goodwill.

| | |
|---|---|
| Good morning | *Selamat pagi* |
| Good afternoon | *Selamat petang* |
| Good evening | *Selamat malam* |
| Good night | *Selamat tidur* |
| Goodbye | *Selamat tinggal* |
| Welcome | *Selamat datang* |
| Bon Appetit | *Selamat makan* |
| Please | *Tolong* |
| Thank you | *Terima kasih* |
| You're welcome | *Sama sama* |
| Sorry/excuse me | *Maaf* |
| Yes | *Ya* |
| No | *Tidak* |
| Do you speak English | *Bisa bercakap bahasa Inggris?* |
| I don't understand | *Saya tidak mengerti* |
| Can you help me? | *Bolekah anda tolong saya?* |
| Where is the...? | *Dimana...?* |
| Stop | *Berhenti* |
| Train station | *Stesen keratapi* |
| Bus station | *Stesen bas* |
| Airport | *Lapangan terbang* |
| Hotel | *Hotel/rumah penginapan* |
| Post office | *Pejabat pos* |
| Restaurant | *Restoran* |
| Shop | *Kedai* |
| Market | *Pasar* |
| Taxi | *Teksi* |
| How much is...? | *Berapa...?* |
| Cheap/expensive | *Murah/mahal* |
| Good | *Bagus* |
| Closed | *Tutup* |
| Ill/sick | *Sakit* |
| Toilet | *Tandas* |
| Water | *Air* |
| Food | *Makan* |
| Drink | *Minum* |

### Numbers

| | |
|---|---|
| 0 | *Nul* |
| 1 | *Satu* |
| 2 | *Dua* |
| 3 | *Tiga* |
| 4 | *Empat* |
| 5 | *Lima* |
| 6 | *Enam* |
| 7 | *Tujuh* |
| 8 | *Lapan* |
| 9 | *Sembilan* |
| 10 | *Sepuluh* |
| 11, 12, 13, etc | *Sebelas, duabelas, tigabelas* |
| 20 | *Duapuluh* |
| 21, 22, etc | *Duapuluh satu, dua puluh dua* |
| 30, 40, 50, etc | *Tigapuluh, empatpuluh, limapuluh* |
| 100, 200, 300, etc | *Seratus, duaratus, tigaratus* |
| 1000 | *Seribu* |

## Food and drink glossary

| | |
|---|---|
| *Menu* | Menu |
| *Sejuk* | Cold |
| *Panas* | Hot (temperature) |
| *Pedasl* | Hot (spicy) |
| *Saya tak makan daging* | I don't eat meat or fish |

### Noodles (mee) and noodle dishes

| | |
|---|---|
| *Bee hoon* | Thin rice noodles |
| *Char kuey* teow | Flat noodles with prawns, sausage, fishcake, egg, vegetables or chilli |
| *Foochow noodles* | Steamed and served in soy and oyster sauce |
| *Hokkien fried mee* | Yellow noodles fried with pork, prawn and vegetables |
| *Kuey teow* | Flat noodles |
| *Laksa* | Noodles, bean sprouts, fishcakes and prawns in a spicy coconut soup |
| *Mee* | Round yellow wheat flour noodles |
| *Mee suah* | Noodles served dry and crispy |
| *Wan ton mee* | Roast pork, noodles and vegetables soup with dumplings |

### Rice (nasi) dishes

| | |
|---|---|
| *Claypot* | Rice topped with meat, cooked in an earthen-ware pot over a fire |
| *Daun pisang* | Banana-leaf curry |
| *Nasi campur* | Rice served with several meat, fish and vegetable dishes |
| *Nasi goreng* | Fried rice with diced meat and veg |
| *Nasi puteh* | Plain boiled rice |

### Meat, fish and basics

| | |
|---|---|
| *Ayam* | Chicken |
| *Babi* | Pork |
| *Daging* | Beef |
| *Garam* | Salt |
| *Gula* | Sugar |
| *Ikan* | Fish |
| *Kambing* | Mutton |
| *Kepiting* | Crab |
| *Sotong* | Squid |
| *Sup* | Soup |
| *Tahu* | Tofu (beancurd) |
| *Telor* | Egg |
| *Udang* | Prawn |

### Desserts

| | |
|---|---|
| *Bubor cha cha* | Sweetened coconut milk with pieces of sweet potato, yam and tapioca balls |
| *Cendol* | Coconut milk, palm syrup and pea-flour noodles poured over shaved ice |
| *Es kachang* | Shaved ice with red beans, jelly, sweet corn, rose syrup and evaporated milk |
| *Pisang murtabak* | Banana pancake |

### Drinks (minum)

| | |
|---|---|
| *Air minum* | Water |
| *Bir* | Beer |
| *Jus* | Fruit juice |
| *Kopi* | Coffee |
| *Kopi-o* | Black coffee |
| *Kopi susu* | Coffee with milk |
| *Lassi* | Sweet or sour yoghurt |
| *Teh* | Tea |
| *Teh susu* | Tea with milk |
| *Teh tarik* | Sweet, frothy, milky tea |

Wiring money to Malaysia is straightforward. In KL, the best bank to use is HSBC, 2 Lebuh Ampang, Little India (☎03/2070 0744).

## OPENING HOURS AND PUBLIC HOLIDAYS

**Shops** are open daily 9am to 7pm and shopping centres 10am to 11pm. **Government office** hours are Monday to Thursday 8am to 12.45pm and 2 to 4.15pm, Friday 8am to 12.15pm and 2.45 to 4.15pm, Sat 8am to 12.45pm; however, in the states of Kedah, Kelantan and Terengganu, on Thursday the hours are 8am to 12.45pm, they're closed on Friday and are open with full working hours on Sunday. **Banking hours** are generally Monday to Friday 10am to 3pm and Saturday 9.30 to 11.30am. **Post offices** are open Monday to Saturday 8am to 6pm.

### Public holidays

The Muslim holidays of Hari Raya Haji, which celebrates the end of the annual Muslim pilgrimage to Mecca, and Hari Raya Puasa, which celebrates the end of the Ramadan fast, change year on year as Islam operates on a lunar calendar, so it's best to check before you go.

**January 1** New Year's Day
**January/February** Chinese New Year (2 days)
**January/February** Thaipusam (depending on the full moon)
**March/April** Maal Hijrah (the Muslim New Year)
**May** Pesta Kaamatan (Sabah only)
**May 1** Labour Day
**May/June** Birthday of the Prophet Mohammed
**June** Gawai Dayak (Sarawak only)
**June 4** Yang di-Pertuan Agong's birthday
**August 31** National Day
**November** Deepavali (the Hindu festival more commonly known as Diwali, the Festival of Light)
**December 25** Christmas Day

## FESTIVALS

Three religions – Islam, Buddhism and Hinduism – are represented in Malaysia, and they play a vital role in the everyday lives of the population. Some religious festivals are celebrated at home or in the mosque or temple. During Ramadan, Muslims fast during the daytime for a whole month, while other festivals are marked with great spectacle. Most of the festivals have no fixed dates, but change annually according to the lunar calendar. Festivals of interest to tourists include:

**Chinese New Year** Jan–Feb. Chinese operas and lion and dragon dance troupes perform in the streets. The festival is actually 15 days long, but in general only the first two and the last are observed with actual events – throughout the rest of the time, a general holiday atmosphere abounds but life continues as normal.

**Thaipusam** Jan/Feb. Entranced Hindu penitents carry elaborate steel arches, attached to their skin by hooks and skewers (especially at KL's Batu Caves). Hospitals are often overwhelmed with people sporting wounds and injuries.

**Gawai Dayak** Sarawak's Iban and Bidayuk people hold extravagant feasts to mark the end of the harvest, best experienced at the Iban longhouses on the Ai, Skrang and Lemanak rivers near Kuching (June) and in Bidayuh communities around Bau.

**Dragon Boat Festival** June/July in Penang, Melaka and Kota Kinabalu, where the traditional dragon boats (long narrow boats decorated with an impressive dragon head at its stern) race. This often attracts international competitors.

**Festival of the Hungry Ghosts** late Aug. Known locally as Yue Lan, this is a festival for appeasing both ancestors and homeless spirits, by providing them with essentials such as food and drink. There are many free performances of Chinese opera and wayang, or puppet shows.

**Navarathiri** Sept–Oct. Hindu temples devote nine nights to classical dance and music in honour of the deities.

**Kota Belud Tamu Besar** Oct/Nov. Sabah's biggest annual market, which features cultural performances.

# Kuala Lumpur and around

Founded in the mid-nineteenth century, **KUALA LUMPUR**, or KL, is a fast-changing super-city, with establishments being opened up and closed down again so fast you're liable to miss something if you so much as blink. The city is permanently awash with building sites manned by gung-ho workers and is an impressive mix of architecture, of which the most famous and iconic is perhaps the awesome Petronas Towers, which rise up from the chaos. As a total mix of cultures, KL manages to combine the best of all worlds, being less frenetic than most Indian cities and friendlier and more laid-back than a lot of Chinese ones. With a population of nearly two million, it has undeniable energy, but still manages to retain a relaxed old-world charm – and the inhabitants' warmth is hard to beat anywhere. From a cultural standpoint, it certainly has enough interesting monuments, galleries, markets and museums to keep visitors busy for at least a week.

## What to see and do

Despite much modernization, much of Kuala Lumpur's appeal – markets, temples and historic mosques – remains intact. The city centre is quite compact, with the **Colonial District** centred on Merdeka Square; close by, across the river and to the north, **Chinatown** and **Little India** are the two main traditional commercial districts. One of the most prominent (and busiest) of KL's central streets, Jalan Tunku Abdul Rahman, or **Jalan TAR** as it's often known, runs due north from Merdeka Square for 2km to Chow Kit Market; closer in, west of the square, are the **Lake Gardens**, while to the south lie the **Masjid Negara** (National Mosque), the new **Islamic Arts Museum**, the landmark **Old KL train station** and the **Muzium Negara** (National Museum).

### Merdeka Square and the National Museum of History

The small **Colonial District** is centred on the beautifully tended **Merdeka Square** on the west bank of the Klang River: Malaysian Independence (*merdeka*, or freedom) from the British was proclaimed here on August 31, 1957. Nearby, to the south, the **National Museum of History** (daily 9am–6pm; free), on the corner of Jalan Raja, provides an informative romp through the main points of the nation's history.

### Masjid Negara and the Museum of Islamic Arts

South, down Jalan Sultan Hishamuddin, is the impressive seventy-metre-high minaret and geometric lattice work of the **Masjid Negara, the National Mosque** (daily 9am–noon, 3–4pm & 5.30–6.30pm; closed Fri am). To enter, you need to be properly dressed; alternatively, full length lilac-coloured robes (that are liable to make you look like a *Lord of the Rings* extra wannabe) can be borrowed from the desk at the entrance. Behind the mosque on Jalan Lembah Perdana is the ultra-modern **Museum of Islamic Arts** (Tues–Sun 10am–6pm; RM12; Ⓦwww.Iamm.org.my). This fascinating collection of textiles, metalwork and ancient Korans is a must-see – check out the calligraphic section, which includes hand-written sections of the Koran. Some date back a thousand years and many of them are intricate and beautiful.

### Old KL train station and National Museum

A hundred metres south is the 1911 **Old KL train station** (the KTM Komuter Railway's Kuala Lumpur station), with its spires, minarets, domes and arches. Similar in concept to the British-era train

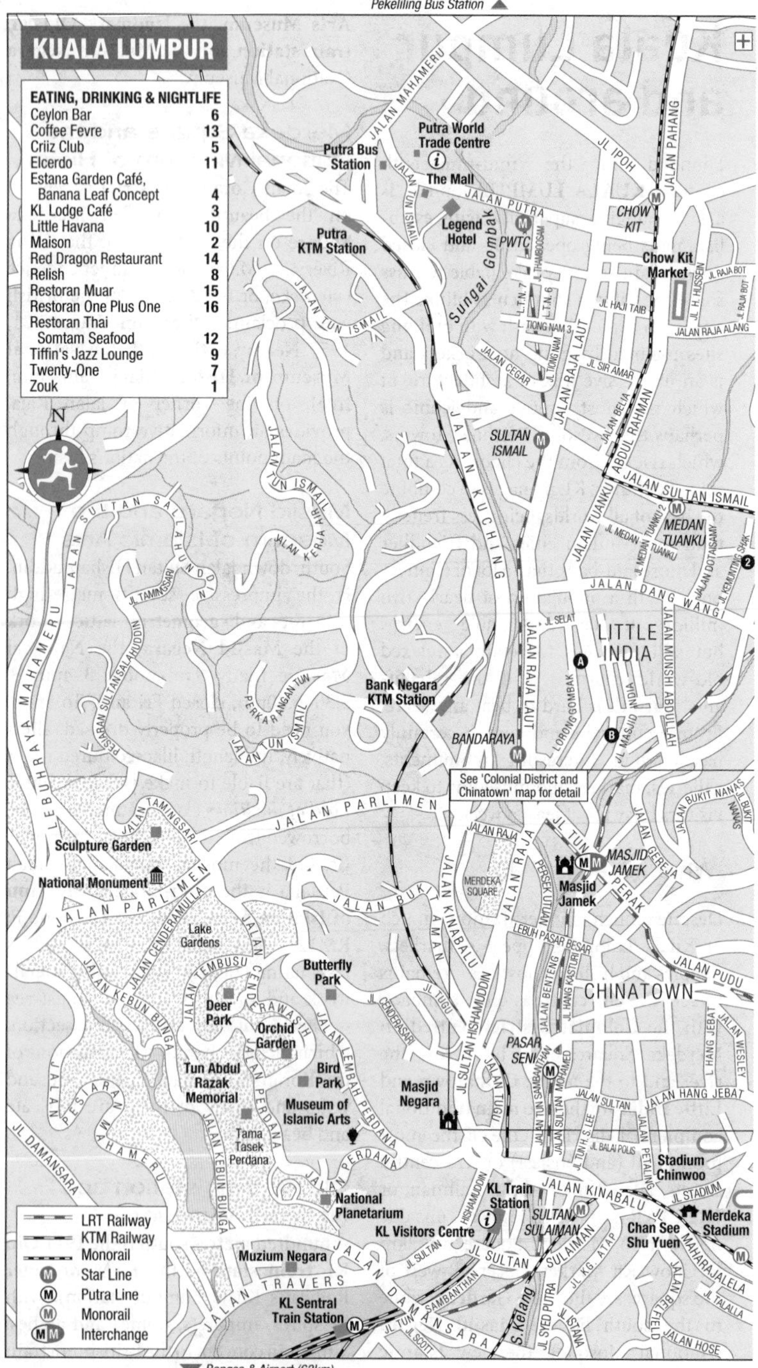
KUALA LUMPUR
EATING, DRINKING & NIGHTLIFE
Ceylon Bar 6
Coffee Fevre 13
Criiz Club 5
Elcerdo 11
Estana Garden Café, Banana Leaf Concept 4
KL Lodge Café 3
Little Havana 10
Maison 2
Red Dragon Restaurant 14
Relish 8
Restoran Muar 15
Restoran One Plus One 16
Restoran Thai Somtam Seafood 12
Tiffin's Jazz Lounge 9
Twenty-One 7
Zouk 1
Pekeliling Bus Station
Putra World Trade Centre
Putra Bus Station
The Mall
Legend Hotel
PWTC
Putra KTM Station
CHOW KIT
Chow Kit Market
SULTAN ISMAIL
MEDAN TUANKU
LITTLE INDIA
Bank Negara KTM Station
BANDARAYA
See 'Colonial District and Chinatown' map for detail
MASJID JAMEK
Masjid Jamek
MERDEKA SQUARE
CHINATOWN
PASAR SENI
Sculpture Garden
National Monument
Lake Gardens
Butterfly Park
Deer Park
Orchid Garden
Tun Abdul Razak Memorial
Bird Park
Museum of Islamic Arts
Masjid Negara
Tama Tasek Perdana
National Planetarium
KL Train Station
KL Visitors Centre
SULTAN SULAIMAN
Chan See Shu Yuen
Stadium Chinwoo
Merdeka Stadium
Muzium Negara
KL Sentral Train Station
Bangsa & Airport (63km)
LRT Railway
KTM Railway
Monorail
Star Line
Putra Line
Monorail
Interchange

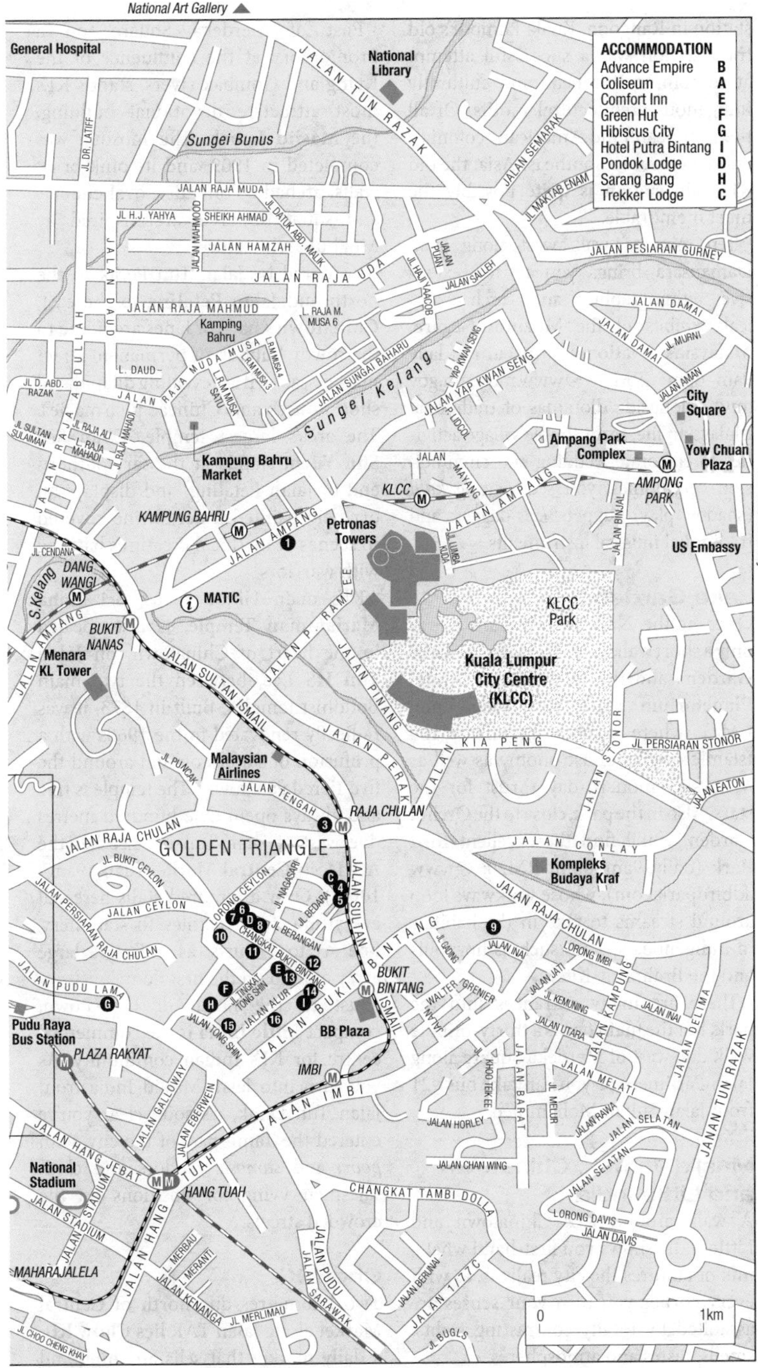
National Art Gallery
Immigration
Thai Embassy
ACCOMMODATION
Advance Empire B
Coliseum A
Comfort Inn E
Green Hut F
Hibiscus City G
Hotel Putra Bintang I
Pondok Lodge D
Sarang Bang H
Trekker Lodge C
General Hospital
National Library
Sungei Bunus
JALAN TUN RAZAK
JALAN SEMARAK
JL MAKTAB ENAM
JALAN PESIARAN GURNEY
JALAN RAJA MUDA
JL H.J. YAHYA
SHEIKH AHMAD
JALAN HAMZAH
JALAN MAHMOOD
JL DATUK ABD. MALIK
JALAN RAJA UDA
JL HAJI YAACOB
JALAN PUAN
JALAN SALLEH
JALAN RAJA MAHMUD
L. RAJA M. MUSA 6
JALAN DAUD
JALAN RAJA ABDULLAH
JL DR. LATIFF
Kamping Bahru
L. DAUD
JALAN RAJA MUDA MUSA
JL D. ABD. RAZAK
JL SULTAN SULAIMAN
JL RAJA ALI
L. RAJA MAHADI
JL RAJA MAHADI
JALAN SUNGAI BAHARU
Sungei Kelang
JALAN YAP KWAN SENG
L. YAP KWAN SENG
P. LIDCOL
JALAN DAMAI
JL MURNI
JALAN AMAN
City Square
Ampang Park Complex
Yow Chuan Plaza
AMPONG PARK
Kampung Bahru Market
KLCC
JALAN MAYANG
JALAN AMPANG
JALAN BINJAI
KAMPUNG BAHRU
Petronas Towers
US Embassy
JL CENDANA
DANG WANGI
S. Kelang
MATIC
JALAN P. RAMLEE
KLCC Park
BUKIT NANAS
Menara KL Tower
JALAN SULTAN ISMAIL
JALAN PINANG
Kuala Lumpur City Centre (KLCC)
JALAN KIA PENG
JALAN STONOR
JL PERSIARAN STONOR
JALAN EATON
JL PUNCAK
Malaysian Airlines
JALAN TENGAH
JALAN PERAK
RAJA CHULAN
JALAN RAJA CHULAN
GOLDEN TRIANGLE
JALAN CONLAY
Kompleks Budaya Kraf
JL BUKIT CEYLON
LORONG CEYLON
JL NAGASARI
JL BEDARA
JALAN CEYLON
CHANGKAT BUKIT BINTANG
JL BERANGAN
JALAN PERSIARAN RAJA CHULAN
JALAN BUKIT BINTANG
JL GADING
JALAN INAI
LORONG IMBI
JALAN PUDU LAMA
JL TINGKAT TONG SHIN
JALAN ALUR
BUKIT BINTANG
JALAN WALTER GRENIER
JALAN JATI
JL KEMUNING
JALAN KAMPUNG
JALAN DELIMA
JALAN TONG SHIN
BB Plaza
JALAN UTARA
Pudu Raya Bus Station
PLAZA RAKYAT
IMBI
JALAN IMBI
JL KHOO TEIK EE
JALAN BARAT
JL MELUR
JALAN MELATI
JALAN RAWA
JALAN SELATAN
JANAN TUN RAZAK
JALAN GALLOWAY
JALAN EBERWEIN
JALAN HORLEY
JALAN CHAN WING
JALAN HANG JEBAT
JALAN HANG TUAH
HANG TUAH
National Stadium
JALAN STADIUM
CHANGKAT TAMBI DOLLA
LORONG DAVIS
JALAN DAVIS
MAHARAJALELA
L. MERBAU
L. MERANTI
JALAN PUDU
JALAN SARAWAK
JALAN BERUNAI
JALAN 1/77C
JALAN KENANGA
JL MERLIMAU
JL BUGIS
JL CHOO CHENG KHAY
0
1km

station in Rangoon, Kuala Lumpur's old train station was a successful attempt at combining European and culturally indigenous architectural motifs. Of all the European (and American) colonial-era structures in Southeast Asia, the old KL train station is quite possibly the most memorable.

Ten minutes' walk west along Jalan Damansara brings you to the extensive ethnographic and archaeological exhibits of the **Muzium Negara, Malaysia's National Museum** (daily 9am–6pm; RM2; ⓦwww.museum.gov.my). Alongside dioramas of traditional Malaysian life, from simple village activities to elaborate wedding and circumcision ceremonies, you see *wayang kulit* (shadow play) puppets, *kris* daggers and traditional musical instruments.

### Lake Gardens

Once at the National Museum you're only a short walk from the extensive **Lake Gardens** and the interesting **National Planetarium** (Tues–Sun 10am–4pm; RM1), where displays illuminate the Islamic origins of astronomy as well as Malaysia's modern-day thrust for the stars. Also in the park, close to the Orchid Garden, you'll find the excellent **Bird Park** (daily 9am–6pm; RM20; ⓦwww.klbirdpark.com), whose walkways loop around streams to take in the habitats of indigenous species such as hornbills and the Brahminy Kite.

There are many entrances into the park, but the main one is a thirty-minute walk due west of Merdeka Square along Jalan Parlimen, or you can take bus #21 from Jalan Sultan Mohammed.

### Masjid Jamek, Chinatown and Little India

A walk around KL's Chinatown and Little India shows you first-hand what a mix of cultures the city really is, as with every corner you turn your senses are assaulted by totally contrasting sights, smells, tastes and atmospheres.

East of Merdeka Square, on a promontory at the confluence of the Klang and Gombak rivers, stands KL's most attractive devotional building, the **Masjid Jemek**. The mosque was completed in 1909, and its pink brick walls, arched colonnades, oval cupolas and squat minarets are inspired by Moghul architecture.

Bordered by Jalan Tun Perak to the north and **Jalan Petaling** to the east, **Chinatown**'s narrow lanes are home to the rowdy hubbub of permanent street markets, as well as revealing dilapidated shop-houses and Chinese pharmacies. The area's largest temple, **Chan See Shu Yuen**, stands at the far southern end of Jalan Petaling, and displays an ornately painted inner shrine covered in scenes of mythical creatures battling with warriors.

KL's main Hindu focus, **Sri Maha Mariamman Temple**, is also located in the heart of Chinatown, on **Jalan Tun HS Lee**, between the two main Buddhist temples. Built in 1873, it was radically renovated in the 1960s with a profusion of statues on and around the five-tiered gate tower. The temple is free and always open. One hundred metres due west of Jalan Tun HS Lee lies the Art Deco **Central Market** (daily 9am–10pm). Over a hundred stalls here sell everything from textiles to stationery, fine art to T-shirts, as well as a large array of food on the first floor.

Just to the north of Chinatown, compact **Little India** is the commercial centre for KL's Indian community. As you turn into Jalan Masjid India from Jalan Tun Perak, it's soon clear you've entered the Tamil part of the city, with *poori* and *samosa* vendors and cloth salesmen vying for positions on the crowded streets.

### Chow Kit

Two kilometres due north of Central Market along Jalan TAR lies **Chow Kit**, a daily market that sells anything and

everything. There are excellent hawker stalls here, a great variety of textiles and clothes, as well as fish, meat and vegetables.

### The Golden Triangle

From Merdeka Square, congested Jalan Tun Perak leads southeast to the Pudu Raya bus station, a kilometre further east of which is the fashionable consumer sector known as the **Golden Triangle**. Many of the city's expensive hotels, nightclubs and modern malls line the three main boulevards of Jalan Bukit Bintang, Jalan Imbi and Jalan Sultan Ismail, and a visit here is a must. If you can make it at night, when the glitz is turned up to max and the area is a glitterball of neon and expensive clothing, all the better. Its main landmarks are the lofty **Petronas Twin Towers** (Ⓦwww.petronastwintowers.com.my), which, at just over 490m high, were the tallest buildings in the world from 1996 until 2003; they form part of the **KLCC (Kuala Lumpur City Centre)** development on the northeast of the Golden Triangle Although until recently you couldn't access its great heights at all, now there are 1400 free tickets issued daily for the **Skybridge** (Tues–Sun 9am–7pm, closed Fri 1–2/30pm) connecting the two towers, 170m above the ground. To nab one, head to the ticket-counter in the basement early in the morning (around 8.30am should guarantee you a ticket on a weekday).

For those who suffer vertigo, there are plenty of other entertainments within

KLCC. Apart from some flash shopping and dining in the Suria complex within the lower levels of the towers, there's also the impressive **Aquaria KLCC** (daily 10am–9pm; RM40; Ⓦwww.klaquaria.com), situated in the Kuala Lumpur Convention Centre on the other side of the park. Highlights include a moving walkway inside a 90m acrylic tunnel, where you can watch sharks and rays swimming around, a hidden shipwreck slowly becoming part of the artificial coral reef, and feeding time, when divers hand-feed sharks, turtles and giant catfish.

If you feel that the Skybridge hasn't taken you quite high enough, head to the **Menara KL Tower**, which though 69m shorter than the Petronas towers, offers a **viewing deck** (daily 9am–10pm; RM20) at 276m. The tower is situated to the west of the Petronas towers, on the other side of Jalan Sultan Ismail.

## Arrival

**By bus and long-distance taxi** Buses from all over Peninsular Malaysia converge on one of four bus stations. Most long-distance buses pull into chaotic Pudu Raya bus station (Ⓣ03/230 0145) on Jl Pudu, just to the east of Chinatown. The ticket counters can be hard to find (you think you've found one, and it turns out to be selling fried chicken) – they are located along the back wall. Long-distance taxis also arrive at Pudu Raya, on the second floor above the bus ticket offices. Some buses from the east coast arrive at Putra bus station (Ⓣ03/4041 1295), to the northwest of the city centre, beside the Putra World Trade Centre. To head downtown, walk down Jalan Putra to The Mall shopping centre, where you should either catch a bus (#B110) to Central Market on Jl Hang Kasturi or walk a little further south to the Putra Komuter station for trains to Bank Negara station and the main train station, signposted as Kuala Lumpur station. Services from Kuantan and the interior arrive at Pekeliling bus station (Ⓣ03/4042 7988), at the northern end of Jl Raja Laut; from here, the Star LRT line connects to Chinatown. Klang bus station (Ⓣ03/3344 8066) on Jl Sultan Mohammed, just south of Central Market, is used by Klang Valley buses to and from Klang and Port Klang.

**By boat** The closest port to Kuala Lumpur is Port Klang, about 40km southwest of KL. The Klang bus stop is located about 1km away from the ferry terminal – it's best to take a taxi if you have lots of luggage and don't fancy the walk. From there, bus #710 goes to Kuala Lumpur's Puduraya Bus station. It's also possible to get a train from Port Klang into KL, as the train station is located just across the road from the ferry terminal. From there, it's a 1hr 10 min train ride on KTM Komuter, Klang Valley's train network, into KL Sentral.

**By train** Inter-city trains all stop at KL Sentral station, from where you can transfer to Kuala Lumpur's city rail systems: the LRT and KL Monorail.

**By air** The ultra-modern Kuala Lumpur International Airport (KLIA) at Sepang is 70km southwest of the centre. The new KLIA express trains make it quick and easy to get into town. There are two classes of trains, "express" and "transit", but the latter are more for local commuters. The KLIA express trains (5am–midnight, every 15–20min; 30min; RM35) terminate at Kuala Lumpur's new transportation hub, KL Sentral station, which conveniently connects inter-city trains with LRT and KL Monorail lines. This is by far the fastest and most efficient way into the city. Airport coaches (6.15am–midnight, every 30min; RM12, 15 or 18 depending on how far you want to go) leave from the bus terminus and take an hour to get to the centre. Follow the clearly marked signs from the Arrivals area at Level 4 to the escalators down to the concourse. The coach will drop you directly at your accommodation. Taxis into the centre cost around RM95–120, depending on the time of day – there's a surcharge from midnight until 6am. You'll need to buy a coupon at the taxi counter in the Arrivals hall; it's best to avoid the taxi touts, who may charge upwards of RM200, and have been known to demand payment in US, rather than Malaysian, dollars. All the major car rental companies have offices at the airport, and there are money exchange outlets here, too. Kuala Lumpur's Domestic Airport is the Low Cost Carrier Terminal, 20km from KLIA. Airport coaches (6am–midnight, every 30 min; RM9) take roughly 45min to the centre of town; alternatively you can get a taxi for around RM60. Taxi coupons are available in the Arrivals hall, where there are also car rental counters and money changers.

## Information

**Tourist information** There are lots of Tourist Information Centres in KL, each of which hands out excellent free maps and bus route details. The biggest is MATIC (Malaysian Tourist Information Complex) at 109 Jl Ampang (daily 9am–6pm; Ⓣ03/2164 3929,

ⓦwww.mtc.gov.my or ⓦwww.tourismmalaysia.gov.my), east of the centre, close to the junction with Jalan Sultan Ismail, which also hosts cultural performances. The KL Visitors Centre (Mon–Fri 8.30am–5pm, Sat 8.30am–12.45pm; ⓣ03/2274 0624) outside the old KL train station's west-side entrance, has a better selection of leaflets and more knowledgeable staff who can also help with accommodation. ⓦwww.kuala-lumpur-city-guide.com is full of useful information, including invaluable practical information such as the addresses of all the foreign embassies in KL.

**Tourist infoline** There is also a Tourist Assistance Infoline for general questions (ⓣ1300/885 776).

**Tourist Police** (ⓣ03/2146 0522) for more urgent matters.

## City transport

An efficient grid of city rail systems are attempting to ease KL's chronic traffic problem. Nearly everything passes through the new transportation hub, **KL Sentral** (ⓣ03/7625 8228), where inter-city trains and Kuala Lumpur's city rail systems interface. Electric notice boards inform passengers of exactly how many seconds remain until the train pulls in, and a squeaky automated voice reminds passengers to "smile, as the station is approaching!". Trains are infamously crowded at rush hour (about 5–7pm), and you may well have to wait for three or four trains to go past before you board. Despite the crush, however, people generally remain friendly and polite.

**LRT** The Light Rail Transit system, a 29-kilometre, mostly elevated metro network, is the most extensive of the city rail systems. There are two lines. LRT1, also known as Star LRT (ⓣ03/4294 2550), runs from Ampang, east of the centre, through the Masjid Jamek hub to Sentul Timur in the north of town and Sri Petaling in the south. LRT2, aka Putra LRT (ⓣ03/7625 8228), runs from west of the centre to the northeast, intersecting with the Star line at Masjid Jamek. Trains on both lines operate every five to fifteen minutes from 6am to midnight (from 70 sen).

**KL Monorail** The KL Monorail (ⓣ03/2267 9888) runs between KL Sentral north to Titiwangsa, making stops at eleven stations (6am–midnight, trains every 4 to 10min). It costs from RM1.20 to RM2.50 depending on distance travelled.

**Buses** ⓣ03/7727 2727. Run from 6am to midnight. Costs range from RM1.20 on the larger, municipal-owned Intrakota buses to 70 sen on the privately run City Liner ones. Fares go up to just above RM2 depending on the length of the journey; for example, you'll be paying RM2.20 to go to the Batu Caves, which, although outside KL, still come under the city bus system. If the bus has no conductor, you'll need the exact change. The main depots are Central Market, the Jalan Sultan Mohammed terminus (opposite Klang bus station), 100m south of the market, and Lebuh Ampang, on the northern edge of Chinatown.

**Komuter train** ⓣ03/2267 1200. Of limited use in central KL, but handy for sights outside the city. There are two lines – one from Rawang to Seremban (for Nilai), the other from Sentul to Port Klang (for Sumatra). Both connect at the central KL stations of Putra, Bank Negara and KL Sentral. Trains run at least every thirty minutes and tickets start at RM1; a RM5 day-ticket (valid Mon–Fri after 9.30am) allows unlimited travel.

**Travel cards** If you're planning to stay in KL for more than a week, consider getting an integrated bus and train card, called Touch And Go, available from the main LRT stations and at KL Sentral. The minimum price is RM20; each fare is electronically deducted from the sum on your card when you go through the turnstiles. The downside is the RM15 deposit for the card, which you're unlikely to see again on account of the form-filling required for a refund.

**Taxis** Fares start at RM2 and rise RM1 per kilometre; recommended cab companies are Mesra Taxis (ⓣ03/4042 1019), City Line (ⓣ03/9222 2828) and Sunlight Radio Teksi (ⓣ03/9057 1111). Many taxi drivers can't speak English, and some don't know their way around the city, so it's best to carry a map.

**TREAT YOURSELF**

Kuala Lumpur is teeming with masseurs keen to give you a foot rub, or more threateningly, to clean out your ears or put you through a course of holistic therapy. One of the best places to do this is **Old Asia** at 14 Jalan Bukit Bintang (ⓣ03/2143 9888). Friendly and professional staff deliver a deliciously relaxing assortment of treatments, including traditional foot massages, body massages (including Japanese Shiatsu massage), body scrubs, facials and the so-called "slimming massage", while you recline on one of their chairs in a luxurious and soothing atmosphere. Half-hour head massage RM25.

## Accommodation

Most travellers head for the hotels of Chinatown, or the budget options close to the Pudu Raya bus station. In general, the Chinese-run hotels tend to be slightly cleaner than the guesthouses, but they can also be somewhat sterile. If you're after a bit of atmosphere and the possibility of meeting other travellers, guesthouses are the way to go.

### Chinatown

**Backpackers Travellers Inn** 1st Floor, 60 Jl Sultan ⓣ03/2078 2473, ⓦwww.backpackerskl.com. Centrally located, with small, clean rooms – though overall it bears more than a passing resemblance to a public toilet. The rooftop bar is a highly convivial spot. The friendly staff go to great lengths to help guests, and provide numerous services. 24hr check-in. Dorm ❶; doubles ❸

**Backpackers Travellers Lodge** 1st Floor, 158 Jl Tun HS Lee ⓣ03/2031 0889. Slightly prison-like, but with a genial atmosphere and convenient location, 5 mins from Puduraya and KL Sentral. It also has internet access. Owner Stevie also runs excellent, inexpensive tours to Kuala Selangor Nature Park and the Village Kuantan fireflies in one trip. Dorm ❶, Doubles ❸, weekly rate available.

**Grocer's Inn** 78 Jl Sultan ⓣ03/2078 7906. Excellent centrally located accommodation, with clean, homely, yellow-painted rooms and lovely roof garden. Staff are cheerful and the communal areas are sunlit and laid-back. ❸

**Lok Ann** 113a Jalan Petaling ⓣ03/2078 9544. Neat, reasonable-value hotel with full facilities, though the rooms are rather charmless. ❸

**Red Dragon Hostel** 80 Jl Sultan ⓣ03/2078 9366, ⓔchinatownlim@yahoo.com. Located just a minute's walk from the buzz of Petaling St, this hostel is supremely convenient, if a little austere. Dorm ❶; doubles ❸.

**Shivani Budget Hotel** 52 Jl Tun HS Lee ⓣ03/2031 5150, ⓔ shivanibudgethotal@yahoo.com. This small hotel within walking distance of Pudu Raya is very basic, but it's clean and staff are friendly and eager to help. ❸

**Travellers Home (Full Moon)** 23 & 25 Jl Tun Tan Siew Sin ⓣ03/2031 6873, ⓔfullmoonhome@hotmail.com. Just south of Jl Tun Perak, this popular lodge includes a dorm, small rooms and a roof terrace. Despite being a little rundown, the space is light and spacious and staff are very friendly. Rates include breakfast. Bring a sarong – the staff expect you to provide your own sheets. Dorm ❶, Double ❷

### Little India and Jalan TAR

**Advance Empire** 48b Jl Masjid India ⓣ03/2693 6890. A good deal, if somewhat lacking in character, with en-suite and a/c rooms, and discounts for stays of over a month. ❹

**Coliseum** 98 Jl TAR ⓣ03/2692 6270. This place is now looking rundown, but still retains its colonial-era charm and saloon-bar atmosphere. The lobby bar is deliciously seedy. ❹

### Around Pudu Raya

**Anuja Backpackers Inn** 1st to 3rd Floor, 28 Jl Pudu ⓣ03/2026 6479. Opposite Hentian Pudu Raya, Anuja is beginning to look run down, but remains a good deal in the middle of the city. All rooms have a/c. Dorm ❶; double ❷

**Casavilla** 60 Jl Pudu ⓣ03/2078 6714, ⓔkameleontravellerslodge@hotmail.com. A sprawling guesthouse with a huge veranda in the front, perfect for socializing and having a game of pool. Bollywood films run constantly, and staff are polite and helpful. International calls available. ❷

**Hibiscus City** 90 Jl Pudu ⓣ03/2070 0780, ⓔhhcity@streamyx.com. Fairly bland, but very clean, with understated and polite staff. All rooms have a/c, and internet is available. The rooms with windows and bathroom are a good deal, at RM80 for a double. ❺

### THE JOY OF BEDBUGS

With a bit of luck, you'll never come across these charming scurrying friends. If you're not sure, however, it might be worth checking before you wake up covered in a raging rash of angry bites guaranteed to have you itching to hell and back. Have a look in the seams of the suspect mattress – if you can see any blood it's probably a good idea not to sleep on it. Try lifting the mattress up and letting it fall – this action, done relatively vigorously, should bring anything living in its cosy recesses to the surface so you can see it. Also remember that the bugs can get into your own clothes and sleeping stuff, so consider carefully before using your jumper as a pillow cover. Delightful.

**Kameleon Travellers Lodge** 35–37 Jl Pudu Lama ⓣ03/2070 7770, ⓔkameleontravellerslodge @hotmail.com. Run by the same people as *Casavilla*, so guests have access to the *Casavilla* services down the street. Rooms are run down and old-style but clean and convenient. ❸

**Kawana Tourist Inn** 68 Jalan Pudu Lama ⓣ03/2078 6714, ⓔkameleontravellerslodge @hotmail.com. Further rooms in the Casavilla/ Kameleon empire are neat, small and very good-value, only two minutes' walk from Pudu Raya bus station. Again, all the facilities of *Casavilla* are available. ❷

### The Golden Triangle

**Comfort Inn** 65 Changkat Bukit Bintang ⓣ03/2141 3636, ⓦwww.hotelcomfort.biz. If this is full, ask to be directed to their sister hotel, at 52 Tengkat Tong Shin (ⓣ03/2145 1818). ❹

**Green Hut** 48 Tengkat Tong Shin ⓣ03/2142 3339, or 019/380 5339, ⓦwww.thegreenhut.com. A backpacker's haven, with a relaxed atmosphere, pool table, internet and bags of information. It's a 15-minute walk from Pudu Raya bus station, opposite *Allson Genesis Hotel*. Single-sex dorms for 4, or mixed dorms for 12. ❷

**Hotel Putra Bintang** 72 Jl Changkat Bukit Bintang ⓣ03/2141 9228. Bog-standard but conveniently located, with friendly Malay staff. ❺

**Pondok Lodge** 20–1B Jl Changkat Bukit Bintang ⓣ03/2142 8449, ⓦwww.pondoklodge.com. Situated in a convenient central location, this guesthouse's rooms are somewhat cramped and a little airless, but this is more than made up for by lovely staff, good breakfast served on the roof terrace and the many other travellers you're guaranteed to meet. The slight drawback is pumping music from the next-door club – light sleepers should bring ear plugs. Rates include breakfast. ❷

**Sarang Bang** 21 Jl Tengkat Tong Shin ⓣ03/2144 6437. Located above a Korean restaurant, with free internet and mixed dorms. Dorm ❸; doubles ❸.

**Trekker Lodge** 1 Jl Angsoka, off Jl Nagasari ⓣ03/2142 4633, or 016/263 1410, ⓦwww .thetrekkerlodge.com. Run by the people behind *Green Hut*, this is a chilled-out guesthouse popular with travellers. Staff are welcoming and helpful, rooms small but clean. Single-sex dorms for ❹, or mixed dorms for 12. ❷

## Eating

The best value (and perhaps best tasting) Chinese food in KL is to be found at the foodstalls on Jalan Alur, just east of the city centre, and the atmosphere is also fantastic. A roaring Indian food market can be found on Jalan Masjid India. Changkat Bukit Bintang serves every nationality of food imaginable, from Thai and Japanese to Russian. The trendiest area in KL to eat and drink is the expat area of **Bangsar**, around 4km west of the centre (take any Bangsar bus from the Central Market, or the Monorail to Bangsar station). All restaurants listed here are open daily from 10am until midnight, unless otherwise stated.

### Chinatown and Little India

**Annexe Nasi Kandar** Jl Benteng, just behind Central Market. Large self-service institution playing tinny music, with plenty of outdoor seating and good, varied food for around RM7 per main dish.

**C U There Café** 29M Jl Cheng Lock, opposite Kota Raya Shopping Complex. Weirdly cutesy if slightly dingy little café with handprints and writing all over the walls, serving standard Chinese-style cooking and coffees. Mains around RM6.

**Central Market** 1st and 2nd Floors, Jl Hang Kasturi. Superb Malay stalls on the top floor where plates of *nasi campur* cost just RM2.50.

**Lakshmi Villas** Lebuh Ampang, Little India. On the edge of Chinatown, this raucous, basic café serves the best South Indian food in KL. The ground floor serves various delicious *dosas*; the first floor has an eye-wateringly large selection of sweets and specializes in banana-leaf curries, a bargain at around RM6 for two. Daily 7.30am–8.30pm.

**Meidi-ya bakery** Jl Cheng Lock. Freshly baked, strangely delicious peculiarities like shredded chicken rolls and pineapple buns. A great place to stock up before a long bus or train trip. Roll RM 1.50.

**Restoran Santa** 9 Jl Tun HS Lee (Little India end). Nicknamed the "chapati house", a lively place, best at midday to mid-afternoon, with delicious *chapatis* and curries for around RM5.

**Sangeetha Vegetarian Restaurant** 65 Jl Lebuh Ampang. The delicious smells wafting from this understated boothed restaurant will be enough to tempt anyone to enter. The place is scrupulously clean and staff are courteous in the extreme. Curries around RM7.

**Shukran** Corner of Jl Pudu and Jl Cheng Lock, just opposite the roundabout. A noisy corner restaurant with lots of windows for looking out onto the chaos of Pudu Raya, popular with locals and serving simple Chinese and Indian dishes. RM8 for mains.

### Golden Triangle

**Coffee Fevre** Replica Inn, 64 Jl Changkat Bukit Bintang. For anyone craving a big Western breakfast, the breakfast buffet, inclusive of tea or coffee and juice, is a great deal at RM9.90.

The covered veranda is also an ideal place for evening people-watching.

**Elcerdo** 43 and 45 Changkat Bukit Bintang ⓣ03/2145 0511, ⓦwww.elcerdokl.com. If you fancy a bit of "nose to tail eating", head to this place, which specializes in pork – and a lot of it. Roasted suckling pig and smoked pork shoulder are among the delicacies on the menu, and there are also non-pork options, such as paella with seafood.

**Estana Garden Café, Banana Leaf Concept** Jl Sultan Ismail. Populated by local businessmen at lunchtime and packed full of locals at any other time, this restaurant is split into two open levels, with fountains downstairs and shisha pipes upstairs. *Nasi goreng* RM7.

**KL Lodge Café** 16 Jl Pudu. The hotel itself is being totally overhauled so is currently closed, but the buzzy and bizarrely resort-themed poolside café can still be enjoyed, with palm leaves overhead and three-course meals for RM21.

**Red Dragon Restaurant** Corner of Changkat Bukit Bingtang and Jl Alur. Raucous 24-hour Chinese restaurant, with outdoor seating, tasty food and efficient service.

**Relish** 22 Changkat Bukit Bintang. Possibly the only place in Malaysia where a burger-craving can be genuinely satisfied. Chic and friendly, this is also a great place to sit out front and watch the multi-national world of Bukit Bintang go by. Beef, chicken or veg burger in any imaginable form RM17.

**Restoran Muar** 6G Tengkat Tong Shin. Friendly family-run restaurant serving home-cooked Muar cuisine with specialities such as crispy dragon-tongue fish and deep-fried salted squid. The set menu is a great deal at RM5.80 per person including limitless Chinese tea.

**Restoran One Plus One** Jl Alur. Savour a wide variety of delicious steamed *dim sum* here, washed down either with fresh fruit juice (the cheapest you'll find on Jalan Alur), or a cold beer.

**Restoran Thai Somtam Seafood** 88 Changkat Bukit Bintang. A basic place with wooden seats and overhead lighting, serving excellent Thai food. Popular with locals and foreigners alike, mains are around RM12, and staff are helpfully flexible with ingredients.

## Bangsar

**Alexis Bistro** 29 Jl Telawi Tiga ⓣ03/2284 2880. Big helpings of beautifully presented local and Western food, often with an upscale twist, for KL's growing cappuccino class. Excellent pastries, too, at a buzzy hangout where jazz singers entertain. Free magazines, open noon–midnight, mains RM15–20.

**Caffé 1920** Lot F12 and 13A, First Floor, Bangsar Shopping Village, ⓦwww.caffe1920.com. Small Italian chain café serving coffee and desserts, including *tiramisu* and various gateaux, along with light pasta dishes. Set (generous) brunch RM17. Daily 10am–10pm.

**Lanna** 17 Jl Telawi Dua. Delicious Thai cuisine served in sumptuous settings, with fountains and attentive staff. RM15–20 for main dishes.

**Restoran Sri Nirwana** 43 Jl Telawi 3. A great cheap option in Bangsar, with massive and tasty banana-leaf meals at RM4 and plenty of buzzy outdoor seating.

**Telawi Street Bistro** 1 and 3 Jl Telawi 3, ⓦwww.telawi.com.my. Enter here and you'll imagine you're in any trendy Western city in the world. Perhaps not ideal for those looking for an authenic Malay experience, but for long-time travellers needing a break and a taste of Western food, this is the place. Pasta dishes, pizzas and burgers around RM20. Open until 1am.

# Nightlife and entertainment

Most bars are open from noon until midnight. The music played at clubs is mostly US house and the lighter styles of techno. Entrance charges are around RM20 including a drink. It's worth checking out *KLue* (RM5, ⓦwww.klue.com.my), the local listings magazine that is chockablock with events, new venues, classifieds and more. It's available from newsagents and news-stands. *KL Lifestyle* (ⓦwww.kl-lifestyle.com.my; free) is also worth a look – it's available in hotels and bars. The best place to see traditional theatre and music is at the Malaysian Tourist Information Complex (MATIC), 109 Jalan Ampang (ⓣ03/2164 3929), which does costumed shows – call for show times.

## Bars and live music

**Ceylon Bar** 20–2 Changkat Bukit Bintang, ⓦwww.theceylonbar.com. A relaxed set-up with chatty staff and an intimate bar area opening up onto a lounge-style veranda. Expect to meet plenty of revelling expats and travellers. Mon & Wed Sat 5pm–1am, Sun 11am–1am.

**D'Haven** 33 Jalan Telawi 3, Bangsar ⓣ03/2287 4282. Lavishly decorated with red lanterns, gold-curtained cubicles and traditional drums serving as tables, this place is popular with the sophisticated ex-pats of KL and a good place to enjoy the high-life. Cocktails RM18, snacks such as crispy squid RM18. Open until 1am weekdays, 2am weekends.

**Little Havana** Changkat Bukit Bintang. Unpretentious cigar bar downstairs with a club

TREAT YOURSELF

**Hush** 61 and 63 Jalan Telawi 3, Bangsar. Newly opened linen-tableclothed bar and restaurant with an exclusive feel but altogether friendly staff. Open for brunch, pastries and coffee in the day, or dinner and cocktails till late in the evening. Open until 2am, mains RM17.

upstairs featuring Friday night salsa. Also serves Latin food at around RM12 for mains.

**Reggae Bar KL** 158 Ground Floor, Jl Tun H.S. Lee, Ⓦwww.reggaebarkl.com.my. A shrine to Bob Marley, this dark and seedy bar plays reggae until 3am, and is usually full of backpackers from the *Backpackers Travellers Lodge* upstairs.

**Tiffin's Jazz Lounge** 4th Floor, Starhill Gallery, 181 Jalan Bukit Bintang. Sophisticated and slightly eccentric in equal measure, the cocktails and jazz on offer in this darkly atmospheric lounge make for an intoxicating mixture.

### Clubs

**Club 11:15** 11 and 15 Jalan Telawi 2, Bangsar. Large, atmospherically dark bar and club with outdoor seating, playing largely R&B music to a mixed expat and local crowd. Open until 2am, no cover charge.

**Criiz Club** Jl Sultan Ismail. A low-key place popular with locals, playing live music every night. Entrance RM15. Open until 1am.

**Maison** 8 Jalan Yap Ah Shak Ⓦwww.maison .com.my. An unexpectedly spacious club housed within a row of shop buildings with an energetic, fun-filled atmosphere.

**Twenty-One** 20-1 Changkat Bukit Bintang. Chic, modern bar and club with restaurant downstairs and a pumping dance floor upstairs. Open until 3am.

**Zouk** 113 Jl Ampang Ⓦwww.zoukclub.com.my. A complete clubbing complex to suit all tastes. The KL branch of this Singapore-based megaclub comprises a two-level beach-themed venue, the smaller bar *Loft* and a 70s-style cheesy club, *Velvet Underground*. Entry to the main *Zouk* venue and *Velvet Underground* RM45, Loft only RM20. Open until 3am.

## Shopping

KL is full of shopping malls, particularly in the Golden Triangle; most are open daily from 10am to 10pm. Elsewhere, shops are usually open daily from 9am to 6pm. A wander around KL's many and varied markets is also a great way to soak up some of the atmosphere of the city.

### Markets

**Central Market** Jl Hang Kasturi. Among the most popular, selling a fair amount of tat in a covered area. Quite innocuous, but nice and air-conditioned.

**Jalan Petaling Market** Daily 9am–10pm. Near Central Market, covered walkways, crowded and lively with people shouting about their wares. Everything seems to jangle and glitter. Stalls are usually open to a bit of haggling, but don't take kindly to being pushed too far.

**Chow Kit market** Jl Haji Hussein, off Jalan TAR Daily 9am–5pm. Quite an experience, with its warren of stalls selling everything from animals' brains to quality *batik* textiles.

### Handicrafts and batik

**Kompleks Budaya Kraf** Jalan Conlay, beside the MISC Museum. Although the wares here aren't as tastefully arranged as they could be and the place has a slight warehouse feel, it does offer all of Malaysia's crafts under one roof.

**Peter Hoe** 2nd Floor, Old Lee Rubber Building, Jl Tun HS Lee. A stone's throw from Central Market, this is a more upmarket outlet specializing in beautiful bags, batik shirts and sarongs, as well as locally made and Indonesian crafts. There's also a nice café.

### English-language books

**Basheer Book Store** 3rd Floor, BB Plaza, Jalan Bukit Bintang.

**MPH** Jl Telawi Lima, Bangsar Ⓦwww.mph.com.my.

### Shopping malls

**BB Plaza** Jl Bukit Bintang. Offering excellent deals on cameras, electronic equipment, shoes and much else besides.

**Lot 10 Shopping Centre** Junction of Jl Bukit Bintang and Jl Sultan Ismail. An awesomely large complex specializing in designer clothes, sportswear and music. Prices aren't all that low, but you can get hold of Western brands (Topshop, Ted Baker, Next and so on) that are like gold dust anywhere else in Asia.

**Bangsar Village** 1 Jalan Telawi 1, Bangsar. This new shopping centre is almost intimidatingly chic and shiny, with marble floors and a beautifully planned interior strolled by KL's well-turned out and beautiful. Every possible commercial fashion and foodie delight, from Starbucks to Gucci, is available here.

## Directory

**Airline offices** Most airlines have offices in and around the Golden Triangle. Major airlines include: Aeroflot, Level 17, Menara HLA, 3 Jl Kia Peng ⓣ03/2141 6000; Air France, Unit 106, 1st Floor Grand Plaza Park Royal, Jl Sultan Ismail ⓣ03/2142 7291; American Airlines, Angkasa Raya Building, 123 Jl Ampang ⓣ03/2078 1168; Berjaya Air, Level 6, Berjaya Times Square, 1 Jalan Imbi ⓣ03/2141 0088 extn 103, ⓦwww.berjaya-air.com; British Airways, 8 Jl Perak ⓣ03/2167 6188; Cathay Pacific, Level 22, Menara IMC, Jl Sultan Ismail ⓣ03/2078 3377; China Airlines, Level 3, Amoda Building, 22 Jl Imbi ⓣ03/2148 9417; Delta Air Lines, UBN Tower, 10 Jl P Ramlee ⓣ03/2691 5490; Emirates, Lot 25, 1st Floor, *Shangri-La Hotel* Annex, UBN Tower, Jl P Ramlee ⓣ03/2072 5288; Garuda Indonesia Airways, 1st Floor, Angkasa Raya Building, 123 Jl Ampang ⓣ03/2162 2811; Japan Airlines, 20th Floor, Menara Citibank, Jl Ampang, Menara Lion ⓣ03/2161 1722; KLM Dutch Airlines, Shop 7, Ground Floor, President House, Jl Sultan Ismail ⓣ03/2711 9811; Lufthansa Malaysia, Kenanga International, Jl Sultan Ismail, ⓣ03/2052 3428; Malaysia Airlines (MAS), MAS Building, Jalan Sultan Ismail ⓣ03/2161 0555; Singapore Airlines, 10th Floor, Menara Multi-Purpose, Capital Square, 8 Jl Munshi Abdullah ⓣ03/2699 6381; Thai International Airways, Wisma Goldhill Building, 67 Jl Raja Chulan ⓣ03/2031 1900; Vietnam Airlines, Lot 146, 1st Floor, Wisma, ⓣ03/2141 2416.

**Banks and exchange** Main branches are: Bank Bumiputra, 6 Jalan Tun Perak ⓣ03/2693 1722; HSBC, 2 Lebuh Ampang, Little India ⓣ03/2070 0744; Standard Chartered Bank, 2 Jalan Ampang ⓣ03/2072 6555. Almost all of their branches change money (Mon–Fri 10am–4pm, Sat 9am–12.30pm), but you get better rates from official moneychangers, of which there are scores in the main city areas; the kiosk below the GPO on Jalan Sultan Hishamuddin also gives good rates.

**Car rental** All main companies have offices at the airport; or contact Avis, Angkasa Raya, Jalan Ampang ⓣ03/2144 4487, ⓦwww.avis.com; Budget, 29 Jalan Yap Kwan Seng ⓣ03/2142 4693; Hertz, International Complex, Jl Sultan Ismail ⓣ03/2148 6433, ⓦwww.hertz.com.my; National Car Rental, 9th Floor, Menara Bausted, 69 Jl Raja Chulan ⓣ03/2148 0522.

**Embassies and consulates** Australia, Jalan Yap Kwan Seng ⓣ03/2146 5555; Brunei, 19th Floor, Menara Tan & Tan, 207 Jl Tun Razak, ⓣ03/2161 2800; Cambodia, 46 Jl U-Thant ⓣ03/4257 1157; Canada, 17th Floor, Menara Tan & Tan, 207 Jl Tun Razak ⓣ03/2718 3333; China, 229 Jl Ampang ⓣ03/2142 8495; France, 196 Jl Ampang ⓣ03/2053 5500; Indonesia, 233 Jl Tun Razak ⓣ03/2145 2011; Laos, 108 Jl Damai ⓣ03/4251 1118; Netherlands, 7th Floor, The Ampwalk, South Block, 218 Jalan Ampang ⓣ03/2168 6200; New Zealand, Menara IMC, 8 Jl Sultan Ismail ⓣ03/2078 2533; Philippines, 1 Jl Changkat Kia Peng ⓣ03/2848 9989; Thailand, 206 Jl Ampang ⓣ03/2148 8222; UK, 185 Jl Ampang ⓣ03/2170 2200; USA, 376 Jl Tun Razak ⓣ03/2168 5000; Vietnam, 4 Persiaran Stonor ⓣ03/2148 8060.

**Emergencies** Dial ⓣ999 for ambulance, police or fire. For the tourist police, call ⓣ03/2140 6590.

**Hospitals and clinics** General Hospital, Jalan Pahang ⓣ03/2615 5555, ⓦwww.hkl.gov.my; Assunta Hospital, Petaling Jaya ⓣ03/7782 3443, ⓦwww.assunta.com.my; Pantai Medical Centre, Jl Pantai, off Jalan Bangsar, Bangsar ⓣ03/2282 5077, ⓦwww.pantai.com.my; Tung Shin Hospital, 102 Jl Pudu ⓣ03/2072 1655, ⓦwww.tungshinhospital.com.my. There are 24hr casualty wards at all of the above.

**Immigration** Block 24G, Pusat Pentadbiran Kerajaan Persekutuan, Putrajaya (Mon–Fri 9am–4.30pm; ⓣ03/8880 1000). This office deals with visa extensions.

**Internet** There are hundreds of internet cafés throughout KL, most of which charge RM3 /hr. There's also internet access in most guesthouses. Free WiFi is available in many cafés, bars and guesthouses.

**Pharmacies** Kota Raya Pharmacy, 1st Floor, Kota Raya Plaza Complex Jalan Cheng Lock, Chinatown; Watson's Pharmacy, on the crossroads between Jl Cheng Lock and Jl Sultan.

**Police** The main tourist police station, where you must report stolen property and claim your insurance form, is 1PK, Jalan Hang Tuah (ⓣ03/2140 6590). It's opposite the old Pudu Jail.

**Post office** Poste restante at the GPO on Jalan Sultan Hishamuddin, opposite Central Market (Mon–Fri 8am–5pm).

**Telephone services** The cheapest places to make international calls are the Telekom Malaysia offices; the largest branch is in Wisma Jothi, Jalan Gereja (daily Mon–Sun 8.30am–9pm).

**Travel agencies** MSL Travel, 66 Jl Putra ⓣ03/4042 4722, ⓦwww.msltravel.com; Reliance Travel, 12 Jl Yap Kwen Seng ⓣ03/2162 8181, ⓦwww.reliancetravel.com; STA, 5th Floor, Magnum Plaza, 128 Jl Pudu ⓣ03/2148 9800, ⓦwww.statravel.com.my.

## Moving on

**By bus and long-distance taxi** Most long-distance buses leave from Pudu Raya bus station

## TRAVELLING BY BOAT TO INDONESIA

You can catch a ferry to Dumai or Tanjung Balai, both in Sumatra, Indonesia from **PORT KLANG**, 38km southwest of KL in Selangor State. To Dumai, there are daily departures at 9am and 10.30am, and the trip takes just under three hours (RM100). To Tanjung Balai, there are daily departures at 11am (apart from Sundays), and the trip takes three and a half hours (RM120). Tickets are available at the jetty, or from *Aero Speed* (for Tanjung Balai; ⓣ03/165 2545/3073) or *Indomal Express* (for Dumai; ⓣ03/167 1058). You can get a visa on arrival at Dumai, but those entering at Tanjung Balai must arrange an Indonesian visa in advance. The best way to get to Port Klang is on the Komuter train (every 30min; 1hr 10min; RM2.20) from KL's train station, which stops directly opposite the main jetty. Bus 58 from Klang bus station on Jalan Sultan Mohammed in KL (hourly; 1hr) stops 200m further along the road. The jetty complex has a small cafe and moneychanger.

(ⓣ03/2070 0145) on Jl Pudu, just to the east of Chinatown. The buses leave from ground-floor bays, and ticket offices are on the floor above, along with a left-luggage office (daily 6am–midnight; RM2). Some buses also operate from outside the terminus – these are legitimate, but may only leave when full. For some destinations you'll need one of the other bus stations: Putra (ⓣ03/4042 9530), near the Putra World Trade Centre, for the east coast; Klang (ⓣ03/3344 8066) on Jl Sultan Mohammed for Klang and Port Klang; and Pekeliling (ⓣ03/4042 1256) at the northern end of Jalan Raja Laut, for Kuantan and the interior.

**Pudu Raya station** to: Alor Setar (9 daily; 9hr); Butterworth (every 30min; 7hr); Cameron Highlands (hourly; 4hr 30min); Ipoh (every 30min; 4hr); Johor Bahru (5 daily; 6hr); Kuala Perlis (6 daily; 9hr); Lumut (8 daily; 5hr 30min); Melaka (every 30min; 2hr); Mersing (1 daily; 7hr); Penang (every 30min; 8hr); Singapore (7 daily; 7hr).

**Pekeliling station** to: Jerantut (4 daily; 3hr 30min); Kuala Lipis (4 daily; 4hr); Mentakab (hourly; 1hr 15min).

**Putra station** to: Kota Bharu (8 daily; 10hr); Kuala Terengganu (3 daily; 7hr); Kuantan (every 30min; 5hr); Temerloh (hourly; 3hr).

**By taxi** Long-distance taxis also use Pudu Raya, arriving and departing from the second floor above the bus ticket offices.

**By ferry** see box above.

**By train** Kuala Lumpur's colonial-era Moorish railway station has been replaced by a new inter-city train station located at nearby KL Sentral. The station's information kiosk (daily during office hours; ⓣ03/2279 8888 for information and reservation) has up-to-date train timetables. You must book, preferably at least three days ahead, for the night sleeper to Singapore or Butterworth; most large hotels can do this for you.

**Destinations:** Alor Setar (1 daily; 13hr 10min); Butterworth (1 daily; 10hr 40min); Gemas (6 daily; 2hr 40min–4hr 10min); Ipoh (1 daily; 5hr 30min); Johor Bahru (4 daily; 5hr 30min–8hr); Singapore (4 daily; 7–9hr); Tapah Rd (1 daily; 4hr).

**By air** For domestic and most international flights, check-in is at KL Sentral, the city's new transportation hub. Check in at the KLIA counter one and a half hours before your flight and then take the new KLIA Express trains for the thirty-minute ride to the airport (RM35). The easiest way to get to the airport is to call a taxi from your hotel (RM70–80); taxis flagged down on the street tend not to want to go out that far. Most of the larger hostels can help arrange transport to the airport for around the same price. Otherwise, call the airport coach service (ⓣ1800/880 737), preferably giving a day's notice, to ensure you're picked up from your hotel in good time. If you're taking a flight with the tiny Berjaya Air to Pulau Tioman, Pulau Redang or Pulau Pangkor, you'll need to get to Sultan Abdul Aziz Shah Airport, 20km west of the city centre.

**Destinations:** Alor Setar (2 daily; 50min); Bandar Seri Begawan, Brunei (1 daily; 2hr 20min); Ipoh (2 daily; 35min); Johor Bahru (4 daily; 45min); Kota Bharu (4 daily; 50min); Kota Kinabalu (10 daily; 1hr 45 min); Kuala Terengganu (3 daily; 45min); Kuantan (4 daily; 40min); Kuching (10 daily; 1hr 45 min); Miri (4 daily; 2hr 15min); Penang (11 daily; 45min); Pulau Langkawi (4 daily; 55min); Pulau Tioman (2 daily; 45min); Sibu (1 daily; 2hr); Singapore (10 daily; 55min), as well as many other destinations.

## DAY-TRIPS FROM KL

The biggest attractions **around KL** are north of the city, where limestone peaks rise up out of the forest and the roads narrow as you pass through small kampungs (villages). There is dramatic scenery just 13km from the city, where the Hindu shrine at the **Batu Caves** attracts enough visitors to make it one of Malaysia's main tourist attractions. Further north, the **Orang Asli Museum** offers a fascinating insight into the Peninsula's native inhabitants. Southwest of KL, a little further north along the coast from Port Klang where ferries go to Sumatra (see p.505), **Kuala Selangor Nature Park** and the **fireflies at Village Kuantan** are worth a visit.

### The Batu Caves

Long before you reach the entrance to the **Batu Caves**, you can see them ahead: small, black holes in the vast limestone hills, 13km north of the city centre. Since 1891, the caves have sheltered Hindu shrines, and today they're surrounded by shops selling religious paraphernalia. By the time you leave there's a strong possibility the endlessly repetitive and extremely loud, clanging Hindu music might be doing your head in. The caves are always packed with visitors, never more so than during the three-day Thaipusam festival held at the beginning of every year.

To the left of the staircase up to the main **Temple Cave**, a small path strikes off to the **Art Gallery** (daily 8.30am–7pm; RM1), which contains dozens of striking multi-coloured statues and murals, portraying scenes from the Hindu scriptures. At the top of the main staircase, **Subramaniam Swamy Temple** (daily 8am–7pm) is set deep in a huge cave, its walls lined with idols representing the six lives of Lord Subramaniam. The whole place is swarming with monkeys and they can turn vicious if you tease them with food. To get to the caves, catch bus 11d (RM2, 30min) from the Bangkok Bank, outside Central Market.

### The Orang Asli Museum

Located 24km north of the city in the quiet village of Gombak, KL's **Orang Asli Museum** (Sun–Thurs 9am–5.30pm; free; ⓦwww.jheoa.gov.my) provides a fine illustration of the cultural richness of the Orang Asli ("the first people"), Malaysia's indigenous inhabitants. Orang Asli groups are found in just about every part of the region, many of them maintaining a virtually pre-industrial lifestyle and pursuing their traditional occupations in some isolation. Bus #174 leaves from Lebuh Ampang street in Little India (RM2, every 30min; 1hr); the museum stop is beside two rundown shops, but ask the driver to tell you when you've arrived.

### Kuala Selangor Nature Park and the fireflies

North of Klang is the small **Taman Alam Kuala Selangor Nature Park** (ⓣ03/289 2294; ⓦwww.mns.org.my), set in partial primary rainforest; the trails are short (taking between 15min and 2 hours to walk) but lead to hides that make perfect **bird-viewing** spots. The park recently set up a breeding programme for the endangered milky stork, and several now live on the lake. The park is accessible by bus 141 from KL's Pudu Raya bus station (hourly; RM5.40, 7am–9.30pm). Spartan but clean chalets in the park are available (❸), and there is also accommodation in nearby Kuala Selangor town at *Hotel Kuala Selangor*, 88 Main St (ⓣ03/3289 2709; ❷). It's basic and not particularly thrilling, but clean.

To view the **fireflies** for which the area is so famous, take a taxi (RM20 return from Kuala Selangor – there's no bus) to **Village Kuantan** ten kilometres away. It costs RM10 to take a ride in a battery-powered *sampan* (small boat) along the river, Sungei Kuantan, at around 8pm, to see the thousands of flies glowing on the riverbank. If you're looking for an unusual and implausibly romantic evening around Kuala Lumpur, this may just fit the bill.

# The west coast

The west coast of the Malaysian Peninsula, from Kuala Lumpur north to the Thai border, is the most industrialized and densely populated part of the country. Chinese towns punctuate the route north, and many of them were founded on the tin economy. This is also the area in which the British held most sway, attracted by the political prestige of controlling such a strategic trading region. Most visitors are too intent on the beckoning delights of Thailand or the lure of the capital to bother stopping at anything other than the major destinations, and there are plenty of ways to **cross into Thailand** – by boat, bus or train. You can get Thai visas in **Georgetown**, the vibrant and stimulating capital of the island of **Penang**, which rewards a few days' stay and is a magnet for travellers of all budgets. But before you leave Malaysia or strike on to KL, you can chill out happily at the **Cameron Highlands** hill station, or sun yourself on the pretty white-sand shores of popular **Pulau Langkawi**, a large and increasingly upmarket island.

## CAMERON HIGHLANDS

Amid the lofty peaks of Banjaran Titiwangsa, the various outposts of the **Cameron Highlands** (1524m) form Malaysia's most extensive hill station, and have been used as a weekend retreat since the 1920s. The hype about the highlands is more than justified – the rolling hills are lush and tranquil in the extreme, and the bright, pure colour of the sky and tea plantations alone is enough to make anybody feel considerably rejuvenated. There's also an appealing sense of community here and locals and travellers alike are laid-back and happy-go-lucky. While **Brinchang** is the principal settlement for locals, **Tanah Rata** is the backpackers' centre, boasting budget accommodation, travel information, plenty of cheap places to eat and conveniences such as internet access. Beware that it's considerably colder here than in the lowlands, and though this is pleasant, it might be wise to bring a sleeping bag as nights get chilly. **Tapah** is the main access point for the region, from where you can reach the other towns, though if you're coming from KL, backpacker hostels can arrange tickets for a direct coach to Tanah Rata (RM14).

### What to see and do

There's plenty to keep you occupied in the Highlands, and activities can either be embarked on alone, armed with the maps and information available at all guesthouses, or as part of a tour. There are **strawberry farms** (8am–6pm), where you can pick your own (at a price); the **Taman Rama Rama butterfly farm** (8am–6pm; RM5), where wonders such as leaf insects and cobras abound; **honey bee farms** (8am–7pm) and the BOH (Best Of the Highlands) **tea plantation.** Guides from local **Orang Asli villages** can also demonstrate how to use a **blow pipe** – this traditional form of hunting uses darts dipped in frog and snake poison, and with the right combination can kill a tiger in ten minutes.

You can also go **jungle trekking**, taking in some of the most spectacular scenery in Malaysia. These can be attempted with the black-and-white sketch map (free from any guesthouse), but some of the trails no longer exist and the ones which do are sometimes badly signposted. As people have been lost in the Highlands for days in recent years it's advisable to take a guide if you want to do any extensive trekking. If you want to attempt any unofficial routes, you must go with a guide from the tourist office and get a permit from the District Office, just north of Tanah Rata (see p.508).

Always inform someone, preferably at your hotel, where you are going and what time you expect to be back. On longer trips, take warm clothing, water, a torch and a cigarette lighter or matches should you get lost. On both the shorter and longer treks, you'll be able to enjoy swimming in **waterfalls** and, if your visit is around January/ February, you can see the infamous and huge (probably the largest you'll ever see in your life) **red flower**, the *Rafflesia arnoldii*, commonly known as the Malaysian monster flower.

If you want to be given a run for your money by a 65-year-old, a tour with **Uncle Kali** is recommended and can be organized through *Kang Hotel and Restaurant*, on Main Street. He knows the surrounding area like the back of his hand, and a jungle trek with him is guaranteed to be tough and beautiful in equal measure.

The best tour operator is the Golden Highland Tours, run by the irrepressible Kumar and his family. Headquarters are located on Main Street next to the post office (ⓣ019/4232 282, ⓦwww.gohighadventure.com), but most guest-houses will be able to arrange tours through them for you. Tours are around RM25 for a half day.

### Tanah Rata

Meaning "Flat Land" in Malay, **TANAH RATA** is the traveller's haven of the Cameron Highlands. Many walks originate here, a couple of waterfalls and three reasonably high mountain peaks are all within hiking distance, and the town itself is festooned with white balustraded buildings, flowers and parks. Comprising little more than one street (officially called Jalan Pasar, but usually known simply as "Main Road"), the location of most hotels, banks and restaurants, Tanah Rata is a cosy and comfortable base for exploring the Highlands.

#### Arrival and information

**By bus** Buses and trains from the lowlands (apart from those organized specifically to take you to a Highland settlement) terminate at Tapah, from where a local bus will take you up the winding mountain road to Tanah Rata (hourly 8.30am – 5.30pm; 2hr; RM5). Buses from Tapah terminate at the bus station about halfway along the main road.

**District Office** Just north of Tanah Rata (Mon–Fri 8am–1pm & 3–4.30pm, ⓣ05/491 1066). To get there, go north towards Brinchang, and take the first major right after about 1km.

**Tourist information** There's no official Tourist Information kiosk, but any of the guesthouses will be able to help you, as will CS Travel on Main Rd (ⓣ05/491 1200) and Golden Highland Tours (see above).

#### Accommodation

**Cameronian Inn** 16 Jl Mentigi ⓣ05/491 1327. This friendly, clean and well-informed place has a motel-like feel, as well as internet access and a library, and is set in a peaceful location. There's a kitchen, a small dorm (RM8) and some double rooms. Trekkers set off from here at 9.30am most mornings; non-guests are welcome to join the treks at no charge. Dorm ❶, doubles ❷

**Cool Point** 891 Persiaran Dayang Endah ⓣ05/491 4914. Just off the main road behind the Shell station. A newish hotel in a quiet location that is well run and very clean. Rates include breakfast. ❺

**Daniel's Lodge** J9 Lorong Perdah ⓣ05/491 5823, ⓦwww.daniels.cameronhighlands.com. The traveller's spiritual home, with a great open-air bar area out the back, a comfortable lounge for watching movies and laid-back, endlessly helpful staff. Buses and tours can be organized from here, and there's a campfire every night. Follow the signs to Brij House off Main St and go 100m past the market area on the left. ❶

**Downtown Café and Hotel** 41 Jl Besar ⓣ05/491 3159. The rooms are considerably nicer than a first glance of the corridors promises, being large and overlooking the main road. It's also located above a buzzy café which serves good breakfasts. ❹

**Father's Guest House** ⓣ05/491 2484, ⓦwww.fathersplace.cjb.net. Three budget guesthouses set on a private hill in the outskirts of Tanah Rata. It's scrupulously clean and very peaceful, with doubles in a stone house, dorm beds in funky, tunnel-like aluminium outhouses and a garden. There's a large collection of books and films, a few internet terminals and very friendly staff. To get there, follow signs which lead off Perisan Camellia to the left, through a gate with "Goodyear" written on it – it's three minutes from the main street and easy to get to. Dorm ❶; doubles ❸

**Hillview Inn** 17 Jl Mentigi ⓣ05/491 2915. Quite chaotic, but with large, carpeted communal areas, including a homely TV lounge that looks like a dodgy grandma's sitting room. There's a clean kitchen and outdoor eating area, and rooms are large, if not particularly well insulated. ❹
**KRS Pines** T7 Jl Mentigi ⓣ05/491 2777, ⓦwww.twinpines.cameronhighlands.com. Run by the same people as *Twin Pines*, this guesthouse is a little more expensive but neater, with a slightly institutional living and dining hall and conveniences such as laundry. ❸
**Seah Meng** 39 Main Rd ⓣ05/491 1618. Clean, thoughtfully furnished and well-kept rooms, some with pleasant views. ❸
**Twin Pines** 2 Jl Mentigi ⓣ05/491 2169. Set back from the main road, this hippy hangout has a garden, book exchange, a spacious lounge area and books full of travellers' tips. At night, the owner leads singalongs around the campfire. There are dorms, a café and internet facilities. Dorm ❶; doubles from ❷.

## Eating and drinking

At night, food stalls set up on the Main Rd, mainly opposite the post office. Many restaurants serve the local steamboat, which involves dipping raw fish, meat, noodles and vegetables in a steaming broth until cooked. In general, Tanah Rata's better known for its Indian food, while Brinchang is better for Chinese dishes.
**Bunga Suria** Jl Perisan Camellia. The best South Indian restaurant in Tanah Rata and a haven for vegetarians as well as meat-eaters.
**Jasmine Restoran** 45 Main Rd. Popular with German and Dutch travellers for its *rijstafel* set meals. It has karaoke in the evenings, which can get a bit rowdy.
**The Jungle Bar** Located behind *Daniel's Lodge*, travellers congregate here every night around the campfire for cheap drinks and a laid-back atmosphere.
**Kumar** Main Rd. Along with *Sri Brinchang* next door, the *Kumar* specializes in claypot rice, tandoori and banana-leaf meals. They're great value (RM6 for a set meal), and delicious.
**The Mayflower** 22 Main St. Serving the best value steamboat in town (RM15 for two), this place is usually packed.
**Orient Restoran** 38 Main Rd. Standard Chinese food in the restaurant below the hotel. The set meals are reasonable value, as are the steamboats.
**The T Café** 4 Main Rd. Cosy second-floor spot on the corner, boasting the only "fruity strawberry scones" in the Cameron Highlands. Western and Chinese comfort food served by friendly staff.
**Traveller's Bistro and Pub** L68A Perisan Camellia 3. The most bar like place in Tanah Rata, with loud music and a good open location on the street corner. Beers are RM9, and food is also served – a South Indian "economy set" is RM8.50.

## Directory

**Bank** CIMB Bank on Perisan Camellia has 24hr ATMs, or try the HSBC on Main Rd.
**Clinic** 48 Main Rd, 8.30am–12.30pm & 2–4.30pm.
**Hospital** At the north end of Main Rd (ⓣ05/491 1966).
**Internet** There are a few places around town; the best is Highlands Computer Centre (ⓣ05/491 5678) at 39 Main Rd or Envonne Internet on Perisan Camellia, which charges only RM3 per hour.
**Police station** Main Rd, opposite the *New Garden Inn*, ⓣ05/491 1222.
**Post office** Main Rd, on the right as you approach from Tapah or Brinchang.
**Travel agent** CS Travel, Main Rd (ⓣ05/491 1200) sells tickets for express buses from Tapah to all major destinations, as well as buses to Ipoh.

## Moving on

**By bus** Local buses go from the bus station, about halfway along the main road, to Brinchang (hourly 6.30am– 6.30pm; 30min) and Village Raja (every 2hr 6.30am–6.30pm; 1hr), the furthest point north. Arrange long-distance buses at CS Travel, to go direct to Ipoh (4 daily; 2 hr) and Kuala Lumpur (5 daily; 4 hr), or to buy an onwards ticket from Tapah to all major destinations. If you want to travel more comfortably, with a/c and more leg room, be sure to ask which are the VIP buses – they're usually the first bus of the day, and there is also one in the afternoon. Buses to Tapah leave hourly (7am–4pm; 2hr; RM5). Most guesthouses can also arrange travel, including connection to popular spots such as Penang (4 daily; 4hr) and Taman Negara (3 daily; 2hr).

### Brinchang

**BRINCHANG**, 5km north of Tanah Rata, is less touristy than its neighbour but not as well-equipped for travellers. However, some of the walks are easily approached from here, and it's closer to the farms and tea estates further north. You can also hike to the summit of Gunung Brinchang (2032m), a steep two- to three-hour climb along a sealed road with wonderful views. To get to Brinchang, get a local bus from Tanah Rata (6.30am–6.30pm, approximately hourly) or a taxi (RM4).

The **Sungai Palas Tea Estate** (Tues–Sun 9am–4.30pm, tours every 10min; free) is set high in the hills and is refreshingly uncrowded. The tea leaves here are no longer hand-picked but cut with shears, after which they go to the factory (which you'll be guided round) to be withered, sifted, rolled, fermented and then fired. Local buses to the estate leave from Brinchang's bus station, just south of the square (8 daily, 6.45am–6.45pm; 25 min; RM2). You can also get back by making your own way to the main road (30-min walk) and picking up one of the more regular Brinchang-bound buses from Village Raja. The last bus back from Sungai Palas leaves at 6pm.

### Accommodation and eating

For food, *OK Tuck*, 26 Main Rd, is one of several good budget Chinese eating houses, and specializes in steamboat.

**Green Garden** Lot 13 Main St ⓣ05/491 5824. A little institutional but very clean, with large rooms. ❹

**Jasmine Hotel** 29 Main St ⓣ05/591 1981. Characterised by big shiny windows, this place is well-run by friendly Indian owners. ❺

**Papillon** 1B Jl Angsana 3 ⓣ013/520 6439. A good budget option, with clean if slightly small and characterless doubles. ❷

### Moving on

**By bus** It's best to head back to Tanah Rata for onwards travel: take a local bus from the bus station on Main St (hourly 6.30am–6.30pm; 30 min; RM2).

## IPOH

Eighty kilometres northwest of Tapah in the Kinta Valley, **IPOH** grew rich on the tin trade and is now the third largest city in Malaysia. This does not, however, really warrant staying here longer than necessary. The muddy **Sungai Kinta** river cuts the centre of Ipoh neatly in two; most of the hotels are situated east of the river, whilst the **old town** is on the opposite side between Jalan Sultan Idris Shah and Jalan Sultan Iskander.

Many Ipoh buildings show the influence of colonial and Straits-Chinese architecture, the most impressive of which is the white stucco **Hong Kong Bank** on Jalan Dato' Maharaja Lela. Turning right from the bank into Jalan Sultan Yusuf, you're on the outskirts of **Chinatown**, many of whose pastel-coloured, nineteenth-century shop-houses are now looking rather tatty. The **Perak Museum** (daily 9.30am–5pm; free) is housed in an elegant former tin miner's mansion, 400m north of the padang on Jalan Panglima Bukit Gantang Wahab, and displays photos of Ipoh's glory days during the tin boom.

The most prominent reminder of Ipoh's economic heyday is the **train station**. Built in 1917, it is a typical example of the British conception of "East meets West", with its Moorish turrets and domes and a two-hundred-metre-long veranda.

### Arrival

**By bus** The local bus station is just south of the train station, at the junction with Jl Tun Abdul Razak. Opposite, you'll find the taxi stand. Express buses operate from behind the ticket booths across the road.

**By train** The train station is on Jl Panglima Bukit Gantang Wahab, west of the old town, next to the GPO.

**Tourist information** The tourist office is on Jl Tun Sambanthan (Mon–Thurs 8am–1pm & 2–4.30pm, Fri 8am–12.15pm & 2.45–4.30pm; closed 1st & 3rd Sat of every month; ⓣ05/241 2959, ⓦwww.ipoh-online.com.my).

### Accommodation

Be careful when choosing accommodation in Ipoh; whereas there are quite a few reasonable options, the town also has more than its fair share of places that charge hourly rates, or are out-and-out brothels.

**New Caspian Hotel** 20-26 Jalan Ali Pitchay ⓣ05/255 1221. This is a decent and welcoming option, with TV, fridge and bathrooms in all the excellent-value rooms. ❸

**Sun Golden Inn** 17 Jalan Che Tak ☎05/243 6255. It may be a little basic and institutional with far too many stairs, but rooms are clean and staff are friendly. ❸

## Eating

Many of Ipoh's restaurants close in the evenings, but there are dozens of excellent hawker stalls at the southern end of Jl Greenhill, east of the *Shanghai Hotel*.

**Greentown Noodle House** 58 Pasan Greenhill. The flat rice-noodles *kway teow*, ubiquitous throughout Malaysia, supposedly originated in Ipoh, and this noodle house is a great place to try them. Mains RM4.

**Rahman** Jalan CM Yusuf. An extremely friendly Indian restaurant where you can fill up on cheap *dosa* and curries. Mains RM5.

## Directory

**Banks** These can be found on Jl Sultan Idris Shah and Jalan Yang Kalsom, and there's an HSBC at Jalan Tun Sambathan.

**Hospital** Jl Hospital.

**Internet** RND Café, 41 Jalan CM Yusuf.

**Post office** Jl Panglima Bukit Gantang Wahab, west of the old town.

## Moving on

**By bus** Local buses to Lumut (the departure point for Pulau Pangkor; see below) leave from a separate forecourt, beside a row of shops and in front of the Shell Petrol Station a little further along Jl Tun Abdul Razak from the bus station. Get a ticket from Perak Roadways under the bill hoardings.

**Destinations:** Butterworth (hourly; 3hr); Kuala Kangsar (every 45min; 3hr); Kuala Lumpur (hourly; 4hr); Lumut (hourly; 90min); Penang (hourly; 3hr); Singapore (4 daily; 10–11hr); Tapah (hourly; 1hr).By train to: Tapah Rd (1 daily; 1hr 25min).

# PULAU PANGKOR

At only 3km by 9km, **PULAU PANGKOR** is one of the most minute of the west coast's islands, with some gorgeous stretches of beach and hardly any people. It's only a forty-minute ferry ride from the port of Lumut (85km southwest of Ipoh), so the perfect place to hop over to if you're after some fairly isolated, low-key relaxation. There's an airport here (flights from Singapore and KL), built to fulfil the demand of weekenders from the mainland and modern-life essentials in Pangkor town. But, by and large, the inhabitants live by fishing rather than tourism and are refreshingly indifferent.

Most villages lie along the east coast, while tourist accommodation and the best beaches are on the west side of the island, at Pasir Bogak and Teluk Nipah. A sealed road runs right round the island and across it from Pangkor Town to Pasir Bogak, 2km away on the west coast. While there isn't all that much in the way of sites, there are a couple of temples worth a peek, such as the madly colourful Lin Je Kong Temple in the north of Teluk Nipah, which includes a devotional figure of Donald Duck, and **Kota Belanda**, the semi-ruined Dutch Fort originally built in 1670, situated 3km south of Pangkor Town.

### Pasir Bogak

**PASIR BOGAK** offers a couple of accommodation options, but has a disappointingly narrow strip of grubby sand. Only a few of the chalets front the beach itself; most line the road that continues north along the west coast, but they're all reasonably close to the sea.

### Teluk Nipah

A few more kilometres to the north is **TELUK NIPAH**, whose beaches are wider and fringed with shade-providing palm trees. The best beach here is **Coral Beach**, a perfect cove with crystal-clear sea and smooth white sand. The bay can be reached either by road, or in five minutes on foot by climbing over the rocks at the northern end of Teluk Nipah's main beach (watch the tide). You can also swim across to "Coral Island" in about ten minutes, though

## TRAVEL TO AND FROM PALAU PANGKOR

**Express ferries** to Pulau Pangkor run from **Lumut** approximately every half hour (daily 6.45am–9pm; RM3 one way), calling at Village Sungei Pinang Kecil before reaching the main jetty at Pangkor Town (7am–8pm for the return journey). Be careful that you don't over-enthusiastically get off too early. You can also catch a catamaran from the same spot for RM5, which will get you to the island in half the time. From Pangkor Town, the island's principal settlement, buses and the bright pink taxis will ferry you to the beaches. Contact Mesra Ferry (☎05/683 5800) or any of the guesthouses for ferry tickets on Pulau Pankor.

**In Lumut** buses arrive at Lumut's bus station, a three-minute walk south of the jetty. The Tourist Office (Mon–Fri 9am–5pm, Sat 9am–1.45pm; ☎05/683 4057) is on the left past the petrol pumps on Jalan Sultan Idris Shah. From Lumut there are bus connections to all major destinations, including: KL (hourly; 4hr), Butterworth (hourly; 3 hr), Kota Bahru (2 daily; 8hr), Johor Bahru (3 daily; 10hr), Kuantan (every 4hr; 6hr), Melaka (2 daily; 6hr 30min).

**To fly** to Pangkor, the tiny airline Berjaya Air (Pangkor office ☎05/685 5828, main number ☎03/7847 6828; Ⓦwww.berjaya-air.com) has flights every day except Tuesday and Thursday (depart from KL at 10.40am, from Pulau Pangkor at 11.40am; 1hr 40min) between KL's Subang airport and Pangkor Airport to the north of the island.

local boatmen will try to convince you the trip is only possible via a RM50 boat ride. Around February there are jellyfish in the water; though the stings are only minor producing a sort of electric shock sensation, and don't leave any discernable mark, swimming through them can be disconcerting.

For boat trips around the island, try Mr Non, located on the beachfront (☎012/437 4679), who'll take you to gorgeous bays such as the aptly named Emerald Bay and Monkey Bay, which, unsurprisingly, is populated by monkeys, and on snorkelling trips (RM30 for a full day).

## Island transport

**Minibus taxis** These manly pink vehicles charge RM5 from Pangkor Town to Pasir Bogak, RM10 to Teluk Nipah and RM40 for a round-island trip.

**Motorbike and bicycle rental** The best way to explore is by motorbike (RM30 for manual or RM40 for a scooter) or bicycle (RM15), available from Pangkor Town and from guesthouses. A full-on exploration of the entire island will only take you a couple of hours and you'll come up against some frustrating privatised bits of land and beach, but it's a great way to spend a morning.

## Accommodation

### Pasir Bogak

For budget accommodation try to avoid Pasir Bogak but if you do end up staying here, the following two aren't bad budget options.

**Ceria Bogak Beach Camp** ☎017/ 503 0350. Rooms are clean and tiled and feature TVs and attached bathrooms. The complex backs straight onto the beach. ❹

**Pangkor Village Beach Resort** ☎05/685 4625 or 685 2227, Ⓦwww.pangkorvillageresort.com. The tents are great value at RM30 per tent (for around 3 or 4 people), just a minute from the beach front. Bring your own sleeping bag. The complex is sprawling and sunny, with volleyball on the stretch in front, watersports such as jet-skiing and kayaking and bicycles for rent. ❹

### Teluk Nipah

**D Lima Chalet** ☎012/567 6923. Run by a charming and relaxed family, this guesthouse, overgrown with flowers, is super laid-back. ❹

**La La Chalet** ☎05/685 3112. The chatty, friendly owner runs a chilled-out guesthouse where rooms are huge with big windows. There's a discount for long stays and the doubles with a/c are good value. Dorm ❷; doubles ❸

**Nazri Nipah Camp** ☎05/685 2014. Laid-back traveller place with kitchen facilities, a dorm, some A-frames and chalets with shower. Jungle trekking tours also arranged. Dorm ❶; doubles ❸

**Ombak Inn Chalet** ⓣ05/685 5223. This guesthouse is quiet, with a cosy little restaurant and garden in the front serving great barbecues in the evening (RM15 gets you a massive set menu, including fish, chicken, crabs and more). Rates include a huge breakfast and are reduced if you stay three nights or longer. ❹
**Purnama Beach Resort** ⓣ05/685 3530, ⓦwww.purnama.com.my. Package-deal development with a good range of plush chalets, quickly snapped up by mainlanders on weekends. There's an internet terminal (one of only two in the village) open to non-guests. Discounts for stays of over three nights. ❺
**Sunset View Chalet** ⓣ05/685 5448. Rooms here are tidy and clean, with little balconies opening out onto an avenue thoughtfully and charmingly shaded by bougainvillea. There are hammocks to chill out in by the outdoor TV and seating area. ❺
**Z-Camp** ⓣ012/537 2701. With cheap, clean A-frames, this place is a good deal and run by a friendly family (though with not much English). ❷

## Eating

### Pasir Bogak

**Pangkor Village Beach Resort** Great seafood at around RM8.50 per dish, with a nice view of the sea.

### Teluk Nipah

**Daddy's Café** Located directly on the beachfront at Coral Bay, in the evening this place is lit with flares and offers a gorgeous moonlit seaview. Prices are slightly above average (around RM14 for a main seafood dish) but well worth it for delicious food in a romantic setting. Owner Vernon is eccentric and friendly and encourages guests to make Daddy's Café a 'home away from home' (if you live on a beach on a tropical island).
**Kakcah** One of the first beach-front eateries you'll come to on Nipah (approaching from Pangkor Town and Pasir Bogak), this tiny raised place has a counter overlooking the sea, and serves delicious *mee goreng* for only RM4. The freshly squeezed lemon and lime juice is refreshing too. Open until 7pm.
**La La Chalet** Great-value barbecues in a peaceful setting with chilled-out music.
**Nipah Bay Villa** The guesthouse itself charges above average, but this place has great breakfasts from RM4, and delicious seafood in the evenings cooked in almost any way you choose, at around RM8 a dish. The outdoor seating also has the distinct advantage of being atmospheric and nicely lit. There's also motorbike rental here.

## Directory

**Bank** There's a Maybank within the *Min Lian Hotel*, Pangkor Town, but for changing money, you'll get much better rates in Lumut.
**Internet** Pangkornet has computer terminals behind its convenience store, with internet access at RM8 for 1 hour; alternatively, *Purnama Beach Resort* has a couple of terminals, at RM6 per hour. Take the first road on the right as you come into Nipah from Pangkor Town.
**Travel agencies** Most guesthouses will help you with onwards travel to the majority of destinations. Try *Nipah Bay Villa* (ⓣ05/685 2198) for reasonable rates on buses from Lumut. For tourist information on Pangkor, go to ⓦwww.pulau-pangkor.com.

# BUTTERWORTH

The industrial town of **BUTTERWORTH** is the port for the island of Penang and its capital, Georgetown, and of no interest except as a transport hub.

## Arrival

The **bus station**, port complex, taxi stand and **train station** (ⓣ04/323 7962) are all next door to each other on the quayside.

## Accommodation

**Sin Tong Ah** (ⓣ04/323 9679). If you get stuck here, try this good, standard option by the port. Walk northeast from the bus station along the main road for a minute or so and follow it left past a huge intersection; the hotel is on the other side of the road. ❸

## Moving on

**By bus** to: Alor Setar (every 30min–1hr; 2hr 30min); Bangkok, Thailand (2 daily; 18hr); Hat Yai, Thailand (2 daily; 5hr 30min); Ipoh (hourly; 3hr); Kota Bharu (2 daily; 6hr); Kuala Lumpur (at least 15 daily; 7hr); Kuala Perlis (5 daily; 3hr 45min); Kuala Terengganu (2 daily; 8hr); Kuantan (3 daily; 12hr); Lumut (4 daily; 4hr); Melaka (1 daily; 6–10hr); Padang Besar (5 daily; 4hr); Singapore (at least 2 daily; 16hr); Surat Thani, Thailand (2 daily; 10hr 30min); Tapah (2 daily; 4hr 30min).
**By train** to: Alor Setar (2 daily; 2hr); Bangkok, Thailand (1 daily; 23hr 30min); Hat Yai, Thailand (2 daily; 4hr 45min–6hr); Ipoh (1 daily; 5hr); Kuala

Kangsar (1 daily; 3hr 30min); Kuala Lumpur (1 daily; 10hr 25min); Tapah Rd (1 daily; 6hr 30min).

**By ferry** The passenger and car ferry service (5am–11pm; RM1 return) runs three times an hour from the port complex to Pengkalan Weld in Georgetown and takes twenty minutes.

## PENANG AND GEORGETOWN

A fair number of people find that **PENANG**, a confusing amalgam of state and island, 370km from Kuala Lumpur on Malaysia's northwestern coast, is not quite what they expect. Skyscrapers greet you as you approach by ferry, and **Georgetown** (the island's capital and Malaysia's second-largest city, often referred to as "Penang") is a busy, bustling town without a beach in sight. However, expectations notwithstanding, the people are extremely friendly, the food is great and this is a fabulous place to take in a substantial amount of Malay culture, with temples, mosques and churches aplenty.

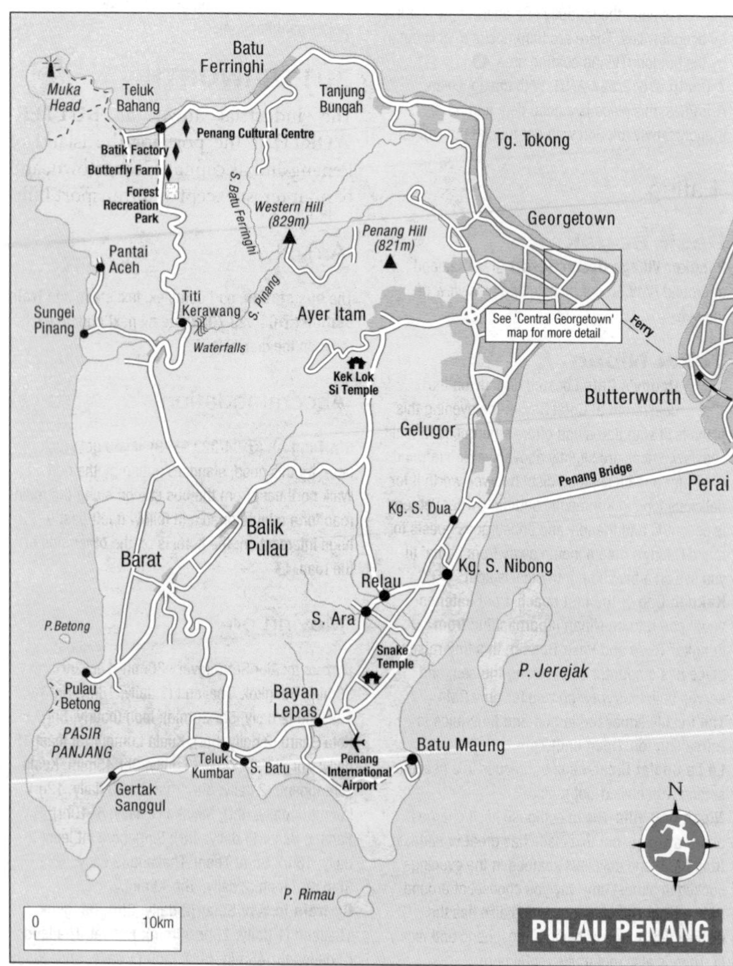

Everything of interest in Penang State is on **Pulau Penang**, a large island of 285 square kilometres connected to the mainland by a bridge and round-the-clock ferry services from Butterworth. In 1791, the island became the **first British settlement** in the Malay Peninsula and a major colonial administrative centre, only declining after the foundation of Singapore in 1819. Most visitors make day-trips out from Georgetown to the island's north-coast beaches of **Batu Ferringhi** and **Tanjung Bungah**, though you can also stay in both these resorts.

## What to see and do

**GEORGETOWN** retains more of its cultural history than virtually anywhere else in the country. The most confusing thing about finding your way around Georgetown is the fact that many **streets** have several names – Penang Road has become Jalan Penang, Penang Street is Lebuh Penang, Weld Quay has become Pengkalan Weld, and Beach Street is now Lebuh Pantai. Lebuh Cinta is almost universally known as Love Lane, and Jalan Masjid Kapitan Kling is often referred to as Lebuh Pitt.

### Fort Cornwallis and around

The site of **Fort Cornwallis** (daily 8.30am–7pm; RM1) on the northeastern tip of Pulau Penang, marks the spot where the British fleet under Captain Francis Light disembarked on July 16, 1786. For all its significance, however it holds little of interest save a replica of a traditional Malay house and an underground bunker detailing the history of Penang. Southwest from the fort, **Lebuh Pantai** holds some fine colonial buildings. West of Lebuh Pantai, on Jalan Masjid Kapitan Kling (or Lebuh Pitt), stands the Anglican **St George's Church** (Sunday services in English at 8.30am & 10.30am), one of the oldest buildings in Penang (1817–19) and as simple and unpretentious as anything built in the Greek style in Asia can be. Next to the church on Lebuh Farquhar, **Penang Museum and Art Gallery** (daily 9am–5pm; RM1) has an excellent collection of rickshaws, press cuttings and black-and-white photographs.

### Little India

The area east of here, enclosed by parallel Lebuh King and Lebuh Queen, forms Georgetown's compact **Little India** district, full of sari and incense shops as well as banana-leaf curry houses. It is also home to the towering **Sri Mariamman Temple** (open early morning to late evening) on the corner of Lebuh Queen and Lebuh Chulia, which is a typical example of Hindu architecture. You're welcome to have a look around if you remove your shoes and join the reflective worshippers gazing at its many brightly coloured statues.

### Khoo Kongsi

To the south, in a secluded square at the end of an alleyway off Lebuh Aceh, stands the **Khoo Kongsi**, one of many *kongsi*, or traditional "clan-houses" in Penang where Chinese families gather to worship their ancestors. The original building was started in 1894 and meticulously crafted by experts from China. Its central hall is dark with heavy, intricately carved beams and pillars and bulky mother-of-pearl inlaid furniture. The hall on the left is a richly decorated shrine to Tua Peh Kong, the god of prosperity; the right-hand hall contains the gilded ancestral tablets. Connecting all three halls is a balcony minutely decorated in carvings of folk tales. Visitors are requested to ask permission and sign in at the adjacent office before entering.

### Cheong Fatt Tze Mansion

On the western edge of Georgetown, on the corner of Lebuh Leith, is the stunning **Cheong Fatt Tze Mansion** (guided tours

Mon–Fri 11am & 3pm, Sat, Sun & public holidays 11am only; RM12; ⓦwww.cheongfatttzemansion.com), commonly known as The Blue House, whose outer walls are painted in a striking rich blue. It's the best example of nineteenth-century Chinese architecture in Penang, built by Thio Thiaw Siat, a Cantonese businessman. The elaborate halls of ceremony, bedrooms and libraries, separated by courtyards and gardens, have been restored and it is now a breathtaking hotel, where complete apartments can be rented as well as rooms and prices

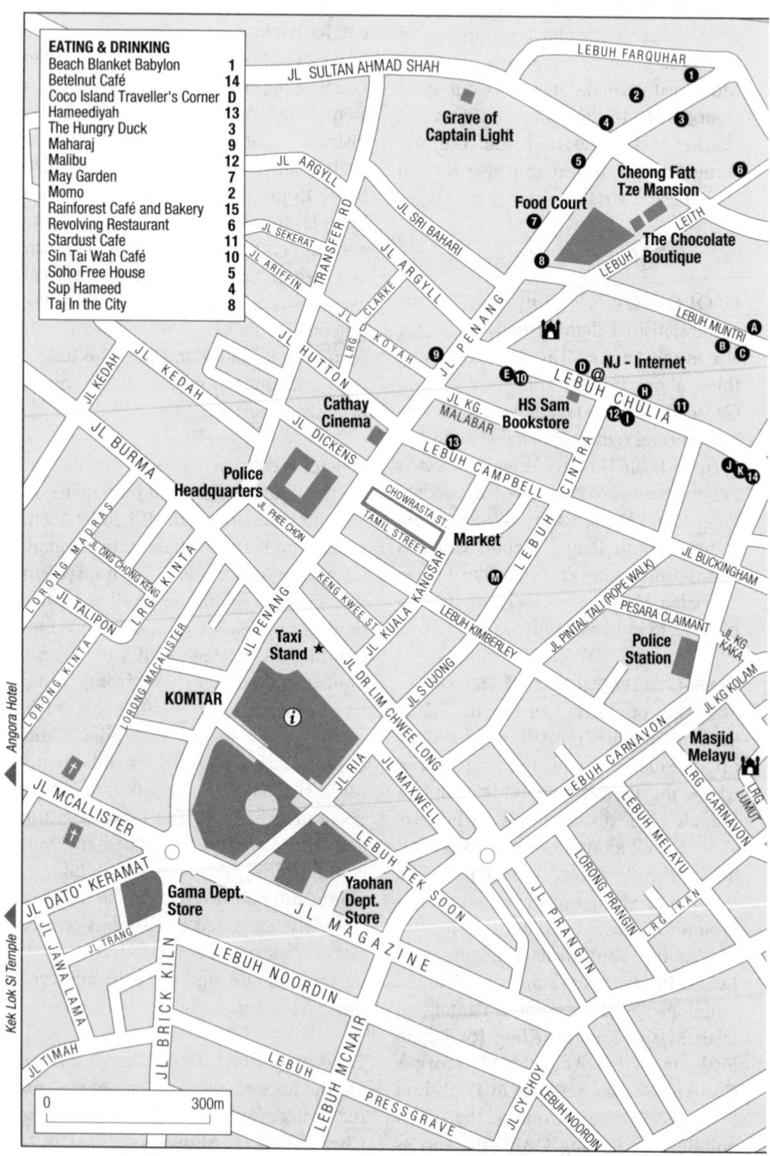

start at RM320. The mansion was used as a set for the film *Indochine*.

### Kek Lok Si Temple

Bedecked with flags, lanterns, statues and pagodas, the sprawling and exuberant **Kek Lok Si Temple** (open 9am–9pm; free) is supposedly the largest Buddhist temple complex in Malaysia and a major tourist spot. The "Million Buddhas Precious Pagoda" is the most prominent feature of the compound, with a tower of simple Chinese saddle-shaped eaves and more elaborate Thai



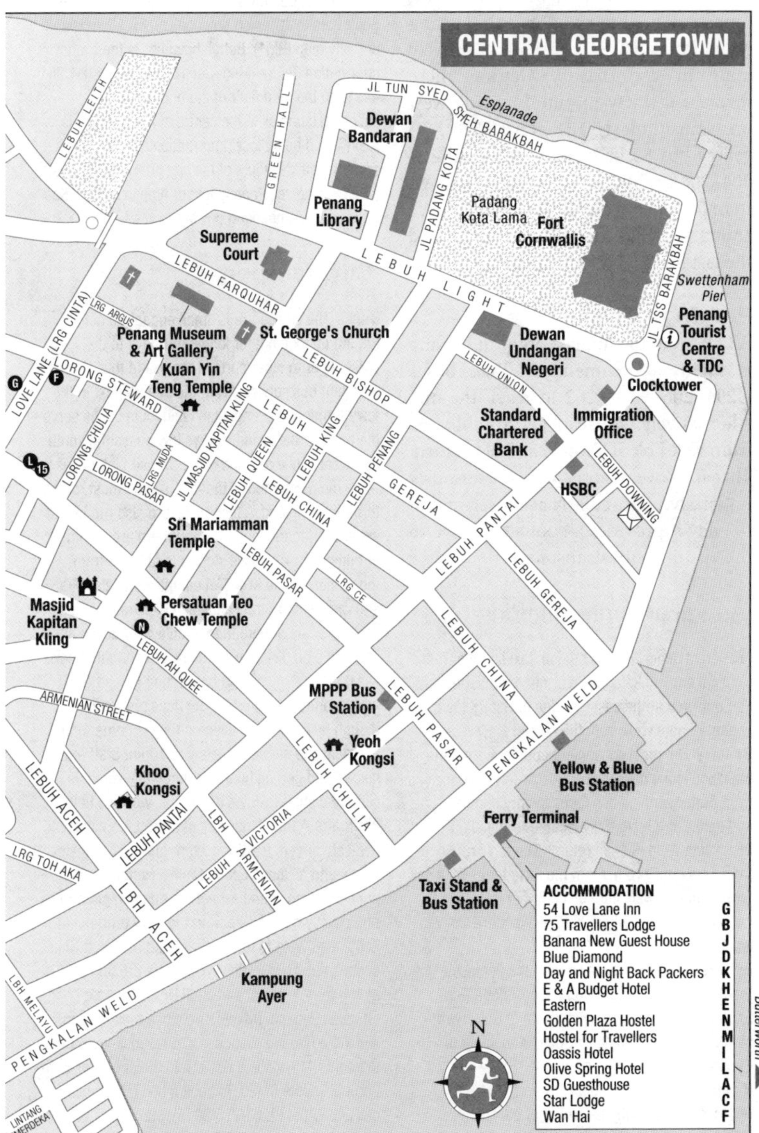

arched windows, topped by a golden Burmese stupa. It costs RM2 to climb the 193 steps to the top, where there is a great view of Georgetown and the bay.

Come in the evening for the most kitsch and impressive lighting spectacle you're likely to witness in a while – in the dark, Kek Lok is so brightly lit with multi-coloured fairy lights and flashing neon it makes Las Vegas look positively tame in comparison. Getting there involves a thirty-minute bus ride west on Transitlink 1, 101, 130, 351, 361, yellow bus 85 or minibus 21, or the U 204, 206 or 203. Ask to be let off at Air Item for the temple. Buses usually leave about every half an hour after 8pm, and the last bus is at about 9.30pm.

### Penang Hill

A trip up to the highest point in Penang is highly recommended. Take buses U204, 206, 93 or 202 to reach the hill. Alternatively, you can get a **cable car** from Kek Lok Si Temple at RM4 return. The views over Georgetown are seriously impressive, particularly at sunset, and in the day it provides a cool alternative to the bustling city atmosphere.

## Arrival and information

Arriving at either the bus station, taxi stand or ferry terminal on Pengkalan Weld or nearby Swettenham Pier puts you at the eastern edge of Georgetown, a twenty-minute walk from the hotels.

**By ferry** The most convenient approach from the mainland is the passenger-and-car ferry service from Butterworth, which takes twenty minutes and docks at the centrally located terminal on Pengkalan Weld (60 sen return). The ferry runs from 5am until 11pm. From the ferry terminal, it's a fifteen-minute walk into the centre of town and the Lebuh Chulia area where backpackers are likely to want to stay.

**By taxi** Long-distance taxis from the Peninsula use the thirteen-kilometre-long Penang Bridge (RM7 toll), which crosses from just south of Butterworth at Perai to a point on Jalan Udini, 8km south of Georgetown on the east coast.

**By air** Penang International Airport (ⓣ04/643 0811) is on the southeastern tip of the island. Yellow bus 83 (hourly on the hour, 6am–10pm) takes about 45 minutes to get into Georgetown, dropping you next to the Pengkalan Weld ferry terminal. A taxi costs RM20 – buy a coupon inside the terminal building.

**Tourist information** On arrival, the most convenient tourist office is the Penang Tourist Centre (Mon–Fri 8.30am–1pm & 2–4.30pm, Sat 8.30am–1pm; ⓣ04/261 6663) on the ground floor of the Penang Port Commission building on Jalan Tun Syed Sheh Barakbah, which produces an excellent island and city map (RM1). Better, however, is the Tourist Information Centre (Mon–Sat 10am–6pm; ⓣ04/261 4461) on the third floor of the huge KOMTAR shopping complex in the centre of town, which is really clued up on local information and can also arrange half-day tours of the city (from RM30) – not a bad way to see Penang if your time is limited. See ⓦwww.tourismpenang.gov.my.

## City transport

**Buses** The city centre is small enough to get around on foot, but for longer journeys to the outskirts or to other parts of the island there is an excellent bus service. From the station next to the ferry terminal on Pengkalan Weld, blue buses serve the north of the island, and yellow buses the south and west, while red-and-white Transit Link buses – the most common of the lot – run on most routes through the island. A few buses are also run by the small Sri Negara company, and there are a number of minibuses. All buses stop at (and leave from) the station by the KOMTAR complex on Jalan Ria and most stop at the Pengkalan Weld station, too. Fares are rarely more than a Malaysian dollar, and are based on distance travelled, but you must have exact change in coins to board the bus – in other words, bring lots of coins. Services are frequent, though by 8pm in the evening they become more sporadic and stop completely at 10pm. Staff are helpful and getting hold of a timetable, which is clear and shows routes and stops, will also help.

**Pedicabs** A traditional way of seeing the city is by pedicab: drivers tout for custom outside the major hotels and all along Lebuh Chulia. Negotiate the price in advance and expect the opening price to be ridiculously high; a ride from the ferry terminal at Pengkalen Weld to the northern end of Lebuh Chulia costs around RM3. Otherwise, there are taxi stands by the ferry terminal and on Jl Dr Lim Chwee Long, off Jalan Penang. Drivers rarely use their meters, so fix the fare in advance – a trip across town runs to about RM5, while a ride out to the airport or Batu Ferringhi costs RM20. To book a taxi in advance, call Jade Auto (ⓣ04/226 3015), Sunshine Taxi (ⓣ04/642 5961) or MCI Taxis (ⓣ04/264 5534).

**Bike and car rental** Useful if you plan to see the rest of the island – check the list of addresses in "Listings'.

## Accommodation

Georgetown is one of the few places in the country where you might experience difficulty in finding a room, so arrive early or book ahead. The budget places are mostly on and around Lebuh Chulia; most have dorm beds as well as rooms, and the majority sell bus tickets to Thailand and can help to obtain Thai visas. No. 1 Lebuh Chulia is at the southern end (nearest the ferry terminal).

**54 Love Lane Inn** 54 Love Lane ⓣ016/419 8409. A chilled-out travellers' hangout, with murals on the wall and cheerfully blue-painted wooden doors, a cosy TV area and communal spaces both upstairs and down. Staff are sweet and friendly. ❶

**75 Travellers Lodge** 75 Lebuh Muntri ⓣ04/262 3378. Run by the jokey Jimmy and his ever-smiling godfather, rooms here are a good and clean deal, if basic. The dorm at the front can be a little noisy, but with an hour's free internet a day for guests, a load of travel information and an informal, friendly atmosphere, it's a good choice. Dorm ❶, Doubles ❷

**Banana New Guest House** 355–59 Lebuh Chulia ⓣ04/262 6171, ⓦwww.banananewguesthouse.com. A large, buzzing travellers' hub with a pool table and internet (RM3/ hr) downstairs. It's always pretty packed, and staff are fairly indifferent so book in advance if you want to guarantee a bed. ❷

**Blue Diamond** 422 Lebuh Chulia ⓣ04/261 1089. Modern frontage hides a traditionally elaborate inner courtyard and a grand staircase. The large, high-ceilinged rooms with showers have luxurious sprung mattresses. There's a dorm (RM8) and the washing machine is free to guests. ❶–❸

**Day and Night Back Packers** 319 Lebuh Chulia ⓣ04/262 5645. A new joint whose cheerful, smiley owner is so laid-back he's practically lying down. Rooms are basic but clean, there's a café downstairs and the location is extremely central, though it can be a little noisy at night. Rates include breakfast. ❷

**E & A Budget Hotel** 380 Lebuh Chulia ⓣ04/262 1311. A standard guesthouse, but very conveniently located, and beds are more than averagely comfortable. ❷

**Eastern** 509 Lebuh Chulia ⓣ04/261 4597. Standard Chinese-run guesthouse. Small, clean rooms with fan or a/c and saloon-style wooden doors. More solidly built than most. ❷

**Golden Plaza Hostel** 1 Pitt Lane, off Lebuh Chulia ⓣ04/263 2388. A traveller-friendly dorm (RM8) with a balcony, sitting area, washing facilities and lockers. There are also simple doubles, a good cafe, internet services and lots of travel info. ❷

**Hostel for Travellers** 100 Cintra St ⓣ04/264 3581 ⓦwww.100cintrastreet.com. Set in a massive, traditional dark-wood mansion, rooms here are huge and very Oriental in feel. There's a small café underneath serving beer at RM7, the dorms are extremely clean if a little sparse and it's worth staying in just to check out the architecture of the building. Dorm ❶, Doubles ❸

**Oassis Hotel** 431 Lebuh Chulia ⓣ04/262 0133. Standard hostel that welcomes a mixture of travellers and holidaying Malays. Set back from the road with parking and an airy café. Dorm ❶ Double ❷

**Olive Spring Hotel** 302 Lebuh Chulia ⓣ04/261 4641. This place is now slightly run-down as the owners are waiting to see if their lease will be renewed before refurbishing. It's still a lovely place to stay, however, being located above a delicious bakery and set in a sprawling colonial-style house full of shuttered windows and attic-like open spaces. ❷

**SD Guesthouse** 28 Muntri St ⓣ04/261 6102. There are two locations of these guesthouses but the one on Muntri St is a slight cut-above the one on Love Lane. Rooms in this tiled hotel are very clean, if slightly lacking in character. Check the room to see if you get a window. There are hot showers though, free internet and a card phone connection. ❷

**Star Lodge** 39 Muntri St ⓣ04/262 6378. A brand-new guesthouse where the owners can't do enough to help, with one free hour of internet access per day and peaceful, spotless rooms, all with attached bathroom and hot showers. Some rooms have balconies. ❸

**Wan Hai** 35 Lrg Cinta ⓣ016/413 7915. Although this place is a pretty big shambles, with decrepit, noisy rooms and a tumbledown building, the owners are friendly and the prices are right. There's a roof terrace and bike rental. ❶

## Eating

A local favourite is Penang *laksa*, noodles in thick fish soup garnished with vegetables, pineapple and *belacan* (shrimp paste). The main travellers' hangouts around Lebuh Chulia serve Western breakfasts, banana pancakes and milkshakes for under a couple of dollars; they usually open from 9am to 5pm. There are also hawker stalls on Lebuh Kimberley and Lebuh Cintra, and a fantastic food court on Lebuh Leith, where in addition to the Malay, Indian, Japanese, Thai and Chinese cuisine, there's a nightly singer and local oldies often head for the dance floor.

**Hameediyah** 164 Lebuh Campbell. Great Indian food at reasonable prices in a century-old building; around RM4 a head for a full meal. The *nan* bread is recommended.

**Maharaj** 132 Jl Penang, next to the Odeon Cinema. A kitschly grand Indian restaurant in a brightly coloured little building, serving delicious food from various provinces, with prices at around RM13 for a main dish.

**Malibu** 433 Lebuh Chulia. A chilled-out café-bar offering cheap food. A good place to have a beer and catch up with other travellers.

**May Garden** 70 Jl Penang. Plush but affordable Cantonese restaurant serving excellent food.

**Rainforest Café and Bakery** 300 Lebuh Chulia. A delicious European-style bakery with a laid-back café attached, this is a great place to come for breakfast or a cake fix.

TREAT YOURSELF

**Revolving Restaurant** The sixteenth floor of the *City Bayview Hotel* is the ideal location for a romantic meal, especially as the service is attentive and friendly. Choose from Western and Oriental dishes during the 45-minute rotation, which offers stunning 360-degree views of Penang – if you time your visit with sunset, the view is especially spectacular. The buffet dinner from 6.30pm costs RM38.

**Stardust Café** 370 Lebuh Chulia. A friendly roadside caff that's good for a beer, or for a cheap-and-cheerful breakfast. Also offers accommodation, with just seven rooms. RM22 for single.

**Sin Tai Wah Café** Lebuh Chulia. A good choice for a casual snack or meal, this atmospheric café is attractively festooned with greenery.

**Soho Free House** Jl Penang. A pub that might have been transported straight from England, with authentic fish and chips, pies and draught Guinness.

**Sup Hameed** 48 Penang Rd. An Indian stall that's grown to become a small empire, serving tandoori and roti at moreish prices (RM1.50 for a *roti*), on a spot with great people-watching.

## Drinking and nightlife

Most of Georgetown's bars are comfortable places to hang out, but when the fleet arrives, a good many turn into rowdy meat markets, so choose carefully. Usual opening hours are 6pm–2am. In Georgetown's discos, there's usually a cover charge of around RM20.

**Beach Blanket Babylon** 2 Jl Penang. Snazzy café and wine bar with curtained-off booths and a mirrored bar. Prices are slightly over the odds, but it's a good spot to watch the beautiful and slightly poseur-ish of Penang go by. RM14 beer, main course RM20.

**Betelnut Café** 360 Lebuh Chulia. A typical traveller's café-bar, with fairy lights, cheap beers and a laid-back atmosphere.

**Coco Island Traveller's Corner** 422 Lebuh Chulia. Live music every night, 'until the neighbours complain' (around 1–2am). The restaurant serves good Mexican food and there's a party atmosphere.

**The Hungry Duck** 3H and 3I Upper Jl Penang. This dark little bar offers the best deal for a girls' night out in the area, with free vodka all night on ladies' night – theoretically this is on Wed, but it seems fairly flexible and to run pretty frequently.

**Momo** The Bungalow, Upper Jl Penang. The biggest "club" in Penang, with a live band full of hyperactive Malaysian Barbies playing more than passable imitations of Western songs. Mon–Thurs free entry; Fri & Sat RM35. Girls with a "sexy miniskirt" on Friday night get a free bottle of vodka. Beer RM11.

**Sin Tai Wah** Lebuh Chulia. This daytime café turns into a lively bar full of Indonesian guest workers in the evening, and has the cheapest beer in town, though avoid upstairs (apparently it runs a brothel when ships dock).

**Taj In the City** 55 Penang Rd. With heavy air-conditioning and an atmosphere like a slightly seedy gentleman's club, this small lounge is slightly weird but a good place for a quiet drink in faded Western surroundings.

## Directory

**Airline offices** Air Asia, 463 Lebuh Chulia, ☎04/261 5642; Cathay Pacific, Menara PSCI, Jl Sultan Ahmed Shah ☎04/226 0411; Malaysia Airlines, Jl Sultan Ahmad Shah, ☎04/217 6323; Singapore Airlines, Wisma Penang Gardens, Jl Sultan Ahmed Shah ☎04/226 3201; Thai International, Wisma Central, Jl Macalister ☎04/226 6000.

**Banks and exchange** Major banks (Mon–Fri 10am–3pm, Sat 9.30–11.30am) are along Lebuh Pantai, including Standard Chartered and the HSBC Bank, but since they charge a hefty commission, the licensed moneychangers on Lebuh Pantai, Lebuh Chulia and Jalan Kapitan Kling (daily 8.30am–6pm) are preferable – they charge no

## THE CHOCOLATE BOUTIQUE

22 Leith Street ⓣ04/250 2488 ⓦwww.thechocolateboutique.com. It isn't what you'd immediately associate with Penang or with Malaysia, but this emporium, offering over sixty varieties of chocolate, is a fun stop if you're craving something sweet. The chocolate is made with local ingredients, and the flavours include tiramisu and coffee. There's even a healthy chocolate room, which explains how dark chocolate lowers blood pressure and prevents heart attacks. With loads of tasting opportunities, you're guaranteed to leave feeling satisfied (and possibly a bit sick).

commission and the rate is often better. Try Noor and Kabeer, at 419 Lebuh Chulia, where there's also a bookshop. It's open until 10pm too. American Express is at Mayflower Acme Tours, MWE Plaza, 8 Lebuh Farquhar, (Mon–Fri 8.30am–5.30pm, Sat 8.30am–1pm; ⓣ04/262 8196). Credit-card and travellers' cheque-holders can use the office as a poste restante/general delivery address.

**Bike rental** Outlets on Lebuh Chulia rent out motorbikes and bicycles: RM20 a day for a motorbike (you need a valid driving licence – in practice, you'll rarely be asked to show it); RM8–10 for a bicycle. Try NJ at no. 425.

**Bookshops** United Books Ltd, Jl Penang, has a large selection of English-language books, including travel books. There are several outlets in the KOMTAR building, including Popular Books on the 2nd floor. In addition, there are several secondhand bookshops on Lebuh Chulia. HS Sam Book Store at no. 473 does exchanges and has a good line in travel guides.

**Car rental** Avis, at the airport (ⓣ04/643 9633) and Batu Ferringhi (ⓣ04/881 1522); Hertz, 38 Lebuh Farquhar (ⓣ04/263 5914); ORIX at the City Bayview Hotel (ⓣ04/261 8608) and at the airport (ⓣ04/644 4772).

**Consulates** Australia, 1c Lorong Hutton ⓣ05/263 3320; Indonesia, 467 Jl Burma ⓣ04/227 4686; Thailand, 1 Jalan Tunku Abdul Rahman ⓣ04/262 8029; UK, Standard Chartered Bank Chambers, Lebuh Pantai ⓣ04/262 5333. For citizens of the USA, Ireland or New Zealand KL has the nearest offices (see p.504).

**Hospitals** Adventist Hospital, 465 Jalan Burma ⓣ04/222 7200, ⓦwww.pah.com.my – take blue bus 93, minibus 26, 31, 88 or Transitlink 202, 212; General Hospital, Jalan Utama ⓣ04/229 3333 – take Sri Negara bus 136, 137.

**Immigration office** Pejabat Imigresen, Lebuh Pantai, on the corner of Lebuh Light ⓣ04/261 5122. For on-the-spot visa renewals.

**Internet** As well as a few places in the KOMTAR building, you'll find no shortage of internet terminals in Lebuh Chulia. Try the ground floor of *Banana New Guesthouse*, RM2/hr, or NJ, RM2/hr, at no.425. Alternatively, try the *Western Oriental Café*, 81 Lebuh Muntri, for a more traditional atmosphere place. RM5/ hr.

**Pharmacy** There are several pharmacies along Jl Penang (10am–6pm).

**Police** In emergencies, dial ⓣ999; the police headquarters is on Jalan Penang.

**Post office** The GPO is on Lebuh Downing (Mon–Fri 8.30am–5pm, Sat 8.30am–4pm). The efficient poste restante/general delivery office is here.

**Sport** You can play golf at *Bukit Jambul Country Club*, 2 Jalan Bukit Jambul (ⓣ04/644 2255; green fees RM74), or the Penang Turf Club Golf, Jalan Batu Gantung (ⓣ04/226 6701; green fees RM84, RM126 weekends); there's horse racing at the Penang Turf Club, Jl Batu Gantung (ⓣ04/226 6701, ⓦwww.penangturfclub.com) – see the local paper for fixtures – and you can swim at the Pertama Sports Complex, Paya Terubong, near Ayer Itam (9–11am & 4–9pm; RM4). It's also possible to have riding lessons at *Batu Ferringhi Country Club* for RM40 an hour. ⓣ012/556 8805, book in advance.

**Telephone services** Calls within Penang made from public telephone booths cost a flat rate of 10 sen and can be dialled direct. For international calls, you can buy a phone card or use the Telekom office at the GPO on Lebuh Downing, open 24hr.

**Travel agencies** Try MSL Travel, *Angora Hotel*, 202 Jalan McAllister, for student and youth travel. There are a large number of other agencies on Lebuh Chulia, including the reliable Happy Holidays at no. 442, ⓣ04/262 9222, and the friendly HS Sam Book Store at no.473.

### Moving on

**By bus** Although some buses to destinations on the Peninsula depart from Pengkalan Weld in Georgetown, most use the long-distance bus terminal at Sungei Nibong, just south of Georgetown. To get to the long-distance bus station, take Minibus 25 from the KOMTAR bus station. From Sungei Nibong there are five buses a day to Tanah Rata, as well as buses to KL, Kota Bharu, Melaka and Kuala Terengganu. However, the majority of long-distance buses use the terminal at Butterworth; any travel agency on Lebuh Chulia will book seats for you. Most long-distance buses from Butterworth depart in the evening, so you can take them overnight.

**By train** The nearest train station is in Butterworth, but there is a booking office in the Pengkalan Weld ferry terminal (Ⓣ04/261 0290).

**By ferry** Ferries to Butterworth are frequent from 5am to 11pm and take twenty minutes. Ferries to Medan in Sumatra, Indonesia (4hr) and Pulau Langkawi (2hr) depart twice daily from Swettenham Pier. Tickets for either route can be purchased in advance from the office next to the Penang Tourist Association and from the tourist information office at the KOMTAR complex. Tickets for Langkawi are sold by the Langkawi Ferry Service (Ⓣ04/264 2088; Ⓦwww.langkawi-ferry.com) and by Ekspres Bahagia (Ⓣ04/263 1943), both at the PPC Shopping Complex. Travel agencies on Lebuh Chulia will also book for you. It's a good idea to book ferries a few days in advance to ensure a seat.

**By air** Penang is quite a hot-spot from which to catch budget flights. To get to Penang International Airport (Ⓣ04/643 0811) take a taxi (RM20) or the yellow bus 83 (hourly on the hour, 6am–10pm; 45min) from Pengkalan Weld or the KOMTAR complex.

**Destinations:** Bangkok, Thailand (3 daily; 1hr 40min); Johor Bahru (at least 3 daily via KL; 1hr 5min–3hr 45min); KL (14 daily; 45min); Kota Bharu (at least 3 daily via KL; 3hr 15min–4hr); Langkawi (2 daily; 30min); Medan, Indonesia (1 daily; 20min); Phuket, Thailand (3 weekly; 30min); Singapore (8 daily via KL; 1hr 10min–3hr 55min);

## Batu Ferringhi

**BATU FERRINGHI**, a thirty-minute bus ride west of Georgetown on Transitlink 202 or Transitlink a/c 93 (but not the standard 93), or U101 or U105, is largely populated by flash resorts, but does have a decent beach and several guesthouses. The road runs more or less straight along the coast for 3km, on which all the hotels and restaurants are lined up side by side. The bus stops in the centre, where you'll find the **Telekom office**, **post office**, **police station** and **clinic.**

The **budget guesthouses** face the beach and are largely towards the western end of Batu Ferringhi. Reliable deals include clean and cool *Ali's* (Ⓣ04/881 1316; ❹ with fan, TV, shared bath), which has a relaxing open-air café and garden as well as a restaurant that spills out onto the beach, but a fair few rules and regulations. It offers laundry, internet and travel advice and tickets.

There's also spotless *Baba Guesthouse* (Ⓣ04/881 1686; ❷), a friendly, low-key, family-run operation with a small roof terrace with beach view. Or try *ET Budget Guest House* (Ⓣ04/881 1553, Ⓦwww.geocities.com/etguesthouse; ❸), which is as peaceful as any hostel you'll find and boasts a huge balcony at the front.

For **eating**, there's the *Sunset Bistro* serving snacks and drinks on the beachfront, with a chilled soundtrack perfect for watching the waves to, and excellent Indian food (around RM15 a dish) at *Jewel of the North.* For internet, Nazzazo's has reliable connection, at RM4 per hour.

### TRAVEL TO THAILAND

Although the eastern routes into Thailand are strongly advised against, the western routes are considered less dangerous, but check the latest travel advice, including for travel through Hat Yai, beforehand. Most guesthouses will arrange your Thai visa for you if you need one. From the central bus station at KOMTAR in Georgetown, there are bus and minibus services to Thailand, including Hat Yai (3hr) and Phuket (10hr). There's likely to be a change of vehicle in Hat Yai while you go through the immigration procedures, sometimes with a fair amount of waiting around, but booking one trip from Penang does at least save you the hassle of having to organize the different legs of the journey yourself.

### Teluk Bahang

Five kilometres west of Batu Ferringhi lies the sleepy fishing village of **TELUK BAHANG**. To get there, stay on any of the buses which go to Batu Ferringhi from Georgetown (see above). There's not a great deal going on, but it's quite interesting to have a stroll around, to get a flavour of exceptionally quiet and laid-back local life. The beaches around the rocky headland of **Muka Head** make a pleasant place for a stroll, and can be reached in about three hours via a trail that runs west from Teluk Bahang. Avoid going in the heat of the day, however, as there isn't a lot of shade.

There's also a **Butterfly Farm** (Mon–Fri 9am–5pm, Sat & Sun 9am–6pm; RM17.50), which boasts over a hundred species of butterflies, and also has resident reptiles and amphibians, and a Batik Factory (9am–6pm; free), where you can watch Malaysian-style batik being made and buy the finished product.

*Restoran Khaleel*, 18 Lorong Hassan Abas, serves basic Indian **food** such as *roti* and *dosa*, as well as a good-value *nasi campur*. The noodles, which they fry at the stall on the front, are delicious and a steal at RM3.

## ALOR SETAR

**ALOR SETAR**, the tiny state capital of Kedah, is the last major stop before the Thai border. It's a city that is keen to preserve its heritage, but in its battle to do so appears to be permanently under construction – numerous impressive-looking buildings such as its Old Royal Palace have been under construction and inaccessible for years. Since Alor Setar has useful transport links to the east coast as well as to Thailand, you're likely to end up spending at least a short time here.

### What to see and do

The main sights are located to the west of the town around the padang, whose west side is dominated by the awe-inspiringly huge and impressive mosque, **Masjid Zahir**, which looks like something out of a children's fable.

South of the padang, across the Sungei Kedah at 18 Lorong Kilang Ais, **Rumah Kelahiran Mahathir** (Tues–Sun 10am–5pm; Fri closed noon–3pm) is the birthplace of Dr Mahathir Mohammed; it's now a museum, documenting the life of the local doctor who became the most powerful Malaysian prime minister of modern times. The **Pekan Rabu** market, held every day from morning to midnight on Jalan Tunku Ibrahim, is a good place to buy handicrafts and sample local foods. North of the padang, beside the roundabout on Jalan Telok Wanjah, the **Nikhrodharam Buddhist Temple** is a glittering complex with numerous statues, mosaics and paintings that shows the continuing influence of Thai culture.

### Arrival and information

**By bus** Long-distance buses arrive at Alor Setar's huge express bus station (Shahab Perdana), 6km north of the centre, well connected to the city by municipal buses (RM1) and taxis (RM7). The local bus station on Jl Langgar runs services to the express terminal.

**By train** The train station is behind the Jl Langar terminus, a five-minute walk east of the centre on Jl Stesyen.

**By air** The domestic airport (☎04/714 4021), 11km north of town, is served by the hourly "Kepala Batas" bus to and from the express bus station. Alternatively, it's a RM10 taxi ride into town.

**Tourist information** The efficient tourist office (daily 9am–5pm; ☎04/922 2078) is on Jl Bukit Kayuhitam.

### Accommodation

Most of the budget hotels are in the vicinity of Jl Langgar.

**Comfort Motel** 2C Jalan Kg Perak ☎04/734 4866. A good-value Chinese-run guesthouse, this is a standard, tiled hotel in a wooden house across the road from the mosque. ❷

**Flora Inn** 8 Kompleks Medan Raja ☎04/732 2376. Built over a small food court with rooms overlooking the town, this small guesthouse has basic but good-value rooms. ❷

## Eating

**Hajjah** Jl Tungku Ibrahim, opposite Citypoint shopping centre. A small, unassuming outlet serving exceptional Thai seafood.
**Queen's Bakery** Jl Tunku Ibrahim. This tiny, bustling café has a decent bakery at the front, and a super-efficient kitchen serving Western options alongside the usual noodles and rice.
**Pekan Rabu Market** Jl Tungku Ibrahim. A wide-ranging choice of excellent dishes all under one roof.

## Directory

**Banks** Most of the major banks are on Jl Raja. There's also a Maybank on Jalan Sultan Badlishah.
**Internet** There are several places at the Citypoint shopping centre.

## Moving on

**By bus** From the express bus station to Butterworth (every 45min; 30min); Ipoh (3 daily; 3hr); Johor Bahru (2 daily; 16hr); Kota Bharu (2 daily; 8–9hr); Kuala Lumpur (2 daily; 5hr); Kuala Perlis (hourly; 1hr 30min); Kuala Terengannu (2 daily; 8hr); Kuantan (2 daily; 9hr 30min). From the local bus station, catch the 106 to Kuala Kedah for the Langkawi ferry.
**By train** to: Bangkok, Thailand (1 daily; 21hr 30min); Butterworth (2 daily; 1hr 45min–2hr 45min); Hat Yai, Thailand (2 daily; 2hr 35min–4hr 10min); Kuala Lumpur (1 daily; 13hr 10min).
**By air** Air Asia (☎1300 889 933) and Malaysia Airlines (☎04/731 1106) have several daily flights to Kuala Lumpur.

# PULAU LANGKAWI

Situated 30km off the coast at the very northwestern tip of the Peninsula is a cluster of 104 tropical islands, the largest of which is **Pulau Langkawi**, a paradise island where it's easy to while away a good few days, taking trips to the various water-spots and jungle areas around the island. The name Langkawi combines the Malay words *helang* (eagle) and *kawi* (strong) – hence the eagle is the symbol for the island, and an impressive statue can be found in Kuah. Langkawi has seen unparalleled development in recent years: some of the country's most luxurious hotels are here, and there's an international airport with flights from Japan, Taiwan and Singapore. Langkawi's principal town is Kuah, on the south-eastern side of the island, but the main tourist developments have been on the west of the island, at **Pantai Tengah** and **Pantai Cenang.**

By far the most popular destination for travellers is **Pantai Cenang,** which offers a long stretch of white sand, bars and cafés on the beachfront and plenty of cheap accommodation. Some of the beaches on the island have been privatised for resorts, but there are still plenty available for lounging and swimming – they're slowly being overtaken by litter, though, so it's vital to be scrupulous about taking everything with you when you leave a place. There is basically one circular road around the island, with the other main road running north and south along with some minor roads.

## Kuah

Lining a large sweep of bay in the southeastern corner of the island,

### JELLYFISH JOY

Beware that in **jellyfish season** (Feb and March) you're likely to experience a sort of electric shock sensation when you're in the water – stings aren't lethal, nor do they leave marks, but it can be a little uncomfortable while bathing. If you do notice that you have a visible or particularly painful sting, avoid putting freshwater on it as this will increase the pain. Instead, a splash of vinegar or alcohol should help alleviate it. Also watch out for the **sandflies**, which attack if you sit directly on the sand – you won't feel them, but might discover the next day that you look like you've developed chicken pox, and it itches like mad.

## TRAVEL TO AND FROM PULAU LANGKAWI

All boat services to Langkawi dock at the jetty on the southeastern tip of the island, two minutes' taxi drive (RM5) from Kuah. The most common approach is by ferry from **Kuala Perlis**, 5km north of Alor Setar and adjacent to the Thai border (hourly; 45min; RM12 one way). Express buses from Padang Besar, Alor Setar and Butterworth are fairly frequent and drop you next to the jetty.

Ferries also operate between Kuah and **Kuala Kedah** (every 30min, leaving Kuala Kedah 7.30am–7pm, last boat from Kuah 5.30pm; 1hr 15min; RM15 one way), 8km from Alor Setar (local buses from the bus station opposite the ferry terminal to Alor Setar cost RM2, but can take ages; a taxi costs RM15); **Penang** (2 daily, leaving Penang 8am & 8.45am; leaving Kuah 2.30pm & 5.30pm; 2hr 30min; RM45) and **Satun in Thailand** (4 daily; 9.30am– 4pm; 1hr; RM25). From Satun, you can make easy onward connections in Thailand. From the jetty at Kuah, a taxi to Cenang will cost RM15 per person, and the driver is unfortunately unlikely to budge on the price.The **airport** (Ⓣ04/955 1311) is 20km west of Kuah, near Pantai Cenang; a taxi is supposed to cost RM15 to Kuah, but drivers tend to ignore the posted fare; be sure to agree on a price before setting off. Air Asia (Ⓣ03/955 7752, Ⓦwww.airasia.com) offers about seven flights daily between Langkawi and KL, as do Malaysia Airlines (Ⓣ03/966 6622, Ⓦwww.malaysiaairlines.com). Silk Air (Ⓣ065/6223 8888, Ⓦwww.silkair.com) has flights to Singapore every day except Monday. There's a MAS office (Ⓣ04/966 6622) on the ground floor of the Langkawi Fair Shopping Complex, 400m from the main jetty.

**KUAH** is easily the largest town on Langkawi, and has a ferry terminal, hotels and shopping complexes. Beside the ferry terminal is Dataran Lang (Eagle Square where, unsurprisingly, Langkawi's namesake eagle statue can be found) and **Lagenda Langkawi Dalan Taman** (daily 9am–7pm; admission free), a landscaped "theme park" of giant sculptures based around the legends of the islands. Although there are several hotels around the bay and many of the island's facilities are here, there isn't really much to detain you since other areas are far more appealing.

## LEGENDARY LANGKAWI

Langkawi is an island surrounded by legends. One of the most popular tells how a beautiful and innocent young girl, Mahsuri, was wrongly accused of infidelity. When she was unjustly executed for her crime, her blood flowed out pure white in protestation and proof of her innocence, staining the beaches of Langkawi the white that they remain today.

### Pantai Tengah and Pantai Cenang

A clearly signed junction 18km west from Kuah points you to the first of the western beaches, **PANTAI TENGAH**, 6km further on from the junction. It's a quiet beach with a few large resorts popular with families – the sand isn't bad, but the water is murky.

Five hundred metres north of Tengah, the development at **PANTAI CENANG** is the most extensive on the island, with small chalet sites side by side, and numerous bars and restaurants. The bay forms a large sweep of wide, white beach with crisp, sugary sand, and it's hugely popular with backpackers. Plenty of places offer **watersports** and **boat rental**, where you can expect to pay RM50 for thirty minutes on a jet ski, the same for fifteen minutes' water-skiing, or RM200 for half a day's fishing (4–6 people). Paragliding over the sea is also a not-too-expensive thrill, at RM70 for the chance to fly suspended above the ocean. You can also check out the huge **Underwater World** (daily 10am–6pm; RM18; www.underwaterworldlangkawi.com.my), where the highlight is a walk-through aquarium.

### Pantai Kok and Telaga Tujuh

**PANTAI KOK**, a secluded beach lined by a woody area and plenty of palm trees, lies on the far western stretch of Langkawi. Accommodation is limited to a few big resorts, only one of which – *Baru Bay* – is actually on the beach. Pantai Kok's seclusion is sufficient for people to feel it necessary to sunbathe there naked; you have been warned.

The road after the turn-off to the *Berjaya Langkawi Beach and Spa Resort* leads up to the island's most wonderful natural attraction, **Telaga Tujuh** or "Seven Wells", where the mossy rocks enable you to slide from one pool to another (although during the dry season it's, obviously, drier), before the fast-flowing water disappears over the cliff to form the ninety-metre waterfall. It's a steep two-hundred-metre climb to the pools from the base of the hill so expect to be delightfully sweaty by the time you get there – in total, it's about a 45-minute walk from the road.

### Gunung Machinchang

This is the vertiginous hilly jungle (708m high at its peak) scaled by the **Langkawi Cable Car** (Mon–Thurs 10am–6pm, Fri–Sun 10am–7pm), well worth the RM25, even for travellers on a tight budget. At the top there are stunning views of the island, and you'll realize there's more jungle on Langkawi than you could have imagined. The cable car ride itself is fifteen minutes each way, but you'll probably want to have an hour or two to spend gazing down once you get up there. The cable car stop is situated in "Oriental Village", a slightly surreal shopping conglomeration built around a series of pagodas and little red bridges. Stopping for food here on the way up or down in the cable car is a good option; *Dolce Vita Café* does great coffees and freshly baked banana-and-chocolate muffins.

### Pantai Pasir Tengorak

On the northwestern coast, this beach is small but perfectly formed, with a small campsite used by Malay visitors sitting unobtrusively next to it. It's much more secluded than, say, Cenang and a lovely place to spend an afternoon, particularly as the rocky outcrops are good for snorkelling. However take note that as Malay visitors are more modest than the Westerners, you may feel a little out of place in a bikini.

### Tanjung Rhu

If you make one trip while on Langkawi, make it to the tiny beach at Tanjung Rhu. It's breathtaking at dusk; the sun

#### MONKEYING AROUND

From Cenang, you can take a boat to the "castaway"-style **Monkey Island** – the irrepressible AC (a friendly Indonesian local with a choice vocabulary in practically any language you care to throw at him) at *Babylon Bar* is more than happy to oblige with a return boat trip for RM15. The island is gorgeously secluded, with beautiful white beaches and clear waters all around – watch your stuff though, because it isn't called "Monkey Island" for nothing. If you ask the day in advance and have a reasonable party, barbecues on the island can also be arranged. The tiny bar there, *Monkey Bar*, does a great line in full-moon parties, although at the time of writing these had been banned by unimpressed Muslim locals. The plan was to restart within a few months though, so it's probably worth making some enquiries.

sets over stunning limestone outcrops which can be viewed from a pure white and almost completely secluded beach, and the spectacle is highly likely to make it into a list of top ten sunsets. It's also a good spot to sunbathe in the day, though the water is very shallow – but very clear.

## Information and island transport

**Tourist information** The Langkawi tourist office (Sat–Thurs 9am–5pm; ⓣ04/966 7789), next to the mosque on the way into Kuah, is very helpful, and there's also an information booth at the airport, open daily. See ⓦwww.langkawi-online.com for useful up-to-date information.

**Island-hopping tours** These begin at RM25 for half a day on a boat and involve going to islands such as Pulau Dayang Bunting in the south to enjoy a swim in the refreshingly freshwater Dayang Bunting Lake (Lake of the Pregnant Maiden, which is supposedly good for fertility). It's a pleasant and fairly stress-free way to check out what Langkawi has to offer.

**Map** The Langkawi Discovery Map, produced by Sunspot Productions, is a good investment at RM3 if you plan to explore the island. Otherwise, despite the lack of major roads, it's mysteriously easy to get lost.

**Car rental** Available from a fair number of travel agencies – try the Tourist Needs Shop on Pantai Cenang (daily 8am–9pm, ⓣ04/955 5551), which is a reliable choice at RM60 per day for a small car.

**Motorbike rental** Many of the chalets and motels offer motorbike rental (RM25 per day). Take a map (and plenty of sunscreen) and enjoy.

**Taxis** There are no bus routes, so this is the only option. Unfortunately taxi rides tend to be fairly pricey: a journey to Pantai Cenang from the jetty will cost you RM15 per person, and from Pantai Cenang to Pantai Kok is around RM25.

## Accommodation

### Kuah

Despite the multitude of hotels, it's not somewhere you're likely to want to stay.

**Langkawi Baron Hotel** 2 Jl Lencongan, ⓣ04/966 2000. A clean, modern hotel that's probably the best of the budget choices in Kuah, and one of the only ones with a dorm. It's conveniently located in the centre of town and has a restaurant. Dorms ❷; doubles ❻

### Pantai Tengah

**Tanjung Malie** ⓣ04/955 1891. A good budget option with quiet and comfortable fan or a/c chalets set in a garden. ❸

### Pantai Cenang

**Big Bro Guesthouse** ⓣ017/254 5746 or ⓣ013/418 4014 A good choice despite its terrible name. Although this is fairly chaotic from the outside, rooms are large and clean with thoughtful additions such as kettles. The beach is just a two-minute walk away and owners are friendly. ❸

**Gecko Guesthouse** ⓣ019/428 3801 By far the most popular budget choice on Cenang (and probably all of Langkawi), this laid-back guesthouse is sprawling and cool, serving breakfasts until 2pm and with a large shady chill-out area off to one side. Run by no-nonsense Brit Rebecca, it's a short walk to the beach and a great place to stay. Dorm ❶; double ❷

**Lagenda Permai Chalet** ⓣ04/955 2806. This place is good value, with basic chalets directly on the beach front, all with attached bathroom (though water pressure in the showers is weak). ❸

**Langkapuri Beach Resort** ⓣ04/955 1202. Located at the southern end of the beach, these brick chalets are sturdier than most, and clustered around an appealingly leafy patch of beach. ❹

**Melati Tanjung Motel** ⓣ04/955 1099. Standard choice of fan and a/c chalets, the more expensive of which are on the beachfront. All rooms come with mini fridges – so if this is slightly pricier than you're used to, you can make up the difference by drinking only cool bargain beers on your very own veranda. ❺

**The Palms** ⓣ017/631 0121. If you're after en-suite bedrooms, this new guesthouse run by Brits Sue and Dave is an excellent choice. Rooms are spotless and spacious, and being set just a little back from the beach it's also a peaceful haven from the hustle and bustle of Cenang. On Jl Madrasah, a track signposted clearly from the main road. ❺

**Rainbow** ⓣ012/513 6103. A new development along the road behind Gecko, this is built around an open area and jauntily painted with stars and moons. It's clean and friendly with a café serving Western breakfasts, and a good place to meet other travellers. Dorm ❶; double ❷

## Eating

### Pantai Tengah

**Boom Boom Corner** This popular food court is at the northern end of the beach, and serves a huge array of Malay and Indian food at around RM4 a dish.

**White Sands Restaurant** A little pricier, but more of a proper restaurant, serving excellent Malay seafood at around RM17 a dish, set a little way from the seafront.

### Pantai Cenang

Most of the resorts also have decent attached restaurants: some don't serve alcohol and won't allow it on the premises, whereas others don't serve it but have no objections to your bringing your own.

**Champor Champor** Located opposite the *AB Motel*, this upmarket restaurant combines Western and Oriental influence to successful effect in an enchanted grove atmosphere, and is well worth the splurge. RM20 for a main course.

**D'Sini Restoran** This nondescript-looking shack serves super-cheap *nasi campur* – RM3 for a plate and delicious. Located thirty seconds from the beachfront at the *Gecko Guesthouse* end.

**H J Jelani's** A completely understated, basic shack serving food on the beachfront at great prices. The fried *koey teow*, at RM7, is delicious, and breakfasts start at RM2 for toast and jam.

> **TREAT YOURSELF**
>
> **Putumayo** ⓣ04/953 2233, ⓔrebeccalook_paul@yahoo.com. This sophisticated place, decorated in minimalist Oriental style, is great for a romantic dinner, with an atmospheric outdoor seating area with a candle-lit approach. Mains are around RM20, and seriously delicious. It's located halfway down the main road behind the beach.

**Rafii's Place** Halfway down the beach, this tiny restaurant is a dream, serving mouthwateringly delicious, traditionally cooked seafood and Thai curries in a pleasant and low-key atmosphere. There's also a chilled-out candle-lit bar on the beachfront where you can enjoy the sound of the sea, and lovely (if slightly pricier) cocktails. The meals are a steal, at RM7 for a main course.

**Rasa** A good place for breakfast a stone's throw from most of the budget accommodation, with muesli and fruit at RM8. It's also good for dinner, where seafood portions are tasty, if a little on the small side (RM12 for a main).

**Red Tomato** A chance to blow a day's budget on some fine Western food with tasty breakfasts, pizzas and very cold beer. Eggs Benedict RM17.50, pasta dishes RM15–20.

**Samba Rio** The restaurant attached to the *Sandy Beach Resort* serves excellent seafood right on the beach. At RM10 for fresh grilled squid or barracuda it's a steal, and even better, you can bring your own alcohol.

### Pantai Kok and Telaga Tujuh

In general, food is served at the big resorts, and the Oriental Village Shopping Complex has a good cluster of restaurants.

**7 Wells Restoran** Just before you reach Telaga Tujuh, on the corner of the road to Datai, is this tiny restaurant offering wonderful home cooking.

## Drinking

Being a tax-free island, beer on Langkawi is seriously cheap, available in convenience stores at RM1.50 a can. Enjoying these on the beach is an affordable way to spend an evening, but take a throw – otherwise you're liable to wake up the next day covered in sandfly bites. Quite a few of the restaurants serve alcohol and most big hotels have bars. For stand-alone bars, Pantai Cenang is by far the buzziest option – the best are listed below.

**Babylon Mat Lounge** Less is sometimes more – some bamboo matting and little tables on the beach, all lit with flares and playing great music – what more could you ask for? There are also often fire poi performers, and the rasta owners are so laid-back they won't mind what time you stay until – they'll just leave and ask you to put away your furniture when you're ready to go.

**Little Lilia's Chillout Bar** Drinks and food right on the seafront, and is a lovely buzzy place to catch up on the day with the sand between your toes.

**Sands Bar** The closest thing you'll get to a club on Cenang, this place has a great vibe and a buzzy dance floor. It's a ten minute taxi-ride from Cenang Beach and closes late (5am).

**Yellow Café** A raised area on the seafront where you can sit on mats (away from the sandflies). Reggae night is on Thursdays, with a live band starting at 9.30pm, and there's a barbecue buffet on Tuesdays from 8pm for RM40. There are also nightly happy hours 5–7pm, with a buy-one-get-one-free offer.

## Directory

**Banks** Three parallel streets behind the MAYA shopping complex in Kuah hold all the banks

### TRAVELLING TO THAILAND

**Kuala Perlis** is one of the best gateways into Thailand, and one of the few places with routes that are still viable considering the political unrest. To get to Kuala Perlis from Langkawi, there are ferries every hour from Kuah between 9am and 6pm. There are then several options for continuing your journey over the border.

**By boat to Satun:** Directly from Kuala Perlis: small boats leave from the jetty en route from Langkawi as soon as they're full and charge RM4 for the thirty-minute journey. This is the quickest cross-border option if you're coming from Langkawi. At weekends, you'll be charged an additional RM1 for the immigration officers' overtime payment.

**By train:** The nearest train station is at Arau, 16km east of Kuala Perlis, where you can catch the **daily train to Hat Yai and Bangkok** (though the train doesn't stop here on the return journey). The northbound train comes to a halt at **PADANG BESAR**, where a very long platform connects the Malaysian service with its Thai counterpart. You don't change trains here, although you must get off and go through immigration and customs at the station. Beware that when the Thai border opens in the morning (at 9am) the queues for immigration are pretty awful.

**By bus:** There are frequent services from the local bus station (1km north of the express terminal) at **Kangar**, 12km east of Kuala Perlis, to the border at Padang Besar. The crossing is open from 6am to 10pm. Buses also ply the North–South Highway, which runs to the Thai border at **Bukit Kayu Hitam**, from where it's about a five-hundred-metre walk to Danok on the Thai side. Once you've passed through immigration, there are regular bus connections from both places with Hat Yai, 60km away (see p.883).Make sure you've had your passport stamped by both sets of border police. Citizens of most countries don't need a visa for stays of up to thirty days, but you need to show a plane ticket departing from Thailand, so if you're departing overland, or staying longer than thirty days, you'll need a visa. Most travel agencies and even guesthouses throughout Malaysia can help – particularly in Penang, Kota Bharu, and Kuala Perlis. Thai Consulates in Malaysia are located at: Penang, no.1, Jalan Tunku Abdul Rahman ⓣ04/226 8029, ⓔthaipg@tm.net.my; Kota Bharu, 4426 Jalan Pengkalan Chepa ⓣ09/744 5266, ⓔthaicg@tm.net.my; Kuala Lumpur, 206 Jalan Ampang ⓣ03/248 8222.

– these are virtually the only places to change money on the whole island. Otherwise, money can be changed at some guesthouses or travel agencies, but rates aren't great.

**Hospital** ⓣ04/966 3333. Jl Bukit Tengah 07000, 7km from Kuah.

**Internet** The quickest connection on Pantai Cenang is *Malati Internet*, which charges RM3.50 an hour. In Kuah, there are plenty of options along Jl Kisap.

**Police station** Jl Kisap, Kua ⓣ04/966 6222.

**Post office** Daily except Fri 9am–5pm. Jl Kisap, Kuah.

**Travel Agencies** Most guesthouses will help you organize tickets for onward travel, and trips around the island. Otherwise, try Seahill Travel ⓣ04/953 1111, ⓦwww.seahilltravel.com.my.

# The interior

Banjaran Titiwangsa (Main Range) forms the western boundary of the interior; to its east is an H-shaped range of steep, sandstone mountains and luxuriant valleys where small towns and villages nestle. The rivers that flow from these mountains – Pahang, Tembeling, Lebir, Nenggiri and Galas – provide the northern interior's indigenous peoples, the Negritos and Senoi, with their main means of transport. Visitors, too, can travel by boat to perhaps the most stunning of all Peninsular Malaysia's delights, **Taman Negara National Park**. Bordering Taman Negara to the south, **Kenong Rimba** is a smaller, quieter, less visited national park, but none the worse for that. And what better way to get from the coasts to these wilderness places than by the **Jungle Railway**, which chugs leisurely through the scenic interior from **Gemas** in the south to **Kota Bharu** on the northwest coast.

## THE JUNGLE RAILWAY

Unless you're in a real hurry to get to either coast, consider a trip on the **Jungle Railway**, which winds through the valleys and round the sandstone hills from Mentakab in southern Pahang to Kota Bharu, 500km to the northeast. It also offers useful stops at Jerantut and Kuala Tembeling, both access points for Taman Negara and at Kuala Lipis, close to Kenong Rimba National Park. The line was completed in 1931 and runs at a snail's pace (it is seldom less than two hours behind schedule) along valley floors where trees and plants almost envelop the track.

It's a great way to encounter rural life, and for the Malays, Tamils and Orang Asli who live in these remote areas, the railway is the only alternative to walking. Most people do this trip from south to north, but going in the opposite direction, from north to south, gives you many more hours of daylight in the jungle. The most useful connection leaves Kota Bharu at 6.35am, supposedly arriving in Jerantut at 1.40pm. Realistically, however, don't expect to arrive any time before 3.30pm, or that it will leave when scheduled. Schedules change frequently, so ask at the train station, or check the Keretapi Tana Melayu Berhad (Malaysian Rail) website at ⓦwww.ktmb.com.my.

### Mentakab

If you approach the Jungle Railway **from Kuala Lumpur**, a convenient option is to take a bus to **MENTAKAB** (every 30min from Pekeliling; 2hr 30min), less than 100km east of KL. To reach the train station, walk from the bus station south onto the main road, Jalan Temerloh, and bear left for 50m to a big junction. Turn right, walk another 200m and watch for a narrow road on your right, marked to the train station – a fifteen-minute walk. There are numerous budget **hotels** on Jalan Temerloh that you'll reach if you carry on walking eastwards. The cleanest is the *London Café and Hotel*, 71 Jalan Temerloh (ⓣ09/277 1119; ❷), which features neat, basic doubles with attached bathrooms.

## JERANTUT

**JERANTUT** is a small, busy town with only one major street, Jalan Besar, that's usually a stop-off on the way to destinations closer to Taman Negara National Park.

### Arrival and information

**By bus** The bus station is a five-minute walk south to Jl Besar and the centre of town. Turn right out of the train station, take the first left, go past the supermarket in the centre and the bus station is opposite the KFC.

**By train** The train station (ⓣ09/266 2219) is off Jl Besar, just behind *Hotel Sri Emas*.

**Tourist information** Beware of the misleading sign for "tourist Information", just outside a central handicraft shop. Nobody seems to have any idea why it's there and the people in the handicraft shop certainly don't have any tourist information. The best places to ask if you're stuck are at the train or bus stations.

### Accommodation and eating

Between the train and bus stations there are plenty of stalls and mini-restaurants serving Thai, Malay and Chinese food. They're very atmospheric, being popular with locals and travellers alike, and serve excellent cheap *rotis*, *nasi goreng* and *kuey teow*, as well as more regional specialities. Open until 3am.

**Cheng Heng Hotel** 24 Jl Besar ⓣ09/266 3693. The friendliest place in town, run by a very helpful family. It's just south of the *Emas* on the opposite side of the road. ❷

**Hotel Sri Emas** ⓣ09/266 4499. Situated at the junction of Jl Besar and the road that leads to the train station, this basic hostel has a dorm (RM7), inexpensive doubles and better a/c rooms, and offers a wealth of information on the park as well as fast internet access. There's also luggage storage here, which is helpful if you're waiting for transport. ❶

**Jerantut Resthouse** ⓣ09/266 6200. A large, rambling and good-value place 1km west of the train station on Jl Benta that offers free pick-up. Extremely friendly and has a dorm (RM8), which is unusual in Jerantut. ❷

## Moving on

**By bus or taxi to Taman Negara** Take either a taxi (RM16) or a local bus (8am, 11am & 1.30pm; 40min; RM1.20) to Tembeling jetty (the 1.30pm bus doesn't get to the jetty in time for the 2pm boat). Alternatively, join the *Hotel Sri Emas* bus trip that leaves Jerantut at 8.30am, stopping at cocoa, rubber and oil palm plantations before reaching Kuala Tahan at around 11am (RM25). Or if you'd rather go straight to Kuala Tahan, the village where most of the accommodation is, you can take a taxi for RM60 (this takes about an hour), or the local bus (9am, 11am, 3.30pm & 5pm; 2hr RM6).

**By bus** Other destinations include: Kuantan (9.30am, 11am & 2.30pm; 4hr), a useful stopover point from which you can get transport to a variety of destinations; Kota Bharu (4 daily, first one at 6.30am; 4hr), Kuala Lumpur (4 daily; 3hr), Melaka (1 daily; 6hr), Johor Bahru (one daily; 8hr), Kuala Lipis (four daily; 6hr 30min). You can also take a local bus to Temerloh (hourly; 8am – 5pm; 1hr) from where there are connections to a variety of places. *Hotel Sri Emas* arranges transport to the Perhentian Islands (5hr) and the Cameron Highlands (2hr) according to demand. Enquire at the reception.

**By train** Local trains make the fifteen-minute run from Jerantut to tiny **Kuala Tembeling** several times a day. As the schedule is both changeable and unreliable, ask at the train station for times. (Village Tembeling is an unscheduled stop, so you'll need to tell the guard you want to get off.) From here, it's a two-kilometre walk west to the jetty.You can pick up the **Jungle Railway** here going in either direction. Southward, it connects with the Singapore–KL railway line at Gemas, making it an easy journey to either of those destinations. There are two express trains a day to Singapore via Johor Bahru, at 2am and 8.50am. Northward, the line heads to Kuala Lipis and Gua Masang.

# TAMAN NEGARA NATIONAL PARK

**Taman Negara** is Peninsular Malaysia's largest and most popular national park and contains perhaps some of the most spectacular jungle scenery you'll ever come across. Trails ranging from short, sunlit strolls to hard-core tropical treks snake through some of the oldest rainforest in the world. Accommodation ranges from luxury resorts and rustic guesthouses to hides and campsites. To catch sight of some of the more impressive mammals, including the resident elephants, mouse deer, tapir and wild ox (and possibly some snake varieties you'd be less keen to catch sight of) you probably need to do a three- or four-day trek, staying in hides along the way, or journey upriver to remote **Kuala Keniam**.

The most popular village for budget accommodation is **Kuala Tahan**, where the park headquarters are also situated. For a quieter experience, there's the more basic **Nusa Camp**, 2km upstream, and the upriver camps at **Kuala Keniam** and **Kuala Trenggan**. The best time to **visit** the park is between February and October, during the "dry" season, although it still rains even then (and then the leeches come out in force). In the wet season (mid-Oct to Feb), there may be restrictions on the trails and boat trips.

## What to see and do

While lots of people come to Taman Negara to do some hard-core **trekking** and wildlife spotting, there are plenty of others who just fancy a meander through the jungle and aren't up for anything too strenuous. There are options galore for both groups, with **hides** to stay in, **waterfalls** to explore and off-the-beaten-track accommodation for the first group, and the tamer (but no less beautiful) man-made **canopy walkway** and shorter walks for the latter. The bat caves of Gua Telinga are also well worth exploring, and a lazy **boat ride** down the Sungei Tahan is a must.

To start off, you'll need to visit the **Taman Negara Park Information Centre,** located in the Mutiara Taman Negara Resort complex on the west bank of the Sungei Tahan river, opposite Kuala Tahan village. Here you can get your **park entry permit** (RM1) and your **camera licence** (RM5). Being caught without one results in a hefty fine so it's worth paying up. They can also provide you with maps and information and book you into hides.

To get around the park along the river, take a **sampan** (boat). It will cost you RM1 to cross the river, and for, say, trips to upriver sites such as the waterfalls of Lata Berkoh, RM80 per boat one-way. Getting one either to, halfway to or back from a destination means you'll be able to see more without necessarily having to go the whole hog and walk for hours at a time.

Sampans can be organized from the park office, the jetty, or almost any of the floating restaurants by Kuala Tahan. It's probably a good idea to organize your return trip as well, since boatmen only operate out of Kuala Tahan and Nusa Camp. Although less reliable, it is, however, possible to flag down boats going in the direction you want, either if they're chartered but not full, or local boats. This is worth bearing in mind if you need to get out of the jungle quickly (for emergencies or because you just can't take the sweat and the leeches anymore).

It's also possible to rent things like sleeping bags (RM5), roll mats (RM3) and walking boots (RM4) from a variety of places, including *Tembeling River View Hostel*, and from the park's

## GETTING TO TAMAN NEGARA

Most visitors approach the park by going to **Jerantut** or **Kuala Tembeling**, then going on to **Tembeling Jetty** from which it's a beautifully scenic boat ride (daily 9am & 2pm, except Fri 9am & 2.45pm; RM25) along the **Sengei Tahan river** to the village of **Kuala Tahan**, where the park headquarters and most of the budget accommodation can be found, or the more quiet **Nusa Camp**, 2km further upstream. The journey takes around three hours. Taking the boat from Tembeling Jetty means that technically speaking you're entering the park already, so you'll have to buy a park entry permit (RM1) and a camera licence (RM5) from Taman Negara Resort ticket office on the jetty. Both Jerantut and Kuala Tembeling are stops on the Jungle Railway, or some people get to Jerantut by bus. From Jerantut it's a forty-five-minute bus-ride to Tembeling Jetty, 15km away, and from Kuala Tembeling it's a half-hour walk. There's no accommodation at Kuala Tembeling, so many stay the night at Jerantut (see p.530).

### From KL and the west coast

**By bus** Buses to Jerantut go from Pekeliling station (4 daily; 3hr 30min).
**By train** A/c express trains from KL into the interior leave from Sentral station at 7am and 8pm. It's also possible to take a bus to Mentakab and take the Jungle Railway from there (see p.530)

### From the east coast

**From Kota Bharu** The Jungle Railway goes directly from **Wakaf Bharu** (7km and an easy taxi ride from Kota Bharu) to either Jerantut or Kuala Tembeling. The most useful connection leaves Wakaf Bharu at 6.38am – as the line doesn't usually run on schedule, it tends to arrive in Jerantut at about 3.30pm. **From Kuantan** Three daily buses (10am, 1pm & 3pm; RM10.50) go straight to Jerantut, or there's an hourly service to Temerloh, where you change for Jerantut.

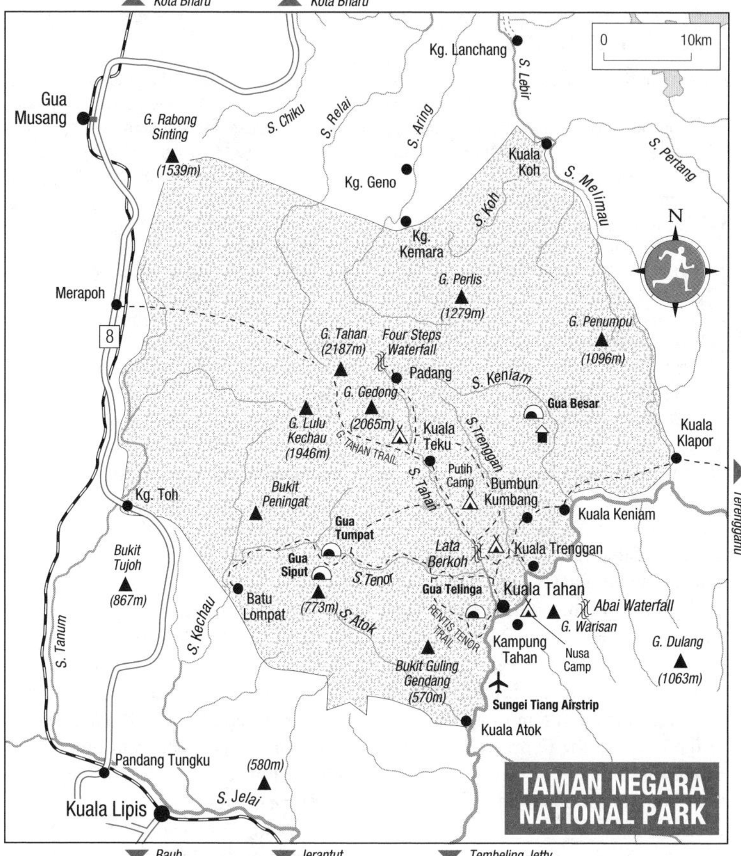


**Recreation Counter** (located next to the Information Centre in the Mutiara Resort). Renting boots is highly advisable, especially if you're going in wet weather, so you don't have to carry around your own soaking shoes afterwards, and the high sides will help protect against the leeches.

## The hides

Spending a night in one of the park's **hides**, situated beside salt licks, doesn't guarantee sightings of large mammals, but the sound of the jungle at night guarantees that it'll be a memorable experience, and you may catch sight of deer, tapir, elephant, leopard or wild ox. The hides offer very (very) basic bunk accommodation in concrete huts for six to eight people and must be booked at the wildlife office in the resort (RM5–8 per person, depending on the hide). They are sturdily built and sufficiently raised up that you don't have to worry about things creeping on you during the night, but they have no washing or cooking facilities, and no electricity, so bring a torch. You'll also need to take all the food and drink you will need, a sleeping bag, rain gear and hat – and don't forget to bring your rubbish back. The guides based in the camps are usually happy to lend you equipment such as a pan, a cook stand and some fuel, and being properly equipped makes for a much more

## LOVELY LEECHES

Don't underestimate the leeches, particularly if you visit just after the monsoon. Rain makes the little bloodsuckers come to the surface with even greater wriggling enthusiasm than usual. It's hard to decide about long socks and trousers – on the one hand, this might stop them getting to you, on the other, if you're wearing shorts and short socks, you've got more chance of being able to pick them off when they do (inevitably) attack you. Deet is a good repellant, as is rubbing wet tobacco all over your legs. It's also not a bad idea to carry some salt or a lighter with you to get them off, as pulling them off can occasionally result in their teeth being left behind and causing infections. If you're squeamish about wiggly little things crawling inside your skin and sucking on your blood supply, you might have to toughen up before attempting a serious walk. Once you've come out of the jungle in once piece, expect locals to find your heroic wounds the most side-splittingly hilarious things they've ever come across. On the upside, leech bites don't hurt at all, and look much worse than they actually are.

pleasant evening after a trek through the jungle.

The closest hide to the resort is the **Bumbun Tahan**, just south of the junction with the Bukit Teresek trail. There's also the **Bumbun Tabing**, on the east bank of Sungei Tahan, about 3km from the start of the trail, and **Bumbun Cegar Anjing**, an hour from the Tabing, on the west bank of Sungei Tahan. The most distant hide to the north of the resort is the six-bed **Bumbun Kumbang**, an eleven-kilometre walk from Kuala Tahan and the best place to catch sight of animals.

### Bukit Teresek trail

Although heavily used, the route to the hill of **Bukit Teresek** is an excellent starter. Follow the path between the chalets east of the resort office, beyond which a trail heads northeast away from the river. It's wide and easy to follow, hitting primary jungle almost immediately; after around twenty minutes, the trail divides, straight on to Bukit Teresek and left for the Tabing hide and Bukit Indah. The climb up 342-metre-high Bukit Teresek (1hr) offers breathtaking views. Along the trail you might hear gibbons or hill squirrels in the trees. Back at the base of the hill, the canopy walkway is just 300m to the north along a clearly marked path.

### The canopy walkway

If you do one thing while you're in Taman Negara, the canopy walkway, located about thirty minutes' walk east from Kuala Tahana along the riverside, would be a good choice. Only a small group of people can gain access to the walkway (daily 9.30am–3.30pm, except Fri 9am–noon; RM5) at any one time, so you may have to wait. The walkway is a swaying bridge made from aluminium ladders bound by rope and set 40m above the ground.

At 450m, it's one of the longest walkways of its kind in the world and guaranteed to give you a great adrenaline rush, gorgeous views and frequent sightings of grey-banded leaf monkeys and white-eyed dusky leaf monkeys swinging determinedly amongst the branches. You reach it by climbing a sturdy wooden tower, and it takes thirty minutes to cross, as long as you don't stop for too long in the middle wondering whether you're about to fall to your death or not.

### The Bukit Indah trail

This is another steep but lovely hill climb, meandering northeast past the canopy. It's a three-hour round-trip from the resort office. Initially, this follows the riverbank, and you stand a chance of spotting monkeys, various birds, squirrels, shrews, a multitude of insects and perhaps tapir or wild ox. The path to Bukit Indah hill itself leaves the main riverside trail (which continues to Kuala Trenggan, 6km away) and climbs at a slight gradient for 200m to give a lovely view over the jungle, and the rapids of Sungei Tembeling.

### Gua Telinga Bat Cave and Kemah Keladong Campsite

Another major trail (the Rentis Tenor) leads south alongside the river, with branches to Gua Telinga and the campsite at Kemah Keladong. From the jetty by the KT Restoran, take a sampan across Sungei Tahan. On the other side, follow the trail through a small village into the trees. After 3km, follow the sign north for a further 200m to reach the limestone cave of **Gua Telinga** (better known simply as "The Bat Cave"), which is teeming with tiny roundleaf and fruit bats, as well as giant toads, black-striped frogs and (non-poisonous) whip spiders. You can follow a guide rope through the eighty-metre long cave, and it's weirdly good fun, even though fitting through some of the cavities requires contortionists' tricks that Houdini would be proud of (and wear clothes you don't mind having covered in bat poo from head to foot).

From Gua Telinga, it's another 500m to the noisy Belau hide, and another 1km to the one at Yong, where the trail divides, north to Kemah Rentis and left to the tranquil **Kemah Keladong** campsite, 1km further on. Given an early start, it's quite possible to reach this point, have a brilliantly refreshing swim, and get back to the resort before dusk; bring at least a litre of water per person and lunch.

### The roaring rapids of Lata Berkoh

Most people visit the rapids of **Lata Berkoh** by boat, but you could walk the trail there and arrange for a boat to pick you up for the return journey. **Sampans** from Kuala Tahan cost around RM80 for four people and take half an hour. The **trail** from the resort (8km; 3hr) starts at the campsite and leads through dense rainforest, passing Lubok Lesong campsite (3km), then crossing gullies and steep ridges, before reaching the river, which must be forded. The final part of the trail runs north along the west side of Sungei Tahan before reaching the falls. The **waterfall** itself is 50m north of Berkoh Lodge. There's a deep pool for swimming, and you may see kingfishers, large fish eagles, bulbul birds and monitor lizards.

### Kuala Trenggan and Kuala Keniam

The upriver lodges are set in tranquil surroundings, and make excellent bases for intrepid explorers wanting to see the less-visited parts of the park. You should pre-book all lodges with the park wildlife office at the resort. *Trenggan Lodge* (10 beds; ❶), situated at **Kuala Trenggan**, is a convenient and charming base, with polished wood chalets and a café. It can be reached either by boat (30min; RM80 per boat), or by one of two trails (6–8hr). The shorter and more direct trail runs alongside Sungei Tembeling (9km), but can be quite hard going; the easier inland route (12km) runs north past the campsite at Lubok Lesong.

A further 20km north along Sungei Tembeling (2hr from the resort; RM140 per boat), *Keniam Lodge* (18 beds; ❶), at **Kuala Keniam**, comprises several chalets and a small café. From here, the **Perkai trail** (3km; 2hr) is rich with banded and dusky leaf monkeys, long-tailed macaques and white-handed gibbons. The more popular hike from here is the **Keniam–Trenggan trail** (13km), a major highlight, combining the possibility of seeing elephants with visits to three caves. It's generally a tough, full day's hike, but can be done in around six hours; there are innumerable streams to wade through and hills to circumvent.

## Information and guides

**Taman Negara Park Information Counter** This is located at the *Mutiara Taman Negara Resort*, on the opposite bank of the river from Kuala Tahan. It deals with all park queries, regardless of where you're staying, offers an excellent free site and park map, and is where you can obtain park and camera permits. This is also the place to rent shoes and sleeping bags and so on, at the Recreation Counter just next door. You can also store your luggage here (RM2 per day).

**Guides** There are numerous guides on hand in Taman Negara. The most interesting, long-standing and jungle-savvy guide in the area, Man, can usually be found in the cafés around *Tembeling Riverview Hostel*. His enthusiasm for everything to do with the jungle (particularly if it relates to virility) is infectious. To contact him with any questions about the park or trekking try ⓔ akbarmmnaturezone@hotmail.com. He can organize almost any style of trek that takes your fancy but beware – he's a slave driver. Expect to pay around RM100 per day. If you'd prefer a slightly more sedately paced and considerably more empathetic guide, ask around for the old-world chivalrous Sulaiman, who can also usually be found around *Tembeling Riverview*, or try contacting him on ⓣ 017/955 2979.

## Accommodation

### Kuala Tahan

If you don't stay in the lovely but somewhat pricey *Mutiara Taman Negara Resort*, it's a RM1 ride across the river from Kuala Tahan to the actual park itself.

**Ekoton Chalets** ⓣ 09/266 9897. The dorms here are slightly airless but clean and functional, and doubles are generously proportioned, some with large balconies. The set-up, with the sturdy wooden chalets built around greenery and being near the local school, is charming. Dorm ❶, double ❺

**Lana Guesthouse** ⓣ 03/266 9322. A barracks-style corridor of four-bed dorms (RM10) – not fantastic, or as good as the *Tembeling*, but fine at the price. ❶

**Mutiara Taman Negara Resort** ⓣ 09/266 3500, ⓦ www.mutiarahotels.com. A luxurious, international-standard resort with accommodation consisting of twin-bed chalets (8) and comfortable two-bedroom bungalows (RM700). You can also camp 300m from the resort office (RM2 per person), and tents can be rented for RM8 a night – the RM45 dorm isn't worth bothering with, as you can get the same standard at half the price across the river (although bear in mind that the village is prone to lengthy power cuts). The resort will also prepare good packed lunches and at the Ayer Spa, a foot massage will put you back RM60, but might be an extremely well-needed treat after a hard trek. ❽–❾

**Tembeling Riverview Hostel and Chalets** ⓣ 09/266 6766. Across the river in Kuala Tahan itself, this is the best place to stay if you don't want to spend too much. The hostel is an attractive complex of thatched, timber chalets and has a café-garden. The doubles with shower are good value and the two dormitories (RM10) are the best around by a long shot. They also have a book exchange. ❶

**Teresek View Motel** ⓣ 09/266 9744. Standard, but with friendly staff, the dorm here at RM10 is fine, and masses of information is available. There's also internet access and a laundry service. ❶

**Yellow Guesthouse** ⓣ 09/266 4243. The cleanest in the area, with huge double rooms and a totally spotless dorm. The guesthouse is small, so it feels rather like staying in a family home, and it's slightly set back from the riverside. Dorm ❶; double ❺

### Nusa Camp

Nusa Camp is 2km further upstream on Sungei Tembeling. Boats from Tembeling jetty will take you straight there, stopping briefly at Kuala Tahan first.

**Nusa Holiday Camp** For the accommodation here, it's best to book in advance at MATIC (ⓣ 03/2164 3929) in KL, or call SPKG Tours who have offices in Jerantut (ⓣ 09/266 2369), Kuala Lumpur (ⓣ 03/230 5401) and Tembeling Jetty (ⓣ 09/266 3043). There are all levels of accommodation available, from camping (tents are provided at RM15), dorms and tiny tepee-like A-frames to twin-bed chalets and full-on houses. Nusa Camp has one small cafeteria (daily 8am–10pm), which does cheap set meals. ❶–❻

## Eating and drinking

**Chess Corner** On the path between *Lana Guesthouse* and *Tembeling Riverview Hostel*. This tiny riverside stall serves great shakes and a small selection of Thai food. It's a great place to watch the river go by and chat to some of the super-friendly locals, one of whom will almost invariably have a guitar out. Wadi, the long-suffering owner, also runs a hairdressing salon on the side.

**Family Restaurant** The food isn't fantastic, but this floating restaurant on the river just below *Lana* and *Tembeling* hostels is a popular place for travellers to hang out and decide what their next trek is going to be.

### TOURS AROUND KENONG RIMBA STATE PARK

Kenong Rimba State Park is situated in the hills at the base of Taman Negara National Park and offers a compact version of the jungle experience – trails, caves, riverside camping and excellent bird-watching – at much reduced prices and considerably less hype. Sightings of large mammals are rare, but there are plenty of monkeys, wild pigs, tapirs and innumerable species of birds. The best way to see Kenong Rimba is as part of an organized tour from Kuala Lipis – nobody is allowed within the park without a guide anyway.

#### Tours

Tours can be organized at either of Kuala Lipis's **Tourist Information Offices**. Tuah Travel and Tours (Mon–Fri 9am–5pm, Sat 9am–1pm; ⓣ09/312 3277, 24hr information on ⓣ09/312 2292) is located just to the left of the train station exit opposite the ticket booth, while Tourist Information (Mon–Fri 9am–5pm, Sat 9am–1pm; ⓣ09/312 5032) is just outside the station. Appu, the owner of *Hotel Lipis* (ⓣ09/312 2619), also offers a good basic tour.

Tours should cost about RM50–60 per day, plus around RM150 for the boat to and from **Jeti Tanjung Kiara**, on the edge of the park, but prices are somewhat negotiable depending on numbers of people and the time of year. A standard tour offers a choice of two to three days, with nights spent in the jungle and all food and equipment included. It will take in a variety of seriously impressive caves including **Gua Batu Tinggi**, which houses orchids and fig trees, and **Gua Hijau**, which is home to thousands of bats. Depending on which tour you choose, you might also see the impressive **Seven Steps Waterfall** and stay near one or more of the **indigenous villages** within the park.

#### Kuala Lipis

Getting to and away from Kuala Lipis is fairly straightforward. Long-distance buses arrive here from several major destinations, and the jungle railway also stops here. From the central bus station, there are buses for KL (six daily; 4hr), Kuantan (four daily; 6hr) and Temerloh (hourly; 2hr), from where there are good connections to major destinations. There are trains to Singapore (2 daily) and KL (1 daily), both of which make stops at Jerantut, useful if you want to carry on to Taman Negara. You can also get long-distance taxis to major destinations such as Kota Bharu, Kuantan and KL from the bus station.

**Woodland Resort** A good place to go if you're dying for a beer (RM10) as none of the other eateries sell any – you'll find this up the small hill slightly inland from the river, and will be able to see it at night as it's the only place that's clearly lit up. There's also a pool table, young customers and refreshingly anonymous service, but don't come here for the food, which is badly cooked and overpriced.

## Directory

**Internet** Rivernet, located between *Tembeling Riverview Hostel* and *Lana Guesthouse* next to *Chess Corner*, offers reliable internet at RM5 an hour.

**Travel agency** Han Travel, located in a riverboat next to *Family Restaurant* in Kuala Tahan, can help you with onwards travel and give plenty of advice. They tend to see what they can get away with price-wise though, so be prepared for some sky-high prices to start with, which will come down if you flatly refuse to pay them.

# The east coast

The four-hundred-kilometre stretch from the northeastern corner of the Peninsula to Kuantan, roughly halfway down the east coast, is the most "Malay" region in Malaysia, with strong cultural traditions – particularly in conservative **Kota Bharu**, the last major town before the Thai border, and one of the only towns in Malaysia with a Muslim majority. Islamic traditions are strictly followed – the call to prayer will wake you up before sunrise, and even hawker stalls in Kota Bharu's market close for twenty minutes during the working day. There are some good beaches along the east coast, including the laid-back traveller's haven of **Cherating**. By far the most beautiful beaches, however, are on **Pulau Perhentian** in the north, with stunningly clear azure waters and white sands fringed with palm trees. Further south, **Pulau Kapas** and **Rantau Abang** also boast fantastic coral reefs and wildlife in idyllic settings – Rantau Abang is one of only five places in the world where giant leatherback turtles come to nest between May and September. The annual monsoon affects the east coast between November and February when many of the east-coast islands are virtually out of bounds.

## KOTA BHARU

At the very northeastern corner of the Peninsula, close to the Thai border, **KOTA BHARU** is the capital of Kelantan State and one of the few **Muslim-governed** states in Malaysia. There's an impressive Cultural Centre and lots of craft workshops and a friendly, relaxed atmosphere, even towards women who aren't sporting traditional Muslim dress. However, there isn't really all that much to detain you (unless you want to form a closer relationship with the town's innumerable resident rodents and stray cats) and a night or two here would be more than sufficient. During the holy month of **Ramadan**, strongly Muslim Kota Bharu virtually shuts up shop.

### What to see and do

Small Padang Merdeka in the north part of town is Kota Bharu's historical heart. Near here, the **Istana Jahar** (daily except Fri 8.30am–4.45pm; RM3) houses the Royal Customs Museum whose ground floor is given over to a display of exquisite *ikat* and *songket* textiles and ornate gold jewellery; upstairs, you'll see life-size reconstructions of various traditional royal ceremonies, from weddings to circumcisions.

As you leave the museum, turn the corner to your left and after a few metres you'll see the sky-blue **Istana Batu** (daily except Fri 8.30am–4.45pm; RM2), now the **Kelantan Royal Museum,** with the sultan's rooms left in their original state. Situated on the corner of Jalan Hospital and Jalan Sultan Ibrahim, the **Museum of Islam** (daily except Fri 8.30am–4.45pm; RM1) is the only organisation of its kind, and features exhibits explaining the importance of Islam to the culture of Kelantan. The **Gelanggang Seni**, Kota Bharu's **Cultural Centre** on Jalan Mahmood, has free performances (March–Oct, Wed & Sat except during Ramadan) that feature many of the traditional pastimes of Kelantan, including the vigorous sport of top-spinning and the playing of giant one-hundred-kilogram *rebana* drums. On Wednesday evenings, there are *wayang kulit* (shadow play) performances, which can last for two to three hours. On Saturday nights, shows combine singing, dancing and comedy, derived from nineteenth-century court entertainment.

### Arrival and information

**By bus** Long-distance buses arrive at one of the two bus stations, inconveniently situated on the southern outskirts of the town. The state bus company, SKMK, operates from the Langgar bus station on Jl Pasir Puteh, as does the MARA company, which runs buses to KL and Singapore; other companies use the larger bus station on Jl Hamzah, which also has a left-luggage facility. If you arrive at night, you're at the mercy of the unofficial taxis at the stations, whose drivers can charge up to RM15 for the 2km drive to the centre: the daytime charge is around RM4. The local bus station, where buses from Kuala Terengganu and Kuala Besut arrive, is on Jl Padong Garong; SKMK also operates some services from here and has an

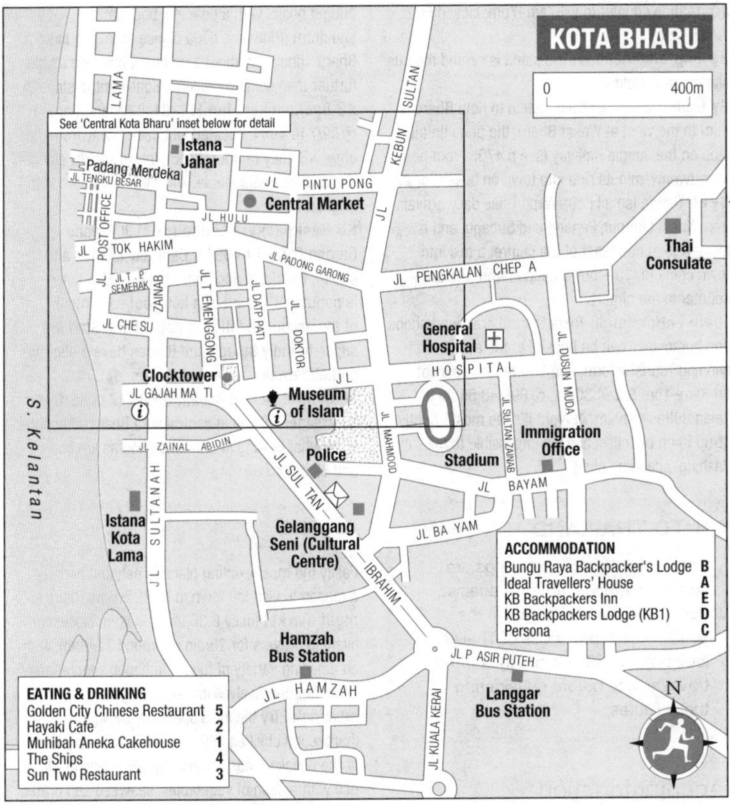

# KOTA BHARU

0 400m

See 'Central Kota Bharu' inset below for detail

LAMA
SULTAN
KEBUN
Istana Jahar
Padang Merdeka
JL TENGKU BESAR
JL PINTU PONG
Central Market
JL HULU
POST OFFICE
JL TOK HAKIM
JL PADONG GARONG
JL PENGKALAN CHEP A
JL T. P SEMERAK
ZAINAB
JL T EMENGGONG
JL DATP PATI
JL DOKTOR
JL CHE SU
General Hospital
JL HOSPITAL
JL DUSUN MUDA
Thai Consulate
Clocktower
JL GAJAH MA TI
Museum of Islam
JL MAHMOOD
JL SULTAN ZAINAB
Immigration Office
Stadium
JL ZAINAL ABIDIN
Police
JL SUL TAN IBRAHIM
JL BAYAM
JL BA YAM
S. Kelantan
Istana Kota Lama
JL SULTANAH
Gelanggang Seni (Cultural Centre)
Hamzah Bus Station
JL HAMZAH
JL P ASIR PUTEH
Langgar Bus Station
JL KUALA KERAI
N
Airport & Pantai Dasar Sabak

**ACCOMMODATION**

| | |
|---|---|
| Bungu Raya Backpacker's Lodge | B |
| Ideal Travellers' House | A |
| KB Backpackers Inn | E |
| KB Backpackers Lodge (KB1) | D |
| Persona | C |

**EATING & DRINKING**

| | |
|---|---|
| Golden City Chinese Restaurant | 5 |
| Hayaki Cafe | 2 |
| Muhibah Aneka Cakehouse | 1 |
| The Ships | 4 |
| Sun Two Restaurant | 3 |

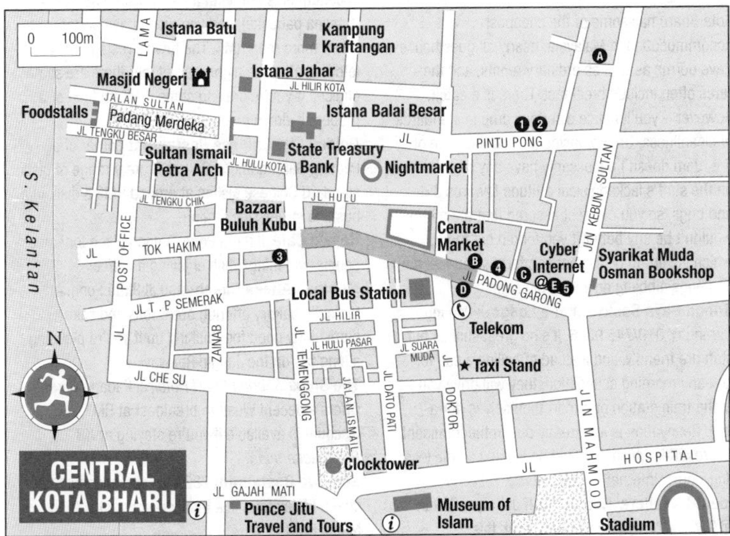


MALAYSIA

THE EAST COAST

information counter (daily 7am–7pm; closed Fri 12.45–2pm).

**By long-distance taxi** The stand is behind the bus station on Jl Doktor.

**By train** The nearest train station to Kota Bharu is 7km to the west at Wakaf Bharu, the penultimate stop on the Jungle Railway (see p.479). From here, it's a twenty-minute ride into town on bus 19 or 27.

**By air** Sultan Ismail Petra Airport has daily arrivals from Kuala Lumpur, Penang and Subang, and is located 9km northeast of the centre; a taxi into town costs RM15 – buy a coupon from the taxi counter in the airport.

**Tourist information** Tours to local craft workshops and homestays can be booked at the award-winning Tourist Information Centre (daily except Fri 8am–1pm & 2–4.30pm; ⓣ09/748 5534) on Jalan Sultan Ibrahim. At night it's the most brightly lit-up thing by miles, and it's impossible to miss its flashing, sparkling bling.

### INTO THAILAND

The eastern border crossings are currently strongly advised against, due to the political unrest in the southeastern provinces of Thailand (see box, p.883). Check the current travel advice before considering these routes.

## Accommodation

Kota Bharu has some of the cheapest accommodation in Malaysia; nearly all guesthouses have dorms as well as ordinary rooms, and the rates often include breakfast. There is a catch, however – you'll notice a serious drop in standards of cleanliness. On the upside (or not) the price of the room doesn't necessarily have any bearing on the staff's lackadaisical attitude towards dirt and bugs, so you can rest assured that the rooms wouldn't be any better if you forked out more, which is sure to be a great comfort as you feel the bed bugs nibbling on you in the night.

**Bungu Raya Backpacker's Lodge** Jl Padang Garong ⓣ019/746 9866. It's no great shakes but staff are friendly, and instead of calling a cab for an early morning connection, they will drive you to the train station or airport themselves (for a fee). Renovation is apparently due in the imminent future, after which it should be looking a little less dog-eared. Internet RM2.50/hr. ❶

**Ideal Travellers' House** 3954f Jl Kebun Sultan ⓣ09/744 2246. Friendly and quiet, this budget hostel with a peaceful beer garden and dorm (RM8) is a good choice for a stay in Kota Bharu, though at about 1km out of town it's a little further than some travellers might want to stay. ❶

**KB Backpackers Inn** 171–81 Jl Padang Garong ⓣ09/744 4944. Located just doors away from the other *KB* (they're not related), this is slightly cleaner, if a little less personable. Walls are decorated with bright murals. ❶

**KB Backpackers Lodge (KB1)** Jl Padang Garong ⓣ09/748 8841. Centrally located and cheap, the dorm accommodation (RM8) here is popular. It's a bit of a hole, but so is most of the accommodation in Kota Bharu. Staff are super-friendly though and it does have a slightly pathetic excuse for a roof garden. ❶

**Persona** Jl Padang Garong ⓣ09/747 0085. By far the cleanest option in central Kota Bharu, although somewhat lacking in character. Rooms are cool and tiled. ❷

## Eating

Easily the most exciting place to eat, and perhaps a reason to visit the town in itself, is Kota Bharu's **night market** (daily 6.30pm–midnight; closes for evening prayers for 20min at around 7.30pm), with an amazing variety of food – although vegetarians could find themselves limited to vegetable *murtabaks*. Try the local speciality *ayam percik* (barbecued chicken with a creamy coconut sauce) or the delicious *nasi kerabu* (purple, green or blue rice with a dash of vegetables, seaweed and grated coconut), finish off with a filling *pisang murtabak* (banana pancake), and you won't have parted with much more than RM5. The town's restaurants are a letdown after the night market, but there are some choices if you're craving some Western food or a proper sit-down meal.

**Golden City Chinese Restaurant** Corner of Jl Padang Garong and Jl Sultan. A great range of tasty, standard Chinese dishes at around RM6 a dish, in a bustling street-side setting.

**Hayaki Café** Jl Pintu Pong. A good place for some people-watching while enjoying a coffee.

**Muhibah Aneka Cakehouse** Jl Pintu Pong. A fantastic bakery offering great rolls and cakes, particularly good for stocking up if you're planning a long trip on the Jungle Railway.

**The Ships** *Sabrina Court Hotel*, Jl Padang Garong. Offers a decent Western breakfast at RM7. A discount is available if you're staying at *KB Backpackers Inn*.

**Sun Two Restaurant** 782A Jl Temenggong. Super-cheap Malay food in a family restaurant setting. Mains RM8.

## Directory

**Airlines** MAS, Kompleks Yakin, Jl Gajah Mati ⓣ09/744 7000.
**Banks and exchange** HSBC Bank, Jl Padong Garong; Standard Chartered Bank, Jl Tok Hakim; Maybank, Jl Pintu Pong, near the night market.
**Bookshops** Syarikat Muda Osman Bookshop, Jl Kebun Sultan.
**Hospital** The General Hospital is on Jl Hospital ⓣ09/748 5533.
**Immigration** On-the-spot visa renewals are available at the Immigration Office, 2nd Floor, Wisma Persekutuan, Jl Bayan (daily 8am–3.30pm except Thurs 8am–12.30pm; ⓣ09/748 2126).
**Internet** It's not hard to find an internet café, most are clustered around the Central Market. The cheapest around is Cyber Internet on Jl Padang Garong which offers quick connection at RM1.80/hr.
**Police** Headquarters on Jl Sultan Ibrahim ⓣ09/748 5522.
**Post office** The GPO is on Jl Sultan Ibrahim (daily except Fri 8.30am–5pm, closed first Sat of every month; ⓣ09/748 4033).
**Telephone services** The Telekom centre is on Jl Doktor (daily 8am–4.30pm).
**Thai visas** From the Royal Thai Consulate, 4426 Jalan Pengkalan Chepa (ⓣ09/748 2545; Mon–Thurs & Sun 9am–noon & 2–3.30pm, closed Fri & Sat). Two-month tourist visas (RM33) are issued within 24 hours.
**Travel agency** Punce Jitu Travel and Tours, Jl Gajah Mati, can help you organize onwards travel.

## Moving on

**By bus** Most long-distance buses go from Langgar bus station, on Jl Patir Puseh to the south of the city. However, there are central bus stations as well, so ask where your bus leaves from when you book. **Destinations:** Kuala Lumpur (2 daily; 8hr), Johor Bahru and Singapore (2 daily; 11hr), Kuala Terengganu (six daily; 3hr), Butterworth (2 daily; 8hr), Penang (2 daily; 9hr), Alor Setar (3 daily; 8hr) and Melaka (2 daily; 9hr).
**By train** Daily to Kuala Lumpur and Singapore. Ask about times, or see ⓦwww.ktmb.com.my, as they're liable to change quite frequently. Wakaf Bharu is also a stop on the Jungle Railway, which stops in Jerantut for Taman Negara National Park, after much scenic meandering.
**By air** The airport is served by Air Asia (ⓣ09/746 1671, ⓦwww.airasia.com) whose offices are on Jl Dusa Raja, and Malaysia Airlines (ⓣ09/744 7000, ⓦwww.malaysiaairlines.com), whose offices can be found on Jl Gajah Mati, opposite the clock tower. Several flights daily go to Kuala Lumpur (55min).

## PULAU PERHENTIAN

**Pulau Perhentian**, just over 20km off the northeastern coast, is actually two islands – **Perhentian Kecil** (Small Island) and **Perhentian Besar** (Big Island). Both are veritable tropical paradises, with clearer water and whiter sand than any other islands in Malaysia. Each is less than 4km in length, neither of the islands has roads or ATMs, there's little or no electricity during daylight and internet is only available at RM20/hr – all of this adds to the laid-back charm of the islands. The harsh east-coast **monsoon** means that the islands, reached by slow and unsophisticated fishing boats from Kuala Besut, are frequently inaccessible between November and February. However, it's worth bearing in mind that if you can get there at the beginning or end of the monsoon season, prices are exceptionally low, you'll have the islands practically to yourself and the rains are in fact fairly few and far between.

There's an excellent choice of budget accommodation, a good range of cafés and restaurants and a few laid-back bars (though be under no illusions – this isn't the place to go if you're looking for a Malaysian version of Ibiza).

The Perhentians are a great place either to learn how to **dive** or to enjoy some breathtaking, fun dives. Dives include **The Three Brothers** (Terumbu Tiga), where you go through three seriously impressive rock formations; **Temple of the Sea**, which everyone raves about for its good visibility, so you can see an almost infinite variety of fish; and the **Sugar Wreck**, one of the few wreck dives in the world suitable for relative beginners. Beyond that, there isn't anything to do – except swim, **snorkel** (RM40 for a day-trip, or RM12 to rent your own equipment), eat, drink and sunbathe.

### TRAVEL TO AND FROM PULAU PERHENTIAN

The ragged little town of **KUALA BESUT**, 45km south of Kota Bharu, is the departure point for Pulau Perhentian. It's reached by taking bus #3 from Kota Bharu's local bus station to Pasir Puteh (every 15min; 1hr), and then bus #96 (every 30min; 30min) to Kuala Besut. Most guesthouses in Kota Bharu also organize share taxis (RM24) direct to Kuala Besut. If you take a bus to the Perhentian Islands from further afield, it will drop you at Jerteh, from where it's a half-hour RM15 taxi ride or RM2 local bus ride to Kuala Besut.

Choose from **slow boats** (1hr 30min; RM30) or **fast boats** (20min; RM40) leaving every hour or so between 7am and 4pm, weather permitting, and there is a whole slew of companies to select from.

On a rough day you might not want to eat before you board a fast boat, unless you have a stomach of steel. Boatmen act as touts for places of accommodation on the islands and will say anything to get you to stay where they'll get a commission – just sit back and enjoy the view. A giant concrete monstrosity of a jetty has been built just in front of Coral Bay on Perhentian Kecil. Boats stop at most of the jetties, but check with the skipper first. **Taxi boats** also shuttle visitors between the two islands. When the weather's rough, boats don't travel to the island – call the companies for an update or have someone from your guesthouse do it for you. Their answers aren't always reliable so it's sometimes a case of waiting on the jetty to see for yourself. If you've paid for a return fast boat, in bad weather not all the companies' boats turn up, so you might well end up having to take a slow boat back anyway, or having yet more money demanded off you to board the fast boat of another company.

Boats **leave the island** at 8am, noon and at 4pm. An operation to beware of is *MD Travelers Holiday* (Ⓣ019/940 0409) who are friendly but insist you pay the return, then frequently don't bother sending boats to the islands at any reasonable time to get you back again.

There is a RM5 **entrance fee** to the islands that is supposed to go to the Department of Fisheries and is paid upon boarding the boat.

There are no banks in Kuala Besut or on the islands so **change money** before you go.

### Perhentian Kecil

This is generally considered to be the livelier of the two islands and very popular with backpackers, having a slightly more ramshackle atmosphere than its larger neighbour. On the south-eastern corner of **Perhentian Kecil** lies the island's only village, **Village Pasir Hantu**, with a jetty, police station, school and clinic – but the littered beach doesn't encourage you to stay. **Coral Bay** is the most popular west-facing cove on the island, lined with friendly guesthouses and shack eateries. The view out to sea remains extremely tranquil despite being somewhat marred by the hideous concrete jetty – many locals bemoan the sunset they can no longer see. East-facing **Long Beach** boasts a wide stretch of white beach and a laid-back atmosphere, with good coral nearby. However, it's much more exposed to the elements, and the crashing surf forces many of the chalet owners to close up from the end of October through to March.

Coral Bay is usually the first drop-off point when coming from the mainland. If the accommodation here doesn't grab you, it's a fairly easy ten-minute walk along the path through the interior to Long Beach. There are also plenty of taxi boats around to take you to the more southerly points of the island – don't attempt to walk there with luggage.

## Perhentian Besar

**Perhentian Besar** somehow seems to have acquired a reputation for being populated solely by the older generation, and many travellers, having esconced themselves on the Little Island, never even make it over for a day-trip. The pace of life is indeed even more laid-back than it is on Kecil, but Besar's got plenty of budget accommodation on gorgeous beaches and more space for lounging about on than Perhentian Kecil. The best place on the islands for turtle-watching is undoubtedly **Three Coves Bay** on the north coast. A stunning conglomeration of three beaches, it is separated from the main area of accommodation by rocky outcrops and is reached only by speed-boat. The bay provides a secluded haven between May and September for green and hawksbill turtles to come ashore and lay their eggs, though sadly, dwindling numbers mean the chances of spotting any are slim (see p.549). Most of the accommodation on Perhentian Besar is on the western half of the island.

### Information and island transport

**Boats** Taxi boats shuttle visitors between the beaches and two islands. On Perhentian Kecil, these usually go from Coral Bay rather than Long Beach as the water tends to be calmer. *Amelia's Chalet* organizes taxi boats, as do several of the other guesthouses and restaurants along the beach. Similarly, on Perhentian Besar, there's at least one clearly signposted taxi-boat point on every bay.

Prices vary from RM5 to beaches on the same island, or between the Fisherman's Village on Kecil and the point directly opposite on Besar, to RM25 to remoter coves on either island.

**Internet** On Perhentian Kecil, there's internet access at *Mohsin's* and *Panorama* on Long Beach and *Senja Bay* on Coral Bay. On Perhentian Besar, it's available at *Paradise Resort* and *Coral View*. It's slow and unreliable in all these places and costs RM20/hr.

**Clinic** There's a very basic one at Village Pasir Hantu on the Perhentian Kecil – otherwise the dive centers can offer some medical care. If it's serious, you're better off returning to the mainland.

## Dive operators

The Perhentians are a good place to get your PADI Open Water certificate and go diving (RM750 for the four-day course, and RM90 for fun dives) as they boast unbelievable crystal-clear waters and great underwater locations such as wrecks and reefs.

### Perhentian Kecil

**Quiver Diveschool** Long Beach Ⓔkin_voon@tm.net.my. This brilliant dive school only operates with small groups and is probably the best bet on either island for friendliness and personal attention. Everybody on the island knows Mark, the English dive instructor who's likely to have you having running circles around yourself with his practical jokes, and he and his lovely team are guaranteed to make you feel comfortable in the water. PADI Open Water RM1100, Fun Dive (3–4 hours) RM90.

**Steffen's Sea Sport** Coral Beach ⓣ016/621 2364. A large, well-kitted-out dive school with friendly staff. PADI Open Water RM1100, Fun Dive RM90.

### Perhentian Besar

**Universal Diver** ⓣ03/7727 8890 or 019/363 1348, Ⓦwww.universaldiver.net. A well-organized new dive centre run by a group of friendly enthusiasts. PADI Open Water RM980, Fun Dive RM90, going down in price the more dives you do.

**Watercolours Dive Centre** ⓣ019/981 1852, Ⓦwww.watercoloursworld.com. Staff here are helpful and free pick-up is available from anywhere on the islands. Watercolours is owned by the same people as *Paradise Resort*, so divers here can get discounts on accommodation at *Paradise*, as well as free entrance to ReefTalk, a twice-weekly presentation on the marine life of the Perhentians. PADI Open Water RM1100 and Fun Dive RM90, going down in price the more dives you do.

## Accommodation

### Perhentian Kecil: Coral Bay

**Amelia Chalets** ⓣ019/9130 742. Basic but clean, with an excellent attached restaurant where mains are RM6–7. ❸

**Aur Beach Chalets** ⓣ013/995 0817. One of the cheapest options on Coral Bay and right on the beach. Run down, but fine. ❷

**Fatimah's** ⓣ019/923 2730 This brand-new guesthouse is a clean, basic budget option, right next to *Aur Bay*. ❸

**Maya Resort** ⓣ017/888 1809. Probably some of the best accommodation on this stretch of beach, with double chalets on the beach. Huts have sliding doors, bathroom and fan and are very clean. Some huts are set around a large green garden area with hammocks, where considerate signs warn "*Awas* - coconut may fall on your head". ❹

**Senja Bay Resort** ⓣ09/691 1799 or ⓣ019/664 3105, Ⓦwww.senjabay.com. On the southern end of the bay, rooms are set up amongst the cliffs and offer stunning views of the sea, unmarred by the jetty. The restaurant also offers great food from a prime location, and has internet access (although like on the rest of the island, it's at an eye-watering RM20/hr). There's also a reputable diveshop, Senja Mantis, attached. ❹–❻

### Perhentian Kecil: Further south

**Mira's Chalet** Located on its own sandy bay a 25-minute walk from Coral Bay, this popular place is a cluster of rustic chalets with a driftwood restaurant attached. Seekers of *The Beach*-style seclusion and atmosphere may want to settle here. ❸

**Petani** ⓣ019/957 1624. Fifteen minutes around the headland from *Mira's* on a superb beach, this has clean, well-built chalets with showers. The easiest way to get here is by boat, otherwise it's a rough 45-minute walk from Coral Bay. ❹

**Sandy Coral** ⓣ019/969 2686. These longhouse rooms on a perfect little cove are already much sought-after. Shared-facilities, hurricane lamps, a family atmosphere, and stunning sunset views from the balcony. ❸

### Perhentian Kecil: Long Beach

**D'Lagoon** ⓣ019/985 7089. Set in a tiny cove at the very northeast tip of the island 1km from Long Beach, with dorms and chalets. From here, you can clamber across the narrow neck of the island to the turtle-spotting beach on the other side. ❶–❷

**Lemon Grass** ⓣ019/938 3893. The cheapest accommodation on Long Beach, with doubles from RM20, these rooms are basic but clean, and the café has a nice view over the beach. *Lemon Grass* also organizes snorkelling tours around the island for RM40 a day. ❷

**Mata Hari** ⓣ014/836 2863, ⓦwww.mataharichalet.com. Simple but well-designed chalets in a garden, complete with hammocks and a good restaurant, just ten seconds from the beach. ❸–❺

**Mohsin's Chalets** ⓣ019/249 6635, ⓦwww.mohsinperhentian.com.my. Slightly set back from the beach, the chalets here are a cut above the rest. The restaurant here, *Rumours,* is also a good place to meet people and watch a film, although the food is seriously over-rated. The dorm is scarcely used however, so its cleanliness is in doubt – go for a chalet if you possibly can. Dorm ❷, doubles ❸.

**Moonlight Chalets** ⓣ091/985 8222. Rustic chalets along with some upmarket units at the northern end of the beach – check the cleanliness of the room before checking in, however, as problems have been reported in the past. ❸–❺

**Panorama** ⓣ09/697 7542 ⓦwww.malaysia-panorama.com. A large, friendly sprawl of chalets providing everything you could wish for – large, clean rooms with mosquito nets and bathrooms, a delicious restaurant and bar area with pool table and films, its own dive school (Seadragon) and a minimarket. Staff are laid-back and friendly. ❸–❹

## Perhentian Besar

**ABC Guesthouse** ⓣ019/920 2875. Rooms in this wooden sea-front building are basic, but the low prices, gorgeous views and the balconies on which you can enjoy them more than make up for it. ❹

**Abdul's** ⓣ09/697 7058. Located on one of the best strips of beach, all chalets are basic A-frames but have a small veranda. The restaurant is right on the sand and open until 11pm, after which it's extremely peaceful here. One of the best places at the low end of the price spectrum. ❸

**Coco Hut Chalets** ⓣ09/691 1811 / 691 1810, ⓦwww.perhentianislandcocohut.com. This place has just undergone a refurb and the new wooden chalets are sturdy with French windows that open straight out on to a white sand and coconut tree garden. The restaurant's beautifully located on a platform built over the ocean and serves a good variety of Western and local food. ❻

**Fauna Beach Chalet** ⓣ019/697 7266. Situated around the water in Flora Bay, an attractive and secluded enclave, these standard chalets are clean and good value with nice views. ❹

**TREAT YOURSELF**

**Coral View** ⓣ09/697 7427. Located on a rocky outcrop with breathtaking views on every side, this sprawling resort offers tastefully designed and very well-furnished chalets connected by little paths and bridges, which are the best accommodation on either island. The best rooms are hotel-style en-suites with a/c, mini-bar and hot water. The restaurant is also well worth a visit, serving delicious seafood and good Western options. You can't drink within the resort, but it's a small price to pay. ❻–❾

**Mama's Chalet** ⓣ019/984 0232, ⓦwww.mamaschalet.com. These chalets are European in feel, perhaps because they're unusually well-built, and boast stained-glass panelling in the windows and doors. The more expensive ones open up on to the beachfront, while others are set in a cool and pleasant garden. There's also cheap food in abundance and a licensed ferry service running to surrounding islands. ❹

**New Coco Huts** ⓣ09/697 7988, ⓦwww.perhentianislandcocohut.com. Previously *Cozy Huts,* this accommodation has been taken over and rebuilt by the *Coco Hut* owners. Built on a headland that separates the beach north and south, the chalets boast a great view and look set to run to *Coco Huts'* high standards. ❻

**Paradise Resort** ⓣ010/981 0930. Next door to *Mama's* and connected with the Watercolours Dive Centre. Seaview chalets are slightly cheaper here than elsewhere (RM90 for a double) and very satisfactory. The scenic restaurant also serves good pizza at RM15. There's also internet at the islands' usual sky-high rates (RM10/ 30min). ❻

**Tuna Bay** ⓣ09/697 7172, or 09/697 9779, ⓦwww.tunabay.com.my. If you want double glazing and solid buildings, this upscale resort is the place to come. The well-built bungalows, on a good southern stretch of beach, boast all the amenities you could want (a/c, hot en-suite showers, TV and so on). Staff are very friendly and all the activities are lined up for you. ❼–❾

## Eating and drinking

Most of the guesthouses on both islands have a restaurant attached, which are mentioned if they're note-worthy; on Besar, there aren't any stand-alone restaurants, just those at guesthouses. Several places serve alcohol, while others don't mind if you bring your own. While there aren't many bars on the islands, Perhentian Kecil offers a couple that stay open late and have a bit of a party atmosphere.

TREAT YOURSELF

**BuBu's Resort** Long Beach, Perhentian Kecil ⓣ03/212 6688, ⓦwww.buburesort .com.my. If you're dying for a taste of something Western that doesn't have the texture of cardboard and look like it's come out of the freezer, chef Salim will cook you up a storm. The green fettucini with smoked salmon and tuna is highly recommended, and other treats such as crème brûlée and the black forest gateau are all genuinely home-made and delicious. At around RM20 for a dish, it's not actually all that expensive, and the rise in standard is phenomenal. It's also a great place to stay if you fancy splashing out (❽), with a circular bar area that's atmospheric and buzzy, and clean, comfortable rooms, the best of which have large balconies.

### Perhentian Kecil

**The Beach** Long Beach. A low-key shack run by Karim, who shakes a cocktail with incredible skill and has the biggest collection of music yet to be seen within Malaysia. All the other outlets rely on the *Beach* for their alcohol, which makes it the original and the best.

**Buffalo Bar** Long Beach. Some mats, some little tables and some candles on the beach. Perfect.

**Palm Tree Café** The closest the Perhentians get to raving, with every evening bringing another excuse for a party. It looks like a rundown children's haunted house, and usually has a roaring campfire going outside. Beers RM10.

**Rumours** The restaurant attached to *Mohsin's*, located high on a hill, often has parties going on, for which you'll see posters around the island. It's a great place to chill out and meet some new people – but eat before you come, as the food is overpriced and tasteless.

## KUALA TERENGGANU

The tiny Muslim metropolis **KUALA TERENGGANU**, 160km south of Kota Bharu, is a traditional town set on an estuary. It's a pleasant and relaxed place to make a stop-over or get stuck. There isn't a great deal to do or see in the town itself, which adds to its laid-back charm, but there are a few workshops and factories you can check out in the surrounding area.

### What to see and do

The **Istana Tengku Long Museum** (daily except Fri 9am–5pm; RM5) is set in landscaped gardens 3km west of the centre, on Bukit Losong. Here you'll find exquisite fabrics and crafts, a fine exhibit of Koranic calligraphy and some reconstructed ancient timber palaces. The supreme example of these is the Istana Tunku Long, built in 1888 with a high, pointed roof and wooden gables fitted with twenty gilded screens, intricately carved with Koranic verses. The museum is easily reached by the regular Losong minibus #7 (20min; 70sen) from the local bus station.

At the west end of Kuala Terengganu, Jalan Bandar forms the centre of **Chinatown**, where you'll find the excellent *Teratai*, at no. 151, selling local arts and crafts. Kuala Terengganu's **Central Market** (daily 7am–6pm), a little further down on the right, close to the junction with Jalan Kota, also deals in batik, *songkets* and brassware.

On the same road, it's also worth taking a peek at the lavish **Ho Ann Kong Temple,** built by Taoist devotees in 1801. Ky Enterprises, about 3km due south of the centre on Jalan Panji Alam, is a good place to watch the *mengkuang* style of **weaving**, using pandanus leaves to make bags, floor mats and fans; take minibus 12, 15, 26 or 13c (70 sen) for the fifteen-minute ride from the local bus station. You can catch **traditional dance** shows at the **Gelanggang Seni Cultural**

**Centre**, a two-kilometre walk or trishaw ride southeast from the centre, facing the town's beach, Pantai Batu Buruk (pick up a timetable of events from the Tourist Information Centre).

## Arrival and information

**By bus** The Express Bus Station, where buses from Kota Bharu pull in, is on Jl Sultan Zainal Abidin; it's a fifteen-minute walk to the centre of town, or a RM4 taxi. Across town is the local bus station, opposite the taxi stand on Jl Masjid Abidin.

**By air** Sultan Mohammed Airport (ⓣ09/666 3666) is located 13km northeast of the centre, a RM20 taxi ride into town; the city bus marked "Kem Seberang Takir" picks up from the road directly outside and runs to the local bus station.

**Tourist Information Centre** Jl Sultan Zainal Abdin, on the seafront near the GPO. Daily except Fri 9am–5pm ⓣ09/622 1553, ⓦwww.terengganutourism.com

## Accommmodation

**Awi's Yellow House** ⓣ09/624 5046. This rickety complex of basic stilted huts built over the water on the tiny island of Duyung is the best place to stay for a taste of relaxing village life, though it's a little out of the way. From the bus station, take minibus #16 or #20 (RM1), and get off at the base of the Sultan Mahmud Bridge, from where *Awi's* is a short walk. If you're travelling after 6pm, you'll probably have to take a taxi (RM5), as buses across the bridge are infrequent and there are very few ferries in the evening. ❷

**Ping Anchorage Travellers' Lodge** 77a Jalan Sultan Sulaiman, ⓣ09/626 2020, ⓦwww.pinganchorage.com.my. A traveller-friendly hostel and the best place to stay in town – rooms are exceptionally spartan (walls are concrete and windows are barred) but clean, and staff are very helpful. There's also a friendly café downstairs that will provide you with a map of the town, and an attached travel agency. Dorm ❶; doubles ❷

## Eating

There are excellent food stalls behind the express bus station, serving the usual Malay dishes (11.30am–midnight).

**MD Curry House** 19c Jl Tok Lam. A buzzing place popular with travellers, serving exceptional South Indian *thalis.*

**Ping Anchorage Travellers' Café** Jl Sultan Sulaiman. Under the same friendly management as the hostel, this café serves a good variety of Western and local food, including excellent breakfasts, though prices are slightly over the odds. It's also a good place to have a drink with other travellers. Pasta dish RM8.

**Restoran Golden Dragon** Jl Bandar. The best Chinese in town, served in a bright and rowdy setting.

**Town City Food Court** Jl Bandar. A cosy, popular food court with outdoor seating by the sea, serving delicious *dim sum* and other delicacies. Mains RM3.

## Directory

**Internet** There are a wealth of inexpensive places on Jl Tok Lam, including the reliable and friendly *Orange Internet Café*, RM3/hr. There's also an internet café next to the Ping Anchorage travel agency on Jl Sultan Sulaiman, RM3/hr.

**Post office** Jl Sultan Zainal Abdin, just in front of the jetty. Daily except Fri 9am–5pm

**Travel agency** Ping Anchorage, 77a Jalan Sultan Sulaiman, ⓣ09/626 2020, ⓦwww.pinganchorage.com.my. Service here is very thoughtful and well-intentioned. Unfortunately this means it can also be maddeningly slow.

## Moving on

**By bus** Ask when buying your ticket whether your bus leaves from the local or express bus station, as long-distance buses depart from both.

**Destinations:** Alor Setar (2 daily; 9hr 30min); Butterworth (2 daily; 9–10hr); Ipoh (1 daily; 11hr); Johor Bahru (2 daily; 10hr); Kota Bharu (5 daily; 4hr); KL (2 daily; 8–9hr); Kuantan (6 daily; 4hr); Marang (every 30min; 30min); Melaka (3 daily; 7hr); Mersing (2 daily; 6hr); Rantau Abang (every 30min; 1hr).

**By air** Kuala Terengganu is served by Malaysia Airlines (13 Jl Sultan Omar, ⓣ09/622 1415) and Air Asia (Jl Sultan Omar, ⓣ09/631 3122), which offer several flights a day to KL.

# MARANG

The small coastal town of **MARANG**, 17km south of Kuala Terengganu, attracts a steady trickle of foreign visitors, though most are simply en route to nearby Pulau Kapas, 6km offshore (see p.548), and the town's charm has been diminished by a modernization scheme. There are a handful of guesthouses, banks and batik shops here, but nothing much else.

### Arrival and Information

**By bus** Any Dungun – or Rhu Muda-bound bus (every 30min, RM4) from Kuala Terengganu, or Kuala Terengganu-bound bus from Cherating (RM1.80), will drop you on the main road at Marang, from where the centre is a short walk down one of the roads towards the sea.

### Accommodation

**Green Mango Inn** ⓣ09/618 2040. A travellers' hangout three-minutes' walk from the main road (follow the sign for *Kapas Island Resort*). It has a dorm (RM10) and very basic A-frame doubles set in a tiny tropical garden. ❶–❷

**Island View Resort** ⓣ09/618 2006. Located five-minutes' walk from the jetty, this outfit offers a range of rooms, including a/c doubles and more basic fan rooms. ❷–❸

### Moving on

**By bus** The ticket office is on Jl Tanjung Sulong Musa ⓣ09/618 2799. For a greater choice of destinations, you might want to go north to Kuala Terengganu (every 30min; RM4; 40min).

**Destinations:** JB (2 daily; 4hr); KL (2 daily; 8hr); Kuantan (5 daily; 4hr)

**By ferry** to Pulau Kapas: All the ferry companies have their offices on the main road, and ferries are RM15 return. Morning, between 8am and 9am, is the usual departure time, or the boat will leave when four or more people are ready to go. There's no service during the monsoon season (Nov–Feb).

## PULAU KAPAS

A thirty-minute ride by fishing boat from Marang takes you to the lovely island of **Pulau Kapas**, less than 2km in length. Coves on the western side are accessible only by sea or by clambering over rocks, but you'll be rewarded by sand and aquamarine water. Like many of its neighbours, Kapas is a designated marine park, and the best snorkelling is around rocky Pulau Gemia, just off the northwestern shore. The northernmost cove is good for **turtle-spotting**. However, the high number of visitors and a local lack of regard for the environment is causing some of the surrounding coral reef to die off.

### Accommodation

The only accommodation is at the two western coves that directly face the mainland.

**Dahimah's Guest House** ⓣ09/845 2843. One km south of the information centre, this is the best of the limited accommodation options, situated in a secluded and pretty spot by a lagoon. It offers a range of rooms, from comfortable fan doubles to riverside a/c family rooms. It has its own restaurant, as do the other, now slightly rundown guesthouses. ❷

**Kapas Island Resort** ⓣ09/631 6468, ⓦwww.kapasislandresort.com. A wooden walkway leads to these Malay-style chalets with a swimming pool and extensive watersports facilities. There are cheaper rooms facing the jungle, and a longhouse dorm sleeping up to thirty. Dorm ❷; doubles ❺

**Lighthouse** ⓣ019/215 3558. This popular and atmospheric place is built in Malay longhouse-style, with dorm beds and only a well shower. ❷

**Zaki Beach Chalet** ⓣ019/956 0513. This is the best-value accommodation on the island, with comfortable A-frames and a buzzing restaurant. ❷

## CHERATING

The travellers' hangout of **CHERATING**, 47km north of Kuantan, hugs the northern end of a windswept bay, protected from the breeze by the shelter of a rocky cliff. Most of the locals have long since moved to a small village further south, so it's not the place to come if you're looking for a genuine taste of Malay *village* life, but it's a good spot for chilling out and enjoying a bit of traveller **nightlife**. Cherating is ideal for **windsurfing**, and you can rent equipment for RM25 an hour. Clambering over the rocks at the eastern end of the bay brings you to a tiny secluded cove, though the beach isn't as good as that belonging to the *Club Med* over the next outcrop.

The main drag is a tiny surfaced road that runs roughly parallel to the beach, and this is where you'll find most of the restaurants and bars, as well as convenience stores and arts and craft shops selling batik, t-shirts

## THE GIANT LEATHERBACK TURTLE

The village of **RANTAU ABANG**, 43km from Marang, is no more than a small collection of guesthouses strung out along two kilometres of dusty road, but it has made its name as one of a handful of places in the world where the increasingly rare **giant leatherback turtle** comes ashore to lay its eggs, returning annually between May and September. Specific nesting areas and hatcheries have been established on the beach, fenced off from curious human beings. When the hatchlings have broken out of their shells, they are released at the top of the beach (4–6am), and their scurry to the sea is supervised to ensure their safe progress. When a female turtle does come ashore to lay eggs, visitors are asked to keep at least 5m away and not to use torches and camera flashes. In reality, however, unfortunately turtle numbers have diminished so much – thought to be because of illegal fishing – that the chances of seeing any are very slim. For interesting background, visit the **Turtle Information Centre** (Ⓣ09/845 8169; daily except Fri, 8am–4.15pm; free), to the north of the central two-kilometre strip. Local **buses** from Kuala Terengganu and Marang run every thirty minutes (7.30am–6pm; 1hr) to Rantau Abang. If you're coming by express bus from the south, you have to change at Dungun, 13km to the south, from where you can easily get a local bus for the remainder of the journey. Buses drop you on the main road, at the R&R Plaza, just a short walk from all the accommodation.

### Save the Turtles

With turtle numbers sadly dwindling, sanctuaries such as the **Ma'Daerah Turtle Sanctuary** (Ⓣ09/845 8169, Ⓦwww.madaerah.org) are becoming increasingly important. Volunteering here is a truly rewarding and worthwhile experience, and can be done for as short a time as a single weekend, or even an afternoon – in April, the beaches are cleaned up ready for the nesting season, and any willing hands for this task are gratefully received. A donation of at least RM250 is required, but meals and accommodation are included for your stay, and your money will be going towards the work of the sanctuary. Alternatively you can adopt a turtle (RM150), or a nest (RM100).

and other trinkets. Limbong Art, in particular, has an excellent range of wood carvings upstairs.

## Arrival and information

**By bus** Any express or local bus between Kuala Terengganu and Kuantan will drop you off at Cherating – tell the driver beforehand. If you're looking out for it, a clear sign to "Pantai Cherating" guides the way. Two rough tracks lead from the road down into the main part of the village, about five minutes away, although the one nearest the bridge is the most direct.

**Travel Post** (Ⓣ09/581 9825) Acts as a travel agency where you can book bus tickets for destinations in Malaysia and to Singapore, as well as local river and snorkelling trips (RM35 including food) and turtle-watching tours (May to August). They also have internet terminals, an international fax line and money-changing services.

## Accommodation

**Cherating Cottage** Ⓣ09/581 9273. A sturdily-built bar and restaurant surrounded by chalets. It caters for every budget and has pleasant, helpful staff. ❷

**Maznah's** Ⓣ09/581 9072. The A-frames and chalets in this traveller's spot are basic, but the atmosphere is laid-back and staff extremely welcoming. ❶–❷

**Matahari** Ⓣ09/581 9835. Excellent value for spacious, sturdy chalets without attached bathrooms, but with a fridge and large veranda, as well as a separate communal area with a TV room, cooking facilities and a batik studio. Batik courses RM30 for t-shirt, RM40 for sarong. ❷

**Payung Guesthouse** Ⓣ09/581 9658. The friendly Scottish owner couldn't be more helpful, and the chalets here back onto a garden by the river. There are hammocks for lounging in, and the guesthouse offers bike and canoe hire (RM10 per day), as well as organizing river trips. ❷

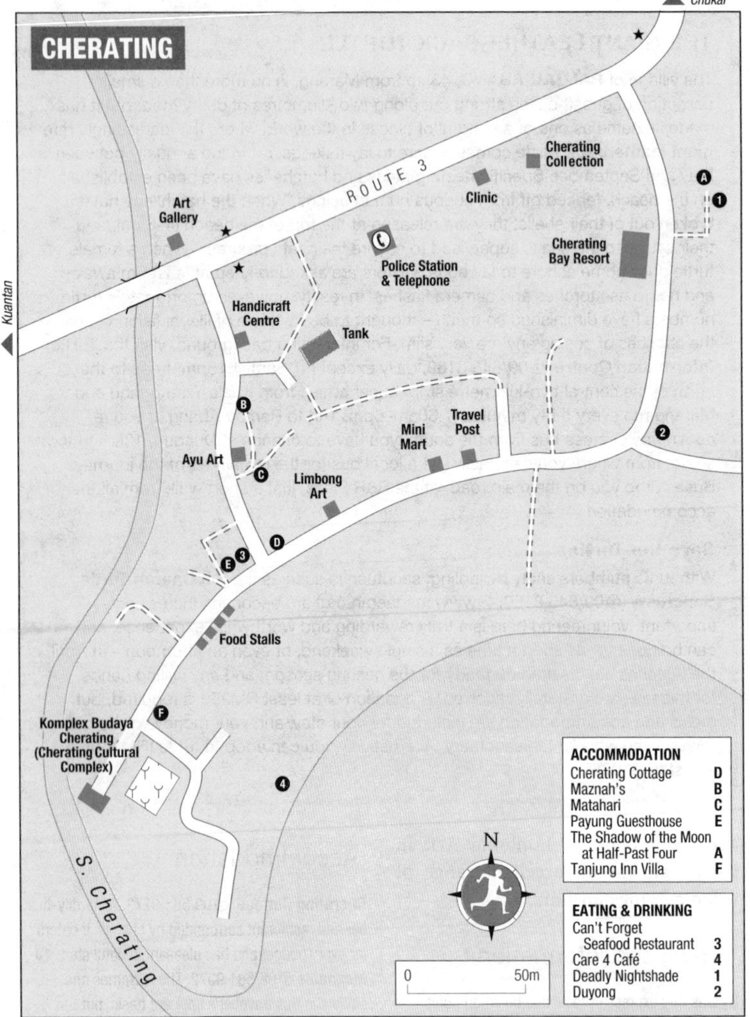


**The Shadow of the Moon at Half-Past Four** ⓣ09/581 9186. Well-designed timber chalets decorated with vintage film posters and tucked away in a ramshackle and lush wooded area, where goblins wouldn't look out of place. Laundry is free and one meal a day is included. All have attached bathrooms, hot water and hand-crafted furniture. There's also a dorm (RM12). ❷

**Tanjung Inn Villa** ⓣ09/581 9081. An attractive range of excellent-value chalets and family rooms set in a scenic, landscaped garden with a lotus-filled lake. ❹–❺

## Eating and drinking

**Can't Forget Seafood Restaurant** Despite the ambiguous name, this informal Chinese-owned eatery serves quality food including delicious claypot noodles (RM15).

**Care 4 Café** A small, laid-back café with a beach view, offering a dartboard, simple food menu, occasional live music and cold beer. Open until midnight.

**Deadly Nightshade** At the *Shadow of the Moon at Half-Past Four*. One of the most imaginatively

designed bars you'll come across. Fairy lights, piles of books, chess sets and home-made furniture add to the atmosphere. The menu embraces local, Western and Portuguese dishes for around RM12.
**Duyong** A stilted restaurant offering tasty, inexpensive Chinese, Western and Thai food, with a panoramic beach view.

### Moving on

From Cherating, you really need to get **to Kuantan** to get anywhere useful. The local bus leaves from the main road at quarter past and quarter to every hour, from 6.15am to 8.15pm. A taxi to Kuantan will set you back RM60. Either way, the journey is around 45min long.
**Travel Post** can arrange long-distance bus tickets to major destinations in the north such as Kuala Terengganu (6 daily; 4hr) and Kota Bharu (5 daily; 6hr). The long-distance buses will be the ones from Kuantan and the drivers will stop on the main road to pick you up.

## KUANTAN

It's virtually inevitable that you'll pass through the dull, concrete town of **KUANTAN** at some stage since it's the region's transport hub, lying at the junction of Routes 2 (which runs across the Peninsula to KL), 3 and 14. Kuantan's one real sight is the stunning **Masjid Negeri** on Jalan Makhota, boasting an impressive pastel exterior (green for Islam, blue for peace and white for purity). Otherwise it's a fairly useful place for facilities such as utilitarian shopping malls.

### Arrival and information

**By bus** The local bus station is on Jl Basar, beside Sungai Kuantan, and the Makmur express bus station is on Jl Stadium, in front of the Darulmakmur stadium. A taxi between the two costs around RM8. Taxis can be found between Jl Besar and Jl Mahkota.
**By air** Kuantan airport is 15km west of town (☎09/538 1291) – a taxi to the centre costs RM20. The MAS office is on the ground floor of the Wisma Bolasepak Pahang, Jl Gambut (☎09/515 6030).
**Tourist information** The Tourist Information Centre (daily 9am–1pm & 2–5pm; ☎09/516 1007) is situated at the end of Jl Mahkota facing the playing fields, and can help you out with accommodation in and around Kuantan. It also organizes day-trips to the surrounding area.

### Accommodation

**Hotel Baru Raya** 134–36 Jl Besar ☎09/513 9746. Conveniently located if a little noisy, with friendly staff and spacious rooms. ❸
**Meian** 78 Jl Teluk Sisek ☎09/552 0949. Basic and clean despite its monstrous exterior, with a communal hot shower for the simplest rooms. ❷

### Eating

The stalls near the mosque on Jl Makhota behind the Ocean Shopping Complex on Jl Tun Ismail are the best bet for endless varieties of cheap and tasty food.
**New Yee Mee** Jl Haji Abdul Aziz. A large, busy, budget Chinese restaurant with a tasty wide-ranging menu.
**Restoran E & E** 219 Jl Tun Ismail. Bizarre but strangely moreish Malay versions of Western food, such as steaks in cashew sauce, pizzas and Cantonese spaghetti.
**Restoran Paruvathy** Jl Bukit Ubi. One of the few Indian restaurants in town, serving especially good *masala dosa* and curries.
**Tjantek Art Bistro** A surprisingly trendy bistro-type place – complete with jazz music playing and modern art adorning the walls – serving Western and local dishes.

### Directory

**Banks and exchange** HSBC has a 24hr ATM and can be found on the corner of Jl Bank and Jalan Mahkota.
**Immigration office** First Floor, Wisma Persekutuan, Jalan Gambut. On-the-spot visa renewals (Mon–Fri 9am–4.15pm; ☎09/514 2155) can be arranged here.
**Internet** There are plenty along Jalan Tun Ismail, or try Mega Tech on Lg Pasar Baru 3, next to the long-distance bus station RM2 per hour.
**Post office** Jl Haji Abdul Aziz.
**Telekom office** Jl Haji Abdul Aziz, next door to post office (8.45am–4.15pm)

### Moving on

**By bus** As Kuantan is a major transport hub, it's possible to get nearly anywhere from here, and quite easily too. Long-distance taxis (☎09/513 4478) leave from the express bus station.

**Destinations:** Butterworth (3 daily; 10hr); Jerantut, for Taman Negara National Park (4 daily; 3hr 30min); Kota Bharu (5 daily; 6hr); Kuala Lipis (2 daily; 6hr); Kuala Lumpur (6 daily; 5hr); Kuala Terengganu (6 daily; 4hr); Melaka (2 daily; 5hr); Mersing (6 daily; 3hr 30min); Singapore (3 daily; 7hr).

**By air** Kuantan is served by Malaysia Airlines, who have an office on Jl Gambut (☎09/515 6030, Ⓦwww.malaysiaairlines.com). There are flights to all major destinations (domestic and international), including Johor Bahru, all of which go via Kuala Lumpur (3 daily; 40min).

# The south

The south of the Malaysian Peninsula, below Kuala Lumpur and Kuantan, has some of the richest history and culture in the country. The west-coast city of **Melaka**, two hours by bus south from KL, retains an enticing mixture of cultures from its Portuguese, Dutch and British colonial days, not to mention its unique Chinese–Malay community of Peranakans. There's plenty to see here, and the city is also just a short boat ride from **Sumatra**. There's little to recommend **Johor Bahru** (or JB) at the tip of the Peninsula, save for its speedy transport links into Singapore, just across the causeway. Don't miss the laid-back island of **Pulau Tioman**, which boasts nice beaches, good diving opportunities and plenty of budget accommodation.

## MELAKA

When Penang was known only for its oysters and Singapore was just a fishing village, **MELAKA** had already achieved worldwide fame. Under the auspices of the Melaka Sultanate, founded in the early fifteenth century, political and cultural life flourished, helping to define what it means to be Malay. The town grew rich by **trading spices** from the Moluccas in the Indonesian archipelago and textiles from Gujarat in northwest India. A levy on all imported goods made it one of the wealthiest kingdoms in the world, and it gradually expanded its territory to include Singapore and most of east-coast Sumatra. A series of takeovers, beginning in 1511, by the Portuguese, Dutch and British, has also substantially characterized Melaka – the architecture, street plans, churches and overall atmosphere are of an eclectic East-meets-West fusion, reminiscent of other colonial Asian ports, such as Cochin.

### What to see and do

Legacies of all phases of Melaka's past remain in the city, constituting the main tourist sights. Of these, the most interesting are the ancestral homes of the **Baba-Nyonya community**, a racial mix also known as Peranakan, that evolved from the sixteenth-century Chinese merchants who settled here and married Malay women. For a one-stop introduction to the city's history, watch the English-language **Sound and Light Show** on Padang Pahlawan Square (also known as Dutch Square; daily 9pm; 1hr; RM5).

The centre of Melaka is split in two by the murky **Sungei Melaka**, the western bank of which is occupied by **Chinatown** and **Village Morten**, a small collection of stilted houses. On the eastern side of the river lies the colonial core with **Bukit St Paul** at its centre, encircled by Jalan Kota. Southeast of here, **Taman Melaka Raya** is a new area with a giant shopping centre and a good selection of budget hotels, restaurants and bars. A relaxing 45-minute **boat trip** up Sungei Melaka takes you to "**Little Amsterdam**", the old Dutch quarter of red-roofed *godowns*, which back directly onto the water. Boats leave from the jetty behind the Tourist Information Centre (hourly, depending on the tide, 10am–2pm; RM8).

#### Around Bukit St Paul

The imposing dark timber palace of **Istana Ke Sultanan** (daily 9am–6pm,

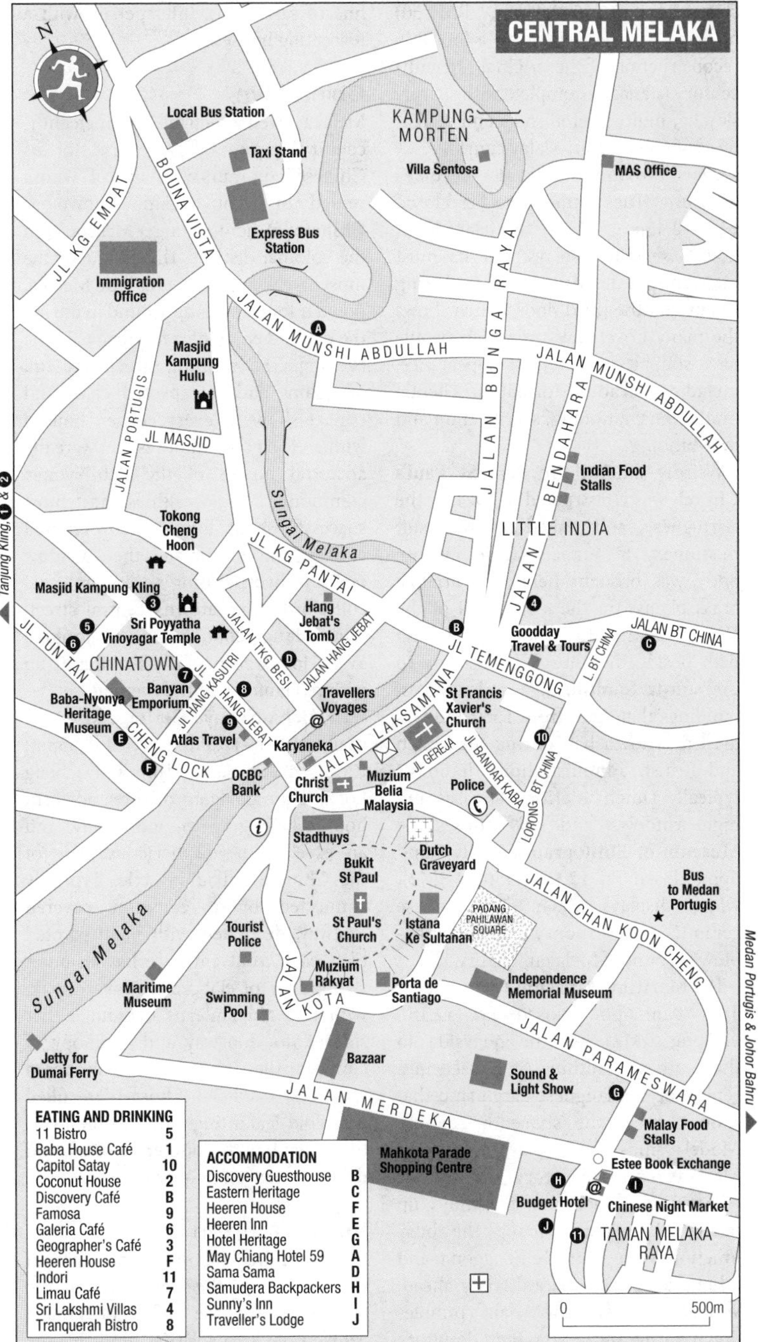
CENTRAL MELAKA
Kuala Lumpur, Airport, Johor Bahru & Ayer Keroh
Tanjung Kling, 1 & 2
Medan Portugis & Johor Bahru
Local Bus Station
Taxi Stand
Express Bus Station
KAMPUNG MORTEN
Villa Sentosa
MAS Office
JL KG EMPAT
BOUNA VISTA
Immigration Office
JALAN MUNSHI ABDULLAH
JALAN BUNGA RAYA
Masjid Kampung Hulu
JALAN PORTUGIS
JL MASJID
JALAN BENDAHARA
Indian Food Stalls
LITTLE INDIA
Sungai Melaka
Tokong Cheng Hoon
JL KG PANTAI
Masjid Kampung Kling
Sri Poyyatha Vinoyagar Temple
Hang Jebat's Tomb
JALAN TKG BESI
JALAN HANG JEBAT
JL TUN TAN
CHINATOWN
Banyan Emporium
JL HANG KASUTRI
HANG JEBAT
Baba-Nyonya Heritage Museum
CHENG LOCK
Atlas Travel
Travellers Voyages
Karyaneka
JALAN LAKSAMANA
St Francis Xavier's Church
JL TEMENGGONG
Goodday Travel & Tours
L. BT CHINA
JALAN BT CHINA
OCBC Bank
Christ Church
Muzium Belia Malaysia
JL GEREJA
JL BANDAR KABA
LORONG BT CHINA
Police
Stadthuys
Dutch Graveyard
Bukit St Paul
St Paul's Church
Istana Ke Sultanan
PADANG PAHLAWAN SQUARE
JALAN CHAN KOON CHENG
Bus to Medan Portugis
Tourist Police
Maritime Museum
Swimming Pool
Muzium Rakyat
Porta de Santiago
JALAN KOTA
Independence Memorial Museum
JALAN PARAMESWARA
Jetty for Dumai Ferry
Bazaar
Sound & Light Show
JALAN MERDEKA
Mahkota Parade Shopping Centre
Malay Food Stalls
Estee Book Exchange
Budget Hotel
Chinese Night Market
TAMAN MELAKA RAYA
0
500m
EATING AND DRINKING
11 Bistro 5
Baba House Café 1
Capitol Satay 10
Coconut House 2
Discovery Café B
Famosa 9
Galeria Café 6
Geographer's Café 3
Heeren House F
Indori 11
Limau Café 7
Sri Lakshmi Villas 4
Tranquerah Bistro 8
ACCOMMODATION
Discovery Guesthouse B
Eastern Heritage C
Heeren House F
Heeren Inn E
Hotel Heritage G
May Chiang Hotel 59 A
Sama Sama D
Samudera Backpackers H
Sunny's Inn I
Traveller's Lodge J

closed Fri 12.15–2.45pm; RM1.50) on Jalan Kota is well worth a look – a reconstruction of the original fifteenth-century istana, it's complete with sharply sloping, multi-layered roofs and recreations of scenes from Malay court life.

The **Muzium Rakyat** (People's Museum; Tues 9am–6pm, Fri closed 12.15–2.45pm; RM2), on Jalan Kota, houses several displays, but its most interesting is the **Museum of Enduring Beauty** on the third floor, which shows the many novel ways in which people have sought to alter their appearance, including head deformation, dental mutilations, tattooing, scarification and foot-binding.

Weirdly ethereal, roofless **St Paul's Church** was constructed in 1521 by the Portuguese, and visited by the Jesuit missionary St Francis Xavier, whose body was brought here for burial; a brass plaque on the south wall of the chancel marks the spot. A winding path beside the church brings you to the sturdy **Stadthuys**, a collection of buildings that dates from 1660 and was used as a town hall during the Dutch and British administrations. It boasts typically Dutch interior staircases and high windows, and now houses the **Museum of Ethnography** (daily 9am–6pm, closed Fri 12.15–2.45pm; RM2), which displays Malay and Chinese ceramics and weaponry and a blow-by-blow account of Melakan history.

The **Maritime Museum** (daily except Tues 9am–6pm, closed Fri 12.15–2.45pm; RM2), on the quayside to the south of Stadthuys, is housed in a replica of a Portuguese cargo ship that sank here in the sixteenth century. Model ships and paintings chart Melaka's maritime history.

If you head north of Stadthuys up Jalan Laksamana, skirting the busy junction with Jalan Temenggong and taking Jalan Bendahara directly ahead, you reach the centre of Melaka's tumble-down **Little India**, a rather desultory line of sari shops, interspersed with a few eating houses.

## Chinatown

Melaka owed much of its nineteenth-century economic recovery to its Chinese community, many of whom settled in what became known as **Chinatown**, across Sungei Melaka from the colonial district. This is one of the most lively, compact areas in Melaka, popular for wandering around in during the day and enjoying a few drinks in the evening. The winding streets are full of quaint and unexpected cafés and trinket shops at every corner, housed within elegant townhouses that were the ancestral homes of the Bab-Nyonya community. The wealthiest and most successful built long, narrow-fronted houses, and minimized the "window tax" by incorporating several internal courtyards. Chinatown's central street, **Jalan Hang Jebat**, known as **Jonkers Walk**, looks particularly striking lit up with red lanterns in the evening.

The **Baba-Nyonya Heritage Museum** (daily 10am–12.30pm & 2–4.30pm; RM8), 48–50 Jalan Tun Tan Cheng Lock, is an amalgam of three adjacent houses belonging to one family, and an excellent atmospheric example of the Chinese Palladian style. Typically connected by a common covered footway, decorated with hand-painted tiles, each front entrance has an outer swing door of elaborately carved teak, with two red lanterns hanging either side of the doorway and a canopy of Chinese tiles around the shuttered windows. Inside, the homes are filled with gold-leaf fittings, blackwood furniture inlaid with mother-of-pearl and delicately carved lacquer screens.

## Village Morten

Seven hundred metres to the north of Chinatown, on the west bank of the Sungei Melaka, the village of **Village Morten** is a surprising find in the heart of the city. To get here, take the footbridge down a small path off Jalan Bunga Raya, one of the principal roads leading north out of town, or take a river trip from the tourist office. The wooden stilted houses here are distinctively Melakan, with their long, rectangular living rooms and kitchens, and narrow verandas approached by ornamental steps. On the left as you cross the footbridge you'll find the **Villa Sentosa** (daily 9am–5pm; voluntary donation), a beautiful old home converted to a small museum, where the welcoming family will gladly show you their artefacts and heirlooms.

### Taman Mini Malaysia

Fourteen kilometres north of central Melaka, in the recreational park area of Ayer Keroh, **Taman Mini Malaysia** and mini **ASEAN** (daily 9am–6pm; RM5) are full-sized reconstructions of typical houses from all thirteen Malay states and from Brunei, Indonesia, the Philippines, Singapore and Thailand. Cultural shows featuring traditional dance are regularly staged here, too. Town buses #19 and #105 run every thirty minutes to Ayer Keroh from the local bus station.

## Arrival and information

**By bus** There are two bus stations, a local and an express, and both are located on the northern outskirts of the city, off Jl Hang Tuah. Buses from Singapore arrive at the local bus station. The chaotic express bus station is beyond the **taxi station**, a block to the south. From either, it's just a ten-minute walk over the bridge to the town centre, or take bus #17 and ask to be let off at Town Square to find yourself in the heart of Melaka.
**By ferry** The daily ferry from Dumai in Sumatra docks at Shah Bandar jetty on Jl Merdeka, close to the historical centre and the budget hostel area.
**By train** There's no train station in Melaka itself, the nearest being at Tampin, 38km north; buses from Tampin drop you at the local bus station.
**Tourist information centre** Jl Kota (Mon–Sat 9am–1pm & 2–5.30pm, Sun 9am–4.30pm; ⓣ06/281 4803, ⓦwww.melaka.gov.my), 400m from the Shah Bandar jetty. Staff are very helpful, and the information board outside displays the times of the river trips to Village Morten.

## City transport

**Trishaws** You should be able to get a trishaw from the Padang Pahlawan Square and outside the Mahkota Parade Shopping Centre. This is understandably a popular tourist option – particularly at night when the cycles, already pimped out with so many flowers, parasols and bells that you can barely get in, are lit up with flashing multi-coloured lights. A sightseeing tour costs RM25 for one hour.
**Taxis** Quite hard to find on the narrow streets, but you can always get one from the taxi stand near the express bus station.
**Buses** Buy a RM2 ticket on any of the local red buses, and you can re-use it for 24 hours.

## Accommodation

Hotel prices are a little higher than in other Malaysian towns, but so are standards.
**Discovery Guesthouse** 3 Jl Bunga Raya, ⓣ06/292 5606. Fairly shambolic with basic, somewhat shabby rooms. However, it's located above the *Discovery Café,* so guests are sure to run into other backpackers and the location is convenient, if a little hazardous being so near a roundabout. Also has internet, pool table and guidebook library. ❷
**Eastern Heritage** 8 Jl Bukit China, ⓣ06/283 3026. Set in an imaginatively decorated dark-wood house that makes the best of its impressive original architectural features. Rooms are clean if a bit worn, with murals on the walls. The owner also offers batik classes, and there is a plunge pool downstairs ideal for a hot day. Curfew midnight. Dorm ❶; doubles ❷

**TREAT YOURSELF**

**Heeren House** 1 Jalan Tun Tan Cheng Lock ⓣ06/281 4241. A cool, peaceful haven at the heart of Melaka, within Chinatown, and two minutes' walk from the Town Square, The rooms are tastefully decorated, some with four-poster beds, the owners are friendly and helpful and there is a classier-than-average book exchange. The very best choice for a small upmarket hotel. Reservations recommended. ❺–❼

**Heeren Inn** 23 Jl Tun Tan Cheng Lock ☎06/288 3600. A sprawling establishment with long, large-windowed corridors and a brisk but pleasant Chinese owner. Rooms are scrupulously clean and quite spacious. Internet (RM3/hr) and bicycle rental (RM7/ day) available. ❺

**Hotel Heritage** Q116 A Jl Merdeka ☎06/281 8688. This hotel is basic and not massively inspiring, but lives up to its promise of being "the friendliest hotel in town". The rooms are clean and the Chinese owner, despite being incomprehensible, is extremely motherly. ❸

**May Chiang Hotel 59** 59 Jl Munshi Abdullah ☎06/282 2101. A little institutional but clean, and the large rooms offer good value. The location, though convenient, is unfortunately marred by the noisy road. ❸

**Sama Sama** 26 Jl Tkg Besi ☎012/305 1980. Run by the eccentric but extremely friendly Gaby, this hippie hangout is very popular and often booked up. Rooms are basic and quite open, but the leafy central courtyard area and relaxed atmosphere more than make up for it. Bookings only accepted for stays of two nights or more. ❶

**Samudera Backpackers** 205B Jl Melaka Raya ☎014/635 5981 or 06/281 5796. Family-run hostel with a large lounge and pleasant balcony. Rooms are somewhat airless, but it's clean and conveniently located. ❷

**Sunny's Inn** 270a Taman Melaka Raya ☎06/227 5446. Somewhat run-down but homely family hostel, which has a cosy communal lounge, a roof garden and bags of tourist information. Dorm ❶; doubles ❷

**Traveller's Lodge** 214b Taman Melaka Raya ☎06/226 5709. As pleasant a hostel as you'll find in Malaysia, with a downstairs café, roof terrace and a raised lounging area, complete with books and board games. There's home cooking, and the wide range of rooms – from dorms to basic fan doubles to a/c en-suites – are all great value. Dorm ❶; doubles ❷

## Eating and drinking

Sampling the spicy dishes of Nyonya cuisine is a must in Melaka, with its emphasis on sour herbs like tamarind, tempered by creamy coconut milk. Usual opening hours are 9am–11pm unless otherwise stated.

**11 Bistro** 11 Jl Hang Lekir. Charming chic bar that plays chilled-out tunes. There's a little bridge at the entrance and it's decked out with Thai chairs for reclining on. Good for a late-night drink; open until 2am.

**Baba House Café** 125 Jl Tun Tan Cheng Lock. A small, cosy café serving breakfasts, coffees and "local delights" (around RM8).

**Capitol Satay** Jl Bukit China. A buzzy, frenetic place popular with local Chinese, where you can experience *satay celup* – take your pick of assorted fish, meat and vegetables skewered on sticks and cook them in a spicy peanut sauce at your table. Drinks served in coconuts are delicious and refreshing. Open 7pm–midnight.

**Coconut House** 128 Jl Tun Tan Cheng Lock. Effortlessly stylish restaurant, bookshop and art gallery housed in a restored shop-house with its own courtyard, where those in the know opt for the excellent woodfire pizzas. The terrace at the back offers peaceful rooftop views. Daily 11am–midnight, closed Wed & Thurs am.

**Discovery Café** 3 Jl Bunga Raya. Decrepit but fun garden bar with pool table and a live band seven days a week.

**Famosa** 28–30 Jl Hang Kasturi. Situated in an incongrously grand old shop-house, Famosa serves traditional food tailored to Western tastes.

**Galeria Café** Entrance through *Hotel Puri*, 118 Jl Tun Tan Cheng Lock. Portuguese and Melakan specialities are served in a gorgeous cool garden, complete with waterfalls and ponds and shaded by trees. It's also a lovely place to enjoy a coffee while making the tour of Chinatown. Coffee RM6, main dishes RM12–18.

**Geographer Café** 83 Jl Hang Jebat. Atmospheric little café, restaurant and bar in a corner shop-house complete with wicker chairs and lazy ceiling fans. Evenings bring on varied entertainment – Thursday is acoustic night, when you can listen to cheesy Western songs being cheerfully murdered. Open until 1am.

**Heeren House** 1 Jl Tun Tan Cheng Lock. This stylish, peaceful café is situated behind the *Archipelago* craft shop, which sells gorgeous antiques and local crafts. Food is reasonably priced, with Nyonya lunches at the weekends for RM15, and tea-time treats such as scones and brownies for RM7.

**Indori** 236–237 Jl Melaka Raya 1. Situated opposite *Traveller's Lodge*, this is a casual roadside café with seating spilling onto the street, good for a bite of breakfast or a coffee. It also serves cheap and tasty *ikan bakar* (grilled fish) for proper meals. Around RM6 for a main meal.

**Limau Café** 49 Jl Hang Jebat. Tiny café with cool, dark interior, popular with travellers, serving fruit shakes and cakes. Open until 6pm.

**Sri Lakshmi Villas** 2 Jl Bendahara. A noisy, basic café on a somewhat desultory strip, serving a range of *dosas* and reliable South Indian *thalis*, with as many top-ups as you can eat. Good for vegetarians.

**Tranquerah Bistro** 18 Jl Hang Jebat. An airy canteen with high ceilings and an outdoor courtyard seating area in Melaka Heritage Square. The food is traditional and delicious. RM8 for a main dish.

## Shopping

**Antiques** Melaka is famed for its antiques, and there are many specialist outlets along Jl Hang Jebat and Jl Tun Tan Cheng Lock, though they are by no means cheap. If it's a genuine antique, check that it can be exported legally and fill in an official clearance form. Interesting places to browse on Jl Hang Jebat include Dragon House at no. 65 for old coins and banknotes, and Wang Naga Antique Centre at no. 88, which specializes in artefacts salvaged from shipwrecks. Malaqa House, 70 Jl Tan Cheng Lock, set up partly as a museum and partly as a shop, is a gorgeous place to browse. The ancient building is in good repair, and features such as a leafy central courtyard have been retained.

**Books** Estee Book Exchange, Taman Melaka Raya, has a good selection of English-language books, as does MPH in the Mahkota Parade Shopping Centre.

**Crafts and souvenirs** Wah Aik at 103 Jl Kubu sells silk shoes like the ones that used to be made to bind feet, whilst Gee's Original on Lorong Hang Kasturi has a shopful of handcrafted wooden articles behind the most attractive shopfront in Melaka. For modern crafts and souvenirs, Tribal Arts Gallery at 27 Jl Hang Kasturi specializes in Sarawakian crafts and Orang Utan, 59 Lorong Hang Jebat, is the outlet for local artist Charles Cham's witty cartoon T-shirts and paintings. For cheap DVDs, shoes and electrical goods, head to the Northern End of Jl Bunga Raya, Little India.

## Directory

**Banks and exchange** HSBC, Jl Hang Tuah, has a 24hr ATM as does OCBC bank, just over the bridge in Chinatown. Moneychangers are often more convenient and offer as good rates as the banks: Try Malaccan Souvenir House and Trading at 22 Jl Tokong.

**Car rental** Avis, Equatorial Hotel, Jl Bandar Hilir ☎06/282 8333. Car rental is around RM200 per day.

**Hospital** Sultan Hospital, Jalan Bendahara ☎06/283 5888; Melaka General Hospital, Jalan Pringgit ☎ 06/282 2344.

**Immigration** The Immigration Office is on the 2nd Floor, Bangunan Persekutuan, Jalan Hang Tuah (☎06/282 4958) for on-the-spot visa renewals.

**Internet** The east end of Jl Merdeka has a string of internet cafés, or try the ground floor of the *Budget Hotel* at 259 Jl Melaka Raya 3, RM3/hour.

**Police** The Tourist Police Office (☎06/282 2222) is on Jl Kota and is open 24hr. The emergency police number is ☎06/285 1999.

**Post office** The GPO is inconveniently situated on the way to Ayer Keroh on Jl Bukit Baru – take town bus #19. A minor branch on Jl Laksamana off Town Square sells stamps and aerograms.

**Telephone services** The Telekom building is on Jl Chan Koon Cheng (daily 8am–5pm).

**Travel agents** Atlas Travel, 5 Jl Hang Jebat (☎06/286 3016). Good Day Travel and Tours, 41 Jl Temenggong, is good for plane tickets.

## Moving on

**By bus** Buses run to all points on the Peninsula, most from the express bus station. Most express services to Singapore leave from the local bus station.

**Destinations:** Alor Setar (11 daily; 8hr); Butterworth (11 daily; 6hr); Ipoh (11 daily; 4hr); Johor Bahru (5 daily; 4hr); Kota Bharu (1 daily; 11hr); Kuala Lumpur (14 daily; 2hr); Kuala Terengganu (1 daily; 8hr); Kuantan (1 daily; 6hr); Mersing (2 daily; 5hr); Singapore (9 daily; 5hr); Tapah (1 daily; 3hr 30min).

**By ferry** A daily boat leaves for Dumai, Sumatra (2hr; RM80) as well as Pekan Baru (RM120) three times weekly. Contact Indomal Express (☎06/283 2506), or call at the Tourist Information Centre, Jl Kota.

**By train** Trains run to Singapore from the train station at Tampin, 38km north of Melaka (☎06/411 1034).

# JOHOR BAHRU

The southernmost Malaysian city of any size, **JOHOR BAHRU** – or simply **JB** – is the gateway into Singapore, linked to the city-state by a 1056-metre causeway which is crossed by around fifty thousand people a day. At weekends in particular, Singaporeans flock to JB to shop, and although a government crackdown means it's a less seedy city than it once was, it still has the grimy underbelly of a transit border town. It also has good links to KL and Melaka, so there's little to detain you whichever direction you're travelling in. JB's one interesting attraction is the **Istana Besar**, the former residence of Johor's royal family. Surrounded by extensive gardens, it is an impressive Victorian-style building set on a hillock overlooking the Johor Straits. It's open to the public as the **Museum Di Raja Abu Bakar** (daily except Fri 9am–4pm; RM7), and is still set out pretty much as it would have been when used as a palace. Exhibits include gifts from foreign dignitaries, such as stuffed tigers and crystal tables and chairs.

## Arrival and information

**By bus** Larkin bus station is 3km away from the centre of JB on Jl Geruda. Plenty of buses run from here to the causeway, or you can catch a taxi for around RM7. There's also a left-luggage counter (7am-11pm, RM2 per bag).
**By train** The train station is slightly east of the city centre, off Jl Tun Abdul Razak.
**By air** Flights to JB land at Senai Airport (T07/599 4500, ⓦ www.senaiairport.com), 30km north of the city, from where a regular shuttle bus service (RM8; 45min) runs to the city centre.
**Tourist Information Centre** There are two: the main one, JOTIC, is on Jl Air Molek (Mon–Fri 9am–5pm, Sat 9am–1pm; ⓣ07/222 3591, ⓦwww.johortourism.com.my), and an office on the Causeway (Mon–Fri 9am–5pm, Sat & Sun 9am–4pm; ⓣ07/224 9485).

## Accommodation

JB attracts more business people than tourists, especially as most travellers only use it as a stopover, but there are a few cheap options, mostly clustered around Jl Meldrum in the centre of town.
**Footloose Homestay** 4h Jl Ismail ⓣ07/224 2881. The cheapest option by far, with a basic dorm at RM15. ❶
**JB Hotel** 80-A Jl Wong Ah Fook ⓣ07/223 4989. It's no great shakes but the rooms are fairly clean and quite spacious, which is more than can be said for most other budget accommodation in JB. ❸

## Eating

The liveliest of the places to eat in JB is the large **night market** across the footbridge from the train station beside the Hindu Temple. In the evenings, a fair number of Singaporeans make it over the Causeway to come and enjoy a cheap bite here. Try the delicious grilled seafood – coconut drenched *laksa* are also a must.

## Directory

**Banks and exchange** There are plenty in the main shopping centres, or try Maybank 11 Jl Selat Tebrau; HSBC Jl Timbalan (this has a 24hr ATM); or OCBC Jl Ibrahim. There is also a brace of cashpoints on the south side of the Merlin Tower.
**Car rental** This is cheaper here than in Singapore, but if you intend to take the car over the border, check that this is allowed. Try Avis at the *Tropical Inn* (ⓣ07/223 7971), or Hertz in the JOTIC building (ⓣ07/223 7520).
**Clinic** Sultana Aminah Hospital 07/223 1666
**Internet** There are plenty of places around City Square and the Komtar building. Or try Meeting Point, 59 Jl Meldrum, RM3/hr.

## Moving on

**By bus** to Alor Setar (2 daily; 16hr); Butterworth (at least 2 daily; 14hr); Ipoh (4 daily; 9hr); Kota Bharu (2 daily; 12hr); Kuala Lumpur (every 30min; 7hr); Kuala Terengganu (2 daily; 9hr); Kuantan (6 daily; 6hr); Melaka (5 daily; 3hr); Mersing (at least 2 daily; 2hr 30min); Singapore (every 30min; 1hr).
**By train** to: Gemas (5 daily; 3–4hr); Kuala Lipis (2 daily; 7hr); Kuala Lumpur (4 daily; 5hr 30min–7hr 10min); Singapore (6 daily; 1hr); Tumpat (1 daily; 12hr 30min).
**By air** Heading out to Senai International Airport, MAS passengers can take the RM4 shuttle bus from outside the Tourist Information Centre. Alternatively, you can get a taxi to the airport for about RM25. The MAS office is at Level 1, Menara Pelangi, Jl Kuning Taman Pelangi (ⓣ07/334 1001). JB is also served by Air Asia and by Riau Airlines (ⓣ07/599 4500, ⓦwww.riau-airlines.com); their office is in the airport.
**Destinations:** Kota Kinabalu (1 daily; 2hr 15min); Kuching (3 daily; 1hr 25min), Kuala Lumpur (at least 6 daily; 45min), Penang (2 daily; 1hr 5min) and other destinations.

## Pulau Tioman

**Pulau Tioman**, 30km east of Mersing, is a popular holiday island scattered with small palm-fringed beach coves. Express boats travel here in less than two hours, and several daily flights arrive from Singapore and Kuala Lumpur – perhaps as a result, locals seem fairly indifferent

## TRAVEL TO SINGAPORE, AND ON TO INDONESIA

Two bus services run throughout the day between JB and **Singapore**. The a/c JB–Singapore Express (every 10min, 6.30am–midnight; RM2.40, or RM4.80 if you have luggage) is the most comfortable, though the city bus (SBS) 170, is cheaper (RM1.70). Confusingly, however, the 170 has two routes: every ten minutes (6am–11.30pm), it runs from Larkin bus station in JB either to the Queen Street terminal in central Singapore, or to Kranji MRT station. You can buy tickets on the bus. You can also catch a bus into Singapore from just outside the train station on the main road at the border. There's an SPS coach run by Malaysian Airlines from JB's Senai Airport to Singapore's *Copthorne Orchid* hotel. (2hr; RM12). Taxis between JB and Singapore departing from Pasar Bakti station, Jalan Trus, cost around RM10 per person, and leave only when they're full. Local city taxis can't cross the causeway into Singapore.

Whichever direction you're travelling, buses drop passengers outside the **immigration points** at either end of the causeway and immigration procedures take around ten minutes. To enter Singapore, visitors must have a passport valid for at least six months. Occasionally, you may be asked to provide evidence of onwards travel and a healthy bank balance, but this is fairly rare. If you want to stay in JB, don't get back on the bus, just take the short walk into town. Similarly, it's possible to board the buses to Singapore at the causeway terminal instead of trekking out to the bus station. The bus will drop you off at the border for the immigration procedures; they won't wait for you, but if you hold onto your ticket you can board any bus of the same number on the other side of the border. To avoid this hassle you can make the journey by train, as the formalities are carried out on board at RM2.90 for a second-class seat on a 1hr journey. You can also take a ferry to Indonesia, to Tanjung Pinang (one way RM82) and Pulau Batam (one way RM57). Tickets can be booked from Sriwani Tours and Travel (Ⓣ07/221 1677) in the Bebas Cukai shopping centre on Jalan Ibrahim Sultan, 2km east of the border crossing. There are also boats departing from Kukup, southwest of JB, which go to Tanjung Balai, Sumatra – contact Fast Ferry Ⓣ07/696 0988 for further details.

to tourists, which can be refreshing or frustrating depending on the circumstance. Damage has unfortunately been inflicted on the surrounding coral and marine life, but Tioman still has some breathtaking natural scenery. Most of the island's facilities are at industrial **Tekek**, on the west coast, and the popular budget places are in the bay of **Air Batang** or livelier (and slightly more expensive) **Salang**. The east coast's sole settlement, **Juara**, is less developed, and **Nipah** and **Mukut** are just opening up to tourism.

Many of Tioman's nearby islets provide excellent opportunities for snorkelling and diving. Most of the chalet operations offer day-trips (RM30) to nearby reefs, and there are numerous dive centres on the island.

The only road wide enough for cars leads to the *Berjaya Tioman Beach Resort*, and a two-metre-wide path runs north from Tekek to Air Batang. Apart from these, the island is criss-crossed by dirt roads and jungle tracks.

Tioman is affected by the **monsoon**, making the island hard to reach by sea between November and February.

### Tekek

The village of **TEKEK** is the main settlement on the island and the least inspiring part of Tioman. It has been overdeveloped and locals aren't hugely friendly, but it's about the only place on the island where you'll find essential services. If you're stuck here for a few hours, you could distract yourself with the large government-sponsored **Marine Centre**

## LAYAK ISLAND

This tiny island is currently uninhabited, but a single resort is set to open here in April 2009. Only 25 people will be allowed on the island at any time, making it an exclusive getaway. The island is as beautiful as any on the east coast, and boasts opportunities for turtle-watching and for catching sight of lobsters and billfish on snorkelling trips. There will also be jungle trekking as well as, of course, plenty of scope for relaxing in paradisiacal surroundings. For further information, contact Wan, who also owns *D. Layak Guesthouse and Adventure Centre* (ⓣ09/413 1215 or 012/963 9109, Ⓔdlayak@hotmail.com).

(daily 8.30am–4pm; free). Situated north of the main jetty at the very end of the bay, it's hard to miss. Set up to protect the coral and marine life around the island, and to patrol the fishing taking place in its waters, it contains an aquarium and samples of coral.

### Air Batang

**AIR BATANG**, commonly referred to as ABC beach, 2km north of Tekek (jetty to jetty), is the most popular choice for backpackers, and essentially a single track running along the long stretch of beachfront, with guesthouses

## TRAVEL TO AND FROM PULAU TIOMAN

### Via Mersing

The east-coast fishing port of **Mersing**, 130km north of Johor Bahru, is the main gateway to **Pulau Tioman** and the smaller islands of the Seribuat archipelago. The town is grouped around two main streets, Jalan Abu Bakar and Jalan Ismail. Express buses drop you off just before the roundabout between the two, and at the R&R Plaza near the jetty, from where they also depart. You can buy tickets from *Restoran Malaysia* and offices at R&R Plaza itself. The local bus station is on Jalan Sulaiman, close to the riverfront. The **Mersing Tourist Information Centre** (Mon–Sat, mornings at the ferry terminal 8am–1pm; afternoons at the office on Jalan Abu Bakar 2–4.30pm; ⓣ07/799 5212) is very helpful and offers impartial advice on the many different island deals.The **jetty** is about ten minutes' walk from the roundabout along Jalan Abu Bakar. Inside the R&R Plaza near the jetty, a large signboard shows which of the thirteen companies' boats sail to Pulau Tioman and when (the last one is about 4.30pm). For the other islands, it's best to book ahead, either at the particular island office itself, around the jetty, or at one of the travel agencies on Jalan Abu Bakar or Jalan Ismail. Make sure that you **change money** before you leave, as rates on the islands are lousy. If you end up having to **stay** overnight (a distinct possibility if you're travelling around monsoon season), try *Omar's Backpackers'* (ⓣ07/799 5096, Dorms RM10) on Jalan Abu Bakar, which offers the cheapest rooms in town in a clean, basic and helpful guesthouse.

**Slow boats from Mersing** include catamarans and the so-called sea buses (which were used for transportation before the tourism boom). These take two to three hours, depending on the tide; tickets are RM40 for the one-way trip. Smaller boats, sometimes referred to as "sea taxis", take two to three people and charge according to destination (RM30–50 per person). A speedboat departs approximately every hour, making the journey in half the time (RM35). In addition, a RM5 entrance fee, which supposedly goes towards marine conservation, is required before you can travel. You'll have to decide in advance which bay you want to stay in since the boats generally make drops only at the major resorts of Genting, Paya, Tekek, Air and restaurants, spread out along it, making for spaciously laid out chalets. However, it lacks a centre, and the jetty dividing the bay roughly in half is a bit of an eyesore. However, there's a good stretch of beach at the southern end (to the right as you get off the jetty), a charming series of bridges linking the chalets at the northern end and a pleasant, laid-back atmosphere to the whole area. A fifteen-minute **jungle trail** leads over the headland to the north, which – after an initial scramble – flattens out into an easy walk, ending up at secluded **Penuba Bay**. From here, it's an hour's walk to gorgeous, secluded Monkey Beach, beyond which is Salang.

### Salang

North of Air Batang, **SALANG** is a livelier option, but there has been a lot of development recently and the string of hostels stretches pretty much the whole length of the seafront. Prices tend to be a little higher than at Air Batang and the sea, because of a combination of rocks, depth and rubbish, isn't all that great for swimming. The southern end of the beach is the more scenic, and Pulau Soyok, the small island off the southern headland, has a pretty reef for snorkelling.

### Juara

Life is simple at **JUARA**, situated across two quiet stretches of beach on the east coast, where the only entertainments



Batang and Salang (in that order); there are only occasional boats from Mersing to Juara on the east coast.

#### Via Tanjung Gemok

The ferries from this tiny town, 35km north of Mersing, are less frequent than from Mersing, but have the advantage of basically leaving in all kinds of weather. It's also a more convenient departure point if you're coming from the north. Between November and early March, there's one ferry a day at 1pm, and from mid-March to October, there are three a day, at 9am, 10am and 1pm. Tickets can be purchased from **Tanjung Gemok Ferry Terminal** (☎07/413 1997; RM60). If you have to **stay** here overnight, *D. Layak Guesthouse and Adventure Centre* (☎09/413 1215) is a good choice – rooms are somewhat basic and showers are "Malay style" (there's a tap and bucket), but it's exceptionally clean and the chatty owner Wan can't do enough to help. To get here, take a bus going to Mersing (or if these are in short supply or booked up, one to Johor Bahru, though that will cost more) and ask the driver to let you off at Tanjung Gemok.

#### By air

There are daily flights from Kuala Lumpur (Subang Airport) and Singapore (Seletar Airport) operated by tiny Berjaya Air (☎03/7846 8228, Ⓦwww.berjaya-air.com). You'll land at the airstrip in Tekek, from where there's a shuttle bus to the *Berjaya Tioman Beach Resort*, 2km to the south. This bus is for arriving and departing guests only, but the locals also run an unofficial RM3 taxi service to the airport according to demand. Otherwise, there are plenty of touts hanging around who'll take you in a sea taxi to the bay of your choice.

#### Returning

On the way back, ask at your guesthouse for the departure times from the particular bay you're staying in – the first boat leaves Salang at 7am, and the last at mid-afternoon (around 4pm). Particularly in uncertain weather, it's a good idea to ask your guesthouse owner to phone ahead to be sure the boats are running that day. If you decide you want to fly off the island, call *Berjaya Tioman Beach Resort* (☎09/419 1303) to reserve a place on a flight to Singapore or KL.

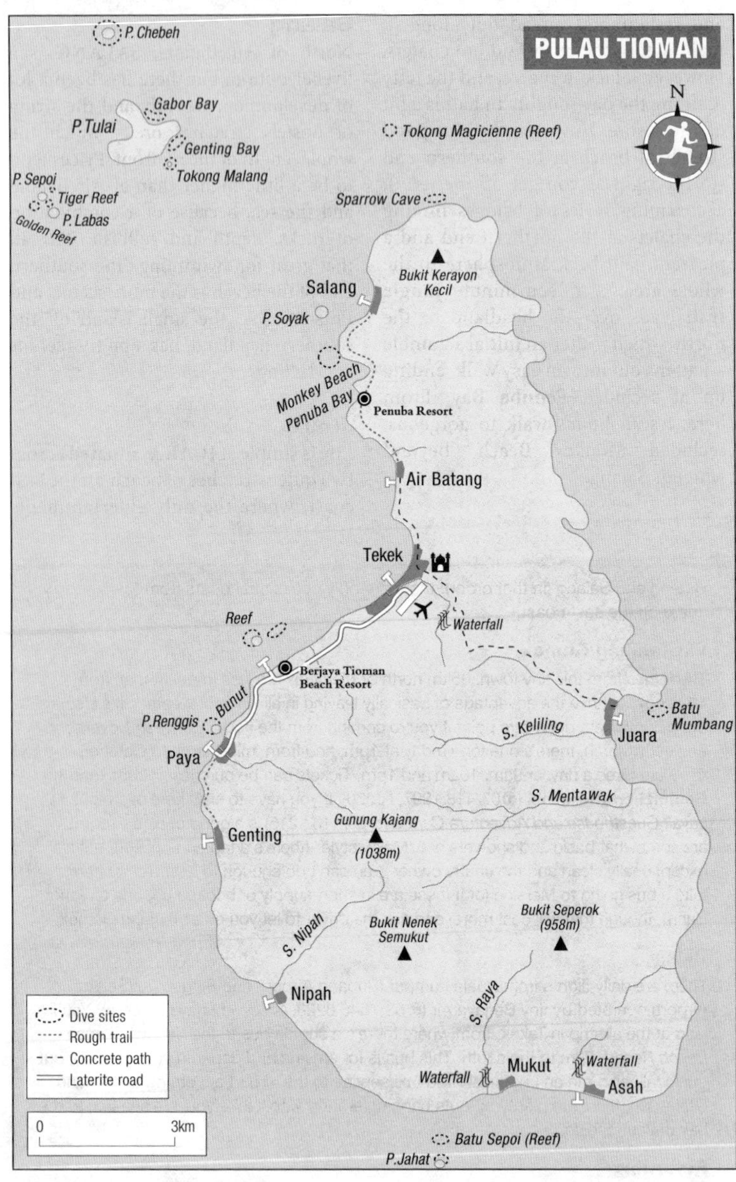


are diving or self-made beach games. As the northern (more populated) bay faces out to open sea, it's more susceptible to bad weather but lovely when the weather is good (which it usually is, outside the monsoon months). The southern bay is more secluded, but does have a couple of chalets. The locals speak less English and are more conservative than elsewhere on the island: officially alcohol isn't served.

There's only one sea bus a day to the *village* from the west coast of Tioman. At any other time the journey to this isolated bay can be made either by **sea taxi** or by **4-wheel-drive** – this costs RM35 per person for a minimum of four people (or simply charter the car for RM140). Alternatively, locals do take their **scooters** through the jungle and will sometimes allow you to ride on the back for a fee, but as the paths are both seriously steep and extremely rocky, this isn't necessarily recommended if you want to come out of the jungle in one piece. There's also a path through the jungle that can be navigated **on foot** from Tekek in about two hours. The start of the trail (a five-minute walk from the airstrip) is easy enough to identify since it's the only concrete path that heads off in that direction, passing the local mosque before hitting virgin jungle after about fifteen minutes. There's no danger of losing your way: cement steps climb steeply through the greenery, tapering off into a smooth, downhill path once you're over the ridge. After 45 minutes, there is a **waterfall** – it's forbidden to bathe here, since it supplies Tekek with water. From the waterfall, it's another hour or so to Juara village.

### Nipah

For almost total isolation, head to **NIPAH** on Tioman's southwest coast. Comprising a clean, empty beach of coarse, yellow sand and a landlocked lagoon, there's no village to speak of here. You might be lucky enough to get a ferry from the mainland to drop you here since there is an adequate jetty, but it's more likely that you'll have to come by sea taxi from Genting; if so, the *Nipah Resort* operates a free service.

## Information and island transport

Transport on the island is somewhat limited. In favourable weather, **foot** and **canoe** are good ways to explore the island

**Bicycle and canoe rental** *Nazri's Place* on Air Batang, *Featherlight Café* (in the Terminal Complex next to the airstrip) in Tekek. RM5/hr for bikes, RM10/hr for canoes. For bicycles, navigable routes are limited, since most bays are separated by rocky jungle paths. If you go through the jungle, be sure to make your return journey before it gets dark and on canoe beware of the conditions and the tides.

**Island sea bus** Operates outside the monsoon season and takes two hours to visit Salang, Air Batang, Tekek, Genting, Paya and the *Berjaya Tioman Beach Resort*. It's very unreliable, but there is usually one departure a day from Salang at 8.30am and the return from Juara at 2.45pm. Salang to Juara will set you back RM20. This service doesn't run during the monsoon, when you'll have to wait for the morning ferry from Mersing or the return afternoon ferry from Salang, depending on your destination.

**Taxi boats** These operate from the majority of guesthouses, with prices starting at RM20 for travel between adjacent bays – it's also possible to travel as part of a round-island trip (RM55), which run from the various chalets. You could also hire a small boat, but a five-seater will set you back RM250–300 per day.

**Tourist infromation** *Mawar's Beach Chalets* on Air Batang run an ad-hoc Tourist Information Centre and can help you with boat tickets and day-trips, as well as onwards travel from the island (though be sure you've got *all* the information you need – they're liable to give you lots of positive sounding information, only to then tell you that actually everything they've just suggested isn't viable for one reason or another).

## Dive operators

Many dive centres on Tioman offer the range of PADI certificates, from the four-day Open Water course (usually around RM800) through to the fourteen-day Divemaster (RM1700); always check that qualified English-speaking instructors are employed, and that the cost includes equipment.

### West coast

**B & J Dive Centre** ⓣ09/419 5555, ⓦwww.divetioman.com. This friendly, longstanding outfit on Air Batang is a good choice, with the advantage of an open-air pool, so skills don't have to be practised in the unpredictable sea currents. PADI Open Water RM800.

**Eco-Divers** ⓣ09/419 1250, ⓦwww.eco-divers.net. Also on Air Batang, this is a slightly smaller centre, with friendly staff and PADI Open Water courses at RM800.

### East coast

**Sunrise Dive Centre** Ⓣ09/419 3102, Ⓦwww.sunrisedivecentre.com. This dive centre in Juara is the best and most popular place to go, with PADI Open Water at RM750.

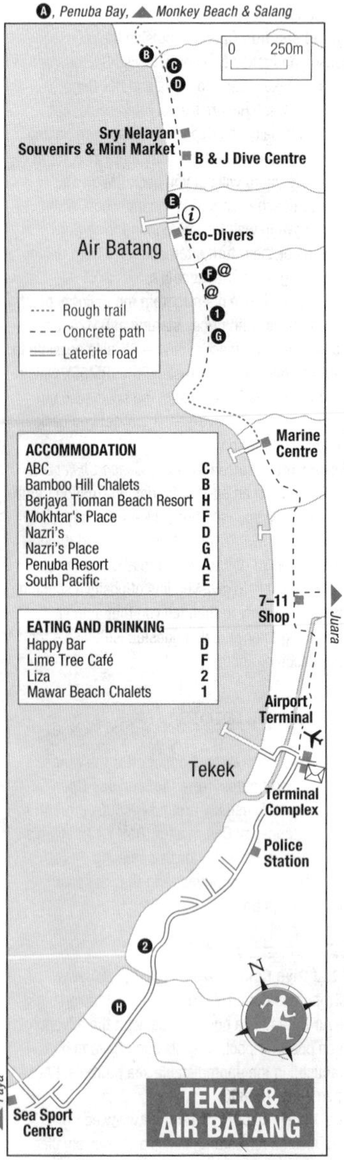

**TEKEK & AIR BATANG**

A, Penuba Bay, Monkey Beach & Salang

Sry Nelayan Souvenirs & Mini Market
B & J Dive Centre
Eco-Divers
Air Batang
Marine Centre
7-11 Shop
Juara
Airport Terminal
Tekek
Terminal Complex
Police Station
Paya
Sea Sport Centre

Rough trail
Concrete path
Laterite road

**ACCOMMODATION**

| | |
|---|---|
| ABC | C |
| Bamboo Hill Chalets | B |
| Berjaya Tioman Beach Resort | H |
| Mokhtar's Place | F |
| Nazri's | D |
| Nazri's Place | G |
| Penuba Resort | A |
| South Pacific | E |

**EATING AND DRINKING**

| | |
|---|---|
| Happy Bar | D |
| Lime Tree Café | F |
| Liza | 2 |
| Mawar Beach Chalets | 1 |

## Accommodation and eating

### Tekek

There's really no reason why you'd need to stay in Tekek as it's not the most scenic town and most of the accommodation options are dilapidated and located next to piles of rubbish.

**Berjaya Tioman Beach Resort** Ⓣ09/419 1000, Ⓦwww.berjayaresorts.com. Two kilometres to the south of Tekek, and sufficiently far away to be a self-sufficient paradise, this is the island's only international-standard hotel. It's a village-sized complex with a nine-hole golf course and stables, offering everything from double rooms to deluxe apartments. The hotel is owned by the Berjaya Corporation, which also runs Berjaya Air, the only airline to fly to and from Tioman island. ❾

### Air Batang

As you get off the boat, a signpost helpfully lists the direction of the numerous guesthouses in the bay. Air Batang likes to keep its nightlife low-key, unlike Salang, which can get rowdy. All of the chalets have restaurants.

**ABC** Ⓣ09/419 1154. At the far northern end of the bay and among the best in Air Batang. Quieter location than most, the inexpensive, pretty chalets are set in a well-tended garden. The beachfront café is ideal for a sunset drink. ❹

**Bamboo Hill Chalets** Ⓣ09/419 1339. These wooden chalets on stilts, perched on the northern headland, are very well equipped and enjoy stunning views. It's a shame about the unhelpful staff. ❺

**Mokhtar's Place** Ⓣ09/419 1148. Rooms are basic but clean and airy. *Mokhtar's* offers booking services for buses on the mainland, water-taxis, fishing and snorkelling trips, which non-guests can use as well as guests. There is also internet at RM10/hr. ❸

**Nazri's** Ⓣ09/419 1375. A great outfit set up in a shaded garden area, with well-built chalets at a variety of prices. The restaurant serves exceptional Indian food, and *Happy Bar* is the place to be in the evening. ❸–❺

**Nazri's Place** Ⓣ09/419 1329. A new venture by the owners of the original Nazri's, boasting a range of chalets from fairly basic doubles to ridiculously luxurious family palaces. Staff are friendly and can organise taxi-boats and snorkel and canoe hire. Plus, the nightly BBQ is delicious. ❸–❺

**Penuba Resort** ⓣ013/772 0454. The only place to stay in Penuba Bay. Its stilted chalets, high up on the rocks, have fantastic views out to sea and a far better beach than Air Batang. It has both the advantage and disadvantage of being fairly secluded and only accessible by a jungle-path, taxi-boat or scrambling over the rocks at low tide. ❺–❼

**South Pacific** ⓣ09/419 1176. Close to the jetty. Clean, good-value chalets with bathrooms, some right on the beach. Although it always looks closed, the kitchen is in fact always open, and the food here is simple and tasty. ❸

## Salang

The budget places to stay are on the right (south) as you leave the jetty.

**Pak Long** ⓣ09/419 5000. Situated over the bridge just behind the little lagoon this is a friendly, sprawling place with well-kept en-suite chalets. Internet RM10/ hr. ❹–❼

**Salang Indah Resort** ⓣ09/419 5015. This resort's restaurant is popular and usually crowded, offering lovely sea views and a wide choice of Western food. They also arrange snorkelling and sightseeing trips. The rooms range from boxes to double-storeyed family complexes, with sea-view ones being right over the ocean. ❷

**Zaid's Place** ⓣ09/419 5020. This boasts attractive hillside and beachfront chalets with great views, as well as a leafy garden, a restaurant, and a moneychanger. ❹–❺

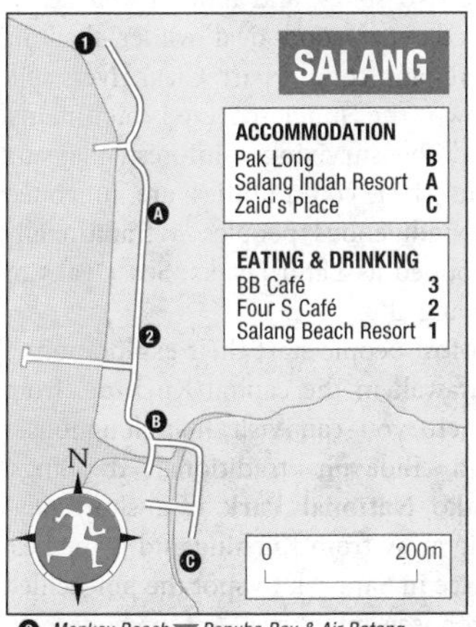


## Juara

**Juara Mutiara** ⓣ09/419 3161. This family-run operation is the biggest in Juara, with a wide variety of room types and prices, including clean dorms at RM15 per person. Staff are friendly and rooms are set in a leafy garden space. These are also the people to see if you want to arrange a boat trip. ❶–❸

**Mizanie Chalet** ⓣ09/547 8445. This is located at the even quieter southern bay, reached by following the path round past the school and permanent fixture football games. ❸

**Paradise Point** ⓣ09/419 3145. Located at the northern end of the beach, this offers clean but basic chalets with shower, many of which open out onto the beach (which here has, unfortunately, been somewhat ruined by the enormous concrete jetty). ❹

**Rainbow** ⓣ09/419 3140. This boasts huge, characterful, painted A-frames right on the beach, though the squat toilets may not necessarily appeal. Good value for money. ❹

**Shack Beach Chalets** A brand-new outfit on the southern bay, offering clean and comfortable rooms in a secluded location. ❸

## Nipah

**Nipah Resort** ⓣ09/799 4287. The only place to stay, offering simple chalets and more expensive A-frames, as well as a nicely designed restaurant. The food can get a little monotonous but it's a small price to play for almost complete seclusion. ❸–❺

# Eating and nightlife

While most places to stay have a restaurant, some of the best, including places to enjoy a drink, are listed below.

## Tekek

**Liza** At the far southern end of the bay, this offers a wide-ranging menu specializing in Chinese food at RM20 a meal.

### Air Batang

**Happy Bar** At *Nazri's*. About the only "buzzing" place on Air Batang, this is a relaxed open-air shack with good music where travellers congregate. English football, which is massively popular in Malaysia, is often shown on the TV here.

**Lime Tree Café** At *Mokhtar's*. This café boasts a raised platform area where you can lounge about on cushions while enjoying drinks and gazing out at sea, and seats around a bar area right on the beach. During happy hour (4.30–7pm) beers are three for RM10. Open until people get bored and leave.

**Mawar Beach Chalets** The food here is probably the best in Air Batang, and the tables on the sand ensure a soothing Eden ambience.

### Salang

**BB Café** A tiny driftwood shack precariously situated amongst the rocks, playing good music and offering a lively atmosphere.

**Four S Café** A fun, laid-back place to come for a long evening of beers or cocktails at reasonable prices (RM5 Tiger beer).

**Salang Beach Resort** The seaview restaurant here serves exceptional Malay cuisine and seafood at around RM10 per dish.

**Salang Indah** This buzzy bar is popular and open until late.

### Juara

While there's less choice for eating here, portions tend to be larger and the menus more imaginative than on the west coast.

**Ali Putra**, **Beach Café** and **Seaview Corner** A row of beachfront cafés by the jetty, all serving a large range of local and Western dishes.

**Bushman's** This cosy, atmospheric shack next to Sunrise Divers is the perfect place to enjoy a sunset drink, or the sound of the sea with an evening meal. It also offers a book exchange.

**Paradise Point** As well as boasting a nice spacious spot on the beach, this offers good *rotis* and unusual dishes such as fish with peanut sauce and fried rice with coconut.

**Santai Bistro** Right on the waterfront next to Juara Mutiara, this outlet boasts comfort Western food and comfy sofas to gossip on, as well as occasional live band performances.

## Directory

**Banks and exchange** Traveller's cheques can be cashed at the *Berjaya Tioman Resort* and there's a moneychangers in the Terminal Complex (though rates are lousy). *Bank Simpanan Nasional* is located opposite the airport. It has an ATM but its opening times (supposedly 6am–midnight) are unreliable.

**Clinic** Poliklinik Komuniti Tekek ⓣ09/419 1800. Situated in a small gated compound a hundred metres south of the jetty in Tekek.

**Internet** Tends to be expensive and slow (RM10/hr) but is available at a few guesthouses and resorts. Try *YP Guesthouse* or *Mokhtar's Place* at Air Batang, *Pak Long* at Salang, or *Featherlight Café* or the bank opposite the airport, at Tekek.

**Police Station** Ten minutes' walk south of the main jetty, Tekek.

**Telephones** There are plenty of public phones around Tekek and ABC beach, but only a select few actually work. *Bamboo Chalets* at Air Batang offer international calls at the same rate as a phonecard, and collect calls and ring back for RM5. Otherwise, try *Featherlight Café* in the terminal complex.

# Sarawak

Separated from Peninsular Malaysia by the South China Sea, the two East Malaysian states of Sarawak and Sabah lie on of the northern side of the island of Borneo. **SARAWAK** is the larger of the two states, and though well developed, is a good deal wilder than its mainland counterpart. Clear rivers spill down the jungle-covered mountains, and the surviving rainforest, plateaux and river communities are inhabited by indigenous peoples – traditionally grouped as Land Dyaks, Sea Dyaks or Orang Ulu.

Most people start their exploration of Sarawak in the capital **Kuching**, from where you can visit Iban longhouses and Bidayuh traditional dwellings. **Bako National Park** is a short day-trip away from Kuching and is the best place in Sarawak to spot the pot-bellied proboscis monkeys. A four-hour boat ride north of Kuching, **Sibu** marks the start of the popular route along **Batang Rajang**, Sarawak's longest river. Most people stop at **Kapit** and from there visit longhouses on the Katibas and

### SARAWAK'S INDIGENOUS PEOPLES

The indigenous peoples of Sarawak make up around half of the state's population and some still live in massive **longhouses**. A typical longhouse is made from brick or timber and might have as many as a hundred doors – each giving access to the private living quarters of one of the families who live there. Visits to these longhouses are one of the highlights of a trip to Sarawak. However, don't expect these longhouse communities to be living some kind of "primitive" lifestyle: almost all longhouses have electricity and that of course means radios and TVs, though not yet computers. Most of the community wander around clutching mobile phones while wearing jeans and t-shirts – a far cry from the scantily clad warriors that some people expect. But this takes nothing away from the enjoyment of being among these people; their warmth, hospitality and humour remain legendary, despite the passing of many traditions.

Baleh tributaries, before making their way up to **Belaga** to explore more of the interior. North of Belaga, **Niah National Park** boasts a vast cave system and accessible forest hikes. On its way north to the Brunei border, the road goes to Miri, from where can either take a boat via Marudi or fly to the spectacular **Gunung Mulu National Park**, Sarawak's chief natural attraction, which features astonishing limestone pinnacles, some of the world's largest caves and a swathe of pristine rainforest.

## KUCHING

**KUCHING** has a magnetic charm, one that many people fall for and find difficult to leave. Sprawled along a lazy waterfront, the city has a laid-back, mellow atmosphere brought alive by its waterside stalls, trinket markets and busy nightlife. Small enough to navigate by foot yet big enough to justify spending a few days here, Kuching is perfect for ambling around. Its courthouse and Istana (palace) lend it a historical air, while the commercial district in the old town is a warren of crowded lanes. Kuching is also a great base from which to explore the surrounding area: Bako National Park, and Iban and Bidayuh dwellings are all within reach, as is the Santubong Peninsula.

### GETTING TO SARAWAK

Most people fly to the Sarawak capital of **Kuching** with either Air Asia or Malaysia Airlines, from Kuala Lumpur (RM200 one-way), Kota Kinabalu or Sabah (RM239). Batavia Airlines flies from Pontianak in Kalimantan (RM340). There are also direct flights to the northern town of Miri from Kota Kinabalu (RM115). Air Asia has the cheapest flights (ⓦwww.airasia.com). MASWings is a subsidiary of Malaysian Airlines and offers cheap internal flights throughout Sarawak and Sabah (ⓦwww.maswings.com.my).

Daily **boat** services run from Brunei (see p.72) to both Lawas and Limbang in north Sarawak. The main overland route into Sarawak is by **bus** from Kuala Belait in Brunei to Miri, a very straightforward crossing that takes approximately four hours. The other main crossing is via Sipitang in Sabah (see p.595) to Lawas, either by local bus, taxi or the daily Lawas Express from Kota Kinabalu. From Indonesian Kalimantan, the easiest overland route is from Pontianak (see p.370) into southwest Sarawak, crossing via Entikong (Indonesia) to Tebedu (Malaysia) and then heading on to Kuching.

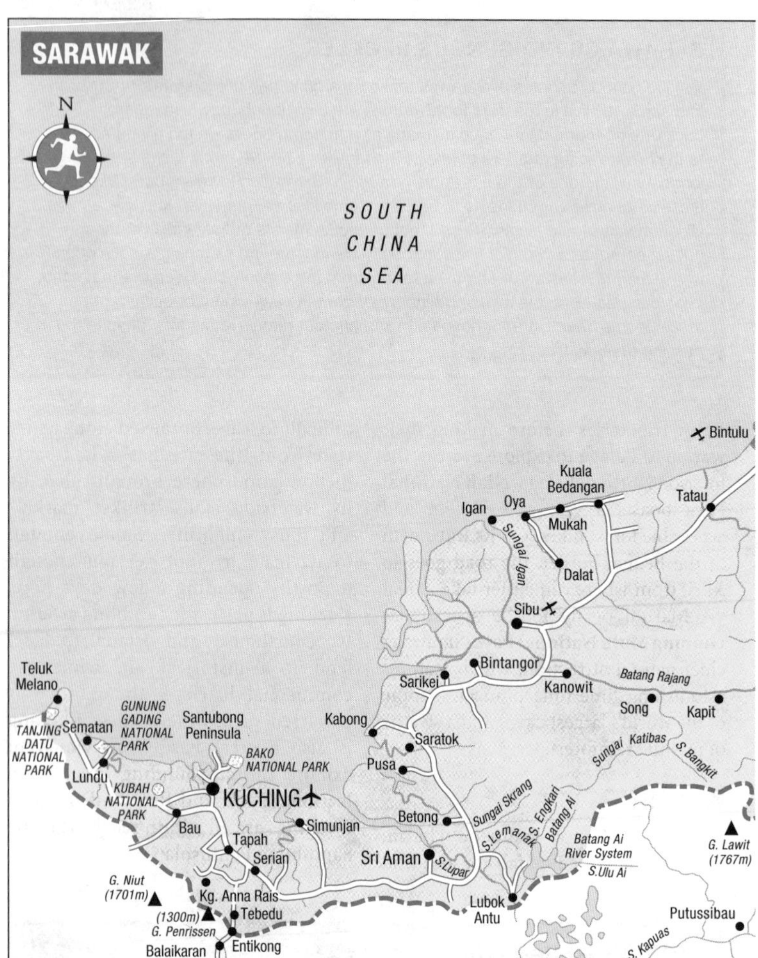


## What to see and do

The city sprawls along the banks of the Sangai Sarawak making the waterfront its main focus. The southern side of the river is flanked by paved walkways, small tidy gardens and numerous food stalls. To the west is the **Main Bazaar**, lined with traditional antique and handicraft shops and still sporting the remains of its original *godowns* (river warehouses). Fruit stalls and the unmistakeable **fish market** are at its far end.

Heading eastwards along the waterfront takes you past the **old courthouse**, with its colonial-Baroque clocktower and Charles Brooke memorial, to the *Holiday Inn* area, which is full of bars, restaurants and plazas. On the waterfront you'll find the jetty to take a boat, known as a *tambang*, over to the other side of the river.

### The Sarawak museums

The **Sarawak Museum** (daily 9am–4:30pm except public holidays; free),

spread across opposite sides of Jalan Tun HaJI Openg, shows you in a nutshell all the things you can expect from a visit to Sarawak. The main building dates from the 1890s and is set in the grounds of the botanical gardens. The ground floor of the museum is a taxidermist's dream, displaying a range of stuffed Sarawak wildlife along with jars of pickled fish. Upstairs, the excellent ethnographic section includes an authentic wooden Iban longhouse, a Penan hut and some traditional tools and weapons. In the same grounds, the **Art Museum** (daily 9am–4:30pm except public holidays; free) houses tribal carvings and local exhibitions.

Crossing over the bridge, you reach the **Islamic Museum** (daily 9am–4:30pm except public holidays; free), which exhibits aspects of Islamic culture, including architecture, weaponry and textiles. The new wing is home to varying exhibitions; check with Sarawak Tourist Board (see p.571) for current listings. On the same side of the road

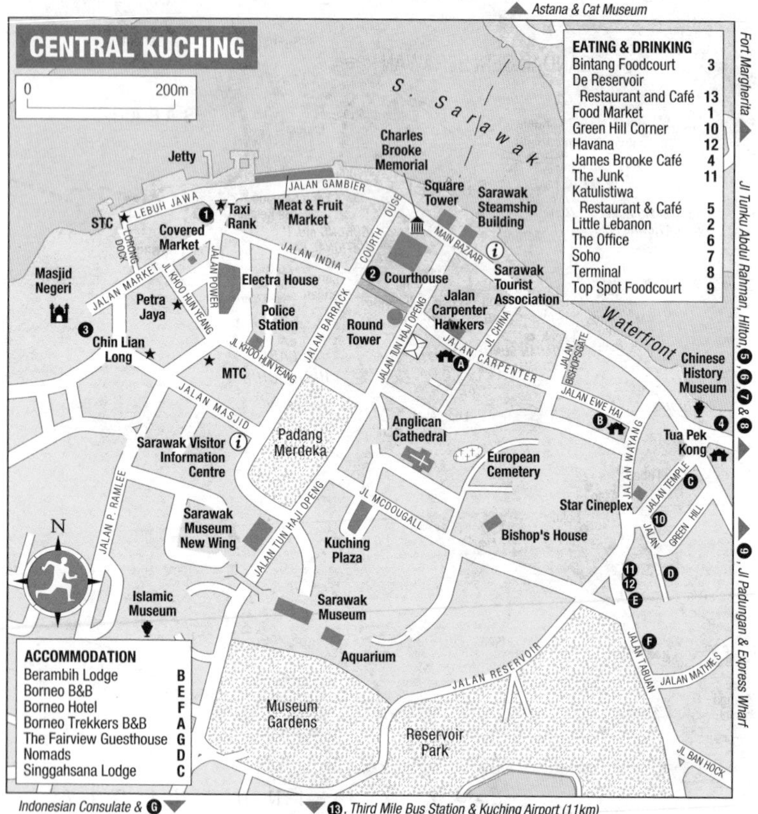


opposite the post office, the new **Textile Museum** shows examples of traditional clothing modelled by startled-looking mannequins. The **Natural History Museum** is under renovation (due to reopen early in 2009).

### Chinatown

The grid of streets running eastwards from Jalan Tun HaJI Openg, past the main Chinese temple Tua Pek Kong, and on to the end of Jalan Padungan constitutes Kuching's **Chinatown**. On busy Main Bazaar and, one block south, on Jalan Carpenter, there are stores and restaurants operating out of renovated two-storey shop-houses, built by Hokkien and Teochew immigrants who arrived in the 1890s.

Overlooking the river on Jalan Temple, **Tua Pek Kong** is the oldest Taoist temple in Sarawak (1876) and attracts a stream of people wanting to pay their respects to Tua Pek Kong, the patron saint of prosperity. You can learn about the history of Sarawak's Chinese community, which dates back to the tenth century, in the **Chinese History Museum** (daily except public holidays 9am–4:30pm; free) across the road.

### North of the river

The north side of the river is lined with some stunning buildings, especially when they're all lit up at night. **Fort Margherita** (daily 9am–4:30pm except public holidays) has good views over the town from the top of the watchpoint. The **Istana** (palace), 1km west of the Fort, is still the official residence of the Governor of Sarawak, and not open to the public. This side of the river is also home to Kuching's **Cat Museum**, which contains a comical collection of feline paraphernalia (take bus #2D, 2C RM1 from outside Kuching Mosque and get off at North City Hall). Even if architecture and cats aren't your thing, it's worth taking a *tambang* (30sen) over to this side of the river to wander around the Malay Kampungs (villages).

## Arrival

**By bus** All express buses from outside the immediate municipality arrive at the Third Mile (Jalan Penrissen) bus station, 5km south of downtown Kuching. To get into town from Third Mile, walk on to the main road, where you'll see a bus shelter to the right. Buses are frequent heading into town, or a taxi will cost you RM15.

**By air** Kuching Airport (Ⓣ082/457373) is 11km south of the city and has a good 24-hour information desk, currency exchange (daily 8am–9pm) and ATMs. A taxi into the centre will cost RM17.50 from the prepaid taxi booth outside the arrivals hall (RM35 after midnight); or the #12a bus takes 30min (daily 7am–3pm; every 20min; RM1.80) and will drop you off at the central STC bus station in the middle of town.

## Information

**Tourist information** The excellent Sarawak Tourism Board (Mon–Fri 8am–6pm, Sat, Sun & public holidays 9am–3pm; Ⓣ082/410944) is in the Old Courthouse on Jl Tun Abang HaJl Openg. The booking desk of the **National Parks and Wildlife Office**, which issues permits for overnight stays at Bako, Gunung Gading and Kubah national parks, is also based here.

**Tours** Kuching tour operators run trips to the longhouses for around RM300 per person per day; reductions are available depending on the size of the group. They can also arrange trips to other parts of the state, including Gunung Mulu National Park. Recommended operators include: Borneo Inbound Tours & Travel, 1st Floor, 40 Main Bazaar (Ⓣ03/87377543); CPH Travel Agencies, 70 Padungan Rd (Ⓣ082/421018); and Borneo Adventures, 55 Main Bazaar (Ⓣ082/245175), which arranges numerous tours throughout the region, as well as mountain-biking trips to the Batang Ai.

## Accommodation

*Singgahsana* and *Nomad* are the best options, the others useful back-ups if they are full.

**Berambih Lodge** 104 Ewe Hai St Ⓣ082/238 589, Ⓦwww.berambih.com A newly decorated place with a large, comfortable communal area. The dorm sleeps just two so can get booked up quickly, and other rooms are quite cramped. Dorms ❷; rooms ❺

**Borneo B&B** 24 Tabuan Rd Ⓣ082/231 200, Ⓔborneobedbreakfast@yahoo.com. Located on the main road just round the corner from Jl Green Hill, this functional hostel provides somewhat cramped dorms and small doubles, some a/c. Internet access available. Dorms ❷; rooms ❷–❺

**Borneo Trekkers B&B** 51 Upper China/Carpenter St, off Main Bazaar Ⓣ082/256 050. In the centre of Chinatown, this hostel has very basic yet affordable rooms, with three-bed dorms. There's a small kitchen and rates include breakfast. The hostel also runs cooking courses. Dorms ❷; rooms ❸

**The Fairview Guesthouse** 6 Jl Taman Budaya Ⓣ082/ 240017 or 013/801 1561, Ⓦwww.thefairview.com.my. Comfy, traditional homestay located near to Reservoir Park – a good diversion from the backpacking scene. Rooms are huge with attached bathrooms. Internet access and laundry available. Dorms ❷; rooms ❹; en-suite a/c double ❻

**Nomad** No 3, 1st Floor, Jl Green Hill Ⓣ082/237831, Ⓦwww.borneobnb.com. A good budget choice with a lively sociable feel. Rooms are clean (although some don't have windows), there's a good communal area and the kitchen can be used to self-cater. The owners' wealth of knowledge is invaluable, and they're happy to impart their pearls of wisdom over a beer or few. Internet access and laundry available. Prices include pancake breakfast. Dorms ❷; rooms ❺

**Singgahsana Lodge** 1 Temple St Ⓣ082/429 277, Ⓦwww.singgahsana.com. This great

**TREAT YOURSELF**

**Borneo Hotel** 30C-F Tabuan Rd Ⓣ082/244 122. Business style hotel with large en-suite rooms, all with TVs. Good if you want to splash out a bit and need a break from staying in backpackers. ❼ place has everything that weary travellers need. Rooms are clean and bright with funky lighting and comfy beds, there's a whole host of services from tour information to phone cards, and a cool rooftop bar with a pool table. Prices include breakfast. Internet access, WiFi, laundry. Dorms ❷; rooms ❺



## Eating

**Bintang Foodcourt** Ji Datuk Ajibah Abol (nr Kuching mosque). Food stalls serving mixture of veg, seafood and chicken dishes. RM3 upwards.
**De Reservoir Restaurant and Café** Reservoir Park. Various stalls serving traditional Malay dishes with a seating area situated on a lovely lakeside location. RM3 upwards. 7–11pm.
**Food market** Jl Market. Located in the western end of town towards the fish market, this covered open-air market is one of the best places in town for both food and atmosphere. Serves fresh seafood and dishes made to order. RM3–RM12.
**Green Hill Corner** Ji Green Hill. Local food stalls in a handy location for hostels in the Jl Temple area. Dishes from RM3, beer buckets RM11.
**James Brooke Café** Located right on the waterfront, this is a fabulous place for people-watching. Serves Asian and some Western dishes at prices between RM9 and RM18.
**The Junk** Jl Wayang, quite pricey, but serves a range of Western dishes and is great if you're having pasta cravings. Portions (from RM20 upwards) are big enough for two. 7–11pm.
**Katulistiwa Restaurant & Café** On the waterfront. This 24-hour café serves fish and chips, steaks etc as well as rice and noodles. Good portion sizes for between RM9 and RM30.
**Little Lebanon** Ji Barrack, behind the tourist office. Downstairs fast food café, and upstairs restaurant with a bigger menu selection. *Little Lebanon* serves fantastic falafel, delicious babaganoush and the chips with garlic sauce will certainly keep mosquitoes away. Dishes cost between RM6 and RM28. Café open lunchtimes; restaurant Tues–Sun 6:30–11pm.
**Top Spot Foodcourt** Jl Bukit Mata. Great for seafood, which is served according to weight; RM6 plus. 5–10pm.

## Drinking and nightlife

**Green Hill Corner** Jl Green Hill. Great for quick and tasty noodles (RM4) along with buckets of Tiger Beer at RM11 each.
**Havana** Tabuan Rd. Relaxed, slightly trendy bar though somewhat quiet. Has beers on draught. Happy hour 5–7pm.
**The Office** 191 Jl Pandugan. Centrally located. Quite quiet but good for the happy hour deals (happy 5–9pm).
**Soho** 64 Jl Padungan. Trendy bar that does Latin/dance-oriented music, popular with locals. Stays open until the early hours.
**Terminal** Jl Chan Chin Ann. New bar located to the eastern side of town. All staff dress like airline crew giving you the impression you're in a terminal. Slightly pricey, but does good gin and tonics.

## Shopping

Kuching is the best place in Sarawak to buy just about anything, although it would be unwise to stock up on tribal textiles and handicrafts before visiting Sibu or Kapit, or the longhouses where you can buy direct.
**Markets** The Sunday Market, southwest of the city on the Jalan Satok/Jalan Palm junction, is the place to go if you want to buy, well, just about anything. Knives, handicrafts, fresh jungle ferns, t-shirts, knickers, live fish and baskets of puppy dogs are all on offer. The market actually begins on Sat and trades through the early hrs until Sun afternoon. It's an easy ten-minute walk from the post office, but if you want to take the bus then #5, #7, #9, #11, #12 from the STC bus station, or #6 or #2b from Petra Jaya station (5min, RM1) will take you there. Jalan India is also a good place to stock up on cheap clothes and buy an umbrella.
**Books** Times Bookstore, 1st floor, Crowne Plaza Riverside; Mohamad Yahiah & Sons, with branches in the *Holiday Inn*; and Bell Books in Sarawak Plaz. The latter also stocks the best maps of the state.
**Handicrafts** For interesting carvings and other handicrafts, try Yeo Hing Chuan, 46 Main Bazaar. Sarakraf in Sarawak Plaza (next to the *Holiday Inn*) is good for baskets, textiles and ironwork; for fine Iban pua kumbu textiles head to Sarawak Batik Art Shop, 1 Jl Temple. The top floor of the Tun Jugah shopping centre, Jin Abell (opposite Sarawak Plaza) has a textile museum and rugs made on the premises.

## Directory

**Airline offices** Air Asia, Wisma Ho Ho Lim, Ground Floor, No. 291 Sub Lot 4, Jin Abell ⓣ082/283222 call centre 03/7651 2222, ⓦwww.airasia.com; Batavia Air, 1 Padungan Arcade, Jl Song Thian Cheok ⓣ082/244299; MAS, Lot 215, Jl Song Thian Cheok ⓣ082/246622/244144, ⓦwww.malaysiaairlines.com; Silk Air, 7th Floor, Gateway Kuching, Jl Bukit Mata ⓣ082/256772, ⓦwww.silkair.com.

**Banks and exchange** HSBC, Jl Padungan ☎082/427 999; Majid & Sons, 45 Jl India ☎082/42 402 – cash only; Maybank, Jl Tunku Abdul Rahman ☎082/24 964; Standard Chartered Bank, Jl Tunku Abdul Rahman ☎082/252 233; Everise Moneychanger, 199 Jl Pandugan (☎082/233 200) offers good rates.
**Bike rental** Borneo Adventures, Main Bazaar ☎082/245 175; Power Action Cycles, 64 Carpenter St ☎082/421 387.
**Embassies and consulates** Australian Honorary Consul, Suite 504, 5th Floor, Wisma Bukit Mata ☎082/233350, Ⓔditing@tm.net.my; British Honorary Consul ☎082/250950; Brunei Consulate, No. 325 Lorong Seladah, Jl Seladah ☎082/456515; Chinese Consulate (PRC), Lot 3719 Dogan Garden, Jl Dogan, off Jl Batu Kawa ☎082/453344; Indonesian Consulate, 111 Jl Tun Abang Hj, Openg ☎082/241734; New Zealand ☎082/482177; South African Honorary Consul ☎082/245587.
**Hospitals** Sarawak General Hospital, Jl Ong Kee Hui (☎082/276666), charges RM50 for A&E consultations; for private treatment, go to Norman Medical Centre, Jl Tun Datuk Patinggi (☎082/440055) or the Timberland Medical Centre, Jl Rock Rd (☎082/234991). You can also try Dr Chan's Clinic, at 98 Main Bazaar (☎082/240307).
**Immigration** 1st Floor, Bangunan Sultan Iskander, Jl Simpang Tiga (Mon–Fri 8am–noon & 2–4.30pm, closed every second Fri; ☎082/245661) for visa extensions; take CLL bus #6, #11 or #14 from outside Kuching Mosque. Get there by noon if you want service the same day.
**Internet** Cyber Corner, Jl Temple; Cyber City, Sarawak Plaza. All hostels offer internet access.
**Pharmacies** There are a lot of pharmacies around the Electra House shopping centre on Jl Power. Apex Phamacy, No 15, Ground Floor, Electra House (☎082/246011), inside the centre, is the most reputable. Watsons Pharmacy, on the lower ground floor inside the Crowne Plaza shopping centre.
**Police** There is a police station on Jl Khoo Hun Yeang (☎082/241222).
**Post office** The GPO on Jl Tun Haji Openg (Mon–Sat 8am–4:30pm, closed Sun, first Sat of every month and public holidays) keeps poste restante.

## Moving on

**By local bus** There are four local bus companies: the Sarawak Transport Company's (STC; ☎082/242966) green-and-yellow buses run from the western end of Lebuh Jawa to the airport, the Indonesian consulate, the immigration office and the express wharf. Chin Liang Long's (CLL) blue-and-white buses run from Jl Masjid towards the airport and express wharf. Petra Jaya Transport's black-and-yellow buses run north from below the open-air market on Lebuh Market to Bako National Park. Matang Transport Company's orange-and-yellow buses (for Matang and Kubah) depart from the north end of Jl P Ramlee. For Damai beach on the Santubong peninsula and the Sarawak Cultural Village, the only service is the shuttle from the *Holiday Inn*, at Jl Tunku Abdul Rahmen (4 daily from 9am; 45min, RM10 one way; ☎082/423111).
**Destinations:** Bako (#6 Petra Jaya; 12 daily; 1hr); Express Boat Wharf (#1A, #17, #19 CLL, every 30min; 30 min); Lundu for Gunung Gading National Park (#EP7 STC, 4 daily; 2hr); Semengoh Wildlife Rehab Centre (#6 STC, 4 daily; 30min); Sunday Market (#5, #7, #9, #11, #12, #6, #2 STC & Petra Jaya, every hour).
**By long-distance bus** All long-distance express buses to destinations in Sarawak and Pontianak in Indonesia leave from Third Mile bus station. You can easily buy tickets when you get to the station, or in advance from Biaramas Express booking office (☎082/429418) on Jl Khoo Hun Yeang (near Electra House). Biaramas also has an office at the terminal (☎082/456999, open 6 am–10pm). Other long-distance bus companies include Vital Focus Transportation (☎082/453190 or 461277), which operates the PB Express, Suria Bus Express, Borneo Highway Express (tickets also available at Borneo Interland, 63 Main Bazaar, ☎082/413595), Kirata & Sapphire Pacific Express and Sri Merah Express bus services; Syarikat Bus Baram (☎082/576700); MTC Express (☎082/463161); Sungei Merah (☎082/571888); Borneo Express Bus (☎082/452717); Lanang Express (☎082/462887); Eva Express (☎082/576761); TransBorneo Resources (☎082/452271) and ATS (☎082/457773). All these companies operate services to a number of destinations throughout Sarawak. Buses to the Third Mile bus station from the STC bus station go every few minutes (from Leboh Jawa at the western end of the fish market; #3A, #6, #8D, #10A, #12A; RM1;).
**Destinations:** Bintulu (several daily; 11hr); Miri (several daily; 15 hr); Mukah (2 daily; 11hr 30min); Pontianak, Indonesia (10 daily; 8–10hr); Sibu (several daily; 7hr); Sri Aman (several daily; 3hr).
**By boat** The wharf is 5km east of the city centre in the suburb of Pending. Ferries go to Sibu (1 daily; 8:30am; 4hr; RM40). Tickets are sold at the wharf in Pending. It's advisable to get to the jetty 30min before departure. Take CCL Bus #17 or #19 (60 sen). Or a taxi is RM10.
**By air** To get to the airport, take a taxi (RM17.50) or the #12a bus from the STC station on Lebuh Jawa (6am–2:20pm).

**Destinations:** Bandar Seri Begawan, Brunei (5 weekly; 1hr 15min); Johor Bahru (4 daily; 1hr 25min); Kota Kinabalu (5 daily; 2hr 15min); Kuala Lumpur (several daily; 1hr 40min); Miri (5 daily; 1hr); Penang (1 daily; 2hr); Pontianak, Indonesia (4 weekly; 1hr); Sibu (8 daily; 40min); Singapore (6 daily; 1hr 25min).



## THE SARAWAK CULTURAL VILLAGE

The **Sarawak Cultural Village** (9am–12.30pm & 2–5.15pm; RM60; ⓣ082/422411) is picturesquely located on the Santubong Peninsula 35km north of Kuching, and provides a worthwhile day-trip from the city. To get here, take the shuttle from the *Holiday Inn*, at Jalan Tunku Abdul Rahman (4 daily from 9am; 45min; RM10 one way). It's very much a show for tourists, but nevertheless the Penan shelter and Iban, Melanau and Bidayuh longhouses are exact replicas of what you'd be lucky to find two weeks upriver in this day and age. Here you'll get a close-up of the fading traditions – dancing, top-spinning, weaving and carving. There's a traditional dance at 11.30am and 4pm and five minutes' walk away is a **beach** where you can swim. The SCV also hosts the annual **Sarawak Rainforest World Music Festival**, held during three days in July and featuring acts from around the globe. Information can be found at ⓦwww.rainforestmusic-borneo.com.

## SEMENGOH NATURE RESERVE

**Semengoh Nature Reserve** (daily 8am–noon & 2–4.15pm, feeding time 3–3.30pm; RM3) is home to semi-wild **orang-utans** who have been orphaned or rescued from captivity. Here they are trained in the vital skills to survive in the wild and fend for themselves. Although the main programme has been transferred to Matang Wildlife Centre, Semengoh still has some younger orang-utans who you can see swinging through the trees. They generally spend most of their time roaming the surrounding forest but do come to the main platform for feeding time, which is the best time to see them.

To get here catch bus #6, #6A, #6B or #6C (45min; RM2 one way) from outside the post office. This will drop you at the entrance to the park; it's then a 1.3km clearly signed walk along a tarmac pathway to the feeding area. Minivans will take you back to town for RM3.

## BAKO NATIONAL PARK

**BAKO NATIONAL PARK** was established in 1957 and is the best place to see wildlife in the state. The rare proboscis monkey, which is found only in Borneo, is resident here and most visitors are guaranteed a sight of its unmistakable hooter. You'll definitely catch sight of cheeky macaque monkeys who hang around here, and it's not uncommon to see vipers, giant monitor lizards and silver leaf monkeys. Bako can easily be visited as a day-trip from Kuching. **To get to the park**, take Petra Jaya bus #6 (hourly 6.40am–4.40pm; 45min; RM2) from Jalan Khoo Hun Yeang in Kuching to the jetty at Kampung Bako. From here, take a motorized boat to the park headquarters (RM30 per boat for up to seven people; 30min). Once at the park headquarters you need to pay the park fee (RM3, plus RM5 camera and RM10 video camera), sign in and collect the informative map of the park.

The park boasts some nineteen miles of **trails**, which all start from park headquarters and are colour-coded with paint splashes every twenty metres. The trails vary in difficulty and length of time. The easiest and shortest walk (and the best to see probiscis monkeys) is the Telok Paku trail. There's a hike to **Tajor Waterfall** (3.5km; about 2hr), which involves climbing the forested cliff through *kerangas,* with plentiful pitcher plants and peat bogs. Leaving the main trail at the wooden hut there's a path that descends to two beautiful beaches,

### LONGHOUSE VISITS

The interior of Sarawak is home to many tribal groups who still live in their longhouse communities, and a visit to a longhouse is a definite highlight. There are many tour operators in Kuching who arrange either day or overnight trips but it's best to shop around – some can be quite touristy, while others will let you absorb the atmosphere and enjoy the hosts' hospitality. A good trip should include an overnight stay with some jungle trekking, and usually involves being offered copious amounts of *tuak* (rice wine). When you're offered *tuak*, it's polite to have at least some, but if you don't want any then just touching the glass will suffice. Also, remember that *tuak* can be pretty lethal and will put paid to many a hardened drinker. Respect the community and accept their hospitality, but don't abuse it.

You may be disappointed if you're expecting the communities to still follow a traditional lifestyle, as many now have jobs in Kuching or live abroad, and TVs and music systems are often in evidence. However, the gregarious Iban and Bidayuh will make a trip at any time of year an enjoyable one, and you may even be offered some local delicacies to try – just watch out for that boiled monkey. Taking presents for the community is the norm – things that they can use such as books and pencils are best rather than anything involving plastic which will just litter the jungle. It's best to find out how many families live in the longhouse, as gifts will get divided equally. Also, when walking through the communal areas, be careful not to walk across any of the mats that are laid out on the floor, as this would similar to walking across someone's couch.

The following **tour companies** are recommended for a longhouse visit: Borneo Adventures, 55 Main Bazaar ⓣ082/245175; Borneo Inbound Tours & Travel, 1st Floor, 40 Main Bazaar ⓣ03/87377543; CPH Travel Agencies, 70 Padungan Rd ⓣ082/421018. If you wish to visit the longhouses independently, the Sarawak Tourism Board in Kuching has a list of longhouses that accommodate travellers and will give you all the details of where to go, how to get there, and the chief's phone number so that you can arrange your visit directly.

**Telok Pandan Kecil** and **Telok Pandan Besar** (30min).

There is **accommodation** at the park for those who wish to stay overnight – though be sure to get a **permit** and reserve your accommodation at the visitor centre in Kuching before you go (see p.571). At park headquarters, you can camp (RM4) or stay at the hostel (RM10.50) or one of the lodges (❹–❺), all of which provide bed linen and cooking facilities. Some hikers prefer to camp on the trails and others have been known to sling a hammock up on the beach somewhere. There's a simple café at headquarters and a provisions shop.

## SIBU

**SIBU**, 60km from the coast up Batang Rajang, is Sarawak's second-largest city and the state's biggest port. Most of the local population is Foochow Chinese (the town is known locally as New Foochow), and its remarkable modern growth is largely attributed to these enterprising immigrants. Sibu is the starting point for trips up the Batang Rajang to Belaga and beyond.

### What to see and do

Other than simply soaking up the atmosphere of the town, there's not much to do here. The town's most striking landmark is the towering, seven-storey **pagoda** at the back of Tua Pek Kong Temple beyond the western, waterfront end of Jalan Khoo Peng Loong. The roof and columns are decorated with traditional dragon and holy bird statues, and murals depict

## INTO INDONESIA

You can travel across the border into Indonesian Kalimantan directly from Kuching. A ten-hour bus ride will take you as far as **Pontianak** (several buses leave either early in the morning or late at night). You must make sure you have your visa before heading over the border; travellers have been known to be turned away, and it's a long way back. The Indonesian consulate in Kuching (6th Floor, HSBC building, 111 Jl Tun Abang Hj; ⓣ082/41734) now issues **thirty-day visas** (RM170). They take about two days to issue and you'll need to take a copy of your passport, evidence of onward flights, sufficient funds and two passport photos.



the signs of the Chinese zodiac. Across the way, in the network of streets between Jalan Market, Jalan Channel and Jalan Central, is **Chinatown**, with its plethora of hardware shops, newspaper stalls, rowdy cafés, food vendors and hotels. The central artery, **Jalan Market**, runs from Jalan Pulau beside the temple, and forms the hub of possibly the most vibrant *pasar malam* (night market) in Sarawak. Beside Jalan Channel, the daily **Lembangan Market** opens before dawn and closes around 5pm; there are hundreds of stalls here, selling anything from edible delicacies such as flying fox, snake and jungle ferns to rattan baskets, beadwork and charm bracelets.

## Arrival and information

**By bus** The bus and taxi station is on Jl Khoo Peng Loong, 200m west of town and close to many budget hotels.

**By boat** Boats dock at the upriver boat wharf, 100m northwest of the bus terminal.

**By air** The airport (ⓣ084/307770) is 25km east of the city centre. Taxis cost RM28 (via pre-paid coupon at the taxi counter in the airport) into the centre. To catch the bus, walk out of the airport, follow the road to the main junction and wait for #3a (every 45min, daily 6am–8pm; RM2.50).

**Information** The helpful Sarawak Tourism Board (Mon–Fri 8am–5pm, Sat 8am–12.50pm, closed first and third Sat of the month; ⓣ084/340980) at Jl Tukang Besi has plenty of information on how to get upriver and to access the Rajang longhouses.

**Tours** Mr Ling How Kang is recommended for tours to nearby longhouses and also up the Rajang to Belaga and beyond (RM80 per day including food and transport; ⓣ084/211243, ⓔsibutour@gmail.com). Metropolitan Travel Services also offers reasonably priced tours to go further upriver (ⓣ084/322251).

## Accommodation

There are plenty of hotels dotted around Sibu, with no shortage of budget places. Listed below are the best budget options; be warned that others can (and do) double up as brothels.

**Plaza Inn** 16–18 Jl Morshidi Sidek (Jl Sanyan) ⓣ084/341218. Situated across the road from Wisma Sanyan, this place has large, clean rooms and is well maintained. Reception is helpful, and there are great food outlets right downstairs. ❹

**River Park Hotel** 51–53 Jl Maju ⓣ084/316688. Close to the bus station over in the west of town, *River Park* offers clean, spacious a/c rooms. Some rooms have TVs, but most of the plugs don't fit the power points. ❺

**Sentosa Inn** 12 Jl Pulau ⓣ084/349875. A bargain basement option which offers bargain basement quality and service. Good location but doesn't score many points for much else. ❸

**Victoria Inn** 80 Jl Market ⓣ084/320099. A good central location right opposite the market. Rooms are clean and spacious, and it's a good idea to book ahead. ❹–❻

**Villa Hotel** 2–4 Jl Central ⓣ084/337833. Good cheapy with sizeable rooms, handily located right in the centre, has a faint whiff of stale smoke but if you can put up with that it's worth the stay. ❸

## Eating and drinking

Hawker stalls at the Lembangan Market are the busiest place in the morning; in the evening, everyone congregates at the *pasar malam* in the town centre, though you can't sit down and eat here.

**Durian market** Jl Chew Geon Lew. If durians are your thing then this place is for you. Follow your nose and head towards the Chinese temple to stock up on these whiffy fruits.

**Emas Corner** Jl Morshidi Sidek. Located underneath the *Plaza Inn*, a good popular local spot with the usual *nasi goreng* dishes and local speciality of foochow noodles. From RM3 upwards.
**Hai Bing Coffee Shop and Restaurant** Jl Maju. An outdoor coffee shop and an indoor restaurant; this two-in-one place will satisfy you whatever mood you're in. Great for eating streetside with the locals or in a/c coolness. Dishes from RM5.
**Night market** Night-time stalls selling delicious freshly made local dishes and a variety of wonderful unidentifiable fried things. RM2 upwards.
**Passar Semtral Sibu** Covered market with Chinese snacks on sale during the day as well as fresh local produce.

## Directory

**Airlines** Air Asia, 1st floor, Sibu Airport Terminal building ☎084/307808; MAS is at 61 Jl Tunku Osman ☎084/326166.
**Banks and exchange** There are plenty of banks dotted around town: Standard Chartered, at Jl Tukang Besi (opposite tourist information); Maybank, at Jl Kampung Nyabor; Public Bank, at Jl Central; Yewon Money Changer, at 8 Jl Tukang Besi.
**Hospital** The nearest hospital is 8km away on Jl Ulu Oya (☎084/276666). There's also the Rejang Medical Centre at Jl Pedada (☎084/330733).
**Internet** Ibrowse Netcafe, 4th floor, Wisam Sayan tower; Cyber café, 1st Floor, Foo Chow Lane, behind the *Premier Hotel*.
**Laundry** Mr Dobi, 5 Jl Bindang.
**Pharmacy** Watsons Pharmacy, ground floor, Wisma Sayan Plaza.
**Police** Jl Kampung Nyabor (☎084/322222).
**Post office** The GPO is on Jl Kampung Nyabar (Mon–Sat 8am–4.30pm).

## Moving on

**By bus** All express services are via the Sibu New Bus Terminal, Jl Pahlawan. To get there, take the #2, #7 or #9 bus from the city bus station. You can book tickets through bus company offices in Sibu.
**Destinations:** Bintulu (several daily; 3hr 30min); Kanowit (12 daily; 1hr 30min); Kuching (several daily; 8hr); Miri (5 daily; 7hr 30min); Mukah (daily; 3hr 30min); Sarikei (several daily; 1hr 30min).
**By boat** The express boats to Kapit depart more or less hourly from 5.30am until 2.30pm from the upriver boat wharf, 100m northwest of the bus terminal. Some boats go direct, others make various stops along the way. From the downriver wharf 100m further northwest, just beside the Chinese temple, Express Bahagia, at 20a Jl Tukang Besi (☎084/319228), runs a daily service to Kuching at 11.30am; Sejahtera Petrama Express, at 2d Jl Kampung Dato (☎084/318885), runs a similar service at 7:30am.
**Destinations:** Kapit (15 daily; 3-4hr); Belaga (1 daily; 6hr); Kuching (1 daily; 5hr); Song (6 daily; 2hr).
**By air** MASWings and Air Asia both have regular flights to and from Sibu.
**Destinations** Bintulu (2 daily; 35min); Johor Bahru (1 daily; 1hr 30min) Kota Kinabalu (2 daily; 1hr 35min); Kuala Lumpur (1 daily; 2hr); Kuching (3 daily; 40min); Miri (3 daily; 5min).

## SONG AND SUNGAI KATIBAS

Two hours upstream from Sibu is **SONG**, at the head of one of the Rajang's major tributaries, Sungai Katibas, which winds and narrows as it runs south towards the mountainous border region with Kalimantan. There's not much to do in Song, as it's little more than a few blocks of waterfront shop-houses, cafés, a small Chinese temple and a few token hotels, but it's a good place to start if you want to venture further up river. On the Katibas are several **Iban longhouses** worth visiting, including the large community at **Nanga Bangkit** and Sungai Bangkit. Sadly, there are plans to replace many

### TRAVELLING UP THE BATANG RAJANG

The 560-kilometre-long **Batang Rajang** lies at the very heart of Sarawak. This is the world of isolated colonial forts, logging wharves and boat trips to busy longhouses. The communities here are used to tourists, but not to the extent of those in the Kuching area. Express boats from Sibu (hourly 5.30am–2.30pm; RM20 economy class) take three hours to reach **Kapit**, stopping first at **Kanowit** and then at the little town of **Song**. Kapit, with its experienced tour operators, is the most popular springboard for the longhouses as well as for trips much further inland.

of these traditional longhouses with concrete ones, so some may not be open to visitors. It's best to check with the Song District Office (Ⓣ084/777221) for the latest on the renovation status and which ones are open to travellers.

### Arrival and information

**By boat** All boats arrive at the small jetty just to the right of Song's main road.

### Accommodation

**Capital Hotel** 8 Song Bazaar Ⓣ084/777264. Offers decent-size rooms and is next door to the *Katibas Inn*. The hotel can also help to arrange local guides. ❸
**Katibas Inn** 7 Song Bazaar Ⓣ084/777323. This smart hotel has basic rooms but is the best in town and is right on the riverfront. ❸
**Mesra Inn** 31 Song Shoplot Ⓣ084/777777. Another good, cheap option whose clean rooms have attached bathroom. ❸

### Eating

**Capital Inn** Has a good café if you need a fill of *mie goreng*. It's popular with locals and serves very simple dishes from RM3. There are a couple of similar cafés serving Malaysian dishes dotted along the main bazaar.

### Directory

**Banks** There are no banks in Song, so be sure to get enough cash in either Kapit or Sibu.
**Hospital** Song Health Clinic (Ⓣ084/777634).
**Police** Ⓣ084/777222.

### Moving on

**By boat** To explore Sungai Katibas, you need to catch the passenger longboat that leaves Song each morning (from RM1); departure times change so ask at the canteen on the jetty. Private charters are a whopping RM300 or so. From Nanga Bangkit, the boat back to Song leaves at around 6am though – as ever – you could charter your own.

## KAPIT

**KAPIT**, around three hours east of Sibu by express boat, is a fast-growing timber town with a frontier atmosphere, where karaoke lounges and snooker halls are very much in evidence. There are lots of good cafés and an excellent night market. It's also the main place to organize trips to local Iban communities with one of the tour operators based in town.

### What to see and do

Close to the jetty is Kapit's main landmark, **Fort Sylvia**. It was built in 1880 in an attempt to prevent the warring Iban attacking smaller groups such as the upriver Ukit and Bukitan. Kapit's main square, simply called **Kapit Square**, is surrounded by shops selling everything from noodles to rope. The walk west along Jalan Temenggong, which forms the square's northern edge, leads to the day market. Back from the jetty, near the pond, the **Civic Museum** (Mon–Sat 8am–1pm & 2–4pm, closed Fri 11.45am–2.15pm; free) has a collection of interesting exhibits on the tribes in the Rajang basin, including a well-constructed longhouse and a mural painted by local Iban.

### Arrival and information

**By boat** Express boats from Sibu and Belaga dock at the jetty, which is a couple of minutes' walk away from the town centre.
**Tours** There are two main tour operators in town, both offering a wide range of trips, including day-visits to a local longhouse, overnight trips upriver and week-long trips to the remote Penan Highlands on the Kalimantan border. The Iban-run *New Rejang Inn* (Ⓣ084/796600 Ⓔjoana_37@hotmail.com) and Mr Tan Teck Chuan, Kapit Adventure Tours, 11 Jl Tan Sit Leong (Ⓣ084/796352) can both arrange these trips. Expect to pay in the region of RM400 per person per night for overnight tours.

### Accommodation

Accommodation in Kapit is somewhat lacklustre, though there are some good deals to be found.
**Ark Hill Inn** Jl Penghulu Gerinang Ⓣ084/796168. Located near to the square, *Ark Hill* has clean en-suite rooms and also offers free Wi-Fi. ❸–❺
**Kapit River View Inn** 1st Floor, 10 Jl Tan Sit Leong Ⓣ084/796310. Another good option with en-suite

rooms located a couple of minutes away from the wharf. ❹

**New Rajang Inn** 104 Jl Teo Chow Beng ☎084/796600. This is a real bargain with en-suite a/c rooms with TV and fridge. ❹

## Eating

At the covered market on Jl Airport there are a dozen stalls serving Chinese, Malay and Dyak dishes. The day market on Jalan Teo Chow Beng also has a number of hawker stalls.

**Friendship Café** A cheap place serving typical Malay dishes and Tiger beer by the bucket. Food from RM4.

**Islamic Café** Jl Airport. Halal café which serves a selection of traditional Malay dishes. Owners are more than willing to cater for special diets including vegetarians. Dishes from RM4.

**Night market** Between Jl Teo Chow Beng and Jl Penghulu Berjaya. Offers a variety of Chinese, Malay and Dyak dishes. Deliciously fresh and tasty dishes for bargain prices from RM2 upwards.

## Directory

**Bank** There is a Maybank with ATM on Jl Teo Chow Beng that can also cash traveller's cheques.

**Hospital** Kapit Health Clinic ☎084/799661.

**Internet** Cyber Café, 17 Jl Tan Sit. RM3/hr.

**Police** ☎084/796222.

**Post office** Near the Maybank on Jl Teo Chow Beng (Mon–Sat 8am–4.30pm).

## Moving on

**By boat** You need a **permit** (free of charge) to travel beyond Kapit up the Batang Rajang to Belaga and beyond. Permits are available from the Resident's Office, 9th Floor, Jalan Bleteh (Mon–Fri 8am–1pm & 2–5pm, closed weekends & Fridays between 11.45am and 2.15pm); to get there take a minivan from outside the Tenesang Market on the corner of Jalan Penghulu. Take your passport with you.

**Destinations:** Belaga (1 daily at 9am; 6hr); Nanga Baleh (4 daily; 2hr); Sibu (several daily; 3hr); Song (10 daily; 2 hr); Sungai Gaat (2 daily; 2hr 30min).

# BELAGA

Further up the Batang Rajang, **BELAGA** is a small remote town perfectly placed for exploring the interior in more depth. Not many tourists make it this far, so it's a great place to go to if you want to experience a more authentic longhouse without feeling as though it's all part of a show. Independent travel to the longhouses depends on a certain amount of luck and basically chatting to someone who will invite you over – try asking around at one of the cafés, where you're sure to find someone who can help. There are various treks that take you further into the jungle, past the Bakun Dam area and into the villages beyond. Mr Daniel of *Daniel's Corner* (☎086/461997 or 013/848 6351, ⓔudiontheroad@yahoo.com) is a local who helps coordinate tours, though as it's the only choice for organizing tours from Belaga make sure you get what you pay for.

## Accommodation and eating

Belaga consists of just two roads and there's only a handful of places to stay.

### BEYOND KAPIT ON THE SUNGAI BALEH

**Sungai Baleh** branches off from the Rajang 10km east of Kapit. Several boats leave Kapit for Sungai Baleh between 7am and noon. Some ply only the 20km to **NANGA BALEH** (1hr 30min; RM8), a large, modern longhouse, where there is also a logging camp; others push on to the junction with the tributaries of Sungai Gaat and Sungai Merirai (2hr 30min; RM10); while others follow the shorter stretch to the Sungai Mujong junction (1hr; RM6) – a large tributary closer to Kapit. The express boat ends its route at **PUTAI**, four hours from Kapit, where there's another logging camp. There are Iban longhouses on the **Gaat and Merirai tributaries**, which can only be reached by renting a longboat (around RM80 one way). The longhouse wharves at the junctions of the Baleh and these smaller rivers are the places to ask for advice on how to travel further, and to find out which longhouses are good to visit.

**Belaga Hotel** Next door to the internet café and right on the main drag, this is a good cheap option. There are also some good cafés below the hotel offering a selection of traditional Malay dishes. ❷
**Hock Chiang Inn** Jl Teo Tua Kheng ☎086/46168. Located right near the jetty, this is a perfectly placed budget option. ❷

## Directory

**Bank** There are no banks in Belaga so be sure to bring enough money to pay for tours and accommodation.
**Internet** Worldwide Exploration Travel & Tours, Jalan Penghulu Hang Nyiipa (Mon–Fri 8am–5pm, Sat 8am–1pm, closed Sun). RM3 per hour.
**Police** ☎086/461318.

## Moving on

**By boat** Express boats from Belaga to Kapit leave from the main jetty at 6am (RM30).
**By road** For those who want to travel on to Bintulu, it's possible to travel overland by 4WD using the local logging routes. The journey can be somewhat hazardous and a bit hair-raising in places, but it's a good way to see more of the interior. Ask at the cafés to find a local driver. It should cost around RM50.

# BINTULU

**BINTULU**, close to Niah National Park, is a boom-town grown rich on offshore gas. The only sights worth visiting are the **markets**: the day market, housed in two large, open-sided circular buildings overlooking the river at the west end of Main Bazaar; the adjacent *pasar tamu;* and across town, the *pasar malam*, which starts at around 6pm in the long-distance bus station.

## Arrival and information

**By bus** The long-distance bus station is 5km out of town at Medan Jaya. A taxi to the centre from here will cost RM10, or you can take any bus from the road behind the ticket booths to the local bus station on Lebuh Ray Abang Galau (60 sen), which becomes Jalan Sri Dagang as it enters town.
**By boat** The jetty is in the centre of town, behind the *pasar utama*.
**By air** The airport (☎086/331073) is 14km out of town and a twenty-minute cab ride away (RM17). There is no public transport to get to or from the airport.
**Tours** Borneo Travel of Bintulu, at 171 Jl Main Bazaar (☎086/315207) can help book tours around Sarawak as well as flights. Similajau Adventure Tours, at Lot 4539 No.5 Medan Jaya Cemmercial Centre (☎086/331552) also arranges tours around Borneo, and as the name suggests can help with trips to Similajau National Park.

## Accommodation

Decent budget accommodation is hard to find in Bintulu. The best options are listed below.
**Faber Inn** Taman Sri Dagang ☎086/313667. Double rooms with TV and kettle. ❹
**Kemena Inn** 78 Jl Keppel ☎086/331533. Good-sized rooms and located close to the night market. ❹
**Kintown Inn** 93 Jl Keppel ☎086/333666 Slightly more upmarket but a better option if you can stretch that extra bit. Has comfy beds, cable TV and power showers. ❺
**Welcome Inn** 1st floor, 186 Taman Sri Damang ☎086/315266. Good, clean budget option located right outside the taxi rank. ❸

## Eating

**Ama Restoran** Jl Keppel. Has an Indian influence and serves excellent curries. *Roti canai* from RM2.
**Hawker stalls** There are hawker stalls at both the day market and the *pasar malam*, though the *pasar malam* is take-away only from RM3.
**Night market** Located behind Jl Abang Galau. The night market is a great place (as always) for fresh, delicious food and the best way to mix with the locals. *Mie goreng* from RM3.
**Popular Corner** Lebuh Raya Abang Galau. Has several outlets under one roof, selling seafood fresh from the tank, claypots, chicken rice and juices. Dishes from RM2.
**Sea View Restoran** 254 Esplanade. An atmospheric Chinese café, overlooking Sungai Kemena and serving quality food. From RM10.

## Directory

**Airline** MAS is at 129 Jl Masjid (☎086/331554).
**Banks** There are two banks on Jl Keppel: an HSBC at the western end and a Standard Chartered just over the road.
**Hospital** Jl Abang Galau (☎086/255899).
**Internet** There are plenty of facilities on Jl Keppel.
**Police** Jl Sommerville (☎086/331129).
**Post office** Jl Tun Razak (Mon–Sat 8am–4.30pm).

## Moving on

**By bus** The long-distance bus station serves Batu Niah, Kuching, Sibu and Miri. Borneo Highway Express (☎086/339855) runs a daily service to Pontianak (7pm; 18hr).
**Destinations:** Kuching (9 daily; 11hr); Miri (every 30min; 3hr); Sibu (8 daily; 4hr).
**By air** to: Kota Kinabalu (5 weekly; 1hr 15min); Kuching (2 daily; 1hr); Miri (2 daily; 35min); Sibu (3 daily; 35min); Kuala Lumpur (3 daily, 3hr).

# NIAH NATIONAL PARK

Visiting **NIAH NATIONAL PARK**, 131km north of Bintulu, is a highly rewarding experience – in less than a day you can see one of the largest caves in the world, as well as prehistoric rock graffiti in the remarkable Painted Cave, and hike along primary forest trails. The Park is one of Sarawak's smaller national parks, but it is recognized as one of the most important archeological sights in the world. In the outer area of the present park, deep excavations have revealed human remains and flake stone tools, mortars and shell ornaments that date back forty thousand years – the first evidence that people lived in Southeast Asia that long ago. The park is roughly halfway between Bintulu and Miri, 11km off the main road and close to the small town of Batu Niah. The caves are 3km north of Batu Niah, and reached either by a half-hour walk, by longboat (around RM25) or taxi (RM20).

## What to see and do

**Niah National Park** is spread over 3102 hectares of peat swamp, forests and gigantic limestone outcrops. The caves are joined by a wooden walkway, which takes you through the lowland forest along to all the caves. Traders Cave comes first, followed by the Great Cave with its little houses and shelters. The marked route takes you into the depths of the cave system, so it's best to take a torch. There are also a couple of trails and a 400-metre limestone ridge which you can scale, both of which are clearly signposted from park headquarters. Local longhouses are also in the vicinity; speak to park headquarters to find out which ones are accessible.

A small information centre covers the geology of the caves and the history of collecting birds' nests – a few locals still venture into the dark interior to collect guano and birds' nests, which then gets turned into birds'-nest soup.

From the park headquarters, it's a thirty-minute walk to the **caves**: take a sampan across the river and then follow a wooden walkway through dense rainforest where you're likely to see monkeys, hornbills, birdwing butterflies, tree squirrels and flying lizards.

### The caves

The main walkway heads up through the **Traders Cave** (so-called because early nest-gatherers would congregate here to sell their harvests) to the vast west mouth of the **Great Cave**. From within the immense, draughty darkness you can hear the voices of the bird's-nest collectors who gather swiftlet nests for use in bird's-nest soup; their thin beanstalk poles snake up from the cave floor. Once inside, the walkway continues, via **Burnt Cave** and **Moon Cave** to the **Painted Cave**, thirty minutes' walk away. Here, early Sarawak communities buried their dead in boat-shaped coffins, arranged around the cave walls; dating of the contents has proved that the caves have been used as a cemetery for tens of thousands of years. One of these wooden coffins is still perched on an incline, its contents long since removed to the Sarawak Museum (see p.568).

### The trails

There are two other **trails** in the park. Jalan Madu splits off the main walkway around 800m from the park headquarters and cuts first east then south across a peat swamp forest, where you can see wild orchids, mushrooms and pandani. The trail crosses Sungai Subis and then follows its south bank to its confluence with Sungai Niah, from where you'll have to hail a passing boat to cross over to Batu Niah.

The more spectacular trail to Bukit Kasut starts at the confluence of these two rivers. After crossing the Niah river, the clearly marked trail winds through forest, round the foothills of Bukit Kasut and up to the summit – a hard one-hour slog, at the end of which there's a view both of the forest canopy and Batu Niah.

### Arrival and information

**By bus** Regular buses run from both Bintulu and Miri. From Miri take any bus going towards Bintulu, Sibu or Sarikei, there should be a bus every hr on the hr until 8pm. Ask to get off at Niah junction (2hr 15mins; RM10). Take a taxi to park headquarters from here (30min; RM20) From Bintulu bus station there are several buses to Batu Niah (3 hr; RM10). The park office is 3km from Batu Niah, either a taxi ride from the bus station (RM20), short boat ride away (RM25) or a 45-minute stroll away.

**By taxi** Taxis from Miri (1hr 45min; RM120). With some decent bartering you may be able to get it cheaper. Taxi from Batu Niah (RM20; 15min).

**Information** Niah National Park HQ (Ⓣ085/737450); visitor information centre in Miri, at Jl Melayu (Ⓣ085 434184).

### Accommodation

Within the park there are various accommodation options, including camping. If there are no beds available in the park, you can stay in Batu Niah. All bookings for park accommodation can be made through Sarawak Forestry (Ⓣ085/737450 or 737454, Ⓦwww.forestry.sarawak.gov.my):

**Forrest Hostel** Consisting of two hostels, namely *Asrama Agathis A* and *Asrama Agathis B*. Dorms with four to ten beds (RM15 per bed, or RM40 for room of four), with basic rooms with attached bathrooms. Dorms ❸

**Forrest Lodge** Two lodges, either with or without a/c, consisting of two rooms with four single beds (you rent a room or lodge). Bedding and utensils are provided. Rooms ❼–❽

**Camping** There is a campsite with enough pitches for 30 tents (RM5 per night).

**The Niah Cave Inn** Batu Niah Bazaar Ⓣ085/737332. The best accommodation option outside the park; although rooms are pretty basic it's a good place to lay your head. ❹

### Eating

**Asrama Agathis Hostels** There's a canteen at the hostel which does rice and noodle dishes. Also sells chocolate treats for those in need. Basic friend rice or noodles from RM4.

**Chinese Cafés** There are a few Chinese cafés near the Niah Cave Inn that serve breakfasts of porridge until noon, as well as basic Malay dishes. From RM4.

## MIRI

**MIRI** is a booming oil town with a significant expat community and a strong Chinese character. For tourists, it's the main departure point for independent and organized trips into Gunung Mulu National Park (see p.585) and the route north to Brunei and Sabah.

### What to see and do

Miri's old town around Jalan China in the west of town has a cluster of cafés, shops and a few cheap hotels. The fish market occupies the top of Jalan China, along with the Chinese Temple. The main artery through town is **Jalan Brooke**, which has a couple of markets selling fresh fruit and veg and some pigs' heads. The wide road running east from here and parallel to the river, **Jalan Bendahara**, is the simplest route into the new town area. The shopping centre Wisma Pelita, south of the old town on Jalan Padang, includes the **Longhouse Handicraft Centre** (Mon–Sat 9am–4.30pm) on the top floor where you can buy rattan bags, *pua kumbu* (tie-dyed) textiles and carvings. Directly south of the adjacent bus station is the padang, on whose border lies **Tamu Muhibbah** (daily 6am–4pm), the town's jungle produce market, where Orang Ulu come downriver to sell rattan mats, tropical fruits, rice wine and even jungle animals.

There's a 50m **swimming pool** in City Fan at Jalan Merpati (RM1; Tues–Sat 9am–9pm, Sun & public hols 9am–7pm; locker 30sen; RM5 deposit).

**Diving** is also possible as there's a reef and a couple of shipwrecks off the coast of Miri; dive excursions may cover these wrecks as well as disused oil rigs, though the dive sites pale in comparison to those in Sabah.

## Arrival and information

**By bus** The long-distance bus station is 4km out of town at Pujut Corner Terminal. Buses from Bintulu will stop here. Arriving from Brunei, the bus will go to the bus station on Jl Padang, a five-minute walk from the city centre.

**By air** The airport (ⓣ085/615433) is 8km west of the town centre: bus #28 (every 45min) runs from outside the terminal to the bus station.

**Tourist information** The visitor information centre (Mon–Fri 8am–6pm, Sat & Sun 9am–3pm; ⓣ085/434180) is next to the bus station. It provides information on all national parks in the area and offers park accommodation booking.

**Tours and diving** Several tour operators organize trips and treks to Gunung Mulu and other destinations. Borneo Jungle Safari, 174A Jl Brooke (ⓣ085/435736), runs caving and climbing trips, as well as excursions to the Kelabit Highlands. Seridan Mulu, 2km west of the centre at Lobby Arcade, *Park City Everly Hotel*, Jl Temenggong (ⓣ085/414300, ⓔinfo@seridanmulu.com), is a very professional outfit that also runs dive trips to the nearby reefs off Miri. Borneo Adventures, Lot 1344, 1st Floor, Miri Waterfront Commercial Centre (ⓣ085/424332), is another reputable company that arranges treks. Tropical Adventures, Ground Floor, *Mega Hotel* (ⓣ082/419337), is also recommended. Tropical Dives, Jl Temenggong Datuk Oyong Lawai, (ⓣ085/415582, ⓦwww.seridanmulu.com), can organize trips to nearby dive sites.

## Accommodation

**Brooke Inn** 14 Brooke Rd ⓣ085/412881. Has a slightly old-fashioned feel, but rooms are clean with attached baths and a/c, plus it's in a good central location. ❸

**De Central Inn** 14 Jl North Yu Seng ⓣ085/424168. Great location for the bars and food stalls along Jl North Yu Seng, but rooms have seen (and smelt of) better days. ❸

**Highlands** 3rd Floor, 1271 Jl Sri Dagang ⓣ085/422327. The best option in town for backpackers. Clean spacious dorms and decent-sized doubles with breakfast included. Staff can be persuaded to help organize tours around the area. Dorms ❷; rooms ❹

**Tai Tong Lodging House** 19 China St ⓣ085/411498. Basic lodging house which is the cheapest but most bizarre option in town: men get to sleep in the reception area in the open-plan dorms, while women get the stark double rooms. Located at the jetty end of Jl China in the old part of town. Dorms ❶; rooms ❷

## Eating

**Bilal Restaurant** Persiaran Kabor, off Jl Maju. Great place for Indian curry, and the Afghani chicken comes highly recommended – watch out for the bones though. Dishes RM4–RM11.

**Hawker Stalls** Jl North Yu Seng. This area really comes alive at night and there are various hawker stalls located on the central reservation. Dishes from R3.

**Ming Café** Jl North Yu Seng. Although its name may suggest otherwise, this place serves tasty options of Malay or Indian food (from RM4), washed down with some cold beers. It even has Guinness on draught.

**Uncle Lai Cafe** Jl Indica. Great indoor café serving the usual *mee goreng* options from RM3, but also does cracking cheese on toast for those who fancy a change.

## Directory

**Airlines** MAS, Jalan South Yu Seng (ⓣ085/414144); Air Asia, Jalan Parry & 1st Floor, Miri Airport (ⓣ03/8775 4000).

**Banks** Maybank, on Jalan Pujut. There are also money-changers and ATMs along Jalan China.

**Books** The Popular Bookstore, 3rd Floor, Bintang Plaza, Jl Bintang Jaya. Sells a range of English-language books from mushy novels to a limited selection of travel guides.

**Hospital** Miri's General Hospital, Jl Cayaha (ⓣ085/420033).

**Immigration** Jl Kipas, Room 3 (Mon–Fri 8am–12.45pm & 2–5pm, closed 1st & 3rd Sat of month, 8am–12.45pm on 2nd & 4th Sat; ⓣ085/442112). Note they will only extend your Sarawak visa by a few days.

**Internet** Planet Café, 1st Floor, Bitang Plaza, RM3 per hour; Cyber Corner, 1st Floor, Wisma Pelita, Jl

### INTO BRUNEI FROM MIRI

Heading straight for Brunei from Miri involves a few changes but it's a pretty straightforward journey. The bus takes you from Miri and will wait while you clear Malaysian immigration. The same bus will then drop you off at Bruneian immigration where you and your luggage disembark (keep your ticket). After the formalities, board another waiting bus to the outskirts of the Bruneian town of Kuala Belait, 6km further on. At Kuala Belait, you change bus again, this time heading to Seria. Once at Seria you pick up a bus to Bandar Seri Begawan. The last bus from Seria that will get you to the Bruneian capital the same day leaves at around 3.30pm. Although this sounds somewhat complicated, the journey only takes four hours, and all buses are timed to meet each connection.



Padang, RM3 per hour; Coffee Bean & Tea Leaf, Bintang Plaza, free WiFi.
**Pharmacy** Guardian Pharmacy, Bintang Plaza.
**Police** Jl Miri Pujut ⓣ085/432533 or 085/433222.
**Post office** Jl Post ⓣ085/438006 (Mon–Sat 8am–4:30pm).

## Moving on

**By bus** All buses towards Kuching leave from the express bus station 8km out of town at Pujut Corner, Jl Miri Pujut; to get there, take the #33 from the local bus station outside the visitor information office (10 min). Syarikat Bus Suria (ⓣ085/434317) operates services to Bintulu and other locations south, including Kuching and Pontianak. Buses to Brunei stop at the local bus station on Jl Padang Miri.
**Destinations:** Bintulu (several daily; 4hr 30min); Batu Niah (8 daily; 2hr); Kuala Belait (5 daily; 2hr 30min); Kuching (2 daily; 15hr); Mukah (2daily; 12hr); Sibu (several daily; 8hr).
**By air** to: Bario (3 daily; 40min); Bintulu (3 daily; 35min); Gunung Mulu (2 daily; 30min); Kota Kinabalu (5 daily; 40min); Kuala Lumpur (3 daily; 2hr 15min); Kuching (5 daily; 1hr); Labuan (3 daily; 40 min); Lawas (3 daily; 45min); Limbang (3daily; 40min); Sibu (4 daily; 1hr).

# MARUDI

**MARUDI**, 80km southeast of Miri on Batang Baram, is the only sizeable town in the whole Baram watershed, and the jetty is the centre of the community. The main reason for coming here is the boat connections. If you have a few hours between boats you can walk to **Fort House**, past the main Bazaar Square, and along Jalan Fort to the top of the hill, which was built in 1901 and is still in good condition. The fort is now a government office, and also houses a Penan handicraft centre (Mon–Fri 9am–2pm).

## Arrival and information

**By boat** Express boats travel from Marudi up to Kuala Baram regularly until 3pm (3hr; RM20).
**By air** The airport is 1km from the town centre so it's possible to walk in just ten minutes, although taxis are usually there to meet the flights (RM3).
**Information** There's no tourist information at Marudi – if you need assistance be sure to ask at the information centre in Miri.

## Accommodation

**Grand Hotel** Lg Lima ⓣ085/755711. Huge hotel with clean, quiet rooms. Has good information on tours to Gunung Mulu National Park. ❸–❹
**Victoria Hotel** Pekan Marudi, Marudi ⓣ085/756067. Clean, functional and a good cheap option with good views of the jetty. ❸

## Eating

**Boon Kee Restoran** Behind the main street on Jalan Newshop. Good for the usual staples of *Mie/Nasi goreng*, all tasty, fresh and cheap (from RM3).
**Restoran Koperselera** For great Indian food (dishes from RM2) try this place on Jalan Cinema.

## Moving on

**By bus** There are no bus services to Marudi.
**By boat** Boats run from here to Long Terawan, where there's a connection for Gunung Mulu

National Park (RM20–50 per person, depending on number of passengers). Boats also go west to Kuala Baram (RM20 per person), where buses wait to take passengers to Miri or Brunei.

**Destinations:** Kuala Baram (7 daily; 3hr); Long Terawan (1 daily; 3hr).

**By air to:** Bario (daily; 40min); Lon Akah (2 weekly; 35min); Long Banga (weekly; 50min); Miri (2 daily; 20min).

## GUNUNG MULU NATIONAL PARK

**GUNUNG MULU NATIONAL PARK** is Sarawak's premier natural attraction. At the last count, it featured over three hundred animal species and nearly three thousand plant species. The park comprises primary rainforest, which is characterized by clear rivers and

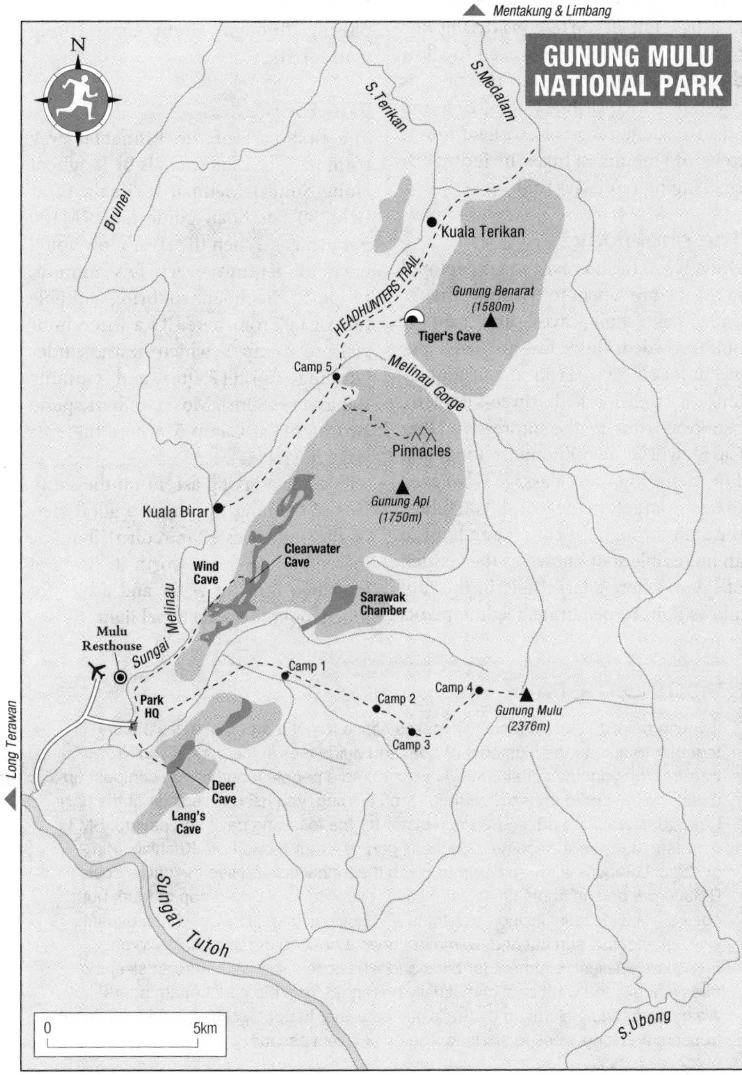

high-altitude vegetation, and three dramatically eroded mountains, including fifty-metre-high limestone spikes known as the **Pinnacles**. Gunung Mulu also has the largest **limestone cave system** in the world, much of which is still being explored.

## What to see and do

It is quite possible to see the main caves in a day, but if you're considering one of the treks as well you'll need to allow three or four days extra. The park is covered in rich primary rainforest and offers a whole range of excellent jungle treks and mountain hikes, including the challenging Pinnacles trail.

### The show caves

Only five of the 25 caves so far explored in Mulu are open to visitors; they're known as "show caves" and can get quite crowded. Guide fees are RM20 per group for all caves. From the headquarters, a well-marked three-kilometre plankway runs to the impressive **Deer Cave**, whose two-kilometre-long and 174-metre-high cave passage is believed to be the largest in the world. You follow the path through the cave for an hour to an incredible spot known as the Garden of Eden, where a large hole in the roof allows light to penetrate, feeding plants and attracting birds, insects and leaf monkeys.

Probing some 107km through Mulu's substratum, **Clearwater Cave**, thought to be the longest in Southeast Asia, is reached by a fifteen-minute longboat journey (RM85 per boat) along Sungai Melinau from park headquarters. You can walk the whole way if you wish (1hr) along a pleasant jungle boardwalk, which has the advantage of passing through **Moon Cave** (bring your torch).

### The Pinnacles

The first part of the **Pinnacles** trek from park headquarters is by longboat along Sungai Melinau to Kuala Birar (RM350 per boat, guide fees RM100 per group). When the river's low you'll have to get out every few minutes to push the boat, so bring suitable footwear. From here, it's a three-hour walk to Camp 5, which nestles under Gunung Api (1750m) and Gunung Benarat (1580m). Most climbers spend two nights at Camp 5, where there's a large hostel (❷).

It's quite a taxing ascent up the south face of Gunung Api to get a good view of the Pinnacles (7hr return), but the incredible views are worth it. Bring at least two litres of water and a bite for lunch, but otherwise travel light.

### VISITING THE PARK

If you're trekking independently, it makes sense to get a group of at least four together to spread the high cost of boat and guide fees in the park; if you're travelling on your own or simply want to get more people together you can post up a note on the board at headquarters. Upon arriving, you need to register at the **park headquarters** (if it's after 5.30pm, register for the following day), and pay the RM3 park fee. Many visitors come to Mulu as part of a tour group from Kuching, Miri or Kuala Lumpur – a four-day trip to climb the Pinnacles and see the caves costs RM600 per person (three times what you'd pay with your own group of four), but covers all incidentals, including permits and guides. Take plenty of water, decent walking shoes, a sun hat and swimming gear, a poncho or rain sheet, a torch, mosquito repellent, ointment for bites and a basic first-aid kit. Mats and sleeping bags (should you want one) can usually be rented from the park headquarters. Wear shorts and T-shirts on the trails (it'll be easier to spot leeches), and bring long trousers and long-sleeved shirts for the dusk insect assault.

### Walks from Camp 5

Once back at the camp, most people rest, swim, eat and sleep, preferring to start the return trip to park headquarters the following day. However, there are some other interesting walks from here. A path from the camp follows the river further upstream and ends at a beautiful spot below the **Melinau Gorge** (2hr return), where a vertical wall of rock rises 100m above the vanishing river. A much longer option from Camp 5 is to follow the so-called **Headhunter's Trail**, a route once traced by Kayan war parties. Cross the bridge, turn left and walk along a wide trail passing a large rock (around 4km). From here, a clearly marked flat trail to **Kuala Terikan**, a small Berawan settlement on the banks of Sungai Terikan, takes four hours (11km). You can stay at basic hut accommodation, bookable at park headquarters (RM15dorm). From here, the trail continues for two hours to Sungai Medalam, where you can take a longboat (RM200–300 per boat) to the Iban longhouse at Bala. It's best to stay here and then continue next day down Sungai Medalam in a longboat into Sungai Limbang and on up to **Limbang,** an all-day trip. This is a good way of getting to Brunei from Mulu, as boats run frequently from Limbang to Bandar Seri Begawan (hourly until 6pm; RM15).

### Gunung Mulu

The route to the summit of **Gunung Mulu** (2376m) is a straightforward climb, though very steep. Park regulations require that you hire a guide (RM250 per group). The first stage is from park headquarters to Camp 3, an easy three-hour walk on a flat trail. The first night is at the open hut at Camp 3, which has cooking facilities. Day two comprises a hard, ten-hour uphill slog, some of it along the southwest ridge, a series of small hills negotiated by a narrow, twisting path. The hut at Camp 4 is at 1800m; it can be cool here, so bring a sleeping bag. Most climbers set off well before dawn for the hard ninety-minute trek to the summit, to arrive at sunrise. Near the top you have to haul yourself up by ropes onto the cold, windswept, craggy peak. From here, the view is exhilarating, looking down on Gunung Api.

## Arrival and information

**By air** The airport is 2km west of park headquarters; minibuses (RM1) and taxis (RM3) meet the planes to take you to the headquarters or accommodation.

**By boat** Reaching Mulu by boat from Miri involves four separate stages and takes all day. The first step is to take an early bus (every 15min; 45min; RM3) or taxi (30min; RM20) to Kuala Baram. From here, take the 7am or 8am express boat upriver to Marudi (2hr 30min; RM18) to connect with the noon express to Long Terawan (3hr; RM20). When the river is low, this boat may only go as far as Long Panai-Kuala Apoh (RM15–18), though you can then take a longboat (RM5) from there to Long Terawan. From Long Terawan, a longboat (RM25–50 per person, depending on numbers; 2hr) will take you to the park.

**Information** Park Headquarters office (ⓣ085/432561, ⓦwww.mulupark.com, 8am–5pm).

## Accommodation

Accommodation for Mulu can be arranged at the visitor information centre in Miri or at the park headquarters, but it's best to arrange in advance. It is possible to camp at the park too (RM5).

**Hostel** There's a large 21-bed dorm in the hostel which has cooking facilities and kettles for tea/coffee. ❷

**Rainforest Chalet Rooms** Can sleep up to four people, have attached bathrooms and rooms come either with a fan or a/c. ❺–❻

## Eating

**Buyun Sipan Lounge** A canteen across the bridge over Sungai Melinau serves basic Malay dishes of noodles and rice porridge from RM3. There's a provisions shop next door too. Daily 8am–8pm.

**Café Mulu** This place near the hostel serves an uninspiring range of meals and snacks from RM3. Daily 7.30am–9pm.

### INTO SABAH AND BRUNEI: LAWAS

Boxed in between Sabah and Brunei, **LAWAS** town sits on Sungai Lawas. Daily **boats** arrive here from Muara in Brunei, Sabah's Pulau Labuan, and Limbang. The jetty is beside the old mosque, 400m east of the town. A daily express **bus** from Kota Kinabalu (4hr; RM30) calls in here via the Sabah border town of Sipitang and then goes on through Brunei's little-known Temburong district before terminating in Limbang. There's also a bus going the other way to Kota Kinabalu at 7.30am and 1.30pm.



### Moving on

**By boat** It's a complicated, time-consuming (8–10hr) process getting back by boat, and can work out more expensive than a flight. Mulu Park HQ can help charter a boat to Long Terawan (RM250 per boat or RM55 per person for big groups; 2hr) – and it's best for the longboat to pick you up at 6am at the latest. This connects with the early morning express or longboat that gets you to Marudi (RM20) by late morning. From Marudi, take another express boat heading to Kuala Baram (departs between 7am & 3pm; 3hr; RM20). From Kuala Baram it's a taxi to get back to Miri (RM50) – or a bus from Kuala Baram.
**By air** Return flights to Miri leave the park twice daily (30min; RM160), and to Kota Kinabalu once daily (50min); it's best to book in advance.

# Sabah

Bordering Sarawak on the northeastern flank of Borneo, **SABAH**'s beauty lies in its wealth of natural resources and abundant wildlife. Its rainforests, spectacular mountains and reef-lined coasts are the region's chief draws. You can watch turtles hatch in **Turtle Islands National Park**, see baby orang-utans at the **Sepilok Orang-utan Rehabilitation Centre** or marvel at forest-dwelling proboscis monkeys along the lower reaches of the **Kinabatangan River**. The diving is good too: **Pulau Sipadan** is rated one of the world's top dive destinations, with turtles, sharks, barracuda and reefs aplenty. Sabah's other major attraction is climbing the granite shelves of 4101-metre-high **Mount Kinabalu**: it's certainly challenging, but the rewards are spectacular.

As well as its natural beauty, Sabah also has a diverse ethnic heritage. Until European powers gained a foothold here in the nineteenth century, the northern tip of this remote land mass was inhabited by **tribal groups** who had only minimal contact with the outside world. The peoples of the Kadazan and Dusun tribes constitute the largest indigenous racial group, along with the Murut of the southwest and Sabah's so-called "sea gypsies", the Bajau. Recently economic migrants from the Philippines and neighbouring Kalimantan have further added to the state's rich ethnic mix.

Like Sarawak, travel is more expensive in Sabah than in peninsular Malaysia. Tourism has been an ongoing project in Sabah for many years and while there are plenty of tour operators, independent travel is completely achievable and a breeze compared to other parts of Borneo.

## KOTA KINABALU

Settled on the South China Sea, **KOTA KINABALU** is the capital of Sabah and for many the main entry point to the region. Sprawled around a maze of shopping malls, KK (as it's often called) offers a range of budget accommodation and plenty of restaurants and bars to suit all moods. Lacking in architectural charm, it's nevertheless pleasant enough to amble around on foot, exploring the various markets, trying local delicacies and soaking up the waterfront atmosphere.

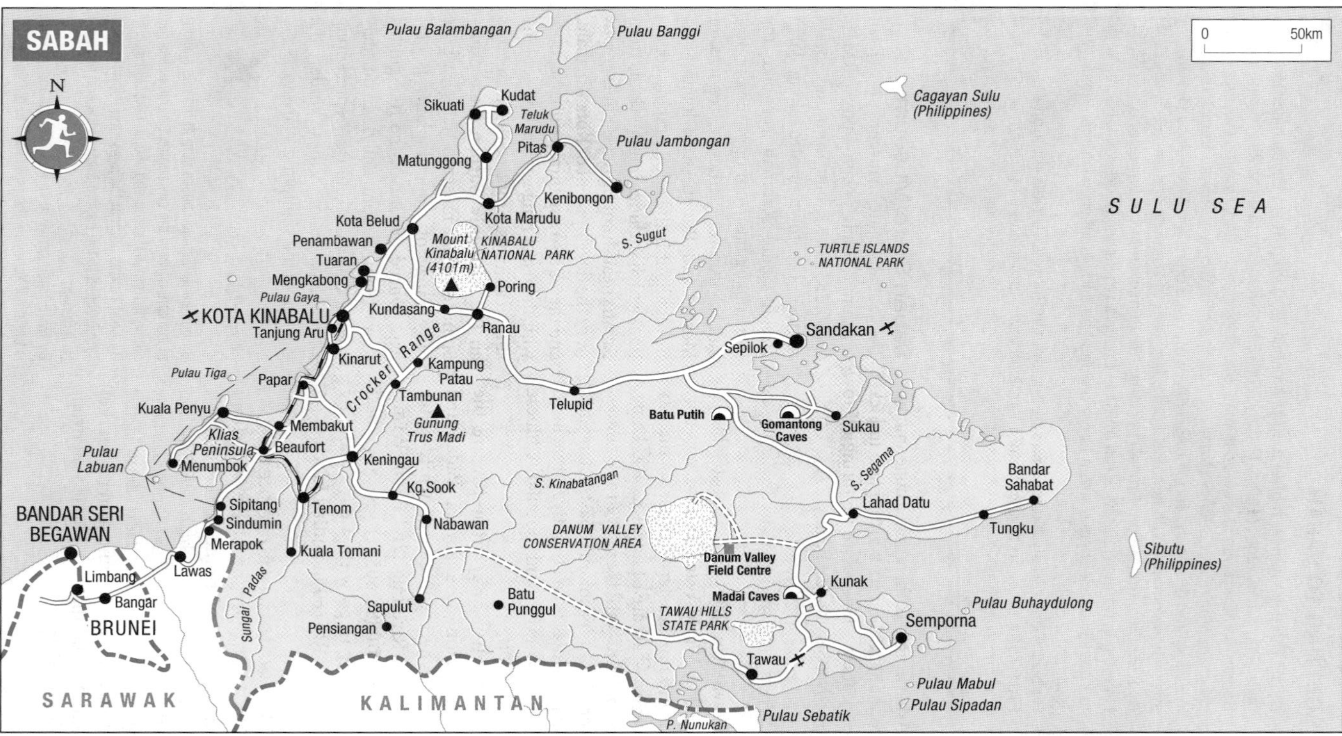
SABAH
N
0 50km
SULU SEA
Pulau Balambangan
Pulau Banggi
Cagayan Sulu (Philippines)
Sikuati
Kudat
Teluk Marudu
Pitas
Pulau Jambongan
Matunggong
Kenibongon
Kota Marudu
Kota Belud
Penambawan
Tuaran
Mengkabong
Pulau Gaya
Mount Kinabalu (4101m)
KINABALU NATIONAL PARK
S. Sugut
TURTLE ISLANDS NATIONAL PARK
Poring
Kundasang
Ranau
KOTA KINABALU
Tanjung Aru
Crocker Range
Kinarut
Kampung Patau
Tambunan
Sandakan
Sepilok
Pulau Tiga
Papar
Telupid
Kuala Penyu
Membakut
Gunung Trus Madi
Batu Putih
Gomantong Caves
Sukau
Klias Peninsula
Beaufort
Pulau Labuan
Menumbok
Keningau
Kg.Sook
S. Kinabatangan
S. Segama
Bandar Sahabat
Lahad Datu
Tungku
Sipitang
Tenom
BANDAR SERI BEGAWAN
Sindumin
Nabawan
DANUM VALLEY CONSERVATION AREA
Merapok
Kuala Tomani
Danum Valley Field Centre
Sibutu (Philippines)
Limbang
Lawas
Kunak
Sungai Padas
Bangar
Madai Caves
Pulau Buhaydulong
Sapulut
Batu Punggul
TAWAU HILLS STATE PARK
Semporna
BRUNEI
Pensiangan
Tawau
Pulau Mabul
Pulau Sipadan
SARAWAK
KALIMANTAN
P. Nunukan
Pulau Sebatik

## GETTING TO SABAH

**By air** There are regular **flights** to Kota Kinabalu (KK) from Kuala Lumpur (several daily ; 2hr 30min), Johor Bahru (2 daily; 2hr 15min), Kuching (6 daily; 2hr 15min), Bandar Seri Begawan (6 weekly; 20min), Manila (2 weekly; 2hr), Penang (several daily; 2hr 50min) and Sydney (1 daily; 11hr). You can also fly to Tawau from Tarakan in Kalimantan (2 weekly; 1hr). Air Asia (Ⓦwww.airasia.com) and MASWings (Ⓦwww.maswings.com.my) both fly to KK from other parts of Sarawak and Sabah.
**By boat** Daily **boats** from Brunei (1–2 daily; 1hr 30min) and from Lawas and Limbang in northern Sarawak run to Pulau Labuan, which has good connections to Kota Kinabalu. There's also a ferry from Tarakan and Nunukan in Kalimantan to Tawau (1–2 daily).
**By bus** A twice-daily express **bus** from Lawas in Sarawak travels through Brunei's Temburong district before terminating at Kota Kinabalu (7.30am and 1.30pm; 4hr; RM30.)

Aside from this, there's not a huge amount to do in KK but it's a great place to kick back for a while before venturing off to discover Sabah's real beauty.

## What to see and do

Downtown KK was almost obliterated by World War II bombs, and only in the northeastern corner of the city centre – an area known as KK Lama, or old KK – are there even the faintest remains of its colonial past. Jalan Gaya in particular is an attractive street lined with colourful and popular Chinese *kedai kopis*.

A day-trip away from KK are the rapids along the Sungai Padas and Klias, where you can go **white-water rafting**. Riverbug (2nd Floor, Wisma Sabah Ⓣ088/260501) is the best company to go with; a day's paddling will cost RM160 including lunch.

### The waterfront markets

The most diverting of the waterfront markets is the **Filipino market** on Jalan Tn Fuad Stephens, which sells Sabahan ethnic wares as well as Filipino baskets, shells and trinkets. Next door is the dark and labyrinthine **general market** and, behind that, the manic waterfront **fish market**.

### Sabah State Museum

The Sabah State Museum on Jalan Muzium (daily 9am–5pm; RM15; Ⓣ088/25319), twenty minutes' walk west of the town centre along Jalan Tunku Abdul Rahman (or take the Penampang bus from opposite the post office), features authentic replicas of Murut- and Rungus-style longhouses. Its highlight is the ethnographic collection, which includes human skulls from Sabah's head-hunting days. Photographs trace the development of Kota Kinabalu, and there's also a natural history section, with the usual range of startled-looking stuffed animals. Fronting the museum is an **Ethnobotanic Garden** (daily 9am–5pm; free with museum ticket), whose huge range of tropical plants is best experienced on one of the free guided tours (9am & 2pm daily). Exquisitely crafted traditional houses representing all Sabah's major tribes border the garden, in the Kampung Warisan.

## Arrival

**By bus** Long-distance buses stop at the bus station at Inanam, north of the city centre. Shuttle buses run regularly from Jl Padang and should take 30min.
**By boat** Ferries dock at the Jesselton Point Ferry Terminal just to the east of town at the end of Jl HaJl Saman.
**By train** Trains arrive at Tanjung Aru station, which is beside Jl Kepayan, the main road to points south

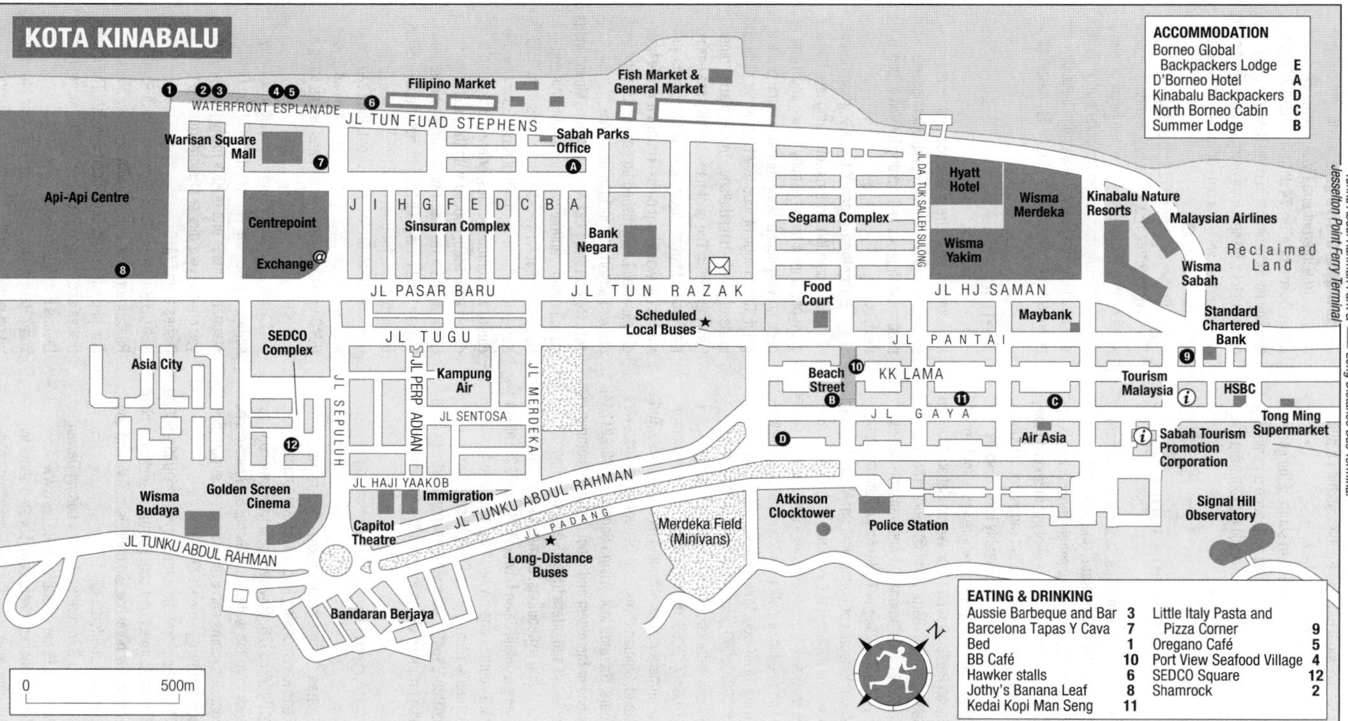
KOTA KINABALU
ACCOMMODATION
Borneo Global Backpackers Lodge E
D'Borneo Hotel A
Kinabalu Backpackers D
North Borneo Cabin C
Summer Lodge B
EATING & DRINKING
Aussie Barbeque and Bar 3
Barcelona Tapas Y Cava 7
Bed 1
BB Café 10
Hawker stalls 6
Jothy's Banana Leaf 8
Kedai Kopi Man Seng 11
Little Italy Pasta and Pizza Corner 9
Oregano Café 5
Port View Seafood Village 4
SEDCO Square 12
Shamrock 2
Tunku Abdul Rahman Park & Jesselton Point Ferry Terminal
Long Distance Bus Terminal
E, Sabah State Museum, Tanjung Aru Train Station & Airport
Filipino Market
Fish Market & General Market
WATERFRONT ESPLANADE
JL TUN FUAD STEPHENS
Warisan Square Mall
Sabah Parks Office
Api-Api Centre
Centrepoint
Exchange
Sinsuran Complex
J I H G F E D C B A
Bank Negara
Segama Complex
JL DA TUK SALLEH SULONG
Hyatt Hotel
Wisma Merdeka
Wisma Yakim
Kinabalu Nature Resorts
Malaysian Airlines
Reclaimed Land
Wisma Sabah
JL PASAR BARU
JL TUN RAZAK
Food Court
JL HJ SAMAN
Standard Chartered Bank
Maybank
Scheduled Local Buses
SEDCO Complex
Asia City
JL TUGU
JL PANTAI
JL PERP ADUAN
Kampung Air
JL MERDEKA
Beach Street
KK LAMA
Tourism Malaysia
HSBC
Tong Ming Supermarket
JL SEPULUH
JL SENTOSA
JL GAYA
Air Asia
Sabah Tourism Promotion Corporation
JL HAJI YAAKOB
Immigration
Wisma Budaya
Golden Screen Cinema
Capitol Theatre
JL TUNKU ABDUL RAHMAN
JL PADANG
Atkinson Clocktower
Police Station
Signal Hill Observatory
Merdeka Field (Minivans)
Long-Distance Buses
Bandaran Berjaya
N
0 500m

of KK, so you'll have no trouble catching a bus heading into town from here.

**By air** KK's airport is 6.5km south of the centre. Walk out to the main road and catch a minibus (RM3) into town, or take a taxi (RM20) from the pre-paid taxi counter.

## Information and tours

**Tourist information** The Sabah Tourism Board (Mon–Fri 8am–5pm, Sat & Sun 9am–4pm; ⓣ088/212121, ⓦwww.sabahtourism.com) is at 51 Jl Gaya and has a range of information on the top tourist destinations. Staff range from extremely knowledgeable to considerably less so, so be armed with questions on where you want to go. Sabah Parks, Ground Floor, Wisma Sabah (Mon–Fri 8am–5pm, Sat 8am–2pm; ⓣ088/211881), can help with accommodation and transport details if you're travelling to Tunku Abdul Rahman Park, Mount Kinabalu or Poring. Tourism Malaysia, at Api Api Centre (Mon–Fri 8am–8pm; ⓣ088/248698, ⓦwww.tourism.gov.my), are a good point of contact if you need information on other parts of Malaysia.

**Tours** River Bug, 2nd Floor, Wisma Sabah (ⓣ088/260501) for rafting on the Klias River; Borneo Authentic Adventure, Wisma Sabah (ⓣ088/773066, ⓔinfo@borneo-authentic.com) for numerous trips including Mount Kinabalu, Turtle Island, Sipidan diving and Danum treks; Discovery Tours, Ground Floor, Wisma Sabah (ⓣ088/221244) is one of the oldest and most reputable companies in Sabah and offers trips all over the region. For diving expeditions, Borneo Divers, 9th Floor, Menara Jubili, Jalan Gaya (ⓣ088/222226) offers PADI courses and diving to Sipadan and Mabul; Borneo Anchor, Ground Floor, Wisma Sabah (ⓣ088/255482, ⓦwww.borneoanchortours.com) also arranges diving to the east-coast islands.

## Accommodation

**Borneo Global Backpackers Lodge** 1st Floor, Karamunsing Godown, Jl Karamunsing ⓣ088/270976, ⓦwww.bgbackpackers.com. Just back from the waterfront, *Global Backpackers* has spacious rooms and even offers free airport pick-ups. Dorms ❷; rooms ❹

**D'Borneo Hotel** Sinsuran Complex ⓣ088/266999, ⓔinfo@borneohotel.com For those seeking a bit of luxury, this hotel has big beds, large TVs and good all-round comforts. ❼

**Kinabalu Backpackers** Lot 4 Lorong Dewan, Australia Place ⓣ088/253385, ⓦwww.kinabalubackpackers.com. Located about five minutes' walk from the mini-van stand near Merdaka fields, this is a good option with comfy doubles, free internet and DVDs. Dorms ❷

**North Borneo Cabin** 74 Jl Gaya ⓣ088 272800, ⓦwww.northborneocabin.com. Newly opened, clean hostel with spacious dorms. Has a great café downstairs as well; the only downside is there's no hot water. Dorms ❷

**Summer Lodge** Lot 120 Jl Gaya ⓣ088/244499, ⓦwww.summerlodge.com.my. Located above Beach St in the heart of town, this is a friendly, relaxed and popular option. Good size doubles, free internet and cheap beer. Can also arrange a number of tours. Dorms ❷; rooms ❹

## Eating

KK is known for its fresh seafood and there are many restaurants where the offerings are swimming in tanks just waiting for you to pick them out.

**Barcelona Tapas Y Cava** Warisan Square, Jl Duapuloh. As the name suggests, this is a great place for a range of tasty tapas, and if you've been craving decent wine then this is the place to get it. Good range of food (RM12 plus per dish) and loads of potato-based dishes for vegetarian diners.

**Hawker stalls** The best hawker stalls are behind the Filipino Market, Jalan Tun Fuad Stephens, just east of the waterfront cafés. There's a whole host of delicacies being dished up here and it's the best place to absorb the local atmosphere.

**Jothy's Banana Leaf** Api Api Centre. Mountainous *daun pisang* (banana leaf) meals, biriyanis and curries – great for vegetarians. Meals from RM5.

**Kedai Kopi Man Seng** 86 Jl Gaya. Busy Chinese eatery with outdoor tables, offering tasty staple dishes from RM3. Popular with the local crowd.

**Little Italy Pasta and Pizza Corner** Under the *Capital* hotel on Jl HaJl Saman, this place does big bowls of pasta for under RM10.

**Oregano Café** On the waterfront, the *Oregano* serves delicious Malay food at reasonable prices (RM6 upwards). Grouper fish and jungle ferns are a speciality.

**Port View Seafood Village** Located in a lovely setting right on the waterfront (off Jl Tun Fuad Stephens), this is one of KK's many places where you choose your dinner straight from the tank. Dishes from RM10.

**SEDCO Square** SEDCO Complex, off Jl Sapuloh. Restaurant-lined square, with outdoor tables; a fine place for barbecued meat and fish. The lobster dishes and jumbo prawns are highly recommended. Dishes RM10 upwards.

**Tong Hing Supermarket** Jl Gaya. Good for stocking up on supplies for the Mount Kinabalu climb.

## Drinking and nightlife

**Aussie Barbeque and Bar** Waterfront Esplanade. A great place for sinking a cool beer and people-watching.
**BB Café** Beach St. If you fancy a game of pool then this is the place to come. Also does buckets of beer for RM18.
**Bed** Waterfront Esplanade. Live bands are a regular set-up here, playing from 9pm onwards. Stays open until the early hours, although (as with most places in KK) it can often be quite empty, so get a gang together if you can.
**Shamrock** Waterfront Esplanade. The *de rigueur* Irish pub, serving Guinness on tap.

## Directory

**Airline offices** Air Asia, Jl Gaya ⓣ088/284669; Dragon Air, Ground Floor, Block C, Kuwasa Complex, Jl Tunku Abdul Rahman ⓣ088/254733; MAS, 11th Floor, Gaya Centre, Jl Tun Fuad Stephens ⓣ088/290600; Philippine Air, Karamunsing Complex, Jl Tuaran ⓣ088/239600; Royal Brunei, Ground Floor, Block C, Kuwasa Complex, Jl Tunku Rahman ⓣ088/242193; Singapore Airlines, Ground Floor, Block C, Kuwasa Complex, Jl Tunku Rahman ⓣ088/255444; Thai Airways, Ground Floor, Block C, Kuwasa Complex, Jl Tunku Rahman ⓣ088/242193.
**Banks and exchange** Among the various moneychangers (Mon–Sat 10am–7pm) in Wisma Merdeka are Ban Loong Money Changer and Travellers' Money Changer, both on the ground floor; there's also an office in the Taiping Goldsmith, Block A, Sinsuran Complex. ATMs are found throughout town – HSBC, Jl Gaya; Maybank, Jl Pantai.
**Books** Times The Bookshop, Ground Floor, Warisan Square (ⓣ03/5628 6999). Sells an excellent selection of English books, novels and travel guides.
**Embassies and consulates** Australian Honorary Consul, Suite 10.1, Level 10, Wisma Great Eastern, 65 Jl Gaya ⓣ088/267151; British Honorary Consul ⓣ088/253333; Brunei Consulate, Lot No 8–4, 8th Floor, Api-Api Centre ⓣ088/236112; Indonesian Consulate, Lorong Kemajuan, Karamunsing, Peti Surat 11595 ⓣ088/218600.
**Hospital** Queen Elizabeth Hospital is beyond the Sabah State Museum, on Jl Penampang (ⓣ088/218166). Sabah Medical Centre is located just off Jl Damai (ⓣ088/211333). In an emergency, dial ⓣ999.
**Immigration office** 4th Floor, Wisma Dang Bandang, Jl Hj Yaakob (Mon–Thurs 8am–1pm & 2–4.30pm, Fri 8–11.30am & 2-4.30pm, Sat 8am–1pm; ⓣ088/216711).
**Internet** Most backpackers' places have internet access. Exchange, at Centre Point (Mon–Fri 8am–10.30pm, Sat & Sun 8–11pm).
**Pharmacy** Apex Pharmacy, 2 Jalan Pantai ⓣ088/255100; UMH Pharmacy, 80 Jalan Gaya ⓣ088/215312.
**Police** Balai Polis KK (ⓣ088/258191 or 258111) is below Atkinson Clocktower on Jl Padang.
**Post office** The general post office (Mon–Sat 8am–4.30pm) is on Jl Tun Razak and keeps poste restante.
**Shopping** Borneo Handicraft (1st Floor, Wisma Merdeka) has a good choice of woodwork,

### TAKING THE TRAIN BETWEEN TENOM AND BEAUFORT

West of KK, Tenom and Beaufort are uneventful towns, and there is little reason to visit apart from experiencing the impressive train journey that runs from KK to Beaufort and then on to Tenom. The journey takes a plodding five hours and is only really worth doing for the Beaufort to Tenom section (2hr 15min). This winds through the Padas River gorge and offers dramatic jungle scenery. Three **types of trains** run along the route: diesel locomotive (from Tenom: Mon–Sat 8am & 2.50pm, Sun 8am, 12.10pm & 2.30pm; from Beaufort: Mon–Sat 10am & 4.50pm; Sun 7am, 10am & 4.20pm; RM2.75); cargo (from Tenom: Mon–Sat 10.15am; from Beaufort: Mon–Sat 1.30pm; RM2.75); and railcar (from Tenom: Mon–Sat 6.40am, Sun 7.25am; from Beaufort: Mon–Sat 8.30am, Sun noon; RM8.35). Train timetables do change so it's best to call for the current schedule (ⓣ088/254611). The fastest and most comfortable of these is the railcar, but you must book ahead for this on ⓣ087/735514 or at the station.

If you want to pick the train up in Beaufort then you can catch a bus from outside Merdeka Field in KK (1hr 30min; RM9); buses leave when full. For a **place to stay,** try the *Hotel Orchid* in Tenom (ⓣ087/737600; ➌) or the *Mandarin Inn* in Beaufort (ⓣ087/211800; ➍).

basketry and gongs; Borneo Handicraft & Ceramic Shop (Ground Floor, Centrepoint) stocks ceramics, antiques and primitive sculptures. Warisan Square opposite the Waterfront Esplanade has a great range of shops including Western high street names.

**Telephone services** There are IDD facilities at Kedai Telekom (daily 8am–10pm) in the Sadong Jaya Complex.

## Moving on

**By bus** Long-distance buses operate from the new bus terminal at Inanam in the northern end of town. Mini-vans to take you to Mount Kinabalu National Park congregate around the Merdeka Field area, just off Jl Tunku Abdul Rahman. Generally, buses leave when full; turn up by 7am to ensure a seat.

**Destinations** Beaufort (15 daily; 1hr); Kinabalu National Park (8 daily; 1hr 45min); Kota Belud (16 daily; 1hr); Lawas (1 daily; 4hr); Ranau (10 daily; 2hr); Sandakan (12 daily; 5hr 30min); Tawau (2 daily; 9hr).

**By ferry** Ferries to Pulau Labuan leave from Jesselton Point ferry terminal; you can book tickets and check departures on the Labuan information line (Ⓣ087/423445). The Labuan Express departs from KK at 8am, 10am, and noon (2 hr; RM32). Tickets can be bought at the jetty or at Rezeki Murni, 1st Floor, Block D, Segama Complex (Ⓣ088/236835). From Palau Labuan you can take another ferry to Muara in Brunei. There are four daily services at 8.30am, 11am, 1pm and 4.30pm (1hr; RM34).

**By train** Trains to Tenom and Beaufort leave from Tanjung Aru station daily (except Sun) at 7.45am (4hr). The steam train to Papar leaves on Wed and Sat. Call Ⓣ088/254611 for updated timetables as the train times are prone to change.

**By air** KK has good connections to areas within Sabah and Sarawak, as well as regular flights to Brunei, mainland Malaysia, Indonesia, the Philippines and Australia.

**Destinations:** Bandar Seri Bagawan (3 daily, 20min); Bintulu (5 weekly; 1hr 15min); Kuching (6 daily; 2hr 15min); Kuala Lumpur (several daily; 3hr); Johor Bahru (2 daily; 2hr 15min); Manila (daily; 3hr) Pulau Labuan (5 daily; 30min); Penang (daily, 3hr); Miri (4 daily; 40min); Sandakan (7 daily; 50min); Sibu (2 daily; 1hr 35min); Sydney (daily; 11hr); Tawau (5 daily; 45min).

# TUNKU ABDUL RAHMAN PARK

Situated within an eight-kilometre radius of downtown KK, the five islands of **TUNKU ABDUL RAHMAN PARK** (TAR Park) represent the most westerly ripples of the undulating Crocker mountain range. The largest of the park's islands is **Pulau Gaya**, where a twenty-kilometre system of trails snakes across the lowland rainforest. Most of these trails start on the southern side of the island at Camp Bay, which also offers pleasant enough swimming, but a more alluring alternative is Police Beach, on the north coast. Boatmen demand extra for circling round to this side of Gaya (RM20 return), but it's money well spent: the dazzling white-sand bay is idyllic. Wildlife on Gaya includes hornbills, wild pigs, lizards, snakes and macaques – which have been known to swim over to nearby **Pulau Sapi**, a ten hectare islet off the northwestern coast of Gaya that's linked with a sandbar at low tide.

### VISITING TUNKU ABDUL RAHMAN PARK

Boats leave KK's ferry terminal at 8am, 9am, 10am, 11am, noon, 2pm and 4.30pm, returning at 7.30am, 9.30am, 10.30am, 11.30am, 3pm and 4pm (RM17 return); each boat calls at all five islands. Chartering a boat to go island-hopping costs RM200. The boatmen can also rent snorkelling gear for RM5 a day.

An entry fee of RM5 is charged on landing at Sapi, Manukan and Mamutik. Expensive resort-style accommodation is available on Manukan and Gaya (from RM400) but it is possible to camp on Gaya, Manukan and Mamutik for RM5. If you don't have your own tent then speak to Sabah Parks at Lot 1–3, Sinsuran Complex, Jl Tun Fuad Stephens (Ⓣ088/211881, Ⓦwww.sabahparks.org.my), for details on renting one, as well as permits required for staying overnight. The resort at Manukan also has the only place to eat on the islands, so make sure you bring ample supplies.

## TRAVELLING ON TO BRUNEI AND SARAWAK

The small island of **Pulau Labuan** is most useful as a transit point between KK and Brunei. **Ferries** to Kota Kinabalu (RM36; 2hr), Limbang (RM20; 2hr 30min), Lawas (RM25; 2hr) and Muara, Brunei (RM27; 2hr) dock at the ferry terminal, below Jalan Merdeka. Plenty of speedboats also run from here to Menumbok (RM10), from where it's a two-hour bus ride to Kota Kinabalu. Tickets can be bought from the Duta Muhibbah Agency (Ⓣ087/413827).

Ferries to Labuan depart from Sipitang (daily 7am; RM20), from where you can also travel overland to Sarawak – take a minibus or taxi from the centre of town (1hr; both RM15). The Lawas Express (RM10) passes through Sipitang (on its way from KK) at around 4pm and gets to Lawas after 5pm; or you can catch a minibus to Sindumin, on the Sabah side of the border, and then connect with a Sarawak bus. Whichever you choose, the driver will wait while you pass through the passport controls flanking the border – one in Sindumin, the other a couple of hundred metres away at Merapok in Sarawak. If you need to stay overnight, try the friendly *Hotel Asanol* (Ⓣ087/821506; ❷). In Labuan, head for the *Pantai View Hotel*, at Jalan Bunga Tanjung (Ⓣ087/411339; ❷).

The park's other islands cluster together 2.5km west of Gaya. Across a narrow channel is tiny **Pulau Mamutik**, which can be crossed on foot in fifteen minutes and has excellent sands on either side of its jetty. **Pulau Sulug** is the most remote of the islands and consequently the quietest.

## THE RAFFLESIA RESERVE

Southeast from Kota Kinabalu, paddy-fields give way to the rolling foothills of the Crocker mountain range. A 58-kilometre ride up to the 1649-metre-high Sinsuron Pass takes you onto the **Rafflesia Reserve** (Mon–Fri 8am–12.30pm & 2–4.30pm, Sat & Sun 8am–5pm; free; Ⓣ011/861499). In the reserve you can see the world's largest flower, the rafflesia: a smelly, parasitic plant whose rubbery, liver-spotted blooms can reach up to one metre in diameter. It was first catalogued in Sumatra in 1818, by Sir Stamford Raffles and the naturalist Dr Joseph Arnold. There's no need to hire one of the guides from the visitor centre, as the park's paths are simple to follow. Someone at the centre should be able to direct you to a plant that's in bloom, though you could phone the visitor centre's hotline before leaving KK as each flower only lasts a few days before dying. To get here, take any Tembunan-bound bus (11 daily from the long-distance bus station in KK; 2hr).

## KINABALU NATIONAL PARK

There's no more astounding sight in Borneo than the cloud-encased summit of **Mount Kinabalu**. Standing at 4101m, Kinabalu's jagged peaks look impossibly daunting from a distance, but the mountain is a relatively easy – if somewhat exhausting – climb. At half the height of Everest, it is plainly visible from Sabah's west coast. The well-defined, 8.7-kilometre path weaves up the mountain's southern side to the bare granite of the summit, where a mile-deep gully known as Low's Gully cleaves the peak in two. The view from the top is awe-inspiring and the blanket of stars which encases you until sunrise will leave you breathless. The aching muscles and creaking joints are well worth the sense of exhilaration you'll achieve at the top.

## STAYING ON THE MOUNTAIN

Accommodation at park headquarters and on the mountain can fill up so it's best to book ahead. Sabah Parks in KK on Wisma Sabah can help with this (Mon–Fri 8am–5pm, Sat 8am–2pm; ☎088/211881). Most people choose to spend their first night at the accommodation in the park headquarters area, either at the basic *Old Fellowship* or *New Fellowship* hostels (❶), or in nearby cabins (❻), or four-person annexe rooms (❼). You can eat at *Kinabalu Balsam* (daily 6am–10pm, Sat until 11pm), near reception, which also has a provisions shop, and at *Liwagu Restaurant* (same hours). Scaling the mountain from here gets you to the basic huts at Gunting Lagadan, Panar Laban or Waras, all of which have electricity and cooking facilities (dorms ❸), or at the more comfortable *Laban Rata Rest House*, which has central heating, hot water and a restaurant (daily 7am–8pm; dorms ❺). *Sayat-Sayat Hut* (❸) is an hour further up the mountain, but has no electricity. The advantage of making it as far as this camp on the first day, however, is that you won't need to get up so early the following morning to reach the summit by sunrise.

## What to see and do

For many, the main attraction of a visit to Sabah is climbing Mount Kinabalu. However, for those not so keen on ascending the 4095m, there are other trails that you can take in the park leading through rich lowland forest to mountain rivers and waterfalls, whilst bringing ample opportunity for bird watching and nature walks. You can also climb the main ascent part way without taking a guide. The park also has its own botanical garden. The park headquarters has details on all the various walks and trails. Poring Hot Springs, whilst a thirty-minute drive away from the main park headquarters, is also part of Kinabalu National Park.

### Climbing Mount Kinabalu

The main climb of Mount Kinabalu takes two days, though rainfall can hamper climbing conditions and make it a tough ascent. There are various **tour operators** in KK who can organize trips to the summit, but it's quite possible to make your own way there and sort out guides and accommodation yourself. Before you leave KK, visit Sabah Parks office on Wisma Sabah (Mon–Fri 8am–5pm, Sat 8am–2pm; ☎088/211881) to book a bed on the mountain for the night of the climb.

Buses stop about 50m from the park reception office (daily 7am–7.30pm), which is the check-in point for accommodation and obtaining guides. On arrival you'll need to pay park entry (RM3 per person), get a climbing permit (RM100 per person), and pay for an obligatory guide (RM92 for up to eight people, RM7 for insurance). It's usually easy to join with others to share the guide fee with at reception. The guides do not try to keep everyone walking at the same pace, so it's fine if you strike out on your own, as long as you stay on the trail.

You should aim to be at the park reception by 11am to make it up to the overnight resthouse before nightfall. The Timpohon Gate at the start of the mountain trail is over an hour's walk, so many people prefer to take the shuttle bus, conserving their energy for what lies ahead (RM10).

Climbing to your first night's accommodation brings you to a height of around 3350m, and takes roughly about five hours, depending on your fitness. The trail is marked out with regular signboards every 500m and there are regular rest-stops with toilets dotted along the way. Two or three hours into the climb, incredible views of the hills, sea and clouds below you start to unfold and the trail changes from lowland forest to dense foliage. After about 5km, the surrounding jungle becomes slightly spartan and there are several large, steep rocks that you need to navigate your way through. The resthouses are located just after 6km at the foot of Panar Laban (see box opposite), from where views of the sun setting over the South China Sea are exquisite. Plan to get up at 2.30am the next morning to join the procession snaking their way to the top for sunrise. Ropes have been strung up to help with the ascent and it can seem a little hairy in places, especially in the dark. Most climbers make it to the summit just before sunrise.

After that, it's back down to Panar Laban for breakfast before the three-hour descent to park headquarters.

### Moving on

**By bus** Several a/c express buses going to Sandakan (4hr) pass park headquarters. There are return buses going back to KK (usually before 3pm), which can be flagged down outside the park entrance. For **Poring Hot Springs** mini-vans leave park headquarters (3 daily; 45min), you can take a taxi for RM38, or you can walk out of the main gate and hail any passing Sandakan-bound bus. They'll drop you off at Ranau (RM5), from where you can take a minibus (RM5) to the springs.

### Poring Hot Springs

The sulphurous waters of **Poring Hot Springs** (daily 7am–6pm; RM5) are situated on the park's southeastern border. It's a place where ailing bones will be grateful of a soak, but if you're expecting a beautiful natural spa location then you'll be disappointed: the springs are man-made and have been designed with purpose rather than luxury or comfort in mind. There are shared open-air baths (open 24hr; admission free), where you simply slip into a tub and just turn on the tap. There are also a couple of "private" baths that are little more than a sunken plastic tub, mostly with broken jacuzzi (RM20 an hour). Although the baths are a disappointment, the park itself is a stunning location and has some lovely walks through natural forest (if you can face more walking). A fifteen-minute trail beyond the baths brings you to Poring's **canopy walk** (daily 6.30am–5.30pm; RM5, with camera RM35), where five tree huts connected by suspended walkways 40m above ground afford you a monkey's-eye view of the surrounding lowland rainforest. A trail strikes off to the right of the baths, reaching 150-metre-high Langanan Waterfall about 90min later. On its way, it passes smaller Kepungit Waterfall, whose icy pool is ideal for swimming. There is also a butterfly reserve in the grounds (RM4), with a garden, nursery and hatchery, which houses some spectacular species.

### Accommodation and eating

No permit is needed to visit Poring, though it's a good idea to book your accommodation beforehand. Sabah Parks office in KK can help (see p.592), as can the park headquarters at Mount Kinabalu. **Camping** is RM6 per person; there are also **dorm beds** (❸) and **rooms** (❼) in the hostels. There's a café at the springs which serves a small selection of Western dishes (RM5 upwards) and two restaurants just outside the gates serving Malay food from RM3.

### Moving on

**By bus** Buses leave from nearby Ranau. The best way to get there is to take a taxi from Poring (RM38).

## SANDAKAN

Sandwiched between sea and cliffs on the northern lip of Sandakan Bay, **SANDAKAN** isn't an appealing city with no particular sights of interest. Most travellers use it as a good base for day-trips to the **Sepilok Orang-utan Rehabilitation Centre**, wildlife-spotting river trips on the Sungai Kinabatangan, **Turtle Islands Park** and the **Gomantong Caves**.

Fifteen minutes' walk west of the dense downtown area along **Jalan Leila** are the blocks of shops that make up Bandar Ramai Ramai, while to the east, running up round the bay, is Jalan Buli Sim-Sim. A fifteen-minute walk east of the town centre, along Jalan Buli Sim-Sim, brings you to Sandakan's modern **mosque**. Beyond this is Kampung Buli Sim-Sim, the water village around which Sandakan expanded in the nineteenth century, its countless photogenic shacks spread like lilies out into the bay. Sandakan's less central addresses are pinpointed according to their distances out of the downtown area – "Mile 1 1/2", "Mile 3" and so on. Mile 4 is a good place to head for night-life, especially karaoke.

## Arrival and information

**By bus** The long-distance bus station is located 4km north out of town.

**By air** The airport (Ⓣ089/273966) serving KK is 11km north of town and connected by minibuses (RM3) and taxis (Rm20) to the southern end of Jl Pelabuhan.

**Tourist information** The tourist information centre, at Wisma Warisan (Ⓣ089/229751), is a mine of information; staff can suggest the best tours and trips to cater to your individual budgets.

**Tours** To visit Turtle Islands Park you'll need to be on an official tour run by Crystal Quest, 12th Floor, Wisma Khoo Siak Chiew (Ⓣ089/212711). This tour company is the only one actually allowed to stay overnight in the park. For trips to the Kinabantangan River, *Uncle Tan's* Wildlife Camp does good-value tours (Ⓣ089/531639, Ⓦwww.uncletan.com) or Sepilok Jungle Resort can also arrange wildlife-spotting trips (Ⓣ089/533031, Ⓦwww.sepilokjungleresort.com).

## Accommodation

**@Ease Boutique** Sandakan Harbour Square Ⓣ089/240888. For those in need of a bit of comfort, this trendy business-style hotel, with king-size beds and plasma TVs, is a good choice. Can offer some cracking discounts. ❻

**MayFair Hotel** 24 Jl Pryer Ⓣ089/219855. The *MayFair* is a unique place to stay and offers some hidden gems behind its stark entrance. Each room has a large TV and DVD player and there's a great stock of films in reception. The seemingly brusque owner has travellers' needs at heart and even offers free umbrellas. ❹

**Sandakan Backpackers** Lot 108, Block SH-11, Sandakan Harbour Square Ⓣ089/221104, Ⓦwww.sandakanbackpackers.com. Located right on the waterfront, it's cheap and clean with bright dorms and good double rooms. Price also includes free breakfast. Dorms ❷; rooms ❹

**Sunset Harbour Botik Hostel** Lot Sandakan Harbour Square Ⓣ089/229875, Ⓔsunset_hostel@yahoo.com. Another good backpackers' place based on the waterfront, with a good kitchen for self-catering. Dorms ❷; rooms ❹

## Eating

For hawker stalls, the market on Jl Pryer is fantastic.

**@Ease Café** Sandakan Harbour Square. Located right on the waterfront underneath the *@Ease Boutique*, this trendy café has a good selection of sandwiches, noodle dishes and Western food from RM3. A good place to go to kick back and relax.

**The English Tea House and Restaurant** Jl Istana. Set up high on a hill overlooking the town, this lovely English teahouse is a good place for jam and scones in a serene garden setting. Also has a great wine list if you're in need of more than cake. 10.30am – midnight.

**Hawaii Restaurant** On the corner of Lebuh Tiga, just underneath the *City View Hotel*. Does a mix of Malay and Western dishes, and Tiger beer. Also serves great breakfasts. Dishes from RM2.

**Restoran Zakira III** Jl Tiga. A popular Indian restaurant, serving great *roti canai* (RM2) and caters well for vegetarians.

**Subway Café** Lot 1, Block 8. Not the American Subway sandwich chain, this place is located at Mile 4 and a lively place for some dinner washed down with cold Tiger beers. Malay dishes from RM4.

## Directory

**Airlines** Air Asia, Terminal Building, Sandakan Airport Ⓣ03/8775 4000; MAS, Sabah Building, Jl Pelabuhan Ⓣ089/273966.

**Bank** HSBC at the junction of Lebuh Tiga and Jl Pelabuhan.

**Hospital** Duchess of Kent Hospital, Jl Utara, Mile 2 (Ⓣ089/219460).

**Immigration** Wisma Persekutuan (Ⓣ089/668328).

**Internet** Point Cyber Café, Centre Pont, Jl Pelabuhan (RM4/hr); Internet Cyber Café, Wisma Sandakan (RM3/hr).

**Police station** Lebuh Empat (Ⓣ089/211222).

**Post office** Five minutes' walk west of town, on Jl Leila (Mon–Fri 8am–4.30pm, Sat 10am–1pm).

### Moving on

**By bus** There are long-distance buses to and from KK (frequently 6.30–10am then 2pm & 8pm; 6hr), Ranau (3 daily; 4hr); Semporana (daily at 8am; 5hr 30min); Tawau (daily; 5hr 30min).
Sandakan's local bus station is situated on the waterfront at Jl Pryer. A short walk west along Jl Pryer brings you to the minibus area.
**By long-distance taxi** Long-distance taxis operate from the area around the bus station.
**By air** to: Kota Kinabalu (7 daily; 1hr 45min); Kuala Lumpur (4 daily; 3hr 30min); Kudat (3 weekly, 50min); Tawau (daily; 40min).

## SEPILOK ORANG-UTAN REHABILITATION CENTRE

One of only three orang-utan sanctuaries in the world, the **Sepilok Orang-utan Rehabilitation Centre** (daily 9–11am & 2–3.30pm; feeding times 10am & 3pm; RM30; ⓣ089/531180), 25km west of Sandakan, is home to semi-wild orang-utans who have been orphaned or rescued from captivity. They generally roam around the surrounding forest, but know exactly when feeding time is and have their body clocks well tuned to those free bananas. At the feeding platform you'll see them dancing along the ropes, fighting with the long-tail macaques to get their fill of fruit and bamboo sticks.

The boardwalk winds through the forest to feeding Station A, and you'll usually hear them swinging in the branches overhead. The cheeky macaques on the trail will grab at anything that catches their eye, so keep a careful hold on your belongings. There are a number of pleasant walks throughout the park; ask at reception for details of the trails and timings.

### Arrival

**By bus** To get to Sepilok from Sandakan take blue bus "Sepilok Batu 14" from the local bus stand on the waterfront (hourly 7.30am–4.30pm; 30min). Mini-vans also go every hour or so from the stop just up from the bus station. All stop just outside the park entrance.

### Accommodation

**Labuk B&B** Jl Rambutan-Sepilok ⓣ089/533190, ⓦwww.sepilok@sepilokforestedge.com. Just 500m away from the rehab centre, *Forest Edge* offers both dorms and private chalets. Also organizes trips up the Kinabantangan. Dorms ❷; rooms ❼
**Sepilok B&B** ⓣ089/532288. Another excellent option, situated 1km before the Centre's entrance. Offers basic accommodation but in a great jungle location. Dorms ❷; rooms ❹
**Sepilok Jungle Resort** Jl Labuk ⓣ089/532288, ⓦwww.sepilokjungleresort.com. Great location just five minutes' walk from the orang-utan centre. Set in the jungle in a lovely lakeside location. Also organizes tours to Kinabatangan. Dorms ❷; rooms ❹–❻
**Uncle Tan's** Mile 16, Jl Gum Gum ⓣ089/531639, ⓦwww.uncletan.com. This excellent guesthouse is around 28km west of Sandakan and quite near the Orang-utan Centre (coming from KK by bus, ask to be dropped outside *Uncle Tan's*, it's about a 30min ride). The guesthouse is actually in Gum Gum village at Mile 16 Labuk Rd. The price for a bed in a room includes three good meals. The guesthouse also arranges wildlife-spotting trips to its jungle camp on Sungai Kinabatangan (see p.601). Dorms ❷

### Moving on

**By bus** To get from Sepilok to Sandakan, the "Sepilok Batu 14" bus will take you back to the waterfront in town (hourly 7.30am–4.30pm; 30min). If you're moving on to other parts of Sabah, the long-distance bus station is en-route back to Sandakan, so ask the driver to drop you there. Mini-vans returning back into town can also be picked up at the park entrance.
**By taxi** Most of the accommodation lodges can arrange taxis. The journey will take 20min and should cost RM30.

## TURTLE ISLANDS NATIONAL PARK

Peeping out of the Sulu Sea some 40km north of Sandakan, three tiny islands comprise Sabah's **TURTLE ISLANDS NATIONAL PARK**, the favoured egg-laying sites of the green and hawksbill turtles, varying numbers of which haul themselves laboriously above the high-tide mark to bury their clutches of eggs. All three of the park's islands (Pulau Selingaan, Pulau Bakkungan Kechil and Pulau Gulisaan) have a hatchery – though only Selingaan has amenities for tourists.

Turtles visit the park every day of the year, but the peak nesting time falls between July and October. They begin to come ashore around 7.30pm, then dig a nesting pit and lay upwards of a hundred eggs. With hatchings a nightly event, you're almost guaranteed the stirring sight of scores of determined little turtles wriggling up through the sand. Note that flash photography of the turtles is prohibited though, as the turtles are confused by the light. In the meantime, Selingaan's quiet beaches are good for swimming and sunbathing, or you can go snorkelling off nearby Bakkungan Kechil (RM15 per person, minimum four people; details from park headquarters).

The only way to **stay overnight** on Selingaan is to come on a tour with Crystal Quest (see p.598), which will cost RM220. Sabah Parks allows no more than twenty visitors a night, all of whom are put up in the island's four comfortable chalets. *Uncle Tan's* and the *Travellers' Rest Hostel* visit Selingaan during the day and then take you to other islands, which are not in the park, for the night. *Rose's Café* inside the visitor centre provides meals for the limited number of people in the evening and for extra visitors during the day.

## GOMANTONG CAVES

Further afield, the **Gomantong Caves**, south of Sandakan Bay, are inspiring enough at any time of the year, though you'll get most out of the trip when the edible nests of their resident swiftlets are being harvested (Feb–April & July–Sept). Bird's-nest soup has long been a Chinese culinary speciality and Chinese merchants have been coming to Borneo to trade for birds' nests for at least twelve centuries. Of the two major caves, **Simud Hitam** is the easiest to visit: follow the trail from behind the staff quarters to the right of the reception building, taking a right fork after five minutes, and continue for a further ten minutes. Simud Hitam supports a colony of black-nest swiftlets, whose nests – a mixture of saliva and feathers – sell for US$40 a kilogram. Above Simud Hitam, the larger but less accessible **Simud Putih** is home to the white-nest swiftlet, whose nests are of pure, dried saliva and can fetch prices of over US$500 a kilograme. To reach Simud Putih, take the left fork, five minutes along the trail behind reception, and start climbing. The easiest way to visit is with a tour agency (from RM80 per person from *Uncle Tan's*). Be sure to bring a torch.

## SEMPORNA

The Bajau fishing town of **SEMPORNA**, 108km east of Tawau, is the departure point for diving trips to Pulau Sipadan. The only feature of note in Semporna itself is the huge water village stretching southwards along the coast from the centre, which incorporates mosques, shops and hundreds of dwellings.

### Arrival and information

**By bus** Mini-vans all arrive near the Shell petrol station. Most of the tourist hotels are a quick cab ride away from here, or a thirty-minute walk.

**Tours** Borneo Divers, Sipadan Dive Centre and Borneo Sea Adventures all have offices at the Semporna Ocean Tourism Centre (SOTC) on the waterfront causeway. *Scuba Junkie*, at 36 Semporna Seafront (Ⓦ www.scuba-junkie.com) doubles up as a backpackers' hostel and dive outfit, and comes highly recommended.

### Accommodation

**Dragon Inn Hotel** Jl Custom Ⓣ 089/781088. The *Dragon Inn Hotel* consists of wooden huts which extend into the sea. Dorms ❷; doubles ❹–❾

## SUNGAI KINABATANGAN

The Kinabatangan River area is dubbed as one of the best places to see **wildlife** in Sabah. Though pygmy elephants and rhinos are rare, you're quite likely to spot wild orang-utans, proboscis monkeys, gibbons, macaques, wild boar, huge water monitors and crocodiles in the forest flanking the river. The resident bird life – hornbills, Brahming kites, crested serpent eagles, egrets, stork-billed kingfishers and oriental darters – is equally impressive.

The best way to appreciate the river is to stay in one of the several jungle camps or lodges on its banks, which can be arranged as a tour in Sepilok. Recommended camps are:

**Sepilok Jungle Resort** (see p.599). Arranges accommodation and tours (RM299 two days/one night). Includes all food and early morning and evening river cruise.

**Uncle Tan's** (see p.599) Also runs great tours. Their accommodation in Sepilok can arrange the tour and charges RM145 and RM150 respectively for the car and riverboat ride to camp, plus two safari boat trips a day. Meals and accommodation are an extra RM15 a day.

**Scuba Junkie** 36 Semporna Seafront ⓣ089/785372. A great, lively hostel completely set up for backpackers. Has a bar downstairs, does great pizza and often has barbecues. Dorms ❷

**Seafest Hotel** Jl Kastam ⓣ089/782333. Although pricier than the other options in town, this traditional business hotel has good-sized rooms, excellent showers and big squashy beds. ❻–❼

### Eating

There are numerous **hawker stalls** dotted along the waterfront serving fresh seafood dishes. From RM3.

**Pearl City Restaurant** Dragon Inn, 1 Jl Custom. The floating restaurant has enviable views over the water and it's possible to sit and watch the fish swim below you. Serves a range of tasty seafood and Malay noodle dishes from RM10. The freshly caught crab comes highly recommended.

### Directory

**Banks** Maybank, Block 1 Lot No 7 (out towards the Shell petrol station where mini-vans arrive in town).

**Internet** *Scuba Junkie* has internet access.

### Moving on

**By bus** Mini-vans all depart from the Shell petrol station whenever they are full.

**Destinations:** Tawau (1hr 30min); Lahad Datu (3hr); Sandakan (2hr).

## PULAU SIPADAN

The waters around tiny **Pulau Sipadan**, 30km south of Semporna in the Celebes Sea, literally teem with giant hawksbill turtles, white-tip sharks, barracuda, vast schools of tropical fish, and a huge diversity of coral; unsurprisingly, Sipadan is listed as one of the top dive sites in the world. Twenty metres from the shore, the bottom plunges to over six hundred feet, delving to a vast wall of coral. Divers will find themselves face to face with large schools of jacks, batfish, parrotfish, and grey- and white-tipped reef sharks. This surrounds nearly ninety percent of the island and the ledges are a common resting point for turtles. **Barracuda Point** is a popular site on the dive circuit and is so called for the myriad of chevron barracuda that lurk in the waters.

Since 2005 it has not been possible to stay on Pulau Sipadan. The damage caused by the large numbers of tourists as well as dynamite-fishing has placed the fragile environment under some strain, and it is now a fully protected conservation zone. Numbers are limited to 120 visitors per day, and the dive operators are responsible for sorting out who gets to go and when. If it's not possible to dive Sipadan on that particular day, there is impressive

**DIVING IN SEMPORNA**

There are various dive options that you can do from Semporna, varying in price and quality. Some involve staying in Semporna going diving as a day-trip, others involve living aboard at sea. A couple of options are:

**Scuba Junkie** 36 Semporna Seafront ⓣ089/785372 ⓦwww.scuba-junkie.com. Not only do *Scuba Junkie* offer backpacker accommodation but they also offer the best-value diving day-trips over to Sipadan and the surrounding islands of Mabul and Kapalai. Three fun dives start at RM250, leaving Semporna at 8am. Two morning dives are followed by a relaxing lunch on the beach. The third and final dive of the day takes place after lunch bringing you back to Semporna by 4:30pm.

**Seaventure** 4th Floor, Room 422–24 Wisma Sabah, Kota Kinabalu, ⓣ088/261 669 or 251669 ⓦwww.seaventuresdive.com. Seaventures diving platform is a live-aboard converted oil rig which sits in the ocean just off the northern shore from Mabul Island. Dive packages start from US$570 for four days, three nights including eight dives to Sipadan and all surrounding islands, as well as all equipment, accommodation in private a/c rooms and as much food as you can eat.

**Kapalai Island Resort** Block C, Ground Floor, Lot 38 & 39, Mile 6, Sandakan ⓣ089/673999 / 674999 / 675999 ⓦwwwsipadan-kapalai.com. For the ultimate luxurious experience, *Kapalai Island Resort* is a romantic paradise. The nearest thing you'll get to the Maldives in Borneo, the resort consists of a number of chalets standing on wooden stilts on a powdery white sand-bar with nothing but ocean, sea-turtles and myriad fish surrounding you for miles. The chalets are a/c luxury with verandas that extend into the sea and bath tubs where you can watch fish below. Dive packages start from $610 for three nights/two days including three boat dives, unlimited dives from the resort where you just plop off the end of the pier, and full-board accommodation.

diving on the surrounding neighbouring islands of Mabul and Kapalai.

Snorkellers accompanying divers to the island can expect to see reef sharks, lion fish, barracudas and scores of turtles, without having to leave the surface.

## TAWAU

**TAWAU**, Sabah's southernmost town of any size, is a major departure point for Indonesian Kalimantan. There's not a great deal to see or do here, though the market beside *Soon Yee* hotel is worthy of a browse if you happen to be there before noon.

### Arrival and information

**By bus** Long-distance buses terminate at Sabindu bus station on the eastern end of Jl Dunlop (which runs parallel to the shore). The local bus and minibus station, serving the airport, is on Jl Stephen Tan (west and one block inland of Sabindu).

**By air** The new airport (ⓣ089/775819) is 28km outside of town and can be reached by minibus (45min; RM10) or taxi (RM38).

### Accommodation

**Sanctuary Hotel** Jl Chester ⓣ089/751155. Offers less than spritely service but it's a good place to lay your head, and rooms are clean as well as affordable. ❸

**Soon Yee** Jl Stephen Tan ⓣ089/772447. This friendly hotel has fan or a/c rooms; most have shared bathrooms. ❷–❸

### Eating

**Hawker stalls** Two blocks below Jl Dunlop in the Sabindo Complex, the two-hundred-metre stretch of open-air restaurants and stalls collectively known as Taman Selera sets up daily.

**Restoran Rasa Sayang** Jl Haji Karim. Good Chinese diner which offers the usual staples and dishes with jumbo prawns from RM5.

**Zayaha** Sabindo Square. Delicious range of curries (from RM3) in this Indian restaurant; a great choice for vegetarians.

## INTO INDONESIA

**Tawau** is the main stepping-stone for onward travel to Kalimantan. **Ferries** to Indonesia depart from the customs wharf, 150m south of Jalan Dunlop's Shell station. There are four departures a day – at 7am and noon for the Indonesian islands of Tarakan (RM85) and 2pm and 4pm for Nunukan (RM35). There is no service on Sundays. Check at Sasaran (☎089/772441) and Perkhidmatan Pelayaran Bumiputra (☎019/8415618) ticket booths north of the jetty by the fish market (Pasar Ikan) on Jalan Pelabuhan. Nunukan is an hour from Tawau, after which it's a further two hours to Tarakan. There are also **flights** on MAS from Tawau to Tarakan in Indonesia. For these crossings Indonesian visas must be obtained before heading into Kalimantan. The Indonesian consulate in KK can help (☎088/218600).



## Directory

**Airlines** Air Asia, Jl Bunga; MAS, Ground and First Floor, TB 319 Block 38, Jl Hj Sahabudin, Fajar Complex.
**Bank** Maybank, 262–264 Fajar Complex, Jl Mahkamah; HSBC, Jl Perbandaran.
**Consulate** Indonesia, Jl Tanjong Batu ☎089/752669.
**Hospital** ☎089/773533.
**Internet** Cyber Café, Kompleks Fajar, Jl Perbandaran (RM2/hr).
**Police station** Jl Dunlop and at the airport.
**Post office** Jl Utara (Mon–Fri 8am–4.30pm, Sat 10am–1pm).

## Moving on

**By bus** There's a bus to Sandakan (6hr) and KK (12hr) at around 7am and another at 6pm. Buses depart from in front of the public library on Jl Chen Fook. Mini-vans depart from Sabindo Square.
**Destinations:** Semporna (2hr); Lahad Datu (3hr); Sandakan (5hr 30min).
**By long-distance taxi** Landcruisers to Keningau leave from the Sabindu bus station whenever they have enough passengers to fill them.
**By air** to: Kota Kinabalu (2 daily; 50min); Kuala Lumpur (3 daily; 3hr 15min); Sandakan (2 daily, 40min).

# The Philippines

## HIGHLIGHTS

**THE CORDILLERAS:** home to ancient hanging coffins at Sagada and Banaue's famous rice terraces

**PARTYING IN MANILA:** for a flambuoyant night on the town, head to Malate, with its fashionable clubs and cafés

**BORACAY:** first stop for most sun-worshippers is the famous White Beach

**BACUIT ARCHIPELAGO:** explore the stunning seascapes and jagged limestone islands

**MALAPASCUA ISLAND:** dive among thresher sharks and relax on the blindingly white beaches of this tiny island

## ROUGH COSTS

**DAILY BUDGET** Basic $20/ Occasional treat $30

**DRINK** San Miguel beer $0.70

**FOOD** Adobo $2.50

**HOSTEL/BUDGET HOTEL** $15

**TRAVEL** Bus: Banaue to Baguio (7hr) $8.50; Ferry: Cebu to Tagbilaran (4hr) $8; Flight: Manila to Puerto Princesa (1hr 15min) $48.

## FACT FILE

**POPULATION** 91 million

**AREA** 300,076 sq km

**LANGUAGE** Filipino/ English

**RELIGION** Majority Roman Catholic

**CURRENCY** Piso (Peso)

**CAPITAL** Manila

**INTERNATIONAL PHONE CODE** ⓣ+63

**TIME ZONE** GMT+8hr

# Introduction

**Travellers on the traditional Asian trails have tended to ignore the Philippines because it often involves an extra flight, albeit a short one, across the South China Sea. Perversely, it is this very lack of mass tourism that makes the Philippines such an attractive destination. If you are ready to cope with some eccentric infrastructure and a distinctly laid-back attitude towards the passage of time, the Philippines has plenty to offer. It is the second-largest archipelago in the world (after Indonesia), with 7107 islands – sixty percent of them uninhabited – and 58,390km of coastline, all in a land mass no bigger than Arizona.**

Most international flights land in the capital, **Manila**, which though dilapidated and traffic-choked, also has some of the ritziest shopping malls and most spectacular nightlife in Asia. For beach connoisseurs, the central **Visayan region** is an island-hopper's paradise. Though Boracay remains the most popular island destination, travellers are discovering quiet islands around Cebu and Bohol; if you're willing to leave the beaten track, it's not hard to find your own deserted tropical beach. **Palawan** is an unforgettable wilderness of diamond-blue lagoons, volcanic lakes and first-rate scuba diving, while in the **Cordillera Mountains** of northern Luzon live tribes whose way of life has barely changed since they first settled here around 500 BC.

Centuries of **colonial rule** have resulted in a delightfully schizophrenic country of potent but conflicting influences. Spain brought Catholicism, European architecture and the *mañana* ethic, while America gave the Philippines both its constitution and its passion for basketball, beauty pageants and pizza. In 1946 the Philippines became Asia's first real democracy, a fact most Filipinos remain fiercely proud of.

Despite the political intrigues and the poverty, Filipinos themselves remain enviably optimistic and gregarious.

## WHEN TO GO

The Philippines has a tropical marine climate characterized by two distinct seasons: the **wet season** (southwest monsoon, or *habagat*) from May to October and the **dry season** (northeast monsoon, or *amihan*) from November to April. During the wet season, the country is hit directly by five or six typhoons. This doesn't necessarily mean the wet season is a bad time to travel, though flights are sometimes cancelled and roads are made impassable by floodwaters, even in the capital – but this only lasts a few days. The first typhoon can hit as early as May, although typically it is June or July before the rains really start, with August the wettest month. The southern Visayas and Palawan are less prone to typhoons.

**Temperatures** are fairly constant throughout the year. November and December are coolest, with daytime highs of around 28°C. March, April and May are very hot: expect temperatures to peak at 36°C.

At **Christmas** and **Easter**, the whole of the Philippines hits the road and getting a seat on a bus or plane can be difficult.

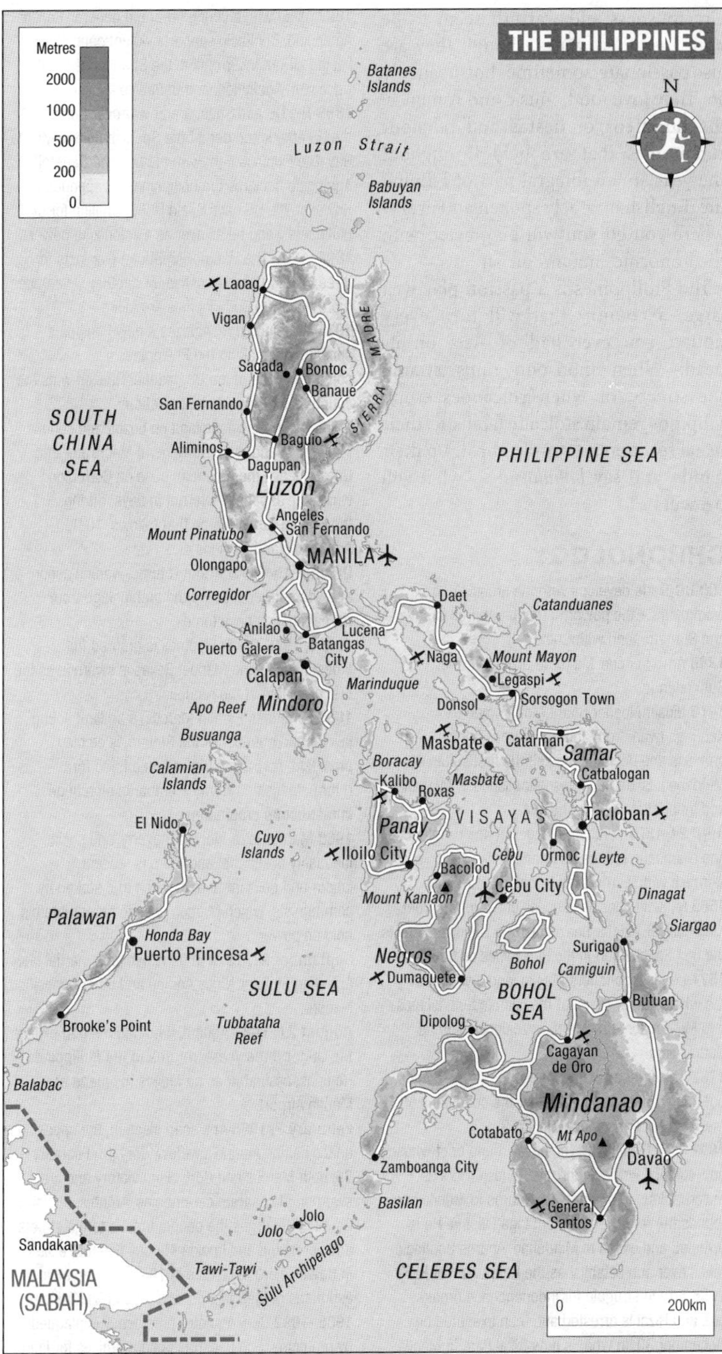


THE PHILIPPINES INTRODUCTION

Graciousness and warmth seem to be built into their genes, though they are also passionate, sometimes hot-headedly so. They love food, music and romance; the hundreds of **fiestas** and religious ceremonies that are held throughout the year are an integral part of Filipino life. English is widely spoken and everywhere you go you will be greeted with the honorific "ma'am" or "sir".

The Philippines is a passion play writ large, a country that will turn every notion you ever had of Asia on its head. When monsoon rains swamp the streets, or when volcanoes erupt, Filipinos remain stoically fatalistic, their usual reaction is to smile, throw up their hands, and say *bahala-na* – "what will be, will be".

## CHRONOLOGY

**500 BC** Trade develops with the archipelago's neighbours – the powerful Hindu empires in Java and Sumatra, and with China.

**1380** Arab scholar Makdam arrives in the Sulu Islands.

**1475** Muslim leader Sharif Mohammed Kabungsuwan, from Johore, marries a local princess and declares himself the first sultan of Mindanao. Islam becomes established in Mindanao, and influential as far as Luzon.

**April 24, 1521** Ferdinand Magellan arrives in Cebu and claims the islands for Spain. He is killed in a skirmish with warriors led by chief Lapu-Lapu.

**1565** Miguel Lopez de Legaspi, under orders from King Philip II, establishes a colony in Bohol and erects the first Spanish fort in the Philippines on Cebu.

**1571** Legaspi conquers Manila, and a year later the whole country, except the Islamic Sulu Islands and Mindanao. Spanish friars zealously spread Catholicism.

**1762** The British occupy Manila for a few months, but hand it back to Spain under the conditions of the Treaty of Paris, signed in 1763.

**1892** Jose Rizal, a lawyer, novelist and poet whose anti-colonial writings portray Spanish friars as unscrupulous and depraved, returns to Manila and founds the reform movement Liga Filipina. He is arrested and exiled to Mindanao. Andres Bonifacio takes over and establishes the Katipunan, or KKK.

**1896** Armed struggle for independence breaks out, and Rizal is arrested and then executed on December 30, in what is now Rizal Park in Manila.

**1897** Allied with a young firebrand general, Emilio Aguinaldo, Bonifacio supports violent opposition. Facing all-out insurrection, the Spanish negotiate a truce with Aguinaldo, and Bonifacio is executed.

**1898** The US and Spain are at war over Cuba, and the US attack and defeat the Spanish fleet in Manila Bay. The Filipinos fight with the US, and General Aguinaldo declares the Philippines independent. However, the US pays Spain US$20 million for the Philippines, and takes over as a colonizing power.

**1898–1902** The Filipino–American War lasts for three years (with skirmishes for another seven), and more than 600,000 Filipinos are killed.

**1935** Washington recognizes a new Philippine constitution, making the Philippines a commonwealth of the US. Manuel Quezon wins the country's first presidential elections.

**1942** Japanese troops land on Luzon and conquer Manila on January 2. US General MacArthur and Quezon leave the American base on Corregidor, which the Japanese overrun in days; during the Bataan Death March that follows, 10,000 Americans and Filipinos die.

**October 1944** MacArthur returns, wading ashore at Leyte and recapturing the archipelago from retreating Japanese forces.

**July 4, 1946** The Philippines is granted full independence and Manuel Roxas is sworn in as the first president of the republic.

**1965** Ferdinand Edralin Marcos, a brilliant young lawyer and member of the Senate, is elected president, portraying himself as a force for reform. In his first term he embarks on a huge infrastructure programme.

**1969** Marcos is re-elected. Poverty, and social inequality is still rife, and there is student, labour and peasant unrest, much of it stoked by communists, which Marcos uses to perpetuate his hold on power.

**September 21, 1972** Marcos declares martial law, arresting Senator Ninoy Aquino and other opposition leaders.

**August 21, 1983** Aquino, who had been in exile in the US for three years, returns to the Philippines. He is assassinated as he leaves his plane at Manila Airport.

**February 7, 1986** At a snap election, the opposition unites behind Aquino's widow, Cory. On February 25, both Marcos and Cory claim victory and are sworn in at separate ceremonies. Archbishop Jaime Cardinal Sin urges the people to take to the streets and Ferdinand and Imelda Marcos flee into exile in Hawaii; Ferdinand dies in 1989. Conservative estimates of their plunder are around $10 billion.

**1986–1992** Cory Aquino's presidency is plagued by problems. She backtracks on promises for land reforms, survives seven coup attempts and makes little headway in tackling the widespread poverty.

**July 1, 1992** Fidel Ramos is elected president.

**1998** Former vice-president Joseph Estrada (universally known as Erap), a popular former tough-guy film actor, becomes president.

**2000** Estrada is accused of receiving P500 million in illegal gambling payoffs. He is impeached, but the trial falls apart. Following protests of half a million people, the military withdraws its support and Estrada is evicted from Malacañang.

**January 20, 2001** Vice-president Gloria Macapagal-Arroyo is sworn in as president.

**2004** Macapagal-Arroyo wins the presidential elections against Fernando Poe Jr, a movie star and friend of Estrada. Poe's supporters claim election fraud.

**November 2007** An attempted coup in Manila is put down. It is similar to one in 2003, and around a dozen others in the past twenty years. Though it lacked popular support, the country is still plagued by endemic corruption, and extra-judicial killings remain high on the list of the human rights abuses allegedly sanctioned by the current administration.

# Basics

## ARRIVAL

Most major Southeast Asian airlines have regular **flights** to Ninoy Aquino International Airport in Manila, with a few also flying to Cebu City and the international airport in Davao. **From Europe** most major European airlines have flights to Manila, though many of them require a stop-over. **Hong Kong** is one of the most convenient gateways to the Philippines; there are also regular flights from many major Asian cities, including Bangkok, Tokyo, Seoul, Shanghai, Beijing, Taipei, Singapore and Kuala Lumpur. Flying via the Middle East is also a good option, with Qatar Airways flying via Doha, Gulf Air via Bahrain and Emirates via Dubai. **From the US**, there are regular Philippine Airlines, Northwest, Continental and American Airlines flights to Manila.

**By ferry** from Malaysia, Weesam Express offers a twice-weekly service between Sandakan, Sabah, and Zamboanga, Mindanao (13hr). There are also a number of smaller, unlicensed boats that ply this route, though check the current situation in Mindanao before considering this (see box, p.682).

## VISAS

Most tourists do not need a visa to enter the Philippines for up to **21 days**, though you need a passport valid for at least six months and an onward ticket to another country. You can apply for longer visas in advance from a Philippine embassy or consulate. A single-entry visa, valid for **three months** from the date of issue, costs around $48, and a multiple-entry visa, valid for **one year** from the date of issue, around $130. Apart from a valid passport and a completed application form (downloadable from some Philippine embassy websites, see below) you will have to present proof that you have enough money for the duration of your stay in the Philippines.

Without a visa in advance, the 21-day stay you're granted on arrival can be extended by 38 days (giving a total stay of 59 days) at immigration offices in major cities and some key tourist destinations, or through many travel agents. The extension fee is P2200, which includes a P500 Express Lane fee, guaranteeing you get your visa within 24 hours (otherwise expect it to take at least one week, possibly longer). A subsequent extension of **three or four months** is possible at the immigration office in Manila or Cebu City. There's nothing to stop you from applying for additional extensions, though once you've stayed more than six months the bureaucracy becomes complicated. See ⓦhttp://immigration.gov.ph for information on visa requirements.

### AIRPORT DEPARTURE TAX

For international flights, Philippine airport **departure tax** is P550. There is a P200 departure tax at the domestic airport in Manila and for domestic flights leaving from Philippine Airlines' NAIA Centennial Terminal Two. Many provincial domestic airports have a nominal departure tax or "terminal fee", usually P10–50.

## GETTING AROUND

The number of **flights** and **ferry services** between major destinations makes it easy to cover the archipelago, even when you're on a budget. One essential however, is a flexible itinerary. Local road transport is mostly limited to **buses** and **jeepneys,** although in cities such as Manila and Cebu City it's still relatively cheap to get around by taxi.

### Planes

Air travel is a godsend for island-hoppers, with a number of airlines both large and small linking Manila to most of the country's major destinations. However, while getting from Manila or Cebu to almost any island is straightforward, it can be difficult to fly between islands, meaning some backtracking is hard to avoid. Philippine Airlines, Air Philippines and Cebu Pacific have the most comprehensive schedules. Asian Spirit and Southeast Asian Airlines (SEAIR) are excellent small airlines offering regular flights to major resort areas and also to interesting destinations often not served by larger airlines. There is little difference in price between these five, and **airfares** in the Philippines are generally inexpensive, especially if you book more than three days in advance: one way to Cebu from Manila shouldn't cost more than $50, Cebu to Puerto Princesa is $40, and from Manila to Caticlan (for Boracay) will set you back about $46.

Cebu Pacific in particular runs frequent promotions, selling flights for as little as one peso, though, needless to say once the taxes are added it's considerably pricier.

### THE BIG FIVE – RESERVATION NUMBERS

Not all routes appear on the websites, it's worth phoning to check.

**Air Philippines** ⓣ02/855 4626, ⓦwww.airphils.com
**Asian Spirit** ⓣ02/855 3333, ⓦwww.asianspirit.com
**Cebu Pacific** ⓣ02/702 0888, ⓦwww.cebupacificair.com
**Philippine Airlines** (PAL) ⓣ02/855 8888, ⓦwww.philippineairlines.com
**SEAIR** ⓣ 02/849 0100, ⓦwww.flyseair.com

### Buses

For Filipinos, the journey is as much a part of the experience as the destination. Nowhere is this truer than on the **buses**. Dilapidated contraptions with no air-conditioning compete with bigger bus lines with all mod cons on hundreds of routes that span out from Manila. Fares are cheap, but journeys can be long. Manila to Baguio, for instance, costs P350 on an air-conditioned bus, but takes anything up to nine hours. You might want to make this type of trip overnight, when traffic is lighter and delays less likely. The longest of long bus trips is Philtranco's Manila to Davao service. It leaves the Pasay City terminal every day at 6pm and snakes ponderously through the Bicol region, Samar, Leyte and eastern Mindanao, arriving in Davao two days later. A one-way ticket costs P2600. For longer trips, advance booking is recommended.

### Ferries

**Boats** are the bread and butter of Philippine travel, with wooden outrigger boats – known as bancas – and luxury ferries ready to take you from one destination to the next in varying degrees of comfort and safety. Remember that even in the dry season, the open ocean can get rough, so think carefully about using small boats that look ill-equipped or overcrowded. Ferry disasters are not unknown, often with great loss of life. Major lines include **Supercat**, **Superferry** and **Negros Navigation**, which have daily sailings throughout the country, but even these have not been accident-free. On less popular routes you might have to take your chances with smaller lines. Ferries are cheap but often crowded, although on overnight journeys you can always keep away from the dormitory crowds by sleeping on the deck, or paying extra for a cabin. For an idea of **fares**: from Manila Superferry charges P1100 to Cagayan de Oro, Negros Navigation charges P2200 to Puerta Princesa, and to get to Dumaguete with Sulpicio will set you back P1960. Without meals, it's about ten percent cheaper, but some of the journeys last two or three days, depending on stops, so you'll have to pack a lot of food.

## Local transport

The stalwart of the transport system is the fabled **jeepney**, a legacy of World War II, when American soldiers left behind army jeeps; these were converted by ingenious locals into factotum vehicles, carrying everything from produce to livestock and people. Over the years, they evolved into today's colourful workhorses of the road, with their fairy lights, boomboxes and cheesy decor. Provincial jeepneys charge as little as P2.50 a ride, while in Manila, prices range from P7.50 for a short hop to P20 for longer distances. Jeepneys ply particular routes, indicated on the side of the vehicle, and stop anywhere, so simply flag one down and hop on. When you want to get off, bang on the roof or shout "para!"

In some cities, Cebu City in particular, old jeepneys are now being replaced with modern Isuzu vans, although they are still decorated in the same ostentatious manner. In Manila, the popular alternative is a **Toyota FX Tamaraw**, or "FXs", cheaper than taxis and more comfortable than jeepneys or buses. The fare is set by the driver – usually P10 for a short trip and anything up to P100 on longer routes.

**Tricycles** are the Filipino equivalent of the Thai tuk-tuk, and while they are not allowed on major roads they can be useful for getting from a bus station to a beach and back again. Most tricycles carry three passengers, and fares tend to increase dramatically when a tourist approaches, so always reach agreement beforehand. Fares are lower, often as little as a few pesos per person, if you are willing to share the tricycle with anyone else who flags it down and can fit on board. To hire the tricycle exclusively for yourself – or for a small group of you – P50 is a reasonable fare for a ten-minute journey.

## Taxis

By international standards, **taxis** in the Philippines are dirt-cheap, making them a viable option for getting around on a daily basis. In larger cities, the flag-down rate is P30 and P2.50 per 200m. Before you get in make sure the driver will use his meter or that you have negotiated a reasonable fare. Never use a taxi if the driver has companions and never use one that isn't clearly marked as a taxi. All taxi registration plates have black letters on a yellow background. Private cars and vans have white letters on a green background, so it's easy to tell the difference. You stand more chance of getting a taxi if you use them at off-peak times. Few taxi drivers will jump at the chance to take you to the airport at five o'clock on a Friday afternoon in a monsoon downpour, so you'll need to be flexible and allow yourself time.

### Vehicle rental

It's easy and relatively cheap to **rent a self-drive car** in the Philippines. The question is whether or not you would want to. Most Filipino drivers seem to have a very relaxed attitude towards the rules of the road. Swerving is common, as is changing lanes suddenly and driving with one hand permanently on the horn, particularly for bus and jeepney drivers. The demands of time and traffic make many drivers belligerent and aggressive, so if you do rent a car you'll require nerve and patience. If you need to get somewhere quickly and have money to spare, you can always hire a **car with a driver** for about P2000 a day, depending on distance (plus a tip for the driver if he gets you there in one piece). Major car rental firms are listed in the *Yellow Pages* under "Automobile Renting and Leasing". They include Avis (ⓦwww.avis.com.ph, ⓣ02/531 2097), Budget (ⓦwww.budget.com.ph, ⓣ02/831 8256) and Filcar (ⓦwww.filcartransport.com, ⓣ02/894 1754). Self-driven cars start from P2200 a day. Hiring a small van for day-trips is also possible for groups. A van big enough for around eight people will cost about P4000 a day.

## ACCOMMODATION

There is **accommodation** for all budgets in the Philippines, from swanky private resorts where Hollywood stars chill out, to humble huts on a stretch of deserted beach. On the outlying islands you can find nipa huts, made from indigenous palms, ranging in price from P400 for a simple room with a shower to P1500 for something a bit more refined with a/c.

In the poorer areas of the country there is no running **water**. Even in the rich enclaves of Manila you'll find that water can be a problem. The water authorities pump water only twice a day into residential areas – many households save it in a purpose-built tank with a small electric pump attached so they can use it when they need it. Households without tanks often keep water in a large plastic dustbin and shower by scooping it over their heads with a plastic scoop known as a *tabo*. In the provinces, this is the normal way to bathe.

**Electricity** is usually supplied at 220 volts, although you may come across 110 volts. Plugs are two pins, with the pins flat and rectangular, as opposed to round. Power cuts ("brownouts") are common, especially in the more rural areas.

## FOOD AND DRINK

The high esteem in which Filipinos hold their **food** is encapsulated by the common greeting "Let's eat!". Filipino cuisine has not been accepted worldwide as Indian and Thai food have, perhaps because it has an unwarranted reputation for being one of Asia's less adventurous cuisines, offering a relatively bland meat and rice diet

### ADDRESSES

It's common in the Philippines for buildings to give an **address** as 122 Legaspi cor. Velasco streets. This means the place you are looking for is at the junction of Legaspi Street and Velasco Street. Streets are sometimes renamed in honour of new heroes or because old heroes have been discredited or boundaries moved. Pasay Road in Makati is now Arnaiz Avenue, but confusingly everyone still calls it Pasay Road. The ground floor of multi-storey buildings is referred to as the first floor and the first floor as the second. Buildings do not have a 13th floor; it is considered unlucky.

with little variety or spice. But those willing to experiment will find even the most simple rural dishes can offer an intriguing blend of the familiar and the exotic. Food is something of a comfort blanket for Filipinos and to be without it is cause for panic. Any Filipino who eats only three meals a day is usually considered unwell because that's simply not considered enough. A healthy appetite is seen as a sign of a robust constitution and sundry smaller meals and snacks – **merienda** – are eaten in between every meal. Not to partake when offered can be considered rude.

Meat dishes, notably of chicken and pork (both cheap and easily available), form the bulk of the Filipino diet. The **national dish**, if there is one, is *adobo*, which is chicken or pork (or both) cooked in soy sauce and vinegar, with pepper and garlic. *Baboy* (pig) is the basis of many coveted dishes such as *pata* (pig's knuckle) and *sisig* (fried chopped pork, liver and onions). At special celebrations, Filipinos are passionate about their *lechon*, roasted pig stuffed with *pandan* (screwpine) leaves and cooked so the skin turns to crackling. *Lechon de leche* is roasted suckling pig. Pork is also the basis of *Bicol Express* (the most well known of the very few spicy local dishes), consisting of pork ribs cooked in coconut milk, soy sauce and vinegar, with hot chillies (a vegetable version is also available). Coconut, soy sauce, vinegar and *patis* (a brown fish sauce, more watery than *bagoong*, a smelly, salty fish paste) are widely used to add flavour. Colonization and migration have resulted in touches of Malay, Chinese, Spanish and American culinary influence, sometimes all within the same meal.

The **beer** of choice in the Philippines is San Miguel, but with meals many Filipinos tend to stick to soft drinks such as iced tea. Fresh *buko* (coconut) or *calamansi* (lime) juice are refreshing alternatives on a hot day. There are also plenty of cheap Philippine-made spirits such as Tanduay rum and San Miguel *ginebra* (gin). For something authentically native, try the strong and pungent *tapuy* (rice wine). *Lambanog* is another potent spirit, made by gathering sap from coconut trees and fermenting it with fruit in a hole in the ground.

### BALUT

Sold at roadside stalls all over the country, **balut** are boiled duck embryos in the shell, a popular type of *merienda*, and reputed aphrodisiac. The preferred method of eating them is to crack open the top and drink the "soup" (embryonic fluid) before devouring the foetus and its eggy surrounds. Depending on the egg's maturity you might get the added crunch of beak and feet, or the tickle of baby feathers as it goes down your throat. Sampling *balut* will practically make you an honorary Pinoy but whether the admiration of the locals is enough of an incentive, is up to you.

## CULTURE AND ETIQUETTE

Filipinos tend to be outgoing people who are not afraid to ask **personal questions** and certainly don't consider it rude; prepare to be interrogated by everyone you meet. They will want to know where you are from, why you are in the Philippines, how old you are, whether you are married – if not, why not – and so on and so forth. They pride themselves on their hospitality and are always ready to share a meal or a few drinks. Don't offend them by refusing outright.

A sense of *delicadeza* is also important to Filipinos. This is what you might refer to as propriety, a simple sense of good behaviour, particularly in the presence of elders or women. Filipinos who don't speak good English will often answer any question you ask them with a smile and a nod. Be careful: a smile and a nod doesn't always mean "yes". It can also mean "no", "maybe" or "I have no idea what you are talking about". It's not advisable to **lose your temper** – Filipinos hate to be embarrassed in front of others and so don't respond well to being shouted at. The general rule is to behave in a manner conducive to what the locals refer to as "SID", or smooth interpersonal relationships.

Colonization by America left its mark on the national psyche, so don't be offended if everyone in the provinces thinks you are a *kano*. Protestations that you are from Britain, France or Australia will often be greeted with the response, "Is that in America?"

Filipinos share the same attitudes to **dress** as other Southeast Asian countries (see p.45).

## SPORTS AND OUTDOOR ACTIVITIES

### Scuba diving

Of the three and a half million tourists who visit the Philippines every year, many come for the scuba diving alone. It's hardly surprising that in a nation made up of 7107 islands there are dive sites all over the place, with the exception perhaps of the far north. Two hours from Manila by road, you can dive on the reefs of **Anilao** in the province of Batangas (see p.643). An hour from Batangas City by ferry is the hugely popular area around **Puerto Galera**, home to many dive schools and fine beaches (see p.643). The **Visayas** has dive sites in Boracay, Apo Island (near Dumaguete), Cebu and Bohol. A one-hour flight or twelve-hour ferry journey from the capital takes you to the "last frontier" of **Palawan**, where you can dive at World War II Japanese wrecks in the company of dolphins and manta rays (see p.680). **Tubbataha Reef** in the Sulu Sea offers some of the best diving in the world, but the only way you can reach it is by live-aboard from Puerto Princesa (see p.678). In short, you can slip into a wet suit just about anywhere.

The Professional Association of Dive Instructors, better known as **PADI**, organizes most scuba tuition in the Philippines. Always pick a PADI dive centre and ask to see their certification. If you haven't been diving before, you can start with a "Discovery Dive" to see if you like it. The full PADI Open Water Diver course takes around four days and costs around US$350. You might want to consider doing a referral course with PADI at home, which involves doing the pool sessions and written tests before you travel, then doing the final checkout dives with a PADI resort in the Philippines. You'll need to bring your PADI referral documents with you, as your instructor in the Philippines will want to see them.

### Trekking

**Trekking** is becoming popular among the urban middle class with a number of clubs organizing regular trips up famous peaks such as Mount Apo, Mount Pulag (see p.694) and Mount Mayon (see p.648). The **Mountaineering Federation of the Philippines** (Ⓦwww.mfpi.org) is an umbrella organization of the country's major mountaineering clubs, who all run regular trips and may be willing to take you along. Before attempting a volcano climb, trekkers should visit the website of the Philippine Institute of Volcanology and Seismology (Ⓦwww.phivolcs.dost.gov.ph).

## COMMUNICATIONS

**Letters** from the Philippines take at least five days to reach other countries by air, sometimes significantly longer. If you have to post anything valuable, use registered mail or pay the extra for a reliable courier. Letters sent in the general post are sometimes rifled and the contents stolen. Major post offices in Manila have a counter for **poste restante**. The country's **telephone** system has made great advances, although outside urban centres it can still be temperamental. Public **payphones** are not common outside big cities; the best place to find them is in malls and hotel lobbies. PLDT cards, known as **Fonkards**, are available in P100, P200, P300 and P500 denominations and can be bought from hotels or convenience stores such as 7/11. When you can find an internet café with headsets, mainly in the larger towns, Skype (ⓦwww.skype.com) is a cheap and convenient way to call home.

The Philippines has embraced the **mobile phone** age like no one else, with over 40 million texts sent daily. Mobile networks provide coverage in areas where landlines are limited, and using them costs next to nothing. A cheaper alternative to using your own service is buying a local SIM card (you'll need to make sure that your phone is unlocked before you travel), available at dozens of mobile-phone outlets in malls for any of the country's three mobile networks: Smart, Globe and Sun Cellular. You can then buy prepaid cards, which come in units of P300 and P500, called "loads", to make calls. Everywhere you go in the Philippines you'll see signs outside sari-sari shops proclaiming "*Load na dito*", meaning credit bundles are sold there. Basic mobile phones in the Philippines are inexpensive, and widely available. Many places listed in the guide only have mobile phone contact numbers, and as such are more likely to change.

**Internet cafés** are all over Manila, Cebu and the provincial cities (about P20–60 an hour). In rural areas internet access is not as readily available.

## CRIME AND SAFETY

The Philippines is a **safe** place to travel as long as you exercise discretion and common sense. There are a number of insurgent groups in the country fighting for causes that range from an independent Muslim homeland in Mindanao to communist rule, and there have been isolated cases of tourists being kidnapped in the west and far southwest areas of Mindanao and the Sulu archipelago, sometimes with tragic consequences. For updates on the situation, you can check foreign ministry, state department and embassy websites.

You'll find the same **con artists** and hustlers here that you'll find anywhere else, but most Filipinos are friendly and helpful. One of the most common scams is for foreigners to be approached by well-dressed young men or women who offer to buy you a coffee or a beer. The next day you wake up from a deep drug-induced sleep to find you have been relieved of your personal belongings. Another scam is to approach you on the street and offer alluring exchange rates for foreign currency before short-changing you and disappearing. Snatching mobile telephones – often while the owner is making a call – has become a problem, so try to make calls in safe places such as shops and restaurants, not on the street. A number of Western men have also fallen into the so-called "honey-trap", finding themselves charged with serious crimes such as rape by local "girlfriends". Needless to say, the charges are quickly dropped once a substantial amount of money is handed over, but not before the victim has languished for a while in some grim local jail.

### THE PHILIPPINES ON THE NET

ⓦ**www.visitmyphilippines.com** The Department of Tourism's website with links to regional sites.
ⓦ**www.wowphilippines.co.uk** Useful tourist information.
ⓦ**www.divephil.com** Everything you need to know before you dive.
ⓦ**www.clickthecity.com** Excellent listings website, and the best source of information on bus schedules.

**Police** in the Philippines are not Asia's finest. Successive governments have made some headway in cleaning up the force, but it is still plagued by accusations of corruption, collusion and an alleged willingness to shoot first and ask questions later. Part of the problem is the low pay police officers receive, making some of them – a tiny minority, according to senior officers – willing to supplement their income with payoffs from anyone from the humblest motorist to the most notorious drug king.

## MEDICAL CARE AND EMERGENCIES

There are pharmacies everywhere in the Philippines, so if you have a minor ailment and need to buy medicine over the counter, finding one should not be a problem. The biggest chain is Mercury, which has branches all over the place, but even the smallest village tends to have some sort of store where you can buy the basics.

In Manila and other major tourist centres, **hospitals** are reasonably well equipped and staffed by English-speaking doctors. Hotels and resorts sometimes have their own doctor on duty, or can at least point you in the direction of a local clinic. In case of serious illness you will need to be evacuated, either to Manila or your home country, so make sure you have arranged health insurance before you leave home. Remember that if you are hospitalized in the Philippines, you won't be allowed to leave the hospital until the bill is settled.

### EMERGENCY NUMBERS

The 24-hour number for **emergency services** (police, fire and ambulance) throughout the Philippines is ⓣ166, but it doesn't always work in the provinces, where ambulances and fire stations are few and far between. Even in Manila the emergency services are not known for their efficiency. In Manila, a ⓣ117 hotline is open for all emergencies, staffed 24 hours a day. Other emergency numbers include police and fire (ⓣ757) and 24-hour tourist police (ⓣ116).

## INFORMATION AND MAPS

The Philippine **Department of Tourism** (DoT) has a small number of overseas offices, where you can pick up glossy brochures and get answers to general pre-trip questions about destinations, major hotels and domestic travel. These offices aren't so helpful, however, when it comes to information about off-the-beaten-track places. It's not their fault: there simply isn't much information about less well-known destinations in the first place. The DoT has offices throughout the Philippines, but most of them have small budgets, poorly trained staff and very little in the way of reliable information or brochures. The best sources of up-to-date information are often guesthouses and hotels that cater to backpackers, many of which have notice boards where travellers can swap tips and ideas. At the DoT Head Office in Manila (ⓣ02/524 1703 or 524 2384; 24hr), room 106 of the Department of Tourism Building, TM Kalaw Street, Ermita (on the eastern edge of Rizal Park), you can claim your free copy of the *Tourist Map of the Philippines*. This useful folding map also includes a street map of Manila, contact numbers for all overseas and domestic DoT offices, and listings of hotels, embassies and bus companies. A range of maps called E-Z Map, covering Manila and other destinations, such as Boracay, Baguio, Batangas, Palawan and Angeles are sold in many bookshops and hotels. Road maps and country maps can be bought at National Book Store branches throughout Manila and in most provincial cities.

## MONEY AND BANKS

The Philippine **currency** is the piso (P), although it is almost always spelt "**peso**". It is divided into 100 centavos, with bills in denominations of P20, P50, P100, P200, P500 and P1000, though the last is uncommon. Coins come in 25 centavos, P1, P5, P10 and P20. The P20 notes are being phased out and replaced by coins. Most banks will not change sterling, euros or anything other than **US dollars** or **dollar traveller's cheques**, although at private moneychangers in tourist areas you should be able to change major foreign currencies. If you're likely to be going in any way off the beaten track, you should bring a ready supply of cash, and keep small denominations of pesos handy for transport and tips. Breaking anything larger than a P100 note can be tricky anywhere other than large businesses. At the time of writing the **exchange rate** had settled at around P42 to US$1 and P84 to £1.

Visa, MasterCard and, to a lesser extent, American Express are widely accepted throughout Manila and other major cities, and also in popular tourist destinations such as Boracay. You can withdraw cash from 24-hour **ATMs** (in the Visa, Plus, MasterCard and Cirrus networks) in all cities and even many smaller towns. Most banks will advance cash against cards (generally Visa and MasterCard) for a commission. If you use credit cards to pay for airline tickets and hotels, there is sometimes an extra charge of around 2.5 percent. Some shops impose a credit card supplement of six percent, so always check first.

## OPENING HOURS AND PUBLIC HOLIDAYS

Most **government offices** are open Monday to Friday 8.30am–5.30pm. Businesses generally keep the same hours, with some also open for half a day on Saturday from 9am until noon. **Post offices** in major cities are open Monday to Friday 8.30am to 5.30pm. Off the beaten track, the hours are less regular. **Banks** open Monday to Friday 9am to 3pm, while **shops** in major shopping centres are generally open 10am to 8pm, seven days a week. Restaurants and cafés are generally open from early morning until 11pm, seven days a week. Those in malls tend to open later and close earlier, in accordance with mall hours.

### Public holidays

**January 1** New Year's Day
**February 25** Anniversary of the overthrow of Marcos
**April 9** Bataan Day
**Maundy Thursday**
**Good Friday**
**May 1** Labour Day
**June 12** Independence Day
**November 1** All Saints' Day
**November 30** Bonifacio Day
**Mid-December** (moveable) Aidilfitri, end of Ramadan
**December 25** Christmas Day
**December 26**
**December 30** Rizal Day

## FESTIVALS

It's at the fiestas that you get a chance to see legendary Filipino hospitality at its best. The beer flows, pigs are roasted and there's dancing in the streets for days on end. More solemn fiestas, usually religious in nature, are a mixture of devotion, drama, passion and reaffirmation of faith.

**Feast of the Black Nazarene** (Jan 9) Quiapo, Manila. Devotees gather in the plaza outside Quiapo Church to touch a miraculous image of Christ.

**Sinulog** (Third Sun in Jan) Cebu City. The second city's biggest annual event, in honour of its patron saint, Santo Niño. Huge street parade, live music and plenty of food and drink.

**Ati-Atihan** (Third week of Jan) Kalibo, Aklan province. Street dancing and wild costumes at arguably the biggest festival in the country, held to celebrate an ancient land pact between settlers and indigenous Atis.

**Dinagyang** (Fourth week of Jan) Iloilo City, Panay Island. Relatively modern festival based on the Ati-Atihan and including a parade on the Iloilo River.

**Baguio Flower Festival** (Third week in Feb) Baguio. The summer capital's largest annual event

## TAGALOG

There are more than 150 languages and dialects in the Philippines. Tagalog, also known as Filipino or Pilipino, is spoken as a first language by 17 million people – mostly on Luzon, and also in some parts of the Visayas – and is the national language. Many English words have been adopted by Filipinos, giving rise to a slang known affectionately as Taglish. Why ask someone to take a photograph when you can ask them to do some "kodaking"?

### Stresses

Tagalog sounds staccato to the foreign ear, with clipped vowels and consonants. It has no tones, and most words are spoken as they are written, though working out which syllable to **stress** is tricky. In words of two syllables, the first syllable tends to be stressed, while in words of three or more syllables the stress is almost always on the final or penultimate syllable; thus Boracay is pronounced Bo-**ra**-kay or sometimes Bo-ra-**kay**, but never **Bo**-ra-kay. Sometimes a change in the stress can drastically alter the meaning. Vowels that fall consecutively in a word are always pronounced individually, as is every syllable; for example, *tao* meaning person or people is pronounced ta-o, while *oo* for yes is pronounced o-o (with each vowel closer to the "o" in "show" than in "bore").

### Pronunciation

| | |
|---|---|
| **a** | as in "apple" |
| **e** | as in "mess" |
| **i** | as in "ditto", though a little more elongated |
| **o** | as in "bore" |
| **u** | as in "put" |
| **ay** | as in "buy" |
| **aw** | in "mount" |
| **iw** | is the sound **ee** continued into the **u** sound of "put" |
| **oy** | as in "noise" |
| **uw** | as in "quarter" |
| **uy** | produced making the sound **oo** and continuing it to the **i** sound in "ditto" |
| **c** | as in "skin" |
| **g** | as in "get" |
| **k** | as in "skin" (unaspirated) |
| **mga** | is pronounced as "mang" |
| **ng** | as in singing |
| **p** | as in "speak" (unaspirated) |
| **t** | as in "stop" (unaspirated) |

### Greetings and basic phrases

| | |
|---|---|
| Hello/how are you? | *Kamusta* (There's no word for hello in Filipino. People usually use Kamusta, which means "how are you?") |
| Fine, thanks | *Mabuti, salamat* |
| Goodbye | *Bye* |
| Good evening | *Magandang gabi* |
| Excuse me | *Iskyus* (to get past) |
| Please | Use the word *paki* before a verb. For example, *upo* means sit, so "please sit" is *paki-upo* |
| Thank you | *Salamat* |
| Yes | *oo* |
| No | *hindi* |
| Stop | *Para* (for a jeepney). Shout this and/or bang on the roof with a coin to let the driver know you wish to get off) |

### Food and drink glossary

| | |
|---|---|
| *Vegetarian ako* or *gulay lang ang kinakain ko* (literally, "I only eat vegetables") | I'm vegetarian |

**Main dishes**

| | |
|---|---|
| *Adobo* | Chicken and/or pork simmered in soy sauce and vinegar, with pepper and garlic |
| *Beef tapa* | Beef marinated in vinegar, sugar and |

| | |
|---|---|
| | garlic, then dried in the sun and fried |
| *Bicol Express* | Fiery dish of pork ribs cooked in coconut milk, soy sauce, vinegar, *bagoong* and hot chillies |
| *Bistek tagalog* | Beef tenderloin with *calamansi* and onion |
| *Daing na bangus* | *Bangus* (milkfish) marinated in vinegar and spices, and fried |
| *Diniguan* | Pork cubes simmered in pig's blood, with garlic, onion and laurel leaves |
| *Lechon (de leche)* | Roast whole (suckling) pig, dipped in a liver-paste sauce |
| *Longganisa/ longganiza* | Small beef or pork sausages, with lots of garlic |
| *Longsilog* | *Longganisa* with garlic rice and fried egg |
| *Pinakbet* | Vegetable stew with *bagoong*, cooked in broth, often with small pieces of meat |
| *Sisig* | Fried chopped pork, liver and onions |
| *Tapsilog* | Beef *tapa* with garlic rice and fried egg |
| *Tocino* | Marinated fried pork |
| *Tosilog* | Marinated fried pork with garlic rice and fried egg |

**Snacks (merienda) and street food**

| | |
|---|---|
| *Adidas* | Chicken's feet; named after the sports-shoe manufacturer, served on a stick with a choice of sauces for dipping |
| *Arroz caldo* | Rice porridge with chicken |
| *Balut* | Raw, half-formed duck embryo |
| *Chicheron* | Fried pork skin, served with a vinegar dip |
| *Pancit* | Noodles |
| *Dilis* | Dried anchovies, dipped in vinegar as a bar snack, or added to vegetable stews |
| *kanin* | Rice (cooked) |
| *Tokneneng* | Hard-boiled *balut* covered in orange dough and deep-fried |

**Fruit (fruitas)**

| | |
|---|---|
| *Buko* | Coconut |
| *Calamansi* | Lime |
| *Lanzones* | Outside, the size and colour of a small potato; inside, sweet, translucent flesh with a bitter seed |
| *Mangga* | Mango (available in sweet and sour varieties) |
| *Saging* | Banana |

**Desserts**

| | |
|---|---|
| *Bibingka* | Cake made of ground rice, sugar and coconut milk, baked in a clay stove and served hot with fresh, salted duck's eggs on top |
| *Halo-halo* | Sweet concoction made from ice cream, crushed ice, jelly, beans or sweetcorn and tinned milk; the name literally means "mix-mix" |
| *Leche flan* | Caramel custard |

**Drinks (inumin)**

| | |
|---|---|
| *Buko juice* | Coconut water |
| *Calamansi juice/soda* | lime juice either cold or hot |
| *Chocolate-eh* | Thick hot chocolate |
| *Ginebra* | Gin |
| *Rum* | Rum; the cheap, popular Tanduay is now almost synonymous with rum |
| *Tapuy* | Rice wine |
| *Tubig* | Water |

includes parades of floats beautifully decorated with flowers from the Cordillera region. There are also flower-related lectures and exhibitions.

**Pasayaw Festival** (Third week of March) Canlaon, Negros. Thanksgiving festival to God and St Joseph, with twelve barangays competing for honours in an outdoor dancing competition. The final "dance-off" is held in the city gym.

**Flores de Mayo** (Throughout May) Countrywide. Religious procession celebrating the coming of the rains, with girls dressed as the various "Accolades of our Lady", including Faith, Hope and Charity. Processions are sometimes held after dark and lit by candles, a lovely sight.

**Carabao Carroza** (May 3–4) Iloilo City, Panay Island. Races held to celebrate the humble *carabao* (water buffalo), beast of burden for many a provincial farmer.

**Ibalong** (Third week of Oct) Legaspi City and throughout the Bicol region. Epic dances and street presentations portraying Bicol's mythical superheroes and gods.

**Lanzones festival** (Third week of Oct) Lambajao, Camiguin. Vibrant and good-natured outdoor party giving thanks for the island's lanzone crop.

**Masskara** (Third week of Oct) Bacolod, Negros Occidental. Modern festival conceived in 1980 to promote the city. Festivities kick off with food fairs, mask-making contests, brass-band competitions, beauty and talent pageants, a windsurfing regatta and so forth. The climax is a Mardi Gras-style parade, where revellers don elaborate masks and costumes and dance to Latin rhythms Rio de Janeiro-style.

# Manila

The capital of the Philippines, an ever-expanding sprawl of six individual cities, eighteen municipalities and fourteen million people, **MANILA** offers an introduction to the country akin to a baptism by fire. A conurbation plagued by the twin evils of traffic and pollution, Manila is also deeply mired in a political atmosphere so inherently corrupt that the infrastructure needed to transform it into a serious destination remains but a twinkle in the eyes of the tourist authorities. Most travellers are in the capital because they have a day or two to kill at the beginning or end of a trip to the rest of the country, but once you've acclimatized to the chaos, you'll discover that Manila has a certain shambolic charm. Boasting some of the world's friendliest people, nightlife unequalled in Asia, cavernous shopping malls and a few historical sights that are worth battling it out with the sea of jeepneys to visit, the raw energy of the capital may just overcome those first impressions of a clamorous, unkempt and vaguely threatening megalopolis. Plunge into the fray and go with the flow as Manileños themselves have learned to do, and you may find that though its days as the "Pearl of the Orient" are long gone, Manila is still something of a rough diamond.

## What to see and do

Manila's reputation as a forbidding city for visitors stems partly from its size and apparent disorder. The relentless growth of the conurbation has not been helped by unchecked urban development and an influx of *provincianos* looking for work, most of whom live in shanties on the periphery, continually encroaching on rainforest and paddy-field. To see the major sights you'll have to sweat it out in heavy traffic and be prepared for delays, but at least the main attractions are close to one another, grouped mostly along the crescent sweep of Manila Bay and Roxas Boulevard, taking in the neighbourhoods of **Ermita** and **Malate**, where budget visitors usually base themselves. From here it's a relatively short hop to **Rizal Park** and the old town of **Intramuros**. Beyond **Chinatown** (Binondo), the gargantuan **Chinese Cemetery** is morbidly interesting, while the rather sterile business districts of **Makati** and **Ortigas** are best known for their malls and restaurants, though pockets of the former retain vestiges of its historic red-light status. By day Makati is the **Central Business District** (CBD), built around the main thoroughfare of Ayala Avenue. A short taxi ride north of Makati is the shopping area of **Rockwell**, built on the site of an old power plant. Beyond it, north through the heaving traffic on Epifano de los Santos Avenue (commonly referred to as **EDSA**), is the commercial district of **Ortigas**, which is trying to out-Makati Makati with its hotels, malls and themed restaurants. Beyond Ortigas is **Quezon City**, which is off the map for most visitors but has some lively nightlife catering to the nearby University of the Philippines.

### Intramuros

**Intramuros**, the old Spanish capital of Manila, is the one part of the metropolis where you get a real sense of history. It was built in 1571 and remains a monumental, if ruined, relic of the Spanish occupation, separated from the rest of Manila by its crumbling walls. It featured well-planned streets, plazas, the Governor's Palace, fifteen churches and six monasteries as well as dozens of cannon that were used to keep the natives in their place. Many buildings were destroyed in World War II, but Intramuros still lays claim to most of Manila's top tourist sights. **Manila Cathedral** (daily 9am–7pm; free), built

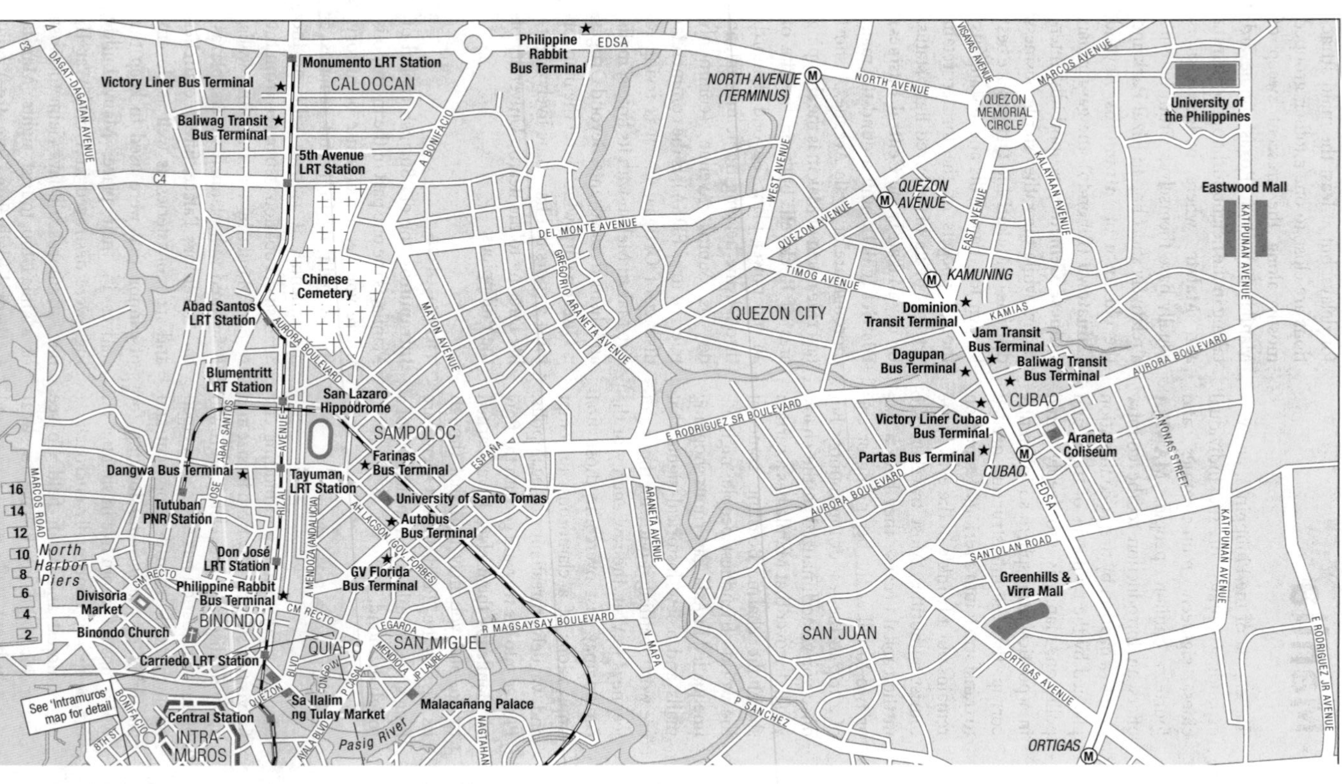
Monumento LRT Station
Victory Liner Bus Terminal
CALOOCAN
Baliwag Transit Bus Terminal
5th Avenue LRT Station
Philippine Rabbit Bus Terminal
EDSA
NORTH AVENUE (TERMINUS)
NORTH AVENUE
QUEZON MEMORIAL CIRCLE
MARCOS AVENUE
VISAYAS AVENUE
University of the Philippines
Eastwood Mall
KATIPUNAN AVENUE
DAGAT-DAGATAN AVENUE
C3
C4
A BONIFACIO
WEST AVENUE
QUEZON AVENUE
KALAYAAN AVENUE
EAST AVENUE
DEL MONTE AVENUE
Chinese Cemetery
GREGORIO ARANETA AVENUE
TIMOG AVENUE
KAMUNING
Dominion Transit Terminal
KAMIAS
Abad Santos LRT Station
AURORA BOULEVARD
MAYON AVENUE
QUEZON CITY
Jam Transit Bus Terminal
Dagupan Bus Terminal
Baliwag Transit Bus Terminal
Blumentritt LRT Station
San Lazaro Hippodrome
CUBAO
E RODRIGUEZ SR BOULEVARD
Victory Liner Cubao Bus Terminal
SAMPOLOC
Araneta Coliseum
Farinas Bus Terminal
ESPAÑA
Partas Bus Terminal
ANONAS STREET
Dangwa Bus Terminal
ABAD SANTOS
Tayuman LRT Station
RIZAL AVENUE
University of Santo Tomas
ARANETA AVENUE
MARCOS ROAD
JOSE
Tutuban PNR Station
AH LACSON (GOV FORBES)
Autobus Bus Terminal
North Harbor Piers
16
14
12
10
8
6
4
2
Don José LRT Station
A MENDOZA (ANDALUCIA)
GV Florida Bus Terminal
SANTOLAN ROAD
Greenhills & Virra Mall
CM RECTO
Divisoria Market
Philippine Rabbit Bus Terminal
BINONDO
Binondo Church
LEGARDA
R MAGSAYSAY BOULEVARD
V MAPA
SAN JUAN
QUIAPO
SAN MIGUEL
MENDIOLA
Carriedo LRT Station
JP LAUREL
QUEZON BLVD
P CASAL
ONGPIN
ORTIGAS AVENUE
See 'Intramuros' map for detail
BONIFACIO
Sa Ilalim ng Tulay Market
Malacañang Palace
Central Station
8TH ST
AYALA BLVD
NAGTAHAN
P SANCHEZ
Pasig River
INTRA-MUROS
ORTIGAS
E RODRIGUEZ JR AVENUE

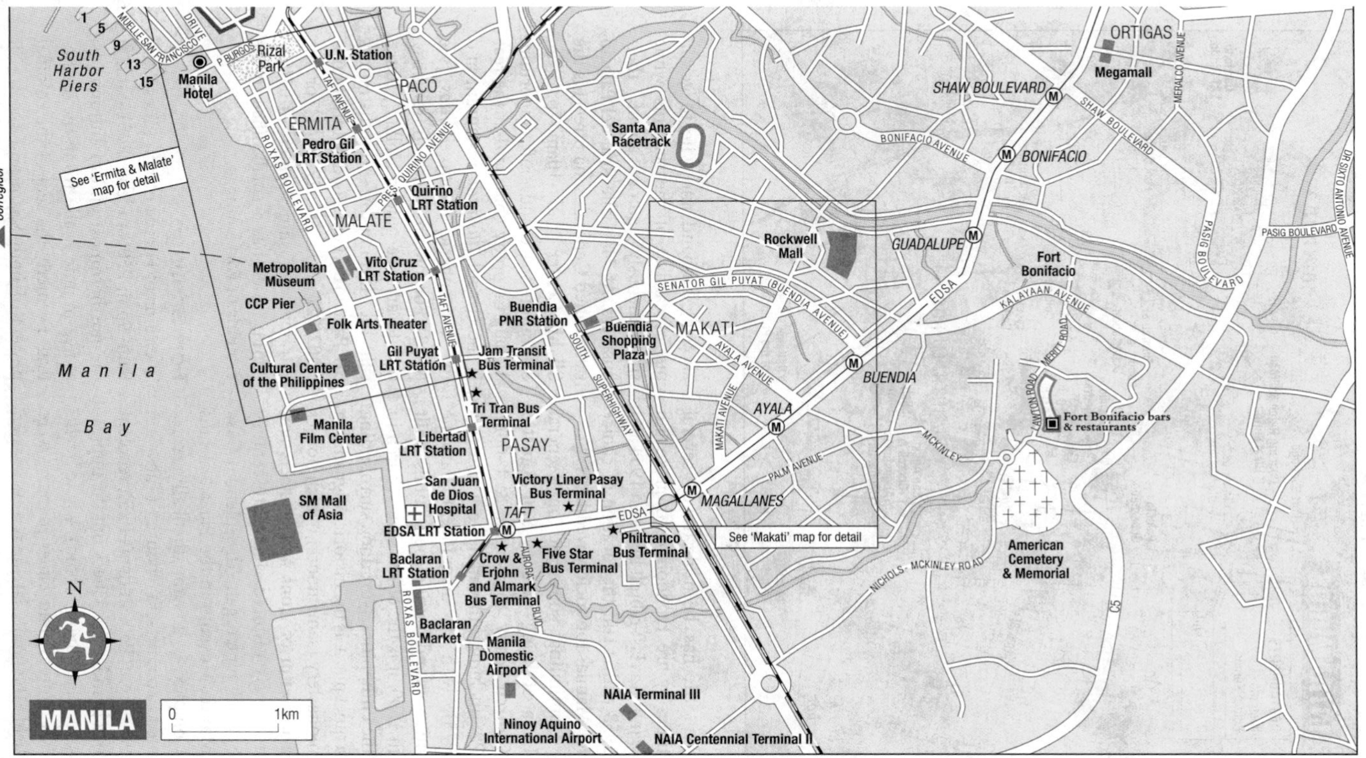
MANILA
0
1km
N
South Harbor Piers
1
5
9
13
15
MUELLE SAN FRANCISCO
DRIVE
Manila Hotel
P BURGOS
Rizal Park
U.N. Station
PACO
ERMITA
TAFT AVENUE
Pedro Gil LRT Station
See 'Ermita & Malate' map for detail
Corregidor
PRES QUIRINO AVENUE
Quirino LRT Station
MALATE
ROXAS BOULEVARD
Metropolitan Museum
Vito Cruz LRT Station
CCP Pier
Folk Arts Theater
Cultural Center of the Philippines
Gil Puyat LRT Station
Jam Transit Bus Terminal
Tri Tran Bus Terminal
Manila Bay
Manila Film Center
Libertad LRT Station
PASAY
San Juan de Dios Hospital
SM Mall of Asia
EDSA LRT Station
TAFT
Victory Liner Pasay Bus Terminal
EDSA
Philtranco Bus Terminal
Baclaran LRT Station
Crow & Erjohn and Almark Bus Terminal
Five Star Bus Terminal
AURORA BLVD
Baclaran Market
Manila Domestic Airport
NAIA Terminal III
Ninoy Aquino International Airport
NAIA Centennial Terminal II
Buendia PNR Station
Buendia Shopping Plaza
SOUTH SUPERHIGHWAY
Santa Ana Racetrack
MAKATI
SENATOR GIL PUYAT (BUENDIA AVENUE)
AYALA AVENUE
MAKATI AVENUE
PALM AVENUE
AYALA
BUENDIA
MAGALLANES
See 'Makati' map for detail
Rockwell Mall
GUADALUPE
EDSA
Fort Bonifacio
KALAYAAN AVENUE
LAWTON ROAD
MERITT ROAD
Fort Bonifacio bars & restaurants
MCKINLEY
American Cemetery & Memorial
NICHOLS - MCKINLEY ROAD
C5
BONIFACIO AVENUE
BONIFACIO
SHAW BOULEVARD
SHAW BOULEVARD
ORTIGAS
Megamall
MERALCO AVENUE
PASIG BOULEVARD
PASIG BOULEVARD
DR SIXTO ANTONIO AVENUE

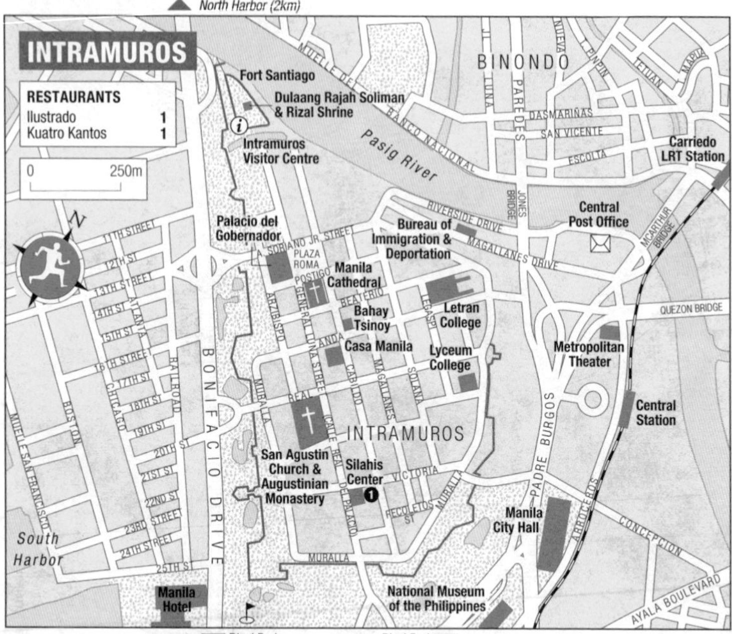


in 1581, has been destroyed several times by fire, typhoon, earthquake and war. It was last rebuilt between 1954 and 1958 and is still the location of choice for Manila's top society weddings.

Continuing southeast on General Luna St brings you to **San Agustin Church** (daily 8am–noon & 1–6pm; P85 including the monastery, students P75), with its magnificent Baroque interiors and trompe-l'oeil murals. Built in 1599, it is the oldest stone church in the Philippines. Next door, surrounding a quiet plaza, is the historic Augustinian monastery (same hours), which houses a **museum** of icons and artefacts and a lovingly restored eighteenth-century Spanish pipe organ. The splendid **Casa Manila Museum** in the Plaza San Luis Complex is a sympathetically recreated colonial-era house (Tues–Sun 9am–6pm; P50, students P25), redolent of a grander age. Check out the impressive *sala* (living room) where *tertulias* (soirees) and *bailes* (dances) were held. The family latrine is a two-seater, allowing husband and wife to gossip out of earshot of the servants while simultaneously going about their business. At 744 Calle Real del Palacio (also called General Luna Street) is the **Silahis Center** (daily 10am–7pm), an exhibition space and craft emporium. Through a pretty courtyard at the rear is the elegant *Ilustrado* restaurant and the atmospheric *Kuatro Kantos* (see p.633). For information on Intramuros, and to arrange guided walking tours, call the Intramuros Administration, 5/F Palacio del Gobernador, Intramuros (☎02/527 3138 or 527 3141) or the Intramuros Visitor Center (☎02/527 2961), which has a small office in the grounds of Fort Santiago.

## Fort Santiago

The ruins of **Fort Santiago** (Tues–Sun, 8am–9pm; P50, students P25) stand at the northernmost end of Intramuros, a five-minute walk from the cathedral. Formerly the seat of the colonial powers of both Spain and the US, it was also a dreaded prison under the Spanish regime and the scene of countless military police atrocities during the Japanese occupation. On the northern side of the fort is the **Dulaang Rajah Soliman** which houses the room where Jose Rizal spent the hours before his execution on Bagumbayan (now Rizal Park), probably the most well-known episode in Philippine history. As well as a small theatre, it also contains one of the country's most significant historical documents – the original copy of Rizal's valedictory poem, *Mi Ultimo Adios*, which was secreted in an oil lamp and smuggled to his family hours before his death. It's possible to walk part of the walls of the fort, but check with the visitor centre first, as some areas are in disrepair.

### Rizal Park

**Rizal Park** (popularly known as the Luneta) was where the colonial-era glitterati used to promenade after church every Sunday. These days, in a city notoriously short of greenery, the park is an early-morning jogging circuit, a weekend repository for children and a refuge for couples and families trying to escape the burning haze of pollution that hangs over much of the city. People take picnics and lounge under trees, or relax in a shady area known as Chess Plaza, gambling a few centavos on the outcome of a game. Hawkers sell everything from balloons and mangoes to plastic bags full of *chicheron*, a local version of pork scratchings served with a little container of vinegar and chilli for dipping. Few visitors to the park report any problems with hustlers or what Filipinos refer to as "scalawags", but if you do need assistance you can call the park hotline on ⓣ117.

The park's sundry attractions include a rundown **planetarium** (P50), an amphitheatre where open-air concerts are held every Sunday at 5pm, a giant relief map of the Philippines, and Chinese and Japanese gardens. At the bay end of the park, close to the *Manila Hotel*, is the **Rizal Memorial** and the flagpole where Manuel Roxas, first President of the Republic, was sworn in on July 4, 1946. Rizal's execution site is also near here, close to a memorial commemorating three priests garrotted by the Spanish for alleged complicity in the Cavite uprising of 1872. One of the park's newer features is the **Orchidarium and Butterfly Pavilion**, designed and operated by the Clean and Green Foundation, and sponsored, somewhat incongruosly, by Nokia (Tues–Sun 8am–5pm; P100, students P60).

### The National Museum

Beyond the Orchidarium lie the country's two major museums, both under the auspices of the National Museum and both worth a visit. The **National Museum of the Philippines** (Tues–Sun 10am–4pm; P70, students P30, free on Sun) is in what used to be the Congress Building and houses Filipino masters' paintings and clearly labelled displays of geology, zoology, botany, crafts and weapons. Directly opposite, the **National Museum of the Filipino People** (same hours; P150, students P50, free on Sun) is in the former Government Finance Building and includes treasures from the *San Diego*, which sank off the coast of Fortune Island in Batangas in 1600. Not all the artefacts recovered from the wreck were intrinsically valuable; you'll see chicken bones and hazelnuts from the ship's store, as well as fine porcelain, rosaries and silver goblets. The anthropology section upstairs is equally enthralling, with reburial jars dating from 5 BC, which held the bones of ancestors, who were buried, exhumed and then stored for safekeeping.

### Manila Bay

When the capital was in its heyday, **Manila Bay** must have been a sight to behold, with its sweeping panorama across the South China Sea and dreamy sunsets. The sunsets are perhaps more vivid than ever, thanks to the ever-present blanket of smog, and Manileños still watch them from the harbour wall, but much of the bay feels as if it's trading on its romantic past. The grand buildings were bombed during the war and have been replaced with uninspiring concrete boxes. Horse-drawn carriages (*calesas*) still tout for business, but the horses look exhausted and even the palm trees that line Roxas Boulevard are drooping from the pollution. A trip north along the boulevard from its southern end in Pasay takes you past the **Cultural Center of the Philippines** and the ruins of Imelda Marcos's infamous **Manila Film Center**, which she hoped would turn the city into the Cannes of the East. Construction was rushed to beat tight deadlines and as a result the building collapsed, allegedly trapping an unknown number of workers inside.

### The Met and the Manila Hotel

While you're in the area, make a beeline for the **Metropolitan Museum**, usually known as the Met, at the Bangko Sentral ng Pilipinas Complex, Roxas Boulevard (Mon–Sat 10am–6pm; P80, free first Mon of the month). This fine arts museum, a Filipino mini-Guggenheim, also houses the Central Bank's collection of prehistoric jewellery and coins. Roxas Boulevard ends at the **Manila Hotel**, home from home over the years for the likes of General Douglas MacArthur (who has a suite named after him), Michael Jackson and Bill Clinton. If you're interested in the hotel's history you can ask the concierge to open the small but fascinating archive, with signed photographs of famous guests and unique images from World War II. Alternatively, you could just soak up the old-world atmosphere with a cocktail in the surprisingly welcoming downstairs piano bar and pretend you can afford to stay here (it helps to not look *too* scruffy).

### Ermita and Malate

Two of the city's oldest neighbourhoods, **Ermita** and **Malate**, are tucked behind Roxas Boulevard, ten minutes' walk east of Manila Bay. Until the late 1980s Ermita was infamous for its go-go bars and massage parlours until tough-guy mayor Alfredo Lim shut them all down in an ostentatious display of reform. New bars eventually took their place, but the bulk of the tourist trade had moved on and Ermita is now a ragbag of budget hotels, choked streets and fast-food outlets. Though a good place to stay, for anything to see and do you'll have to walk north to Intramuros or southeast along **M Adriatico Street** to **J Nakpil Street** in Malate, where a lively café scene thrives. Modish restaurants and bars have spread like a rash along Adriatico, Nakpil and neighbouring **Maria Orosa Street**, and on Friday and Saturday nights this is the place to be seen. Don't bother getting there early: at weekends, things rarely get going before 10pm and the pavements are still bustling at dawn. A five-minute walk towards the sea from Remedios Circle brings you to **Malate Church**, on MH del Pilar Street, where British soldiers took refuge during their brief and ill-advised occupation of the Philippines from 1762 to 1763. There are also a couple of major **malls** in the area, including Robinson's Place on Adriatico Street, and Harrison Plaza, across A Mabini Street from the Metropolitan Museum.

### Chinatown (Binondo)

The Chinese-Filipino (Tsinoy) community have created their own niche in **Chinatown** (Binondo). It's fascinating to wander through the mercantile hubbub of Ongpin Street, past the thriving apothecaries. Urban legend speaks of the enigmatic Soup Number Five, sold in the neighbourhood's restaurants and

| ACCOMMODATION | |
|---|---|
| Bianca's Garden Hotel | I |
| Ermita Tourist Inn | D |
| Friendly's Guesthouse | G |
| Iseya Hotel | A |
| Joward's Pension | F |
| Mabini Pension | C |
| Malate Pension | H |
| Midtown Inn | B |
| Pension Natividad | E |

| EATING, DRINKING & NIGHTLIFE | |
|---|---|
| Anthology | 10 |
| Aristocrat | 14 |
| Bed | 8 |
| Bedrock Bar & Grill | 9 |
| Café Adriatico Premier | 11 |
| Café Havana | 13 |
| Hobbit House | 2 |
| Kamayan | 3 |
| Kashmir | 4 |
| Koko's Nest | 7 |
| LA Café | 5 |
| Library | 6 |
| Seafood Market Restaurant | 1 |
| Tia Maria's | 12 |

said to cure everything from colds to impotence. Its contents remain a closely guarded secret, though many conjecture that the soup pot is the final resting place for many of the area's stray dogs. **Binondo Church**, at the west end of Ongpin, is where the first Filipino saint, Lorenzo Ruiz, served as a sacristan. Built in 1614 by the Dominicans, it quickly became the hub of the Catholic Chinese community.

At the eastern end of Chinatown, across Rizal Street, you reach **Quiapo Church**, the centre of celebrations of the Feast of the Black Nazarene, when eighty thousand barefooted Catholic faithful come together every January 9 to worship a revered crucifix bearing a black figure of Christ.

Quiapo is also a good area for bargain-hunters, with handicrafts at local prices sold in an area under Quiapo Bridge known, imaginatively, as Sa Ilalim ng Tulay ("Under the Bridge"). Two kilometres north of Chinatown, a short walk from the Abad Santos LRT station, is the morbidly impressive **Chinese Cemetery**. The tombs resemble mini-houses, with fountains, balconies, bathrooms and, for at least one, a small swimming pool. It has become a sobering joke in the Philippines that this necropolis, now numbering over thirty thousand tombs, is among the best accommodation in the city. Tour guides are on hand to offer their services for a negotiable fee.

### Malacañang Palace

The shoes are long gone, but you can still take a tour of the place the president of the Philippines calls home. The area open to the public is known as the **Malacañang Museum** (Mon–Fri 9am–4pm; P50) and the entrance is in JP Laurel Street, San Miguel; use the entrance at Gate Six.

**Malacañang** was once a relatively simple stone house, bought by Colonel Luis Miguel Formento in 1802. In 1825, the Spanish government purchased it, and designated it the summer residence of the Governor General in the Philippines in 1849. In the great tremor of 1863, the Governor General's palace in Intramuros was destroyed, and he became a full-time resident of Malacañang. Over the years rooms were added and renovations made, but on a number of occasions the building was damaged either by earthquake or typhoon. During the last major renovation in 1978, it underwent extensive interior and exterior changes, and was expanded to its present size – only a portion of the basement remains from the original structure. Malacañang will forever be associated with the horrifying excesses of the **Marcos years**. When Cory Aquino became president she wanted to distance herself from her profligate predecessors and refused to use the palace as a home. She opened the Malacañang Museum of Marcos Memorabilia, but when Fidel Ramos took over the museum focused instead on general Philippine presidential history, although the Marcos Room does contain some of the late dictator's personal belongings. In its current incarnation the Museum takes up about a third of the palace, while beleaguered president Gloria Macapagal-Arroyo (or GMA, as she styles herself) uses the rest for her official functions and duties.

### Makati

**Makati** was a vast expanse of malarial swampland until the Ayala family, one of the country's most influential business dynasties, started developing it at the beginning of the last century. Now Manila's business district, it's chock-full of plush hotels, expensive condominiums and monolithic air-conditioned malls housing everything from cinemas and bowling alleys to cacophonous food courts and international luxury emporiums. The main triangle of Makati is delineated by Ayala Avenue, Paseo de Roxas and Makati Avenue, and this is

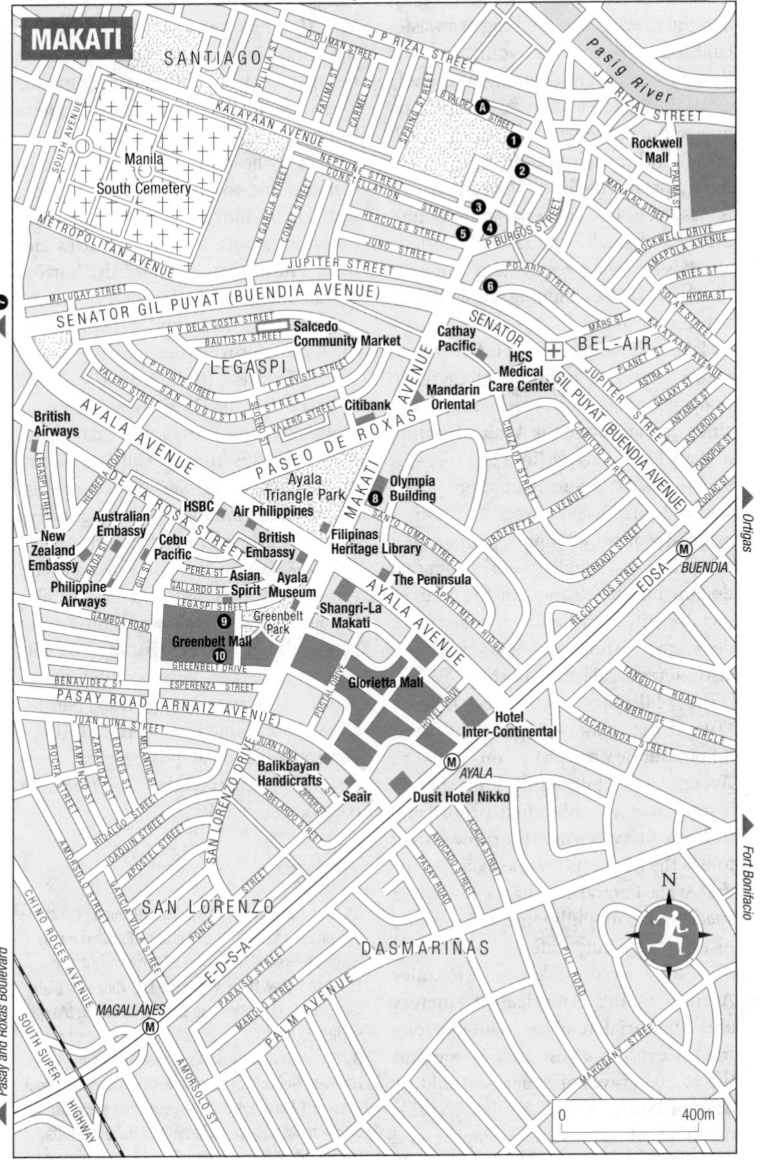


**EATING & DRINKING**

| | | | | | |
|---|---|---|---|---|---|
| Barrio Fiesta | 1 | Ice Vodka Bar | 9 | Oody's | 10 |
| Club Government | 2 | New Bombay Canteen | 7 | Wasabi Bistro and Sake Bar | 8 |
| Heckle and Jeckle | 6 | Next Door Noodles | 4 | | |
| Hossein's Persian Kebab | 5 | North Park Noodles | 3 | | |

**ACCOMMODATION**

| | |
|---|---|
| Robelle House | A |

where most of the banks and multinational corporations are situated. In terms of sights, Makati is something of a wasteland, but if all that's on your agenda is shopping, eating and drinking, it's the holy grail. The biggest mall by far is **Glorietta**, opposite the *Shangri-La Makati*, which heaves with people seeking refuge from the traffic and the heat. The central area is reserved for concerts, promotions, events and small-scale shows. Glorietta also has a seven-screen cinema complex (ⓣ02/752 7880), including one dedicated to arthouse films.

Makati's other main mall is **Greenbelt**, with a similarly mind-boggling selection of shops, bars, restaurants and cinemas. Next door, the **Ayala Museum**, Makati Ave cnr Dela Rosa St (Tues–Fri 9am–6pm, Sat & Sun 10am–7pm; P350; ⓦwww.ayalamuseum.org), houses original works by Filipino painters and a multimedia "People Power" room that documents the turmoil of the Marcos dictatorship and the restoration of democracy – not to be missed. There's also a terrific café and gift shop.

The **Filipinas Heritage Library** (Tues–Sat 9am–4.30pm; ⓦwww.filipinaslibrary.org.ph), on Makati Avenue, is an interesting little slice of history: it was Manila's first airport, and Paseo de Roxas is where the runway used to be. The library is privately owned (by the Ayala family) but has a bookshop specializing in Philippine culture and history, and a quiet café.

On the edge of Makati on McKinley Avenue is the **American Cemetery and Memorial** (daily 6.30am–4.30pm; free). Covering a vast area, it contains the 17,206 graves of American military dead of World War II. A short taxi ride north of Makati is the shopping and entertainment mecca of **Rockwell Mall**.

### Corregidor

The small tadpole-shaped island of **Corregidor** lies in the mouth of Manila Bay and makes a fascinating side trip from the city. A visit to the Island, which was going on over bitterly during World War II, offers a unique perspective on the Philippine struggle against Japanese occupation. It's worth making time for a visit to the Malinta tunnels, where General Douglas MacArthur set up temporary headquarters, and the site of vicious hand-to-hand combat. You can walk the island's trails, rent mountain bikes or explore the gun batteries and other ghostly reminders of the horrors of war. There is also a Japanese cemetery, a sobering museum and a memorial to the thousands who died here.

Sun Cruises (ⓣ02/813 8140, 524 8140 or 524 0333, ⓦwww.corregidorphilippines.com) organizes day- and overnight trips from the Cultural Center of the Philippines pier every morning. Accommodation for the overnight trips is in the *Corregidor Inn*, formerly owned by the Marcos family as a weekend retreat and guesthouse. It has an airy restaurant and views towards the Bataan peninsula. A day-trip package usually costs P1770 per person although to drum up trade during lean periods tickets are sometimes reduced (daily 7am, also 11am at peak times; reservations recommended). Overnight packages start at P2880.

## Arrival

**By bus** The majority of Manila's plethora of bus stations are located in and around Epifanio de los Santos Avenue (EDSA). The MRT runs west along EDSA to Pasay, from where the LRT runs to Malate. The closest LRT station to the tourist belt in Malate is Quirino Ave.

**By ferry** Superferry docks at Pier 15, South Harbour; Sulpicio Lines and Negros Navigation dock at piers 12 and 2, North Harbour. Both areas are easily accessible by taxi from Malate and Ermita.

**By air** Ninoy Aquino International Airport, widely known as NAIA, is in Parañaque, on the southern fringes of the city. In the arrivals hall there's a small 24-hour Department of Tourism (DoT) reception desk, where you can get maps, but not much else. There are several banks that will change dollars and traveller's cheques.

The easiest and safest way to get into the city is to take an official airport taxi; they charge P440 to Malate and P330 to Ermita. You pay in advance at a small booth in the arrivals hall, then present your receipt to the driver. Taking a non-official taxi from the airport guarantees you'll be ripped off, and you should never get into a taxi that is unmarked or has other people in it. All international and domestic Philippine Airlines (PAL) flights arrive next door at NAIA Centennial Terminal Two, which is cleaner, better lit and more salubrious than its neighbour. Go to the taxi booths outside the arrivals hall and buy a ticket to your destination. The fare to Makati and Manila Bay is P400.

An enormous new terminal for international arrivals has been built at the northern end of the airport, about 11km from Makati and 9km from Manila Bay, but its opening has been delayed for the past several years due to alleged corruption. The government recently expressed "hope" that it would open in 2009.

## Information and tours

**Tourist information** The Department of Tourism head office (24hr hotline ⓣ02/524 1703 or 524 2384) is in Room 106 of the Department of Tourism Building, TM Kalaw St, Ermita. The entrance is through a double door at the rear. The staff try to be helpful, but resources are thin on the ground. They do have some general information and a useful folding map with telephone numbers for airlines and embassies. Opposite Room 106 is the Tourist Police office (ⓣ02/524 1728 or 524 1660) where you should report problems such as theft, lost property, or overcharging by taxi drivers.

**Walking tours** For something different, try Carlos Celdran (ⓦhttp://celdrantours.blogspot.com; ⓣ0920 909 2021 for tour timetable) who runs weekly history lesson-cum-magical mystery tours around the city. As well as the classic Intramuros circuit, there are tailormade trips through different Manila moments – join in "Living La Vida Imelda", a trip through the city of the notorious shoe-collecting First Lady that Celdran describes as "a little bit disco, a little bit New Society, and completely Imeldific".

## City transport

Manila's roads are in a perpetual state of chaos bordering on anarchy. There are so many vehicles fighting for every inch of road space that at peak times it can be a sweaty battle of nerves just to get a few hundred metres. Walking is usually out of the question, except for short distances, because buses and jeepneys belch smoke with impunity, turning the air around major thoroughfares into a poisonous miasma.

**MetroStar Express** (5.30am–10.30pm) Runs the length of EDSA from Taft Ave in the south to North Ave, Quezon City. Key stations are Taft, from where you can get a taxi, a jeepney or the LRT to Malate; Ayala, which is close to Makati's malls and hotels; and Cubao for bus stations heading north. A single-journey ticket ranges from P10 to P15, and a pre-paid ticket costs P100 and is valid for three months.

**LRT** (Light Rail Transit; 5.30am–9pm) An elevated railway that runs from Baclaran in the south (near the airport) to Monumento in Caloocan in the north. Trains run frequently and all journeys cost P12. You can use it to get to places in the north of Manila, such as Rizal Park (exit at United Nations station), Intramuros (Central Station), and the Chinese Cemetery (Abad Santos station). Pedro Gil station is a ten-minute walk from Ermita, while Quirino station is closest to Malate.

**Jeepneys** Jeepneys go back and forth all over the city. Fares start at P4 for the shorter journeys and

### TRAVELLING SAFELY IN MANILA

Manileños take every oppurtunity to warn visitors about travelling around their city, but as long as you exerise common sense, there's little to worry about. MetroStar and LRT platforms are patrolled by armed security guards, and there are separate waiting areas for female passengers, minimizing opportunities for muggers, though of course it pays to remain alert. Official taxis are perfectly safe, but take the precaution of sitting in the back, and lock your doors, as you are likely to sit in traffic for long stretches of any journey. For complaints about taxis in Manila, contact the traffic police (ⓣ02/877 1791). Taking the bus in Manila is a potentially risky business; bus drivers are extraordinarily reckless, swerving from lane to lane and blocking busy junctions while they pick up passengers. The hours are long and the authorities have become worried that some are resorting to drugs to stay awake.

increase by P2 for each kilometre after. Pass your fare to the passenger sitting closest to the driver. A useful route runs the length of Taft Avenue from Baclaran in the south to Bindondo in the north. From Baclaran, you can get jeepneys to the bus terminals in Pasay. Jeepneys heading to Cubao will take you past a number of bus terminals at the northern end of EDSA, where you can get buses to destinations in the north.

**Taxis** It is extremely cheap and easy to get around Manila by taxi as long as you don't mind the occasional bout of wearisome haggling. Many taxi drivers are happy to turn on their meters, while others insist on starting even the shortest journey with a long negotiation. Needless to say, the metered option is always cheaper. Most taxis are a/c and charge an initial P30, plus P2.50 for every 200m. Trips of a couple of kilometres cost P50–60. From the Manila Bay area to the business district of Makati, the metered fare will be P100–120.

**Buses** Local buses in Manila bump and grind their way along all major thoroughfares. The destination is written on a sign in the front window, and fares start at P8, but they are the least reliable form of city transport (see box, p.631).

## Accommodation

Most of Manila's budget accommodation is in the Manila Bay area, in the enclaves of Ermita and Malate, which also have a high density of restaurants, bars and tourist services. In Makati, there is some reasonably priced accommodation in and around P. Burgos St at the northern end of Makati Ave. Budget places nearly always offer both fan and more expensive a/c rooms.

### Ermita and Malate

**Bianca's Garden Hotel** 2139 Adriatico St, Malate ⓣ02/526 0351, ⓔbiancasg@skyinet.net. On the seamier end of Adriatico past Remedios Circle, but gated and with 24hr security. Rooms are spacious and elegant, decorated with Filipino antiques evoking the building's former incarnation as a wealthy family home. There's a small swimming pool in the shady garden. ❺–❻

**Ermita Tourist Inn** 1549 A Mabini St, Ermita ⓣ02/521 8770. Clean and tiled a/c doubles with private baths. The staff are friendly and helpful, and there's a travel agent downstairs for flights and visas. Rates include a continental breakfast. ❺

**Friendly's Guesthouse** J Adriatico St, Malate ⓣ0917 333 1418, ⓦwww.friendlysguesthouse.com. Don't be put off by the lugubrious exterior and dimly lit stairs, the large balcony common area, with internet access (including free Wi-Fi) and bird's-eye views over Malate more than compensate. Self-catering cooking facilities available. Dorms and rooms with shared or private bathrooms available. Dorms ❷; rooms ❹–❺

**Iseya Hotel** 1241 MH del Pilar St, Ermita ⓣ02/523 8166, ⓦwww.iseyahotel.com. Dusty old pension house close to the noisy junction with Padre Faura and surrounded by moneychangers and *halal carinderias* (canteens). Expensive for what you get, but central. ❻

**Joward's Pension** 1730 Adriatico St, Malate ⓣ02/338 3191. If you're really strapped for cash and don't mind providing your own blankets, towels and sheets, you could do worse than *Joward's*, which is at least close to the action and has friendly staff. ❷

**Mabini Pension** 1337 A Mabini St, Ermita ⓣ02/523 3930, ⓦwww.mabinipension.com. Convenient, friendly and well established, though in rather close proximity to a number of karaoke joints; unless you consider late-night power ballads an atmospheric addition, get a room at the back. Also offers internet access, tourist information, visa extensions and flight reservations. ❹–❺

**Malate Pensionne** 1771 M Adriatico St, Malate ⓣ02/523 8304, ⓦwww.mpensionne.com.ph. Tucked into a colourful courtyard behind *Starbucks*, this popular guesthouse is furnished in Spanish colonial style and boasts an unbeatable position for nightlife. Rooms have varying facilities; there's internet access and a small café downstairs. Reservations recommended. Dorms ❷; doubles ❹

**Midtown Inn** 551 Padre Faura St, Ermita. ⓣ02/521 2602, ⓔmidtown_inndinner@yahoo.com. Not the friendliest place in town, but the location is central, if a little noisy. The attached diner does basic budget meals from P65. ❹

**Pension Natividad** 1690 MH del Pilar St, Malate ⓣ02/521 0524. Choice of spacious, plain rooms in an old family house that was built before the war and partially destroyed by bombing. The pleasant terrace café serves a small but reasonably priced range of drinks and snacks, including coffee (P25) and breakfast (from P80). Luggage storage is P10 per bag per day. One of the best budget places to stay in the area. Dorms ❷; rooms ❺

### Makati

**Robelle House** 4402 B Valdez St ⓣ02/899 8209. This rambling family-run pension at the P. Burgos end of Makati Ave has been in business for years and is still the most atmospheric Filipino budget accommodation in Makati. There's the advantage of a small pool, though the rooms, for the price, are no more than serviceable. ❹–❺

## Eating

### Intramuros, Ermita and Malate

**Aristocrat** 432 San Andres St, Malate. An institution among Filipinos looking for comfort food such as *arroz con caldo* (rice porridge with entrails, P76) and *dinuguan* (blood stew, P98). The less adventurous can settle for barbecue chicken or pork, noodles, sandwiches or *adobo*. They have a food shop and bakery next door. Opposite Malate Church, close to the seafront. 24hr.

**Kamayan** 532 Padre Faura cnr M Adriatico St, Ermita. The word *kamayan* means "with your hands", which is how you eat, without knife and fork. The staff are dressed in great Filipino costumes and the dudes in shades work the tables doing musical requests for the many lively family parties that keep this place bustling. If you want a whole roast suckling pig, order it a day ahead. Set prices for buffets range from P325 to 465 per head, although if you are "below four feet", you eat for P210.

TREAT YOURSELF

**Ilustrado** 744 Calle Real del Palacio (Gen. Luna St) Intramuros ⓣ02/527 3674, ⓔilustrado_restaurant@yahoo.com. Nothing compares to *Ilustrado* if you're looking for the ambience of colonial Manila. The floors are polished wood, the tables are set with starched linen, ceiling fans whirr quietly, and the cuisine is rich and grand. Signature dishes include paella (P600), *kaldereta* (Filipino beef stew, P420), tuna belly (P420) and a four-course set dinner (P1200) or lunch (P720) including an aperitif. Reservations recommended.

**Kashmir** Merchants Center Building, Padre Faura St, Ermita, next door to *Kamayan*. Authentic chicken tikka, a mouthwatering selection of breads, and wonderfully cheesy ersatz Raj decor make this one of the best Indian places in Manila. They do a fantastic version of *calamansi*, the Filipino lime soda, just the thing to put out the fire in your mouth – the *Kashmir* chefs can be liberal with the spices. There's another branch at Fastejo Building, 816 Pasay Rd. Chicken tikka masala P435.

**Kuatro Kantos** 744 Calle Real del Palacio (same old building as *Ilustrado*). Charming little bar and café, which starts with extremely hearty breakfasts and stays open until 9.30pm – perfect for a good cup of coffee or a bite to eat while you're wandering around Intramuros. The hot *pan de sal* with *adobo* or sardines and *kesong purti* (a type of white cheese) makes an excellent and very affordable snack. They also do a wide range of flavoured coffees for P75–140.

**Seafood Market Restaurant** J Bocobo St, opposite cnr Arquiza St, Malate. Typical of the many seafood restaurants in the area where the day's catch is laid out on ice and you pick and pay by weight. The extensive choice normally includes giant prawns, lapu-lapu, lobster, fish lips and sea slug, all cooked as you watch by wok chefs in a glass-fronted kitchen. If fish lips (P70) aren't your thing there's also chicken feet dim sum (P60).

### Makati

**Barrio Fiesta** Makati Ave, cnr Valdez St. There are various branches of this popular and colourful Filipino restaurant dotted around the metropolis, all serving indigenous food such as *adobo* and *lechon* with hefty portions of rice and daily buffet options. The Makati branch incorporates a franchise of *Ihaw-Ihaw Kalde Kaldero* upstairs where the menu is the same but the waiters and waitresses sing as they work.

**Hossein's Persian Kebab** 7857 LKV Building, Makati Ave. Enormous Middle Eastern and Indian menu served in frou-frou surroundings. If you're not in the mood for fried brain, or "homos with meat" choose from dozens of curry and kebab dishes. Mains around P450.

**New Bombay Canteen** G/F Sagittarius Building III, HV de la Costa St, opposite the *Grand Stamford Hotel*, a few minutes' walk from the *Mandarin Oriental*. Exceptional Indian food, including an impressive vegetarian range, all at consistantly low prices. Lentil curry P110. Daily 9.30am–10pm.

**Next Door Noodles** 1200 Makati Ave. Cheap and cheerful Chinese place, almost opposite its sister restaurant, *North Park Noodles*, which has a similar menu at the same low prices. Excellent value – almost everything on the menu is under P200.

**Oody's** Level Two, Greenbelt 3, Makati Ave. There are dozens of inexpensive restaurants serving all sorts of cuisine on the second level of this mall. *Oody's* specializes in Thai, with a reasonable choice for vegetarians. Unusual desserts include "water chestnuts, toddy palm and *langka* in ice". Thai chicken curry P228. Daily until 11pm.

**Wasabi Bistro & Sake Bar** Olympia Building, 7912 Makati Ave. Minimalist, trendy Japanese restaurant with a relaxed ambience. Excellent Sunday buffet from P700, featuring suberb mahi-mahi and tuna sashimi, creamy baked scallops and asparagus maki. The early-bird bento specials from 6 to 7.30pm are also good value at P443. Daily noon–11pm.



## Nightlife and entertainment

### Ermita and Malate

JM Nakpil St late on a Friday night is a sight to behold. Beatnik poets mingle with film stars, models, swaggering transvestites and a smattering of expats to create an amazingly good-natured outdoor rave.

**Anthology** M Adriatico St, Malate. Live music and drink deals; local beers are just P38 all night. Closed Sun.

**Bed** J Nakpil St. Malate's biggest and boldest gay club draws an uninhibited crowd of gay and straight revellers. Thurs–Sat, and doesn't kick off properly until after midnight.

**Bedrock Bar & Grill Restaurant** 1782 M Adriatico St, Malate. A vaguely Flinstones-esque interior, lack of a cover charge and better-than-average music have established this place as an Adriatico St institution. Two live bands play three sets each of hip hop/pop nightly until 4am or until the last punter stumbles off the dance floor. Mon–Wed & Sun 6pm–4am, Thurs–Sat 6pm–5am.

**Café Adriatico Premier** 1900 M Adriatico St, Malate. This chic and casual stalwart of the Malate nightlife scene has been going since 1979 and has benefited from recent renovation. It does wonderful breakfasts and is a favourite of Manila ladies-who-lunch, but at night it gets down to serious business – excellent cocktails.

**Café Havana** 1903 M Adriatico St, Malate. The modus operandi here is to get drunk and dance to live samba music. It also features the Ché Guevara cigar room. There's another *Café Havana* on the ground floor of the Greenbelt mall on Makati Avenue in Makati. Daily 5pm–2am (Adriatrico St), 11am–2am (Greenbelt).

**Hobbit House** 1212 MH del Pilar St, Ermita. Twenty years ago, a young Manila entrepreneur decided to open a bar that would pay homage to his favourite book, *The Lord of the Rings*. As a tribute to Bilbo Baggins he staffed it with twenty dwarves, and a legend was born. *Hobbit House* still employs short people, and boasts nightly appearances by bluesy local groups, cheap drinks and a large range of imported lagers. The menu includes Filipino, international and grilled food. Happy hour is 5–9pm. There's another, less atmospheric branch in D'Mall on Boracay.

### THE BARS OF P. BURGOS STREET

Manila's notorious strip of girlie bars in Makati is still thriving and writhing, with haunts such as *Blushes*, *Tickles* and *Bottoms* doing a roaring trade with foreigners. Though prostitution is officially illegal, bars openly advertise their "guest relations officers" (GROs), who are expected to leave with any patron who buys ten "ladies drinks" at the bar. One of the (relatively) less seedy joints is *Rogues* (P. Burgos St cnr Makati Ave), where, if you can stomach the sight of lonely old Western men bumping and grinding with young Filipinas, you can drink all the free San Miguel you want between 4 and 8pm every Wednesday. There's a pool table and they show American and Premiership football, but, as in many of the bars on Burgos, female patrons are not made overly welcome.

**Koko's Nest** Adriatico St, Malate. Friendly little bar next door to *Malate Pensionne*, which makes a great first stop on a night out. The pavement-side tables offer some of the best people-watching in Malate, and a San Miguel will set you back just P25.

**LA Café** 1429 MH del Pilar St, Ermita. *LA Café* has its share of GROs and single customers on the make, but the waitresses are friendly, the San Miguel is on draught, and there are live bands upstairs at 9pm most evenings. 24hr.

**Library** 1739 Maria Orosa, Malate. Nightly stand-up/karaoke from veteran Manila drag queens where audience participation is very much part of the show. P100 cover charge.

**Tia Maria's** 532 Remedios St, Malate. Branch of a popular Mexican restaurant chain that has become known less for its food, which is average, and more for its drinks promotions (a pitcher of San Miguel costs P205, a "barrel" costs P548). The music starts at 9pm every night and goes on until the small hours, by which time most of the young audience have abandoned their seats and taken enthusiastically to the dance floor. The live bands are a walking Filipino cliché: four-piece combos with two pretty girls sharing lead vocals on a standard selection of American pop and R&B.

### Makati

**Club Government** 7840 Makati Ave. Box-like gay club hosting different theme nights such as a a "Sexercise" gym party and a "Kylie-ton". Plays mostly hard house on regular nights. Mon–Sat; Saturday cover charge of P200, other nights vary.

**Heckle and Jeckle** Jupiter St. A haven for sports fans with two pool tables and live Premiership football every weekend. They even serve popcorn to enjoy it with (P40). Other bar snacks include chicken satay (P160), pizzas (P150), and Filipino specialities (P250). The generous happy "hour" runs from 4 till 10pm, with all local beers and spirits half price.

**Ice Vodka Bar** Level 3, Greenbelt 3. Watering hole of choice for Manila's beautiful people; it can seem a touch pretentious at first, but with limitless freeflowing Vodkatinis for P395 between 7 and 10pm nightly (and a free pizza thrown in for good measure), the atmosphere tends not to stay frosty for long. When the Vodkatinis stop there's a huge range of designer cocktails to get stuck into.

## Shopping

### Traditional crafts

In Intramuros, opposite San Agustin Church, is a complex of small art and tribal shops, selling everything from carved rice gods and oil paintings to native basketware and jewellery.

**Balikbayan Handicrafts** The biggest branch is at 290–298 C Palanca St, Quiapo, with others in Pasay Rd, Makati and A Mabini St, Ermita. Sells an inspiring range of native jewellery, ethnic carvings and household pieces at bargain prices.

**Silahis** 744 General Luna St, Intramuros. One of the best places in Manila for unusual gifts, including cigars, hand-carved chess sets and coconut oil soaps. Daily 10am–7pm.

### Markets

**Baclaran Market** Southern tip of Roxas Blvd. This is the granddaddy of flea markets where haggling is the order of the day and the delights on offer include live puppies, quail eggs, caged finches and the ubiquitous pirate DVDs. Take the LRT to Baclaran, and allow plenty of time.

**Divisoria Market** CM Recto St, Binondo, open every day from 10am. Fake Converse trainers, pirated DVDs, bags, wallets and all manner of household paraphernalia crowd the stalls at this immense Chinatown market. Divisoria can get overwhelmingly busy, and while it's safe it's best to dress down and leave valuables at your hotel, just in case. You also stand a better chance of picking up a bargain if you don't look too well-off.

**Salcedo Community Market** Jaime Velasquez Park, Bel-Air, Makati, Sat 7am–2pm. Undoubtedly one of the city's culinary highlights, Salcedo features a dazzling display of gastronomic delights from all corners of the Philippines and further afield to take away or savour on one of the market's communal tables. Leave some room for the *tarte tatin* at the Cuisine Francaise stall.

**San Andres Market** San Andres St, cnr Guerrero St, close to Quirino Ave LRT station. For the cheapest and most mind-boggling choice of fruit in the archipelago, take a wander through this labyrinth. Twenty-four hours a day, seven days a week, hundreds of stalls groan under the weight of mango, pomelo, jackfruit, cantaloupe, watermelon, mangosteen, rambutan and more.

**"Under the Bridge" Market** (Sa Ilalim ng Tulay) Quezon Bridge, Quiapo. A good place to pick up handicrafts – the pretty lanterns (*parols*) made from capiz seashells that you see all over the country at Christmas cost P750, half what you would pay in a mall. There's also a selection of surprisingly cool vintage-style clothes, mainly T-shirts, at a fraction of what you'd pay for the same kind of thing at home.

### Books

**Filipino Bookstore** G-72, Ground Floor, Glorietta 1, Ayala Center, Makati. A small but interesting range of Filipino books and environmental videos.

**National Bookstore** Branches in Greenbelt and Rockwell, level 2. Chainstore found everywhere, selling books, maps and stationery.

**Power Books** 4/L Greenbelt 4. Good-value chain bookstore.

**Solidaridad Bookshop** 531 Padre Faura. (Mon–Sat 9am–6pm). Owned by celebrated Filipino novelist F. Sionil Jose.

### Malls

With their dazzling array of goods and services, Manila's malls offer a major source of entertainment in the city. Many are the size of small towns, so expect to get lost inside. International brands, especially clothing, are roughly 25 percent cheaper than in Western countries. Opening hours are usually Mon–Fri 10am–9pm, Sat and Sun 10am–10pm.

**Glorietta** (Ayala Center), Makati Ave, Makati; see p.630.

**Greenbelt** Malls 1, 2 3 and 4. Makati Ave. Part of the Ayala Center complex. Paseo de Roxas, cnr Legaspi and Esperanza streets, Makati. Fast food, upscale boutiques, bars, theatres, cinemas etc. Big name clothing stores, including Topshop.

**Harrison Plaza** Between Adriatico and Mabini, Malate.

**Mall of Asia** Bay Blvd cnr EDSA extension, Pasay City. The largest mall in the Philippines, and the third largest in the world. Has everything you'd expect, and more you wouldn't, including an Olympic sized ice-skating rink and an internal tram to ferry shoppers around its citadel-like interior.
**Robinson's Place** Adriatico St, cnr Padre Fauna, Malate.
**Rockwell Center** Rockwell Drive, Makati. The mall here is officially called the Power Plant mall, but everyone just refers to it as Rockwell.

## Directory

**Airline offices** Air Canada, c/o Supersonic Services, G/F Colonnade Condominium, 132 Palanc St, Makati ⓣ02/840 4626; Air Philippines, 472 Padre Fauna Center, Padre Fauna St cnr MH del Pilar St, Malate ⓣ02/524 0540, also G/F Charter House, 114 Legaspi St, Makati 02/551 7991; American Airlines, Olympia Condominium, Makati ⓣ02/817 8645; Asian Spirit, LPL Towers, 112 Legaspi St, Makati ⓣ02/855 3333; British Airways, Dela Rosa cnr Legaspi St, Legaspi Village, Makati ⓣ02/817 0361; Cebu Pacific, Express Ticket Office, Beside Gate 1, Terminal Building 1, Manila Domestic Airport, or Robinson's Place, Level 1, Pedro Gil St, Ermita ⓣ02/702 0888; PAL, PNB Financial Centre, Pres. Diosdado Macapagal Ave, CCP Complex, Pasay City, 24hr reservations ⓣ02/855 8888; South East Asian Airlines (SEAIR), 2/F Dona Concepcion Building, 1020 Pasay Rd, Makati ⓣ02/849 0100; Thai Airways, Country Space 1 Building, Senator Gil Puyat Ave, Makati ⓣ02/817 4044; Vietnam Airlines, Imex Travel, Ground Floor, Colonnade Building, 132 Carlos Pelanca St, Makati ⓣ02/810 3406, 810 3653 or 893 2083.
**Banks and exchange** Most major bank branches have 24hr ATMs for Visa and MasterCard cash advances. American Express, 1810 A Mabini St, Malate; Citibank, 8741 Paseo de Roxas, Makati; HSBC, Ayala Ave, Makati and 648 Remedios St, Malate; Solidbank, 777 Paseo De Roxas, Makati; Standard Chartered Bank, 6756 Ayala Ave, Makati.
**Embassies and consulates** Australia, Level 23, Tower 2, RCBC Plaza, 6819 Ayala Ave, Makati ⓣ02/757 8100; Canada, Levels 6–8, Tower 2, RCBC Plaza, 6819 Ayala Ave, Makati ⓣ02/857 9000; Ireland, 3rd Floor, 70 Jupiter St, Bel-Air 1, Makati ⓣ02/896 4668; New Zealand, 23rd Floor, Far East Bank Center, Sen Gil Puyat Ave, Makati ⓣ02/891 4625; South Africa, 29th Floor, Yuchengco Tower, RCBC Plaza, 6819 Ayala Ave Makati ⓣ 02/889 9383; UK, 15th–17th Floor, LV Locsin Building 6752 Ayala Ave cnr Makati Ave, Makati ⓣ02/580 8700; US, 1201 Roxas Blvd, Ermita ⓣ02/301 2000.
**Emergencies** The Department of Tourism has two assistance lines (ⓣ02/524 1703 or 524 2384) and two Tourist Hotlines (ⓣ02/524 1660 and 524 1728).
**Hospitals and clinics** Makati Medical Center, 2 Amorsolo St, Makati (ⓣ02/888 8908), is the largest and one of the most modern hospitals in Manila. It has a 24-hr emergency department and dozens of specialist clinics (10am–noon & 2–4pm). You can't make an appointment for the clinics – just turn up and join the queue. An initial consultation costs around P1000. Manila Doctors' Hospital (ⓣ02/524 3011) is at 667 United Nations Ave, and the Medical Center Manila (ⓣ02/523 8131) is at 1122 General Luna St, Ermita.
**Immigration** Bureau of Immigration and Deportation, Magellanes Drive, Intramuros (ⓣ02/527 3260 or 527 3248). 8am–noon & 1–5pm.
**Internet** Internet access is very easy to find in all tourist areas and there are internet cafés in all malls: Rty B connected internet café Greenbelt 4; Mailstation, 30-A Park Square 1, Ayala Center, Makati; Ecafé, 1415, MH del Pilar St, Ermita.
**Pharmacies** You're never far from a Mercury Drug outlet in Metro Manila; at the last count, there were two hundred. In Ermita, there's one at 444 TM Kalaw St and another at Robinson's Place in M Adriatico. In Makati, there's a big branch in the Glorietta mall on the ground floor near Tower Records.
**Police** Tourist Police, Room 112, Department of Tourism Building, Teodoro Valencia Circle, TM Kalaw St, Ermita (ⓣ02/524 1660 or 524 1728); Western District Police, United Nations Ave, Ermita.
**Post office** In the Manila Bay area there's a small post office opposite the *Manila Hotel* and a general post office at Liwasang Bonifacio, Intramuros, near MacArthur Bridge on the Pasig River. The closest LRT station is Central. In Makati, there is a post office at the junction of Gil Puyat and Ayala avenues, next to Makati Fire Station. Look out also for the numerous Mailstation outlets, where you can post letters, make telephone calls and often find internet services.
**Telephones** Pre-paid PLDT Fonkards are available from 7–11 stores and allow you to make local or international (IDD) calls from PLDT cardphones.
**Travel agents** There are plenty of travel agents around Malate and Ermita. The Filipino Travel Center, 15555 Adriatico St (ⓣ 02/538 4504, ⓦwww.filipinotravel.com.ph), is a helpful one-stop shop, and is particularly useful for organizing day-trips. There are several branches around the

country, incuding at White Beach, Boracay. Other options include: Bridges Travel, Liberty Center Bldg, 104 HV Dela Costa St cnr Leviste St, Makati (ⓣ02/889 6654, ⓦwww.bridgestravel.com); Century Travel & Tours, 1991 A. Mabini St, Malate (ⓣ02/526 8633, ⓔcentury@abacus.com.ph); Danfil Express, 635 Casa Catalina Bldg, Gen. Malvar St, Malate (ⓣ02/524 8703).

## Moving on

**By bus** There is no single bus station for Manila, timetables are hard to come by and in a constant state of flux, all of which can make getting out of Manila by bus a bit of a headache. Often if you tell your taxi driver your destination, he'll bring you to the right station. The good news is that departures are frequent to almost everywhere, so if you miss the bus you were planning to catch, you won't be waiting too long for another. A good resource is the "getting around" section of ⓦwww.philippines-travel-guide.com. A number of competing bus companies have terminals either in the Pasay area of EDSA (one of the major terminals is behind Araneta Coliseum), or the Cubao end of EDSA – see box below.

**Destinations south:** Batangas City (18–20 daily; 3hr); Calamba (10–12 daily; 2hr); Daet (6–8 daily; 7–8hr); Legaspi (8–10 daily; 8–10hr); Naga (6–8 daily; 6–8hr); Nasugbu (6–8 daily; 3hr); Pagsanjan (10–12 daily; 3hr); Sorsogon Town (2–3 daily; 24hr); Taal (10–12 daily; 2–3hr); Tagaytay (10–12 daily; 2–3hr).

**Destinations north:** Baguio (12–15 daily; 6–8hr); Banaue (5–6 daily; 7–9hr); Dau (for Clark; frequent; 2hr); Iba (3–4 daily; 6hr); Laoag (6–8 daily; 8–10hr); Lingayen (8–10 daily; 6–7hr); Olongapo (8–10 daily; 4–5hr); San Fernando (La Union; 4–6 daily; 6–8hr); Vigan (6–8 daily; 8–10hr).

**By ferry** Most inter-island departures sail from the north harbour, a few km north of Intramuros beyond the *Manila Hotel,* except SuperFerry, which uses pier 15, south harbour, close to the *Manila Hotel.* It's best to take a taxi. You can book tickets through a number of agents, including 2GO, who have branches in most malls. The three main ferry companies, which all serve most destinations

### MANILA BUS COMPANIES AND TERMINALS

Below is a list of major bus companies, their Manila terminals, and the destinations they cover.

**Auto Bus** (ⓣ02/735 8098) cnr Tolentino and España Sts, Sampoloc. Direct to Banaue and Vigan.

**Crow** (ⓣ 02/804 0632) and **Erjohn & Almark** (no phone) behind Taft MRT. Frequent services to all areas in the Batangas region including Tagayaty and Nasugbu.

**Dagupan** (ⓣ02 727 2330 or 02/929 6123) New York St cnr EDSA, Cubao. North to Aliminos and Baguio.

**Dangwa** (ⓣ02/731 2879) 1600 Dimasalang, Sampoloc. Overnight services to Baguio and Banaue.

**Dominion Transit** (ⓣ02/741 4146) EDSA, cnr East Ave, Cubao. Hourly to Vigan and San Fernando (La Union).

**Farinas Transit Company** (ⓣ02 731 4507), Cnr Laoag Laan and M del a Fuente streets, Sampaloc. Vigan and Laoag.

**GV Florida** (ⓣ02/731 5358) cnr Extremadura and Earnshaw sts, Sampoloc. Direct services to Banaue.

**Five Star** (ⓣ 02/833 8339) Aurora Blvd, Pasay. South to Batangas and the Bicol region.

**JAM Transit** (ⓣ 02/541 4409) EDSA, Cubao. Batangas and Laguna.

**Partas** (ⓣ02 725 7303 or ⓣ 02/725 1740) 816 Aurora Blvd, Cubao Deluxe services to Baguio, Laoag, San Fernando (La Union), Vigan, La Union and Ilocos Sur.

**Philippine Rabbit** (ⓣ02/734 9836) 1240 EDSA, Quezon City. Destinations north such as Angeles, Baguio, Vigan, Laoag, and San Fernando (La Union).

**Philtranco** (ⓣ02/832 2456) EDSA cnr Apelo Cruz St, Pasay and behind Araneta Coliseum. Daily runs as far afield as Quezon, Bicol, Leyte, Samar and even Davao, through Daet, Naga, Legaspi and Sorsogon.

**Tritran** (ⓣ02/925 1758) EDSA cnr East Ave. Batangas province.

**Victory Liner** (ⓣ02/727 4534 or 02/833 0293) EDSA, Pasay, and EDSA, Cubao. North to various destinations, including Baguio, Aliminos and Banaue.

below, are: Negros Navigation (numerous ticket offices including the Ayala Center, Makati and at Pier 2, north harbour; ⓣ02/243 5231 or 244 0408, ⓦwww.negrosnavigation.ph); Superferry (also known as WG&A; ticket offices at Robinson's Place Mall, Pier 15 & 7/F Times Plaza Building, UN Ave, cnr Taft Ave, Ermita; ⓣ02/528 7209, ⓦwww.superferry.com.ph); and Sulpicio Lines (Pier 12, north harbour; ⓣ02/241 9701 or 241 9801, ⓦwww.sulpiciolines.com).

**Destinations:** Bacolod (8–10 weekly; 7hr/9hr 30min); Cagayan de Oro (5 weekly; 33/42hr); Cebu (5 weekly; 12hr); Coron (1 weekly; 12hr); Dumaguete (1 weekly; 36hr); Iloilo (6 weekly; 19hr); Puerto Princesa (1 weekly; 13hr 30min); Tagbilaran (1 weekly; 18hr).

**By train** The government-funded Philippine National Railways (PNR) only has one line running from Manila through the Bicol region but the service is shambolic and information erratic. The trains are slow, uncomfortable and occasionally involved in fatal accidents. The main station in Manila, Tutuban PNR, is the best source of what little information there is. It's on Dagupan St, a twenty-minute walk west of Tayuman LRT station.

**By air** All international flights except PAL's leave from Ninoy Aquino International Airport (ⓣ02/877 1109) in Parañaque. PAL's international flights and all domestic flights go from either NAIA Centennial Terminal Two (ⓣ02/877 1109) or the smaller domestic terminal next door. Domestic departure tax from Manila is P200; international is P550.

**Destinations:** Bacolod (up to 8 daily; 1hr 10min); Baguio (daily; 1hr 10min); Busuanga (up to 3 daily; 1hr); Cagayan de Oro (up to 10 daily; 1hr 25min); Caticlan (up to 46 daily; 1hr); Cebu City (up to 16 daily; 1hr 10min); Dumaguete (up to 5 daily; 1hr 15min); Iloilo City (up to 11 daily; 1hr); Kalibo (up to 6 daily; 50min); Laoag (up to 3 daily; 50min); Legaspi (up to 4 daily; 1hr 10min); Naga (2–3 daily; 1hr); Puerto Princesa (2 daily; 1hr 10min); Tacloban (5 daily; 1hr 10min); Tagbilaran ( 4 daily; 2hr).

# Southern Luzon and Mindoro

Leaving the sprawl of Manila behind and heading south takes you along the South Luzon Expressway (known to Filipinos as the South Luzon Distressway), and into the provinces of Cavite, Laguna and Batangas. Traffic can be grim, particularly on weekends and holidays, so try to time your journey for a weekday if at all possible. **Laguna**, known for hot springs and mountain pools, is the first province south of the capital. Laguna de Bay, the lake that forms its northern boundary, has a few resorts, clustered around the hot springs of Los Baños, but they are catered towards company outings and day-trippers, and have little to offer the budget traveller. A better option by far is to explore the province of **Batangas**, Manila's weekend playground, with tropical-style beach resorts and alluring **Taal Volcano** to climb. The provincial capital, **Batangas City**, is a polluted port town but its ferry pier offers escape to the island of **Mindoro** and the lively diving resorts of **Puerto Galera**. The region south of Batangas and Quezon (Region V) is commonly known as **South Luzon** or **Bicol**, home of the Philippines' fieriest cuisine, whose staple is the creamy, delicious Bicol Express, contender with *adobo* for the finest native dish. From Batangas City the National Highway meanders through the provinces of Camarines Norte, Camarines Sur and Albay. The main towns of **Daet**, **Naga** and **Legaspi** are typically provincial, with their jumbled traffic, concrete malls and occasional Spanish-era relics – Legaspi, as the jumping-off point for the active volcano **Mount Mayon**, is the only one covered by our guide. Continuing further south still, you reach the coastal town of **Sorsogon**, from where it's a fifty-kilometre ride to the bucolic backwater of **Donsol**, popular because of the concentration of plankton-eating whale sharks that congregate here. The opportunity to swim with these gentle giants is probably the single biggest draw for visitors to this area of the country. From **Matnog** in **Sorsogon**

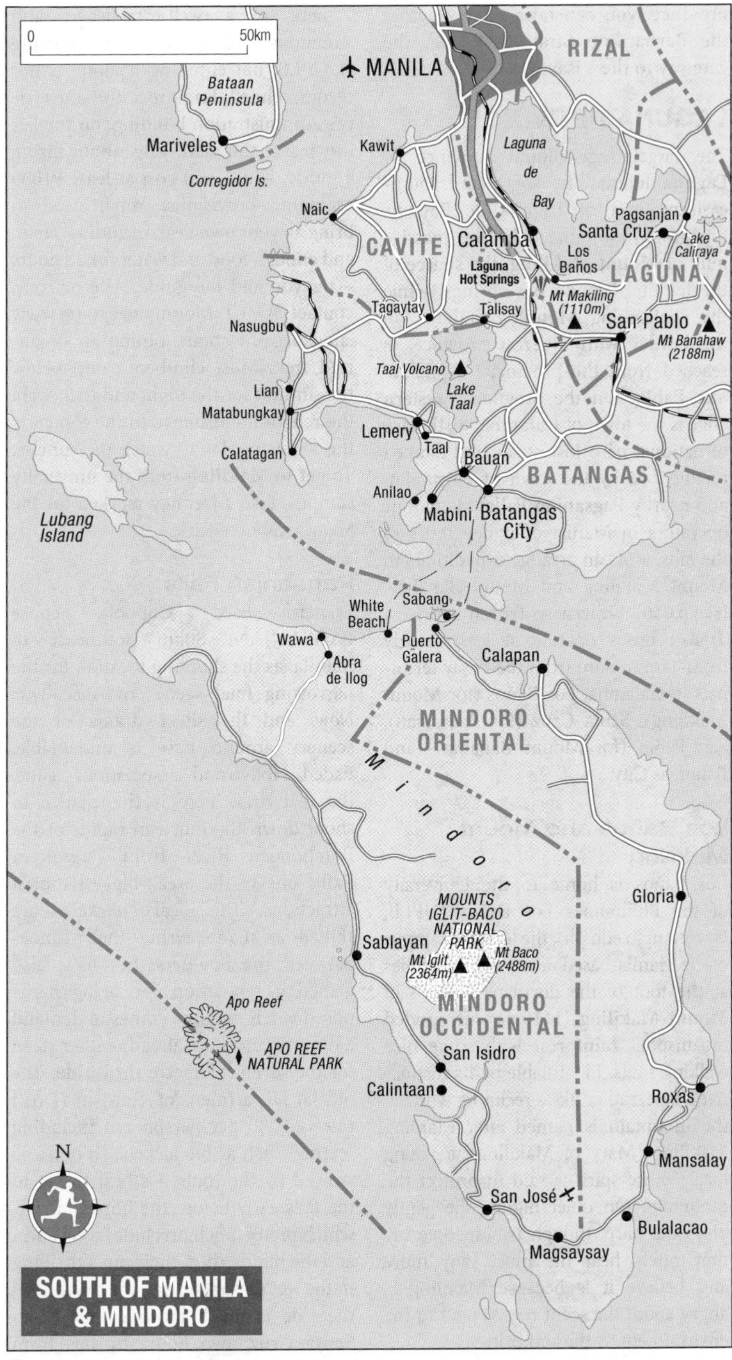

SOUTH OF MANILA & MINDORO

THE PHILIPPINES

SOUTHERN LUZON AND MINDORO

province, you can take a ferry across the Bernardino Strait to Samar, the gateway to the Visayas.

## LAGUNA PROVINCE

The largely agricultural province of **Laguna** follows the south and south-eastern coast of Laguna de Bay, its topography dominated by the massive hulk of **Mount Makiling**, the source of the famous Laguna hot springs, while the challenging **Mount Banahaw**, on the border with Quezon province, is reached from the provincial capital of **San Pablo**. On the province's western edge is the town of **Calamba**, birthplace of national hero José Rizal, and flanked on the east by the town of **Pagsanjan** and nearby **Pagsanjan Falls**. Many tour operators in Manila offer day tours to the falls, and can arrange expeditions to Mount Makiling and Mount Banahaw (see p.636). Otherwise Tritran and JAM Transit buses operate at least hourly from 4am to 8pm from the Pasay terminals to Calamba, Los Baños (for Mount Makiling), Santa Cruz (for Pagsanjan), San Pablo (for Mount Banahaw) and Batangas City.

### Los Baños and Mount Makiling

Los Baños is home to the University of the Philippines Los Baños (UPLB; Ⓦwww.uplb.edu.ph), the forestry campus of the Manila-based university, which lies at the foot of the dormant volcano of **Mount Makiling** (1110m), surrounded by unspoilt **rainforest** with some nice walking trails. Identifiable by its distinctive shape, rather like a reclining woman, the mountain is named after Mariang Makiling (Mary of Makiling), a young local whose spirit is said to protect the mountain. On quiet nights, she gently plays the harp, though tribespeople say they rarely hear the music any more and believe it is because Makiling is angry about the scant regard paid to the environment by the authorities.

There is a well-established and strenuous trail to the summit starting at UPLB, but climbing it alone is not recommended. Enquire at the university's administration building, on the left just inside the main gate, about hiring a **guide**, which will cost at least P1000 excluding provisions. You'll need to bring all your own gear, including a tent, and enough food and water for 48 hours – for you and the guide. Alternatively, contact AMCI Mountaineers (Ⓦwww.amci.org.ph) about joining an organized trek. Most climbers camp below the summit for the night and then walk the remaining distance to the top early the following day to watch the sunrise. To **get to Makiling** from the university campus, take a jeepney marked for the Scout Jamboree Park.

### Pagsanjan Falls

Francis Ford Coppola chose **PAGSANJAN**, 80km southeast of Manila, as the shooting location for the harrowing final scenes of *Apocalypse Now*, and the sheer drama of the scenery around here is undeniable. Faded Hollywood associations aside, the real draw here is the chance to shoot down the fourteen rapids of the Bombongan River from **Pagsanjan Falls**, one of the area's biggest tourist attractions. The local *bangkeros* are skilled at manoeuvring their canoes between the boulders, but have also gained a reputation for being hard-nosed when the time comes to demand a tip, and prices are already rather steep for the seven-kilometre thrill ride. The official Department of Tourism (DoT) rate is P580 per person not including "extras" such as life jackets, so don't be swayed by the touts. It's best to get to the falls early before the hordes arrive, which pretty much precludes weekends, and the rapids are at their most thrilling in the wet season; during the dry season the ride is much more sedate. From **Santa Cruz**, two hours by bus from

Manila, you'll be offered "special rides" to the falls, but there's no need as it's an easy ten minutes in a jeepney, which run regularly from the little square in the centre of town to the river (P15). The last rapids trip is usually a couple of hours before sundown, at around 4pm.

### Accommodation

**Pagsanjan Youth Hostel** 237 General Luna St, Santa Cruz ⓣ049/645 2347. Has basic dorm beds with fan and slightly more expensive singles and doubles. ❷–❸

**Willy Flores Guesthouse** 821 Garcia St, Santa Cruz ⓣ049/500 8203. A simple but clean guesthouse offering singles and doubles with fan and bath. ❷

### Mount Banahaw

About 130km southeast of Manila, near Dolores in Quezon province, is 2188-metre **Mount Banahaw**. Considered sacred by seventeen religious sects with different beliefs and rituals, it draws thousands of visitors every year, especially around Easter, when huge crowds of pilgrims flock to the mountain. Banahaw has spawned a vast number of legends and superstitions: one says that every time a foreigner sets foot on the mountain it will rain. If you don't mind being the catalyst for a few showers, Banahaw is a challenging but rewarding climb, its slopes thick with verdant jungle and with panoramic views of the surrounding landscape from the crater rim. To get to the start of the trail, take a **jeepney** from **San Pablo** to the barangay of **Kinabuyahan**, where you will need to visit the barangay hall to hire a **guide** and sign a logbook before you are allowed to proceed. Treat this mountain seriously because although the early part of the trail looks wide and well-trodden it soon peters out into inhospitable rainforest – even experienced climbers allow three days to reach the summit and get back down safely, and a crater descent should only be attempted by expert climbers. If you haven't got time to reach the summit you can trek to **Kristalino Falls** ("Crystalline Falls") and back in a day. An hour and a half further along from the falls is a second waterfall, an ideal spot to **camp**. The Department of Environment and Natural Resources is a good source of information on the trek, (ⓦwww.denr.gov.ph).

## TAAL VOLCANO

Rising majestically from the centre of picturesque Taal lake and perennially popular with day-trippers, **Taal Volcano** offers infinitely gentler trekking than either Banahaw or Makiling. **Taal** is still active – there have been signs of unrest since 1991 – and the authorities are occasionally forced to issue evacuation warnings to local inhabitants. A team of seismologists are permanently based on the lakeshore and continue to monitor the situation. The volcano last erupted in 1977 without causing major damage, but when it blew its top in 1754, thousands died and surrounding villages were largely destroyed. **Tagaytay**, 70km south of Manila, is the nearest town, perched out of harm's way on a 600-metre-high ridge above the lake. Because of its cool climate – on some days it even gets foggy – Tagaytay is a popular retreat from the heat of the nearby capital. Unfortunately, rash development and abuse of building restrictions have turned Tagaytay into the tourist town from hell, with menacing shoals of tricycles and overpriced accommodation. The views from the ridge are admittedly stunning but staying beside the lake in the little barangay of **Talisay**, is a far more affordable option. This is also the jumping-off point if you want to climb the volcano; you can hire a boat and guide in Talisay for around P1500, and then there's a P50 entry fee. If you make an early start, it's possible to climb to either the new crater or the old crater (both are active) and be back in Talisay in time for a good fish lunch at one of the many native-cuisine restaurants along the shore. There is not much shade on the volcano and it can get hot, so don't go without sunblock, a good hat, food and plenty of water. There are horses for hire (P350) if you feel like enjoying the view without expending any energy. You can find out more about Taal Volcano and other volcanoes at the **Philippine Institute of Volcanology and Seismology**, 5km west of Talisay in Buco.

## Arrival and information

**By bus** Crow Transit and JAM liner buses run frequently from Manila (Pasay) to Tagaytay and Lemery-Batangas. The latter stops at Tanauan from where you can catch a jeepney to Talisay (30min). Jeepneys between Tagaytay and Talisay (40min) run only until 4pm, after which time you'll need to take a tricycle (P200), a long bumpy ride down an unlit hill to get back to Talisay. From Batangas City, some buses bound for Pasay in Manila pass through Tanuaun and others take a route through Tagaytay. Make sure you ask the driver before you get on.

## Accommodation

All places below are in Talisay and rent boats to the volcano.

**Gloria de Castro's** ⓣ043/773 0138 or 0928 504 5170. Gloria herself is as friendly as you could wish, and she whips up simple and tasty Filipino dishes at rock bottom prices. Boat rental is also competitively priced. ❻

**Rosalina's Place** ⓣ 0927 565 8221. The cheapest place in Talisay. Lex, Rosalina's son, rents boats to the volcano at P1000, slighty less than the going rate, but there's no denying that the fan rooms here are dingy and small. ❷

**San Roque Beach Resort** ⓣ043/773 0271 or 0905 417 9179, ⓔsanroquebeachresort@yahoo.com. A warm and welcoming place right on the lakeshore with magnificent views across to the volcano. Owned by the charming Lita and Leo Merkx, a Filipina/Dutch couple who delight visitors with their combined skills as professional chef and raconteur respectively. Rooms are spotless, spacious and adorned with pleasing little touches such as plants and reading lamps. ❻

## Eating

**Josephine's** On the main ridge road in Tagaytay. Hugely popular with a menu of affordable dishes including tuna steak (P295), sizzling gambas (P240) and a decadent Bailey's cheesecake (P110). Seating in the pretty outside garden catches a refreshing breeze from the lake, and the views are magnificent.

**Sonya's Garden** ⓦwww.sonyasgarden.com. Fifteen kilometres outside Tagaytay on the way to Nasugbu, this stunning restaurant and B&B is worth every effort – catch a jeepney towards Lian and ask the driver to let you off at *Sonya's* junction, where a tricycle will take you the rest of the way. The set menus (P560) feature home made pesto, olive tapenade, inventive salads, pastas and no less than three desserts (per person), including a wonderfully sticky sweet-potato confection, all served in a dining room-cum-greenhouse swathed in flowering plants. Bring your appetite, the portions are immense.

## Directory

**Banks and exchange** There's a BPI with ATM at the Tagaytay roundabout.

**Internet** Several internet cafés around Olivarez Plaza in Tagaytay. There is no internet access in Talisay.

## Moving on

Tagaytay is well connected by jeepney to Nasugbu, for Batangas' beaches and is a stop on the Manila-Taal-Leery route (for Anilao). Erjohn & Almark buses to Lian (for Nasugbu and Matabungkay) can be flagged down at the Tagaytay roundabout.

# BATANGAS BEACH RESORTS

For many hardworking city-dwellers, the first stop at the weekend is one of the many **beach resorts in Batangas**. The beaches are far from the country's finest specimens, but they are at least relatively close to Manila. Three hours after leaving the smog you can be breaking out the suntan oil. From **NASUGBU** and neighbouring Matabungkay on the west coast, the resorts stretch south to Calatagan.

Further south **ANILAO** has not only sea and sand, but also some of the best diving in Batangas, though getting here is trickier. It's worth making a reservation in advance so that you can be picked up from Anilao; the resorts here are spread out along the coast and it's not always easy to get around. If you haven't made a reservation try not to arrive later than 3pm as tricycles will be scarce. Note that Bauan is the last ATM outpost before Batangas city.

## Arrival

**By bus** Crow Transit and Erjohn & Almark buses leave from Pasay terminals in Manila **for Nasugbu** (hourly; 2hr). Tricycles from Nasugbu and Matabungkay will take you to your resort. **For Anilao** take a bus from Cubao or Pasay to Batangas City (3hr) and ask to be let off in Bauan. From here you can take a jeepney to Anilao. Or, from Batangas City take a regular Batangas–Anilao or Batangas–Mabini jeepney from outside *McDonald's* on P. Burgos St. From Matabungkay or Nasugbu, catch a jeepney to Lemery, change for Bauan then catch a jeepney to Anilao.

## Accommodation

### Nasugbu area

**Alfresco Beach Resort** Matabungkay Beach ⓣ0932 285 43139 or 0917 830 0038, ⓦwww.alfrescoresort.com. Warm and welcoming, it's the little touches that make this place special – outdoor cabanas with day beds and billowing white curtains, fantastic seafood and a romantic deck bar facing the sunset. The resort has its own *balsas,* the floating picnic rafts that dot the seashore at Matabungkay. ❻

**Mar-Lou Beach Resort** Nasugbu Beach Rd (no phone). Family-run place, complete with kids and chickens running around. Rooms are basic, but have a/c and private bathrooms. The resort opens straight onto the beach, and next door is *Concepto* bar and disco, the only sign of nightlife in Nasugbu itself. ❹

**Villa Rebekah Resort and Restaurant** Nasugbu Beach Rd ⓣ043/031 1108. The rooms are nothing special, but they're set in a lush compound with a swimming pool and billiard tables. The restaurant occasionally hosts live folk bands. ❻

### Anilao area

It's worth booking ahead, so you can arrange a pickup from Anilao.

**Anilao Outrigger Resort** ⓣ 02/890 6778 or 02/807 4574. ⓦwww.outrigger.com.ph. Good range from standard doubles to spacious rooms opening onto a veranda and family rooms for five people. Offers kayaking, windsurfing and snorkelling equipment for rent. Significant midweek discounts, otherwise ❻

**Aquaventure Reef Club** ⓣ0927 387 7485, ⓦwww.aquareefclub.com. Comfortable, unpretentious scuba resort 3km along the coastal road beyond Anilao. Also offers island-hopping and snorkelling trips in rented bancas. Bamboo-built rooms come with fan and hot water and buffet-style meals are served in a nice open restaurant overlooking the sea. Three-day dive packages start at $160 otherwise ❺

**Planet Dive** The last of the resorts along the Anilao strip ⓣ02/906 3898/0927 230 8008, ⓦwww.planetdive.net. Tastefully decorated native-style cottages opposite the Twin Rocks dive site, where the bay is sheltered enough for good snorkelling. You can have candlelit dinners on the wooden deck, from where you can take in Anilao's wonderful sunsets. Dive packages (from P3000 per person) can be best value. It's essential to specify your diving level while making your booking, so you can be matched with your own knowledgeable and friendly in-house scuba master. ❻ including three meals.

## Moving on

Leaving Anilao, a convenient option is to hire a private van – from your resort to Batangas pier will cost P1500.

# BATANGAS CITY

**BATANGAS CITY** (as opposed to Batangas province) is a transit point for tourists on their way to Puerto Galera. As a destination in its own right, it has nothing to offer; the only sight most visitors see in Batangas City is the ferry terminal. If you get stranded overnight, try *Avenue Pension House*, 150 Rizal Ave (ⓣ 043/300 1964; ❷).

# PUERTO GALERA

**PUERTO GALERA** on the northern coast of **Mindoro**, 80km south of Manila, has become one of the Philippines' most popular tourist attractions, and rightly so. It has a stunning natural harbour, countless coves and beaches, a good range of affordable accommodation and excellent scuba diving, with around thirty listed **dive sites**. As well as being

## TRAVEL TO AND FROM PUERTO GALERA

The most convenient way to reach Puerta Galera from Manila is a combined **bus-and-ferry** service (3hr to Batangas pier, then 2hr by boat; P600 one-way). Si-Kat (Manila: ⓣ 02/521 3344; Batangas City: ⓣ 02/521 3344) leaves at 9am sharp from the *City State Tower Hotel* at 1315 A Mabini St, Ermita. Coming back, the service leaves Puerto at 8.15am, stopping in Sabang at 9am. There's a similar service run by ZCL Shipping Lines, from the *Swagman Hotel* in Malate, Manila (ⓣ02/523 8541). **From Batangas Pier** there are numerous, competitive **ferry** options, with regular departures for Puerto Galera town (Muelle Pier), Sabang and White Beach until 5pm. Fares are around P180 plus P25 terminal fee (2hr). On the way back from Puerto Galera, numerous buses wait at Batangas pier for the trip to Manila. Try to take a direct bus marked for Pasay or Cubao – some buses go through the barrios, making it a long journey.



the name of a small town, "Puerto Galera" is generally used to refer to the area between Sabang, 5km to the east, and White Beach, 8km to the west.

The area's extensive and diverse coral reefs have been declared a UNESCO Man and the Biosphere Marine Reserve – a marine environment of global importance. The direct protection that comes from such a declaration is minimal, but the reefs remain intact thanks to the efforts of local people, hotel owners and dive operators, who all co-operate to ensure the undersea riches are not frittered away.

Even arriving at Puerto Galera is memorable, the ferry from Batangas City slipping gently through aquamarine waters past a series of headlands fringed with haloes of sand and coconut trees. Brilliant white yachts lie at anchor in Muelle Bay, and in the background looms the brooding hulk of **Mount Malasimbo**, invariably crowned with a ring of cumulus. There's plenty on offer in addition to diving, including excellent snorkelling, trekking into the mountains and beach-hopping by banca, perhaps with a packed lunch so you can picnic in the deserted cove of your choice.

**Sabang** is the busiest beach, with a mind-boggling variety of accommodation dotted haphazardly along the shoreline, some above-average

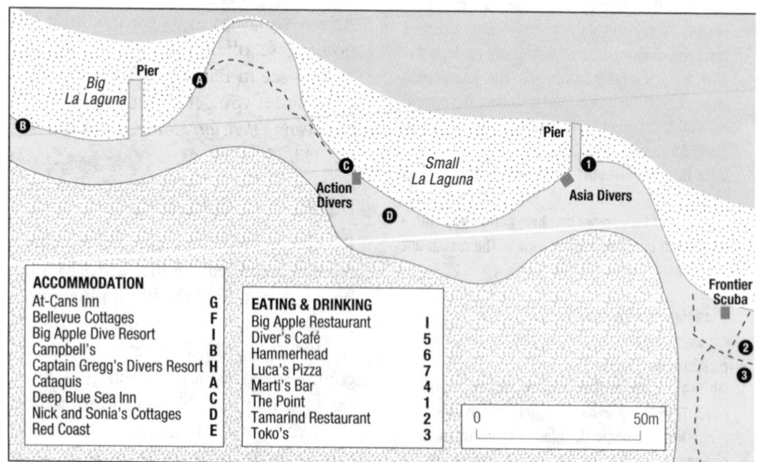

restaurants and a couple of go-go bars. Neighbouring **Small La Laguna** and **Big La Laguna** are rather more laid-back and family-oriented. Twenty minutes by jeepney on the other side of Puerto Galera town is **White Beach**, which has no girlie bars and fewer boorish scuba divers than Sabang. It gets busy at peak times, especially Easter, when backpackers from Manila hold all-night raves on the sand. Five minutes beyond White Beach by jeepney is quiet **Talipanan Beach**. Both are good bases for **trekking** in the mountains.

## Information and transport

**Tourist information** There's a small travel agent on Muelle pier. In Sabang, to arrange trekking, kayaking tours or overnight trips into the tribal hinterland, go to either Tarzan Trek Tours, beside the *Sunset* "disco" on the main drag or Jungle Trek Adventure Tours, on the main road to Puerto Galera. Next door to Jungle Trek is a small tourist office with currency exchange.

**Local transport** Travelling between the tourist areas is relatively easy. A **tricycle** from Puerto to White Beach costs P100. For the **jeepney** to Sabang from Puerto (a cheaper, quicker, option than hiring a banca) you have to walk up the hill to the left for about 150m. A **pumpboat** from Big/Small La Laguna to Sabang costs P200 during the day, P400 at night.

## Dive operators

There are dozens of dive operators in the area, so take time to shop around and get the best deal. You'll find an incredible range of dives to suit all abilities all around the coast of northern Mindoro. A single dive is in the region of $25, an open water course is at least $300.

**Action Divers** Small La Laguna ⓦwww.actiondivers.com.

**Asia Divers** Between Sabang and Small La Laguna ⓦwww.asiadivers.com.

**Captain Gregg's** (see p.646) Sabang.

**Frontier Scuba** Sabang ⓣ043/287 3077, ⓦwww.frontierscuba.com.

**Marco Vincent's** White Beach towards the main road ⓦwww.mvdive.com.

**Pacific Divers** White Beach, at the east end of the beach ⓣ0912 888 6763. Rents scuba and snorkelling gear and you can rent jet-skis from *Wave Jetski* next door.

**Titan Divers** at *Badladz* (see below) Puerto Galera ⓣ0906 221 4972 ⓦwww.titandivers.info. Will set you up with all the water-based activity you could want.

## Accommodation

### Puerto Galera

**Badladz** ⓣ043/283 3184, ⓦwww.badladz.com. The best budget accommodation in Puerto. This backpacker favourite is right beside Muelle pier, and does fantastic Mexican food. Incorporates Titan Divers (see above). ❹

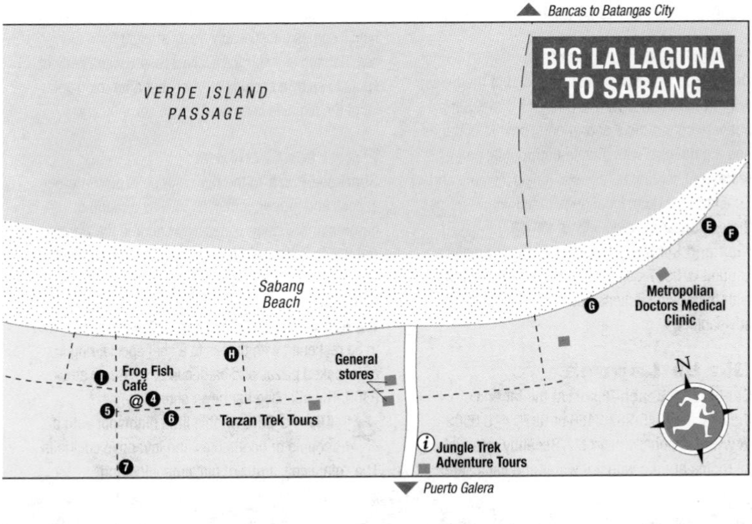

Bancas to Batangas City

BIG LA LAGUNA TO SABANG

VERDE ISLAND PASSAGE

Sabang Beach

Metropolian Doctors Medical Clinic

Frog Fish Café

General stores

Tarzan Trek Tours

Jungle Trek Adventure Tours

N

Puerto Galera

**El Cañonero Mariveles** Directly opposite Muelle pier ☎0905 278 5851. The restaurant downstairs does decent Italian, but some of the rooms suffer from jeepney noise early in the morning. *John and Jayne's* across the road changes cash and traveller's cheques, and offers long-distance phone calls. 4

### Sabang

**At-Cans Inn** ☎0918 799 7303 or 0920 406 1885. Good budget option right on the beach just to the left of where the bancas dock. Nipa huts with kitchens. 4

**Bellevue Cottages** ⓔbellevue_viewpoint@hotmail.com. Up a long flight of steps just past *Red Coast*. Six cottages, all with spectacular views of the whole bay and their own hammocks. 4–5

**Big Apple Dive Resort** Middle of the beach ☎043/287 3134, ⓦwww.divebigapple.com. *Big Apple* is one of Sabang's most popular resorts, with a dive centre, 24-hr bar and swimming pool. Perfect if you're looking for somewhere lively – the bar and disco never stop and there's an ongoing pool tournament – but the rooms are noisy as a result. Free welcome drink at the bar. There's a Manila booking office at 1505 MH del Pilar St, Ermita (☎02/526 7592). 3–4

**Captain Gregg's Divers Resort** Right on the shore, middle of the beach ☎0917 540 4570, ⓦwww.captngreggs.com. Popular, well-established resort catering mainly to divers. Acceptable rooms, decent grub in the restaurant – there's a nightly barbecue 6–9pm – and good advice from the resident divers in the dive shop, many of whom have lived in Sabang for years. 5

**Red Coast** (formerly *Gold Coast*) Far eastern edge of the beach, close to the ferry dock (no phone). Bright clean rooms with their own balconies, as well as kitchen and TVs. A good long-stay option. 4–5

### Small La Laguna

**Deep Blue Sea Inn** On the west end of the beach, 30m from Action Divers ☎043/287 3209. Simple but very comfortable apartments, private cottages and a/c doubles with private bathrooms, and a restaurant serving an eclectic Italain, Filipino and Thai menu. A quiet location with fine views across the sea towards Verde Island. 4–6

**Nick and Sonia's Cottages** Centre of Small La Laguna ☎0917 803 8156. Five simple rooms with their own kitchens and hot water. Booking advisable. 4

### Big La Laguna

**Campbell's Beach Resort** At the far end of the beach ☎043/287 3466 or 0920 416 0502, ⓦwww.campbellsresort.biz. Recently refurbished, all rooms are a/c with hot water and cable, and boast ocean views. It has its own bar, *Fat Bastards*, and the café does fantastic breakfasts. 5

**Cataquis** ☎ 0916 316 9877. The first accommodation you reach on Big La Laguna Beach as you walk down the path from Small La Laguna. Very simple cottages but they're clean and cheap and the location is exceptional. 4

### White Beach

Don't let the touts tie you down. Take time to wander up and down the beach; accommodation is most expensive in the centre, and prices increase at weekends. White Beach is a beautiful spot for extended R&R, so for longer stays negotiate a discount.

**Delgado's** Just after *The White Beach Resort* close to the path to the main road ☎0912 357 0803 or 0918 352 6001. The rooms have seen better days but you'd be hard pushed to find cheaper on White Beach. Concrete and bamboo cottages are set a little back from the beach, quiet, but in a great location close to everything. 3–4

**Summer Connection** At the western edge of the beach ☎0920 230 5098 or 0917 926 5943 ⓦhttp://summerconnection.multiply.com. Friendly, laid-back and comfortable lodge and restaurant with nipa huts set in a lovely compound right on the sand and dotted with hammocks. There's also an outdoor grill area where guests can cook locally-caught seafood. The same company own *Lagundian Hills*, the resort on the hill above *Summer Connection*, where for similar prices you can get a room with a great view of the bay. 6

## Eating, drinking and nightlife

If you're not sure what to eat in Puerto Galera, eat fish: it comes unbelievably fresh, straight from the sea. Sabang is by far the liveliest resort, with plenty of spots to enjoy a cocktail or three, but after midnight a lot of the nightlife is centred on the sex industry.

### Puerta Galera

**Sharkeez Pizza** To the right of Muelle pier. Internet access and proper coffee, as well as a menu of burgers and sizzling plates. Next door is the *Hangout Bar* which is the height of Puerta Galera's nightlife.

### Sabang

**Big Apple Restaurant** *Big Apple Dive Resort*. A force to be reckoned with thanks to a chef specializing in oven-baked pizzas and barbecue grills. Rump steak P400. The attached bar never shuts.

**Diver's Café** Affable little nightspot with a couple of pool tables and inventive cocktails. The "ginjuice", a mix of gin, lime juice and calamansi soda, is dangerously addictive.

**Hammerhead** Upstairs from *Broadway* bar. The only disco in Sabang that isn't a strip club. P80 entrance includes your first drink, and it fills up late.

**Luca's Pizza** Up the little alley beside *Broadway* this tiny, evening-only takeaway joint serves possibly the best pizza in Mindoro.

**Marti's Bar** ⓔ martis_bar_sabangbeach@yahoo.com. A chilled, friendly bar with armchairs, chess sets and a book exchange. Happy hour 4–7pm. Marti is thinking of expanding the premises to include a backpacker's dorm, an option definitely worth investigating.

**Tamarind Restaurant** For tropical charm right on the water with wonderful views *Tamarind* can't be beat. One of the longest established places in Sabang. Seafood and pasta dishes are around P240.

**Toko's** Part of the upmarket *Atlantis Resort Hotel* with prices to match, but the international, Asian-fusion food is good and the daily buffet option (P896) means you can get your money's worth.

### Small La Laguna

**The Point** A Puerto favourite, *The Point* sits between Small La Laguna and Sabang. Two-for-one cocktails during its popular happy hour get the punters in, and it rocks 'til midnight.

### White Beach

**Coco Aroma** Next to *Summer Connection*, ⓔ coco_aroma5203@yahoo.com. This hippyish hangout has rustic wooden tables on the sand, good music and a wide chice of Filipino and world dishes at reasonable prices. The budget meals like pork spring rolls with rice and ice tea (P100), are particularly good value. Mid-range rooms are available, though there is one fan double (❻).

**Foodtrip sa Galera Snack Bar** Near *Delgado's*. Budget meals with "eat all you can" rice (P100–150).

## Directory

**Banks and exchange** Puerto Galera Rural Bank changes cash, but the closest ATMs are in Calapan.

**Internet** In Sabang, try the *Frog Fish Café*, on the main beach path opposite *Diver's Café* or *Mindoro Net Café* opposite *Broadway*. In Sabang, try *Sharkeez* near the pier.

**Medical centre** Misereor Health Clinic, Puerta Galera, beside the church, at the junction with road to Sabang.

# LEGASPI

The port city of **LEGASPI** (often spelt Legazpi), four hours south of Naga, is the place to base yourself if you fancy climbing **Mount Mayon**, but otherwise there's really no reason to visit. Legaspi is a fairly charmless provincial town with one main thoroughfare, Peñaranda Street, which connects the port area (Legaspi city proper) with the district of Albay, where most of the accommodation and restaurants are. The town itself has little in the way of tourist attractions, but one sight worth seeing are the **Cagsawa Ruins** (daily 7am–7pm), the eerie remains of a church that was buried in the devastating eruption of Mayon in 1814. The best time to see the ruins is at dawn before the vendors and hawkers stake a claim to it and the clouds roll in and obscure the view of the volcano. Take a jeepney bound for Daraga and change for Camalig; ask the driver to let you off near the ruins. The nearby **National Museum of the Philippines, Cagsawa** (Mon–Fri 9am–4pm; free) has exhibits about Mount Mayon and many other volcanoes in the Philippines. If you want a clear view of Mayon from a safe vantage point, head to Kupuntukan Hill in the port area of Legaspi.

## Arrival and information

**By bus** The bus station is 1.5km west of the town centre. Victory Liner, Five Star and Philippine Rabbit all make the long trek from Manila daily. Philtranco goes all the way from Manila to Davao, using ferries where it has to: it stops at Daet, Naga and Legaspi, before heading on to the port of Matnog at the southernmost tip of South Luzon for the Samar ferry.

**By air** Legaspi Airport lies 3km northwest of the town centre, off Washington Drive; private cars meet incoming flights for the ride into Legaspi (P200).

**Tourist Information** Albay Provincial Tourist Office, F. Aquenda Drive, close to City Hall (ⓣ 052/820 6314 or 820 6316, ⓔ tourism@albay.gov.ph). Enquire here about arranging a guide for Mount Mayon.

**Tour operators** Bicol Adventure and Tours, Suite 20, V&O Bldg, downstairs from the *Legaspi Tourist Inn*, Quezon Ave (ⓣ 052/480 2266) is the best company to organize a trip up Mayon.

## Accommodation

**Legazpi Tourist Inn** 3rd Floor, V&O Building, cnr Quezon Ave and Lapu-Lapu St ⓣ052/480 6147. Very clean and bright with friendly staff and a central location; fan rooms. ❸

**Magayon Hotel** Peñaranda St ⓣ052/480 7770 or 052/414 3121. A little long in the tooth but staff are very friendly, and the a/c doubles with TV are a steal. You can book Cebu Pacific flights downstairs. ❹

**Sampaguita Tourist Inn** Rizal St (Albay district end) ⓣ052/480 6258. Set back from the street behind an out-of-use petrol station. Has acceptable fan or a/c rooms, with luxurious add-ons such as hot water and television for a little extra. ❷–❸

## Eating

*Jollibee*, *McDonald's* and *Chow King* are pervasive; the population of Legaspi seem to be devoted to fast food.

**Graceland** Branches on Peñaranda St, the Albay end of Rizal St and in Pacific Mall. For something (marginally) different, try this Bicol-only fast-food restaurant serving barbecue pork, barbecue chicken and adobo with rice, all for around P95.

**Legaspi Four Seasons** Upstairs at 205 Magallanes St. The best restaurant in town, a simple, clean Chinese place: portions are freshly cooked, huge, and cheap so choose a few different dishes and share them around.

**Waway** Peñaranda St. Serves native Bicol cuisine in a cavernous dining room reminiscent of a suburban convention centre circa 1983, with all the atmosphere that implies. The food is good though, with daily meat-based specials.

## Directory

**Airlines** Air Philippines has a ticket office on Lapu-Lapu St.

**Banks and exchange** There are a number of banks with ATMs on Quezon Ave and upper Rizal St.

**Internet** *Sweetheart Internet Café*, 122 Magallanes St. Half a block north of Silverscreen Cinemas.

**Post office** On the nothern end of Lapu-Lapu St at the junction with Quezon Ave.

**Shopping** LCC Mall is at the junction of Lapu-Lapu St and Quezon Ave.

## Moving on

**By bus/minivan** to: Donsol (frequent; 2hr); Naga (frequent; 4hr); Sorsogon (frequent; 1hr 30min).

**By air** to Manila: (3–4 daily; 1hr 10min).

## MOUNT MAYON

The perfectly triangular cone of **Mount Mayon** (2421m) in Albay province makes it look, from a distance, like a child's drawing of a mountain, but don't be deceived, Mayon has claimed the lives of a number of climbers in rock avalanches in recent years. It is the most active volcano in the country and has erupted more than 47 times in the last four centuries – 1984 and 1993 saw significant eruptions. As recently as late 2006 hundreds were killed by mudslides of volcanic ash loosened by Typhoon Durian. It's no wonder the locals spin fearful stories around it. The most popular legend says Mayon was formed when a beautiful native princess eloped with a brave warrior. Her uncle, Magayon, pursued the young couple, who prayed to the gods for help. A terrible landslide halted Magayon, burying him alive, and he is said to still be inside the mountain, his irrepressible anger bursting forth in the form of volcanic eruptions.

Mayon has an adverse effect on Legaspi's weather conditions; the only window of opportunity for an ascent is **March to May**, and even then you should be prepared for cold nights at altitude and showers. At other times, you could be hanging around for days waiting for a break in the weather. The slopes of Mayon are not as silky smooth as they look from a few miles away. It takes at least two days to reach the summit, working your way through forest, grassland and deserts of rock-sand boulders, and another day to descend. A **guide** is essential, arranged at the tourist offices in Legaspi or through Mayon Mountaineers Club (ⓦwww.mfpi.org, or ask the tourist office to put you in touch). You can also arrange for a tent and sleeping bag; it can be chilly on the higher slopes, so don't bank on sleeping outside. You'll have to bring all your food with you from Legaspi; there are sources of water on the volcano, but you'll need purifying tablets.

The **safest approach** is from the northwestern slope, which starts at 762m above sea level on a ledge where the Philippine Institute of Volcanology and Seismology (PHIVOLCS) research station is located, and where you'll need to register. See ⓦwww.phivolcs.dost.gov.ph for the latest updates on the status of the volcano.

## SORSOGON TOWN AND GUBAT

Near the southeastern tip of the Bicol peninsula, **SORSOGON TOWN**, capital of the eponymous province, makes a good base for visiting Donsol and exploring the beaches of the eastern seaboard, where waves hammer in from the Pacific and surfing is a burgeoning industry. One gem waiting to be discovered is **Rizal Beach** in the barrio of **GUBAT**, a twenty-minute jeepney ride from Sorsogon. There's little development here; you won't find loungers, sunset cocktails and other trappings of beach life, but it is wildly beautiful.

In Sorsogon there are a number of ATMs and internet cafés stretched along Rizal Street.

### Arrival and information

**By bus and jeepney** All buses, jeepneys, minivans and tricycles congregate around the market square in Sorsogon. There are frequent departures to Gubat and Donsol, as well as services to Manila and Legaspi.

**Tourist information** *Fernando's Hotel* is the headquarters of the local tourism council (ⓦwww.sorsogontourism.com) and can arrange local tours, including excursions to see the whale sharks. The owner, David Duran, is a mine of information about the area.

### Accommodation

**Fernando's Hotel** Pareja St ⓣ056/211 1357, ⓔfernandohotel@hotmail.com By far the most attractive accommodation in Sorsogon itself, with a quaint, antique ambience and the small patio restaurant is easily the best place to eat in town. ❻

**Rizal Beach Resort Hotel** Gubat ⓣ056/211 1056. Ageing but adequate rooms by the beach. ❹

## DONSOL

The peaceful fishing community of **DONSOL** lies almost equidistant between Legaspi and Sorsogon Town; you can get there by frequent bus or jeepney from either in less than two hours. The area around Donsol is best known for one of the greatest concentrations of **whale sharks** in the world, and your first stop in town should be the **Visitor Centre** (daily 7am–4pm) next to the town hall, where you can complete all the formalities of hiring a boat for a whale shark-watching trip. The number of sightings varies: during peak season (Dec–Jan), there's a good chance of seeing ten or fifteen whale sharks – known locally as *butanding* – a day, but on some days you might strike out and see none. The other busy time of the year in Donsol is April, when the town holds its annual Butanding Festival.

Tourists intent on seeing the sharks are not allowed to board a boat without first being briefed by a **Butanding Interaction Officer** (BIO), who explains how to behave in the water near one of these huge creatures. The number of snorkellers around any one whale shark is limited to six; flash photography is not permitted, nor is scuba gear, and don't get anywhere near the animal's tail because it's powerful enough to do you some serious damage. Take plenty of protection against the sun and a good book. Once a whale shark has been sighted you'll need to get your mask, snorkel and flippers on and get in the water before it dives too deep to be seen.

Boats **cost** P3500 for up to seven people, and there's also a registration fee of P300 for foreigners and P100 for Filipinos. Each boat has a crew of three, the captain, the BIO and the spotter, each of whom will expect a token of your appreciation (at least P100 to each person) at the end of a successful day (and even an unsuccessful one). Renting snorkelling equipment is P300. All this makes it an expensive day out by Philippine standards, but take heart from the fact that your money is helping the conservation effort.

If you want to stay overnight in Donsol, try the *Santiago Lodging House* (☎ 056/411 8311 or 0920 388 1218; ❷), a simple, clean homestay right in the centre of town, with great-value rooms.

# The Visayas

No one seems entirely sure how many islands there are in **the Visayas**, but it certainly runs into the thousands. Everywhere you turn there's a patch of tropical sand or coral reef, with a ferry or banca to take you there. There are nine major islands – Cebu, Bohol, Guimaras, Samar, Leyte, Panay, Negros, Romblon and Siquijor – but it's the hundreds of others in between that make this part of the archipelago so irresistible. A lazy boat journey can take you from the glitzy, wallet-damaging hotels and shopping malls of the bigger islands to enchantingly bucolic islets.

Despite recent efforts to turn **Cebu City** into a major international freeport, most of the islands remain lost in their own little world. Vast areas of **Bohol**, **Leyte**, **Panay** and **Samar** and the sugar plantation island of **Negros** are relatively undiscovered, while the island of **Siquijor** is said to be home to witches and faith healers. Of the smaller islands, some are famous for their beaches – **Boracay's White Beach**, off the northern tip of Panay, still holds its own amongst the world's finest – some for their fiestas, some for sugar and some for their folklore. No one can accuse the Visayas, and Visayans, of being a uniform lot. A huge variety of dialects are spoken here, including Cebuana, Ilonggo, Waray Waray and Aklan, and while English is less readily understood in some places, visitors won't find a warmer welcome anywhere in the Philippines.

Getting around the Visayas is fairly easy. The major islands are accessible by air from Manila, and, increasingly, from Cebu City, but the **ferry network** is so extensive that it doesn't really matter if you can't get a flight. The beauty of the Visayas is that there's no need to make formal plans. There's always another island, another beach, another place to stay.

## SAMAR

The large island of **Samar**, 320km from top to toe, lies between Bicol and Leyte. It's a short hop by ferry from Matnog, on the southern tip of Bicol, and is connected to Leyte by the two-kilometre-long San Juanico Bridge. There are several daily departures from Matnog to both Allen and San Isidro, though the former is better served by transport to the rest of the island.

Samar has never quite taken off as a major tourist destination, which is a shame, because large parts of the coast are unspoiled and the beaches of the east, especially, are wild and beautiful. Perhaps the lack of visitors is something to do with the **weather**. Samar has a different climate from the rest of the country, with dry periods only in May and June. Apart from that, rainfall is possible throughout the year, although never for long periods. Most of the rain falls from the beginning of November until February, and from early October to December fierce typhoons are not uncommon, a boon only to the growing number of surfers who come here to take advantage of the swells that rip in from the Pacific. Most people find the best time to visit is from May to September when the island is bathed in sunshine.

One reason to visit Samar is the marvellous **Sohoton Natural Bridge National Park**, a prehistoric wilderness full of caves, waterfalls and underground rivers. The park is in the southern part of the island, so access is quickest and easiest from Tacloban on Leyte. For many visitors, Sohoton is scheduled only as a day-trip before they loop back to to Leyte and continue through the Visayas. From Tacloban, you'll have to start early in the morning – catch a jeepney to **Basey** (1hr), then a pedicab to the **Municipal Tourism Information Office** (Mon–Fri 8am–5pm, Sat & Sun, 8am–1pm; ⓣ053/276 1471), where you can arrange guides and accommodation, though the tourist office in Tacloban itself is also very helpful in this respect (see below).

## LEYTE

In the sixteenth century, Magellan passed through Leyte before his celebrated arrival on Cebu, striking a blood compact with the local chieftain as he did so and marking the fateful first contact between the natives of the archipelago and a series of foreign conquistadors. But it was **World War II** that really brought Leyte fame – or infamy – as the scene of brutal fighting in its jungle hinterlands. On October 20, 1944, General Douglas MacArthur landed at Leyte, fulfilling the famous promise he had made to Filipinos, "I shall return." He brought with him the first President of the Commonwealth, Sergio Osmeña.

### Tacloban

On the northeast coast, the capital of Leyte (and unofficially of Samar), **TACLOBAN** is the hometown of that tireless collector of shoes, Imelda Marcos, who was born here to a humble family called Romualdez. The Daniel Z. Romualdez airport and numerous streets and buildings bearing the name testify to the enduring power of the nepotism and self-promotion that characterized her years in Malacañang. In her youth, Imelda was a local beauty queen, and referred to herself in later life as "the rose of Tacloban". As dubious a claim as this is, the town itself has little else to recommend it; there's not much to see and it's dirty, run-down and noisy. Around Tacloban there are a number of sights associated with the war, including the **Leyte Landing Memorial**, marking the spot where General MacArthur waded ashore on Red Beach, Palo, and nearby, on **Hill 522**, foxholes still remain. Palo is just south of Tacloban and easily reached by jeepney. From Tacloban you can also go on trips to Sohoton Natural Bridge National Park (see opposite) and Ormoc and around (see p.654).

#### Arrival and information

**By bus and jeepney** The terminal is at the junction of Quezon Blvd and Rizal Ave, on the northeastern edge of Tacloban. Philtranco uses a station 2km outside the city. A tricycle from here to the town centre costs P100. From Bicol buses meet the ferries at Allen for the long, arduous journey to Tacloban, with stops at Calbayog and Catbalagan. Sorsogon in Bicol to Tacloban takes about fourteen hours.

**By ferry** The wharf runs parallel to Bonifacio St.

**By air** Daniel Z. Romualdez Airport is 12km outside the town, served by regular jeepneys. A tricycle will cost P100.

**Tourist information** The tourist information office is at 141 Santo Niño St (Mon–Fri 8am–5pm; ⓣ053/321 2048 or 523 0295).

#### Accommodation

**Cecilia's Lodge** 178 Paterno St ⓣ053/523 1759. Set a little back from the street and easy to miss. Plain, dark fan rooms with shared bathrooms, and the staff have very limited English, but at this price, who's complaining? ❶

**Hotel Alejandro** P. Paterno St ⓣ053/321 7033, ⓦwww.alejandro.tacloban.biz. A well-managed, bright hotel two blocks from Santo Niño Park. Rooms are spacious and have a/c, hot showers and TVs as standard and there's a popular café downstairs serving Spanish and Filipino dishes. Don't miss the "Remembering Leyte" photo exhibition on the 2nd floor, detailing MacArthur's landing and the historic events of 1944. ❺

**San Juanico Lodge** J. Romualadez St ⓣ053/523 4442. Rather woebegone and almost devoid of atmosphere, but dirt-cheap and central. ❶–❷

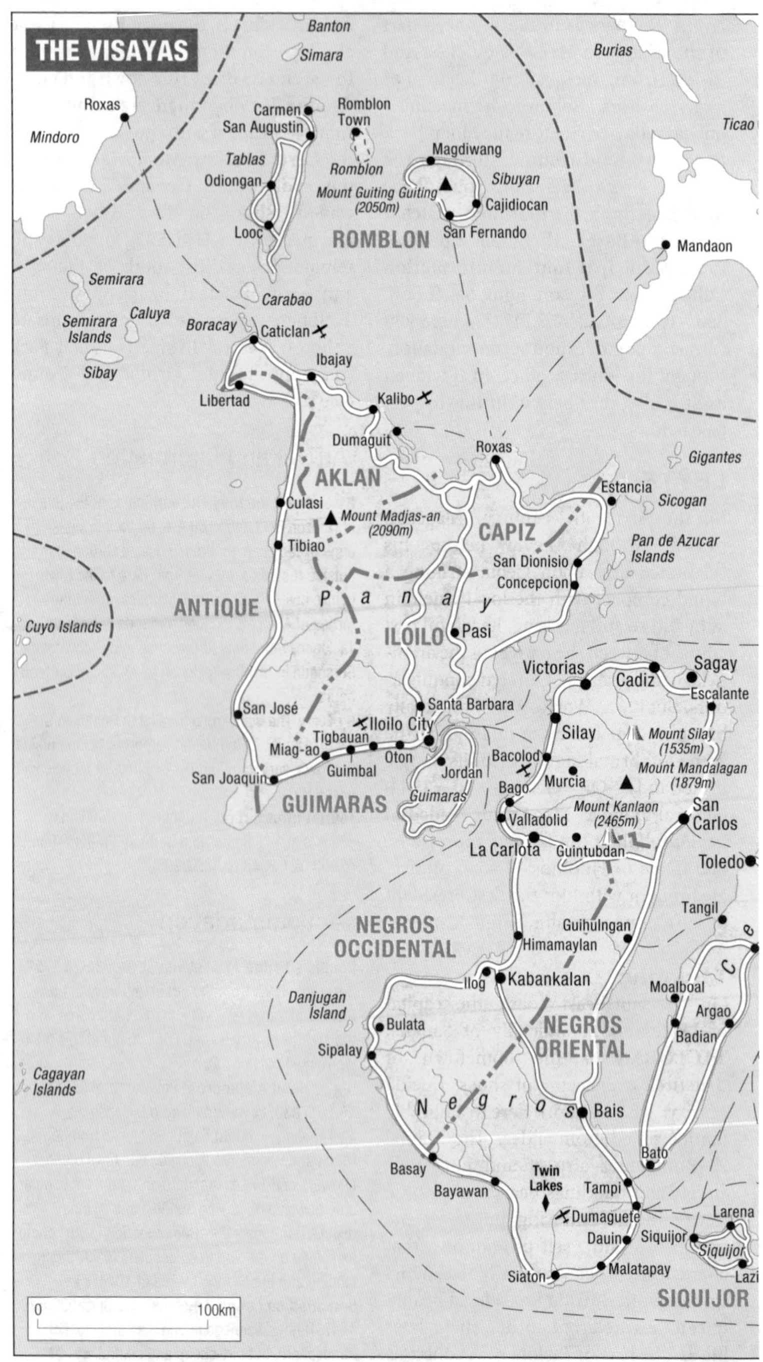
THE VISAYAS
Banton
Simara
Burias
Roxas
Mindoro
Carmen
San Augustin
Romblon Town
Ticao
Tablas
Romblon
Magdiwang
Sibuyan
Odiongan
Mount Guiting Guiting (2050m)
Cajidiocan
Looc
ROMBLON
San Fernando
Mandaon
Semirara
Carabao
Semirara Islands
Caluya
Boracay
Caticlan
Sibay
Ibajay
Libertad
Kalibo
Dumaguit
Roxas
Gigantes
AKLAN
Estancia
Sicogan
Culasi
Mount Madjas-an (2090m)
CAPIZ
Tibiao
Pan de Azucar Islands
San Dionisio
Concepcion
ANTIQUE
P a n a y
Cuyo Islands
ILOILO
Pasi
Victorias
Sagay
Cadiz
Escalante
San José
Santa Barbara
Silay
Iloilo City
Mount Silay (1535m)
Tigbauan
Miag-ao
Oton
Bacolod
Mount Mandalagan (1879m)
Guimbal
Jordan
Murcia
San Joaquin
Bago
GUIMARAS
Guimaras
Mount Kanlaon (2465m)
San Carlos
Valladolid
La Carlota
Guintubdan
Toledo
Tangil
NEGROS OCCIDENTAL
Guihulngan
Himamaylan
Ilog
Kabankalan
Moalboal
Danjugan Island
Argao
Bulata
NEGROS ORIENTAL
Badian
Sipalay
Cagayan Islands
N e g r o s
Bais
Bato
Basay
Twin Lakes
Tampi
Bayawan
Dumaguete
Larena
Dauin
Siquijor
Siquijor
Malatapay
Siaton
Lazi
SIQUIJOR
0
100km

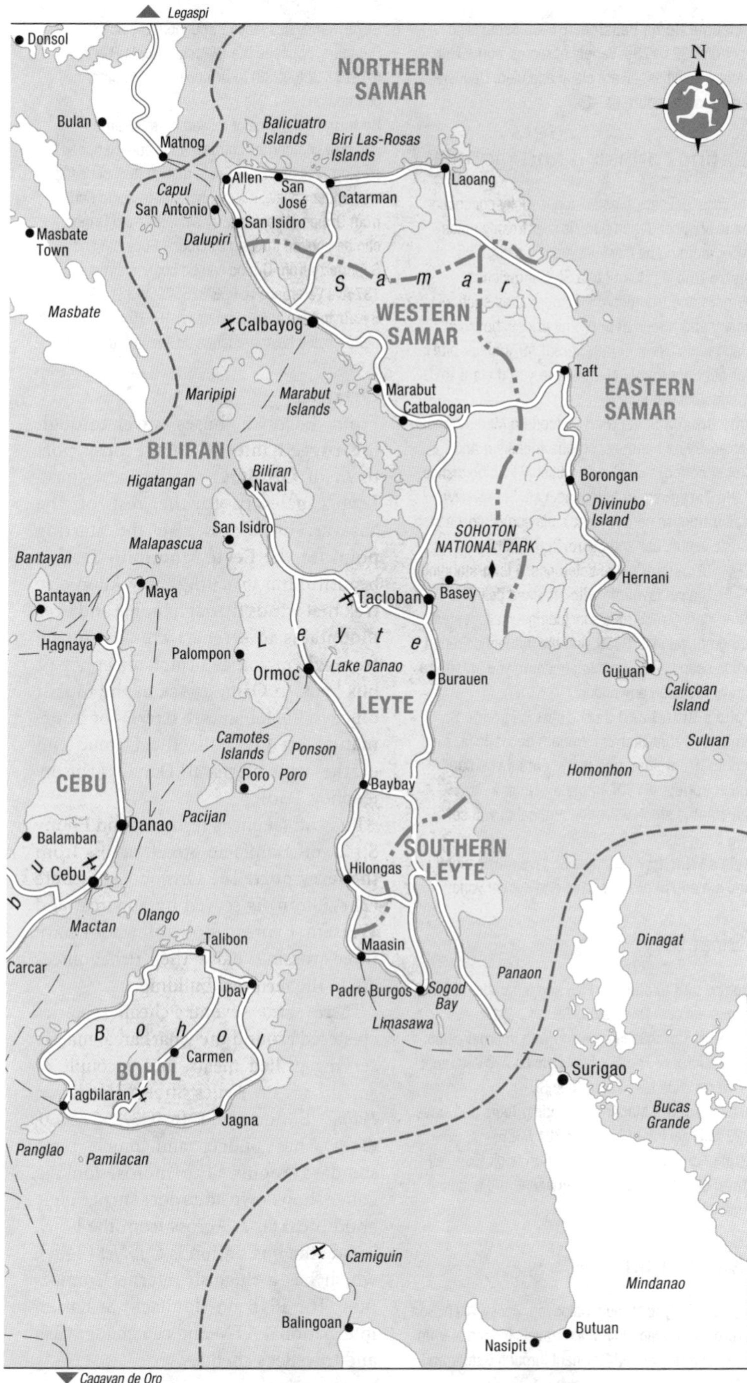
Legaspi
Donsol
NORTHERN SAMAR
Bulan
Matnog
Balicuatro Islands
Biri Las-Rosas Islands
Allen
San José
Catarman
Laoang
Capul
San Antonio
San Isidro
Masbate Town
Dalupiri
Samar
WESTERN SAMAR
Masbate
Calbayog
Taft
EASTERN SAMAR
Marabut
Maripipi
Marabut Islands
Catbalogan
BILIRAN
Higatangan
Biliran
Naval
Borongan
Divinubo Island
San Isidro
SOHOTON NATIONAL PARK
Malapascua
Bantayan
Bantayan
Maya
Basey
Hernani
Tacloban
Hagnaya
Palompon
Leyte
Ormoc
Lake Danao
Burauen
Guiuan
Calicoan Island
LEYTE
Camotes Islands
Ponson
Suluan
Poro
Poro
Homonhon
CEBU
Baybay
Danao
Pacijan
Balamban
SOUTHERN LEYTE
Cebu
Hilongas
Olango
Mactan
Dinagat
Talibon
Maasin
Carcar
Ubay
Padre Burgos
Sogod Bay
Panaon
Limasawa
Bohol
Carmen
BOHOL
Surigao
Tagbilaran
Jagna
Bucas Grande
Panglao
Pamilacan
Camiguin
Mindanao
Balingoan
Butuan
Nasipit
Cagayan de Oro
N

**Welcome Home Pension** 161–63 Santo Niño St ⓣ053/321 2739. Variety of rooms, some with kitchen facilities; all are clean and tiled. Opposite Duptours Transport. ❹–❺

## Eating, drinking and nightlife

The local delicacy *binagul*, a hot sticky concoction made of coconut and nuts, is sold freshly made every morning by hawkers around town.

**Bistro Uno** 41 Juan Luna St. Sandwiches, burgers and traditional Filipino dishes such as *pancit* and *adobo* at very low prices, but this place feels like a garage; great for a quick bite but not necessarily somewhere you'd want to spend your evening.

**Café Urbana** Santo Niño St. Modern Mediterranean oasis serving hummus, croque-monsieur and proper coffee, as well as traditional Filipino dishes.

**Calle Zaragosa** 39 Independencia St (ⓦwww.callezaragosa.com for who's playing). Laid-back music venue, bar and bistro. 7pm until late.

**Giuseppi's** Ave Veteranos. A long-standing Italian favourite with attached deli. The three-part combo meals including excellent steak are great value at P450, and the authentic French onion soup is just the thing to warm you up after a heavy Tacloban downpour.

**Julio's Buffet and Jazz Joint** P. Paterno St. From Wed–Sat there's "smooth acoustic jazz nights" from 9pm, and daily "eat all you can" lunch buffets (P130). In the evening, a substantial steak with rice and salad will set you back just P160.

**Kyle's Wine Bar** P. Gomez St. Live music nightly and a menu of pasta, salads and decent wine.

## Directory

**Banks and exchange** PNB and a number of other banks are on J Romualdez St.

**Internet** Tacloban is crowded with internet cafés. Try Explorer or The Net Surf Café on Ave Veteranos, or World Wide Net, Santo Niño St.

**Travel agents** MacArthur Landing Tours and Travel, 222 M.H del Pilar St, ⓣ053 321 5685, ⓔpbc–cruz888@yahoo.com. Can book tours, all travel services and is also an agent for Philippine Airlines.

## Moving on

**By bus** Daily to Ormoc, Calbayog, Basey, Allen, San Isidro and Davao. Philtranco travels to Manila from its own terminal (a 24-hr haul through Samar and Bicol). Minibuses leave throughout the day from Duptours, opposite the *Welcome Home Pension* (ⓣ0917 306 3233) to Ormoc (2hr) and other Leyte destinations.

**By ferry** At the time of research Cebu Ferries (ⓦwww.cebuferries.com) was the only company serving Tacloban from Cebu, though their schedule was under review. It's much faster to get to Cebu from Ormoc. Weesam ferry services from Ormoc can be booked through Duptours. Supercat and Superferry from Ormoc can be booked through 2GO, 137 Ave Veteranos ⓣ053/325529 or 321 3982.

**By air** to Manila (several daily; 1hr 10min). PAL and Cebu Pacific have branches on Ave Veteranos.

## Ormoc

From Tacloban, buses travel through the rugged interior to the busy port town of **ORMOC** on the west coast, Leyte's gateway to the rest of the Visayas. Ormoc is also the starting point for the **Leyte Mountain Trail**, a beautiful but gruelling forty-kilometre trek that winds through jungle and over mountains to serene Lake Mahagnao, from where you can catch a jeepney or bus back to Ormoc. Ask at the tourist office in Tacloban (see p.651) for information on the trail. The Ormuc end of the trail starts at Danao (1hr by jeepney, P30).

Bus and jeepneys terminate on Ebony Street off Bonifacio Street, across from the **ferry port**. The Ormoc-Cebu route (2hr 50min) is served by Supercat and Weesam Express, both of whom have three crossings daily. Their ticket offices are in the terminal building.

There are several cheap eateries clustered around the wharf area, mainly serving grilled meats, and a couple of small bars on Aviles Street. *Hotel Don Felipe*, Bonifacio St (ⓣ053/255 2460; ❸–❻), has budget and much nicer standard rooms. The morose-looking coffee shop downstairs does surprisingly good breakfasts. Across from the hotel, beside the bus station is *CupNet* (24hr), which has a sluggish internet connection. The PNB on Bonifacio St has an international ATM and can change cash and traveller's cheques.

## CEBU

The island of **Cebu** is the ninth largest in the Philippines and is considered, at least by Cebuanos themselves, as the beating heart of the Visayas. It's certainly the main hub of the hundreds of shipping arteries that crisscross the region. Any island-hopping trip will inevitably take you through **Cebu City**, the Philippines' second city, which despite its clamour is a great place to get a fix of shopping and shiny clubs before returning to lazy tropical living. When you've had your fill of the city head north to the idyllic island of **Malapascua**, where the sand is as fine as Boracay's, or to tranquil **Bantayan** off the northwest coast. South of Cebu City, on the opposite coast, lies the diving and drinking haven of **Moalboal** where the sites around Pescador Island are a mecca for divers and snorkellers.

### Cebu City

The "Queen City of the South", **CEBU CITY** has, like many Philippine municipalities, become something of an urban nightmare in the past decade, with an increasing number of jeepneys and taxis clogging up the terminally inadequate road network. The good news is that it's not half as chaotic as some parts of Manila; it's possible, at least, to get from one side of the city to the other without completely losing the will to live. Cebu has some great restaurants, lively nightlife and so many malls that it's a wonder Cebuanos ever see daylight, but the big annual attraction here is the **Sinulog Festival**, which culminates on the third Sunday of January with a wild Mardi Gras-style street parade and an outdoor concert at Fuente Osmeña. The festival, in honour of Cebu's patron saint the Santo Niño, is similar to, and almost as popular as, Kalibo's Ati-Atihan and hotels are usually full, particularly for the climax of the festivities. Check out Ⓦwww.sinulog.ph for details.

#### What to see and do

Cebu City is defined at its northern limit by **Fuente Osmeña**, also known as Osmena Circle, the large traffic roundabout at the far end of Osmeña Boulevard, which serves as the city's main north–south artery. Here you'll find all manner of hotels, restaurants, massage centres and pungent barbecue stalls as well as the usual *Jolibees* and huge department stores. At night it's full of skaters and promenaders, and is the closest thing Cebu has to a city centre. The coastal end of Osmeña Boulevard is the business district, with banks and airline offices.

The old part of Cebu City ("downtown") is, for the most part, a seething cobweb of sunless avenues and murky streams; half a day is enough to see all the sights. (The only other reason to come downtown is to catch a ferry.) **Colon Street** is said to be the oldest mercantile thoroughfare in the country, though there's nothing in its appearance to lend it any kind of historical ambience. About ten minutes' walk south is **Carbon Market**, where the range of goods on offer, edible, sartorial and unidentifiable, will leave you reeling. Abandon your sense of direction in the maze of alleys and allow yourself to get lost in the throng.

The city's spiritual heart is a small crypt opposite the town hall containing the **Cross of Magellan**. It's a modern hollow replica said to hold fragments of the original crucifix brought by the infamous conquistador in 1521. Next to the cross is the towering, dusty **Basilica del Santo Niño**, where vendors hawk tawdry religious icons and amulets. Throughout the Sinulog festival the area heaves with crowds of the faithful and it can be difficult to get inside.

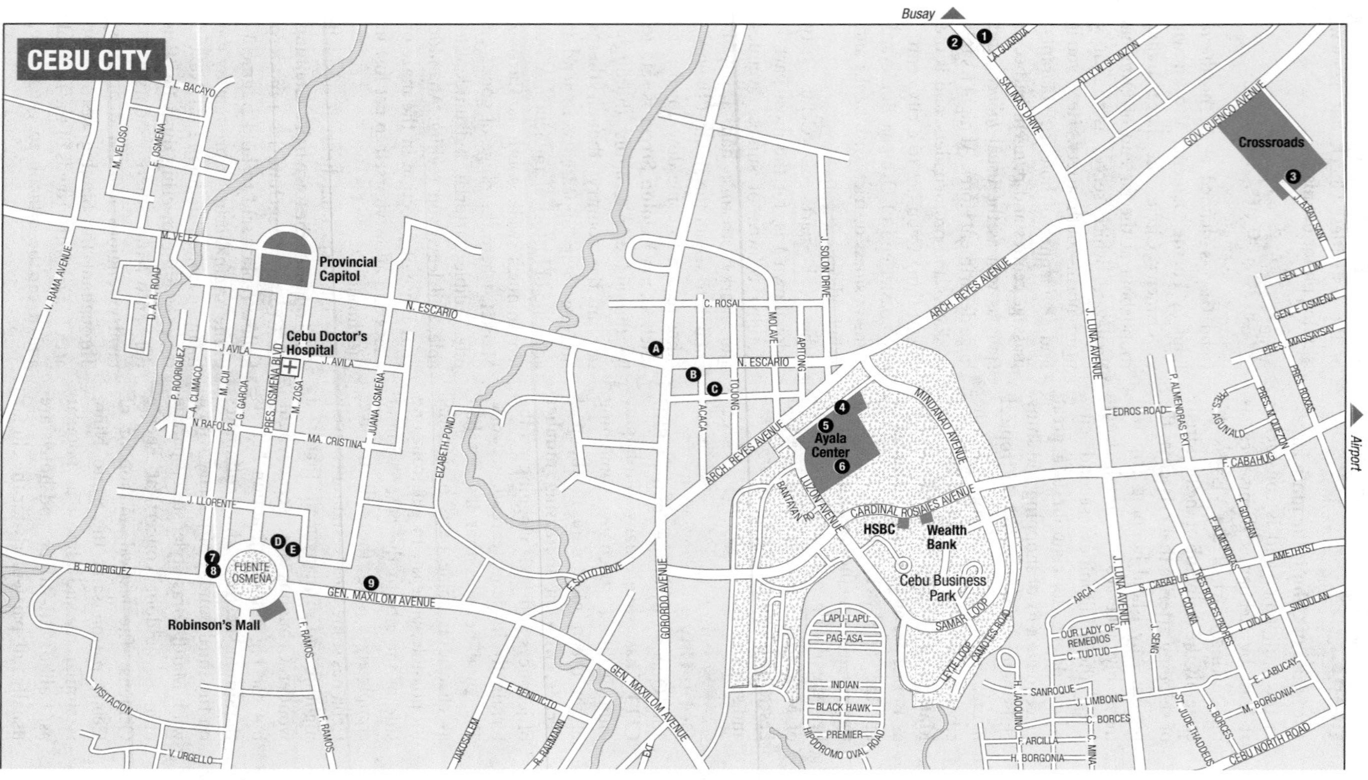
CEBU CITY
Busay
Airport
Crossroads
Provincial Capitol
Cebu Doctor's Hospital
Ayala Center
HSBC
Wealth Bank
Cebu Business Park
FUENTE OSMEÑA
Robinson's Mall
L. BACAYO
M. VELOSO
E. OSMEÑA
M. VELEZ
V. RAMA AVENUE
D. A. R. ROAD
N. ESCARIO
J. AVILA
PRES. OSMEÑA BLVD
M. ZOSA
P. RODRIGUEZ
A. CLIMACO
M. CUI
G. GARCIA
N RAFOLS
MA. CRISTINA
JUANA OSMEÑA
ELIZABETH POND
J. LLORENTE
B. RODRIGUEZ
GEN. MAXILOM AVENUE
F. RAMOS
VISITACION
V. URGELLO
E. BENEDICTO
JAKOSALEM
R. RAHMANN
F. SOTTO DRIVE
GORORDO AVENUE
C. ROSAL
MOLAVE
APITONG
TOJONG
ACACA
J. SOLON DRIVE
ARCH. REYES AVENUE
LA GUARDIA
SALINAS DRIVE
ATTY W GEONZON
GOV. CUENCO AVENUE
J. ABAD SANT
J. LUNA AVENUE
MINDANAO AVENUE
LUZON AVENUE
BANTAYAN RD
CARDINAL ROSALES AVENUE
SAMAR LOOP
LEYTE LOOP
CAMOTES ROAD
LAPU-LAPU
PAG-ASA
INDIAN
BLACK HAWK
PREMIER
HIPODROMO OVAL ROAD
EDROS ROAD
P. ALMENDRAS EXT
PRES. AGUINALDO
PRES. M. QUEZON
PRES. ROXAS
PRES. MAGSAYSAY
GEN. E. OSMEÑA
GEN. V. LIM
F. CABAHUG
F. GOCHAN
P. ALMENDRAS
AMETHYST
S. CABAHUG
R. COLINA
TRES BORCES PADRES
I. DIDLA
SINDULAN
ARCA
OUR LADY OF REMEDIOS
C. TUDTUD
J. SENG
H. JAOQUINO
SANROQUE
J. LIMBONG
C. BORCES
F. ARCILLA
C. MINA
H. BORGONIA
ST. JUDE THADDEUS
S. BORCES
M. BORGONIA
E. LABUCAY
CEBU NORTH ROAD

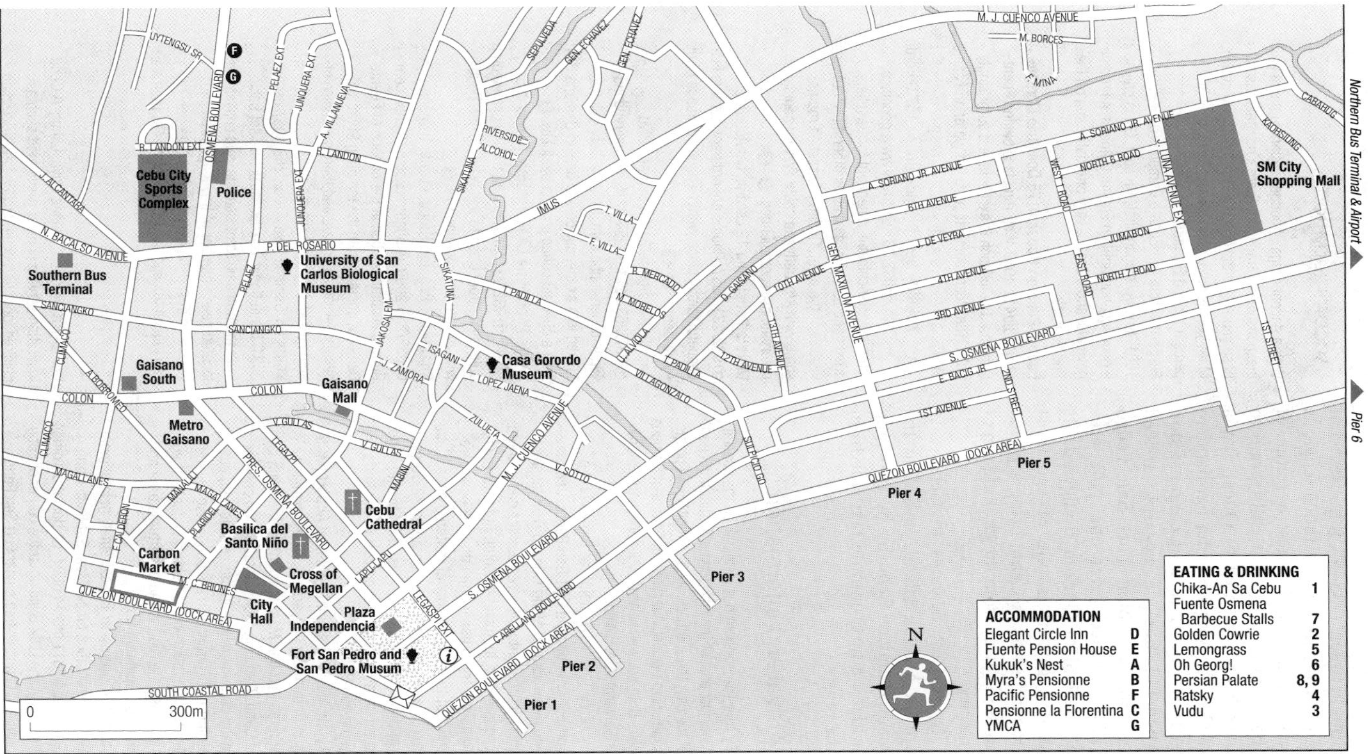
Northern Bus Terminal & Airport
Pier 6
SM City Shopping Mall
ACCOMMODATION
Elegant Circle Inn D
Fuente Pension House E
Kukuk's Nest A
Myra's Pensionne B
Pacific Pensionne F
Pensionne la Florentina C
YMCA G
EATING & DRINKING
Chika-An Sa Cebu 1
Fuente Osmena Barbecue Stalls 7
Golden Cowrie 2
Lemongrass 5
Oh Georg! 6
Persian Palate 8, 9
Ratsky 4
Vudu 3
N
Pier 1
Pier 2
Pier 3
Pier 4
Pier 5
Cebu City Sports Complex
Police
Southern Bus Terminal
University of San Carlos Biological Museum
Casa Gorordo Museum
Gaisano South
Gaisano Mall
Metro Gaisano
Cebu Cathedral
Basilica del Santo Niño
Cross of Megellan
Carbon Market
City Hall
Plaza Independencia
Fort San Pedro and San Pedro Musum
M. J. CUENCO AVENUE
M. BORCES
E. MINA
A. SORIANO JR. AVENUE
J. LUNA AVENUE EXT
NORTH 6 ROAD
NORTH 7 ROAD
WEST 1 ROAD
EAST ROAD
JUMABON
6TH AVENUE
J. DE VEYRA
4TH AVENUE
3RD AVENUE
S. OSMENA BOULEVARD
E. BACIG JR.
1ST AVENUE
2ND STREET
1ST STREET
QUEZON BOULEVARD (DOCK AREA)
GEN. MAXILOM AVENUE
10TH AVENUE
12TH AVENUE
13TH AVENUE
D. GAISANO
SULPICIO GO
UYTENGSU SR
PELAEZ EXT
JUNQUERA EXT
A. VILLANUEVA
R. LANDON EXT
F. LANDON
OSMENA BOULEVARD
J. ALCANTARA
N. BACALSO AVENUE
P. DEL ROSARIO
SIKATUNA
RIVERSIDE
ALCOHOL
IMUS
SEPULVEDA
GEN. ECHAVEZ
T. VILLA
F. VILLA
B. MERCADO
M. MORELOS
I. PADILLA
L. ALVIOLA
P. PADILLA
VILLAGONZALO
SANCIANGKO
PELAEZ
JAKOSALEM
ISAGANI
J. ZAMORA
LOPEZ JAENA
ZULUETA
V. SOTTO
COLON
CLIMACO
A. BORROMEO
V. GULLAS
LEGAZPI
PRES. OSMENA BOULEVARD
MABINI
MAGALLANES
MANALILI
PLARIDEL
F. CALDERON
M. C. BRIONES
LEGASPI EXT
C. ARELLANO BOULEVARD
SOUTH COASTAL ROAD
0
300m

Built between 1735–37, it houses what is probably the most famous religious icon in the Philippines, a statue of the Santo Niño (Christ child), said to have been presented to Queen Juana of Cebu by Magellan after her baptism in 1521. The succeeding conquistador, Miguel Lopez de Legaspi, arrived in 1565 and built **Fort San Pedro** (P21 entrance) near the port area at the end of Quezon Boulevard. Its shaded garden is one of the most tranquil spots in Cebu; bring a picnic and hide away from the choking din of the city.

The closest **beaches** to Cebu City are on Mactan Island, linked to the main island of Cebu by by two long bridges, a forty-minute taxi ride from the centre.

## Arrival and information

**By bus** The northern bus terminal, on the coastal road, just east of the city, serves destinations north of the city; the southern bus terminal for all points south, is in Bacalso Ave, west of President Osmeña Blvd. Both are well served by jeepneys and there are always taxis waiting.

**By ferry** The arrival point for ferries is the harbour area beyond Fort San Pedro. Jeepneys and buses line up along Quezon Blvd for the short journey into the city. Look for one marked Osmeña Blvd (uptown) or Colon St (downtown). Touts will try to usher you into a "special fare" taxi, but there are plenty of metered ones. Cebu taxi fares start at P30 and go up by P2.50 every km thereafter: a metered taxi from the ferry port to the northern bus station costs P55, touts will quote you P150.

**By air** Mactan Cebu International Airport (MCIA) is 8km from the city, across the suspension bridges that link Mactan Island to the main island of Cebu. There's a tourist information counter (daily 6am–midnight) in the arrivals hall; outside, airport taxis (around P180, depending on your destination) take you to Cebu City itself, or you can cross the road to the departures area and pick up a metered taxi.

**Tourist information** The extremely helpful main tourist information office (Mon–Sat 8am–6pm; ⓣ032/254 2811 or 254 6007, ⓔ dotcebu@gmail.com) is in the LDM Building at the corner of Lapu-Lapu and Legaspi streets near Fort San Pedro.

## Accommodation

With a decent range of budget options uptown and inexpensive city transport, there's no real reason to base yourself in the grime and noise of downtown. Many places put up their prices by roughly 30 percent around Sinulog.

**Elegant Circle Inn** Fuente Osmeña ⓣ032/254 1601, ⓦwww.elegantcircleinn.com. Glass edifice in a good location right on Fuente Osmeña. All rooms have a/c, and there's a very affordable spa on the 2nd floor. ⑤

**Fuente Pension House** 0175 Don Julio Llorente St ⓣ032/412 4989. Well-run place behind Fuente Osmeña. The location is excellent and surprisingly quiet. The clean rooms all have hot water and cable TV. ⑤

**Kukuk's Nest Pension House** 157 Gorordo Ave ⓣ032/231 5180, ⓦwww.geocities.com/kukuksnestcebu. A hangout for travellers, artists and beatniks, as well as other more dubious visitors of the night. Quaintly furnished rooms, some with a/c, bath and cable TV. Very popular so reservations recommended. ③–④

**Myra's Pensionne** 12 Escario, cnr Acacia St ⓣ032/231 5557. Rooms are ordinary, but this is a peaceful family place within walking distance of the Ayala Center. ⑤–⑥

**Pacific Pensionne** 313-A Osmeña Blvd ⓣ032/253 5271 or 254 9216, ⓔreservations@pacificpensionne.com. Bright yellow building tucked into a quiet cul-de-sac behind Osmeña Blvd with a cheerful coffee shop in the lobby. ④

**Pensionne La Florentina** 18 Acacia St ⓣ032/231 3318 or 232 6738. Located on a quiet side street close to the Ayala Center. Doubles with private bathroom and TV. ④

**Shamrock Pension House** Fuente Osmeña ⓣ032/255 2999, ⓔshamrockotap@yahoo.com. Budget accommodation in the hubbub of Fuente Osmeña, upstairs from the tempting Shamrock bakery. All rooms are a/c and there's a choice of standard, deluxe or studio. ⑤

**YMCA** 51 Osmeña Blvd ⓣ032/253 4057 or 253 0691. Institutional, box-like structure set back from the traffic noise of Osmeña, and conveniently located near a number of travel agencies and internet cafés. Ostensibly for members only but you can join on the spot for P100. Dorms ①; rooms ③

## Eating

**Chika-An Sa Cebu** Salinas Drive, Lahug. A Cebu institution serving popular rustic food such as chicken, pork barbecue, *lechon kawali*, sizzling *bangus* and *bulalo* (beef bone stew). Unmissable for affordable native Cebuano cuisine.

**Fuente Osmeña barbecue stalls** A cluster of stalls on Fuente Osmeña, even the smoke from them smells good. Cooking tends to start with a vengeance at dusk. Cheap and tasty, but strictly for carnivores.

**Golden Cowrie** Salinas Drive, Lahug. Traditional but chic Filipino cuisine, including first-class seafood dishes such as tuna jaw and grilled *lapu-lapu*, served on banana leaf platters. The hospitable servers in native costume wander between tables up topping up your banana leaf from buckets of limitless rice. Try the sticky grilled ribs (P198). Busy, especially at weekends. Daily 11am–2pm & 6–10pm.

**Lemongrass** Food court, Ayala Center. Authentic Thai and Vietnamese cuisine, with almost all dishes under P200. Highlights of the light and healthy menu are the spicy beef salad and home-made spring rolls. You can listen to the band at *Ratsky* next door from the outside tables, though whether this is a blessing or a curse depends on who's playing. Thai curries P185.

**Oh Georg!** Level 1, Ayala Center. This coffee shop and dessert bar deserves special mention for its indulgent cakes, old-fashioned soda floats (P110) and strong Batangas coffee. For something more substantial there are plenty of home-made dishes to choose from, such as bean and vegetable soup, Greek salad and an enormous Mexican platter that's big enough to share.

**Persian Palate** Mango Square Complex, Maxilom Ave. When you positively can't face eating another part of a pig in one form or another, *Persian Palate* comes to the rescue. Fiery Malaysian, Indian, Middle Eastern and halal dishes offer great choices for vegetarians and the health conscious. Veggie paella serving two to three people is P160. There's another branch on the ground floor of Robinsons Plaza, Fuente Osmeña.

## Nightlife and entertainment

Cebu City, like its big brother Manila, is a city that never – or rarely – sleeps. A great resource for what's on is ⓦwww.cebucentral.com. There are **cinemas** showing the latest Hollywood films in SM City Cebu and the Ayala Center (tickets P130).

**Ratsky's** Ayala Center. Cavernous space with a vaguely tropical theme, and live bands belting out the usual American R&B. Friendly atmosphere and a young crowd uninhibited about showing off their dance moves. Free; Mon–Fri until 2am, Sat & Sun until 4am.

**Vudu** Crossroads, Archbishop Reyes Ave ⓦwww.vudu.com.ph. Swanky place where bar snacks include baked oysters, but frequent promotions make it affordable. Wed is ladies' night, Thurs is band night, Fri is R&B, and Sat is house. There are several other fun nightspots in the Crossroads development. Thurs P50, Sat & Sun P100; cover charge includes a beer. Tues–Sat 9pm until late.

## Directory

**Banks and exchange** ATMs are everywhere, and there's no shortage of places to change currency, particularly along the main drag of Osmeña Blvd, where there are branches of HSBC, Citibank and Metrobank. There's a Travelex located next to *Lemongrass*, ground floor Ayala Center.

**Hospital** Cebu Doctor's Hospital, Osmeña Blvd. ⓣ032/253 7511.

**Immigration** Cebu Immigration District Office, P.Burgos St, Mandaue City (Mon–Fri 8–11am, 1–4pm).

**Internet** Internet cafés are everywhere. Try Netopia, top floor Ayala Center.

**Police** Cebu City police (ⓣ032/231 5802 or 253 5636) are located south of Fuente Osmeña, on R. Landon St.

**Post office** On Quezon Blvd close to the port area; offers a poste restante service.

**Shopping** The three main malls in Cebu are the Ayala Center (Cebu Business Park) Robinson's Plaza (Fuente Osmeña) and SM City (north Reclamation area). All are open 10am to 9pm, and have a huge range of shops and sevices. The SM Mall in particular, like its counterpast in Manila, is one of the largest in Asia. The Crossroads development in Lahug is of interest to visitors largely as a nightspot.

## Moving on

**By bus:**

**Destinations north** (from northern bus terminal): Hagnaya, for Bantayan (7 daily; 3hr); Maya, for Malapascua (up to 24 daily; 4hr)

**Destinations south** (from southern bus terminal): Bato, via Moalboal (5–6 daily; 3hr).

**By ferry** A great place to get up-to-date ferry information (schedules and pier numbers often change) is at SM City shopping mall, where the SM travellers' lounge (ⓣ032/232 0291) has schedules and booking facilities. You can also check the *Cebu Daily News* and the *Sun Star Cebu* for schedules.

**Fast boats:** OceanJet (ⓦwww.oceanjet.net), Supercat (ⓣ032/233 7000, ⓦwww.supercat.com.ph), Superferry (ⓦwww.superferry.com.ph) and Weesam Express (ⓦwww.weesamexpress.com) serve the following daily: Dumaguete (4hr); Larena (Siquijor; 5hr); Ormoc (2hr 50min); Tagbilaran (1hr 30min).

**Slow boats:** Cebu Ferries (Ⓣ032/232 4394), Negros Navigation (Ⓣ032/245 4394), Sulpicio Lines (Ⓣ032/241 9701 or 9801), Trans-Asia Shipping Lines (Ⓣ032/254 6491, Ⓦwww.transasiashipping.com) and Palacio Shipping (Ⓣ032/255 4538) serve destinations including Manila (1–2 daily; 21hr), Cagayan de Oro (3 weekly; 8hr) and Banyatan (2 weekly; 9hr).
**By air** Cebu Pacific, SEAIR, PAL, Asian Spirit and Philippine Airlines have ticket offices at the airport, as well as in the malls.
**Destinations:** Bacolod (1 daily; 35min); Cagayan de Oro (1 daily; 1hr); Camiguin (3 weekly; 40m); Caticlan (1 daily; 1hr); Clark (1 daily; 2hr 50min), Iloilo City (1 daily; 40 min); Manila (16 daily; 1hr 10min); Puerta Princesa (3 weekly; 1hr 15min).

## Moalboal

Almost 100km from Cebu City on the island's southwestern flank lies the sleepy coastal village of **Moalboal**, a relaxed, rather boozy divers' hangout. It's hardly surprising (the diving, not the drinking that is): the sea is crystal clear, and while many reefs along the mainland coast have been damaged by successive typhoons, the enigmatic Pescador Island has survived, and remains one of the most alluring **dive sites** in the Philippines. Located just a few miles offshore, it's a haven for sharks, mantas and moray eels; regular sightings are all but guaranteed. Sun-worshippers looking for a Boracay-style sandy beach will be disappointed, though, there isn't one. In fact, if you're not planning on diving, there's little reason to visit, though in its favour the town does boast a great range of cheap accommodation (with discounts on diving and rooms if you hang around long enough) and marvellous views of the sun setting over distant Negros.

### Arrival and information

**By bus** From Cebu City you'll be dropped off on the main road, from where a tricycle will take you down the partially paved track to Panagsama Beach where all the resorts are (P40).
**Tour operators** In the unlikely event that you get fed up of diving, pay Planet Action a visit (Ⓣ0916 653 7608 or 032/474 0068, Ⓦwww.action-philippines.com), next to *The Last Filling Station*, where you can arrange climbing, trekking and mountain biking trips. Adventure day-trips from P1500. *Chili's Bar* also rents motorbikes.
**Internet** Hotline Internet Café, just off the beach path towards Moalboal town. There are no banks or ATMs.

### Dive operators

Dive Operators are stretched along the beach; shop around before you commit.
**Ocean Safari** Ⓣ032/474 0010, Ⓔoceansafariphilippines@hotmail.com. Run by Nelson, the brother of Eve of the eponymous *Kiosk*, which is right next door.
**Savedra Dive Centre** Ⓦwww.savedra.com. This five-star operation offers plenty of choice for all levels of ability.
**Visaya Divers** *Quo Vadis* resort Ⓣ032/474 0018, Ⓦwww.visayadivers.info. German owned and operated since 1997.

### Accommodation

It's best to book accommodation in advance, especially at weekends.
**Eve's Kiosk** Ⓣ0917 950 5249, Ⓔeveskiosk@hotmail.com. Just to the left of the path to the main road. Clean, tiled rooms set around a quiet garden, some overlooking the pool. There's a terrace restaurant and staff can arrange transport to the airport in Cebu. ❸–❺
**Pacita's Beach Resort** Ⓣ 0910 858 7222. Towards the southern end of the beach, just past where the path begins to break up, *Pacita's* has a range of cottages, set back from the seafront. Generally quiet, except on Sat nights when the disco next door can be horribly intrusive. ❹
**Sunshine Pension House** Next door to the Blue Abyss Dive Shop off the beach path Ⓣ032/474 0049, Ⓔsunshinepension@yahoo.com. The excellent Swiss restaurant and large swimming pool elevate this place out of the ordinary. Double cottages ❸–❹

### Eating, drinking and nightlife

**Beach Bar** Chilled-out upstairs place overlooking the middle of the beach path with beanbags, table football, pool and an English-language book swap.
**Chili's Bar** Midway along the beach path. "The liver is evil and it must be punished" states a sign over the pool table, and when you can get a shot of Jaegermeister and a beer for just P90, such punishment seems inevitable. Cheap drinks, pool, music and the exhortation to "slip

out of that wetsuit and into a dry Martini" Who could resist?

**Hannah's Place** Just to the right of the main road to Moalboal. Some of the best seafood on the beach, along with Indonesian and Filipino specialities. The wooden terrace is a peaceful place to watch the sunset with a cold San Miguel.

**The Last Filling Station** Just north of *Pacita's*, this quaint little European-owned restaurant does everything from pizza and spicy Thai curry to home-made yogurt and crêpes. Fish curry P170.

**Lipay Lipay Coffee Shop and Bar** Midway along the beach path. Proper coffee and home-made bread make this place a favourite breakfast stop, though it morphs into a cocktail bar when the sun goes down.

**Ocean Globe Japanese Restaurant** Above Ocean Globe Divers. Cheap, tasty set meals for P200, and a great view of the sunset.

### Moving on

Buses back to Cebu City (5–6 daily until 5pm; 3hr) from the main road are often full by the time they reach Moalboal; it's often standing room only.

## BANTAYAN ISLAND

**Bantayan Island**, just off the northwest coast of Cebu, is flat and arable; here tropical topography replaces the moody mountains of the mainland. Though it's a great place to explore, divers will be disappointed by the paucity of coral left along the shore. Most of the island's resorts and beaches are around the attractive little town of **SANTA FE** on Bantayan's southeast coast, whose beach is exquisite but not a patch on Bounty Beach on Malapascua. It's fun to rent a motorbike or moped and tour the island by the coastal road, but be careful, some of the bike owners are hustlers and will try to charge you for scratches that were already there. Inspect the bike thoroughly beforehand and get the renter to sign an agreement that details all existing damage, however insignificant. Bantayan is besieged by Filipino tourists every Easter, with rooms booked out for weeks in advance, but for the rest of the year, it's one of the most blissful spots in the Visayas.

### TRAVEL TO AND FROM BANTAYAN

The easiest option is to hop on a bus from Cebu City's northern bus terminal to the northern port town of **Hagnaya** (7 daily; 3hr) where you can catch one of the six daily crossings to **Santa Fe** (P120; 1 hr); the last departures are 6.30pm from Hagnaya and 3pm from Santa Fe. Palacio Shipping has twice-weekly overnight ferry services leaving from Pier One at Cebu port at 9pm arriving in Santa Fe at 6am (P175–275). Days of departure are seasonal, so check ahead. From further afield, there are intermittent big banca to **Bantayan** town on the west coast from **Cadiz** on Negros, depending on the tide. You can also hire a banca to take you directly to Bantayan from **Malapascua** for around P3500 per group, but the journey can be stormy.

### Accommodation and eating

Don't miss dinner at *White Sands*, north of the pier, the best restaurant on Bantayan by several nautical miles.

**Budyong Beach Resort** Santa Fe Beach ⓣ032/438 9040. The pleasant nipa huts are in the best position on the island and have unbeatable views. Needless to say, rooms are much in demand, so be sure to book ahead. ❹

**Kota Beach Resort** ⓣ032/254 2726. A short ride west of Santa Fe, *Kota* has basic rooms and cottages with fans and baths. It's expensive for what you get, but the restaurant serves up excellent seafood and has memorable views. ❹–❺

**St Bernard Beach Resort** ⓣ0917 963 6162, ⓦwww.bantayan.dk. Five minutes from the pier, *St Bernard* offers something out of the ordinary with quaint little circular cottages right on the beach. ❹

## MALAPASCUA ISLAND

Eight kilometres off the northern tip of Cebu, the island of **Malapascua** is one of Southeast Asia's finest scuba-diving destinations. Anyone staying more than a few days is almost guaranteed a sighting of manta rays and thresher sharks. Nearby **Gato Island** is a marine sanctuary and a breeding place for black-and-white banded sea snakes, which are potentially deadly but don't attack divers, and overnight trips can be arranged to the tiny volcanic island of **Maripipi**, where reef sharks and dolphins are common. At 2.5km long and about 1km wide, and with some of the warmest, most welcoming people you'll meet in the Philippines, Malapascua has been touted as a potential baby brother to Boracay, largely because of the charms of **Bounty Beach**, a blindingly white stretch of sand on the island's south coast that's home to a dozen simple resorts and several excellent restaurants.

Though Boracay-style development has yet to transpire, changes are afoot, and for the past few years rumours have been circulating about a proposed new pier and paved road, which would dramatically alter the island's influx of visitors. Though a slew of beach-front properties were demolished in preparation in 2005, the threatened developments have yet to materialize, and, for the time being, Malapascua remains a perfect low-key travellers' paradise.

### TRAVEL TO AND FROM MALAPASCUA

You can get to Malapascua direct from **Cebu City**. From the northern bus terminal, take a Rough Riders or Ceres Liner bus to **Maya** (4hr). Competition between the two companies is fierce, so be prepared to be manhandled towards one bus or another. Buses run half-hourly from 6am and it's best to set off early to avoid traffic and the heat. There are frequent bancas from Maya to Malapascua from dawn until 6pm (30min; P200), though the price can depend on the number of other passengers waiting. Bancas pull in to the centre of the Bounty Beach, right opposite *Cocobana*. The first banca of the day leaves Malapascua at 6.30am. Coming from **Bantayan**, you can hire a banca (P3500 per group).

## Accommodation

All the places listed below are on Bounty Beach.

**Blue Water Beach Resort** Just west of *Cocobana* ⓣ032/437 1053 or 0918 919 9128, ⓔjanetmalapascua@hotmail.com. Clean, wooden-floored rooms are pleasant if ordinary and the beachside dining area is undeniably atmospheric, though service moves at a glacial pace. Standard fan room ❺; cottages ❻

**Cocobana Beach Resort** ⓣ032/437 1007, ⓦwww.cocobana.ch. Right in the heart of Bounty Beach, the welcoming *Cocobana* comprises spacious cottages. Hammocks, pool tables and a laid-back bar complete the deliciously relaxed ambience. ❹ including breakfast at their excellent restaurant.

**Daño Beach Resort** Eastern end of Bounty Beach ⓣ0915 666 1584 or 0928 463 5032. Cottages are clean and fresh, but this place has little going for it in terms of amenities. ❺ including breakfast.

**Hippocampus** Eastern end of the beach ⓣ0915 400 1005, ⓦwww.hippocampus-online.com. Romantic, native-style rooms with private tiled bathroom and mosquito nets. Staff are very friendly and there's a cosy little bar and restaurant. ❺–❻

## Eating, drinking and nightlife

Happy hours are a feature almost everywhere, and rarely last less than two hours.

**Floating Island Internet and Restaurant** Directly behind *Cocobana*. Has a not-so-speedy connection (P30/30min). Also serves inexpensive Chinese and Japanese dishes (10am–2pm & 5.30–9pm). Drinks are a steal: rum and coke P40, San Miguel P30; daily 8am–10pm.

**Ging-Ging's Flower Garden** Opposite *Floating Island*, behind *Cocobana*. Some of the cheapest meals on Malapascua including various sandwiches (P40) and chicken dishes (P120). Their chocolate and banana pancakes (P50) are outstanding. Daily 6.30am–9pm.

**La Dolce Vita** Poblacion Beach; take the path inland beside *Mabuhay Foods*. Red-checked tablecloths, thin-crust pizza, proper espresso and home-made tiramisu. Try to get an outside table overlooking Poblacion beach where you'll catch the best of Malapascua's sunsets. Be warned – the portions are so generous you may not need to add weights to your dive belt the next day. Set breakfasts P190, pasta Arrabiata P225.

**La Isla Bonita** Located directly behind *Sunsplash* on the inland path. The menu covers world cuisines from Greek to Italian, Filipino to Thai, but the seafood dishes are the star turn, all wonderfully fresh and imaginatively prepared. Try the grilled shrimp with just a squeeze of *calamansi* (native lime) for P110.

**Mabuhay Foods** next to *Blue Coral*. Simple place with a few tables, some fairy lights and a sound system powered off a motorbike parked in the sand. Serves whatever's been caught that day, as part of an "eat all you can" deal for P180.

**Maldito's** Next door to *La Dolce Vita*, inland. This large drinking-and-dancing restaurant-bar was temporarily closed at time of research, but is set to reopen bigger and brasher than ever in early 2009.

**Sunsplash Bar and Resort** Western end of Bounty Beach. A convivial place to hang out, with pool tables, movies and sofas, not to mention the opportunity to represent your country in a drinking league table (at the time of research Germany were in the lead). Happy hour 5–7pm. They also have an offshore floating bar, open 11am–7pm.

## Dive operators

**Malapascua Exotic Island Dive and Beach Resort** ⓣ032/437 0983; ⓦwww.malapascua.net. This resort has the most established dive shop on the island; open-water course $370, one dive with equipment P1500. Thurs is Coral reef watch day. It has expensive and intermittent internet connection (P100/hr).

**Sea Explorers** Next door to *Hippocampus* ⓔfabienneandsven@gmail.com, ⓦwww.sea-explorers.com. One dive is P1320 though the more you do the cheaper it is. Full equipment rental per day is P720. Sea Explorers also have branches in Alona (Panglao), Dumaguete, Moalboal and Siquijor.

**Thresher Shark Divers** ⓣ0927 936 0029, ⓦwww.thresherdivers.com. Runs early morning shark-spotting dives, and can arrange liveaboard trips to Apo and Tubbataha. One dive is P1600, open water P18,000, Nitrox P13,000 (discounts if you pay cash).There's also a little rooftop bar with a happy hour 4–6pm and glorious views.

# BOHOL

It's hard to imagine that idyllic, sleepy **Bohol**, a two-hour hop south of Cebu by fast ferry, has a bloody past. The only reminder is a memorial stone in the barrio of **Bool**, marking the spot where Rajah Sikatuna and Miguel Lopez de Legaspi concluded hostilities in 1565 by signing a compact in blood. These days, however, apart from some mercantile activity in the capital, **Tagbilaran**, Bohol is a dozy sort of place. The only serious activity is on the beautiful beaches of **Panglao Island**, connected to the main island by a bridge from the capital and another from Bool, where scuba divers gather. Everywhere else, Bohol is firmly on Filipino time and runs at Filipino pace. Even the *carabao* chew slowly.

## What to see and do

The main transit hub for Bohol and several other islands is **Tagbilaran**, somewhere you may well pass through at some stage, though there's not a whole lot of reason to base yourself here when you could be on **Panglao's Alona beach**, a powdery strip of sand 1.5km long, with some great diving and laid-back nightlife, in less than twenty minutes. For most visitors, the only obligatory sortie away from Panglao's beaches is into Bohol's hinterland to see the island's most iconic tourist attraction, the **Chocolate Hills**. Some geologists believe that these unique forty-metre mounds were formed from deposits of coral and limestone sculpted by centuries of erosion. The locals, however, will tell you the hills are the calcified tears of a giant, whose heart was broken by the death of a mortal lover. The best time to see the Chocolate Hills – there are allegedly 1268 of them – is at dawn, when the rising sun plays spectacular tricks with light, shadow and colour. Aficionados recommend the end of the dry season (April or May), when the grass has turned brown, and with a short stretch of the imagination, the hills really do resemble chocolate drops. Most people see the hills as part of an organized trip, which you can arrange through your accommodation or through the tourist office. Otherwise, you can catch a bus to Carmen from the Dau terminal (hourly; P55) and tell the driver you're going to the hills.

More and more people are visiting Bohol for its world-class **scuba diving** – not only at Panglao, but at the lesser-known islands of Cabilao, Ajo, Mahanay and Lapinin, all off the northern coast. There's also excellent diving around the exquisite little island of **Balicasag**, southwest of Panglao, which you can reach by renting a banca; it's just 35 minutes from Poblacion, Panglao.

Experienced divers should not miss a trip to **Pamilacan Island**, where it's possible to see short-finned pilot whales, long-snouted spinner, spotted, bottlenose and melon-headed dolphins. You can organize a day-trip to Pamilacan Island from any resort, or rent your own banca.

## Arrival and information

**By bus** Dao integrated bus terminal is in E. Butalid St, ten minutes north of Tagbilaran along Clarin Ave by tricycle. Buses and jeepneys heading for Panglao are marked for Alona. At Panglao buses drop passengers on the main road above the beach, from where it's a short stroll to the resorts. Private taxis from Tagbilaran will take you directly to your resort.
**By ferry** The pier is in the northwest of Tagbilaran off Gallares St, a ten-minute tricycle ride to the centre.
**By air** Tagbilaran Airport is under 2km from the city. A tricycle will cost P50 to the centre of town. Private taxis will take you to Alona beach for P300.
**Tourist information** (Mon–Fri 8am–noon & 1–5pm; ⓣ038/501 9136, ⓦwww.bohol.gov.ph). The tourist office is located in the New Capitol Commercial Complex. Hopelessly understaffed, but they can at least organize tours to the Chocolate Hills (P2000). There's also a small tourist office at the ferry dock (daily 8am–6pm). Most resorts are well geared up for tourists and can offer better information. On Panglao, Sunshine Travel (daily 9am–10pm) where the beach path meets the main road, can arrange transport to Tagbilaran pier and day-trips to the Chocolate Hills. The tourist centre (daily 8am–8pm), next door to Sunshine Travel has a postal service, currency exchange and internet access.

## Accommodation

There are a couple of decent accommodation choices in Tagbilaran, only useful if you're very pushed for time and can't make it to Alona, where most of the budget beach accommodation on Panglao Island is.

### Tagbilaran

**Nisa Traveller's Inn** 2nd floor, 14 Carlos P. Garcia Ave ⓣ038/411 3731. The best value in town and handily located a short walk from the BQ Mall and close to banks and ticket agents. Rooms are small and those overlooking the main road can be noisy; ask for one at the back. Rates are for 24hr, regardless of your check in time. ❷–❸
**Taver's Pension House** Remolador St ⓣ038/411 4896 or 411 3983 ⓦwww.geocities.com/taverspension. The rooms are a little on the chintzy side, but all are clean, with hot water and cable TV as standard. Rates include a transfer to the airport or ferry, and they also have internet access. ❹

### Panglao Island

**Alonaland** ⓣ038/502 9007, ⓦwww.alonaland.ch. Across the road from *Alona Tropical* (through which guests can access the beach), *Alonaland* has decent private garden cottages, but is let down by the incompetence of its staff. An adequate budget choice if everywhere else is full. ❺
**Alona Tropical** ⓣ038/502 9024. Well run and extremely popular; staff here are happy to arrange day-trips and transportation. The large grounds stretching down from the main road to the beach feature lush tropical vegetation and a swimming pool. ❺
**Oops Cottages** ⓣ 0920 461 7895. Tucked behind the *Oops Bar* in a surprisingly quiet garden, these pretty native cottages are great value with clean bathrooms, balconies with wooden sun loungers and complimentary mineral water. Breakfasts at the attached restaurant are perhaps the best on the beach – their freshly squeezed mango juice has mysterious hangover-curing properties. ❹–❺
**Peter's** Genesis Divers ⓦwww.genesisdivers.com. Simple rooms attached to this friendly and well-established dive shop. There's also a small pizza restaurant. ❸

### Balicasag Island

**Balicasag Dive Resort** ⓣ02/812 1984 (Manila). Very expensive, but it's the only place to stay on the island, with ten lovely duplex cottages. ❽

## Eating, drinking and nightlife

### Tagbilaran

**BQ mall** Carlos P. Garcia Ave. Has the usual chain cafés inside.
**Joving's** Cheap, if not exactly cheerful seafood shack near the pier, offering Filipino favourites at budget prices.

### Panglao island

**Jasz** Everyone heads to this beachside place on Friday nights for live music sessions.

**Oops Bar** Right in the centre of Alona Beach, *Oops* serves a varied menu from 7am to 9.30pm, including deliciously assertive Thai curries (P200); later it fills up with divers looking for cheap drinks and a good time. Hosts a beach disco every Saturday night, every other night there's chilled-out acoustic reggae.

**Roderick and Vivian** You'd never guess by its appearance, but this brightly lit place near the *Alona Kew* does some of the best seafood on the beach, all at lower prices than the resorts.

**Safety Stop Bar** Part of the *Alona Pyramid Resort*. Another of the big names on Alona. Pool, fairy lights and nightly live music.

## Directory

Facilities at the beach revolve around the tourist centre and Sunshine Travel.

**Banks** PNB is on the junction of CPG Ave and Clarin St, while there's a BPI with an ATM in Carlos Garcia Ave.

**Police** Near City Hall, behind St Joseph's Cathedral.

**Post office** Near City Hall, behind St Joseph's Cathedral. Same complex as the police station.

**Internet** There are a number of cheap internet cafés near the market in Grupo St.

**Left luggage** Facility on the ground floor of BQ mall, Carlos P. Garcia Ave (P50).

## Moving on

**By bus** Dau Integrated Terminal, E. Butalid St is the departure point for all other destinations on Bohol. For the Chocolate Hills, catch a bus to Carmen (hourly; 2hr). Buses from Alona to Tagbilaran pick up on the main road, but aren't particularly frequent. Sharing a taxi/private transfer back to Tagbilaran from Alona can be a good-value option.

**By ferry** Frequent daily fast ferries to Cebu City and Dumaguete. Supercat, Weesam Express and Oceanjet all have offices at Tagbilaran pier. The terminal fee is P11.25 and checking in luggage is P50.

**By air** Cebu Pacific and PAL both have daily flights from Tagbilaran to Manila (1hr 15min).

# NEGROS

The island of **Negros** lies at the heart of the Visayas, between Panay to the west and Cebu to the east. Shaped like a boot, it is split diagonally into Negros Occidental and Negros Oriental. The demarcation came when early missionaries decided the central mountain range was too formidable to cross, even in the name of God. It's an island many tourists skip and as a result is largely unspoilt: it has miles of untouched coastline, some pleasant towns – **Dumaguete**, the capital of Negros Oriental is one of the stateliest in the Philippines – and dormant **volcanoes**. Negros is known as "Sugarlandia", producing fifty percent of the country's **sugar**, an industry that has defined its history in sometimes bloody ways. Around **Bacolod**, the capital of Negros Occidental, authentic steam locomotives from 1912 and well-preserved Spanish ancestral homes serve as reminders of the rich sugar barons of the past.

## Bacolod

The city of **BACOLOD**, like so many Philippine provincial capitals, is big, hot, noisy and there's not all that much to see or do. A notable exception is The Old Capitol Building, one of the few architectural highlights, and home to the excellent **Negros Museum** (Tue–Sun, 10am–6pm; P40), which details five thousand years of local history. The third week of October sees everybody who is anybody joining in with Bacolod's flamboyant **Masskara Festival**, a jamboree of street dancing and beauty pageants where the participants' inventive masks are the stars of the show.

### Arrival and information

**By bus** Ceres Liner, which dominates transport in the area, has two bus terminals, one for northern and one for southern destinations, located next to each other on Lopez Jaena St on the eastern edge of the city. Jeepneys run regularly to city plaza (P10).

**By ferry** Reclamation Port is 500m west of the plaza. This is the arrival and departure point for most major ferries with the exception of Negros

Navigation, which uses the old Banago wharf 8km north of Bacolod. Jeepneys into town from Banago are frequent (P20)

**By air** The long-awaited Bacolod-Silay airport, 15km outside the city, opened in early 2008. PAL, Air Philippines and Cebu Pacific all have ticket offices here. A taxi to the centre of town costs around (P150)

**Tourist Information** Negros Occidental Tourism Center, Provincial Capitol Building (Mon–Sat 8.30am–5.30pm; ⓣ034/433 2515, ⓔtourism@negros-occ.gov.ph), is a good source of information for taking a tour of the region's sights. The City Tourism Office, San Juan St (ⓣ034/435 1001 or 433 2517), can offer brochures and maps, but little else.

## Accommodation

**Pension Bacolod** 11th St ⓣ034/433 3377 or 434 7065. Probably the most popular place to stay in Bacolod, this place is great value with sparse rooms and a decent restaurant. ❷–❸

**Star Plus Pension House** Lacson St ⓣ034/433 2949. Small but clean rooms. Fan ❷; a/c ❸

## Eating

You can nibble on sweet delicacies such as *piyaya* (a hardened pancake with sugar melted inside) and *bay ibayi* (sugar and coconut served in a coconut shell), sold by vendors all over the city.

**Bacolod Chicken House** Araneta St. You can hardly get away from barbecue chicken in Bacolod, and this place does some of the best.

**Kaisei** Corner Lacson and 10th sts. An affordable little Japanese place, which does noodles, tempura and some excellent sushi. P200 set menus are excellent value.

**Vienna Kaffeehaus** Mayfair Plaza, Lacson St. A good Teutonic breakfast, lunch or dinner will cost P120–200 a head.

## Directory

**Banks and exchange** PNB Lacson St has an ATM and foreign exchange.

**Immigration** Bureau of Immigration 2nd Floor, G&M Villacor Building, San Juan Lusuriaga St (ⓣ034/433 8581).

**Internet** Try the trendy Cyberheads Café on the junction of Lacson and 7th streets. Also no shortage of internet cafés around the university.

**Post office** Gatuslao St, near the junction with Burgos St.

## Moving on

**By bus** to: Cebu City (frequent daily 1am–8.15am; 11hr including ferry); Dumaguete (every 30min until 7pm; 6hr).

**By ferry** All companies have ticket offices at their respective departure points (Reclamation Port, 500m from the plaza, for all except Negros Navigation, which uses the old Banago wharf 8km north of Bacolod). There are also many 2GO outlets in the city itself, which sell ferry tickets.

**Destinations:** Iloilo City (8 daily; 2hr); Manila (3 weekly; 15hr).

**By air** Air Philippines, PAL and Cebu Pacific all fly daily to Manila (1hr) and Cebu City (30min).

## Mount Kanlaon National Park

**Mount Kanlaon** – sometimes spelt Canlaon – two hours from Bacolod by jeepney, is the tallest peak and most active volcano in the central Philippines. Climbers have died scaling it, so don't underestimate its fury, especially considering it's been rumbling ominously since 2006. The surrounding forest contains all manner of wonderful fauna, including pythons, monitor lizards, tube-nosed bats and the dahoy pulay, a poisonous green tree snake, among whom President Manuel Quezon hid from invading Japanese forces during World War II. The best way to get here is by jeepney via Murcia, southeast of Bacolod. There are several routes up the volcano, one of the best is from the village of **Guintubdan** on the western slopes, and most involve three tough days of walking and two nights of camping. Before you set out you must visit the Park Superintendent's office in Bacolod (Penro compound, South Capitol Rd, ⓣ0917 301 1410) to put your name down for a park permit (P500) and a compulsory guide (P700). The numbers of visitors allowed to the summit is limited, and there's often a waiting list. For up-to-date information about the safety of climbing Kanlaon, contact either of the tourist offices in Bacolod (see above).

## Dumaguete and around

**DUMAGUETE** (pronounced "dum-a-get-eh"), the elegant capital of Negros Oriental, lives up to its reputation as "The City of Gentle People". Lying on the southeast coast of Negros, within sight of the most southerly tip of Cebu Island, it's a perfect jumping-off point for the beach resorts of nearby Dauin and the marine sanctuary of Apo Island, where the scuba diving is superb.

### Arrival and information

**By bus** The bus terminal is on Governor Perdices St on the southern side of the Banica River. A jeepney into the city costs P10, but if you haven't got much luggage you can walk it almost as quickly.
**By ferry** The ferry pier is near the northern end of Rizal Blvd, within easy walking distance of the centre. A tricycle costs P20.
**By air** The airport is a few km northwest of the city centre. Tricycles make the trip for about P50.
**Tourist information** The tourist office (Mon–Sat 8.30am–6pm; ⓣ035/422 3561, ⓔtourismdgte@gmail.com) is in the City Hall complex on Colon St, near Quezon Park. *Why Not*, Rizal St, organizes international and domestic air tickets, passport and visa assistance, and tour and hotel reservations.
**Internet** *Cyberbox* (8am–2am), part of the Why Not complex, and charges P45 per hour. The internet cafés around the Silliman University complex, at the northern end of Hibbard St, are plentiful and cheap.

### Accommodation

**Harold's Mansion** 205 Hibbard Ave ⓣ035/225 8000, ⓦwww.haroldsmansion.com. Backpacker-friendly establishment where the spotless rooms are remarkably spacious and modern for the price. All have hot water and cable TV. Rates include a (rather unimpressive) continental breakfast, and free pick-up from the airport or port. Dorms ❷; doubles ❷–❸
**Honeycomb Tourist Inn** Rizal Blvd, cnr Dr V Locsin St ⓣ035/225 1181. Large, cool house with wide staircases and a vaguely colonial ambience, though the rooms a little stuffy and past their best ❹–❺
**OK Pensionne House** Santa Rosa St ⓣ035/225 5925 or 225 5702, ⓔo.k.pensionne@eudoramail.com. Nondescript but centrally located and you probably won't find cheaper in town. ❷–❸
**Private Garden Resort** Noreco Rd, Mangnao ⓣ035/422 1759. A little outside town, this beach resort is quiet and laid-back. The beach itself isn't great but guests can take solace in the fully stocked bar. Cottages from P800.

### Eating, drinking and nightlife

**Cocoamigos** Rizal Blvd. Second only to *Why Not* as Dumaguete's hangout of choice. The diverse menu runs the gamut from traditional Filipino to Hungarian goulash and coq au vin, as well as the usual pizzas and curries. Happy hour (4–6pm) is a popular time to watch the promenaders on Rizal Ave from one of the pretty outdoor tables.
**Why Not** Rizal Ave. Dumaguete's premier expat hangout and a good place to find out what's going on locally. As well as internet and travel facilities it's home to a bar, disco, a small Swiss café and *Chicos Pizza and Deli*. The complex is open 6am–2am.

### Moving on

**By bus** For bus departures to the north of the island, it's worth making sure you get on an express bus, shaving a few painful hours from journey times. The Ceres terminal is in Governor Perdices St. For Cebu island, take a morning bus to Tampi (45min), from where you can get a fast ferry to Bato. From here buses go to Moalboal and Cebu City.
**By ferry** to: Cagayan de Oro (several weekly; 6hr 30min); Cebu City (1–2 daily; 3hr); Larena (3 daily; 45min); Manila (4 weekly; 22–25hr); Tagbilaran (1–2 daily; 1hr 30min); Siquijor Town (2 daily; 4hr).
**By air** PAL and Cebu Pacific fly to Manila (2–3 daily; 1hr 15min).

### APO ISLAND

Accessible by banca from Damaguete (45min; P50) the **Apo Island Marine Reserve and Fish Sanctuary** is said by those in the know to be one of the world's top ten diving sites. For a taste of the simple life stay at *Apo Island Beach Resort* (ⓣ035/422 9663 or 035/422 9663; ❸–❻), which stands on an isolated sandy cove hemmed in by rocks. You can inquire and make reservations at Paradise Travel Centre, Rizal Blvd, Dumaguete (ⓣ035/225 5490 and 422 9663).

## SIQUIJOR

**Siquijor**, a laid-back little island where life is simple and tourists are made very welcome, lies slightly apart from the rest of the Visayas off the southern tip of Cebu and about 22km east of Negros. The Spanish sailors nicknamed Siquijor the Isla del Fuego ("Island of Fire") because of eerie luminescence generated by swarms of fireflies at night. Even today, the island is suffused with a lingering sense of mystery, with many Filipinos believing Siquijor to be a centre of witchcraft and black magic, a superstition reinforced by the staging of the Folk Healing Festival in the mountain village of San Antonio every Easter on Black Saturday. You can circumnavigate Siquijor by bus and jeepney along the coastal road and most resorts can also arrange motorbike rental or guided tours.

**SIQUIJOR TOWN**, the capital, lies twenty minutes by jeepney southwest of Larena, the main port (served by up to six fast ferries daily from Dumaguete with OceanJet and Delta; 45min) where the island's only ATM is located.

The most popular beaches on Siquijor are **Sandugan**, half an hour by jeepney north of Larena, and **Paliton** and **San Juan** beaches on the west coast, which you can reach easily by jeepney from Siquijor Town and most places along the coastal road.

### Accommodation

There is plenty of rustic beach accommodation on the island.

**Coral Cay Resort** San Juan Beach ⓣ0919 269 1269 or 035/481 5024 ⓦwww.coralcayresort.com. A relaxed but well-managed place with budget rooms at the back and beach cottages right on the sand ❹–❻

**Islander's Paradise Beach Resort** Sandugan ⓣ0918 332 0906, ⓦwww.islandersparadisebeach.com. Rustic doubles on a beautiful beach with excellent snorkelling. ❸–❹

**Kiwi Dive Resort** Sandugan ⓦwww.kiwidiveresort.com. Cheap dorm beds or nipa cottages at the water's edge with great discounts on stays of three nights or longer. Dorms ❷; rooms ❸

**TREAT YOURSELF**

**Villa Marmarine** (ⓣ035/480 9167, ⓦwww.marmarine.jp; ❻–❼), about five minutes from Siquijor town, is something special. Tucked away in a secluded cove with its own beach, its tropical grounds are transformed nightly into a magical playground for fireflies. The rooms have delightful touches like outdoor showers or marble baths, and even the most luxurious won't put too much of a strain on your budget. What's more, the Japanese owner, Dagpan, has pledged ten percent of all his revenue to the upkeep of local schools.

## PANAY

The big heart-shaped island of **Panay** has been largely bypassed by tourism, perhaps because everyone seems to get sucked towards Boracay off its northern tip instead. Panay comprises four provinces: Antique on the west coast, Aklan in the north, Capiz in the north-east and Iloilo along the east coast to **Iloilo City** in the south. The province of most interest to tourists is Aklan, whose capital **Kalibo** is the home of the big and brash **Ati-Atihan Festival**, held every year in the second week of January. The northeast coast from Concepcion to Estancia offers access by banca to a number of unspoilt islands, the largest of which is Sicogon, eleven square kilometres, fringed by white sandy beaches and habitation of monkeys, wild pigs and eagles. Most of these islands have few places to stay, so if you want to spend the night take a sleeping bag, water and food. On the other side of Panay, Antique is a poor, bucolic province of beaches and precipitous cordillera mountains.

### Iloilo City

**ILOILO CITY** is a useful transit point for Guimares and other Visayan islands, but otherwise of little interest. There's something drearily homogenous about the ramshackle nature of Philippine port cities and, apart from some graceful old houses in its sidestreets and a handful of interesting churches, the city has little to distinguish it from other horrors of urban planning found throughout the archipelago. A stopover here is partially redeemed by some excellent places to eat, drink and hang out, thanks to a lively student population. West of the city in Molo district is **Molo Church**, a splendid nineteenth-century Gothic Renaissance structure made of coral. The Dinagyang Festival on the fourth weekend in January adds some extra frenzy to the city. Iloilo City is known for a number of delicacies, including **pancit Molo soup**, a garlicky concoction of pork dumplings and noodles in rich broth. It is named after the Molo area of the city and is sold at numerous street stalls. **Batchoy**, an artery-hardening combination of liver, pork and beef with thin noodles, is also available everywhere you look.

## Arrival and information

**By bus** The bus terminal is on Rizal St.

**By ferry** Ferries from Guimaras are served by Oritz wharf, other domestic services use the nearby wharf off San Pedro Drive, at the eastern end of the city.

**By air** Iloilo International Airport is 19km northwest of the city; a taxi to the centre will cost about P200. There is an infrequent airport shuttle serving SM City mall and Jaro Plaza.

**Tourist information** The city's tourist information office is on Bonifacio Drive (Mon–Sat 9.30am–5.30pm; ⓣ033/337 5411 or 335 0245. The post office is in the same building and has poste restante.

**Internet** Widely available, including the ubiquitous Netopia, Robinson's Place.

## Accommodation

**Chito's Hotel** 180 Jalandoni St cnr de Leon St ⓣ033/337 6415, ⓔchitoshotel@yahoo.com. Very pleasant accommodation in a/c en-suite rooms with cable TV. The outdoor *Lobby Café*, surrounded by greenery and overlooking a small swimming pool, is a civilized place to eat. ❺

**Family Pension House** General Luna St ⓣ033/335 0070. One of the city's few good budget options, boasting a helpful travel office with good local information and simple singles and doubles with private shower. ❷–❸

**Iloilo Midtown Hotel** Yulo St ⓣ033/336 6688. Ordinary rooms, though all are well kept and have a/c and hot shower. ❺

## Eating, drinking and nightlife

There are a number of lively bar-clubs in the hip Smallville complex on Diversion Rd, including *Flow Bar, M02* and the peerless *Pier 16.* All have live bands and/or DJs nightly.

**Tatoy's Manukan and Seafoods** Villa Beach in the area of Arevalo, ten minutes west of the city by taxi. A favourite with locals for fresh oysters and other seafood, and should be your first stop if you're looking for something with an authentic Visayan flavour.

**Ted's Oldtimer La Paz Batchoy** Ted's *batchoy* is as original and tasty as it comes in Iloilo. There are seven branches around the city, including one on the ground floor of Robinson's Place. Meals from P49.

## Moving on

**By bus** Buses connect Iloilo City to other towns in Panay. The Ceres bus terminal on Tanza St is the departure point for Caticlan (for Boracay) and Kalibo, via Concepcion and Roxas. Non-stop minivans are slightly more expensive, but make the trip in 4–5 hours. Bus services are most frequent until 1pm.

**Destinations:** Caticlan (10 daily; 7hr); Kalibo (2–3 daily; 5hr). Philtranco serves Manila, using the roll on, roll off (RoRo) ferries.

**By ferry** Iloilo City is a busy port with numerous daily ferry services to Manila and parts of the Visayas. Superferry and Negros Navigation sail to Manila, Bacolod, Cebu City and Cagayan de Oro from the wharf near San Pedro. Fast ferry services to Bacolod leave from the river wharf, and services to Guimaras leave from tiny Oritz wharf.

**By air** Cebu Pacific and Air Philippines have several daily fights to both Manila and Cebu. PAL serves Manila daily.

### Kalibo

**KALIBO** lies on the well-trodden path to Boracay and for most of the year is

## ATI-ATIHAN FESTIVAL

Every January, the Filipino town of **Kalibo** on the island of Panay erupts into Southeast Asia's biggest street party, **Ati-Atihan** (Ⓦwww.ati-atihan.net). This exuberant festival celebrates the original inhabitants of the area, the Atis, and culminates with choreographed dances through the streets by locals daubed in black paint (Ati-Atihan means "to make like the Atis"). Thousands of revellers dress up in outrageous outfits, blacken their faces with soot (in honour of the aboriginal Ati, whose descendants still live on Panay), and salsa through the streets amid cries of "*hala bira, puera pasma*" ("keep on going, no tiring"). It is said that the festival originated when ten Malay chieftains chanced upon the island and persuaded the Ati to sell it to them; the deal was naturally sealed with a party, where the Malays darkened their faces to emulate their new neighbours. Centuries later, the Spanish incorporated Catholic elements into Ati-Atihan and the modern festival is now dedicated to the Santo Niño (Holy Infant Jesus). The event comes to a climax with a huge Mass in the cathedral, and the three-day party ends with a masquerade ball and prizes for the best dressed.

Good accommodation can be hard to find during the Ati-Atihan and prices increase by up to a hundred percent. Direct flights to Kalibo from Manila are often fully booked.

an uninteresting town, but every third Sunday of January it becomes the epicentre of probably the biggest street party in the country, **Ati-Atihan** (see box above).

Kalibo is a compact place with most amenities within walking distance of each other. The major thoroughfare is Roxas Avenue, which runs into town from the **airport** in the south-east, with most streets leading off it to the southwest.

### Arrival

**By bus** There are terminals on Laserna St and Roxas Ave, both served by tricycles.
**By ferry** The new Washington port is 20 minutes from Kalibo. An alternative is Dumaguit, 50 minutes away.
**By air** The ten-minute tricycle ride into town from the airport costs around P10. There are direct FX vans from the airport to Caticlan, P200.

### Accommodation

**Garcia Legaspi Mansion** 159 Roxas Ave Ⓣ036/262 5588. Monastic but clean rooms. ❹–❺
**Gervy's Gourmet & Lodge** R. Pastrada St, east of the *Glowmoon* Ⓣ036/262 4190. Quiet rooms with fan and baths. ❸
**Glowmoon Hotel & Restaurant** Martelino St, near the market and cathedral. Ⓣ036/262 4190. Small and dark rooms, but cheap, and home to a nice restaurant with a surprisingly good range of local and continental dishes. If it's full try the offshoot *Little Glowmoon*, run by the children of the owners, on F. Quimpo St (Ⓣ036/ 262 3072). ❷–❸

### Eating

**Café Latte** Just out from the centre on the way to the airport. Light meals, great coffee and speedy internet access makes this place a favourite with students.
**Peking House Restaurant** Martyr's St. An ever-popular place for cheap Chinese food.

### Directory

**Banks** Several, including BPI and PNB, on Martyr's St, which runs along the southern edge of Pastrana Park, close to Kalibo Cathedral. There's also a BPI on Ryes St.
**Post office** In the Provincial Capitol Building, on Mabini St, off Roxas Ave.
**Internet** Plenty of internet cafés along Roxas Ave, and at *Café Latte*.

### Moving on

**By bus and FXs** For Caticlan (the jumping-off point for Boracay), buses and FX vans both leave the terminal on Roxas Ave every hour; jeepneys, also from this terminal, leave when they are full, often taking as much as four hours to complete the journey as they stop dozens of times along the way. A/c vans and FX taxis also leave from the Ceres Liner bus terminal, 1km south of Kalibo on Laserna St.

**Destinations:** Caticlan (10 daily; 2–2hr 30min); Iloilo City (several daily; 6hr).

**By ferry** From Dumaguit, there are several ferries weekly to Manila and Cebu. You can book ferry tickets at the 2GO outlet right in Kalibo town centre at the junction of Burgos and Luis Barrios sts.

**By air** Several daily to Manila (55min).

## BORACAY

It may be only 7km long and 1km wide at its narrowest point, but **BORACAY**, 350km south of Manila off the north-eastern tip of Panay, is a big tropical island in a small package. With thirty beaches and coves to discover and some of the most chilled-out nightlife in the country, this is an island no backpacker should miss. The sunsets alone are worth the journey.

Boracay is a thrill-seekers' paradise, with horse riding, kiteboarding, beach volleyball, mountain biking, motorcycling, kayaking and diving all on offer. There are 24 official **dive sites** in and around the island, and because of the calm waters near the shore outside the rainy season it's a good place to learn. This said, probably the most popular activity here is doing nothing at all, other than sitting on the beach at dusk watching the sun drift towards the horizon with a cocktail in hand, or having an outdoor massage. Boracay is no longer the sleepy hippy hangout that island veterans reminisce about. There's hardly a patch of beachfront that has not been appropriated for some sort of development, and it's always crowded with vendors. Stray dogs are also a problem. Tourism has begun to encroach on the ecosystem, though many resort owners are aware of how fragile Boracay is and organize beach cleanups and recycling seminars. You can do your bit by taking all your plastic bags and batteries with you when you leave, and not putting cigarettes out on the beach.

### White Beach

The most famous of Boracay's, and quite possibly the country's, beaches is **White Beach** on the island's western shore: 4km of the kind of powder-white sand that you thought only existed in Martini ads. It really does merit the hype. The word Boracay is said to have come from the local word *borac*, meaning cotton, a reference to the sand's colour and texture. **Main Road** runs the western length of Boracay, from Yapak in the north, through White Beach and down to the old Banca Dock on its southern tip. Not surprisingly, most of the development on the island is here, and for the majority of visitors, White Beach *is* Boracay. Before the new ferry system came into place, bancas from Caticlan used to dock directly onto the beach, in three "stations", still used to indicate the south (3) middle (2) and north (1) of the beach. The northern end, beyond the old boat station 1, is the quietest area and home to the more expensive resorts. **D'Talipapa Market** is just north of the tourist centre, while **D'Mall** is a little south of station 1. As a general rule, accommodation at the southern end is cheapest, increasing in price as you move north.

### The rest of the island

The best way to get around the island is to hire a banca from local boatmen on White Beach; you should pay around P1000 for half a day per group. An underused alternative is to rent a bike (see p.672). To the north of White Beach, accessible via a path carved out of the cliffs sits the little village of **Diniwid** with its tranquil, snorkeller-friendly seashore. At the end of a steep path over the next hill is the tiny Balinghai Beach, enclosed by walls of rock, while on the north coast, quiet **Puka Beach**, the second longest on the island, evokes the Boracay of thirty years ago, not least because the shiny white seashells that are found here became a Seventies jewellery craze made famous by Elizabeth Taylor. On the northeast side of the island, Ilig-Iligan Beach has caves and coves to explore, as well as jungle full of fruit bats. From here, a path leads a short way up the hill to **Bat Cave**, a fantastic place to be at dusk when the indigenous flying foxes emerge in immense flocks.

**Mount Luho** in the north of the island is an easy ascent, and the reward is terrific 360-degree views of the island and neighbouring Romblon. There's a P50 entry fee for the final leg of the climb. One of the nicest stretches of island to cycle is from **Punta Bunga** to **Tambisaan Beach**, where the shoreline is dotted with installation art, including the famous Boracay Sandcastle.

From Boracay you can also rent a banca to take you to nearby idyllic **Carabao Island**, part of the **Romblon** group. With wonderful beaches, affordable seafront accommodation at Inobahan on the island's east coast (where the bancas arrive), and a few simple restaurants, tranquil Carabao amply rewards a side trip from Boracay

## Information and transport

**Tourist information** The Boracay Tourist Center (daily 9am–11pm; ⓣ036/288 3704), about halfway along White Beach between stations 2 and 3, is a one-stop shop for all practicalities. As well as tourist information, services include visa assistance, money transfer, currency and travellers' cheque exchange, long-distance telephone, postal and internet facilities and all travel services.

**Tricycles** Fares for the tricycles that run along the length of the Main Road are P10 per person for a trip if you're willing to share the tricycle with others, which means it will pick up passengers along the way. For most foreigners, the flat rate for a private trip is P50 per tricycle, not per person. Make sure you agree the fare in advance. Fares increase at night.

**Bike rental** Boracay Fun & Sports Shop, D'Mall (ⓣ036 288 5941) rents bikes for P75 per hour, P450 per day.

## Dive and sports operators

### Diving

There are over thirty dive shops on Boracay, ensuring fierce competition, and plenty of deals.

### TRAVEL TO AND FROM BORACAY

It's a twenty-minute boat journey to Boracay from the ferry terminal at **Caticlan** (every 10min 6am–6pm, limited sevice 6–10pm). Tickets are P19.50, plus a P50 terminal fee, and another P50 environmental fee. Arrival is at the new **Cagban Jetty Port**, which has replaced the old boat station system. Tricycles meet all boats to take you to your accommodation (P100 flat fee). Occasionally during the monsoon, boats set sail from Tabon and arrive at the eastern side of Boracay, at Tambisaan.

The two closest **airports** to Boracay are **Kalibo** and **Caticlan**. The latter is much closer and the best airport to head for, only five minutes by tricycle from the pier (P50), and Asian Spirit and SEAIR have over fifty daily flights to there from Manila and Cebu. SEAIR has a Thursday morning flight between Busuanga and Caticlan. Kalibo Airport is served by over twenty flights daily by PAL, Air Philippines, and Cebu Pacific with a/c shuttles taking passengers the final two hours by road to Caticlan ferry terminal.

**From Puerta Galera** you can take a daily RoRo vessel leaving Roxas, Mindoro for Caticlan at 2pm.

**From Manila** Superferry and Negros Navigation serve Dumaguit in Aklan, from where you can travel by bus to Caticlan. Negros Navigation also serves Roxas (Panay), leaving Manila on Sunday at 2.30pm. MBRS Shipping Lines sails directly to Caticlan from Manila three times a week (ⓣ02/435888).

**From Iloilo City** Catch a Ceres Liner or GM Liner bus or a/c van from their terminal on Rizal Street to Caticlan (5–7hr).

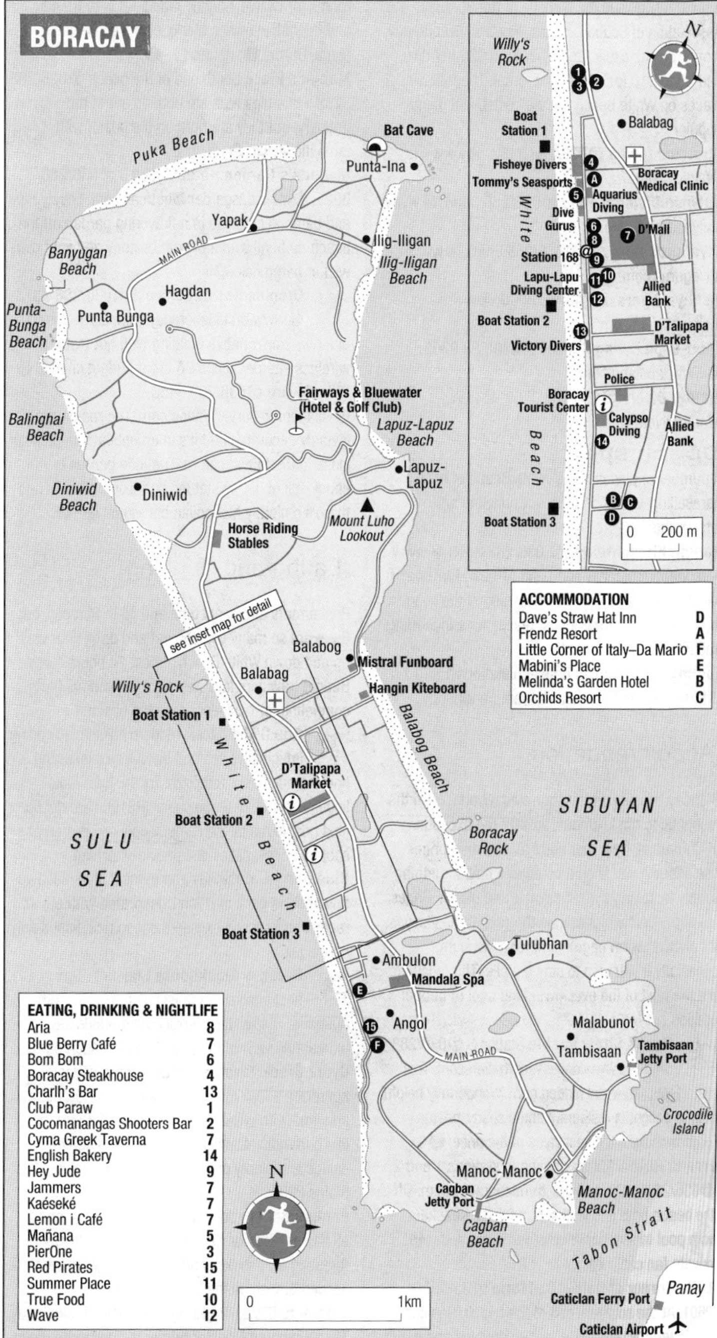
BORACAY
Puka Beach
Bat Cave
Punta-Ina
Yapak
MAIN ROAD
Ilig-Iligan
Ilig-Iligan Beach
Banyugan Beach
Hagdan
Punta-Bunga Beach
Punta Bunga
Fairways & Bluewater (Hotel & Golf Club)
Balinghai Beach
Lapuz-Lapuz Beach
Lapuz-Lapuz
Diniwid Beach
Diniwid
Mount Luho Lookout
Horse Riding Stables
see inset map for detail
Balabog
Mistral Funboard
Balabag
Hangin Kiteboard
Willy's Rock
Boat Station 1
White Beach
Balabog Beach
D'Talipapa Market
Boat Station 2
SULU SEA
SIBUYAN SEA
Boracay Rock
Boat Station 3
Tulubhan
Ambulon
Mandala Spa
Angol
Malabunot
Tambisaan
Tambisaan Jetty Port
Crocodile Island
Manoc-Manoc
Cagban Jetty Port
Manoc-Manoc Beach
Cagban Beach
Tabon Strait
Panay
Caticlan Ferry Port
Caticlan Airport
N
0
1km
Willy's Rock
Boat Station 1
Balabag
Fisheye Divers
Tommy's Seasports
Boracay Medical Clinic
Aquarius Diving
Dive Gurus
D'Mall
Station 168
Lapu-Lapu Diving Center
Allied Bank
Boat Station 2
D'Talipapa Market
Victory Divers
Police
Boracay Tourist Center
Calypso Diving
Allied Bank
Beach
Boat Station 3
0
200 m
ACCOMMODATION
Dave's Straw Hat Inn D
Frendz Resort A
Little Corner of Italy–Da Mario F
Mabini's Place E
Melinda's Garden Hotel B
Orchids Resort C
EATING, DRINKING & NIGHTLIFE
Aria 8
Blue Berry Café 7
Bom Bom 6
Boracay Steakhouse 4
Charlh's Bar 13
Club Paraw 1
Cocomanangas Shooters Bar 2
Cyma Greek Taverna 7
English Bakery 14
Hey Jude 9
Jammers 7
Kaéseké 7
Lemon i Café 7
Mañana 5
PierOne 3
Red Pirates 15
Summer Place 11
True Food 10
Wave 12

A good resource is the website of the Boracay Association of Scuba Schools, ⓦwww.diveboracay.com. You can expect to pay around $25 per dive, and $5 to $10 for equipment rental. The following places on White Beach are well established and popular:

**Aquarius Diving** ⓣ036/288 3132, ⓦwww.phildive.com.
**Calypso Diving School** ⓣ036/288 3206, ⓦwww.calypso-asia.com.
**DiveGurus Boracay** ⓣ036/288 5486, ⓦwww.divegurus.com.
**Fisheye Divers** ⓣ036/288 6090, ⓦwww.fisheyedivers.com
**Lapu-Lapu Diving School** ⓣ036/288 3302, ⓦwww.lapulapu.com.
**Victory Divers** ⓣ036/288 3209, ⓦwww.victorydivers.com.

### Ocean sports

A number of places along White Beach offer parasailing, wakeboarding, waterskiiing and kitesurfing:

**Hangin Kiteboarding** (ⓣ 036/288 3663 ⓦwww.kiteboardingboracay.com) and **Mistral Funboard** (ⓣ036/288 3876), on the other side of the island to White Beach, are the best places for windsurfing and kiteboarding.
**Tommy's Sea Sports** Between stations 1 and 2. Offers plenty to keep aqua adventurers happy.

## Accommodation

Boracay boasts over two hundred resorts, from the monastic to the luxurious, so with the exception of Christmas, New Year and Easter (when prices rise sharply) you should be able to find something simply by taking a stroll down White Beach. Prices are significantly higher than the rest of the Visayas; it's always worth negotiating for a discount, especially if you plan to stay a while. The following are the best of the ever-dwindling pool of budget options.

**Dave's Straw Hat Inn** Station 3 ⓣ036/288 5465, ⓦwww.davesstrawhatinn.com. This place feels like a real hidden gem. Wonderfully helpful staff, a delightful restaurant and a shady, private location make it the best value at the price. ❻
**Frendz** Resort Midway between stations 1 and 2. ⓣ03[…]88 3903, ⓦwww.frendzboracay.com. Off […] path and well set up for backpackers […]bles, hammocks and dorm beds. ❸; […]abin ❻
[…] of Italy – Da Mario ⓣ036/288 […]uthern end of the beach. Besides […]), there are a/c doubles and group rooms for twelve. Slightly faded but very friendly, and the Italian owner, Mario, cooks some mean pasta. Dorms ❶; rooms ❺–❻
**Mabini's Place** South end of the beach ⓣ036/288 3238. Plain nipa huts are nothing out of the ordinary, but they are right on the beach with fantastic views. ❺
**Melinda's Garden Hotel** Station 3 ⓣ036/288 3021, ⓔmelindasgarden@hotmail.com. Lovely nipa and bamboo cottages in a flowering garden off the beach path, all with a private balcony and your own wicker hammock. ❹
**Orchids Resort** Station 3 ⓣ036/288 3313 ⓦwww.orchidsboracay.com. Large rooms in a two-storey native building with hot water and wireless internet access. A great budget choice. ❺
**Villa de Oro** ⓣ036/288 5456, ⓔvilladeororesorts@yahoo.com. The rooms are lovingly decorated and it's in an unbeatable position close to the tourist centre. The little garden is chock-full of quirky statues and woodcarvings and there's a nightly Mongolian barbeque. ❻–❼

## Eating and drinking

Restaurants and bars come and go in Boracay, but there are so many you can eat and drink your way up and down White Beach almost 24 hours a day. Budget travellers fare well from the various buffets competing for business along the beach.

**Aria** D'Mall. Sleek, modern Italian place doing imaginative seafood as well as comforting home-made pasta and pizza. Try the crab-flake linguine in a Pinot Grigio sauce (P210). *Café del Sol* next door is run by the same people and is a great spot for coffee, cakes and people-watching.
**Blue Berry Café** Shady and modest little hideaway towards the back of D'Mall, decorated with ethnic regalia and serving excellent cheap rice dishes and herbal teas.
**Boracay Steakhouse** Station 1. The best steaks on the island, imported from Australia. The upstairs terrace commands an unbeatable view of the action on the beach path.
**Cyma Greek Taverna** D'Mall. Try the *sagnaki* appetiser, a dish of flaming cheese, brandy, butter and lime with crusty bread for dipping. Great meze like hummous, tzatziki and htipiti, plus healthy salads and plenty of veggie options to choose from. Mains P200.
**English Bakery** Just north of Station 3. Open all day but famous for breakfast, especially their tempting fruit shakes and cinnamon rolls. There's a second branch on the Bulabog road.
**Jammers** D'Mall. 24-hr burger meals to take away. Their signature Monster Burger is a favourite dawn

snack for revellers stumbling along the beach path towards home.

**Kaéseké** D'Mall. Tasty Japanese noodles, sashimi and sushi. The unusual interior is almost entirely crafted from native wood.

**Lemon i Café** D'Mall. A favourite for gourmet sandwiches, light Mediterranean meals and sweet treats.

**Mañana** Teeny beachside Mexican place with a seemingly endless menu, and tables in the sand. Their Margaritas are highly recommended. Chicken chimichangas P280.

**Summer Place** Best known as a buzzing all-night bar and disco, but from 8 to 11pm it does the best Mongolian buffet on the island.

**True Food** Take off your shoes and relax on floor cushions at Boracay's most authentic Indian restaurant. Mouthwatering curries, including many vegetarian options. Aloo palak P280.

## Nightlife

Nightlife on Boracay starts with drinks at sunset and carries on well into the following morning. You'll find everything from swanky resort bars to convivial beach shacks to downright raucous dives.

**Bom Bom** Boracay's best nightspot. This convivial little beach bar has everything you could want – beanbags around low tables in the sand, excellent cocktails served by the ever-accommodating Gilbert and great live music. Once you sink into the beanbags you may never make it to another bar.

**Charlh's Bar** Small outdoor place near *Nigi's* with live acoustic music on the beach from dusk and a popular happy hour.

**Club Paraw** Snazzy double-decker club right on the sand between *PierOne* and *Cocomangas*. Plays house and R&B. Happy hour 4–9pm.

**Cocomangas Shooters Bar** Very lively bar at the back of the *Cocomangas Beach Resort* at Balabag (northern end of White Beach), infamous for its drinking games involving potent cocktails, which get rowdier as the night wears on.

**Hey Jude** Entrance to D'Mall. Slick DJs and slicker cocktails attract the beautiful people to this hip hangout. Occasionally hosts beach parties.

**PierOne** (formerly *Beachcomber*). One of Boracay's most longstanding and well-known discos. Plays mainly hip-hop, with occasional visiting performers from Manila.

**Red Pirates** At the southern end of the beach. *Red Pirates* is the most chilled-out beach bar after *Bom Bom*. Plays host to Boracay's full moon parties, considerably lower key entities than many of their Southeast Asian equivalents.

**Summer Place** Big nipa establishment on the beach path where dancing and drinking go on all night. There's a stage for live acts and DJ sets.

**Wave** *Boracay Regency Beach Resort*. An underground cave decked out as an aquarium. Popular with Korean tour groups, and a little expensive, even by Boracay standards.

**TREAT YOURSELF**

**Mandala Spa** (daily 10am–10pm; ⓣ036/288 5857, ⓦwww.mandalaspa.com). Winner of a slew of awards, this romantic, luxurious spa is one of Southeast Asia's finest, and worth every penny. Splash out on a cleansing massage and all memories of living out of a rucksack for weeks on end will be washed away in a stream of warm scented oil, as you snack on fresh fruit and cleansing teas in your private cabaña. There's a huge variety of treatments available from P5600, but for four hours of utter decadence the "Princess" package (P9500) has no equal.

## Directory

**Airlines** Inside the Boracay Tourist Center is a branch of Filipino Travel Center where you can book tickets for PAL, Air Philippines, SEAIR, Asian Spirit, and Cebu Pacific. Asian Spirit and Seair also have branches inside D'Mall.

**Banks and exchange** Allied Bank on the main road near the access path to the Tourist Center and Landbank near Boat Station 1 change traveller's cheques, and the former has an ATM. Many resorts also act as de facto currency changers. In D'Mall, there's a small branch of BPI with an ATM. Visa, MasterCard and American Express are widely accepted, although sometimes with a small surcharge.

**Hospitals and clinics** The main facility is the Boracay Island Hospital, Main Rd (ⓣ036/288 3041). Metropolitan Doctors Medical Clinic is also on Main Rd (ⓣ036/288 6357), by *Cocomangas*, open 24hr. The small Bysshe Medical Clinic and pharmacy is in D'Mall. In the event of serious injury, treatment at the Aklan Baptist Hospital in Caticlan is recommended.

**Internet** There are dozens of internet cafés on Boracay, most with reasonably fast dedicated connections (around P50/hr) – among the mo popular are at the Boracay Tourist Center, and Station 168, open 24hr.

**Post office** The post office in Balabag, the small community halfway along White Beach, is open Mon–Fri 9am–5pm. The Boracay Tourist Center on White Beach has full postal services.

**Pharmacies** There are pharmacies selling most necessities in D'Mall, Boracay Tourist Center and D'Talipapa Market.

**Police** The Philippine National Police have a small facility a short walk inland between Boat Stations 2 and 3, immediately behind the Boracay Tourist Center. Dial ⓣ135 in an emergency.

**Shopping** Dozens of small *sari-sari* stores line White Beach selling beachwear, T-shirts and souvenirs, and at D'Talipapa Market you can buy fruit and fish. D'Mall has an ever-expanding range of shops selling clothes, souvenirs and handicrafts. Boracay Budget Mart, at the back of D'Mall is an inexpensive supermarket.

# Palawan

If you believe the travel agent clichés, **Palawan** is the Philippines' last frontier. For once, it's almost true. Tourism has yet to penetrate much of this long, sword-shaped island to the southwest of Luzon, and travellers willing to take the rough with the smooth will find a Jurassic landscape of coves, beaches, lagoons and razor-sharp limestone cliffs that rise from crystal-clear water. Palawan province encompasses 1780 islands and islets, many of which are surrounded by a coral shelf that acts as an enormous feeding ground and nursery for marine life. It is sometimes said that Palawan's **Tubbataha Reef** is so ecologically important that if it dies, the Philippines will perish also. If you're looking for varied and challenging d... you won't find better anywhere ...rld.

...tal and main gateway, **Puerto** ...nakes a good starting point ...g the northern half of the ...h is where all the tourist attractions are. A typical journey through Palawan might take you from Puerto Princesa, north to **Honda Bay** and the **Underground River**, then onwards up the coast to **Port Barton**, **San Vicente** and **El Nido** and across to **Busuanga** and the rest of the Calamian Islands. The southern half of Palawan, from Puerto Princesa downwards, is relatively unexplored, one reason being that during the wet season the southern roads become almost impassable.



## PUERTO PRINCESA

The provincial capital and only major town in Palawan, **PUERTO PRINCESA** is a pleasant, clean place that most visitors treat as a one-night stop on the way to or from the beaches, islands and coral reefs of the north. It does, however, boast a handful of exceptionally good **restaurants**, and is the administrative centre of the island – all your banking and travel arrangements will have to be made here before you move on.

Twenty-three kilometres to the northwest of Puerto Princesa is the **Iwahig Penal Colony** also known as the Prison Without Bars (daily 8am–7pm; free). Prisoners live here as if in a normal village, fishing and cultivating rice and root crops. The "inmates" are identifiable by scraps of orange cloth pinned to their T-shirts (money for uniforms being scarce), returning to the prison halls only to eat and sleep. Some long-term residents – those deemed least likely to make a run for it – are allowed to stay in small nipa huts with their families. Tourists are also welcome at the small souvenir shop selling handicrafts made by the prisoners. Officials claim the rate of re-offence among those released from Iwahig is significantly lower than among those incarcerated in the country's traditional jails. To get to the colony, catch a jeepney from Malvar Street at 9.30am (P35).

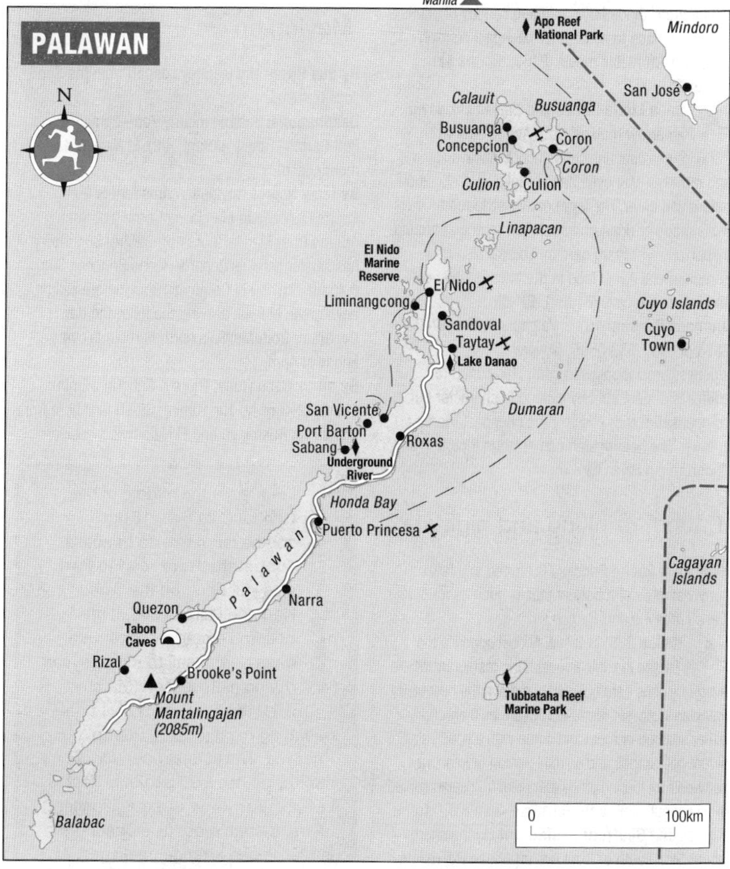


## Arrival and information

**By bus and jeepney** The terminal is at San José, 7km north of the centre. A tricycle will cost P50.

**By ferry** The pier is at the eastern end of Malvar St, a short walk to Rizal Ave.

**By air** The airport is at the eastern end of Rizal Ave, within walking distance of most accommodation, though there are always tricycles waiting it's cheaper to flag one down on the road outside.

**Tourist information** The tourist office (Mon–Sat 9am–5pm; ⓣ048/433 2968, ⓦwww.palawantourism.com) is in the Provincial Capitol Building on Rizal Ave. A good place to plug into the travellers' grapevine is the *Casa Linda Inn*, where the staff are helpful and knowledgeable. A growing number of tour companies on Rizal Ave offer tailored trips to the Underground River, the average rate per person is P1300.

## Accommodation

**Amelia Pensionne** 420 Rizal Ave ⓣ048/433 7029, ⓔamelia_pensionne@yahoo.com. Within walking distance of the airport and offering a good range of rooms, from basic a/c doubles with bathroom to larger deluxe doubles with cable TV. ❸

**Badjao Inn** 350 Rizal Ave ⓣ048/433 2761, ⓔbadajo_inn@yahoo.com. Unattractive brick structure facing the road, and close to the airport, but behind the facade there's a lovely garden and a good choice of spacious rooms overlooking the greenery. The efficient travel desk can book transport for you, and there's internet access. Double fan rooms ❸

**Banwa Art House Pension** Liwanag St cnr Mendoza St ⓣ048/434 8963, ⓦwww.banwa.com. A bohemian oasis set back from th road and decorated with local artwork. The eating area, shaded by a hanging canopy of plants, is a great place to meet other backpackers over tasty and affordable meals (P100). Dorms ❷; rooms ❸

**Casa Linda Inn** Behind *Badjao Inn*, down a narrow road off Rizal Ave ⓣ048/433 2606, ⓔcasalindainn@gmail.com. Always clean and orderly – you even have to take your shoes off before you enter. The large native-style rooms have walls made of dried grass and are arranged around a spacious courtyard garden. There's also good European and Asian food in the little bamboo café and internet access (P40/hr). ❸–❹

**Duchess Pension** 107 E. Valencia St ⓣ048/433 2873 or 0917 553 0605, ⓦwww.duchesspensionpalawan.com. This concrete edifice is almost entirely lacking in character but compensates with possibly the cheapest rooms in town. The helpful staff can arrange trips to the Underground River. ❷

## Eating, drinking and nightlife

Nightlife in Puerto Princesa is limited to a few convivial and quiet bars at places such as *Ka Lui's*, *Casa Linda Inn* and *Badjao Inn*.

**Ka Lui** 369 Rizal Ave. Almost opposite the *Badjao Inn*, this atmospheric restaurant where everyone goes barefoot is hands down the best in Palawan. Daily set meals (P150) are built around either seafood or meat and come with a good salad, sweet potato fries and a small portion of fresh, raw seaweed, all topped off by a tropical fruit salad served in a coconut shell. Mon–Sat 11am–2pm & 6–11pm.

**Badjao Inn Seafront Restaurant** On the shore about 5km south of Rizal Ave off Abueg Rd, reached on foot across a short, dainty bamboo bridge through mangroves. A classy but informal native-style restaurant It's a little more expensive than *Ka Lui*; expect to pay about P500 a head for fresh, wonderfully tasty grilled seafood. If you're here in the evening, take a tricycle and pay the driver P100 to take you out there, wait while you eat and then take you back.

## Directory

**Banks** Rizal Ave is the best place for ATMs and moneych[illegible]ers; PNB lies at the western end, just [illegible]'oza Park.

[illegible]'s an internet café attached to the [illegible] there are small places stretched [illegible] though they are usually filled with [illegible]g computer games.

[illegible]rgos St at its junction with

## Moving on

**By bus** Buses and jeepneys depart from the San José terminal.

**Destinations:** Sabang (hourly 7am–2pm; 3hr); Port Barton (1 daily at 9am; 4hr). El Nido (3 daily, mornings: 8hr)

**By ferry** Negros Navigation runs ferries from Puerto Princesa to Manila via Coron (Sat 9am, returns from Manila Thurs 4pm; 25hr). Superferry has similar service: departs Puerta Princesa Sun 8.45am, arriving in Coron at 10pm, before sailing onwards to Manila, arriving the following day. Departure from Manila's north harbour is every Friday at 4pm.

**By air** to: Cebu (Tues, Thurs & Sat; 1hr 15min); Manila (2–3 daily; 1hr 10min); SEAIR flies here from Manila via Busuanga and El Nido twice weekly.

**TREAT YOURSELF**

Located in the middle of the Central Sulu Sea, 181km southeast of Puerto Princesa, **Tubbataha Reef Marine Park** was inscribed on the World Heritage List in 1993. It has become a magnet for **scuba divers**, who sail to it every year during high season (March–June) on liveaboard dive boats operating mostly out of Puerto Princesa. The largest operator in the Philippines is Expedition Fleet Liveaboards (ⓦwww.expeditionfleet.com), though most dive operators in Manila can arrange packages. At around US$1200 for one week it's not cheap, but if you're willing to – literally – push out the boat you'll be rewarded with superlative diving at one of the best reefs in the world, with sightings of sharks and manta rays a daily occurrence.

## HONDA BAY

Picturesque **Honda Bay** sits 10km north of Puerto Princesa by road and makes a good day-trip, though there's the option to stay overnight. There are seven islands in the bay, including **Snake Island**, with a good reef for snorkelling, and **Starfish Island**, which has a rustic restaurant where the seafood, when it's still available, is as fresh as it comes. Look out for **Bat Island** in the late afternoon, as scores of bats suddenly fly away on their nocturnal hunting trips.

Any jeepney or bus going north from Puerto Princesa in the direction of Roxas (the only decent stretch or road on the island) will take you to Honda Bay. You'll need to get off at **Santa Lourdes wharf** (this may involve a tricycle ride from where the bus or jeepney leaves you) and sign in at the little tourist office and book a banca. A boat will cost anything from P500 to P800 depending on which island you plan to visit and for how long. Some islands ask visitors to pay a small fee. On Starfish Island, the *Starfish Sandbar Resort* has rustic huts that sleep four (❸–❹), but bring your own tinned food because the small restaurant often runs out.

## THE UNDERGROUND RIVER

The **Underground River**, or to give it its proper name, St Paul's Subterranean National Park, is another UNESCO World Heritage Site and is top of the list of wonders visitors to Palawan want to see. The longest underground river in the world, it meanders for more than 8km through a bewildering array of stalactites, stalagmites, caverns, chambers and pools. The formations are made even more eerie on your ride through by the shadows cast by the boatmen's kerosene lamp (trips daily 7am–5pm), though their inane running commentary takes away somewhat from the atmosphere.

The park is some way northwest of Puerto Princesa – up to three hours by road and another twenty minutes by banca. Buses and jeepneys make regular trips to **Sabang**, the jumping-off point for the Underground River. You can also club together and hire your own jeepney (about P1000). At the **Visitors Assistance Centre** in Sabang, close to the pier, you pay P200 per person to enter the cave, plus another P700 for six passengers in the boat. If you're feeling energetic, you can hike to the mouth of the river, a 5km trip through lush scenery. When you arrive at the park, look out for the famous resident monitor lizards (bayawak), and monkeys that are tame (and cheeky) enough to take food from your hand. Sabang has beaches stretching either side where there a growing number of quiet **places to stay**, all of similar price and with their are own simple restaurants. All have electricity from 6 to 10pm only. Try *Taraw Beach Resort*, a convenient five-minute walk north of the pier along Sabang Beach, with plain bamboo cottages (❷–❸).

## PORT BARTON AND AROUND

On the northwest coast of Palawan, roughly halfway between Puerto Princesa and El Nido, **Port Barton** has become something of a travellers' rest stop in recent years. There are several white-sand islands in the bay and Port Barton itself has a short stretch of beach that is home to half-a-dozen resorts. **Buses** and **jeepneys** from Puerto Princesa arrive on Rizal Street, very close to the beach and the town centre. Alternatively, you can travel up the coast by banca (see p.680) About 15km north along a rough coastal road from Port Barton is the sleepy fishing village of **SAN VICENTE**, which has a market and a pier where bancas can be chartered. The marvellous beaches around San Vicente make a fantastic day-trip from Port Barton. **Long Beach**, an undeveloped fourteen-kilometre stretch of stunning sand ranks as one of the most extraordinary beaches in the country – you can see both ends only on a brilliantly clear day.

### Accommodation and eating

All the places below are in Port Barton.

**Greenview Resort** ⓣ0921 326 0565, ⓦwww.palawandg.clara.net. Cottages right on the be
at its eastern end in a secluded, idyllic lo

Though the resort has few amenities, it does boast an excellent restaurant. ③

**Princesa Michaella's** Close to *Ysobelle's*, right on the beach (no phone). Offers basic, fan-cooled huts. ②

**Ysobelle's Beach Resort** (formerly *Swissippini Lodge and Resort*) ⓣ0928 503 0388, ⓔysobellepalawan@yahoo.com.ph. A short walk from Rizal St, this is the best-equipped resort here, with big A-frame cottages, all with balconies and private bathrooms, internet access and a decent restaurant. ⑥ including breakfast.

## EL NIDO AND THE BACUIT ARCHIPELAGO

In the far northwest of Palawan is the small coastal town of **EL NIDO**, departure point for excursions to the innumerable islands of the **BACUIT ARCHIPELAGO**, undoubtedly one of the highlights of any trip to the Philippines. This is spectacular limestone-island country, with jaw-dropping formations rising from the sea everywhere you look. These iconic karst cliffs with their fearsomely jagged rocky outcrops are believed to have been formed over sixty million years ago, emerging from the sea as a result of India colliding with mainland Asia. Weathering and erosion have produced deep crevices, caves, underground rivers and sinkholes in endlessly strange and wonderful permutations. The result is one of the most beautiful island seascapes on earth, despite being peppered with a number of exclusive and expensive resorts. If US$200 a night for a taste of air-conditioned paradise is too much for you, then you can stay in rustic El Nido itself – where electricity cuts off at one in the morning – and island-hop by day. All day banca trips cost around P700 per person, and the best place to arrange [illegible] ping is the *El Nido Boutique* [illegible] *fé* on Palerma St.

### [illegible] d information

[illegible] near *Rosanna's Cottages*, at the [illegible] bay.

**By air** It's a straightforward jeepney or tricycle ride from El Nido airport into town, though you'll be charged an extortionate P150.

**Tourist information** The *El Nido Boutique & Art Café* on Palmera St is a wonderful resource for tourist information. You can also change money and make travel arrangements here, and they do great coffee.

### Accommodation and eating

It's easy to walk from the bus arrival point to all the town's accommodation. Apart from the restaurants at resorts, there are a cluster of cheap eateries around Del Pilar and Real streets.

**Alternative Centre** Serona Rd, ⓣ0917 896 3406, ⓦwww.palawan-elnido.com. Offering a bevy of "welllness packages" and boasting a fantastic vegan and vegetarian-friendly restaurant, this place is really special. ④–⑤

**Marina Garden Beach Resort** Middle of the beach ⓣ048/723 0876, ⓔmarinagarden.elnido@gmail.com. Spacious, neatly furnished cottages with balcony and private bathrooms. Staff here are a good source of info on travelling to the Calamians or south by banca. ③

**Rosanna's Beach Cottages** Hama St ⓣ0929 605 4631. Right on the beach, the cottages are clean and good value, though there are better views from the rooms in the main building. ③–⑤

**Tandikan Cottages** ⓣ0927 562 6350. Fan cottages in a pretty garden leading back from the beach and a quaint little restaurant offering simple food. ③

### Moving on

**By bus** There are two early morning departures for Puerto Princesa (9hr)

**By banca** In high season, bancas ply the Sabang–Port Barton–El Nido route roughly three times a week, with early morning departures and hefty "special ride" fares of P1500–2000 per person. For similar prices you can take a twice-weekly ferry from El Nido to Coron (8hr)

**By air** SEAIR flies to: Busuanga (2 weekly; 1hr 5min); Manila (3 weekly; 2hr 15m); Puerto Princesa (2 weekly; 45min).

## THE CALAMIAN ISLANDS

Access to the beautiful Calamian Islands, the largest of which is **Busuanga**, followed in size by **Culion** and **Coron**, is through the increasingly popular little fishing community of **CORON TOWN**, which confusingly is on Busuanga, not Coron. The presence of several Japanese World War II wrecks in the bays near Coron Town has made it a point of pilgrimage for **wreck divers**, and the rest of the Calamians have plenty to occupy island-hoppers and regular divers. The centre of Coron Town is huddled around the pier (there's no beach) where you can hire bancas for island trips and get information on diving; most of the other tourist facilities are no more than a short walk or tricycle ride away. **Landbank**, halfway between the market and the port, has an ATM, and the Sea Dive Internet Café is on Don Pedro Street.

The precipitous limestone cliffs of **Coron Island**, twenty minutes by boat from Coron Town, are absolutely spectacular – it's only when you get close to them in a banca that they reveal dozens of perfect little coves, hidden in the folds of the mountains. Tribes, including the Tagbanua, still live in the interior, where a short, steep climb takes you to the island's volcanic **Cayangan Lake**, a great place to swim and one of the area's favourite dive sites (admission P200). You could spend a lifetime on Coron and still not get to see every hot spring, hidden lake or pristine cove. South of Coron Town is the large island of **Culion**, home to a former leper colony and a fascinating **museum** (Mon–Sat 10am–5pm; P25) detailing the colony's history.

From Coron Town, you can also catch a bus or jeepney to take you west along the **south Busuanga coast** to the villages of Concepcion, Salvacion and Old Busuanga, where there are a number of resorts, and piers with bancas for hire.

## Accommodation and eating

Most of the accommodation on Busuanga is around the pier in Coron Town and can be noisy. If you want quieter accommodation you'll have to stay out of town, which means taking a tricycle back and forth to the pier when you dive or go island hopping. Resorts are mushrooming, and prices are rising accordingly. **The Bistro**, Don Pedro St, is easily the best place to eat in Coron, with mouthwatering European and local dishes freshly cooked by French expat Bruno.

### TRAVEL TO AND FROM THE CALAMIAN ISLANDS

Asian Spirit and SEAIR both have regular **flights** from Manila to Busuanga, the latter also connects Busuanga with El Nido and Puerto Princesa. The airport is an hour by jeepney (P150) from Coron Town, where both airlines have offices. WG&A (Superferry) have a weekly sailing from Manila to Coron Town (13hr) and then onwards to Puerto Princesa. The WG&A ticket office (ⓣ0919 540 1695) is on Real Street. A private-hire banca to El Nido for up to six people costs P18000; there are also two ferry services a week during high season (8hr).

### Coron Town

**Crystal Lodge** ⓣ0920 801 6058. Built right out over the water, this place is hard to miss. Run by expat Zimbabwean John, this place has lovely cottages and a pleasantly ramshackle ambience. ❹–❺

**KokusNuss Resort** ⓣ0919 448 7879, ⓦwww.kokosnuss.info. The first accommodation as you approach Coron Town from the airport, on the left-hand side about 1km before the town. If you haven't had your fill of diving, one of the cottages is decorated as an underwater world. ❸–❻

**Michelangelo Hotel and Restaurant** ⓣ0921 451 5503, ⓦwww.hotelmichelangelo-coron.com. Close to where the Superferry docks, five minutes from the centre of town. At the time of writing the hotel was in the midst of an expansion from 9 rooms to 52, but even if you can't stay, the restaurant here serves great Italian and is one of the best in the area. Room rates include welcome drinks and breakfast. ❻

**Sea Dive Resort** ⓣ0920 945 8714. Right in the centre of town, this American-run resort has a nice bar, and is a great place to swap diving tips. First-rate dive and accommodation packages fr P10,000, otherwise ❹

# Mindanao

The signals **Mindanao** sends to the rest of the Philippines and the rest of the world are nothing if not mixed. This massive island at the foot of the archipelago is in many ways a cultural and artistic faultline, a place where tribalism and capitalism clash head on, a refuge for those fleeing Manila's pollution in search of cleaner air and greener pastures. All of this has led to something of a cultural and economic boom in cities such as **Davao**, Mindanao's de facto capital and gateway to the southern half of the region but Mindanao is also a troubled island, with various indigenous Islamic or Moro groups agitating, sometimes violently, for autonomy (see box below) Some parts of the island are considered unsafe for tourists, and only the volcanic island of **Camiguin**, and the busy portal city of **Cagayan de Oro** on Mindanao's north coast are covered here.

## CAGAYAN DE ORO

**CAGAYAN DE ORO** on the north coast of Mindanao is the starting point for many travellers for a trip to dazzling Camiguin island, though the city itself is generally unimpressive, a noisy mish-mash of busy streets and fast-food restaurants, hardly enough to tempt you to stay longer than a day or night before moving on. You'll find few memorable sights, apart from the eighteenth-century **San Augustine Cathedral**, a pretty, off-white stone edifice just south of Gaston Park, with a gold-plated altar and immense stained-glass windows.

If you pass through the eastern suburbs of the city (on the road to Balingoan, for instance), you'll notice the sweet smell of the source of much of Cagayan de Oro's income today: pineapples from enormous plantations inland, mostly owned by Del Monte, which are brought here for canning.

### THE MINDANAO PROBLEM

Mindanao has been a nagging thorn in the side of successive governments, with repeated attempts by the island's Muslims (or Moros) to establish autonomy on the island, while the indigenous Lumad peoples also assert rights to their traditional lands.

The **Moro National Liberation Front** (MNLF) started a war for independence in the 1970s. Meanwhile, a communist-led rebellion spread from the northern Philippines to Mindanao, drawing many majority Filipinos. In the early 1990s, one disaffected group left the MNLF and formed **Abu Sayyaf** ("Bearer of the Sword"), whose centre of operations is largely Basilan Island, part of the Sulu Archipelago off Mindanao's southern coast. The group is said to have ties to a number of Islamic fundamentalist organizations around the world, including al-Qaeda.

In 1996, the Philippine government signed a peace pact with the MNLF granting a certain degree of autonomy to four provinces. But this peace is by no means final or universal and splinter groups are still engaged in conflict, including Abu Sayyaf, who are believed to have been responsible for the bombing of the WG&A *Superferry 14* in February 2004, which sank off the coast of Manila with the loss of 116 lives. In early 2007 there were several bombings on the same day in General San... City, Kidapawan City and Cotabato City, killing seven people and injuring ...7 others, and in November 2007, a bomb exploded in a shopping mall in ...n City. Public transport is a common target for attacks and kidnapping ... threat.

...ook went to press, the British Foreign and Commonwealth Office was ...ainst all travel to Mindanao. However, most of the northern coast and ... Christian and Visayan speaking, and is more like part of the Visayas.

## Arrival and information

**By bus** Buses arrive at the Integrated Bus Terminal on the northeastern outskirts next to Agora Market, from where it's an easy tricycle or jeepney ride into town.

**By ferry** Macabalan Wharf is 5km north of the centre, with regular jeepneys back and forth; a taxi from here into the city costs about P70.

**By air** The airport is 10km outside the city – a taxi ride in will cost about P120. A much larger airport, 46km outside the city, is set to open in 2010.

**Tourist information** The tourist office (Mon–Sat 8am–noon & 1–5pm; ⓣ088/857 3164) is on A Velez St, a short walk north of the city centre close to the library, and has maps, details of guided tours and lists of accommodation in and around the city, including on Camiguin.

## Accommodation

The area around T Neri St in the south of the city, near Gaston Park, is home to most of the town's budget accommodation.

**Hotel Ramon** Burgos St ⓣ088/857 4084. Within walking distance of everything; get a river-view room if you can. ❹

**Parkview Hotel** T Neri St ⓣ088/227 2855. In a quiet area right next to the park. One of the better options, with adequate a/c or fan rooms. ❷

## Eating, drinking and nightlife

Try the barbecue stalls around Xavier University, where you can get hot and spicy barbecue and rice for under P50.

**Bigby's Café** Limekai Center. Bright, friendly place serving great coffee and light lunches.

**Divisoria Market** Golden Friendship Park. On weekend evenings, this is a great place to hang out, with lively outdoor food stalls selling all manner of treats, and informal communal tables.

**Persian Palate** SM City Mall. Branch of the popular chain doing tasty and healthy Middle Eastern food, with great vegetarian options.

**Thrives** Capistrano St. This hybrid music lounge and comedy club is a favourite venue for visiting bands, and fills up with students from 9pm.

## Directory

**Banks** BPI and Equitable PCI have branches on JR Borja St.

**Internet** There are a number of small internet cafés along T Chavez St.

## Moving on

**By bus** There are several daily buses to Butua (4hr) which pass through Balingoan (2hr), the departure point for Camiguin.

**By boat** Superferry and Negros Navigation both run ferries to Manila (1 weekly; 32hr); Bacolod (1 weekly; 17 hr); Iloilo (2 weekly; 10hr) and Cebu City (3 weekly; 8hr).

**By air** to: Cebu City (daily; 1hr); Davao (4 weekly; 50min); Manila (daily; 1hr 30min).

# CAMIGUIN ISLAND

Sitting about 20km off the north coast of mainland Mindanao, the pint-sized island of **Camiguin** is one of the country's most appealing tourist spots, offering ivory beaches, iridescent lagoons and undulating scenery. It's a peaceful, almost spiritual island, where residents are proud of their faith, though there's no shortage of adventure either, with reasonable scuba diving and some tremendous trekking and climbing in the rugged interior, especially on volcanic **Mount Hibok-Hibok**. Camiguin is home to six other volcanoes, a multitude of hot springs, a spring that gushes natural soda water, and a submerged cemetery for divers to explore near the coastal town of **Bonbon**. Another major tourist draw is the annual **Lanzones Festival**, held in the fourth week of October when revellers stomp and dance in the streets as a tribute to this humble fruit, one of Camiguin's major sources of income. The festival is one of the liveliest and most welcoming in the country, and this on an island already renowned for the friendliness of its people.

The beauty of Camiguin is that it doesn't really matter where you stay because you can see all the sights easily from anywhere. The **coastal road** is almost 70km long, making it feasible to circle the island in a day. If you don't want to depend on public transport, consider hiring your own private jeepney or tricycle for the trip. M resorts also offer motorcycle

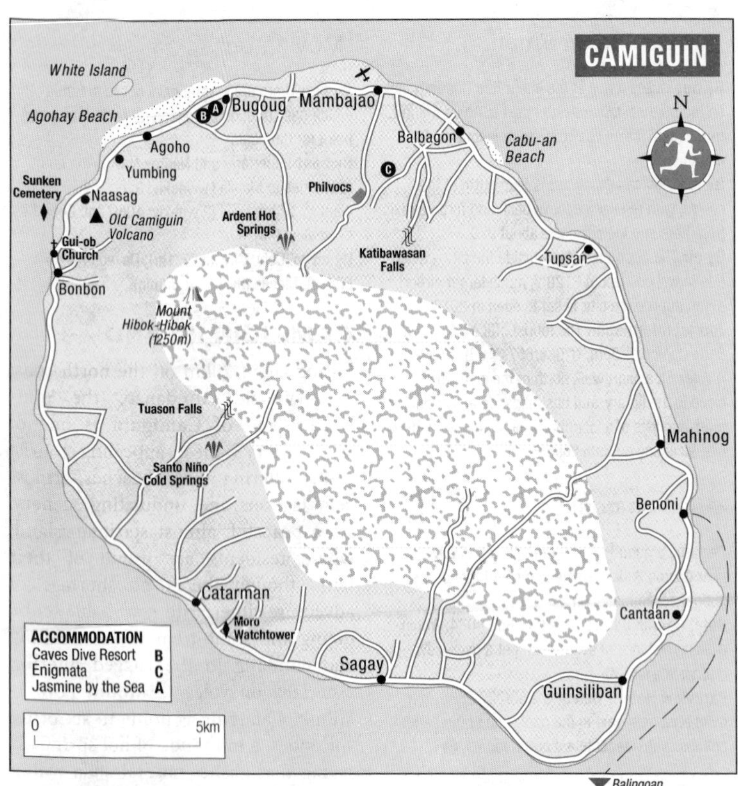


## TRAVEL TO AND FROM CAMIGUIN ISLAND

From **Cagayan de Oro**, catch a regular bus to **Balingoan** about 80km northeast (2hr) from where ferries depart hourly for **Benoni** on Camiguin's southeast coast. From here, jeepneys (P30) run roughly every hour to **Mambajao**, the bustling little capital on the north coast. If you want to bypass Cagayan de Oro altogether, you can **fly from Cebu**. SEAIR fly to Camiguin from Cebu City and back on W[...]esday, Friday and Sunday [...] (45min). The airstrip is [...]metres to the west of [...], from where it's an easy [...] into town or to your [...]any cases, the resort will [...]le to meet you.

and can help you arrange all manner of adventurous activities.

## Accommodation

Most of the best beach accommodation is west of Mambajao between the small towns of Bug-ong and Naasag. The resorts here are well prepared for foreign tourists and have lots of information about diving and trekking; resorts near the town of Agoho, a little west of Bug-ong, are popular because it gives quickest access to White Island, a dazzling serpentine ribbon of sand only visible at low tide.

**Caves Dives Resort** ⓣ 088/387 0077, ⓦ www.cavesdiveresort.com. Beachfront resort in a tropical garden with bungalow or cottage accommodation and one of the best restaurants on Camiguin. ❹–❺

**Enigmata** 2km east of Mambajao ⓣ 0918 230 4184, ⓦ www.mindanaoculture.com/enigmata. This place is something different: an eco-lodge built around a giant acacia tree in the middle of a sculpture garden, and managed by an artists' collective. There's also a great restaurant serving budget meals. Backpacker heaven. ❸–❹

**Jasmine by the Sea** Bug-ong ⓣ088/387 9015. Excellent value, with spacious fan cottages on the shore and a restaurant that serves fantastic organic dishes. ❸

# Northern Luzon

The provinces of Luzon that lie immediately **northwest of Manila** are so diverse in geographical character that leaving the city behind you can go from the volcanic landscape of **Zambales** to the tropical beaches and islands of the **Lingayen Gulf** in a single day. Major attractions of the region include the testing **Mount Pinatubo** and **Mount Arayat**, the island-hopper's heaven of **One Hundred Islands National Park** and the chance to surf the breaks of **San Fernando** and **San Juan** on the La Union coast.

There's only one way to get out of Manila heading north and that's on the **North Luzon Expressway**, which runs north through the provinces of Bulacan, Pampanga, Tarlac and Pangasinan. Victory Liner and Philippine Rabbit have dozens of departures daily for all points north of Manila, including Angeles, Dau (for Clark) and Aliminos (for One Hundred Islands National Park).

## CLARK

Some 70km north of Manila, **CLARK**, formerly the site of an American air base, is popular with visitors for two things: sex and adventure sport. Prostitution in Clark and neighbouring Angeles is rife, with many male visitors flying in from Europe for one reason only, lending this former military base town a seedy atmosphere that may well put you off lingering, especially if you are unlucky enough to encounter evidence of the endemic child-sex trade. The one thing Clark does have going for it is its proximity to the volcanic mountains of **Pinatubo and Arayat**.

### Arrival

**By bus** Buses arrive at Dau, from where you can take a tricycle (P50) for the short ride to Fields Ave or Don Juico Ave, where all tourist services are.

**By air** There's a free shuttle bus that takes passengers between the airport and a number of hotels on Fields Ave, a trip of about fifteen minutes.

### Accommodation

**Clarkton Hotel** 620 Don Juico Ave ⓣ045/892 6272, ⓦwww.clarkton.com. Very friendly staff, internet facilities and a swimming pool make this worth paying a little extra for. It also has the advantage of distance from the seedier bars. ❻

**La Casa Hotel** 511 Tamarind St, Clarkview Subdivision ⓣ045/322 7984. Quiet rooms with bath or shower in a family home. To get there, take a jeepney (P5) to the far end of Don Juico Ave. ❺

### ADVENTURE ACTIVITIES

Besides climbing Pinatubo and Arayat, there are an increasing number of other **adventurous activities** in and around Clark, including mountain biking, trekking, microlight flying and parachuting. The Tropical Asia Parachute Center at 940 Fields Ave has been operating at Clark since 1996 and does courses for US$240. At the Angeles City Flying Club (ⓣ0918 920 3039 or 0917 335 5073; ⓦwww.angelesflying.com), about forty-five minutes east of Clark by road in Sitio Talimundok, Magalang, you can have a thirty-minute introductory **microlight** flight along the Pampanga River and over the lower slopes of Mount Arayat for around P1000, where you'll see fields of lahar, a mass of volcanic debris and water that has solidified into gargantuan cliffs and spires.

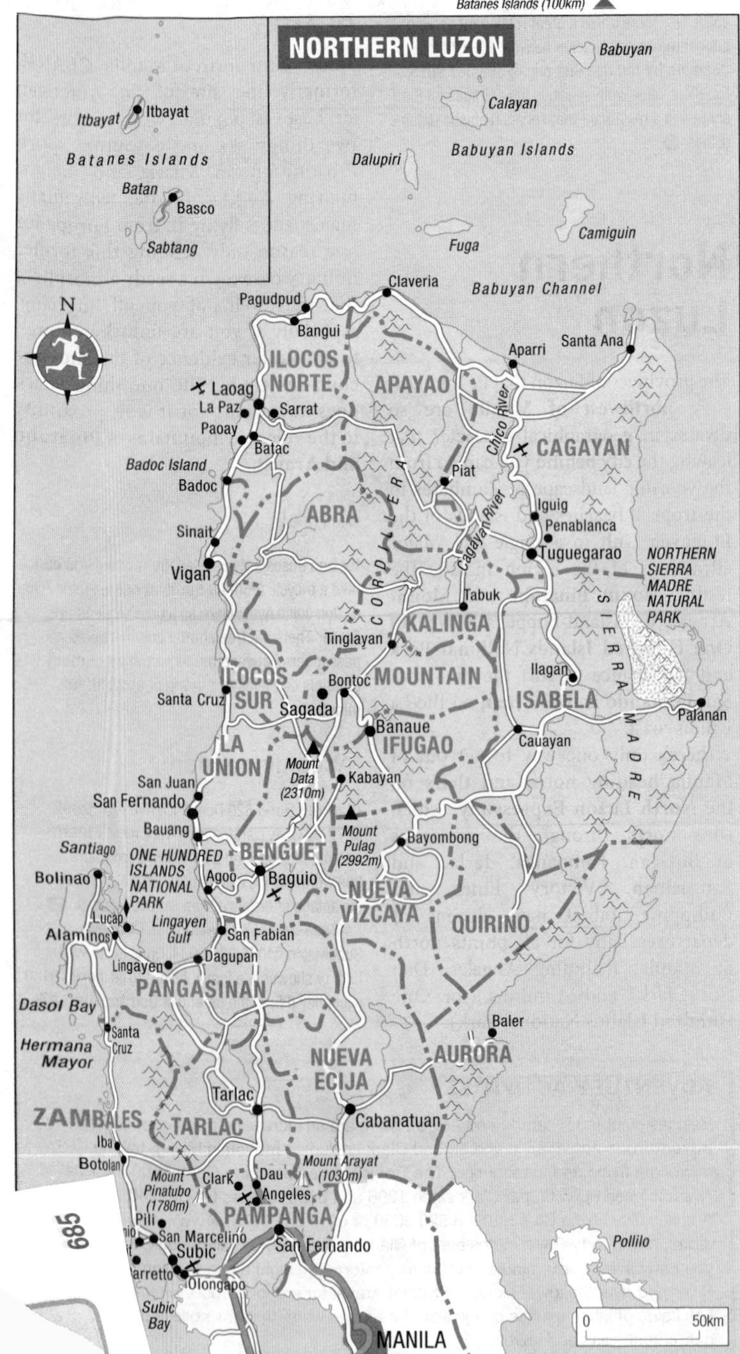
NORTHERN LUZON
Batanes Islands (100km)
Itbayat
Itbayat
Batanes Islands
Batan
Basco
Sabtang
Babuyan
Calayan
Dalupiri
Babuyan Islands
Camiguin
Fuga
Claveria
Babuyan Channel
Pagudpud
Bangui
N
Santa Ana
Aparri
ILOCOS NORTE
APAYAO
Laoag
La Paz
Sarrat
Paoay
Batac
Chico River
CAGAYAN
Badoc Island
Badoc
Piat
CORDILLERA
ABRA
Iguig
Penablanca
Cagayan River
Sinait
Tuguegarao
NORTHERN SIERRA MADRE NATURAL PARK
Vigan
Tabuk
SIERRA MADRE
KALINGA
Tinglayan
Ilagan
ILOCOS SUR
Bontoc
MOUNTAIN
Santa Cruz
Sagada
ISABELA
Palanan
Banaue
LA UNION
IFUGAO
Cauayan
Mount Data (2310m)
Kabayan
San Juan
San Fernando
Mount Pulag (2992m)
Bauang
Bayombong
Santiago
ONE HUNDRED ISLANDS NATIONAL PARK
BENGUET
Bolinao
Agoo
Baguio
NUEVA VIZCAYA
Lucap
Lingayen Gulf
QUIRINO
Alaminos
San Fabian
Lingayen
Dagupan
PANGASINAN
Dasol Bay
Santa Cruz
Baler
Hermana Mayor
NUEVA ECIJA
AURORA
Tarlac
ZAMBALES
TARLAC
Cabanatuan
Iba
Botolan
Mount Pinatubo (1780m)
Clark
Dau
Mount Arayat (1030m)
Angeles
PAMPANGA
Pili
San Marcelino
San Fernando
Subic
Olongapo
Subic Bay
Pollilo
MANILA
0
50km

## Eating

**Salvatore's** Fields Ave. Popular Italian restaurant on the first floor above a bar called *Roadhouse*. The bulk of the menu consists of pizza, but there are also some good pasta dishes and the honey-roast chicken is tangy and delicious.

**Zapata's** 480 Don Juico Ave. Good-value and popular Mexican restaurant with tacos, burritos, enchiladas and tortillas, along with a number of vegetarian dishes.

## Directory

**Banks and exchange** There are dozens of moneychangers on Fields Ave and banks on the nearby MacArthur Highway.

**Internet** There are plenty of places offering internet access along Fields Ave.

**Travel agents** At the City Airport Terminal (which is no longer an airport terminal), on Fields Ave, you'll find convenience stores, ticketing offices and tour operators.

## Moving on

**By bus (from Dau)** to: Baguio (5–6 daily; 5–6hr); Manila (frequent; 2hr); Olongapo (frequent; 2hr).

**By jeepney** The main jeepney station in Clark is at the MacArthur Highway end of Fields Ave. You can catch jeepneys from here to Angeles, Pinatubo, Arayat and San Fernando. Jeepneys up and down Fields Ave cost P7, no matter where you get on and off.

**By air** SEAIR and Cebu Pacific fly daily to Manila (50min) and Cebu (1hr 20min). SEAIR also has a flight every Thurs to Busuanga, and daily to Caticlan (1hr 30min) via Manila.

## MOUNT PINATUBO AND MOUNT ARAYAT

On April 2, 1991, people from the village of Patal Pinto on the lower slopes of **Mount Pinatubo** (1780m) saw small explosions followed by steaming and the smell of rotten eggs coming from the upper slopes of the supposedly dormant volcano, whose last known eruption was six hundred years ago. Much worse was to follow, and on June 12, the first of several major explosions took place, an eruption so violent that shockwaves could be felt in the Visayas. A giant ash cloud rose 35km into the sky, red-hot blasts seared the countryside and nearly twenty million tonnes of sulphur dioxide were blasted into the atmosphere, causing red skies for months afterwards. Ash paralysed Manila, closing the airport for days and turning the capital's streets into an eerie post-apocalyptic landscape. More than 350 people were killed.

Pinatubo is quiet once again, except for tourist activity. Regulations require all trekkers to be accompanied by a **guide**; the usual tourist crater trek begins at your hotel at 5am, when a car picks you up for the drive north to the jump-off point in Santa Juliana, where you must register with the Barangay office. You then transfer to a 4WD jeep that takes you another forty minutes to the start of the climb proper in Crow Valley. It takes three hours of strenuous walking to get to the crater and the same to get back down. Overnight treks can also be arranged through your hotel, or any of the travel agencies in Angeles or Manila. Try Charinas Travel Centre at the *Clarkton Hotel* (see p.685), or travel agents in Manila (see p.636). Tours cost in the region of P3000 to P3500.

It takes between seven and nine hours to reach the top of **Mount Arayat**, making it an even more strenuous climb than nearby Pinatubo. A 1030-metre extinct volcano, Arayat rises from the lowlands of Pampanga in solitary and dramatic fashion. It's said to be inhabited by Mariang Sinukuan (Maria the Abandoned), the sister of Mariang Makiling (Maria of Makiling; see p.640).

Arayat National Park, at the foot of the mountain, features picnic sheds and swimming pools for some well deserved post-climb relaxation. To **get to Mount Arayat** from Clark, take a jeepney (45min; P30) from the terminal in Fields Avenue. A taxi w cost about P100.

## ONE HUNDRED ISLANDS NATIONAL PARK

It's actually 123, but who's counting? These emerald-like tiny islands make up a **national park** covering almost twenty square kilometres, nestled in the Lingayen Gulf. Some islands have beaches, but many are no more than coral outcrops crowned by scrub. Sadly, much of the underwater coral in the park has been damaged by a devastating combination of cyanide and dynamite fishing, typhoons and the El Niño weather phenomenon. On a positive note, the authorities are going all out to protect what coral is left and help it regenerate, meaning you can only snorkel in approved areas. Marine biologists from the University of the Philippines have been at the forefront of the protection movement, replanting hundreds of *taklobos* (giant clams), which attract other marine life, notably in the area of Taklobos Reef, making this the nicest area in the park for snorkelling. The best place to base yourself for exploring the islands is **Lucap**, which is right on the shore and from where you can island-hop by day (you'll need to take your own food and water), returning to a shower and a comfy bed in the evening. Don't expect Robinson Crusoe solitude, especially at weekends when many of the islands are overrun by day-trippers. You *can* find your own piece of paradise here (try Marta, Marcos or Cuenco islands), but you'll have to make it clear to the boatman that you're not interested in the bigger islands.

The only three islands with any form of development are **Governor's Island**, **Children's Island** and **Quezon Island**, where there's basic accommodation.

### information and boat

sest bus terminal is in the nearby
', where you'll also find ATMs and
From here it's a fifteen-minute
'ap.

**Information** The park is accessible year-round: the only restriction is that you have to register and pay a fee (P20/P40) at the National Park /Philippine Tourist Authority office at the end of the pier at Lucap (daily 6am–9pm ⓣ 075/5512145, ⓦ www.alaminoscity.gov.ph or ⓦ www.hundredislands.ph).

**Boats** The tourist office is the best place to arrange a boat, as prices are set by the DoT. A motorboat for up to five people is P1400 for the day, while a three-island hop costs P800. The latest pick-up time from the islands back to Lucap is 5.30pm. If you fancy touring the islands by kayak, contact Hundred Islands Ocean Sports in Lucap (ⓦ www.hundredislandsoceansports.com) or Hundred Islands Eco-Tours Association (ⓣ 075/552 0773, ⓔ hieta_phils@yahoo.com).

### Accommodation and eating

#### On the islands

You can pitch a tent on the three islands below for P200, payable at the park office.

**Children's Island** There are nipa huts with bathrooms for two to four travellers. You can also rent picnic tables for the day (P300). ❻

**Governor's Island** The large concrete *Big Brother House* sleeps ten people for P10,000 a night, including the use of a generator 6am–6pm. It has two bedrooms, a living room, dining room, water, and cooking facilities.

**Quezon Island** Thirty minutes from Lucap at the northern edge of the park, this island has a range of nipa accommodation. ❹–❻

#### Lucap

Other than dinner at one of the little restaurants, the only nightlife in Lucap is based around the ubiquitous karaoke machines blaring out of a couple of shops where locals gather of an evening.

**Helden Resthouse** ⓣ 075/654 1657 or 0918 731 2151. Very basic fan cottages with shared bathrooms. ❸

**Hundred Islands Pension House** Lucap pier ⓣ 075/551 2505. This government-run place is clean and functional, and great value for groups. P1650 for a group of up to six.

**Maxine by the Sea** ⓣ 075/551 2537. Clean, tiled doubles with either a/c or fan and private bathrooms. The seafood restaurant here is justifiably popular, not least for the romantic views. ❺

**Sweet Honey Hotel** ⓣ 0927 922 3498, ⓔ SweetHoneyHotel@yahoo.com. Small and welcoming family-run place. All rooms have cable TV and a/c. ❹

### Moving on

**By bus** From Aliminos there are regular Victory Liner buses to Baguio (4hr) until 5pm. Several bus companies serve Manila (hourly; 6hr).

## SAN FERNANDO (LA UNION) AND SAN JUAN

**SAN FERNANDO**, the capital of La Union province and a shortish hop up the coast from Hundred Islands is a good place to rest up for a night during a tour of the north. The city itself comprises the usual jumble of jeepneys and fast-food restaurants, but nearby, especially to the north, there are some nice little resorts on the beach and from October to March the area is home to much of the Philippines' nascent surf scene. Quezon Avenue, the main road which runs through the city from south to north, has a number of internet cafés and ATMs. Outside the city limits, Quezon Avenue becomes the National Highway.

**San Juan**, 7km north of San Fernando, has a marvellous crescent of a beach, pounding surf and some quaint, quiet resorts. Buses northbound for Laoag, Vigan or Abra pass through San Juan; ask the driver to let you off at one of the resorts, which are all signposted along the road. You can also catch a jeepney, marked for Bacnotan, to San Juan from the junction of P Burgos Street and Quezon Avenue in San Fernando.

### Arrival and information

**By bus** Buses from Manila heading north stop at one of a number of terminals. The Philippine Rabbit terminal lies a few km south of the city, while Dominion stops near *McDonald's* just before the city centre, and Partas terminates on the northern fringe of the city in Quezon Ave beyond the Town Plaza.

**Tourist information** The tourist information office (ⓣ072/888 2411) is in the *Oasis Country Resort*, a few kilometres south of the city.

### Accommodation

**San Juan Surf Resort** San Juan ⓣ072/720 0340. This Australian-run place is where most of the die-hard surfers stay. It's on the beach and has a lively bar, restaurant and a popular surf school. Dorms ❷; rooms ❸–❹

**Sunset German Beach Resort** San Juan ⓣ0917 921 2420, ⓦwww.sunsetgermanbeachresort.com. Pleasant little rustic resort at the northern end of the beach, with a touch of European efficiency courtesy of the friendly German owner. Rooms are spotless, the food is consistently good and there are surfboards and body boards for rent. ❹

# The Cordilleras and the far north

To Filipino lowlanders, brought up on sunshine and beaches, the mountainous north is still seen as a mysterious Shangri-La full of enigmatic tribes and their unfamiliar gods. **Baguio**, the traditional mountain retreat for Manileños during the fierce heat of Easter week, is about as far north as many southerners get. But it's not until you get beyond Baguio that the adventure really begins. The Benguet, Ifugao and Mountain provinces are the **tribal heartlands** of the northern Philippines, settled first by indigenous Negritos and then during the Spanish regime by hunter-gatherers from neighbouring areas who were on the move looking for food and water. Life for many of these tribal people has changed little in hundreds of years, with traditional customs and values still very much in evidence, though an increasing number of tribal folk are making more from the sale of handicrafts than th do from the production of rice. One of the challenges faced by the government is to make the highlands accessible to travellers, without causing the breakup of a social and economic structure that is unique to the region and culturally important to the country as a whole.

In the early twentieth century a group of mummies, possibly dating as far back as 2000 BC, were discovered in the caves of **Kabayan**, an Ibaloi village north of Baguio. Kabayan is also a base for scaling **Mount Pulag**, the highest mountain in Luzon. A swing through the north shouldn't miss out the mountain village of **Sagada**, with its caves and hanging coffins; the riverside town of **Bontoc**, capital of Mountain province; and the magnificent **rice terraces at Banaue**. To the west of Baguio, on the western seaboard, are the provinces of **Ilocos Sur** and **Ilocos Norte**, perhaps best known as die-hard Marcos country, but with some real hidden gems such as the old Spanish colonial outpost of **Vigan**.

## BAGUIO AND AROUND

**BAGUIO** is known as "City of Pines" or "City of Flowers", but chronic traffic congestion in recent years has greatly diminished its appeal as a northern oasis. Lying on a plateau 1400m above sea level, Baguio was built by the colonizing Americans as a recreational and administrative centre, from where they could preside over their dubiously gained tropical colony without working up too much of a sweat. Baguio is also etched on the Filipino consciousness as the site of one of the country's worst natural disasters, the earthquake of July 16, 1990, which caused terrible devastation and claimed hundreds of lives. The majority of the damage was to shanty towns, which have either been cleared or, unfortunately, rebuilt.

Although for many visitors it's little more than a stopping-off point en route to Sagada and the mountain provinces, Baguio has a few secrets worth discovering, such as its parks and excellent bohemian cafés. The climate also offers

### TRIBES OF THE CORDILLERAS

The Cordilleras are home to six main indigenous Filipino tribes: the Ibaloi, the Kankanay, the Ifugao, the Kalinga, the Apayao and the Bontoc, collectively known as **Igorots**. There are also smaller sub-tribes among these six. The Ibaloi, a large ethnic group of around 85,000, comprises Ibaloy, Ibadoy, Igodot, Benguet and Nabaloi.

Tribes began to gather in small, isolated communities in the archipelago during pre-Spanish times when lowland Filipinos, both Muslim and Christian, expanded into the interiors of Luzon, isolating upland tribes into pockets in which they still exist today. Like other Filipinos, these **upland tribes** were a blend of various ethnic origins, ranging from the highly skilled Bontoc and Ifugao to the more primitive groups. Some have intermarried with lowlanders for more than a century, but others, like the **Kalinga**, choose to remain isolated from lowland influences. The **Ifugao**, creators of the famous rice terraces, mostly live in and around Banaue and are the tribe visitors to the north are most likely to come into contact with.

Tribal disputes are less common than they used to be but by no means unknown; they ... st frequently arise over land and water resources, and they are no longer ... through headhunting, as they were up until the beginning of the twentieth ... nstead other tribes help mediate between the two factions. After reaching ... ent, both sides celebrate by throwing a lavish party, known as a *canao*, ... ch food, rice wine and blood flow freely. A typical *canao* will involve the ... f a carabao, a pig, and half a dozen chickens, whose bladders are "read" ... good fortune, in much the same way other cultures read tea leaves.

pleasant respite from the searing heat of the south.

## What to see and do

**Burnham Park** is the city's centrepiece, a sort of hilltop version of Rizal Park in Manila. It's a nice place for a stroll, with a boating lake and strange little three-wheeled bicycles for rent. The park area was designed by Daniel Burnham, who was also responsible for parts of Chicago, Washington DC and much of colonial American Manila. On the eastern edge of the park is Harrison Road and immediately behind that and running almost parallel to it is the city's congested main artery, Session Road, lined with shops and restaurants. Standing imperiously above it all, and reached by a flight of a hundred steep steps, is **Baguio Cathedral**, an example of "wedding cake gothic" in an eye-catching shade of rose pink.

The northern end of Session Road leads to Magsaysay Drive and the **City Market**, one of the liveliest and most colourful in the country, selling strawberries, peanut brittle, sweet wine, honey, textiles, handicrafts and jewellery, all produced in the Cordilleras. The best museum in Baguio is the **St Louis University Museum of Arts and Culture** (Mon–Sat 9am–4.30pm;



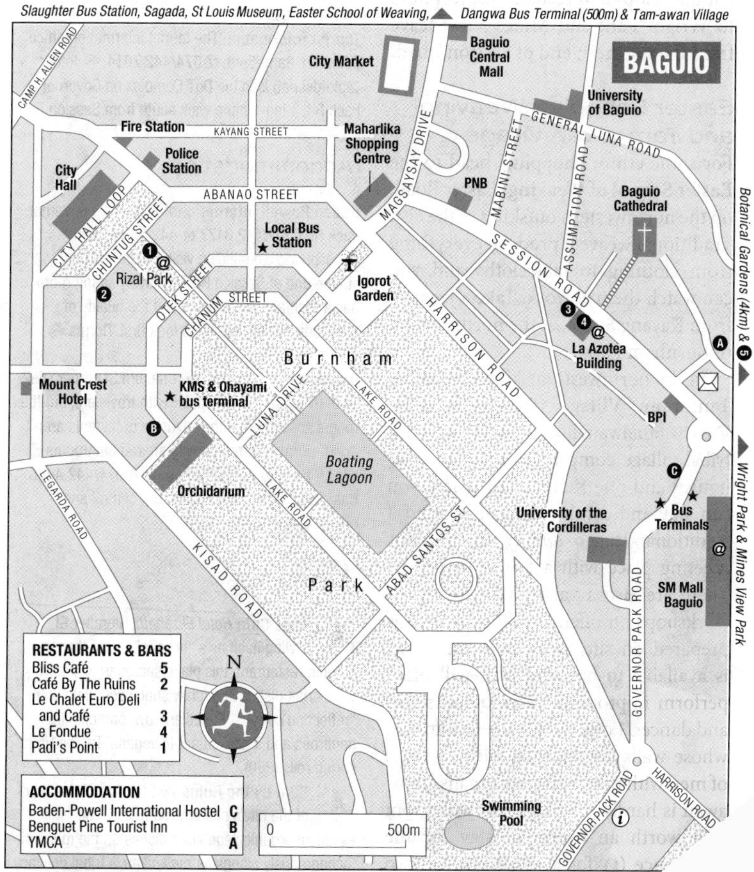

free), near St Louis Hospital on Bonifacio Street, a fifteen-minute walk north of Session Road; it has hundreds of artefacts from the region, including tribal houses, weapons and costumes, on display.

### East of Baguio

Around 4km east along Leonard Wood Road are the **Botanical Gardens** (daily 7am–8pm; P10), also known as the **Igorot Village** because it contains replica native huts typical of Igorot dwellings in the Cordilleras. A little further on is **Wright Park**, where you can go horse-riding, and **Mines View Park**, which has a few souvenir stalls, antique shops and restaurants. Jeepneys to Wright Park and Mines View leave from the northern end of Session Road.

### Easter School of Weaving and Tam-awan Village

For some ethnic shopping, head to the **Easter School of Weaving**, Easter Road, on the northwestern outskirts of the city. Traditional weavers produce everything from clothing to tablecloths and you can watch them at work. Take a jeepney from Kayang Street, at the northern end of Burnham Park.

On the northwest outskirts of Baguio, **Tam-awan Village** (ⓣ074/446 2949, ⓦwww.tamawanvillage.com) is a replica tribal village comprised of eight Ifugao houses and one Kalinga hut where you can stay and drink rice wine around a traditional Ifugao *dap-ay*, an outdoor meeting place with a fire at its centre. There are also a variety of native craft workshops on offer. Cordilleran food is prepared on site, work by local artists is available to buy and staff will often – mpromptu ceremonies, songs s. Look out for the fertility hut 's are adorned with carvings impressive sex organs. Tam- lly the height of luxury, but in overnight stay for the for a small hut for two people with shared toilets and showers). Lunch and dinner costs P250 per head, while breakfast is P150. Take a jacket because it can get surprisingly cold. You can reach Tam-awan Village by taxi for less than P100; it's past the Easter School of Weaving on the road to La Trinidad.

## Arrival and information

**By bus** Buses including Victory Liner, Partas, Dagupan and Philippine Rabbit drop passengers on the eastern edge of the city, where Session Rd 2 meets Governor Pack Rd. KMS and Oyehami buses arrive on the far side of Burnham Park.

**By air** Loakan Airport is 7km south of the city beyond Camp John Hay. Asian Spirit (ⓣ074/447 3912) flies daily from Manila to Baguio at 8.30am. Jeepneys run regularly from the airport to Burnham Park and Session Rd.

**Tourist information** The tourist information office (Mon–Fri, 8am–5pm; ⓣ074/442 7014, ⓔdotcar@pldtdsl.net) is in the DoT Complex on Governor Pack Rd, a ten-minute walk south from Session Rd.

## Accommodation

**Baden Powell International Hostel** 26 Governor Pack Rd ⓣ02/442 8177 or 442 5836. In an atmospheric old building visible from the bus station end of Session Rd. The lovely sitting room has a fireplace and a piano, but the quality of the rooms varies widely, so look first. Dorms ❷; rooms ❻

**Benguet Pine Tourist Inn** Chanum St corner Otek St ⓣ074/442 7325. Popular with travellers, but the rooms are tatty, and the inclusive breakfasts aren't great. Dorms ❸; rooms with shared bathrooms ❹

**YMCA Baguio** Post Office Loop ⓣ 074/442 4666. Basic and rather institutional, but central and cheap. Dorms ❷

## Eating

**Bliss Café** *Hotel Elizabeth*, Gibralter St. Styling itself as a "holistic" rather than organic restaurant, this place serves truly superb vegetarian dishes in a funky space complete with "reflection corner". Prices are low, portions are generous and it also caters to vegans. Try the Ubud spring rolls (P60).

**Café by the Ruins** 25 Chuntug St. Another of the city's culinary highlights. The excellent organic vegetarian dishes on the menu sit incongruously alongside *pinikpikan*, a tribal delicacy that's also known as "killing me softly" because the chicken is beaten slowly to death with a hammer to make the meat bloody and tender (P175). They also do outstanding soups, including an unusual one made from watercress, shitake mushrooms and ginger (P90).

**Le Chalet Euro Deli and Café** Next to La Azotea Building, Session Rd. European-style bistro with a chic, modern interior. Try the highly recommended "world famous Swiss burger" with home-made fries (P160). It also offers fillet steaks, gourmet sandwiches and very drinkable house wines by the glass (P47), a rarity in the beer-mad Philippines.

**Le Fondue** 4th Floor, La Azotea Building, Session Rd. Folksy live music, cheap drinks and Swiss fondue at P900 for two, including soup, salad, rice and dessert. The Asian dishes are less successful. Try for a table on the pretty balcony overlooking Session Rd.

## Drinking and nightlife

With half the population under thirty and a quarter of a million college students, it's surprising that Baguio doesn't have better nightlife. It's somewhat livelier at weekends, with the hub of the action centred around the bars of **Nevada Square**, a short taxi ride from the city centre.

**Padi's Point** Rizal Park. Like its Manila counterpart, this place bangs out live hip hop and pop until the wee hours. P50 cover charge, and it often doesn't warm up until at least 10pm.

## Directory

**Banks and exchange** PNB at the northern end of Session Rd has an ATM, while PCI on Magsaysay Ave will give cash advances on MasterCard or Visa. BPI has a number of branches, including one in Session Rd close to the *Baden Powell* hostel.

**Internet** Internet cafés are common, especially along Session Rd. Try South Park Internet, ground floor of La Azotea Building, Session Rd. There's a branch of Netopia, 3rd level SM City Mall, and Horayzen Internet is beside *Padi's Point*, Rizal Square.

**Hospitals** Baguio Medical Center (☎074/442 4216) lies on Governor Pack Rd and Baguio General Hospital is at the city end of the Marcos Highway; you pass it as you approach Baguio by bus from the south.

**Police** The station is located near City Hall, next to the fire station off Abanao St.

**Post office** Situated, unsurprisingly, on Post Office Loop, at the junction of Session and Governor Pack rds. Offers a poste restante service.

## Moving on

**By bus** Buses for Sagada and Bontoc (from where you can get an onward bus to Banaue), leave hourly 6am–1pm from the Dangwa terminal off Magsaysay Ave (6–8hr). Kabayan is served by Norton Trans buses (9am, 11am & noon; 5hr) from the Slaughter bus terminal in Slaughterhouse Rd, a five-minute taxi ride from the city centre. Buses for all other destinations leave from the terminal in Governor Pack Rd outside the *Baden Powell* hostel, near Session Rd: San Fernando (La Union; 4–5 daily; 2hr); Manila (hourly until 11pm; 6hr); Vigan (5hr; 5 daily). Note that Victory Liner buses terminate just past the Governor Pack Rd terminal on Upper Session Rd.

**By air** to Manila (1 daily; 50 min). There's an Asian Spirit booking office on the ground floor, La Azotea Building, Session Rd.

# KABAYAN

The isolated mountain village of **KABAYAN**, 50km or five hours by bus north of Baguio, gained some notoriety in the early twentieth century when a group of mummies was discovered in surrounding caves. The mummies are believed by some scientists to date back as far as 2000 BC. When the Spanish arrived, mummification was discouraged and the practice died out. Controversy still surrounds the Kabayan mummies, some of which have "disappeared" to overseas collectors. One was said to have been stolen by a Christian pastor in 1920 and wound up as a sideshow in a Manila circus. Some mummies remain, however, and you can see them in their mountaintop caves and also in the small Kabayan branch of the National Museum, which displays the so-called Smiling Mummy and the Laughing Mummy. The museum doesn't keep regular opening hours, although the curator is usually around during the day and will let you in. Admission is free, but leave a donation. Officials know of dozens of other mummies in the area, but will not give their locations for fear of desecration.

You can hire a guide to trek up to some of the mummy caves: ask at the museum for details. **Timbak Cave** is one of the best, but it's high on a mountaintop and a strenuous four- to five-hour climb.

*Kabayan Coop Lodge* has rooms with bunk beds for two people with a shared bath and toilet (❶). It's a clean and friendly place, built mostly of pine. If the *Lodge* is full, which is unlikely, the municipal building up the road has a hall with bunk beds. There are half a dozen *sari-sari* stores in Kabayan where you can get snacks and basic meals. Kabayan is dry: local officials have banned the sale of alcohol, so if you're likely to want a quick restorative after a long day's hiking, bring your own from Baguio.

## MOUNT PULAG

Standing 2992m above sea level, **Mount Pulag** is the highest mountain in Luzon and classified by the Metropolitan Mountaineering Society of the Philippines as a Level III strenuous climb. which means unless you're experienced, don't try it alone. Villagers in Kabayan, where many climbers spend a night before setting off, will tell you it's possible to go without a guide and to get up and down in a day, but their familiarity with these mountains means they tend to overestimate the skill and stamina of city dwellers. Pulag is a challenge: the terrain is steep, there are gorges and ravines and, in the heat of the valleys below, it's easy to forget it's bitterly cold on top.

The two best **trails** for first-timers are those that start from Ambangeg and Kabayan. Both are accessible from Baguio on the Norton Trans bus. In Ambangeg, the trail begins near the police sub-station in **Bokod**: ask the bus driver to let you off in Ambangeg itself, which is a regular stop on the route. The main ranger station and the Department of Environment and Natural Sources (DENR) office are both a short way along this trail, close to the gate that marks the entrance to Mount Pulag National Park. You must **register** here and it's a good place to get a guide. There are no lodgings in Bokod, but if you need to rest up for a night the staff at the municipal building will find you a room in the school or a private home. The Kabayan trail, known as the Akiki or Killer Trail, starts 2km south of Kabayan on the Baguio–Kabayan road. Most climbers on this route rest up for a night in Kabayan beforehand. Whichever way you choose to climb Pulag, take a tent and expect to spend the night on top. The next morning wake early to watch the sun rise and to marvel at the whole of Luzon at your feet.

## SAGADA

The village of **SAGADA**, 160km north of Baguio, has oodles of charm and mystery, much of it connected with the hanging coffins that can be seen perched high in the surrounding limestone cliffs. A number of ancient traditions survive today; the dead are still sometimes positioned outside their house in a death chair, allowing the soul a chance to escape before the remains are disposed of. Sagada began to open up as a destination with the arrival of electricity in the early 1970s, and intellectuals – many of whom had been made internal refugees by the Marcos dictatorship – flocked here to write and paint. They didn't produce anything of note, perhaps because they are said to have spent much of their time drinking *tapuy*, the local rice wine. European hippies followed and so did the military, who thought the *turistas* were supplying funds for an insurgency. Indeed, an informal 9pm curfew remains in place today. The artistic influence has left its mark in the form of quaint little cafés and inns and a distinctly bohemian feel, an atmosphere no doubt enhanced by the ready availability of potent local marijuana. Most of Sagada's restaurants and guesthouses are stretched along the nameless main street, which runs through the town centre.

Sagada can get very chilly, especially at night, and the streets are poorly lit; bring a sweater, scarf and torch if you have one.

## What to see and do

About 500m from the centre of the village heading towards Bontoc is the **Eduardo Masferré Studio** (no set hours, just knock on the door; free), where you can see fascinating old photographs of tribal life in the early twentieth century, maintained by the photographer's widow, who is a mine of information. Prints are for sale from P200. At nearby **Sagada Weaving**, a five-minute walk past the hospital on the road to Bontoc, you can watch distinctive coloured fabrics being produced using traditional tribal designs.

The area's cool forest paths and extensive cave network make for some excellent **treks**, although you must register first with the Sagada Environmental Guides Association (SEGA) at the town hall; the tourist information office and police outpost are also here. A typical five-hour trek for one to four people costs P700 for the group. One of the most popular day-hikes, taking about five hours in all, is to the **hanging coffins** in **Echo Valley**, high on the surrounding limestone cliffs. There are dozens of sinuous paths leading off through deep foliage in all directions, so a guide from SEGA is essential.

**Caving** in Sagada's labyrinth network of channels and caverns is an exhilarating but potentially risky activity. A small number of tourists have died in these caves, so don't risk going alone. The highlight is Sumaging Cave, a forty-five-minute walk south of town, an old burial cave whose chambers and rock formations are an eerie sight. A guided tour costs P250.

## Arrival

**By bus** Buses terminate close to the town hall on the main street. These buses are rudimentary to say the least with uncomfortable seats and no glass in the windows and the journey can be hair-raising. The Halsema Highway to Sagada traverses the coldest point on the Philippine highway system, so bring warm clothing for the trip.

## Accommodation

Reservations are highly recommended, especially at weekends.

**Rock Inn and Café** ⓣ0920 909 5899 or 0920 902 8608, ⓔrockfarm_sagada@yahoo.com. A twenty-minute walk from Sagada proper, though they do offer a free shuttle service. Set amongst flowering orange trees overlooking a gorge, this place is an absolute delight, and Bang, the owner, is the perfect host. Home-made pastries are just one of the treats available at the terrace café. Attic rooms ❷; dorms with hot water ❸

**Sagada Guesthouse and Café** ⓣ0919 357 4377. Right in the centre of town, and one of the cheapest options (if you don't mind the faint smell of petrol that permeates the whole house). The rooms, though small, are very clean. ❶–❷

**St Joseph's Resthouse** Bright, alpine-style hostel set in flowering garden with great views of the surrounding countryside. The rooms vary from basic dorms to private cottages. ❸–❻

## Eating

**Café St Jo** Grounds of *St Joseph's Resthouse*. Service here can be a little reluctant, but portions are generous and the upstairs terrace is a convivial place to swap stories about your day's hiking.

**Kimchi** Part of the *Igorot Inn*, just past the municipal hall. Serves a mix of Korean and native Ilocano dishes, most of which are under P200. The atmosphere of the bare, brightly lit dining room is considerably improved by the presence of an excellent guitar duo playing rock and blues favourites including their jazzy ode to the Philippines' favourite snack, *balut*.

**The Log Cabin Café** The best restaurant for miles around, this place fills up quickly and it's essential to call in and reserve a spot for dinner or lunch. If you can't manage a whole baked chicken with mountain herbs the aubergine in tomato sauce is equally delicious. There's a Saturday night buffet at 7pm, reserve by Friday night. P290, or P100 for vegetarians.

**Yogurt House** Main St, downhill past the town hall. Hugely popular for breakfast, though they're open for other meals also. The strong coffee, fruit pancakes and creamy home-made yogurt are perfect fuel for a day's trekking, and a pot of ginger tea (P25) is just the thing to combat altitude sickness. They also sell secondhand books.

## Directory

**Banks and exchange** There are no ATMs in Sagada and credit cards are not accepted so stock up on pesos in Baguio. The Rural Bank of Sagada underneath the municipal hall (closed Sun and lunchtimes) will change dollars and traveller's cheques at an unfavourable rate.
**Internet** The fastest connection is at *Golinsan* opposite the municipal hall (P40/hr). They also have a payphone.

## Moving on

**By bus** Departures to Baguio (hourly 5–10am, then 1pm) from the marketplace. Cable Tours have a daily 3pm departure for Manila (P600).
**By jeepney** Jeepneys leave Sagada half-hourly 6–9am, then hourly 10am–noon for Bontoc (where you can change for Banaue).

# BONTOC

The capital of Mountain province, **BONTOC** is the first major town in the north beyond Baguio. It lies on the banks of the Chico River, about an hour east of Sagada by jeepney. Jeepneys and buses arrive at the terminal opposite the town plaza, close to the market.

Bontoc is primarily a commercial town used by tourists as a rest-stop on the circuit to Banaue. It is, however, gaining a reputation as a good place for **trekking**; contact the Bontoc Ecological Tour Guides Association at the *Pines Kitchenette and Inn*, behind the market in Rizal Plaza (guides P300–500 per day). Don't miss the small but well-run **Bontoc Museum** (daily 8am–noon & 1–5pm; P50) behind *Pines*. It features photographs of headhunting victims and of zealous American missionaries trying to persuade incredulous warriors to choose the path of righteousness. Check out the replica tribal village built in the grounds of the museum.

## Accommodation and eating

**Cable Café** Main St. This is Bontoc's only nightspot, meaning there's occasional live music to go with your meal, and they serve half-decent Margaritas. Mains P80–110.
**Churya-a Hotel** Main St ☎0909430853. Unremarkable dorms and doubles, but there's a nice balcony eating area with a view over the mountains and it's right in the centre of town. Dorms ❶; rooms ❸
**Pines Kitchenette and Inn** Behind the market ☎074/602 1408. Big doubles with private showers or cheaper rooms with shared facilities. Live music at weekends in the downstairs café, where most meals are under P100. ❷

## Directory

**Banks and exchange** PNB opposite the town plaza has an ATM and will change traveller's cheques.
**Internet** The grandly named Bontoc Micro Computer and Entertainment just past *Churya-a* has internet access for just P20 per hour.
**Post office** The post office is next door to the Bontoc Museum.

## Moving on

**By bus** Hourly to Baguio until 4pm (GL Lizardo and D'Rising Sun). Buses for Manila, via Banaue, leave daily at 3pm from outside the *Cable Café*. There are two other Manila departures (Kasilen Transport and KMJ Transit; 4pm & 8.30pm; 12hr).
**By jeepney** Departures for Banaue from beside the town hall, ostensibly at 8am, 10am and 1pm, but in reality they leave when they're full (3hr; P50).

# BANAUE AND AROUND

It's a rugged but spectacular three-hour trip south from Bontoc to **BANAUE** in Ifugao province, along a winding road that leads up into the misty Cordilleras, across a mountaintop pass, then down precipitous mountainside. It may only be 300km north of Manila, but Banaue is a world away, 1300m above sea level and far removed in spirit and topography from the beaches and palm trees of the south. This is the heart of **rice-terrace** country: the terraces in Banaue itself are some of the most impressive and well known, although there are hundreds of others in the area, some of the best of which are at nearby **BATAD**, where there is also rustic accommodation, so you can stay overnight and hike back the next morning.

Banaue itself is a small town centred on a marketplace, where there are a few guesthouses and some souvenir shops. Two kilometres up the road from the marketplace are the four main **lookout points** for the rice terraces. Tricycle drivers angle constantly to take you there, which can be irritating, but the views are truly superb. A tricycle will cost around P200, but be sure to agree the price beforehand. Ifugao in traditional costume will ask for a small fee if you want to take their photograph, and there's a handful of souvenir stalls surrounding the lookouts selling carved wooden bowls and woven blankets at bargain prices. Don't miss the remarkable little **museum** (daily 8am–5pm; free) at the *Banaue View Inn*, which documents the extraordinary life of Henry Otley Beyer, an American anthropologist who came to study Ifugao tribes at the beginning of the twentieth century and, after marrying an Ifugao woman, settled and died in the region. The **Museum of Cordilleran Sculpture** (9am–5pm), beside the *Spring Village Inn,* which includes quite a variety of erotic tribal artefacts is an interesting place to while away a rainy afternoon, though the P100 entrance fee is a little steep for what you get.

## Arrival and information

**By bus and jeepney** They terminate at the main road above the marketplace, reached by a flight of steep stone stairs.

**Tourist information** The tourist information office is near the town hall (daily 6.30am–6pm), where you can get maps of the area for trekking (P15). They'll also help you find a guide for half-day treks to local Ifugao communities or longer treks through the rice terraces to isolated communities, such as Batad (P650–1200).

## Accommodation and eating

**Banaue View Inn** ⓣ074/386 4078. Set in a pretty flower garden with an unsurpassable view, next door to the Banaue Museum. Amenities are simple, but rooms are spick and span; you can also arrange a guide here. ❸–❹

**Greenview Lodge and Restaurant** Just down the hill from the market square ⓣ074/386 4021, ⓔugreenview12@yahoo.com.ph. Homely doubles with shared or private baths. The pleasant restaurant is excellent value, with huge three-course set meals for P180, and it boasts rice-terrace views, as do a couple of the rooms. ❷–❹

**People's Lodge and Restaurant** Next door to the *Greenview* ⓣ074/386 4014. *People's* is the best

### THE STAIRWAYS TO HEAVEN

The **rice terraces** at Banaue are one of the great icons of the Philippines. They were hewn from the land over two thousand years ago by Ifugao tribespeople using primitive tools, an achievement in engineering terms that ranks alongside the building of the pyramids. Called the "Stairways to Heaven" by the Ifugaos, the terraces would stretch 20,000km if laid out end to end.

The future of the terraces, added to the United Nations' World Heritage list in 1995, is closely tied to the future of the tribespeople themselves. Part of the problem, it must be said, is tourism. Locals who would otherwise have been working on the terraces are now making a much easier buck selling reproduction tribal artefacts or rare orchids from the surrounding forests. What's more, rice farming has little allure for the young tribespeople of the Cordilleras. Tired of the subsistence livelihood that their parents eked out from the land, they are packing their bags and leaving in droves for Manila. The resulting labour shortage means the terraces are producing a mere 35 percent of the area's rice needs when they should be producing a hundred percent.

choice in town if you're travelling in a group; a room for eight costs just P1500. What the attached restaurant lacks in atmosphere it makes up in portion size. Internet access is available for P50 an hour. ❷

**Sanafe Lodge and Restaurant** ⓣ074/386 4085, ⓦwww.sanafelodge.com. This welcoming wooden lodge offers the best food in Banaue, served on an atmospheric outdoor patio overlooking the rice terraces. Dorm beds are rather close together; the upstairs doubles are more spacious and come with the luxury of hot water. Dorms ❶; rooms ❹

## Directory

**Banks and exchange** There are no banks or ATMs in Banaue, though some hotels will accept dollars if you're desperate.

**Internet** The cheapest place in town is Nico's Internet, next door to *People's Lodge and Restaurant*. (P35/hr)

**Post office** Has poste restante, but it's a ten-minute jeepney ride from the marketplace near the *Banaue Hotel & Youth Hostel*. You can also make telephone calls here. There's another post office in the municipal town hall.

## Moving on

**By bus** Several companies offer a direct Banaue–Manila route (9hr), including GV Florida, Victory Liner and Auto Bus. Each has just one trip daily, departure times vary according to the season. There are eight daily departures to Baguio (6.45am–7pm); Banaue Bus Lines, with departures at 5 and 7pm, offers a discounted fare to students. Buses will often leave earlier than advertised, especially first thing in the morning.

**By jeepney** There are several morning jeepneys for the long, uncomfortable journey to Bontoc, where you can change for Sagada. Buses and jeepneys leave from the main road above the market.

## BATAD

The fifteen-kilometre trek from Banaue to the remote little village of **BATAD** has become something of a pilgrimage for visitors looking for rural isolation and unforgettable rice-terrace scenery. You'll need to take a jeepney from the market in Banaue for the first (bumpy) 12km before starting a tiring walk up a steep trail, but the spectacular views more than compensate for any discomfort. Jeepneys run hourly until 1pm from Banaue to Batad Junction; the standard fare is P60. Alternatively, you can arrange private transportation at the visitors' centre in Banaue – including a guide it will set you back P900, a better value option than the services of the freelance "tour guides" who incessantly tout for business on the streets.

Batad nestles in a natural amphitheatre, close to the glorious **Tappia Waterfall**, which is 21m high and has a deep, bracing pool for swimming. Village life here remained virtually unchanged for centuries until the development of tourism, but its influence hasn't been too insidious, with just half a dozen primitive **guesthouses** catering to the recent influx. Rooms in Batad, while not as dirt-cheap as they once were, are still very reasonable (all ❶). Choose from *Foreigner's Inn*, which has a nice balcony restaurant, the wonderful *Hillside Inn*, with its majestic views, and *Simon's Inn*, which has a good cosy café offering the widest choice of dishes in town.

## VIGAN

About 135km north of San Fernando in La Union lies the old Spanish town of **VIGAN**, an obligatory stop on any trip through the northern provinces. It has become a bit of a cliché to describe Vigan as a living museum, but it does do some justice to the tag. One of the oldest towns in the Philippines, it was called Nueva Segovia in Spanish times and was an important political, military, cultural and religious centre. Having narrowly escaped bombing in World War II, it has retained its pavements of cobbled stones and some of the finest **Spanish colonial architecture** in the country, including impressive homes that once belonged to friars, merchants and colonial officials. Inscribed onto the UNESCO world heritage list in 1999, it remains the finest example of a planned Spanish colonial city in Asia. Vigan can thank Juan de Salcedo for its glorious architecture. The grandson of conquistador Miguel de Legaspi and ruler of Ilocos province in the late sixteenth century, he set about replicating his grandfather's design of Intramuros. Various organizations have joined forces to preserve the old buildings; many are still lived in, others are used as curio shops and a few have been converted into museums.

## What to see and do

Vigan's time-capsule ambience is enhanced by the decision to allow only pedestrians and **calesas** (one-pony, two-seat traps) on some streets. A ride in a calesa makes for a romantic tour of the town (P150 per hour). Vigan is one of the easier Philippine towns to negotiate because its streets follow a fairly regular grid. Mena Crisologo Street runs south from Plaza Burgos and is lined with quaint old antique shops and cafés. Running parallel to it is the main thoroughfare, Governor A. Reyes Street. Between Plaza P. Burgos and Plaza Salcedo stands **St Paul's Metropolitan Cathedral** (daily 6am–9pm), dating back to 1641 – one of the oldest cathedrals in the country. Next to the cathedral, the **Father José Burgos House and Museum** (Mon–Fri 8.30–11.30am & 1.30–4.30pm; P10) is a captivating old colonial house that was once home to one of the town's most famous residents, Padre José Burgos, whose martyrdom in 1872 galvanized the revolutionary movement. It houses Burgos memorabilia, as well as fourteen paintings by the artist Villanueva, depicting the violent 1807 Basi Revolt, prompted by a Spanish effort to control the production of *basi* (sugar-cane wine).

Souvenir-hunters after something more than the usual bulk-produced tourist knick-knacks should head for **Rowilda's Hand Loom**, on Mena Crisologo Street near the *Cordillera Inn*, which offers the kind of old-style textiles that used to be traded during colonial times. Vigan is also known for its **pottery**. The massive wood-fired kilns at the Pagburnayan Potteries in Rizal Street, at the junction with Liberation Boulevard, turn out huge jars, known as *burnay*, in which northerners store everything from vinegar to fish paste. Carabao (water buffalo) are still used to squash the clay under hoof.

## Arrival and information

**By bus** Philippine Rabbit buses pull in just off the national highway, a short jeepney or tricycle ride from the hotels and attractions. Partas buses arrive at the Partas terminal near the Vigan Public Market in Alcantara St at the southern end of town. Dominion buses arrive at the corner of Quezon Ave (the main street running south to north) and Liberation Blvd.

**Tourist information** The tourist office (daily 8am–5pm; ⓣ077/732 8772) is in Leona Florentina House, near *Café Leona* in Plaza Burgos. You can also get information at the nearby Provincial Capitol Building.

## Accommodation

**Cordillera Inn** Crisologo St, cnr Gen. Luna St ⓣ077/722 2727. Ordinary doubles with fan, private bath and cable TV. Slightly pricey, but rates include a huge breakfast, and there's a pleasant rooftop garden. ❻

**El Juliana Hotel** Liberation cnr Quirino Blvd ⓣ077/722 2994. Small a/c rooms come with a toilet, shower and cable TV. There's a swimming pool, also open to the public. ❹–❺

**Grandpa's Inn** 1 Bonifacio St ⓣ077/722 2118. Rather tired old place on the eastern edge of Bonifacio St, but the staff are friendly and it's full of curios. Inspect the rooms before you commit yourself because some are better than others. ❹

**Villa Angela Heritage House** Quirino Blvd ⓣ077/722 2914, ⓦwww.villangela.com. The most colonial of all the colonial hotels, this beautiful old museum of a place is the billet of choice if you want to wallow in history and don't mind paying a little extra for the privilege. You can ask for the room Tom Cruise slept in: he stayed here for a few weeks when *Born on the Fourth of July* was being filmed on the sand dunes near Laoag. Even the dorm (P500) has Spanish-style wooden bunkbeds and billowing mosquito nets and curtains. ❻–❼

## Eating and drinking

One of Vigan's specialities is *empanada*, a type of tortilla that you can pick up for a few pesos from one of the many street stalls and small bakeries, where they are freshly baked.

**Café Leona** Plaza Burgos. The most popular restaurant in Vigan, *Café Leona* serves native Ilocano dishes, from less than P200; try the Special Vigan Sinanglaw, a dish of pork entrails sautéed with ginger, vinegar, fish sauce, onion and pepper.

**Café Uno** Next door to *Grandpa's*. Great light meals and all manner of quality teas, coffees, iced drinks and home-made cookies. Pasta dishes from P70.

**Sitio Bar** Cnr Plaza Burgos, next door to the *Vigan Plaza*. Nightlife in Vigan is pretty low-key – watching the world go by with a beer in hand is the height of the action. *Sitio* obliges with outside tables right in the centre of town and San Miguel happy hour promotions.

**Uno Grille** 2 Bonifacio St. Across the road from *Café Uno*, the menu at this friendly outdoor place is dominated by barbecued meats, with a few classic Filipino and European dishes.

## Directory

**Banks and exchange** Equitable PCI is on Plaza Maestro, and there are several ATMs along Quezon Ave.

**Hospital** The Gabriela Silang General Hospital (Ⓣ077/722 2722) is on Quirino Blvd, and there's a Mercury Drug outlet Cnr Quezon Ave and Bonifacio St.

**Internet** There are a couple of places with internet access around Plaza Burgos, though they are mostly filled with schoolchildren. Calle Uno on Bonifacio St opposite the post office has a speedy DSL connection.

**Police** The police station is at the eastern end of Florentino St.

**Post office** At the junction of Governor A. Reyes and Bonifacio sts.

## Moving on

**By bus** See arrival for location of bus terminals. For the long trip back to Manila, Parats buses offer the most comfort. You can also catch a/c minibuses north from the Caltex station on the highway to Laoag where there's an airport.

**Destinations**: Laoag (3–4 daily; 3hr). Baguio (3 daily; 5hr); Manila (hourly; 10hr)

# Singapore

## HIGHLIGHTS

BUKIT TIMAH: escape the city in Singapore's pocket of primary rainforest
SINGAPORE ZOOLOGICAL GARDENS: spend the day with over 2000 animals housed in a humane environment
LITTLE INDIA: ornate temples, manic markets and fine restaurants
CHINATOWN: traditional shop-houses, fiery red temples and venerable restaurants proliferate
SENTOSA: a theme-park island with beaches and an historic fort

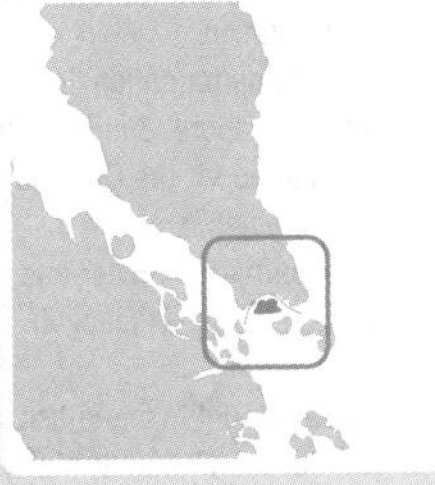

## ROUGH COSTS

**DAILY BUDGET** Basic US$35/ Occasional treat US$50

**DRINK** Tiger beer (US$7 pint)

**FOOD** Chicken rice (US$3)

**HOSTEL/BUDGET HOTEL** US$13–16/ US$18–25

**TRAVEL** Bus and MRT (whole island; US$1.50); taxi airport to downtown (US$18)

## FACT FILE

**POPULATION** 4.5 million

**AREA** 700 sq km

**LANGUAGE** English, Malay, Mandarin and Tamil

**RELIGIONS** Buddhism, Islam, Christianity

**CURRENCY** Singapore Dollar (S$)

**INTERNATIONAL PHONE CODE** ⓣ+65

**TIME ZONE** GMT+8hr

# Introduction

**Conveniently linked by a kilometre-long causeway to the southern tip of Malaysia, the tiny city-state of Singapore makes a gentle gateway for many first-time travellers to Asia, providing Western standards of comfort and hygiene alongside traditional Chinese, Malay and Indian enclaves. Its downtown areas are dense with towering skyscrapers and gleaming shopping malls, yet the island retains an abundance of nature reserves and lush, tropical greenery.**

Singapore is a wealthy nation compared to the rest of Southeast Asia. Outsiders have traditionally bridled at the country's somewhat extreme regulations (neglecting to flush a public toilet carries a sizeable fine), but with plans to lure in over a million new citizens by 2010, there are suggestions that the government is starting to loosen its grip on the population, and as Singapore begins to change, it is transforming into the social hub of Southeast Asia. The conscious effort to liberalize the island has led to a growing **arts scene** and a vibrant **nightlife**.

Although the city is a beacon of modernization in the region, it is still possible to get lost in the diverse districts – **Chinatown**, **Little India** and the **Colonial District** – that make up the leafy island. Much of the country's appeal springs from its multicultural population: of the 3.7 million residents, 74 percent are Chinese (a figure reflected in the predominance of Chinese shops, restaurants and temples across the island), sixteen percent are Malay, and nine percent are Indian, while the remaining one percent comprise other ethnic groups.

## CHRONOLOGY

**Third century AD** The earliest known mention of Singpapore is a Chinese reference to Pu-luo-chung, or "island at the end of a peninsula".

**Eleventh century** The tiny island is known as "Singa Pura" (Lion City) – according to legend because a prince mistook a local animal for a lion.

**Late thirteenth century** Marco Polo reports seeing a place called Chiamassie, possibly Singapore, which was known locally as Temasek – "sea town" – and was a minor trading outpost of the Sumatran Srivijaya Empire.

**c. 1390** A Sumatran prince, Paramesvara, flees to present-day Singapore, murders his host and rules the island until a Javanese offensive forces him to flee north to the Peninsula. He and his son, Iskandar Shah, found the Melaka Sultanate.

**1613** A Portuguese account describes the razing of an unnamed Malay outpost at the mouth of Sungei Johor, an event that marks the beginning of two centuries of historical limbo for Singapore.

**1819** Thomas Stamford Raffles, lieutenant-governor of Bencoolen (in Sumatra), arrives in Singapore to establish a British trading station.

**1822** Raffles draws up the demarcation lines that divide present-day Singapore. South of the Singapore River is earmarked for the Chinese; the commercial district is established on a filled in swamp at the mouth of the river; and Muslims settle around the Sultan's Palace in today's Arab Quarter.

**1824** Singapore is ceded outright to the British, and the island's population reaches 10,000 as Malays, Chinese, Indians and Europeans arrive in search of work.

**1826** The fledgling state unites with Penang and Melaka (now under British rule) to form the Straits Settlements.

**1860** The population reaches 80,000. Arabs, Indians, Javanese and Bugis all came, but most populous of all are the Chinese from the southern provinces of China.

**1877** Henry Ridley introduces the rubber plant into Southeast Asia; Singapore becomes the world centre of rubber exporting, helped as British control of the Malay Peninsula expands, completed in 1913.

**1887** The Armenian Sarkies brothers open the *Raffles Hotel*. It becomes the social hub of a booming and cosmopolitan Singapore.

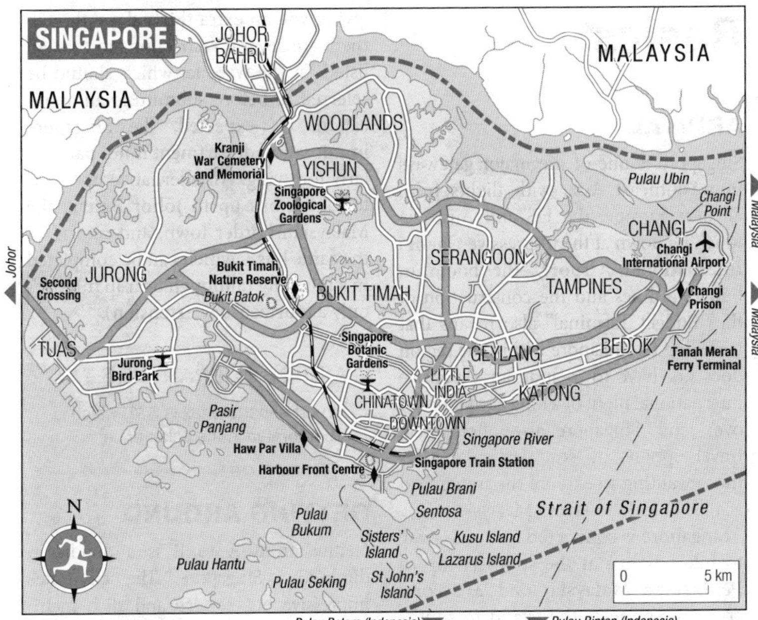


**1926** The pro-independence Singapore Malay Union is established, but grumblings of independence are no more than a faint whisper.

**1942–45** Singapore is occupied by the Japanese during World War II. Thousands of civilians are executed in vicious anti-Chinese purges and Europeans are either herded into Changi Prison, or marched up the Peninsula to work on Thailand's infamous "Death Railway".

**1945** Singapore returns to British control.

**May 1959** The People's Action Party (PAP), led by Cambridge law graduate Lee Kuan Yew, wins 43 of the 51 seats for the new legislative assembly, which Britain had agreed to two years earlier. Lee became Singapore's first prime minister.

**1963** Singapore, Malaya, Sarawak and British North Borneo (modern-day Sabah) form the Federation of Malaysia, but within two years Singapore falls out with Kuala Lumpur and leaves the federation.

**August 9, 1965** Singapore independence, described by Lee Kuan Yew as "a moment of anguish".

**1970s** Under Lee, Singapore is transformed into an Asian economic heavyweight, but at a price: in an apparent trade-off between freedoms and economic efficiency, media is censored and political opponents suppressed.

**1990** Lee retires and is succeeded as prime minister by Goh Chok Tong; Lee remains senior minister.

**1997** The Asian economic crisis hits Singapore.

**2004** Lee Hsien Loong, son of Lee Kuan Yew, becomes Prime Minister.

**March 15, 2008** Twelve people, including the leader of the opposition Singapore Democratic Party (SDP), Chee Soon Juan, are arrested for protesting outside parliament against fast-rising prices.

### WHEN TO VISIT

Singapore is just 136km north of the equator, which means that you should be prepared for a hot and sticky time whenever you go; **temperatures** hover around 30°C throughout the year. November, December and January are usually the coolest and wettest months, but rain can fall all year round. July usually records the lowest annual rainfall.

# Basics



## ARRIVAL

Singapore is one of the major gateways into Southeast Asia, with flights from all over Europe, the US and Australia touching down at the impressive **Changi International Airport**. The boom in budget airlines and the construction of the "Budget Terminal" also means that travelling to Singapore within the region does not have to include an expensive international flight or a long hard journey over land. Singapore also offers great travel options by sea, particularly for those wanting to explore the untouched islands of Indonesia and Malaysia.

Singapore is connected by a causeway to Johor Bahru at the southern tip of **Peninsular Malaysia**, and a second crossing connects the island to southwestern Johor state. There are excellent road and rail connections with numerous Malaysian cities. In addition, there are daily ferries to Singapore from **Indonesia**. Check out the Tiger Airways (ⓦwww.tigerairways.com) for cheap flights in and out of Singapore. For information on the airport, bus and train terminals see p.719.

## VISAS

Citizens of Western Europe, the USA and Commonwealth countries automatically receive a visa on arrival in Singapore; but check with the relevant embassy before departure (see p.57). Arriving by land or sea, you will be given a **fourteen-day visa**; arriving by air, you will receive a **thirty-day visa**. Check with the "Visa Requirements" section of the Singapore Immigration and Registration Department (Mon–Fri 9am–5pm; ⓣ6391 6100, ⓦwww.ica.gov.sg) for a list of nationals who need to obtain a visa before entering Singapore.

You can **extend your visa** online at the immigration department's website, giving you an extra thirty days, though there are several restrictions to this, all listed on the website, which should be referred to before submitting an application. As expected, the Singapore immigration department is not particularly forgiving. An alternative option is to take a bus up to **Johor Bahru**, the Malaysian border town, and return on the same bus – which can be completed in a morning (although bear in mind it's only a fourteen-day extension).

### AIRPORT DEPARTURE TAX

Airport departure tax is S$2, which is incorporated in the ticket price.

## GETTING AROUND

Getting from A to B is a doddle in diminutive Singapore. The city-state's impressive bus service and slick metro rail network system – the **MRT** (Mass Rapid Transport) – have all corners of the island covered. Bus and MRT **fares** are extremely reasonable, though if you aren't watching the pennies too closely, you might consider hailing a **taxi** in order to buy yourself some time. Singaporean taxis are ubiquitous and so affordable as to make car rental hardly worthwhile, unless you are planning to drive into Malaysia. However, getting around **on foot** is the best way to do justice to the central areas. Full transport listings are given on p.722.

## ACCOMMODATION

Room rates take a noticeable leap when you cross the causeway from Malaysia into Singapore, but it is possible to find a room at a reasonable price, particularly if you don't mind sharing. The **Singapore Hotel Association** has booking counters at Changi Airport, and touts circle the arrivals hall handing out flyers.

The cheapest beds are in the communal dormitories of many resthouses, where you'll pay S$20 or less a night. These resthouses tend to be a bit gritty;

bedbugs can be a problem and the lights are left burning all night. They also serve as cheap accommodation for many of Singapore's guest workers, so if you want to practise your Thai or Tagalog, you'll have ample opportunity.

The next best deals are at guesthouses; the most affordable of which are situated in Little India. Guesthouses aren't nearly as cosy as their name suggests: costing S$35–50, the rooms are tiny, bare, and divided by paper-thin partitions, toilets are shared, and showers are cold. However, another S$10–20 secures a bigger, a/c room, and often TV, laundry and cooking facilities, lockers and breakfast are included. Always check that the room is clean and secure, and that the shower and a/c work before you hand over any money, and it's worth speaking to hotel owners on arrival to see if they are offering promotion prices on any of their rooms.

In more modern, mid-range hotels, an en-suite room for two with a/c and TV will cost around S$80–120. while at the upper end of the accommodation scale, you'll find that Singapore has an enormous range of hotels of varying levels of splendour. Electricity is supplied at 220 volts. For full accommodation listings, see p.723.

### ADDRESSES

With so many of Singapore's shops, restaurants and offices located in vast high-rise buildings and shopping centres, deciphering **addresses** can sometimes be tricky; an address containing 10-08 refers to room 8 on the 10th floor (ground level is denoted #01).

## FOOD AND DRINK

Eating is one of the most profound pleasures that Singapore affords its visitors, and ranks alongside shopping as one of the national pastimes. An enormous number of food outlets cater for this obsession, and strict government regulations ensure that they are consistently hygienic. By far the cheapest and most fun place to dine is in a **hawker centre** or **food court**, where scores of stalls let you mix and match Asian dishes, fast-food style, at really low prices; it's possible to eat like a king for S$5. Otherwise, there's a whole range of **restaurants** to visit, ranging from no-frills, open-fronted eating-houses and coffee shops to sumptuously decorated establishments. Even in restaurants, you'll be hard-pressed to spend more than S$30–40 a head, including drinks, unless you opt for one of the island's more exclusive addresses.

All types of cuisine can be found here, from North and South Indian to Malay, Indonesian, Korean, Japanese and Vietnamese food. Chinese restaurants are some of the most popular, which reflects the fact that three-quarters of the population is Chinese. The closest Singapore comes to an indigenous cuisine is Nonya, a hybrid of Chinese and Malay food developed by the Peranakan community, formed as a result of the intermarrying of nineteenth-century Chinese immigrants and Malay women. For a guide to local cuisine, see the food and drink section in the Malaysia chapter (p.482).

Vegetarians need to tread carefully, as chicken and seafood will appear in a whole host of dishes unless you make it perfectly clear that you don't want them. The best bests are specialist Chinese and Indian restaurants, and a few stalls at hawker centres serve **vegetarian food**.

Most restaurants are open daily between 11.30am and 2.30pm and 6 to 10.30pm though cheaper places tend to open longer hours. Tap water is drinkable throughout Singapore.

## CULTURE AND ETIQUETTE

Though relatively liberal in outlook, Singapore shares the same basic attitudes to dress and social taboos as other Southeast Asian cultures (see p.45).

Bargaining is de rigueur in Singapore, especially when shopping outside the major stores, or getting a room for the night – it's always worth trying to haggle, though you don't bargain for meals. Although the city is definitely going through a period of liberalization, Singapore is still synonymous with strict rules, including ones about failing to flush toilets after use, littering, jaywalking, the sale of chewing gum and the possession of pornography. Also note that sexual activity (including oral sex) between men is illegal. Although all these rules are still enforced, the city is no longer as fearful of the government as in bygone years. In general, people are outgoing and friendly and service is usually excellent.

## SPORTS AND OUTDOOR ACTIVITIES

Despite its urban reputation, Singapore is a great spot to enjoy the outdoors. Head down to the East Coast for some beachfront cycling or rollerblading (rental S$3–6). Also situated on the East Coast is Singapore's first cable ski park, Ski360 (ⓦwww.ski360degrees.com), which offers an affordable (and safe) way to have a go at the growing sports of wakeboarding or waterskiing. Try to get down there midweek as the weekends tend to be crowded and noticeably more expensive. Golf is becoming a popular sport in Singapore with driving ranges popping up everywhere. If you fancy hacking up some of Singapore's prime real estate, head down to the Royal Tanglin Golf Club (ⓣ9636 3380, ⓔgolfcr@pacific.net.sg) next to the US Embassy. At S$16 a round, it's a great way to spend an afternoon. Those who would prefer not to spend any money on their exercise should enjoy a run around one of Singapore's many parks. The Bukit Timah Nature Reserve houses several good running routes.

Singapore's recent boom has paved the way for several new international sporting events. The first ever Singapore Motor Racing Grand Prix is being held in September 2008; the route weaves between the Central Business District and some of the countries major attractions, and is being hailed as the Monaco Grand Prix – but held at night. Other major events include the Singapore Barclays Golf Open (November) and the Singapore Airlines International Horse Riding Cup (May). Singapore has also recently won the bid to host the 2010 Youth Olympic Games.

## COMMUNICATIONS

Singapore's postal system is predictably efficient (even during Christmas), with letters and cards often reaching their destination within three days. There are an abundance of post offices across the state, with usual hours of Monday to Friday 8.30am–5pm and Saturday 8.30am–1pm, though postal services are available until 9pm at the Singapore Singapore Telecom Comcentre Complex, on Killiney Road.

**Local calls** from public phones cost 10¢ for three minutes, with the exception of Changi Airport's free courtesy phones. Singapore has no area codes – the only time you'll punch more than eight digits for a local number is if you're dialling a toll-free (ⓣ1800) number. Cards for cardphones are available from the Comcentre and post offices, as well as 7–11s, stationers and bookshops, come in denominations of S$5 upwards.

**International calls** (IDD) can be made from all public card-phones. Otherwise,

### SINGAPORE ON THE NET

**ⓦwww.sistic.com** A good website for finding and booking tickets for events going on across the island.
**ⓦwww.timeout.com/sg** A great guide to the city's bars and clubs. Allows you to do a keyword search on events In Singapore.
**ⓦwww.visitsingapore.com** The official tourist website with general details on Singapore's major sights.

use a credit-card phone. Singapore prides itself on being among the most connected of societies – **internet cafés** can be found across the island; see p.731 for a selection of the most central ones.

## CRIME AND SAFETY

Singapore is a very safe place for travellers, though you shouldn't become complacent – muggings have been known to occur and theft from dormitories by other tourists is a common complaint. Follow the advice peppered all over Singapore's taxis and billboards – "Low Crime doesn't mean no crime".

It's with some irony that Singaporeans refer to the place as a "**fine city**". There's a fine of S$500 for smoking in public places such as cinemas, trains, lifts, air-conditioned restaurants and shopping malls, and one of S$50 for jaywalking – here defined as crossing a main road within 50m of a pedestrian crossing or bridge. Littering carries a S$1000 fine, with offenders forced to do litter-picking duty, while eating or drinking on the MRT could cost you S$500. Other fines include those for urinating in lifts (some lifts are supposedly fitted with urine detectors), not flushing a public toilet and chewing gum (which is outlawed in Singapore). It's worth bearing all these offences in mind, since foreigners are not exempt from the various Singaporean punishments – as American Michael Fay discovered in 1994, when he was given four strokes of the cane for vandalism.

In Singapore, the possession of **drugs** – hard or soft – carries a hefty prison sentence and trafficking is punishable by the death penalty. If you are caught smuggling drugs into or out of the country, at the very best you are facing a long stretch in a foreign prison; at worst, you could be hanged.

### EMERGENCY NUMBERS

Police ⓣ999
Ambulance and Fire Brigade ⓣ995

Singapore's police, who wear dark blue, are generally polite and helpful when approached. Although they appear to maintain a low profile, they are usually not far from major attractions. For details of the main police station, see p.732.

## MEDICAL CARE AND EMERGENCIES

Medical services in Singapore are excellent, with hospital staff almost everywhere speaking good English and using up-to-date techniques and facilities. **Pharmacies** (Mon–Sat 9am–6pm) are well stocked with familiar brand-name drugs and pharmacists can recommend products for skin complaints or simple stomach problems, though if you're in any doubt you should contact a local doctor (see p.731). Pharmacists also stock oral contraceptives, spermicidal gels and condoms.

Larger hotels have doctors on-call at all times. Dentists are listed in the *Singapore Buying Guide* (equivalent to the *Yellow Pages*) under "Dental Surgeons", and "Dentist Emergency Service". For details of hospital casualty departments, see p.731.

## MONEY AND BANKS

The currency is Singapore dollars, usually written simply as $, though throughout the chapter we have used S$. The Singapore dollar is divided into 100 cents. Notes are issued in denominations of S$2, S$5, S$10, S$50, S$100, S$500, S$1000 and S$10,000; coins are in denominations of 5, 10, 20 and 50 cents, and S$1. At the time of writing, the exchange rate was around S$2.70 to £1, S$1.40 to US$1. Singapore dollars are legal tender in Brunei and can be used interchangeably at the same value.

Sterling or US dollar traveller's cheques can be cashed at Singaporean banks, licensed moneychangers and some hotels. Major credit cards (preferably MasterCard and Visa over American Express) are widely accepted in the more upmarket hotels, shops and restaurants, but beware the illegal surcharges levied by some establishments. Banks will often advance cash against major credit cards; with American Express, Visa and MasterCard; it's possible to withdraw money from ATMs in Singapore. For lost or stolen traveller's cheques or credit cards contact: Visa ⓣ1800/448 1250; MasterCard ⓣ1800/110 0113; American Express ⓣ6880 1111; Diners Card ⓣ6294 4222. There are also moneychangers in shopping centres and at hotels. No black market operates in Singapore, nor are there any restrictions on carrying currency in or out of the state. This means that rates at moneychangers are as good as you'll find at the banks.

## OPENING HOURS AND PUBLIC HOLIDAYS

Shopping centres officially open daily 10am to 7.30pm but opening times are far from set in stone. Banks open at least Monday to Friday 10am to 3pm, Saturday 9.30am to 1pm; while offices generally work Monday to Friday 8.30am to 5.30pm and sometimes on Saturday mornings. In general, Chinese temples open daily from 7am to around 6pm, Hindu temples from 6am to noon and 5 to 9pm and mosques from 8.30am to noon and 2.30pm to 4pm.

### Public holidays

**January 1** New Year's Day
**January/February** Chinese New Year (two days)
**March/April** Good Friday
**May 1** Labour Day
**May** Vesak Day
**August 9** National Day
**November** Deepavali
**December** Hari Raya Puasa
**December 25** Christmas Day

## FESTIVALS

With so many ethnic groups and religions represented in Singapore, you'll be unlucky if your trip doesn't coincide with some sort of **festival**, secular or religious. Most of the festivals have no fixed dates, but change annually according to the lunar calendar; check with the tourist office (see p.722). Bear in mind that the major festival periods may play havoc with travel plans.

**Chinese New Year** (Jan/Feb 2 days) Chinese operas and dragon dances in China Town
**Thaipusam** (Jan/Feb) Watch Hindu devotees pierce their own flesh with elaborate steel cages and walk from the Sri Srinivasa Perumal Temple to the Chettiar Hindu Temple
**Birthday of the Monkey God** (Sept) Similar to Thaipusam but on a smaller scale. Best witnessed at the Monkey God Temple on Seng Poh Rd.
**Singapore Food Festival** (July) Singapore celebrates its oldest pastime and the island goes food crazy.
**Festival of the Hungry Ghosts** (July) Catch a free performance of a Chinese opera, or *wayang*, in which characters act out classic Chinese legends, accompanied by cymbals, gongs.
**Moon Cake Festival** or Mid-Autumn Festival (July-Aug). Celebrate with children's lantern parades after dark in the Chinese Gardens and try to stomach a traditional Chinese moon cake.
**Navarathiri** (Oct) Chettiar Hindu Temple stages classical dance and music, and at the Sri Mariamman Temple.
**Thimithi** (Oct) Watch Hindu devotees running across a pit of hot coals.
**Diwali** (Oct/Nov) The Hindu festival celebrating the victory of Light over Dark is marked by the lighting of oil lamps outside homes.

### LANGUAGE

English, Mandarin, Malay (for more on which, see p.490) and Tamil all have the status of official languages, and you should have no problem getting by in English. One intriguing by-product of Singapore's ethnic melting pot is **Singlish**, or Singaporean English, a patois that blends English with the speech patterns, exclamations and vocabulary of Chinese and Malay. Look out for the word "lah" when conversing with Singapore locals – it doesn't actually mean anything, and was originally used to add emphasis to the point being made, however, more commonly, it is just used to round off a sentence.

# Downtown Singapore

Ever since Sir Stamford Raffles first landed on its northern bank, in 1819, the area around the Singapore River, which strikes into the heart of the island from the south coast, has formed the hub of Singapore. All the city's central districts lie within a 3km radius of the mouth of the river – which makes **Downtown Singapore** an extremely convenient place to tour.

## What to see and do

The entire state is compact enough to be explored exhaustively in just a few days. Forming the core of downtown Singapore is the **Colonial District**, around whose public buildings and lofty cathedral the island's British residents used to promenade. Each surrounding enclave has its own distinct flavour, from the aromatic spice stores of **Little India** to the tumbledown backstreets of **Chinatown**, where it's still possible to find calligraphers and fortune-tellers, or the **Arab Quarter**, whose cluttered shops sell fine cloths and silks.

### The Colonial District

As the colony's trade grew, the **Singapore River** became its main artery, clogged with traditional cargo boats (known as "bumboats"), which ferried coffee, sugar and rice to the *godowns*, or warehouses. A recent campaign to clean up the river relocated the bumboats to the west coast, though a handful still remain, offering trips downriver and around Marina Bay. Start your tour at the elegant **Cavenagh Bridge**. Stepping off the bridge, you're just a stone's throw away from the **landing site** where Stamford Raffles, Singapore's founder, took his first steps on Singaporean soil. Now the lower end of North Boat Quay, the site is marked with a statue of Raffles. Singapore River cruise boats (see box below) depart from a tiny jetty a few steps along from Raffles' statue. North of the statue up Parliament Lane, the dignified white Victorian building on the left ringed by fencing is **Parliament House**, built as a private dwelling for a rich merchant in 1833. It has since been converted into a centre for the arts, The Arts House (Ⓦwww.theartshouse.com.sg).

### Asian Civilisations Museums

Between Cavenagh Bridge and Raffles Landing Site, sits the **Asian Civilisations Museum** (Mon 1–7pm, Tues–Sun 9am–7pm; S$8; Ⓦwww.acm.org.sg). The robust Neoclassical structure was constructed with Indian convict labour in 1864. Today, each of the museum's ten galleries is devoted to the art and culture of a particular region of Asia, including China, India and Southeast Asia.

There is also a smaller Asian Civilisations Museum (same times and

#### SINGAPORE RIVER, ISLAND AND HARBOUR CRUISES

Fleets of cruise boats ply Singapore's southern waters every day and night. The best of these, the Singapore River Cruises (Ⓣ6336 6111), cast off from North Boat Quay, Raffles Landing Site, Riverside Point Landing Steps and Clarke Quay (daily 9am–11pm; every 10min). Cruises on a traditional bumboat (S$13 for 30min) will take you past the old *godowns* upriver where traders once stored their merchandise. Several cruise companies also operate out of Clifford Pier and the HarbourFront Centre, offering everything from luxury catamaran trips around Singapore's southern isles to dinner on a Chinese sailing boat.

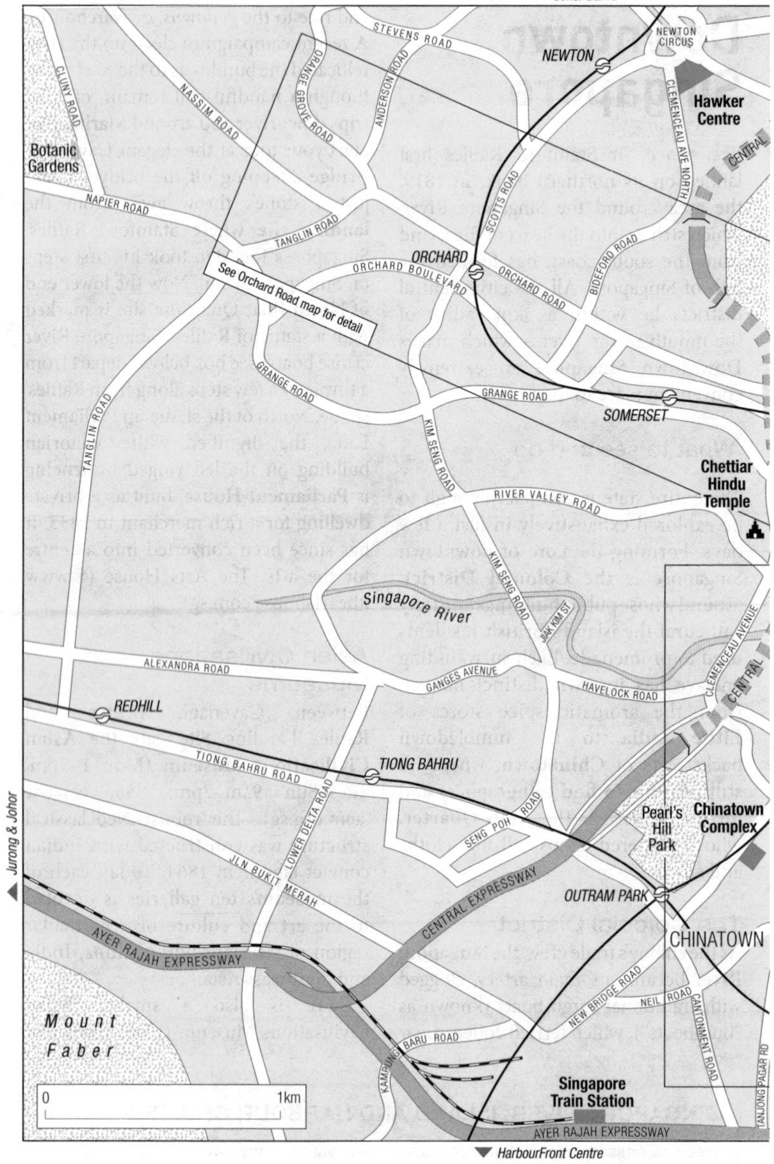


entrance fee as the flagship ACM) at 39 Armenian St, just around the corner, which features exhibits highlighting the hybrid nature of the Peranakan culture. A joint ticket for both museums for S$12 can be purchased at either museum.

## The Padang and Esplanade

The very essence of colonial Singapore, the **Padang** was earmarked by Raffles as a recreation ground shortly after his arrival. At the southwestern end, the **Singapore Cricket Club**, founded in the 1850s, was

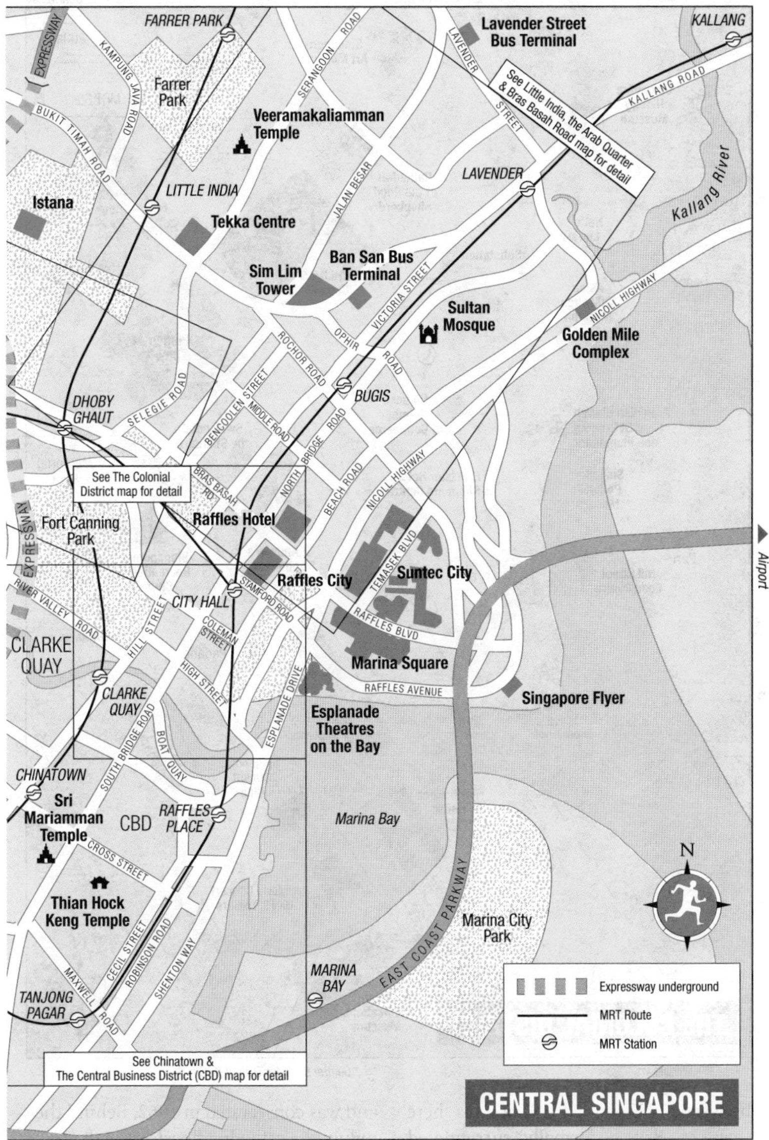


the hub of colonial British society and still operates a "members-only" rule; its brown-tiled roof, whitewashed walls and dark green blinds have a certain nostalgic charm. If you are visiting on a weekend, you might be fortunate enough to catch the members indulging in a lazy game of cricket, completing the colonial picture. You can watch the action from outside the Padang itself.

Just to the west sits Singapore's Neoclassical **Supreme Court**. Built

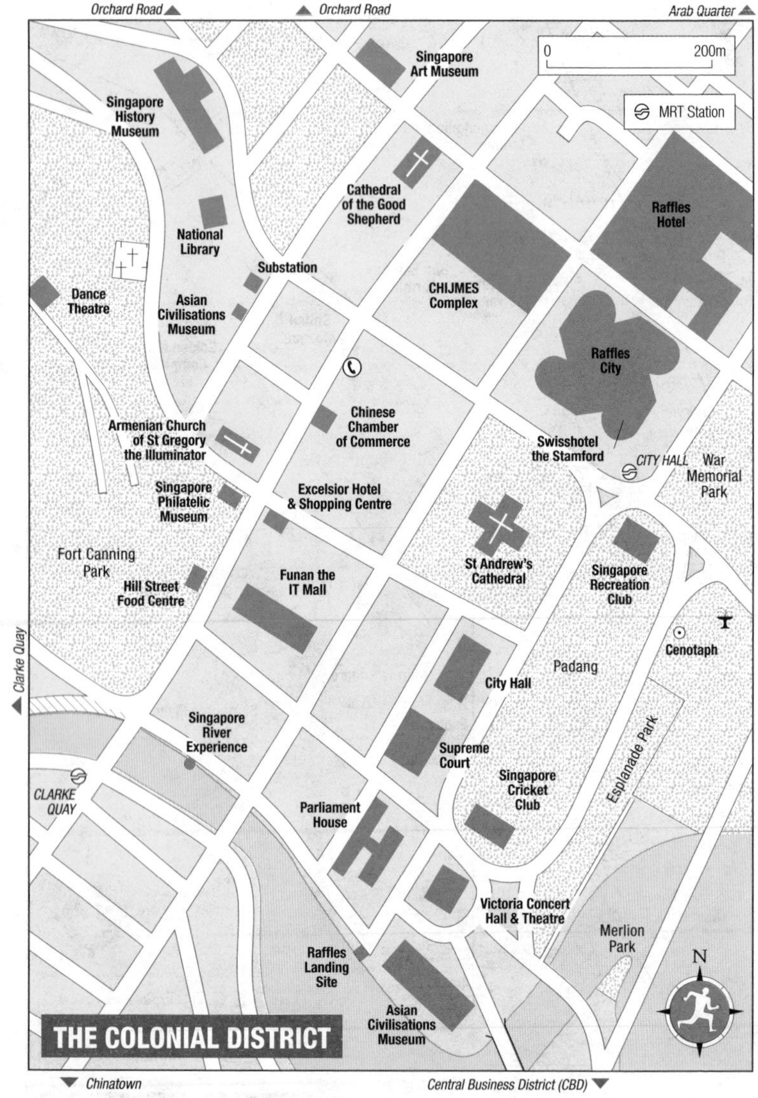


between 1937 and 1939, it was here that the British formally surrendered to the Japanese in 1942. Uniform rows of grandiose Corinthian columns mark the older **City Hall**, next door. The final building on the west side of the Padang, **St Andrew's Cathedral** on Coleman Street, was built in high-vaulted, Neo-Gothic style, using Indian convict labour, and was consecrated in 1862. Behind the pulpit, the cathedral boasts a small cross crafted from two fourteenth-century nails salvaged from the ruins of England's Coventry Cathedral, which was razed during World War II.

Due east of the Padang lie the iconic twin Esplanade buildings. In much the way that Sydney's Opera House has become Australia's most recognized building, the futuristic **Esplanade Theatres on the Bay** may become architectural symbols of the city; in a city obsessed with high-rises, the Esplanade Theatres, dubbed "the durians" by the locals due to their resemblance in shape and texture to the stinking fruit, look like nothing else in Asia. The juxtaposition of the modern spiked domes against the ancient Padang and Cricket Club reflect both Singapore's progressive future and proud colonial past. The buildings house several theatres and various restaurants and boutiques.

## Raffles City and Raffles Hotel

Immediately north of St Andrew's Cathedral, across Stamford Road, is **Raffles City**, a huge development comprising two enormous hotels, a multi-level shopping centre and floor upon floor of offices. Completed in 1985, the complex was designed by Chinese-American architect I.M. Pei – the man behind the glass pyramid which fronts the Louvre in Paris. On the top floor of **Swissotel The Stamford** is the *New Asia Bar*, a popular bar and restaurant with a spectacular view of the city. The imposing **Civilian War Memorial** stands on the open land east of Raffles City, comprising four seventy-metre-high white columns, and is known locally as "the chopsticks".

The lofty halls, restaurants, bars and peaceful gardens of the legendary **Raffles Hotel** all conspire to evoke an aching nostalgia for British colonialism (sorry, cuffing the punkah wallah, the old colonial fanning boy, is no longer allowed). The hotel opened for business on December 1, 1887, and quickly began to attract some impressive guests, including Joseph Conrad, Rudyard Kipling and Herman Hesse. In 1915, the legendary "Singapore Sling" cocktail was created here by bartender Ngiam Tong Boon. During World War II, the hotel became a Japanese officers' quarters, then a transit camp for liberated Allied prisoners. Postwar deterioration ended with a S$160-million facelift in 1991, which retained much of its colonial grace. An upscale shopping arcade was also added, which, though in keeping with the hotel's architecture, for some it takes away from the charm of the *Raffles* experience.

Non-guests are welcome to visit the free **museum** (daily 10am–7pm) located upstairs, at the back of the hotel complex, which is crammed with memorabilia.

## CHIJMES and the Singapore Art Museum

**Bras Basah Road** cuts west from Raffles, crossing North Bridge Road and then passing one of Singapore's most aesthetically pleasing eating and shopping

### THE SINGAPORE FLYER

Singapore's newest landmark, the **Singapore Flyer** (daily 8.30am–10.30pm; Ⓦwww.singaporeflyer.com), on Raffles Avenue, east of the Esplanade Theatres, made its maiden voyage on Valentine's Day 2008 and is currently the world's largest Ferris wheel. With a diameter of 165m, the wheel offers 360-degree views of everything from the bustling business district to the surrounding Indonesian and Malaysian islands. The standard thirty-minute "round trip" is surprisingly affordable (adult S$29.50, child S$20.65, senior S$23.60); however, those who want to make a night of it might try the "cocktail flight" (adult S$69.50, senior S$55.20), which includes a free cocktail en route (and you get to keep the glass). The best way to reserve a spot in one of the pods is to book online, but it's also possible to just turn up and jump the queue for a nominal fee (adult S$52, child S$36.40, senior S$41.60).

places, CHIJMES (ⓦwww.chijmes.com.sg). Based around the Neo-Gothic husk of the former Convent of the Holy Infant Jesus (from whose name the complex's acronymic title is derived), CHIJMES is a rustic version of London's Covent Garden, with lawns, courtyards, waterfalls, fountains and a sunken forecourt. Some argue that there is too much going on at CHIJMES, giving it a somewhat contrived feeling.

Northwest of CHIJMES, at 71 Bras Basah, is the new **Singapore Art Museum** (Mon–Sun 10am–7pm; S$8, free Fri 6–10pm and weekdays noon–2pm; ⓦwww.nhb.sg/SAM/home), which is housed in the venerable St Joseph's Institution, Singapore's first Catholic school, many of whose original rooms survive. SAM's strength lies in its contemporary regional and pan-Asian exhibitions, mapping the modern Asian experience by drawing on a permanent collection of 5500 artworks. The museum's Cyber Gallery incorporates experimental forms, and guides conduct free **tours** around the museum's major works.

## National Museum of Singapore

The **National Museum of Singapore** (daily 10am–6pm; the Singapore Living Galleries, daily 10am–8pm; S$10, free 6–8pm; ⓦwww.nationalmuseum.sg) is housed in one of Singapore's most distinguished colonial buildings. Formerly the Raffles Library, it has undergone major renovation and is now the country's largest museum. As well as having permanent collections relating to the history of Singapore, the museum offers several interactive exhibits where local Singaporeans can share their stories of island life. Modern multimedia devices are used effectively and will keep you interested all afternoon.

## Bugis Village

One block east of Waterloo Street's shops and temples, at the junction of Rochor Road and Victoria Street, sits **Bugis Village** – a rather tame manifestation of infamous Bugis Street. Until the area was remodelled to make way for an MRT station, Bugis Street embodied old Singapore: after dark it was a chaotic place, crawling with rowdy sailors (who euphorically referred to it as "Boogie Street"), transvestites and prostitutes – anathema to a Singapore government keen to clean up its country's reputation. Singaporean public opinion demanded a replacement and Bugis Village duly opened in 1991. However, with its beer gardens, seafood restaurants and pubs, it is a sad shadow of its former self, though the covered and air-conditioned "streets" of nearby PARCO Bugis Junction Shopping Centre are a welcome escape from the heat.

## Fort Canning Park and Clarke Quay

When Raffles first caught sight of Singapore, **Fort Canning Park** was known locally as Bukit Larangan (Forbidden Hill). Singapore's first British Resident, William Farquhar – a political officer appointed by London – displayed typical colonial tact by promptly having the hill cleared and building a bungalow on the summit. The bungalow was replaced by a fort in 1859. An early European **cemetery** survives, however, on whose stones are engraved intriguing epitaphs to nineteenth-century sailors, traders and residents.

There's a back entrance to the park which involves climbing the exhausting flight of steps that runs next to the Hill Street Food Centre on Hill Street. Once you reach the top, you're greeted by a brilliant view along High Street towards the Merlion monument at the mouth of the Singapore River. The highlight of Fort Canning, however, is the **Battle Box** (ⓣ6333 0510; daily 10am–6pm, last admission 5pm; S$8), an underground museum of sorts which uses audio and video effects and animations to bring to life the last hours before the Japanese occupation began in February 1942.

On the other side of River Valley Road, which skirts the southwestern slope of Fort Canning Park, lies a chain of nineteenth-century *godowns* (warehouses) which have been renovated into the popular night spot, **Clarke Quay**. In recent years a huge emphasis has been put developing the area and making it a choice alternative to Boat Quay. There's a river taxi for Clarke Quay (daily 11am–11pm; S$4 return) which departs every five minutes from the quayside above the Standard Chartered Bank, two minutes' walk from Raffles Place MRT.

### Chinatown

The two square kilometres of **Chinatown**, located just south of the Singapore River, once constituted the focal point of Chinese life and culture in Singapore. Although nowadays the area is on its last traditional legs, a wander through the surviving nineteenth-century streets unearths aged craft shops and restaurants.

Until the middle of the twentieth century, the area was populated by Chinese immigrants working mainly as small traders and manual labourers. However, in the 1950s, the government embarked on a catastrophic **redevelopment campaign** that saw whole roads bulldozed to make way for new shopping centres. Only recently has public opinion finally convinced the Singaporean authorities to restore the area. The **Chinatown Heritage Centre** (daily 9am–8pm; S$10; ⓣ6325 2878), at 48 Pagoda Street, is located in a row of restored shop-houses which give visitors an idea of what the whole neighbourhood once looked like.

The enormous **Thian Hock Keng Temple** (the "Temple of Heavenly Happiness") on McCallum Street is a hugely impressive Hokkien building; dragons stalk its broad roofs, while the temple compound's entrance bristles with ceramic flowers, foliage and sculpted figures.

**Amoy Street** is another Hokkien enclave from the colony's early days. Long terraces of shop-houses flank the street, all featuring characteristic **five-foot ways**, simply covered verandas that were so-called because they jut five feet out. It's worth walking down to the **Sian Chai Kang Temple**, 66 Amoy St, its eaves painted a shade of red every bit as fiery as the dragons on its roof.

Turn right out of Ann Siang Hill and you'll see **Eu Yan Sang Medical Hall**, 267–71 South Bridge Road (Mon–Sat 8.30am–6pm), opened in 1910 and geared up, to an extent, for the tourist trade. The shop has been beautifully renovated and sells a weird assortment of ingredients, from herbs and roots to various dubious remedies derived from endangered species.

Across the road, the compound of the **Sri Mariamman Hindu Temple** bursts with wild-looking statues of deities and animals in primary colours. To the left of the main sanctum there's a patch of sand; once a year during the festival of Thimithi, it is covered in red-hot coals which male Hindus run across to prove the strength of their faith.

### The Central Business District (CBD)

**Raffles Place** forms the nucleus of the **Central Business District** (commonly referred to as the CBD) – the commercial heart of the state, home to many of its banks and financial institutions. The most striking way to experience the giddy heights of the CBD is by surfacing from Raffles Place MRT. A dizzying stroll will reveal the soaring metallic triangle of the OUB Centre (Overseas Union Bank), the rocket-shaped UOB Plaza 2 (United Overseas Bank); the rich brown walls of the Standard Chartered Bank; and the almost Art Deco Caltex House. The three roads that run southwest from Raffles Place

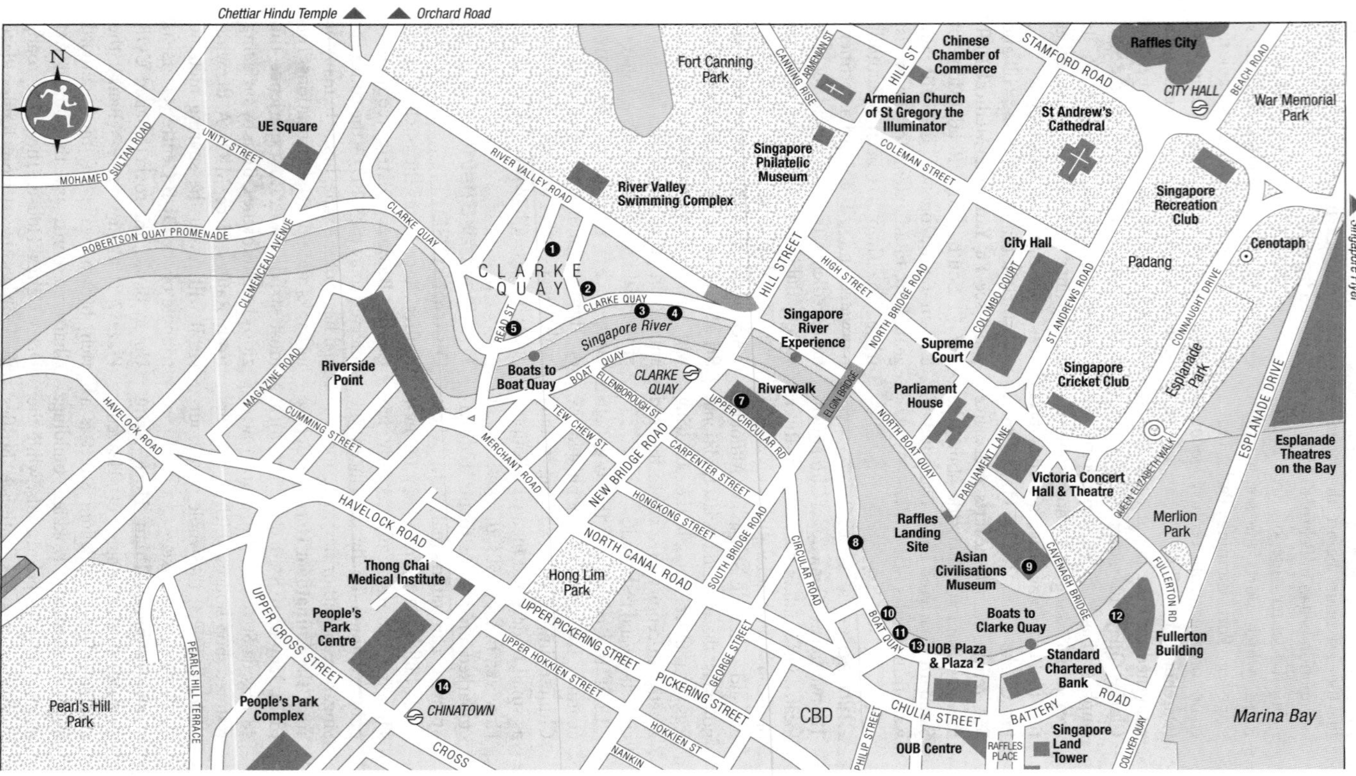
Chettiar Hindu Temple
Orchard Road
Singapore Flyer
N
UE Square
Sultan Road
Mohamed
Unity Street
Robertson Quay Promenade
Clemenceau Avenue
River Valley Road
River Valley Swimming Complex
Fort Canning Park
Canning Rise
Armenian St
Hill St
Chinese Chamber of Commerce
Armenian Church of St Gregory the Illuminator
Singapore Philatelic Museum
Coleman Street
Stamford Road
Raffles City
City Hall
Beach Road
War Memorial Park
St Andrew's Cathedral
Singapore Recreation Club
Padang
Cenotaph
Connaught Drive
Esplanade Park
Esplanade Drive
Esplanade Theatres on the Bay
City Hall
Colombo Court
St Andrews Road
Supreme Court
Singapore Cricket Club
Queen Elizabeth Walk
Clarke Quay
Clarke Quay
Read St
Singapore River
Boats to Boat Quay
Boat Quay
Clarke Quay
Ellenborough St
Hill Street
High Street
North Bridge Road
Singapore River Experience
Riverwalk
Upper Circular Rd
Elgin Bridge
Parliament House
North Boat Quay
Parliament Lane
Victoria Concert Hall & Theatre
Merlion Park
Riverside Point
Magazine Road
Cumming Street
Havelock Road
Merchant Road
Tew Chew St
New Bridge Road
Carpenter Street
Hongkong Street
South Bridge Road
Circular Road
Raffles Landing Site
Asian Civilisations Museum
Cavenagh Bridge
Fullerton Rd
Fullerton Building
Havelock Road
North Canal Road
Hong Lim Park
Thong Chai Medical Institute
People's Park Centre
Upper Cross Street
Pearls Hill Terrace
Pearl's Hill Park
People's Park Complex
Chinatown
Cross
Upper Pickering Street
Upper Hokkien Street
Hokkien St
Nankin
Pickering Street
George Street
CBD
Philip Street
Boat Quay
UOB Plaza & Plaza 2
Boats to Clarke Quay
Standard Chartered Bank
Chulia Street
OUB Centre
Raffles Place
Battery Road
Singapore Land Tower
Collyer Quay
Marina Bay

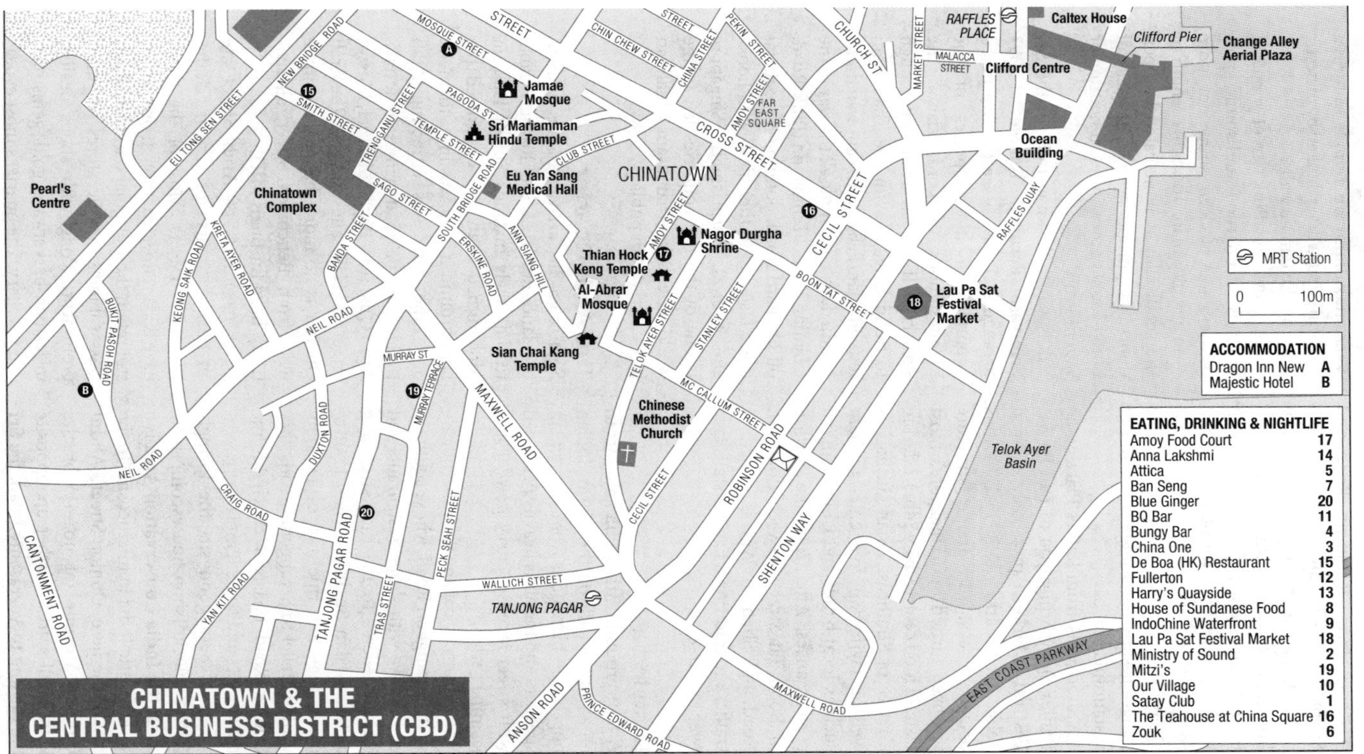
CHINATOWN & THE
CENTRAL BUSINESS DISTRICT (CBD)
ACCOMMODATION
Dragon Inn New A
Majestic Hotel B
EATING, DRINKING & NIGHTLIFE
Amoy Food Court 17
Anna Lakshmi 14
Attica 5
Ban Seng 7
Blue Ginger 20
BQ Bar 11
Bungy Bar 4
China One 3
De Boa (HK) Restaurant 15
Fullerton 12
Harry's Quayside 13
House of Sundanese Food 8
IndoChine Waterfront 9
Lau Pa Sat Festival Market 18
Ministry of Sound 2
Mitzi's 19
Our Village 10
Satay Club 1
The Teahouse at China Square 16
Zouk 6
MRT Station
0
100m
CHINATOWN
Pearl's Centre
Chinatown Complex
Jamae Mosque
Sri Mariamman Hindu Temple
Eu Yan Sang Medical Hall
Nagor Durgha Shrine
Thian Hock Keng Temple
Al-Abrar Mosque
Sian Chai Kang Temple
Chinese Methodist Church
Lau Pa Sat Festival Market
Ocean Building
Clifford Centre
Caltex House
Clifford Pier
Change Alley Aerial Plaza
RAFFLES PLACE
TANJONG PAGAR
Telok Ayer Basin
FAR EAST SQUARE
MOSQUE STREET
STREET
CHIN CHEW STREET
CHINA STREET
PEKIN STREET
CHURCH ST
MARKET STREET
MALACCA STREET
NEW BRIDGE ROAD
EU TONG SEN STREET
SMITH STREET
TRENGGANU STREET
PAGODA ST
TEMPLE STREET
CLUB STREET
AMOY STREET
CROSS STREET
CECIL STREET
RAFFLES QUAY
SAGO STREET
SOUTH BRIDGE ROAD
ERSKINE ROAD
ANN SIANG HILL
BANDA STREET
KRETA AYER ROAD
KEONG SAIK ROAD
BUKIT PASOH ROAD
NEIL ROAD
MURRAY ST
MURRAY TERRACE
TELOK AYER STREET
STANLEY STREET
BOON TAT STREET
MC CALLUM STREET
ROBINSON ROAD
SHENTON WAY
MAXWELL ROAD
DUXTON ROAD
CRAIG ROAD
PECK SEAH STREET
WALLICH STREET
TANJONG PAGAR ROAD
TRAS STREET
YAN KIT ROAD
CANTONMENT ROAD
ANSON ROAD
PRINCE EDWARD ROAD
EAST COAST PARKWAY

– Cecil Street, Robinson Road and Shenton Way – are all choc-a-bloc with more high-rise banks and financial houses. Just north of Raffles Place, and beneath the "elephant's trunk" curve of the Singapore River, the pedestrianized row of shop-houses known as **Boat Quay** is Singapore's most fashionable hangout, sporting a huge collection of restaurants and bars.

A short walk from Raffles Place along Raffles Quay brings you to **Lau Pa Sat Festival Market**, previously named Telok Ayer Market. Built in 1884, this octagonal cast-iron frame structure has been turned into Singapore's most tasteful food centre (daily 24hr), offering a range of Southeast Asian cuisines as well as laying on free entertainment such as local bands and Chinese opera performances. After 7pm, the portion of Boon Tat Street between Robinson Road and Shenton Way is closed to traffic, and traditional hawker stalls take over the street.

### Little India

A tour around **Little India** amounts to an all-out assault on the senses. Indian pop music blares out from gargantuan speakers and the air is heavily perfumed with sweet incense, curry powder and jasmine garlands.

The district's backbone is the north–south Serangoon Road, whose southern end is alive with shops, restaurants and fortune-tellers. To the east, stretching as far as Jalan Besar, is a tight knot of roads that are ripe for exploration; while parallel to Serangoon Road, Race Course Road boasts a clutch of fine restaurants and some temples.

East of Serangoon sits the lovingly restoredblockofshop-housescomprising the **Little India Conservation Area** is a sort of Little India in microcosm. To the east of the here, Dunlop Street's **Abdul Gaffoor Mosque** (at no. 41) bristles with small spires. Further up, opposite the turning to Veerasamy Road, the **Sri Veeramakaliamman Temple** features a fanciful gopura that's flanked by majestic lions on the temple walls.

You won't find **Pink Street** – one of the most incongruous and sordid spots in the whole of clean, shiny Singapore – on any city map. The entire length of the small alley is punctuated by open doorways, inside which gaggles of bored-looking prostitutes sit knitting or watching TV.

It is worth heading over to the **Sri Srinivasa Perumal Temple** at 397 Serangoon Road to see the five-tiered gopura with its sculptures of the manifestations of Lord Vishnu the Preserver. If you are fortunate enough to be in Singapore for the Thaipusam festival (Jan/Feb), you can watch the Hindu devotees parade all the way to the Chettiar Hindu Temple on Tank Road, off Orchard Road, donning huge metal cages fastened to their flesh with hooks and prongs. Surprisingly, Singapore is one of the few countries left in the world where the Thaipusam ritual can be carried out in public.

### The Arab Quarter

Soon after his arrival, Raffles allotted the land north of the Rocher Canal to the newly installed Sultan Hussein Mohammed Shah and designated the land around it as a Muslim settlement. Soon the zone was attracting Arab traders, as the road names in today's **Arab Quarter** – Baghdad Street, Muscat Street and Haji Lane – suggest. The Arab Quarter is no more than a ten-minute walk from Bencoolen Street; alternatively, head for Bugis MRT.

The pavements of **Arab Street** are an obstacle course of carpets, cloths, baskets and bags. Most of the shops have been renovated, though one or two still retain their original dark-wood and glass cabinets. Textile stores are most prominent, along with shops dealing in leather, basketware, gold, gemstones and jewellery. The quarter's most evocative patch is the stretch of **North Bridge Road** between Arab Street and Jalan Sultan. Here, the men sport long sarongs and long beards and the women wear fantastically colourful shawls and robes.

Squatting between Kandahar and Aliwal streets, is the **Istana Kampong Glam,** which houses a **Malay Heritage Centre** (Mon 1–6pm, Tues–Sun 10am–6pm; S$3). It was built as the royal palace of Sultan Ali Iskandar Shah, son of Sultan Hussein, who negotiated with Raffles to hand over Singapore to the British. A few steps further on, Baghdad Street crosses pedestrianized Bussorah Street, from where you get the best initial views of the golden domes of the **Sultan Mosque** or Masjid Sultan (daily 9am–1pm & 2–4pm; all visitors must keep shoulders and legs covered).

A ten-minute walk down Beach road stands the Thai-themed **Golden Mile Complex.** On route notice the Gateway Office Blocks, designed by I.M. Pei to appear two-dimensional from the roadside.

Numerous bus firms selling tickets to Thailand operate out of the Golden Mile Complex, while inside the shops sell Thai foodstuffs, Singha beer and Mekong whisky.

### Orchard Road

**Orchard Road** is synonymous with shopping – indeed, tourist brochures refer to it as the "Fifth Avenue, the Regent Street, the Champs Elysées, the Via Veneto and the Ginza of Singapore". The road runs northwest from Fort Canning Park and is served by three **MRT stations** – Dhoby Ghaut, Somerset and Orchard; the last of these is the most central for shopping expeditions.

Huge **malls** line the streets selling everything under the sun. Those not looking to spend their monthly budget on Calvin Klein or Armani might like to try Lucky Plaza or Far East Plaza (located on the perpendicular Scotts Road). Both offer good prices on fashion, tailoring and, particularly at Lucky Plaza, electronic goods. Bargaining is expected.

Three minutes' walk west along Orchard Road from Dhoby Ghaut MRT, at its eastern extremity, takes you past the gate of the **Istana Negara Singapura**, the official residence of the president of Singapore. Continuing west, **Emerald Hill Road** holds a number of exquisitely crafted houses built in the late nineteenth century. Several of the houses now serve as an ideal rest stop for an afternoon drink and a bite to eat.

By the time you reach the western end of Orchard Road, you'll be glad of the open space afforded by the **Singapore Botanic Gardens** (daily 5am–midnight; free; ⓦwww.sbg.org.sg) on Cluny Road, a ten-minute walk from the western end of Orchard Road. Founded in 1859, the fifty-odd hectares of land feature a mini-jungle, rose garden, topiary, fernery, palm valley and lakes. There's also the **National Orchid Garden** (daily 8.30am–7pm; S$5; ⓣ6471 7138) containing 60,000 flower varieties and one of the world's most prestigious collections of orchids. The Garden also sells orchid jewellery, made by plating real flowers with gold (S$100 per piece). If you get to the gardens early, enjoy a delicious breakfast in one of the jungle restaurants.

## Arrival

**By bus** Singapore has three bus terminals. The Singapore-KL Express and local buses from Johor Bahru and arrive at Ban San terminal at the junction of Queen and Arab sts. Buses from elsewhere in Malaysia and from Thailand terminate at one of two sites, Lavender St terminal (near Lavendar MRT) and the Golden Mile Complex.

**By train** Trains to and from Malaysia use the Singapore train station on Keppel Rd, southwest of Chinatown. If you want to avoid taking the train down to its terminus in the south of the island, get off in Johor Bahru, clear Malaysian immigration and get back on bus #160 or #170.

**By boat** Boats to and from the Indonesian Riau archipelago dock at two different piers. Boats from Pulau Batam arrive at the HarbourFront Centre,

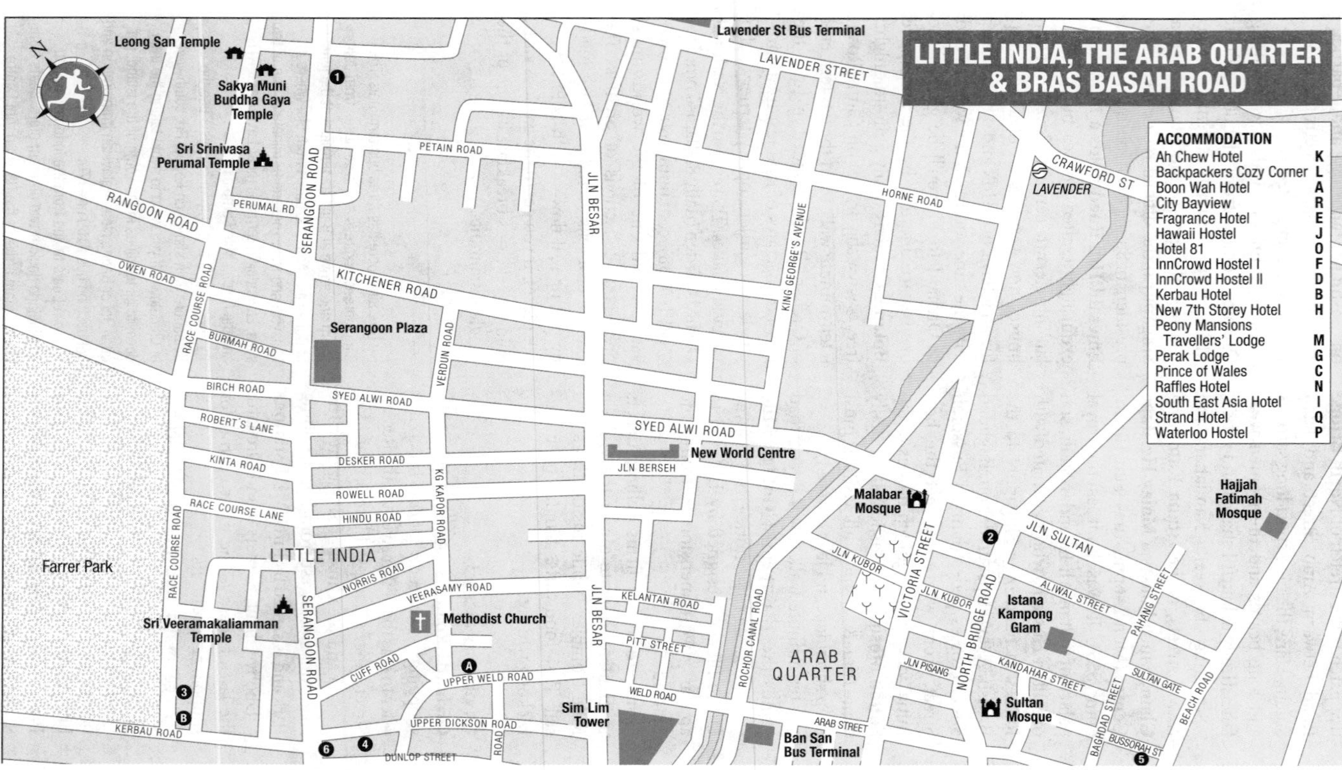
LITTLE INDIA, THE ARAB QUARTER & BRAS BASAH ROAD
ACCOMMODATION
Ah Chew Hotel K
Backpackers Cozy Corner L
Boon Wah Hotel A
City Bayview R
Fragrance Hotel E
Hawaii Hostel J
Hotel 81 O
InnCrowd Hostel I F
InnCrowd Hostel II D
Kerbau Hotel B
New 7th Storey Hotel H
Peony Mansions Travellers' Lodge M
Perak Lodge G
Prince of Wales C
Raffles Hotel N
South East Asia Hotel I
Strand Hotel Q
Waterloo Hostel P
Leong San Temple
Sakya Muni Buddha Gaya Temple
Sri Srinivasa Perumal Temple
Lavender St Bus Terminal
LAVENDER STREET
LAVENDER
CRAWFORD ST
HORNE ROAD
KING GEORGE'S AVENUE
PETAIN ROAD
PERUMAL RD
RANGOON ROAD
SERANGOON ROAD
JLN BESAR
OWEN ROAD
KITCHENER ROAD
RACE COURSE ROAD
Serangoon Plaza
VERDUN ROAD
BURMAH ROAD
BIRCH ROAD
SYED ALWI ROAD
ROBERT'S LANE
KINTA ROAD
DESKER ROAD
KG KAPOR ROAD
ROWELL ROAD
HINDU ROAD
RACE COURSE LANE
New World Centre
JLN BERSEH
Malabar Mosque
Hajjah Fatimah Mosque
JLN SULTAN
JLN KUBOR
VICTORIA STREET
NORTH BRIDGE ROAD
ALIWAL STREET
PAHANG STREET
Istana Kampong Glam
Farrer Park
LITTLE INDIA
NORRIS ROAD
VEERASAMY ROAD
KELANTAN ROAD
Methodist Church
Sri Veeramakaliamman Temple
PITT STREET
ROCHOR CANAL ROAD
ARAB QUARTER
JLN PISANG
KANDAHAR STREET
SULTAN GATE
BEACH ROAD
CUFF ROAD
UPPER WELD ROAD
WELD ROAD
Sim Lim Tower
Sultan Mosque
UPPER DICKSON ROAD
ARAB STREET
BAGHDAD STREET
BUSSORAH ST
KERBAU ROAD
DUNLOP STREET
Ban San Bus Terminal

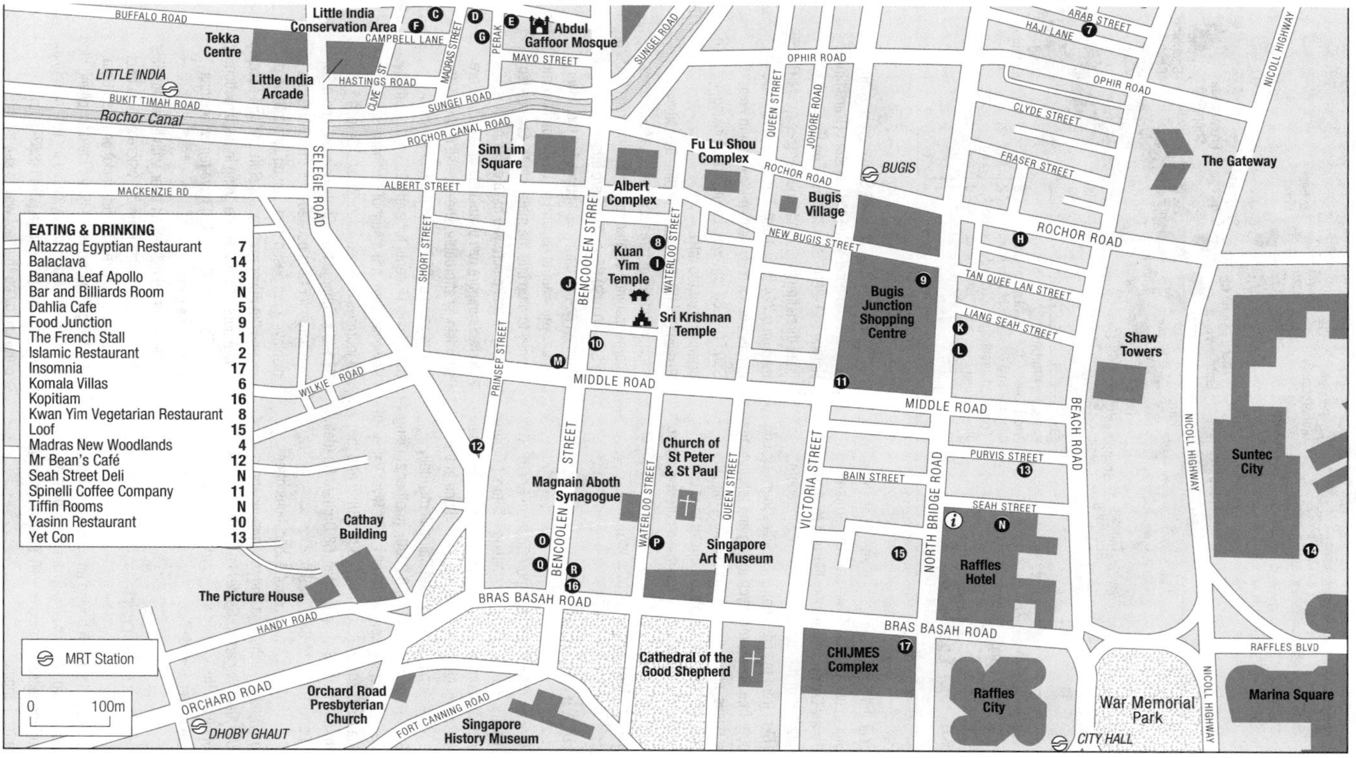
EATING & DRINKING
Altazzag Egyptian Restaurant 7
Balaclava 14
Banana Leaf Apollo 3
Bar and Billiards Room N
Dahlia Cafe 5
Food Junction 9
The French Stall 1
Islamic Restaurant 2
Insomnia 17
Komala Villas 6
Kopitiam 16
Kwan Yim Vegetarian Restaurant 8
Loof 15
Madras New Woodlands 4
Mr Bean's Café 12
Seah Street Deli N
Spinelli Coffee Company 11
Tiffin Rooms N
Yasinn Restaurant 10
Yet Con 13
MRT Station
0 100m
Little India Conservation Area
Tekka Centre
Little India Arcade
LITTLE INDIA
Abdul Gaffoor Mosque
Rochor Canal
Sim Lim Square
Albert Complex
Fu Lu Shou Complex
Kuan Yim Temple
Sri Krishnan Temple
BUGIS
Bugis Village
Bugis Junction Shopping Centre
The Gateway
Shaw Towers
Suntec City
Church of St Peter & St Paul
Magnain Aboth Synagogue
Singapore Art Museum
Cathay Building
The Picture House
Cathedral of the Good Shepherd
CHIJMES Complex
Raffles Hotel
Raffles City
War Memorial Park
CITY HALL
Marina Square
Orchard Road Presbyterian Church
Singapore History Museum
DHOBY GHAUT
BUFFALO ROAD
CAMPBELL LANE
MADRAS STREET
PERAK
MAYO STREET
HASTINGS ROAD
CLIVE ST
BUKIT TIMAH ROAD
SUNGEI ROAD
ROCHOR CANAL ROAD
SELEGIE ROAD
MACKENZIE RD
ALBERT STREET
SHORT STREET
PRINSEP STREET
BENCOOLEN STREET
WATERLOO STREET
QUEEN STREET
JOHORE ROAD
OPHIR ROAD
ROCHOR ROAD
NEW BUGIS STREET
ARAB STREET
HAJI LANE
CLYDE STREET
FRASER STREET
NICOLL HIGHWAY
TAN QUEE LAN STREET
LIANG SEAH STREET
MIDDLE ROAD
BEACH ROAD
PURVIS STREET
BAIN STREET
SEAH STREET
VICTORIA STREET
NORTH BRIDGE ROAD
BRAS BASAH ROAD
RAFFLES BLVD
WILKIE ROAD
HANDY ROAD
ORCHARD ROAD
FORT CANNING ROAD

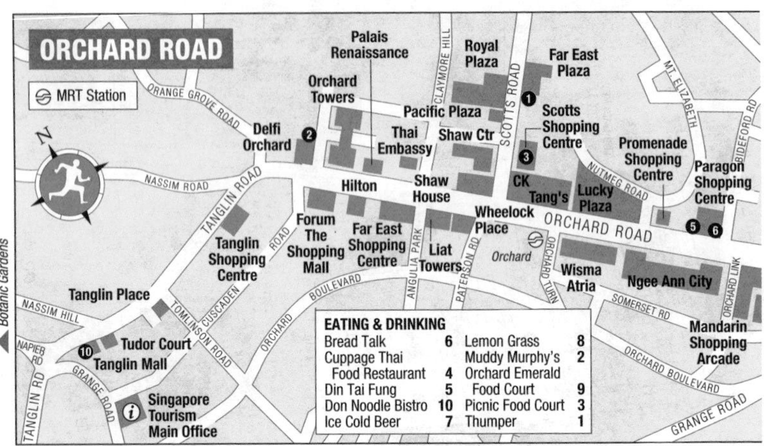


near the MRT of the same name. Boats from Pulau Bintan use the Tanah Merah ferry terminal.

**By air** Changi International Airport (☎1800/542 4422) is at the far eastern end of Singapore, 16km from the city centre. Facilities there include duty-free shops, moneychanging and left-luggage services, hotel reservations counters and, in Terminal One's basement, a cheap food centre. Either take a taxi into town (make sure the driver uses his meter, should be no more than S$25) or take the MRT from any of the terminals.

## Information

**Tourist office** The Singapore Tourism Board (STB) maintains five Tourist Information (visitors') Centres, including one in the arrivals area of each terminal at Changi Airport. In town, you'll find one at the intersection of Orchard and Cairnhill rds (daily 8am–10pm; ☎1-800/736 2000); another at Liang Court Shopping Centre, Level 1, 177 River Valley Rd (daily 10.30am–9.30pm; ☎6336 2888); and the third at Plaza Singapura Mall, 68 Orchard Rd (daily 10am–10pm; ☎6332 9298).

**Publications** A number of publications offer a "What's On" listings and recommendations. *Uniquely Singapore Guide* is a free handout but best of all are the weekly *8 Days magazine* ($1.50) and the newer, weekly *I-S*.

## City transport

**Tickets** It's worth buying an ez-link card, a stored-value card valid on all MRT and bus journeys in Singapore; it's sold at MRT stations and bus interchanges.

**MRT (Mass Rapid Transit)** Singapore's clean, efficient and good-value MRT system (Transitlink Hotline ☎1-800/767 4333) runs on three main lines threading the island together (see the MRT map on p.724 for details). Trains run every five minutes or so, daily 6am–midnight, and cost S$0.80–1.80 one-way. Eating and drinking are both prohibited on the MRT.

**Buses** Call the Transitlink Hotline (see above) for information about fares and routes. Most buses charge distance-related fares, ranging from S$0.70 to S$1.40 (S$0.80–1.70 for a/c buses). If you don't have an ez-link card (see above), tell the driver where you want to go, and he'll tell you how much money to drop into the metal chute. Change isn't given, so make sure you have enough coins.

**Taxis** Singapore has thousands of taxis that are surprisingly affordable. They are all metered, the fare starting at S$2.80 for the first kilometre, then rising 10 cents for every 225m thereafter. However, there are a host of surcharges, including on journeys between midnight and 6am, a S$3–5 surcharge from Changi Airport, and a S$3 surcharge for taxis booked over the phone. If a taxi displays a red destination sign on its dashboard, it means the driver is changing shift and will accept customers only if they are going in his direction. TIBS Taxis (☎6555 8888) have ten wheelchair-accessible cabs.

**Bicycle rental** (S$4–8 an hour, with ID) is possible along the East Coast Parkway, where a cycle track skirts the seashore. The dirt tracks on Pulau Ubin, off Changi Point (see p.734), are ideal for biking, and there's a range of bikes available for rent next to the ferry terminal on Sentosa Island (S$3–8 an hour), providing by far the best way to see the island.

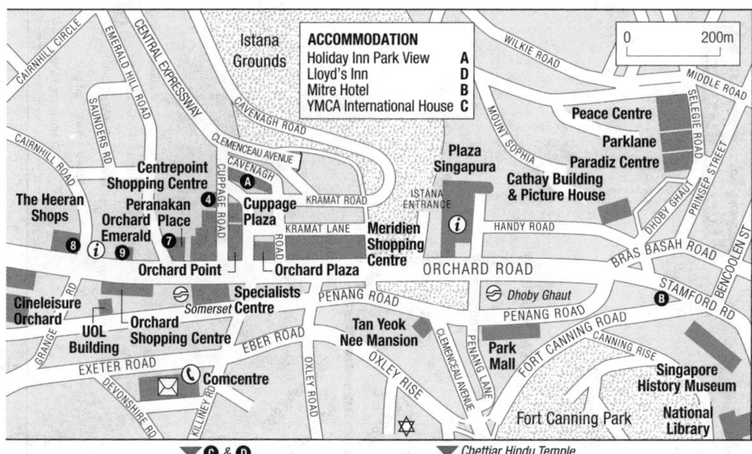


## Accommodation

### Little India

Little India's hotels and guesthouses are attracting an increasing number of backpackers. Buses along Jl Besar connect Little India with the rest of central Singapore. See the map pp.720–721 for locations.

**Boon Wah Hotel** 40–43 Upper Weld Rd ⓣ6339 6561. Formerly called *Goh Homestay*, the rooms in this well-established guesthouse are clean and well maintained. Its location away from the backpacker strip means that it lacks some ambience, but with a cosy canteen area, it's still possible to meet like-minded travellers. No dorm options. 6

**Fragrance Hotel** 63 Dunlop St ⓣ6295 6888, ⓦwww.fragrancehotel.com. One of the newer hostels in the area, the clean rooms and well-lit lobby are a welcome change for the seasoned traveller. It only offers dorms (S$22). Affordable and sociable internet room on the ground floor. 3

**InnCrowd Hostel I** 35 Campbell Ln ⓣ6296 9169, ⓦwww.the-inncrowd.com. In a renovated century-old shop-house, this hostel goes way above and beyond as far as amenities, comfort and cleanliness is concerned. Exceptionally friendly and helpful staff, too. The S$18 dorm beds include breakfast and free internet access. Very popular, so advanced booking is a good idea. 4–7

**InnCrowd Hostel II** 73 Dunlop St ⓣ6296 9169, ⓦwww.the-inncrowd.com. Just around the corner from the original, this place is just as well run with spotless common areas and comfortable dorm beds. 4–7

**Kerbau Hotel** 54–62 Kerbau Rd ⓣ6297 6668. Friendly hotel, if starting to show its age a little. The tidy and welcoming rooms all have TV. 6

**Perak Lodge** 12 Perak Rd ⓣ6299 7733, ⓦwww.peraklodge.com. Located in a back street behind the Little India arcade, the *Perak Lodge* is one of the new breed of upper-bracket guesthouses which looks like it's trying to discourage the budget traveller. The rooms are secure, well appointed and welcoming, and the price includes breakfast. Internet access available. 8

**Prince of Wales** 101 Dunlop St ⓣ6299 0130, ⓦwww.pow.com.sg. Cheap backpackers option with a great bar and live music most nights. The rooms are a little small and scruffy, but as one of the cheapest options in the area, this shouldn't phase the hardcore backpacker. Dorms S$18. 6

### Between Bras Basah Road and Rochor Road

Rochor Rd and the western part of the Rochor Canal broadly divide Little India and the Arab Quarter from the old-time backpacker centres of Bencoolen St and the southern part of Beach Rd. There are still some good options in Bencoolen St, while Beach Rd boasts a mixture of charismatic old Chinese hotels and smart new guesthouses. See map pp.720–721.

**Ah Chew Hotel** 496 North Bridge Rd ⓣ6837 0356. Simple and a bit grubby but functional enough rooms in a good location. Doubles up as a resthouse for overseas contracted workers so space can be a problem. Despite its address, it's just around the corner from North Bridge Rd, on Liang Seah St. 4

**Backpacker Cozy Corner** 3rd Floor, 490 North Bridge Rd ⓣ6338 8826, ⓦwww.cozycornerguest.com. Formerly *Waffles Home*

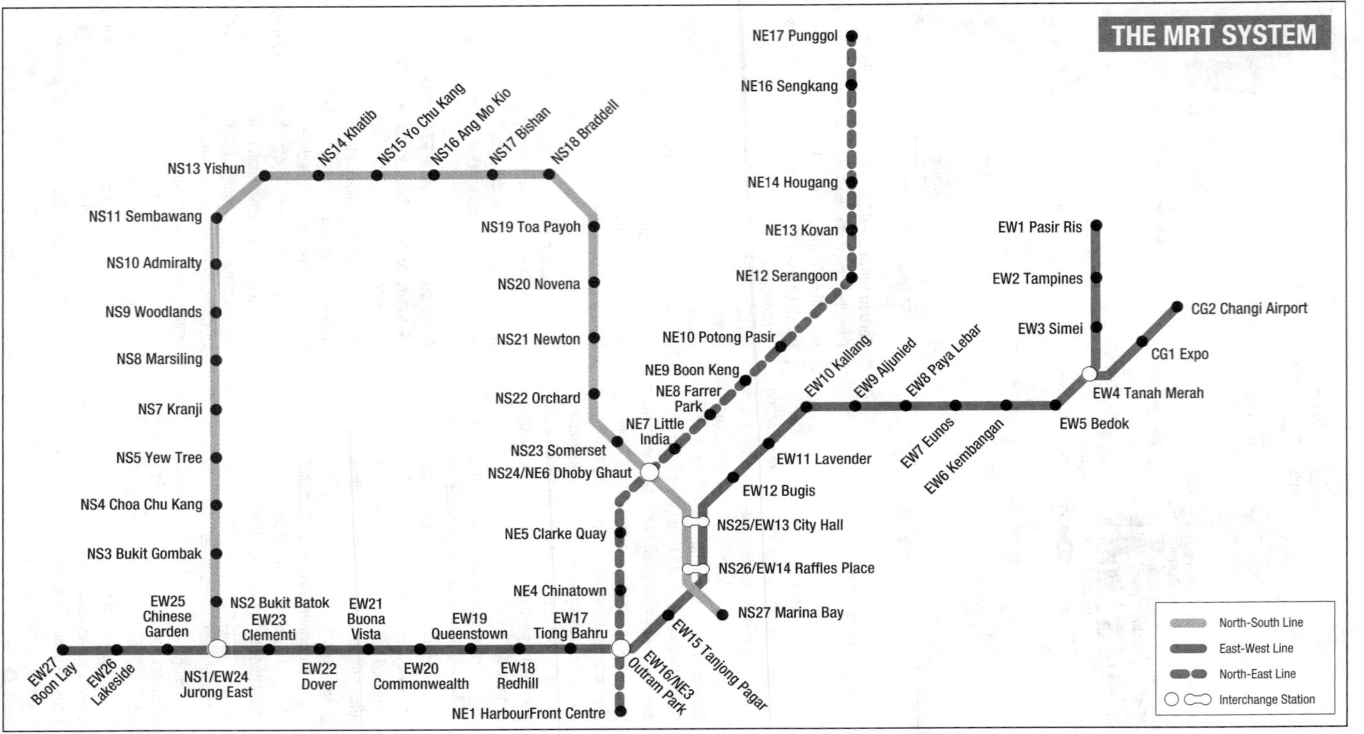
THE MRT SYSTEM
NE17 Punggol
NE16 Sengkang
NE14 Hougang
NE13 Kovan
NE12 Serangoon
NE10 Potong Pasir
NE9 Boon Keng
NE8 Farrer Park
NE7 Little India
NS13 Yishun
NS14 Khatib
NS15 Yo Chu Kang
NS16 Ang Mo Kio
NS17 Bishan
NS18 Braddell
NS11 Sembawang
NS10 Admiralty
NS9 Woodlands
NS8 Marsiling
NS7 Kranji
NS5 Yew Tree
NS4 Choa Chu Kang
NS3 Bukit Gombak
NS2 Bukit Batok
NS19 Toa Payoh
NS20 Novena
NS21 Newton
NS22 Orchard
NS23 Somerset
NS24/NE6 Dhoby Ghaut
NE5 Clarke Quay
NE4 Chinatown
NE1 HarbourFront Centre
EW1 Pasir Ris
EW2 Tampines
EW3 Simei
CG2 Changi Airport
CG1 Expo
EW4 Tanah Merah
EW5 Bedok
EW6 Kembangan
EW7 Eunos
EW8 Paya Lebar
EW9 Aljunied
EW10 Kallang
EW11 Lavender
EW12 Bugis
NS25/EW13 City Hall
NS26/EW14 Raffles Place
NS27 Marina Bay
EW15 Tanjong Pagar
EW16/NE3 Outram Park
EW17 Tiong Bahru
EW18 Redhill
EW19 Queenstown
EW20 Commonwealth
EW21 Buona Vista
EW22 Dover
EW23 Clementi
NS1/EW24 Jurong East
EW25 Chinese Garden
EW26 Lakeside
EW27 Boon Lay
North-South Line
East-West Line
North-East Line
Interchange Station

## USEFUL BUS ROUTES

Note that many of the services heading out of the centre from the Orchard Road area actually leave from Penang Road or Somerset Road.

**#2** passes along Eu Tong Sen Street (in Chinatown) and Victoria Street (past the Arab Quarter) en route to Changi Prison and Changi Village.

**#7** runs along Orchard Road, Bras Basah Road and Victoria Street; its return journey takes in North Bridge Road, Stamford Road, Penang Road and Somerset Road en route to Holland Village.

**#36** loops between Orchard Road and Changi Airport.

**#65** terminates at the HarbourFront Centre, after passing down Jalan Besar, Bencoolen Street, Penang Road and Somerset Road.

**#97** runs along Stamford Road to Little India, then on to Upper Serangoon Road; returns via Bencoolen Street and Collyer Quay.

**#103** runs between New Bridge Road terminal (Chinatown) and Serangoon Road (Little India).

**#124** connects Scotts Road, Orchard Road and North Bridge Road with South Bridge Road, Upper Cross Street and New Bridge Road in Chinatown; in the opposite direction, travels along Eu Tong Sen Street, Hill Street, Stamford Road and Somerset Road.

**#139** heads past Tai Gin Road, via Dhoby Ghaut, Selegie Road, Serangoon Road and Balestier Road.

**#167** passes down Scotts Road, Orchard Road and Bras Basah Road, Collyer Quay, Shenton Way and Neil Road (for Chinatown).

**#170** starts at the Ban San terminal at the northern end of Queen Street, passing Bukit Timah Nature Reserve and Kranji War Cemetery on its way to Johor Bahru in Malaysia.

**#190** is the most direct service between Orchard Road and Chinatown, via Scotts Road, Orchard Road, Bras Basah Road, Victoria Street, Hill Street and New Bridge Road; returns via Eu Tong Sen Street, Hill Street, Stamford Road, Penang Road, Somerset Road and Scotts Road.

*Stay*. Recommended crashpad. Breakfast and internet included, friendly staff and discounts if you introduce new guests. Good notice boards. Dorms S$14. ❸

**City Bayview** 30 Bencoolen St ⓣ6337 2882, ⓦwww.bayviewhotels.com. One of Bencoolen Street's smarter hotels, with very comfortable rooms, a compact rooftop swimming pool and a friendly, modern café. ❾

**Hawaii Hostel** 2nd Floor, 171b Bencoolen St ⓣ6338 4187, ⓦwww.hawaiihostel.com.sg. Welcoming staff maintain small, tidy, a/c rooms. Considering its location, the S$14 dorms are not a bad option. ❺

**Hotel 81** 41 Bencoolen St ⓣ6336 3611, ⓦwww.hotel81.com.sg. Part of the ever-growing *Hotel 81* chain. Bare but safe rooms and overpriced for the services provided. Synonymous with room rental by the hour. A good option if the smarter Bencoolen hotels are all full. ❼

**New 7th Storey Hotel** 229 Rochor Rd ⓣ6337 0251, ⓦwww.nsshotel.com. Classy, tastefully furnished rooms at a fraction of what you'd pay elsewhere. Spotless dorms have a/c and TV, and even a deluxe double won't break the bank. An old-fashioned elevator running down the middle of the hotel adds a touch of sophistication. Dorms S$18. ❺

**Peony Mansions Travellers' Lodge** 2nd Floor, 131a Bencoolen St ⓣ6334 8697. Singapore's classic guesthouse address, a cluster of establishments shoehorned into several floors of a decrepit apartment building. The rent increase seems to have affected *Peony Mansions* and the number of rooms available has been reduced. ❹

**Raffles Hotel** 1 Beach Rd ⓣ6337 1886, ⓦwww.raffleshotel.com. The flagship of Singapore's tourism industry, *Raffles* takes shameless advantage of its reputation but is still a beautiful place, dotted with frangipani trees and palms, and the suites are as tasteful as you would expect at these prices. ❾

**South East Asia Hotel** 190 Waterloo St ⓣ6338 2394, ⓦwww.seahotel.com.sg. Spotless doubles with a/c, TV and phone. Downstairs is a vegetarian restaurant serving Western breakfasts. ❼

**Strand Hotel** 25 Bencoolen St ⓣ6338 1866, ⓦwww.strandhotel.com.sg. A smart, central hotel.

Rooms and staff are welcoming, but a rent increase has had a dramatic effect on prices. 8

**Waterloo Hostel** 55 Waterloo St, Catholic Welfare Building, 04-02 ⓣ6336 6555, ⓦwww.waterloohostel.com.sg. Large but characterless rooms at decent rates. Despite the central locality, this hostel lacks the ambience and warmth of surrounding spots. For better or worse, quiet in the evenings. 7

### Chinatown and around

Despite being such a big tourist draw, Chinatown doesn't have a lot of budget accommodation. The places listed below are marked on the map on pp.716–717.

**Dragon Inn** 18 Mosque St ⓣ6222 7227. Sizeable, comfortable double rooms in the middle of Chinatown, all with a/c, TV, fridge and bathroom, and set in attractive shop-houses. 7

**New Majestic Hotel** 31–37 Bukit Pasoh Rd ⓣ6222 3377, ⓦwww.newmajestichotel.com. Incredibly clean and friendly hotel. All rooms have a/c and private bathrooms, while those at the front boast little balconies. Room rates include American-style breakfast. 9

### Orchard Road and around

Sumptuous hotels abound in the Orchard Rd area (see map on pp.722–723), with most double rooms here costing at least S$100.

**Holiday Inn Park View** 11 Cavenagh Rd ⓣ6733 8333, ⓦwww.holidayinn.com. Smart hotel with all the trimmings, across the road from Singapore's presidential residence. 9

**Lloyd's Inn** 2 Lloyd Rd ⓣ6737 7309, ⓦwww.lloydinn.com. Motel-style building boasting attractive rooms and a fine location, just 5min from Orchard Rd. 7

**Mitre Hotel** 145 Killiney Rd ⓣ6737 3811. Ramshackle old Chinese hotel, set amid overgrown grounds, and with an endearingly shabby air about it; there's a great lobby bar downstairs. 4

**YMCA International House** 1 Orchard Rd ⓣ6336 6000, ⓦwww.ymcaih.com.sg. Plush but overpriced rooms and dorms, with a rooftop pool and a branch of *McDonald's* linked to the lobby. Rooms seem expensive for such an organization, but this may be down to the prime location. Dorms start at S$48. 8

## Eating

### Breakfast, brunch and snacks

Western breakfasts are available, at a price, at all bigger hotels, most famously at the *Fullerton* or *Raffles*. For a really cheap fry-up, you can't beat a Western food stall in a hawker centre, where S$8 buys steak, chops and sausage. The classic Chinese breakfast is *congee*, a watery rice porridge augmented with strips of meat, though *dim sum* tend to be more palatable to Western tastes.

> TREAT YOURSELF
>
> **Champagne Brunch at The Fullerton** Fullerton Hotel, 581 Orchard Rd ⓣ6737 2233. Admittedly at around S$140 this might mean you can't afford to eat again in Singapore, but it is still worth every penny. Free-flowing delicacies include lobster, kobe beef, oysters – all washed down with litres of champagne and orange juice. Head over to the Post Bar for a Bloody Mary if you have any change. Reservations are essential. Sun 11.30am–2.30pm only.

**Bread Talk** The Paragon, B1-11/12, Orchard Rd ⓣ6733 4434. The *Bread Talk* chain has over twenty stores across Singapore. An ideal spot for some food on the go, the hi-tech bakery offers delicious sweet and savoury snacks at an affordable price. Several other bakery chains have recently sprung up but none of them are in the same league.

**De Boa (HK) Restaurant** 42 Smith St, Chinatown. Right opposite the Chinatown Complex, this smashing little coffee shop offers *dim sum*, *pow* and Chinese tea. Daily 7.30am–5pm.

**Mr Bean's Café** 30 Selegie Rd, Colonial District. Based in the same wedge-shaped colonial building as the Selegie Arts Centre, *Mr Bean's Café* draws a crowd with its muffins, croissants, toast and coffee.

**Spinelli Coffee Company** 01–15 Bugis Junction Shopping Centre, 230 Victoria St, Colonial District. San Francisco-based franchise riding on the local mania for fresh coffee; the narrow bar is ideal for a quick espresso.

**Tiffin Rooms** *Raffles Hotel*, 1 Beach Rd, Colonial District ⓣ6412 1190. Have your buffet breakfast here and you won't eat again until dinner; S$35 per adult, children S$20. Daily 7–10am.

**Yasinn Restaurant** 945 Bencoolen St, Colonial District. Does a roaring trade in *roti pratha* each morning; the *murtabak* also has plenty of devotees.

### Hawker centres and food courts

The unprepossessing, functional buildings that house most **hawker centres** tend to get extremely hot, so an increasing number of smaller, a/c **food courts** are popping up, where eating is a slightly more civilized, if less atmospheric, affair. Hawker centres and food courts are open from lunchtime through to dinnertime and sometimes beyond. Avoid the peak lunching (12.30–1.30pm) and dining (6–7pm) periods, and you should avoid a confrontation with a band of hungry Singaporean ties.

**Amoy Food Court** Corner of Telok Ayer and Amoy sts. A huge range of dishes, all cheap and delicious. Check out *Bake Of* on the top floor; try to find a better muffin in Southeast Asia.

**Food Junction** B1, Seiyu Department Store, Bugis Junction Shopping Centre, 200 Victoria St, Colonial District. Buzzing, newly renovated food court where Thai and Japanese cuisines are represented, as are *nasi padang* (highly spice Sumatran cuisine) and claypot options.

**Kopitiam** Corner of Bencoolen St and Bras Basah Rd, Colonial District. Glitzy hawker centre gleaming with chrome and neon, where the food is as colourful and varied as the furniture.

**Lau Pa Sat Festival Market** 18 Raffles Quay. The smartest hawker stalls in Singapore and open around the clock. Try the mutton curry set meal at *Andhra Curry* (stall 3). S$4 has never tasted so good.

**Orchard Emerald Food Court** Basement, Orchard Emerald, 218 Orchard Rd. Smart food court where the Taiwanese counter is the pick of a varied bunch.

**Picnic Food Court** Scotts Shopping Centre, 6 Scotts Rd, off Orchard Rd. Squeaky clean, and with lots of choice.

**Satay Club** Clarke Quay, Singapore River. A Singapore institution not to be missed, serving inexpensive chicken and mutton satay. Open evenings only, from around 7pm.

## Chinese restaurants

**Ban Seng** B1–44 The Riverwalk, 20 Upper Circular Rd, Chinatown ⓣ6534 3435. Traditionally prepared Teochew dishes, including steamed crayfish, braised goose and stuffed sea cucumber; mid-priced.

**Din Tai Fung** The Paragon, Orchard Rd ⓣ6291 2350. Conveniently located *dim sum* restaurant in the heart of Orchard Rd. Great place to take a break from shopping and all the food is reasonably priced. The Paragon arm is just one of several *Din Tai Fung* restaurants dotted around the island.

**Kwan Yim Vegetarian Restaurant** 190 Waterloo St, near Bencoolen St, Colonial District ⓣ6338 2394. A huge display of sweet and savoury *pow* is the highlight of this unfussy veggie establishment. Daily 8.30am–9pm.

**Mitzi's** 24–26 Murray Terrace, Chinatown ⓣ6222 0929. The cracking Cantonese food in this simple place, situated in a row of restaurants known as "Food Alley", draws the crowds, so be prepared to wait in line. Two can eat for S$30, drinks extra. Daily 11.30am–3pm & 5.30–10pm.

**The Teahouse at China Square** 145 Telok Ayer St, China Square Food Court, Level 3, Chinatown ⓣ6533 0660. Authentic Cantonese food served on old-fashioned trollies. Try their delicious and traditional *dim sum*, or go out on a limb and take on the jelly fish and sea cucumber. Not for the faint hearted. Tues–Sun 10am–9pm.

**Yet Con** 25 Purvis St, off Beach Rd ⓣ6337 6819. Cheap and cheerful, old-time Hainanese restaurant: try "crunchy, crispy" roast pork with pickled cabbage and radish, or S$10 buys classic chicken rice, washed down with barley water, to feed two. Daily 10.30am–9.30pm.

## Indian restaurants

**Anna Lakshmi** 133 New Bridge Rd, B1-02, Chinatown Point ⓣ6339 9993. Terrific North and South Indian vegetarian food, all the profits from which go to an Indian cultural association. Many of

### CHINESE FOOD

The majority of the **Chinese** restaurants in Singapore are Cantonese, from Guangdong in southern China, though you'll also come across northern Beijing (or Peking) and western Szechuan cuisines, as well as the Hokkien specialities of the southeastern province of Fujian, and Teochew dishes from the area east of Canton. Whatever the region, it's undoubtedly the real thing – Chinese food as eaten by the Chinese – which means it won't always sound particularly appealing to foreigners: the Chinese eat all parts of an animal, from its lips to its undercarriage. Fish and seafood is nearly always outstanding, but for something a little more unusual, try a steamboat, a Chinese-style fondue filled with boiling stock in which you cook meat, fish, shellfish, eggs and vegetables; or a **claypot** – meat, fish or shellfish cooked over a fire in an earthenware pot. In many Cantonese restaurants (and in other regional restaurants, too), lunch consists of **dim sum** – steamed and fried dumplings served in little bamboo baskets.

the staff are volunteers from the Hindu community, so your waiter might just be a doctor or a lawyer. Dishes from S$10. Mon 6–10pm, Tues–Sun 11am–10pm.

**Banana Leaf Apollo** 54–58 Race Course Rd, Little India ⓣ6293 8682. Pioneering fish-head-curry restaurant where South Indian dishes are all served on banana leaves. Reckon on S$40 for two people. Daily 10.30am–10pm.

**Islamic Restaurant** 791–797 North Bridge Rd, Arab Quarter ⓣ6298 7563. Muslim restaurant serving the best traditional chicken *biriyani* in Singapore. S$10 for two. Daily 10am–10pm.

**Komala Villas** 76–78 Serangoon Rd, Little India ⓣ6293 6980. A cramped, inexpensive and popular vegetarian establishment specializing in fifteen varieties of *dosai*. The vegetarian *thali* is justifiably popular, featuring various curries, pickles and condiments spread across a huge banana leaf, and served with rice. Daily 7am–10pm.

**Madras New Woodlands** 12–14 Upper Dickson Rd, Little India ⓣ6297 1594. Recommended, canteen-style place serving decent vegetarian food at bargain prices (there's an upmarket sister operation in nearby Belilios Lane). *Thali* set meals from around S$5. Daily 8am–11pm.

**Our Village** 46 Boat Quay (top floor). Our Village is one of the few eateries worth visiting on Boat Quay. Located on the roof of one of the shop houses, the restaurant serves up the best view of Boat Quay alongside some decent Indian and Sri Lankan food. There are definitely cheaper and better Indian restaurants in Singapore, but *Our Village* is hard to beat on a warm, balmy night.

### Southeast Asian restaurants

**Blue Ginger** 97 Tanjong Pagar Rd, Chinatown ⓣ6222 3928. Trendy Peranakan restaurant offering *ikan masal assam gulai* (mackerel simmered in a tamarind and lemongrass gravy), and *ayam buah keluak* – braised chicken with Indonesian black nuts. Daily noon–2.30pm & 6.30–10.30pm.

**Cuppage Thai Food Restaurant** 49 Cuppage Terrace, behind Centrepoint Shopping Centre, off Orchard Rd ⓣ6734 1116. Cheap and cheerful restaurant serving quality Thai dishes at around the S$8 mark. Daily 6–11pm.

**Dahlia Cafe** 68 Bussorah St, near Arab St ⓣ6297 7472 Authentic Indonesian-influenced Malay food at very reasonable prices. Either stick to the simple but delicious assortment of curries or go out on a limb and try the lamb's lung. The restaurant gets busy around lunch time so you should plan accordingly.

**House of Sundanese Food** 75 Boat Quay, Singapore River ⓣ6534 3775; and Suntec City Mall ⓣ6345 5020. Spicy salads and barbecued seafood characterize the cuisine of Sunda (West Java). Try the tasty *ikan sunda* (grilled fish) – an S$18 fish serves two to three people. Mon–Fri 11am–2pm & daily 6–10pm.

**IndoChine Waterfront** Asian Civilization Museum, 1 Empress Place ⓣ6339 1720. Looking over the Singapore River, there is no doubt that this is one of the best located restaurants in Singapore. The Indochinese food is reasonable, as are the prices, but you are really there for the ambience and view. There several other restaurants from the same chain scattered around the prime locations of Singapore.

**Lemon Grass** The Hereen Bldg, 260 Orchard Rd ⓣ6736 1998. Thai cuisine that tends to be on the sweet side, but nice ambience and snappy service. Daily 3–11pm.

### American and international food

**Altazzag Egyptian Restaurant** 24 Haji Lane, Arab Quarter ⓣ6295 5024. Authentic Egyptian food down a quiet, narrow street in the Arab quarter. Ideal stop for a quick snack and drink before continuing on with your tour.

**Don Noodle Bistro** 01-16 Tanglin Mall, Tanglin Rd, on the way out to the Botanic Gardens ⓣ6738 3188. Something of a paradox: a Western-style take on the noodle bar, imported back to the East with a non-country-specific menu. Daily 11.30am–10.30pm.

**The French Stall** 544 Serangoon Rd ⓣ 6299 3544. Excellent French restaurant located in the heart of Little India. The chef and manager are both French and know how to cook a steak. Despite the odd location, it is not uncommon to hear thick Parisian accents discussing (and enjoying) the finer sides of life. Incredible selections of desserts including a profiterole the size of a football.

**Seah Street Deli** *Raffles Hotel*, 1 Beach Rd ⓣ6412 1816. New York-style deli boasting some of the most mountainous sandwiches in Asia, at around S$10 each. Daily 11am–10pm, Fri & Sat until 11pm.

## Nightlife

Singapore's burgeoning **bar and pub** scene means there's a wide range of drinking holes to choose from, with the Colonial District, Boat Quay and Orchard Rd areas offering particularly good pub-crawl potential. More and more bars are turning to **live music** to woo punters, though this is usually no more than cover versions performed by local bands. **Clubs** also do brisk business; glitzy yet unpretentious, they feature the latest imported pop, rock and dance music, though don't expect anything like a rave scene – Ecstasy isn't in the Singaporean dictionary.

## Bars and pubs

It's possible to buy a small glass of beer in most bars and pubs for around S$8, but prices can be double or treble that, especially around Orchard Rd or on the Quays. During happy hour in the early evening, bars offer local beers and house wine either at half price, or "one for one" – you get two of whatever you order, but one is held back for later. Most places close around 2am.

**Balaclava** Suntec City Convention Centre T 6339 1600. Don't be put off by the location, as this stylish place is worth seeking out for its unique ambience. Can get very crowded on weekends. Daily noon–2am.

**Bar and Billiards Room** *Raffles Hotel*, 1 Beach Rd. A Singapore Sling (S$25), in the colonial elegance of the hotel where it was invented in 1915, is required drinking on a visit to Singapore. Daily 11.30am–midnight.

**BQ Bar** 39 Boat Quay T 6536 9722, W www.bqbar.com. Well-located bar in the heart of Boat Quay. Get there early to enjoy happy hour prices on the river. Mon & Tues 11am–1am, Wed–Fri 11am–3am, Sat 5pm–4am.

**Bungy Bar** 01-07 Traders Market, River Valley Rd T 63395707 W www.bungybar.com. Located at the end of Clarke Quay, Bungy Bar serves as a good outdoor drinking hole. Pluck up the Dutch courage to have a ride on the onsite Reverse Bungy (S$40). Daily 11am–3am.

**China One** Block 3E River Valley Rd, 02-01, (upstairs), Clark Quay T 6339 0280 W www.baize.com.sg. Clarke Quay's best bar, playing decent rock music on the turntable between live sessions by various bands. Start the night with a relaxed game of pool in either of the bar's two pool halls. Open till late.

**Harry's Quayside** 28 Boat Quay T 6538 3029. Live jazz Tues–Sat, with an all-day happy hour on Monday, when a Latin band adds to the fun.

**Ice Cold Beer** 9 Emerald Hill, off Orchard Rd T 6735 9929. Noisy, hectic and happening place, very popular with expats – and the beer really is ice cold. Daily 5pm–2am; happy hour daily until 9pm.

**Loof** Odeon Towers Extension Rooftop, 331 North Bridge Rd, 03-07 T 6338 8035. A trendy rooftop bar overlooking the famous *Raffles Hotel*. Relaxed Zen decor and an assortment of cocktails make it a hot spot for Singapore's hipster crowd. Sun–Thurs 5pm–1.30am, Fri & Sat 5pm–3am.

**Insomnia** 82a/b30 Victoria, 01-21, CHIJMES T 6338 6883. The best bar in CHIJMES, offering affordable beer and live music. Wed nights prove particularly popular with very reasonable all-you-can-drink options for both men and women. Sun–Tues 11am–3am, Wed–Sat 11am–5am. Happy hour 11am–9pm.

**Muddy Murphy's** Orchard Hotel Arcade, Orchard Rd T 6735 0400. One of those prefab Irish pubs that gets better with each pint of Guinness. Very friendly staff and a good mix of both expats and locals. Daily 5pm–2am; happy hour until 9pm.

## Clubs

Singapore's clubs have become increasingly sophisticated in recent years: European and American dance music dominates and many feature live cover bands. Clubs tend to open around 9pm, and can stay open until 5 or 6 in the morning. Most clubs have a cover charge of S$10–30, although this is usually less for women. Singapore also has a plethora of extremely seedy, extortionately priced hostess clubs, worked by [illegible]e hostesses.

**Attica** 3A River Valley Rd, 01-03, Clark Quay T 6333 9973, W www.attica.com.sg. One of Singapore's most popular clubs with the expat crowd. The outside bar offers a welcome alternative to the chaos of the dance floor. Not for the faint-hearted, Attica is generally still pumping at 6am.

**Ministry of Sound (MOS)** Block 3, The Cannery, Clark Quay T 62352292 W www.ministryofsound.com.sg. The London-based nightclub arrived in Singapore in 2005 and the long lines and busy bars suggest it is still as popular as the day it opened. Guest DJs, sophisticated light shows and a diverse music range attract both locals and foreigners.

**St James' Power Station** 3 Sentosa Gateway T 6270 7676, W www.stjamespowerstation.com. A revolution in clubbing. The refurbished power station has been converted into an insomniac's dream; with more than six bars and clubs under one roof, punters can move between salsa, canto pop and R&B without getting wet. The beauty of the Power Station? One cover-charge gives you free reign the whole night. A good option after soaking up the Sentosa beaches.

**Thumper** Located in the *Goodwood Park Hotel* on Scotts Rd (off Orchard Rd). *Thumper* boasts some of the best bartenders, and cocktails, in Singapore. The restaurant-cum-club offers more space than some of Singapore's other big clubs and the understated ambience makes it a popular spot for Singapore's top international models.

**Zouk** 17–21 Jiak Kim St ⓣ6738 2988. Still one of Singapore's trendiest venues, with different-themed sub-clubs within the club to keep things interesting. DJs from Europe and the US often guest here. There is a substantial cover charge to keep out the riff raff. Happy hour 11pm–midnight; open Tue–Sat 9pm–3am.

## Entertainment

In an effort to increase tourism, the Singaporean government is making a conscious effort to turn Singapore into the arts capital of Southeast Asia. Along with the opening of the Esplanade Theatre, more and more funky music bars are opening up in popular night spots. All this compliments Singaporeans' obsession with cinema, reflected by the thirty plus cineplexes around the island, two of which are located in the bustling malls of Orchard Rd.

### Cinema

**Gold Class Cinemas** For those prepared to part with a little more cash (S$30) it is well worth checking out one of the two Gold Class Cinemas (ⓦwww.gv.com.sg) at either Golden Village Vivocity (Harbour Front MRT) or Golden Village Grand (located within Great World City). Here you can watch the latest blockbuster hits from the comfort of a first class reclining chair. Try to stay awake long enough to order food and drinks (alcohol included) from one of the roaming servers.

### Live music

**Timbre** The Arts House, 1 Old Parliament Lane, #01-04, ⓦwww.timbre.com.sg. A good alternative to the crowded bars of Boat Quay on the other side of the river. The trendy but mellow bar plays live music every night except Sun. A great spot to grab a pizza and listen to some of Singapore's finest up-and-coming musicians playing a healthy mix of their own creations and some classic covers.

### Theatre

**Esplanade Theatre** 1 Esplanade Drive ⓣ6828 8377, ⓦwww.esplanade.com Its arrival has breathed some much needed life into Singapore's theatre scene. With more than eight venues within the two domes, there is something going on every night, including plays from Europe, Australia and other parts of Asia. Check out listings on the Esplanade website for the full lowdown.

**Repertory Theatre** DBS Arts Centre, 20 Merbau Rd near Clarke Quay ⓦwww.srt.com.sg. This understated, refurbished warehouse shows some of the best international and local plays in Singapore, however you need to keep checking the website as plays come and go without much notice. There is also a sprinkling of smart bars and restaurants in the vicinity.

## Shopping

For many stopover visitors, Singapore is synonymous with **shopping**, though prices aren't rock bottom across the board. Good deals can be found on watches, cameras, electrical and computer equipment, fabrics and antiques, however, many other articles offer no substantial saving. The free monthly, *Where Singapore*, has plenty of suggestions as to what you can buy and where. Usual **shopping hours** are daily 10am–9pm, though some shopping centres, especially those along Orchard Rd, stay open until 10pm (except CK Tang's, which closes on Sun). Note that there is a goods and services **tax** (GST) of seven percent, but tourists can claim a refund on purchases of S$300 or over at retailers displaying a blue and grey **Tax-Free Shopping** sticker. Ask retailers to draft you a Tax-Free Shopping Cheque, which you can then redeem at the airport.

### CHINESE OPERA

If you walk around Singapore's streets for long enough, you're likely to come across a wayang, or Chinese opera, played out on tumbledown outdoor stages that spring up overnight next to temples and markets, or just at the side of the road. Wayangs are highly dramatic and stylized affairs, in which garishly made-up and costumed characters enact popular Chinese legends to the accompaniment of the crashes of cymbals and gongs. Wayangs take place throughout the year, but the best time to catch one is during the Festival of the Hungry Ghosts (see p.708) when they are held to entertain passing spooks. An alternative is to pop along to the Chinese Opera Teahouse, 5 Smith Street, near the Chinatown Complex (ⓣ6323 4862), where S$30 buys you Chinese tea and an opera performance with English subtitles.

For designer clothes, tailor-made suits, sports equipment, electronic goods or antiques, head for the shopping malls of **Orchard Road** (see p.719).

**Books** Books Kinokuniya, #03-10/15 Ngee Ann City, 391 Orchard Rd, is the island's biggest bookshop. MPH shops are also well stocked, especially the flagship store on #73 Stamford Rd. For secondhand books go no further than Sunny Bookshop, #03-58 Far East Plaza on Scotts Rd.

**Camping equipment** Campers' Corner, 11 Stamford Rd.

**Computers and software** Funan the IT Mall, 109 North Bridge Rd; Square, 1 Rocher Canal Rd.

**Electronic equipment** The intersection of Bencoolen St and Rochor Rd, is known for electrical goods; also Sim Lim Square, 1 Rocher Canal Rd.

**Fabrics and silk** On Arab St (p.718), you'll find exquisite textiles and batiks, and some good deals on jewellery. From here, make a beeline for the silk stores and goldsmiths of Little India (see p.718). Also good is: Jim Thompson Silk Shop, #01-07 Raffles Hotel Arcade, 328 North Bridge Rd; Aljunied Brothers, 91 Arab St. Dakshaini Silks, 87 Serangoon Rd.

**Music** There is a four-storey HMV in the Heeran Centre on Orchard Rd. Although there are smaller shops dotted around the island, none of them can compete with HMV's prices. If you are looking for something a little different check out That CD Shop (01-01 Pacific Plaza, Scotts Rd).

**Souvenirs** As well as its souvenir shops, Chinatown (see p.715) boasts some more traditional outlets.Eng Tiang Huat, 284 River Valley Rd, for Oriental musical instruments, wayang costumes and props; Funan Stamp and Coin Agency, #03-03 Funan the IT Mall, 109 North Bridge Rd; Sai Artefacts, 18 Kerbau Rd, for ethnic furniture and Indian curios; Selangor Pewter, #02-38 Raffles City, 252 North Bridge Rd, for fine pewterwork; Singapore Handicraft Centre, Chinatown Point, 133 New Bridge Rd, with around fifty souvenir shops under one roof; Zhen Lacquer Gallery, 1 Trengganu St.

## Directory

**Airline offices** Air Canada, #02-43/46 Meridien Shopping Centre, 100 Orchard Rd ⓣ6256 1198; Air India, #17-01 UIC Building, 5 Shenton Way ⓣ6225 9411; Air New Zealand, #24-08 Ocean Building, 10 Collyer Quay ⓣ6535 8266; American Airlines, #15 Cairnhill Rd ⓣ1800/616 2113; Cathay Pacific, #16-01 Ocean Building, 10 Collyer Quay ⓣ6533 1333; Garuda, #01-68 United Sq, 101 Thomson Rd ⓣ6250 2888; KLM, #12-06 Ngee Ann City Tower A, 391a Orchard Rd ⓣ6737 7545; Lufthansa, #05-07 Palais Renaissance, 390 Orchard Rd ⓣ6245 5600; Malaysia Airlines, #02-09 Singapore Shopping Centre, 190 Clemenceau Ave ⓣ6336 6777; Philippine Airlines, #01-10 Parklane Shopping Mall, 35 Selegie Rd ⓣ6336 1611; Qantas British Airways, #15 Cairnhill Rd ⓣ6589 7000; Royal Brunei, #03-11/12 UE Square, 81 Clemenceau Ave ⓣ6235 4672; Royal Nepal Airlines, #03-09 Peninsula Shopping Centre, 3 Coleman St ⓣ6339 5535; Scandinavian Airways, #2108/10 Shaw House, 350 Orchard Rd ⓣ6235 8211; Silkair, T:6225 4488; Singapore Airlines, #08-02 Temasek Tower, 8 Shenton Way ⓣ6223 6666, and also at #02-26/28 The Paragon, 290 Orchard Rd ⓣ6224 4122; Sri Lankan Airlines, #13-01a/b, 133 Cecil St ⓣ6223 6026; Thai Airways, #02-00 The Globe, 100 Cecil St ⓣ6224 9977; Tiger Airways, T65384437; United Airlines, #01-03 Hong Leong Building, 16 Raffles Quay ⓣ6873 3533.

**Banks and exchange** All Singapore's banks change traveller's cheques. Licensed moneychangers abound on Arab St, at the Serangoon Road's Mustafa Centre, and in Orchard Road's shopping centres. American Express is at #18-01 The Concourse, 300 Beach Rd ⓣ1800/732 2244.

**Embassies and consulates** Australia, 25 Napier Rd ⓣ6737 9311; Brunei, 325 Tanglin Hill ⓣ6733 9055; Canada, #11-01 One George St ⓣ6854 5900; Indonesia, 7 Chatsworth Rd ⓣ6737 7422; Ireland, #08-06 Tiong Bahru Plaza, 298 Tiong Bahru ⓣ6276 8935; Laos, 179B, Goldhill Centre, Thompson Rd, ⓣ6250 6044; Malaysia, 301 Jervois Rd ⓣ6235 0111; New Zealand, #15-06, Ngee Ann City Tower A, 391a Orchard Rd ⓣ6235 9966; Philippines, 20 Nassim Rd ⓣ6737 3977; Thailand, 370 Orchard Rd ⓣ6737 2644; UK, Tanglin Rd ⓣ6473 9333; USA, Napier Rd ⓣ6476 9100; Vietnam, 10 Leedon Park ⓣ6462 5938.

**Hospitals** Singapore General, Outram Rd ⓣ6222 3322; Alexandra Hospital, Alexandra Rd ⓣ6473 5222; and National University Hospital, Kent Ridge ⓣ6779 5555.

**Internet** Cyberian City, #01-01 *Hotel Rendezvous*, 9 Bras Basah Rd ⓣ6883 2383; DotCom Online Services, 53 Dunlop St, Little India ⓣ6296 0760; Travel Café, 50 Prinsep St ⓣ6338 9001.

**Laundry** Washington Dry Cleaning, 2 Bukit Batok St (Mon–Sat 9am–7.45pm); Washy Washy, #01-18 Cuppage Plaza, 5 Koek Rd, off Orchard Rd (Mon–Sat 10am–7pm).

**Pharmacy** Guardian Pharmacy has over forty outlets, including ones at Centrepoint Shopping Centre, 176 Orchard Rd, and Raffles City, 252 North Bridge Rd.

**Police** Report theft at Orchard Neighbourhood Police Station, 51 Killiney Rd, off Orchard Rd (☎1800/735 9999); in an emergency, dial ☎999.

**Post office** Poste restante c/o the GPO, beside Paya Lebar MRT (Mon–Fri 8am–6pm, Sat 8am–2pm).

**Telephone services** IDD calls can be made from any public cardphone or credit-card phone.

**Travel agents** The following agents are good for discounted air fares and buying bus tickets to Malaysia and Thailand: Airpower Travel, 131a Bencoolen St ☎6334 6571; Phya Travel Service, Golden Mile Complex, 5001 Beach Rd, ☎6294 5415; STA Travel, Cuppage Terrace ☎6737 7188; Sunny Holidays, Bugis Junction, 200 Victoria St, ☎6292 7927.

## Moving on

**By bus** The easiest way across the causeway to **Malaysia** is to get the #170 Johor Bahru-bound bus from the Ban San terminal (every 15min, 6am–12.30am; S$1.20). The plusher a/c Singapore–Johor Express (every 10min, 6.30am–11.30pm) from Ban San costs S$2.40. Both buses take around an hour (including border formalities); both stop at JB bus terminal. The Singapore–Kuala Lumpur Express leaves from the Ban San terminal frequently and takes approximately six hours (S$25). For Kuala Lumpur (S$15–30) there are both morning and night departures from the Lavender St terminal. It's slightly cheaper to travel to JB and then catch an onward bus from the bus terminal there – though it still pays to make an early start from Singapore. Buses to **Thailand** leave early morning from the Golden Mile Complex at 5001 Beach Rd. You can buy a ticket all the way to Bangkok or to Hat Yai, but check the latest travel advice on southern Thailand (see box, p.883) before taking this route. Don't forget to allow two working days for securing a Thai visa (needed for stays of over thirty days).

**Destinations:** Ban San terminal to: Kuala Lumpur, Malaysia (Pudu Raya station; 7 daily; 6hr).

Golden Mile Complex to: Hat Yai, Thailand (several daily; 14hr). Lavender St terminal to: Butterworth, Malaysia (at least 2 daily; 16hr); Ipoh, Malaysia (4 daily; 10–11hr); Johor Bahru, Malaysia (every 30min; 1hr); Kota Bharu, Malaysia (at least 1 daily; 10hr); Kuala Lumpur, Malaysia (7 daily; 7hr); Kuantan, Malaysia (3 daily; 7hr); Melaka, Malaysia (9 daily; 5hr); Mersing, Malaysia (4 daily; 3hr 30min).

**By train** Trains from the Singapore Train Station on Keppel Rd run either to Kuala Lumpur or up through the interior of Malaysia to Tumpat in the northeast, near Kota Bharu. Unfortunately, none of the trains to Kuala Lumpur connects conveniently with northbound services up the west coast, including the international express to Bangkok. Singapore to Bangkok is a tiring journey done in one go, particularly if you don't book a berth on the overnight leg between Butterworth and Bangkok, but it is the quickest way (other than flying) to travel right through Malaysia.

**Destinations:** Jhor Bahru (6 daily; 1hr); Kuala Lumpur (4 daily; 7–9hr); Wakaf Bharu (for Kota Bharu; 1 daily; 13hr).

**By boat** Boats to Pulau Batam in **Indonesia**'s Riau archipelago (see p.277) depart throughout the day from the HarbourFront Centre (7.30am–7pm; S$35 one-way), docking at Sekupang, from where you take a taxi to Hangnadim Airport for internal Indonesian flights. It's also possible to travel between Singapore and **Malaysia** by boat. Reliable Ferrylink ferries depart from Changi ferry terminal for Tanjung Belungkor, in Johor, a little way east of Changi Village, leaving daily at 7.30am, 11.30am, 4pm and 8pm (45min; S$32 return; ☎6545 3600); check in one hour before departure.

**Destinations:** Changi ferry terminal to: Tanjung Belungkor (Johor Bahru), Malaysia (4 daily; 45min).

Changi Point to: Kampung Pengerang (Johor Bahru), Malaysia (hourly; 45min).

HarbourFront Centre to: Pulau Batam, Indonesia (every 30min; 40min).

Tanah Merah ferry terminal to: Pulau Bintan, Indonesia (4 daily; 1hr); Pulau Tioman, Malaysia (March–Oct 1 daily; 4hr 30min).

**By air** There are good deals on plane tickets from Singapore to Australia, Bali, Bangkok, Hong Kong and Jakarta through either Tiger Airways (Ⓦwww.tigerairways.com) or Jet Star (Ⓦwww.jetstar.com); see above, for agents. However, if you're planning to head for **Malaysia** by air, it can be cheaper going to Johor Bahru (p.557), across the causeway and buying a domestic flight from there.

**Destinations:** Kota Kinabalu, Sabah (1 daily; 2hr 30min); Kuala Lumpur, Malaysia (10 daily; 55min); Kuching, Sarawak (2 daily; 1hr 20min); Langkawi, Malaysia (3 weekly; 1hr 25min); Penang, Malaysia (at least 5 daily; 1hr 10min); Pulau Tioman, Malaysia (1 daily; 30min).

# Day-trips

Beyond the downtown area, Singapore still retains pockets of greenery in between its sprawling new towns. Most rewarding are the **Bukit Timah Nature Reserve**, and the excellent **Singapore Zoological Gardens**, both in the north of the island. Dominating the eastern tip of the island is Changi Airport and, beyond that, **Changi Village**, in whose prison the Japanese interned Allied troops and civilians during World War II. From Changi Point it's possible to take a boat to picturesque **Pulau Ubin**, a small island with echoes of pre-development Singapore. Western Singapore, notoriously the manufacturing heart of the state, is growing in popularity, boasting a quiet coastline and some open parks. It is also the home of the popular **Jurong BirdPark**.

## BUKIT TIMAH NATURE RESERVE

Bukit Timah Road shoots northwest from the junction of Selegie and Serangoon roads, arriving 8km later at the faceless town of **BUKIT TIMAH**, and then on to Singapore's last remaining pocket of primary rainforest, which now comprises **Bukit Timah Nature Reserve** (daily 8.30am–6pm; free). Tigers roamed the area in the mid-eighteenth century, but now the 81-hectare reserve provides a refuge for the dwindling numbers of species still extant in Singapore – only 25 types of mammal now inhabit the island. Creatures you're most likely to see here are long-tailed macaques, butterflies, insects and birds like the dark-necked tailorbird, which builds its nest by sewing together leaves. Scorpions, snakes, flying lemurs and pangolins (anteaters) can be found here, too. Four well-signposted, colour-coded **paths** lead out from the informative **Visitor Centre** (daily 8.30am–6pm) to the top of Bukit Timah Hill. **Bus** #171 passes down Somerset and Scotts roads en route to Bukit Timah Reserve, while the #961 can be picked up on North Bridge Road, South Bridge Road or New Bridge Road; a third option is to take the #170 from the Ban San terminal on Queen Street.

## SINGAPORE ZOOLOGICAL GARDENS AND NIGHT SAFARI

The **Singapore Zoological Gardens** (daily 8.30am–6pm; S$16.50; ⓦwww.zoo.com.sg) on Mandai Lake Road is an open zoo, where moats are preferred to cages. Though leopards, pumas and jaguars still have to be kept behind bars, this is a thoughtful, humane place, which manages to approximate the natural habitats of the animals it holds. There are over two thousand animals here, representing more than 240 species, so it's best to allow a whole day for your visit. A **tram** (S$5) circles the grounds on a one-way circuit. Highlights include the Komodo dragons, the polar bears (which you view underwater from a gallery) and the primate kingdom. You can take your pick of **animal shows**, especially enjoyable for children; there are four during weekdays, with additional performances on weekends and holidays.

Naturally enough, kids also take to the **Children's World** section of the zoo. Supposedly the largest colony of **orang-utans** from Borneo and Sumatra are here. It's also possible to go on a **Night Safari** (daily 7.30pm–midnight; S$22; ⓦwww.nightsafari.com.sg) where you can watch over a hundred species of animals – including elephants, rhinos, giraffes, leopards, hyenas, otters and incredibly cute (but shy) fishing cats – play out their nocturnal routines.

Buy the S$1 *Guide to S'pore Zoo* on arrival: besides riding and feeding times and a map, the booklet suggests itineraries that take in all the major shows and attractions. To get to the zoo, take

**bus** #171 from either Stamford Road or Orchard Boulevard to Mandai Road, then transfer to #138. Alternatively, take the MRT to Ang Mo Kio and connect with bus #138.

## CHANGI PRISON MUSEUM

Bus #2 from Victoria Street, or from Tanah Merah MRT, drops you right outside **Changi Prison**, the infamous site of a World War II POW camp in which Allied prisoners were subjected to the harshest of treatment by their Japanese jailers. The prison itself is still in use (drug offenders are periodically executed here), but on its north side, through the outer gates, is the hugely moving prison **museum** (daily 9.30am–5pm; free), where sketches and photographs plot the Japanese invasion of Singapore and the fate of the soldiers and civilians subsequently incarcerated here and in nearby camps. Beyond the museum is a replica of a simple wooden chapel, typical of those erected in Singapore's wartime prisons; its brass cross was crafted from spent ammunition casings, while the north wall carries poignant messages, penned by former POWs and relatives.

Journey's end for bus #2 is at the terminal at **CHANGI VILLAGE**, ten minutes further on from the prison. There's little to bring you out here, save to catch a boat from **Changi Point**, behind the bus terminal, for **Pulau Ubin**, or to the coast of Johor in Malaysia. The left-hand jetty is for Ubin, the right-hand one for bumboats to Johor.

## PULAU UBIN

With the recent shelving of a plan to reclaim land on **Pulau Ubin** for military use, this lazy backwater situated 2km offshore in the Straits of Johor is suddenly a fashionable destination for Singaporeans wishing to discover what their island would have been like fifty years ago. It's a great place to head for when you get tired of shops, high-rises and traffic and it's almost worth coming for the ten-minute boat trip alone, made in an old, oil-stained bumboat, which departs from Changi Point throughout the day, leaving when full (S$2 each way). The last boat back to Changi may leave as late as 11pm, but plan to be at the jetty by 8.30pm at the latest, just in case. The boats dock at **Ubin Village**, where Malay stilt houses teeter over the sludgy, mangrove beach.

The best, and most enjoyable, way to explore the dirt tracks of Ubin is by **mountain bike**, which can be rented for S$5–15 per day from Universal Adventure on the left-hand side of the road leading west from the jetty. You'll be given a baffling map of the island's labyrinthine network of tracks, though it's more fun to strike off and see where you end up – Ubin is only a small island (just 7km by 2km) so you won't get lost. Ride through the village until you come to a basketball court, where a **right turn** takes you past raised kampung houses and rubber trees to the eastern side of the island.

Turning left instead takes you to the centre of the island, past a quarry, to a rather incongruous **Thai Buddhist Temple**, complete with portraits of the King and Queen of Thailand, and murals telling the story of the life of Buddha. If you follow the **left track** out of Ubin Village for twenty or thirty minutes, you'll come to a steep slope: a right turn at the top takes you straight to the temple, just beyond which is another quarry where you can swim. Ignoring the right turn to the temple at the top of the steep slope and continuing straight ahead takes you towards the *Ubin Restaurant* (☎6543 2489), the island's best; it's a bit tricky to find, though – you'll have to look out for a taxi taking Singaporean diners there to discover which track to turn down.

## TELOK BLANGAH, THE HARBOURFRONT CENTRE AND MOUNT FABER

A twenty-minute walk west of Chinatown is the area known as **Telok Blangah**, in which stands Singapore's **HarbourFront Centre**, itself a splendid shopping centre-cum-marine terminal, where boats depart Singapore for Indonesia's Riau archipelago. Lots of buses come this way: #97 and #166 travel down Bencoolen Street; from Scotts and Orchard roads, take bus #143. You'll know when to get off, because you'll see cable cars rocking across the skyline in front of you, on their way to and from Mount Faber.

**Mount Faber** – 600m north of the HarbourFront Centre – was named in 1845 after Government Engineer Captain Charles Edward Faber; the top of the "mount" (hillock would be a better word) commands fine views of Keppel Harbour and, to the northeast, central Singapore – views that are even more impressive at night, when the city is lit up. It's a long, steep walk from Telok Blangah Road up to the top of Mount Faber – it's better to take the **cable car** from the HarbourFront Centre complex (daily 8.30am–9pm; S$8.90 return).

## JURONG BIRDPARK

The twenty hectares of land that comprise the **Jurong BirdPark** (daily 9am–6pm; S$18), on Jalan Ahmad Ibrahim in the Jurong Lake area, has more than eight thousand birds from over six hundred species, ranging from Antarctic penguins to New Zealand kiwis. This makes it one of the world's largest bird collections and the biggest in Southeast Asia. A ride on its **Panorail** (S$4) is a good way to get your bearings and the running commentary points out the attractions. Be sure at least to catch the **Waterfall Walk-in Aviary**, which allows visitors to walk among 1500 free-flying birds in a specially created patch of simulated rainforest, dominated by a thirty-metre-high waterfall.

Other exhibits to seek out are the colourful **Southeast Asian Birds**, where a tropical thunderstorm is simulated daily at noon; the **Penguin Chitchat** (feeding times 10.30am & 3.30pm); and the **World of Darkness**, a fascinating exhibit that simulates night for its nocturnal residents. The best of the **bird shows** is undoubtedly the "Kings of the Skies" (4pm) – a tour de force of speed-flying by a band of trained eagles, hawks and falcons. Entrance to this, and to the similar "World of Hawks" show (10am) and "JBP All Stars Bird Show" (11am & 3pm), is included with your ticket. To get to the BirdPark, take a ten-minute ride on **bus** #194 or #251 from the bus interchange outside Boon Lay MRT station.

## SENTOSA

Heavily promoted for its beaches, sports facilities, hotels and attractions, and ringed by a speeding monorail, the theme park island of **Sentosa**, 3km by 1km in size, is a contrived but enjoyable place. It's linked to the southern shore of downtown Singapore by a five-hundred-metre causeway and by a necklace of cable cars. Avoid coming at the weekend and don't even think about visiting on public holidays.

Two nature-oriented attractions outshine all others on Sentosa. At the **Underwater World** (daily 9am–9pm; S$17) and **Dolphin Lagoon** (daily 10.30am–6pm; S$17 for both) near monorail station 2, a moving walkway carries you along a tunnel between two large tanks: sharks lurk menacingly on all sides, huge stingrays drape themselves languidly above you and immense shoals of gaily coloured fish dart to and fro. Equally fascinating is the nearby **Butterfly Park and Insect Kingdom** (daily 9am–6pm; S$10)

### VISITING SENTOSA

Basic **admission** to Sentosa costs S$3, which includes transport to the island on the Sentosa bus that departs frequently from the **HarbourFront Centre** in Telok Blangah. You can save a buck by walking across the bridge; if you drive yourself, admission is S$2 per person plus an additional S$2 entrance fee for the car. The most spectacular way there, however, is by one of the **cable cars** (daily 8.30am–9pm) that travel between mainland Mount Faber and Sentosa, via the HarbourFront Centre. Tickets cost S$11 to S$18 per person, depending on what kind of cable car you take – the higher fare will get you a glass-bottomed car and a vertigo-inducing view. The cable car fare doesn't include the basic admission fee to the island. A cable car dining experience has recently been introduced; although it is a little pricey and the food has much to be desired. Free maps showing the various attractions and transport routes can be picked up at the main entry gate.

Sentosa's basic admission fee gives unlimited rides on the island's **monorail and bus systems** – there's a colour-coded system of four bus lines that link the island's attractions, while the monorail runs from 9am until 10pm. But the best way to get about is to **rent a bike** for the day (S$3–8 an hour, S$50 deposit) from the kiosk beside the old ferry terminal. There are lots of options for **eats** on Sentosa, including *Warung Pantai*, serving local cuisine as fast food, and even a *Burger King*.

where you can wander through a virtual blizzard of tropical butterflies, or witness the magical twinkling of thousands of fireflies. Another major-league attraction is the **Images of Singapore Exhibition** (daily 9am–7pm; S$10), near monorail station 2. Here, life-sized dioramas present the history and heritage of Singapore from the fourteenth century through to the surrender of the Japanese in 1945. The highlight is the Surrender Chambers, where audio-visuals and dioramas recount the events of World War II.

A trip up to **Fort Siloso** (monorail station 3), on the far western tip of the island, ties in nicely with a visit to the Surrender Chambers. The fort – actually a cluster of buildings and gun emplacements above a series of tunnels bored into the island – guarded Singapore's western approaches from the 1880s until 1956, but was rendered obsolete in 1942, when the Japanese invaded Singapore from the north. Today, the recorded voice of Battery Sergeant Major Cooper talks you through a mock-up of a nineteenth-century barracks, complete with living quarters, laundry and assault course.

The rest of Sentosa is crammed with less interesting options and it's probably best to head for the three **beaches** (monorail station 2 or 5, or take bus A or bus M) on its southwestern coast. Although the beaches might not compare to Malaysia or Thailand, they are still a good option if you want to escape the city haze. A new *Café Del Mar* has recently opened up on Siloso Beach. Singapore's hip crowd can usually be found lulling around the bar's swimming pool on a Sunday afternoon. The ambience makes up for the high prices and slow service.

# Thailand

## HIGHLIGHTS

**CHIANG MAI:** Thailand's trekking capital also has superb old-town temples and fine crafts

**KANCHANABURI:** sleep in a rafthouse on the River Kwai

**AYUTTHAYA:** crumbling relics of an ancient kingdom

**THE GRAND PALACE, BANGKOK:** home of the country's holiest and most dazzling temple, Wat Phra Kaeo

**KHAO SOK NATIONAL PARK:** mist-clad cliffs and whooping gibbons make for a memorable stay

**KRABI REGION:** sea-kayaking is a great way to explore the extraordinary Andaman coast

**KO LANTA:** choose from several fine beaches on this long, laid-back island

## ROUGH COSTS

**DAILY BUDGET** Basic US$15/ Occasional treat US$30

**DRINK** Singha beer (US$2)

**FOOD** *Kway tiaw pad thai* (US$1)

**HOSTEL/BUDGET HOTEL** US$5–12

**TRAVEL** Bangkok–Chiang Mai (713km): Bus 10hr, US$12–24; Train 12hr, US$28–41

## FACT FILE

**POPULATION** 64 million

**AREA** 514,000 sq km

**LANGUAGE** Thai

**RELIGIONS** Buddhism and Islam

**CURRENCY** Baht (B)

**CAPITAL** Bangkok

**INTERNATIONAL PHONE CODE** ⓣ66

**TIME ZONE** GMT +7hr

# Introduction

**With nearly twelve million foreigners flying into the country each year, Thailand is Asia's primary holiday destination and a useful and popular first stop on any overland journey through Southeast Asia. Despite the influx of tourist cash and influence, Thailand's cultural integrity remains largely undamaged. Some ninety percent of Thais are practising Theravada Buddhists, and King Bhumibol remains a revered figure. The country remains mainly traditional and rural, and though some cities boast modern high-rises and neon lights, tiered temple rooftops and saffron-robed monks still predominate.**

Most journeys start in **Bangkok**, which can be an overwhelming introduction to Southeast Asia, but there are traveller-oriented guesthouses aplenty, as well as heaps of spectacular temples to visit. A popular side-trip is to **Kanchanaburi**, home of the infamous Bridge over the River Kwai. After Bangkok, most travellers head north, sometimes via the ancient capitals of **Ayutthaya** and **Sukhothai**, to the enjoyably laid-back city of **Chiang Mai**, where they organize treks to nearby hilltribe villages. To the **northwest**, the beautiful highlands around **Mae Hong Son** and **Pai** are idyllic, while Thailand's **northeast**, its least visited region, offers ancient Khmer ruins at **Phimai** and **Phanom Rung** and is home to the country's most accessible national park, **Khao Yai**.

After trekking and temples in the north, most visitors head for the **beach**. Thailand's **eastern and southern coasts** are lined with gorgeous white-sand shores, aquamarine seas and kaleidoscopic reefs. The most popular of these are the east-coast backpacker resorts of **Ko Samet** and **Ko Chang**, the **Gulf coast islands** of Ko Samui, Ko Pha Ngan and Ko Tao, and the **Andaman coast** idylls of Laem Phra Nang, Ko Lanta, Ko Tarutao and Ko Lipe. The southern island of **Phuket** is a more expensive, package-tour-oriented spot.

## CHRONOLOGY

**c. Third or second century BC** Theravada Buddhism is introduced to the region by Indian missionaries.

**c. Sixth century AD** The Theravada Buddhist Dvaravati civilization occupies northern Thailand.

**Eighth century** Peninsular Thailand comes under the control of the Srivijaya Empire, a Mahayana Buddhist state centred on Sumatra.

**Ninth century** The Khmer Empire, based at Angkor, conquers Thailand. Their administrative centre is at modern-day Lopburi.

**1238** The Thais in the upper Chao Phraya Valley capture the Khmer outpost at Sukhothai and establish a kingdom there.

### WHEN TO VISIT

The **climate** of most of Thailand is governed by three seasons: rainy (roughly June–Oct), caused by the southwest monsoon; cool (Nov–Feb); and hot (March–May). The cool season is the most pleasant time to visit and the most popular; during the hot season, temperatures can rise to 40°C. The rainy season hits the Andaman coast (Phuket, Krabi, Phi Phi) harder than anywhere else in the country – heavy rainfall usually starts in May and persists until November. The Gulf coast (Ko Samui, Ko Pha Ngan and Ko Tao) gets much less rain from the southwest monsoon, but is also hit by the northeast monsoon, which brings rain between October and January.

**1278–99** The reign of King Ramkhamhaeng. He seizes control of much of the Chao Phraya Valley and establishes the capital of the first kingdom of Siam at Sukhothai. Following his death the empire declines.
**1351** King Ramathibodi founds the city of Ayutthaya and who adopts Angkor's elaborate court rituals. Ayutthaya prospers as a centre for trade and by 1540 it rules most of the area of modern-day Thailand.
**1568** The Burmese invade and occupy for twenty years.
**Seventeenth century** Ayutthaya makes a spectacular comeback, as its foreign trade booms, first with Portugal, then Spain, England and Holland.
**1767** Ayutthaya is recaptured by the Burmese, who raze it to the ground, take tens of thousands of prisoners and abandon the city to the jungle.
**1768** Phraya Taksin, a charismatic general, emerges out of the lawless mess, and is crowned king at his new capital of Thonburi, on the opposite bank to modern-day Bangkok. Within two years, he conquers all of Ayutthaya's territories, plus Cambodia and Laos.
**1782** Taksin is ousted in a coup led by his military commander, Chao Phraya Chakri.
**1782–1809** Chakri – reigning as Rama I – moves the capital across the river to Bangkok and builds a new royal palace and monasteries in Ratanakosin.
**1809** Rama 1's son, Rama II, succeeds the throne, securing the Chakri dynasty, still in place today.
**1851–68** The reign of Rama IV, known as Mongkut. He signs trade treaties with the British, then France and the US. By avoiding a close relationship with just one power, he protects Thailand from annexation.
**1868** Mongkut's son, fifteen-year-old Chulalongkorn (who had been educated by Mrs Anna Leonowens, subject of *The King and I*) takes the throne as Rama V.
**1893** Thailand comes under increasing pressure from Western powers, most notably during the Franco–Siamese Crisis when the French send gunboats as far as Bangkok. France claims Laos and Chulalongkorn cedes almost half of Siam's territory.
**June 24, 1932** Lawyer Pridi Phanomyong and an army major, Luang Phibunsongkhram (Phibun), lead a coup. Siam's absolute monarchy comes to an end as King Rama VII is sidelined to a symbolic position.
**1938** Phibun is elected prime minister. A year later he renames the country Thailand ("Land of the Free").
**December 8, 1941** The Japanese invade, and, after initially resisting, Phibun's government allies with Japan. Pridi secretly coordinates the resistance movement. Over 100,000 people (POWs and Asian labourers) die constructing the notorious Death Railway linking Thailand and Burma.
**January 1946** Pridi is elected prime minister.
**June 9, 1946** Rama VII's successor, King Ananda, is shot dead in his bed. Three palace servants are convicted, but the murder has never been satisfactorily explained. He is succeeded by King Bhumibol, the current king.
**April 1948** Phibun becomes prime minister, and allies with the US against the communist threat.
**1957** Phibun narrowly wins a general election, but only by vote-rigging and coercion. After a public outcry he is overthrown by army chief General Sarit, who encourages the monarchy into a more active role.
**1963** Sarit dies and is succeeded by General Thanom. The Thais, with US backing, conduct covert military operations in Laos. By 1968, around 45,000 US military personnel are in Thailand, and the economy swells with dollars. One result is the proliferation of prostitution – centred on Bangkok's Patpong district.
**1971** As a left-wing coalition gains popular support, and Muslim dissidents gain hold in the south, Thanom imposes military rule.
**October 1976** Students demonstrate in Bangkok, and hundreds are brutally beaten by the police; the military take control and suspend the constitution.
**1980** General Prem Tinsulanonda becomes prime minister, with broad popular and parliamentary support, and rules with a unique mixture of dictatorship and democracy. He stands down in 1988 to allow for a democratic prime minister.
**February 23, 1991** Prem's successor, Chatichai Choonhavan, is overthrown in a coup. General Suchinda becomes premier.
**May 1992** Mass demonstrations against Suchinda are brutally crushed, with hundreds killed or injured, but Suchinda is forced to resign when King Bhumibol expresses his disapproval.
**1997** Foreign-exchange dealers mount speculative attacks on the baht, and the currency collapses, causing a currency crisis across the region.
**2001** One of Thailand's wealthiest men, telecoms tycoon Thaksin Shinawatra, and his new party, Thai Rak Thai (Thai Loves Thai), win the elections.
**2004** Violence in the Islamic southern provinces escalates sharply, with frequent attacks on police, soldiers, and also Buddhist monks.
**September 2006** Thaksin's government is overthrown in a bloodless army coup.
**December 2007** The pro-Thaksin People Power Party wins parliamentary elections. In February 2008 Thaksin returns to Thailand to face corruption charges.

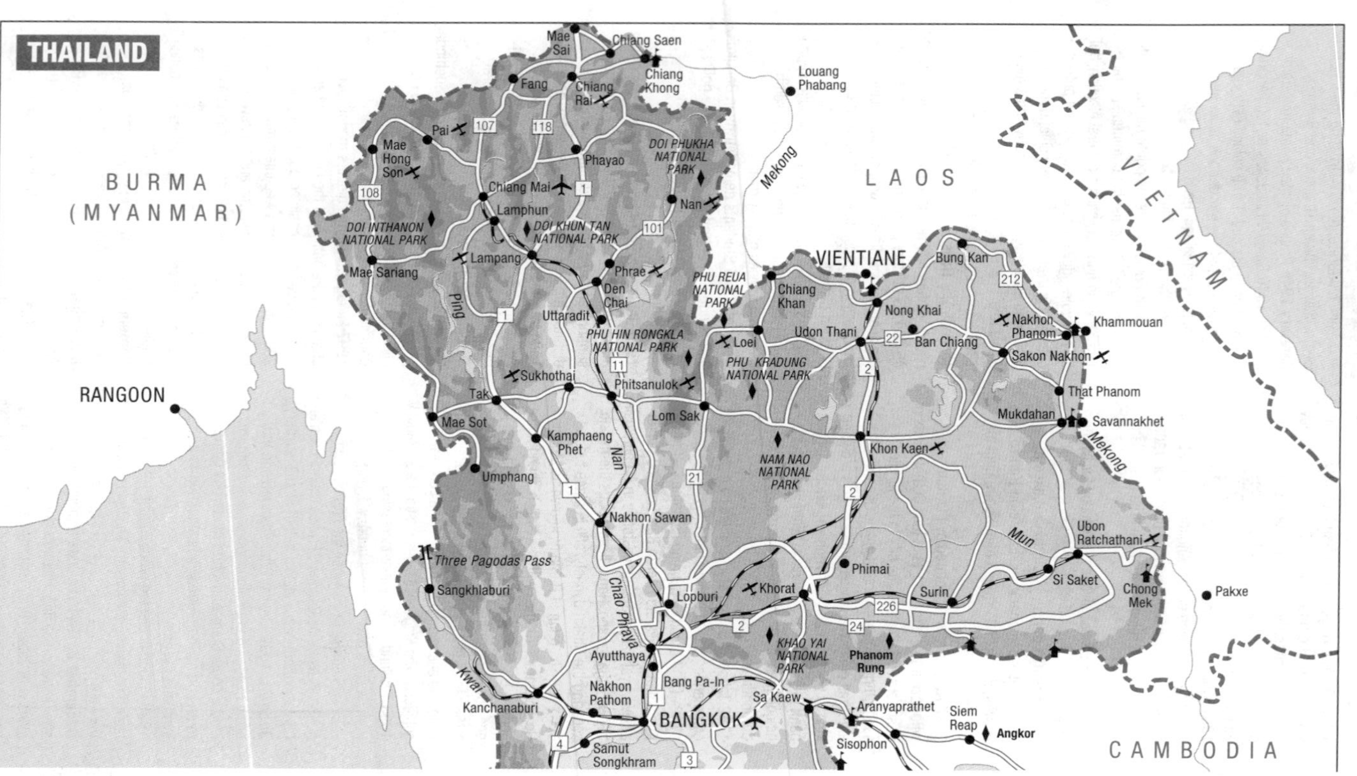
THAILAND
BURMA (MYANMAR)
LAOS
VIETNAM
CAMBODIA
RANGOON
VIENTIANE
BANGKOK
Louang Phabang
Pakxe
Khammouan
Savannakhet
Siem Reap
Angkor
Sisophon
Mekong
Mae Sai
Chiang Saen
Chiang Khong
Fang
Chiang Rai
Pai
Mae Hong Son
Phayao
Chiang Mai
Lamphun
Lampang
Mae Sariang
Nan
Phrae
Den Chai
Uttaradit
Sukhothai
Phitsanulok
Tak
Mae Sot
Umphang
Kamphaeng Phet
Lom Sak
Nakhon Sawan
Three Pagodas Pass
Sangkhlaburi
Kanchanaburi
Kwai
Ping
Nan
Chao Phraya
Mun
Lopburi
Ayutthaya
Bang Pa-In
Nakhon Pathom
Samut Songkhram
Sa Kaew
Aranyaprathet
Khorat
Phimai
Surin
Si Saket
Ubon Ratchathani
Chong Mek
Phanom Rung
Khon Kaen
Udon Thani
Loei
Chiang Khan
Nong Khai
Ban Chiang
Bung Kan
Nakhon Phanom
Sakon Nakhon
That Phanom
Mukdahan
DOI INTHANON NATIONAL PARK
DOI KHUN TAN NATIONAL PARK
DOI PHUKHA NATIONAL PARK
PHU HIN RONGKLA NATIONAL PARK
PHU REUA NATIONAL PARK
PHU KRADUNG NATIONAL PARK
NAM NAO NATIONAL PARK
KHAO YAI NATIONAL PARK
1
2
3
4
11
21
22
24
101
107
108
118
212
226

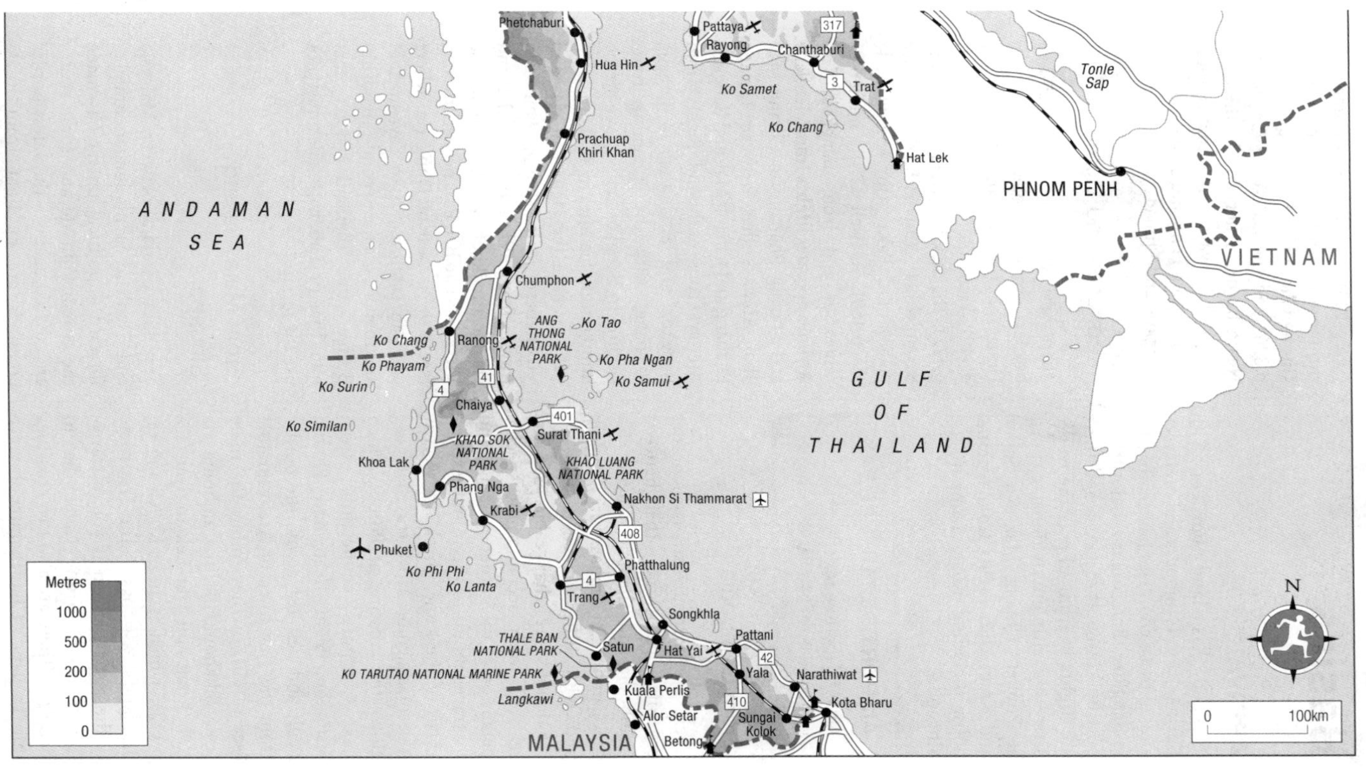
ANDAMAN SEA
GULF OF THAILAND
PHNOM PENH
VIETNAM
MALAYSIA
Tonle Sap
Phetchaburi
Hua Hin
Prachuap Khiri Khan
Pattaya
Rayong
Chanthaburi
Trat
Hat Lek
Ko Samet
Ko Chang
Chumphon
Ranong
Ko Chang
Ko Phayam
Ko Surin
Ko Similan
ANG THONG NATIONAL PARK
Ko Tao
Ko Pha Ngan
Ko Samui
Chaiya
Surat Thani
KHAO SOK NATIONAL PARK
KHAO LUANG NATIONAL PARK
Khoa Lak
Phang Nga
Krabi
Nakhon Si Thammarat
Phuket
Ko Phi Phi
Ko Lanta
Phatthalung
Trang
Songkhla
THALE BAN NATIONAL PARK
Satun
Hat Yai
Pattani
Yala
Narathiwat
KO TARUTAO NATIONAL MARINE PARK
Langkawi
Kuala Perlis
Alor Setar
Betong
Sungai Kolok
Kota Bharu
317
3
41
4
401
408
4
42
410
Metres
1000
500
200
100
0
N
0
100km

# Basics

## ARRIVAL

Thailand has **land borders** with Burma, Laos, Cambodia and Malaysia, and all these countries have embassies in Bangkok. Bangkok is a major transport hub in Southeast Asia and there are **flights** in from all over the world. There are also international airports at Phuket, Chiang Mai, Ko Samui and Krabi with flights from regional hubs, including Kuala Lumpur and Singapore.

### AIRPORT DEPARTURE TAX

Airport departure tax on international flights is B700.

### From Cambodia

There are currently six legal border crossings open to non-Thais between Cambodia and Thailand. Check with the Cambodian Embassy in Bangkok and with other travellers first, as regulations are changeable. See the relevant town accounts for specific details on all the border crossings, and for travellers' up-to-the-minute experiences of the same, check out ⓦwww.talesofasia.com. Most travellers use either the crossing at **Poipet**, which has transport connections from Sisophon, Siem Reap and Phnom Penh and lies just across the border from the Thai town of Aranyaprathet (see p.120); or they follow the route from Sihanoukville in Cambodia via Koh Kong and **Hat Lek** to Trat (see p.127), which is near Ko Chang on Thailand's east coast – the Trat route is the fastest option if you're travelling non-stop from Cambodia to Bangkok. There are also two crossings into Thailand's **Chanthaburi** province (see p.120) from Pailin in Cambodia, the more recently opened crossing at **Chong Chom** into Surin province (see p.826) and the little-used Choam–Sa Ngam border. Alternatively, there are Bangkok Airways **flights** that connect both Phnom Penh and Siem Reap with Bangkok and Phuket.

### From Laos and Vietnam

There are currently five Thai–**Lao border crossings** open to tourists: Houayxai (for Chiang Khong; see p.449); Vientiane (for Nong Khai; see p.422); Thakhek (for Nakhon Phanom; Savannakhet (for Mukdahan; see p.453); and Pakxe (for Chong Mek; see p.460). As well as the numerous routes to and from Bangkok, Lao Airlines operates **flights** from Vientiane and Louang Phabang to Chiang Mai; Thai Airways flies between Louang Phabang and Chiang Mai; and Bangkok Airways runs outbound flights from Bangkok and Sukhothai to Louang Phabang, with the incoming route landing in Bangkok only (there are no immigration facilities in Sukhothai).

If you have the right Lao visa and Vietnamese exit stamp, you can travel from **Vietnam** to Thailand via Savannakhet; you'll need to use Vietnam's Lao Bao Pass border crossing (see p.967), west of Dong Ha, where you can catch a bus to Savannakhet and then across the Second Friendship Bridge to Thailand; note that non-Thai or Lao nationals must not use the ferry.

### From Malaysia and Singapore

Travelling overland between Malaysia and Thailand is no longer straightforward – political unrest has made the crossing unsafe and some routes are advised against. The safest border crossings are by **boat** from Kuala

Perlis (which can be reached by train or bus services from Butterworth; see p.529) and Pulau Langkawi to Satun. Many people still choose to travel by **long-distance bus** from KL and Butterworth to Bangkok, Krabi, Surat Thani or Hat Yai, but these bus routes pass through volatile territory (see p.883), and most Western governments advise citizens not to do so. The same goes for the **train** routes from Singapore to Bangkok via Malaysia. Lines run along both Malaysia's east and west coasts – the former is the safer route – but at the time of writing both were inadvisable.

In addition to the numerous daily **flights** on any number of international airlines from Malaysia and Singapore to Bangkok, Bangkok Airways operates daily flights between Singapore and Ko Samui, while Phuket is served by flights from Singapore with Silk Air. There are also flights to Krabi through Thai/Air Asia from Kuala Lumpur and Tiger Airways from Singapore. Both Silk Air (3 weekly) and Tiger Air (4 weekly) operate flights from Singapore to Chiang Mai.

## VISAS

Most foreign passport holders are allowed to enter the country for **stays of up to thirty days** without having to apply for a visa, but in theory must show proof of having adequate funds while in the country (B10,000 per person). It's easy enough to get a new thirty-day pass by hopping across the border into a neighbouring country. You're only allowed to stay up to ninety days in the country over a six-month period; if you wish to stay longer you will need to visit a Thai embassy and apply for a sixty-day tourist visa. Your application – which generally takes several days to process – must be accompanied by your passport, two passport photos and evidence of travel on from Thailand (with air ticket paid in full). If you're fairly certain you want to stay longer than thirty days, you may wish to apply for the **sixty-day tourist visa** from the outset. The sixty-day visa currently costs B1000 per entry – multiple-entry versions are available, which are handy if you're going to be leaving and re-entering Thailand.

It's not a good idea to **overstay** your visa limits. Once at the airport or the border, you'll be required to pay a fine of B500 per day before you leave. And if you get involved with police or immigration officials whilst in possession of an expired visa, they're obliged to take you to court, possibly imprison you, and deport you.

Thirty-day stays can be **extended** in Thailand for a further seven days, sixty-day tourist visas for thirty days, at the discretion of officials; extensions cost B1900 and are issued within the hour over the counter at immigration offices (*kaan khao muang*) in nearly every provincial capital – most offices ask for one or two photos as well, plus two photocopies of the main pages of your passport, including your Thai arrival card and arrival stamp or visa. Many tour agents on Bangkok's Thanon Khao San offer to get visa extensions for you, but beware: they are reputedly faking the stamps.

For the latest information, see the Thai Ministry of Foreign Affairs' **website** at Ⓦwww.mfa.go.th/web/2637.php; for further, unofficial details, such as the perils of overstaying your visa, see Ⓦwww.thaivisa.com.

If you need a visa for China, you might want to apply at the consulate in Chiang Mai. Laos and Vietnam have consulates in Khon Kaen as well as in Bangkok.

## GETTING AROUND

The wide range of efficient **transport** options makes travelling around Thailand very easy and inexpensive.

## Buses, songthaews and minibuses

**Ordinary orange buses** (*rot thammadaa*) are state-run, incredibly inexpensive and cover most short-distance routes between main towns (up to 150km) very frequently during daylight hours. They can get packed and are usually quite slow because they stop frequently and often wait until they have enough passengers to make the journey worthwhile.

The **state-run blue a/c buses** (*rot air*) are faster and more comfortable, but cost up to twice as much, depart less frequently, and don't cover nearly as many routes. In a lot of cases they're indistinguishable from **privately owned a/c buses** (often known as *rot tua*), which ply the most popular long-distance routes and often operate out of government bus terminals.

On some longer routes, there are also more expensive **VIP buses**, with fewer seats and more legroom. Major private companies, such as Nakorn Chai and Win Tour, are generally reliable, but many smaller companies on the main travellers' routes, especially from Thanon Khao San to Chiang Mai and Surat Thani, have a poor reputation for service and comfort despite attracting customers with bargain fares and convenient timetables. Travellers have reported a frightening lack of safety awareness and frequent thefts from luggage on these routes, too (see p.751 for more).

**Tickets** for all buses can be bought from the departure terminals, but for ordinary buses it's normal to buy them onboard. A/c buses may operate from a separate station, and tickets for the more popular routes should be booked a day in advance. As a rough indication of **prices**, a trip from Bangkok to Chiang Mai (713km) costs B805 VIP, B518/403 by a/c bus (first/second class) and B215 by ordinary bus.

In rural areas, the bus network is supplemented or replaced by **songthaews** (see opposite). Often overloaded, cramped and uncomfortable, share taxis, in the form of **a/c minibuses**, also now feature on popular routes in the deep south, central plains and elsewhere.

## Trains

Managed by the State Railway of Thailand (SRT; Ⓦwww.railway.co.th), the **rail network** consists of four main lines and a few branch lines. **Fares** depend on the class of seat, whether or not you want a/c and on the speed of the train. Hard, wooden, third-class seats are very cheap (Bangkok–Chiang Mai B271); in second class, you can often choose between reclining seats or berths, with or without a/c, on long journeys (Bangkok–Chiang Mai B431–881); and in first class (B1353) you get a private two-person a/c compartment. Nearly all long-distance trains have dining cars. The speed supplements are as follows: Special Express (B120), Express (B80) and Rapid (B60). **Advance booking** of at least one day is strongly recommended for first- and second-class seats on all lengthy journeys, and for sleepers needs to be done as far in advance as possible; at least 24hr ahead of departure. It should be possible to make bookings at the station in any major town. The SRT has a 24-hour hotline (Ⓣ1690) and publishes clear and fairly accurate free **timetables**; the best place to get hold of one is over the counter at Hualamphong, or from their website.

## Car and motorbike rental

Nearly all tourist centres rent **cars** (B800–1400 per day) and **motorbikes** (B150–400 per day), for which a national driver's licence is usually acceptable; helmets are obligatory on bikes. Thais drive on the left, and the speed limit is 60km/hr within built-up areas and 90km/hr outside them; a major road doesn't necessarily have right of way over a minor, but the bigger vehicle always has right of way. Avoid driving at night, which can be very dangerous.

## Boats

Plenty of **boats**, in all shapes and sizes, connect the islands of southern Thailand to the mainland and each other. Large ferries with interior seating and decks often jammed with fellow sun-kissed tourists serve the bigger islands. Vehicle ferries are also common.

A rough-and-ready overnight **ferry**, equipped with roll-out beds and sheets for sleeping, connects the islands of the Ko Samui archipelago, which are also served by slick **Lomprayah Catamarans** offering speed, a/c luxury and comfortable seating (140 in total). Large, equally speedy and powerful three-engine **speedboats** (seating up to 36 people) serve most islands, except those around the Krabi and Phuket area. The most pleasurable water vessels to travel in, however, are the traditional, small, arching-timber **longtail boats** (seating up to ten), so named for their long-stick propellers that make shallow coastal navigation a doddle. Longtails cover mainland coastal, or coast to island hops and short inter-island journeys.

## Planes

Thai Airways (Ⓦwww.thaiair.com) still dominates the internal **flight** network, which extends to all parts of the country, using some two-dozen airports. Bangkok Airways (Ⓦwww.bangkokair.com), Nok Air (Ⓦwww.nokair.com), PBair (Ⓦwww.pbair.com) and One-Two-Go (Ⓦwww.fly12go.com) provide useful additional services, often at cheaper rates than Thai Airways. Book early if possible – you can reserve online with most companies – though fares generally don't fluctuate. As for **fares**, Bangkok to Chiang Mai costs B1545 with Thai Airways, B1850 with One-Two-Go, B3170 with Bangkok Air and B1490 with Nok Air. If you're planning to make lots of domestic flights, consider the **airpass** offered by Thai or Bangkok Airways – their complex conditions and prices are posted on their websites.

## Local transport

Most sizeable towns have some fixed-fare transport network of **local buses**, **songthaews** or even **longtail boats**, often with set routes, but never with rigid timetabling; within towns songthaews act as communal taxis, picking up people heading in the same direction and usually taking them to their destination, with set prices (around B10–30). It's sometimes possible to charter a whole songthaew as a private taxi (notably in Chiang Mai), though this makes it much more expensive. In most towns, you'll find the songthaew "terminal" near the market; to pick one up between destinations, just flag it down, and to indicate to the driver that you want to get out, press the bell, shout, or rap hard with a coin on the ceiling.

Named after the noise of its excruciatingly unsilenced engine, the three-wheeled open-sided **tuk-tuk** is the classic Thai vehicle. They are fast, fun and inexpensive: fares start at around B20 (B30 in Bangkok), regardless of the number of passengers. Tuk-tuks are also sometimes known as samlors ("three wheels"), but the real **samlors** are tricycle rickshaws propelled by pedal power alone. Samlors still operate in many towns, though not in Bangkok, and drivers usually charge a minimum fee of around B10, adding B10 per kilometre, possibly more for a heavy load. Even faster and more precarious than tuk-tuks, **motorbike taxis** feature both in big towns and out-of-the-way places; prices are higher but they can halve journey times during rush hour. Motorbike taxis should come with helmets for the pillion passenger.

With all types of taxi, bar Bangkok's metered taxis, always establish the fare before you get in.

## ACCOMMODATION

While the number of budget, traveller-orientated **guesthouses** in Thailand is thinning rapidly, it is still possible in most places to find simple double rooms with shared bathrooms for B150–350. If you're travelling on your own, expect to pay anything between sixty and one hundred percent of the double-room price. Checkout time is usually noon, so during high season (roughly Nov–Feb, July & Aug) you should try and arrive to check in at about 11.30am. However, waiting lists and advance bookings are becoming more common in the Christmas/New Year period, and worth attempting.

With just twenty officially registered **youth hostels** in the whole country (ⓦwww.tyha.org), it's not worth becoming a YHA member just for your trip to Thailand. There's little point in lugging a tent around Thailand either, unless you're planning an extensive tour of national parks: accommodation is generally too inexpensive to make **camping** a necessity, and anyway there are no campsites inside town perimeters; camping is allowed on nearly all islands and beaches, however. Many **national parks** offer basic hut accommodation: they aren't always cheap, but advance booking is unnecessary except on weekends and holidays; book online at ⓦwww.thaiforestbooking.com.

Few Thais use guesthouses, opting instead for Chinese–Thai-run **budget hotels**, often located near bus stations, with rooms in the B200–600 range. They're generally clean and en suite, but usually lack any communal area. Beds in these places are large enough for a couple, and it's quite acceptable for two people to ask and pay for a single room (*hong diaw*). **Mid-range hotels** (B600–1200) are often much more comfortable and come equipped with extras such as TV, fridge, a/c and pool; they generally work out to be good value.

**Electricity** is supplied at 220 volts AC and available at all but the most remote villages and basic beach huts. Several **plug** types are commonly in use, most usually with two round pins, but also with two flat-blade pins, and sometimes with both options.

## FOOD AND DRINK

Thai **food** is renowned for its fiery but fragrant dishes, flavoured with lemon grass, basil and chilli, and you can eat well and cheaply even in the smallest provincial towns. **Hygiene** is a consideration when eating anywhere in Thailand, but there's no need to be too cautious: wean your stomach gently by avoiding excessive amounts of chilli and too much fresh fruit in the first few days and always drink bottled (or boiled) water. You can be pretty sure that any noodle stall or curry shop that's permanently packed with customers is a safe bet.

### Where to eat

Throughout the country most inexpensive Thai **restaurants** specialize in one general food type or preparation method – a "noodle shop", for example, might do fried noodles and noodle soups plus a basic fried rice, but nothing else; a restaurant displaying whole roast chickens and ducks will offer these sliced or with chillies and sauces served over rice; and "curry shops" serve just that. As often as not, the best and most entertaining places to eat are the local **night markets** (*talaat yen*), where "specialist" pushcart kitchens congregate from about 6pm to 6am on permanent patches in most towns, often close to the fruit and vegetable market or the bus station. Each stall is fronted by tables and stools, and you can choose your food from wherever you like.

At a cheap stall or café, you'll get a main course for under B60, while upmarket, expensive restaurants can charge over B130.

## What to eat and drink

Thais eat **noodles** when Westerners would dig into a sandwich – for lunch, as a late-night snack or just to pass the time – and at B20–30 they're the cheapest hot meal you'll find anywhere. They come in assorted varieties (wide and flat, thin and transparent, made with eggs, soybean flour or rice flour) and get boiled up as soups, doused in sauces, or stir-fried. The usual practice is to order the dish with extra chicken, beef, pork or shrimps. The most popular noodle dish is *kway tiaw pat thai*, usually abbreviated to *pat thai*, a delicious combination of fried noodles, beansprouts and egg, sprinkled with ground peanuts and lime juice, and often spiked with dried shrimps. Fried **rice** is the other faithful standby. Although very few Thais are **vegetarian** (*mangsawirat*), you can nearly always ask for a vegetable-only fried rice or noodle dish – though many places will routinely add fish sauce as a salt substitute. All traveller-oriented restaurants are veggie-friendly.

Aside from fiery **curries** and **stir-fries**, restaurant menus often include spicy Thai **soup**, which is eaten with other dishes, not as a starter. Two favourites are *tom kha kai*, a creamy coconut chicken soup, and *tom yam kung*, a prawn soup without coconut milk. Food from the northeastern **Isaan** region is popular throughout the country, particularly sticky rice, which is rolled up into balls and dipped into chilli sauces and other side dishes, such as the local dish *som tam*, a spicy green-papaya salad with garlic, raw chillies, green beans, tomatoes, peanuts and dried shrimps. Barbecued chicken on a stick (*kai yaang*) is the classic accompaniment. Raw minced pork is the basis of another popular Isaan and northern dish called *larb*, subtly flavoured with mint and served with vegetables.

**Sweets** (*khanom*) don't really figure on most restaurant menus, but a few places offer bowls of *luk taan cheum*, a jellied concoction of lotus seeds floating in a syrup, and coconut custard (*sangkaya*) cooked inside a small pumpkin. Cakes are sold on the street and tend to be heavy, sticky affairs made from glutinous rice and coconut cream pressed into squares and wrapped in banana leaves.

Thais don't drink **water** straight from the tap, and nor should you: plastic bottles of drinking water are sold countrywide, even in the smallest villages. Night markets, guesthouses and restaurants do a good line in freshly squeezed **fruit juices** and shakes, as well as fresh coconut water and freshly squeezed sugar-cane juice, which is sickeningly sweet.

**Beer** is comparatively expensive at around B60 for a 330ml bottle; the most famous beer is the slightly acrid locally brewed Singha, but Kloster, Carlsberg and Heineken, which are also brewed locally, are more palatable. At about B60 for a 375ml bottle, the local **whisky** is a lot better value and Thais think nothing of consuming a bottle a night. The most drinkable and widely available of these is the 35 percent proof Mekhong. Sang Thip is an even stronger **rum**. Bars aren't an indigenous feature, as Thais rarely drink out without eating, but you'll find a fair number in Bangkok and the tourist centres.

# CULTURE AND ETIQUETTE

Tourist literature has so successfully marketed Thailand as the "Land of Smiles" that a lot of tourists arrive in the country expecting to be forgiven any outrageous behaviour. This is just not the case: there are some things so universally sacred in Thailand that even a hint of disrespect will cause deep offence. The worst thing you can possibly do is to bad-mouth the universally revered **royal family**. The king's anthem is always played before every film screening in the cinema, during which the audience is expected to stand up.

Thais very rarely shake hands, using the **wai**, a prayer-like gesture made with raised hands, to greet and say goodbye and to acknowledge respect, gratitude or apology. The *wai* changes according to the relative status of the two people involved: as a farang (foreigner) your safest bet is to go for the "stranger's" *wai*, raising your hands close to your chest and placing your fingertips just below your chin. Although all Thais have a first name and a family name, everyone is addressed by their first name – even when meeting strangers – prefixed by the title "**Khun**" (Mr/Ms).

Thailand shares the same attitudes to dress and social taboos as other Southeast Asian cultures (see p.45).

## SPORTS AND OUTDOOR ACTIVITIES

Thailand's natural environment is well exploited by numerous tour agencies cashing in on the tourist dollar. While this can lead to dodgy, often dangerous practices, the range of outdoor activities available – from snorkelling and scuba diving, river rafting and inner-tube riding, sea-kayaking, jet-skiing, whitewater rafting, waterskiing and parasailing to rock-climbing, spelunking (caving), bungy jumping, elephant trekking, jungle trekking and bike riding – is astonishing. Always choose your tour operator carefully however.

### Trekking

**Trekking** is concentrated in the north around Chiang Mai and Chiang Rai (see p.798) but there are smaller, less touristy trekking operations in Kanchanaburi (see p.778), Mae Hong Son, Pai and Umphang (p.797), all of which are worth considering. Treks in the north usually include an overnight stay in a hilltribe village, a visit to hot springs, elephant riding and bamboo or whitewater rafting, plus around three hours' walking per day. See the box on p.798 for more. Some **national parks**, such as Khao Yai (see p.822) and Khao Sok (p.862), offer shorter trails for unguided walks; most national parks charge a B400 entrance fee.

### Diving

You can **dive** all year round in Thailand, as the coasts are subject to different monsoon seasons: the diving seasons are from November to April along the Andaman coast, from January to October on the Gulf coast, and all year round on the east coast. See Ⓦwww.divethailand.net for dive reports and links.

Major dive centres include Ko Chang (see p.838) on the east coast; Phuket (see p.869), Ao Nang near Krabi and Ko Lanta (see p.876) on the Andaman coast; and Ko Tao (see p.858), Ko Samui

### THAI BOXING

**Thai boxing** (*muay Thai*) enjoys a following similar to football in Europe: every province has a stadium, and whenever it's shown on TV you can be sure that large noisy crowds will gather round the sets in streetside restaurants and noodle shops. The best place to see live Thai boxing is at one of Bangkok's two stadiums (see box on p.772). There's a strong spiritual and ritualistic dimension to *muay Thai*, adding grace to an otherwise brutal sport. Any part of the body except the head may be used as an offensive weapon, and all parts except the groin are fair targets. Kicks to the head are the blows that cause most knockouts.

### MEDITATION CENTRES AND RETREATS

Of the hundreds of **meditation** temples in Thailand, a few cater specifically for foreigners by holding meditation sessions and retreats in English. The meditation is mostly Vipassana, or "insight", which emphasizes the minute observation of internal physical sensation. Novices and practised meditators alike are welcome. To join a session in Bangkok, drop in at Wat Mahathat (see p.758). Longer retreats are for the serious-minded only and generally last 21 or 26 days: there's usually around eight hours of meditation per day; tobacco, alcohol, drugs and sex are forbidden; there's generally no talking and no eating after midday; and conditions are spartan. In the south, frequent ten-day retreats led by foreign teachers are held at Wat Khao Tham on Ko Pha Ngan (see p.851). For options in the north, head to the Northern Insight Meditation Centre at Wat Ram Poeng or The International Buddhism Center at Doi Suthep, both just outside Chiang Mai (see p.799).

(see p.845) and Ko Pha Ngan (see p.851) on the Gulf coast. The diving off islands of the Ko Tarutao National Marine Park (see p.881) is also very impressive. You can organize dive expeditions and undertake a certificated diving course (B12,000–24,000 for four-day PADI Open Water courses) at all these places; Ko Tao dive centres offer the cheapest courses. For beginners with not much cash or time, Discover Scuba dives, which involve diving with the accompaniment of a Dive Master, who regulates your equipment (leaving you to focus on breathing steadily and equalizing) – are a wonderful introduction to the underwater world. Always verify the dive instructors' PADI or equivalent credentials and check Ⓦwww.padi.com to see if the dive shop is a member of PADI's International Resorts and Retailers Association (IRRA) as this guarantees a certain level of professionalism. There are currently **recompression chambers** in Pattaya (north of Ko Samet), on Ko Samui (p.845), on Ko Tao (see p.858) and on Phuket (p.869).

## Other outdoor activities

**Mountain bike** rental is usually available, but most islands are considerably mountainous, so be prepared for a workout and bring lots of water. At Railay, in the south, you will find one of the best **rock-climbing** destinations in the world, with towering limestone cliffs. **Sailing** and **windsurfing** courses are offered on most of the main islands and some (like Phuket and Samui) offer **treetop walks** and **cable rides**. **Fishing tours** are also plentiful. For those with more obscure tastes there's **paintball** warfare on Ko Tao, **bungy jumping** and **Go Kart racing** in Patong, on Phuket, and **archery** near Chaloklum in Ko Pha Ngan. But to truly appreciate your surroundings while working up a sweat, **beach volleyball and football**, a sunset phenomenon on most island beaches, are a great way to make new friends; there's truly nothing like freshening up after a big game with a sunset swim in the ocean.

## COMMUNICATIONS

**Mail** takes around a week to get from Bangkok to Europe or North America, longer (up to two weeks) from more isolated areas. Almost all main post offices across the country operate a **poste restante** service and will hold letters for two to three months. All parcels must be officially boxed and sealed at main post offices – you can't just turn up with a package and buy stamps for it. Surface packages take three months.

**Internet access** is available at private outlets almost everywhere in Thailand, averaging B2 per minute in tourist centres, and as little as B20 per hour upcountry, especially in Bangkok. There's also a public internet service, Catnet, at most government telephone offices; you need to buy a B100 card with a Catnet PIN, which gives you about three hours of internet time.

There are **payphones** dotted around all Thai towns, especially near 7-11s and the post office. They come in several colours. Red and pale-blue phones are for **local calls** and take B1 coins. Dark-blue and stainless steel ones are for any calls anywhere **within Thailand**, but they gobble up B1, B5 and B10 coins over long distances, so you're better off buying a TOT phonecard for domestic calls (B25–240), available from hotels and many shops; they come with a PIN number and can be used in designated orange cardphones or the stainless-steel payphones. Thai area codes have recently been incorporated into the subscriber number so even when phoning from the same city, you must dial the entire number. For directory enquiries within Thailand, call ⓣ1133.

There are various pre-paid cards for good-value **international** calling. For government IDD rates, you'll need a Thaicard, issued by the CAT in B50–3000 denominations; they can be used either in designated purple cardphones or at government telephone centres (usually within, or adjacent to, the main post office). For cheaper tariffs, you can use CAT's internet-based Phone Net Cards (B300, B500 or B1000). Calling **via the internet** is the cheapest option, and you'll find that many internet cafés in touristy areas dramatically undercut government phone rates. Skype, which has extremely low rates, is available in most internet cafés.

Collect or **reverse-charge** calls can be made free of charge at government phone centres, or from many guesthouses and private phone offices, usually for a fee of B100. From the government phone centres, as well as from some payphones and fixed telephones, you can make "Home Country Direct" calls to your own international operator, who will arrange for you to make a credit-card or reverse-charge call. For international directory enquiries, call ⓣ100.

Not all foreign **mobile phone** networks have links with Thai networks so you should check before you leave home. As global roaming rates are exorbitant, you may wish to purchase a Thai prepaid SIM card (1-2-Call is the biggest network with the best coverage), available for as little as B250, and charge it accordingly with top-up cards.

### THAILAND ON THE NET

**ⓦwww.bangkoktourist.com** Smart website packed with information.

**ⓦwww.tourismthailand.org** Official TAT (Tourist Authority of Thailand) website.

**ⓦwww.khaosanroad.com** Good site with comprehensive listings: hotels, restaurants, employment opportunities and the like.

**ⓦwww.2bangkok.com** Local and national news from Thai-language papers.

**ⓦwww.travelfish.org** Good information on lesser-visited towns, focusing especially on accommodation.

## CRIME AND SAFETY

As long as you keep your wits about you and follow the usual precautions, you shouldn't encounter much trouble in Thailand. **Theft** and **pickpocketing** are two of the main problems, but the most common cause for concern are the **con-artists** who dupe gullible tourists into parting with their cash: be suspicious of anyone who makes an unnatural effort to befriend you, never buy anything from a tout, and heed specific warnings given throughout the Guide. The most notorious scam entails flogging low-grade **gems** at vastly inflated prices:

read ⓦwww.2bangkok.com/2bangkok/Scams/Sapphire.shtml before you shell out any cash at all.

Theft from some long-distance **overnight buses** is also a problem, with the majority of reported incidents taking place on the temptingly cheap buses run by private companies direct from Bangkok's Thanon Khao San (as opposed to those that depart from the government bus stations) to destinations such as Chiang Mai and the southern beach resorts. The best solution is to go direct from the bus stations. On any bus or train, be wary of accepting food or drink from strangers, especially on long overnight journeys: it may be drugged so as to knock you out while your bags are stolen. Violent crime against tourists is not common but it does occur.

There have been several serious attacks on **women travellers** in the past few years, but bearing in mind the millions of tourists visiting the country every year, the statistical likelihood of becoming a victim is extremely small. Unfortunately, it's also necessary for female tourists to think twice about spending time alone with a monk, as there have been rapes and murders committed by men wearing the saffron robes of the monkhood.

**Drug-smuggling** carries a maximum penalty of death in Thailand, dealing will get you anything from four years to life in a Thai prison, and possession of Category 1 drugs (heroin, amphetamines, LSD and ecstasy) for personal use can result in a life sentence; travellers caught with even the smallest amount of drugs at airports and international borders are prosecuted for trafficking.

## MEDICAL CARE AND EMERGENCIES

Thai **pharmacies** (*raan khai yaa*; typically open daily 8.30am–8pm) are well stocked with local and international branded medicaments, and most pharmacists speak English. All provincial capitals have at least one **hospital** (*rong phayaabahn*). Cleanliness and efficiency vary, but generally hygiene and healthcare standards are good; most doctors speak English. In the event of a major health crisis, get someone to contact your embassy or insurance company – it may be best to get yourself flown to Bangkok or even home.

### EMERGENCY NUMBERS

In any emergency, contact the English-speaking **tourist police** who maintain a 24-hour toll-free nationwide line (ⓣ1155) and have offices within many regional TAT offices. TAT has a special department for tourist-related crimes and complaints called the **Tourist Assistance Center (TAC)**, which is based in the TAT headquarters on Thanon Rajdamnoen Nok, Bangkok (daily 8.30am–4.30pm; ⓣ02/281 5051).

## INFORMATION AND MAPS

For impartial **information** on local attractions and transport, call in at the efficient **Tourism Authority of Thailand** (TAT; ⓦwww.tourismthailand.org), which has offices in Bangkok and 23 regional towns, all open daily 8.30am–4.30pm, except where noted in the Guide. You can also contact the TAT Call Centre from anywhere in the country on ⓣ1672 (daily 8am–8pm). For a decent **map** of the country, try either Rough Guides' 1:1,200,000 rip-proof map of Thailand or the 1:1,500,000 maps produced by Nelles and Bartholomew. In addition, Nancy Chandler's maps of Bangkok and Chiang Mai are interesting and quirky; they are available from bookshops.

## MONEY AND BANKS

Thailand's unit of **currency** is the baht (abbreviated to "B"), which is divided into 100 satang. Notes come in B10, B20, B50, B100, B500 and B1000

## THAI LANGUAGE

Most Thais who deal with tourists speak some English, but off the beaten track you'll probably need a few words of Thai. Thai is extremely tonal difficult for Westerners to master. Five different tones are used – low (syllables marked ˋ), middle (unmarked), high (marked ˊ), falling (marked ^), and rising (marked ˇ) Thus, using four of the five tones, you can make a sentence from just one syllable: mái mài mâi mǎi – "New wood burns, doesn't it?"

Street signs in tourist areas are nearly always written in Roman script as well as Thai. Because there's no standard system of transliteration of Thai script into Roman, Thai words and names in this book will not always match the versions written elsewhere. Ubon Ratchathani, for example, could come out as Ubol Rajatani, while Ayutthaya is synonymous with Ayudhia.

### Pronunciation

| | |
|---|---|
| a | as in "dad" |
| aa | is pronounced as it looks, with the vowel elongated |
| ae | as in "there" |
| ai | as in "buy" |
| ao | as in "now" |
| aw | as in "awe" |
| e | as in "pen" |
| eu | as in "sir", but heavily nasalized |
| i | as in "tip" |
| ii | as in "feet" |
| o | as in "knock" |
| oe | as in "hurt", but more closed |
| oh | as in "toe" |
| u | as in "loot" |
| uay | "*u*" plus "*ay*" as in "pay" |
| uu | as in "pool" |
| r | as in "rip"; in everyday speech, it's often pronounced like "l". |
| kh | as in "keep" |
| ph | as in "put" |
| th | as in "time" |
| k | is unaspirated and unvoiced, and closer to "g" |
| p | is also unaspirated and unvoiced, and closer to "b" |
| t | is also unaspirated and unvoiced, and closer to "d" |

### Greetings and basic phrases

Whenever you speak to a stranger in Thailand, it's polite to end your sentence in *khráp* if you're a man, *khâ* if you're a woman. *Khráp* and *khâ* are also often used to answer "yes" to a question, though the most common way is to repeat the verb of the question (preceded by *mâi* for "no").

| | |
|---|---|
| Hello | *sawàt dii* |
| Where are you (used a general greeting) | *pai nǎi?* |
| I'm out having fun / I'm travelling (answer to *pai nǎi*) | *pai thîaw* |
| Goodbye | *sawàt dii/la kàwn* |
| Excuse me | *khǎw thâwt* |
| Thank you | *khàwp khun* |
| What's your name? | *khun chêu arai?* |
| My name is… | *phǒm (men)/diichǎn (women) chêu…* |
| I don't understand | *mâi khâo jai* |
| Do you speak English? | *khun phûut phasǎa angkrìt dâi mǎi?* |
| Can you help me? | *chûay phǒm/ diichǎn dâi mǎi?* |

### Getting around

| | |
|---|---|
| Where is the… ? | *…yùu thîi nǎi?* |
| How far? | *klai thâo rai?* |
| I would like to go to… | *yàak jà pai…* |
| When will the bus leave? | *rót jà àwk mêua rai?* |
| Train station | *sathàanii rót fai* |
| Bus station | *sathàanii rót meh* |
| Airport | *sanǎam bin* |
| Ticket | *tu˜a* |
| Hotel | *rohng raem* |
| Restaurant | *raan ahǎan* |
| Market | *talàat* |
| Hospital | *rohng pha-yaabaan* |
| Motorbike | *rót mohtoesai* |
| Taxi | *rót táksîi* |
| Boat | *reua* |
| How much is… ? | *…thâo rai/kìi bàat?* |

| | |
|---|---|
| Cheap/expensive | *thùuk/phaeng* |
| A/c room | *hãwng ae* |
| Bathroom/toilet | *hãwng nám* |
| Telephone | *thohrásàp* |
| Fan | *phát lom* |
| Today | *wan níi* |
| Tomorrow | *phrûng níi* |
| Yesterday | *mêua wan* |
| Now | *diãw níi* |
| Morning | *cháo* |
| Afternoon | *bài* |
| Evening | *yen* |
| Night | *kheun* |

## Numbers

| | |
|---|---|
| 0 | *su˜un* |
| 1 | *nèung* |
| 2 | *sãwng* |
| 3 | *sãam* |
| 4 | *sìi* |
| 5 | *hâa* |
| 6 | *hòk* |
| 7 | *jèt* |
| 8 | *pàet* |
| 9 | *kâo* |
| 10 | *sìp* |
| 11 | *sìp èt* |
| 12, 13, etc | *sìp sãwng, sìp sãam…* |
| 20 | *yîi sìp/yiip* |
| 21, 22, etc | *yîi sìp èt, yîi sìp sãwng…* |
| 30, 40, etc | *sãam sìp, sìi sìp…* |
| 100, 200, etc | *nèung rói, sãwng rói…* |
| 1000 | *nèung phan* |
| 10,000 | *nèung mèun* |

## Food and drink glossary

| | |
|---|---|
| *Khãw...* | I would like... |
| *Khãw check bin?* | Can I have the bill please? |
| *phõm* (male) / *diichãn* (female) *kin ahãan mangsàwirát/jeh* | I am vegetarian/ vegan |

**Noodle dishes**

| | |
|---|---|
| *ba mìi* | egg noodles |
| *ba mìi kràwp* | crisp fried egg noodles |
| *kwáy tiãw* | white rice noodles |
| *...haêng* | ...fried with egg, meat and vegetables |
| *nám (mu˜u)* | ...with chicken broth (and pork balls)... |
| *...rât nâ (mu˜u)* | ... fried in sauce with vegetables (and pork) |
| *pàt thai* | thin noodles fried with egg and beansprouts, topped with ground peanuts |

**Rice (khâo) dishes**

| | |
|---|---|
| *...man kài* | ...with chicken |
| *...nâ kài/pèt ...* | with chicken/duck with sauce |
| *...rât kaeng* | ...with curry |
| *khâo niãw* | sticky rice |
| *khâo pàt kài/ muũ/kûng/ néua/phàk* | fried rice with chicken/pork/ shrimp/ beef/vegetables |
| *Khâo tôm* | Rice soup |

**Curries, soups and other dishes**

| | |
|---|---|
| *Kaeng phèt* | Hot, red curry |
| *Kaeng phánaeng* | Thick, savoury curry |
| *Kaeng khiãw wan* | Green curry |
| *Kài pàt nàw mái* | Chicken with bamboo shoots |
| *Kài pàt mét mámûang* | Chicken with cashew nuts |
| *Kài pàt khĩng* | Chicken with ginger |
| *Mũu prîaw wãan* | Sweet and sour pork |
| *Néua pàt krathiam phrík thai* | Beef fried with garlic and pepper |
| *Néua pàt nám man hõy* | Beef in oyster sauce |
| *Pàt phàk lãi yàng* | Stir-fried vegetables |
| *Plaa rât phrík* | Whole fish cooked with chillies |
| *Plaa thâwt* | Fried whole fish |
| *Sôm tam* | Spicy papaya salad |
| *Tôm khàa kài* | Chicken coconut soup |
| *Tôm yam kûng* | Hot and sour prawn soup |
| *Yam néua* | Spicy beef salad |

**Drinks (khreûang deùm)**

| | |
|---|---|
| *Bia* | Beer |
| *Chaa ráwn* | Hot tea |
| *Chaa yen* | Iced tea |
| *Kaafae ráwn* | Hot coffee |
| *Nám klûay* | Banana shake |
| *Nám mánao/sôm* | Fresh, bottled or fizzy lemon/orange juice |
| *Nám maprao* | Fresh coconut water |
| *Nám awy* | Fresh sugar-cane juice |
| *Nám plaò* | Drinking water (boiled or filtered) |
| *Nom jeùd* | Milk |
| *Sohdaa* | Soda water |

denominations. At the time of writing, the **exchange rate** was averaging B63 to £1 and B32 to US$1. The exchange counters at Suvarnabhumi and Don Muang airports operate 24 hours, so there's little point arranging to buy baht before you arrive. You should also be able to withdraw cash from hundreds of 24-hour **ATMs**.

## OPENING HOURS AND HOLIDAYS

Most **shops** open at least Monday to Saturday from about 8am to 8pm, while **department stores** operate daily from around 10am to 9pm. **Banking hours** are Monday to Friday 8.30am to 3.30 or 4.30pm, but exchange kiosks in the main tourist centres are often open till 10pm, and upmarket hotels change money 24 hours a day. **Post offices** are generally open Monday to Friday 8.30am to 4.30pm, Saturday 9am to noon. **Private office** hours are generally Monday to Friday 8am to 5pm and Saturday 8am to noon, though in tourist areas these hours are longer, with weekends worked like any other day. **Government offices** work Monday to Friday 8.30am to noon and 1 to 4.30pm, and national **museums** tend to stick to these hours, too, but some close on Mondays and Tuesdays rather than at weekends. Most shops and tourist-oriented businesses, including TAT, stay open on national holidays. The only time an inconvenient number of shops, restaurants and hotels do close is during **Chinese New Year**, which, though not marked as an official national holiday, brings many businesses to a standstill for several days in late January or early February.

### Public holidays

**January 1** International New Year's Day
**February** (day of full moon) Maha Puja. Commemorates the Buddha preaching to a spontaneously assembled crowd of 1250.
**April 6** Chakri Day. The founding of the Chakri dynasty.
**April** (usually 13–15) Songkhran. Thai New Year
**May 5** Coronation Day.
**May** (early) Royal Ploughing Ceremony. Marks the start of the rice-planting season.
**May** (day of full moon) Visakha Puja. The holiest of all Buddhist holidays, celebrating the birth, enlightenment and death of the Buddha.
**July** (day of full moon) Asanha Puja. Commemorates the Buddha's first sermon.
**July** (the day after Asanha Puja) Khao Pansa. The start of the annual three-month Buddhist rains retreat, when new monks are ordained
**August 12** Queen's Birthday/Mothers' Day
**October 23** Chulalongkorn Day. The anniversary of Rama V's death.
**December 5** King's Birthday/Fathers' Day.
**December 10** Constitution Day.
**December 31** Western New Year's Eve.

## FESTIVALS

Thais use both the Western Gregorian **calendar** and a Buddhist calendar – the Buddha is said to have died (or entered Nirvana) in the year 543 BC, so Thai dates start from that point: thus 2009 AD becomes 2552 BE (Buddhist Era). Dates for religious festivals are often set by the lunar calendar, so check specifics with TAT or consult Ⓦwww.thailandgrandfestival.com. The most spectacular festivals include:

**Songkhran** (usually April 13–15) Thai New Year is welcomed in with massive public waterfights in the street, at their most exuberant in Chiang Mai and on Bangkok's Thanon Khao San.
**Candle Festival** (July) For three days around the full moon enormous wax sculptures are paraded through Ubon Ratchathani to mark the beginning of the annual Buddhist retreat period.
**Vegetarian Festival** (Oct) Chinese devotees in Phuket and Trang become vegetarian for a nine-day period and then parade through town performing acts of self-mortification.
**Loy Krathong** (late Oct or early Nov) Baskets of flowers and lighted candles are floated on rivers, canals and ponds nationwide to celebrate the end of the rainy season. It's best in Sukhothai and Chiang Mai.
**Elephant Roundup** (third weekend of Nov) The main tourist-oriented festival is in Surin: two hundred elephants play team games, and parade in battle dress.

# Bangkok and around

Manic, thrilling, dynamic, exhausting, overpowering, titillating – the one thing **BANGKOK** (Krung Thep in Thai; the "City of Angels") is not, is boring. Whether you spend two days here or two weeks you'll always find something to invigorate your senses, kick-start your enthusiasm and drive you crazy: frenetic markets and bustling temples, zinging curries and cutting-edge clubs. Bring patience, a sense of adventure and comfy shoes; leave your Western expectation of aesthetics behind and you'll not be disappointed.

Bangkok began life as a largely amphibious city in 1782 after the Burmese sacked the former capital of Ayutthaya. The first king of the new dynasty, Rama I, built his palace at Ratanakosin, which remains the city's spiritual heart. The capital was modernized along European lines in the late nineteenth century, and since World War II has undergone a dramatic transformation. Long gone are the exotic costumes and pageantry of ancient Siam; most of the city's waterways have been concreted over, its citizens no longer live on floating bamboo rafts and the charmless urban sprawl is spiked by skyscrapers. Yet in amongst the chaotic jumble of modern Bangkok there remains a city fiercely proud of its traditions. As such it is a perfect microcosm of Southeast Asia, and the perfect place to begin your adventures.

## What to see and do

Bangkok's traveller heart is **Banglamphu**, with its myriad guesthouses, bars and restaurants. From here, it's a short walk to **Ratanakosin**, the royal island on the east bank of the Chao Phraya that is home to the **Grand Palace**, **Wat Pho** and the **National Museum**. To the east, **Chinatown** is noteworthy for its markets and street food, while across the river **Thonburi**'s appeal lies in its traditional canal-side life and boat rides. The amorphous sprawl of **downtown** Bangkok offers several impressive historical residences amongst its rampant commercialism, though with over ten malls it's primarily a shopper's paradise. At weekends, don't miss the enormous **Chatuchak Weekend Market**, on the city's outskirts, which sells just about everything under the sun. There are thousands of **bars and restaurants** in Bangkok, with tastes and prices to suit everybody, or you can escape the chaos and float on the river for a **dinner cruise**.

### Wat Phra Kaeo and the Grand Palace

Built as a private royal temple in 1782, the dazzling and sumptuous **Wat Phra Kaeo** (Ⓦwww.palaces.thai.net) is the holiest site in the country and houses its most important icon, the Emerald Buddha. The temple is located within

### A WORD OF WARNING

If you're heading for the major sights, beware of **scams**. Tuk-tuk drivers or well-dressed people pretending to be students or officials may lie and tell you that the sight is closed, because they want to lead you on a shopping trip, invariably to purchase gems or silk that are often fake or on sale at vastly inflated prices (for which they'll receive a hefty commission). These sights are rarely closed for national holidays or state occasions, so play it safe and check it out for yourself. Similarly, steer clear of tuk-tuk or taxi drivers who offer to take you on a tour of the city; gem shops are often in the itinerary.

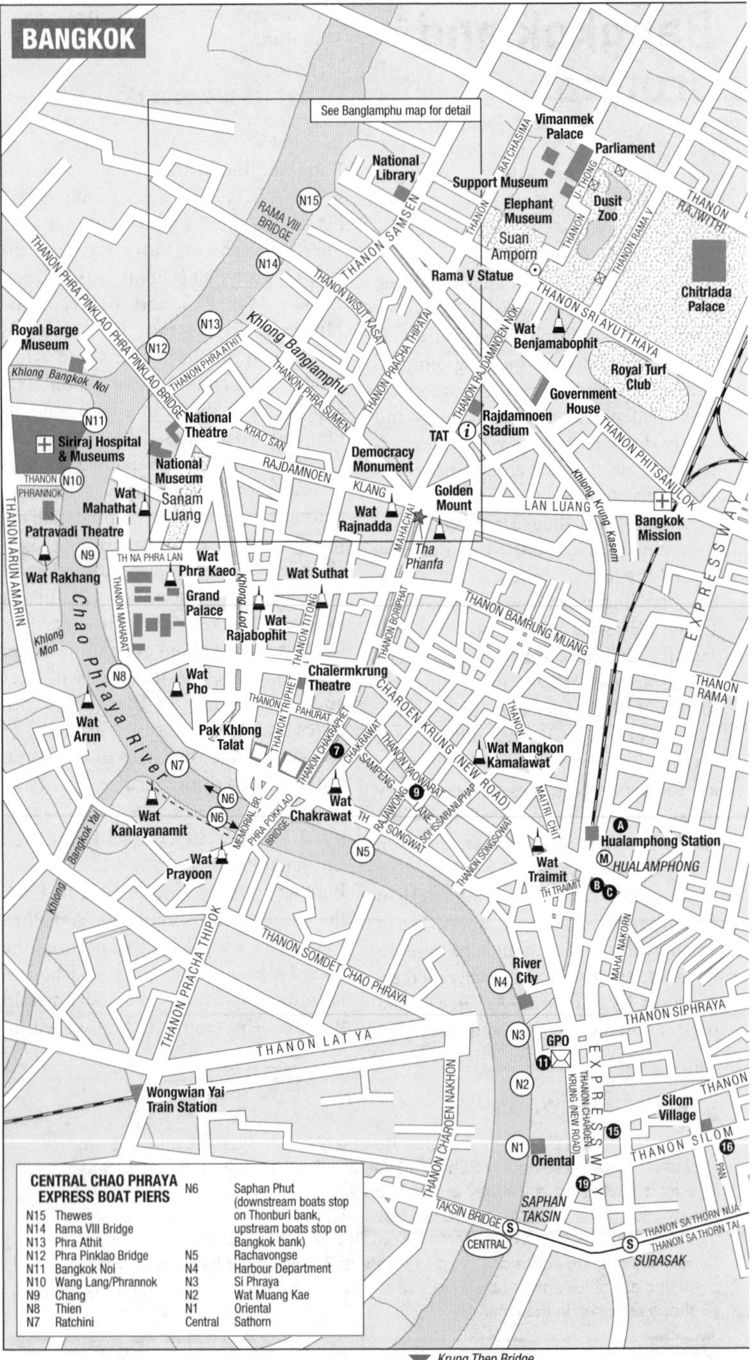
BANGKOK
Nonthaburi
Southern Bus Terminal
Thonburi Tain Station
Krung Thep Bridge
See Banglamphu map for detail
Vimanmek Palace
Parliament
National Library
Support Museum
Elephant Museum
Dusit Zoo
Suan Amporn
Rama V Statue
Chitrlada Palace
THANON RAJWITHI
THANON SAMSEN
THANON RATCHASIMA
THANON U-THONG
THANON RAMA V
RAMA VIII BRIDGE
THANON WISUT KASAT
THANON PRACHA THIPATAI
THANON RAJDAMNOEN NOK
THANON SRI AYUTTHAYA
Wat Benjamabophit
Royal Turf Club
Government House
Rajdamnoen Stadium
TAT
THANON PHITSANULOK
Royal Barge Museum
Khlong Bangkok Noi
Khlong Banglamphu
THANON PHRA PINKLAO PHRA PINKLAO BRIDGE
THANON PHRA ATHIT
THANON PHRA SUMEN
National Theatre
KHAO SAN
RAJDAMNOEN KLANG
Democracy Monument
Golden Mount
Siriraj Hospital & Museums
National Museum
THANON PHRANNOK
Wat Mahathat
Sanam Luang
Wat Rajnadda
MAHACHAI
Tha Phanfa
LAN LUANG
Khlong Krung Kasem
Bangkok Mission
Patravadi Theatre
Wat Rakhang
TH NA PHRA LAN
Wat Phra Kaeo
Wat Suthat
Grand Palace
Khlong Lord
Wat Rajabophit
THANON TITONG
THANON BORIPHAT
THANON BAMRUNG MUANG
EXPRESSWAY
THANON ARUN AMARIN
THANON MAHARAT
Khlong Mon
Chao Phraya River
Wat Pho
Chalermkrung Theatre
THANON TRIPHET
THANON PAHURAT
CHAROEN KRUNG (NEW ROAD)
THANON RAMA I
Wat Arun
Pak Khlong Talat
THANON CHAKRAPHET
CHAKRAWAT
SAMPENG LANE
THANON YAOWARAT
Wat Mangkon Kamalawat
Wat Kanlayanamit
MEMORIAL BR.
PHRA POKKLAO BRIDGE
Wat Chakrawat
TH SONGWAT
RAJAWONG
SOI ISSARANUPHAP
THANON SONGSOWAT
MAITRI CHIT
Hualamphong Station
HUALAMPHONG
Wat Traimit
TH TRAIMIT
Bangkok Yai
Khlong
Wat Prayoon
THANON PRACHA THIPOK
THANON SOMDET CHAO PHRAYA
MAHA NAKORN
River City
THANON SIPHRAYA
THANON LAT YA
GPO
THANON CHAROEN KRUNG (NEW ROAD)
Wongwian Yai Train Station
THANON CHAROEN NAKHON
Silom Village
THANON SILOM
PAN
Oriental
SAPHAN TAKSIN
TAKSIN BRIDGE
CENTRAL
THANON SA THORN NUA
THANON SA THORN TAI
SURASAK
CENTRAL CHAO PHRAYA EXPRESS BOAT PIERS
N15 Thewes
N14 Rama VIII Bridge
N13 Phra Athit
N12 Phra Pinklao Bridge
N11 Bangkok Noi
N10 Wang Lang/Phrannok
N9 Chang
N8 Thien
N7 Ratchini
N6 Saphan Phut (downstream boats stop on Thonburi bank, upstream boats stop on Bangkok bank)
N5 Rachavongse
N4 Harbour Department
N3 Si Phraya
N2 Wat Muang Kae
N1 Oriental
Central Sathorn

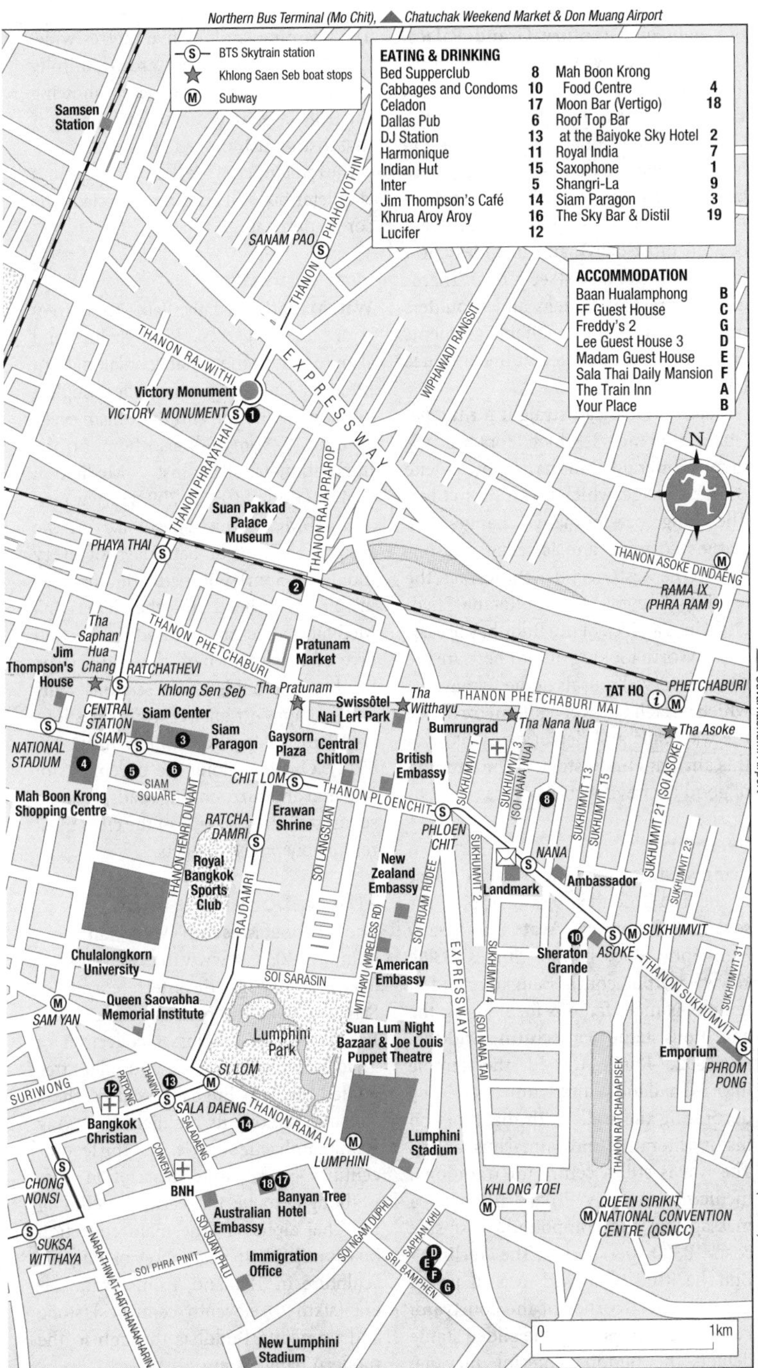
Northern Bus Terminal (Mo Chit), Chatuchak Weekend Market & Don Muang Airport
BTS Skytrain station
Khlong Saen Seb boat stops
Subway
EATING & DRINKING
Bed Supperclub 8
Cabbages and Condoms 10
Celadon 17
Dallas Pub 6
DJ Station 13
Harmonique 11
Indian Hut 15
Inter 5
Jim Thompson's Café 14
Khrua Aroy Aroy 16
Lucifer 12
Mah Boon Krong Food Centre 4
Moon Bar (Vertigo) 18
Roof Top Bar at the Baiyoke Sky Hotel 2
Royal India 7
Saxophone 1
Shangri-La 9
Siam Paragon 3
The Sky Bar & Distil 19
ACCOMMODATION
Baan Hualamphong B
FF Guest House C
Freddy's 2 G
Lee Guest House 3 D
Madam Guest House E
Sala Thai Daily Mansion F
The Train Inn A
Your Place B
Samsen Station
SANAM PAO
THANON PHAHOLYOTHIN
THANON RAJWITHI
EXPRESSWAY
WIPHAWADI RANGSIT
Victory Monument
VICTORY MONUMENT
THANON PHRAYATHAI
THANON RAJAPRAROP
Suan Pakkad Palace Museum
PHAYA THAI
THANON ASOKE DINDAENG
RAMA IX (PHRA RAM 9)
THANON PETCHABURI
Pratunam Market
Tha Saphan Hua Chang
Jim Thompson's House
RATCHATHEVI
Khlong Sen Seb
Tha Pratunam
Tha Witthayu
THANON PHETCHABURI MAI
TAT HQ
PHETCHABURI
Suvarnabhumi Airport
CENTRAL STATION (SIAM)
Siam Center
Siam Paragon
Swissôtel Nai Lert Park
Bumrungrad
Tha Nana Nua
Tha Asoke
NATIONAL STADIUM
Gaysorn Plaza
Central Chitlom
British Embassy
SIAM SQUARE
CHIT LOM
THANON PLOENCHIT
Mah Boon Krong Shopping Centre
RATCHADAMRI
Erawan Shrine
PHLOEN CHIT
SUKHUMVIT 1
SUKHUMVIT 3 (SOI NANA NUA)
SUKHUMVIT 13
SUKHUMVIT 15
SUKHUMVIT 21 (SOI ASOKE)
SUKHUMVIT 23
THANON HENRI DUNANT
Royal Bangkok Sports Club
SOI LANGSUAN
New Zealand Embassy
SUKHUMVIT 2
NANA
Landmark
Ambassador
RAJDAMRI
WITHAYU (WIRELESS RD)
SOI RUAM RUDEE
EXPRESSWAY
SUKHUMVIT 4 (SOI NANA TAI)
SUKHUMVIT
ASOKE
Sheraton Grande
Chulalongkorn University
American Embassy
SOI SARASIN
THANON SUKHUMVIT
SUKHUMVIT 31
SAM YAN
Queen Saovabha Memorial Institute
Lumphini Park
Suan Lum Night Bazaar & Joe Louis Puppet Theatre
Emporium
PHROM PONG
Eastern Bus Terminal (Ekamai)
SURIWONG
PATPONG
THANIYA
SI LOM
SALA DAENG
THANON RAMA IV
Bangkok Christian
SALADAENG
CONVENT
Lumphini Stadium
LUMPHINI
THANON RATCHADAPISEK
CHONG NONSI
BNH
Banyan Tree Hotel
KHLONG TOEI
QUEEN SIRIKIT NATIONAL CONVENTION CENTRE (QSNCC)
Australian Embassy
SOI NGAM DUPHLI
SAPHAN KHU
SUKSA WITTHAYA
SOI SUAN PHLU
Immigration Office
SRI BAMPHEN
SOI PHRA PINIT
NARATHIWAT-RATCHANAKHARIN
New Lumphini Stadium
0
1km
N

the eighteenth-century **Grand Palace**, now used solely for state functions. The main entrance is on Thanon Na Phra Lan, near to Banglamphu and Tha Chang express-boat pier. Admission is B250 (daily 8.30am–3.30pm, palace halls closed Sat & Sun; free tours in English at 10am & 1.30pm, plus 10.30am & 2pm most days), and includes entry to Vimanmek Palace (see p.762). There's a strict dress code (legs and shoulders must be covered) but suitable garments and shoes can be rented at the entrance (B100 deposit).

Most visitors head straight for the *bot* (main sanctuary) which contains the sacred Emerald Buddha, a tiny, jadeite Buddha image, which is just 75cm high. The king ceremonially changes the statue's costume and jewellery seasonally. At the western end of the terrace, the eye-boggling gold Phra Si Ratana Chedi enshrines a piece of the Buddha's breastbone. Worth looking out for here are the well-preserved murals of the Ramayana, which stretch for over a kilometre inside the wat walls and depict every blow of this ancient Hindu story of the triumph of good over evil in 178 panels.

## Wat Pho

Lying south of the Grand Palace, close to the Tha Thien express-boat pier, the seventeenth-century **Wat Pho** (daily 8am–6pm; B50; private guides B300; Ⓦwww.watpho.com), Bangkok's oldest temple, is most famous for housing the enormous statue of a **reclining Buddha**. In 1832, Rama turned the temple into "Thailand's first university" by decorating the walls with diagrams on history, literature and animal husbandry. The wat is still a centre for traditional medicine, notably Thai massage: a massage on the compound's east side costs B300 per hour. The reclining Buddha itself is housed in a chapel in the northwest corner of the courtyard. Forty-five metres long, the gilded statue depicts the Buddha entering nirvana. The beaming smile is five metres wide, and the vast black feet are beautifully inlaid with mother-of-pearl showing the 108 lakshanas or auspicious signs that distinguish the true Buddha.

The remainder of the temple compound is quieter but still striking, especially the coronation hall.

## Wat Mahathat

**Wat Mahathat** (daily 9am–5pm; free) is one of Bangkok's oldest shrines and also houses the Mahachulalongkorn Buddhist University, which offers English talks on meditation and Buddhism every evening (8–9pm). It's also home to the International Buddhist Meditation Centre (Room 105 or 209; Ⓦwww.mcu.ac.th/IBMC), which has talks on the second and fourth Saturdays of every month (3–5pm). For meditation practice in English, head to the Vipassana Meditation Centre, located in Section Five of the wat, where the enthusiastic head monk holds three sessions daily and is happy to answer your questions (7–10am, 1–4pm & 6–8pm; Ⓣ02/222 6011). Outside, along the pavements of Maharat and surrounding roads, vendors set up stalls to sell some of the city's most reasonably priced amulets.

## The National Museum

The **National Museum** (Wed–Sun 9am–4pm; B40; Ⓦwww.thailandmuseum.com), at the northwestern corner of Sanam Luang, the park near the Grand Palace, houses a colossal collection of Thailand's artistic riches, and offers free guided tours in English (Wed & Thurs 9.30am). Among its highlights are King Ramkhamhaeng's stele, a thirteenth-century black stone inscription that is thought to be the earliest record of the Thai alphabet. The main collection boasts a chronological survey of religious sculpture in Thailand, from Dvaravati-era (sixth to eleventh centuries) stone and terracotta Buddhas through to the modern Bangkok era.

Elsewhere in the museum compound, Wang Na, a former palace, contains a fascinating array of Thai objets d'art, including an intricately carved ivory howdah, theatrical masks, and a collection of traditional musical instruments. The Phra Sihing Buddha, the second holiest image in Thailand after the Emerald Buddha, is housed in the beautifully ornate Buddhaisawan Chapel, the vast, muralled hall in front of the entrance to the Wang Na. Elaborate teak funeral chariots belonging to the royal family are stored in a large garage behind the chapel.

## Chinatown

The sprawl of narrow alleyways, temples and shops packed between Charoen Krung (New Road) and the river is Bangkok's **Chinatown** (Sampeng). Easiest access is by Chao Phraya Express boat to Tha Rachavongse (Rajawong) at the southern end of Thanon Rajawong, by subway to Hualamphong Station, or by Hualamphong-bound bus #53 or #507. The ethnic Chinese arrived in Thailand before the ethnic Thais and they've always played a fundamental role in the economic and commercial life of the kingdom. Spend some time in **Sampeng Lane** (also signposted as Soi Wanit 1), a kilometre-long alley off Thanon Songsawat that's packed with tiny, bargain-basement shops grouped together according to their merchandise. About halfway down Sampeng Lane on the right, **Soi Issaranuphap** (also signed in places as Soi 16) is good for more unusual fare such as ginseng roots, fish heads and cockroach-killer chalk. Soi Issaranuphap ends at the Thanon Plaplachai intersection with a knot of shops specializing in paper funeral art: Chinese people buy miniature paper replicas of necessities (like houses, cars, suits and money) to be burned with the body. Aim to be here in the early evening when **Thanon Yaowarat** explodes into life and street stalls are set up selling delicious and cheap Chinese-influenced food, especially around Soi 11; fish is a speciality.

## The Golden Buddha

**Wat Traimit**, 250m west of Hualamphong Station on Thanon Tri Mit (daily 9am–5pm; B30), houses the world's largest solid-gold Buddha. Over 3m tall and weighing five and a half tons, the **Golden Buddha** was cast in the thirteenth century and completely encased in stucco for several hundred years, probably to protect it from the marauding Burmese. No one realized what was underneath until 1955 when the image was accidentally knocked in the process of being moved nearer $140 million at today's price of gold.

## Wat Arun

Almost directly across the river from Wat Pho, in the **Thonburi** district, rises the enormous five-pranged **Wat Arun** ("Temple of Dawn"; daily 8am–6pm; B50). It's Bangkok's most distinctive landmark, and you'll recognize it from the TAT logo. To get here, take a cross-river ferry (B3.50) from Tha Thien. The temple has been reconstructed numerous times, but Wat Arun today is a classic prang (tower) built as a representation of Mount Meru, the home of the gods in Khmer mythology. The prangs are decorated with flowers made from donated porcelain as well as mythical figures. The terrace depicts Buddha at the four most important stages of his life: at birth (north), in meditation (east), preaching his first sermon (south) and entering nirvana (west). Wat Arun hosts a yearly festival in August which celebrates traditional Thai art and dance, games and sports. See ⓦwww.watarun.org for more information.

## The Royal Barge Museum

**Royal Barge Museum** on the north bank of Khlong Bangkok Noi (daily 9am–5pm; B30, plus B100 camera fee) houses eight

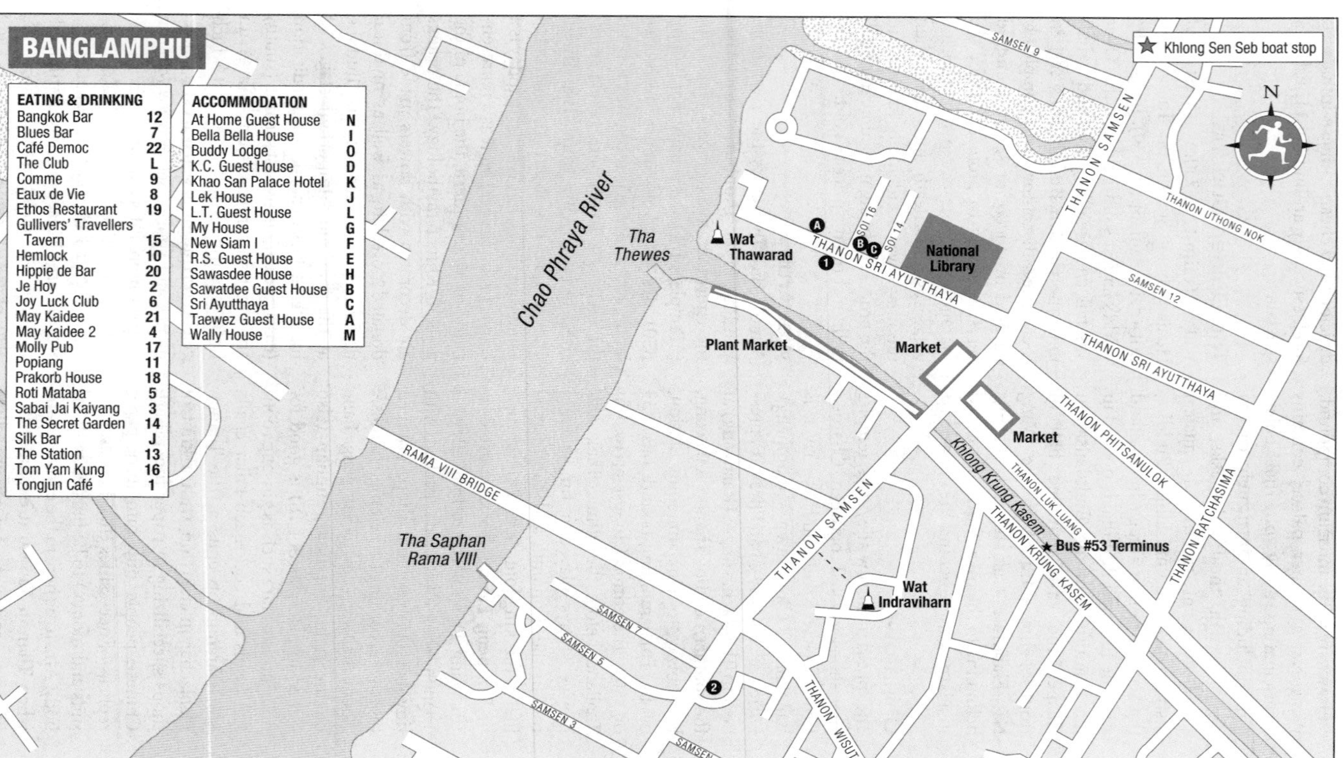
BANGLAMPHU
EATING & DRINKING
Bangkok Bar 12
Blues Bar 7
Café Democ 22
The Club L
Comme 9
Eaux de Vie 8
Ethos Restaurant 19
Gullivers' Travellers Tavern 15
Hemlock 10
Hippie de Bar 20
Je Hoy 2
Joy Luck Club 6
May Kaidee 21
May Kaidee 2 4
Molly Pub 17
Popiang 11
Prakorb House 18
Roti Mataba 5
Sabai Jai Kaiyang 3
The Secret Garden 14
Silk Bar J
The Station 13
Tom Yam Kung 16
Tongjun Café 1
ACCOMMODATION
At Home Guest House N
Bella Bella House I
Buddy Lodge O
K.C. Guest House D
Khao San Palace Hotel K
Lek House J
L.T. Guest House L
My House G
New Siam I F
R.S. Guest House E
Sawasdee House H
Sawatdee Guest House B
Sri Ayutthaya C
Taewez Guest House A
Wally House M
Khlong Sen Seb boat stop
N
Chao Phraya River
Tha Thewes
Wat Thawarad
National Library
THANON SRI AYUTTHAYA
SOI 16
SOI 14
SAMSEN 9
THANON SAMSEN
THANON UTHONG NOK
SAMSEN 12
Plant Market
Market
Market
THANON PHITSANULOK
THANON RATCHASIMA
Khlong Krung Kasem
THANON LUK LUANG
THANON KRUNG KASEM
Bus #53 Terminus
RAMA VIII BRIDGE
Tha Saphan Rama VIII
Wat Indraviharn
SAMSEN 7
SAMSEN 5
SAMSEN 3
SAMSEN
THANON WISUT

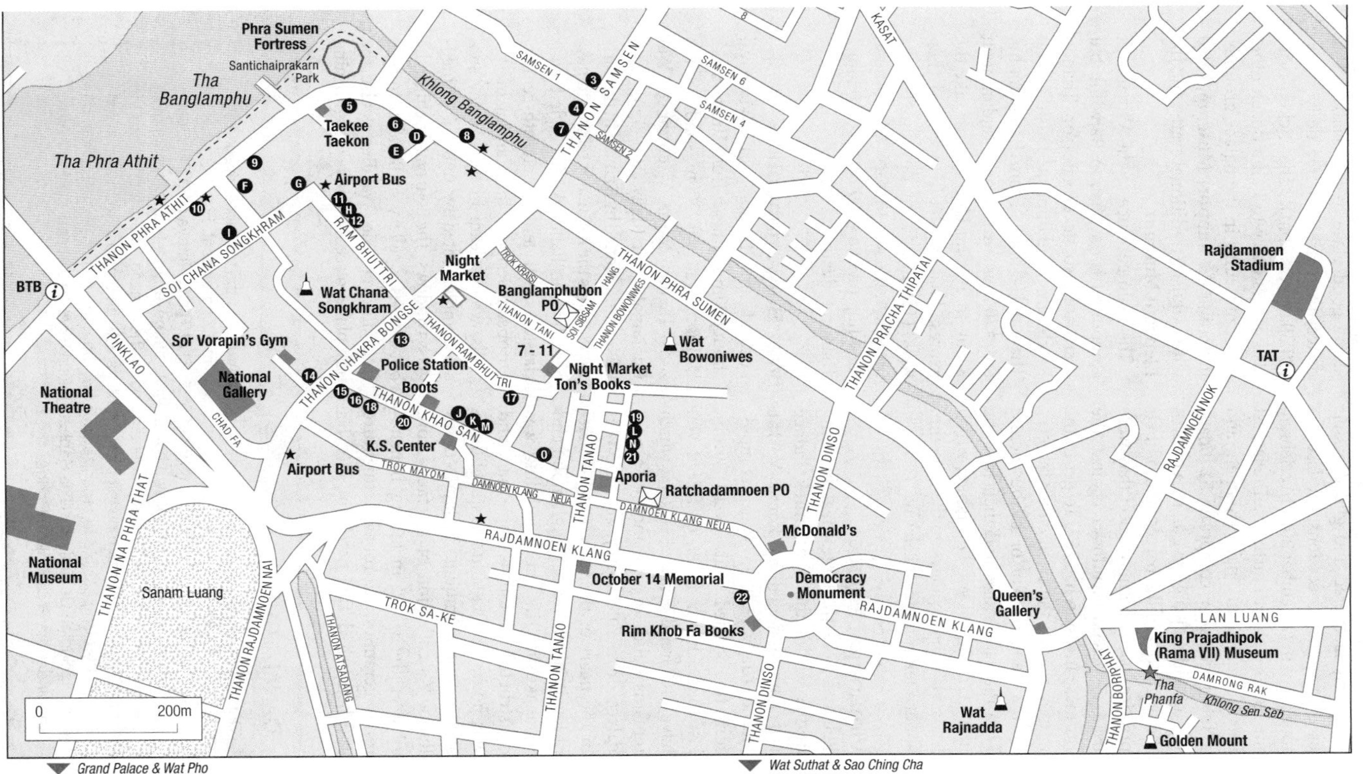
Royal Barge Museum
Phra Sumen Fortress
Santichaiprakarn Park
Tha Banglamphu
Tha Phra Athit
Khlong Banglamphu
Taekee Taekon
Airport Bus
THANON PHRA ATHIT
SOI CHANA SONGKHRAM
RAM BHUTTRI
BTB
Wat Chana Songkhram
Night Market
Banglamphubon PO
TROK KRAISI
THANON TANI
SOI SIBSAM HANG
THANON BOWONIWES
THANON PHRA SUMEN
Wat Bowoniwes
THANON PRACHA THIPATAI
SAMSEN 1
SAMSEN 2
SAMSEN 4
SAMSEN 6
THANON SAMSEN
KASAT
Rajdamnoen Stadium
TAT
RAJDAMNOEN NOK
PINKLAO
Sor Vorapin's Gym
National Gallery
National Theatre
CHAD FA
THANON CHAKRA BONGSE
Police Station
THANON RAM BHUTTRI
7 - 11
Night Market
Ton's Books
Boots
THANON KHAO SAN
K.S. Center
Airport Bus
TROK MAYOM
DAMNOEN KLANG NEUA
THANON TANAO
Aporia
Ratchadamnoen PO
THANON DINSO
McDonald's
RAJDAMNOEN KLANG
October 14 Memorial
Democracy Monument
Rim Khob Fa Books
Queen's Gallery
LAN LUANG
King Prajadhipok (Rama VII) Museum
DAMRONG RAK
Tha Phanfa
Khlong Sen Seb
THANON BORIPHAT
Golden Mount
Wat Rajnadda
National Museum
THANON NA PHRA THAT
Sanam Luang
THANON RAJDAMNOEN NAI
TROK SA-KE
THANON ATSADANG
0
200m
Grand Palace & Wat Pho
Wat Suthat & Sao Ching Cha

intricately lacquered and gilded vessels used for royal processions; the last one took place in December 2007 to celebrate the King's eightieth birthday. The largest barges require fifty navy oarsmen, and a full procession comprises 52 boats. Photos and drawings give an idea both of the splendour of the barges, and of their practical use and importance; they were used to defend Ayutthaya against the Burmese invasion in 1767. To get to the museum, cross the river, either by ferry to Tha Bangkok Noi or by bus across Phra Pinklao Bridge, and then take the first left along Soi Wat Dusitaram, which leads, via winding alleys, to the museum, about a ten-minute walk away.

### Vimanmek Palace

Believed to be the largest teak building in the world, the **Vimanmek Palace** was commissioned by Rama V. The palace (daily 9.30am–4pm; compulsory free guided tours every 30min, last tour 3.15pm; B100, or free if you have a Grand Palace ticket, which remains valid for one month; Grand Palace dress rules apply, see p.758) is in the heart of the leafy royal district of Dusit, northeast of Banglamphu and Ratanakosin. The entire building was constructed without a single nail, and was home to Thailand's first lightbulb and indoor plumbing. Today it holds Rama V's collection of artefacts from all over the world including bencharong ceramics, European furniture and bejewelled Thai betel-nut sets. It's also a good place to see classical Thai dance; there are two free daily shows (10.30am & 2pm). The ticket price also covers entry to half a dozen other small museums in the palace grounds, including the **Support Museum**, filled with exquisite traditional crafts, and the **Elephant Museum**.

The main entrance to the Vimanmek compound is on Thanon Rajwithi, but there are also ticket gates on Thanon Ratchasima, and opposite Dusit Zoo on Thanon U-Thong. From Banglamphu, the #70 bus runs from Rajdamnoen Klang to Thanon U-Thong, or take the express boat to Tha Thewes and then walk (15min). From downtown, take the Skytrain to Victory Monument, then hop on bus #509 or #510/10 along Thanon Rajwithi.

### Wat Benjamabophit

Located on Thanon Sri Ayutthaya, about 600m southeast from Vimanmek's U-Thong gate, or 200m south of the zoo's Thanon Rama V entrance, **Wat Benjamabophit** (daily 7am–5pm; B20) was commissioned by Rama V in the early 1900s and is the last major temple to have been built in Bangkok. The style blends classical Thai and nineteenth-century European design – the Carrara marble walls, which gleam in the midday sun, are complemented by unusual stained-glass windows. The courtyard behind the bot houses a gallery of Buddha images from all over Asia. Wat Ben is also the best place to see the daily early-morning

#### CANAL TOURS

One of the most popular ways of seeing Wat Arun and the traditional riverine neighbourhoods is to embark on a **canal tour** in a longtail boat. Fixed-priced trips with The Boat Tour Centre (☎02/235 3108) at Tha Si Phraya cost B500 per boat for one hour or B800 for two hours, while the government-run Mitchaopaya Travel Service (☎02/623 5340), operating out of Tha Chang, offers a one-hour trip for B900 per boat (max 6 people), or two hours with an orchid farm thrown in for B1500. It's also possible to organize your own boat trip around Thonburi from other piers, including Central Pier (Tha Saphan Taksin Skytrain station), Tha Phra Athit and under the Phra Pinklao Bridge.

ritual arms-giving ceremony (between about 6 and 7.30am); in contrast to the usual parade of monks around the locality, the temple's monks line up and await donations from local citizens.

### Wat Indraviharn

The temple complex of **Wat Indraviharn** is dominated by an enormous standing Buddha, 32m high. The striking image, commissioned in the mid-nineteenth century and covered in gold mirror-mosaic, is the tallest representation in the world of the Buddha holding an alms bowl from beneath his robes. His toes peep out through flower garlands, and you can climb the stairs supporting the statue to get a decent view over the area. The temple compound is an interesting amalgam of religious architectural styles and includes a Chinese shrine. Wat In is an easy ten-minute walk north of Banglamphu, along Thanon Samsen; bus #53 stops nearby on Thanon Samsen. Be aware that the complex has become a favourite hangout for con-artists (see box, p.755).

### Jim Thompson's House

Decades after his death, Jim Thompson remains Thailand's most famous farang (foreigner). A former agent of the OSS (later to become the CIA), Thompson moved to Bangkok after World War I and later disappeared mysteriously in Malaysia's Cameron Highlands in 1967. He is most famous for introducing Thai silk to the world and for his collection of traditional art, much of which is now displayed at his former home, Jim Thompson's House (daily from 9am, last tour 5pm; B100, under-25s and students B50; National Stadium or Siam Central Skytrain stations or on the Khlong Saen Seb Canal taxi; Ⓦwww.jimthompson.com), near Siam Square at 6 Soi Kasemsan 2, Thanon Rama I. The grand, rambling house was constructed – without nails – from six two-hundred-year-old teak houses that Thompson shipped to Bangkok from around the kingdom. The tasteful interior has been left as it was during Thompson's life.

### Erawan Shrine

Located on the congested corner of Thanons Ploenchit and Rajdamri, sitting conspicuously next to the *Grand Hyatt Erawan*, the garishly ornate **Erawan Shrine** is well worth a visit. It is dedicated to Brahma, the Hindu creation god, and Erawan, his elephant. Buddhists, largely from Singapore, Hong Kong and Taiwan, come in droves to pray and offer thanks to each of Brahma's heads – luckily for the flower and incense hawkers. Thai dance troops can be hired to perform thanksgiving routines here when a prayer has been answered; the number of dancers depends on the magnitude of the wish fulfilled.

### Suan Pakkad Palace Museum

The **Suan Pakkad Palace Museum** (daily 9am–4pm; B100; Ⓦwww.suanpakkad.com), five minutes' walk from Phaya Thai Skytrain station at 352–4 Thanon Sri Ayutthaya, is the former palace of Prince and Princess Chumbhot of Nagara Svarga, and visitors can view their private collection of antiquities. The palace is constructed of groups of individual buildings clustered around a garden. Highlights include four-thousand-year-old pottery and jewellery, and the interior of the Lacquer Pavilion, which is decorated with Ramayana panels in gilt on black lacquer. Elsewhere you'll find Thai and Khmer sculptures, ceramics and some fine theatrical *khon* masks. The attached **Marsi Gallery** showcases contemporary art (Ⓣ02/246 1775 for details).

### Chatuchak Weekend Market

With eight thousand open-air stalls to peruse, the enormous **Chatuchak**

**Weekend Market** (Sat & Sun 7am–6pm; Ⓦwww.jjmarketplace.com), about 5km north of Banglamphu, is Bangkok's most enjoyable shopping experience. It's the place to make for if you want to get handicrafts and cheap northern and northeastern textiles and products, including axe pillows, silk, farmers shirts and *benja* pottery, which are clustered in sections 22–26. Other best buys include lacquerware, jeans, musical instruments, jewellery and baskets. The market occupies a huge patch of ground between the Northern Bus Terminal and Mo Chit Skytrain and subway stations, and can also be reached by a/c buses #503/#3 or #509/#9 from Rajdamnoen Klang in Banglamphu (1hr). *Nancy Chandler's Map of Bangkok* shows the location of all the specialist sections within Chatuchak, and TAT hands out a free map of the market from their counter in the building on the southwest edge of the market, across the car park. You can change money (7am–7pm) in the market building, and there's an ATM here, too.

### Chao Mae Tubtim Shrine

If you've seen enough of the glimmer and spectacle of traditional temples, head to the five-star **Nai Lert Park Hotel**, where, hidden incongruously in a corner of the car park, you'll find Bangkok's most intriguing and confusing shrine, dedicated to **Chao Mae Tubtim**, an ancient fertility spirit. Hundreds of penises (phalluses) – ranging from diminutive carvings to ten-foot-tall stone sculptures – crowd haphazardly around a central spirit house, to which women who are trying to conceive leave offerings of lotus and jasmine flowers. If their wish is fulfilled, the women return, leaving another phallus at the shrine to offer thanks. The origins of the shrine are mysterious, but the phallic symbol (the lingam) has its basis in the fabled Hindu god Shiva and can be seen at Hindu temples throughout Thailand. Phalluses are frequently sold as good luck or protecting amulets, and are believed to influence the cashflow of businesses, though how exactly is a mystery. *Lai Nert Park Hotel* is at 2 Thanon Witthayu (Wireless Rd; Chit Lom or Phloen Chit Skytrain station, or Khlong Saen Saeb canal boat).

## Arrival

**By bus** Bangkok has three long-distance bus terminals. Services from Malaysia and the south come in at the Southern Bus Terminal, about 5km into Thonburi. The following buses serve Phra Pinklao Bridge (for Banglamphu): #124, #507 (Th Yaowarat/Hualamphong station) and #511 (Democracy Monument/Th Sukhumvit). Services from the north and northeast use the Northern Bus Terminal on Th Kamphaeng Phet 2, near Chatuchak Weekend Market; either take a short taxi ride to Mo Chit Skytrain station or use bus #3 (Th Samsen/Th Phra Athit) or #512 (Democracy Monument). Buses from the east coast pull into the Eastern Bus Terminal at Soi 40, Th Sukhumvit (a few east-coast services also use the Northern Bus Terminal). Either take the Skytrain from Ekamai station, or bus #24 (Siam/Hualamphong station/Wat Pho) or #512 (Sanum Luang/Democracy Monument).

**By train** Nearly all trains to Bangkok arrive at Hualamphong station, which is at the southern end of the subway line and served by buses #53 and #507 to Banglamphu (#53 continues to Thewes), #25 to Siam Square (for Skytrain connections) and Th Sukhumvit, and #29 for Th Rama IV and Siam Square. Tuk-tuks are more reliable and cost around B60. Trains from Kanchanaburi arrive at Bangkok Noi station in Thonburi, from which it's easiest to take a taxi into the centre.

**By air** Bangkok boasts two airports: Suvarnabhumi Airport (BKK) and Don Muang (DMK). Always check with your airline which airport you'll arrive at. Suvarnabhumi Airport (Ⓣ02/132 3888, Ⓦwww.bangkokairportonline.com) is 30km east of Bangkok and handles its main international flights and some domestic. A tourist information service and currency exchange is located in the arrivals hall on Level 2, and ATMs are found throughout the airport. A free shuttle bus transports passengers to the Transport Centre within the airport grounds where public buses, taxis and rental cars can be found. Taxis can also be found on Level 1 at arrivals; they cost between B500 and B700, plus B40 expressway toll. The airport bus (frequent departures; B150; 1hr 30min) leaves from outside the arrivals hall on Level 2, and serves four main areas of the city; route AE2 serves Banglamphu and AE4 heads to Hualamphong Station. Don Muang handles domestic flights operated by Thai Airways, Nok Air and One-Two-Go, and is 25km north of the city. There are 24-hour exchange booths, ATMs, two TAT information desks (daily 9am–midnight; ⓣ02/523 8973, ⓦwww.donmuangairportonline.com), an accommodation booking desk (24hr) and several left-luggage offices (B90 per day). Trains run from Don Muang Station, opposite the airport, to Hualamphong Station in central Bangkok (14 daily, mostly at night; 1hr). There are also public buses to Hualamphong and other main destinations in the city; #551 terminates at Victory Monument (from whence take bus #59 or #509 to Sanum Luang). A taxi from Don Muang costs around B350, including B70 expressway toll. Never take an unlicensed taxi as robberies are not unknown.

## Information and tours

**Tourist information** Bangkok Tourist Bureau (BTB), 17/1 Th Phra Athit in Banglamphu (daily 9am–7pm; ⓣ02/225 7612, ⓦwww.bangkoktourist.com), provides a decent information service and has twenty or so booths around the capital. Tourism Authority of Thailand (TAT) 4 Rajdamnoen Nok (Mon–Fri 8.30am–4.30pm; ⓣ02/282 9773, 24hr freephone tourist assistance ⓣ1672, ⓦwww.tourismthailand.org) is a good stop for destinations further afield.

**Publications** Useful monthly magazines include *Metro*, aimed at expats, which has useful listings and is available in bookstores across the city (B100), and *Farang*, which targets backpackers (B100), and is sold mainly in Banglamphu.

**Maps** All bookshops stock a wide range of maps, most of which include a bus map. The idiosyncratic *Nancy Chandler's Map of Bangkok* (ⓦwww.nancychandler.net) is great for shopping.

**Tour operators** Th Khao San is a notorious centre of fly-by-night operations, some of which have been known to flee with travellers' money overnight, so check that the travel agent belongs to the Association of Thai Travel Agents (ATTA; ⓣ02/237 6046, ⓦwww.atta.or.th). Many travel agents can also arrange visas for neighbouring countries. Recommended agents include: Educational Travel Centre (ETC; ⓦwww.etc.co.th), inside the *Royal Hotel*, Room 318, 2 Th Rajdamnoen Klang, Banglamphu (ⓣ02/224 0043), at 180 Th Khao San, Banglamphu (ⓣ02/282 2958), and at 5/3 Soi Ngam Duphli (ⓣ02/286 9424); NS Tours (ⓔnstravel@hotmail.com), inside the *Vieng Tai Hotel*, Th Ram Bhuttri, Banglamphu (ⓣ02/629 0509), and at 46/1 Th Khao San (ⓣ02/282 1900); and STA Travel, 14th Floor, Wall Street Tower, 33/70 Th Suriwong (ⓣ02/236 0262, ⓦwww.statravel.co.th), the Bangkok branch of the worldwide travel agent, which can organize round-the-world tickets and hotel booking.

## City transport

**Bus** There are three types of bus services in the city: ordinary (non-a/c; B3.50–5.50), which come in various colours and run either from around 4am to 10pm or 24hr; the blue, white or orange a/c buses (B8–24), most of which stop at around 8.30pm; and the pink, daytime-only a/c microbuses (B10/20). Note that an attempt to clarify the numbering of the main a/c buses by adding a "5" on the front has so far not been fully enforced – you're likely to find, for example, both a/c #11 and a/c #511 plying the same route between the Southern Bus Terminal and Th Sukhumvit. Of the several bus maps sold at bookshops and hotels, the best and most useful is Bangkok Guide's *Bus Routes & Map.*

**Boats** Bangkok's network of canals is one of the fastest ways to get around the city. The Chao Phraya Express runs large water buses in daylight hours between Krung Thep Bridge in the south and Nonthaburi in the north, stopping at numbered piers (*tha*) all along its course; prices are staggered depending on distance and speed; "standard" boats with no flag (roughly 6am–7pm; every 15min; B8–11) do not necessarily stop at every landing, but will pull in if people want to get on or off. During busy periods (roughly Mon–Fri 6–9am & 3–7pm, "orange flag" also Sat 7–9am & 4–6pm), there are extra limited-stop "special express" services, flying either a yellow (B30) or orange (B15) flag; a sign on each pier shows which service stops there. The important central Chao Phraya Express stops are outlined in the box on p.767 and marked on our city map (see pp.756–757). Chao Phraya Express tourist boats (ⓦwww.chaophrayaboat.co.th), distinguished by light-blue flags, with on-board guides, run between Phra Athit (every 30min; 9.30am–3pm) and Sathorn, stopping at all piers close to tourist attractions, on both side of the river. A one-day ticket with unlimited stops costs B120. Longtail boats (*reua hang yao*) run every fifteen minutes during daylight hours along Khlong Saen Seb canal from Tha Phanfa, near Democracy Monument (handy for Banglamphu, Ratanakosin and Chinatown), and head way out east, with useful stops at Th Phrayathai, aka Saphan Hua Chang (for Jim Thompson's House and Ratchathevi Skytrain stop), Pratunam (for the Erawan Shrine), Th Witthayu (Wireless Rd), and Soi Nana Nua (Soi 3), Soi Asoke (Soi 21, for TAT headquarters and

## USEFUL BUS ROUTES

**#3** (ordinary and a/c, 24hr): Northern Bus Terminal–Chatuchak Weekend Market–Th Samsen–Th Phra Athit–Th Sanam Chai–Th Triphet–Memorial Bridge–Wat Suwan.
**#25** (ordinary and a/c, 24hr): Eastern Bus Terminal–Th Sukhumvit–Siam Square–Hualamphong Station–Th Yaowarat (for Chinatown and Wat Traimit)–Wat Pho–Tha Chang (for the Grand Palace).
**#29** (ordinary and a/c, 24hr): Don Muang Airport–Chatuchak Weekend Market–Victory Monument–Siam Square–Th Rama IV–Hualamphong Station.
**#53** circular (also anti-clockwise; ordinary): Thewes–Th Krung Kasem–Hualamphong Station–Th Yaowarat–Th Maharat (for Wat Pho and the Grand Palace)–Sanam Luang–Th Phra Athit and Th Samsen (for Banglamphu guesthouses)–Thewes.
**#159** (ordinary): Southern Bus Terminal–Phra Pinklao Bridge–Democracy Monument–Hualamphong Station–MBK Shopping Centre–Th Ratchaprarop–Victory Monument–Chatuchak Weekend Market–Northern Bus Terminal.
**#507** or **#7** (a/c): Southern Bus Terminal–Phra Pinklao Bridge (for Banglamphu guesthouses)–Sanam Luang–Th Charoen Krung–Th Chakraphet–Th Yaowarat (for Chinatown and Wat Traimit)–Hualamphong Station–Th Rama IV (for Soi Saphan Khu guesthouses)–Pak Nam (for Muang Boran Ancient City).
**#511** or **#11** (a/c): Southern Bus Terminal–Phra Pinklao Bridge–Rajdamnoen Klang–Wat Bowoniwes (for Banglamphu guesthouses)–Democracy Monument–Th Lan Luang–Th Phetchaburi–Th Sukhumvit–Eastern Bus Terminal–Pak Nam (for Muang Boran Ancient City buses).

Phetchaburi subway stop), Soi Thonglo (Soi 55) and Soi Ekamai (Soi 63), all off Th Sukhumvit. This is your quickest and most interesting way of getting across town, if you can stand the stench of the canal; fares cost B10–20.

**Skytrain** Although their networks are limited, the BTS Skytrain and the subway provide much faster alternatives to the bus. There are two Skytrain lines (Ⓦwww.bts.co.th), both running daily every few minutes from 6am to midnight, with fares of B15–40 per trip depending on distance travelled. The Sukhumvit Line runs from Mo Chit (stop N8, right next to Chatuchak Weekend Market and near the Northern Bus Terminal) in the northern part of the city to the interchange, Central Station (CS), at Siam Square, and then east along thanons Ploenchit and Sukhumvit, via Ekamai (E7, a couple of minutes' walk from the Eastern Bus Terminal) to Soi On Nut (E9). The Silom Line runs from the National Stadium (W1) through Siam Square Central station, and then south and west along thanons Rajdamri, Silom and Sathorn, via Sala Daeng near Patpong (S2), to Saphan Taksin (Taksin Bridge; S6) to link up with express boats on the Chao Phraya River.

**Subway** The subway runs frequently (up to every 2min in rush hour) from Hualamphong train station, heading east along Th Rama IV with useful stops at Silom (near the Sala Daeng Skytrain station) and Lumphini (near Th Sathorn). The line then turns north up Soi Asoke/Th Ratchadapisek via Sukhumvit Station (near Asoke Skytrain station), before looping around via Chatuchak Park (near Mo Chit Skytrain station) and Kampaeng Phet (best stop for the Chatuchak Weekend Market) to terminate at Bang Sue train station in the north of the city. Fares are B14–36, and trains run from 6am to midnight.

**Taxis** Fares in Bangkok's metered, a/c taxi cabs start at B35 (look out for the "TAXI METER" sign on the roof, and a red light in the windscreen by the passenger seat, which means that the cab is free). Insist that the taxi use its meter; some taxis refuse especially for late night or inconvenient journeys. Try to have change with you as cabs tend not to carry a lot of money or will pretend not to; tipping of up to ten percent is common, though occasionally a cabbie will round down the fare on the meter. Don't expect taxi drivers to know Bangkok particularly well; many are Isaan farmers only working to supplement a failed harvest. Pick up a business card from your guesthouse; it will most likely have directions in Thai.

**Tuk-tuks** The unmetered buggies known as tuk-tuks are nippier than cabs but be warned that there have been cases of robberies and attacks on solo women in tuk-tuks late at night, and see p.755 about cons. Also, the drivers prey on rookie tourists and often overcharge; always agree a price before you set off. In many cases it's cheaper (and more pleasant) to use a taxi. It's worth asking your guesthouse for advice on price guidelines; estimate B50 between Thewes

## CENTRAL STOPS FOR THE CHAO PHRAYA EXPRESS BOAT

Piers are marked on the map on pp.756–757.

| | |
|---|---|
| **N15** | Thewes (all boats) – for Thewes guesthouses. |
| **N14** | Rama VIII Bridge (standard) – for Samsen Soi 5. |
| **N13** | Phra Athit (standard and orange flag) – for Th Phra Athit, Th Khao San and Banglamphu guesthouses. |
| **N12** | Phra Pinklao Bridge (all boats) – for Royal Barge Museum. |
| **N11** | Bangkok Noi (Thonburi) Railway Station; standard) – for trains to Kanchanaburi. |
| **N10** | Wang Lang (or Prannok; all boats) – for Siriraj Hospital. |
| **N9** | Tha Chang (standard and orange flag) – for the Grand Palace. |
| **N8** | Thien (standard) – for Wat Pho, and the cross-river ferry to Wat Arun. |
| **N7** | Ratchini (standard). |
| **N6** | Saphan Phut (Memorial Bridge; standard and orange flag) – for Pahurat. Boats going downstream stop on the Thonburi bank, upstream boats on the Bangkok side; cross-river ferries connect the two. |
| **N5** | Rachavongse (all boats) – for Chinatown. |
| **N4** | Harbour Department (standard and orange flag). |
| **N3** | Si Phraya (all boats) – for River City. |
| **N2** | Wat Muang Kae (standard) – for GPO. |
| **N1** | Oriental (standard and orange flag) – for Th Silom. |
| **Central** | Sathorn (all boats) – for the Skytrain and Th Sathorn. |

and Th Khao San; B100 Th Khao San to Siam; B50 Hualamphong Station to Th Khao San.

**Motorbike taxis** Faster still are motorbike taxis, which can only carry one passenger and generally do shortish local journeys. The riders wear numbered, coloured vests; crash helmets are now compulsory on all main thoroughfares in the capital. Always agree a price before you set off.

## Accommodation

If you're only in Bangkok a short amount of time, the best place to base yourself is around Th Khao San (better known as Khao San Road); even though the road itself is noisy and chaotic, you're close to the action, avoiding the city's appalling traffic jams. Most bus routes stop near to Khao San, and the area is crammed with tuk-tuks (most will overcharge so haggle hard) and metered taxis. Unless you pay a cash deposit in advance, bookings of any kind are rarely accepted by budget guesthouses; from November to February, you may have difficulty getting a room after noon.

**TREAT YOURSELF**

**Buddy Lodge** 265 Th Khao San ⓣ02/629 4477, ⓦwww.buddylodge.com. Banglamphu's most stylish and expensive hotel offers charming, colonial-style rooms, a rooftop pool, a gym and a spa. ❼

### Thanon Khao San and Banglamphu

Th Khao San has become progressively more upmarket and really cheap accommodation is no longer plentiful. The cheapest places share cold-water bathrooms; expect to pay B200–400 for a double. These places are marked on the map on pp.760–761.

**At Home Guest House** 117 Th Tanao (opposite *Mai Kaidee's*) ⓣ02/281 4056, ⓔathome117@hotmail.com. Immaculately clean but slightly cramped rooms on a quiet soi within 2min of Khao San. ❷

**Bella Bella House** 74 Soi Chana Songkhram ⓣ02/629 3090. Delightful guesthouse with immaculate pale-pink rooms; the cheapest fan rooms share bathrooms, and the priciest have a/c. ❷–❹

**K.C. Guesthouse** 64 Trok Kai Chae ⓣ02/282 0618, ⓦwww.kcguesthouse.com. Just 5min from Khao San, this cheery guesthouse has cheap rooms with shared bathrooms; some have a/c. ❷–❹

**Khao San Palace Hotel** 139 Th Khao San ⓣ02/282 0578. Well-appointed hotel with a rooftop pool. All rooms have bathrooms and windows and some also have a/c, TV and panoramic views; good value for money. ❸

**Lek House** 125 Th Khao San ⓣ02/281 8441. Friendly, classic old-style Khao San guesthouse, with cramped spartan rooms and shared facilities that could be cleaner; can be noisy. ❷

**L.T. Guest House** Th Tanao (opposite *Mai Kaidee's*) ⓣ02/282 1022. Old-fashioned wooden house set above a cheap restaurant; just twelve simple rooms with shared bathroom for a bargain B100. ❶

**My House** 37 Soi Chana Songkhram, Th Phra Athit ⓣ02/829263. Cheap and simple rooms with shared bathrooms, above a cavernous café with chill-out areas with axe pillows and evening film-showings. ❶–❷, plus a B500 key deposit

**New Siam I** 21 Soi Chana Songkhram ⓣ02/282 4554, ⓦwww.newsiam.net. Well-organized place offering decent hotel-style rooms – the cheapest share bathrooms, the priciest have a/c – and access to a nearby pool (B90); they accept online bookings. ❷–❸

**R.S. Guest House** 8 Trok Kai Chae ⓣ02/282 4875, ⓔrs_guesthouse@hotmail.com. More a homestay than a guesthouse; just eight simple rooms with shared bathroom, and a friendly owner. ❷

**Sawasdee House** 147 Soi Ram Bhuttri ⓣ02/281 8138, ⓦwww.sawasdeehouse.com. Standard but noisy rooms set above a busy restaurant, with attentive staff and good value for money set menus. Offers lockers, internet and tourist information. ❷–❹

**Wally House** 189/1–2 Th Khao San ⓣ02/282 7067. Small guesthouse, where the simplest rooms are among the cheapest in the area, or you can pay a bit extra for a bathroom and fan. ❶–❷

## Thewes

The guesthouses clustered behind the National Library on Th Sri Ayutthaya are more charming and laid-back than their Khao San counterparts, appealing to a mixed crowd of travellers and families; it's an interesting 25-minute walk to Khao San, or just a few stops on the Chao Phraya river boat. These places are marked on the map on pp.760–761.

**Sawatdee Guest House** 71 Th Sri Ayutthaya, corner of Soi 16 ⓣ02/281 0757. Nice, airy, wood-panelled rooms with shared hot-water bathrooms, set behind a concrete front. The chatty owner may discount long-term stays. ❷–❸

**Sri Ayutthaya** Soi 14, 23/11 Th Sri Ayutthaya ⓣ02/282 5942. The most attractive guesthouse in Thewes with elegant, wood-panelled rooms, some of them en suite, though the staff win no prizes. ❷–❸

**Taewez Guesthouse** 23/12 Th Sri Ayutthaya ⓣ02/280 8856, ⓦwww.taewez.com. Basic, bare rooms in a modern annexe with spotless shared bathrooms and especially friendly staff; popular with the French and good for solo travellers. ❷

## Chinatown and Hualamphong Station area

The guesthouses below are convenient for Hualamphong station but are away from points of interest. Chinatown's maze of streets is noisy and not particularly backpacker-friendly. See the map on pp.756–757.

**Baan Hualamphong** 336/20 Soi Chalongkrung, off Th Rama IV ⓣ02/639 8095. Custom-built wooden house with hanging plants and a stylish modern decor. The double rooms are big and there are four-person dorms (B200); all rooms share facilities. ❹

**FF Guest House** 338/10 Trok La-O, off Th Rama IV ⓣ02/233 4168. The cheapest accommodation in the area has a homestay atmosphere. It's at the end of an alley just 5min from the station and subway, and offers ten basic rooms with dingy shared bathrooms. ❶–❷

**The Train Inn** 428 Th Rong Mueang ⓣ02/215 3055, ⓦwww.thetraininn.com. Located a minute's walk behind Hualamphong (exit from platform 3), the Train Inn has smart en-suite rooms with cable TV and a/c. ❸–❹

**Your Place** 336/17 Soi Chalongkrung, off Th Rama IV, ⓣ02/639 8034, ⓦwww.yourplaceguesthouse.com. Bright, tidy rooms, some with a/c and en-suite, others with fan and shared hot-water bathrooms. ❸–❺

## Downtown

There are some decent guesthouses south of Rama IV close to Lumphini metro station, although quite far from the main travellers' hangouts. The area attracts an older expat crowd. These places are marked on the map on pp.756–757.

**Freddy's 2** 27/40 Soi Sri Bamphen ⓣ02/286 7826. Popular, clean, though rather noisy guesthouse with shared bathrooms, and a small café at the rear. ❶–❷

**Lee Guest House 3** 13 Soi Saphan Khu ⓣ02/679 7045. The pick of the Lee establishments dotted around the neighbourhood; spacious rooms with en-suite cold showers and a charming owner. ❶–❷

**Madam Guest House** 11 Soi Saphan Khu ⓣ02/286 9289. Characterful but cramped rooms set in a warren of an old wooden house, most with shared cold-water bathroom; the cheapest on the soi. ❶

**Sala Thai Daily Mansion** 15 Soi Saphan Khu ⓣ02/287 1436. A cluttered but spotlessly clean and friendly place at the end of this quiet alley, with shared hot-water bathrooms and a roof terrace. ❸–❹

## Eating

Bangkok boasts an astonishing fifty thousand places to eat – that's almost one for every hundred citizens – ranging from B3 chicken on a stick to world-class haute cuisine. There are food stalls on almost every corner (expect to pay B20–50) so you could easily spend a week here without stepping foot inside a restaurant. The basic rule of thumb is to do as the Thais do; if there's a stall crammed with locals, go there. Don't bother going to a restaurant where no locals are eating; chances are the food will be bland and overpriced. Most places are open from around 7/8am until 10pm; exceptions are noted below.

### Banglamphu

**Ethos Restaurant** opposite *Mai Kaidee's*. A non-preachy vegetarian/vegan restaurant with low tables, a fabulously varied menu, a huge selection of teas including a delicious iced mint tea with lemon, inexpensive exotic cocktails and a laid-back atmosphere and fantastic staff – the perfect antidote to Th Khao San. Nothing is artificial and dishes are guaranteed MSG-free. Free Wi-Fi and a good book selection are also on offer.

**Hemlock** 56 Th Phra Athit ⓣ02/282 7507. Small, stylish restaurant that offers a long, mid-priced menu of unusual Thai dishes, including some great ancient specialities, and a good veggie selection. Mon–Sat 5pm–midnight; worth reserving on Fri and Sat nights.

**Je Hoy** Th Samsen, corner of Soi 8/1. Pavement restaurant that draws big Thai crowds, with a sumptuous menu specializing in freshly-cooked fish. Open from 5pm.

**Joy Luck Club** Th Phra Sumen; look for the greenery on the pavement. An intriguing oasis of calm in the chaos of Th Khao San, this café/restaurant has plants inside and out, hanging fish traps, interesting Afghan beads and stylish art. The ultra-friendly owner does Thai and fusion food.

**May Kaidee** ⓦwww.maykaidee.com. May Kaidee is something of a Bangkok institution and now serves her vegetarian food at two locations, as well as running cookery courses (B1200). The original and still popular street restaurant is behind 111 Th Tanao (open till 9pm), while *May Kaidee 2* (the a/c restaurant with the cookery school out back; open till 10pm) is at 33 Th Samsen (opposite Soi 2). Try the tasty green curry with coconut or the sticky black-rice pudding.

**Popiang** Soi Ram Bhuttri. Very popular place serving freshly cooked seafood for rock-bottom prices; plates of mussels, cockles and squid cost just B50–70. Testament to the rule that the worse the decor is, the better the food.

**Prakorb House** Th Khao San. Archetypal travellers' haven, with an emphasis on wholesome ingredients instead of decor. Herbal teas, mango shakes, delicious pumpkin curry and lots more besides, all at inexpensive prices.

**Roti Mataba** 136 Th Phra Athit. Famous outlet for very cheap fried Indian breads (under B30), or *rotis*, served here in lots of sweet and savoury varieties, including with vegetable and meat curries, and with bananas and condensed milk. A good place to watch the world go by. Closed Sun.

**Sabai Jai Kaiyang** no English sign, corner of Samsen 1, Th Samsen. A no-nonsense, open restaurant serving all the Isaan favourites at rock-bottom prices, with a tantalizing selection of *som tam*, salads and *larb*. Equally popular with Thais and farangs. Not to be missed. Open 11am–10pm.

**The Secret Garden** Th Chakra Bongse. Escape into this a/c café with tall bamboo plants and indulge in some tasty Middle Eastern food: falafel, baba ganoush, salads and sandwiches, washed down with a delicious coconut shake. Prices B50–120.

**Tom Yam Kung** Th Khao San. Delicious, fairly expensive, authentic Thai food, served in a beautiful early twentieth-century villa that's hidden behind Khao San's modern clutter. Well worth paying the extra for; the fried snapper with spicy salad is outstanding, or try the spicy fried catfish and coconut-palm curry with tofu. There's a lively mixture of Thais and farangs. Open 24hr.

**Tongjun Café** Th Sri Ayutthaya, opposite Soi 16. Fabulous fruit shakes (mango is a speciality) and tasty coffee at this little street-side café with the best and friendliest service in Thailand.

### Chinatown and Pahurat

The best place to eat in Chinatown is on the street; night stalls set up along Th Yaowarat, especially around Soi 11, mostly selling fish served in imaginative ways to an eager and appreciative Thai crowd. Bring your phrasebook or pointing finger as little English is spoken.

**Royal India** Just off Th Chakraphet at 392/1. Famously good mid-priced curries served in the heart of Pahurat, Bangkok's most Indian neighbourhood, to an almost exclusively South Asian clientele.

**Shangri-La** 306 Th Yaowarat (corner of Th Rajawong). Cavernous place serving mid-priced Chinese classics, including lots of seafood, and lunchtime dim sum. Very popular.

## Downtown

**Cabbages & Condoms** 6-8 Soi 12 Th Sukhumvit ⓦwww.pda.or.th/restaurant. Run by the Population and Community Development Association of Thailand, all proceeds from this fun, atmospheric open-air restaurant go to community projects. The menu features all the Thai classics (B100–300).

**Celadon** *Sukhothai Hotel*, 13/3 Th Sathorn Tai ⓣ02/287 0222. Consistently rated as the best Thai hotel restaurant in Bangkok, in an elegant setting among lotus ponds; well worth a splurge. Seafood is a great choice: both *plaa thalay prikpao* (seafood salad) and green curry with prawns (B320) come highly praised.

**Harmonique** 22 Soi 34, Th Charoen Krung, on the lane between Wat Muang Kae express-boat pier and the GPO ⓣ02/237 8175. Relaxing, moderately priced restaurant, where tables are scattered throughout several old houses and a leafy courtyard, and the Thai food is varied and delicious. Closed Sun.

**Indian Hut** 311/2–5 Th Suriwong. Bright, moderately expensive, North Indian restaurant, with plenty of veggie options, that's justly popular with local Indians.

**Inter** 432/1–2 Soi 9, Siam Square. Honest, popular Thai restaurant equally popular with office workers as with shoppers, serving cheap one-dish meals (B50), good-value three-course lunch deals with jelly and ice cream (B100), and a great range of curries, salads and Isaan food, in a no-nonsense canteen atmosphere.

**Jim Thompson's Café** 120/1 Soi 1, Th Saladaeng. A civilized, moderately priced haven with delicious Thai daily specials and desserts, pasta, cakes and other Western food.

**Khrua Aroy Aroy** 3/1 Th Pan. In a fruitful area for cheap food (there is also a night market across Th Silom on Soi 20), this simple shop-house stands out for its choice of tasty dishes from around the kingdom. Roughly Mon–Fri 8am–6pm, Sat & Sun 8am–4pm.

**Mah Boon Krong Food Centre** Floor 5, 6 and 7, MBK shopping centre, corner of Rama I and Phrayathai roads. MBK is the place to come if you're hungry in Siam – it has over 80 eating choices. Floor 5 boasts the swanky new International Food Hall, where a huge range of delicious food is prepared in front of you at mini-kitchenettes; choose from among Vietnamese, Indian, Greek, Japanese or Italian. Floor 6 is a more standard food court serving inexpensive one-dish meals from all over Thailand. Floor 7 is packed with joints; the best choice is the fantastic *MK Restaurant* which serves *suki* (DIY Thai fondue), where you pick your own ingredients and cook them in a hot pot in front of you on the table; the roast duck is also a must.

**Siam Paragon** Surprisingly inexpensive, tempting food court in the ultra-chic Siam Paragon serving everything from one-dish Thai standards to steaks and pizzas, with seating laid out around brightly lit fish tanks. There's also a delicatessen area with outstanding pastry snacks and cakes.

**TREAT YOURSELF**

A great way to see Bangkok's beautifully illuminated riverside temples at night is on a dinner cruise. Chomping on Thai green curry whilst gliding past the Grand Palace is an experience you'll never forget. Several companies offer evening cruises (leaving around 7pm and lasting around 2hr), with either a set menu or buffet, many featuring Thai music or dance. Prices are around B1200–1600 but it is well worth the splurge. Always book in advance.

**Grand Pearl of Siam** ⓣ089/110 5719. Departs River City at 7pm, with an international buffet dinner and live music.

**Manohra** ⓣ02/477 0770, ⓦwww.manohracruises.com. Beautifully converted rice barges and live traditional music. Departs the Manohra Pier in front of *Bangkok Marriott Resort* at 7pm (alternative pick-ups available).

**Wan Fah** ⓣ02/222 8679, ⓦwww.wanfah.in.th. Traditional open-air boats and Thai dance, with a fabulous four-course Thai or seafood set menu. Departs River City at 7pm.

## Drinking and nightlife

Bangkok's nightlife has become more sophisticated and stylish in the last few years. Silom 4 (Soi 4, Th Silom), just east of Patpong, is one of Bangkok's most happening after-dark haunts, along with the high-concept clubs and bars of Sukhumvit, studenty Siam Square and the lively, teeming venues of backpacker-orientated Banglamphu, which is a great place to meet other travellers and enjoy live music. Many bars in Banglamphu show nightly films and most big football games. Though Silom 4 started out as a purely gay area, it now offers a

## RED-LIGHT BANGKOK

More than a thousand sex-related businesses operate in Bangkok: they dominate Thanon Sukhumvit's Soi Cowboy (between Sois 21 and 23), Clinton Entertainment Plaza (between Sois 13 and 15) and Nana Plaza (Soi 4), but the city's most notorious zone is **Patpong**, between the eastern ends of thanons Silom and Suriwong. Here, girls cajole passers-by in front of lines of go-go bars, with names like *French Kiss* and *Love Nest*, while insistent touts proffer printed menus detailing the degradations of the sex shows upstairs. If you do end up at a sex show, be warned that you'll be charged exorbitant prices for drinks, and will have to face a menacing bouncer if you refuse to pay. In amongst the bars Patpong also has a night market, which mainly sells fake designer clothes – and attracts all sorts to the strip after dark, including demure tourists of both sexes (see p.774).

mixed range of styles, while the city's other main gay area is the more exclusive Silom 2 (towards Th Rama IV). Note that the current government's Social Order Policy has involved clampdowns on illegal drugs, including urine testing of bar customers, and ID checks to curb under-age drinking – you're supposed to be over 21 in bars and clubs, though Thais seem to be more rigorously checked than foreigners.

### Banglamphu

**Bangkok Bar** 149 Soi Ram Bhuttri. This small, narrow dance bar is fronted by a different DJ every night and draws capacity crowds of drinkers and clubbers. Open 5pm–2am.

**Blues Bar** (aka *Ad Here the 13th*) 13 Th Samsen. Chilled-out bar where you can relax with musos and enjoy popular live music from the in-house jazz and blues quartet from about 10pm onwards. Good cocktails too. Open 6pm–midnight.

**Café Democ** 78 Th Rajdamnoen Klang, overlooking Democracy Monument. Fashionable, dark bar offering lots of cocktails, with nightly sessions from up-and-coming Thai DJs and regular hip-hop evenings. Open 4pm–2am; closed Mon.

**The Club** Th Khao San. If all the Chang Beer's gone straight to your feet, grab your dancing shoes and head to *The Club*. Resident DJs pump thumping house tunes through the two bars and relatively spacious dance floor until late.

**Comme** Th Phra Athit. This open-fronted bar-restaurant draws big crowds with its laid-back atmosphere and lively cover bands.

**Eaux de Vie** 67 Th Phra Sumen. It's no wonder that this dinky bar draws a lively Thai crowd: it's atmospherically decked out in dark wood with iconic artwork and has a great range of spirits. Look for the cinema sign overhead.

**Gullivers' Travellers Tavern** Th Khao San. Backpacker-oriented a/c sports pub with two pool tables, sixteen TV screens, masses of sports memorabilia and reasonably priced beer. Daily 11am–2am.

**Hippie de Bar** About 30m south along Khao San, near to the neon illumination of *Tom Yam Kung Restaurant*. An eclectic and laid-back patio restaurant-bar with an extensive cocktail menu; the mojitos are well worth the trip. Popular with local Thais, especially for food; mains B85–120.

**Molly Pub** Th Ram Bhuttri. With its attractive, colonial-style facade, and comfy low-slung wooden chairs, this is a great place to kick back, though the beer's not cheap.

**Silk Bar** 129–131 Th Khao San. The two-tiered outdoor decks are a popular spot for sipping cocktails – the blended mojitos are unmissable – while watching the nightly Khao San fashion parade; inside, there's a pool table and a DJ. Daily 6am–2am.

**The Station** Th Chakra Bongse. Either deplore its tackiness or love the concept (and the menu littered with petrol puns) – this bar is in a disused petrol station. Grab a "tank" (bucket) of Sang Som and coke, then sit back and watch the world go by. Its mix-and-match menu is good value for money, and tasty fresh fruit cocktails are on offer. Also shows big football matches.

### Downtown

**Bed Supperclub** 26 Soi 11, Th Sukhumvit ⑦02/651 3537. Seductively curvaceous spacepod bar whose futuristic all-white interior is furnished with bed-style couches. DJs, cocktails and a surprisingly cosy atmosphere. Daily 8pm–2am.

**Dallas Pub** Soi 6, Siam Square. Typical dark, noisy "songs for life" (Thai folk-rock) hangout – buffalo skulls, American flags – but a lot of fun: singalongs to decent live bands, dancing and friendly staff.

**DJ Station** Soi 2, Th Silom. Highly fashionable but unpretentious gay disco, packed at weekends, attracting an interesting mix of Thais and farangs.

Cabaret show at 11.30pm; B300 including two drinks Fri & Sat.

**Lucifer** 76/1–3 Patpong 1. Popular dance club in the dark heart of Patpong, done out with mosaics and stalactites like a satanic grotto; no admission charge except on Fri & Sat (B150). *Radio City*, the bar downstairs, features famous Elvis and Tom Jones impersonators.

**Saxophone** 3/8 Victory Monument (southeast corner), Th Phrayathai ⓣ02/246 5472. Lively bar that hosts nightly jazz, blues, folk and rock bands and attracts a relaxed mix of Thais and farangs.

**TREAT YOURSELF**

Bangkok can be monstrously ugly by day, but when the sun sets and the smog dissolves the city can reveal a magical charm. The best way to take advantage of this is to head to one of the enormously tall skyscraper hotels that have rooftop bars; drinks are expensive but the views are unbeatable.

**Moon Bar (Vertigo)** at the *Banyan Tree Hotel*, Thanon Sathorn Tai. 61st-floor rooftop bar which overlooks bustling downtown. 6.30–11pm.

**Roof Top Bar** at the *Baiyoke Sky Hotel* 222 Th Rajaprarop. Thailand's tallest building has a bar on floor 83 but head up to the revolving 84th floor for truly awesome, vertigo-inducing views. 10pm–1am.

**The Sky Bar & Distil** at *Lebua at State Tower*, corner of Thanon Silom and Thanon Charoen Krung. Incredible river views and live jazz. 5pm–1am.

## Culture shows, theatre and puppetry

**Baan Thai Restaurant** Soi 32, Th Sukhumvit ⓣ02/258 5403. The nightly culture show at the *Baan Thai* is a hotchpotch of Thai dancing and classical music, accompanying a set dinner. Performances at 8.30pm; B550.

**The Joe Louis Puppet Theatre** Suan Lum Night Bazaar, Th Rama IV ⓣ02/252 9683. Magical retelling of the Rama story using all manner of puppets, including the dying art of shadow puppetry. Mon–Fri 7.30pm; Sat & Sun 5pm & 7.30pm; arrive 30min early for mask-making demonstration. B600, kids B300.

**Patravadi Theatre** 69/1 Soi Wat Rakang ⓣ02/412 7287, ⓦwww.patravaditheatre. The free performances at the Patravadi Theatre blend contemporary and classical Thai dancing, with a busy schedule of evening performances by both Thailand's top performers and up-and-coming stars. There are also Thai classical dance and drum classes (B150 for foreigners). Also features an excellent garden restaurant (dishes B60–200).

### THAI BOXING

**Thai boxing matches** (*muay Thai*) can be very violent, but also very entertaining (see p.748). Sessions usually feature ten bouts of five three-minute rounds and are held in the capital every night of the week at either the Rajdamnoen Stadium, next to the TAT office on Rajdamnoen Nok (ⓣ02/281 4205; Mon, Wed & Sun 6pm, Thurs 5pm), and at Lumphini Stadium on Thanon Rama IV (ⓣ02/252 8765; Tues & Fri 6.30pm, Sat 5pm & 8.30pm). Tickets go on sale one hour beforehand and range from B1000 to B2000. To partake in *muay Thai* yourself, head to Sor Vorapin's Gym at 13 Trok Kasap, off Thanon Chakra Bongse in Banglamphu; he holds classes twice daily (B400 per session, B2500 for seven sessions; ⓣ02/282355, ⓦwww.thaiboxings.com).

## Shopping

Department stores and tourist-oriented shops in the city open at 10 or 11am and close at about 9pm.

### Books

**Aporia** Th Tanao, Banglamphu. One of Banglamphu's main outlets for new books, and also sells secondhand books. Wide and fantastic selection of fiction and lots of maps.

**Asia Books** ⓦwww.asiabooks.com. English-language bookshop recommended for its books on Asia. Has 13 branches in Bangkok including: in Siam Paragon, level 2; in *Landmark Hotel* between sois 4 and 6, Tha Sukhumvit; and in Siam Discovery Centre on Th Rama I.

**Bookazine** Huge range of foreign newspapers and magazines plus a decent selection of English-language books and maps; the most convenient

## TRADITIONAL DRAMA

Drama pretty much equals dance in Thai theatre, and many of the traditional dance-dramas are based on the Hindu epic, the Ramayana (in Thai, Ramakien), a classic adventure tale of good versus evil that is known across Southeast Asia. The most spectacular form of traditional Thai theatre is **khon**, a stylized drama performed in masks and elaborate costumes by a troupe of highly trained classical dancers whose every graceful, angular gesture depicts a precise event, action or emotion that will be familiar to educated *khon* audiences. The story is chanted and sung by a chorus, accompanied by a classical orchestra.

Serious and more refined, **lakhon** is derived from *khon*, but is used to dramatize a greater range of stories, including Buddhist Jataka tales and local folk dramas as well as the Ramayana. The form you're most likely to come across is *lakhon chatri*, which is performed at shrines such as Bangkok's Erawan as entertainment for the spirits and as a token of gratitude from worshippers. Dancers wear decorative costumes but no masks.

**Likay** is a much more popular derivative of *khon*, with lots of comic interludes, bawdy jokes and over-the-top acting. Most *likay* troupes adapt potboiler romances or write their own, and travel around the country doing shows on makeshift outdoor stages and at temple fairs.

branch is at 58 Th Khao San. Other branches include those on Th Silom in the CP Tower (Patpong) and in the Silom Complex; Siam Square; All Seasons Place on Th Witthayu; and at the mouth of Sukhumvit Soi 5.

**Shaman Books** Two branches on Th Khao San (one opposite *Susie's Pub*; the other on Th Tanao). A goldmine of interesting non-fiction books (especially travel writing, Thai literature and religion) as well as a good selection of English-language fiction. Don't expect bargains, though.

**Ton's Bookseller** 327/5 Th Ram Bhuttri. One of Banglamphu's best-stocked outlets for non-fiction books about Thailand and Southeast Asia including essential reading Do's and Don'ts guides. It also sells some maps and a limited selection of English-language fiction.

### Crafts

**Chatuchak Weekend Market** See p.763.

**The Legend** Floor 3, Amarin Plaza, Th Ploenchit; and Floor 3, Thaniya Plaza, Th Silom. Stocks well-made Thai handicrafts at reasonable prices. Its subsidiary Tamnan Mingmuang, Floor 3, Thaniya Plaza, concentrates on unusual basketry from all over the country.

**Suan Luam Night Bazaar** Over 3000 outlets and stalls; some have handicraft sections but it's more focused on contemporary design. Best from 6 to 10pm.

### Gems

Bangkok is a good place to buy cut and uncut rubies, blue sapphires and diamonds, but never accompany touts, "guides" or tuk-tuk drivers to the shops they recommend (there are no TAT-endorsed jewellery shops): many a gullible traveller has wasted thousands of dollars on worthless stones. See ⓦwww.2bangkok.com/2bangkok/scams/sapphire.shtml for a detailed description of the typical scam and advice on what to do if you get done.

**Johnny's Gems** 199 Th Fuang Nakhon, near Wat Rajabophit. Reputable gem and jewellery shop.

### Malls

**Mah Boon Krong (MBK)** Rama I/Phrayathai intersection; National Stadium Skytrain stop ⓦwww.mbk-center.co.th. Labyrinthine shopping centre that houses hundreds of small, mostly inexpensive outlets, including plenty of high-street fashion shops. Floor 3 is the best place to buy anything to do with mobile phones; floors 5 and 6 have extensive food courts and floor 7 has a cinema with daily English-language film showings.

**Siam** Siam is packed full of malls; check out Siam Centre and Siam Discovery Centre, both good for trendy local labels. In Siam Square, head to what's styled as the area's "Centerpoint" between Sois 3 and 4, with hundreds of inexpensive boutiques selling colourful street gear. Siam Paragon is the newest addition to Siam's shopping family, with the most expensive shops in Bangkok in a luxurious mall and an incredible food centre.

**Silom/Ploenchit** Around Silom you'll find more the upmarket malls, including Central Chitlom (arguably the city's best shopping centre) and Gaysorn Plaza, which are glossier than their Siam counterparts, and boast chic design shops.

## Markets

**Chatuchak Weekend Market** See p.763.
**Pak Khlong Talat** Sprawling flower and vegetable market that's been in business since the nineteenth century. The most interesting approach is from Old Siam Plaza along Th Banmo. Best visited before dawn.
**Patpong Night Market** The place to stock up on fake designer goods, from pseudo-Rolex watches to Burberry shirts. Daily 5pm–1am.
**Suan Lum Night Bazaar** corner of thanons Rama IV and Witthayu. This place is aiming to become a night-time Chatuchak, with some interesting clothes and handicrafts stalls, as well as an open-air food and beer garden, with nightly live music. If you're shopped-out, absorb some culture at the Joe Louis puppet theatre (see p.772). Daily 3pm–midnight.
**Thanon Khao San** An open market both day and night with traders plying cheap clothes, iconic Khao San Road t-shirts, sunglasses and fake identity cards. The competition brings prices down but haggle hard as they're used to travel rookies.

## Directory

**Airlines, domestic** Bangkok Airways, 1111 Th Ploenchit ⓣ02/254 2903; One-Two-Go, 18 Th New Rachadapisek, Khlongtoey, ⓣ02/229 4260; PBair, UBC 2 Bldg, 591 Sukhumvit Soi 33 ⓣ02/261 0220; Thai Airways, 485 Th Silom ⓣ02/232 8000, and 6 Th Lan Luang near Democracy Monument ⓣ02/280 0060, 24hr reservations ⓣ02/628 2000.
**Airlines, international** Aeroflot ⓣ02/254 1180; Air Asia ⓣ02/515 9999; Air Canada ⓣ02/670 0400; Air France ⓣ02/635 1186; Air India ⓣ02/235 0557; Air New Zealand ⓣ02/254 8440; Biman Bangladesh Airlines ⓣ02/233 3640; British Airways ⓣ02/636 1747 or 02/236 2800; Cathay Pacific ⓣ02/263 0616; China Airlines ⓣ02/253 4242; Druk Air ⓣ02/535 1960; Egyptair ⓣ02/231 0505; Emirates ⓣ02/664 1040; Eva Air ⓣ02/240 0890; Finnair ⓣ02/635 1234; Garuda ⓣ02/679 7371; Gulf Air ⓣ02/254 7931; Japan Airlines ⓣ02/234 9114; KLM ⓣ02/679 1100; Korean Air ⓣ02/635 0465; Lao Airlines ⓣ02/237 6982; Lauda Air ⓣ02/267 0873; Lufthansa ⓣ02/264 2400; Malaysia Airlines ⓣ02/263 0565; Nok Air ⓣ1318 or ⓣ02/900 9955; Olympic Airways ⓣ02/237 6141; Pakistan International (PIA) ⓣ02/234 2961; Philippine Airlines ⓣ02/633 5713; Qantas ⓣ02/636 1747; Royal Brunei ⓣ02/637 5151; Singapore Airlines ⓣ02/236 0440; Sri Lankan Airlines ⓣ02/236 4981; Swiss ⓣ02/636 2150; Thai Airways ⓣ02/280 0060, 24hr reservations ⓣ02/628 2000; Tiger Airways ⓣ02/351 8333; United Airlines ⓣ02/253 0558; Vietnam Airlines ⓣ02/655 4137.
**Banks and Exchange** ATMs are dotted all around Bangkok – especially outside 7/11 stores. Nearly all accept foreign cards. You can take out cash advances (take your passport for identification) at banks; most offer money exchange into baht.
**Embassies and consulates** Australia, 37 Th Sathorn Tai ⓣ02/287 2680; Cambodia, 518/4 Th Pracha Uthit ⓣ02/957 5851; Canada, 15th floor, Abdulrahim Place, 990 Th Rama IV ⓣ02/636 0540; China, 57 Th Rajadapisek ⓣ02/245 7043; Indonesia, 600–602 Th Phetchaburi ⓣ02/252 3135; Ireland (Republic of), 28th Floor, Q House, Lumphini Building, 1 Th Sathorn Tai ⓣ02/677 7500; Laos, 520, 502/1-3 Th Pracha-Uthit ⓣ02/539 6667; Malaysia, 33-35 Th Sathorn Tai ⓣ02/679 2190; New Zealand, 14th Floor, M Tower, All Seasons Place, 87 Th Witthayu ⓣ02/254 2530; Philippines, 760 Th Sukhumvit, opposite Soi 47 ⓣ02/259 0139; Singapore, 129 Th Sathorn Tai ⓣ02/286 2111; South Africa, 124th Floor, M Thai Tower, All Seasons Place, Lumphini ⓣ02/659 2900; Vietnam, 83/1 Th Witthayu ⓣ02/251 7202; UK, 1031 Th Witthayu ⓣ02/305 8333; US, 120–122 Th Witthayu ⓣ02/205 4000.
**Emergencies** For all emergencies, either: call the tourist police (free 24hr phoneline ⓣ1155), who also maintain a 24hr booth in the Suan Lum Night Bazaar on Th Rama IV; visit the Banglamphu Police Station at the west end of Th Khao San; or contact the Tourist Police Headquarters, CMIC Tower, 209/1 Soi 21 (Asoke), Th Sukhumvit (ⓣ02/664 0222).
**Hospitals, clinics and dentists** Most expats rate the private Bumrungrad Hospital, 33 Sukhumvit Soi 3 (ⓣ02/667 1000, emergency ⓣ02/667 1175), as the best and most comfortable in the city, followed by: the Bangkok Nursing Home (BNH) Hospital, 9 Th Convent (ⓣ02/686 2700); the Bangkok General Hospital, 2 Soi Soonvijai 7, Th Phetchaburi Mai, ⓣ02/310 3102; and the Samitivej Sukhumvit Hospital, 133 Sukhumvit Soi 49 (ⓣ02/392 0011). You can get vaccinations and malaria advice, as well as rabies advice and treatment, at the Thai Red Cross Society's Queen Saovabha Memorial Institute (QSMI) and Snake Farm on the corner of Th Rama IV and Th Henri Dunant (Mon–Fri 8.30–noon & 1–4.30pm; ⓣ02/252 0161 or 0167, ⓦwww.redcross.or.th). Among general clinics, the Australian-run Travmin Bangkok Medical Centre, 8th Floor, Alma Link Building, next to the Central Chitlom department store at 25 Soi Chitlom, Th Ploenchit (ⓣ02/655 1024; B650 per consultation),

is recommended. For dental problems, try the Bumrungrad Hospital's dental department on ⓣ02/667 2300, or the following dental clinics (not 24hr): Dental Hospital 88/88 Sukhumvit Soi 49 ⓣ02/260 5000; Siam Family Dental Clinic 292/6 Siam Square Soi 4 ⓣ02/255 6664.

**Immigration office** About 1km down Soi Suan Phlu, off Th Sathorn Tai (Mon–Fri 8.30am–4.30pm; ⓣ02/287 3101); you can extend a 30-day tourist visa by seven days, and a 60-day tourist visa by thirty days for B1900 in less than an hour. They also send a weekly mobile office to the *Emerald Hotel*, Th Ratchadaphisek near the Huay Khwang intersection, in the northeast of the city (Wed 9am–noon). Check on ⓦwww.immigration.go.th for the latest information. Be very wary of any Khao San tour agents who offer to organize a visa extension for you: some are reportedly faking the relevant stamps, which has caused problems at immigration. If you can't extend your visa, travel agents arrange visa runs into Cambodia, crossing at Aranyaprathet (B500 for transport plus B1200/US$20 for the Cambodian visa). Note that the Thai government has capped the number of days it is possible to spend in the kingdom at 90 within a six-month period; if you go over 90 days you must leave the country and apply for a visa in a Thai embassy abroad. You will be charged B500 for each day you overstay your visa.

**Internet** You can find internet at most guesthouses and dotted all around Bangkok, especially on Th Khao San. The Thais' penchant for computer games keeps prices down; expect to pay B20–40 an hour. The Ratchadamnoen Post Office on Banglamphu's Soi Damnoen Klang Neua (daily 8am–7pm) also has very cheap public Catnet Internet booths. There are Catnet centres in the 24hr public telephone office adjacent to the GPO on Th Charoen Krung, and at Don Muang Airport.

**Laundry** Nearly all guesthouses offer a one-day turnaround laundry service for around B30 per kilo (including ironing); many other shops around Bangkok offer the same service.

**Left luggage** At Don Muang Airport (international and domestic; B90 per day); Don Muang train station (B15 per day); Eastern Bus Terminal (B30 per day), Hualamphong Station (B10–30 per day), and at most hotels and guesthouses (B10–20 per day).

**Post offices** The GPO is at 1160 Th Charoen Krung, a few hundred metres left of the exit for Wat Muang Kae express-boat pier. Poste restante can be collected here Mon–Fri 8am–8pm, Sat, Sun & hols 8am–1pm; letters are kept for three months. The parcel-packing service at the GPO operates Mon–Fri 8am–4.30pm, Sat 9am–noon. If you're staying in Banglamphu, it's more convenient to use the poste restante service at one of the two local post offices: the one closest to Khao San is Ratchadamnoen Post Office on Soi Damnoen Klang Neua (Mon–Fri 8am–5pm, Sat 9am–noon), and Banglamphu's other post office is on Soi Sibsam Hang, just west of Wat Bowoniwes (Mon–Fri 8.30am–5.30pm, Sat 9am–noon); You can also send and receive faxes here on ⓣ02/281 1579.

**Pharmacies** There are English-speaking staff at most of the capital's pharmacies, including the citywide branches of Boots the Chemist (most usefully on Th Khao San, in the Siam Centre on Th Rama I and inside the Emporium on Th Sukhumvit), which are also the easiest places to buy tampons.

**Telephones** International cardphones are dotted all over the city, and there are public telephone offices in or adjacent to major post offices, including the GPO on Th Charoen Krung (24hr), which also offers a free collect-call service, and the post offices (all 8am–7pm) at Hualamphong Station, on Th Sukhumvit, and in Banglamphu. Skype, with headphones, is widely available at internet cafés.

## Moving on

**By bus** Seats on long-distance a/c bus services to Chiang Mai, Krabi, Phuket and Surat Thani should be reserved ahead either at the relevant bus station or through guesthouses. If you go by bus from Banglamphu, you'll need at least ninety minutes (outside rush hour) to get to the Eastern Bus Terminal, and a good hour to reach the Northern or Southern terminals; taxis are faster.

There are two Southern Bus Terminals (*sai tai mai*) at the time of writing, though all routes are intended to leave from the swanky new one, about 5km further west. From Phra Pinklao Bridge catch bus #124, #159, #507 or #511. The Southern Bus Terminals handle services to all points south as well as destinations west of Bangkok. Services to the north and northeast (and a few to places on the east coast) use the Northern Bus Terminal (*sathaanii mo chit*), on Th Kamphaeng Phet 2, near Chatuchak Weekend Market. Either take the Skytrain to Mo Chit Station and hop on a taxi for the last section or take bus #3 from Phra Athit, #159 from Phra Pinklao Bridge or #512 from Democracy Monument. The Eastern Bus Terminal (*sathaanii ekamai*), at Soi 40, Th Sukhumvit, serves east-coast destinations; it's near the metro stop Ekamai, or can be reached by bus #511 from Democracy Monument or #25 from Siam Square.

**Eastern Bus Terminal** to: Ban Phe (12 daily; 3hr); Rayong (every 15min; 2hr 30min); Trat (at least hourly; 5–6hr).

**Northern Bus Terminal** to: Aranyaprathet (10 daily; 4hr 30min); Ayutthaya (every 15min; 2hr); Ban Phe (12 daily; 3hr); Chiang Khong (10 daily; 13–14hr); Chiang Mai (19 daily; 10–11hr); Chiang Rai (16 daily; 12hr); Chong Mek (2 daily; 12hr); Khon Kaen (23 daily; 6–7hr); Khorat (every 20min; 4–5hr); Lampang (10 daily; 8hr); Lopburi (every 20min; 3hr); Mae Hong Son (2 daily; 18hr); Mae Sai (8 daily; 13hr); Mae Sot (10 daily; 8hr 30min); Mukdahan (13 daily; 11hr); Nakhon Phanom (17 daily; 12hr); Nong Khai (17 daily; 10hr); Pak Chong (every 15min; 3hr); Phitsanulok (up to 19 daily; 5–6hr); Sukhothai (17 daily; 6–7hr); Surin (up to 20 daily; 8–9hr); Trat (5 daily; 4–5hr); Ubon Ratchathani (19 daily; 10–12hr); Udon Thani (for Nong Khai; every 15min; 9hr).

**Southern Bus Terminal** to: Chumphon (12 daily; 6hr 30min–9hr); Damnoen Saduak (every 20min; 2hr); Hat Yai (21 daily; 12–15hr); Kanchanaburi (every 15min; 2–3hr); Ko Samui (5 daily; 15hr); Krabi (9 daily; 12–14hr); Nakhon Pathom (every 10min; 40min–1hr 20min); Nakhon Si Thammarat (11 daily; 12hr); Phang Nga (4 daily; 11hr–12hr 30min); Phetchaburi (every 30min; 2hr); Phuket (at least 10 daily; 14–16hr); Ranong (2 daily; 8hr).

**By budget transport** Many Bangkok outfits offer budget transport on small and large buses to Chiang Mai, Surat Thani, Krabi, Ko Samet and Ko Chang. This often works out cheaper than a public a/c bus, and is often handier as departures are usually from Th Khao San. However many of the buses are cramped and airless, drivers often race, and drop-off points can be miles from the town centre, despite adverts to the contrary. Security on large buses is also a big problem, so keep everything of value on your person at all times and lock other luggage. If you're heading for an island, check whether your bus ticket covers the ferry ride. Consult other travellers before booking any budget transport and consider taking the train or a public a/c bus instead.

**By train** All trains depart from Hualamphong station except the service to Kanchanaburi, which leaves from Bangkok Noi station, about an 850m walk west of the Bangkok Noi express-boat pier. All north- and northeast-bound trains from Hualamphong make a stop at the Don Muang Airport station. The 24-hour Information booth at Hualamphong Station keeps English-language timetables, or you can try phoning the Train Information Hotline on ⓣ1690; the State Railway of Thailand website (ⓦwww.railway.co.th) carries a fare chart. Tickets for overnight trains should be booked at least a day in advance and are most reliably bought from Hualamphong; get them either from the advance booking office (daily 8.30am–4pm), which also sells joint rail-and-boat or rail-and-bus tickets via Surat Thani (B650 second-class a/c sleeper) to Ko Samui (plus B150), Ko Pha Ngan, Ko Tao and Krabi (plus B200), or from ticket counter #2 (daily 5–8.30am & 4–10pm); counters #1 and #2 deal with ticket refunds and alterations. You can also buy train tickets through travel agents (booking fee charged).

**Hualamphong Station** to: Aranyaprathet (2 daily; 5hr 30min); Ayutthaya (20 daily; 1hr 30min); Butterworth, Malaysia (daily; 23hr); Chiang Mai (7 daily; 12–14hr); Chumphon (12 daily; 7hr–9hr 30min); Don Muang Airport (30 daily; 50min); Hat Yai (5 daily; 14–16hr); Khon Kaen (5 daily; 7hr 30min–10hr 20min); Khorat (9 daily; 4–5hr); Lampang (7 daily; 11hr); Lopburi (15 daily; 2hr 30min–3hr); Nakhon Pathom (12 daily; 1hr 20min); Nakhon Si Thammarat (2 daily; 15hr); Nong Khai (4 daily; 11–12hr); Pak Chong (11 daily; 3hr 30min–4hr 45min); Phetchaburi (8 daily; 2hr 45min–3hr 45min); Phitsanulok (10 daily; 5hr 40min–8hr); Sungai Kolok (2 daily; 20hr); Surat Thani (11 daily; 9hr–11hr 30min); Surin (10 daily; 7–10hr); Trang (2 daily; 16hr); Ubon Ratchathani (7 daily; 8hr 30min–14hr); Udon Thani (for Nong Khai; 5 daily; 9hr–12hr 30min).

**Bangkok Noi Station** to: Kanchanaburi (2 daily; 3hr); Nakhon Pathom (2 daily; 1hr 10min); Nam Tok (2 daily; 5hr).

**By air** For general enquiries to Suvarnabhumi Airport, call ⓣ02/132 1888, for departures ⓣ02/132 9324 and for arrivals ⓣ02/132 9328. Check ⓦwww.donmuangairportonline.com for Don Muang. Because of the traffic in Bangkok, timings for getting to the airport are unreliable; it's best to leave an hour for Don Muang, more for Suvarnabhumi. The easiest way of getting to the airports is by metered taxi; Don Muang costs around B350, including B70 expressway toll, and Suvarnabhumi B500–700, plus B40 expressway toll. It's cheaper to book a taxi through your guesthouse. Guesthouses and travel agents can also book tickets on private minibuses to both airports (B130–150); they run hourly between 4am and 10pm. Alternatively, the B150 airport bus service to Suvarnabhumi departs hourly between 5am and midnight from outside the *Sawasdee Khao San Inn* at the southern end of Th Chakra Bongse. For Don Muang it's faster to take the Skytrain or subway to Mo Chit/Chatuchak Park and pick up a taxi for the last few kilometres to the airport from there. Orange public bus #551 (B35) leaves hourly for Don Muang from Victory Monument; it runs 24 hours but it's unreliable.

**Destinations**: Chiang Mai (22 daily; 1hr); Chiang Rai (10 daily; 1hr 20min); Hat Yai (7 daily; 1hr 25min); Khon Kaen (4 daily; 55min); Ko Samui

(15 daily; 1hr 20min); Krabi (4 daily; 1hr 20min); Lampang (daily; 1hr); Nakhon Phanom (2 daily; 1hr 5min); Nakhon Si Thammarat (2–3 daily; 1hr 15min); Phitsanulok (2 daily; 45min); Phuket (20 daily; 1hr 25min); Ranong (daily; 1hr 20min); Sukhothai (2 daily; 1hr 10min); Surat Thani (2 daily; 1hr 10min); Trang (1–2 daily; 1hr 30min); Trat (2 daily; 50min); Ubon Ratchathani (3 daily; 1hr 5min); Udon Thani (for Nong Khai; 7 daily; 1hr).

## DAY-TRIPS FROM BANGKOK

There are a few day-trips out of Bangkok that provide a happy respite from the smog and mayhem. Tour companies offer combined trips to **Damnoen Saduak Floating Market** and **Nakhon Pathom**, which are good value for money. They're worth doing for the ease of transport (avoiding the early morning trek to the Southern Bus Terminal), but most tours don't arrive at the market much before 9am, by which time it's lost much of its charm.

### Muang Boran Ancient City

A day-trip out to the **MUANG BORAN ANCIENT CITY** open-air museum (daily 8am–5pm; B300; Ⓦwww.ancientcity.com), 33km southeast of Bangkok, is a great way to explore Thailand's history and architecture, especially if you don't have time to visit the real sights. There are 112 immaculately reproduced traditional buildings dotted around the Thailand-shaped 320 acres of landscaped grounds. The best way to do the site justice is to rent a bike (B50), or hop on a tram tour (B75 with guide). To get here, take a/c bus #511/11 from Banglamphu/Thanon Rama I/Thanon Sukhumvit to Samut Prakan on the edge of Greater Bangkok (1hr 30min; B25), then change onto songthaew (pick-up) #36 for Muang Boran. A faster alternative (around 2hr) is to take a Chao Phraya Express boat down to Tha Sathorn, change on to the Skytrain as far as Ekamai and then pick up the #511/11 from there.

### Damnoen Saduak floating markets

To get an idea of what shopping in Bangkok used to be like before all the canals were tarmacked over, many people take an early-morning trip to the floating markets of **DAMNOEN SADUAK**, 109km southwest of Bangkok. Vineyards and orchards back onto a labyrinth of narrow canals thick with paddle boats, and floating farmers in traditional dress sell fresh fruit and vegetables and whip up steaming bowls of noodles over burning fires. It's richly atmospheric but feels increasingly manufactured; there are hordes of tour groups and some visitors have complained of seeing more tourists than vendors. You can avoid the worst of the crowds if you arrive before 9am (the market kicks off at 6am and closes down at 11am). The target for most groups is the main **Talat Khlong Ton Kem**, 2km west of the tiny town centre at the intersection of Khlong Damnoen Saduak and Khlong Thong Lang. However, **Talat Khlong Hia Kui** (a little further south down Khlong Thong Lang) feels a little more authentic. Touts congregate at the Ton Kem pier to sell boat trips (hourly rates from B200 per person); a quieter alternative is to explore on foot along the canalside walkways.

To make a trip worthwhile you'll need to catch an early bus from Bangkok's Southern Bus Terminal (from 5.40am; 2hr 30min). Frequent yellow songthaews will carry you the 2km to Ton Kem; alternately, follow the walkway alongside the canal (from Thanarat Bridge), or cross the bridge and take the road to the right (west), following Th Sukhaphiban 1 through the orchards. Nearly all travel agents run tours to Damnoen Saduak (usually leaving at 7am) either as a half-day tour (B250) or combined with Nakhon Pathom (B400).

### Nakhon Pathom

**NAKHON PATHOM**, 56km west of Bangkok, has little of interest to most travellers, but if you're into your temple chedis, this is the *crème de la crème*. Measuring a staggering 120m – the same height as St Paul's Cathedral in London – **Phra Pathom Chedi** is the tallest in the world. Legend has it that the Buddha rested in Nakhon Pathom, and the original Indian-style chedi may have been erected to commemorate this. It was rebuilt with a Khmer prang (tower) between the eighth and twelfth centuries, which was later encased in the enormous plunger-shaped chedi that exists today. The inner and outer chambers at the cardinal points each contain a tableau of the life of the Buddha, and there are two **museums** within the chedi compound: the newer Phra Pathom Chedi National Museum (Wed–Sun 9am–noon & 1–4pm; B30), which is clearly signposted from the bottom of the chedi's south staircase, displays historical artefacts excavated nearby, while the Phra Pathom Chedi Museum (same hours; free), halfway up the steps near the east viharn, contains a beguiling selection of curios.

Arriving at Nakhon Pathom's train station (12 daily from Bangkok Hualumphong, 1hr 10min; 2 daily from Bangkok Noi, 1hr), a two-hundred-metre walk south across the khlong and through the market will get you to the chedi's north gate. **Buses** (every 10min from the Southern Bus Terminal; 1hr) terminate 1km east of the town centre, but most circle the chedi first, dropping you near its southern gate. For inexpensive Thai and Chinese food, head for any of the restaurants along the eastern arm of Thanon Phraya Gong which runs along the south (chedi) side of the canal.

Nakhon Pathom is easily done as a day-trip from Bangkok either independently or through a travel agency; it's often combined with an early-morning floating market trip for around B400.

# The central plains

North and west of the capital, the unwieldy urban mass of Greater Bangkok peters out into the vast, well-watered **central plains**, a region that for centuries has grown the bulk of the nation's food and been an irrisistible temptation for neighbouring power-mongers. The riverside town of **Kanchanaburi** has long attracted visitors to the notorious Bridge over the River Kwai and is now well established as a budget-travellers' hangout. Few tourists venture further west except to travel on the Death Railway, but the tiny hilltop town of **Sangkhlaburi** is worth the trip for its idyllic remoteness. On the plains north of Bangkok, the historic heartland of the country, the major sites are the ruined ancient cities of **Ayutthaya**, **Lopburi** and **Sukhothai**. **Mae Sot** makes a therapeutic change from old monuments and is the departure point for **Umphang**, a remote border region that's becoming increasingly popular for trekking and rafting.

## KANCHANABURI AND AROUND

Nestled among limestone hills 121km northwest of Bangkok, the peaceful riverside rafthouses of **KANCHANABURI** make it a popular and pleasant travellers' hangout. Aside from the town's main sights – the Bridge over the River Kwai and several moving memorials to the town's role in World War II – there are caves, waterfalls and historical sites to explore. A very popular commemorative *son-et-lumière* River Kwai Bridge Festival is held here for ten days every November.

### What to see and do

The town of Kanchanaburi is dusty and full of package tourists snapping photos

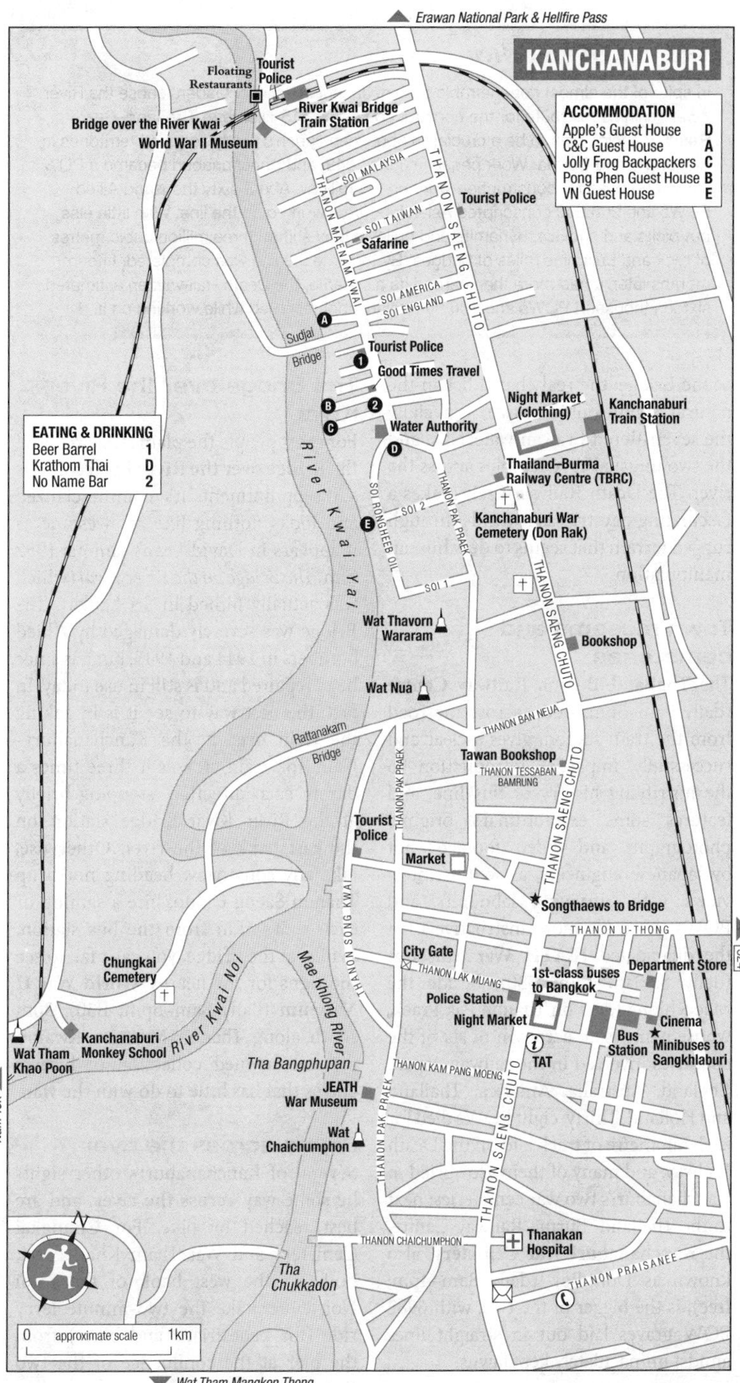

Erawan National Park & Hellfire Pass
KANCHANABURI
ACCOMMODATION
Apple's Guest House D
C&C Guest House A
Jolly Frog Backpackers C
Pong Phen Guest House B
VN Guest House E
EATING & DRINKING
Beer Barrel 1
Krathom Thai D
No Name Bar 2
Floating Restaurants
Tourist Police
River Kwai Bridge Train Station
Bridge over the River Kwai
World War II Museum
SOI MALAYSIA
SOI TAIWAN
SOI AMERICA
SOI ENGLAND
THANON MAENAM KWAI
THANON SAENG CHUTO
Tourist Police
Safarine
Sujdai Bridge
Tourist Police
Good Times Travel
Night Market (clothing)
Kanchanaburi Train Station
Water Authority
Thailand–Burma Railway Centre (TBRC)
River Kwai Yai
SOI RONGHEEB OIL
SOI 2
SOI 1
THANON PAK PRAEK
Kanchanaburi War Cemetery (Don Rak)
Wat Thavorn Wararam
Bookshop
Wat Nua
THANON BAN NEUA
Rattanakarn Bridge
Tawan Bookshop
THANON TESSABAN BAMRUNG
Tourist Police
Market
Songthaews to Bridge
THANON SONG KWAI
THANON U-THONG
324
City Gate
THANON LAK MUANG
1st-class buses to Bangkok
Department Store
Chungkai Cemetery
Police Station
Night Market
Cinema
Bus Station
Minibuses to Sangkhlaburi
TAT
Mae Khlong River
River Kwai Noi
Wat Tham Khao Poon
Kanchanaburi Monkey School
Tha Bangphupan
THANON KAM PANG MOENG
JEATH War Museum
Nam Tok
Wat Chaichumphon
THANON CHAICHUMPHON
Thanakan Hospital
Tha Chukkadon
THANON PRAISANEE
N
0 approximate scale 1km
Wat Tham Mangkon Thong

## THE DEATH RAILWAY

In spite of the almost impenetrable terrain, Japanese military leaders chose the River Kwai basin as the route for the construction of the 415-kilometre **Thailand–Burma Railway**, which was to be a crucial link between Japan's newly acquired territories in Singapore and Burma. Work began in June 1942, and Kanchanaburi became a POW camp and base for construction work on the railway. About sixty thousand Allied POWs and 200,000 conscripted Asian labourers worked on the line. With little else but picks and shovels, dynamite and pulleys, they shifted three million cubic metres of rock and built nine miles of bridges. By the time the line was completed, fifteen months later, it had more than earned its nickname, the Death Railway: an estimated sixteen thousand POWs and 100,000 Asian labourers died while working on it.



of the Bridge; the real charm lies in the natural sights out of town, especially the seven-tiered Erawan waterfalls, and the two unusual cave temples across the river. The Death Railway itself makes a fascinating day-trip as it winds through rugged terrain that seems to defy human manipulation.

### Town musems and cemeteries

The **Thailand–Burma Railway Centre** (daily 9am–5pm; B60), across the road from the train station, gives a clear and successfully impartial introduction to the horrifying history of this line, and features some extraordinary original photographs and video footage shot by Japanese engineers, as well as interviews with surviving labourers and POWs. It's a lot more instructive than the dilapidated **JEATH War Museum** (daily 8.30am–6pm; B30), beside the Mae Khlong River on Thanon Pak Praek, whose name is an acronym of six of the countries involved in the railway: Japan, England, Australia, America, Thailand and Holland. Thirty-eight POWs died for each kilometre of track laid on the Death Railway, and many of them are buried in Kanchanaburi's two war cemeteries: next to the Thailand–Burma Railway Centre, the **Kanchanaburi War Cemetery**, also known as Don Rak (daily 8am–4pm; free), is the bigger of the two, with 6982 POW graves laid out in straight lines amidst immaculately kept lawns.

### The Bridge over the River Kwai

For most people the plain steel arches of the **Bridge over the River Kwai** come as a disappointment: it's commercialized and looks nothing like as awesome as it appears in David Lean's famous 1957 film, *The Bridge on the River Kwai* (which was actually filmed in Sri Lanka). The Bridge was severely damaged by Allied bombers in 1944 and 1945, but has since been repaired and is still in use today. In fact, the best way to see it is by taking the train over it: the Kanchanaburi–Nam Tok train crosses it three times a day in each direction, stopping briefly at the River Kwai Bridge station on the east bank of the river. Otherwise, take any songthaew heading north up Thanon Saeng Chuto, hire a samlor, or cycle – it's 5km from the bus station. Whilst at the Bridge, you can't fail to see the signs for the nearby **World War II Museum** (daily 8am–6pm; B30), 30m south along Thanon Maenam Kwai, a privately owned collection of bizarre curios that has little to do with the war.

### Sights across the river

Several of Kanchanaburi's other sights lie some way **across the river**, and are best reached by bike. For Chungkai Cemetery and Wat Tham Khao Poon, both on the west bank of the Kwai Noi, either take the two-minute ferry ride (for pedestrians and bikes) from the pier at the confluence of the two rivers on Thanon Song Kwai, or cycle over Rattanakarn Bridge 1km north of the pier. After about 2km you'll reach **Chungkai Cemetery**, built on the banks of the Kwai Noi at the site of a former POW camp, and final resting place for some 1750 POWs. One kilometre on from Chungkai Cemetery, at the top of the road's only hill, sits the cave temple **Wat Tham Khao Poon** (daily 8am–6pm; donation), a fascinating labyrinthine grotto presided over by a medley of religious icons.

Luscious greenery and craggy limestone cliffs make a trip across to the east bank of the River Kwai Noi an equally worthwhile bike trip, but the main attraction at Wat Tham Mangkon Thong (6am–6pm), otherwise known as the "Floating Nun Temple", is fairly tacky: a nun will get into the temple pond and float there, meditating – if tourists give her enough money to make it worth her while. More interestingly, head up an enormous naga staircase behind the pond to the claustrophia-inducing cave temple. To get here by bicycle or motorbike, take the ferry across the Mae Khlong River at Tha Chukkadon and then follow the road on the other side for about 4km.

### MONKEYING AROUND

**Kanchanaburi Monkey School**, on the west bank of the River Kwai Noi, is a training school for abandoned monkeys; when they've "graduated", they work as coconut pickers in the jungle. If you want to get up close and personal with our primate cousins, there are daily shows and coconut-harvesting demonstrations (open 9am–5pm; ⓣ01/857 5518).

## The Death Railway and Hellfire Pass

The scenic two-hour rail journey from Kanchanaburi to **Nam Tok** (three trains daily in each direction) travels the POW-built **Death Railway**. Highlights include crossing the Bridge over the River Kwai, squeezing through ninety-foot solid rock cuttings at Wang Sing (Arrow Hill), and the Wang Po viaduct, where a three hundred-metre trestle bridge clings to the cliff face as it curves with the Kwai Noi.

At **Konyu**, 18km beyond Nam Tok, seven separate cuttings were dug over a three-kilometre stretch. The longest and most brutal of these was Hellfire Pass, which got its name from the hellish lights of the fires the POWs used when working at night. Hellfire Pass has now been turned into a circular, ninety-minute memorial walk (4km), which follows the old rail route through the eighteen-metre-deep cutting and on to Hin Tok creek. At the trailhead, the beautifully designed Hellfire Pass Memorial Museum (daily 9am–4pm; donation), the best and most informative of all Kanchanaburi's World War ll museums, movingly documents the POWs' story. Most Kanchanaburi tour operators feature visits to Hellfire Pass, or any bus from Kanchanburi (1hr 5min) or Nam Tok (20min) that's bound for Thong Pha Phum will drop you outside; the last bus back to Kanchanaburi passes the museum at about 4.45pm.

## Erawan National Park

Chances are that when you see a poster of a waterfall in Thailand, you'll be looking at a picture of the seven-tiered falls in **Erawan National Park** (daily 8am–4pm; B400), 65km northwest of Kanchanaburi. The falls are a popular day-trippers' destination, although it's possible to stay overnight (tents cost B50 and bungalows B800; book ahead on ⓣ034/574222). From the entrance there's a fairly easy trail up to the fifth tier (2km), beyond which you have to scramble (wear strong shoes); the best pools for swimming are at levels two and seven. Most Kanchanaburi guest-houses arrange songthaew transport to the falls for B80 per person, or take a bus to Srinakarind market (#8170; every 50min, 8am–5.20pm; 1hr 30min), then walk 500m to the national park headquarters, food stalls and trailhead; the last bus home leaves at 4pm.

## Arrival and town transport

**By bus** Buses from Bangkok's Southern Bus Terminal arrive at the bus station, 5km southeast of the Bridge on Th Saeng Chuto.

**By train** Trains from Bangkok Noi (Thonburi) station arrive at Kanchanaburi train station just east of the town centre; some guesthouses send free transport.

**Songthaews** For transport between the bus station, Maenam Kwai guesthouses and the Bridge, use the songthaews that run along Th Saeng Chuto via the Kanchanaburi War Cemetery (Don Rak) and then up Th Maenam Kwai to the Bridge (every 15min; 15min; B5). They start from outside the Bata shoe shop on Th Saeng Chuto, one block north of the bus station.

**Bicycle rental** The best way to explore Kanchanaburi and its countryside is by renting a bicycle from one of the many outlets along Th Maenam Kwai, or your guesthouse (B50).

## Information and tour operators

**Tourist information** The TAT office (Ⓣ034/511200, Ⓔtatkan@tat.or.th) is a ten-minute songthaew ride (B50) from the Soi Rongheeb Oil and Maenam Kwai guesthouses.

**Tour operators** Many tour operators offer reasonably priced day-trips and overnight excursions to local caves, waterfalls and sights, plus elephant-riding, trekking and rafting. Operators include: AS Mixed Travel at *Apple's Guest House*, 52 Soi Rongheeb Oil 3 (Ⓣ034/512017, Ⓦwww.applenoi-kanchanaburi.com), which does all the standard tours including bamboo rafting and elephant trekking; Good Times Travel at 63/1 Th Maenam Kwai (Ⓣ034/624441; Ⓦwww.good-times-travel.com) which offers local day excursions, trekking and fishing trips; and Safarine at 4 Soi Taiwan, off Th Maenam Kwai (Ⓣ034/624140, Ⓦwww.safarine.com), a kayaking specialist that does both package and custom-built tours.

## Accommodation

The stretch of river alongside Th Song Kwai is noisy and overdeveloped, but several hundred metres upriver the accommodation along Soi Rongheeb Oil and Th Maenam Kwai enjoys a much more peaceful setting. Many of the guesthouses have cheaper floating raft rooms; these have again become a peaceful option after an 11pm curfew was placed on karaoke boats.

**Apple's Guest House** 52 Soi Rongheeb Oil 3 Ⓣ034/512017, Ⓦwww.applenoi-kanchanaburi.com. Welcoming place, with spotless en-suite fan and a/c rooms, in a quiet garden location. ❷

**C&C Guest House** Soi England, 265/2 Th Maenam Kwai Ⓣ034/624547, Ⓔcctrekking@yahoo.com. Quiet, riverside compound of basic rafts and idiosyncratic huts, some with bathrooms and a/c set in a garden. ❶–❷

**Jolly Frog Backpackers** 28 Soi China, just off Th Maenam Kwai Ⓣ034/514579, Ⓦwww.jollyfrog.net. This large complex of comfortable fan and a/c bamboo huts ranged around a riverside garden with hammocks and deck-chairs is most backpackers' first choice, though it can be noisy. A great place for solo travellers; rooms are just B70. ❶–❷

**Pong Phen** Soi Bangladesh, just off Th Maenam Kwai Ⓣ034/512981, Ⓦwww.pongphen.com. A great budget hotel with a swimming pool set in an attractive terrace overlooking the river. Listen out for the wolf-whistling parrot. ❸

**VN Guest House** 44 Soi 2, Th Rongheeb Oil, Ⓣ034/514082, Ⓦwww.vnguesthouse.net. Big, spacious floating rooms set amongst lilies with seating overlooking the water. ❷

## Eating and drinking

At dusk, the ever-reliable night market sets up alongside Th Saeng Chuto on the edge of the bus station; its range of choices will satisfy even the pickiest eater. The night market outside the train station sells predominately clothes and knock-off CDs, but has a few hot food stalls.

**Beer Barrel** Th Maenam Kwai. Rustic-styled outdoor beer garden where you sit amid a jungle of low-lit trees. Serves some snacks to accompany the ice-cold draught beer. Watch out for the emu.

**Krathom Thai** *Apple's Guest House*, 52 Soi Rongheeb Oil 3. Delicious mid-priced Thai food, including mouthwatering curries and huge set dinners. Cookery classes available on request.

**No Name Bar** 53 Th Maenam Kwai. Popular farang-run travellers' hangout, with international sport on the satellite TV and a pool table, serving cheap beer and classic British pub grub including bangers and mash; open early till midnight.

## Directory

**Banks and exchange** There are several banks with ATMs and moneychanging facilities on Th Saeng Chuto, and Th Maenam Kwai, including outside 7–11.
**Bookshops** For the town's best selection of books about Thailand, visit Tawan bookshop on Th Saeng Chuto. *Jolly Frog*'s bookshop is a goldmine, and there are a handful of other good bookshops on Th Maenam Kwai.
**Hospitals** The private Thanakan Hospital is at 20/20 Th Saeng Chuto (Ⓣ034/622366) and the government-run Phahon Phonphayulasena Hospital is further south at 572/1 Th Saeng Chuto (Ⓣ034/511233).
**Internet** Available at most guesthouses and there are Catnet terminals at the CAT telephone office on Soi Praisanee/Soi 38 off Th Saeng Chuto (daily 8.30am–8pm).
**Tourist police** Booths right beside the Bridge, near *Beer Barrel* on Th Maenam Kwai, and on Th Song Kwai (Ⓣ034/512795).

## Moving on

**By bus:** The cheapest (but most convoluted) way to get to Ayutthaya is to take a public bus to Suphanburi (every 20min; 2hr), then change onto an Ayutthaya-bound bus (hourly; 3hr 30min).
**Destinations**: Ayutthaya (via Suphanburi; every 20min; around 5hr 30min); Bangkok (every 15min; 2hr); Lopburi (via Suphanburi; hourly; 5hr); Sangkhlaburi (7 daily; 4–5hr).
**By private bus:** A quicker option to get to Ayutthaya is to book an a/c minibus through your guesthouse (1.30pm; B350). Minibuses to Sangkhlaburi leave from east of main bus station; note that they do not accept large bags.
**Destinations**: Ayutthaya (1 daily; 3hr); Sangkhlaburi (hourly; 3hr).
**By train to:** Bangkok Noi Station, Thonburi (2 daily; 3hr).

# SANGKHLABURI

Located right at the northernmost tip of the 73-kilometre-long Khao Laem Reservoir, the tiny hilltop town of **SANGKHLABURI**, 220km north of Kanchanaburi, is a charming if uneventful hangout. It lies close to the Burmese border, though at the time of writing the border crossing at the Three Pagodas Pass was officially closed.

## What to see and do

You can boat across the reservoir in search of the submerged temple **Wat Sam Phrasop** in canoes rented from *P. Guest House* (B150 per hour); during the dry season it's possible to swim through the temples' windows. Alternatively, join a sunset longtail boat trip (B350–500 per boat).

Across the reservoir stands the Mon village of Ban Waeng Ka, which grew up in the late 1940s after the outbreak of civil war in Burma forced the country's ethnic minorities to flee across the border. To reach it, walk across the lake via the spider's web of a wooden bridge, said to be the longest hand-made wooden bridge in the world and reputedly visible from space: the approach is from beside *Burmese Inn*. You'll need to catch a motorbike taxi to get to **Wat Wang Wiwekaram** which stands 2km away at the edge of the village; its massive, golden chedi is modelled on the centrepiece of India's Bodh Gaya, the sacred site of the Buddha's enlightenment.

## Arrival

**By bus** Minibuses from Kanchanaburi terminate about 100m east of the market; buses stop directly in front.

## Accommodation

**Burmese Inn** 700m down the hill from the bus station then right down Soi 1 Ⓣ034/595146, Ⓔburmeseinn@yahoo.com. This place has fan and a/c bungalows, organizes tours and has good free maps. ❷–❸
**P. Guest House** Ⓣ034/595061, Ⓦwww.pguesthouse.com. Flintstones-inspired, prehistoric-style rooms, a garden leading down to the lake and a stunning view make this a worthwhile choice. The fan rooms have great shared bathrooms and the a/c rooms are en suite. Motorbikes (B200/day), bicycles (B20/hr, B70/day), canoes and kayaks (B150/hr, B600/day) can all be rented. ❷–❸

## Eating and drinking

**Floating restaurant** on the lake (no English name); follow Soi 1 down behind *Burmese Inn* – it's under the red archway. Good prices, delicious food and pretty views across the lake to the Mon village.
**Market stalls** by the bus station at the northern end of town. The food stalls around the market are the cheapest place to eat. The stall under the sign reading "tourist information" next to the minibus terminus does particularly good coffee.
**Wild Wild West** opposite the temple between Soi 1 and 3. Boasts a few books and a few rooms, and guarantees a few laughs. The owner is an enthusiastic and upbeat expat; it serves mean banana daiquiris.

## Directory

**Bank** The bank behind the market (open Mon–Fri 8.30am–3.30pm) has an exchange (though the ATM doesn't work with foreign cards, cash advances are available inside).
**Post office** Just south of the bus station, with a Catnet terminal.

## Moving on

**By bus** You can reach Kanchanaburi by government bus (4 daily; 4hr) or by a/c minibus (6 daily; 6.30am–3.30pm; 3hr). Minibuses leave from east of the market at the corner towards the exit of the town.

# AYUTTHAYA

The city of **AYUTTHAYA**, 80km north of Bangkok, was founded in 1351 and was the capital of King U-Thong's empire, which covered most of modern-day Thailand. By 1685 this wealthy city had a population of one million people – roughly double the population of London at the same time – living largely on houseboats in a 140-kilometre network of waterways. In 1767, the city was sacked by the Burmese and today its ruins are a designated UNESCO World Heritage Site.

## What to see and do

The heart of this ancient city was a narrow river island and the majority of the ancient remains are spread out across its western half; the small modern town rests on its northeast bank. The only way to do justice to the ruins is to rent out a bicycle (B30–50 per day) or motorbike (B250 per day), available from most guesthouses. There are plenty of tuk-tuks and motorbike taxis around; the going rate for hiring a tuk-tuk is B200 per hour.

### Wat Phra Magathat and Wat Ratburana

One kilometre west out of the new town centre along Thanon Chao Phrom (which becomes Thanon Naresuan), the overgrown **Wat Phra Mahathat**, on the left (daily 8am–6pm; B30), is the epitome of Ayutthaya's atmospheric decay, and the home of the oft-photographed Buddha head serenely trapped in gnarled tree roots. Across the road, towering **Wat Ratburana** (daily 8am–6pm; B30) retains some original stuccowork, including fine statues of garudas swooping down on nagas. It's possible to go down steep steps inside the prang to the crypt, where you can make out fragmentary murals of the early Ayutthaya period.

### Wat Phra Si Sanphet and Viharn Phra Mongkol Bopit

Further west, the grand, well-preserved **Wat Phra Si Sanphet** (daily 8am–6pm; B30) was built in 1448 as a private royal chapel, and its three grey chedis have become the most hackneyed image of Ayutthaya. Save for a few bricks in the grass, the wat is all that remains of the huge walled complex of royal pavilions that extended north as far as the Lopburi River.

Viharn Phra Mongkol Bopit (Mon–Fri 8.30am–4.30pm, Sat & Sun 8.30am–5.30pm), on the south side of Wat Phra Si Sanphet, boasts a pristine replica of a typical Ayutthayan viharn (assembly hall), complete with characteristic chunky lotus-capped columns. It was built in 1956, with help from the Burmese to atone for their flattening of the city two centuries earlier, in order to shelter the revered Phra Mongkol Bopit. This powerfully austere bronze statue, with its flashing mother-of-pearl eyes, was cast in the fifteenth century, then sat exposed to the elements from the time of the Burmese invasion until its new home was built.

### Wat Na Phra Mane

Across on the north bank of the Lopburi River, **Wat Na Phra Mane** (daily 8am–6pm; B20) is Ayutthaya's most rewarding temple, as it's the only one from the town's golden age that survived the ravages of the Burmese. The main bot, built in 1503, shows the distinctive outside columns topped with lotus cups, and slits in the walls instead of windows to let the wind pass through. Inside, underneath a rich red-and-gold coffered ceiling representing the stars around the moon, sits a powerful six-metre-high Buddha in the disdainful, overdecorated style characteristic of the later Ayutthaya period. It's worth walking behind the bot where there's a surreal sight of a tree growing out of a chedi.

### Wat Chai Watthanaram

About 2km southwest of central Ayutthaya, the striking riverside **Wat Chai Watthanaram** (daily 8am–6pm; B30) is one of the most imposing ancient Buddhist monasteries. The main Khmer-style prang measures 35m and is surrounded by twelve lesser prangs; the structure reflects that of Mount Sumeru, the central Universe, as dictated by Khmer mythological design. Inside its walled gallery is the unnerving sight of hundreds of beheaded Buddha statues. Initially established in 1630 and beautifully conserved, it is a great place to watch the sunset.

### Museums

Ten minutes' walk south of Viharn Phra Mongkol Bopit, the large **Chao Sam Phraya National Museum** (Wed–Sun 9am–4pm; B30) holds numerous Ayutthaya-era Buddhas and gold treasures. The **Historical Study Centre** (daily 9am–4.30pm; B100), five minutes' walk away along Thanon Rojana, showcases the broad social history of Ayutthaya with the help of videos and reconstructions. The centre's **annexe** (same times, same ticket), 500m south of Wat Phanan Choeng across the Chao Phraya River, tells the story of Ayutthaya's relations with foreign powers.

### Wat Yai Chai Mongkol and Wat Phanan Choeng

The colossal and celebrated chedi of the ancient but still functioning **Wat Yai Chai Mongkol** (daily 8am–6pm; B20), across the bridge to the southeast of the island, was built to mark a major victory over the Burmese in 1593. By the entrance, a reclining Buddha, now gleamingly restored in toothpaste white, dates from the same time. To the west of Wat Yai Chai Mongkol, at the confluence of the Chao Phraya and Pasak rivers, stands the city's oldest and liveliest working temple, **Wat Phanan Choeng** (daily 8am–6pm; B20), whose nineteen-metre-high Buddha has survived since 1324, and is said to have wept when Ayutthaya was sacked by the Burmese. The stunning murals in the ordination hall are beautifully restored. The Chinese believe that the temple protects those who sail the seas and the temple compound is cluttered by colourful and ostentatious religious paraphernalia, elaborate tapestries featuring dragons and birds and flashing fairy lights.

## Arrival and information

**By bus and minibus** Most government and private buses from Bangkok stop on Th Naresuan just west of the centre of the modern town, though some government buses, mainly those on long-distance runs, will only stop at Ayutthaya's Northern Bus Terminal, 2km to the east of the centre on Th Rojana. A tuk-tuk to the main guesthouse area costs around B50.

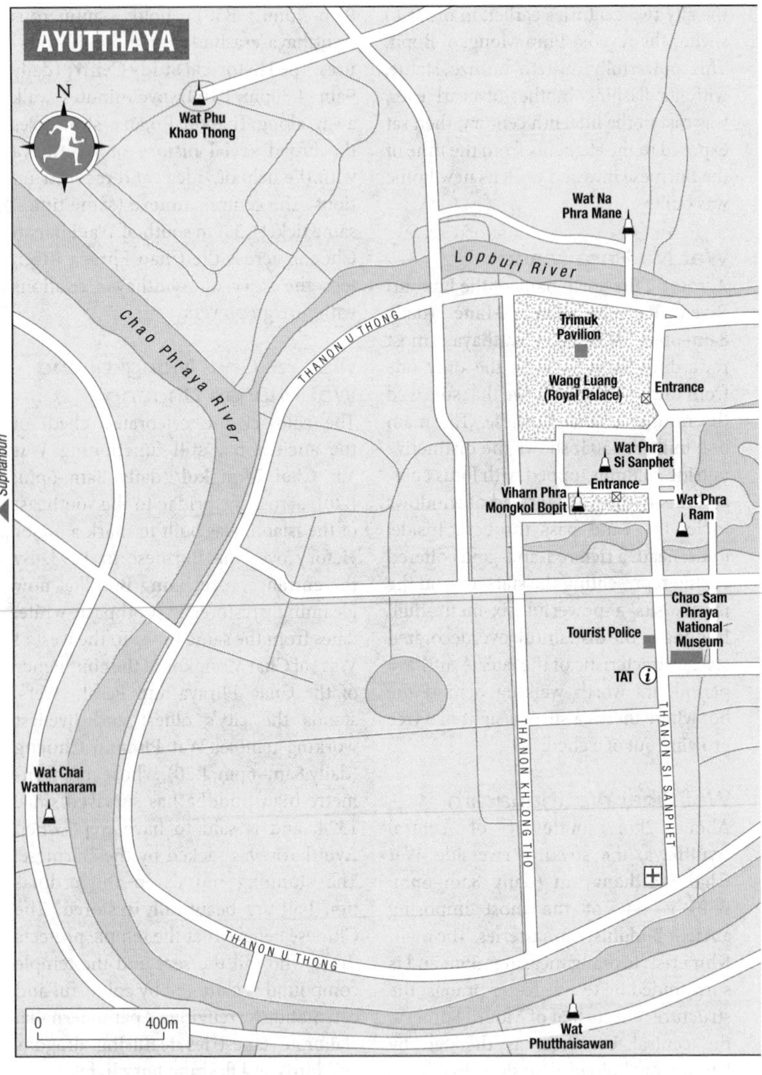




**By train** The train station is just east of the river; take the ferry (B2) from the pier 100m west (last ferry 7pm) up to Chao Phrom pier, then walk five minutes to the junction of U Thong and Chao Phrom roads to reach the centre. The station has a left-luggage service (supposedly 24hr; B10 per piece per day). A tuk-tuk to most guesthouses costs B30–50.

**Tourist information** The TAT office (☎035/246076) and tourist police are opposite the Chao Sam Phraya National Museum on Th Si Sanphet; at the former, it's well worth heading upstairs to the smartly presented multimedia exhibition on Ayutthaya (daily except Wed 9am–5pm).

## Accommodation

Most of the guesthouses and tourist amenities are crowded into an area that's become known as

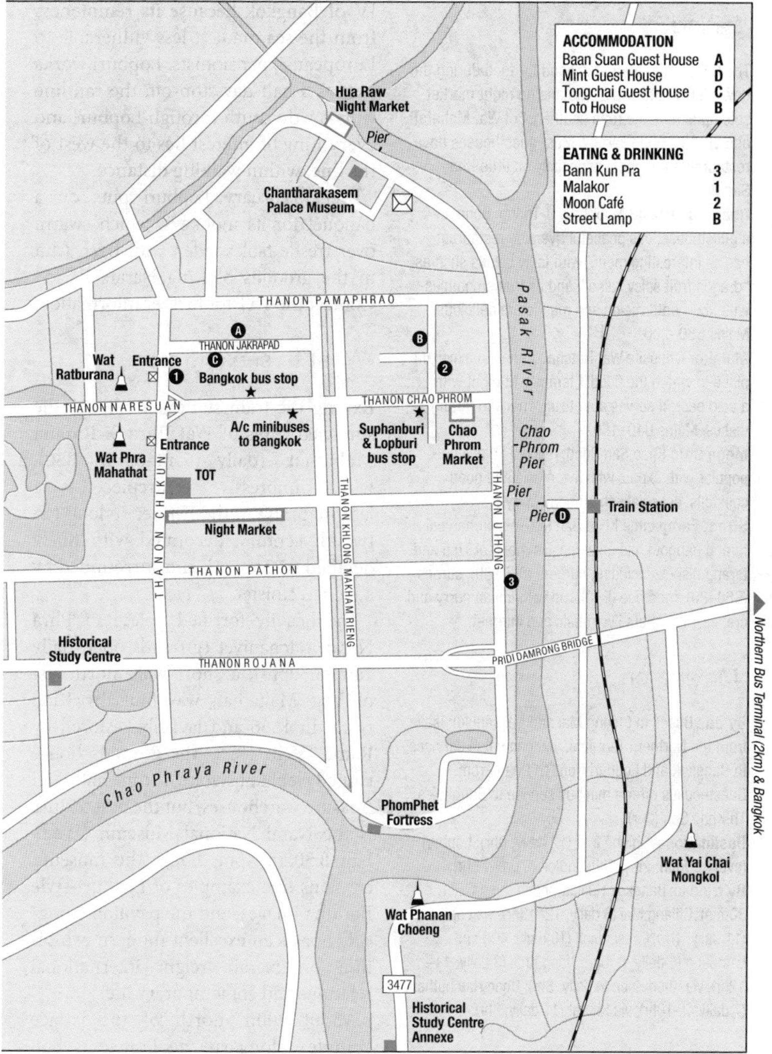




"little Khao San Road", which just runs north from Chao Prom market.

**Baan Suan Guest House** (formerly *P.S. Guesthouse*) 23/1 Th Jakraprad ⓣ035/242394, ⓦwww.baansuanguesthouse.com. Pretty bungalows set in a peaceful garden, newer airy rooms out back in a quiet spot near Wat Ratchaburana. ❶–❷

**Mint Guest House** Th Kramung Pranakornsi ⓣ081/290 7095 or 035/234791, ⓔmint-guesthouse@hotmail.com. Very convenient for the train station, singles start at just B100; also has a restaurant and rents out bikes and motorbikes. ❶

**Tongchai Guest House** Th Jakrapad ⓣ035/245210. Tidy rooms lacking in atmosphere but very clean. ❷

**Toto House** above *Street Lamp* ⓣ035/232658. Run by the same family as *Street Lamp*, this is a cheap option in the heart of "little Khao San". ❶

## Eating

The Chao Prom market is good for food during the day, while Ayutthaya's outstanding night market sets up across the road southeast of Wat Mahatat and offers a huge variety. Most guesthouses have restaurants attached, especially on little Khao San Road.

**Baan Kun Pra** 48 Moo 3, Th U-Thong. Beneath a guesthouse, this peaceful riverside restaurant has an interesting menu, with tasty salads such as "dragon fruit spicy salad", and its fruit smoothies with kiwi, watermelon and mango are delicious. Mains B50–200.

**Malakor** Opposite Wat Ratchaburana. An excellent place to watch the floodlit temples at night with a cold beer; it serves appetizing Thai and farang dishes. Mains B40–150.

**Moon Café** Khao San Road, relaxed little venue popular with expats with live music and good cocktails, especially the Bloody Mary.

**Street Lamp** Little Khao San Rd. This archetypal farang hangout has an extensive menu of Thai and farang dishes, including burgers (B70–80), curries (B60–80), fried rice (B40), roti with Indian curry and crepes. Also offers live music and internet.

## Moving on

**By bus** Buses to Chiang Mai and Phitsanulok leave from the Northern Terminal; you can catch services to Bangkok and Lopburi from Th Chao Prom. Guesthouses offer a minibus service to Bangkok's Th Khao San (2hr).

**Destinations**: Chiang Mai (12 daily; 8hr); Lopburi (every 20min; 2hr); Phitsanulok (9 daily; 5hr).

**By train** to: Bangkok Hualamphong (26 daily; 1hr 30min); Chiang Mai (6 daily; 12–13hr), via Lopburi (11 daily; 1hr), Phitsanulok (10 daily; 4hr) and Lampang (6 daily; 8–9hr); Nong Khai (3 daily; 11–12hr), via Khon Kaen (4 daily; 8hr); Ubon Ratchathani (7 daily; 9–10hr), via Khorat (11 daily; 3hr).

# LOPBURI

**LOPBURI**, 150km due north of Bangkok, is famous for its historically important but rather unimpressive Khmer ruins, and for the large pack of tourist-baiting monkeys that swarm all over them. The ruins date back to the eleventh century, when Lopburi was the local capital for the extensive Khmer Empire. The town was later used as a second capital both by King Narai of Ayutthaya and Rama IV of Bangkok because its remoteness from the sea made it less vulnerable to European expansionists. Lopburi works best as a half-day stop-off; the rail line runs north–south through Lopburi and everything of interest lies to the west of the line, within walking distance.

Every February Lopburi puts on a banquet for its monkeys, which swarm over trestle tables laden with fresh fruit in the grounds of King Narai's Palace. Contact the TAT for further information.

## What to see and do

Exiting the train station, you'll see the sprawled ruins of **Wat Phra Si Ratana Mahathat** (daily 6am–6pm; B30), whose impressive centrepiece is a laterite prang in the Khmer style of the twelfth century, decorated with finely detailed stuccowork and surrounded by a ruined cloister.

The heavily fortified palace of Phra Narai Ratchanivet (grounds open daily 7am–5.30pm), a short walk northwest of Wat Mahathat, was built by King Narai in 1666 and lavishly restored by Rama IV in 1856. The grounds house ruined elephant stables, throne halls and treasure warehouses, but the best feature is the Narai National Museum (Wed–Sun 8.30am–4pm; B30). The museum contains fine examples of Lopburi-style Buddha images, and the pavilion alongside boasts an excellent modern exhibition on Narai's reign, international relations and contemporary life.

About 200m north of the palace complex along rue de France is Ban Vichayen (daily 8.30am–4.30pm; B30); originally built as a residence for foreign ambassadors, its Christian chapel is incongruously stuccoed with Buddhist motifs. Around 150m east along Thanon Vichayen, the striking Phra Prang Sam Yod (daily 6am–6pm; B30) is a Hindu temple, later converted to Buddhism under the Khmers. The three chunky prangs, made of dark laterite with some restored stuccowork are a favourite haunt of Lopburi's fierce monkeys. Just east at San Phra Karn, there's even a monkeys' adventure playground beside the ruins of a huge Khmer prang.

### Arrival and information

**By bus** Buses from Bangkok's Northern Terminal pull in 2km east of the town centre: a blue city bus or red songthaew will save you the walk.
**By train** The train station is directly opposite Wat Phra Si Ratana Mahathat; there are left-luggage facilities.
**Tourist information** TAT's office (☎036/422768) is on Th Wat Phra That, on the north side of Wat Phra Si Ratana Mahathat and 50m from the train station.

### Accommodation

**Nett Hotel** 17 1-2 Th Ratchadamnoen ☎036/411738. Slightly sterile but friendly and good value. ❷
**Noom Guest House** 15–17 Th Phayakamjad ☎036/427693. Simple wooden rooms with some newer ones, all en-suite with a/c, in a garden. The friendly staff offer Western breakfasts, tourist advice and a free map; rock climbing and jungle trips can also be organized. ❶–❸

### Eating

There are food stalls dotted around the centre of Lopburi, especially south of Tesco Lotus, and a good night market sets up on the road leading north of the train station.
**Coffee House** Th Ratchadamnoen. Serves delicious bowls of noodles for only B10 to an exclusively Thai clientele; order a few like the locals do. Also a great place for a quick snack and cheap coffee.
**Sixty Coffee** Shopping St, opposite the entrance to Tesco Lotus. A varied coffee menu and inexpensive fruit juices in some unusual flavours. Open 8.30am–7pm.

### Moving on

**By train** to: Bangkok (11 daily; 3hr), via Ayutthaya (1hr); Chiang Mai (6 daily; 10–12hr), via Phitsanulok (10 daily; 3–4hr) and Lampang (6 daily; 8–9hr).
**By bus** to: Bangkok (every 30min 4.30am–10pm; 4hr); Phitsanulok (4 daily; 4hr).

## PHITSANULOK

Pleasantly located on the east bank of the Nan River, **PHITSANULOK** (locally called "Phitlok") makes a handy base for exploring the Sukhothai area, but only holds a couple of sights itself.

### What to see and do

Standing at the northern limit of town, the fourteenth-century **Wat Phra Si Ratana Mahathat** (aka Wat Mahathat or Wat Yai) is home to the country's second most important Buddha image; because the image is so sacred, shorts and skimpy clothing are forbidden, and there's an entrance fee of B10. The holy statue itself, Phra Buddha Chinnarat, is a lovely example of late Sukhothai style, with a distinctive halo; it is said to have wept tears of blood during a thirteenth-century war. Come at the weekend when the temple comes alive with Thais rattling fortune sticks and pious devotion gives way to religious mayhem.

Across town on Thanon Wisut Kasat, southeast of the train station (bus #8 will drop you close by), the small **Sergeant Major Thawee Folklore Museum** (daily except Mon 8.30am–4.30pm; B50) is one of the best ethnology museums in the country and includes a reconstruction of a typical village house, as well as traditional musical instruments. About 50m south of the museum, located behind a big green metal gate at 26/43 Th Wisut Kasat, is the **Buranathai Buddha Bronze-Casting Foundry** (roughly 9am–5pm). The foundry gives you a rare chance to see Buddha images being forged; anyone can drop in to watch the stages involved in moulding and casting an image.

### Arrival

**By bus** All buses pull into the regional (government) bus station, 2km east of Phitsanulok; local buses #1, #2 and #8 shuttle into the city bus centre.
**By train** The train station is to the east of town centre, less than 500m from the accommodation

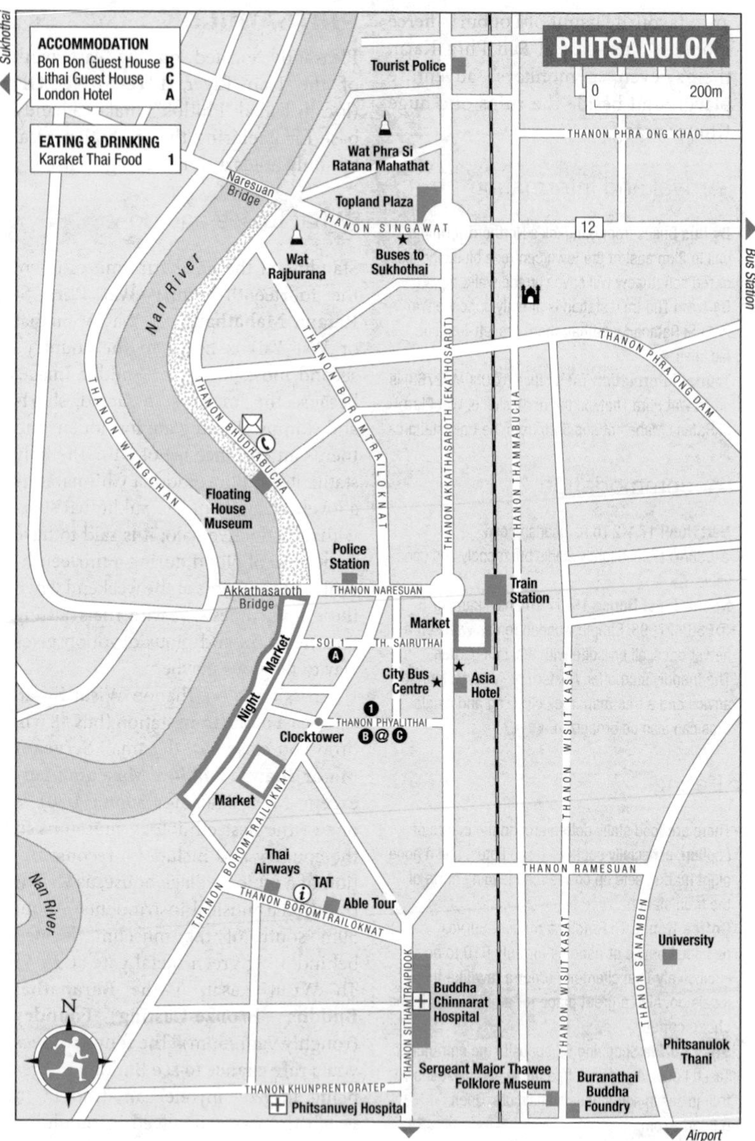


listed below. Left-luggage costs B20 (open 7am–11pm).

**By air** The airport is on the southern edge of town; Thai Airways share-taxis charge B50 per person to any Phitsanulok accommodation, or you can walk 100m north from the airport gates and take city bus #4 into town from Th Sanambin.

## Information and agencies

**Tourist information** The TAT office is on the eastern arm of Th Boromtrailoknat (known to local taxi drivers as Surasi Trade Centre; ⓣ 055/252742, ⓔ tatphs@loxinfo.co.th).

**Travel agents** Able Tour and Travel is also on the eastern arm of Th Boromtrailoknat (ⓣ 055/242206,

ⓔ abletour_phs@yahoo.com), and rents cars with driver (B1200 a day).

## Town transport

In the town centre, most **city buses** (B8–16) start from the city bus centre, 150m south of the train station, where southbound buses pick up outside the *Asia Hotel,* and northbound ones from across the road. Useful routes include: #1, from the regional bus station to the train station and Wat Mahathat; #5 and #11, from the train station to Topland Plaza (for buses to Sukhotai) and Wat Mahathat; and #8, from the regional bus station to the Folklore Museum, train station, Topland Plaza and Wat Mahathat.

## Accommodation

Budget accommodation in Phitlok is scarce and unimpressive, apart from:

**Bon Bon Guest House** 77 Th Phayalithai ⓣ055/219058. A nicer choice than *Lithai*; full of character with an enthusiastic and personable manager (who speaks little English though) The en-suite rooms boast cable TV and balconies. It's just minutes from the night bazaar and walkable from train station. ❸

**Lithai Guest House** 73/1-5 Th Phayalithai ⓣ055/219629. A hotel with guesthouse prices; en-suite rooms are spacious and clean but drab; all have TV. ❷–❹

**London Hotel** at 21–22 Soi Buddhabucha (Phuttabucha) 1 ⓣ055/225145. Cheap but slightly grimy and shabby rooms with shared Thai toilet-bathroom in a converted family home. ❶

## Eating and drinking

**Karaket Thai Food** Th Phaylithai. Popular, cheap cafeteria-style Thai curry shop with a wide selection of curries, fish and meat dishes, costing around B40. Shuts around 8.30pm.

**Markets** There are two fresh day markets in Phitsanulok; one just south of the train station off Th Ekathosarot, and the other off Th Boromtrailokanat, one block south of the clocktower. In the evening head to the lively night market, which sets up along the east bank of the river at about 6pm: several stall-holders serve "flying vegetables", a strong-tasting morning-glory (*phak bung*), which is stir-fried before being tossed flamboyantly some considerable distance into the air.

## Directory

**Hospital** Buddha Chinnarat Hospital on the road leading southeast from the clocktower (ⓣ055/219844).

**Internet** There is internet at various locations across town, and an internet café that does coffee and breakfasts underneath *Lithai Guest House.*

**Post office** Next to the CAT telecoms office on Th Bhudhabucha ⓣ055/258013.

**Telephone** Catnet inside the telephone office on Th Bhudhabucha (ⓣ055/243116; open daily 8am–6pm).

**Tourist police** north of Wat Mahathat on Th Akkathasaroth (Ekathosarot) ⓣ055/245357.

## Moving on

**By bus:** You can pick up a Sukhothai-bound bus (daily every 30min: 5.20am–7pm; 1hr 30min) as it passes near the Topland Plaza shopping centre on Th Singawat (northbound local buses #5, #8 and #11 run past the Topland Plaza roundabout), or from the regional bus station (take local buses #1 or #8 (southbound). All other buses leave from the bus station, 2km east.

**Destinations:** Ayutthaya (9 daily; 5hr); Bangkok (every 20min; 5–6hr); Chiang Khong (5 daily; 5hr); Chiang Mai (20 daily; 6–7hr); Chiang Rai (26 daily; 7–8hr); Khon Kaen (15 daily; 6hr); Khorat (15 daily; 7hr); Mae Sai (12 daily; 8hr 30min); Mae Sot (by private minibus; 9 daily; 5hr); Nakhon Phanom (7 daily; 10hr); Sukhothai (every 30min; 1hr 30min); Ubon Ratchathani (7 daily; 12hr); Udon Thani (for Nong Khai) (7 daily; 7hr).

**By train** Book sleeper trains to Bangkok in advance.

**Destinations:** Ayutthaya (10 daily; 5hr); Bangkok (12 daily; 6–8hr). Chiang Mai (6 daily; 7hr); Lopburi (10 daily; 4hr).

**By air**: Thai Airways has an office in the airport (ⓣ055/301002), as well as on Th Boromtrailoknat. To get to the airport take city bus #4 from the city bus stand.

**Destination:** Bangkok (2 daily; 1hr).

# SUKHOTHAI

For a brief but brilliant hundred and forty years (1238–1376), the walled city of **SUKHOTHAI** presided as the capital of Thailand. Now an impressive assembly of elegant ruins, Muang Kao Sukhothai (Old Sukhothai), 58km northwest of Phitsanulok, has been designated a historical park and is the most famous place in Thailand to celebrate the **Loy Krathong Festival** (Ⓦwww.grandfestivalthailand.com) in October/November. Most travellers stay in lively "New" Sukhothai, 12km to the east, which has good travel links and is better for accommodation; frequent songthaews shuttle between the two.

## What to see and do

Cycling around **Old Sukhothai** is a great way to spend a day; its collapsed ruins are evocative of a glorious time gone by. Some of its temples are exquisitely restored; others have been left to crumble. Grab a map and a bicycle to avoid the worst of the snap-happy package crowds. In its prime, Old Sukhothai boasted some forty separate temple complexes and covered an area of about seventy square kilometres. At its heart stood the walled royal city, protected by a series of moats and ramparts. **Sukhothai Historical Park** (daily 6am–6pm) covers all this area and is divided into five zones: entry to the central zone is B40, plus B10–50 per vehicle; all other zones cost B30 each, inclusive.

### The central zone

Just outside the entrance to the central zone, the **Ramkhamhaeng National Museum's** (daily 9am–4pm; B30) collection is not very inspiring, but it does include a copy of King Ramkhamhaeng's famous stele. Turn left inside the gate to the central zone for Sukhothai's most important site, the enormous **Wat Mahathat** compound, packed with the remains of scores of monuments and surrounded, like a city within a city, by a moat. It was the spiritual epicentre of the city, the king's temple and symbol of his power.

A few hundred metres southwest, the triple corn-cob-shaped prangs of Wat Sri Sawai indicate that this was once a Hindu shrine for the Khmers; the square base inside the central prang supported the Khmer Shiva lingam (phallus). Just west, Wat Trapang Ngoen rises gracefully from an island in the middle of the eponymous "silver pond". North of the chedi, notice the fluid lines of the walking Buddha mounted onto a brick wall – a classic example of Sukhothai sculpture. Taking the water feature one step further, Wat Sra Sri commands a fine position on two connecting islands north of Wat Trapang Ngoen; its bell-shaped chedi with a tapering spire and square base shows a strong Sri Lankan influence.

### The outer zones

There are also interesting outlying temples in the north, west and east zones. Continuing north of Wat Sra Sri, cross the city walls into the north zone and you'll find **Wat Sri Chum**, which boasts Sukhothai's largest surviving Buddha image. The enormous brick-and-stucco seated Buddha, measuring over 11m from knee to knee and almost 15m high, peers through the slit in its custom-built temple.

Around 8km west of the city walls, **Wat Saphan Hin** sits atop a hill, affording decent views of the surrounding countryside. About 1km east of the city walls, the best temple in the east zone is Wat Chang Lom, just off the road to New Sukhothai, near *Thai Village Hotel*. Chang Lom translates as "surrounded by elephants": the main feature here is a large, Sri Lankan-style, bell-shaped chedi encircled by a frieze of pachyderm.

## Arrival and information

**By bus** Buses pull into the terminal 3km west of New Sukhothai's town centre (Ⓣ055/613296); purple songthaew #1 (roughly every 20min: 6am–6pm; B8) runs into New Sukothai, stopping opposite 7/11 before the river and in front of Wat Ratchathani after the bridge. A tuk-tuk to the centre costs B40–50.

**By air** The airport is about 15km north of town; flights are met by shuttle buses that head into the centre (B80).

**Tourist information** There is no TAT but most guesthouses organize local tours, and rent out bicycles and motorcycles.

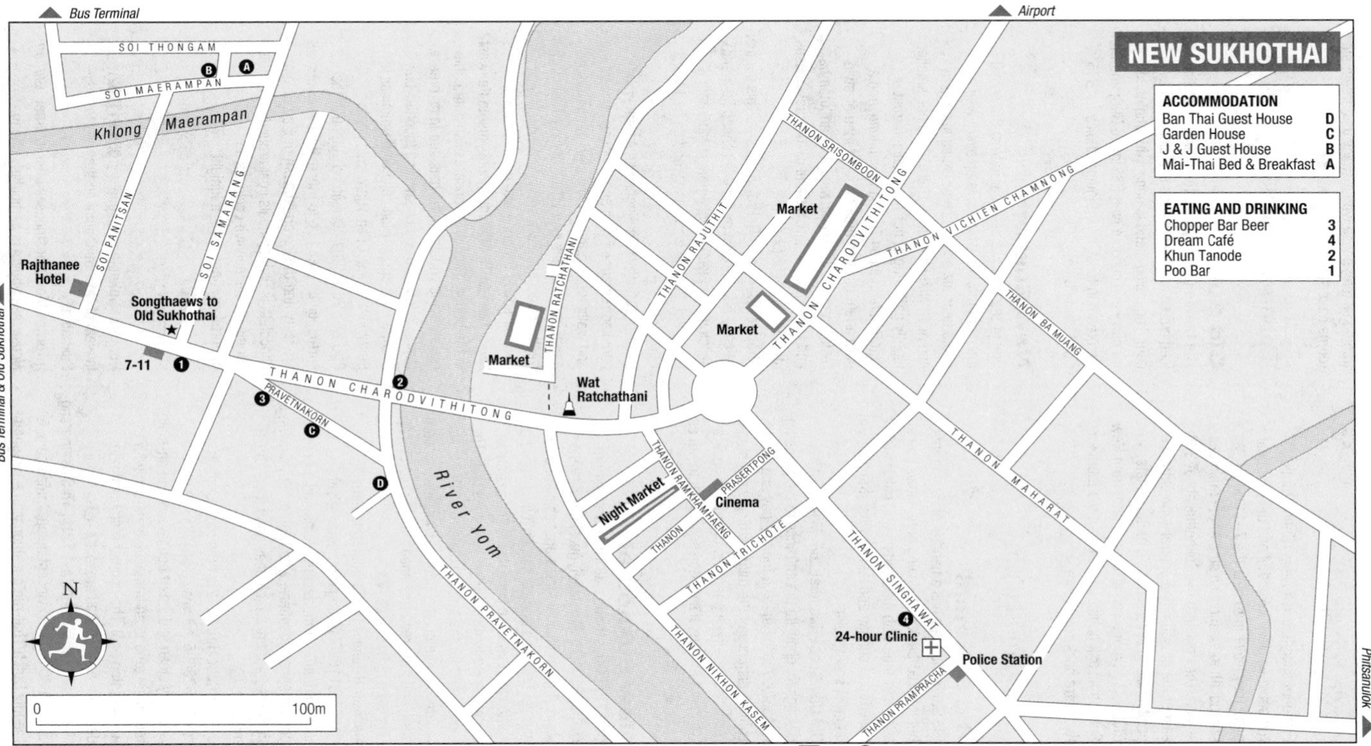
NEW SUKHOTHAI
ACCOMMODATION
Ban Thai Guest House D
Garden House C
J & J Guest House B
Mai-Thai Bed & Breakfast A
EATING AND DRINKING
Chopper Bar Beer 3
Dream Café 4
Khun Tanode 2
Poo Bar 1
Bus Terminal
Airport
Bus Terminal & Old Sukhothai
Phitsanulok
, CAT (200m) & Night Market
SOI THONGAM
SOI MAERAMPAN
Khlong Maerampan
SOI PANITSAN
SOI SAMARANG
Rajthanee Hotel
Songthaews to Old Sukhothai
7-11
THANON CHARODVITHITONG
PRAVETNAKORN
River Yom
THANON PRAVETNAKORN
Market
THANON RATCHATHANI
Wat Ratchathani
THANON RAJUTHIT
THANON SRISOMBOON
Market
THANON VICHIEN CHAMNONG
THANON BA MUANG
THANON MAHARAT
THANON RAMKHAMHAENG
PRASERTPONG
Cinema
Night Market
THANON
THANON TRICHOTE
THANON NIKHON KASEM
THANON SINGHAWAT
24-hour Clinic
Police Station
THANON PRAMPRACHA
N
0
100m

## Town transport

Frequent songthaews (every 15min; 25min) run between New Sukhothai and the historical park; they leave from near the 7–11 on Th Charodvithitong, and also stop at the main bus station. They pull into Old Sukhothai about 300m east of the museum and central zone entrance point, close to several bicycle rental outlets (B30–50/day). You can also cycle here from New Sukhothai: ask guesthouses about the fourteen-kilometre back-road route.

## Accommodation

### Old Sukothai

Old Sukhothai only has a handful of restaurants, but it is laid-back and staying here allows you to take your time with the sights – and catch them deserted at sunrise and sunset when the light's at its most spectacular.

**Old City Guest House** at 28/7 Moo 3, Th Muangkao, opposite the entrance to the museum ⓣ055/697515. Run by a friendly guy and within spitting distance of the ruins with spotless modern rooms set around a garden with outdoor carved-wooden furniture. It's worth shelling out for an en suite. ❶–❷

### New Sukhothai

**Ban Thai Guesthouse** 38 Th Pravetnakhorn ⓣ055/610163, ⓔbanthai_gueshouse@yahoo.com. A great choice: rooms are basic but clean, and set around a tropical garden, which also has some smart wooden bungalows. The restaurant is a good place to meet people and does tasty Thai food tamed for the farang palate. *Ban Thai* is also a reliable source of local information, with wonderful staff, and runs recommended evening bicycle trips (2hr 30min; B150). ❶–❸

**Garden House** 11/1 Th Pravetnakhorn ⓣ055/611395, ⓔtuigardenhouse@yahoo.com. Friendly staff, decent rooms and a great communal atmosphere, with regular film showings in the restaurant, which does good food. Cheap internet. ❷

**J & J Guest House** 122/1 Soi Maeramphan ⓣ055/620095, ⓦwww.jj-guesthouse.com. Squeaky clean and smart bungalows and en-suite rooms set around an immaculate garden with a swimming pool. The popular restaurant does delicious home-baked bread. ❷–❺

**Mai-Thai Bed & Breakfast** 121/1 Th Sirisamarang ⓣ087/680 3876, ⓔvincent.deleu@gmail.com. A friendly Dutch/Thai-run guesthouse in a beautiful traditional teak house with a spacious garden; all rooms have shared bathroom. ❷

## Eating and drinking

### Old Sukhothai

**The Coffee Cup** Opposite the museum. Delicious iced coffee and fruit shakes in a clean and airy café. The mixed menu is huge, with photos to help: try curry in a coconut (veg B65/meat B90) and fried ice cream in toast, an intriguing choice for B45. Open 7am–10pm.

### New Sukhothai

One of the best places to eat in New Sukhothai is the night market, which sets up every Wed and Thurs near the post office at the southeastern end of Th Nikhon Kasem. There's another, smaller nightly gathering of hot-food stalls in front of Wat Ratchathani on Th Charodvithitong, and a permanent covered area for night market-style restaurants on the soi between Th Ramkhamhaeng and Th Nikhon Kasem. Several of the guesthouses also do excellent food.

**Chopper Bar Beer** Th Pravetnakhorn. This popular balcony bar with live music does cheap beer and delicious *tom yam kung*, amongst other things, and is a great place to watch the world go by. Mains from B50.

**Dream Café** 88/1 Th Singhawat. A dark wood-panelled restaurant with an art-house atmosphere and walls full of curios. It has a great mid-priced menu (most dishes over B100) of fiery Thai curries, fresh Vietnamese-style spring rolls, deep-fried banana-flower fritters – and gin and tonics.

**Khun Tanode** Th Charodvithitong, just to the west of the bridge. Though it appears dilapidated, this restaurant is popular with Thais due to its breezy riverside location and cheap food (noodles only B30); try the crispy-fried chicken drumsticks in Sukhothai sauce. Open 10am–midnight.

**Poo Bar** 26 Th Charodvithitong. Although the surroundings aren't up to much, the cheap curries are tasty and the ice cream with melted Belgian chocolate is divine; meals cost around B50. It also serves up inexpensive cocktails and rents out motorbikes. Open 8am–midnight.

## Directory

**Hospital** Sukhothai Hospital (ⓣ055/611782) is west of New Sukhothai on the road to Old Sukhothai.

**Internet** Most guesthouses offer internet; *Garden House* (see above) is particularly cheap.

**Post office** Th Nikon Kasem, about 1km south of the bridge (Mon–Fri 8.30am–4.30pm).
**Telephones** CAT is on Th Nikhon Kasem (Mon–Fri 8.30am–4.30pm, Sat 8.30am–noon).

## Moving on

**By bus** Private bus services to Bangkok are run by Wintour (☎055/378477).
**Destinations:** Ayutthaya (12 daily; 6hr); Bangkok (Mo Chit Northern Terminal; 12 public buses and 10 with Wintour; 7hr); Chiang Mai (13 daily, via Lampang; 6hr); Chiang Rai (3 daily, via Sri Satchanalai; 9hr); Khon Kaen (7 daily; 6–7hr); Mae Sot (8 daily; 3hr); Phitsanulok (every 30min 6am–8pm; 1hr 30min); Tak (for Mae Sot every 1hr 30min; 2hr).
**By air** The local Bangkok Airways office (☎055/647224) is located at 99 Moo 4 Klong Krajong, Sawankaloke. A tuk-tuk to the airport costs B100–150.
**Destination:** Bangkok (2 daily; 1hr 15min).

# MAE SOT

Located only 6km from the Burmese border, **MAE SOT** boasts a thriving trade in gems and teak and a rich ethnic mix of Burmese, Karen, Hmong and Thai, plus a lively injection of committed NGO expats working with the thousands of refugees from Burma. It's a relaxed place to hang out before heading down to Umphang for some trekking (see p.797) – treks can be arranged from Mae Sot – and chances are you'll meet some interesting people at one of the many excellent places to eat.

**Donations** of clothes and medicines for the refugees living at the nine camps along the Burmese border can be left at *Krua Canadian* and *Bai Fern* restaurants (see below).

## What to see and do

There's little to see in the small town apart from several glittering Burmese-style temples and an ornate Chinese temple. Frequent songthaews (B10) run from just west of the market on Thanon Prasat Vithi to the Burmese border at **Rim Moei**, 6km from Mae Sot, where a large, slightly tacky market for Burmese handicrafts and other goods crowds the banks of the River Moei, and Burmese men stick their heads through the bars demarking the territories and sell cheap cigarettes. Look out for shops selling exquisite woodcarvings to the east of the market. At the time of writing, access to the Burmese village of Myawaddy on the opposite bank of the River Moei is only open to farangs for a day's shopping (B500 entry); visitors are allowed no further into Burma. When coming back through Thai customs (6.30am–6.30pm) you will automatically be given a new thirty-day Thai visa.

## Arrival and information

**By bus** To reach Mae Sot from Sukhothai, you need to change in Tak. Buses from Chiang Mai, Chiang Rai, Mae Sai and Lampang use the stand on Th Indharakhiri, about 150m east of the police station. Those from Bangkok use the bus station 2km east of town near the Highway 105/1090 intersection; songthaews (B10) run into the market place.
**By songthaew and minibus** Government minivans from Tak use a depot north off Th Indharakhiri, about 200m behind the police station. Those to and from Phitsanulok and Sukhothai arrive at a terminus on Th Banthung, about 300m south of the police station.
**By air** Although there's an airport in Mae Sot there are currently no flights.
**Tourist information** There is no TAT office here, but both *Bai Fern* and *Khrua Canadian* restaurants are good sources of local information; the latter has a great map and can point you in the right direction for volunteering in a Burmese school. See the "Trekking around Umphang" box on p.797 for details of operators in Mae Sot that organize treks around Umphang.

## Accommodation

**Bai Fern Guest House** 660/2 Th Indharakiri ☎055/531349. Popular place with simple rooms in the centre of town. The helpful owner rents out motorbikes and bicycles. *Bai Fern* also has a restaurant with a wide range of Western and Thai favourites (B40–120). ❶

**Green Guest House** 406/8 Th Indharakiri, behind the police station and across the stream from the Tak bus station ⓣ055/533207. Clean and bright rooms with shared bathrooms set around a garden. ❷

**Krung's** about 200m west of *Bai Fern* on Th Indharakiri. Clean but cluttered en-suite rooms behind a bar. ❶–❷

## Eating and drinking

**Aiya** opposite *Bai Fern Guesthouse*. Popular with expats, *Aiya* does tasty Burmese food in an art-house setting. Mains from B60.

**Casa Mia** Th Don Kaew. A varied menu of Thai and Italian dishes, specializing in pasta (such as ravioli with spinach), pizzas and salads; mains from B50. Very popular with local volunteers. Open 8am–10pm.

**Khao Mao Khae Fang** 382 Mu 5 Mae Pa, north of town between km1 and km2 markers ⓣ055/533607. This extraordinary restaurant was designed by a Thai botanist, who has created a tropical jungle complete with rocky pools, waterfalls, vines and giant carp fish ponds. A surreal dining experience, with delicious authentic Thai food at reasonable prices (B60–250). A tuk-tuk to the restaurant costs B60.

**Khrua Canadian** 3 Th Sriponit, diagonally across from the police station. Delicious breakfasts, bagels, and deli sandwiches served on a range of breads (such as seven-grain or rye bread). The hilltribe coffee is refreshingly not Nescafé, and cheese and imported wines by the bottle or box are on sale. There are English-language newspapers to peruse, or talk to the owner: he's a great source of local knowledge and has detailed maps. Open 7am–9pm.

**T-Corner 557/2** Th Intarakiri. Nice café set-up with hanging plants and poinsettias. There's a good inexpensive menu with ample veggie options and ice creams (including banana split for B25).

## Directory

**Banks** There are banks dotted all about Mae Sot, especially on thanons Indharajiri and Prasat Vithit. Note that Umphang doesn't have exchange facilities, so change money at Mae Sot if you're headed there.

**Internet** Internet is available at many places around Mae Sot, especially on Th Indharakiri.

**Motorbike rental** From most guesthouses (around B150 per day), or from Mr Park, 304/17 Th Indharakiri opposite the Government Savings Bank, (ⓣ055/533900; 8am–5pm). If you plan to bike to Umphang you can rent them for multiple days, leaving your passport as insurance.

**Post office** To the east of the police station on Th Indharakiri.

## Moving on

**By songthaew**: Songthaews headed for Umphang leave Mae Sot from a shop front two blocks south of Th Prasat Vithi (hourly 7.30am–3.30pm). The drive takes about four hours and the breathtaking road – dubbed the "Sky Highway" – careers round the edges of endless steep-sided valleys.

**By bus** to: Chiang Rai (2 daily; 11hr); Mae Sai (2 daily; 12hr); Phitsanulok (7 daily; 3hr 15min–5hr); Sukhothai (via Tak; 6 daily; 3hr); Tak (every 30min; 1hr 30min).

# UMPHANG

Even if you don't fancy joining a trek, it's worth considering making the spectacular 164-kilometre trip south from Mae Sot to the village of **UMPHANG**, both for the fine mountain scenery and for the buzz of being in such an isolated part of Thailand. Chances are your songthaew will be crammed full of people from varied ethnic and tribal backgrounds. About halfway, the road passes past U-Thien, a refugee camp for fifteen thousand or so Burmese.

Surrounded by mountains and sited at the confluence of the Mae Khlong and Umphang rivers, Umphang itself is small and quiet; it takes no more than twenty minutes to walk from one end to the other. It has few signposted roads, but the two main points of orientation are the river at the far western end of the village, and the wat – about 500m east of the river – that marks its centre.

## Arrival

Songthaews drop people at the bus station, just east of the village centre; most places are within walking distance, though there are also motorbike taxis.

## Accommodation

Bungalow accommodation is also available at Trekker Hill (see box opposite).

## TREKKING AROUND UMPHANG

The focus of most treks from Umphang is the three-tiered **Tee Lor Su Waterfall**. It's at its most thunderous just after the rainy season in November, when you can also swim in the beautifully blue lower pool, though trails can still be muddy at this time. During the dry season (Dec–April), you can get close to the falls by road and it's usually possible to climb up to one of the upper tiers. At other times, the falls are reached by a combination of rafting and walking. It's possible to arrange your trek in Mae Sot, but the best place to set up a trip is in Umphang itself. A typical trek lasts three days and features rafting, hot springs, three or four hours' walking per day, a night in a Karen village, and an elephant ride (sometimes at an extra cost). Guides should provide tents, bedrolls, mosquito nets and sleeping bags, plus food and drinking water; trekkers may be asked to help carry some of the gear. Bring a fleece as nights can get pretty chilly. Costs range from B3500 for a three-day trek to US$400 for seven days, and are always cheaper if you're with a bigger group. From June through October, other trips feature whitewater rafting from the Karen village of Umphang Khi via the forty-plus rapids of the Umphang River, as well as one- and two-day rafting outings to Thi Lor Leh Falls.

### Trekking operators in Mae Sot

**Khun Om** c/o *Number 4 Guest House*, 736 Th Indharakiri ⓣ055/544976, ⓦwww.geocities.com/no4guesthouse. The treks run by the taciturn Khun Om get rave reviews, particularly his seven-day expedition. Book ahead by email if possible.

**Max One Tour** In the *DK Hotel* plaza at 296/1 Th Indharakiri ⓣ055/542942, ⓦwww.maxonetour.com. A Mae Sot outlet for the Umphang-based Umphang Hill trek operator (see below).

### Trekking operators in Umphang

**Awe Umphang Tour** 214 M.1 Th Umphang ⓣ089/568 5273. Based at *Boonyaporn Garden House* and run by the disarmingly friendly Deth, this tour agency not only does treks with the usual waterfall/hilltribes/trekking itinerary but also plans to run an exhilarating cycling tour from Mae Sot along the "Sky Highway" for those looking to push their athleticism to its limits.

**BL Tour** West of the wat at 1/438 Th Umphang-Palata ⓣ055/561021. Enthusiastic and well-informed guides earn this outfit lots of good reviews.

**Trekker Hill** 700m northeast of the wat, off Thanon Pravitpaiwan ⓣ055/561090. Mr Tee and his "jungle team" of five guides get good reviews. Offers accommodation for trekkers in en-suite double bungalows. ❶–❷

**Umphang Hill** At *Umphang Hill Resort* on Thanon Umphang-Palata, but can also be booked through Max One Tour in Mae Sot ⓣ055/561063, ⓦwww.umphanghill.com. Very efficiently run, this reputable place often undercuts rival outfits and has English-speaking staff at the office throughout the day.

**Boonyaporn Garden House** On the main road leading northwest from the wat ⓣ055/561093, ⓦwww.boonyapornresort.com. Smart, airy en-suite rooms, including some simple, cheaper wood-panelled ones with shared bathroom. ❷

**Phu Doi Campsite Resort** ⓣ055/561049, ⓦwww.phudoi.com. Dark wood-panelled rooms with spotless bathrooms in log buildings overlooking a lotus pond; free tea, coffee and internet. ❷–❸

**Umphang House** Northwest of the wat along the main road ⓣ055/561073. Spacious basic rooms for B200 with shared bathroom in a large elevated wooden house with glorious mountain views. ❷

## Eating

Food options are limited in Umphang. Food stalls set up around the wat every day, and there are a few noodle and rice places in the centre. When you do a trek, the tour operator will provide food (some at extra cost).

**Boonyaporn Garden House** (see above). Does delicious set Thai menus for tour groups (around B200 per person); ring in advance to book.

## Moving on

Umphang is a dead-end so you must return to Mae Sot before heading on; songthaews leave hourly from 7.30am to 2.30pm (4hr; B120), though if there are no other passengers the price will be higher.



# The north

Beyond the northern plains, the climate becomes more temperate, nurturing the fertile land that gave the old kingdom of **the north** the name of **Lanna**, "the land of a million rice fields". Until the beginning of the last century, Lanna was a largely independent region, with its own styles of art and architecture. Its capital, the cool, pleasant city of **Chiang Mai**, is now a major travellers' centre and the most popular base from which to organize treks to nearby hilltribe villages. Another great way of exploring the scenic countryside up here is to rent a jeep or motorbike and make the six hundred-kilometre loop over the forested western mountains, via the backpackers' honeypot of **Pai**, to **Mae Hong Son** and back. Heading north from Chiang Mai towards the Burmese border brings you to the charming but increasingly upmarket town of **Chiang Rai**, and then on to the frontier settlement of **Mae Sai**, the so-called **"Golden Triangle"** at Sop Ruak, and the atmospheric ruined temples of **Chiang Saen**.

## TREKKING

**Trekking** in the mountains of northern Thailand differs from trekking in most other parts of the world, in that the emphasis is not primarily on the scenery but on the region's inhabitants. Northern Thailand's **hilltribes**, now numbering over 800,000 people living in around 3500 villages, have so far preserved their way of life with little change over thousands of years (you'll increasingly hear the more politically correct term "mountain people" used). Over a hundred thousand travellers now trek each year, most heading to well-trodden areas such as the Mae Tang Valley, 40km northwest of Chiang Mai, and the hills around the Kok River west of Chiang Rai. This steady flow of trekkers creates pressures for the traditionally insular hilltribes. Foreigners unfamiliar with hilltribe customs can easily cause grave offence, especially those who go looking for drugs. Most tribespeople are genuinely welcoming to foreigners; nonetheless, it is important to take a responsible attitude.

The hilltribes are big business in northern Thailand: in **Chiang Mai**, there are over two hundred agencies that between them cover just about all the trekkable areas in the north. **Chiang Rai** is the second-biggest trekking centre, and agencies can also be found in **Mae Hong Son** and **Pai**, although these usually arrange treks only to the villages in their immediate area. Guided trekking on a much smaller scale than in the north is available in **Umphang** (see p.797).

### The basics

On any trek, you'll need walking boots or training shoes, long trousers (against thorns and wet-season leeches), a hat, a sarong or towel, a sweater or fleece, plus insect repellent and, if possible, a mosquito net. On an organized trek, water, blankets or a sleeping bag, and possibly a small backpack, should be supplied. It's wise not to take anything valuable with you; most guesthouses in Chiang Mai have safes, but check their reputation with other travellers, and sign an inventory – theft and credit-card abuse are not uncommon.

### Trekking etiquette

As guests, it's up to farangs to adapt to the customs of the hilltribes and not to make a nuisance of themselves.

**Chiang Khong**, on the Mekong River, is an important crossing point to Laos.

The best map of the area is *Thailand North* (Berndtson & Berndtson; 1:750,000), which shows accurately the crisscross of dirt tracks and minor roads, and also contains insets of the Golden Triangle and Chiang Mai area.

## CHIANG MAI

Despite becoming a fixture on the package-tourist itinerary, **CHIANG MAI** – Thailand's second city – manages to preserve a little of the atmosphere of an overgrown village and a laid-back traveller vibe, especially in the traditional old quarter, set within a two-kilometre-square moat. Chiang Mai is a fun and historic city, packed with culture and bustling markets, but its real charm lies in the staggering range of tours, treks, courses and activities available. You can spend a week in Chiang Mai and do something completely different every day. The choices are endless: elephant-riding, hilltribe homestays, waterfalls, massage, cooking, hot-air ballooning, mountain biking, rock climbing, bungy jumping, river cruises, unlimited shopping experiences and national parks on its doorstep. On top of that, there are fabulous temples, delicious food, unparalleled night markets and an energetic nightlife that caters for everyone, from laid-back reggae bars to thumping techno-clubs. It's impossible to get bored here.

- Dress modestly, avoiding skimpy shorts and vests. Try to keep your shoulders covered. Wear a sarong when showering; no bikinis or swim suits.
- Before entering a hilltribe village, look out for taboo signs of woven bamboo strips on the ground outside the village entrance, which mean a special ceremony is taking place and that you should not enter. Be careful about what you touch. In Akha villages, keep your hands off cult structures such as the entrance gates and the giant swing. Do not touch or photograph any shrines, or sit underneath them. You'll have to pay a fine for any violation of local customs.
- Most villagers do not like to be photographed in keeping with their spiritualist and animist beliefs. Be particularly careful with pregnant women and babies – most tribes believe cameras affect the soul of the foetus or new-born. Always ask first, and accept that you may have to offer a "donation" for any photos taken.
- Taking gifts is dubious practice: ask your guide what the village actually *needs* and follow their advice; clothes are always useful but avoid sweets and cigarettes as they may encourage begging.

### Organized treks

**Organized treks** usually last for three days, have six to twelve people in the group, and follow a route regularly used by the agency. There will be a few hours' walking every day, plus the possibility of an elephant ride and a trip on a bamboo raft. The group usually sleeps on the floor of the village headman's hut, and the guide cooks communal meals. A typical three-day trek costs B1800–2500 in Chiang Mai, sometimes less in other towns, and much less without rafting and elephant rides.

Word of mouth is often the best way to choose a trekking agency. If you want to trek with a small group, get an assurance that you won't be tagged onto a larger group. Meet the guides, who should speak reasonable English, know about hilltribe culture and have a certificate from the Tourism Authority of Thailand (TAT). Check how much walking is involved per day, and ask about the menu. Also enquire about transport from base at the beginning and end of the trek, which sometimes entails a long public bus ride. Before setting off, each trek should be registered with the tourist police.

## What to see and do

The main sights within Chiang Mai are mostly situated within the ancient city walls, which are surrounded by a moat, and intersected at the cardinal points by elaborate gates. Tha Pae Gate, on the east side of old Chiang Mai, leads out to the sprawling new town and the river. Just 16km west of town, the striking Wat Phra That Doi Suthep is set on a mist-shrouded mountain.

### Wat Phra Singh

If you see only one temple in Chiang Mai it should be **Wat Phra Singh**, at the far western end of Thanon Ratchdamnoen in the old town. Its largest structure, a colourful modern viharn fronted by naga balustrades, hides from view the beautiful Viharn Lai Kam, a wooden gem of early nineteenth-century Lanna architecture, with its squat, multi-tiered roof and exquisitely carved and gilded pediment. Inside sits a portly, radiant and much-revered bronze Buddha in fifteenth-century Lanna style. The walls are enlivened by murals depicting daily life in the north a hundred years ago.

### Wat Chedi Luang

The nearby **Wat Chedi Luang** on Thanon Phra Pokklao is an enormous crumbling pink-brick chedi, which

### THE HILLTRIBES

There are at least ten different **hilltribes** in northern Thailand, many of them divided into distinct subgroups. Migrating from various parts of China and Southeast Asia, most arrived in Thailand in the twentieth century and many have tribal relatives in other parts of Southeast Asia. The tribes have sophisticated systems of customs, laws and beliefs, and are predominantly animists. They often have exquisitely crafted costumes, though many men and children now adopt Western clothes for everyday wear. To learn more about the tribes, visit the Tribal Museum in Chiang Mai (see above) or the Hilltribe Museum in Chiang Rai (see p.817).

**Karen**

The largest hilltribe group (pop. 500,000), the **Karen** began to arrive in the seventeenth century, though many are recent refugees from Burma. Most of them live west of Chiang Mai, stretching all the way down to Kanchanaburi. Unmarried Karen women wear loose V-necked shift dresses, often decorated with grass seeds at the seams. Married women wear blouses and skirts in bold red or blue. Perhaps the most famous of all hilltribe groups are the **Paduang**, a small subgroup of the Karen. Paduang women wear columns of heavy brass rings around their necks (see box, p.813)

**Hmong**

The **Hmong** (or Meo; pop. 110,000) are found widely in northern Thailand, and are also the most widespread minority group in south China. The Blue Hmong subgroup live to the west of Chiang Mai, while the White Hmong are found to the east. Most Hmong live in extended families in traditional houses with a roof descending almost to ground level. Blue Hmong women wear intricately embroidered pleated skirts decorated with bands of red, pink, blue and white. White Hmong women wear white skirts for special occasions, black baggy trousers for everyday use. All the Hmong are famous for their chunky silver jewellery.

**Lahu**

The **Lahu** (pop. 80,000) originated in the Tibetan highlands. The Lahu language has become the lingua franca of the hilltribes, since the Lahu often hire out their labour. About one-third of Lahu have been converted to Christianity. The remaining animist Lahu believe in a village guardian spirit, who is often worshipped at a central temple. Houses are built on high stilts and thatched with grass. Some Lahu women wear a once housed the Emerald Buddha (now in Bangkok's Wat Phra Kaeo) but was toppled by an earthquake in 1545. In the early evening resident bats flit around. On the north side of the chedi, "Monk Chat" is advertised (Mon–Sat noon–6.30pm), giving you a chance to meet and talk to the monks in English.

### Chiang Mai City Arts and Cultural Centre

Housed in an elegant 1920s former provincial office, the **Chiang Mai City Arts and Cultural Centre** (daily except Mon 8.30am–5pm; free) is an informative museum of the history, customs and culture of the city and the region that's well worth a visit. It's just off Thanon Phra Pokklao, north of Thanon Ratchadmnoen.

### National Museum

For a comprehensive picture of Lanna art, head for the **National Museum** (Wed–Sun 9am–4pm; B30), on the north-western outskirts of Chiang Mai, which houses a wealth of Buddha images and a fine collection of ceramics. To get here, charter a tuk-tuk (B40) or songthaew (B20) from the centre of town.

### Tribal Museum

One kilometre north of the Superhighway, off Thanon Chotana, the very worth-

distinctive black cloak with diagonal white stripes, decorated in bold red and yellow on the sleeve, but many now wear Thai dress. The tribe is famous for its richly embroidered shoulder bags.

#### Akha

The poorest of the hilltribes, is the **Akha** (pop. 50,000). Every Akha village is entered through ceremonial gates decorated with carvings of human attributes – even cars and aeroplanes – to indicate to the spirit world that only humans should pass. Akha houses are recognizable by their low stilts and steeply pitched roofs. Women wear elaborate headgear consisting of a conical wedge of white beads interspersed with silver coins, topped with plumes of red taffeta and framed by dangling silver balls.

#### Mien

The **Mien** (or Yao; pop. 42,000) consider themselves the aristocrats of the hilltribes. Originating in central China, and widely scattered throughout the north, they are the only people to have a written language, and a codified religion, based on medieval Chinese Taoism, although many have converted to Christianity and Buddhism. Mien women wear long black jackets with bright scarlet lapels, and heavily embroidered loose trousers and turbans.

#### Lisu

The **Lisu** (pop. 30,000), who originated in eastern Tibet, are found mostly in the west, particularly between Chiang Mai and Mae Hong Son. They are organized into patriarchal clans, and their strong sense of clan rivalry often results in public violence. The Lisu live in extended families in bamboo houses. The women wear a blue or green knee-length tunic, with a wide black belt and blue or green pants. Men wear green, pink or yellow baggy pants and a blue jacket.

#### Lawa

The **Lawa** people (pop. 17,000) have inhabited Thailand since at least the eighth century and most Lawa villages look no different from Thai settlements. But between Hot, Mae Sariang and Mae Hong Son, the Lawa still live a largely traditional life. Unmarried Lawa women wear strings of orange and yellow beads, white blouses edged with pink, and tight skirts in parallel bands of blue, black, yellow and pink. All the women wear their hair tied in a turban.

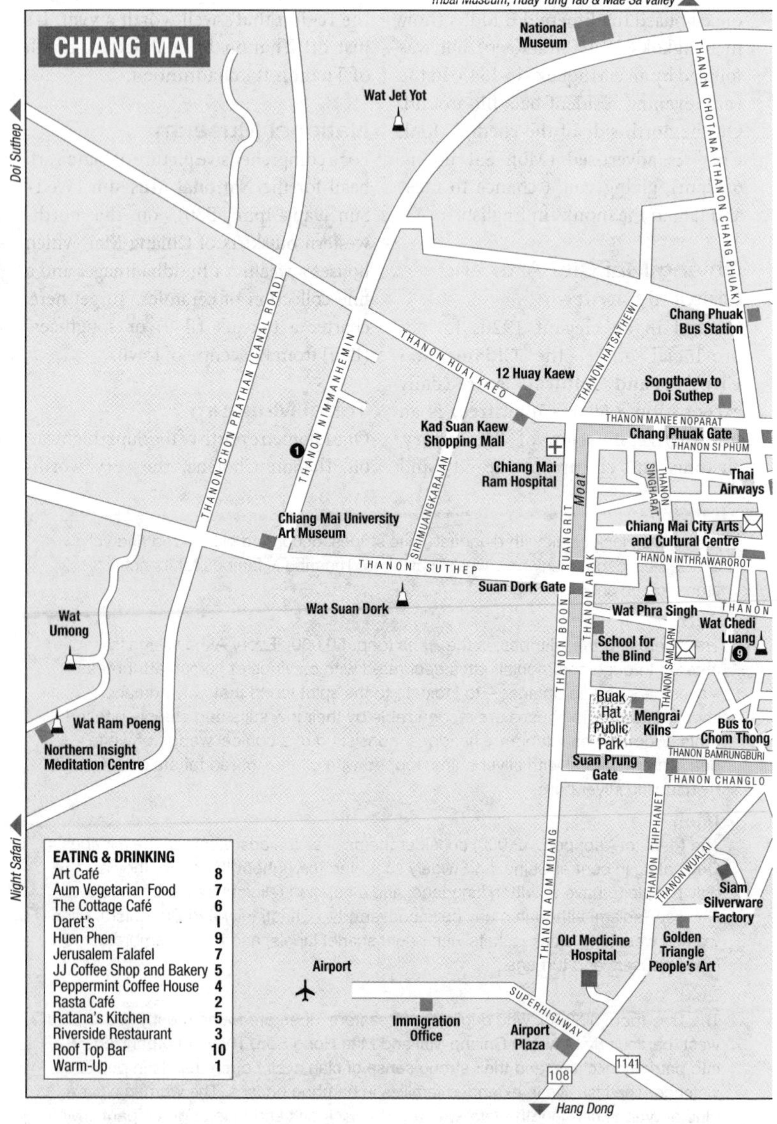


while **Tribal Museum** (daily 9am–4pm; free) stands in the artfully landscaped Ratchamangkla Park. The exhibition introduces the major hilltribes with photos, artefacts and models, and there's a chance to hear tapes of traditional music. It's about a ten-minute walk from the park gate on Thanon Chotana to the museum entrance; songthaews leave from the Chang Phuak bus station, 500m north of the moat along Thanon Chotana; they can drop you at the museum, but only pick up from the gate.

## Wat Suan Dork

Midway along Thanon Suthep, the

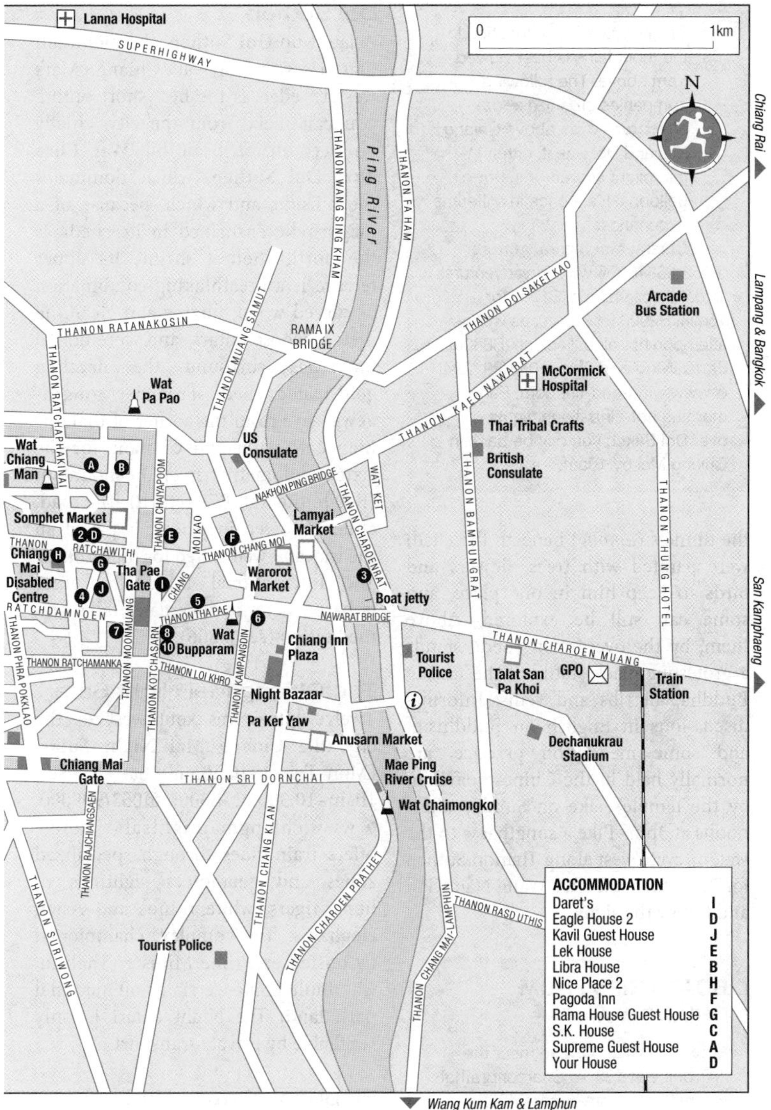




brilliantly whitewashed chedi of **Wat Suan Dork** sits next to a garden of smaller, equally dazzling chedis that contain the ashes of the old Chiang Mai royal family – framed by Doi Suthep to the west, this makes a photogenic sight, especially at sunset. More "Monk Chat" (Mon, Wed & Fri 5–7pm) gives you a chance to meet and talk to the monks in English here.

## Wat Umong

More of a park than a temple, **Wat Umong** was built in the 1380s for a brilliant monk who was prone to wandering off into the forest to meditate;

TREAT YOURSELF

Chiang Mai's idyllic location in the mountains is best viewed from above. The following companies organize **aerial adventure trips** above Chiang Mai and Doi Saket, either in microlight aircraft or in hot-air balloons. It's a once in a lifetime experience.

**Chiang Mai Sky Adventure** ⓣ053/868460, ⓦwww.skyadventures.info. Microlight trips (B1700 for 15min; B2900 for 30min), as well as afternoon hot-air ballooning (B8800).

**Earth Wind and Fire** ⓣ053/292224, ⓦwww.wind-and-fire.com. Early-morning hot-air balloon flights over Doi Saket; you can be back in Chiang Mai by 10am.

the tunnels (*umong*) beneath the chedi were painted with trees, flowers and birds to keep him in one place, and some can still be explored. Above them, by the overgrown chedi, stands a grotesque black statue of the fasting Buddha, all ribs and veins. Informal discussions in English on Buddhism, and some meditation practice, are normally held in the Chinese pavilion by the temple's lake on Sunday afternoons at 3pm. Take a songthaew to the wat, or cycle west along Thanon Suthep for 2km, turn left after Wang Nam Gan and follow the signs.

## BOAT TRIPS FROM CHIANG MAI

**Mae Ping River Cruise**, near the TAT office at 133 Th Chareonprathat (every 2hr 8.30am–5pm; B400; ⓣ053/274822, ⓦmaepingrivercruise.com), runs two-hour cruises through lush countryside on converted rice barges, with a stop at a local farmer's house and a herbal drink and snack included. They also offer ninety-minute evening dinner cruises, with a set Thai menu (7pm; B450; pick-up from hotel available).

### Doi Suthep

A jaunt up **Doi Suthep**, the mountain that rises steeply at Chiang Mai's western edge, is the best short outing you can make from the city, chiefly on account of beautiful **Wat Phra That Doi Suthep**, which dominates the hillside, and which, because of a magic relic enshrined in its chedi, is the north's holiest shrine. Its upper terrace is a breathtaking combination of carved wood, filigree and gleaming metal, whose altars and ceremonial umbrellas surround the dazzling gold-plated chedi. Frequent **songthaews** leave from the corner of thanons Manee Noparat and Chotana for the sixteen-kilometre trip up the mountain (B40 to the wat, B70 return). The road, although steep in places, is paved all the way and well suited for motorbikes. The International Buddhist Center is based here; it does daily talks and meditation (see p.806).

### The Chiang Mai Night Safari

Twelve kilometres southwest of the city, the **Chiang Mai Night Safari** (Mon–Fri 1–10.30pm, Sat & Sun 10am–10.30pm; B500; ⓣ053/999000, ⓦwww.chiangmainightsafari.com), offers train rides through specialized zones and guarantees sightings of lions, tigers, white rhinos and Asian elephants. The complex, championed by ousted ex-Prime Minister Thaksin, was built controversially on national park land. The Night Safari is only reachable by private transport.

### Elephant Nature Park

About an hour north of Chiang Mai, the **Elephant Nature Park** (ⓣ053/272855, ⓦwww.thaifocus.com/elephant) is essentially a hospital for sick elephants, but hands-on pre-arranged educational – and recreational – visits by the public are encouraged. Either opt for a full-day trip (pick-up at 8.30am from Chiang Mai), or sign up as a paying volunteer for a week

**LISU HILL TRIBE**
For a more thorough appreciation of the hilltribes, head to the hills. Situated 90km from Chiang Mai on the road towards Pai, **Lisu Hill Tribe** (☎089/998 4886, Ⓦlisuhilltribe.com) offers the chance of spending the night in a Lisu village (B300), and an array of courses (B1000/day) from jewellery-making to cooking. To get there, take a minibus to Pai, then a public bus to Soppong; alternatively, hire your own transport from Chiang Mai or Pai.

or two (B2500/day, B12,000/week; fee includes transport from Chiang Mai).

## Arrival

**By bus** The long-distance Arcade bus station on Th Kaeo Nawarat is 3km northeast of Chiang Mai; tuk-tuks cost around B50 to the landmark Tha Pae Gate or take a shared songthaew. Beware that many of the low-cost private buses from Bangkok's Th Khao San stop on a remote part of the Superhighway, where they "sell" their passengers to various guesthouse touts; tuk-tuks from here cost around B40.
**By train** The train station is on Th Charoen Muang, just over 2km east of the Tha Pae Gate; a tuk-tuk into the centre cost B50.
**By air** The airport is 3km southwest of the centre; here you'll find banks, a post office and taxis (around B150 to the city centre, including an official airport flat fee of B60; to avoid this walk to the main road and catch a tuk-tuk from there, which will cost around B60 to Tha Pae gate).

## Information

**TAT** First port of call should be the TAT office at 105/1 Th Chiang Mai-Lamphun on the east bank of the river (☎053/248604, Ⓦwww.tatchiangmai.org), which can point you in the best direction for courses and has useful transport information. *Nancy Chandler's Map of Chiang Mai* (B140) is very handy for a detailed exploration.

## City transport

**Bicycle** Most guesthouses rent bicycles for B30–50 per day, and you can also pick them up around Tha Pae Gate.
**Motorbike and car rental** Many places around Tha Pae Gate rent out motorbikes (from B150 a day) and cars (from B800). The latter should come with insurance included: check before you set off. Petrol costs extra.
**Songthaews** Red songthaews act as shared taxis within the city, picking up people heading in roughly the same direction and taking each to their specific destination. Fares to most places should cost around B20 but arrange a price before you get in.
**Tuk-tuk and songthaews** The city is stuffed with tuk-tuks and songthaews, ready to take advantage of tourists – haggle hard. Expect to pay around B50 from the train station to Tha Pae Gate, and the same from the bus station.

## Activities and tour operators

One-day tours are not recommended unless you're desperately short of time; you'll spend more time waiting in queues and sitting in transport than actually viewing the sights. Three-day/two-night treks are best, and usually include an overnight stop in a hilltribe vilage, elephant trekking, rafting and a few hours' walking a day.

### Trekking tour operators

**Chiangmai Green Alternative Tours** 31 Th Chiangmai-Lamphun ☎053/247374, Ⓦwww.chiangmaigreen.com. Offers treks, nature field trips, birdwatching and mountain-biking.
**Chiang Mai Mountain Biking** 1 Th Samlarn, 50m south of Wat Phra Singh ☎081/024 7046, Ⓦwww.mountainbikingchiangmai.com. A wide range of routes for all level of fitness and experience, all of which start from the summit of Doi Suthep.
**Chiang Mai Rock Climbing Adventures** 55/3 Th Ratchapakhinai ☎053/207102, Ⓦwww.thailandclimbing.com. Climbing trips based at the striking "Crazy Horse Buttress" 35km from Chiang Mai. Runs lead climbing top-roping, and caving courses, with a partner-finding service and extensive equipment for rent. Its in-town bouldering wall is a good place to meet and train.
**Contact Travel** 420/3 Th Chang Klang ☎053/277178, Ⓦwww.activethailand.com. Also offer treks, lake- and river-kayaking and whitewater rafting trips on the Pai River.
**Eagle House** (see p.806) A reliable trekking operator that passes on a proportion of its revenue towards funding projects in hilltribe villages.
**The Peak** 302/4 Chiang Mai–Lamphun ☎053/800567, Ⓦwww.thepeakadventure.com. Highly recommended trips with enthusiastic staff. They teach basics to beginners at their fifteen-metre rock-climbing wall in town (B400/hr; also

three-day courses), and offer thrilling out-of-town combination trips with rock-climbing, kayaking, caving, quad-biking, whitewater rafting and canyoning at the mighty Vachiratharn waterfall.

### Adventure tour operators

**Flight of the Gibbon** ⓣ089/970 5511, ⓦwww.treetopasia.com. Zoom through the tropical rainforest on zip wires and sky bridges in this exhilarating trip high above the jungle floor. Free pick-up/drop-off from central Chiang Mai.
**Jungle Bungy Jump** ⓣ053/297700, ⓦwww.junglebungy.com. Experienced bungy jump specialists offering 50-metre jumps over water. B1500 including insurance, pick-up and certificate.

## Courses

The courses listed below are only a taster of the huge range on offer.

### Cookery lessons

**Baan Thai Cookery School** 11 Th Ratchadamnoen Soi 5 ⓣ053/357339, ⓦwww.cookinthai.com. Based in central Chiang Mai, Baan Thai has interesting menu choices and offers both full-day (B800) and evening courses (B700).
**Chiang Mai Thai Cookery School** 1–3 Th Moonmuang ⓣ053/206388, ⓦwww.thaicookeryschool.com. Though many guesthouses now offer lessons, this is the original – and still the best. Courses range from one to five days (B900–4200), covering common Thai and traditional Lanna dishes; book ahead.
**Chiang Mai Thai Farm Cooking School** 2/2 Th Ratchadamnoen Soi 5 ⓣ081/288 5989, ⓦwww.thaifarmcooking.com. A good way to escape the city: you can pick your own organic vegetables, herbs and fruits for cooking on their farm thirty minutes' drive from town (B900/day). Alternatively visit their in-town office.

### Massage

Massages in Thailand are considered more an essential part of daily life than a luxurious pampering treat so they're readily available all over Chiang Mai, with prices ranging from B150 to 300/hr. For something a little different, you can get a massage by extremely competent blind masseurs at the School for the Blind, 41 Th Arak (ⓣ053/278009; open 9am–5pm; B150/hr), and by disabled masseurs at the Chiang Mai Disabled Centre, 133/1 Th Ratchapakinai (ⓣ053/213941, ⓦwww.disabled.infothai.com); proceeds from the latter go towards local physical therapy and wheelchair projects.
**Old Medicine Hospital** 78/1 Soi Mo Shivagakomarpaj, off Th Wualai ⓣ053/275085, ⓦwww.thaimassageschool.ac.th. Highly respected massage courses running 1–10 days; herbal compress courses are also available.
**Thai Massage School of Chiang Mai** 203/6 Th Mae Jo Road ⓣ053/854330, ⓦwww.tmcschool.com. Runs shorter five-day courses fully accredited by the Ministry of Education, as well as longer professional courses.

### Meditation

These meditation courses are serious undertakings: conditions are sparse, the routine is strict and there's often no reading or music, and speaking must be kept to a minimum. White-only clothing must be worn, and men are often expected to shave their heads.
**International Buddhism Center** at Doi Suthep ⓦwww.fivethousandyears.org. The IBC (open 9am–5pm) offers daily monk chat (12.30–2.30pm), library resources and group meditation instruction (book ahead). It also offers an evening Dharma talk and Pali chanting session, twenty one-day meditation courses, and three-day meditation practice retreats.
**Northern Insight Meditation Centre** Wat Ram Poeng (aka Wat Tapotaram),Th Canal near Wat Umong ⓣ053/278620 ext 13, ⓔwatrampoeng@hotmail.com. Disciplined Vipassana courses; the minimum stay is ten days, with a basic course lasting 26 days.

## Accommodation

The main concentrations of guesthouses are in the surprisingly quiet sois around the eastern side of the moat, close to all the sights and amid a larder of restaurants. Many guesthouses make their bread and butter from trekking and will encourage you to use their service; though this can be convenient it's always worth shopping around. None of the places listed should hassle you to trek, though some may limit the number of nights you can stay; ask when you check in.
**Daret's** 4/5 Th Chaiyapoom ⓣ053/252292. Cheap basic rooms with friendly staff, set above the popular restaurant; can be noisy. ❶
**Eagle House 2** 26 Soi 2, Th Ratchawithi ⓣ053/210620, ⓦwww.eaglehouse.com. Decent guesthouse with garden café and en-suite rooms, plus dorms; well-organized treks and cookery courses are on offer, plus free pick-ups from train or bus stations or airport. ❶–❷
**Kavil Guest House** 10/1 Soi 5, Th Ratchdamnoen, near Somphet Market ⓣ053/224740. Smallish, friendly, well-run place in a quiet soi with fan and a/c rooms; all have hot-water bathrooms. ❶–❷

**Lek House** 22 Th Chaiyapoom ⓣ053/252686. Central and set back from the road, with clean, en-suite rooms around a small garden and some cheaper ones out back. ❷

**Libra House** 28 Soi 9, Th Moonmuang ⓣ053/210687, ⓔlibra_guesthouse@hotmail.com. Decent, modern trekking-oriented guesthouse. All rooms are en suite, some with hot water, some a/c. ❶–❷

**Nice Place 2** 133 Th Ratchaphakinai ⓣ053/418305. *Nice Place 2* has a great swimming pool and smart clean en-suite rooms with hot shower. ❷–❸

**Pagoda Inn** Soi Wat Chomphu, 49 Th Chang Moi ⓣ053/233290. Nice en-suite rooms with great communal areas, slightly away from the fray. ❷–❸

**Rama House Guest House** 8 Soi 5, Th Moonmuang ⓣ053/225027. Cheap rooms overlooking a peaceful garden complex with table-tennis tables and water fountains. Just behind *Rama Bar*, which has snooker and darts. ❶

**S.K. House** Soi 9, 20 Th Moonmuang. Large complex of rooms set around a pool with hanging flowers and seating areas with traditional Thai art work. However, staff aren't especially friendly and there are reports of trek-pushing. ❸–❹

**Supreme Guest House** 44/1 Soi 9, Th Moonmuang ⓣ053/222480. A charismatic Scot runs this friendly guesthouse, popular with long-stays, in a modern concrete block. Rooms have en-suite hot showers, and there's a pleasant roof veranda with a chill-out zone with TV and Playstation, and a useful library/secondhand bookshop. ❶.

**Your House** 8 Soi 2, Th Ratchawithi ⓣ053/217492, ⓦwww.yourhouseguesthouse.com. Welcoming old-town teak house. Big rooms with shared hot-water bathrooms, plus some smaller en-suite ones in a modern annexe, some a/c. Fabulous, inexpensive breakfasts; free pick-ups are sometimes possible from train or bus stations or airport. ❶–❸.

### NORTHERN FOOD

Northern food has been strongly influenced by Burmese cuisine, especially in curries such as the spicy *kaeng hang lay*, made with pork, ginger and tamarind. Another favourite local dish, especially for lunch, is *khao soi*, a thick broth of curry and coconut cream, with both soft and crispy egg noodles and meat.

## Eating and drinking

There are several markets with good street food stalls: Anusarn, off Th Chang Klan; along Th Bamrungburi by Chiang Mai Gate; and at Talat San Pa Khoi, out towards the train station on the south side of Th Charoen Muang.

### Cafés and restaurants

**Art Café** 263/1 Th Tha Pae. Popular though slightly overpriced farang hangout with all the café favourites and a big veggie menu. Dishes B60–200.

**Aum Vegetarian Food** On the corner of thanons Ratchdamnoen and Moonmuang. Small and relaxing long-time favourite, serving cheap and interesting veggie dishes and salads, and Thai desserts (dishes from B40). Peruse their eclectic books selection over a steaming cup of organic hilltribe coffee. Open 8.30am–2pm & 5–8pm.

**The Cottage Café** 1/1 Soi 4 Th Tha Pae. A relaxed café with a British-trained chef, serving delicious, mostly veggie, international food at good prices (jacket potatoes B60), toasties (B55–60), with daily specials, tasty desserts and invigorating juices.

**Daret's** 4/5 Th Chaiyapoon. Generous portions with great prices make this place a must-visit. Delicious curries and soups, vegetable salad a bargain B15, fruit shakes B20, and a moreish *khao soi*. Rice dishes B30, noodles B39.

**Huen Phen** 112 Th Ratchamanka. Probably Chiang Mai's most authentic northern restaurant, with bags of ambience. Try the selection of local appetizers, and specialities such as *sai ooua* (sausage), and *khao soi* (noodle curry). Prices B60-200.

**Jerusalem Falafel** 35/3 Th Moonmuang. Small and simple a/c café serving pitta bread, home-made cheeses and yoghurts, and Israeli food, right near Tha Pae Gate; prices around B100 a plate.

**JJ Coffee Shop and Bakery** Th Tha Pae. In bustling, a/c surroundings, all kinds of very popular Thai, Western and veggie food are served (mains B30–80), but it's best for breakfast, with home-baked croissants, buckwheat pancakes, multi-grain bread, and great home-made muesli and yoghurt. Open 7am–5pm.

**Peppermint Coffee House** 1/1 Soi 5 Th Rachadamnoen. Friendly relaxed English/Thai-run café/restaurant with an appetizing international and Thai menu; the fish and chips are delicious, and it's the perfect place for a cuppa, with real milk, and tasty banana cake. There's also an interesting selection of curios for sale.

**Ratana's Kitchen** 320–322 Th Tha Pae. A favourite among locals both for northern specialities, such as *kaeng hang lay* and *khao soi*, and for tasty Western breakfasts, sandwiches and steaks, all at good prices (B40–120). Open 7.30am–11pm.

**Riverside Restaurant** 9 Th Charoenrat ⓣ053/243239. Archetypal farang bolthole: candle-lit terraces by the water, mid-priced Western and Thai food, live bands and reasonable draught beer.

### Bars

Chiang Mai boasts a huge number of bars, most of which serve food. Beware of the beautiful bar girls; the sex trade in Chiang Mai is booming.

**Rasta Café** Behind Soi 2, Th Ratchwithi. One of a handful of chilled-out places in a gravelled car park tucked behind the soi. Has a reggae vibe, and often features live music.

**Roof Top Bar** Opposite Thai Pae Gate. Hugely popular with backpackers, this rooftop terrace has low tables, axe pillows and a laid-back atmosphere, making it a good place to meet people. Daily drinks offers, often gin and tonic.

**Warm-Up** Th Nimmanhemin. Typical Thai club where girls in dangerously short skirts dance around their handbags to pulsating techo beats. Either chill out at the tables out front or tackle the madness of the masses within. No admission charge but pricey drinks.

## Shopping

Chiang Mai is a shopper's paradise, selling everything from touristy slogan t-shirts to unique hilltribe handicrafts. It's worth shopping around as quality and prices vary, and don't forget to haggle in the night market, but be prepared to pay out for quality handmade products.

### Books

Gecko Books sells secondhand books at 2/6 Th Chang Moi Kao (just off Th Tha Pae). On the same street there's Backstreet Books and Annex, both well stocked. Book Zone, 318 Th Tha Pae, has a wide selection of new books, and also sells maps, while *Aum Vegetarian* restaurant has an eclectic selection. Most guesthouses offer a book-swap scheme, or have books for sale.

### Clothes

Fishermen's trousers, generic cotton garb, silk and slogan-printed t-shirts are extensively available at all tourist markets. For a selection of trendy and chic boutique clothes head to Th Nimmanhemin, northwest of the town centre.

### Hilltribe handicrafts and silver

The road to San Kamphaeng, which extends due east for 13km from the end of Th Charoen Muang, is lined with craft shops and factories, including silverware and jade. The biggest concentrations are at Bo Sang, the "umbrella village", 9km from town, and at San Kamphaeng itself, dedicated chiefly to silk-weaving. Frequent white songthaews to San Kamphaeng leave Chiang Mai from the central Lamyai market. In Chiang Mai, try the following places:

**John's Gallery** 340 Th Tha Pae (and the shop a few doors down). An eclectic and interesting selection of crafts in an overgrown shop, including Karen knives and elephant bells; the gallery has fun art on postcards and bags.

**Pa Ker Yaw** 180 Th Loikroh. An incredible shopping experience: a huge range of handicrafts from many different tribes are on sale in this atmospheric shop. Prices can be justly astronomical but there are some good buys, such as the stunning silver jewellery and beetle-shell earrings.

**Siam Silverware Factory** Soi 3, Th Wualai. In the heart of the old silversmiths' quarter, the factory is noisy, sulphurous and well worth a visit.

**Thai Tribal Crafts** 204 Th Bamrungrat. Good selection of embroidered shoulder bags and non-profit-making.

### Markets

**Chiang Mai Night Bazaar** Spread expansively around the junction of thanons Chang Klan and Loi Khro is the main shopper's playground, where bumper-to-bumper street stalls and shops sell just about anything produced in Chiang Mai (from 5pm). Highlights are the hilltribe jewellery and bags, and buffalo-hide shadow puppets.

**Sunday night market** Th Ratchdamnoen turns into a walking street on Sunday evenings, moving west from Tha Pae Gate; it's a tamed and friendlier version of the night bazaar.

**Warorot Market** Bustling day-time market with lots of cheap cotton, linen and ceramics; it turns into a late-night flower market.

## Directory

**Banks and exchange** There are banks all over Chiang Mai; most of which offer exchange facilities.

**Consulates** Canada c/o Raming Tea Co. Ltd., 151 Moo 3, Superhighway ⓣ053/850147; UK, 198 Th Bumrungrat ⓣ053/263015; USA, 387 Th Witchayanon ⓣ053/252629.

**Hospitals** 24hr emergency service (and dentistry) at Lanna Hospital, 103 Superhighway (ⓣ053/357234), east of Th Chotana; McCormick Hospital on Th Kaeo Nawarat (ⓣ053/241010) and Chiang Mai Ram Hospital at 8 Th Boon Ruangrit (ⓣ053/224851) also have good reputations.

**Immigration office** 300m east of the airport ☎053/277510.
**Internet** Most guesthouses offer internet access, and there are dozens of places dotted around the city; around B30/hr.
**Laundry** Laundry is available at most guesthouses (around B30 per kilo) or at small shops and hairdressers across town.
**Post office** The GPO is near the train station on Th Charoen Muang (Mon–Fri 8.30am–4.30pm, Sat & Sun 9am–noon). Poste restante is available.
**Telephones** International phones at the Chiang Mai Telecommunication Center (open 24hr) on the Superhighway, just south of the east end of Th Charoen Muang, and at the GPO.
**Tourist police** Down a soi behind the *Lanna Palace Hotel*, off Th Chang Klan ☎053/247318 or nationwide helpline ☎1155.

## Moving on

**By bus** Both government and private buses leave from Arcade bus station (☎053/242664).
**Destinations:** Bangkok (19 daily; 10hr); Chiang Khong (3 daily; 6hr); Chiang Rai (11 daily; 3hr); Chiang Saen (2 daily; 4hr); Khon Kaen (13 daily; 12hr); Khorat (12 daily; 12hr); Mae Hong Son (5 daily; 9hr); Mae Sai (8 daily; 4hr); Mae Sot (4 daily; 6hr); Pai (6 daily; 4hr); Phitsanulok (10 daily; 6hr); Rayong (8 daily; 17hr); Sukhothai (12 daily; 6hr); Ubon Ratchasima (6 daily; 17hr); Udon Thani (for Nong Khai; 4 daily; 12 hr).
**By train** to: Ayutthaya (6 daily; 10–12hr); Bangkok (6 daily; 12–14hr); Lampang (7 daily; 2hr 30min); Lopburi (6 daily; 9–10hr); Phitsanulok (6 daily; 7hr).
**By air** Call ☎053/270222 for airport information.
**Destinations:** Bangkok (22 daily; 1hr 10min); Chiang Rai (daily; 35min); Kuala Lumpur, Malaysia (daily; 2hr 50min); Louang Phabang, Laos (daily; 2hr); Mae Hong Son (3 daily; 35min); Pai (daily; 20min); Phuket (5 daily; 2hr); Samui (daily; 1hr 40min); Siem Riep, Cambodia (2 weekly; 2hr 20min); Singapore (8 weekly; 3–4hr); Udon Thani (daily; 1hr); Vientiane, Laos (4 weekly; 1hr).

# LAMPANG AND THE THAI ELEPHANT CONSERVATION CENTRE

The north's second-largest town and an important transport hub, **LAMPANG**, 100km southeast of Chiang Mai, boasts a sedate, traditional charm and a few key attractions, such as temples and an elephant conservation centre.

## What to see and do

Lampang is unique in Thailand for its horse-drawn carriages, which act as charming if bumpy taxis (rides from B150. The majority of the town is south of the river, which curls west to east; the clocktower is considered the central point.

### Wat Phra Kaeo Don Tao

The imposing, Burmese-influenced **Wat Phra Kaeo Don Tao** on Thanon Phra Kaeo, northeast of the river, about 3km from the clocktower, is noteworthy for its high, gilded roof. From 1434 to 1468 it was the home for the Emerald Buddha, now housed in Bangkok at Wat Phra Kaeo.

### Wat Si Rong Mueng

West of the clocktower on Thanon Wang Khwa, **Wat Si Rong Mueng** is a Burmese-style temple built in 1905. Its wooden viharn has a beautifully tiered roof, and its interior is elaborately decorated with coloured glass in patterns of animals, flowers, leaves and guardian angels. The nine spires represent the nine families who donated generously for the building of the temple.

### Wat Phra That Lampang Luang

It's also well worth heading 18km southwest of town to **Wat Phra That Lampang Luang**, a grand and well-preserved capsule of beautiful Lanna art and architecture. One of the oldest wooden temples in Thailand, dating back to 1486, the wat features elaborate, well-preserved carvings; note the entwined dragon heads over the entrance arched gateway. Take a songthaew from outside the Thai Farmers Bank on Thanon Robwiang (songthaews leave 8am–6pm; 45min).

### Thai Elephant Conservation Centre

The **Thai Elephant Conservation Centre** (shows daily 10am & 11am plus Sat & Sun 1.30pm; bathing at 9.45am and 1.15pm; B70, B30 for children, price includes bananas and sugar cane for the elephants; ⓣ054/228034, ⓦwww.changthai.com), 37km northwest of Lampang on Highway 11 towards Chiang Mai, is the most authentic place to see elephants displaying their skills; it also cares for abandoned and sick elephants in its elephant hospital. An interpretive centre has exhibits on the history of the elephant in Thailand, cheap elephant rides are available, and there is a homestay programme, on which you spend usually three days learning how to care for and control elephants for around B3000 a day. The centre is best visited en route between Chiang Mai and Lampang; any Chiang Mai-bound bus from the bus station will drop you off on the way (30min). If coming by bus, allow for the two-kilometre walk from the entrance gates to the centre.

## Arrival and information

**By bus** The bus station is around 1km southwest of the city, though many buses also stop on Th Phaholyothin in the centre; shared songthaews will drop you off near your destination (B20).

**By train** The train station is about 50m further west than the bus station, on Th Prasanmaitri.

**By air** The airport (ⓣ054/226483) is just southeast of town centre; shared songthaews run into town (B20).

**TAT** There's a small but helpful tourist information centre (Mon–Fri 8.30am–noon & 1–4.30pm; ⓣ054/237229), just east of the clocktower and next to the fire station on Th Takrao Noi.

## Accommodation

**Riverside Guest House** 286 Th Talat Khao ⓣ054/227005, ⓔriversidefamily@yahoo.com. Traditional compound of elegant, mostly en-suite rooms, whose helpful owner rents out motorbikes. ❷–❸

**Tip Inn** Th Talat Khao, just east of *Riverside Guest House* ⓣ054/221821. The best budget place to stay: it has simple rooms from just B150, offers internet and rents bikes. The café downstairs does good breakfasts and coffees. ❶

## Eating and drinking

There is a vibrant night market off Th Thakhrao, and food in the evening on the pedestrian street outside Seri Department Store, northeast of the clocktower.

**Aroy One Bath** corner of thanons Sichum and Tipchang. Phenomenally busy restaurant catering to an exclusively Thai clientele. Main rice dishes cost around B30; "Pork leg soup with or without pork organs" sounds particularly appetizing. Open 4pm–midnight.

**Huen Chom Wang** 276 Th Talat Kao. A beautiful riverside restaurant serving northern specialities, amongst other tasty dishes, accompanied by a Thai wine selection, at the steeper end of the budget (B80–300). Open 11am–midnight.

**I love coffee** Th Chatchai, near the clocktower. Sells snacks, beer, coffee and American breakfasts (7am–10pm).

**Riverside Restaurant** 328 Th Tipchang. This big restaurant on the riverfront offers a delicious fresh cake selection, huge mid-priced menu, live music and serves fresh pizzas at the weekend.

## Moving on

**By bus** to: Bangkok (3 daily; 8hr 30min); Chiang Mai (every 30min 2am–9pm; 1hr 30min); Sukhothai (hourly 5.30am–4.30pm; 4hr).

**By train** to: Ayutthaya (6 daily; 8–9hr); Bangkok (6 daily; 11hr); Chiang Mai (6 daily; 3hr); Lopburi (6 daily; 7hr 30min); Phitsanulok (6 daily; 5hr).

**By air** to: Bangkok (2 daily; 50min).

# DOI INTHANON NATIONAL PARK

Covering a huge area to the southwest of Chiang Mai, **Doi Inthanon National Park**, with its hilltribe villages, dramatic waterfalls and fine panoramas, is a popular destination for naturalists and hikers. The park supports about 380 bird species and, near the summit of Doi Inthanon itself, the only red rhododendrons in Thailand (in bloom Dec–Feb). Night-time temperatures can drop below freezing, so bring warm clothing. The park is best explored as a day-trip from Chiang Mai using private transport, but set out early because there's a lot to see and the distances are deceptive.

## What to see and do

Three sets of **waterfalls** provide the main roadside attractions on the way to the park headquarters: overrated and overcrowded Mae Klang Falls, 8km in; Vachiratharn Falls, a long misty drop 11km beyond; and the twin cascades of Siriphum Falls, behind the park headquarters; The Peak tour agency in Chiang Mai organizes canyoning up these falls (see p.805). The more beautiful **Mae Ya Falls**, believed to be the highest in Thailand, are accessed by a road that heads west off the main park road 3km north of Chom Thong.

The paved Mae Chaem road skirts yet more waterfalls: 7km after the turn-off, look for a steep, unpaved road to the right, leading down to a ranger station and, just to the east, the dramatic long drop of **Huai Sai Luaeng Falls**. A circular two-hour **walking trail** from the ranger station takes in some smaller waterfalls, such as Mae Pan Falls.

For the most spectacular views in the park, head for the twin chedis on the summit road. Near the chedis lies the trailhead of Kew Mae Pan Trail, an easy two-hour circular walk through beautiful forest and savannah – home of the red rhododendrons – around the steep, western edge of **Doi Inthanon**; you need to hire a guide from headquarters to walk the trail (B200 per group; maximum 10 people). Doi Inthanon's summit (2565m), 6km beyond the chedis, is a disappointment.

## Information

The park's **visitor centre** is 9km up the main park road from Chom Thong, while the **park headquarters** are 22km further on. Both sell park maps. **Entrance** to the park costs B400 per person, plus B20–30 per vehicle.

## Accommodation

You can stay in the national park **bungalows** (bookings ⓣ053/268550, ⓦwww.dnp.go.th; ❻–❽) near the headquarters, or **camp** near the headquarters and at Huai Sai Luaeng Falls (B30 per person per night). Fully equipped two-person tents (B225) can be rented at the headquarters.

## Eating and drinking

**Food stalls** operate at Mae Klang, Vachiratharn and Mae Ya Falls (daytime only) and at the park headquarters and Mae Pan Falls, and there's a daytime **canteen** by the twin chedis. The food at Mae Ya falls can be packed up like a picnic and eaten sitting on stones in the middle of the river.

### GETTING TO DOI INTHANON NATIONAL PARK

The best way to access Doi Inthanon is by using private transport rented in Chiang Mai; the roads, though winding, are well paved and the views are stunning. If you want to use public transport, however, you'll need to get to the village of Chom Thong, 58km southwest of Chiang Mai on Highway 108. Buses run from the bottom of Thanon Phra Pokklao in Chiang Mai to Chom Thong (every 30min; 1hr), from where you can catch a songthaew towards Mae Chaem through the park, leaving you to hitch the last 10km to the summit, or you can charter a whole songthaew from Chom Thong's temple (from B800 round trip). The main road through the park leaves Highway 108 1km north of Chong Thong, winding northwestwards for 48km to the top of Doi Inthanon; a second paved road forks left 10km before the summit, reaching the riverside market of Mae Chaem, southwest of the park, after 20km, and Highway 108 towards Mae Hong Son after a further 45km.

## MAE HONG SON AND AROUND

Set deep in a mountain valley, **MAE HONG SON** is often billed as the "Switzerland of Thailand", and has enjoyed a recent boost in tourism, due in part to the villages of long-necked Paduang women nearby. Most travellers come here to trek in the beautiful countryside and cool climate, but crowds are also drawn here every April for the spectacular parades of the **Poy Sang Long Festival**, which celebrates local Thai Yai/Shan boys' temporary ordination into the monkhood.

### What to see and do

Mae Hong Son's main Thanon Khunlumprapas, lined with shops and businesses, runs north–south and is intersected by Singhanat Bamrung at the traffic lights in the centre of town.

To the southeast of the Thanon Khunlumprapas/Singhanat Bamrang junction, the town's classic picture-postcard view is of its twin nineteenth-century Burmese-style temples, **Wat Chong Kham** and **Wat Chong Klang**, from the opposite bank of Jong Kham Lake. The latter temple is famous for its paintings on glass, depicting stories from the lives of the Buddha.

The town's vibrant, smelly morning market is a magnet for hilltribe traders and worth getting up at dawn for. Next door, the many-gabled viharn of Wat Hua Wiang shelters the beautiful bronze Burmese-style Buddha image, Chao Palakeng. For a godlike overview of the area, especially at sunset, climb up to Wat Doi Kong Mu on the steep hill to the west.

#### Local treks

**Trekking** up and down Mae Hong Son's steep inclines is tough, but the hilltribe villages are generally unspoilt and the scenery is magnificent. To the west, trekking routes tend to snake along the Burmese border and can sometimes get a little crowded; the villages to the east are more traditional. Many guesthouses and travel agencies run treks out of Mae Hong Son (see opposite), though many villages can be reached independently by motorbike.

#### Pha Sua Falls and Mae Aw

North of Mae Hong Son, a trip to **Pha Sua Falls** and the border village of Mae Aw takes in some spectacular and varied countryside, best visited by motorbike or on a tour (around B600). Head north for 17km on Highway 1095 (ignore the first signpost for Pha Sua, after 10km) and then, after a long, steep descent, turn left onto a side road, paved at first, which passes through the village of Ban Bok Shampae. About 9km from the turn-off, you'll reach the wild, untidy Pha Sua Falls; take care when swimming, as several people have been swept to their deaths here.

Above the falls, the paved road climbs 11km to the village of Naphapak, from where it's another 7km to **Mae Aw** (aka Ban Ruk Thai), a settlement of Kuomintang (anti-communist Chinese) refugees. It's the highest point on the Burmese border that visitors can reach, and provides a fascinating window on Kuomintang life. Bright-green tea bushes line the slopes, and Chinese ponies wander the streets of long bamboo houses. In the marketplace on the north side of the village reservoir, shops sell Oolong and Chian Chian tea, and dried mushrooms.

### Arrival

**By bus** Buses and minibuses from Chiang Mai's Arcade bus station arrive at the bus station on Th Khunlumprapas (☎053/611318), about 1km north of TAT, though this is due to move. It's a B40 tuk-tuk ride to most of the guesthouses. Buses from Bangkok run by Sombat tour arrive further south down Th Khunlumprapas (☎053/613211).

**By air** The tiny airport is on the east side of town behind the market, a B60 tuk-tuk ride from most guesthouses.

## NAI SOI AND THE LONG-NECK WOMEN

The most famous – and notorious – sight in the Mae Hong Son area is its contingent of **"long-neck" women**, members of the Paduang tribe of Burma who fled to Thailand to escape repression. Though the women's necks appear to be stretched to 30cm and more by a column of brass rings, the pressure of eleven pounds of brass actually squashes the collarbones and ribs; to remove a full stack would cause the collapse of the neck and suffocation. Girls of the tribe start wearing the rings from about the age of 6, adding one or two each year until they are 16. Only half of the Padaung women now lengthen their necks; left to its own course, the custom would probably die out, but the influence of tourism may well keep it alive for some time yet.

The original village of long-neck Paduang women in the Mae Hong Son area, **Nai Soi**, 28km northwest of town, has effectively been turned into a human zoo for snap-happy tourists, with an entrance fee of B250 per person. At least much of the entrance fee is used to support the Karenni National People's Party in their fight for the independence of Burma's Kayah state (where the Paduang come from), and the "long necks" themselves get paid a living wage. Without your own transport, you'll have to join a **tour** (about B800, including the entrance fee) from Mae Hong Son. By motorbike, head north along Highway 1095 for 2km and turn left after the police box; cross the bridge over the Pai River, turn left at the next village and continue for another 10km.



## Information and tours

**Information** TAT have a helpful office (Mon–Fri 8.30am–4.30pm, plus Sat & Sun same times in high season; ⓣ053/612982, ⓦwww.travelmaehongson.org) opposite the post office on Th Khunlumprapas.

**Tour operators** There are over thirty registered tour agencies in Mae Hong Son, each of which can arrange all the local treks; TAT can point you in the right direction. Sunflower Café and Tours, 2/1 Soi 3, Th Khunlumprapas (ⓣ053/620549) is the best fixer for boating and rafting on the Pai river and elephant rides, and also has a good café. Nam Rin Tour, based in the post office car park (ⓣ053/614454), does a five-day trek to Pai.

## Accommodation

**Jean's Guest House** 6 Th Prachautith ⓣ053/611662. The simple but clean rooms (from B100) here are the cheapest in town, though about 1km from town centre. ❶

**Jongkum Guest House** 7 Moo 7, Th U-Domchaonitesh ⓣ053/613885. A choice of basic rooms or nicer bungalows around a pretty garden with a relaxed seating area overlooking the lake. ❶–❷

**Mae Hong Son Guest House** 295 M.11 Pangmoo, to the west of the town ⓣ053/612510, ⓔlotee@hotmail.com. The longest-running guesthouse in Mae Hong Son with standard rooms and attractive bungalows in a large peaceful garden, situated about 3km northwest of town centre. It also has a restaurant and runs tours. ❷–❸

## Eating and drinking

Nightly stalls set up in front of the illuminated temples selling a tantalizing array of Thai food including cheap noodle and rice dishes. The views of the temples are stunning and the atmosphere is great.

**Fern Restaurant** 87 Th Khunlumprapas, south of the TAT office. Upmarket and tourist-oriented, with a good menu of local specialities and European dishes; prices B70–120.

**Kai Mook** 23 Th U-Domchaonitesh ⓣ053/612092. Very popular with locals, with an appealing variety of dishes, including spicy salads and delicious roasted duck; prices B60–200.

## Directory

**Car and motorbike rental** The most reliable place to rent a four-wheel drive is Avis at the airport (ⓣ053/611367; B1200 per day). Bicycles (B80) and motorbikes (B200) can be rented from guesthouses, or from opposite *Friend House* on Th Praditjongkham.

## Moving on

**By bus and minivan** Non-a/c buses and a/c minivans run from the bus station (☎053/611318) via Pai to Chiang Mai (6hr; B150/B250) roughly hourly from 7am to 2pm. Ordinary and a/c buses go via Mae Sariang to Chiang Mai (8hr; 7 daily including 3 overnight services; B100/B337). Sombat Tours (☎053/613211) run direct buses to Bangkok (2 daily; 16hr). Note that the bus station is due to move to the southwest of Mae Hong Son.
**By air** Flights to Chiang Mai are surprisingly inexpensive; Thai Airways (☎053/611220, office on Hospital Rd) and Nok Air (☎02/664 6099 or ☎1318; office at the airport) both have daily flights (30min). PBair (☎025/354843; office at the airport) has daily flights to Bangkok.

# PAI

Once just a stopover on the tiring journey to Mae Hong Son, **PAI**, 135km from Chiang Mai is now a tourist honeypot, especially favoured by Thais. The laid-back New-Agey feel that once drew travellers in for weeks has changed substantially with this influx of tourists; the hippies are leaving and big commercial money is coming in. However, it still retains its outdoorsy charm, despite a burgeoning bar scene. There's all manner of **outdoor activities** to tempt you, plus courses and therapies – including retail therapy at the art studios, leather and jewellery shops – and a hugely popular yearly reggae festival in February; check out Ⓦwww.paifestival.com.

## What to see and do

Pai itself is a cute but rambling town. Most points of interest lie southwest of the river on a square gridlock of roads, although the most tranquil guesthouses are north of the river. The charm of Pai lies in its surrounding countryside; rent a motorbike or join a trek to appreciate its undulating beauty. For keen anglers, Mhor Peng Fishing Park, near the Mhor Peng Waterfall, northwest of Pai, offers a day's fishing, including tackle and bait, from B150.

### Trekking and rafting

Pai is a centre both for undemanding valley walks and for **trekking** (around B500 per day, plus B250 each for rafting and elephant-riding) through varied terrain to Karen, Lisu and Lahu villages. These can be arranged either through guesthouses or via Back Trax (see opposite) There are several **elephant camps** around town; Thom's, at 5/3 Moo 4, Th Rungsiyanon (☎053/698084, Ⓦwww.thomelephant.com), arranges mountain and river rides with playful elephants.

From July to January, you can take an impressive two-day **rubber-raft trip** down the Pai River to Mae Hong Son with Thai Adventure Rafting (see opposite). Back Trax can also arrange one- or two-day white-water rafting trips, which include muddy hot springs; August is the best month.

### Spas and massage

On the east side of town is a large open-air **swimming pool** (daily 10.30am–8.30pm; B50). About 7km down the same minor road, the **hot springs** aren't up to much, but nearby **spas** put the piped hot water to much better use. Thapai Spa Camping (☎09/557 6079), down a side road about 1km north of the springs, has a large pool (B50) and offers massages and other treatments.

## Arrival and information

**By bus and minibus** Buses and faster a/c minibuses from Mae Hong Son and Chiang Mai stop at the minute bus station near the junction of Th Rungsiyanon and Th Chaisongkhram; motorbike taxis are available on the junction itself, a/c minibus taxis on the east side of the bus station.
**By air** Pai's tiny airport is just north of town. Take a taxi into town.
**Tourist information** A booth adjacent to the Bangkok Bank ATM machine on Th Chaisongkhram gives out tourist information.

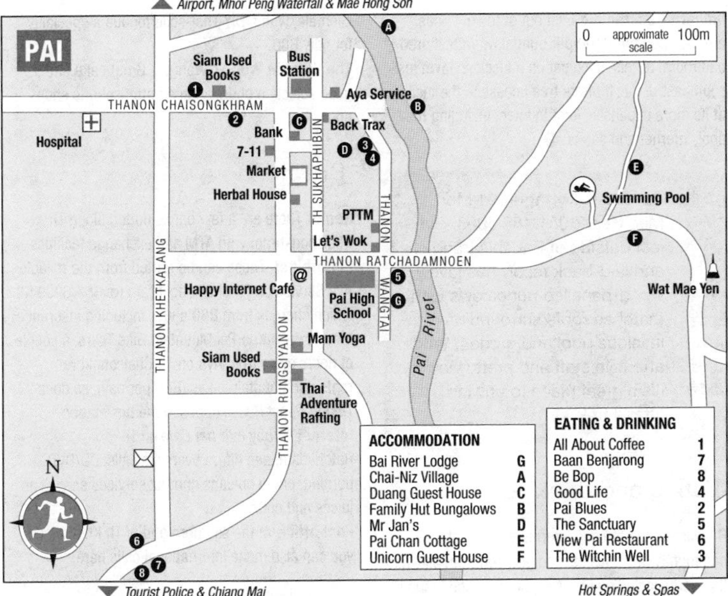


## Activities and courses

**Trekking and rafting** Back Trax, 17 Th Chaisongkhram (ⓣ053/699739, ⓔbacktraxinpai @yahoo.com), which gives up to 25 percent of the price to the hilltribe villages it visits, can arrrange trekking trips, and one- or two-day whitewater rafting trips, which include muddy hot springs. The reliable Thai Adventure Rafting, based on Thanon Rungsiyanon (ⓣ053/699111, ⓦwww.activethailand.com/rafting) offer a two-day rubber-raft trip for B2000.

**Massage and massage courses** *Mr Jan's* is famous for its Thai and Burmese/Shan massages (B150/hr), while Herbal House (ⓣ053/699964, ⓔtiger_healing@hotmail.com), offers massages and other treatments. A government-certified training centre, Herbal House also lays on massage courses (B800 per day; ⓣ01/883 7020), as well as live-in courses (B2000 per day) at a retreat 2.5km outside town, which feature meditation and yoga practice. Pai Traditional Thai Massage on Thanon Wangtai (PTTM; ⓣ053/699121) also does a three-day course as well as giving massages.

**Yoga** There's guided yoga at the *Good Life* restaurant on Thanon Wangtai (ⓣ081/031 3171; Mon, Wed & Fri 11am), or with Mam Yoga on Thanon Rangsiyanon (t089/9544981); all levels of experience are catered for.

**Cookery classes** At Let's Wok (ⓣ086/114 9921), Tee holds friendly and relaxed Thai cooking courses of one (B750) or two (B1500) days, with a market tour and a shared communal dinner to which you can invite friends at the end of each day. The day after your course you can go and practise for free.

## Accommodation

**Bai River Lodge** On soi alongside high school, next to *Baan Tawan* (no phone). Inexpensive bungalows set around a tranquil lawn on the riverbank; check out the quirky sign pointing to heaven. ❶

**Chai-Niz Village** Just north of the river ⓣ087/193 6314, ⓦwww.myspace.com /chai_niz. Traditional teepees and bamboo huts scattered around a beautiful garden, and terrific staff. The fantastic bathrooms are open-air and full of flowers; a top choice. ❶–❷

**Duang Guest House** Opposite the bus station. This guesthouse has cheap rooms and nicer bungalows in a garden space, but it can be noisy. It also has a popular restaurant and does recommended treks. ❶–❷

**Family Hut Bungalows** ⓣ084/949 9132 or 085/709 1306. Has spacious bungalows with shared hot shower in a charming location north of the river. ❶–❷

**Mr Jan's** 3 Th Sukhaphibun ⓣ053/699554. In a mess of alleys behind Th Chaisongkhram, *Mr Jan's* offers quiet, simple rooms set in a medicinal herb garden, plus some dorm rooms. ❶

**Unicorn Guesthouse** East out of town. Prices are rock bottom (B100 per bungalow with shared bathroom) at this place set on a luscious lawn just southeast of Pai. It offers free access to the facilities at its more expensive joint in town, including the pool, internet and sauna. ❶

TREAT YOURSELF

**Pai Chan Cottage** 191 Moo 1, Mae Hee ☎081/180 3063. Set just outside of Pai, this tranquil and laid-back resort has lovely wood-panelled bungalows with thatched roofs surrounding a luscious pool and garden. With attentive staff and pretty views, it's a great place to unwind after a trek. ❹

## Eating and drinking

Because of the thriving international expat community in Pai it's easy to get food from all over the world, including Mexican, German and French. Pai is no Khao San Road however; its scene is more laid-back and music-oriented so don't expect drunken revelry.

**All About Coffee** Th Chaisongkhram. A tantalizing array of coffee and cakes (from B30) in an atmospheric art-gallery/café.

**Baan Benjarong** Th Rungsiyanon, to the south of town ☎053/698010. An understandably popular restaurant that serves the best Thai food in town. The mid-priced menu (B60–200) is varied and imaginative, and the *larb* is divine. Serves 11am–2pm & 5–9.30pm.

**Be-Bop** Th Rungsiyanon, at the south end of town. A popular bar for travellers that hosts live music in the evenings.

**Good Life** Th Wangtai. *Good Life* encapsulates Pai. As well as offering guided meditation (see p.815), it serves homegrown wheatgrass and has a tantalizing range of filling breakfasts, bagels and teas. There's also a large book selection.

**Pai Blues** Th Chaisongkhram. An easy-going place where, as well as Western dishes, you can sample tasty Thai Yai cuisine whilst listening to regular live music.

**The Sanctuary** 115/1 Moo 4, Th Wangtai. A great café/restaurant which uses organic and local produce, in a relaxed setting on the riverbank. The bakery selection is tasty and the exilir juices invigorating.

**View Pai Restaurant** opposite *Baan Benjarong* on the road out of town. Caters for an exclusively Thai clientele, with a DIY Thai-style fondue a speciality for only B80.

**The Witchin Well** Th Wangtai. Great cake and a good selection of drinks in an atmospheric shop-house.

## Directory

**Banks** There are a few banks dotted along Th Chaisongkhram with ATM and exchange facilities.

**Motorbikes** These can be rented from the reliable Aya Service on Th Chaisongkhram (☎053/699940), which charges from B80 a day, including insurance.

**Mountain bikes** Pai Mountain Bike Tours, a couple of doors away from Aya on Th Chaisongkhram, rents out mountain bikes (B80 per day), as does *Duang Guest House* opposite the bus station.

**Internet** *Happy Internet Café* on Th Ratchadamnoen offers overseas calls, CD/DVD burning, photo uploads and fax services as well as juices and coffees.

**Post office** At the southern end of Th Khetkalang; you can also make international calls here.

## Moving on

**By bus** Aya runs a minibus service to Chiang Mai (3hr: B150; ☎053/699888). Otherwise you can get to Chiang Mai by ordinary bus (5 daily; 3hr 30min) or a/c minibus (11 daily; 3hr). Services also run to Mae Hong Son (7 daily; 3hr).

**By air** to: Chiang Mai (2 daily; 20min), operated by Nok Air (☎1318); you can pay for the flights at the 7-11 on Th Rungsiyanon.

# THA TON AND THE KOK RIVER

Leafy **THA TON**, 176km north of Chiang Mai, sits clustered either side of the **Kok River**, which flows out of Burma 4km upstream. The main attractions here are boat and raft rides, which offer a novel way of getting to Chiang Rai.

Travelling down the hundred-kilometre stretch of the Kok River to Chiang Rai gives you the chance to soak up a rich diversity of typical northern landscapes, through rice-fields and orchards, past riverside wats and over rapids. Noisy, canopied longtail boats leave from the south side of the bridge in Tha Ton every day at 12.30pm for the four-hour trip to Chiang Rai (B250, plus B300 for motorbikes). Return boats from Chiang Rai leave at 10.30am (☎053/750009). If you have more time, choose the peaceful bamboo rafts, which glide downriver to Chiang Rai in two days. These can be organized via *Thip's Traveller House* (see below; B2000 each for a group of four, including food and soft drinks). You sleep on the raft, and a visit to hot springs and an optional elephant ride are included. Alternately hire a private longtail from Tha Thon for around B3000.

Buses between Chiang Mai's Chang Phuak bus station and Tha Ton take about four hours (7 daily). **Accommodation** options in town include *Thip's Traveller House* (☎081/981 1780, Ⓦwww.thiptravel.com; ❷–❹), on the south side of the bridge, which has decent en-suite rooms (some with a/c) and good food, and *Garden Home Nature Resort* on the north side of the river, (☎053/373015), with cheap rooms (❶) and attractive en-suite a/c bungalows (❷) in an orchard, some with hot water and a/c; they also rent bikes.

## CHIANG RAI

The long arm of the package-tour industry has reached **CHIANG RAI**, but it still retains its rustic charm once you move away from the package-holiday fray. Villagers from different hilltribes mingle seamlessly, their elaborate costumes a fascinating backdrop to a laid-back town with



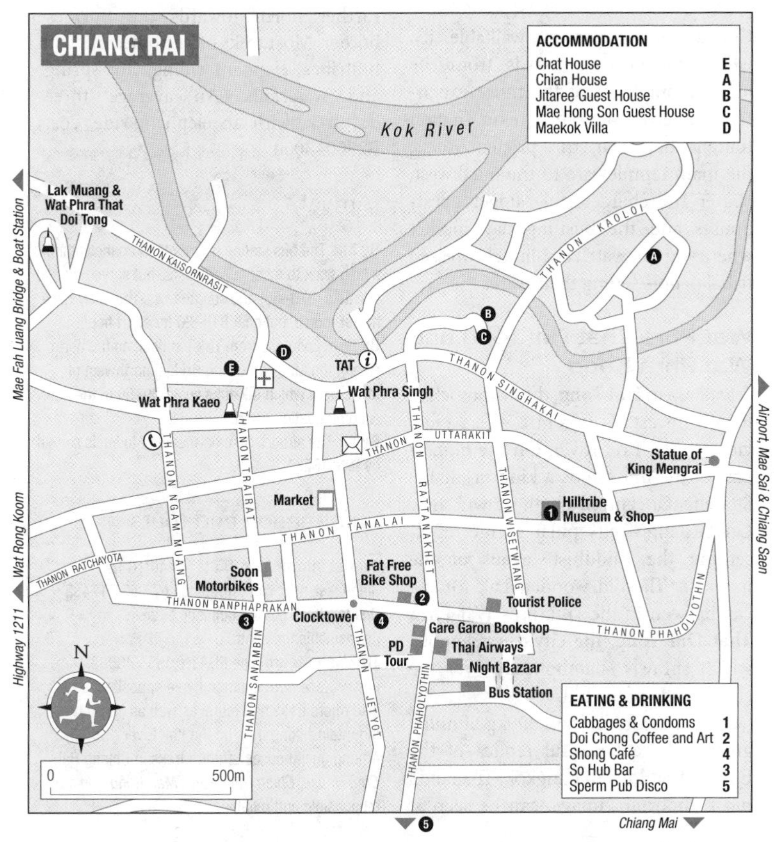

### AKHA HILL HOUSE

A more authentic and rewarding way of spending time in a hilltribe village is offered by the *Akha Hill House* (☎089/997 5505, Ⓦwww.akhahill.com; B120–1500); situated just 23km from Chiang Rai (with free pick-up) amongst stunning mountain scenery, within walking distance of waterfalls, hot springs and other hilltribe villages. You can either trek independently or take an organized tour with the award-winning village chief, Mr Apae.

some splendid temples and excellent trekking opportunities.

## What to see and do

Chiang Rai is a compact, walkable city, which spreads northwards from the bus station. Most of the more expensive Western restaurants are on Thanon Rattanakhet near the pricier hotels; the main temples are to the northwest, nearer the characterful budget guesthouses and the bustling day market where you can watch elaborately dressed tribal people selling their wares.

### Wat Phra That Doi Tong and Wat Phra Kaeo

A walk up to **Doi Tong**, the hummock to the northwest of the centre, offers a fine view up the Kok River. On the highest part of the hill stands a kind of phallic Stonehenge centred on the town's new **Lak Muang** – city pillar shrine representing the Buddhist layout of the universe. The old wooden Lak Muang can be seen in the viharn of **Wat Phra That Doi Tong**, the city's first temple, which sprawls shambolically over the eastern side of the hill.

Carved in China from 300kg of milky green jade, a beautiful replica of the Emerald Buddha in Bangkok, Thailand's most important image, can be seen at **Wat Phra Kaeo**, back into town on Thanon Trairat.

### Wat Rong Koom

It's well worth hiring a motorbike and heading to the stunning **Wat Rong Koom** (8am–6pm; free) 13km southwest of Chiang Rai, where a zealous renowned local artist has dedicated his life to building a new dazzling all-white stucco temple with fragments of reflective glass that sparkle in the sun. Check out the disturbing mural artwork inside the viharn.

### Trekking and mountain-biking

The Chiang Rai region offers a range of **treks**, from gentle walking trails near the Kok River to tough mountain slopes further north towards the Burmese border. Most treks offer homestays with hilltribes, elephant riding, hot springs and waterfalls. An average three-day trek, with an elephant ride, costs B2500–3000.

## Arrival

**By bus** The bus station is just off Th Phaholyothin, a long walk to most guesthouses, but served by tuk-tuks (B30–50) and songthaews. The latter have no set routes, but cost B10–20 for short hops.

**By boat** Longtails from Tha Ton dock on the north side of the Mae Fah Luang Bridge, northwest of town, from which tuk-tuks cost B30–50 to the accommodation listed.

**By air** The airport, 8km northeast of town, is served by taxis (B200).

## Information and tours

**Tourist information** TAT is at 448/16 Th Singhakai, near Wat Phra Singh (☎053/717433). Online, check out the fantastic Ⓦwww.tourismchiangrai.com.

**Treks and tours** The PDA (☎053/740088, Ⓦwww.pda.or.th/chiangrai; see opposite) also offers treks and tours, as well as one-day mountain-biking trips up the Kok River (B2200). Among guesthouses offering treks in Chiang Rai, *Chat House*, *Chian House* and *Mae Hong Son* are responsible and reliable.

## Accommodation

**Chat House** 3/2 Soi Sangkaew, Th Trairat ⓣ053/711481. Chiang Rai's longest-running travellers' hangout, just behind Wat Phra Kaeo, has a laid-back atmosphere and fantastic staff. The attached restaurant does great breakfasts and Thai herbal whisky that will put hairs on your chest. ❶–❷

**Chian House** 172 Th Sriboonraung ⓣ053/713388. Pleasant en-suite rooms, some with a/c, and bungalows in a fun and lively garden compound around a pool. It offers internet access, tours and motorbike rental. ❶–❷

**Jitaree Guest House** 246/3 Soi Santirat, Th Singhaklai ⓣ053/719348. Big, spotless en-suite rooms in a concrete block with hanging plants. Soap/paper/towel included. ❶

**Mae Hong Son Guest House** 126 Th Singhaklai ⓣ053/715367. Friendly courtyard establishment with bar and café in a quiet street about a 10min walk from TAT. Good rooms, some en suite. ❶–❷

**Maekok Villa** 445 Th Singhaklai ⓣ053/711786, ⓔmaekokvilla@thai.com. Basic rooms in a spacious villa; the characterful owner can arrange tours and trekking, and rents out bikes, motorbikes and jeeps. ❶

## Eating, drinking and nightlife

For cheap Thai food there's a wide selection of food stalls in the night bazaar selling everything from roasted crickets to *tom yam kung*. The block west of the clocktower on Th Banphaprakan is jam-packed with shop-front restaurants selling curries, noodles and rice dishes in the evening.

**Cabbages and Condoms** 320/25 Th Tanalai. Run by the family planning and HIV/AIDS prevention organization, on the ground floor of the Hilltribe Museum (see below), this popular restaurant does some traditional northern and veggie dishes and hosts regular live music. Decor features some quirky condom-inspired artwork.

**Doi Chong Coffee and Art** 82 Th Uttarakit ⓣ053/744741. Serves delicious Doi Chong hilltribe coffee in a fun and relaxing garden space with a running waterfall, as well as tasty cakes and pastries.

**Shong Café** 531/5 Th Banphaprakan, just east of the clocktower. Does a wide range of teas and coffees and has free Wi-Fi. The atmosphere is laid-back, with comfy sofas in the a/c café, with a garden area out back.

**So Hub Bar** corner of Th Trairat and Banphaprakan. Popular Thai bar with outside seating and good cocktails from an extensive list. Open from 5pm till late.

**Sperm Pub Disco** 555 Th Phaholyotin, about 2km south of centre. Very popular with Thai locals, this fun club has thumping live music, some of it in farcical cabaret style; no entrance fee but drinks aren't cheap – bring in your own from outside and pay for corkage. Open till 2am.

## Shopping

**Gare Garon** 869/18 Th Phaholyothin. Stocks a small range of new and used books.

**The Hilltribe Museum and Shop** 620/25 Th Tanalai, run by the Population and Community Development Association (PDA) has the most authentic selection of handicrafts and is non-profit-making. The upstairs museum (Mon–Fri 9am–6pm, Sat & Sun 10am–6pm; B50) is a good place to find out about the local hilltribes before going on a trek.

**Night bazaar** off Th Phaholyothin, next to the bus station. Sells handicrafts and other tourist-enticing paraphernalia; there's also a stage for cabaret shows and live music, and a popular food court.

## Directory

**Car, motorbike and bicycle rental** Guesthouses can rent out motorbikes (B200) and bicycles (B80). Fat Free Bike Shop at 542/2 Th Banpapragarn (ⓣ097/554676) rents out both mountain bikes (B200) and aluminium city bikes (B80), and stocks all the parts and accessories you're ever likely to need. Soon Motorbikes, at 197/2 Th Trairat (ⓣ053/714068), has the best choice of motorbikes (from B150 plus B50 insurance) and mountain bikes (B100). PD Tour at 869/108 Th Pemavipat, near the *Wangcome Hotel* (ⓣ053/712829), rents out jeeps (B700) and saloon cars (B1200); it's optional B300 extra for a driver.

**Tourist police** Th Phaholyothin (ⓣ1155).

## Moving on

**By bus** to: Chiang Khong (hourly 6am–5pm; 2–3hr); Chiang Mai (roughly every 30min; 3–4hr); Chiang Saen (every 15min; 1hr 30min); Khon Kaen (5 daily; 12hr); Khorat (6 daily; 12hr 30min); Lampang (every 20min; 5hr); Mae Sai (every 15min; 1hr 30min); Mae Sot (2 daily; 10hr); Phitsanulok (4 daily; 7hr).

**By air** At time of writing the Thai Airways office was closed for renovation; make enquiries to the airport or call ⓣ053/711179. Flights to Bangkok (10 daily; 1hr 30min) are operated by Thai Airways, Air Asia and Nok Air.

## MAE SAI

**MAE SAI**, with its bustling border crossing, is Thailand's northernmost town, 61km from Chiang Rai. Thanon Phaholyothin is the town's single north–south street, which ends at the bridge over the Mae Sai River, the frontier with Burma.

Farangs can make a day-trip across to **Thakhilek** (6am–6pm; note that Burma is 30min behind Thailand), though the frontier is sporadically closed during disputes between the two countries. Thai immigration on the bridge will exit-stamp your passport; on the Burmese side it costs B500 or US$10 for a one-day stay. Returning to Thailand you'll automatically be given a new thirty-day visa. If, however, you don't want to affect your existing visa, photocopy the relevant pages of your passport at one of the handy copying booths by the frontier, leave your passport at Thai immigration at the bridge, and pay the Burmese B500 for a one-day stamp on the photocopies. Thakhilek's sprawling **market** (on the right after the bridge) is the town's main attraction and is dominated by cheap knock-off goods and cigarettes.

**Buses** to Mae Sai stop 4km south of the frontier at the bus station, from where frequent songthaews (B10) shuttle into town. There's a **tourist police** booth (☎1155) at the frontier bridge. There's no reason to **stay** in Mae Sai; if you get stuck, however, try the friendly but grotty *Chad Guest House* (☎053/732054; ❶) on Soi Wiengpan, about 1 km south of the border.

## SOP RUAK

For the benefit of tourists, the "**Golden Triangle**" (see box, below) has been artificially concentrated into the precise spot where the Thai, Lao and Burmese borders meet, at the confluence of the Ruak and Mekong rivers, 70km northeast of Chiang Rai: **SOP RUAK**. Don't expect to run into sinister drug-runners, addicts or even poppy-fields here – instead, you'll find souvenir stalls and much-photographed "Golden Triangle" signs. A giant Buddha sits opulently surveying the scene. Behind his back, you can boost your luck by whirling pennies down the fairground-esque money chute that carries your wishes into the belly of a fat Buddha. The ambitious **Hall of Opium**, about 2km out of the village towards Mae Sai (daily except Mon 10am–5.30pm, last tickets 4pm; B300), gives an imaginatively presented, balanced picture of the use and abuse of opium, and its history over five thousand years. For uninterrupted views of the meeting of the rivers and of Burma and Laos beyond, climb up to **Wat Phra That Phu Khao**, a 1200-year-old temple perched on a small hill above the village. For B400, you can take

### THE GOLDEN TRIANGLE

Opium growing has been illegal in Thailand since 1959, but during the 1960s and 70s, rampant production and refining of the crop in the lawless region on the borders of Thailand, Burma and Laos earned the area the nickname "the **Golden Triangle**". Two "armies" have traditionally operated most of the trade within this area: the Shan United Army from Burma, led by the notorious warlord Khun Sa, and the Kuomintang (KMT) refugees from communist China. The Thai government's concerted attempt to eliminate opium growing within its borders has been successful, but Thailand still has a vital role to play as a conduit for heroin; most of the production and refinement of opium has simply moved over the borders into Burma and Laos. More worryingly for the Thai authorities, factories just across the Burmese border are now also producing vast quantities of **ya baa**, or methamphetamines, destined for consumption in Thailand itself.

## INTO LAOS AT CHIANG KHONG

**Chiang Khong**, 70km downriver from Chiang Saen, is the only crossing point into Laos in this part of Thailand. The journey from Chiang Saen is convoluted and time-consuming; irregular green songthaews run when they're full and you've got to change to a red songthaew halfway at the village of Ban Hat Bai. The journey can take up to four hours. Alternately, you can hire a songthaew for B800 (or B400 each step). The scenic journey would be easy on motorbikes though, or an exciting alternative is to run the rapids on a private longtail boat (B2000; 4 people; 1hr 30min). Regular buses run to Chiang Khong from Chiang Rai (2–3hr; B173), and there are direct a/c minibuses from Chiang Mai, available through travel agents, or from the bus station (3 daily; 6hr). Chiang Khong's best guesthouse is the helpful, easy-going *Ban Tam-Mi-La*, down a riverside lane off the main street at 113 Soi 1 Th Banwatkaeo (ⓣ053/791234, ⓔbaantammila@hotmail.com), which has charming en-suite wooden bungalows and rooms (❷), an excellent daytime restaurant with an awesome view across into Laos, and bike and motorbike rental (B150).

Thirty-day **visas for Laos** are available on arrival across the river at **Houayxai** (open 8am–5.30pm; prices range from US$30–42 depending on nationality); note, however, that visa regulations change frequently. Frequent boats to Houayxai (B20, plus B20 "overtime" at lunchtime and after 4pm) depart from Chiang Khong's main pier, Hua Wiang, at the north end of town, and from Houayxai (see p.449) you can get slow boats down the Mekong to Louang Phabang.

a longtail **boat** from the pier in the centre of the village for a whistle-stop tour of the "Golden Triangle", which takes in a market on the Laos side (B20 admission).

To get to Sop Ruak you'll have to go via Chiang Saen (see below) or Mae Sai first. From Chiang Saen, you have a choice of regular songthaew, rented bicycle (an easy 10km ride on a paved road) or longtail boat tour up the Mekong (B300 per person). From Mae Sai, blue songthaews make the 45-minute trip (B40) from outside the 7-11 on Thanon Phaholyothin, about 800m south of the border.

## CHIANG SAEN

Combining tumbledown ruins with sweeping Mekong River scenery, **CHIANG SAEN**, 60km northeast of Chiang Rai, makes a relaxing base camp for the border region east of Mae Sai.

### What to see and do

The **National Museum** (Wed–Sun 8.30am–4.30pm) is an informative starting point, housing some impressive locally cast Buddha images and architectural features rescued from the ruins. **Wat Phra That Chedi Luang** next door is worth looking in on for its imposing, overgrown octagonal chedi. **Wat Pa Sak** (daily 8am–6pm; B30) is the most impressive of Chiang Saen's many temple ruins. The central chedi owes its eclectic shape largely to the grand temples of Pagan (Phukam) in Burma and displays some beautiful carved stucco decoration, as well as Chinese and Sukhothai influences.

### Arrival and transport

**By bus** There is no bus station in Chiang Saen. Buses from Chiang Rai stop just west of the T-junction of the main Th Phaholyothin and the river road.

**By songthaew** Songthaews from Sop Ruak stop near the disembarkation point for Chiang Rai buses; those from Chiang Khong stop on the river road to the south of the T-junction.

**Transport** Bicycles (B80), motorbikes (B180/250) and four-wheel drives (B900) can be rented at *Gin's Guest House*.

## Tour operators

**Gin's Guest House** Offers trekking and tours, and can arrange transport on passenger boats to Jing Hong in China, passing through stunning scenery (overnight; B4000), and Louang Phabang in Laos (either 6hr or overnight; from B1590) It's best to get your Chinese visa yourself in Bangkok or Chiang Mai, but *Gin's* can arrange this if necessary in anything from four days to a day (B1200–3200). They can also arrange visas for Vietnam and Cambodia.

## Accommodation

**Chiang Saen Guest House** 45 Th Rimkrong, on the riverfront ⓣ053/650196. Decent en-suite rooms from B150, and closer to the sights than *Gin's*. ❶
**Gin's Guest House** outside the ramparts 2km north of the T-junction ⓣ053/650847. Large A-frame bungalows in a lychee orchard, or pricier rooms in the main house. There's also a restaurant, and they offer treks and tours (see above). ❶–❹

## Eating and drinking

At night, street stalls specializing in *suki (*Thai fondue) set up on the illuminated riverfront north of the pier. During both day and night there's a range of street stalls set up on Th Phaholyothin. *Mong Doo Nam* on Th Rimkrong sells fancy coffees and delicious cakes; the carrot cake is especially good.

# The northeast: Isaan

Bordered by Laos and Cambodia on three sides, the tableland of **northeast** Thailand, known as **Isaan,** is the least-visited region of the kingdom and the poorest, but also its most traditional. Most northeasterners speak a dialect that's more comprehensible to residents of Vientiane than Bangkok, and Isaan's historic allegiances have tied it more closely to Laos and Cambodia than to Thailand. Between the eleventh and thirteenth centuries, the all-powerful Khmers covered the northeast in magnificent stone temple complexes, which can still be admired at **Phimai** and **Phanom Rung**. The mighty **Mekong River** forms 750km of the border between Isaan and Laos, and there are four points along it in this region where foreigners are allowed to cross the border (there's also a little-used border crossing into Cambodia from Isaan, see p.826). The river makes a popular backpackers' trail, not least because of the laid-back waterfront guesthouses in **Chiang Khan** and **Nong Khai.** Inland scenery is rewarding too, with good hiking trails at **Khao Yai National Park.**

## KHAO YAI NATIONAL PARK

Only 120km northeast of Bangkok, **Khao Yai** is Thailand's most popular national park. It offers a realistic chance of seeing white-handed (lar) gibbons, pig-tailed macaques, hornbills, civets and barking deer, plus the possibility of sighting an elephant or a tiger. The park has lots of waterfalls and several undemanding walking trails. The best way to see Khao Yai is to stay in or just on the edge the park, or in the nearby town of Pak Chong. You have the choice of exploring the trails yourself or joining a backpackers' tour; bring warm clothes as it gets cool at night.

### What to see and do

You're most likely to spot the animals if you join a tour with an expert guide, but if you're short on time or money you can always take your chances and follow the trails. Fifteen well-worn **trails** radiate from the area around the park's visitor centre and headquarters (at kilometre stone 37), and a few more branch off from the roads that cross the park. The main trails are numbered and should be easy to follow; sketch maps are available at the visitor centre. The most popular include **Trail 5** to Nong Pak Chee observation tower (4.5km one-way; 2hr

30min) and **Trail 1** to Haew Suwat Falls (8.3km one-way; 3–4hr), which featured in the 1999 film, *The Beach*.

### Guided tours

The good thing about joining a **tour** of Khao Yai is that you're accompanied by an expert wildlife-spotter, and you have transport between the major sights of the park; book ahead if possible. As Khao Yai has recently been plagued with unscrupulous, fly-by-night tour operators, we are recommending only three companies (see below), all of which run budget tours lasting for a day and a half (around B1300), with the middle night spent outside the park: some include the accommodation and the B400 entrance fee – check before you book.

### Night safaris

A much-touted park attraction is the hour-long **night safaris** ("night lightings") that take truckloads of tourists round Khao Yai's main roads in the hope of sighting wildlife. Some tours include a night safari, whereas others visit the bat cave instead. If you're on your own, book a place on one of the trucks at the national park headquarters; they leave from here every night at 7pm and 8pm and cost B400 for up to eight people.

## Accommodation and tours

### Around the national park

To stay at the national park lodges, you'll need to reserve ahead through the Royal Forestry Department office in Bangkok (Ⓣ02/579 5734, Ⓦwww.thaiforestbooking.com), but if you want to **camp** you can just turn up at the park headquarters (Ⓣ09/424 7698) and arrange to rent a tent, bedding and cooking equipment (B250 inclusive) there. Avoid weekends, which get booked out well in advance. There's a cafeteria complex opposite the HQ and visitor centre. ❺

**Green Leaf Tour** At kilometre stone 7.5 on the park road, 12.5km out of Pak Chong Ⓣ044/365073, Ⓦwww.greenleaftour.com. Offers sparse though brightly decorated rooms and one-and-a-half-day tours including visiting the bat cave and waterfall swimming (B1500; entrance included). ❶–❷

**Khao Yai Garden Lodge** At kilometre stone marker 7 on the road into the park Ⓣ044/365178, Ⓔkhaoyaigarden@gmail.com. Fifty rooms set around a beautiful garden with a swimming pool. Tours cost B950 (1 day), B1200 (1.5 days); price excludes entrance fee and accommodation. ❸–❹

**Wildlife Safari** 39, Th Pak Chong, Subsanun, Non Kaja, 2km from Pak Chong Ⓣ096/288224, Ⓦwww.khaoyaiwildlife.com. This friendly family-run business offers jungle trekking and birdwatching, as well as smart en-suite rooms. One-day tours cost B1300 including accommodation, one-and-a-half days cost B1900. Call for free transfer. ❸

### Pak Chong

**Phubade Hotel** Tesaban Soi 15, just 50m south of the train station Ⓣ044/314964. This is a spartan choice in Pak Chong itself, with slightly grimy en-suite rooms.

If you're doing a tour, you'll stay at the tour operators' accommodation (see above). ❶

## Eating

Pak Chong's exceptionally good **night market** sets up on the edge of the main road, between Tesaban Sois 17 and 19.

# KHORAT (NAKHON RATCHASIMA)

Ninety kilometres from Pak Chong, bustling and non-touristy **KHORAT** (officially known as Nakhon Ratchasima) can be used as a base for exploring Phimai and Phanom Rung.

The town's most important statue is of Ya Mo, the mayor's feisty wife whose bravery and cunning genius were an inspiration to the people of Khorat when it was attacked by Laos in 1826. People come in their droves in the evening to offer her thanks and pray for protection. It's also worth checking out the city shrine on Thanon Chumphon, which features a lingam, shimmering with applied gold leaf and festooned with colourful garlands.

## Arrival and information

**By bus** Buses from other provinces (including from Phimai, Pak Chong, Ban Tako (for Phanum Rung),

Bangkok, Chiang Mai, Surin, Khon Kaen and Nong Khai) arrive at Bus Terminal 2, just north of the city on Th Mitraphap. The best way to get to and from town is with a tuk-tuk (around B60). Bus Terminal 1, just off Th Suranari, is closer to the town centre and runs a few buses to Bangkok.

**By train** The train station is 1km to the west of town centre on Th Mukkhamontri, midway between the TAT office and the commercial centre. If you don't want to walk, take a tuk-tuk (around B30) or shared songthaew #1, #2 or #3.

**Tourist information** The TAT office (☎044 213666) is on the western edge of town on Th Mitraphap.

## City transport

Local **buses** (B10) and **songthaews** (B8) travel most of Khorat's main roads. Yellow route #1 heads west along Th Chumphon, past the train station, returning east via Th Yommarat; route #2 runs between the main TAT office in the west, via the train station, and thanons Suranari and Assadang, to the east; and route #3 also runs right across the city, via thanons Mahathai and Jomsurangyat, past the train station. **Tuk-tuks** swarm the streets.

## Accommodation

**Chumpol Hotel** 124 Th Phoklang ☎044/242453. This friendly hotel offers clean though slightly institutional rooms, an on-site coffee shop, a barber and massage. It's right next to the market, so near to the hustle and bustle. ❷

**Sakon Hotel** 46–48 Th Asadrang, just east of the Ya Mo statue ☎044/241260. Set above a car park this spotless hotel has basic en-suite rooms; it's especially good for single travellers. ❶–❷

**Siri Hotel** 688–690 Th Pho Klang ☎044/241556. Recently upgraded budget hotel offering outstanding value for money; all its very en-suite smart rooms have a/c and cable TV.

## Eating and drinking

There's a night market on Th Manat with a few hot-food stalls, and a large food plaza, and more food stalls about 800m further east near the *Iyara Hotel* on Th Chumphon. Around the market and along Th Pho Klang, there are noodle and rice stalls.

**Bibi's** 786 Th Pho Klang. Very cheap Muslim food shop serving halal curries and standard one-dish Thai meals for around B30.

**The Mall** 124/2 Th Mittrapap. Generic selection of Western fast-food chains, as well as more appealingly the fantastic *MK Suki*, serving Thai-style fondue.

**Rabiang Keaw** Just off Th Yommarat. This smart restaurant comes highly recommended for its authentic Thai dishes (around B100), though it's best to bring a phrasebook as English is not always spoken.

## Directory

**Car rental** Korat Car Rental, 136 Th Phonsaen ☎044/393730, Ⓦwww.koratcarrental.com; Budget Car Rental, Tesco Lotus car park, Th Mitraphap ☎044/341654.

**Hospital** St Mary's Hospital, Th Mitraphap, just southwest of Bus Terminal 2 ☎044/261261.

**Internet** There are internet places all over town: near *Tokyo Hotel* on Th Suranari; at 352 Th Pak Chong, 600m east of *Siri Hotel*; and on the second floor of The Mall (see above).

**Telephones** The CAT office is on Th Chomsurang Yard just west of the city moat (open Mon–Fri 8.30am–4.30pm).

**Tourist Police** Opposite Bus Terminal 2 ☎044/341777, ☎1155.

## Moving on

**By bus** to: Chiang Mai (7 daily; 12–14hr); Chiang Rai (5 daily; 14–16hr); Lopburi (11 daily; 3hr 30min); Nong Khai (7 daily; 6–8hr); Pak Chong (for Khao Yai; every 20min; 1hr 30min); Phimai (every 30min; 1hr); Phitsanulok (7 daily; 7–9hr); Surin (every 30min; 4–5hr); Ubon Ratchathani (7 daily; 5–7hr); Udon Thani (for Nong Khai; every 45min; 3hr 30min–5hr).

**By train** to: Ayutthaya (11 daily; 4hr); Bangkok (11 daily; 6hr); Khon Kaen (daily; 3hr 30min); Nong Khai (daily; 6hr 30min); Pak Chong (10 daily; 2hr); Surin (10 daily; 2–3hr); Ubon Ratchathani (7 daily; 4hr 30min–6hr); Udon Thani (daily; 5hr 30min).

# PHIMAI

Tiny **PHIMAI**, 60km northeast of Khorat, is a much more appealing overnight stop than Khorat. The town is dominated by the exquisitely restored eleventh-century Khmer temple complex of **Prasat Hin** Phimai (daily 6am–6pm; B40), considered by many to be the blueprint for Angkor Wat itself. Built mainly of dusky pink and greyish-white sandstone, it was connected by a direct road to the Khmer capital of Angkor and follows the classic symbolic precepts of Khmer temple design: the moat represented the cosmic ocean, the surrounding walls the mountains, and the sanctuary tower (main prang) Mount Meru, the mythological axis of the world according to Hindu cosmology. Phimai's magnificent main prang has been restored to its original cruciform groundplan, complete with an almost full set of carvings, mostly picking out episodes from the Ramayana. Those around the outside of the prang depict predominantly Hindu themes: Shiva – the Destroyer – dances above the main entrance to the southeast antechamber heralding the end of the world and the creation of a new order. By the early thirteenth century, Phimai had been turned into a Buddhist temple, and the main prang now houses Phimai's most important image – the Buddha sheltered by a seven-headed naga (snake). Many other stonecarvings can be seen at the well-presented Phimai National Museum (Mon–Wed & Sun 8.30am–4pm; ⓣ044/471167; B30) 50m northeast of the ruins.

### Arrival

**By bus** Buses from Khorat's Bus Terminal 2 (every 30min; 1hr) stop near the ruins; the last return bus departs Phimai around 7pm. If coming from the north (for example, Khon Kaen) take any bus towards Bangkok and get off at Ban Talat Kaew, from where you can hop on a local bus (B12) for the last 10km.

### Accommodation and eating

**Bunsiri Guest House** 228 Th Chomsudasadet ⓣ089/4249942. Two large, clean, en-suite dorm rooms costing B180 per person; there's also a nice planted roof terrace with seating. ❷

**Old Phimai Guest House** 214 Th Chomsudasadet, behind the AGFA photo shop ⓣ044/471918, ⓦwww.phimaigh.com. An old-fashioned wooden house with internet and bike rental and runs day-trips to Phanum Rung (B1400 each for 2 people). The friendly owner has an excellent free map of Phimai. ❶–❷

### Eating

As always, the cheapest place to eat is at the handful of **food stalls** that set up in the evenings on the eastern road.

**Bai Toei** Th Chomsudasadet. serves tasty fresh fish dishes (English menu).

## HIN KHAO PHANOM RUNG AND PRASAT MUANG TAM

Built during the same period as Phimai, the temple complexes of Prasat Hin Khao Phanom Rung (often shortened to just Phanom Rung) and Prasat Muang Tam form two more links in the chain that once connected the Khmer capital with the limits of its empire. It's best to visit the ruins as a day-trip from either Khorat or Surin.

### Prasat Hin Khao Phanom Rung

**Prasat Hin Khao Phanom Rung** (daily 6am–6pm; B40) dates back to the tenth century and stands as the finest example of Khmer architecture in Thailand, its every surface ornamented with exquisite carvings and its buildings so perfectly aligned that on the morning of April's full-moon day you can stand at the

#### GETTING TO THE RUINS

To get to the ruins, you first need to take a bus to the small town of **Ban Tako**, located on Highway 24, 115km southeast of Khorat or 83km southwest of Surin; bus #274 travels between the two provincial capitals (every 30min). From Ban Tako, it's 12km south to Phanom Rung and another 8km south to Muang Tham, so you'll either have to hitch or rent a motorbike taxi (B300 per person for the round trip). The last bus back to Khorat ieaves around 5pm.

westernmost gateway and see the rising sun through all fifteen doors. This day marks Songkhran, the Thai New Year, which is celebrated here with a day-long festival of huge parades.

Before entering the temple, it's well worth visiting the excellent, museum-like **Phanom Rung Tourist Information Centre** (daily 9am–4pm; free) inside the Gate 1 car park to bone up on symbolism and background. You approach the temple compound along a dramatic two-hundred-metre-long avenue flanked with lotus-bud pillars, going over the first of three naga (snake) bridges, and past four small purification ponds. This constitutes the symbolic crossing of the abyss between earth and heaven. Part of the gallery that runs right round the inner compound has been restored to its original covered design, with arched roofs, small chambers inside and false windows. Above the entrance to the main prang (corn-cob shaped tower) are carvings of a dancing ten-armed Shiva, and of a reclining Vishnu, who is dreaming up a new universe.

### Prasat Muang Tam

Down on the well-watered plains 8km to the southeast of Phanom Rung, and accessed via a scenic minor road that cuts through a swathe of rice-fields lies the small but elegant temple complex of **Prasat Muang Tam** (daily 7.30am–6pm; B30). It sits behind a huge kilometre-long *baray* (Khmer reservoir), which was probably constructed at the same time as the main part of the temple, in the early eleventh century. Like Phanom Rung, Muang Tam is based on the classic Khmer design of a central prang, flanked by minor prangs and encircled by a gallery punctuated with gateways. The four stone-rimmed L-shaped ponds between the gallery and the outer wall may have been used to purify worshippers as they entered the complex.

## SURIN

The quiet, typically northeastern town of **SURIN** is best known for the much-hyped elephant round-up held here every year on the third weekend of November when hundreds of elephants congregate from the surrounding countryside (information on ⓣ044/213666, ⓦwww.tat.or.th/festival). Situated 197km east of Khorat, Surin makes a good base for Phanom Rung and has a fine guesthouse. It's also an excellent place to buy silk, either from the women around the Tannasarn–Krungsrinai intersection, or from the Ruen Mai Silk Shop at 52 Th Chitramboong.

Trains from Bangkok and Ubon pull in at the northern edge of town, and **b**uses stop one block east. For **accommodation**, head to *Pirom's Guest House*, 55-326 Soi Arunee, Thanon Thung Poh, (ⓣ044/515140; ❶), about 1.5km northwest of the train station, run by Pirom, a knowledgeable ex-social worker and his friendly wife Aree; they also serve food. Their fascinating tours give tourists an

### INTO CAMBODIA: CHONG CHOM–O'SMACH

**Buses** leave Surin approximately once an hour from dawn until 4.30pm for the ninety-minute journey via Prasat to Kap Choeng's **Chong Chom** border pass. You can get one on arrival at the Chong Chom–O'Smach checkpoint (daily 7am–8pm; US$20 or B1200), from where you can get transport to Anlong Veng. Arriving from Cambodia, songthaews and motorbike taxis ferry travellers from the border checkpoint to the bus stop for Prasat and Surin. For travellers' accounts of the border crossing, see ⓦwww.talesofasia.com/cambodia-overland.htm; for details on other overland routes into Cambodia, see p.837.

unusual glimpse into rural northeastern life; most itineraries feature the Ban Ta Klang elephant trainers' village.

For fiery Isaan **food**, you can't beat Surin's lively night market, which occupies the eastern end of Thanon Krungsrinai. Buses run from Surin to: Bangkok (10 daily; 7–8hr); Khon Kaen (8 daily; 4hr); Khorat (every 30min; 1hr).

## UBON RATCHATHANI

Almost always referred to simply as Ubon, **UBON RATCHATHANI**, 168km east of Surin, is Thailand's fifth-largest city, but only really worth stopping at en route to the Lao border. If you're here in early July though, drop by for the **Ubon Candle Festival**, when huge beeswax sculptures are paraded through the streets. If you're in Ubon in the evening, head to Thung Si Muang Park for some spectator sports; the park comes alive with activity.

There's little to see in Ubon, but Wat Thung Si Muang, 300m east of the park along Thanon Sri Narong, is noteworthy for its well-preserved teak library – raised on stilts over an artificial pond to keep book-devouring insects at bay – and its murals in the bot, to the left of the library, which display lively scenes of nineteenth-century life. The Ubon Ratchathani National Museum (Wed–Sun 9am–4pm; B30), south from the park across Thanon Sri Narong, has decent displays on the region's geology, history and folk crafts.

### Arrival and information

**By bus** The long-distance bus terminal is about 3km north of Ubon city centre on Th Chayangkun, from where songthaews #2 and #3 run into town. Private a/c buses run by Nakorn Chai use the terminal just south of the River Mun, on the road to the suburb of Warinchamrab, served by city buses #1, #2, #3 and #6 (B10); a taxi costs around B80.
**By train** The train station is in Warinchamrab, south across the Mun River. White city bus #2 (B10) runs from the train station across the river into central Ubon; a taxi costs around B50.
**By air** Ubon Airport is just north of the town centre; it costs B40 in a tuk-tuk or B70 in a shared limousine to city centre.
**Information** The TAT office is on Th Khuenthani (☎045/243770).

### Accommodation

**Tokyo Hotel** 178 Th Auparat ☎045/241739. Accommodation is severely limited in Ubon and the *Tokyo Hotel* is the best of a bad bunch. Rooms in its old building are dingy; some in the newer block have a/c. It's about a five-minute walk north of the museum. ❷–❸

### Eating and drinking

Ubon has two night markets, both of which are great places to eat. One sets up on Th Khuang Thani, just west of TAT, and sells a wide variety of food including the Isaan classics – sticky rice and *som tam*; the other, more rambling covered market, sets up on the north bank of the River Mun. There are also street stalls on Th Chayangkun, north of the Th Suriyat intersection.
**Chiokee** Th Khuenthani. Inexpensive Thai and Western food across from the museum.
**Teemnauychock** Th Sappasit. This cavernous restaurant is phenomenally busy with locals and the best place to eat in Ubon. The menu (dishes B40–80), which is also in English, features some unusual specialities such as frog meat and wild boar, and the spicy prawn salad is outstanding.

### Directory

**Hospital** Rom Kao Hospital is near the museum on Thanon Upparat (☎045/244658).
**Internet** You can get online at the CAT telephone office, next to the main post office on the Th Srinarong/Luang intersection, though only during office hours (Mon–Fri 8.30am–4.30pm).
**Police** The police station is on Th Suriyat (☎045/244941).

### Moving on

**By bus** to: Bangkok (at least hourly; 10hr); Khon Kaen (18 daily; 5hr); Pakxe, Laos (2 daily; 4hr); Phibun (every 40min; 1hr); Surin (12 daily; 2hr 30min); Udon Thani (for Nong Khai; 2 daily; 8hr).
**By train** to: Ayutthaya (10hr); Bangkok (7 daily; 12hr), via Surin (3hr); Khorat (5hr);
**By air** Thai Airways have a town office at 364 Th Chayanggoon (☎045/313343) and another at the airport. There are three flights daily to Bangkok (2hr).

## INTO LAOS: CHONG MEK

Ninety-nine kilometres east of Ubon, Highway 217 hits the **Lao border** at **Chong Mek**, site of a busy Thai-Lao market, and one of the five legal border crossings for foreigners. The border **market** here is well worth a browse, especially at weekends when it's at its liveliest. Among the stalls are traditional herbalists, lots of basketware sellers and vendors of cheap jeans, combat gear and sarongs; foreign shoppers can cross over to the Lao-side market in Vangtao simply by paying B5 at the checkpoint.

There are no direct buses from Ubon to Chong Mek; you must go via the town of Phibun. Catch a bus from the central bus station to Phibun (every 40min 6am–4pm; 1hr; B30), then on to Chong Mek (hourly 8am–4pm; 1hr; B35). On reaching Chong Mek you first need to get a Thai exit stamp from the office hidden behind the market on the Thai side (officially daily 6am–6pm). It's possible to get a Lao **visa** on arrival at Vangtao, on the Lao side of the Chong Mek border crossing (official hours Mon–Fri 8am–4pm; US$1 "surcharge" hours Mon–Fri 4–6pm, Sat, Sun & hols 8.30am–6pm); you'll be charged $30 for a thirty-day visa and will need two passport photos.

A faster and easier alternative is to use the Thailand International Transport Company Ltd's service that runs direct from Ubon's bus station to Pakxe (2 daily; B200; 4hr).

## KHON KAEN

The lively studenty city of **KHON KAEN**, 188km northeast of Khorat, makes a decent resting point on the Bangkok–Nong Khai rail line and, crucially, it also has both a Lao and a Vietnamese consulate, the only ones outside Bangkok. The farang centre is around the *Sofitel Hotel*; here's where you'll find most English spoken and restaurants with English menus. The exuberantly lit plaza just behind often shows open-air films.

### What to see and do

The striking, modern, nine-tiered, red- white-and-gold pagoda at Wat Nongwang is well worth a visit; it's at the far southern end of Thanon Klang Muang and served by city songthaews #8 (light blue) from the central stretch of Thanon Klang Muang and #14 (blue) from the train station, Thanon Si Chan and south-central Thanon Klang Muang. In keeping with its status as a university town, Khon Kaen boasts several fine collections in its museum on Thanon Lung Soon Rachakarn (Wed–Sun 9am–4pm; B30), including Bronze Age pots, Buddha sculptures, and local folk art.

### Arrival and information

**By bus** The a/c bus station is right in the city centre, while the non-a/c bus station is a five-minute walk northwest of the hotels on Thå Klang Muang.

**By train** Khon Kaen's train station is about fifteen minutes' walk southwest of Th Klang Muang on Th Darunsamran.

**By air** The airport is 10km west of the city centre; the airport "limousine" is B50 to most town addresses.

**Information** The TAT office is on Th Prachasamoson (☎043/244498). The tourist police are also based here.

### City transport

**City buses and songthaews** The most useful bus routes are: #3 (yellow; train station–non-a/c bus station); #8 and #9 (both light blue; regular bus terminal–a/c bus station–Th Klang Muang); #10 (blue; non-a/c bus station–TAT–Lao consulate–Vietnamese consulate–a/c bus station– Th Klang Muang); #11 (red; train station–Th Si Chan–a/c bus station–TAT–Lao consulate); and #15 (yellow)

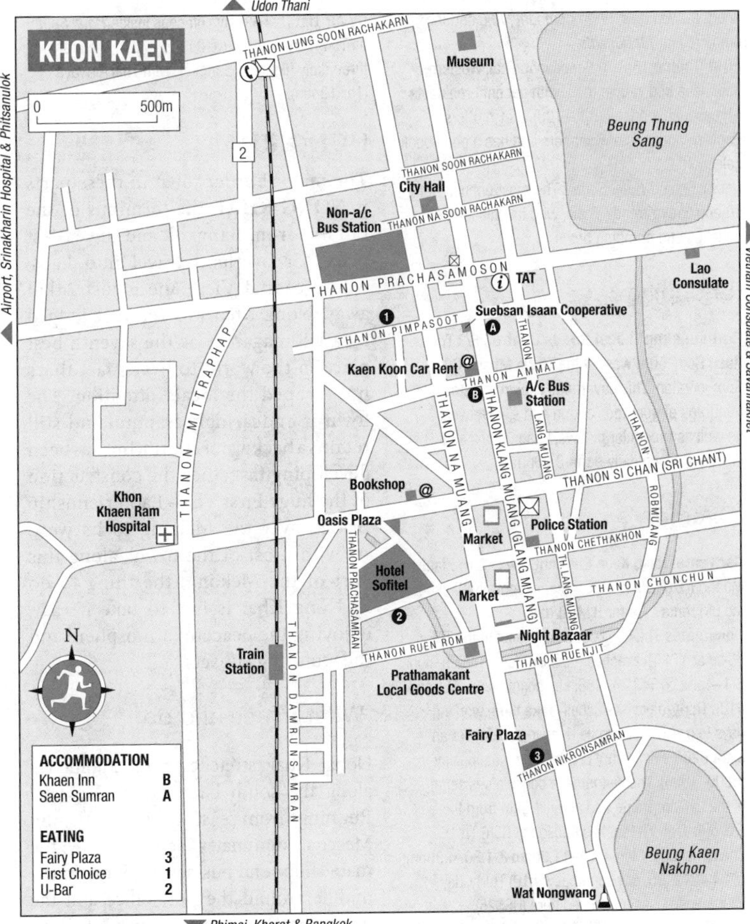




and #21 (brown), which both run up and down Th Klang Muang at least as far as Thanon Chonchun. Songthaews (B8) also run the streets.

**Tuk-tuks** Khon Kaen's limited number of tuk-tuks and taxis congregate around the transport hubs, but are expensive; unlike in the rest of Thailand they don't drive around picking up fares.

## Accommodation

There is very little budget accommodation in Khon Kaeng.

**Kaen Inn** 56 Th Klang Muang ☎043 245420. A more luxurious option than the *Saen Sumran*: all the smart, modern rooms are en-suite and a/c with cable TV. ❻

**Saen Sumran** 55 Th Klang Muang ☎043/239611. The most traveller-oriented hotel in town, with a useful noticeboard. Its spacious wooden-floored en-suite rooms are good value, if slightly dilapidated. ❶–❷

## Eating and drinking

Khon Kaen has a reputation for very spicy food, particularly sausages (*sai krog isaan*), served at stalls along Th Klang Muang (around *Saen Sumran Hotel)*. The same street boasts a large variety of cheap noodle and curry stalls both day and night.

**Fairy Plaza** at the south end of Th Klang Muang. Head here (on songthaew #8) when you're bored of noodle soup. It has all the fast food you'll ever need: *Daidomon's, Pizza Company, KFC* and the omnipresent *McDonalds*.

**First Choice** 18/8 Th Pimpasoot. Thai, Western, Japanese and veggie food, with decent breakfasts at reasonable prices (B30–100). It also offers English-language newspapers and has a good book selection.

**U-bar** Behind *Hotel Sofitel*. The most popular bar among young trendy Thais, with its chic leather couches and pumping beats.

### Shopping

**Prathamakant Local Goods Centre** 75/3 Th Ruen Rom, 50m west of the Th Na Muang/Ruen Rom junction. This cavernous showroom stocks hundreds of gorgeous cotton and silk weaves, as well as triangular pillows, khaen pipes and jewellery. Open daily 9am–8.30pm.

### Directory

**Car rental** Kaen Koon Car Rent, 54/1–2 Th Klang Muang (Ⓣ043/239458, Ⓔkaenkoontravel@yahoo.co.uk) rents cars for B1400/day.

**Consulates** The Lao consulate is east of the TAT office at 171 Th Prachasamoson (Mon–Fri 8am–noon & 1–4pm; Ⓣ043/242856; city songthaews #11 and #10). Thirty-day visas usually take three working days to process or can be done in one day for an extra B200. Prices vary depending on nationality (B800–1600). The Vietnamese consulate is south of the Lao consulate and about 1.5km from the TAT office, off Th Prachasamoson at 65/6 Th Chaiaphadung (Mon–Fri 8–11.30am & 1.30–4.30pm; Ⓣ043/242190; city songthaew #10) Thirty-day Vietnamese visas are issued here (US$25).

**Hospital** Khon Kaen Ram Hospital, on the far western end of Th Si Chan, is the main private hospital in town (Ⓣ043/333900).

**Internet** is available at various locations on Th Klang Muang, including next to 7/11.

### Moving on

**By bus** to: Bangkok (23 daily; 6–7hr); Chiang Mai (8 daily; 10hr); Chiang Rai (5 daily; 12hr); Khorat (hourly; 2hr 30min–3hr); Nakhon Phanom (12 daily; 5hr); Nong Khai (10 daily; 2–3hr); Phitsanulok (6 daily; 5–6hr); Surin (hourly; 4hr 30min–6hr); Ubon Ratchathani (15 daily; 6hr); Udon Thani (for Nong Khai; every 30min; 2hr).

**By train** to: Ayutthaya (4 daily; 7hr); Bangkok (4 daily; 9hr); Khorat (1 daily; 3hr); Nong Khai (3 daily; 3hr 20min); Udon Thani (4 daily; 2hr).

**By air** The Thai Airways office is inside *Hotel Sofitel* on Th Prachasumran (Ⓣ043/227701). There are three daily flights to Bangkok with Thai Airways (1hr 10min).

## NONG KHAI

The major border town in these parts is **NONG KHAI**, the terminus of the rail line from Bangkok and the easiest place for overland travel into Laos, whose capital Vientiane is just 24km away. Nong Khai was recently judged by a US magazine as the seventh best place in the world to live, a fact that's not escaped the locals' attention. The town is endearingly tranquil and still retains a backwater charm, but has been developing fast since the construction of the huge First Thai–Lao Friendship Bridge over the Mekong to its west. As with most of the towns along this part of the Mekong, the thing to do in Nong Khai is just to take it easy, enjoying the peaceful atmosphere and the stunning sunsets.

### What to see and do

Nong Khai stretches four kilometres along the south bank of the Mekong. Running from east to west, Thanon Meechai dominates activity, with the main shops and businesses plumb in the middle around the post office and the main pier, Tha Sadet. The town is famous for the Mekong Fireballs; pink points of light which rise noiselessly from the river after dusk on the last day of Buddhist lent in October. Despite eager attempts to disprove it as a hoax, no evidence of misdoing has been found and thousands of people amass every year to gawp at this mysterious phenomenon. One of the best places to see Nong Khai's famous sunset is from aboard a cruise run from *Mut Mee Guest House* (leaves 5pm; 1hr; B100) on their floating restaurant, *Nagarina*, which docks at the pier beneath (food is available at extra cost).

Just off the main highway, 5km east of Nong Khai, **Sala Kaeo Kou** (daily

7am–5pm; B20) is best known for its bizarre sculpture garden, which looks like the work of a giant artist on acid. The temple was founded by the unconventional and charismatic holy man, Luang Phu Boonlua Surirat, who believed, somewhat controversially, in a fusion of the teachings from all religions. The garden bristles with Buddhist, Hindu, Christian and secular figures, all executed in concrete with imaginative abandon by unskilled followers under Luang Phu's direction, and continued after his death in 1996. He also established a similarly weird "Buddha Park" (Xiang Khouan) across the Mekong near Vientiane in Laos (see p.425). The best way to get here is to rent a bike (B30) or motorbike (B200) from your guesthouse or from opposite the entrance to *Mut Mee* on Thanon Kaew Worawut.

## Arrival and information

**By bus** The bus terminal is on the east side of town off Th Prajak; tuk-tuks abound and cost around B30 to the centre. If you're coming into Nong Khai by bus from the north (Chiang Mai, for example) you'll need to change buses at Udon Thani (every 30min 7am–8pm; 1hr; B38).

**By train** The train station is 3km west of the town centre; a B40 tuk-tuk ride will take you into town.

**By air** Nong Khai doesn't have an airport itself but is less than an hour from Udon Thani (7 flights from Bangkok daily). Frequent limousine minivans run from Udon airport to Nong Khai; buy your ticket in the foyer (50min; B100).

**Information** TAT has an information booth on the road leading up to the Friendship Bridge (Ⓣ042/467844) but no branch in town; *Mut Mee Guest House* is a great source of information.

## Accommodation

**Esan Guest House** 538 Soi Srikunmuang Ⓣ086/242 1860, Ⓔe-san07@hotmail.com. A welcoming, traditional wooden house looking onto a neat ornamental garden. The rooms are beautifully wood-panelled, some with balconies, and have shared hot bathrooms. ❷

**Mut Mee Guest House** 1111 Th Keawworut, on the west side of town Ⓣ042/460717, Ⓦwww.mutmee.com. *Mut Mee* is by far the best place to stay in town. It's a magnet for travellers with its attractive riverside garden, well-kept rooms and B80 dorm beds, plus yoga and mountain bikes. Its incredibly friendly owners are charming and the service faultless. It also has a fish restaurant serving delicious and authentic Thai food (see below), and a floating bar, *Gaia*, with live music and a laid-back atmosphere. It's always busy so aim to arrive early. ❶–❷

**Rimkhong Guesthouse** 815/1-4 Th Rimkhong (about 100m west of Tha Sadet). Nice rooms around a well-planted garden with seating areas. ❶–❷

**Ruan Thai Guest House** 1126 Th Rimkhong, near Tha Sadet Ⓣ042/412519. *Ruan Thai* occupies a quiet planted compound of attractive wooden houses, with cheaper basic rooms with shared bathrooms also on offer. It rents bikes, serves breakfast and has internet available. ❷–❸

## Eating and drinking

**Daeng Naem-Nuang** 1062/1-2 Th Banterngjit, near Tha Sadet. This place is stupendously popular with the locals for its delicious Vietnamese food, particularly the *nam nueng* – make-them-yourself fresh spring rolls with barbecued pork.

**German Bakery** Tasty pastries from B15 and bread for those needing a carbohydrate fix.

**Nagarina** *Mut Mee*'s floating fish restaurant serves tasty authentic Thai food in an atmospheric setting.

### INTO LAOS ON THE FIRST FRIENDSHIP BRIDGE

The border crossing at Nong Khai is the First Friendship Bridge (open daily 6am–10pm), where you get a thirty-day visa on arrival (US$30 or B1500). To cross the border from downtown Nong Khai, take a tuk-tuk to the foot of the bridge (about B30–50), then a minibus (B20) across the span itself (every 15min; 8am–7.30pm), before catching a bus (B10), a tuk-tuk (about B100) or a taxi (about B200) to Vientiane, 24km away (see p.418). A cheaper and easier alternative is to catch a direct bus to Vientiane, leaving from the bus station (7.30am–6pm; 6 daily; B55) run by Thailand International Transport Company Ltd.

## INTO LAOS: MUKDAHAN

A hundred kilometres downriver of Nakhon Phanom, **Mukdahan** is the last stop on the Mekong trail before Highway 212 heads off inland to Ubon Ratchathani, 170km to the south. Buses run to Mukhadan from Nakhon Phanom (every 30min; 3hr); Bangkok (5 daily; 10hr); Ubon (every 30min; 4hr) and Khon Kaen (roughly hourly; 3hr). The Second Friendship Bridge opened in 2007, and is now the only way for foreigners (not Thai or Lao) to cross the border; foreigners must not use the ferry. The bridge is 8km north of Mukdahan; direct buses to Pakxe leave Mukdahan bus station roughly hourly from 8.15am to 7pm (B45). The border is open 6am–10pm and you can get a thirty-day visa on arrival (around $30).



**Warm-Up** On the riverfront just east of Tha Sadet. This trendy and upmarket bar, with a lively selection of tunes, is popular with the locals.

### Shopping

**Hornbill Bookshop** near *Mut Mee Guest House*. Stocks new and secondhand books and offers internet access, plus a phone and fax service.

**Village Weaver Handicrafts** 1151 Soi Chitapanya. Th Prajak ⓣ042/411236. On the south side of the centre with a branch at 1020 Thanon Prajak, on the corner of Thanon Haisoke, sells *mut mee* cotton, silk and axe pillows made under a local self-help project.

### Directory

**Motorbikes** Motorbikes (from B200) and bicycles (B30) can be rented on Th Keawworut opposite *Mut Mee Guest House*, and from most guesthouses.

### Moving on

**By bus** to: Bangkok (4 daily; 10hr); Chiang Mai (via Udon Thani; 4 daily; 12hr); Nakhon Phanom (5 daily; 6hr); Udon Thani (for Nong Khai; every 30min; 1hr).
**By train** to: Bangkok (4 daily; 11–12hr), via Udon Thani (1hr), Khon Kaen (3hr) and Ayutthaya (10hr).
**By air** Thai Airways, Air Asia and Nok Air all operate daily flights to Bangkok from Udon Thani. Travel agents can arrange transport to the airport (50min).

## NAKHON PHANOM

**NAKHON PHANOM**, 313km from Nong Khai, affords stunning views of the Mekong and the mountains behind but is chiefly of interest as a point of access to Laos, via the town of Thakhek across the river. Ferries cross to Thakhek roughly half-hourly in the morning and hourly in the afternoon from 8.30am to 6pm (B60), from the ferry pier opposite the market in the centre of town: thirty-day Lao visas can be bought on arrival for around US$30. There's a TAT office 700m north of the ferry pier at 184/1 Th Sunthon Vichit, on the corner with Thanon Salaklang (ⓣ042/513490). The best place to stay is *Grand Hotel*, at 210 Th Sri Thep (ⓣ042/511526), a block back from the river just south of the passenger ferry and market. The clean rooms are en-suite, the staff lively and the snow-themed decor surprising. ❷

Buses arrive at the bus station about 2km west of the centre from Nong Khai (5 daily; 6hr), Mukdahan (every 30min; 3hr) and Bangkok (12 daily; 11hr). Both Thai Airways and PBair operate daily 75-minute flights to and from Bangkok; the airport is 5km from town, and served by tuk-tuks.

# The east coast

Thailand's **east coast** is a five-hundred-kilometre string of fairly dull beaches and over-packaged family resorts, the largest and most notorious of which is Pattaya (omitted from this guide). Offshore, the tiny island of **Ko Samet** attracts backpackers and Bangkokians to its pretty white-sand beaches, while further east the much larger, forested island of **Ko Chang** is developing into a mainstream destination, leaving budget travellers to explore the quieter islands of **Ko Whai** and **Ko Mak**. East of Ko Chang lies the Cambodian border post of Hat Lek, one of two points in this region – the other being Aranyaprathet, a little way north – where it is currently legal to **cross overland into Cambodia** (see p.837).

## KO SAMET

The dazzling white-sand beaches of pretty little **Ko Samet** draw big crowds of backpackers, package tourists and Bangkokians. But, despite being declared a national park in 1981, a building ban has had little effect and the island is suffering under a glut of development. Away from the two main beaches however, Ko Samet remains quaint, with a comparative absence of cement, plentiful plant life and a coastal dirt road and tracks joining the beaches. At just 6km long, distances aren't great and you can easily walk to most destinations; there are also motorbikes for rent on every beach, and a sporadic **songthaew** service starts at Na Dan pier continuing down the track as far as Wong Duan. There's a B200 national park entrance fee on arrival, payable at the checkpoint near Hat Sai Kaew or at Ao Wong Duan pier.

### The beaches

**Hat Sai Kaew**, or Diamond Beach, so called afer its beautiful long stretch of luxuriant sand, lies ten minutes' walk south from Na Dan. It's the most popular – and congested – beach on Samet and sits under a mass of bungalows, restaurants and beachwear stalls.

Separated from Hat Sai Kaew by a low promontory, **Ao Hin Kok** combines equally fine sand with a laid-back village feel and a leafy, relatively unsullied natural environment. There's a pleasant travellers' vibe here and the charming beachside restaurants serve delicious food.

Past the next rocky divide, **Ao Phai** is one of the livelier places to stay on

### TRANSPORT TO AND FROM KO SAMET

The mainland departure point for Ko Samet is the fishing port of **Ban Phe**, about 200km from Bangkok.

**Buses** from Bangkok's Eastern Bus Terminal run hourly to Ban Phe pier (B112), or you can take a bus to Rayong instead (every 15min) and then change onto a songthaew to Ban Phe pier (30min).

**Tourist minibuses** run direct from Thanon Khao San to Ban Phe (about B250). Buses from Chanthaburi and Trat drop you on Thanon Sukhumvit, from which songthaews or motorbike taxis will take you on a 5km ride to the pier. If you need to stay in Ban Phe, make for the traveller-oriented *Tan Tan Too* (Ⓣ038/653671, ❹) on Soi 2, across the road from the main Taruaphe pier.

**Boats** go from Ban Phe to Ko Samet (Nov–Feb; approximately hourly 8am–6pm; 30min; B50) and back again to the same schedule. Most go to **Na Dan pier**, but if you're headed for Ao Wong Duan, Ao Cho or Ao Thian, it's more convenient to take the boat to **Ao Wong Duan** (every 2hr 8.30am–4.30pm; 40min; B60). Boats for both destinations leave from Ban Phe's Saphaan Nuan Tip pier, opposite the 7–11. In low season, there should be up to four boats daily to both piers. There are also two companies running small **speedboats** (seating up to 10) between Ban Phe and the island. Prices start at B600 to Na Dan pier. Customers share the cost; boats leave when the price is covered.

Tourist minibuses **depart** across the road from *Tan Tan Too* to Thanon Khao San (Bangkok) and Laem Ngop (for Ko Chang); otherwise, take a songthaew from Ban Phe to Rayong bus station and make onward connections there.

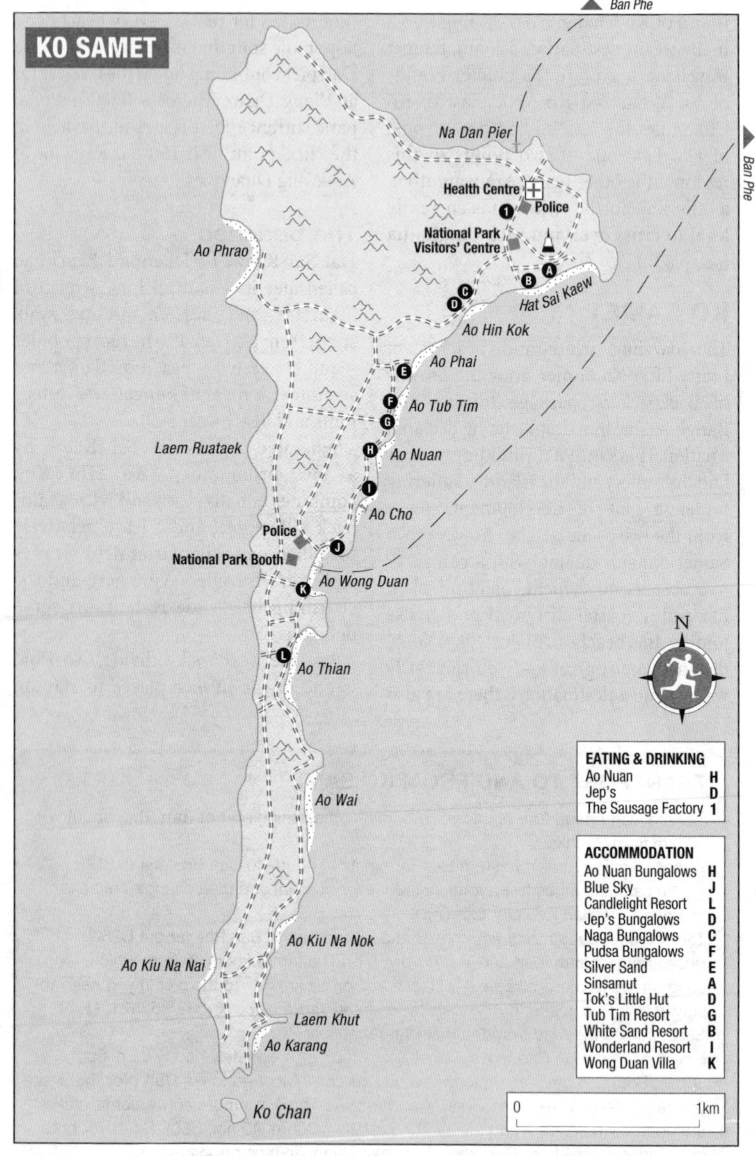




the island. By day, a relaxed beach-life atmosphere pervades, but by night sleep is elusive as *Silver Sand*'s nightly parties thump out tunes until the small hours of the morning. For the best of both worlds stay at Ao Hin Kok or Ao Tub Tim and make the short walk to Ao Phai when the party mood takes you.

Moving further south, **Ao Tub Tim**, also known as Ao Pudsa, is a small white-sand bay sandwiched between rocky promontories. Trees are plentiful, bungalows are tasteful and there's a charming, dilapidated shantytown feel to its non-resort midsection, back from the beach.

**Ao Nuan**, a quick clamber over the next steep headland, is a pretty little getaway. While the small sand beach is strewn with big rocks, there is easy swimming among the beautiful natural surroundings: the one, all-timber, bungalow operation is here, blending into the forested and rocky hillside.

A five-minute walk south along the track from Ao Nuan brings you to **Ao Cho**, which has a wide stretch of beach but development that's a bit of an eyesore. The pier that cuts down halfway along does nothing to improve things.

Around the next headland, the horseshoe bay of **Ao Wong Duan** is the second most popular beach on the island and is dominated by pricey bungalow resorts. Unfortunately its sand, while white and fine, is almost lost under a plethora of deck chairs, stalls, innumerable inflatables and crowds of sunbathers.

**Ao Thian** (also known as Candlelight Beach), a couple of minutes' walk over the hill, has none of the commerce of Wong Duan, though its lovely, scenic shorefront is fronted by an unbroken line of bungalows and little restaurants.

## Accommodation

### Hat Sai Kaew

**Sinsamut** Central Hat Sai Kaew ⓣ038/644134. Though the location isn't great – a two-storey building cramped behind an unappealing beachfront restaurant – inside the rooms at *Sinsamut* are quaint and clean and most en-suite bathrooms are pleasantly decorated with loose pebble floors and stepping-stones. ❺–❻

**White Sand Resort** At the south end of the beach, ⓣ038/644004. The cheapest rooms are small and plain, but come with en suite and hot water. The garden compound is nice enough and the beach is less congested at this point. ❺–❽

### Ao Hin Kok and Ao Phai

**Jep's Bungalows** South-central Ao Hin Kok ⓣ038/644112. This rocky, tropical garden compound encompasses seven cheap but high-quality rooms with TV and shared facilities in a timber two-storey building. Pay a little more for the three with en-suite and hot water, and pay a lot more for the attractive stained wooden bungalows that climb the hillside. ❸–❻

**Naga Bungalows** Ao Hin Kok ⓣ038/644167. This popular place provides cheap rooms in simple plank huts with shared facilities, as well as pricier stone en-suite ones; it also has a pool table, a large selection of secondhand books and bakes its own bread and cakes. ❸–❺

**Silver Sand** Ao Phai ⓣ038/644300. Set in a pleasant compound, the cheapest rooms, in two long timber buildings at the back, are spacious, clean and tiled with fan, fridge and hot shower. ❻

**Tok's Little Hut** Ao Hin Kok, next door to *Naga Bungalows* ⓣ038/644072. The faded, light blue bungalows here have grubby wall interiors and very basic bathrooms, but the beds are soft, the linen is fresh and some have ocean views from their balconies. ❸–❺

### Ao Tub Tim and Ao Nuan

**Ao Nuan Bungalows** Cute wooden bungalows of varying designs dot the forested hillside. The cheapest, but by no means cheap, rooms have just a mattress on the floor and a mosquito net. All have shared bathrooms. ❺–❽

**Pudsa Bungalows** Ao Tub Tim ⓣ038/644030. Small and welcoming, offering a range of pretty nice, large and sturdy huts with wood interiors. The dirt garden compound is poorly maintained however. ❹–❻

**Tub Tim Resort** Ao Tub Tim ⓣ038/644025, ⓦwww.tubtimresort.com. Around sixty attractive, wooden bungalows on stilts with a range of interiors (reflected in the price), on a grassy hillside leading down to the beach. ❹–❾

### Ao Cho, Ao Wong Duan and Ao Thian (Candlelight Beach)

**Blue Sky** North Ao Wong Duan ⓣ089/936 0842. Reasonable quality bamboo thatched bungalows or pricier wood and cement numbers in a scruffy compound on the northern headland. A pleasant restaurant with a deck sits on the northern rocks with a good view over the beach. ❹–❻

**Candlelight Resort** Central Ao Thian ⓣ087/149 6139. A long line of pretty decent bungalows facing the water with a charming sandy bar/restaurant on a mid-beach promontory. ❻

**Wonderland Resort** North Ao Cho ⓣ038/644102, ⓦwww.samedlungwang.com. These ugly cement bungalows in a dishevelled compound on the northern headland are by no means good value, but offer the cheapest accommodation on Ao Cho. ❺–❾

**Wong Duan Villa** South Ao Wong Duan ☎038/644260. Characterful white-plank huts built on stilts with picture windows and decks, with both fan and a/c rooms. ❻–❾

## Eating

**Ao Nuan** Ao Nuan. The mellow restaurant at *Ao Nuan Bungalows* has some of the best veggie food on the island.

**Jep's** Hin Kok. Deservedly the most popular restaurant on Ao Hin Kok. Serves up a great menu of travellers' fare at its tables on the beach, under trees prettily decorated with paper lanterns.

**The Sausage Factory** On the Na Dan–Sai Kaew Rd. This charming, British-run, rustic timber and plant-filled restaurant serves up a top-notch full English breakfast (B130).

## Directory

**Banks and exchange** There's an ATM at the 7-11 on the Na Dan–Hat Sai Kaew road; the island's biggest resorts will change money,

**Diving** You can organize dive trips through Ploy Scuba (☎038/644212) on Hat Sai Kaew.

**Health** Ko Samet Health Centre (☎038/644123) is midway along the Na Dan– Hat Sai Kaew road.

**Internet and phones** There are international phone services and internet access on the Na Dan–Hat Sai Kaew road and at almost every beach.

**Police** Next door to the Health Centre (☎038/644111; 24hr).

**Post office** Ko Samet post office is run out of *Naga Bungalows*.

**Travel agents** CP Travel (☎038/644136) on Hat Sai Kaew, beside the main track on the edge of the *White Sand* complex, sells air, train, bus and minibus tickets as well as package tours.

# CHANTHABURI

There's not a lot to see in the provincial capital of **CHANTHABURI**, 80km east of Ban Phe, but you may find yourself stranded here, however, as this is a transit point for most Rayong–Trat buses and a handy terminus for services to and from the northeast. Eight daily buses make the scenic six-hour Chanthaburi–Sa Kaew–Khorat journey in both directions, with Sa Kaew (3hr) being a useful interchange for buses to Aranyaprathet and **the Cambodian border** (see box, opposite). Buses to and from all these places, as well as Bangkok's Eastern and Northern bus terminals, use the Chanthaburi bus station on Thanon Saritidet, about 750m northwest of the town centre and a five- minute songtheaw trip (B40) from *The River Guest House* (☎039/348211, ❶–❸), at 3/5–8 Th Srichan, which has sizeable clean, fan and a/c rooms, some with good views of the river.

# TRAT

The small, engaging market town of **TRAT**, 68km east of Chanthaburi, with its charming historic neighbourhood of narrow lanes, old wooden shop houses and characterful bars, cafes and restaurants, is a good place to while away time and stock up on essentials before heading, via local ports, to Ko Chang and the outer islands, or moving on to **Cambodia**.

## Arrival and information

**By bus** Private and government a/c buses from Bangkok's Eastern and Northern bus terminals, Ban Phe and Chanthaburi all drop their passengers at the bus station 1km northeast of Trat centre. Songthaews charge B60 into Trat's centre and around B180 to island ferry ports. With more passengers, the price is reduced dramatically.

**By air** Taxis ferry air-passengers the 16km to Laem Ngop (B400–500).

**Tourist information** The best sources of local information are the Tratosphere bookshop, 200m east along Th Lak Muang from Th Sukhumvit, at 23 Soi Kluarimklong, and *Cool Corner* restaurant (see p.838).

## Accommodation

**Ban Jaidee** 200m walk east across from Th Sukhumvit's Trat Department Store, then a short walk north up Th Chaimongkon ☎039/520678. A bright, inviting and rather stylish guesthouse, with a pleasant ground-floor seating area and just seven simple upstairs bedrooms; has overseas call service. ❶–❷

**Guy Guest House** Th Thoncharoen, east of *Cool Corner* ☎085/841 8958. Popular guesthouse with well-priced if thin-walled rooms. Rooms with shared bathrooms are very cheap (B80), then price gradations apply according to what's added: TV, en suite, hot water, a/c. Internet, overseas calls and transport tickets are also available. ❶–❷

**Trat Guesthouse** Up a small soi that leads north off Th Thoncharoen, about 50m west of *Cool Corner* ⓣ085/393 8327. Characterful, stone and timber place with lush plant life, clean cosy rooms and hot water; shared bathrooms. ❶

## INTO CAMBODIA

Visas for Cambodia are issued to travellers on arrival at Phnom Penh and Siem Reap airports, and at the Aranyaprathet–Poipet, Hat Lek–Koh Kong and Ban Pakkard–Pailin land borders; you need US$20 and two photos.

### Via Aranyaprathet, Poipet and Chanthaburi province

The most commonly used overland crossing into Cambodia is at **Poipet**, which lies just across the border from the Thai town of **Aranyaprathet**. The border here is open daily from 7am to 8pm and officials will issue thirty-day Cambodian visas on arrival (see p.78 for details). Once through the border, hop on whatever's available for the quick trip to Poipet's transport depot, from which it's a gruelling eight to twelve hours to Siem Reap. Share-taxis are the most hassle-free mode of transport, but expensive at up to US$60 a taxi (or US$15/person). If you need a hotel in Aranyaprathet, try the comfortable fan or a/c rooms at *Inter Hotel* on Thanon Chatasingh (ⓣ037/231291; ❸–❹).

Travelling to Poipet from east-coast towns, the easiest route is to take a bus from Chanthaburi to the town of Sa Kaew, 130km to the northeast, and then change to one of the frequent buses for the 55km ride east to Aranyaprathet. From Bangkok, the easiest way to get to Aranyaprathet is by train (2 daily; 6hr): you'll need to catch the one at 5.55am to ensure reaching the border before 5pm. Tuk-tuks or motorcycle taxi will take you the 4km from the train station to the border post. Alternatively, take a first-class (B200–220) or second-class (B150–170) bus from Bangkok's Northern bus terminal to Aranyaprathet, then take a tuk-tuk to the border.

There are also two lesser used crossings in Chanthaburi province, giving access to the Cambodian town of **Pailin**, just east of the border: the Daung Lem border crossing at **Ban Laem**, 88km northeast of Chanthaburi, and the Phsa Prom border crossing at **Ban Pakkard** (aka Chong Phakkat), 72km northeast of Chanthaburi. Share taxis leave Chantaburi (3 daily) from the opposite side of the river from *River Guest House* to Ban Pakkard (1h; B140 one way and return) or you can take a songthaew from Chanthaburi to Pong Nam Ron, 42km north of Chanthaburi on Highway 317 (1hr 30min), then charter another to either border post. The borders are open daily from 7am to 8pm; at the time of writing you can get visas on arrival only at Ban Pakkard.

### Via Hat Lek to Koh Kong

Many travellers use the **Hat Lek–Koh Kong** border crossing (daily 7am–8pm) for overland travel into Cambodia, not least because thirty-day visas on arrival are issued here and Koh Kong has reasonable transport connections to Sihanoukville and, via Sre Ambel, Phnom Penh. The only way to get to Hat Lek is by minibus from Trat, 91km northwest. Minibuses leave Trat approximately every 45 minutes between 6am and 5pm (1hr–1hr 30min; B120) from the bus station. Hat Lek (on the Thai side) and Koh Kong (in Cambodia) are on opposite sides of the Dong Tong River estuary, but a bridge connects the two banks. If you want to reach Sihanoukville in one day, you'll need to catch the 6am minibus from Trat, which should give you just enough time to connect with the daily 8am boat to Sihanoukville from Koh Kong. To reach Koh Kong pier, you need to take a motorcycle or car taxi from the Hat Lek immigration post at Cham Yeamto Koh Kong on the east bank of the estuary. If you leave Trat later in the day and need to overnight in Koh Kong, simply follow the route described above to Koh Kong pier.

## Eating

The day market, on the ground floor of the Th Sukhumvit shopping centre, and the atmospheric night market, north of the historic centre, between Soi Vichidanya and Soi Kasemsan (east of Th Sukhumvit) are good places to eat.

**Cool Corner** by the river on Th Thoncharoen, west of *Guy Guest House*. An enjoyably arty spot to chill out over home-made bread, real coffee and veggie specials.

**Joy's Pizza** Opposite *Guy Guest House*. Top-notch pizza.

**Kluarimkong** 100m east of *Guy Guest House*. Stylish place dishing out delicious Thai standards.

## Directory

**Hospital** Bangkok-Trat Hospital (☎039/532735) on the Sukhumvit Highway, 1km north of Trat Department Store.

**Internet** There's internet access at many guesthouses and restaurants and at Cybercafé on Th Sukhumvit.

**Post office** On Th Chaimongkon, a 10-minute walk on the road running northeast from *Ban Jaidee*.

## Moving on

**By bus** Government and a/c buses leave from the bus station, 1km northeast of Trat's centre. For connecting boats to Ko Samet, there are 4 buses daily to Ban Phe (3hr). Minibuses also leave here for Hat Lek (every 45min; 1hr–1hr 30min) and Chanthaburi (hourly; 1hr 30min). There are two main bus companies, Cherdchai Tour (☎023/912237) and Tanakawee (☎023/912331) that run routes from Trat to Bangkok's Eastern Bus Terminal (Ekamai; 17 daily) and northern terminal (Morchit; 6 daily); both take 4–6hr.

**By air** Bangkok Airways flies to Bangkok (3 daily; 1hr).

# KO CHANG

The focal point of a national marine park archipelago of 52 islands, **Ko Chang** is Thailand's second-largest island (after Phuket) and an increasingly popular destination, drawing crowds to its mountainous, dense jungle interior and beautiful white sand beaches. During peak season, accommodation on the west coast fills up very fast, but it gets quieter (and cheaper) from May to October, when fierce storms can make the sea too rough for swimming. Though mosquitoes are not much in evidence, Ko Chang is one of the few areas of Thailand still considered to be **malarial**, so it's advisable to take prophylactics before you arrive; for on-the-spot advice contact Ko Chang International Clinic on Hat Sai Khao (☎039/551555; 24hr).

A wide road runs almost all the way round the island, served – between Tha Dan Kao and Hat Kai Bae – by frequent public **songthaews**; you can also rent cars, motorbikes and mountain bikes on most beaches, and should be able to arrange a motorbike taxi from the same places.

### Sai Khao (White Sand Beach)

Framed by a broad band of fine white sand at low tide, **Hat Sai Khao** (White Sand Beach) is the island's longest beach but also its most commercial, with over thirty unattractive hotel-style developments and bungalow operations squashed in between the road and the shore. The atmosphere is more laid-back and traveller-oriented at the northern end of the beach, however, where through a maze of haphazard boardwalks (a high tide necessity) you'll find the most budget-priced accommodation. Currents can get very strong on Hat Sai Khao, so be careful when swimming.

### Hat Khlong Phrao and Hat Kai Bae

Just south of the khlong fed by **Khlong Phu Waterfall** (B200 entry), the long sandy beach of central **Hat Khlong Prao** remains a beauty. Behind a thin line of casuarinas there's a scattering of cheap and charming bungalow operations nestled in a huge coconut grove. About 5km further south, the narrow, once beautiful beach at **Hat Kai Bae**, while almost ruined by breakneck development, remains quaint at its southern extremity.

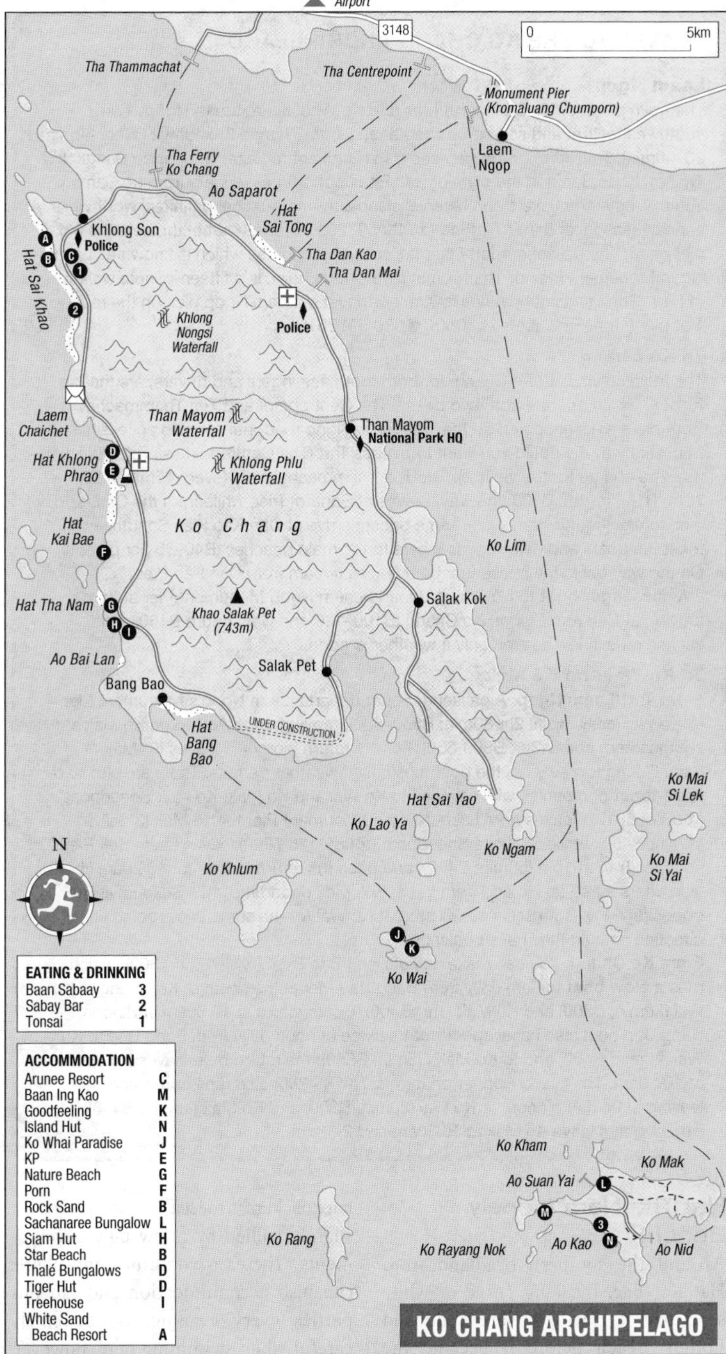
Airport
3148
0
5km
Tha Thammachat
Tha Centrepoint
Monument Pier
(Kromaluang Chumporn)
Trat
Laem
Ngop
Tha Ferry
Ko Chang
Ao Saparot
Hat
Sai Tong
Khlong Son
Police
Tha Dan Kao
Tha Dan Mai
Hat Sai Khao
Khlong
Nongsi
Waterfall
Police
Laem
Chaichet
Than Mayom
Waterfall
Than Mayom
National Park HQ
Hat Khlong
Phrao
Khlong Phlu
Waterfall
Hat
Kai Bae
Ko Chang
Ko Lim
Hat Tha Nam
Khao Salak Pet
(743m)
Salak Kok
Ao Bai Lan
Salak Pet
Bang Bao
Hat
Bang
Bao
UNDER CONSTRUCTION
Ko Mai
Si Lek
Hat Sai Yao
Ko Lao Ya
Ko Ngam
Ko Mai
Si Yai
Ko Khlum
Ko Wai
N
EATING & DRINKING
Baan Sabaay 3
Sabay Bar 2
Tonsai 1
ACCOMMODATION
Arunee Resort C
Baan Ing Kao M
Goodfeeling K
Island Hut N
Ko Whai Paradise J
KP E
Nature Beach G
Porn F
Rock Sand B
Sachanaree Bungalow L
Siam Hut H
Star Beach B
Thalé Bungalows D
Tiger Hut D
Treehouse I
White Sand
Beach Resort A
Ko Kham
Ko Mak
Ao Suan Yai
Ko Rang
Ko Rayang Nok
Ao Kao
Ao Nid
KO CHANG ARCHIPELAGO
Ko Kud

## TRAVEL TO THE KO CHANG ARCHIPELAGO

### Laem Ngop

The main piers for Ko Chang, Ko Mak and Ko Whai are at **Laem Ngop**, 17km southwest of Trat and served by songthaews from Thanon Sukhumvit (every 30min; 20–40min). **Tourist minibus** services also run direct to Laem Ngop from Bangkok's Thanon Khao San and the piers at Ban Phe (for boat passengers from Ko Samet). You can buy ferry tickets and reserve island accommodation (definitely worthwhile in peak season) at the **TAT office** (Ⓣ039/597259, Ⓔtattrat@tat.or.th), near the old pier head. The passenger-ferry pier (for foot-passengers), which is known as Laem Ngop Monument Pier, or Tha Kromaluang Chumphorn, is a fifteen-minute walk west of here. The immigration office is 3km northeast of Laem Ngop pier, on the road to Trat pier (Mon–Fri 8.30am–4.30pm; Ⓣ039/597261).

### To Ko Chang

The main services to Ko Chang, for both foot passengers and drivers, are the **car ferries**, which operate from two piers – Tha Centrepoint and Tha Thammachat. Both piers are signposted off the Trat–Laem Ngop road, but are also accessible from Highway 3, should you want to bypass Trat (Tha Centrepoint is preferable, with no extra charge for the vehicle). The Tha Thammachat ferry (every 45min: 6.30am–7pm; B160 return; B100 one way) arrives at Saparot Pier, while from the Centrepoint pier, ferries (hourly: 6am–7pm; same prices) arrive at Dan Kao Pier. Songthaews meet the boats and deliver passengers to the main beaches (B40–80 per person). On the way back, the passenger boat leaves at 9am from Dan Kao Pier.

A **passenger boat** to Ko Chang departs Laem Ngop Monument Pier at 3pm, arriving at Dan Kao Pier on Ko Chang (B100–120 one way; return B160). This service runs in low season only if weather is good.

### To Ko Wai and Ko Mak

**From Trat/Laem Ngop:** A passenger boat departs Laem Ngop's Monument Pier to Ko Wai (daily; 3pm; 2hr 30min; B250–300), moving on to Ao Nid on Ko Mak's southeastern coast (3hr; B300-350). For the return journey it leaves Ko Mak at 8am. During low season, the boat runs only if weather permits. There are also two **speedboat** companies with services to Ko Wai and Ko Mak: Ko Mak Speedboat (Ⓣ039/538122) leaves from Laem Ngop's Monument Pier for Ko Mak (3 daily; 50min; B450), while Siriwhite Speedboat (Ⓣ086/126 7860) leaves Laem Sok Pier, south of Trat, at 1pm (50min; B400), and does the return journey at 10.20am (it also offers a free taxi to and from Laem Sok pier, departing Trat's Sukhumvit Rd, opposite 7-11). Both services will stop at Ko Wai for the same price, going either direction (should they have bookings).

**From Ko Chang:** You can make use of Bang Bao Boat (Ⓣ087/054 4300), which runs a **slow boat** at 9am daily from Bang Bao Pier in the south of Ko Chang to Ko Wai (30min; B300) and Ko Mak (1hr; B400). Boats return at 10.30am and noon. Bang Bao boat also has a **speedboat** service at noon daily from Bang Boa to Ko Wai (20min; B400) and to Ko Mak (35min; B550); the return boat leaves Ko Mak at 10.30am. The Island Hopper boat (Ⓣ087/054 4300) also runs from Bang Bao, leaving at 9am and noon, to Ko Wai (20min; B300) and Ko Mak (40min; B400). Return boats leave Ko Mak at 10.30am and 2.30pm.

### Hat Tha Nam (Lonely Beach)

Around the southern headland from Hat Kai Bae, the long curve of white sand bay at **Hat Tha Nam** – dubbed **Lonely Beach** before it became the backpackers' mecca – is lovely, if slightly sullied by a few ugly developments. There's a youthful atmosphere, cheapish accommodation and raucous parties every evening. Be extremely careful when swimming here, however, especially around *Siam Beach* at the far northern end, as the steep shelf and dangerous current result in a sobering number of **drownings** every year; do your swimming further south and don't go out at all when the waves are high.

## Dive operators

**Ko Chang Dive Point** Bai Lan, the small bay south of Hat Tha Nam ⓣ087/142 2948, ⓔarnhelm @gmx.de. Charges around B3000 for "Discover Scuba" dives, around B2200–2500 for certified diver day expeditions (2 dives) and about B13,000 for the four-day PADI Open Water course.
**Ploy Scuba** Has offices on all main beaches ⓣ039/558038, ⓦwww.ployscuba.com.
**Sea Horse Diving** Hat Kai Bae ⓣ081/996 7147, ⓦwww.ede.ch/seahorse.

## Accommodation and eating

### Hat Sai Khao

Many of the bungalow restaurants have nightly fish barbecues. *Tonsai* has a predominantly Thai and vegetarian menu and seating is Thai-style on cushions in a breezy treehouse. Down on the beach, *Sabay Bar* is the place for cocktails and rave music.
**Arunee Resort** ⓣ039/551075. These cute, clean wooden rooms, with mozzie nets, fans and en-suite bathrooms, occupy a long balconied building stretching inland from the road. The yard is a little unkempt, but it's only at a thirty-metre walk from a nice stretch of beach. A very good budget option. ❸
**Rock Sand** ⓣ087/580 7474. A travellers' favourite with a charming, if somewhat kitsch, rustic restaurant jutting over the water below a few cheap, comfortable, woven bamboo-wall rooms, with shared facilities. Also offers a number of simple timber huts (fan and a/c), perched on the rocky escarpment. ❹–❻
**Star Beach** ⓣ0847/805341. Dilapidated plywood huts, precariously perched on a steep rocky hillside. ❹–❺
**White Sand Beach Resort** ⓣ018/637737. Located in a secluded, very attractive spot at the far north end of the beach, this place offers a range of nicely spaced huts. Many are quite basic, others are upmarket and made of ugly cement, but most have uninterrupted sea views. ❻–❽

### Hat Khlong Phrao and Hat Kai Bae

**KP** Khlong Phrao ⓣ084/099 5100. Traveller-oriented set-up, featuring log cabin-style bungalows (en-suite or shared facilities) and some tree-houses fronting the beach. The shared facilities are top-notch and the management rents out kayaks and organizes snorkelling and fishing day-trips. ❸–❺
**Porn** At the southern end of the beach, Hat Kai Bae ⓣ089/535 2037. The only cheap place to stay here, offering both basic huts with shared facilities and classy en-suite wooden bungalows. Its massive shoreside restaurant is a phenomenon (and serves great food) – reason enough, in fact, to stay here. ❸–❻
**Thalé Bungalows** Khlong Phrao ⓣ081/901 0346. This beautiful grassy palm grove, occupied by basic bamboo huts fronting a tranquil stretch of beach and flanked by a lagoon estuary, is a great budget option. Its thatched restaurant, with dangling shell mobiles, plays laid-back blues and reggae music. ❶–❷
**Tiger Hut** Khlong Phrao ⓣ084/109 9660. A pleasant, sandy, palm-filled compound, with a scattering of ferns. Has simple, attractive bamboo bungalows and a relaxed restaurant, with pool table and deck, on the beach. ❷–❹

### Hat Tha Nam

**Nature Beach** ⓣ018/038933. In the central beach area, this popular place has a vibrant, youthful atmosphere. Choose between basic huts flanking sandy paths and lush gardens, and pricier, attractively furnished options. ❹–❼
**Siam Hut** ⓣ086/609 7772. Rows and rows of primitive, split-bamboo huts, all of which are en suite, located in the central beach area. Also has a big restaurant/bar deck for watching the sunset. ❹
**Treehouse** ⓣ081/847 8215. Set on the rocky headland at the southern end of the bay, this German/Thai-managed place put this beach on the map and is the most chilled spot on Hat Tha Nam. Its forty shaggy-thatched huts all contain just a mattress, a mosquito net and a paraffin lamp (there's no electricity in the huts) and all of them share bathrooms; there's also a massive seaside deck area with hammocks and floor cushions. ❶–❷

## Directory

Most main beaches offer ATMs, currency exchange and internet access but the bulk of the island's facilities are centred in Hat Sai Khao.
**Books** There's a bookshop with a reasonable selection of titles at the Thai market next to White Sand's southern 7–11.
**Pharmacy** Opposite *Arunee Resort*, a few doors down from the 7-11, and further south, three doors down from the Bank of Ayuthaya.

**Police** Northern White Sand, opposite the 7-11 (☎039/551544). The tourist police have an office on central Hat Khlong Phrao (☎019/828381)
**Post office** On the road between White Sand and Khlong Phrao (Mon–Fri 10am–noon and 1–6pm, Sat 10am–1pm).

## KO WAI

Sparkling with ripples of refracted light, the luminous turquoise waters of little **Ko Wai** (3km long and 1.5km wide), with its palm-fringed beaches and laid-back atmosphere, were, until recently, the perfect escape from the commercial chaos of Ko Chang. Now, massive crowds of day-trippers descend every day on its northwestern, and most attractive beach. Here *Koh Wai Paradise* (☎081/762 2548; ❷), which plays culinary host to the daily onslaught, offers basic bamboo huts along an escarpment looking over a slightly dishevelled palm grove. Further east, on a brown sand beach, Ko Wai, *Goodfeeling* (☎081/850 3410; ❷), with its reception off the main pier, offers seven cheap, basic en-suite bungalows spread across the rocky coast, with a few fronting a small, secluded beach. Electricity on the island functions generally between 6pm and 11.30pm.

## KO MAK

**Ko Mak** (sometimes spelt "Maak"), is 20km southeast of Ko Chang, and, while larger than Ko Wai and developing rapidly, still offers pockets of relaxed charm. An interior of palm and rubber plantations makes road journeys a pleasure and the colourful reefs and fishes of nearby islands are a treat for scuba divers and snorkellers (contact Koh Mak Divers, ☎085/922 5262). The palm-fringed **Ao Kao** on the southwest coast has sadly seen some recent ugly development (and a steep rise in accommodation prices) – though there remain some attractive places to stay – while long, curvy, **Ao Suan Yai**, on the northwest coast, is a beauty though also pricey. Most bungalows offer, or can arrange, motorbike (B350–400 a day) or mountain bike (B150 a day) rental and there's a small health clinic, up a lane off the road heading inland from the Ao Nid pier.

### Accommodation and nightlife

Should you be wanting to party, *Baan Sabaay*, on the Ao Kao road, has been known to get quite lively now and then.
**Baan Ing Kao** ☎0871/430020. Away from it all, on Ao Kao's far western extremity, this place exudes a quaint, village-like atmosphere and has adorable shaggy bamboo bungalows on a steep escarpment up from a pretty if rocky beach. ❸
**Island Hut** Ao Kao ☎0871/395537 A contrast to most of the developments on Ao Kao, with basic log-wall bungalows with brightly painted doors and windows, hammocks and colourful deck chairs. ❷–❸
**Sachanaree Bungalow** Ao Suan Yai ☎089/606 2413. The stand-out place to stay on Ao Suan Yai, with relatively cheap, beautifully designed bungalows in a gorgeous beachfront compound. The island post office service, internet access, money change and cash advance are all offered at *Koh Mak Resort* next door. ❹

# Southern Thailand: the Gulf coast

**Southern Thailand's Gulf coast** is famous chiefly for the three fine islands of the Samui archipelago: large and increasingly upmarket **Ko Samui**, laid-back **Ko Pha Ngan**, site of monthly full-moon parties at **Hat Rin**, and tiny **Ko Tao**, which is encircled by some of Thailand's best dive sites. Other attractions seem minor by comparison, but the historic town of **Phetchaburi** has a certain charm, and the grand old temples in **Nakhon Si Thammarat** are worth a detour.

## PHETCHABURI

Straddling the River Phet about 120km south of Bangkok, the provincial capital of **PHETCHABURI** flourished as a seventeenth-century trading post. Now a centre for sweet manufacturing, it retains much of its old-world charm, with fine historic wats, wooden shophouses and a fabulous hilltop palace.

### What to see and do

The town's central sights cluster around Chomrut Bridge (**saphaan Chomrut**) and the River Phet. About 700m east of the bridge, the still-functioning seventeenth-century **Wat Yai Suwannaram** contains a remarkable set of old faded murals, depicting divinities ranged in rows of ascending importance, and a well-preserved scripture library built on stilts over a pond. Fifteen minutes' walk east and then south from Wat Yai Suwannaram, the five crumbling stone prangs of **Wat Kamphaeng Laeng** are elegant structures of weathered earth-tone beauty. Built to enshrine Hindu deities, they were later adapted for Buddhist use. Turning west across the river, you reach Phetchaburi's most fully restored and important temple, **Wat Mahathat**, probably founded in the fourteenth century. The five landmark prangs at its heart are adorned with stucco figures of mythical creatures, while miniature angels and gods embellish the roofs of the main viharn and bot.

About thirty minutes' walk from Wat Mahathat, **Khao Wang** (B40), Rama IV's hilltop palace, is a great place to explore. Quaint brick paths undulate and wind through a forest of gnarled and twisted frangipanis, some covered in brilliant flowering vines, to a number of whitewashed, or now peeling and pleasingly mottled, wats, chedis and gazebos, as well as the king's observatory (now a moderately interesting museum) and summer house. It's reached on foot from near the western end of Thanon Rajwithi or by cable car from the western base of the hill off Highway 4 (daily 8.30am–4.30pm; B70); songthaews from Chomrut Bridge should drop you close to either access point. The hill is populated by a large number of monkeys, who can be very aggressive, so keep your distance.

### Arrival and information

**By bus** The main non-a/c bus station is on the southwest edge of Khao Wang, about thirty minutes' walk or a ten-minute songthaew ride west of the town centre. From the a/c bus terminal just off Th Rajwithi, it's about ten minutes' walk south to Chomrut Bridge.

**By train** The train station is about 500m northwest of the a/c bus terminal.

**Internet** There is an internet café 100m west of *Rabieng Rimnum Guest House* (9am–2pm).

### Accommodation

**Rabieng Rimnum (Rim Nam) Guest House** Beside Chomrut Bridge at 1 Th Chisa-in ⓣ032/425707. This is the most traveller-oriented hotel here, offering simple rooms in an old wooden house, a great restaurant looking over the river, bicycle and motorbike rental, tourist maps of Phetchaburi and tours to the nearby Kaengkrachan National Park. It can get a little loud so bring your earplugs and ask for a room away from the road. ❷

### Moving on

**By bus** to: Bangkok (every 30min; 2hr); Chumpon (3 daily; 5hr); Krabi (daily; 11hr); Phang Nga (daily; 10hr); Phuket (6 daily; 10–12hr); Ranong (daily; 7hr); Surat Thani (2 daily; 7hr), Trang (daily; 10hr).

**By train** to: Chumpon (1 morning train, 1 afternoon train, multiple evening trains; 4hr) and Surat Thani (6hr); Bangkok (3hr) there are many impossibly early trains, then one at 5am and two afternoon trains.

## CHUMPHON

**CHUMPHON** is a useful departure point for Ko Tao, but of little other interest. Thanon Sala Daeng, running north–south, is the city's main stem and a good place to orient yourself. Thanon Lomluang Chumphon, which intersects at its north, bustles to the east among the smoky food stalls and intoxicating aromas of the night market, which, should you find yourself staying overnight, is definitely worthy of an evening stroll and a feed. Fame Tour and Services (see below) offers overseas phone, money exchange, motorbike rental, fax, internet services, minibus and boat bookings and local activity/nature tours.

## Arrival

**By bus** From Bangkok or the Andaman coast, Chokeanan Tour's Bangkok–Phuket buses drop you at the Chokeanan Tour office, a few hundred metres southeast of Th Sala Daeng on the diagonally intersecting Th Phacha U-Thit. Government buses from Surat Thani and Ranong stop at the bus station, 10km south of town (B200 taxi).
**By minibus** Minibuses arrive in various parts of the city, within walking distance of Th Sala Daeng.
**By train** The train station is a few hundred metres west of Th Sala Daeng on Th Lomluan Chumphon.

## Accommodation

Chumphon's guesthouses are used to accommodating Ko Tao-bound travellers, so it's generally no problem to check into a room for half a day before catching the night boat. Most places will also store luggage.
**Chumphon Guest House** Kromluang Soi 1 ⓣ077/502900, ⓔkakaekooki@hotmail.com. Friendly place on a quiet soi, just north of the night market, with a pleasant outdoor seating area. Rooms all share facilities and the price depends on the size of the room. ❷
**Fame** 188/20-21 Th Sala Daeng ⓣ077/571077. Very basic rooms consisting of a fan, four walls, a window and mattress on the floor. The staff in the restaurant/reception downstairs are very cheerful, offering multiple travel services, and the food is good. ❶–❷
**Paradorn (Inn) Hotel** Sala Daeng Soi 4, 50m east of Th Sala Daeng ⓣ077/511500. This big, well-run place is great value. The cheapest rooms come with a/c, TV and en suite with hot water. ❸–❻

## Directory

**Banks** The main banks, with exchange counters and ATMs, are on Th Sala Daeng and Th Pracha U-Thit.
**Hospital** Viarasin Hospital (ⓣ077/503238) is west of the southern end of Th Sala Daeng, on the intersecting Th Phorramin Mankha.
**Police** North Th Sala Daeng ⓣ077/511300. For emergencies contact the tourist police (ⓣ1155).
**Post office** East of Th Sala Daeng on Th Phorramin Mankha (ⓣ077/511012).

## Moving on

**By bus** Seven Bangkok-bound government buses pass the bus station daily. Chokeanan Tour buses leave for Bangkok (3 daily), Ranong (2 daily) and Surat Thani (3 daily). Minibuses to Krabi (4hr), Ko Lanta (6hr), Railay (bus and boat; 5hr) and Ko Phi Phi (bus and boat; 5hr 30min) can be arranged at Fame (see above) and leave at 6am and/or 1pm daily.
**By train** to: Bangkok (1 around noon, then regularly 7.20pm–2.30am; 7–10hr), Phetchaburi (1 around noon, then regularly 7.20pm–2.30am; 4–5hr); Surat Thani (6 daily; 2–3hr).
**By boat** Most guesthouses sell tickets for boats to Ko Tao; otherwise, try Lomprayah (ⓣ077/570085), or Songserm (ⓣ077/506205). Passengers get free transport from Chumphon to the piers at Ao Thung Makham, Pak Nam and Noi Tha Yang. There are also slow, cheaper overnight boats: the Ko Jaroen car ferry (ⓣ077/580030) departs at 11pm daily and there's an infrequent midnight boat (ⓣ081/894 5488); both offer minibus pick ups from guesthouses for an extra B50. See p.856 for details of boats to Ko Tao.

# SURAT THANI

Uninspiring **SURAT THANI**, is of use only as the main jumping-off point for trips to Ko Samui and Ko Pha Ngan; for details on island boats, see boxes on p.846 & p.851. The east–west Thanon Ban Don hugs the river Tapi to the north of town. Here you will find Ban Don Pier, a couple of friendly restaurants and an atmospheric night market. Two blocks south, parallel Thanon Namuang bustles with retail trade while multi-laned Thanon Taladmai, the next block along, is the town's main thoroughfare with the bus terminals, Talat Kaset 1 and Talat Kaset II, a few hundred metres east of the centre.

## Arrival and information

**By bus** Most buses to Surat Thani arrive on Th Taladmai, either at Talat Kaset II, on the south side of the road, or opposite at Talat Kaset I. The bus terminal 2km southwest of the centre handles most buses from Bangkok. Small share-songthaews buzz around town, charging around B20 per person for most journeys.

**By train** The train station is at Phunphin, 13km to the west. Here you can buy a boat ticket to Ko Samui and Ko Pha Ngan, including a connecting bus to the relevant pier. Buses run into town every ten minutes till 8pm.

**By air** A minibus (B70) connects Surat Thani Airport, 21km west, with the town centre, or you can buy a bus/boat combination ticket to Ko Samui (B280) or Ko Pha Ngan (B420).

**Information** TAT (☎077/288817) is at the western end of town at 5 Th Taladmai. In front of Talat Kaset I, Phantip Travel, 293/6–8 Th Taladmai (☎077/272230, www.phantip.co.th), can arrange most of your onward travel needs.

## Accommodation

**Ban Don Hotel** 268/2 Th Namuang ☎077/272167. Offers clean en-suite rooms above a decent restaurant. ❸

**In Town Hotel** 276/1 Th Namuang ☎077/210145. Equipped with TV and en-suite bathrooms in both its fan and a/c rooms. ❸

## Eating

The outdoor night market at Ban Don Pier, on Th Ban Don, overlooking the Tapi River, has English menus and serves up delicious and very cheap Thai dishes,

**Milano** Across the road from the night market, and east a little. Authentic and reasonably priced Italian pizzas, pastas, salads and wines.

**Sweet Kitchen** A few doors west, of Milano. Passable Western breakfasts with complimentary mixed fresh apple, carrot and pineapple juices.

## Moving on

**By public bus** All long-distance buses pick up passengers at Talat Kaset II, and many heading west out of Surat also make a stop at Phunphin train station.

**Destinations**: Bangkok (1st class and VIP buses, 8.50–11am & 7.15–9pm; 10hr; 5 2nd class buses, noon–7.30pm; 10hr); Chumpon (hourly 6.30am–3pm; 3hr 30min); Krabi (hourly 5.30am–4.30pm; 3–4hr); Phang Nga (almost hourly 7am–3pm; 3hr); Phuket (almost hourly 6.40am–3pm; 5–6hr); Ranong (hourly 6am–3pm; 4hr).

**By private bus** These also leave from Talat Kaset II. Beware of scams on the more tourist-oriented routes, notably to Khao Sok and Malaysia.

**Destinations**: Chumphon (hourly 6am–5pm; 3hr); Khao Sok (every 30min; 2hr); Krabi (hourly; 3hr); Nakhon Si Thammarat (every 30min 6.30am–6pm; 1hr 30min); Phang Nga (hourly 8am–6pm; 2hr); Phuket (hourly 8am–6pm; 4hr 30min–6hr); Ranong (hourly; 3hr); Trang (hourly 7am–5.30pm; 3hr).

**By train** Train tickets can be booked through Phantip Travel (see above). Trains leave from Phunphin train station, to which a minibus departs every 5min from Talat Kaset 1.

**Destinations**: Bangkok (overnight sleepers every 1–2 hr 4.40pm–11.06pm; 11–12hr); Butterworth, Malaysia (1 daily; 10hr); Nakhon Si Thammarat (3 daily; 3hr 50min); Trang (1 daily 4hr).

**By boat** See box p.846 for transport to Ko Samui. Tickets for the Seatran Ferry are available from Seatran Holiday, Th Kanchanavithee (the east section of Thanon Talad Mai), about 1.5 km east of Talat Kaset 1 and II (☎077/275 0602, www.seatranferry.com), which also has vehicle ferries to Samui (with connecting buses), both sailing from Don Sak pier, 68km east of Surat. Phantip Travel (see above) also sells Seatran Ferry tickets and organizes buses to Dan Sak pier; Samui Tour, 326/12 Th Taladmai (☎077/282352), handles buses to Ko Samui, Ko Pha Ngan and Ko Tao via the Raja Vehicle Ferries at Don Sak. Contact Phangan Tour, also on Th Taladmai (☎077/205799) and ADV on Th Namuang (☎077/205 4189) for Songserm Express Boats to Ko Samui, Ko Pha Ngan and Ko Tao (and from there to Chumphon), departing from the pier at Pak Nam Tapi, on the east side of Surat town.

**By air** Thai Airways and Air Asia run flights to Bangkok and beyond from Surat Thani airport, which can booked with Phantip Travel (see above). Minibuses to the airport leave from Phantip Travel, with one departure for each flight.

# KO SAMUI

An ever-widening cross-section of visitors, from globetrotting backpackers to suitcase-toting fortnighters, comes to southern Thailand just for the beautiful beaches of **Ko Samui**, 80km from Surat Thani. At 15km across and down, Samui is generally large enough to cope with this diversity, except during the Christmas and New Year rush. The island's paradise sands and clear blue seas are fringed by palm trees, but development behind the beaches is extensive and often thoughtless. Frequent ferries serve the island: for details, see the box below.

The northeast monsoon blows heaviest here in November, but can bring rain at any time between October and January. January is often breezy, March and April are very hot, and between May and October the southwest monsoon blows mildly onto Samui's west coast and causes a little rain.

### Na Thon

The island capital, **NA THON** is a frenetic half-built town that most travellers use only for stocking up with supplies en route to the beaches. The two piers come to land at the promenade, Thanon Chonvithi, which is paralleled first by narrow Thanon Ang Thong, then by Thanon Taweeratpakdee (or Route 4169), the round-island road.

### Maenam

The four-kilometre arced bay of **Maenam**, 13km from Na Thon, with its leafy, relatively unadulterated beachfront, is an attractive location for a day or two of sand, sun and relaxation. Inland, the village is ugly, but a number of quiet, budget beachside accommodations, offering great views of the bay, make Maenam Samui's most popular destination for budget travellers. There is a post office and a police station on the highway, east of the pier.

### Bophut, Bangrak (Big Buddha Beach) and Choeng Mon

The next beach east of Maenam, quiet, 2km-long **Bophut**, with a wider beach and welcoming clear water, is becoming steadily more upmarket, with a plethora of expensive resorts and a distinct absence of budget accommodation. Its

#### TRAVEL TO AND FROM KO SAMUI

The most obvious way of getting to Ko Samui is on a **boat** from the **Surat Thani** area.

**The night boat**: The longest established boat, it leaves **Ban Don pier** in Surat Thani for Na Thon – the main port on Samui – at 11pm daily (7hr); tickets (B200) are sold at the pier on the day of departure.

**Express boat**: From **Pak Nam Tapi pier**, on the east side of Surat, one Songserm Express Boat a day runs to Na Thon, Ko Samui (8am; 2hr 30min; B200 including transport from ADV's office in Surat). Travel agents at the train station sell ADV tickets, with commission – price includes transportation from the station to the pier.

**Vehicle ferries**: Seatran vehicle ferries run from **Don Sak pier**, 68km east of Surat, to Na Thon (hourly 5am–7pm; buses leave 1hr 30min before boat departure from Surat and 1hr 45min before from the train station; B110, or B180 including bus from Surat. Raja vehicle ferries run hourly between Don Sak and Thong Yang pier, on Ko Samui, 9km south of Na Thon (hourly 5am–7pm; 1hr 30min; B110 for passenger only, B325 with vehicle); buy tickets from Samui Tour (Surat Thani office ⓣ077/282353; Ko Samui office ⓣ077/415230). Samui Tour also run buses from Surat or the train station to Don Sak, and, once on Ko Samui, from Thong Yang Pier to Na Thon, charging B200 total. Note that the total journey time from Surat using the vehicle ferries from Don Sak is much the same as with Songserm from Pak Nam Tapi.

**From Ko Samui**: For information about boats from Ko Samui to **Ko Pha Ngan** and **Ko Tao**, see p.851 & p.856; all offer the same service in the return direction.

**By air**: You can fly to Samui direct from Bangkok (1hr 30min) with Bangkok Airways (24 daily; Bangkok ⓣ022/655555; Samui Airport ⓣ077/245 6018) or Thai Airways (2 daily). Bangkok Airways also flies from Samui to Phuket (1–2 daily), Singapore (Mon, Wed, Fri & Sat), Hong Kong (Mon, Wed & Fri) and Kuala Lumpur (Tues & Sun).

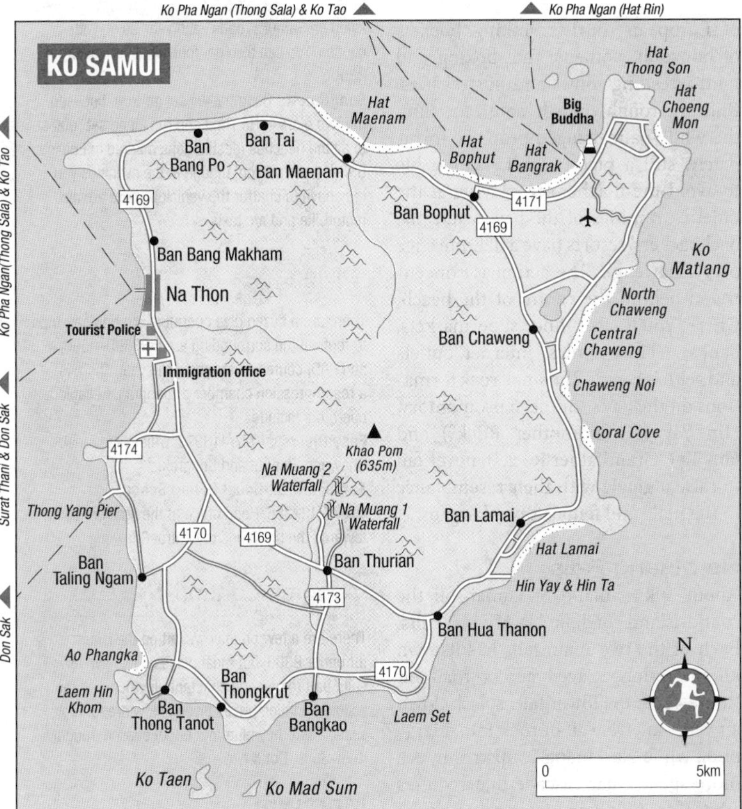


narrow beach road is surprisingly quaint however, with a number of attractive, traditional Thai wooden buildings.

**Bangkrak** is also known as Big Buddha Beach, after the huge **Big Buddha** statue on a small island in the bay, which gazes down on the sunbathers populating its less than perfect beach. A short causeway leads to a clump of souvenir shops and food stalls in front of the temple, and ceremonial dragon-steps lead to the terrace around the statue, from where there's a fine view of the sweeping north coast. After Bangrak comes the high-kicking boot of the northeastern cape and beautiful **Choeng Mon**, whose white sandy beach is lined with casuarina trees and served by songthaews.

## Chaweng

For sheer natural beauty, none of the other beaches can match **Chaweng**, with its gently sloping six-kilometre strip of white sand framed between the small island of Ko Matlang at the north end and the headland above Coral Cove in the south. Of course, such beauty has heavy development and high accommodation prices. There is also a thumping nightlife and diverse watersports. An ugly village of amenities stretches for two kilometres behind the central section.

## Lamai and around

Although **Lamai** is less heavily developed than Chaweng, its nightlife is if anything tawdrier, with planeloads of European tourists sinking buckets of booze at women's Thai boxing and mud-wrestling shows and hostess bars. Running roughly north–south for 4km, the white palm-fringed beach is, fortunately, still a picture, and it's possible to avoid the mayhem by staying at the quiet extremities of the bay, where the backpackers' resorts have a definite edge over Chaweng's. The action is concentrated behind the centre of the beach, where you'll also find supermarkets, banks, ATMs, clinics, internet outlets and vehicle rental. The small rock formations on the bay's southern promontory, Hin Yay ("Grandmother Rock") and Hin Ta ("Grandfather Rock"), never fail to raise a giggle with their resemblance to the male and female sexual organs.

### Na Muang Falls

About 10km inland of Lamai, off the round-island road, lie **Na Muang Falls**. Each of the two main falls has its own kilometre-long paved access road off Route 4169: the lower falls splash down a twenty-metre wall of rock into a large pool, while Na Muang 2, upstream, is a more spectacular cascade that requires a bit of foot-slogging from the car park (about 15min uphill); alternatively, you can walk up there from Na Muang 1, by taking the 1.5km trail that begins 300m back along the access road from the lower fall. From the entrance to Na Muang 1, you can also take forty-minute elephant rides that take in Na Muang 2 Falls (B700 per person).

## Information and island transport

**Tourist information** TAT runs a small but helpful office (Ⓣ077/420504), tucked away on an unnamed side road in Na Thon, north of the pier and inland from the post office. Another useful source of information is Ⓦwww.samui.sawadee.com, which allows direct booking at a range of hotels on the island.

**Motorbikes** You can rent motorbikes (from B200) at all main beaches, though note that dozens are killed on Samui's roads each year, so go with caution. You can also get four-wheel drives (from B800).

**Songthaews** Songthaews set off from between the two piers in Na Thon and run along set routes to all the beaches (destinations marked in English; B30–50 per person, though in the evenings you may have to charter the vehicle). There are also motorbike and a/c taxis.

## Diving

There are a dozen dive operators offering day-trips to reefs in the surrounding area (B3800–4500) and PADI courses throughout the year. There is a recompression chamber at Bangrak. Reliable operators include:

**Easy Divers** Ⓣ077/413373. Offices in Lamai, Chaweng, Bophut and Bangrak.

**Samui International Diving School** Ⓣ077/422386. Head office at the *Malibu Resort* towards the north end of central Chaweng.

## Accommodation

There are a few bungalows left on the island for under B300, but most places now have en-suite bathrooms and constant electricity. All the accommodation prices given below are for high season, but they plummet out of season (roughly April–June, Oct & Nov).

### Maenam

The eastern end of the bay offers the best choice of budget accommodation.

**Moonhut** Near the village, just east of the pier Ⓣ077/425247, Ⓦkohsamui.com/moonhut. Sits in a sandy plot, with lush gardens and substantial bungalows, all en-suite, some with hot water and a/c. ❹–❼

**Morning Glory** At the east end of the bay Ⓣ087/277 5476. This place is a laid-back old-timer, with basic wooden huts in a shady compound. There's a characterful bar/restaurant/reception with a pool table and live bands on Mon and Thurs eves. It's poorly signed – turn towards the beach at the sign advertising *Rainbow Bungalow.* ❸

**New Star Villa** On the far eastern end of the bay Ⓣ077/332001, Ⓔnewstarapartments@hotmail.com. Basic, slightly musty bungalows, but redeemed by the cool shade of the large restaurant/bar area, with its pool table, cushioned "movie zone" and ocean view. ❷

**SR** On the same access road as *New Star Villa* Ⓣ077/427529. Clean, quiet and welcoming with abundant plant life, nice views of the bay and a very good restaurant. Cement bungalows with fan or a/c, all en suite. ❸–❺

**Shangrilah** On an access road 500m west of the village ⓣ077/425189, ⓦwww.geocities.com/pk_shangrilah. Friendly place in a grassy compound on the nicest stretch of sand on Maenam. Smart, en-suite bungalows with rustic balconies, plus a hidden cluster of ugly cement luxury villas. ❸–❽

### Bophut, Bangrak and Choeng Mon

**Cactus** Access from the highway, west of Bophut ⓣ077/245565, ⓔcactusbung@hotmail.com. Cacti, earth tones and organic contours combine to generate an inviting beachfront restaurant and selection of beautiful bungalows in a lovely garden. ❺–❼

**O'Soleil** ⓣ077/425239, ⓔosoleil@loxinfo.co.th. Cement bungalows with interiors ranging from functional, clean and basic to the semi-luxurious. The elegant Thai/French design of the beachside timber restaurant/reception building, with its casuarina shaded deck and good European food, is a bonus. ❸–❼

**Shambala** Bangrak ⓣ077/425330. Well-designed and maintained timber bungalows; the relaxed restaurant fronts a lush green garden filled with cushioned decks and gazebos. Proximity to Bangrak pier makes it a good base for the return speedboat service to full-moon parties. ❹–❺

### Chaweng

Over fifty bungalow resorts and hotels at Chaweng are squeezed into thin strips running back from the beachfront.

**Lucky Mother Bungalows** North Chaweng ⓣ077/230931. Simple, attractive, log cabin-style bungalows, with slightly decrepit but bearable interiors. They face the dirt path perpendicular to the beach. Pay more for the stylish modern numbers at the back. ❹–❼

**Rattana Guest House and Bungalow** North Chaweng, 50m back from the beach, behind Marine Resort ⓣ077/422441, ⓦwww.rattanaguesthouse.com. Three-storey buildings around a palm-filled garden. The cheapest rooms are rather plain, with bathroom and fan. ❹–❼

**Samui Coconut Grove Mandalay** North central Chaweng ⓣ077/422340. This long but rather ugly building stretching down to the beach offers beautifully furnished, relatively cheap rooms. There are also two rows of wonderfully designed but expensive polished wooden bungalows to its side. ❻

**Somwang House** ⓣ077/422269. Basic but clean wooden bungalows, all en suite, in a long line running back from the beach – unfortunately looking over the unpretty exterior of *Samui Coconut Grove Mandalay*. ❹–❻

**Your Place Resort** At the far north of Chaweng ⓣ077/230039. The best budget accommodation going, with very clean and comfortable bungalows set around a grassy palm grove. The tiered restaurant has tables and chairs on the beach. ❸–❺

### Lamai and around

Lamai's budget accommodation is concentrated around the beach's northern and southern ends.

**Beer House** In the central section of the northern part of the beach ⓣ077/230467. A hidden, single-storey cement building at the back holds a row of down-at-heel but very cheap rooms. Pay more for the very appealing bungalows in its lush, shaded compound. ❷–❺

**Green Villa** 150m inland, at the far southern end of the bay ⓣ077/424296, ⓦEresagreenvilla@hotmail.com. Offers a selection of cute wooden en-suite bungalows with dilapidated interiors, compensated by its tranquil, tropical garden and central, clear-blue swimming pool. ❸–❹

**New Hut** *Beer House's* northern neighbour ⓣ077/424298. A rustic restaurant/reception area combines with cheap, attractive but cramped thatched bungalows with mattress, fan and mosquito net. Located in a sandy, palm-filled compound wedged between the beach and a lagoon. ❸

**Sunrise Bungalow and Soul Spa** At the far southern tip of the beach, on the access road to Hat Yai and Hat Yin ⓣ077/424433, ⓦwww.sunrisebungalow.com. A luxury resort offering three clean, and very appealing, budget huts in green and sumptuous surrounds. Be sure to book in advance. ❸–❽

**Surat Palm Resort** A few hundred metres further north than *Sunrise Bungalow* ⓣ077/418608, ⓔkjorlux@yahoo.com. Immaculate and beautifully furnished wooden bungalows tightly packed into a garden. ❹–❼

**White Sand** On the same access road as *Green Villa* ⓣ077/424298. Long-established, laid-back budget place with attractive but very basic beachside wooden huts, the cheapest with shared (somewhat inadequate) bathroom facilities. ❶–❺

## Eating

### Chaweng

For cheap Thai food, join local workers at the evening food stalls of Laem Din market, on the road between the heart of central Chaweng and Ban Chaweng.

**Betelnut** Soi Colibri, to the south. It's a long trek from listed accommodation but the exceptional (if a little expensive) Californian/Thai fusion here makes any effort worthwhile. Furthermore, the Samui Institute of Thai Culinary Arts (across the road from *Betelnut*) offers a fantastic Thai cookery course (Ⓣ077/413172).

**Ninja Crepes** Central/south Chaweng. This ugly, tiled, place has a dedicated expat clientele and offers cheap, good quality Western and Thai meals along with sweet and savoury crepes.

**Via Via** Central Chaweng. This authentic Italian restaurant's sleek modern design of polished wood and stone boasts a wood-fired brick oven, which produces delicious thin-crust pizzas for a very appreciative public. There is tasty pasta and plenty of ice cream as well.

### Lamai

**Eldorado** Just west of the central crossroads. Good-value Swedish restaurant, serving a few Thai favourites and all manner of tasty international mains.

**Ninja Crepes** Similar in appearance and quality to its twin in Chaweng (see above). The eponymous crepe is a sweet milky rice and fresh mango crepe sensation.

**The Spa Resort Restaurant** North Chaweng, on Highway 4169. With a strong health focus, this place offers a wide selection of delicious, reasonably priced Western, Mexican and Thai meals and lots of vegetarian options.

## Drinking and nightlife

The best place to drink in Chaweng is on the beach, especially towards its north end.

**Bauhaus** Near the central crossroads, Lamai. This sprawling barn-like entertainment complex was once the nightlife's core, but its popularity is waning.

**Green Mango** North-central Chaweng. A long-standing megaclub in a massive multi-zoned industrial shed with tropical garden touches. From midnight.

**The Reggae Pub** Bang in the heart of central Chaweng, inland from the main road. Samui's oldest nightclub is an unpretentious good-time venue that kicks off around midnight.

**Samui Shamrock** Next door to *Bauhaus*, Lamai. Very popular place with live music, generally consisting of reasonable quality local cover bands with the occasional original group passing through.

## Directory

**Books** Nathon Book Stores on Thanon Na Amphoe, Na Thon, is a good secondhand bookshop.

**Car rental** Budget car-rental outlet on Highway 4169, opposite the gas station (Ⓣ077/413384, Ⓦwww.budget.co.th).

**Hospital** 3km south of Na Thon on Route 4169 and right on to Route 4172 (Ⓣ077/421230).

**Immigration office** Na Thon (Ⓣ077/421069), and also on Route 4172.

**Pharmacy** Boots, opposite Starbucks, Chaweng.

**Post office** At the northern end of the promenade, Na Thon (Mon–Fri 8.30am–4.30pm, Sat & Sun 9am–noon); also has an international phone service and Catnet internet access upstairs (8.30am–4.30pm). At Chaweng, there is another post office 1km inland on Highway 4169 (the round-island road).

**Tourist police** 1km south of town on Route 4169, Na Thon (Ⓣ1699, or 077/421281), and near Chawengburi Resort, Chaweng (Ⓣ1699).

**Travel agent** Travel Solutions, Chaweng (Ⓣ077/230203, Ⓦwww.travelsolutions.co.th).

# ANG THONG NATIONAL MARINE PARK

It's possible to buy tickets at any of the beaches on Samui for boat trips to **Ang Thong National Marine Park** (B1200 including entry to the national park, or B1800 all-in by speedboat – most include snorkelling), a gorgeous group of 42 small islands, 30km west of Samui. Boats generally leave Na Thon or Bophut at 8.30am and return at 5.30pm. First stop on any boat tour is usually Ko Wua Talab, site of the park headquarters, from where it's a steep 430-metre climb (about 1hr return; bring walking sandals or shoes) to the island's peak and fine panoramic views. The feature that gives the park the name Ang Thong, meaning "Golden Bowl", is a landlocked lake, 250m in diameter, on Ko Mae Ko to the north of Ko Wua Talab; it was the inspiration for the setting of Alex Garland's cult bestseller, *The Beach*. A well-laid path (30min return) leads from the beach through natural rock tunnels to the rim of the cliff wall encircling the lake, which is connected to the sea by an underground tunnel. Most day-trip boats now carry a few desultory kayaks on board, but if you are interested in **kayaking**, it's best to go to one of the two dedicated operators (see p.874).

## KO PHA NGAN

In recent years, backpackers have tended to move over to Ko Samui's little sibling, **Ko Pha Ngan**, 20km to the north, but the island still has a simple atmosphere, mostly because the lousy road system is an impediment to the developers. With dense jungle covering its inland mountains and rugged granite outcrops along the coast, Pha Ngan lacks sweeping beaches, but it does have some coral and a few beautiful, sheltered bays, including **Hat Rin**, a pilgrimage site for ravers.

### Thong Sala and Wat Khao Tham

**THONG SALA** is a port of entrance and little more. In front of the piers, transport to the rest of the island (songthaews, jeeps and motorbike taxis) congregates by a dusty row of banks, travellers' restaurants, supermarkets, dive centres and motorbike and jeep rental places.

The island's south coast is lined with bungalows, but it's hard to recommend staying here as the beaches are mediocre by Thai standards. On a quiet hillside above Ban Tai, 4km east of Thong Sala, however, **Wat Khao Tham** holds ten-day meditation retreats with farang teachers most months of the year (B4500 per person to cover food; min age 20). Space is limited, so pre-register. For further information, go to Ⓦwww.watkowtahm.org.

### Hat Rin

Although known for its **full-moon parties** (see box, p.853), there's a more sedate side to **Hat Rin**'s alternative scene, with old and new-age hippies packing out the t'ai chi, yoga and meditation classes. It's not all so chilled out unfortunately, as drugs are rife and dodgy pills and mushroom teas send an average of two farangs a month into psychiatric care. The local authorities have set up a permanent police box at Hat Rin, and instigate regular bungalow searches and roadblocks, drafting in scores of police, both uniformed and plain-clothed, on full-moon nights.

### TRAVEL TO AND FROM KO PHA NGAN

**From Surat Thani** An overnight ferry leaves Ban Don pier in Surat Thani at 11pm every night for Thong Sala (7hr; B200); tickets are available from the pier on the day of departure.
**From Don Sak** There are five vehicle ferries daily (7am–5.50pm; 2hr 30min; B200) and one Songserm Express Boat a day (via Ko Samui; 8am; 4hr; B200). There's also one extra boat a day for the three days before and three days after the full moon party, departing at 2pm. All the above include bus transport to the pier from Surat Thani.
**From Ko Samui** two Songserm Express Boats a day do the 45-minute trip from Na Thon to Thong Sala (11am & 5pm; B200), while Seatran does the same voyage in thirty minutes (8am & 1pm; B250). A car ferry departs Na Thon for Thong Sala at 5pm (passenger B110; 1hr) while an express boat leaves Bangrak Pier for Thong Sala at 8am and 1.30pm (B350). Speedboats from Bangrak, Bophut and Maenam (depart 8.30am; B250) and the Lomprayah catamaran from Maenam (8am & 12.30pm; B250) call in at Thong Sala on their way to Ko Tao. From Bangrak, four passenger boats a day (10.30am, 1.30pm, 4pm & 6.30pm) take an hour to cross to Hat Rin (B150).
**From Ko Tao** Five kinds of vessel currently run between Ko Pha Ngan and Ko Tao: one Songserm Express Boat a day (12.30am; 2hr; B250); the Ko Tao Express Boat (10am; B350); the Lomprayah catamaran twice a day (9.30am & 3pm; 1hr; B350); and Samui Marine Recreation, once a day (12.30pm; 3hr 30min; B200); and at least one speedboat a day (50min–1hr; B350).

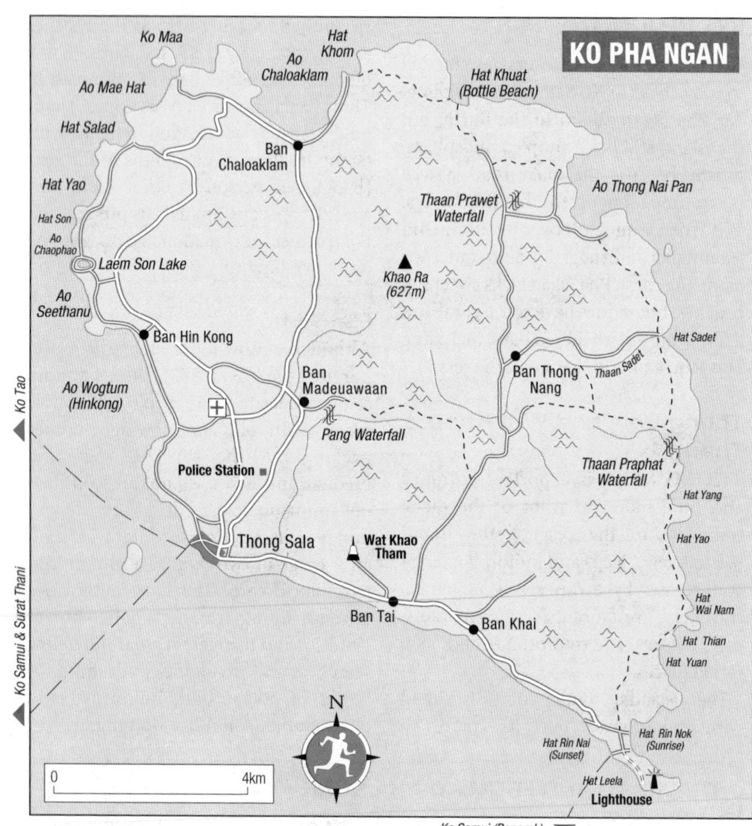


Hat Rin comprises two back-to-back beaches, joined by transverse roads at the north and south ends. The main, eastern beach, usually referred to as **Sunrise** or Hat Rin Nok and lined with bars, restaurants and bungalows, is a classic curve of fine sand between two rocky slopes. With so much boat traffic and its disturbing role as a public urinal at full-moon time, though, these days its waters are far from limpid. **Sunset** beach (Hat Rin Nai) is usually littered with flotsam, but has plenty of quieter accommodation.

## The east coast

North of Hat Rin, no roads run along the rocky, exposed **east coast**, only a rough, steep, fifteen-kilometre trail, which starts from Hat Rin's northern transverse road (signposted). About ninety minutes up the trail (also accessible in 10–15min by longtail boats from Sunrise), the small, sandy bays of Hat Yuan and the picturesque **Hat Thian** make a quiet alternative to Hat Rin.

**Ao Thong Nai Pan** is a beautiful, sandy bay, good for swimming and backed by steep, green hills. It supports a few shops, dive outfits and restaurants. Jeeps connect with boats at Thong Sala every day and a bumpy dirt road winds the 12km from Ban Tai on the south coast, though not if there's very heavy rain.

## The north coast

**Ao Chaloaklam** is the largest bay on the **north coast,** with a vibrant fishing

## THE FULL MOONERS

The monthly **full-moon parties** on Hat Rin are famous around the world, attracting up to ten thousand revellers to the beach. As there are only around three thousand rooms on the whole island, you should arrive a day or more early. Alternatively, forget about sleep altogether and join one of the many **party boats** from Ko Samui (about B450 per person), which usually leave between 9pm and midnight and return between 3.30am and dawn.

On the night, *Paradise* styles itself as the party host, but the mayhem spreads along most of Sunrise Beach, fuelled by hastily erected drinks stalls and sound systems. For somewhere to chill, head for *Mellow Mountain Bar*, which occupies a great position up in the rocks on the north side of Sunrise; the *Back Yard* club, up the hill behind the southern end of Sunrise, hosts the morning-after.

village and fine sweep of white sand to its east, where most of the budget accommodation is. To the west, the village has ramshackle charm and, free of tourist clutter you might find yourself in the company of local Thais with very little concern for the tourist dollar. Ao Chaloaklam can easily be reached by songthaew or motorbike taxi from Thong Sala, 10km away. If the sea is not too rough, longtail boats run three times a day for most of the year from the village of **Ban Chaloaklam** to the lovely, secluded **Hat Khuat** (Bottle Beach); you could also walk there in about ninety minutes along a testing trail from Hat Khom.

### The west coast

Pha Ngan's **west coast** is lush and mountainous with good sunset views over the islands to the west; reefs, enclosing most of the bays, keep the sea too shallow for a decent swim, however, especially between May and October. **Ao Seethanu**, while nondescript to its south, has a wide stretch of sand to the north, with a number of budget bungalows operations and an invariably relaxed atmosphere. Round the next headland, **Ao Chaophao**, with its narrow beach and densely foliaged beachfront, is a nice place to relax, but tends to accumulate a line of seaweed along the shore.

Beyond Chaophao, the long, gently curved beach of **Hat Yao**, with its soft white sand and clear waters, is becoming deservedly, and detrimentally, more popular – it's suffering from overcrowding and an increase in ugly cement development. Here you will find several bars and restaurants, diving outfits, supermarkets and Jeep (about B1000 per day) and bike (B200 per day) rental.

## Information

The *Koh Phangan Guide* (ⓦwww.phangan.info) booklet is available at the pier and most travel agents. While very much a commercial venture, it has a lot of useful info. Also check out ⓦwww .kohphangan.com.

## Accommodation

### Hat Rin

On the west side of the headland, palm-fringed Hat Leela, a twenty-minute walk along a well-signposted route from *Paradise* is a slightly quieter alternative to Sunset and Sunrise beaches.

**Coco Hut Village** Hat Leela ⓣ077/375368, ⓦwww.cocohut.com. A bit like a Coca-Cola commercial, with crowds of hip twenty-somethings parading about the wide stretch of sandy beach, vast, multi-tiered decking and palm-ringed pool. The stylish bungalows here are exorbitant but the much cheaper shared facility rooms are good value. ❹–❽

**Leela Beach Bungalows** Hat Leela ⓣ019/951304, ⓦwww.leelabeach.com. With plenty of space under the palm trees and half of the beach to themselves, these sturdy, no-frills bungalows have mosquito nets and en-suite bathrooms – a good travellers' option. ❸

**Paradise** Southern Sunrise ⓣ077/375 2445. Site of the first full moon party, with a continuing central role in the proceedings, this well-established place is best suited to vampires and party animals as night-time sleep is near impossible. All rooms and bungalows are en suite and some of the hillside options offer fine views. ❸–❻
**Sarikantang** Hat Leela ⓣ077/375055. A boutique resort with spa, swimming pool and luxurious accommodation; offers seventeen good-value "budget option" bungalows. ❹–❾
**Sun Cliff Resort** High up on the tree-lined slope above the south end of Sunset ⓣ077/375134. Friendly place with great views and a range of well-maintained bungalows, some with hot water and a/c. ❸–❽

## The east coast

**Haad Tien Resort** Hat Thian ⓣ086/953 7122. In a massive palm tree grove, with quaint wooden bungalows with cute open-air bathrooms. ❷
**Pingjun** South Beach, Ao Thong Nai Pan ⓣ077/445062. Large en-suite bungalows with wrap-around balconies on a green, palm-filled lawn stretching back from the beach. ❸
**The Sanctuary** Hat Thian ⓣ081/271 3614, ⓦwww.thesanctuarythailand.com. This magical fairyland, connected by a labyrinth of dirt paths, offers a huge range of basic to luxury en-suite bungalows built into the lush promontory, along with dorm accommodation (B100). It also hosts courses in yoga and meditation, and has a massage and beauty spa as well as a fasting and cleansing centre. The beautiful timber restaurant, built into massive granite boulders, serves up great Thai and Western food. ❸–❾
**Star Huts** North Beach, Ao Thong Nai Pan ⓣ077/299005. This place has attractive bamboo/timber bungalows with spacious, furnished balconies and immaculate interiors. ❺–❼

## The north coast

**Coral Bay** On a grassy promontory that divides Chaloaklam from Hat Khom ⓣ077/374245. Offers beautifully designed stained timber bungalows, most with great views of Hat Khom. ❷–❸
**North Beach Bungalow** East Ao Chaloaklam ⓣ077/374258. Situated in a beachfront grove, with gorgeous woven bamboo bungalows equipped with hammocks and shell mobiles hanging from spacious balconies. There are also free snorkelling equipment, fishing expeditions and an atmospheric restaurant and bar. ❺–❻
**Smile Resort** Bottle Beach ⓣ081/956 3133. Set on a rocky, flower-strewn slope on the western side of the beach; has basic, yellow-bamboo bungalows with en-suite bathrooms. ❸–❹

## The west coast

**Ibiza** Hat Yao ⓣ077/349121, ⓦwww.ibizabungalows.com. A soft, white-sand beach meets spacious green lawns filled with palm trees and shrubs and clusters of bamboo, timber and cement en-suite bungalows, some with hot water and a/c. ❷–❺
**Loy Fah** Ao Seethanu ⓣ077/377319. A well-run place, commanding fine views from its position on the southern promontory. There's also a pool table, fuzz ball, free snorkelling equipment, kayak rental and an agent offering transport, boat trips, scuba diving and fishing expeditions. ❹–❽
**Sea Flower** Ao Chaophao ⓣ077/349090. In a spectacular tropical garden palm grove with an expansive octagonal timber restaurant that serves great food. The cheapest rooms are charming thatched bungalows and there's a bar hut by the beach. ❷–❽
**Seaview Rainbow** Ao Seethanu ⓣ077/349084. A wide stretch of beach greets spacious and clean timber and brick en-suite bungalows. There's a laid-back backpackers atmosphere here and friendly young staff. ❷

## Directory

In the dense tourist village of **Hat Rin** you will easily find clinics, supermarkets, travel agents, motorbike rental places (from B200 per day), overseas phone facilities, dozens of internet outlets and plenty of ATMs and currency exchange booths. All facilities below are in Thong Sala, unless otherwise stated.
**Books** Try the two Book Corners; one behind Sunrise, near the school, the other on the southern transverse.
**Diving** Phangan Divers (ⓣ077/375117, ⓦwww.phangandivers.com) near the Sunset pier, has trips to Sail Rock and the Ang Thong Marine Park – also has outlets in Thong Nai Pan, Hat Yao and Ko Ma, just north of Hat Yao.
**Hospital** In Hat Rin, the Bandon International Hospital lies on the southern transverse, near the pier (ⓣ077/375471; open 24hr); also 3km north of Thong Sala, on the road towards Mae Hat (ⓣ077/377034).
**Kitesurfing** Cuttlebone Kitesurfing, Ao Ban Taii (ⓣ081/940 1902), runs great kitesurfing classes.
**Police station** Nearly 2km up the Ban Chaloaklam Rd from Thong Sala (ⓣ077/377114).
**Post office** One (barely recognizable) on the southern transverse near the pier on Sunset, and

another on the coastal road heading east to Hat Rin (Mon–Fri 8.30am–noon & 1–4.30pm, Sat 9am–noon).

**Travel agent** The English-Thai Backpackers Information Centre, behind *Paradise* (10am–11pm; ⓣ089/471 7419, ⓦwww.backpackersthailand.com), provides a friendly, reliable service.

## KO TAO

Forty kilometres north of Ko Pha Ngan, small, forested **Ko Tao** is the last and most remote island of the archipelago, with a long curve of classic beach on its west side and secluded rocky coves along its east coast. Famed for its low-

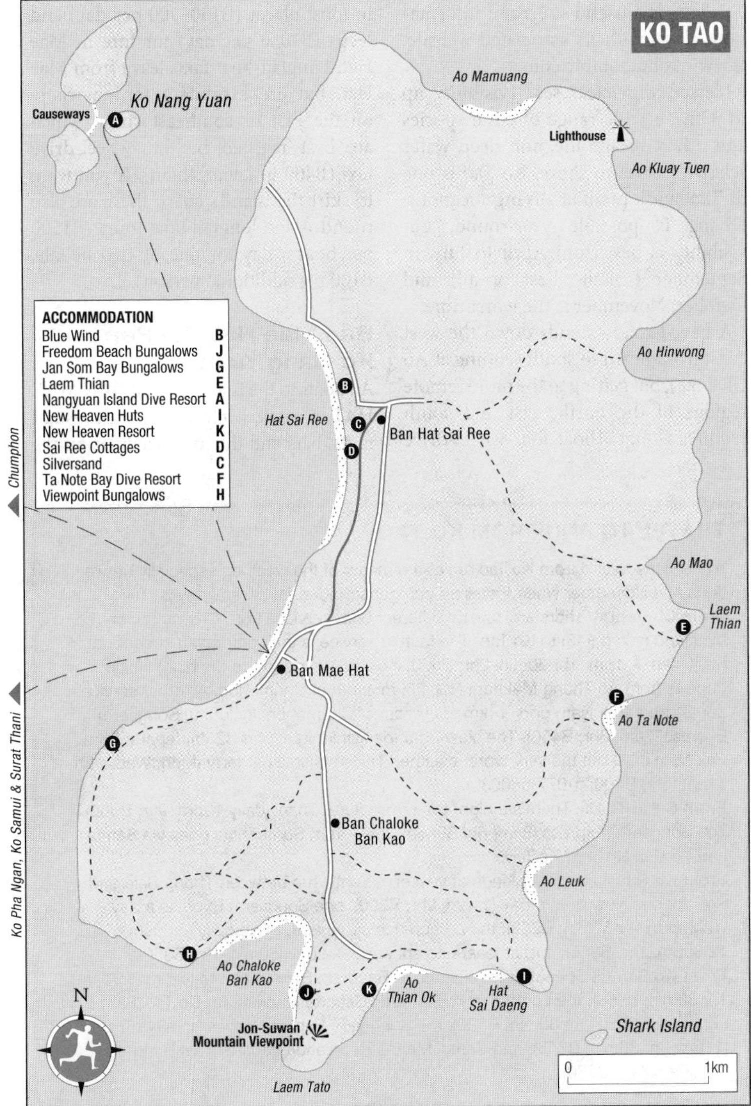

key bungalows, it's a popular travellers' destination, especially from December to March. Ko Tao feels the southwest monsoon more than Samui and Pha Ngan, so June to October can have strong winds and rain; some of its hundred or so bungalow operations close from June to August. The regularly updated and widely available free booklet, *Ko Tao Info*, is a useful source of information, along with its associated website, Ⓦwww.kohtaoonline.com.

Blessed with clear seas (visibility up to 35m), a wide range of coral species and other marine life, and deep water relatively close to shore, Ko Tao is one of Thailand's premier **diving** locations. Diving is possible year-round, but visibility is best from April to July, in September (usually best of all) and October; November is the worst time.

A paved road extends down the west coast from north to south (ending at Ao Chaloke), but getting to the more remote regions of the north, east and south requires a longtail boat, four-wheel-drive taxi, quad-bike (B800 per day) or trail bike (B300 per day). Only experienced trail bike riders should attempt these tortuous and steep dirt paths, however: 50-degree ascents and descents do not treat inexperience kindly. For paved road transport, motorbike taxis and pickups are available (B50–100 per person, more late at night) as well as mopeds for rent in most places (B150–200 per day) and Jeeps (B1000 per day) for hire in Mae Hat. Longtail-boat taxis leave from Mae Hat, but are exorbitant for anywhere on the east or southeast coast, which are best reached by four-wheel-drive taxi (B400 to Laem Thian). If you want to skirt the island's coast, there are also round-island longtail boat tours (B1500 per boat a day for one or two people, B100 per additional person).

## Ban Mae Hat, Sai Ree and Ko Nang Yuan

All boats to the island dock at **BAN MAE HAT**, a small, lively village with restaurants, bars and the most facilities on the

### TRAVEL TO AND FROM KO TAO

All services to and from Ko Tao are at the mercy of the weather, especially between June and November when travellers can get stranded for several days.

**From Chumpon:** There are several different boat services from Chumphon on the mainland (see p.843) to Ko Tao. The fastest service is the Lomprayah speedboat (daily 7am & 1pm; 1hr 30min–2hr; B550, including transport to the pier), which departs from Ao Thung Makham Noi, 25km south of Chumphon. All other services depart from Pak Nam port, 14km southeast of Chumphon, including Songserm Express (7am; 3hr; B450). The slow boat (daily midnight; 6hr; B250) departs from Pak Nam in all but the very worst weather. There's also a car ferry (Mon, Wed & Fri 11pm; 6hr; B300; Ⓣ077/580030).

**From Surat Thani:** There's a night boat from Surat Thani (daily 10pm; 9hr; B500). The Songserm Express (8am; 6hr 30min; B550) from Surat Thani goes via Samui and Ko Pha Ngan to Ko Tao.

**From Ko Pha Ngan:** Four kinds of vessel currently run between Thong Sala and Ko Tao: one slow boat a day (11am; 3hr; B200); one Songserm Express a day (12.30pm; 1hr 30min; B250); the Lomprayah catamaran twice daily (8.30am & 12:30pm; 1hr; B350); and at least one speedboat a day (50min–1hr; B350).

**From Ko Samui:** Speedboats originate at Bangrak, Bophut and Maenam (8.30am; 1hr 30min; B550); the Lomprayah catamaran departs Maenam for Ko Tao (8am & noon; 1hr 30min–2hr 30min; B580); the Songserm Express leaves from Na Thon (11am; 2hr 30min; B345); and Samui Marine Recreation departs from Bangrak (10.30am; 2hr; B550).

island. On the roads leading inland from the main pier and the neighbouring Seatran pier, and on the narrow coastal road that extends north and south of them, you'll find bars, restaurants, cafes, bakeries, internet, motorbike rental, ATMs, photoprinting facilities and more.

To the north of Mae Hat, **Hat Sai Ree**'s two-kilometre strip of white sand is Ko Tao's only long beach. While the beach is almost lost at high tide the water sparkles and shines and there's ample beachfront foliage. Over twenty attractive bungalow resorts have set up shop here, and a small village, **BAN HAT SAI REE**, with bars, restaurants, internet outlets, clinics, supermarkets and a bank with ATM, has evolved at its northern end.

One kilometre off the northwest of Ko Tao, the three tiny islands of **Ko Nang Yuan**, arguably one of the prettiest sites in Thailand, are encircled by a ring of coral, and joined by a causeway of fine white sand. Boats from Mae Hat run back and forth three times a day; day-trippers are charged B100 to land on the island, and cans and plastic bottles are banned.

**TREAT YOURSELF**

The **Jamahkiri Spa and Resort** (Ⓣ066/7745 6400, Ⓦwww.jamahkiri.com) in Ban Mae Hat, on the road leading inland from the Seatran pier, offers top-notch spa treatments in a paradise setting on the south coast. It's a truly exceptional coastal resort, with organic architecture and landscaping, luxury bungalows and a tiered pool that blend with the arching coastline, vast blue ocean and the granite boulders that grace the coastal slope. A two-and-a-half hour treatment including steam sauna, aloe vera body wrap, facial massage and Thai massage, and four-wheel-drive transfer is B1550.

### The east and south coasts

The sheltered inlets of the **east coast**, most of them containing one or two sets of bungalows, can be reached by boat, pick-up or four-wheel-drive. In the middle of the coast, the dramatic tiered promontory of **Laem Thian** shelters a tiny beach and a reef on its south side, which stretches down towards **Ao Ta Note**, a horseshoe inlet with the best snorkelling just north of the bay's mouth.

The **southeast corner** of the island sticks out in a long, thin area of land, which shelters sandy **Hat Sai Daeng** on its west side. **Ao Thian Ok** is the next pretty bay along the south coast. Ko Tao's coast is protected from the worst of both monsoons, and consequently the main bay, **Ao Chaloke Ban Kao**, has seen a fair amount of development. It does however have some gorgeous rock formations and undulating, palm-clad hillocks on its eastern headland.

## Information

A five-minute walk north of Ban Mae Hat, opposite the school, the gregarious Mr J (Ⓣ077/456 0667) is an all-purpose fixer, from booking trips to renting motorbikes to selling unwanted air tickets.

## Accommodation and eating

### West coast

**Blue Wind** North of Sai Ree village, off the main east coast road Ⓣ077/457015. Offers smart bungalows in a shady compound. Fronting the beach is a very stylish modern, timber, two-storey restaurant with delicious home-made pastries, bread and cakes and Thai, Indian and Western food. The yoga courses here come highly recommended (B400; 2hr). ❸–❼

**Jan Som Bay Bungalows** A 15-minute walk south of Ban Mae Sat Ⓣ077/456883. A characterful place overlooking a rocky beach with a pleasant garden. It has spacious and immaculate en-suite bungalows with wide balconies. ❺

**Nangyuan Island Dive Resort** Ko Nang Yuan Ⓣ077/456088, Ⓦwww.nangyuanisland.com. Makes the most of its beautiful location with swanky fan and a/c bungalows (unfortunately painted a sickly green) spreading over all three islands. ❼–❾

**Sai Ree Cottages** Towards the midpoint of Sai Ree beach Ⓣ081/372 3427. Has well-maintained en-suite timber, brick and cement huts and bungalows

## DIVING ON KAO TAO

Ko Tao has forty or so **dive companies**, making this the largest training centre in Southeast Asia. PADI Five-Star Dive Centres, all of which are committed to looking after the environment, include Big Blue Diving (Ⓣ077/456415, Ⓦwww.bigbluediving.com) and Scuba Junction (Ⓣ077/456164, Ⓦwww.scuba-junction.com) at Hat Sai Ree; and Easy Divers (Ⓣ077 456010, Ⓦwww.thaidive.com) and Planet Scuba (Ⓣ077/456110, Ⓦwww.planet-scuba.net) at Mae Hat.

### Costs

PADI's four-day Open Water course costs B9000–10,000; at a reliable company such as Easy Divers you can expect to pay around B9800, with reduced-cost accommodation and insurance. For qualified divers, one dive typically costs B1000, a ten-dive package B7000.

### Recompression chamber

There's a one-person recompression chamber and diving medicine centre, Badalveda, in Mae Hat (Ⓣ077/456580, Ⓦwww.badalveda.com).



in a flower-strewn garden by the beach. There's also good food in its atmospheric restaurant. ❸–❽

**Silversand** Accessed from Sai Ree village Ⓣ077/456603. Two facing rows of beautifully designed, clean timber bungalows in a verdant garden. ❺–❼

### East coast

**Laem Thian** Laem Thian Ⓣ077/456477, Ⓔpingpong_laemthian@hotmail.com. With the headland to itself, this place offers simple but comfy bungalows and hotel-style rooms, decent food and a remote, castaway feel. It also offers kayak rental, runs snorkelling and fishing trips and provides pick-up from the pier (free) and morning and afternoon transport to the east coast (B50–60). ❹–❻

**Ta Note Bay Dive Resort** Ao Ta Note Ⓣ077/456757, Ⓔtanote@hotmail.com. The pick of the resorts here, with plenty of well-designed, en-suite wooden bungalows set among thick bougainvillea. ❹–❽

### South coast

**Freedom Beach Bungalows** Ao Chaloke Ban Kao Ⓣ077/456596. Offers stilt wood bungalows with big decks on a steep escarpment with a wonderful view down, through palm trees, to a perfect beach. Also has a great decked bar over the water. ❸–❼

**New Heaven Huts** Hat Sai Daeng Ⓣ087/933 1329, Ⓔnewheavenhut@yahoo.com. Straddling the headland, this is a laid-back place with a good kitchen, a dive school and snorkelling equipment; its pleasantly idiosyncratic en-suite bungalows enjoy good views. ❹–❺

**New Heaven Resort** Ao Thian Ok Ⓣ077/456462, Ⓦwww.newheavenkohtao.com. A piece of paradise carved into a steep hillside with terraced gardens, ponds and stunning bungalows. Has its own little beach and great views from its restaurant. ❼–❾

**Viewpoint Bungalows** Ao Chaloke Ban Kao Ⓣ077/456444, Ⓦwww.kohtaoviewpoint.com. A delightful tropical garden fantasyland with wrap-around balcony timber bungalows and stone and cement numbers with jaw-dropping views. ❻–❼

## Directory

**Books** On the road leading inland from the main pier in Ban Mae Hat. Has a good selection of reasonably priced secondhand books and sells current Western newspapers and magazines. Also does book exchange.

**Health centre** Mae Hat, on the same road as the post office (8am–9pm; Ⓣ077/456930).

**Money exchange** On the same road at Siam City Bank, Ban Mae Hat (daily 9am–4.30pm).

**Police** A 10-minute walk on the narrow coast path heading north from Mae Hat (Ⓣ077/456631).

**Post office** Up the road leading inland from the Seatran Pier (Mon–Sat 8.30am–5pm, Sun 9.30–5pm).

## NAKHON SI THAMMARAT

**NAKHON SI THAMMARAT**, the south's religious capital, is an absorbing place, well known for traditional handicrafts, shadow plays and especially its festivals. The biggest of these is Tamboon Deuan Sip every September/October, which is marked by a ten-day fair at Sri Nakharin park, processions, shadow plays and other theatrical shows.

## What to see and do

The town runs 7km from north to south, to either side of Thanon Ratchadamnoen (the third parallel street, east of the rail line), which is served by frequent songthaews. The south's most important temple, **Wat Mahathat**, is on this road, about 2km south of the town centre. Its courtyard is dominated by the huge Sri Lankan-style chedi enshrining relics of the Buddha, around which are arrayed row upon row of smaller chedis, an Aladdin's cave of a temple museum, and local handicraft stalls. A few minutes' walk south of Wat Mahathat, the **National Museum** (Wed–Sun 9am–4pm; B30) houses a small but diverse collection covering prehistoric finds, Buddha images and ceramics. For the best possible introduction to southern Thailand's **shadow puppet theatre**, head for 110/18 Soi 3, Th Si Thammasok, ten minutes' walk from Wat Mahathat (☎075 346394) – walk north, take your first right (past *Khanom Jiin Muangkon*), turn right again, then left onto Thanon Si Thammasok. Here, Suchart Subsin, one of the south's leading exponents of *nang thalung*, and his son have opened their workshop to the public and, for a small fee (around B100), will show you scenes from a shadow play. You can also buy puppets here and see them being made.

## Arrival and information

**By bus** Nakhon's bus terminal, slightly southwest of the train station, on the other side of the river, is a cheap songthaew or motorbike taxi ride from town. Minibuses arrive at a number of different locations around town.

**By train** Nakhon's train station is in the town centre, three streets west of Th Ratchadamnoen

**By air** The airport is around 20km northwest of Nakhon. A/c minibuses ferry passengers into town (B80 per person).

**Tourist information** The TAT office is south of the centre in Sanam Na Muang Park, on Th Ratchadamnoen – towards Wat Mahathat (☎075/346 5156).

## Accommodation

**Nakor Garden Inn** 1/4 Th Pak Nakhon (the road running east from the train station) ☎075/313333. Tastefully decorated and cosy rooms come with cable TV, fridge, a/c and en suite with hot water. There's also a tranquil garden. ❸

**Thai Lee Hotel** 1130 Th Ratchadamnoen ☎075/356948. Offers ultra-cheap, en-suite clean rooms with tiled floors and plush furniture – very good value. ❶

## Eating

**Bovorn Bazaar** This courtyard complex off central Th Ratchadamnoen, just north of *Thai Lee Hotel* (down a sheltered soi flanking the bright green Fuji Film Station) offers: open-air *Krua Nakhon* which serves tasty local dishes; *Hao Coffee*, a traditional Chinese-style coffee shop with good Thai eats and great iced cappuccinos; and *Rock 99 Bar and Grill* (4pm–1am), a popular place that hosts live bands between 9pm and midnight.

**Hua Thale** 1204/29-30 Th Pak Bakhon, opposite *Nakor Garden Inn* (no English sign). This place is renowned among locals for its excellent, varied and inexpensive seafood. Daily 4–10pm.

**Khanom Jiin Muangkorn** on Th Panyon, first right when heading north from Wat Mahathat (no English sign). Famous for *khanom jiin* (noodles topped with hot, sweet or fish sauce). Lunchtime only.

## Moving on

**By bus** to: Bangkok (every 10min 8–9am & 5–6.30pm; 12hr); Krabi (6.30am & 1.30pm; 3hr); Phuket (approx hourly 5.20–11am; 8hr); Ranong (7.30am; 6hr); Surat Thani (frequent; 2hr 30min); Trang (1pm; 2hr).

**By minibus** Minibuses leave hourly between 7am and 4pm daily to Trang (3hr), Krabi (4hr), Phuket (5hr) and Surat Thani (2hr), departing from various parts of the city centre. Departure points are variable.

**By train** There are two first-class sleeper trains daily to Bangkok (1pm & 3pm; 15hr), via Surat Thani (4hr).

**By air** There are 4 flights daily from Nakhon to Bangkok with Nok Air; One-Two-Go has one flight daily.

# The Andaman coast

The landscape along the Andaman coast is lushly tropical and spiked with dramatic limestone crags, best appreciated by staying in **Khao Sok National Park** or taking a boat trip around the bizarre **Ao Phang Nga Bay**. Most people, however, come here for the beaches and the coral reefs: **Phuket** is Thailand's largest island and this stretch of coast's place to learn to dive, but it's package-tour-oriented, so backpackers usually head straight for the beaches around **Krabi**, or to the island of **Ko Lanta**. Unlike the Gulf coast, the Andaman coast is hit by the southwest monsoon from May to October, when the rain and high seas render some of the outer islands inaccessible and litter many beaches with debris; prices drop significantly during this period. The Andaman Coast was severely battered by the devastating **tsunami** of December 26, 2004, though nearly all tourist facilities have now been rebuilt.

## RANONG

The multi-ethnic provincial capital of **RANONG** is chiefly of interest as a stepping-off point for boats to Ko Chang and Ko Phayam, and for visa runs to Kaw Thaung, Burma, just a few kilometres away. Thanon Ruangrat has half a dozen places offering internet access, and the CAT international phone office on Thanon Tha Muang also has Catnet Internet terminals.

### Arrival and information

**By bus** All west-coast buses from Bangkok to Phuket or Krabi pass through Ranong, stopping at the bus terminal on Highway 4 (Th Phetkasem), 1.5km southeast of the centre; songthaews ferry passengers on to Th Ruangrat in the town centre or to the port at Saphan Pla.

**By air** Ranong Airport is 20km south of town on Highway 4, served by share taxis charging up to B200 per person.

**Tourist information** Both *Kiwi Orchid*, at the bus terminal, and *Pon's Place* restaurant, 300m north of the *Asia Hotel* on Th Ruangrat, are good sources of info on buses, flights, tours and the islands.

### Accommodation

**Asia Hotel** 39/9 Th Ruangrat, about 70m south of the market ⓣ077/811113. Has decent, clean fan and a/c en-suite rooms off its rather prison-like hallways. ❶–❹

**Kiwi Orchid and PL Guest House** 19/20 Moo 1, Phetchakasem Rd, in the bus terminal compound ⓣ077/832812. A ramshackle place occupying two

### VISA RUN TO BURMA

The quickest and easiest way to get a **new visa** is the "visa run" service offered by hotels and restaurant all over town (B300–350 plus visa fee). Alternatively, an actual visa run to Burma and back is a relatively simple affair. Take the Saphan Pla-bound songthaew no. 3 (20min; B10–15) from the market on Thanon Ruangrat, north of *Asia Hotel*, and jump off at the Thai immigration office (daily 8.30am–6pm). Once you have your stamp, continue down the road for 10–15 minutes until you reach the PTT petrol station, where you turn right to find a quay choked with longtails.

The longtails leave for Kaw Thaung when they have enough custom: the fare should be B100 one-way per person, possibly B50 if you're lucky enough to get a lot of people on board. Longtail drivers will take you through the steps of the visa procedure. Before leaving you will need to exchange B500 for US$10 in order to pay for your Burmese visa – black-market money changes are often found at the quayside. When back across the border, return to the Thai immigration office for your new thirty-day Thai visa. The whole process takes 2–3 hours. As with everything in Burma, the situation could change so check in advance; also note that paying for a Burmese visa is giving money to the Burmese military government.

properties, with basic fan rooms, shared bathrooms and a friendly travellers' atmosphere. Has a big lounge/dining area with book exchange, info on local attractions, food and movies. ❷

## Eating

**Coffee House** 173 Th Ruangrat. A no-frills place with cheap, tasty, freshly baked filled baguettes, pancakes and real coffee. 7am–6pm.
**Pon's Place** Th Ruangrat. Serves cheap Western breakfasts and standard Thai offerings with flair. 7.30am–9pm.

## Moving on

**By bus** A/c government buses to Bangkok leave every 2–3hr from 5am to 8.30pm with Newmit Tour, while Chockeanan Tour run VIP buses daily at 8am & 8pm. Services to Phuket and Krabi run via Ta Kuapa and Khao Lak. Change at Ta Kuapa for a Surat Thani-bound bus – tourist minibuses run this route but approach with caution (see p.744).
**Destinations**: Bangkok (8 daily; 9hr); Khao Sok (change at Ta Kuapa; 2hr 30min); Krabi (3 daily; 4hr); Phuket (3 daily; 5–6hr); Surat Thani (2 daily; 3hr).
**By boat** Take songthaew #3 (20min; B10–15) from the market on Th Ruangrat, north of *Asia Hotel*, to Saphan Pla. Boats leave for Ko Chang at 9.30am, noon & 2pm (B100).
**Destinations**: Ko Chang (3 daily; 1–2hr); Ko Phayam (1–2 daily; 2–3hr).
**By air** Air Asia runs flights from Ranong to Bangkok (Tues, Fri & Sun; 4.45pm; 55min).

# KO CHANG

Not to be confused with the much larger Ko Chang on Thailand's east coast (see p.838), Ranong's **Ko Chang** is a forested little island about 5km offshore, with a charmingly low-key atmosphere. The beaches are connected by tracks through the trees; there are no cars and only sporadic electricity. At the moment, there's barely any commercial activity on Ko Chang save for a couple of local minimarkets, a dive operator, and foreign exchange and an overseas phone service at *Cashew Resort* (see below). The prettiest (and longest) beach on the island is **Ao Yai,** which arches its way along the mid-west coast. **Boats** to Ko Chang depart from Saphan Pla (see above), returning from Ko Chang at 7.30am and 2pm. In the rainy season services are erratic and only go to Ko Chang's east coast, from where it's a 3km hike to Ao Yai.

## Accommodation

The dozen or so family-run bungalow operations are mostly scattered along the west coast, many of them hidden amongst the shorefront trees on Ao Yai; they nearly all close June–Oct.
**Cashew Resort** North of the lagoon on central Ao Yai ⓣ077/820116. The largest outfit, comprising both simple and more comfortable wooden huts. ❷
**Ko Chang Resort** South of the lagoon ⓣ077/820176, ⓔsound_of_sea@lycos.com. Many of these en-suite bungalows occupy a fabulous spot high on the rocks. There is also an atmospheric bar, with a good selection of cocktails and music. ❷–❹
**Sawasdee** At the far south of Ao Yai ⓣ077/820177. An ingeniously designed set of bungalows with sliding walls for ventilation. Its eye-catching restaurant is spread out among a cool, sandy, beachfront grove. ❸
**Sunset Bungalows** Towards the far north end of Ao Yai ⓣ077/820171. Arguably the nicest place to stay on the island with cute, cheap, bamboo bungalows and a gorgeous rustic restaurant/reception that blends into the beach surroundings. There's a raised deck to relax on and enjoy a massage. ❶–❷

# KO PHAYAM

Diminutive **KO PHAYAM,** measuring just 4 by 7km, is home to some fine white-sand beaches and relaxing beachfront bungalows connected by a network of narrow, winding, concrete paths. Behind the beaches, the island is covered in forests and overgrown rubber, cashew and palm plantations. Slightly more developed than Ko Chang, it has sporadic electricity, a fledgling though still very low-key bar scene, and a **village** at the port comprising several small shops and restaurants – including *Oscar's*, a favourite expat watering hole and excellent source of island info, internet access, motorbike rental and a dive shop. Most bungalow operations offer motorbike rental (B200) but close down during the wet season (June–Oct).

Ko Phayam's nicest beach is the three-kilometre-long **Ao Yai** on the southwest coast, a beautiful sweep of soft white sand that occasionally gets pounded by large waves. Across on the northwest coast, the prettiest stretch of beach is the northern part of **Ao Kao Kwai** (also known as Ao Kao Fai, or Buffalo Bay).

Motorbike taxis meet incoming boats from Ranong's port Saphan Pla (see p.861) at the pier in Ko Phayam village and charge B70 to most bungalows. The boat returns from Ko Phayam to Saphan Pla at 8.30am and 2pm, but are less regular during the rainy season.

## Accommodation

### Ao Yai

**Aow Yai Bungalow Gilles and Phatchara** Southern end of the beach ⓣ077/870216, ⓔgilles_phatchara@hotmail.com. Beautiful bamboo bungalows with balconies and en-suite bathrooms. ❷–❹

**Bamboo Bungalows** In the centre of the bay ⓣ077/820012. This place has been lovingly created from bamboo, timber, shells and abundant plant life. The attractive restaurant/reception area fronting the beach has a good travellers' vibe, and offers internet access as well as kayak, boogie board, flippers and snorkel and mask rental. Open all year round. ❷–❻

**Smile Hut** Next door to *Bamboo Bungalows* ⓣ077/820335. A charming, scruffy little place, with tightly packed rows of basic bungalows and good food. Internet and Wi-Fi also available. ❷

**Ao Kao Kwai Jansom Koh Phayam** North of *Saithong* ⓣ081/968 5720. Clean, well-furnished bungalows in a garden above a rocky part of the beach. Also has an attractive multi-tiered restaurant. ❸

**Saithong** Buffalo Bay ⓣ080/141131, ⓔsaithong_ranongth@yahoo.com. Simple bamboo bungalows in a great setting. *Mr Gao* (ⓣ077/823995) next door offers snorkelling expeditions to Ko Surin. ❷

**Mountain Resort** At the beach's northern end ⓣ077/820098. Five tasteful cement bungalows in a palm tree grove fronting a thin stretch of beach. ❸

## Eating

**Hippy Bar** Next door to *Mountain Resort*, Ao Kao Kwai. Put together from all manner of timber detritus, this is a kind of hippy saloon, with multiple swinging doors and a pool table in one of the many chill-out zones outside. It serves basic cocktails and beer.

# KHAO SOK NATIONAL PARK

Whether you're heading down the Andaman or the Gulf coast, the stunning jungle-clad karsts of **Khao Sok National**

### TRANSPORT TO AND FROM KHAO SOK

Most Surat Thani-bound **buses** from Khao Lak pass the park entrance, which is located at kilometre-stone marker 109 on Highway 401 – less than an hour by bus from Ta Kuapa, ninety minutes from Khao Lak, or two hours from Surat Thani. Coming from Ranong, get a Phuket- or Krabi-bound bus and change at Takua Pa. Buses run at least every ninety minutes in both directions; at the park entrance, you'll be met by guesthouse staff offering free lifts to their accommodation, the furthest of which is 3km away. Coming by bus from Bangkok or Chumphon, take a Surat Thani-bound bus, but ask to be dropped off at the junction with the Takua Pa road, about 20km before Surat Thani, and then change onto a Takua Pa bus.
If coming direct from Surat Thani, think twice about using the **tourist minibus** services to Khao Sok that leave at or after 3pm as they have a reputation for dumping passengers at the wrong guesthouse.
**Moving on** buses run past the highway at least every ninety minutes, stopping at 5.30pm. The first to Surat Thani arrives at 7.30am, the first to Phuket, 8.30am.
**Minibuses** go to to Krabi (daily 8.30am; 2hr) and Surat Thani (hourly 6.30am–5pm; 2hr 30min).

**Park** (B200 entry, valid for 24hr) are well worth veering inland for.

## What to see and do

Much of the park is carpeted in impenetrable rainforest – home to pythons, cobras, scorpions, tarantulas, sun bears, gibbons, leopards, tigers and almost two hundred species of bird – but nine fairly easy **treks** radiate from the visitor centre (daily 8am–6pm), which hands out sketch maps showing their routes and sells a good guidebook to the park, *Waterfalls and Gibbon Calls* (B520).

### Treks

The most popular treks run to **Ton Gloy Waterfall** (7km from the national park visitor centre; 3hr each way; 6hr round-trip) and to the eleven-tiered **Sip-et Chan Waterfall**, which can be tricky to reach and involves some climbing plus half a dozen river crossings (4km; 3hr each way; 6hr round-trip). Take plenty of water, as Khao Sok is notoriously humid. Longer **guided treks** into the jungle can be arranged through most guesthouses (B700–1200; day hike) or, for variety, take to the water in a tube (B250; 2hr) or canoe (B800, 2hr), try an elephant trek (B800–1000, 2hr) or a night safari (B600–700, 2hr).

The most popular outings are to **Cheow Lan Lake**, with its spectacular limestone crags regularly shrouded in morning mists. Day tours to the lake include a boat ride and a swim/hike through the **Nam Talu** river-cave (B1500). Be warned, however, that nine people died in the cave in a flash flood in October 2007, at the end of the wet season. The cave is considered safe in the driest months of December, January and February. You can also opt for two- (B2500–3000) and three- (B3400) day tours, which include night safaris; you spend the nights on a raft house on the lake.

### The village

An attractive tourist **village** has grown up along the north–south access road to the national park visitor centre and trailheads, and along the main east–west track that bisects it. As well as around twenty sets of **bungalows**, all of which serve food, you'll find minimarkets and internet centres, currency exchange, and motorbike rental.

## Accommodation

**Baan Khao Sok Resort** The sign is 700m north of the highway, on the north–south access road; follow the dirt path from here ⓣ081/958 0185. For a few days of relaxation, it's worth paying a little extra for these beautifully designed bamboo bungalows set in a enchanting garden, right on the river, with glimpses of towering karsts above. It's a 5min walk into town. ❹

**Khao Sok Bungalow** On the north–south access road, 150m south of the river ⓣ086/627 0526, ⓔlekkhaosokbungalow@hotmail.com. The best budget option, with eight attractive and very clean bamboo bungalows set in a lovely garden, full of orchids, flowering shrubs and quaint timber bridges. ❷

**Khaosok Evergreen House** Turn left after *Nirvana* bar, on the east–west sidetrack ⓣ084/745 8220, ⓦwww.evergreenhouse2007.net. Four immaculate high-stilt timber bungalows (each with bathroom, mosquito net, fan and balconies with timber furniture) set in a spacious, yet secluded garden. ❷

**Nung House** 300m along the quieter east–west sidetrack ⓣ077/395147, ⓦwww.nunghouse.com. Clean wood and cement bungalows set around a regularly mown lawn, bordered by rambutan trees and ferns. Serves good, cheap Thai food in its elegant open-air restaurant. ❷–❹

## Nightlife

**Funky Monkey** 100m southeast of *Nirvana Bar*. This two-storey bamboo structure, composed of multiple decks with low tables, plus mats and cushions for seating, occasionally explodes into party mode when the funky Thai staff spin out Western alternative rock, funk and reggae music.

**Nirvana Bar** 300m down the east/west sidetrack, next door to *Nung House*. A great place to stargaze while sipping on a tasty margarita; the small gazebo bar sits in the corner of a big lawn, surrounded by palm trees, which is pleasantly illuminated by small lights and candles. Cushioned decks, low tables, and mats are set around a central fire.

## KHAO LAK

Thirty kilometres south of Takua Pa and ninety minutes by bus from Khao Sok National Park, the area usually referred to as **Khao Lak** is in fact three separate beaches, consisting, from north to south, of **Bang Niang**, **Nang Thong** and **Khao Lak** proper. The area suffered horrendous damage and loss of life as a result of the 2004 tsunami. The reconstruction process has been slow and favoured the privileged. Consequently, plush resorts dominate the beachfront with budget accommodation relegated to the less than idyllic, and still recovering, inland tourist village areas.

### Nang Thong

Inland **Nang Thong** is the business centre, an unattractive clutter of banks, ATMs, money exchanges, dive shops, restaurants, bars and internet places on Highway 4, the main inland road.

#### TSUNAMI MEMORIALS AND ORGANIZATIONS

In Bang Niang, on Highway 4, the small and informative **International Tsunami Museum** traces the geographical cause and aftermath of the tsunami. In a vacant lot, 100m south of here, a **beached police boat** stands as a memorial to the tsunami's power – it was propelled up here, 2km inland, while patrolling Bang Niang beach.

The **Tsunami Volunteer Center** (Ⓣ084/898 7554, Ⓦwww.tsunamivolunteer.net) situated in the Khao Lak–Lamru National Park, on the headland between Khao Lak and Nang Thong accepts donations and offers educational day tours, snorkelling trips, trekking, canoeing, language lessons, cooking classes and homestays with sea gypsies and local community representatives.

The beach is nice enough, however, with soft yellow sand, unfortunately black in parts, winding its way along the coast, with boulders populating the shallows.

### Bang Niang

**Bang Niang** beach, 2km north, is a beauty, but the luxury resorts dominating the beachfront can be a little off-putting. To the north of the main resort cluster however, an undeveloped palm grove facing the beach marks a nice spot to swim, while to its south, a number of thatched Thai-run bars and restaurants, with tables, chairs and parasols on the sand provide an alternative, relaxed beachside experience. Inland, empty lots are still numerous and construction is underway in many places.

### Khao Lak

**Khao Lak** proper is the least developed part of the resort, separated from Nang Thong by an inspiring 5km winding drive through jungle-clad headland. Budget accommodation is available in its southern, most attractive, section, where palm groves, casuarinas and rubber plantations greet soft yellow sand dotted with granite boulders.

### Arrival and local transport

**By bus** All buses running from Phuket to Takua Pa and Ranong (and vice versa), as well as some of the Phhuket–Surat Thani services, pass through Khao Lak; if you're coming from Krabi or Phan Nga, take a Phket–bound bus to Khokkloi and change. Most bus drivers will drop you near your chosen accommodation.

**Songthaews** connect the beaches, charging upwards of B50 per person.

**Motorbikes** Available for rent on all beaches (B200 per day).

### Activities

Tour agents offer **jungle elephant treks**, **rafting** and **biking tours**. Alternatively, on the road to Chong Fah Falls (which heads east from Bang Niang) there's a jungle garden authentically overgrowing a Khmer-style city-themed eighteen-hole **mini-golf course** (ⓣ076/486728).

## Diving and snorkelling

There are plenty of snorkelling and diving trips to the spectacular reefs off Ko Similan and Ko Surin (Nov–April). Prices waver from B12,000 to B17,000 for three-day trips. Some operators also offer day-trips in speedboats (2 dives B5100; snorkelling B2900) and they all offer PADI dive courses (B14,500–17,000 for four-day PADI Open Water).

**Poseidon Bungalows** Runs fantastic three-day trips to the Similans; these are for snorkellers only, cost B7400 and depart twice weekly (Tues & Fri), so book ahead.

**Sea Dragon Dive Center** ⓣ076/485420, ⓦwww.seadragondivecenter.com. Across from Nang Thong supermarket. Highly regarded, the longest-running Khao Lak dive operator.

## Accommodation

### Nang Thong

**Father & Son** On Highway 4, 50m north of the beach access road ⓣ076/485277. Nang Thong's best budget option: a lovely place with cute, clean bamboo bungalows, plus bigger, pricier numbers in a verdant tropical garden. ❷–❹

**Jai** Another 50m north on the opposite side of the highway ⓣ076/485390, ⓔjairestaurant&bungalows@hotmail.com. Twelve baby-blue bungalows around a central, unkempt, overgrown garden. Interiors are clean but a little musty with kitsch wall hangings. The restaurant is popular. ❸

**Phu Khao Lak Resort** 150m south of the beach access road ⓣ076/420141, ⓔphukhaolak@hotmail.com. Set in a spacious, well-tended coconut grove at the foot of a thickly foliaged mountain. The cheapest rooms are in white-walled four-room blocks with immaculate interiors – or you can splash out on the stylish, minimalist bungalows to the side. ❹–❼

**Sri Guesthouse** 300m north of the beach access road ⓣ089/867 0807. For the diehard budgeter, there are some very basic, cheap rooms here, plus pricier, slightly more salubrious quarters. ❷–❹

### Bang Niang

**Amsterdam Resort** ⓣ081/857 5881. Brick bungalows with plain interiors; the cheapest rooms in the main two-storey structure are a little stuffy but good value considering the area. There is an open-air restaurant/bar area with cable TV. ❸–❺

**Sanuk Resort** ⓣ076/420800. Set in a small, leafy compound with quaint paths fanning out from a timber arch entrance. The wood/brick bungalows have spacious interiors and come with a basin, fridge and hot water shower and there's a gorgeous little outdoor, jungle spa. ❻

### Khao Lak

**Khao Lak Mountain Hill Bungalow** Get off bus at the turn-off between 53km and 54km and walk 300m ⓣ089/593 2495. Pretty, plant-rimmed bungalows with rustic timber facades, big front windows and woven bamboo wall interiors. Has a lagoon below and rubber plantation on the hillside behind. A pleasant 1km walk or motorbike-ride to the beach. ❹

**Poseidon Bungalows** Either get off the bus at the village of Laem Kaen and take a motorbike taxi, or get off at the turn-off between 53km and 54km and walk the 1km to the bungalows ⓣ076/443258. Solid bungalows on a thickly vegetated, rocky headland with idyllic ocean views and easy access to beautiful beaches. Also has a pleasing restaurant, internet access and motorbike rental. Try to book weeks, if not, months in advance. ❻

**Pramote Bungalow** Across the road from *Khao Lak Mountain Hill Bungalow* ⓣ095/929660. Set around a scruffy but strangely appealing yard. Features simple timber en-suite bungalows with fan, a little on the grubby side, most with TV and fridge. ❸

## Eating and drinking

### Nang Thong

**Jai** On Highway 4, 100m north of the beach access road. A popular place with well-priced curries and seafood.

**Khao Lak Seafood** A little further north than *Jai*. An open-air restaurant with cheap, flavoursome Thai and Western dishes.

**Tarzan Bar** A few doors north of the beach access road. Has a slick, rustic, tropical beach bar theme with a breezy timber balcony over the street and a good selection of cocktails (B150).

### Bang Niang

**Songs Bar** On the beach access road. Set far back from the beach but with a rustic, sandy-floored, all-bamboo, beach bar aesthetic; has elevated platforms with low tables and cushions and serves good cocktails – all that's missing is the water.

**Tekieng** On Highway 4, next to the police boat memorial. An all-timber shack with numerous wood carvings, earthy artworks, Thai artefacts and plentiful plant life; serves delicious seafood dishes, hot and spicy salads (B80–100), curries (B100) and rice and noodle standards.

### Khao Lak

There are a few bamboo bars, serving basic refreshments at the southern extremity of the beach which will sometimes rustle up a meal if you ask nicely.

**Poseidon Bungalows** A thatched roof gazebo restaurant on stilts extends over rocks and a winding ocean-bound canal, and has marvellous views south over the beach. The Thai (*pat thai* B100) and Western food (pepper steak B310) is not cheap but the quality is good.

## Directory

**Cinema** European Cinema is in Bang Niang, just south of the bridge and consists of one main cinema (seating 12) with a big-screen projector, Thai back rests and cushions (B150 per person) and two bamboo hut structures out the back with TVs and DVD players (2–3 people; B150 per person). Big-screen movies are shown at 8pm and 10pm or you can choose your own private viewing experience from a vast movie library.

**Doctor** Dr Chusak (5.30–8.30pm), across the road from *Jai Bungalows*, speaks good English and does routine examinations (B300–500 fee). Khuk Kaak Health Centre lies on Highway 4–4.5 km north of Bang Niang.

**Markets** Bang Niang market (Wed & Sat pm) opposite the police boat memorial has stalls selling fresh vegetables, meat, clothes and household items.

**Police** There is a police box on the Khao Lak/Nang Thong headland, at the main entrance to the Khao Lak-Lamru National Park.

**Post office** Lies 700m south of the Khuk Kaak Health Centre.

## Moving on

**By bus** Buses can be flagged down on Highway 4 (preferably at a bus stop gazebo), heading north to Ranong (3 daily) and Surat Thani (3 daily) and heading south to Phuket (every 2hr; 3hr). You can also get a minibus to Krabi (8am; 2hr).

# PHUKET

Thailand's largest island and a province in its own right, **Phuket** (pronounced "Poo-ket") ranks second in tourist popularity only to Pattaya. Thoughtless developments have scarred much of the island, particularly along the central west coast, and the trend on all the beaches is upmarket, with very few budget possibilities. Parts of the island were badly damaged by the 2004 tsunami but reconstruction was swift.

## What to see and do

Phuket is Thailand's most important **diving** centre, offering easy access to some of the most spectacular reefs and islands in the world. The sea gets quite rough from May to October, when diving is less rewarding and swimming can be dangerous. Aside from the beaches and the reefs, the island's main attractions include the dramatic headland of **Laem Promthep** at Phuket's southernmost tip – a popular coach-tour stop for sunset – and the **Gibbon Rehabilitation Centre** (daily 10am–4pm, last tour at 3.15pm; donation; ⓦwww.warthai.org), which is near Bang Pae in Phra Taew National Park, 10km northeast of the Heroines' Monument, off Route 4027. It's accessible by songthaew from Phuket Town (most frequent in the mornings; 40min), then a 1km walk.

Although Phuket's west-coast beaches are connected by road, to get from one beach to another by public transport you generally have to go back into Phuket Town. **Motorbikes** can be rented on all the beaches but be sure to wear a helmet as the compulsory helmet law is strictly enforced on Phuket.

### Phuket Town

Most visitors only remain in **PHUKET TOWN** long enough to jump on a beach-bound songthaew; they run regularly throughout the day from Thanon Ranong in the town centre to all the main beaches (B15–30). While not the most beautiful of places, this is an authentic Thai town in striking contrast to the tailor-made tourist settlements that make up the rest of the island. The

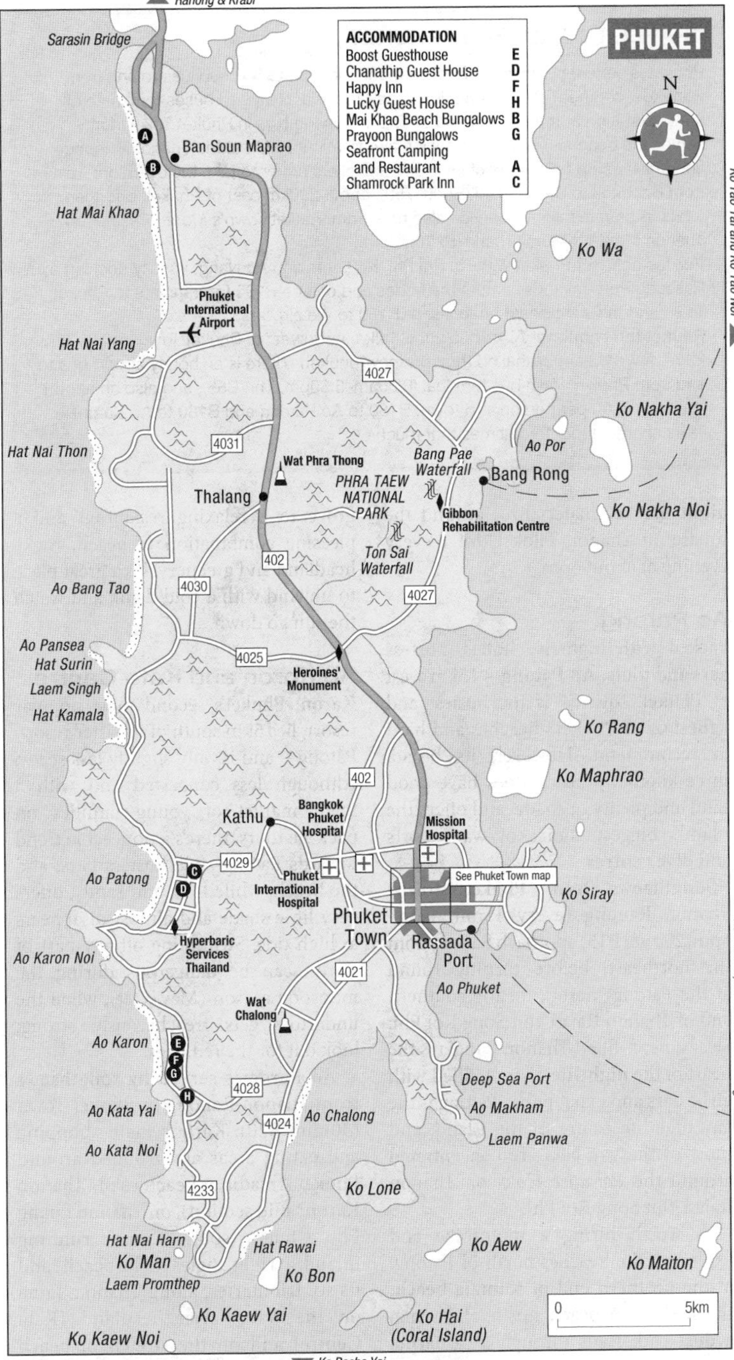
PHUKET
ACCOMMODATION
Boost Guesthouse E
Chanathip Guest House D
Happy Inn F
Lucky Guest House H
Mai Khao Beach Bungalows B
Prayoon Bungalows G
Seafront Camping and Restaurant A
Shamrock Park Inn C
N
Ranong & Krabi
Sarasin Bridge
Ban Soun Maprao
Hat Mai Khao
Phuket International Airport
Hat Nai Yang
Hat Nai Thon
Wat Phra Thong
Thalang
PHRA TAEW NATIONAL PARK
Bang Pae Waterfall
Bang Rong
Gibbon Rehabilitation Centre
Ton Sai Waterfall
Ao Por
Ko Wa
Ko Nakha Yai
Ko Nakha Noi
Ko Yao Yai and Ko Yao Noi
4027
4031
402
4030
4025
Ao Bang Tao
Ao Pansea
Hat Surin
Laem Singh
Hat Kamala
Heroines' Monument
Ko Rang
Ko Maphrao
Kathu
Bangkok Phuket Hospital
Mission Hospital
4029
Ao Patong
Phuket International Hospital
See Phuket Town map
Ko Siray
Phuket Town
Rassada Port
Hyperbaric Services Thailand
Ao Karon Noi
4021
Ao Phuket
Wat Chalong
Ao Karon
Ko Phi Phi, Ko Lanta & Ao Nang
Deep Sea Port
Ao Makham
4028
Ao Kata Yai
4024
Ao Chalong
Laem Panwa
Ao Kata Noi
4233
Ko Lone
Hat Nai Harn
Ko Man
Hat Rawai
Ko Aew
Ko Maiton
Laem Promthep
Ko Bon
Ko Kaew Yai
Ko Hai (Coral Island)
Ko Kaew Noi
0
5km
Ko Racha Yai

## TRAVEL TO AND FROM PHUKET

Phuket is served by dozens of government and private **bus** services to and from Bangkok, southern Thai destinations and Malaysia. Nearly all buses terminate at the bus station at the eastern end of Thanon Phang Nga in Phuket Town (none serves the beaches), from where it's a fifteen-minute walk to the Thanon Ranong songthaew stop for the beaches. Some travellers prefer to take the overnight train from Bangkok to Surat Thani (B500–750), about 290km east of Phuket, and then a bus. A private minibus service also runs from Phuket Town's *Montri Resotel* on Thanon Montri to Surat Thani. (B270).

**Ferries** connect Phuket with Ko Phi Phi, Ko Lanta and Ao Nang, usually docking at Rassada Port; minibuses meet the ferries and charge B100 for transfers to Phuket Town and the west-coast beaches, or B150 to the airport.

**Phuket International Airport** is about 32km northwest of Phuket Town (Ⓣ076/327 2307, Ⓦwww2.airportthai.co.th/airportnew/phuket). There is an hourly airport bus to and from Phuket Town bus terminal (6.30am–5.30pm; 1hr; B55), and also an airport minibus (B100 per person into town, B150 to Ao Patong and B180 to Ao Karon). Taxis charge about three times that much.

**night market** materializes around the square off Thanon Tilok Uthit 1 every evening at about 6pm.

### Ao Patong

Packed with high-rise hotels, hostess bars and touts, **Ao Patong** – 15km west of Phuket Town – is the busiest and ugliest of all Phuket's beaches and hard to recommend. However, its broad, three-kilometre beach does have good sand and plenty of shade, and offers the island's biggest choice of watersports and **dive centres**.

**Songthaews** from Phuket Town's Thanon Ranong (every 15min 6am–6pm; 20min; B15) approach Patong from the northeast, before turning round at the Patong Merlin, on the southern end of Thanon Raja Uthit Song Roi Phi. Sleazy, neon-filled Thanon Bangla is the heart of the **nightlife** district, filled with girlie bars and expat pubs. Patong is the **gay** nightlife centre of the island, and most of the gay bars are concentrated around the *Paradise Hotel* on Thanon Raja Uthit Song Roi Phi.

It's worth hiring a motorbike and exploring the beaches north of Patong: at the northern end of **Kamala beach**, the first main beach north of Patong, a dust path leads through a casuarina grove to a relaxing restaurant and a pleasing combination of beach, rocky headland and greenery. It's a great place to unwind with a cold drink and watch the sun go down.

### Ao Karon and Kata Centre

**Karon**, Phuket's second most popular resort, lies 5km south of its sister resort, Patong – and is only slightly less seedy. Although less congested and with a main market of young families on package tours, there's a noticeable trend towards Patong-style hostess bars, and the beach, while long and sandy, offers very little shade and almost disappears at high tide. Swimming off any part of Karon can be dangerous during the monsoon season (May–Oct), when the undertow gets treacherously strong; look out for the red flags.

Ao Karon is served by songthaews from Thanon Ranong in Phuket Town (30min; B20). Karon's main shopping and eating areas are grouped around Phuket Arcadia at beach road (Thanon Karon's mid section), on Thanon Luang Pho Chuan (south Karon, running inland, at right angles to the beach) and its soi tributaries, along Thanon Taina on the Kata/Karon headland (Kata Centre) and on the stretch of beach road (Thanon Karon) between the latter two.

### Hat Mai Khao

Should all the hustle and seediness become too much, Phuket's longest and least developed beach, **Hat Mai Khao**, 34km northwest of Phuket Town, offers a serene contrast. It still harbours just a couple of discreet, though not particularly cheap, bungalow operations. The almost deserted beach seems to stretch on forever, and the hammocks that swing between the trees provide a comfortable means to properly appreciate the soothing sights and sounds of the natural environment. The easiest way to get to Hat Mai Khao is by long-distance bus to the Ta Cha Chi Police Checkpoint, through which all buses travelling between Phuket Town bus station and the mainland must pass. Having given prior notification of your arrival, contact your chosen accommodation supplier on the public phone here and they will pick you up free of charge.

## Accommodation

### Phuket Town

**On On Hotel** 19 Th Phang Nga ⓣ076/211154. Has 49 basic, just adequate rooms and internet access in its sprawling colonial-style 1920s building. Cheaper rooms come without shower; the most expensive have a/c. ❷–❸

**Thalang Guest House** 37 Th Talang ⓣ076/214225, ⓦwww.thalangguesthouse.com. Large, comfortable en-suite rooms in an old wooden house on one of Phuket's more traditional streets. ❸

### Ao Patong

**Chanathip Guest House** Th Raja Uthit Song Roi Phi, Soi Neung ⓣ081/787 2537, ⓔbaby-ing-far@hotmail.com. This small building has a handful of plain en-suite rooms, most with balconies, and walls that could do with a fresh coat of paint. Fan ❹, a/c ❺

**Shamrock Park Inn** Th Raja Uthit Song Roi Phi ⓣ076/342275, ⓔshamrock340991@hotmail.com. A small, friendly little hotel with pleasant a/c rooms in a two-storey complex. ❻

### Ao Karon/Kata Centre

**Boost Guesthouse** Karon Plaza, off Th Luang Pho Chuan ⓣ076/398451. Has the cheapest rooms

## DIVING IN PHUKET

See ⓦwww.phuket.com/diving/guide.htm for links to Phuket's dive shops, all of which offer Discover Scuba dives (B3100–4600), day-trips for certified divers (B2200–4800) and diving courses (B12,000–16,250 for a four-day PADI Open Water). Always check the equipment and staff credentials carefully and ask whether the dive centre has membership for one of Phuket's recompression chambers. Reliable **dive centres** include:

### Ao Patong

Santana 49 Th Thavee Wong ⓣ076/294220, ⓦwww.santanaphuket.com.

Scuba Cat 94 Th Thavee Wong ⓣ076/293120, ⓦwww.scubacat.com.

### Ao Karon/Ao Kata

Dive Asia 24 Th Karon ⓣ076/396199, and on Karon/Kata headland near Dino Park, 24 Th Karon ⓣ076/330598.

Marina Divers 45 Th Karon, next to the Marina Phuket Resort on the Karon/Kata headland ⓣ076/330272, ⓦwww.marinadivers.com.

### Recompression chambers

There are three recompression chambers on Phuket:

Hyperbaric Services Thailand (HST) 233 Th Raja Uthit Song Roi Phi, Ao Patong ⓣ076/342518 or 076/342519 and in emergencies ⓣ089/871 2335, ⓦwww.sssnetwork.com.

Badalveda Diving Medicine Centre At Bangkok Phuket Hospital, 2/1 Th Hongyok Utis, on the outskirts of Phuket Town ⓣ076/254425, ⓦwww.badalveda.com.

Wachira Hospital Soi Wachira, Th Yaowarat, Phuket Town ⓣ076/211114 or 076/217294.

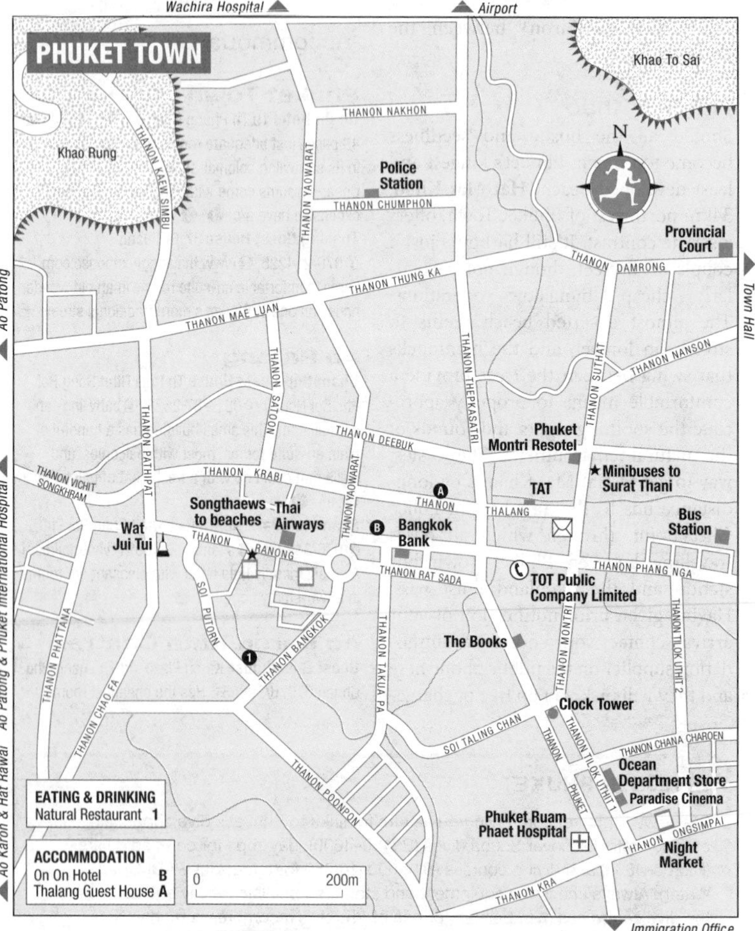


going. They're basic, and a little cramped with ugly views, but most are clean and liveable. ③–⑤

**Happy Inn** Th Luang Pho Chuan, Soi 1, further north and down the hill a bit ⓣ076/396260. Attractive bungalows in a peaceful environment. ⑥

**Lucky Guest House** Kata Centre, Th Taina, ⓣ076/330572, ⓔluckyguesthousekata@hotmail.com. Has large bright rooms in a block and good value en-suite, prefabricated huts in regimented rows – looks a little like US military accommodation. ④–⑥

**Prayoon Bungalows** Th Luang Pho Chuan, Soi 2, a short walk from the beach (behind *Andaman Sea View Hotel*) ⓣ076/396196. A beautiiful oasis with seven tasteful bungalows set in a circle around a cool grassy incline, shaded by casuarina trees. ⑥

## Hat Mai Khao

Both places close during the monsoon season (May–Oct).

**Mai Khao Beach Bungalows** ⓣ081/895 1233, ⓔbmaikhao_beach@hotmail.com. Has just a few exorbitantly priced but attractive en-suite bungalows and five tents available (B350 each or B100 for a pitch if you bring your own); the quaint restaurant serves good, cheap Thai cuisine. Electricity 6pm–6am only. ⑥

**Seafront Camping and Restaurant** ⓣ081/538 0781. Offers four very small, squat bungalows with shared bathroom and expensive tents for B400 and B300. All prices include breakfast. ④

## Eating, drinking and nightlife

### Phuket Town

**Natural Restaurant** 62/5 Soi Putorn (Phoo Thon). Atmospheric, open-air timber structure full of hanging plants and vines (plus an amusing fish tank television). Serves good, inexpensive seafood (from B150) and Thai specialities, and also does deep-fried ice cream (B50) and sundaes (B40).

### Ao Patong

Consisting of hundreds of bars, Ao Patong is like one big bar in itself. If you're making a night of it, your best bet is to start on Th Bangla and go wherever whim takes you. For food:

**Baan Sukhothai** At eastern end of Soi Bangla. This elegant hotel restaurant serves fine Thai cuisine (meals B120–300).

**Restaurant 4** At the back of the most easterly soi heading north off Th Bangla. A no-frills place with plastic tables and chairs; has very cheap seafood with the right blend of spices.

### Ao Karon

The string of five **street-side restaurants** just north of the *Ruam Thep Inn* on Th Karon, a convenient stroll across the road from the beach, serve a decent spread of cheapish tasty seafood. For a **drink**, the bars on Karon Plaza, off the eastern end of Th Luang Pho Chuan, can get quite lively, but are becoming increasingly seedy.

### Kata Centre

**Café del Mar** Th Taina. This small café offers some respite from its seriously ugly surroundings – and the cocktails aren't bad either. There are Thai paintings, paper lanterns, numerous rustically fashioned board games and ambient musical accompaniment.

**Easy Rider Bar** Th Taina. Flashing fairy lights front a dimly lit, log cabin-style bikers' bar. The beer is exorbitantly priced, but come 11pm a bunch of alternative Thai rockers bash out popular hard rock classics with gut-stirring, crowd-pleasing aplomb.

**Kampong-Kata Hill Restaurant** Th Taina. This hilltop traditional Chinese/Thai pagoda-style building, with hanging lanterns and Buddha statues, serves classy Thai dishes.

**Kwong Seafood Shop** Th Taina. Mid-priced barbecued fish and other Thai favourites (including vegetarian options) in an unassuming but unceasingly popular place. Walls are adorned with informative posters on fish of the sea and tropical fruits.

## Directory

**Airlines** All offices are in Phuket Town. Bangkok Airways, 158/2–3 Th Yaowarat ⓣ076/225033; China Airlines ⓣ076/327099; Dragon Air ⓣ022/630367; Korean Air ⓣ076/328540; Malaysia Airlines, 1/8 Th Thungka ⓣ076/213749 or 076/216675; Silk Air/Singapore Airlines, 183 Th Phang Nga ⓣ076/213895; Thai Airways, 78 Th Ranong, international ⓣ076/211 1195 or ⓣ076/212499.

**Banks and exchange** These are plentiful in Phuket Town. In Ao Karon, try the Siam Commercial Bank on Th Karon, south of Th Luang Pho Chuan. In Ao Patong, most banks are a short walk north of the post office on Th Thawewong.

**Books** The Books (daily 11am–9.30pm), just north of The Clock Tower on Th Thepkasatri, Phuket Town.

**Cinema** At the Paradise Multiplex next to Ocean Department Store on Th Tilok Uthit 1, Phuket Town.

**Health** Phuket International Hospital (ⓣ076/249400, emergencies ⓣ076/210935 or 1321), near the Big C on the airport bypass road, just west of Phuket Town, at 44 Th Chalermprakiat Ror 9, is considered to have Phuket's best facilities. In Ao Karon, there's a health centre on Th Patak, just north of Th Luang Pho Chuan.

**Immigration office** At the southern end of Th Phuket, near Ao Makham (ⓣ076/221905; Mon–Fri 8.30am–4.30pm).

**Police station** South Thanon Karon, Ao Karon.

**Post office** On Th Montri, Phuket Town (with poste restante), on Th Patak, just south of Thai Na Rd, in Ao Karon, and on beachfront Th Thawewong, south of its intersection with Th Bang La, in Ao Patong.

**TAT** 191 Th Thalang, Phuket Town (daily 8.30am–4.30pm; ⓣ076/212213).

**Telephones** International calls from the public phone office on Th Phang Nga, Phuket Town (daily 8am–midnight).

**Tourist police** 24hr help available on ⓣ1155 or contact the police station on ⓣ076/355015.

## AO PHANG NGA

Covering some four hundred square kilometres of coast between Phuket and Krabi, the mangrove-lined bay of **Ao Phang Nga** is littered with dramatic limestone karst formations of up to 300m in height.

## What to see and do

The best, and most affordable, way of seeing the bay is to join one of the longtail **boat trips** arranged from the nearby unappealing town of **Phang Nga** (see below). There are half-day tours (daily 8.30am & 2pm; 3–4hr; B300) and full-day tours (8.30am; until 4pm; B600). Overnight trips with a stay on the Muslim stilt village of Ko Panyi cost an extra B250. All prices exclude the B200 national park entry fee. The standard itinerary follows a circular or figure-of-eight route around the bay, passing weirdly shaped karst silhouettes including "James Bond Island" which was Scaramanga's hideaway in *The Man With the Golden Gun*. Most boats return to the mainland via Ko Panyi. **Kayaking** tours of the bay are a lot more expensive and should be arranged from Khao Lak, Phuket, Krabi or Railay.

## Arrival and tours

**By bus** The bus station is on Th Phetkasem, a few minutes' walk from the hotels, banks (with ATMs and exchange) and restaurants along the same road. Phang Nga town has frequent bus connections with Phuket, Krabi and Trang, and some to Surat Thani.

**Boat tour operators** Sayan Tour (Ⓣ076/430348, Ⓦwww.sayantour.com) and Mr Kean Tour (Ⓣ076/430619) in Phang Nga town both have offices inside the bus station and offer similar itineraries. They will also store your baggage for a few hours; they also sell bus and boat tickets to Krabi, Ko Phi Phi, Ko Lanta and Ko Samui.

## Accommodation and eating

For a good feed the restaurant next door to Bangkok Bank (no English title) is very popular with locals for its cheap and tasty Chinese rice and noodle dishes.

**Phang-nga Guest House** 99/1 Th Phetkasem Ⓣ076/411358. A step up from *Thawisuk*, with clean, tastefully decorated en-suite rooms, equipped with cable TV. ❷–❸

**Thawisuk Hotel** 77 Th Phetkasem Ⓣ076/412100. Phang Nga's main budget gig, a few hundred metres north of the bus station. ❶

# KRABI

The small estuary town of **KRABI** is the transport hub for the islands of Ko Phi Phi and Ko Lanta and makes a nice spot for a couple of nights.

Although the town has no beaches of its own, it's only a 45-minute boat ride to the stunning bays of **Laem Phra Nang** and about the same time in a songthaew to **Ao Nang**, a busy mainland beach resort. Every Krabi travel agent sells **sea-kayaking** expeditions (see box, p.874) and snorkelling trips, and many also offer tours of Krabi's mangrove swamps. Krabi River runs north to south on the eastern flank of the town. Thanon Utrakit, west of the river, provides most tourist facilities, with restaurants, a night market and the longtail-boat pier.

## Arrival and information

From Bangkok, the most comfortable option is to get an overnight sleeper train to Surat Thani and then pick up a Krabi bus.

**By bus** Nearly all buses terminate at the Krabi bus station 5km north of town at Talat Kao, from where there's a frequent songthaew service to Th Maharat in the town centre.

**By air** Krabi Airport (Ⓣ075/636541) is 18km east of town, just off Highway 4. Flights are met by private minibuses (B90 per person) and taxis (B400–500 to Krabi or B700 to Ao Nang).

**Tourist information** The TAT office (daily 8.30am–noon & 1pm–4.30pm; Ⓣ075/622163) is beside the estuary on Th Utrakit at the northern edge of the town centre.

## Accommodation

**Chan-Cha-Lay** 55 Th Utrakit Ⓣ075/620952. This stylish blue and white place is a good option. Pay a little extra for the en suites, with fan or a/c, facing onto the stylish back garden. Shared bathroom ❷, en-suite fan ❸, a/c ❺

**K Guest House** 15–25 Th Chao Fah Ⓣ075/623166. This old wooden long house is one mass of timber, with upstairs timber balconies, wooden shutters and bright clean rooms. ❷–❹

**Lipstic** 20 Soi 2, Th Maharat Ⓣ075/612392. Offers very cheap, basic rooms with fan and shared bathroom, and has a warm, earthy bar/restaurant downstairs serving a big selection of Thai and Western dishes. ❶

## Eating

Krabi has plenty of traveller-oriented restaurants. For something more interesting try either the riverside night market near the longtail-boat pier on Th Kong Ka, or the inland night market on Soi 10, Th Maharat, off the northern end of Th Utrakit.

**Ko Tung** Opposite the riverside nightmarket. Makes up for its dull decor with some excellent Thai dishes; popular with locals and travellers alike.

**Pizzeria Firenze** North Th Kong Ka, near its intersection with Th Utrakit. Offers a great selection of authentic Italian cuisine, from pizzas (B150–230) and pasta (B130–160) to tasty tiramisu.

**Raan Ahaan Jeh (Vegetarian Café)** At the northern end of Th Pruksa Uthi, the first parallel road west of Th Utrakit. May not be particularly attractive but it's a good veggie option with meat-substitute curries and stir-fries over rice. Daily 6.30am–2pm.

## Directory

**Airline offices** Bangkok Airways, Th Maharat ⓣ075/701608; Nok Air ⓣ075/76061; One-Two-Go ⓣ075/701539; Thai/Air Asia ⓣ075/701551; Tiger Airways ⓣ022/062222.

**Hospital** Krabi Hospital is about 1km north of the town centre at 325 Th Utrakit (ⓣ075/611212) and also has dental facilities.

**Immigration office** About 150m south of the post office at 116 Th Utrakit (Mon–Fri 8.30am–4.30pm; ⓣ075/611097).

**Police** The police station is 200m south of the immigration office (ⓣ075/611222).

**Post office** A short walk south of *Chan-Cha-Lay* on Th Utrakit.

**Telephones** The CAT international phone office is 2km north of the town centre on Th Utrakit (Mon–Fri 8am–8pm, Sat & Sun 8.30am–4.30pm), reached by any songthaew heading up that road.

## Moving on

**By bus** A/c and non-a/c buses depart for Phang Nga (frequent; 1hr 30min–2hr); Phuket (every 30min; 3–5hr); Ranong (4 daily; 5hr); Surat Thani (hourly; 2hr) and Trang (hourly; 2–3hr). There are also minibuses to: Ko Lanta (2 daily; 2–4hr); Nakhon Sri Thammarat (every 30min 8.30am–4pm; 3hr); Phuket (11.30am; 3hr) and Surat Thani (hourly 7.30am–4.30pm; 2hr).

**By boat** Ferries to Ko Phi Phi (daily 9.30am & 2.30pm; 1hr 30min–2hr) and Ko Lanta (mid-Oct to mid-May 11am; 2hr 30min) use the Krabi Passenger Port outside Krabi town, 2km to the southwest. Ferry tickets, bought from tour operators in town, should include a free transfer from central Krabi, though any Ao Nang-bound songthaew (from Maharat Soi 10, off Th Utrakit, north of the town centre) will also go via the port if requested (about 10min). Longtail boats for East Railay on Laem Phra Nang (45min) leave on demand from the town-centre piers on Th Kong Ka and nearby Th Utrakit. For Ao Ton Sai and West Railay get a songthaew to Ao Nang and jump on a longtail there.

**By air** The listed airlines (see above) collectively supply numerous daily flights to Bangkok; contact offices for flight times and prices. Bangkok Airways also has flights to Samui (Tues, Thurs & Sat; 1.50pm); Thai Air Asia flies to Kuala Lumpur (Mon, Wed, Fri & Sun; 12.45pm) and Tiger Airways flies to Singapore (Mon, Wed, Thurs, Fri & Sun; 9.25pm).

# LAEM PHRA NANG (RAILAY)

The stunning headland of **Laem Phra Nang** is accessible only by longtail boat from Krabi (45min) or Ao Nang (10min), so staying on one of its four beaches feels like being on an island. The sheer limestone cliffs, pure-white sand and emerald waters make it a spectacular spot, though bungalows have now been built on almost every inch of available land so the whole place feels congested.

The beaches are all within ten minutes' walk of each other. **Ao Phra Nang** is the prettiest, with luxuriously soft sand, reefs close to shore, and just one discreet super-luxury hotel. Ao Phra Nang is flanked by **Hat Railay**, technically one bay, but in fact composed of opposing east and west beaches: **East Railay** is not suitable for swimming because of its fairly dense mangrove growth and a tide that goes out for miles, but accommodation here is cheaper. **West Railay**, on the other hand, enjoys impressive karst scenery, crystal-clear water and a much longer stretch of good sand. On the other side of a rocky promontory from northern West Railay, the beach at

**Ao Ton Sai** is coarse and littered with rocks that make it impossible to swim at low tide. Leafy and wedged between towering limestone cliffs this is the travellers' beach, with scores of budget bungalows set amongst the palms several hundred metres back from the shore, and regular all-night beach parties at the beachfront *Freedom Bar* and *Chillout Bar*.

## Activities

**Longtail boat trips** to the cape depart from various spots along the Krabi riverfront and dock at East Railay, from where it's easy to cut across to West Railay along any of the through-tracks. Krabi boats do run during the rainy season, but it's safer to go via Ao Nang instead. Ao Nang is much closer to Laem Phra Nang, and longtails run from the beachfront here to West Railay and Ao Ton Sai (10min) year-round. During high season, there's one direct boat a day to Ko Phi Phi (9.15am; B350).

**Rock climbing** Laem Phra Nang is Thailand's premier rock-climbing centre, with six hundred bolted sport-climbing routes on the cape alone. Check with other tourists before choosing a climbing guide, as operators' safety standards vary (Wee's Climbing School at Ao Ton Sai is highly recommended; ⓣ087/107 8367). A typical half-day introduction costs B800.

## Accommodation

During high season (Nov–Feb), it's essential to arrive on the beaches as early in the morning as possible to get a room.

**Andaman Nature Resort** Ao Ton Sai, on the inland road parallel to the beach ⓣ081/402 0812 (no bookings). Offers small but cosy bungalows that are clean and colour coordinated. Also has a big, rustic, multi-roofed restaurant built into the trees. ❸

**Banyan Tree Resort** Ao Ton Sai, next door to *Andaman Nature Resort* ⓣ075/621644. Two opposing rows of attractive, en suite, spacious bungalows in a cool banyan grove. ❸–❺

### SEA-KAYAKING IN THE KRABI AREA

By far the most enjoyable way of exploring the glories of the Krabi coastline is by **sea kayak**. Paddling silently and stealthily into the eerie mangrove swamps and secret tidal lagoons, or **hongs**, hidden inside the limestone karsts is a fantastic experience and gives you close-up views of birds, animals and plants that would be impossible from a roaring longtail.

*Hongs* can only be accessed at certain tides in canoes small enough to travel along the narrow tunnels that lead into the karst's central pool. Once inside a *hong* you are enclosed by a ring of cliff faces hung with strange plants that nourish a local population of flying foxes and monkeys and support an ecosystem that has remained unchanged for millennia.

The most popular kayaking destination is **Ao Thalen** (also called Ao Talin or Talane), about 25km northwest of Krabi town, where you can paddle out to the *hongs* and beaches of Ko Hong and Ko Bileh. Another 25km north up the Krabi coast, the Ban Bor Tor (aka Ban Bho Tho) area of **Ao Luk** bay is famous for its caves, in particular Tham Lod, which has a long tunnel hung with stalagmites and stalactites, and Tham Phi Hua Toe, whose walls display around a hundred prehistoric cave-paintings.

Kayaking **trips** to any of the above destinations usually cost about B1500–1700 for a full day or B600–900 for half a day; the better companies will take groups of two and limit their numbers to fourteen. Trips can be arranged through any tour operator in Krabi town, Laem Phra Nang or Ao Nang, or with reputable, though more expensive, kayaking operators such as John Gray Sea Canoe (ⓣ076/254505, ⓦwww.johngray-seacanoe.com) and Sea Canoe (ⓣ076/212172, ⓦwww.seacanoe.net) in Phuket Town. Tour leaders should give you full kayaking instruction; if asked, most tour operators can arrange for someone else to paddle you around for an extra B300.

**Rapala Rock Wood Resort** Northern end of East Railay ⓣ081/4763379. The most traveller-friendly place on Railay; has nice wooden huts with mattress-beds set around a garden high above the beach. The cheapest rooms, with shared bathroom, are in a thin bamboo-walled longhouse to the side. ❸–❺

**Railay Cabana** Northern East Railay; follow the path behind *Diamond Cove Resort* on Northern East Railay and turn right at the cave ⓣ075/621733. Set beneath dramatic cliffs on a verdant slope, this place offers cheap, basic huts with en-suite bathrooms or more expensive and extravagant options. ❸–❻

**Tiew Khao Bungalow** Ao Ton Sai, right at the back, on the path leading north into the jungle ⓣ075/621644. Very basic and very cheap stilt bamboo bungalows with no fans and shared bathroom, residing on a steep, leafy escarpment. ❷

**Ya Ya Resort** Central East Railay ⓣ075/622593, ⓦwww.yaya-resort.com. Cosy, wooden, en-suite rooms in elegant three-storey traditional timber buildings set around a tropical garden compound. ❹–❽

## KO PHI PHI

One of southern Thailand's most famous destinations, the two spectacular **Ko Phi Phi** islands, 40km south of Krabi and 48km east of southern Phuket, leapt to international notoriety as the location for the 1999 film, *The Beach*. Then, in December 2004, they became headline news again as the tsunami wreaked inconceivable destruction on the two main beaches of the larger island, **Ko Phi Phi Don**, and on the densely packed tourist village connecting them. The island has made a fast recovery, however, and despite a few barren lots, Ko Phi Phi is very much a thriving tourist hub again. Phi Phi Don's sister island, **Ko Phi Phi Leh**, home to the magnificent Maya Bay, is an uninhabited national marine park and can only be visited on day-trips.

Detailed maps are available at the tourist information centre at the pier, and at any number of travel agents in the village.

### Ao Ton Sai, Laem Hin and Ao Loh Dalum

Ko Phi Phi Don would itself be two islands were it not for the narrow isthmus that connects the hilly expanses to the east and west, separating the stunningly symmetrical double bays of **Ao Ton Sai** to the south and **Ao Loh Dalum** to the north. The land between the two bays is occupied by an ugly tourist village, crammed with guesthouses, tour operators, restaurants, bars, internet cafés and dive centres.

East along the coast from the pier, about ten minutes' walk down the main track, the **Laem Hin** promontory overlooks a quieter patch of swimmable beach. Just a few minutes' walk north through Ton Sai village, seductively curvaceous **Ao Loh Dalum** is much better for swimming and sunbathing, though the tide here goes out for miles.

### Hat Yao (Long Beach)

With its luxurious white sand and large reefs just 20m offshore, **Hat Yao** (Long Beach), east along the coast from Ao Ton Sai, is the best of Phi Phi's main beaches. Longtail boats do the ten-minute shuttle from Hat Yao to Ao Ton Sai between 8am to 8pm, and from Ao Ton Sai to Hat Yao till all hours of the morning, but it's also possible to walk between the two in half an hour. At low tide you can get to Hat Yao along the rocky shore, from Laem Hin, past many quaint secluded beaches; otherwise, a pleasant path feeding off and into these beaches, through forests and resorts, also weaves its way there – while much of the path is lit, at night a flashlight is advisable.

### Diving

Ko Phi Phi is an exceptionally good diving and snorkelling site, and you can arrange day-dives (from B1800) and four-day PADI courses (B10,000) through **Moskito** in Ao Ton Sai (ⓣ076/283208, ⓦwww.moskitodiving.com) or the friendly and professional **Long Beach Divers** on Hat Yao (ⓣ085/783 2043, ⓦwww.longbeachdivers.com).

## TRAVEL TO AND FROM KO PHI PHI

Scheduled **ferries** connect Ko Phi Phi Don with Krabi (2 daily; 1hr 30min–2hr) and Phuket (3 daily; 1hr 30min–2hr 30min). There is at least one a day in low season.

From November to May, there are also daily boats to Ao Nang (1 daily; 2hr) and Ko Lanta Yai (3 daily; 1hr 30min). All boats dock at Ao Ton Sai. From here, you can catch a **longtail** to any of the other beaches or walk – there are no roads or vehicle tracks on Phi Phi Don, just a series of paths across the steep and at times rugged interior.



## Accommodation

Ko Phi Phi is one of Thailand's most expensive locations, with Ao Ton Sai the most exorbitant.

### Ao Ton Sai

**Gypsy Bungalow** On the path leading inland from *Phi Phi Rimlay Resort* at Laem Hin Promontory, east of Ton Sai ⓣ075/601045. This is one of very few open spaces in Ton Sai: overpriced identikit pink plywood huts form a U-shape around a grass football field. There are also five very basic, relatively cheap, shared facility bamboo bungalows with mosquito net and fan. ❹–❺

**Valentine Bungalows** Further up the same path, a short walk from Ao Loh Dalum ⓣ086/962 8496. Quaint, cream wood bungalows, with cosy interiors and basic functional bathrooms, line a hedge and fern-flanked village path. ❹

### Hat Yao

**Long Beach Bungalows** Central Hat Yao ⓣ089/973 6425. Occupying a fine stretch of beach, the twelve cheapest bungalows here have shared bathroom facilities and climb an escarpment at the back. En-suite rooms are a small step up, and closer to the water. ❹–❻

**Paradise Pearl Bungalow** Next door to *Long Beach Bungalows* ⓣ075/618050. The cheapest rooms are spacious bungalows with a mattress on the floor and spotless shared bathrooms, set around a pleasant garden. The ugly cement villas with a/c are overpriced. ❹–❽

**Phi Phi Hill Resort** On the northern tip of Hat Yao, up a very steep stairway ⓣ075/618203, ⓦwww.phiphihill.com. Occupying a large headland plateau, this place offers bungalows with a choice of three different views, the cheapest with shared bathroom facing south over a cliff to the ocean. The restaurant, with ample decking, looks over Hat Yao, southern Phi Phi Don and Phi Phi Ley. ❸–❼

**Viking Resort** On a small beach over the western headland of Hat Yao ⓣ075/829398. The secluded, white-sand beach, the modern art-filled, twisted-timber restaurant and the uniquely designed bungalows nestled in steep forested slopes make staying here well worth the price tag. ❻–❽

## Eating

For cheap, tasty Thai food it's worth trying one of the sit-down restaurants in the market, west of the village centre.

**Cosmic** In two locations: one on the main road heading north from Island Divers; the other down a small soi flanking *Breakers Bar & Grill*. This popular Italian restaurant has all the classics, from bruschettas (B50) to pastas (B140), thin-crust pizzas (from B160) and steaks (B150–250). It also serves authentic Italian desserts, some basic cocktails and has a good selection of wines.

**Papaya** In the village centre, next door to *Tiger Bar* – near the Bank of Ayudhya. Very popular with Thais and expats: serves up delicious Thai standards – its curries being particularly sensational.

## Nightlife

Ko Phi Phi is a Thai party capital. In high season Ao Ton Sai teems with young, hormonal Westerners out for a good time. Four main bars juggle the mantle of party host: **Reggae Bar**, in the heart of the village, and **Carlito's**, **Apache Bar** and **Hippies Bar** on the coastal path running east from the village centre. On any given night, one or two of these bars will be brimming with people.

# KO LANTA

Forested, **Ko Lanta** (full name Ko Lanta Yai), 25km long, offers plenty of fine sandy beaches along its west coast and is a deservedly popular destination. It's also within easy day-tripping distance of the stunning beaches and reefs of Ko Rok Nai and Ko Rok Nok, 47km south (B1300 through any tour agent). In the

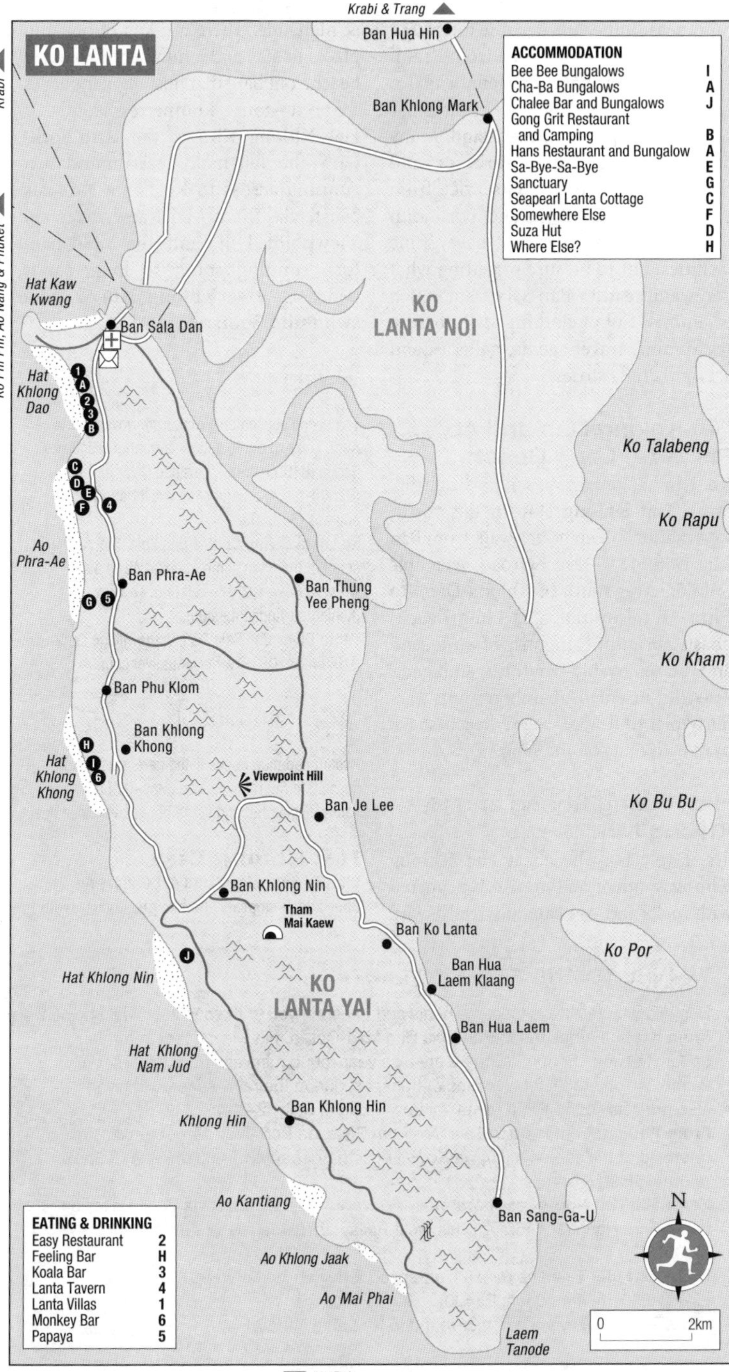

KO LANTA
Krabi & Trang
Krabi
Ko Phi Phi, Ao Nang & Phuket
Ko Rok
ACCOMMODATION
Bee Bee Bungalows I
Cha-Ba Bungalows A
Chalee Bar and Bungalows J
Gong Grit Restaurant and Camping B
Hans Restaurant and Bungalow A
Sa-Bye-Sa-Bye E
Sanctuary G
Seapearl Lanta Cottage C
Somewhere Else F
Suza Hut D
Where Else? H
EATING & DRINKING
Easy Restaurant 2
Feeling Bar H
Koala Bar 3
Lanta Tavern 4
Lanta Villas 1
Monkey Bar 6
Papaya 5
Ban Hua Hin
Ban Khlong Mark
KO LANTA NOI
Hat Kaw Kwang
Ban Sala Dan
Hat Khlong Dao
Ao Phra-Ae
Ban Phra-Ae
Ban Thung Yee Pheng
Ban Phu Klom
Ban Khlong Khong
Hat Khlong Khong
Viewpoint Hill
Ban Je Lee
Ban Khlong Nin
Tham Mai Kaew
Ban Ko Lanta
Ban Hua Laem Klaang
Ban Hua Laem
Hat Khlong Nin
KO LANTA YAI
Hat Khlong Nam Jud
Khlong Hin
Ban Khlong Hin
Ao Kantiang
Ban Sang-Ga-U
Ao Khlong Jaak
Ao Mai Phai
Laem Tanode
Ko Talabeng
Ko Rapu
Ko Kham
Ko Bu Bu
Ko Por
N
0 2km

rainy season the seas become too rough for boats to get to Ko Lanta from Krabi.

A road runs the entire length of Ko Lanta's west coast, but there's no regular songthaew service on the island. Many bungalows rent out **motorbikes**, and there is a motorbike taxi service from the commercial centre and port, **Ban Sala Dan**. Most beaches have some facilities, but to be sure of getting what you want head to Ban Sala Dan, which is jammed full of clothing stalls, banks, restaurants, travel agents, galleries and arts and crafts stores.

### Hat Khlong Dao and Ao Phra-Ae (Long Beach)

Ko Lanta's longest beach is beautiful, broad **Hat Khlong Dao** in the northwest, about half an hour's walk from Ban Sala Dan, or 2–3km by road. A couple of kilometres south of Khlong Dao, **Ao Phra-Ae** (also known as **Long Beach**) boasts a beautiful long strip of white sand and an enjoyably youthful ambience. Traveller-oriented bamboo huts are fairly plentiful here, as are beach-shack **bars** with mats on the sand.

### Hat Khlong Khong and Hat Khlong Nin

The lovely long beach at **Hat Khlong Khong**, south of Ao Phra-Ae, is peppered with rocks and you can only really swim at high tide. There are lots of beautiful places to stay and a number of colourful beachfront bars that host regular parties.

About four kilometres south of Hat Khlong Khong, the road forks, with the left-hand, east-bound arm running across to Ko Lanta Yai's east coast, via Tham Mai Kaew caves and Viewpoint Hill, and the right-hand fork running south to long, sandy, laid-back **Hat Khlong Nin**, a good swimming spot.

## Diving

The diving season only runs from November to April. The two outfits below both offer Discover Scuba (B4000–4500), Certified Diver day-trips (B2600–3100) and four-day PADI Open Water courses (B13,500)

**Ko Lanta Diving Centre** Ban Sala Dan. A little south of the town centre, behind *Nang Sabai German Bakery* ⓣ075/684065, ⓦwww.kohlantadivingcenter.com.

**Lanta Diver** Ban Sala Dan, in the village centre ⓣ075/684208, ⓦwww.lantadiver.com.

## Accommodation

Accommodation prices listed here are for high season; in the rainy season (May–Oct) rates are vastly discounted and some bungalows close down.

### Hat Khlong Dao

**Cha-Ba Bungalows and Art Gallery** An über-kitsch dinosaur-themed guesthouse, with

### TRAVEL TO AND FROM KO LANTA

Bungalow touts always meet the boats and transport you to the beach of your choice.

**From Krabi:** Ferries run to Ban Sala Dan (mid-Oct to mid-May: 11am, returning at 8am & 1pm; 2hr 30min). There are also year-round minivans from Krabi (2 daily; 2–4hr), which are the only means of transport during the rainy season. Minivans also run year-round to Ko Lanta Yai from Trang (3 daily; 2–4hr).

**From Phuket:** Ferries go to Sala Dan from Rassada Port (Nov–May; 8am & 1pm, returning at the same times), via Ko Phi Phi (1hr; departing 11.30am, 2pm & 3pm; returning 8am & 1pm).

**From Tha Hat Nopparat Thara (near Ao Nang):** Ferries travel via West Railay on Laem Phra Nang (2hr 15min; pass West Railay at 10.45am & 12.45pm; return at 1.30pm).

**From Ko Lipe:** Tigerline runs a high-speed ferry service between Ko Lanta and Ko Lipe (10.30am; 4hr 30min; B1400).

**From Trang:** Minivans run year-round to Ko Lanta (4 daily).

salmon-pink, yellow and baby-blue huts, the cheapest with basic interiors and loud, clashing wallpaper. Has a bright blue, Flintstones-esque restaurant/bar. 5–7

**Gong Grit Restaurant and Camping** ⓣ089/592 5844, ⓔgonggrit@hotmail.com. Has small and slightly larger tents (with mattress, blanket and pillows) behind its sandy, rustic timber restaurant. It's behind a small canal, so beware of the mosquitoes. 2

**Hans Restaurant and Bungalow** ⓣ075/684152, ⓦwww.krabidir.com/hansrestaurant. The cheapest and arguably most pleasant place to stay on Hat Klong Dao with shaggy bungalows in a long casuarina grove. 3

## Ao Phra-Ae (Long Beach)

For cheap accommodation, try the small operations in the area behind *Funky Fish*.

**Sa-Bye-Sa-Bye** Behind *Funky Fish* ⓣ087/905 9677. Tiny bamboo huts with immaculate bathrooms in a cool, shady grove. 3

**Sanctuary** Southern end of the beach. Elegant bamboo bungalows with pretty interiors and open-air bathrooms, set in two rows leading back from the beach. The Batak/Thai-style restaurant roof is impressive and there is a cute bar hut on the beachfront. 4–6

**Seapearl Lanta Cottage** North Long Beach ⓣ075/684504, ⓔseapearllanta_@hotmail.com. Standard-issue bamboo bungalows, roomy with good en-suites, in two opposing well spaced out rows occupying a sandy palm grove. 4–6

**Somewhere Else** North Long Beach ⓣ015/360858. Attractive, en-suite bamboo bungalows of octagonal design with tasteful interiors and immaculate bathrooms on a lively part of the beach. 4–6

**Suza Hut** North Long Beach ⓣ081/537 7220, ⓔsuzahutlanta@gmail.com. There are only four dishevelled little bungalows in this sandy little place by the sea. Very laid-back. 3

## Hat Khlong Khong and Hat Khlong Nin

**Bee Bee Bungalows** Hat Khlong Khong ⓣ081/537 9932, ⓦwww.diigii.de. Immaculate en-suite huts, each individual and a beautiful experiment in bamboo architecture. The restaurant/bar is equally special. 3–5

**Chalee Bar & Bungalows** Hat Khlong Nin ⓣ087/685 0080. A rambling, rickety restaurant with cheap rooms in its second storey, which offers a good view of the beach. It also has slightly more expensive wooden huts clustered in the cute garden out the back. 2

**Where Else?** Hat Khlong Khong ⓣ081/536 4870, ⓦwww.lanta-where-else.com. A beachside hippy village utopia, creatively built from all natural products. Has idiosyncratic bamboo and coconut-wood bungalows with beautifully decorated interiors and a fabulous beachfront restaurant/bar. 4–7

# Eating, drinking and nightlife

## Hat Khlong Dao

**Easy Restaurant** Popular for its consistently tasty Thai standards.

**Koala Bar** Considered to have the best cocktails on the island with everything from scrumptious strawberry daiquiris (B150) to potent originals, like the pan galactic gargle blaster (B350).

**Lanta Villas** The nightly seafood barbecues here are very popular.

## Ao Phra-Ae (Long Beach)

Bars take turns putting on parties so there's usually something going on somewhere. Check the *Ko Lanta Chronicle* events calender or simply ask around. Try *Ozone Bar* on Thursday evenings (north of *Somewhere Else*), *Chillout Bar* on Sundays and Tuesdays (behind *Somewhere Else*), *Klapa Klum* on Fridays (100m south of *Ozone*) and *Irie Bar* on Saturdays (inland from *Klapa Klum*). *The Earth Bar* and *Opium* (inland and south on the island road) are both popular for their regular dance music parties.

**Lanta Tavern** On the island road, south of the *Funky Fish* turn-off. While not cheap, this cute British-run restaurant is considered by many to be the best place on the island for Western food, with tasty dishes like chicken breast stuffed with ham, asparagus and cheese served with creamy white sauce (B260), pastas (B180) and triple-decker sandwiches (B100–120).

**Papaya** On the island road, south Long Beach, just north of the 7-11. Very popular with expats for its tasty Thai food at considerably cheaper prices than the beachfront restaurants.

## Hat Khlong Khong and Hat Khlong Nin

There is a burgeoning nightlife that revolves around the ten or so little beach bars here.

**Feeling Bar** At *Where Else?* Featuring driftwood sculptures and multiple chill-out zones – many quirkily boat-shaped, including one housing a pool table – this place puts on regular parties.

**Monkey Bar** At *New Coconut Bungalows*. Known to put on a good party.

## Directory

**Health Centre** Just south of the town centre is Saladan Health Centre (☎075/684170; doctors available Mon–Fri 9am–noon & 1–3pm).
**Post office** Unsigned, in a long strip mall of basic shopfronts, opposite the canopied stalls of the market, south of the village centre (Mon-Fri 8.30am–4.30pm, Sat 9am–noon).



# The deep south

As Thailand drops down to meet Malaysia, the cultures of the two countries begin to merge. Many inhabitants of the **deep south** are ethnically more akin to the Malaysians, and a significant proportion of the 1,500,000 followers of Islam here speak Yawi, an old Malay dialect. Some also yearn for secession from Thailand, and in 2004 there was an escalation in violent militancy, leading the Thai government to introduce special security measures in certain parts of Pattani, Yala and Narathiwat provinces – for up-to-the-minute advice, consult your government travel advisory. The safest **border crossings to Malaysia** are detailed below.

## TRANG AND AROUND

**TRANG** hosts a **vegetarian festival** every October, but is chiefly of interest for the string of gorgeous **beaches and islands** nearby. Travel agents offer a number of snorkelling day-trips to the islands of Ko Hai, Ko Mook, Ko Kradan and Ko Libong, which provide a perfect getaway, and also have some accommodation. Trang province's coastline, from Ban Pak Meng down to Ban Chao Mai, offers some exceptional beaches, well worth exploring on motorbike, by car or as a part of a tour. Trang town's main thoroughfare is the Rama VI, where you will find all the restaurants, bars, accommodation, banks and travel agents you're likely to need – most cluster near the train station at its western extremity. Internet is available at Gigabyte (9am–9pm), opposite and a little west from *Ko Teng Hotel.*

## Arrival and information

**By bus** All buses arrive at the terminal on Th Huay Yod, to the north of the centre, a tuk-tuk (B50) or motorbike taxi (B30) into town
**By train** The train station is at the western end of Th Rama VI.
**By air** Trang Airport is around 3km south of town. World Travel Services Ltd on Th Rama VI, 50m from the train station, runs a flight-correlated minibus service to and from the airport (B90 per person).
**Tourist information and travel agents** TAT has a small tourist office up a small soi off Th Rama VI, opposite the city hall 100m east of the clocktower (☎075/215867). Further information on the town and area is available at Ⓦwww.trangonline.com. Near the station, at 22 Th Sathanee, staff at Trang Island Hopping (☎075/211457, Ⓦwww.sukorn-island-trang.com) provide an excellent booking service and source of information. KK Travel, around the corner at 44 Th Sanathee, also gives out extensive information on Trang island accommodation.

## Accommodation

**Ko Teng Hotel** 77–79 Th Rama VI ☎075/218622. This ancient run-down place has a certain olde-world quality. The spacious rooms all come with en suites; a few extra baht will get you cable TV and a/c. ❸
**Yamawa** 94 Th Visetkul, north from the clock tower on Th Rama VI ☎075/216617. The stairwell here is beautifully decorated, with woven walls, hanging vines and pot plants. All rooms come with en suite and cable TV, and many have balconies. The B200 single bedrooms are in fact better than their double-bed neighbours. ❸

## Eating

For a cheap feed, try the night markets on Th Ruenrom.
**Meeting Point** Th Sanathee, near the train station. Smart, well-run place; caters largely to foreigners, with espresso coffee, pancakes, pasta, burgers, pizzas, steaks and a large Thai menu. 7am–8pm.

**Wunderbar** Rama VI, around the corner. Has cheap and tasty Thai standards and well-executed Western fare – pizza, pastas and burgers. Doubles as a small travel agent and has one internet station.

## Moving on

**By bus** to: Krabi (hourly; 2–3hr); Nakhon Si Thammarat (3 daily; 2–3hr); Phuket (hourly; 5hr); Satun (every 30min; 3hr). Travel agents sell tickets for minibus services to Ko Lanta (hourly; 3hr) and Pak Bara (2 daily; 1hr 30min) and bus/longtail packages to the Islands.

**By train** 2 trains depart for Bangkok daily (14–16hr).

**By boat** Tigerline (☎081/092 8800, Ⓦwww.tigerlinetravel.com) runs a high-speed ferry service from nearby Hat Yao Pier to Ko Lanta (2hr 30min), via Ko Mook (30min) and Ko Ngai (1hr), departing at 1pm daily; and to Langkawi in Malaysia (4hr 30min), via Ko Lipe (3hr), departing at 12.30pm,

**By air** Nok Air flies twice-weekly to Bangkok's Don Muang airport (Fri & Sun 4.10pm).

# KO TARUTAO NATIONAL MARINE PARK

The unspoilt **Ko Tarutao National Marine Park** is probably the most beautiful of all Thailand's accessible beach destinations. The park covers 51 mostly uninhabited islands, of which three – Tarutao, Adang and Lipe – are easy to reach and have accommodation. The park's forests and seas support a fascinating array of wildlife, including **turtles**, which lay their eggs on Ko Tarutao between September and April. Snorkelling gear can be rented at Pak Bara visitor centre or on Ko Adang for B50 per day, and is widely available from the private bungalow outfits or dive shops on Ko Lipe. The park amenities on Tarutao and Adang are closed to tourists from mid-May to mid-November, while getting to Lipe at the height of the monsoon in September and early October is an unlikely – or at the very least unappealing – proposition.

## Ko Tarutao

Hilly **Ko Tarutao**, the largest of the islands, is covered in rainforest and has perfect beaches all along its 26-kilometre west coast. Boats dock at **Ao Pante**, on the northwestern side, where the admission fee (B200) is collected; here you'll find the park headquarters (☎086/956 9540) and a visitor centre, restaurant and a small shop, all of which give off a distinct feeling that you've entered a military facility. You can stay here in the overpriced national park bungalows, longhouses (B500–1000), or tents (B225; no bedding or mattress provided), or pitch your own tent (B30 per person

### TRAVEL TO AND FROM KO TARUTAO

In season, **ferries** leave **Pak Bara** (daily 10.30am & 1.30pm) for the roughly ninety-minute voyage to Ao Pante on Ko Tarutao (B250 one way); they then continue on to Ko Adang (B550 from Pak Bara), about two hours west of Ko Tarutao, from where it's a short longtail hop (B50) to any of the beaches on Ko Lipe. Ferries make the return journey from Ko Lipe at 10am and 2pm daily. Bundaya and Lipeh Ferry **speedboats** depart at 11.30am and 1.30pm to Ko Tarutao and Ko Lipe (1hr 30min; B650, return B1200). Call the Pak Bara National Park Visitor Centre (☎074/783485 or 074/783597) for up-to-date information.

To get to Pak Bara from Trang, either take the direct high-season **minibus** run by *Sukorn Beach Bungalows and Tours*, or catch a Satun-bound bus (2hr 30min) or share-taxi (1hr 30min) to Langu and change to a red songthaew for the ten-kilometre hop to the port.

From Satun, frequent buses and taxis travel the 50km to Langu.

If you miss the boat in Pak Bara, try the friendly **Bara Guesthouse** (☎089/654 2801; ❷–❸), a row of rough cement-rendered en-suite huts, 500m before the pier.

per night). Behind the settlement, the steep, half-hour Tolkienesque climb to **To-Boo Cliff** is a must, especially at sunset, for its fine island, river, beach and offshore island views. Boat trips, arranged at the park headquarters (1hr; B450 per boat; fits 10 people), venture up a bird-filled, mangrove-lined canal to Crocodile Cave. A half-hour walk south from Ao Pante brings you to the quiet, white-sand bays of **Ao Jak** and **Ao Molae**, the latter with bungalows (B1000) and a restaurant; beyond (2hr from Ao Pante; look out for the road behind the house at the south end of Ao Molae) lies **Ao Sone**, a timeless, all natural beach environment, backed by a steep forested escarpment.

In the 1930s and 1940s Tarutao was used as a penal colony. At **Ao Taloh Wow**, a rocky bay on the east side of the island (12km by road from Ao Pante; B40 per person in a car), are the remains of a penal colony for common criminals. There are also prison remains at **Ao Taloh Udang**, a sandy bay on the south side. Political prisoners were kept here under conditions far more favourable. The trail to Ao Taloh Udang is now overgrown, leaving longtails, seating ten people and hired at the Park Headquarters for B3000 a day, as the only means of access.

## Ko Adang

**Ko Adang**, a wild, untamed island covered in rainforest, has a **national park station** at Laem Sone beach, the luxurious white-sand curve of its southeast coast. Facilities include a cafeteria-style restaurant, a visitor centre and en-suite rooms in bungalows (B800) and longhouses (B400); both sleep four. There are also tents for rent (B150–300 for 3–4 people), with pillows and mattresses (B50 per person), that can be pitched in a pleasant casuarina grove fronting the beach (pitch your own for B30 per person). Should you wish to venture further afield, contact the visitor centre for information on forest trails, waterfalls and excellent snorkelling trips to nearby islands (B1200–2000 for 6–8 people, price depending on the selected tour).

## Ko Lipe

Covered in coconut plantations and forests, and home to upwards of seven hundred *chao ley* or sea gypsies (a traditionally nomadic group, with animistic beliefs and their own language), **Ko Lipe** has become considerably more commercial and expensive in recent years. There is now a cluster of exorbitantly priced bungalow resorts, restaurants and bars and an excess of longtails now tainting **Pattaya beach**, the beautiful crescent of soft white sand on the island's south coast.

Between Ocean Pro Divers and *Baracuda Bar*, at the centre of Pattaya beach, a dirt trail lined with a low-key string of restaurants, cafés, travel agents and clothing stalls leads northeast to the charmingly ramshackle **Chao Ley village** and **Sunlight beach**, on the east coast. There's plenty of foliage, crystal-clear water, good snorkelling at small offshore islands and a laid-back atmosphere here, but the beach's northern and southern extremities are perhaps its finest assets.

Northwest of the village, a sandy trail leads inland, through grass lands and forest, past the popular bar/restaurant, *Jack's Jungle Bar*, to pretty little **Sunset beach**, where there are sunsets aplenty.

For **diving**, contact Sabye Sports at *Porn Resort* (Ⓣ089/464 5884, Ⓦwww.sabye-sports.com), or Forra Diving on Sunlight, south of the village (Ⓣ089/673 1121, Ⓦwww.forradiving.com)

## Accommodation

### Pattaya beach

**De Zee Hut** Ⓣ089/761 6266. Has funky yellow bamboo bungalows with attached open-air bathrooms, set back from an attractive stretch of beach. ❹

## INTO MALAYSIA FROM SOUTHERN THAILAND

Because of ongoing violence in the deep south, all major Western governments are currently advising people not to travel to or through the Thai provinces of Songkhla, Pattani, Yala and Narathiwat. This includes the city and transport hub of Hat Yai and several of the main border crossings to Malaysia: by rail from Hat Yai (and Bangkok) to Butterworth via Padang Besar, and down the east coast to Kota Bahru. The provinces of Phatthalung, Trang and Satun, however, are not affected, leaving the border crossings from Satun and Ko Lipe as the safest route into Malaysia.

### From Satun

Remote Satun, in the last wedge of Thailand's west coast, has boat and overland passages to Malaysia. Satun's bus terminal is at the town's southeastern periphery, but many buses also make a detour through the town centre. Should you need to stay here, try *Rian Thong* (☎074/711036; ❶), 4 Th Saman Pradit, the best budget hotel. *On's*, 48 Th Bureewanit (☎081/097 9783), serves Thai and Western food, rents out motorbikes (B250 per day) and acts as a tourist information service.

It is possible to cross by road into Malaysia at Thale Ban National Park, either on your own transport or by share taxi to Alor Setar (contact *On's*). Songtheaws to Thammalang pier, 10km south of Satun, leave in front of the 7-11 on Thanon Sulakanukul (the southern continuation of Thanon Bureewanit). From Thammalang pier, longtail boats leave, when full, to Kuala Perlis (45min; B100) on the northwest tip of Malaysia, from where there are plentiful transport connections down the west coast. Ferries from Thammalang to the Malaysian island of Langkawi depart at 9.30am, 1.30pm and 4pm (50min; B300, B600 return).

### From Ko Lipe

There's a ferry to Langkawi (daily 3.30pm, 2hr; B900 one way), and a speedboat service (4pm; 1hr; B1200 one way). An immigration officer lives permanently on Ko Lipe and can be contacted via the island's travel agents.

### From Hat Yai

It is not recommended to travel to **Hat Yai**, but being a major transport hub and stop-off point to or from Malaysia, you might find yourself stuck here. If so, make your way to *Cathay Guesthouse/Tour* (93/1 Th Niphat-Uthit 2, ☎074/243815; ❷), a short walk east from the train station, which has a small café, basic en-suite rooms, provides information on train timetables and organizes onward flight, bus and a/c minibus transportation.

### Sunlight beach

**Andaman Resort** To the north ☎074/ 728017. Ask for one of the basic bamboo bungalows in two long rows behind the resort's northern casuarina grove. ❹–❻

**Coco Bungalow** To the south ☎084/407 8071. Charming, the cheapest accommodation on the island. ❸

**Viewpoint Bungalows** To the south ☎03/193 3362. Made up of stilt en-suite bungalows climbing an escarpment above a gorgeous boulder-bordered beach. ❹–❺

### Sunset beach

**Porn Resort** ☎089/464 5765. Offering simple bungalows and tents (B150) in a slightly dishevelled hillside compound. ❸–❻

## Ko Bulon Lae

Tiny **Ko Bulon Lae**, a lovely undeveloped island, has one beautiful arc of white-sand beach on its southeast coast and a hilly interior of forests, rubber plantations and small fishing communities. It's actually just outside Ko Tarutao National Park but easily reached from Pak Bara, 20km to the east.

In high season, **ferries** leave Pak Bara for Ko Bulon daily at 1.30pm (1hr; B350 one way, B600 return) while every two days a speedboat does the same journey (30min; B350, return B600). Services are reduced, sometimes to

**TREAT YOURSELF**

On a gorgeous stretch of Sunlight beach, south of the village, **Castaway Beach Resort** (Ⓣ083/138 7472, Ⓦwww.castaway-resorts.com; ❾) is a perfect place to splurge for one or two nights of luxury accommodation. The hardwood bungalows are spacious and elegant, with large, cushioned balconies, and the modern Thai architecture of the restaurant/bar and decking area fronting the beach is exquisite. Food, while expensive, is likely to make you drool (the menu consists of local specialties, Thai standards and a few Western meals – an English breakfast will not disappoint) and the well-stocked bar delivers plenty of excellent cocktails.

nothing, during the monsoon season; contact *Pansand Resort's* agent in Trang, First Andaman Travel, 82–84 Th Wisetkul (Ⓣ075/218035), for the latest information. From Ko Lipe a ferry leaves for Ko Bulon daily at 3pm (2hr; B550), while a speedboat does the same journey every two days, departing at 9am and stopping at Ko Bulon (1hr; B600) before continuing on to Ko Muk, Ko Ngai, then Ko Lanta (5hr; B1500).

## Accommodation

**Jungle Hut Resort** True budget travellers should head for the middle of the island (15min walk from the beach – take the path behind *Marina Resort*) to a peaceful rubber plantation, where the cheap stilt huts immaculately kept are a welcome escape from it all. ❶

**Marina Resort** Ⓣ081/598 2420. More costly, but great value, consisting of fabulous stilt huts, with spacious, beautifully furnished interiors and set in a lush, tropical garden (a short walk inland), this place is worth forking out for. ❺

**School Bungalows** The cheapest accommodation available on the beach, a row of bamboo-woven en-suite bungalows 50m from the beach – ask at the school. ❷

# Vietnam

## HIGHLIGHTS

**SA PA:** the perfect mountain base for trekking through paddy-fields and villages

**HA LONG BAY:** sail through grottoes, islands and jagged limestone outcrops

**HANOI, OLD QUARTER:** wander through the city's narrow, fascinating streets

**HUE:** the hillside mausoleums of former emperors can be reached by slow boat along Hue's Perfume River

**HOI AN:** have a new silk wardrobe run up in this charming ancient town

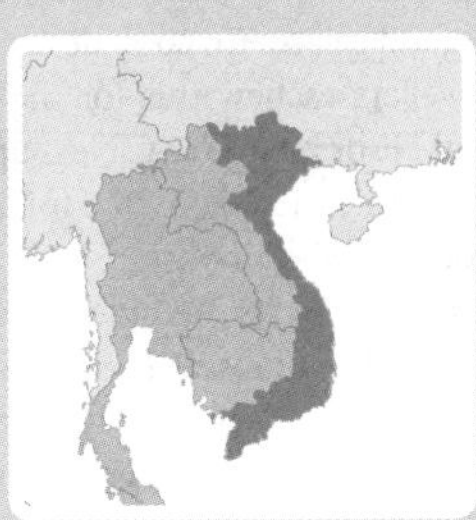

**MEKONG DELTA:** a network of slender, shaded canals, floating markets and fruit orchards

## ROUGH COSTS

**DAILY BUDGET** Basic US$15–25/ Occasional treat US$30

**DRINK** Bottle of beer (US$1)

**FOOD** Pho (noodle soup) (US$0.50–1)

**BUDGET HOTEL** US$5–10

**TRAVEL** Hanoi to Hue (660km): Train 14hr, US$15; tourist bus 16hr, US$10

## FACT FILE

**POPULATION** 85.2 million

**AREA** 329,560 sq km

**LANGUAGE** Vietnamese

**RELIGIONS** Two-thirds Mahayana Buddhism.

**CURRENCY** Vietnamese dong (VND) or US$

**CAPITAL** Hanoi

**INTERNATIONAL PHONE CODE** ⓣ084

**TIME ZONE** GMT + 7hr

# Introduction

**History weighs heavily on Vietnam, but over thirty years after the end of its infamous war, this incredibly resilient nation is finally emerging from its shadows. As the number of tourists soars, the word is out that this is a land not of bomb craters and army ordnance, but of shimmering paddy-fields and sugar-white beaches, full-tilt cities and venerable pagodas. The speed with which Vietnam's population has been able to transcend the recent past comes as a surprise to visitors who are generally met with warmth and curiosity. Average monthly incomes remain at about $50 for city dwellers, but drop to $15 in the poorest provinces.**

For the majority of visitors, the furiously commercial southern city of **Ho Chi Minh City** (HCMC) provides a head-spinning introduction to Vietnam, so a trip out into the rice fields and orchards of the nearby **Mekong Delta** makes a welcome next stop. If you then head north, the quaint hill-station of **Da Lat** provides a good place to cool down, but some travellers eschew this for the **beaches** of **Mui Ne** or **Nha Trang**. Next up comes the enticing little town of **Hoi An**, full of wooden shop-houses, and aristocratic **Hue**, with its temples, palaces and imperial mausoleums. **Hanoi** has served as Vietnam's capital for close on a thousand years and is a rapidly developing but absorbing city of pagodas and dynastic temples, where life proceeds – for now – at a relatively gentler pace than in Ho Chi Minh. From here, most visitors strike out east to the labyrinth of limestone outcrops in **Ha Long Bay**. The market town of **Sa Pa**, set in spectacular uplands close to the Chinese border in the far northwest, makes a good base for exploring nearby ethnic minority villages.

## CHRONOLOGY

**c. 2000 BC** A highly organized society of rice-farmers, the Lac Viet, emerge in the region.

**111 BC** The Chinese Han emperors take over the Red River Delta; they introduce Confucianism and a rigid, feudalistic hierarchy.

**938 AD** Vietnamese forces defeat the Chinese at the battle of the Bach Dang River, heralding nearly ten centuries of Vietnamese independence (in the north) under a series of dynasties.

**c. Third century onwards** The kingdom of Champa dominates the south, and builds numerous temples, including My Son. From the end of the eleventh century onwards, it loses territory to the Viets from the north.

**Sixteenth century** Two powerful clans split the country in two: the Trinh lords in Hanoi and the north, and the Nguyen in Hue down to the Mekong Delta.

**1771** The Tay Son rebellion led by three brothers with a message of equal rights, justice and liberty gains broad support. By 1788 they have overthrown both the Trinh and Nguyen lords.

**1802** Vietnam comes under a single authority when Emperor Gia Long captures the throne and establishes his capital at Hue, building its magnificent citadel and reimposing feudal order.

**1858** A French armada captures Da Nang. By 1862, they control the Mekong Delta, and by 1887 the whole country, creating the Union of Indochina.

**1930** Ho Chi Minh establishes the Indochinese Communist Party, its goal an independent Vietnam governed by workers, peasants and soldiers.

**1941** Ho Chi Minh returns to Vietnam after thirty years, joining other resistance leaders and forging a nationalist coalition, known as the Viet Minh.

**1941–1945** Vietnam is controlled by Japan; in March 1945 they establish a nominally independent state under Bao Dai, the last Nguyen emperor.

**1945** Following Japanese surrender Ho Chi Minh calls for a national uprising, known as the August Revolution, and on September 2 proclaims an independent Vietnam. It is not recognized by the Allied countries, and Vietnam is put under British

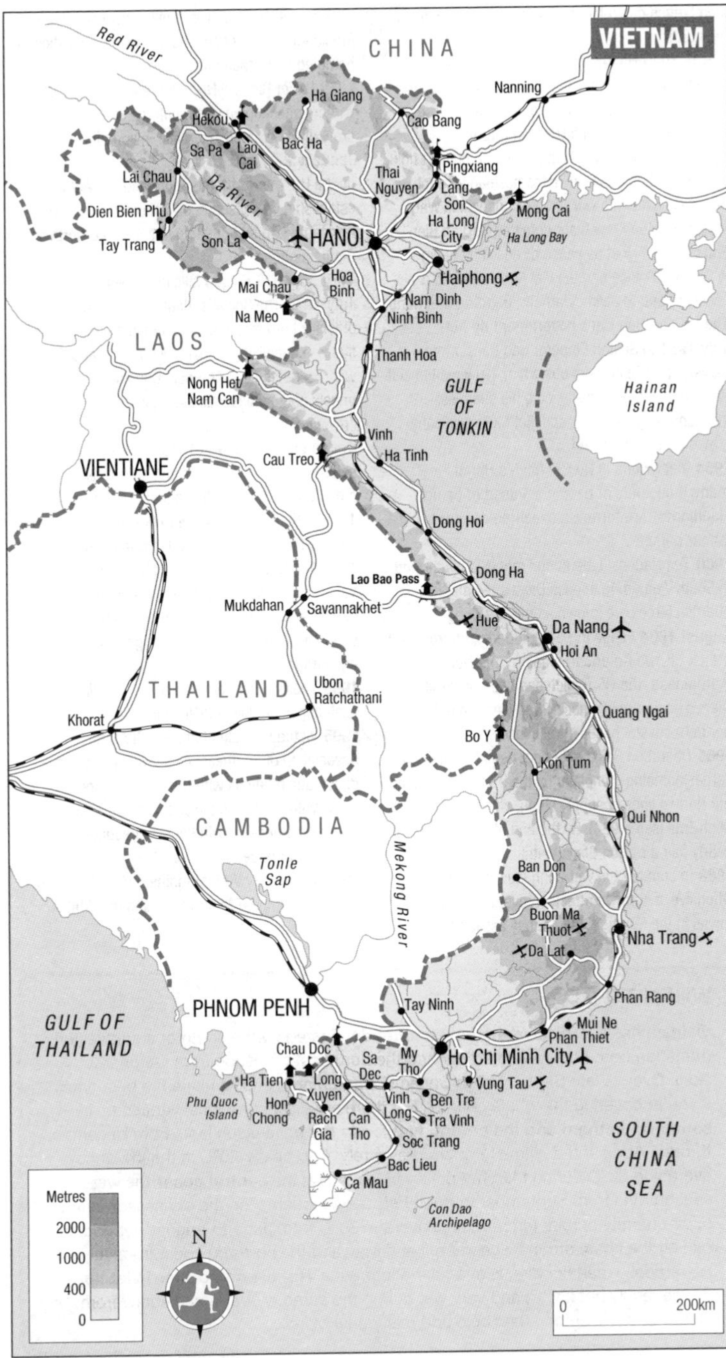
VIETNAM
CHINA
Red River
Nanning
Ha Giang
Hekou
Cao Bang
Sa Pa
Lao Cai
Bac Ha
Pingxiang
Lai Chau
Da River
Thai Nguyen
Lang Son
Mong Cai
Dien Bien Phu
Ha Long City
Ha Long Bay
Tay Trang
Son La
HANOI
Haiphong
Mai Chau
Hoa Binh
Nam Dinh
Na Meo
Ninh Binh
LAOS
Thanh Hoa
GULF OF TONKIN
Hainan Island
Nong Het/ Nam Can
Vinh
Cau Treo
Ha Tinh
VIENTIANE
Dong Hoi
Dong Ha
Lao Bao Pass
Mukdahan
Savannakhet
Hue
Da Nang
Hoi An
THAILAND
Ubon Ratchathani
Quang Ngai
Khorat
Bo Y
Kon Tum
Qui Nhon
CAMBODIA
Mekong River
Tonle Sap
Ban Don
Buon Ma Thuot
Nha Trang
Da Lat
Phan Rang
PHNOM PENH
Tay Ninh
Mui Ne
Phan Thiet
GULF OF THAILAND
Chau Doc
Sa Dec
My Tho
Ho Chi Minh City
Ha Tien
Long Xuyen
Vung Tau
Phu Quoc Island
Hon Chong
Vinh Long
Ben Tre
Rach Gia
Can Tho
Tra Vinh
SOUTH CHINA SEA
Soc Trang
Bac Lieu
Ca Mau
Con Dao Archipelago
Metres
2000
1000
400
0
N
0
200km

then French control in the south and Chinese in the north.

**March 1946** Ho Chi Minh agrees on a limited French force to replace the Chinese, with France recognizing the Democratic Republic as a "free state" within the French Union in return.

**1946–1954** The treaty with the French doesn't hold, and skirmishes between Vietnamese and French troops escalate into war (the First Indochina War).

**May 1954** The French are defeated at Dien Bien Phu on May 7, just as peace discussions begin in Geneva. France and the Viet Minh agree to a ceasefire and to divide Vietnam, pending elections. The US and Bao Dai's government do not.

**July 1954** In Saigon Emperor Bao Dai's prime minister Ngo Dinh Diem ousts him, declares himself President, and begins silencing his enemies, including religious sects and Viet Minh dissidents – over 50,000 are killed.

**1954** Meanwhile In Ho Chi Minh's Hanoi many thousands of people accused of being "landlords" are tortured, executed or sent to labour camps.

**1960** The National Liberation Front (NLF) is formed in South Vietnam to oppose Diem's regime; its guerrilla forces are known as the Viet Cong.

**August 1964** Following an, allegedly, unprovoked attack on two American ships by the North Vietnamese, the US (which had been bankrolling Diem's government since 1950) starts bombing northern coastal bases in response.

**1965** Operation Rolling Thunder begins, a massive carpet-bombing campaign by the US to try and stop the North's lines of supply south, along the Ho Chi Minh Trail (see p.934). By the end of 1967 there are nearly half a million GIs in Vietnam.

**1968** In January the Viet Cong launch the Tet Offensive, a surprise attack on over a hundred towns in the South. In March they assault the US Embassy in Saigon, and five Americans die. President Johnson announces a virtual cessation of bombing and peace talks begin.

**1969** Under Richard Nixon there is a gradual US withdrawal coupled with reinforcing the South's army and a dramatic increase in bombing.

**January 27, 1973** The Paris Accords are signed by the US, the North, the South and the Viet Cong, establishing a ceasefire; all American troops are repatriated, though fighting between the North and South continues.

**April 30, 1975** Saigon falls to the North.

**July 1976** The Socialist Republic of Vietnam is officially born, and Hanoi ushers in a rigid socialist state, nationalizing land, industry and trade. Those with connections to America, Buddhist monks, priests and intellectuals are interned in "re-education camps".

**December 25, 1978** In 1975, the Khmer Rouge seized power in Cambodia and soon after make cross-border forays into Vietnam. On Christmas Day 1978, 120,000 Vietnamese troops invade Cambodia and oust Pol Pot, remaining there until 1989.

**1986** The new reformist general secretary Nguyen Van Linh introduces sweeping economic reforms, known as *doi moi* or "renovation". A market economy is embraced, and foreign investment encouraged.

**1993** The US lifts their veto on aid, and Western cash begins to flow into Vietnam.

**1995** Vietnam is admitted into ASEAN (the Association of Southeast Asian Nations), and full diplomatic relations with the US are restored.

**1997** With the economic crisis across Southeast Asia Vietnamese growth flags, but economic reforms continue.

**2007** In January Vietnam joins the WTO; in July President Nguyen Minh Triet visits the White House.

## WHEN TO GO

Vietnam has a tropical **monsoon climate**, dominated by the south or southwesterly monsoon from May to September and the northeast monsoon from October to April. Overall, late September to December and March and April are the best times if you're covering the whole country, but there are distinct regional variations. In **southern Vietnam and the central highlands** the dry season lasts from December through April, and daytime temperatures rarely drop below 20°C in the lowlands, averaging 30°C during March, April and May. Along the **central coast** the wet season runs from September through February, though even the dry season brings a fair quantity of rain; temperatures average 30°C from June to August. Typhoons can hit the coast around Hue in April and May and the northern coast from July to November, when flooding is a regular occurrence. **Hanoi and northern Vietnam** are generally hot (30°C) and very wet during the summer, warm and sunny from October to December, then cold and misty until March.

# Basics

## ARRIVAL

Vietnam has three **international airports**: Noi Bai in Hanoi, Tan Son Nhat in HCMC and Da Nang in central Vietnam. The national airline is Vietnam Airlines, which also has a controlling stake in Pacific Airlines, with pricey flights to and from Asia, Europe, Australia and the US. The cheapest option to get to Vietnam from outside Asia is to take a budget flight to Bangkok or Singapore, and travel overland or take a cheap connecting flight from there.

Current routes within Asia include Hanoi to Kunming, Beijing, Hong Kong, Tokyo, Louang Phabang, Vientiane and Bangkok; and HCMC to Phnom Penh, Singapore, Kuala Lumpur and Bangkok. Low-cost airfares are offered by Tiger Air (Singapore to Hanoi and HCMC) Air Asia (Bangkok to Hanoi), Nok Air (Bangkok to Hanoi), and Bangkok Air (Bangkok to HCMC).

An increasing number of travellers, especially backpackers, arrive overland through one of Vietnam's **borders** with Cambodia, Laos and China. **Visas** for Vietnam must be arranged in advance (see below).

### Overland from Cambodia

Tourist buses ply the route between Phnom Penh and **HCMC**, via the **Moc Bai** border crossing (see p.100). Alternatively, take a local bus from Phnom Penh to the border, then continue by share taxi to HCMC. Foreigners can also cross at a popular border crossing at **Vinh Xuong**, near Chau Doc in the Mekong Delta; some tour operators run boats from Phnom Penh down the Mekong River through to Chau Doc in Vietnam (see p.100). There is another border checkpoint near Chau Doc at **Tinh Bien** (see p.100). The newest crossing open to foreigners is at **Ha Tien** (see p.130) near Kep and Kampot on the Cambodian side and just 10km from Ha Tien in Vietnam.

### Overland from Laos

There are six border points between **Laos** and Vietnam where tourists can cross overland. The **Lao Bao Pass** (see p.458), roughly 240km from Savannakhet, is the most popular. There's also an international bus link between Savannakhet and Da Nang, which can take up to 24hr (see p.452). New border crossings have recently opened at **Bo Y** near Kon Tum in the Central Highlands (see p.472) and **Tay Trang** near Dien Bien Phu in the far northwest (see p.999), which offer two interesting but challenging routes. There are additional crossings close to the Vietnamese city of Vinh at **Cau Treo** (see p.453) and **Nong Het** Nam Can (east of Phonsavan in Laos; see p.439), and the more remote, seldom used **Na Meo** (east of Xam Nua; see p.439).

There have been several complaints from travellers using buses coming from Laos to the Vietnam border about tour operators; ask fellow travellers about the more reliable ones.

### Overland from China

At the time of writing, the Chinese border was open to foreigners at three points: at **Lao Cai** (from Kunming on the Chinese side; see p.993), **Mong Cai** (from Guangzhou; see p.989) and, busiest of all, at **Huu Nghi** (from Pingxiang or Nanning; see p.981). There is one **direct train service** between China and Vietnam from Beijing to Hanoi (see p.981 for details). The Kunming–Hanoi service was suspended in 2004; you can take the bus to Lao Cai, and then take the train from there to Hanoi.

## VISAS

All foreign nationals need a **visa** to enter Vietnam. **Tourist visas** are generally valid for **thirty days** from your specified arrival date and cost about $30–70, depending on where you apply. **Three-month visas** are also available for about $90–130; both types take three to ten days to process, though some agencies and consulates offer an express one-day service. See p.57 for a list of Vietnamese embassies abroad. In Southeast Asia, Bangkok and Phnom Penh are the cheapest, quickest and most popular places to apply for a Vietnamese visa (1–5 working days).

On arrival, you will need to complete an **Arrival and Departure Card.** You must hand back this card at Customs when you leave the country, so keep it somewhere safe. If you're arriving with more than $7000, you'll need to declare it on this form.

There are now a few **authorized agents** in Vietnam – including Ann Tours and Exotissimo Travel in HCMC (see p.908) – who can issue **visas on arrival** (contact the agent five days before to secure paperwork; costs start at $25 plus $20 "stamp fee"); this is especially helpful for people with no Vietnamese consulate in their home country, or simply those strapped for time. The agent will send you a special clearance fax to show upon arrival in Vietnam and will inform the relevant airline for boarding clearance; they will then meet you off your flight and hand over the official documents at immigration.

At the time of writing, **thirty-day visa extensions** were being issued through tour agents and travellers' cafés in HCMC, Nha Trang, Hoi An, Hue, Da Nang and Hanoi (around $25; 1–3 days), but the situation changes frequently, so check with the embassy before you leave. The **fine** for overstaying your visa can also vary, ranging from no charge for up to a week's overstay to a maximum of $50 for longer.

### AIRPORT DEPARTURE TAX

Airport departure tax is $14 for international flights departing from HCMC and Hanoi, $8 from Da Nang. Tax for domestic flights is 10,000–25,000VND (dependent on the individual airports). All taxes are now included in the price of your airline ticket.

## GETTING AROUND

Vietnam's main thoroughfare is Highway 1, which runs from Hanoi to HCMC and is shadowed by the country's main rail line. **Public transport** has improved considerably in the past few years, with many upgraded trains and state-run buses, fleets of "open-tour" buses run by travellers' cafés, and an increasing amount of high-quality, privately owned minibuses. Having said that, there's still much room for improvement: local bus timetables are often unreliable and some travellers find themselves overcharged for tickets, or forced to change buses mid-route and pay a second time. Many tourists opt for internal flights in order to avoid these hassles, but as everywhere, nothing beats local transport as a way to see the country and interact with locals.

### Planes

Vietnam Airlines (Ⓦwww.vietnamairlines.com.vn) operates a reasonably cheap, efficient and comprehensive network of **domestic flights** and has branch offices in many towns; addresses and contact details are given in the Directory sections for towns. The two-hour journey between Hanoi and HCMC ($70), for instance, compares favourably with the thirty or more hours you might spend on the train. Book as far ahead as you can.

### Buses, minibuses and open-tour buses

Vietnam's **national bus network** offers daily services between all major towns.

The government is slowly introducing a national upgrading of state buses, but for now many remain unbearably cramped with hard seats; breakdowns are frequent and progress slow. All towns have a bus station, and larger places have both a local and a long-distance station. Most buses depart early, from 5am through to mid-morning, waiting only as long as it takes to get enough passengers. For longer journeys, tickets are best bought a day in advance, since many routes are heavily over-subscribed. Prices at certain tourist hot spots can be over the odds – always try to ascertain the correct price (most bus stations now have a board displaying timetables and fares) and buy a ticket before boarding. Fares for shorter distances (2–4hr) should be around 30–50,000VND; overnight journeys 80–160,000VND.

Privately owned **minibuses** compete with public buses on most routes; they sometimes share the local bus station, or simply congregate in the centre of a town, and you can also flag them down along the major highways. Though generally even more cramped than ordinary buses, they do at least run throughout the day. There are also an increasing number of privately owned "high-quality" **air-conditioned minibuses** run by the recognizable white and green Mai Linh taxi company – particularly in the south – that operate from their own offices as well as some bus stations; these usually stick to a timetable, don't pick up passengers en route, and provide free bottled water. Fares are surprisingly similar to those charged on public buses.

Special **"open-tour" buses** shuttling between major tourist destinations are the most popular and comfortable way for foreigners to travel in Vietnam. Competition is fierce, so prices are coming down, though they are still more expensive than local buses. The best thing to do is buy a one-way through-ticket, for example from HCMC to Hue ($16) or Hanoi ($23), which enables you to stop off at specified destinations en route: heading north, the main stops are Da Lat, Nha Trang, Phan Thiet/Mui Ne, Hoi An, Da Nang and Hue. Phone a day in advance to secure your seat. You can also buy separate sector tickets between certain destinations. Tickets and onward reservations are available from agents in each town.

## Trains

Though Vietnamese **trains** (Ⓦwww.vr.com.vn) can be slow on some services, they generally provide a comfortable, inexpensive and pleasant way to travel the country. The country's main line shadows Highway 1 on its way **from HCMC to Hanoi** (1726km), passing through Nha Trang, Da Nang and Hue en route. **From Hanoi**, one branch goes northwest to Lao Cai; another runs north to Dong Dang, which is the route taken by the two weekly trains from **Hanoi to Beijing**; and the third goes to **Hai Phong**.

The most popular lines with tourists are the shuttle from Da Nang to Hue, which offers some of the most stunning views in the country, and the overnighters from Hue to Hanoi and from Hanoi up to Lao Cai, for Sa Pa. Four "**Reunification Express**" trains depart each day from Hanoi to HCMC and vice versa. They are labelled S1 to S8; odd-numbered trains travel south, even ones north, hence the S2 (34hr), S4, S6 and S8 (all 40hr) depart daily from HCMC, and the S1 to S7 (same times) make the trip in the opposite direction.

When choosing which **class** to travel in, it's worth paying extra for more comfort. Hard seats are bearable for short journeys (and can make for interesting encounters with local people), but even soft seats can be rather uncomfortable for long hauls. On overnight journeys, you should go for a **berth**: cramped hard-sleeper berth compartments have six bunks (cheapest at the top) and soft-sleeper berths have only four bunks. S3–S8 trains have a choice of soft-sleeper berths and soft seats with a/c or fan; hard-sleeper berths and hard seats have fan only. On the modern S1 and S2 (faster) trains, all compartments, even hard-sleeper, have a/c, and reclining soft seats are located in new double-decker carriages. Simple meals are included in the price of the ticket on overnight journeys. Booking ahead is essential, and you may need your passport when you buy a ticket.

**Fares** vary according to the class and the speed of the train. On the slowest services from HCMC to Hanoi (S4, S6 & S8), HCMC to Nha Trang costs around $7 for a hard seat, $14 for a soft berth; from HCMC to Da Nang, the same classes cost $11 and $26; and from HCMC to Hanoi they cost $36 and $50. On S1 and S2 express trains, soft seats from HCMC to Hanoi cost $38 and soft-sleepers $58.

## Vehicle rental

For most foreign visitors to Vietnam self-drive car rental is still not an option. However, it's easy to hire a **car, jeep or minibus with driver** from tour agencies and tourist offices ($20–60 per day). Check who pays for the driver's accommodation and meals, fuel, tolls, parking fees and repairs, and what happens in the case of a major break-down. Sign a contract showing this and the agreed itinerary, and arrange to pay half before and the balance at the end.

**Bicycles** are available from hotels and tour agencies in most towns; main tourist spots usually charge around $1 per day. **Motorbike** ($6–10 per day) or **moped** ($4–7) rental is possible in most major towns, but the appalling road discipline of most Vietnamese drivers means that the risk of an accident is very real (see box opposite). Organized motorbike tours can be a better option (see p.896). If you go it alone, check everything carefully, especially brakes, lights and horn. Also check the small print on your **insurance** policy, and consider taking out local **accident insurance** anyway. The biggest local insurer is Bao Viet, with offices in HCMC and Hanoi; their policies cost $14 for the basic three-month cover and are easy to obtain. **Repair shops** are fairly ubiquitous – look for a Honda sign or ask for *sua chua xe may* (motorbike repairs) – but you should still carry at least a puncture-repair kit, pump and spare spark plug. Fuel (*xang*) is around $0.80 (13,000VND) per litre and widely available; many roadside vendors keep a few bottles handy. Always leave your bike in a parking compound (*gui xe*) or pay someone a dollar or two to keep an eye on it.

The theory is that you **drive on the right**, though in practice motorists and cyclists swerve and dodge wherever they want, using no signals and their **horn** as a surrogate brake. **Right of way** invariably goes to the biggest vehicle on the road; note that overtaking vehicles assume you'll pull over onto the hard shoulder to avoid them. It's best to avoid driving after dark, since many vehicles don't use headlights. Road conditions can be extremely poor in rural areas off the national highways; livestock cause serious hazards and landslides are very common. If you are involved in an **accident** and it was deemed to be your fault, the penalties can involve fairly major fines.

## Local transport

**Taxis** are becoming increasingly common in big cities, and there are also some useful city **bus** services, which are especially handy for transport between major bus stations and shuttling to and from the airports. Elsewhere, you'll have to rely upon a host of two- and three-wheeled vehicles, the most ubiquitous being the **xe om** or motorbike taxi, also known as the **Honda om**. Drivers wait at bus stations and along the roadside in even the remotest of towns to take you and your luggage to your chosen destination. A ten-minute journey should cost around 10,000VND.

Cheap, ubiquitous and fun, **cyclo** – three-wheeled bicycle rickshaws – can carry one person (two at a push) and cost a dollar or less for a five- to ten-minute hop, depending on your bargaining prowess. However, now cyclo are more commonly used for sightseeing rather than getting around, and they are banned from many city centre roads. The motorized version of the cyclo, found in the south, is known as the **cyclo mai**. In the Mekong Delta, the **xe dap loi** is also a variation on the cyclo theme, and the motorized version is known as a **Honda loi**.

There's a growing **safety problem** with hiring cyclo, xe om and taxis across the country, particularly in cities. As a general guideline, avoid using them after dark and always agree a price before setting off, ensuring you know which currency you are dealing in (five fingers could mean 5000VND or $5), and whether you're negotiating for one passenger or two; it's best to write the fare down before you start your journey. With taxis, if you don't agree the fare upfront, make sure that the meter is on before you start your journey. Be wary of some meters that suddenly race ahead, or drivers insisting that your hotel is "closed" or "full," and taking you to another one; this is usually part of a commission scam – always be firm with your directions. It's best to try and get your hotel to recommend you a taxi.

**Xe lam** (also known as **Lambros**) are three-wheeled, motorized buggies whose drivers squeeze in more passengers than you'd believe possible. These act as a local bus service outside Hanoi and HCMC, and rows of them are usually found either at the local bus station, or outside the local market. A typical xe lam ride of a few kilometres costs around 5000VND.

## ACCOMMODATION

Compared to other Southeast Asian countries, **accommodation** in Vietnam can be poor quality and pricey, though better in the main tourist spots. The cheapest option is a bed in a **dormitory**; an increasing number of budget guesthouses (*nha khach*) and rooms for rent in Hanoi, HCMC, and other tourist centres, offer dorms at around $3–6 per bed per night. Next up is a simple fan room with shared washing facilities, in either a **state-run hotel** (*khach san*) or **guesthouse** for around $4–7. In the main tourist destinations, **rooms**, **mini-hotels** (a modest, privately owned hotel) and **hotels** now offer fairly decent rooms with fans, private bathroom, hot water and phone, for around $6–10; add a/c and satellite TV and they can range from $10 to $30. **Rates** are often negotiable in budget hotels, especially for stays of more than

### WEAR A HELMET

A shocking 11,000 people die every year on Vietnamese roads, and a further 30,000 are seriously injured. An estimated forty per cent of those injuries could have been prevented by wearing a helmet. Traffic accidents are the leading cause of death, severe injury and evacuation for foreigners. Insist on a helmet before renting a motorbike or getting on the back of a *xe om*, and check that the chin straps are properly adjusted and fastened before taking off. Since December 2007, it has been mandatory to wear a helmet when travelling on all Vietnamese roads, major and minor, with fines of up to 200,000VND for violation. Helmets can be bought in Hanoi and HCMC for $20–35.

one night, and during low season prices can drop by up to fifty percent. Some places add a government **tax** and service charge of fifteen percent.

Hotel **security** can be a problem, so never leave valuables in your room, and use your own padlock on the door if possible. **Prostitution** is rife in Vietnam, and in less reputable budget hotels it's not unknown for Western men to be hassled at night. Hotels often close their shutters between 10 and 11pm – however most have a porter sleeping inside the door, so knock politely to be let in.

Not all places are permitted to take foreigners: if the staff merely smile and shake their heads, chances are this is the case. On the whole there's no need to book ahead, except during the festival of Tet (early spring).

## FOOD AND DRINK

The cheapest and most fun places to eat are the **street kitchens**, which range from makeshift food stalls set up on the street to open-fronted eating houses. They are permanent, with an address if not a name, and most specialize in one type of food, generally indicated on a signboard, or offer the ubiquitous *com pho* rice dishes and noodle soups. **Com binh dan**, "people's meals", comprise an array of prepared dishes like stuffed tomatoes, fried fish, tofu, pickles and eggs, plus rice; expect to pay from around 20,000VND for a good plateful. Outside the major cities, street kitchens rarely stay open beyond 8pm.

Western-style **Vietnamese restaurants** (*nha hang*) have chairs and menus and usually serve a wide range of meat and fish dishes. Menus often don't show prices and overcharging is a regular problem. Peanuts, hot towels and tissues on the table will be added to the bill even if untouched; ask for them to be taken away if you don't want them. A modest meal for two will cost roughly $8–10. The more expensive restaurants tend to stay open until 9.30 or 10.30pm, have menus priced in dollars and, in some cases, accept credit cards; a meal for two will cost around $10 and up.

Catering primarily to budget travellers, **travellers' cafés** tend to serve reasonably priced but mediocre Western and Vietnamese dishes, from banana pancakes to steak and chips or fried noodles – and usually open from 7am to 11pm. They're mainly found in Hanoi, HCMC, Hoi An, Hue, Nha Trang and Da Lat.

### Vietnamese food

Though closely related to Chinese cuisine, **Vietnamese food** is quite distinct, using herbs and seasoning rather than sauces, and favouring boiled or steamed dishes over stir-fries. The staple of Vietnamese meals is **rice** (com), with **noodles** a popular alternative. Typically, rice will be accompanied by a fish or meat dish, a vegetable dish and soup. Vietnamese food tends not to be overly spicy, as chilli sauces are served separately. Vietnam's most popular seasoning is *nuoc mam*, a fermented **fish sauce**. The use of monosodium glutamate (**MSG**) can be excessive, and what looks like salt on the table may be MSG, so taste it first. You can try asking for no MSG in your food: "*khong co my chinh*".

### ADDRESSES

Where two numbers are separated by a slash, such as 110/5, you simply make for no. 110, where an alley will lead off to a further batch of buildings – you want the fifth one. Where a number is followed by a letter, as in 117a, you're looking for a single block encompassing several addresses, of which one will be 117a.

The most famous Vietnamese dish has to be **spring rolls**, known as *cha gio, cha nem, nem ran* or just plain *nem*. Various combinations of minced pork, shrimp or crab, rice vermicelli, onions, beansprouts and fragrant herbs are rolled in rice-paper wrappers, and then eaten fresh or deep-fried, usually dipped in the ubiquitous chilli-fish sauce. The other great staple is **pho** (pronounced "fur"), a noodle soup eaten at any time of day but primarily at breakfast. The basic bowl of pho consists of a light beef or chicken broth flavoured with ginger and coriander, to which are added broad, flat rice-noodles, spring onions and slivers of chicken, pork or beef. **Lau** is more of a main meal than a soup, where the vegetable broth arrives at the table in a **steamboat** (a ring-shaped dish on live coals or, nowadays, often electrically heated) and you cook slivers of beef or prawns in it, and then afterwards drink the flavourful liquid that's left.

Most restaurants offer a few **meat-free dishes**, such as stewed spinach or similar greens, or a mix of onion, tomato, bean sprouts, various mushrooms and peppers; places used to foreigners may do **vegetarian** spring rolls (*nem an chay*, or *nem khong co thit*). At street kitchens you're likely to find tofu and one or two dishes of pickled vegetables. However, soups are usually made with beef stock, morsels of pork fat sneak into many dishes and animal fat tends to be used for frying. The phrase to remember is *nguoi an chay* (vegetarian), or seek out a vegetarian rice shop (*tiem com chay*) – Buddhist restaurants that serve faux-meat dishes. On the 1st and 14th/15th days of every lunar month, many Vietnamese spurn meat, so you'll find more veggie options then.

Vietnam is blessed with dozens of tropical and temperate **fruits**. Pineapple, coconut, papaya, mangoes, longan and mangosteen flourish in the south. A fruit you might want to give a miss is the **durian**, a spiky, yellow-green football-sized fruit with an unmistakably pungent odour reminiscent of mature cheese and caramel, but tasting like an onion-laced custard.

## Drinks

Don't drink the **water** in Vietnam, including **ice** which is frequently added (no ice, thanks, is "*dung bo da, cam on*"). Most guesthouses and hotels provide thermos flasks of boiled water, hot tea is always on offer, and cheap, **bottled water** (10,000VND or less per litre) and carbonated drinks are widely available. *Giai khat* means "quench your thirst", and you'll see the signs everywhere.

Other good thirst-quenchers include fresh coconut milk, orange and lime **juices**, and sugar-cane juice (*mia da*). Somewhere between a drink and a snack is **chè**, sold in glasses at the markets. Made from taro flour and green bean, it's served over ice with chunks of fruit, coloured jellies and even sweetcorn or potato. Small cups of refreshing, strong **green tea** are presented to all guests or visitors in Vietnam: the well-boiled water is safe to drink.

As one of the leading exporters of **coffee**, the Vietnamese are proud of their brew. The **coffee** is very strong and served in small quantities, prepared using a stainless steel "dripper" that sits on the top of the glass, black with sugar (*ca phe den*), iced (*ca phe da*) or with a large dollop of condensed milk (*ca phe sua*).

Several foreign **beers** are brewed under licence in Vietnam, but good local brews include 333 (Ba Ba Ba), Halida and Saigon. **Bia hoi** ("fresh" or draught beer) is served warm from the keg and then poured over ice. Its quality varies, but it's unadulterated by chemicals. *Bia hoi* has a 24-hour shelf life, so the better places sell out by early evening. There are dozens of lively *bia hoi* outlets in Hanoi and HCMC; most offer snacks of some sort. The stronger, pricier **bia tuoi** comes in a light or dark brew. The most common local **wine** is rice alcohol; the ethnic minorities drink stem alcohol (*ruou can*).

## CULTURE AND ETIQUETTE

Vietnam shares the same **attitudes to dress and social taboos** (see p.45) as other Southeast Asian cultures. In a pagoda or temple you are also expected to leave a small **donation**. Passing round **cigarettes** (to men only) is always appreciated and is widely used as a social gambit aimed at progressing tricky negotiations and bargaining. If you have been invited to dinner, always wait for your host to be seated first, and never refuse food that is placed in your bowl during the meal; it will be taken as a sign of ingratitude.

**Tipping**, while not expected, is always appreciated; a few thousand dong should suffice. However, sometimes, especially in rural areas away from the tourist trail, it is not unusual for a waiter to chase after you down the street to give you your "change" – their reciprocal act of hospitality towards you.

Although officially deemed a "social evil" on par with drug use and prostitution, **homosexuality** is largely ignored in Vietnam, though discretion is advised. The gay scene is slowly emerging in Hanoi and HCMC, but athough the number of openly gay men is on the increase, lesbianism is still very much underground. Visit Ⓦwww.utopia-asia.com for more information and advice.

## SPORTS AND ACTIVITIES

Outdoor pursuits and adventure sports have really taken off in Vietnam over the past few years, and specialist tour agencies now offer a wide range of options for adventurous travellers.

### Trekking and rock climbing

Compared to other countries in Asia, **trekking** in Vietnam remains relatively low key, but one-day hikes and longer treks incorporating overnight stays in minority villages are a popular way to explore the countryside. Sa Pa and Mai Chau in the north, and to a lesser extent Da Lat and Kon Tum in the Central Highlands, provide good bases for treks into the hills. A guide is strongly recommended for longer treks into more remote areas, especially if you intend to stay the night, as many places are sensitive to the presence of foreigners, and some require a permit or may even be out of bounds altogether. As the tallest mountain in Vietnam, Mount Fan Xi Pan (p.995) offers the most challenging hike in the country, but easier, very pleasant treks can be taken around the country's national parks, including Cat Ba (see p.989), Cuc Phuong (see p.984) and Yok Don.

The rivers and waterfalls around Da Lat provide good conditions for **canyoning** and **rock climbing**, and the limestone karsts and caves around Ha Long Bay have begun to attract international attention for their climbing and bouldering opportunities.

### Biking and motorbiking

**Mountain-biking** and **motorbiking** are becoming increasingly popular means of travel for tourists visiting Vietnam. The most popular routes include Hanoi to HCMC through the Central Highlands along the Ho Chi Minh Highway, the Northwestern circuit (see p.999), the Mekong Delta, and numerous mountain-to-coast routes starting in Da Lat and ending in Mui Ne, Nha Trang or Hoi An. You can rent your own bike or motorbike, but make sure you have adequate insurance cover; a guide is highly recommended. **Tours** can be booked with independent guides, travel agencies or outfits such as the legendary Easy Riders in Da Lat (see p.932).

## Diving and watersports

An increasing number of **watersports** operators are opening up along Vietnam's 3000-kilometre coastline, though classes and equipment rental aren't cheap. Mui Ne is the country's premier **kitesurfing** and **windsurfing** destination, hosting an international kitesurfing competition every spring (usually February). Several operators in Nha Trang and Hoi An can organize **wakeboarding, waterskiing, kitesurfing** and **sea-kayaking**, while the surf is up on China Beach near Da Nang from September to December. **Sea-kayaking** between the karsts around Cat Ba Island is one of the most rewarding ways to experience Halong Bay.

The waters around Phu Quoc, Nha Trang and Hoi An are popular places for **scuba diving** and **snorkelling**, and established outfits such as Rainbow Divers offer certified courses to suit all levels.

# COMMUNICATIONS

**Mail** can take anywhere from four days to four weeks in or out of Vietnam; from major towns, eight to ten days is the norm. Rates for all post office services are posted up in the main halls. **Poste restante** services are available in major towns, including Hanoi, HCMC, Da Nang, Hue, Hoi An and Da Lat. Mail is held for between one and two months; you will need to show your passport.

When **sending a parcel** take it to the post office parcel counter (often open mornings only; take your passport as well) unwrapped and keep it small. After inspection, and a good deal of form-filling, the parcel will be wrapped for you. **Receiving parcels** is not such a good idea – they are subject to customs inspections and import duty and some simply go astray.

There are **internet cafés** in virtually all towns and cities, and most provide a variety of services, including cheap international calls (around 5000VND/min, available at some in the main cities, although the connection can be poor; better is Skype) and document scanning, which is cheaper than faxing. Most hotels and guesthouses have internet access, usually free for guests, and an increasing number of restaurants, travellers' cafés and hotels offer free WiFi.

The **post office** is cheapest for conventional international and long-distance domestic calls from private booths, as well as receiving faxes (they charge 1100–500VND to receive one). Add the prefix **171** or **177** (so ⓣ171+00 + country code + area code) for international calls – this gives you a flat rate of 11,500VND per minute to over fifty countries. There's no facility for reverse-charge calls, but you can almost always get a "**call-back**" to the post

### VIETNAM ON THE NET

ⓦ **www.vietcourses.com** Informative website about learning Vietnamese, with audio pronunciation, online tests and a dictionary.

ⓦ **www.saigonesl.com** Teachers' website with information on living, working and culture in Vietnam.

ⓦ **www.vietnamadventures.com** Regularly updated articles on travel in Vietnam, including a question-answering service.

ⓦ **www.vietnamtourism.com** Official tourist information site, lists basic background information about the country and its main tourist attractions, and also provides an expensive hotel and tour booking service.

ⓦ **vietnamnews.vnagency.com.vn** Online version of the national English-language daily newspaper, with brief snippets of local, regional and international news.

office you're calling from, for the price of a one-minute call.

In theory, you can dial abroad direct from a **public telephone**, but they're usually unbearably noisy. Calling direct from **hotel** rooms costs at least an extra ten percent and there's a minimum charge even if the call goes unanswered.

The general enquiries numbers are: International Operator ⓣ110; Directory Enquiries ⓣ116. **Public phones** (all card phones) are only in the main cities. Phonecards (international: 150,000VND or 300,000VND; domestic: 30,000VND or 50,000VND) can be purchased at the post office.



## CRIME AND SAFETY

Violent **crime** against tourists in Vietnam is extremely rare, but there are a few things to be wary of. Some tourist destinations, such as HCMC and Nha Trang, now have a fairly bad reputation for thieves, pickpockets and con-artists, and some cases of **bag snatching** – day or night – have caused a few serious injuries. Always take care when carrying valuables and money, and wherever possible leave them in a secure place at your hotel. You should also be careful with taxis and cyclo (see p.893). At night, there is a fair amount of **drug selling** on the streets of HCMC, Hanoi, Nha Trang and even Sa Pa. In some places, cyclo drivers may sell you **drugs** and then turn you in to the police. A substantial bribe might persuade them to drop the matter, otherwise, you're looking at fines and jail sentences for lesser offences, or the death penalty for smuggling large quantities.

Vietnam is generally a safe country for **women** to travel around alone; most Vietnamese will simply be curious as to why you are on your own. That said, it pays to take the normal precautions, especially late at night, when you should avoid taking a cyclo by yourself; take a taxi instead. Asian women travelling with a white man have reported cases of harassment – probably because they are assumed to be prostitutes. Men should also be careful travelling alone at night as they may become targets for petty thieves or **prostitutes**, who are renowned for pickpocketing unsuspecting men, customers or not.

If you have anything **stolen**, go to the nearest **police** station and ask for a report for your insurance company; try to recruit an English-speaker to come with you – and be prepared to pay a few dollars (usually around $20) as a "fee". Corruption among police and other officials can be a problem: very occasionally, trumped-up fines are imposed on bus, cyclo or other drivers seen carrying a Westerner – fines you'll often be expected to pay. But with patience, plus a few cigarettes to hand round, you should be able to bargain fines down considerably.

Not surprisingly, the Vietnamese authorities are sensitive about **military installations**, border regions, military camps, bridges, airports and train stations. Anyone taking photographs near such sites may be stopped, or receive the ubiquitous "fine". **Unexploded mines** still pose a serious threat: the problem is most acute in the Demilitarized Zone, where each year a few local farmers are killed or injured. Always stick to well-trodden paths and never touch any shells or half-buried chunks of metal.

## MEDICAL CARE AND EMERGENCIES

**Pharmacies** can generally help with minor injuries or ailments, and provide some medication without prescription; in major towns you may well find a pharmacist who speaks French or even English; HCMC and Hanoi have reasonably well-stocked pharmacies. That said, drugs past their shelf life and even counterfeit medicines are rife, so inspect packaging carefully, check use-by dates – and bring

> **EMERGENCY NUMBERS**
>
> Try to get a Vietnamese-speaker to phone for you.
> Police ⓣ113
> Fire ⓣ114
> Ambulance ⓣ115

anything you know you're likely to need from home.

Local **hospitals** will treat minor problems, but in a real emergency your best bet is to head for Hanoi or HCMC, where excellent international medical centres can provide diagnosis and treatment. Hospitals expect immediate cash payment for health services rendered, so if you can, bring a credit card with you as fees, especially in the international clinics, may exceed the ATM transaction limit. Keep all receipts in order to seek reimbursement from your insurance company.

## INFORMATION AND MAPS

Your best bet for **information** are reception desks at guesthouses and hotels, or the many **travellers' cafés** and tour operators across the country, but especially in Hanoi and HCMC. The Vietnamese government maintains a handful of **tourist promotion offices** around the globe, but state-owned tourist offices in Vietnam itself are profit-making concerns and not information bureaux. The biggest of these is Vietnamtourism (ⓦwww.vietnamtourism.com), with offices in Hanoi, HCMC and other major tourist centres. There's also a general **information telephone number**, government-run and in English – dial ⓣ1080 (free).

The best **maps** of Vietnam are the International 1:1,000,000 *Travel Map of Vietnam*, and several covering Vietnam, Laos and Cambodia, including Rough Guides' (1:1,200,000), and Nelles' (1:1,500,000).

## MONEY AND BANKS

Vietnam's **currency** is the **dong**, usually abbreviated as "VND" or "d". Notes come in denominations of 200VND, 500VND, 1000VND, 2000VND, 5000VND, 10,000VND, 20,000VND, 50,000VND, 100,000VND and 200,000VND; coins – the first in Vietnam for 25 years – were issued in 2003 in denominations of 200VND, 500VND, 1000VND, 2000VND and 5000VND. The **US dollar** operates in parallel to the dong as unofficial tender, and most travellers carry some dollars as back-up. Dong are not available outside the country, though if you take in some small-denomination US dollars you'll have no problems getting by until you reach a bank. At the end of your trip, you can change leftover dong back into dollar bills. At the time of writing, the **exchange rate** was 16,000VND to $1; 31,000VND to £1; and 23,100VND to €1. A black market of sorts exists in Vietnam, but is best avoided, especially as the mark-up is tiny.

Major **credit cards** – Visa, MasterCard and, to a lesser extent, American Express – are becoming more accepted. There is a growing network of 24-hour ATMs (in the Visa, Plus, MasterCard, Maestro and Cirrus networks) in all main tourist centres (dong only). Even outside the major cities, banks and some travellers' cafés and hotels can now advance cash against cards (generally Visa and MasterCard) for a small commission.

**US dollar traveller's cheques** can be cashed at major banks (Vietcombank usually charges the lowest rates), but often not at banks in smaller towns. If you need to have **money wired**, contact the Vietcombank in Hanoi or HCMC, though some provincial branches can also now handle transfers. Vietcombank has arrangements with selected banks across the world; payment can be made to you in dong or dollars, but hefty charges are levied at both ends. Vietcombank and major post offices also accept the faster, more expensive, Moneygram and Western Union. Again, this has to come from a designated bank; contact any branch of Vietcombank for details. Charges are levied at the sender's end, and to collect the money all you need is the sender's eight-digit reference number. To wire money from Vietnam, you will need a wage slip, certificate or bank receipt to prove that the money has a legal source.

### Prices and bargaining

Vietnam's old **two-tier pricing** system, whereby foreigners paid more than locals for transport and accommodation, has been officially phased out, with most hotels, public buses and the national train system now having standardized prices. However, unofficially, the old system is still very much in place, especially in smaller, privately run businesses, and the Vietnamese have a reputation for a particularly voracious attitude to making money, which tourists unfortunately fall easy victim to. Private transport companies charge you twice the local fare, tour guides demand tips, xe om and taxi drivers take you on a circuitous route, have tampered meters or take you to places where they can glean a commission, and most taxing of all, street vendors and market stalls increase the price of goods up to ten fold when they see a foreigner approaching. Ask around before visiting the market to find out what locals would pay for fruit and vegetables, or a fair price for your coveted souvenir. Remember that unless a price is displayed on an item or service (say at a supermarket, a bus station or a food stall), it is usually negotiable, and almost everything can be bargained down. **Bargain** hard but fair – pleasantness and good humour will get you further than aggression.

**DOLLARS OR DONG?**

In Vietnam, most of the larger costs (such as accommodation and transport) are quoted in US **dollars**, but can be paid for in either currency; smaller amounts (for a street meal or a museum entrance ticket) change hands in **dong**. Prices are given in the currency quoted in each case.

## OPENING HOURS AND HOLIDAYS

Basic **hours of business** are 7.30–11.30am and 1.30–4.30pm. Most offices close on Sunday, and many also close on Saturdays. State-run **banks** and government offices usually open Monday to Friday, closing at weekends, though there are exceptions. **Banking hours** are usually Monday–Friday 7.30–11.30am and 1–4pm, though in major cities you can change cash outside these hours at registered exchange counters, some travellers' cafés, and hotels. Most main **post offices** are open daily, usually from 6.30am to 9.30pm. **Travellers' cafés** and tour agents tend to open early to late every day; state-run **tourist offices** usually open daily until the early evening, sometimes closing Sunday. As a general rule, **museums** open daily; core opening hours are usually 8–11am and 1.30–4.30pm; however these vary at the weekend. Hanoi museums tend to close Monday or Friday. Temples and pagodas occasionally close for lunch but are otherwise open all week and don't close until late evening. Tourist **restaurants** tend to open around 10am and stay open right through until 10pm; local restaurants and food stalls serve from 6am until 9pm. Bars are generally open until 11pm, with later opening hours and lock-ins common in the bigger cities and tourist hotspots. Restaurants and bars listed in the text are open daily for approximately these hours unless otherwise stated.

## Public holidays

**January 1** New Year's Day
**Late January/mid-February** (dates vary each year) Tet, Vietnamese New Year (three days, though increasingly offices tend to close down for a full week)
**February 3** Founding of the Vietnamese Communist Party
**April 30** Liberation of Saigon, 1975
**May 1** International Labour Day
**May 19** Birthday of Ho Chi Minh
**June** Birthday of Buddha (eighth day of the fourth moon)
**September 2** National Day
**December 25** Christmas Day

# FESTIVALS

Most Vietnamese **festivals** are fixed by the lunar calendar: most take place in spring, and the days of the full moon (day one) and the new moon (day fourteen or fifteen) are particularly auspicious. All Vietnamese calendars show both the lunar and solar (Gregorian) months and dates. On the eve of the full moon, every month, Hoi An celebrates a **Full-Moon Festival**. Electricity is switched off, silk lanterns light up traffic-free streets, and traditional games, dance and music are performed in the streets.

**Tet Nguyen Dan** Or simply Tet ("festival"). Seven days between the last week of January and the third week of February, on the night of the new moon. Vietnam's most important annual event, it's is a time when families get together to celebrate renewal and hope for the New Year, when ancestral spirits are welcomed back to the household, and when everyone in Vietnam becomes a year older – age is reckoned by the new year and not by individual birthdays. Everyone cleans their house from top to bottom, pays off debts and makes offerings to Ong Tau, the Taoist god of the hearth. The eve of Tet explodes into a cacophony of drums and percussion, and the subsequent week is marked by feasting on special foods. For tourists, Tet can be a great time to visit Vietnam, but most of Vietnam closes down for the week after the New Year, and either side of the holiday local transport services are stretched to the limit.
**Water Puppet Festival** At Thay Pagoda, west of Hanoi.
**Buddhist full moon festival** (March–April; see p.982). Two-week festival at the Perfume Pagoda, west of Hanoi.
**Tet Doan Ngo** (late May to early June). Summer solstice, marked by festivities and dragon boat races.
**Trung Thu** also known as Children's Day (Sept–Oct). Dragon dances take place and children are given lanterns in the shape of stars, carp or dragons.

## VIETNAMESE

Vietnamese is tonal and is extremely tricky for Westerners to master – luckily, some English is increasingly spoken in tourist areas and the script is Romanized. Vietnam's minority peoples have their own languages, and may not understand standard Vietnamese.

### Pronunciation

Six tones are used, which change the meaning of a word: the mid-level tone (syllables with no marker), the low falling tone (marked ă), the low rising tone (marked à), the high broken tone (marked ã), the high rising tone (marked á) and the low broken tone (marked ạ).

| | |
|---|---|
| a | 'a' as in father |
| ă | 'u' as in hut (slight 'u' as in unstressed English 'a') |
| â | 'uh' sound as above only longer |
| e | 'e' as in bed |
| ê | 'ay' as in pay |
| i | 'i' as in -ing |
| o | 'o' as in hot |
| ô | 'aw' as in awe |
| o' | 'ur' as in fur |
| u | 'oo' as in boo |
| u' | 'oo' closest to French 'u' |
| y | 'i' as in -ing |
| ai | 'ai' as in Thai |
| ao | 'ao' as in Mao |
| au | 'a-oo' |
| âu | 'oh' as in oh! |
| ay | 'ay' as in hay |
| ây | 'ay-i' (as in 'ay' above but longer) |
| eo | 'eh-ao' |
| êu | 'ay-oo' |
| iu | 'ew' as in few |
| iêu | 'i-yoh' |
| oa | 'wa' |
| oe | 'weh' |
| ôi | 'oy' |
| o'i | 'uh-i' |
| ua | 'waw' |
| uê | 'weh' |
| uô | 'waw' |
| uy | 'wee' |
| u'a | 'oo-a' |
| u.u | 'er-oo' |
| u'o'i | 'oo-uh-i' |
| c | 'g' |
| ch | 'j' as in jar |
| d | 'y' as in young |
| v | 'd' as in day |
| g | 'g' as in goat |
| gh | 'g' as in goat |
| gi | 'y' as in young |
| k | 'g' as in goat |
| kh | 'k' as in keep |
| ng/ngh | 'ng' as in sing |
| nh | 'n-y' as in canyon |
| ph | 'f' |
| q | 'g' as in goat |
| t | 'd' as in day |
| th | 't' |
| tr | 'j' as in jar |
| x | 's' |

### Greetings and basic phrases

How you speak to somebody depends on their sex, age and social standing. Addressing a man as ông, and a woman as bà, is being polite. With someone of about your age, you can use anh (for a man) and chi (for a woman).

| | |
|---|---|
| Hello | chào ông/bà |
| Goodbye | chào, tạm biêt |
| Excuse me | xin lôi |
| Excuse me (to get past) | xin ông/bà thú' lôi |
| Please | làm o'n |
| Thank you | cám o'n ông/bà |
| Do you speak English? | ông/bà biê't nói tiê'ng không? |
| I don't understand | tôi không hiê'u |
| Yes | vâng (N); dạ (S) |
| No | không |
| Can you help me? | ông/bà có thê' giúp tôi không? |
| hospital | bê'nh viê'n |
| police station | don cong an |
| Where is the...? | ....ò' đâu? |
| ticket | vé |
| aeroplane | máy bay |
| airport | sân bay |
| boat | tàu bè |
| bus | xe buýt |
| bus station | bê'n xe buýt |
| train station | bê'n xe lù'a |
| taxi | tăc xi |
| car | xe ho'i |

| | |
|---|---|
| bicycle | xe đạp |
| bank | nhà băng |
| post office | sô bu' điên |
| passport | hô chiê'u |
| hotel | khách sạn |
| restaurant | nhà hàng |
| left/right | bên trái/bên phài |
| Do you have any rooms? | ông/bà có phòng không? |
| How much is it? | bao nhiêu tiên? |
| cheap/expensive | rè/đàt |
| air conditioner | máy lạnh |
| fan (electric) | quạt máy |
| open/closed | mò' cù'a/vóng cù'a |

### Numbers

For numbers ending in 5, from 15 onwards, lăm is used in the north and nhăm in the south, rather than the written nạm. An alternative for numbers that are multiples of 10 is chaục – so, 10 can be môt chục etc.

| | |
|---|---|
| 0 | không |
| 1 | môt |
| 2 | hai |
| 3 | ba |
| 4 | bô'n |
| 5 | năm |
| 6 | sáu |
| 7 | bày |
| 8 | tám |
| 9 | chín |
| 10 | mùò'i |
| 11, 12, 13 etc | mu'ò'i môt, mu'ò'i hai, mu'ò'i ba |
| 20, 30 etc | hai mu'ò'i, ba mu'ò'i, |
| 100 | mot trăm |
| 1000 | mot ngàn |

### Food and drink glossary

Some names differ in the north (N) and south (S).

| | |
|---|---|
| cheers! | *can chen* (N); *can ly* (S) |
| delicious | *rat ngon* |
| vegetarian | *nguoi an chay* |
| I don't eat meat or fish | *toi khong an thit* |

**Rice and noodles**

| | |
|---|---|
| *bun* | round rice noodles |
| *com* | rice |
| *com rang; com chien* | fried rice |
| *chao* | rice porridge |
| *mi xao* | fried noodles |
| *pho* | flat rice noodles in soup |
| *pho bo tai/ bo chin* | pho with rare/ medium beef |

**Fish, meat and vegetables**

| | |
|---|---|
| *ca* | fish |
| *cua* | crab |
| *luon* | eel |
| *muc* | squid |
| *tom* | shrimp |
| *thit* | meat |
| *bo* | beef |
| *ga* | chicken |
| *lon* (N); *heo* (S) | pork |
| *vit* | duck |
| *rau co or rau cac loai* | vegetables |
| *mang* | bamboo shoots |
| *ngo* (N); *bap* (S) | sweetcorn |

**Miscellaneous**

| | |
|---|---|
| *banh* | cake |
| *banh mi* | bread |
| *bo* | butter |
| *duong* | sugar |
| *pho mat, fo mat* | cheese |
| *lac* (N); *dau phong* (S) | peanuts |
| *muoi* | salt |
| *ot* | chilli |
| *tao pho* (N); *dau hu* (S) | tofu |
| *trai cay* | fruit |
| *trung* | egg |
| *trung om let or op lep* | omelette |

**Drinks**

| | |
|---|---|
| *bia* | beer |
| *ca phé den* | black coffee |
| *ca phé sua* | coffee with milk |
| *tra* | tea |
| *khong da* | no ice |
| *nuoc* | water |
| *nuoc khoang* | mineral water |
| *nuoc cam* | orange juice |
| *nuoc chanh* | lime juice |
| *nuoc dua* | coconut milk |
| *sua tuoi* | fresh milk |

# Ho Chi Minh City

Washed ashore above the Mekong Delta, some 40km north of the South China Sea, **HO CHI MINH CITY** (HCMC) is a city on the march, a boomtown where the rule of the dollar is absolute. Fuelled by the sweeping economic changes wrought by *doi moi*, this effervescent city, perched on the west bank of the Saigon River, now boasts fine restaurants, immaculate hotels, and glitzy bars among its colonial villas, venerable pagodas and austere, Soviet-style housing blocks.

Formerly **Saigon**, it was renamed Ho Chi Minh City in 1976, a year after the communists rolled through the gates of the Presidential Palace and took control of the city. Happily, however, the evocative old name lives on: the city's central District 1 is invariably referred to as Saigon, and the name is also listed in railway timetables.

## What to see and do

**Ho Chi Minh City** is divided into eighteen districts, though tourists rarely travel beyond districts 1, 3 and 5. The city proper hugs the west bank of the Saigon River, and its central area, District 1, nestles in the hinge formed by the confluence of the river with the silty Ben Nghe Channel; traditionally the French Quarter of the city, this area is still widely known as **Saigon**. Dong Khoi is its backbone, and around the T-shape it forms along with Le Duan are scattered most of the city's museums and colonial remnants. Except for **Cho Lon**, HCMC's frenetic Chinatown, the city doesn't carve up into homogeneous districts, so visitors have to do a dot-to-dot between sights. These are almost invariably places that relate to the American War, but there are many religious sights too, most notably the **Jade Emperor Pagoda**.

### The Ho Chi Minh City Museum

Of all the stones of empire thrown up in Vietnam by the French during their rule, few are more eye-catching than the former **Gia Long Palace,** 65 Ly Tu Trong, built in 1886. Ngo Dinh Diem – the President of the Republic of South Vietnam – decamped here in 1962, and it was in the tunnels under the building that he spent his last hours of office, before fleeing to the church in Cho Lon, and meeting his death nearby. Nowadays, it houses the **Ho Chi Minh City Museum** (daily 8am–4pm; 15,000VND; Ⓦwww.hcmc-museum.edu.vn), one of the city's more user-friendly museums, clearly labelled with English-language signs. The ground floor focuses on archeology and the environment, with exhibits including a thousand-year-old stone *pesari*. There's also a gallery dedicated to the history of HCMC and its ethnic communities, with some interesting photos of early twentieth-century Saigon. Upstairs, the focus predictably

### CRIME IN HCMC

Sadly, HCMC is full to bursting with people for whom progress hasn't yet translated into food, lodgings and employment, so begging, stealing and prostitution are all facts of life here. Petty crime has increased dramatically in the past few years, particularly bag snatching, so you should take care at all times with personal belongings whilst walking the streets, or travelling on cyclo and motorbikes – especially after dark and around tourist nightspots. There is a **Tourist Police** kiosk at the junction of Pham Ngu Lao and De Tham where you can report any incidents and seek advice, or call the Tourist Hotline on Ⓣ08/925000.

turns to anti-French and anti-American resistance in the twentieth century.

### The Reunification Palace

A red flag billows proudly above the **Reunification Palace** (135 Nam Ky Khoi Nghia; daily 7.30–11am & 1–4pm; 15,000VND including guided tour), which occupies the site of the Norodom Palace, a colonial mansion erected in 1871 to house the governor-general of Indochina. With the French departure in 1954, Ngo Dinh Diem commandeered this extravagant monument as his presidential palace, but after the February 1962 assassination attempt, it was pulled down. The palace, known as Independence Palace, was reconstructed in 1966, and remained home and office of the president. On April 30, 1975, a North Vietnamese tank stormed the palace's gates, becoming the defining moment in the fall of Saigon; it was renamed Reunification Hall. A replica of the tank stands just inside the entrance and serves as an imposing reminder of the victory. Spookily unchanged from its working days, much of the building's interior is a veritable time-capsule of 1960s and 1970s kitsch. Most interesting is the third floor, with its presidential library, projection room and entertainment lounge. The basement served as the former command centre and displays archaic radio equipment and vast strategic wall maps.

### The War Remnants Museum

One block northwest of the palace, at 28 Vo Van Tan, the **War Remnants Museum** (daily 7.30am–noon & 1.30–5pm; 15,000VND) is probably the city's most popular attraction. Its exhibits speak for themselves, a distressing compendium of the horrors of modern warfare. On display in the courtyard outside are a 28-tonne howitzer, a ghoulish collection of bomb parts and a renovated Douglas Skyraider plane. A series of halls present a grisly portfolio of photographs of mutilation, napalm burns and torture. One gallery details the effects of the 75 million litres of defoliant sprays dumped across the country, including hideously malformed foetuses preserved in pickling jars; another looks at international opposition to the war as well as the American peace movement. There's also a moving exhibition of children's artwork on the atrocities of war, and an excellent photographic display of war photographs from the countless photojournalists who lost their lives working during the French and American wars. The museum rounds off with a grisly mock-up of the tiger cages, the prison cells of Con Son Island.

### The History Museum

An attractive, pagoda-style roof crowns the city's **History Museum** (Mon–Sat 8–11am & 1.30–4.30pm, Sun 8.30am–4.30pm; 15,000VND, 8000VND extra for the gardens), whose main entrance is tucked just inside the gateway to the Botanical Gardens. To visit the museum only, use the side entrance at 2 Nguyen Binh Khiem. The museum houses a series of galleries illuminating Vietnam's past from primitive times to the end of French rule by means of a decent if predictable array of artefacts and pictures. There's also a **water puppetry theatre** (30,000VND), with six shows a day.

### Jade Emperor Pagoda

The spectacular **Jade Emperor Pagoda,** 73 Mai Thi Lu (daily 6am–6pm), was built by the city's Cantonese community in around 1900, and is still the city's most captivating pagoda, with its exquisite panels of carved gilt woodwork and a panoply of Taoist and Buddhist deities beneath a roof that groans under the weight of dragons, birds and animals. A statue of the Jade

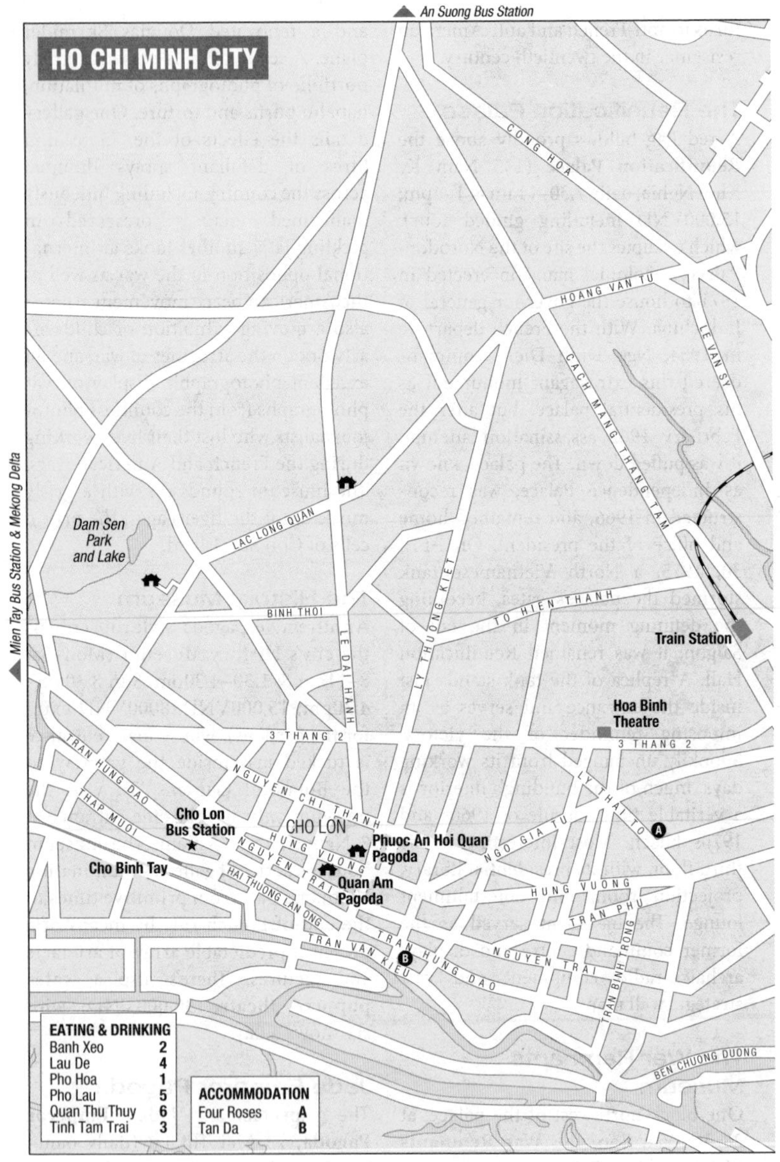


Emperor lords it over the main hall's central altar, monitoring entry into Heaven, and his two keepers – one holding a lamp to light the way for the virtuous, the other wielding an ominous-looking axe – are on hand to aid him. To the right of the main hall, a rickety flight of steps runs up to a balcony, behind which is set a neon-haloed statue of Quan Am, a female saint in Buddhist tradition, known as Quan Yin in Chinese. Left

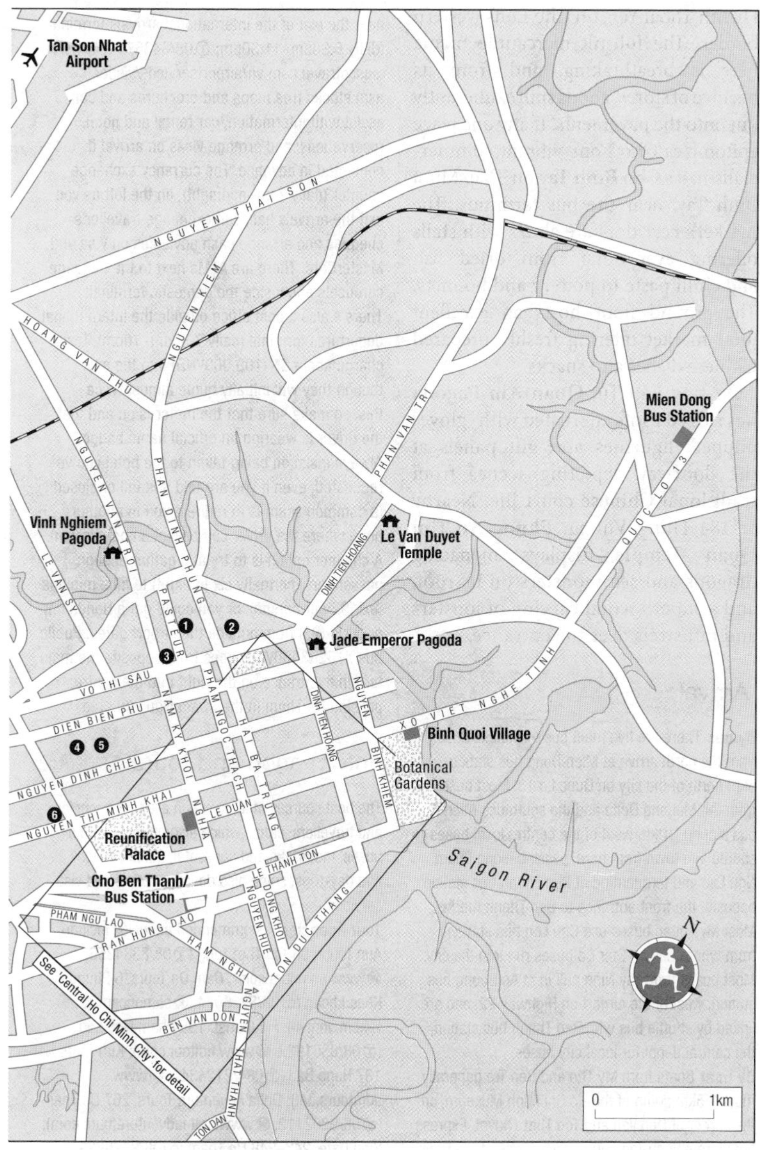


out of the main hall stands Kim Hua, to whom women pray for children, and in the larger chamber behind you'll find the Chief of Hell alongside ten dark-wood reliefs depicting all sorts of punishments.

## Cho Lon

The dense cluster of streets comprising the Chinese ghetto of **Cho Lon** is linked to the city centre by five-kilometre-long Tran Hung Dao and best reached by cyclo or a Saigon Star Co bus to

Huynh Thoai Yen, on Cho Lon's western border. The full-tilt mercantile mania here is breathtaking, and from its beehive of stores, goods spill exuberantly out onto the pavements. If any one place epitomizes Cho Lon's vibrant commercialism, it's **Cho Binh Tay** on Thap Muoi Binh Tay, near the bus terminus. The market's corridors are abuzz with stalls offering everything from dried fish and chilli paste to pottery and bonnets. The ground floor hosts an excellent food market offering freshly prepared Chinese dishes and snacks.

On tiny Lao Tu, **Quan Am Pagoda** has ridged roofs encrusted with "glove-puppet" figurines and gilt panels at the doorway depicting scenes from traditional Chinese court life. Nearby at 184 Hung Vuong, **Phuoc An Hoi Quan Temple** displays menacing dragons and sea monsters on its roof, and a superb wood carving of jousters and minstrels over the entrance.

## Arrival

**By bus** There are five main bus terminals. Buses from the north arrive at Mien Dong bus station, 5km north of the city on Quoc Lo 13. Most buses from the Mekong Delta and the south use Mien Tay bus station, 10km west of the centre; local buses shuttle into town from here, passing along Pham Ngu Lao and terminating at Ben Thanh bus station opposite the front entrance to Ben Thanh market. Most My Thuan buses use Cho Lon bus station, from where Saigon Star Co buses run into the city. Most buses from Tay Ninh pull in at An Suong bus station, west of the airport on Highway 22, and are linked by shuttle bus with Ben Thanh bus station, the central depot for local city buses.

**By boat** Boats from My Tho and Ben Tre generally moor 1.5km south of the Ho Chi Minh Museum, on the corner of Den Van and Ton That Thuyet. Express boats from Vung Tao and Can Tho dock at the Bach Dang Wharf at the eastern end of Ham Nghi.

**By train** The train station, Ga Saigon, is 3km northwest of town at 1 Nguyen Thong. Cyclo or xe om will take you to the centre for 15,000VND (15min); a taxi is about 25,000VND.

**By air** Tan Son Nhat Airport (Ⓣ08/8456654) is 7km northwest of the centre. The excellent SASCO Visitors Information and Services Centre near the exit of the international arrivals terminal (daily 6.30am–11.30pm; Ⓣ08/8486711, Ⓦwww.sascotravel.com.vn/airportservices/visitor.asp) stocks free maps and brochures and can assist with information, car rental and hotel reservations, and arrange visas on arrival if contacted in advance. The currency exchange counter (daily 7am–midnight), on the left as you exit the arrivals hall, can exchange traveller's cheques and arrange cash advances on Visa and MasterCard. There are ATMs next to the baggage carousels and inside the domestic terminal. There's also a post office outside the international departures terminal (daily 7.30am–10pm). Taxis charge about $6 (100,000VND) into the city, though they will initially quote almost twice this, so make sure that the meter is on and that the driver is wearing an official name badge. Always insist on being taken to the hotel you've requested, even if you are told it is full or closed (a common scam is to redirect you to another hotel where the driver can collect a commission). A cheaper option is to try and gather enough passengers (normally six to eight) to fill a minibus taxi ($2 per person), or you could get a Honda om or cyclo ($3) from outside the airport gates. Public bus #152 (3000VND) goes from opposite the main terminal entrance on the right into the centre, passing De Tham in the Pham Ngu Lau area.

## Information and tours

The best sources of information are tour agencies and travellers' cafés, which also offer open-tour buses, motorbike and car rental, guide services and day-trips; some also do longer tours and visa services.

**Tour agencies** Recommended agencies include: Ann Tours, 58 Ton That Tung (Ⓣ08/8334356, Ⓦwww.anntours.com); Cam On Tours, 6 Phung Khac khoan (Ⓣ08/8256074, Ⓔcamoncom@hcm.vnn.vn); Fiditourist, 195 Pham Ngu Lao (Ⓣ08/8361922, Ⓦwww.fiditour.com); Kim Tours 137 Hang Bac (Ⓣ084/9124340, Ⓦwww.kimtours.net); Delta Adventure Tours, 267 De Tham (Ⓣ08/9202112, Ⓦwww.deltaadventuretours.com); Sinh Café, 246–248 De Tham (Ⓣ08/8376833, Ⓦwww.sinhcafevn.com); Sinhbalo, 283/20 Pham Ngu Lao (Ⓣ08/8376766, Ⓦwww.sinhbalo.com). Larger, more upmarket outfits include Exotissimo Travel, Saigon Trade Centre, 37 Ton Duc Thang (Ⓣ08/8251723, Ⓦwww.exotissimo.com); Saigontourist, 49 Le Thanh Ton (Ⓣ08/8298914, Ⓦwww.saigontourist.net); and Vietnamtourism, Room 303, Mondial Centre, 203 Dong Khoi

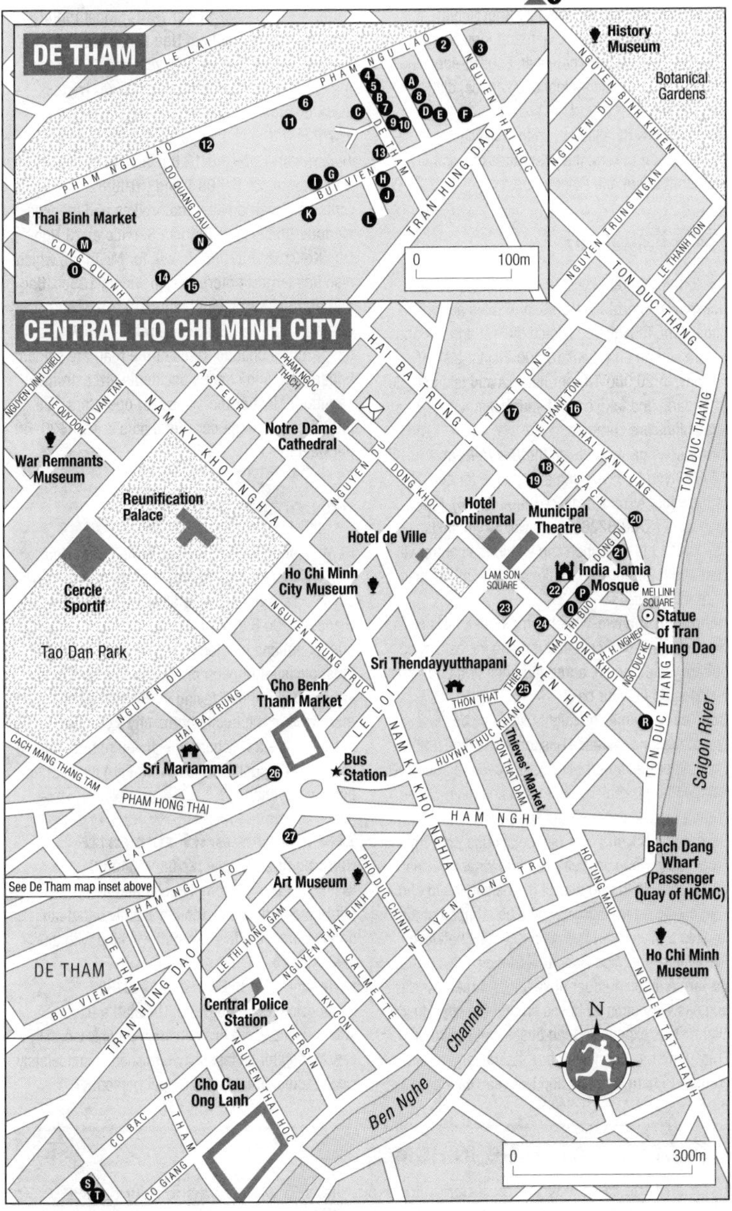


**ACCOMMODATION**

| | | | | | |
|---|---|---|---|---|---|
| Hong Kong | F | Madame Cuc 64 | G | Quan San | L |
| Hong Vinh | E | Madame Cuc 127 | O | Tan Mai Phai | D |
| Hotel 97 | K | Madame Cuc 184 | M | Thang Long | Q |
| Hotel 265 | C | Majestic | R | Thanh Guesthouse | S |
| Lan Anh | B | Miss Loi | T | Thao Nhi | A |
| Linh Hotel | P | Ngoc | N | Yellow House | H |
| Luan Vu | J | Phan Lan | I | | |

**EATING & DRINKING**

| | | | | | | | |
|---|---|---|---|---|---|---|---|
| Allez-Boo | 4 | Cay Xoai | 18 | Long Phi Café | 12 | Sinh Café | 7 |
| Akbar Ali | 14 | Coriander | 15 | Malee Thai | 21 | Taj Mahal | 11 |
| Apocalypse Now | 20 | Cyclo Bar | 2 | Mai Thai | 25 | Tan Nam | 22 |
| Bao | 3 | Eden Bar | 9 | O'Briens | 19 | Tin Nghia | 27 |
| Binh Quoi I | 1 | Go2 | 13 | Pho 2000 | 26 | Underground Basement | 24 |
| Blue Gecko | 17 | Kim Café | 5 | Saigon Café | 6 | Zen | 10 |
| Bread and Butter | 8 | Lemon Grass | 23 | Sheridan's Irish House | 16 | | |

(☎08/8242000) & 234 Nam Ky Khoi Nghia (☎08/8292442), Ⓦwww.vietnamtourism.com.

**Tourist informaton** There's an English-speaking, state-run information telephone service; dial ☎1080 (free).

**Maps** A fairly detailed city map is available from street hawkers, the post office or from Vietnamtourism and Saigontourist.

## City transport

**Cyclo** Over 50,000 cyclo (three-wheeled cycle-rickshaws) operate in HCMC, and rates are pretty consistent, though you should always agree a price before setting off (about 10,000VND for a short journey, or 20,000VND per hour). Avoid taking cyclo after dark, and take care of your belongings – bag snatchings are common.

**Taxis** Taxis gather outside the *Rex Hotel* at 141 Nguyen Hue; you can also phone for one of the white Airport Taxis (☎08/8446666), Mai Linh taxis (☎08/8226666) or yellow Vinataxis (☎08/8111111). A short trip within the centre will cost about 25,000VND; make sure the meter is on from the start.

**Honda om** The two-wheeled motorbike taxis or Honda om (xe om) cost about the same as a cyclo but are faster; again, agree the price first and keep a close grip on your bag.

**Bus** The only time you might use a city bus is for one of the long-distance bus terminals (see p.908), Cho Lon or the airport (#152). All fares are 3000VND. Saigon Star Co runs buses to Cho Lon (daily 5am–10pm), looping between the south side of Mei Linh Square and Huynh Thoai Yen, below Cho Binh Tay. From Pham Ngu Lao, head south to where Bui Vien meets Tran Hung Dao to pick up the service to Cho Lon; on the return journey, you'll be dropped at the far side of Tran Hung Dao. Bus #26 runs between Ben Thanh and Mien Dong Bus Station.

**Xe lam** A small number of xe lam – three-wheeler buggies – function as buses around the city. They're slightly less expensive than buses, but crowded. They gather at Ben Thanh bus station, and at the corner of Pham Ngu Lao and Nguyen Thai Hoc.

**Bike, motorbike and car rental** Most rental places are around Pham Ngu Lao; prices per day average around $1 for a bicycle and $5–10 for a moped or medium-sized motorbike. Try the kiosk outside the *Que Huong-Liberty 3 Hotel*, 187 Pham Ngu Lao; *Hotel 265*, 265 De Tham; or *Huong Mini-Hotel*, 40/19 Bui Vien. In the centre, Getrantours, 24 Hai Ba Trung (☎08/8292366), rents cars with drivers, motorbikes and mopeds, as does Tuan-Thuat Tourism Service at 23 Ngo Duc Ke (☎090/3709589; ask for Mr Tuan), which also has larger motorbikes, including 125cc. Bao Viet at 23–25 Thai Van Lung (☎08/8251500) offers motorbike insurance. Traffic in HCMC is dangerously chaotic; rules of the road are seldom adhered to, and serious accidents are extremely common. Most of the city's tour operators (see p.908) can arrange car rental plus driver ($30–60 per day).

## Accommodation

HCMC's budget enclave centres on Pham Ngu Lao, Bui Vien and De Tham, 1km west of the city centre. The charming alleyways between Co Giang and Co Bac offer some excellent family-run budget options just ten minutes' walk away. The most pleasant (though pricey) area to stay in is around Dong Khoi. Staying in Cho Lon leaves you marooned in the bustle of the city's Chinatown, but there are a few bargains. If you're hitting town around Tet (usually late Jan/mid-Feb) it's best to book in advance.

### De Tham and around

**Hong Kong** 22 Bui Vien ☎08/9204089, Ⓔnthutan@yahoo.com. Popular and friendly mini-hotel, with clean, though slightly dated fan or a/c rooms; the friendly staff will help with tour bookings. ❹

**Hong Vinh** 28/1 Bui Vien ☎08/9201382, Ⓔhongvinh28@yahoo.com. The staff are a little unfriendly, but this new mini-hotel is worth considering for its tastefully furnished, immaculately clean rooms. Breakfast is $1 per person. ❹

### PEOPLE-WATCHING IN HCMC

One of the best ways to experience local city life is to while away an hour or two in one of the city's **public parks**, such as the strip running adjacent to Pham Ngu Lao, or Cong Vien Van Hoa Park next to the Reunification Palace. Early morning t'ai chi and badminton keep the older folk in shape, evening aerobics classes are open to all, and young romancing couples whisper sweet nothings on their parked motorbikes at dusk. The parks are especially lively on Sunday afternoons.

**Hotel 97** 97 Bui Vien ⓣ08/8368801. The lobby may look a little worse for wear, but the fan rooms are spacious and clean with quirky chequered floor tiles; excellent value. ❷

**Hotel 265** 265 De Tham ⓣ08/8367512, ⓔhotelduy@hotmail.com. Great-value budget option with immaculate fan and a/c quarters all with en-suite bathrooms, fridges and hot water. Breakfast included. ❸

**Lan Anh** 252 De Tham ⓣ08/8365197, ⓔlan-anh-hotel@hcm.vnn.vn. A relative newcomer, but already a favourite, this is a friendly, family-run hotel, with bright a/c and fan rooms; breakfast included. ❸

**Luan Vu** 35/2 Bui Vien ⓣ08/8377185, ⓔphanlan@hcm.vnn.vn. Helpful staff and pleasantly furnished rooms with WiFi access make this hotel a good bet. ❸

**Madame Cuc** 127 Cong Quynh ⓣ08/836 8761; 184 Cong Quynh ⓣ08/8361679; 64 Bui Vien ⓣ08/8365073; ⓦwww.madamcuchotels.com. Hugely popular and unfailingly friendly, this fantastic trio of family-run guesthouses offer a range of comfortable rooms, some sleeping up to four, with satellite TV and fridges, plus free breakfast, refreshments, internet access and airport transfers. ❸

**Ngoc** 30 Do Quang Dau ⓣ08/8377241. Good for those on the tightest of budgets, this little place offers tiny but decent rooms. A few extra dollars buys natural light and a/c. ❶–❷

**Phan Lan** 70 Bui Vien ⓣ08/8369569, ⓔphanlan36@yahoo.com. A popular and expanding veteran, offering a choice of a/c and fan rooms, most of them airy and pleasant, plus one four-bed room. Hot drinks, breakfast, and internet access are included. A sister-hotel has recently opened at 283/6 Pham Ngu Lao ⓣ08/8378749. Both ❸–❹

**Quan San** 35/10 Bui Vien ⓣ848/8364745, ⓔquansan_guesthouse@yahoo.com. This new family-run guesthouse, nestled down the end of a quaint alley away from the bustle of De Tham, offers spacious, immaculately clean rooms sleeping up to four, with all amenities; the outstandingly friendly service is the best in the area. Hot drinks, breakfast and internet access are included. ❸

**Tan Mai Phai** 40/14a Bui Vien ⓣ848/8367438. The bright and airy rooms are excellent value. There are over forty similar budget guesthouses crammed along this alley and its continuation, 185 Pham Ngu Lao. ❷

**Thao Nhi** 185/20 Pham Ngu Lao ⓣ848/9201262, ⓔthaonhihotel@hcm.vnn.vn. Clean, spacious rooms with all amenities and free internet. ❸–❹

**Yellow House** 31 Bui Vien ⓣ848/8368830 ⓔyellowhousehotel@yahoo.com Most of the rooms in this budget hotel are a little jaded and lack natural light, but beds in the eight-person a/c dormitory are good value at $5.50 per night, including free breakfast and internet access. ❷–❸

### Co Giang area

**Miss Loi** 178/20 Co Giang ⓣ848/8379589, ⓔmissloi@hcm.fpt.vn. This charmingly quirky little guesthouse with a communal dining area complete with colourful statuettes, pool table and welcoming staff has become somewhat of an institution amongst backpackers in recent years. The rooms are clean and well equipped, and breakfast is included. ❸

**Thanh Guesthouse** 171/1e Co Bac ⓣ848/368469. Quiet and comfortable rooms with private balconies, satellite TV and hot water. ❷

### Dong Khoi and around

**Linh Hotel** 16 Mac Thi Buoi ⓣ848/8243954, ⓔlinhhotel@hcm.vnn.vn. This newly refurbished mini-hotel is good value given the central location; there is WiFi access in all rooms and breakfast is included. ❻–❼

**Thang Long** 48 Mac Thi Buoi ⓣ08/8222595. One-star mini-hotel in mock-traditional style, with dark-panelled, slightly gloomy rooms of varying sizes, all with a/c, breakfast and satellite TV. ❻

### Cho Lon and around

**Four Roses** 790/5 Nguyen Dinh Chieu ⓣ08/8325895. Located in no-man's land between Cho Lon and the city centre, this is a peaceful, family-run home-from-home: seven pleasant rooms with balconies, plus a terraced garden and professional beauty salon. ❸–❹

**Tan Da** 22–24 Tan Da ⓣ08/8555711. Fairly quiet hotel, with straightforward if slightly overpriced no-frills fan and a/c rooms. ❷

## Eating

The culinary capital of Vietnam, HCMC offers everything from fine French cuisine in the Dong Khoi area, to noodle soups and fresh spring rolls at the makeshift street-kitchens scattered around the city. Cho Lon has the best Chinese restaurants, and average but reasonably priced backpacker cafés predominate around Pham Ngu Lao. Most restaurants open daily from around 10am to 10pm unless otherwise stated, and where phone numbers are given, it's best to book ahead.

TREAT YOURSELF

**Majestic** 1 Dong Khoi ⓣ08/8295514, ⓦwww.majesticsaigon.com.vn. Historic riverfront hotel, built in 1925 and still oozing character. Rooms are charming with original artwork adorning every wall, some have river views, and all include breakfast; the impeccably professional staff fall over themselves to be helpful, but starting at $235 for a standard double, luxury doesn't come cheap. ⑨

## De Tham and around

**Akbar Ali** 240 Bui Vien. Sumptuously authentic Indian curries, including an extensive vegetarian selection, dished up with a lively Bollywood soundtrack accompaniment. Mains 24–50,000VND.

**Bao** 132 Nguyen Thai Hoc. Popular with locals, who tuck into grilled goat, rabbit, bird, boar and kangaroo at red-clothed trestle tables. Mains 20–50,000VND. Daily 6am–late.

**Bread and Butter** 40/24 Bui Vien. The Australian trained chefs here produce mouthwatering, hearty portions of home favourites such as bangers and mash. The Sunday roast (90,000VND) is served with real gravy and golden roast potatoes, and the hot chocolate pudding is simply divine.

**Coriander** 185 Bui Vien. Flavoursome Thai favourites at reasonable prices, with two streetside tables to watch the world go by. The duck red curry (38,000VND) is particularly good.

**Kim Café** 268 De Tham. As well as breakfasts, fresh juices and veggie meals galore, there's guacamole, garlic bread, mashed potatoes and a fantastic Malay-style chicken curry. Mains 35,000VND. Daily 7am–1am.

**Pho 2000** 1–3 Phan Chu Trinh. Next to Ben Cho Thanh. Tuck into big bowls of delicious noodle soup for 25,000VND at gleaming aluminium tables; there's another branch at 1 Phan Van Dat, near Mei Linh Square. Daily 6am–1am.

**Quan Thu Thuy** 26 Cach Mang Thang Tam. Banana-leaf parcels of cured pork hang along the frontage of this excellent *nem* (spring roll) specialist, a short walk north of Pham Ngu Lao. Daily 6.30am–10pm.

**Saigon Café** 195 Pham Ngu Lao. No-nonsense expat hangout with commanding streetside position, good music, beer and excellent menu that runs to Western, Indian and Thai dishes, all at reasonable prices. Daily 6.30am–midnight. Mains 30–50,000VND.

**Sinh Café** 246–248 De Tham. The big daddy of the traveller scene, doling out average but affordable meals in bright surroundings. Mains 40–60,000VND. Daily 6am–11pm.

**Taj Mahal** 241/1 Pham Ngu Lao. An unfussy little snug with just five tables tucked down an alley. They offer delicious halal Indian and Pakistani dishes, and also have a takeaway and catering service. Mains 25–45,000VND.

**Tin Nghia** 9 Tran Hung Dao. Mushrooms, tofu and homemade soups provide the backbone to the inventive menu in this genial Buddhist "pure vegetarian" restaurant, established 80 years ago. Soups 15,000VND; mains 11–17,000VND. Daily 7am–2pm & 4–9pm.

**Zen** 185/30 Pham Ngu Lao. Bargain-priced, imaginative veggie dishes ranging from European and Indian to southern Vietnamese. Pizzas 45,000VND; soups and stir-fries 16,000VND. Daily 6.30am–11pm.

## Around Dong Khoi and Thi Sach

**Cay Xoai** 15a Thi Sach. One of several restaurants along this strip, which gets lively by evening, and is popular with locals. Good-value seafood is guaranteed.

**Lemon Grass** 4 Nguyen Thiep ⓣ08/8220496. Located off Dong Khoi, this stylish hundred-seater restaurant serves highly rated Vietnamese food to the strains of traditional music recitals every night. Mains $3–6. Daily 11am–2pm & 5–10pm.

**Malee Thai** 37 Dong Du ⓣ08/8293029. Superbly presented, eye-wateringly spicy Thai dishes served in sumptuous surroundings. The three-course set-lunch (45,000VND) is particularly good value. Evening mains 60–90,000VND. They have recently opened a sister restaurant, *Mai Thai* (ⓣ08/8212920) nearby at 13 Ton That Thiep.

### FOOD FAIRS

Buffets of traditional Vietnamese cuisine, with around seventy dishes such as roasted young chicken wrapped in glutinous rice and pig skin cake with saffron, are held in the lush, coconut-tree gardens of Binh Quoi I Tourist Village (1147 Bình Quoi; ⓣ08/5565891; Fri & Sat 5–8pm, Sun 11am–2pm & 5–8pm; 109,000VND). Saigontourist (49 Le Thanh Ton; ⓣ08/8298914) can provide information and assist with arrangements.

## STREET FOOD

Informal local eating-houses, makeshift **street-kitchens** and market **food-stalls** offer the cheapest, most authentic dining experience. As they come and go regularly, it's difficult to recommend any in particular, but generally those packed with locals are your best bet. At night, the stalls around Ben Thanh Market buzz with life, as locals and foreigners alike tuck into steaming bowls of soup, barbecued meat skewers and delectable seafood dishes.

**Tan Nam** 60–62 Dong Du ⓣ08/8298634. Top-notch Vietnamese meat dishes and sumptuous seafood hotpots, plus veggie alternatives and set menus ($6–10) in traditional, open-fronted surroundings. Daily 7am–10.30pm.

### Around Dien Bien Phu

**Banh Xeo** 46a Dinh Cong Trang. Cheap, filling Vietnamese pancakes stuffed with shrimps, pork, beans and egg for around 15,000VND are the speciality at this streetside place off Hai Ba Trung.
**Lau De** 45 Ngo Thoi Nhiem. Goat meat – boiled, fried or barbecued at your table – is the order of the day at this cavernous, dimly lit local restaurant. Mains 20–30,000VND.
**Pho Hoa** 260c Pasteur. Heaving with locals and decorated with striking bamboo murals, this restaurant serves up generous portions of *pho* (26,000VND) with big chunks of beef or chicken and piles of fresh greens. Daily 5am–10pm.
**Pho Lau** Bo Minh 107/P Truong Dinh. *Lau* (steamboat) and *pho* (15,000VND) are the staples at this streetside, no-frills restaurant. 6am–11pm.
**Tinh Tam Trai** 170a Vo Thi Sau. Friendly restaurant dishing up flavoursome, if unidentifiable, vegetables in imaginative combinations. Mains 15–30,000VND. Daily 6am–1pm & 3–9pm.

## Drinking and nightlife

The area around Pham Ngu Lao is lined with lively, cheap bars, whilst Dong Khoi and around plays host to most of the city's nightclubs, which shut in the early hours of the morning; take care of your bag when leaving, and be aware, too, that quite a few bars have upfront prostitution.
**Allez-Boo** 187 Pham Ngu Lao. Pham Ngu Lao's largest bar, busy most nights and popular for its good music, award-winning reasonably priced menu (including excellent Thai food and decent burgers) and selection of cocktails served in traditional bamboo surroundings. Daily 6.30am–late.
**Apocalypse Now** 2c Thi Sach. One of the original Saigon nightspots, attracting travellers, locals and expats with its party atmosphere and eclectic mix of danceable music. Always heaving and sweaty at weekends, though it can be a little dull during the week. No cover charge. Daily 7pm–late.
**Blue Gecko** 31 Ly Tu Trong. Popular Aussie sports bar with several screens, a pool table, dartboard and a rowdy crowd.
**Cyclo Bar** 163 Pham Ngu Lao. Intimate little bar with nightly live music, laid-back atmosphere and friendly staff.
**Eden Bar** 236 De Tham. Heaving with backpackers and expats every night, with a small and sweaty dance floor, bamboo bar and pool room upstairs. Happy hour (6–9pm) cocktails are just 25,000VND. Daily 6am–late.
**GO2** 187 De Tham. Fabulously cheesy backpacker hangout run by the owners of *Allez Boo*. Vietnamese and Western snacks are served all day in the neon-lit downstairs bar, to a soundtrack of forgotten classics. There are two pool tables and the upstairs dance floor hosts a nightly DJ and live music at weekends. Daily 7am–late.
**Long Phi Café** 325 Pham Ngu Lao. Stylish, slightly more expensive bar than its neighbours, but relaxing and popular, with Italian food and table footie. Happy hour 5–9pm. Daily 10am–late.
**O'Briens** 74 A2 Hai Ba Trung. Not a world away from an intimate London Irish pub and deservedly popular with expats and travellers alike for its cool music, good bar food and pool room. Daily 10am–midnight.
**Sheridan's Irish House** 17/13 Le Thanh Ton. Cosy Irish pub in the heart of town with nightly live music. Daily 10am–midnight.
**Underground Basement** Lucky Plaza, 69 Dong Khoi. A winning blend of international food, live

## BIA HOA

A Vietnamese beer at a streetside café won't come to more than 12,000VND, but you can multiply that by four in a more upmarket bar. Far cheaper though is a **bia hoi bar**, spit-and-sawdust roadside set-ups where locals glug cheap local beer over ice for just 2000VND per glass.

## WHAT'S ON

Several publications carry listings information: the *Vietnam Economic Times'* ($4.50 monthly) supplement *The Guide*, which can also be purchased separately ($1), the weekly *Vietnam Investment Review*'s ($2) *Time Out*, and the monthly *Vietnam Discovery* magazine ($1). *Asia Life* and *Vietnam Pathfinder* are free publications with HCMC listings, reviews and useful travel tips, which are widely available in bars and backpacker cafés around the city.

sports coverage, weekly live bands, lunch buffets, Sunday barbecues and an extended happy hour (daily 10am–9pm) has made this new bar-restaurant a hit with expats and tourists alike. Daily 10am–midnight.

## Traditional entertainment

**Hoa Binh Theatre** 3 Thang 2 ⓣ08/8655199. Regular performances of modern and traditional Vietnamese music, as well as traditional theatre and dance.
**Le Van Duyet Temple** Northern end of Dinh Tien Hoang. Festivals held on the first and eighth days of every lunar month include performances of Vietnamese opera.

## Shopping

Shops open daily from around 10am to dusk, with some larger stores and shops in the tourist areas staying open beyond 8pm.
**Art** Paintings on silk and rice paper from Workshop Hai, 239 and 241 De Tham. Good art galleries include Gallerie Lotus, 55 Dong Khoi, and Vietnam Oil Painting at 158a Dong Khoi. Galleries specializing in replicas of famous originals abound in HCMC – The Sun Gallery at 9 Bui Vien is particularly good.
**Books** HCMC's best bookshops are on Dong Khoi: Xuan Thu at no. 185 or Bookazine at no. 28 have a large secondhand range; Lao Dong, opposite the Rex at 104 Nguyen Hue, stocks magazines and newspapers. Women hawking metre-high stacks of copied popular novels for $2–5 stalk the Pham Ngu Lao area.
**Electronics** Some of the country's best-value electronics outlets jostle for attention along Huynh Thuc Khang.
**Handicrafts** For lacquerware, ceramics and other souvenirs, try Art Arcade,151 Dong Khoi; Precious Qui, 27–29a Dong Khoi; Bich Lien, 125a Dong Khoi; or Butterfly 26, 26b Le Thanh Ton. Kim Phuong, 77 Le Thanh Ton and 110 Nguyen Hue, Minh Huong, 85 Mac Thi Buoi, or Authentique Boutique, 6 Dong Khoi, are all good for hand-embroidered household goods and clothes.
**Malls and department stores** Diamond Plaza, 34 Le Duan, is the city's newest and most exclusive department store. Saigon Square, 77–89 Nam Ky Khoi Nghia, is good for fake designer clothes and watches, as well as a couple of shops selling trekking boots, raingear and other outdoor equipment. The Tax Trading Centre, 135 Nguyen Hue, hosts shops selling reasonably priced clothing and electronic goods.
**Markets** The city's biggest market is Cho Ben Thanh, at the junction of Tran Hung Dao, Le Loi and Ham Nghi, with everything from conical hats, basketware bags, Da Lat coffee and Vietnam T-shirts to buckets of eels and pigs' ears and snouts. Cho Lon's equivalent is Cho Binh Tay (see p.908), below Thap Muoi. For American and Vietnamese army surplus, try Dan Sinh Market at 336 Nguyen Cong Tru. The spacious courtyard of Vinh Nghiem Pagoda, at 339 Nam Ky Khoi Nghia, turns into a bustling market on religious holidays.
**Musical instruments** For traditional musical instruments, try the shops along Nguyen Thien Thuat.
**Supermarkets** The Citimart, 189c Cong Quynh, and Maxi-Mart, 3c Ba Thang Hai, are both centrally located, Western-style supermarkets selling food, clothes, cosmetics and electronic goods.
**Tailors** For tailoring, try Albert at 22 Vo Van Tan or Zakka at 134 Pasteur; for *ao dai* head to Bich Son, 135 Dong Khoi (custom-made clothing is cheaper in Hoi An).

## Directory

**Airline offices** Air France, 130 Dong Khoi ⓣ08/8290981; British Airways, 1st Floor, 114a Nguyen Hue ⓣ08/8292262; Cathay Pacific, Jardine House, 58 Dong Khoi ⓣ08/8223203; China Airlines, 132–134 Dong Khoi ⓣ08/8251388; China Southern Airlines, Somerset Chancellor House, 1st Floor, 21–23 Nguyen Thi Minh Khai ⓣ08/8235588; Emirates, 1st Floor, 114a Nguyen Hue ⓣ08/8256575; Japan Airlines, Sun Wah Tower, Ground Floor, 115 Nguyen Hue

℡08/8219099; KLM, Saigon Riverside, 2A–4A Ton Duc Thang ℡08/8231990; Lao Airlines, 93 Pasteur ℡08/8226990; Lufthansa, 132–134 Dong Khoi ℡08/8298529; Malaysia Airlines, 132–134 Dong Khoi ℡08/8292529; Pacific Airlines, 177 Vo Thi Sau ℡08/9325978; Philippine Airlines, 229 Dong Khoi ℡08/8272105; Qantas, 1st Floor, 114a Nguyen Hue ℡08/8238844; Siem Reap Airways, 132–134 Dong Khoi ℡08/8239288; Singapore Airlines, 101 Saigon Tower, 29 Le Duan ℡08/8236211; Thai Airways, 65 Nguyen Du ℡08/8223365; United Airlines, 7th Floor, Jardine House, 58 Dong Khoi ℡08/8234755; Vietnam Airlines, 116 Nguyen Hue ℡08/832 0320.

**Banks and exchange** ANZ, 11 Me Linh Square; HSBC, 235 Dong Khoi; Vietcombank, 29 Chuong Duong and 17 Chuong Duong; Vietcombank, 1st Floor, 79a Ham Nghi. Outside normal banking hours, try the Vietcombank bureaux either inside the *Rex Hotel* lobby (daily 8.30am–7.30pm) or at Fiditourist, 187a Pham Ngu Lao (Mon–Sat 7.30am–8.30pm); the airport exchanges (daily 7am–midnight); or Sacombank's foreign exchange annexe on the corner of Pham Ngu Lao at 211 Nguyen Thai Hoc (Mon–Fri 7.30–11.30am & 1–4.30pm, Sat 7.30–11.30am; closed Sun).

**Cinemas** The Diamond Plaza Cinema (13th floor, 34 Le Duan) and Galaxy Cinema (116 Nguyen Du) screen the latest foreign releases. Tickets 30–50,000VND.

**Embassies and consulates** Australia, Landmark Building, 5b Ton Duc Thanh ℡08/8296035; Cambodia, 41 Phung Khac Khoan ℡08/8292751; Canada, 235 Dong Khoi ℡08/8279899; China, 39 Nguyen Thi Minh Khai ℡08/8292457; Indonesia, 18 Phung Khac Khoan ℡08/8251888; Laos, 93 Pasteur ℡08/8297667; Malaysia, Room 1208, Mei Linh Point Tower, 2 Ngo Duc Ke ℡08/8299023; New Zealand, 5th Floor, 41 Nguyen Thi Minh Khai ℡08/8226907; Singapore, Saigon Centre, 65 Le Loi ℡08/8225173; Thailand, 77 Tran Quoc Thao ℡08/9327637; UK (and British Council), 25 Le Duan ℡08/8232604; USA, 4 Le Duan ℡08/8229433.

**Hospitals and clinics** International SOS Clinic, 65 Nguyen Du (℡08/8298424), has international doctors with consultation fees starting at $80; they also have a dental clinic, can arrange emergency evacuation and have a 24hr emergency service (℡08/8298520). Columbia Asia, Saigon International Clinic, 8 Alexandre De Rhodes (℡08/8238455) and 1 No Trang Long, Binh Thanh (℡08/8030678), have multinational doctors, a 24hr A&E unit, emergency cover and evacuation, charging from $45 for consultations. HCM City Family Medical Practice, Diamond Plaza, 34 Le Duan (℡08/8227848), is an international clinic with multinational doctors, a dental surgery and a specialist knowledge in vaccinations, as well as 24hr emergency cover and evacuation (℡09/1234911); consultations start at $50 ($85 after office hours). International Medical Centre, 1 Han Thuyen (℡08/8272366), is a French-run, non-profit 24hr hospitalization centre with inpatient wards, intensive care and emergency surgery; general consultations start at $40, with profits subsidizing heart operations for underprivileged children. Cho Lon's Cho Ray Hospital, at 201 Nguyen Chi Thanh (℡08/8558074), has an outpatients' room for foreigners ($3.60 per consultation) and a foreigners' ward ($27 per night). Grand Dentistry, Ground Floor, Sun Wah Tower, 115 Nguyen Hue (℡08/8219446), is an international-standard dental clinic; basic check-ups start from $30; 24hr emergency line ℡090/3647156.

**Immigration** For re-entry visas: the Ministry of the Interior, 254 Nguyen Trai, at the junction with Nguyen Cu Trinh. For extension visas: Immigration of HCMC, 161 Nguyen Du.

**Immigration Office** 254 Nguyen Trai ℡08/8392221 (Mon–Fri 9–11am & 1–4pm). For a nominal extra fee, it is much quicker and less hassle to apply for visa extensions through one of the budget travel agencies.

**Internet** Most budget hotels provide free internet access, and there are countless outlets around De Tham and Pham Ngu Lao; rates are currently 100–300VND per minute, printing and scanning costs approximately 1000VND and 2000VND respectively per page. Try Dai Ly Internet at 177 & 220 De Tham, or FPT Internet, 239 Pham Ngu Lao. CyberCafe Saigon, 232 De Tham, has internet phone to all countries. Cheapest Internet access in the area is downstairs at the *Phi Long Hotel*, 38 Bui Vien (4000VND/hr). Downtown, the CyberCafe at 48 Dong Du is an a/c business centre which has a colour printer, fax and scanner.

**Pharmacies** There are several around Pham Ngu Lao area, including 214 De Tham and 81 Bui Vien. Downtown, there are pharmacies at 197–199 Dong Khoi, 199 and 205 Hai Ba Trung and 14a Nguyen Dinh Chieu.

**Post offices** The main post office (daily 6.30am–10pm) is beside the cathedral at the head of Dong Khoi; its impressive architecture makes it a tourist attraction in its own right. Poste restante is held here, and incoming faxes are accepted both here (Ⓕ08/8225662) and at nearby 230 Hai Ba Trung (Ⓕ08/8298540); there's a 2200VND pick-up fee for first page, 1100VND for each remaining page. International parcel dispatch is located behind the main post office at 117 Hai Ba Trung; parcels are received next door at no. 119 – bring your passport and 3000VND for the customs fee (Mon–Fri 7am–7pm; Sat & Sun 7.30am–4.30pm). There are also post offices at 303 Pham Ngu Lao, at 156 Cong Quynh (with poste restante), outside the arrivals terminal at Tan Son Nhat Airport, and at Ga Saigon train station.

**Telephone services** There are IDD, fax and telex facilities at the post office and numerous IDD telephone kiosks around De Tham and Pham Ngu Lao, plus IDD facilities at most hotels. Most Internet cafés offer Skype or an alternative Internet call service which works out much cheaper than IDD.

## Moving on

**By bus** Buses north leave from Mien Dong bus station. Buy a ticket in advance from the large, blue hangar-type building marked "Booking office – Phong Ve" (daily 4am–6pm). Express a/c buses depart regularly for Da Lat, Buon Me Thuot and Nha Trang. Most buses for the south (exceptions include some buses to My Thuan) use Mien Tay bus station – express buses to My Tho, Can Tho, Long Xuyen and Chau Doc. To get to Mien Tay, catch a shuttle bus from Ben Thanh bus station. Buses for My Thuan depart from Cho Lon bus station. Saigon Star Co buses run to near here from the city (see p.910 for the route), or you can catch a xe lam from Ben Thanh bus station. Buses for My Tho no longer leave from Cho Lon.

Open-tour buses of varying quality run from most budget travel companies in De Tham; Kim Travel and Sinh Café buses are recommended (see p.908). All run to the main tourist destinations north of HCMC such as Da Lat, Mui Ne, Nha Trang, Hoi An, Da Nang, Hue and Hanoi. See opposite for details on getting to Phnom Penh.

**Destinations:** Buon Ma Thuot (7–8hr); Can Tho (4hr); Chau Doc (6hr); Da Lat (5–7hr); Da Nang (21hr); Hanoi (42hr); Ha Tien (8hr); Hue (27hr); Mui Ne (4hr); My Tho (1hr 30min); Nha Trang (9hr); Rach Gia (5–6hr).

**By boat** Boats for My Tho (6hr) and Ben Tre (8hr) depart irregularly from the mooring on the corner of Den Van and Ton That Thuyet, 1.5km south of the Ho Chi Minh Museum. Hydrofoils to Vung Tao (1hr, 6 daily, 120,000VND) depart from the Bach Dang Wharf at the eastern end of Ham Nghi. Express boats to Can Tho (3hr 15min, 160,000VND) depart at 7.15am and 1.15pm from the same quay.

**By train** Always book train tickets as far ahead as possible, through a travel agent, Saigon Railways Tourist Service, 275c Pham Ngu Lao (daily 7.30am–8pm; ⓣ08/8367640), or in person at counters no. 5 and 6 on the first floor at the train station (daily 7am–11pm; ⓣ08/9310666).

**Destinations:** Da Nang (10 daily; 15hr–23hr); Hanoi (10 daily; 30–41hr); Hue (10 daily; 17hr 40min–24hr 30min); Nha Trang (10 daily; 6hr 20min–10hr); Ninh Binh (6 daily; 34hr 40min–36hr); Vinh (10 daily; 24hr 30min–35hr 30min).

**By air** The easiest way to get to Tan Son Nhat Airport is by taxi ($6), but you can also take a shared car from one of the many tour operators in the Pham Ngu Lao area ($2). Public bus no.152 runs to the airport, and picks up passengers on De Tham (3000VND). International destinations include Bangkok, Kuala Lumpur, Phnom Penh, Singapore.

**Destinations:** Buon Ma Thuot (10 weekly; 1hr); Da Lat (2 daily; 50min); Da Nang (5 daily; 1hr 10min); Hai Phong (2 daily; 1hr); Hanoi (3 daily; 2hr); Hue (3 daily; 1hr 20min); Nha Trang (4 daily; 1hr); Phu Quoc (5 daily; 1hr); Rach Gia (1 daily; 40min); Plei Ku (1 daily, 1hr 15min); Quy Nhon (10 weekly; 1hr 25min); Vinh (1 daily; 1hr 45min).

# DAY-TRIPS FROM HO CHI MINH CITY

The single most popular trip out of the city takes in two of Vietnam's most memorable sights: the **Cu Chi tunnels**, for twenty years a bolt hole, first for Viet Minh agents, and later for Viet Cong cadres; and the weird and wonderful **Cao Dai Holy See** at Tay Ninh, the fulcrum of the country's most charismatic indigenous religion. Most HCMC travel agents combine these two sights, with tours costing $5 (not including entrance to the tunnels).

## The Cu Chi tunnels

During the American War, the villages around the district of Cu Chi supported a substantial Viet Cong (VC) presence. Faced with American attempts to neutralize them, they quite literally dug themselves out of harm's way, and the legendary **Cu Chi tunnels** were the result. Today, the tunnels have been widened to allow passage for Western tourists, but it's still a dark, sweaty, claustrophobic experience. The most popular site is **Ben Dinh** (daily 7.30am–5pm; 70,000VND), 40km from HCMC and best visited on a tour.

## INTO CAMBODIA: MOC BAI

### Moc Bai

At present, the main overland entry and exit point between Cambodia and Vietnam for foreigners is at **Moc Bai**, which is northwest of HCMC, the usual overland departure point for this crossing. The Moc Bai border is open daily 7am–5pm. Sinh Café and Kim Travel (see p.908) both run daily a/c buses ($10) **to Phnom Penh** from their respective offices in De Tham, departing at 6.30am and 9am, arriving at around 1pm and 3pm respectively. More expensive, but with no change of bus at the border, direct state-run buses for Phnom Penh depart from Saigon Passenger Transport Company, 309 Pham Ngu Lao (daily 8am–5pm; ⓣ08/9203623), on Tuesdays, Thursdays and Saturdays at 6am, arriving around 2pm in Phnom Penh; tickets ($12) can be purchased here. All bus tickets can be bought in advance or on the day. Another option is to sign up with a tour operator for a **share taxi** in Pham Ngu Lao ($15–25 for a full car); this will take you as far as the Moc Bai border crossing, from where you can walk over the border and negotiate onward transport to Phnom Penh. Cambodian visas are available on the border for $25 including the "processing fee".

By 1965, 250km of tunnels criss-crossed Cu Chi and surrounding areas. Tunnels could be as small as 80cm wide and 80cm high, and were sometimes four levels deep; there were latrines, wells, meeting rooms and dorms here, as well as rudimentary hospitals, where operations were carried out by torchlight using instruments fashioned from shards of ordnance. At times inhabitants stayed below ground for weeks on end, and they often had to lie on the floor to get enough oxygen to breathe. American attempts to flush out the tunnels proved ineffective. They evacuated villagers into strategic hamlets and then used defoliant sprays and bulldozers to rob the VC of cover, in "scorched earth" operations. GIs known as tunnel rats would go down themselves, but faced booby traps and bombs. Finally, they sent in the B52s to level the district with carpet-bombing.

### The Cao Dai Holy See

Northwest of Cu Chi at Tay Ninh lies the fantastical confection of styles that is the **Cao Dai Holy See**. The Cao Dai religion was founded in October 1926 as a fusion of oriental and occidental religions. Though its beliefs centre on a universal god and it borrows the structure and terminology of the Catholic Church, Cao Dai is primarily influenced by Buddhism, Taoism and Confucianism, and looks to hasten the evolution of the soul through reincarnation.

The cathedral's central portico is topped by a bowed, first-floor balcony and a Divine Eye, the most recurrent motif in the building. Two figures in semi-relief emerge from either side of the towers: Cao Dai's first female cardinal, Lam Huong Thanh, on the left; and on the right, Le Van Trung, Cao Dai's first pope. Men enter through an entrance in the right wall, women by a door to the left. Tourists can wander through the nave as long as they remain in the aisles and don't stray between the rows of pink pillars, entwined by green dragons. The papal chair stands at the head of the chamber, its arms carved into dragons. Dominating the chamber, though, and guarded by eight silver dragons, a vast, duck-egg-blue sphere, speckled with stars, rests on a polished, eight-sided dais. **Services** are held daily at 6am, noon, 6pm and midnight and are well worth attending. A traditional band plays as robed worshippers chant, pray and sing.

# The Mekong Delta

The orchards, paddy-fields and swamplands of the **Mekong Delta** stretch from Ho Chi Minh's city limits southwest to the Gulf of Thailand, crisscrossed by nine channels of the Mekong River – Asia's third-longest river after the Yangtse and Yellow rivers. Here at the Mekong's delta, not only does it water "Vietnam's rice bowl", but it also serves as a crucial transportation artery, teeming with rowing boats, sampans, ferries and floating markets.

The most enjoyable way to experience delta life is by boat: most people rent boats in **My Tho**, but from here a ferry traverses the uppermost strand of the Tien Giang to laid-back **Ben Tre**, a more rewarding and less touristy town. **Can Tho**, on the west bank of the Hau Giang, holds the delta's most famous floating markets; access to the city is by ferry until the much anticipated Can Tho Bridge is finally completed. From here, a road runs to the Cambodian border towns of **Chau Doc** and **Ha Tien**. Foreigners can cross into Cambodia near Chau Doc at **Vinh Xuong**, most conveniently by organized boat transfer (see p.925); another border crossing is also open at nearby **Tinh Bien**. Off the coast near here, a boat ride from **Rach Gia**, is the idyllic island of **Phu Quoc**.

## MY THO

Nestled on the north bank of the Tien Giang channel, 70km southwest of HCMC, the amiable market town of **MY THO** attracts crowds of tourists and day-trippers from HCMC for boat trips around the region's narrow waterways, who throng around the waterfront at lunchtime. However, the city itself has little to offer in the way of attractions or amenities, so it's best to pass through My Tho and venture further into the delta.

### What to see and do

The lower of the two bridges spanning the Bao Dinh canal marks the start of waterfront Phan Thanh Gian, home to My Tho's modest **Chinese quarter**, where shop fronts are piled to the rafters with sugar-cane poles, watermelons and fish awaiting transportation up to HCMC. A cyclo journey east of Phan Thanh Gian, Nguyen Trung Truc's attractive **Vinh Trang Pagoda** (daily 7am–noon & 2–5pm), with its Rajah's palace-style front facade, has become rather a tourist trap in recent years, but is of interest to many as it is said that VC soldiers hid here in the 1960s.

### Boat trips

Taking a **boat trip** on the Mekong is the undoubted highlight of a stay in My Tho. Of the four nearby islands, Tan Long, Phung Island and Thoi Son are all regularly visited by tourist boats. Beyond its chaotic shoreline of stilthouses and boatyards, **Tan Long** ("Dragon Island") boasts bounteous sapodilla, coconut and banana plantations. **Phung Island** (daily 7am–5pm) is famed as the home of an offbeat religious sect set up three decades ago by the eccentric Coconut Monk, Ong Dao Dua, but only the skeleton of the open-air complex he established remains. Beyond the compound stretch acres of orchards, whose fruits can be sampled at the several cafés dotted around the island. **Thoi Son** ("Unicorn Island") is the largest of the four islands. Slender canals, their banks shaded by water coconut trees, allow boats to weave through its interior.

The cheapest way of getting onto the water is to take a **public ferry**. Ferries to Tan Long depart from Trung Trac; Thoi Son ferries leave from either Vong Nho or Binh Duc markets. Public

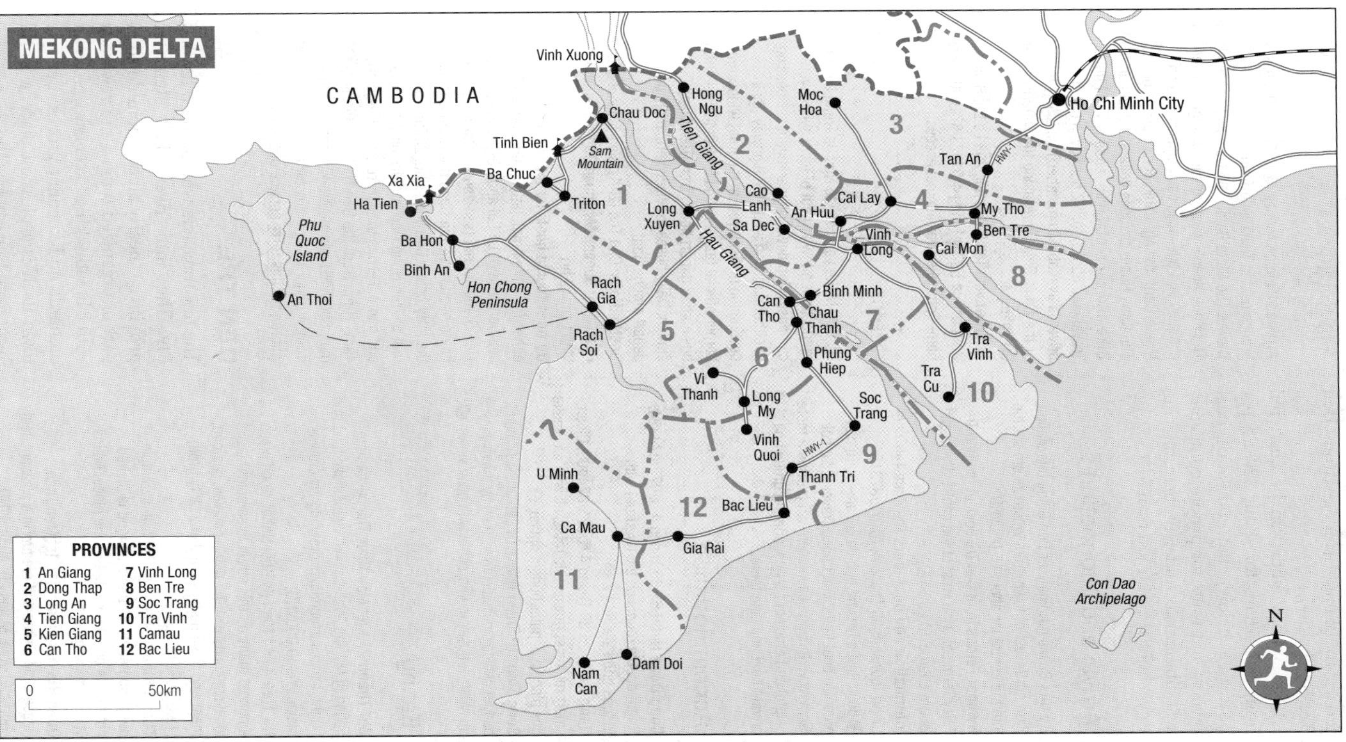
MEKONG DELTA
CAMBODIA
Vinh Xuong
Hong Ngu
Moc Hoa
Ho Chi Minh City
Chau Doc
Tinh Bien
Sam Mountain
Tien Giang
Xa Xia
Ba Chuc
Ha Tien
Triton
Long Xuyen
Cao Lanh
Cai Lay
Tan An
HWY-1
My Tho
Ben Tre
An Huu
Sa Dec
Vinh Long
Cai Mon
Phu Quoc Island
Ba Hon
Binh An
Hon Chong Peninsula
Hau Giang
An Thoi
Rach Gia
Rach Soi
Binh Minh
Can Tho
Chau Thanh
Tra Vinh
Phung Hiep
Vi Thanh
Long My
Tra Cu
Soc Trang
Vinh Quoi
Thanh Tri
U Minh
Bac Lieu
Ca Mau
Gia Rai
Con Dao Archipelago
N
Nam Can
Dam Doi
1
2
3
4
5
6
7
8
9
10
11
12
PROVINCES
1 An Giang
2 Dong Thap
3 Long An
4 Tien Giang
5 Kien Giang
6 Can Tho
7 Vinh Long
8 Ben Tre
9 Soc Trang
10 Tra Vinh
11 Camau
12 Bac Lieu
0
50km

ferries to Phung Island go from Ben Tre (see below).

Boats with a guide can be chartered from tour agents for about $20–25 per boat (see below), but individual boat owners and touts for private companies will substantially undercut them, offering three-hour trips for less than $10.

## Arrival and information

**By bus** Buses terminate at Tien Giang bus station, 3km northwest of town, from where xe om shuttle into the centre for about 15,000VND.
**By boat** Ferries from Ben Tre dock at the Ben Tre Ferry Terminal, 1km west of the centre. Cyclo and xe om charge 10,000VND.
**Information and boat tours** The state-run Tien Giang Tourist (8 30 Thang 4; ⓣ073/873184; ⓔdulichtg@bdvn.vnd.net; daily 7am–5pm) can organize boat tours. Viet Phong Travel (2 Le Loi; ⓦwww.vietphongmekong.com.vn) provide a more helpful and efficient service, offering group and private boat and bike tours.

## Accommodation

**Cong Doan Hotel** 61 30 Thang 4 ⓣ073/874324. Bright double rooms on the riverfront with a/c, fridges and satellite TV. ❷
**Rang Dong** 25 30 Thang 4 ⓣ073/874400. Clean, smart rooms at reasonable rates, all with a/c, make this place a popular budget option. ❷
**Song Tien** 101 Trung Trac ⓣ073/872009. A sound budget choice, conveniently located by the river, with 36 clean, unfussy rooms, some with good views. ❷

## Eating

**Chi Thanh** 279 Tet Mau Than. The best eating option in My Tho. Well-cooked Vietnamese food and bright, clean surroundings draw nightly crowds. Mains 20–40,000VND.
**Hu Tieu 44** 44 Nam Ky Khoi Nghia. Good place amongst many on this street to sample the local speciality dish *hu tieu* – noodles, seafood, meat and fresh herbs served in a tasty broth (15,000VND).
**Thuan Kieu** 47 Nam Ky Khoi Nghia. Simple but flavoursome Vietnamese food is dished out in this popular canteen-style place. Mains 10–15,000VND.
**Quan Bia Hai Xuan** 141b Tet Mau Than. Reasonable dishes and *bia tuoi* in a pleasant, leafy courtyard area. Mains 20–40,000VND.

## Directory

**Airlines** Vietnam Airlines (ⓣ073/872006) has a branch next to Tien Giang Tourist.
**Banks** The State Bank, 15b Nam Ky Khoi Nghia, at Thu Khoa Huan's western end, changes traveller's cheques and advances cash against Visa and MasterCard; the Agribank, corner of Le Loi and Thu Khoa Huan, changes dollars and has an ATM.
**Bike and car rental** Bike rental at Viet Phong Travel (see above) for $2 per day; a car plus driver is available from either Tien Giang Tourist or the *Cong Duan Hotel* along the waterfront on 30 Thang 4.
**Internet** Vinh Tan Computer, 203 Le Dai Hanh.
**Post office** 59 30 Thang 4 ⓣ073/871000 (daily 6am–9pm); also has internet access.

## Moving on

**By bus** Make your way to Nga Ba Trung Luong roundabout a few km out of town, where you can easily flag down regular minibuses passing in either direction along the highway (their destination is displayed on the front windscreen). Larger official buses bound for HCMC's Mien Tay bus station depart hourly from Tien Giang bus station. Daily buses for elsewhere in the delta depart around 5am.
**Destinations**: Can Tho (2hr); Mien Tay bus station, HCMC (1hr 30min); My Thuan Bridge (1hr 30min); Vinh Long (2 hr).
**By boat** Tourist boats for the islands leave either from the small jetty at the corner of the southern end of Le Loi and 30 Thang 4, or at Tien Giang Tourist (see above). Cargo/passenger boats heading to Tan Chau (for Chau Doc) use the jetty below Cho Vong Nho, 200m west of the foot of Tran Hung Dao (1 daily, between 11am and noon). Ferries to Ben Tre depart regularly 4am–10pm from the Ben Tre Ferry Terminal (20 min; 5000VND per motorbike, foot passengers free). A major bridge, due for completion in 2009, will render this ferry service obsolete.

# BEN TRE

The few travellers who push on beyond My Tho into riverlocked **Ben Tre province** – nearly all of whom do so as part of organized tours – are rewarded with breathtaking scenery of fruit orchards and coconut groves. Ben Tre town itself is a pleasant place, a world away from touristy My Tho.

Once you've scanned Ben Tre's buzzing **market** in the centre of town, you'll want to pass over the quaint bridge leading to Ben Tre channel's more rustic south bank, where scores of boats moor in front of thatch houses. With a bicycle (bring one from My Tho, or ask at your hotel), you can explore the maze of dirt tracks and visit the riverside **wine factory**, 450m west of the bridge, where *ruou trang* (rice wine) fizzes away in earthenware jars.

### Cai Mon

Honda om congregate outside the post office in the centre of Ben Tre, and for $6 (100,000VND) they'll whisk you off on a three-hour round-trip to the **fruit orchards of Cai Mon**. Ten minutes' ride west of town you cross a river on the Ham Luong ferry, then head off into waxy green paddy-fields to the coconut village of Ba Vat (20min). Twenty-five minutes later, the road reaches Cai Mon, a sleepy community whose residents make a living by cultivating fruit in the vast plain of orchards, veined by miles of canals and paths.

### Arrival and information

**By bus** Buses either terminate at the bus station 2km out of town (10,000VND to the centre by xe om), or nearer the centre at Truc Giang Lake.

**By boat** Ferries from My Tho (20min) disgorge their passengers at Ben Tre's Hongvan port, 1km north of the town centre; a xe om will take you into town for less than 10,000VND.

**Tourist information** Ben Tre Tourism, 65 Dong Khoi (☎075/829618) can help with tours.

### Accommodation

**Hung Vuong Hotel** 166 Hung Vuong ☎075/822408. The all-new riverside hotel has spotlessly clean rooms, all with satellite TV, bathtub and hot water. Rooms at the front of the hotel offer views of the bustling waterfront below. ❸

**Thao Nhi Guest House** in Tan Thach Village ☎075/860009. Located 10km north of town near the Tien Giang River, this charming guesthouse has six basic fan and a/c rooms set amongst quiet fruit gardens; to get here, turn left immediately after leaving the ferry terminal and continue parallel to the river for about 500m until you see a sign for the guesthouse on the right. There is a good restaurant too, and the helpful staff can arrange bike rental and boat tours. ❷

### Eating

The stalls around the market (along Nguyen Trai) offer the best food and the best prices in town.

**Ben Tre Floating Restaurant** near the bridge. It's seen better days but remains a good spot for a sunset drink, and boasts a reasonably priced menu with mains starting at 40,000VND.

### Moving on

**By bus** Buses leave early in the morning for some Delta towns, but a more reliable service runs from My Tho. Public transport services to towns south of Ben Tre do not depart from here – you must return to My Tho.

**By boat** Regular ferries depart from Hongvan port to My Tho (20min) between 4am and 10pm.

## CAN THO

Sited at the confluence of the Can Tho and Hau Giang rivers, **CAN THO** is the delta's biggest city, a major trading centre and transport interchange. However, abundant rice fields are never far away, and boat trips along the canals and rivers, through memorable floating markets, are undoubtedly Can Tho's star attraction.

### What to see and do

Broad Hoa Binh is the city's backbone, and the site of the **Ho Chi Minh Museum** (Mon–Fri 7.30–11.30am, 1.30–4.30pm; free), where photographs and army ordnance are displayed. Can Tho was the last city to succumb to the North Vietnamese Army, on May 1, 1975, a day after the fall of Saigon and the date that has come to represent the absolute reunification of the country. The impressive **Can Tho Museum**, 1 Hoa Binh (Tues, Wed & Thurs 8–11am & 2–5pm, Sat & Sun 8–11am & 6.30–9pm; free), presents a history of local resistance, and economic and social achievements.

The city's **central market** swallows up the entire central segment of waterfront Hai Ba Trung, with piles of fruit and fresh shellfish for sale. North of the market, past the silver-coloured statue of Ho Chi Minh, the **Ong Pagoda** is a prosperous and perfectly preserved nineteenth-century temple financed by a wealthy Chinese townsman, Huynh An Thai.

### Boat trips

Every morning an armada of boats takes to the web of waterways spun across Can Tho province, and makes for one of its **floating markets**, which are still unbeatable as snapshots of Mekong life. Everything your average villager could need is on sale, from haircuts to coffins, though predictably fruit and vegetables make up the lion's share of the wares. Each boat's produce is identifiable by a sample hanging off a bamboo mast in its bow.

Of the three major markets in the province, **Cai Rang** – the busiest and largest – and the more modest but still interesting **Phong Dien** are both visited by tour groups but remain relatively friendly and uncommercialized. Most organized tours take in one of the markets and return to Can Tho via the maze of surrounding canals; tours can be organized through your hotel or at the Can Tho Tourist Office (see below) for $15–20; or negotiate your own itinerary with any of the many touts along the waterfront for a maximum of $10 per small boat. The markets are at their busiest between 6 and 8am, so it's best to make a really **early start**.

## Arrival and information

**By bus** Long-distance buses take you across the Hau Giang estuary and into Can Tho's bus station, 1200m northwest of town at the junction of Nguyen Trai and Hung Vuong. Most buses terminate here, where a xe om can take you into the centre for 10,000VND.

**By boat** Express boats from HCMC dock at the Ninh Kieu jetty at the northern end of Hai Ba Trung. It is a five-minute walk from here along the river to the city's main tourist hub.

**Tourist information** Can Tho Tourist, 20 Hai Ba Trung (Ⓣ 071/821853, Ⓦ www.canthotourist.com.vn), has a Vietnam Airlines branch and can help with car rental and boat tours, though for the latter, you'll do better to book an unofficial boat through a tout on Hai Ba Trung. They also assist with bus ticket reservations, and organize homestays with local families for $10 per person including dinner and breakfast.

## Accommodation

Most hotels are on Hai Ba Trung and Chau Van Liem, though there's some much cheaper accommodation of a similar standard a short walk south of the main drag.

**Hotel 31** 31 Ngo Duc Ke Ⓣ 071/825287. A family-run hotel with very basic but comfortable double rooms. The restaurant is popular with tour groups and offers Vietnamese specialities for 15–30,000VND. ❶–❷

**Huy Hoang** 35 Ngo Duc Ke Ⓣ 071/825833. A pleasant mini-hotel with lean and bright rooms and helpful staff. ❷–❸

**Tay Ho** 36 Hai Ba Trung Ⓣ 071/823392, Ⓔ kstayho-ct@hcm.vnn.vn. Sitting in an aged row of shop-houses, this recently refurbished mini-hotel offers reasonably priced double, triple and family rooms. ❷–❸.

**Xuan Mai** 17, 94 Nguyen An Ninh Ⓣ 071/823578. This popular hotel has raised the bar with its scrupulously clean, business-like rooms with free WiFi and a/c. Its sister hotel of the same name at 17 Dien Bien Phu Street (Ⓣ 071/823578) has similarly well-furnished double rooms with fans for half the price. ❸ & ❷

## Eating

**Mekong Restaurant** 38 Hai Ba Trung. This established favourite is hard to top for cheap, flavoursome Vietnamese and Chinese meals; the fried fish in sweet-and-sour sauce (around 25,000VND) is highly recommended.

**Nambo Café** 50 Hai Ba Trung Ⓣ 071/823908. A popular place, *Nambo* serves French-influenced dishes in colonial-style elegance and has a pleasant balcony overlooking the riverfront.

Advance reservations are recommended for the evening sitting. Daily 9am–2pm & 5–11pm. Mains 25–55,000VND.

**Phuong Nam** 48 Hai Ba Trung. Next door to *Nambo*, this little restaurant offers quality cooking at reasonable rates; house specialities include fried squid in tamarind sauce for around 25,000VND.

**Thien Hoa** 26 Hai Ba Trung. Large portions of sour soups and other local and Chinese food for under 20,000VND are popular with locals and tourists alike. Daily 9am–2pm & 5–11pm.

## Directory

**Bank** Vietcombank, 7 Hoa Binh (Mon–Fri, 7.30–10.45am & 1.30–4pm), changes cash and traveller's cheques and cash advances against Visa and MasterCard

**Internet** Phuc Thai, 161 Ly Tu Trong; 9 Chau Van Liem.

**Pharmacy** 88–90 Ly Tu Trong.

**Post office** 2 Hoa Binh (daily 6am–9pm).

**Supermarket** Co-Op Mart, 1 Dai Lo Hoa Binh. Stocks a good selection of dry goods, breads, dairy products, fresh fruit and vegetables.

## Moving on

**By bus** Express high-quality minibuses to Chau Doc and HCMC depart from 75a Tran Phu (or arrange a hotel pick-up on ☎071/761761); ask the driver to stop en route for My Tho. Regular public buses run from the Can Tho bus station to elsewhere in the delta.

**Destinations**: Chau Doc (2hr 30min); Ha Tien (7hr); Mien Tay bus station, HCMC (4hr); My Tho (2hr); Rach Gia (2hr 30min).

# CHAU DOC

Snuggled against the west bank of the Hau Giang River, next to the Cambodian border (see box p.925), **CHAU DOC** was under Cambodian rule until the mid-eighteenth century and still sustains a large Khmer community. Forays by Pol Pot's genocidal Khmer Rouge into this corner of the delta led to the Vietnamese invasion of Cambodia in 1978, but today Chau Doc is a bustling, friendly port town that's well worth a visit.

## What to see and do

First stop should be the town's **market**, roughly between Quang Trung, Doc Phu Thu, Tran Hung Dao and Nguyen Van Thoi, which offers the usual fruit and vegetables alongside baskets piled high with a pungent selection of glassy-eyed dried fish. One or two colonial relics are on parade in nearby Doc Phu Thu, some of whose grand shop-house terraces flaunt arched upper-floor windows and wrought-iron struts. A grand, four-tiered gateway deep in the belly of the market announces **Quan Cong Temple**, ornamented with two rooftop dragons and some vivid murals.

Northwest up Tran Hung Dao, long boardwalks lead to sizeable stilthouse communities, and from here, at the junction with Thuong Dang Le, you can take a ferry across the Hau Giang River to the stilthouses of **Con Tien Island**. Cham-dominated **Chau Giang district** lies across the Hau Giang River, 2km northeast of the town. Kampung-style wooden houses, sarongs and white prayer caps betray the influence of Islam, as do the twin domes and minaret of the Mubarak Mosque. Xe om and xe dap loi will take you there and back for about 30,000VND, including waiting time.

### Sam Mountain

Arid, brooding **Sam Mountain** rises dramatically from an ocean of paddy-fields 5km southwest of Chau Doc, and Vietnamese tourists flock here to worship at its clutch of pagodas and shrines. From town, a road runs straight to the foot of the mountain, reached by xe dap loi and xe lam, or easily covered by bicycle. Steep steps lead **up the mountain** for 1km in a clockwise direction from beyond a large, mustard-coloured school. After fifteen minutes, an observatory affords fine views of the patchwork of fields below, but if you carry on for another twenty minutes to the top, there are spectacular 360-degree views from the summit.

## Arrival and Information

**By bus** Buses offload 2km southeast of town, on Le Loi, from where xe dap loi and xe om run into town for about 10,000VND; some minibuses drop off in the centre on Thu Khoa Nghia.
**By boat** Boats from Cambodia and other points on the Vinh Te Canal dock at a small jetty at the northern end of Tran Hung Dao, 1km from the centre.
**Tourist information** Mekong Tours, 14 Nguyen Huu Canh ⓣ076/868222, offers half-day trips to a fish farm and Cham village ($6) as well as longer trips through the delta, and can assist with onward travel arrangements including overland routes and boats to Cambodia (see opposite).

## Accommodation

**Hang Chau 2** 10 Nguyen Van Thoai ⓣ076/868891, ⓔhangchau2agg@hcm.vnn.vn. Smart, spotless rooms with wooden floors and crisp white sheets all come with satellite TV and hot water. ❷
**Hoa Hung Motel** 5 Qaung Trung ⓣ076/866417. Kitsch but comfortable fan and a/c rooms, with plastic flowers and technicolour walls, are good value. ❷
**Thuan Loi Hotel** 18 Tran Hung Dao ⓣ076/866134, ⓔhotelthuanloi@hcm.vnn.vn. The choice of spacious, clean rooms in this waterfront guesthouse includes bargain fan quarters, some of which have absorbing views of river life drifting by; there's also a stilt restaurant. Fan ❷; a/c ❸
**Thanh Nam 2** 10 Quang Trung ⓣ076/562265, ⓔthanhnamhotel@yahoo.com. Offering spotlessly clean, colourful rooms at rock bottom rates, this mini-hotel is the best deal in Chau Doc. Fan ❶; a/c ❷
**Trung Nguyen** 86 Bach Dang ⓣ076/868674, ⓔtrunghotel@yahoo.com. Bustling, conveniently located mini-hotel popular with tour groups that offers good value for money. ❸

## Eating

Stalls at the market offer delicious pho, fresh spring rolls and other Vietnamese dishes for less than 10,000VND. At night, vendors set up food stalls around the pagoda at the central square between Nguyen Huu Canh and Chi Lang.
**Bay Bong** 22 Thuong Dang Le. Try the local speciality of pork or fish cooked in a clay pot for 35,000VND.
**Lam Hung Ky** 71 Chi Lang. Serves the town's most imaginative menu, featuring dishes like beef with bitter melon and black beans for 25,000VND.
**Truong Van** 15 Quang Trung. Tasty, inexpensive Vietnamese and Chinese dishes make this little place popular with both tourists and locals.

## Directory

**Bank** Vietcombank opposite the bus station changes traveller's cheques.
**Bike rental** *Trung Nguyen Hotel* offers bike rental for $2 per day, and motorbikes for $8.
**Internet** 16/2 Nui Sam; 40 Nguyen Van Thoai.
**Post office** 73 Le Loi (daily 6am–10pm). Also provides international phone and fax service.

## Moving on

**By bus** Public buses to HCMC depart hourly from the bus station on Le Loi; regular express minibuses to elsewhere in the delta can be booked through your hotel.
**Destinations**: Can Tho (2hr 30min); HCMC (5–6hr); Hat Tien (3 hr); Long Xuyen (1hr 15min).
**By boat** Express boats to HCMC ($10; 3hr 15min) depart from the Ninh Kieu jetty at 7.15am and 1.15pm daily. Tickets are available from the Thanh Nhan booking office at 2 Hai Ba Trung (ⓣ071/817817).

# RACH GIA

Teetering precariously over the Gulf of Thailand, **RACH GIA** is home to a farming and fishing community of almost 150,000 people. A small islet in the mouth of the Cai Lon River forms the hub of town, its central area shoehorned tightly between Le Loi and Tran Phu. Although the town is mainly visited as a jumping off point for Phu Quoc, the charming riverfront, bustling market and quaint back streets hold enough charm to keep you entertained for a half day. The small **museum** at 27 Nguyen Van Troi (Mon–Wed, Sat & Sun 7–11am & 1–5pm; free) holds a small collection of wartime souvenirs, photographs and relics from the nearby ancient city of Oc Eo, including shards of pottery, coins and bones.

## INTO CAMBODIA: VINH XUONG AND TINH BIEN

### Vinh Xuong

It's possible to cross into Cambodia from Chau Doc via the **Vinh Xuong border crossing** (daily 8am–5pm), 30km north of Chau Doc. The overland route to the border and on to Phnom Penh is still fairly difficult; much easier than slogging it out overland is to take a boat. *Victoria Chau Doc Hotel*, 32 Le Loi (Ⓣ076/865010), operates direct taxi-service speedboats – subject to availability – up the Mekong River to Phnom Penh (daily 7am; 4hr; minimum 2 people; $35). A cheaper option is offered by Mekong Tours, who run a daily express boat ($18; 5hr) and daily slow boat ($8; 9hr) direct to Phnom Penh. The Delta Adventure Tours office in HCMC at 267 De Tham (Ⓣ08/9202110) organizes an all-in transfer from HCMC to Phnom Penh for $26 which includes one night's accommodation in Chau Doc. Cambodian visas are available at the border for $22.

### Tinh Bien

Another border crossing near Chau Doc is at **Tinh Bien**, 25km west of Sam Mountain. The thirty-kilometre road from Chau Doc to Tinh Bien is poor; take a car (1hr; $25) motorbike ($8; 1hr 30min) or local bus ($1.30; 1hr 30min). For onward travel to Phnom Penh, take a private taxi (2–3 hours) from Phnom Den on the Cambodian side for about $25.

## Arrival and information

**By bus** Buses from points north pull up 500m above town, at Nguyen Binh Khiem's station, next to the covered market. Arrivals from Long Xuyen and beyond hit the coast at Rach Soi, 7km southeast of Rach Gia. Some, including those from Can Tho, continue into town, dropping you along central Tran Phu; others terminate at Rach Soi bus station, from where a shuttle minibus, xe lam or xe om will get you to the centre.

**By boat** Boats arriving from Phu Quoc dock at Ben Tau Khach Bien quay, 200m west of the Nguyen Trung Truc Temple on Nguyen Cong Tru. It is a ten-minute walk west along the river to the centre. Boats from elsewhere arrive at Ben Tau Rach Meo quay, 5km south of the town on Ngo Quyen, where xe om await your arrival.

**By air** Flights from HCMC and Phu Quoc arrive in Rach Soi airport, 7km from Rach Gia. From the airport, you can take a xe om direct to Rach Gia (25–30,000VND), or catch a xe lam to Rach Soi centre and then a minibus to Rach Gia.

**Tourist information** Kien Giang Tourism at 12 Ly Tu Trong (Ⓣ077/862081) can arrange tours, car rental and flight reservations.

## Accommodation

**Kim Co Hotel** 141 Nguyen Hung Son Ⓣ077/879611, Ⓔkhachsankimco@yahoo.com.vn. Spacious and clean doubles with a/c. ❸

**Nhat Quang** 16 Duong Tu Ⓣ077/863433. The cheapest and most basic rooms in town; cramped and a little dingy, but adequate for a one-night stopover if you're on a tight budget. ❷

**Wild Rose** 19 Tran Quang Dieu Ⓣ077/920325. Although a little more expensive than others here, the spacious, bright rooms with all amenities and river views are excellent value. The largest rooms sleep up to six, and rates are negotiable. ❸

## Eating

**Ao Dai Moi** 26 Ly Tu Trong. Offers cheap, local rice and noodle dishes in a warm family atmosphere. Daily 6.30am–1pm.

**Tay Ho** 6 Nguyen Du. Always packed with locals, this place serves standard Vietnamese dishes at reasonable prices.

**Thao Phan** corner of Hung Vuong and Duy Tan. Friendly family-run place offering simple rice and noodle dishes and delicious iced coffees in a quaint courtyard setting.

**Vinh Hong 1** 39b Tran Hung Dao. The ingredients of the seafood dishes on the menu eye you warily from tanks mounted on the walls at this place, which enjoys a good reputation for its imaginative and fresh food.

## Directory

**Airline** Vietnam Airlines has a branch at 180 Nguyen Trung Truc (Ⓣ077/8618480).

**Banks** Vietcombank, 2 Mac Cu, exchanges traveller's cheques and cash and can advance cash against Visa and MasterCard. The bank at 44 Pham Hong Thai can also exchange cash.
**Internet** 135 and 143 Nguyen Hung Son; 170 and 257 Tran Phu.

## Moving on

**By bus** Xe lam and minibuses heading back to Rach Soi can be picked up on Tran Phu. Buses for Ha Tien and elsewhere in the delta depart from Nguyen Binh Khiem's bus station, departing as demand dictates; more comfortable luxury a/c minibuses (35,000VND) can be organized through your hotel or directly with the Mai Linh Express office (☎077/929292). If you're taking one of the three nightly express buses to HCMC, you'll board in town: tickets cost $4 and should be bought in advance from the booth marked "Toc Hanh" in front of the Vietcombank on Mac Cuu.
**Destinations**: Can Tho (3hr); Ha Tien (3hr); Mien Tay bus station in HCMC (7hr).
**By boat** Boats for Phu Quoc depart from Ben Tau Khach Bien quay daily at 8am and 12.45pm. Tickets can be bought in advance from offices at 14 Tu Dao (☎077/877742) and 18 Nguyen Cong Tru (☎077/879765), or various other outlets dotted along Nguyen Cong Tru. From the Ben Tau Rach Meo terminal, 5km south of town on Ngo Quyen, passenger/cargo boats leave early in the morning for destinations in the delta.
**Destinations**: Ca Mau (hourly express boats, 2 hr); Can Tho (1 daily; 8 hr); Ha Tien (1 daily; 4 hr); Long Xuyen (1 daily; 4 hr); Phu Quoc (2 daily; 2hr 30min).
**By air** HCMC (1 daily; 50 min); Phu Quoc (1 daily; 40 min).

# PHU QUOC

Lying in the Gulf of Thailand 45km west of Ha Tien and just 15km from the coast of Cambodia, **PHU QUOC** is a quiet, relatively undeveloped tropical island of almost 600 square kilometres. Fringed with golden and powder-white sandy beaches and pretty fishing villages, with a tropical forested interior, and an archipelago of fifteen small islands off the southern tip perfect for diving, snorkelling and fishing, it's no wonder Cambodia contests ownership of such a paradisal place. However, there are plans for major development along the west coast, and billboards announcing mega-luxury resorts stand proud along the roadsides; visit Phu Quoc quick before it loses its unique charm.

## What to do and see

Most tourists visiting Phu Quoc fall easily from one lazy beach day to another. However, Phu Quoc is attracting an increasing number of young backpackers, drawn by the **diving** and **snorkelling** opportunities, and the network of dirt tracks that are perfect for **motorbike excursions** through the island's protected forest and beach-hopping around the deserted sandy coast.

### Duong Dong

The island's main town, **Duong Dong**, is a rather unattractive place with little for the visitor save for the bustling port-side market, on the northern side of the Duong Dong channel, just over the Nguyen Trung Truc bridge. The bridge itself provides a good vantage point over the market and the fleet of pretty blue fishing boats jostling in the harbour. Phu Quoc is famous for its **fish sauce** (*nuoc mam*). A visit to one of the factories can while away an interesting hour or two, if only for the olfactory onslaught; the Hung Thanh factory on Nguyen Van Troi (daily 8–11am & 1–5pm) welcomes visitors.

### The beaches

The palm fringed, twenty-kilometre stretch of golden grainy sand sweeping down the island's west coast, aptly named **Bai Truong** (Long Beach), is the most accessible and well known of Phu Quoc's beaches. Though the northern end is crammed with hotels and luxury resorts all jostling for their section of the beachfront, the southern 10km is deserted, for the moment at least. Flotsam is a problem here however, but it is natural refuse,

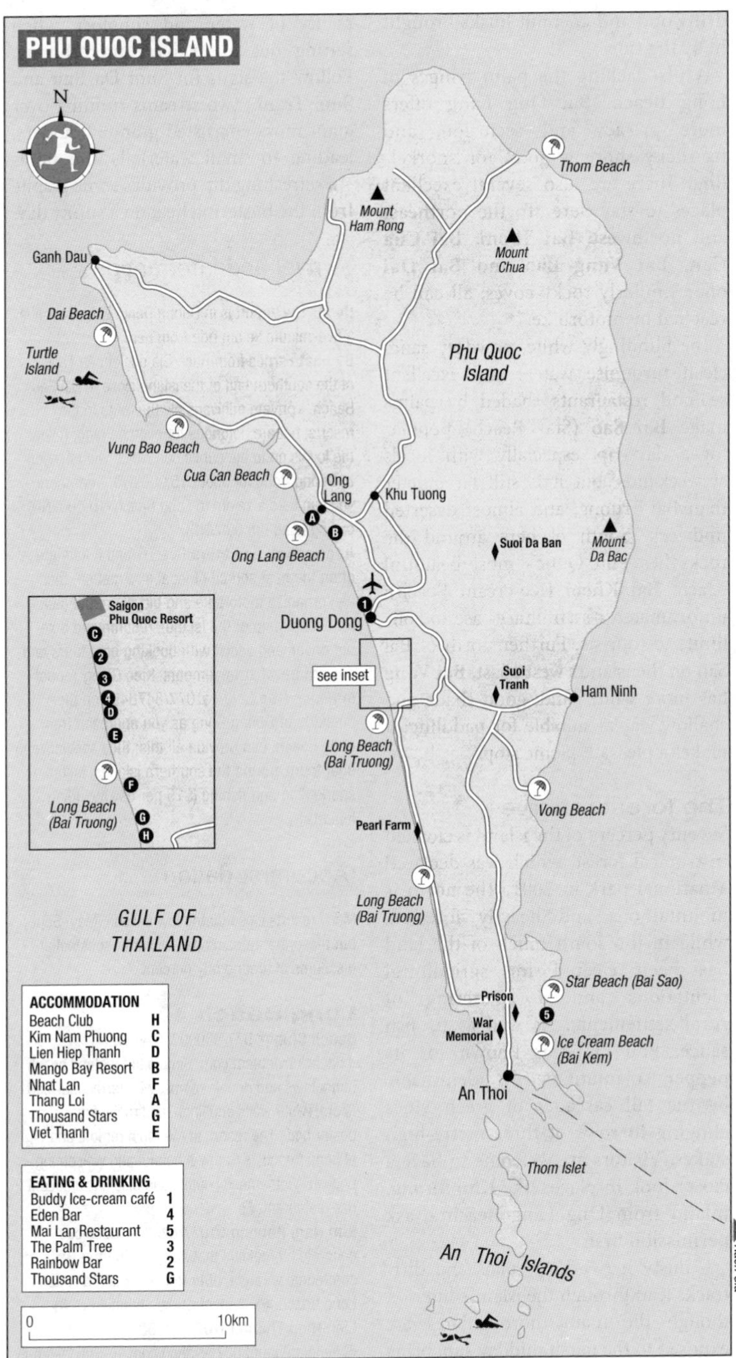
PHU QUOC ISLAND
N
Thom Beach
Mount
Ham Rong
Mount
Chua
Ganh Dau
Dai Beach
Turtle
Island
Phu Quoc
Island
Vung Bao Beach
Cua Can Beach
Ong
Lang
Khu Tuong
Ong Lang Beach
Suoi Da Ban
Mount
Da Bac
Saigon
Phu Quoc Resort
Duong Dong
see inset
Suoi
Tranh
Ham Ninh
Long Beach
(Bai Truong)
Vong Beach
Long Beach
(Bai Truong)
Pearl Farm
Long Beach
(Bai Truong)
GULF OF
THAILAND
Star Beach (Bai Sao)
Prison
War
Memorial
Ice Cream Beach
(Bai Kem)
An Thoi
Thom Islet
An Thoi Islands
Rach Gia
ACCOMMODATION
Beach Club H
Kim Nam Phuong C
Lien Hiep Thanh D
Mango Bay Resort B
Nhat Lan F
Thang Loi A
Thousand Stars G
Viet Thanh E
EATING & DRINKING
Buddy Ice-cream café 1
Eden Bar 4
Mai Lan Restaurant 5
The Palm Tree 3
Rainbow Bar 2
Thousand Stars G
0
10km

driftwood and coconut husks brought in by the tide.

Whilst lacking the palm fringes of Long Beach, **Bai Ong Lang** offers more privacy and seclusion, and its rocky shore is good for snorkelling. There are also several excellent places to stay here. To the northeast and northwest, **Bai Thom**, **Bai Cua Can**, **Bai Vung Bao** and **Bai Dai** offer similarly rocky coves; all can be reached by motorbike.

The blindingly white, powdery sand, clean turquoise waters and excellent seafood restaurants shaded by palms make **Bai Sao** (Star Beach) popular for a day-trip, especially with locals at weekends, but it is still far quieter than Bai Truong, and almost deserted midweek. South of here around the rocks lies Phu Quoc's most beautiful beach, **Bai Khem** (Ice-cream Beach); unfortunately it's a military base and off-limits to tourists. Further north of Bai Sao on the island's west coast, **Bai Vong** has more white sand, good shade and shallow waters suitable for paddling; it makes a pleasant picnic stop.

### The forest reserve

Seventy percent of the island is cloaked in tropical forest, which was declared a national park in 2001. The north is mountainous and heavily forested, while in the south much of the land has been cleared for agricultural plantations and a spattering of rural settlements. As well as its fish sauce, Phu Quoc is known for its pepper plantations – identifiable by the tall cascades of green vines clinging to rows of three-metre-high stakes. Visitors are welcome to have a closer look in places like **Khu Tuong**, inland from Ong Lang Beach – ask permission first.

A dusty network of roads and dirt-tracks lead through the island's interior, though the main thoroughfares are exposed to the harsh midday sun; bring plenty of water and sunblock when setting out for a day's motorbiking. Follow the signs for **Suoi Da Ban** and **Suoi Tranh**, two streams running over giant moss-encrusted granite boulders, leading to small waterfalls and pools – a refreshing dip provides some respite from the blistering heat on a sunny day.

## Arrival and information

**By air** The airport is in Duong Dong. Long Beach is a five-minute xe om ride from here.

**By boat** Ferries from Rach Gia dock in An Thoi at the southern end of the island close to Bai Sao Beach – private minivans ply the route to the resorts, but are notorious for overcharging; follow the locals on to the public bus which will take you to Duong Dong for about 15,000VND; from there you can take a xe om to Long Beach (10,000VND) or Ong Lang (25,000VND).

**Information and tours** Resorts and hotels are often the best source of local information; most can organize motorbike and bicycle rental (ask for a local map of the island), recommend a xe om driver, and assist with booking boat tours and onward travel arrangements. Kien Giang Tourist in *Huong Bien Hotel* (Ⓣ077/847649), on the outskirts of Duong Dong as you approach from Long Beach, can provide all this; they specialize in boat tours around the southern islands, including snorkelling and fishing ($15 per day including lunch).

## Accommodation

Many resorts close during low season (May–Sept), but those that remain open will offer substantial discounts of around fifty percent.

### Long Beach

**Beach Club** Ⓣ077/980998, Ⓦwww.beachclubvietnam.com. Simple but tasteful beach bungalows and double rooms, with terracotta-tiled floors, white walls and linen, and rustic four-poster beds The resort, at the most remote end of Long Beach, is run by a helpful and welcoming English–Vietnamese couple, and also has a decent bar-restaurant. ❹

**Kim Nam Phuong** Ⓣ077/846319. Spacious concrete bungalows that sleep up to three, with a communal veranda, offer the best budget option on Long Beach. ❷; beachfront a/c bungalows ❺

**Lien Hiep Thanh** (Ⓣ077/847583) Ⓔlienhiepthanh2007@yahoo.com.vn. The tastefully

## DIVING AND SNORKELLING AROUND PHU QUOC

When Nha Trang's waters become too murky to dive, Phu Quoc's dive centres are open (September to April), ferrying divers and snorkellers to **Turtle Island** to the north and the **An Thoi** archipelago to the south, where you can see hard and soft corals, and a spectacular array of reef fish including scorpion fish, butterfly fish, parrot fish, fairy basslets, damsel fish and huge sea urchins. Rainbow Divers (Ⓣ091/3400964, Ⓦwww.divevietnam.com) offers well-organized and highly recommended diving and snorkelling trips; a day-trip with two fun-dives and lunch costs $75. They also offer half-day "discover diving" beginners' courses ($30), and PADI certification courses for all levels. Their office is on the main roundabout coming into Duong Dong from the south (Long Beach road), or pay a visit to the *Rainbow Bar* on Long Beach from about 7 to 9pm each evening. Other dive operators include Coco Dive Center (58 Tran Hung Dao, Ⓣ077/9821000, Ⓦwww.cocodivecenter.com), and Vietnam Explorer (36 Tran Hung Dao, Ⓣ077/3846372, Ⓔvietnam_explorer@yahoo.com).

furnished bungalows with private balconies with hammocks right on the beach are beautiful but slightly overpriced; rooms furnished to a similar standard set away from the seafront offer better value. Rooms ❹; bungalows ❻

**Nhat Lan** Ⓣ077/847663, Ⓔnhatlanpq@yahoo.com. There's not much English spoken here, but the simply furnished, clean bungalows set in a manicured tropical garden are very good value. ❸–❹

**Viet Thanh** Ⓣ0773/847716. Spacious bungalows with wooden-slatted balconies in a friendly family-run compound on the beach. ❸–❹

### Ong Lang Beach

**Thang Loi** Ⓣ077/985002, Ⓦwww.phu-quoc.de. Wonderfully friendly resort with rustic wooden and bamboo bungalows of various sizes dotted around the spacious, grassy compound on a hill stretching down to the sea. The large terraced restaurant serves very decent food (try the hot pot) with stunning sunset views. ❹–❻

### Bai Sao

**Mai Lan Restaurant** Ⓣ077/3990779. At Bai Sao there is simple bungalow accommodation here at the southern end of the beach. ❸

## Eating and drinking

Most resorts have bar-restaurants – particularly good at *The Beach Club* and *Thousand Stars Resort*. Places close very early; with the exception of *Eden* very little is open past 10pm, even at weekends, though this is likely to change. For the island's best, cheapest seafood head for the food stalls along Vo Thi Sau in Duong Dong every evening. The small restaurants at the northern end of Tran Hung Dao offer similarly excellent, reasonably priced seafood (mains 15–30,000VND) in a convivial al fresco dining area.

**Buddy's Ice-cream Café** 26 Nguyen Trai. Try their imported New Zealand ice cream and sublime fruit shakes; also offers free internet to customers.

**Eden Bar Long Beach** With tables and pretty red lights set up on the sand and a large bar and dance floor inside, this new bar is ready for the onslaught of tourists expected to arrive with the upcoming development. Sister bar to the *Eden* in HCMC, this is the only place here open late. Free taxi boats shuttle up and down the beach to take you there

TREAT YOURSELF

**Mango Bay Resort** Ⓣ077/981693, Ⓦwww.mangobayphuquoc.com. This beautiful compound of wooden and rammed-earth thatched bungalows, enclosed by deserted beaches and protected forest, is the island's first eco-friendly resort. There are no TVs, phones or a/c in the rooms, all hot water is solar powered, and the manicured exotic garden yields organic fruit and vegetables for use in the excellent restaurant. The bungalows themselves are elegantly furnished with four-poster beds, white linen and soft lighting; all have tasteful alfresco bathrooms and a private verandah. The perfect place to switch-off – literally. ❼–❽ and home again; they also offer basic bungalow accommodation for $10. Open till 3am.

**The Palm Tree Long Beach** This popular beachfront restaurant is always busy, serving cheap fresh seafood under a bamboo canopy on the sand. Try the stir-fried glass noodles with seafood for 30,000VND.

**Rainbow Bar Long Beach** Pool table, cheap beer and tasty barbecues make this beachfront terrace bar a popular hangout for a young crowd in the evenings. They also do good breakfasts.

## Directory

**Airline** Vietnam Airlines, 291 Nguyen Trung Truc (☎077/980779), 200m east of the airport, and, more conveniently, at the *Saigon Phu Quoc Resort* on Long Beach (☎077/846510).

**Bank** There is an ATM in the reception of the *Saigon Phu Quoc Resort*; they also exchange cash and traveller's cheques. Another ATM is on the roundabout in Duong Dong centre opposite the Rainbow Divers office, and there's an Agribank at 2 Trang Hung Dao.

**Internet** At the post office or Net Café, 5 Nguyen Dinh Chieu. *Buddy Ice-cream Café* offers free Internet to customers.

**Pharmacies** Several near the market on Ngo Quyen.

**Post office** 10, 20 Thang 4.

## Moving on

**By boat** Several operators run twice-daily hydrofoils to Rach Gia at around 8am and 12.30pm from An Thoi; tickets can be booked through your hotel or from one of the kiosks on Tran Hung Dao in Duong Dong. There can be serious delays and frequent cancellations during low season – a flight is more reliable.

**By air** Reserve air tickets as far in advance as possible, as the small aircraft are always heavily booked.

**Destinations**: HCMC (4 daily; 1hr; Rach Gia (1 daily; 40min).

# HA TIEN

Many visitors find **Ha Tien**, with its shuttered terraces, crumbling colonial buildings and seafood drying in the sun, the quaintest and most beautiful town in the delta. Lapped by the Gulf of Thailand, 93km northwest of Rach Gia and only a few kilometres from the Cambodian border, the town has a real end-of-the-line feel.

## What to do and see

Ha Tien is big on atmosphere, if a little short on sights beyond the lively waterfront **market** on Tran Hau, and a temple dedicated to **Mac Cuu**, the seventeenth-century feudal lord who founded Ha Tien – walk up Mac Thien Tich and west along Mac Cuu to find it. Mac Cuu and his relatives lie buried here in semicircular Chinese graves. Mac Cuu's grave is uppermost on the hill, daubed with a yin and yang symbol, and guarded by two swordsmen, a white tiger and a blue dragon. From this vantage point, there are good views down to the river.

### Biking around Ha Tien

A full day can be spent **biking** through the countryside around Ha Tien on a convenient circular route. Strike off west along Lam Son, through rice fields, coconut groves and water palm, past a war cemetery (2.5km from town), from where it's 1.5km to the first of three marked turnings – all with toll gates (2000VND) – to **Mui Nai** peninsula, a relatively peaceful, dark-sand cove, somewhat marred, however, by ongoing development. The beach has numerous cafés and restaurants running alongside a promenade.

You'll see the 48-metre-high granite outcrop housing **Thach Dong** cave long before you reach it – 3–4km past Mui Nai, a right turn deposits you at its base. A monument shaped like a clenched fist and commemorating the 130 people killed by the Khmer Rouge near here in 1978 marks the entrance (daily 7am–5pm) to Thach Dong, beyond which steps lead up to a cave-pagoda that's home to a colony of bats. To your right is Cambodia. From here, another 3km brings you back to Ha Tien.

## Arrival and information

At the time of writing, the boat service between Ha Tien and Chau Doc had stopped, but it may restart in the future, so ask around locally for up-to-date information.

**By bus** Buses terminate 1km south of the town centre over the new Cau To Chau bridge. Xe om will take you for 10,000VND. Long-distance minibuses terminate at a tiny enclosure on the riverside at the west end of Tran Hau. From here, it's a short walk up to town.

**Tourist information** Most hotels are happy to provide local information, maps and assistance with onward travel.

## Accommodation

**Dong Tam** 12–14 Tran Hau ⓣ077/3950555, ⓔduhunghotel@yahoo.com.vn. The 54 rooms in this smart, business-class hotel are excellent value for the quality and comfort. Free WiFi access, a/c, hot water and satellite TV are provided in every room. The largest room sleeps eight. ❸–❻

**Hai Van** 55 Lam Son ⓣ077/852872. A convivial choice offering immaculate, spacious rooms with satellite TV; superior doubles are available in a new mid-range annexe (ⓣ077/852001). ❸

**Hai Yen** 15 Duong To Chau ⓣ077/3851580. Rather lacking in charm, and the staff speak no English, but the rooms are spacious and clean, with a/c, hot water and TV. ❸

**To Chau Hotel** 56 Dong Ho ⓣ077/852148. Adjacent to the pontoon bridge at the southern end of To Chau, this hotel offers spartan, though clean, fan and a/c rooms. Those at the front have unrivalled views of the waterfront. ❷

**Viet Toan** 74 Chi Lang ⓣ077/850109, ⓔksviettoan_hatien@yahoo.com. Friendly English-speaking staff offer restful lilac rooms that sleep up to four. ❸

## Eating

The stalls around the bustling market on Tran Hau offer cheap and cheerful Vietnamese dishes from early morning to around 9pm.

**Huong Bien** To Chau. A wide range of reliable seafood and meat staples averaging around 25,000VND.

**Thuy Tien** Dong Ho. This little café built on a floating river raft is the perfect place to enjoy the sunset over an iced coffee after a tiring day's cycling.

**Xuan Thanh** 20 Ben Tran Hau. This cheery place is the best eating option in town, serving cheap Chinese and Vietnamese dishes and making good use of fresh local seafoods. Mains 25,000VND.

## Directory

**Bank** The local Vietcombank at 4 Phuong Thanh has an ATM and the best rates for exchanging dollars.

**Bike rental** From the *To Chau Hotel* (see above).

**Internet** Outlets are cropping up around town, with two on Tran Hau, at nos. 54 and 72.

**Post office** 3 Duong To Chau (daily 6.30am–9pm); also has internet access.

## Moving on

**By bus** Local buses to elsewhere in the delta depart early in the morning from the bus station over the Cau To Chau bridge. Regular private a/c minibuses can be booked through your hotel, or directly with the Mai Linh office (ⓣ08/9292929).

**Destinations**: Can Tho (5–6hr); HCMC (8hr); Long Xuyen (4hr); Rach Gia (3hr).

**By boat** It is possible to catch a cargo boat to Phu Quoc from the harbour at Ba Hon, 20km from Ha Tien (55,000VND, one daily). Xe om drivers charge 120,000VND for the ride. However, the boats are very old and have been known to sink; the hydrofoil from Rach Gia is safer, quicker and much more reliable.

Currently there's no boat service between Ha Tien and Chau Doc but ask your hotel for up-to-date information on the service.

### INTO CAMBODIA: HA TIEN

A new border crossing (daily 7am–6pm) has recently opened at **Xa Xia**, 10km from **Ha Tien**. There are no organized trips for tourists as yet, but xe om will make the trip for about $5. From **Prek Chang** on the Cambodian side, it's an hour's drive by xe om to Kep/Kampot ($8–12). Visas are not available at the border, so must be organized in advance at the Cambodian Consulate in HCMC (see p.915).

# The southern and central highlands

After a hot and sticky stint labouring across the coastal plains, the little-visited **southern and central highlands**, with their host of ethnic minorities, mist-laden mountains, vast plantations and crashing waterfalls, can provide an enjoyable contrast – though the region is not as spectacular nor ethnically diverse as the far north. Many of the highlands' 2.5 million inhabitants are *montagnards* ("mountain folk") from Bah Nar, E De, Jarai, Sedang, Koho and Mnong **ethnic minorities**, but visiting their villages independently can be difficult and is best done by basing yourself at the highland towns of **Buon Ma Thuot** and **Kon Tum**, from where you can either book a tour or take a Honda om with a local guide. For most tourists, the main target is **Da Lat**, a former French mountain retreat that, with its dreary tourist trappings, is not as idyllic as it sounds, though it does have its charms, and provides a good starting point for exploring the rest of the region.

## DA LAT AND AROUND

Nestled at an elevation of around 1500m, the city of **DA LAT** is Vietnam's premier hill station, an amalgam of maze-like streets and picturesque churches, spliced unfortunately with ugly new constructions and touristy kitsch. In 1897, the Governor-General of Indochina ordered the founding of a convalescent hill station here, where Saigon's hot-under-the-collar *colons* could recharge their batteries. By tacit agreement during the American War, both Hanoi and Saigon refrained from bombing the city and it remains much as it was half a century ago, a great place to chill out, literally and metaphorically.

### What to see and do

Da Lat's major attractions are all easily seen in one day on foot or by bicycle. **Day-trips** to outlying attractions, best seen on the back of a xe om with a good guide (see p.935), usually take in a minority village, silk worm hamlet and factory, Lien Khuong and Prenn waterfalls, a rice wine factory and a cut-flower farm.

### Cho Da Lat

**Cho Da Lat market** is housed in a charmless reinforced concrete structure, but offers the usual entertainment in its staggering range of fruit and vegetables, as well as a spectacularly colourful array of locally grown flowers, some interesting souvenirs such as watergourds, lacquer-ware, and hilltribe backpacks and fabrics on its upper level, linked by a raised walkway to the top of Le Dai Hanh.

### Lake Xuan Huong and Ga Da Lat

Cycling or walking round glassy, man-made **Lake Xuan Huong** is a pleasant pastime and takes in Da Lat's **flower gardens** (daily 7.30am–4pm; 5000VND) at its northeastern corner, from where you continue south down Ba Huyen Thanh Quan, with the option of striking east up Nguyen Trai to **Ga Da Lat**, the city's Art Deco train station, built in 1938. Only one tourist train is operational, running a shuttle service (departures on demand; 70,000VND return) through market gardens to the village of **Trai Mat**, a few kilometres away; the train idles for thirty minutes – time enough to take a look at **Linh Phuoc Pagoda** – before returning to Da Lat. Back at the southwest corner of the lake on Tran Phu, Da Lat's charming pink Venetian-style **cathedral**, completed in 1942, is dedicated to Saint Nicholas, protector of the poor; its seventy stained-glass windows were mostly crafted in Grenoble.

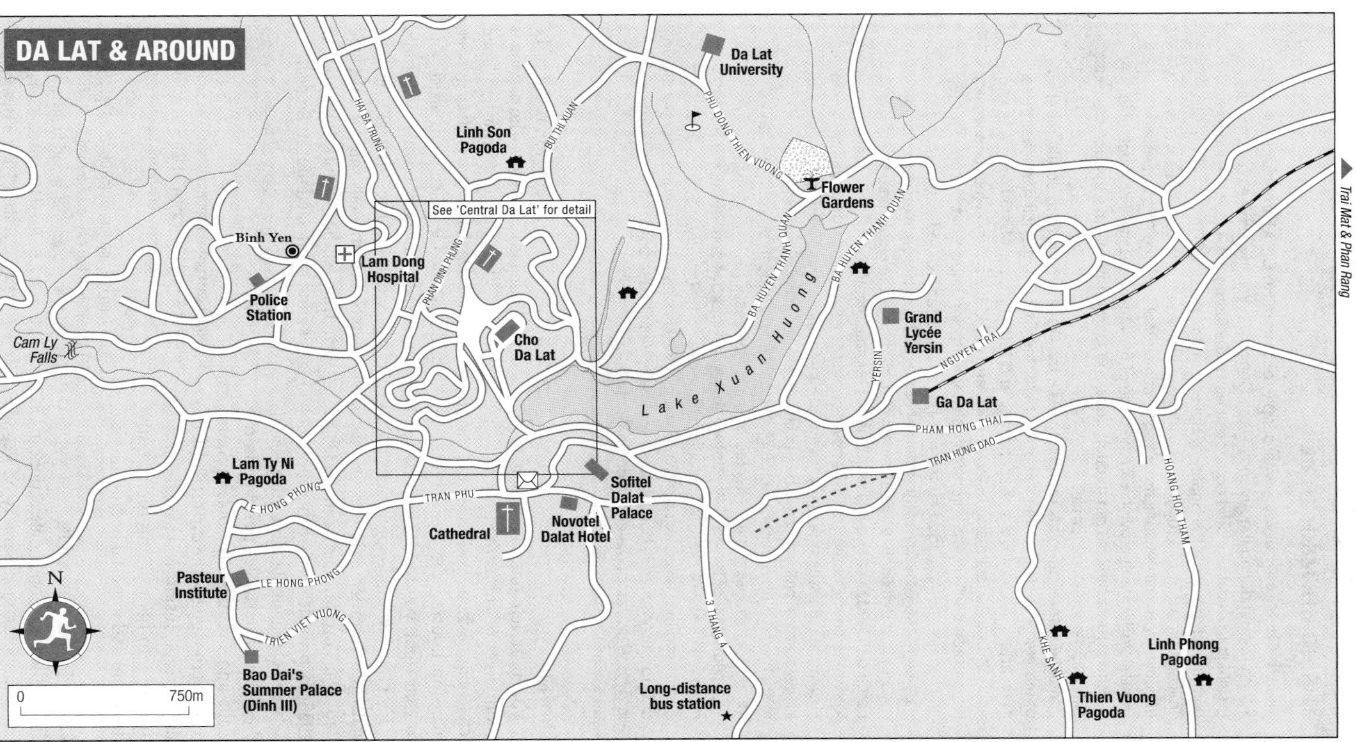
DA LAT & AROUND
Trai Mat & Phan Rang
Highway 20, Airport, Datanla Falls & Lake Tuyen Lam
Da Lat University
Linh Son Pagoda
Flower Gardens
See 'Central Da Lat' for detail
Binh Yen
Lam Dong Hospital
Police Station
Cam Ly Falls
Cho Da Lat
Lake Xuan Huong
Grand Lycée Yersin
Ga Da Lat
Lam Ty Ni Pagoda
Sofitel Dalat Palace
Novotel Dalat Hotel
Cathedral
Pasteur Institute
Bao Dai's Summer Palace (Dinh III)
Long-distance bus station
Linh Phong Pagoda
Thien Vuong Pagoda
HAI BA TRUNG
BUI THI XUAN
PHU DONG THIEN VUONG
BA HUYEN THANH QUAN
PHAN DINH PHUNG
NGUYEN TRAI
YERSIN
PHAM HONG THAI
TRAN HUNG DAO
TRAN PHU
LE HONG PHONG
TRIEN VIET VUONG
3 THANG 4
HOANG HOA THAM
KHE SANH
N
0
750m

### THE HO CHI MINH TRAIL

The **Ho Chi Minh Trail** was a vital supply route from Ho Chi Minh's North Vietnam into the South during the American War. Conceived in early 1959 as a safe route by which to direct men and equipment down the length of Vietnam in support of communist groups in the South, by the end of its "working" life the Ho Chi Minh Trail had grown from a rough assemblage of jungle paths to become a highly effective logistical network stretching from near Vinh, north of the Seventeenth Parallel, to Tay Ninh province on the edge of the Mekong Delta. For much of its southerly route the Trail ran through **Laos** and **Cambodia**, always through the most difficult, mountainous terrain.

Initially, it took up to six months to walk the Trail from north to south, most of the time travelling at night, but by 1975, the Trail – comprising at least three main arteries plus several feeder roads and totalling over **15,000km** – was wide enough to take tanks and heavy trucks, and could be driven in just one week. It was protected by anti-aircraft emplacements and supported by fuel depots, ammunition dumps, food stores and hospitals, often located underground.

By early 1965, **aerial bombardment** of the Trail had begun in earnest, using napalm and defoliants as well as conventional bombs. In eight years the US Air Force dropped over two million tonnes of bombs, mostly over Laos, in an effort to cut the flow. But the Trail was never completely severed. In Vietnam the Central Highlands suffered particularly badly, with Vietnamese and American soldiers and locals alike severely affected by the chemicals, resulting in respiratory illness, miscarriage, birth defects, neurological disease and cancer; an estimated three million Vietnamese remain affected by such illnesses.

Construction of the **Ho Chi Minh Highway**, an improvement of the old Route 14 road, to link Hanoi to HCMC through the centre of the country, began in 2000, and certain sections are now open. The new highway is often presumed to shadow the old Ho Chi Minh Trail, but it snakes within the Vietnamese border and never crosses into Laos or Cambodia as the original network did.

### Dinh III

If you bear left onto Le Hong Phong 500m west of the cathedral, and then left again when you see the wide mansion housing the Pasteur Institute to your right, you reach **Dinh III** (daily 7.30–11am & 1.30–5pm; 5000VND), erstwhile summer palace of Emperor Bao Dai. Erected between 1933 and 1938 to provide him with a bolt hole between elephant-slaughtering sessions, the nautical portholes punched into its walls and the mast-like pole sprouting from its roof give it the distinct look of a ship's bridge. Inside, you have the chance to nose into his working room, festivities room and imperial bedrooms.

### Lam Ty Ni Pagoda

One of the most popular attractions in Da Lat is dropping in at **Lam Ty Ni Pagoda** at the western edge of town, north of Le Hong Phong on Thien My. The pagoda is home to Vien Thuc, the so-called "mad monk" of Da Lat, who is also a poet, gardener, builder, sculptor, artist and somewhat astute businessman. His studio is stacked with over 100,000 abstract watercolours and oils, all for sale, and Vien Thuc relishes visitors, for whom he gives a full conducted tour in English.

## Arrival

**By bus** Buses arrive five minutes' walk south of the centre at Da Lat bus station, at the western edge of Xuan Hong Lake. Open-tour buses usually drop you off at your hotel.

**By air** Lien Khuong Airport (☎063/843373) is 29km south of the city, off the road to HCMC: Vietnam Airlines buses ($3) depart from here to their offices at 2 Ho Tung Mau (☎063/833499); a taxi or xe om will cost about $10 or $3 respectively.

## Information and tours

**Tourist offices** Several tourist offices can organize tours, guides and cars with drivers ($25–30 per day); try Dalat Travel Service, at *Thuy Tien Hotel*, 7 3 Thang 2 (☎063/822125), or Dalat Tourist at 1 Nguyen Thi Minh Khai (☎063/510104, Ⓦwww.dalattourist.com.vn).

**Motorbike tours** Honda om drivers charge $10–15 for a day-long tour to local pagodas, waterfalls and ethnic villages; if they don't find you first, ask for the Easy Riders or visit them at their new office (70 Phan Dinh Phung; mornings only; Ⓦwww.dalat-easyrider.com.vn), a group of war veterans who have been conducting highly rated tours of the area for the past fifteen years. English-, French- and German-speaking guides are available, and their local knowledge is unrivalled, especially about the central highlands' war-torn history, which many have personal experience of. Each Easy Rider carries an official identification and wears a black and blue jacket to distinguish them from the many impersonators in town. They can also take you on trips of up to five days through the Central Highlands, ending up in Hoi An, HCMC, Nha Trang or Mui Ne (approx $50 per day). Either go to their office where you can meet your guide over a coffee and discuss your itinerary, or book in advance through their website.

**Taxis** Taxis charge $20 upwards for a day-long tour; they congregate beside the food stalls on Le Dai Hanh and two blocks above the cinema.

**Activities** Phat Tire Ventures at 73 Truong Cong Dinh (☎063/829422, Ⓦwww.phattireventures.com) and Groovy Gecko Tours at 65 Trong Cong Dinh (☎063/836521) both organize adventure trips including hiking, mountain biking, climbing and canyoning; prices start at $14 for a day's hike to $135 for a two-day all-included off-road mountain-bike trip. Groovy Gecko also assists with visa extensions ($25).

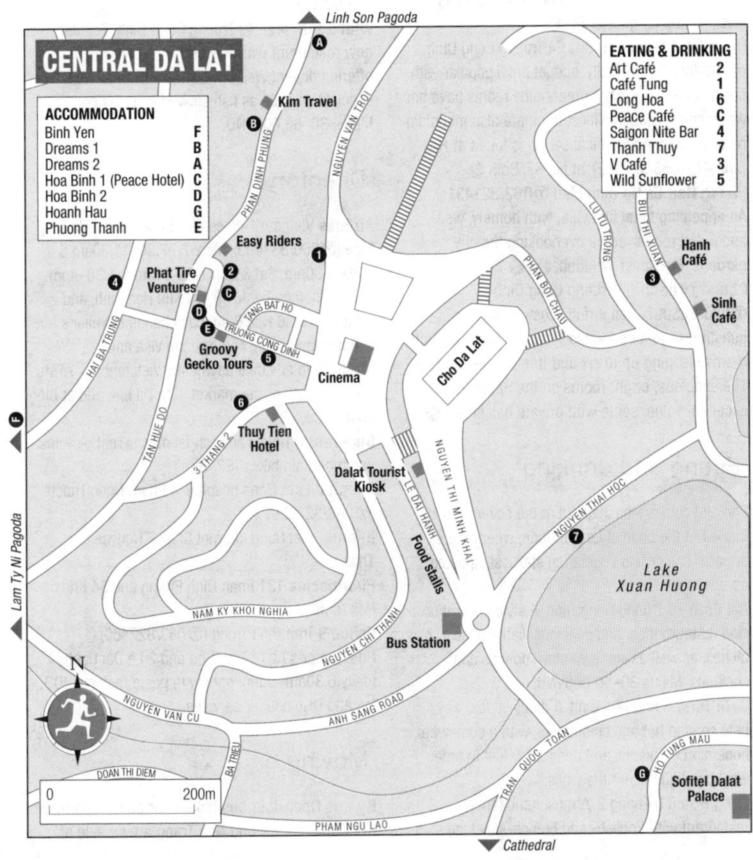

## Accommodation

The best streets for budget accommodation are Trung Hong Dinh, 3 Thang 2 and Phan Dinh Phung. Check that prices include hot water and heating in winter, necessities in Da Lat.

**Binh Yen** 7/2 Hai Thuong ⓣ063/823631. Nicely tucked away at the top of Hai Thuong, offering functional double and triple rooms, all with hot water, TVs and breakfast. Mountain bikes available for rent. ❹

**Dreams 1 and 2** 151 and 164b Phan Dinh Phung ⓣ063/833748, ⓔdreams@hcm.vnn.vn. Two neighbouring mini-hotels with well-equipped and spotlessly clean en-suite rooms, all with massaging power showers and some with jacuzzi bathtubs. Generous free breakfasts, friendly staff and free internet access have made these a hit with travellers. The recently refurbished *Dreams 1* has smaller rooms than no. 2, but boasts a sauna, steamroom and communal jacuzzi on the upper level, all free for guests. ❹–❺

**Hoa Binh I (Peace Hotel)** 64 Truong Cong Dinh ⓣ063/822787. Friendly, budget hotel popular with backpackers. Basic but great-value rooms have hot water and private facilities; there are also mountain bikes for rent. An identical set-up is found at *Hoa Binh II* (ⓣ063/822982), at no. 67. Both ❷

**Hoang Hau** 8a Ho Tung Mau ⓣ063/821431. An appealing hotel in a villa, with homely, well-appointed rooms, some overlooking the city gardens. Breakfast included. ❸–❹

**Phuong Thanh** 65 Truong Cong Dinh ⓣ063/825097. Delightfully cosy family-run guesthouse in a converted French townhouse with rooms sleeping up to six and free internet access. The spacious, bright rooms on the upper level are excellent value, some with private balconies. ❷

## Eating and drinking

Pho and com are bashed out at the covered food market at the base of Le Dai Hanh, where there are also one or two vegetarian stalls, signposted as *com chay*.

**Art Café** 70 Truong Cong Dinh. A stylish, bamboo-clad restaurant serving delicious Vietnamese dishes, as well as some Western options and cocktails. Mains 30–50,000VND.

**Café Tung** 6 Khu Hoa Binh. A dimly lit, low-key café serving hot and cold drinks, with a somewhat bohemian ambience and decor truly lost in time; local paintings adorn the walls.

**Long Hoa** 6 3 Thang 2. Atmospheric family-run restaurant with English- and French-speaking staff and a good range of thoughtfully prepared Western and Vietnamese dishes. Mains 40–70,000VND.

**Peace Café** 64 Truong Cong Dinh. Popular travellers' café adjoining Hoa Binh 1, serving decent breakfasts (12,000VND) and cheap Vietnamese food in a friendly, home-kitchen atmosphere. Great place to pick up tips from fellow travellers over a beer or a warming cup of tea. A second café under the same management is due to open down the street at number 58.

**Saigon Nite Bar** 11a/1 Hai Ba Trung. A reassuringly dark and shabby Western-style bar, with friendly staff, pool, darts and sports on TV.

**Thanh Thuy** 2 Nguyen Thai Hoc. Elegant and romantic lakeside restaurant, sometimes deluged with tour groups. The menu boasts over 300 Vietnamese and Western dishes, all reasonably priced (30–50,000VND).

**V Café** 1/1 Bui Thi Xuan. A few minutes' walk east of the market, this American-run restaurant near the lake has good Western food, pastries and a relaxed atmosphere. Mains 60,000VND, desserts 15,000VND.

**Wild Sunflower** 49 Truong Cong Dinh. Popular new restaurant with French bistro-style decor, offering decent Western dishes and local specialities such as fish stewed in a clay pot. Mains 30–60,000VND.

## Directory

**Airlines** Vietnam Airlines has an office at 2 Ho Tung Mau (ⓣ060/833499), Mon–Fri 7.30–11.30am & 1.30–4.30pm, Sat & Sun 7.30–11am & 1.30–4pm.

**Banks** Vietcombank, 46–48 Khu Hoa Binh, and Agribank at 36 Hoa Binh, can change traveller's cheques and cash, and arrange Visa and MasterCard advance payments; Vietcombank ATMs are just south of the market, Cho Da Lat, and at the post office.

**Bike rental** Hotels and tourist offices rent bicycles and mountain bikes ($2–3).

**Hospital** Lam Dong hospital, 4 Pham Ngoc Thach (ⓣ063/827529).

**Internet** Viet Hung Internet Café, 7 Nguyen Chi Thanh.

**Pharmacies** 131 Phan Dinh Phung and 34 Khu Hoa Binh.

**Police** 9 Tran Binh Trong (ⓣ063/822460).

**Post offices** At 14 Tran Phu and 2 Le Dai Hanh (daily 6.30am–9pm), both with poste restante, IDD, fax and DHL courier services.

## Moving on

**By bus** Open-tour bus tickets for daily departures to HCMC, Mui Ne and Nha Trang are on sale at most hotels; otherwise, contact the operators: Sinh Café inside the *Trung Cang Hotel* at 4a Bui Thi Xuan (☎063/822663, ⓦwww.sinhcafevn.com); Dalat Tourist Transportation Service, 9 Le Dai Hanh (☎063/822479, dltoseco@hcm.vnn.vn); and TM Brothers at 7/2 Hai Thuong (☎63/823631). Your hotel can arrange onward travel by public bus – most departures leave early in the morning.

**Destinations:** Buon Ma Thuot (5–6hr); Da Nang (14–17hr); HCMC (5–7hr); Mui Ne (4hr); Nha Trang (5–6hr).

**By air** Vietnam Airlines runs a shuttle bus to the airport from their office on Ho Tung Mau for $3. A taxi will cost about $15.

**Destinations:** Hanoi (6 weekly; 1hr 40min); HCMC (2 daily; 50min).

## BUON MA THUOT

In recent years coffee production in the highlands has grown rapidly, elevating Vietnam to the position of second largest coffee producer in the world after Brazil. The largely unattractive, sprawling modern highland town of **BUON MA THUOT** holds a deserved reputation for the best (and strongest) coffee in Vietnam, and the town boasts many **streetside cafés** serving endless cups of the syrupy brew. The town is also chiefly of interest for its outlying **minority villages**. However, following protests by local ethnic minority groups in 2004 against the government's policies towards them and their ancestral lands, there are restrictions in place and tourists are currently forbidden from visiting most of the surrounding villages; you need a permit to visit those you may. How stringently these restrictions are enforced depends on the current political climate, so it's worth checking with Dak Lak Tourist Office (see p.939).

### What to see and do

The one ethnic minority village you can easily visit from Buon Ma Thuot is the E De village of **Ban Don**. However, it's now very touristy and the highlight of a visit to the area seldom lies in an encounter with minority culture, but with the spectacular **waterfalls** and **wildlife**.

If you need to while away a few hours in town, try the **history museum** (daily 7.30–10.30am & 2–5pm; 10,000VND) on Le Duan, chronicling the struggles against the French and the Americans, and the more interesting **ethnographic museum**, a little further down the road on the opposite side (entrance 4 Nguyen Du; same times; 10,000VND), with its exhibits about local minority peoples, including a scale model of an E De longhouse, rice-wine jars and instruments for taming elephants.

### The Dray Sap and Trinh Nu Falls

The splendid crescent-shaped **Dray Sap Falls** (7am–5pm; 8000VND), 20km from Buon Ma Thuot, are reached by heading southwest out of town along Doc Lap. A Honda om return trip will cost around $6 (100,000VND). Almost 15m high and over 100m wide, the "waterfall of smoke" can be reached by clambering through bamboo groves and over rocks to the right of the pool formed by the falls. A few kilometres south of here, **Trinh Nu Falls** (7am–5pm; 7000VND) are not as spectacular as Dray Sap, though you can **stay** nearby: Dak Lak Tourist runs the low-key *Trinh Nu Falls Resort* (☎050/882587), dramatically perched above the Serepok River, with a bamboo bar-restaurant, good-value, well-equipped bungalows (❷), and basic longhouse accommodation (❶). Trekking, elephant riding, fishing and abseiling can also be arranged from here. To get there, turn left off the road to Dray Sap at the sign for "Trinh Nu" and continue along a dirt track for about 2km.

### Yok Don National Park

The entrance to Vietnam's largest wildlife reserve – the 580-square-kilometre

**Yok Don National Park** – lies 45km west of Buon Ma Thuot. Over sixty species of animals, including tigers, leopards and bears, and around two hundred types of birds, from peacocks to hornbills, populate Yok Don Park, but **elephant rides** are the park's main attraction ($30 for 1hr). One-day walking tours and overnight safaris ($40 for two) are available, as are longer tours penetrating deeper into the forest where animals still preside. The park is best visited in the dry season when wildlife is more visible, For enquiries and bookings, phone the park HQ (T050/783020), or arrange through a tour operator (see below), who can organize transport and combined day-tours to visit the park and Ban Don. There's also a range of basic **accommodation** available at the park HQ (❶–❷).

### Ban Don

The three sub-hamlets that comprise the much-visited village of **BAN DON** lie 2km beyond Yok Don's Park HQ on the bank of the crocodile-infested Serepok River. Khmer, Thai, Lao, Jarai and Mnong live in the vicinity, though it's the **E De** who form the majority. They adhere to a matriarchal social system, and build their houses on stilts. As you explore, you may be invited to share tea or rice wine ($5 or 80,000VND a jar). The two Buon Ma Thuot travel agents (see below) arrange tours here, but you could just as well hire a Honda om ($10 return).

Both the Ban Don Tourist Centre (T050/783019), in the centre of the village, and the Yok Don park HQ (see above) can organize **cultural programmes** of E De dance, music and wine ($55–65) with the option of spending the night in a nearby longhouse (❶–❷); Ban Don Tourist Centre can organize elephant rides ($20 per hour); and basic **accommodation** (❷).

## Arrival and information

**By bus** Buon Ma Thuot's bus station (T050/876833) is 4km north of town on Nguyen Tat Thanh, where xe om await to take you into town. Buses to and from Lak Lake stop at the Victory Monument in the centre of town.

**By air** The airport is 8km down the road towards Nha Trang; Vietnam Airlines (67 Nguyen Tat Thanh, T050/954442) has a shuttle bus running to its office (30,000VND); a taxi into town costs around 100,000VND.

**Travel agents** Both the helpful Dak Lak Tourist, 53 Ly Thuong Kiet (T050/852108, Wwww.daklaktourist.com), and Highland Travel, 24 Ly Thuong Kiet (T050/855009, Wwww.vietnamhighlandtravel.com.vn), can arrange tours and treks in the surrounding hills and jungles, such as a three-day trek in Yok Don National Park ($70) with nights spent in traditional villages, and the permits you need for visiting the villages.

## Accommodation

**Anh Vu** 7 Hai Ba Trung T050/814045. Offers a range of good-value, clean fan and a/c rooms. ❷

**Damsan Hotel** 212 Nguyen Cong Tru T050/851234, Edamsantour@dng.vnn.vn. The best quality accommodation in town, 1km out of the centre, with comfortable rooms (some overlooking a green valley), a tennis court and pool. ❻

**Thanh Binh** 24 Ly Thuong Kiet T050/853812. Basic but very clean rooms with a/c and hot water baths. The rooms in the centre of the building are cheaper but windowless and less spacious. ❷

**Thanh Phat** 41 Ly Thuong Kiet T050/854857, Ethanhphat@pmail.vnn.vn Popular budget hotel with the cheapest rates in town if you're willing to forego windows and clean sheets. Some of the more spacious rooms have a balcony for a few extra dollars. ❷

## Eating and drinking

Streetside cafés are dotted around the centre, serving the infamously strong local coffee; those clustered around the main roundabout or along Phan Chu Trinh are ideally located to watch the city bustle go by. In the evenings, locals converge on Nguyen Duc Canh to consume platefuls of seafood and vast quantities of Tiger beer. Most of the restaurants along here are simply called *Bia Lanh* (cold beer), followed by the street number. A popular local dish on offer in the street-kitchens lining the western end of Ly Thuong Kiet is *com tam* (broken rice) served with barbecued pork or chicken and fresh vegetables.

**Bon Trieu** 33 Hai Ba Trung. Perennially popular breakfast joint serving *bon me* (sizzling beef and egg on a hot-plate).

**Thanh Hung** 14 Ly Thuong Kiet Friendly family run eatery serving excellent *nem* (fresh spring rolls) in spotless, bright surroundings.

## Directory

**Airlines** Vietnam Airlines, 67 Nguyen Tat Thanh ⓣ050/954442

**Banks** Vietcombank, at 121 Y-Jut, can change traveller's cheques, foreign currencies and advance cash on Visa, MasterCard and JCB cards; it has an ATM outside the *Thang Loi Hotel* on Phan Chu Trinh (opposite the Victory Monument).

**Hospital** Mai Hac De. Provincial hospital, providing a 24hr emergency service (ⓣ095/5917375).

**Internet** The post office has cheap high-speed access.

**Post office** 6 Le Duan (daily 6.30am–9pm).

## Moving on

**By bus** There are regular local buses running to elsewhere in the Highlands, and several a/c buses depart daily to Nha Trang ($2) and to HCMC ($5) from the main bus station. Note that Buon Ma Thuot is often indicated as "Dak Lak" on buses.

**Destinations:** Da Lat (4hr); Da Nang (15hr); Lak Lake (2hr); HCMC (7–8hr); Nha Trang (4hr); Plei Ku (4hr).

**By air** Vietnam Airlines runs a shuttle-bus to the airport ($3 per person). A taxi will cost about 100,000VND.

**Destinations:** Da Nang (4 weekly; 1hr 10min); Hanoi (1 daily; 1hr 40min); HCMC (10 weekly; 55min).

# LAK LAKE AND JUN VILLAGE

About 60km south of Buon Ma Thuot, Highway 27 passes **Lak Lake**, a beautiful and peaceful spot. Along the lake's shoreline, Emperor Bao Dai's palace, which has recently been converted into a three-star resort, enjoys a prime vantage point. Beyond this sits **JUN VILLAGE**, a thriving Mnong community, whose impressive longhouses clustered on the shore have remained little changed, although the hordes of tourists visiting detract slightly.

Although Lak Lake is mostly geared towards organized tour groups – it gets very busy at weekends – it's possible to arrive here independently either by xe om or by one of the ten daily buses from Buon Ma Thuot; it's best to reserve accommodation in advance.

## Information and activities

**Dak Lak Tourist** ⓣ050/886184, ⓦwww.daklaktourist.com. Has one branch by the lake and one inside the village gate, both of which organize homestays with a family at a Jun longhouse in the village ($5), gong shows and rice wine feasts ($60 per group), guided treks or elephant rides around the lake ($30 per hour for two), and dug-out canoe excursions ($10 per hour for two).

## Accommodation

**Lak Resort** ⓣ050/586550. A new compound next to Dak Lak office on the lake offering elegantly furnished bungalows with private riverside decks and a couple of longhouses where it's possible to overnight; there is also a simple stilt restaurant built out on the lake, which offers magnificent views. Bungalows ❹ including breakfast; longhouses ❶

**Moi Truong Hotel** ⓣ050/586795. A five-minute walk up the hill from the lake, this offers cheaper, simply furnished fan rooms. It also has a popular restaurant serving local delicacies such as fried silk-worm larvae with chilli and garlic. ❷–❸

# KON TUM

Some 250km north of Buon Ma Thuot, northbound Highway 14 crosses the Dakbla River and runs into the southern limits of diminutive **KON TUM**, a sleepy, friendly town that serves as a springboard for jaunts to its outlying **Bah Nar villages**.

## What to see and do

Phan Dinh Phung forms the western edge of town; running east above the river is Nguyen Hue, and between these two axes lies the town centre. Scrap metal yards piled high with bomb shells and rusting weapons betray the hardships endured during the American War, and yet a stroll along Nguyen Hue still reveals some red-tile terraces of shop-houses left over from the French era. At the base of Tran Phu stands the grand, whitewashed bulk of Tan Huong Church. Further east is the so-called **Wooden Church**, built by the French in 1913. In the grounds, there's a scale model of a communal house.

### Kon Ko Tu

There are dozens of Bah Nar villages encircling Kon Tum, but one of the most accessible is **KON KO TU**, a relatively timeless community only 5km east of Kon Tum. Follow Tran Hung Dao east, crossing Duong Dao Duy Tu and passing an impressive high-roofed *rong* (communal house) just before you cross Dakbla River over the suspension bridge. Turn left at the first crossing after the bridge and continue for 3–4km to reach the village. Many of the dwellings are still made of bamboo and secured with rattan string, but it's the village's immaculate *rong*, with its impossibly tall thatch roof, that commands the most attention. Constructed with wood and bamboo, and without the use of any nails, the *rong* is used for festivals and village meetings, and as a village court at which anyone found guilty of a tribal offence must apologize in front of the village and ritually kill a pig and a chicken.

## Arrival, information and tours

**By bus** Buses approaching Kon Tum from the south pass over the main bridge, which signals the start of town, before terminating at Kon Tum's bus station, 3km north of the bridge along Phan Dinh Phung. Take a xe om back into the centre from the bus station, or ask the driver to let you off at the bridge, from where it's a 250-metre walk east along riverside Nguyen Hue to the foot of Le Hong Phong, and another 150m to Tran Phu; both run up into the town centre.

**Tours** Kon Tum Tourist (ⓣ060/861626, ⓦwww.kontumtourist.com.vn), in the *Dakbla Hotel*, 2 Phan Dinh Phung, and with a branch office in the *Quang Trung Hotel*, 168 Ba Trieu, offers tailor-made tours; ask for Mr Huynh, who is a mine of information on the area. A popular two-day tour combines a jungle trek with a night in a Bah Nar village stilt house and a riverboat trip; expect to pay about $40 for two. Local xe om drivers offer tours of outlying minority villages for about $15 for a full day, which is the best way to experience the area. Agree your itinerary in advance and ensure that your guide speaks good English.

## Accommodation

**Bac Huong Hotel** 88 Trang Hung Dao ⓣ060/200424. Run by the same people as the *Family Hotel*, this bright establishment offers well-furnished, spacious a/c double rooms at very reasonable rates. ❷

**Family Hotel** 55 Tran Hung Dao ⓣ060/862448, ⓔphongminhkt@yahoo.com. Friendly family-run hotel with good-value, sky-blue rooms. The staff speak good English, internet is free and motorbike rental is also available. There is a beautiful courtyard restaurant linked with the hotel (entrance at no. 53) complete with pond and wooden ethnic sculpture. ❷

**Viet Tram** 162 Nguyen Hue ⓣ060/869269. This hotel conveniently located close to the market has clean rooms with high ceilings. The rooms at the front have a balcony overlooking the street, and internet is free. ❷

## Eating

Restaurants in Kon Tum specialize in grilled meat such as boar and deer (but it is most often illegally poached).

**Dakbla** 168 Nguyen Hue. Friendly restaurant serving surprisingly sophisticated local and Western dishes. Also sells local handicrafts. Mains 25–35,000VND.

**Dakbla Hotel Restaurant** 2 Phan Dinh Phung. Enjoys idyllic river views from its terrace and the extensive menu is reasonably priced. Mains 25–50,000VND.

**Hiep Thanh** 129 Nguyen Hue. A reliable choice for simple food such as chicken fried rice with garlic and other local specialities. Mains 15–30,000VND.

## Directory

**Airlines** Vietnam Airlines, 129 Phan Dinh Phung (ⓣ060/862282), can arrange tickets for flights from Plei Ku.

**Bank** The Agribank at 88 Tran Phu does currency exchange and also has an ATM.

### INTO LAOS: BO Y

A new border crossing into Laos opened to tourists in 2006 at **Bo Y**, 80km north of Kon Tum. The easiest option is to catch a direct bus from Kon Tum to Attapu in Laos which depart at 10am on Thursday, Friday, and Sunday (5hr; $20). Buses bound for the Lao town of Pakxe depart from Quy Nhon on Monday, Tuesday, Thursday and Sunday, passing through Kon Tum bus station en route (12hr from Kon Tum; $16). Alternatively, take one of the regular minibuses to Ngoc Hoi (2hr), from where you can pick up another mini-van to the border at Bo Y and another from the border onwards to Attapu. Leave plenty of time for these connections, as the service between Ngoc Hoi and Bo Y is notoriously irregular and unreliable. Lao visas are not available at the border.

**Hospital** Kon Tum General Hospital is on the corner of Phan Dinh Phung and Ba Trieu (℡060/862573).
**Internet** 21 Nguyen Hue.
**Post office** 205 Le Hong Phong (daily 7–11am & 1–5pm).

### Moving on

**By bus** Kon Tum bus station is refreshingly orderly, with a ticket booth, displayed timetable and a distinct lack of touts.
**Destinations:** Buon Ma Thuot (3 daily; 5hr); Da Lat (1 at 5am daily; 8hr); Da Nang (hourly; 5hr); Hanoi (1 at 7am daily; 24hr); HCMC (2 daily; 11hr); Plei Ku (frequently; 1hr); Nha Trang (1 daily; 9hr).

# The south-central coast

Extending from the wetlands of the Mekong Delta right the way up to the central provinces, Vietnam's south-central coast was, from the seventh to the twelfth century, the domain of the Indianized trading empire of Champa. A few communities of Cham people still live in the area, and there are some fine relics of their ancestors' temple complexes near **Nha Trang**, which also boasts an attractive municipal beach and some good snorkelling trips to nearby islands. The other beach option along this stretch of coast is the wonderful **Mui Ne**, a 21-kilometre-long arc of fine sand lapped by aquamarine waters.

## MUI NE

In the space of just a few years, **MUI NE** has established itself as a major tourist and beach destination – unsurprising given the laid-back, low-key atmosphere and its endless palm-shaded, golden sands. Only low-rise development is allowed, and Mui Ne is still very much a quiet, relaxing place.

### What to see and do

The best stretch of Mui Ne beach starts just before you arrive at Mui Ne village. From here onwards, a large cluster of guesthouses and hotels vie for beach frontage along Nguyen Dinh Chieu, the main drag. Mui Ne is justifiably famous for its impressive Sahara-esque red and white **sand dunes**, best seen in late afternoon, which can be visited as part of a guided tour or independently by bicycle or motorbike. Local youths await your arrival with homemade plastic sand-sleds. En route to the dunes, it is worth a stop at **Mui Ne village** for a scenic vantage point from the road, high over the bevy of blue fishing boats jostling in the harbour, and the fishmongers preparing their wares on the sand below.

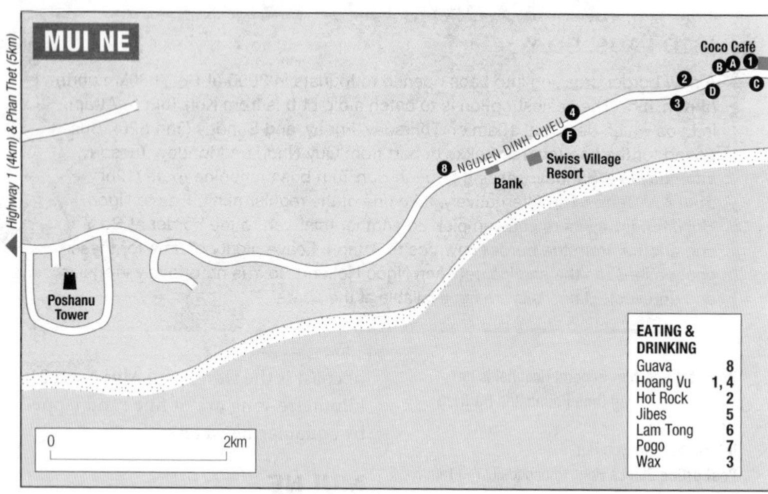


Mui Ne is rapidly becoming one of the hottest **windsurfing** and **kitesurfing** destinations in Southeast Asia. There are several reputable watersports schools offering lessons and equipment rental (see below), but neither comes cheap.

## Arrival

**By bus** Open-tour buses arrive around noon. Kim Travel and Hanh Café buses end up at the *Hanh Café 2* (ⓣ062/847347), near the *Full Moon Beach* resort. Sinh Café buses terminate at their office in the grounds of *Mui Ne Resort* (ⓣ062/847542). Long-distance buses drop you at Phan Thiet, 20km inland from Mui Ne; a Honda om from here should cost around $3, a taxi $5.

## Information and activities

**Tourist information** Most hotels have an information desk which can assist with tour bookings. ⓦwww.muinebeach.net has independent information on hotels, activities and local events.
**Bike and motorbike rental** The area is best seen independently by rented bicycle ($2) or motorbike ($6), both available from Hanh Café and several other tour operators and hotels on the strip.
**Tours** The Hot Rock Information Centre opposite the *Sun Sea Resort* at Km12 (ⓣ062/847608) offers sunrise and sunset tours ($5) and private jeep or motorbike day-trips to attractions including the red and white dunes ($28 per jeep with driver). Sinh Café and Hanh Café offer similar packages. Many hotels also run private tours, but shop around as prices differ greatly, and agree an itinerary beforehand.
**Watersports** There are several watersports operators here; check they hold the relevant accreditations, and offer full insurance for lessons and equipment rental. C2Sky, 64–66 Nguyen Dinh Chieu (ⓣ091/6655241, ⓦwww.muinebeach.net), right on the beach behind the *Sunny Beach Resort*, is a friendly kitesurfing school that offers two-, five- and seven-hour instruction packages, as well as hourly/daily rental ($30/95 including insurance). Jibes, 90 Nguyen Dinh Chieu (ⓣ062/847405, ⓦwww.windsurf-vietnam.com) offers watersport lessons and equipment rental, including windsurfers, kitesurfers, surfboards and kayaks.
**Sand-buggies** Dune Riders runs 150cc engine sand-buggy races on a 26,000 square-metre purpose-built sand track; $15–20 for a four-lap race. The booking office is at *Mellow* (see opposite) or contact ⓔpaul_clayton@hotmail.com.

## Accommodation

Several budget places are clustered at the centre of the strip. Noise pollution from the main road and construction can be an issue, and the beach at the eastern end disappears completely during high tide. In low season (May–Nov), rates drop by up to 30 per cent. Addresses in Mui Ne are sometimes denoted by distance from Phan Thiet.
**Gio Bien** 117b Nguyen Dinh Chieu ⓣ062/210567. The four rooms in this building on the non-beach side of the road are pleasantly cool, and come with

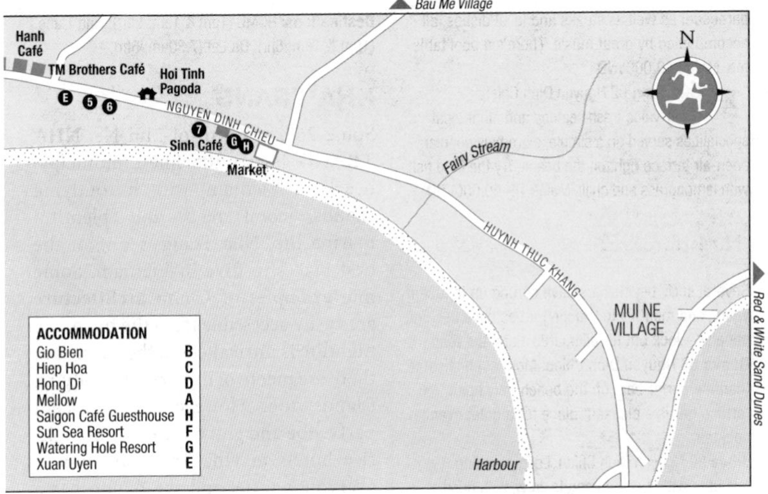


hot water, TV and fan or a/c. The staff are full of smiles. ❷

**Hiep Hoa** 80 Nguyen Dinh Chieu ⓣ062/847262 ⓔhiephoatourism@yahoo.com. Tastefully furnished, spacious rooms and bungalows, all with massive bathrooms, TVs and a/c, set in an attractive tropical flower garden. ❹

**Hong Di** 70 Nguyen Dinh Chieu ⓣ062/847014, ⓔhdqnhdi@yahoo.com. Bamboo bungalows encircle an attractive communal area with hammocks strewn amongst the coconut palms. There's a private beach and small restaurant. ❸

**Mellow** 117c Nguyen Dinh Chieu ⓣ062/743086. Popular place with the kitesurfing crowd, this laid-back compound has ten simple but elegantly furnished thatched-roof bungalows, including cheapies with shared bathroom. Free WiFi, and there's a friendly bar-restaurant and adjoining watersports shop. ❷–❸

**Saigon Café Guesthouse** 170 Nguyen Dinh Chieu ⓣ062/847848. Located a little away from the action at the eastern end of the strip. Simple, rustic bamboo and woven grass huts with private bathrooms are the cheapest accommodation option in Mui Ne. ❷

**Watering Hole Resort** 150 Nguyen Dinh Chieu ⓣ062/847327, ⓔthewateringhole_resort@yahoo.com. Popular resort with bungalows in a range of sizes with fan or a/c, and are tastefully decorated, very clean and well equipped. There's a private beach, bar-restaurant with pool table, Internet and even an in-house beauty salon. A bizarre glass-fronted bungalow displaying vintage Vespas near the entrance completes the picture. ❷

**Xuan Uyen** km13.3 ⓣ062/847476. Spacious bamboo bungalows in an intimate, shady compound with a private beach and tiny restaurant serving cold drinks and simple, cheap snacks. ❸

## Eating

Most hotels and guesthouses have pleasant, albeit pricey, beachside restaurants, but the numerous independent places lining Nguyen Dinh Chieu are better value.

**Hoang Vu** 93 & 121 Nguyen Dinh Chieu. Both branches of this popular restaurant offer delicious, reasonably priced Vietnamese dishes with a Western twist. The staff are friendly and the terrace setting is luxuriously romantic. Mains 30–60,000VND.

**Hot Rock** km12.5. Australian-run bar-restaurant serving excellent seafood (try the table

**TREAT YOURSELF**

**Sun Sea Resort** 50 Nguyen Dinh Chieu, km12.5,Mui Ne ⓣ062/847700, ⓦwww.sunsearesort-muine.com. A boutique resort with tastefully furnished rooms facing the pool, and round traditional-style thatched cottages facing the sea. Located next to the spot where local fishermen picturesquely drag their coracles and catch ashore. Breakfast included. ❽ barbecue) as well as steaks and local dishes, all accompanied by great music. There's a pool table too. Mains 40,000VND.

**Lam Tong** 92 Nguyen Dinh Chieu. Great-value fresh seafood and other local specialities served on a simple, extremely popular open-air terrace right on the beach. Try the fried fish with lemongrass and chilli. Mains 15–50,000VND.

## Nightlife

Several surfy beach-bars have sprung up in recent years, and monthly full-moon parties have become popular – look out for billboards along the road.

**Guava** 55 Nguyen Dinh Chieu. More sophisticated than the surfer bars on the beach, this open terrace bar is a pleasant place for a quiet evening cocktail.

**Jibes** 90 Nguyen Dinh Chieu. Long-standing favourite with the watersports crew, with good music and free pool table.

**Pogo** Lively bar at the eastern end, with a pool table, bean bags and loud music till late most nights.

**Wax** 68 Nguyen Dinh Chieu. The most popular late-night bar on the beach, this lively place attracts the kitesurfers and backpackers with themed party nights and drinks specials.

## Directory

**Bank** Bank next to the *Swiss Village Resort* (Mon–Fri 7.30am–noon & 1–4.30pm) changes cash and traveller's cheques and gives advances against Visa and MasterCard at better rates than the hotels. There's an ATM at the front of the *Saigon Mui Ne Resort*, 56 Nguyen Dinh Chieu.

**Bike rental** Most hotels and tour operators can arrange motorbike ($6) and bike ($2) rental.

**Hospital** There is an international medical clinic with an English-speaking doctor in the *Swiss Village Resort*, 44 Nguyen Dinh Chieu (ⓣ062/847497, daily 11.30am–1.30pm & 5.30pm–9pm). 24hr emergency service also available (ⓣ0918/210504).

**Internet** In most resorts, and at the *Hot Rock Café*.

**Post office** 348 Huynh Thuc Chang, and a small branch at the *Swiss Village Resort*.

**Pharmacy** Several next to the market.

## Moving on

**By bus** Open-tour buses can be booked from Hanh Café and Sinh Café (see p.942), as well as several other tour operators along the strip.

**Destinations:** HCMC (1pm & 1am; 5hr;); Nha Trang (1pm & 1am; 5hr); Da Lat (7.30am; 5hr).

# NHA TRANG

Some 260km north of Mui Ne, **NHA TRANG** boasts the finest municipal beach in Vietnam; with its outlying islands, coral reefs and plentiful marine life, Nha Trang is one of the best places to **dive** in Vietnam. Some fine examples of **Cham architecture** are easily accessible from the town, the nightlife is unrivalled on the coast, and there are plenty of day-trips to outlying islands too. However, the nascent party vibe and glut of beachfront high-rise hotels in Nha Trang are not to everyone's taste, and the region has a **rainy season** lasting from November through to early January when the sea becomes choppy, the beach windy and rather dirty, and the waters too murky to dive. Xe om are ubiquitous around town, but the best way to see Nha Trang is by rented bicycle.

## What to see and do

Most new arrivals in the city make a beeline for the **municipal beach**, a grand six-kilometre scythe of soft yellow sand that's only five minutes' stroll east of Cho Dam.

The Pasteur Institute at the top of Tran Phu Boulevard, which runs parallel to the beach, houses the **Alexandre Yersin Museum** (Mon–Sat 8–11am & 2–4.30pm, Sat 8–11am; 25,000VND). It profiles the Swiss–French scientist who settled in Nha Trang in 1893 and became a local hero, thanks to his educational work, and his ability to predict typhoons. The work of internationally acclaimed photographer Long Thanh is on display at **Long Thanh Gallery**, 126 Hoang Van Thu (Mon–Sat 8.30–11.30am & 1–6pm; ⓦwww.elephantguide.com/longthanh); the photographer, whose work captures poignant vignettes of Vietnamese life, is often available to talk to visitors.

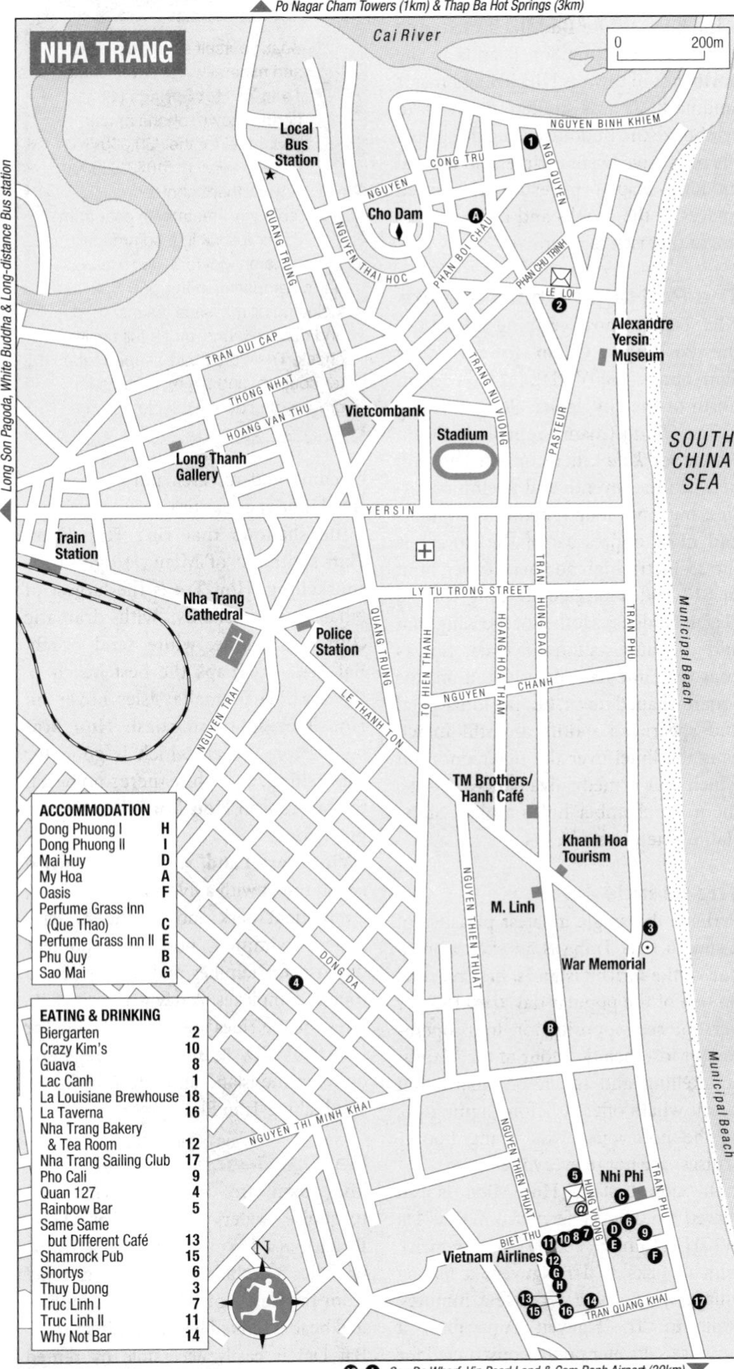
NHA TRANG
Po Nagar Cham Towers (1km) & Thap Ba Hot Springs (3km)
Cai River
0 200m
Long Son Pagoda, White Buddha & Long-distance Bus station
Local Bus Station
Cho Dam
NGUYEN BINH KHIEM
CONG TRU
NGUYEN
NGO QUYEN
QUANG TRUNG
NGUYEN THAI HOC
PHAN BOI CHAU
PHAN CHU TRINH
LE LOI
Alexandre Yersin Museum
TRAN QUI CAP
THONG NHAT
HOANG VAN THU
Vietcombank
Stadium
TRANG NU VUONG
PASTEUR
SOUTH CHINA SEA
Long Thanh Gallery
YERSIN
Train Station
LY TU TRONG STREET
TRAN HUNG DAO
TRAN PHU
Nha Trang Cathedral
Police Station
QUANG TRUNG
TO HIEN THANH
HOANG HOA THAM
Municipal Beach
NGUYEN CHANH
LE THANH TON
NGUYEN TRAI
TM Brothers/ Hanh Café
Khanh Hoa Tourism
M. Linh
NGUYEN THIEN THUAT
War Memorial
DONG DA
ACCOMMODATION
Dong Phuong I H
Dong Phuong II I
Mai Huy D
My Hoa A
Oasis F
Perfume Grass Inn (Que Thao) C
Perfume Grass Inn II E
Phu Quy B
Sao Mai G
EATING & DRINKING
Biergarten 2
Crazy Kim's 10
Guava 8
Lac Canh 1
La Louisiane Brewhouse 18
La Taverna 16
Nha Trang Bakery & Tea Room 12
Nha Trang Sailing Club 17
Pho Cali 9
Quan 127 4
Rainbow Bar 5
Same Same but Different Café 13
Shamrock Pub 15
Shortys 6
Thuy Duong 3
Truc Linh I 7
Truc Linh II 11
Why Not Bar 14
NGUYEN THI MINH KHAI
NGUYEN THIEN THUAT
HUNG VUONG
Nhi Phi
TRAN PHU
BIET THU
Vietnam Airlines
TRAN QUANG KHAI
Municipal Beach
N
18, I, Cau Da Wharf, Vin Pearl Land & Cam Ranh Airport (30km)

The huge **White Buddha** seated on a hillside above Long Son Pagoda in the northwest of town is Nha Trang's major landmark. It was crafted in 1963 to symbolize the Buddhist struggle against the repressive Diem regime, and around its lotus-shaped pedestal are carved images of the monks and nuns that set fire to themselves in protest.

### The Po Nagar Cham towers

Nha Trang's most gripping attraction, the **Po Nagar Cham towers** (daily 6am–6pm; 4500VND), stand 1.5km north of the city centre along 2 Thang 4. The Hindu Cham probably built ten towers, or *kalan*, here on Cu Lao Hill between the seventh and twelfth centuries, but only four remain. The largest and most impressive of the towers is the 23-metre-high northern tower, built in 817 and dedicated to Yang Ino Po Nagar, Goddess Mother of the Kingdom and a manifestation of Uma, Shiva's consort. Time has taken its toll on this square-shaped tower, but the lotus-petal and spearhead motifs are still intact, as is the lintel over the outer door, on which four-armed Shiva dances. Inside, the main chamber holds a black stone statue of ten-armed Uma.

### The islands

Perhaps the single greatest pleasure of a stay in Nha Trang is an excursion to one of the nearby **islands**, best reached on one of the popular day-trips ($6 per person; see opposite for tour operators). Most include a tour of the islands, snorkelling and lunch on board, but check what's offered before signing up, as the notorious "Nha Trang booze-cruises" are not to everyone's taste.

The closest island, **Hon Mieu**, is also served by a local ferry from Cau Da Wharf (15min; 20,000VND return), which docks at Tri Nguyen, a fishing village. From here it's a few minutes' walk to Tri Nguyen Aquarium, a series of saltwater ponds constructed for breeding and research purposes and a small indoor aquarium.

> **TREAT YOURSELF**
>
> Soak yourself in organic mud and mineral water baths at the **Thap Ba Hot Springs** (4km north of town, phone or ask your hotel for their 30,000VND pick-up service; ⓣ058/830090, ⓦwww.thapbahotspring.com.vn). Treatments cost from $4 for a soak in a communal mineral pool to $105 for a full day's pampering in the "VIP Spa", including oil massage, sauna, mud and mineral baths, and a full health check. There are heart-shaped tubs for couples, and big mud baths for groups of up to six people.

The shallows that ring **Hon Tam**, 2km southeast of Mieu, are good for snorkelling. **Hon Tre** is the largest of Nha Trang's islands, with dramatic cliffs and a fine, white sand beach, Bai Tru – perhaps the best beach in the area. Two smaller isles hover off Hon Tre's southern coast: **Hon Mot** has a stony beach which is good for snorkelling, and while there's no beach to speak of on **Hon Mun** there's some great coral.

**Vin Pearl Land**, a privately owned island resort with a five-star hotel, disco, amusement park and Southeast Asia's largest swimming pool, is a popular day-trip for families and fans of kitsch tourist complexes. A day pass costs $20; fares for the rides are extra. A cable car (100,000VND return) runs regularly between the island and a terminal 6km south along Tran Phu.

### Bai Dai Beach

The 10km arc of golden sand and turquoise waters at Bai Dai (Long Beach), just 19km south of Nha Trang, provides a secluded and tranquil relief from the bustle of Nha Trang's municipal beach. Linked by a new direct road, Bai Dai is easily accessible by rented motorbike, making it perfect for a day-trip. Cheap and cheerful seafood restaurants line the northern end of the beach. To get there, head south on Nguyen Tat Thanh for 10km from Cam Ranh, and follow the dirt-track for 200m after passing Dong Bo Mountain.

## Arrival

**By bus** The long-distance bus station is 500m west of the train station on Thai Nguyen. Open-tour buses usually stop at a selection of hotels in town, before terminating at their respective offices.
**By train** Nha Trang's train station is just west of the centre along Thai Nguyen.
**By air** Cam Ranh Airport is 30km south of town; Vietnam Airlines (Ⓣ058/826768) runs buses to and from its office at 91 Nguyen Thien Thuat ($3); a taxi to town will cost about $15.

## Activities and tours

**Tour operators** Tour operators can arrange car rental ($30–35 per day), motorbike tours ($15–35 per day, depending on distance), open-tour buses, and tours of the region, as well as boat trips to nearby islands. Companies include: Hanh Café, 22 Tran Hung Dao (Ⓣ058/827814, Ⓔhaphuongnt1@dng.vnn.vn); Khanh Hoa Tourism, 1 Tran Hung Dao (Ⓣ058/822753); Mama Linh, 2a Hung Vuong (Ⓣ058/826693, Ⓔmamalinhvn@yahoo.com); Nhi Phi (Sinh Café), 2A Biet Thu (Ⓣ058/522982, Ⓦwww.sinhcafevn.com); TM Brothers Café, 22b Tran Hung Dao (Ⓣ058/814556, Ⓔhuuhanhnguyen@yahoo.com).
**Diving** During the rainy season, visibility can be very low, and dives are often cancelled. The most reliable operators are Octopus Diving Club, 62 Tran Phu Boulevard (Ⓣ058/810629), and Rainbow Divers, 90a Hung Vuong (Ⓣ058/829946, Ⓦwww.divevietnam.com). Expect to pay about $50 for two fun dives, including lunch on the boat. Both offer PADI Open Water beginner and advanced courses, and Rainbow Divers offers longer Instructor and Emergency Response courses.
**Watersports** Mana Mana, 6 Tran Quang Kai (Ⓣ058/524362, Ⓦwww.manamana.com/travel_vietnam.html), organizes wakeboarding, waterskiing, windsurfing, kitesurfing and sea-kyaking. They are also based at Sailing Club, 72–74 Tran Phu and the *Louisiane Brewhouse* on the same street at no. 29.
*The Shamrock Pub*, 56a Nguyen Thien (Ⓣ058/527548, Ⓦwww.raftingvietnam.com), specializes in small-group activities and tours, including sea and lake fishing, white-water rafting on the Serapok River, sea-kayaking and mountain biking. Prices average $30 per day, all-inclusive.

## Accommodation

The best place for budget accommodation is the centrally located alleyway at 64 Tran Phu. Prices drop about 30 percent in low season.
**Dong Phuong I** 103 Nguyen Thien Thuat Ⓣ058/825986, Ⓔdongphuongnt@dng.vnn.vn. Large and popular family-run hotel, with an elevator, and good-value, functional and spacious rooms, most with bathtubs. The *Dong Phuong II*, along the seafront at 96a 6/1 Tran Phu Boulevard (Ⓣ058/814580), has slightly larger rooms for a few dollars more, some with a sea view. Free train and bus station pick-up. ❷–❹
**Mai Huy** 7h Hung Vuong Ⓣ058/527553. Friendly family-run guesthouse in a quiet but central alleyway, offering warmly decorated fan and a/c rooms. ❷
**My Hoa** 7 Hang Ca Ⓣ058/810111, Ⓔmyhoahotel@dng.vnn.vn. Family-run mini-hotel at the other end of town with tidy, reasonably priced rooms; those at the top have private balconies with great city views. ❷–❹
**Oasis** 64b/12 Tran Phu Ⓣ058/524181. Friendly family-run hotel offering spacious, brightly decorated rooms, most with sea view. A/c optional. ❷
**Perfume Grass Inn (Que Thao)** 4a Biet Thu Ⓣ058/524286, Ⓦwww.perfume-grass.com. One of the best budget guesthouses in Vietnam; lovely staff, a good café, and tastefully

### CRIME IN NHA TRANG

Nha Trang seems to have more **petty crime** than elsewhere, so take care of your possessions (particularly after dark) in bars and on cyclo. Leave all valuables in the hotel safe when you're heading out. There have been reports of attacks on young men coming home alone late at night – be especially wary of women who approach you coming out of bars and nightclubs. Taxis and licensed xe om drivers wearing blue, numbered shirts wait outside venues to take you home safely. Dial Ⓣ113 for an emergency police unit.

furnished en-suite rooms equipped with cable TV and a/c or fan – and not lit by glaring neon, for a change. The upper rooms have sea views. A second branch has recently opened at 64b/8 Tran Phu (ⓣ058/523209). ❸–❺

**Phu Quy** 54 Hung Vuong ⓣ058/810609, ⓔphuquyhotel@dng.vnn.vn. Friendly hotel with an elevator and a range of reasonably priced, clean a/c and fan rooms; extra dollars secure more space and a balcony. There's a large rooftop terrace, too, and free train and bus station pick-up. ❸

**Sao Mai** 99 Nguyen Thien Thuat ⓣ058/526412, ⓔsaomai2ht@dng.vnn.vn. Small, friendly, family-run hotel with basic, clean en-suite rooms, a small rooftop terrace and a dorm ($3 per bed). The receptionist and guide Mr Mai Loc is an accomplished photographer and sells beautiful postcards. A second hotel of a similar standard has opened at 96b/1 Tran Phu (ⓣ058/524055). ❶–❸

## Eating

**Lac Canh** 44 Nguyen Binh Khiem. Set in the quiet streets east of Cho Dam *Lac Canh* is renowned for its mouth- and eye-watering cooked-at-table barbecues for about 70,000VND per person.

**La Taverna** 115 Nguyen Thien Thuat. Excellent pizza, pasta, steaks and Vietnamese dishes made using fine imported ingredients are served up by the Italian–Swiss owner in an atmospheric, trattoria-style setting. Pizzas 60,000VND, meat dishes 40–70,000VND.

**Nha Trang Bakery & Tea Room** 99b Nguyen Thien Thuat. The best place in backpackers-ville to stock up on pastries or have a decent breakfast before a long bus ride. Open from 5.30 am.

**Pho Cali** 7g Hung Vuong. Cheap and delicious Vietnamese food in a modern, deli-style café. The two-course set menu of soup, choice of a fish or pork dish, rice and vegetables is excellent value for 30,000VND.

**Quan 127** 127 Hong Bang. Local noodle restaurant serving excellent *mi quang nam* – fat rice noodles in a tasty broth served with crispy rice crackers and fresh leaves. Mornings only.

**Rainbow Bar** 90a Hung Vuong, ⓣ058/524351. An excellent travellers' café with foreign beers, Western and local food and early breakfasts (but higher than average prices), plus a welcoming atmosphere. Also Rainbow Divers' (see p.947) main office. Daily 7am–late.

**Same Same but Different Café** 111 Nguyen Thien Thuat. Popular backpacker café offering an extensive range of Vietnamese, Thai and Western dishes. There's also a good vegetarian selection, and the owner is an excellent source of local information. Mains 15–50,000VND.

**Shortys** 1 Biet Thu. Excellent home-style chips, hamburgers and full English breakfast at this pub-style place, plus pool, happy hour (6–10.30pm) and book exchange. Daily 8am–late.

**Thuy Duong** Tran Phu Beach. Near the memorial, this popular beachside restaurant serves excellent fish, fresh from the tank. Mains 35–80,000VND.

**Truc Linh I & II** 11 & 21 Biet Thu. Great Vietnamese food at two locations; a simple corner restaurant at no. 11 and a more upmarket seafood restaurant at no. 21. Daily 6am–10pm and 6am–11pm respectively.

## Drinking and nightlife

**Biergarten** 7c Le Loi. German-run beergarden with a breakfast menu, German and international dishes, and San Miguel draught beer for under $1. 9am–late.

**Crazy Kim's** 19 Biet Thu. Enjoy the huge cocktails during the 10am to 10pm happy "hour", or drop by for a hangover breakfast. A percentage of the profits go towards Kim's campaign to assist vulnerable street children, and accommodation is offered to volunteers who wish to teach English in her free education scheme. 10am-1am.

**Guava** 17 Biet Thu. Modern and sophisticated cocktail bar with comfortable couches, afternoon movies, themed drinks specials and loud dance music in the evenings. Happy hour 5–9pm. Daily 11am–1am.

**La Louisiane Brewhouse** 29 Tran Phu, ⓦwww.louisianebrewhouse.com.vn. Inexpensive beach club with a free pool, patrolled beach, restaurant and pastry bar; the microbrewery offers a range of beers made with all natural ingredients. Also has a watersports centre and travel agent. Open from 7.30am.

**Nha Trang Sailing Club** 7 Tran Phu, ⓦwww.sailingclubvietnam.com. Draws a well-heeled expat crowd and hordes of tourists to its refined beachfront bar and dance floor, which gets less refined as the night wears on. Monthly full-moon parties are held on the beach with live DJ sets. As well as bar food, there's a decent Italian and Japanese restaurant, plus an excellent "Seafood Corner" in the club compound. Happy hour 8.30–10.30pm; open daily noon–2am.

**Shamrock Pub** 56a Nguyen Thien. Relaxed Irish bar good for a quiet drink or an authentic full Irish breakfast. They have all day sports coverage and also offer a range of good tours and activities (see p.947).

**Why Not Bar** 24 Tran Quang Khai. Relative newcomer to the Nha Trang night scene, this bar now rivals the *Sailing Club* for the hottest late-night spot in town. Fresh coconut cocktails, a pool table, dance floor and outdoor terraced seating area attract nightly crowds. Happy hour 4–10pm. Daily till 4am.

## Directory

**Banks** Vietcombank ATMs are outside the upmarket hotels along Tran Phu Boulevard; the Vietcombank office at 17 Quang Trung changes cash and traveller's cheques, and can also advance cash against Visa, MasterCard and JCB cards; Nhi Phi (Sinh Café) also offers these services at slightly higher rates.
**Hospital** 19 Yersin (Ⓣ058/822168). A resident French GP, Dr Catherine Bonnotte, has a small surgery at 37b Dong Da (Ⓣ058/512308; $15 per consultation).
**Internet** At the post offices, in hotels and in several cafés around Biet Thu.
**Police** 2 Le Thanh Ton Ⓣ058/510144.
**Post office** The main post office, 4 Le Loi (daily 6.30am–10pm), has fax, poste restante, DHL courier and IDD phone facilities; IDD is also available at the smaller post offices at 50 Le Thanh Ton (6.30am–midnight), and at 23c Biet Thu (6.30am–9.30pm).
**Pharmacy** 23d Biet Thu.

## Moving on

**By bus** There are several morning minibus departures from the bus station (which can also be booked through your hotel) for Buon Ma Thuot (4hr) and HCMC (9hr). Open-tour companies have daily departures for Buon Ma Thuot (4hr); Da Lat (5–6hr); Da Nang (12hr); Hanoi (32hr); HCMC (9hr); Hue (17hr).
**By train** The train station ticket office at 17 Thai Nguyen (Ⓣ058/822113), is open daily 6.30–11.30am & 1.30–10pm. A new luxury train service runs from Nha Trang to HCMC – tickets can be booked in the office to the right of the main station. **Destinations:** Da Nang (10 daily; 8hr 30min–13hr); Hanoi (10 daily; 23hr–34hr); HCMC (10 daily; 6hr 20min–10hr); Hue (10 daily; 11hr 30min–26hr 20min).
**By air** Da Nang (2 daily; 1hr 20min); Hanoi (2 daily; 1hr 40min); HCMC (4 daily; 55min).

# The central provinces

Vietnam's narrow waist comprises a string of provinces squeezed between the long, sandy coastline and the formidable barrier of the Truong Son Mountains, which mark the border between Vietnam and Laos. Just south of **Da Nang** – a useful transport hub but not much more – the much visited riverside town of **Hoi An** is one of Vietnam's most charming destinations and a highlight of the region. Renowned for its hundreds of tailor shops, crafts, traditional Chinese merchants' houses and temples, it also makes a good base for visiting the beach and exploring the fine ruins of the Cham temple complex at nearby **My Son**. The former Vietnamese capital of **Hue** is equally impressive, and its nineteenth-century palaces, temples and royal mausoleums constitute another of Vietnam's highlights. In 1954, Vietnam was divided at the Seventeenth Parallel, only 100km north of Hue, where the **Demilitarized Zone (DMZ)** marked the border between North and South Vietnam until reunification in 1975. The desolate battlefields of the DMZ and the extraordinary complex of residential tunnels at nearby **Vinh Moc** are a poignant memorial to those, on both sides, who fought here and to the civilians who lost their lives in the bitter conflict.

## HOI AN

The ancient core of seductive, charming **HOI AN** – recognized as a UNESCO World Cultural Heritage Site in 1999 – is a rich architectural fusion of Chinese, Japanese, Vietnamese and European influences dating back to the sixteenth century. In its heyday the port town attracted vessels from the world's great trading nations, and many Chinese merchants stayed on. Today its charming two-hundred-year-old wooden-fronted shop-houses are among its chief attractions.

### What to see and do

The **historic core** of Hoi An consists of just three short parallel streets:

### JUNGLE BEACH

Located 60km north of Nha Trang, *Jungle Beach Resort* (ⓣ058/622384, ⓔsyl@dng.vnn.vn; 300,000VND including all meals, snacks and activities) is an isolated eco-friendly getaway run by a Canadian–Vietnamese couple, with very basic homestay accommodation, bamboo huts and al fresco mosquito-net covered mattresses. Hammocks are strewn amongst the trees for lazy days, and the jungle-clad mountains offer great trekking opportunities, with possible sightings of rare langurs, three species of eagles and many varieties of indigenous birds and butterflies. A communal ethos is fostered, and all home-cooked meals are eaten together. To get there, take an open-tour bus between Nha Trang and Hoi An, and ask to be dropped off at the Doc Let petrol station. From there, take a xe om (60,000VND) to Jungle Beach.



Tran Phu is the oldest and, even today, the principal commercial street, with plenty of crafts shops and galleries; one block south, Nguyen Thai Hoc has many wooden townhouses and some galleries; while riverfront Bach Dang holds the market and several waterside cafés. There are also a couple of attractive **beaches** nearby, and a cluster of **islands** that make excellent day-trips from the town.

## Japanese Covered Bridge

The western end of Tran Phu is marked by a small bridge known as the **Japanese Covered Bridge**, which has been adopted as Hoi An's emblem. It has been reconstructed several times since the mid-sixteenth century to the same simple design. Inside the bridge's narrow span are a collection of stelae and four statues, two dogs and two monkeys, usually said to record that work began in the year of the monkey and ended in that of the dog. Motorized traffic can't use the bridge, and pedal bikes must be pushed across.

## The Chinese Assembly Halls

Historically, Hoi An's ethnic Chinese population organized themselves according to their place of origin (Fujian, Guangdong, Chaozhou or Hainan), and each group maintained its own assembly hall as both community centre and house of worship. The most populous group hails from Fujian, and their **Phuoc Kien Assembly Hall**, at 46 Tran Phu, is an imposing edifice with an ostentatious, triple-arched gateway. The hall is dedicated to Thien Hau, Goddess of the Sea and protector of sailors. She stands, fashioned in 200-year-old papier mâché, on the main altar flanked by her green- and red-faced assistants, who between them can see or hear any boat in distress over a range of a thousand miles.

### VISITING HOI AN'S SIGHTS

A **combined ticket** (75,000VND) gives access to five of the major sights in Hoi An, one from each of the following groups: one of the three museums (Trade Ceramics, Sa Huynh Culture or Historical and Cultural); one of the four participating merchants' houses; one of the three participating Chinese assembly halls; a traditional music concert or a handicraft workshop; the temple on the Japanese Covered Bridge or Quang Cong Temple. Tickets are valid for two days and can be purchased at seven clearly marked **outlets** in and around the historic centre. All offices and relevant sights are open daily from 6.30am to 6pm; a **guide** is available for an additional 50,000VND.

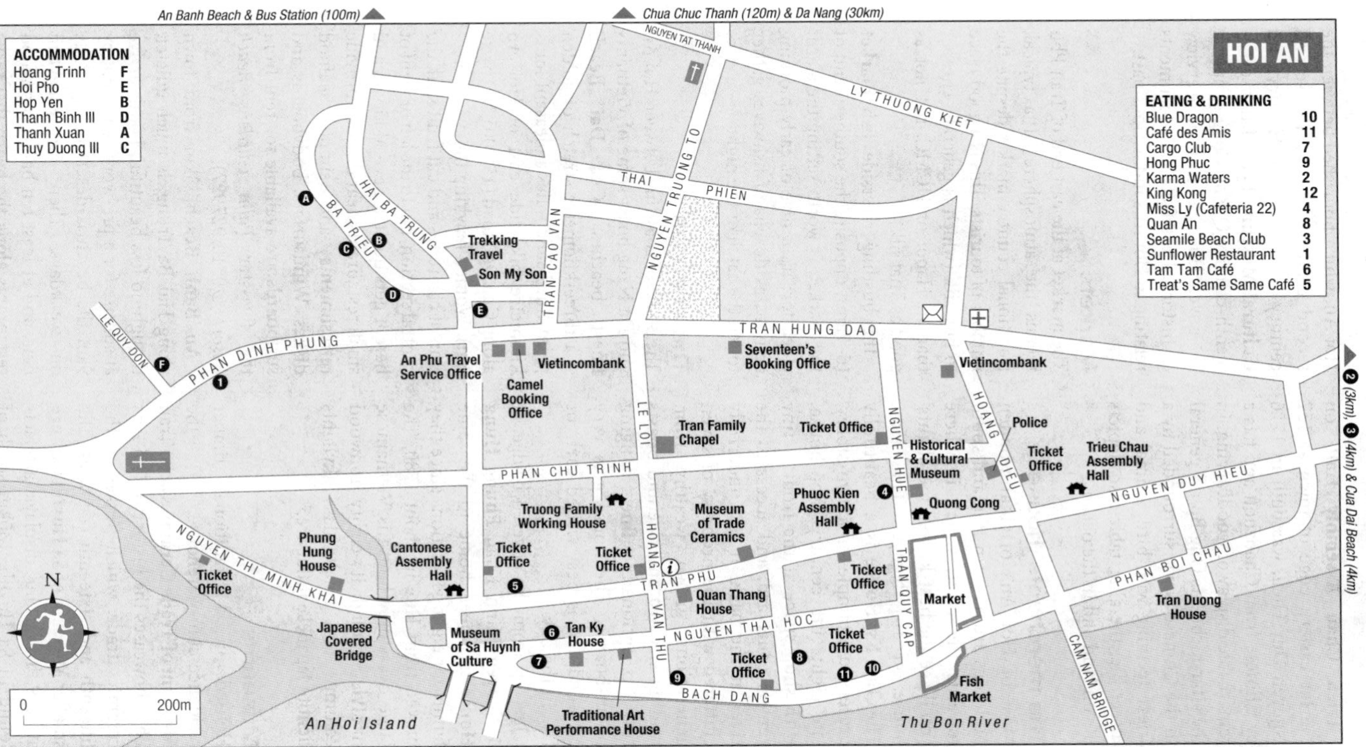
HOI AN
ACCOMMODATION
Hoang Trinh F
Hoi Pho E
Hop Yen B
Thanh Binh III D
Thanh Xuan A
Thuy Duong III C
EATING & DRINKING
Blue Dragon 10
Café des Amis 11
Cargo Club 7
Hong Phuc 9
Karma Waters 2
King Kong 12
Miss Ly (Cafeteria 22) 4
Quan An 8
Seamile Beach Club 3
Sunflower Restaurant 1
Tam Tam Café 6
Treat's Same Same Café 5
An Banh Beach & Bus Station (100m)
Chua Chuc Thanh (120m) & Da Nang (30km)
My Son (40km)
2 (3km), 3 (4km) & Cua Dai Beach (4km)
12 & Cam Nam Island
NGUYEN TAT THANH
LY THUONG KIET
THAI PHIEN
NGUYEN TRUONG TO
HAI BA TRUNG
BA TRIEU
TRAN CAO VAN
LE QUY DON
PHAN DINH PHUNG
TRAN HUNG DAO
LE LOI
PHAN CHU TRINH
NGUYEN HUE
HOANG DIEU
NGUYEN DUY HIEU
PHAN BOI CHAU
CAM NAM BRIDGE
NGUYEN THI MINH KHAI
HOANG VAN THU
TRAN PHU
NGUYEN THAI HOC
TRAN QUY CAP
BACH DANG
Trekking Travel
Son My Son
An Phu Travel Service Office
Vietincombank
Camel Booking Office
Seventeen's Booking Office
Vietincombank
Tran Family Chapel
Ticket Office
Police
Historical & Cultural Museum
Ticket Office
Trieu Chau Assembly Hall
Phuoc Kien Assembly Hall
Quong Cong
Truong Family Working House
Museum of Trade Ceramics
Phung Hung House
Cantonese Assembly Hall
Ticket Office
Ticket Office
Ticket Office
Ticket Office
Market
Tran Duong House
Quan Thang House
Tan Ky House
Japanese Covered Bridge
Museum of Sa Huynh Culture
Ticket Office
Ticket Office
Fish Market
Traditional Art Performance House
An Hoi Island
Thu Bon River
N
0
200m

**Trieu Chau Assembly Hall**, on the far eastern edge of town at 157 Nguyen Duy Hieu, was built in 1776 by Chinese from Chaozhou and has a remarkable display of woodcarving. In the altar-niche sits Ong Bon, a general in the Chinese Navy, surrounded by a frieze teeming with bird, animal and insect life; the altar table also depicts life on land and in the ocean.

### The merchants' houses

Most of Hoi An's original wooden buildings are on Tran Phu and south towards the river, which is where you'll see the best-known merchants' house, at 101 Nguyen Thai Hoc. The **Tan Ky House** is a beautifully preserved example of a two-storey, late eighteenth-century shop-house, with shop space at the front, a tiny central courtyard, and access to the river at the back. It is wonderfully cluttered with the property of seven generations grown wealthy from trading silk, tea and rice and boasts two exceptionally fine hanging poem-boards. The house gets very crowded and is best visited early or late in the day.

Just up from the covered bridge, at 4 Nguyen Minh Khai, **Phung Hung House** has been home to the same family for eight generations since they moved from **Hue** in about 1780. The large two-storey house is Vietnamese in style although its eighty ironwood columns and small glass skylights denote Japanese influence.

### Museums

Housed in a traditional timber residence-cum-warehouse, the **Museum of Trade Ceramics** at 80 Tran Phu showcases the history of Hoi An's ceramics trade, which peaked in the fifteenth and sixteenth centuries. The smaller **Museum of Sa Huynh Culture** at 149 Tran Phu displays artefacts found in Sa Huynh, 130km south of Hoi An, which flourished between the second century BC and the second century AD, while the **History and Cultural Museum**, behind the seventeenth-century Quang Cong temple at 7 Nguyen Hue, has a small overview of historical artefacts and documents relating to Hoi An's industrious past.

### Markets

The **market** at the east end of Tran Phu retains the atmosphere of a typical, traditional country market despite the number of tourists. This is a good place to buy **silk** (which is generally cheaper than in Hanoi or HCMC, but not as good as Thai silk).

The bustling riverside **fish market** (6–7am), opposite the southern end of the market, is worth setting the alarm clock for; it's a hive of early-morning activity, as dozens of fishwives gather to sell the catch of the night.

### The beaches

The 30km of coastline between Hoi An and Da Nang boast some of Vietnam's finest beaches. **Cua Dai Beach** – a three-kilometre stretch of golden palm-lined sand – lies a pleasant four-kilometre bike-ride east of Hoi An along Cua Dai Road (15,000VND by xe om). Women hawking the usual selection of cigarettes and cut fruit stalk the central section, but to the left or right of here it gets quieter. Several kiosks and small restaurants near the road provide refreshments and simple seafood dishes. Windsurfers, bodyboards and surfboards are available for rent from the five-star *Palm Gardens Beach Resort* (☎0510/927927).

**An Banh Beach**, 3km from town along Hai Ba Trung, is much quieter, though no less beautiful. Locals arrive at sunrise for a pre-work swim, but by 9am the beach is deserted, especially on weekdays. There are volleyball nets, and at least ten bamboo seafood restaurants along the beach that serve cheap fresh seafood dishes from the local fishing village.

### The islands

Touring the outlying islands on a rented bicycle makes a good day out. **Cam Nam Island** lies over the Cam Nam Bridge, offering a great view of Hoi An across the water. The row of waterfront restaurants to the south of the island specializes in *hen tron* (fried fresh clams).

From Hoi An ferry station on Bach Dang, you can take a ferry (10,000VND) to **Cam Kim**, a large island famous for its specialist craft villages. The island's wood-carving workshops are a popular stopover for tourist boats returning from My Son, but the maze of sandy tracks, bamboo "monkey" bridges and picturesque little villages make the island a beautiful place to explore independently. A main road bisects the island from the western to eastern shore, where there is a small jetty with boats to ferry you back to Hoi An.

The mountainous **Cham Islands**, 10km offshore from Cua Dai Beach, are renowned for their swallows' nests, a culinary delicacy that can fetch up to $2500 per kilo. The islands' main attraction for tourists, however, is the coral reefs and marine life in the surrounding waters; diving is possible mainly between April and September, and you can also go on day-trips here (see below).

## Arrival

**From Da Nang** People generally arrive in Hoi An by car, or Honda om from Da Nang Airport or train station (30km) – see p.955 for details.

**By bus** Open-tour buses drop you off at central hotels. Local buses drop you at the corner of Nhi Trung and Le Hong Phong.

## Information and activities

**Tourist information** The friendly, state-run Tourist Information Office at 45 Le Loi (daily 7am–7pm, ⓣ0510/910919, ⓦwww.hoianworldheritage.org.vn) sells maps and books and can help with information about sights, tours and hotels, though you can't book here.

**Tours** Hoi An has plenty of agencies offering tours, visas, train and air tickets, try: Camel Travel at 23 Phan Dinh Phung (ⓣ0510/861203); Trekking Travel, 621 Hai Ba Trung (ⓣ0510/917770, ⓦwww.trekkingtravel.com.vn); Seventeen's, 17 Tran Hung Dao (ⓣ0510/861947, ⓔseventeenstours@yahoo.com); or Sinh Café, 11 Le Loi (ⓣ0510/863948, ⓦwww.sinhcafevn.com). They can all arrange car hire, and book open-tour buses to Hue and Nha Trang. *Karma Waters* vegetarian restaurant (see p.954) offers eco-tours to the Cham Islands, including snorkelling, hiking, dinghy sailing, kayaking and windsurfing; they can also arrange homestays in Bai Huong fishing village.

**Diving** Rainbow Divers (99 Le Loi ⓣ0914/224102, ⓦwww.divevietnam.com) and the Cham Island Diving Centre (98 Bach Dang ⓣ0510/910782, ⓦwww.chamislanddiving.com) both offer snorkelling and diving trips around Cham Island; a one-day trip including two fun-dives costs approximately $70. Cham Island Diving Centre also has simple guesthouse accommodation and camping facilities (❷).

## Accommodation

Outside of high season, you should be able to negotiate the room rate down by 10–20 percent.

**Hoang Trinh** 45 Le Quy Don ⓣ0510/916579, ⓔkshoangtrinhhoian@yahoo.com. All rooms in this friendly hotel have a bathtub and balcony; those at the front have views of the Confucius Temple. There's a communal rooftop terrace for breakfast, and Internet is free. ❸

### STREET NAMES

There have been a number of changes in street names between the bus station and the town centre, but the locals continue to use the old names on signs and business cards. Nhi Trung is now called Hai Ba Trung, and the road looping west of it is now Ba Trieu; Le Hong Phong is now Nguyen Tat Thanh, but is called Ly Thuong Kiet east of the crossing with Hai Ba Trung.

TREAT YOURSELF

**Thuy Duong III** Ba Trieu ⓣ0510/916565, ⓦwww.thuyduonghotel-hoian.com. The 45 elegant rooms in this French colonial-style hotel range from a superior room overlooking the pool to a deluxe suite complete with kingsize bed, jacuzzi bathtub and a large balcony with a magnificent view of the neighbouring paddy-fields. There is a spa next to the pool, with massage, sauna and jacuzzi. All prices include a fantastic buffet breakfast, free Internet and Wi-Fi. ❻–❽

**Hoi Pho** 627 Hai Ba Trung ⓣ0510/916382, ⓔhoiphohotel@yahoo.com. Bright, unfussy rooms in this quiet little hotel are great value. ❷

**Hop Yen** 103 Hai Ba Trung ⓣ0510/863153, ⓔhopyenhotel@yahoo.com. Basic and friendly hostel offering simple double and twin rooms and two a/c three-bed dorms in the attic. Breakfast included. Dorm ❶; rooms ❷–❸

**Thanh Binh III** Ba Trieu ⓣ0510/916777. One of several similar hotels in the Hai Ba Trung cluster, with spacious a/c rooms and a small swimming pool. The cheapest rooms with private balcony or patio offer the best value. ❹

**Thanh Xuan** (*Long Life Hotel*) 26 Ba Trieu ⓣ0510/916696, ⓦwww.longlifehotels.com. Exceptionally helpful staff do their utmost to make a stay in this tastefully decorated hotel a pleasure. Every room comes with bathtub, balcony, WiFi access, and touching extras like fresh flowers in the bathrooms and a small gift on check-out. Breakfast in the poolside garden restaurant is also included. ❺

## HOI AN SPECIALITIES

Hoi An has excellent food of all kinds, including local **specialities** such as *banh bao vac* ("white rose"), a shrimp dumpling made from translucent manioc-flour dough bunched to look like a rose; *hoanh thanh chien*, crispy Chinese-style wantons; and *cao lau*, thick rice-flour noodles, beansprouts and pork-rind croutons in a light soup topped with thin slices of pork.

## Eating

**Blue Dragon** 46 Bach Dang. With a pretty terrace overlooking the river, big colourful cushions and over a hundred cheap dishes to choose from – try the delicious "wrap and roll" spring rolls – this place is perfect for lunch on a sunny day. A percentage of the profits go to the Blue Dragon Foundation, assisting street kids in Hoi An. Mains 10–25,000VND.

**Café des Amis** 52 Bach Dang. Renowned for its "Vietnamese cuisine plus imagination" and charismatic host Mr Kim, there's no menu, just four dishes that change every evening. The veggie and seafood specialities are all great. Try the Vietnamese set menu (90,000VND) to sample a bit of everything.

**Cargo Club** 107 Nguyen Thai Hoc. A colonial-style, Vietnamese and international restaurant with speciality teas and coffees, cooking classes and rooftop dining. If the dinner menu is out of your budget, it's worth saving your pennies for their delicious homemade cakes, ice cream and pastries. Mains 25–80,000VND, desserts 15–30,000VND.

**Hong Phuc** 86 Bach Dang. A friendly, good-value eatery in a great waterside location, run by two multilingual female cousins who niftily fillet your fish at the table. The fish in banana leaf with lemon sauce is highly recommended. Happy hour 5–7pm.

**Karma Waters** Cua Dai Bridge (ⓦwww.karmawaters.com). Located just five minutes' walk from Cua Dai Beach, this vegan restaurant serves vegetarian versions of Vietnamese staples, as well as a good selection of salads and sandwiches. They also offer highly rated eco-tours to the Cham Islands.

**Miss Ly (Cafeteria 22)** 22 Nguyen Hue. This well-established restaurant, run by a delightful family, serves great Hoi An specialities, such as *cau lau* (12,000VND).

**Quan An** 19 Hoang Van Thu. The guestbook testifies as to the popularity of this little restaurant, with outside seating, friendly service and cold *bia hoi* for just 3000VND per glass; the chilli duck is highly recommended. Morning cookery classes ($10) are also available.

**Sunflower Restaurant** 165 Tran Hung Dao (Phan Dinh Phung). The decor has definitely seen better days but this roadside restaurant, run by a charming local family, serves very reasonably priced seafood and local specialities. Mains 12–40,000VND.

## Drinking and nightlife

**King Kong** Cam Nam Island. With free rum and coke 10–11pm, a pool table and loud music you can pick yourself, this tiny bar packed with backpackers nightly descends into mayhem. Open 10pm till very late.

**Seamile Beach Club** Cua Dai Beach. Themed party nights, happy-hour cocktail specials, beach bonfires, a swimming pool and a sweaty dance floor to bop to cheesy pop tunes, make this place a popular late-night alternative to *King Kong*. A free hourly shuttle bus runs from 23A Le Loi to the *Seamile*. A xe om should cost 15,000VND. Daily 9pm–4am.

**Tam Tam Café** 110 Nguyen Thai Hoc. Stylish French-run bar-restaurant with good music, pool table and upscale international cuisine served on balconies overlooking the street.

**Treat's Same Same Café** 158 Tran Phu. Popular backpacker bar-restaurant with two-for-one cocktails 4–9pm, a pool table, and a selection of Vietnamese dishes as well as burgers, steaks, salads and pizzas; two other outlets at 31 Phan Dinh Phung and 69 Tran Hung Dao enigmatically promise to be "same same, not different".

## Entertainment

**Performance House of Traditional Arts** 75 Nguyen Thai Hoc. One-hour evening performances of traditional folk music and dance. Mon–Sat 9pm; 40,000VND.

## Shopping

**Books** There are several secondhand bookshops along Le Loi (try no. 52 for the best selection) and at no. 81 and 83 Tran Phu.

**Handicrafts** The trio of streets running parallel to the river, Bach Dang, Nguyen Thai Hoc and Tran Phu, are the best places to search for lacquerware, original and copied artwork, pottery and ceramics, and shops selling colourful silk lanterns, a Hoi An speciality.

**Tailors** Lining the streets are scores of tailors that can knock up beautiful garments in a matter of hours and at minimal cost. They can make (or copy) just about any item of clothing. Ask around to find out price levels and reliable companies, and try having one item made before you order a complete wardrobe. Recommended places include: the shop at 36 Le Loi and Bi Bi Silk at 13 Phan Chu Trinh for women; and flamboyant Mr Xe's shop at 71 Nguyen Thai Hoc for men. Impressions Boutique, 166 Tran Phu (and eight other locations around town) also has a deservedly high reputation. You can buy your own materials locally, or choose from the silk and cotton the tailor has in stock; take examples or photos if you have something specific in mind. There are also dozens of workshops that can make shoes and bags to your specifications, though again, quality varies greatly.

## Directory

**Bank** Vietcombank, 35 Tran Hung Dao, has an ATM and can change cash and traveller's cheques, and arrange cash advances against Visa and MasterCard. The post office also has a Vietcombank ATM.

**Bike rental** Bicycles (15,000VND) and motorbikes ($5–6 per day) are available for rent from guesthouses and the stall opposite 6 Le Loi.

**Hospital** 4 Tran Hung Dao ☎0510/861218

**Internet** There are Internet cafés on Hai Ba Trung, Phan Dinh Phung and Nguyen Duy Hieu.

**Police** 8 Hoang Dieu.

**Pharmacy** Bac Ali, 68 Nguyen Thai Hoc.

**Post office** 4b Tran Hung Dao and 89 Phan Chu Trinh. Most tailors and hotels can arrange for a post office worker to come to assist with packaging and paying for overseas shipping; very useful for sending home your new tailored clothing.

## Moving on

**By bus** The bus station in Hoi An has twice-hourly buses to Da Nang, but they are notoriously slow, and overcharge tourists. Open-tour buses (2 daily) provide the easiest and quickest way out of Hoi An, stopping at all major destinations north and south. There are also once-daily buses departing for Savannakhet and Vientiane. Tickets can be booked from any of the listed travel agencies or in your hotel.

**Destinations:** Da Lat (18hr); Da Nang (1hr); Hanoi (21hr); HCMC (22hr); Hue (4hr); Mui Ne (17hr).

**By train and by air** The closest train station and airport are in Da Nang. To get there from Hoi An,

### FULL-MOON FESTIVAL

On the eve of the full moon every lunar calendar month, the centre of Hoi An celebrates a **Full-Moon Festival**. Vehicles are banned, the streets are taken over by traditional entertainment and performances, and the only lights allowed are a mass of coloured silk lanterns.

hire a car ($10) or Honda om ($4), or arrange to be dropped off in town on an open-tour bus ($2), as local buses (every 30min until 5pm; 1–2hr; 10,000VND) are slow, and happy to overcharge.

## MY SON

The mouldering, overgrown World Heritage-listed ruins of Vietnam's most evocative Cham site, **MY SON** (daily 6.30am–5pm; 60,000VND), lie 40km southwest of Hoi An in a bowl of lushly wooded hills. Most visitors come on a **tour** from Hoi An, which often return part of the way by boat, visiting traditional villages along the river ($3–6).

Cham kings were buried here as early as the fourth century, but the ruined sanctuaries you see today were erected between the seventh and thirteenth centuries. My Son was considered the domain of gods and god-kings, and in its prime, comprised some seventy buildings, which weathered well until the 1960s when the Viet Cong based themselves here and were pounded by American B52s. There are **unexploded mines** in the area, so don't stray from main paths.

Archeologists regard **Group B** as the spiritual epicentre of My Son. Of the eleventh-century central *kalan* (sanctuary), **B1**, only the base remains; stone epitaphs reveal that it was dedicated to the god-king Bhadresvara, a hybrid of Shiva and King Bhadravarman. **B5**, the impressive **repository room**, boasts a bowed, boat-shaped roof still in reasonably good shape. The outer walls support ornate columns and statues of deities, and, on the western side, a bas-relief depicting two elephants with their trunks entwined around a coconut tree. Next door in **Group C**, the central *kalan*, **C1**, is fairly well preserved; statues of gods stand around the walls and a carved lintel runs across the entrance.

East of B and C, the two long, windowed meditation halls that comprise **Group D** now house modest galleries: **D1** contains a lingam, the remains of a carving of Shiva and a statue of Nandi, Shiva's Bull; **D2** houses a fine frieze depicting many-armed Shiva dancing, and, below the steps up to its eastern entrance, a statue of Garuda. Bomb damage was particularly cruel near **Group A**, reducing the once-spectacular *kalan*, **A1**, to a heap of toppled columns and lintels. Within, a huge lingam base is ringed by a number of detailed, small figures at prayer.

## DA NANG

Central Vietnam's dominant port and its fourth largest city, **DA NANG** harbours few sights beyond the exceptional Cham Museum, but is a major transport hub with air connections as well as road and rail links. In the American War it served as a massive South Vietnamese airbase and played host to thousands of US troops as well as refugees searching for work. But walking around today, it's the earlier, French presence that is more apparent in the leafy boulevards and colonial-style houses. Day-trips to My Son and Hoi An by rented motorbike or as part of an organized tour can be arranged from here.

### What to see and do

The **Cham Museum**, at the southern end of Bach Dang (daily 7am–5.30pm; 30,000VND), is the most comprehensive exhibit of Cham art in the world. The display of graceful, sometimes severe, terracotta and sandstone figures gives a tantalizing glimpse of an artistically inspired culture that ruled most of southern Vietnam for a thousand years. Exhibits are grouped according to their place of origin: My

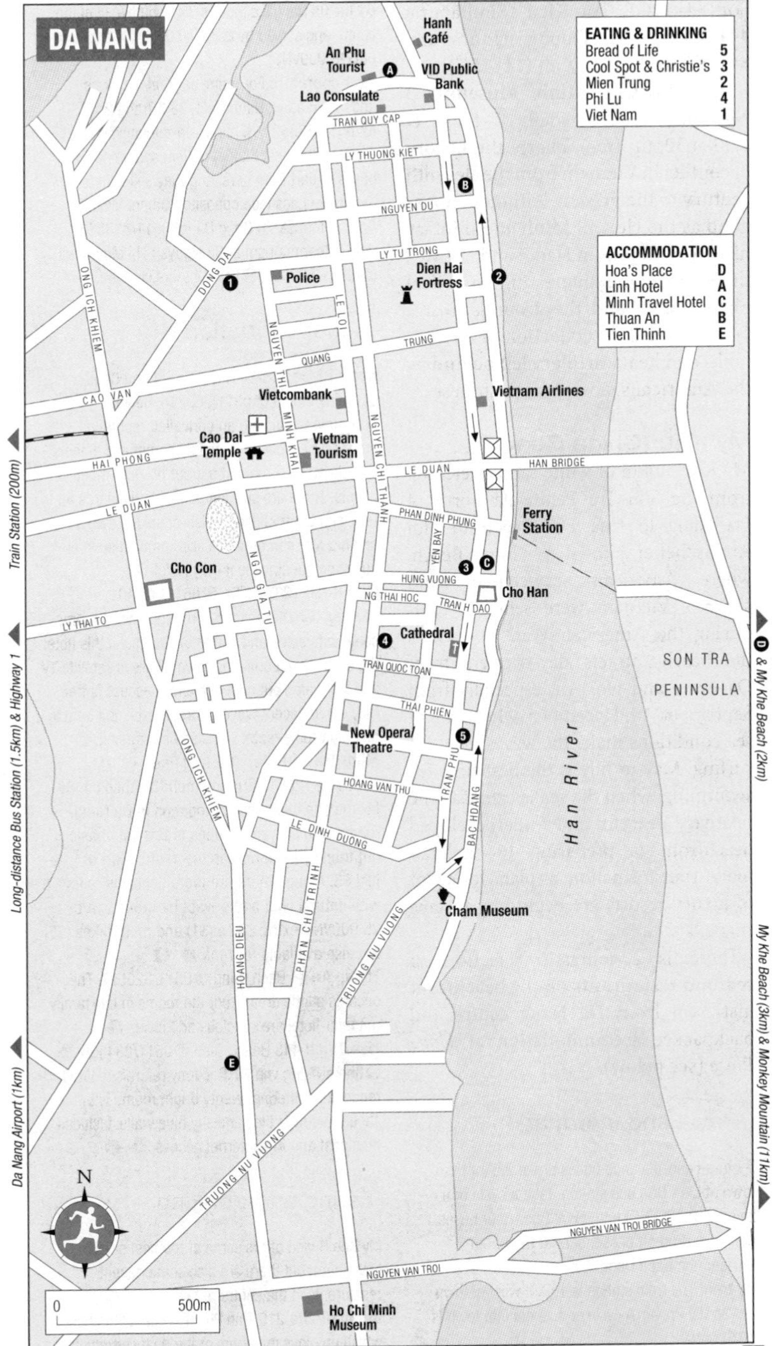
DA NANG
EATING & DRINKING
Bread of Life 5
Cool Spot & Christie's 3
Mien Trung 2
Phi Lu 4
Viet Nam 1
ACCOMMODATION
Hoa's Place D
Linh Hotel A
Minh Travel Hotel C
Thuan An B
Tien Thinh E
Hanh Café
An Phu Tourist
VID Public Bank
Lao Consulate
TRAN QUY CAP
LY THUONG KIET
NGUYEN DU
LY TU TRONG
Dien Hai Fortress
Police
DONG DA
ONG ICH KHIEM
LE LOI
NGUYEN THI MINH KHAI
QUANG TRUNG
CAO VAN
Vietcombank
Vietnam Airlines
Cao Dai Temple
Vietnam Tourism
HAI PHONG
NGUYEN CHI THANH
LE DUAN
HAN BRIDGE
PHAN DINH PHUNG
Ferry Station
YEN BAY
Cho Con
NGO GIA TU
HUNG VUONG
Cho Han
NG THAI HOC
TRAN H DAO
LY THAI TO
Cathedral
TRAN QUOC TOAN
SON TRA
PENINSULA
THAI PHIEN
New Opera/ Theatre
TRAN PHU
Han River
HOANG VAN THU
BAC HDANG
LE DINH DUONG
PHAN CHU TRINH
Cham Museum
TRUONG NU VUONG
HOANG DIEU
N
NGUYEN VAN TROI BRIDGE
NGUYEN VAN TROI
0
500m
Ho Chi Minh Museum
Train Station (200m)
Long-distance Bus Station (1.5km) & Highway 1
Da Nang Airport (1km)
D & My Khe Beach (2km)
My Khe Beach (3km) & Monkey Mountain (11km)
Marble Mountains (15km), Non Nuoc Beach & Hoi An (32km)

Son (4–11C), Tra Kieu (Simhapura; 4–10C), Dong Duong (Indrapura; 8–10C), and Binh Dinh (11–15C).

The **Ho Chi Minh Museum**, 3 Nguyen Van Troi (daily 7–11am & 1.30–4.30pm; free), charts the history of conflict in Vietnam from the eleventh century to the present. Although not as good as the Ho Chi Minh and military history museums in Hanoi and HCMC, there are some interesting historical photographs, and the grounds host a fantastic outdoor collection of aircraft, tanks and heavy artillery left behind by the Americans, Soviets and Chinese.

### My Khe (China Beach)

**My Khe**, 30km of white sand stretching from the Son Tra Peninsula north of Da Nang to Cua Dai Beach in Hoi An, is better known as China Beach, where American servicemen from all over Vietnam were sent for R&R during the American War. Nowadays, the beach attracts day-trippers from Da Nang and Hoi An, especially from September to December when rough sea conditions make the waves ideal for surfing. May to July is the best time for swimming, when the sea is calmest. The relatively peaceful and underdeveloped beachfront is preparing to undergo major transformation, as plans for a glut of luxury resorts are beginning to take shape.

There is a fantastic selection of **seafood restaurants** on the beachfront just 3km from Da Nang centre and backpacker accommodation at *Hoa's Place* (see below).

## Arrival and information

**By bus** Long-distance buses arrive 2.5km from town at Lien Tinh bus station. Take a cyclo or a xe om (10,000VND) into town. Open-tour buses generally drop off passengers at the Cham Museum on Bach Dang.

**By train** The train station is 1.5km west of town at 128 Hai Phong. A cyclo or a xe om into town is 10,000VND.

**By air** Da Nang's airport is 3km southwest of the centre and served by taxis (30,000VND) and Honda om (15,000VND).

**Tour operators** For tours, car rental, tickets and information, Hanh Café, 28 3 Trang 2 (ⓣ0511/538627, ⓔhanhcafe-danang@yahoo.com), is the best budget option; some open-tour buses depart from here, and they sell tickets for the bus to Laos (see opposite). Others include An Phu Tourist, 20 Dong Da (ⓣ0511/818366), and Vietnamtourism at 83 Nguyen Thi Minh Khai (ⓣ0511/823660, ⓦwww.vitours.com.vn).

## Accommodation

**Hoa's Place** 215/14 Huyen Tran Cong Chua St, China Beach ⓣ0511/969216. Beach accommodation with an unrivalled reputation amongst backpackers; nightly communal dinners and cheap beer make it a great place to meet people. There are surfboards and bodyboards for rent, and the friendly, English-speaking owner Hoa and his wife can organize accommodation in an adjoining guesthouse if they're full. ❷

**Linh Hotel** 12 Dong Da ⓣ0511/820401, ⓔhongphan248@yahoo.com. Huge clean rooms, some with sofas and coffee tables, make this hotel the best budget option in town. There is satellite TV and hot water, but no a/c. Internet access is free, they serve decent Western breakfasts, and bicycle and motorbike rental can also be arranged. ❷

**Minh Travel Hotel** 105 Tran Phu ⓣ0511/812661, ⓔmtjraymond@yahoo.ca. By far the cheapest accommodation in Da Nang, rooms with shared facilities in this very basic but friendly hotel right in the centre start at just $3, though there are more spacious rooms with natural light and private bathrooms; a/c 25,000VND extra. Bikes ($1) and motorbikes ($5) are also available for rent. ❶–❷

**Thuan An** 14 Bach Dang ⓣ0511/820527. The decor is a little dreary, but the rooms in this family-run mini-hotel are spacious and clean. ❷

**Tien Thinh** 448 Hoang Dieu ⓣ0511/834566, ⓔtthotel@dng.vnn.vn. Recently refurbished mid-range hotel offering twenty bright rooms with chequered floor tiles and sky blue walls. Includes breakfast and free Internet access. ❹–❺

## Eating and drinking

My Khe Beach offers some of the best seafood in Vietnam, but there are also some decent restaurants in the centre of town.

**Bread of Life** 215 Tran Phu. Excellent little bakery, which employs members of the deaf community, selling cakes, decent sandwiches and Italian coffee. Closed Sunday.

**Cool Spot & Christie's** 112 Tran Phu. Japanese/ Australian-run expat hangout where the upstairs restaurant serves spicy curries from across Asia, as well as pizzas, burgers and Japanese dishes; the ground-floor bar shows sports on TV. The food is a little overpriced (mains from 40,000VND), but it's a good spot for a drink on a Friday or Saturday night.

**Mien Trung** 9 Bach Dang. This riverside eatery won't win any prizes for decor, but it does serve excellent regional food to a mostly local clientele.

**Phi Lu** 225 Nguyen Chi Thanh. Award-winning Chinese restaurant serving thoughtfully prepared dishes at very reasonable prices – the fresh seafood is particularly recommended. There's an all-you-can-eat buffet every Sunday for 95,000VND. Mains 20–50,000VND.

**Viet Nam** 53–55 Ly Tu Trong. Popular with locals and visitors alike, this busy restaurant serves excellent mud-trout cooked in a clay pot and other local specialities such as pigeon, eel and frog. There are chicken, pork and vegetarian options for the less adventurous. Mains 15–40,000VND.

## Directory

**Airlines** Pacific Airlines, 169 Tran Phu ⓣ0511/817374; PB Air, Da Nang International Airport ⓣ0511/656060; Siem Reap Airways, 84 Nguyen Van Linh ⓣ0511/582361; Vietnam Airlines, 39 Tran Phu ⓣ511/821130.

**Bike rental** *Linh Hotel* and *Minh Travel Hotel* both rent bicycles ($1–2) and motorbikes ($5–7).

**Bank** Vietcombank, 147 Le Loi, has exchange facilities, including an ATM, credit-card transactions and traveller's cheques. There's an ATM at the crossing of Le Loi and Tran Quoc Toan.

**Hospital** Benh Vien Da Khoa, 124 Hai Phong ⓣ0511/821118, opposite the Cao Dai Temple. There's also a 24hr service with English-speaking staff at the Family Medical Practice, 50-02 Nguyen Van Linh ⓣ0511/582699.

**Immigration police** 1 Nguyen Thi Minh Khai.

**Internet** At several places along Tran Quoc Toan, and at Club Internet, 90 Hai Phong.

**Lao consulate** 16 Tran Quy Cap (Mon–Fri 8–11am & 2–4pm; ⓣ0511/821208), for tourist visas for Laos.

**Post office** 60 Bach Dang. Poste restante is across the street at no. 64.

**Pharmacy** 5 Le Duan.

## Moving on

**By bus** Local buses leave from the main Lien Tinh bus station. An Phu Tourist and Hanh Café (see opposite) both organize open-tour bus tickets (2 daily north and south) and once-daily buses to Laos (see box below).

**Destinations:** Da Lat (14–17hr); Hanoi (16hr); Hoi An (45min–1hr); HCMC (24hr); Hue (3hr); Nha Trang (12hr); Savannakhet (22hr); Vientiane (24hr).

**By train** To avoid travel agencies' extortionate commissions, book your tickets directly at the train station (128 Hai Phong). The train journey from Da Nang to Hue, the railway hugging the cliff over the dramatic Hai Van Pass with the vast expanse of the ocean to your right, is one of the most impressive stretches of railway in Vietnam, a journey well worth taking in itself.

**Destinations:** Hanoi (10 daily; 12–19hr); HCMC (10 daily; 15–23hr); Hue (10 daily; 2hr 30min–4hr 40min); Nha Trang (10 daily; 9–12hr).

**By air** Da Nang airport is served by Vietnam Airlines, Pacific Airlines, PB Air (to Bangkok), and Siem Reap Airways (to Siem Reap).

**Destinations:** Bangkok (3 weekly; 1hr 40min); Buon Ma Thuot (4 weekly; 1hr 10min); Hanoi (4 daily; 1hr 10min); HCMC (5 daily; 1hr 10min); Nha Trang (2 daily; 1hr 20min); Plei Ku (1 daily; 50min); Siem Reap (5 weekly).

# HUE

**HUE** is a small, peaceful city, full of lakes, canals and lush vegetation, and some magnificent historical sights – including the nineteenth-century walled citadel, the remnants of its once-magnificent Imperial City, and seven palatial Royal Mausoleums. With all this to offer, Hue is inevitably one of Vietnam's pre-eminent

### INTO LAOS: LAO BAO AND CAU TREO

Daily a/c buses run from Da Nang via the Lao Bao and Cau Treo border crossings **to Savannakhet** (12.30pm; 22hr), and **Vientiane** (2.30pm; 24hr); tickets ($20 and $23) are available at An Phu Tourist and Hanh Café (see opposite). Thirty-day tourist visas for Laos (about $30 depending on your nationality) are available at the border.

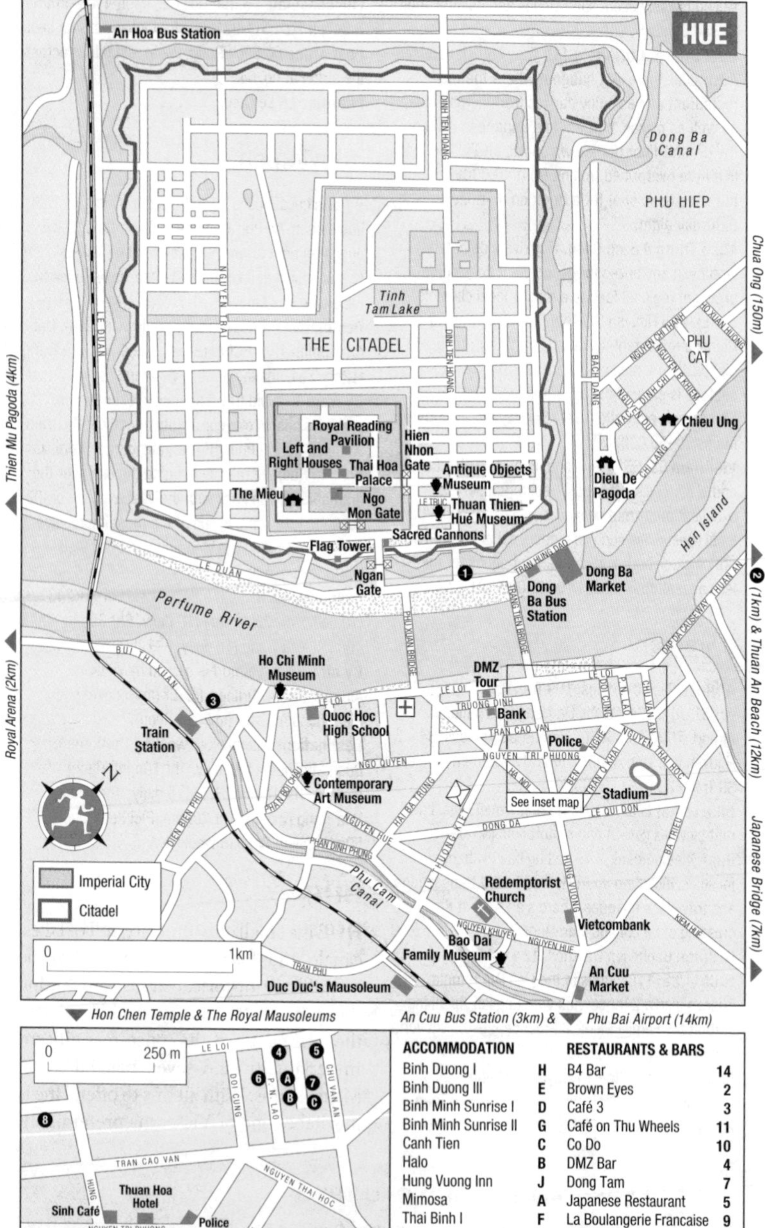


| ACCOMMODATION | |
|---|---|
| Binh Duong I | H |
| Binh Duong III | E |
| Binh Minh Sunrise I | D |
| Binh Minh Sunrise II | G |
| Canh Tien | C |
| Halo | B |
| Hung Vuong Inn | J |
| Mimosa | A |
| Thai Binh I | F |
| Thang Long | I |

| RESTAURANTS & BARS | |
|---|---|
| B4 Bar | 14 |
| Brown Eyes | 2 |
| Café 3 | 3 |
| Café on Thu Wheels | 11 |
| Co Do | 10 |
| DMZ Bar | 4 |
| Dong Tam | 7 |
| Japanese Restaurant | 5 |
| La Boulangerie Francaise | 9 |
| Lac Thien | 1 |
| Mandarin Café | 8 |
| Omar Khayyam's Tandoori | 6 |
| Violon Bar | 13 |
| Xuan Trang | 12 |

tourist destinations. It's also the main jumping-off point for day-tours of the DMZ (see p.966), as well as a springboard for buses to Savannakhet in Laos, via the Lao Bao border (see p.967).

During the 1968 **Tet Offensive**, the North Vietnamese Army (NVA) held the city for 25 days, and in the ensuing counter-assault the city was all but levelled. The huge task of rebuilding received a boost in 1993 when UNESCO listed Hue as a World Heritage Site.

## What to see and do

**Built astride the enchanting Perfume River,** with its pleasant, tree-lined boulevards, abundance of historic sights, beautiful buildings and picturesque surrounding countryside, Hue repays exploration at a leisurely pace. The imperial **citadel** stands on the northern bank of the river, where you can wander through the manicured gardens and the grid of narrow residential and commercial streets within its walls for hours. The southern bank hosts the majority of the city's hotels and restaurants. The city is easily navigated on foot, whilst the best way to visit outlying **temples** and **mausoleums** and enjoy the surrounding countryside is by renting a bicycle or motorbike, or on the back of a xe om.

### The citadel

Hue's days of glory kicked off in the early nineteenth century when Emperor Gia Long, founder of the **Nguyen dynasty,** moved the capital here and laid out a vast **citadel**, comprising three concentric enclosures. In its heyday, the city must have been truly awe-inspiring, but out of the original 148 buildings, only twenty have survived.

Ten gates pierce the citadel wall: enter through Ngan Gate, east of the flag tower. A second moat and defensive wall inside the citadel guard the **Imperial City** (daily 6am–5.30pm; 55,000VND), which follows the same symmetrical layout along a north–south axis as Beijing's Forbidden City. By far the most impressive of its four gates is south-facing **Ngo Mon**, the Imperial City's principal entrance and a masterpiece of Nguyen architecture. The gate itself has five entrances: the central one for the emperor; two for civil and military mandarins, and two for the royal elephants. Perched on top is an elegant pavilion called the **Five Phoenix Watchtower** as its nine roofs are said to resemble five birds in flight.

North of Ngo Mon, **Thai Hoa Palace,** dating from 1883, boasts a spectacular interior glowing with sumptuous red and gold lacquers, and this was where major ceremonies were held. The **Forbidden Purple City**, enclosed by a low wall, was reserved for residential palaces, many of which were destroyed in a fire in 1947, but a handful remain. The **Royal Reading Pavilion** is an appealing, two-tier structure surrounded by bonsai; the nearby Royal Theatre holds daily court music and theatre **performances** (9am, 10am, 2.30pm & 3.30pm; 20,000VND). **The Mieu** dynastic temple, a decorous low, red-lacquerwork building, has a row of thirteen altar tables dedicated to the Nguyen Royal Emperors.

### Thien Mu Pagoda

Founded in 1601 by Nguyen Hoang, **Thien Mu Pagoda** (free) is the oldest in **Hue** and has long been a focus for Buddhist protest against repression. In 1963, it hit international headlines when one of its monks, Thich Quang Duc, burned himself to death in Saigon in protest at the excesses of President Diem's repressive regime. The monk's powder-blue Austin car is now on display here, with a copy of the famous photograph that shocked the world. The seven tiers of the octagonal, brick stupa each represent one of Buddha's incarnations on earth. Thien Mu Pagoda is included on most boat trips along the

## BOAT TRIPS

A boat trip on the **Perfume River** is in theory one of the city's highlights, puttering in front of the citadel, past row-boats heading for Dong Ba market. The standard **boat trip** takes you to Thien Mu Pagoda, Hon Chen Temple and the most rewarding royal mausoleums, and it's usually possible to take a bicycle on the boat and cycle back to Hue. Most tour agents and hotels offer river tours starting at $2 per person (though this does not include entrance to the tombs or Hon Chen Temple). Ask around and book with a reputable agent, as there have been many reports of the boat crew constantly hassling people to purchase souvenirs on the cheaper tours, making for a thoroughly unenjoyable trip. Agents can also arrange charter boats at $20–25 for the day; alternatively, go direct to the wharf east of the Trang Tien Bridge, where the going rate should be $2–3 per hour.

### Folksong performances

A more unusual way to enjoy the Perfume River is to attend a traditional **folksong performance** on its waters. Under the Nguyen emperors Hue was also the cultural capital of Vietnam, and artists would entertain the gentry with poetry and music from sampans on the river. Tourist offices and hotels can sell you tickets for nightly performances on the river ($3–5). Minh-Hai Boat Company (☎054/845060) can also organize dinner cruises with traditional music for $22, which includes a boat for up to six people and the musicians; food is another $3 per person.

river (see box above), but is also within **cycling** distance of Hue (6km; 30min). Follow Le Duan (Highway 1) west along the river.

## Hon Chen Temple

**Hon Chen Temple** (20,000VND) is most memorable for its scenery of russet temple roofs among towering trees. Of several shrines and temples that populate the hillside, the most interesting is the main sanctuary, Hue Nam, up from the landing stage and to the right, with its unique nine-tier altar table and small, upper sanctuary room accessible via two steep staircases. The temple is 9km from Hue and is only accessible from the river. If you don't want to take a **tour** (see box above), hire a sampan either from the ferry station (accessible from the riverside road, near Thieu Tri Mausoleum; 5000VND per person), from Minh Mang pier (around 25,000VND per person return) or from boat stations off Le Loi in Hue (100,000VND per boat return).

## The Mausoleum of Tu Duc

Emperor Tu Duc was a romantic poet and a weak king, who ruled Vietnam from 1847 to 1883. The **Mausoleum of Tu Duc** is the most harmonious of all the mausoleums, with elegant pavilions and pines reflected in serene lakes. It took only three years to complete (1864–67), allowing Tu Duc a full sixteen years here for boating and fishing, meditation, and composing some of the four thousand poems he is said to have written. From the southern gate, brick paths lead alongside a lake and a couple of waterside pavilions, from where steps head up through a triple-arched gateway to a second enclosure containing the **main temple**, Hoa Khiem, which Tu Duc used as a palace. Behind the temple stands the colourful royal theatre. The second group of buildings, to the north, is centred on the **emperor's tomb**, preceded by the salutation court and stele-house. Tu Duc's Mausoleum is 7km from central Hue by road. From the boat jetty, it's a two-kilometre walk from the river, or take one of the Honda om waiting on the river bank (20,000VND return).

### The Mausoleum of Khai Dinh

The **Mausoleum of Khai Dinh** is a monumental confection of European Baroque and ornamental Sino-Vietnamese style, set high up on a wooded hill. Khai Dinh was the penultimate Nguyen emperor and his mausoleum has neither gardens nor living quarters. Though he only reigned for nine years (1916–25) it took eleven (1920–31) to complete his mausoleum. The approach is via a series of dragon-ornamented stairways leading first to the salutation courtyard and the stele-house. Climbing up a further four terraces brings you to the **principal temple**, built of concrete with slate roofing imported from France, whose walls, ceiling and furniture are all decorated to the hilt in glass and porcelain mosaic that writhes with dragons and is peppered with symbolic references and classic imagery. A life-size statue of the emperor holding his sceptre sits under the canopy. Khai Dinh's Mausoleum is 10km from Hue by road, or a 1.5-kilometre walk or Honda om ride from the boat, heading eastwards with a giant Quan Am statue on your right until you see the mausoleum on the opposite hillside.

### The Mausoleum of Minh Mang

Court officials took fourteen years to find the location for the **Mausoleum of Minh Mang** and then only three years to build it (1841–43), using ten thousand workmen. Minh Mang, the second Nguyen emperor (1820–41), was a capable, authoritarian monarch who was passionate about architecture, and he designed his mausoleum along traditional Chinese lines, with fifteen hectares of superb landscaped gardens and plentiful lakes to reflect the red-roofed pavilions. Inside the mausoleum a processional way links the series of low mounds bearing all the main buildings. After the salutation courtyard and stele-house comes the crumbling principal temple where Minh Mang and his queen are worshipped. Continuing west you reach **Minh Lau**, the elegant, two-storey "Pavilion of Pure Light" standing among frangipani trees, symbols of longevity.

You can reach Minh Mang's Mausoleum from Khai Dinh's by following the **road** west until you hit the Perfume River

### VISITING THE ROYAL MAUSOLEUMS

The Nguyens built themselves magnificent **Royal Mausoleums** in the valley of the Perfume River among low, forested hills to the south of Hue. Each one is a unique expression of the monarch's personality, usually planned in detail during his lifetime to serve as his palace in death. Though the details vary, all the mausoleums consist of three elements: the **main temple** is dedicated to the worship of the deceased emperor and his queen, and houses their funeral tablets and possessions; a large, stone **stele** records details of his reign, in front of which spreads a paved courtyard, where ranks of stone mandarins line up to honour their emperor; and the royal **tomb** itself is enclosed within a wall.

The contrasting mausoleums of Tu Duc, Khai Dinh and Minh Mang are the most attractive and well preserved. They are easily accessible. and visited by the boat trips, so they can get crowded; everywhere gets packed at weekends. **Entry** to the mausoleums (daily 7am–5.30pm) is 55,000VND each for the main three, 20,000VND for the majority of the others. To **get to the mausoleums** you can either rent a bicycle or motorbike, or take a Perfume River boat trip (see opposite), which entails a couple of longish walks or Honda om ride (20,000VND). A good compromise is to take a bike on board a tour boat and cycle back to Hue from the last stop.

(1.5km); turn left along the bank and you'll find sampans to take you across the river (10,000VND return; a new bridge is due to open in 2008). The entrance is then 200m away on the other side. This is also where you pick up sampans for Hon Chen Temple (see p.962).

## Arrival

**By bus** Hue has two long-distance bus stations: services from the south pull into An Cuu station (sometimes called Phai Nam station), 3km southeast of the centre along Highway 1; buses from Hanoi and the north dump you at An Hoa station, 4km northwest on Highway 1: cyclo and xe om are on hand to take you into the centre. Open-tour buses from Hanoi and Hoi An stop at the cluster of travel agent offices and hotels along Hung Vuong or the northern end of Le Loi; expect persistent hotel touts when you step off the bus – it's a good idea to have decided on a hotel in advance.
**By train** The train station lies about 1.5km from the centre of town at the far western end of Le Loi. Cyclo and xe om will bring you into town for 10,000VND.
**By air** Flights into Hue's Phu Bai Airport, 15km southeast of the city, are met by an airport bus run by Vietnam Airlines (25,000VND), which goes to central hotels, and by metered taxis (about $9).

## Information and tours

**Tour operators** Sinh Café, 12 Hung Vuong (ⓣ 054/845022, ⓦ www.sinhcafevn.com), Hanh Café, 60 Nguyen Tri Phuong (ⓣ 054/837279), and Trekking Travel, 66 Nguyen Tri Phuong (ⓣ 054/829839, ⓦ www.trekkingtravel.com.vn) arrange Perfume River boat trips and DMZ tours, and tickets for buses to Laos and Thailand. Both the *Café on Thu Wheels* (see opposite) and the *Stop & Go café* at 10 Ben Nghe (ⓣ 054/827051) are recommended for their motorcycle tours around the area ($7). Mrs Thuy, proprietor of *Café on Thu Wheels* for the past 16 years, is a mine of local information. The recently relocated *Mandarin Café* (see opposite) also enjoys a long-standing reputation for decent tours in Hue. Call in for a delicious fruit shake and pick up their *Hue Walking-Tour* map, a helpful guide to seeing the city by yourself.

## Accommodation

**Binh Duong I** 7/34 Nguyen Tri Phuong, ⓣ 054/829990 ⓔ binhduong1@dng.vnn.vn. The budget rooms in this bright and friendly mini-hotel are outstanding value, equipped with IDD phone, satellite TV and a/c, and all but the cheapest have their own computer with Internet access. Its sister hotel, *Binh Duong III* (4/34 Nguyen Tri Phuong; ⓣ 054/830145), has more upmarket accommodation, but still at remarkably competitive rates. *Binh Duong I* ❷–❸; *Binh Duong III* ❸–❹
**Binh Minh Sunrise II** 45 Ben Nghe, ⓣ 054/849007, ⓦ www.binhminhhue.com. Bright, popular hotel with a range of clean, homely rooms, some with balconies. Free Internet and a generous breakfast are included. A 20 percent discount is offered for online reservations. A similar, slightly pricier set-up can be found at *Binh Minh I* (36 Nguyen Tri Phuong; ⓣ 054/825526). *Binh Minh I* ❷–❸; *Binh Minh II* ❹–❻
**Canh Tien** 9/66 Le Loi ⓣ 054/831540. One of several budget guesthouses on an alley leading off northern Le Loi, this newly built mini-hotel offers simply decorated, spotlessly clean rooms with all amenities, free breakfast and Internet access. ❷
**Halo** 10a/66 Le Loi ⓣ 054/829371, ⓔ huehalo@yahoo.com. *Halo* offers friendly service and excellent-value rooms complete with lacy curtains and flowery bedspreads. There's a communal rooftop with a chair-swing and seating area, and free Internet in the lobby. ❷–❸
**Hung Vuong Inn** 20 Hung Vuong ⓣ 054/821068, ⓔ truongdung2000@yahoo.com. This centrally located mini-hotel offers bright and sunny rooms with simple pine furniture and all amenities. Pastries from the *Boulangerie Francaise* are served for breakfast. ❸
**Mimosa** 12/66 Le Loi ⓣ 054/828068. This sweet, family-run place next door to *Halo* has the cheapest and most basic accommodation in Hue. Windowless singles with fan are just $3, and a few extra dollars can get you natural light and a/c. A communal balcony rounds out the picture. ❶–❷
**Thai Binh I** 10/9 Nguyen Tri Phuong ⓣ 054/828058, ⓦ www.thaibinhhotel-hue.com. Spotlessly clean, popular hotel with a good range of well-equipped rooms, some with balconies, down an alleyway opposite the perennially popular *Café on Thu Wheels*. ❷–❸
**Thang Long** 18 Hung Vuong ⓣ 054/826462, ⓔ dinhxuanlong@dng.vnn.vn. A friendly hotel with well-equipped homely rooms, a tour information centre, and free station or airport pickups. There's no lift, so rates drop the higher you climb. ❸

## Eating

**Café 3** 3 Le Loi. A cheap-and-cheerful streetside café near the train station serving the standard

## BANH KHOAI

The most famous Hue dish is **banh khoai**, a small, crispy yellow pancake, fried up with shrimp, pork and bean sprouts, and served with peanut and sesame sauce, starfruit, green banana, lettuce and mint.

range of Western and Vietnamese dishes. They also have a variety of tours on offer. Mains 10–25,000VND.

**Co Do** 22 Ben Nghe. A small, no-frills corner restaurant serving cheap and tasty squid, chicken or shrimp dishes, predominantly flavoured with lemongrass and chilli.

**Dong Tam** 48/7 Le Loi. A vegetarian restaurant with a garden courtyard down an alley off Le Loi, run by a Buddhist family who offer a short menu, including vegetarian *banh khoai* (15,000VND) and a good-value set menu (50,000VND).

**Japanese Restaurant** 12 Chu Van An, ⓦwww.001.upp.so-net.ne.jp/jass. The short menu offers sushi and other simple Japanese dishes, with proceeds going to Jass, a foundation set up by Japanese man Michio Koyama which has provided shelter, education and vocational training to disadvantaged, at-risk children in Hue since 1994. Dishes $1–8.

**La Boulangerie Francaise** 46 Nguyen Tri Phuong. Sells fresh croissants, brown bread, pastries and cakes – perfect for that early open-tour bus departure. Profits go to local charities.

**Lac Thien** 6 Dinh Tien Hoang. On the citadel side, this is probably Hue's friendliest and most interesting eatery, run by a deaf family, who only communicate by a highly developed sign language. The food is excellent, taking in the Hue staples; not to be confused with similarly named restaurants along this street. Mains 10–25,000VND.

**Mandarin Café** at 24 Tran Cau Van ⓣ054/821281. Recently relocated popular backpacker café serving Western breakfasts, sandwiches and good travel advice.

**Omar Khayyam's Tandoori** 22 Pham Ngu Lao. Recently relocated from Nguyen Tri Phuong, this Indian restaurant is deservedly popular for its North Indian menu, which includes a good vegetarian and thali selection. Mains 40–80,000VND, thalis 75–95,000VND.

**Xuan Trang** 14a Hung Vuong. Above-average backpackers' place with an extensive and reasonably priced menu. The ice creams and Hue speciality dishes are recommended – try the *nem lui*, grilled pork with peanut sauce, fresh veggies and rice paper (25,000VND).

## Drinking and nightlife

**B4 Bar** 75 Ben Nghe. Relaxed bar with pool, local Huda beer on tap and bottled Belgian beers; Bruno, the congenial Flemish owner, is a good source of travel tips.

**Brown Eyes** 55 Nguyen Sinh Cung. Late night bar-club with sizeable dance floor, pool table, seating area with floor cushions and an attractively lit garden area facing onto the Perfume River.

**Café on Thu Wheels** 10/2 Nguyen Tri Phuong. This tiny bar-café, run by the charmingly nutty Mrs Thu, has loud music, good food and friendly staff that run excellent motorbike tours – attested to by the recommendations scribbled on the walls.

**DMZ Bar** 44 Le Loi. Popular with travellers for its pool tables and dancing, this bar forms the epicentre of Hue's nightlife.

**Violon Bar** 65 Ben Nghe. Popular with locals and romantics, this is one of the few candlelit places in the country, with upmarket drinks and nightly live music under a thatched roof.

## Directory

**Airline** Vietnam Airlines, 3 Nguyen Van Cu ⓣ054/824709 (Mon–Sat, 7.15–11.15am & 1.30–4.30pm).

**Bank** Vietcombank is at 78 Hung Vuong; more convenient is its exchange office outside the *Saigon Morin Hotel*, 30 Le Loi (Mon–Sat 7am–10pm), which also has an ATM and can deal with traveller's cheques and Visa and MasterCard cash advances.

**Bike rental** Bicycles (10,000VND per day), motorbikes ($4–6) and cars ($30 with driver) can be rented from hotels, guesthouses and cafés.

**Hospital** 16 Le Loi ⓣ054/822325.

**Internet** In all hotels and along Hung Vuong and at the northern end of Le Loi.

**Immigration police** 77 Ben Nghe.

**Pharmacies** At nos. 33 and 36 Hung Vuong.

**Post office** 14b Ly Thuong Kiet. Also provides Internet access and IDD service.

## Moving on

**By bus** Open-tour buses to Hanoi and Hoi An depart from the cluster of travel agent offices and hotels along Hung Vuong or the northern end of Le Loi. Long-distance southbound buses depart from An Cuu Bus Station, 3km southeast of the centre on Highway 1. Buses for the north depart from An Hoa station, 4km northwest on Highway 1.

**Destinations:** Da Nang (3hr); Dong Ha (1hr 30min); Hanoi (16–17hr); HCMC (26hr).

**By train** Trains out of Hue get booked up quickly, so make onward travel arrangements as early as possible.

**Destinations:** Da Nang (10 daily; 2hr 30min–4hr 40min); Hanoi (10 daily; 12hr 30min–16hr 30min); HCMC (10daily; 17hr 40min–24hr 30min); Nha Trang (10 daily; 11hr 30min–26hr 20min); Ninh Binh (8 daily; 13hr).

**By air** The airport bus (30,000VND) departs from the Vietnam Airlines branch office at 3 Nguyen Van Cu (☎054/824709), or you can arrange a pick-up from your hotel reception.

**Destinations:** Hanoi (3 daily; 2hr); HCMC (3 daily; 1hr 20min).

## THE DMZ

Under the terms of the 1954 Geneva Accords, Vietnam was split in two along the Seventeenth Parallel; the demarcation line ran along the Ben Hai River and was sealed by a strip of no man's land 5km wide on each side known as the **Demilitarized Zone**, or DMZ. The two provinces either side of the DMZ were the most heavily bombed and saw the highest casualties, civilian and military, American and Vietnamese, during the American War. So much firepower was unleashed over this area, including napalm and herbicides, that for years nothing would grow in the chemical-laden soil, but the region's low, rolling hills are now mostly reforested and green. There's not that much to see here nowadays, except for the occasional bunker or rusting tank, though just visiting such infamous sites is worth the trip for most.

### What to see and do

You can explore the DMZ independently, but it's highly recommended to take a local **guide**, who will be able to show you the unmarked sites and will know which paths are free from **unexploded mines**. The daily **DMZ bus** day-trip starting in Hue (from 6am-6pm, $11 including entrance fees and breakfast) is the easiest way to see the most important places, and can be booked at most travel agents. As well as the sights detailed below, the day-trip takes in the **Rockpile**, a 230m-high hill used by the US as an artillery base, the **Ho Chi Minh Trail** and the touristy **Van Kieu Bru minority village**. Keep in mind this tour is very long, with short stops for photographs, and your understanding of the area depends a lot on how good the guide is. For an in-depth tour of the area, it's better to spend a few dollars more and hire a car or motorbike and guide from Hue or Dong Ha.

#### Doc Mieu Firebase

The American front line comprised a string of firebases looking north across the DMZ. The most accessible of these is **Doc Mieu Firebase**, where a number of bunkers built by the North Vietnamese Army (NVA) still stand amid a landscape pocked with craters. Before the NVA overran Doc Mieu in 1972, the base played a pivotal role in the South's defence, and for a while, this was the command post for calling in airstrikes along the Ho Chi Minh Trail.

#### Vinh Moc tunnels

The highlight of the DMZ tour, the **Vinh Moc** tunnels are an impressive feat. To provide shelter from constant American air-raids, from 1966 villagers spent two years digging more than fifty tunnels, which were constructed on three levels at 10, 15 and 20–23m deep, with freshwater wells, a generator and lights. The underground village had a school, clinics, and a maternity room where seventeen children were born. Each family was allocated a tiny cavern, and were only able to emerge at night; the lack of fresh air and sunlight was a major problem, especially for young children. In 1972, the villagers were finally able to abandon their tunnels and rebuild their homes above ground. A section of the tunnels has been restored and opened to visitors, with a small museum at the entrance (daily 7am–5pm; 25,000VND including guide and flashlight).

### Con Thien Firebase

The largest American installation along the DMZ was **Con Thien Firebase**, which, in the lead-up to the 1968 Tet Offensive, became the target of prolonged shelling. The Americans replied with everything in their arsenal, but the NVA finally overran the base in the summer of 1972. From the US-built bunker in the ruined lookout post on Con Thien's highest point you get a great view over the DMZ and directly north to former enemy positions on the opposite bank of the Ben Hai River.

### The Truong Son Cemetery

The **Truong Son War Martyr Cemetery** is dedicated to the estimated 25,000 men, women and children – some soldiers were as young as 12 – who died on the Truong Son Trail, better known in the west as the Ho Chi

## INTO LAOS: LAO BAO, CAU TREO AND NAM CAN

It's possible to cross into Laos at three border crossings in the central provinces. Long-distance tourist buses depart from Da Nang, Hue and Hanoi. Thirty-day tourist visas for Laos are available at all three crossings (about $30 depending on your nationality).

### The Lao Bao border crossing

The **Lao Bao** border crossing (daily 7am–5pm) is the most popular of Vietnam's overland routes into Laos. The public bus **to Savannakhet** in Laos via the Lao Bao border departs from Hue daily at 5.30pm, arriving at around 5pm after a night in Dong Ha (tickets $13, including hotel); there's a connecting bus to Vientiane ($9 extra), arriving there in the early morning. A quicker and more comfortable option is the a/c tourist bus ($16), leaving Hue at 6am every second day with a change of bus in Dong Ha at 8am, and arrival in Savannakhet around 4pm; in Hue, you can buy tickets through to Vientiane ($26, arrival around 3pm the following day, includes a night in a hotel in Savannakhet) or for the connecting night bus to Bangkok ($55 including the Thai border ferry; arrival at 6am the following day).

### The Cau Treo border crossing

Although Lao Bao is by far the most popular land crossing into Laos, it is also possible to cross the border at **Cau Treo** (daily 7.30am–5pm), 105km west of the city of **Vinh** on Highway 8. Open-tour buses to or from Hue can set down passengers in Vinh en route; however, make sure you reconfirm onward travel with the relevant office before arrival. From Vinh's provincial bus station (Ben Xe Cho Vinh), about 500m from Vinh's market, several morning buses depart for Trung Tram (formerly known as Huong Son), the last settlement of any size before the border. From here, you'll either have to pick up a motorbike taxi for the last 35km to Cau Treo, or catch one of the regular shuttle buses that ferry locals to the border. Alternatively, hotels in Vinh can arrange a share taxi all the way to the border (105km) for around $30, or a xe om for $18. An easier option are the Laos-bound buses, booked in Hanoi, that trundle through this border en route to Vientiane. Facilities at Cau Treo amount to about half a dozen pho stalls, so sort out money and anything else you need before leaving.

### The Nam Can / Nong Het border crossing

The **Nam Can** border crossing (daily 8am–5pm) is also accessible from Vinh, and near Nong Het in Laos, convenient for Phonsavan and the Plain of Jars (see p.440). Direct buses depart from Vinh to Phonsavan at 6am on Tuesdays, Thursdays, Saturdays and Sundays (150,000VND; 12hr) and to Louang Phabang at 6am on Wednesdays and Sundays (340,000VND; 20hr).

Minh Trail. Many bodies were never recovered, but a total of 10,036 graves lie in this cemetery; each headstone announces *liet si* ("martyr").

### Khe Sanh

The **battle of Khe Sanh** attracted worldwide media attention and, along with the simultaneous Tet Offensive, demonstrated the futility of the US's efforts to contain its enemy. The North Vietnam Army's (NVA) attack on the US base at Khe Sanh began in the early hours of January 21, 1968, and the battle lasted nine weeks, during which time the US pounded the area with nearly 100,000 tonnes of bombs, averaging one airstrike every five minutes, backed up by napalm and defoliants. The NVA were so well dug in that they continued to return fire, despite horrendous casualties. By the middle of March, the NVA had all but gone, having successfully diverted American resources away from southern cities prior to the Tet Offensive. Three months later, the Americans also withdrew, leaving a plateau that resembled a lunar landscape, contaminated for years to come with chemicals and explosives, although that's hard to imagine now, with widespread greenery and coffee and rubber plantations.

# Hanoi

Vietnam's small, elegant capital, **HANOI**, lies in the heart of the northern delta. Given the political and historical importance of Hanoi and its burgeoning population of three million, it's a surprisingly low-key city – though with a dramatic rise in motorbike ownership, increased traffic and Western-style shops, it's catching up fast with the brash, young HCMC. The city has also seen an explosion in travellers' cafés, and mini-hotels, especially around Hang Bac, one of the Old Quarter's main drags. The big question now is how much of central Hanoi will survive the onslaught of modernization, though for now, at least, it remains relatively laid-back.

## What to see and do

At the heart of Hanoi lies **Hoan Kiem Lake**, around which you'll find the banks, airlines and main post office, plus many hotels, restaurants, shopping streets and markets. The lake lies between the cramped but endlessly diverting **Old Quarter** in the north, and the tree-lined boulevards of the **French Quarter** to the south. West of this central district, across the rail tracks, some of Hanoi's most impressive monuments occupy the wide, open spaces of the former **Imperial City**, grouped around Ho Chi Minh's Mausoleum on Ba Dinh Square and extending south to the ancient, walled gardens of the Temple of Literature. The large **West Lake** sits north of the city, harbouring a number of interesting temples and pagodas.

### Hoan Kiem Lake

**Hoan Kiem Lake** itself is small – you can walk round it in thirty minutes – but to Hanoians this is the soul of their city, a point of social convergence for groups of power-walkers, families, older folk practising Tai Chi and young courting couples. A squat, three-tiered pavilion known as the **Tortoise Tower** ornaments a tiny island in the middle of Hoan Kiem, "Lake of the Restored Sword". The names refer to a legend of the great fifteenth-century Vietnamese hero, Le Loi, whose miraculous sword was swallowed by a golden turtle/tortoise in this lake. Cross the red-lacquered Huc Bridge to a second island on which stands **Den Ngoc Son** temple (daily 8am–6pm; 3000VND), founded in the fourteenth century and rebuilt in the 1800s in typical Nguyen dynasty style. National hero General Tran Hung

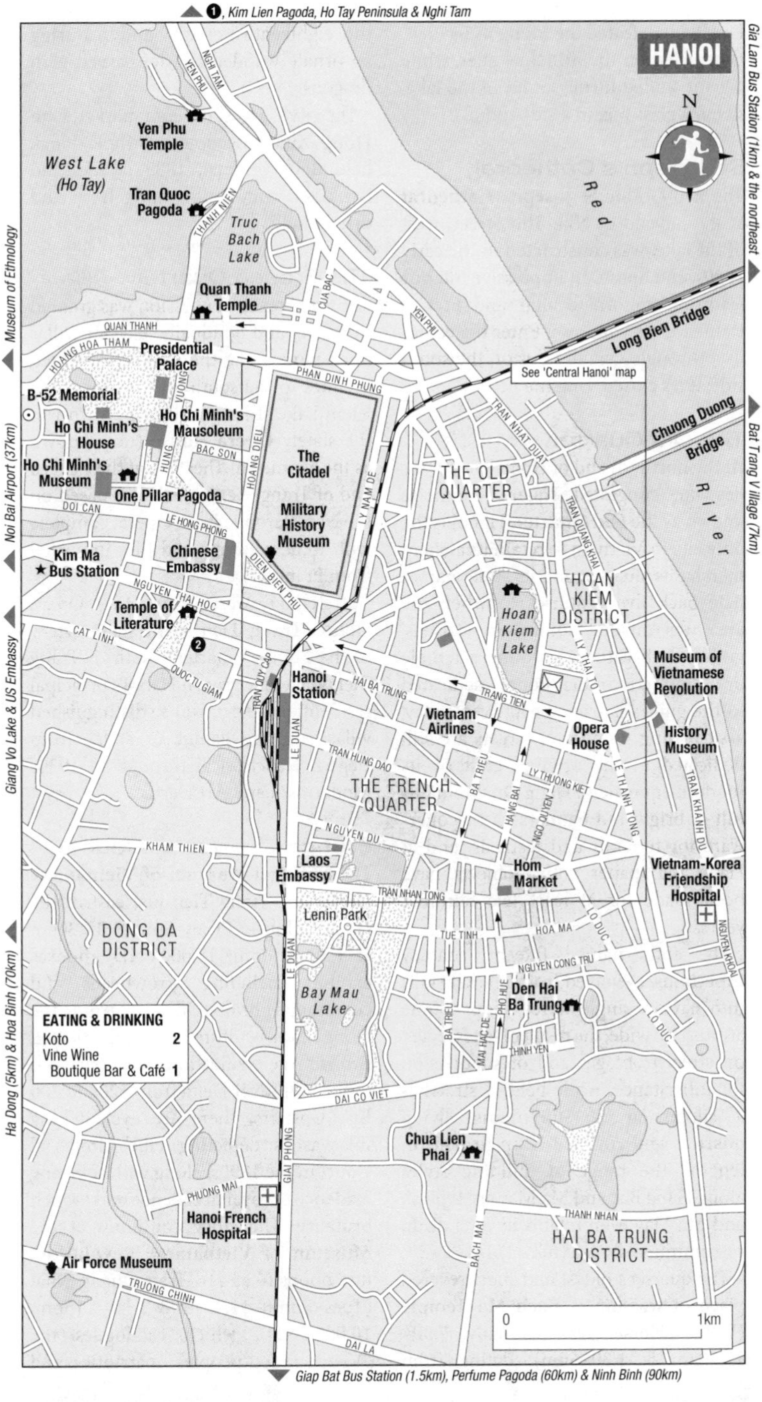

# HANOI

1, Kim Lien Pagoda, Ho Tay Peninsula & Nghi Tam

Gia Lam Bus Station (1km) & the northeast

Bat Trang Village (7km)

Museum of Ethnology

Noi Bai Airport (37km)

Giang Vo Lake & US Embassy

Ha Dong (5km) & Hoa Binh (70km)

Giap Bat Bus Station (1.5km), Perfume Pagoda (60km) & Ninh Binh (90km)

See 'Central Hanoi' map

West Lake (Ho Tay)
Truc Bach Lake
Red River
Hoan Kiem Lake
Bay Mau Lake

Yen Phu Temple
Tran Quoc Pagoda
Quan Thanh Temple
Presidential Palace
B-52 Memorial
Ho Chi Minh's House
Ho Chi Minh's Mausoleum
Ho Chi Minh's Museum
One Pillar Pagoda
The Citadel
Military History Museum
Chinese Embassy
Kim Ma Bus Station
Temple of Literature
Hanoi Station
THE OLD QUARTER
HOAN KIEM DISTRICT
Museum of Vietnamese Revolution
History Museum
Opera House
Vietnam Airlines
THE FRENCH QUARTER
Laos Embassy
Hom Market
Vietnam-Korea Friendship Hospital
Lenin Park
DONG DA DISTRICT
Den Hai Ba Trung
Chua Lien Phai
Hanoi French Hospital
Air Force Museum
HAI BA TRUNG DISTRICT
Long Bien Bridge
Chuong Duong Bridge

NGHI TAM, YEN PHU, THANH NIEN, CUA BAC, QUAN THANH, HOANG HOA THAM, PHAN DINH PHUNG, VUONG, HUNG, BAC SON, HOANG DIEU, LY NAM DE, TRAN NHAT DUAT, TRAN QUANG KHAI, DOI CAN, LE HONG PHONG, DIEN BIEN PHU, NGUYEN THAI HOC, CAT LINH, QUOC TU GIAM, TRAN QUY CAP, HAI BA TRUNG, TRANG TIEN, LY THAI TO, LE DUAN, TRAN HUNG DAO, BA TRIEU, LY THUONG KIET, HANG BAI, NGO QUYEN, LE THANH TONG, TRAN KHANH DU, KHAM THIEN, NGUYEN DU, TRAN NHAN TONG, TUE TINH, HOA MA, LO DUC, NGUYEN KHOAI, NGUYEN CONG TRU, PHO HUE, MAI HAC DE, THINH YEN, DAI CO VIET, GIAI PHONG, PHUONG MAI, THANH NHAN, BACH MAI, TRUONG CHINH, DAI LA

0 — 1km

| EATING & DRINKING | |
|---|---|
| Koto | 2 |
| Vine Wine Boutique Bar & Café | 1 |

Dao, who defeated the Mongols in 1288, is depicted on the principal altar, while a giant stuffed turtle, found in the lake, sits in a glass box in a side room.

### St Joseph's Cathedral

The neo-Gothic **St Joseph's Cathedral** at the far end of Nha Tho Street, west of the lake, was constructed in the early 1880s, and boasts an impressive interior featuring an ornate altar and French stained-glass windows. Enter the cathedral through a small door on the south side; if it's closed, ring the bell.

### The Old Quarter

At the northern end of Hoan Kiem Lake lies the congested square kilometre known as the **Old Quarter**. Hanoi is the only city in Vietnam to retain its ancient merchants' quarter, and its street names date back five centuries to when the area was divided among 36 artisans' guilds, each gathered around a temple or a *dinh* (communal house) dedicated to the guild's patron spirit. Even today, a surprising number of streets are still dedicated to the original craft or its modern equivalent: Hang Quat remains full of bright red banners and lacquerware for funerals and festivals, and at Hang Ma, paper votive objects have been made for at least five hundred years.

The aptly named fifteenth-century **tube-houses** evolved from market stalls into narrow single-storey shops. Some are just 2m wide, the result of taxes levied on street-frontages and of subdivision for inheritance, while behind stretches a succession of storerooms, living quarters and courtyards up to 60m in length. The range of building styles along Hang Bac and Ma May are typical, and Ma May even retains its own **dinh**, or communal house (no. 64).

The quarter's oldest and most revered place of worship is **Bach Ma Temple** (White Horse Temple; daily 7.30–11.30am & 1.30–6pm), dating from the eighteenth century and featuring an ornate wooden chariot carved with dragons.

The city's largest covered market, **Cho Dong Xuan**, occupies a whole block behind its original, 1889 facade, and is packed with stalls selling fresh and dried food.

### The French Quarter

The first French concession was granted in 1874, and gradually elegant villas filled plots along the grid of tree-lined avenues to the south and east of Hoan Kiem Lake. The jewel in the crown was the stately **Opera House** (now known as the Municipal Theatre), at the eastern end of Trang Tien, which was based on the Neo-Baroque Paris Opéra, complete with Ionic columns and tiles imported from France.

Stretching west from the Opera House, **Trang Tien** is the main artery of the French Quarter. South of Trang Tien you enter French Hanoi's principal residential district, whose distinguished villas run the gamut of styles from elegant Neoclassical through to 1930s Modernism and Art Deco.

### French Quarter museums

The **National Museum of Vietnamese History**, 1 Trang Tien just east of the Opera House (Tues–Sun 8–11.30am & 1.30–4.30pm; 15,000VND), houses exhibits including arrowheads and ceremonial bronze drums from the Dong Son culture, a sophisticated Bronze Age civilization that flourished in the Red River Delta from 1200 to 200 BC. Upstairs, there are eye-catching ink-washes depicting Hue's Imperial Court in the 1890s, along with sobering evidence of royal decadence and French brutality. The story continues at the **Museum of Vietnamese Revolution**, just opposite at 216 Tran Quang Khai (Tues–Sun 8–11.45am & 1.30–4.15pm; 10,000VND), which catalogues the "Vietnamese people's patriotic and revolutionary struggle" from the first anti-French movements of the late nineteenth century to post-1975 reconstruction. The **Museum of Vietnamese Women**, at 36 Ly Thuong Kiet (daily 8am–4.30pm; 10,000VND), houses some engaging exhibits on the role played by female revolutionaries in the national struggle, and also a display of ethnic minority dress and craftwork.

Further west, at 1 Hoa Lo, the **Hoa Lo Prison** (daily 8–11am & 1.30–4.30pm; 5000VND) deals with the pre-1954 period when the French incarcerated and tortured thousands of patriots and revolutionaries here. The exhibition includes the French guillotine used, and mock-ups of the conditions here, prisoners shackled to the ground in tiny, cramped cells. Following the liberation of the North in October 1954, Hoa Lo became a state prison, and from 1964 to 1973 it was used to detain American prisoners of war, who nicknamed it the **Hanoi Hilton**; one small room is dedicated to portraying this section of the prison's history.

### Ho Chi Minh Mausoleum complex

The wide, open spaces of **Ba Dinh Square**, 2km west of Hoan Kiem Lake, are the nation's ceremonial epicentre. It was here that Ho Chi Minh read out the Declaration of Independence to half a million people on September 2, 1945, and here that independence is commemorated each National Day with military parades. Cyclo and xe om will bring you to Ba Dinh Square from the centre for 10–15,000VND. The square's west side is dominated by **Ho Chi Minh's Mausoleum** (April–Sept Tues–Thurs 7.30–10.30am, Sat & Sun 7.30–11am; Dec–March Tues–Thurs 8–11am, Sat & Sun 8–11.30am; closed for two months each year while Ho undergoes maintenance, usually Oct & Nov; free). In the tradition of great communist leaders, Ho Chi Minh's embalmed body is displayed under glass in a cold, dark room. Huge crowds come here to pay their respects to "Uncle Ho", especially at weekends: sober behaviour and appropriate dress is required (no shorts or vests).

Nearby is **Ho Chi Minh's house**, 3 Ngoc Ha (Tues–Thurs, Sat & Sun 7.30–11am & 2–4pm; 5000VND), built by the president in 1954 and modelled on an ethnic minority stilthouse. The ground-level meeting area was used by Ho and the politburo; upstairs, his study and bedroom are sparsely furnished and unostentatious. **Ho Chi Minh's Museum** (Tues–Thurs, Sat & Sun 8–11.30am & 2–4pm, Mon & Fri 8–11.30am; 10,000VND) contains many photographic displays and symbolic art installations celebrating Ho Chi Minh's life and the pivotal role he played in the nation's history.

Close by the mausoleum, the tiny **One Pillar Pagoda** rivals the Tortoise Tower as a symbol of Hanoi and represents a flowering of Vietnamese art. Founded in the eleventh century (and reconstructed in 1954), it is supported on a single column rising from the middle of a lake, the whole structure designed to resemble a lotus blossom, the Buddhist symbol of enlightenment.

### Military History Museum

The **Military History Museum**, 28 Dien Bien Phu (Tues–Thurs, Sat & Sun 8–11.30am & 1–4.30pm; 20,000VND; ⓦwww.btlsqsvn.org.vn), chronicles military history from the 1930s to the present day, a period dominated by the French and American wars, well documented in two separate halls. Unlike HCMC's War Remnants Museum, the captions here are still clogged with outdated communist rhetoric – "spies", "bandits" and "puppet-regime soldiers" are everywhere.

### Temple of Literature

The **Temple of Literature**, or **Van Mieu,** is Vietnam's principal Confucian sanctuary and its historical centre of learning (daily: summer 7.30am–5.30pm; winter 7.30am–5pm; 5000VND; guides available on request). The temple is one of the few remnants of Thang Long, the Ly kings' original eleventh-century city, and consists of five walled courtyards, modelled on that of Confucius's birthplace in Qufu, China. As you enter the third courtyard, via an imposing double-roofed gateway, you'll see the central Well of Heavenly Clarity (a walled pond), flanked by the temple's most valuable relics: 82 stone **stelae** mounted on tortoises. Each stele records the results of a state examination held at the National Academy between 1442 and 1779, and gives biographical details of successful candidates. The fourth courtyard leads to the **ceremonial hall**, a long, low building whose sweeping, tiled roof is crowned by two lithe dragons bracketing a full moon. Here, the king and his mandarins would make sacrifices before the altar of Confucius. Directly behind the ceremonial hall lies the temple sanctuary, where Confucius sits with his four principal disciples. The fifth courtyard was formerly the site of the National Academy, Vietnam's first university, which was destroyed by French bombs in 1947.

### West Lake

North of the city, cool breezes drift off **West Lake (Ho Tay)**. In the seventeenth century, villagers built a causeway across the lake's southeast corner, creating a small fishing lake, still in use today and now called **Truc Bach**. The eleventh-century **Quan Thanh Temple** (daily 8am–4.30pm, 3000VND) stands on the lake's south-east bank, and is dedicated to the Guardian of the North, Tran Vo, whose statue, cast in black bronze in 1677, is nearly 4m high and weighs four tonnes. The shrine room also boasts a valuable collection of seventeenth- and eighteenth-century poems and parallel sentences (boards inscribed with wise maxims and hung in pairs). The gate of Quan Thanh is just a few paces south of the causeway, Thanh Nien, which leads to Hanoi's oldest religious foundation, **Tran Quoc Pagoda**, occupying a tiny island in West Lake (daily 7–11.30am & 1.30–6pm; no shorts allowed). The pagoda probably dates back to the sixth century, and the sanctuary's restrained interior is typical of northern Vietnamese pagodas. West of Quan Thanh in Ngoc Ha (Flower Village), down the alley next to 55 Hoang Hoa Tham, lies the **B-52 Memorial**. The remains of the downed bomber, half-submerged in a lake, form a poignant memorial tribute to the victims of the 1972 "Christmas Bombing" raids.

### Museum of Ethnology

The highly recommended **Museum of Ethnology**, or Bao Tang Toc Hoc Viet Nam, situated on the western outskirts of Hanoi in the Cau Giay district along Nguyen Van Huyen (Tues–Sun 8.30am–5.30pm; 20,000VND), is a bit of a trek out of town, but worth the effort for its informative exhibitions on all the country's major ethnic groups. Musical instruments, games, traditional dress and other items of daily life fill the showcases, alongside excellent life-size displays on, amongst other things, funerary ceremonies, conical-hat production and traditional sacrificial spears. Outside in the museum grounds, there are detailed replicas of various ethnic dwellings and burial statues. The museum is 6km from the centre, signposted left off Hoang Quoc Viet Street (also known as Nghia Do). A taxi from the Old Quarter will cost around 70,000VND, or hop on city bus #14 from the west side of Hoan Kiem Lake to the Hoang Quoc Viet stop, from where it's a 500m walk.

## Arrival

**By bus** Long-distance buses from the south use Giap Bat station, 6km south of town on Giai Phong. Services from the northeast arrive at

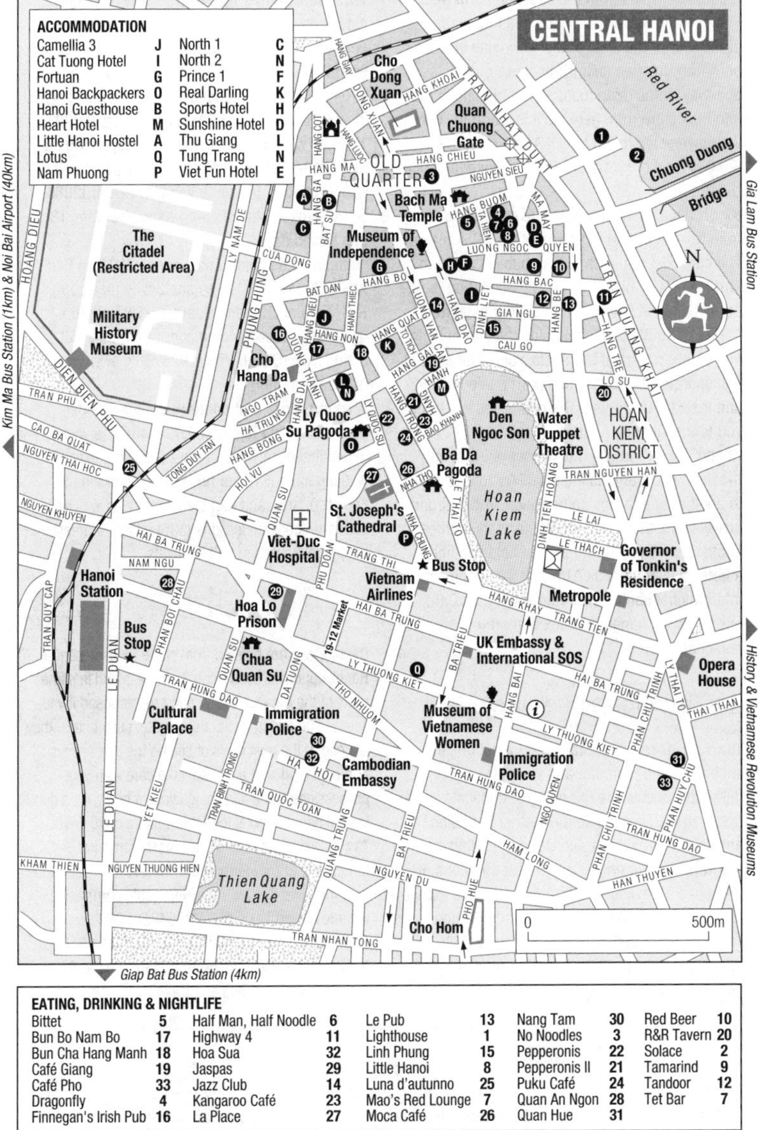


Gia Lam station, 4km away on the east bank of the Red River. Buses to and from the northwest and some northeast points use Kim Ma station, 2km west of the centre. A xe om ride from any of these bus stations to the centre will cost less than 15,000VND. Some buses, particularly private services, drop passengers at more central spots in the city.

**By train** Arriving by train from HCMC, all points south and from China, you'll exit the main station onto Le Duan (exit A). Look out for the uniformed Mai Linh taxi drivers who have a good reputation. Trains from the east and north (Hai Phong, Lang Son and Lao Cai) pull into platforms at the rear of the main station, bringing you out onto Tran Quy Cap (exit B); because of the one-way traffic restrictions, it is a circuitous route into the centre from here, so it is worth making your own way around to exit A to pick up a taxi (20,000VND) or xe om (10,000VND) directly to the Old Quarter.

**By air** It's a 45-minute ride into central Hanoi from Noi Bai Airport (Ⓣ04/5844427), 35km away. The cheapest option is to take public bus #7 to Kim Ma station or #17 to Long Bien station (both 3500VND), and take a xe om to your hotel from there (10,000VND). Just outside the international and domestic arrival terminals, you'll find Noi Bai Transport (Ⓣ04/8865615) airport minibuses ($2) and taxis ($10) waiting. The minibuses will bring you to the Vietnam Airlines office at 1 Quang Trung. If taking a taxi, always insist on the hotel you want, as many will try to take you to another one for the commission. In the airport arrivals hall, there's a tourist information office booth (daily 8am–7pm) that can help you find a hotel, a Vietcombank ATM that accepts most international bank cards, Visa and MasterCard, and a few exchange bureaux that offer reasonable rates.

## Information and tours

**Tourist information** State-run tourist offices such as Vietnamtourism and Vinatour are unreliable, as too are the batch of duplicate-name travel agencies, such as the plethora of "Sinh" and "Kim" cafés in the Old Quarter, trading on the reputation of the originals. It's best go to one of the reliable travellers' cafés, such as *Love Planet* or *Kangaroo Café* (see below) for information on visas, tours and transport. For an English-language, state-run telephone information service, dial Ⓣ1080.

**Travellers' cafés and tours** Many travellers' cafés organize bargain-basement tours to the Perfume Pagoda ($9–16), Ha Long Bay/Cat Ba Island (3 days; $35–120) and Sa Pa (3–4 days; $70–120). Recommended reliable agencies include: Ann Tours, 18 Duong Thanh (Ⓣ04/923 1366, Ⓦwww.anntours.com); Handspan, 80 Ma May (Ⓣ04/9332377, Ⓦwww.handspan.com); Hanoi Toserco, 18 Luong Van Can (Ⓣ04/9286631, Ⓦwww.tosercohanoi.com); *Kangaroo Café*, 18 Bao Khanh (Ⓣ04/8289931, Ⓦwww.kangaroocafe.com); *Love Planet*, 25 Hang Bac (Ⓣ04/8284864, Ⓔloveplanet8@hotmail.com); *Real Darling*, 33 Hang Quat (Ⓣ04/8269386, Ⓔdarling_cafe@hotmail.com); *Sinh Café*, 52 Luong Ngoc Quyen (Ⓣ04/9261568, Ⓦwww.sinhcafevn.com).

**Walking tours and cookery classes** Hidden Hanoi, 137 Nghi Tam (Ⓣ091/2254045, Ⓦwww.hiddenhanoi.com.vn), organizes several excellent walking tours ($10 per hr), among others in the French Quarter and Kim Lien district, as well as hands-on cooking lessons ($35) and Vietnamese language classes to suit all levels.

## City transport

**Cyclo** Cyclo are banned from some roads in central Hanoi, notably around Hoan Kiem Lake and in some parts of the Old Quarter, so don't be surprised if you seem to be taking a circuitous route; despite this, they are one of the best ways of seeing the city. Always agree on a price in advance, take care with your possessions and avoid using cyclo at night; it's a good idea to get your hotel to recommend a cyclo driver.

**Taxis** Taxis wait outside the more upmarket hotels and at the north end of Hoan Kiem Lake and cost just over $1 per 2km. Reputable companies include Airport Taxis Ⓣ04/8254250; CP Taxis Ⓣ04/8262626; and Mai Linh Taxis Ⓣ04/8616161.

**Bicycles** Bicycles can be rented for around $1 per day from many hotels and travellers' cafés in the

### SCAMS IN HANOI

Though few cities in Vietnam are scam-free, Hanoi seems to play host to more hotel racketeers, phone tour operators and downright schemesters determined to make you part with your cash. Check the authenticity of any establishment before booking a tour (check the real address using a guidebook or the Internet) as imitations are common, and be very sceptical of taxi drivers telling you a hotel or restaurant has closed down or relocated. Be wary also of "students" who approach you around Hoan Kiem Lake wishing to practise their English – it is a renowned scam that could land you with a restaurant or bar bill of a few hundred dollars. Such incidents should be reported to the Hanoi Administration of Tourism, 3 Le Lai Ⓣ04/9341449, Ⓦwww.hanoitourism.gov.vn.

Old Quarter. It's best to pay the minuscule charge at a supervised bike park (*gui xe dap*), rather than run the risk of a stolen bike. Parking is banned on Trang Tien and Hang Khay; elsewhere, it's only allowed within designated areas.

**Motorbike and car rental** Motorbikes are available from guesthouses and small tour agencies, and also from the *Meeting Café*, 59b Ba Trieu, and *Memory Café*, 33b Tran Hung Dao. Prices start from $4 per day, including use of a helmet. Park in supervised motorbike parks (*gui xe may*). Bao Viet at 15c Tran Khanh Du (ⓣ04/8267664) can arrange motorbike insurance. Any tour agency will rent you a car with driver ($35–50 per day).

**Buses** Hanoi's new a/c city buses are mainly useful for transport between the long-distance bus stations (every 15min, 5am–5.30pm; flat fare of 3500VND). Tourist maps on sale in bookshops and travel agencies often have bus routes marked on them, or see ⓦwww.hanoibus.com.vn/InfobusVN/hanoibus/homeE.asp.

## Accommodation

Several hotels adopt the same name, so you'll need an exact address if arriving by cyclo or taxi. Beware of being dropped off at the wrong hotel; insist on being taken to the hotel of your choice.

### The Old Quarter and west of Hoan Kiem Lake

**Cat Tuong Hotel** 10d Dinh Liet ⓣ04/8266054. Don't let the shabby lobby put you off; the rooms in this very friendly mini-hotel are very clean, and though basic and a little cramped, offer excellent value for money given the location. ❷

**Camellia 3** 31 Hang Dieu ⓣ04/8285704. Plush rooms with satellite TV and generous bathrooms with bathtub. Rates are reasonable and include breakfast and free Internet access. ❹

**Fortuan** 68 Hang Bo ⓣ04/8281324, ⓦwww.fortuanhotel.com. This once-grand, French colonial-style hotel is now desperately in need of renovation, but the high-ceilinged, spacious rooms are still reasonably good value, some with rattan furniture and dwarf-sized bathtubs. ❹–❺

**Hanoi Backpackers Hostel** 48 Ngo Huyen ⓣ04/8285372, ⓦwww.hanoibackpackershostel.com. Australian-run, standard-setting hostel west of Hoan Kiem Lake, offering private double rooms or bunks in mixed or women-only dormitories. Private lockers are provided, breakfast and Internet access are included, there's a cinema area and kitchenette, and the rooftop bar hosts regular barbecues and parties. The laid-back, social vibe makes it a great place for solo travellers, and there's also a budget travel service. Dorms ❷; double rooms ❻

**TREAT YOURSELF**

**Heart Hotel** 11b Hang Hanh ⓣ04/9286682, ⓦwww.heart-hotel.com. Newly built hotel located down a bustling alleyway off Hoan Kiem lake. The rooms are elegantly decorated in French colonial style with shuttered windows and cream-coloured furnishings, some with a small balcony offering lake or city views – perfect for a romantic treat. Breakfast and Internet access included. ❻–❼

**Hanoi Guesthouse** 14 Bat Su ⓣ04/8245732, ⓔhanoiguesthouse@yahoo.com. Wonderfully welcoming family-run guesthouse which enjoys a deservedly popular, word-of-mouth reputation amongst travellers. The rooms are clean, comfortable and quiet with heavy wooden furniture, satellite TV and WiFi; the deluxe rooms have balconies. ❸–❹

**Little Hanoi Hostel** 48 Hang Ga ⓣ04/8284461, ⓦlittlehanoihostel.com. Brand-new hotel with modern superior rooms with bathtubs and balconies, and cheaper windowless doubles. The six-bed dormitory is excellent value (❷) including breakfast. ❹–❺

**Nam Phuong** 26 Nha Chung ⓣ04/8246894 ⓦwww.namphuonghotel.com. This friendly, small hotel in the cathedral area has good-value bright and airy rooms facing a busy street, some with a/c and balcony. The larger rooms sleep up to four. ❸–❺

**North 1** 15 Hang Ga ⓣ04/8267242 ⓔnorth-hotel@fpt.vn. Family-run mini-hotel with basic but good-value accommodation, and a communal balcony and free Internet. The genial French- and English-speaking owner Hoang Hai is a retired doctor, and offers free medical advice for guests. His daughter's hotel, *North 2*, down a quiet alleyway at 5 Tam Thuong (ⓣ04/8285030) has similar rooms. ❸–❹

**Prince 1** 51 Luong Ngoc Quyen ⓣ04/8280155, ⓦwww.hanoiprincehotel.com. A smart hotel with spotlessly clean rooms, in the heart of the Old Quarter. The pricier rooms are decorated with heavy Chinese furniture and lacy curtains, but there are some cheap ones with no windows. Includes breakfast and Internet access. ❸–❺

**Real Darling** 33 Hang Quat ⓣ04/8269386, ⓔdarling_cafe@hotmail.com. Friendly, honest travellers' café with Internet access and a range of spotlessly clean budget rooms, all with private bathrooms and a/c (charged extra). A dormitory (❶) is also available. ❷

**Sports Hotel** 96 Hang Bac ⓣ04/9260154 ⓔhanoisportshotel@gmail.com. In the heart of the Old Quarter. The rooms here are very clean, cheerful and tastefully furnished, but the cheaper ones are rather small. A couple of extra dollars buys you more space and a balcony. Breakfast and Internet access included. ❸–❺

**Sunshine Hotel** 42 Ma May ⓣ04/9261559, ⓦwww.hanoisunshinehotel.com. Rooms are spacious and elegantly decorated in French classical style, and all have ADSL computer, complimentary fruit basket and satellite TV. A generous breakfast is included, and the service is unfailingly friendly and professional. ❻

**Thu Giang** 5a Tam Thuong ⓣ04/828 5734, ⓔthugiangn@hotmail.com. A peaceful, welcoming family guesthouse near *North 2*. The no-frills, basic rooms can be very small but all have private bathrooms and balconies. (Not to be confused with the inferior *Thu Giang* guesthouse on Thuoc Bac). ❷–❸

**Tung Trang** 13 Tam Thuong ⓣ04/8266267 ⓔtungtranghotel@yahoo.com. Attractive, ochre-fronted guesthouse run by a welcoming, chatty family. The cheaper rooms are a little cramped but spotlessly clean and pleasantly furnished, while the more spacious and bright rooms at the front have pretty balconies with a leafy view of the quaint alley below. Free Internet and WiFi. ❸–❺

**Viet Fun Hotel** 48 Ma May ⓣ04/9262113, ⓦwww.vietfunhotels.com. Spacious and bright rooms, all with satellite TVs and ADSL computers, friendly service and a complimentary breakfast. ❹–❻

### The French Quarter

**Lotus** 42v Ly Thuong Kiet ⓣ04/8268642 ⓔlotus-travel@hn.vnn.vn. Entered through the funky *Safari* bar, the *Lotus* guesthouse has small, quaint rooms with private bathrooms, some with balconies, and apartments for longer stays. Popular for its prime location in the quieter French Quarter and friendly staff, it's best to book ahead. ❷–❸

## Eating

You'll need to get to restaurants early: local places stop serving around 9pm, while Western-style restaurants and top hotels tend to allow an extra hour or two. Most restaurants open up early to serve breakfast. Phone numbers are given where it's advisable to book.

### The Old Quarter and west of Hoan Kiem Lake

**Bittet** 51 Hang Buom. Hidden down a long, dark passage, this small and bustling restaurant probably represents the best bargain in the Old Quarter. Around $2 will buy you a plate of *bittet* – a Vietnamese corruption of traditional French *biftec* and chips served with lashings of garlic, a salad, crusty bread and beer. Daily 5am–9pm.

**Bun Bo Nam Bo** 67 Hang Dieu. Deservedly popular place serving generous portions of rice noodles topped with lean beef, minty greens, roasted peanuts and garlic, all swimming in a delicious broth for around 20,000VND.

**Bun Cha Hang Manh** 1 Hang Manh. This local eatery draws crowds of locals for its excellent *bun cha* and *nem cua be* (crabmeat spring rolls).

**Café Giang** 7 Hang Gai. A café famous for its Vietnamese take on cappuccino, *café trung* – delicious and extremely rich coffee frothed up with whipped egg. This little hole-in-the-wall café also offers *cacao trung* or even *bia trung* for a few thousand dong.

**Highway 4** 5 Hang Tre. The Old Quarter's most atmospheric restaurant/bar, with a warren of rooms on three floors culminating in a great rooftop terrace. Known for its excellent Vietnamese dishes and traditional medicinal liquors. Mains 30–80,000VND. Daily 9am–2am; food served until 9pm.

**Kangaroo Café** 18 Bao Khanh. Australian-run travellers' café that serves giant portions of Vietnamese staples and home comforts such as bangers and mash, juicy burgers, decent salads of organic vegetables, and individually baked cottage pies. The service is impeccably friendly and helpful, and they also run a reliable travel service (see p.974). Mains 30–60,000VND.

**Koto** 59 Van Mieu ⓣ04/7470337, ⓦwww.koto.com.au. "Know One Teach One" restaurant overlooking the Temple of Literature, with reasonably

#### FOOD STALLS

For sheer value for money and atmosphere, it's hard to beat the rock-bottom, stove-and-stools **food stalls** or the slightly more upmarket **street kitchens**; try streets such as Mai Hac De, Hang Dieu and Duong Thanh. Look out for two Hanoi specialities: the ubiquitous pho noodle soup, and *bun cha*, small barbecued pork burgers served with a bowl of rice noodles and minty greens.

priced, thoughtfully considered lunch and dinner menus, accompanied by a decent wine list. Their cakes and Western breakfasts are also excellent. The staff are disadvantaged children and former streetkids being trained to work in restaurants by an Australian-run charity. Mains 60,000VND. Daily 7.30am–10pm, closed Monday evening.

**La Place** 4 Au Trieu. Cosy open-fronted French café looking out on to the cathedral, serving good espresso, giant lattes and tasty filled baguettes for around 30,000VND.

**Linh Phung** 7 Dinh Liet. Friendly family-run café-restaurant serving cheap Western breakfasts, toasted sandwiches and roast chicken, amongst the usual selection of Vietnamese staple dishes. Mains 15–35,000VND.

**Little Hanoi** 9 Ta Hien ⓣ04/9260168. Small, friendly and great-value restaurant on a quiet sidestreet, serving traditional Vietnamese food: try the fried tofu in tomato sauce and pork with lemon and chilli. Usually busy with tourists, so book ahead. Mains 20–40,000VND. Daily 7am–11pm.

**Luna d'autunno** 11b Dien Bien Phu. Excellent pizzas and fresh pasta make this Italian restaurant a good option, despite the trek from the Old Quarter and the slightly higher prices. There's a garden courtyard, upstairs lounge and a/c dining room. Delivery service available (ⓣ04/8237338). Mains from 60,000VND. Daily 11am–11.30pm.

**Moca Café** 14–16 Nha Tho. Located in the hippest part of town near the cathedral, this lofty bar-café is something of a favourite with expats, with its colonial-style decor, decent Western food, good coffee and great breakfast selection. Mains 60–100,000VND. Daily 8am–11pm.

**No Noodles** 18 Dao Duy Tu. Reasonably priced deli-style café with a good selection of salads and sandwiches for around 20–30,000VND to eat in or take-away.

**Pepperonis** 29 Ly Quoc Su. This good-value Western-style pizza chain has pasta, salads and vegetarian specials. Buffet lunches ($2) and evening meal deals are available on weekdays. Free pizza delivery service (ⓣ04/9285246). There's another outlet, *Pepperonis II*, at 31 Bao Khanh. Mains from 40,000VND.

**Puku Café** 2f/60 Hang Trong. Bohemian, homely café hidden down an alleyway, with a relaxed atmosphere, good music, comfy couches and free WiFi access. The food is very good – homebaked muffins, cookies and hearty lunches such as giant salads, bangers and mash and aubergine lasagne. Sandwiches 40,000VND; mains 50,000VND.

**Quan An Ngon** 18 Phan Boi Chau. Popular alfresco food court known as *the* place to sample traditional Vietnamese street food in more salubrious surroundings; choose your dish from the menu, or take your pick from what's on offer at the various food stalls around the courtyard seating area. Mains 30–60,000VND.

**Tamarind** 80 Ma May. A cut above most vegetarian restaurants, serving innovative, delicious food with a Japanese-Vietnamese slant; Western dishes such as the mushroom burger and vegetable gratin are also excellent. Head for the back, where there are Asian-style wooden dining platforms. Mains $3–5. Daily 6am–11pm.

**Tandoor** 24 Hang Be. A well-established, popular Indian restaurant, renowned for its authentic curries: fish tikka, tandoori chicken and plenty of vegetarian options. *Tandoor*'s sister all-vegetarian restaurant *Dakshin* (94 Hang Trong, same hours) is also highly recommended. Mains 30–80,000VND. Daily 11.30am–2.30pm & 6–10.30pm.

TREAT YOURSELF

**Vine Wine Boutique Bar and Café** 1a Xuan Dieu ⓣ04/7198000. Widely regarded as one of the best restaurants in Hanoi, *Vine* serves fine Mediterranean cuisine such as pasta, pizza and steak done every way, accompanied by excellent wine in a warmly decorated, refined dining space. The service is impeccable. Mains 100–240,000VND.

## The French Quarter

**Café Pho** 15 Ly Thuong Kiet. A delightful garden café popular with locals, offering good coffee, a selection of teas and juices, and simple but tasty Vietnamese dishes at very reasonable prices. Mains 15–30,000VND. Daily 8am–10pm.

**Hoa Sua** 28A Ha Hoi (walk down Xom Ha Hoi alley from Tran Hung Dao and turn right) ⓣ04/9424448 ⓦwww.hoasuaschool.com. Excellently presented food and superb desserts with a heavy French influence, served inside or on the garden terrace. *Hoa Sua* is part of a non-profit training school giving disadvantaged children a start in the restaurant trade. Mains 50–100,000VND. Daily 7am–10.30pm.

**Nang Tam** 79a Tran Hung Dao ⓣ04/9429184. Small, elegant Buddhist vegetarian restaurant down a quiet alleyway off Tran Hung Dao, and named after a Vietnamese Cinderella character. *Goi bo*, a main-course salad of banana flower, star fruit and pineapple, is recommended, or try one of the well-priced set menus (20–30,000VND). No MSG is used. Daily 11am–1.30pm & 5–10pm.

**Quan Hue** 6 Ly Thuong Kiet. A simple restaurant with open-air seating, *Quan Hue* serves authentic, reasonably priced Hue cuisine. Don't miss the banana-flower salad, and pep it up with eel fried in chilli and lemongrass. Mains 30–50,000VND. Daily 8am–10pm.

## Drinking and nightlife

Venues open and close quickly and popularity wavers, so check the English-language press such as *Vietnam Pathfinder* for the latest information. Legally, all bars in Hanoi should close by 11pm, but many host nightly lock-ins – the shutters go down and the drinking continues late into the night. Police raids are common – but there should be another venue still open close by.

### Bars

**Dragonfly** 15 Hang Bong. Recently relocated, longstanding expat drinking den that also draws crowds of backpackers for its free pool, foosball, sheesha and themed nights. There's a DJ downstairs but you can choose your own music upstairs. Open till 2am.

**Finnegan's Irish Pub** 16a Duong Thanh. Rowdy Irish bar popular with expats, with a flatscreen TV for the sports coverage, and a games room to the rear with a pool table and darts board. Decent pub-grub and weekly pub quizzes every Thursday night complete the picture.

**Half Man, Half Noodle** 52 Dao Duy Tu. Intimate bar with a quirky atmosphere, known for its late-night lock-ins. There's also a $4 dorm if you can't face the journey home.

**Jaspas** 4th Floor Hanoi Towers, 49 Hai Ba Trung. Preppy sports bar offering nightly sports coverage on giant screens, and decent but expensive bar food.

**Jazz Club** 31 Luong Van Can. Live jazz music every night led by the charismatic Mr Quyen Van Minh.

**Le Pub** 25 Hang Be. Relaxed and welcoming by day, atmospheric and crowded by night, this popular little bar with streetside seating to watch Hanoian life go by draws a regular crowd of backpackers and expats, with nightly drinks specials and the coldest beer in the capital. You can pick your own music too.

**Mao's Red Lounge** 7 Ta Hien. Wonderfully chilled, friendly little bar in the heart of the Old Quarter, with cheap beer, good music, and comfortable couches to lounge about on.

**Red Beer** 97 Ma May. Microbrewery serving home-brewed beers from giant silver vats in a high-ceilinged space.

**R&R Tavern** 47 Lo Su. American bar serving cheap beer and decent pub-grub. There are big couches upstairs, a pool table and live rock music at the weekends, including a popular open-mic session at 9pm every Friday.

**Tet Bar** 2a Ta Hien. Formerly *Le Maquis*, Tet is a multi-levelled yet intimate little bar, particularly popular with French expats and visitors to the city. Open very late.

### Clubs

**The Lighthouse** 51 Phuc Tan. Rowdy club with an outdoor terrace facing the Red River, popular with backpackers as one of the only late-night places in Hanoi with a big dance floor. The music is poppy, the toilets are doorless and filthy (although there are rumours of refurbishment) but it still draws nightly crowds.

**Solace** Boat moored on the Red River at the end of Chuong Duong Do. Lounge on deck with a cocktail, or walk the gangplank to the busy dance floor playing mostly house music on this upmarket party-boat (formerly called *Titanic*) open till very late, especially on weekends. Your xe om driver should know where it is, otherwise cross Tran Nhat Duat and go down Bao Linh, turn right at the end and continue until you see the boat's brightly lit pier.

### BIA HOI

Serious beer drinking tends to be an all-male preserve in Vietnam, but don't be put off as the local **bia hoi** outlets are fun, friendly and extremely cheap. The best-known and popular with locals is at **59 Ly Thuong Kiet**. Right in the heart of backpackersville, the large *bia hoi* at **27 Hang Be** serves the more alcoholic, pressurized beer, *bia tuoi*, and a variety of more sophisticated dishes, such as pan-fried prawns in coconut milk and honey ginger chicken, all at bargain prices. The four small *bia hoi* joints at the crossroads of Ta Hien and Luong Ngoc Quyen are known as **International Bia Hoi Corner**, drawing crowds of backpackers, expats and locals for their glasses of 25,000VND beer and convivial atmosphere.

### WHAT'S ON

A number of publications carry **listings** information and maps for Hanoi and the surrounding area, best of which is the monthly *Vietnam Pathfinder*, which has restaurant and bar reviews. Others include the monthly *Vietnam Economic Times*' supplement *The Guide*; the weekly *Vietnam Investment Review's Time Out*; and the monthly tourist magazine, *Vietnam Discovery*. They can be picked up for free in hotel lobbies or at travellers' cafés. The excellent **website** for expats in Hanoi ⓦwww.newhanoian.com carries reliable restaurant and bar reviews, as well as listings, upcoming events, job opportunities and housing ads.

## Shopping and markets

Hanoi has perhaps the best value, quality and choice when shopping for traditional silk clothes, accessories and souvenirs in Vietnam. The best areas to browse are Hang Gai in the Old Quarter, and around the southeastern edge of Hoan Kiem Lake.

**Art** The Apricot Gallery, 40b Hang Bong, is a well-established gallery with a range of works by local artists.

**Books** The best for English-language books are the Bookworm, 15a Ngo Van So (Tues–Sun 10am–7pm), and Love Planet (see p.974), which also has an extensive library and book exchange.

**Clothing** For vintage clothing and once-off pieces try the boutiques at the eastern end of Ly Thuong Kiet. Clothes shops scattered around the Old Quarter aimed at tourists are more likely to stock larger Western sizes. Look out for the Made in Vietnam stores, which stock end-of-the-line designer gear at rock-bottom prices.

**Communist memorabilia** Several small shops on Hang Bong supply Communist Party banners and badges and Vietnamese flags, while the gallery at 17 Nha Chung sells pricey old propaganda posters.

**Handicrafts** The non-profit Craft Link, 43–45 Van Mieu, sells traditional crafts made by ethnic minorities, including lacquerware, paper goods, baskets and clothes. For embroideries and drawn threadwork try Song, Hoa Sua at 63 Trang Thi, and Tan My at 66 Hang Gai – which has a three-level showhouse shop packed with handmade bed-linens, tablecloths and quilts. Minh Tam, 2 Hang Bong, sells lacquerware.

**Markets** Hanoi has over fifty markets, selling predominantly foodstuffs: Cho Dong Xuan on Dong Xuan Street is a good place to buy cheap bags, shoes, hats and materials; also try Cho Hom, 81 Pho Hue, which has clothing upstairs. All around Cho Hom are specialist shopping streets: Tran Nhan Tong focuses on shirts and jackets, while Phung Khac Khoan, off Tran Xuan Soan, is a riot of colourful fabrics.

**Musical instruments** Traditional Vietnamese instruments are on sale at 11 Hang Non, or 1a and 1c Hang Hanh.

**Silk** Compared with Thailand, Vietnamese silk is of slightly inferior quality, but prices are lower and the tailoring is great value. So many silk shops are concentrated on Hang Gai, at the southern edge of the Old Quarter, that it's now known as "Silk Street". The best known is Khai Silk at 96 Hang Gai, but try also Thanh Ha at no. 114, and Kenly Silk at no. 108. For a large selection of exquisite silk bags and shoes, go to Ha Dong Silk at 102 Hang Gai. The Tailoring Shop Co, 18 Nha Tho, and Song – probably Hanoi's most famous shop – opposite at 5 Nha Tho, have the best handmade clothes in town.

**Supermarkets** Citimart in the Hanoi Towers, 49 Hai Ba Trung, Fivimart, 210 Tran Quang Khai and 10 Trang Vu, Intimex, 26–32 Le Thai To, and Vinaconex in the Trang Tien Plaza on Trang Tien all stock cosmetics, toiletries and a decent selection of Western food.

## Directory

**Airlines** Air Asia, 30 Le Thai To ⓣ04/9288282; Air France, 1 Ba Trieu ⓣ04/8253438; British Airways, 25 Ly Thuong Kiet, ⓣ04/9347239; Cathay Pacific, 49 Hai Ba Trung ⓣ04/8267290; China Airlines, 18 Tran Hung Dao ⓣ04/8242688; China Southern Airlines, Ground Floor, Dae Ha Business Centre, 360 Kim Ma ⓣ04/7716611; Emirates, 25 Ly Thuong Kiet ⓣ04/9347240; Lao Airlines, 41 Quang Trung ⓣ04/8229951; Malaysia Airlines, 49 Hai Ba Trung ⓣ04/8268820; Pacific Airlines, 152 Le Duan ⓣ04/5181503; Qantas, 4 Pham Ngu Lao ⓣ04/9333025; Singapore Airlines, 17 Ngo Quyen ⓣ04/8268888; Thai International, 44b Ly Thuong Kiet ⓣ04/8266893; Vietnam Airlines, 1 Quang Trung ⓣ04/8320320 for domestic and international services; sales agents at 112 Cau Go ⓣ04/9343144 and 46 Ly Thuong Kiet ⓣ04/8243606.

**Banks and exchange** Vietcombank's main branch is at 198 Tran Quang Khai, and provides all major services; there's another branch at 78 Nguyen Du, and agents all over town. There's a

## WATER PUPPETRY

Most people don't leave Hanoi without seeing a performance by the traditional **water puppets**, *mua roi nuoc* – literally, puppets that dance on the water – a uniquely Vietnamese art form that originated in the Red River Delta. Traditional performances consist of short scenes depicting rural life or historic events accompanied by musical narration. Puppeteers stand waist-deep in water, manipulating the heavy, colourfully painted wooden puppets attached to long underwater poles. The Thang Long Water Puppet Troupe give tourist-oriented performances of their updated repertoire at **Kim Dong Theatre**, 57b Dinh Tien Hoang (6 daily, 1st performance 2.45pm, last 9.15pm; ⓣ04/8249494; 20–40,000VND); the view from the pricier front seats isn't that much better, but you get a free cassette of traditional music.



24hr Vietcombank ATM, which accepts Visa and MasterCard, outside the main post office. ANZ Bank, 14 Le Thai To, has a 24hr ATM for Visa, Visa Plus and MasterCard holders. VID Public Bank at 2 Ngo Quyen will also change traveller's cheques and cash. Money-changers in and around the main post office offer higher rates than banks, but will try to befuddle you with stacks of small denominations – watch out for notes folded to count twice.

**Cinemas** The Megastar Cinema (5f Vincom Towers, 191 Ba Trieu; tickets 50,000VND, 30,000VND on Wed) is the newest cineplex, screening the latest foreign releases. The Cinematheque (22a Hai Ba Trung) is a members-club showing mostly arthouse films; membership costs 100,000VND, tickets by further donation; there's also a courtyard café making it a pleasant place to spend a lazy day.

**Embassies and consulates** Australia, 8 Dao Tan, Van Phuc ⓣ04/8317755; Cambodia, 71 Tran Hung Dao ⓣ04/9424788; Canada, 31 Hung Vuong ⓣ04/8235500; China, 48 Hoang Dieu ⓣ04/8453736; India, 58–60 Tran Hung Dao ⓣ04/8244990; Indonesia, 50 Ngo Quyen ⓣ04/8253353; Ireland, 191 Ba Trieu, ⓣ04/9743291; Lao PDR, 22 Tran Binh Trong ⓣ04/9424576; Malaysia, 43-45 Dien Bien Phu ⓣ04/7343836; New Zealand, 63 Ly Thai To ⓣ04/8241481; Philippines, 27b Tran Hung Dao ⓣ04/9437948; Singapore, 41–43 Tran Phu ⓣ04/8233965; Thailand, 63–65 Hoang Dieu ⓣ04/8235092; UK, 5th Floor, 31 Hai Ba Trung ⓣ04/9360500; USA, 7 Lang Ha ⓣ04/7721500.

**Hospitals and clinics** Emergency Ambulance ⓣ115. Hanoi French Hospital, 1 Phuong Mai, offers international-class doctors and facilities at their outpatients clinic (daily 8am–7pm for GP consultations; $55 consultation fee; ⓣ04/5740740), plus surgery and a 24hr emergency and ambulance service (ⓣ04/5741111). Hanoi Family Medical Practice in Van Phuc, Building A1, 109–112 Kim Ma (Mon–Fri 8.30am–5.30pm, Sat 8.30am–12.30pm; ⓣ04/8430748), has multinational doctors and an outpatients clinic ($50 standard consultation fee), plus intensive care and 24hr emergency service and evacuation (ⓣ90401919); they also have an international-standard dental surgery in Building A2 (ⓣ04/8230281). The emergency assistance company, International SOS, at Central Building, 31 Hai Ba Trung, provides routine care to travellers (Mon–Fri 8am–7pm, Sat 8am–2pm; $59 consultation fee, $10 more for a foreign doctor; ⓣ04/9340666), and 24hr emergency care and evacuation (ⓣ04/9340555).

**Immigration office** 40 Hang Bai (ⓣ04/8257941), with a branch office at 89 Tran Hung Dao.

**Internet** Most hotels provide free Internet access, and Internet cafés are numerous in the Old Quarter.

**Pharmacies** 119 Hang Gai, and near Hoan Kiem Lake at 29 Dinh Tien Hoang and 3 Trang Tri. The latter stocks a good range of US and French supplies.

**Police** 89 Tran Hung Dao and 40b Hang Bai; police reports should be made at the nearest station to the scene of the crime. Emergency ⓣ113.

**Post offices** The main post office occupies a whole block at 75 Dinh Tien Hoang (daily 6.30am–9.30pm). International postal services, including parcel dispatch and poste restante are located in the southernmost hall (Mon–Fri 7.30–11.30am & 1–4.30pm). The next entrance up is for telephone and fax services; call between 10pm–7am or on Sunday for lower rates; dial prefix ⓣ171 for substantial savings (see p.897). Useful sub-post offices are at 66 Trang Tien, 66 Luong Van Can, 20 Bat Dan and at Hanoi train station.

## Moving on

**By public bus** Long-distance public buses to the south, including Ninh Binh and Hue, use Giap Bat station, 6km south of town on Giai Phong. Services to the northeast (Hai Phong, Bai Chay/Ha Long Bay and Cao Bang) depart from Gia Lam station, 4km away on the east bank of the Red River; express buses to Lang Son also leave from here. Buses to the northwest (Lao Cai) use Kim Ma station, 2km west of the centre; there are also regular express buses here for Ha Long and Hai Phong. Long Bien station, just beneath Long Bien Bridge, has express buses to Lang Son; whilst Ha Dong station, 10km west of the centre, has buses bound for Mai Chau. Always check at the station a day or two before you want to travel, especially for destinations north and west of Hanoi.

**Destinations:**Bai Chay (4 hourly; 3hr–3hr 30min); Hai Phong (2hr); Hue (16–17hr); Lang Son (3hr); Mai Chau (4hr); Ninh Binh (2hr); Son La (7–10hr).

**By open-tour bus and minibus** For tickets and information on long-distance tourist buses, contact reliable operators such as Sinh Café, Real Darling or Love Planet (see p.974). Direct one-way overnight buses for Savannakhet and Vientiane (daily, 17hr and 20hr; $25) depart from Hanoi at 6pm, crossing the border at Lao Bao for Savannakhet and Cau Treo. Minibuses organized by travellers' cafés in the Old Quarter depart for Bai Chay (Ha Long Bay) early every morning; Sinh Café also has buses departing daily at 7am from the northwest corner of Hoan Kiem Lake.

**By train** The main station is at 120 Le Duan (☎04/9423697), 1km southwest of the Old Quarter. Tickets and information are available at the window marked "Booking Office for Foreigners and International Express Train" (daily 7.30am–12.30pm & 1–8.45pm). Book early, especially for sleeping berths to Hue (berths $9–27) and HCMC (berths $23–60). Services to the east and north, including trains for Hai Phong (22,000VND or $1.50) and Lao Cai (berths $9–15), leave from the back of the station on Tran Quy Cap.

**Destinations:** Beijing, China (Tues & Fri; 43hr); Da Nang (13 daily; 12–19hr); Dong Dang (Tues & Fri; 4–5hr); Hai Phong (2 daily; 2hr 30min); HCMC (13 daily; 30–41hr); Hue (13 daily; 11–16hr); Lao Cai (4 daily; 7hr 30min–10hr 15min); Nha Trang (13 daily; 23–34hr); Ninh Binh (6 daily; 2hr 15min–4hr); Vinh (13 daily; 5hr–6hr 40min).

**By air** To get to the airport, take the Noi Bai Airport minibus, which departs from their office at 2 Quang Trung (daily 5am–7pm; ☎04/9344070) every half an hour (5am–6pm); you can buy tickets ($2) at this office, or from the minibus driver. A taxi from your hotel costs $10, or sign up at one of the travellers' cafés for a shared car or bus ($3–5 per person). International destinations include Bangkok, Beijing, Hong Kong, Kunming, Louang Phabang, Tokyo, Vientiane.

**Destinations:** Buon Ma Thuot (1 daily; 1hr 40min–5hr 20min); Da Nang (4 daily; 1hr 15min); Dien Bien Phu (2 daily; 1hr); HCMC (15 daily; 2hr); Hue (3 daily; 1hr 10min); Nha Trang (2 daily; 1hr 40min).

## INTO CHINA

### The train to China

Tickets should be booked well in advance for the direct train service from Hanoi to China, and you'll need your passport with a valid China visa when you buy them. The **Hanoi–Beijing** service (43hr; $120) leaves Hanoi main station on Tuesdays and Fridays at 6.30pm and goes via Dong Dang, but cannot be boarded anywhere other than Hanoi; in China, you can get off at Pingxiang just across the border, or at Nanning, Guilin and so on. The Hanoi–Kunming service was suspended in 2004 due to landslide damage on the Chinese side, and it's still unclear if the tracks will be repaired at all; you can take the train to Lao Cai, and take a bus from there to Kunming (see p.993).

### Huu Nghi and on to Nanning

The road crossing known as the **Huu Nghi ("Friendship") border gate** is 164km northeast of Hanoi at the end of Highway 1. Local trains from Hanoi (hard seat only) terminate at Dong Dang station, 800m south of the main town, from where you can take a xe om up to the border (10,000VND). The Huu Nghi border gate (daily 7am–6pm) is just a small road checkpoint and has no exchange facilities; there's a walk of less than 1km between the two checkpoints. On the Chinese side, taxis and rickshaws (from ¥15–30) will take you to **Pingxiang**, 15km away, for the nearest accommodation and the trains to **Nanning** (3 daily; 4hr–5hr 30min; $2–4).

# Around Hanoi

The fertile and densely populated landscape of the Red River Delta that surrounds Hanoi is crisscrossed by massive ancient dykes and studded with temples and pagodas, including the **Perfume Pagoda** – the city's most popular day-trip. The magnificent karst scenery at **Tam Coc**, 90km south of Hanoi, can also be visited as a day-trip from the capital, but many travellers choose to explore the area at a more leisurely pace: the sleepy town of **Ninh Binh** makes an excellent base for Tam Coc and the nearby ancient capital of **Hoa Lu.**

## THE PERFUME PAGODA

Sixty kilometres southwest of Hanoi, a forested spur shelters north Vietnam's most famous Buddhist pilgrimage site, the **Perfume Pagoda**, Chua Huong, said to be named after spring blossoms that scent the air. Though a popular day-trip from Hanoi, many travellers are disappointed by the low-key nature of the grotto, combined with the long walk and the barrage of hawkers en route. The easiest way to visit the pagoda is on an all-inclusive tour (approx. $15) or in a rental car.

The pagoda occupies a grotto over 50m high; the journey there begins with a pleasant, half-hour sampan ride up a flooded valley among karst hills, then a path brings you to the seventeenth-century Chua Thien Chu ("Pagoda Leading to Heaven"), in front of which stands a magnificent, triple-roofed bell pavilion. Quan Am, Goddess of Mercy, takes pride of place on the pagoda's main altar. To the right of the pagoda, a three-kilometre path leads steeply uphill (1–2hr) at the end of which a gaping cavern is revealed beneath the inscription "supreme cave under the southern sky". The Perfume Pagoda is also dedicated to Quan Am and a flight of 120 steps descends into the dragon's mouth-like entrance, where gilded Buddhas emerge from dark recesses wreathed in clouds of incense (bring a torch). You must wear long trousers and long-sleeve shirts to Chua Thien Chu, and shoes with good grip are highly recommended.

## NINH BINH AND AROUND

The dusty provincial capital of **Ninh Binh**, 90km from Hanoi, has little to detain you, but serves as a good base for trips to nearby **Tam Coc** and **Hoa Lu**, and many travellers rate the local people and guesthouse owners here amongst the most welcoming in the country. Two radio masts provide convenient landmarks in town: the taller stands over the post office in the south, while the shorter signals the northern extremity 2km away up Highway 1 (Tran Hung Dao). Exactly halfway between the two, Le Hong Phong shoots off east at a major junction, taking traffic to join the Nam Dinh road.

The Vietincombank, on the main strip on Tran Hung Dao, has an ATM and can **exchange** cash and traveller's cheques, and arrange Visa and MasterCard cash advances.

### What to see and do

The most rewarding way to see the area is by **renting a bicycle**; the surrounding landscape, with giant limestone karsts dramatically rising from glistening rice paddies, makes the journey to **Tam Coc** worthwile, and the temples of **Hoa Lu** are an easy day-trip.

#### Tam Coc

It's hard not to be won over by the mystical, watery beauty of the Tam Coc region, which is a miniature, landlocked version of Ha Long Bay. Journey's end for the three-hour sampan-ride through the flooded landscape is **Tam Coc**, three long, dark tunnel-caves eroded through the limestone hills with barely sufficient clearance for the sampan in places.

**Starting point is** the dock in Van Lam village, and **boats** leave here between 6.30am and 5pm (go early or late to avoid the crowds), and cost 70,000VND per person, including entry to Bich Dong Pagoda. However, many tourists complain of constant hassle on the boats to buy refreshments and handicrafts; be firm from the outset.

Follow the road another 2km beyond the boat dock to visit the cave-pagoda of **Bich Dong**, where stone-cut steps lead up a cliff face peppered with shrines to the cave entrance. Three Buddhas sit unperturbed on their lotus thrones beside a head-shaped rock, which bestows longevity if touched.

The most enjoyable way to reach Tam Coc is to rent a **bicycle** ($1) or **motorbike** ($5–6) from a Ninh Binh guesthouse, which should also be able to provide a photocopied map. The turning, marked by four large pillars, is 4km south of the town centre on Highway 1. A **xe om** from Ninh Binh will cost about $4–7 all-in. If your next stop is Hoa Lu, you can take a back road for a spectacular ten-kilometre ride through rice fields, karst scenery and villages; the thirty-kilometre round trip is easily done in a day. This back road starts in the village halfway down the road between Highway 1 and the boat landing; follow the signs for Troung Yen village to reach Hoa Lu.

### Hoa Lu

Thirteen kilometres northwest of Ninh Binh stands **Hoa Lu** (entrance 10,000VND), site of the tenth-century capital of an early, independent Vietnamese kingdom called Dai Co Viet. The fortified royal palaces of the Dinh and Le kings are now in ruins, but their dynastic temples, seventeenth-century copies of eleventh-century originals, still rest quietly in a narrow valley surrounded by hills. Opposite the temples, steps lead up "Saddle Mountain" for a panoramic view of Hoa Lu. It's also possible to take a **boat trip** (2–3hr; 50,000VND per person) along the Sao Khe River.

The quickest way out to Hoa Lu is by xe om ($5–8 round trip), but going by **bicycle** is more fun. After the first five unnerving kilometres on Highway 1, it's a pleasant ride on paved back roads west of the highway, following signs to Truong Yen village and Hoa Lu (13km in total). You can then cycle back along the Sao Khe River: take the paved road heading east directly in front of the temples, turn right over the bridge and follow the dirt track for about 4km to the first village. Here, a left turn leading to a concrete bridge will take you back to Ninh Binh, while the road straight ahead continues for another 6km to Tam Coc.

## Arrival and information

**By bus** The bus station is east of the Van River, less than 1km by xe om from Tran Hung Dao. Open-tour buses en route to and from Hanoi (2hr) pick up and drop off at their associated hotels along Tran Hung Dao.

**By train** The train from Hanoi takes just over two hours; the station is also east of the Van River, a short xe om ride from Tran Hung Dao.

## Accommodation

All the listed hotels can assist with tours, car and motorbike rental, as well as onward open-tour buses.

**Queen Mini Hotel** 21 Hoang Hoa Tham ⓣ030/871874, ⓔluongvn2001@yahoo.com. Very decent budget hotel with a spacious six-bed dorm and well-equipped private rooms with satellite TV. There is a simple selection of local dishes available in the restaurant. Dorm ❶; rooms ❷–❸

**Thanh Binh Hotel** 31 Luong Van Tuy ⓣ030/872439, ⓔtbhotelnb@yahoo.com. Family-run hotel offering clean and spacious accommodation with breakfast and free Internet included; the rooms in the new wing are excellent value, and the food is also recommended. Good-quality mountain bikes for rent ($2–4). ❷–❸

**Than Thuy's Guesthouse** 128 Le Hong Phong ⓣ030/871811, ⓦwww.hotelthanhthuy.com. Friendly place with decent older rooms in the guesthouse, and spacious, fully equipped rooms in the newer hotel at the back. There's a central courtyard restaurant, and their tailor-made motorbike tours to outlying villages are popular. 2–5

**Xuan Hoa Hotel 1 & 2** 31D Minh Khai, Nam Thanh ⓣ030/880970, ⓦwww.xuanhoahotel.com. Two neighbouring hotels owned by Xuan and his wife Hoa, offering spotless, modern and well-equipped rooms, friendly service and excellent home-cooking. 2–3

### Eating

There are very few decent independent restaurants in Ninh Binh, but most hotels offer good food as well.

**Com Pho 1.2.3** 112 Le Hong Phong near *Than Thuy's Guesthouse*. Good for simply prepared, tasty Vietnamese dishes.

**Thuy Anh** 36 Truong Han Sieu. Has excellent fish steamboat (*lau ca*).

### Moving on

**By bus** Public buses depart hourly for Hanoi from the bus station east of the Van River. They can also be flagged down on their way through town. Open-tour buses west to Hanoi (2 daily) or south to Hue, Da Nang, Hoi An and HCMC (all 2 daily) pick up along Tran Hung Dao; tickets can be organized through your hotel.

## CUC PHUONG NATIONAL PARK

Established as Vietnam's first national park in 1962, **Cuc Phuong**, 200 square kilometres of tropical evergreen forest surrounded by limestone mountains, now attracts approximately forty thousand visitors a year who flock to see the prehistoric caves and the myriad species of wildlife that live among the forest's ancient trees – some of which are over a thousand years old. There are over three hundred bird and ninety mammal species, including bats, bears, leopards, rare butterflies, and one of the world's most endangered monkeys, Delacour's langur. At the entrance gate (40,000VND, plus 10,000VND for a mandatory guide), the **visitors' centre** (daily 9.30–11am & 1.30–4pm; ⓣ030/848006, ⓦwww.cucphuongtourism.com) can organize biking, hiking, bird-watching, night-spotting and overnight accommodation either in the park headquarters, bamboo bungalows or stilthouses in a Muong village in the park ($5–20 per person). Beyond the visitors' centre stands the **Endangered Primate Rescue Center** (daily 9–11am & 1.30–4pm; ⓦwww.primatecenter.org), where you can see the park's research, conservation and breeding programmes to save endangered langurs, lorises and gibbons.

Tourist agencies in Hanoi arrange day-trips to Cuc Phuong for about $15 per person (not including entrance fees). If coming from Ninh Binh, rent a motorbike or hire a xe om (about 120,000VND return including waiting time). Head north along Highway 1 for about 10km, and take the left at the sign for Cuc Phuong. From here it's another 18km to the park entrance.

# Ha Long Bay

Nearly two thousand bizarrely shaped limestone outcrops jut out of the emerald **Ha Long Bay**, its hidden coves, echoing caves and needle-sharp ridges providing the inspiration for dozens of local legends and poems. Navigating the silent channels and scrambling through caves is a hugely popular activity, but with so much hyperbole, some find Ha Long disappointing: this stretch of coast is an industrialized region, and views in February and March can be poor.

The vast majority of visitors to Ha Long Bay come on **organized tours** from Hanoi, with most overnighting in Cat Ba (three days/two nights; $28–100). For the best experience, choose an operator offering one or two nights sleeping on the boat (with the chance of a midnight dip in the phosphorescent waters) and a guided hike though Cat Ba National Park. If you're not coming on a tour, the epicentre of tourism in Ha Long Bay itself is **Ha Long City**, which offers rather mediocre accommodation and overpriced restaurants plus hordes of boatmen. **Cat Ba Island**, accessible from Ha Long City, and the port city of **Hai Phong** make slightly less touristy bases for bay trips.

## THE BAY

Ha Long Bay is split in two by a wide channel running north–south: the larger, western portion contains the most dramatic scenery and best caves, while to the east lies an attractive area of smaller islands, known as Bai Tu Long. Independent visitors to the bay need to buy a $2 **excursion ticket** at the tourist wharf, which includes insurance and entrance to the caves along your route.

The bay's most famous cave is **Hang Dau Go** ("Grotto of the Wooden Stakes"). In 1288, General Tran Hung Dao amassed hundreds of wooden stakes here; these were driven into the Bach Dang River estuary mud, skewering the boats of Kublai Khan's Mongol army as the tide went out. The same island also boasts the beautiful **Hang Thien Cung** cave, whose rectangular chamber, 250m long and 20m high, holds a textbook display of sparkling stalactites and stalagmites. To the south, you should single out **Ho Dong Tien** ("Grotto of the Fairy Lake") and the enchanting **Dong Me Cung** ("Grotto of the Labyrinth").

Of the far-flung sights, **Hang Hanh** is one of the more adventurous day-trips from Bai Chay: the tide must be exactly right (at half-tide) to allow a coracle ($10 extra, or $1 per person) access to the two-kilometre-long tunnel-cave; a powerful torch is very useful. Dau Bo Island, on the south-eastern edge of Ha Long Bay, encloses **Ho Ba Ham** ("Three Tunnel Lake"), a shallow lagoon wrapped round with limestone walls and connected to the sea by three low-ceilinged tunnels that are only navigable by sampan at low tide. This cave can be included in a one- or two-day excursion out of Bai Chay and can also be arranged from Cat Ba Island.

## BAI CHAY AND HONG GAI (HA LONG CITY)

In 1994, Hong Gai and Bai Chay were amalgamated into **Ha Long City**, but locals still stick to the old names – as do ferry services and minibuses – since this is a useful way to distinguish between the two towns, which lie on either side of the narrow Cua Luc channel. Neon signs blaze out at night along the **BAI CHAY** waterfront, advertising north Vietnam's most developed resort, whose main business is boat tours around the bay. **HONG GAI**, on the other hand, is a bustling working harbour.

### HA LONG BAY TOURS

Cruises around Ha Long Bay are available from every hotel and travel agency in Hanoi, but despite their popularity, many travellers complain about the standard of service on both budget and luxury tours. Travel agencies seldom commission their own boats, merely acting as agents for larger operators, who shift passengers mid-tour from boat to boat to cram as many on board as possible, making it impossible to work out which agency to book with. The best you can do is ask as many questions as you can before booking, such as the size of group, standard of accommodation and planned activities, so you have some comeback at the end if the tour fails to live up to what was promised. Report any unsatisfactory experiences to the Administration of Tourism in Hanoi (see p.974). Kangaroo Café (p.974) receives consistently good reviews as one of the only operators who commission their own boats and deliver on their promises.

## Arrival and information

**By bus** Buses from Hanoi and Hai Phong use the western bus station (Bai Chay), at the far end of Ha Long Avenue. Buses from Mong Cai and the north arrive at the eastern bus station (Hong Gai); from here, Hong Gai centre is 1km back down Le Thanh Tong, or you can cross over the new road bridge to Bai Chay by xe om (5000VND).

**By train and boat** A slower and more expensive, but far more scenic approach, is to take the train from Hanoi to Hai Phong and then the public ferry to Hong Gai (2 daily; 2hr). Ferries from Hai Phong, Quan Lan and Cat Ba arrive at Ben Tau Pier south of the market in Hong Gai. Ferries from Mong Cai arrive at the Bai Chai Hydrofoil Jetty at the northern end of Ha Long Avenue. Tourist boats dock at the Tourist Wharf halfway along Ha Long Avenue, 2km from the tourist centre.

**Information and boat trips** Most hotels in Bai Chay can help with boat trips, as can the information office at Bai Chay Tourist Wharf, 2km west of town; they have several itineraries, including a rushed standard four-hour tour (60,000VND).

## Accommodation

Hong Gai accommdation is basic, but the atmosphere of the town has a certain charm. Bai Chay has a bigger choice, most along Ha Long Avenue and Vuon Dao, but quality is variable (many of the seedier hotels double up as massage parlours). Most hotels can arrange boats for hire.

### Hong Gai

**Hien Cat** 252 Ben Tau ☎033/827417. Welcoming guesthouse, conveniently located right by the ferry pier, and with the most scenic bathrooms in Ha Long City. ❷

### Bai Chay

**Hoa Binh** 39 Vuon Dao ☎033/846009. This friendly family-run place is one of the better mini-hotels on Vuon Dao, with some of its bright rooms affording spectacular sea views. ❷

**Huyen Long** Ho Xuan Huong ☎033/845777. Family-run mini-hotel close to Minh Tuan with reasonably priced, clean rooms and friendly service. ❷

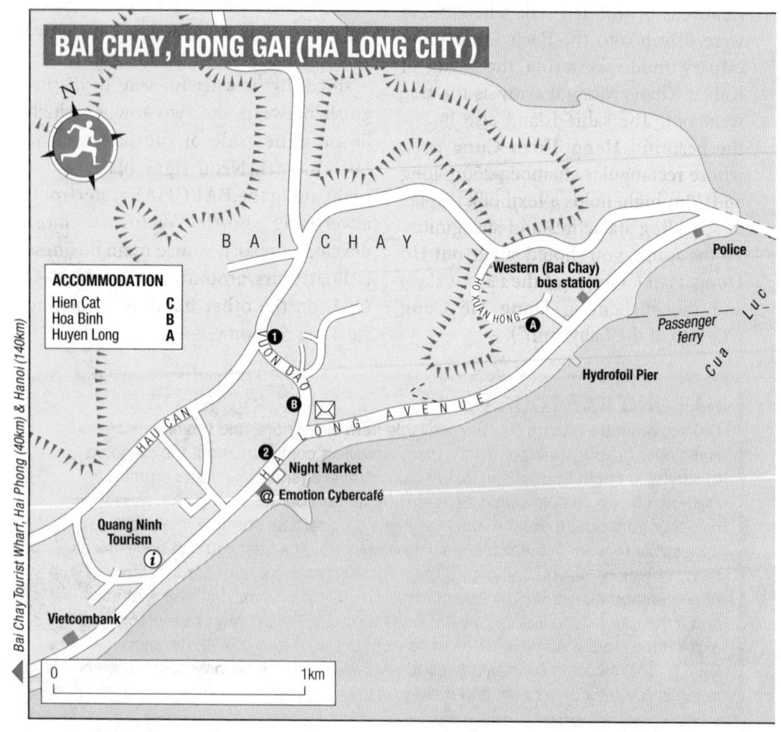

## Eating

The restaurants on Ha Long Avenue in Bai Chay tend to cater for tour groups. In Hong Gai the best food is at the market stalls.

**Quang Vinh** 24 Vuon Dao. Serves decent, cheap Vietnamese and Western food; the German-speaking owner can help with boat tours. Mains 20–35,000VND.

**Thuy Hien** Ha Long Avenue. Fresh seafood, noodle and rice dishes at reasonable prices; popular with tour groups. Mains 20–45,000VND.

## Directory

**Bank** Bai Chay's Vietcombank on Ha Long Avenue can change cash and traveller's cheques, and also has ATMs both here and opposite Hong Gai post office.

**Internet** At the Emotion Cybercafé on Ha Long Avenue in Bai Chay, and at the post office.

**Pharmacy** In Bai Chay at 59 Vuon Dao.

**Post office** Bai Chay Post Office: Ha Long Road at the junction with Vuon Dao; Hong Gai Post Office: Le Thanh Tong at the junction with Tran Nhat.

## Moving on

**By bus** Buses to Hanoi and Hai Phong depart from the western bus station; you can also flag down buses during the day on Ha Long Avenue around the main post office or at the junction of Ha Long Avenue and Cai Lau Road (around 35,000VND for an a/c bus to Hanoi, negotiate direct with the driver). Tour buses to Hanoi leave from Bai Chay's Tourist Wharf, between noon and 1pm. Buses for Mong Cai and the north use the Hong Gai bus station.

**Destinations:** Hai Phong (2hr); Hanoi (3hr); Lang Son (5hr); Mong Cai (3hr 30min).

**By boat** There are no direct public ferries to Cat Ba Island, but you can hop on one of the tourist boats (100,000VND), which will include a five-hour cruise to Cat Ba through the bay, a glut of which depart at about 11am every morning from the Tourist Wharf. Ferries and hydrofoils for Hai Phong depart from the Ben Tau Pier beside the market in Hong



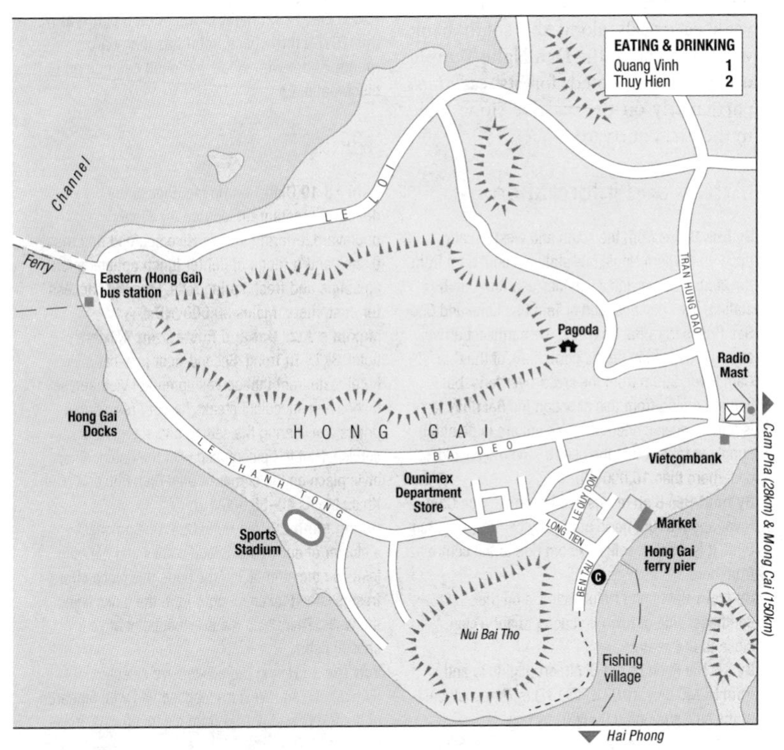

Gai. Hydrofoil services to Mong Cai depart from the hydrofoil jetty near Bai Chay bus station.
**Destinations:** Hai Phong (hydrofoil, 1 daily, 1hr; ferries 3 daily, 3hr); Mong Cai (2 daily; 3hr).

## HAI PHONG

Located 100km east of Hanoi, **HAI PHONG** is north Vietnam's principal port – a small, orderly city of broad avenues and subtle, cosmopolitan charms, with good hydrofoil and ferry links to Cat Ba Island, Mong Cai and Hong Gai (for Ha Long Bay), but not much else of interest.

The city's crescent-shaped nineteenth-century core lies between the curve of the Tam Bac River and the loop of the train tracks. To the north of the main artery, **Dien Bien Phu**, you'll find broad avenues and colonial architecture. To the south is the merchants' quarter, these days a dilapidated area of street markets between Tran Trinh Street and the market, Cho Sat; immediately below here is Tam Bac Lake. A ten-minute walk eastwards along the south bank will bring you to the **Den Nghe Temple on** Me Linh, noted for its carvings, particularly on the massive stone table in the first courtyard.

### Arrival and information

**By bus** Buses from the south and west usually pitch up at Niem Nghia bus station, about 3km from the centre. Some Hanoi services use Tam Bac bus station, near the west end of Tam Bac Lake and Cho Sat. Buses from Bai Chay and the northeast arrive at Binh bus station on the north bank of the Cua Cam River, 300m from the cross-river ferry, but if you're coming from this direction the Bai Chay ferry is a more scenic alternative. Xe om are in plentiful supply to take you to the centre – no trip should cost more than 10,000VND.
**By boat** Ben Binh ferry station is on the Cua Cam River about 500m north of the city centre along Ben Binh. It is a short walk or xe om ride to the centre from here.
**By train** Hai Phong train station is on the southeast side of town on Luong Khanh Thien, close to the centre.
**By air** Hai Phong's Cat Bi Airport (flights to and from HCMC only; Ⓣ031/921137) is 7km southeast of the city, around 60,000VND by taxi.
**Tourist information** Vietnamtourism, 15 Le Dai Hanh (Ⓣ031/822516, Ⓔvntourism.hp@bdvn.vnmail.vnd.net), has information about tours, car rental and air tickets.

### Accommodation

Budget accommodation is in short supply in Hai Phong.
**Hotel du Commerce** 62 Dien Bien Phu Ⓣ031/842790. A once grand French colonial-style hotel now offering shabby, cheap rooms and acceptable mid-range doubles with high ceilings and slatted shutters. ❸–❹
**Maxim's** 3k Ly Tu Trong Ⓣ031/746450, Ⓔmaximhotelvn@yahoo.com. Tasteful new mini-hotel offering well-equipped, clean rooms, free Internet access and an excellent jazz restaurant on the second floor (see below). ❸–❺
**Monaco** 103 Dien Bien Phu Ⓣ031/746468, Ⓔmonacohotel@hn.vnn.vn. This fine hotel outshines the competition in Hai Phong by some way, with a warped Egyptian theme and large, luxurious rooms. The VIP suites have full kitchen facilities, sitting room and separate single bedroom. ❺–❼
**Thanh Long** 75 Luong Khanh Thien Ⓣ031/3921282. Right in the station courtyard, this 1970s throwback hotel has dingy a/c rooms, some with wood-panelled ceilings and disco balls. ❷

### Eating

**Café 10** 10 Dinh Tien Hoang. Pleasantly decorated restaurant located on a leafy boulevard, offering inexpensive seafood and meat dishes and a range of lighter lunch options such as soups and fresh spring rolls. Free WiFi access for customers. Mains 30,000VND.
**Maxim's Jazz Bar and Restaurant** *Maxim's* hotel, 3k Ly Tu Trong. Second-floor jazz-bar style hotel restaurant that serves upmarket Vietnamese dishes and succulent steaks for very reasonable prices considering the setting and standard of service. (Not to be confused with the dated, diner-style place on the corner of Dien Bien Phu and Minh Khai.) Mains 40–55,000VND.
**Quang Minh** 26 Tran Hung Dao. One amongst a cluster of decent local food places and *bia hoi* joints on the strip facing the park, this place offers fresh seafood taken straight from the tanks lining the walls. There's no menu – just point at your chosen fish.
**Van Tue** 1a Hoang Dieu. Extensive selection of Vietnamese and Western food, served with tankards of home-brewed pilsner from gleaming vats, make

this bustling beer-hall style restaurant popular with locals, tourists and expats alike. Mains from 35,000VND.

## Directory

**Airline** Vietnam Airlines, 30 Tran Phu ☎031/921242.
**Banks** Various banks change currency and traveller's cheques: Techcombank, 16 Tran Hung Dao; VID Bank, 56 Dien Bien Phu. Vietcombank, 11 Hoang Dieu, can also arrange Visa and MasterCard cash advances and has an ATM.
**Hospital** Ben Vien Viet-Tiep, 1 Nha Thuong ☎031/700570.
**Internet** 133 Dien Bien Phu, or nearer to the train station at 36 Minh Khai.
**Pharmacy** 61 Dien Bien Phu.
**Supermarket** Intimex, 23 Minh Khai. Small but well stocked with Western dairy products, confectionary and dry goods.
**Post office** At the junction of Nguyen Tri Phuong and Hoang Van Thu, with a smaller office at 36 Quang Trung.

## Moving on

**By bus** Hanoi-bound minibuses hang around the ferry station and Tam Bac bus station, where you'll also find public buses to Hanoi; it's also possible to flag down the Hanoi bus on the riverfront. All other buses to the south and west depart from Niem Nghia bus station, whilst northeast and Bai Chay buses depart from Binh station.
**Destinations:** Bai Chay (2hr); Hanoi (2hr); Ninh Binh (3hr).
**By boat** The main ticket office for ferries is at the front of the ferry terminal, while hydrofoil tickets can be purchased from four different boat companies on Ben Binh. At the train station, next to the train ticket counters, there's a desk where you can buy ferry tickets for Cat Ba Island, Bai Chay and Mong Cai.
**Destinations:** Bai Chay (Ha Long City; hydrofoils 1 daily, 1hr; ferries 3 daily, 3hr); Cat Ba Island (hydrofoils 3–6 daily, 45min–1hr; ferries 2 daily, 2hr 30min); Hong Gai (Ha Long City; ferries 2 daily; 2hr); Mong Cai (1 daily; 4hr).
**By train** Hanoi (2 daily; 2hr 15min); Long Bien (3 daily; 2hr 30min)
**By air** There are 2 daily flights to HCMC (2hr).

# CAT BA ISLAND

Dragon-back mountain ranges mass on the horizon 20km out of Hai Phong as boats approach **Cat Ba Island**, the largest member of an archipelago sitting on the west of Ha Long Bay.

## What to see and do

The island's main settlement is Cat Ba Town, from where it's 30km across a landscape of forested peaks or along the coast to tiny Phu Long village.

**Cat Ba Town** consists of a much depleted original fishing village and

### INTO CHINA: MONG CAI

**Hydrofoils** from Ha Long City and Hai Phong go to **Mong Cai**, the border town for China. They land 16km outside town: complimentary shuttle bus brings you to the centre. **Buses** from Hanoi (9hr; 75,000VND) arrive at Mong Cai bus station, 500m west of the centre. The blue, space-age building northwest of the roundabout identifies Mong Cai's focal point, the covered market. The **Chinese border** is just 1km away: walk north along Tran Phu and turn left at the end of the road to reach the border gate (daily: summer 7am–4.30pm; winter 7.30am–4pm; visas must be arranged in advance). Once in Dongxing on the Chinese side, take a xe om to the bus station, from where regular buses depart for Nanning and Guilin.

For somewhere to stay in Mong Cai, try the *Tuan Thanh* mini-hotel, near the post office at 4 Nguyen Du (☎033/881481; ❷), with clean, comfortable rooms, some with balconies, and English-speaking staff. Streets near the market turn into open-air food stalls in the evening. Vietcombank has a branch with a 24hr ATM north of the market, on Van Don.

**Arriving in Mong Cai**, hydrofoil tickets to Bai Chay (2 daily; 3hr including shuttle bus; $6) can be purchased from the Mui Ngoc office at 1 Tran Phu (☎033/883988); tickets for Hai Phong (1 daily; 4hr including shuttle bus; $15) are available from the Greenlines office, 43 Tran Phu (☎033/881214).

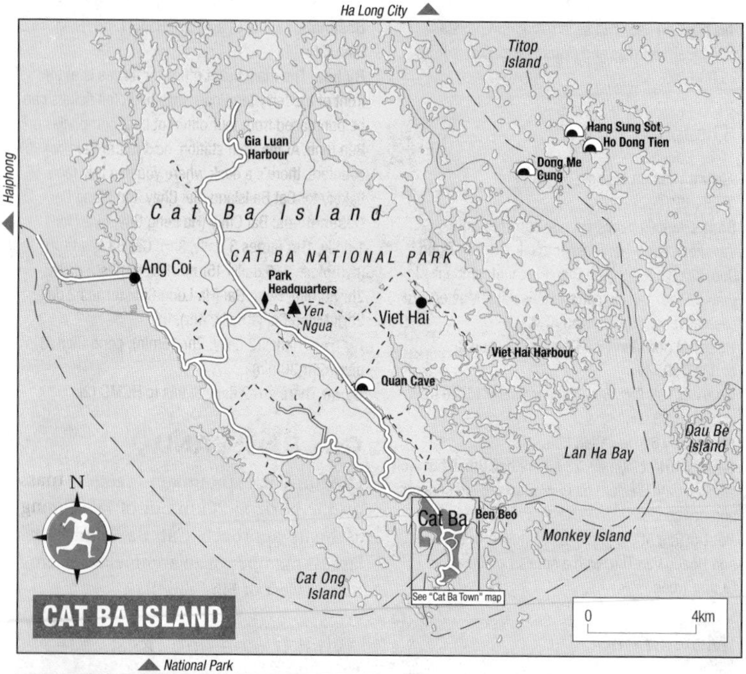

## CAT BA ISLAND

Ha Long City
Haiphong
Titop Island
Hang Sung Sot
Ho Dong Tien
Dong Me Cung
Gia Luan Harbour
Cat Ba Island
CAT BA NATIONAL PARK
Ang Coi
Park Headquarters
Yen Ngua
Viet Hai
Viet Hai Harbour
Quan Cave
Dau Be Island
Lan Ha Bay
Cat Ba
Ben Beo
Monkey Island
Cat Ong Island
See "Cat Ba Town" map
0 4km
N

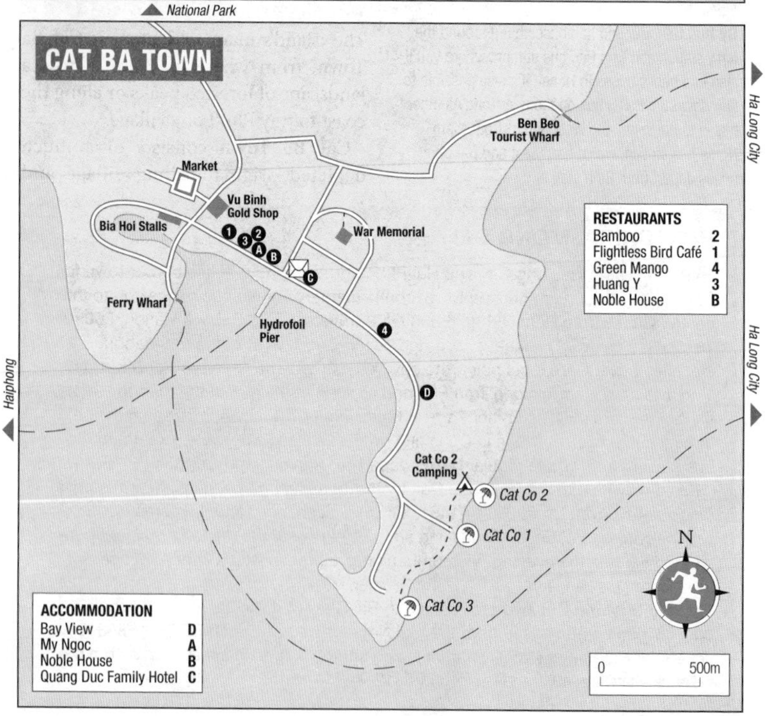

## CAT BA TOWN

National Park
Ha Long City
Haiphong
Ben Beo Tourist Wharf
Market
Vu Binh Gold Shop
Bia Hoi Stalls
War Memorial
Ferry Wharf
Hydrofoil Pier
Cat Co 2 Camping
Cat Co 2
Cat Co 1
Cat Co 3
0 500m
N

| RESTAURANTS | |
|---|---|
| Bamboo | 2 |
| Flightless Bird Café | 1 |
| Green Mango | 4 |
| Huang Y | 3 |
| Noble House | B |

| ACCOMMODATION | |
|---|---|
| Bay View | D |
| My Ngoc | A |
| Noble House | B |
| Quang Duc Family Hotel | C |

market and, 800m to the east across a small headland, the main ferry pier, Ben Ca. A steep road just east of the waterfront leads to a small, sandy **beach, Cat Co 1**; from here, a ten-minute walk further along a cliff-hugging boardwalk leads you to a second, quieter and more secluded beach, **Cat Co 2**, where it is also possible to overnight (see p.992). A third beach, **Cat Co 3**, is located over the headland to the right of Cat Co 1. All three have beach facilities, including toilets, sun-loungers and lockers, as well as restaurants selling snacks and drinks.

In 1986, almost half the island and adjacent waters were declared a **national park** (entrance fee 15,000VND), the entrance to which is 19km along the road from Cat Ba Town. It's worth hiring an experienced and English-speaking guide to explore the park (around $5–7 for up to one day), as people have got seriously lost on the unmarked paths. You'll need good boots, lots of water, mosquito repellent and a compass. The going can be quite tough, and trekking should be avoided after heavy rains, when the paths can be slippery and treacherous.

## Arrival and island transport

**By boat** Tourist boats drop you at the Gia Luan pier, a 30min bus or xe om ride to town. The hydrofoil from Hai Phong docks either at the pier in the centre of Cat Ba Town, or at Ang Coi pier at the island's western point, from where a bus will take you to Cat Ba Town.

**Island transport** Two buses per day ply the route between Cat Ba Town and the Cat Hai Island ferry terminal in Phu Long village (45min; 20,000VND), but the best way to get around is by xe om or by renting a motorbike from one of the hotels.

## Tours and activities

**Tours and treks** Most Cat Ba hotels can help arrange boat tours and treks in the national park. The most popular option is a full-day trip with a trek through the national park, lunch in a village, and a boat trip back to Cat Ba town via Lan Ha Bay, with a swimming stop and a visit to a pearl farm. Cat Ba Tourism Information Centre (Ⓣ0313/688285) along the main waterfront offers impartial advice on available tours and transport options in the area, and Hanoi's Handspan travel company has a representative at *Giang Son Hotel* (Ⓣ031/888214), on the waterfront, offering a trek/boat trip package for $12 per person. A half-day boat trip into Lan Ha Bay with snorkelling, swimming and pearl farm visit costs around $8. Other boat trips venture up into Ha Long Bay itself, or to one of the bay's more dramatic caves, Ho Ba Ham.

**Sea kayaking** Some shops and hotels near the seafront can rent out two-person sea kayaks ($6 per day) for self-powered paddling around the bay.

**Climbing** Cat Ba Island and the surrounding limestone outcrops have become internationally renowned sites for amateur and professional climbers. Slo Pony Adventures, Noble House Mezzanine (222), Ⓣ0913760025, Ⓦwww.slopony.com) is run by two experienced American climbers, who have developed an extensive network of rock climbing routes and bouldering sites in the area suitable for all skill levels. They can also incorporate boat trips (necessary to access some of the climbing sites), kayaking, trekking, camping and the occasional beach party into their highly recommended, tailor-made packages.

## Accommodation

The summer months can get very busy with domestic tourists, so it's best to book in advance. In low season, most hotels offer a 40–50 percent discount. The main waterfront strip, where almost all budget accommodation is, is known by several names, but a new numbering system has been introduced (given in brackets below).

### Hostels and hotels

**Bay View** (246) Ⓣ031/3488241. Laid-back mini-hotel popular with rock climbers. Accommodation ranges from luxury doubles with sea views to bunk beds in the two eight-person dormitories. Free cooking lessons, regular communal dinners, and use of the kitchen facilities, lounge area and pool table have lured many travellers into staying much longer than intended. Dorm ❷; rooms ❹–❻

**My Ngoc** (212) Ⓣ031/388842. Perennially popular with young budget travellers, this friendly mini-hotel offers the cheapest rooms on Cat Ba. All are spacious and spotlessly clean, and most have sea views. There's also a decent seafood restaurant and a travel service offering very reasonably priced private boat tours. ❷; a/c $2 extra.

**Noble House** (222) ☎031/3888570; ⓔthenoblehousevn@yahoo.com. A member of Hostelling International, this welcoming place offers just six modest rooms, all with a balcony overlooking the bay. There's a ground-floor restaurant, and a busy 2nd-floor bar (see below). ❸–❹

**Quang Duc Family Hotel** ☎031/888231. Opposite the hydrofoil pier, this welcoming, family-run hotel with a helpful, English-speaking owner offers excellent value for money. The rooms are spacious and clean, and the front balconies have great views of the waterfront. ❷–❸

### Camping

**Cat Co 2** The family-run restaurant on Cat Co 2 has tents complete with mattresses for those who would like to overnight on the beach; check the weather forecast in advance though, as tropical monsoon storms in the midst of the night can quickly turn a romantic alfresco sleeping experience into a miserable nightmare. ❷–❸

**National Park** Slo Pony Adventures (see p.991) can recommend sites around the National Park where camping is permitted, though you'll need your own camping gear.

## Eating

At night, you'll find a cluster of neon-lit *bia hoi* stands at the western end of the strip – an atmospheric place for a snack and a cheap beer (2000VND per glass).

**Bamboo** (199). Delicious, reasonably priced fresh seafood dishes (25–50,000VND).

**Flightless Bird Café** (189) Kiwi-run bar serving a good range of international drinks and cheap local spirits. There's a small book exchange, darts and a pool table.

**Huang Y** (195). This busy restaurant enjoys a well-deserved reputation for its excellent crab spring rolls, grilled shrimp with lemon and garlic, and fried whole fish with tomato, lemon and ginger. Mains 30–60,000VND.

**Noble House** (222).The popular restaurant doles out very average Western food, but the streetside tables and 2nd-floor bar with pool table, board games, table football and a decent cocktail list make it a great place to hang out with other travellers in the evenings. Mains 40,000VND.

## Directory

**Banks and exchange** There's no bank or ATM on Cat Ba Island, so it's best to change money before arrival. Hotels and restaurants will change money, but cash only and at poor rates. *The Flightless Bird Café* (see above) can change cash and traveller's cheques, and Vu Binh Jewellers opposite the market can do cash advances on credit card for a 5 percent commission.

**Internet** Access on the island is slow and pricey. Try the *Nam Phuong Hotel* at number 188.

**Post office** On the waterfront next to the *Noble House* (daily 7am–10pm); has IDD phones.

## Moving on

**By boat** Tickets for hydrofoils to Hai Phong (with onward bus connections to Hanoi also available) can be bought from the Hoang Long ticket office (☎031/3887224) or the Cat Ba Tourism Information Centre (☎0313/688285) along the main waterfront. Alternatively, you could try and catch a tourist boat to Bai Chay (Ha Long City), departing around 8am from Ben Bao (4hr; 100,000VND).

**Destinations:** Hai Phong (6 daily in high season, 4 daily in low season; 2hr 30min); boat and bus to Hanoi (5 daily; 4hr).

# The far north

Vietnam fans out above Hanoi, the majority of it a mountainous zone wrapped around the Red River Delta. The region is mostly wild and inaccessible, sparsely populated by a fascinating mosaic of **ethnic minorities**, whose presence is the chief tourist attraction for the area. The hill station of **Sa Pa** is the main departure point for treks to minority villages. **Mai Chau**

**TREAT YOURSELF**

**Green Mango** Trendy upmarket restaurant serving deliciously innovative Western and Asian dishes – try the imported "Oz sesame tuna" or home-smoked duck. In the evenings, there's relaxed music and soft couches to lounge on whilst enjoying a happy hour cocktail from their imaginative drinks list. Mains 70–200,000VND.

and **Bac Ha** are less-visited centres, but attract travellers seeking an alternative to the well-worn tourist trail, while the **northwestern circuit** is a difficult but rewarding trip that takes you far off the beaten track.

## LAO CAI

Follow the Red River Valley northwest from Hanoi and after 300km, pushing ever deeper into the mountains, you eventually reach the border town of **LAO CAI**, of little interest in itself except as the **railhead for Sa Pa** and as the place to catch the bus **into China** for travellers heading to Kunming.

Most people arrive on the night train from Hanoi; the **train station** is on the east bank of the Red River, just 3km due south of the Chinese border. Several travel agents and hotels hook their own a/c, soft-berth carriages up to the three nightly trains between Hanoi and Lao Cai ($16/berth). Vietnam Railways' (VR) carriages are almost as good; buy your tickets (hard a/c sleeper $8–10, soft a/c sleeper $10–15) in Hanoi, purchasing the return ticket at Sa Pa's VR office, or the train station in Lao Cai. The four-berth soft sleeper carriages are very comfortable for an overnight trip.

Tourist buses **to Sa Pa** (1hr; 30,000VND) meet the morning Hanoi trains, as do minibuses (25,000VND), which also depart regularly for Sa Pa from the bus station. If you've booked a room in Sa Pa, your hotel may include a pick-up. Otherwise, your options are to take a jeep or a xe om ($4–6 per person).

There's no need to stay in Lao Cai, but if you wish to, try *Hiep Van*, 342 Nguyen Hue, opposite the train station (Ⓣ020/835470; ❷ including breakfast), which has clean, spacious rooms. The road outside the train station is lined with food stalls and **restaurants**: *Nhat Linh* and *Thai Du* are good. Alternatively, try *Than Son Restaurant* five minutes' walk away at 346 Nguen Hue, which can also assist with onward travel to Sa Pa and Kunming in China.

## SA PA AND AROUND

Forty kilometres from Lao Cai, the small market town of **SA PA** perches dramatically on the western edge of a high plateau, overshadowed by the imposing **Fan Xi Pan**, Vietnam's highest peak. A former hilltop retreat for French rulers, Sa Pa enjoys a refreshing climate set in magnificent scenery, with plenty of walks out to **minority villages** of Hmong, Dao and Giay peoples. Accommodation and restaurants get rather overrun at weekends throughout the year as tour groups head in; if you have the chance to visit during the week, you'll find Sa Pa a lot quieter and more interesting.

### INTO CHINA: LAO CAI

The border crossing from Lao Cai into China is via the **Hekou border gate** (daily 7am–5pm), on the east bank of the Red River. Queues at immigration are longest in the early morning. Inside the Vietnamese border post building, there's an exchange desk that deals in dong, dollars and yuan, but not traveller's cheques. There's a bank across the street, and plenty of women hanging around who are eager to change cash. Travellers **entering Vietnam** at Lao Cai may have to pay a small "fee" for paperwork. Across on the Chinese side, several high-quality a/c buses depart for **Kunming**, 520km away, from Hekou bus station, 100m from the border crossing (four in the morning, five sleeper services in the evening; 12hr; $10). Visas for both countries must be arranged in advance.

## What to see and do

In a move to protect Sa Pa's vulnerable minority areas, tourists are only allowed to visit the area around Sa Pa (including Ta Phin, Hoang Lien valley and Fan Xi Pan) with a **permit and guide**; some villages are out of bounds altogether. Cat Cat village and waterfall can be explored without a guide but you still need a permit. Permits are free of charge and can be arranged quickly by licensed tour agents (see p.996).

### Weekend market

Sa Pa itself is ethnically Vietnamese, but the **weekend market**, which runs from noon on Saturday to noon on Sunday, draws in minority villagers from all around and has become a major tourist attraction, not least for the chance to see minority women clad in their colourful finery. In peak season, however, tourists can outnumber locals and some visitors may find the market slightly disappointing – a day-trip to one of the outlying markets in Can Cau

### ETHNIC MINORITY VILLAGES

Historically, all the peoples of northern Vietnam migrated from southern China at various times throughout history: those who arrived first, notably the Tay and Thai, settled in the fertile valleys, where they now lead a relatively prosperous existence, whereas late arrivals, such as groups of Hmong and Dao, were left to eke out a living on the inhospitable higher slopes. Around five million minority people (nearly two-thirds of Vietnam's total minority population) now live in the northern uplands, mostly in isolated villages. The largest ethnic groups are **Thai** and **Muong** in the northwest, **Tay** and **Nung** in the northeast, and **Hmong** and **Dao** dispersed throughout the region. Despite government efforts to integrate them into the Vietnamese community, many of the minorities in these remote areas continue to follow a way of life little changed over the centuries.

#### Visiting minority villages

A popular, hassle-free way of visiting the minority villages in the north is to join an **organized trip** from a Hanoi tour agency, whose usual destinations are Sa Pa for the weekly market (4 days; from $25 per person), and Mai Chau (2 days; from $25). The standard package includes guided walks to at least two different minority villages – with Sa Pa tours, the Sunday market at Bac Ha is included – and in the case of Mai Chau, a night in a stilthouse. You'll need strong boots or training shoes, socks and long trousers (against thorns and leeches), a hat, sunblock and warm clothing; take plenty of water. You might also want a sleeping bag, mosquito net and food – though these may be provided.

Otherwise, you could try and arrange an individual programme through a Hanoi tour agent or guesthouses in Sa Pa.

#### Etiquette

There's a whole debate about the **ethics of cultural tourism** and its negative impact on traditional ways of life. Most villagers are genuinely welcoming, appreciating contact with Westerners and the material benefits which they bring. Nonetheless, it's important to take a responsible attitude, and try not to cause offence. It's preferable to visit the minority villages as part of a **small group**, ideally four people or fewer, as this causes least disruption and allows for greater communication. Dress modestly (no shorts or vests), never take photographs without asking and only enter a house when invited, removing your shoes first. Small gifts, such as fresh fruit, are always welcome. However, there is a view that even this can foster begging, and that you should only ever give in return for some service or hospitality. A compromise is to buy craftwork produced by the villagers. Take litter back to the towns.

(Saturdays) and Bac Ha (Sundays) is often better (see p.997).

### Cat Cat village

**CAT CAT** village, a huddle of wooden houses hidden among fruit trees and bamboo, is a three-kilometre walk from town (5000VND entrance fee). Follow the track west from the market square, past the steeple-shaped building, then turn left onto a path that drops steeply down to the river. The hike itself offers spectacular vistas over the valley's terraced rice paddies. Look out for tubs of indigo dye outside the houses, used to colour the hemp cloth typical of Hmong dress. **Cat Cat waterfall** is just below the village.

### Ta Van and Lao Chai

With a guide, several more ethnic minority villages in the area can be visited. One of the most enjoyable guided treks is along the newly resurfaced road from the *Auberge* south down the Muong Hoa valley for 12km to a wooden suspension bridge and **TA VAN** village, on the opposite side of the river. Ta Van actually consists of two villages: immediately across the bridge is a Giay community, while further uphill to the left is a Dao village. From here, it's possible to walk back towards Sa Pa on the west side of the river, as far as another Hmong village, **LAO CHAI**, before rejoining the main track.

### Fan Xi Pan

Rising dramatically above the rest of the Hoang Lien Son mountain range and lording over Sa Pa is **Mount Fan Xi Pan**, Vietnam's highest peak at 3143m. The mountain lies within Hoang Lien Son Nature Reserve, a thirty-square-kilometre national park established in 1986 to protect the forest habitat southwest of Sa Pa. It

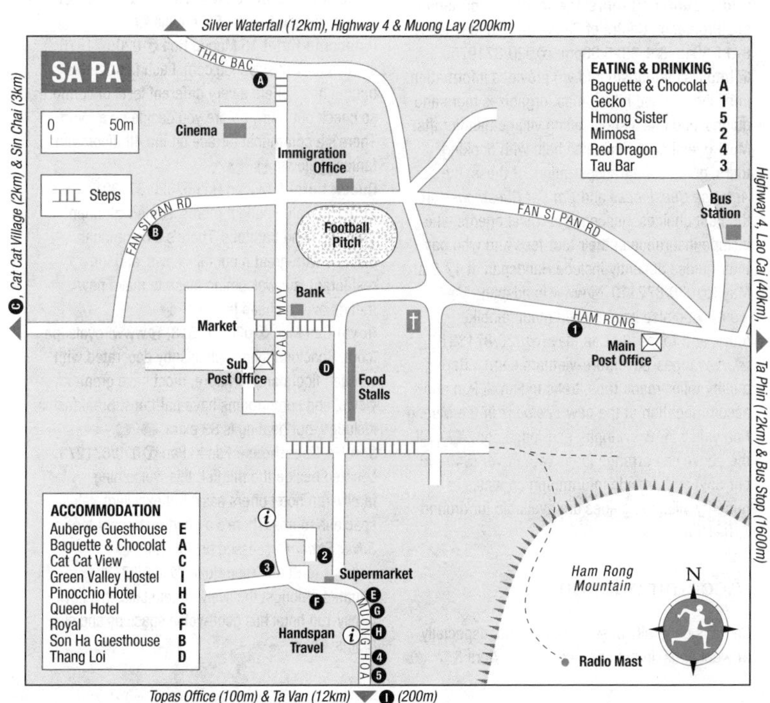

takes three to five days to tackle the mountain, a challenging climb to the summit (19km from Sa Pa) – climbers often have to turn back due to perilous weather conditions. However, the view from the summit on a clear day rewards those who make it to the top, taking in the whole mountain range of northwest Vietnam, south to Son La province, and north to the peaks of Yunnan in China. There are no facilities as yet on the mountain, so you will need to bring your own sleeping bag, tent and food supplies. A local guide is strongly recommended; organized group excursions with all necessary equipment can be arranged by most hotels and travel agencies in Sa Pa (about $60 per person).

## Arrival, information and tours

**By bus** The bus from Lao Cai (connecting from the Hanoi train) drops you at various hotels or along the main street, Cau May.

**Information and tours** The Tourism Information and Promotion Centre of Sa Pa, 28 Cau May (daily 8–11.30am & 1.30–5.30pm; ⓣ020/871975, ⓦhttp://sapatourism.info.vn) provides information, publishes a good hiking map, organizes tours and guides, and has a shop selling village handicrafts. Most guesthouses can also help with booking tours, guides and transportation; of these, the *Auberge Guesthouse* and *Cat Cat Guesthouse* are the best choices. Responsible travel agents who include insurance in their tour fees and who pay their guides decently include Handspan at 17 Cau May (ⓣ020/872110, ⓦwww.handspan.com), who also have guided mountainbike tours, and Topas, 20 Cau May (ⓣ020/871331, ⓦwww.topas-adventure-vietnam.com), offering quality tailor-made trips, treks to Fan Si Pan and accommodation at the new *Ecolodge* in the Muong Hoa valley (ⓦwww.topas-eco-lodge.com; ❾). All the above can arrange jeeps with driver ($45–60 per day) and provide information on walks to minority villages; guides are available for around $10–15 per day.

## Accommodation

Sa Pa is generally busy all year round, especially at weekends. In high season (March, April & Sept–Nov) and at weekends, rooms can be in short supply.

**Auberge Guesthouse** 7 Muong Hoa ⓣ020/871243, ⓦwww.sapanowadays.com. The rooms set around a pleasant central courtyard in this popular hotel are a little worn for the price, but there are good views from the higher rooms, recommended tours and decent food. Breakfast and Internet access included. ❹–❻

**Baguette & Chocolat** Thac Bac ⓣ020/871766, ⓦwww.hoasuaschool.com. Up the steps at the top end of Cau May, the small guesthouse above the popular training restaurant (see below) has just four elegant guest rooms with a delicious bakery breakfast included. ❹

**Cat Cat View** 46 Fan Xi Pan ⓣ020/871946, ⓦwww.catcathotel.com. A popular terraced guesthouse just below the market, boasting budget and mid-range rooms with fireplaces and panoramic views of Fan Xi Pan from the spacious balconies. There's now a lift for the top floors and the decent restaurant. ❷–❻

**Green Valley Hostel** 45 Muong Hoa ⓣ020/871449, ⓔsapawelcomes@vnn.vn. Hostelling International member offering decent dorm and private accommodation with stunning views of the valley below. Breakfast and Internet access included. Dorm ❶; double ❷

**Pinocchio Hotel** 15 Muong Hoa ⓣ020/871876, ⓔquysapa1978@yahoo.com. Each floor in this budget hotel offers a very different level of comfort, so check out a few before you decide on a room. There's a communal terrace on the 4th floor with fantastic views. ❷–❸

**Queen Hotel** 9 Muong Hoa ⓣ020/871301. Excellent-value budget rooms, some with open fireplaces and bathtubs. There's a communal balcony with great mountain views, and the restaurant is a welcoming place to make new friends over a cheap beer. ❷–❸

**Royal** Cau May ⓣ020/871313, ⓦwww.royalsapa.com. Spacious rooms, pleasantly decorated with wooden floors and furniture; most have great views, and some rooms have bathtubs. Breakfast is included, but heating is $3 extra. ❸–❺

**Son Ha Guesthouse** Fan Xi Pan ⓣ020/871273. Located beside the market, this welcoming family-run hotel offers basic but excellent-value, spacious rooms. There's a good restaurant too, *Silver Stream*, accessed on Tue Tinh. ❷

**Thang Loi** Pham Xuan Huan ⓣ020/871331. Situated amongst the lively street stalls, this new family-run hotel has good-value spacious and clean rooms. ❷

## Eating and drinking

**Baguette & Chocolat** Thac Bac. For delicious bakery snacks and decent sandwiches, pizza and Vietnamese favourites, look no further than this cosy branch of the Hanoian Hoa Sua training school for disadvantaged youth. They also sell lunch packets for gourmet hikers. Mains 40,000VND.

**Gecko** Ham Rong. Upmarket restaurant with street-side terraced seating, serving excellent French and Vietnamese food. Set menus from 100,000VND.

**Hmong Sister** 31 Muong Hoa. Newly established, cosy little bar with plenty of board games to while away the evening.

**Mimosa** Off Cau May. Set in a small garden villa and serving great-value, tasty Vietnamese and European dishes that are hard to beat; there's a decent selection of vegetarian options too. Mains 15–35,000VND.

**Red Dragon** 23 Muong Hoa. British-run pub, where you can wash down your shepherd's pie with a pint. The downstairs tearoom is a pleasant place for Vietnamese dishes and a selection of English favourites such as bangers and mash or roast beef with all the trimmings. Mains 40–60,000VND; three-course set menu 75,000VND.

**Tau Bar** Beneath the Hoang Mai Hotel on Cau May. Popular hangout in the evenings, where Hmong girls practise their pool skills most nights and challenge unsuspecting travellers to a game.

## Directory

**Bank** There is an Agribank at 1 Cau May (though the ATM only accepts Vietnamese bank cards); it is possible to advance cash on Visa for an additional 3 percent commission. Some hotels and guesthouses can also change money, and the *Auberge* can arrange cash advances against Visa and MasterCard, but rates are better in Hanoi.

**Internet** Below the *Auberge* and several outlets along Cau May.

**Pharmacies** Several on Cau May.

**Motorbike rental** At several shops near the *Auberge Guesthouse* ($5–8 per day). Keep in mind that road conditions are treacherous around Sa Pa, landslides are common and fog can make visibility extremely poor. Alcohol-induced accidents are also common, so drive with caution and always wear a helmet.

## Moving on

**By bus and train** Local buses to Lao Cai leave all day from near the church on the main square, and will tout for business up and down Cau May. The Lao Cai Railway Station Office at 24 Cau May (daily 7.30–11am & 1.30–4pm; ⓣ020/871480) is the main ticket office for buses and trains; tourist buses for Lao Cai station depart from here at 7.30am, 4.30pm and 6.30pm (30,000VND; 1hr). Tickets for the night trains are in short supply at Lao Cai station, so book as far ahead as possible in Sa Pa, either at the Lao Cai Railway Station Office, or (more expensively) through your guesthouse. Guesthouses can also organize jeeps back to Lao Cai for $10 per vehicle, and arrange motorbike taxis.

# BAC HA AND AROUND

The small town of **BAC HA**, nestling in a high valley 40km northeast of Highway 7, makes a long but popular day excursion from Sa Pa, especially on Sunday for the lively and colourful local market. The town is much less touristy than Sa Pa and worth lingering in, if you have time.

## What to see and do

Recently Bac Ha has attempted to emulate Sa Pa's success by developing its own trekking business to minority villages and nearby rural markets. Regulations for permits and guides are not as stringent here as in Sa Pa, but permits are required for overnight stays in minority villages; these are free and can be organized by your guide or through your hotel.

Bac Ha's own **Sunday market** (8am–2pm) sees villagers of the Tay, Dao, Nung, Giay and Flower Hmong ethnic minorities – and day-trippers from Sa Pa – converging on the town, transforming the otherwise rather drab centre into a mass of colour and activity. Everything – from haircuts to suits, vats of rice wine and corn liquor to bundles of incense, and of course the usual vegetables, meat and dried fish – is on sale. The stunningly adorned Flower Hmong women trade embroidery, cloth and silver, and there's a large livestock fair to the rear of the market. Hotels in Sa Pa can organize a long day-trip to the Sunday market for about $10 per person.

## Ban Pho and Can Cau villages

The picturesque Hmong hamlet of **BAN PHO**, 3km from town, makes a pleasant stroll. Take the road half left at the hammer and sickle sign and head down past the *Sao Mai Hotel*, turning left immediately after the next big building, which is the local hospital. The road continues up the hill for 2km after the village, and affords good views of the valley.

The village of **CAN CAU**, 18km north of Bac Ha, hosts a market each Saturday, which is well worth visiting. The emphasis is on livestock, especially buffalo, with traders trekking in from as far afield as China in search of bargains. Relatively few visitors get here, and the fair retains much of its authenticity. You can book a day-trip to Can Cau in Sa Pa for about $12 per person, or slightly cheaper from hotels in Bac Ha.

### Arrival

**By bus** Local buses terminate at Bac Ha's bus station, near the market's south entrance in the centre of town. If you are coming direct from Hanoi, get off the bus or train at Pho Lu, from where there are two buses a day to Bac Ha (5.30am & 6.30am; 1hr 20min; 20,000VND) from the bus station on the highway, just across from the train station. Minibuses depart from outside Lao Cai train station (6.30am & 1pm; 2hr; 30,000VND). From Sa Pa, it's easier and quicker to join a tour ($10), which will include the market and a short trek, with the option of being dropped off at Lao Cai on the way back. A motorbike from Sa Pa takes three hours and costs about $15, from Lao Cai $10.

### Accommodation

The town's hotels and restaurants are clustered around the square near the post office. Places to stay are basic, and prices are usually about 20 percent lower during the week.

**Dang Khoa** On the main street near the post office ⓣ020/880290. Mini-hotel offering clean, bright rooms with balcony. ❷–❸

**Hoang Vu Hotel** ⓣ020/880264. Basic but friendly hotel with ten en-suite rooms. To find it, go past the post office on your right along the main street and walk up the hill until you come to a road leading left at a hammer and sickle sign – the hotel is immediately on your left. The owners can arrange tours and transport. ❷

**Sao Mai Hotel** At the end of the road past Hoang Vu ⓣ020/880288, ⓦwww.saomaibacha.com. Imposing hotel frequented by tour groups, with somewhat overpriced rooms in a new wooden stilt-house block, or cheaper, smaller rooms in the old quarter. Breakfast included. ❻

### Eating

Many of the hotels in town double up as restaurants.

**Cong Fu Restaurant** Just off the main road along the same street as the bus station. This little restaurant is popular with the Sunday tourists and serves good, cheap rice and noodle dishes. 15–30,000VND.

**Sao Mai Hotel Restaurant** A more sophisticated menu than most places in town, serving decent European and Vietnamese dishes at reasonable prices. Mains 30–40,000VND.

**Tran Sin Hotel** Next to the market entrance. Popular place offering local specialities. 15–25,000VND.

### Moving on

**By bus** Buses for Pho Lu and Lao Cai depart from either the bus station or along the main street; departure times depend on the day so ask at one of the local hotels or restaurants. Tourist buses for Sa Pa depart from the main square outside the post office at around 2.30pm on Sundays, or you can take a xe om. Alternatively, take the bus to Lao Cai from where regular minibuses depart for Sa Pa.

## MAI CHAU

The minority villages of the fertile **Mai Chau Valley**, inhabited mainly by White Thai people, are close enough to Hanoi (150km) to make this a popular destination, particularly at weekends. The valley is still largely unspoilt, a peaceful scene of rice fields and jagged mountains. **MAI CHAU** is the valley's main village, a friendly, quiet place that suddenly bursts into life for its **Sunday market**, when minority people – who, unlike in Sa Pa, have largely forsaken their traditional dress – trek in. You can overnight in Mai Chau, but it's more interesting to head for the outlying villages.

### INTO LAOS: TAY TRANG

A new border crossing has opened at **Tay Trang** (8am–4pm), 31km from Dien Bien Phu. There are no tourist buses plying the route yet, but it is possible to catch a local bus from the bus station in Dien Bien Phu (Mon, Wed & Fri, 5.30am, 7hr) to the town of Muang Khoua on the Laotian side, from where you can catch a boat down the Nam Ou River to Muang Ngoi or Nong Khiaw. Several daily buses depart from Muang Khoua for elsewhere in the region; for onward travel to Louang Phabang, take a bus to Udom Xai and from there a bus to Louang Phabang. Lao visas are available on arrival for around $35, including "administration" fees.

The most accessible village in the Mai Chau Valley is **BAN LAC**, a White Thai settlement of seventy houses where you can buy hand-woven textiles, watch performances of traditional dancing and sleep overnight in a stilthouse; expect to pay around 50,000VND per person per night, plus around 20,000VND per meal. For a less touristy stilthouse village, head for pretty **POM COONG**, marooned on a small hill in a sea of rice paddies; several stilthouses here offer accommodation. **BAN VAN** village is less visited, hemmed in by the hills; the first house you see is the friendly *Ban Van Guesthouse* (Ⓣ018/867182; ❶).

Most people visit the Mai Chau Valley on an organized tour from Hanoi. Alternatively, take one of the regular public buses to Hoa Binh (2hr), from where several buses depart for Mai Chau (2hr). Tell the driver in advance that you are going to Mai Chau; you will be dropped at Tong Dau junction where xe om will take you into the centre for 15,000VND.

## THE NORTHWESTERN CIRCUIT

**Highway 6** loops around Vietnam's northwest, skimming the borders of Laos and China, and passing through some of the country's most dramatic landscapes. The journey from Hanoi typically passes through **Mai Chau**, **Moc Chau**, **Son La**, **Dien Bien Phu** and **Muong Lay** before finishing in Sa Pa or Lao Cai. Terraced rice paddies, tropical rainforests, stilthouse minority villages and markets bursting with colour make a journey around the northwestern circuit one of the most spectacular in Southeast Asia. However, there is a reason why the route attracts so few tourists: the bumpy, unpaved road swerves around hairpin bends, and landslides are common, causing serious delays even after a short spell of rain. Public transport takes the form of ancient minivans crowded to twice their capacity, so the best way to travel is by motorbike. You can then detour off Highway 6 and on to smaller backroads, with even more stunning scenery and many Hmong, Black and White Thai, Dao and Muong villages, where it is usually possible to overnight in a local house. It takes at least a week to make the journey, and ten days to do so comfortably. **Guided motorbike** and **mountain bike tours** of the region are offered by Sinh Balo (Ⓦwww.cyclingvietnam.net), and in Hanoi through agencies such as Offroad Vietnam (36 Nguyen Huu Huan; Ⓣ049/045049, Ⓦwww.offroadvietnam.com) for about $70 per day all inclusive. Guesthouses in Ninh Binh (see p.982) offer guides, motorbike rental and xe om with drivers for less.

# Travel store

Laos
Vietnam
Cambodia
Malaysia
Thailand
Japan
South Korea
Carefully Crafted Tours
SOUTH EAST ASIA
• Unique small group holidays
• Three & Four star hotels
• Informative, knowledgeable tour leaders
• Cultural Tours, Active Adventures
• Over 130 countries worldwide
• All tours are fully escorted
ADVENTURESABROAD
info@adventures-abroad.co.uk
www.smallgroup.travel
0114 247 3400
ABTA
W3508

www.roughguides.com

INTREPID

# NOTES

Small print and

# Index

## A Rough Guide to Rough Guides

Published in 1982, the first Rough Guide – to Greece – was a student scheme that became a publishing phenomenon. Mark Ellingham, a recent graduate in English from Bristol University, had been travelling in Greece the previous summer and couldn't find the right guidebook. With a small group of friends he wrote his own guide, combining a highly contemporary, journalistic style with a thoroughly practical approach to travellers' needs.

The immediate success of the book spawned a series that rapidly covered dozens of destinations. And, in addition to impecunious backpackers, Rough Guides soon acquired a much broader and older readership that relished the guides' wit and inquisitiveness as much as their enthusiastic, critical approach and value-for-money ethos.

These days, Rough Guides include recommendations from shoestring to luxury and cover more than 200 destinations around the globe, including almost every country in the Americas and Europe, more than half of Africa and most of Asia and Australasia. Our ever-growing team of authors and photographers is spread all over the world, particularly in Europe, the USA and Australia.

In the early 1990s, Rough Guides branched out of travel, with the publication of Rough Guides to World Music, Classical Music and the Internet. All three have become benchmark titles in their fields, spearheading the publication of a wide range of books under the Rough Guide name.

Including the travel series, Rough Guides now number more than 350 titles, covering phrasebooks, waterproof maps, music guides from Opera to Heavy Metal, reference works as diverse as Conspiracy Theories and Shakespeare, and popular culture books from iPods to Poker. Rough Guides also produce a series of more than 120 World Music CDs in partnership with World Music Network.

Visit www.roughguides.com to see our latest publications.

Rough Guide travel images are available for commercial licensing at www.roughguidespictures.com

## Rough Guide credits

**Text editors**: Alice Park, Edward Aves, Lucy White, Christina Valhouli
**Layout**: Ankur Guha
**Cartography**: Miles Irving
**Picture editor**: Mark Thomas
**Production**: Rebecca Short
**Proofreaders**: Stewart Wild, Susannah Wight
**Cover design**: Chloë Roberts
**Editorial**: **London** Ruth Blackmore, Alison Murchie, Andy Turner, Keith Drew, Jo Kirby, James Smart, Natasha Foges, Róisín Cameron, Emma Traynor, James Rice, Emma Gibbs, Kathryn Lane, Monica Woods, Mani Ramaswamy, Joe Staines, Peter Buckley, Matthew Milton, Tracy Hopkins, Ruth Tidball; **New York** Andrew Rosenberg, Steven Horak, AnneLise Sorensen, April Isaacs, Ella Steim, Anna Owens, Sean Mahoney, Paula Neudorf, Courtney Miller; **Delhi** Madhavi Singh, Karen D'Souza
**Design & Pictures**: **London** Scott Stickland, Dan May, Diana Jarvis, Nicole Newman, Sarah Cummins, Emily Taylor; **Delhi** Umesh Aggarwal, Ajay Verma, Jessica Subramanian, Pradeep Thapliyal, Sachin Tanwar, Anita Singh, Nikhil Agarwal
**Production**: Vicky Baldwin
**Cartography**: **London** Maxine Repath, Ed Wright, Katie Lloyd-Jones; **Delhi** Jai Prakash Mishra, Rajesh Chhibber, Ashutosh Bharti, Rajesh Mishra, Animesh Pathak, Jasbir Sandhu, Karobi Gogoi, Alakananda Bhattacharya, Swati Handoo, Deshpal Dabas
**Online**: **London** George Atwell, Faye Hellon, Jeanette Angell, Fergus Day, Justine Bright, Clare Bryson, Aine Fearon, Adrian Low, Ezgi Celebi, Amber Bloomfield; **Delhi** Amit Verma, Rahul Kumar, Narender Kumar, Ravi Yadav, Debojit Borah, Rakesh Kumar, Ganesh Sharma
**Marketing & Publicity**: **London** Liz Statham, Niki Hanmer, Louise Maher, Jess Carter, Vanessa Godden, Vivienne Watton, Anna Paynton, Rachel Spracket, Libby Jellie, Holly Dudley; **New York** Geoff Colquitt, Nancy Lambert; Katy Ball; **Delhi** Ragini Govind
**Manager India**: Punita Singh
**Reference Director**: Andrew Lockett
**Operations Manager**: Helen Phillips
**PA to Publishing Director**: Nicola Henderson
**Publishing Director**: Martin Dunford
**Commercial Manager**: Gino Magnotta
**Managing Director**: John Duhigg

## Publishing information

This first edition published November 2008 by
**Rough Guides Ltd**,
80 Strand, London WC2R 0RL
345 Hudson St, 4th Floor,
New York, NY 10014, USA
14 Local Shopping Centre, Panchsheel Park,
New Delhi 110017, India
**Distributed by the Penguin Group**
Penguin Books Ltd,
80 Strand, London WC2R 0RL
Penguin Group (USA)
375 Hudson Street, NY 10014, USA
Penguin Group (Australia)
250 Camberwell Road, Camberwell,
Victoria 3124, Australia
Penguin Group (Canada)
195 Harry Walker Parkway N, Newmarket, ON,
L3Y 7B3 Canada
Penguin Group (NZ)
67 Apollo Drive, Mairangi Bay, Auckland 1310,
New Zealand
Cover concept by Peter Dyer.

Typeset in Bembo and Helvetica to an original design by Henry Iles.

Printed and bound in China



1024pp includes index

A catalogue record for this book is available from the British Library

ISBN: 978-1-85828-953-3



1 3 5 7 9 8 6 4 2

## Help us update

We've gone to a lot of effort to ensure that the first edition of **The Rough Guide to Southeast Asia on a Budget** is accurate and up to date. However, things change – places get "discovered", opening hours are notoriously fickle, restaurants and rooms raise prices or lower standards. If you feel we've got it wrong or left something out, we'd like to know, and if you can remember the address, the price, the hours, the phone number, so much the better.

Please send your comments with the subject line "**Rough Guide Southeast Asia on a Budget Update**" to ⓔmail@roughguides.com. We'll credit all contributions and send a copy of the next edition (or any other Rough Guide if you prefer) for the very best emails.

Have your questions answered and tell others about your trip at ⓦcommunity.roughguides.com

## Acknowledgements

Thanks to all the writers who updated this edition: Laura Bennitt (Hong Kong and Macau), Tom Burns (Singapore), Emily Butler (Thailand), Róisín Cameron (The Philippines), Ben Connor (Thailand), Michelle Doran (Brunei, Indonesia and Malaysia), Hilary Heuler (Cambodia), Ciara Kenny (Vietnam), Lorna North (Laos), Emily Paine (Malaysia), Nicholas Owen (Indonesia), Lesley Reader (Indonesia), Lucy Ridout (Indonesia) and Henry Stedman (Indonesia).

## Photo credits

All photos © Rough Guides except the following:

**Introduction**
Boats, Ko Pada © Ellen Rooney/Axiom

**Architectural wonders**
Borobudur Temple © Jill Gocher/Getty Images

**The great outdoors**
Emerald dove in Tamen Negara National Park © David J Slater/Alamy
Ha Long Bay © Nik Wheeler/Alamy
Orangutan © Anup Shah/Getty Images
Khao Sok National Park © Andrew Bain/Alamy

**Activities**
Diver, Indonesia © Jeff Hunter/Getty Images
Mount Kinabalu © Robert Harding Picture Library/Alamy
Full Moon Party, Thailand © Benjamin Lowy/Corbis

# Index

Map entries are in colour

**ABBREVIATIONS**
Brunei (B)
Cambodia (C)
Hong Kong (H)
Indonesia (I)
Laos (L)
Macau (Mc)
Malaysia (M)
The Philippines (P)
Singapore (S)
Thailand (T)
Vietnam (V)

## A



## B

INDEX

# E



# F



# G



# H

## I



## J

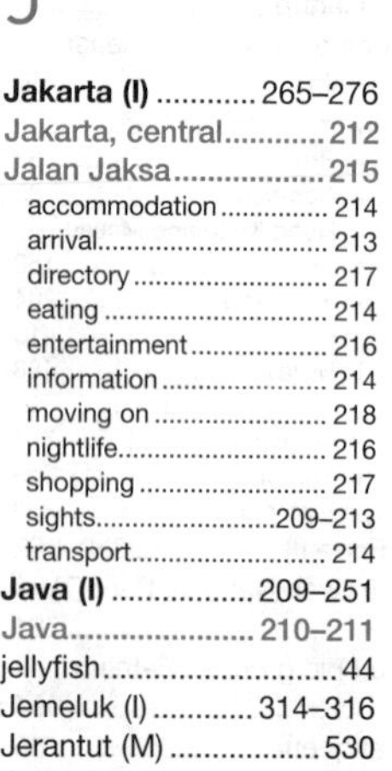

# M

# N



# O



# P

# Q



# R

# T

## U



## V



## W



## X